W9-BFN-130

M I C R O S O F T ®

Office 2003

Introductory Concepts and Techniques

Gary B. Shelly
Thomas J. Cashman
Misty E. Vermaat

Contributing Authors
Steven G. Forsythe
Mary Z. Last
Philip J. Pratt
James S. Quasney
Jeffrey J. Quasney
Susan L. Sebok
Jeffrey J. Webb

THOMSON COURSE TECHNOLOGY
25 THOMSON PLACE
BOSTON MA 02210

SHELLY CASHMAN SERIES®

Australia • Canada • Denmark • Japan • Mexico • New Zealand • Philippines • Puerto Rico • Singapore • South Africa
Spain • United Kingdom • United States

THOMSON
COURSE TECHNOLOGY

Microsoft Office 2003: Introductory Concepts and Techniques, School Edition

Gary B. Shelly
Thomas J. Cashman
Misty E. Vermaat

Managing Editor:
Alexandra Arnold

Product Manager:
Reed Cotter

Associate Product Manager:
Selena Coppock

Editorial Assistant:
Klenda Martinez

Series Consulting Editor:
Jim Quasney

Print Buyer:
Justin Palmeiro

Production Editor:
Marissa Falco

Copy Editor:
Lyn Marcowicz

Proofreader:
Marc Masse

Interior Designer:
Becky Herrington

Cover Image:
John Still

Compositor:
GEX Publishing Services
Pre-Press Company, Inc.

Indexer:
Liz Cunningham

Printer:
Banta Menasha

Printed in the United States of America

2 3 4 5 6 7 8 9 10 BM 08 07 06

For more information, contact Thomson Course Technology
25 Thomson Place
Boston, Massachusetts 02210

Or find us on the World Wide Web at: www.course.com

ISBN-13: 978-1-4188-5968-8 (hardcover, spiral bound)
ISBN-10: 1-4188-5968-0 (hardcover, spiral bound)
ISBN-13: 978-1-4188-5967-1 (hardcover)
ISBN-10: 1-4188-5967-2 (hardcover)

MICROSOFT®
Office
Introductory Concepts
and Techniques
2003
SCHOOL EDITION

Contents

INTRODUCTION TO THE

World Wide Web

Project One

Browsing and Searching the World Wide Web

MICROSOFT OFFICE

Word 2003

Project One

Creating and Editing a Word Document

Project Two

Creating a Research Paper

Project Three

Creating a Resume Using a Wizard and a Cover Letter with a Table

Web Feature

Creating Web Pages Using Word

MICROSOFT OFFICE
Excel 2003

Project One

Creating a Worksheet and an Embedded Chart

Project Two

Formulas, Functions, Formatting, and Web Queries

Project Three

What-If Analysis, Charting, and Working with Large Worksheets

Web Feature

Creating Static and Dynamic Web Pages Using Excel

MICROSOFT OFFICE

Access 2003

Project One

Creating and Using a Database

Project Two

Querying a Database Using the Select Query Window

Project Three

Maintaining a Database Using the Design and Update Features of Access

Integration Feature

Sharing Data among Applications

MICROSOFT OFFICE
PowerPoint 2003

Project One

Using a Design Template and Text Slide Layout to Create a Presentation

Project Two

Using the Outline Tab and Clip Art to Create a Slide Show

Web Feature

Creating a Presentation on the Web Using PowerPoint

MICROSOFT OFFICE
Outlook 2003

Project One

E-Mail and Contact Management with Outlook

Project One

Integrating Office 2003 Applications and the World Wide Web

Appendix A

Microsoft Office Help System

Appendix B

Speech and Handwriting Recognition and Speech Playback

Appendix C

Publishing Office Web Pages to a Web Server

Appendix D

Changing Screen Resolution and Resetting the Word Toolbars and Menus

Appendix E

Microsoft Office Specialist Certification

Preface

The Shelly Cashman Series® offers the finest textbooks in computer education. With each new edition of our Office books, we have made significant improvements based on the software and comments made by the teachers and students.

In this *Microsoft Office 2003, School Edition* book, you will find an educationally sound, highly visual, and easy-to-follow pedagogy that combines a vastly improved step-by-step approach with corresponding screens and a reading level that is appropriate for high school learners. The Q&A feature, new to the Office 2003 series of texts, offers students a way to solidify important application concepts. The new Skill Builder feature enables students to reinforce and to practice skills presented in each project. A new Career Corner element and new You're Hired! online learning game help students focus on the practicality of the skills taught for a career in the computer industry. The Learn It Online page presents a wealth of additional exercises to ensure your students have all the reinforcement they need. The project material is developed to ensure that students will see the importance of learning how to use the Office applications for future coursework.

Objectives of This Textbook

Microsoft Office 2003: Introductory Concepts and Techniques, School Edition is intended for a course that includes an in-depth introduction to Office 2003. No experience with a computer is assumed, and no mathematics beyond the high school freshman level is required. The objectives of this book are:

- To teach the fundamentals of Microsoft Office 2003, Microsoft Windows XP, and browsing and searching the World Wide Web
- To expose students to practical examples of the computer as a useful tool
- To acquaint students with the proper procedures to create documents, worksheets, databases, and presentations suitable for coursework, professional purposes, and personal use
- To help students discover the underlying functionality of Office 2003 so they can become more productive
- To develop an exercise-oriented approach that allows learning by doing
- To serve as courseware in combination with the companion book *Microsoft Office 2003: Advanced Concepts and Techniques* for students interested in Microsoft Office Specialist certification
- To introduce students to new input technologies
- To encourage independent study, and help those who are working alone

International Society for Technology in Education (ISTE), National Educational Technology Standards (NETS)

The ISTE National Educational Technology Standards for Students is designed to provide teachers, technology planners, teacher preparation institutions, and educational decision-makers with frameworks and standards to guide them in establishing enriched learning environments supported by technology. The NETS-S outlines six major standards and related performance indicators, indicating what students should know about and be able to do with technology to support their learning, communications, research, problem-solving, and productivity. The six standards are: Basic Operations and Concepts; Social, Ethical, and Human Issues; Technology Productivity Tools; Technology Communications Tools; Technology Research Tools; Technology Problem-Solving and Decision-Making Tools. For more information, visit www.iste.org and click NETS. A document mapping *Microsoft Office 2003: Introductory Concepts and Techniques, School Edition* to the ISTE NETS is available on the Teacher Resources CD-ROM (ISBN 1-4188-5969-9) or on the Web at course.com.

Approved by Microsoft as Courseware for Microsoft Office Specialist Certification

Microsoft Office 2003: Introductory Concepts and Techniques, School Edition, when used in combination with the companion textbook *Microsoft Office 2003: Advanced Concepts and Techniques* in a two-course sequence, has been approved by Microsoft as courseware for Microsoft Office Specialist certification. After completing the projects and exercises in this book and its companion book, students will be prepared to take the specialist-level exams for the five basic Office applications. See Appendix E for additional information about obtaining Microsoft Office Specialist certification.

The Shelly Cashman Approach

Features of the Shelly Cashman Series *Microsoft Office 2003*, *School Edition* book include:

- **Project Orientation:** Each project in the book presents a practical problem and complete solution in an easy-to-understand approach.
- **Step-by-Step, Screen-by-Screen Instructions:** Each of the tasks required to complete a project is identified throughout the project. Full-color screens with call outs accompany the steps.
- **Thoroughly Tested Projects:** Unparalleled quality is ensured because every screen in the book is produced by the author only after performing a step, and then each project must pass Course Technology's award-winning Quality Assurance program.
- **Quick Reference Summary:** In Office 2003, a task can be completed in a number of ways. The Quick Reference Summary at the back of this book lists the different ways (mouse, menu bar, shortcut menu, and keyboard) to invoke a command.
- **Q&A Feature:** These marginal annotations provide answers to common questions that complement the topics covered, adding depth and perspective to the learning process.

Q & A

Q: Where can a user learn more about Windows XP?

A: A vast amount of information about Microsoft Windows XP is available on the Internet. For additional information about Microsoft Windows XP, visit the Office 2003 Q&A Web Page (scsite.com/off2003sch/qa) and then click Microsoft Windows XP.

- **Skill Builder Feature:** Reinforcement is the key to learning the Office applications. Skill Builders are short, step-by-step exercises strategically placed in the margins of the projects so that the reader can practice recently covered tasks before moving on.
- **Career Corner Feature:** Each project ends with a Career Corner feature that introduces students to a computer-career opportunity.
- **Integration of the World Wide Web:** The World Wide Web is integrated into the Office 2003 learning experience by (1) Q&A annotations that send students to Web sites for up-to-date information and alternative approaches to tasks; (2) Web-based Skill Builder exercises tactically placed throughout the projects to reinforce topics covered; (3) a Microsoft Office Specialist Certification Web page so students can prepare for the certification examinations; (4) a Quick Reference Summary Web page that summarizes the ways to complete tasks (mouse, menu, shortcut menu, and keyboard); and (5) the Learn It Online page at the end of each project, which has project reinforcement exercises, learning games, and other types of student activities.

Skill Builder 1-2

To practice the following tasks, visit scsite.com/off2003sch/skill, locate Windows XP Project 1, and then click Skill Builder 1-2.

- ❑ Start Windows Explorer
- ❑ Create a folder
- ❑ Expand a drive and a folder
- ❑ Display drive and folder contents

Organization of This Textbook

Microsoft Office 2003: Introductory Concepts and Techniques, School Edition consists of a brief introduction to computers, an introduction to the World Wide Web, a project that introduces Microsoft Windows XP and Office 2003, three projects each on Microsoft Office Word 2003, Microsoft Office Excel 2003, and Microsoft Office Access 2003, two projects on Microsoft Office PowerPoint 2003, four special features emphasizing Web related topics, one project on Microsoft Office Outlook 2003, one project on integrating Office 2003 applications and the World Wide Web, five appendices, and a Quick Reference Summary. A short description of each follows.

Essential Introduction to Computers

Many students taking a course in the use of Microsoft Office 2003 will have little previous experience with computers. For this reason, this book begins with a completely updated 40-page section titled Essential Introduction to Computers that covers essential computer hardware and software concepts and information on how to purchase, install, and maintain a computer.

Introduction to Microsoft Windows XP and Office 2003

In this project, students learn about user interfaces, Windows XP, Windows Explorer, and each Office 2003 application. Topics include using the mouse; minimizing, maximizing, and restoring windows; closing and reopening windows; sizing and scrolling windows; launching and quitting an application; displaying the contents of a folder; expanding and collapsing a folder; creating a folder; selecting and copying a group of files; renaming and deleting a file and a folder; Windows XP Service Pack 2; using Windows XP Help and Support; and shutting down Windows XP. Topics pertaining to Office 2003 include a brief explanation of Word 2003; Excel 2003; Access 2003; PowerPoint 2003; Publisher 2003; FrontPage 2003; and Outlook 2003 and examples of how these applications take advantage of the Internet and World Wide Web.

Introduction to the World Wide Web

In this 48-page project, students learn how to browse and search the World Wide Web. Topics include the Internet Explorer window, browsing the World Wide Web, stopping a page transfer, refreshing a page, using the history and favorites list, saving and printing a Web page, Internet Explorer help, types of Web resources, and searching the Web using a directory and keywords.

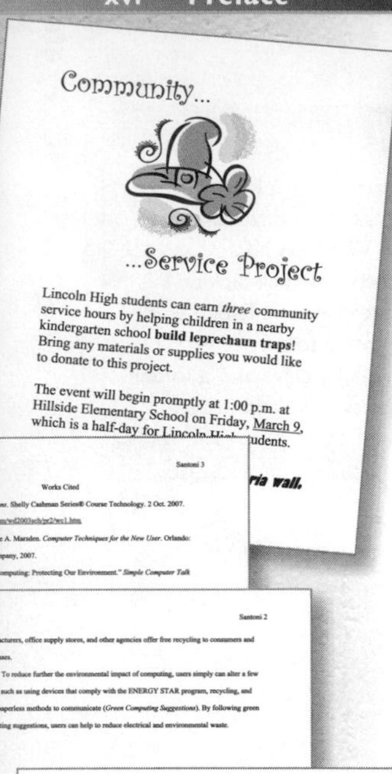

Microsoft Office Word 2003

Project 1 – Creating and Editing a Word Document In Project 1, students are introduced to Word terminology and the Word window by preparing an announcement. Topics include starting and quitting Word; entering text; checking spelling while typing; saving a document; selecting characters, words, lines, and paragraphs; changing the font and font size of text; centering, right-aligning, bolding, and italicizing text; undoing commands and actions; inserting clip art in a document; resizing a graphic; printing a document; opening a document; correcting errors; and using the Word Help system.

Project 2 – Creating a Research Paper In Project 2, students use the MLA style of documentation to create a research paper. Topics include changing margins; adjusting line spacing; using a header to number pages; entering text using Click and Type; first-line indenting paragraphs; using the AutoCorrect feature and AutoCorrect Options button; adding a footnote; modifying a style; inserting a symbol automatically; inserting a manual page break; creating a hanging indent; creating a text hyperlink; sorting paragraphs; moving text; using the Paste Options button; finding a synonym; counting and recounting words in a document; checking spelling and grammar at once; e-mailing a document; and using the Research task pane.

Project 3 – Creating a Resume Using a Wizard and a Cover Letter with a Table In Project 3, students create a resume using Word's Resume Wizard and then create a cover letter with a letterhead. Topics include personalizing the resume; using print preview; adding color to characters; setting and using tab stops; collecting and pasting; adding a bottom border; clearing formatting; inserting the current date; inserting a nonbreaking space; creating and inserting an AutoText entry; creating a bulleted list while typing; inserting a Word table; entering data into a Word table; and formatting a Word table. Finally, students prepare and print an envelope address, use smart tags, and modify the document summary.

Web Feature – Creating Web Pages Using Word In the Web feature, students are introduced to creating Web pages in Word. Topics include saving a Word document as a Web page; formatting an e-mail address as a hyperlink; applying a theme to a Web page; previewing a Web page; creating and modifying a frames page; and inserting and modifying hyperlinks.

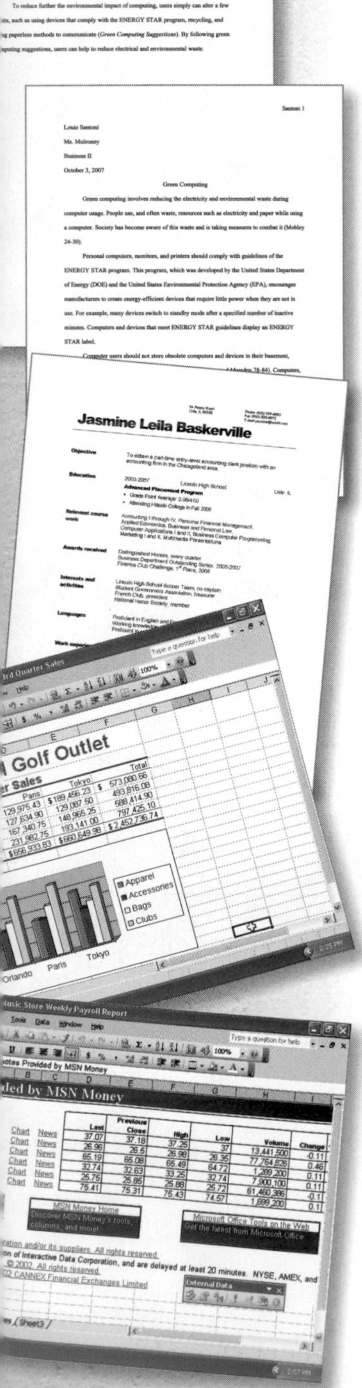

Microsoft Office Excel 2003

Project 1 – Creating a Worksheet and Embedded Chart In Project 1, students are introduced to starting Excel, quitting Excel, Excel terminology, the Excel window, and the basic characteristics of a worksheet and workbook. Topics include entering text and numbers; selecting a range; using the AutoSum button; copying using the fill handle; changing font size; formatting in bold; centering across columns; using the AutoFormat command; charting using the ChartWizard; saving and opening a workbook; editing a worksheet; using the AutoCalculate area; and using the Excel Help system.

Project 2 – Formulas, Functions, Formatting, and Web Queries In Project 2, students use formulas and functions to build a worksheet and learn more about formatting and printing a worksheet. Topics include entering formulas; using functions; verifying formulas; formatting text and numbers; conditional formatting; drawing borders; changing the widths of columns and rows; spell checking; previewing a worksheet; printing a section of a worksheet; and displaying and printing the formulas in a worksheet. This project also introduces students to accessing real-time data using Web Queries and sending the open workbook as an e-mail attachment directly from Excel.

Project 3 – What-If-Analysis, Charting, and Working with Large Worksheets In Project 3, students learn how to work with larger worksheets, how to create a worksheet based on assumptions, how to use the IF function and absolute cell references, charting techniques, and how to perform what-if analysis. Topics include assigning global formats; rotating text; using the fill handle to create a series; deleting, inserting, copying, and moving data on a worksheet; displaying and formatting the system date; displaying and docking toolbars; creating a 3-D Pie chart on a chart sheet, enhancing a 3-D Pie chart; freezing titles; changing the magnification of worksheets; displaying different parts of the worksheet using panes; and simple what-if analysis and goal seeking.

Web Feature – Creating Static and Dynamic Web Pages Using Excel In the Web feature, students are introduced to creating static Web pages (noninteractive pages that do not change) and dynamic Web pages (interactive pages that offer Excel functionality). Topics include saving and previewing an Excel workbook as a Web page; viewing and manipulating a Web page created in Excel using a browser; file management tools in Excel; and using the Spreadsheet toolbar.

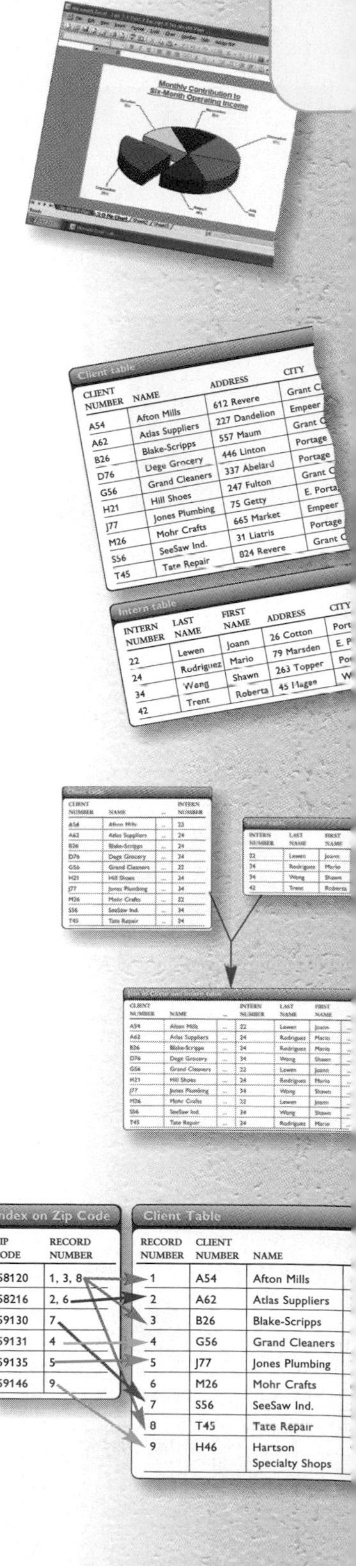

Microsoft Access Office 2003

Project 1 – Creating and Using a Database In Project 1, students are introduced to the concept of a database and shown how to use Access to create a database. Topics include creating a database; creating a table; defining the fields in a table; opening a table; adding records to a table; closing a table; and previewing and printing the contents of a table. Other topics in this project include creating a query using the Simple Query Wizard, using a form to view data, using the Report Wizard to create a report, and using Access Help. Students also learn how to design a database to eliminate redundancy.

Project 2 – Querying a Database Using the Select Query Window In Project 2, students learn to use queries to obtain information from the data in their databases. Topics include creating queries, running queries, saving queries, and printing the results. Specific query topics include displaying only selected fields; using character data in criteria; specifying parameter queries; using wildcards; using numeric data in criteria; using comparison operators; and creating compound criteria. Other related topics include sorting, joining tables, and restricting records in a join. Students also learn to use calculated fields, statistics, and grouping. They also learn how to create top-values queries and how to format fields in queries. Finally, they learn to create and use crosstab queries.

Project 3 – Maintaining a Database Using the Design and Update Features of Access In Project 3, students learn the crucial skills involved in maintaining a database. These include using Datasheet view and Form view to add new records, to change existing records, to delete records, and to locate and filter records. Students also learn the processes of changing the structure of a table, adding additional fields, and changing characteristics of existing fields. They learn ways to change the appearance of a datasheet. They learn to create a variety of validation rules and to specify referential integrity. Students perform mass changes and deletions using queries, create single-field and multiple-field indexes, and use subdatasheets to view related data.

Integration Feature – Sharing Data among Applications In this Integration feature, students learn how to embed an Excel worksheet in an Access database and how to link a worksheet to a database. Students also learn how to prepare Access data for use in other applications. Topics include embedding worksheets; linking worksheets; using the resulting tables; using the Export command to export database data to an Excel worksheet; using drag-and-drop to export data to a Word document; and using the Export command to create a snapshot of a report. They also learn how to export and import XML data.

Microsoft Office PowerPoint 2003

Project 1 – Using a Design Template and Text Slide Layout to Create a Presentation In Project 1, students are introduced to PowerPoint terminology, the PowerPoint window, and the basics of creating a bulleted list presentation. Topics include choosing a design template by using a task pane; creating a title slide and text slides with single and multi-level bulleted lists; changing the font size and font style; ending a slide show with a black slide; saving a presentation; viewing the slides in a presentation; checking a presentation for spelling errors; printing copies of the slides; and using the PowerPoint Help system.

Project 2 – Using the Outline Tab and Clip Art to Create a Slide Show In Project 2, students create a presentation from an outline, insert clip art, and add animation effects. Topics include creating a slide presentation by indenting paragraphs on the Outline tab; changing slide layouts; inserting clip art; changing clip art size; adding an animation scheme; animating clip art; running an animated slide show; printing audience handouts from an outline; and e-mailing a slide show from within PowerPoint.

Web Feature – Creating a Presentation on the Web Using PowerPoint In the Web feature, students are introduced to saving a presentation as a Web page. Topics include saving an existing PowerPoint presentation as an HTML file; viewing the presentation as a Web page; editing a Web page through a browser; and viewing the editing changes.

Microsoft Office Outlook 2003

Project 1 – E-Mail and Contact Management with Outlook In Project 1, students learn to read and send e-mail messages and work with Contacts. Topics include reading, replying to, forwarding, and deleting e-mail messages; composing, formatting, and inserting a file attachment; sending new e-mail messages; flagging, sorting, and configuring e-mail options; generating and maintaining a contact list; and creating a personal folder for contacts.

Microsoft Office 2003 Integration

Project 1 – Integrating Office 2003 Applications and the World Wide Web In Project 1, students are introduced to the seamless partnership of the Microsoft Office 2003 applications, which allows the sharing of information among Word, Excel, Access, PowerPoint, Outlook, and the World Wide Web. Topics include embedding an Excel chart into a Word document; creating a Web site home page from a Word document; creating a Web page from a PowerPoint presentation; creating a data access page Web page from an Access database; and creating hyperlinks from the home page created in Word to the Web pages created in PowerPoint and Access, as well as adding an e-mail hyperlink.

Appendices

The book includes five appendices. Appendix A presents an introduction to the Microsoft Office Help system. Appendix B describes how to use the Office speech and handwriting recognition and speech playback capabilities. Appendix C explains how to publish Web pages to a Web server. Appendix D shows how to change the screen resolution and reset the menus and toolbars. Appendix E introduces students to Microsoft Office Specialist certification.

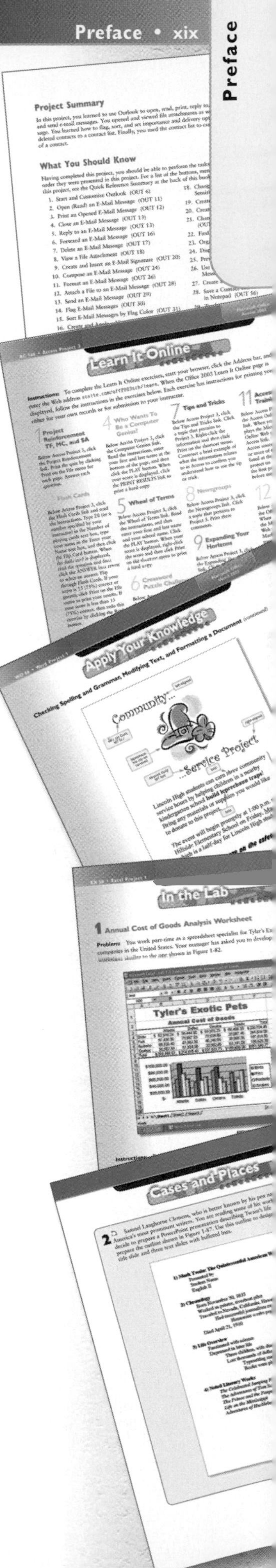

Quick Reference Summary

In Office 2003, you can accomplish a task in a number of ways, such as using the mouse, menu, shortcut menu, and keyboard. The Quick Reference Summary at the back of the book provides a quick reference to each task presented.

End-of-Project Student Activities

A notable strength of the Shelly Cashman Series *Microsoft Office 2003*, *School Edition* book is the extensive student activities at the end of each project. The activities in the Shelly Cashman Series Office books include the following.

- What You Should Know   A listing of the tasks completed within a project together with the pages on which the step-by-step, screen-by-screen explanations appear.
- Learn It Online   Every project features a Learn It Online page that comprises thirteen exercises. These exercises include True/False, Multiple Choice, Short Answer, Flash Cards, Practice Test, Learning Games, Tips and Tricks, Newsgroup usage, Expanding Your Horizons, Search Sleuth, Office Online Training, and Office Marketplace.
- Apply Your Knowledge   This exercise usually requires students to open and manipulate a file on the Data Disk that parallels the activities learned in the project. To obtain a copy of the Data Disk, follow the instructions on the inside back cover of this textbook.
- In the Lab   Three in-depth assignments per project require students to utilize the project concepts and techniques to solve problems on a computer.
- Cases and Places   Five unique real-world case-study situations, including one small-group activity. Each case-study has a cross-curricular designation: Math; Social Studies; Science; Language Arts; Art and Music; Business; and Health.

Teacher Resources CD-ROM

The Shelly Cashman Series is dedicated to providing you with all of the tools you need to make your class a success. Information on all supplementary materials is available through your Course Technology representative or by calling 1-800-824-5179.

The Teacher Resources CD-ROM for this textbook includes both teaching and testing aids. The contents of each item on the Teacher Resources CD-ROM (ISBN 1-4188-5969-9) are described below.

TEACHER'S MANUAL   The Teacher's Manual is made up of Microsoft Word files, which include detailed lesson plans with page number references, lecture notes, teaching tips, classroom activities, discussion topics, projects to assign, and transparency references. The transparencies are available through the Figure Files on the next page.

LECTURE SUCCESS SYSTEM   The Lecture Success System consists of intermediate files that correspond to certain figures in the book, allowing you to step through the creation of an application in a project during a lecture without entering large amounts of data.

SYLLABUS Four sample syllabi, which can be customized easily to any course, are included. The syllabi cover policies, class and lab assignments and exams, and procedural information. Sample syllabi are built for the varying class schedules of High Schools, with the following syllabi offerings: (1) block schedule for a semester-long course, (2) hour-long classes for a semester-long course, (3) block schedule for a full-year course and (4) hour-long classes for a full-year course.

FIGURE FILES Illustrations for every figure in the textbook are available in electronic form. Use this ancillary to present a slide show in lecture or to print transparencies for use in lecture with an overhead projector. If you have a personal computer and LCD device, this ancillary can be an effective tool for presenting lectures.

POWERPOINT PRESENTATIONS PowerPoint Presentations is a multimedia lecture presentation system that provides slides for each project. Presentations are based on project objectives. Use this presentation system to present well-organized lectures that are both interesting and knowledge based. PowerPoint Presentations provides consistent coverage at schools that use multiple lecturers.

SOLUTIONS TO EXERCISES Solutions are included for the end-of-project exercises, the Skill Builder exercises, as well as the Project Reinforcement exercises.

RUBRICS AND ANNOTATED SOLUTION FILES The grading rubrics provide a customizable framework for assigning point values to the laboratory exercises. Annotated solution files that correspond to the grading rubrics make it easy for you to compare students' results with the correct solutions whether you receive their homework as hard copy or via e-mail.

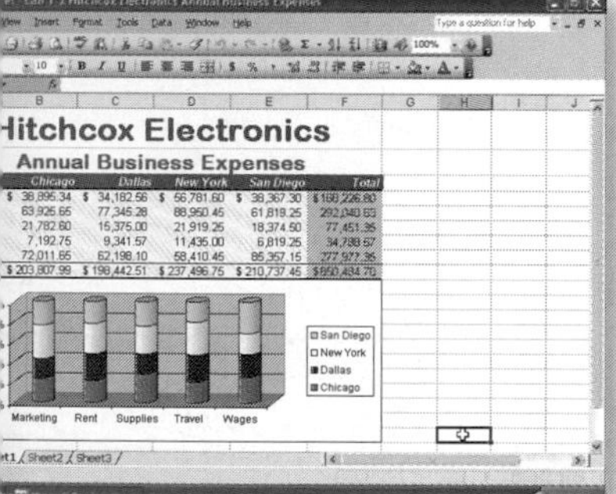

TEST BANK & TEST ENGINE The ExamView test bank includes 110 questions for every project (25 multiple-choice, 50 true/false, and 35 completion) with page number references, and when appropriate, figure references. A version of the test bank you can print also is included. The test bank comes with a copy of the test engine, ExamView, the ultimate tool for your objective-based testing needs. ExamView is a state-of-the-art test builder that is easy to use. ExamView enables you to create paper-, LAN-, or Web-based tests from test banks designed specifically for your Course Technology textbook. Utilize the ultra-efficient QuickTest Wizard to create tests in less than five minutes by taking advantage of Course Technology's question banks, or customize your own exams from scratch.

Part-Time Jobs...
...Available Now!

District 221 Transportation Department

Part-time jobs available to students 16 to 18 years old include assisting staff with office work, Web site maintenance, newsletter development, bus care, and yard upkeep.

Hours are flexible. Work schedule *can vary* weekly depending on after school or summer activities.

Call 555-2817 to interview.

LAB TESTS/TEST OUT The Lab Tests/Test Out exercises parallel the In the Lab assignments and are supplied for the purpose of testing students in the laboratory on the material covered in the project or testing students out of the course.

DATA FILES FOR STUDENTS All the files that are required by students to complete the exercises are included. You can distribute the files on the Teacher Resources CD-ROM to your students over a network, or you can have them follow the instructions on the inside back cover of this book to obtain a copy of the Data Files.

ADDITIONAL ACTIVITIES FOR STUDENTS These additional activities consist of Project Reinforcement Exercises as well as Word document versions of the Skill Builders exercises. The Project Reinforcement Exercises are true/false, multiple choice, and short answer questions that help students gain confidence in the material learned. The Skill Builder exercises are short, step-by-step exercises enabling the reader to practice recently covered tasks before moving on.

ADDITIONAL TEACHER FILES Grids map the text to common technology standards, showing skills required for the ISTE National Educational Technology Standards (ISTE NETS) and the SCANS (Secretary's Commission on Achieving Necessary Skills) workplace competencies and skills.

SAM 2003

SAM 2003 helps you energize your class exams and training assignments by allowing students to learn and test important computer skills in an active, hands-on environment.

SAM 2003 ASSESSMENT With SAM 2003 Assessment, you create powerful interactive exams on critical applications such as Word, Excel, Access, PowerPoint, Windows, Outlook, and the Internet. The exams simulate the application environment, allowing your students to demonstrate their knowledge and think through the skill by performing real-world tasks. Build hands-on exams that allow students to work in the simulated application environment.

SAM 2003 TRAINING Invigorate your lesson plan with SAM 2003 Training. Using highly interactive text, graphics, and sound, SAM 2003 Training gives your students the flexibility to learn computer applications by choosing the training method that fits them best. Create customized training units that employ various approaches to teaching computer skills.

SAM 2003 ASSESSMENT AND TRAINING Designed to be used with the Shelly Cashman Series, SAM 2003 Assessment and Training includes built-in page references so students can create study guides that match the Shelly Cashman Series textbooks you use in class. Powerful administrative options allow you to schedule customized exams and assignments, secure your tests, and choose from more than one dozen reports to track testing and learning progress.

Online Content

Course Technology offers textbook-based content for Blackboard, WebCT, and MyCourse 2.1

BLACKBOARD AND WEBCT As the leading provider of IT content for the Blackboard and WebCT platforms, Course Technology delivers rich content that enhances your textbook to give your students a unique learning experience.

MYCOURSE 2.1 MyCourse 2.1 is Course Technology's powerful online course management and content delivery system. Completely maintained and hosted by Thomson, MyCourse 2.1 delivers an online learning environment that is completely secure and provides superior performance.

To the Student... Getting the Most Out of Your Book

Welcome to *Microsoft Office 2003: Introductory Concepts and Techniques, School Edition*. You can save yourself a lot of time and gain a better understanding of the Office 2003 applications if you spend a few minutes reviewing the figures and callouts in this section.

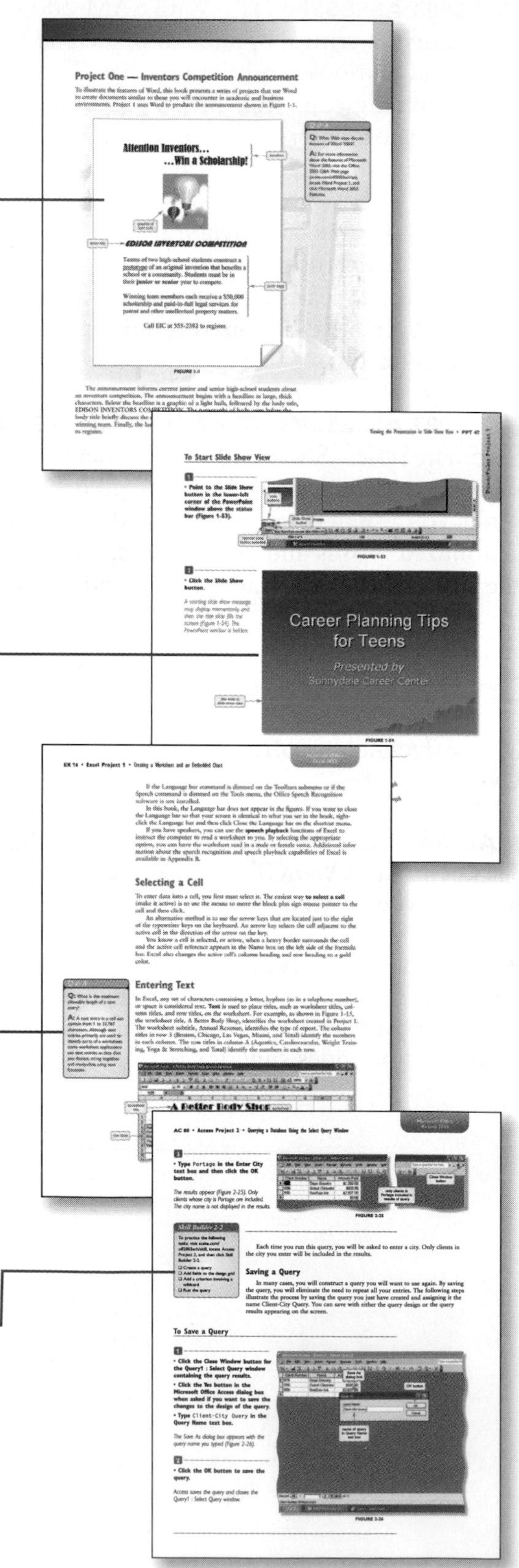

1 Project Orientation

Each project presents a practical problem and shows the solution in the first figure of the project. The project orientation lets you see first-hand how problems are solved from start to finish using application software and computers.

2 Consistent Step-by-Step, Screen-by-Screen Presentation

Project solutions are built using a step-by-step, screen-by-screen approach. This pedagogy allows you to build the solution on a computer as you read through the project. Generally, each step is followed by an italic explanation that indicates the result of the step.

3 More Than Just Step-by-Step

Q&A annotations in the margins of the book and substantive text in the paragraphs provide background information, tips, and answers to common questions that complement the topics covered, adding depth and perspective. When you finish with this book, you will be ready to use the Office applications to solve problems on your own.

4 Skill Builder Boxes

Skill Builder boxes provide opportunity to further reinforce and practice the skills taught in each step sequence. Follow the link in each box to the Web and complete the Skill Builder exercise.

5 Quick Reference Summary

A Quick Reference Summary at the back of the book explain the other ways to complete the task presented, such as using the mouse, menu, shortcut menu, and keyboard.

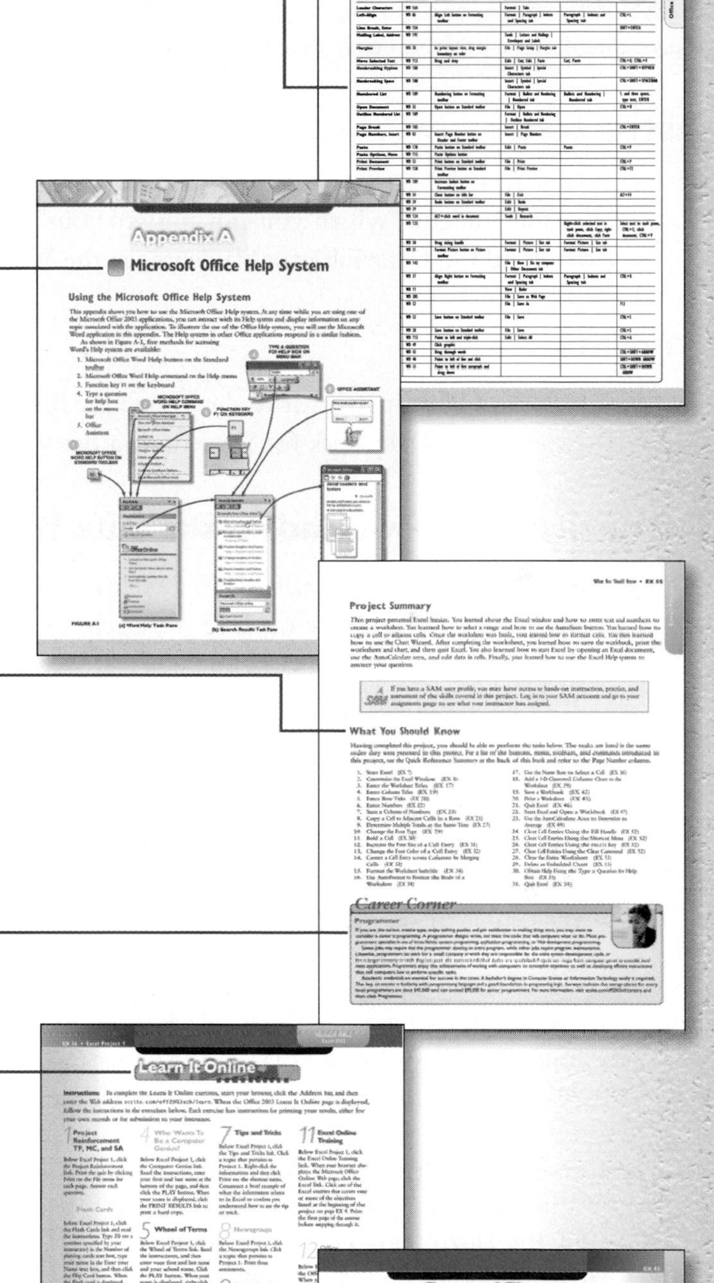

6 Emphasis on Getting Help When You Need It

The first project of each application and Appendix A show you how to use all the elements of the Office Help system. Being able to answer your own questions will increase your productivity and reduce your frustrations by minimizing the time it takes to learn how to complete a task.

7 Review

After you successfully step through a project, a section titled What You Should Know summarizes the project tasks with which you should be familiar. Terms you should know for test purposes are bold in the text.

8 Career Corner

The Career Corner box at the end of each project introduces the student to a computer-career opportunity.

9 Reinforcement and Extension

The Learn It Online page at the end of each project offers reinforcement in the form of review questions, learning games, and practice tests. Also included are Web-based exercises that require you to extend your learning beyond the book.

10 Laboratory Exercises

If you really want to learn how to use the applications, then you must design and implement solutions to problems on your own. Every project concludes with several carefully developed laboratory assignments that increase in complexity.

Obtaining the Data Files for Students

A few of the exercises in this book require that you begin by opening a data file. Choose one of the following methods to obtain a copy of the Data Files for Students.

Instructors

- A copy of the Data Files for Students is on the Instructor Resources CD-ROM below the category Data Files for Students, which you can copy to your school's network for student use.
- Download the Data Files for Students via the World Wide Web by following the instructions below.

Students

- Check with your instructor to determine the best way to obtain a copy of the Data Files for Students.
- Download the Data Files for Students via the World Wide Web by following the instructions below.

Instructions for Downloading the Data Files for Students from the World Wide Web

1. Insert your removable media (USB flash drive, floppy disk, or Zip disk) into your computer.
2. Start your browser. Enter the URL scsite.com in the Address box and then click Go.
3. When the scsite.com home page displays, locate your book using one of the methods below.
   - Browse: Using the Browse by Subject navigation bar on the left side of the screen, click the subject category to which your book belongs. For example, click Office Suites, and then Office 2003.
   - Search: Using the Find Your Book feature at the top of the screen, enter the title of your book, or other identifying information, and then click Go.
   - Quick Link: If your book is featured in the Quick Link area on the right side of the screen, you may click your book title and proceed directly to your material. Skip to Step 5 below.
4. In the center of the screen, locate your book and click the title. For example, click Microsoft Office 2003: Introductory Concepts and Techniques, Premium Edition. Note: You may need to scroll down or navigate to the next Results Page.
5. When the page for your textbook displays, click the appropriate data files link.
6. If Windows displays a File Download – Security Warning dialog box, click the Run button. If Windows displays an Internet Explorer – Security Warning dialog box, click the Run button.
7. When Windows displays the WinZip Self-Extractor dialog box, type in the Unzip to folder box the portable storage media drive letter followed a colon, backslash, and a sub-folder name of your choice (for example, f:\Office 2003).
8. Click the Unzip button.
9. When Windows displays the WinZip Self-Extractor dialog box, click the OK button.
10. Click the Close button on the right side of the title bar in the WinZip Self-Extractor dialog box.
11. Start Windows Explorer and display the contents of the folder that you specified in Step 7 to view the results.
12. Repeat Steps 5–11 to download another set of files.

ESSENTIAL

Introduction to Computers

and How to Purchase a Personal Computer

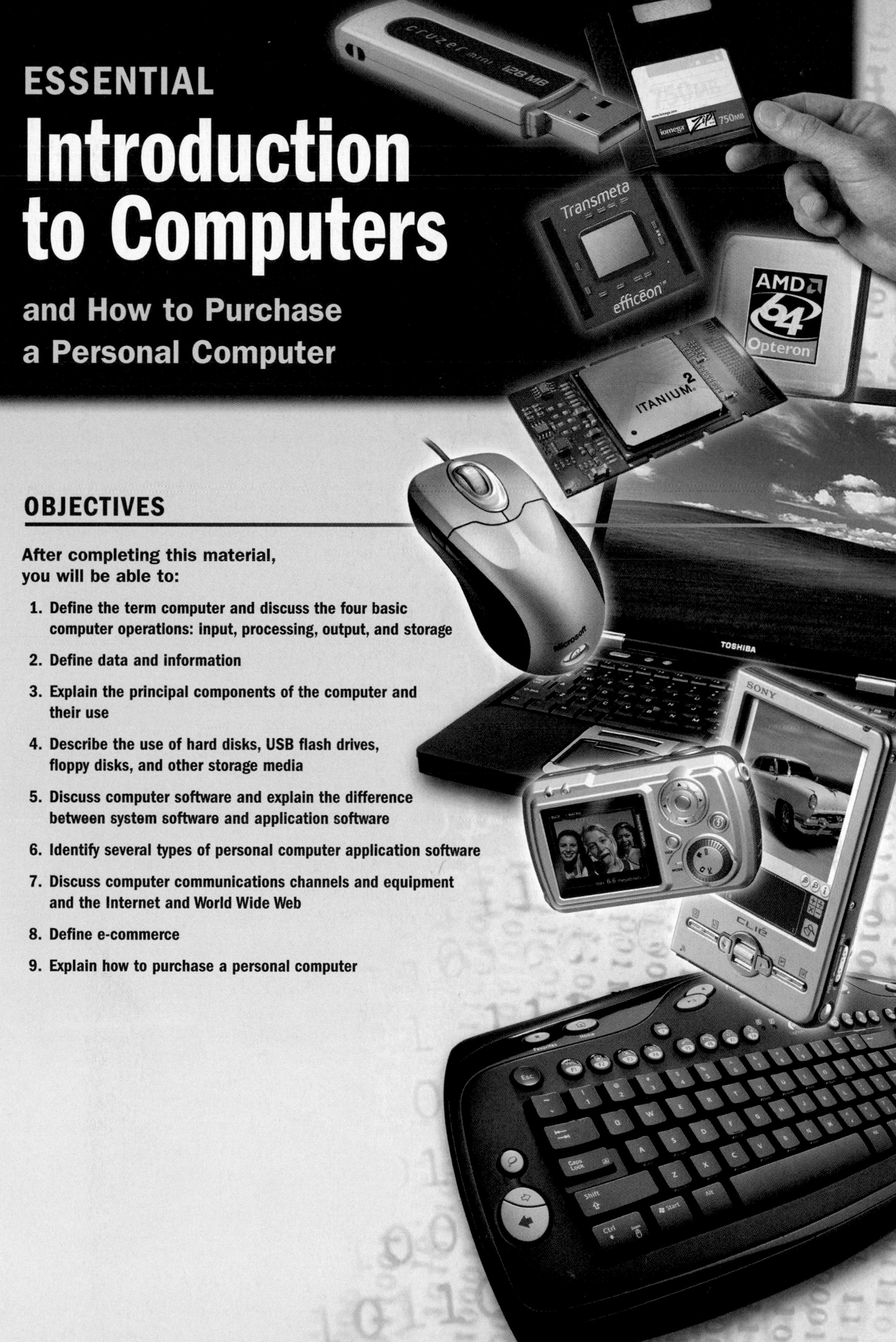

OBJECTIVES

After completing this material, you will be able to:

1. Define the term computer and discuss the four basic computer operations: input, processing, output, and storage
2. Define data and information
3. Explain the principal components of the computer and their use
4. Describe the use of hard disks, USB flash drives, floppy disks, and other storage media
5. Discuss computer software and explain the difference between system software and application software
6. Identify several types of personal computer application software
7. Discuss computer communications channels and equipment and the Internet and World Wide Web
8. Define e-commerce
9. Explain how to purchase a personal computer

Computers are everywhere: at work, at school, and at home. In the workplace, employees use computers to create correspondence such as e-mail, memos, and letters; calculate payroll; track inventory; and generate invoices. At school, teachers use computers to assist with classroom instruction. Students complete assignments and do research on computers. At home, people spend hours of leisure time on the computer. They play games, communicate with friends and relatives using e-mail, purchase goods online, chat in chat rooms, listen to music, watch videos and movies, read books and magazines, research genealogy, compose music and videos, retouch photographs, and plan vacations. At work, at school, and at home, computers are helping people do their work faster, more accurately, and in some cases, in ways that previously would not have been possible.

WHAT IS A COMPUTER?

WEB LINK

Computers

For more information, visit scsite.com/ic6/weblink and then click Computers.

A **computer** is an electronic device, operating under the control of instructions stored in its own memory, that can accept data (input), process the data according to specified rules (process), produce results (output), and store the results (storage) for future use. Generally, the term is used to describe a collection of hardware components that function together as a system. An example of common hardware components that make up a personal computer is shown in Figure 1.

FIGURE 1 Common computer hardware components.

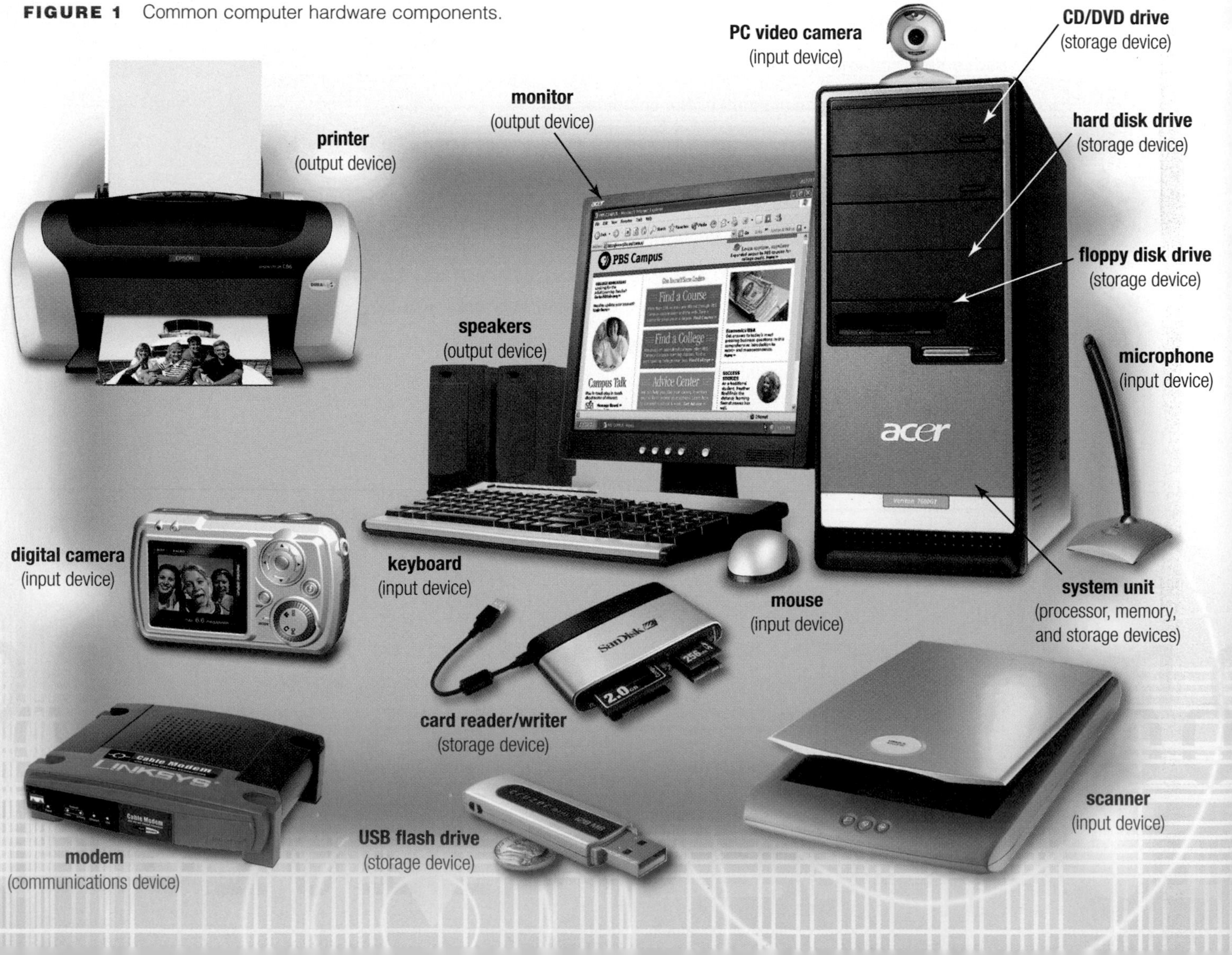

printer (output device)
monitor (output device)
PC video camera (input device)
CD/DVD drive (storage device)
hard disk drive (storage device)
floppy disk drive (storage device)
speakers (output device)
microphone (input device)
digital camera (input device)
keyboard (input device)
mouse (input device)
system unit (processor, memory, and storage devices)
card reader/writer (storage device)
scanner (input device)
USB flash drive (storage device)
modem (communications device)

WHAT DOES A COMPUTER DO?

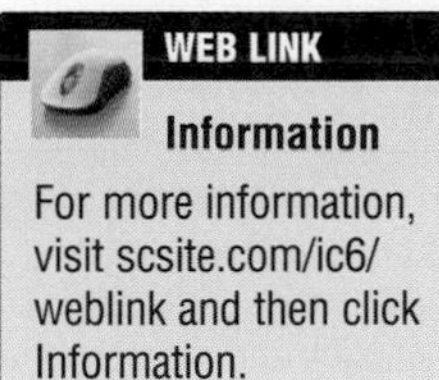

WEB LINK

Information

For more information, visit scsite.com/ic6/weblink and then click Information.

Computers perform four basic operations — input, process, output, and storage. These operations comprise the **information processing cycle**. Collectively, these operations change data into information and store it for future use.

All computer processing requires data. **Data** is a collection of unprocessed items, which can include text, numbers, images, audio, and video. Computers manipulate data to create information. **Information** conveys meaning and is useful to one or more people. During the output operation, the information that has been created is put into some form, such as a printed report, or it can be written on computer storage for future use. As shown in Figure 2, a computer processes several data items to produce a paycheck. Another example of information is a grade report, which is generated from data items such as a student name, course names, and course grades.

People who use the computer directly or use the information it provides are called **computer users**, **end users**, or sometimes, just **users**.

FIGURE 2 A computer processes data into information. In this example, the employee's name and address, hourly rate of pay, and hours worked all represent data. The computer processes the data to produce the payroll check (information).

Computer Programs

For more information, visit scsite.com/ic6/weblink and then click Computer Programs.

WHY IS A COMPUTER SO POWERFUL?

A computer derives its power from its capability to perform the information processing cycle with amazing speed, reliability (low failure rate), and accuracy; its capacity to store huge amounts of data and information; and its ability to communicate with other computers.

HOW DOES A COMPUTER KNOW WHAT TO DO?

For a computer to perform operations, it must be given a detailed set of instructions that tells it exactly what to do. These instructions are called a **computer program**, or **software**. Before processing for a specific job begins, the computer program corresponding to that job is stored in the computer. Once the program is stored, the computer can begin to operate by executing the program's first instruction. The computer executes one program instruction after another until the job is complete.

WHAT ARE THE COMPONENTS OF A COMPUTER?

To understand how computers process data into information, you need to examine the primary components of the computer. The six primary components of a computer are input devices, the processor (control unit and arithmetic/logic unit), memory, output devices, storage devices, and communications devices. The processor, memory, and storage devices are housed in a box-like case called the **system unit**. Figure 3 shows the flow of data, information, and instructions between the first five components mentioned. The following sections describe these primary components.

FIGURE 3 Most devices connected to the computer communicate with the processor to carry out a task. When a user starts a program, for example, its instructions transfer from a storage device to memory. Data needed by programs enters memory either from an input device or a storage device. The control unit interprets and executes instructions in memory and the ALU performs calculations on the data in memory. Resulting information is stored in memory, from which it can be sent to an output device or a storage device for future access, as needed.

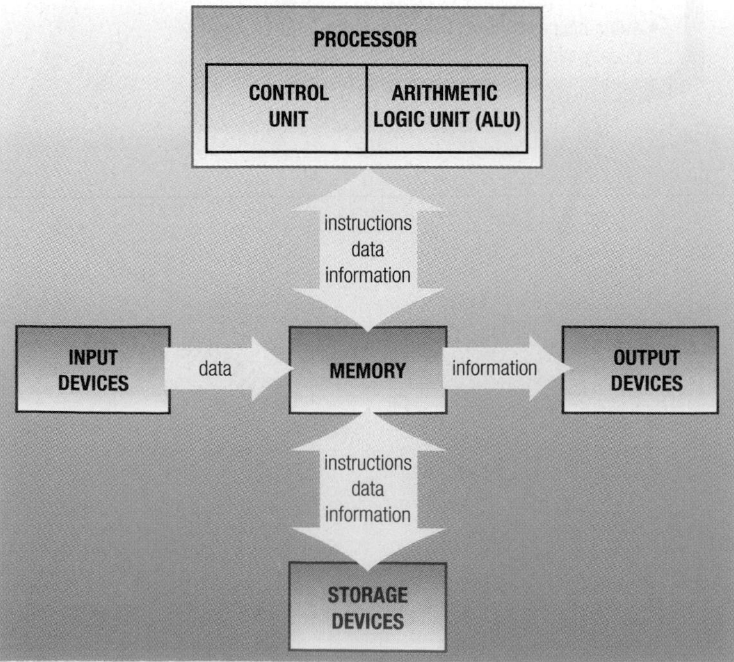

INPUT DEVICES

An **input device** is any hardware component that allows you to enter data, programs, commands, and user responses into a computer. Depending on your particular application and requirement, the input device you use may vary. Popular input devices include the keyboard, mouse, digital camera, scanner, and microphone. The two primary input devices used are the keyboard and the mouse. This section discusses both of these input devices.

WEB LINK

Input Devices

For more information, visit scsite.com/ic6/weblink and then click Input Devices.

The Keyboard

A **keyboard** is an input device that contains keys you press to enter data into the computer. A desktop computer keyboard (Figure 4) typically has 101 to 105 keys. Keyboards for smaller computers, such as notebooks, contain fewer keys. A computer keyboard includes keys that allow you to type letters of the alphabet, numbers, spaces, punctuation marks, and other symbols such as the dollar sign ($) and asterisk (*). A keyboard also contains other keys that allow you to enter data and instructions into the computer.

FIGURE 4 On a desktop computer keyboard, you type using keys in the typing area and on the numeric keypad.

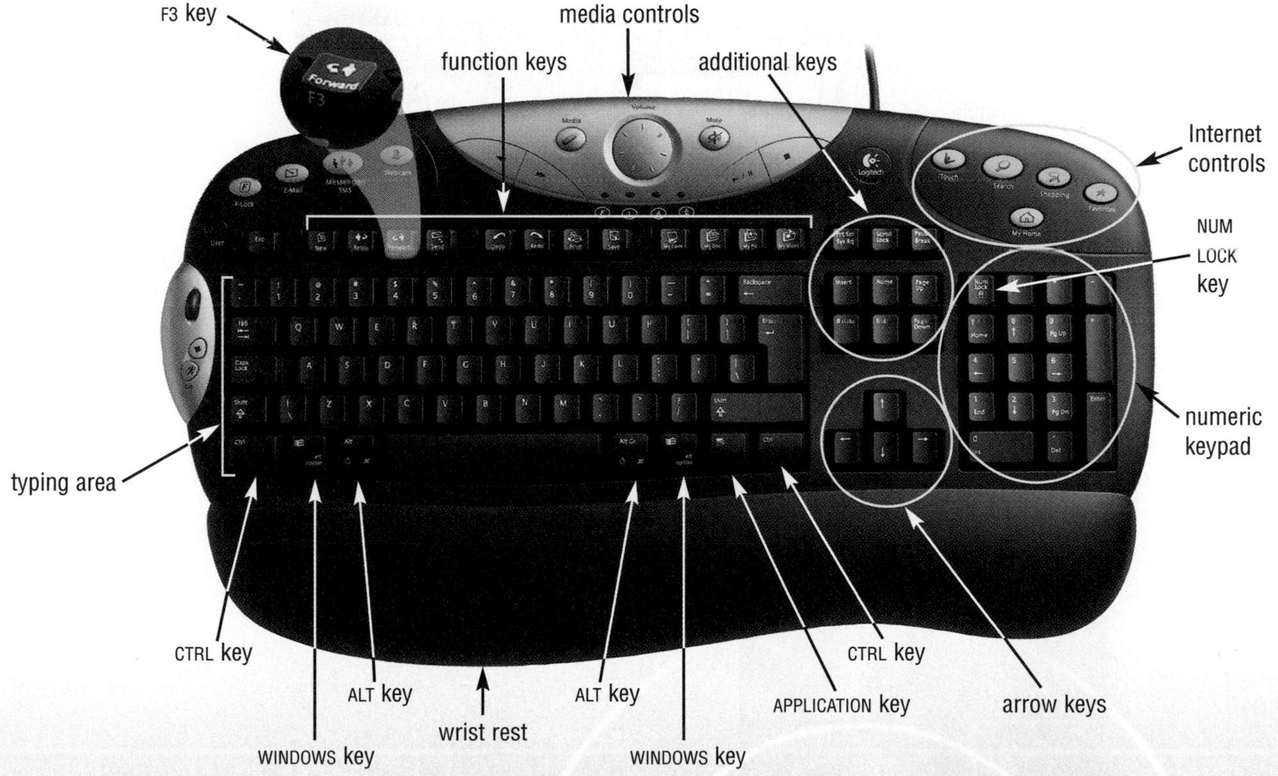

Most handheld computers, such as smart phones, PDAs, and Tablet PCs, use a variety of alternatives for entering data and instructions (Figure 5). One of the more popular handheld computer input devices is the stylus. A **stylus** is a small metal or plastic device that looks like a ballpoint pen, but uses pressure instead of ink to write, draw, or make selections.

Smart phones often include a digital camera so users can send pictures and videos to others (Figure 6).

FIGURE 5 Users enter data and instructions into a PDA using a variety of techniques.

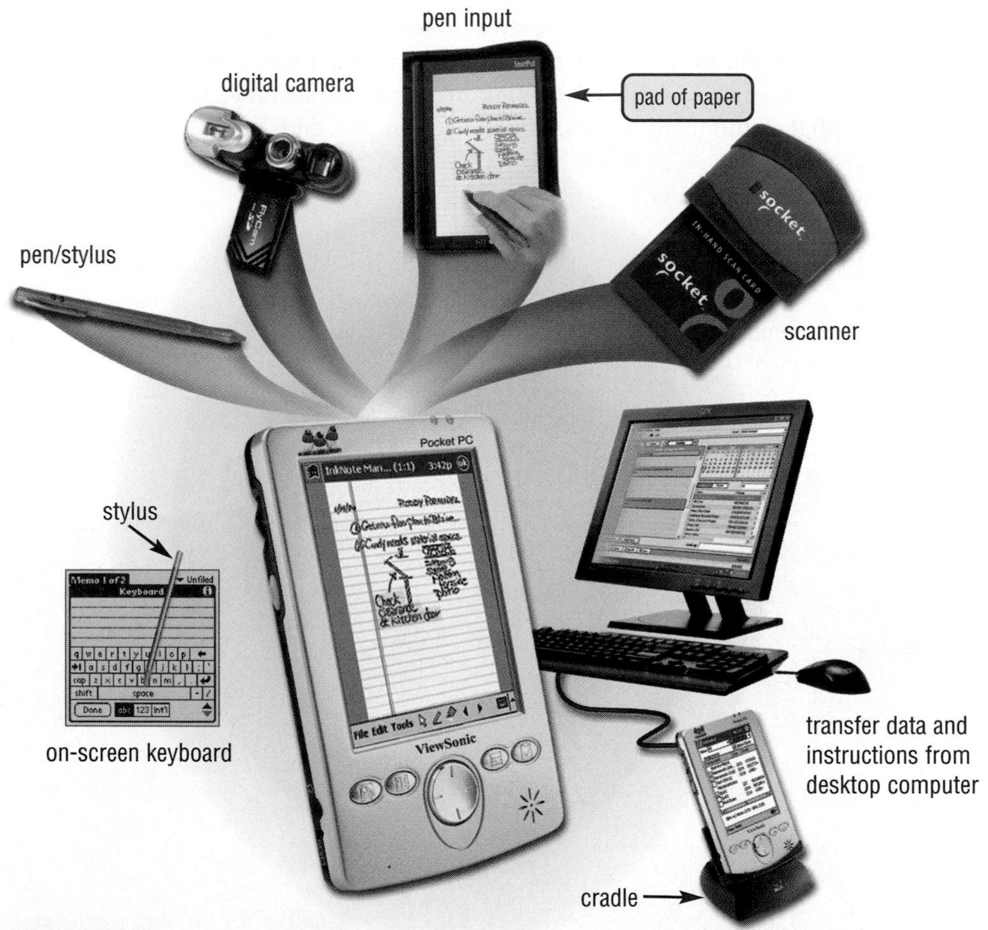

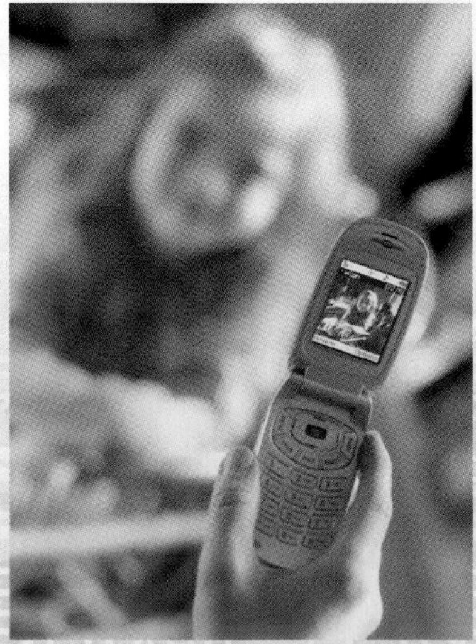

FIGURE 6 Many smart phones include a digital camera so users can send pictures and videos to others.

The Mouse

A **mouse** (Figure 7) is a pointing device that fits comfortably under the palm of your hand. With a mouse, you control the movement of the **pointer**, often called the **mouse pointer**, on the screen and make selections from the screen. A mouse has one to five buttons. The bottom of a mouse is flat and contains a mechanism (ball, optical sensor, or laser sensor) that detects movement of the mouse.

Notebook computers come with a pointing device built into the keyboard (Figure 8) so that you can select items on the screen without requiring additional desktop space. Notice in Figure 8 that the notebook computer has the keyboard built into the unit.

FIGURE 7 A mechanical mouse (a) contains a small ball. The optical mouse (b) uses an optical sensor. The laser mouse (c) uses a laser sensor. They all include a wheel you roll to scroll and zoom. The optical mouse and laser mouse contain additional buttons that enable forward and backward navigation through Web pages. The laser mouse is the most precise.

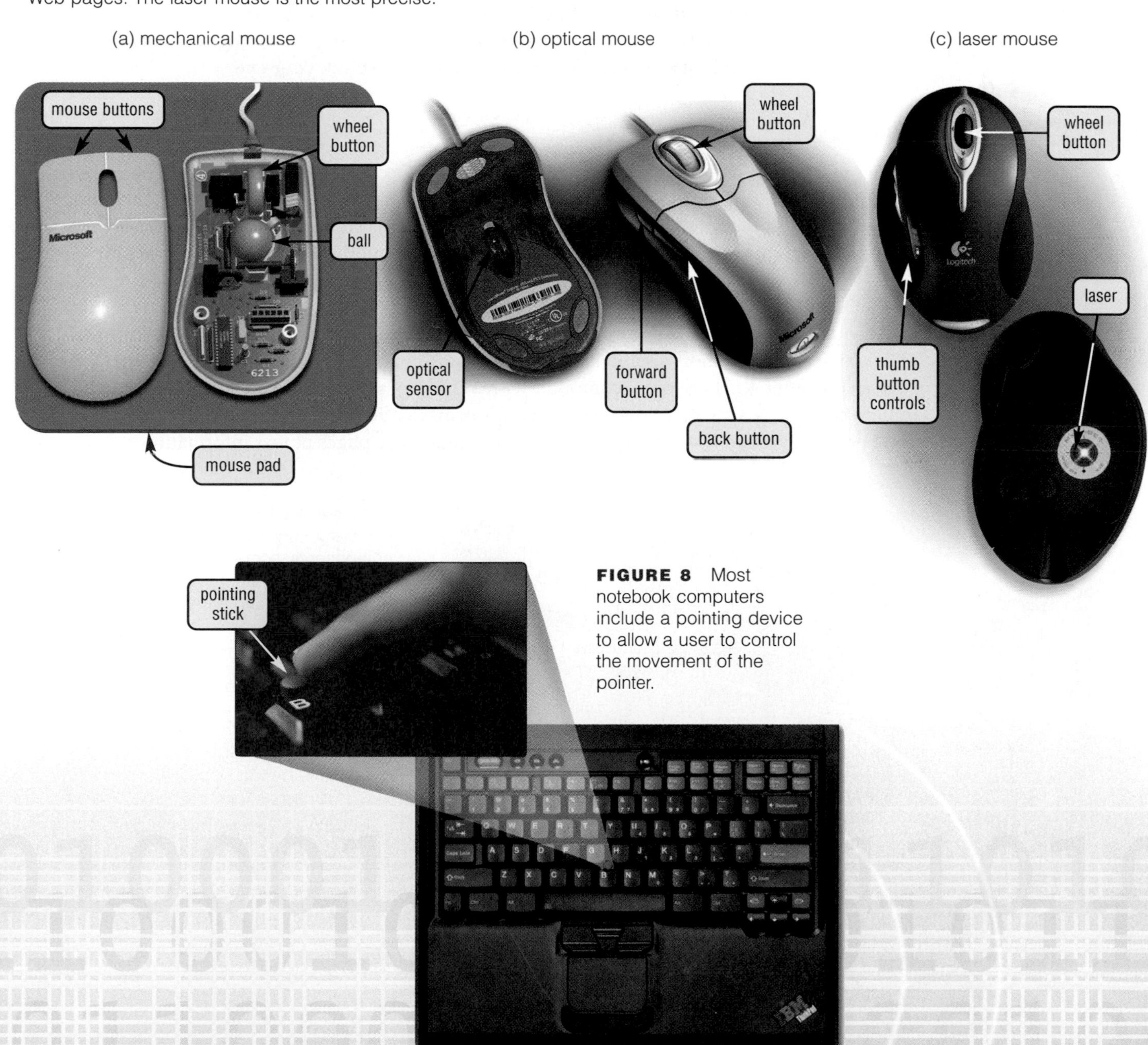

FIGURE 8 Most notebook computers include a pointing device to allow a user to control the movement of the pointer.

SYSTEM UNIT

The **system unit** (Figure 9) is a case that contains electronic components of the computer used to process the data. System units are available in a variety of shapes and sizes. The case of the system unit, also called the chassis, is made of metal or plastic and protects the internal electronic parts from damage. The **motherboard**, sometimes called a system board, is the main circuit board of the system unit. Many electronic components attach to the motherboard, such as the processor, memory, and expansion slots. The sound card and video card shown in Figure 9 are examples of adapter cards, which allow a user to enhance the computer system with add-on products.

WEB LINK

Processor

For more information, visit scsite.com/ic6/weblink and then click Processor.

Processor

The **processor** (top right in Figure 9), also called the **central processing unit** (**CPU**), interprets and carries out the basic instructions that operate a computer. The processor is made up of the control unit and arithmetic/logic unit (Figure 3 on page COM-4). The **control unit** interprets the instructions. The **arithmetic/logic unit** performs the logical and arithmetic processes. High-end processors contain over 100 million transistors and are capable of performing some operations 10 million times in a tenth of a second, or in the time it takes to blink your eye.

WEB LINK

Memory

For more information, visit scsite.com/ic6/weblink and then click Memory.

Memory

Memory, also called **random access memory**, or **RAM**, consists of electronic components that temporarily stores instructions waiting to be executed by the processor, data needed by those instructions, and the results of processed data (information). Memory consists of chips on a memory module (right side of Figure 9) that fits in a slot on the motherboard in the system unit.

The amount of memory in computers typically is measured in kilobytes, megabytes, or gigabytes. One **kilobyte** (**K or KB**) equals approximately 1,000 memory locations and one **megabyte** (**MB**) equals approximately one million memory locations. One **gigabyte** (**GB**) equals approximately one billion memory locations. A **memory location**, or **byte**, usually stores one character such as the letter A. Therefore, a computer with 512 MB of memory can store approximately 512 million characters. One megabyte can hold approximately 500 letter-size pages of text information and one gigabyte can hold approximately 500,000 letter-size pages of text information.

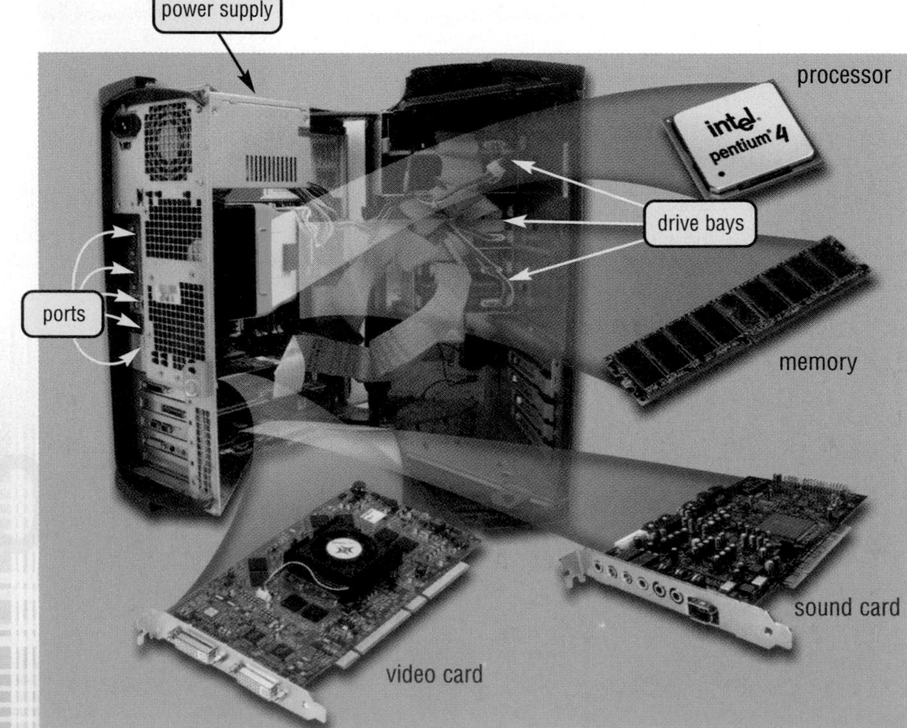

FIGURE 9 The system unit on a typical computer consists of numerous electronic components, some of which are shown in this figure. The sound card and video card are two types of adapter cards.

OUTPUT DEVICES

Output devices make the information resulting from processing available for use. The output from computers can be presented in many forms, such as a printed report or displaying it on a screen. When a computer is used for processing tasks such as word processing, spreadsheets, or database management, the two output devices more commonly used are the printer and a display device.

Printers

Printers used with computers are impact or nonimpact. An **impact printer** prints by striking an inked ribbon against the paper. One type of impact printer used with personal computers is the dot-matrix printer (Figure 10).

Nonimpact printers, such as ink-jet printers (Figure 11) and laser printers (Figure 12), form characters by means other than striking a ribbon against paper. One advantage of using a nonimpact printer is that it can print higher-quality text and graphics than an impact printer, such as the dot-matrix. Nonimpact printers also do a better job of printing different fonts, are quieter, and can print in color. The popular and affordable ink-jet printer forms a character or graphic by using a nozzle that sprays tiny drops of ink onto the page.

Ink-jet printers produce text and graphics in both black and white and color on a variety of paper types and sizes. Some ink-jet printers, called **photo printers**, produce photo-quality pictures and are ideal for home or small-business use. The speed of an ink-jet printer is measured by the number of pages per minute (ppm) it can print. Most ink-jet printers print from 3 to 19 pages per minute. Graphics and colors print at the slower rate.

A laser printer (Figure 12) is a high-speed, high-quality nonimpact printer that employs copier-machine technology. It converts data from the computer into a beam of light that is focused on a photoconductor drum, forming the images to be printed. Laser printers for personal computers can cost from a couple hundred dollars to thousands of dollars. Generally, the more expensive the laser printer, the more pages it can print per minute.

FIGURE 10 A dot-matrix printer is capable of handling wide paper and printing multipart forms. It produces printed images when tiny pins strike an inked ribbon.

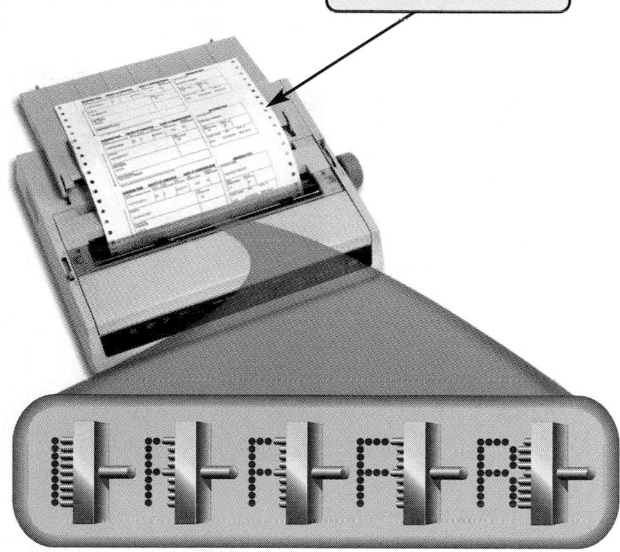

FIGURE 11 Ink-jet printers are a popular type of color printer used in the home. Many photo printers, which can produce photo-lab quality pictures, use ink-jet technology.

FIGURE 12 Laser printers, which are available in both black and white and color, are used with personal computers, as well as larger computers.

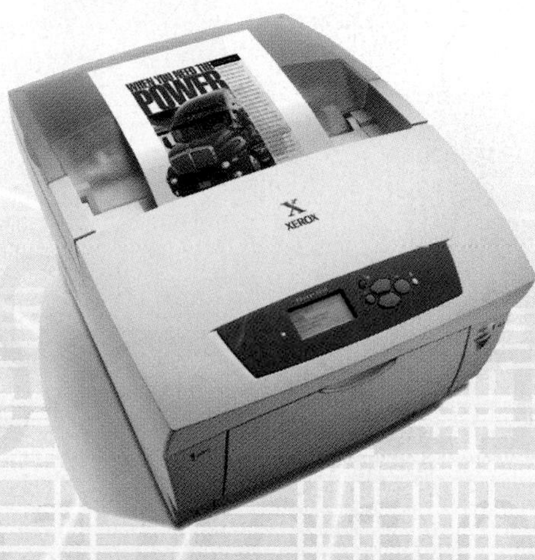

WEB LINK

Output Devices

For more information, visit scsite.com/ic6/weblink and then click Output Devices.

Display Devices

A **display device** is an output device that visually conveys text, graphics, and video information. A **monitor** is a plastic or metal case that houses a display device. Two basic types of monitors are the LCD and CRT. The **LCD monitor**, also called a **flat panel monitor**, shown on the left in Figure 13, uses a liquid display crystal, similar to a digital watch, to produce images on the screen. The flat panel monitor, although more expensive than the CRT monitor, takes up much less desk space and has gained significant popularity over the past few years. The television-like **CRT (cathode ray tube)** monitor is shown on the right in Figure 13. The surface of the screen of either a CRT monitor or LCD monitor is composed of individual picture elements called **pixels**. A screen set to a resolution of 800 x 600 pixels has a total of 480,000 pixels. Each pixel can be illuminated to form parts of a character or graphic shape on the screen.

Mobile computers, such as notebook computers and Tablet PCs, and mobile devices, such as PDAs and smart phones, have LCD screens (Figure 14).

FIGURE 13 The LCD monitor (left), also called a flat-panel monitor, and the CRT monitor (right) are used with desktop computers. The LCD monitor is thin, lightweight, and far more popular today than the CRT monitor.

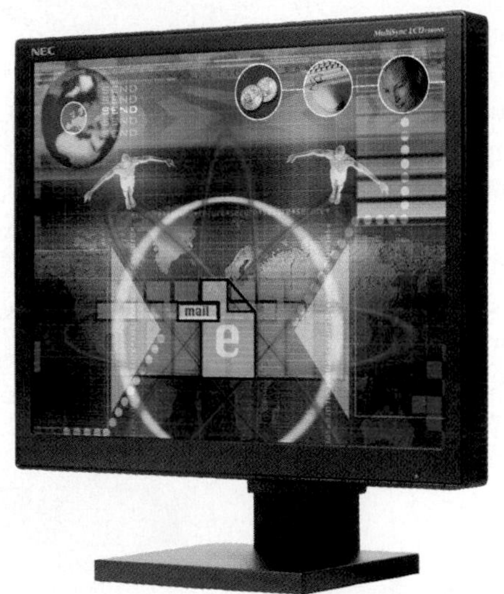

FIGURE 14 Notebook computers and Tablet PCs have color LCD screens. Some PDAs and smart phones also have color displays.

STORAGE DEVICES

A **storage device**, also called a **secondary storage device**, is used to store instructions, data, and information when they are not being used in memory. Four common types of storage devices are magnetic disk, optical discs, tape, and miniature mobile storage media. Figure 15 shows how different types of storage media and memory compare in terms of relative speeds and uses.

Magnetic Disks

Magnetic disks use magnetic particles to store items such as data, instructions, and information on a disk's surface. Before any data can be read from or written on a magnetic disk, the disk must be formatted. **Formatting** is the process of dividing the disk into tracks and sectors (Figure 16), so the computer can locate the data, instructions, and information on the disk. A **track** is a narrow recording band that forms a full circle on the surface of the disk. The disk's storage locations consist of pie-shaped sections, which break the tracks into small arcs called **sectors**. On a magnetic disk, a sector typically stores up to 512 bytes of data.

Three types of magnetic disks are floppy disks, Zip disks, and hard disks. Some of these disks are portable, others are not. **Portable storage medium** means you can remove the medium from one computer and carry it to another computer. The following sections discuss specific types of magnetic disks.

FIGURE 15 Comparison of different types of storage media and memory in terms of relative speed and uses. Memory is faster than storage, but is expensive and not practical for all storage requirements. Storage is less expensive but is slower than memory.

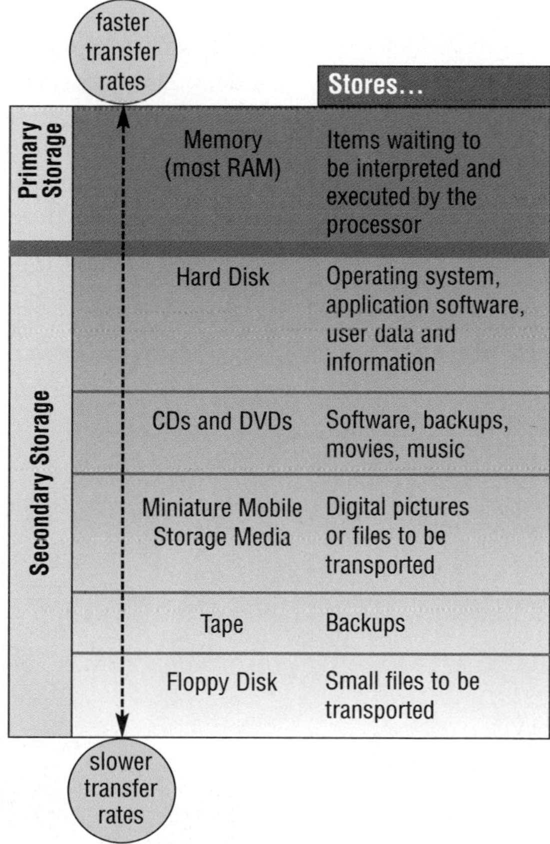

faster transfer rates
Stores...
Primary Storage
Memory (most RAM)
Items waiting to be interpreted and executed by the processor
Secondary Storage
Hard Disk
Operating system, application software, user data and information
CDs and DVDs
Software, backups, movies, music
Miniature Mobile Storage Media
Digital pictures or files to be transported
Tape
Backups
Floppy Disk
Small files to be transported
slower transfer rates

FIGURE 16 Tracks form circles on the surface of a magnetic disk. The disk's storage locations are divided into pie-shaped sections, which break the tracks into small arcs called sectors.

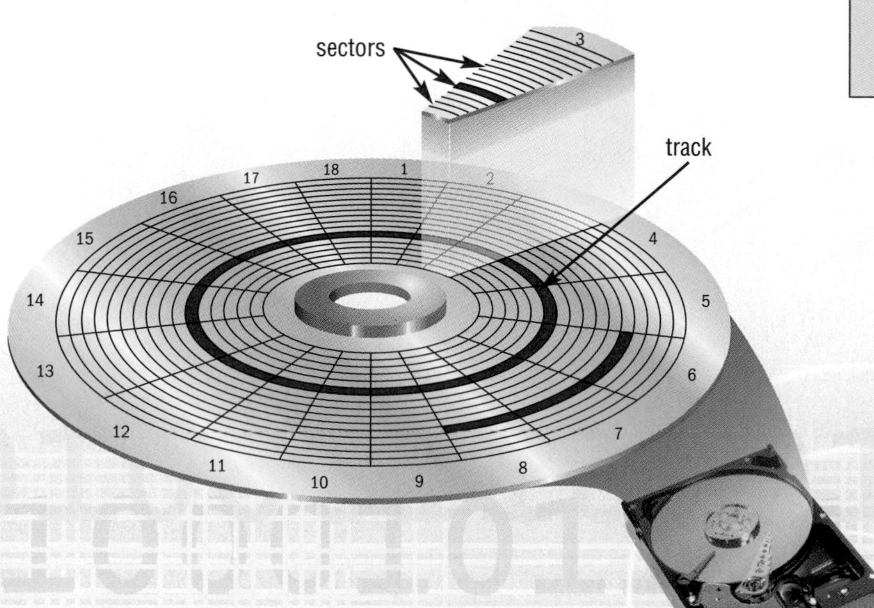

FLOPPY DISKS A **floppy disk**, or **diskette**, is an inexpensive portable storage medium that consists of a thin, circular, flexible plastic disk with a magnetic coating enclosed in a square-shaped plastic shell (Figure 17a). The most widely used floppy disk is 3.5 inches wide and typically can store up to 1.44 megabytes of data, or 1,474,560 characters. Although the exterior of the 3.5-inch disk is not floppy, users still refer to them as floppy disks.

A **floppy disk drive** is a device that can read from and write on a floppy disk. Floppy disk drives are either built-into the system unit (Figure 17a) or are external to the system unit and connected to the computer via a cable (Figure 17b).

Data stored on a floppy disk must be retrieved and placed into memory to be processed. The time required to access and retrieve data is called the **access time**. The access time for floppy disks varies from about 175 milliseconds to approximately 300 milliseconds (one millisecond equals 1/1000 of a second). On average, data stored in a single sector on a floppy disk can be retrieved in approximately 1/15 to 1/3 of a second.

ZIP DISKS A **Zip disk** is a type of portable storage media that can store from 100 MB to 750 MB of data. Zip disks can be built-in to the system unit or it can be external (Figure 18). The larger capacity Zip disk can hold about 500 times more than a standard floppy disk. These large capacities make it easy to transport many files or large items such as graphics, audio, or video files. Another popular use of Zip disks is to back up important data and information. A **backup** is a duplicate of a file, program, or disk that you can use in case the original is lost, damaged, or destroyed.

FIGURE 17 On a personal computer, you insert and remove a floppy disk from a floppy disk drive.

(a) Floppy disk drive installed inside a desktop computer

(b) External floppy disk drive attached to computer with a cable

WEB LINK

Hard Disks

For more information, visit scsite.com/ic6/weblink and then click Hard Disks.

HARD DISKS Another form of storage is a hard disk. A **hard disk**, also called a hard disk drive, is a storage device that contains one or more inflexible, circular patterns that magnetically store data, instructions, and information. As with floppy disks, the data on hard disks is recorded on a series of tracks located on one or more platters. The tracks are divided into sectors when the disk is formatted. Figure 19 shows how a hard disk works.

The hard disk platters spin at a high rate of speed, typically 5,400 to 7,200 revolutions per minute. When reading data from the disk, the read head senses the magnetic spots that are recorded on the disk along the various tracks and transfers that data to memory. When writing, the data is transferred from memory and is stored as magnetic spots on the tracks on the recording surface of one or more of the disk platters. When reading or writing, the read/write heads on a hard disk drive do not actually touch the surface of the disk.

The number of platters permanently mounted on the spindle of a hard disk varies. On most drives, each surface of the platter can be used to store data. Thus, if a hard disk drive uses one platter, two surfaces are available for data. If the drive uses two platters, four sets of read/write heads read and record data from the four surfaces. Storage capacities of internally mounted fixed disks for personal computers range from 10 GB to more than 200 GB.

The system unit on most desktop and notebook computers contains at least one hard disk. Although hard disks are available in removable cartridge form, most hard disks cannot be removed from the computer.

FIGURE 18 An external Zip drive and Zip disk.

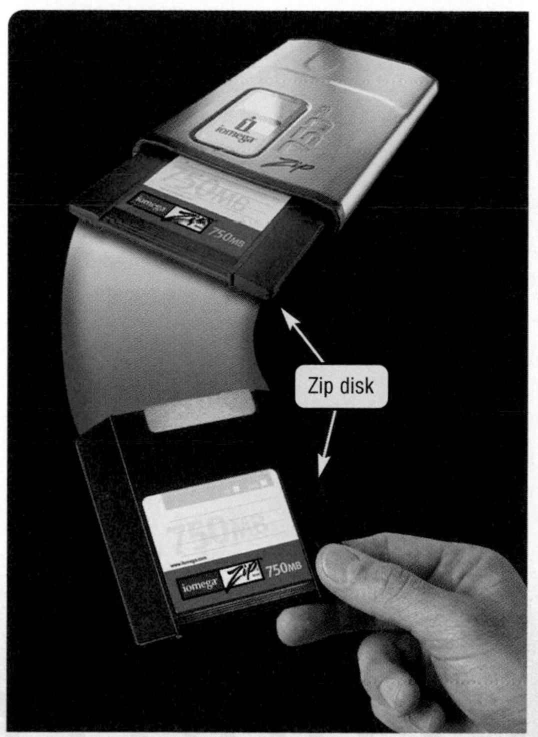

FIGURE 19 How a hard disk works.

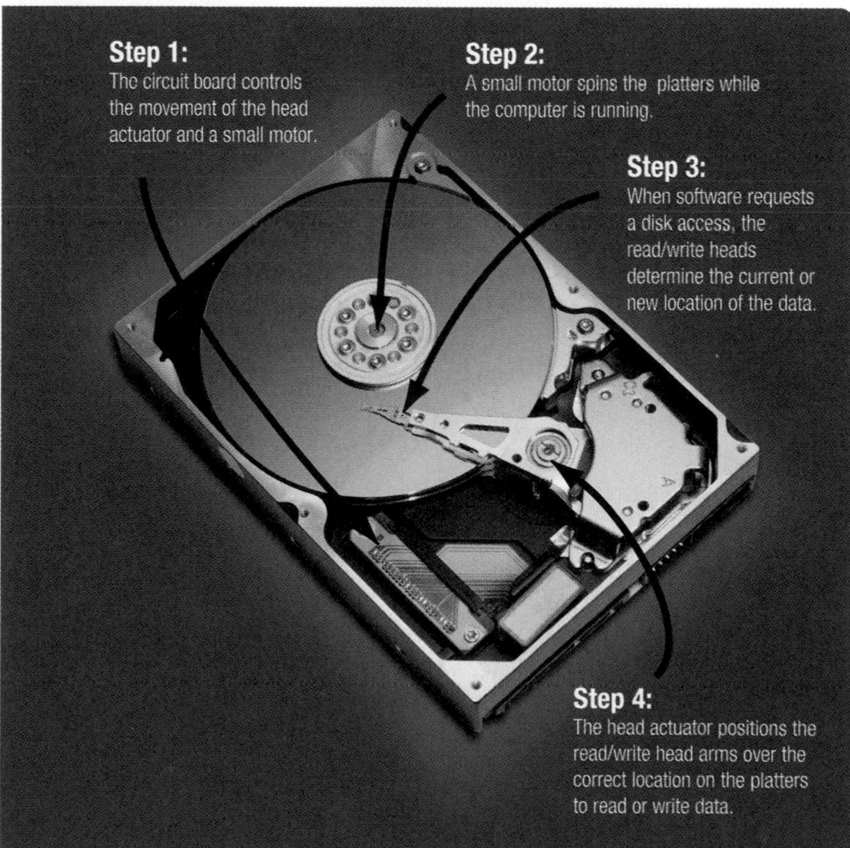

Step 1:
The circuit board controls the movement of the head actuator and a small motor.
Step 2:
A small motor spins the platters while the computer is running.
Step 3:
When software requests a disk access, the read/write heads determine the current or new location of the data.
Step 4:
The head actuator positions the read/write head arms over the correct location on the platters to read or write data.

WEB LINK

CDs

For more information, visit scsite.com/ic6/weblink and then click CDs.

Optical Discs

An optical disc is a portable storage medium that consists of a flat, round, portable disc made of metal, plastic, and lacquer that is written and read by a laser. Optical discs used in personal computers are 4.75 inches in diameter and less than 1/20 of an inch thick. Nearly every personal computer today has some type of optical disc drive installed in a drive bay. On these drives, you push a button to slide the tray out, insert the disc, and then push the same button to close the tray (Figure 20).

Many different formats of optical discs exist today. These include CD-ROM, CD-R, CD-RW, DVD-ROM, DVD-R, DVD+R, DVD-RW, DVD+RW, and DVD+RAM. Figure 21 identifies each of these optical disc formats and specifies whether a user can read from the disc, write on the disc, and/or erase the disc.

A **CD-ROM** (compact disc read-only memory) is a type of optical disc that users can read but not write on (record) or erase — hence, the name read-only. A typical CD-ROM holds from 650 MB to 1 GB of data, instructions, and information. This is equivalent to about 450 high-density 3.5-inch floppy disks. Software manufacturers often distribute their programs using CD-ROMs.

To read a CD-ROM, insert the disc in a **CD-ROM drive** or a CD-ROM player. Because audio CDs and CD-ROMs use the same laser technology, you may be able to use a CD-ROM drive to listen to an audio CD while working on the computer. Some music companies, however, configure their CDs so the music will not play on a computer. They do this to protect themselves from customers illegally copying and sharing the music.

Push the button to slide out the tray.
Insert the disc, label side up.
Push the same button to close the tray.

FIGURE 20 On optical disc drives, you push a button to slide out a tray, insert the disc, and then push the same button to close the tray.

A **CD-R** (compact disc-recordable) is an optical disc onto which you can record your own items such as text, graphics, and audio. With a CD-R, you can write on part of the disc at one time and another part at a later time. Once you have recorded the CD-R, you can read from it as many times as you wish. You can write on each part only one time, and you cannot erase the disc's contents. Most CD-ROM drives can read a CD-R.

A **CD-RW** (compact disc-rewriteable) is an erasable optical disc you can write on multiple times. Originally called an erasable CD (CD-E), a CD-RW overcomes the major disadvantage of CD-R discs, which is that you can write on them only once. With CD-RWs, the disc acts like a floppy or hard disk, allowing you to write and rewrite data, instructions, and information onto it multiple times.

Although CDs have huge storage capacities, even a CD is not large enough for many of today's complex programs. Some software, for example, is sold on five or more CDs. To meet these tremendous storage requirements, some software companies have moved from CDs to the larger DVD — a technology that can be used to store large amounts of text and even cinema-like videos (Figure 22).

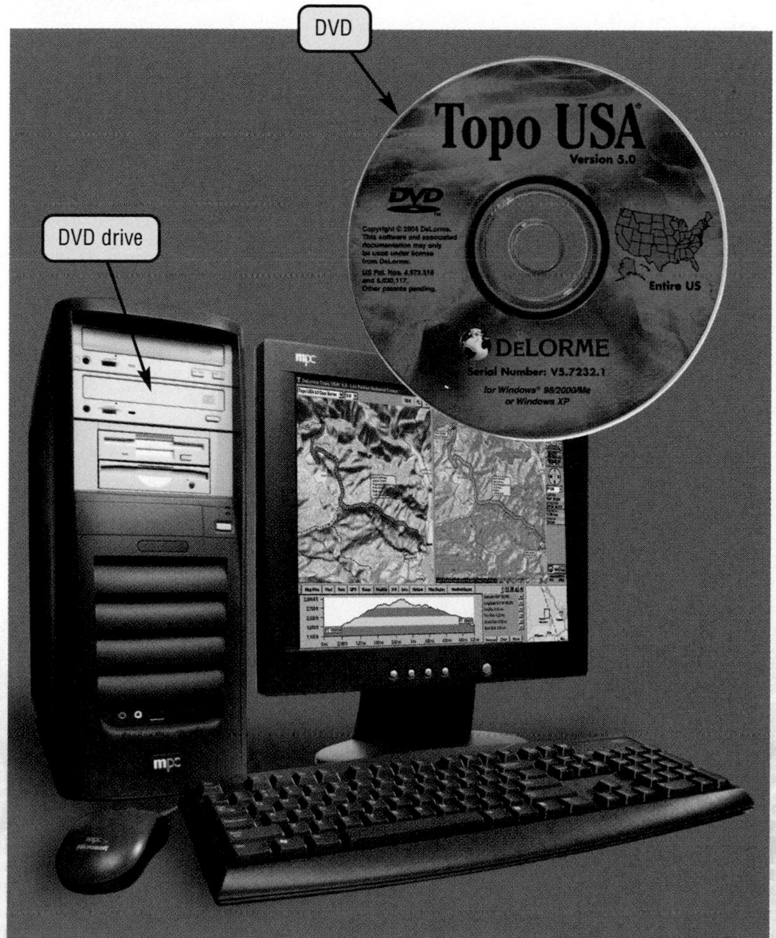

FIGURE 22 A DVD is an extremely high-capacity optical disc.

OPTICAL DISC FORMATS

Optical Disc	Read	Write	Erase
CD-ROM	Y	N	N
CD-R	Y	Y	N
CD-RW	Y	Y	Y
DVD-ROM	Y	N	N
DVD-R DVD+R	Y	Y	N
DVD-RW DVD+RW DVD+RAM	Y	Y	Y

FIGURE 21 Manufacturers sell CD-ROM and DVD-ROM media prerecorded (written) with audio, video, and software. Users cannot change the contents of these discs. Users, however, can purchase the other formats of CDs and DVDs as blank media and record (write) their own data, instructions, and information on these discs.

WEB LINK

DVDs

For more information, visit scsite.com/ic6/weblink and then click DVDs.

A **DVD-ROM** (digital versatile disk-read-only memory) is a very high capacity optical disc capable of storing from 4.7 GB to 17 GB — more than enough to hold a telephone book containing every resident in the United States. As with the CD-ROM format, you cannot write on an optical disc that uses the DVD-ROM format. You can only read from it. To read a DVD-ROM, you need a **DVD-ROM drive**.

DVD-R and **DVD+R** are competing DVD-recordable formats, each with up to 4.7 GB storage capacity. Both allow users to write on the disc once and read (play) it many times. **DVD-RW**, **DVD+RW**, and **DVD+RAM** are three competing DVD formats, each with storage capacities up to 4.7 GB per side, that allow users to erase and write (record) many times. To write to a DVD, you need a recordable or rewriteable DVD-ROM drive.

Tape

Tape is a magnetically coated ribbon of plastic housed in a tape cartridge (Figure 23) capable of storing large amounts of data and information at a low cost. A **tape drive** is used to read from and write on a tape. Tape is primarily used for long-term storage and backup.

WEB LINK

Miniature Mobile Storage Media

For more information, visit scsite.com/ic6/weblink and then click Miniature Mobile Storage Media.

Miniature Mobile Storage Media

Miniature mobile storage media are rewriteable media usually in the form of a flash memory card, USB flash drive, or a smart card. Miniature mobile storage media allow mobile users to transport digital images, music, or documents easily to and from computers and other devices (Figure 24).

FIGURE 23 A tape drive and a tape cartridge.

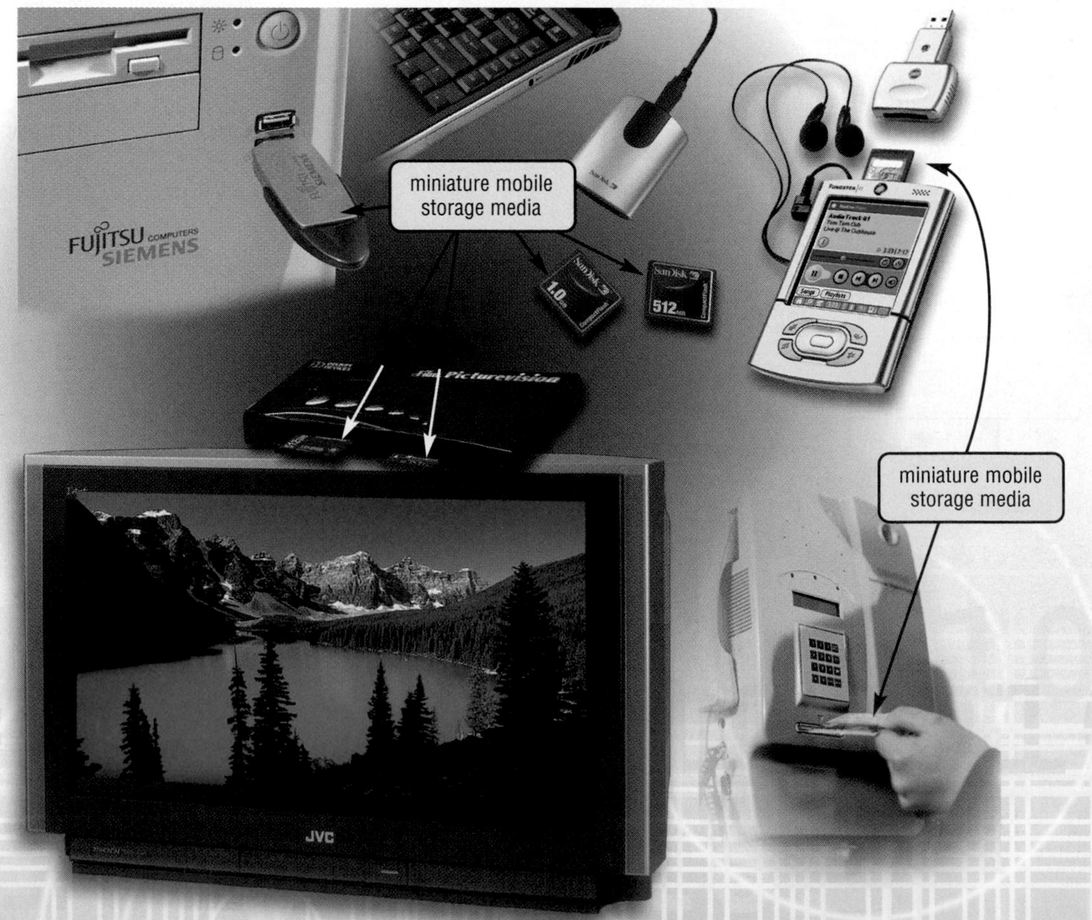

FIGURE 24 Many types of computers and devices use miniature mobile storage media.

Flash memory cards are solid-state media, which means they consist entirely of electronics (chips, wires, etc.) and contain no moving parts. Common types of flash memory include CompactFlash, SmartMedia, Secure Digital, xD Picture Card, and Memory Stick (Figure 25).

A **USB flash drive** (Figure 26), sometimes called a pen drive, is a flash memory storage device that plugs into a USB port on a computer or mobile device. USB flash drives are the portable storage media of choice among users today because they are small, lightweight, and have such large storage capacities. Capacities typically range from 16 MB to 4 GB.

VARIOUS FLASH MEMORY CARDS

Media Name	Storage Capacity	Use
CompactFlash 	32 MB to 4 GB	Digital cameras, PDAs, smart phones, photo printers, music players, notebook computers, desktop computers
SmartMedia 	32 MB to 128 MB	Digital cameras, PDAs, smart phones, photo printers, music players
Secure Digital 	64 MB to 1 GB	Digital cameras, digital video cameras, PDAs, smart phones, photo printers, music players
xD Picture Card 	64 MB to 512 MB	Digital cameras, photo printers
Memory Stick 	256 MB to 2 GB	Digital cameras, digital video cameras, PDAs, photo printers, smart phones, notebook computers

FIGURE 25 A variety of flash memory cards.

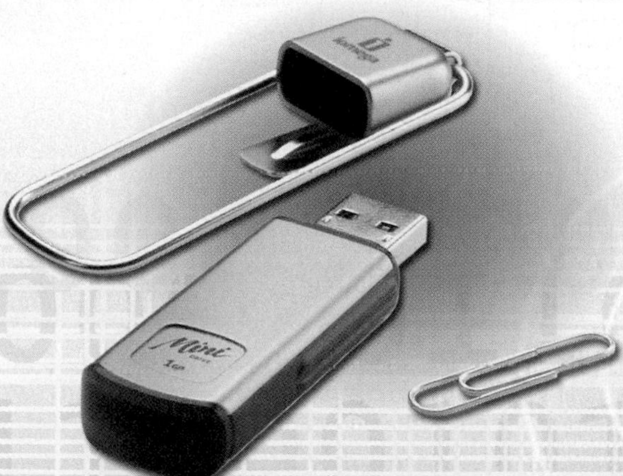

FIGURE 26 A USB flash drive next to a paper clip.

A **smart card**, which is similar in size to a credit card or ATM card, stores data on a thin microprocessor embedded in the card. When you insert the smart card in a specialized card reader, the information on the card is read and, if necessary, updated (Figure 27). Use of smart cards include storing medical records, tracking customer purchases, storing a prepaid amount of money, and authenticating users, such as for Internet purchases.

COMMUNICATIONS DEVICES

A **communications device** is a hardware component that enables a computer to send (transmit) and receive data, instructions, and information to and from one or more computers. A widely used communications device is the telephone or cable modem (Figure 1 on page COM-2).

Communications occur over **transmission media** such as telephone lines, cables, cellular radio networks, and satellites. Some transmission media, such as satellites and cellular radio networks, are **wireless**, which means they have no physical lines or wires. People around the world use computers and communications devices to communicate with each other using one or more transmission media.

COMPUTER SOFTWARE

Computer software is the key to productive use of computers. With the correct software, a computer can become a valuable tool. Software can be categorized into two types: system software and application software.

WEB LINK

Operating Systems

For more information, visit scsite.com/ic6/weblink and then click Operating Systems.

System Software

System software consists of programs to control the operations of computer equipment. An important part of system software is a set of programs called the operating system. Instructions in the **operating system** tell the computer how to perform the functions of loading, storing, and executing an application program and how to transfer data. For a computer to operate, an operating system must be stored in the computer's memory. When a computer is turned on, the operating system is loaded into the computer's memory from auxiliary storage. This process is called **booting**.

Today, most computers use an operating system that has a **graphical user interface** (**GUI**) that provides visual cues such as icon symbols to help the user. Each **icon** represents an application such as word processing, or a file or document where data is stored. Microsoft Windows XP (Figure 28) is a widely used graphical operating system. Apple Macintosh computers also have a graphical user interface operating system.

FIGURE 27 A smart card and smart card reader.

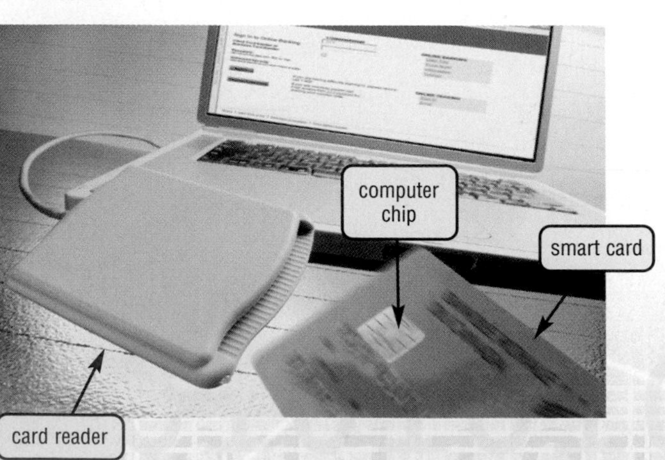

FIGURE 28 A graphical user interface such as Microsoft Windows XP makes the computer easier to use. The small pictures, or symbols, on the screen are called icons. An icon represents a program or data the user can choose. A window is a rectangular area of the screen that is used to display a program, data, and/or information.

Application Software

Application software consists of programs that tell a computer how to produce information. Some widely used application software includes personal information manager, project management, accounting, computer-aided design, desktop publishing, paint/image editing, audio and video editing, multimedia authoring, Web page authoring, personal finance, legal, tax preparation, home design/landscaping, educational, reference, and entertainment (games, simulations, etc.). Often, application software is available for purchase from a Web site or store that sells computer products (Figure 29).

Personal computer users regularly use application software. Some of the more commonly used applications are word processing, electronic spreadsheet, database, and presentation graphics.

WORD PROCESSING **Word processing software** (Figure 30) is used to create, edit, format, and print documents. A key advantage of word processing software is that users easily can make changes in documents, such as correcting spelling; changing margins; and adding, deleting, or relocating entire paragraphs. These changes would be difficult and time consuming to make using manual methods such as a typewriter. With a word processor, documents can be printed quickly and accurately and easily stored on a disk for future use. Word processing software is oriented toward working with text, but word processing packages also support features that enable users to manipulate numeric data and utilize graphics.

WEB LINK

Word Processing Software

For more information, visit scsite.com/ic6/weblink and then click Word Processing Software.

SPREADSHEET **Electronic spreadsheet software** (Figure 31) allows the user to add, subtract, and perform user-defined calculations on rows and columns of numbers. These numbers can be changed, and the spreadsheet quickly recalculates the new results. Electronic spreadsheet software eliminates the tedious recalculations required with manual methods. Spreadsheet information frequently is converted into a graphic form, such as charts. Graphics capabilities now are included in most spreadsheet packages.

WEB LINK

Spreadsheet Software

For more information, visit scsite.com/ic6/weblink and then click Spreadsheet Software.

FIGURE 29 Stores that sell computer products have shelves stocked with software for sale.

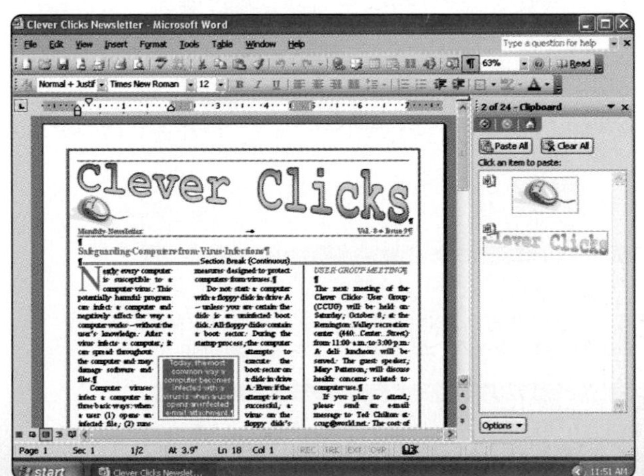

FIGURE 30 Word processing software is used to create letters, memos, newsletters, and other documents.

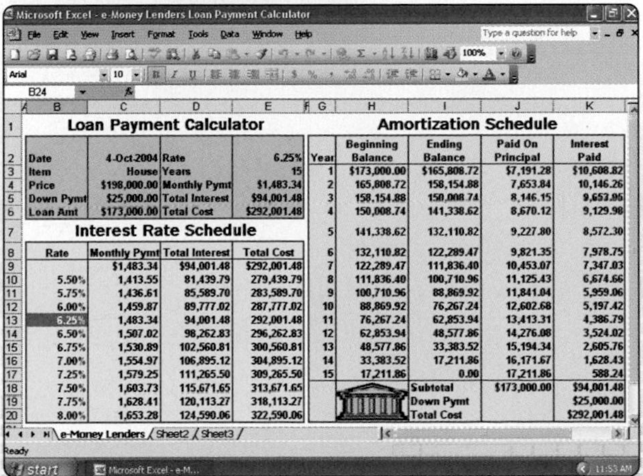

Microsoft Excel - e-Money Lenders Loan Payment Calculator

Loan Payment Calculator

Date	4-Oct-2004	Rate	6.25%
Item	House	Years	15
Price	$198,000.00	Monthly Pymt	$1,483.34
Down Pymt	$25,000.00	Total Interest	$94,001.48
Loan Amt	$173,000.00	Total Cost	$292,001.48

Interest Rate Schedule

Rate	Monthly Pymt	Total Interest	Total Cost
	$1,483.34	$94,001.48	$292,001.48
5.50%	1,413.55	81,439.79	279,439.79
5.75%	1,436.61	85,589.70	283,589.70
6.00%	1,459.87	89,777.02	287,777.02
6.25%	1,483.34	94,001.48	292,001.48
6.50%	1,507.02	98,262.83	296,262.83
6.75%	1,530.89	102,560.81	300,560.81
7.00%	1,554.97	106,895.12	304,895.12
7.25%	1,579.25	111,265.50	309,265.50
7.50%	1,603.73	115,671.65	313,671.65
7.75%	1,628.41	120,113.27	318,113.27
8.00%	1,653.28	124,590.06	322,590.06

Amortization Schedule

Year	Beginning Balance	Ending Balance	Paid On Principal	Interest Paid
1	$173,000.00	$165,808.72	$7,191.28	$10,608.82
2	165,808.72	158,154.88	7,653.84	10,146.26
3	158,154.88	150,008.74	8,146.15	9,653.95
4	150,008.74	141,338.62	8,670.12	9,129.98
5	141,338.62	132,110.82	9,227.80	8,572.30
6	132,110.82	122,289.47	9,821.35	7,978.75
7	122,289.47	111,836.40	10,453.07	7,347.03
8	111,836.40	100,710.96	11,125.43	6,674.66
9	100,710.96	88,869.92	11,841.04	5,959.06
10	88,869.92	76,267.24	12,602.68	5,197.42
11	76,267.24	62,853.94	13,413.31	4,386.79
12	62,853.94	48,577.86	14,276.08	3,524.02
13	48,577.86	33,383.52	15,194.34	2,605.76
14	33,383.52	17,211.86	16,171.67	1,628.43
15	17,211.86	0.00	17,211.86	588.24
		Subtotal	$173,000.00	$94,001.48
		Down Pymt		$25,000.00
		Total Cost		$292,001.48

e-Money Lenders / Sheet2 / Sheet3

FIGURE 31 Electronic spreadsheet software frequently is used by people who work with numbers. The user enters the data and the formulas to be used on the data, and the computer calculates the results.

WEB LINK

Database Software

For more information, visit scsite.com/ic6/weblink and then click Database Software.

DATABASE **Database software** (Figure 32) allows the user to enter, retrieve, and update data in an organized and efficient manner. These software packages have flexible inquiry and reporting capabilities that let users access the data in different ways and create custom reports that include some or all of the information in the database.

WEB LINK

Presentation Graphics Software

For more information, visit scsite.com/ic6/weblink and then click Presentation Graphics Software.

PRESENTATION GRAPHICS **Presentation graphics software** (Figure 33) allows the user to create slides for use in a presentation to a group. Using special projection devices, the slides are projected directly from the computer.

NETWORKS AND THE INTERNET

A **network** is a collection of computers and devices connected via communications media and devices such as cables, telephone lines, modems, or other means.

Computers are networked together so users can share resources, such as hardware devices, software programs, data, and information. Sharing resources saves time and money. For example, instead of purchasing one printer for every computer in a company, the firm can connect a single printer and all computers via a network (Figure 34); the network enables all of the computers to access the same printer.

Most business computers are networked together. These networks can be relatively small or quite extensive. A network that connects computers in a limited geographic area, such as a school computer laboratory, office, or group of buildings, is called a **local area network** (**LAN**). A network that covers a large geographical area, such as one that connects the district offices of a national corporation, is called a **wide area network** (**WAN**) (Figure 35).

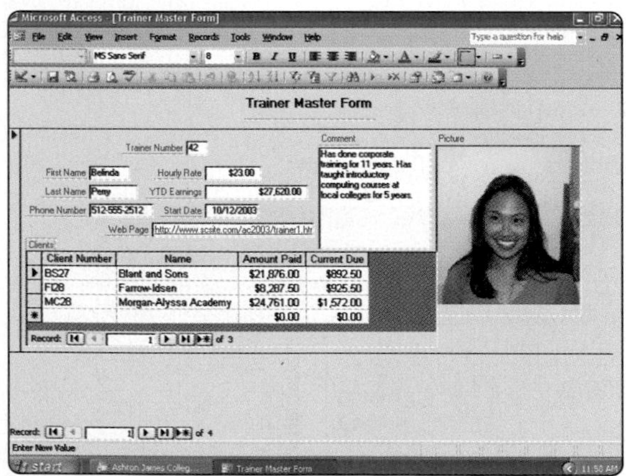

FIGURE 32 Database software allows the user to enter, retrieve, and update data in an organized and efficient manner.

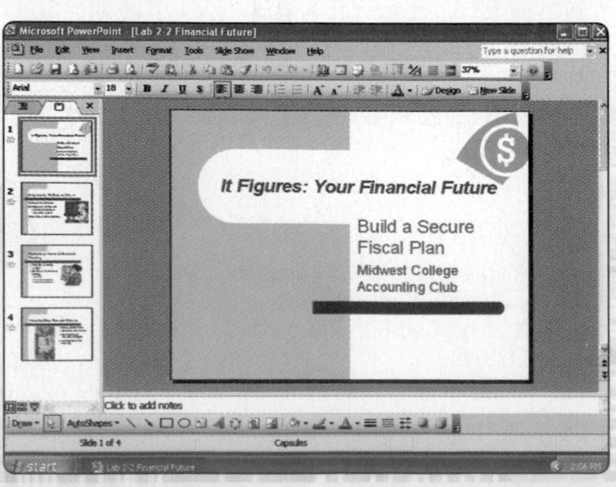

FIGURE 33 Presentation graphics software allows the user to produce professional-looking presentations.

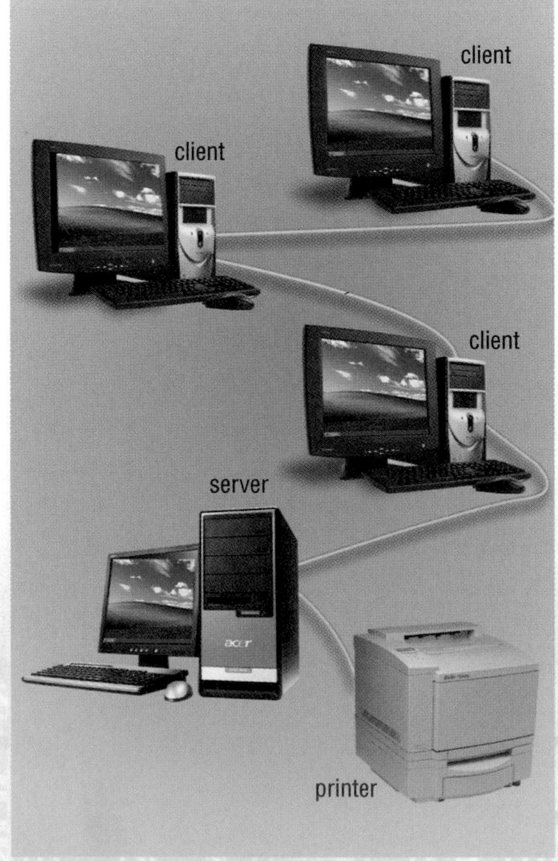

FIGURE 34 The local area network (LAN) enables two or more separate computers to share the same printer.

The Internet

The world's largest network is the **Internet**, which is a worldwide collection of networks that links together more than 200 million host computers by means of modems, telephone lines, cables, and other communications devices and media. With an abundance of resources and data accessible via the Internet, more than 1 billion users around the world are making use of the Internet for a variety of reasons. Some of these reasons include the following:

- Sending messages to other connected users (e-mail)
- Accessing a wealth of information, such as news, maps, airline schedules, and stock market data
- Shopping for goods and services
- Meeting or conversing with people around the world via chat rooms, online collaboration, and instant messaging
- Accessing sources of entertainment and leisure, such as online games, magazines, and vacation planning guides

Most users connect to the Internet in one of two ways: through an Internet service provider or through an online service provider. An **ISP** (**Internet service provider**) is an organization, such as a cable company or telephone company, that supplies connections to the Internet for a monthly fee. Like an ISP, an **online service provider** (**OSP**) provides access to the Internet, but it also provides a variety of other specialized content and services such as financial data, hardware and software guides, news, weather, legal information, and other similar commodities. For this reason, the fees for using an online service usually are slightly higher than fees for using an ISP. Two popular online services are America Online (AOL) and The Microsoft Network (MSN).

The World Wide Web

One of the more popular segments of the Internet is the **World Wide Web**, also called the **Web**, which contains billions of documents called Web pages. A **Web page** is a document that contains text, graphics, sound, and/or video, and has built-in connections, or hyperlinks, to other Web documents. Figure 36 on the next page shows the different types of Web pages found on the World Wide Web today. Web pages are stored on computers throughout the world. A **Web site** is a related collection of Web pages. Visitors to a Web site access and view Web pages using a software program called a **Web browser**. A Web page has a unique address, called a **Uniform Resource Locator** (**URL**).

FIGURE 35 A wide area network (WAN) can be quite large and complex connecting users in district offices around the world.

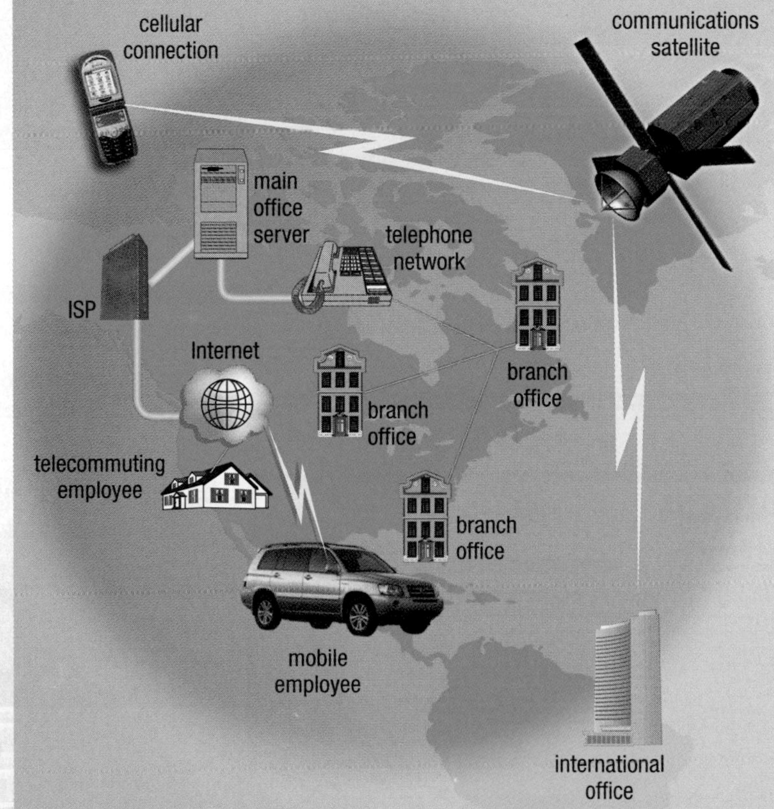

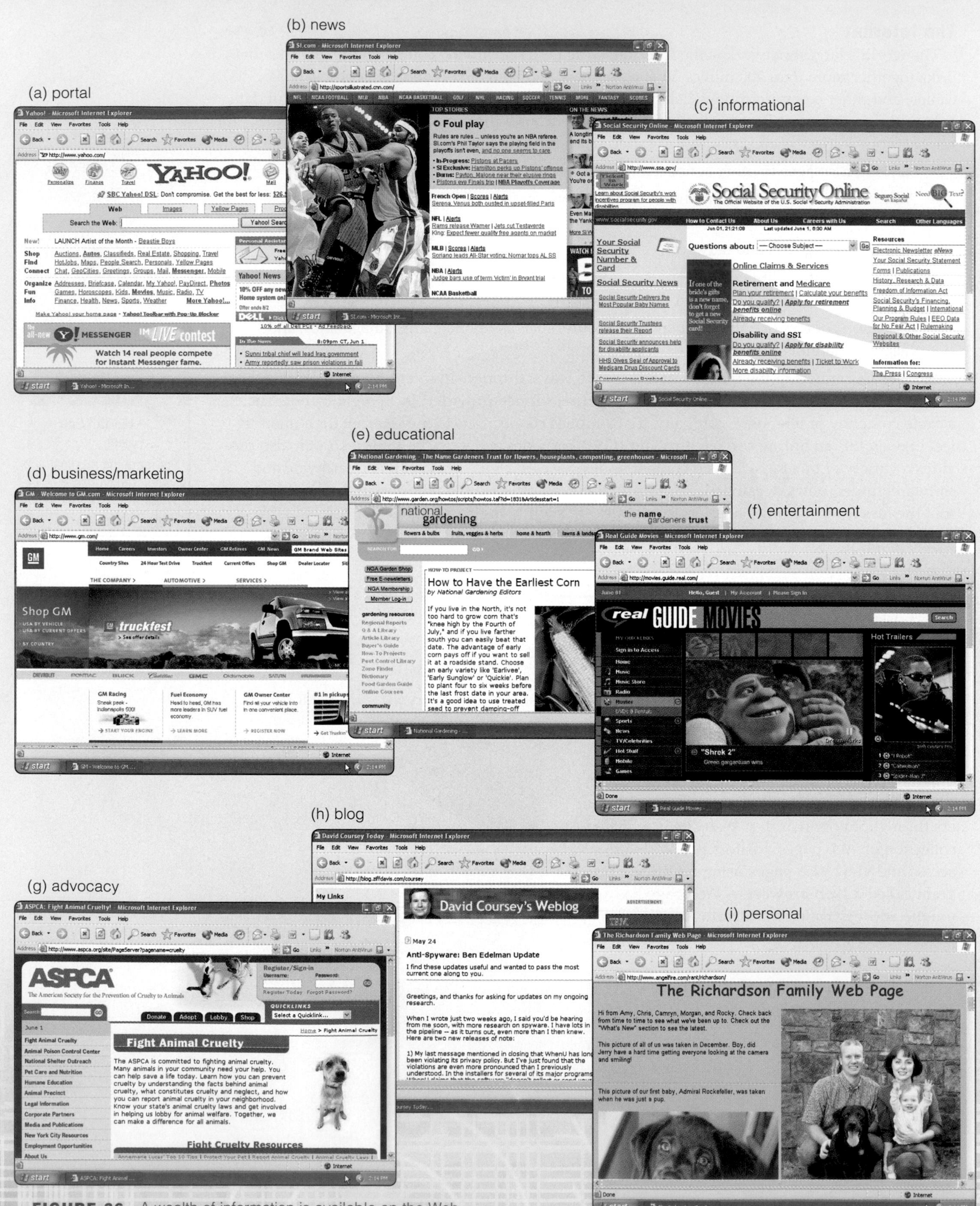

FIGURE 36 A wealth of information is available on the Web.

As shown in Figure 37, a URL consists of a protocol, a domain name, sometimes the path to a specific Web page or location in a Web page, and the Web page name. Most Web page URLs begin with **http://**, which stands for **hypertext transfer protocol**, the communications standard used to transfer pages on the Web. The domain name identifies the Web site, which is stored on a Web server. A **Web server** is a computer that delivers (serves) requested Web pages.

Electronic Commerce

When you conduct business activities online, you are participating in **electronic commerce**, also known as **e-commerce**. These commercial activities include shopping, investing, and any other venture that represents a business transaction. Today, three types of e-commerce exist: business to consumer, consumer to consumer, and business to business. **Business to consumer** (**B2C**) involves the sale of goods to the general public. **Consumer to consumer** (**C2C**) involves one consumer selling directly to another. **Business to business** (**B2B**) provides goods and services to other businesses.

WEB LINK

E-Commerce

For more information, visit scsite.com/ic6/weblink and then click E-Commerce.

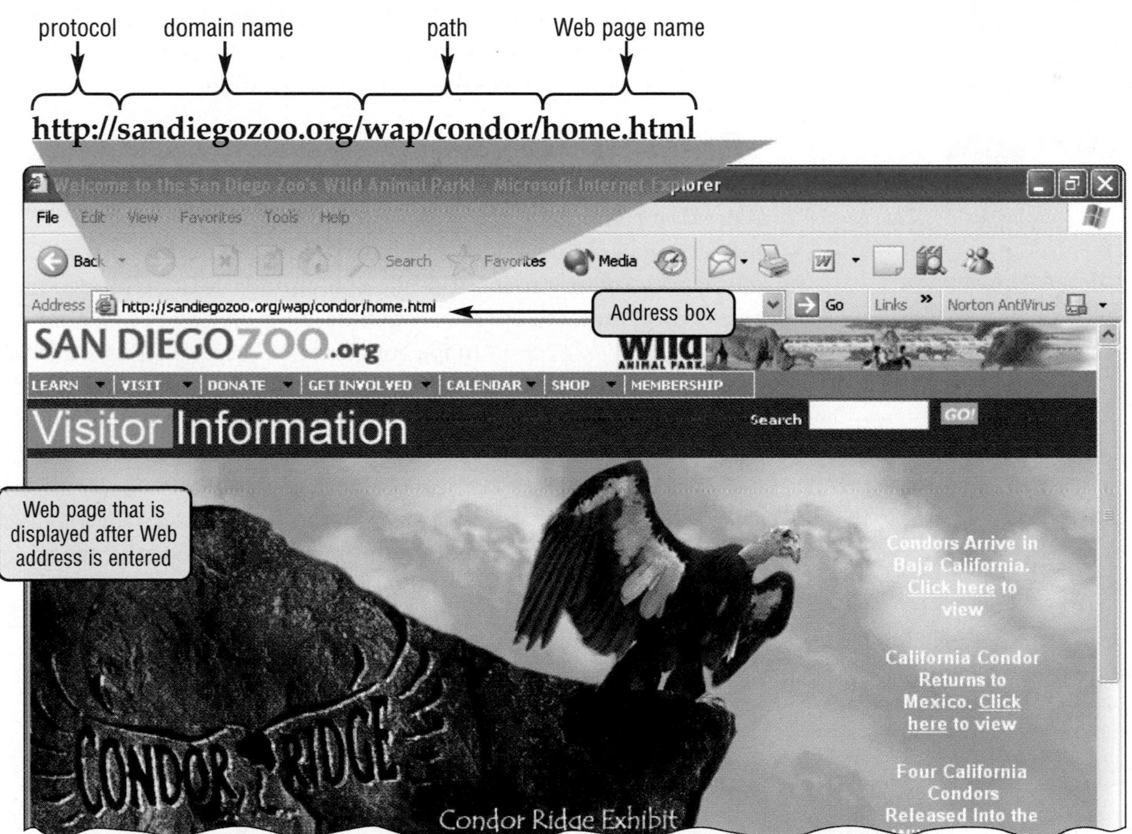

FIGURE 37 After entering the Web address http://www.sandiegozoo.org/wap/condor/home.html in the Address box, this Web page at the San Diego Zoo Web site is displayed. Notice the www portion of the domain name does not appear in the Address box after the Web page downloads.

How to Purchase a Personal Computer

(a) desktop computer

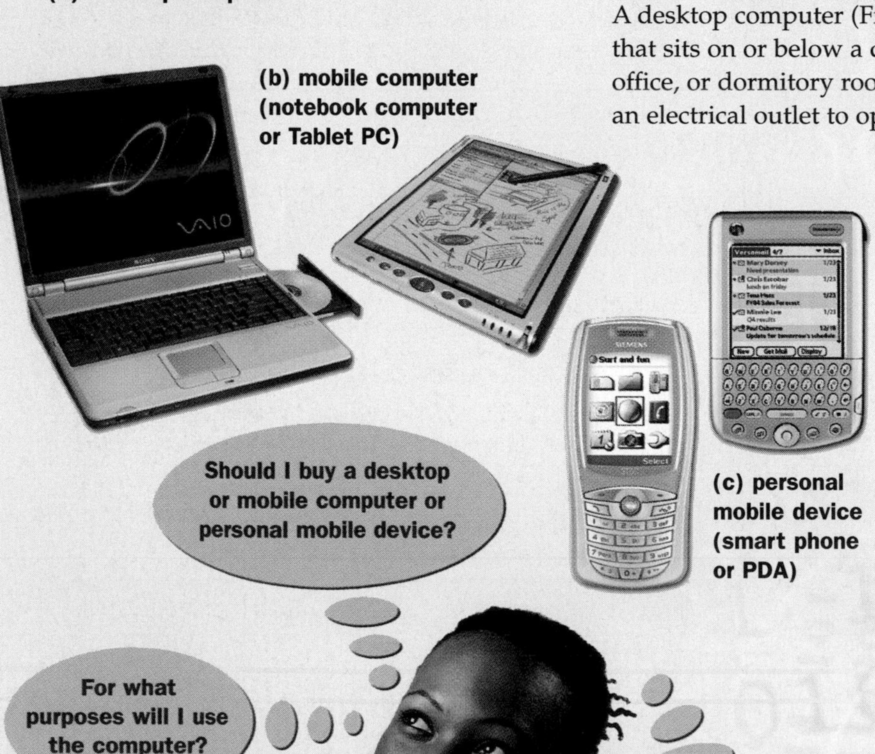

Should I buy a desktop or mobile computer or personal mobile device?
For what purposes will I use the computer?
Should the computer I buy be compatible with the computers at school or work?
Should I buy a Mac or PC?

(b) mobile computer (notebook computer or Tablet PC)

(c) personal mobile device (smart phone or PDA)

FIGURE 38

At some point, perhaps while you are taking this course, you may decide to buy a personal computer. The decision is an important one and will require an investment of both time and money. Like many buyers, you may have little computer experience and find yourself unsure of how to proceed. You can get started by talking to your friends, coworkers, and instructors about their computers. What type of computers did they buy? Why? For what purposes do they use their computers? You also should answer the following four questions to help narrow your choices to a specific computer type, before reading this Buyer's Guide.

1 Do you want a desktop computer, mobile computer, or personal mobile device?

A desktop computer (Figure 38a) is designed as a stationary device that sits on or below a desk or table in a location such as a home, office, or dormitory room. A desktop computer must be plugged into an electrical outlet to operate. A mobile computer, such as a notebook computer or Tablet PC (Figure 38b), is smaller than a desktop computer, more portable, and has a battery that allows you to operate it for a period without an electrical outlet. A personal mobile device (Figure 38c) runs on a battery for a longer period of time than a notebook computer or Tablet PC and can fit in your pocket.

Desktop computers are a good option if you work mostly in one place and have plenty of space in your work area. Desktop computers generally give you more performance for your money.

Increasingly, more desktop computer users are buying mobile computers to take advantage of their portability to work in the library, at school, while traveling, and at home. The past disadvantages of mobile computers, such as lower processor speeds, poor-quality monitors, weight, short battery life, and significantly higher prices, have all but disappeared when compared with desktop computers.

If you are thinking of using a mobile computer to take notes in class or in business meetings, then consider a Tablet PC with handwriting and drawing capabilities. Typically, note-taking involves writing text notes and drawing charts, schematics, and other illustrations. By allowing you to write and draw directly on the screen with a digital pen, a Tablet PC eliminates the distracting sound of the notebook keyboard tapping and allows you to capture drawings. Some notebook computers can convert to Tablet PCs.

A personal mobile device, such as a smart phone or a PDA, is ideal if you require a pocket-size computing device as you move from place to place. Personal mobile devices provide personal organizer functions, such as a calendar, appointment book, address book, and many other applications. The small size of the processor, screen, and keyboard, however, limit a personal mobile device's capabilities when compared with a desktop or notebook computer or a Tablet PC. For this reason, most people who purchase personal mobile devices also have a desktop or notebook computer to handle heavy-duty applications.

Drawbacks of mobile computers and personal mobile devices are that they tend to have a shorter useful lifetime than desktop computers and lack the high-end capabilities. Their portability makes them susceptible to vibrations, heat or cold, and accidental drops, which can cause components such as hard disks or display devices to fail. Also, because of their size and portability, they are easy to lose and are the prime targets of thieves.

2 For what purposes will you use the computer?

Having a general idea of the purposes for which you want to use your computer will help you decide on the type of computer to buy. At this point in your research, it is not necessary to know the exact application software titles or version numbers you might want to use. Knowing that you plan to use the computer primarily to create word processing, spreadsheet, database, and presentation documents, however, will point you in the direction of a desktop or notebook computer. If you want the portability of a smart phone or PDA, but you need more computing power, then a Tablet PC may be the best alternative. You also must consider that some application software runs only on a Mac, while others run only on a PC with the Windows operating system. Still other software may run only on a PC running the UNIX or Linux operating system.

3 Should the computer be compatible with the computers at school or work?

If you plan to bring work home, telecommute, or take distance education courses, then you should purchase a computer that is compatible with those at school or work.

Compatibility is primarily a software issue. If your computer runs the same operating system version, such as Microsoft Windows XP, and the same application software, such as Microsoft Office, then your computer will be able to read documents created at school or work and vice versa. Incompatible hardware can become an issue if you plan to connect directly to a school or office network using a cable or wireless technology. You usually can obtain the minimum system requirements from the Information Technology department at your school or workplace.

4 Should the computer be a Mac or PC?

If you ask a friend, coworker, or instructor, which is better — a Mac or a PC — you may be surprised by the strong opinion expressed in the response. No other topic in the computer industry causes more heated debate. The Mac has strengths, especially in the areas of graphics, movies, photos, and music. The PC, however, has become the industry standard with 95 percent of the market share. Figure 39 compares features of the Mac and PC in several different areas.

Area	Comparison
Cost and availability	A Mac is priced slightly higher than a PC. Mac peripherals also are more expensive. The PC offers more available models from a wide range of vendors. You can custom build, upgrade, and expand a PC for less money than a Mac.
Exterior design	The Mac has a more distinct and stylish appearance than most PCs.
Free software	Although free software for the Mac is available on the Internet, significantly more free software applications are available for the PC.
Market share	The PC dominates the personal computer market. While the Mac sells well in education, publishing, Web design, graphics, and music, the PC is the overwhelming favorite of businesses.
Operating system	Users claim that Mac OS X provides a better all-around user experience than Microsoft Windows XP. Both the Mac and PC supports other operating systems, such as Linux and UNIX.
Program control	Both have simple and intuitive graphical user interfaces. The Mac relies more on the mouse and less on keyboard shortcuts than the PC. The mouse on the Mac has one button, whereas the mouse on a PC has a minimum of two buttons.
Software availability	The basic application software most users require, such as Microsoft Office, is available for both the Mac and PC. More specialized software, however, often is available only for PCs. Many programs are released for PCs long before they are released for Macs.
Speed	The PC provides faster processors than the Mac.
Viruses	Dramatically fewer viruses attack Macs. Mac viruses also generally are less infectious than PC viruses.

FIGURE 39 Comparison of Mac and PC features.

Overall, the Mac and PC have more similarities than differences, and you should consider cost, compatibility, and other factors when choosing whether to purchase a Mac or PC.

After evaluating the answers to these four questions, you should have a general idea of how you plan to use your computer and the type of computer you want to buy. Once you have decided on the type of computer you want, you can follow the guidelines presented in this Buyer's Guide to help you purchase a specific computer, along with software, peripherals, and other accessories.

Many of the desktop computer guidelines presented also apply to the purchase of a notebook computer, Tablet PC, and personal mobile device. Later in this Buyer's Guide, sections on purchasing a notebook computer or Tablet PC or personal mobile device address additional considerations specific to those computer types.

HOW TO PURCHASE A DESKTOP COMPUTER

Once you have decided that a desktop computer is most suited to your computing needs, the next step is to determine specific software, hardware, peripheral devices, and services to purchase, as well as where to buy the computer.

Determine the specific software you want to use on your computer.

Before deciding to purchase software, be sure it contains the features necessary for the tasks you want to perform. Rely on the computer users in whom you have confidence to help you decide on the software to use. The minimum requirements of the software you select may determine the operating system (Microsoft Windows XP, Linux, UNIX, Mac OS X) you need. If you have decided to use a particular operating system that does not support software you want to use, you may be able to purchase similar software from other manufacturers.

Many Web sites and trade magazines, such as those listed in Figure 40, provide reviews of software products. These Web sites frequently have articles that rate computers and software on cost, performance, and support.

Your hardware requirements depend on the minimum requirements of the software you will run on your computer. Some software requires more memory and disk space than others, as well as additional input, output, and storage devices. For example, suppose you want to run software that can copy one CD's or DVD's contents directly to another CD or DVD, without first copying the data to your hard disk. To support that, you should consider a desktop computer or a high-end notebook computer, because the computer will need two CD or DVD drives: one that reads from a CD or DVD, and one that reads from and writes on a CD or DVD. If you plan to run software that allows your computer to work as an entertainment system, then you will need a CD or DVD drive, quality speakers, and an upgraded sound card.

Type of Computers	Web Site	Web Address
PC	CNET Shopper	shopper.cnet.com
	PC World Magazine	pcworld.com
	BYTE Magazine	byte.com
	PC Magazine	zdnet.com/reviews
	Yahoo! Computers	computers.yahoo.com
	MSN Shopping	eshop.msn.com
	Dave's Guide to Buying a Home Computer	css.msu.edu/PC-Guide
Mac	Macworld Magazine	macworld.com
	Apple	apple.com
	Switch to Mac Campaign	apple.com/switch

For an updated list of hardware and software reviews and their Web site addresses, visit scsite.com/ic6/buyers.

FIGURE 40 Hardware and software reviews.

2 Look for bundled software.

When you purchase a computer, it may come bundled with software. Some sellers even let you choose which software you want. Remember, however, that bundled software has value only if you would have purchased the software even if it had not come with the computer. At the very least, you probably will want word processing software and a browser to access the Internet. If you need additional applications, such as a spreadsheet, a database, or presentation graphics, consider purchasing Microsoft Works, Microsoft Office, OpenOffice.org, or Sun StarOffice, which include several programs at a reduced price.

3 Avoid buying the least powerful computer available.

Once you know the application software you want to use, you then can consider the following important criteria about the computer's components: (1) processor speed, (2) size and types of memory (RAM) and storage, (3) types of input/output devices, (4) types of ports and adapter cards, and (5) types of communications devices. The information in Figures 41 and 42 can help you determine what system components are best for you. Figure 41 outlines considerations for specific hardware components. Figure 42 (on page COM-29) provides a Base Components worksheet that lists

PC recommendations for each category of user discussed in this book: Home User, Small Office/Home Office User, Mobile User, Power User, and Large Business User. In the worksheet, the Home User category is divided into two groups: Application Home User and Game Home User. The Mobile User recommendations list criteria for a notebook computer, but do not include the PDA or Tablet PC options.

Computer technology changes rapidly, meaning a computer that seems powerful enough today may not serve your computing needs in a few years. In fact, studies show that many users regret not buying a more powerful computer. To avoid this, plan to buy a computer that will last you for two to three years. You can help delay obsolescence by purchasing the fastest processor, the most memory, and the largest hard disk you can afford. If you must buy a less powerful computer, be sure you can upgrade it with additional memory, components, and peripheral devices as your computer requirements grow.

CD/DVD Drives: Most computers come with a 32X to 48X speed CD-ROM drive that can read CDs. If you plan to write music, audio files, and documents on a CD, then you should consider upgrading to a CD-RW. An even better alternative is to upgrade to a DVD+RW combination drive. It allows you to read DVDs and CDs and to write data on (burn) a DVD or CD. A DVD has a capacity of at least 4.7 GB versus the 650 MB capacity of a CD.

Card Reader/Writer: A card reader/writer is useful for transferring data directly to and from a removable flash memory card, such as the ones used in your camera or music player. Make sure the card reader/writer can read from and write to the flash memory cards that you use.

Digital Camera: Consider an inexpensive point-and-shoot digital camera. They are small enough to carry around, usually operate automatically in terms of lighting and focus, and contain storage cards for storing photographs. A 2- to 4-megapixel camera with an 8 MB or 16 MB storage card is fine for creating images for use on the Web or to send via e-mail.

Digital Video Capture Device: A digital video capture device allows you to connect your computer to a camcorder or VCR and record, edit, manage, and then write video back to a VCR tape, a CD, or a DVD. The digital video capture device can be an external device or an adapter card. To create quality video (true 30 frames per second, full-sized TV), the digital video capture device should have a USB 2.0 or FireWire port. You will find that a standard USB port is too slow to maintain video quality. You also will need sufficient storage: an hour of data on a VCR tape takes up about 5 GB of disk storage.

Floppy Disk Drive: If you plan to use a floppy disk drive, then make sure the computer you purchase has a standard 3.5", 1.44 MB floppy disk drive. A floppy disk drive is useful for backing up and transferring files.

Hard Disk: It is recommended that you buy a computer with 40 to 60 GB if your primary interests are browsing the Web and using e-mail and Office suite-type applications; 60 to 80 GB if you also want to edit digital photographs; 80 to 100 GB if you plan to edit digital video or manipulate large audio files even occasionally; and 100 to 160 GB if you will edit digital video, movies, or photography often; store audio files and music; or consider yourself to be a power user.

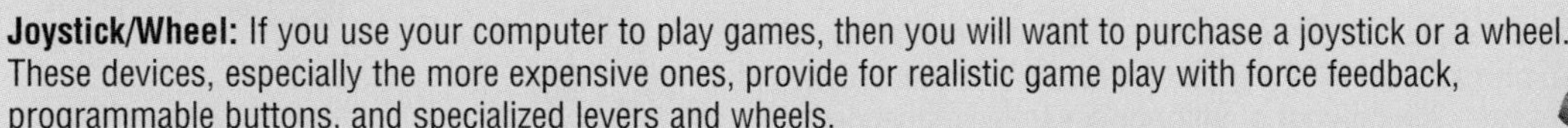

Joystick/Wheel: If you use your computer to play games, then you will want to purchase a joystick or a wheel. These devices, especially the more expensive ones, provide for realistic game play with force feedback, programmable buttons, and specialized levers and wheels.

Keyboard: The keyboard is one of the more important devices used to communicate with the computer. For this reason, make sure the keyboard you purchase has 101 to 105 keys, is comfortable and easy to use, and has a USB connection. A wireless keyboard should be considered, especially if you have a small desk area.

Microphone: If you plan to record audio or use speech recognition to enter text and commands, then purchase a close-talk headset with gain adjustment support.

Modem: Most computers come with a modem so that you can use your telephone line to dial out and access the Internet. Some modems also have fax capabilities. Your modem should be rated at 56 Kbps.

Monitor: The monitor is where you will view documents, read e-mail messages, and view pictures. A minimum of a 17" screen is recommended, but if you are planning to use your computer for graphic design or game playing, then you may want to purchase a 19" or 21" monitor. The LCD flat panel monitor should be considered, especially if space is an issue.

FIGURE 41 Hardware guidelines.

(continued next page)

(Figure 41 continued from previous page)

Mouse: As you work with your computer, you use the mouse constantly. For this reason, spend a few extra dollars, if necessary, and purchase a mouse with an optical sensor and USB connection. The optical sensor replaces the need for a mouse ball, which means you do not need a mouse pad. For a PC, make sure your mouse has a wheel, which acts as a third button in addition to the top two buttons on the left and right. An ergonomic design is also important because your hand is on the mouse most of the time when you are using your computer. A wireless mouse should be considered to eliminate the cord and allow you to work at short distances from your computer.

Network Card: If you plan to connect to a network or use broadband (cable or DSL) to connect to the Internet, then you will need to purchase a network card. Broadband connections require a 10/100 PCI Ethernet network card.

Printer: Your two basic printer choices are ink-jet and laser. Color ink-jet printers cost on average between $50 and $300. Laser printers cost from $200 to $2,000. In general, the cheaper the printer, the lower the resolution and speed, and the more often you are required to change the ink cartridge or toner. Laser printers print faster and with a higher quality than an ink-jet, and their toner on average costs less. If you want color, then go with a high-end ink-jet printer to ensure quality of print. Duty cycle (the number of pages you expect to print each month) also should be a determining factor. If your duty cycle is on the low end — hundreds of pages per month — then stay with a high-end ink-jet printer, rather than purchasing a laser printer. If you plan to print photographs taken with a digital camera, then you should purchase a photo printer. A photo printer is a dye-sublimation printer or an ink-jet printer with higher resolution and features that allow you to print quality photographs.

Processor: For a PC, a 2.8 GHz Intel or AMD processor is more than enough processor power for application home and small office/home office users. Game home, large business, and power users should upgrade to faster processors.

RAM: RAM plays a vital role in the speed of your computer. Make sure the computer you purchase has at least 512 MB of RAM. If you have extra money to invest in your computer, then consider increasing the RAM to 1 GB or more. The extra money for RAM will be well spent.

Scanner: The most popular scanner purchased with a computer today is the flatbed scanner. When evaluating a flatbed scanner, check the color depth and resolution. Do not buy anything less than a color depth of 48 bits and a resolution of 1200 x 2400 dpi. The higher the color depth, the more accurate the color. A higher resolution picks up the more subtle gradations of color.

Sound Card: Most sound cards today support the Sound Blaster and General MIDI standards and should be capable of recording and playing digital audio. If you plan to turn your computer into an entertainment system or are a game home user, then you will want to spend the extra money and upgrade from the standard sound card.

Speakers: Once you have a good sound card, quality speakers and a separate subwoofer that amplifies the bass frequencies of the speakers can turn your computer into a premium stereo system.

PC Video Camera: A PC video camera is a small camera used to capture and display live video (in some cases with sound), primarily on a Web page. You also can capture, edit, and share video and still photos. The camera sits on your monitor or desk. Recommended minimum specifications include 640 x 480 resolution, a video with a rate of 30 frames per second, and a USB 2.0 or FireWire connection.

USB Flash Drive: If you work on different computers and need access to the same data and information, then this portable miniature mobile storage device is ideal. USB flash drive capacity varies from 16 MB to 4 GB.

Video Graphics Card: Most standard video cards satisfy the monitor display needs of application home and small office users. If you are a game home user or a graphic designer, you will want to upgrade to a higher quality video card. The higher refresh rates will further enhance the display of games, graphics, and movies.

Wireless LAN Access Point: A Wireless LAN Access Point allows you to network several computers, so they can share files and access the Internet through a single cable modem or DSL connection. Each device that you connect requires a wireless card. A Wireless LAN Access Point can offer a range of operations up to several hundred feet, so be sure the device has a high-powered antenna.

Zip Drive: Consider purchasing a Zip disk drive to back up important files. The Zip drive, which has a capacity of up to 750 MB, is sufficient for most users. An alternative to purchasing a backup drive is to purchase a CD-RW or DVD+RW and burn backups of key files on a CD or DVD.

BASE COMPONENTS

	Application Home User	Game Home User	Small Office/Home Office User	Mobile User	Large Business User	Power User
HARDWARE						
Processor	Pentium® 4 at 2.66 GHz	Pentium® 4 at 3.0 GHz	Pentium® 4 at 3.0 GHz	Pentium® M at 2.2 GHz	Pentium® 4 at 3.0 GHz	Multiple Itanium® at 2.8
RAM	512 MB	1 GB	512 MB	512 MB	1 GB	2 GB
Cache	256 KB L2	512 KB L2	512 KB L2	512 KB L2	512 KB L2	2 MB L3
Hard Disk	60 GB	120 GB	80 GB	80 GB	160 GB	250 GB
Monitor/LCD Flat Panel	17" or 19"	21"	19" or 21"	15.4" Wide Display	19" or 21"	23"
Video Graphics Card	256 MB	512 MB	256 MB	32 MB	128 MB	256 MB
CD/DVD Bay 1	48x CD-ROM	48x CD-RW Drive	48x CD-ROM	24X CD-RW/DVD	48x CD-RW Drive	16x DVD-ROM
CD/DVD Bay 2	8x DVD+RW	12x DVD+RW	8x DVD+RW	4x DVD+RW/+R	12x DVD+RW	8x DVD+RW
Floppy Disk Drive	3.5"	3.5"	3.5"	3.5"	3.5"	3.5"
Printer	Color Ink-Jet	Color Ink-Jet	18 ppm Laser	Portable Ink-Jet	50 ppm Laser	10 ppm Laser
PC Video Camera	Yes	Yes	Yes	Yes	Yes	Yes
Fax/Modem	Yes	Yes	Yes	Yes	Yes	Yes
Microphone	Close-Talk Headset With Gain Adjustment	Close-Talk Headset With Gain Adjustment	Close-Talk Headset With Gain Adjustment	Close-Talk Headset With Gain Adjustment	Close-Talk Headset With Gain Adjustment	Close-Talk Headset With Gain Adjustment
Speakers	Stereo	Full-Dolby Surround	Stereo	Stereo	Stereo	Full-Dolby Surround
Pointing Device	IntelliMouse or Optical Mouse	Optical Mouse and Joystick	IntelliMouse or Optical Mouse	Touchpad or Pointing Stick and Optical Mouse	IntelliMouse or Optical Mouse	IntelliMouse or Optical Mouse and Joystick
Keyboard	Yes	Yes	Yes	Built-In	Yes	Yes
Backup Disk/Tape Drive	250 MB Zip®	External or Removable Hard Disk	External or Removable Hard Disk	External or Removable Hard Disk	Tape Drive	External or Removable Hard Disk
USB Flash Drive	128 MB	256 MB	256 MB	128 MB	4 GB	1 GB
Sound Card	Sound Blaster Compatible	Sound Blaster Audigy 2	Sound Blaster Compatible	Built-In	Sound Blaster Compatible	Sound Blaster Audigy 2
Network Card	Yes	Yes	Yes	Yes	Yes	Yes
TV-Out Connector	Yes	Yes	Yes	Yes	Yes	Yes
USB Port	6	8	6	2	8	8
FireWire Port	2	2	2	1	2	2
SOFTWARE						
Operating System	Windows XP Home Edition with Service Pack 2	Windows XP Home Edition with Service Pack 2	Windows XP Professional with Service Pack 2	Windows XP Professional with Service Pack 2	Windows XP Professional with Service Pack 2	Windows XP Professional with Service Pack 2
Application Suite	Office 2003 Standard Edition	Office 2003 Standard Edition	Office 2003 Small Business Edition	Office 2003 Small Business Edition	Office 2003 Professional	Office 2003 Professional
AntiVirus	Yes, 12-Mo. Subscription	Yes, 12-Mo. Subscription	Yes, 12-Mo. Subscription	Yes, 12-Mo. Subscription	Yes, 12-Mo. Subscription	Yes, 12-Mo. Subscription
Internet Access	Cable, DSL, or Dial-up	Cable or DSL	Cable, DSL, or Dial-up	Wireless or Dial-up	LAN/WAN (T1/T3)	Cable or DSL
OTHER						
Surge Protector	Yes	Yes	Yes	Portable	Yes	Yes
Warranty	3-Year Limited, 1-Year Next Business Day On-Site Service	3-Year Limited, 1-Year Next Business Day On-Site Service	3-year On-Site Service	3-Year Limited, 1-Year Next Business Day On-Site Service	3-year On-Site Service	3-year On-Site Service
Other		Wheel	Postage Printer	Docking Station Carrying Case Fingerprint Scanner Portable Data Projector		Graphics Tablet Plotter or Large-Format Printer

Optional Components for all Categories	
802.11g Wireless Card	Graphics Tablet
Bluetooth™ Enabled	iPod Music Player
Biometric Input Device	IrDa Port
Card Reader/Writer	Mouse Pad/Wrist Rest
Digital Camera	Multifunction Peripheral
Digital Video Capture	Photo Printer
Digital Video Camera	Portable Data Projector
Dual-Monitor Support with Second Monitor	Scanner
Ergonomic Keyboard	TV/FM Tuner
External Hard Disk	Uninterruptible Power Supply

FIGURE 42 Base desktop and mobile computer components and optional components. A copy of the Base Components worksheet is on the Data Disk. To obtain a copy of the Data Disk, see the inside cover of this book for instructions.

Consider upgrades to the mouse, keyboard, monitor, printer, microphone, and speakers.

You use these peripheral devices to interact with your computer, so you should make sure they are up to your standards. Review the peripheral devices listed in Figure 41 and then visit both local computer dealers and large retail stores to test the computers on display. Ask the salesperson what input and output devices would be best for you and whether you should upgrade beyond what comes standard. Consider purchasing a wireless keyboard and wireless mouse to eliminate bothersome wires on your desktop. A few extra dollars spent on these components when you initially purchase a computer can extend its usefulness by years.

Determine whether you want to use telephone lines or broadband (cable or DSL) to access the Internet.

If your computer has a modem, then you can access the Internet using a standard telephone line. Ordinarily, you call a local or toll-free 800 number to connect to an ISP (see Guideline 6 on the next page). Using a dial-up Internet connection is relatively inexpensive but slow.

DSL and cable connections provide much faster Internet connections, which are ideal if you want faster file download speeds for software, digital photos, and music. As you would expect, they also are more expensive. DSL, which is available through local telephone companies, also may require that you subscribe to an ISP. Cable is available through your local cable television provider and some online service providers (OSPs). If you get cable, then you would not use a separate Internet service provider or online service provider.

6 If you are using a dial-up or wireless connection to connect to the Internet, then select an ISP or OSP.

You can access the Internet via telephone lines in one of two ways: an ISP or an OSP. Both provide Internet access for a monthly fee that ranges from $6 to $25. Local ISPs offer Internet access to users in a limited geographic region, through local telephone numbers. National ISPs provide access for users nationwide (including mobile users), through local and toll-free telephone numbers and cable. Because of their size, national ISPs generally offer more services and have a larger technical support staff than local ISPs. OSPs furnish Internet access as well as members-only features for users nationwide. Figure 43 lists several national ISPs and OSPs. Before you choose an ISP or OSP, compare such features as the number of access hours, monthly fees, available services (e-mail, Web page hosting, chat), and reliability.

Company	Service	Web Address
America Online	OSP	aol.com
AT&T Worldnet	ISP	www.att.net
Comcast	OSP	comcast.net
CompuServe	OSP	compuserve.com
EarthLink	ISP	earthlink.net
Juno	OSP	juno.com
NetZero	OSP	netzero.com
MSN	OSP	msn.com
SBC Prodigy	ISP/OSP	prodigy.net

For an updated list of national ISPs and OSPs and their Web site addresses, visit scsite.com/ic6/buyers.

FIGURE 43 National ISPs and OSPs.

7 Use a worksheet to compare computers, services, and other considerations.

You can use a separate sheet of paper to take notes on each vendor's computer and then summarize the information on a worksheet, such as the one shown in Figure 44. You can use Figure 44 to compare prices for either a PC or a MAC. Most companies advertise a price for a base computer that includes components housed in the system unit (processor, RAM, sound card, video card), disk drives (floppy disk, hard disk, CD-ROM, CD-RW, DVD-ROM, and DVD+RW), a keyboard, mouse, monitor, printer, speakers, and modem. Be aware, however, that some advertisements list prices for computers with only some of these components. Monitors and printers, for example, often are not included in a base computer's price. Depending on how you plan to use the computer, you may want to invest in additional or more powerful components. When you are comparing the prices of computers, make sure you are comparing identical or similar configurations.

PC or MAC Cost Comparison Worksheet

Dealers list prices for computers with most of these components (instead of listing individual component costs). Some dealers do not supply a monitor. Some dealers offer significant discounts, but you must subscribe to an Internet service for a specified period to receive the dicounted price. To compare computers, enter overall system price at top and enter a 0 (zero) for components included in the system cost. For any additional components not covered in the system price, enter the cost in the appropriate cells.

Items to Purchase	Desired System (PC)	Desired System (Mac)	Local Dealer #1	Local Dealer #2	Online Dealer #1	Online Dealer #2	Comments
OVERALL SYSTEM							
Overall System Price	< $1,500	< $1,500					
HARDWARE							
Processor	Pentium(R) 4 at 2.8 GHz	PowerPC G4 at 800 MHz					
RAM	512 MB	512 MB					
Cache	256 KB L2	256 KB L2					
Hard Disk	80 GB	80 GB					
Monitor/LCD Flat Panel	17 Inch	17 Inch					
Video Graphics Card	128 MB	128 MB					
Floppy Disk Drive	3.5 Inch	NA					
USB Flash Drive	128 MB	128 MB					
CD/DVD Bay 1	48x CD-ROM	4x DVD+RW					
CD/DVD Bay 2	8x DVD+RW	NA					
Speakers	Stereo	Stereo					
Sound Card	Sound Blaster Compatible	Sound Blaster Compatible					
USB Ports	6	6					
FireWire Port	2	2					
Network Card	Yes	Yes					
Fax/Modem	56 Kbps	56 Kbps					
Keyboard	Standard	Apple Pro Keyboard					
Pointing Device	IntelliMouse	Intellimouse or Apple Pro Mouse					
Microphone	Close-Talk Headset with Gain Adjustment	Close-Talk Headset with Gain Adjustment					
Printer	Color Ink-Jet	Color Ink-Jet					
Backup	250 MB Zip®	250 MB Zip®					
SOFTWARE							
Operating System	Windows XP Home Edition	Mac OS X					
Application Software	Office 2003 Small Business Edition	Office 2004 for Mac					
Antivirus	Yes - 12 Mo. Subscription	Yes - 12 Mo. Subscription					
OTHER							
Card Reader							
Digital Camera	4-Megapixel	4-Megapixel					
Internet Connection	1-Year Subscription	1-Year Subscription					
Joystick	Yes	Yes					
PC Video Camera	With Microphone	With Microphone					
Scanner							
Surge Protector							
Warranty	3-Year On-Site Service	3-Year On-Site Service					
Wireless Card	Internal	Internal					
Wireless LAN Access Point	LinkSys	Apple AirPort					
Total Cost			$ -	$ -	$ -	$ -	

FIGURE 44 A worksheet is an effective tool for summarizing and comparing components and prices of different computer vendors. A copy of the Computer Cost Comparison worksheet for the PC and Mac is on the Data Disk. To obtain a copy of the Data Disk, see the inside cover of this book for instructions.

8 If you are buying a new computer, you have several purchasing options: buying from your school bookstore, a local computer dealer, a local large retail store, or ordering by mail via telephone or the Web.

Each purchasing option has certain advantages. Many college bookstores, for example, sign exclusive pricing agreements with computer manufacturers and, thus, can offer student discounts. Local dealers and local large retail stores, however, more easily can provide hands-on support. Mail-order companies that sell computers by telephone or online via the Web (Figure 45) often provide the lowest prices, but extend less personal service. Some major mail-order companies, however, have started to provide next-business-day, on-site services. A credit card usually is required to buy from a mail-order company. Figure 46 lists some of the more popular mail-order companies and their Web site addresses.

9 If you are buying a used computer, stay with name brands such as Dell, Gateway, Hewlett-Packard, and Apple.

Although brand-name equipment can cost more, most brand-name computers have longer, more comprehensive warranties, are better supported, and have more authorized centers for repair services. As with new computers, you can purchase a used computer from local computer dealers, local large retail stores, or mail order via the telephone or the Web. Classified ads and used computer sellers offer additional outlets for purchasing used computers. Figure 47 lists several major used computer brokers and their Web site addresses.

10 If you have a computer and are upgrading to a new one, then consider selling or trading in the old one.

If you are a replacement buyer, your older computer still may have value. If you cannot sell the computer through the classified ads, via a Web site, or to a friend, then ask if the computer dealer will buy your old computer. An increasing number of companies are taking trade-ins, but do not expect too much money for your old computer. Other companies offer free disposal of your old PC.

11 Be aware of hidden costs.

Before purchasing, be sure to consider any additional costs associated with buying a computer, such as an additional telephone line, a cable or DSL modem, an uninterruptible power supply (UPS), computer furniture, a USB flash drive, paper, and computer training classes you may want to take. Depending on where you buy your computer, the seller may be willing to include some or all of these in the computer purchase price.

FIGURE 45 Mail-order companies, such as Dell, sell computers online.

Type of Computer	Company	Web Address
PC	CNET Shopper	shopper.cnet.com
	Hewlett-Packard	hp.com
	CompUSA	compusa.com
	Dartek	dartek.com
	Dell	dell.com
	Gateway	gateway.com
Macintosh	Apple Computer	store.apple.com
	ClubMac	clubmac.com
	MacConnection	macconnection.com
	PC & MacExchange	macx.com

For an updated list of new mail-order computer companies and their Web site addresses, visit scsite.com/ic6/buyers.

FIGURE 46 Computer mail-order companies.

Company	Web Address
Amazon.com	amazon.com
Off-Lease Computers	off-leasecomputers.com
American Computer Exchange	www.amcoex.com
U.S. Computer Exchange	usce.org
eBay	ebay.com

For an updated list of used computer mail-order companies and their Web site addresses, visit scsite.com/ic6/buyers.

FIGURE 47 Used computer mail-order companies.

12 Consider more than just price.

The lowest-cost computer may not be the best long-term buy. Consider such intangibles as the vendor's time in business, the vendor's regard for quality, and the vendor's reputation for support. If you need to upgrade your computer often, you may want to consider a leasing arrangement, in which you pay monthly lease fees, but can upgrade or add on to your computer as your equipment needs change. No matter what type of buyer you are, insist on a 30-day, no-questions-asked return policy on your computer.

13 Avoid restocking fees.

Some companies charge a restocking fee of 10 to 20 percent as part of their money-back return policy. In some cases, no restocking fee for hardware is applied, but it is applied for software. Ask about the existence and terms of any restocking policies before you buy.

14 Use a credit card to purchase your new computer.

Many credit cards offer purchase protection and extended warranty benefits that cover you in case of loss of or damage to purchased goods. Paying by credit card also gives you time to install and use the computer before you have to pay for it. Finally, if you are dissatisfied with the computer and are unable to reach an agreement with the seller, paying by credit card gives you certain rights regarding withholding payment until the dispute is resolved. Check your credit card terms for specific details.

15 Consider purchasing an extended warranty or service plan.

If you use your computer for business or require fast resolution to major computer problems, consider purchasing an extended warranty or a service plan through a local dealer or third-party company. Most extended warranties cover the repair and replacement of computer components beyond the standard warranty. Most service plans ensure that your technical support calls receive priority response from technicians. You also can purchase an on-site service plan that states that a technician will come to your home, work, or school within 24 hours. If your computer includes a warranty and service agreement for a year or less, think about extending the service for two or three years when you buy the computer.

CENTURY COMPUTERS
Performance Guarantee
(See reverse for terms & conditions of this contract)

Invoice #: 1984409
Invoice Date: 10/12/07

Effective Date: 10/12/07
Expiration Date: 10/12/10

Customer Name: Leon, Richard
Date: 10/12/07
Address: 1123 Roxbury
Sycamore, IL 60178
Day phone: (815) 555-0303
Evening Phone: (728) 555-0203

System & Serial Numbers
IMB computer
S/N: US759290C

John Smith
Print Name of Century's Authorized Signature

10/12/07
Date

HOW TO PURCHASE A NOTEBOOK COMPUTER

If you need computing capability when you travel or to use in lecture or meetings, you may find a notebook computer to be an appropriate choice. The guidelines mentioned in the previous section also apply to the purchase of a notebook computer. The following are additional considerations unique to notebook computers.

1 Purchase a notebook computer with a sufficiently large active-matrix screen.

Active-matrix screens display high-quality color that is viewable from all angles. Less expensive, passive-matrix screens sometimes are difficult to see in low-light conditions and cannot be viewed from an angle. Notebook computers typically come with a 12.1-inch, 13.3-inch, 14.1-inch, or 15.7-inch display. For most users, a 14.1-inch display is satisfactory. If you intend to use your notebook computer as a desktop computer replacement, however, you may opt for a 15.7-inch display. Notebook computers with these larger displays weigh seven to ten pounds, however, so if you travel a lot and portability is essential, you might want a lighter computer with a smaller display. The lightest notebook computers, which weigh less than 3 pounds, are equipped with a 12.1-inch display. Regardless of size, the resolution of the display should be at least 1024 x 768 pixels. To compare the monitor size on various notebook computers, visit the company Web sites in Figure 48.

Type of Notebook	Company	Web Address
PC	Acer	global.acer.com
	Dell	dell.com
	Fujitsu	fujitsu.com
	Gateway	gateway.com
	Hewlett-Packard	hp.com
	IBM	ibm.com
	NEC	nec.com
	Sony	sony.com
	Toshiba	toshiba.com
Mac	Apple	apple.com

For an updated list of companies and their Web site addresses, visit scsite.com/ic6/buyers.

FIGURE 48 Companies that sell notebook computers.

2 Experiment with different keyboards and pointing devices.

Notebook computer keyboards are far less standardized than those for desktop computers. Some notebook computers, for example, have wide wrist rests, while others have none. Notebook computers also use a range of pointing devices, including pointing sticks, touchpads, and trackballs. Before you purchase a notebook computer, try various types of keyboard and pointing devices to determine which is easiest for you to use. Regardless of the pointing device you select, you also may want to purchase a regular mouse to use when you are working at a desk or other large surface.

3 Make sure the notebook computer you purchase has a CD and/or DVD drive.

Loading and installing software, especially large Office suites, is much faster if done from a CD-ROM, CD-RW, DVD-ROM, or DVD+RW. Today, most notebook computers come with an internal or external CD-ROM drive. Some notebook computers even come with a CD-ROM drive and a CD-RW drive or a DVD-ROM drive and a CD-RW or DVD+RW drive. Although DVD drives are slightly more expensive, they allow you to play CDs and DVD movies using your notebook computer and a headset.

4 If necessary, upgrade the processor, memory, and disk storage at the time of purchase.

As with a desktop computer, upgrading your notebook computer's memory and disk storage usually is less expensive at the time of initial purchase. Some disk storage is custom designed for notebook computer manufacturers, meaning an upgrade might not be available in the future. If you are purchasing a lightweight notebook computer, then it should include at least a 2.4 GHz processor, 512 MB RAM, and 80 GB of storage.

5 The availability of built-in ports on a notebook computer is important.

A notebook computer does not have a lot of room to add adapter cards. If you know the purpose for which you plan to use your notebook computer, then you can determine the ports you will need. Most notebooks come with common ports, such as a mouse port, IrDA port, serial port, parallel port, video port, and USB port. If you plan to connect your notebook computer to a TV, however, then you will need a PCtoTV port. If you want to connect to networks at school or in various offices, make sure the notebook computer you purchase has a built-in network card. If your notebook computer does not come with a built-in network wireless card, then you will have to purchase an external network card that slides into an expansion slot in your notebook computer, as well as a network cable. If you expect to connect an iPod portable digital music player to your notebook computer, then you will need a FireWire port.

6 If you plan to use your notebook computer for note-taking at school or in meetings, consider a notebook computer that converts to a Tablet PC.

Some computer manufacturers have developed convertible notebook computers that allow the screen to rotate 180 degrees on a central hinge and then fold down to cover the keyboard and become a Tablet PC (Figure 49). You then can use a stylus to enter text or drawings into the computer by writing on the screen.

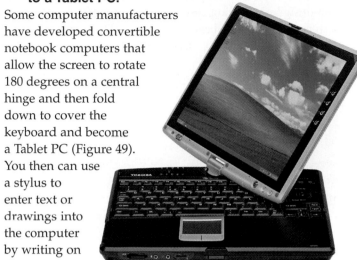

FIGURE 49 The Toshiba Protégé M200 notebook computer converts to a Tablet PC.

7 Consider purchasing a notebook computer with a built-in wireless card to connect to your home network.

Many users today are setting up wireless home networks. With a wireless home network, the desktop computer functions as the server, and your notebook computer can access the desktop computer from any location in the house to share files and hardware, such as a printer, and browse the Web. If your notebook computer does not come with a built-in wireless card, you can purchase an external one that slides into your notebook computer. Most home wireless networks allow connections from distances of 150 to 800 feet.

8 If you are going to use your notebook computer for long periods without access to an electrical outlet, purchase a second battery.

The trend among notebook computer users today is power and size over battery life, and notebook computer manufacturers have picked up on this. Many notebook computer users today are willing to give up longer battery life for a larger screen, faster processor, and more storage. In addition, some manufacturers typically sell the notebook with the lowest capacity battery. For this reason, you need to be careful in choosing a notebook computer if you plan to use it without access to electrical outlets for long periods, such as an airplane flight. You also might want to purchase a second battery as a backup. If you anticipate running your notebook computer on batteries frequently, choose a computer that uses lithium-ion batteries, which last longer than nickel cadmium or nickel hydride batteries.

9 Purchase a well-padded and well-designed carrying case.

An amply padded carrying case will protect your notebook computer from the bumps it will receive while traveling. A well-designed carrying case will have room for accessories such as spare floppy disks, CDs and DVDs, a user manual, pens, and paperwork (Figure 50).

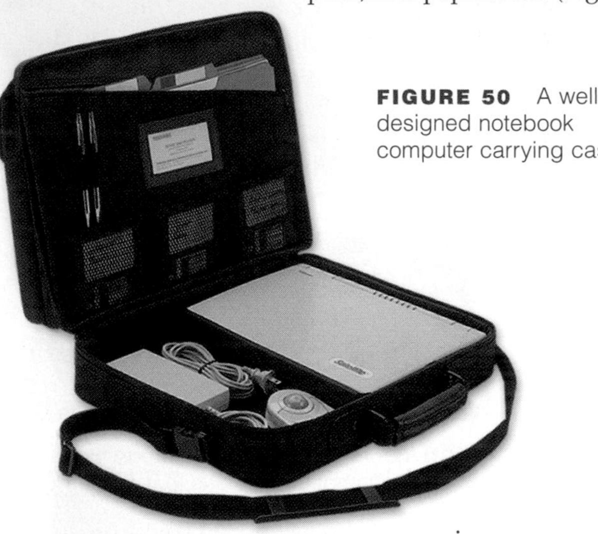

FIGURE 50 A well-designed notebook computer carrying case.

10 If you travel overseas, obtain a set of electrical and telephone adapters.

Different countries use different outlets for electrical and telephone connections. Several manufacturers sell sets of adapters that will work in most countries.

FIGURE 51 A notebook computer connected to a video projector projects the image displayed on the screen.

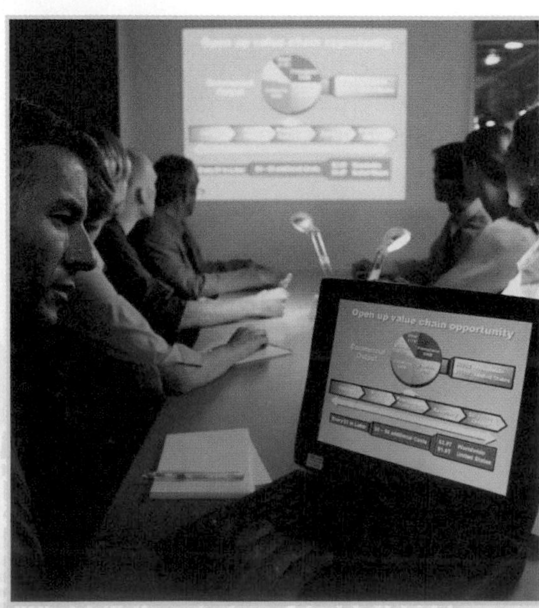

11 If you plan to connect your notebook computer to a video projector, make sure the notebook computer is compatible with the video projector.

You should check, for example, to be sure that your notebook computer will allow you to display an image on the computer screen and projection device at the same time (Figure 51). Also, ensure that your notebook computer has the ports required to connect to the video projector.

12 For improved security, consider a fingerprint scanner.

More than a quarter of a million notebook computers are stolen or lost each year. If you have critical information stored on your notebook computer, then consider purchasing one with a fingerprint scanner (Figure 52) to protect the data if your computer is stolen or lost. Fingerprint security offers a level of protection that extends well beyond the standard password protection.

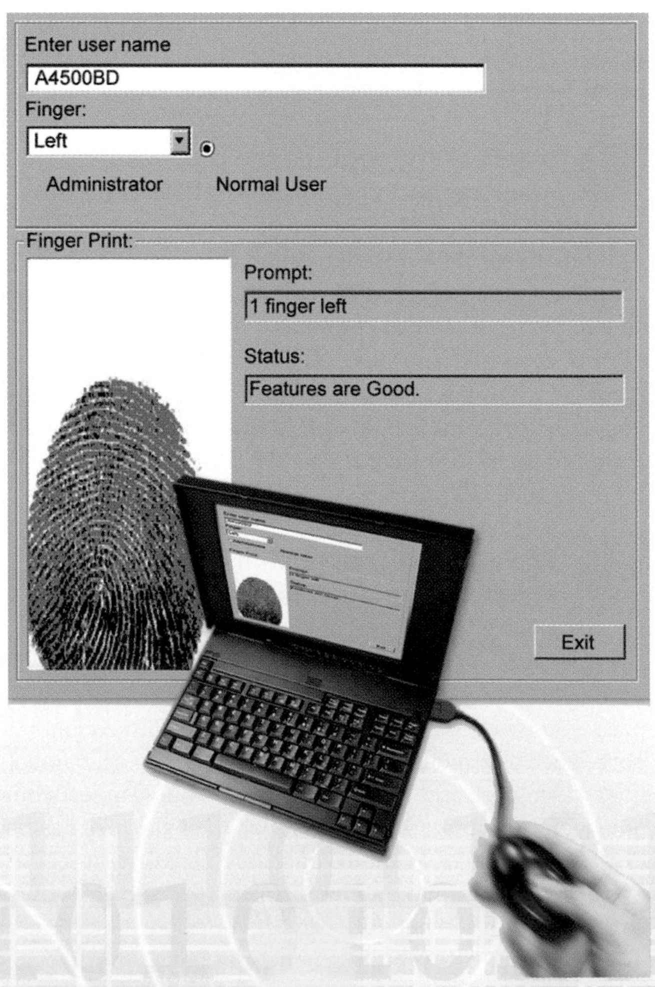

FIGURE 52 Fingerprint scanner technology offers greater security than passwords.

HOW TO PURCHASE A TABLET PC

The Tablet PC (Figure 53) combines the mobility features of a traditional notebook computer with the simplicity of pencil and paper, because you can create and save Office-type documents by writing and drawing directly on the screen with a digital pen. Tablet PCs use the Windows XP Tablet PC Edition operating system, which expands on Windows XP Professional by including digital pen and speech capabilities. A notebook computer and a Tablet PC have many similarities. For this reason, if you are considering purchasing a Tablet PC, review the guidelines for purchasing a notebook computer, as well as the guidelines below.

FIGURE 53 The lightweight Tablet PC, with its handwriting capabilities, is the latest addition to the family of mobile computers.

Make sure the Tablet PC fits your mobile computing needs.

The Tablet PC is not for every mobile user. If you find yourself in need of a computer in class or you are spending more time in meetings than in your office, then the Tablet PC may be the answer. Before you invest money in a Tablet PC, however, determine the programs you plan to use on it. You should not buy a Tablet PC simply because it is a new and interesting type of computer. For additional information on the Tablet PC, visit the Web sites listed in Figure 54. You may have to use the search capabilities on the home page of the companies listed to locate information about the Tablet PC.

Company	Web Address
Fujitsu	fujitsu.com
Hewlett-Packard	hp.com
Microsoft	microsoft.com/windowsxp/tabletpc
ViewSonic	viewsonic.com

For an updated list of companies and their Web site addresses, visit scsite.com/ic6/buyers.

FIGURE 54 Companies involved with Tablet PCs and their Web sites.

Decide whether you want a convertible or pure Tablet PC.

Convertible Tablet PCs have an attached keyboard and look like a notebook computer. You rotate the screen and lay it flat against the computer for note-taking. The pure Tablet PCs are slim and lightweight, weighing less than four pounds. They have the capability of easily docking at a desktop to gain access to a large monitor, keyboard, and mouse. If you spend a lot of time attending lectures or meetings, then the pure Tablet PC is ideal. Acceptable specifications for a Tablet PC are shown in Figure 55.

TABLET PC SPECIFICATIONS

Dimensions	12" × 9" × 1.2"
Weight	Less than 4 Pounds
Processor	Pentium III processor-M at 1.33 GHz
RAM	512 MB
Hard Disk	40 GB
Display	12.1" XGA TFT
Digitizer	Electromagnetic Digitizer
Battery	4-Cell (3-Hour)
USB	2
FireWire	1
Docking Station	Grab and Go with CD-ROM, Keyboard, and Mouse
Bluetooth Port	Yes
Wireless	802.11b/g Card
Network Card	10/100 Ethernet
Modem	56 Kbps
Speakers	Internal
Microphone	Internal
Operating System	Windows XP Tablet PC Edition
Application Software	Office Small Business Edition
Antivirus Software	Yes – 12 Month Subscription
Warranty	1-Year Limited Warranty Parts and Labor

FIGURE 55 Tablet PC specifications.

Be sure the weight and dimensions are conducive to portability.

The weight and dimensions of the Tablet PC are important because you carry it around like a notepad. The Tablet PC you buy should weigh four pounds or less. Its dimensions should be approximately 12 inches by 9 inches by 1.5 inches.

4 Port availability, battery life, and durability are even more important with a Tablet PC than they are with a notebook computer.

Make sure the Tablet PC you purchase has the ports required for the applications you plan to run. As with any mobile computer, battery life is important especially if you plan to use your Tablet PC for long periods without access to an electrical outlet. A Tablet PC must be durable because if you use it the way it was designed to be used, then you will be handling it much like you handle a pad of paper.

5 Experiment with different models of the Tablet PC to find the digital pen that works best for you.

The key to making use of the Tablet PC is to be comfortable with its handwriting capabilities and on-screen keyboard. Not only is the digital pen used to write on the screen (Figure 56), you also use it to make gestures to complete tasks, in a manner similar to the way you use a mouse. Figure 57 compares the standard point-and-click of a mouse unit with the gestures made with a digital pen. Other gestures with the digital pen replicate some of the commonly used keys on a keyboard.

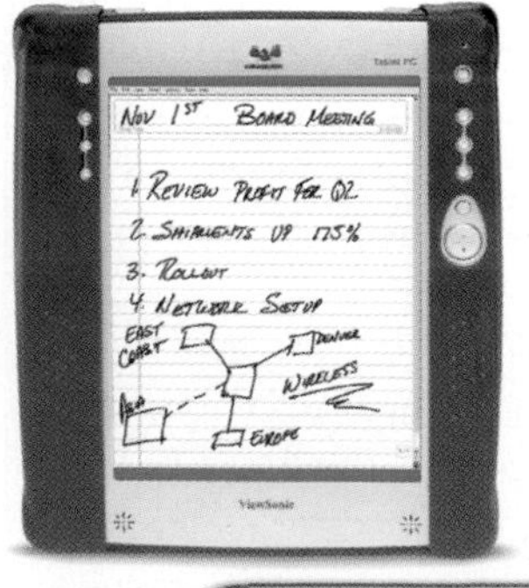

FIGURE 56 A Tablet PC lets you handwrite notes and draw on the screen using a digital pen.

Mouse Unit	Digital Pen
Point	Point
Click	Tap
Double-click	Double-tap
Right-click	Tap and hold
Click and drag	Drag

FIGURE 57 Standard point-and-click of a mouse unit compared with the gestures made with a digital pen.

6 Check out the comfort level of handwriting in different positions.

You should be able to handwrite on a Tablet PC with your hand resting on the screen. You also should be able to handwrite holding the Tablet PC in one hand, as well as with it sitting in your lap.

7 Make sure the LCD display device has a resolution high enough to take advantage of Microsoft's ClearType technologies.

Tablet PCs use a digitizer under a standard 10.4-inch motion-sensitive LCD display to make the digital ink on the screen look like real ink on paper. To ensure you get the maximum benefits from the new ClearType technology, make sure the LCD display has a resolution of 800 × 600 in landscape mode and a 600 × 800 in portrait mode.

8 Test the built-in Tablet PC microphone and speakers.

With many application software packages recognizing human speech, such as Microsoft Office, it is important that the Tablet PC's built-in microphone operates at an acceptable level. If the microphone is not to your liking, you may want to purchase a close-talk headset with your Tablet PC. Increasingly more users are sending information as audio files, rather than relying solely on text. For this reason, you also should check the speakers on the Tablet PC to make sure they meet your standards.

9 Consider a Tablet PC with a built-in PC video camera.

A PC video camera adds streaming video and still photography capabilities to your Tablet PC, while still allowing you to take notes in lectures or meetings.

10 Review the docking capabilities of the Tablet PC.

The Microsoft Windows XP Tablet PC Edition operating system supports a grab-and-go form of docking, so you can pick up and take a docked Tablet PC with you, just as you would pick up a notepad on your way to a meeting (Figure 58).

FIGURE 58 A Tablet PC docked to create a desktop computer with the Tablet PC as the monitor.

11 Wireless access to the Internet and your e-mail is essential with a Tablet PC.

Make sure the Tablet PC has wireless networking, so you can access the Internet and your e-mail anytime and anywhere. Your Tablet PC also should include standard network connections, such as dial-up and Ethernet connections.

12 Review available accessories to purchase with your Tablet PC.

Tablet PC accessories include docking stations, mouse units, keyboards, security cables, additional memory and storage, protective handgrips, screen protectors, and various types of digital pens.

HOW TO PURCHASE A PERSONAL MOBILE DEVICE

Whether you choose a PDA, smart phone, or smart pager depends on where, when, and how you will use the device. If you need to stay organized when you are on the go, then a PDA may be the right choice. PDAs typically are categorized by the operating system they run. If you need to stay organized and in touch when on the go, then a smart phone or smart pager may be the right choice. Just as with PDAs, smart phones, and smart pagers are categorized by the operating system they run. The six primary operating systems for these devices are the Palm OS, Windows Mobile for Pocket PC, Windows Mobile for Smartphone, Symbian OS, Blackberry, and Embedded Linux.

This section lists guidelines you should consider when purchasing a PDA, smart phone, or smart pager. You also should visit the Web sites listed in Figure 59 on the next page to gather more information about the type of personal mobile device that best suits your computing needs.

1 Determine the programs you plan to run on your device.

All PDAs and most smart phones and smart pagers can handle basic organizer-type software such as a calendar, address book, and notepad. The availability of other software depends on the operating system you choose. The depth and breadth of software for the Palm OS is significant, with more than 20,000 basic programs and over 600 wireless programs. Devices that run Windows-based operating systems, such as Windows Mobile or Windows Smartphone, may have fewer programs available, but the operating system and application software are similar to those with which you are familiar, such as Word and Excel. Some Symbian-based smart phones also include the capability to read and/or edit Microsoft Office documents.

2 Consider how much you want to pay.

The price of a personal mobile device can range from $100 to $800, depending on its capabilities. Some Palm OS devices are at the lower end of the cost spectrum, and Windows-based devices often are at the higher end. For the latest prices, capabilities, and accessories, visit the Web sites listed in Figure 59.

3 Determine whether you need wireless access to the Internet and e-mail or mobile telephone capabilities with your device.

Smart pagers give you access to e-mail and other data and Internet services. Smart phones typically include these features, but also include the ability to make and receive phone calls on cellular networks. Some PDAs and smart phones include wireless networking capability to allow you to connect to the Internet wirelessly. These wireless features and services allow personal mobile device users to access real-time information from anywhere to help make decisions while on the go.

4 For wireless devices, determine how and where you will use the service.

When purchasing a wireless device, you must subscribe to a wireless service. Determine if the wireless network (carrier) you choose has service in the area where you plan to use the device. Some networks have high-speed data networks only in certain areas, such as large cities or business districts. Also, a few carriers allow you to use your device in other countries.

When purchasing a smart phone, determine if you plan to use the device more as a phone, PDA, or wireless data device. Some smart phones, such as those based on the Pocket PC Phone edition or the Palm OS, are geared more for use as a PDA and have a PDA form factor. Other smart phones, such as those based on Microsoft Smartphone or Symbian operating systems, mainly are phone devices that include robust PDA functionality. RIM Blackberry-based smart phones include robust data features that are oriented to accessing e-mail and wireless data services.

5 Make sure your device has enough memory.

Memory (RAM) is not a major issue with low-end devices with monochrome displays and basic organizer functions. Memory is a major issue, however, for high-end devices that have color displays and wireless features. Without enough memory, the performance level of your device will drop dramatically. If you plan to purchase a high-end device running the Palm OS operating system, the device should have at least 16 MB of RAM. If you plan to purchase a high-end device running the Windows Mobile operating system, the PDA should have at least 48 MB of RAM.

6 Practice with the touch screen, handwriting recognition, and built-in keyboard before deciding on a model.

To enter data into a PDA or smart phone, you use a pen-like stylus to handwrite on the screen or a keyboard. The keyboard either slides out or is mounted on the front of the device. With handwriting recognition, the device translates the handwriting into a computerized font. You also can use the stylus as a pointing device to select items on the screen and enter data by tapping on an on-screen keyboard. By practicing data entry before buying a device, you can learn if one device may be easier for you to use than another. You also can buy third-party software to improve a device's handwriting recognition.

7 Decide whether you want a color display.

Pocket PC devices usually come with a color display that supports as many as 65,536 colors. Palm OS devices also have a color display, but the less expensive models display in 4 to 16 shades of gray. Symbian- and Blackberry-based devices also have the option for color displays. Having a color display does result in greater on-screen detail, but it also requires more memory and uses more power. Resolution also influences the quality of the display.

8 Compare battery life.

Any mobile device is good only if it has the power required to run. For example, Palm OS devices with monochrome screens typically have a much longer battery life than Pocket PC devices with color screens. The use of wireless networking will shorten battery time considerably. To help alleviate this problem, most devices have incorporated rechargeable batteries that can be recharged by placing the device in a cradle or connecting it to a charger.

9 Seriously consider the importance of ergonomics.

Will you put the device in your pocket, a carrying case, or wear it on your belt? How does it feel in your hand? Will you use it indoors or outdoors? Many screens are unreadable outdoors. Do you need extra ruggedness, such as would be required in construction, in a plant, or in a warehouse?

10 Check out the accessories.

Determine which accessories you want for your personal mobile device. Accessories include carrying cases, portable mini- and full-sized keyboards, removable storage, modems, synchronization cradles and cables, car chargers, wireless communications, global positioning system modules, digital camera modules, expansion cards, dashboard mounts, replacement styli, hands-free headsets, and more.

11 Decide whether you want additional functionality.

In general, off-the-shelf Microsoft operating system-based devices have broader functionality than devices with other operating systems. For example, voice-recording capability, e-book players, MP3 players, and video players are standard on most Pocket PC devices. If you are leaning towards a Palm OS device and want these additional functions, you may need to purchase additional software or expansion modules to add them later. Determine whether your employer permits devices with cameras on the premises, and if not, do not consider devices with cameras.

12 Determine whether synchronization of data with other devices or personal computers is important.

Most devices come with a cradle that connects to the USB or serial port on your computer so you can synchronize data on your device with your desktop or notebook computer. Increasingly, more devices are Bluetooth and/or wireless networking enabled, which gives them the capability of synchronizing wirelessly. Many devices today also have an infrared port that allows you to synchronize data with any device that has a similar infrared port, including desktop and notebook computers or other personal mobile devices.

Web Site	Web Address
Hewlett-Packard	hp.com
CNET Shopper	shopper.cnet.com
palmOne	palmone.com
Microsoft	windowsmobile.com pocketpc.com microsoft.com/smartphone
PDA Buyers Guide	pdabuyersguide.com
Research in Motion	rim.com
Danger	danger.com
Symbian	symbian.com
Wireless Developer Network	wirelessdevnet.com
Sharp	myzaveus.com

For an updated list of reviews and information about personal mobile devices and their Web addresses, visit scsite.com/ic6/pda.

FIGURE 59 Web site reviews and information about personal mobile devices.

Learn It Online

INSTRUCTIONS

To complete these exercises, start your browser, click the Address box, and then enter scsite.com/ic6/learn. When the Introduction to Computers Web page displays, follow the instructions in the exercises below.

1 Project Reinforcement — True/False, Multiple Choice, and Short Answer

Click Project Reinforcement. Select the type of quiz and print it by clicking Print on the File menu. Answer each question. Write your first and last name at the top of each page, and then hand in the printout to your instructor.

2 Practice Test

Click Practice Test. Answer each question, enter your first and last name at the bottom of the page, and then click the Grade Test button. When the graded practice test is displayed on your screen, click Print on the File menu to print a hard copy. Continue to take practice tests until you score 80% or better. Hand in a printout of the final practice test to your instructor.

3 Who Wants To Be a Computer Genius?

Click Computer Genius. Read the instructions, enter your first and last name at the bottom of the page, and then click the PLAY button. Submit your score to your instructor.

4 Wheel of Terms

Click Wheel of Terms. Read the instructions, and then enter your first and last name and your school name. Click the PLAY button. Submit your score to your instructor.

5 Visiting Web Link Sites

Visit 10 of the 18 Web Link sites in the margins of pages COM-2 to COM-23. Print the main Web page for each of the 10 Web sites you visit and hand them in to your instructor.

6 Crossword Puzzle Challenge

Click Crossword Puzzle Challenge. Read the instructions, and then enter your first and last name. Click the PLAY button. Work the crossword puzzle. When you are finished, click the Submit button. When the crossword puzzle redisplays, click the Print button. Hand in the printout to your instructor.

7 Making Use of the Web

Click Making Use of the Web. Read 1 of the 15 areas of interest, visit each of the Web sites listed, print the first page of each Web site, and then complete the Web exercises. Hand in the printouts and your answers to the Web exercises to your instructor.

8 Scavenger Hunt

Click Scavenger Hunt. Print a copy of the Scavenger Hunt page. Use a search engine to answer the questions. Hand in your completed page to your instructor.

9 Search Sleuth

Click Search Sleuth to learn search techniques that will help make you a research expert. Hand in your completed assignment to your instructor.

10 Install and Maintain a Personal Computer

(a) Click Install Computer, visit the Ergonomics links in Figure 1, and write a brief report outlining what you learned. (b) Click Maintain Computer, choose one of the step topics. Use the Web to learn more about the topic. Write a brief report on what you learned.

Case Studies

1. Computers are ubiquitous. Watching television, driving a car, using a charge card, ordering fast food, and the more obvious activity of typing a term paper on a personal computer, all involve interaction with computers. Make a list of every computer you can recall that you encountered over the past week (be careful not to limit yourselves just to the computers you see). Consider how each computer is used. How were the tasks the computers performed done before computers existed? Write a brief report and submit it to your instructor.

2. The Internet has had a tremendous impact on business. For some businesses, that influence has not been positive. For example, surveys suggest that as a growing number of people make their own travel plans online, travel agents are seeing fewer customers. Use the Web and/or printed media to research businesses that have been affected negatively by the Internet. What effect has the Internet had? How can the business compete with the Internet? Write a brief report and submit it to your instructor.

INDEX

PHOTO CREDITS

Figure 1a, Computer, Courtesy of Acer America Corp.; Figure 1b, PC video camera, Courtesy of Logitech, Inc.; Figure 1c, Microphone, Courtesy of Logitech, Inc.; Figure 1d, Open flatbed scanner, Courtesy of Umax Systems GmbH; Figure 1e, External card reader, Courtesy of Sandisk Corporation; Figure 1f, USB flash drive, Courtesy of Sandisk Corporation; Figure 1g, External cable modem, Courtesy of Linksys, a Division of Cisco Systems Inc.; Figure 1h, digital camera, Courtesy of Umax Systems GmbH; Figure 1i, Ink-jet printer, Courtesy of Epson America, Inc.; Figure 2, payroll check, © C Squared Studios/Getty Images; Figure 4, Internet keyboard, Courtesy of Logitech; Figure 5a, PDA, Courtesy of ViewSonic® Corporation; Figure 5b, PDA scanner, Courtesy of Socket Communications, Inc.; Figure 5c, pen/stylus combination, Courtesy of Belkin Corporation; Figure 5d, stylus, Courtesy of ViewSonic® Corporation; Figure 5e, PDA digital camera, Courtesy of LifeView, Inc.; Figure 5f, pen input , Courtesy of Seiko Instruments USA Inc.; Figure 5g, PDA, Courtesy of ViewSonic® Corporation; Figure 5h, desktop computer, Courtesy of IBM; Figure 6, smart phone with picture or video on it, © Edward Bock/CORBIS; Figure 7a, mechanical mouse, Courtesy of Microsoft Corporation; Figure 7b, optical mouse, Courtesy of Microsoft Corporation; Figure 7c, laser mouse, Courtesy of Logitech; Figure 8a, laptop pointing stick, Courtesy of IBM; Figure 8b, finger using laptop mouse, © Getty Images; Figure 9a, system unit opened, © Gary Herrington; Figure 9b, Pentium 4 processor, Courtesy of Intel Corporation; Figure 9c, memory chips on a module, Courtesy of SMART Modular Technologies, Inc. © 2002; Figure 9d, sound card, Courtesy of Creative Labs, Inc. Copyright © 2003 Creative Technology Ltd. (SOUND BLASTER AUDIGY 2S). All rights reserved.; Figure 9e, video card, Courtesy of Matrox Graphics Inc.; Figure 10, dot matrix printer, Courtesy of Oki Data Americas, Inc.; Figure 11a - f, ink-jet printer with output, Courtesy of Epson America, Inc.; Figure 12, color laser printer, Courtesy of Xerox Corporation; Figure 13a, LCD monitor, Courtesy of NEC-Mitsubishi Electronics Display of America Inc.; Figure 13b, CRT monitor, Courtesy of NEC-Mitsubishi Electronics Display of America Inc.; Figure 14a, notebook computer, Courtesy of Acer America Corp.; Figure 14b, Tablet PC, Courtesy of Acer America Corp.; Figure 14c, PDA with color screen, Courtesy of Sony Electronics Inc.; Figure 14d, smart phone, Siemens press picture; Figure 17a, person inserting floppy disk into PC (tower model), © Masterfile (Royalty-Free Div.) www.masterfile.com; Figure 17b, external floppy disk drive plugged into a laptop computer, Photo Courtesy of Iomega Corporation. Copyright (c) 2003 Iomega Corporation. All Rights Reserved. Zip is a registered trademark in the United States and/or other countries. Iomega, the stylized "i" logo and product images are property of Iomega Corporation in the United States and/or other countries; Figure 18a, Iomega 750 MB Zip disk sticking out of a Zip drive, Photo Courtesy of Iomega Corporation; Figure 18b, product shot of a 750 MB Zip disk, Photo Courtesy of Iomega Corporation; Figure 19, SATA hard disk, Courtesy of Maxtor Corporation. © 2004 Maxtor Corporation. All Rights Reserved; Figure 20, opening CD-ROM drive, © Gary Herrington; Figure 21a, CD-ROM (with software program), Courtesy of Merriam-Webster; Figure 21b, CD-R (box shot), Courtesy of Memorex Products, Inc.; Figure 21c, CD-RW box shot, Courtesy of Memorex Products, Inc.; Figure 21d, DVD-ROM, © 2004 DeLorme (www.delorme.com) Topo USA®; Figure 21e, DVD-R (box shot), Courtesy of Memorex Products, Inc.; Figure 21f, DVD+R (box shot), Courtesy of Memorex Products, Inc.; Figure 21g, DVD-RW (box shot), Courtesy of Memorex Products, Inc.; Figure 21h, DVD+RW (box shot), Courtesy of Memorex Products, Inc. Figure 21i, DVD-RAM (box shot), Courtesy of Memorex Products, Inc.; Figure 21j, screen shot for LCD monitor, © 2004 DeLorme (www.delorme.com) Topo USA®; Figure 22, DVD software disc , © 2004 DeLorme (www.delorme.com) Topo USA®; Figure 23, tape cartridge and tape drive, Courtesy of Sony Electronics Inc.; Figure 24a, flash, Courtesy of Sandisk Corporation; Figure 24b, miniature storage media and PDA, Courtesy of palmOne, Inc.; Figure 24c, flash memory cards & USB flash drives in desktop computers, laptop computers, and mobile, Siemens Press Picture; Figure 24d, USB flash drive in desktop computer, Courtesy of Fujitsu Siemens Computers; Figure 24e, digital photo viewer with a card sticking out, Courtesy of Delkin Devices, Inc.; Figure 24f, JVC TV, Courtesy of JVC Company of America; Figure 24g, landscape for TV, © Digital Vision/Getty Images; Figure 24h, CompactFlash 4.0 Sandisk, Courtesy of Sandisk Corporation; Figure 25a, SmartMedia, Courtesy of Sandisk Corporation; Figure 25b, SecureDigital card, Courtesy of Sandisk Corporation; Figure 25c, 1G xD-Picture Card, Courtesy of Lexar Media, Inc.; Figure 25d, memory stick, Courtesy of Sandisk Corporation; Figure 26, USB flash drive, Photo Courtesy of Iomega Corporation. Copyright (c) 2003 Iomega Corporation. All Rights Reserved. Zip is a registered trademark in the United States and/or other countries. Iomega, the stylized "i" logo and product images are property of Iomega Corporation in the United States and/or other countries; Figure 27, smart card in use, © Jean-Yves Bruel/Masterfile; Figure 29, software aisle at a computer store, ©Bonnie Kamin/Photo Edit; Figure 38a, desktop computer,Courtesy of IBM Corporation; Figure 38b1, mobile computer, Courtesy of Sony Electronics, Inc.; Figure 38b2, notebook computer\ tablet pc, Courtesy of Motion Computing; Figure 39c, personal mobile device, Courtesy of palmOne, Inc.; Figure 38c2, smart phone/PDA, Siemens press picture; Figure 38d, thinking female, © Digital Vision/Getty Images; Figure 41a, CD\ DVD drives, Courtesy of JVC; Figure 41b, Card Reader\ Writer, Courtesy of Sandisk; Figure 41c, Digital Camera, Courtesy of UMAX; Figure 41d, Digital Video Capture Device, Courtesy of Pinnacle Systems, Inc.; Figure 41f, Hard Disk, Courtesy of Seagate; Figure 41g, Joystick\ Wheel, Courtesy of Logitech; Figure 41h, keyboard, Courtesy of Microsoft; Figure 41j, Modem, Courtesy of US Robotics; Figure 41k, Monitor, Courtesy of ViewSonic Corporation; Figure 41l, Mouse, Courtesy of Microsoft; Figure 41m, Network Card, Courtesy of 3Com Corporation; Figure 41n, Printer, Courtesy of EPSON America, Inc.; Figure 41o, Processor, Courtesy of Intel Corporation; Figure 41p, RAM, Courtesy of Kingston Technology; Figure 41q, Scanner, Courtesy of UMAX; Figure 41s, Speakers, Courtesy of Logitech; Figure 41t, PC Video Camera, Courtesy of Logitech; Figure 41u, USB Flash Drive, Courtesy of Sandisk; Figure 41v, Video Graphics Card, Courtesy of 3Com Corporation; Figure 41x, Zip Drive, Courtesy of Iomega; Figure 39, notebook computer converts to a Tablet PC, Courtesy of Toshiba America; Figure 50, A well designed notebook computer carrying case, Courtesy of Toshiba America; Figure 51, a notebook computer connected to a video projector, © Britt Erlanson/Getty Images; Figure 53, light weight Tablet PC, © Thomas Barwick/PhotoDisc Collection/Getty Images; Figure 56, a Tablet PC and pen, Courtesy of ViewSonic Corporation; Figure 58, Tablet PC docked, Courtesy of Fujitsu Siemens Computers.

MICROSOFT
Windows XP and Office 2003

Microsoft Windows XP and Office 2003

MICROSOFT
Windows XP and Office 2003

Introduction to Microsoft Windows XP and Office 2003

PROJECT

CASE PERSPECTIVE

After weeks of planning, your school finally installed Microsoft Windows XP Professional on all workstations. Because of your experience with computers and previous versions of Windows, your principal has asked you to present an after-school seminar for the faculty and staff. Since installing Windows XP Professional, many teachers have come to you with questions. You have taken the time to answer their questions by sitting down with them at their computers and searching for the answers using the Help and Support feature.

From their questions, you determine that you should customize the after-school seminar to cover the basics of Windows XP Professional, including basic mouse operations, working with windows, starting an application, and searching for answers using Help and Support. Your goal is to become familiar with Microsoft Windows XP Professional in order to teach the seminar more effectively to the faculty and staff.

As you read through this project, you will learn how to use the Windows XP operating system to perform basic operating system tasks and become familiar with the Microsoft Office 2003 applications.

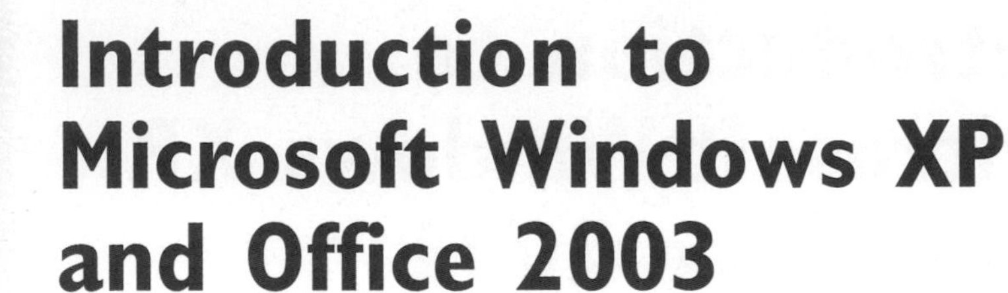

Introduction to Microsoft Windows XP and Office 2003

PROJECT

Objectives

You will have mastered the material in this project when you can:

- Launch Microsoft Windows XP, log on to the computer, and identify the objects on the desktop
- Perform the basic mouse operations: point, click, right-click, double-click, drag, and right-drag
- Display the Start menu and start an application program
- Open, minimize, maximize, restore, move, size, scroll, and close a window
- Display drive and folder contents
- Create a folder in Windows Explorer and Microsoft Word
- Type, name, and save a Word document
- Download folders from scsite.com
- Copy, move, rename, and delete files
- Search for files using a word or phrase in the file or by name
- Use Help and Support
- Log off the computer and turn it off

Introduction

An **operating system** is the set of computer instructions, called a computer program, that controls the allocation of computer hardware such as memory, disk devices, printers, and CD and DVD drives, and provides the capability for you to communicate with the computer. The most popular and widely used operating system is **Microsoft Windows. Microsoft Windows XP**, the newest version of Microsoft Windows, allows you to communicate with and control your computer easily.

Microsoft Office 2003, the latest edition of the world's best-selling office suite, is a collection of the more popular Microsoft application software products that work similarly and together as if they were one program. Microsoft Office 2003 integrates these applications and combines them with the power of the Internet so you can move quickly among applications, transfer text and graphics easily, and interact seamlessly with the World Wide Web. The **Internet** is a worldwide group of connected computer networks that allows public access to information on thousands of subjects and gives users the means to use this information, send messages, and obtain products and services. An explanation of each of the application software programs in Microsoft Office 2003 is given at the end of this project.

Microsoft Windows XP Operating Systems

The Microsoft Windows XP operating systems consist of Microsoft Windows XP Professional, Microsoft Windows XP Home Edition, Microsoft Windows XP Media Center Edition, Microsoft Windows XP Tablet PC Edition, and Microsoft Windows XP 64-Bit Edition. **Microsoft Windows XP Professional** is the operating system designed for businesses of all sizes and for advanced home computing. Windows XP is called a **32-bit operating system** because it uses 32 bits for addressing and other purposes, which means the operating system can address more than four gigabytes of RAM (random-access memory) and perform tasks faster than older operating systems.

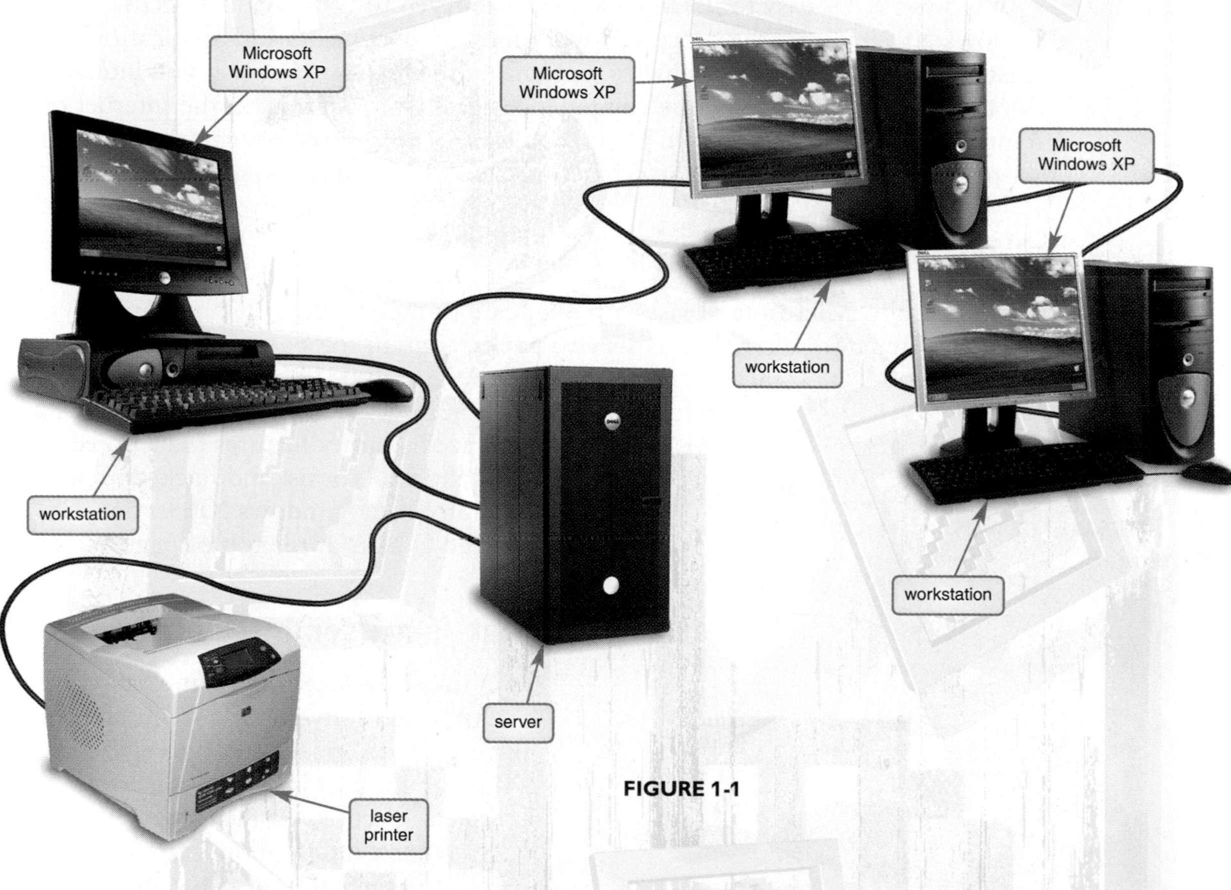

FIGURE 1-1

In business, Windows XP Professional commonly is used on computer workstations and portable computers. A **workstation** is a computer connected to a server. A **server** is a computer that controls access to the hardware and software on a network and provides a centralized storage area for programs, data, and information. Figure 1-1 illustrates a simple computer network consisting of a server and three computers (called workstations) and a laser printer connected to the server.

Microsoft Windows XP Home Edition is designed for entertainment and home use. Home Edition allows you to establish in the home a network of computers that share a single Internet connection, share a device such as a printer or a scanner, share files and folders, and play multicomputer games.

Microsoft Windows XP Media Center Edition is designed for use with a Media Center PC. A **Media Center PC** is a home entertainment desktop personal computer that includes a mid- to high-end processor, large-capacity hard disk, CD and DVD drives, a remote control, and advanced graphics and audio capabilities. **Microsoft Windows XP Tablet PC Edition** is designed for use on a special type of notebook

Q & A

Q: Where can a user learn more about Windows XP?

A: A vast amount of information about Microsoft Windows XP is available on the Internet. For additional information about Microsoft Windows XP, visit the Office 2003 Q&A Web Page (scsite.com/off2003sch/qa) and then click Microsoft Windows XP.

computer, called a Tablet PC. A **Tablet PC** allows you to write on the device's screen using a digital pen and convert the handwriting into characters the Tablet PC can process. A **Windows XP 64-Bit Edition** also is available for individuals solving complex scientific problems, developing high-performance design and engineering applications, or creating 3-D animations.

Microsoft Windows XP Professional

Microsoft Windows XP Professional (called **Windows XP** for the rest of the book) is an operating system that performs every function necessary for you to communicate with and use the computer.

Windows XP is easy to use and can be customized to fit individual needs. Windows XP simplifies the process of working with documents and applications by transferring data between documents, organizing the manner in which you interact with the computer, and using the computer to access information on the Internet or an intranet. Windows XP is used to run **application programs**, which are programs that perform an application-related function such as word processing.

Windows XP Service Pack 2

Periodically, Microsoft releases a free update to the Windows XP operating system. These updates, referred to as **service packs**, contain fixes and enhancements to the operating system. In August 2004, Microsoft released the Windows XP Service Pack 2. **Windows XP Service Pack 2** (**SP2**) contains advanced security features that protect a computer against viruses, worms, and hackers. For more information about Windows XP Service Pack 2, see the Q & A at the top of page WIN 7.

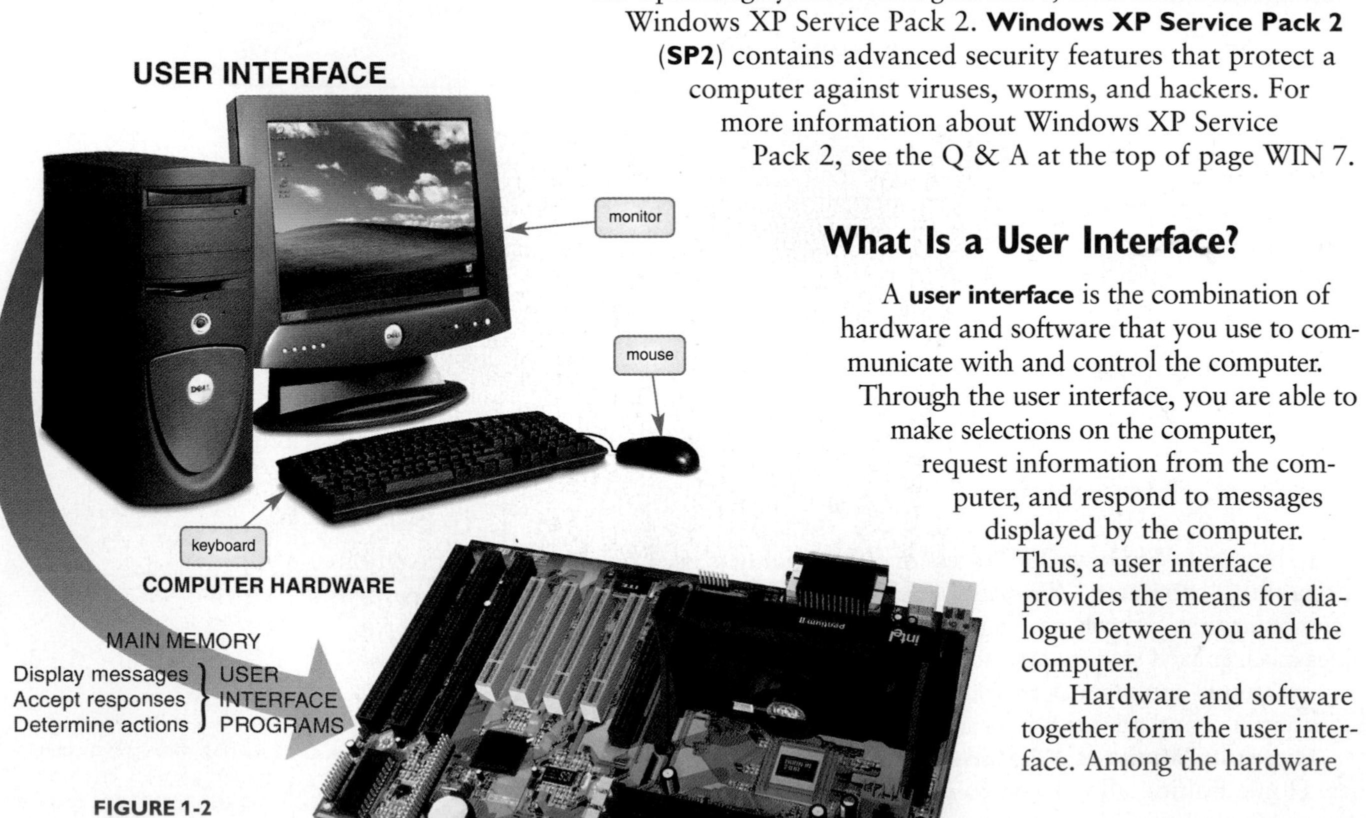

FIGURE 1-2

What Is a User Interface?

A **user interface** is the combination of hardware and software that you use to communicate with and control the computer. Through the user interface, you are able to make selections on the computer, request information from the computer, and respond to messages displayed by the computer. Thus, a user interface provides the means for dialogue between you and the computer.

Hardware and software together form the user interface. Among the hardware devices associated with a user interface are the monitor, keyboard, and mouse (Figure 1-2). The **monitor** displays messages and provides information. You respond by entering data in the form of a command or other response using the **keyboard** or **mouse**. Among the responses available to you are ones that specify which application program to run, what document to open, when to print, and where to store data for future use.

The computer software associated with the user interface consists of the programs that engage you in dialogue (Figure 1-2). The computer software determines the messages you receive, the manner in which you should respond, and the actions that occur, based on your responses.

The goal of an effective user interface is to be **user-friendly**, which means the software can be used easily by individuals with limited training. Research studies have indicated that the use of graphics can play an important role in aiding users to interact effectively with a computer. A **graphical user interface**, or **GUI** (pronounced gooey), is a user interface that displays graphics in addition to text when it communicates with the user.

The Windows XP graphical user interface was designed carefully to be easier to set up, simpler to learn, faster, more powerful, and better integrated with the Internet.

Q & A

Q: What are the features of Windows XP Service Pack 2?

A: A table summarizing the new features contained in the Windows XP Service Pack 2 is available on the Internet. For additional information about Windows XP Service Pack 2, visit the Office 2003 Q&A Web Page (scsite.com/off2003sch), locate Windows XP Project 1, and then click Windows XP Service Pack 2.

Launching Microsoft Windows XP

When you turn on the computer, an introductory black screen consisting of the Microsoft Windows XP logo, progress bar, copyright messages (Copyright © Microsoft Corporation), and the word, Microsoft, are displayed. The progress bar indicates the progress of the Windows XP operating system launch. After approximately one minute, the Welcome screen is displayed (Figure 1-3).

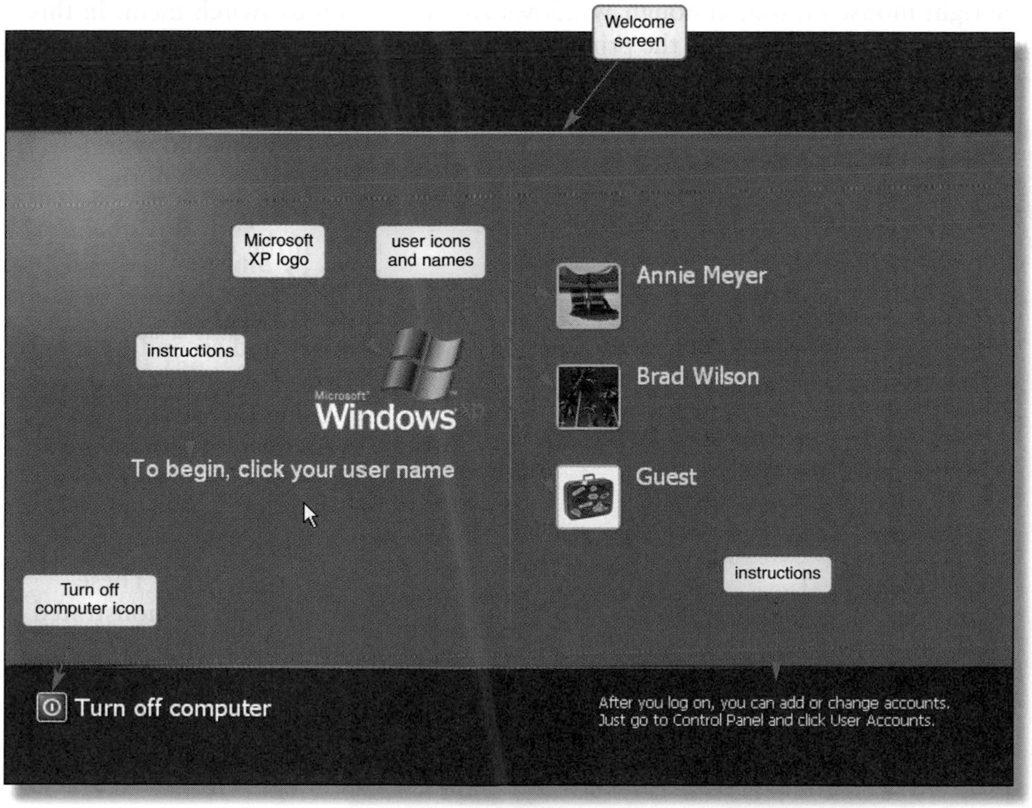

FIGURE 1-3

Q & A

Q: What type of interface preceded the Windows graphical user interface?

A: Some older interfaces, called command-line interfaces, required you to type keywords (special words, phrases, or codes the computer understood) or press special keys on the keyboard to communicate with the interface. Today, graphical-user interfaces incorporate colorful graphics, use of the mouse, and Web browser-like features, which make them more user-friendly.

2

• **Click the icon by pressing and releasing the left mouse button, type** `lakers` **(or your password) in the Type your password text box, and then point to the Next button.**

Windows XP highlights the Brad Wilson icon and name, displays the Type your password text box containing a series of bullets (••••••) and an insertion point, and the Next and Help buttons (Figure 1-7). A ***text box*** *is a rectangular area in which you can enter text. The bullets in the text box hide the password entered by the user.*

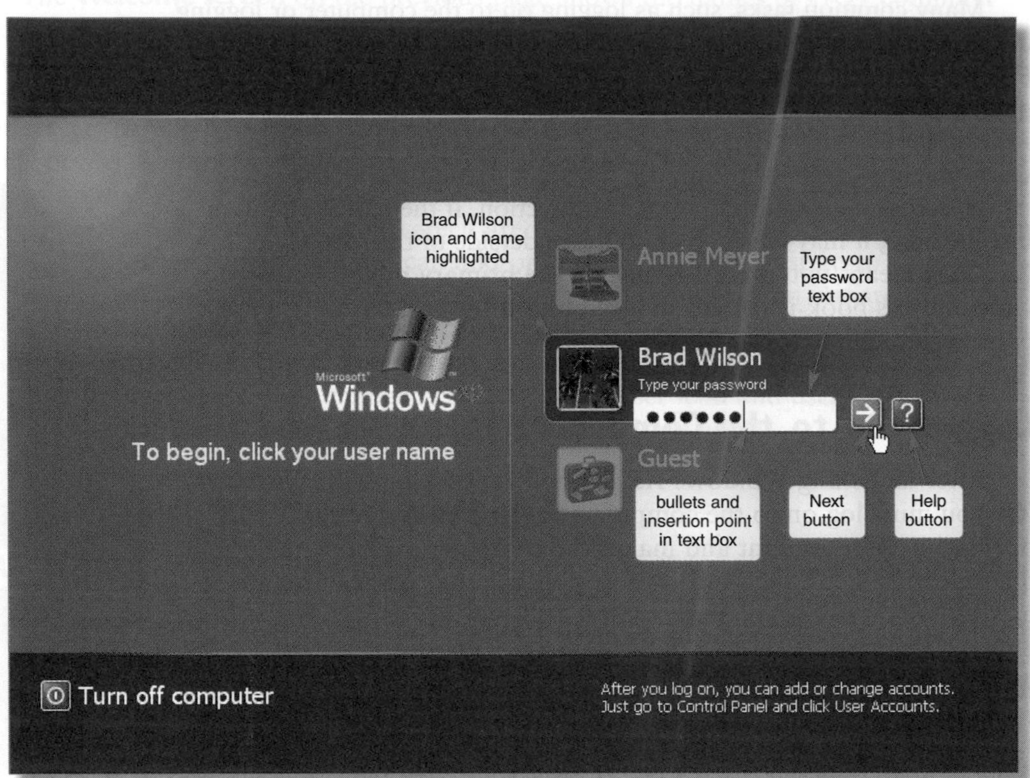

FIGURE 1-7

3

• **Click the Next button.**

The contents of the Welcome screen change to contain the word, Welcome, on the left side of the screen and the user name, user icon, and message, Loading your personal settings..., on the right side. This screen appears momentarily while the user is logged on to the computer and then several items appear on a background called the desktop (Figure 1-8). The background design of the desktop is Bliss, but your computer may display a different design.

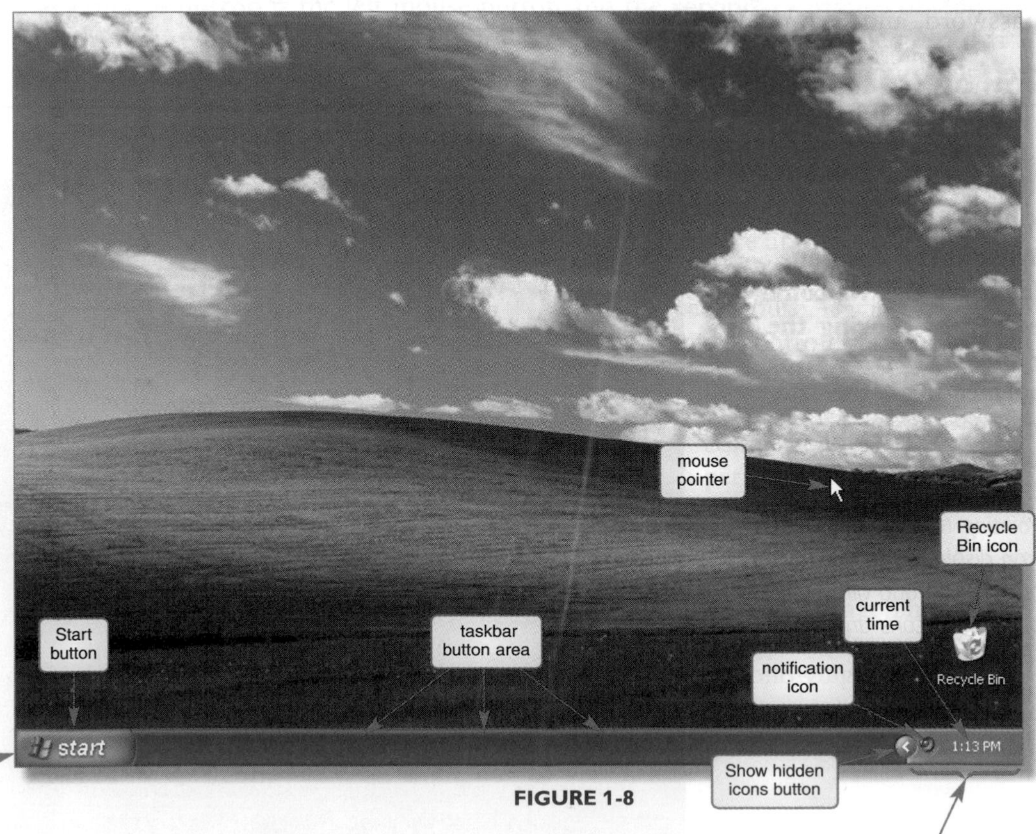

FIGURE 1-8

The items on the desktop in Figure 1-8 include the Recycle Bin icon and its name in the lower-right corner of the desktop and the taskbar across the bottom of the desktop. The Recycle Bin icon (Recycle Bin) allows you to discard unneeded objects. Your computer's desktop may contain more, fewer, or different icons because you can customize the desktop of the computer.

The **taskbar** shown at the bottom of the screen in Figure 1-8 contains the Start button, taskbar button area, and notification area. The **Start button** allows you to start a program quickly, find or open a document, change the computer's settings, obtain Help, shut down the computer, and perform many more tasks. The **taskbar button area** contains buttons to indicate which windows are open on the desktop. In Figure 1-8, no windows are displayed on the desktop and no buttons appear in the taskbar button area.

The **notification area** contains the Show hidden icons button, one notification icon, and the current time. The **Show hidden icons button** indicates that one or more inactive icons are hidden from view in the notification area. The **notification icon** in the notification area provides quick access to programs on the computer. Other icons that provide information about the status of the computer appear temporarily in the notification area. For example, the Printer icon appears when a document is sent to the printer and is removed when printing is complete. The notification area on your desktop may contain more, fewer, or different icons because the contents of the notification area can change.

The mouse pointer appears on the desktop. On the desktop, the **mouse pointer** is the shape of a block arrow. The mouse pointer allows you to point to objects on the desktop and may change shape when it points to different objects. A shadow may be displayed behind the mouse pointer to make the mouse pointer appear in a three-dimensional form.

When you click an object, such as the Brad Wilson icon or the Next button shown in Figure 1-7, you must point to the object before you click. In the steps that follow, the instruction that directs you to point to a particular item and then click is, Click the particular item. For example, Click the Next button means point to the Next button and then click.

Q & A

Q: How does a user display hidden icons in the notification area?

A: The Show hidden icons button is displayed on the left edge of the notification area if one or more inactive icons are hidden from view in the notification area. Clicking the Show hidden icons button returns the hidden icons to the notification area and replaces the Show hidden icons button with the Hide button. Moving the mouse pointer off the Hide button removes, or hides, the inactive icons in the notification area and displays the Show hidden icons button again.

The Windows XP Desktop

Nearly every item on the Windows XP desktop is considered an object. Even the desktop itself is an object. Every **object** has properties. The **properties** of an object are unique to that specific object and may affect what can be done to the object or what the object does. For example, a property of an object may be the color of the object, such as the color of the desktop.

The Windows XP desktop and the objects on the desktop emulate a work area in an office. You may think of the Windows desktop as an electronic version of the top of your desk. You can place objects on the desktop, move the objects around on the desktop, look at them, and then put them aside, and so on. In this project, you will learn how to interact and communicate with the Windows XP desktop.

Q & A

Q: Can you change the appearance of the desktop?

A: Yes. You may use a different background design and icons on the desktop and in the notification area, and you may display additional toolbars on the taskbar. To change the background design, right-click an open area of the desktop and click Properties on the shortcut menu. To change the contents of the taskbar and notification area, right-click the Start button or taskbar and then click Properties on the shortcut menu.

Displaying the Start Menu

A **menu** is a list of related commands, and each **command** on a menu performs a specific action, such as searching for files or obtaining Help. The **Start menu** allows you to access easily the most useful items on the computer. The Start menu contains commands that allow you to connect to and browse the Internet, start an e-mail program, start application programs, store and search for documents, customize the computer, and obtain Help on thousands of topics.

The steps on the following pages show how to display the Start menu.

To Display the Start Menu

1

- **Point to the Start button on the taskbar.**

The mouse pointer on the Start button causes the color of the Start button to change to light green and displays a ToolTip (Click here to begin) (Figure 1-9). The ToolTip provides instructions for using the Start button.

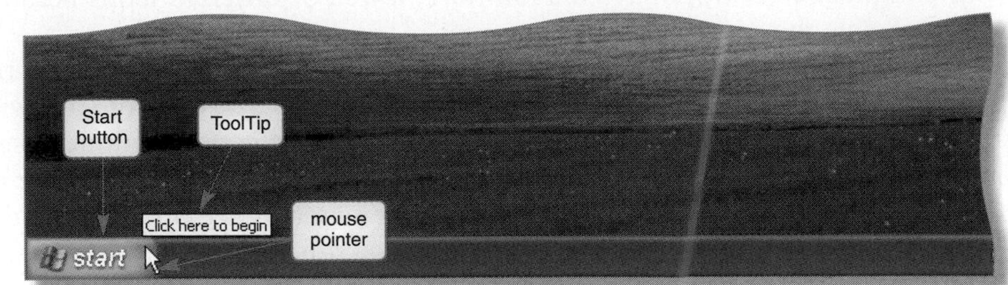

FIGURE 1-9

2

- **Click the Start button.**

The Start menu appears, the color of the Start button changes to dark green, and the Start button becomes recessed (Figure 1-10). The top section of the Start menu contains the user icon and name, the middle section contains two columns of commands, and the bottom section contains two icons (Log Off and Turn Off Computer).

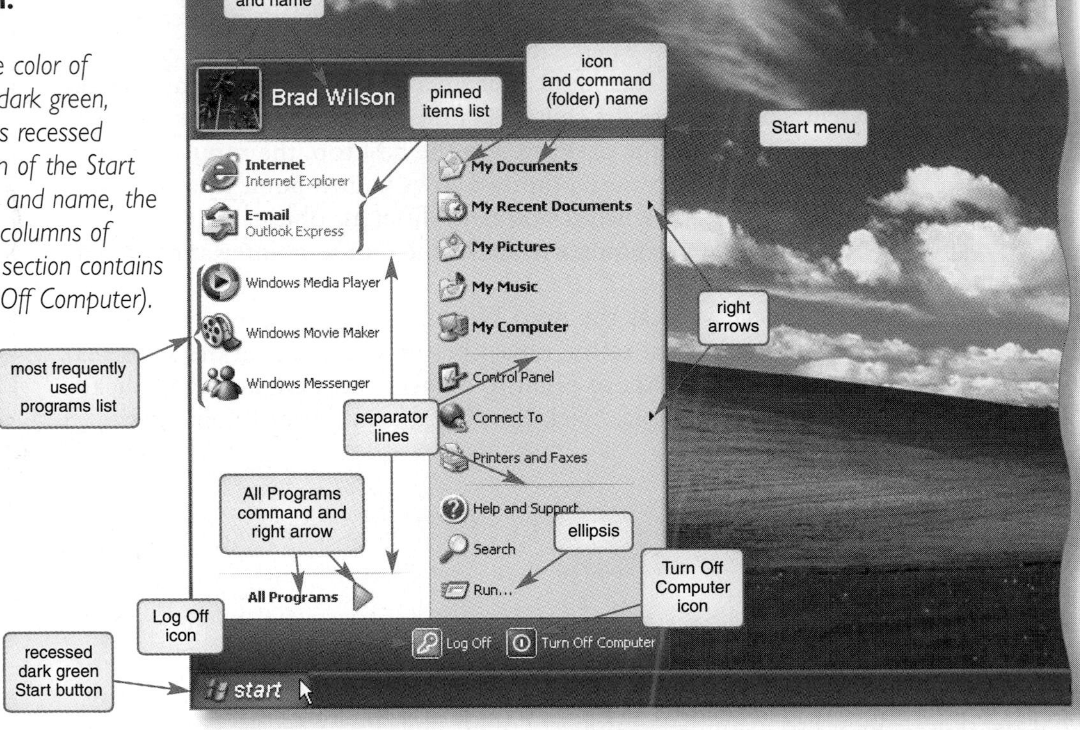

FIGURE 1-10

3

- **Point to All Programs on the Start menu.**

When you point to All Programs, Windows XP highlights the All Programs command on the Start menu by displaying the All Programs command name in white text on a blue background and displays the All Programs submenu (Figure 1-11). A submenu is a menu that appears when you point to a command followed by a right arrow. Whenever you point to a command on a menu or submenu, the command name is highlighted.

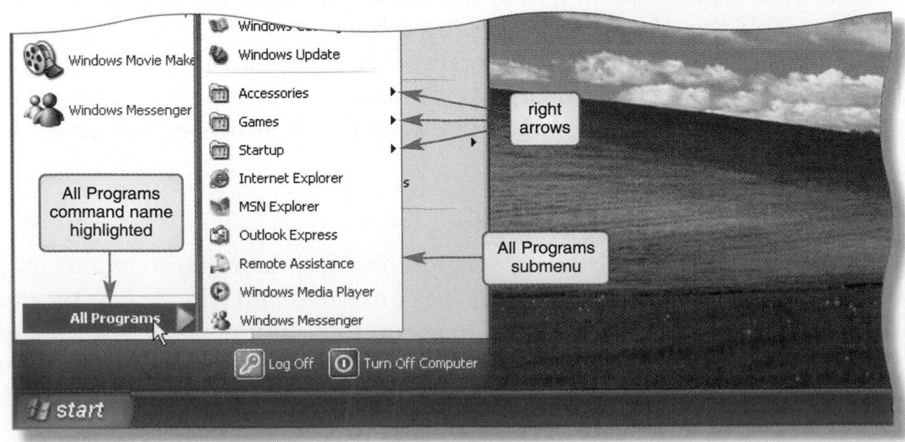

FIGURE 1-11

4

• **Point to Accessories on the All Programs submenu.**

When you point to Accessories, Windows XP highlights the Accessories command on the All Programs submenu and displays the Accessories submenu (Figure 1-12). Clicking a command on the Accessories submenu that contains an application name starts that application. For example, to start Notepad, you would click the Notepad command on the Accessories submenu.

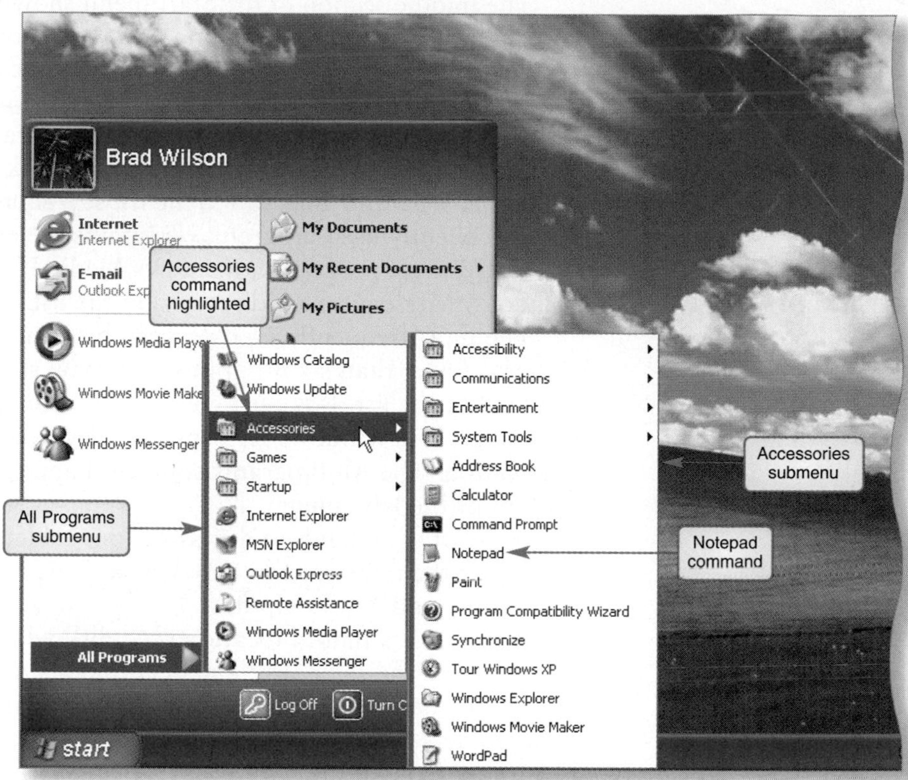

FIGURE 1-12

5

• **Point to an open area of the desktop and then click the open area to close the Start menu, Accessories submenu, and All Programs submenu.**

The Start menu, Accessories submenu, and All Programs submenu close, and the recessed dark green Start button changes to its original light green color (Figure 1-13). The mouse pointer points to the desktop. To close a menu, click any area of the desktop except the menu itself.

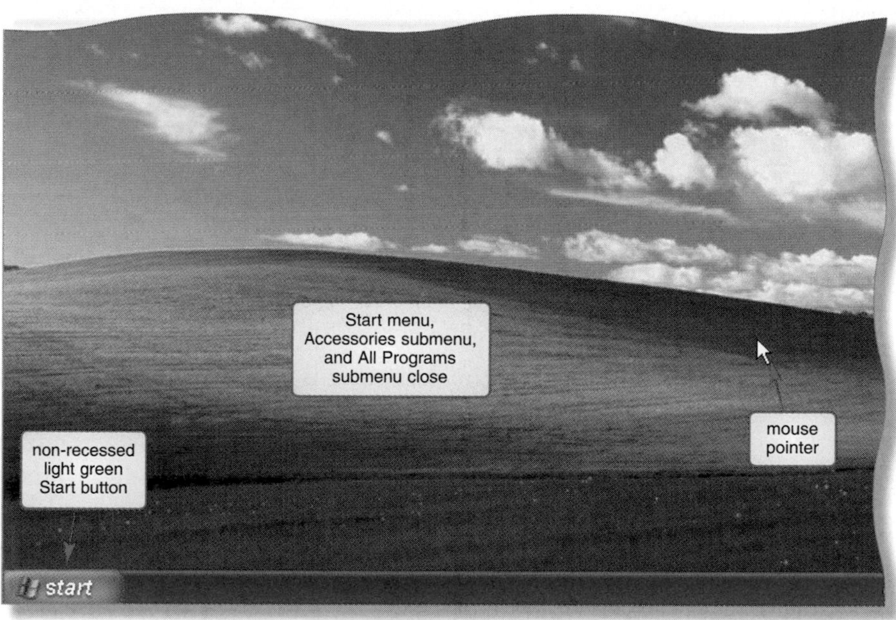

FIGURE 1-13

The middle section of the Start menu shown in Figure 1-10 on page WIN 12 consists of two columns of commands. Each command is identified by a unique icon and name. Commands may represent an application program, folder, or operation.

The list of commands above the separator line at the top of the left column, called the **pinned items list**, consists of the default Web browser program (Internet Explorer) and default e-mail program (Outlook Express). The list of commands below the separator line, called the **most frequently used programs list**, contains the most frequently used programs. Programs are added to the list when you use them. Currently, three programs (Windows Media Player, Windows Movie Maker, and Windows Messenger) are displayed in the list.

The most frequently used program list can contain up to six programs. If the list contains fewer than six programs when you start a new program, the program name is added to the list. If the list contains six names when you start a program that is not on the list, Windows XP replaces a less frequently used program with the new application. The All Programs command appears below the separator line at the bottom of the left column.

A list of commands to access various folders appears above the separator line at the top of the right column (My Documents, My Recent Documents, My Pictures, My Music, and My Computer).

A **folder** is a named location on a disk where files are stored. A folder contains files in much the same way a manila folder stores important documents, such as a class schedule or syllabus. Each folder is identified by a folder icon and folder name. Some folders include a symbol. In Figure 1-14, the Freshman folder consists of a yellow folder icon and folder name (Freshman) and the My Music folder consists of a yellow folder icon, folder name (My Music), and symbol (musical note).

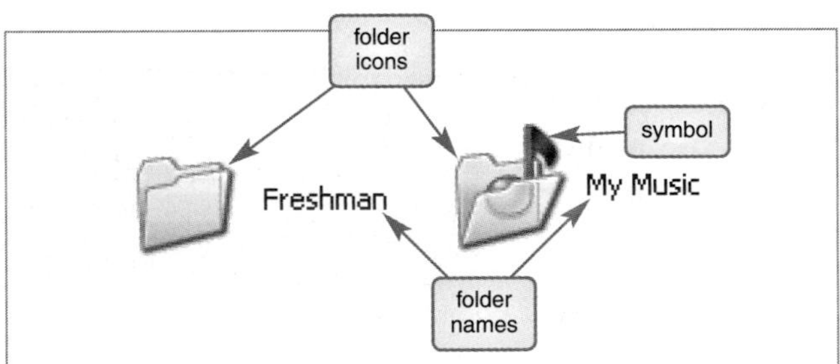

FIGURE 1-14

If the computer is connected to a network, the My Network Places command may appear below the My Computer command. Below the separator line are other commands. They are commands to customize the computer (Control Panel), connect to the Internet (Connect To), and add printers and fax printers to the computer (Printers and Faxes). Below the separator line at the bottom of the right column are commands to obtain Help (Help and Support), search for documents and folders (Search), and start programs (Run). The commands on your Start menu may be different.

A **right arrow** following a command on the Start menu indicates that pointing to the command will display a submenu. The All Programs command is followed by a green right arrow, and the My Recent Documents and Connect To commands are followed by smaller black arrows. One command (Run) is followed by an **ellipsis** (…) to indicate more information is required to execute the command.

Windows XP provides a number of ways in which to accomplish a particular task. In the remainder of this book, a specific set of steps will illustrate how to accomplish each task. These steps may not be the only way in which the task can be completed. In each case, the method shown in the steps is the preferred method, but it is important for you to be aware that you can use other techniques.

> **Q & A**
>
> **Q:** What is the purpose of the right mouse button?
>
> **A:** The earliest versions of Microsoft Windows made little use of the right mouse button. In Windows XP, the right mouse button makes it easy to display a list of commands for an object (called a shortcut menu) and to copy and move objects on the desktop.

Adding an Icon to the Desktop

Although the Windows XP desktop may contain only the Recycle Bin icon (see Figure 1-8 on page WIN 10), you may want to add additional icons to the desktop. For example, you may want to add the My Computer icon to the desktop so you can view the contents of the computer easily. One method of viewing the contents of the computer is to click the My Computer command on the Start menu to open the My Computer window. If you use My Computer frequently, you may want to place the My Computer icon on the desktop where it is easier to find.

One method of adding the My Computer icon to the desktop is to right-click the My Computer command on the Start menu. **Right-click** means you press and release the secondary mouse button, which in this book is the right mouse button. As directed when using the primary mouse button to click an object, normally you will point to the object before you right-click it. The following steps illustrate how to add the My Computer icon to the desktop.

To Add an Icon to the Desktop

1

- **Click the Start button, point to My Computer on the Start menu, and then press and release the right mouse button.**

Windows XP highlights the My Computer command and displays a shortcut menu containing nine commands (Figure 1-15). Right-clicking an object, such as the My Computer command, displays a shortcut menu that contains commands specifically for use with that object.

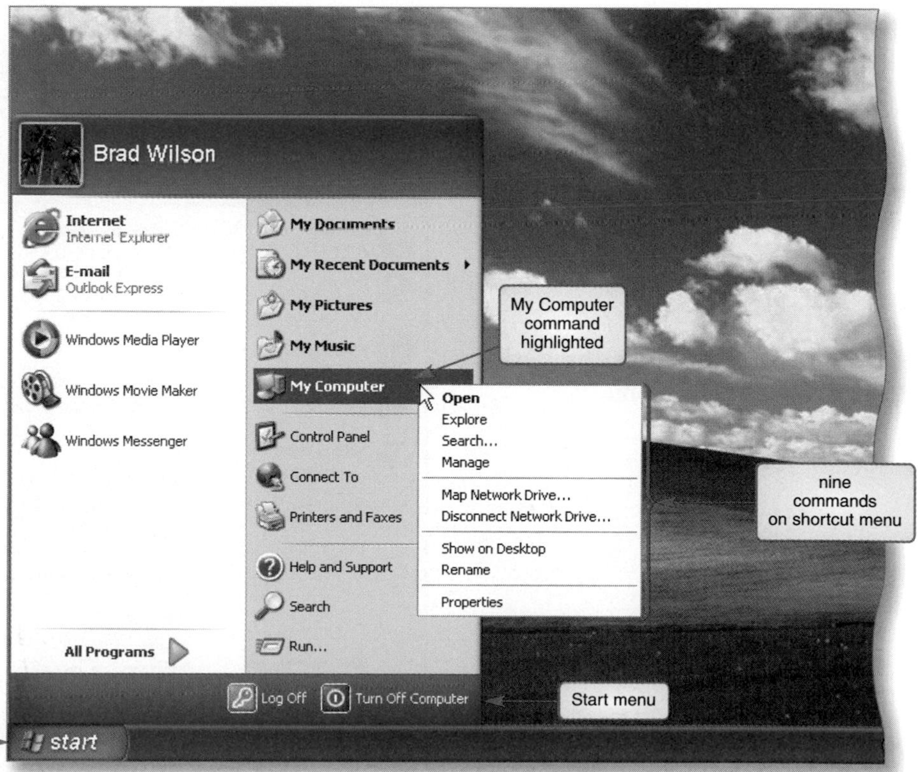

FIGURE 1-15

2

• **Point to Show on Desktop on the shortcut menu.**

When you point to Show on Desktop, Windows XP highlights the Show on Desktop command (Figure 1-16).

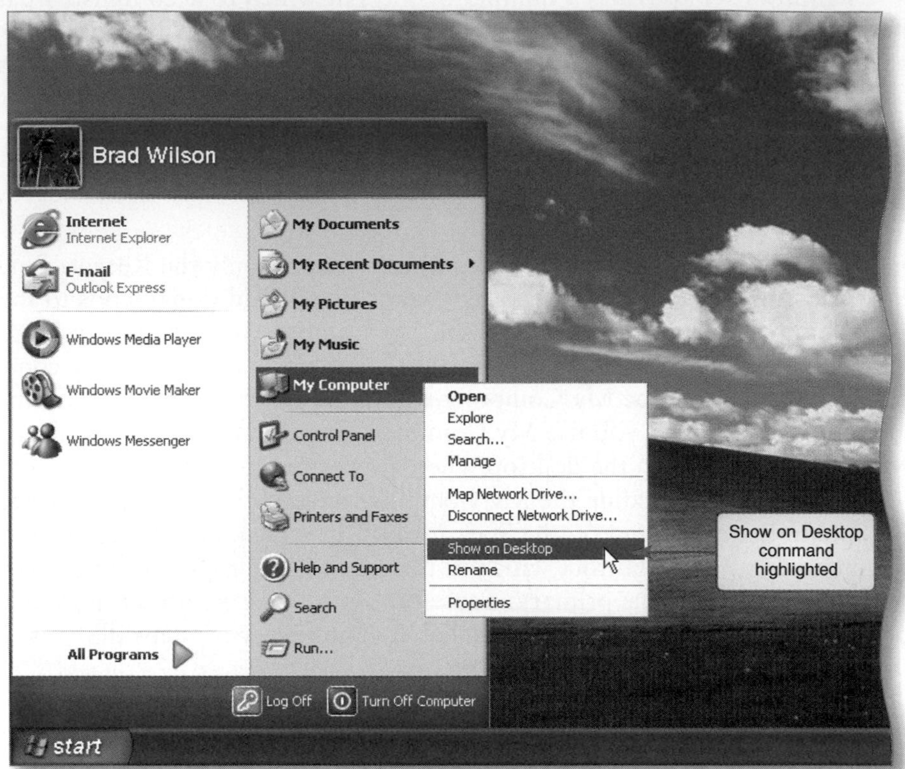

FIGURE 1-16

3

• **Click Show on Desktop.**

The shortcut menu closes and the My Computer icon is displayed on the desktop (Figure 1-17). The Start menu remains on the desktop.

4

• **Click an open area on the desktop to close the Start menu.**

The Start menu closes.

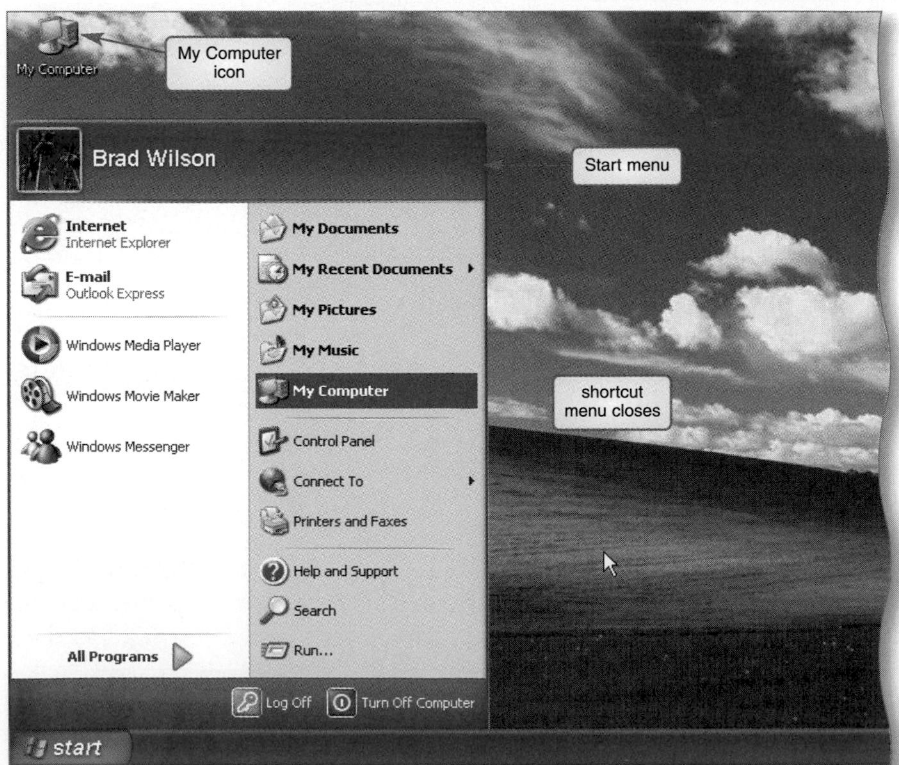

FIGURE 1-17

Whenever you right-click an object, a shortcut menu is displayed. As you will see, the use of shortcut menus speeds up your work and adds flexibility to your interaction with the computer.

Opening a Window Using a Desktop Icon

Double-click means you quickly press and release the left mouse button twice without moving the mouse. In most cases, you must point to an item before you double-click. The following step shows how to open the My Computer window on the desktop by double-clicking the My Computer icon on the desktop.

To Open a Window Using a Desktop Icon

1

- **Point to the My Computer icon on the desktop and then double-click by quickly pressing and releasing the left mouse button twice without moving the mouse.**

The My Computer window opens and the recessed dark blue My Computer button is displayed in the taskbar button area (Figure 1-18). The My Computer window allows you to view the contents of the computer.

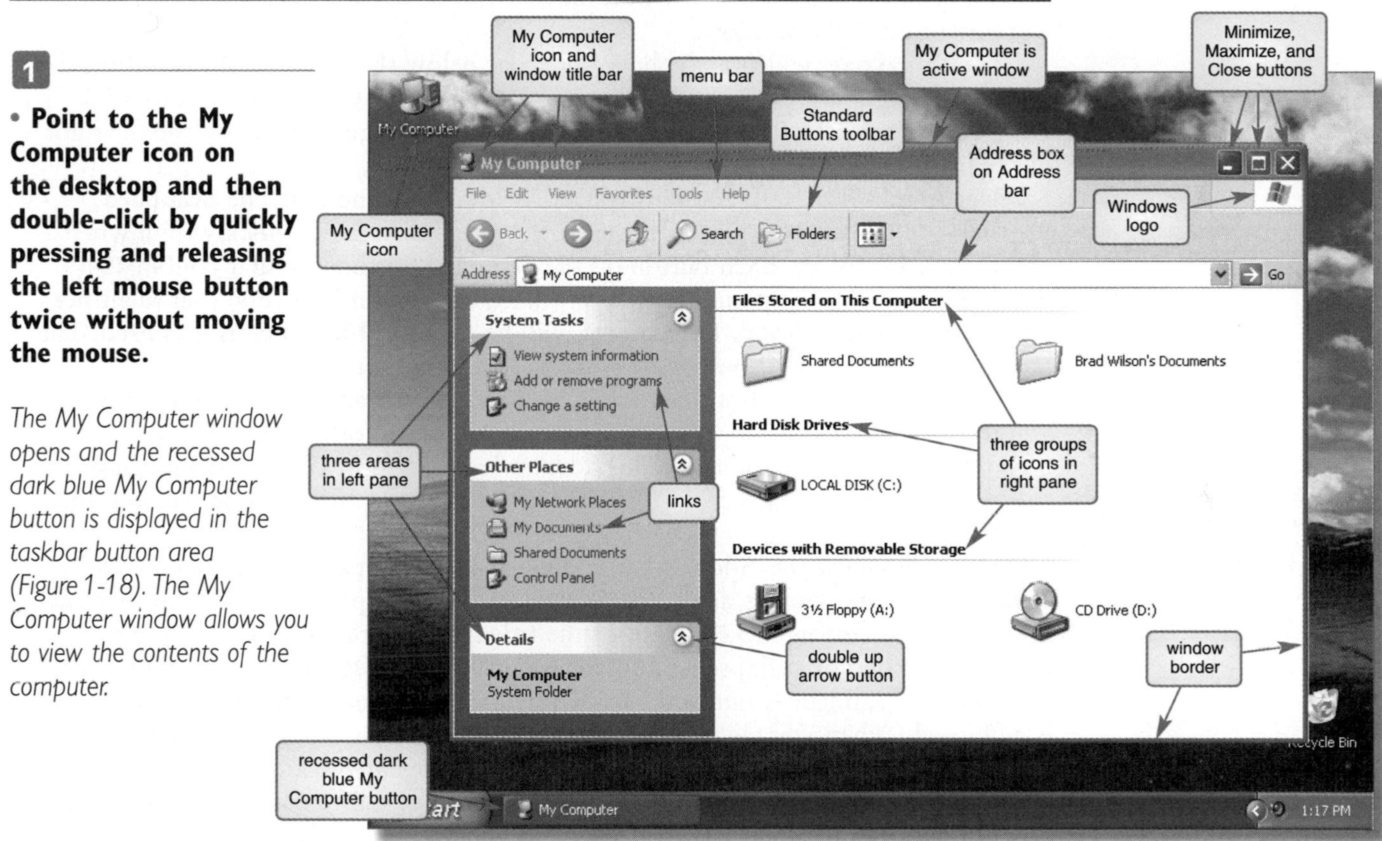

FIGURE 1-18

The My Computer window, the only open window, is the active window. The **active window** is the window you currently are using or that currently is selected. Whenever you click an object that opens a window, such as the My Computer icon, Windows XP will open the window and a recessed dark blue button in the taskbar button area will identify the open window. The recessed dark blue button identifies the active window. The contents of the My Computer window on your computer may be different from the contents of the My Computer window shown in Figure 1-18.

Q & A

Q: Why is double-clicking the most challenging mouse skill to learn?

A: Many people have a tendency to move the mouse before they click a second time, even when they do not want to move the mouse. With a little practice, you should find double-clicking without moving the mouse becomes quite natural.

The My Computer Window

The thin blue line, or **window border**, surrounding the My Computer window shown in Figure 1-18 on the previous page determines its shape and size. The **title bar** at the top of the window contains a small icon that is similar to the icon on the desktop, and the **window title** (My Computer) identifies the window. The color of the title bar (dark blue) and the recessed dark blue My Computer button in the taskbar button area indicate that the My Computer window is the active window. The color of the active window on your computer may be different from the color shown in Figure 1-18.

Clicking the icon at the left on the title bar will display the **System menu**, which contains commands to carry out the actions associated with the My Computer window. At the right on the title bar are three buttons (the Minimize button, the Maximize button, and the Close button) that can be used to specify the size of the window or close the window.

The **menu bar**, which is the horizontal bar below the title bar of a window, in Figure 1-18 contains a list of menu names for the My Computer window: File, Edit, View, Favorites, Tools, and Help. The Windows logo appears on the far right of the menu bar.

The Standard buttons toolbar displays below the menu bar. The **Standard Buttons toolbar** allows you to perform often-used tasks more quickly than when you use the menu bar. Each button on the Standard Buttons toolbar contains an icon. Three buttons contain a **text label** (Back, Search, and Folders) that identifies the function of the button. Each button will be explained in detail as it is used. The buttons on the Standard Buttons toolbar on your computer may be different.

Below the Standard Buttons toolbar is the Address bar. The **Address bar** allows you to start an application, display a document, open another window, and search for information on the Internet. The Address bar shown in Figure 1-18 displays the Address box containing the My Computer icon, window title, box arrow, and the Go button.

The area below the Address bar is divided into two panes. The System Tasks, Other Places, and Details areas are displayed in the left pane. A title identifies each area. A button appears to the right of the title in each area to indicate whether the area is expanded or collapsed. A button identified by a **double up arrow** indicates the area is expanded. A button identified by a **double down arrow** indicates the area is collapsed. When you click the double up arrow button, the area collapses and only the title and the double down arrow button appear. When you click the double down arrow button, the area expands and the entire contents of the area are visible.

All three areas in the left pane are expanded. The **System Tasks area** contains a title (System Tasks) and three tasks (View system information, Add or remove programs, and Change a setting) associated with the My Computer window. The **Other Places area** contains a title (Other Places) and links to four folders (My Network Places, My Documents, Shared Documents, and Control Panel) associated with the My Computer folder. The **Details area** contains a title (Details), the window title (My Computer), and the folder type (System Folder) of the My Computer window. Clicking the double up arrow collapses the area and leaves only the title and arrow button.

Pointing to a task in the System Tasks area or a folder name in the Other Places area underlines the task or folder name and displays the task or folder name in light blue. Underlined text, such as the task and folder names, is referred to as a **hyperlink**, or simply a **link**. Pointing to a link changes the mouse pointer to a hand icon, and clicking a link displays information associated with the link. For example, clicking the Add or remove programs task in the System Tasks area allows you to install or remove application programs, and clicking the My Documents link in the Other Places area opens the My Documents window.

The right pane of the My Computer window in Figure 1-18 on page WIN 17 contains three groups of icons. The top group, Files Stored on This Computer, contains Shared Documents and Brad Wilson's Documents icons. The **Shared Documents folder** contains documents and folders that are available (shared) to other computer users on the network, and the Brad Wilson's Documents folder contains his personal documents. On your computer, your name will replace the Brad Wilson name in the Brad Wilson's Documents icon.

The middle group, Hard Disk Drives, contains the LOCAL DISK (C:) drive icon. A title to the right of the icon identifies the drive name, LOCAL DISK (C:). The bottom group, Devices with Removable Storage, contains the 3½ Floppy (A:) and CD Drive (D:) icons and labels. The three icons in the Hard Disk Drives and Devices with Removable Storage sections, called **drive icons**, represent a hard disk drive, 3½ floppy disk drive, and a Compact Disc drive. The number of groups in the right pane and the icons in the groups on your computer may be different.

Clicking a drive or folder icon selects the icon in the right pane and displays details about the drive or folder in the areas in the left pane. Double-clicking a drive or folder icon allows you to display the contents of the corresponding drive or folder in the right pane and details about the drive or folder in the areas in the left pane. You may find more, fewer, or different drive and folder icons in the My Computer window on your computer.

Minimizing a Window

Two buttons on the title bar of a window, the Minimize button and the Maximize button, allow you to control the way a window is displayed or is not displayed on the desktop. When you click the **Minimize button** (see Figure 1-19 on the next page), the My Computer window no longer is displayed on the desktop and the recessed dark blue My Computer button in the taskbar button area changes to a non-recessed medium blue button. A minimized window still is open but is not displayed on the screen. To minimize and then redisplay the My Computer window, complete the steps on the next page.

Q & A

Q: Why minimize a window?

A: Windows management on the Windows XP desktop is important in order to keep the desktop uncluttered. You will find yourself frequently minimizing windows and then later reopening them with a click of a button in the taskbar button area.

To Minimize and Redisplay a Window

1

• **Point to the Minimize button on the title bar of the My Computer window.**

The mouse pointer points to the Minimize button on the My Computer window title bar, the color of the Minimize button changes to light blue, a ToolTip is displayed below the Minimize button, and the recessed dark blue My Computer button appears on the taskbar (Figure 1-19).

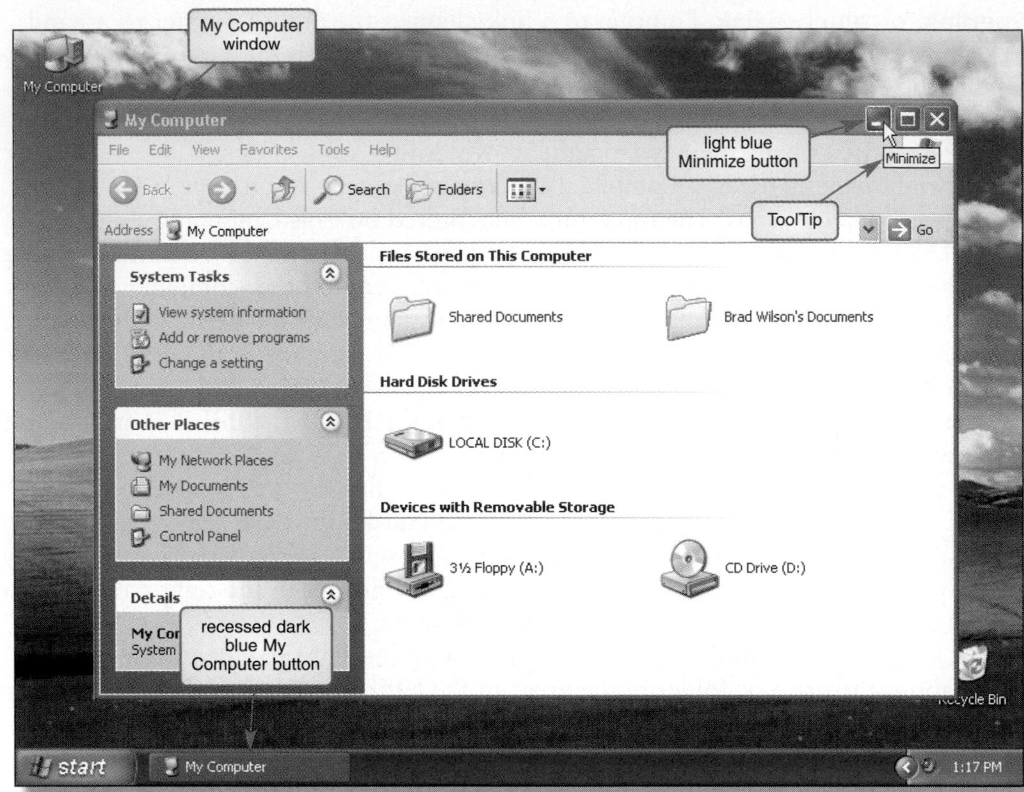

FIGURE 1-19

2

• **Click the Minimize button.**

When you minimize the My Computer window, Windows XP removes the My Computer window from the desktop, the My Computer button changes to a non-recessed button, and the color of the button changes to medium blue (Figure 1-20).

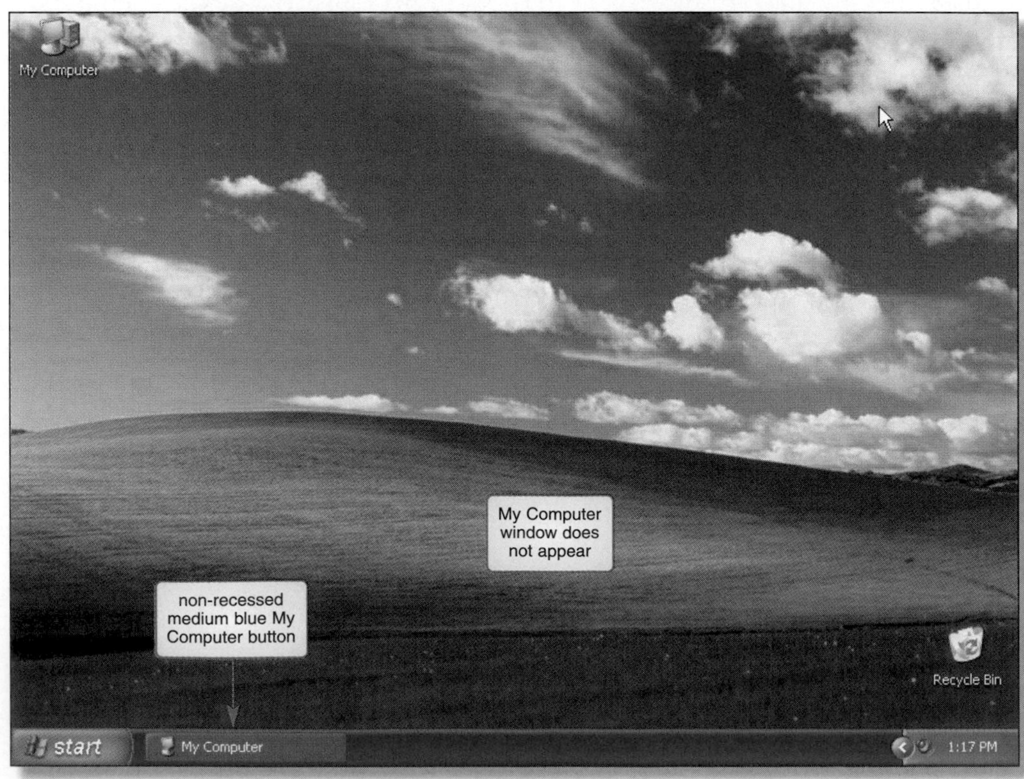

FIGURE 1-20

3

• **Click the My Computer button in the taskbar button area.**

The My Computer window is displayed in the same place with the same size as it was before being minimized, and the My Computer button on the taskbar is recessed (Figure 1-21). With the mouse pointer pointing to the My Computer button, the color of the button is medium blue. Moving the mouse pointer off the button changes its color to dark blue. The My Computer window is the active window because it contains the dark blue title bar.

FIGURE 1-21

Whenever a window is minimized, it is not displayed on the desktop, but a non-recessed dark blue button for the window is displayed in the taskbar button area. Whenever you want a minimized window to display and be the active window, click its button in the taskbar button area.

As you point to many objects, such as a button or command, when you work with Windows XP, Windows XP displays a ToolTip. A **ToolTip** is a short on-screen note associated with the object to which you are pointing. ToolTips display on the desktop for approximately five seconds. Examples of ToolTips are shown in Figure 1-9 on page WIN 12, Figure 1-19, Figures 1-22 and 1-24 on the next page, and Figure 1-26 on page WIN 23. To reduce clutter on the screen, the ToolTips will not be shown on the remaining screens in this book.

Maximizing and Restoring a Window

Sometimes when information is displayed in a window, the information is not completely visible. One method of displaying the entire contents of a window is to enlarge the window using the **Maximize button**. The Maximize button maximizes a window so the window fills the entire screen, making it easier to see the contents of the window. When a window is maximized, the **Restore Down button** replaces the Maximize button on the title bar. Clicking the Restore Down button will return the window to its size before maximizing. To maximize and restore the My Computer window, complete the steps on the next page.

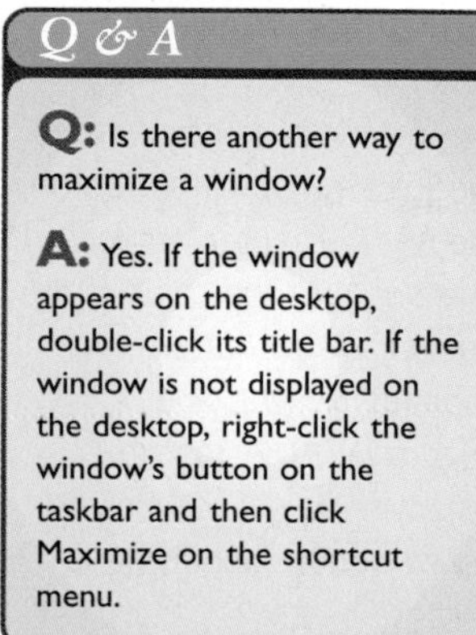

Q & A

Q: Is there another way to maximize a window?

A: Yes. If the window appears on the desktop, double-click its title bar. If the window is not displayed on the desktop, right-click the window's button on the taskbar and then click Maximize on the shortcut menu.

To Maximize and Restore a Window

1

• **Point to the Maximize button on the title bar of the My Computer window.**

The mouse pointer points to the Maximize button on the My Computer window title bar, and the color of the Maximize button changes to light blue (Figure 1-22). A ToolTip identifying the button name is displayed below the Maximize button.

FIGURE 1-22

2

• **Click the Maximize button.**

The My Computer window expands so it and the taskbar fill the desktop (Figure 1-23). The Restore Down button replaces the Maximize button, the My Computer button in the taskbar button area does not change, and the My Computer window still is the active window.

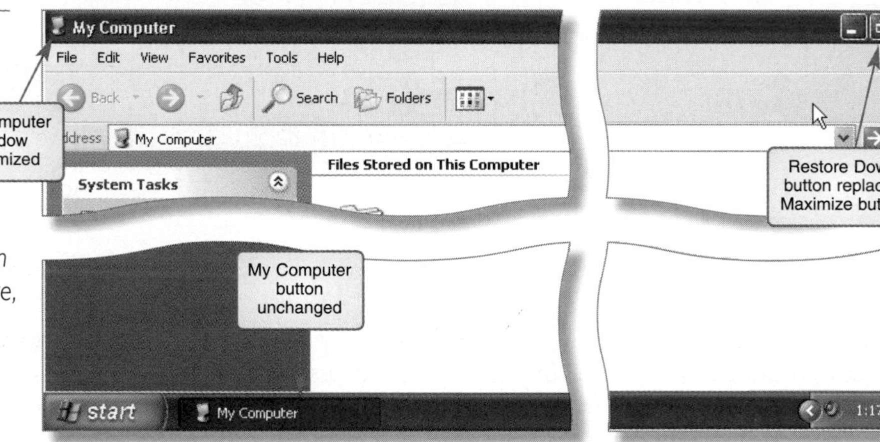

FIGURE 1-23

3

• **Point to the Restore Down button on the title bar of the My Computer window.**

The mouse pointer points to the Restore Down button on the My Computer window title bar, and the color of the Restore Down button changes to light blue (Figure 1-24). A ToolTip is displayed below the Restore Down button identifying it.

FIGURE 1-24

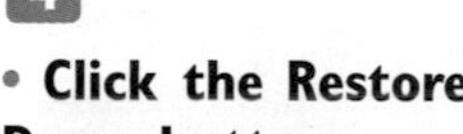

• **Click the Restore Down button.**

The My Computer window returns to the size and position it occupied before being maximized (Figure 1-25). The My Computer button does not change. The Maximize button replaces the Restore Down button.

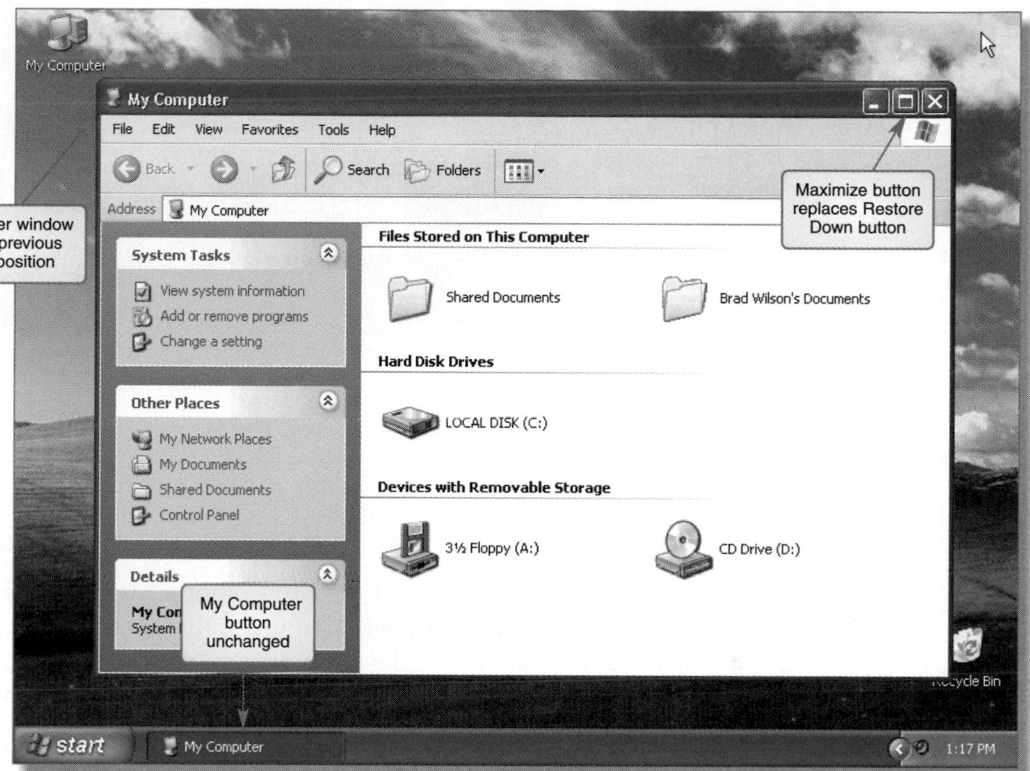

FIGURE 1-25

When a window is maximized, such as in Figure 1-23, you also can minimize the window by clicking the Minimize button. If, after minimizing the window, you click its button in the taskbar button area, the window will return to its maximized size.

Q & A

Q: Does Windows always reopen a closed window in a maximized state?

A: Windows XP remembers the size of a window when you close the window. When you reopen the window, it will display in the same size you closed it.

Closing a Window

The **Close button** on the title bar of a window closes the window and removes the taskbar button from the taskbar. The following steps show how to close the My Computer window.

To Close a Window

• **Point to the Close button on the title bar of the My Computer window.**

The mouse pointer points to the Close button on the My Computer window title bar, and the color of the Close button changes to light red (Figure 1-26). A ToolTip is displayed below the Close button.

FIGURE 1-26

2

• **Click the Close button.**

The My Computer window closes, and the My Computer button no longer is displayed in the taskbar button area (Figure 1-27).

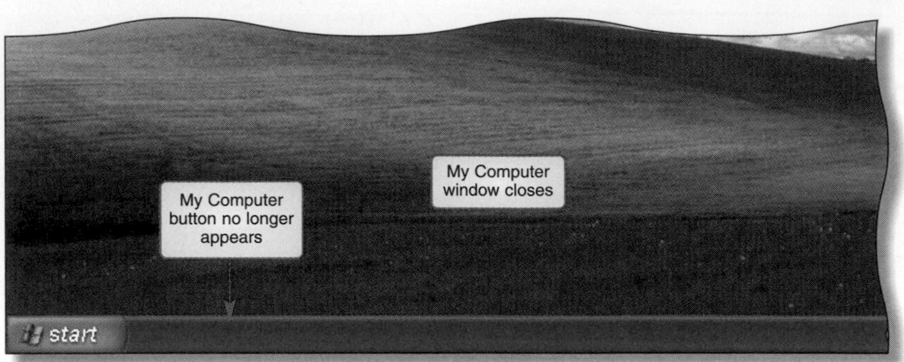

FIGURE 1-27

Opening a Window Using the Start Menu

Previously, you opened the My Computer window by double-clicking the My Computer icon on the desktop. Another method of opening a window and viewing the contents of the window is to click a command on the Start menu. The steps below show how to open the My Documents window using the My Documents command on the Start menu.

To Open a Window Using the Start Menu

1

• **Click the Start button on the taskbar and then point to the My Documents command on the Start menu.**

The Start menu is displayed, the Start button is recessed on the taskbar, the color of the button changes to dark green, and the mouse pointer points to the highlighted My Documents command on the Start menu (Figure 1-28).

FIGURE 1-28

2

• **Click My Documents on the Start menu.**

The My Documents window opens, the recessed dark blue My Documents button is displayed in the taskbar button area, and the My Documents window is the active window (Figure 1-29). You may find more, fewer, or different folder icons in the right pane on your computer.

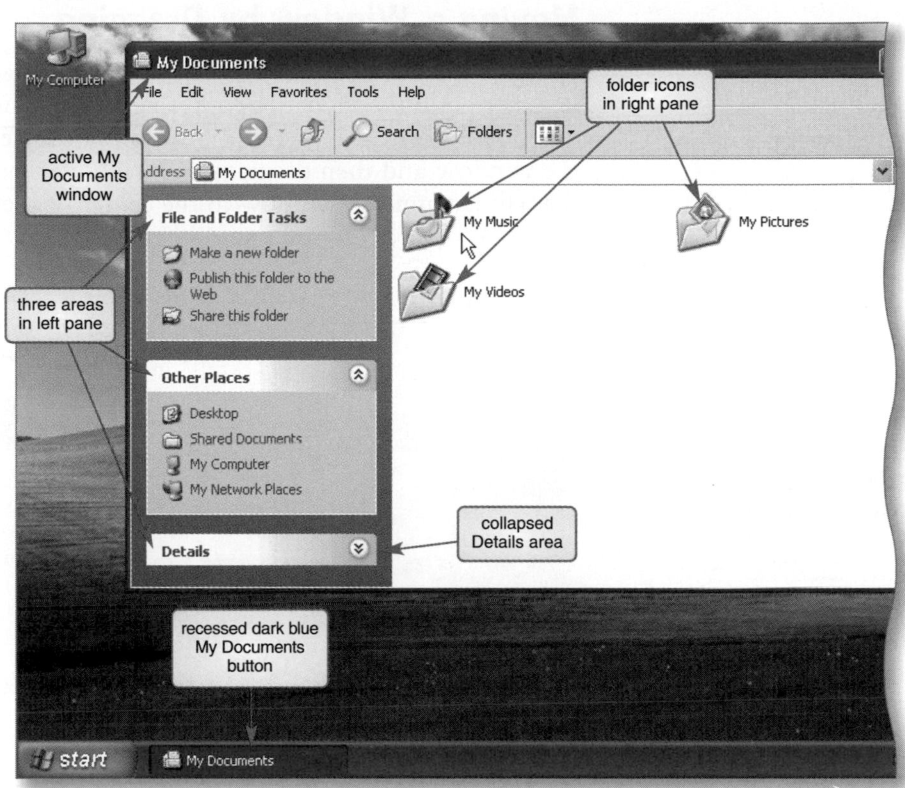

FIGURE 1-29

The My Documents Window

The **My Documents window** shown in Figure 1-29 is a central location for the storage and management of documents. The title bar at the top of the My Documents window identifies the window and the color of the title bar (dark blue), and the recessed dark blue My Documents button in the taskbar button area indicates the My Documents window is the active window.

The File and Folders Tasks, Other Places, and Details areas are displayed in the left pane. The **File and Folders Tasks area** contains three tasks (Make a new folder, Publish this folder to the Web, and Share this folder). The **Other Places area** contains links to four folders (Desktop, Shared Documents, My Computer, and My Network Places). The **Details area** is collapsed and only the title and a double down arrow button appear in the area.

The right pane of the My Documents window contains the My Music, My Pictures, and My Videos folders. Clicking a folder icon in the right pane highlights the icon in the right pane and changes the files and folder tasks in the File and Folder Tasks area in the left pane. Double-clicking a folder icon displays the contents of the corresponding folder in the right pane, adds another area to the folder (My Music Tasks area, My Pictures Tasks area, or My Videos Tasks area) in the left pane, and changes the file and folder information in the left pane.

Moving a Window by Dragging

Drag means you point to an item, hold down the left mouse button, move the item to the desired location, and then release the left mouse button. You can move any open window to another location on the desktop by pointing to the title bar of the window and then dragging the window. The following steps illustrate dragging the My Documents window to the center of the desktop.

To Move a Window by Dragging

• **Point to the My Documents window title bar (Figure 1-30).**

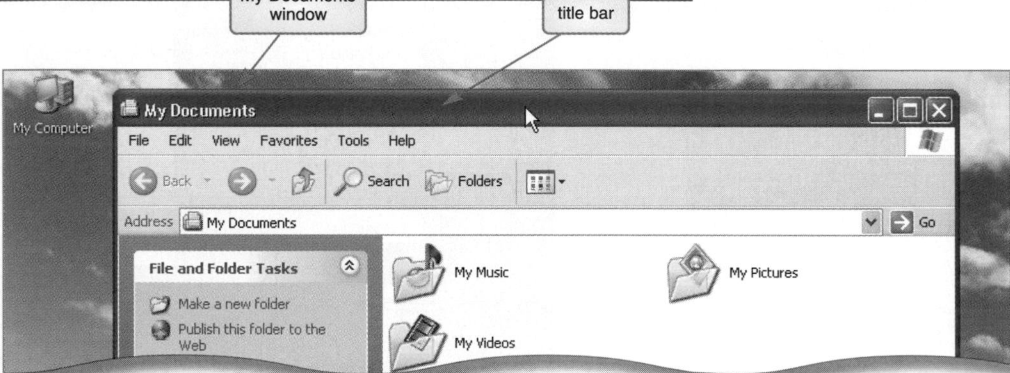

FIGURE 1-30

• **Hold down the left mouse button, move the mouse down so the window moves to the center of the desktop, and then release the left mouse button.**

As you drag the My Documents window, the window moves across the desktop. When you release the left mouse button, the window is displayed in its new location on the desktop (Figure 1-31).

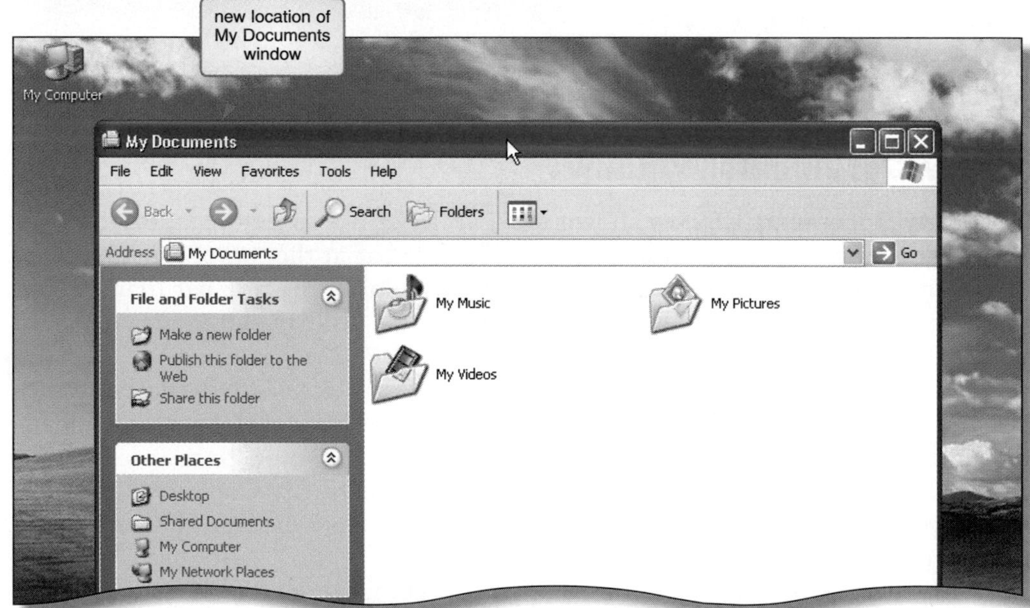

FIGURE 1-31

Expanding an Area

The Details area in the My Documents window is collapsed, and a double down arrow button appears to the right of the Details title (see Figure 1-32). Clicking the button or the area title expands the Details area and reveals the window title (My Documents) and folder type (System Folder) in the Details area. Similarly, clicking the double up arrow button or the area title collapses the area so only the area title and double down arrow button appear in the area. The steps on the next page illustrate how to expand the Details area in the left pane of the My Documents window.

To Expand an Area

1

• **Point to the double down arrow button in the Details area.**

The mouse pointer changes to a hand icon and points to the double down arrow button in the Details area, and the color of the Details title and button changes to light blue (Figure 1-32).

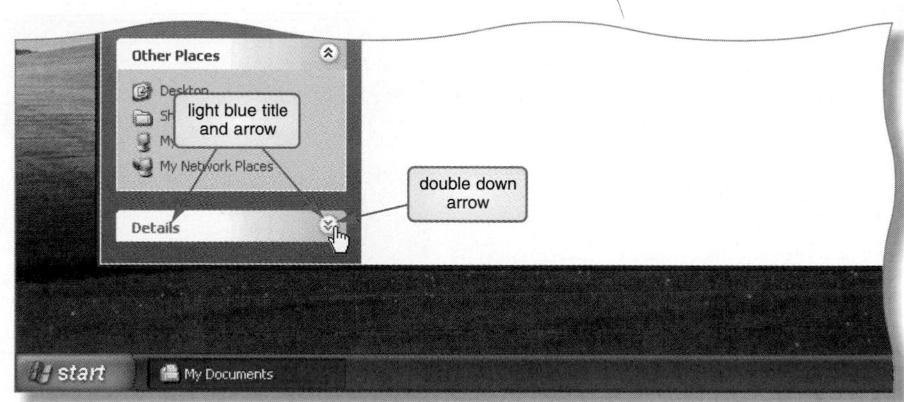

FIGURE 1-32

2

• **Click the double down arrow button.**

The Details area expands, the window title (My Documents) and folder type (System Folder) is displayed in the area, the double down arrow on the button changes to a double up arrow, a portion of the left pane is not visible, and a scroll bar is displayed in the area (Figure 1-33).

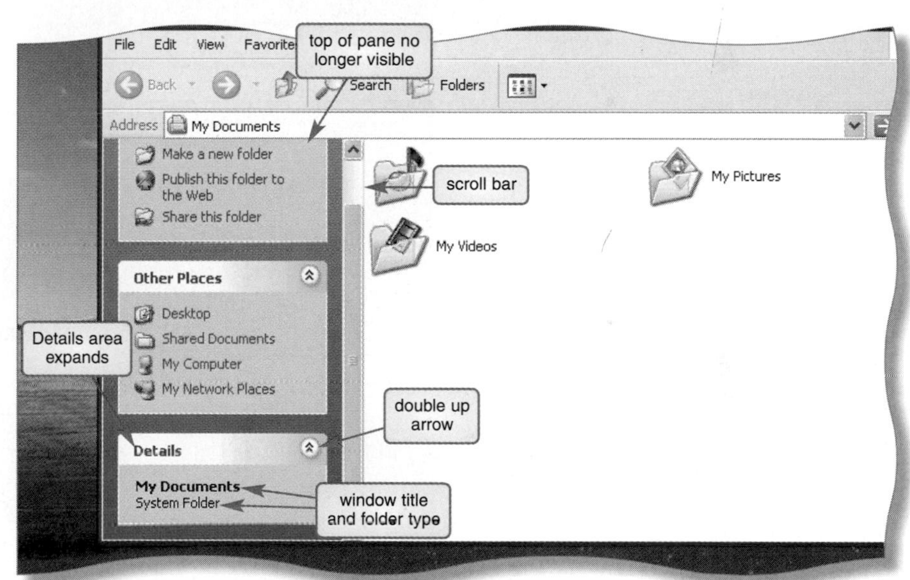

FIGURE 1-33

A **scroll bar** is a bar that appears when the contents of a pane or window are not completely visible. A vertical scroll bar contains an **up scroll arrow**, a **down scroll arrow**, and a **scroll box** that enable you to view areas that currently are not visible. A vertical scroll bar is displayed along the right side of the left pane in the My Documents window shown in Figure 1-33. In some cases, the vertical scroll bar also may appear along the right side of the right pane in a window.

Q & A

Q: Is scrolling a window the most efficient way to view objects in a window?

A: No. Other methods are more efficient. You can either maximize a window or size it so that all the objects in the window are visible. It is better to avoid scrolling because scrolling takes time.

Scrolling in a Window

Previously, the My Documents window was maximized to display information that was not completely visible in the My Documents window. Another method of viewing information that is not visible in a window is to use the scroll bar.

Scrolling can be accomplished in three ways: (1) click the scroll arrows; (2) click the scroll bar; and (3) drag the scroll box. On the following pages, you will use the scroll bar to scroll the contents of the left pane of the My Documents window. The steps on the next page show how to scroll the left pane using the scroll arrows.

To Scroll Using Scroll Arrows

1

• **Point to the up scroll arrow on the vertical scroll bar.**

The color of the up scroll arrow changes to light blue (Figure 1-34).

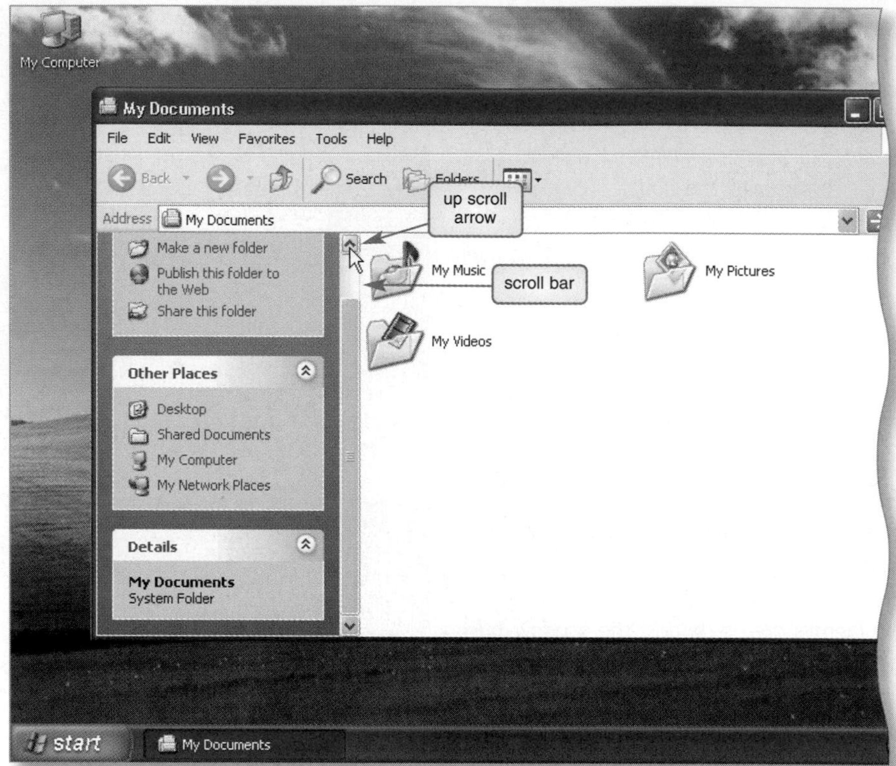

FIGURE 1-34

2

• **Click the up scroll arrow two times.**

The left pane scrolls down (the contents in the left pane move up) and displays a portion of the text in the File and Folder Tasks area at the top of the pane that previously was not visible (Figure 1-35). Because the size of the left pane does not change when you scroll, the contents in the left pane will change, as seen in the difference between Figures 1-35 and 1-34.

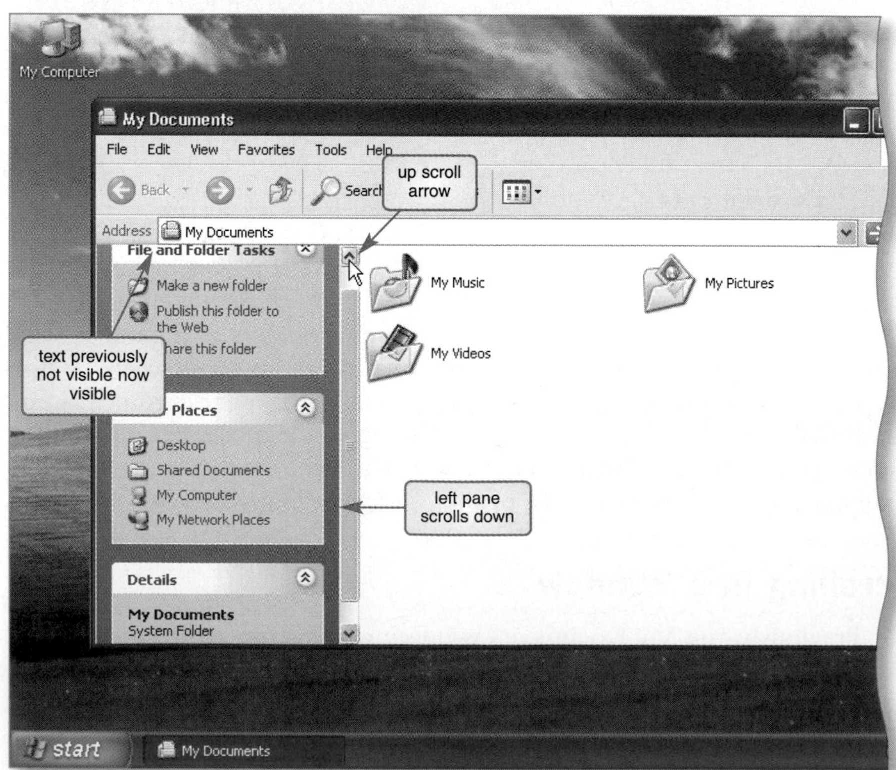

FIGURE 1-35

3

• **Click the up scroll arrow three more times.**

The scroll box moves to the top of the scroll bar and the remaining text in the File and Folder Tasks area is displayed (Figure 1-36).

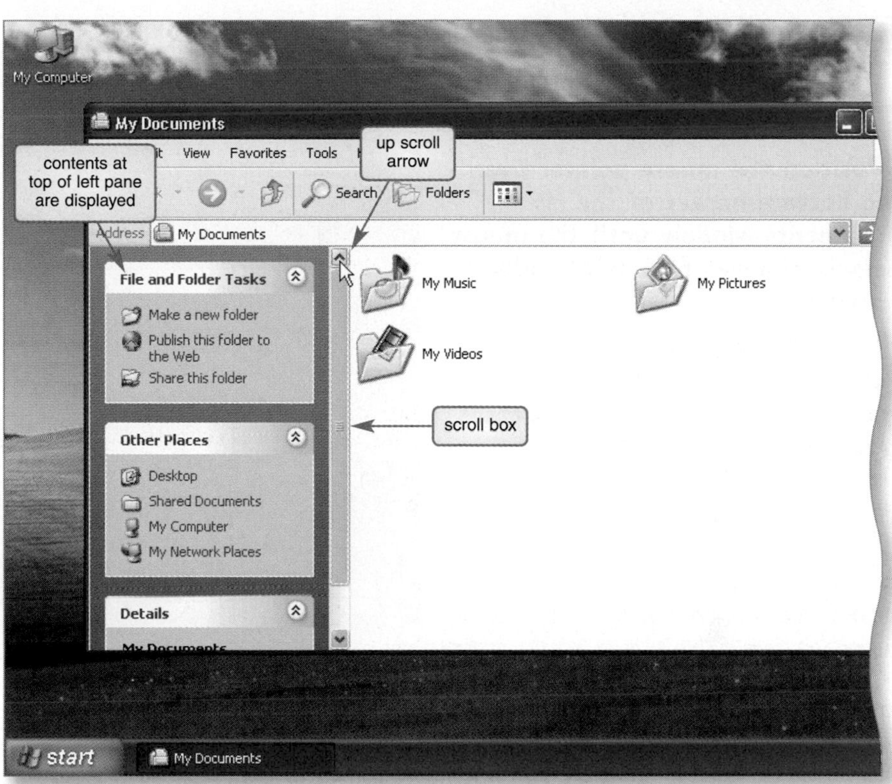

FIGURE 1-36

You can scroll continuously using scroll arrows by pointing to the up or down scroll arrow and holding down the left mouse button. The area being scrolled continues to scroll until you release the left mouse button or you reach the top or bottom of the area. You also can scroll by clicking the scroll bar itself. When you click the scroll bar, the area being scrolled moves up or down a greater distance than when you click the scroll arrows.

The third way in which you can scroll is by dragging the scroll box. When you drag the scroll box, the area being scrolled moves up or down as you drag.

Being able to view the contents of a window by scrolling is an important Windows XP skill because in many cases, the entire contents of a window are not visible.

Sizing a Window by Dragging

As previously mentioned, sometimes when information is displayed in a window, the information is not completely visible. A third method of displaying information that is not visible is to change the size of the window by dragging the border of a window. The step on the next page illustrates changing the size of the My Documents window.

To Size a Window by Dragging

1

- **Position the mouse pointer over the bottom border of the My Documents window until the mouse pointer changes to a two-headed arrow.**
- **Drag the bottom border downward until the Details area on your desktop resembles the Details area shown in Figure 1-37.**

As you drag the bottom border, the My Documents window, vertical scroll bar, and scroll box change size. After dragging, the Details area is visible and the vertical scroll bar no longer is visible (Figure 1-37).

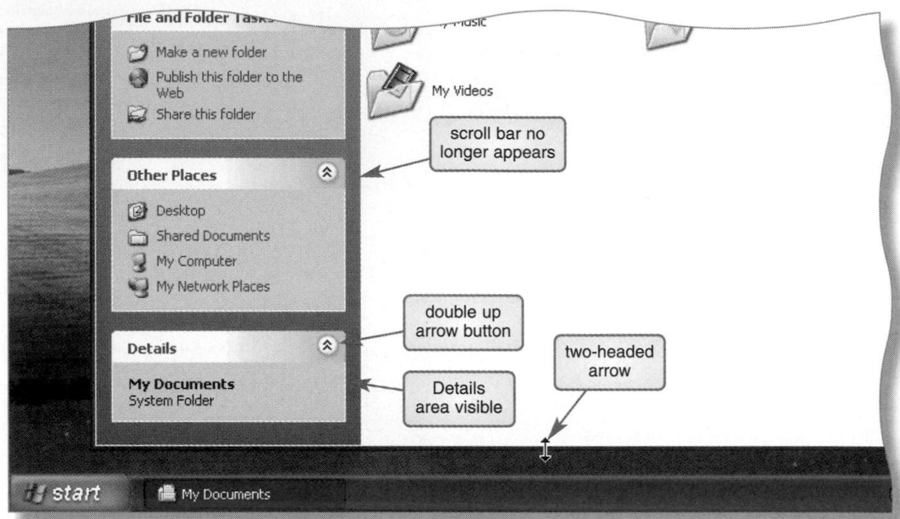

FIGURE 1-37

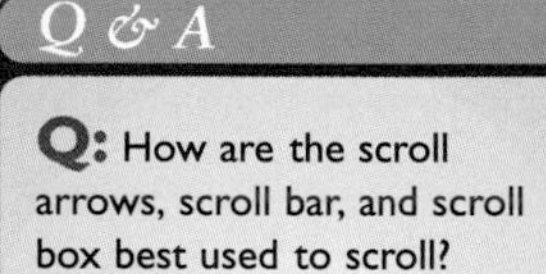

Q & A

Q: How are the scroll arrows, scroll bar, and scroll box best used to scroll?

A: General scrolling guidelines: (1) To scroll short distances (line by line), click the scroll arrows; (2) To scroll one screen at a time, click the scroll bar; and (3) To scroll long distances, drag the scroll box.

In addition to dragging the bottom border of a window, you also can drag the other borders (left, right, and top) and any window corner. If you drag a vertical border (left or right), you can move the border left or right. If you drag a horizontal border (top or bottom), you can move the border of the window up or down. If you drag a corner, you can move the corner up, down, left, or right.

Collapsing an Area

The Details area in the My Documents window is expanded and a double up arrow button displays to the right of the Details title (Figure 1-37). Clicking the button or the area title collapses the Details area and removes the window title (My Documents) and folder type (System Folder) from the Details area. The following steps show how to collapse the Details area in the My Documents window.

To Collapse an Area

1

- **Point to the double up arrow button in the Details area.**

The mouse pointer changes to a hand icon, points to the double up arrow button in the Details area, and the color of the Details title and button changes to light blue (Figure 1-38).

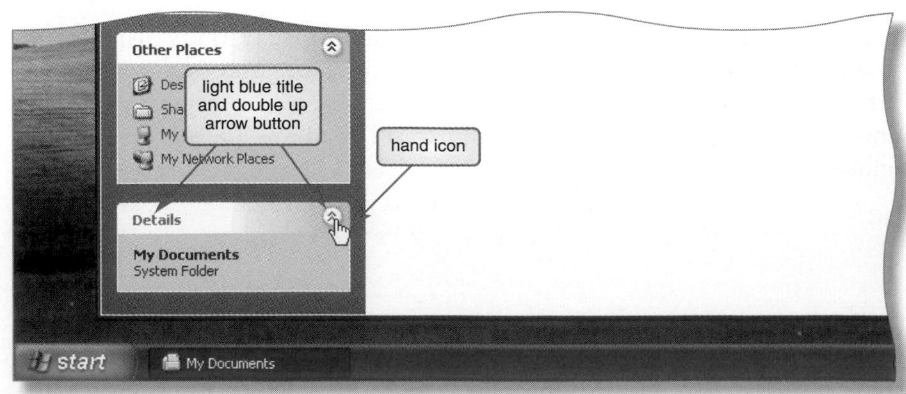

FIGURE 1-38

2

• **Click the double up arrow button.**

The Details area collapses and only the Details title and the double down arrow button are displayed (Figure 1-39).

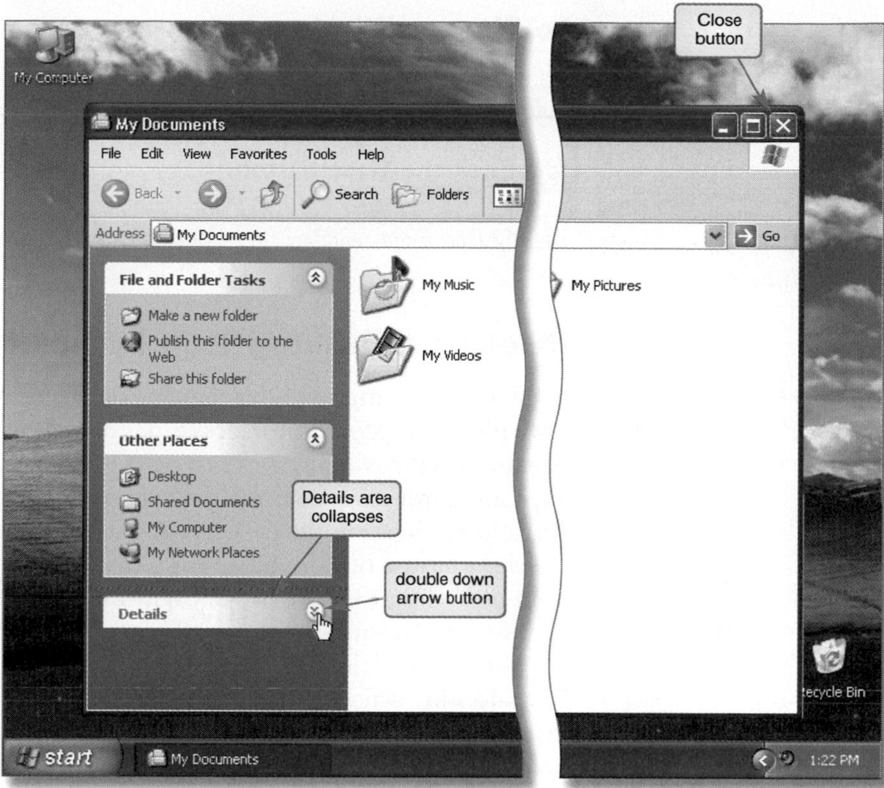

FIGURE 1-39

Resizing a Window

After moving and resizing a window, you may wish to return the window to approximately its original size. To return the My Documents window to about its original size, complete the following steps.

To Resize a Window

1. **Position the mouse pointer over the bottom border of the My Documents window border until the mouse pointer changes to a two-headed arrow.**
2. **Drag the bottom border of the My Documents window up until the window is the same size as shown in Figure 1-29 on page WIN 25 and then release the mouse button.**

The My Documents window is approximately the same size as it was before you made it smaller.

Closing a Window

After you have completed work in a window, normally you will close the window. The steps on the next page show how to close the My Documents window.

To Close a Window

1. **Point to the Close button on the right of the title bar in the My Documents window.**
2. **Click the Close button.**

The My Documents window closes and the desktop contains no open windows.

Deleting a Desktop Icon by Right-Dragging

The My Computer icon remains on the desktop. In many cases after you have placed an icon on the desktop, you will want to delete the icon. Although Windows XP has many ways to delete desktop icons, one method of removing the My Computer icon from the desktop is to right-drag the My Computer icon to the Recycle Bin icon on the desktop. **Right-drag** means you point to an item, hold down the right mouse button, move the item to the desired location, and then release the right mouse button. When you right-drag an object, a shortcut menu is displayed. The shortcut menu contains commands specifically for use with the object being dragged.

When you delete an icon from the desktop, Windows XP places the item in the **Recycle Bin**, which is an area on the hard disk that contains all the items you have deleted not only from the desktop but also from the hard disk. When the Recycle Bin becomes full, you can empty it. Up until the time you empty the Recycle Bin, you can recover deleted items from the Recycle Bin. The following steps illustrate how to delete the My Computer icon by right-dragging the icon to the Recycle Bin icon.

To Delete a Desktop Icon by Right-Dragging

1

- **Point to the My Computer icon on the desktop, hold down the right mouse button, drag the My Computer icon over the Recycle Bin icon.**
- **Release the right mouse button and then point to Move Here on the shortcut menu.**

The My Computer icon is displayed on the desktop as you drag the icon. When you release the right mouse button, a shortcut menu is displayed on the desktop (Figure 1-40). Pointing to the Move Here command on the shortcut menu highlights the Move Here command.

FIGURE 1-40

2

• **Click Move Here and then point to the Yes button in the Confirm Delete dialog box.**

The shortcut menu closes, and the Confirm Delete dialog box is displayed on the desktop (Figure 1-41). A dialog box is displayed whenever Windows XP needs to supply information to you or wants you to enter information or select among several options. The Confirm Delete dialog box contains a question, a message, and the Yes and No buttons.

3

• **Click the Yes button.**

The Confirm Delete dialog box closes, the My Computer icon no longer is displayed on the desktop, and the My Computer icon now is contained in the Recycle Bin.

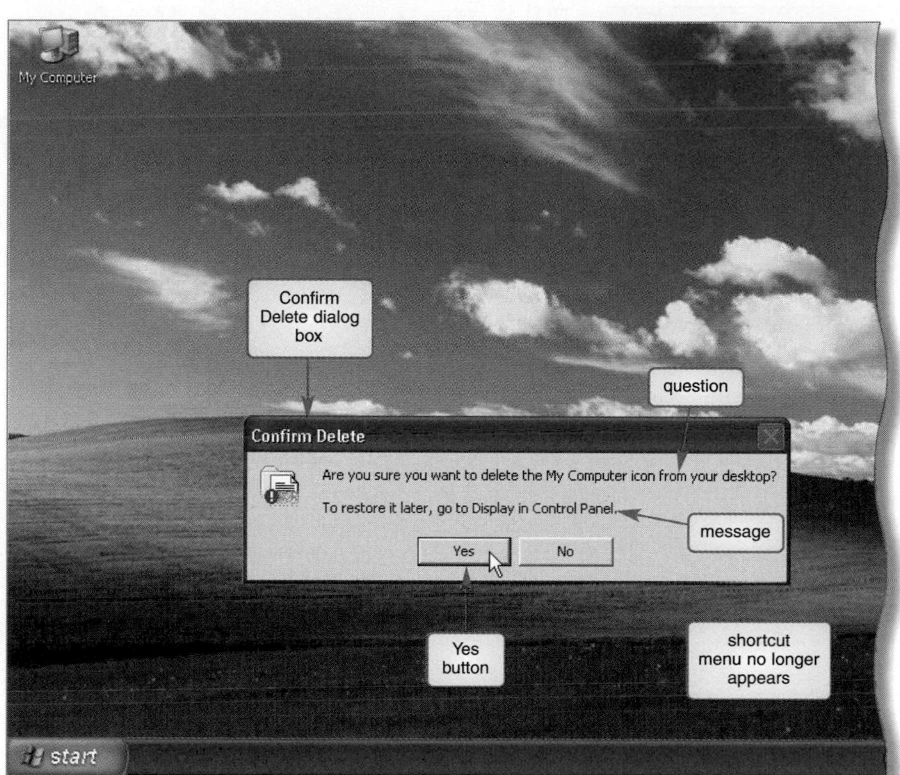

FIGURE 1-41

If you click **Move Here** on the shortcut menu shown in Figure 1-40, Windows XP will move the icon from its current location to the new location. If you click Cancel, the operation will be terminated, and the **Cancel command** will reset anything you have done during the operation.

In Figure 1-41, the Confirm Delete dialog box contains the Yes button and the No button. Clicking the Yes button completes the operation and clicking the No button terminates the operation.

Although you can move icons by dragging with the primary (left) mouse button and by right-dragging with the secondary (right) mouse button, it is strongly suggested you right-drag because a shortcut menu appears and, in most cases, you can specify the exact operation you want to occur. When you drag using the left mouse button, a default operation takes place and that operation may not be the operation you intended to perform.

Skill Builder 1-1

To practice the following tasks, visit scsite.com/off2003sch/skill, locate Windows XP Project 1, and then click Skill Builder 1-1.

- ❑ Log on to the computer
- ❑ Display Start menu
- ❑ Manipulate a window
- ❑ Add an icon to and delete an icon from the desktop

Summary of Mouse and Windows Operations

You have seen how to use the mouse to point, click, right-click, double-click, drag, and right-drag in order to accomplish certain tasks on the desktop. The use of a mouse is an important skill when using Windows XP. In addition, you have learned how to move around and use windows on the Windows XP desktop.

Q & A

Q: How do right-handed mouse users position their hands when using the Single Touch pad?

A: When using the Single Touch pad, Microsoft Office users place their left hand on the pad and their right hand on the mouse. These hand positions allow them to get more work done in less time. They also report that when using Hot Keys, they can increase productivity because they do not have to take their hand off the keyboard as frequently to use a mouse.

The Keyboard and Keyboard Shortcuts

The **keyboard** is an input device on which you manually key in, or type, data. Figure 1-42 shows the Microsoft Office keyboard designed specifically for use with Microsoft Office and the Internet. The Single Touch pad along the left side of the keyboard contains keys to browse the Internet, copy and paste text, and switch between applications. A scroll wheel allows you to move quickly within a document window. The Hot Keys along the top of the keyboard allow you to start a Web browser or e-mail program, play multimedia, and adjust the system volume.

FIGURE 1-42

Many tasks you accomplish with a mouse also can be accomplished using a keyboard. To perform tasks using the keyboard, you must understand the notation used to identify which keys to press. This notation is used throughout Windows XP to identify a **keyboard shortcut**.

Keyboard shortcuts consist of: (1) pressing a single key (such as press the ENTER key); or (2) pressing and holding down one key and pressing a second key, as shown by two key names separated by a plus sign (such as press CTRL+ESC). For example, to obtain help about Windows XP, you can press the F1 key and to display the Start menu, hold down the CTRL key and then press the ESC key (press CTRL+ESC).

Often, computer users will use keyboard shortcuts for operations they perform frequently. For example, many users find pressing the F1 key to start Help and Support easier than using the Start menu as shown later in this project. As a user, you probably will find the combination of keyboard and mouse operations that particularly suits you, but it is strongly recommended that generally you use the mouse.

Starting an Application Program

One of the basic tasks you can perform using Windows XP is starting an application program. A **program** is a set of computer instructions that carries out a task on the computer. An **application program** is a set of specific computer instructions that is designed to allow you to accomplish a particular task. For example, a **word processing program** is an application program that allows you to create written documents; a **presentation graphics program** is an application program that allows you to create graphic presentations for display on a computer; and a **Web browser program** is an application program that allows you to search for and display Web pages.

The **default Web browser program** (Internet Explorer) appears in the pinned items list on the Start menu shown in Figure 1-43. Because the default **Web browser** is selected during the installation of the Windows XP operating system, the default Web browser on your computer may be different. In addition, you easily can select another Web browser as the default Web browser. Another frequently used Web browser program is **MSN Explorer**.

Starting an Application Using the Start Menu

The most common activity performed on a computer is starting an application program to accomplish specific tasks. You can start an application program by using the Start menu. To illustrate the use of the Start menu to start an application program, the default Web browser program (Internet Explorer) will be started. The following steps illustrate starting Internet Explorer using the Internet command on the Start menu.

To Start an Application Using the Start Menu

1

- **Click the Start button on the taskbar and then point to Internet on the pinned items list on the Start menu.**

The Start menu is displayed (Figure 1-43). The pinned items list on the Start menu contains the Internet command to start the default Web browser program and the name of the default Web browser program (Internet Explorer). The default Web browser program on your computer may be different.

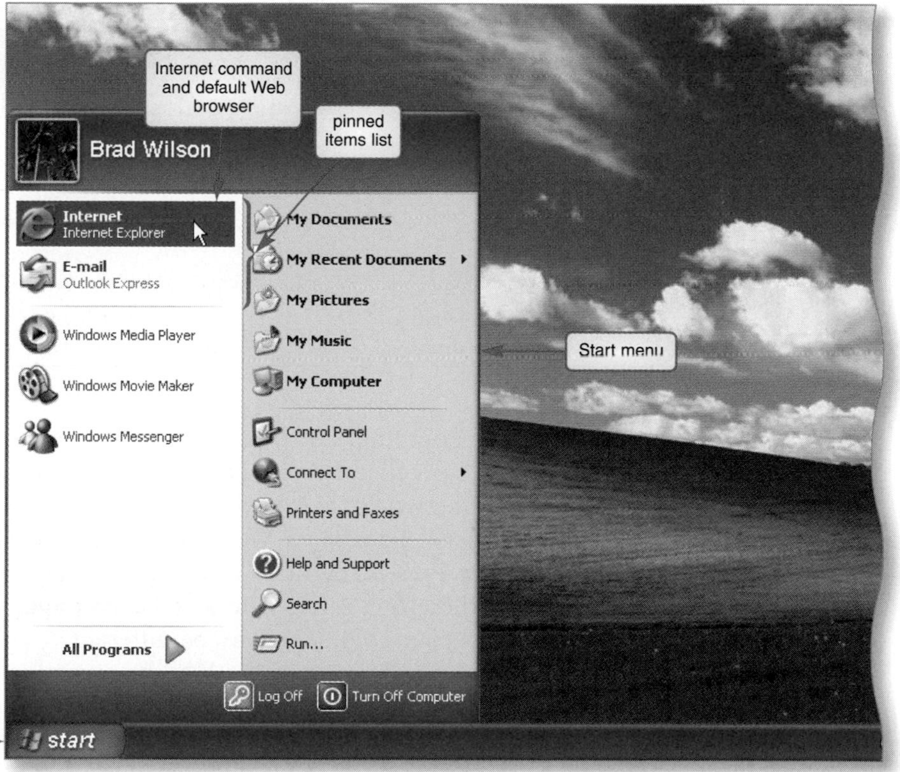

FIGURE 1-43

• **Click Internet.**

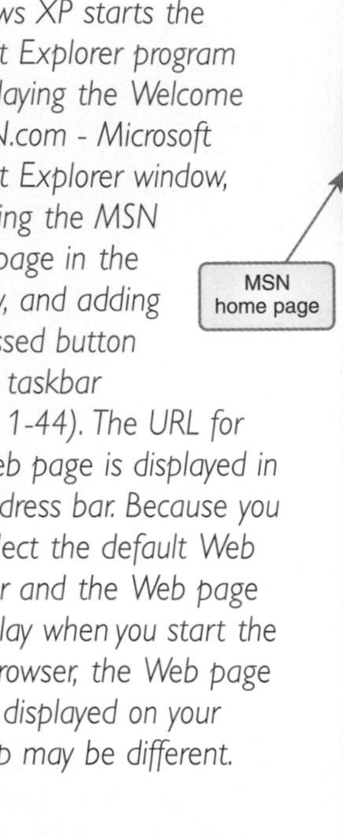

Windows XP starts the Internet Explorer program by displaying the Welcome to MSN.com - Microsoft Internet Explorer window, displaying the MSN home page in the window, and adding a recessed button on the taskbar (Figure 1-44). The URL for the Web page is displayed in the Address bar. Because you can select the default Web browser and the Web page to display when you start the Web browser, the Web page that is displayed on your desktop may be different.

FIGURE 1-44

• **Click the Close button in the Microsoft Internet Explorer window.**

The Microsoft Internet Explorer window closes.

Any computer connected to the Internet that contains Web pages you can reference is called a **Web site**. The **MSN.com Web site**, one of millions of Web sites around the world, is stored on a computer operated by Microsoft Corporation and can be accessed using a Web browser. The Welcome to MSN.com **Web page** shown in Figure 1-44 is the first Web page you see when you access the MSN.com Web site and is, therefore, referred to as a **home page**, or **start page.** The Web page that displays on your computer may be different.

After you have started a Web browser, you can use the program to search for and display additional Web pages located on different Web sites around the world.

In the preceding section, you started Internet Explorer and then quit the Internet Explorer program by closing the Microsoft Internet Explorer window. In the next section, you will learn about hierarchical format, USB flash drives, and the Windows Explorer application program.

Windows Explorer

Windows Explorer is an application program included with Windows XP. It allows you to view the contents of the computer, the hierarchy of drives and folders on the computer, and the files and folders in each folder. In this project, you will use Windows Explorer to: (1) expand and collapse drives and folders; (2) display drive and folder contents; (3) create a new folder; (4) copy a file between folders; and (5) rename and then delete a file. These are common operations that you should understand how to perform.

Starting Windows Explorer

As with many other operations, Windows XP offers a variety of ways to start Windows Explorer. The following steps show how to start Windows Explorer using the Folders button in the My Computer window.

To Start Windows Explorer and Maximize Its Window

1

- **Click the Start button on the taskbar and then click My Computer on the Start menu.**
- **Maximize the My Computer window.**
- **If the status bar does not appear at the bottom of the My Computer window, click View on the menu bar and then click Status Bar.**
- **Point to the Folders button on the Standard Buttons toolbar.**

The maximized My Computer window is displayed (Figure 1-45). The status bar is located at the bottom of the window. Pointing to the Folders button on the Standard Buttons toolbar displays a three-dimensional button.

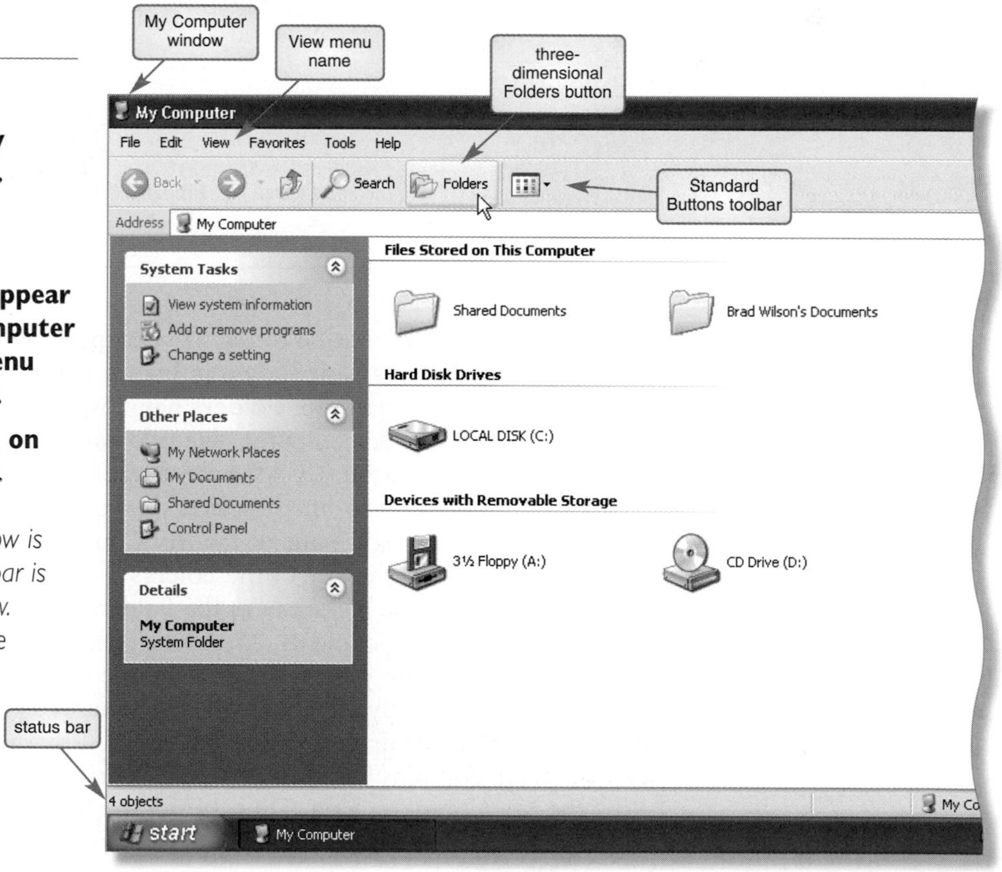

FIGURE 1-45

2

• **Click the Folders button.**

The Folders pane is displayed in place of the left pane in the My Computer window (Figure 1-46).

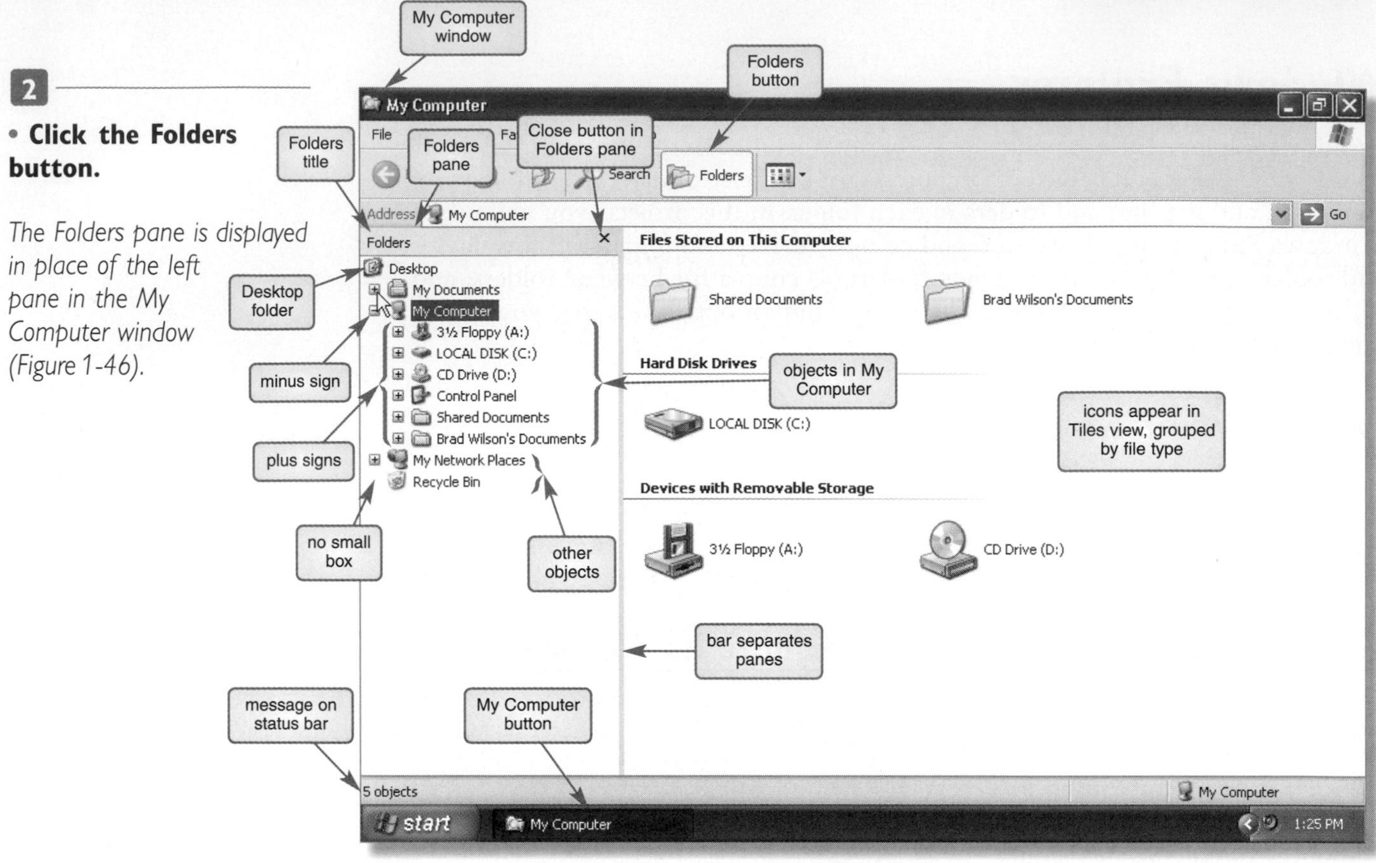

FIGURE 1-46

Clicking the Folders button in the My Computer window selects the Folders button, displays the Folders pane shown in Figure 1-46, and allows you to use Windows Explorer. The **Folders pane** (or **Folders bar**) displays the **hierarchical structure** of folders and drives on the computer. The title bar in the Folders pane contains a title (Folders) and Close button. Clicking the Close button removes the Folders pane from the My Computer window and deselects the Folders button. A bar separates the Folders pane and the right pane of the My Computer window. You can drag the bar left or right to change the size of the Folders pane.

The top level of the hierarchy in the Folders pane is the Desktop. Below the Desktop are the My Documents, My Computer, My Network Places, and Recycle Bin icons. The icons on your computer may be different.

To the left of the My Computer icon is a minus sign in a small box. The **minus sign** indicates that the drive or folder represented by the icon next to it, in this case My Computer, contains additional folders or drives and these folders or drives appear below the My Computer icon. Thus, below the My Computer icon are the 3½ Floppy (A:), LOCAL DISK (C:), CD Drive (D:), Control Panel, Shared Documents, and Brad Wilson's Documents icons. Each of these icons has a small box with a plus sign next to it. The **plus sign** indicates that the drive or folder represented by the icon has more folders within it but the folders do not appear in the Folders pane. As you will see shortly, clicking the box with the plus sign will display the folders within the drive or folder represented by the icon. If an item contains no folders, such as the Recycle Bin, no hierarchy exists and no small box is displayed next to the icon.

The right pane in the My Computer window illustrated in Figure 1-46 contains three groups of icons. The Files Stored on This Computer group contains the Shared Documents icon and Brad Wilson's Documents icon. The Hard Disk Drives group contains the LOCAL DISK (C:) icon. The Devices with Removable Storage group contains the 3½ Floppy (A:) and CD Drive (D:) icons.

The **status bar** appears at the bottom of the window and contains information about the documents, folders, and programs in a window. A message on the left of the status bar located at the bottom of the window indicates the right pane contains five objects.

Windows Explorer displays the drives and folders on the computer in hierarchical structure in the Folders pane. This arrangement allows you to move and copy files and folders using only the Folders pane and the contents of the right pane.

As mentioned earlier, being able to create and organize folders on the computer is an important skill that every student should understand. On the following pages, you will learn about removable media and DOS paths, plug a USB flash drive into a USB port on the computer, create and name a folder on a removable drive, and download the remaining folders in the hierarchical structure (see Figure 1-47) into the Freshman folder.

Using a Hierarchical Format to Organize Files and Folders

One of the more important tasks for a beginning student is to be able to create and organize the files and folders on the computer. A file may contain a spreadsheet assignment given by the computer teacher, a research paper assigned by the English teacher, an electronic quiz given by the Business teacher, or a study sheet designed by the Math teacher. These files should be organized and stored in folders to reduce the possibility of misplacing or losing a file and to find a file quickly.

Assume you are a freshman and are taking four classes (Business, Computer, English, and Math). You want to design a series of folders for the four classes you are taking in the first semester of the freshman year. To accomplish this, you arrange the folders in a **hierarchical format**. The hierarchical structure of folders for the Freshman year is shown in Figure 1-47.

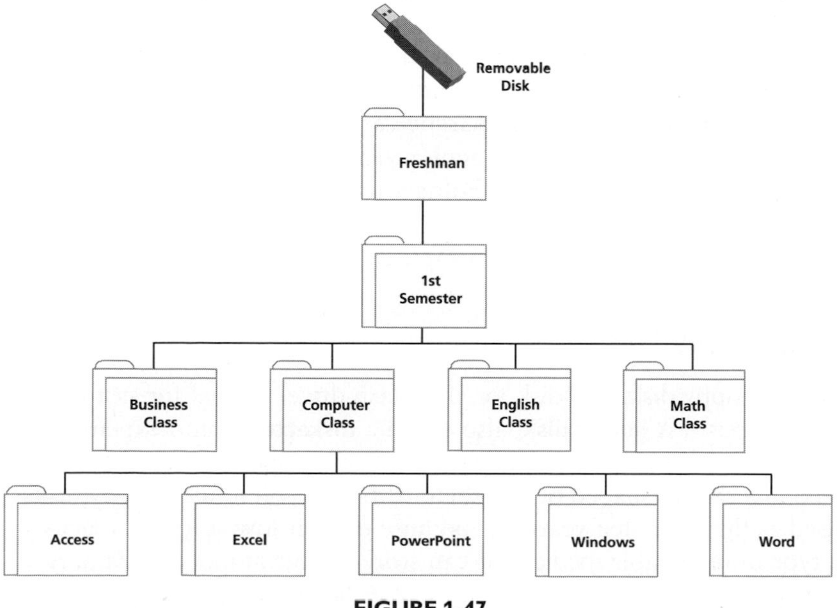

FIGURE 1-47

The hierarchy contains five levels. Each rectangular box is represented by a folder icon and vertical and horizontal lines connect the folders. The first level contains the

Removable Disk drive, the second level contains the Freshman folder, the third level contains the 1st Semester folder, the fourth level contains four folders (Business Class, Computer Class, English Class, and Math Class), the fifth level contains five folders (Access, Excel, PowerPoint, Windows, and Word).

The vertical and horizontal lines in the hierarchy chart form a pathway that allows you to navigate to a drive or folder. Each pathway, or **DOS path**, is a means of navigation to a specific location on a computer or network. The acronym, DOS, comes from the name of Microsoft's first operating system (**D**isk **O**perating **S**ystem). A path consists of a drive letter and colon (C:), a backslash (\), and one or more folders. Each drive or folder in the hierarchy chart has a corresponding path. When you click a drive or folder icon in the Folders pane, the corresponding path appears in the Address box on the Address bar. Table 1-1 contains examples of path names and their corresponding drives and folders.

Table 1-1 Path Names and Corresponding Drives and Folders

PATH	DRIVE AND FOLDER
E:\	Drive E (Removable Disk)
E:\Freshman	Freshman folder on drive E
E:\Freshman\1st Semester	1st Semester folder in Freshman folder on drive E
E:\Freshman\1st Semester\Computer Class\Word	Word folder in Computer Class folder in 1st Semester folder in Freshman folder on drive E

In Table 1-1, the E:\ path represents the Removable Disk (E:) drive, the E:\Freshman folder represents the Freshman folder on the Removable Disk (E:) drive, the E:\Freshman\1st Semester folder represents the 1st Semester folder in the Freshman folder on the Removable Disk (E:) drive, and so on.

When this hierarchy is created on the computer, the Removable Disk drive is said "to contain" the Freshman folder, the Freshman folder is said "to contain" the 1st Semester folder, and so on. In addition, this hierarchy can easily be expanded to include folders for the Sophomore, Junior, and Senior years and additional semesters.

When clicking a drive or folder icon in the Folders pane while performing the steps in this project, look at the path in the Address box to better understand the relationship between the folders and drives on the computer.

Removable Media and Network Drives

A removable media (floppy disk, Zip disk, or USB flash drive) is ideal for storing files and folders on a computer. A **floppy disk**, also called a **diskette**, is an inexpensive, portable storage medium that consists of a thin, circular, flexible plastic disk with a magnetic coating enclosed in a square-shaped plastic shell. Although still in use, floppy disks are not as widely used as they were ten years ago because of their low storage capacity.

A **Zip disk** is a type of removable media that can store a large amount of data. A Zip disk stores 500 times more than a floppy disk. A **USB flash drive**, sometimes called a **pen drive**, is a flash memory storage device that plugs into a USB port on a computer. A **USB port**, short for universal serial bus port, can be found on either the front or back of most computers. USB flash drives are convenient for mobile users because they are small and lightweight enough to be transported on a keychain or in a pocket.

A **network** is a collection of computers and devices connected together for the purpose of sharing information between computer users. In some cases, students might be required to store their files on a network drive found on the school's computer network. A **network drive** is a storage device that is connected to the server on the computer network. A **server** controls access to the hardware, software, and other resources on the network and provides a centralized storage area for programs, data, and information. If student files reside on the network drive on the school's network, files may be accessed from a school computer, or from a personal computer with permission from the school. Ask your teacher if the school requires students to use a network drive.

Connecting a USB Flash Drive to a USB Port

Although other removable media may be used for storage, the USB flash drive is one of the more popular drives (Figure 1-48). To store files and folders on the USB flash drive, you must connect the USB flash drive to a USB port on the computer. Connecting a USB flash drive to a USB port causes the Removable Disk (E:) window to be displayed on the desktop. The removable media drive name on your computer may be different.

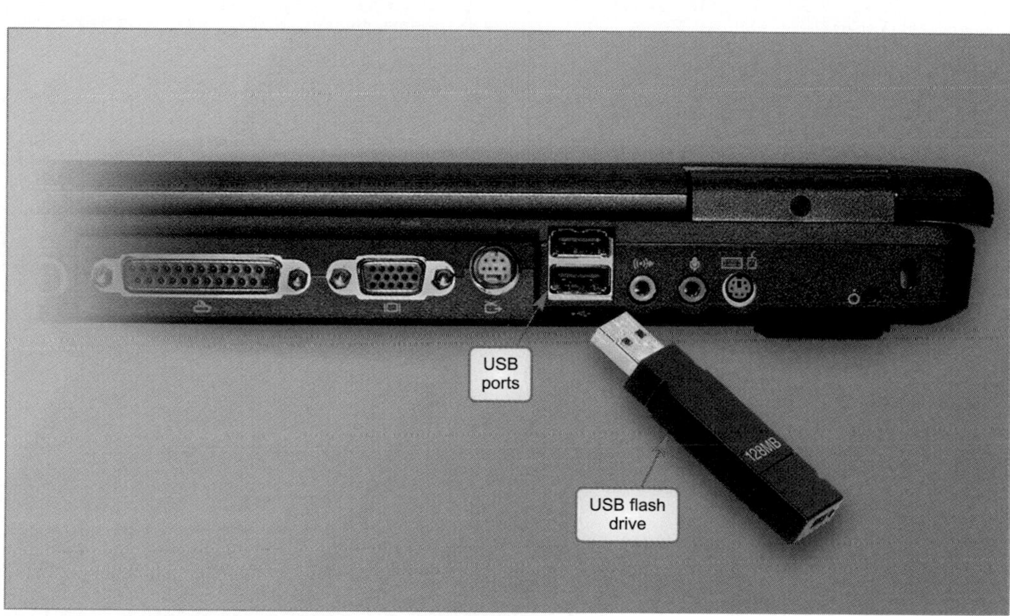

FIGURE 1-48

To Connect a USB Flash Drive to a USB Port

1

• **Connect the USB flash drive to a USB port on the computer.**

When you connect the USB flash drive to the USB port, the Auto Play dialog box appears momentarily, the Removable Disk (E:) icon is displayed in the Folders pane, the Removable Disk (E:) dialog box is displayed, and the Play command is selected in the dialog box (Figure 1-49). The My Computer button and Removable Disk (E:) button appear on the taskbar.

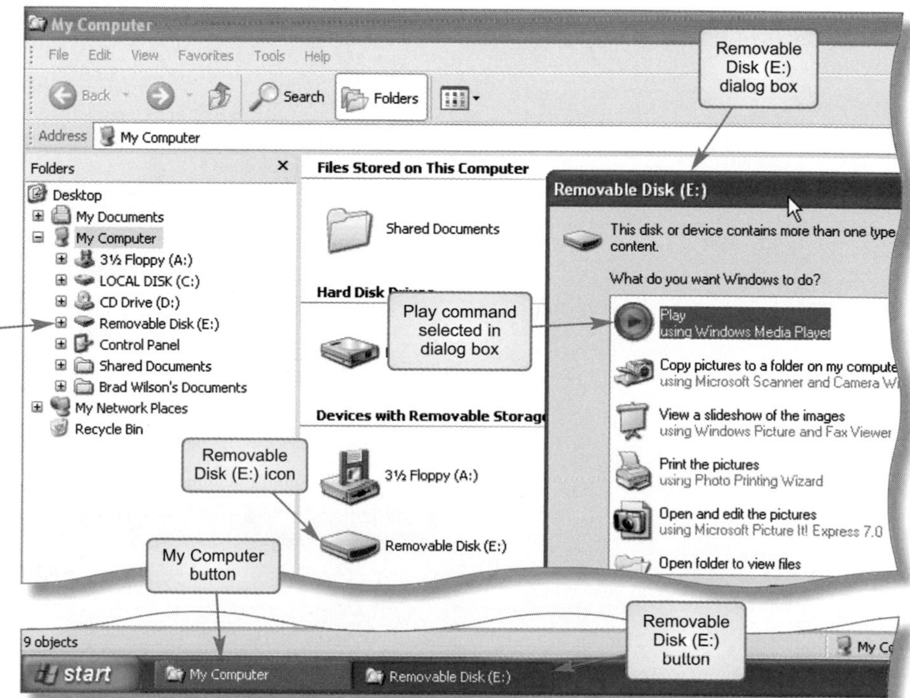

FIGURE 1-49

2

• **Scroll to the bottom of the What do you want Windows to do? list box and click the Take no action command.**

The Take no action command is selected in the What do you want Windows to do? list box (Figure 1-50).

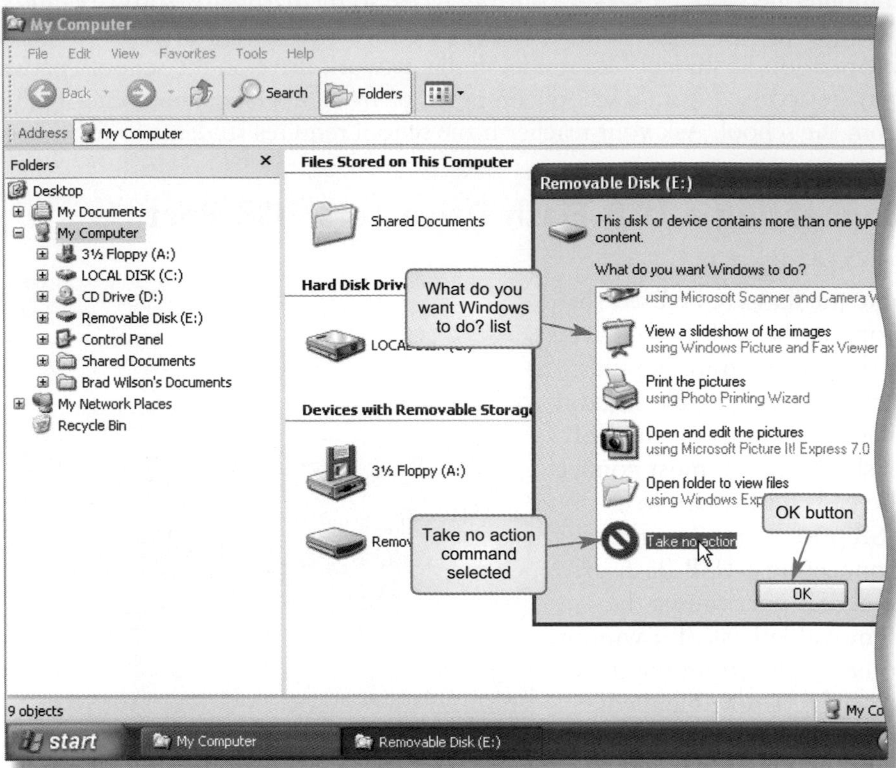

FIGURE 1-50

3

• **Click the OK button in the What do you want Windows to do? list box.**

The Removable Disk (E:) dialog box closes, and the Removable Disk (E:) icon is displayed in the right pane (Figure 1-51).

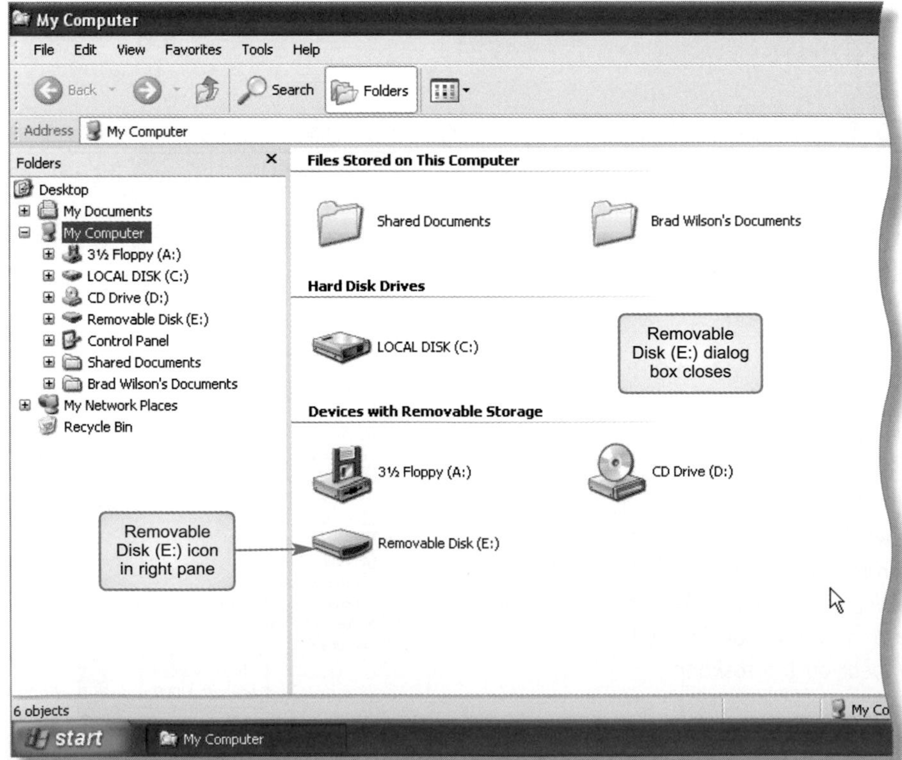

FIGURE 1-51

The USB flash drive is connected to the USB port, the Removable Disk (E:) drive entry is displayed in the Folders pane, and the Removable Disk (E:) drive icon displays in the right pane.

After connecting the USB flash drive to the USB port, the next step is to create the Freshman folder on the Removable Disk (E:) drive (see Figure 1-47 on page WIN 39). The next two sections explain the rules for naming a folder and illustrate how to create the Freshman folder on the Removable Disk (E:) drive.

Naming a Folder

When you create a folder, you must assign a name to the folder. A folder name should be descriptive of the folder. Examples of folder names are Word 2003 Student Data Files, Windows XP Features, and Office Supplies. A folder name can contain up to 255 characters, including spaces. Any uppercase or lowercase character is valid when creating a folder name, except a backslash (\), slash (/), colon (:), asterisk (*), question mark (?), quotation marks ("), less than symbol (<), greater than symbol (>), or vertical bar (|). Folder names cannot be CON, AUX, COM1, COM2, COM3, COM4, LPT1, LPT2, LPT3, PRN, or NUL. The same rules for naming folders also apply to naming files.

Creating a Folder on a Removable Drive

To create a folder on a removable drive, you must select the Removable Disk (E:) drive icon in the Folders pane and then create the folder in the right pane. The following steps show how to create the Freshman folder on the Removable Disk (E:) drive.

To Create a Folder on a Removable Drive

1

• **Click the Removable Drive (E:) icon in the Folders pane, right-click an open area of the right pane to display a shortcut menu, point to New on the shortcut menu, and then point to Folder on the New submenu.**

A shortcut menu containing the highlighted New command and the New submenu containing the highlighted Folder command are displayed (Figure 1-52). The path to the Removable Disk (E:) drive is displayed in the Address box.

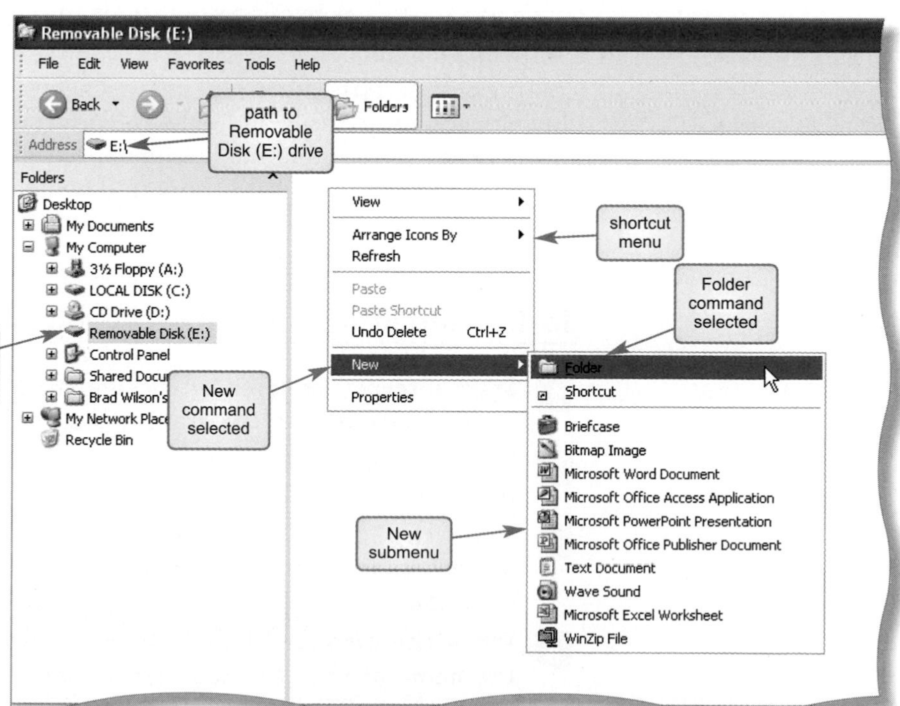

FIGURE 1-52

2

• **Click Folder on the New submenu, type** `Freshman` **in the icon title text box, and then press the ENTER key.**

The shortcut menu and Folder submenu close, the Freshman folder is selected in the right pane, and the Freshman folder is created on the Removable Disk (E:) drive (Figure 1-53).

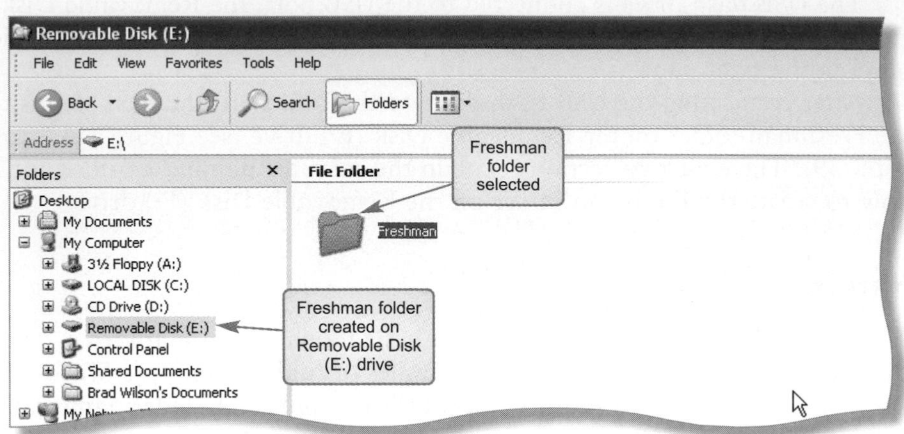

FIGURE 1-53

Downloading a Hierarchy of Folders to the Freshman Folder

After creating the Freshman folder on the Removable Disk (E:) drive, the remaining folders in the hierarchical structure (see Figure 1-47 on page WIN 39), starting with the 1st Semester folder, should be downloaded to the Freshman folder. **Downloading** is the process of a computer receiving information, such as a set of files or folders from a Web site, from a server on the Internet.

The remaining folders could be created by double-clicking the Freshman folder and then creating the 1st Semester folder in the Freshman folder, double-clicking the 1st Semester folder and then creating the next four folders (Business, Computer, English, and Math) in the 1st Semester folder, and so on. To make the task of creating the folders easier, the folders have been created and stored in a hierarchical structure on the SCSITE.COM Shelly Cashman Series Student Resources Web site.

While downloading the structure, a program called WinZip is used. **WinZip** compresses, or **zips**, larger files into a single smaller file, allowing the folders to be downloaded more easily and quickly. Performing the download causes the hierarchy of folders to be stored in the Freshman folder.

The following steps show how to download the folders in the hierarchical structure to the Freshman folder.

To Download a Hierarchy of Folders to the Freshman Folder

1. **Start Internet Explorer by clicking the Start button on the taskbar and then clicking Internet on the Start menu.**
2. **Click the Address box on the Address bar, type** `scsite.com` **in the Address box, and then click the Go button.**
3. **When the SCSITE.COM Shelly Cashman Series Student Resources Web page is displayed, scroll down to view the Browse by Subject area, and then click the Office Suites link.**
4. **When the expanded Office Suites link is displayed, click the link containing the name of your textbook (for example, Microsoft Office 2003: Introductory Concepts and Techniques).**
5. **Scroll down to display the Data Files for Students (Windows) area, and then click the Windows XP Project 1 Folders and Files link.**

6 **When the File Download - Security Warning dialog box is displayed, click the Run button.**

7 **When the Internet Explorer - Security Warning dialog box is displayed, click the Run button.**

8 **When the WinZip Self-Extractor dialog box is displayed, type the removable media drive letter of your removable media drive followed by a colon, backslash, and folder name (Freshman) (for example, E:\Freshman).**

9 **Click the Unzip button in the WinZip Self-Extractor dialog box.**

10 **When a smaller WinZip Self-Extractor dialog box is displayed, click the OK button.**

11 **Click the Close button in the WinZip Self-Extractor dialog box.**

12 **Click the Close button in the SCSITE.COM Shelly Cashman Series Student Resources window.**

The Windows XP Project 1 Folders and Files are downloaded from the SCSITE.COM Shelly Cashman Series Student Resources Web site to the Freshman folder in the right pane (Figure 1-54). Even though you cannot see the folders and files in the Freshman folder, the folders and files are contained in the Freshman folder. Some folders contain files to be used later in this project.

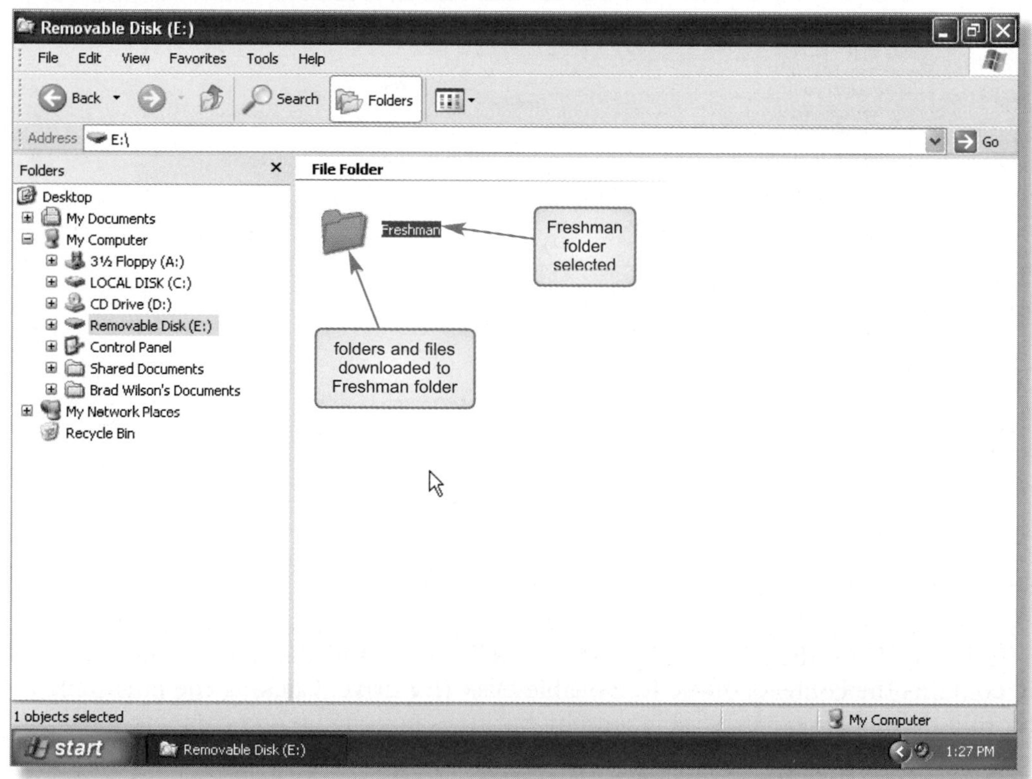

FIGURE 1-54

Expanding a Drive

Explorer displays the hierarchy of items in the Folders pane and the contents of drives and folders in the right pane. To expand a drive or folder in the Folders pane, click the plus sign in the small box to the left of the drive or folder icon. Clicking the plus sign expands the hierarchy in the Folders pane. The contents of the right pane remain the same. The steps on the next page show how to expand a drive.

To Expand a Drive

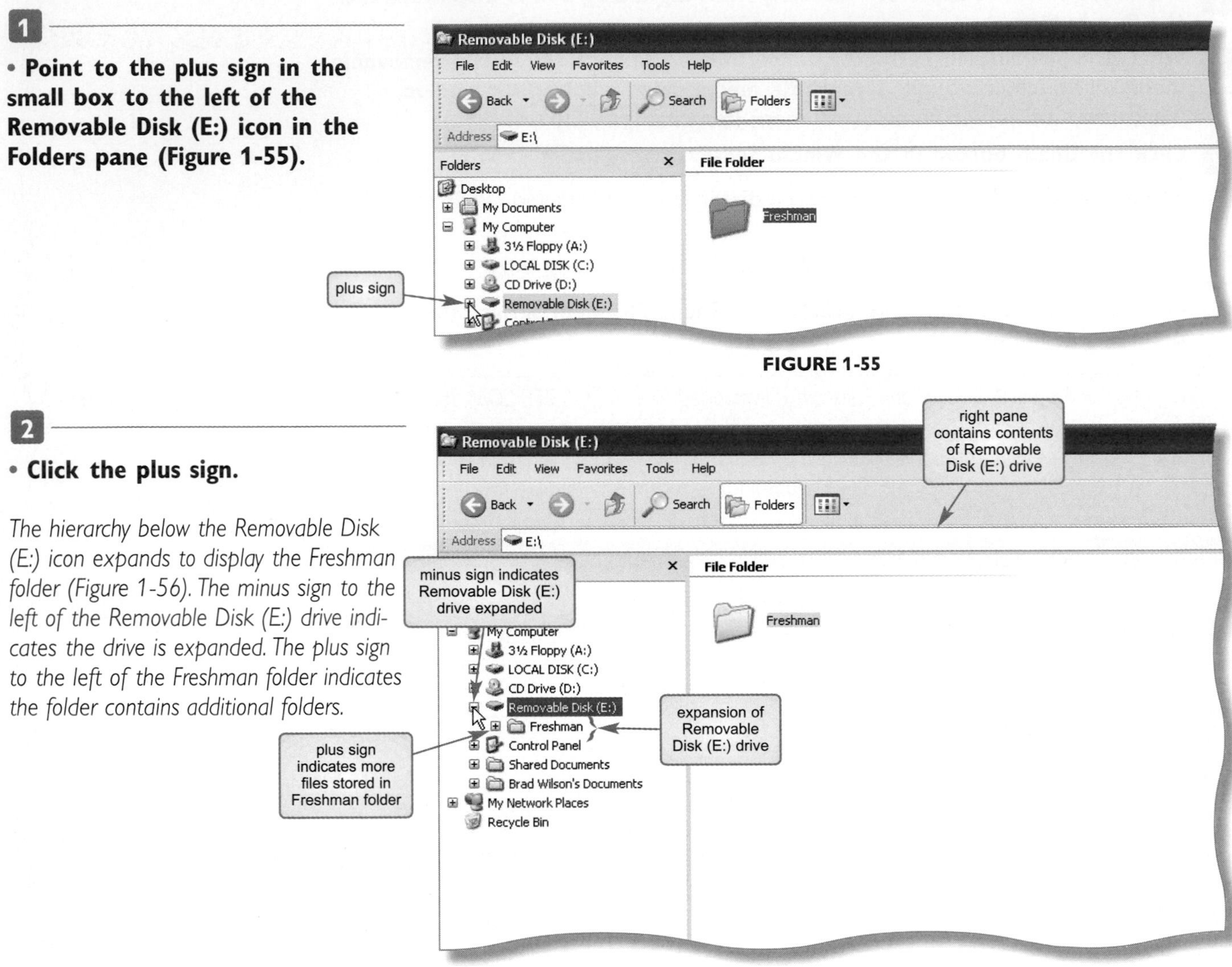

1

- **Point to the plus sign in the small box to the left of the Removable Disk (E:) icon in the Folders pane (Figure 1-55).**

FIGURE 1-55

2

- **Click the plus sign.**

The hierarchy below the Removable Disk (E:) icon expands to display the Freshman folder (Figure 1-56). The minus sign to the left of the Removable Disk (E:) drive indicates the drive is expanded. The plus sign to the left of the Freshman folder indicates the folder contains additional folders.

FIGURE 1-56

In Figure 1-56, the Removable Disk (E:) drive is expanded and the right pane still contains the contents of the Removable Disk (E:) drive. Clicking the plus sign next to a drive icon expands the hierarchy but does not change the contents of the right pane.

Expanding a Folder

When a plus sign in a small box displays to the left of a folder icon in the Folders pane, you can expand the folder to show all the folders it contains. The steps on the next page illustrate expanding the Freshman folder to view its contents.

To Expand a Folder

1

• **Point to the plus sign in the small box to the left of the Freshman icon (Figure 1-57).**

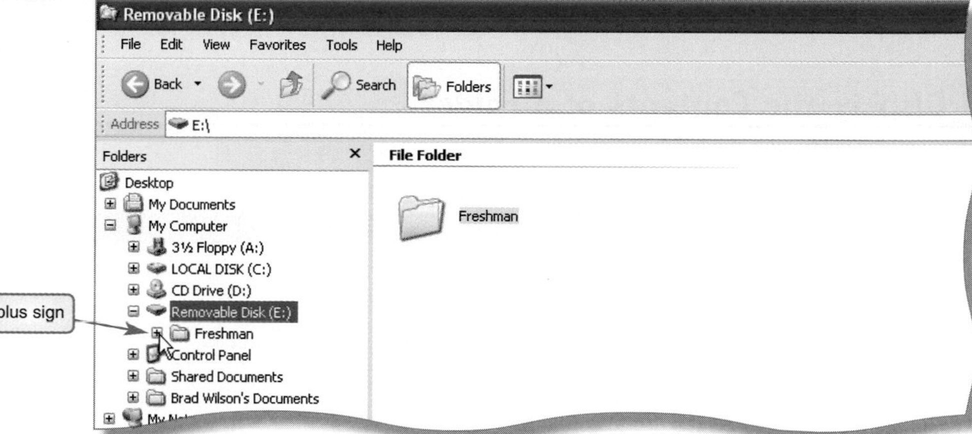

FIGURE 1-57

2

• **Click the plus sign.**

The hierarchy below the Freshman icon expands to display the 1st Semester folder contained in the Freshman folder (Figure 1-58). The folder is indented below the Freshman icon, and the minus sign to the left of the Freshman icon indicates the folder has been expanded. A folder with a plus sign contains more folders.

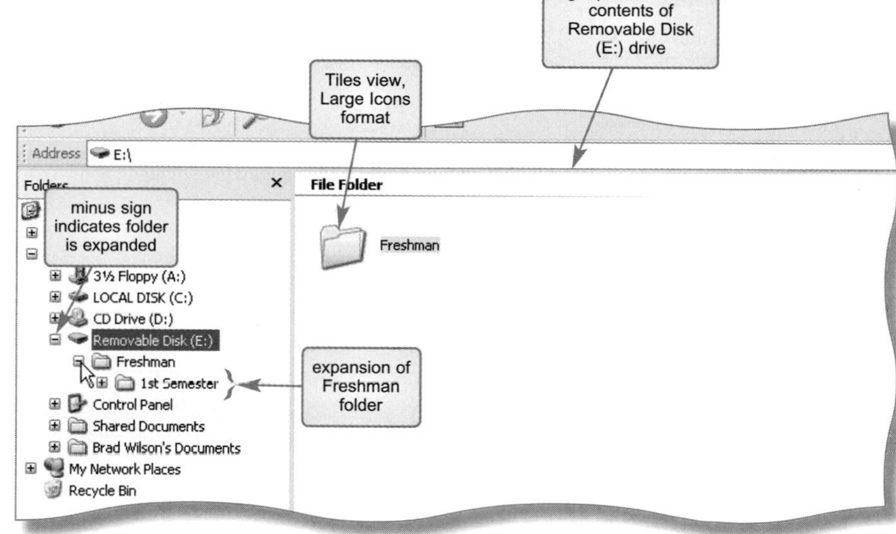

FIGURE 1-58

In Figure 1-58, the Freshman folder is expanded and the right pane still contains the contents of the Removable Disk (E:) folder. Clicking the plus sign next to a folder icon expands the hierarchy but does not change the contents of the right pane.

When a folder is expanded, the folders contained within the expanded folder display in the Folders pane. You can continue this expansion to view further levels of the hierarchy.

You can display files and folders in the right pane in several different views. Currently, the Freshman folder displays in Tiles view using Large Icons format.

Displaying Drive and Folder Contents

Explorer displays the hierarchy of items in the left, or Folders, pane and the contents of drives and folders in the right pane. To display the contents of a drive or folder in the right pane, click the drive or folder icon in the Folders pane. Clicking the icon displays the contents of the drive or folder in the right pane, expands the hierarchy in the Folders pane, and displays the path in the Address box. The following step shows how to display the contents of the 1st Semester folder.

To Display the Contents of a Folder

1

- **Click the 1st Semester icon in the Folders pane.**

The highlighted 1st Semester name is displayed in the Folders pane, the hierarchy below the 1st Semester icon expands, and the right pane contains the contents of the 1st Semester folder (Figure 1-59). The window title changes to 1st Semester, the 1st Semester button replaces the My Computer button on the taskbar, the status bar indicates four objects are displayed in the right pane, and the path to the 1st Semester folder is displayed in the Address box.

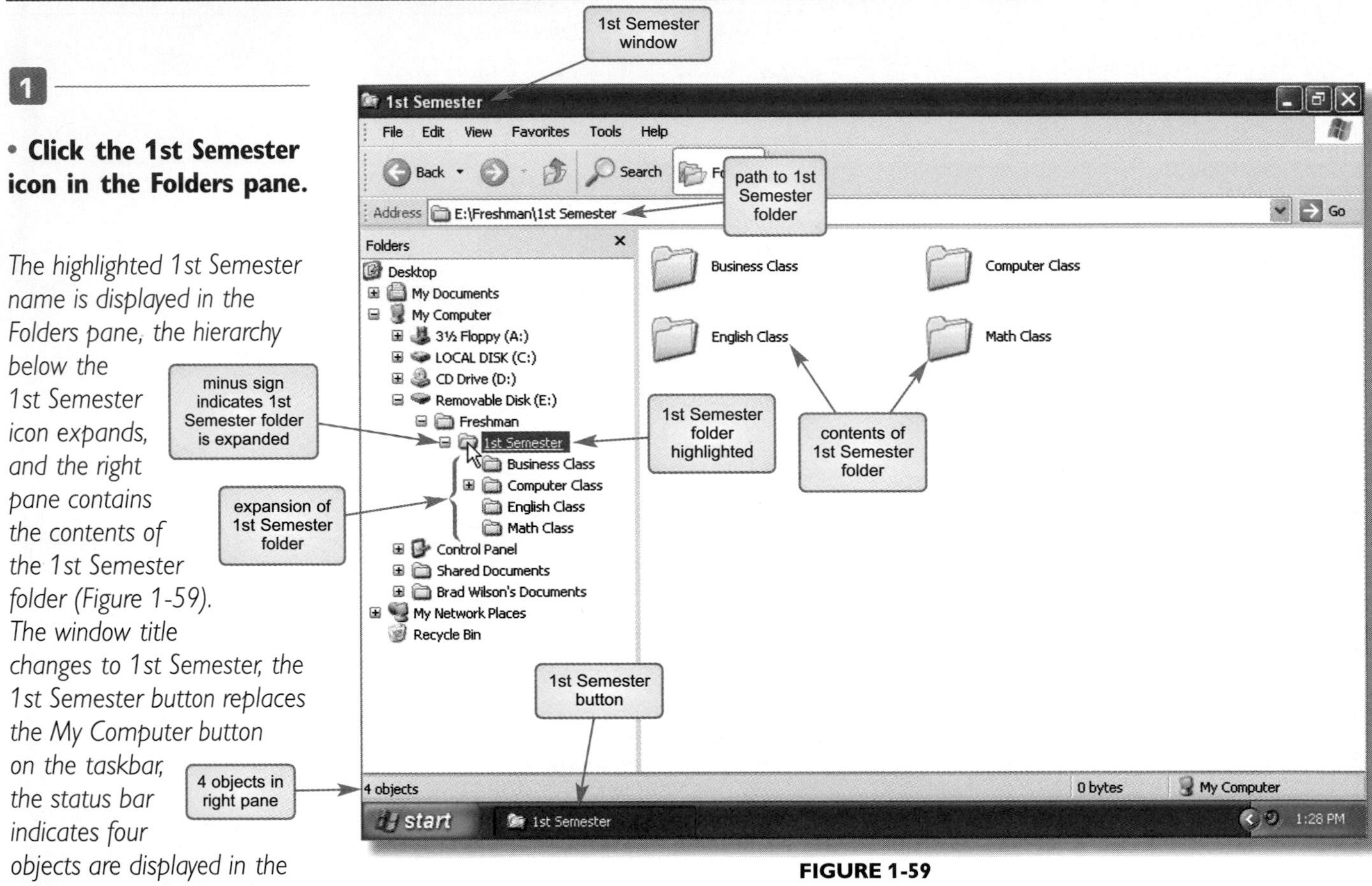

FIGURE 1-59

Skill Builder 1-2

To practice the following tasks, visit scsite.com/off2003sch/skill, locate Windows XP Project 1, and then click Skill Builder 1-2.

- ❑ Start Windows Explorer
- ❑ Create a folder
- ❑ Expand a drive and a folder
- ❑ Display drive and folder contents

Whenever files or folders are displayed in the right pane of a window, you can display the contents of the file or folder by double-clicking the icon of the file or folder.

Creating a Document and Folder in Microsoft Word

Previously, the Freshman folder was created in the Removable Disk (E:) drive using Windows Explorer. You also can create a folder anytime you save a file in a Windows application. For example, you can use Microsoft Office Word 2003 to create a document and then save the document in a folder. Microsoft Office Word 2003 is one of the five basic applications included in Microsoft Office 2003. Word is a full-featured word processing program that allows you to create a variety of personal and business documents.

The following section illustrates how to start Word, type text into a Word document, save the document in a new folder, and verify the document was saved in the folder. For example, you may want to type the Monday, April 10 assignment for your computer class in a Word document and then save the document in a newly created Homework folder.

Starting Word

To create the Monday, April 10 document, you must start Word. You may need to ask your instructor how to start Word on your system.

To Start Word

1

- **Click the Start button on the Windows taskbar, point to All Programs on the Start menu, point to Microsoft Office on the All Programs submenu, and then point to Microsoft Office Word 2003 on the Microsoft Office submenu.**

The Start menu, All Programs submenu, and Microsoft Office submenu are displayed (Figure 1-60). The Microsoft Office submenu contains the Microsoft Office Word 2003 command to start the Microsoft Word program.

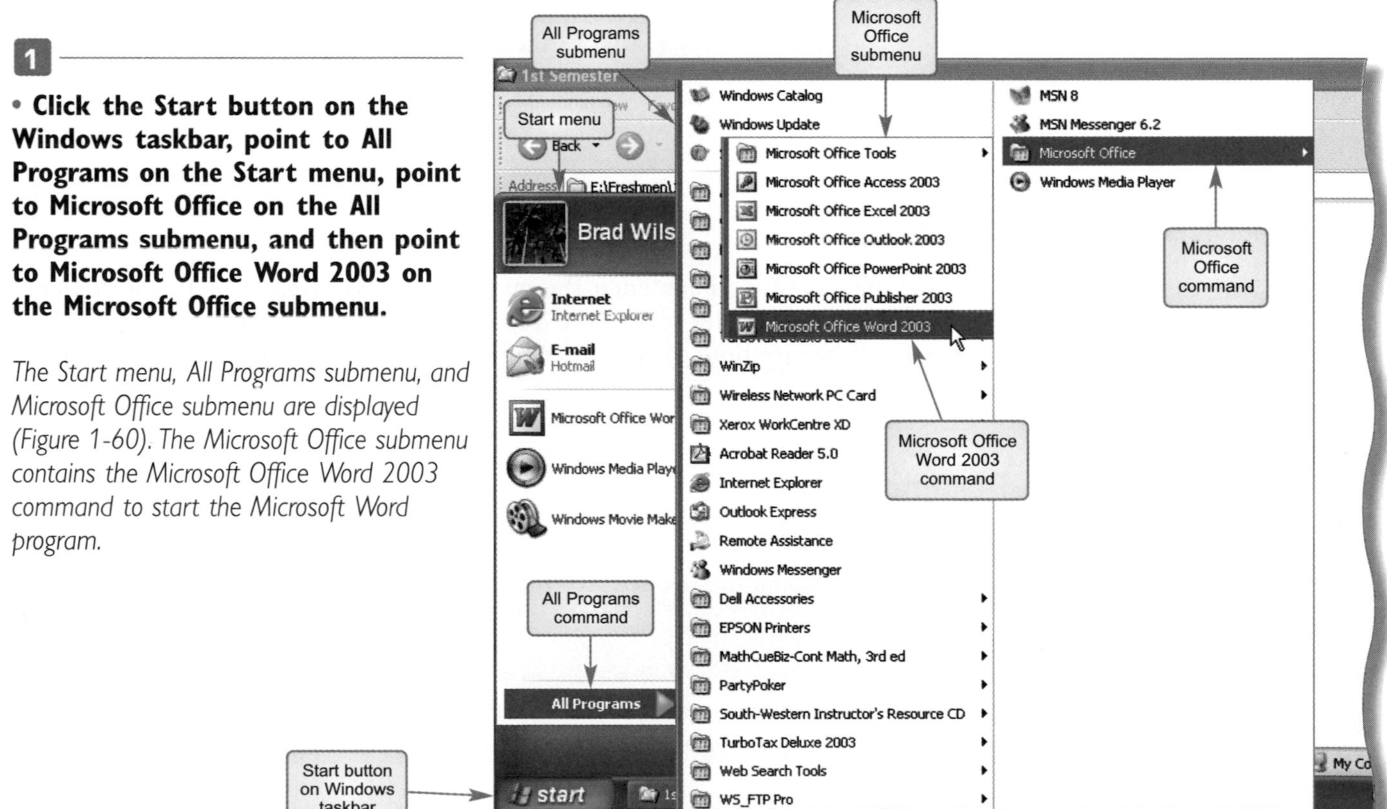

FIGURE 1-60

2

• **Click Microsoft Office Word 2003.**

Word starts. After a few moments, Word displays a blank document titled Document1 in the Microsoft Word window (Figure 1-61). The Windows taskbar displays the Microsoft Word program button, indicating Word is running.

3

• **If the Microsoft Word window is not maximized, double-click its title bar to maximize it.**

• **If the Office Assistant appears, right-click it and then click Hide on the shortcut menu.**

• **If the Getting Started task pane appears, click the Close button in the upper-right corner of the Getting Started task pane.**

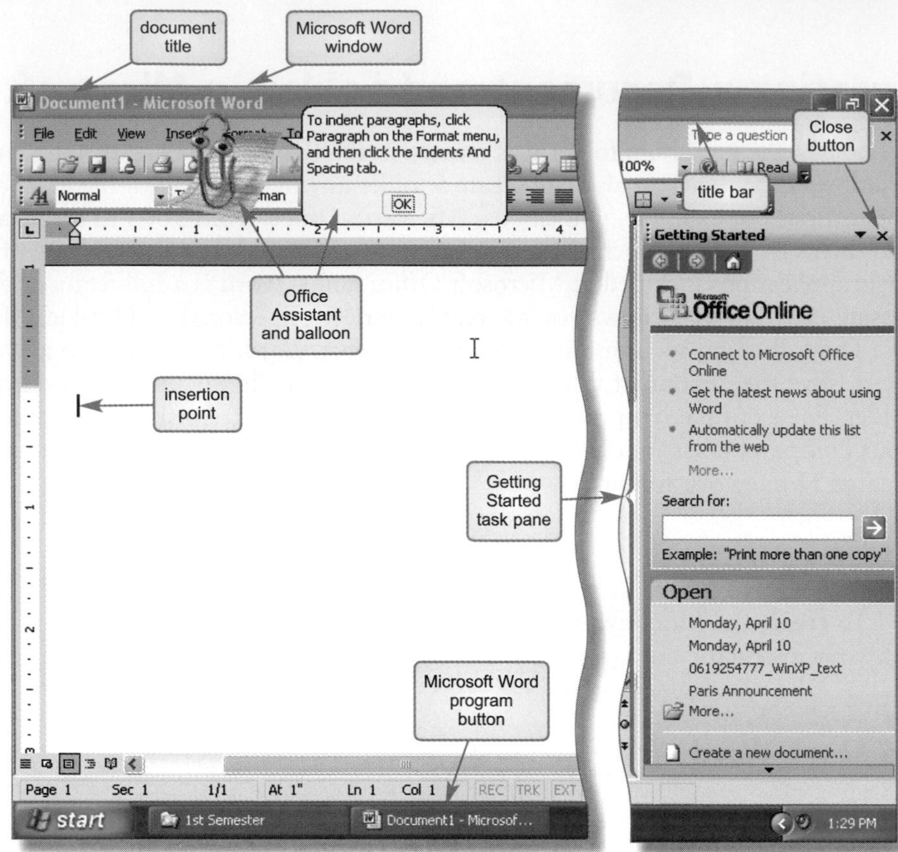

FIGURE 1-61

Typing Text

After starting Word, you can enter the text for the Monday, April 10 assignment in a Word document. To enter text in the document, you type on the keyboard. The following step illustrates how to type the text of the Monday, April 10 assignment in a Word document.

To Type Text in a Word Document

1

• **Type** `Monday, April 10` **and then press the ENTER key twice. Type** `Finish - More Birds Database` **and then press the ENTER key. Type** `Read - Next Project` **and then press the ENTER key.**

The Word document is complete (Figure 1-62).

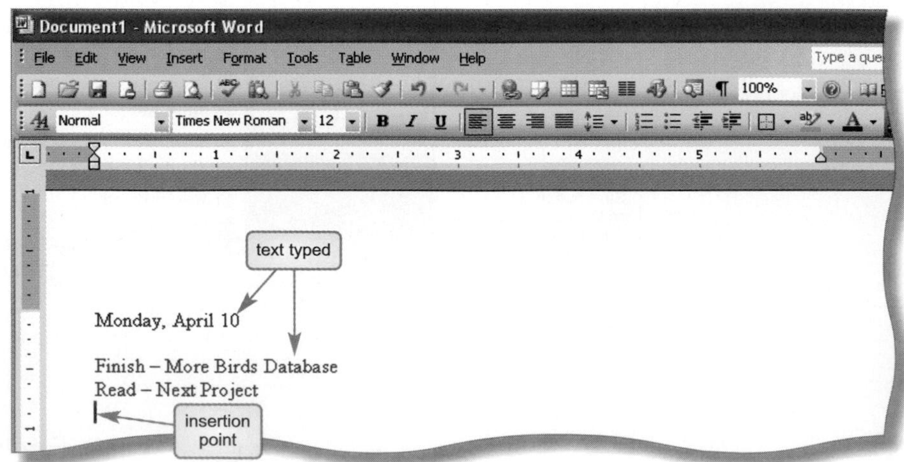

FIGURE 1-62

Saving a Document in a New Folder

After typing text in the Word document, you should name the document using the Monday, April 10 name, create the Homework folder in the Computer Class folder, (see the hierarchy in Figure 1-47 on page WIN 39), and save the Monday, April 10 document in the Homework folder. The following steps show how to create the Homework folder and save the Monday, April 10 document in the Homework folder.

To Save a Word Document in a New Folder

1

- **Click the Save button on the Standard toolbar.**

Word displays the Save As dialog box (Figure 1-63). The first word from the document (Monday) is selected in the File name text box as the default file name. You can change this selected file name by immediately typing the new name.

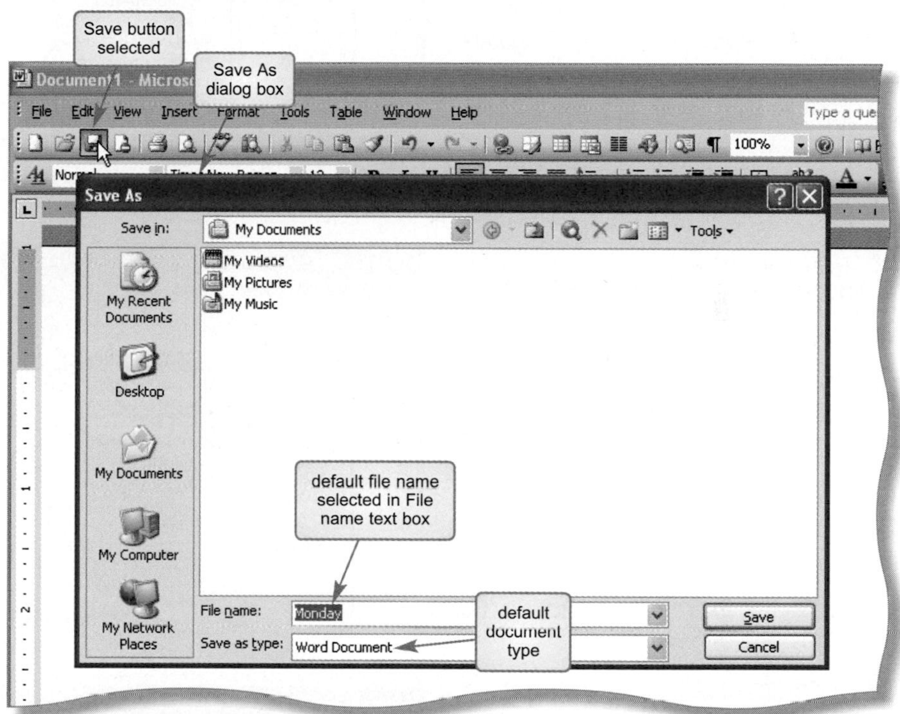

FIGURE 1-63

2

- **Type** `Monday, April 10` **in the File name text box. Do not press the ENTER key after typing the file name.**

The file name, Monday, April 10, replaces the text, Monday, in the file name text box (Figure 1-64).

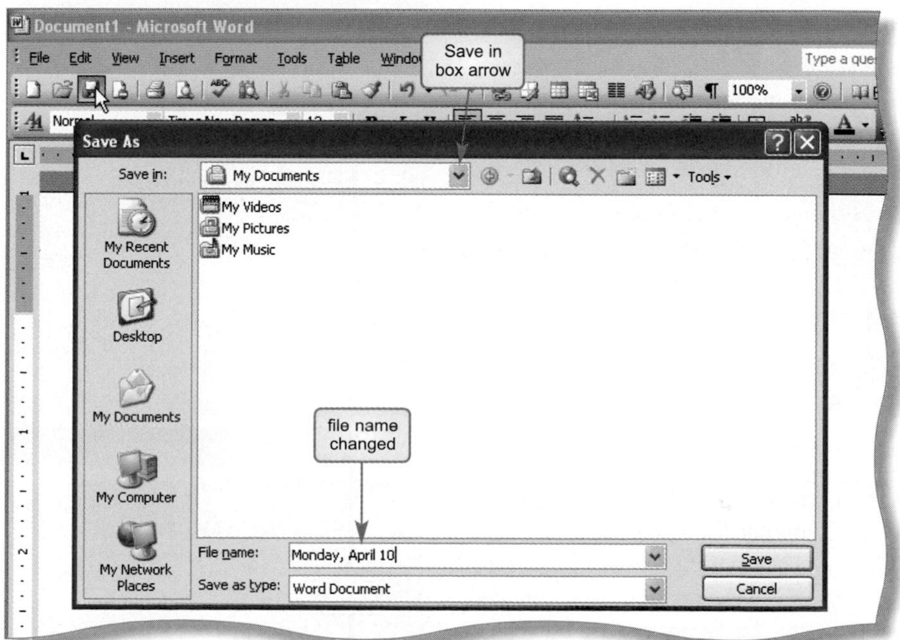

FIGURE 1-64

• **Click the Save in box arrow.**

Word displays a list of the available drives and folders in the Save in list (Figure 1-65). The Brad Wilson's Documents folder is selected in the Save in list. The Brad Wilson's Documents folder displays in the Save in list because a computer administrator previously created a user account for Brad Wilson. Your list may differ depending on your computer's configuration.

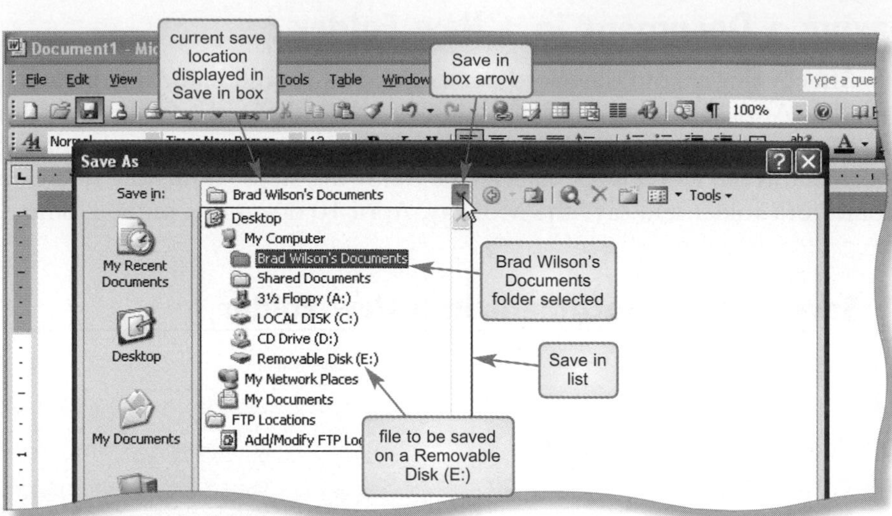

FIGURE 1-65

• **Click Removable Disk (E:) in the Save in list.**

Drive E becomes the new save location (Figure 1-66). The Save As dialog box now shows names of existing folders stored on drive E. In Figure 1-66, the Freshman folder is stored on drive E.

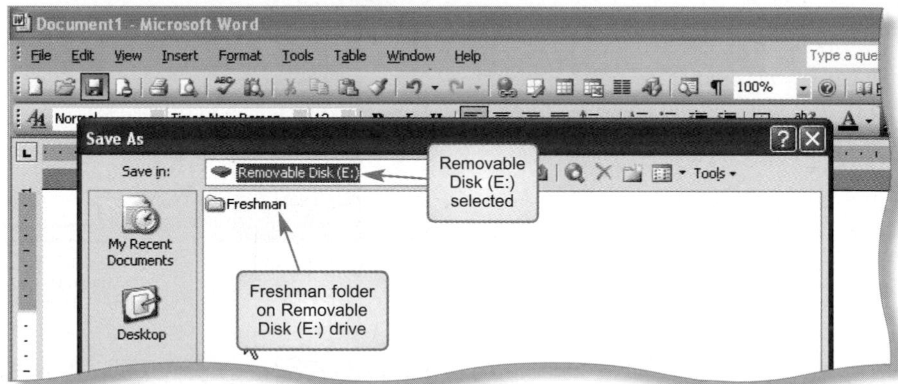

FIGURE 1-66

• **Double-click Freshman in the Save As dialog box.**

The Freshman folder is displayed in the Save in box, and the 1st Semester folder is displayed in the Save As dialog box (Figure 1-67). The 1st Semester folder is contained in the Freshman folder.

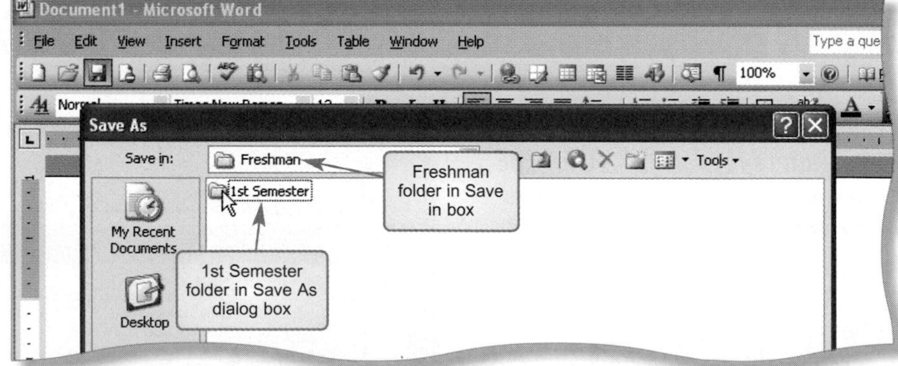

FIGURE 1-67

• **Double-click 1st Semester in the Save As dialog box.**

The 1st Semester folder is displayed in the Save in box and the Math Class, English Class, Computer Class, and Business Class folders are displayed in the Save As dialog box (Figure 1-68). The four folders are contained in the 1st Semester folder.

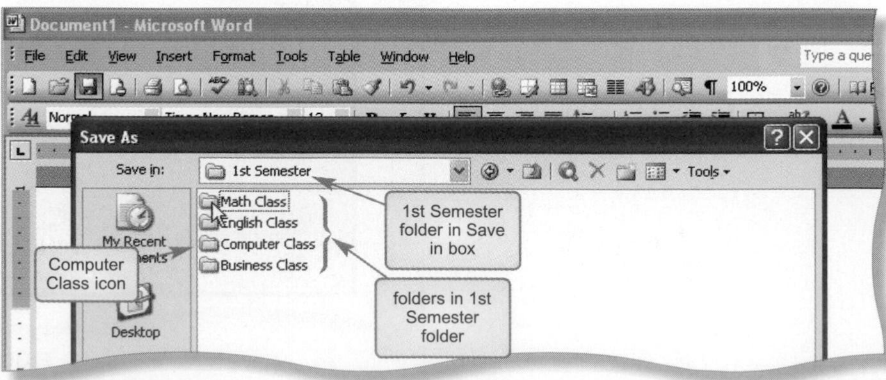

FIGURE 1-68

7

• **Double-click Computer Class in the Save As dialog box.**

The Computer Class folder is displayed in the Save in box and the Word, Windows, PowerPoint, Excel, and Access folders are displayed in the Save As dialog box (Figure 1-69). The five folders are contained in the Computer Class folder.

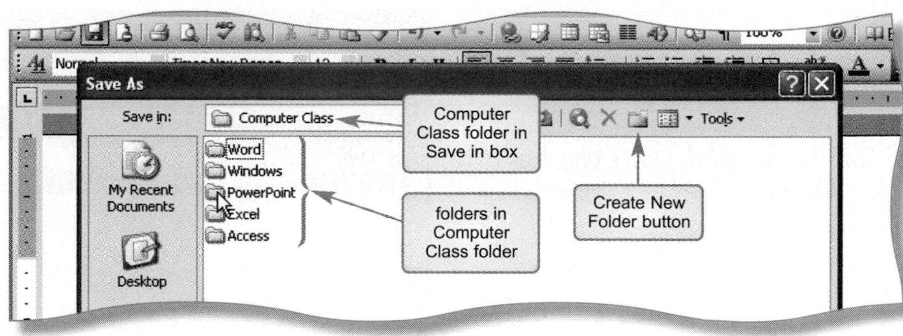

FIGURE 1-69

8

• **Click the Create New Folder button on the Save As dialog box toolbar. Type** `Homework` **in the Name text box in the New Folder dialog box.**

The New Folder dialog box is displayed, and the Homework folder name appears in the Name text box (Figure 1-70).

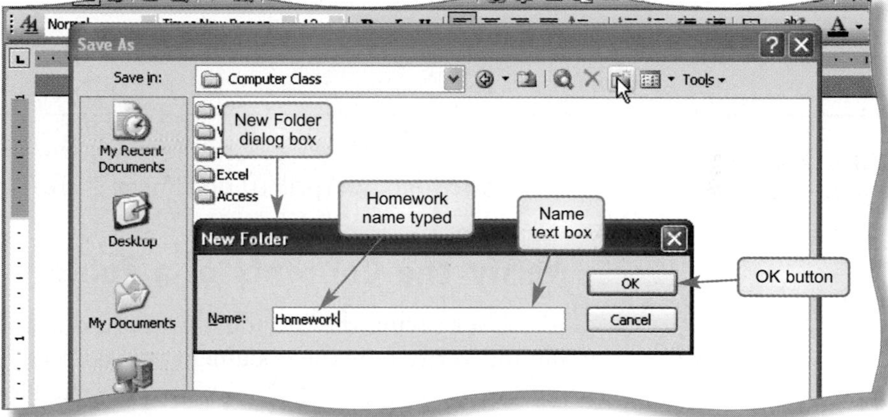

FIGURE 1-70

9

• **Click the OK button in the New Folder dialog box.**

The New Folder dialog box closes, and the Homework folder is displayed in the Save in box (Figure 1-71).

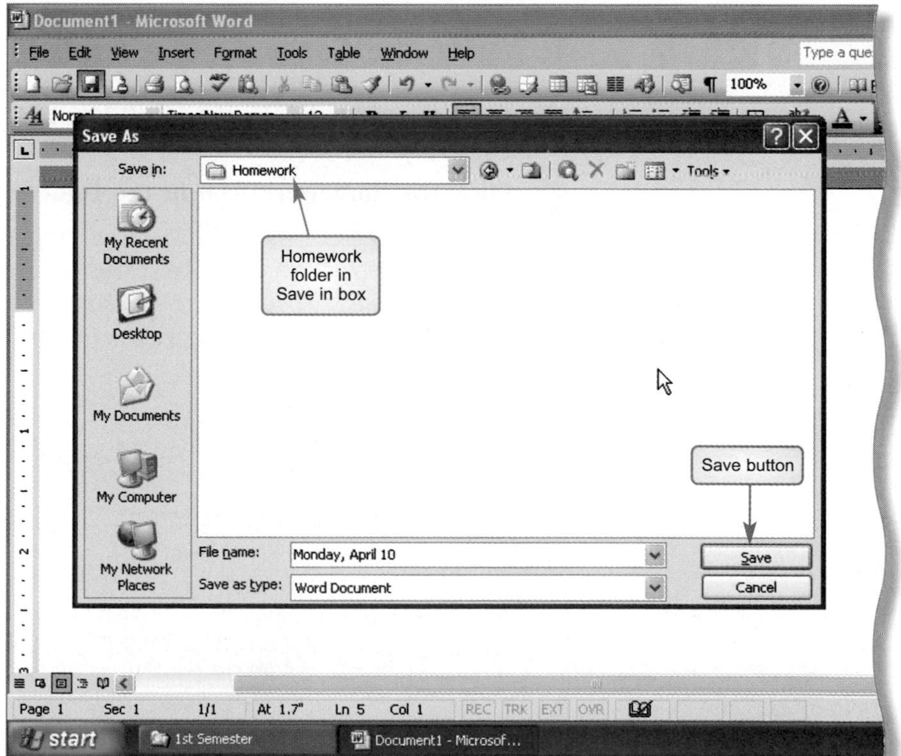

FIGURE 1-71

• **Click the Save button in the Save As dialog box.**

The Save As dialog box closes and the Monday, April 10 - Microsoft Word window is displayed (Figure 1-72).

• **Click the Close button in the Monday, April 10 - Microsoft Word window.**

The Microsoft Word window closes.

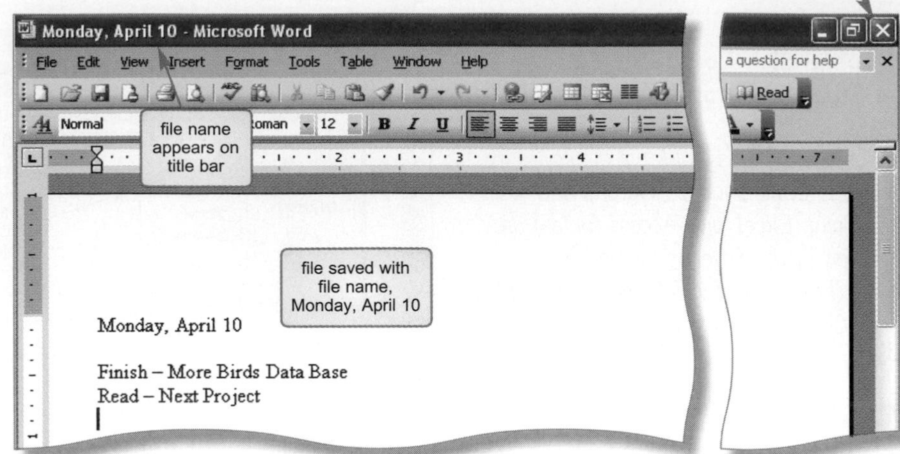

FIGURE 1-72

The Monday, April 10 document is created and stored in the Homework folder.

Verify the Contents of a Folder

After saving the Monday, April 10 document in the Homework folder, you should verify that the document was correctly saved in the Homework folder. The following steps illustrate how to verify the Homework folder contains the Monday, April 10 document.

To Verify the Contents of a Folder

1. **Click the plus sign in the small box next to the Computer Class icon in the Folders pane.**
2. **Click the Homework icon in the Folders pane.**

The Homework folder is selected in the Folders pane, the Monday, April 10 document is displayed in the right pane, Monday, April 10 is correctly saved in the Homework folder, and the path to the Homework folder displays in the Address box (Figure 1-73).

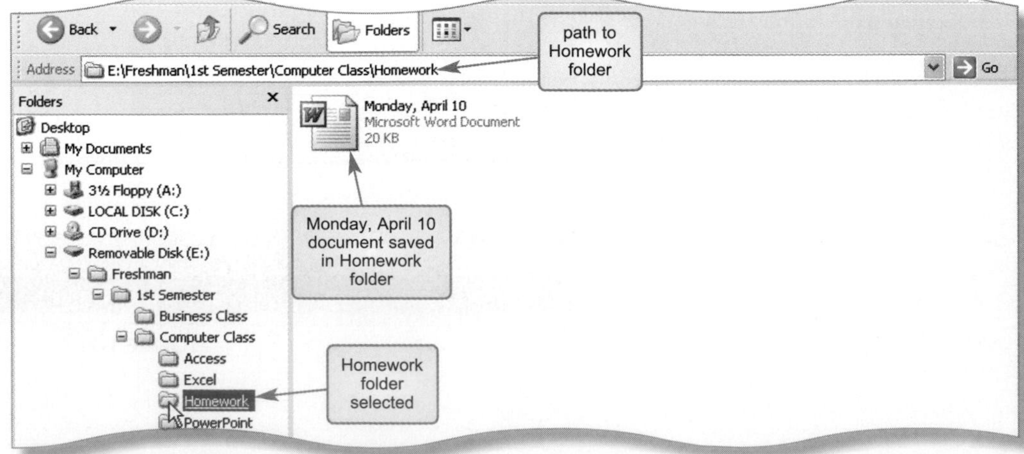

FIGURE 1-73

File Management in Windows Explorer

Being able to manage the files on the computer is one of the more important computer skills a student can have. **File management** includes copying, moving, renaming, and deleting files and folders on the computer. These are common operations that you should understand how to perform. The following pages show how to copy a file between folders, display the contents of a folder, rename a file, and then delete a file.

Copying Files in Windows Explorer

When copying files, the drive and folder containing the files to be copied are called the **source drive** and **source folder**, respectively. The drive and folder to which the files are copied are called the **destination drive** and **destination folder**, respectively. In the following steps, the Access folder is the source folder, the Homework folder is the destination folder, and the Removable Disk (E:) drive is both the source drive and the destination drive. The Access folder contains two of the nine Access database files (Begon Pest Control and More Birds) required to perform the lab assignments in the Access section of this book.

One method of copying files in Windows Explorer is to right-drag a file icon from the right pane to a folder or drive icon in the Folders pane. The following steps show how to copy the More Birds file in the Access folder (source folder) to the Homework folder (destination folder).

To Copy a File in Windows Explorer by Right-Dragging

1

• **Click the Access icon in the Folders pane.**

The Access folder is selected, the contents of the Access folder, including the Begon Pest Control and More Birds files, are displayed in the right pane, and the path to the Access folder appears in the Address box (Figure 1-74).

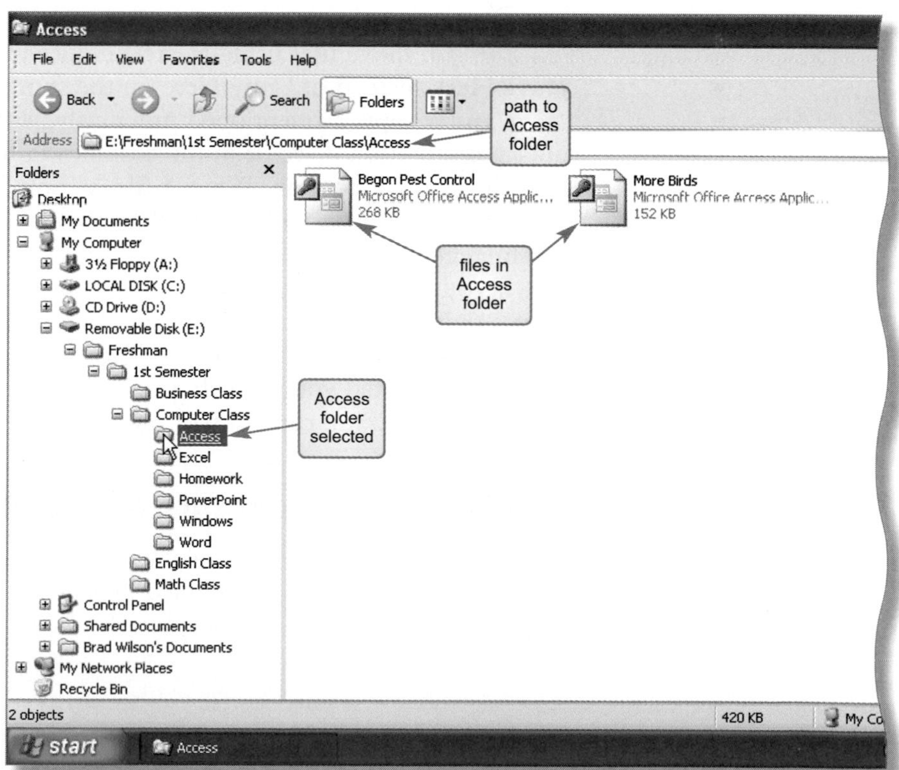

FIGURE 1-74

2

• **Right-drag the More Birds icon onto the top of the Homework folder.**

The dimmed image of the More Birds icon is displayed as you right-drag the icon on top of the Homework folder, the shortcut menu appears, and the dimmed image no longer is displayed (Figure 1-75).

3

• **Click Copy Here on the shortcut menu.**

The More Birds file is copied to the Homework folder.

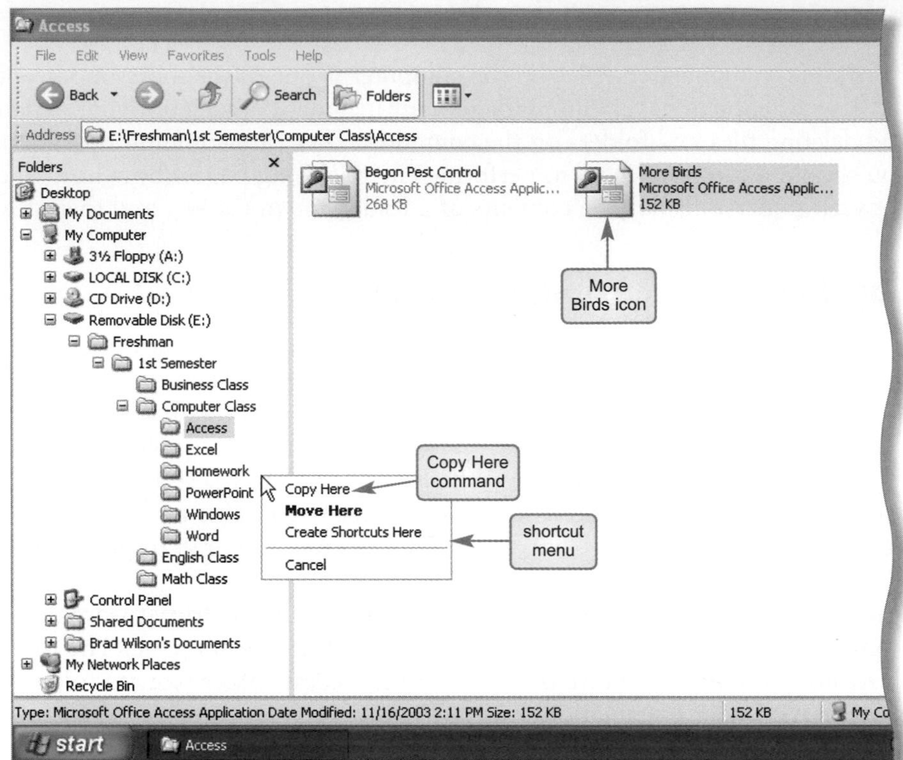

FIGURE 1-75

You can move files using the techniques just discussed, except that you click **Move Here** instead of Copy Here on the shortcut menu. The difference between a move and a copy, as mentioned previously, is that when you move a file, it is placed on the destination drive or in the destination folder and is permanently removed from its current location. When a file is copied, it is placed on the destination drive or in the destination folder as well as remaining stored in its current location.

In general, you should right-drag to copy or move a file instead of dragging a file. If you drag a file from one folder to another on the same drive, Windows XP moves the file. If you drag a file from one folder to another folder on a different drive, Windows XP copies the file. Because of the different ways this is handled, it is strongly suggested you right-drag when moving or copying files.

In addition, you can copy or move a folder using the techniques just discussed.

Displaying the Contents of the Homework Folder

After copying a file, you might want to examine the folder or drive where the file was copied to ensure it was copied properly. The following step illustrates how to display the contents of the Homework folder.

To Display the Contents of a Folder

1

- **Click the Homework icon in the Folders pane.**

The Homework folder name is selected in the Folders pane, the More Birds file is displayed in the right pane, and the Homework name replaces the Access name in the window title and on the taskbar button (Figure 1-76). The path to the Homework folder displays in the Address box.

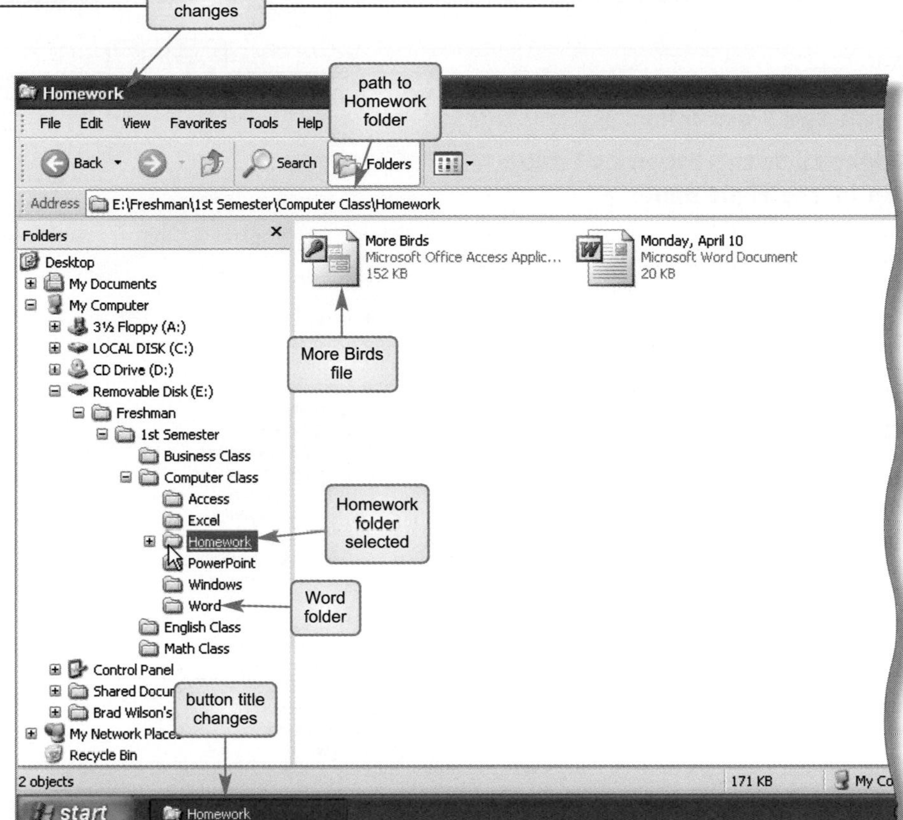

FIGURE 1-76

Renaming Files and Folders

In some circumstances, you may want to **rename** a file or a folder. This could occur when you want to distinguish a file in one folder or drive from a copy, or if you decide you need a better name to identify a file.

The Word folder in Figure 1-77 on the next page contains the three Word document files (Authentication Paragraph, Expenses Table, and Paris Announcement) required to perform the lab assignments in the Word section of this book. In this case, you decide to personalize the Expenses Table name by adding the word, Personal, to the beginning of the name. The following steps illustrate how to change the name of the Expenses Table file in the Word folder to Personal Expenses Table file.

To Rename a File

1

- **Click the Word folder.**
- **Right-click the Expenses Table icon in the right pane.**

The Expenses Table file name is selected, a shortcut menu appears, and the Word name replaces the Access name in the window title and taskbar button (Figure 1-77). The path to the Word folder displays in the Address box.

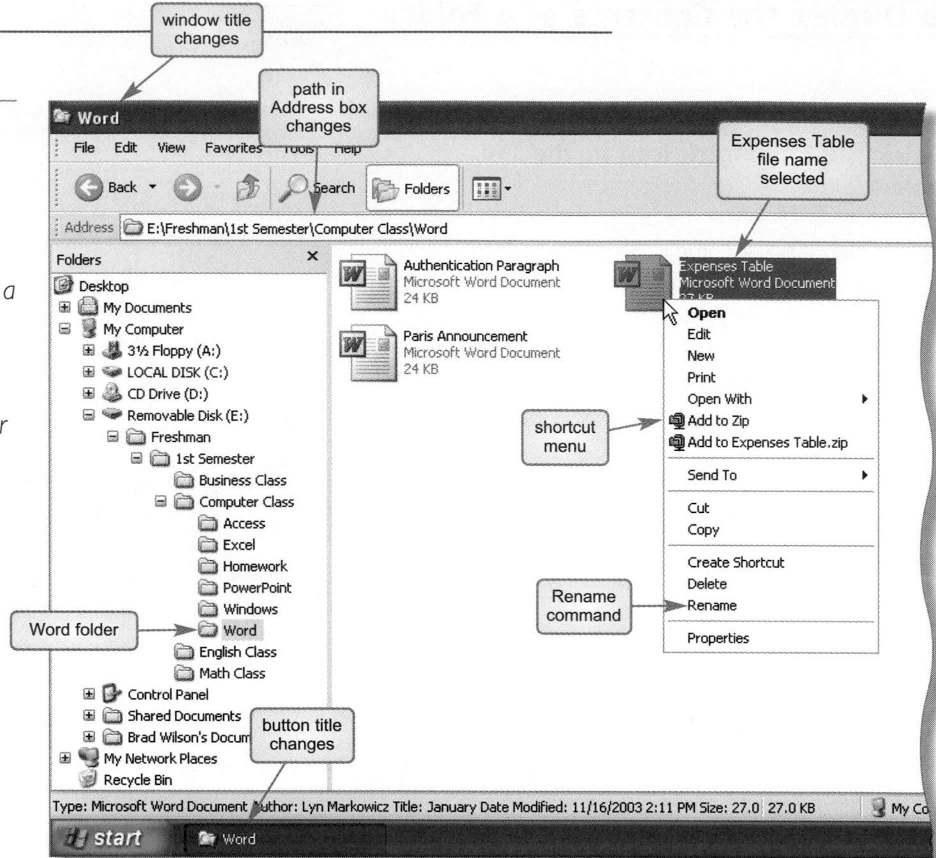

FIGURE 1-77

2

- **Click Rename on the shortcut menu.**
- **Type** `Personal Expenses Table` **and then press the ENTER key.**

The file is renamed Personal Expenses Table (Figure 1-78).

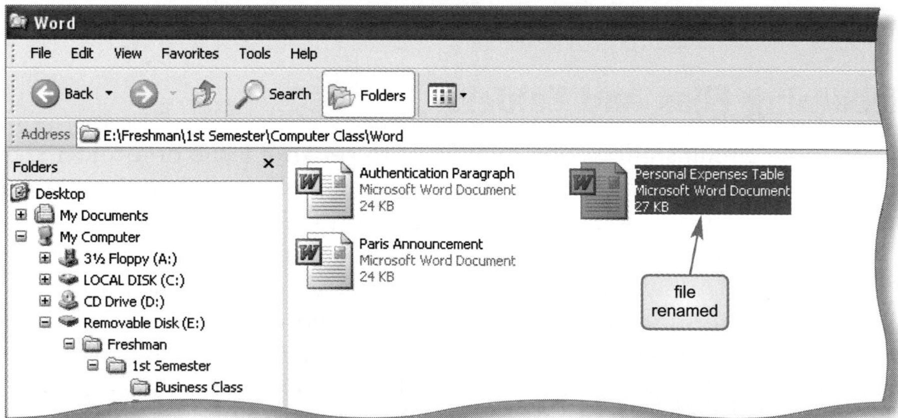

FIGURE 1-78

You can rename a folder using the techniques just discussed. To rename a folder, right-click the folder icon, click Rename on the shortcut menu, type the new folder name, and then press the ENTER key.

Deleting Files in Windows Explorer

A final operation that you may want to perform in Windows Explorer is to delete a file. Exercise extreme caution when deleting a file or files. When you delete a file from a hard drive, the deleted file is stored in the Recycle Bin where you can recover it until you empty the Recycle Bin. If you delete a file from removable media, the file is gone permanently once you delete it.

Assume you have decided you no longer want the Paris Announcement file and would like to delete the file from the Word folder. The following steps show how to delete the Paris Announcement file by right-clicking the Paris Announcement icon.

To Delete a File by Right-Clicking

1

• **Right-click the Paris Announcement icon in the right pane.**

The Paris Announcement icon in the right pane is selected and a shortcut menu is displayed (Figure 1-79).

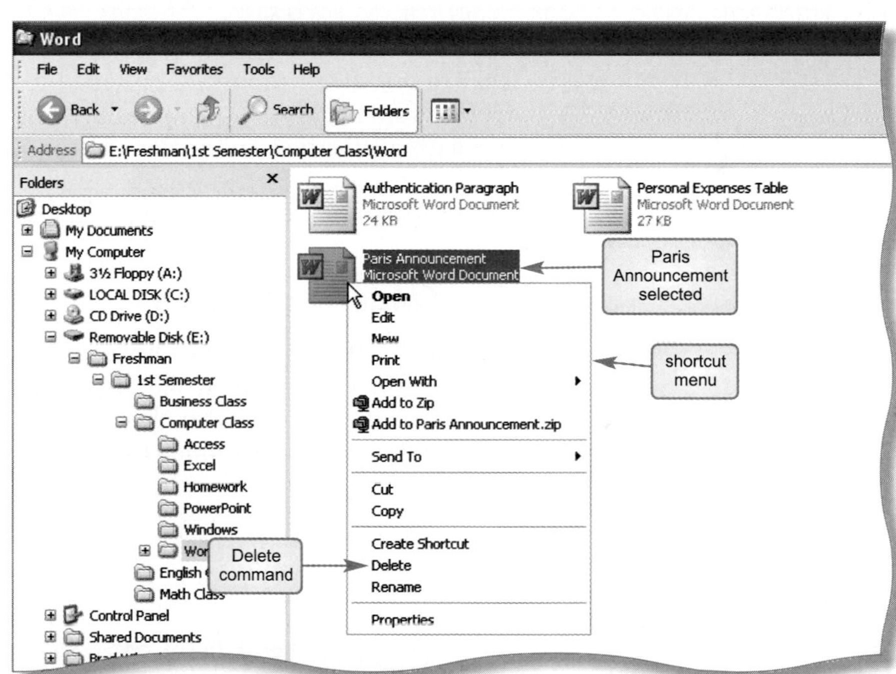

FIGURE 1-79

2

• **Click Delete on the shortcut menu.**

Windows displays the Confirm File Delete dialog box (Figure 1-80). The dialog box contains the question, Are you sure you want to delete 'Paris Announcement'?, and the Yes and No buttons.

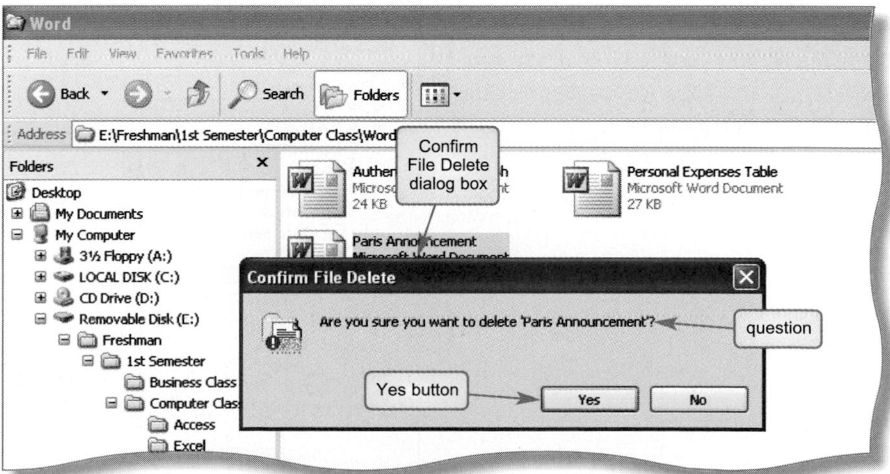

FIGURE 1-80

3

• **Click the Yes button in the Confirm File Delete dialog box.**

The Paris Announcement icon is removed from the right pane (Figure 1-81). Remember — if you delete a file on removable media (flash drive), the file is gone permanently once you delete it.

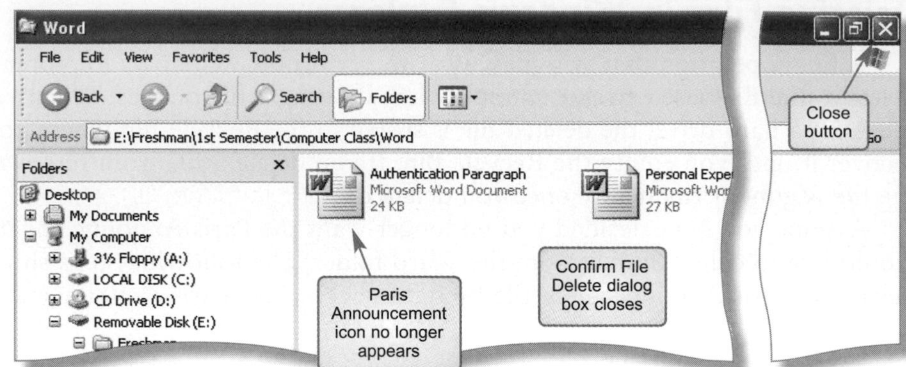

FIGURE 1-81

You can use the methods just specified to delete folders on a disk drive. When you delete a folder, all the files and folders contained in the folder you are deleting, together with all the files and folders on the lower hierarchical levels, are deleted.

Again, you should use extreme caution when deleting files and folders to ensure you do not delete something you may not be able to recover.

Closing Folder Expansions

Sometimes, after you have completed work with expanded folders, you will want to close the expansions while still leaving the Explorer window open. The following steps illustrate how to close the Computer Class folder, 1st Semester folder, Freshman folder, and Removable Disk (E:) drive.

To Close Expanded Folders

1

• **Click the minus sign to the left of the Computer Class icon.**

The expansion of the Computer Class folder collapses and the minus sign changes to a plus sign (Figure 1-82). The contents of the right pane do not change.

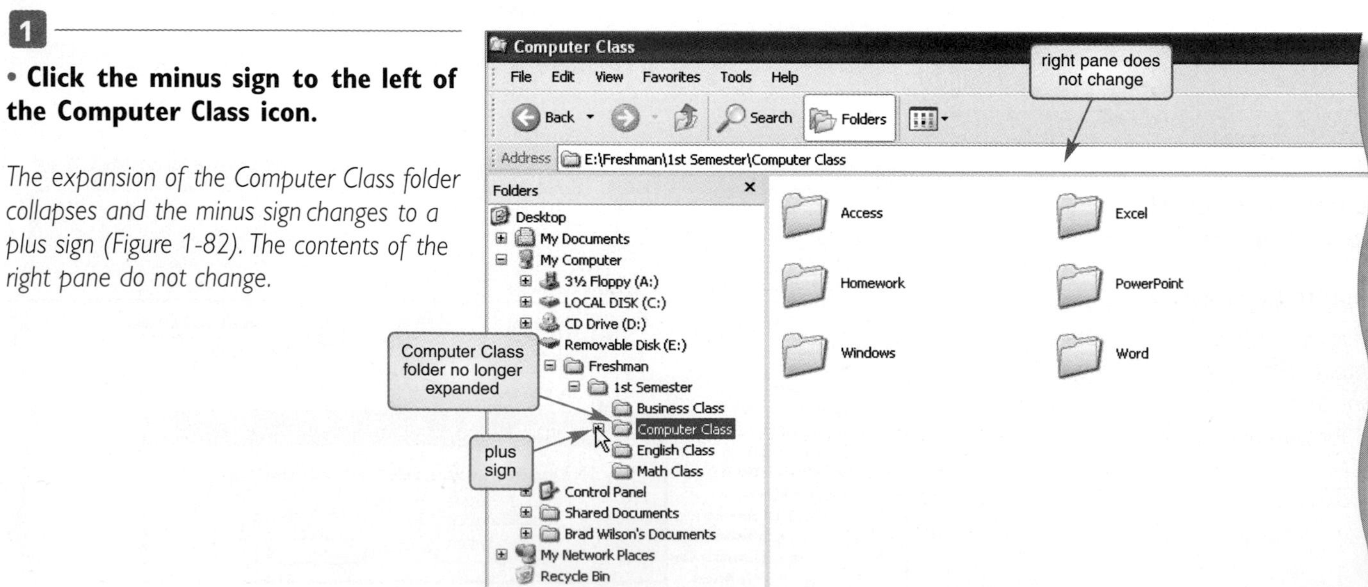

FIGURE 1-82

To Close All Expanded Folders

1 **Click the minus sign to the left of the 1st Semester icon.**

2 **Click the minus sign to the left of the Freshman icon.**

3 **Click the minus sign to the left of the Removable Disk (E:) icon.**

The expansion of the 1st Semester folder, Freshman folder, and Removable Disk (E:) drive collapses and the minus signs change to a plus sign.

Moving through the Folders pane and right pane is an important skill because you will find that you use Windows Explorer to perform a significant amount of file maintenance on the computer.

Quitting Windows Explorer

When you have finished working with Windows Explorer, you can quit Windows Explorer by closing the Folders pane or by closing the Windows Explorer (Removable Disk (E:)) window. The following step illustrates how to quit Windows Explorer by closing the Removable Disk (E:) window.

Skill Builder 1-3

To practice the following tasks, visit scsite.com/off2003sch/skill, locate Windows XP Project 1, and then click Skill Builder 1-3.

- ❑ Save a document in a folder
- ❑ Verify the contents of a folder
- ❑ Copy files
- ❑ Rename files and folders
- ❑ Delete files
- ❑ Close folder expansions

To Quit Windows Explorer

1 **Click the Close button on the Removable Disk (E:) window title bar.**

Windows XP closes the Removable Disk (E:) window and quits Windows Explorer.

Finding Files or Folders

You know the location of files you use often and can locate the folder that contains them. In some cases, however, you may know you have a certain file on the computer but you have no idea in what folder it is located. To search every folder manually on the computer to find the file would be time consuming and almost impossible. Fortunately, Windows XP provides Search Companion.

Search Companion allows you to search for files and folders by name, type, or size. You can search for a file based on when you last worked on the file or search for files containing specific text. You also can choose to search with the help of an animated character.

Searching for a File by Name

If you know the name or partial name of a file, you can use Search Companion to locate the file. For example, a file named Personal Expenses Table exists on the Removable Disk (E:) drive. The following steps show how to search for a file on the Removable Disk (E:) drive knowing only a part of the file name.

To Search for a File by Name

1

• **Click the Start button on the taskbar.**

The Start menu and Search command are displayed (Figure 1-83).

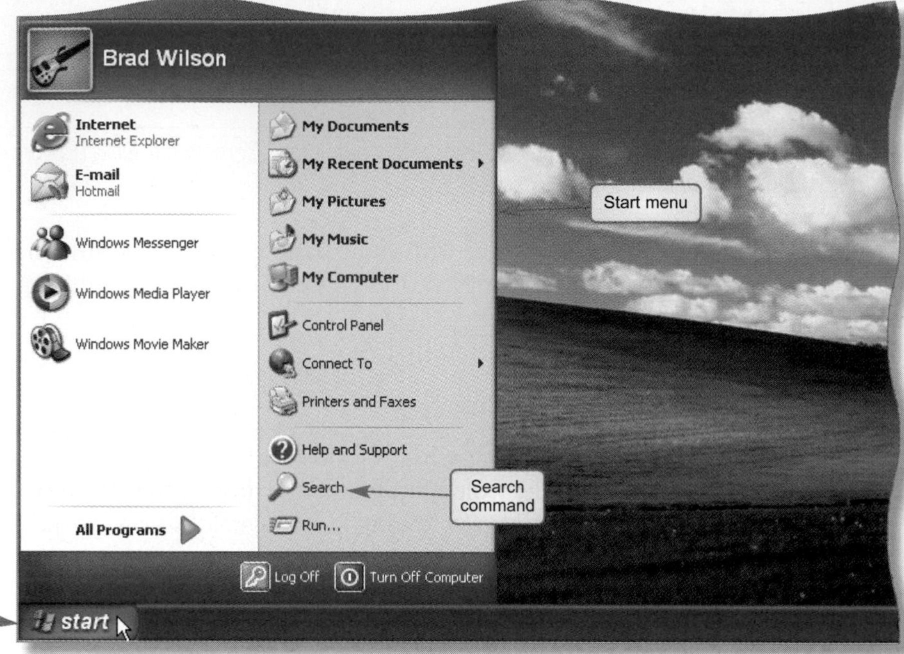

FIGURE 1-83

2

• **Click Search on the Start menu. If necessary, maximize the Search Results window.**

The Search Companion pane is displayed in the Search Results window (Figure 1-84). The pane contains the Search Companion balloon and an animated dog named Rover. The right pane contains a message about starting a search.

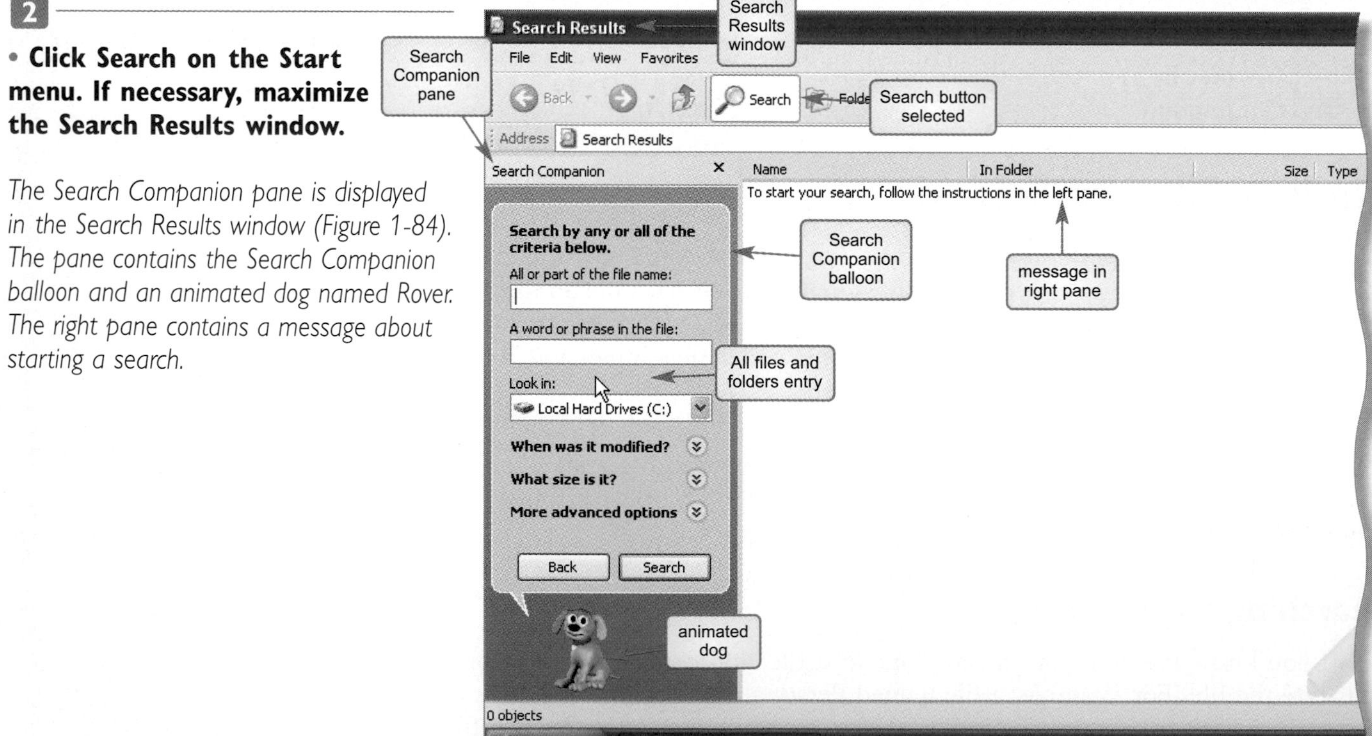

FIGURE 1-84

3

• **Click All files and folders in the Search Companion balloon. Type** `Expenses Table` **in the All or part of the file name text box.**

The contents of the Search Companion balloon change (Figure 1-85). The keywords, Expenses Table, appears in the All or part of the file name text box. The Local Hard Drives (C:) entry in the Look in box indicates all of Local Hard Drives (C:) will be searched.

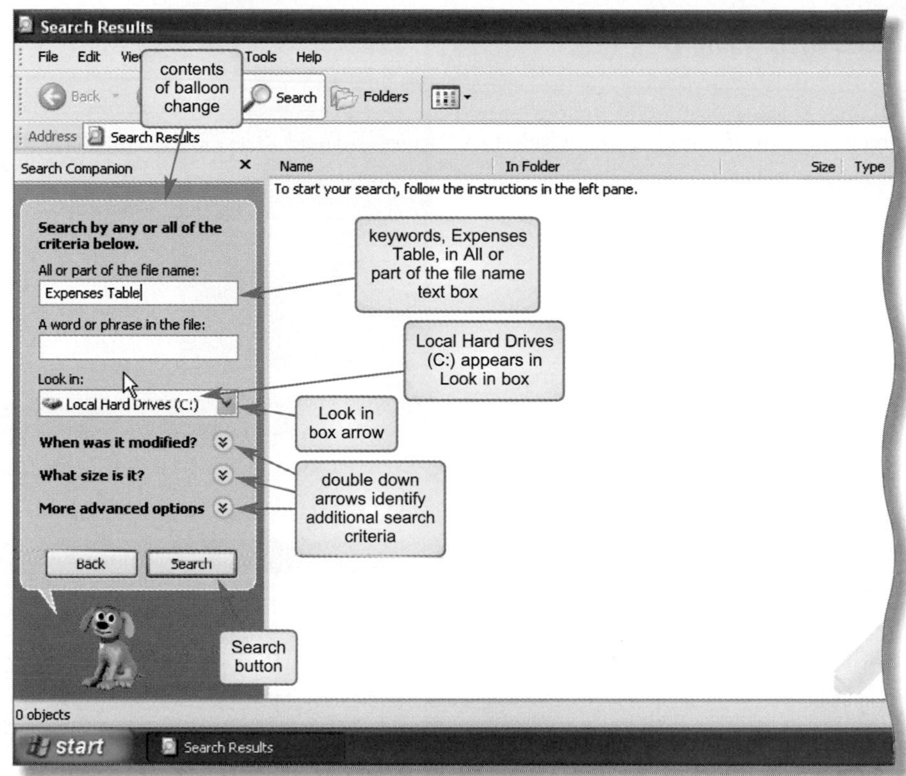

FIGURE 1-85

4

• **Click the Look in box arrow in the Search Companion pane.**

The Look in list is displayed, the Local Hard Drives (C:) entry is selected, and the Removable Disk (E:) drive name appears (Figure 1-86).

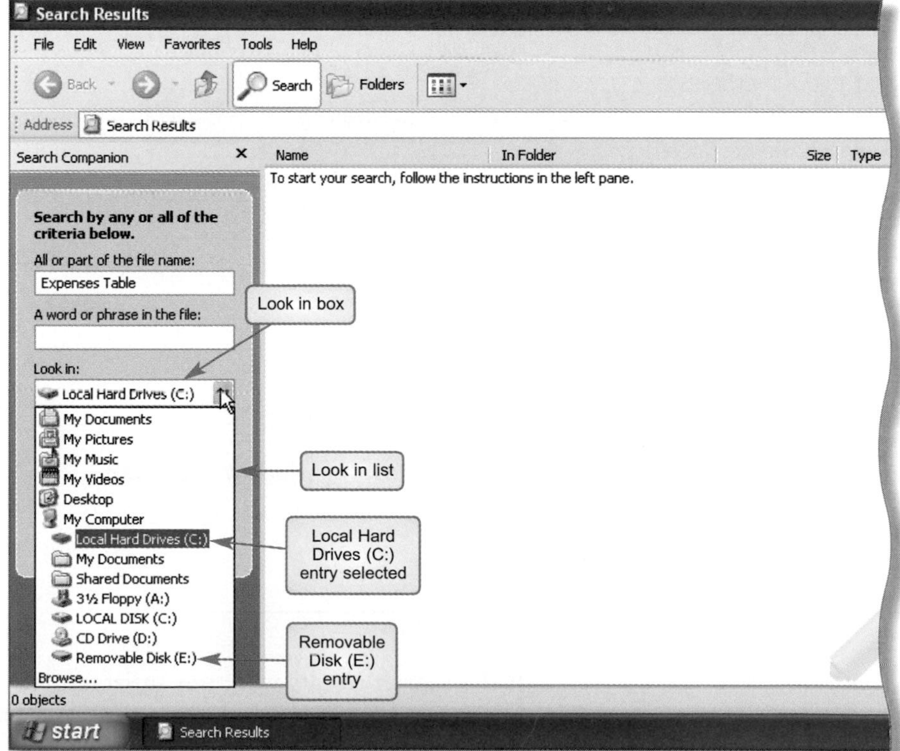

FIGURE 1-86

• **Click Removable Disk (E:).**

The Look in list is closed and the highlighted Removable Disk (E:) drive name is selected in the Look in box (Figure 1-87).

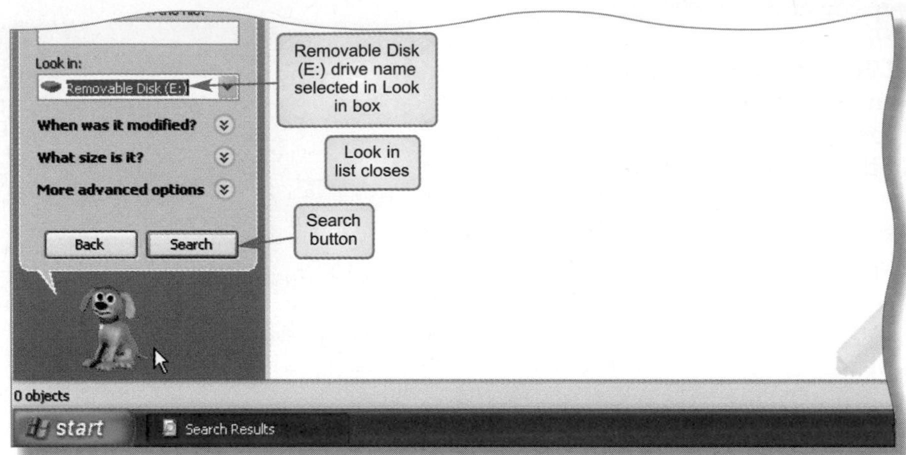

FIGURE 1-87

• **Click the Search button.**

While the search continues, Windows momentarily displays a message, locations being searched, a progress bar, and a Stop button in the balloon. Windows XP searches drive E for the Expenses Table file (Figure 1-88). One file is found, and the right pane displays the file name (Personal Expenses Table), folder path (E:\Freshman\1st Semester\Computer Class\Word), file size (27KB), file type (Microsoft Word Document), and modification date (10/25/2006). The modification date is not visible in the right pane.

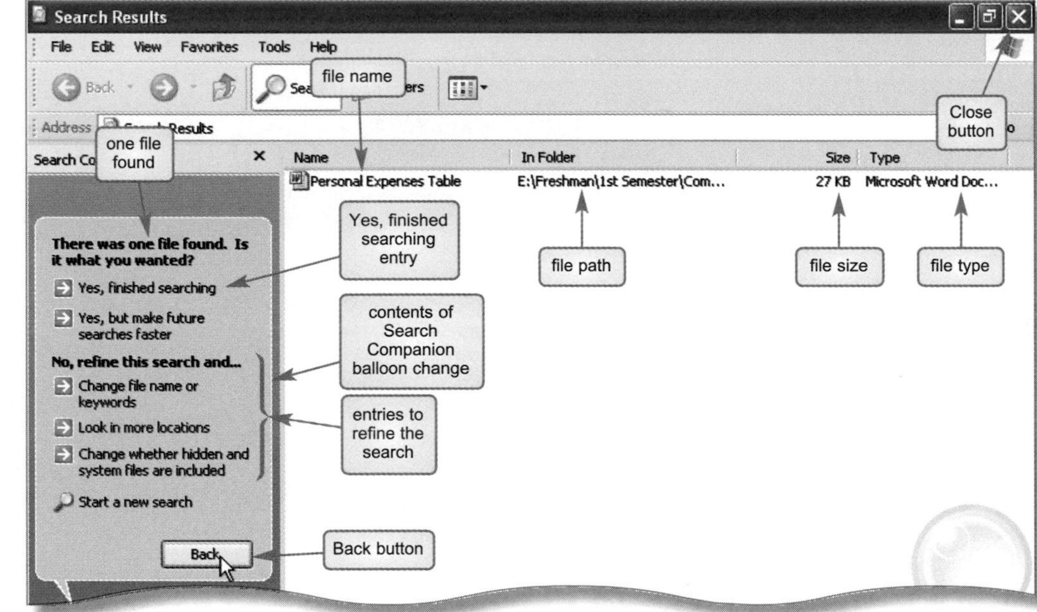

FIGURE 1-88

• **Click the Close button on the Search Results window title bar.**

The Search Results window is closed.

If the search results were not satisfactory, you can refine the search by changing the file name, looking in more locations, or changing whether hidden and system files are included in the search.

In the right pane of the Search Results window shown in Figure 1-88, after the search is complete, you can work with the files found in any manner desired. For example, you can open the file by double-clicking the file icon, or by right-clicking the file icon and then clicking Open on the shortcut menu. You can print the file by right-clicking the file icon and then clicking Print on the shortcut menu. You can copy or move the file with the same method as shown for files in My Computer or Windows Explorer. In summary, any operation you can accomplish from My Computer or from Windows Explorer can be performed on the files displayed in the right pane of the Search Results window.

If the file you are searching for is an executable program file, such as Microsoft Word, you can start the program by double-clicking the file icon in the right pane of the Search Results window.

If you know only a portion of a file's name, you can use an asterisk in the name to represent the remaining characters. For example, if you know a file starts with the letters WIN, you can type **win*** in the All or part of the file name text box. All files that begin with the letters win, regardless of what letters follow, will be displayed.

You may use three additional criteria when searching for all files and folders: modification date, file size, and advanced options. These criteria are identified by double down arrow buttons at the bottom of the balloon shown in Figure 1-85 on page WIN 63. Searching by modification date allows you to display all files that were created or modified within the last week, past month, past year, or on a specific date. Searching by file size allows you to search for files based on file size in kilobytes. Advanced options allow you to search system folders, hidden files or folders, subfolders, and tape backup, and perform case-sensitive searches. If no files are found in the search, a message (Search is complete. There are no results to display.) appears in the right pane of the Search Results window. In this case, you may want to check the file name you entered or examine a different drive to continue the search.

Searching for a File by Using a Word or Phrase in the File

If you want to search for a file knowing only a word or phrase in the file, you can search by typing the word or phrase in the A word or phrase in the file text box in the Search Companion balloon. Assume you want to find all files containing the word, apply, on the Removable Disk (E:) drive. The following steps illustrate how to search for all files containing the word, apply.

To Search for a File Using a Word or Phrase in the File

1

- **Click the Start button on the taskbar. Click Search on the Start menu. If necessary, maximize the Search Results window. Click All files and folders in the Search Companion balloon.**

The Search Companion balloon is displayed in the maximized Search Results window (Figure 1-89). The insertion point is blinking in the All or part of the file name box.

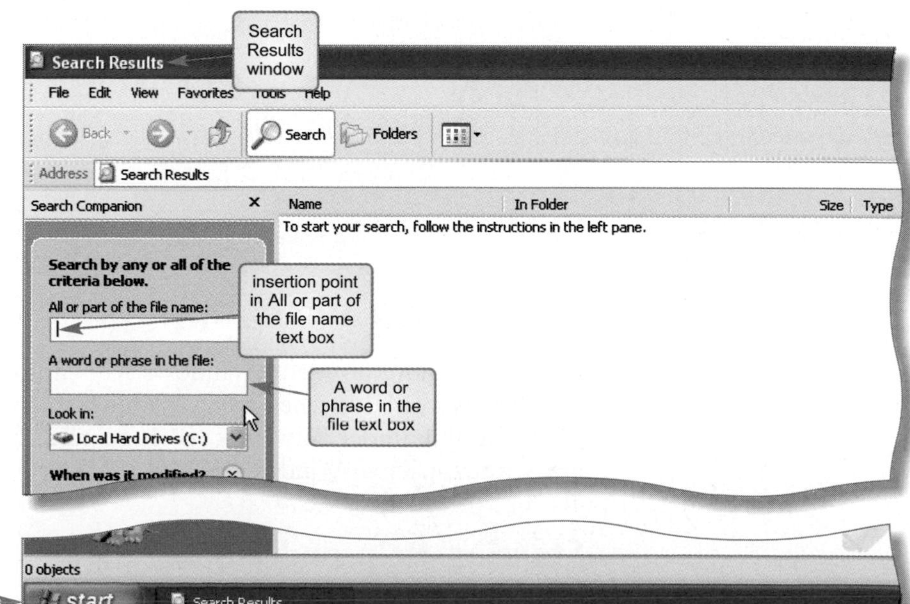

FIGURE 1-89

2

• Click the A word or phrase in the file text box.

• Type `apply` **in the A word or phrase in the file text box, click the Look in box arrow, and then click Removable Disk (E:) in the Look in list.**

The word, apply, is displayed in the A word or phrase in the file text box, and Removable Disk (E:) is displayed in the Look in box (Figure 1-90).

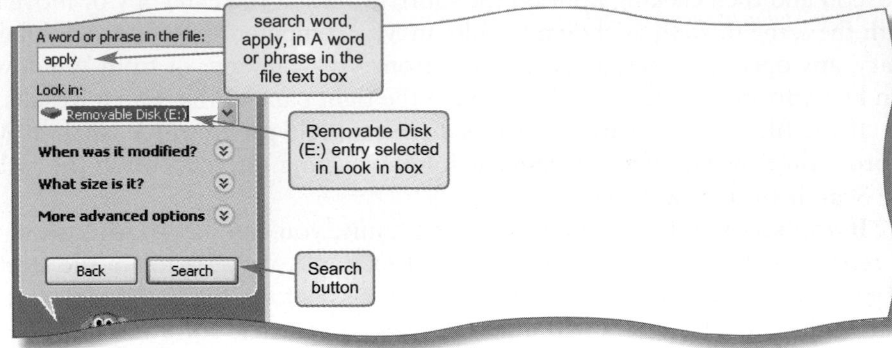

FIGURE 1-90

3

• Click the Search button in the Search Companion balloon.

While the search progresses, Windows displays the search criteria and locations being searched in the balloon along with the path of the folder currently being searched. When the search is complete, four Word document files containing the word, apply, on the Removable Disk (E:) drive are displayed in the Search Results window (Figure 1-91). Different files may appear on your computer.

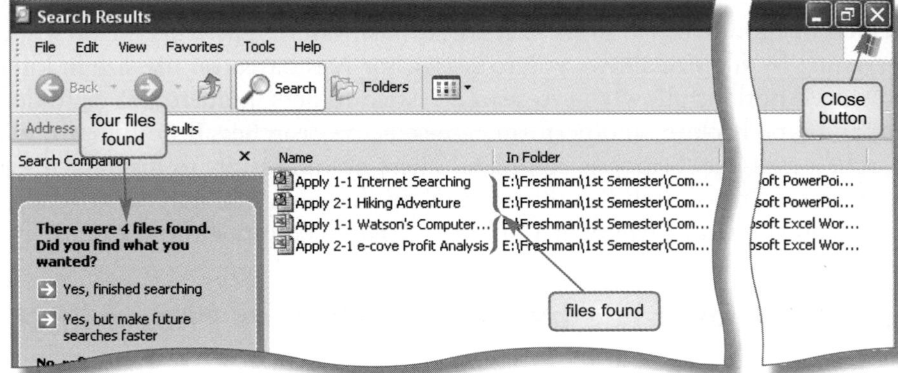

FIGURE 1-91

• Click the Close button on the Search Results window title bar.

The Search Results window closes.

• Remove the USB flash drive from the USB port.

When you remove the USB flash drive, a sound indicating the flash drive has been removed may sound.

Using Help and Support

One of the more powerful Windows XP features is Help and Support. **Help and Support** is available when using Windows XP or when using any application program running under Windows XP. It contains answers to many questions you may ask with respect to Windows XP.

Starting Help and Support

Before you can access the Help and Support Center services, you must start Help and Support. One method of starting Help and Support uses the Start menu. The following steps show how to start Help and Support.

To Start Help and Support

1

• **Click the Start button on the taskbar and then point to Help and Support on the Start menu.**

Windows XP displays the Start menu and highlights the Help and Support command (Figure 1-92).

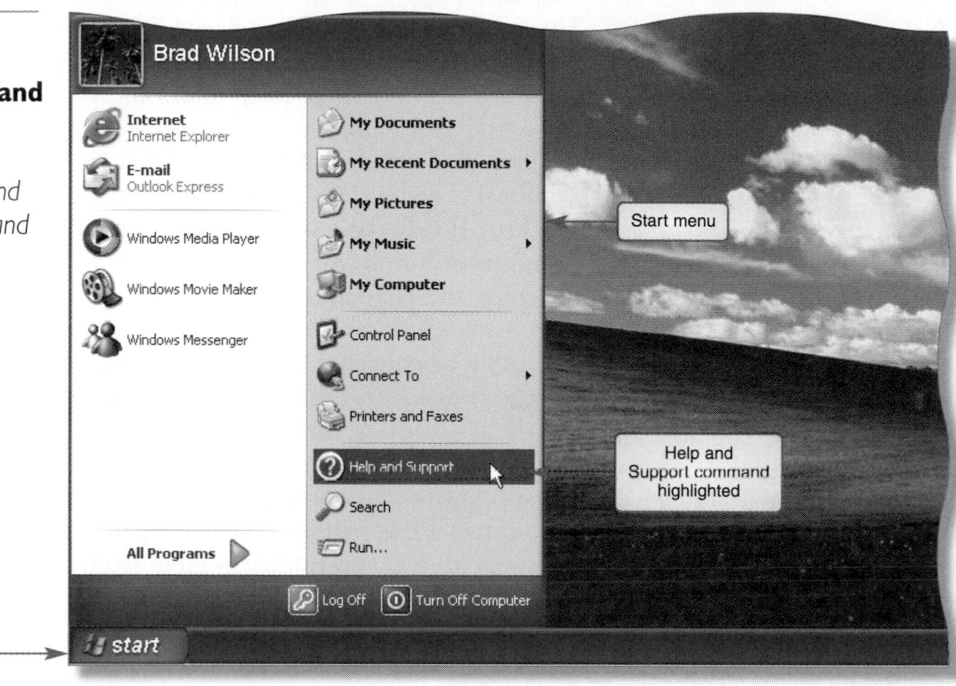

FIGURE 1-92

2

• **Click Help and Support and then click the Maximize button on the Help and Support Center title bar.**

The Help and Support Center window opens and maximizes (Figure 1-93). The window contains the Help viewer. The Help viewer includes the navigation toolbar, Search text box and Set search options link, and table of contents. The table of contents contains four areas (Pick a Help topic, Ask for assistance, Pick a task, and Did you know?).

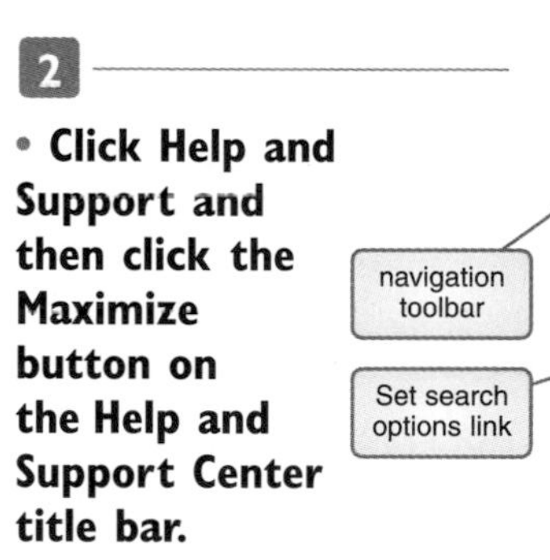

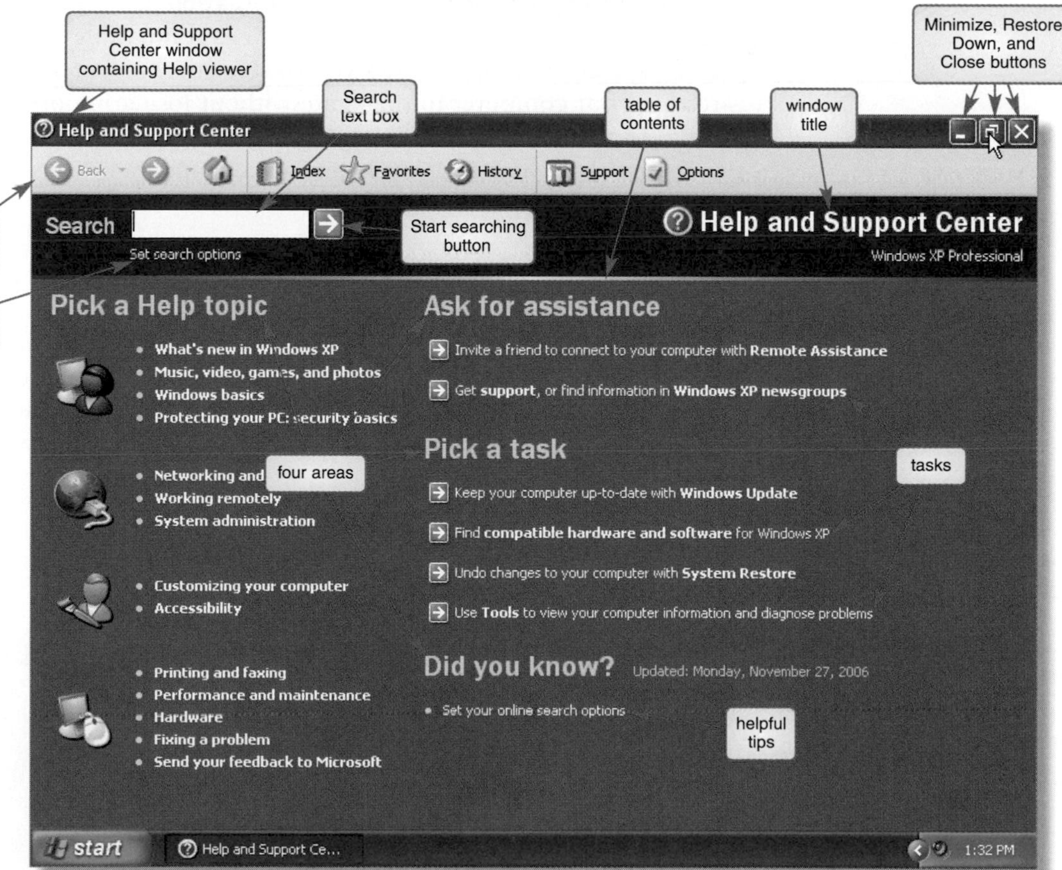

FIGURE 1-93

The Help and Support Center title bar shown in Figure 1-93 on the previous page contains a Minimize button, Restore Down button, and Close button. You can minimize or restore the Help and Support Center window as needed and also close the Help and Support Center window.

The navigation toolbar is displayed below the title bar. The **navigation toolbar** allows you to navigate through Help topics and pages, browse and save Help topics and pages, view previously saved Help topics and pages, get online support for questions and problems, and customize the Help viewer. An icon identifies each button on the navigation toolbar. Six buttons contain a text label (Back, Index, Favorites, History, Support, and Options). The buttons on the navigation toolbar on your computer may be different.

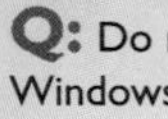

Q & A

Q: Do manuals come with Windows XP?

A: If you purchased an operating system or application program several years ago, you received at least one, and more often several, heavy, thick technical manuals that explained the software. With Windows XP, you receive a booklet with only 34 pages. The Help and Support feature of Windows XP replaces the reams and reams of printed pages in hard-to-understand technical manuals.

The area below the navigation toolbar contains the Search text box and Start searching button used to search for help, the Set search options link to set the criteria for searching the Help and Support Center, and the window's title (Help and Support Center).

The **table of contents** contains four areas. The **Pick a Help topic area** contains four category groups. A unique icon identifies each group. Clicking a category in a group displays a list of subcategories and Help topics related to the category.

The **Ask for assistance area** contains two tasks. The first task (**Remote Assistance**) allows an individual at another computer to connect and control your computer while helping to solve a problem. The second task (**Windows XP newsgroups**) allows you to obtain Help from product support experts or discuss your questions with other Windows XP users in newsgroups.

The **Pick a task area** contains four tasks. The first task (**Windows Update**) allows you to access a catalog of items, such as device drivers, security fixes, critical updates, the latest Help files, and Internet products, that you can download to keep your computer up-to-date. The second task (**compatible hardware and software**) allows you to search for hardware and software that are compatible with Windows XP. The third task (**System Restore**) allows you to store the current state of your computer and restore your computer to that state without losing important information. The fourth task (**Tools**) contains a collection of eight helpful tools to keep your computer running smoothly. The **Did you know? area** is updated daily with helpful tips for using Windows XP.

Browsing for Help Topics in the Table of Contents

After starting Help and Support, the next step is to find the Help topic in which you are interested. Assume you want to know more about finding information using the Help and Support Center. The following steps illustrate how to use the table of contents to find a Help topic that describes how to find what you need in the Help and Support Center.

To Browse for Help Topics in the Table of Contents

1

• **Point to Windows basics in the Pick a Help topic area.**

The mouse pointer changes to a hand icon when positioned on the Windows basics category, and the category is underlined (Figure 1-94).

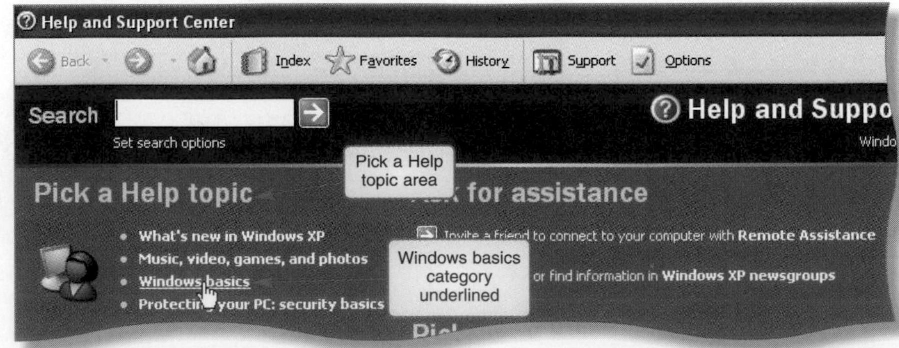

FIGURE 1-94

2

• **Click Windows basics and then point to Tips for using Help.**

The navigation pane and topic pane are displayed in the Help and Support Center window (Figure 1-95). The Windows basics area in the navigation pane contains five categories and the underlined Tips for using Help category. The See Also area contains four Help topics. The topic pane contains the Help and Support toolbar and the Windows basics page.

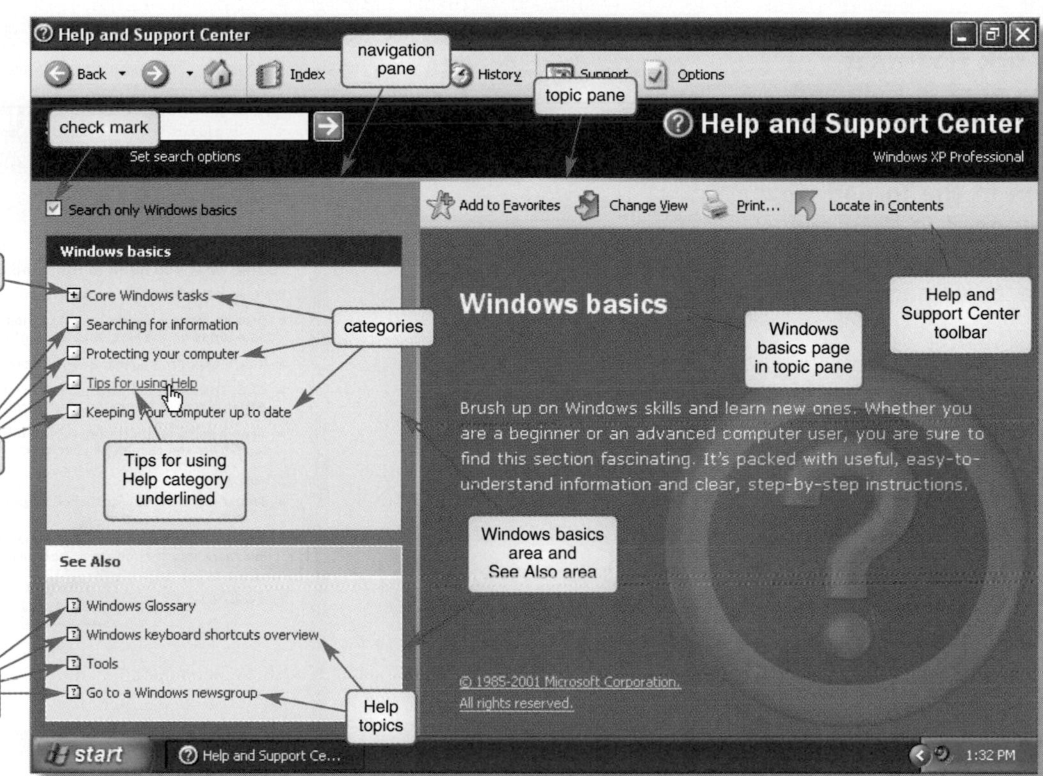

FIGURE 1-95

3

• **Click Tips for using Help and then point to Find what you need in Help and Support Center in the topic pane.**

Windows XP highlights the Tips for using Help category in the Windows basics area, displays the Tips for using Help page in the topic pane, and underlines the Find what you need in Help and Support Center task (Figure 1-96). The Add to Favorites button and Print button on the Help and Support Center toolbar are dimmed to indicate the page cannot be added to the favorites list or printed.

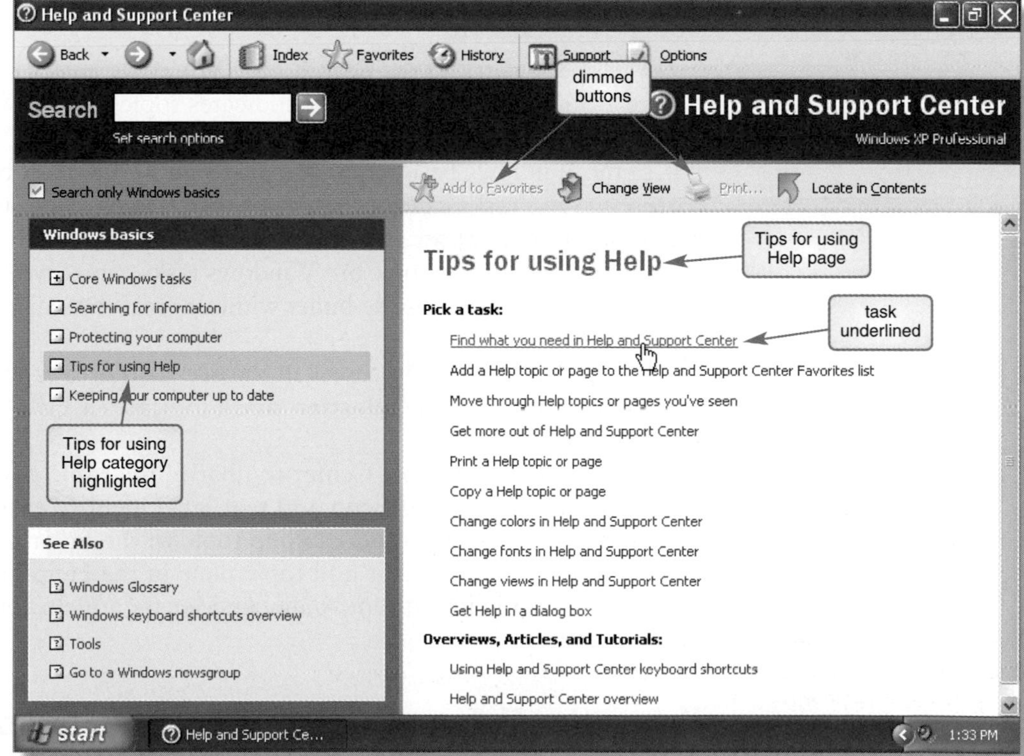

FIGURE 1-96

4

• **Click Find what you need in Help and Support Center and then read the information in the To find what you need in Help and Support Center topic in the topic pane.**

Windows XP removes the dotted rectangle surrounding the Tips for using Help category in the Windows basics area and displays the To find what you need in Help and Support Center topic in the topic pane (Figure 1-97). Clicking the Related Topics link displays a list of related Help topics.

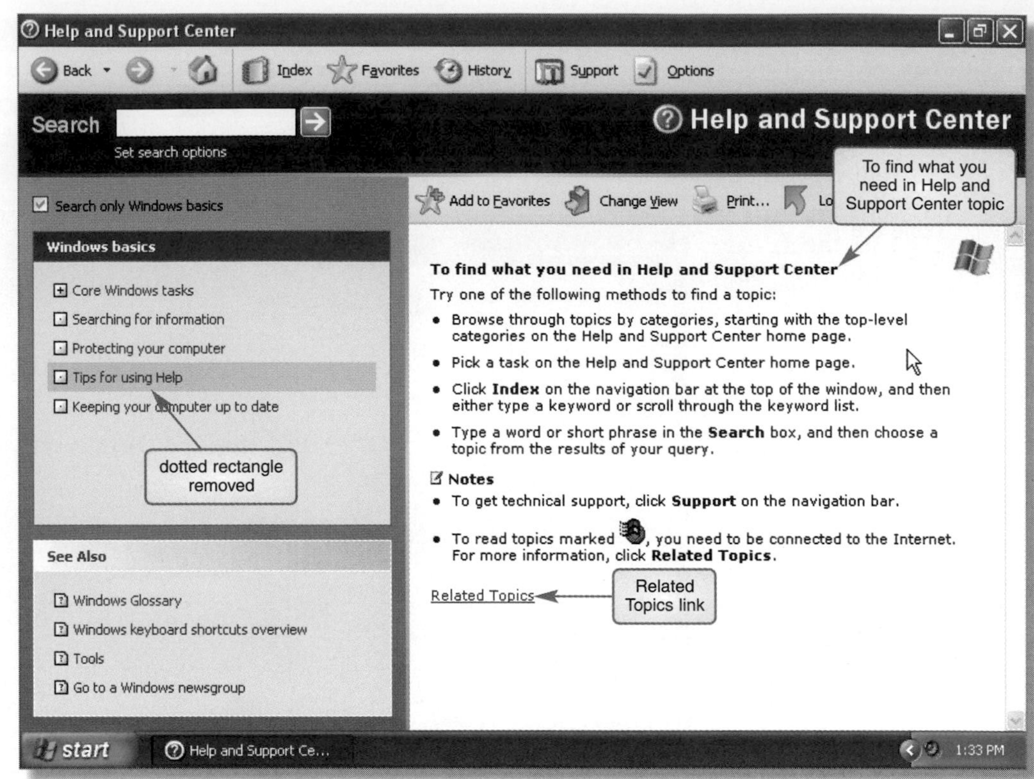

FIGURE 1-97

The check mark in the Search only Windows basics check box shown in Figure 1-95 on the previous page indicates topics in the Windows basics category will be searched.

In the Windows basics area, the **plus sign** in the small box to the left of the Core Windows tasks category indicates the category contains subcategories but the subcategories do not appear in the area. Clicking the box with the plus sign displays a list of subcategories below the Core Windows tasks category. A **bullet** in a small box indicates a category. Clicking the bullet within a small box displays a list of tasks in the topic pane.

Each of the four Help topics in the See Also area is identified by a question mark in a document icon. The **question mark** indicates a Help topic without further subdivision.

The Help and Support Center toolbar in the topic pane shown in Figure 1-95 contains four buttons. An icon and text label identify each button on the toolbar. The buttons allow you to add a Help topic to the favorites list, display only the Help and Support Center toolbar and topic pane in the Help and Support Center window, print a Help topic in the topic pane, and locate a Help topic in the topic pane in the table of contents.

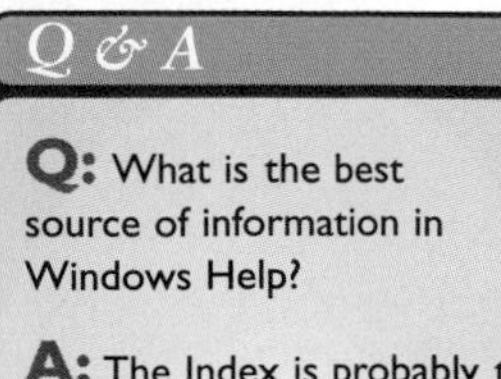

Q & A

Q: What is the best source of information in Windows Help?

A: The Index is probably the best source of information in Windows Help and Support, because you can enter the name of the subject in which you are interested. Sometimes, however, you will have to be creative to discover the index entry that answers your question, because the most obvious entry will not always lead to your answer.

Using the Help and Support Center Index

A second method of finding answers to your questions about Windows XP is to use the Help and Support Center Index. The **Help and Support Center Index** contains a list of index entries, each of which references one or more Help topics. Assume you want more information about home networking. The following steps illustrate how to learn more about home networking.

To Search for Help Topics Using the Index

1

- **Click the Index button on the navigation toolbar, type** `home networking` **in the Type in the keyword to find text box, and then point to overview in the list.**

The Index area, containing a text box, list, and Display button, is displayed in the navigation pane and the Index page is displayed in the topic pane (Figure 1-98). When you type an entry in the text box, the list of index entries in the list automatically scrolls, and the entry you type is highlighted in the list. Several entries appear indented below the home networking entry.

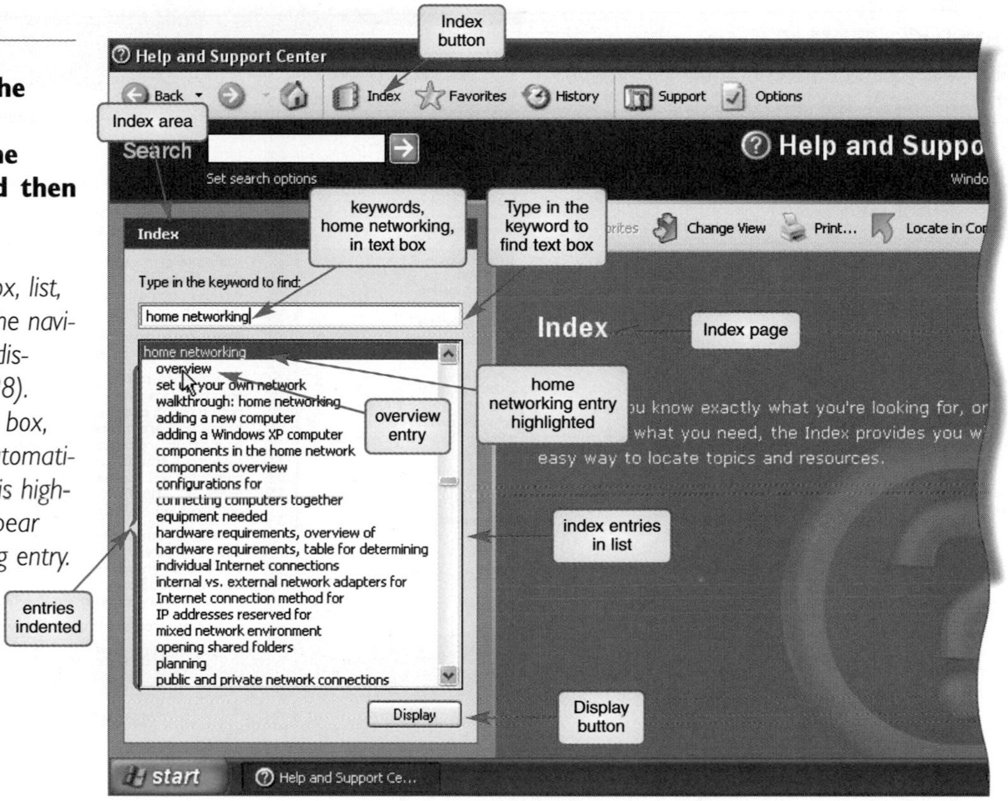

FIGURE 1-98

2

- **Click overview in the list and then point to the Display button.**

Windows XP displays the overview entry in the text box and highlights the overview entry in the list (Figure 1-99). The yellow outline surrounding the Display button indicates the button is selected.

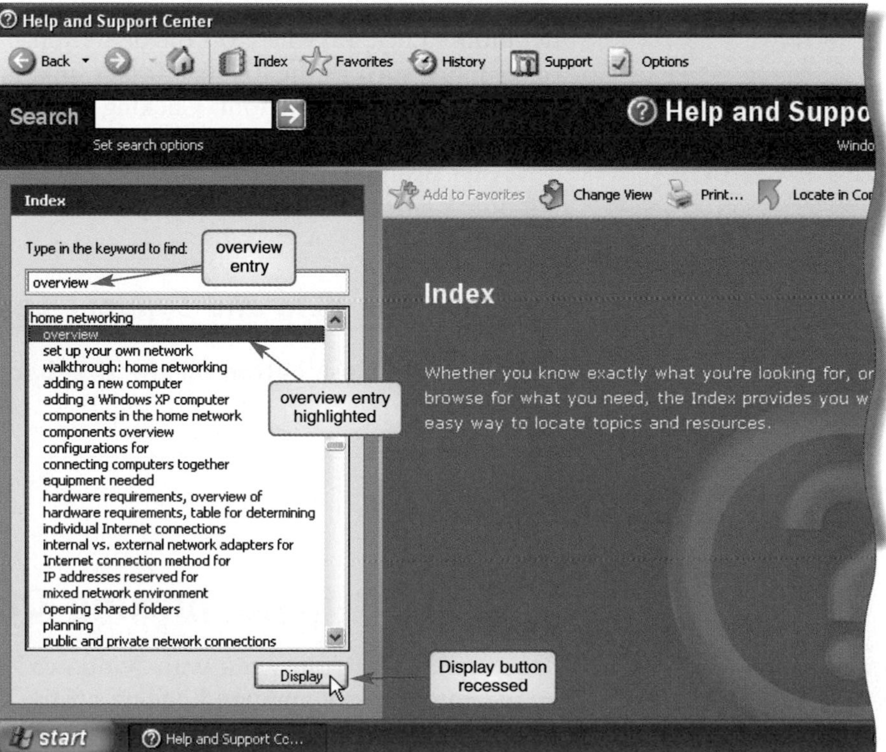

FIGURE 1-99

3

• **Click the Display button.**

The Home or small office networking overview topic is displayed in the topic pane (Figure 1-100). The topic contains an overview of home and small office networks. Additional information is available by using the vertical scroll bar in the topic pane.

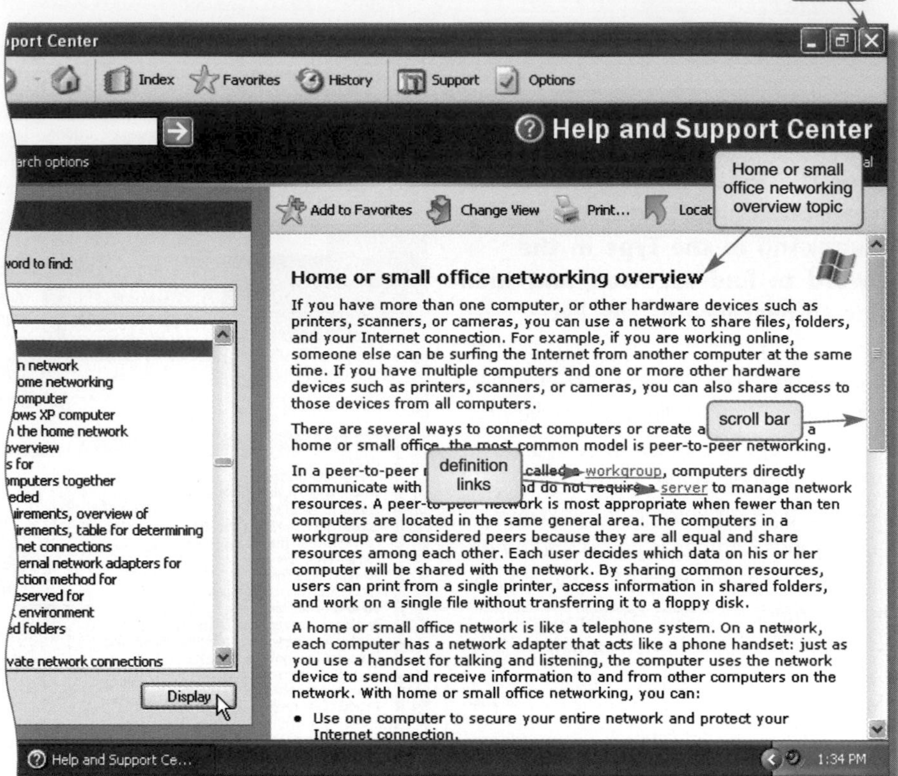

FIGURE 1-100

In Figure 1-100, the workgroup and server links are underlined and displayed in green font to indicate that clicking the link will display its definition. To remove the definition, click anywhere off the definition. Although not visible in Figure 1-100, other links, such as the Related Topics link, appear at the bottom of the page, underlined, and in blue font. Clicking the Related Topics link displays a pop-up window that contains topics related to the home or small office network overview.

After using the Help and Support Center, normally you will close the Help and Support Center. The following step shows how to close the Help and Support Center.

To Close the Help and Support Center

Click the Close button on the title bar of the Help and Support Center window.

Windows XP closes the Help and Support Center window.

Logging Off and Turning Off the Computer

After completing your work with Windows XP, you should close your user account by logging off the computer. Logging off the computer closes any open applications, allows you to save any unsaved documents, ends the Windows XP session, and makes the computer available for other users. Perform the following steps to log off the computer.

To Log Off the Computer

- **Click the Start button on the taskbar and then point to Log Off on the Start menu.**

Windows XP displays the Start menu and highlights the Log Off command (Figure 1-101).

FIGURE 1-101

- **Click Log Off.**
- **Point to the Log Off button in the Log Off Windows dialog box.**

Windows XP displays the Log Off Windows dialog box (Figure 1-102). The dialog box contains three buttons (Switch User, Log Off, and Cancel). Pointing to the Log Off button changes the color of the button to light orange and displays the Log Off balloon. The balloon contains the balloon name, Log Off, and the text, Closes your programs and ends your Windows session. The Cancel button is hidden behind the balloon.

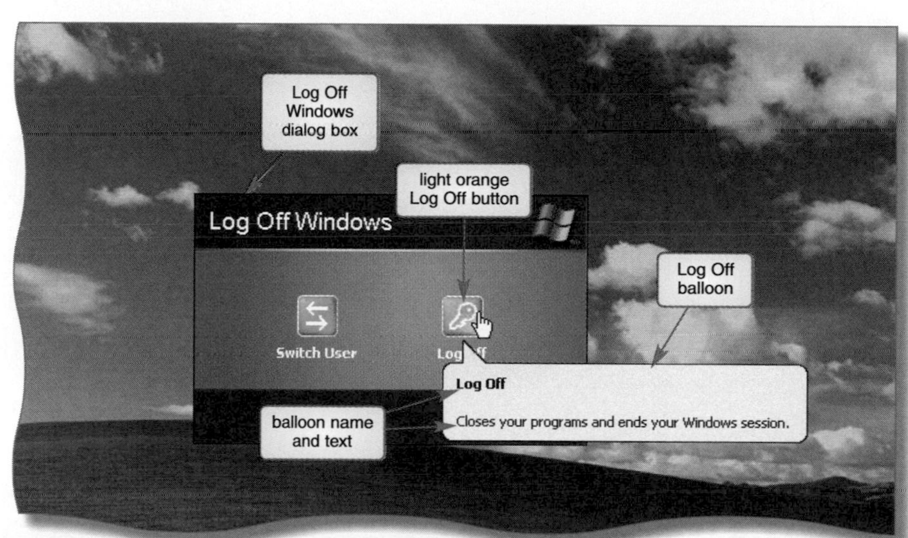

FIGURE 1-102

3

- **Click the Log Off button.**

Windows XP logs off the computer and displays the Welcome screen (Figure 1-103). A message is displayed below the Brad Wilson name on the Welcome screen to indicate the user has unread e-mail messages. Your user name will be displayed instead of the Brad Wilson name on the Welcome screen.

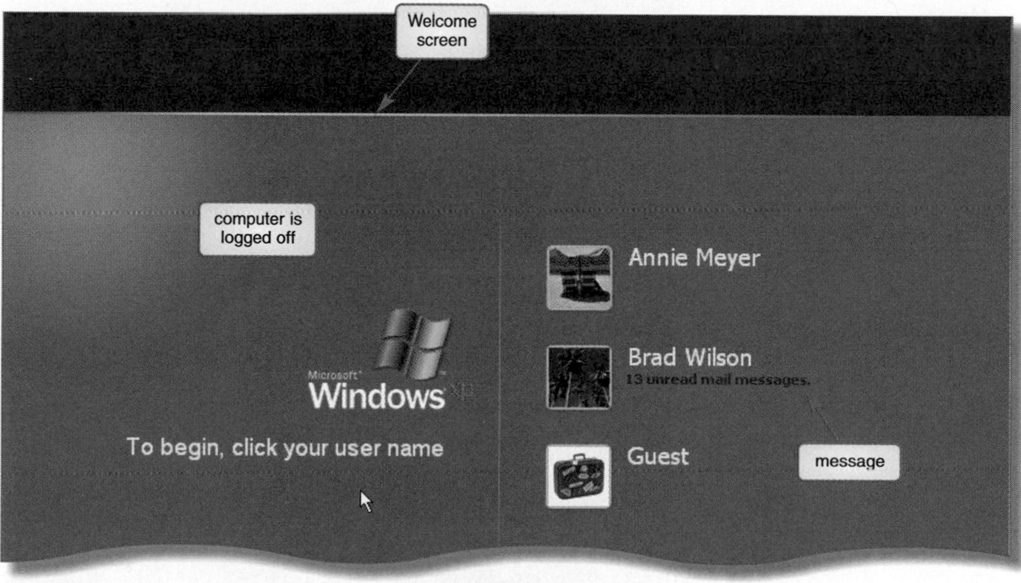

FIGURE 1-103

Q & A

Q: Why is it important to log off the computer?

A: It is important to log off the computer so you do not lose your work. Some users of Windows XP have turned off their computers without following the log off procedure only to find data they thought they had stored on disk was lost.

While Windows XP is logging off, a blue screen containing the word, Welcome, appears on the desktop and the messages, Logging off..., and Saving your settings..., appear on the screen momentarily. The blue screen closes and the Welcome screen (Figure 1-103 on the previous page) appears on the desktop. At this point, another user can log on.

If you accidentally click Log Off on the Start menu as shown in Figure 1-101 on the previous page and you do not want to log off, click the Cancel button in the Log Off Windows dialog box to return to normal Windows XP operation.

After logging off, you also may want to turn off the computer using the **Turn off computer link** on the Welcome screen. Turning off the computer shuts down Windows XP so you can turn off the power to the computer. Many computers turn the power off automatically. The following steps illustrate how to turn off the computer. If you are not sure about turning off the computer, simply read the steps.

To Turn Off the Computer

- **Point to the Turn off computer link on the Welcome screen.**

Pointing to the Turn off computer link underlines the Turn off computer link (Figure 1-104).

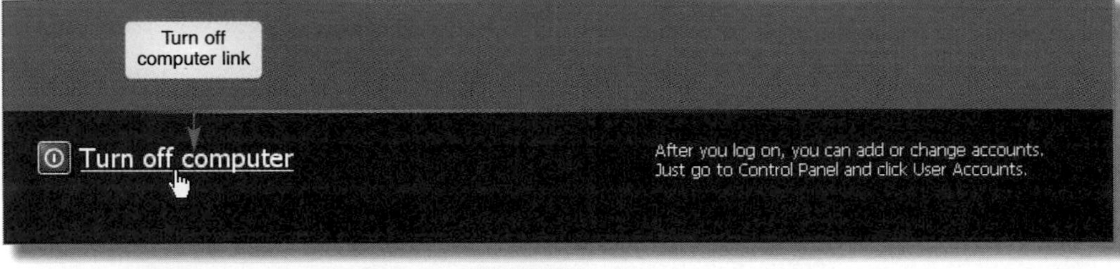

FIGURE 1-104

2

- **Click Turn off computer.**

The Welcome screen darkens, and the Turn off computer dialog box is displayed (Figure 1-105). The dialog box contains four buttons (Stand By, Turn Off, Restart, and Cancel). The buttons allow you to perform different operations, such as placing the computer in stand by mode (Stand By), shutting down Windows XP (Turn Off), restarting the computer (Restart), and canceling the process of shutting down Windows XP (Cancel).

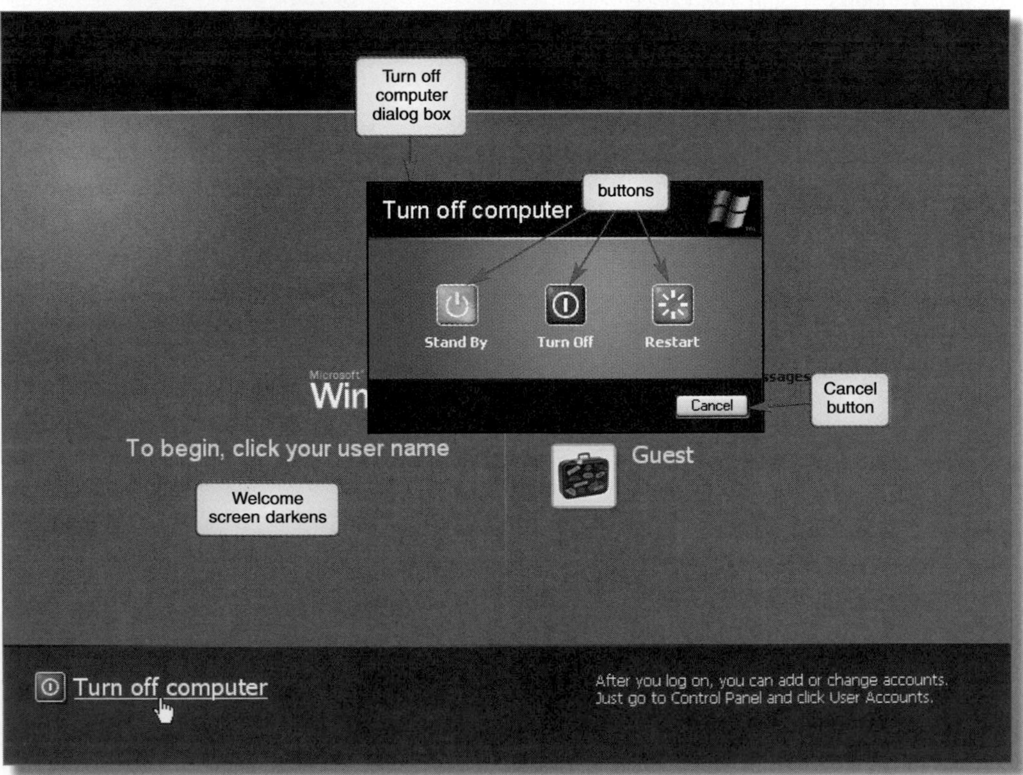

FIGURE 1-105

• **Point to the Turn Off button in the Turn off computer dialog box.**

The color of the Turn Off button changes to light red and the Turn Off balloon is displayed (Figure 1-106). The balloon contains the balloon name, Turn Off, and the text, Shuts down Windows so that you can safely turn off the computer.

4

• **Click the Turn Off button.**

Windows XP is shut down.

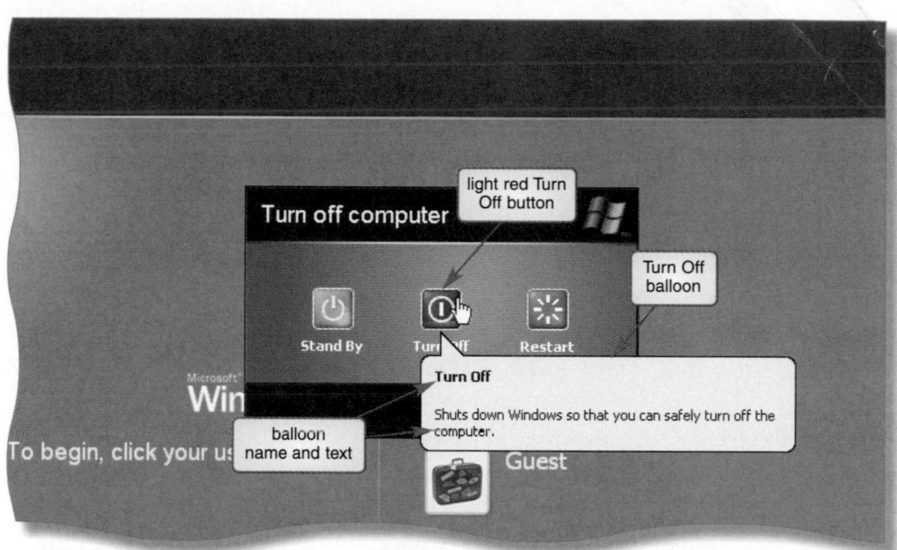

FIGURE 1-106

While Windows XP is shutting down, a blue screen containing the word, Welcome, is displayed on the desktop and the message, Windows is shutting down..., appears momentarily. At this point, you can turn off the computer. When shutting down Windows XP, you should never turn off the computer before these messages appear.

If you accidentally click Turn off computer on the Welcome screen as shown in Figure 1-104 and you do not want to shut down Windows XP, click the Cancel button in the Turn off computer dialog box shown in Figure 1-105 to return to normal Windows XP operation.

Skill Builder 1-4

To practice the following tasks, visit scsite.com/off2003sch/skill, locate Windows XP Project 1, and then click Skill Builder 1-4.

- ❑ Search for a file by name
- ❑ Search for a file using a word or phrase
- ❑ Use Help
- ❑ Log off the computer

What Is Microsoft Office 2003?

Microsoft Office 2003 is a collection of the more popular Microsoft application software products and is available in Standard, Small Business, Professional, Student and Teacher, and Developer editions. The **Microsoft Office Professional Edition 2003** includes the five basic applications, which are Microsoft Office Word 2003, Microsoft Office Excel 2003, Microsoft Office Access 2003, Microsoft Office PowerPoint 2003, and Microsoft Office Outlook 2003. Office allows you to work more efficiently, communicate more effectively, and improve the appearance of each document you create.

Office contains a collection of media files (art, sound, animation, and movies) that you can use to enhance documents. **Microsoft Clip Organizer** allows you to organize the media files on your computer and search for specific files, as well as search for and organize media files located on the Internet. Clip art and media files are accessible from the Microsoft Office Online Web site, which contains thousands of additional media files.

With the **Office Speech Recognition** software installed and a microphone, you can speak the names of toolbar buttons, menus, and menu commands, and list items, screen alerts, and dialog box controls, such as OK and Cancel. You also can dictate text and numbers to insert them as well as delete them. If you have speakers, you can instruct the computer to speak a document or worksheet to you. In addition, you can translate a word, phrase, or an entire document from English into Japanese, Chinese, French, Spanish, or German.

Menus and toolbars adjust to the way in which you work. As Office detects which commands you use more frequently, these commands are displayed at the top of the menu, and the infrequently used commands are placed in reserve. A button at the bottom of the menu allows you to expand the menu in order to view all its commands. More frequently used buttons on a toolbar appear on the toolbar, while less frequently used buttons are not displayed.

In addition, Office integrates its applications with the power of the Internet so you can share information, communicate and collaborate on projects over long distances, and conduct online meetings.

The Internet, World Wide Web, and Intranets

Office allows you to take advantage of the Internet, the World Wide Web, and intranets. The **Internet** is a worldwide network of thousands of computer networks and millions of commercial, educational, government, and personal computers. The **World Wide Web** is an easy-to-use graphical interface for exploring the Internet. The World Wide Web consists of many individual Web sites. A **Web site** consists of a single **Web page** or multiple Web pages linked together. The first Web page in the Web site is called the **home page** and a unique address, called a **Uniform Resource Locator** (**URL**), identifies each Web page. Web sites are located on computers called Web servers.

A software tool, called a **browser**, allows you to locate and view a Web page. One method of viewing a Web page is to use the browser to enter the URL for the Web page. A widely used browser, called **Internet Explorer**, is included with Office. Another method of viewing a Web page is clicking a hyperlink. A **hyperlink** is colored or underlined text or a graphic that, when clicked, connects to another Web page.

An **intranet** is a special type of Web site that is available only to the users of a particular type of computer network, such as a network used within a company or organization for internal communication. Like the Internet, hyperlinks are used within an intranet to access documents, pages, and other destinations on the intranet.

Office and the Internet

Office was designed in response to customer requests to streamline the process of information sharing and collaboration within their organizations. Organizations that, in the past, made important information available only to a select few, now want their information accessible to a wider range of individuals who are using tools such as Office and Internet Explorer. Office allows users to utilize the Internet or an intranet as a central location to view documents, manage files, and work together.

Each of the Office applications makes publishing documents on a Web server as simple as saving a file on a hard disk. Once the file is placed on the Web server, users can view and edit the documents, and conduct Web discussions and live online meetings.

An explanation of each Office application along with how it is used to access an intranet or the Internet is given on the following pages.

Microsoft Office Word 2003

Microsoft Office Word 2003 is a full-featured word processing program that allows you to create many types of personal and business communications, including announcements, letters, resumes, business documents, and academic reports, as well as other forms of written documents. Figure 1-107 illustrates the top portion of a word processing document created using Microsoft Word.

FIGURE 1-107

The Word AutoCorrect, Spelling, and Grammar features allow you to proofread documents for errors in spelling and grammar by identifying the errors and offering corrections as you type. As you create a specific document, such as a business letter or resume, Word provides wizards, which ask questions and then use your answers to format the document before you type the text of the document.

Word automates many often-used tasks and provides you with powerful desktop publishing tools to use as you create professional-looking brochures, advertisements, and newsletters. The drawing tools allow you to design impressive 3-D effects by including shadows, textures, and curves.

Word makes it easier for you to share documents in order to collaborate on a document. The Send for Review and Markup features allow you to send a document for review and easily track the changes made to the document.

Word and the Internet

Word makes it possible to design and publish Web pages on an intranet or the Internet, insert a hyperlink to a Web page in a word processing document, as well as access other Web pages to search for and retrieve information and pictures from them. Figure 1-108 on the next page illustrates the top portion of a cover letter that contains a hyperlink (e-mail address) that allows you to send an e-mail message to the sender.

Clicking the hyperlink starts the Outlook mail program, through which you can send an e-mail message to the author of the cover letter. In Figure 1-109, the Resume and Cover Letter - Message window that allows you to compose a new e-mail message contains the recipient's e-mail address (okamoto@earth.net), subject of the e-mail message (Resume and Cover Letter), and a brief message.

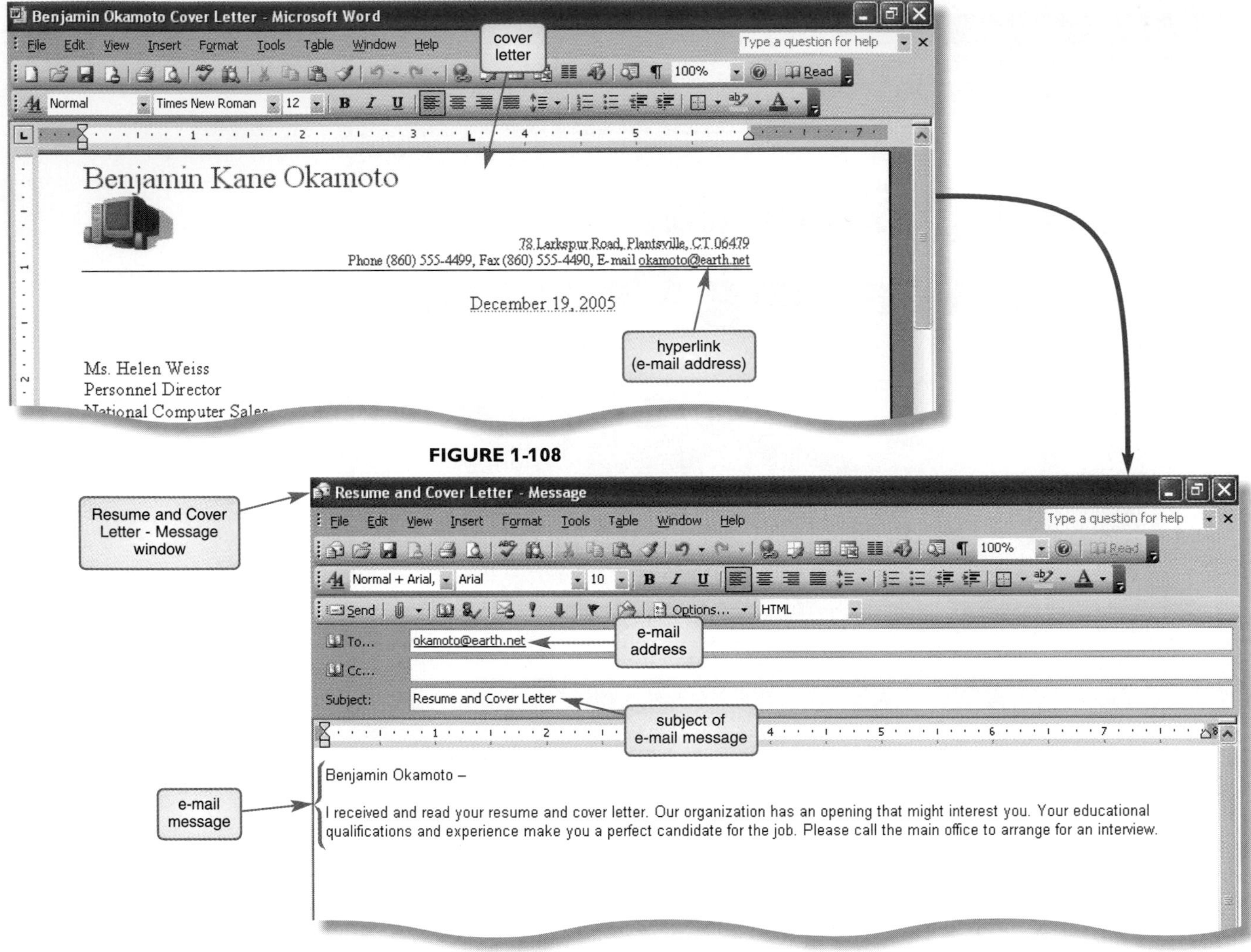

FIGURE 1-108

FIGURE 1-109

Microsoft Office Excel 2003

Microsoft Office Excel 2003 is a spreadsheet program that allows you to organize data, complete calculations, graph data, develop professional-looking reports, publish organized data to the Web, access real-time data from Web sites, and make decisions. Figure 1-110 illustrates a worksheet and 3-D Column chart created using Microsoft Excel.

Excel and the Internet

Using Excel, you can create hyperlinks within a worksheet to access other Office documents on the network, an organization's intranet, or the Internet. You also can save worksheets as static or dynamic Web pages that can be viewed using a browser.

Static Web pages cannot be changed by the person viewing them. Dynamic Web pages give the person viewing them in their browser many capabilities to modify them using Excel. In addition, you can create and run queries to retrieve information from a Web page directly into a worksheet.

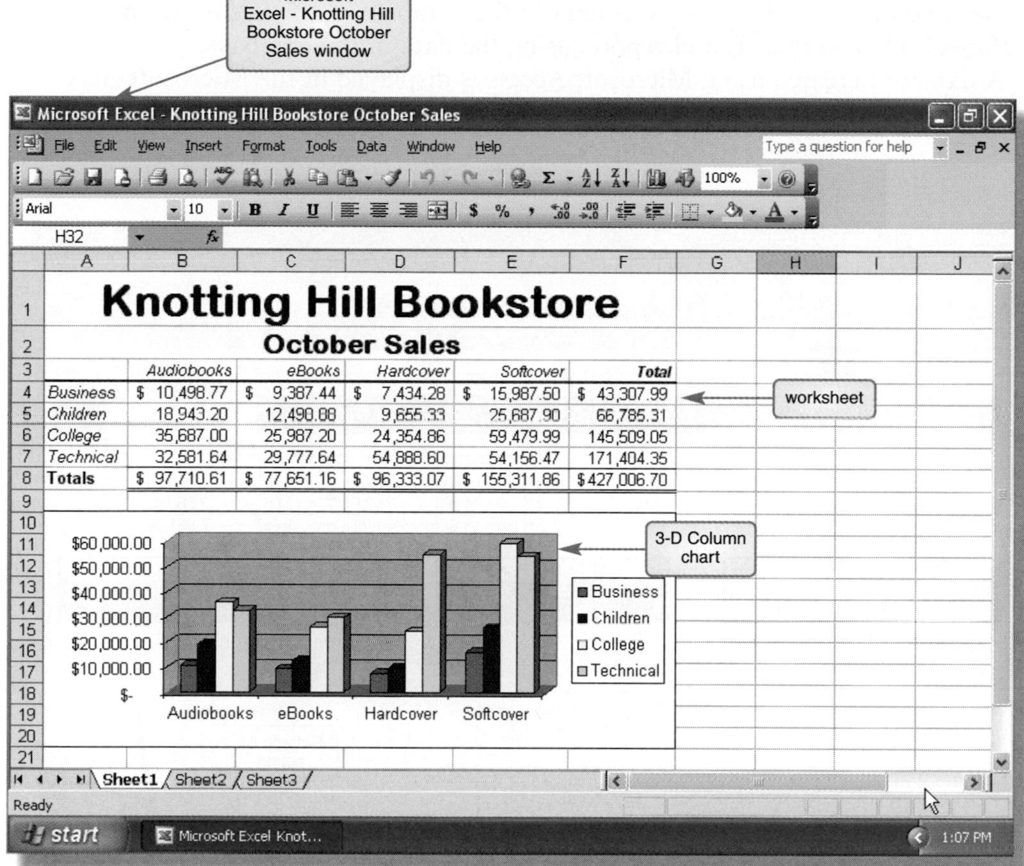

FIGURE 1-110

Figure 1-111 on the next page illustrates a worksheet created by running a Web query to retrieve stock market information for two stocks (XM Satellite Radio Holdings Inc. and Sirius Satellite Radio Inc.). The two hyperlinks were created using the Insert Hyperlink button on the Standard toolbar, and the information in the worksheet was obtained from the MSN Money Web site.

The Refresh All button on the External Data toolbar allows you to update the last price of the stocks (Last). Clicking the Refresh All button locates the MSN Money Web site, retrieves current information for the stocks listed in the worksheet, and displays the updated information in the worksheet (Figure 1-112 on the next page). Notice that the stock prices and information in this worksheet differ from what was displayed in the worksheet shown in Figure 1-111.

Microsoft Office Access 2003

Microsoft Office Access 2003 is a comprehensive database management system (DBMS). A **database** is a collection of data organized in a manner that allows access, retrieval, and use of that data. Access allows you to create a database; add, change, and delete data in the database; sort data in the database; retrieve data from the database; and create forms and reports using the data in the database.

A database created using Microsoft Access is displayed in the Microsoft Access - [Client : Table] window illustrated in Figure 1-113.

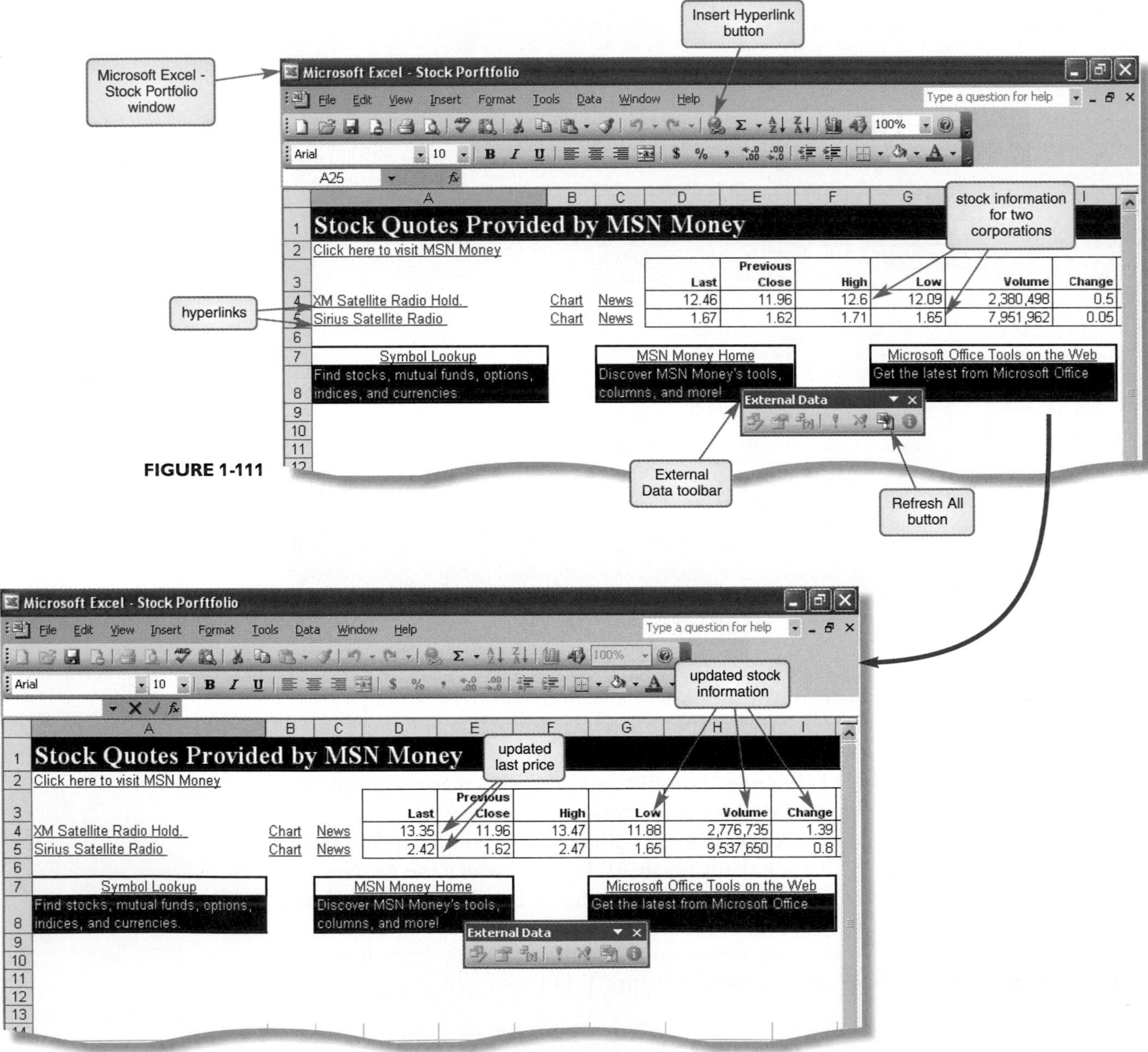

FIGURE 1-111

FIGURE 1-112

Access and the Internet

Databases provide a central location to store related pieces of information. Access simplifies the creation of a database with a wizard that quickly can build one of more than a dozen types of databases. You also can transform lists or worksheets into databases using Access wizards. Data access pages permit you to share a database with other computer users on a network, intranet, or over the Internet, as well as allowing the users to view and edit the database. The database shown in Figure 1-114 contains information (order number, customer number, order date, product number, and quantity) about three orders entered over the Internet using the Internet Explorer browser.

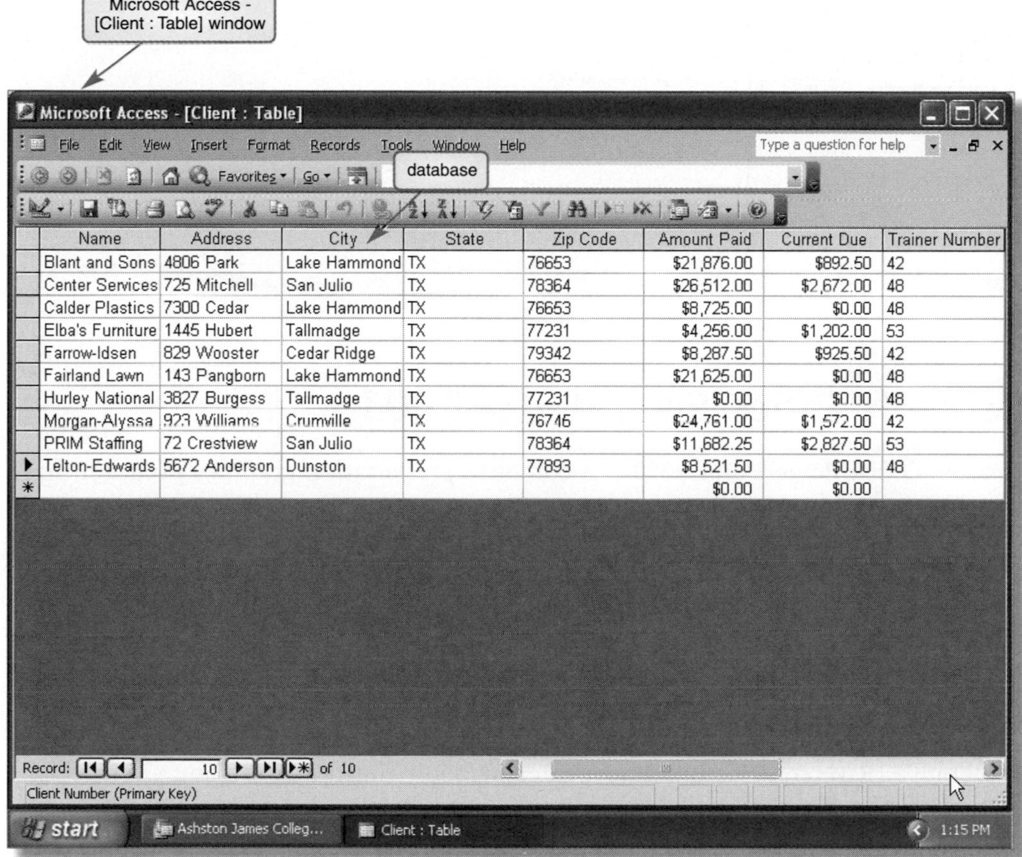

Name	Address	City	State	Zip Code	Amount Paid	Current Due	Trainer Number
Blant and Sons	4806 Park	Lake Hammond	TX	76653	$21,876.00	$892.50	42
Center Services	725 Mitchell	San Julio	TX	78364	$26,512.00	$2,672.00	48
Calder Plastics	7300 Cedar	Lake Hammond	TX	76653	$8,725.00	$0.00	48
Elba's Furniture	1445 Hubert	Tallmadge	TX	77231	$4,256.00	$1,202.00	53
Farrow-Idsen	829 Wooster	Cedar Ridge	TX	79342	$8,287.50	$925.50	42
Fairland Lawn	143 Pangborn	Lake Hammond	TX	76653	$21,625.00	$0.00	48
Hurley National	3827 Burgess	Tallmadge	TX	77231	$0.00	$0.00	48
Morgan-Alyssa	923 Williams	Crumville	TX	76745	$24,761.00	$1,572.00	42
PRIM Staffing	72 Crestview	San Julio	TX	78364	$11,682.25	$2,827.50	53
Telton-Edwards	5672 Anderson	Dunston	TX	77893	$8,521.50	$0.00	48
					$0.00	$0.00	

FIGURE 1-113

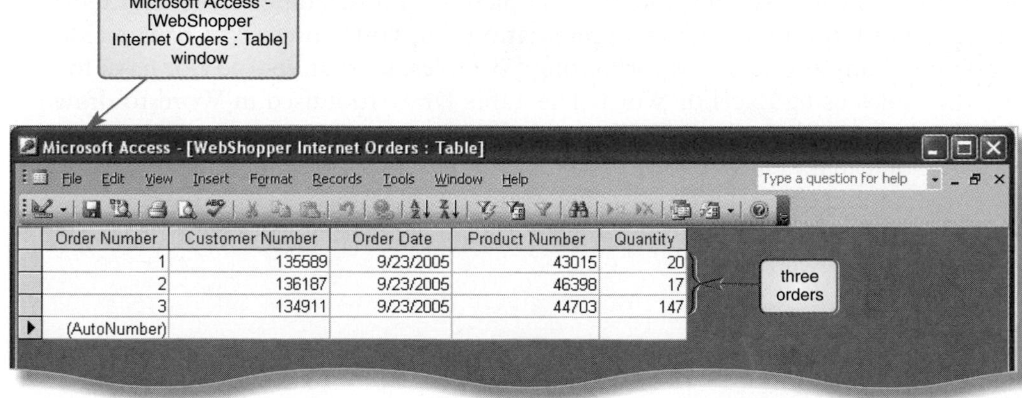

Order Number	Customer Number	Order Date	Product Number	Quantity
1	135589	9/23/2005	43015	20
2	136187	9/23/2005	46398	17
3	134911	9/23/2005	44703	147
(AutoNumber)				

FIGURE 1-114

Figure 1-115 illustrates a simple online order form created to enter order information into the database shown in Figure 1-114 on the previous page. The order form, containing information about order number 4, is displayed in the WebShopper Internet Orders - Microsoft Internet Explorer window.

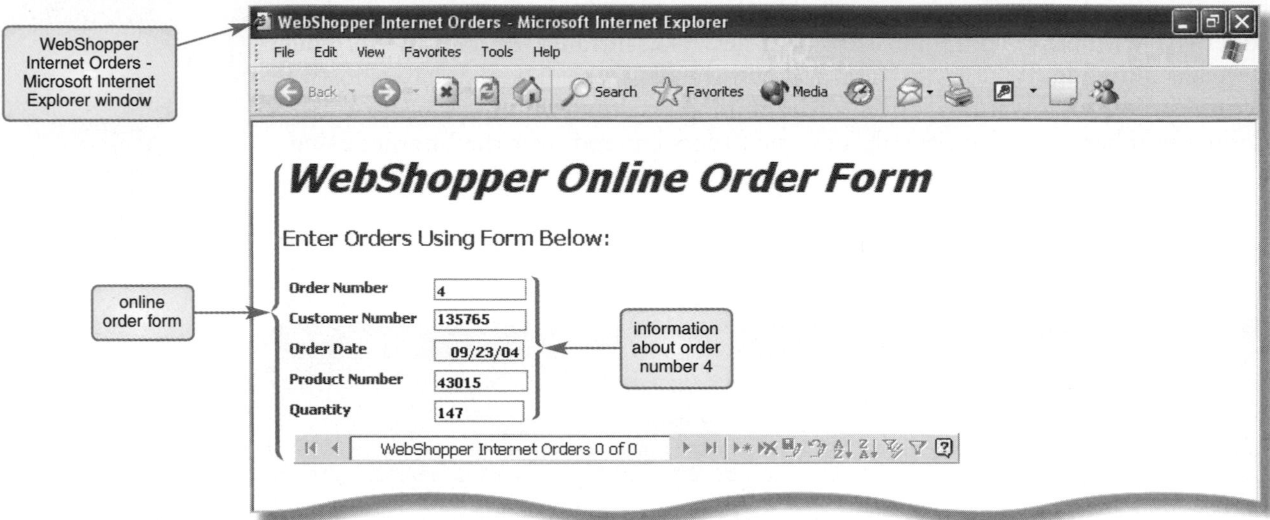

FIGURE 1-115

Microsoft Office PowerPoint 2003

Microsoft Office PowerPoint 2003 is a complete presentation graphics program that allows you to produce professional-looking presentations. PowerPoint provides the flexibility that lets you make informal presentations using overhead transparencies, make electronic presentations using a projection device attached to a personal computer, make formal presentations using 35mm slides or a CD, or run virtual presentations on the Internet.

In PowerPoint, you create a presentation in Normal view. **Normal view** allows you to view the tabs pane, slide pane, and notes pane at the same time. The first slide in a presentation created using Microsoft PowerPoint appears in the Microsoft PowerPoint - [Rivercrest Community Center] window illustrated in Figure 1-116. The full window contains the Outline tab with the presentation outline, the slide pane displaying the first slide in the presentation, and the notes pane showing a note about the presentation.

PowerPoint allows you to create dynamic presentations easily that include multimedia features such as sounds, movies, and pictures. PowerPoint comes with templates that assist you in designing a presentation that you can use to create a slide show. PowerPoint also contains formatting for tables, so that you do not have to create the tables using Excel or Word. The Table Draw tool used in Word to draw tables also is available in PowerPoint.

PowerPoint makes it easier for you to share presentations and collaborate on those presentations. The Send for Review feature and Compare and Merge feature allow you to send a presentation for review and easily merge comments and revisions from multiple reviewers.

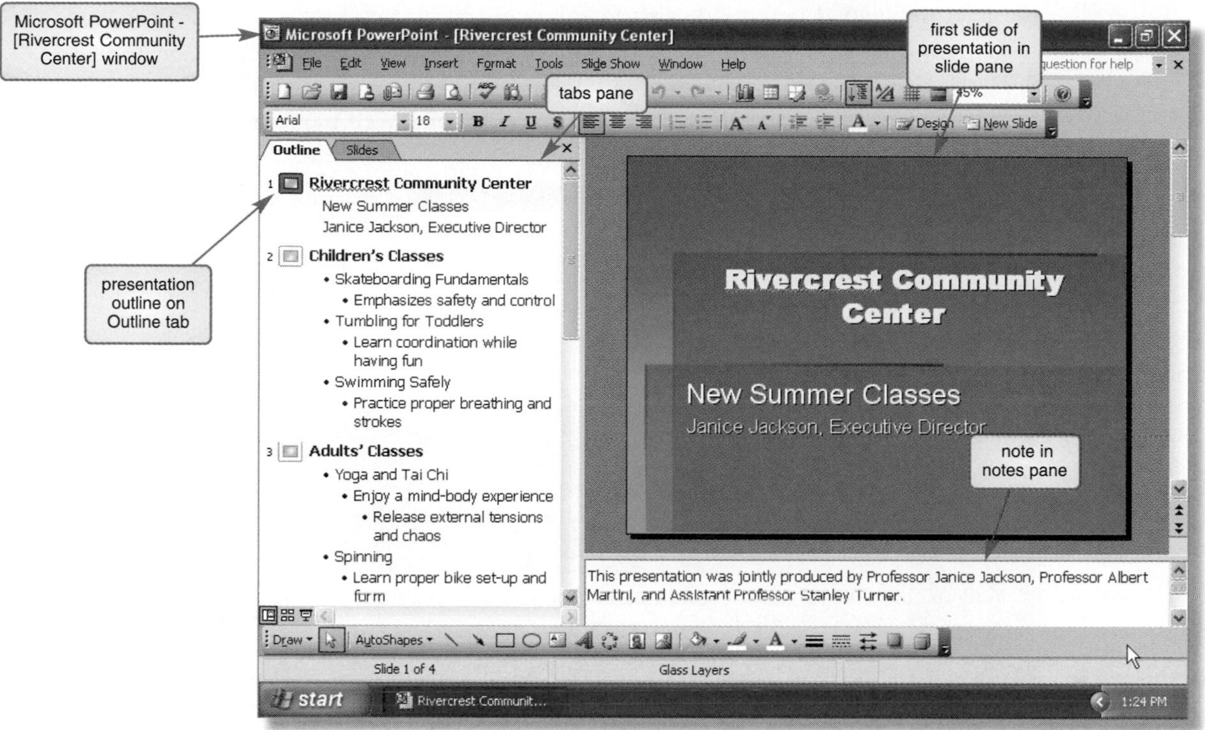

FIGURE 1-116

PowerPoint and the Internet

PowerPoint allows you to publish presentations on the Internet or an intranet. Figure 1-117 illustrates the first slide in a presentation to be published on the Internet. The slide appears in slide view and contains a title (Computers 4 U), a subtitle (Complete Repairs and Service), and a presenter message (Elliott Dane and Lynn Verone). The additional slides in this presentation do not appear in Figure 1-117.

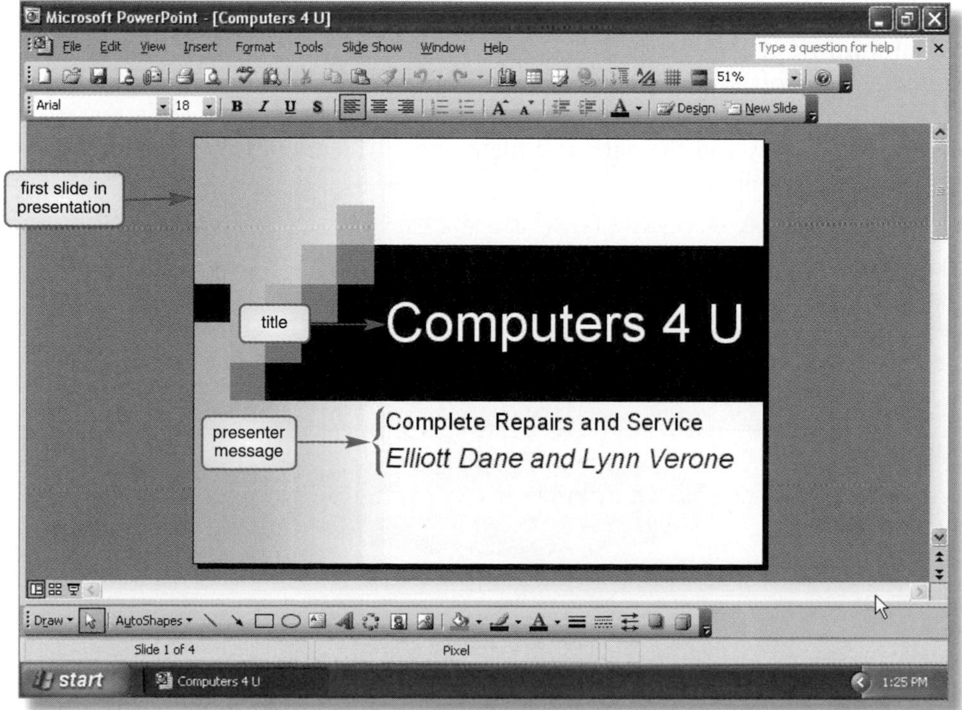

FIGURE 1-117

Figure 1-118 shows the first Web page in a series of Web pages created from the presentation illustrated in Figure 1-117 on the previous page. The Web page appears in the Computers 4 U window in the Internet Explorer browser window. Navigation buttons below the Web page allow you to view additional Web pages in the presentation.

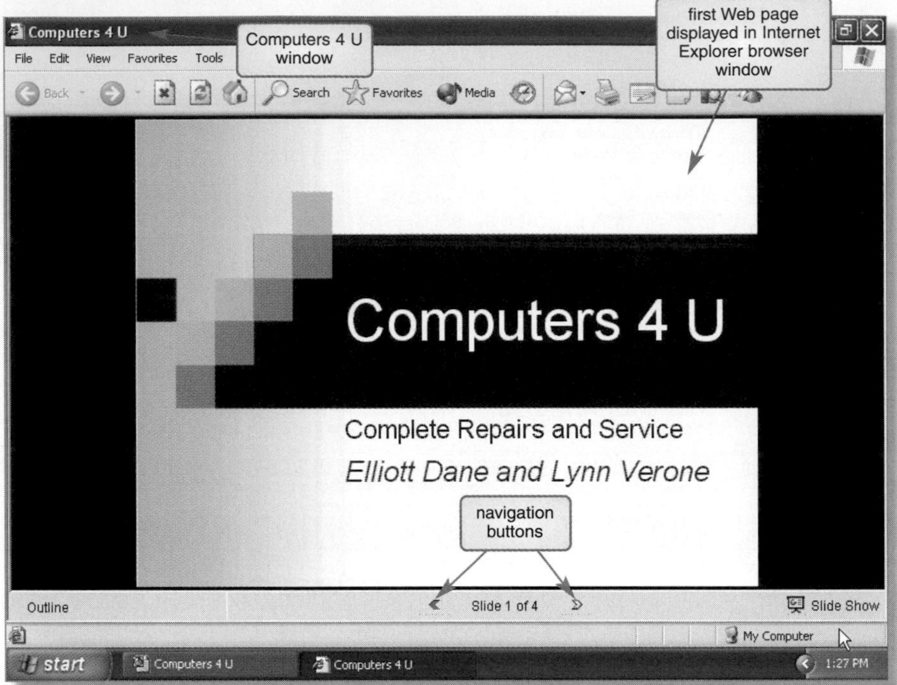

FIGURE 1-118

The Web Toolbar

The easiest method of navigating an intranet or the Internet is to use the Web toolbar. The Web toolbar allows you to search for and open Office documents that you have placed on an intranet or the Internet. The Web toolbar in the Benjamin Okamoto Cover Letter - Microsoft Word window shown in Figure 1-119 is available in all Office applications except FrontPage. Currently, a Word document (cover letter) is displayed in the window, and the path and file name of the document appear in the text box on the Web toolbar.

FIGURE 1-119

The buttons and text box on the Web toolbar allow you to jump to Web pages you have viewed previously, cancel a jump to a Web page, update the contents of the current Web page, or replace all other toolbars with the Web toolbar. In addition, you can view the first Web page displayed, search the Web for new Web sites, and add any Web pages you select to the Favorites folder, so you can return to them quickly in the future.

Microsoft Office Publisher 2003

Microsoft Office Publisher 2003 is a desktop publishing program (DTP) that allows you to design and produce professional-quality documents (newsletters, flyers, brochures, business cards, Web sites, and so on) that combine text, graphics, and photographs. Desktop publishing software provides a variety of tools, including design templates, graphic manipulation tools, color schemes or libraries, and various page wizards and templates. For large jobs, businesses use desktop publishing software to design publications that are **camera ready**, which means the files are suitable for production by outside commercial printers. Publisher also allows you to locate commercial printers, service bureaus, and copy shops willing to accept customer files created in Publisher.

Publisher allows you to design a unique image, or logo, using one of more than 45 master design sets. This, in turn, permits you to use the same design for all your printed documents (letters, business cards, brochures, and advertisements) and Web pages. Publisher includes 60 coordinated color schemes, more than 10,000 high-quality clip art images, 1,500 photographs, 1,000 Web-art graphics, 175 fonts, 340 animated graphics, and hundreds of unique Design Gallery elements (quotations, sidebars, and so on). If you wish, you also can download additional images from the Microsoft Office Online Web page on the Microsoft Web site.

In the Business Card - Hank Landers - Microsoft Publisher window illustrated in Figure 1-120, a business card that was created using the Business Card wizard and the Arcs design set is displayed.

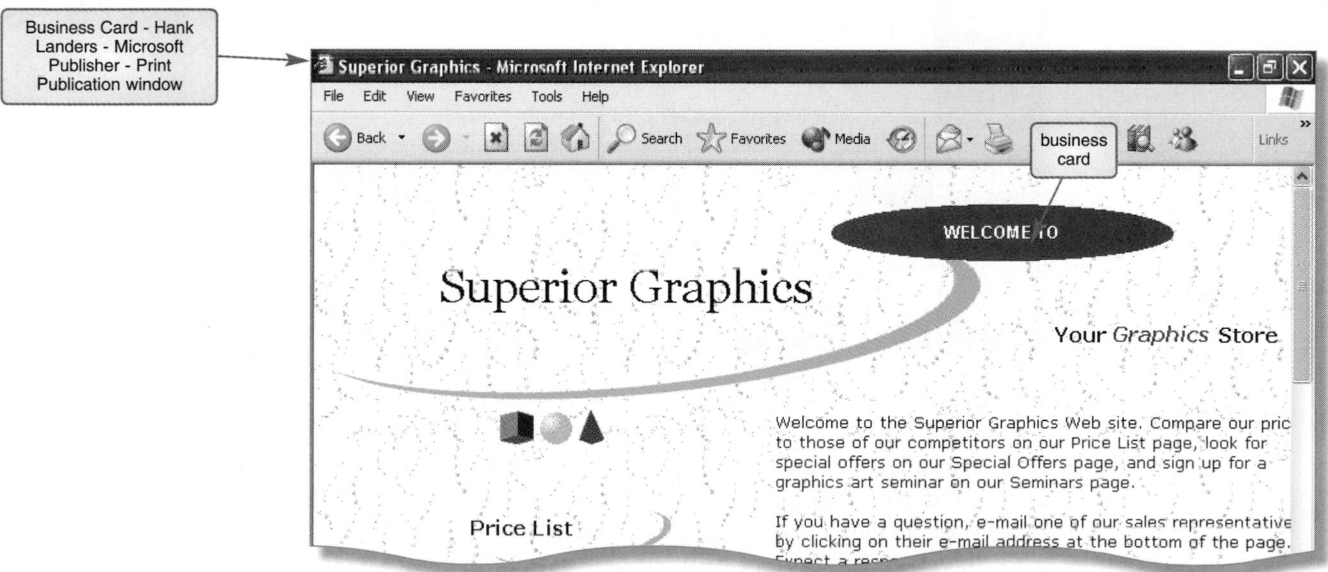

FIGURE 1-120

Publisher and the Internet

Publisher allows you easily to create a multipage Web site with custom color schemes, photo images, animated images, and sounds. Figure 1-121 illustrates the Superior Graphics - Microsoft Internet Explorer window displaying the top portion of the home page in a Web site created using the Web page wizard and Arcs design set.

The home page in the Superior Graphics Web site contains text, graphic images, animated graphic images, and displays using the same design set (Arcs) as the business card illustrated in Figure 1-120 on the previous page.

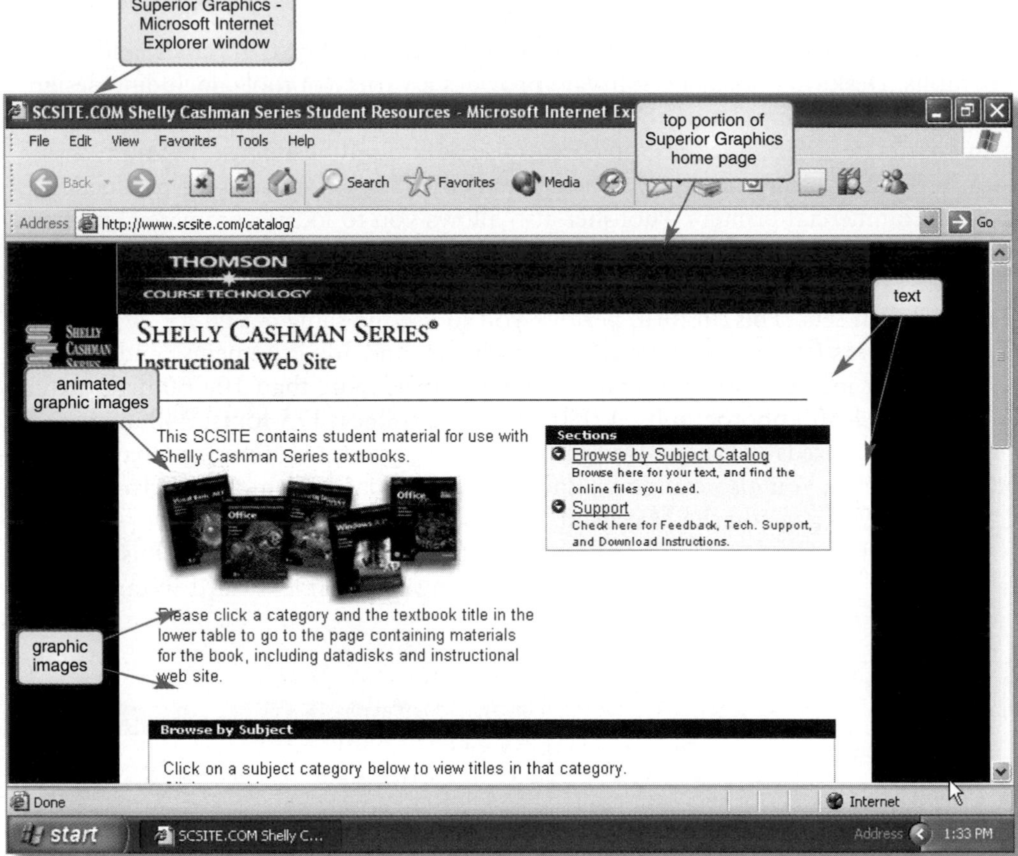

FIGURE 1-121

Microsoft Office FrontPage 2003

Microsoft Office FrontPage 2003 is a Web page authoring and site management program that lets you create and manage professional-looking Web sites on the Internet or an intranet. You can create and edit Web pages without knowing Hypertext Markup Language (HTML), view the pages and files in the Web site and control their organization, manage existing Web sites, import and export files, and diagnose and correct problems. A variety of templates, including the Workgroup Web template that allows you to set up and maintain the basic structure of a workgroup Web, are available to facilitate managing the Web site.

Figure 1-122 illustrates the top portion of a Web page created using FrontPage that contains information about the Shelly Cashman Series developed by Course Technology. It appears in the SCSITE.COM Shelly Cashman Series Student Resources - Microsoft Internet Explorer window.

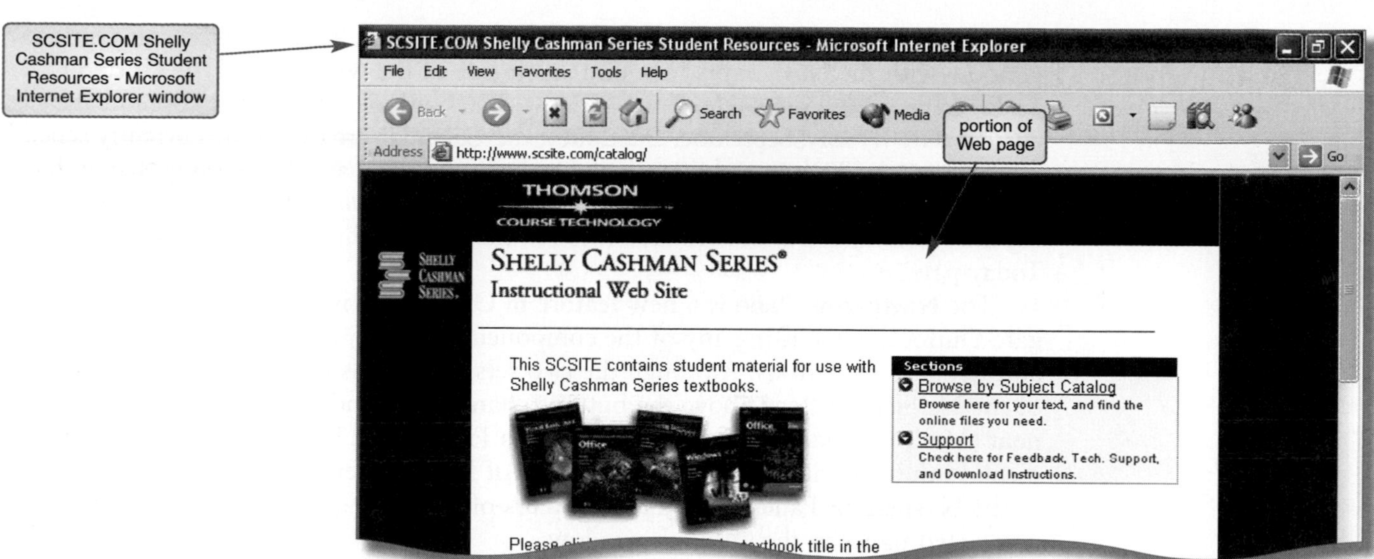

FIGURE 1-122

Microsoft Office Outlook 2003

Microsoft Office Outlook 2003 is a powerful communications and scheduling program that helps you communicate with others, keep track of your contacts, and organize your busy schedule. Outlook allows you to send and receive electronic mail and permits you to engage in real-time messaging with family, friends, or coworkers using instant messaging. Outlook also provides you with the means to organize your contacts. Users easily can track e-mail messages, meetings, and notes with a particular contact. Outlook's Calendar, Contacts, Tasks, and Notes components aid in this organization. Contact information readily is available from the Outlook Calendar, Mail, Contacts, and Task components by accessing the Find a Contact feature.

Personal information management (**PIM**) programs such as Outlook provide a way for individuals and workgroups to organize, find, view, and share information easily.

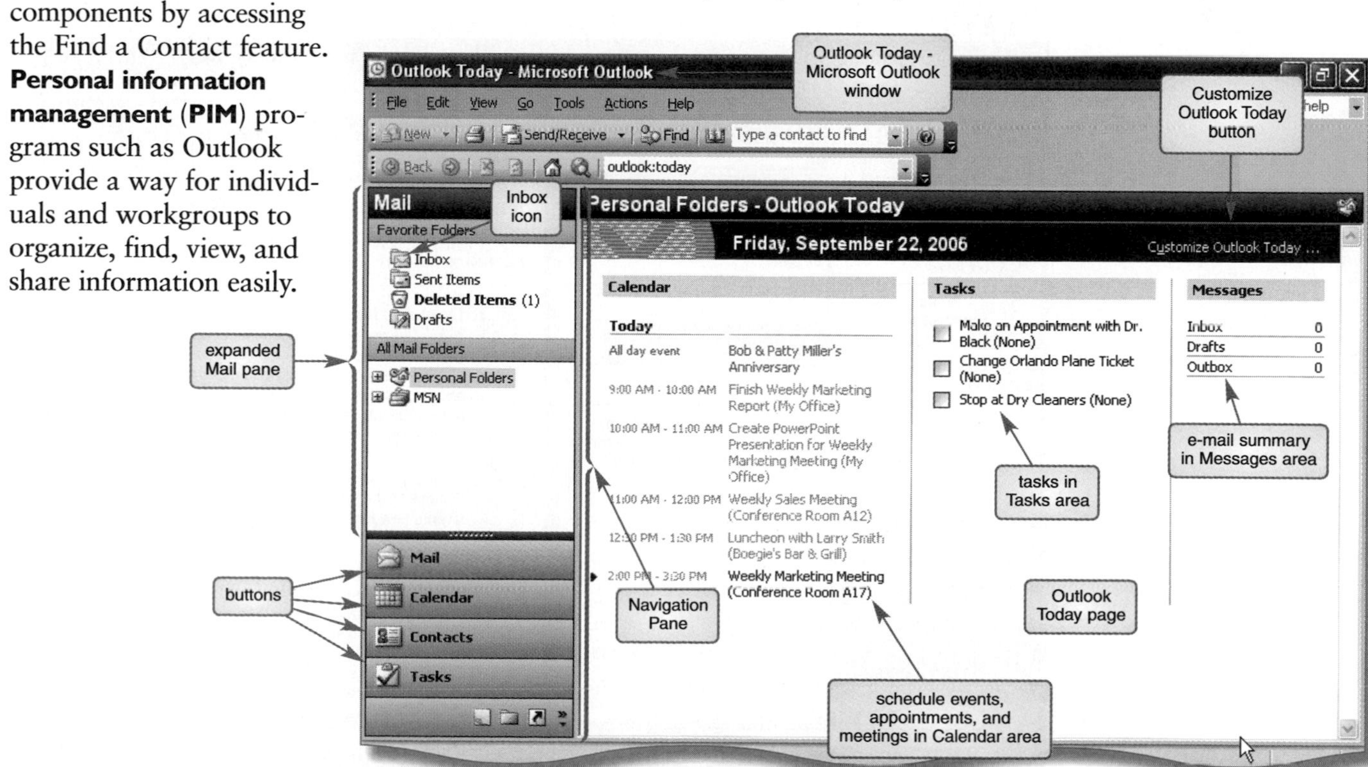

FIGURE 1-123

Figure 1-123 on the previous page shows the Outlook Today - Microsoft Outlook window with the Navigation Pane on the left side of the window and the **Outlook Today page** on the right side of the window. The Outlook Today page contains the current date (Friday, September 22, 2006); the Calendar area with the currently scheduled events; the Tasks area with a list of tasks to perform; and the Messages area that summarizes the users e-mail messages by folder. You can customize this page by clicking the Customize Outlook Today button in the upper-right corner of the Outlook Today page.

The **Navigation Pane** is a new feature in Outlook. It is set up to help you navigate Outlook while using any of the components. It comprises one or more panes and two sets of buttons. Although the two sets of buttons remain constant, the area of the Navigation Pane above the buttons changes, depending on the active component (Mail, Calendar, Contacts, or Tasks). In Figure 1-123, the expanded Mail pane displays the Favorite Folders pane and the All Mail Folders pane. Clicking a button in the Navigation Pane displays the contents of the component's folder with its associated panes in the Outlook window.

Outlook allows you to click the Mail button in the Navigation Pane to view e-mail messages, click the Calendar button to schedule activities (events, appointments, and meetings), click the Contacts button to maintain a list of contacts and e-mail addresses, and click the Tasks button to view a detailed list of tasks.

When you click the Inbox icon in the Mail pane, the Inbox - Microsoft Outlook window is displayed and the contents of the Inbox folder (your e-mail messages) and the Reading Pane are displayed in the window (Figure 1-124).

The Inbox message pane contains two e-mail messages. The second e-mail message is highlighted. The contents of the highlighted e-mail message are displayed in the Reading Pane.

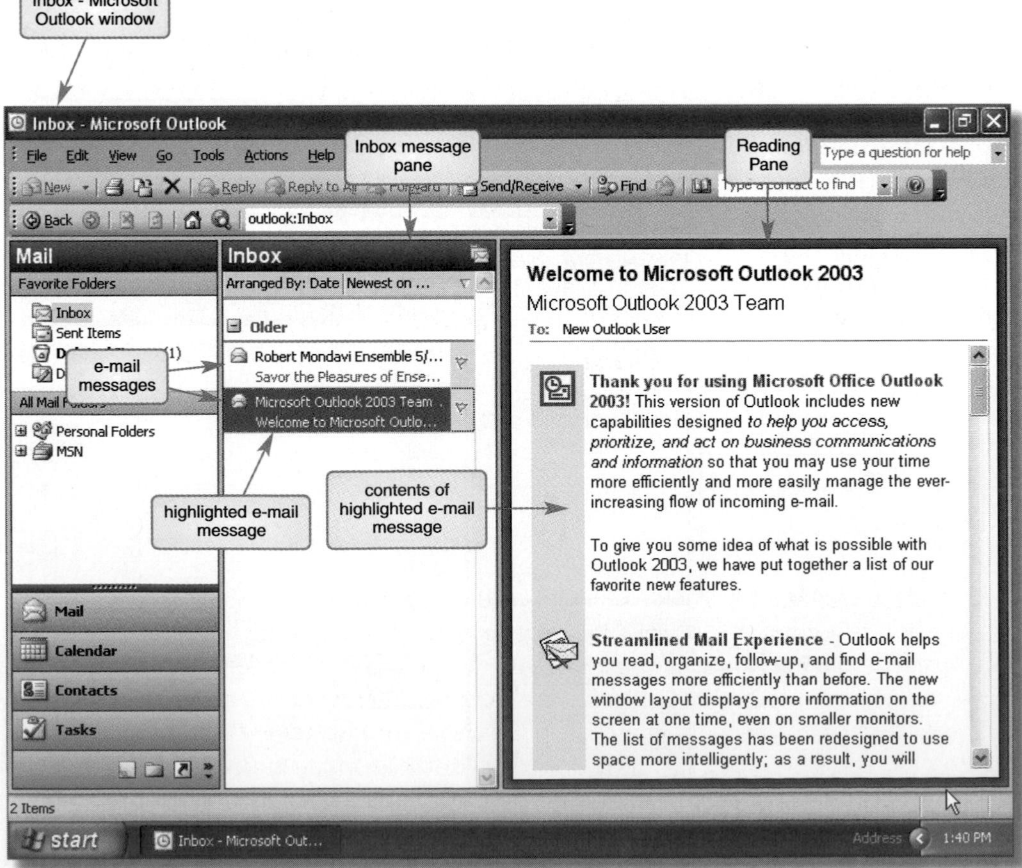

FIGURE 1-124

The Microsoft Office 2003 Help System

At any time while you are using one of the Office applications, you can interact with the **Microsoft Office 2003 Help system** for that application and display information on any topic associated with the application. Several categories of help are available to you. One of the easiest methods to obtain help is to use the Type a question for help box. The **Type a question for help box** on the right side of the menu bar lets you type free-form questions, such as how do I save or how do I create a Web page, or you can type terms, such as template, smart tags, or speech. The Help system responds by displaying a list of topics relating to the question or term in the Search Results task pane. The Type a question for help box that appears in the Grand Prix Announcement - Microsoft Word window is illustrated in Figure 1-125.

When you type the question, How do I check Spelling, in the Type a question for help box shown in Figure 1-125, the Help system displays a list of topics relating to the question. Clicking a topic in the list opens a Help window that provides Help information about spell checking. Detailed instructions for using the Type a question for help box and the other categories of Help are explained in Appendix A of this book.

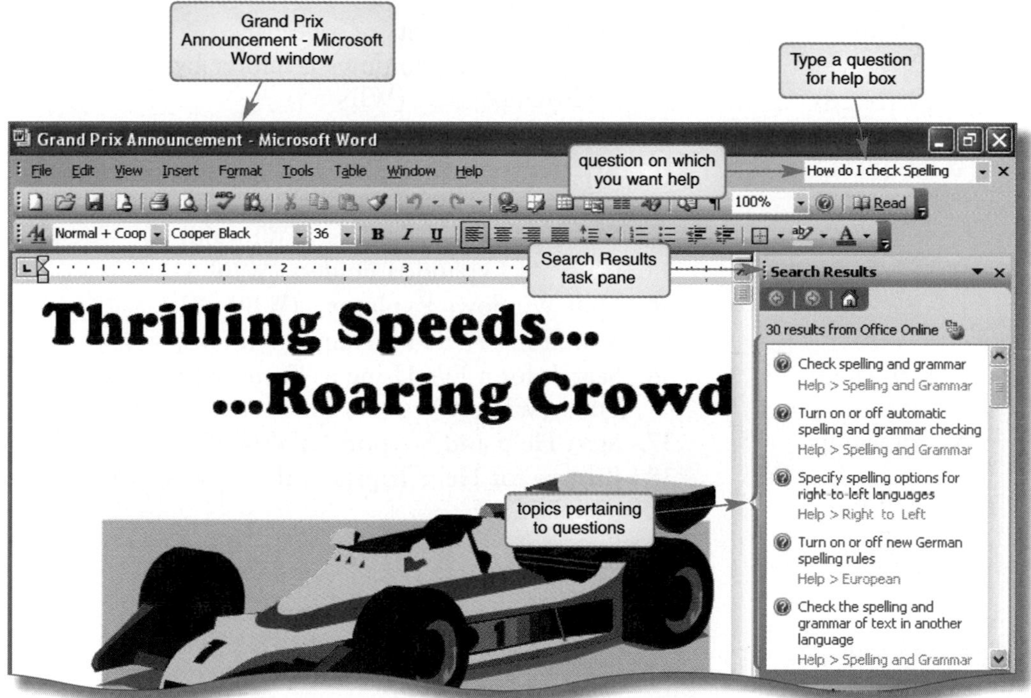

FIGURE 1-125

Project Summary

Project 1 illustrated the Microsoft Windows XP graphical user interface and the Microsoft Office 2003 applications. You launched Windows XP, learned the components of the desktop and the six mouse operations. You opened, closed, moved, resized, minimized, maximized, and scrolled a window. You used Windows Explorer to expand and collapse drives and folders, display drive and folder contents, create a folder, copy a file between folders, and rename and then delete a file. You learned about hierarchical format, removable media, flash drives, and used Microsoft Word to type and save a document in a newly created folder. You searched for files using a word or phrase in the file or by name, you obtained help about using Microsoft Windows XP, and shut down Windows XP.

Brief explanations of the Word, Excel, Access, PowerPoint, Publisher, FrontPage, and Outlook applications and examples of how these applications interact with the Internet were given. With this introduction, you now are ready to begin a more in-depth study of each Office application explained in this book.

If you have a SAM user profile, you may have access to hands-on instruction, practice, and assessment of the skills covered in this project. Log in to your SAM account and go to your assignments page to see what your instructor has assigned.

What You Should Know

Having completed this project, you should be able to perform the tasks below. The tasks are listed in the same order they were presented in this project. For a list of the buttons, menus, toolbars, and commands introduced in this project, see the Quick Reference Summary at the back of this book and refer to the Page Number column.

1. Log On the Computer (WIN 9)
2. Display the Start Menu (WIN 12)
3. Add an Icon to the Desktop (WIN 15)
4. Open a Window Using a Desktop Icon (WIN 17)
5. Minimize and Redisplay a Window (WIN 20)
6. Maximize and Restore a Window (WIN 22)
7. Close a Window (WIN 23, WIN 32)
8. Open a Window Using the Start Menu (WIN 24)
9. Move a Window by Dragging (WIN 26)
10. Expand an Area (WIN 27)
11. Scroll Using Scroll Arrows (WIN 28)
12. Size a Window by Dragging (WIN 30)
13. Collapse an Area (WIN 30)
14. Resize a Window (WIN 31)
15. Delete a Desktop Icon by Right-Dragging (WIN 32)
16. Start an Application Using the Start Menu (WIN 35)
17. Start Windows Explorer and Maximize Its Window (WIN 37)
18. Connect a USB Flash Drive to a USB Port (WIN 41)
19. Create a Folder on a Removable Drive (WIN 43)
20. Download a Hierarchy of Folders to the Freshman folder (WIN 44)
21. Expand a Drive (WIN 46)
22. Expand a Folder (WIN 47)
23. Display the Contents of a Folder (WIN 48, WIN 57)
24. Start Word (WIN 49)
25. Type Text in a Word Document (WIN 50)
26. Save a Word Document in a New Folder (WIN 51)
27. Verify the Contents of a Folder (WIN 54)
28. Copy a File in Windows Explorer by Right-Dragging (WIN 55)
29. Display the Contents of a Folder (WIN 57)
30. Rename a File (WIN 58)
31. Delete a File by Right-Clicking (WIN 59)
32. Close Expanded Folders (WIN 60)
33. Close all Expanded Folders (WIN 61)
34. Quit Windows Explorer (WIN 61)
35. Search for a File by Name (WIN 62)
36. Search for a File Using a Word or Phrase in the File (WIN 65)
37. Start Help and Support (WIN 67)
38. Browse for Help Topics in the Table of Contents (WIN 68)
39. Search for Help Topics Using the Index (WIN 71)
40. Close the Help and Support Center (WIN 72)
41. Log Off the Computer (WIN 73)
42. Turn Off the Computer (WIN 74)

Career Corner

Help Desk Specialist

A Help Desk specialist position is an entryway into the information technology (IT) field. A Help Desk specialist deals with problems in hardware, software, or communications systems. Job requirements may include the following: solve procedural and software questions both in person and over the telephone, develop and maintain Help Desk operations manuals, and assist in training new Help Desk personnel.

Usually, a Help Desk specialist must be knowledgeable about the major programs in use. Entry-level positions primarily involve answering calls from people with questions. Other positions provide additional assistance and assume further responsibilities, often demanding greater knowledge and problem-solving skills that can lead to more advanced IT positions. This job is ideal for people who must work irregular hours, because many companies need support people to work evenings, weekends, or part-time.

Educational requirements are less stringent than they are for other jobs in the computer field. In some cases, a high school diploma is sufficient. Advancement requires a minimum of a two-year degree, while management generally requires a bachelor's degree in IT or a related field. Certification is another way Help Desk specialists can increase their attractiveness in the marketplace. Entry-level salaries range from $27,500 to $56,500 per year. Managers range from $49,000 to $72,500. For more information, visit scsite.com/off2003sch/careers and then click Help Desk Specialist.

Learn It Online

Instructions: To complete the Learn It Online exercises, start your browser, click the Address bar, and then enter the Web address `scsite.com/off2003sch/learn`. When the Windows XP Learn It Online page is displayed, follow the instructions in the exercises below. Each exercise has instructions for printing your results, either for your own records or for submission to your instructor.

1 Project Reinforcement TF, MC, and SA

Below Project 1, click the Project Reinforcement link. Print the quiz by clicking Print on the File menu for each page. Answer each question.

2 Flash Cards

Below Project 1, click the Flash Cards link and read the instructions. Type 20 (or a number specified by your instructor) in the Number of playing cards text box, type your name in the Enter your Name text box, and then click the Flip Card button. When the flash card is displayed, read the question and then click the ANSWER box arrow to select an answer. Flip through Flash Cards. If your score is 15 (75%) correct or greater, click Print on the File menu to print your results. If your score is less than 15 (75%) correct, then redo this exercise by clicking the Replay button.

3 Practice Test

Below Project 1, click the Practice Test link. Answer each question, enter your first and last name at the bottom of the page, and then click the Grade Test button. When the graded practice test is displayed on your screen, click Print on the File menu to print a hard copy. Continue to take practice tests until you score 80% or better.

4 Who Wants To Be a Computer Genius?

Below Project 1, click the Computer Genius link. Read the instructions, enter your first and last name at the bottom of the page, and then click the PLAY button. When your score is displayed, click the PRINT RESULTS link to print a hard copy.

5 Wheel of Terms

Below Project 1, click the Wheel of Terms link. Read the instructions, and then enter your first and last name and your school name. Click the PLAY button. When your score is displayed, right-click the score and then click Print on the shortcut menu to print a hard copy.

6 Crossword Puzzle Challenge

Below Project 1, click the Crossword Puzzle Challenge link. Read the instructions, and then enter your first and last name. Click the SUBMIT button. Work the crossword puzzle. When you are finished, click the Submit button. When the crossword puzzle is redisplayed, click the Print Puzzle button to print a hard copy.

7 Tips and Tricks

Below Project 1, click the Tips and Tricks link. Click a topic that pertains to Project 1. Right-click the information and then click Print on the shortcut menu. Construct a brief example of what the information relates to in Windows XP to confirm you understand how to use the tip or trick.

8 Newsgroups

Below Project 1, click the Newsgroups link. Click a topic that pertains to Project 1. Print three comments.

9 Expanding Your Horizons

Below Project 1, click the Expanding Your Horizons link. Click a topic that pertains to Project 1. Print the information. Construct a brief example of what the information relates to in Windows XP to confirm you understand the contents of the article.

10 Search Sleuth

Below Project 1, click the Search Sleuth link. To search for a term that pertains to this project, select a term below the Project 1 title and then use the Google search engine at google.com (or any major search engine) to display and print two Web pages that present information on the term.

11 Windows XP Online Training

Below Project 1, click the Windows/Office Online Training link. When your browser displays the Microsoft Office Online Web page, click the Windows XP link. Click one of the Windows XP courses that covers one or more of the objectives listed at the beginning of the project on page WIN 4. Print the first page of the course before stepping through it.

12 Office Marketplace

Below Project 1, click the Office Marketplace link. When your browser displays the Microsoft Office Online Web page, click the Office Marketplace link. Click a topic that relates to one of the Office 2003 applications. Print the first page.

13 You're Hired!

Below Project 1, click the You're Hired! link to embark on the path to a career in computers. Directions about how to play the game will be displayed. When you are ready to play, click the begin the game button. If required, submit your score to your instructor.

1 Taking the Windows XP Tour

Instructions: Use a computer to perform the following tasks.

Part 1: Starting the Windows XP Tour

1. If necessary, launch Microsoft Windows XP and log on to the computer.
2. Click the Start button and then click Help and Support on the Start menu.
3. Click the Maximize button on the Help and Support Center title bar.
4. Click What's new in Windows XP in the navigation pane.
5. Click Taking a tour or tutorial in the navigation pane. The Taking a tour or tutorial page appears in the topic pane.
6. Click Take the Windows XP tour in the topic pane. The Windows XP Tour dialog box appears.
7. If your computer does not have speakers or earphones, follow the steps in Part 3. If your computer has speakers or earphones, follow the steps in Part 2.

Part 2: Taking the Windows XP Tour with Sound and Animation

1. Verify the Play the animated tour that features text, animation, music, and voice narration button is selected in the Windows XP Tour dialog box and then click the Next button.
2. Listen to the voice narration of the introduction to the Windows XP tour.
3. Click the gray Windows XP Basics button and answer the following questions.
   a. What is the narrow band at the bottom of the desktop called? ______________________
   b. What identifies a shortcut icon? ______________________
   c. What icons appear on the desktop the first time you launch Windows? ______________________
   d. What is contained in the notification area? ______________________
   e. How does Windows keep the taskbar tidy? ______________________
   f. What does a right-facing arrow on a Start menu command signify? ______________________
   ____
   g. In which folders are text, image, and music files placed? ______________________
   ____
   h. What does the Restore Down button do? ______________________
   i. What appears when a program needs some information from you before it can complete a command?
   ____
   j. What do you use to set up user accounts? ______________________
   k. Where do you go when you want to interrupt your Windows session and let someone else use the computer? ______________________
4. Click the Skip Intro button in the lower corner of the desktop to skip the introduction to the Windows XP tour.
5. Click the yellow Best for Business button and listen to the narration.
6. Click the red Safe and Easy Personal Computing button and listen to the narration.
7. Click the green Unlock the World of Digital Media button and listen to the narration.
8. Click the blue The Connected Home and Office button and listen to the narration.
9. Click the red Exit Tour button on the desktop to exit the Windows XP tour.
10. Click the Close button in the Help and Support center window.

Part 3: Taking the Windows XP Tour without Sound or Animation

1. Click the Play the non-animated tour that features text and images only button in the Windows XP Tour dialog box and then click the Next button.

2. Click the Start Here button to read about the basics of the Windows XP operating system.
3. Scroll the Windows XP Basics window and read the paragraph below the Windows Desktop heading. Click the Next button to display the next topic.
4. Scroll the Windows XP Basics window and read the paragraph below the Icons heading. Answer the following questions.
   a. What icon displays on the desktop the first time you launch Windows? ______________________
   b. Does deleting a shortcut icon affect the actual program or file? ______________________
5. Click the Next button to display the next topic. Scroll the Windows XP Basics window and read the paragraphs below the Taskbar heading. Answer the following question.
   a. Where is the notification area located? ______________________
6. Click the Next button to display the next topic. Scroll the Windows XP Basics window and read the paragraph below the Start Menu heading. Answer the following question.
   a. What does a right-facing arrow mean? ______________________
7. Click the Next button to display the next topic. Scroll the Windows XP Basics window and read the paragraph below the Files and Folder heading. Answer the following question.
   a. In which folders are text, image, and music files placed?

      ____
8. Click the Next button to display the next topic. Scroll the Windows XP Basics window and read the paragraphs below the Windows heading. Answer the following question.
   a. What appears if a program needs some information from you before it can complete a command?

      ____
9. Click the Next button to display the next topic. Scroll the Windows XP Basics window and read the paragraphs below the Control Panel heading. Answer the following questions.
   a. What Windows feature do you use to customize computer settings? ______________________
   b. Where is this feature located? ______________________
10. Click the Next button to display the next topic. Scroll the Windows XP Basics window and read the paragraphs below the Ending Your Session heading. Answer the following question.
    a. What do you do when you want to interrupt your Windows session and let someone else use the computer? ______________________
11. Click the Next button repeatedly to display the topics in the remaining four sections of the Windows XP tour.
12. Click the Close button in the window to end the tour.
13. Click the Close button in the Help and Support Center window.

2 Windows Explorer

Instructions: Use a computer to perform the following tasks.

1. Launch Microsoft Windows XP and connect to the Internet.
2. Right-click the Start button on the Windows taskbar, click Explore on the shortcut menu, and then maximize the Start Menu window.
3. If necessary, scroll to the left in the Folders pane so the Start Menu and Programs icons are visible.
4. Click the Programs icon in the Start Menu folder.
5. Double-click the Internet Explorer Shortcut icon in the Contents pane to start the Internet Explorer application. What is the URL of the Web page that appears in the Address bar in the Microsoft Internet Explorer window? ______________________

(continued)

Windows Explorer *(continued)*

6. Click the URL in the Address bar in the Internet Explorer window to select it. Type `scsite.com` and then press the ENTER key.
7. Scroll the Web page to display the Browse by Subject area containing the subject categories. Clicking a subject category displays the book titles in that category.
8. Click Operating Systems in the Browse by Subject area.
9. Click the Microsoft Windows XP Comprehensive Concepts and Techniques link.
10. Right-click the Microsoft Windows XP textbook cover image on the Web page, click Save Picture As on the shortcut menu, type `Windows XP Cover` in the File name box, and then click the Save button in the Save Picture dialog box to save the image in the My Pictures folder.
11. Click the Close button in the Microsoft Internet Explorer window.
12. If necessary, scroll to the top of the Folders pane to make the drive C icon visible.
13. Click the minus sign in the box to the left of the drive C icon. The 3½ Floppy (A:) and My Documents icons should be visible in the Folders pane.
14. Click the plus sign in the box to the left of the My Documents icon.
15. Click the My Pictures folder name in the Folders pane.
16. Right-click the Windows XP Cover icon and then click Properties on the shortcut menu.
    a. What type of file is the Windows XP Cover file? ____________________
    b. When was the file last modified? ______________________________
    c. With what application does this file open? ______________________
17. Click the Cancel button in the Windows XP Cover Properties dialog box.
18. Connect a USB flash drive to a USB port on your computer.
19. Right-drag the Windows XP Cover icon to the USB flash drive icon in the Folders pane. Click Move Here on the shortcut menu. Click the USB flash drive icon in the Folders pane.
    a. Is the Windows XP Cover file stored on Usb flash drive? ____________________
20. Click the Close button in the 3½ Floppy (A:) window.

3 Using the Help and Support Center

Instructions: Use Windows Help and Support to perform the following tasks.

Part 1: Using the Question Mark Button

1. If necessary, launch Microsoft Windows XP and then log on to the computer.
2. Right-click an open area of the desktop to display a shortcut menu.
3. Click Properties on the shortcut menu to display the Display Properties dialog box.
4. Click the Desktop tab in the Display Properties dialog box.
5. Click the Help button on the title bar. The mouse pointer changes to a block arrow with a question mark.
6. Click the list in the Desktop sheet. A pop-up window appears explaining the list. Read the information in the pop-up window and then summarize the function of the list.

   ____

7. Click an open area of the Desktop sheet to remove the pop-up window.
8. Click the Help button on the title bar and then click the Customize Desktop button. A pop-up window appears explaining what happens when you click this button. Read the information in the pop-up window and then summarize the function of the button.

   ____

9. Click an open area in the Desktop sheet to remove the pop-up window.

10. Click the Help button on the title bar and then click the monitor icon in the Desktop sheet. A pop-up window appears explaining the function of the monitor. Read the information in the pop-up window and then summarize the function of the monitor.

    ____

11. Click an open area in the Desktop sheet to remove the pop-up window.
12. Click the Help button on the title bar and then click the Cancel button. A pop-up window appears explaining what happens when you click the button. Read the information in the pop-up window and then summarize the function of the Cancel button.

    ____

13. Click an open area in the Desktop sheet to remove the pop-up window.
14. Click the Cancel button in the Display Properties dialog box.

Part 2: ***Finding What's New in Windows XP***

1. Click the Start button and then click Help and Support on the Start menu.
2. If necessary, click the Maximize button on the Help and Support Center title bar.
3. Click What's new in Windows XP in the navigation pane.
4. Click What's new topics in the navigation pane. Ten topics appear in the topic pane.
5. Click What's new on your desktop in the topic pane.
6. Click Start menu (or the plus sign in the small box preceding Start menu) to expand the entry. Read the information about the Start menu.
7. Click the Using the Start menu link.
8. Click the Print button on the Help and Support toolbar to print the topic. Click the Print button in the Print dialog box.
9. If necessary, scroll the topic pane to display the Related Topics link. Click the Related Topics link to display a pop-up window containing three related topics. List the three topics.

    ____

    ____

10. Click Display a program at the top of the Start menu in the pop-up window.
11. Click the Print button on the Help and Support toolbar to print the topic. Click the Print button in the Print dialog box.

Part 3: ***Viewing Windows XP Articles***

1. Click Windows XP articles: Walk through ways to use your PC in the What's new in Windows XP area in the navigation pane. A list of overviews, articles, and tutorials appears in the topic pane.
2. Click Walkthrough: Making music in the topic pane. Read the Making music article in the topic pane. List four ways in which you can use Windows XP musically.

    ____

    ____

3. Click Play music in the Making Music area. Scroll to display the Display details about a CD area. List the three steps to display details about a CD.

    ____

    ____

4. Scroll to the top of the window to display the Making Music area.

(continued)

Using the Help and Support Center *(continued)*

5. Click Create CDs in the Making Music area. Scroll to display the steps to burn your own CD. List the six steps to burn a CD.

   ____

   ____

   ____

   ____

   ____

   ____
6. Read other articles of interest to you in the Making Music area.
7. Click the Close button in the Help and Support Center window.

4 Downloading the Word 2003 Project 1-3 Data Files

Instructions: Use the SCSITE.COM Shelly Cashman Series Student Resources Web site to download the Word 2003 Project 1-3 Data Files into the Word folder.

Part 1:* *Plug the USB Flash Drive into the USB Port

1. If necessary, launch Microsoft Windows XP and log on to the computer.
2. Plug the USB flash drive into the USB port on the computer. The removable disk window should display on the desktop and should contain the Freshman folder.
3. If the Freshman folder does not display in the removable disk window, follow the steps in Project One to create the hierarchy of folders shown in Figure 1-47 on page WIN 39.

Part 2:* *Download the Word 2003 Project 1-3 Data Files into the Word Folder

1. Start Internet Explorer by clicking the Start button on the taskbar and then clicking Internet on the Start menu.
2. Click the Address box on the Address bar, type `scsite.com` in the Address box, and then click the Go button.
3. When the SCSITE.COM Shelly Cashman Series Student Web page is displayed, scroll down to view the Browse by Subject area, and then click the Office Suites link.
4. When the expanded Office Suites link appears, click the link containing the name of your textbook (for example, Microsoft Office 2003: Introductory Concepts and Techniques.
5. Scroll down to display the Data Files for Students (Windows) area and then click the Word 2003 Project 1-3 Data Files link.
6. When the File Download - Security Warning dialog box is displayed, click the Run button.
7. When the Internet Explorer - Security Warning dialog box is displayed, click the Run button.
8. When the WinZip Self-Extractor dialog box displays, click the Browse button.
9. Click the plus sign to the left of the removable drive, click the plus sign to the left of the Freshman folder, click the plus sign to the left of the 1st Semester folder, click the plus sign to the left of the Computer Class folder, and then click the Word folder.
10. Click the OK button in the Browse for Folder dialog box.
11. Click the Unzip button in the WinZip Self-Extractor dialog box.
12. When a smaller WinZip Self-Extractor dialog box appears, click the OK button.
13. Click the Close button in the WinZip Self-Extractor dialog box.
14. Click the Close button in the SCSITE.COM Shelly Cashman Series Student Resources window.
15. Verify the Word 2003 Student Data Files folder is contained in the Word folder.
16. Close the Word window.
17. Remove the USB flash drive from the USB port.

INTRODUCTION TO THE

World Wide Web

Browsing and Searching the World Wide Web

PROJECT 1

CASE PERSPECTIVE

As an art history buff and president of your high school's Art Club, you have found that you can enhance your knowledge of art if you learn more about using the Internet. In fact, your art teacher has recommended you take a short course to help you understand how to search for articles and pictures on the Internet.

You browse through your local library's course schedule and find an Introduction to the Internet class offered. The course description emphasizes that the course is for anyone who has little or no experience using the Internet. The topics listed in the course description include connecting to the Internet using Microsoft Internet Explorer, searching the Internet for information, and saving information you find on a Web page. You decide this is the perfect course for you to learn about the Internet.

After completing the course, you decide to use your knowledge of Internet Explorer to earn money by performing Internet research for teachers and local businesses. Instead of the usual resume/cover letter approach to obtaining a job, you decide to take out an advertisement in the local newspaper that advertises your Internet search skills.

Among the responses you receive from the advertisement is one from the manager of the Livingston Gallery. She hires you to identify the origin and authenticity of a piece of Asian art, titled *Three Leaves*, that the gallery wants to purchase. You agree to search for information about the Asian art and supply the gallery with pictures associated with the art.

As you read through this project, you will learn how to use Internet Explorer to connect to the Internet, search the Web, and save and organize information you find on Web pages.

PROJECT

Browsing and Searching the World Wide Web

Objectives

You will have mastered the material in this project when you can:

- Define the Internet and the World Wide Web
- Explain a link and Uniform Resource Locator
- Describe key Internet Explorer features and the Internet Explorer window
- Enter a Uniform Resource Locator (URL)
- Browse the World Wide Web using the Favorites list or URLs
- Display Web pages using the Back, Forward, and Home buttons
- Add and remove a Web page from the Favorites list
- Save a picture from a Web page or an entire Web page
- Print a Web page
- Describe the nine general categories of Web sites
- Describe the three basic types of search tools
- Search the Web using either a directory or keywords
- Use the Keyword system and the Address bar to search the Web
- Use Internet Explorer Help

Introduction

The Internet is the most popular and fastest growing area in computing today. Using the Internet, you can do research, get a loan, shop for services and merchandise, hunt for a job, buy and sell stocks, display weather maps, obtain medical advice, watch movies, listen to high-quality music, and converse with people worldwide.

Once considered mysterious, the Internet is now accessible to the general public because personal computers with user-friendly tools have reduced its complexity. The Internet, with its millions of connected computers, continues to grow with thousands of new users coming online everyday. Schools, businesses, newspapers, television stations, and government services all can be found on the Internet. Service providers are popping up all around the country providing inexpensive access to the Internet from home; but, just exactly what is the Internet?

The Internet

The **Internet** is a worldwide collection of networks (Figure 1-1), each of which is composed of a collection of smaller networks. A **network** is composed of several computers connected together to share resources and data. For example, at a high school, the network in the student lab can connect to the teachers' computer network, which is connected to the administration network, and they all can connect to the Internet.

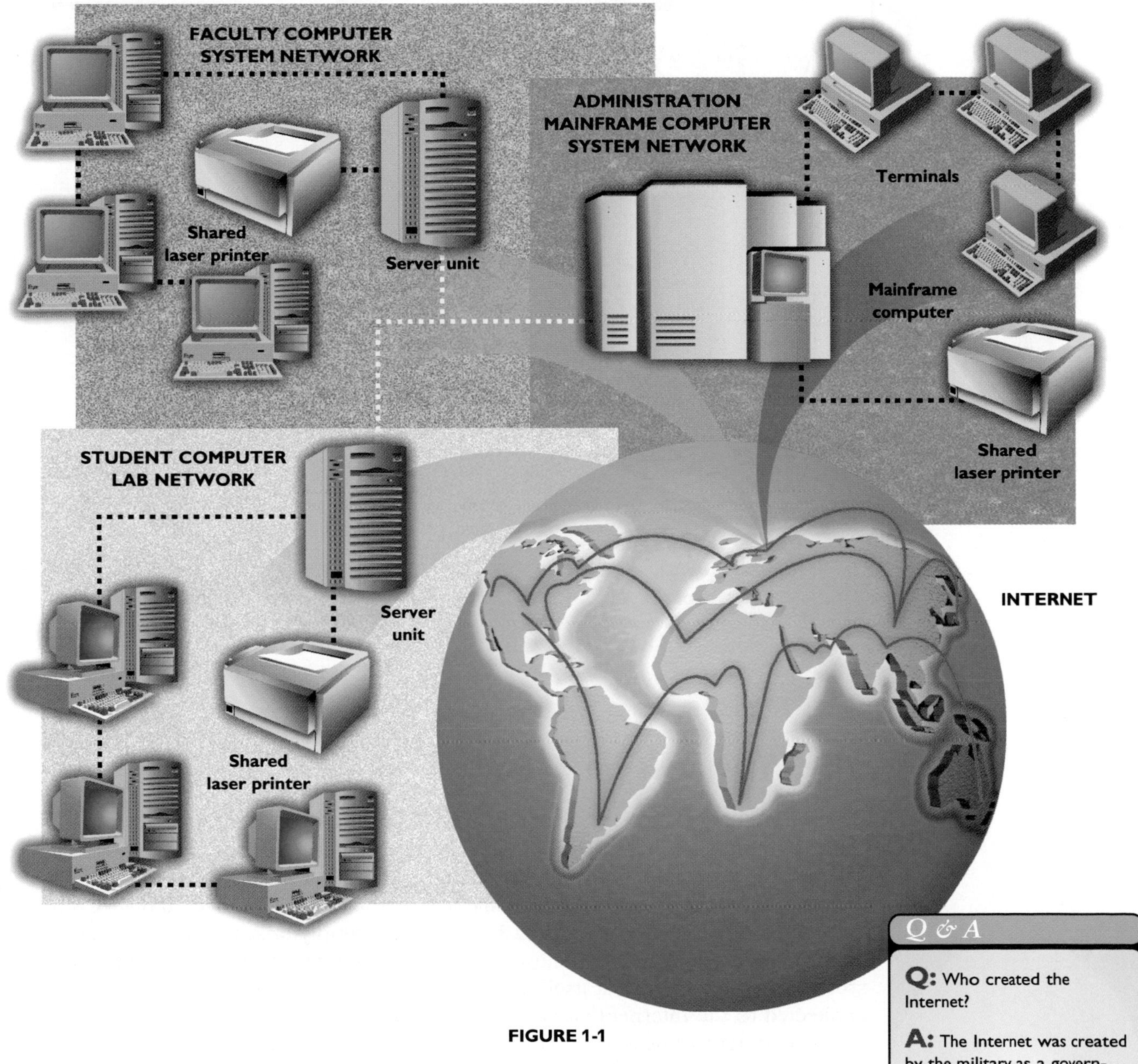

FIGURE 1-1

Networks are connected with high-, medium-, and low-speed data lines that allow data to move from one computer to another (Figure 1-2). The Internet has high-speed data lines that connect major computers located around the world, which form the **Internet backbone**. Other, less powerful computers, such as those used by local ISPs (Internet service providers) often attach to the **Internet backbone** using medium-speed data lines. Finally, the connection between your computer at home and your local ISP, often called **the last mile**, employs low-speed data lines such as telephone lines. In many cases today, cable is replacing telephone lines over the last mile, which significantly improves access to information on the Internet.

Q & A

Q: Who created the Internet?

A: The Internet was created by the military as a government experiment. The military wanted a communication technique that would connect different computers running different operating systems. From this experiment, a communication technique originated called Transmission Control Protocol/Internet Protocol, or TCP/IP.

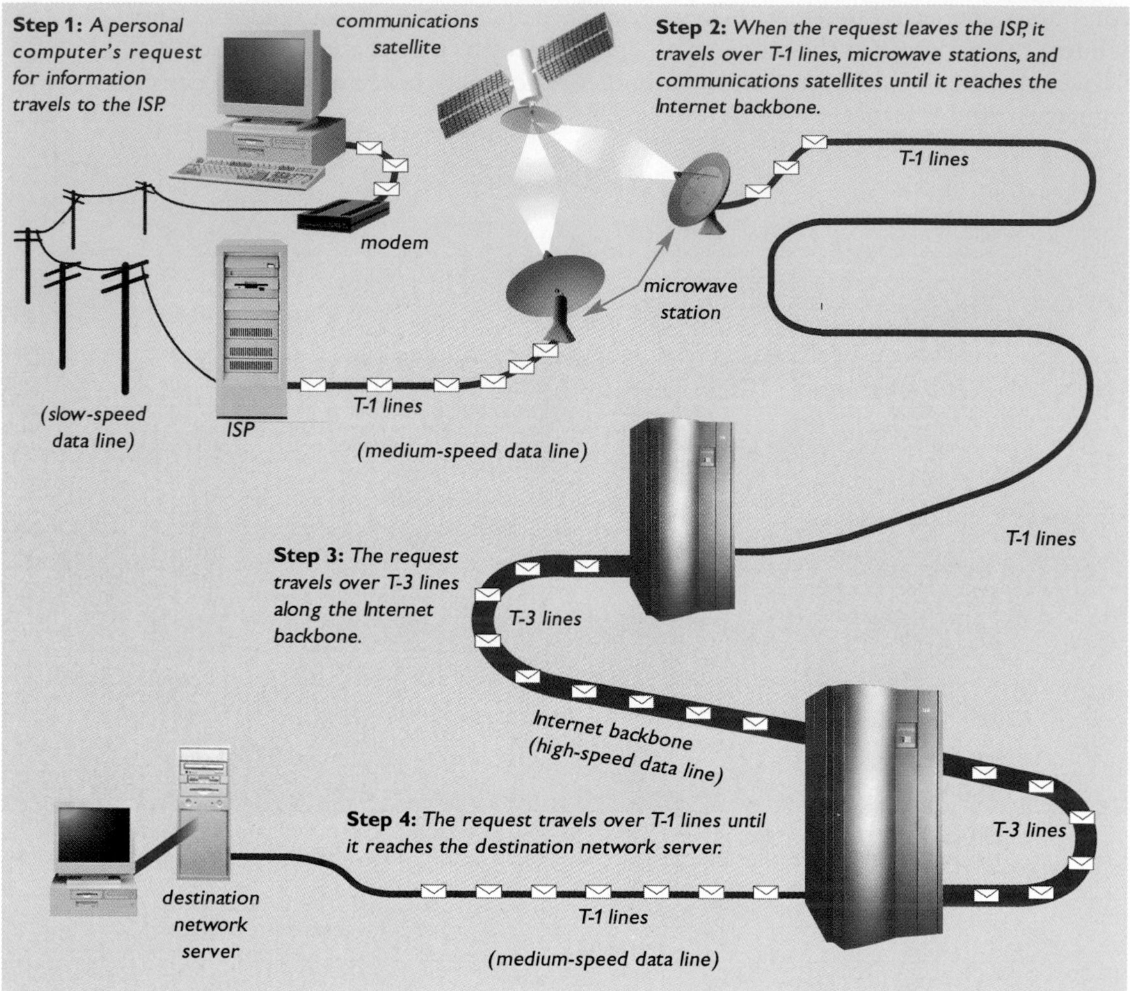
Step 1: A personal computer's request for information travels to the ISP.
communications satellite
Step 2: When the request leaves the ISP, it travels over T-1 lines, microwave stations, and communications satellites until it reaches the Internet backbone.
T-1 lines
modem
microwave station
(slow-speed data line)
ISP
T-1 lines
(medium-speed data line)
T-1 lines
Step 3: The request travels over T-3 lines along the Internet backbone.
T-3 lines
Internet backbone (high-speed data line)
Step 4: The request travels over T-1 lines until it reaches the destination network server.
T-3 lines
destination network server
T-1 lines
(medium-speed data line)

FIGURE 1-2

The World Wide Web

Modern computers have the capability of delivering information in a variety of ways, such as graphics, sound, video clips, animation, and, of course, regular text. On the Internet, this multimedia capability is available in a form called **hypermedia**, which is any variety of computer media, including text, graphics, video, sound, and virtual reality.

You access hypermedia using a **hyperlink**, or simply **link**, which is a special software pointer that points to the location of the computer on which the hypermedia is stored and the hypermedia itself. A link can point to hypermedia on any computer connected to the Internet that is running the proper software. Thus, clicking a link on a computer in Los Angeles could display text and graphics located in New York.

The collection of links throughout the Internet creates an interconnected network called the **World Wide Web**, which also is referred to as the **Web**, or **WWW**. Each computer within the Web containing hypermedia that you can reference with a link is called a **Web site**. Millions of Web sites around the world are accessible through the Internet.

Graphics, text, and other hypermedia available at a Web site are stored in a file called a **Web page**. Therefore, when you click a link to display a picture, read text, view a video, or listen to music, you actually are viewing a Web page.

Figure 1-3 illustrates a Web page at the Disney Online Web site. This Web page contains numerous links. For example, the seven graphics on the Web page are links.

Clicking a link, such as Disney Destinations, could display a Web page from a travel agency located on the other side of the world.

> *Q & A*
>
> **Q:** Can an organization have more than one Web site?
>
> **A:** Yes. Separate departments may have their own Web computers, allowing faster response to requests for Web pages, and local control over the Web pages stored at that Web site.

FIGURE 1-3

Uniform Resource Locator (URL)

Each Web page has a unique address, called a **Uniform Resource Locator** (**URL**), which distinguishes it from all other pages on the Internet. The URL in Figure 1-3 is http://disney.go.com/home/today/index.html.

A URL often is composed of four parts (Figure 1-4). The first part is the protocol. A **protocol** is a set of rules. Most Web pages use the Hypertext Transfer Protocol. **Hypertext Transfer Protocol** (**HTTP**) describes the rules used to transmit Web pages electronically over the Internet. You enter the protocol in lowercase as http followed by a colon and two forward slashes (http://). If you do not begin a URL with a protocol, Internet Explorer will assume it is http, and automatically will append http:// to the front of the URL.

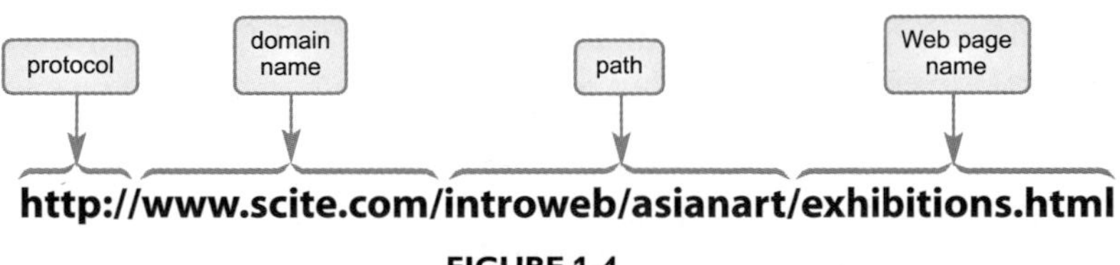

FIGURE 1-4

The second part of a URL is the domain name. The **domain name** is the Internet address of the computer on the Internet where the Web page is located. Each computer on the Internet has a unique address, called an **Internet Protocol address**, or **IP address**. The domain name identifies where to forward a request for the Web page referenced by the URL. The domain name in the URL in Figure 1-4 is www.scsite.com.

The last part of the domain name (com in Figure 1-4) indicates the type of organization that owns the Web site. For example, com indicates a commercial organization, usually a business or corporation. Educational institutions have edu at the end of their domain names. Government entities use gov at the end of their domain names. Table 1-1 shows some types of organizations and their extensions.

Table 1-1 Organizations and Their Domain Name Extensions

TYPES OF ORGANIZATIONS	ORIGINAL DOMAIN NAMES
Commercial organizations, businesses, and companies	.com
Educational institutions	.edu
Government agencies	.gov
Military organizations	.mil
Network providers	.net
Nonprofit organizations	.org
TYPES OF ORGANIZATIONS	NEWER DOMAIN NAMES
Accredited museums	.museum
Businesses of all sizes	.biz
Businesses, organizations, or individuals providing general information	.info
Individuals or families	.name
Certified professionals such as doctors, lawyers, and accountants	.pro
Aviation community members	.aero
Business cooperatives such as credit unions and rural electric co-ops	.coop

The optional third part of a URL is the file specification of the Web page. The **file specification** includes the file name and possibly a directory or folder name. This information is called the **path**. If no file specification of a Web page is specified in the URL, a default Web page appears. This means you can display a Web page even though you do not know its file specification. The fourth part of a URL is the **Web page name**. The Web page name identifies the currently displayed Web page.

You can find URLs that identify interesting Web sites in magazines or newspapers, on television, from friends, or even from just browsing the Web.

URLs of well-known companies and organizations usually contain the company's name and institution's name. For example, ibm.com is IBM Corporation, and umich.edu is the University of Michigan.

Home Pages

No main menus or any particular starting points exist in the World Wide Web. Although you can reference any page on the Web when you begin, most people start with specially designated Web pages called home pages. A **home page** is the introductory page for a Web site. All other Web pages for that site usually are accessible from the home page via links. In addition, the home page is the page that is displayed when you enter a domain name with no file specification, such as nbc.com or disneyland.com.

Because it is the starting point for most Web sites, designers try to make a good first impression and display attractive, eye-catching graphics, specially formatted text, and a variety of links to other pages at the Web site, as well as to other interesting and useful Web sites.

Q & A

Q: Can a Web site consist of numerous home pages?

A: Yes. For example, a computer used by faculty members or students for their hypertext documents could have many home pages: one for each person.

Q & A

Q: Can I select another Web page as my home page?

A: Yes. Display the Web page you want as your home page in the display area, click Tools on the menu bar, click Internet Options on the Tools menu, click the General tab, and then click the Use Current button in the Home page area.

Web Browsers

Just as graphical user interfaces (GUIs), such as Microsoft Windows, simplify working with a computer by using a point-and-click method, a Web browser makes using the World Wide Web easier by removing the complexity of having to remember the syntax, or rules, of commands used to reference Web pages at Web sites. A **Web browser**, or **browser**, takes the URL associated with a link or the URL entered by a user, locates the computer containing the associated Web page, and then displays a starting Web page. The initial home page that is displayed is one selected by the Web browser. Some of the more widely used Web browsers include Microsoft Internet Explorer, Firefox, Macintosh, Safari, and Opera.

Internet Explorer

Internet Explorer 6 is a Web browsing program that allows you to search for and view Web pages, save pages you find for use in the future, maintain a list of the pages you visit, send and receive e-mail messages, use newsgroups, edit Web pages, and listen to radio stations. The Internet Explorer 6 application program is included with most Microsoft Windows operating system software (Windows XP, Windows 2000, and Windows 98) and Microsoft Office software (Office 2003, Office XP, and Office 2000), or you can download it from the Internet. The projects in this book illustrate the use of the Internet Explorer 6 browser.

Starting Internet Explorer

If you are stepping through this project on a computer and you want your screen to match the figures in this book, then you should change your computer's resolution to 800 × 600. For more information on how to change the resolution on your computer, see your instructor. The steps on the next page show how to start Internet Explorer.

To Start Internet Explorer

1

• **Click the Start button on the Windows taskbar, point to All Programs on the Start menu, and then point to Internet Explorer on the All Programs submenu.**

Windows displays the Start menu and the All Programs submenu (Figure 1-5).

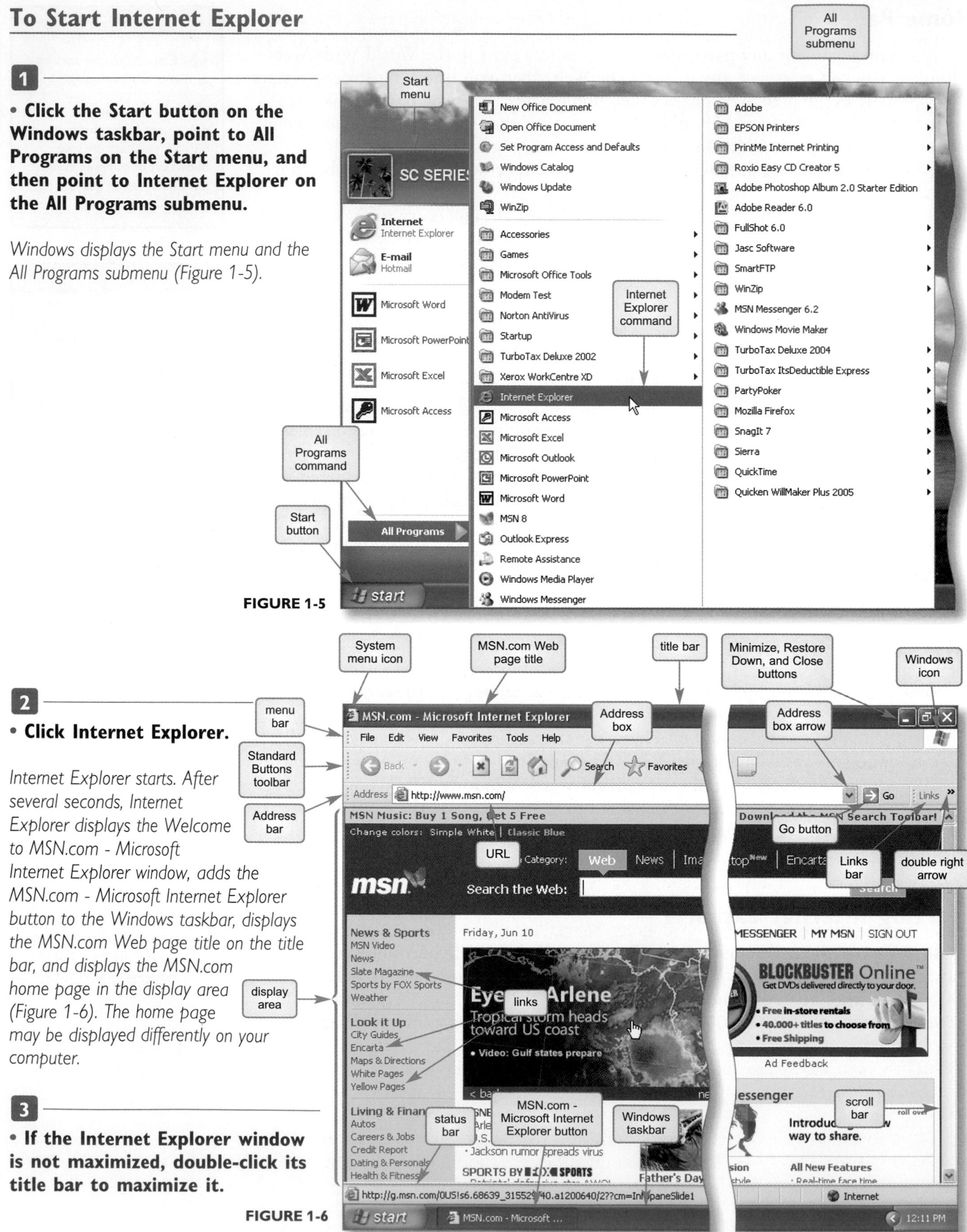

FIGURE 1-5

2

• **Click Internet Explorer.**

Internet Explorer starts. After several seconds, Internet Explorer displays the Welcome to MSN.com - Microsoft Internet Explorer window, adds the MSN.com - Microsoft Internet Explorer button to the Windows taskbar, displays the MSN.com Web page title on the title bar, and displays the MSN.com home page in the display area (Figure 1-6). The home page may be displayed differently on your computer.

3

• **If the Internet Explorer window is not maximized, double-click its title bar to maximize it.**

FIGURE 1-6

Normally, when Internet Explorer starts, the MSN.com home page is displayed. Because it is possible to change the page that initially is displayed through the Internet Options command on the Tools menu, the home page shown in Figure 1-6 may be different on your computer. For example, some schools and businesses have their own Web site home page display when starting Internet Explorer.

The Internet Explorer Window

The **Internet Explorer window** (Figure 1-6) consists of innovative features that make browsing the Internet easy. It contains a title bar, a menu bar, the Standard Buttons toolbar, an Address bar, a Links bar, a scroll bar, the status bar, and a display area where pages from the World Wide Web are displayed. The menu bar, Standard Buttons toolbar, Address bar, and Links bar appear at the top of the screen just below the title bar. The Address bar and Links bar appear on the same row below the Standard Buttons toolbar. The status bar appears at the bottom of the screen.

DISPLAY AREA Only a portion of most pages will be visible on the screen. You view the portion of the page displayed on the screen in the **display area** (Figure 1-6). To the right of the display area is a scroll bar, scroll arrows, and a scroll box, which you can use to move the text in the display area up and down and reveal other parts of the page.

Notice the links on the Internet Explorer home page shown in Figure 1-6. When you position the mouse pointer on one of these links, the mouse pointer changes to a pointing hand. This change in the shape of the mouse pointer identifies these elements as links. Clicking a link retrieves the Web page associated with the link and displays it in the display area.

TITLE BAR The title bar appears at the top of the Microsoft Internet Explorer window. As shown at the top of Figure 1-6, the **title bar** includes the System menu icon on the left, the title of the window, and the Minimize, Restore Down (or Maximize), and Close buttons on the right. Clicking the **System menu icon** on the title bar will display the System menu, which contains commands to carry out the actions associated with the Microsoft Internet Explorer window. Double-click the System menu icon or click the Close button to close the Microsoft Internet Explorer window and quit Internet Explorer.

Click the **Minimize button** to minimize the Microsoft Internet Explorer window. When you minimize the Microsoft Internet Explorer window, the window no longer appears on the desktop, and the Microsoft Internet Explorer taskbar button becomes inactive (a lighter color). The minimized window still is open but it does not appear on the desktop. After minimizing, clicking the taskbar button on the Windows taskbar displays the Microsoft Internet Explorer window in the previous position it occupied on the desktop and changes the button to an active state (a darker color).

Click the **Maximize button** to maximize the Microsoft Internet Explorer window so it expands to fill the entire desktop. When the window is maximized, the Restore Down button replaces the Maximize button on the title bar. Click the **Restore Down button** to return the Microsoft Internet Explorer window to the size and position it occupied before being maximized. The Restore Down button changes to the Maximize button when the Microsoft Internet Explorer window is in a restored state.

You also can double-click the title bar to restore and maximize the Microsoft Internet Explorer window. If the window is in a restored state, you can drag the title bar to move the window on the desktop.

MENU BAR The **menu bar**, which is located below the title bar, displays six menu names (Figure 1-6). Each **menu name** represents a menu of commands you can use

Q & A

Q: Can I change the home page in the Internet Explorer window?

A: Yes. You can change the home page by clicking Tools on the menu bar, clicking Internet Options on the Tools menu, and then clicking the Use Current, Use Default, or Use Blank button. You also can change the home page by dragging the Internet Explorer icon in the Address box to the Home button on the Standard Buttons toolbar. The Web page in the display area becomes the home page.

Q & A

Q: Can I hide the Standard Buttons toolbar, Address bar, and Links bar?

A: Yes. To hide the Standard Buttons toolbar, Address bar, or Links bar, right-click the toolbar you want to hide and then click the toolbar name on the shortcut menu. To display a hidden toolbar, right-click any toolbar and then click the toolbar name on the shortcut menu.

Q & A

Q: How can I increase the size of the display area shown in Figure 1-6?

A: You can increase the size of the display area by moving and resizing the Standard Buttons toolbar, Address bar, or Links bar, or by removing a toolbar.

Q & A

Q: How do I display a text label on a button on the Standard Buttons toolbar if no text label is displayed?

A: To display a text label, right-click the toolbar, click Customize on the shortcut menu, click the Text options box arrow, click Show text labels, and then click the Close button. You also can change the size of the icons on the toolbar buttons using the Icon options box arrow.

to perform actions, such as saving Web pages, copying and pasting, customizing toolbars, sending and receiving e-mail, setting Internet Explorer options, quitting Internet Explorer, and so on. To display a menu, click the menu name on the menu bar. To select a command on a menu, click the command name or press the **shortcut keys** shown to the right of some commands on the menu.

The **Windows icon** at the right end of the menu bar goes into motion (animates) when Internet Explorer transfers a Web page from a Web site to the Microsoft Internet Explorer window and stops moving when the transfer is complete. Another icon may be displayed in place of the Windows icon on your computer.

STANDARD BUTTONS TOOLBAR The **Standard Buttons toolbar** (Figure 1-6) contains buttons that allow you to perform often-used tasks more quickly than using the menu bar. For example, to print the Web page in the Microsoft Internet Explorer window, click the Print button on the Standard Buttons toolbar.

Each button on the Standard Buttons toolbar contains an icon. Three buttons contain text labels (Back, Search, and Favorites) describing the function of the button. Table 1-2 illustrates the buttons on the Standard Buttons toolbar. The table also briefly describes the functions of the buttons. Each of the buttons will be explained in detail as it is used. The buttons on the Standard Buttons toolbar may be different on your computer.

By right-clicking the Standard Buttons toolbar, you can customize its buttons. You can show or remove the text label on each button, or you can remove the entire toolbar by clicking the appropriate toolbar name on the shortcut menu.

Table 1-2 Standard Buttons Toolbar Buttons and Functions

BUTTON	FUNCTION
	Retrieves the previous page, (provided it was previously just viewed). To go more than one page back, click the Back button arrow, and then click a Web page title in the list.
	Retrieves the next page. To go more than one page forward, click the Forward button arrow and then click a Web page title in the list.
	Stops the transfer of a Web page.
	Requests the Web page in the display area to be retrieved from the Web site again.
	Requests the default home page to be displayed.
Search	Displays the Search Companion bar.
Favorites	Displays the Favorites bar.
Media	Displays the Media bar.
	Displays the History bar.
	Displays a menu containing commands to access e-mail messages and Internet newsgroups.
	Prints the Web page shown in the display area.
	Edits the Web page shown in the display area.
	Initiates discussions.

ADDRESS BAR The **Address bar** (Figure 1-6) contains a move handle, toolbar title (Address), Address box, and Go button. The **move handle** allows you to change the size of a toolbar. If a move handle does not appear, read the Q&A on this page to learn how to display the move handle. The **Address box** contains the Internet Explorer icon and holds the Uniform Resource Locator (URL) for the page currently shown in the display area. The URL updates automatically as you browse from page to page. If you know the URL of a Web page you want to visit, click the URL in the Address box to highlight the URL, type the new URL, and then click the Go button (or press the ENTER key) to display the corresponding page.

You can type an application name in the Address box and click the Go button to start the corresponding application, type a folder name and click the Go button to open a folder window, type a document name and click the Go button to start an application and display the document in the application window, and type a keyword or phrase (search inquiry) and click the Go button to display Web pages containing the keyword or phrase. In addition, you can click the **Address box arrow** at the right end of the Address box to display a list of previously displayed Web pages. Clicking a URL in the Address box list displays the corresponding Web page.

Q & A

Q: Move handles are not displayed at the left end of my menu bar and toolbars. How can I display the move handles?

A: In some cases, the move handles at the left end of the menu bar and toolbars (Standard Buttons, Address bar, and Links bar) do not appear because the Lock the Toolbars command has been selected. To display the move handles, right-click an open area on any toolbar and then click Lock the Toolbars on the shortcut menu.

LINKS BAR The **Links bar**, which appears to the right of the Address bar on the same row, allows you to click an icon to display a favorite Web site. The Address bar toolbar and Links bar are preset to display on the same row immediately below the Standard Buttons toolbar (Figure 1-6). Because both of these bars cannot fit entirely on a single row, only a portion of the Links bar appears.

The Links bar contains a move handle, toolbar title (Links), and a button identified by a double right arrow. Clicking this button displays a menu containing all the buttons on the Links bar. Clicking the button a second time removes the menu. Double-clicking the move handle or toolbar title displays the entire Links bar.

When you display the entire Links bar, only a portion of the Address bar toolbar appears. Each button on the Links bar contains an icon and text label. Table 1-3 illustrates the Links bar buttons and briefly describes the functions of the buttons. Additional buttons or different buttons may appear on the Links bar on your computer. Double-clicking the move handle or toolbar title a second time displays the entire Address bar toolbar and only a portion of the Links bar.

Q & A

Q: How can I move the insertion point to the Address box when the box is empty?

A: To move the insertion point to the Address box when the box is empty, or to highlight the URL in the Address box, press ALT+D.

Table 1-3 Links Bar Buttons and Functions

BUTTON	FUNCTION
Customize Links	Displays tips for customizing the buttons on the Links bar.
Free HotMail	Displays the Hotmail Web site to set up and access free e-mail accounts.
Microsoft	Displays the Microsoft home page.
Windows Media	Displays the WindowsMedia.com site that contains the Windows Media Guide.

Q & A

Q: Can I store links to Web pages on the Links bar?

A: Yes. The Links bar is a good place to store links to the Web pages you use frequently. You can add a Web page to the Links bar by dragging an icon from the Address bar or dragging a link from a Web page to the Links bar. Clicking the link on the Links bar displays the associated Web page.

Browsing the World Wide Web

The most common way to browse the World Wide Web is to obtain the URL of a Web page you want to visit and then enter it into the Address box on the Address bar. It is by visiting various Web sites that you can begin to understand the enormous appeal of the World Wide Web. The steps on the following pages show how to

> **Q & A**
>
> **Q:** Why is the domain name (scsite.com) of the publishing company in the URL you enter for the Asian Arts page?
>
> **A:** The Asian Arts site has been stored on the publishing company's server to guarantee that the content of the site is the same for all students. To view the real Asian Arts site, type `asianart.com` in the Address box.

contact a Web site provided by Web Art Publishing in Santa Fe, New Mexico, and visit the Web page titled Asian Arts, which contains information and pictures of artwork from various countries in Asia. The URL for the Asian Arts page is:

```
www.scsite.com/introweb/asianart.htm
```

You are not required to provide the leading http:// protocol when initially typing the URL in the Address box. Internet Explorer will insert http:// and assume the www automatically, if you do not supply it. The following steps show how to browse the Web by entering a URL.

To Browse the Web by Entering a URL

1

• **Click the Address box.**

Internet Explorer highlights the URL in the Address box and the mouse pointer changes to an I-beam (Figure 1-7).

FIGURE 1-7

2

• **Type** `scsite.com/introweb/asianart.htm` **in the Address box.**

The new URL appears in the Address box and the Search for text box, containing the new URL in quotes displays below the Address box (Figure 1-8).

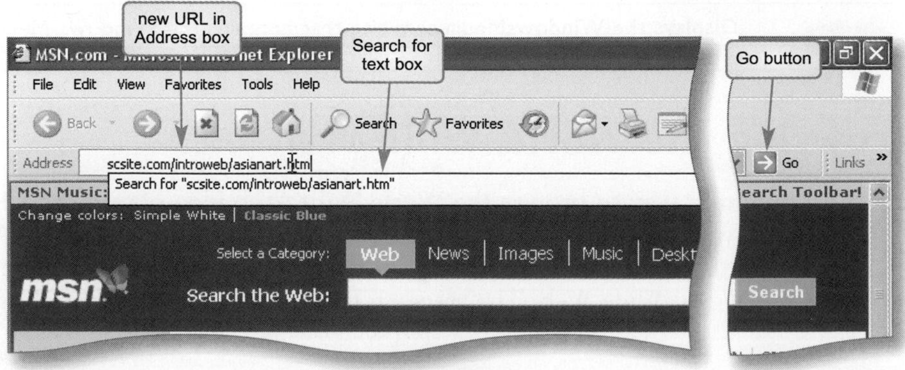

FIGURE 1-8

3

• **Click the Go button.**

The Windows icon on the menu bar goes into motion (animates) while the Asian Arts Web page is displayed and then stops moving when the Asian Arts Web page appears. The Asian Arts Web page title appears on the title bar and on the active button on the taskbar, and the URL of the Web page appears in the Address box (Figure 1-9).

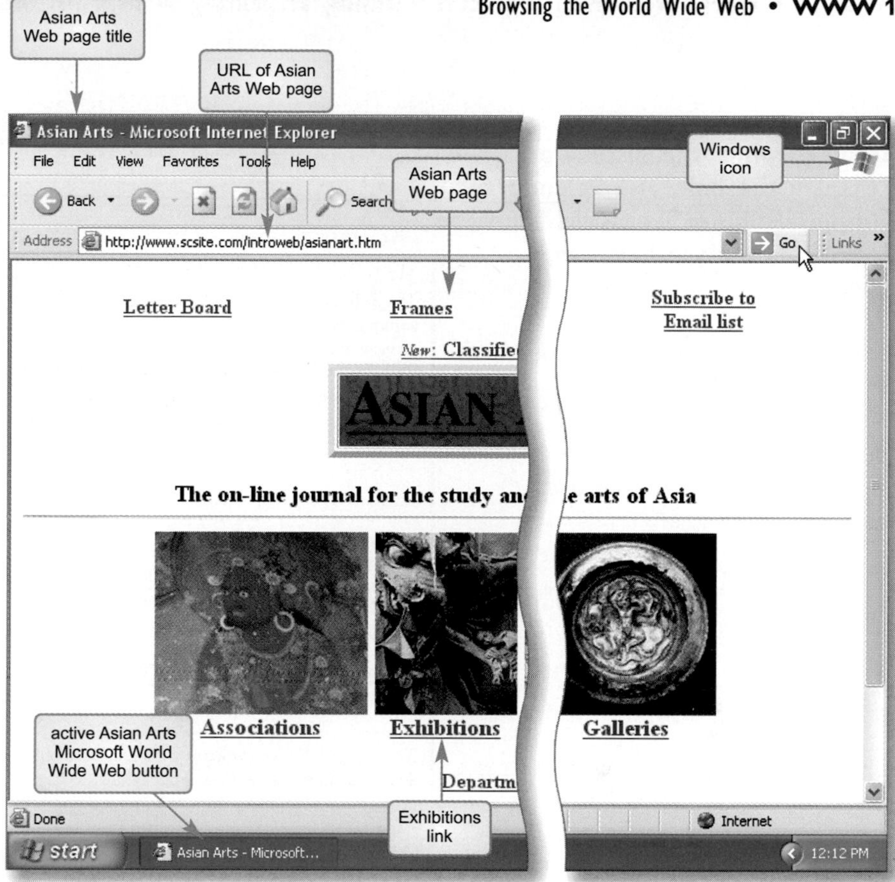

FIGURE 1-9

4

• **Click the Exhibitions link.**

After a brief interval, the Exhibitions page appears (Figure 1-10). The URL of the Web page appears in the Address box, and the Exhibitions Web page title appears on the title bar and on the taskbar button. A vertical scroll bar on the right side of the display area indicates the page is larger than the display area. You will have to scroll to view additional information and pictures on the page.

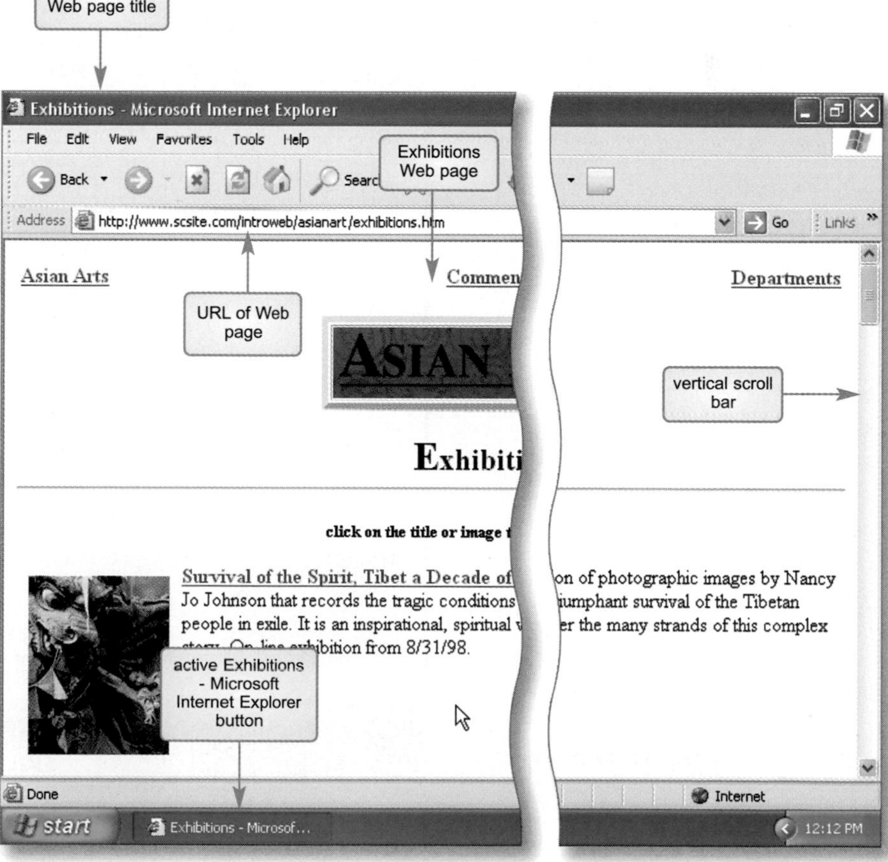

FIGURE 1-10

5

• Scroll through the display area to display the link, The Splendors of Imperial China: Treasures from the National Palace Museum, Taipei.

The display area scrolls and The Splendors of Imperial China: Treasures from the National Palace Museum, Taipei link appears (Figure 1-11). The picture at the right of the display area also is a link to the same page.

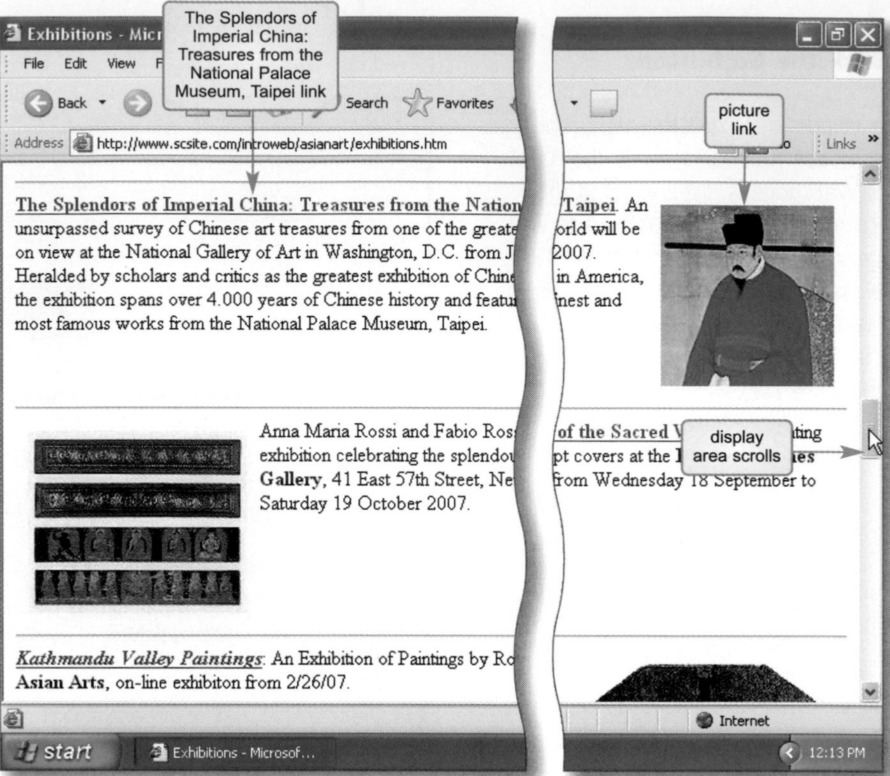

FIGURE 1-11

6

• Click The Splendors of Imperial China: Treasures from the National Palace Museum, Taipei link.

After a brief interval, The Splendors of Imperial China Web page appears (Figure 1-12). The URL of the Web page appears in the Address box, and the Web page title is displayed on the title bar and on the taskbar button. The Web page contains pictures and descriptions of the Chinese art located in the National Place Museum in Taipei, China.

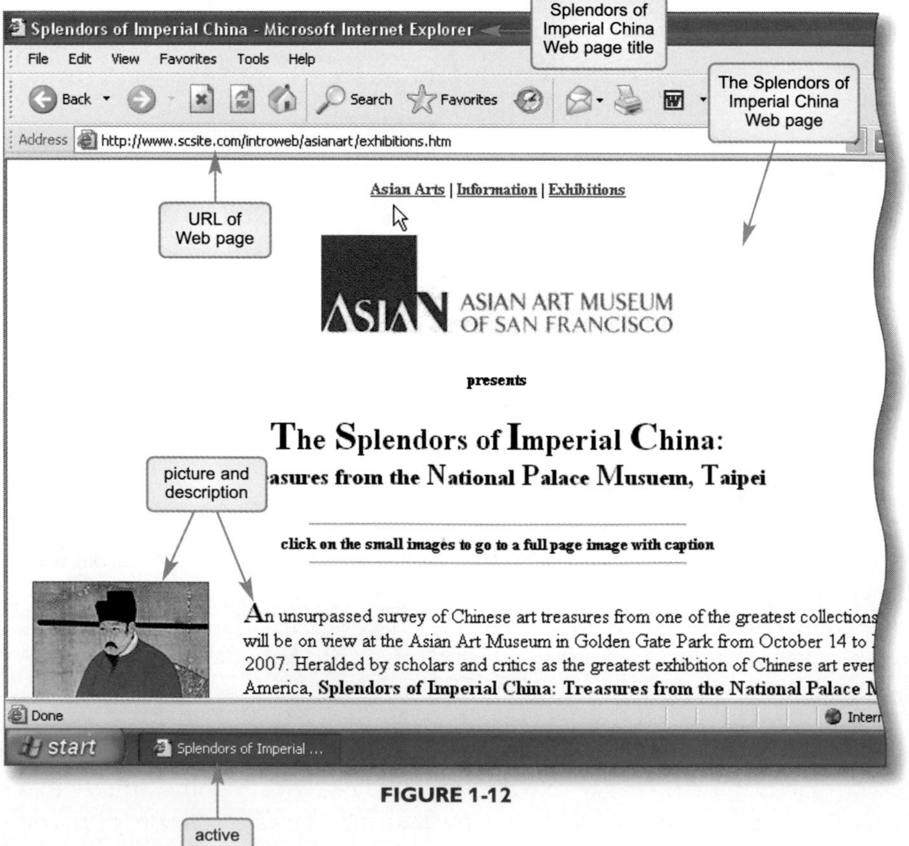

FIGURE 1-12

7

- **Scroll through the display area to view the three pictures numbered 8, 9, and 10.**

The display area scrolls to display the pictures of a stem cup, various leaves and flowers, and a globe vase (Figure 1-13). The title, Three leaves from Landscapes and Flowers, appears below the center picture.

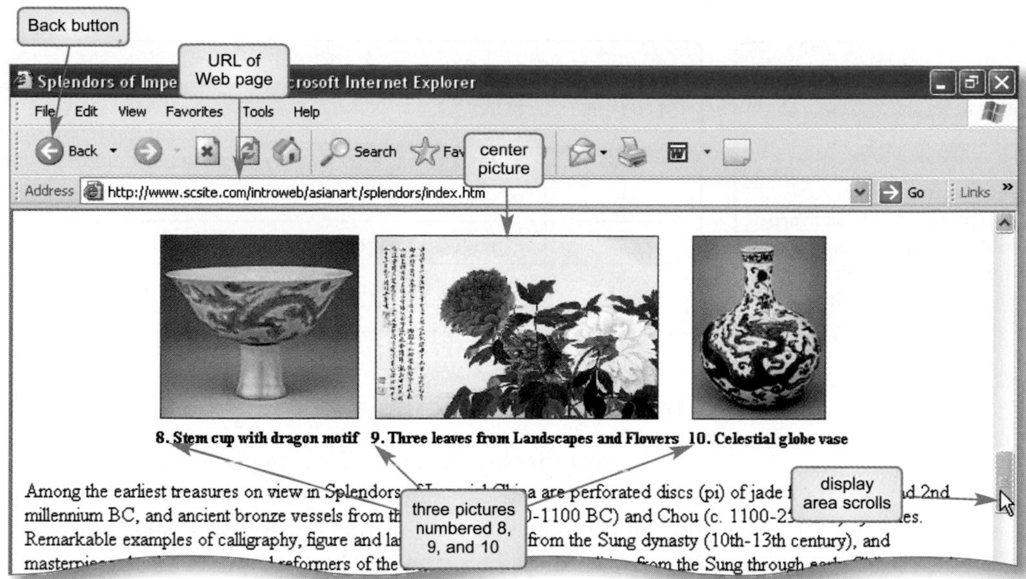

FIGURE 1-13

8

- **Click the center picture (numbered 9).**
- **Point to the larger version of the Three Leaves from Landscapes and Flowers picture.**

The Splendors of Imperial China - Image 9 Web page containing a larger version of the Three leaves from Landscapes and Flowers picture appears (Figure 1-14). Pointing to the picture displays the Image toolbar in the upper-left corner of the image.

FIGURE 1-14

The preceding steps illustrate how simple it is to browse the World Wide Web. Displaying a Web page associated with a link is as easy as clicking a text or picture link.

Pointing to an image on a Web page displays the Image toolbar in the upper-left corner of the image (Figure 1-14). The **Image toolbar** allows you to save, print, or e-mail images you find on the Web and display the contents of the My Pictures folder. The **My Pictures folder** is a central location for the storage of images you find on the Web. Each button on the Image toolbar contains an icon. Table 1-4 on the next page illustrates the buttons on the Image toolbar and briefly describes their function. The buttons on the Image toolbar may be different on your computer.

Q & A

Q: If I type the wrong URL and notice the error before clicking the Go button, how do I correct the error?

A: If you notice the error before clicking the Go button, use the BACKSPACE key to erase all the characters back to and including the one that is wrong. If the error is easier to retype than correct, click the URL and retype it.

Q & A

Q: Can I stop the transfer of an image?

A: Yes. You can click the Stop button on the Standard Buttons toolbar, click the Stop command on the View menu, press the ESC key on the keyboard, or press ALT+V and then press the P key.

Table 1-4 Image Toolbar

BUTTON	FUNCTION
[Save]	Saves an image to the My Pictures folder unless another location is specified.
[Print]	Prints an image.
[E-mail]	E-mails an image using the default e-mail program.
[My Pictures]	Displays the contents of the My Pictures folder.

Finding a Previously Displayed Web Page

As you display different Web pages, Internet Explorer keeps track of the pages you visit, so you can find those pages quickly in the future. Internet Explorer stores the Web pages you visit in the **Temporary Internet Files folder** on the hard disk. When you display a previously displayed Web page, the page is displayed quickly because Internet Explorer is able to retrieve the page from the Temporary Internet Files folder on the hard disk instead of from a Web site on the Internet.

Several methods exist to find a previously displayed Web page. One method is to use the Back button and Forward button on the Standard Buttons toolbar. When you start Internet Explorer, the Back and Forward buttons and their arrows appear dimmed and are unavailable. When you visit the first Web page after starting Internet Explorer, the Back button no longer is dimmed and is available for use. Pointing to the button changes the button to a three-dimensional button, indicating the button is active.

The following steps show how to use the Back and Forward buttons to find previously displayed Web pages.

Q & A

Q: How do I refresh a Web page?

A: You can refresh a Web page by clicking the Refresh button on the Standard Buttons toolbar. Refreshing is particularly useful with Web pages that dynamically change every few minutes, such as stock quotes, and the news.

To Use the Back and Forward Buttons to Find Recently Displayed Web Pages

1

- **Click the Back button on the Standard Buttons toolbar.**

A ScreenTip appears momentarily when you point to the Back button and then the Splendors of Imperial China Web page is displayed (Figure 1-15). The Back button is three-dimensional, the Forward button is active, and The Splendors of Imperial China Web page no longer is the last Web page visited in this session.

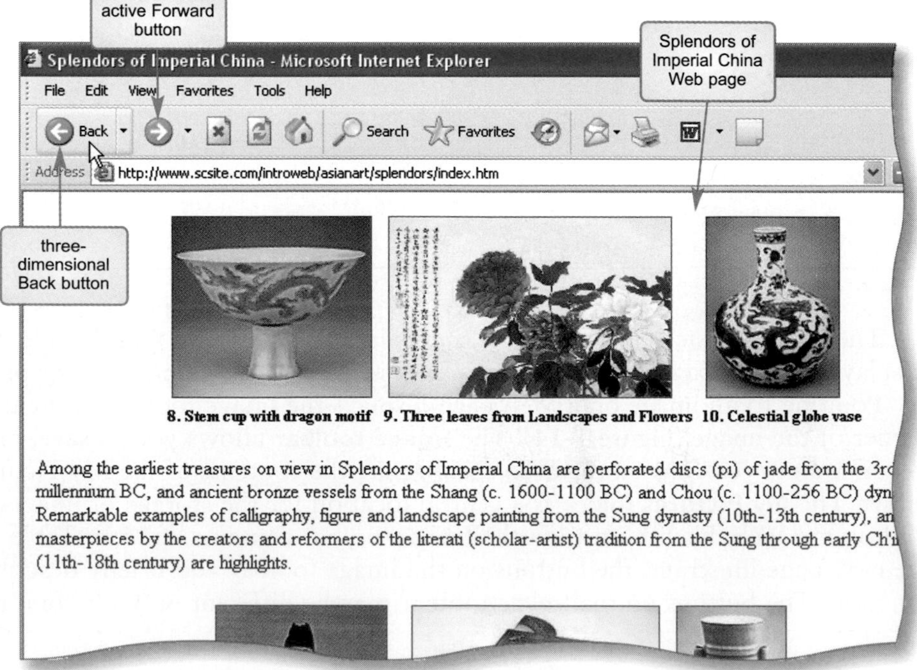

FIGURE 1-15

2

• **Click the Back button again.**

The Exhibitions Web page appears (Figure 1-16).

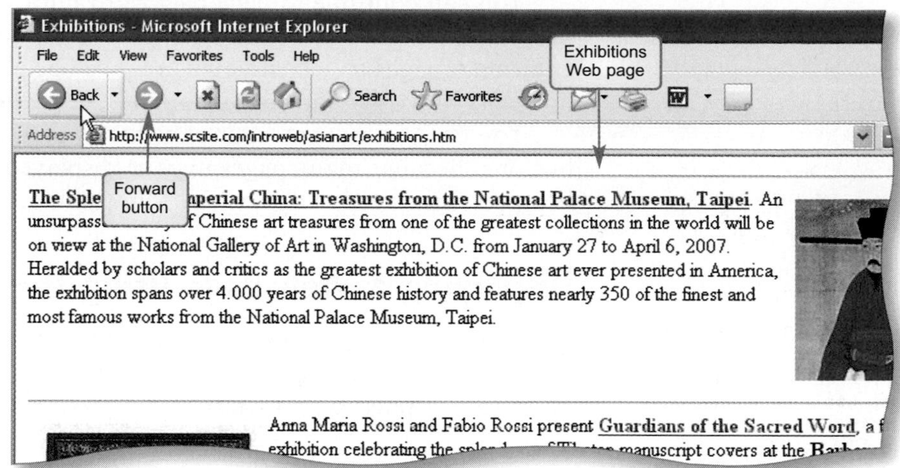

FIGURE 1-16

3

• **Click the Forward button on the Standard Buttons toolbar.**

The Splendors of Imperial China Web page appears again, and the Forward button is three-dimensional (Figure 1-17).

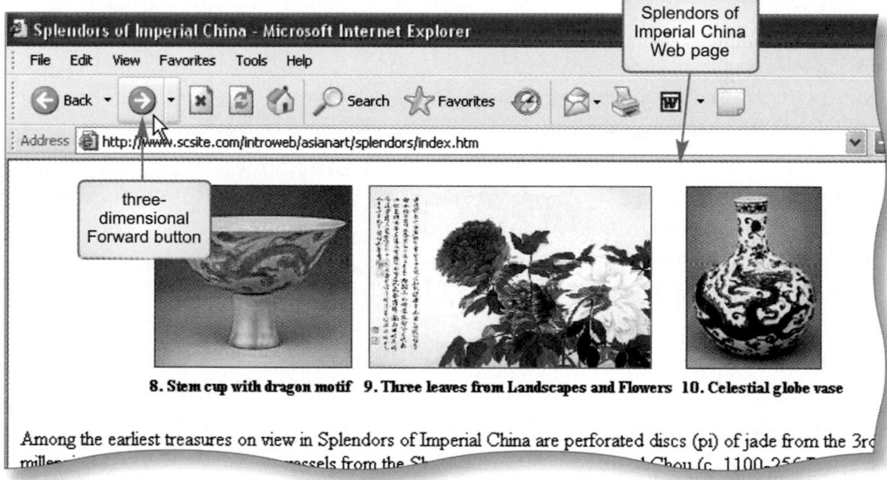

FIGURE 1-17

4

• **Click the Forward button again.**

The Splendors of Imperial China - Image 9 Web page appears (Figure 1-18). The Forward button now is inactive, which indicates no additional pages are available to which you can move forward.

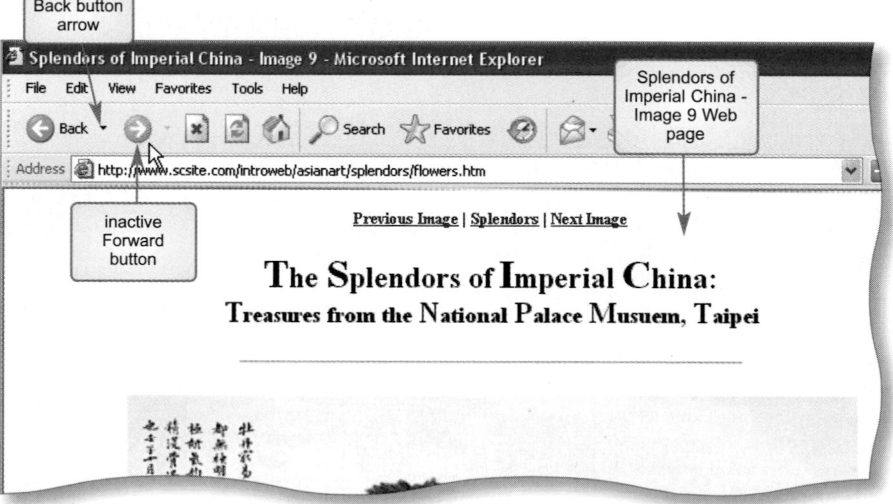

FIGURE 1-18

You can continue to page backward until you reach the beginning of the Back button list. At that time, the Back button becomes inactive, which indicates that no additional pages to which you can move back are contained in the list. You can, however, move forward by clicking the Forward button.

You can see that traversing the list of pages is easy using the Back and Forward buttons. Because many pages may be displayed before the one you want to view, however, this method can be time-consuming.

Displaying a Web Page Using the Back Button List

It is possible to skip to any previously visited page by clicking its title in the Back button list. Thus, you can find a recently visited page without displaying an intermediate page, as shown in the following steps.

To Display a Web Page Using the Back Button List

1

- **Click the Back button arrow on the Standard Buttons toolbar.**

The Back button list displays a list of titles of Web pages you visited during this session beginning with the most recent (Figure 1-19). The Back button list may be different on your computer.

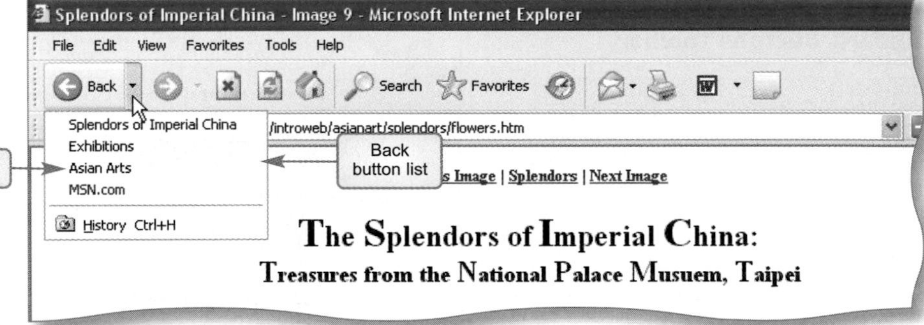

FIGURE 1-19

2

- **Click Asian Arts in the Back button list.**

Internet Explorer displays the Asia Arts Web page (Figure 1-20). Both the Back and Forward buttons are active, indicating that Web pages are available to which you can move backward or forward.

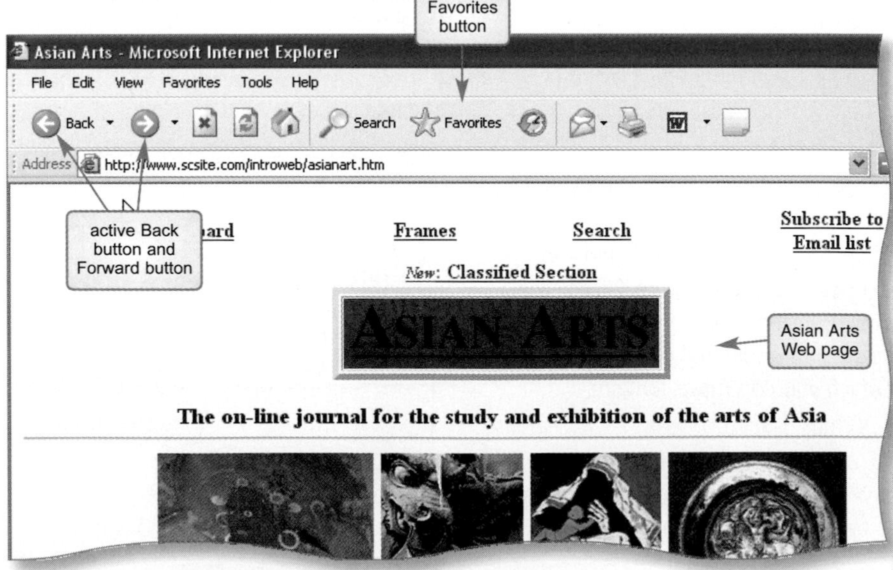

FIGURE 1-20

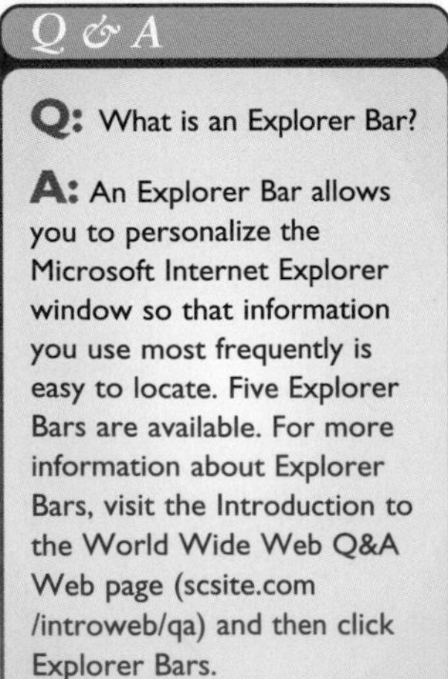

Q & A

Q: What is an Explorer Bar?

A: An Explorer Bar allows you to personalize the Microsoft Internet Explorer window so that information you use most frequently is easy to locate. Five Explorer Bars are available. For more information about Explorer Bars, visit the Introduction to the World Wide Web Q&A Web page (scsite.com /introweb/qa) and then click Explorer Bars.

If you have a small list of pages you have visited, or the Web page you wish to view is only one or two pages away, using the Back and Forward buttons to traverse the lists probably is faster than displaying the Back button list and selecting the correct title. If you have visited a large number of pages, however, the list will be long, and it may be easier to use the Back button list to select the exact page.

> *Q & A*
>
> **Q:** Can I change the title that identifies a favorite?
>
> **A:** Yes. Click the Favorites button on the Standard Buttons toolbar, click Organize in the Favorites list, right-click a favorite in the Organize favorites list, click Rename, type the new title, and then click the Close button. You also can rearrange the order of your favorites by dragging a favorite to another location on the Favorites list.

Keeping Track of Favorite Web Pages

The Favorites feature of Internet Explorer allows you to save the URLs of favorite Web pages. A **favorite** consists of the title of the Web page and the URL of that page. The title of the Web page is added to the Favorites menu. The following steps show how to add the Asian Arts Web page to the Favorites list.

To Add a Web Page to the Favorites List

1

• **Click the Favorites button on the Standard Buttons toolbar.**

The Add button, Organize button, and Favorites list appear on the Favorites bar (Figure 1-21). The Add button adds the title of the page and the URL in the Address box to the Favorites list. Additional or different folders and favorites may display in the Favorites list on your computer.

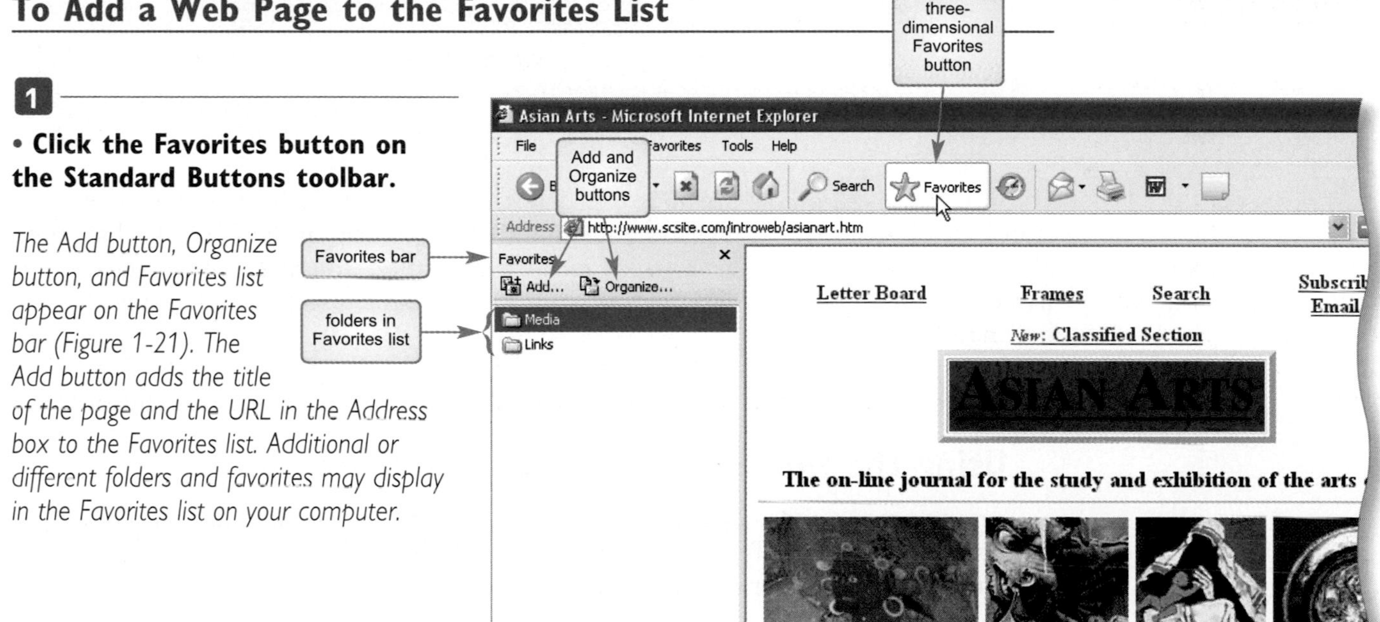

FIGURE 1-21

2

• **Click the Add button above the Favorites list.**

Internet Explorer displays the Add Favorite dialog box (Figure 1-22). The Name text box contains the title of the Asian Arts Web page, and the Address box on the Address bar contains the URL.

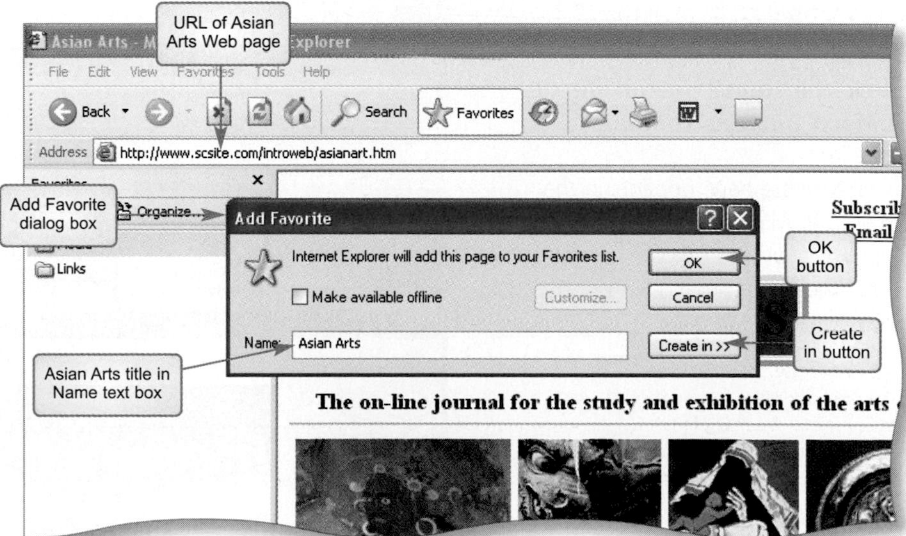

FIGURE 1-22

3

• **Click the OK button in the Add Favorite dialog box.**

The Asian Arts favorite appears in the Favorites list (Figure 1-23).

4

• **Click the Close button on the Favorites bar.**

The Favorites bar containing the Favorites list closes.

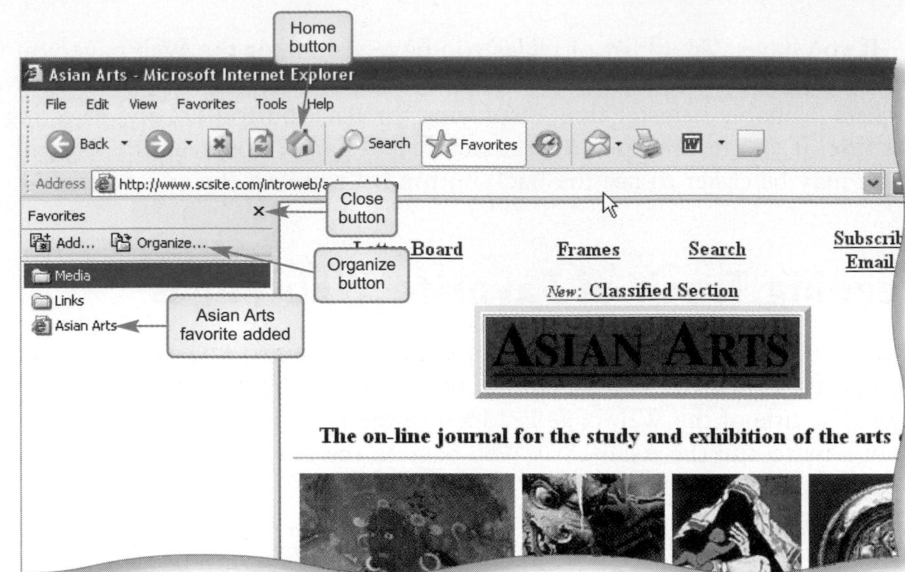

FIGURE 1-23

In Figure 1-22 on the previous page, clicking the Create in button expands the Add Favorite dialog box, displays a hierarchy of the folders in the Favorites list, and allows you to select a folder in which to store a favorite. You also can change the name of a favorite by highlighting the name in the Name text box and typing the new name.

In Figure 1-23, clicking the Organize button allows you to manage the Favorites list. The folders in the Favorites list display below the Add and Organize buttons.

Using the Home Button to Display a Web Page

At any time, you can display the home page in the display area using the Home button on the Standard Buttons toolbar. The following step shows how to display the Internet Explorer home page (MSN home page).

To Display the Home Page Using the Home Button

1

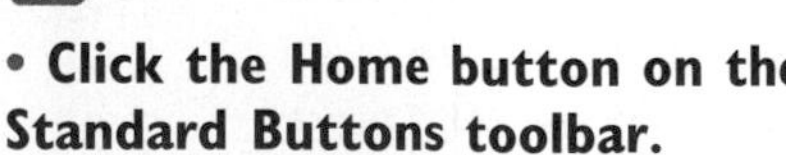

• **Click the Home button on the Standard Buttons toolbar.**

The MSN home page appears in the Welcome to MSN.com - Microsoft Internet Explorer window, and the URL for the home page is displayed in the Address box (Figure 1-24).

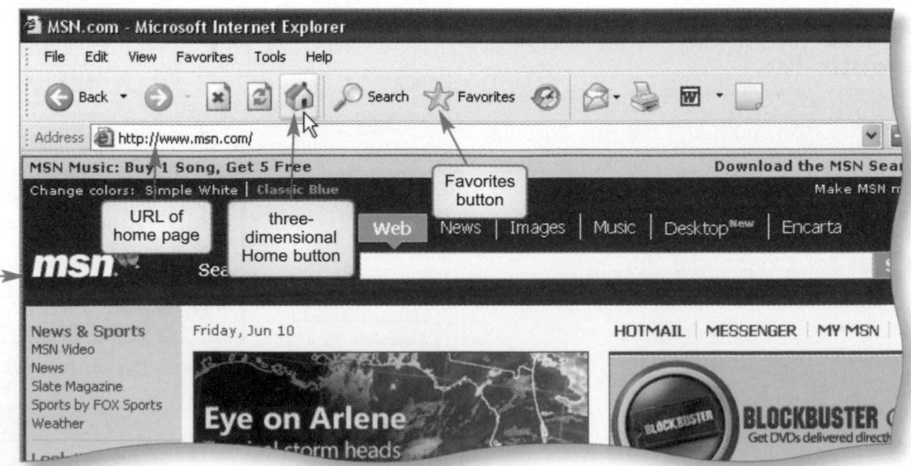

FIGURE 1-24

Displaying a Web Page Using the Favorites List

The Favorites list is used to display favorite or frequently accessed Web pages quickly, without having to navigate through several unwanted pages. The following steps show how to use the Favorites list to display the Asian Arts Web page.

To Display a Web Page Using the Favorites List

1

- **Click the Favorites button on the Standard Buttons toolbar.**

The Favorites list appears (Figure 1-25). The newly added favorite (Asian Arts) is the only favorite in the list in the left pane, and the MSN home page continues to be displayed in the right pane.

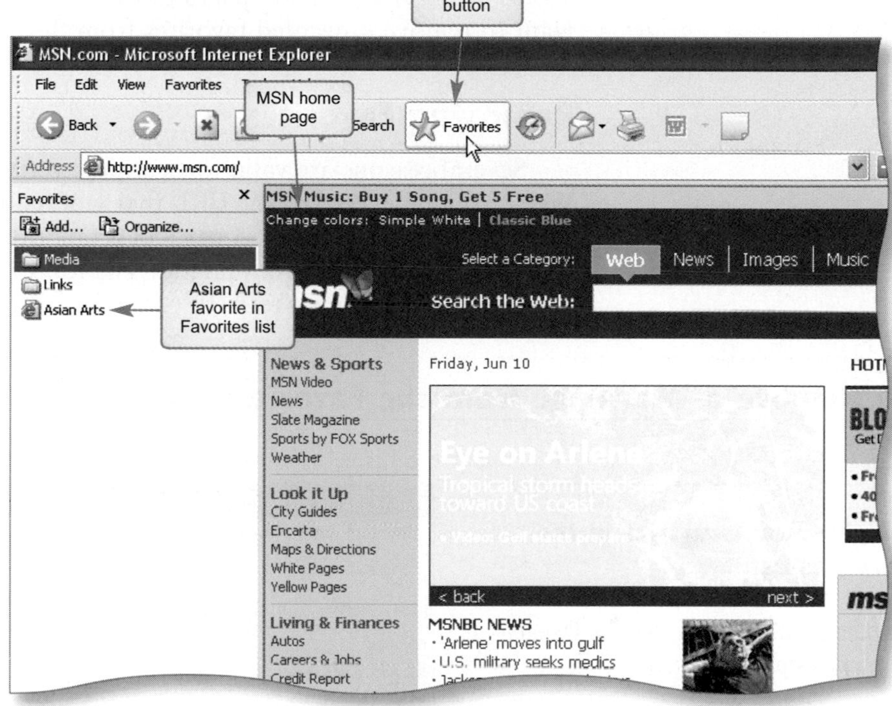

FIGURE 1-25

2

- **Click Asian Arts in the Favorites list.**

The Asian Arts Web page again is visible in the right pane, and the Asian Arts URL appears in the Address box (Figure 1-26). A pointing hand icon points to the highlighted Asian Arts title (white text) in the Favorites list.

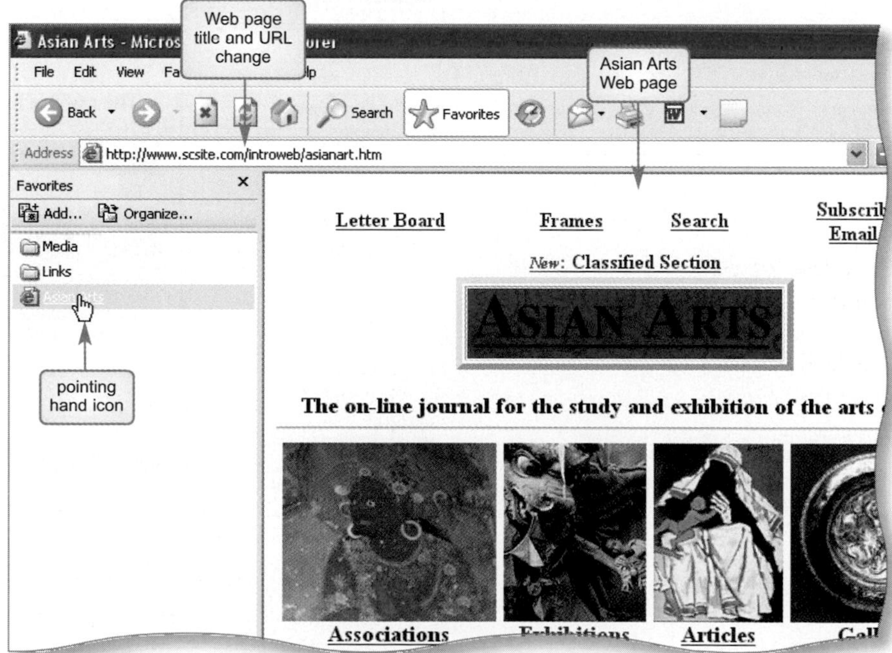

FIGURE 1-26

Additional favorites are displayed in the Favorites list in Figure 1-26 on the previous page. Among the favorites are the Links folder that contains entries corresponding to the buttons on the Links bar and the Media folder that contains a list of interesting media sources (news, sports, music, and so on). Below the two folders is the Asian Arts favorite. Other folders and favorites may appear in the Favorites list on your computer.

You have learned how to add a URL to the Favorites list and how to retrieve a Web page using the Favorites list. As you gain experience and continue to browse the World Wide Web and add pages to the Favorites list, it is likely that in time you will want to remove unwanted favorites from the list.

Removing Favorites

Several reasons are valid for wanting to remove a favorite. With the World Wide Web changing everyday, the URL that worked today may not work tomorrow. Perhaps you just do not want a particular favorite in the list anymore, or maybe the list is getting too big to be meaningful. The following steps show how to remove a favorite from the Favorites list.

To Remove a Web Page from the Favorites List

1

- **Right-click Asian Arts in the Favorites list.**

A shortcut menu containing the Delete command appears (Figure 1-27).

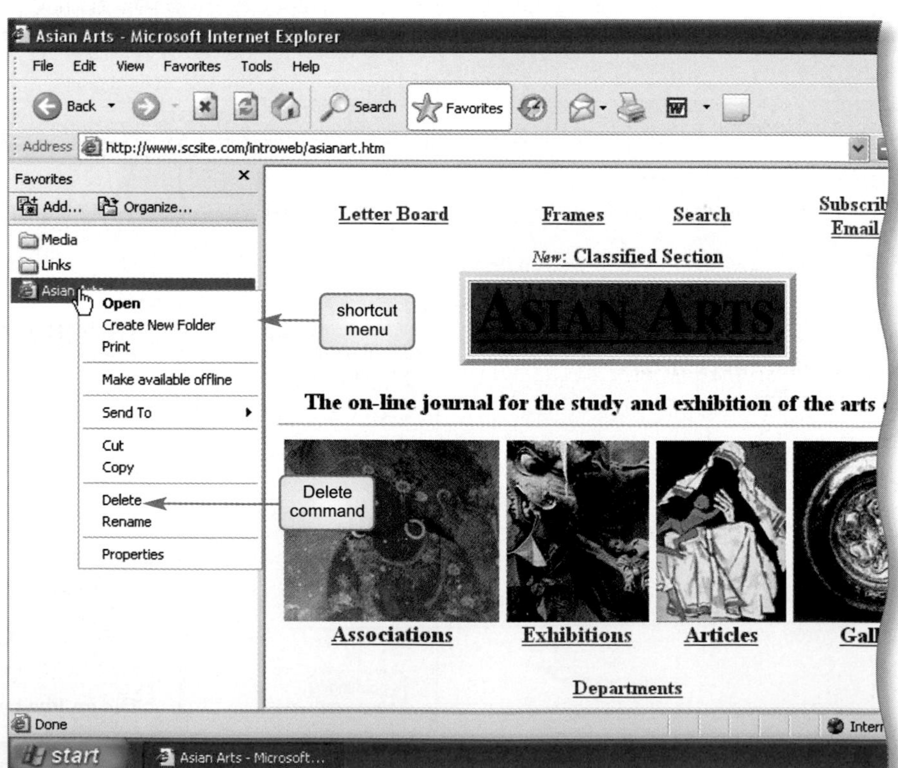

FIGURE 1-27

2

• **Click Delete on the shortcut menu.**

Internet Explorer displays the Confirm File Delete dialog box (Figure 1-28). A message asks if you are sure you want to send the Asian Arts favorite to the Recycle Bin.

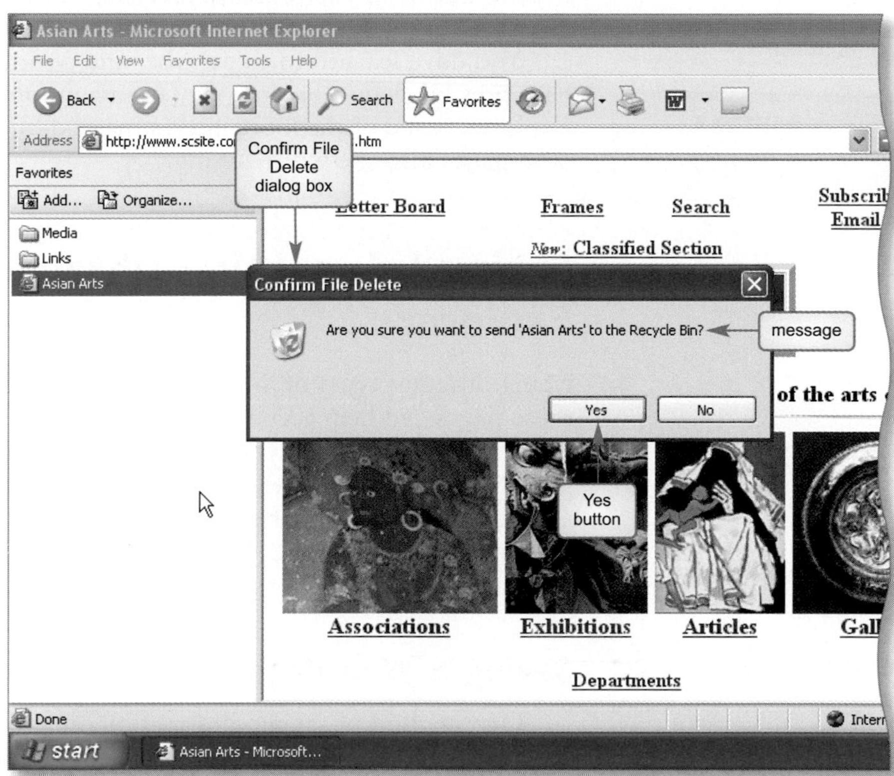

FIGURE 1-28

3

• **Click the Yes button in the Confirm File Delete dialog box.**

The Confirm File Delete dialog box closes, the Deleting dialog box is displayed momentarily, and the Asian Arts favorite is removed from the Favorites list (Figure 1-29).

4

• **Click the Close button on the Favorites bar.**

The Favorites bar closes.

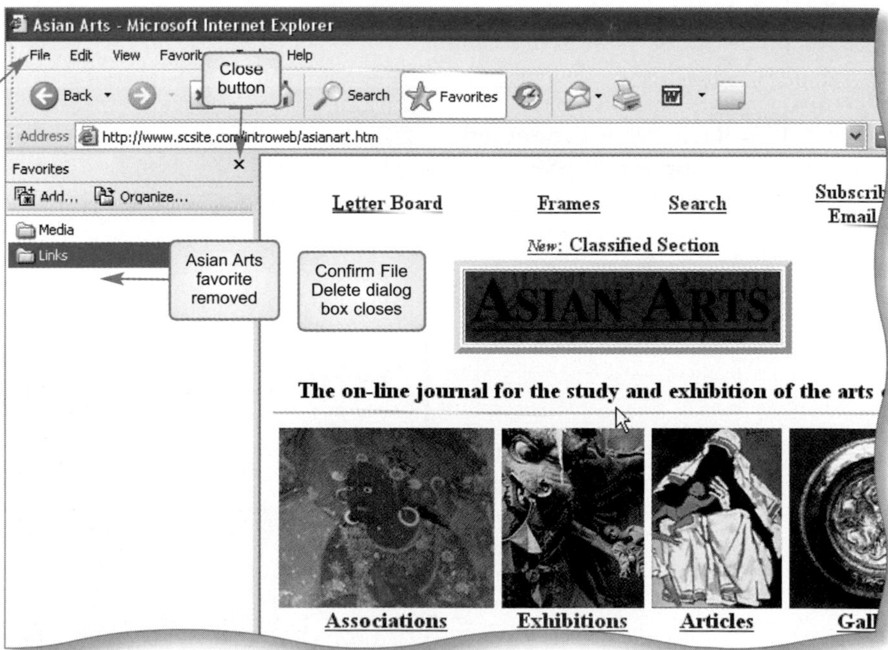

FIGURE 1-29

Using the commands on the shortcut menu can help you manage favorites. Internet Explorer also provides advanced features for handling favorites. For example, you can create folders that allow you to organize the Favorites list into categories. In Figure 1-25 on page WWW 21, Internet Explorer created two folders (Links and

Media) that help you organize favorites. You can create additional folders using the Organize Favorites button on the Favorites bar.

You have learned to create, use, and remove favorites. Saving URLs in the Favorites list is not the only way to save information you obtain using Internet Explorer. Some of the more interesting text and pictures you locate while displaying Web pages also are worth saving.

Saving Information Obtained with Internet Explorer

Many different types of Web pages are accessible on the World Wide Web. Because these pages can help accumulate information about areas of interest, you may wish to save the information you discover for future reference. The different types of Web pages and the different ways you may want to use them require different methods of saving. Internet Explorer allows you to save an entire Web page, individual pictures, or selected pieces of text. The following pages illustrate how to save an entire Web page and how to save a single picture.

Saving a Web Page

One method of saving information on a Web page is to save the entire Web page. The following steps show how to save the Asian Arts Web page on a USB flash drive.

To Save a Web Page

1

- **With a USB flash drive connected to one of the computer's USB ports, click File on the menu bar.**

The File menu appears (Figure 1-30). The Save As command is displayed on the File menu.

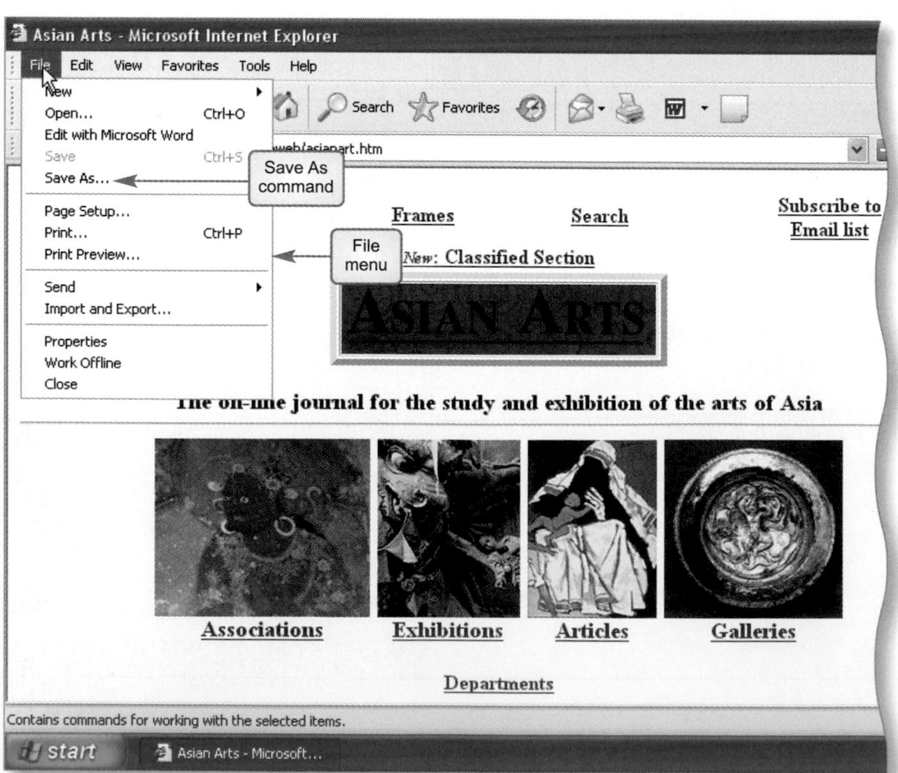

FIGURE 1-30

2

• **Click Save As on the File menu.**

Internet Explorer displays the Save Web Page dialog box. The Save in box contains the My Documents entry, and the File name text box contains the highlighted Web page title, Asian Arts (Figure 1-31). You can change the file name in the File name box by typing a new file name. The My Documents entry in the Save in box may be different on your computer.

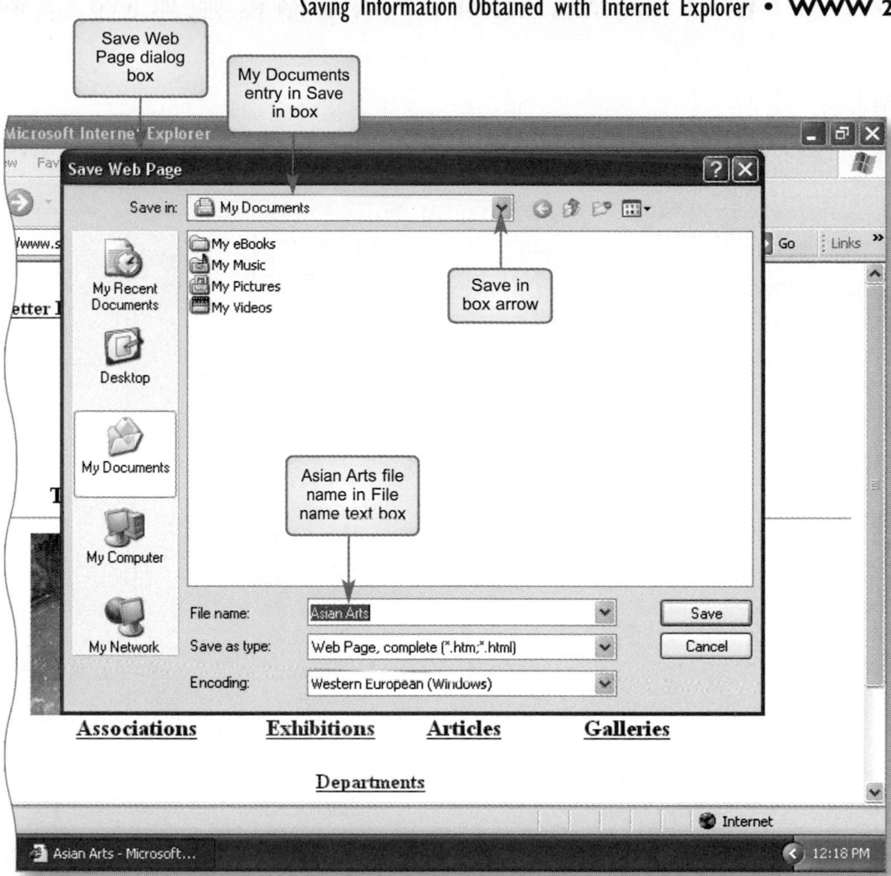

FIGURE 1-31

3

• **Click the Save in box arrow in the Save in box.**

The Save in list contains various components of the computer. My Documents is highlighted (Figure 1-32).

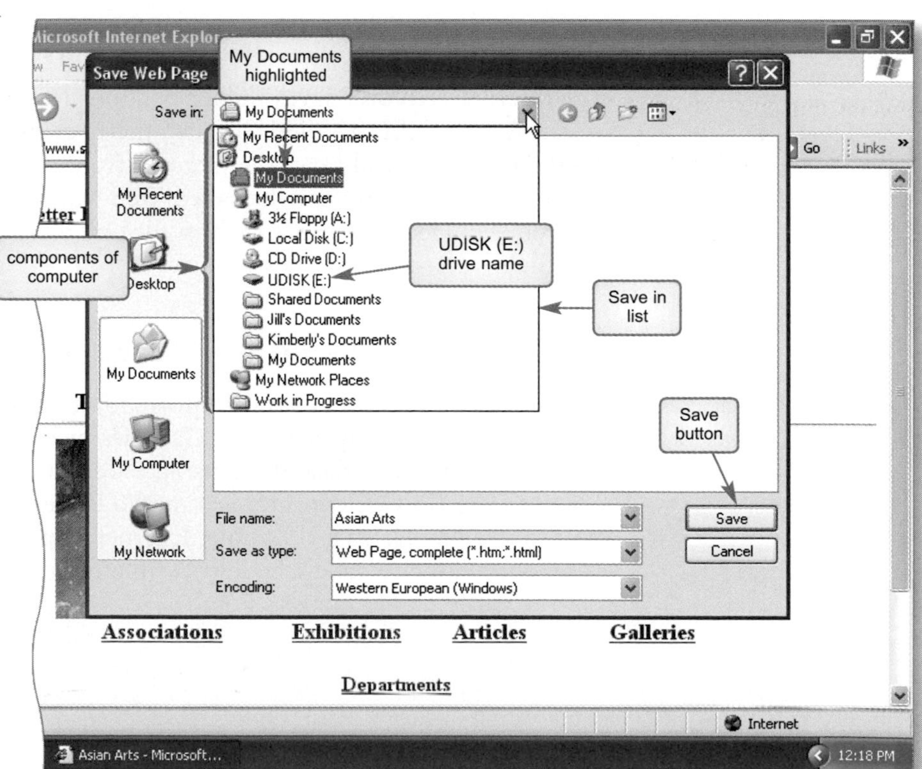

FIGURE 1-32

4

• **If necessary, click UDISK (E:) in the Save in list.**

The highlighted UDISK (E:) drive name appears in the Save in box (Figure 1-33). (Your USB flash drive may have a different name and letter.) The entry in the Save as type box, Web Page, complete (.htm;*.html), determines how the Web page is saved.*

5

• **Click the Save button in the Save Web Page dialog box.**

The Save Web Page dialog box closes and a smaller Save Web Page dialog box appears while the Asian Arts Web page is saved using the file name, Asian Arts.htm, on the USB flash drive.

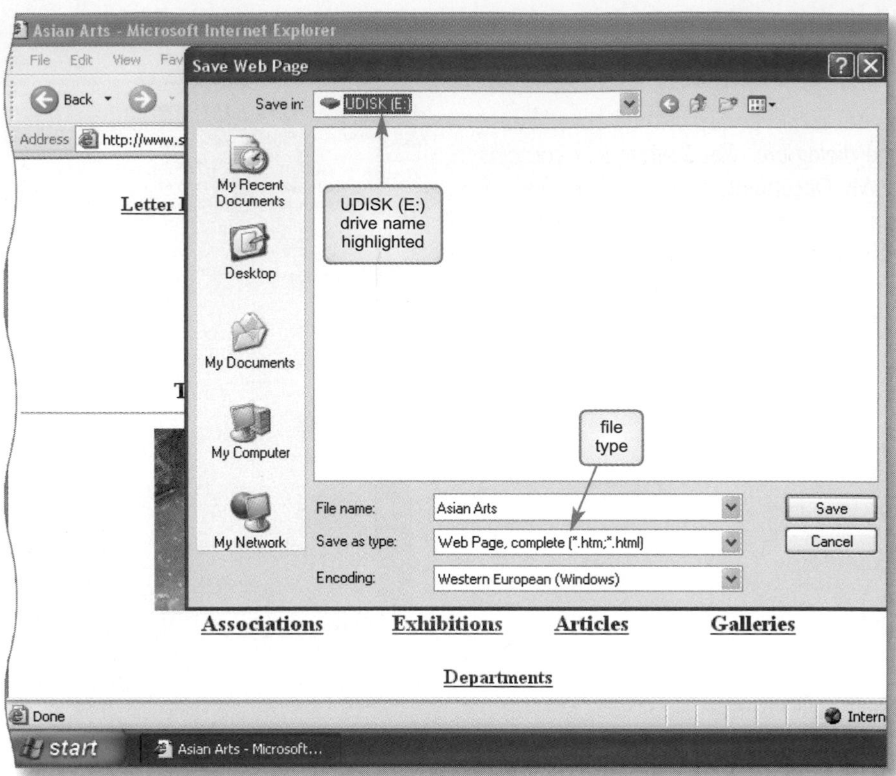

FIGURE 1-33

Internet Explorer saves the instructions to display the saved Web page in the Asian Arts.htm file on the USB flash drive, creates the Asian Arts_files folder on the USB flash drive, and saves the pictures from the Web page in the folder on the USB flash drive. You can view the saved Web page in the Internet Explorer window by double-clicking the Asian Arts.htm file and view a list of saved pictures by double-clicking the Asian Arts_files folder.

Q & A

Q: In addition to saving a picture, can I set a picture as a background on my desktop?

A: Yes. Right-click the image and then click Set as Background on the shortcut menu. The image will be displayed on the desktop.

Saving a Picture on a Web Page

A second method of saving information is to save a picture located on a Web page. In the following steps, the Galleries picture located on the Asian Arts Web page is saved on the USB flash drive using the **Joint Photographic Experts Group** (**JPEG**) format. The JPEG file format is a method of encoding pictures on a computer. When you save a picture as a JPEG file, Internet Explorer can display it. The following steps show how to save the Galleries picture on a USB flash drive in the JPEG format using the file name, image06.jpg.

To Save a Picture on a Web Page

1

- **Right-click the Galleries picture on the Asian Arts Web site.**

A shortcut menu, containing the Save Picture As command, appears (Figure 1-34).

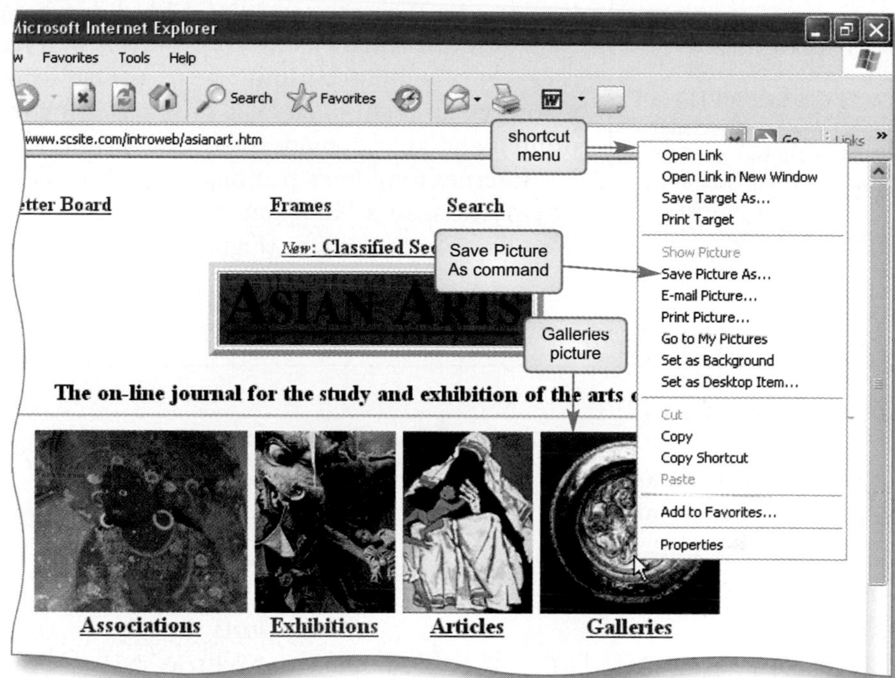

FIGURE 1-34

2

- **Click Save Picture As on the shortcut menu.**
- **Click the Save in box arrow in the Save Picture dialog box.**
- **Click UDISK 2.0 (E:) in the Save in box.**

The Save Picture dialog box appears (Figure 1-35). The Save in box contains the highlighted UDISK 2.0 (E:) drive name, the File name text box contains the image06 file name, and the Save as type text box contains the JPEG (.jpg) file type. The Asian Arts_files folder contains the saved Asian Arts Web page.*

3

- **Click the Save button in the Save Picture dialog box.**

The picture is saved using the image06.jpg file name on the USB flash drive, and the Save Picture dialog box closes.

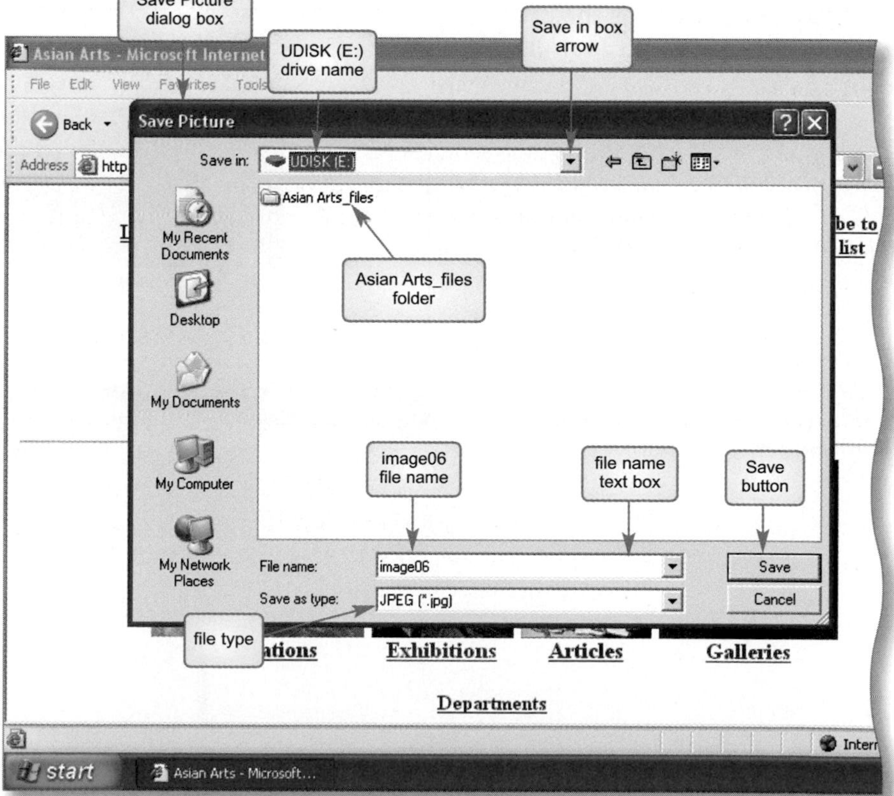

FIGURE 1-35

Q & A

Q: Where should I store my pictures?

A: You should store your pictures in the My Pictures folder. You can use folders to organize your pictures, and you easily can back up the folders in the My Pictures folder to another storage device for safekeeping.

Printing a Web Page in Internet Explorer

As you visit Web sites, you may want to print some of the pages you view. A printed version of a Web page is called a **hard copy** or **printout**. You might want a printout for several reasons. First, to present the Web page to someone who does not have access to a computer, it must be in printed form. Second, persons other than those who prepare them often keep Web pages for reference. In some cases, Web pages are printed and kept in binders for use by others.

Internet Explorer's printing capability allows you to print both the text and picture portions of a Web page. In the following steps, you will print the Exhibitions Web Page on the printer (Figure 1-37).

To Print a Web Page

1

- **Ready the printer according to the printer instructions.**
- **Click the Print button on the Standard Buttons toolbar (Figure 1-36).**

2

- **When the printer stops printing the document, retrieve the printout, which should look like Figure 1-37.**

The URL of the Web page (www.scsite.com/introweb/asianart.htm) prints as a footer in the lower-left corner of the printout (Figure 1-37). The Web page title (Asian Arts) appears in the upper-left corner, the page number (1) and total number of pages (1) in the Web site appear in the upper-right corner, and the date (6/15/2007) is displayed in the lower-right corner.

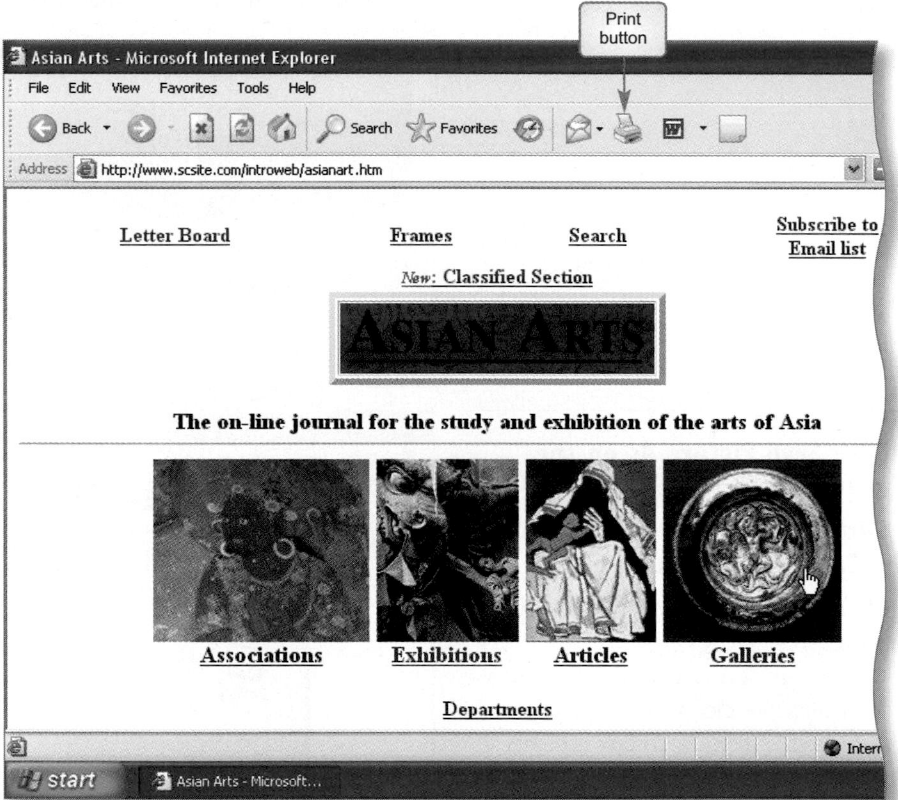

FIGURE 1-36

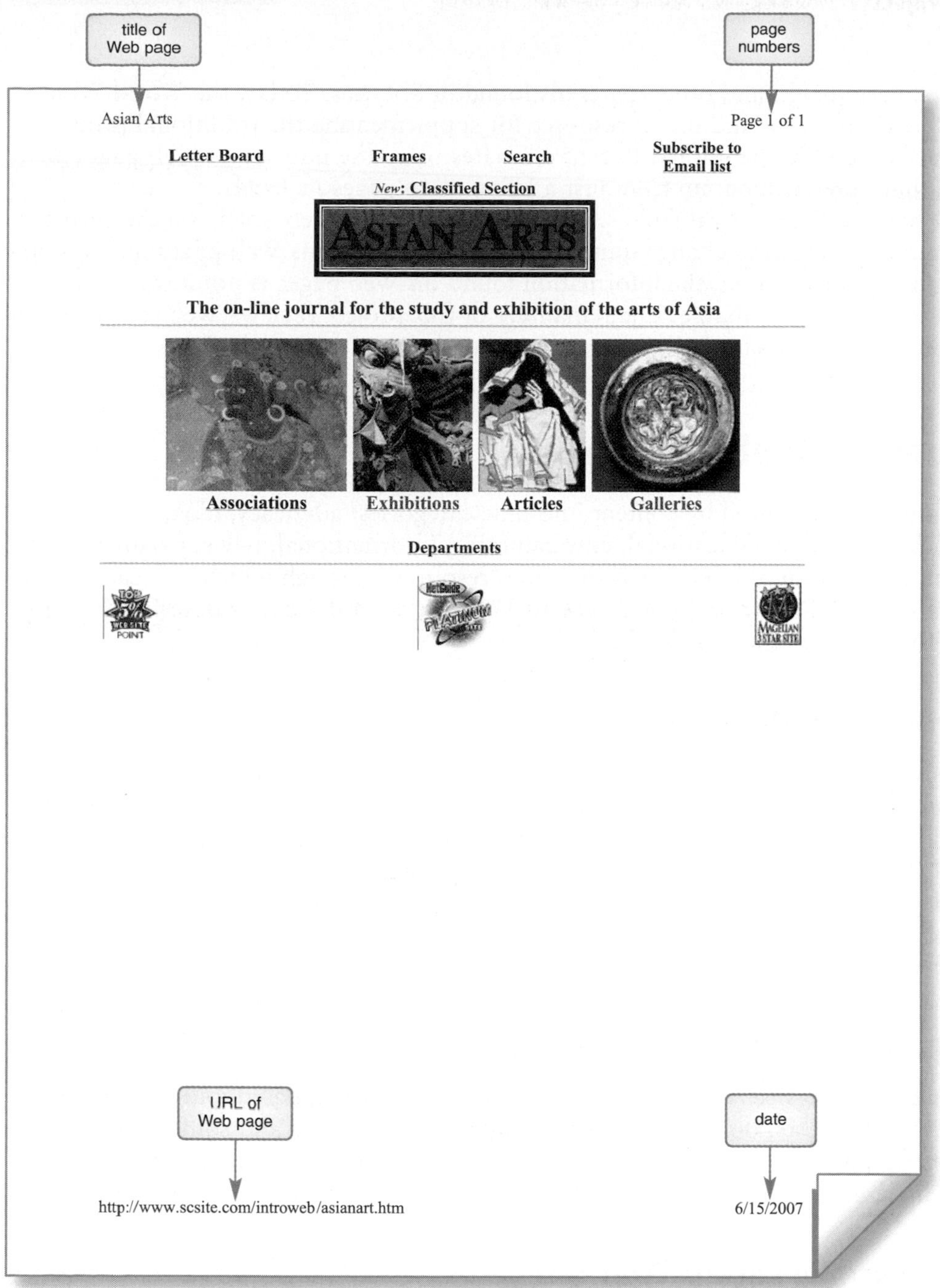

FIGURE 1-37

Q & A

Q: Sometimes a title and URL display at the top of my printed Web page. Can I remove the title and URL?

A: Yes. You can remove the title and URL by clicking File on the menu bar, clicking Page Setup, and removing the text in the Header and Footer text boxes.

Q & A

Q: How can I print a table containing a list of all links on the Web page I am printing or all documents with links on the Web page?

A: In the Print dialog box, click the Options tab, and then click the Print all linked documents check box or Print table of links check box to print the documents or table.

You also can click Print on the File menu to print a Web page. When you do this, a Print dialog box displays. The printing options available in the Print dialog box allow you to print the entire document, print selected pages of a document, print to a disk file, print multiple copies, change the printer properties, and cancel the print request.

Web Searching

For a student, the World Wide Web is an important tool that can be used to search for and find information to write research papers, prepare speeches, and complete homework assignments. In the past, these tasks were accomplished using books, papers, periodicals, and other materials found in libraries. Today, the World Wide Web provides a new and useful resource for supplementing the traditional print materials found in the library. Recent estimates place the number of Web pages at more than three trillion, up from just a few million pages in 1994.

While the Web is a valuable resource, you should not rely solely on the Web for information. Web sites change quite frequently, which means Web pages may become unavailable. In addition, the information found on Web pages is not always up-to-date, accurate, or verifiable. The remainder of this project reviews Web resources and demonstrates successful techniques for locating information on the Web.

Types of Web Resources

Web sites are organized by content into nine categories: advocacy, blog, business/marketing, educational, entertainment, informational, news, personal, and portal. In addition, the Web provides other resources through which you can access useful information when doing research. The next several sections describe the types of Web sites and other resources.

Advocacy Web Sites

An **advocacy Web site** contains content that describes a cause, opinion, or idea (Figure 1-38a). The purpose of the advocacy Web page is to convince the reader of the validity of a cause, opinion, or idea. These Web sites usually present views on a particular group or association. Sponsors of advocacy Web sites include the American Association of Retired Persons (AARP), the Democratic National Committee, the Republican National Committee, the Society for the Prevention of Cruelty to Animals, and the American Civil Liberties Union.

Q & A

Q: What other examples of Web sites are available?

A: More examples of advocacy, blog, business/marketing, educational, entertainment, informational, news, personal, and portal Web sites can be found on the World Wide Web. For more information about other Web sites, visit the Introduction to the World Wide Web Q&A Web page (scsite.com/introweb/qa) and then click Other Types of Web Resources.

Blog Web Sites

A **blog Web site**, short for Web log, uses a regularly updated journal format to reflect the interests, opinions, and personalities of the author and sometimes Web site visitors (Figure 1-38b). A blog has an informal style (similar to a diary) that consists of a single individual's ideas or a collection of ideas and thoughts among visitors.

Business/Marketing Web Sites

A **business/marketing Web site** contains content that tries to promote or sell products or services (Figure 1-38c). Nearly every business maintains a business/marketing Web site. Dell Inc., 21st Century Insurance Company, General Motors Corporation, Kraft Foods Inc., and Walt Disney Company all have business/marketing Web sites. Many of these companies also allow you to purchase their products or services online.

Educational Web Sites

An **educational Web site** offers exciting, challenging avenues for formal and informal teaching and learning (Figure 1-38d). On the Web, you can learn how to sail a boat or how to cook a meal. For a more structured learning experience, companies provide online training to employees, and colleges offer online classes and degrees. Instructors often use the Web to enhance classroom teaching by publishing course materials, grades, and other pertinent class information.

Figure 1-38a (advocacy)

Figure 1-38b (blog)

Figure 1-38c (business/marketing)

Figure 1-38d (educational)

Figure 1-38e (entertainment)

Figure 1-38f (informational)

Figure 1-38g (news)

Figure 1-38h (personal)

Figure 1-38i (portal)

FIGURE 1-38

Entertainment Web Sites

An **entertainment Web site** offers an interactive and engaging environment (Figure 1-38e). Popular entertainment Web sites offer music, videos, sports, games, ongoing Web episodes, sweepstakes, chats, and more. Sophisticated entertainment Web sites often partner with other technologies. For example, you can cast your vote about a topic on a television show.

Informational Web Sites

An **informational Web site** contains factual information (Figure 1-38f). Many United States government agencies have informational Web sites providing information such as census data, tax codes, and the congressional budget. Other organizations provide information such as public transportation schedules and published research findings.

News Web Sites

A **news Web site** contains newsworthy material including stories and articles relating to current events, life, money, sports, and the weather (Figure 1-38g). Many magazines and newspapers sponsor Web sites that provide summaries of printed articles, as well as articles not included in the printed versions. Newspapers and television and radio stations are some of the media that maintain news Web sites.

Personal Web Sites

A private individual or family not usually associated with any organization may maintain a **personal Web site** or just a single Web page (Figure 1-38h). People publish personal Web pages for a variety of reasons. Some are job hunting. Others simply want to share life experiences with the world.

Portal Web Sites

A **portal Web site** offers a variety of Internet services from a single, convenient location (Figure 1-38i). Most portals offer the following free services: search engine and/or subject directory; news; sports and weather; Web publishing services; reference tools such as yellow pages, stock quotes, and maps; shopping malls and auctions; and e-mail and other forms of online communication.

Many portals have Web communities. A **Web community** is a Web site that joins a specific group of people with similar interests or relationships. These communities may offer online photo albums, chat rooms, and other service to facilitate communications among members. Table 1-5 shows the popular portals and their URLs.

Table 1-5 Popular Portals and Their URLs

PORTAL	URL	PORTAL	URL
AltaVista	altavista.com	HotBot	hotbot.com
America Online	aol.com	LookSmart	looksmart.com
Euroseek.com	euroseek.com	Lycos	lycos.com
Excite	excite.com	Microsoft Network	msn.com
Go.com	go.com	Netscape	netscape.com
Google	google.com	Yahoo!	yahoo.com

For more information about other Web resources, visit the Introduction to the World Wide Web Q&A Web page (scsite.com/introweb/qa) and then click Other Web Resources.

> **Q & A**
>
> **Q:** Are newsgroups a type of Web resource?
>
> **A:** Yes. Newsgroups provide a forum for finding current information on a topic. You can access a newsgroup using Internet Explorer, search for a newsgroup, read newsgroup articles, expand a thread, print and post an article, and subscribe and unsubscribe to a newsgroup.

Summary of Types of Web Resources

Determining the exact category into which a Web resource falls sometimes is difficult because of the overlap of information on the page. You will find advertising on news Web pages. Personal Web pages may be advocating some cause or opinion. A business/marketing Web page may contain factual information that is verifiable from other sources. In spite of this overlapping, identifying the general category in which the Web page falls can help you evaluate the usefulness of the Web page as a source of information for a research paper.

Web Search Resources

The World Wide Web includes trillions of Web pages, and bibliographic control does not exist. To find information for a term paper, learn more about a topic of interest, or display the home page of a governmental agency, you must know either the URL of the Web page with the information you are after or you must use a search tool. A **search tool** is a software program that helps you find Web pages containing the desired information. Search tools fall into three general categories:

- Subject directory
- Search engine
- Keyword system

The first type of search tool, called a **subject directory**, uses a directory to organize related Web resources. Figure 1-39 on the next page shows a directory (Google directory) that is organized into broad categories. You must decide into which category the search topic falls and then click the corresponding link. When you click the link, another page of links is displayed that contains more specific categories from which to choose. You continue following the links until you find the information you are seeking.

> **Q & A**
>
> **Q:** Can a search engine provide access to more than just Web pages?
>
> **A:** Yes. Some search engines allow you to search a newsgroup, periodical or newspaper, business directory, or personal directory.

Because directories allow you to choose from a list of categories, you do not have to provide any keywords to find information. You may have to spend considerable time traveling through several levels of categories, however, only to discover that no pages on the topic are available.

A second type of search tool, called a **search engine**, retrieves and displays a list of links to Web pages based on a query. A **query** is a **keyword** or **search term** (a word, set of words, or phrase) you enter to tell the search engine the topic about which you want information. The search engine uses the keyword to search an index of Web resources in its database. Some of the more popular search engines are MSN Search, Google, Yahoo!, Ask Jeeves, AltaVista, and Excite.

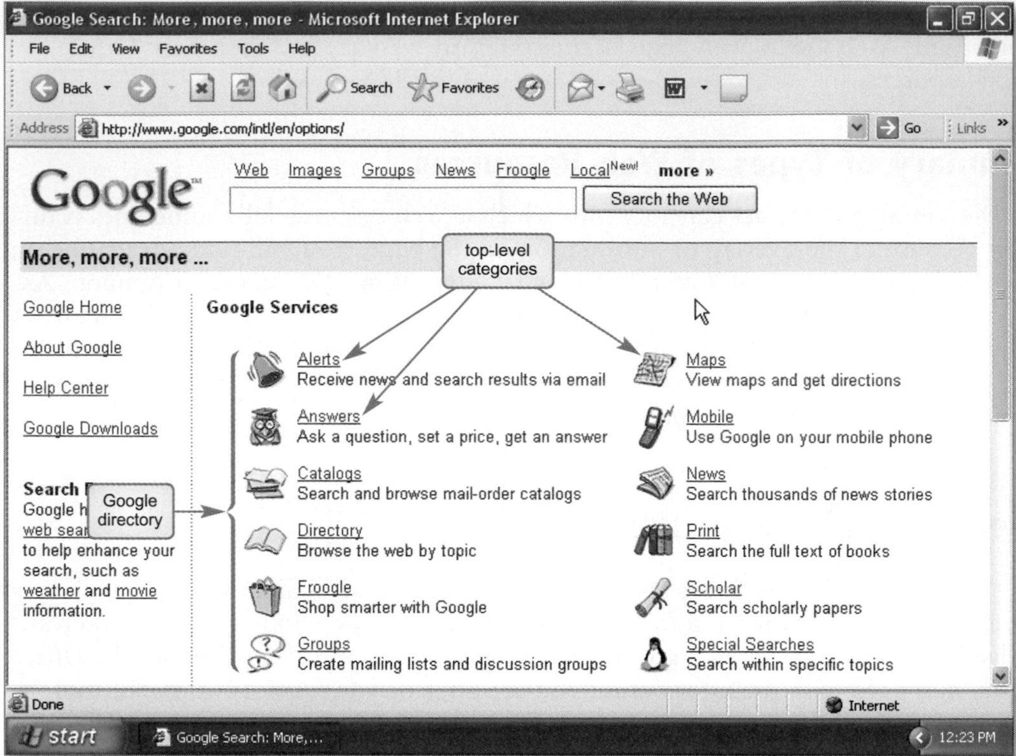

FIGURE 1-39

Figure 1-40 shows a typical **keyword search form** (Google Advanced Search) used to enter keywords to search the Web. You provide one or more relevant keywords about the topic, and the search engine will return links that point directly to Web pages that contain those keywords.

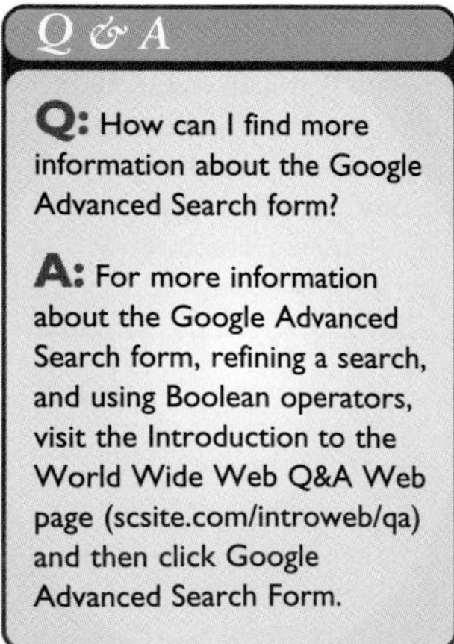
Q & A

Q: How can I find more information about the Google Advanced Search form?

A: For more information about the Google Advanced Search form, refining a search, and using Boolean operators, visit the Introduction to the World Wide Web Q&A Web page (scsite.com/introweb/qa) and then click Google Advanced Search Form.

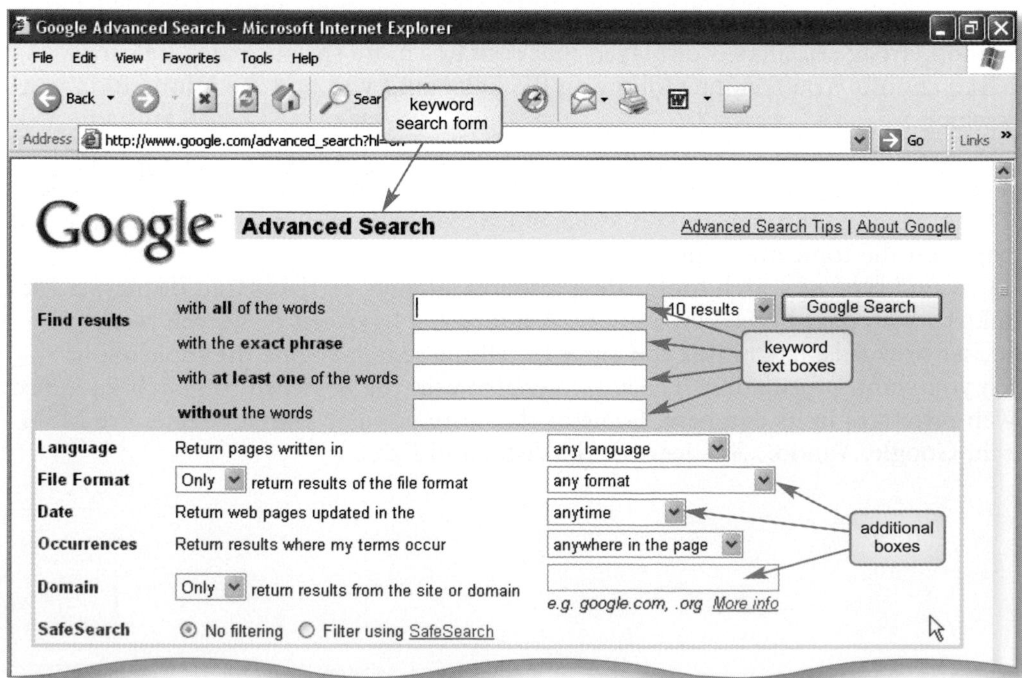

FIGURE 1-40

The index used by a search engine is created using several techniques. An automated program, called a **robot** or **spider**, travels around the Web, automatically following links and adding entries to the index. Individuals also can request that their Web pages be added to a directory or index.

All the popular portal Web sites listed in Table 1-5 on page WWW 32 have both a search engine and a subject directory. Most portals also include specialized search tools that display maps and directions (Expedia), provide information about businesses (Yellow Pages), and help find people (People Finder).

The third type of search tool, a Keyword system, is part of the Internet Explorer browser. A **Keyword system** allows you to enter a name or word in the Address box to display a corresponding Web page. The Keyword system is shown in detail in Figure 1-50 through Figure 1-54 on pages WWW 41–43 in this project.

Why study different search tools? Just as it is impossible for a card catalog to contain an entry for every book in the world, it is impossible for each search tool to catalog every Web page on the World Wide Web. In addition, different search tools on the Web perform different types of searches. Some search for keywords in the title of a Web page, while others scan links for the keywords. Still others search the entire text of Web pages. Because of the different searching techniques, the results of a search vary surprisingly.

When developing Internet Explorer, Microsoft realized the importance of using search tools and made several search tools accessible via the Search button on the Standard Buttons toolbar. To practice doing research on the Web, assume you are interested in Astronomy and want to find information on meteorites from Antarctica. The following section shows how to start Internet Explorer and use the Google directory to search for information on meteors from Antarctica.

Searching the Web Using a Directory

Google is one of the most widely used search engines. As with most search engines, Google has a simple search form, an advanced search form (see Figure 1-40 on page WWW 34), and a subject directory. Starting with general categories and becoming increasingly more specific as links are selected, the Google directory provides a menu-like interface for searching the Web. Because the Google directory uses a series of menus to organize links to Web pages, you can perform searches without entering keywords. The step on the next page illustrates how to display the Google home page.

Q: Do most search engines provide only a directory?

A: No. Most search engines provide both a directory and the capability of performing keyword searches.

To Display the Google Home Page

1

• **Click the Address box, type** `www.google.com` **as the URL, and then click the Go button.**

Internet Explorer displays the URL for the Google home page (http://www.google.com/) in the Address box and displays the Google home page (Figure 1-41).

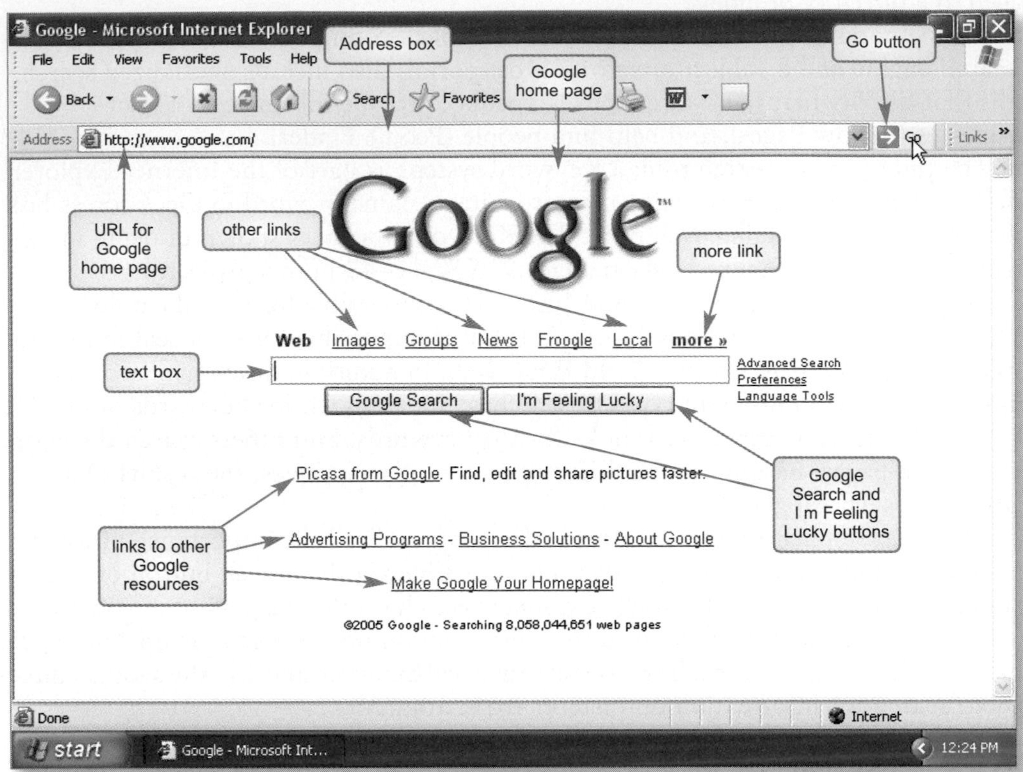

FIGURE 1-41

When you type a URL in the Address box and then click the Go button, **AutoComplete** remembers the URL you typed. As a result, when you type the URL for the Google home page in the Address box in Figure 1-41, AutoComplete may display a list of previously entered URLs in a box below the Address box. If this happens, you can select a URL from the list in the Address box by clicking the URL, or you can continue to type the URL from the keyboard.

The text box and Google Search button below the Google title allow you to perform a keyword search. Clicking the more link below the Google title displays a list of 18 Google services (Alerts, Answers, Catalogs, Directory, and so on). Clicking the Directory link in the list of services allows you to browse the topics in the Google directory.

Web pages in the Google directory are organized into the broad categories. You must decide into which category the search topic falls and then select the corresponding link. When you select a general link, another page of links is displayed with more specific topics from which to choose. You continue following the links until you find the information you are seeking.

Because astronomy is part of the major category, Science, this category is appropriate to start the search. The steps in Figure 1-42 through Figure 1-49 on pages WWW 37–40 illustrate how to navigate through the Google directory to retrieve information about the meteors found on the continent of Antarctica.

To Search Using the Google Directory

1

• Click the more link on the Google home page.

The Google title, Google text box, and Google Services area appear in the display area (Figure 1-42). The Directory link is displayed in the Google Services area.

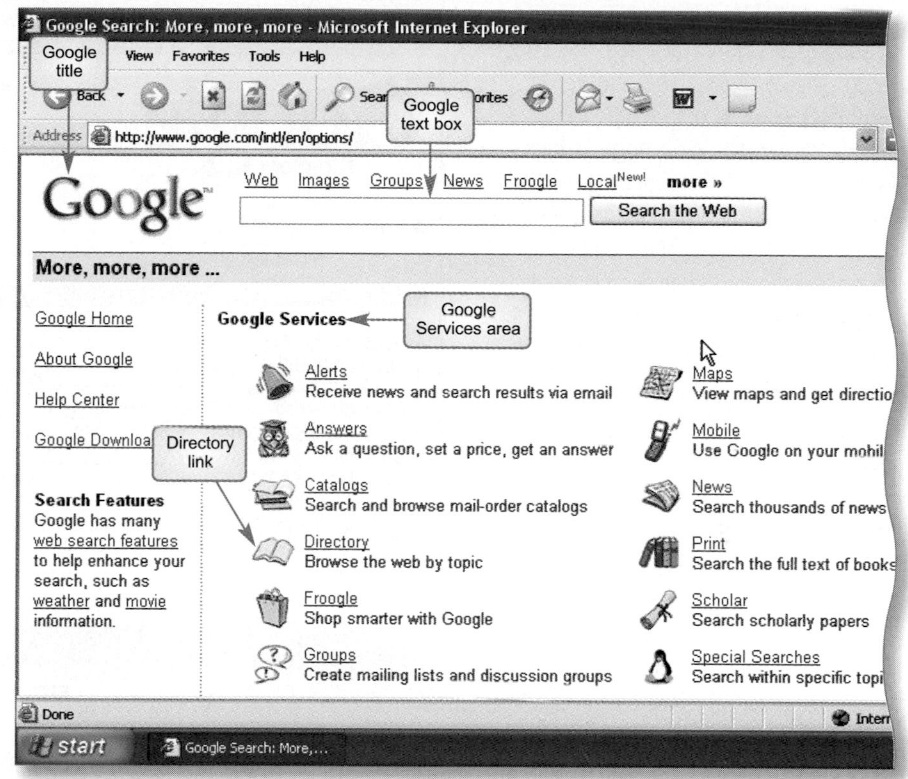

FIGURE 1-42

2

• Click Directory in the Google Services area to view the Google directory.

A portion of the Google directory appears in the display area (Figure 1-43).

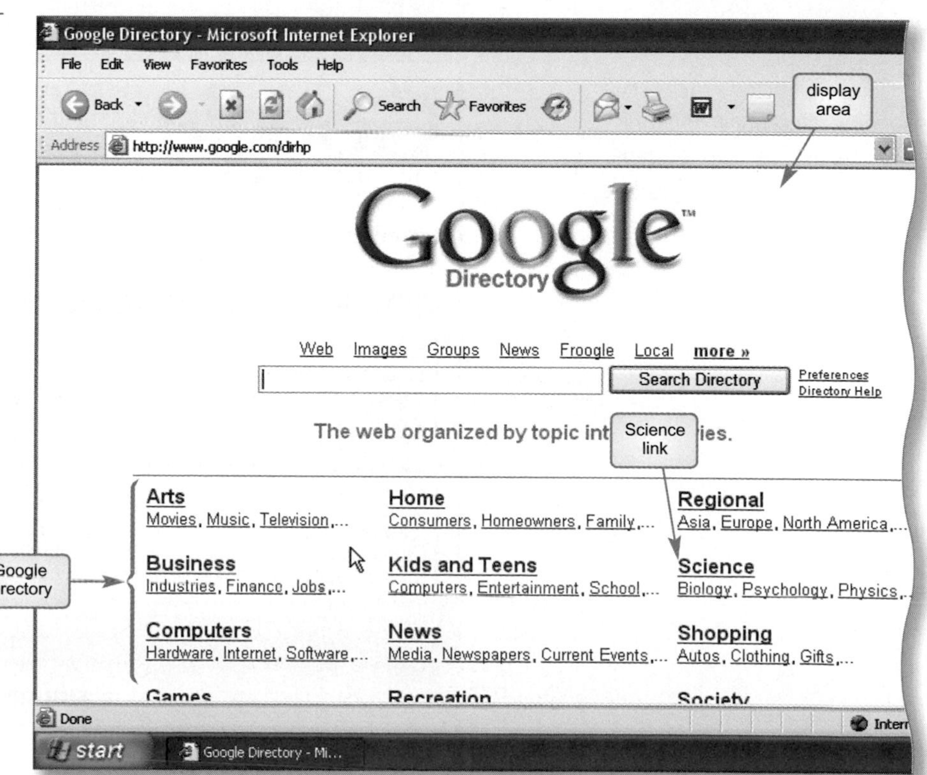

FIGURE 1-43

3

• Click Science to view the links in the Science category.

The Google Directory - Science Web page appears (Figure 1-44). The number in parentheses next to a subcategory indicates how many Web page listings you will find if you click the subcategory. For example, the Astronomy subcategory contains 4,279 listings. The number of Web page listings and/or search results on your computer may be different.

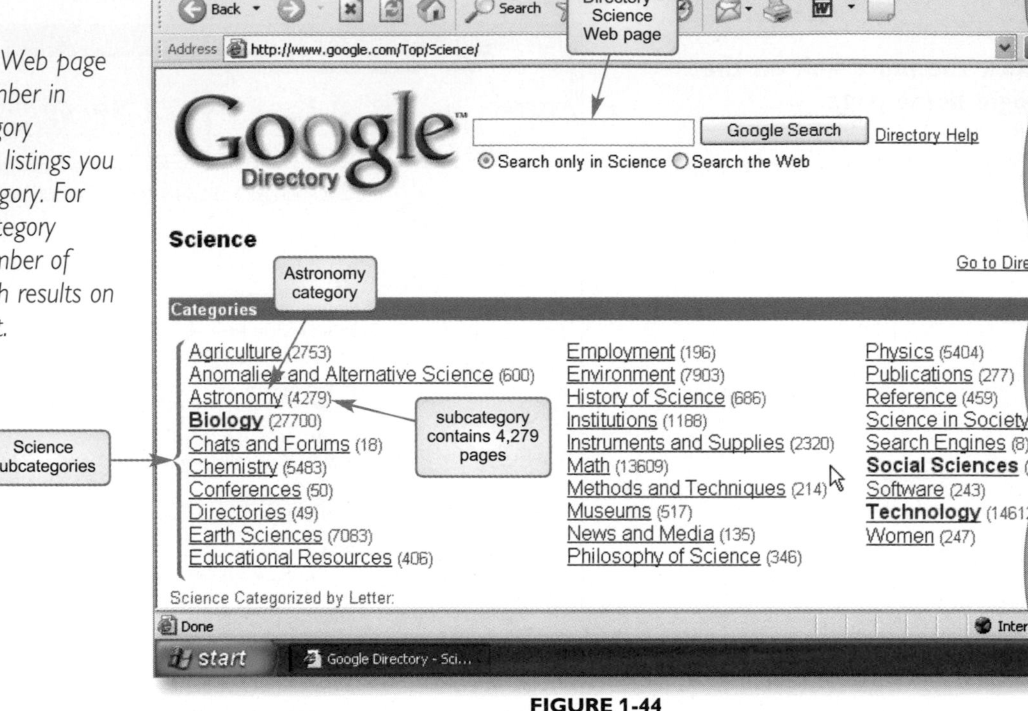

FIGURE 1-44

4

• Click Astronomy to view the links in the Astronomy subcategory.

The Google Directory - Science > Astronomy Web page appears (Figure 1-45). The Solar System subcategory contains 825 listings.

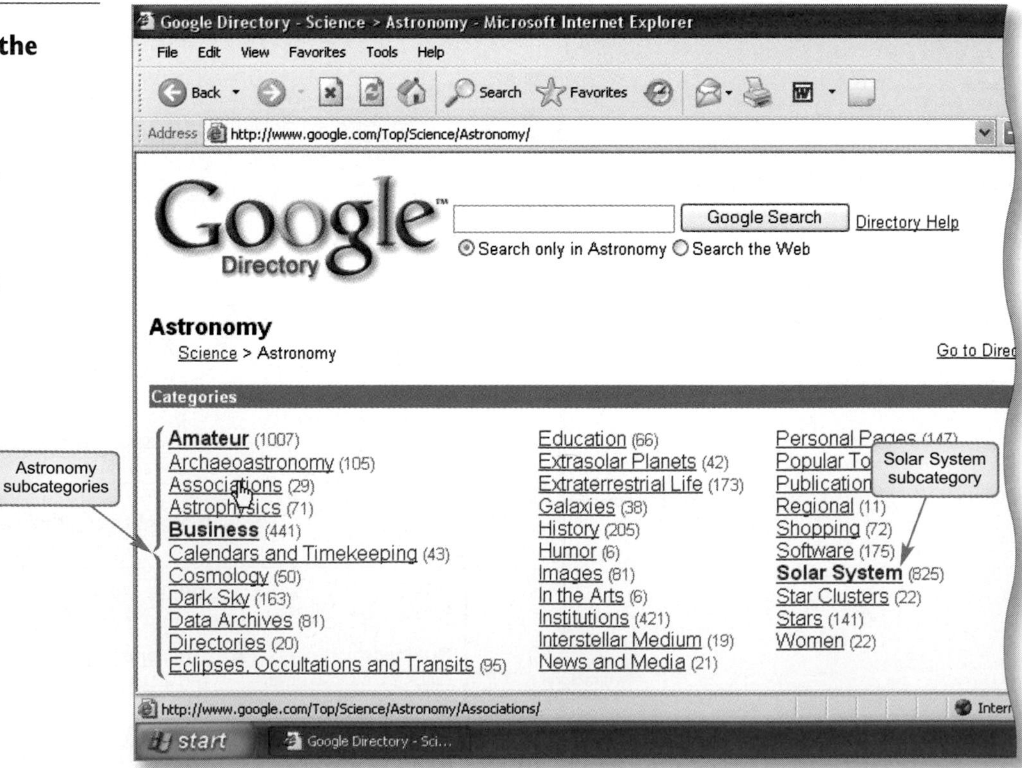

FIGURE 1-45

5

• Click Solar System to view the links in the Solar System subcategory.

The Google Directory - Science > Astronomy > Solar System Web page appears (Figure 1-46). The Asteroids, Comets and Meteors subcategory contains 211 listings.

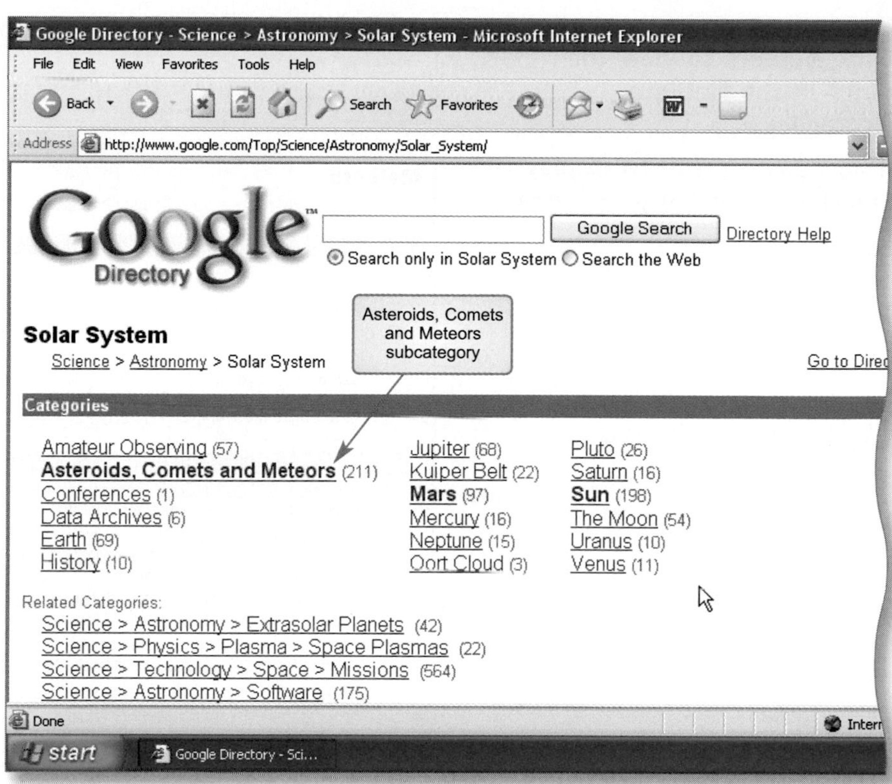

FIGURE 1-46

6

• Click Asteroids, Comets and Meteors to view the links in the Asteroids, Comets and Meteors subcategory.

The Google Directory - Science > Astronomy > Solar System > Asteroids, Comets and Meteors Web page appears (Figure 1-47). The Meteors subcategory contains 43 listings, and a list of Web pages appears in the Web Pages area.

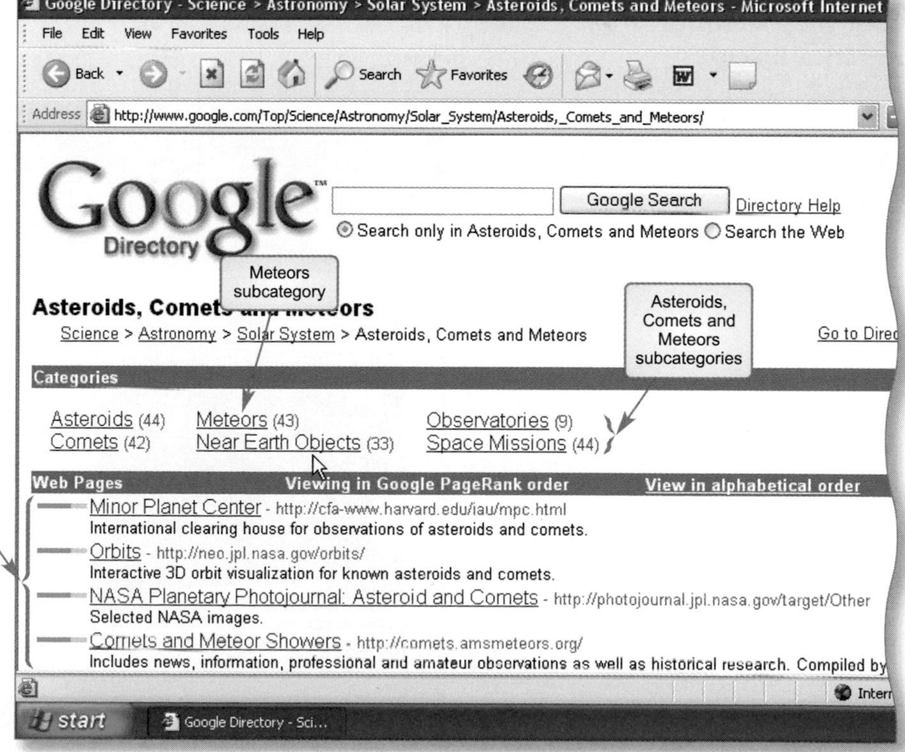

FIGURE 1-47

7

- **Click Meteors to view the listings in the Meteors subcategory.**
- **If necessary, scroll to display the Meteorites from Antarctica link.**

The Google Directory - Science > Astronomy > Solar System > Asteroids, Comets and Meteors > Meteors Web page appears (Figure 1-48). The Meteorites from Antarctica link is displayed in the Web Pages area.

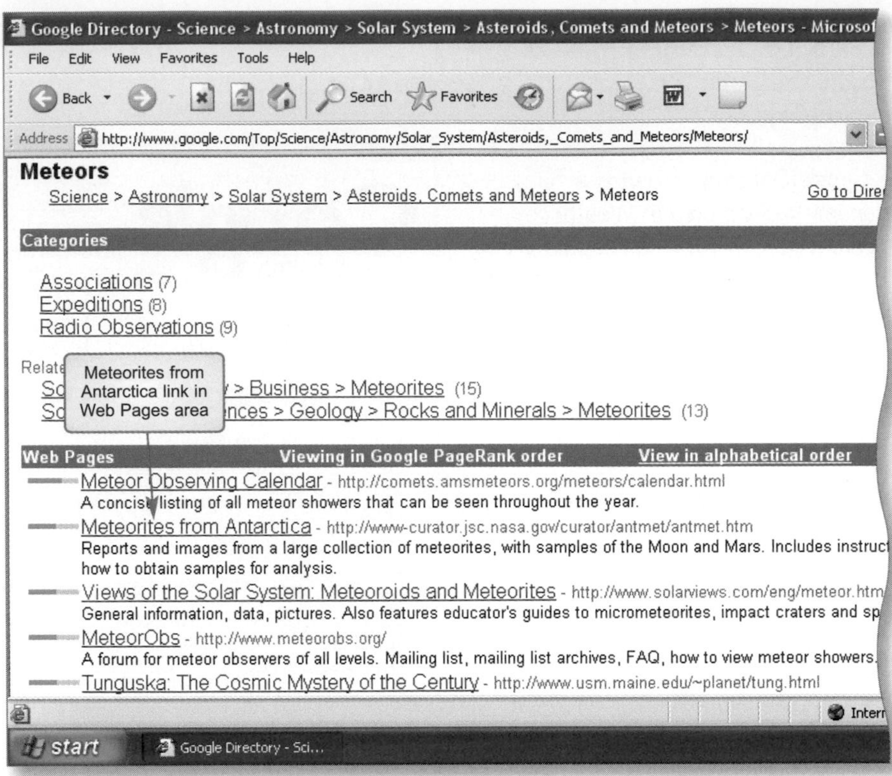

FIGURE 1-48

8

- **Click the Meteorites from Antarctica link.**

The Meteorites from Antarctica Web page containing the Meteorites from Antarctica article appears (Figure 1-49).

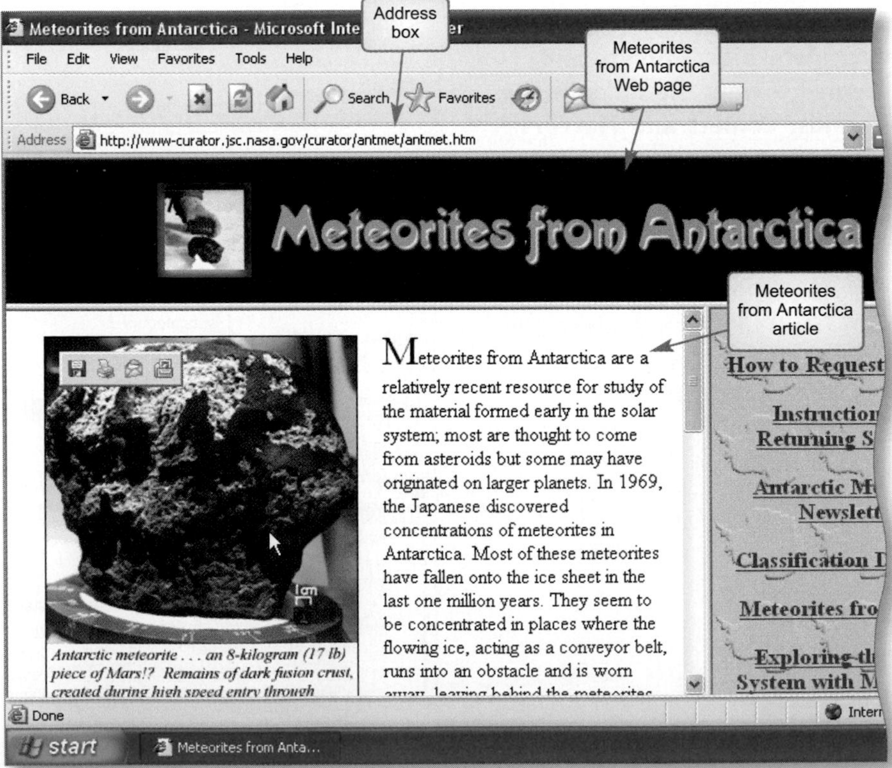

FIGURE 1-49

Searching the Web Using a Keyword System

Previously, this project used the Google Directory to search for information about meteors from Antartica. Using the Address bar also allows you to search for information on the Web. As mentioned previously, this type of search tool is called a Keyword system. A **Keyword system** allows you to enter a name or word on the Address bar to display a list of corresponding Web pages.

You can use the Address bar to type an address (URL) and display the associated Web page or type a keyword or phrase (search inquiry) to display a list of Web pages relating to the keyword or phrase. In addition, you can type a folder location (path) to display the contents of the folder, type an application program name to start a program, and type a document name to start an application and display the document in the application window. Two of these operations are illustrated in the following sections.

Q & A

Q: Can I use Search Companion or Search Assistant to search the Web?

A: Yes, you can use either one. For more information about Search Companion and Search Assistant, visit the Introduction to the World Wide Web Q&A Web page (scsite.com/introweb/qa) and then click Search Companion and Search Assistant.

Using the Address Bar and a Keyword to Display a Home Page

If you type a specific product, trademark, company name, or institution name in the Address box and then click the Go button, MSN Search will search for and display a list of Web pages relating to the entry in the Address box. Any Address box entry that does not end with a .com, .net, .org, .de, or .jp is passed to the Keyword system.

Assume you want information on the University of Michigan, but do not know the university's URL. After entering the phrase, university of michigan, MSN Search searches for and displays a list of Web pages.

The following steps show how to display the home page of the University of Michigan using the Keyword system.

To Search for a Home Page Using the Keyword System

1

• **Click the Address box and then type** `university of michigan` **in the Address box.**

The Address box contains the entry, university of michigan, and the Search for text box below the Address box contains the entry, Search for "university of michigan" (Figure 1-50).

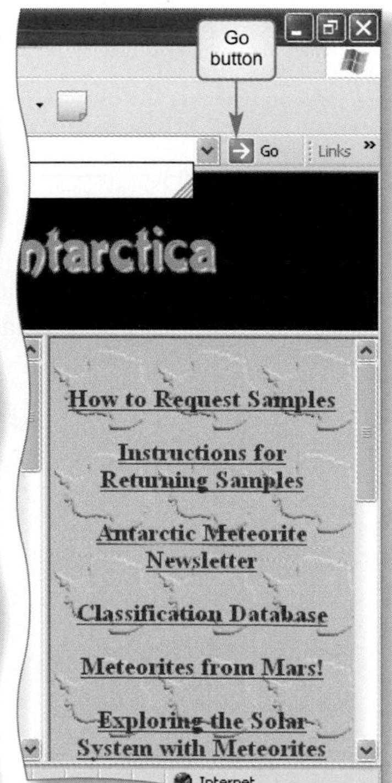

FIGURE 1-50

2

• **Click the Go button.**

Because the university of michigan entry does not have a www. or .com or .org, Internet Explorer sends the keywords (university of michigan) to the Keyword system. The Keyword system matches the keywords to its database of keywords and displays a list of links containing the keywords (Figure 1-51). The University of Michigan link and the www.umich.edu URL identifies the Web page as the home page.

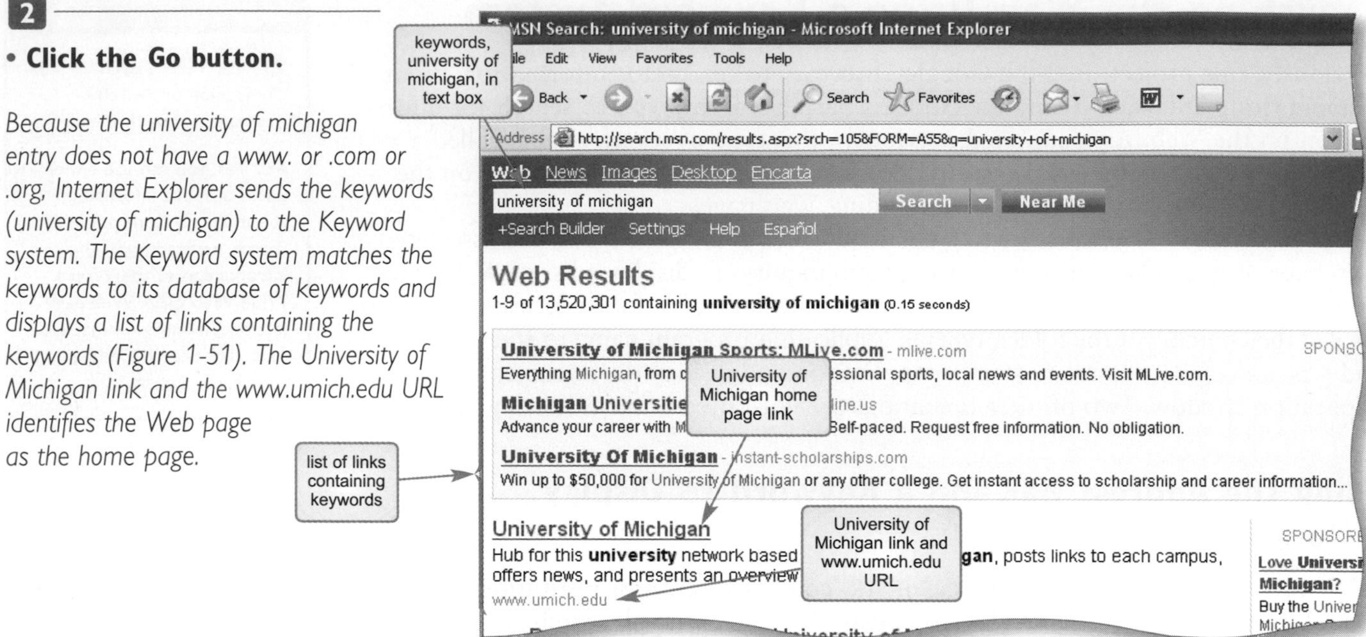

FIGURE 1-51

3

• **Click the University of Michigan link identified by the www.umich.edu URL.**

The University of Michigan home page appears (Figure 1-52).

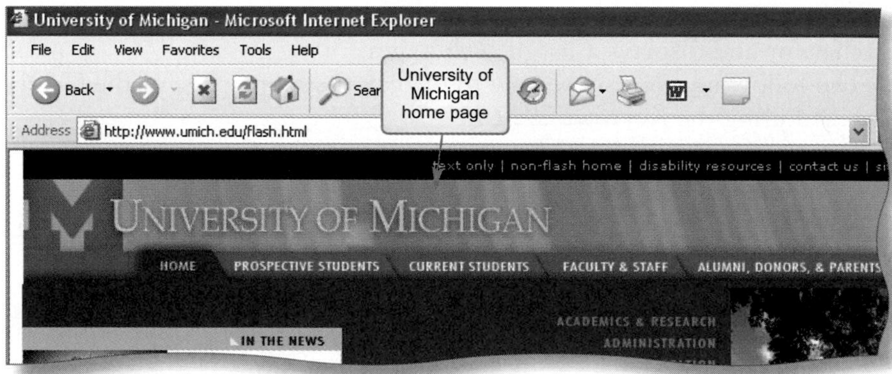

FIGURE 1-52

Because there is only one University of Michigan home page, the Keyword system identifies one Web page as the home page. Thus, this system works well with company names, organization names, association names, and specific products and services.

Using the Address Bar to Display a List of Related Web Pages

More often than not, however, the topic on which you want information is much more general. If you enter a general keyword, such as concerts, home gardening, or construction jobs, the Keyword system passes the keyword to MSN Search, which returns a Web page with several related links from which you can choose. MSN Search is Internet Explorer's default search engine.

As an example, assume you need information on the topic, stem cell research, for a term paper. The following steps show how the Keyword system passes the general topic, stem cell research, to MSN Search, which displays a page of links from which you can choose.

To Search for Related Web Pages Using the Keyword System

1

- **Click the Address box and then type** `stem cell research` **in the Address box.**

The keywords, stem cell research, appear in the Address box, and the Search for text box below the Address box contains the entry, Search for "stem cell research" (Figure 1-53).

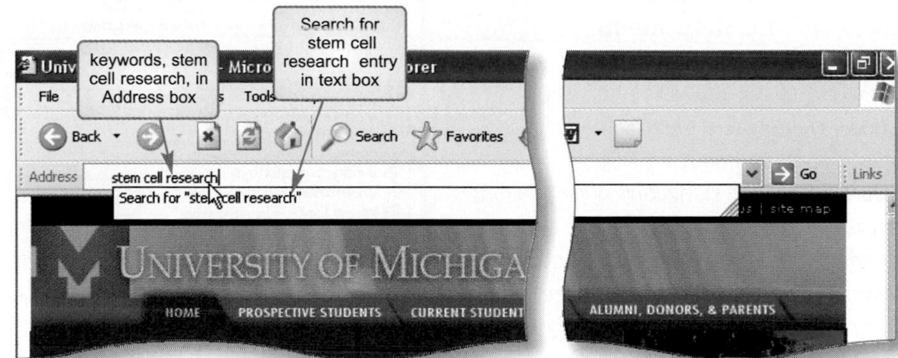

FIGURE 1-53

2

- **Click the Go button.**

Because the keywords, stem cell research, have no specific Web page, the Keyword system passes the entry to MSN Search, which displays a list of related links (Figure 1-54). The window contains several links to other Web pages containing information about stem cell research.

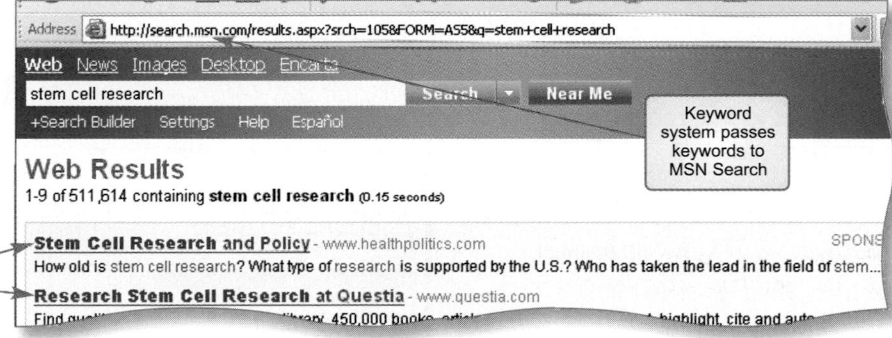

FIGURE 1-54

Internet Explorer Help

Internet Explorer is a program with many features and options. Although you will master some of these features and options quickly, it is not necessary for you to remember everything about each one of them. Reference materials and other forms of assistance are available within **Internet Explorer Help**. You can display these materials and learn how to use the multitude of features available with Internet Explorer. The following steps illustrate how to use Internet Explorer Help to find more information about Uniform Resource Locators (URLs).

To Access Internet Explorer Help

1

- **Click Help on the menu bar.**

The Help menu appears (Figure 1-55). Several commands are available to provide helpful information about Internet Explorer.

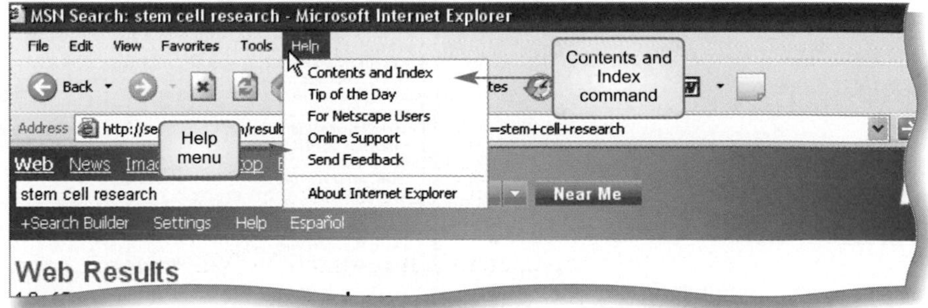

FIGURE 1-55

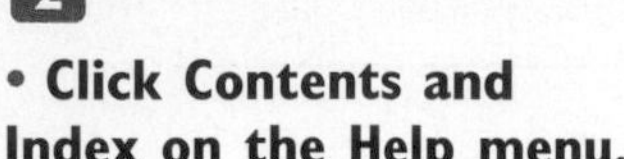

2

• Click Contents and Index on the Help menu.

The Microsoft Internet Explorer window contains the Help toolbar and two panes (Figure 1-56). The navigation pane contains four tabs (Contents, Index, Search, and Favorites) and the display pane contains Help information. The Contents sheet contains topics organized into categories, the Index sheet contains an index of Help topics, the Search sheet allows you to search for specific Help topics, and the Favorites sheet contains a list of favorite Web sites.

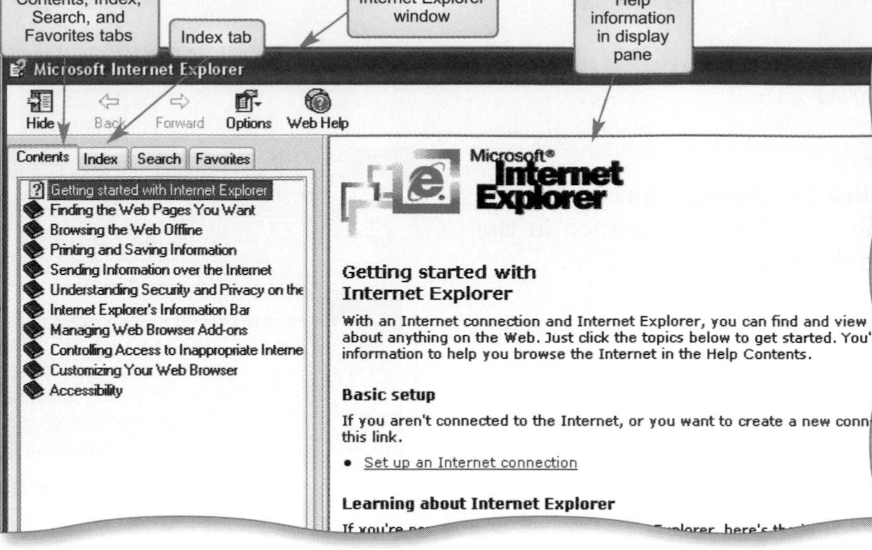

FIGURE 1-56

3

• Click the Index tab in the navigation pane.

The Index sheet appears in the navigation pane (Figure 1-57). The Index sheet contains a text box and a list of Help topics.

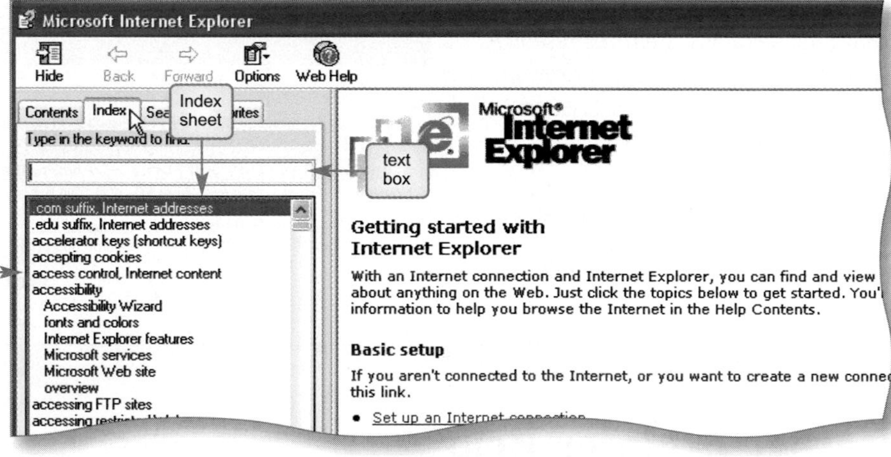

FIGURE 1-57

4

• Type `url` **in the text box in the navigation pane.**

When you type the letters, url, the list automatically scrolls and the first entry beginning with the characters, u-r-l, is highlighted (Figure 1-58). To see additional entries in the list, use the scroll bar at the right of the list. To highlight an entry in the list, click the entry. To view the entry, double-click the entry.

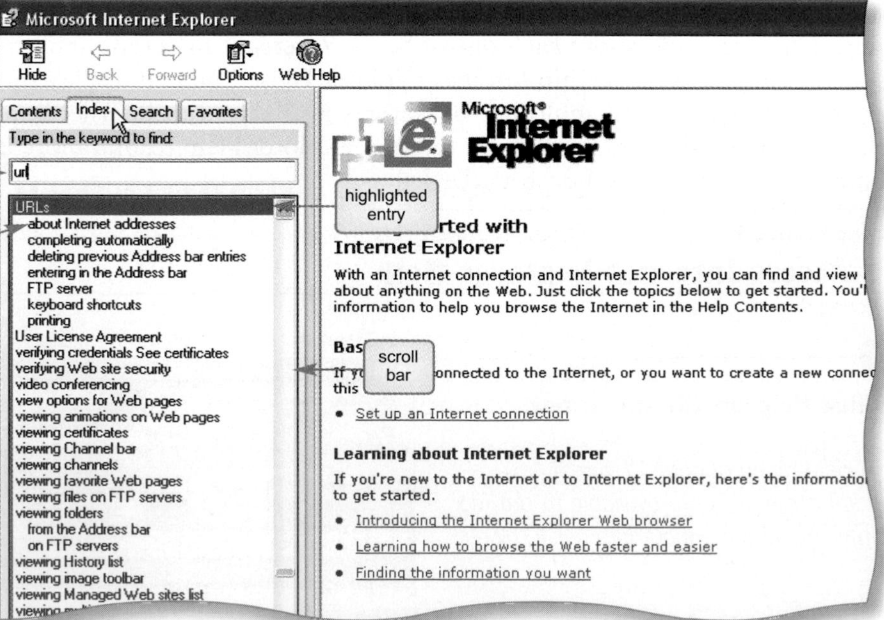

FIGURE 1-58

5

• **Double-click about Internet addresses in the list of Help topics.**

The Understanding Internet addresses Help information appears in the display pane (Figure 1-59). Additional information about Internet addresses can be found by clicking the Related Topics link at the bottom of the screen.

6

• **When you are finished viewing the information, click the Close button on the right side of the title bar to close the Microsoft Internet Explorer window.**

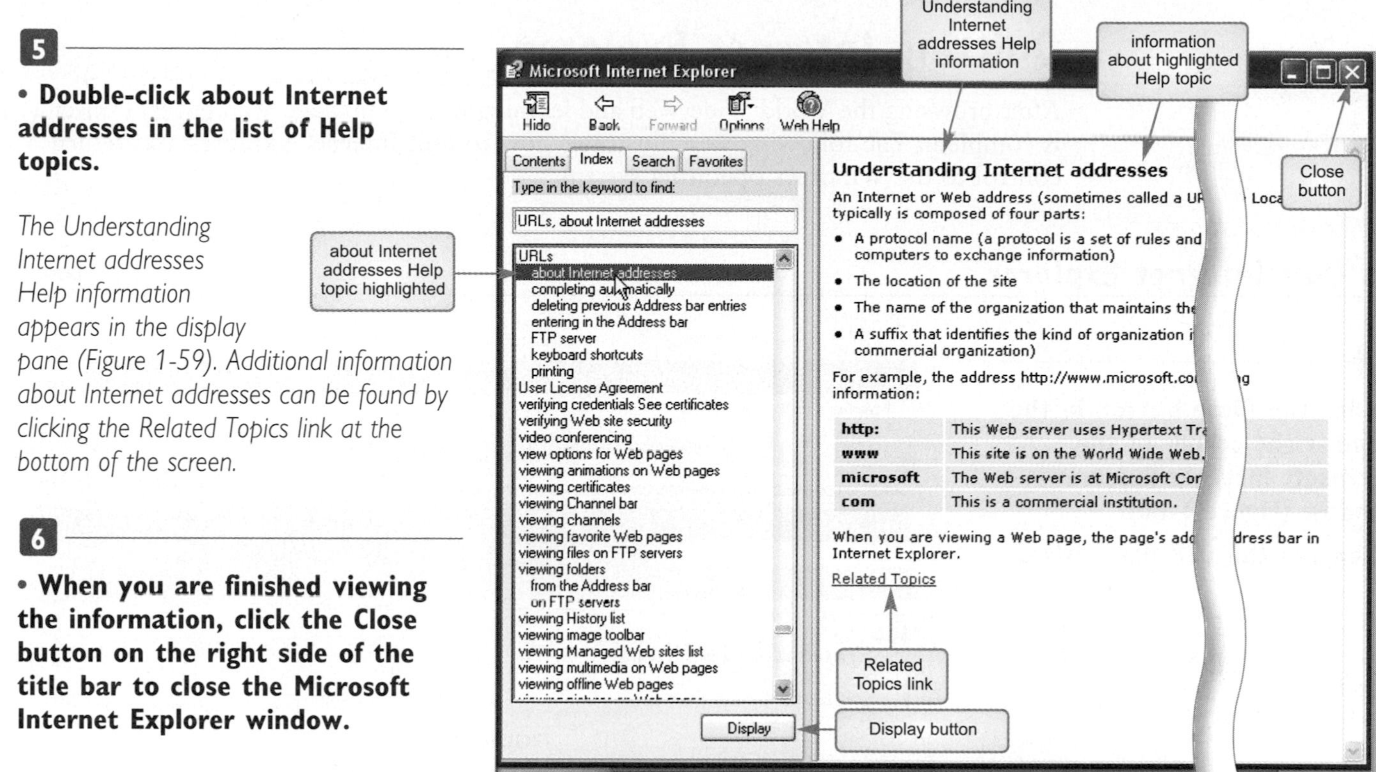

FIGURE 1-59

The Help menu shown in Figure 1-55 on page IE 44 contains several other commands, which are summarized in Table 1-6.

Table 1-6 Commands on the Help Menu

MENU COMMAND	FUNCTION
Contents and Index	Displays Contents, Index, Search, and Favorites tabs.
Tip of the Day	Displays the tip of the day at the bottom of the Microsoft Internet Explorer window. Click the Close button to remove tip.
For Netscape Users	Displays tips for Netscape browser users.
Online Support	Displays Microsoft Product Support Services Web site.
Send Feedback	Displays Contact Us Web site to obtain technical support, ask a question, report a bug, or send comments.
About Internet Explorer	Displays version, cipher strength, product ID, license information, copyright, and acknowledgements about Internet Explorer.

In Figure 1-56 on page WWW 44, buttons on the Help toolbar in the Microsoft Internet Explorer window allow you to perform activities such as hiding the navigation pane, navigating among previously displayed Help topics, changing Internet options, and obtaining Help from the Microsoft Product Support Services Web site. In Figure 1-59, clicking the Display button at the bottom of the navigation pane displays information in the display pane about the highlighted Help topic in the navigation pane.

Quitting Internet Explorer

After browsing the World Wide Web and learning how to manage Web pages, Project 1 is complete. The following step illustrates how to quit Internet Explorer and return control to the Windows operating system.

To Quit Internet Explorer

1

- **Click the Close button in the upper-right corner of the Microsoft Internet Explorer window (Figure 1-60).**
- **Remove the USB flash drive.**

The Microsoft Internet Explorer window closes, and the Windows desktop is displayed.

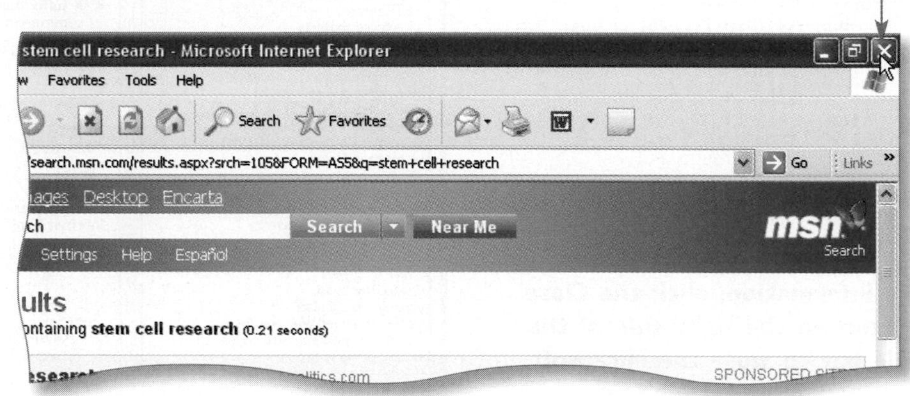

FIGURE 1-60

Project Summary

Project 1 introduced you to the Internet and World Wide Web. You learned how to start Internet Explorer, enter a URL to browse the World Wide Web, find a recently displayed Web page, and use the Favorites list and the buttons on the Standard Buttons toolbar. You learned how to add and remove Web pages on the Favorites list, save and print a document, and save a picture and Web page on a USB flash drive. You learned about the nine general types of Web sites and the three general types of search tools. You searched using the Internet and the Google directory, learned how to use Google simple search, and searched the Web using the Address bar and the Keyword system. In addition, you learned how to use Internet Explorer Help to obtain help.

What You Should Know

Having completed the project, you now should be able to perform the tasks listed below. The tasks are listed in the same order they were presented in this project. For a list of the buttons, menus, toolbars, and commands introduced in this project, see the Quick Reference Summary at the back of this book and refer to the Page Number column.

1. Start Internet Explorer (WWW 8)
2. Browse the Web by Entering a URL (WWW 12)
3. Use the Back and Forward Buttons to Find Recently Displayed Web Pages (WWW 16)
4. Display a Web Page Using the Back Button List (WWW 18)
5. Add a Web Page to the Favorites List (WWW 19)
6. Display the Home Page Using the Home Button (WWW 20)
7. Display a Web Page Using the Favorites List (WWW 21)
8. Remove a Web Page from the Favorites List (WWW 22)
9. Save a Web Page (WWW 24)
10. Save a Picture on a Web Page (WWW 27)
11. Print a Web Page (WWW 28)
12. Display the Google Home Page (WWW 36)
13. Search Using the Google Directory (WWW 37)
14. Search for a Home Page Using the Keyword System (WWW 41)
15. Search for Related Web Pages Using the Keyword System (WWW 43)
16. Access Internet Explorer Help (WWW 44)
17. Quit Internet Explorer (WWW 47)

Learn It Online

Instructions: To complete the Learn It Online exercises, start your browser, click the Address bar, and then enter the Web address scsite.com/introweb/learn. When the Introduction to the World Wide Web Learn It Online page is displayed, follow the instructions in the exercises below. Each exercise has instructions for printing your results, either for your own records or for submission to your instructor.

1 Project Reinforcement TF, MC, and SA

Below Introduction to the World Wide Web, click the Project Reinforcement link. Print the quiz by clicking Print on the File menu for each page. Answer each question.

2 Flash Cards

Click the Flash Cards link and read the instructions. Type 20 (or a number specified by your instructor) in the Number of playing cards text box, type your name in the Enter your Name text box, and then click the Flip Card button. When the flash card is displayed, read the question and then click the ANSWER box arrow to select an answer. Flip through Flash Cards. If your score is 15 (75%) correct or greater, click Print on the File menu to print your results. If your score is less than 15 (75%) correct, then redo this exercise by clicking the Replay button.

3 Practice Test

Click the Practice Test link. Answer each question, enter your first and last name at the bottom of the page, and then click the Grade Test button. When the graded practice test is displayed on your screen, click Print on the File menu to print a hard copy. Continue to take practice tests until you score 80% or better.

4 Who Wants To Be a Computer Genius?

Click the Computer Genius link. Read the instructions, enter your first and last name at the bottom of the page, and then click the PLAY button. When your score is displayed, click the PRINT RESULTS link to print a hard copy.

5 Wheel of Terms

Click the Wheel of Terms link. Read the instructions, and then enter your first and last name and your school name. Click the PLAY button. When your score is displayed, right-click the score and then click Print on the shortcut menu to print a hard copy.

6 Crossword Puzzle Challenge

Click the Crossword Puzzle Challenge link. Read the instructions, and then enter your first and last name. Click the SUBMIT button. Work the crossword puzzle. When you are finished, click the Submit button. When the crossword puzzle is redisplayed, click the Print Puzzle button to print a hard copy.

7 Tips and Tricks

Click the Tips and Tricks link. Click a topic that pertains to Project 1. Right-click the information and then click Print on the shortcut menu. Construct a brief example of what the information relates to in Excel to confirm you understand how to use the tip or trick.

8 Newsgroups

Click the Newsgroups link. Click a topic that pertains to issues regarding the World Wide Web. Print three comments.

9 Expanding Your Horizons

Click the Expanding Your Horizons link. Print the information concerning Internet 2. Construct a brief example of what the information relates to in regards to the World Wide Web to confirm you understand the contents of the article.

10 Making Use of the Web

Click Making Use of the Web. Read 2 of the 15 areas of interest, visit each of the Web sites listed, print the first page of each Web site, and then complete the Web exercises.

11 Scavenger Hunt I

Click Scavenger Hunt I. Print a copy of the Scavenger Hunt I page. Use a search engine to answer the questions. Submit your completed page to your instructor.

12 Scavenger Hunt II

Click Scavenger Hunt II. Print a copy of the Scavenger Hunt II page. Use a search engine to answer the questions. Submit your completed page to your instructor.

13 Search Sleuth I

Click Search Sleuth I to learn more about advanced search techniques. Print a copy of the Search Sleuth I page and then step through the exercises. Submit your answers to your instructor.

14 Search Sleuth II

Click Search Sleuth II to learn more about advanced search techniques. Print a copy of the Search Sleuth II page and then step through the exercises. Submit your answers to your instructor.

Index

Photo Credits

Case Perspective photos, Man pointing at painting on wall in front of people, Courtesy of Manchan/Getty Images; Woman in gallery, smiling, portrait, Courtesy of Mark Scott/Getty Images; Group of high school students using computers in school library, Courtesy of F64/Getty Images; woman reading newspaper in front of computer with flowchart on the screen, Courtesy of Myrleen Ferguson/Photo Edit.

MICROSOFT OFFICE

Word 2003

MICROSOFT OFFICE WORD

MICROSOFT OFFICE
Word 2003

Creating and Editing a Word Document

PROJECT 1

CASE PERSPECTIVE

Teachers and students proclaim the Edison Inventors Competition (EIC) is one of the more rewarding and challenging national high-school competitions. The competition is open to teams of two high-school juniors and seniors. Team members use school grant money to design and build a prototype of an original invention. The invention must benefit a school or a community.

The inventions are judged on their originality, ease of use, and their social, environmental, and/or economic benefit to society. Each member of the winning team receives a $50,000 scholarship, a trophy, and a membership in the Edison Inventors Society. They also receive paid-in-full legal services for patent and other intellectual property matters. Members of 10 finalist teams receive runner-up scholarships, as well as memberships in the Edison Inventors Society.

Teams must be led by a teacher or industry partner. Your computer teacher, Mr. Parker, led last year's winning team. His assignment for each student in his current class is to prepare a one-page flier announcing this year's Edison Inventors Competition. Mr. Parker said the student with the best flier will earn 30 bonus points that can be used at any time during the current school year. The best flier will be posted on every school bulletin board and in local business window fronts. You decide to use thick, bold characters to emphasize the headline and title. To attract attention to the announcement, you plan to include a graphic of a light bulb — to symbolize idea generation.

As you read through this project, you will learn how to use Word to create, save, and print a document that includes an image.

Creating and Editing a Word Document

PROJECT

Objectives

You will have mastered the material in this project when you can:

- Start and quit Word
- Describe the Word window
- Enter text in a document
- Check spelling as you type
- Save a document
- Format text and paragraphs
- Undo and redo commands or actions
- Insert clip art in a document
- Print a document
- Open a document
- Correct errors in a document
- Use Word's Help to answer questions

What Is Microsoft Office Word 2003?

Microsoft Office Word 2003 is a full-featured word processing program that allows you to create professional looking documents and revise them easily. With Word, you can develop announcements, letters, memos, resumes, reports, fax cover sheets, mailing labels, newsletters, and many other types of documents. Word also provides tools that enable you to create Web pages with ease. From within Word, you can place these Web pages directly on a Web server.

Word has many features designed to simplify the production of documents and make documents look visually appealing. Using Word, you easily can change the shape, size, and color of text. You also can include borders, shading, tables, images, pictures, and Web addresses in documents. With proper hardware, you can dictate or handwrite text instead of typing it in Word. You also can speak instructions to Word.

While you are typing, Word performs many tasks automatically. For example, Word detects and corrects spelling and grammar errors in several languages. Word's thesaurus allows you to add variety and precision to your writing. Word also can format text such as headings, lists, fractions, borders, and Web addresses as you type them. Within Word, you can e-mail a copy of a Word document to an e-mail address.

This latest version of Word has many new features to make you more productive. It supports XML documents, improves readability of documents, supports ink input from devices such as the Tablet PC, provides more control for protecting documents, allows two documents to be compared side by side, and includes the capability to search a variety of reference information.

Project One — Inventors Competition Announcement

To illustrate the features of Word, this book presents a series of projects that use Word to create documents similar to those you will encounter in academic and business environments. Project 1 uses Word to produce the announcement shown in Figure 1-1.

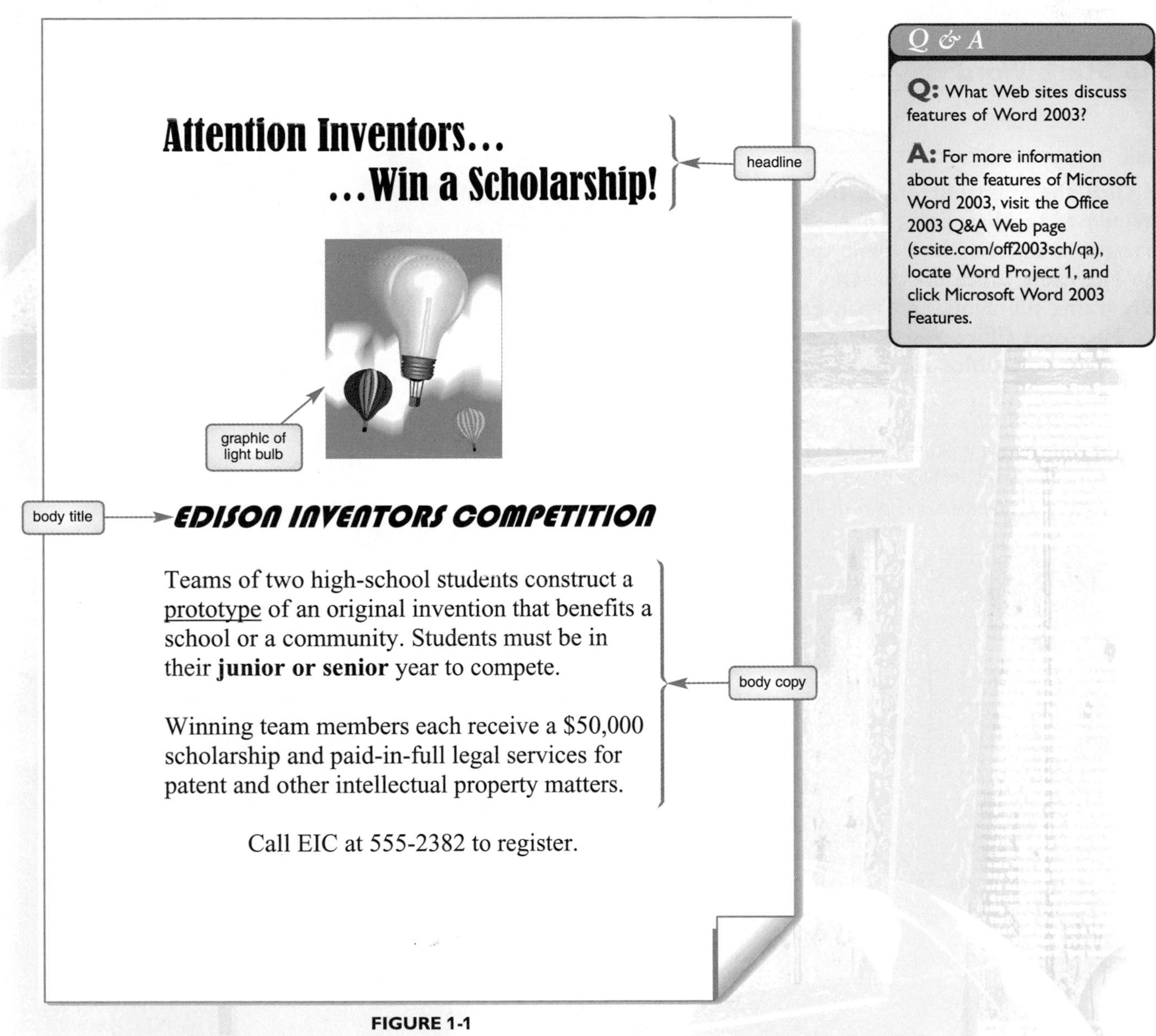

FIGURE 1-1

Q & A

Q: What Web sites discuss features of Word 2003?

A: For more information about the features of Microsoft Word 2003, visit the Office 2003 Q&A Web page (scsite.com/off2003sch/qa), locate Word Project 1, and click Microsoft Word 2003 Features.

The announcement informs current junior and senior high-school students about an inventors competition. The announcement begins with a headline in large, thick characters. Below the headline is a graphic of a light bulb, followed by the body title, EDISON INVENTORS COMPETITION. The paragraphs of body copy below the body title briefly discuss the rules of the competition and the prizes awarded to the winning team. Finally, the last line of the announcement lists the telephone number to register.

Starting and Customizing Word

If you are stepping through this project on a computer and you want your screen to match the figures in this book, then you should change your computer's resolution to 800 × 600. For more information about how to change the resolution on your computer, read Appendix D.

To start Word, Windows must be running. The following steps show how to start Word. You may need to ask your instructor how to start Word for your system.

To Start Word

1

- **Click the Start button on the Windows taskbar, point to All Programs on the Start menu, point to Microsoft Office on the All Programs submenu, and then point to Microsoft Office Word 2003 on the Microsoft Office submenu.**

Windows displays the commands on the Start menu above the Start button and then displays the All Programs and Microsoft Office submenus (Figure 1-2).

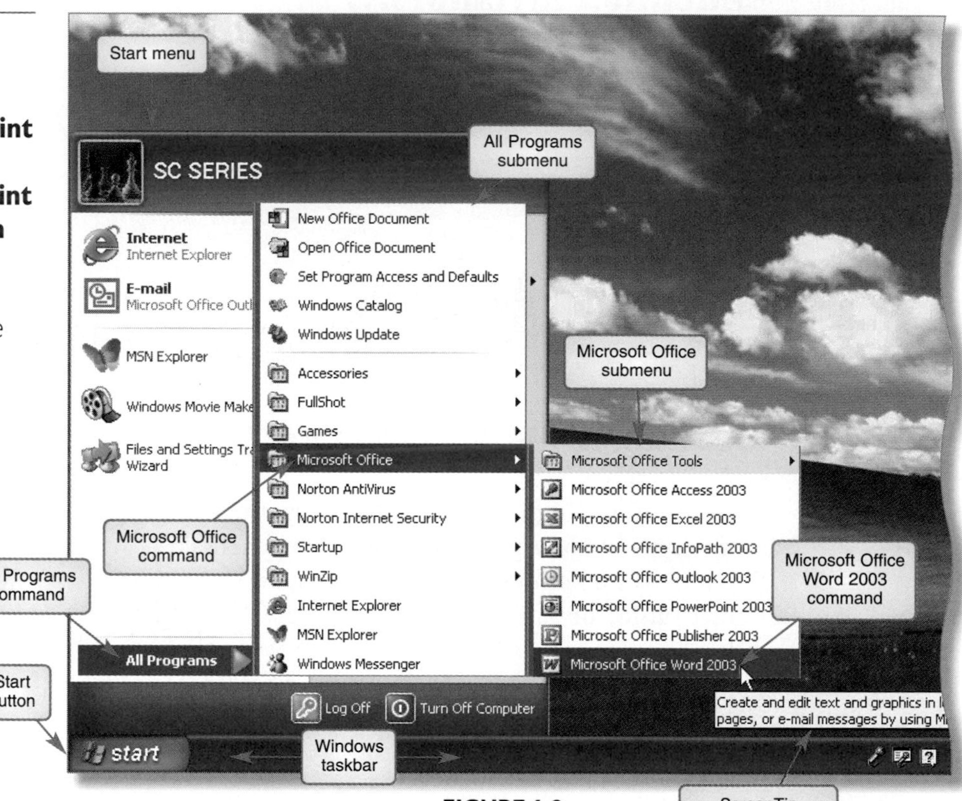

FIGURE 1-2

2

• **Click Microsoft Office Word 2003.**

Word starts. After a few moments, Word displays a new blank document titled Document1 in the Word window (Figure 1-3). The Windows taskbar displays the Word program button, indicating Word is running.

3

• **If the Word window is not maximized, double-click its title bar to maximize it.**

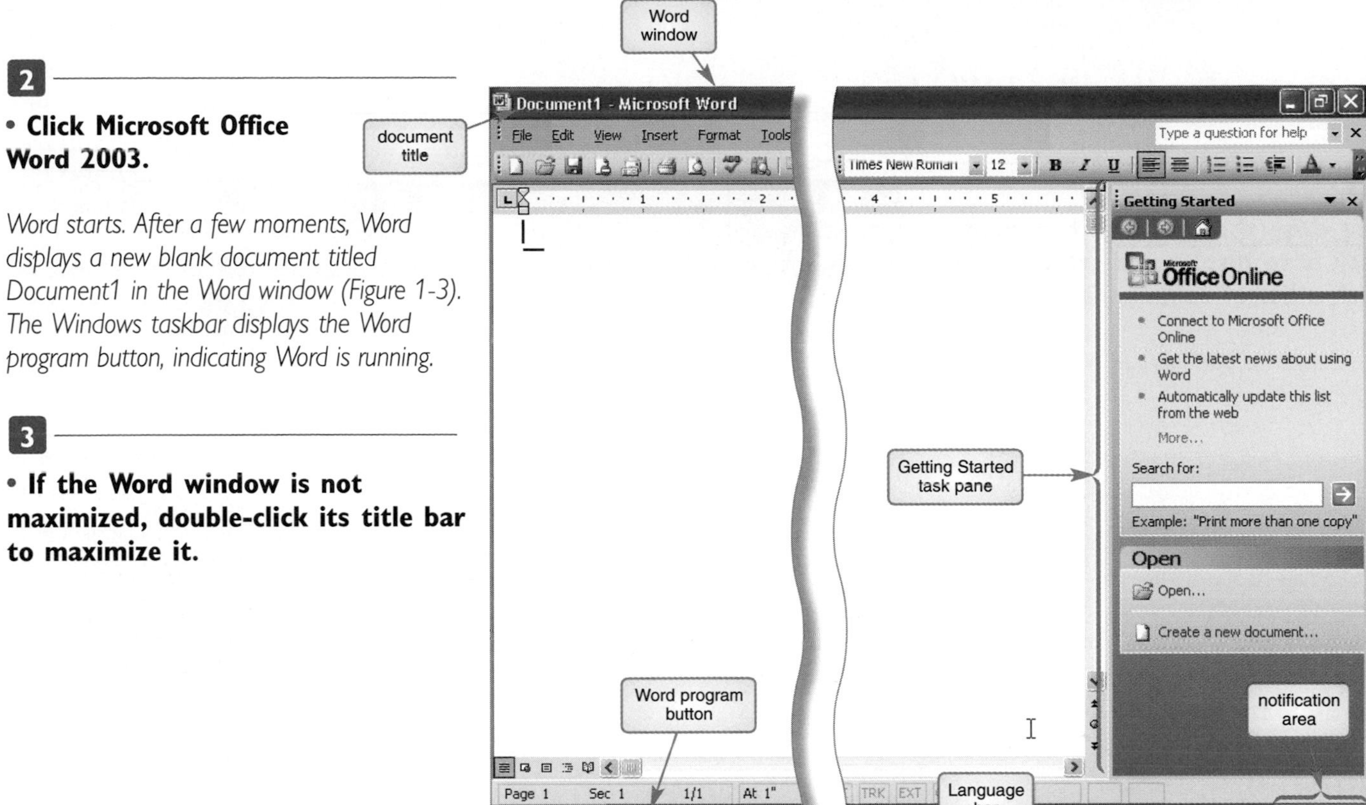

FIGURE 1-3

The screen in Figure 1-3 shows how the Word window looks the first time you start Word after installation on most computers. If the Office Speech Recognition software is installed and active on your computer, then when you start Word the Language bar is displayed on the screen. The **Language bar** contains buttons that allow you to speak commands and dictate text. It usually is located on the right side of the Windows taskbar next to the notification area, and it changes to include the speech recognition functions available in Word. In this book, the Language bar is closed because it takes up computer resources and with the Language bar active, the microphone can be turned on accidentally by clicking the Microphone button, causing your computer to act in an unstable manner. For additional information about the Language bar, see page WD 16 and Appendix B.

As shown in Figure 1-3, Word may display a task pane on the right side of the screen. A **task pane** is a separate window that enables users to carry out some Word tasks more efficiently. When you start Word, it automatically may display the Getting Started task pane, which is a task pane that allows you to search for Office-related topics on the Microsoft Web site, open files, or create new documents. In this book, the Getting Started task pane is closed to allow the maximum typing area in Word.

After installation, Word displays the toolbar buttons on a single row. A **toolbar** contains buttons and boxes that allow you to perform frequent tasks quickly. For more efficient use of the buttons, the toolbars should be displayed on two separate rows instead of sharing a single row.

The steps on the next page show how to customize the Word window by closing the Language bar, closing the Getting Started task pane, and displaying the toolbar buttons on two separate rows.

To Customize the Word Window

1

- **To close the Language bar, right-click it to display a shortcut menu with a list of commands.**

The Language bar shortcut menu appears (Figure 1-4).

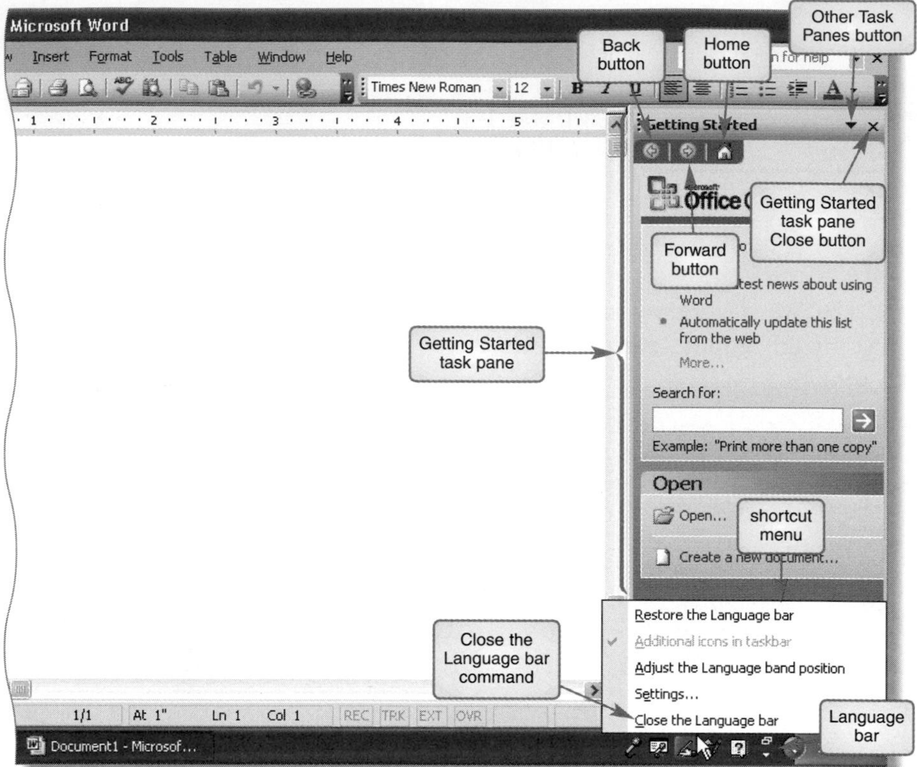

FIGURE 1-4

2

- **Click Close the Language bar on the shortcut menu.**
- **If the Getting Started task pane is displayed, click the Close button in the upper-right corner of the task pane.**

The Language bar disappears. Word removes the Getting Started task pane from the screen (Figure 1-5).

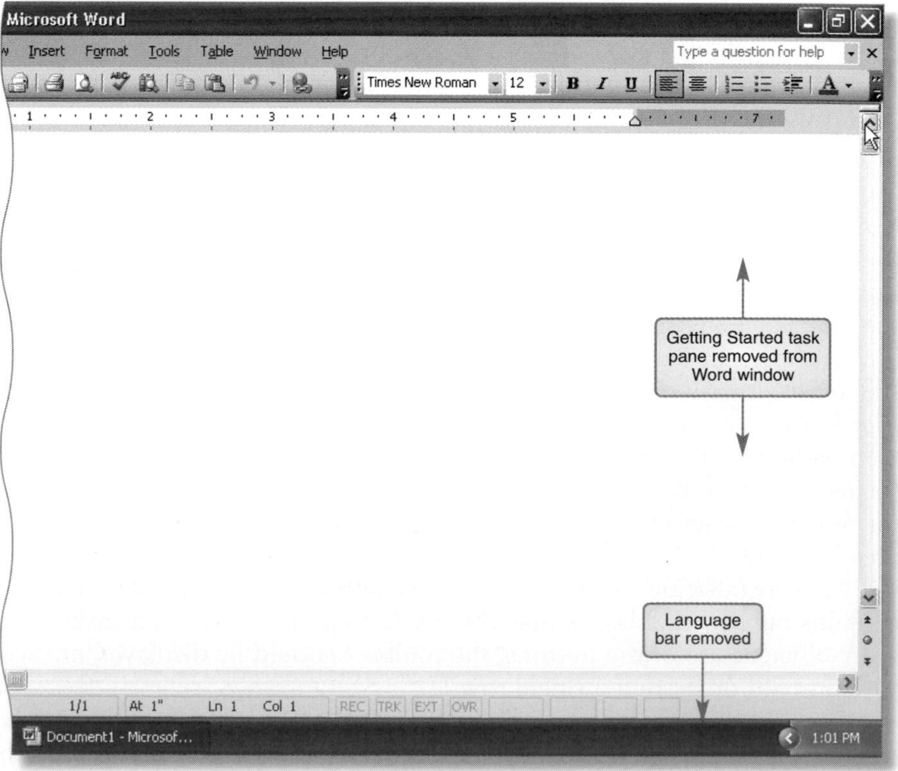

FIGURE 1-5

3

- **If the toolbar buttons are displayed on one row, click the Toolbar Options button.**

Word displays the Toolbar Options list, which shows the buttons that do not fit on the toolbars when they are displayed on one row (Figure 1-6).

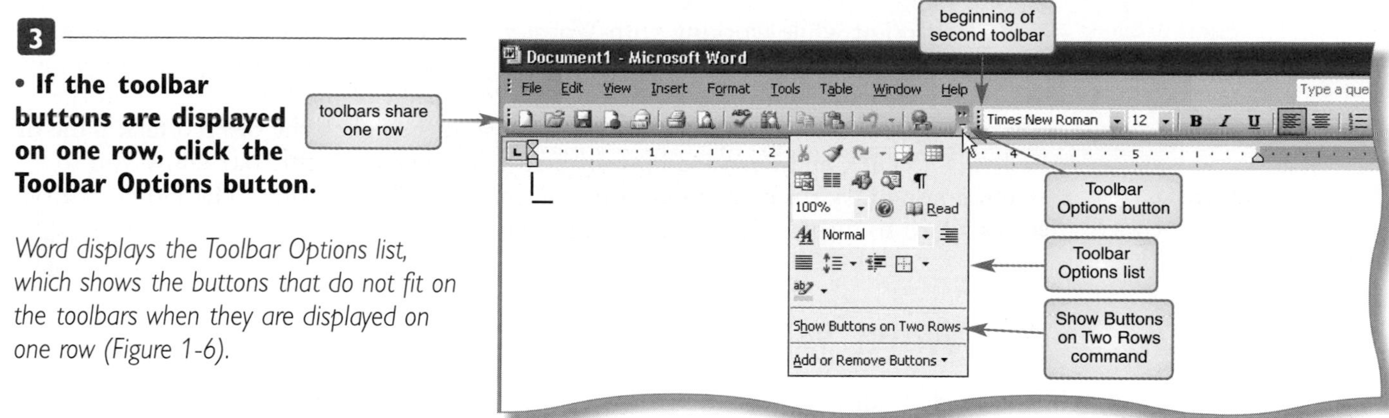

FIGURE 1-6

4

- **Click Show Buttons on Two Rows in the Toolbar Options list.**
- **If your screen differs from Figure 1-7, click the Normal View button on the horizontal scroll bar.**

Word displays the toolbars on two separate rows (Figure 1-7). The Toolbar Options list now is empty because all of the buttons fit on the toolbars when they display on two rows.

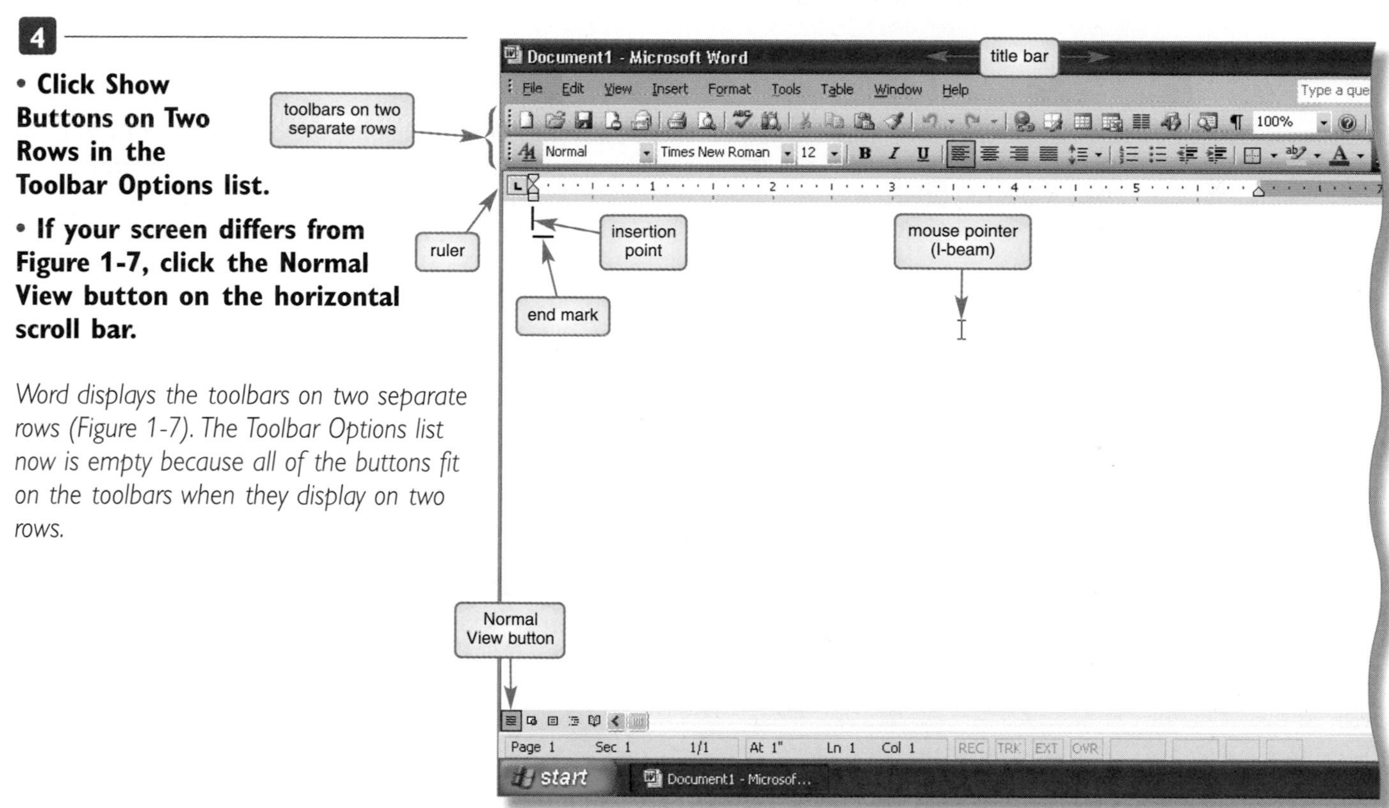

FIGURE 1-7

As an alternative to Steps 3 and 4 above, you can point to the beginning of the second toolbar (Figure 1-6), and when the mouse pointer changes to a four-headed arrow, drag the toolbar down to create two rows of toolbars.

Each time you start Word, the Word window appears the same way it did the last time you used Word. If the toolbar buttons are displayed on one row, then they will be displayed on one row the next time you start Word.

As you work through creating a document, you will find that certain Word operations automatically display a task pane. In addition to the Getting Started task pane shown in Figure 1-4, Word provides 13 other task panes. Some of the more important ones are the Help, Clip Art, Clipboard, and Research task panes. These task panes are discussed as they are used throughout the book.

At any point while working with Word, you can open or close a task pane by clicking View on the menu bar and then clicking Task Pane. To display a different task pane, click the Other Task Panes button to the left of the Close button on the task pane title bar (Figure 1-4 on page WD 8) and then click the desired task pane in the list. The Back and Forward buttons below the task pane title bar allow you to switch among task panes you have opened during a Word session. The Home button causes Word to display the Getting Started task pane.

The Word Window

The Word window consists of a variety of components to make your work more efficient and documents more professional. The following sections discuss these components, which are identified in either Figure 1-7 on the previous page or Figure 1-8.

Document Window

The **document window** displays text, tables, graphics, and other items as you type or insert them in a document. Only a portion of a document, however, appears on the screen at one time. You view the portion of the document displayed on the screen through a document window (Figure 1-8).

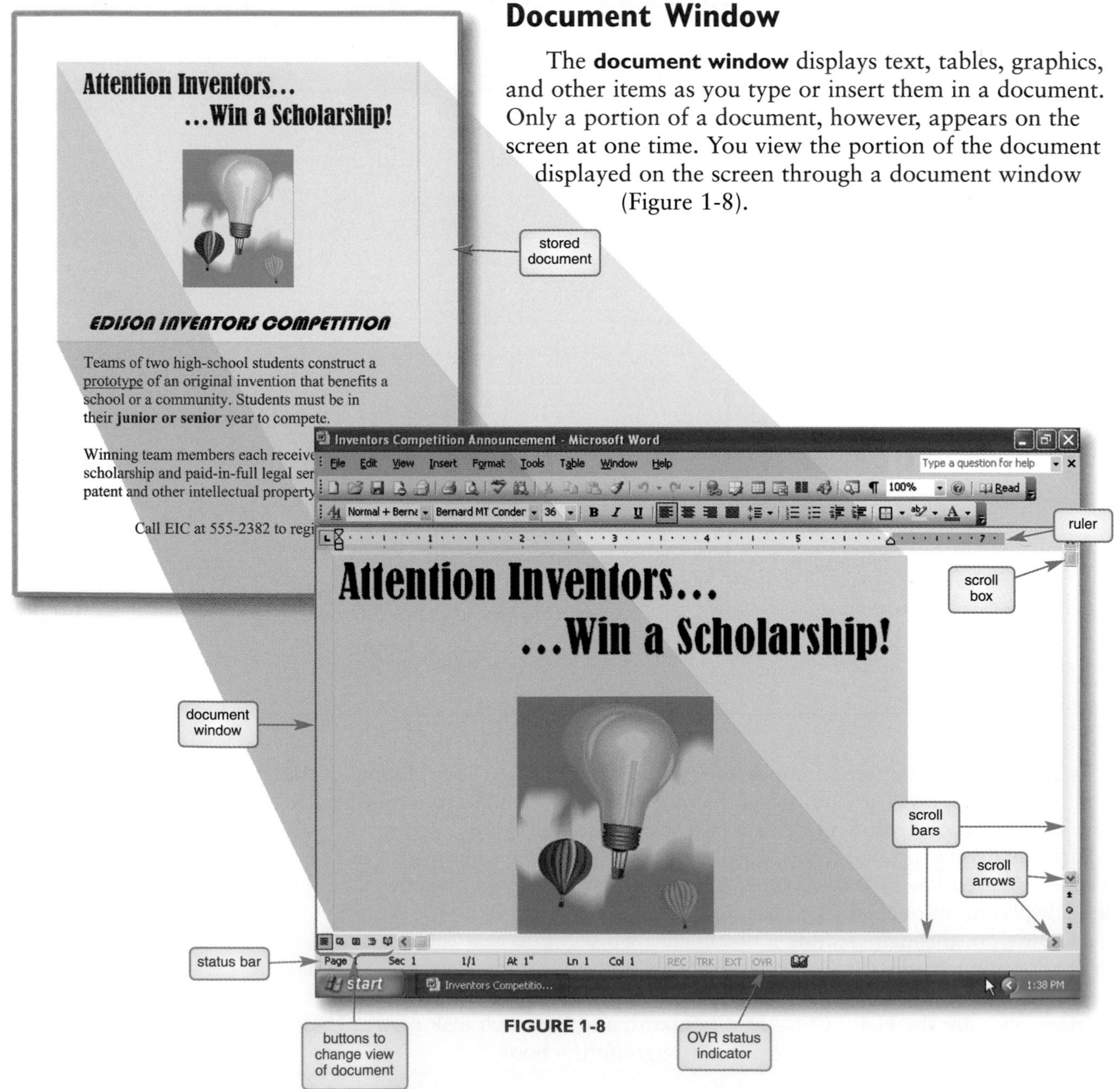

FIGURE 1-8

A document window contains several elements commonly found in other application software, as well as some elements unique to Word. The main elements of the Word document window are the insertion point, end mark, mouse pointer, rulers, scroll bars, and status bar.

INSERTION POINT The **insertion point** (Figure 1-7 on page WD 9) is a blinking vertical bar that indicates where text will be inserted as you type. As you type, the insertion point moves to the right and, when you reach the end of a line, it moves downward to the beginning of the next line. You also insert graphics, tables, and other items at the location of the insertion point.

END MARK The **end mark** (Figure 1-7) is a short horizontal line that indicates the end of the document. Each time you begin a new line, the end mark moves downward.

MOUSE POINTER The **mouse pointer** becomes different shapes depending on the task you are performing in Word and the pointer's location on the screen (Figure 1-7). The mouse pointer in Figure 1-7 has the shape of an I-beam. Other mouse pointer shapes are described as they appear on the screen during this and subsequent projects.

RULERS At the top edge of the document window is the horizontal ruler (Figure 1-8). You use the **horizontal ruler**, usually simply called the **ruler**, to set tab stops, indent paragraphs, adjust column widths, and change page margins.

An additional ruler, called the **vertical ruler**, sometimes is displayed at the left edge of the Word window when you perform certain tasks. The purpose of the vertical ruler is discussed in a later project. If your screen displays a vertical ruler, click View on the menu bar and then click Normal.

SCROLL BARS By using the **scroll bars**, you display different portions of your document in the document window (Figure 1-8). At the right edge of the document window is a vertical scroll bar. At the bottom of the document window is a horizontal scroll bar. On both the vertical and horizontal scroll bars, the position of the **scroll box** reflects the location of the portion of the document that is displayed in the document window.

On the left edge of the horizontal scroll bar are five buttons that change the view of a document. On the bottom of the vertical scroll bar are three buttons you can use to scroll through a document. These buttons are discussed as they are used in later projects.

STATUS BAR The **status bar** displays at the bottom of the document window, above the Windows taskbar (Figure 1-8). The status bar presents information about the location of the insertion point and the progress of current tasks, as well as the status of certain commands, keys, and buttons.

From left to right, Word displays the following information on the status bar in Figure 1-8: the page number, the section number, the page containing the insertion point followed by the total number of pages in the document, the position of the insertion point in inches from the top of the page, the line number and column number of the insertion point, and then several status indicators.

Q & A

Q: What if the horizontal ruler is not on the screen?

A: If the horizontal ruler is not displayed on your screen, click View on the menu bar and then click Ruler. To hide the ruler, also click View on the menu bar and then click Ruler.

You use the **status indicators** to turn certain keys or modes on or off. Word displays the first four status indicators (REC, TRK, EXT, and OVR) darkened when they are on and dimmed when they are off. For example, the dimmed OVR indicates overtype mode is off. To turn these four status indicators on or off, double-click the status indicator on the status bar. Each of these status indicators is discussed as it is used in the projects.

The remaining status indicators display icons as you perform certain tasks. For example, when you begin typing in the document window, Word displays a Spelling and Grammar Status icon. When Word is saving your document, it displays a Background Save icon. When you print a document, Word displays a Background Print icon. If you perform a task that requires several seconds (such as saving a document), the status bar usually displays a message informing you of the progress of the task.

Menu Bar and Toolbars

The menu bar and toolbars display at the top of the screen just below the title bar (Figure 1-9).

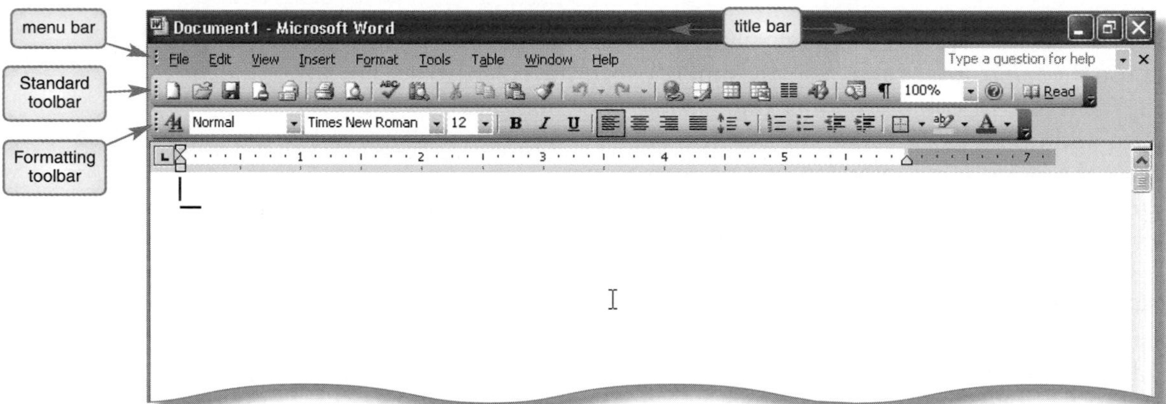

FIGURE 1-9

MENU BAR The **menu bar** is a special toolbar that displays the Word menu names. Each menu name represents a menu. A **menu** contains a list of commands you use to perform tasks such as retrieving, storing, printing, and formatting data in a document.

When you point to a menu name on the menu bar, the area of the menu bar containing the name is displayed as a selected button. Word shades selected buttons in light orange and surrounds them with a blue outline.

To display a menu, click the menu name on the menu bar. For example, to display the Edit menu, click the Edit menu name on the menu bar. When you click a menu name on the menu bar, Word initially displays a **short menu** listing your most recently used commands (Figure 1-10a). If you wait a few seconds or click the arrows at the bottom of the short menu, it expands into a full menu. A **full menu** lists all the commands associated with a menu (Figure 1-10b). You also can display a full menu immediately by double-clicking the menu name on the menu bar.

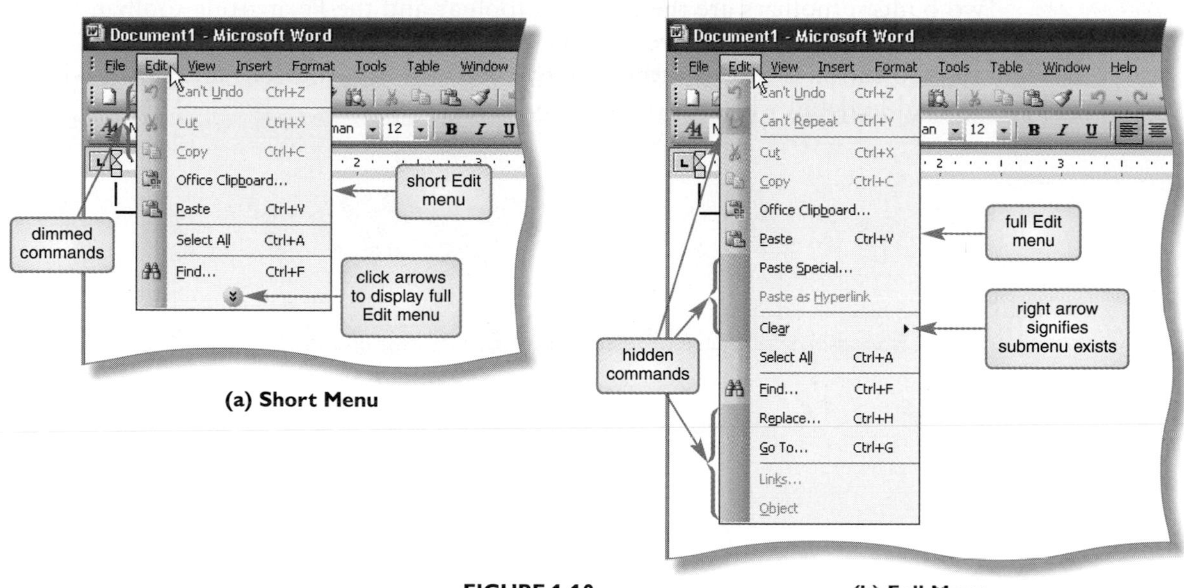

(a) Short Menu

FIGURE 1-10

(b) Full Menu

In this book, when you display a menu, use one of the following techniques to ensure that Word always displays a full menu:

1. Click the menu name on the menu bar and then wait a few seconds.
2. Click the menu name on the menu bar and then click the arrows at the bottom of the short menu.
3. Click the menu name on the menu bar and then point to the arrows at the bottom of the short menu.
4. Double-click the menu name on the menu bar.

Both short and full menus may display some dimmed commands. A **dimmed command** appears gray, or dimmed, instead of black, which indicates it is not available for the current selection. A command with medium blue shading in the rectangle to its left on a full menu is called a **hidden command** because it does not appear on a short menu. As you use Word, it automatically personalizes the short menus for you based on how often you use commands. That is, as you use hidden commands on the full menu, Word *unhides* them and places them on the short menu.

Some commands have an arrow at the right edge of the menu. If you point to this arrow, Word displays a **submenu**, which is a list of additional commands associated with the selected command.

TOOLBARS Word has many predefined, or built-in, toolbars. A toolbar contains buttons, boxes, and menus that allow you to perform tasks more quickly than using the menu bar. For example, to print a document, you can click the Print button on a toolbar instead of navigating through the File menu to reach the Print command.

Each button on a toolbar displays an image to help you remember its function. Also, when you position the mouse pointer on, or point to, a button or box, Word displays the name of the button or box in a ScreenTip. A **ScreenTip** is a short on-screen note associated with the object to which you are pointing.

Two built-in toolbars are the Standard toolbar and the Formatting toolbar. Figure 1-11a shows the **Standard toolbar** and identifies its buttons and boxes. Figure 1-11b shows the **Formatting toolbar**. Each of these buttons and boxes will be explained in detail when it is used in this book.

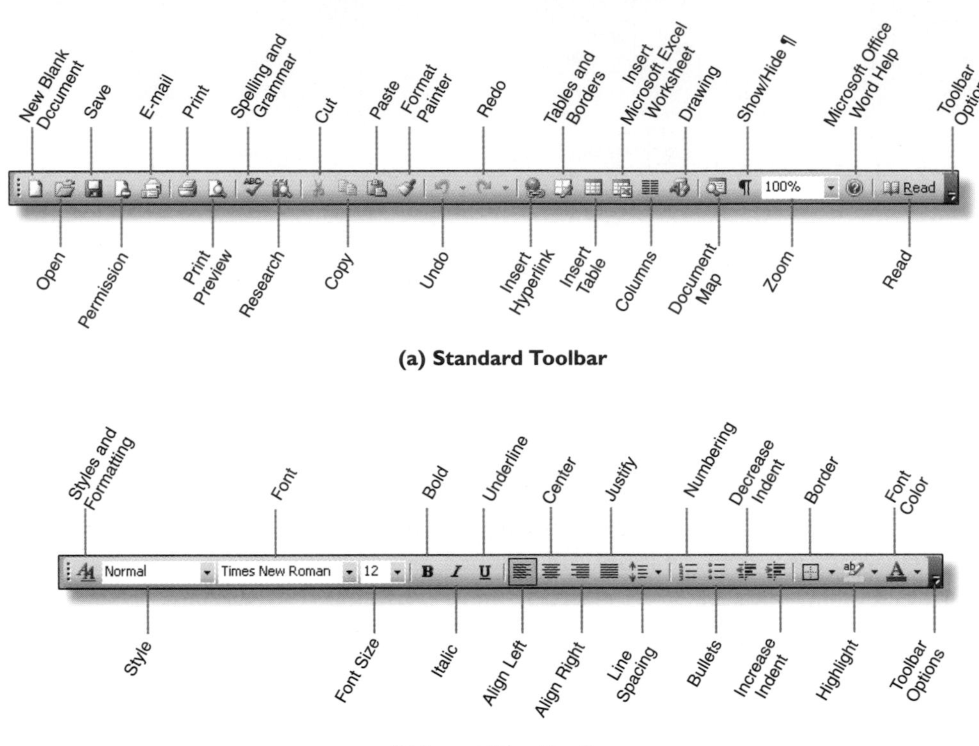

(a) Standard Toolbar

(b) Formatting Toolbar

FIGURE 1-11

When you first install Word, the buttons on both the Standard and Formatting toolbars are preset to display on the same row immediately below the menu bar (Figure 1-12a). Unless the resolution of your display device is greater than 800 × 600, many of the buttons that belong to these toolbars are hidden when the two toolbars share one row. The buttons that display on the toolbar are the more frequently used buttons. Hidden buttons display in the Toolbar Options list (Figure 1-12b). You can display all the buttons on either toolbar by double-clicking the **move handle**, which is the vertical dotted line on the left edge of the toolbar.

As an alternative, you can instruct Word to display the buttons on the Standard and Formatting toolbars on separate rows, one below the other, by clicking the Show Buttons on Two Rows command in the Toolbar Options list (Figure 1-12b). In this book, the Standard and Formatting toolbars are shown on separate rows so that all buttons are displayed on a screen with the resolution set to 800 × 600 (Figure 1-12c).

In the previous figures, the Standard and Formatting toolbars are docked. A **docked toolbar** is a toolbar that is attached to an edge of the Word window. Depending on the task you are performing, Word may display additional toolbars on the screen. These additional toolbars either are docked or floating in the Word window. A **floating toolbar** is not attached to an edge of the Word window; that is, it appears in the middle of the Word window. You can rearrange the order of docked toolbars and can move floating toolbars anywhere in the Word window. Later in this book, steps are presented that show you how to float a docked toolbar or dock a floating toolbar.

Q & A

Q: Need help with Word?

A: Help with Word is no further away than the Type a question for help box on the menu bar in the upper-right corner of the window. Click the box that contains the text, Type a question for help (Figure 1-12c), type `help`, and then press the ENTER key. Word responds with a list of topics you can click to learn about obtaining help on any Word-related topic. To find out what is new in Word 2003, type `what is new in Word` in the Type a question for help box.

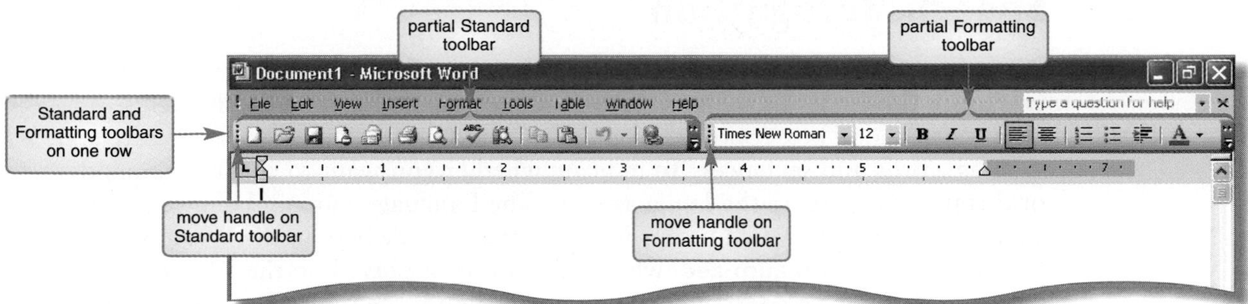

(a) Standard and Formatting Toolbars on One Row

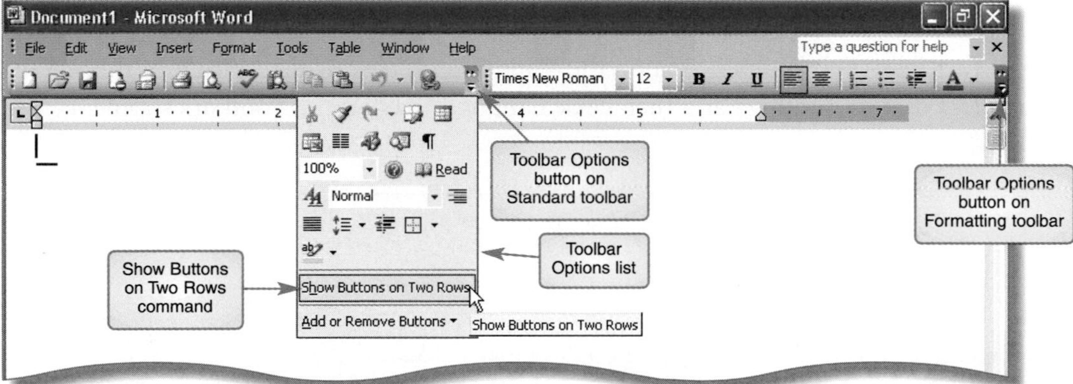

(b) Toolbar Options List

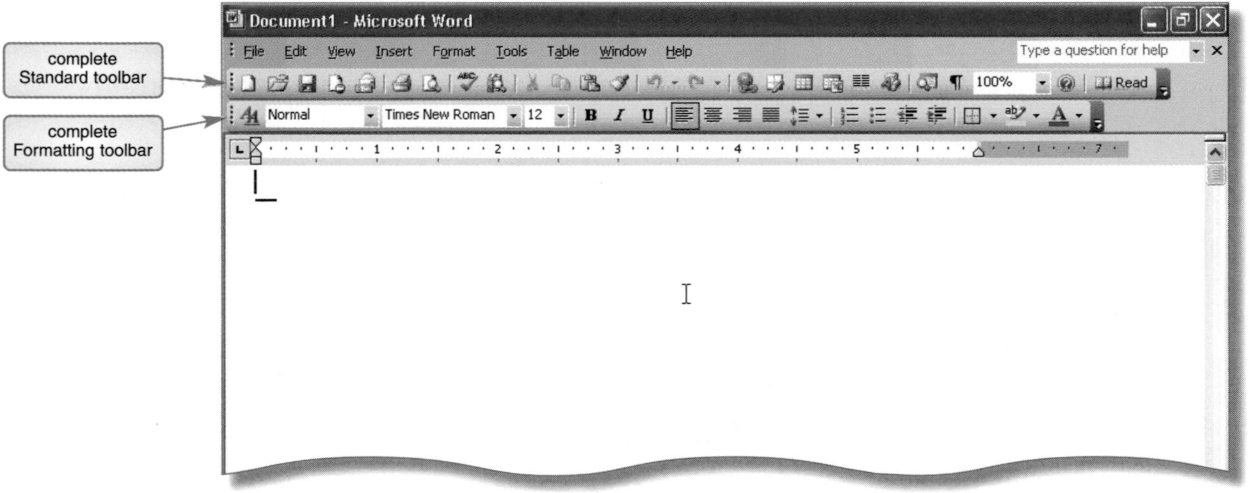

(c) Standard and Formatting Toolbars on Two Rows

FIGURE 1-12

Resetting Menus and Toolbars

Each project in this book begins with the menus and toolbars appearing as they did at the initial installation of the software. If you are stepping through this project on a computer and you want your menus and toolbars to match the figures in this book, then you should reset your menus and toolbars. For more information about how to reset menus and toolbars, read Appendix D.

Speech Recognition

With the **Office Speech Recognition software** installed and a microphone, you can speak the names of toolbar buttons, menus, menu commands, list items, alerts, and dialog box controls, such as OK and Cancel. You also can dictate text, such as words and sentences. To indicate whether you want to speak commands or dictate text, you use the Language bar. The Language bar can be in one of four states: (1) **restored**, which means it is displayed somewhere in the Word window (Figure 1-13a); (2) **minimized**, which means it is displayed on the Windows taskbar (Figure 1-13b); (3) **hidden**, which means you do not see it on the screen but it will be displayed the next time you start your computer; or (4) **closed**, which means it is hidden permanently until you enable it. If the Language bar is hidden and you want it to be displayed, then do the following:

1. Right-click an open area on the Windows taskbar at the bottom of the screen.
2. Point to Toolbars and then click Language bar on the Toolbars submenu.

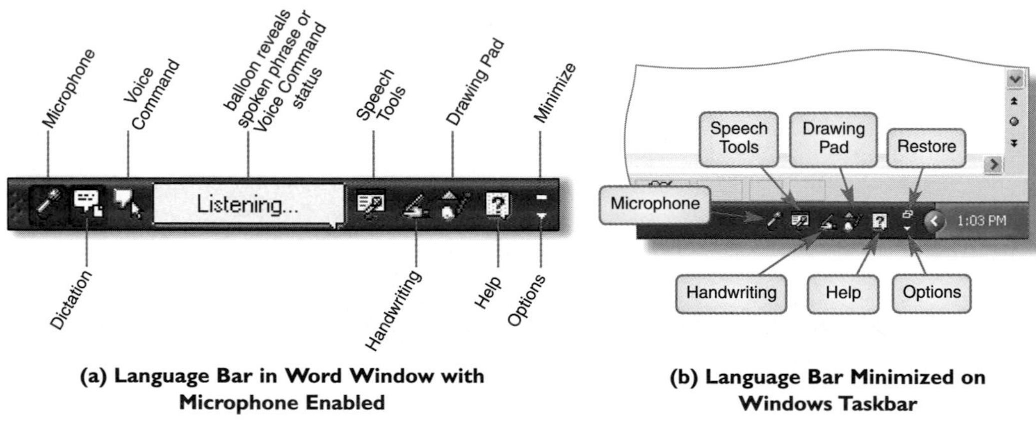

(a) Language Bar in Word Window with Microphone Enabled

(b) Language Bar Minimized on Windows Taskbar

FIGURE 1-13

If the Language bar command is dimmed on the Toolbars submenu or if the Speech command is dimmed on the Tools menu, the Office Speech Recognition software is not installed.

In this book, the Language bar does not appear in the figures. If you want to close the Language bar so that your screen is identical to what you see in the book, right-click the Language bar and then click Close the Language bar on the shortcut menu. Additional information about the speech recognition capabilities of Word is available in Appendix B.

Q & A

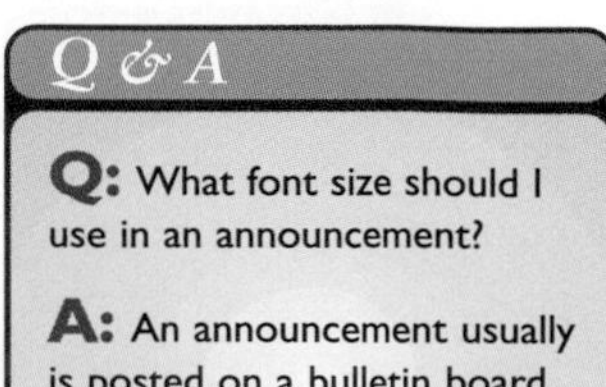

Q: What font size should I use in an announcement?

A: An announcement usually is posted on a bulletin board. Thus, its font size should be as large as possible so that all potential readers easily can see the announcement.

Entering Text

Characters that display on the screen are a specific shape, size, and style. The **font**, or typeface, defines the appearance and shape of the letters, numbers, and special characters. The preset, or **default**, font is Times New Roman (Figure 1-14). **Font size** specifies the size of the characters and is determined by a measurement system called points. A single **point** is about 1/72 of one inch in height. Thus, a character with a font size of 12 is about 12/72 or 1/6 of one inch in height. On most computers, the default font size in Word is 12.

If more of the characters in your document require a larger font size than the default, you easily can change the font size before you type. In Project 1, many of the characters in the body copy of the announcement are a font size of 22. The following steps show how to increase the font size before you begin typing text.

To Increase the Font Size before Typing

1

- **Click the Font Size box arrow on the Formatting toolbar.**

Word displays a list of available font sizes in the Font Size list (Figure 1-14). The available font sizes depend on the current font, which is Times New Roman.

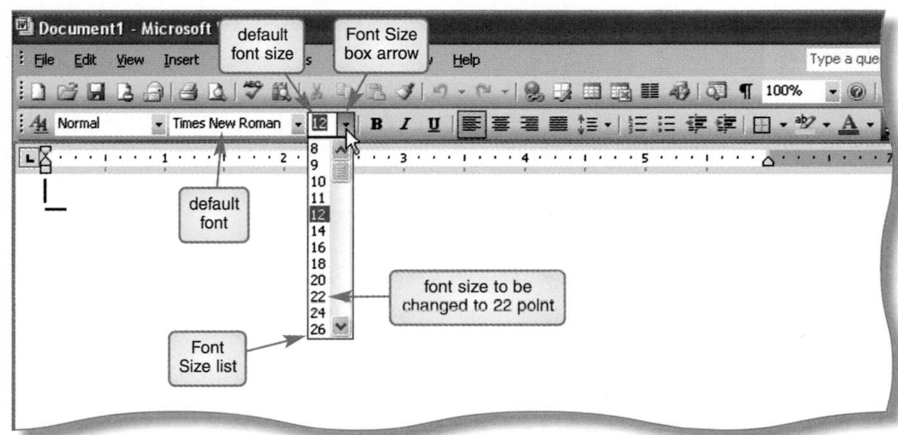

FIGURE 1-14

2

- **Click 22 in the Font Size list.**

The font size for characters to be entered in this document changes to 22 (Figure 1-15). The size of the insertion point increases to reflect the new font size.

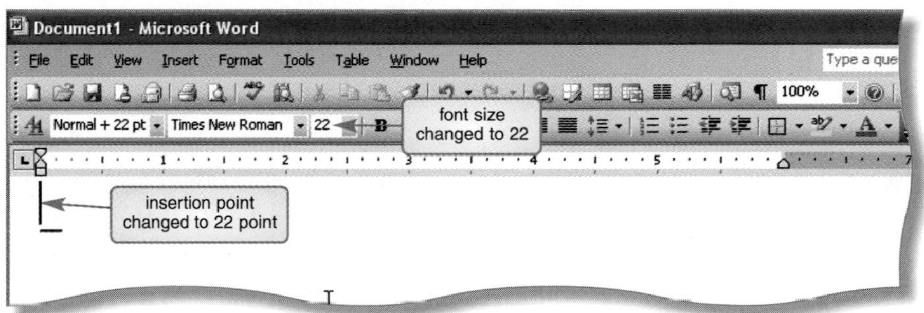

FIGURE 1-15

The new font size takes effect immediately in the document. Word uses this font size for characters you enter in this announcement.

Typing Text

To enter text in a document, you type on the keyboard or speak into the microphone. The example on the next page illustrates the steps required to type both lines of the headline in the announcement. By default, Word positions these lines at the left margin. In a later section, this project will show how to make all of the characters in the headline larger and thicker and how to position the second line of the headline at the right margin.

The steps on the next page show how to begin typing text in the announcement.

To Type Text

1

• **Type** `Attention Inventors` **and then press the PERIOD (.) key three times. If you make an error while typing, press the BACKSPACE key until you have deleted the text in error and then retype the text correctly.**

As you type, the insertion point moves to the right (Figure 1-16).

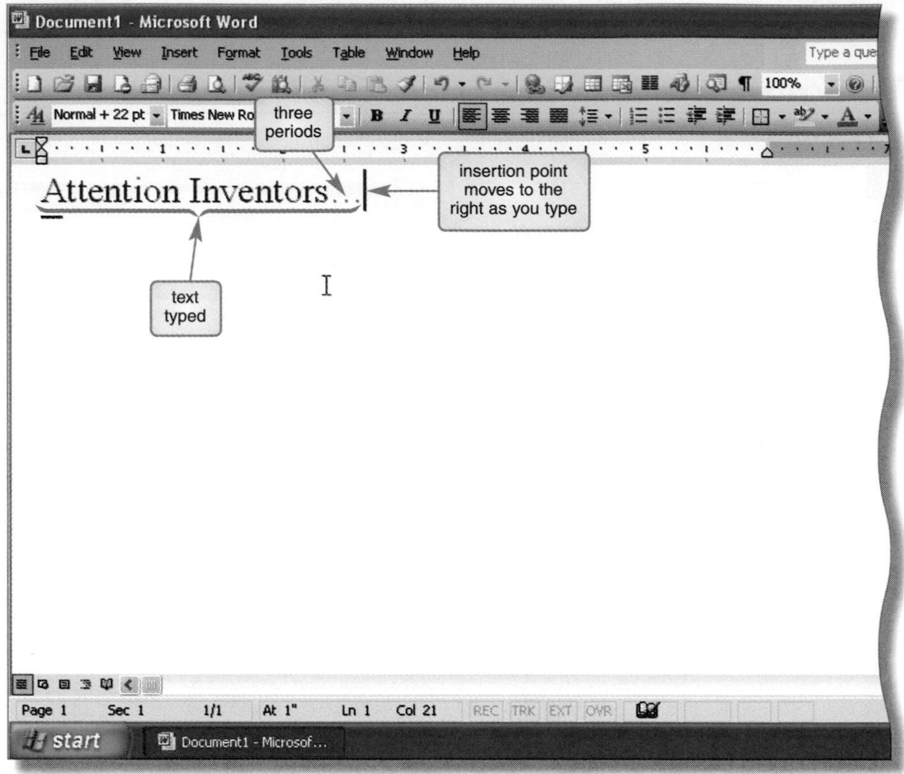

FIGURE 1-16

2

• **Press the ENTER key.**

Word moves the insertion point to the beginning of the next line (Figure 1-17). Notice the status bar indicates the current position of the insertion point. That is, the insertion point currently is on line 2, column 1.

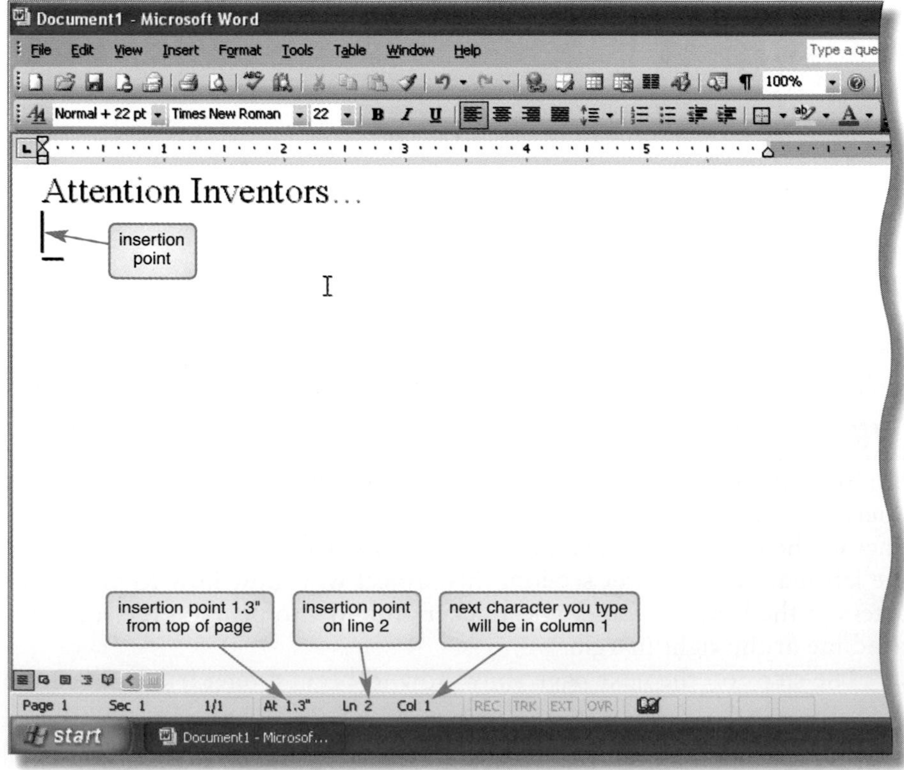

FIGURE 1-17

3

- **Press the PERIOD key three times.**
- **Type** `Win a Scholarship!` **and then press the ENTER key.**

The headline is complete (Figure 1-18). The insertion point is on line 3.

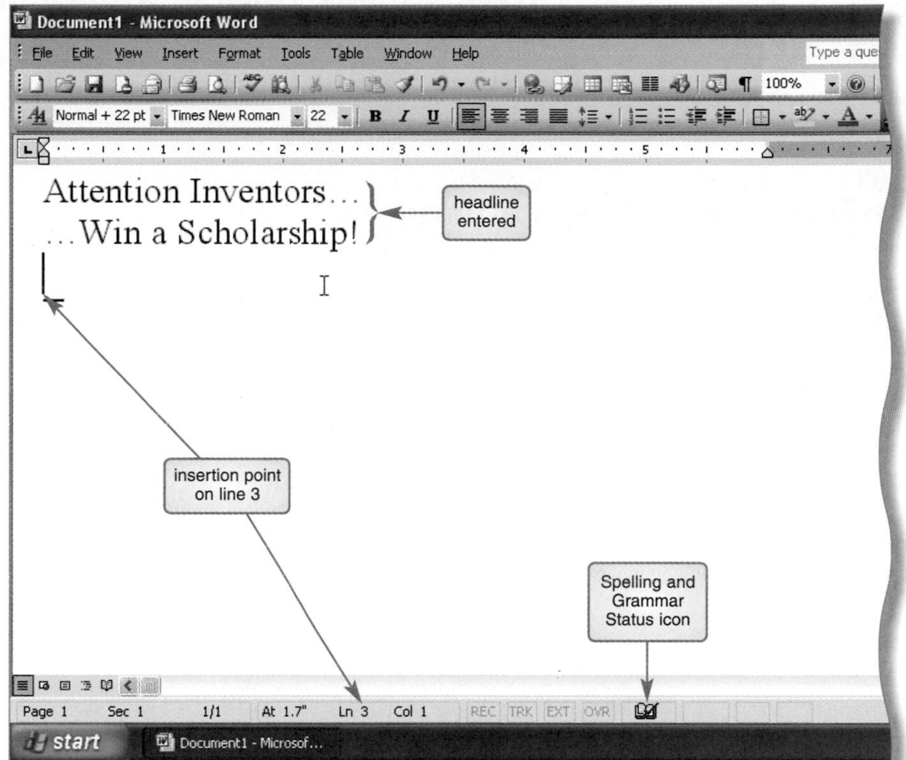

FIGURE 1-18

When you begin entering text in a document, the **Spelling and Grammar Status icon** appears at the right of the status bar (Figure 1-18). As you type, the Spelling and Grammar Status icon shows an animated pencil writing on paper, which indicates Word is checking for possible errors. When you stop typing, the pencil changes to either a red check mark or a red X. In Figure 1-18, the Spelling and Grammar Status icon contains a red check mark.

In general, if all of the words you have typed are in Word's dictionary and your grammar is correct, the Spelling and Grammar Status icon contains a red check mark. If you type a word not in the dictionary (because it is a proper name or misspelled), a red wavy underline appears below the word. If you type text that may be incorrect grammatically, a green wavy underline appears below the text. When Word flags a possible spelling or grammar error, it also changes the red check mark on the Spelling and Grammar Status icon to a red X. As you enter text in a document, your Spelling and Grammar Status icon may show a red X instead of a red check mark. Later, this project will show how to check the spelling of these flagged words. At that time, the red X returns to a red check mark.

Entering Blank Lines in a Document

To enter a blank line in a document, press the ENTER key without typing any text on the line. The following example shows how to enter three blank lines below the headline.

To Enter Blank Lines in a Document

1

- **Press the ENTER key three times.**

Word inserts three blank lines in the document below the headline (Figure 1-19).

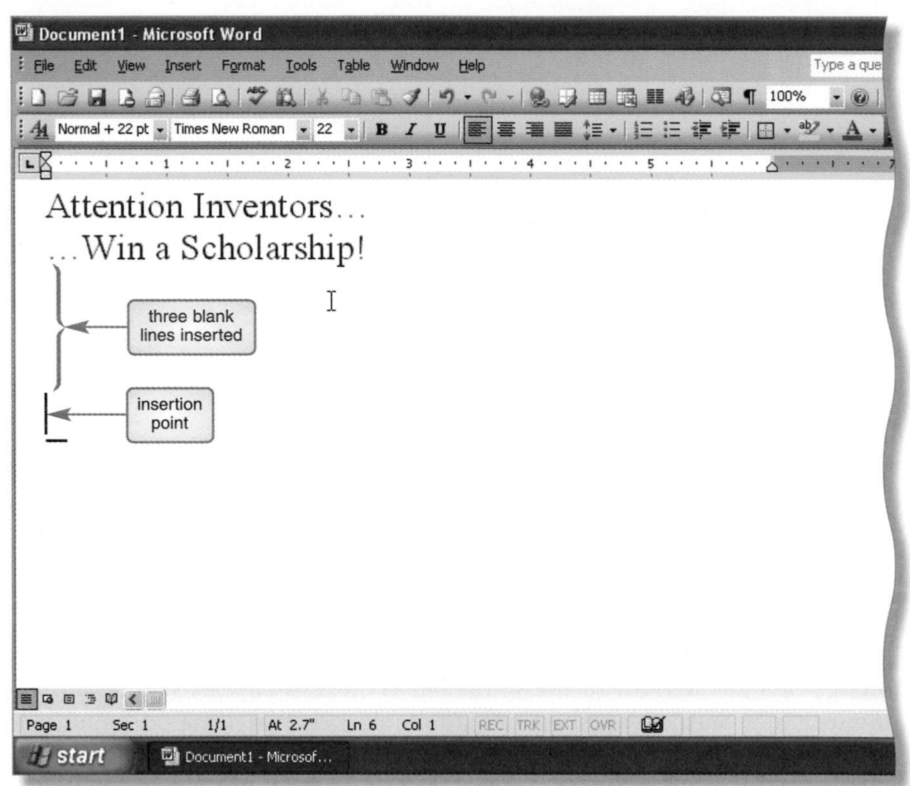

FIGURE 1-19

Displaying Formatting Marks

To indicate where in a document you press the ENTER key or SPACEBAR, you may find it helpful to display formatting marks. A **formatting mark**, sometimes called a **nonprinting character**, is a character that Word displays on the screen but is not visible on a printed document. For example, the paragraph mark (¶) is a formatting mark that indicates where you pressed the ENTER key. A raised dot (•) shows where you pressed the SPACEBAR. Other formatting marks are discussed as they appear on the screen.

Q & A

Q: What is hidden text?

A: When you display formatting marks, Word also displays hidden text. Text formatted as hidden shows on the screen but does not print. Hidden text is useful if you want to write a note to yourself in a document. To format text as hidden, select the text, click Format on the menu bar, click Font, click the Font tab, place a check mark in the Hidden check box, and then click the OK button.

Depending on settings made during previous Word sessions, the Word screen already may display formatting marks (Figure 1-20). The following step shows how to display formatting marks, if they are not displayed already on the screen.

To Display Formatting Marks

1

- **If it is not selected already, click the Show/Hide ¶ button on the Standard toolbar.**

Word displays formatting marks on the screen (Figure 1-20). The Show/Hide ¶ button is selected. That is, the button is light orange and surrounded with a blue outline.

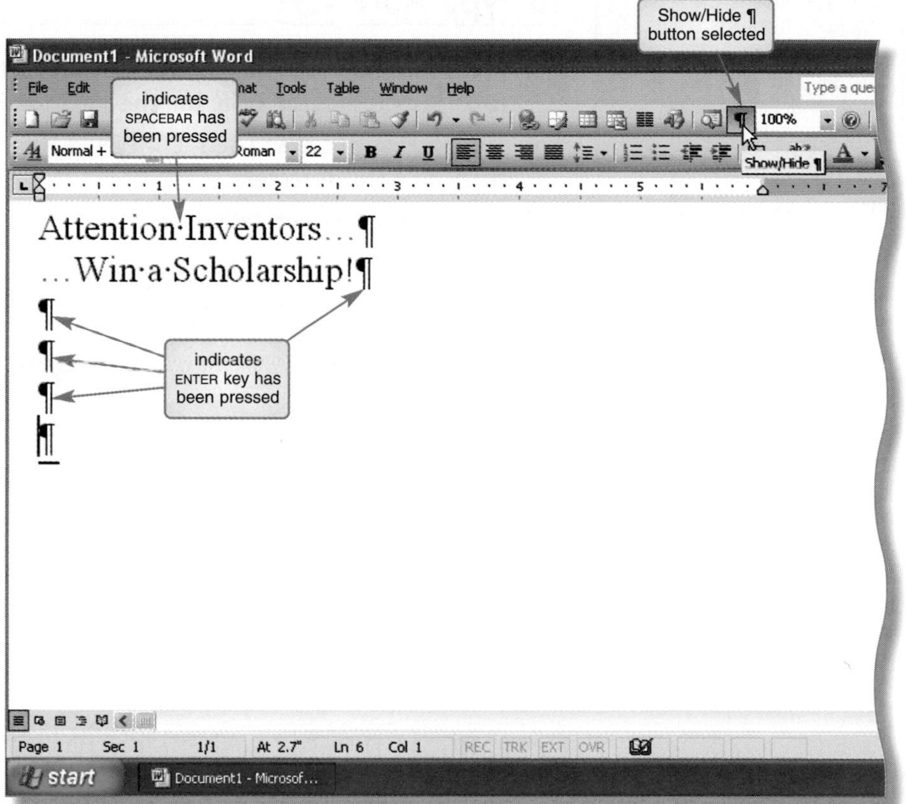

FIGURE 1-20

Notice several changes to the Word document window (Figure 1-20). A paragraph mark appears at the end of each line to indicate you pressed the ENTER key. Each time you press the ENTER key, Word creates a new paragraph. The size of paragraph marks is 22 point because the font size was changed earlier in the project. Between each word, a raised dot appears, indicating you pressed the SPACEBAR. Finally, the Show/Hide ¶ button changes from blue to light orange and has a blue outline, which indicates it is selected.

If you feel the formatting marks clutter the screen, you can hide them by clicking the Show/Hide ¶ button again. It is recommended that you display formatting marks; therefore, the document windows presented in this book show the formatting marks.

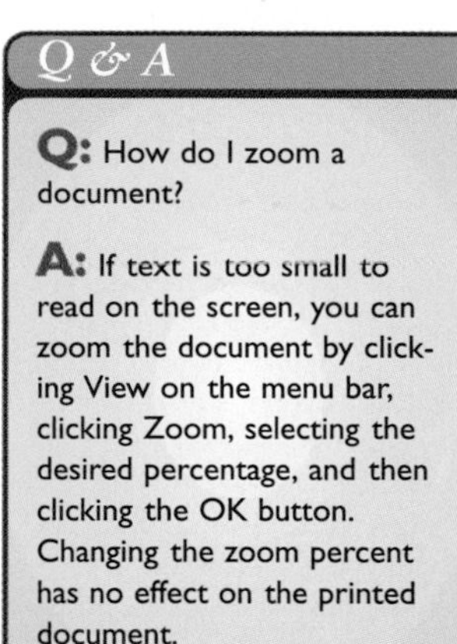

Q & A

Q: How do I zoom a document?

A: If text is too small to read on the screen, you can zoom the document by clicking View on the menu bar, clicking Zoom, selecting the desired percentage, and then clicking the OK button. Changing the zoom percent has no effect on the printed document.

Entering More Text

Every character in the body title (EDISON INVENTORS COMPETITION) of the announcement is in capital letters. The next step is to enter this body title in all capital letters in the document window, as explained below.

> *Q & A*
>
> **Q:** What if I leave the CAPS LOCK key engaged?
>
> **A:** If you leave the CAPS LOCK key on and begin typing a new sentence, Word automatically corrects the problem for you. That is, it disengages the CAPS LOCK key and capitalizes only the first letter of the first word in the next sentence.

To Type More Text

1. **Press the CAPS LOCK key on the keyboard to turn on capital letters. Verify the caps lock indicator is lit on the keyboard.**
2. **Type** EDISON INVENTORS COMPETITION **and then press the CAPS LOCK key to turn off capital letters.**
3. **Press the ENTER key twice.**

Word displays the body title on line 6 (Figure 1-21).

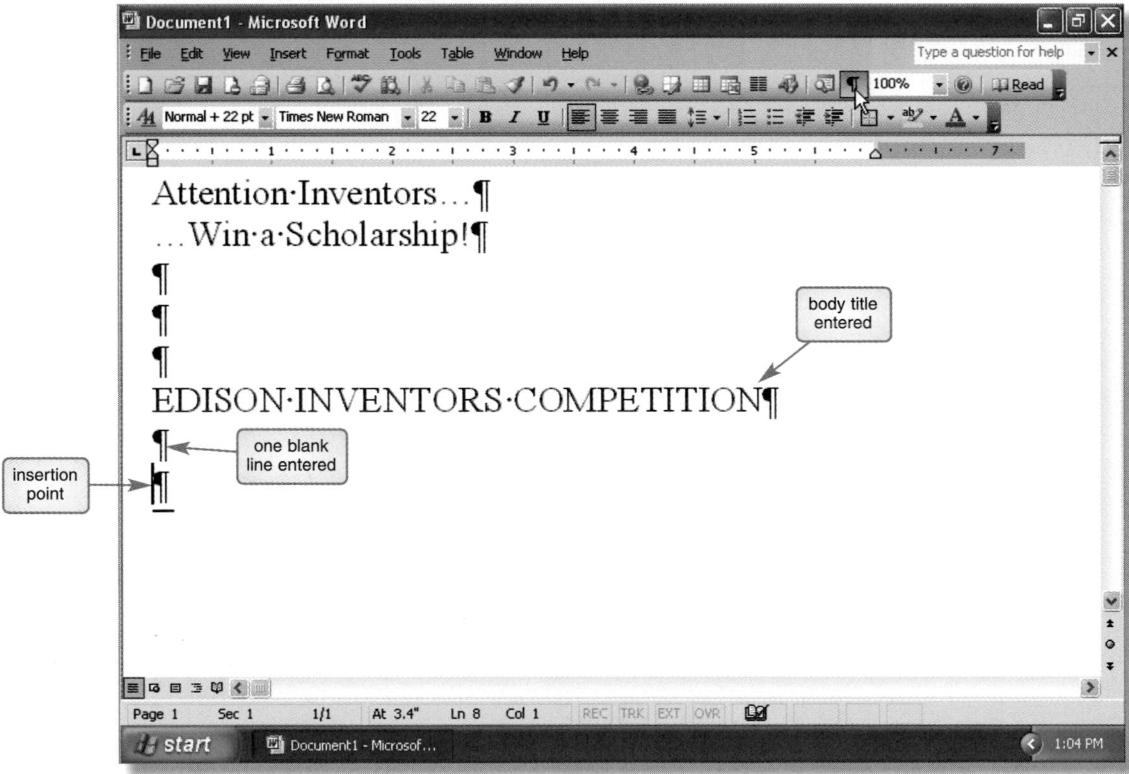

FIGURE 1-21

Using Wordwrap

Wordwrap allows you to type words in a paragraph continually without pressing the ENTER key at the end of each line. When the insertion point reaches the right margin, Word automatically positions the insertion point at the beginning of the next line. As you type, if a word extends beyond the right margin, Word also automatically positions that word on the next line with the insertion point.

As you type text in the document window, do not press the ENTER key when the insertion point reaches the right margin. Word creates a new paragraph each time you press the ENTER key. Thus, press the ENTER key only in these circumstances:

1. To insert blank lines in a document
2. To begin a new paragraph
3. To terminate a short line of text and advance to the next line
4. In response to certain Word commands

The following step illustrates wordwrap.

Q & A

Q: Will words always wrap the same?

A: Not necessarily. Your printer controls where wordwrap occurs for each line in your document. For this reason, it is possible that the same document could wordwrap differently if printed on different printers.

To Wordwrap Text as You Type

1

• **Type** `Teams of two high-school students construct a prototype` **and then press the SPACEBAR.**

The word, prototype, wraps to the beginning of line 9 because it is too long to fit on line 8 (Figure 1-22). Your document may wordwrap differently depending on the type of printer you are using.

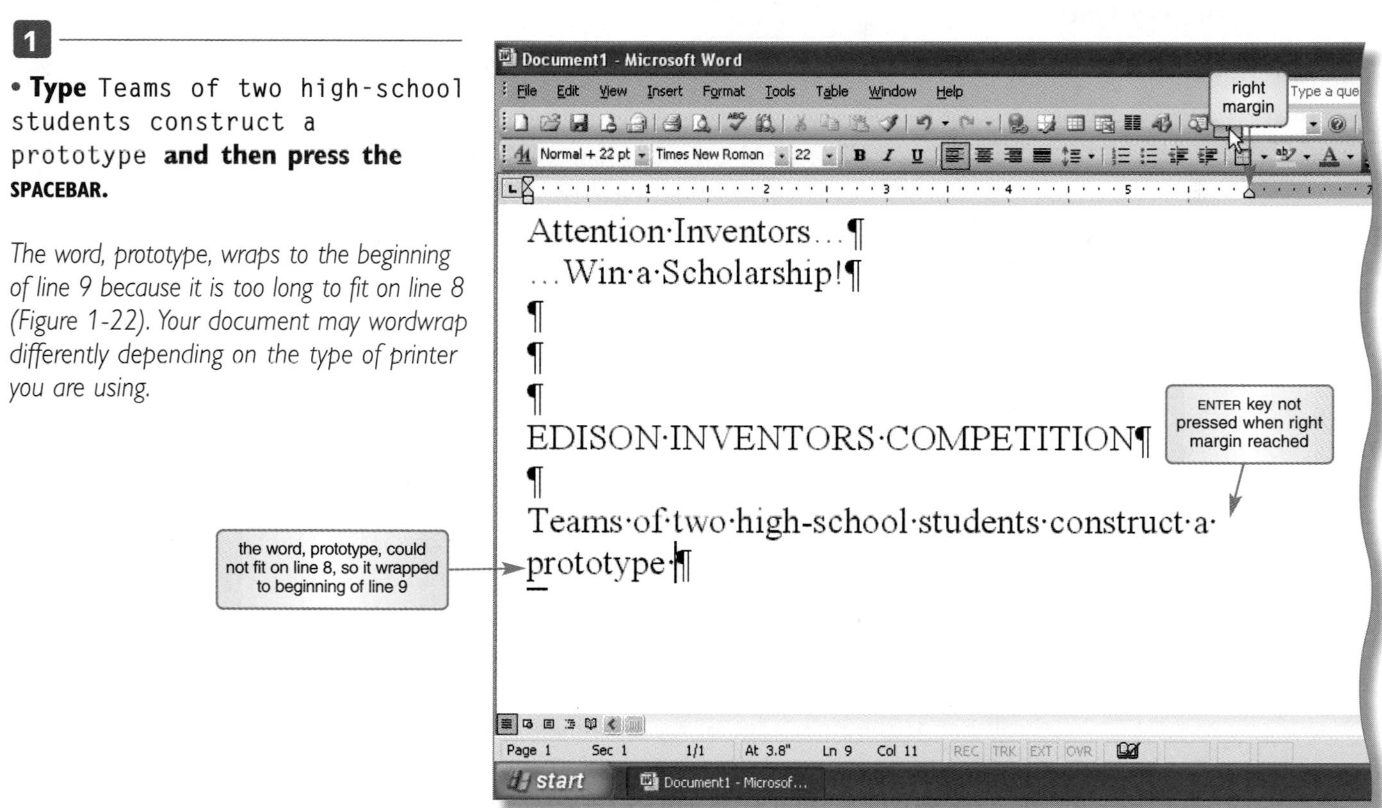

FIGURE 1-22

Entering Text that Scrolls the Document Window

As you type more lines of text than Word can display in the document window, Word **scrolls** the top portion of the document upward off the screen. Although you cannot see the text once it scrolls off the screen, it remains in the document. As previously discussed, the document window allows you to view only a portion of your document at one time (Figure 1-8 on page WD 10).

The following step shows how Word scrolls text through the document window.

To Enter Text that Scrolls the Document Window

1

- **Type** `of an original invention that benefits a school or a community. Students must be in their junior or senior year to compete.`
- **Press the ENTER key twice.**

Word scrolls the headline off the top of the screen (Figure 1-23). Your screen may scroll differently depending on the type of monitor you are using.

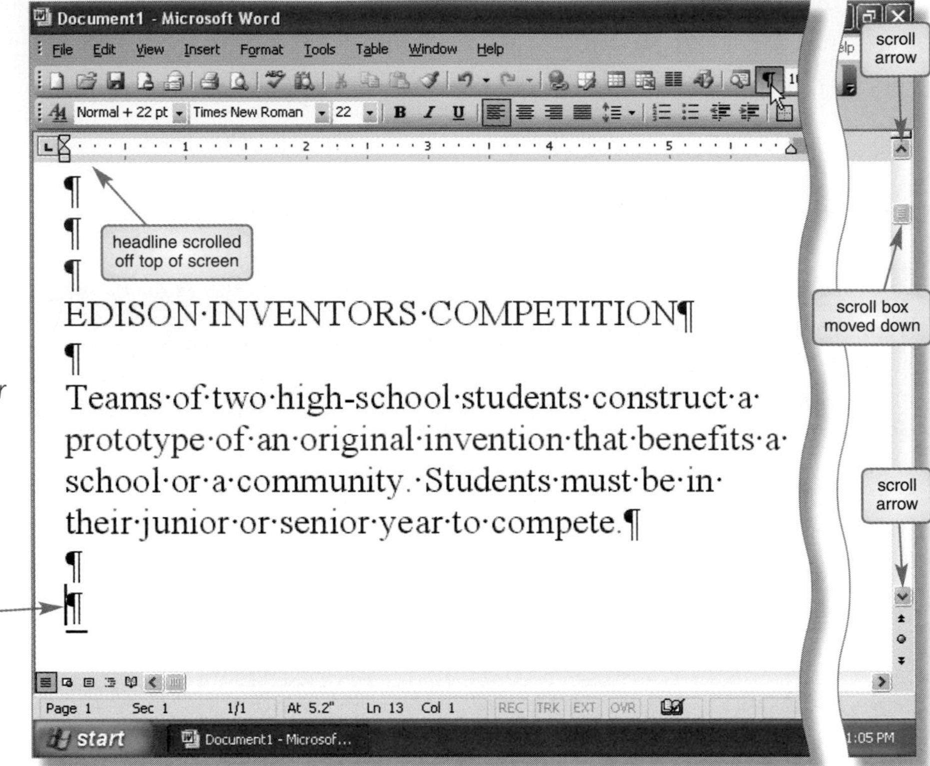

FIGURE 1-23

When Word scrolls text off the top of the screen, the scroll box on the vertical scroll bar at the right edge of the document window moves downward (Figure 1-23). The scroll box indicates the current relative location of the portion of the document that is displayed in the document window. You may use either the mouse or the keyboard to scroll to a different location in a document.

With the mouse, you can use the scroll arrows or the scroll box on the scroll bar to display a different portion of the document in the document window, and then click the mouse to move the insertion point to that location. Table 1-1 explains various techniques for using the scroll bar to scroll vertically with the mouse.

Q & A

Q: How can I learn more about healthy computing?

A: For more information about healthy computing, visit the Office 2003 Q&A Web page (scsite.com/off2003sch/qa), locate Word Project 1, and click Healthy Computing.

Table 1-1 Using the Scroll Bar to Scroll with the Mouse

SCROLL DIRECTION	MOUSE ACTION
Up	Drag the scroll box upward.
Down	Drag the scroll box downward.
Up one screen	Click anywhere above the scroll box on the vertical scroll bar.
Down one screen	Click anywhere below the scroll box on the vertical scroll bar.
Up one line	Click the scroll arrow at the top of the vertical scroll bar.
Down one line	Click the scroll arrow at the bottom of the vertical scroll bar.

When you use the keyboard to scroll, the insertion point automatically moves when you press the appropriate keys. Table 1-2 outlines various techniques to scroll through a document using the keyboard.

Table 1-2 Scrolling with the Keyboard

SCROLL DIRECTION	KEY(S) TO PRESS
Left one character	LEFT ARROW
Right one character	RIGHT ARROW
Left one word	CTRL+LEFT ARROW
Right one word	CTRL+RIGHT ARROW
Up one line	UP ARROW
Down one line	DOWN ARROW
To end of a line	END
To beginning of a line	HOME
Up one paragraph	CTRL+UP ARROW
Down one paragraph	CTRL+DOWN ARROW
Up one screen	PAGE UP
Down one screen	PAGE DOWN
To top of document window	ALT+CTRL+PAGE UP
To bottom of document window	ALT+CTRL+PAGE DOWN
To beginning of a document	CTRL+HOME
To end of a document	CTRL+END

Q & A

Q: How can I help prevent wrist injury while working on a computer?

A: Typical computer users frequently switch between the keyboard and the mouse during a word processing session, an action that strains the wrist. To help prevent wrist injury, minimize switching. If your fingers already are on the keyboard, use keyboard keys to scroll. If your hand already is on the mouse, use the mouse to scroll.

Checking Spelling and Grammar as You Type

As you type text in the document window, Word checks your typing for possible spelling and grammar errors. If a word you type is not in the dictionary, a red wavy underline appears below the word. Similarly, if text you type contains a possible grammar error, a green wavy underline appears below the text. In both cases, the Spelling and Grammar Status icon on the status bar shows a red X, instead of a check mark. Although you can check the entire document for spelling and grammar errors at once, you also can check these flagged errors immediately.

To verify that the check spelling as you type feature is enabled, right-click the Spelling and Grammar Status icon on the status bar and then click Options on the shortcut menu. When Word displays the Spelling & Grammar dialog box, be sure Check spelling as you type has a check mark and Hide spelling errors in this document does not have a check mark.

When a word is flagged with a red wavy underline, it is not in Word's dictionary. To display a list of suggested corrections for a flagged word, right-click the word. A flagged word, however, is not necessarily misspelled. For example, many names, abbreviations, and specialized terms are not in Word's main dictionary. In these cases, you tell Word to ignore the flagged word. As you type, Word also detects duplicate words. For example, if your document contains the phrase, to the the store, Word places a red wavy underline below the second occurrence of the word, the.

In the example on the next page, the word, members, has been misspelled intentionally as mebbers to illustrate Word's check spelling as you type. If you are doing this project on a personal computer, your announcement may contain different misspelled words, depending on the accuracy of your typing.

To Check Spelling and Grammar as You Type

1

- **Type** `Winning team mebbers` **and then press the SPACEBAR.**
- **Position the mouse pointer in the flagged word (mebbers, in this case).**

Word flags the misspelled word, mebbers, by placing a red wavy underline below it (Figure 1-24). The Spelling and Grammar Status icon on the status bar now contains a red X, indicating Word has detected a possible spelling or grammar error.

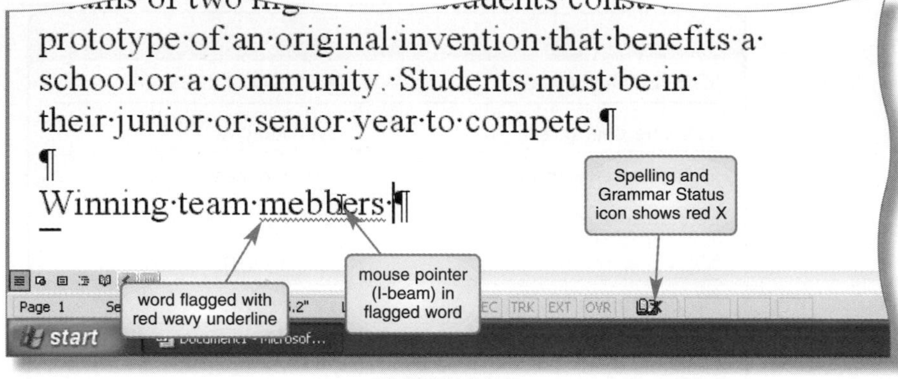

FIGURE 1-24

2

- **Right-click the flagged word, mebbers.**

Word displays a shortcut menu that lists suggested spelling corrections for the flagged word (Figure 1-25).

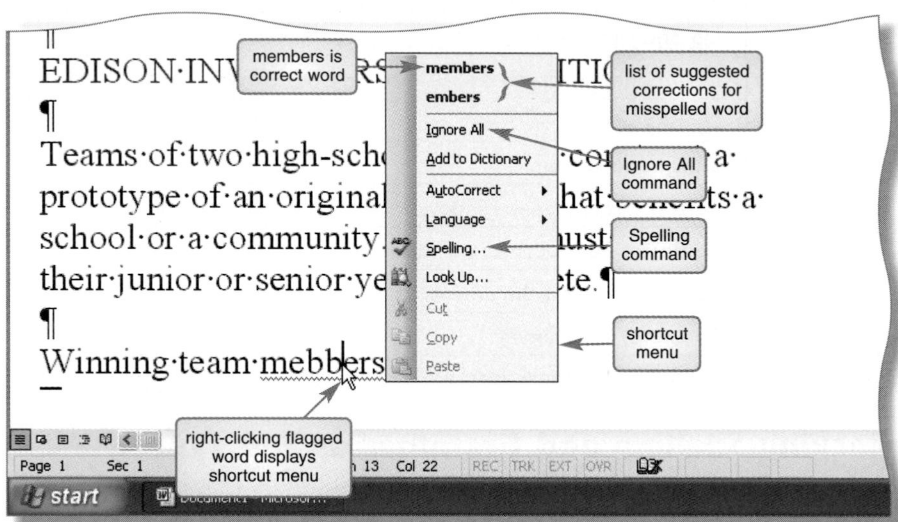

FIGURE 1-25

3

- **Click members on the shortcut menu.**

Word replaces the misspelled word with the word selected on the shortcut menu (Figure 1-26). The Spelling and Grammar Status icon once again contains a red check mark.

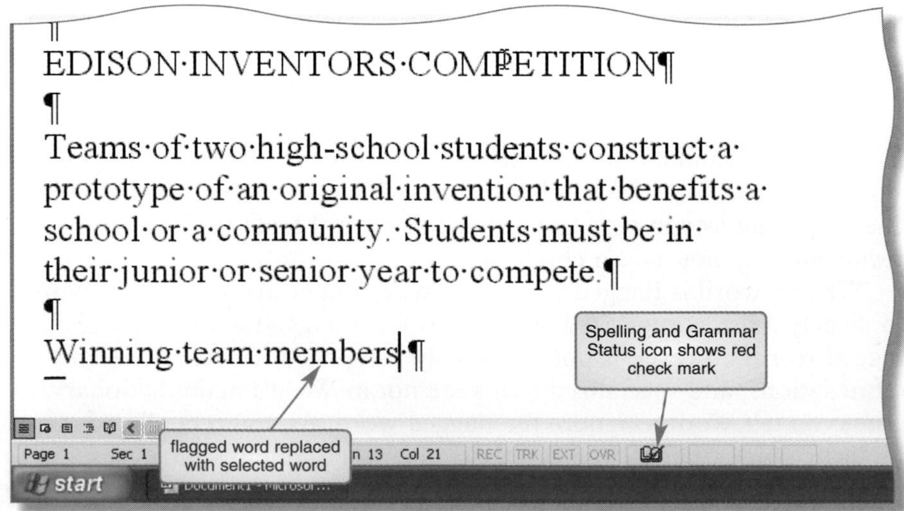

FIGURE 1-26

If a flagged word actually is spelled correctly and, for example, is a proper name, you can right-click it and then click Ignore All on the shortcut menu (Figure 1-25). If, when you right-click the misspelled word, your desired correction is not in the list on the shortcut menu, you can click outside the shortcut menu to close the menu and then retype the correct word, or you can click Spelling on the shortcut menu to display the Spelling dialog box. Project 2 discusses the Spelling dialog box.

If you feel the wavy underlines clutter the document window, you can hide them temporarily until you are ready to check for spelling and grammar errors. To hide spelling errors, right-click the Spelling and Grammar Status icon on the status bar and then click Hide Spelling Errors on the shortcut menu. To hide grammar errors, right-click the Spelling and Grammar Status icon on the status bar and then click Hide Grammatical Errors on the shortcut menu.

The next step is to type the remainder of text in the announcement, as described in the following steps.

Q & A

Q: Does Word automatically correct spelling errors?

A: As you type, Word automatically corrects some misspelled words. For example, if you type recieve, Word automatically fixes the misspelling and displays the word, receive, when you press the SPACEBAR or type a punctuation mark. To see a complete list of automatically corrected words, click Tools on the menu bar, click AutoCorrect Options on the Tools menu, click the AutoCorrect tab, and then scroll through the list of words near the bottom of the dialog box.

To Enter More Text

1. **Press the END key to move the insertion point to the end of the line.**
2. **Type** `each receive a $50,000 scholarship and paid-in-full legal services for patent and other intellectual property matters.`
3. **Press the ENTER key twice.**
4. **Type** `Call EIC at 555-2382 to register.`

The text of the announcement is complete (Figure 1-27).

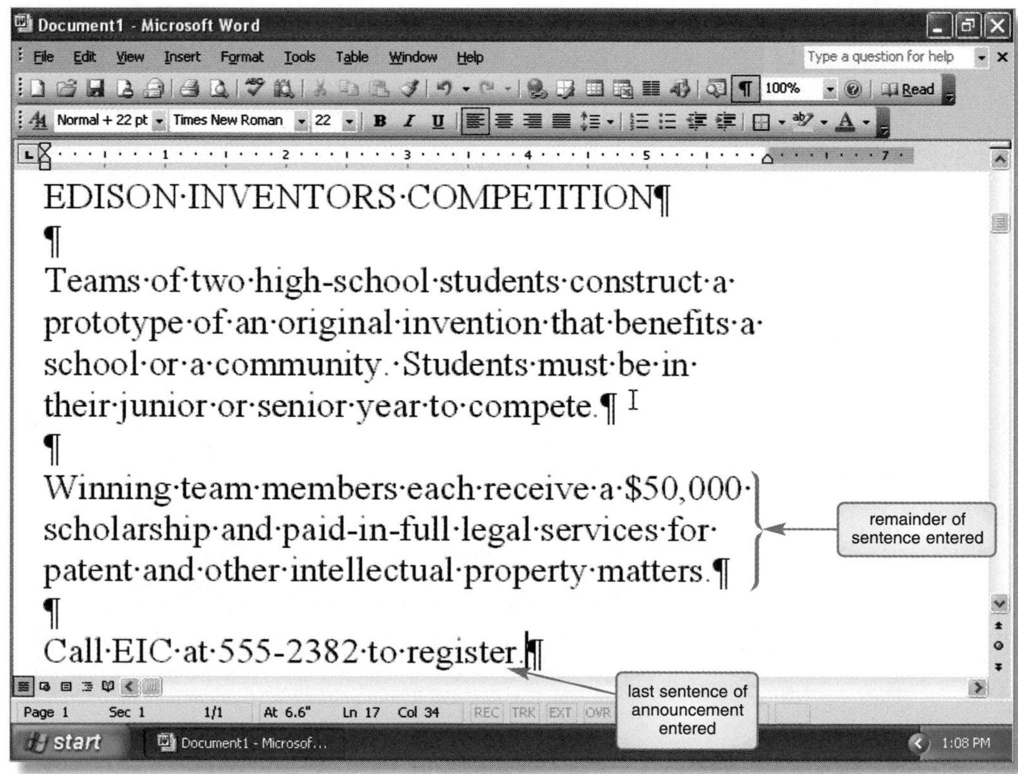

FIGURE 1-27

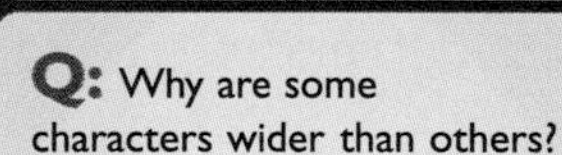

Q: Why are some characters wider than others?

A: Word processing documents use variable character fonts; for example, the letter w takes up more space than the letter i. With these fonts, it often is difficult to determine how many times someone has pressed the SPACEBAR between sentences. Thus, the rule is to press the SPACEBAR only once after periods, colons, and other punctuation marks.

Skill Builder 1-1

To practice the following tasks, visit scsite.com/off2003sch/skill, locate Word Project 1, and then click Skill Builder 1-1.

- ❑ Start Word
- ❑ Enter text
- ❑ Check spelling and grammar as you type

Saving a Document

As you create a document in Word, the computer stores it in memory. If the computer is turned off or if you lose electrical power, the document in memory is lost. Hence, if you plan to use the document later, you must save it on a floppy disk, USB flash drive, or hard disk.

A saved document is called a **file**. A **file name** is the name assigned to a file when it is saved. This project saves the announcement with the file name, Inventors Competition Announcement. Depending on your Windows settings, the file type .doc may appear immediately after the file name. The file type **.doc** indicates the file is a Word document.

The following steps illustrate how to save a document on a USB flash drive using the Save button on the Standard toolbar.

To Save a New Document

1

• **With a USB flash drive connected to one of the computer's USB ports, click the Save button on the Standard toolbar.**

Word displays the Save As dialog box (Figure 1-28). The first line from the document (Attention Inventors) is selected in the File name text box as the default file name. You can change this selected file name by immediately typing the new name.

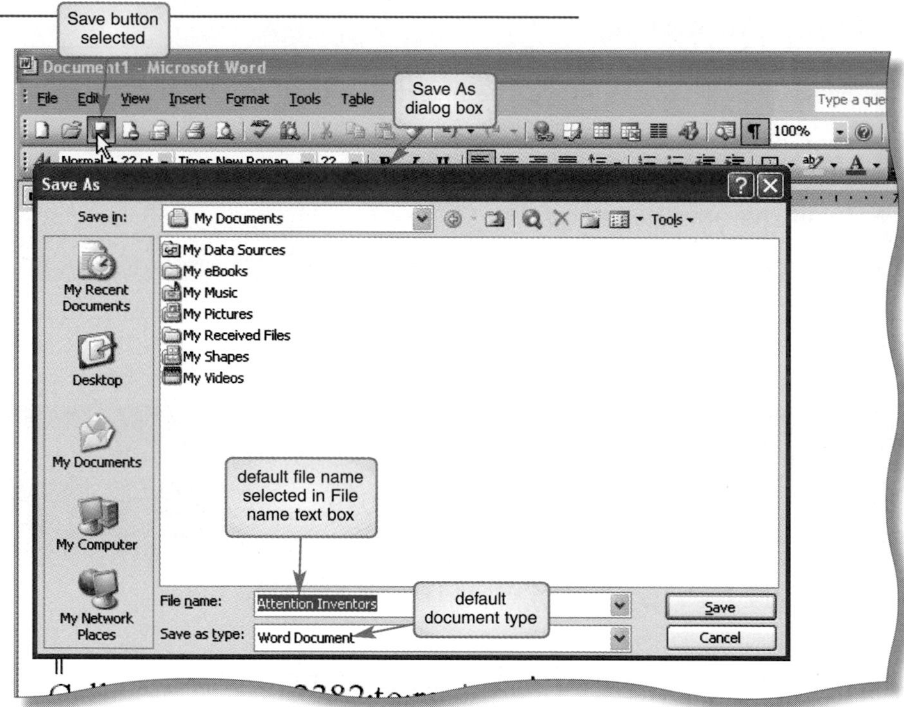

FIGURE 1-28

2

• **Type** Inventors Competition Announcement **in the File name text box. Do not press the ENTER key after typing the file name.**

The file name, Inventors Competition Announcement, replaces the text, Attention Inventors, in the File name text box (Figure 1-29).

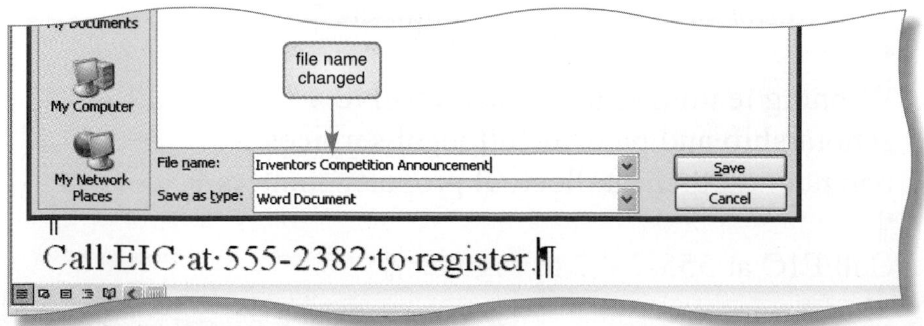

FIGURE 1-29

3

• **Click the Save in box arrow.**

Word displays a list of the available drives and folders in which you can save the document (Figure 1-30). A ***folder*** *is a specific location on a disk. Your list may differ depending on your computer's configuration.*

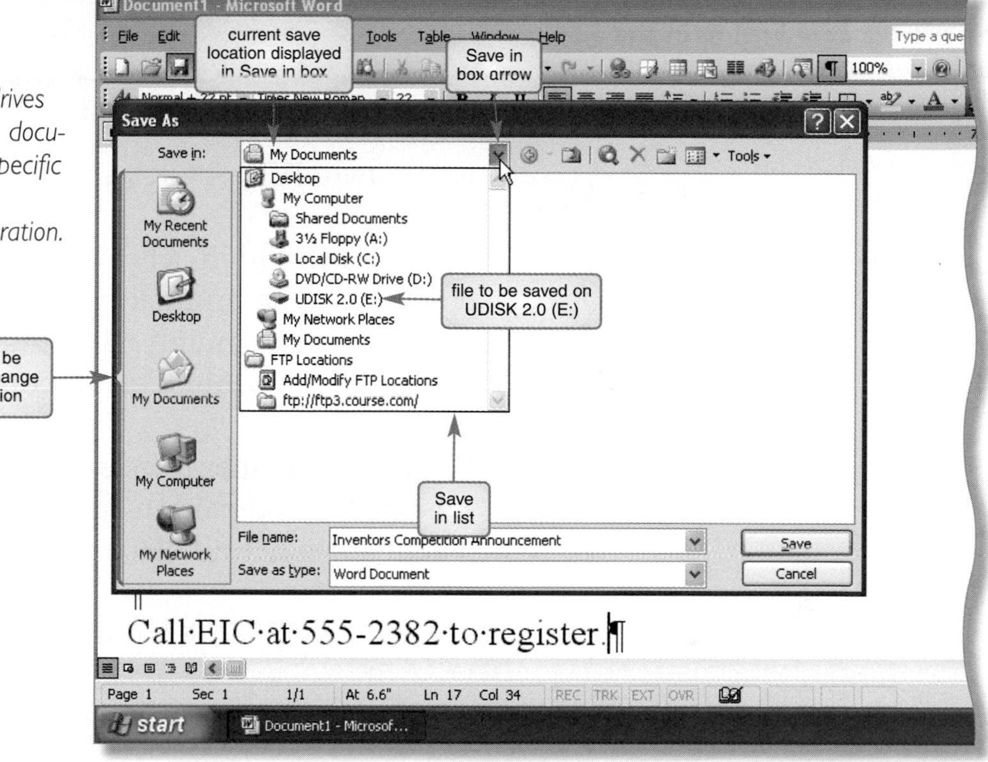

FIGURE 1-30

4

• **Click UDISK 2.0 (E:) in the Save in list. (Your USB flash drive may have a different name and letter.)**

The USB flash drive becomes the new save location (Figure 1-31). The Save As dialog box now shows names of existing files stored on the USB flash drive. In Figure 1-31, the list is empty because no Word files currently are stored on the USB flash drive.

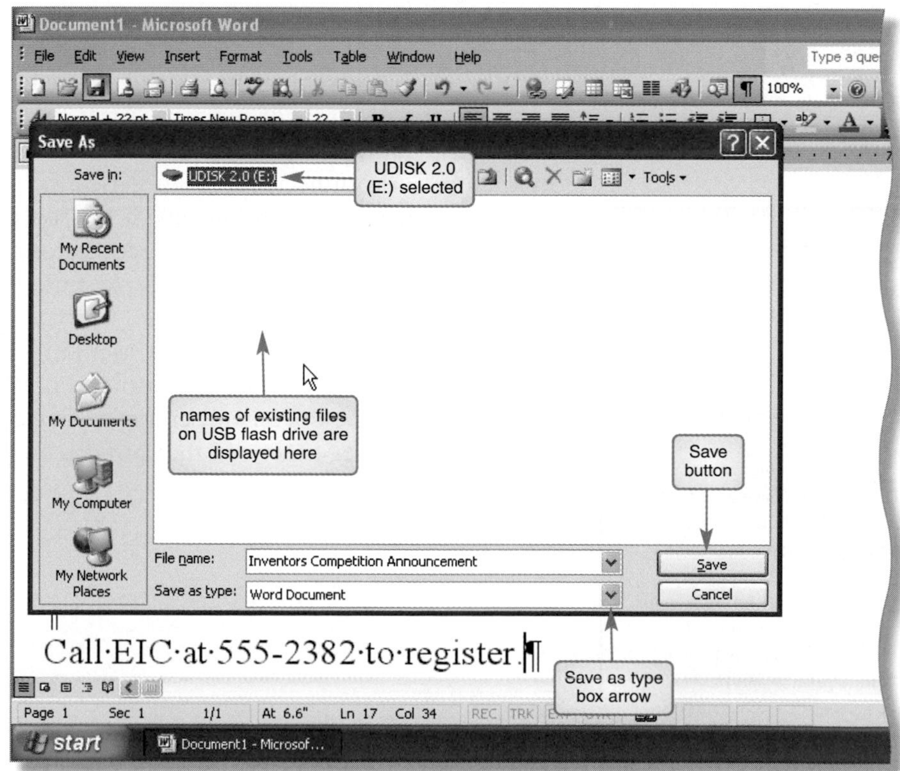

FIGURE 1-31

5

• **Click the Save button in the Save As dialog box.**

Word saves the document on the USB flash drive with the file name, Inventors Competition Announcement (Figure 1-32). Although the announcement is saved on a USB flash drive, it also remains in main memory and on the screen.

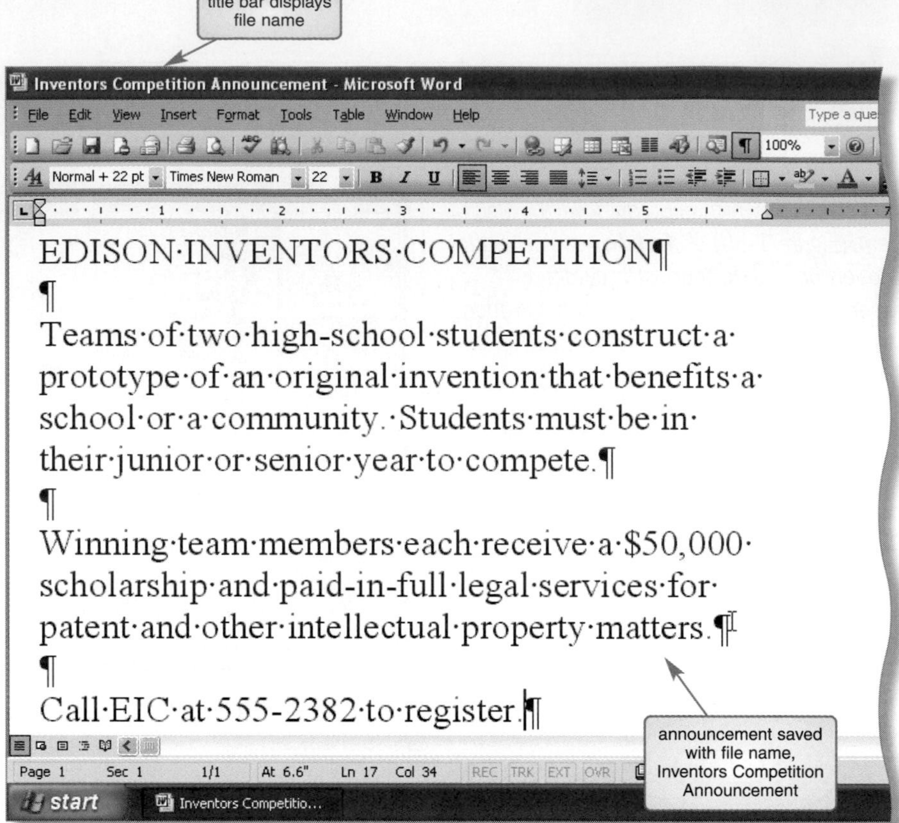

FIGURE 1-32

While Word is saving the document, it displays a message on the status bar indicating the progress of the save. After the save operation is complete, Word changes the name of the document on the title bar from Document1 to Inventors Competition Announcement (Figure 1-32).

You can use the seven buttons at the top of the Save As dialog box (Figure 1-30 on the previous page) and the five icons along the left edge to change the save location and other tasks. Table 1-3 lists the function of the buttons and icons in the Save As dialog box.

When you click the Tools button in the Save As dialog box, Word displays the Tools menu. The Save Options command on the Tools menu allows you to save a backup copy of the document, create a password to limit access to the document, and carry out other functions that are discussed later.

Q & A

Q: Can a Word document be saved in alternative file formats?

A: Yes. Word allows you to save a document in more than 10 different file formats. Choose the file format by clicking the Save as type box arrow at the bottom of the Save As dialog box (Figure 1-31 on the previous page). Word Document is the default file format. When you save a document, use meaningful file names. A file name can be up to 255 characters, including spaces. The only invalid characters are the backslash (\), slash (/), colon (:), asterisk (*), question mark (?), quotation mark ("), less than symbol (<), greater than symbol (>), and vertical bar (|).

Table 1-3 Save As Dialog Box Buttons and Icons

BUTTON OR ICON	BUTTON OR ICON NAME	FUNCTION
	Default File Location	Displays contents of default file location
	Up One Level	Displays contents of folder one level up from current folder
	Search the Web	Starts Web browser and displays search engine
	Delete	Deletes selected file or folder
	Create New Folder	Creates new folder
	Views	Changes view of files and folders
Tools	Tools	Lists commands to print or modify file names and folders
My Recent Documents	My Recent Documents	Displays contents of My Recent Documents in Save in list (you cannot save to this location)

Table 1-3 Save As Dialog Box Buttons and Icons

BUTTON OR ICON	BUTTON OR ICON NAME	FUNCTION
Desktop	Desktop	Displays contents of Windows desktop folder in Save in list to save quickly to the Windows desktop
My Documents	My Documents	Displays contents of My Documents in Save in list to save quickly to the My Documents folder
My Computer	My Computer	Displays contents of My Computer in Save in list to save quickly to another drive on the computer
My Network Places	My Network Places	Displays contents of My Network Places in Save in list to save quickly to My Network Places

Formatting Paragraphs and Characters in a Document

The text for Project 1 now is complete. The next step is to format the paragraphs and characters in the announcement.

Paragraphs encompass the text up to and including a paragraph mark (¶). **Paragraph formatting** is the process of changing the appearance of a paragraph. For example, you can center or indent a paragraph.

Characters include letters, numbers, punctuation marks, and symbols. **Character formatting** is the process of changing the way characters appear on the screen and in print. You use character formatting to emphasize certain words and improve readability of a document. For example, you can italicize or underline characters.

In many cases, you apply both paragraph and character formatting to the same text. For example, you may center a paragraph (paragraph formatting) and bold the characters in a paragraph (character formatting).

With Word, you can format paragraphs and characters before you type, or you can apply new formats after you type. Earlier, this project showed how to change the font size (character formatting) before you typed any text. This section shows how to format existing text.

Q & A

Q: What is the difference between character formatting and paragraph formatting?

A: Character formatting includes changing the font, font style, font size; adding an underline, color, strikethrough, shadow, or outline; embossing; engraving; making a superscript or subscript; and changing the case of the letters. Paragraph formatting includes alignment; indentation; and spacing above, below, and in between lines.

Figure 1-33a shows the announcement before formatting its paragraphs and characters. Figure 1-33b shows the announcement after formatting. As you can see from the two figures, a document that is formatted is easier to read and looks more professional.

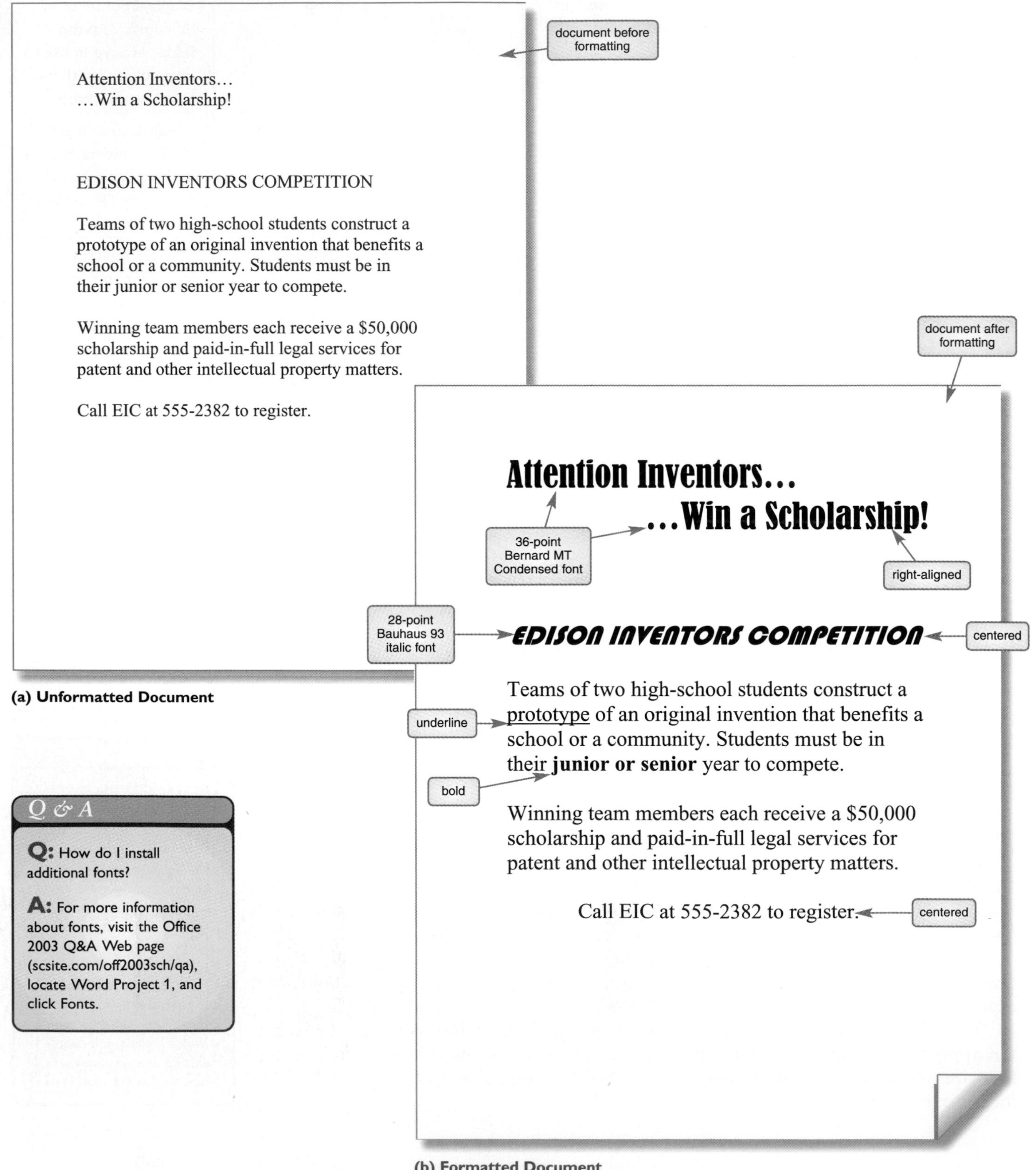

(a) Unformatted Document

(b) Formatted Document

FIGURE 1-33

Q & A

Q: How do I install additional fonts?

A: For more information about fonts, visit the Office 2003 Q&A Web page (scsite.com/off2003sch/qa), locate Word Project 1, and click Fonts.

Selecting and Formatting Paragraphs and Characters

To format a single paragraph, move the insertion point in the paragraph and then format the paragraph. That is, you do not need to select a single paragraph to format it. To format *multiple* paragraphs, however, you first must select the paragraphs you want to format and then format them. In the same manner, to format a single word, position the insertion point in the word and then format the word. To format multiple characters or words, however, you first must select the characters or words to be formatted and then format the selection.

Selected text is highlighted text. If your screen normally displays dark letters on a light background, then selected text displays light letters on a dark background.

Selecting Multiple Paragraphs

The first formatting step in this project is to change the font size of the characters in the headline. The headline consists of two separate lines, each ending with a paragraph mark. As previously discussed, Word creates a new paragraph each time you press the ENTER key. Thus, the headline actually is two separate paragraphs.

To change the font size of the characters in the headline, you first must **select** (highlight) both paragraphs in the headline, as shown in the following steps.

To Select Multiple Paragraphs

1

- **Press CTRL+HOME; that is, press and hold down the CTRL key, press the HOME key, and then release both keys.**
- **Move the mouse pointer to the left of the first paragraph to be selected until the mouse pointer changes to a right-pointing block arrow.**

CTRL+HOME is a keyboard shortcut that positions the insertion point at the top of the document. The mouse pointer changes to a right-pointing block arrow when positioned to the left of a paragraph (Figure 1-34).

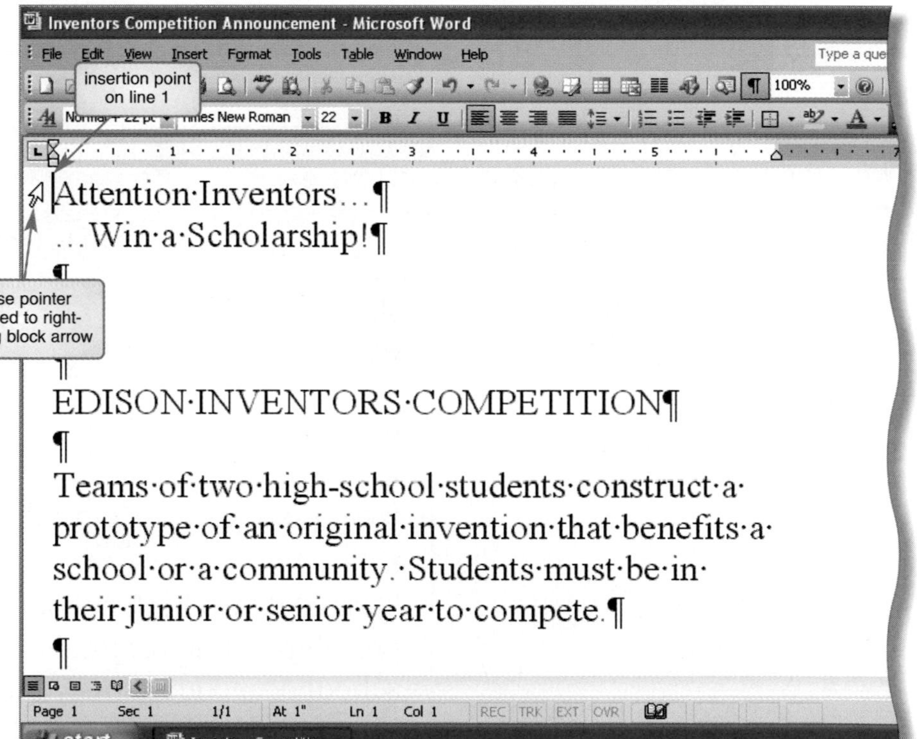

FIGURE 1-34

2

• **Drag downward until both paragraphs are selected.**

Word selects (highlights) both of the paragraphs (Figure 1-35). Dragging is the process of holding down the mouse button while moving the mouse and then releasing the mouse button.

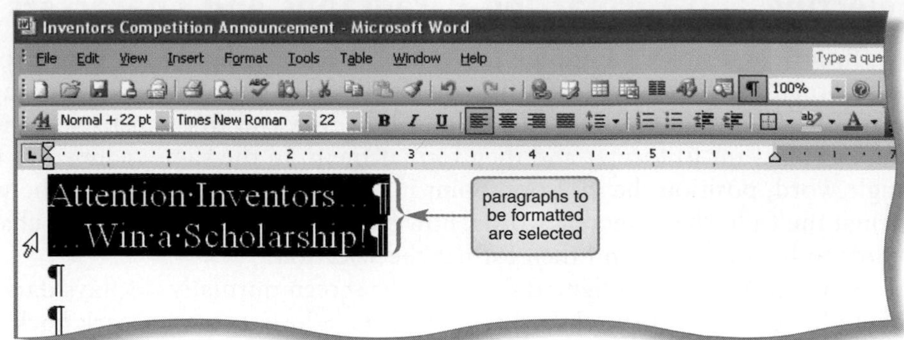

FIGURE 1-35

Changing the Font Size of Text

The next step is to increase the font size of the characters in the selected headline. Recall that the font size specifies the size of the characters. Earlier, this project showed how to change the font size to 22 for characters typed in the entire announcement. To give the headline more impact, it has a font size larger than the body copy. The following steps show how to increase the font size of the headline from 22 to 36 point.

To Change the Font Size of Text

1

• **With the text selected, click the Font Size box arrow on the Formatting toolbar.**

Word displays a list of available font sizes (Figure 1-36). Available font sizes vary depending on the current font and the printer driver.

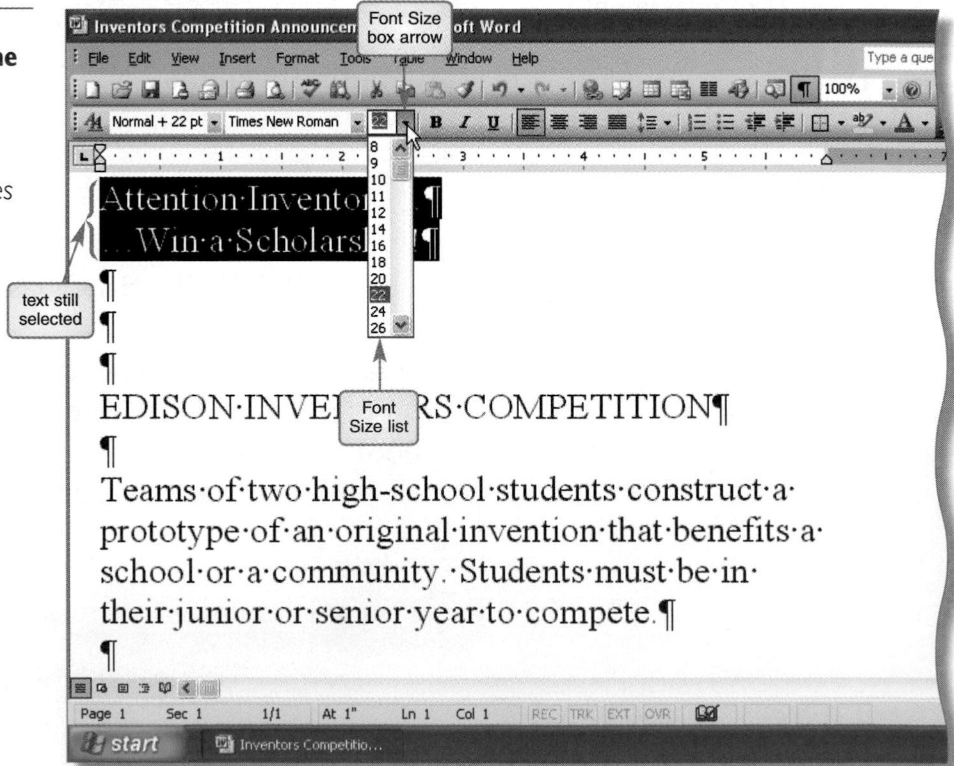

FIGURE 1-36

2

• Click the down scroll arrow on the Font Size scroll bar until 36 appears in the list (Figure 1-37).

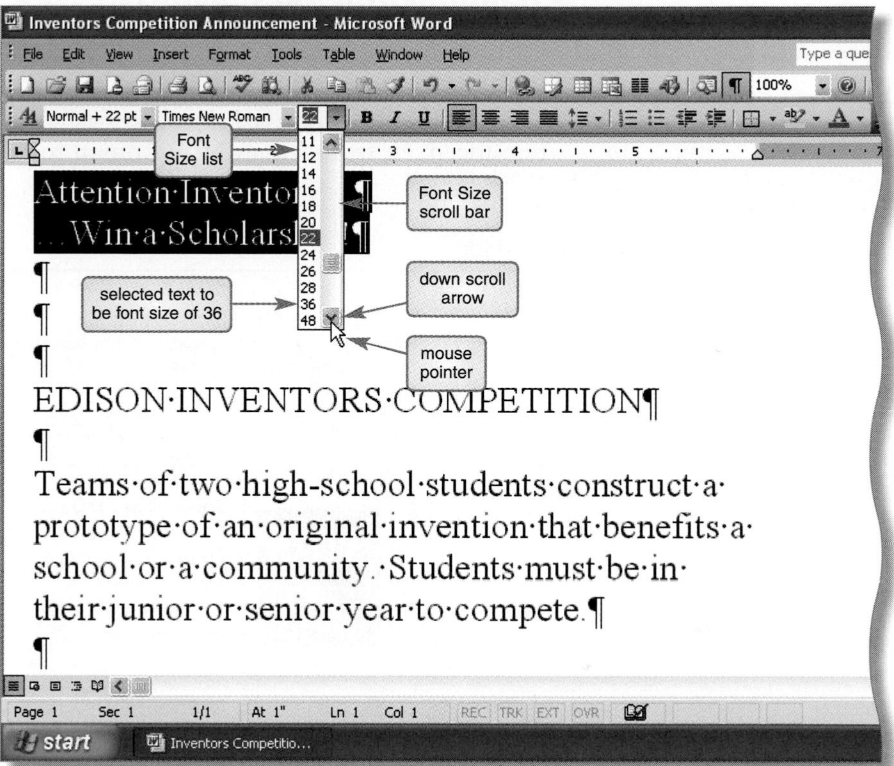

FIGURE 1-37

3

• Click 36 in the Font Size list.

Word increases the font size of the headline to 36 (Figure 1-38). The Font Size box on the Formatting toolbar displays 36, indicating the selected text has a font size of 36. Notice that when the mouse pointer is positioned in selected text, its shape is a left-pointing block arrow.

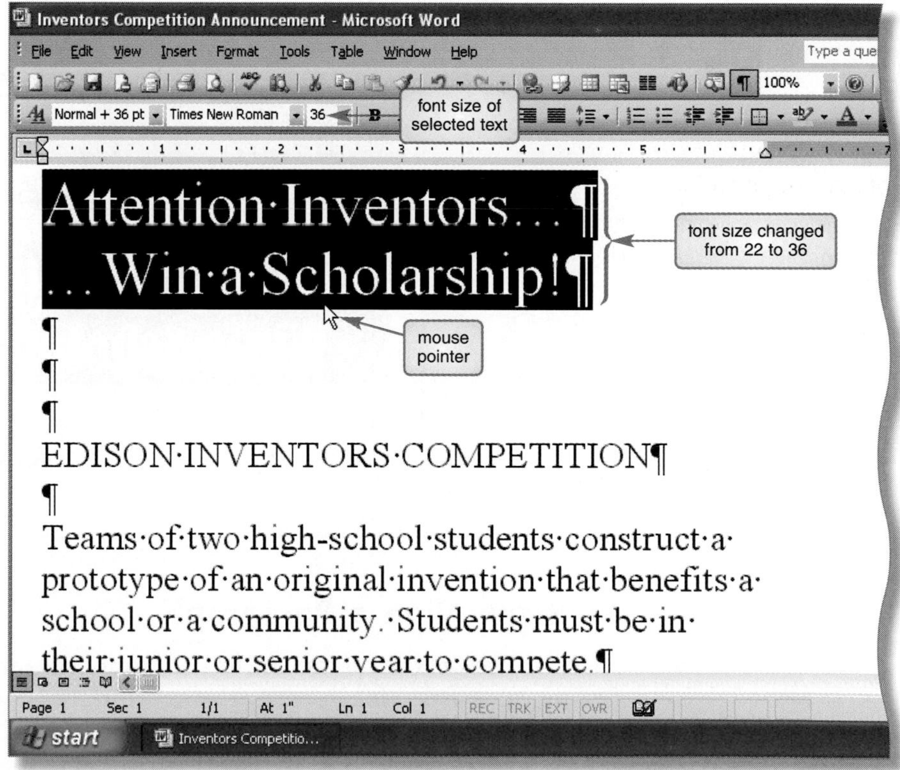

FIGURE 1-38

Changing the Font of Text

As mentioned earlier in this project, the default font in Word is Times New Roman. Word, however, provides many other fonts to add variety to your documents. The following steps show how to change the font of the headline in the announcement from Times New Roman to Bernard MT Condensed.

To Change the Font of Text

1

- **With the text selected, click the Font box arrow on the Formatting toolbar and then scroll through the Font list until Bernard MT Condensed (or a similar font) is displayed.**

Word displays a list of available fonts (Figure 1-39). Your list of available fonts may differ, depending on the type of printer you are using.

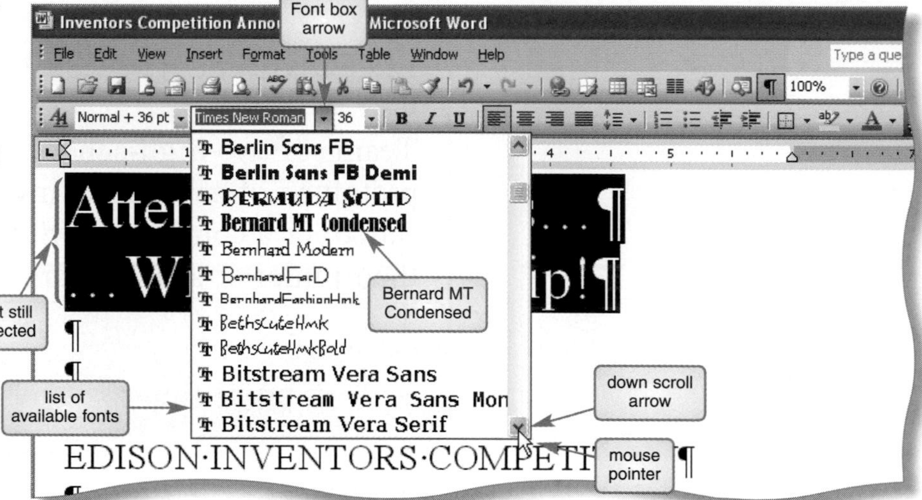

FIGURE 1-39

2

- **Click Bernard MT Condensed (or a similar font).**

Word changes the font of the selected text to Bernard MT Condensed (Figure 1-40).

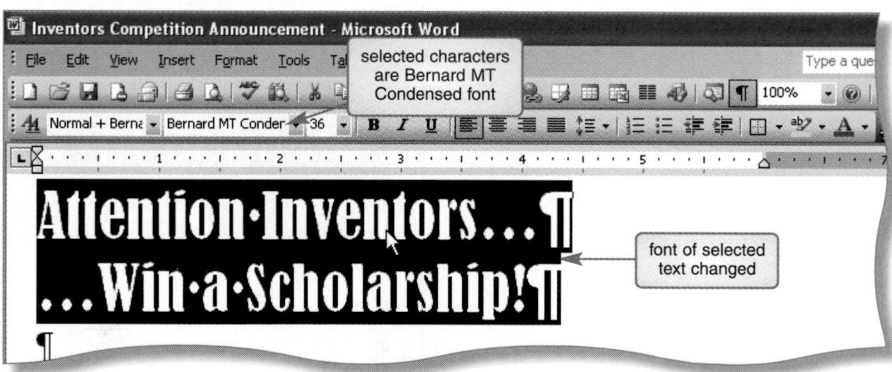

FIGURE 1-40

Right-Align a Paragraph

The default alignment for paragraphs is **left-aligned**, that is, flush at the left margin of the document with uneven right edges. In Figure 1-41, the Align Left button is selected to indicate the paragraph containing the insertion point is left-aligned.

The second line of the headline, however, is to be **right-aligned**, that is, flush at the right margin of the document with uneven left edges. Recall that the second line of the headline is a paragraph, and paragraph formatting does not require you to select the paragraph prior to formatting. Just position the insertion point in the paragraph to be formatted and then format it accordingly.

The following steps show how to right-align the second line of the headline.

To Right-Align a Paragraph

1

- **Click somewhere in the paragraph to be right-aligned.**

Word positions the insertion point at the location you clicked (Figure 1-41).

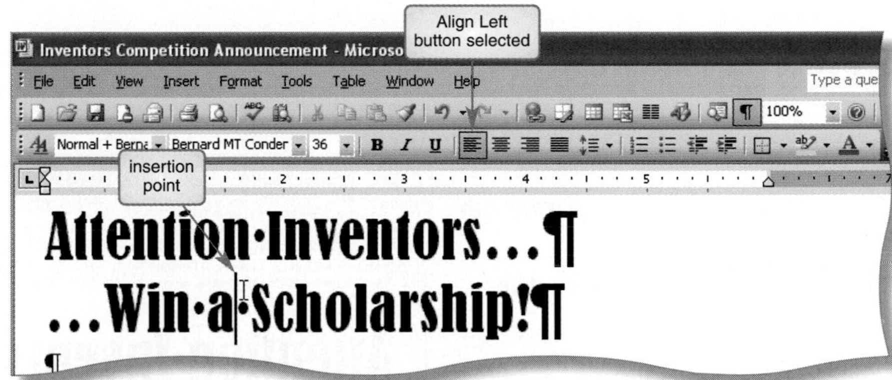

FIGURE 1-41

2

- **Click the Align Right button on the Formatting toolbar.**

The second line of the headline now is right-aligned (Figure 1-42). Notice that you did not have to select the paragraph before right-aligning it. Formatting a single paragraph requires only that the insertion point be positioned somewhere in the paragraph.

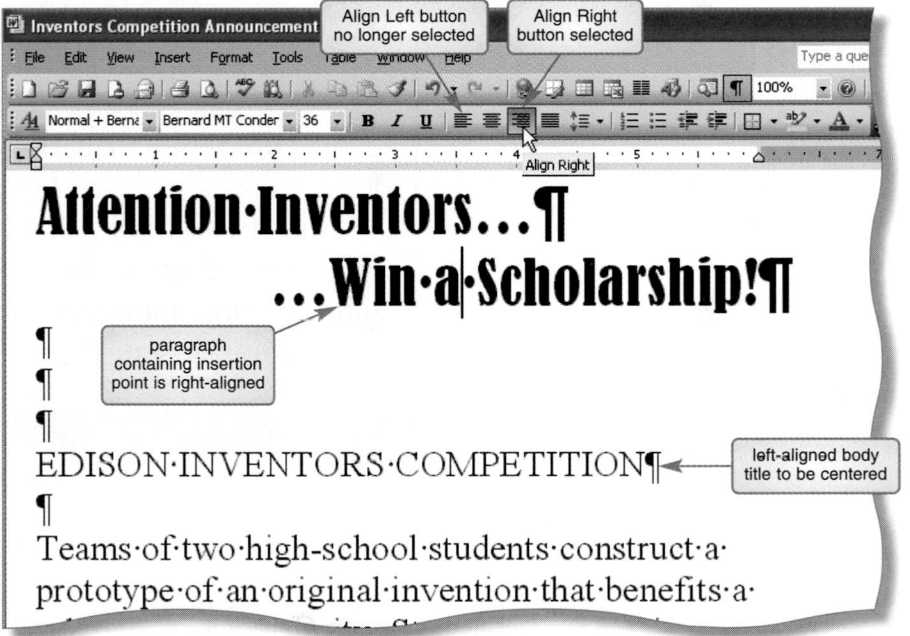

FIGURE 1-42

When a paragraph is right-aligned, the Align Right button on the Formatting toolbar is selected. If, for some reason, you wanted to return the paragraph to left-aligned, you would click the Align Left button on the Formatting toolbar.

Center a Paragraph

The body title currently is left-aligned (Figure 1-42 on the previous page). The following step shows how to **center** the paragraph, that is, position its text horizontally between the left and right margins on the page.

To Center a Paragraph

1

- **Click somewhere in the paragraph to be centered.**
- **Click the Center button on the Formatting toolbar.**

Word centers the body title between the left and right margins (Figure 1-43). The Center button on the Formatting toolbar is selected, which indicates the paragraph containing the insertion point is centered.

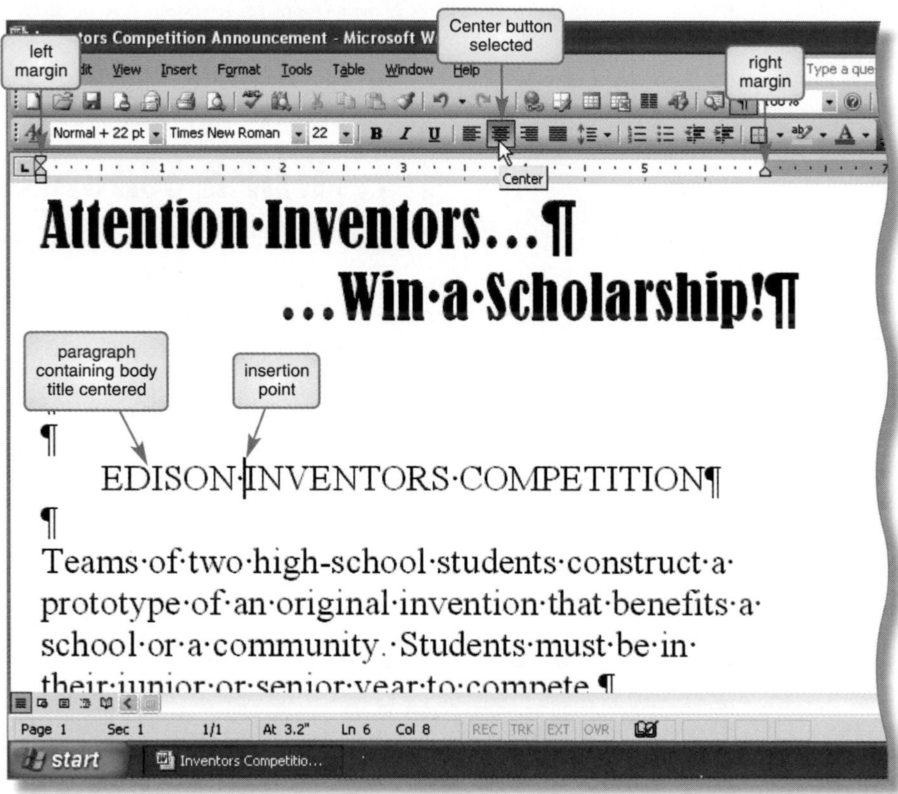

FIGURE 1-43

When a paragraph is centered, the Center button on the Formatting toolbar is selected. If, for some reason, you wanted to return the paragraph to left-aligned, you would click the Align Left button on the Formatting toolbar.

> *Q & A*
>
> **Q:** Can I center text horizontally and vertically?
>
> **A:** Yes. The Center button on the Formatting toolbar centers text horizontally between the left and right margins. You also can center text vertically between the top and bottom margins. To do this, click File on the menu bar, click Page Setup, click the Layout tab, click the Vertical alignment box arrow, click Center in the list, and then click the OK button.

Undoing, Redoing, and Repeating Commands or Actions

Word provides an Undo button on the Standard toolbar that you can use to cancel your recent command(s) or action(s). For example, if you format text incorrectly, you can undo the format and try it again. If, after you undo an action, you decide you did not want to perform the undo, you can use the Redo button to redo the undo. Word prevents you from undoing or redoing some actions, such as saving or printing a document.

The following steps show how to undo the center format to the body title using the Undo button and then re-center it using the Redo button.

To Undo and Redo an Action

1

• **Click the Undo button on the Standard toolbar.**

Word returns the body title to its formatting before you issued the center command (Figure 1-44). That is, Word left-aligns the body title.

2

• **Click the Redo button on the Standard toolbar.**

Word reapplies the center format to the body title (shown in Figure 1-43).

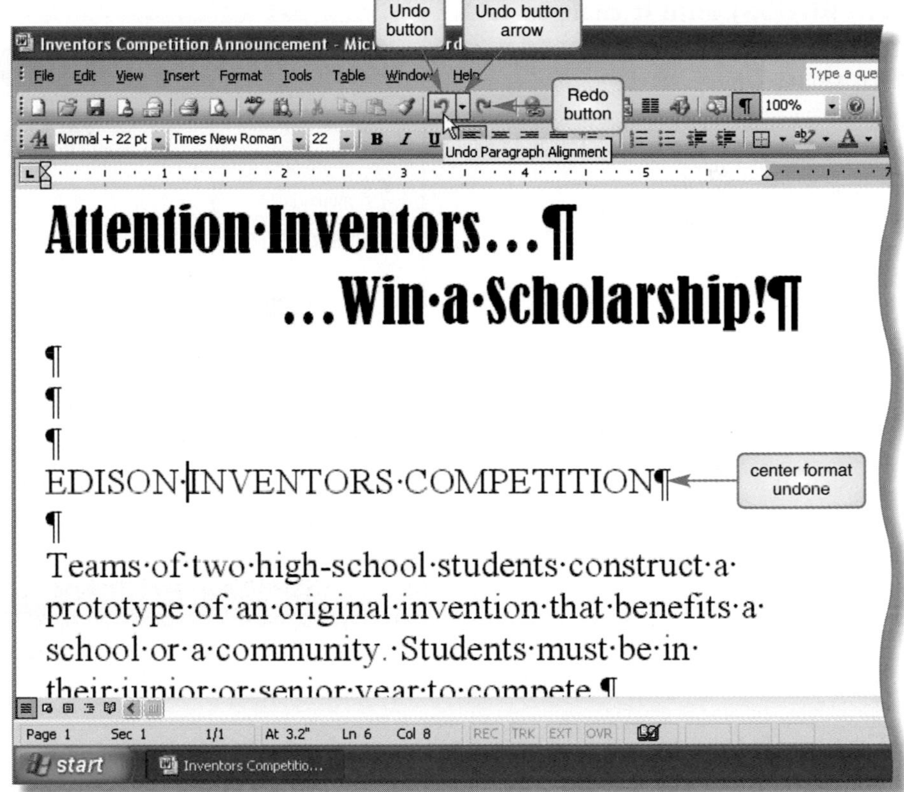

FIGURE 1-44

You also can cancel a series of prior actions by clicking the Undo button arrow on the Standard toolbar (Figure 1-44) to display the list of undo actions and then dragging through the actions you wish to undo.

Whereas the Undo command cancels an action you did not want to perform, Word also provides a **Repeat command** on the Edit menu, which duplicates your last command so you can perform it again. For example, if you centered a paragraph and wish to format another paragraph the exact same way, you could click in the second paragraph to format, click Edit on the menu bar, and then click Repeat Paragraph Alignment. The text listed after Repeat varies, depending on your most recent action. If the action cannot be repeated, Word displays the text, Can't Repeat, on the Edit menu.

Selecting a Line and Formatting It

The characters in the body title, EDISON INVENTORS COMPETITION, are to be a different font, larger font size, and italicized. To make these changes, you must select the line of text containing the body title, as shown in the following step.

To Select a Line

1

- **Move the mouse pointer to the left of the line to be selected (in this case, EDISON INVENTORS COMPETITION) until it changes to a right-pointing block arrow and then click.**

Word selects the entire line to the right of the mouse pointer (Figure 1-45).

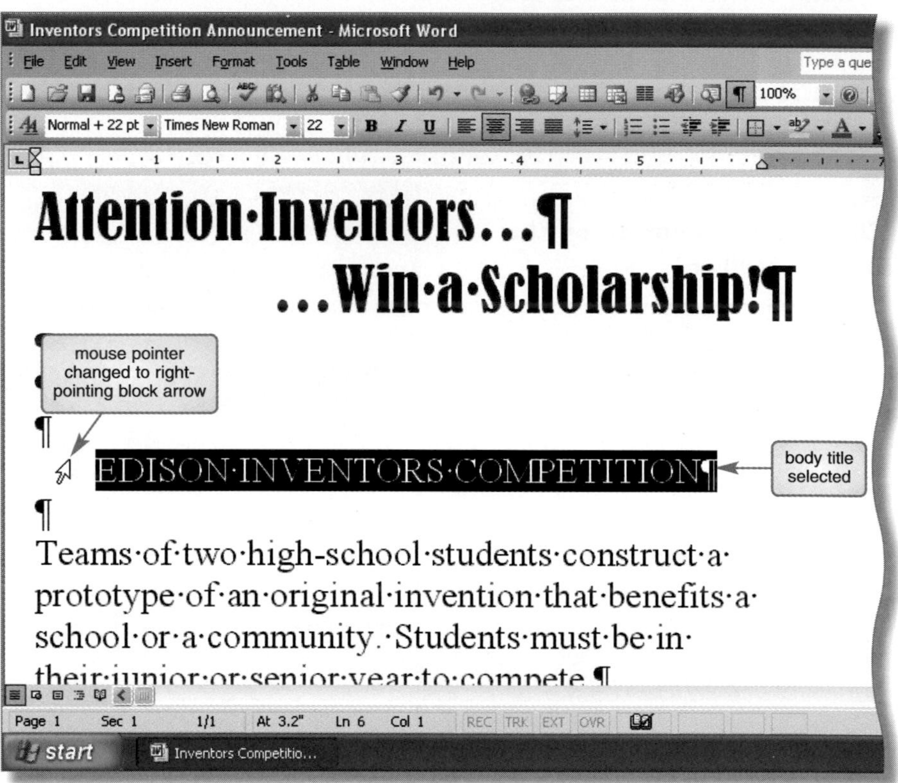

FIGURE 1-45

The next step is to change the font of the selected characters from Times New Roman to Bauhaus 93 and increase the font size of the selected characters from 22 to 28, as explained below.

To Format a Line of Text

1. **With the text selected, click the Font box arrow on the Formatting toolbar and then scroll to Bauhaus 93 (or a similar font) in the list. Click Bauhaus 93 (or a similar font).**
2. **With the text selected, click the Font Size box arrow on the Formatting toolbar and then click 28 in the list.**

Word changes the characters in the body title to 28-point Bauhaus 93 (Figure 1-46).

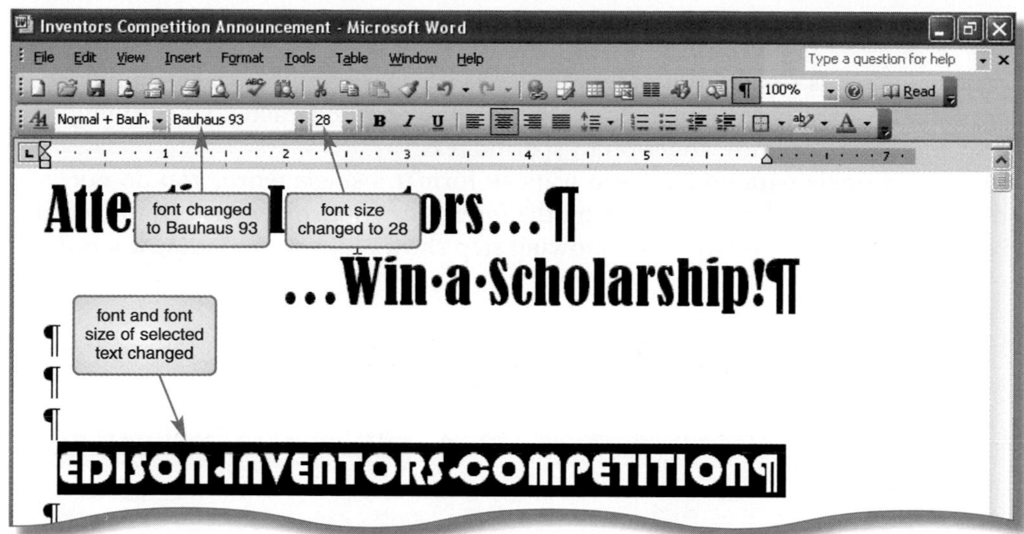

FIGURE 1-46

Q & A

Q: Why do strange formatting marks appear on my screen?

A: With some fonts, the formatting marks are not displayed on the screen properly. For example, the raised dot in each space may be displayed behind a character instead of in the space between two characters, causing the characters to look incorrect. Notice in Figure 1-46 that the formatting marks in the body title run into the characters. Recall that formatting marks do not print. Thus, the line will print fine.

Italicizing Text

Italicized text has a slanted appearance. The following step shows how to italicize the selected characters in the body title.

To Italicize Text

1

- **With the text still selected, click the Italic button on the Formatting toolbar.**

Word italicizes the text (Figure 1-47). The Italic button on the Formatting toolbar is selected.

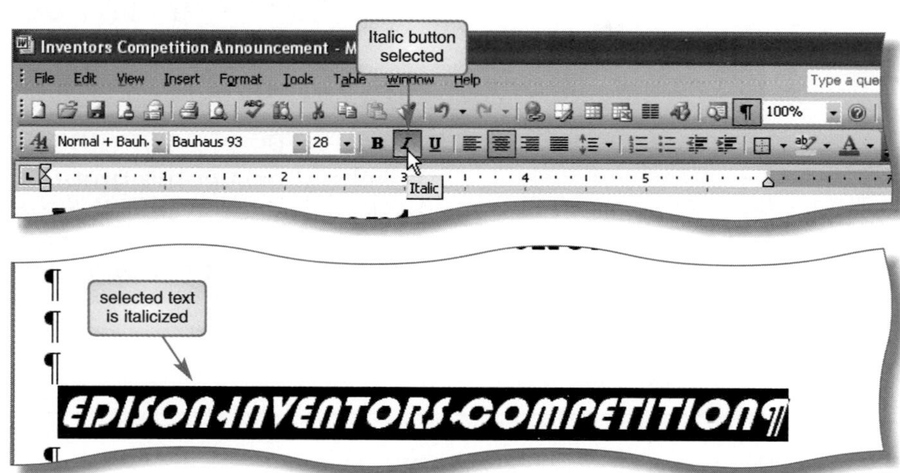

FIGURE 1-47

When the selected text is italicized, the Italic button on the Formatting toolbar is selected. If, for some reason, you wanted to remove the italic format from the selected text, you would click the Italic button a second time, or you immediately could click the Undo button on the Standard toolbar.

Underlining Text

The next step is to underline a word in the first paragraph below the body title. **Underlined** text prints with an underscore (_) below each character. Underlining is used to emphasize or draw attention to specific text.

As with a single paragraph, if you want to format a single word, you do not need to select the word. Simply position the insertion point somewhere in the word and apply the desired format. The following step shows how to underline a word.

To Underline a Word

1

- **Click somewhere in the word to be underlined (prototype, in this case).**
- **Click the Underline button on the Formatting toolbar.**

Word underlines the word containing the insertion point (Figure 1-48). The Underline button on the Formatting toolbar is selected.

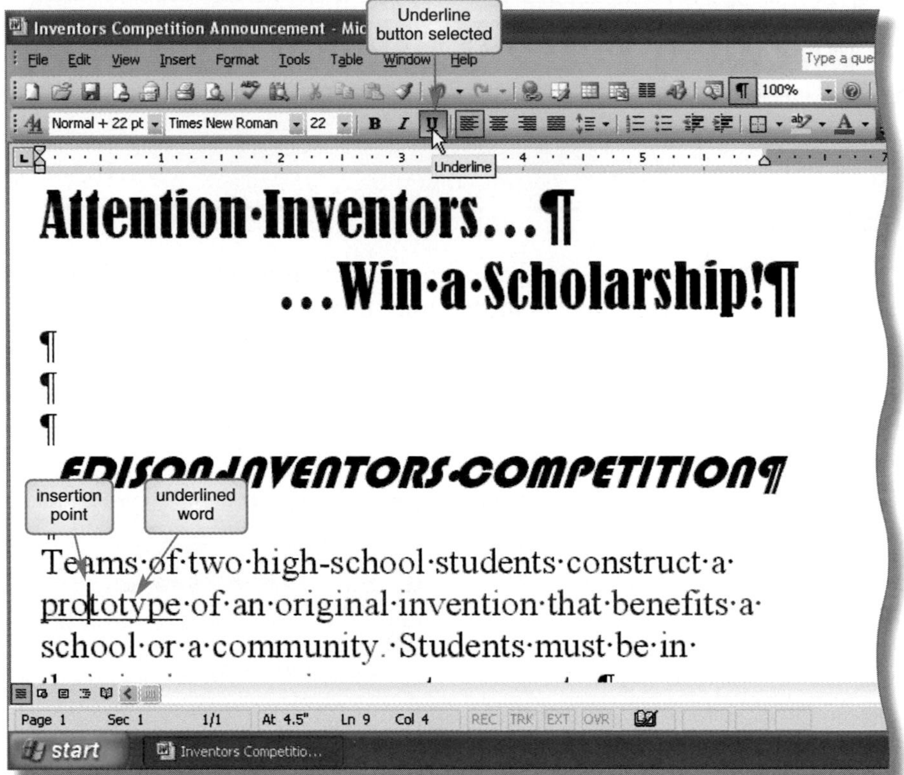

FIGURE 1-48

When the text containing the insertion point is underlined, the Underline button on the Formatting toolbar is selected. If, for some reason, you wanted to remove the underline from the text, you would click the Underline button a second time, or you immediately could click the Undo button on the Standard toolbar.

In addition to the basic underline shown in Figure 1-48, Word has many decorative underlines that are available through the Font dialog box. For example, you can use double underlines, dotted underlines, and wavy underlines. In the Font dialog box, you also can change the color of an underline and instruct Word to underline only the words and not the spaces between the words. To display the Font dialog box, click Format on the menu bar and then click Font.

Scrolling

The next text to format is in the lower portion of the announcement, which currently is not showing in the document window. To continue formatting the document, scroll down so the lower portion of the announcement is displayed in the document window, as shown in the following step.

To Scroll through a Document

1

- **Click the down scroll arrow on the vertical scroll bar nine times.**

Word scrolls through the document (Figure 1-49). Depending on your monitor type, your screen may scroll differently.

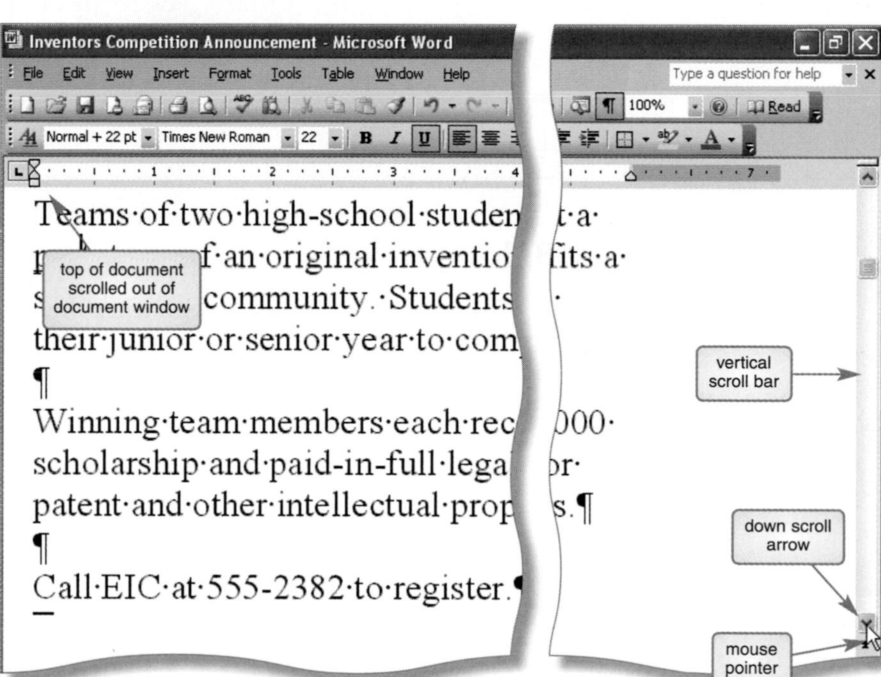

FIGURE 1-49

Selecting a Group of Words

The next step is to bold the words, junior or senior, in the announcement. To do this, you first must select this group of words. The following steps show how to select a group of words.

To Select a Group of Words

1

- **Position the mouse pointer immediately to the left of the first character of the text to be selected (in this case, the j in junior).**

The mouse pointer's shape is an I-beam when positioned in unselected text in the document window (Figure 1-50).

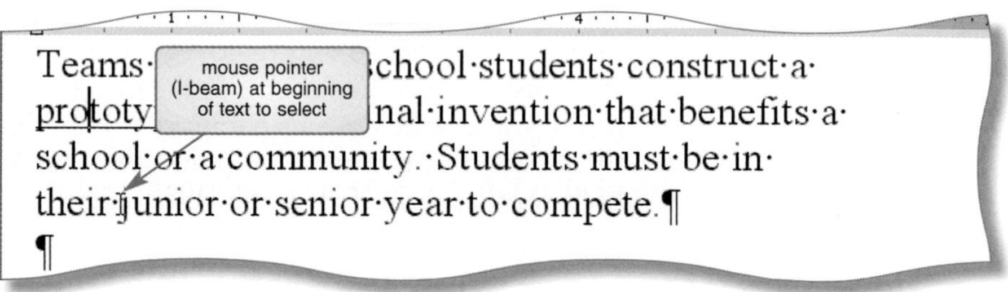

FIGURE 1-50

2

• **Drag the mouse pointer through the last character of the text to be selected (in this case, the r in senior).**

Word selects the phrase, junior or senior (Figure 1-51).

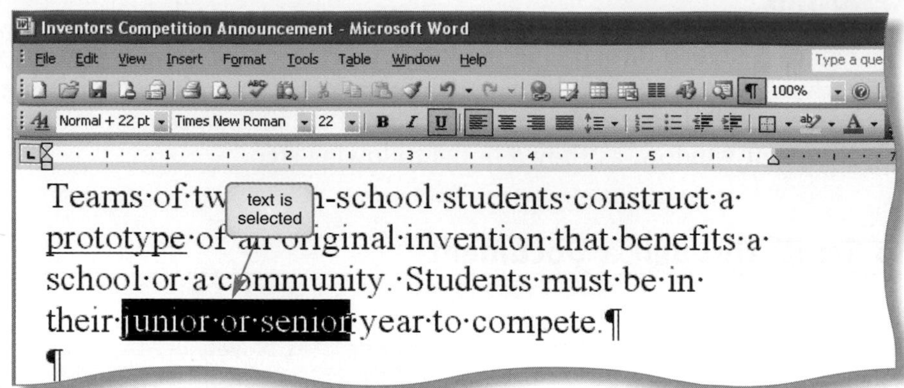

FIGURE 1-51

Bolding Text

Bold characters display somewhat thicker and darker than those that are not bold. The following step shows how to bold the selected phrase, junior or senior.

To Bold Text

1

• **With the text selected, click the Bold button on the Formatting toolbar.**

• **Click inside the selected text to remove the selection (highlight).**

Word formats the selected text in bold and positions the insertion point inside the bold text (Figure 1-52). The Bold button on the Formatting toolbar is selected.

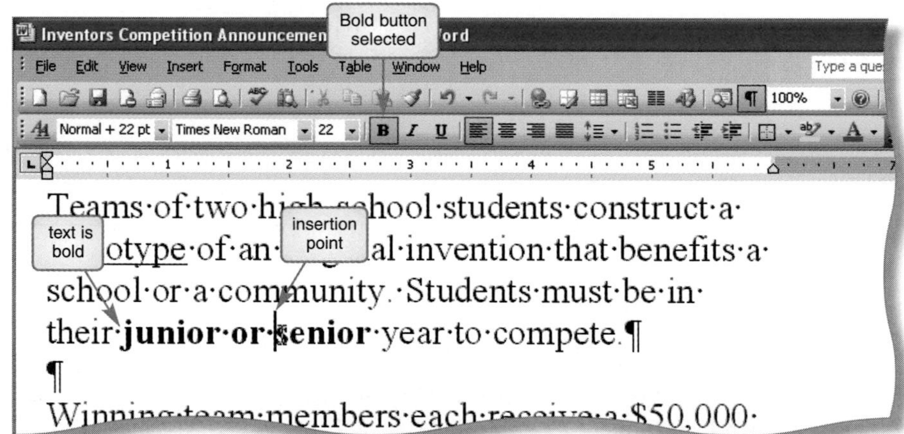

FIGURE 1-52

When you click in the document, Word positions the insertion point at the location you clicked and removes the selection (highlight) from the screen. If you click inside the selection, the Formatting toolbar displays the formatting characteristics of the characters and paragraphs containing the insertion point. For example, at the location of the insertion point, the characters are a 22-point Times New Roman bold font, and the paragraph is left-aligned.

When the selected text is bold, the Bold button on the Formatting toolbar is selected. If, for some reason, you wanted to remove the bold format from the selected text, you would click the Bold button a second time, or you immediately could click the Undo button on the Standard toolbar.

The next step is to center the last line of the announcement, as described in the following steps.

To Center a Paragraph

1. **Click somewhere in the paragraph to be centered (in this case, the last line of the announcement).**
2. **Click the Center button on the Formatting toolbar.**

Word centers the last line of the announcement (Figure 1-53).

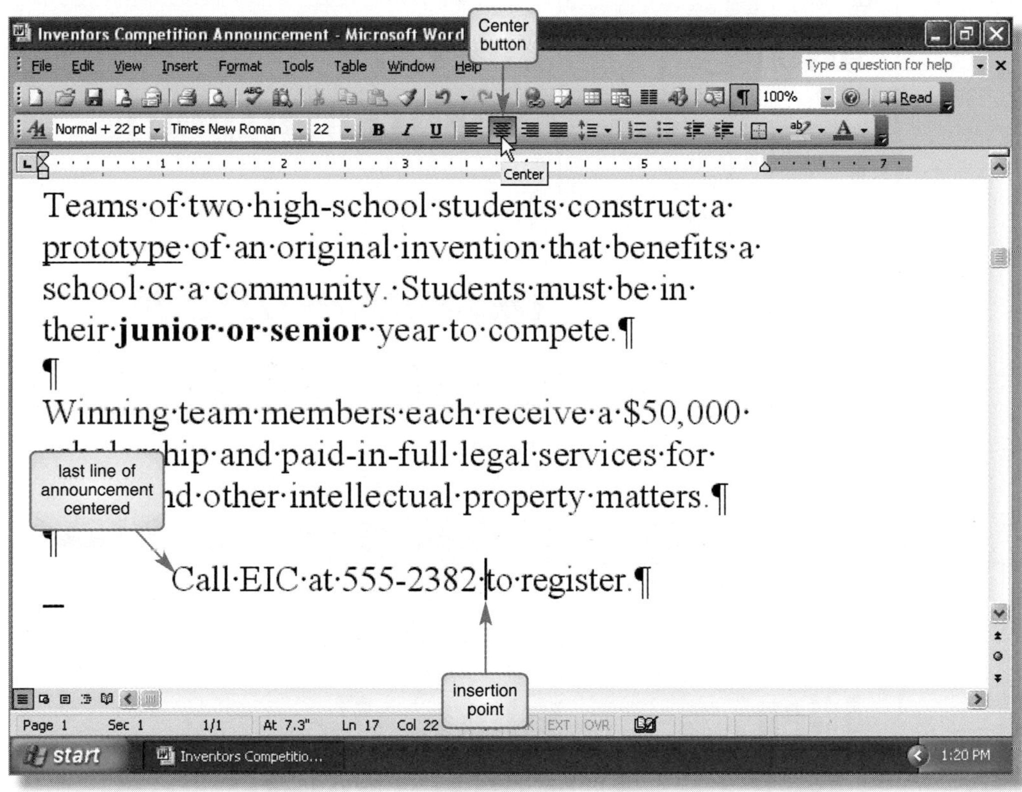

FIGURE 1-53

The formatting for the announcement now is complete.

> ***Skill Builder 1-2***
>
> To practice the following tasks, visit scsite.com/off2003sch/skill, locate Word Project 1, and then click Skill Builder 1-2.
> - ❏ Select characters and paragraphs
> - ❏ Format characters and paragraphs

Inserting Clip Art in a Word Document

Files containing graphical images, also called **graphics**, are available from a variety of sources. Word includes many predefined graphics, called **clip art**, that you can insert in a document. Clip art is located in the **Clip Organizer**, which contains a collection of clips, including clip art, as well as photographs, sounds, and video clips.

Inserting Clip Art

The next step in the project is to insert clip art of a light bulb in the announcement between the headline and the body title. Recall that Word has 14 task panes, some of which automatically appear as you perform certain operations. When you use the Clip Art command, Word automatically displays the Clip Art task pane. The following steps show how to use the Clip Art task pane to insert clip art in a document.

To Insert Clip Art in a Document

1

- **To position the insertion point where you want the clip art to be located, press CTRL+HOME and then press the DOWN ARROW key three times.**
- **Click Insert on the menu bar.**

Word positions the insertion point on the second paragraph mark below the headline, and displays the Insert menu (Figure 1-54). Remember that a short menu initially displays, which expands to a full menu after a few seconds.

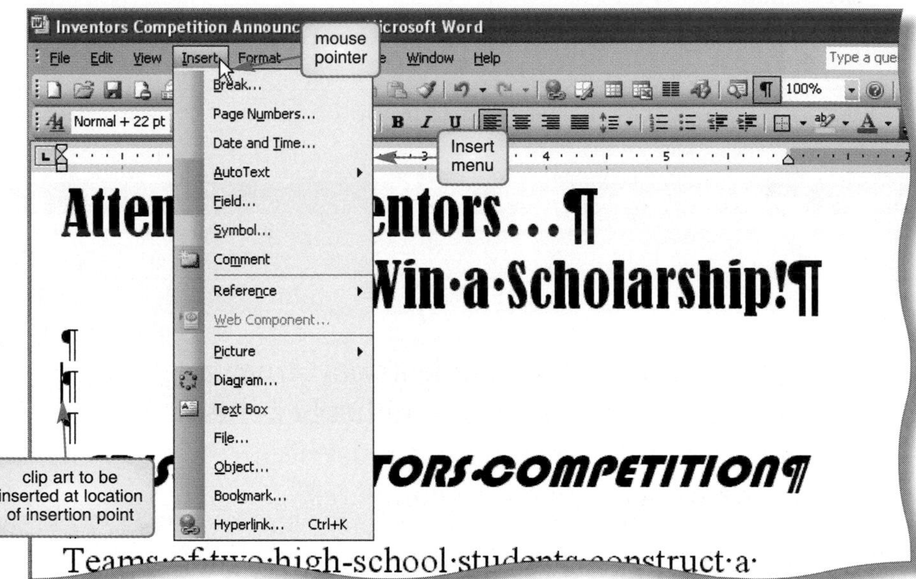

FIGURE 1-54

2

- **Point to Picture on the Insert menu.**

Word displays the Picture submenu (Figure 1-55). As discussed earlier, when you point to a command that has a small arrow to its right, Word displays a submenu associated with that command.

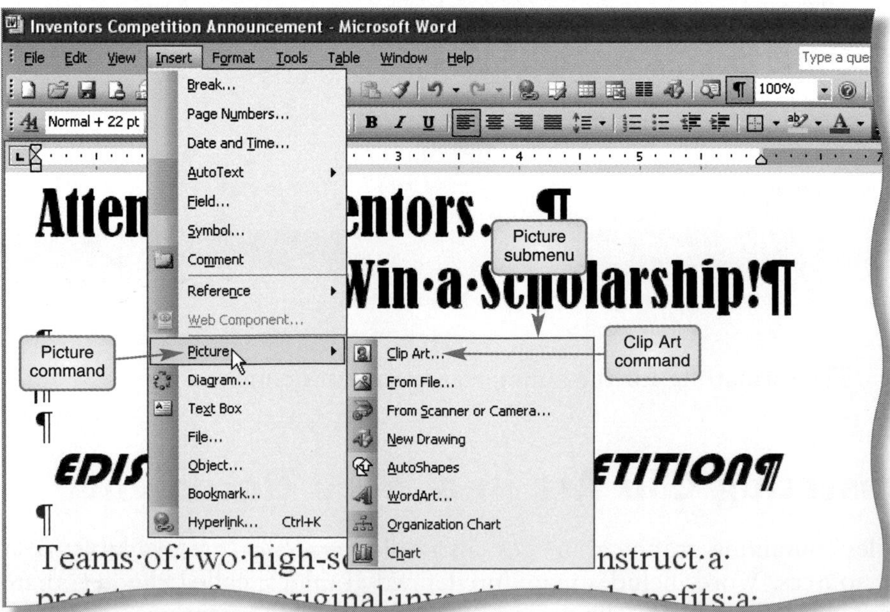

FIGURE 1-55

3

- **Click Clip Art on the Picture submenu.**
- **If the Search for text box contains text, drag through the text to select it.**
- **Type** `light bulb` **in the Search for text box.**

Word displays the Clip Art task pane at the right edge of the Word window (Figure 1-56). Recall that a task pane is a separate window that enables you to carry out some Word tasks more efficiently. When you click the Go button, Word searches the Clip Organizer for clips that match the description you type in the Search for text box.

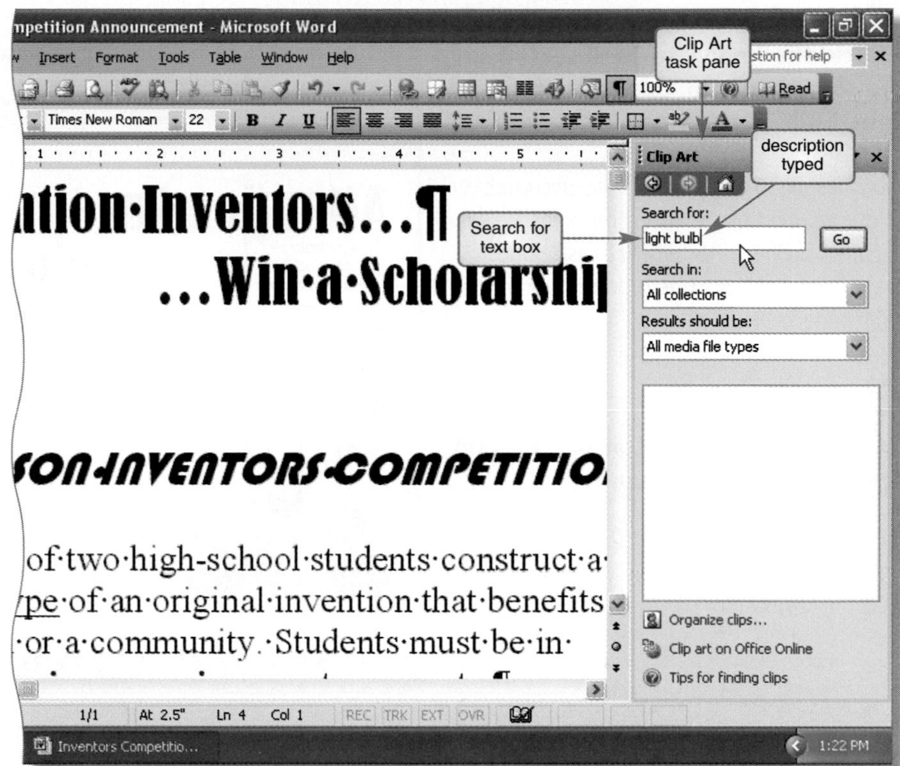

FIGURE 1-56

4

- **Click the Go button.**

Word displays a list of clips that match the description, light bulb (Figure 1-57). If you are connected to the Web, the Clip Art task pane displays clips from the Web, as well as those installed on your hard disk.

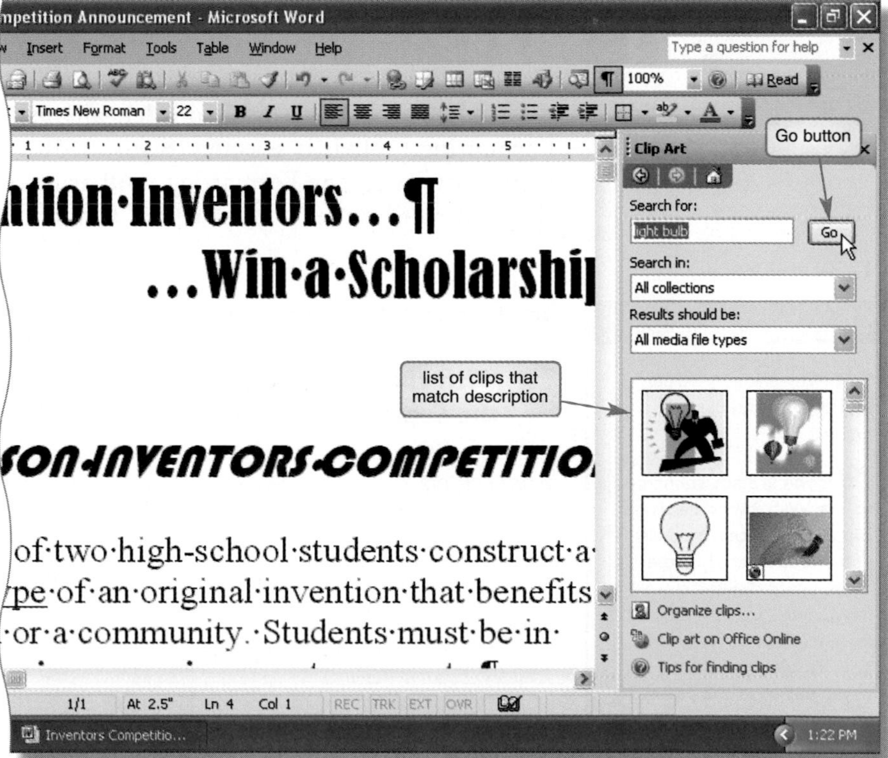

FIGURE 1-57

5

• **Click the image to be inserted in the document (in this case, the light bulb in the sky).**

Word inserts the clip art in the document at the location of the insertion point (Figure 1-58). In the Clip Art task pane, the selected clip art has a box arrow at its right edge.

6

• **Click the Close button on the Clip Art task pane title bar.**

Word removes the Clip Art task pane from the screen.

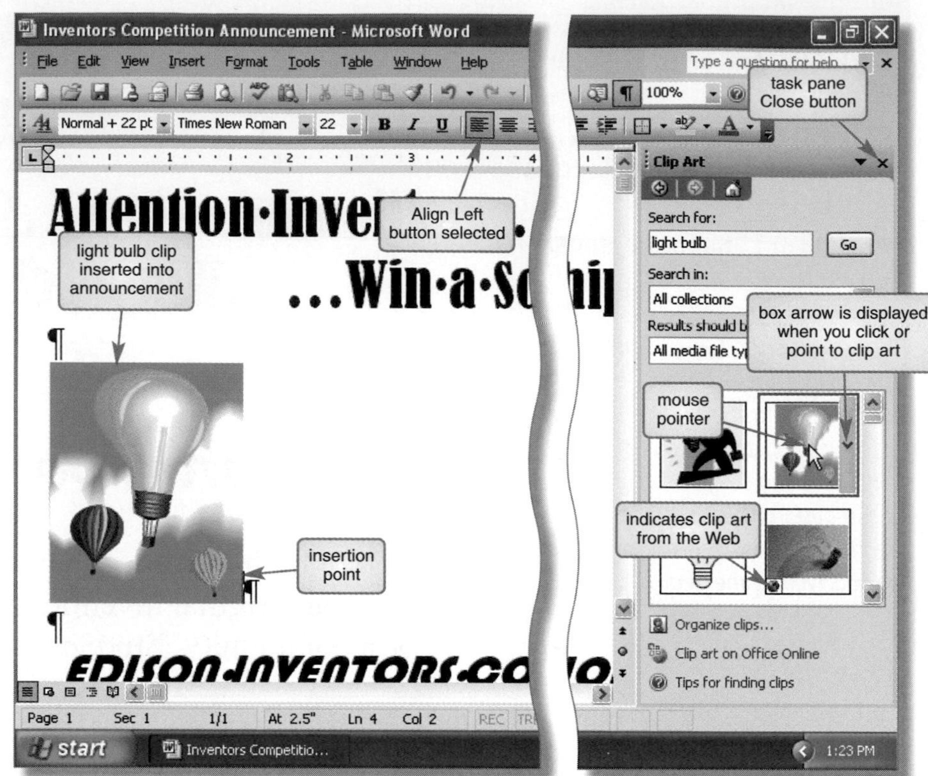

FIGURE 1-58

The clip art in the announcement is part of a paragraph. Because that paragraph is left-aligned, the clip art also is left-aligned. Notice the Align Left button on the Formatting toolbar is selected (Figure 1-58). You can use any of the paragraph alignment buttons on the Formatting toolbar to reposition the clip art. The following step shows how to center a graphic that is part of a paragraph.

To Center a Paragraph Containing a Graphic

1 **With the insertion point on the paragraph mark containing the clip art, click the Center button on the Formatting toolbar.**

Word centers the paragraph, which also centers the graphic in the paragraph (Figure 1-59).

Q & A

Q: Why does my screen display different clip art images?

A: If you are not connected to the Web, Word displays clip art from your hard disk. If you are connected to the Web, Word displays clip art from your hard disk and also from Microsoft's Web site. Your results may differ from those shown in the preceding steps if you are not connected to the Web. When clip art images display in the Clip Art task pane, Web clips are identified by a small globe displayed in their lower-left corner (Figure 1-58).

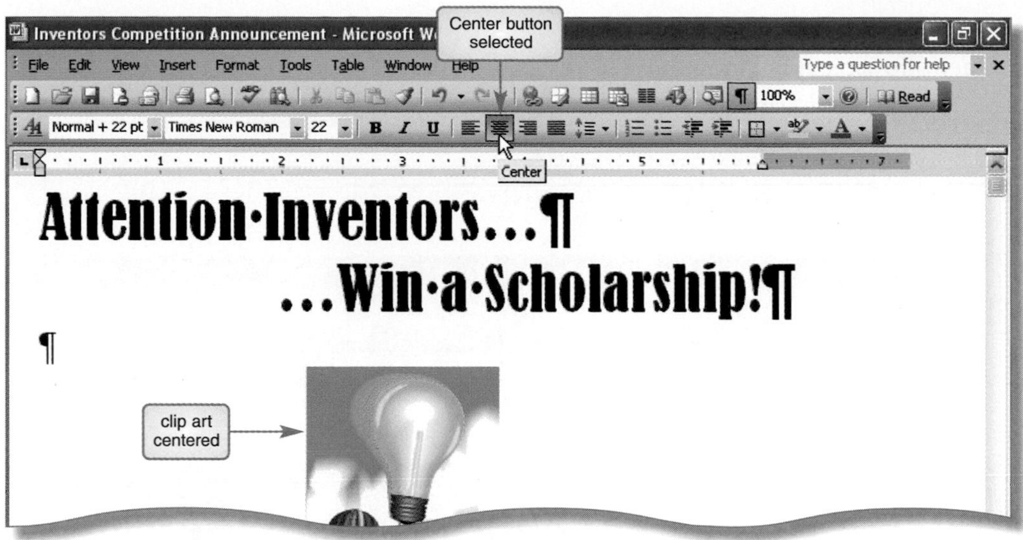

FIGURE 1-59

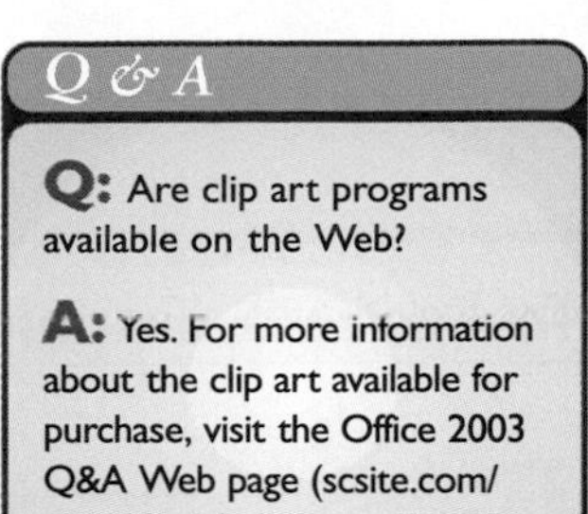

Q & A

Q: Are clip art programs available on the Web?

A: Yes. For more information about the clip art available for purchase, visit the Office 2003 Q&A Web page (scsite.com/off2003sch/qa), locate Word Project 1, and click Clip Art.

Q & A

Q: Where should a graphic be positioned in an announcement?

A: Emphasize a graphic by placing it at the optical center of the page. To determine optical center, divide the page in half horizontally and vertically. The optical center is located one third of the way up the vertical line from the point of intersection of the two lines.

Resizing a Graphic

The clip art in this announcement is to be a larger size. Once you have inserted a graphic in a document, you easily can change its size. **Resizing** includes both enlarging and reducing the size of a graphic. To resize a graphic, you first must select it. Thus, the following step shows how to select a graphic.

To Select a Graphic

1

- **Click anywhere in the graphic.**
- **If your screen does not display the Picture toolbar, click View on the menu bar, point to Toolbars, and then click Picture.**

Word selects the graphic (Figure 1-60). A selected graphic is displayed surrounded by a ***selection rectangle****, which has small squares, called* ***sizing handles****, at each corner and middle location. You use the sizing handles to change the size of the graphic. When a graphic is selected, the Picture toolbar automatically should appear on the screen.*

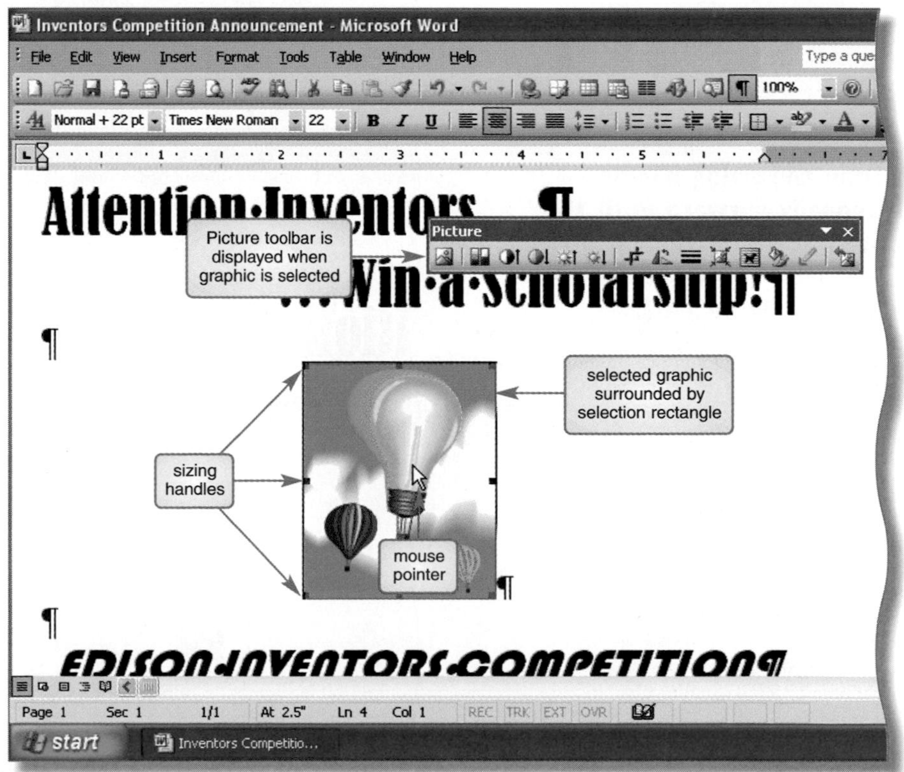

FIGURE 1-60

The following steps show how to resize the graphic just inserted and selected.

To Resize a Graphic

1

• **With the graphic still selected, point to the upper-left corner sizing handle.**

The mouse pointer shape changes to a two-headed arrow when it is on a sizing handle (Figure 1-61). To resize a graphic, you drag the sizing handle(s) until the graphic is the desired size.

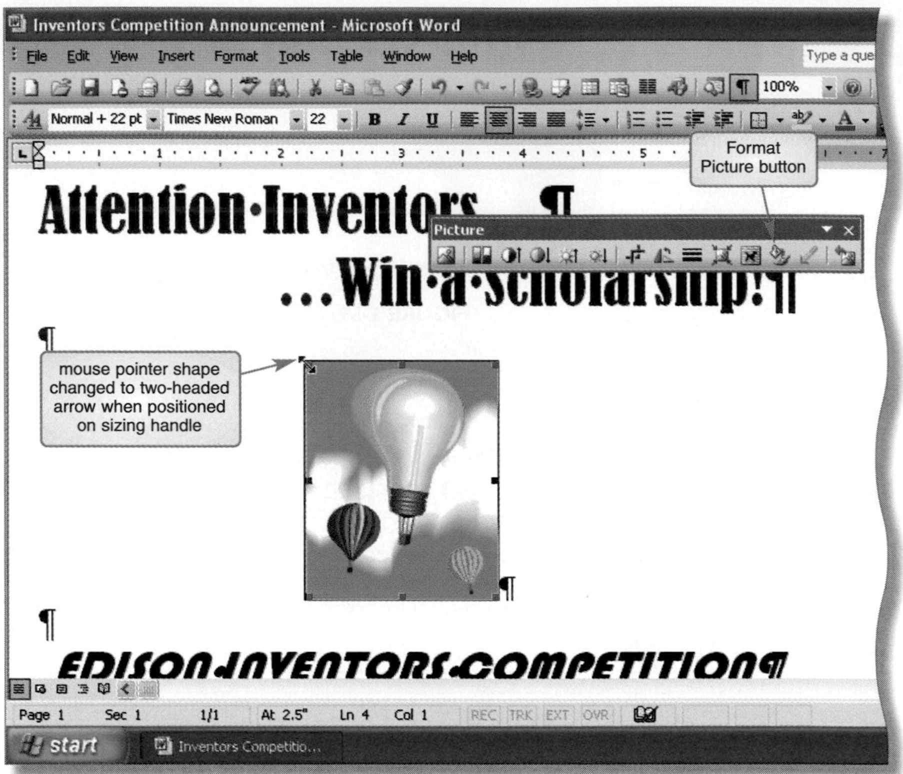

FIGURE 1-61

2

• **Drag the sizing handle diagonally outward until the dotted selection rectangle is positioned approximately as shown in Figure 1-62.**

When you drag a corner sizing handle, the proportions of the graphic remain intact.

FIGURE 1-62

3

• **Release the mouse button. Press CTRL+HOME.**

Word resizes the graphic (Figure 1-63). When you click outside of a graphic or press a key to scroll through a document, Word deselects the graphic. The Picture toolbar disappears from the screen when you deselect a graphic.

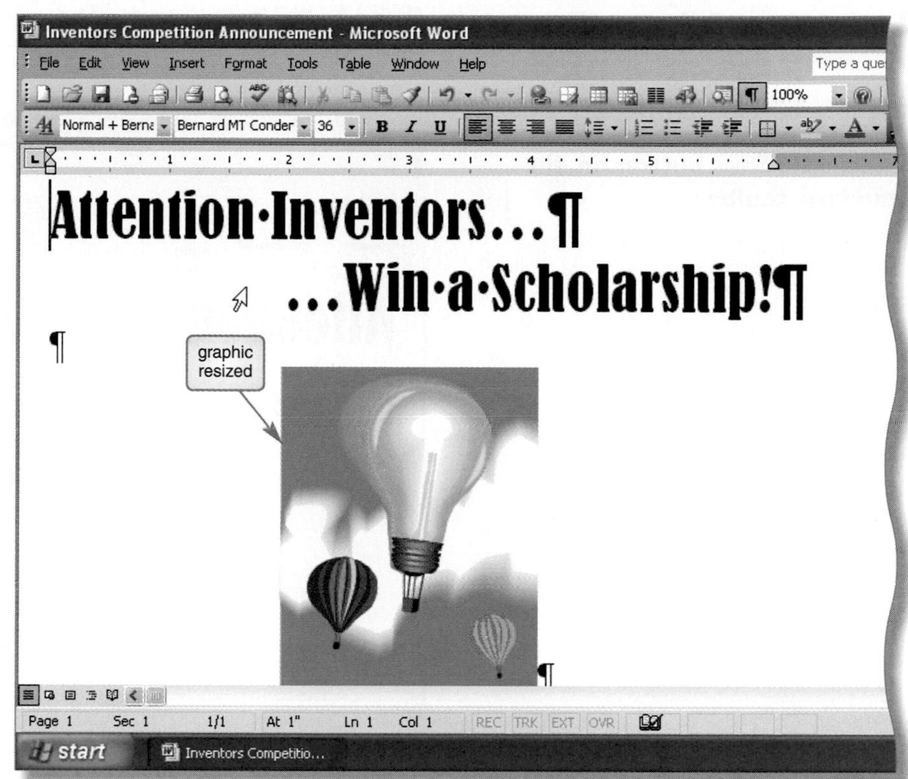

FIGURE 1-63

Instead of resizing a selected graphic by dragging a sizing handle with the mouse, you also can use the Format Picture dialog box to resize a graphic by clicking the Format Picture button on the Picture toolbar (Figure 1-61) and then clicking the Size tab. In the Size sheet, you can enter exact height and width measurements. If you have a precise measurement for a graphic, use the Format Picture dialog box; otherwise, drag the sizing handles to resize a graphic.

Sometimes, you might resize a graphic and realize it is the wrong size. In this case, you may want to return the graphic to its original size and start again. To restore a resized graphic to its exact original size, click the graphic to select it and then click the Format Picture button on the Picture toolbar to display the Format Picture dialog box. Click the Size tab, click the Reset button, and then click the OK button.

Skill Builder 1-3

To practice the following tasks, visit scsite.com/off2003sch/skill, locate Word Project 1, and then click Skill Builder 1-3.
- ❑ Insert clip art
- ❑ Resize a graphic

Saving an Existing Document with the Same File Name

The announcement for Project 1 now is complete. To transfer the modified document with the formatting changes and graphic to the USB flash drive, you must save the document again. When you saved the document the first time, you assigned a file name to it (Inventors Competition Announcement). When you use the procedure on the next page, Word automatically assigns the same file name to the document each time you subsequently save it.

To Save an Existing Document with the Same File Name

1

- **Click the Save button on the Standard toolbar.**

Word saves the document on a USB flash drive using the currently assigned file name, Inventors Competition Announcement (Figure 1-64).

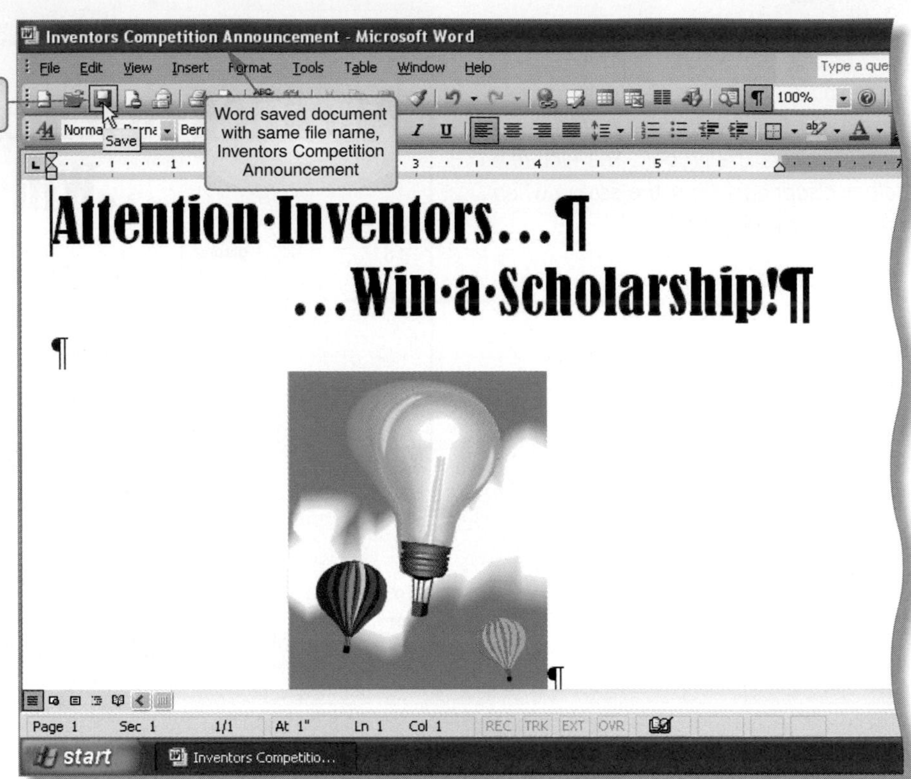

FIGURE 1-64

While Word is saving the document, the Background Save icon appears near the right edge of the status bar. When the save is complete, the document remains in memory and on the screen.

If, for some reason, you want to save an existing document with a different file name, click Save As on the File menu to display the Save As dialog box. Then, fill in the Save As dialog box as discussed in Steps 2 through 5 on pages WD 28 through WD 30.

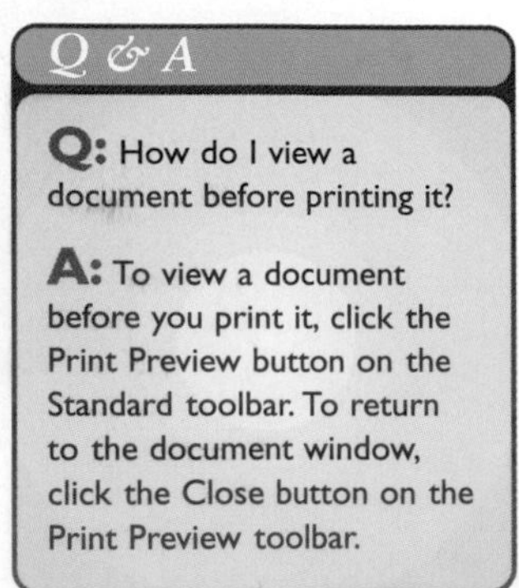

Q & A

Q: How do I view a document before printing it?

A: To view a document before you print it, click the Print Preview button on the Standard toolbar. To return to the document window, click the Close button on the Print Preview toolbar.

Printing a Document

The next step is to print the document you created. A printed version of the document is called a **hard copy** or **printout**. The following steps show how to print the announcement created in this project.

To Print a Document

1

- **Ready the printer according to the printer instructions.**
- **Click the Print button on the Standard toolbar.**

The mouse pointer briefly changes to an hourglass shape as Word prepares to print the document. While the document is printing, a printer icon appears in the notification area on the Windows taskbar (Figure 1-65).

2

- **When the printer stops printing the document, retrieve the printout, which should look like Figure 1-1 on page WD 5.**

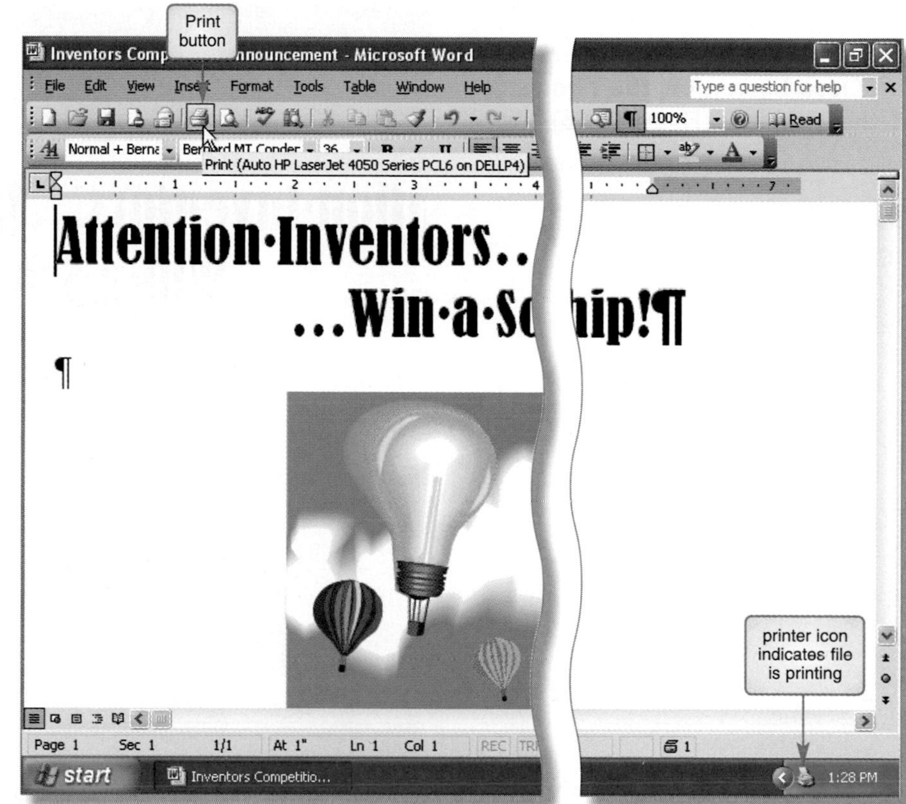

FIGURE 1-65

When you use the Print button to print a document, Word prints the entire document automatically. You then may distribute the printout or keep it as a permanent record of the document.

If you wanted to print multiple copies of the document, display the Print dialog box by clicking File on the menu bar and then clicking Print. In addition to the number of copies, the Print dialog box has several printing options.

If you wanted to cancel your job that is printing or one you have waiting to be printed, double-click the printer icon on the taskbar (Figure 1-65). In the printer window, click the job to be canceled and then click Cancel on the Document menu.

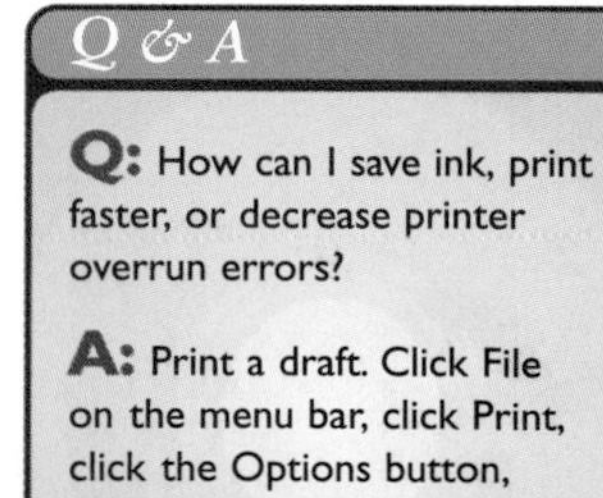

Q & A

Q: How can I save ink, print faster, or decrease printer overrun errors?

A: Print a draft. Click File on the menu bar, click Print, click the Options button, place a check mark in the Draft output check box, and then click the OK button in each dialog box.

Quitting Word

After you create, save, and print the announcement, Project 1 is complete. The following steps show how to quit Word and return control to Windows.

To Quit Word

1

• **Position the mouse pointer on the Close button on the right side of the title bar (Figure 1-66).**

2

• **Click the Close button.**

The Word window closes.

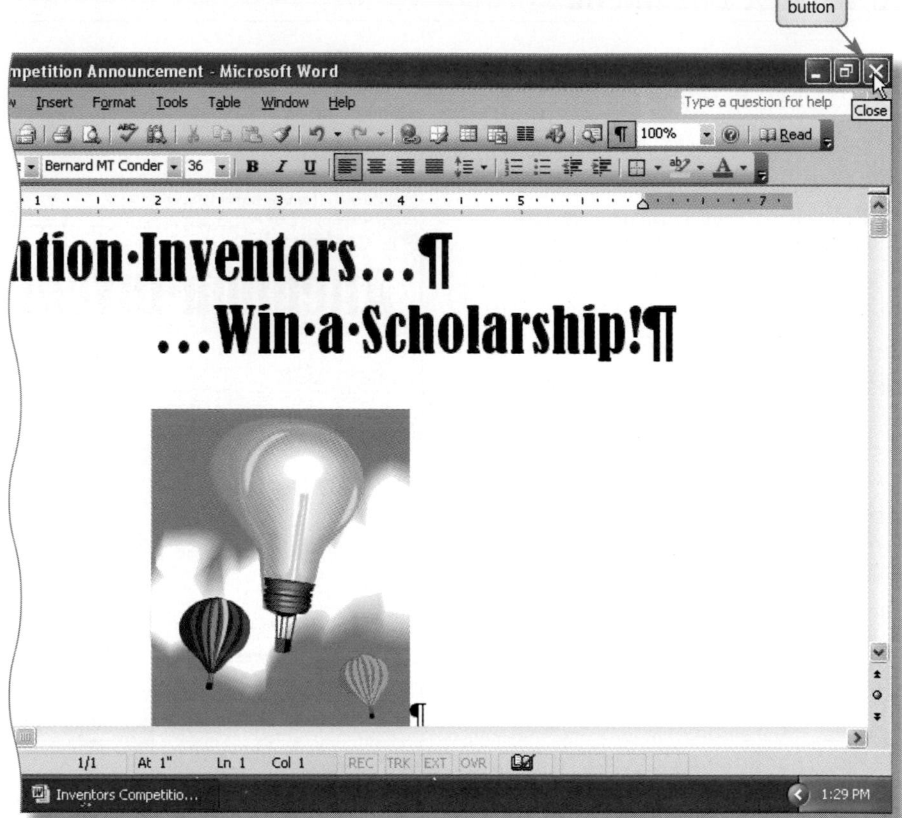

FIGURE 1-66

When you quit Word, a dialog box may display asking if you want to save the changes. This occurs if you made changes to the document since the last save. Clicking the Yes button in the dialog box saves the changes; clicking the No button ignores the changes; and clicking the Cancel button returns to the document. If you did not make any changes since you saved the document, this dialog box usually is not displayed.

Starting Word and Opening a Document

Once you have created and saved a document, you often will have reason to retrieve it from disk. For example, you might want to revise the document or print it again. Earlier, you saved the Word document created in Project 1 on a USB flash drive using the file name, Inventors Competition Announcement.

The following steps, which assume Word is not running, show how to open the Inventors Competition Announcement file from a USB flash drive.

To Open a Document

1

- **With your USB flash drive connected to one of the computer's USB ports, click the Start button on the Windows taskbar, point to All Programs on the Start menu, point to Microsoft Office on the All Programs submenu, and then click Microsoft Office Word 2003 on the Microsoft Office submenu.**

Word starts. The Open area of the Getting Started task pane lists up to four of the most recently used files (Figure 1-67).

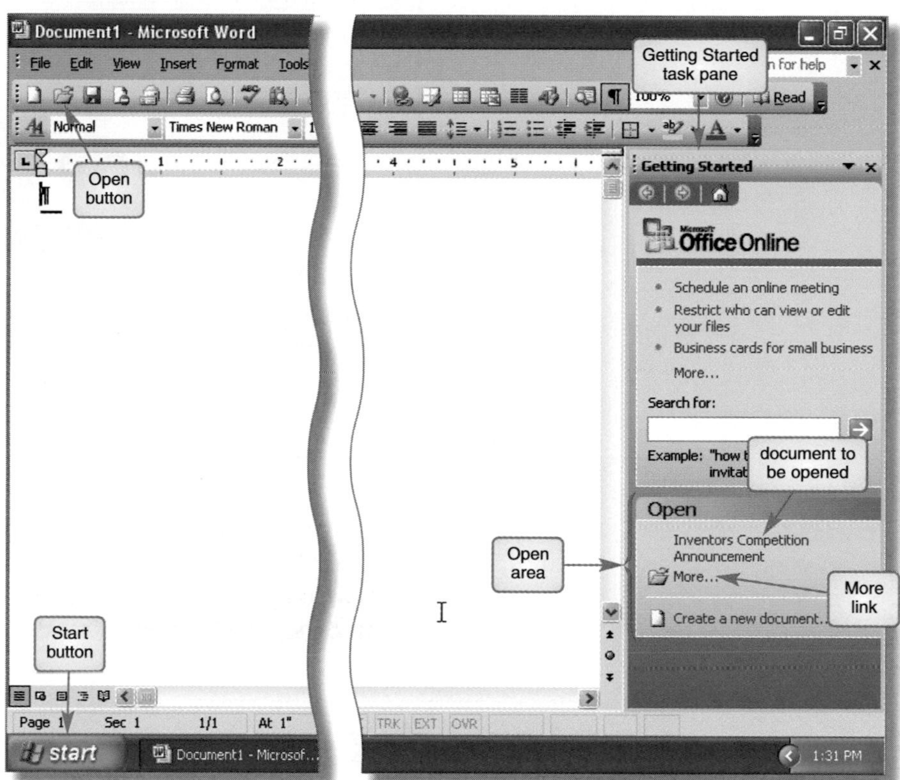

FIGURE 1-67

2

• Click Inventors Competition Announcement in the Getting Started task pane.

Word opens the document, Inventors Competition Announcement, from the USB flash drive and displays it in the Word window (Figure 1-68). The Getting Started task pane closes.

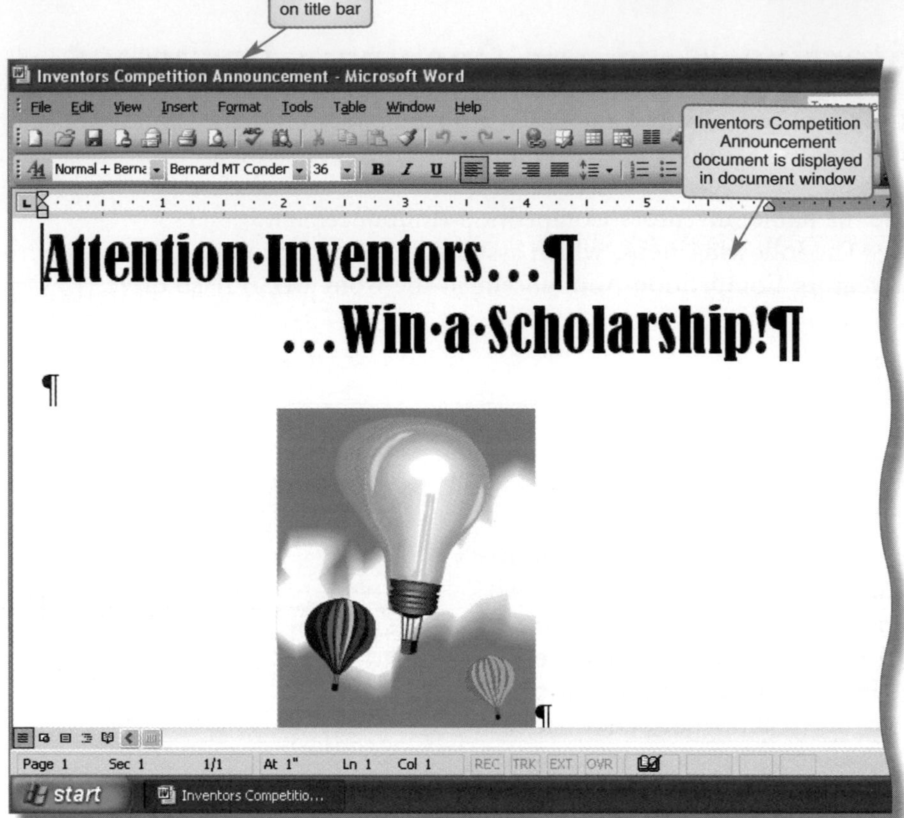

FIGURE 1-68

If you want to open a document other than one of the four most recently opened ones, click the Open button on the Standard toolbar or the More link in the Getting Started task pane. Clicking the Open button or the More link displays the Open dialog box, which allows you to navigate to a document stored on disk.

Correcting Errors

After creating a document, you often will find you must make changes to it. For example, the document may contain an error or new circumstances may require you add text to the document.

Types of Changes Made to Documents

The types of changes made to documents normally fall into one of the three following categories: additions, deletions, or modifications.

ADDITIONS Additional words, sentences, or paragraphs may be required in a document. Additions occur when you omit text from a document and want to insert it later. For example, additional prizes may be listed for the winning team members.

DELETIONS Sometimes, text in a document is incorrect or is no longer needed. For example, the competition may be limited to seniors. In this case, you would delete the words, juniors and, from the announcement.

MODIFICATIONS If an error is made in a document or changes take place that affect the document, you might have to revise a word(s) in the text. For example, the Edison Inventors Society might change the team composition from two high-school students to three high-school students.

Inserting Text in an Existing Document

Word inserts text to the left of the insertion point. The text to the right of the insertion point moves to the right and downward to fit the new text. The following steps show how to insert the word, school, to the left of the word, year, in the announcement.

To Insert Text in an Existing Document

1

- **Scroll through the document and then click to the left of the location of text to be inserted (in this case, the y in year).**

Word positions the insertion point at the clicked location (Figure 1-69).

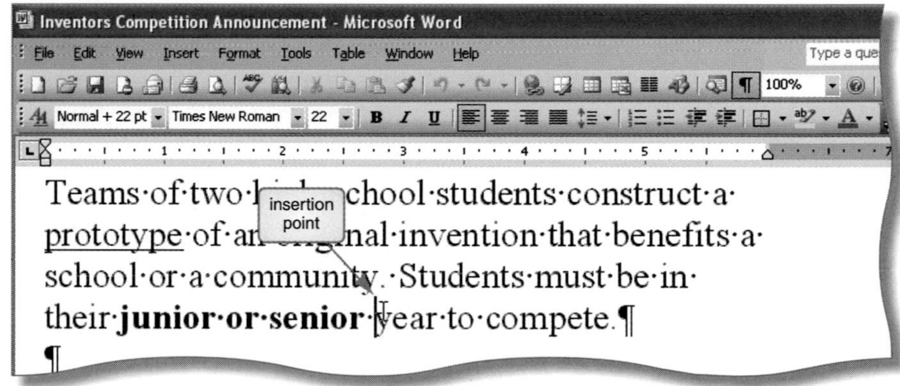

FIGURE 1-69

2

- **Type** `school` **and then press the SPACEBAR.**

Word inserts the word, school, to the left of the insertion point (Figure 1-70).

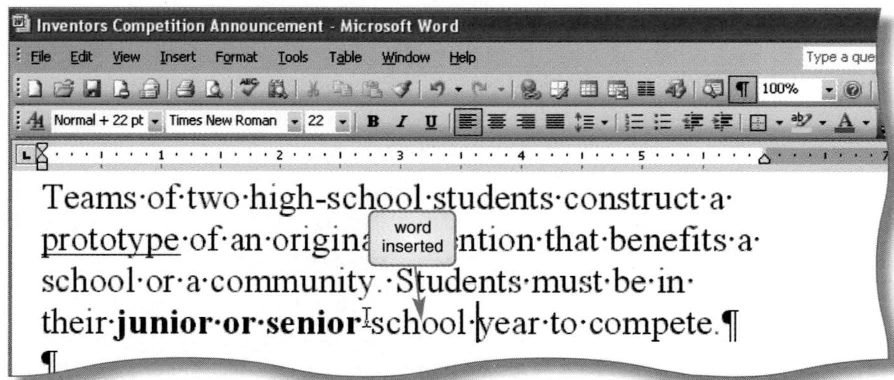

FIGURE 1-70

In Word, the default typing mode is insert mode. In **insert mode**, as you type a character, Word inserts the character and moves all the characters to the right of the typed character one position to the right. You can change to overtype mode by double-clicking the OVR status indicator on the status bar (Figure 1-8 on page WD 10). In **overtype mode**, Word replaces characters to the right of the insertion point. Double-clicking the OVR status indicator again returns Word to insert mode.

Deleting Text from an Existing Document

It is not unusual to type incorrect characters or words in a document. As discussed earlier in this project, you can click the Undo button on the Standard toolbar to immediately undo a command or action — this includes typing. Word also provides other methods of correcting typing errors.

To delete an incorrect character in a document, simply click next to the incorrect character and then press the BACKSPACE key to erase to the left of the insertion point, or press the DELETE key to erase to the right of the insertion point.

To delete a word or phrase, you first must select the word or phrase. The following steps show how to select the word, school, that was just added in the previous steps and then delete the selection.

To Select a Word

1

- **Position the mouse pointer somewhere in the word to be selected (in this case, school), as shown in Figure 1-71.**

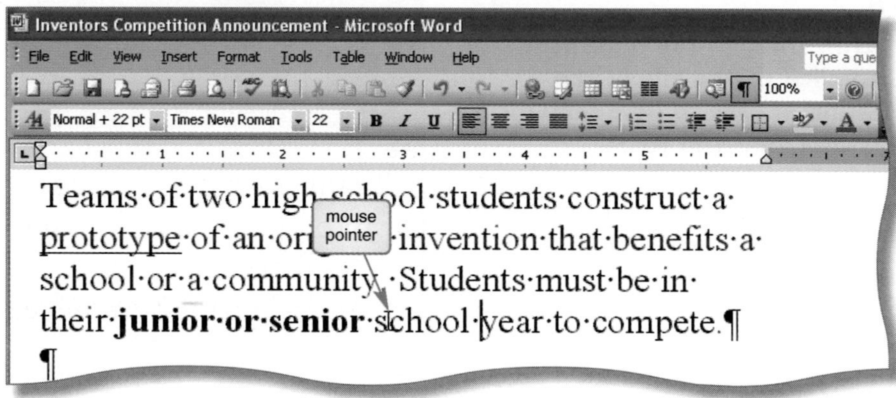

FIGURE 1-71

2

- **Double-click the word to be selected.**

The word, school, is selected (Figure 1-72).

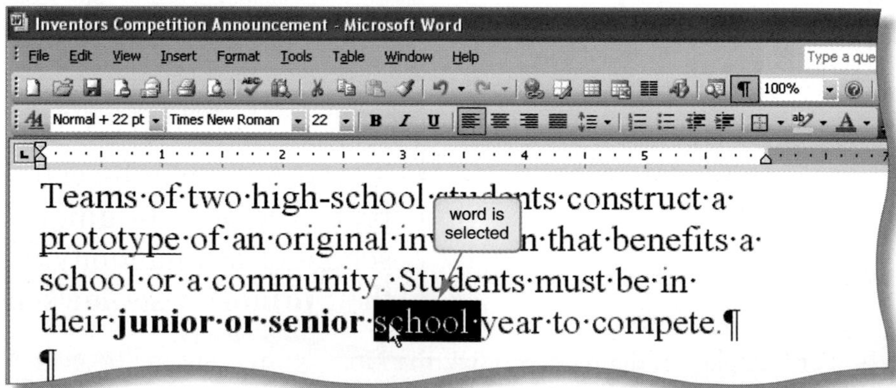

FIGURE 1-72

The next step is to delete the selected text.

To Delete Text

1

- **With the text selected, press the DELETE key.**

Word deletes the selected word from the document (Figure 1-73).

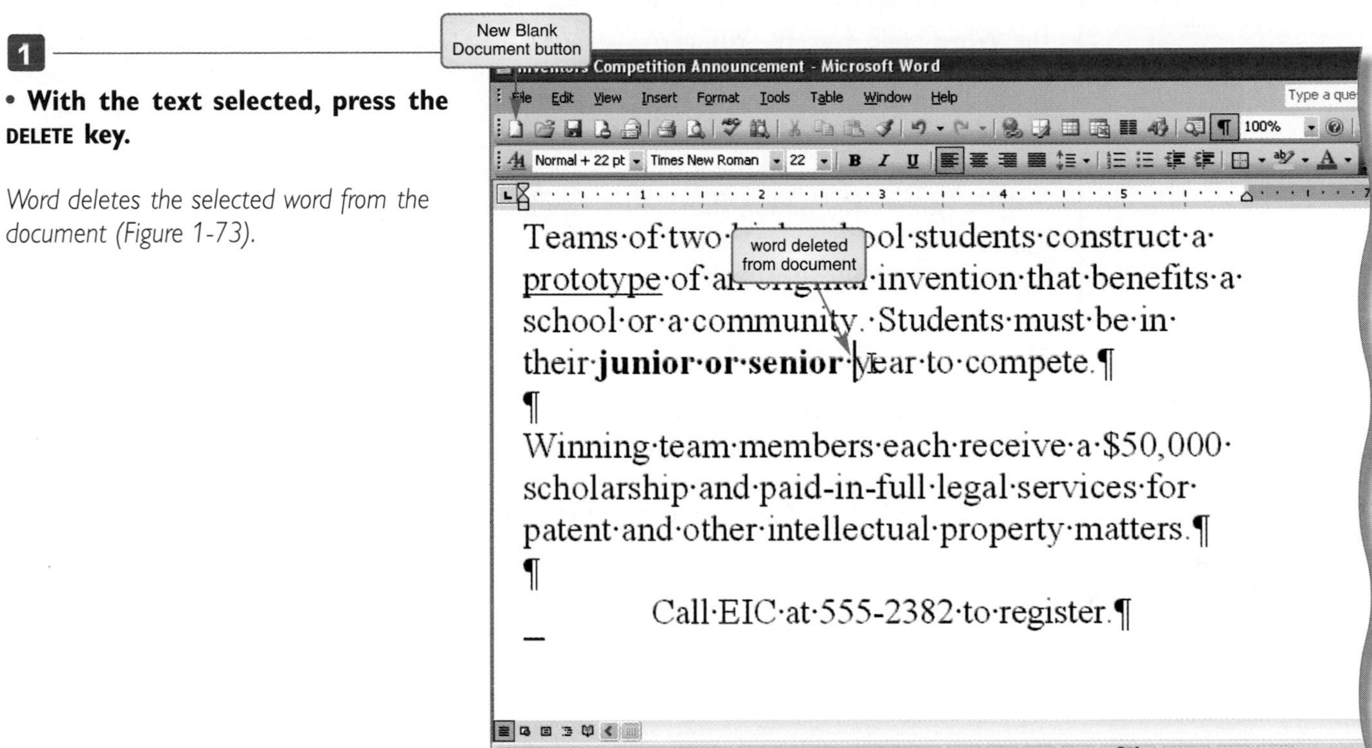

FIGURE 1-73

Closing the Entire Document

Sometimes, everything goes wrong. If this happens, you may want to close the document entirely and start over. You also may want to close a document when you are finished with it so you can begin your next document.

To Close the Entire Document and Start Over

1. Click File on the menu bar and then click Close.
2. If Word displays a dialog box, click the No button to ignore the changes since the last time you saved the document.
3. Click the New Blank Document button (Figure 1-73) on the Standard toolbar.

You also can close the document by clicking the Close button at the right edge of the menu bar.

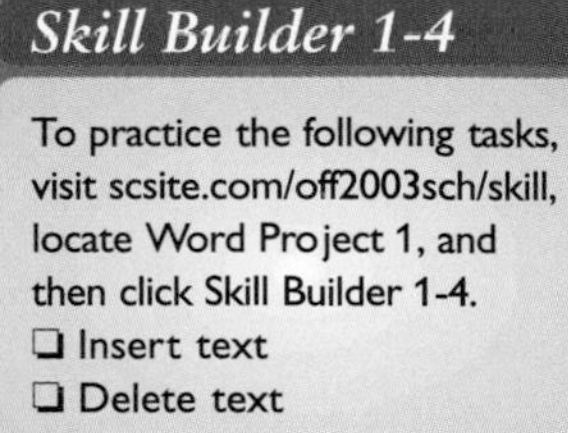

Skill Builder 1-4
To practice the following tasks, visit scsite.com/off2003sch/skill, locate Word Project 1, and then click Skill Builder 1-4.
❑ Insert text
❑ Delete text

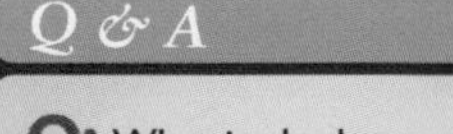

Q: What is the best way to become familiar with the Word Help system?

A: The best way to become familiar with the Word Help system is to use it. Appendix A includes detailed information about the Word Help system and exercises that will help you gain confidence in using it.

Word Help System

At anytime while you are using Word, you can get answers to questions through the **Word Help system**. You activate the Word Help system by using the Type a question for help box on the menu bar, the Microsoft Office Word Help button on the Standard toolbar, or the Help menu (Figure 1-74). Used properly, this form of online assistance can increase your productivity and reduce your frustrations by minimizing the time you spend learning how to use Word.

The following section shows how to obtain answers to your questions using the Type a question for help box. Additional information about using the Word Help system is available in Appendix A.

Using the Type a Question for Help Box

Through the Type a question for help box on the right side of the menu bar (Figure 1-74), you type free-form questions, such as *how do I save* or *how do I create a Web page*, or you type terms, such as *copy*, *save*, or *format*. Word responds by displaying a list of topics related to the word or phrase you typed. The following steps show how to use the Type a question for help box to obtain information about shortcut keys.

To Use the Type a Question for Help Box

1

• **Click the Type a question for help box on the right side of the menu bar and then type** `shortcut keys` **(Figure 1-74).**

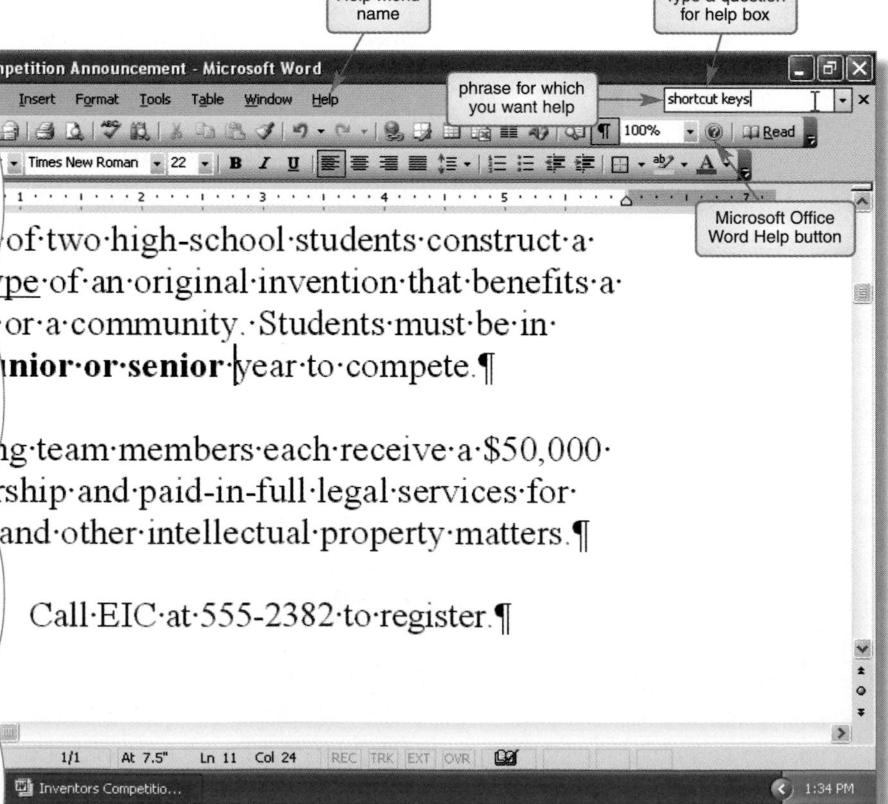

FIGURE 1-74

2

- **Press the ENTER key.**
- **When Word displays the Search Results task pane, if necessary, scroll to display the topic, About shortcut keys.**
- **Click About shortcut keys.**
- **If the Microsoft Office Help window has an Auto Tile button, click it so the Word window and Help window are displayed side-by-side.**

Word displays the Search Results task pane with a list of topics relating to the phrase, shortcut keys. When the About shortcut keys link is clicked, Word opens the Microsoft Office Word Help window on the right side of the screen (Figure 1-75).

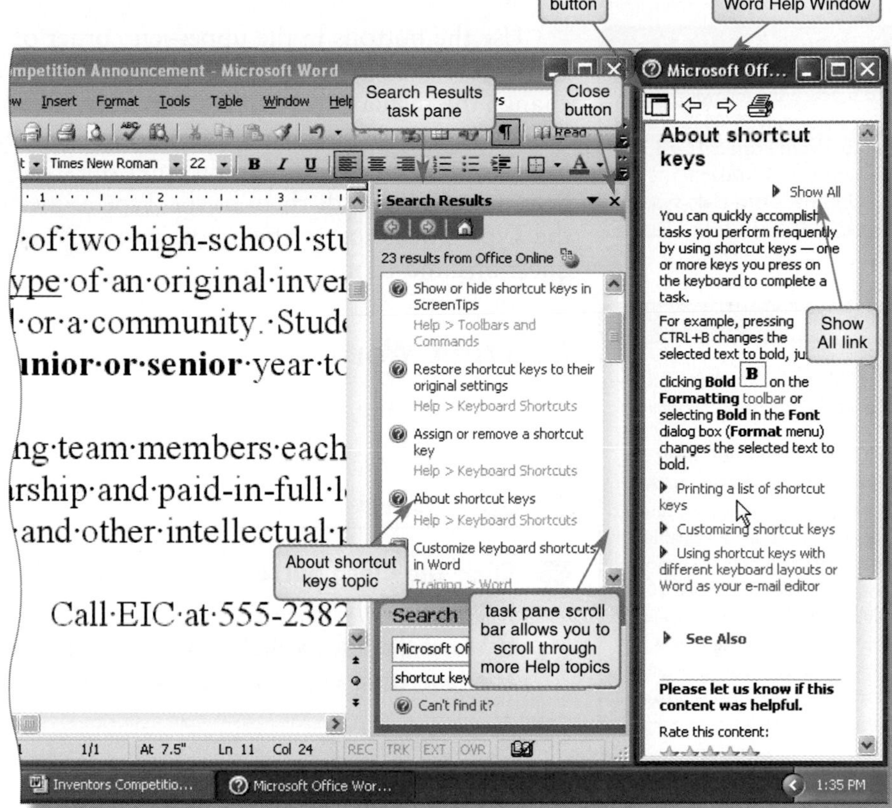

FIGURE 1-75

3

- **Click the Show All link on the right side of the Microsoft Office Word Help window to expand the links in the window.**
- **Double-click the Microsoft Office Word Help window title bar to maximize the window.**

The links in the Microsoft Office Word Help window are expanded and the window is maximized (Figure 1-76).

4

- **Click the Close button on the Microsoft Office Word Help window title bar.**
- **Click the Close button on the Search Results task pane.**

Word closes the Microsoft Office Word Help window. The Word document window again is active.

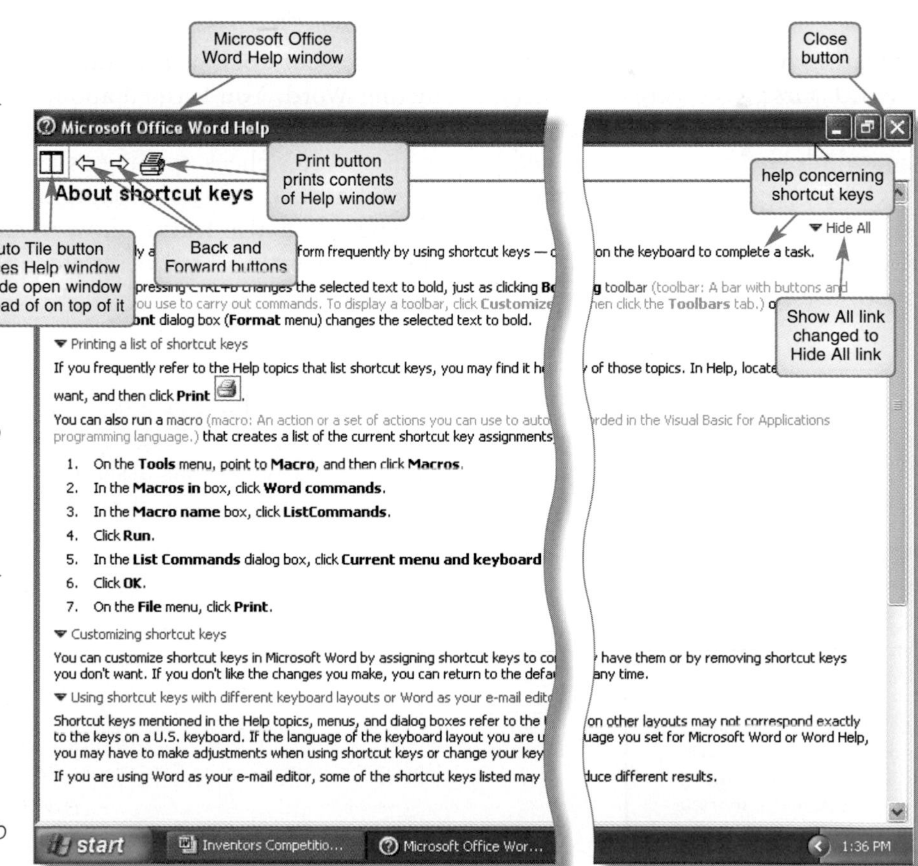

FIGURE 1-76

Skill Builder 1-5

To practice the following task, visit scsite.com/off2003sch/skill, locate Word Project 1, and then click Skill Builder 1-5.
❑ Use the Word Help system

Use the buttons in the upper-left corner of the Microsoft Office Word Help window (Figure 1-76 on the previous page) to navigate through the Help system, change the display, or print the contents of the window.

You can use the Type a question for help box to search for Help about any topic concerning Word. As you enter questions and terms in the Type a question for help box, Word adds them to the Type a question for help list. Thus, if you click the Type a question for help box arrow, Word displays a list of previously typed questions and terms.

Q & A

Q: What is the Microsoft Office Certification program?

A: The Microsoft Office Specialist Certification program provides an opportunity for you to obtain a valuable industry credential — proof that you have the Word 2003 skills required by employers. For more information, see Appendix E or visit the Office 2003 Certification Web page (scsite.com/off2003sch/cert).

Quitting Word

The final step in this project is to quit Word.

To Quit Word

1. **Click the Close button on the right side of the Word title bar (Figure 1-66 on page WD 54).**
2. **If Word displays a dialog box, click the No button to ignore the changes since the last time you saved the document.**

The Word window closes.

Project Summary

In creating the Inventors Competition Announcement document in this project, you gained a broad knowledge of Word. First, you were introduced to starting Word. You learned about the Word window. Before entering any text in the document, you learned how to change the font size. You then learned how to type in the Word document window. The project showed how to use Word's check spelling as you type feature.

Once you saved the document, you learned how to format its paragraphs and characters. Then, the project showed how to insert and resize a clip art image. You also learned how to save the document again, print it, and then quit Word. You learned how to open a document, and insert, delete, and modify text. Finally, you learned how to use the Word Help system to answer questions.

If you have a SAM user profile, you may have access to hands-on instruction, practice, and assessment of the skills covered in this project. Log in to your SAM account and go to your assignments page to see what your instructor has assigned.

Q & A

Q: Is there more than one way to invoke a command in Word?

A: Yes. For a table that lists how to complete the tasks covered in this book using the mouse, menu, shortcut menu, and keyboard, see the Quick Reference Summary at the back of this book, or visit the Office 2003 Quick Reference Web page (scsite.com/ off2003sch/qr).

What You Should Know

Having completed this project, you should be able to perform the tasks below. The tasks are listed in the same order they were presented in this project. For a list of the buttons, menus, toolbars, and commands introduced in this project, see the Quick Reference Summary at the back of this book and refer to the Page Number column.

1. Start Word (WD 6)
2. Customize the Word Window (WD 8)
3. Increase the Font Size before Typing (WD 17)
4. Type Text (WD 18)
5. Enter Blank Lines in a Document (WD 20)
6. Display Formatting Marks (WD 21)
7. Type More Text (WD 22)
8. Wordwrap Text as You Type (WD 23)
9. Enter Text that Scrolls the Document Window (WD 24)
10. Check Spelling and Grammar as You Type (WD 26)
11. Enter More Text (WD 27)
12. Save a New Document (WD 28)
13. Select Multiple Paragraphs (WD 33)
14. Change the Font Size of Text (WD 34)
15. Change the Font of Text (WD 36)
16. Right-Align a Paragraph (WD 37)
17. Center a Paragraph (WD 38)
18. Undo and Redo an Action (WD 39)
19. Select a Line (WD 40)
20. Format a Line of Text (WD 40)
21. Italicize Text (WD 41)
22. Underline a Word (WD 42)
23. Scroll through a Document (WD 43)
24. Select a Group of Words (WD 43)
25. Bold Text (WD 44)
26. Center a Paragraph (WD 45)
27. Insert Clip Art in a Document (WD 46)
28. Center a Paragraph Containing a Graphic (WD 48)
29. Select a Graphic (WD 49)
30. Resize a Graphic (WD 50)
31. Save an Existing Document with the Same File Name (WD 52)
32. Print a Document (WD 53)
33. Quit Word (WD 54, WD 62)
34. Open a Document (WD 55)
35. Insert Text in an Existing Document (WD 57)
36. Select a Word (WD 58)
37. Delete Text (WD 59)
38. Close the Entire Document and Start Over (WD 59)
39. Use the Type a Question for Help Box (WD 60)

Career Corner

Data Entry Clerk

Data entry clerks have an essential role in today's information-producing industry. A data entry clerk enters data into documents, databases, and other applications using computer keyboards and visual display devices. Duties can include manipulating, editing, and maintaining data to ensure that it is accurate and up-to-date, and researching information.

Some data entry clerks telecommute. Although they generally use keyboards, they also work with other input from scanners or electronically transmitted files. Because of the nature of their job, data entry clerks often sit for hours typing in front of monitors. They can be susceptible to repetitive stress injuries and neck, back, and eye strain. To prevent these injuries, many offices use ergonomically designed input devices and incorporate regularly scheduled exercise breaks.

Data entry clerks usually are high school graduates with keyboarding skills. Some employers require an associate's degree or at least two years of post–high-school education plus two years of office experience. Data entry training, basic language skills, and familiarity with word processing, spreadsheet, and database programs are important. Data entry often serves as a stepping-stone to other administrative positions. The average annual salary for data entry clerks is around $23,000. Salaries start at about $18,000 and, with experience, can exceed $31,000. For more information, visit scsite.com/off2003sch/careers and then click Data Entry Clerk.

Learn It Online

Instructions: To complete the Learn It Online exercises, start your browser, click the Address bar, and then enter the Web address `scsite.com/off2003sch/learn`. When the Office 2003 Learn It Online page is displayed, follow the instructions in the exercises below. Each exercise has instructions for printing your results, either for your own records or for submission to your instructor.

1 Project Reinforcement TF, MC, and SA

Below Word Project 1, click the Project Reinforcement link. Print the quiz by clicking Print on the File menu for each page. Answer each question.

2 Flash Cards

Below Word Project 1, click the Flash Cards link and read the instructions. Type 20 (or a number specified by your instructor) in the Number of playing cards text box, type your name in the Enter your Name text box, and then click the Flip Card button. When the flash card is displayed, read the question and then click the ANSWER box arrow to select an answer. Flip through Flash Cards. If your score is 15 (75%) correct or greater, click Print on the File menu to print your results. If your score is less than 15 (75%) correct, then redo this exercise by clicking the Replay button.

3 Practice Test

Below Word Project 1, click the Practice Test link. Answer each question, enter your first and last name at the bottom of the page, and then click the Grade Test button. When the graded practice test is displayed on your screen, click Print on the File menu to print a hard copy. Continue to take practice tests until you score 80% or better.

4 Who Wants To Be a Computer Genius?

Below Word Project 1, click the Computer Genius link. Read the instructions, enter your first and last name at the bottom of the page, and then click the PLAY button. When your score is displayed, click the PRINT RESULTS link to print a hard copy.

5 Wheel of Terms

Below Word Project 1, click the Wheel of Terms link. Read the instructions, and then enter your first and last name and your school name. Click the PLAY button. When your score is displayed, right-click the score and then click Print on the shortcut menu to print a hard copy.

6 Crossword Puzzle Challenge

Below Word Project 1, click the Crossword Puzzle Challenge link. Read the instructions, and then enter your first and last name. Click the SUBMIT button. Work the crossword puzzle. When you are finished, click the Submit button. When the crossword puzzle is redisplayed, click the Print Puzzle button to print a hard copy.

7 Tips and Tricks

Below Word Project 1, click the Tips and Tricks link. Click a topic that pertains to Project 1. Right-click the information and then click Print on the shortcut menu. Construct a brief example of what the information relates to in Word to confirm you understand how to use the tip or trick.

8 Newsgroups

Below Word Project 1, click the Newsgroups link. Click a topic that pertains to Project 1. Print three comments.

9 Expanding Your Horizons

Below Word Project 1, click the Expanding Your Horizons link. Click a topic that pertains to Project 1. Print the information. Construct a brief example of what the information relates to in Word to confirm you understand the contents of the article.

10 Search Sleuth

Below Word Project 1, click the Search Sleuth link. To search for a term that pertains to this project, select a term below the Project 1 title and then use the Google search engine at google.com (or any major search engine) to display and print two Web pages that present information on the term.

11 Word Online Training

Below Word Project 1, click the Word Online Training link. When your browser displays the Microsoft Office Online Web page, click the Word link. Click one of the Word courses that covers one or more of the objectives listed at the beginning of the project on page WD 4. Print the first page of the course before stepping through it.

12 Office Marketplace

Below Word Project 1, click the Office Marketplace link. When your browser displays the Microsoft Office Online Web page, click the Office Marketplace link. Click a topic that relates to Word. Print the first page.

13 You're Hired!

Below Word Project 1, click the You're Hired! link to embark on the path to a career in computers. Directions about how to play the game will be displayed. When you are ready to play, click the begin the game button. If required, submit your score to your instructor.

Apply Your Knowledge

1 Checking Spelling and Grammar, Modifying Text, and Formatting a Document

Instructions: Start Word. Open the document, Apply 1-1 Community Service Announcement Unformatted. See page xxiv at the front of this book for instructions for downloading the Data Files for Students, or see your instructor for information about accessing the files required in this book.

The document you open is an unformatted announcement that contains some spelling errors. You are to fix the spelling mistakes, modify text, format paragraphs and characters, and insert clip art in the announcement, so it looks like Figure 1-77 on the next page.

1. Correct each spelling and grammar error by right-clicking the flagged word and then clicking the appropriate correction on the shortcut menu, so the announcement text matches Figure 1-77 on the next page. The unformatted announcement contains several spelling errors (red wavy underline) and grammar errors (green wavy underline). Word may flag some proper names that are spelled correctly. In these cases, click Ignore Once or Ignore All on the shortcut menu. If your screen does not display the wavy underlines, right-click the Spelling and Grammar Status icon on the status bar and be sure Hide Spelling Errors and Hide Grammatical Errors do not have check marks beside them. If they do, remove the check mark(s) by the appropriate command. If your screen still does not display the wavy underlines, right-click the Spelling and Grammar Status icon on the status bar, click Options on the shortcut menu, click the Recheck Document button, and then click the OK button.
2. At the end of the first sentence of body copy, change the period to an exclamation point. The sentence should end: ...build leprechaun traps!
3. Delete the word, afternoon, in the first sentence of the second paragraph of body copy.
4. Insert the word, promptly, between the text, begin at, in the second paragraph of body copy. The text should read: The event will begin promptly at...
5. Change the font and font size of the first line of the headline to 48-point Curlz MT, or a similar font. Bold the text in the headline.
6. Change the font and font size of the second line of the headline to 48-point Curlz MT, or a similar font. Bold the text in the headline.
7. Right-align the second line of the headline.
8. Change the font size of the two paragraphs of body copy to 22 point.
9. Change the font and font size of the last line of the announcement to 24-point Gil Sans Ultra Bold Condensed.
10. Italicize the word, three, in the first paragraph of body copy.
11. Bold the phrase, build leprechaun traps, in the same paragraph.
12. Underline the date, March 9, in the next paragraph of body copy.
13. Italicize the text in the last line of the announcement.
14. Center the last line of the announcement.
15. Insert the clip art between the first and second lines of the headline. Use the search text, luck, to locate this, or a similar, clip art image. Center the paragraph containing the inserted graphic. Resize the graphic so it is about 75 percent of its original size or until the entire announcement fits on a single page. ***Hint***: Use Help to learn about print preview, which is a way to see the page before you print it. To exit print preview and return to the document window, click the Close button on the Print Preview toolbar.
16. Click File on the menu bar and then click Save As. Save the document using Apply 1-1 Community Service Announcement Formatted as the file name.
17. Print the revised document, shown in Figure 1-77.

(continued)

Apply Your Knowledge

Checking Spelling and Grammar, Modifying Text, and Formatting a Document *(continued)*

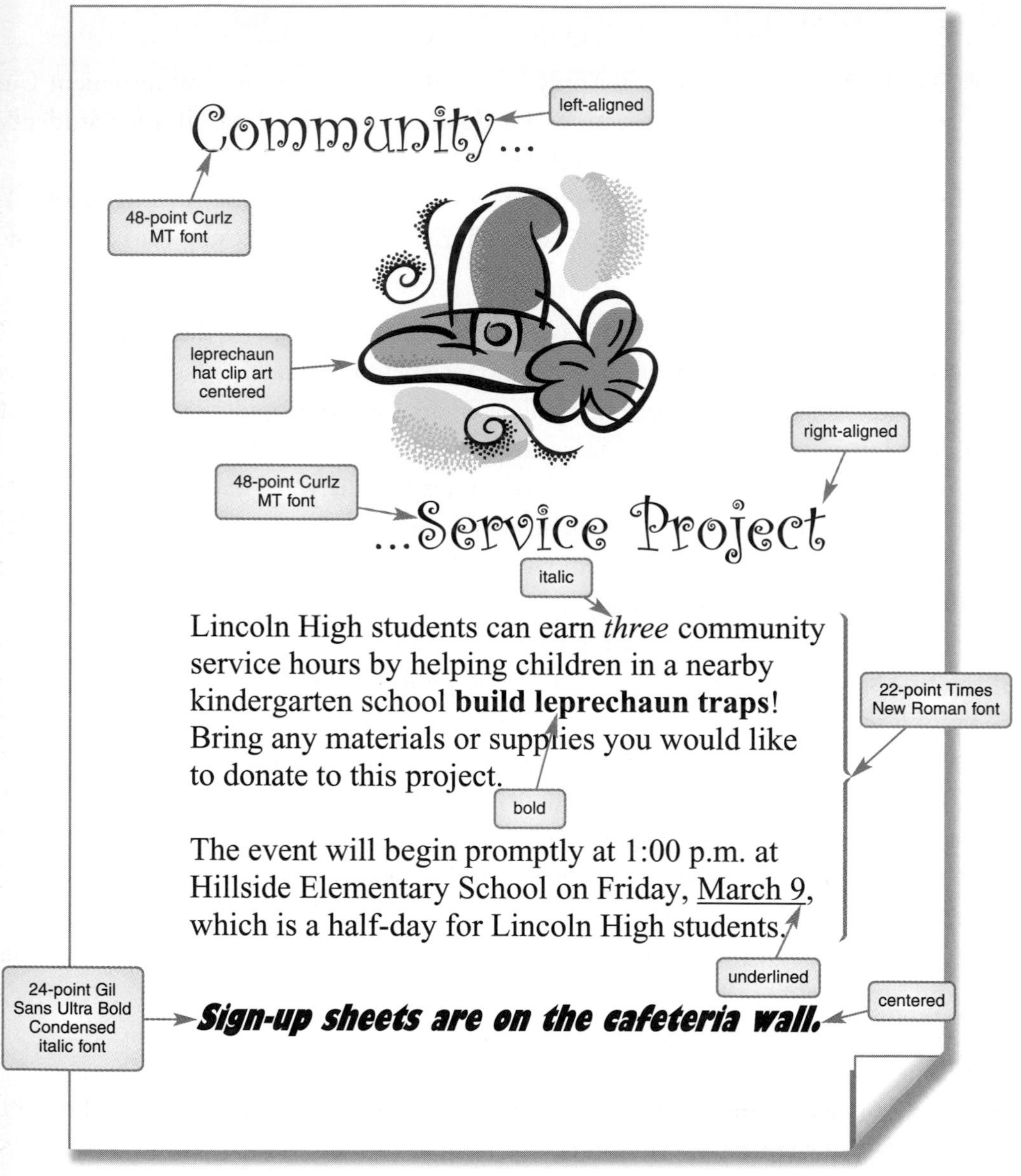

FIGURE 1-77

In the Lab

1 Creating an Announcement with Clip Art

Problem: You work part-time in the Counselors Office at school. Your boss has asked you to prepare an announcement for an upcoming time management program. First, you prepare the unformatted announcement shown in Figure 1-78a, and then you format it so it looks like Figure 1-78b on the next page. ***Hint:*** Remember, if you make a mistake while formatting the announcement, you can click the Undo button on the Standard toolbar to undo your last action.

1. Before entering any text, change the font size from 12 to 22.
2. Display formatting marks on the screen.
3. Type the unformatted announcement shown in Figure 1-78a. If Word flags any misspelled words as you type, check the spelling of these words and correct them.
4. Save the document on a USB flash drive with Lab 1-1 Time Management Announcement as the file name.

Never Be Late Again…
…Manage Your Time!

Time Management Program

Learn how to manage time so you can balance schoolwork and extracurricular activities. Class also shows how to set up and maintain schedules using a variety of digital technologies.

Program runs for six weeks starting Tuesday, September 25. Class meets in Room 23 for one hour each week beginning promptly at 3:30 p.m.

Call 555-2858 to sign up.

FIGURE 1-78a Unformatted Document

5. Change the font of both lines of the headline to Haettenschweiler, or a similar font. Change the font size from 22 to 48.
6. Right-align the second line of the headline.
7. Center the body title line.

(continued)

In the Lab

Creating an Announcement with Clip Art *(continued)*

8. Change the font of the body title line to Forte, or a similar font. Change the font size to 36. Bold the body title line.
9. In the first paragraph of the body copy, bold the text, schoolwork and extracurricular.
10. In the second sentence of the same paragraph, italicize the word, and.
11. In the next paragraph, underline the word, promptly.
12. Center the last line of the announcement.
13. Insert the clip art of an alarm clock between the headline and the body title line. Search for the text, alarm clock, in the Clip Art task pane to locate this, or a similar, graphic.
14. Center the clip art.
15. Save the announcement again with the same file name.
16. Print the formatted announcement, as shown in Figure 1-78b.

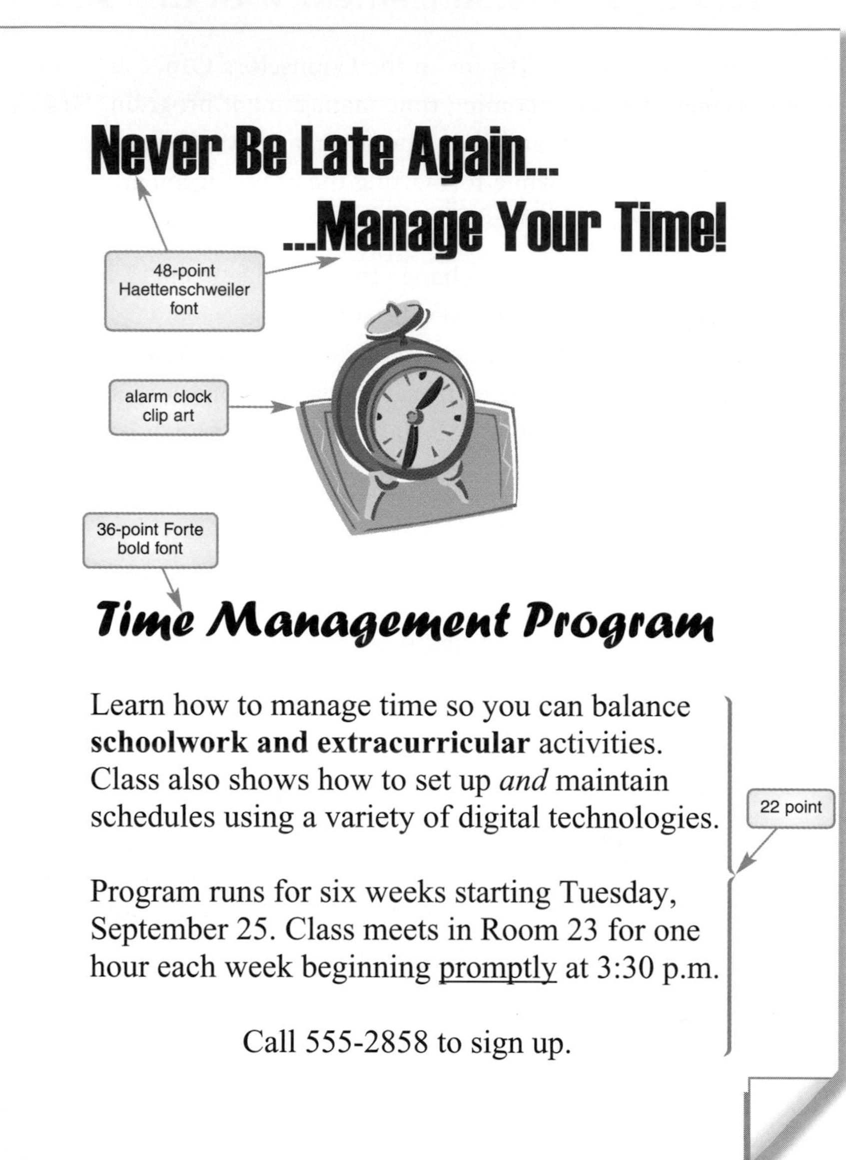

FIGURE 1-78b Formatted Document

2 Creating an Announcement with Resized Clip Art

Problem: Your computer teacher has requested that you prepare an announcement about part-time jobs at your school's transportation department. You prepare the announcement shown in Figure 1-79. ***Hint:*** Remember, if you make a mistake while formatting the announcement, you can click the Undo button on the Standard toolbar to undo your last action.

1. Before entering any text, change the font size from 12 to 22.
2. Display formatting marks on the screen.

In the Lab

3. Create the announcement shown in Figure 1-79. Enter the text of the document first without the clip art and unformatted; that is, without any bold, underlined, italicized, right-aligned, or centered text. If Word flags any misspelled words as you type, check the spelling of these words and correct them.
4. Save the document on a USB flash drive with Lab 1-2 Part-Time Jobs Announcement as the file name.
5. Change the font of both lines of the headline to Bauhaus 93, or a similar font. Change the font size from 22 to 36.
6. Right-align the second line of the headline.
7. Center the body title line.
8. Change the font and font size of the body title line to 28-point Bernard MT Condensed. Bold the body title line.
9. Underline the word, flexible, in the second paragraph of the body copy.
10. In the same paragraph, italicize the text, can vary.

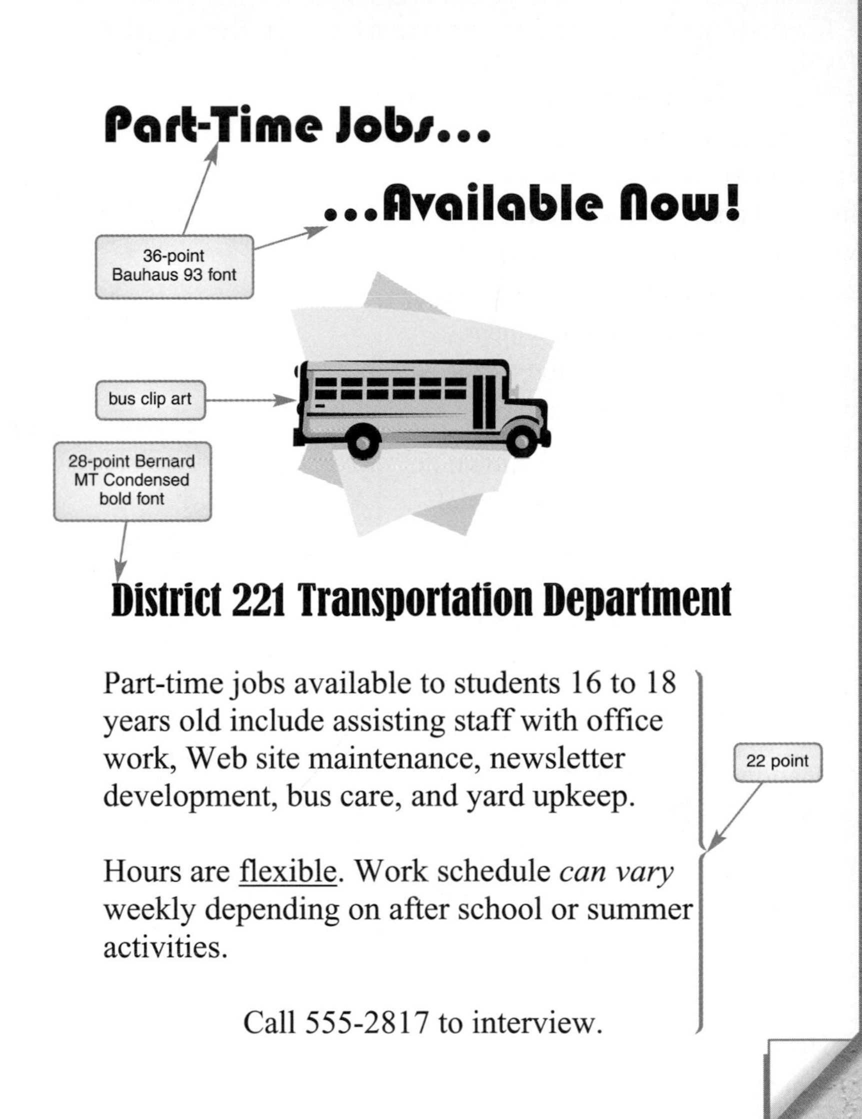

FIGURE 1-79

11. Center the last line of the announcement.
12. Insert the clip art between the headline and the body title line. Search for the text, bus, in the Clip Art task pane to locate this, or a similar, graphic. Center the graphic.
13. Enlarge the graphic. If you make the graphic too large, the announcement may flow onto two pages. If this occurs, reduce the size of the graphic so the announcement fits on a single page. ***Hint:*** Use Help to learn about print preview, which is a way to see the page before you print it. To exit print preview and return to the document window, click the Close button on the Print Preview toolbar.
14. Save the announcement again with the same file name.
15. Print the announcement.

In the Lab

3 Creating an Announcement with Resized Clip Art, a Bulleted List, and Color

Problem: As a member of the student government, you have been asked to prepare an announcement about homecoming events. You prepare the announcement shown in Figure 1-80. *Hint:* Remember, if you make a mistake while formatting the announcement, you can click the Undo button on the Standard toolbar to undo your last action.

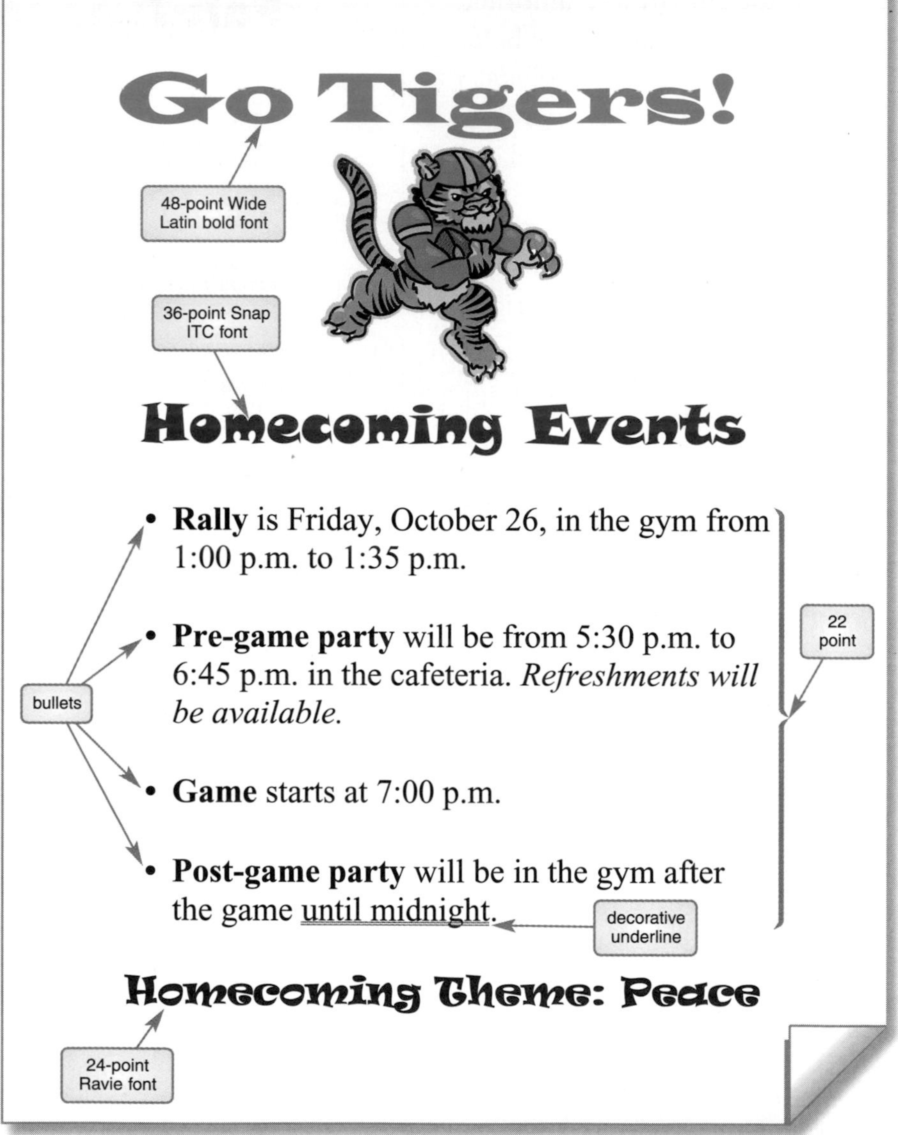

FIGURE 1-80

1. Type the announcement shown in Figure 1-80, using the fonts and font sizes indicated in the figure. Check spelling as you type.
2. Save the document on a USB flash drive with Lab 1-3 Homecoming Announcement as the file name.
3. Change the font color of the headline to green, the body title to red, and the last line of the announcement to blue. *Hint:* Use Help to learn how to change the font color of text.
4. Add a brown double underline below the text, until midnight. *Hint:* Use Help to learn how to add a decorative underline to text.
5. Add bullets to the four paragraphs of body copy. *Hint:* Use Help to learn how to add bullets to a list of paragraphs.
6. Insert clip art related to football between the headline and the body title line. If you have access to the Web, select the clip art from the Web. Otherwise, select the clip art from the hard disk. In the Clip Art task pane, images from the Web display an icon of a small globe in their lower-left corner.
7. Enlarge the football graphic. If you make the graphic too large, the announcement may flow onto two pages. If this occurs, reduce the size of the graphic so the announcement fits on a single page. *Hint:* Use Help to learn about print preview, which is a way to see the page before you print it. To exit print preview and return to the document window, click the Close button on the Print Preview toolbar.
8. Save the announcement again with the same file name.
9. Print the announcement.

Cases and Places

The difficulty of these case studies varies:

are the least difficult and are more difficult.

Each exercise has a cross-curricular designation:

Math Social Studies Science Language Arts Art/Music Business Health

1 You have been assigned the task of preparing an announcement for the Knoxville High Astronomy Club. The announcement is to contain clip art related to astronomy. Use the following text: first line of headline – Join Us...; second line of headline – ...See the Stars; body title – Knoxville High Astronomy Club; first paragraph of body copy – The first Astronomy Club meeting of the school year is scheduled for Wednesday, September 19, after school in Room 42. The meeting will last one hour.; second paragraph of body copy – The guest speaker is Mr. Patella, head of our science program. He will demonstrate how to use the planetarium software available in the computer lab room.; last line – Call 555-8271 with questions. Use the concepts and techniques presented in this project to create and format this announcement. Be sure to check spelling and grammar in the announcement.

2 You have been assigned the task of preparing an announcement for high school students interested in shadowing paramedic technology students at a local technical college. The announcement is to contain clip art related to health. Use the following text: first line of headline – Interested in Health Care?; second line of headline – Be a Paramedic!; body title – Ohio Technical College; first paragraph of body copy – High school students interested in becoming a paramedic are invited to shadow one of our paramedic technology sophomores on Thursday, October 11, or Friday, October 12, from 9:30 a.m. to 2:30 p.m.; second paragraph of body copy – Shadowing provides potential students with firsthand classroom and clinical experiences so they can see our program in action.; last line – Call Juan at 555-5839 to sign up. Use the concepts and techniques presented in this project to create and format this announcement. Be sure to check spelling and grammar in the announcement.

3 As a member of your high school's Drama Club, you have been asked to prepare an announcement for upcoming performances of *The Wizard of Oz*. You are to include appropriate clip art. You have the following information for the announcement. There will be four performances in the Yellville High School auditorium: two on Saturday, November 17, and two on Sunday, November 18. The curtains open each day at 3:00 p.m. and at 7:00 p.m. Admission is $5.50 per person. Tickets can be purchased in advance during lunch hour from Ms. Peterson. Tickets also may be purchased at the door. For more information, call 555-3928. Use the concepts and techniques presented in this project to create the announcement. Change the color of text in the headline, body title, and last line of the announcement. Use a decorative underline in the announcement. Add bullets to the paragraphs of the body copy. Be sure to check spelling and grammar in the announcement.

Cases and Places

4 You have been assigned the task of preparing an announcement for an eleventh-grade field trip to Bodie Island Lighthouse. You are to include appropriate clip art. These details have been provided. The field trip to Bodie Island Lighthouse will be on Tuesday, November 13. It is for all eleventh-grade social studies classes. Bodie Island Lighthouse is at Cape Hatteras National Seashore. Permission slips must be turned in by November 12. The buses will leave Morris High School at 9:00 a.m. Attendees will return to school at 11:30 a.m. See Mr. Li in Room 10 if you have questions. Use the concepts and techniques presented in this project to create the announcement. Change the color of text in the headline, body title, and last line of the announcement. Use a decorative underline in the announcement. Add bullets to the paragraphs of the body copy. Be sure to check spelling and grammar in the announcement.

5 **Working Together** Schools have bulletin boards in offices, classrooms, the cafeteria, the library, the gym, and other locations for announcements and other postings. Often, these bulletin boards have so many announcements that some go unnoticed. Look at a bulletin board at your school and find a posted announcement that you think might be overlooked. Copy the text from the announcement and distribute it to each team member. Each member then independently should use this text, together with the techniques presented in this project, to create an announcement that would be more likely to catch a reader's eye. Be sure to check spelling and grammar. As a group, critique each announcement and have each member redesign their announcement based on the group's recommendations. Hand in printouts of each team member's original and final announcements.

MICROSOFT OFFICE

Word 2003

Creating a Research Paper

PROJECT

2

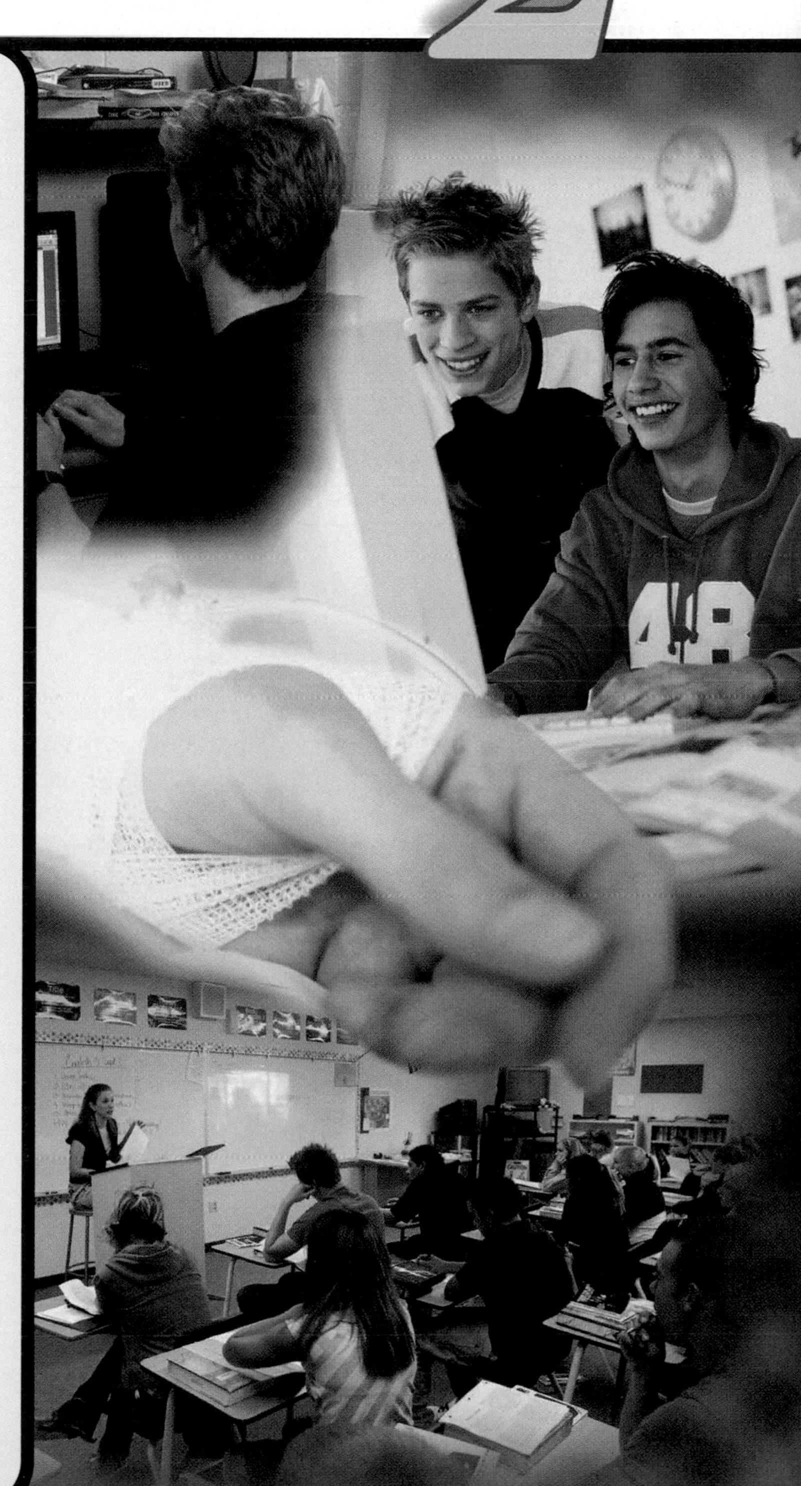

CASE PERSPECTIVE

Ryan Krause recently began the first semester of his senior year at Montrose High School. Ms. Lopez, the instructor in his English 7 class, has assigned a short research paper that should contain a minimum of 325 words. The paper must discuss some aspect of health risks. It also must be written according to the MLA documentation style, which specifies guidelines for report preparation. The paper is to contain one footnote and three references — one of which must be obtained from the World Wide Web. Finally, all students are to submit their papers electronically via e-mail to Ms. Lopez.

When Ryan graduates from high school, he plans to major in computers at a local college. An avid computer user, Ryan is interested in the effects that prolonged computer use can have on one's health. He recently read a short article in one of his computer magazines that mentioned computer users often complain about aching wrists or hands and strained eyes. The article cited references that discuss the prevention and treatment of computer-related health problems. Ryan decides to write his research paper about healthy computing. He intends to review the references in his computer magazine, browse the Web, and e-mail a few keyboard and monitor vendors for suggestions they have about proper use of their devices. He also plans to use the Internet to obtain the guidelines for the MLA style of documentation. Knowing you have a high-speed Internet connection at home, Ryan asks if you could assist him with the Web searches. You immediately agree to help your friend.

As you read through this project, you will learn how to use Word to create a research paper and e-mail a copy of the finished paper.

Creating a Research Paper

PROJECT

Objectives

You will have mastered the material in this project when you can:

- Describe the MLA documentation style for research papers
- Change the margin settings and line spacing in a document
- Use a header to number pages of a document
- Apply formatting using shortcut keys
- Modify paragraph indentation
- Add a footnote to a document
- Count the words in a document
- Insert a manual page break
- Create a hyperlink
- Sort selected paragraphs
- Proof and revise a document
- Display the Web page associated with a hyperlink
- E-mail a copy of a document
- Use the Research task pane to locate information

Introduction

In both academic and business environments, you will be asked to write reports. Business reports range from proposals to cost justifications to five-year plans to research findings. Academic reports focus mostly on research findings. Whether you are writing a business report or an academic report, you should follow a standard style when preparing it.

Many different styles of documentation exist for report preparation, depending on the nature of the report. Each style requires the same basic information; the differences among styles relate to how the information is presented. For example, one documentation style may use the term bibliography, whereas another uses references, and yet a third prefers works cited. Two popular documentation styles for research papers are the **Modern Language Association of America** (**MLA**) and **American Psychological Association** (**APA**) styles. This project uses the MLA documentation style.

Project 2 — Healthy Computing Research Paper

Project 2 illustrates the creation of a short research paper about healthy computing. As shown in Figure 2-1, the paper follows the MLA documentation style. The first two pages present the research paper, and the third page alphabetically lists the works cited.

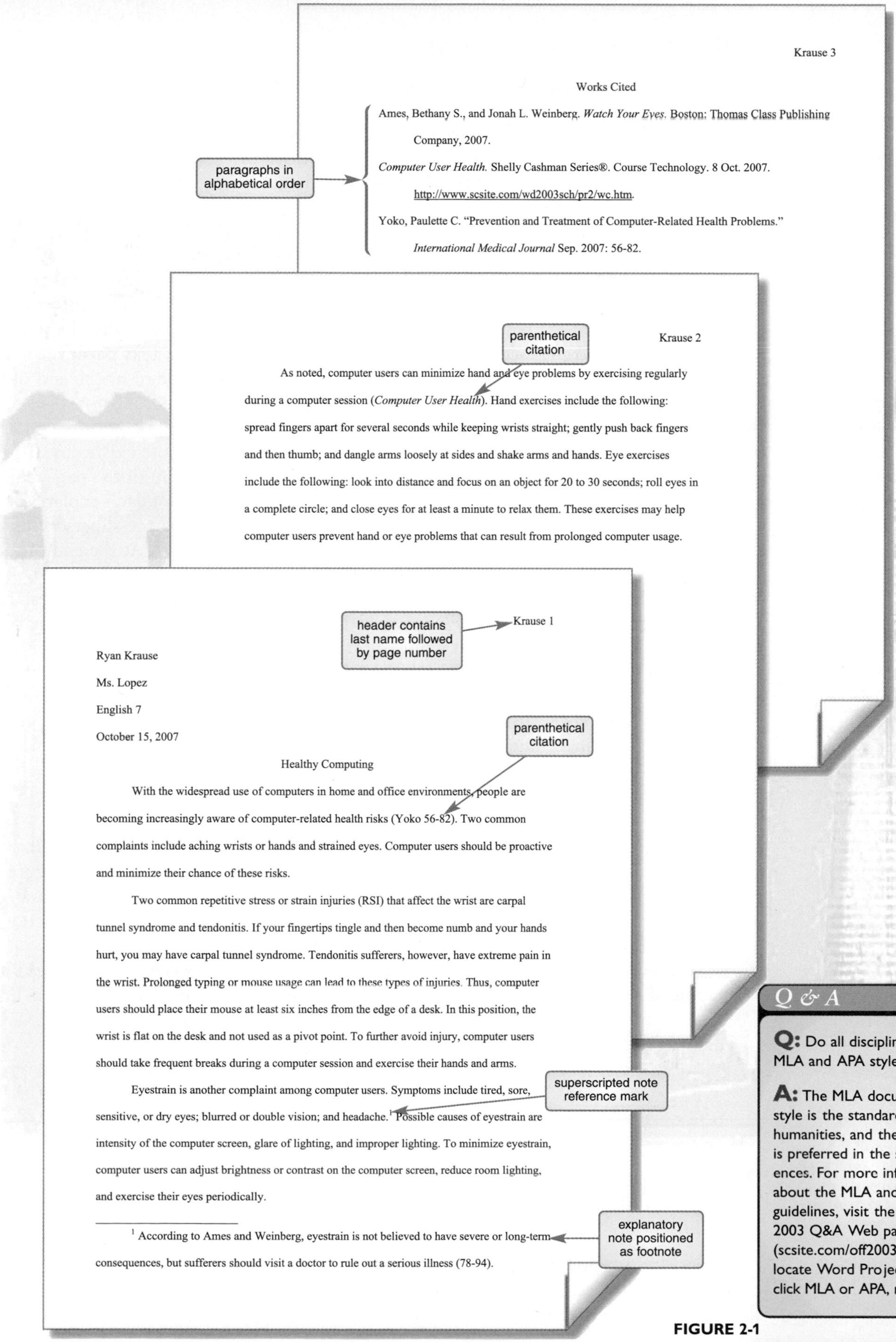

Krause 3

Works Cited

Ames, Bethany S., and Jonah L. Weinberg. *Watch Your Eyes.* Boston: Thomas Class Publishing Company, 2007.

Computer User Health. Shelly Cashman Series®. Course Technology. 8 Oct. 2007. http://www.scsite.com/wd2003sch/pr2/wc.htm.

Yoko, Paulette C. "Prevention and Treatment of Computer-Related Health Problems." *International Medical Journal* Sep. 2007: 56-82.

paragraphs in alphabetical order

Krause 2

parenthetical citation

As noted, computer users can minimize hand and eye problems by exercising regularly during a computer session (*Computer User Health*). Hand exercises include the following: spread fingers apart for several seconds while keeping wrists straight; gently push back fingers and then thumb; and dangle arms loosely at sides and shake arms and hands. Eye exercises include the following: look into distance and focus on an object for 20 to 30 seconds; roll eyes in a complete circle; and close eyes for at least a minute to relax them. These exercises may help computer users prevent hand or eye problems that can result from prolonged computer usage.

header contains last name followed by page number

Krause 1

Ryan Krause

Ms. Lopez

English 7

October 15, 2007

parenthetical citation

Healthy Computing

With the widespread use of computers in home and office environments, people are becoming increasingly aware of computer-related health risks (Yoko 56-82). Two common complaints include aching wrists or hands and strained eyes. Computer users should be proactive and minimize their chance of these risks.

Two common repetitive stress or strain injuries (RSI) that affect the wrist are carpal tunnel syndrome and tendonitis. If your fingertips tingle and then become numb and your hands hurt, you may have carpal tunnel syndrome. Tendonitis sufferers, however, have extreme pain in the wrist. Prolonged typing or mouse usage can lead to these types of injuries. Thus, computer users should place their mouse at least six inches from the edge of a desk. In this position, the wrist is flat on the desk and not used as a pivot point. To further avoid injury, computer users should take frequent breaks during a computer session and exercise their hands and arms.

Eyestrain is another complaint among computer users. Symptoms include tired, sore, sensitive, or dry eyes; blurred or double vision; and headache.[1] Possible causes of eyestrain are intensity of the computer screen, glare of lighting, and improper lighting. To minimize eyestrain, computer users can adjust brightness or contrast on the computer screen, reduce room lighting, and exercise their eyes periodically.

superscripted note reference mark

[1] According to Ames and Weinberg, eyestrain is not believed to have severe or long-term consequences, but sufferers should visit a doctor to rule out a serious illness (78-94).

explanatory note positioned as footnote

FIGURE 2-1

Q & A

Q: Do all disciplines use the MLA and APA styles?

A: The MLA documentation style is the standard in the humanities, and the APA style is preferred in the social sciences. For more information about the MLA and APA guidelines, visit the Office 2003 Q&A Web page (scsite.com/off2003sch/qa), locate Word Project 2, and click MLA or APA, respectively.

MLA Documentation Style

When writing papers, you should adhere to some style of documentation. The research paper in this project follows the guidelines presented by the MLA. To follow the MLA style, double-space text on all pages of the paper using one-inch top, bottom, left, and right margins. Indent the first word of each paragraph one-half inch from the left margin. At the right margin of each page, place a page number one-half inch from the top margin. On each page, precede the page number by your last name.

The MLA style does not require a title page. Instead, place your name and course information in a block at the left margin beginning one inch from the top of the page. Center the title one double-space below your name and course information.

In the body of the paper, place author references in parentheses with the page number(s) of the referenced information. The MLA style uses in-text **parenthetical citations** instead of noting each source at the bottom of the page or at the end of the paper. In the MLA style, notes are used only for optional explanatory notes.

If used, explanatory notes elaborate on points discussed in the body of the paper. Use a superscript (raised number) to signal that an explanatory note exists, and also sequence the notes. Position explanatory notes either at the bottom of the page as footnotes or at the end of the paper as endnotes. Indent the first line of each explanatory note one-half inch from the left margin. Place one space following the superscripted number before beginning the note text. Double-space the note text. At the end of the note text, you may list bibliographic information for further reference.

The MLA style uses the term **works cited** for the bibliographical references. The works cited page alphabetically lists works that are referenced directly in the paper. List works by each author's last name, or, if the author's name is not available, by the title of the work. Italicize or underline the title of the work. Place the works cited on a separate numbered page. Center the title, Works Cited, one inch from the top margin. Double-space all lines. Begin the first line of each entry at the left margin, indenting subsequent lines of the same entry one-half inch from the left margin.

Q & A

Q: What are the guidelines for formatting titles?

A: Titles of books, periodicals, and Web sites typically are underlined when a research paper is submitted in printed form. Some instructors require that Web addresses be hyperlinks for online access. Word formats hyperlinks with an underline. To distinguish hyperlinks from titles, the MLA allows titles to be italicized, if approved by the instructor.

Starting and Customizing Word

To start and customize Word, Windows must be running. If you are stepping through this project on a computer and you want your screen to match the figures in this book, then you should change your computer's resolution to 800 × 600 and reset the toolbars and menus. For information about changing the resolution and resetting toolbars and menus, read Appendix D.

The next steps show how to start Word and customize the Word window. You may need to ask your instructor how to start Word for your system.

Q & A

Q: How does the APA style differ from the MLA style?

A: In the APA style, double-space all pages of the paper with 1.5" top, bottom, left, and right margins. Indent the first word of each paragraph .5" from the left margin. In the upper-right margin of each page, place a running head that consists of the page number double-spaced below a summary of the paper title.

To Start and Customize Word

1. **Click the Start button on the Windows taskbar, point to All Programs on the Start menu, point to Microsoft Office on the All Programs submenu, and then click Microsoft Office Word 2003 on the Microsoft Office submenu.**
2. **If the Word window is not maximized, double-click its title bar to maximize it.**
3. **If the Language bar appears, right-click it and then click Close the Language bar on the shortcut menu.**
4. **If the Getting Started task pane is displayed in the Word window, click its Close button.**
5. **If the Standard and Formatting toolbar buttons are displayed on one row, click the Toolbar Options button and then click Show Buttons on Two Rows in the Toolbar Options list.**
6. **If your screen differs from Figure 2-2 on the next page, click View on the menu bar and then click Normal.**
7. **If your zoom percent is not 100 (shown in Figure 2-2), click View on the menu bar, click Zoom on the View menu, click 100%, and then click the OK button.**

Word starts and, after a few moments, displays an empty document titled Document1 in the Word window (shown in Figure 2-2).

Q & A

Q: Where can I find help about writing papers?

A: The Web contains numerous sites with information, tips, and suggestions about writing research papers. College professors and high-school teachers develop many of these Web sites. For links to Web sites about writing research papers, visit the Office 2003 Q&A Web page (scsite.com/off2003sch/qa), locate Word Project 2, and click one of the Writing Research Papers links.

Displaying Formatting Marks

As discussed in Project 1, it is helpful to display formatting marks that indicate where in the document you pressed the ENTER key, SPACEBAR, and other keys. The following step discusses how to display formatting marks.

To Display Formatting Marks

1. **If the Show/Hide ¶ button on the Standard toolbar is not selected already, click it.**

Word displays formatting marks in the document window, and the Show/Hide ¶ button on the Standard toolbar is selected (shown in Figure 2-2).

Changing the Margins

Word is preset to use standard 8.5-by-11-inch paper, with 1.25-inch left and right margins and 1-inch top and bottom margins. These margin settings affect every page in the document.

Periodically, you may want to change the default margin settings. The MLA documentation style, for example, requires one-inch top, bottom, left, and right margins throughout the paper. Thus, the steps on the next page show how to change the margin settings for a document when the window is in normal view. To verify the document window is in normal view, click View on the menu bar and then click Normal.

Q & A

Q: How can I change the margins in print layout view?

A: In print layout view, you can change margin settings using the horizontal and vertical rulers. Current margin settings are shaded in gray. The margin boundary is located where the gray meets the white. To change a margin setting, drag the margin boundary on the ruler. To see the numeric margin settings, hold down the ALT key while dragging the margin boundary on the ruler.

To Change the Margin Settings

1

- **Click File on the menu bar (Figure 2-2).**

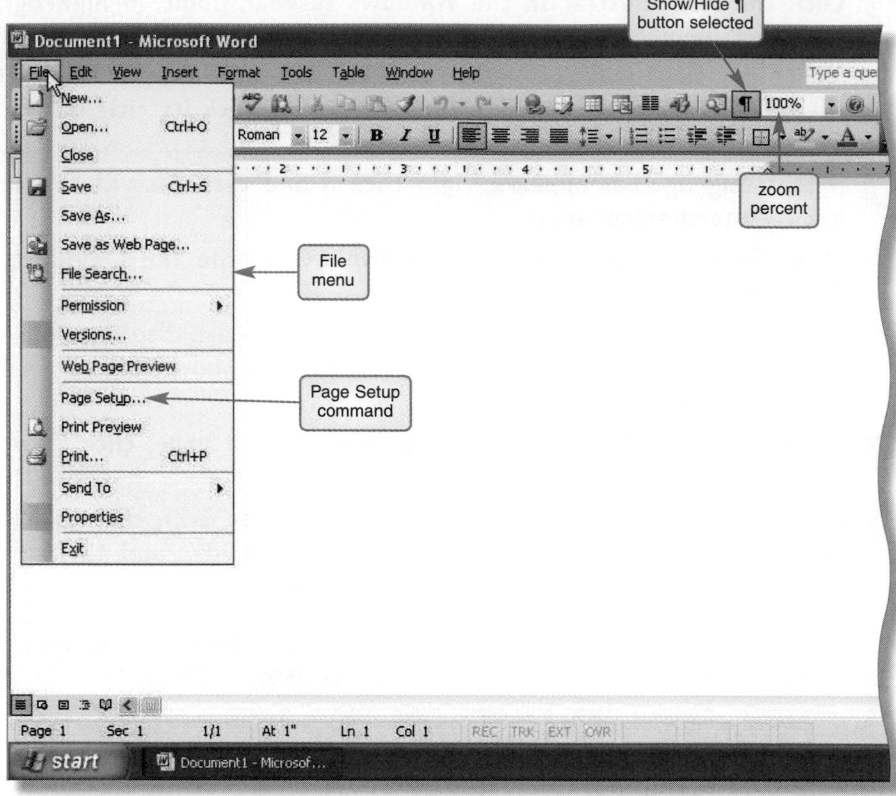

FIGURE 2-2

2

- **Click Page Setup on the File menu.**
- **When Word displays the Page Setup dialog box, if necessary, click the Margins tab.**

Word displays the current margin settings in the text boxes of the Page Setup dialog box (Figure 2-3).

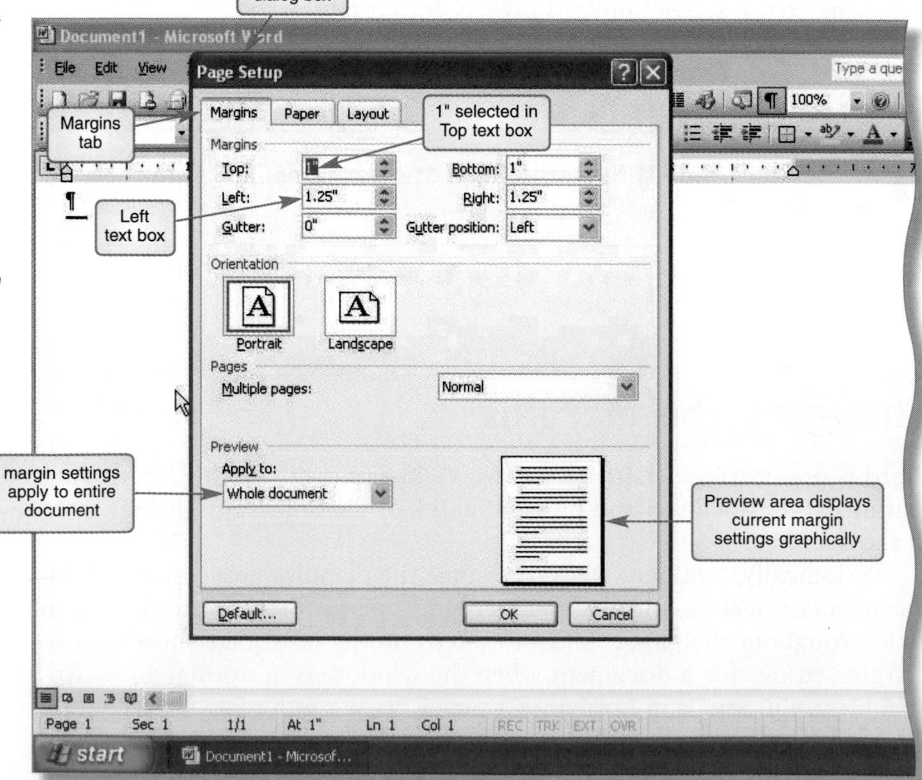

FIGURE 2-3

3

• **With 1" selected in the Top text box, press the TAB key twice to select 1.25" in the Left text box.**

• **Type 1 and then press the TAB key.**

• **Type 1 in the Right text box.**

The new left and right margin settings are 1 inch (Figure 2-4). Instead of typing margin values, you can click the text box arrows to increase or decrease the number in the text box.

4

• **Click the OK button in the Page Setup dialog box.**

Word changes the left and right margins.

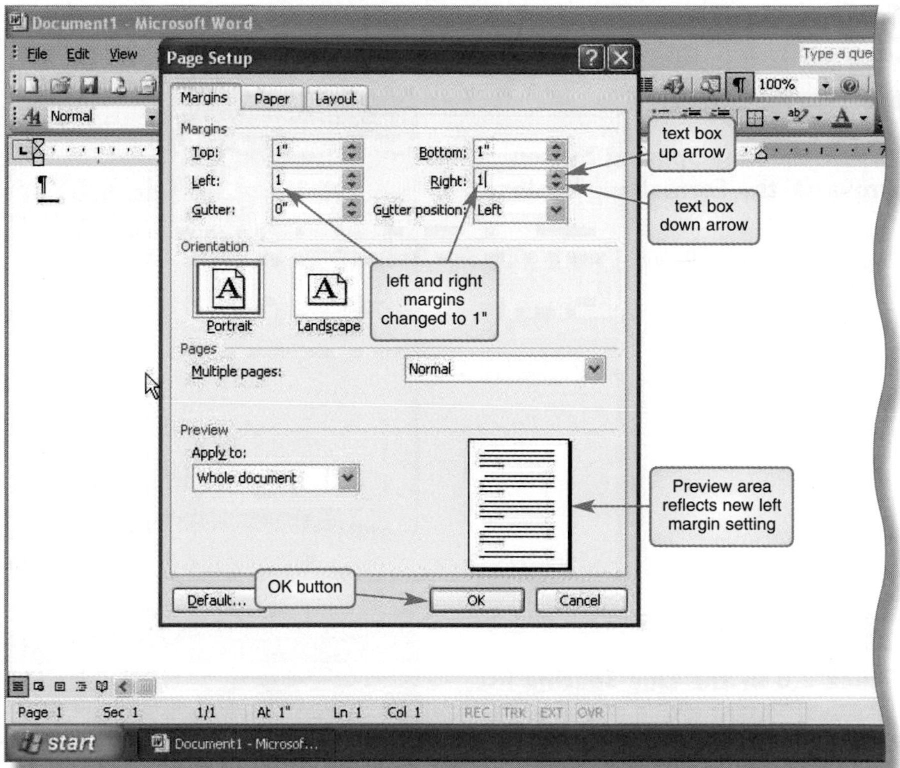

FIGURE 2-4

The new margin settings take effect immediately in the document. Word uses these margins for the entire document.

When you change the margin settings in the text boxes in the Page Setup dialog box, the Preview area (Figure 2-4) does not adjust to reflect a changed margin setting until the insertion point leaves the respective text box. That is, you must press the TAB or ENTER key or click another text box if you want to view a changed margin setting in the Preview area.

Q & A

Q: How do I change the way a document prints?

A: A document printed in portrait orientation is taller than it is wide. A document printed in landscape orientation is wider than it is tall. If you want to change the orientation of a printout from portrait to landscape, click Landscape in the Orientation area in the Page Setup dialog box (Figure 2-4).

Adjusting Line Spacing

Line spacing is the amount of vertical space between lines of text in a document. By default, Word single-spaces between lines of text and automatically adjusts line height to accommodate various font sizes and graphics.

The MLA documentation style requires that you **double-space** the entire paper; that is, one blank line should be between each line of text. The steps on the next page show how to adjust the line spacing from single to double.

To Double-Space Text

1

• **Click the Line Spacing button arrow on the Formatting toolbar.**

Word displays a list of line spacing options (Figure 2-5).

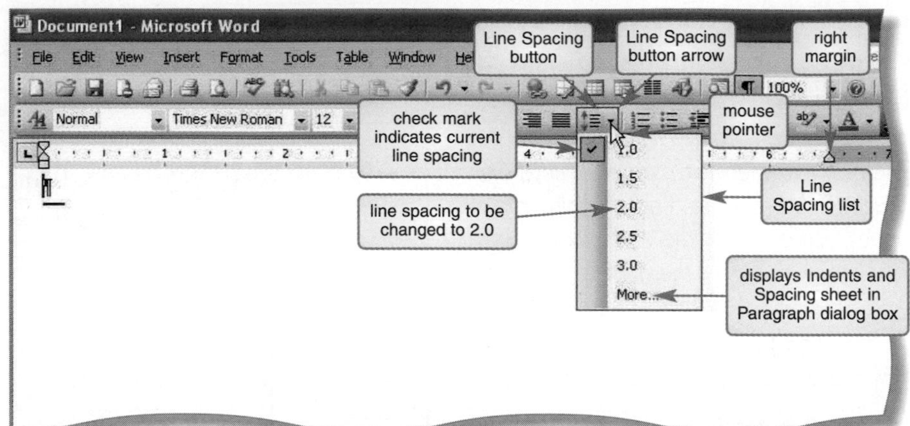

FIGURE 2-5

2

• **Click 2.0 in the Line Spacing list.**

Word changes the line spacing to double at the location of the insertion point (Figure 2-6).

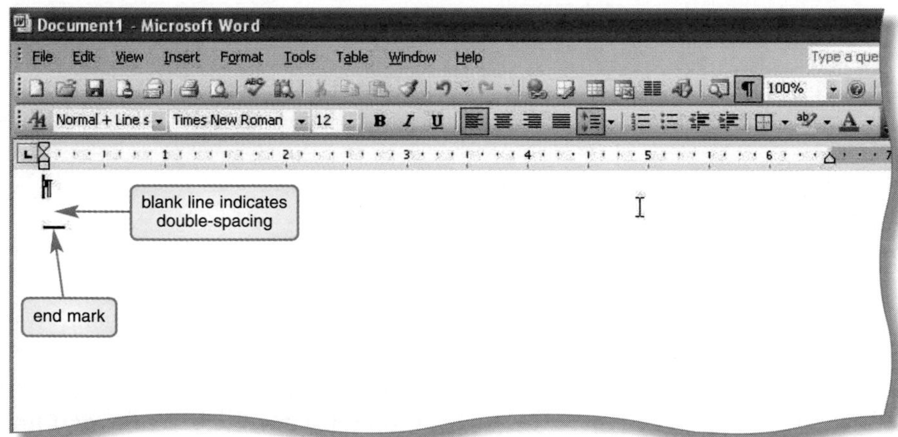

FIGURE 2-6

Notice when line spacing is double (Figure 2-6), the end mark displays one blank line below the insertion point.

The Line Spacing list (Figure 2-5) contains a variety of settings for the line spacing. The default, 1 (for single), and the options 1.5, 2 (for double), 2.5, and 3 (for triple) instruct Word to adjust line spacing automatically to accommodate the largest font or graphic on a line. For additional line spacing options, click More in the Line Spacing list and then click the Line spacing box arrow in the Indents and Spacing sheet in the Paragraph dialog box.

If you wanted to apply the most recently set line spacing to the current or selected paragraphs, you would click the Line Spacing button instead of the Line Spacing button arrow.

To change the line spacing of existing text, select the text first and then change the line spacing. For example, to change an existing paragraph to double-spacing, triple-click the paragraph to select it, click the Line Spacing button arrow on the Formatting toolbar, and then click 2.0 in the list.

Using a Header to Number Pages

In Word, you easily can number pages by clicking Insert on the menu bar and then clicking Page Numbers. Using the Page Numbers command, you can specify the location (top or bottom of the page) and alignment (right, left, or centered) of the page numbers.

The MLA style requires that your last name display to the left of the page number on each page. The Page Numbers command, however, does not allow you to enter text along with the page number. Thus, to place your name to the left of the page number, you must create a header that contains the page number.

Headers and Footers

A **header** is text you want printed at the top of each page in a document. A **footer** is text you want printed at the bottom of every page. In Word, headers print in the top margin one-half inch from the top of every page, and footers print in the bottom margin one-half inch from the bottom of each page, which meets the MLA style. Headers and footers can include text and graphics, as well as the page number, total number of pages, current date, and current time.

In this project, you are to precede the page number with your last name placed one-half inch from the top of each page. Your last name and the page number should print right-aligned; that is, at the right margin.

To create the header, first you display the header area in the document window. Then, you can enter the header text into the header area. The procedures on the following pages show how to create the header with page numbers, according to the MLA documentation style.

To Display the Header Area

1

- **Click View on the menu bar (Figure 2-7).**

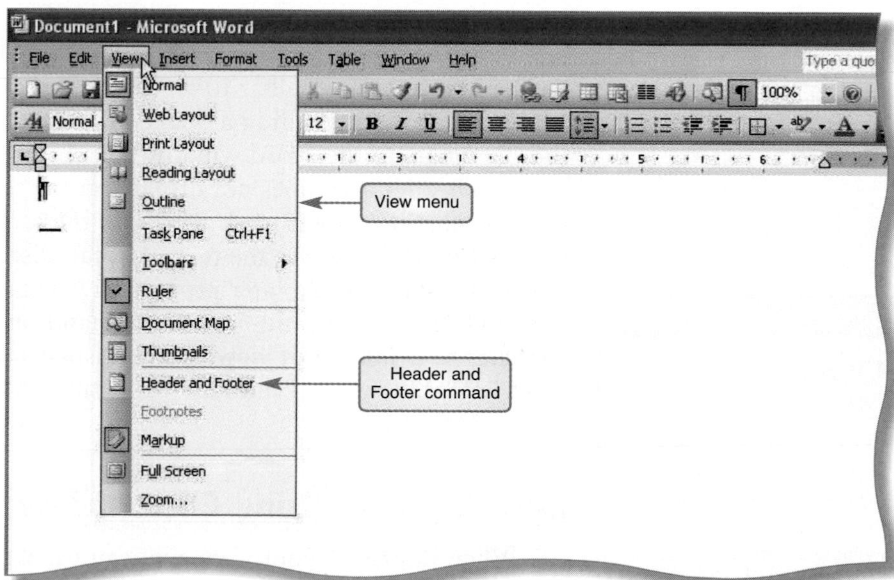

FIGURE 2-7

2

• Click Header and Footer on the View menu.

• If your zoom percent is not 100, click View on the menu bar, click Zoom on the View menu, click 100%, and then click the OK button.

Word switches from normal view to print layout view and displays the Header and Footer toolbar (Figure 2-8). You type header text in the header area.

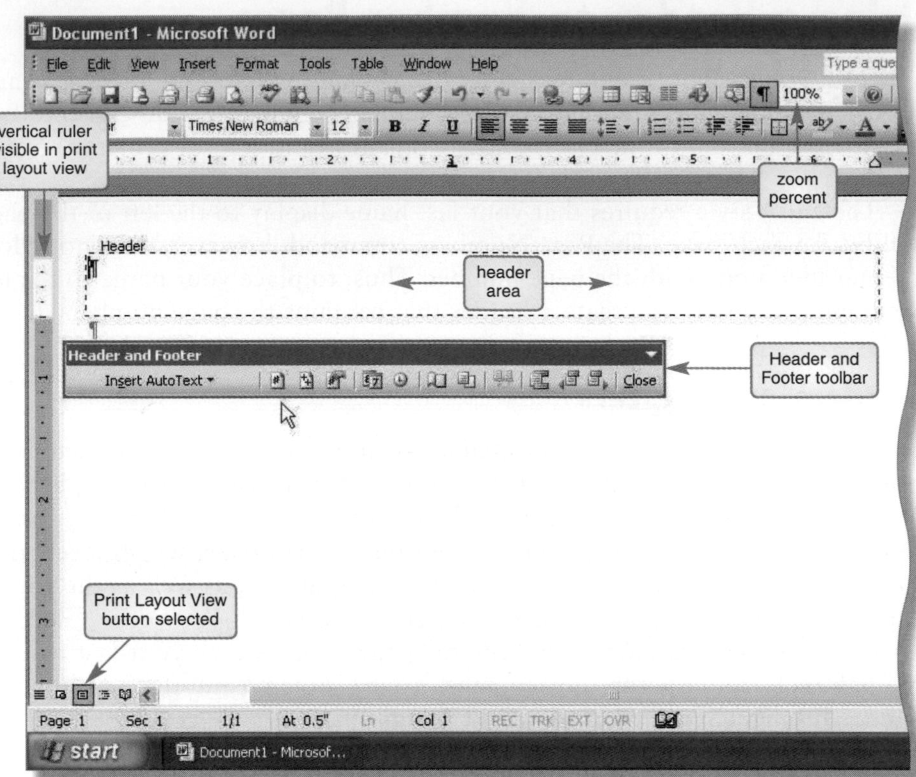

FIGURE 2-8

The Header and Footer toolbar initially floats in the document window. To move a floating toolbar, drag its title bar. You can **dock**, or attach, a floating toolbar above or below the Standard and Formatting toolbars by double-clicking the floating toolbar's title bar. To move a docked toolbar, drag its move handle. Recall that the move handle is the vertical dotted bar to the left of the first button on a docked toolbar. If you drag a floating toolbar to an edge of the window, the toolbar snaps to the edge of the window. If you drag a docked toolbar to the middle of the window, the toolbar floats in the Word window.

The header area does not display on the screen when the document window is in normal view because it tends to clutter the screen. To see the header in the document window with the rest of the text, you can display the document in print preview, which is discussed in a later project, or you can switch to print layout view. When you click the Header and Footer command on the View menu, Word automatically switches to **print layout view**, which displays the document exactly as it will print. In print layout view, the Print Layout View button on the horizontal scroll bar is selected (Figure 2-8).

Q & A

Q: Why won't Click and Type work?

A: Click and Type is not available in normal view, in a bulleted or numbered list, or in a document formatted as multiple columns. In print layout view, use the ruler to click at a specific location in the document (e.g., 2 inches from the top or bottom).

Entering Text Using Click and Type

When in print layout view, you can use **Click and Type** to format and enter text, graphics, and other items. To use Click and Type, you double-click a blank area of the document window. Word automatically formats the item you enter according to the location where you double-click. The next steps show how to use Click and Type to right-align and then type the last name into the header area.

To Click and Type

1

• **Position the mouse pointer at the right edge of the header area to display a right-align icon next to the I-beam.**

As you move the Click and Type pointer around the window, the icon changes to represent formatting that will be applied if you double-click at that location (Figure 2-9).

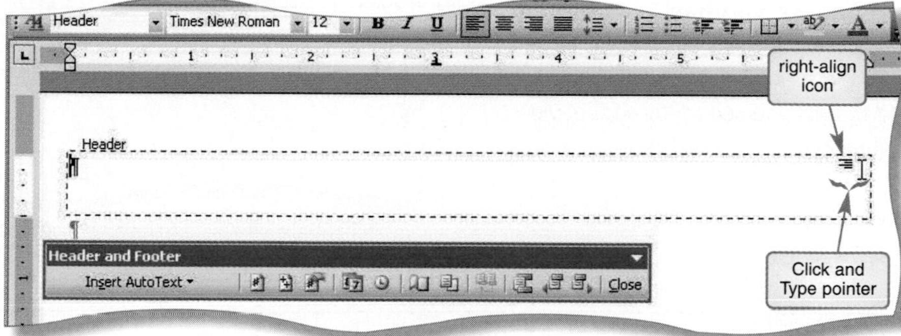

FIGURE 2-9

2

• **Double-click.**

• **Type** `Krause` **and then press the SPACEBAR.**

Word displays the last name, Krause, right-aligned in the header area (Figure 2-10).

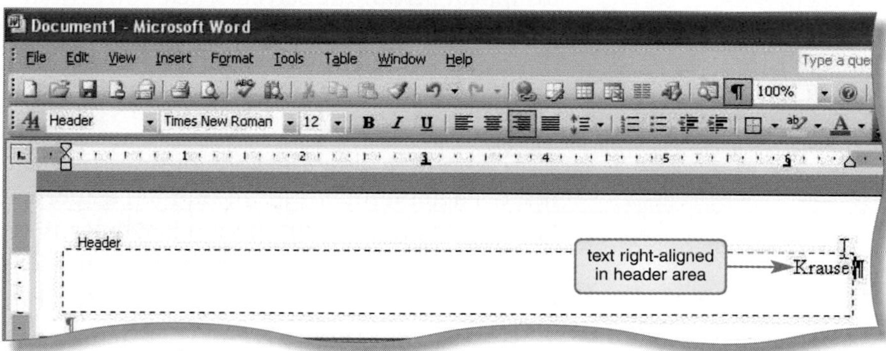

FIGURE 2-10

Entering a Page Number into the Header

The next task is to enter the page number into the header area, as shown in the following steps.

To Enter a Page Number

1

• **Click the Insert Page Number button on the Header and Footer toolbar.**

Word displays the page number 1 in the header area (Figure 2-11).

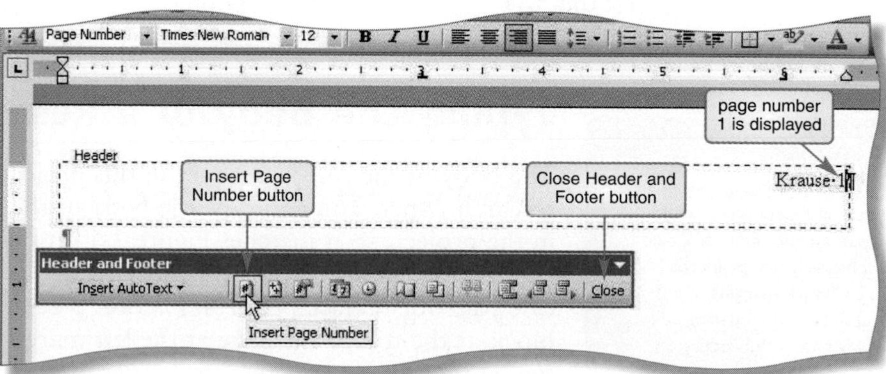

FIGURE 2-11

2

• Click the Close Header and Footer button on the Header and Footer toolbar.

Word closes the Header and Footer toolbar and returns the screen to normal view (Figure 2-12).

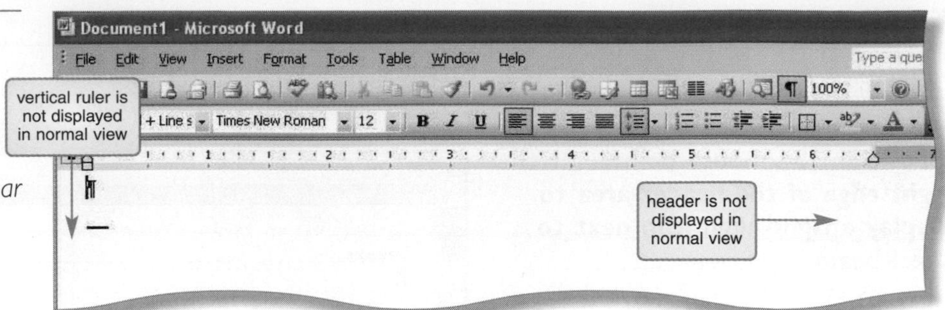

FIGURE 2-12

Word does not display the header on the screen in normal view. Although it disappears from the screen when you switch from print layout view to normal view, the header still is part of the document. To view the header, you can click View on the menu bar and then click Header and Footer; you can switch to print layout view; or you can display the document in print preview. Project 3 discusses print layout view and print preview.

Figure 2-13 identifies the buttons on the Header and Footer toolbar. Just as the Insert Page Number button on the Header and Footer toolbar inserts the page number into the document, three other buttons on the Header and Footer toolbar insert items into the document. The Insert Number of Pages button inserts the total number of pages in the document; the Insert Date button inserts the current date; and the Insert Time button inserts the current time.

To edit an existing header, you can follow the same procedure that you use to create a new header. That is, click View on the menu bar and then click Header and Footer to display the header area. If you have multiple headers, click the Show Next button on the Header and Footer toolbar until the appropriate header is displayed in the header area. Edit the header as you would any Word text and then click the Close Header and Footer button on the Header and Footer toolbar.

To create a footer, click View on the menu bar, click Header and Footer, click the Switch Between Header and Footer button on the Header and Footer toolbar, and then follow the same procedure as you would to create a header.

Later projects explain other buttons on the Header and Footer toolbar.

Header and Footer
Insert AutoText
Close
Insert Page Number
Format Page Number
Insert Time
Show/Hide Document Text
Switch Between Header and Footer
Show Next
Insert AutoText
Insert Number of Pages
Insert Date
Page Setup
Link to Previous
Show Previous
Close Header and Footer

FIGURE 2-13

Typing the Body of a Research Paper

The body of the research paper in this project encompasses the first two pages of the research paper. You will type the body of the research paper and then modify it later in the project, so it matches Figure 2-1 on page WD 75.

As discussed earlier in this project, the MLA style does not require a separate title page for research papers. Instead, place your name and course information in a block at the top of the page at the left margin. The next steps describe how to begin typing the body of the research paper.

Skill Builder 2-1

To practice the following tasks, visit scsite.com/off2003sch/skill, locate Word Project 2, and then click Skill Builder 2-1.

- ❑ Change margins
- ❑ Adjust line spacing
- ❑ Work with headers

To Enter Name and Course Information

1. **Type** `Ryan Krause` **and then press the ENTER key.**
2. **Type** `Ms. Lopez` **and then press the ENTER key.**
3. **Type** `English 7` **and then press the ENTER key.**
4. **Type** `October 15, 2007` **and then press the ENTER key.**

Word displays the student name on line 1, the instructor name on line 2, the course name on line 3, and the paper due date on line 4 (Figure 2-14). Depending on your Word settings, the smart tag indicator may not appear below the date on the screen.

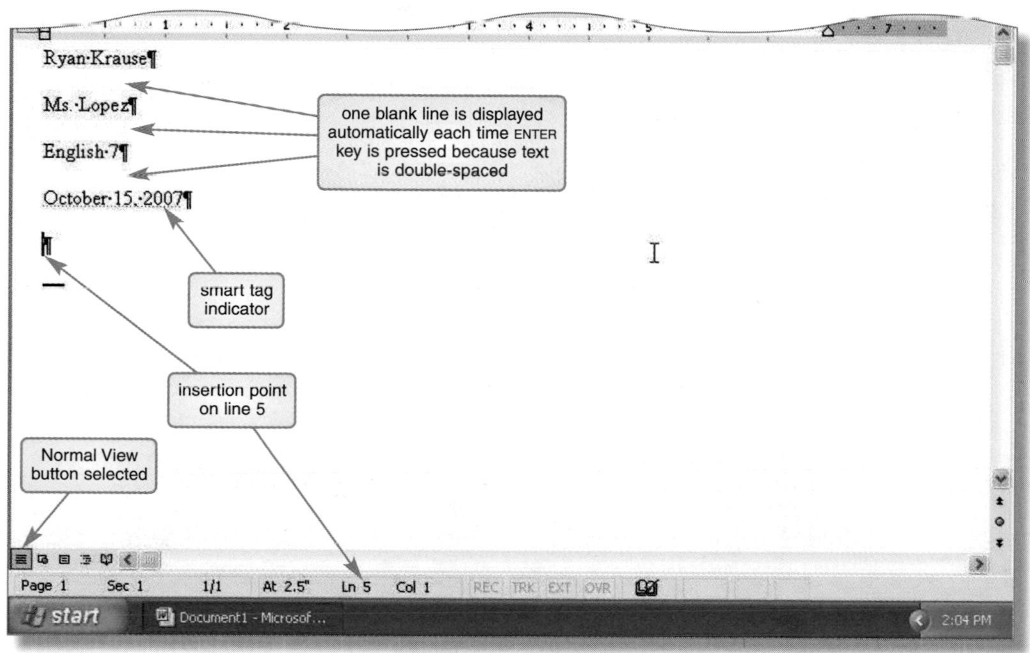

FIGURE 2-14

Q & A

Q: Does the APA style require a title page?

A: Yes, a separate title page is required instead of placing name and course information on the paper's first page. The running head (header), which contains a brief summary of the title and the page number, also is on the title page.

Q & A

Q: What is a smart tag?

A: Word notifies you of a smart tag by displaying a smart tag indicator, such as the purple dotted underline shown in Figure 2-14. You then can use the smart tag to perform tasks more efficiently. For example, you can schedule an appointment on the underlined date in Outlook Calendar. Smart tags are discussed later in this project.

Notice in Figure 2-14 that the insertion point currently is on line 5. Each time you press the ENTER key, Word advances two lines on the screen. The line counter on the status bar is incremented by only one, however, because earlier you set line spacing to double.

If you watch the screen as you type, you may have noticed that as you typed the first few characters in the month, Octo, Word displayed the **AutoComplete tip**, October, above the characters. To save typing, you could press the ENTER key while the AutoComplete tip appears, which instructs Word to place the text of the AutoComplete tip at the location of your typing.

Q & A

Q: How should I take notes for a paper I plan to write?

A: One method is to summarize the information. Another method is to paraphrase, or rewrite the information in your own words. A third method is to quote the exact words of the original. Be sure to use quotation marks when directly quoting a source.

Applying Formatting Using Shortcut Keys

The next step is to enter the title of the research paper centered between the page margins. As you type text, you may want to format paragraphs and characters as you type them, instead of typing the text and then formatting it later. In Project 1, you typed the entire document, selected the text to be formatted, and then applied the desired formatting using toolbar buttons. When your fingers are already on the keyboard, it often is more efficient to use **shortcut keys**, or keyboard key combinations, to format text as you type it.

The following steps show how to center a paragraph using the shortcut keys CTRL+E and then left-align a paragraph using the shortcut keys CTRL+L. (Recall from Project 1 that a notation such as CTRL+E means to press the letter e on the keyboard while holding down the CTRL key.)

To Format Text Using Shortcut Keys

1

- **Press CTRL+E.**
- **Type** `Healthy Computing` **and then press the ENTER key.**

Word centers the title between the left and right margins (Figure 2-15). The paragraph mark and insertion point are centered because the formatting specified in the previous paragraph is carried forward to the next paragraph.

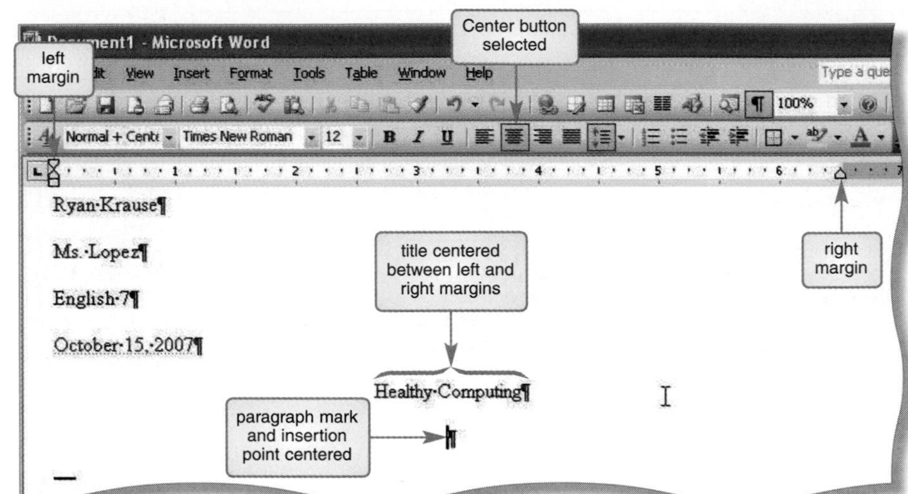

FIGURE 2-15

2

- **Press CTRL+L.**

Word positions the paragraph mark and the insertion point at the left margin (Figure 2-16). The next text you type will be left-aligned.

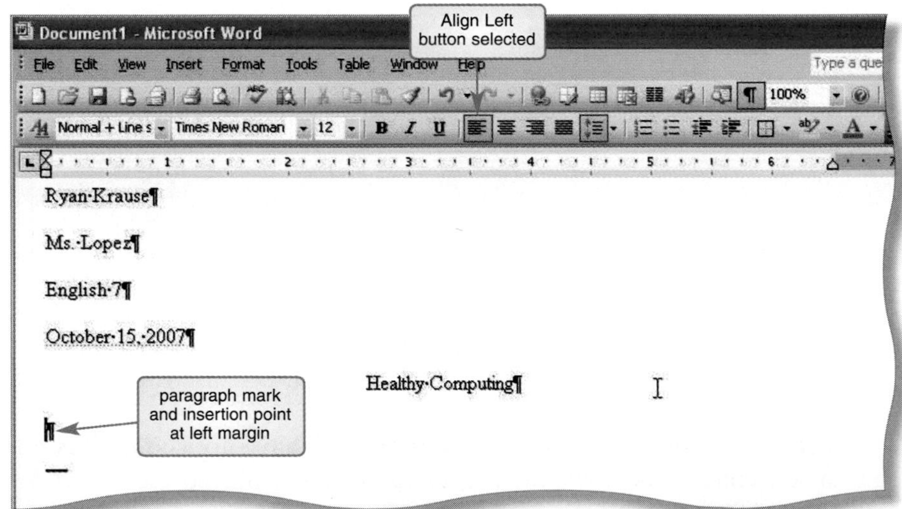

FIGURE 2-16

Word has many shortcut keys for your convenience while typing. Table 2-1 lists the common shortcut keys for formatting characters. Table 2-2 lists common shortcut keys for formatting paragraphs.

Table 2-1 Shortcut Keys for Formatting Characters

CHARACTER FORMATTING TASK	SHORTCUT KEYS
All capital letters	CTRL+SHIFT+A
Bold	CTRL+B
Case of letters	SHIFT+F3
Decrease font size	CTRL+SHIFT+<
Decrease font size 1 point	CTRL+[
Double-underline	CTRL+SHIFT+D
Increase font size	CTRL+SHIFT+>
Increase font size 1 point	CTRL+]
Italic	CTRL+I
Remove character formatting (plain text)	CTRL+SPACEBAR
Small uppercase letters	CTRL+SHIFT+K
Subscript	CTRL+=
Superscript	CTRL+SHIFT+PLUS SIGN
Underline	CTRL+U
Underline words, not spaces	CTRL+SHIFT+W

Table 2-2 Shortcut Keys for Formatting Paragraphs

PARAGRAPH FORMATTING TASK	SHORTCUT KEYS
1.5 line spacing	CTRL+5
Add/remove one line above	CTRL+0 (zero)
Center paragraph	CTRL+E
Decrease paragraph indent	CTRL+SHIFT+M
Double-space lines	CTRL+2
Hanging indent	CTRL+T
Increase paragraph indent	CTRL+M
Justify paragraph	CTRL+J
Left-align paragraph	CTRL+L
Remove hanging indent	CTRL+SHIFT+T
Remove paragraph formatting	CTRL+Q
Right-align paragraph	CTRL+R
Single-space lines	CTRL+1

Saving the Research Paper

You now should save the research paper. For a detailed example of the procedure summarized below, refer to pages WD 28 through WD 30 in Project 1.

To Save a Document

1. **Connect a USB flash drive to one of the computer's USB ports.**
2. **Click the Save button on the Standard toolbar.**
3. **Type** `Healthy Computing Paper` **in the File name text box.**
4. **Click the Save in box arrow and then click UDISK 2.0 (E:). (Your USB flash drive may have a different name and letter.)**
5. **Click the Save button in the Save As dialog box.**

Word saves the document with the file name, Healthy Computing Paper (shown in Figure 2-17 on the next page).

Indenting Paragraphs

According to the MLA style, the first line of each paragraph in the research paper is to be indented one-half inch from the left margin. You can instruct Word to indent just the first line of a paragraph, called **first-line indent**, using the horizontal ruler. The left edge of the horizontal ruler contains two triangles above a square. The **First Line Indent marker** is the top triangle at the 0" mark on the ruler (Figure 2-17). The bottom triangle is discussed later in this project. The small square at the 0" mark is the Left Indent marker. The **Left Indent marker** allows you to change the entire left margin, whereas the First Line Indent marker indents only the first line of the paragraph.

Q & A

Q: How do I print a list of all shortcut keys?

A: To print a complete list of shortcut keys in Word, type `keyboard shortcuts` in the Type a question for help box on the right side of the menu bar. In the Search Results task pane, click the Keyboard shortcuts link. In the upper-right corner of the Office Word Help window, click the Show All link. Click the Print button in the Help window and then click the Print button in the Print dialog box.

Q & A

Q: Can I use a dialog box to indent paragraphs?

A: Some users may find it confusing to use the ruler to indent paragraphs. In this case, you can use the Paragraph dialog box to first-line indent a paragraph. To do this, click Format on the menu bar, click Paragraph, click the Indents and Spacing tab, click the Special box arrow, click First line, and then click the OK button.

The following steps show how to first-line indent paragraphs in the research paper.

To First-Line Indent Paragraphs

1

- **If the horizontal ruler is not displayed on your screen, click View on the menu bar and then click Ruler.**
- **With the insertion point on the paragraph mark in line 6, point to the First Line Indent marker on the ruler (Figure 2-17).**

FIGURE 2-17

2

- **Drag the First Line Indent marker to the .5" mark on the ruler.**

As you drag the mouse, Word displays a vertical dotted line in the document window, indicating the proposed location of the first line of the paragraph (Figure 2-18).

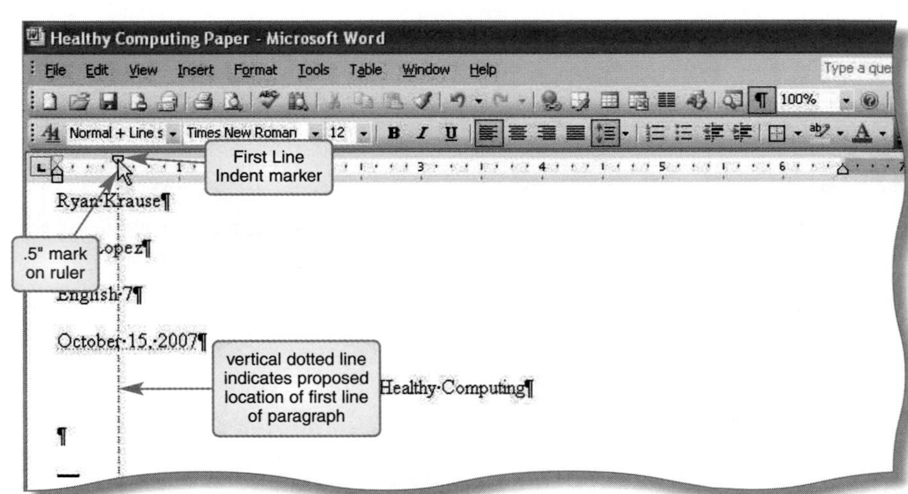

FIGURE 2-18

3

- **Release the mouse button.**

Word displays the First Line Indent marker at the .5" mark on the ruler, or one-half inch from the left margin (Figure 2-19). The paragraph mark containing the insertion point in the document window also moves one-half inch to the right.

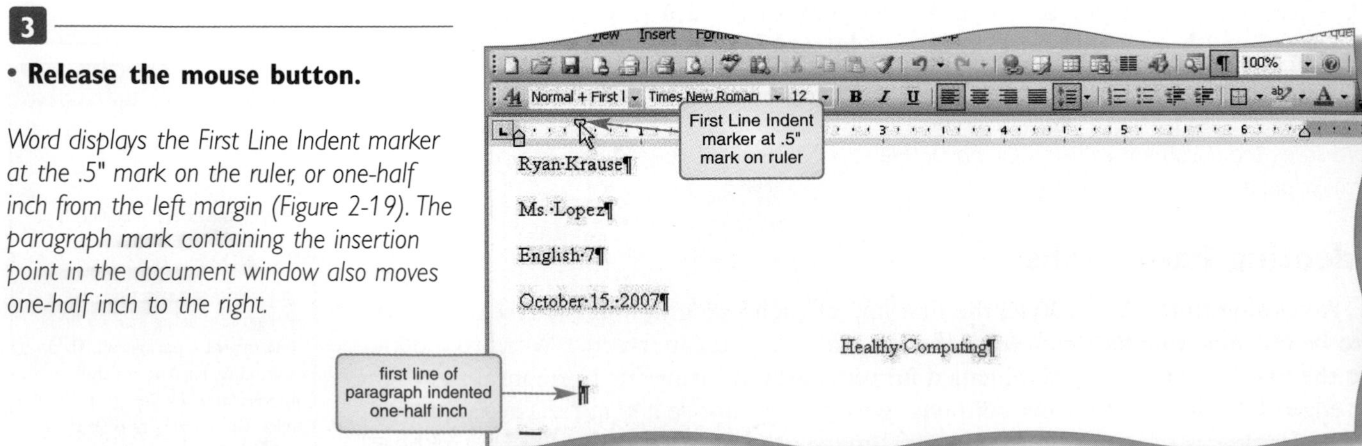

FIGURE 2-19

4

- **Type the first paragraph of the research paper body, as shown in Figure 2-20.**
- **Press the ENTER key.**
- **Type** `Two common repetitive stress or strain injuries (RSI) that affect the wrist are carpal tunnel syndrome and tendonitis.`

Word automatically indents the first line of the second paragraph by one-half inch (Figure 2-20).

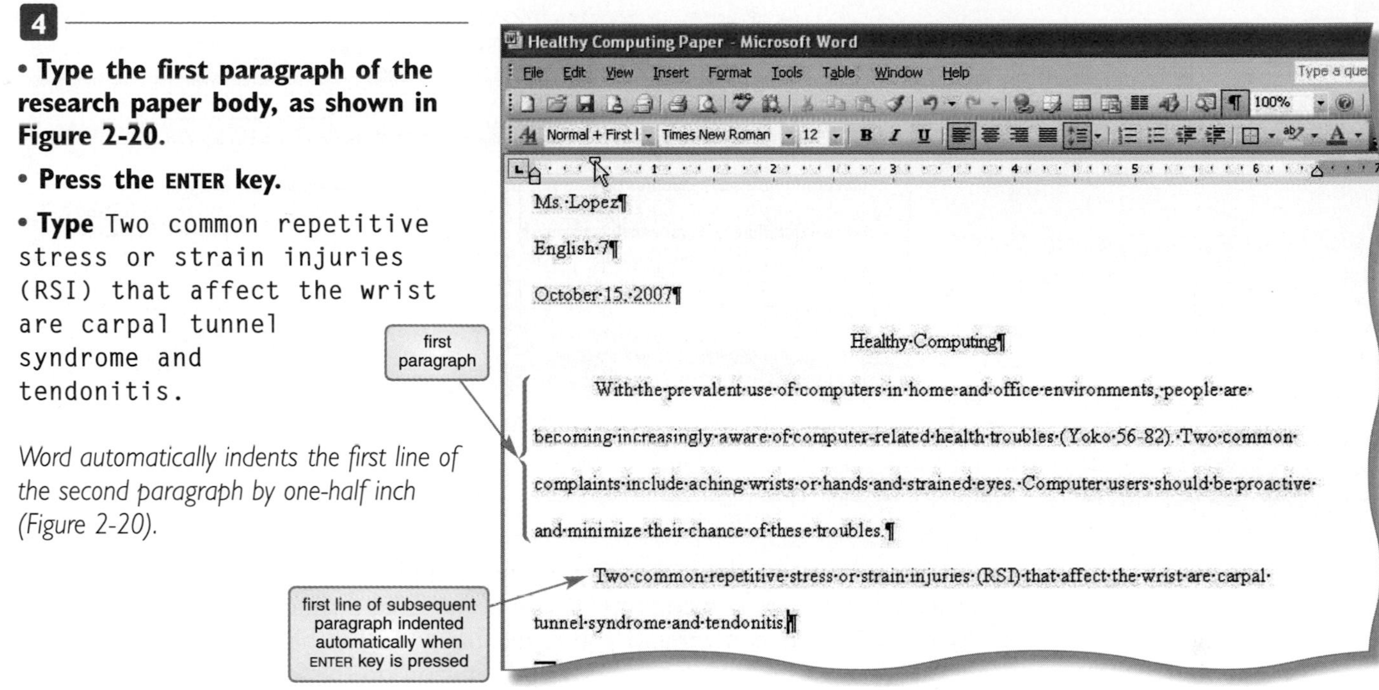

FIGURE 2-20

Recall that each time you press the ENTER key, the paragraph formatting in the previous paragraph is carried forward to the next paragraph. Thus, once you set the first-line indent, its format carries forward automatically to each subsequent paragraph you type.

Using Word's AutoCorrect Feature

As you type, you may make typing, spelling, capitalization, or grammar errors. For this reason, Word provides an **AutoCorrect** feature that automatically corrects these kinds of errors as you type them in the document. For example, if you type the text, ahve, Word automatically changes it to the correct spelling, have, when you press the SPACEBAR or a punctuation mark key such as a period or comma.

Word has predefined many commonly misspelled words, which it automatically corrects for you. In the following steps the word, and, is misspelled intentionally as adn to illustrate the AutoCorrect as you type feature.

To AutoCorrect as You Type

1

- **Press the SPACEBAR.**
- **Type the beginning of the next sentence, misspelling the word, and, as follows:** `If your fingertips tingle and then become numb adn` **(Figure 2-21).**

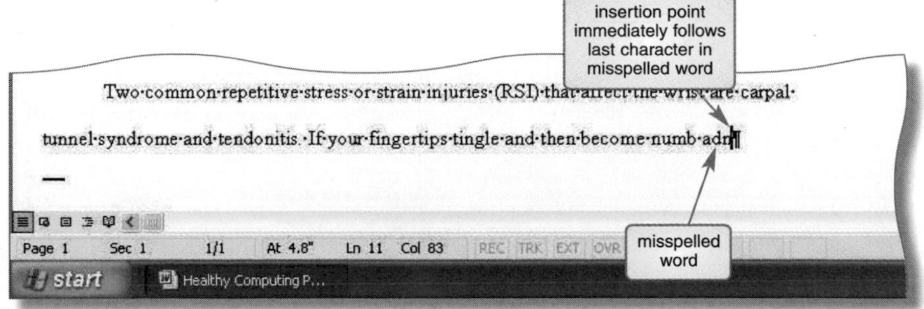

FIGURE 2-21

2

- **Press the SPACEBAR.**
- **Type the rest of the sentence:** `your hands hurt, you may have carpal tunnel syndrome.`

As soon as the SPACEBAR is pressed, Word's AutoCorrect feature detects the misspelling and corrects the misspelled word (Figure 2-22).

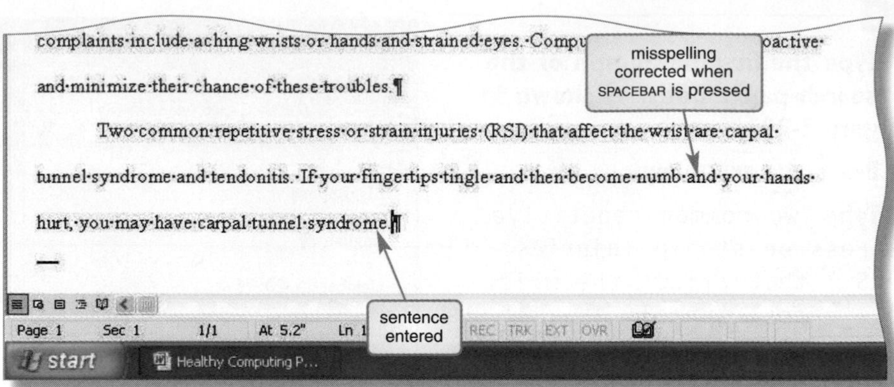

FIGURE 2-22

Word has a list of predefined typing, spelling, capitalization, and grammar errors that AutoCorrect detects and corrects. If you do not like a change that Word automatically makes in a document and you immediately notice the automatic correction, you can undo the change by clicking the Undo button on the Standard toolbar; clicking Edit on the menu bar and then clicking Undo; or pressing CTRL+Z.

If you do not immediately notice the change, you still can undo a correction automatically made by Word through the AutoCorrect Options button. When you position the mouse pointer on text that Word automatically corrected, a small blue box appears below the text. If you point to the small blue box, Word displays the AutoCorrect Options button. When you click the **AutoCorrect Options button**, Word displays a menu that allows you to undo a correction or change how Word handles future automatic corrections of this type. The following steps show how to use the AutoCorrect Options button and menu.

To Use the AutoCorrect Options Button

1

- **Position the mouse pointer at the beginning of the text automatically corrected by Word (in this case, the a in and).**

Word displays a small blue box below the automatically corrected word (Figure 2-23).

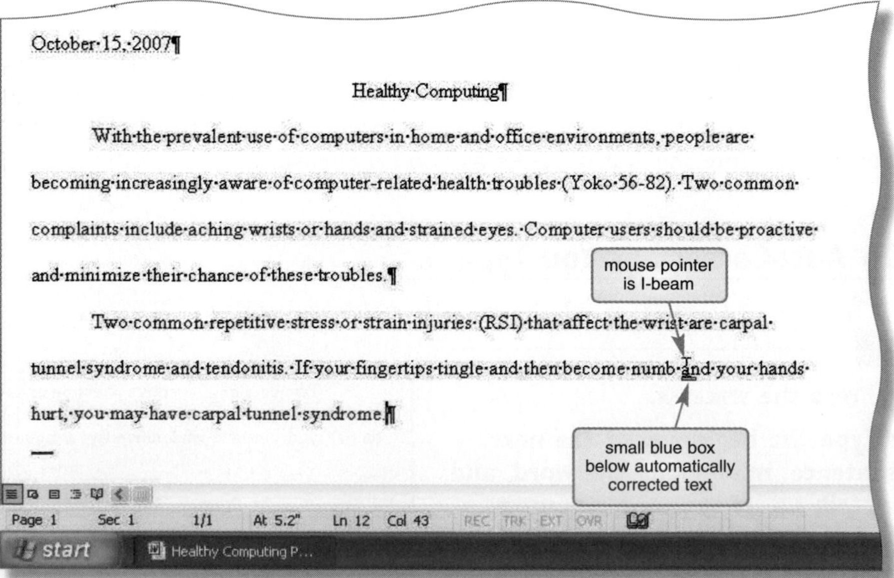

FIGURE 2-23

2

- **Point to the small blue box to display the AutoCorrect Options button.**
- **Click the AutoCorrect Options button.**

Word displays the AutoCorrect Options menu (Figure 2-24).

3

- **Press the ESCAPE key to remove the AutoCorrect Options menu from the screen.**

When you move the mouse pointer, the AutoCorrect Options button disappears from the screen, or you can press the ESCAPE key a second time to remove the AutoCorrect Options button from the screen.

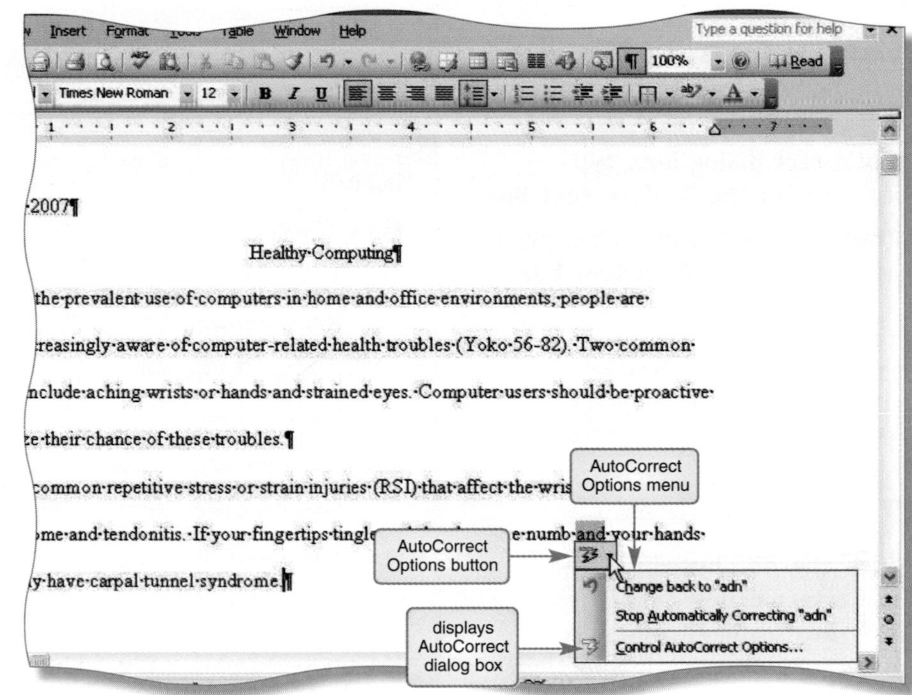

FIGURE 2-24

In addition to the predefined list of AutoCorrect spelling, capitalization, and grammar errors, you can create your own AutoCorrect entries to add to the list. For example, if you tend to type the word, computer, as comptuer, you should create an AutoCorrect entry for it, as shown in these steps.

To Create an AutoCorrect Entry

1

- **Click Tools on the menu bar (Figure 2-25).**

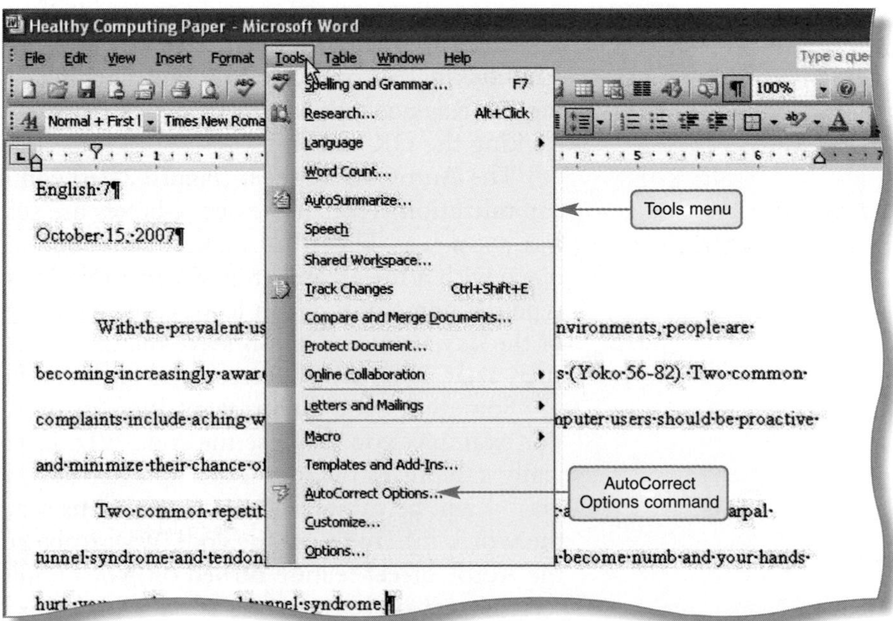

FIGURE 2-25

2

- **Click AutoCorrect Options on the Tools menu.**
- **When Word displays the AutoCorrect dialog box, type** `comptuer` **in the Replace text box.**
- **Press the TAB key and then type** `computer` **in the With text box.**

In the AutoCorrect dialog box, the Replace text box contains the misspelled word, and the With text box contains its correct spelling (Figure 2-26).

3

- **Click the Add button in the AutoCorrect dialog box. (If your dialog box displays a Replace button instead, click it and then click the Yes button in the Microsoft Office Word dialog box.)**
- **Click the OK button.**

Word adds the entry alphabetically to the list of words to correct automatically as you type.

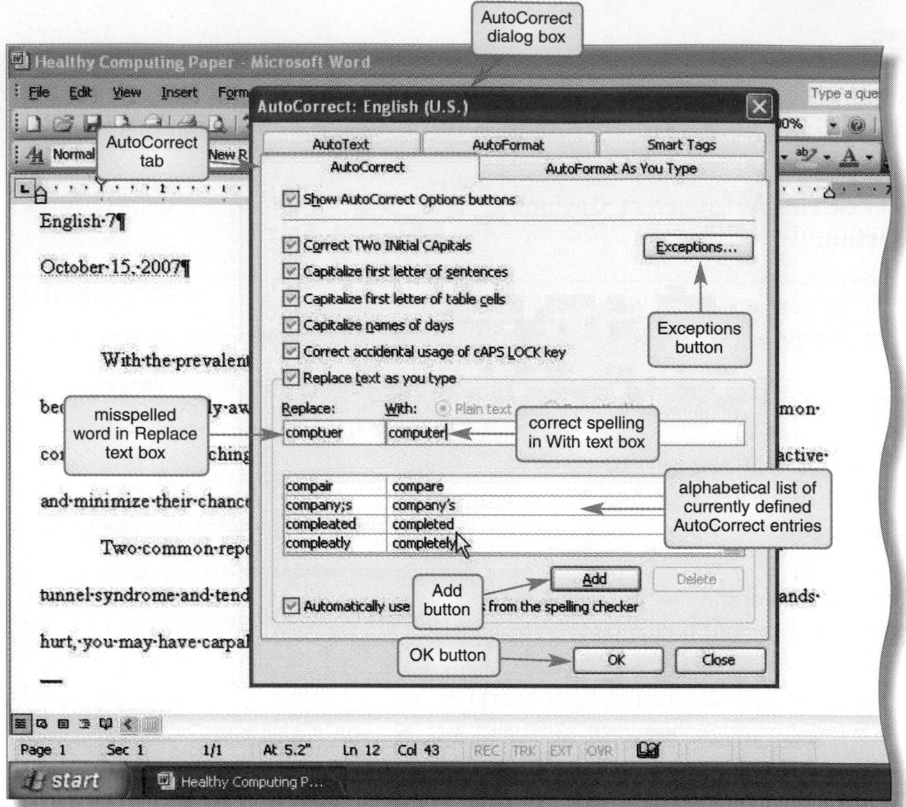

FIGURE 2-26

In addition to creating AutoCorrect entries for words you commonly misspell or mistype, you can create entries for abbreviations, codes, and so on. For example, you could create an AutoCorrect entry for asap, indicating that Word should replace this text with the phrase, as soon as possible.

If, for some reason, you do not want Word to correct automatically as you type, you can turn off the Replace text as you type feature by clicking Tools on the menu bar, clicking AutoCorrect Options, clicking the AutoCorrect tab (Figure 2-26), clicking the Replace text as you type check box to remove the check mark, and then clicking the OK button.

The AutoCorrect sheet (Figure 2-26) contains other check boxes that correct capitalization errors if the check boxes are selected. If you type two capital letters in a row, such as TH, Word makes the second letter lowercase, Th. If you begin a sentence with a lowercase letter, Word capitalizes the first letter of the sentence. If you type the name of a day in lowercase, such as tuesday, Word capitalizes the first letter of the day, Tuesday. If you leave the CAPS LOCK key on and begin a new sentence, such as aFTER, Word corrects the typing, After, and turns off the CAPS LOCK key.

Sometimes you do not want Word to AutoCorrect a particular word or phrase. For example, you may use the code WD. in your documents. Because Word automatically capitalizes the first letter of a sentence, the character you enter following the period will be capitalized (in the previous sentence, it would capitalize the letter i in the word, in). To allow the code WD. to be entered into a document and still leave the AutoCorrect feature turned on, you should set an exception. To set an exception to an AutoCorrect rule, click Tools on the menu bar, click AutoCorrect Options, click the AutoCorrect tab, click the Exceptions button in the AutoCorrect sheet (Figure 2-26), click the appropriate tab in the AutoCorrect Exceptions dialog box, type the exception entry in the text box, click the Add button, click the Close button in the AutoCorrect Exceptions dialog box, and then click the OK button in the AutoCorrect dialog box.

The next step is to continue typing text in the body of the research paper up to the location of the footnote, as described below.

To Enter More Text

1. **Press the SPACEBAR. Type the remaining five sentences in the second paragraph of the paper as shown in Figure 2-27.**

2. **Press the ENTER key. Type the first two sentences in the third paragraph of the paper as shown in Figure 2-27.**

Word displays the entered text in the document window (Figure 2-27).

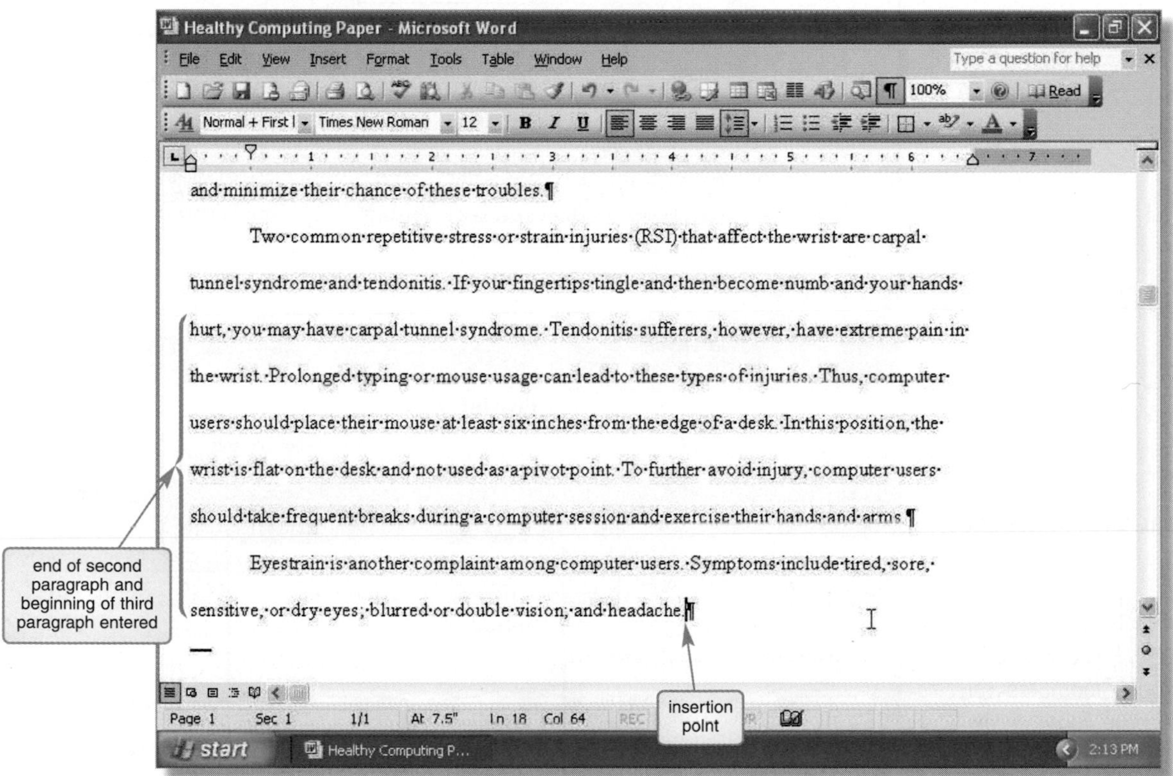

FIGURE 2-27

Adding Footnotes

As discussed earlier in this project, explanatory notes are optional in the MLA documentation style. They are used primarily to elaborate on points discussed in the body of a research paper. The MLA style specifies that a superscript (raised number) be used for a **note reference mark** to signal that an explanatory note exists either at the bottom of the page as a **footnote** or at the end of the document as an **endnote**.

Word, by default, places notes at the bottom of each page as footnotes. In Word, **note text** can be any length and format. Word automatically numbers notes sequentially by placing a note reference mark in the body of the document and also to the left of the note text. If you insert, rearrange, or remove notes, Word renumbers any subsequent note reference marks according to their new sequence in the document.

Q & A

Q: Should I footnote sources in a research paper?

A: Both the MLA and APA guidelines suggest the use of in-text parenthetical citations, instead of footnoting each source of material in a paper. These parenthetical acknowledgments guide the reader to the end of the paper for complete information about the source.

The following steps show how to add a footnote to the research paper.

To Add a Footnote

1

• With the insertion point positioned as shown in Figure 2-28, click Insert on the menu bar and then point to Reference (Figure 2-28).

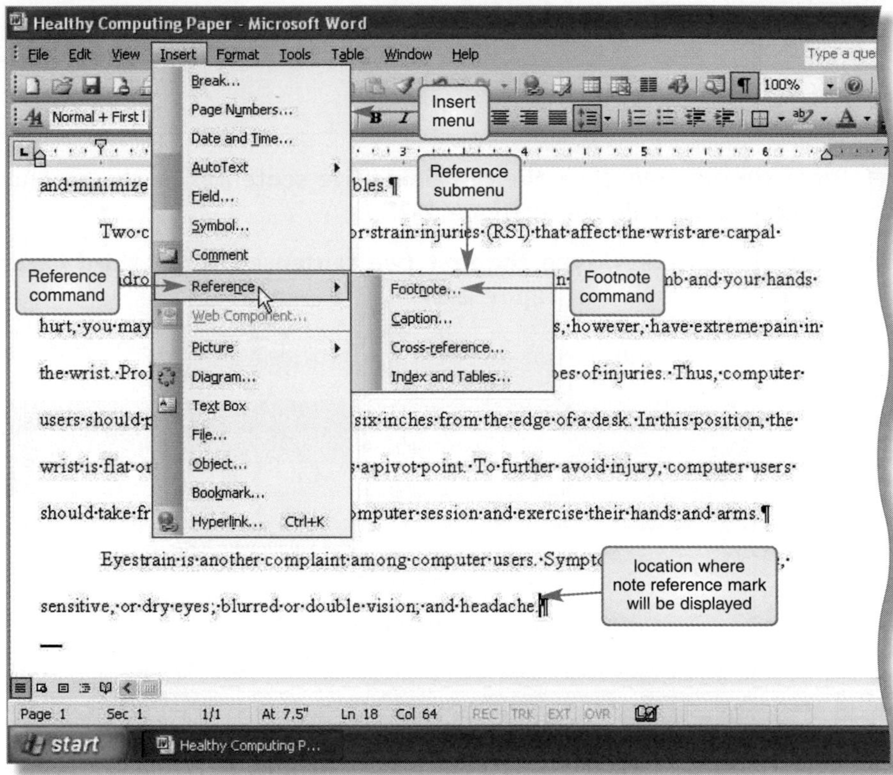

FIGURE 2-28

2

• Click Footnote on the Reference submenu.

Word displays the Footnote and Endnote dialog box (Figure 2-29). If you wanted to create endnotes instead of footnotes, you would click Endnotes in the Footnote and Endnote dialog box.

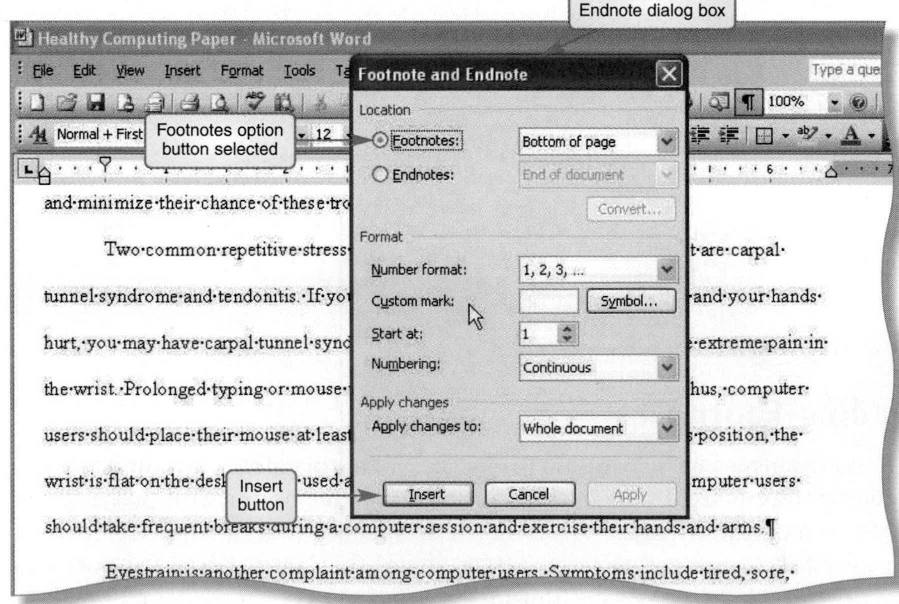

FIGURE 2-29

3

• **Click the Insert button in the Footnote and Endnote dialog box.**

Word opens a note pane in the lower portion of the Word window with the note reference mark (a superscripted 1) positioned at the left margin of the note pane (Figure 2-30). Word also displays the note reference mark in the document window at the location of the insertion point. Note reference marks are, by default, superscripted; that is, raised above other letters.

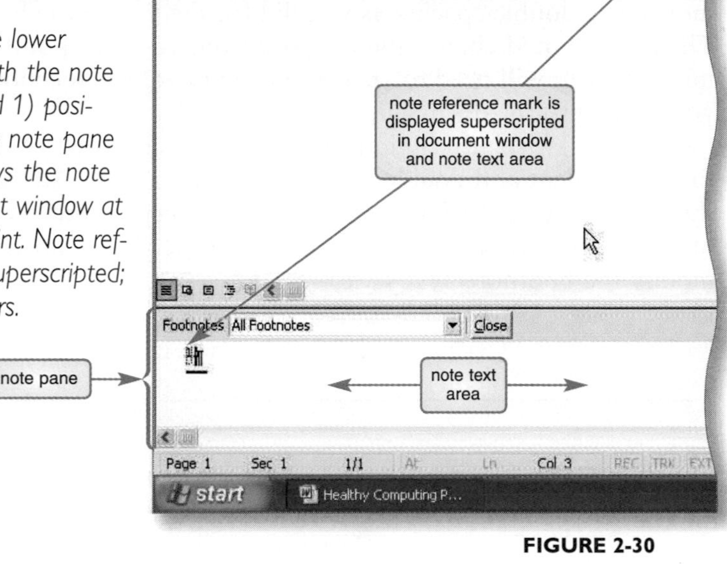

FIGURE 2-30

4

• **Type** `According to Ames and Weinberg, eyestrain is not believed to have severe or long-term consequences, but sufferers should visit a doctor to rule out a serious illness (78-94).`

Word displays the note text in the note pane (Figure 2-31).

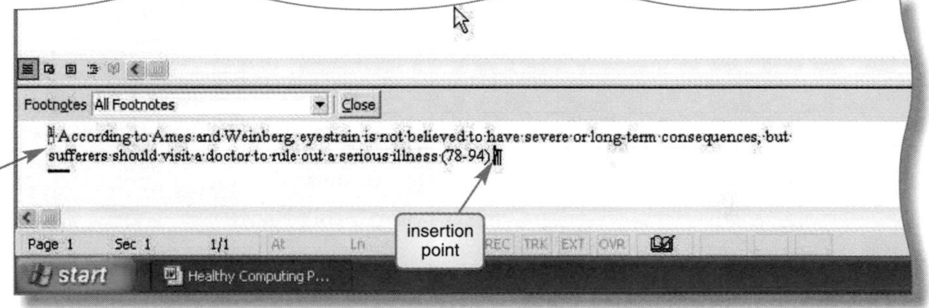

FIGURE 2-31

The footnote is not formatted according to the MLA requirements. Thus, the next step is to modify the style of the footnote.

Modifying a Style

A **style** is a named group of formatting characteristics that you can apply to text. Word has many built-in, or predefined, styles that you may use to format text. The formats defined by these styles include character formatting, such as the font and font size; paragraph formatting, such as line spacing and text alignment; table formatting; and list formatting.

Whenever you create a document, Word formats the text using a particular style. The underlying style, called the **base style**, for a new Word document is the Normal style. For a new installation of Word 2003, the **Normal style** most likely uses 12-point Times New Roman font for characters and single-spaced, left-aligned paragraphs. As you type, you can apply different predefined styles to the text or you can create your own styles. A later project discusses applying and creating styles.

Q & A

Q: How can I view and apply styles?

A: To view the list of styles associated with the current document, click the Style box arrow on the Formatting toolbar or display the Styles and Formatting task pane by clicking the Styles and Formatting button on the Formatting toolbar. To apply a style, click the desired style name in the Style list or in the Styles and Formatting task pane.

When the insertion point is in the note text area, the entered note text is formatted using the Footnote Text style. The Footnote Text style defines characters as 10-point Times New Roman and paragraphs as single-spaced and left-aligned.

You could change the paragraph formatting of the footnote text to first-line indent and double-spacing as you did for the text in the body of the research paper. Then, you would change the font size from 10 to 12 point. If you use this technique, however, you will need to change the format of the footnote text for each footnote you enter into the document.

A more efficient technique is to modify the format of the Footnote Text style to first-line indent and double-spaced paragraphs and a 12-point font size. By changing the formatting of the Footnote Text style, every footnote you enter into the document will use the formats defined in this style. The following steps show how to modify the Footnote Text style.

To Modify a Style

1

• **Right-click the note text in the note pane.**

Word displays a shortcut menu related to footnotes (Figure 2-32).

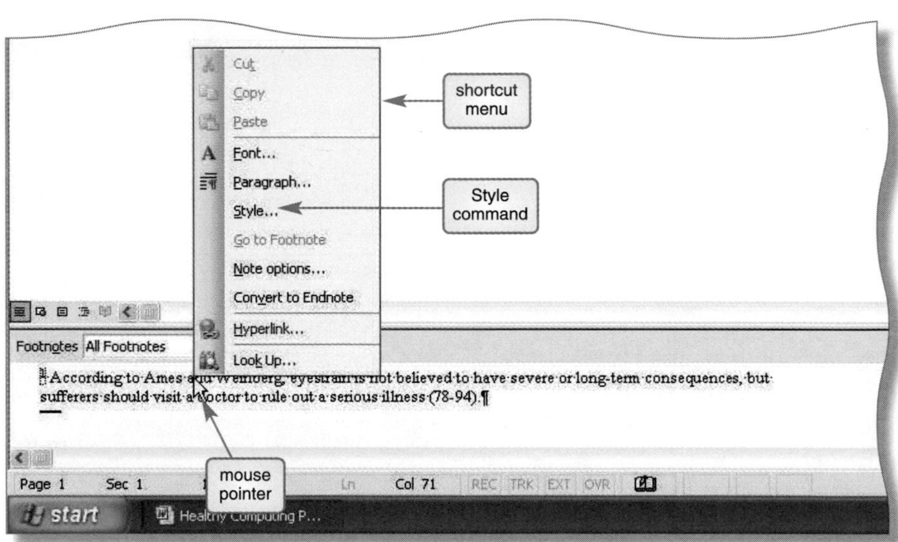

FIGURE 2-32

2

• **Click Style on the shortcut menu.**

• **When Word displays the Style dialog box, if necessary, click Footnote Text in the Styles list.**

The Preview area of the Style dialog box shows the formatting associated with the selected style (Figure 2-33). The selected style is Footnote Text.

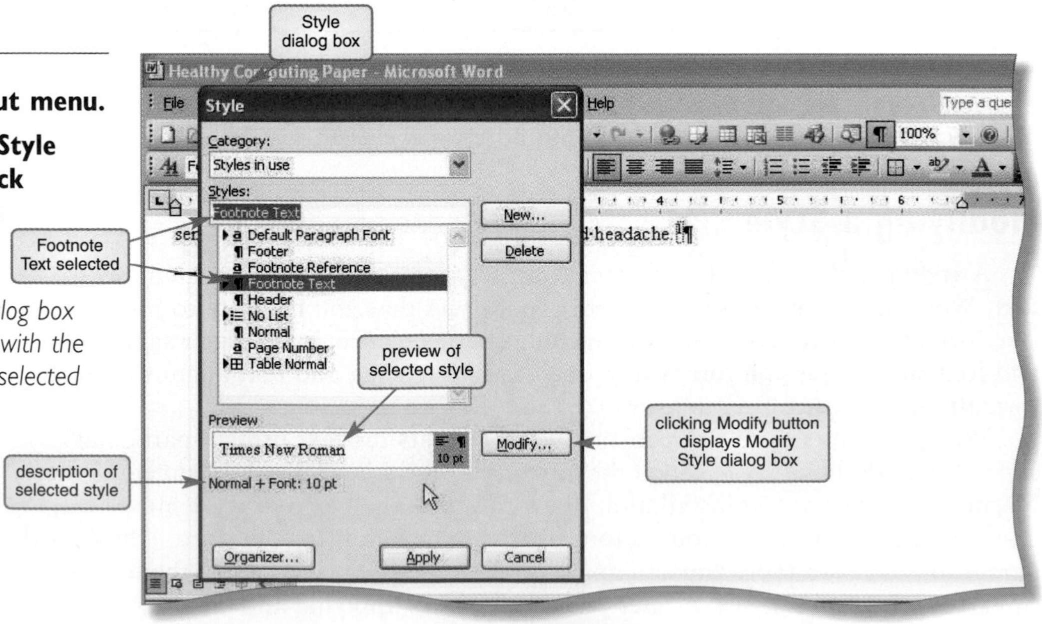

Style dialog box

Footnote Text selected

preview of selected style

clicking Modify button displays Modify Style dialog box

description of selected style

FIGURE 2-33

3

- **Click the Modify button in the Style dialog box.**
- **When Word displays the Modify Style dialog box, click the Font Size box arrow in the Formatting area and then click 12 in the Font Size list.**
- **Click the Double Space button in the Modify Style dialog box.**

In the Modify Style dialog box, the font size for the Footnote Text style is changed to 12, and paragraph spacing is changed to double (Figure 2-34). The first-line indent still must be set.

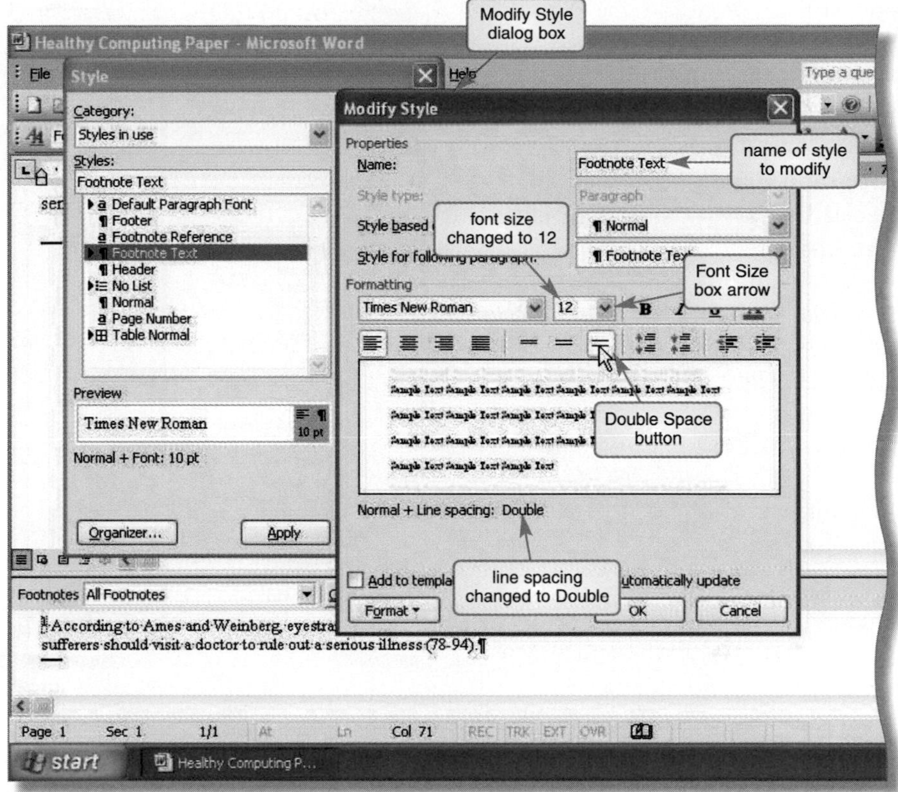

FIGURE 2-34

4

- **Click the Format button in the Modify Style dialog box.**

Word displays the Format button menu above the Format button (Figure 2-35).

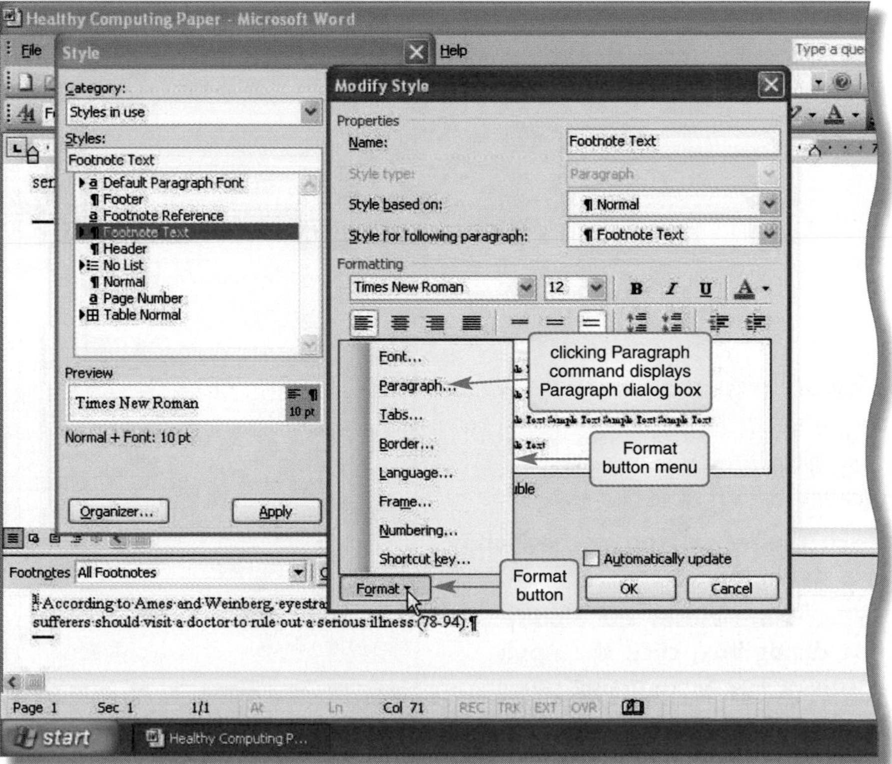

FIGURE 2-35

5

• **Click Paragraph on the Format button menu.**

• **When Word displays the Paragraph dialog box, click the Special box arrow and then click First line.**

In the Paragraph dialog box, Word displays First line in the Special box (Figure 2-36). Notice the default first-line indent is 0.5".

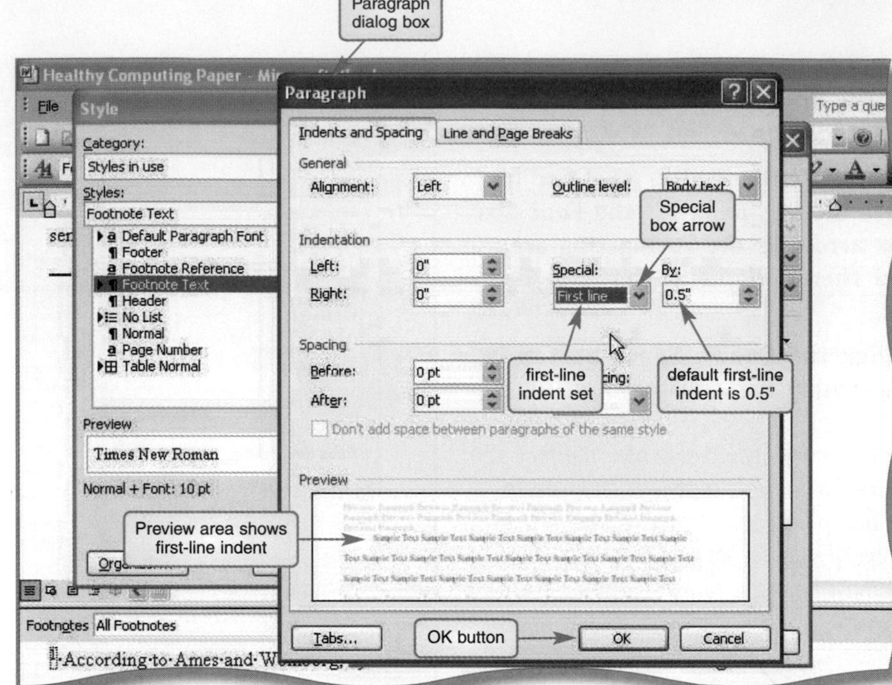

FIGURE 2-36

6

• **Click the OK button in the Paragraph dialog box.**

Word modifies the Footnote Text style to first-line indented paragraphs and closes the Paragraph dialog box (Figure 2-37). The Modify Style dialog box is visible again.

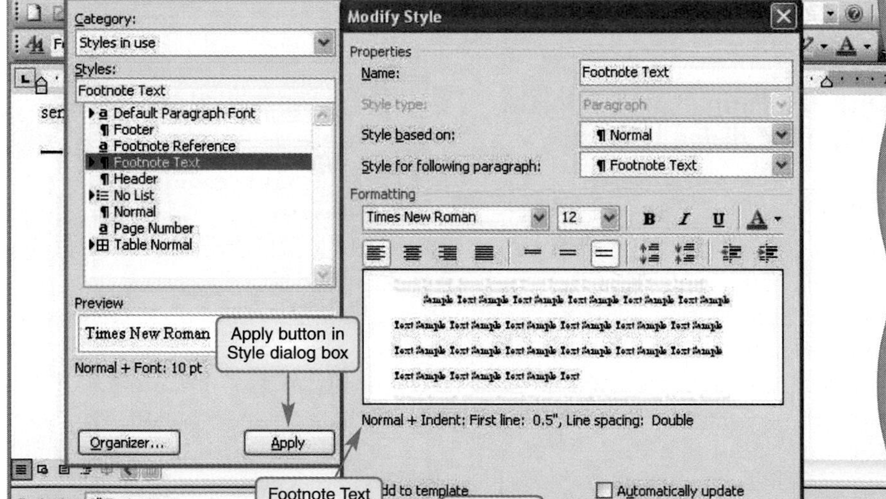

FIGURE 2-37

7

• **Click the OK button in the Modify Style dialog box.**

• **When Word closes the Modify Style dialog box, click the Apply button in the Style dialog box.**

Word displays the note text using the modified Footnote Text style, that is, the font size of the note text is changed to 12, the line spacing for the note is set to double, and the first line of the note is indented by one-half inch (Figure 2-38).

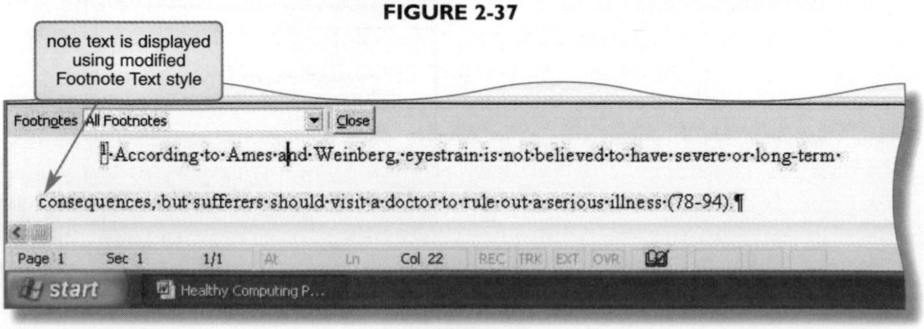

FIGURE 2-38

Any future footnotes entered into the document will use a 12-point font with the paragraphs first-line indented and double-spaced. The footnote now is complete. The next step is to close the note pane.

To Close the Note Pane

1

• **Position the mouse pointer on the Close button in the note pane (Figure 2-39).**

2

• **Click the Close button to remove the note pane from the document window.**

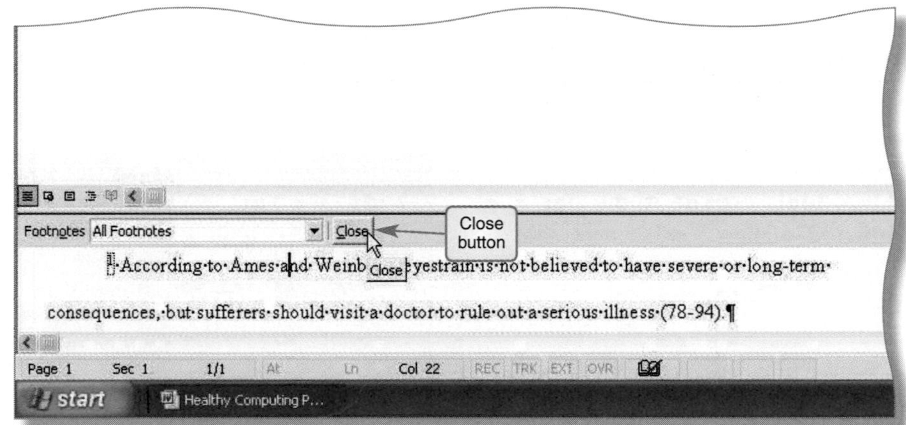

FIGURE 2-39

When Word closes the note pane and returns to the document window, the note text disappears from the screen. Although the note text still exists, it usually is not visible as a footnote in normal view. If, however, you position the mouse pointer on the note reference mark, the note text displays above the note reference mark as a ScreenTip. To remove the ScreenTip, move the mouse pointer.

If you want to verify that the note text is positioned correctly on the page, you must switch to print layout view or display the document in print preview. Project 3 discusses print preview and print layout view.

To delete a note, select the note reference mark in the document window (not in the note pane) by dragging through the note reference mark and then click the Cut button on the Standard toolbar. Another way to delete a note is to click immediately to the right of the note reference mark in the document window and then press the BACKSPACE key twice, or click immediately to the left of the note reference mark in the document window and then press the DELETE key twice.

To move a note to a different location in a document, select the note reference mark in the document window (not in the note pane), click the Cut button on the Standard toolbar, click the location where you want to move the note, and then click the Paste button on the Standard toolbar. When you move or delete notes, Word automatically renumbers any remaining notes in the correct sequence.

You edit note text using the note pane that is displayed at the bottom of the Word window. To display the note text in the note pane, double-click the note reference mark in the document window, or click View on the menu bar and then click Footnotes. In the note pane, you can edit the note as you would any Word text. When finished editing the note text, click the Close button in the note pane.

If you want to change the format of note reference marks in footnotes or endnotes (i.e., from 1, 2, 3, to A, B, C), click Insert on the menu bar, point to Reference, and then click Footnote. When Word displays the Footnote and Endnote dialog box, click the Number format box arrow, click the desired number format in the list, and then click the OK button.

Q & A

Q: How do I convert footnotes to endnotes?

A: To convert existing footnotes to endnotes, click Insert on the menu bar, point to Reference, and then click Footnote. Click the Convert button in the Footnote and Endnote dialog box. Make sure the Convert all footnotes to endnotes option button is selected and then click the OK button. Click the Close button in the Footnote and Endnote dialog box.

Using Word Count

Often when you write papers, you are required to compose the papers with a minimum number of words. The minimum requirement for the research paper in this project is 325 words. Word provides a command that displays the number of words, as well as the number of pages, characters, paragraphs, and lines in the current document. The following steps show how to use word count and display the Word Count toolbar, which allows you easily to recount words as you type more text.

To Count Words

1

- **Click Tools on the menu bar (Figure 2-40).**

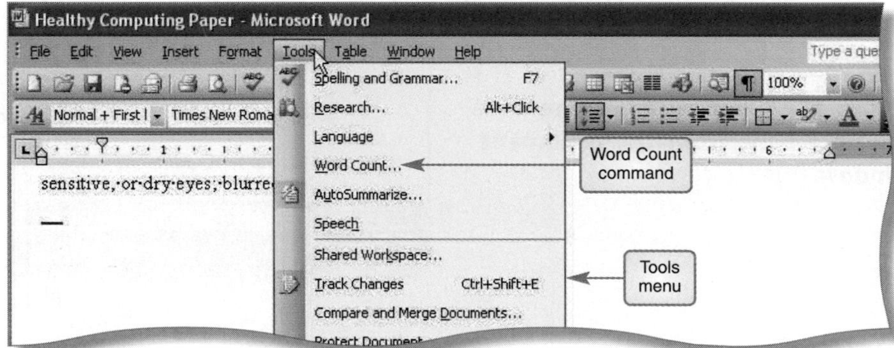

FIGURE 2-40

2

- **Click Word Count on the Tools menu.**
- **When Word displays the Word Count dialog box, if necessary, click Include footnotes and endnotes to place a check mark in the check box.**
- **Click the Show Toolbar button in the Word Count dialog box.**

In the Word Count dialog box, the number of pages, words, characters, paragraphs, and lines is displayed (Figure 2-41). The Word Count toolbar is displayed floating in the Word window. Depending on the accuracy of your typing, your word count may differ.

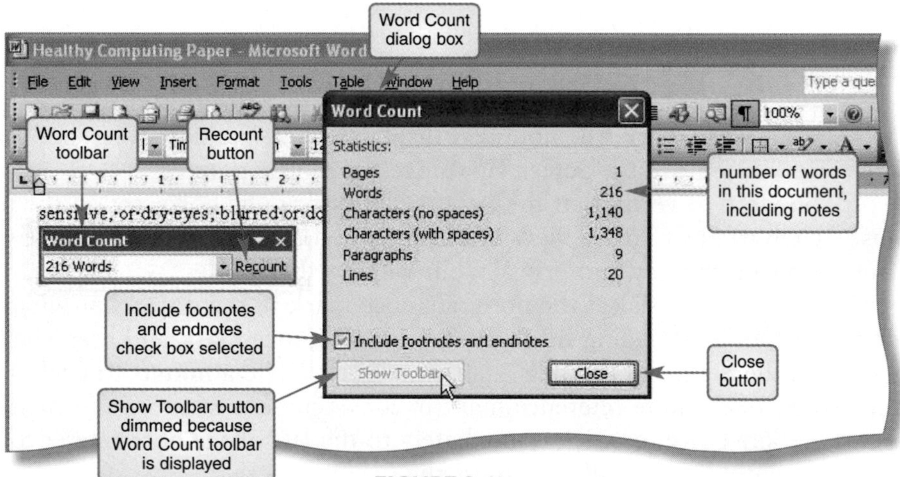

FIGURE 2-41

3

- **Click the Close button in the Word Count dialog box.**

Word removes the Word Count dialog box from the screen, but the Word Count toolbar remains on the screen (Figure 2-42). Your Word Count toolbar may be displayed at a different location on the screen.

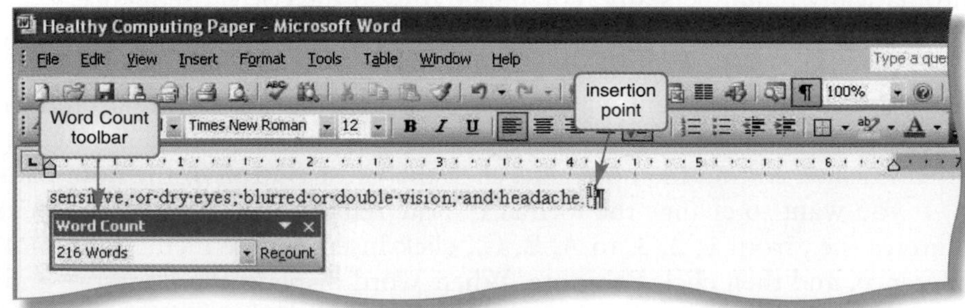

FIGURE 2-42

The Word Count toolbar floats on the screen. As discussed earlier in this project, you can move a floating toolbar by dragging its title bar.

The Word Count dialog box (Figure 2-41) presents a variety of statistics about the current document, including number of pages, words, characters, paragraphs, and lines. You can choose to have note text included or not included in these statistics. If you want statistics on only a section of the document, select the section and then issue the Word Count command.

At anytime, you can recount the number of words in a document by clicking the Recount button on the Word Count toolbar.

Q & A

Q: How can I view statistics about a document?

A: You can display statistics about a document by clicking File on the menu bar, clicking Properties, and then clicking the Statistics tab. This information, however, does not include words and characters in the footnotes or endnotes.

Automatic Page Breaks

As you type documents that exceed one page, Word automatically inserts page breaks, called **automatic page breaks** or **soft page breaks**, when it determines the text has filled one page according to paper size, margin settings, line spacing, and other settings. If you add text, delete text, or modify text on a page, Word recomputes the location of automatic page breaks and adjusts them accordingly.

Word performs page recomputation between the keystrokes, that is, in between the pauses in your typing. Thus, Word refers to the automatic page break task as **background repagination**. In normal view, automatic page breaks display on the Word screen as a single dotted horizontal line. The following step illustrates Word's automatic page break feature.

To Page Break Automatically

1

- **With the insertion point positioned as shown in Figure 2-42, press the SPACEBAR and then type the last two sentences of the third paragraph of the paper, as shown in Figure 2-43.**
- **Press the ENTER key and then type the fourth paragraph. Italicize the text in the parenthetical citation.**
- **Drag the title bar of the Word Count toolbar to the location shown in Figure 2-43.**

As you type, Word places an automatic page break between the third and fourth paragraphs in the paper (Figure 2-43). The status bar now displays Page 2 as the current page.

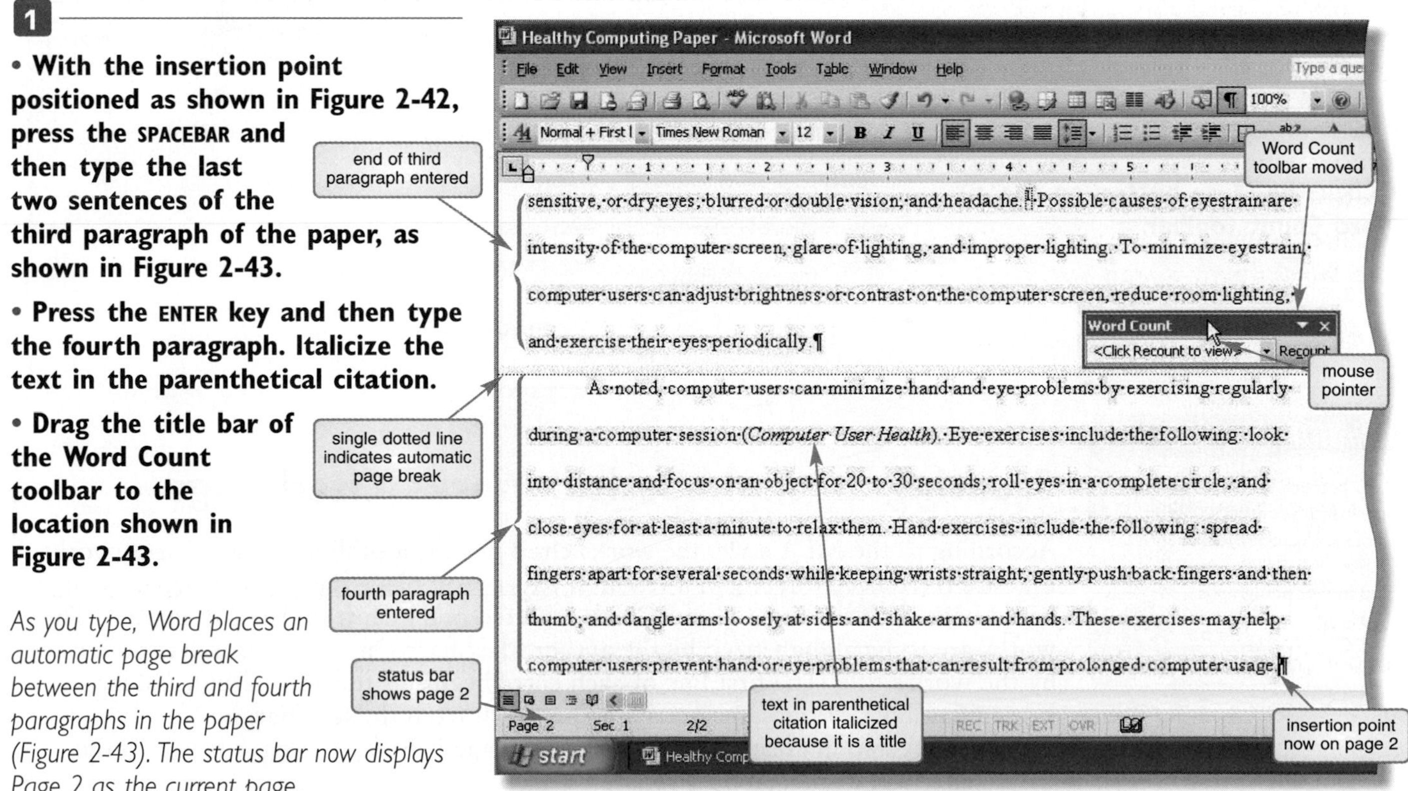

FIGURE 2-43

Q & A

Q: Do I need to cite common knowledge?

A: Information that commonly is known or accessible to the audience constitutes common knowledge and does not need to be listed as a parenthetical citation or in a bibliography. If, however, you question whether certain information is common knowledge, you should document it — just to be safe.

Your page break may occur at a different location, depending on the type of printer connected to the computer.

The header, although not shown in normal view, contains the name, Krause, followed by the page number 2. If you wanted to view the header, click View on the menu bar and then click Header and Footer. Then, click the Close Header and Footer button on the Header and Footer toolbar to return to normal view.

Recounting Words in a Document

Now that the last paragraph of the body of the paper is typed, you want to recount the number of words to see if you have met the minimum requirement of 325 words. The following steps show how to use the Word Count toolbar to recount words in a document.

To Recount Words

1

• **Click the Recount button on the Word Count toolbar.**

The Word Count toolbar displays the number of words in the document (Figure 2-44). You now close the Word Count toolbar because the research paper contains the required minimum of 325 words. Depending on the accuracy of your typing, your word count may differ.

2

• **Click the Close button on the Word Count toolbar.**

Word removes the Word Count toolbar from the screen.

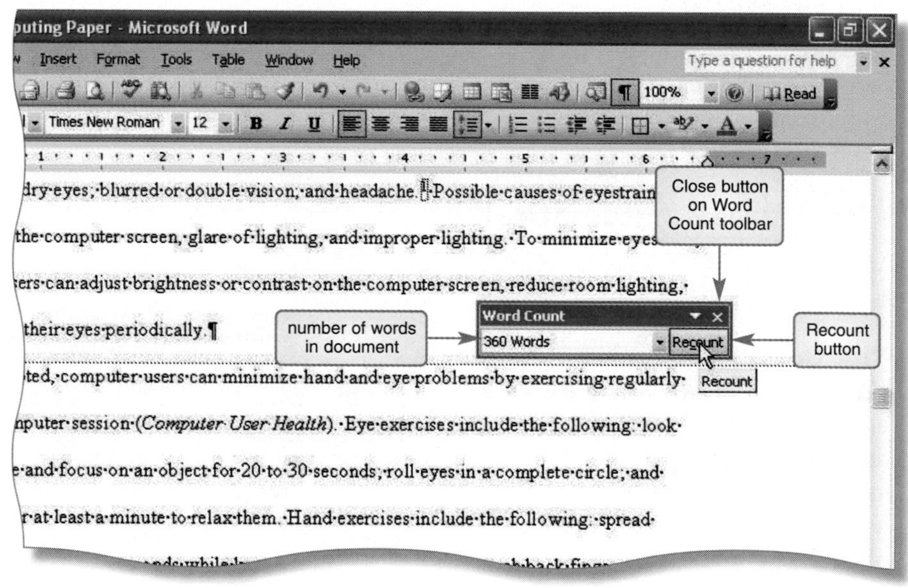

FIGURE 2-44

Skill Builder 2-2

To practice the following tasks, visit scsite.com/off2003sch/skill, locate Word Project 2, and then click Skill Builder 2-2.
- ❑ Indent paragraphs
- ❑ Add a footnote
- ❑ Count words

Creating an Alphabetical Works Cited Page

According to the MLA style, the **works cited page** is a bibliographical list of works that are referenced directly in a research paper. You place the list on a separate numbered page with the title, Works Cited, centered one inch from the top margin. The works are to be alphabetized by the author's last name or, if the work has no author, by the work's title. The first line of each entry begins at the left margin. Indent subsequent lines of the same entry one-half inch from the left margin.

The first step in creating the works cited page is to force a page break so the works cited are displayed on a separate page.

Manual Page Breaks

The works cited are to be displayed on a separate numbered page. Thus, you must insert a manual page break following the body of the research paper. A **manual page break**, or **hard page break**, is one that you force into the document at a specific location. Word displays a manual page break on the screen as a horizontal dotted line, separated by the words, Page Break. Word never moves or adjusts manual page breaks; however, Word adjusts any automatic page breaks that follow a manual page break. Word inserts manual page breaks just before the location of the insertion point.

The following step shows how to insert a manual page break after the body of the research paper.

To Page Break Manually

1

- **With the insertion point at the end of the body of the research paper, press the ENTER key.**
- **Then, press CTRL+ENTER.**

*The shortcut keys, **CTRL+ENTER**, instruct Word to insert a manual page break immediately above the insertion point and position the insertion point immediately below the manual page break (Figure 2-45). The status bar indicates the insertion point now is on page 3.*

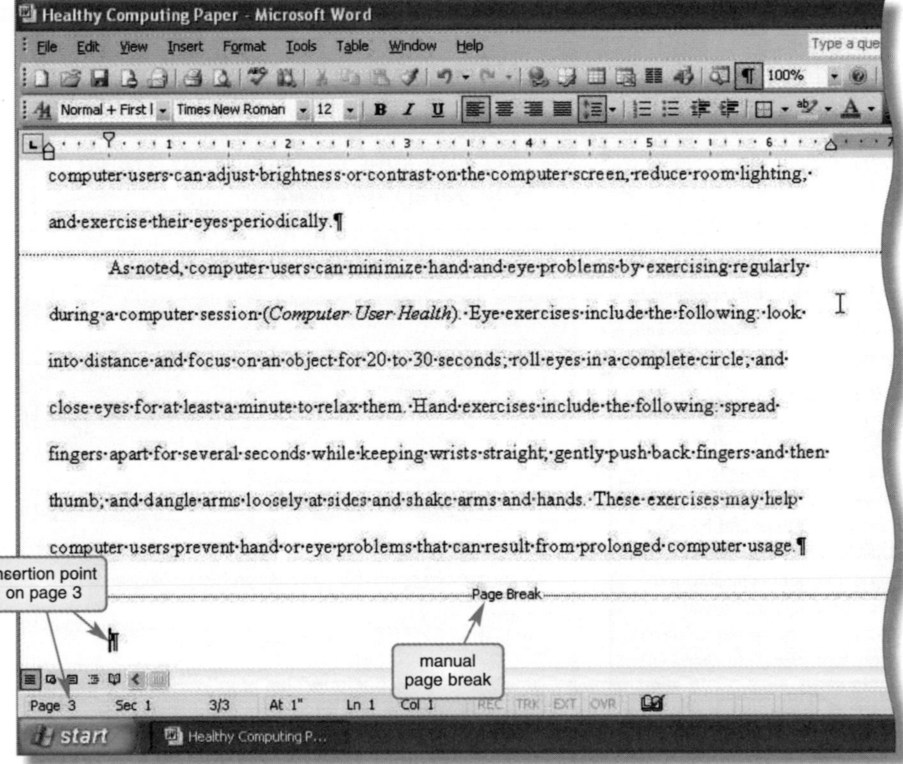

FIGURE 2-45

Word displays the manual page break as a horizontal dotted line with the words, Page Break, in the middle of the line. The header, although not shown in normal view, contains the name Krause followed by the page number 3. If you wanted to view the header, click View on the menu bar and then click Header and Footer. Then, click the Close Header and Footer button on the Header and Footer toolbar to return to normal view.

If, for some reason, you wanted to remove a manual page break from a document, you must first select the page break by double-clicking it. Then, press the DELETE key; or click the Cut button on the Standard toolbar; or right-click the selection and then click Cut on the shortcut menu.

> **Q & A**
>
> **Q:** Are bibliographical references presented similarly in the MLA and APA styles?
>
> **A:** The MLA documentation style uses the title, Works Cited, for the page containing bibliographical references, whereas the APA style uses the title, References. APA guidelines for preparing the reference list entries differ significantly from the MLA style. Refer to an APA handbook or the Web for specifics.

Centering the Title of the Works Cited Page

The works cited title is to be centered between the margins of the paper. If you simply click the Center button on the Formatting toolbar, the title will not be centered properly. Instead, it will be one-half inch to the right of the center point because earlier you set first-line indent at one-half inch. That is, Word indents the first line of every paragraph one-half inch.

To properly center the title of the works cited page, you must move the First Line Indent marker back to the left margin before clicking the Center button, as described in the following steps.

To Center the Title of the Works Cited Page

1. **Drag the First Line Indent marker to the 0" mark on the ruler, which is at the left margin.**
2. **Click the Center button on the Formatting toolbar.**
3. **Type** `Works Cited` **as the title.**
4. **Press the ENTER key.**
5. **Because your fingers already are on the keyboard, press CTRL+L to left-align the paragraph mark.**

Word centers the title properly, and the insertion point is left-aligned (Figure 2-46).

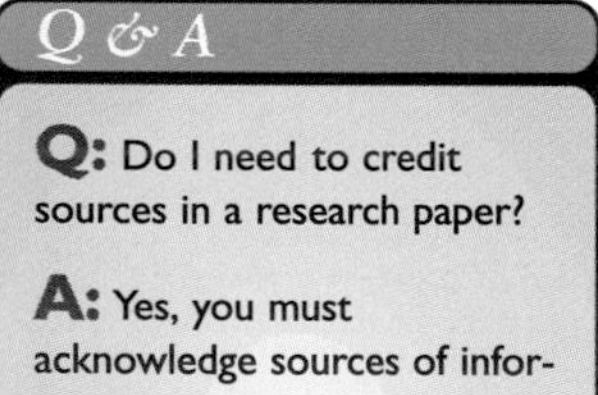

> **Q & A**
>
> **Q:** Do I need to credit sources in a research paper?
>
> **A:** Yes, you must acknowledge sources of information. Citing sources is a matter of ethics and honesty. Use caution when summarizing or paraphrasing a source. Do not plagiarize, which includes using someone else's words or ideas and claiming them as your own.

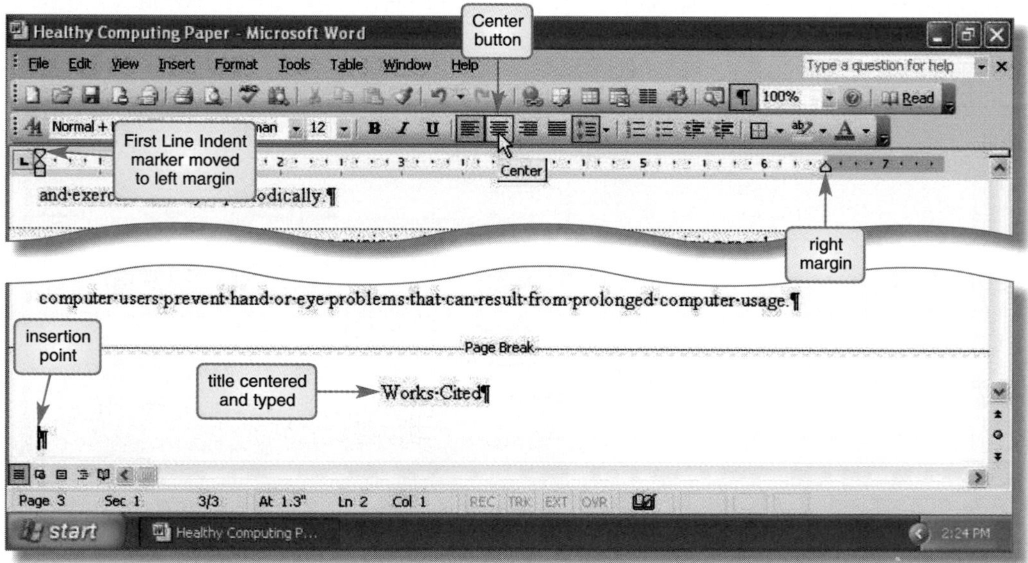

FIGURE 2-46

Creating a Hanging Indent

On the works cited page, the first line of each entry begins at the left margin. Subsequent lines in the same paragraph are to be indented one-half inch from the left margin. In essence, the first line hangs to the left of the rest of the paragraph; thus, this type of paragraph formatting is called a **hanging indent**.

One method of creating a hanging indent is to use the horizontal ruler. The **Hanging Indent marker** is the bottom triangle at the 0" mark on the ruler (Figure 2-47). The next steps show how to create a hanging indent using the horizontal ruler.

To Create a Hanging Indent

1

- **With the insertion point in the paragraph to format, point to the Hanging Indent marker on the ruler (Figure 2-47).**

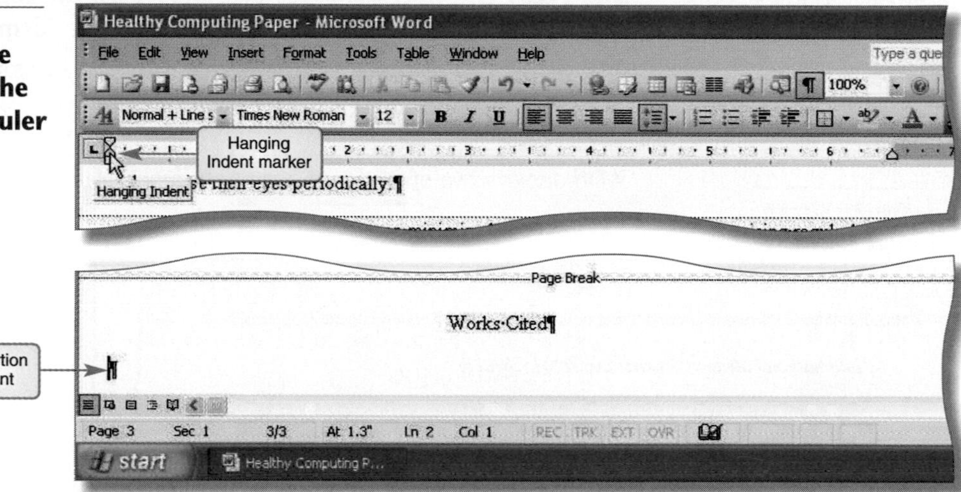

FIGURE 2-47

2

- **Drag the Hanging Indent marker to the .5" mark on the ruler.**

The Hanging Indent marker and Left Indent marker display one-half inch from the left margin (Figure 2-48). When you drag the Hanging Indent marker, the Left Indent marker moves with it. The insertion point in the document window remains at the left margin because only subsequent lines in the paragraph are to be indented.

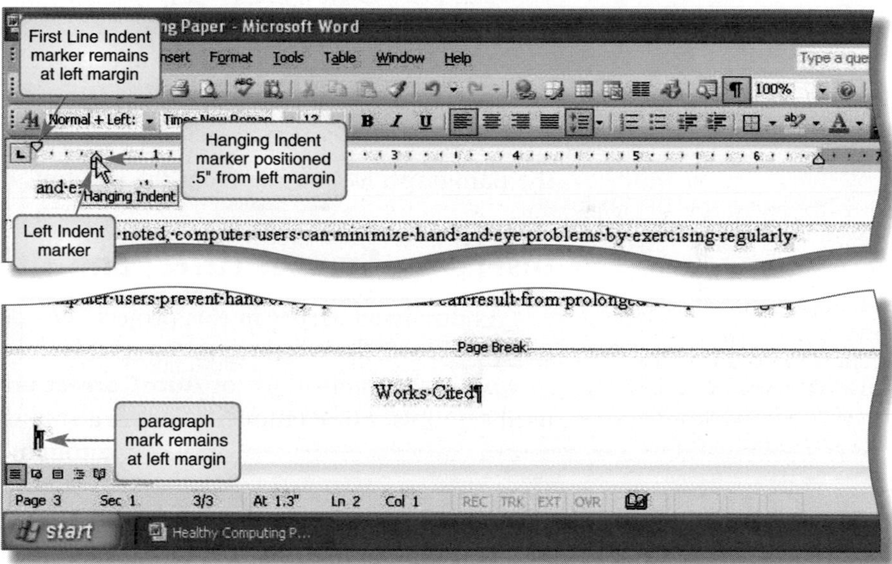

FIGURE 2-48

The next step is to enter the works in the works cited. As you type the works, Word will format them with a hanging indent. The following steps describe how to type the first two works in the works cited.

To Enter Works Cited Paragraphs

1. **Type** `Yoko, Paulette C. "Prevention and Treatment of Computer-Related Health Problems."`
2. **Press the SPACEBAR. Press CTRL+I to turn on the italic format. Type** `International Medical Journal` **and then press CTRL+I to turn off the italic format.**
3. **Press the SPACEBAR. Type** `Sep. 2007: 56-82.`

4 **Press the ENTER key.**

5 **Type** Ames, Bethany S., and Jonah L. Weinberg.

6 **Press the SPACEBAR. Press CTRL+I to turn on the italic format. Type** Watch Your Eyes. **Press CTRL+I to turn off the italic format.**

7 **Press the SPACEBAR. Type** Boston: Thomas Class Publishing Company, 2007.

8 **Press the ENTER key.**

Word displays two of the works cited paragraphs in the document window (Figure 2-49).

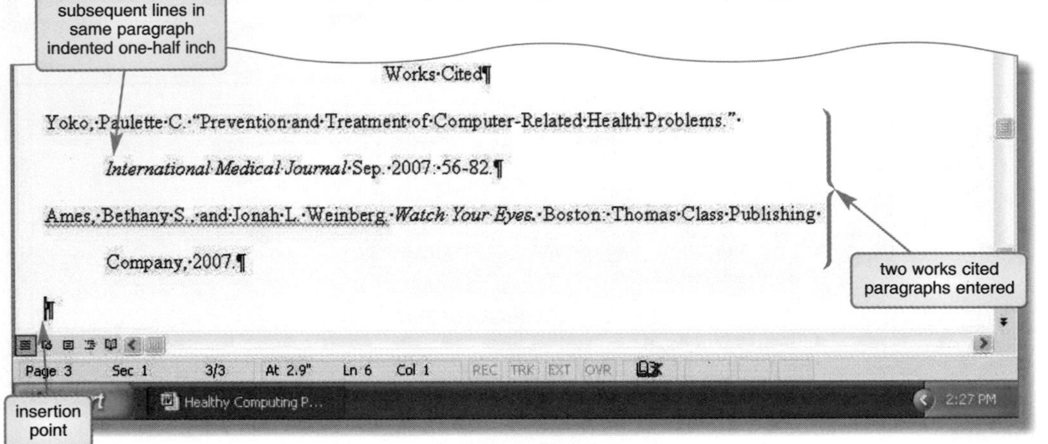

FIGURE 2-49

When Word wraps the text in each works cited paragraph, it automatically indents the second line of the paragraph by one-half inch. When you press the ENTER key at the end of the first paragraph of text, the insertion point returns automatically to the left margin for the next paragraph. Recall that each time you press the ENTER key, Word carries forward the paragraph formatting from the previous paragraph to the next paragraph.

Inserting Arrows, Faces, and Other Symbols Automatically

As discussed earlier in this project, Word has predefined many commonly misspelled words, which it automatically corrects for you as you type. In addition to words, this built-in list of **AutoCorrect entries** also contains some commonly used symbols. For example, to insert a smiling face in a document, you type :) and Word automatically changes it to ☺. Table 2-3 lists the characters you type to insert arrows, faces, and other symbols in a Word document.

Table 2-3 Word's Automatic Symbols

TO DISPLAY	DESCRIPTION	TYPE
©	copyright symbol	(c)
®	registered trademark symbol	(r)
™	trademark symbol	(tm)
…	ellipsis	...
☺	smiling face	:) or :-)
😐	indifferent face	:| or :-|
☹	frowning face	:(or :-(
→	thin right arrow	-->
←	thin left arrow	<
➔	thick right arrow	==>
🡐	thick left arrow	<==
⇔	double arrow	<=>

You also can enter the first four symbols in Table 2-3 and other symbols by clicking Insert on the menu bar, clicking Symbol, clicking the Special Characters tab, clicking the desired symbol in the Character list, clicking the Insert button, and then clicking the Close button in the Symbol dialog box.

As discussed earlier in this project, if you do not like a change that Word automatically makes in a document and you immediately notice the automatic correction, you can undo the change by clicking the Undo button on the Standard toolbar; clicking Edit on the menu bar and then clicking Undo; or pressing CTRL+Z.

If you do not immediately notice the change, you can undo a correction automatically made by Word using the AutoCorrect Options button. Figures 2-23 and 2-24 on pages WD 90 and WD 91 illustrated how to display and use the AutoCorrect Options button.

The next step in the research paper is to enter text that uses the registered trademark symbol. The following steps show how to insert automatically the registered trademark symbol in the research paper.

To Insert a Symbol Automatically

1

- **With the insertion point positioned as shown in Figure 2-49, press CTRL+I to turn on the italic format.**
- **Type** `Computer User Health.`
- **Press CTRL+I to turn off the italic format.**
- **Press the SPACEBAR.**
- **Type** `Shelly Cashman Series(r` **as shown in Figure 2-50.**

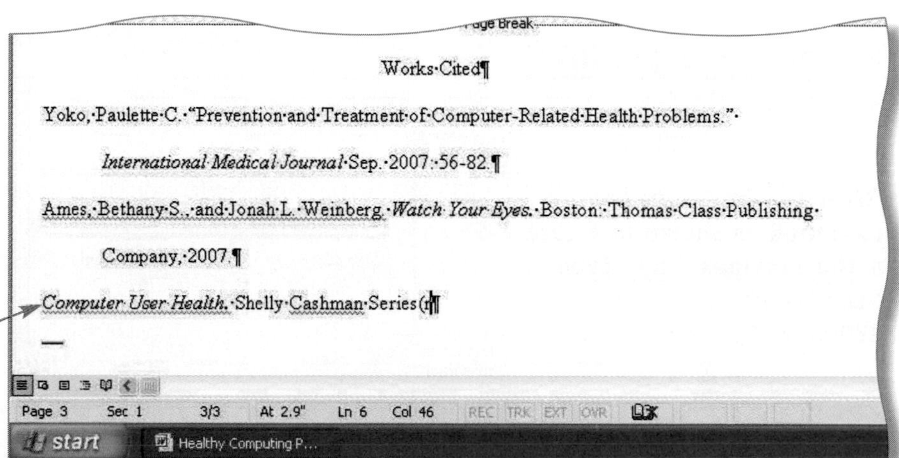

FIGURE 2-50

2

- **Press the RIGHT PARENTHESIS key.**

Word automatically converts the typed (r) to ®, the registered trademark symbol (Figure 2-51).

3

- **Press the PERIOD key.**
- **Press the SPACEBAR.**
- **Type** `Course Technology. 8 Oct. 2007.`
- **Press the SPACEBAR.**

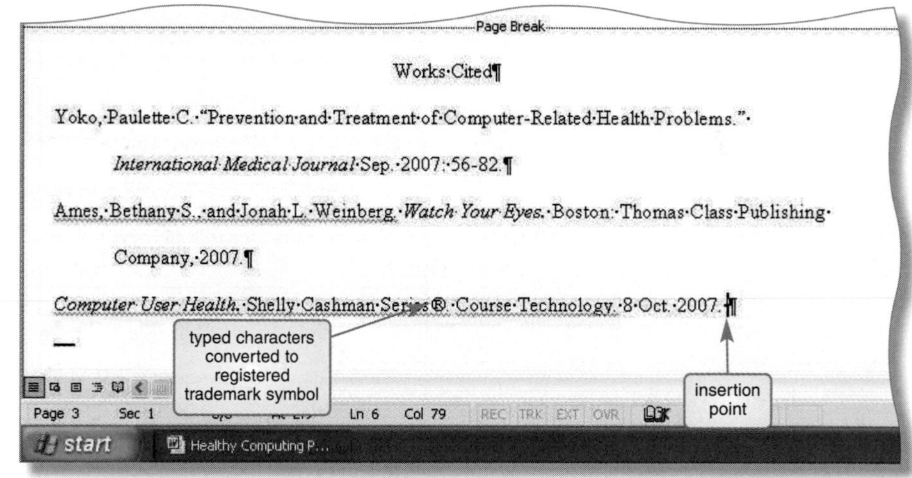

FIGURE 2-51

Creating a Hyperlink

A **hyperlink** is a shortcut that allows a user to jump easily and quickly to another location in the same document or to other documents or Web pages. **Jumping** is the process of following a hyperlink to its destination. For example, by clicking a hyperlink in the document window while pressing the CTRL key (called **CTRL+clicking**), you jump to another document on your computer, on your network, or on the World Wide Web. When you close the hyperlink destination page or document, you return to the original location in your Word document. In Word, you can create a hyperlink simply by typing the address of the file or Web page to which you want to link and then pressing the SPACEBAR or the ENTER key.

In this project, one of the works cited is from a Web page on the Internet. When someone displays your research paper on the screen, you want him or her to be able to CTRL+click the Web address in the work to jump to the associated Web page for more information.

To create a hyperlink to a Web page in a Word document, you do not have to be connected to the Internet. The following steps show how to create a hyperlink as you type.

To Create a Hyperlink

1

- **With the insertion point positioned as shown in Figure 2-51 on the previous page, type** `http://www.scsite.com/wd2003sch/pr2/wc.htm.`

Word does not format the entry as a hyperlink until you press the ENTER key or SPACEBAR (Figure 2-52).

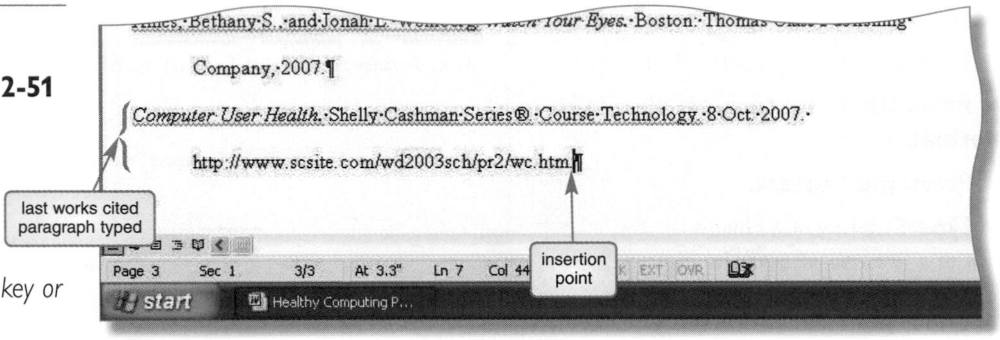

Company, 2007.¶

Computer User Health. Shelly Cashman Series®. Course Technology. 8 Oct. 2007.

http://www.scsite.com/wd2003sch/pr2/wc.htm

last works cited paragraph typed

insertion point

FIGURE 2-52

2

- **Press the ENTER key.**

As soon as you press the ENTER key after typing the Web address, Word formats it as a hyperlink (Figure 2-53). That is, the Web address is underlined and colored blue.

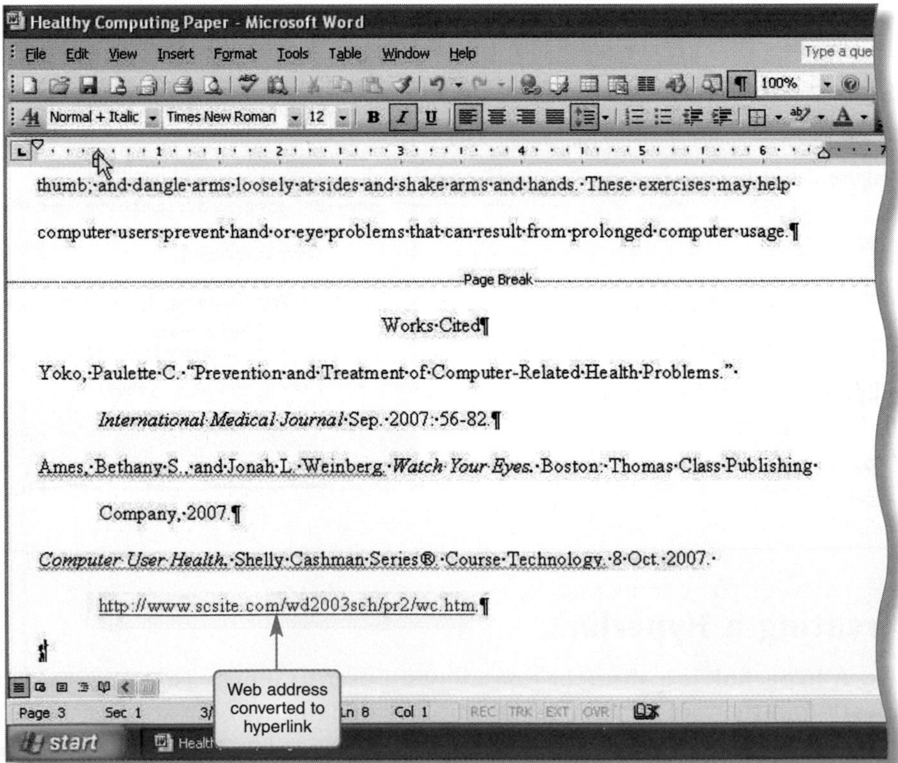

FIGURE 2-53

Later, this project will show how to jump to the hyperlink you just created.

Sorting Paragraphs

The MLA style requires that the works cited be listed in alphabetical order by the first character in each work. In Word, you can arrange paragraphs in alphabetic, numeric, or date order based on the first character in each paragraph. Ordering characters in this manner is called **sorting**.

The following steps show how to sort the works cited paragraphs alphabetically.

> *Q & A*
>
> **Q:** How can I fix a hyperlink?
>
> **A:** If Word does not convert Web addresses to hyperlinks automatically, click Tools on the menu bar, click AutoCorrect Options, click the AutoFormat As You Type tab, select the Internet and network paths with hyperlinks check box, and then click the OK button.

To Sort Paragraphs

1

- **Select all the works cited paragraphs by pointing to the left of the first paragraph and then dragging down.**
- **Click Table on the menu bar.**

Word displays the Table menu (Figure 2-54). All of the paragraphs to be sorted are selected.

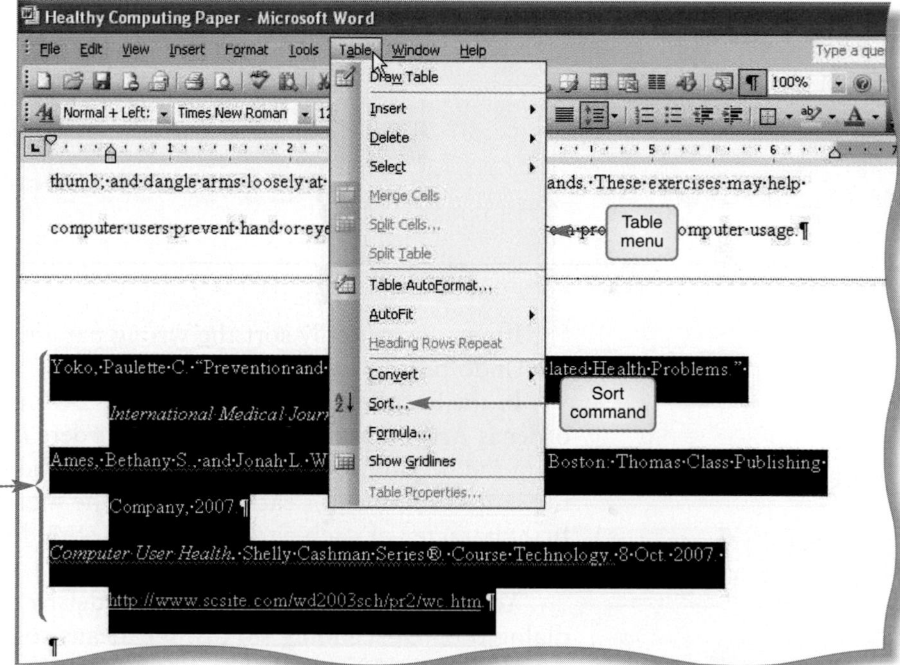

FIGURE 2-54

2

- **Click Sort on the Table menu.**

Word displays the Sort Text dialog box (Figure 2-55). In the Sort by area, Ascending, the default, is selected. The term, ascending, means to sort in alphabetic, numeric, or earliest to latest date order.

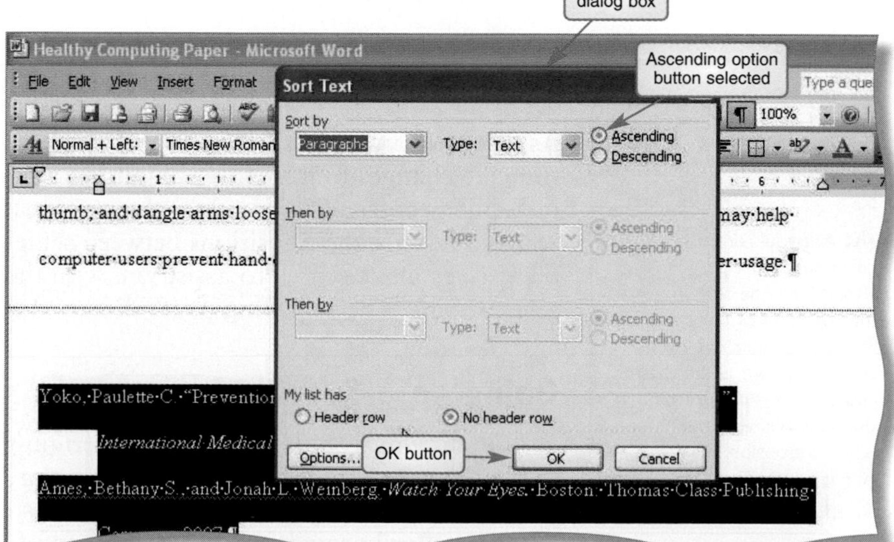

FIGURE 2-55

3

- **Click the OK button in the Sort Text dialog box.**
- **Click inside the selected text to remove the selection.**

Word sorts the works cited paragraphs alphabetically (Figure 2-56).

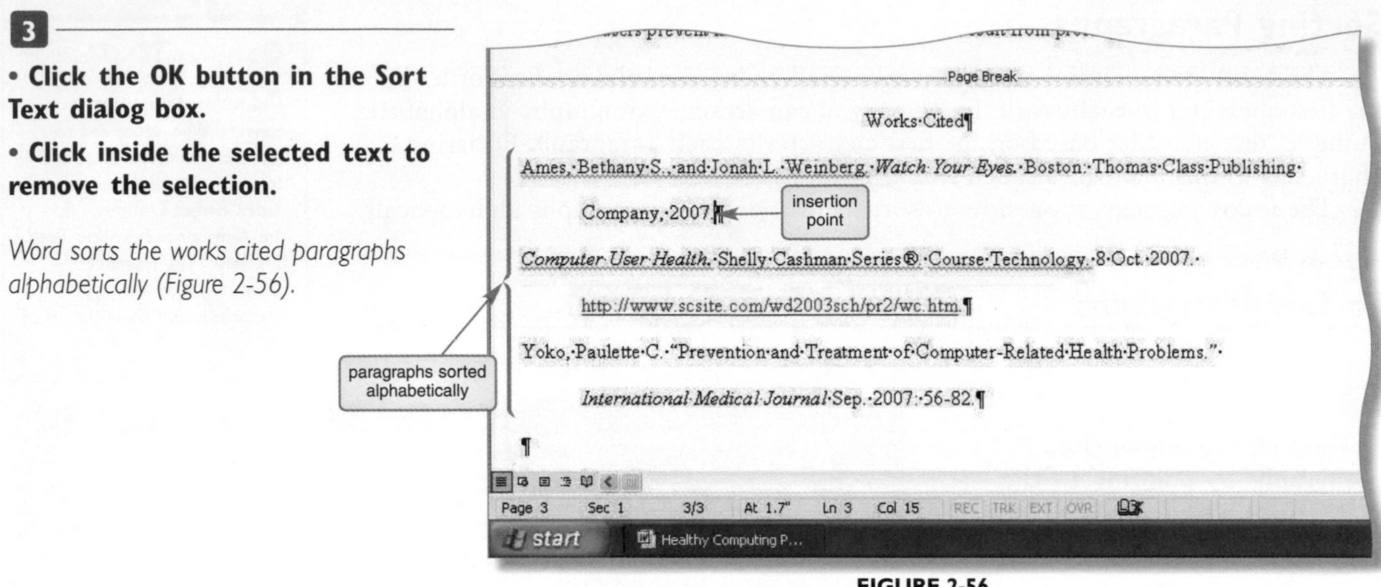

FIGURE 2-56

If you accidentally sort the wrong paragraphs, you can undo a sort by clicking the Undo button on the Standard toolbar.

In the Sort Text dialog box (Figure 2-55 on the previous page), the default sort order is Ascending. By default, Word orders in **ascending sort order**, which means from the beginning of the alphabet to the end of the alphabet, smallest number to the largest number, or earliest date to the most recent date. For example, if the first character of each paragraph to be sorted is a letter, Word sorts the selected paragraphs alphabetically.

You also can sort in descending order by clicking Descending in the Sort Text dialog box. **Descending sort order** means sorting from the end of the alphabet to the beginning of the alphabet, the largest number to the smallest number, or the most recent date to the earliest date.

Q & A

Q: How should I go about proofreading a research paper?

A: Ask yourself these questions: Is the purpose clear? Does the title suggest the topic? Does the paper have an introduction, body, and conclusion? Is the thesis clear? Does each paragraph in the body relate to the thesis? Is the conclusion effective? Are all sources acknowledged?

Proofing and Revising the Research Paper

As discussed in Project 1, once you complete a document, you might find it necessary to make changes to it. Before submitting a paper to be graded, you should proofread it. While **proofreading**, you look for grammatical errors and spelling errors. You want to be sure the transitions between sentences flow smoothly and the sentences themselves make sense. To assist you with the proofreading effort, Word provides several tools. The following pages discuss these tools.

Going to a Specific Location in a Document

Often, you would like to bring a certain page, footnote, or other object into view in the document window. To accomplish this, you could scroll through the document to find a desired page, footnote, or item. Instead of scrolling through the document, however, Word provides an easier method of going to a specific location via the Select Browse Object menu.

The next steps show how to go to the top of page two in the research paper using the Select Browse Object menu.

To Browse by Page

1

- **Click the Select Browse Object button on the vertical scroll bar.**
- **When Word displays the Select Browse Object menu, position the mouse pointer on the Browse by Page icon.**

When you point to an icon on the Select Browse Object menu, Word displays the associated command name at the bottom of the menu (Figure 2-57).

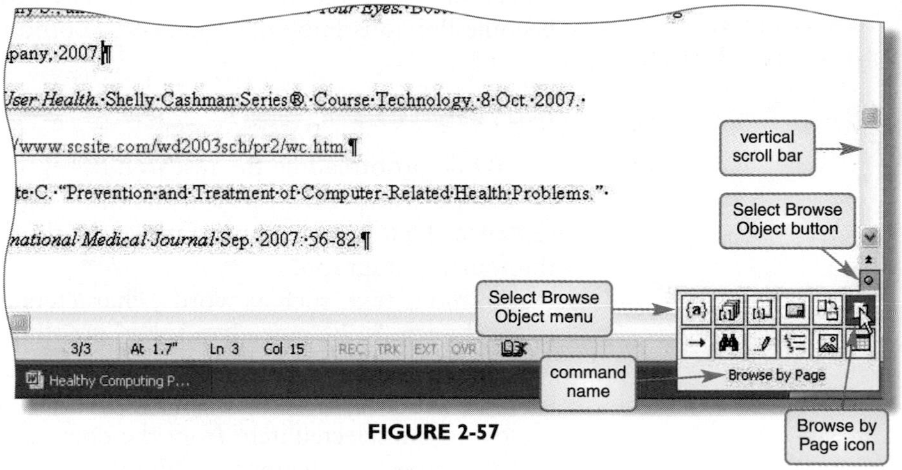

FIGURE 2-57

2

- **Click the Browse by Page icon.**
- **Position the mouse pointer on the Previous Page button on the vertical scroll bar.**

Word closes the Select Browse Object menu and displays the top of page 3 at the top of the document window (Figure 2-58).

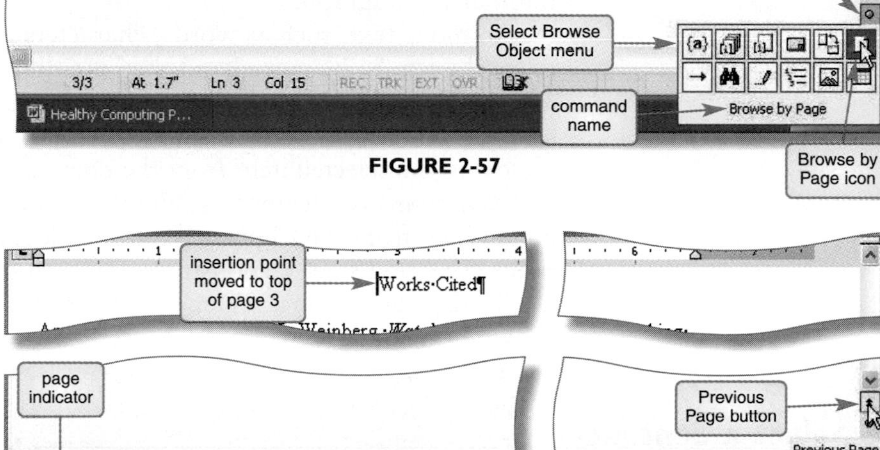

FIGURE 2-58

3

- **Click the Previous Page button.**

Word places the top of page 2 (the previous page) at the top of the document window (Figure 2-59).

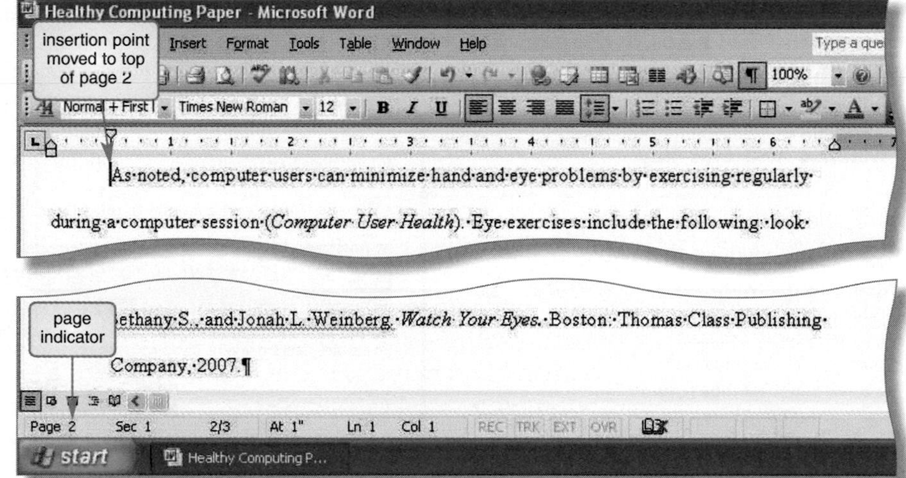

FIGURE 2-59

Depending on the icon you click on the Select Browse Object menu, the function of the buttons above and below the Select Browse Object button on the vertical scroll bar changes. When you select Browse by Page, the buttons become Previous Page and Next Page buttons. If you select Browse by Footnote, however, the buttons become Previous Footnote and Next Footnote buttons, and so on.

Moving Text

While proofreading the research paper, you realize that text in the fourth paragraph would flow better if the third sentence was moved so it followed the first sentence. That is, you want to move the third sentence so it is the second sentence in the fourth paragraph.

To move text, such as words, characters, sentences, or paragraphs, you first select the text to be moved and then use drag-and-drop editing or the cut-and-paste technique to move the selected text. With **drag-and-drop editing**, you drag the selected item to the new location and then insert, or *drop*, it there. **Cutting** involves removing the selected item from the document and then placing it on the Clipboard. The **Clipboard** is a temporary Windows storage area. **Pasting** is the process of copying an item from the Clipboard into the document at the location of the insertion point. The next steps demonstrate drag-and-drop editing.

To drag-and-drop a sentence in the research paper, first select a sentence as shown in the next step.

To Select a Sentence

1

- **Position the mouse pointer (an I-beam) in the sentence to be moved (shown in Figure 2-60).**
- **Press and hold down the CTRL key. While holding down the CTRL key, click the sentence.**
- **Release the CTRL key.**

Word selects the entire sentence (Figure 2-60). Notice that Word includes the space following the period in the selection.

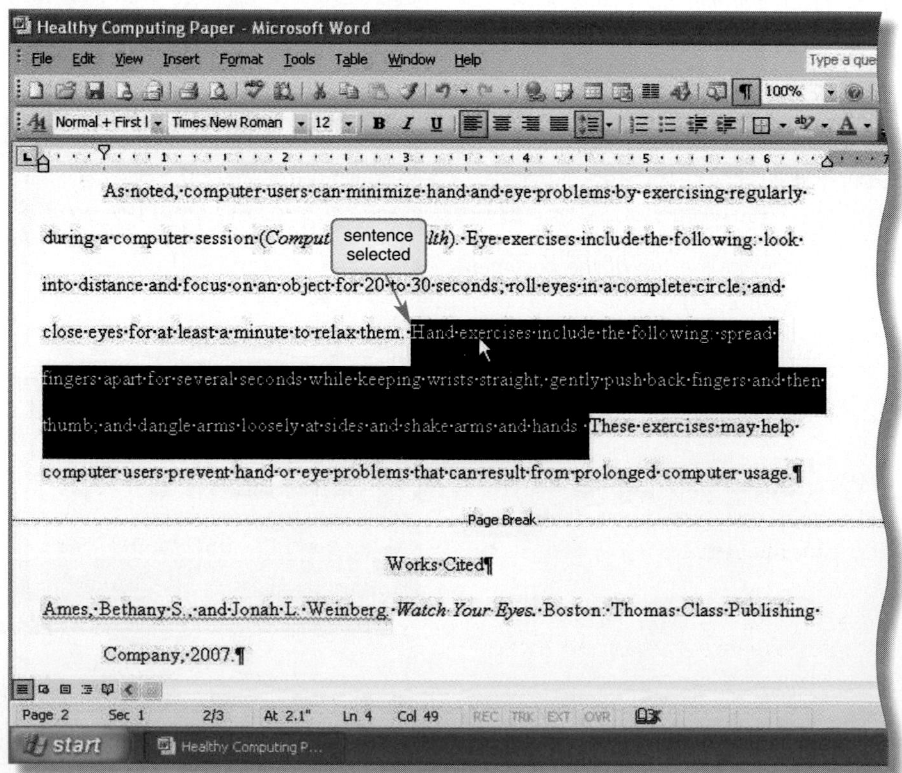

FIGURE 2-60

In the previous steps and throughout Projects 1 and 2, you have selected text. Table 2-4 summarizes the techniques used to select various items with the mouse.

Table 2-4 Techniques for Selecting Items with the Mouse

ITEM TO SELECT	MOUSE ACTION
Block of text	Click at beginning of selection, scroll to end of selection, position mouse pointer at end of selection, hold down SHIFT key and then click; or drag through the text
Character(s)	Drag through character(s)
Document	Move mouse to left of text until mouse pointer changes to a right-pointing block arrow and then triple-click
Graphic	Click the graphic
Line	Move mouse to left of line until mouse pointer changes to a right-pointing block arrow and then click
Lines	Move mouse to left of first line until mouse pointer changes to a right-pointing block arrow and then drag up or down
Paragraph	Triple-click paragraph; or move mouse to left of paragraph until mouse pointer changes to a right-pointing block arrow and then double-click
Paragraphs	Move mouse to left of paragraph until mouse pointer changes to a right-pointing block arrow, double-click, and then drag up or down
Sentence	Press and hold down CTRL key and then click sentence
Word	Double-click the word
Words	Drag through words

With the sentence to be moved selected, you can use drag-and-drop editing to move it. You should be sure that drag-and-drop editing is enabled by clicking Tools on the menu bar, clicking Options, clicking the Edit tab, verifying the Drag-and-drop text editing check box is selected, and then clicking the OK button.

The following steps show how to move the selected sentence so it becomes the second sentence in the paragraph.

To Move Selected Text

1

- **With the mouse pointer in the selected text, press and hold down the mouse button.**

When you begin to drag the selected text, the insertion point changes to a dotted insertion point (Figure 2-61).

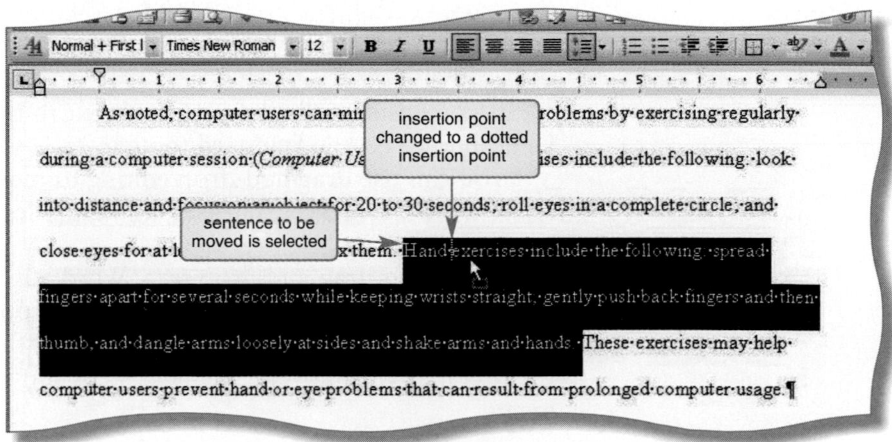

FIGURE 2-61

2

• **Drag the dotted insertion point to the location where the selected text is to be moved, as shown in Figure 2-62.**

The dotted insertion point follows the space after the first sentence in the paragraph (Figure 2-62).

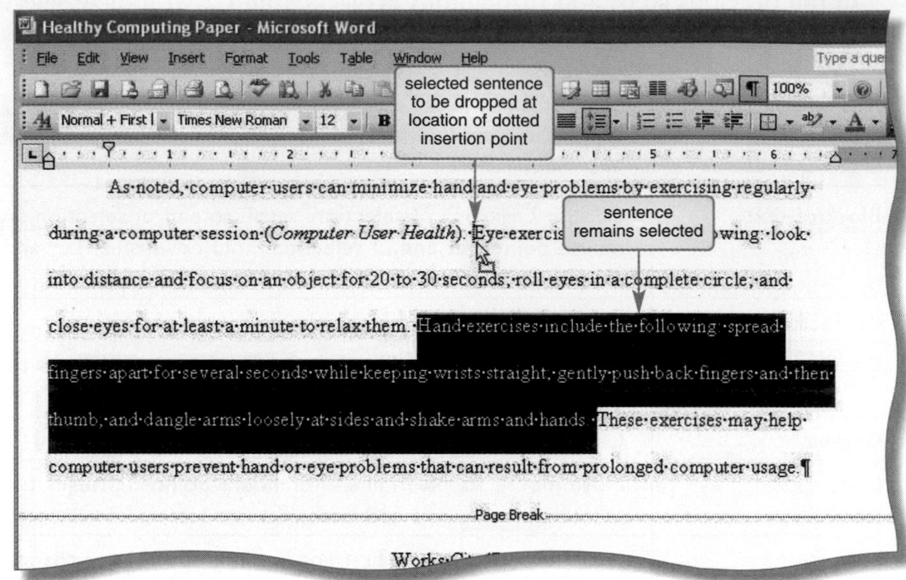

FIGURE 2-62

3

• **Release the mouse button. Click outside the selected text to remove the selection.**

Word moves the selected text to the location of the dotted insertion point (Figure 2-63).

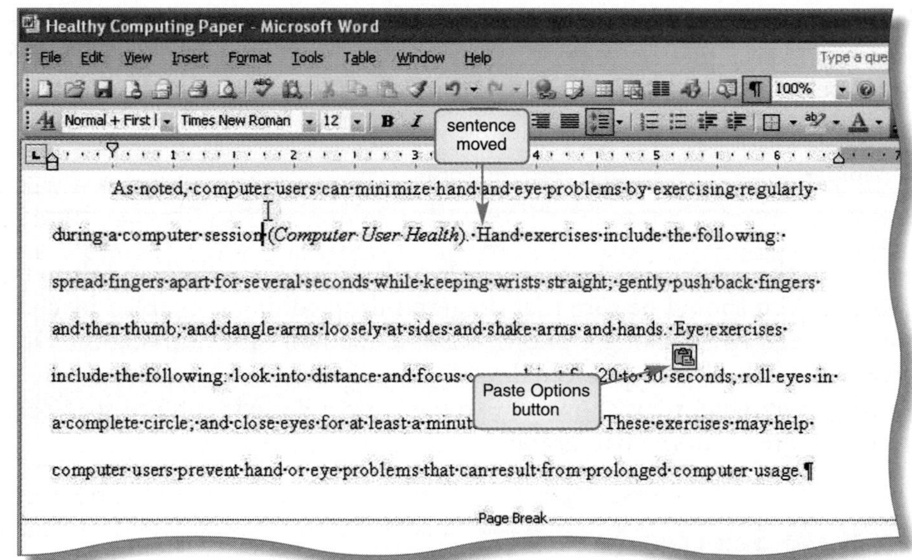

FIGURE 2-63

If you accidentally drag selected text to the wrong location, you can click the Undo button on the Standard toolbar.

You can use drag-and-drop editing to move any selected item. That is, you can select words, sentences, phrases, and graphics and then use drag-and-drop editing to move them.

When you drag-and-drop text, Word automatically displays a Paste Options button near the location of the drag-and-dropped text (Figure 2-63). If you click the **Paste Options button**, a menu is displayed that allows you to change the format of the text that was moved. The next steps show how to display the Paste Options menu.

To Display the Paste Options Menu

1

- **Click the Paste Options button.**

Word displays the Paste Options menu (Figure 2-64).

2

- **Press the ESCAPE key to remove the Paste Options menu from the window.**

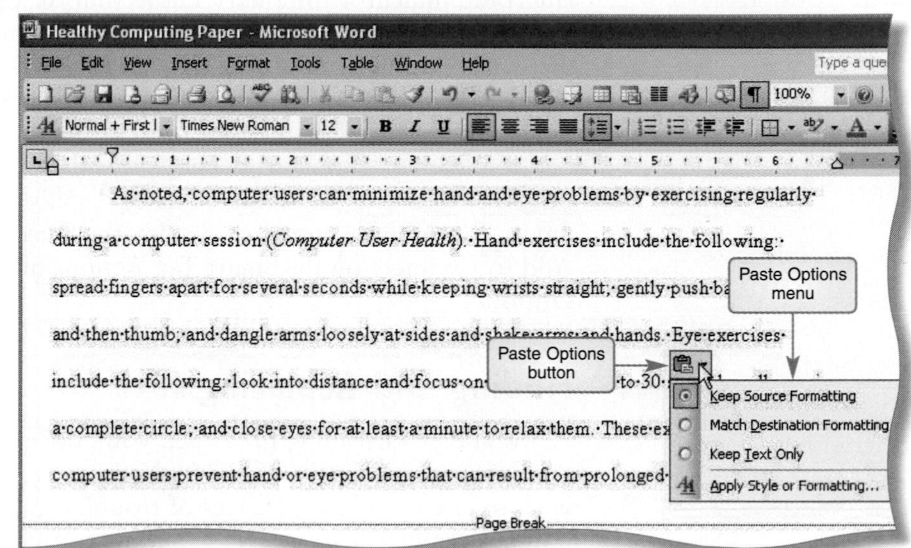

FIGURE 2-64

Smart Tags

A **smart tag** is a button that automatically appears on the screen when Word performs a certain action. In this project, you used two smart tags: AutoCorrect Options (Figures 2-23 and 2-24 on pages WD 90 and WD 91) and Paste Options (Figure 2-64). In addition to AutoCorrect Options and Paste Options, Word provides other smart tags. Table 2-5 summarizes the smart tags available in Word.

Table 2-5 Smart Tags in Word

BUTTON	NAME	MENU FUNCTION
	AutoCorrect Options	Undoes an automatic correction, stops future automatic corrections of this type, or displays the AutoCorrect Options dialog box
	Paste Options	Specifies how moved or pasted items should display, e.g., with original formatting, without formatting, or with different formatting
	Smart Tag Actions	
	• Person name	Adds this name to Outlook Contacts folder, sends an e-mail, or schedules a meeting in Outlook Calendar with this person
	• Date or time	Schedules a meeting in Outlook Calendar at this date or time or displays your calendar
	• Address	Adds this address to Outlook Contacts folder or displays a map or driving directions
	• Place	Adds this place to Outlook Contacts folder or schedules a meeting in Outlook Calendar at this location

Q & A

Q: What if smart tags are not displayed?

A: If your screen does not display smart tag indicators, click Tools on the menu bar, click AutoCorrect Options, click the Smart Tags tab, select the Label text with smart tags check box, and then click the OK button. If AutoCorrect Options buttons do not appear on your screen, click Tools on the menu bar, click AutoCorrect Options, click the AutoCorrect tab, select the Show AutoCorrect Options buttons check box, and then click the OK button.

With the AutoCorrect Options and Smart Tag Actions, Word notifies you that the smart tag is available by displaying a **smart tag indicator** on the screen. The smart tag indicator for the AutoCorrect Options smart tag is a small blue box. The smart tag indicator for Smart Tag Actions is a purple dotted underline, as shown in Figure 2-14 on page WD 85. To display a smart tag button, you point to the smart tag indicator.

Clicking a smart tag button displays a menu that contains commands relative to the action performed at the location of the smart tag. For example, if you want to add a name in your Word document to the Outlook Contacts folder, point to the purple dotted line below the name to display the Smart Tag Actions button, click the Smart Tag Actions button to display the Smart Tag Actions menu, and then click Add to Contacts on the Smart Tag Actions menu to display the Contact window in Outlook.

Finding and Replacing Text

While proofreading the paper, you notice that it contains the word, troubles, in the first paragraph (Figure 2-65). You prefer to use the word, risks. Therefore, you wish to change all occurrences of troubles to risks. To do this, you can use Word's find and replace feature, which automatically locates each occurrence of a word or phrase and then replaces it with specified text, as shown in these steps.

To Find and Replace Text

1

- **Press** CTRL+HOME **to position the insertion point at the top of the document.**
- **Double-click the status bar anywhere to the left of the status indicators.**
- **When Word displays the Find and Replace dialog box, click the Replace tab.**
- **Type** `troubles` **in the Find what text box.**
- **Press the** TAB **key. Type** `risks` **in the Replace with text box.**

Word displays entered text in the Find and Replace dialog box (Figure 2-65).

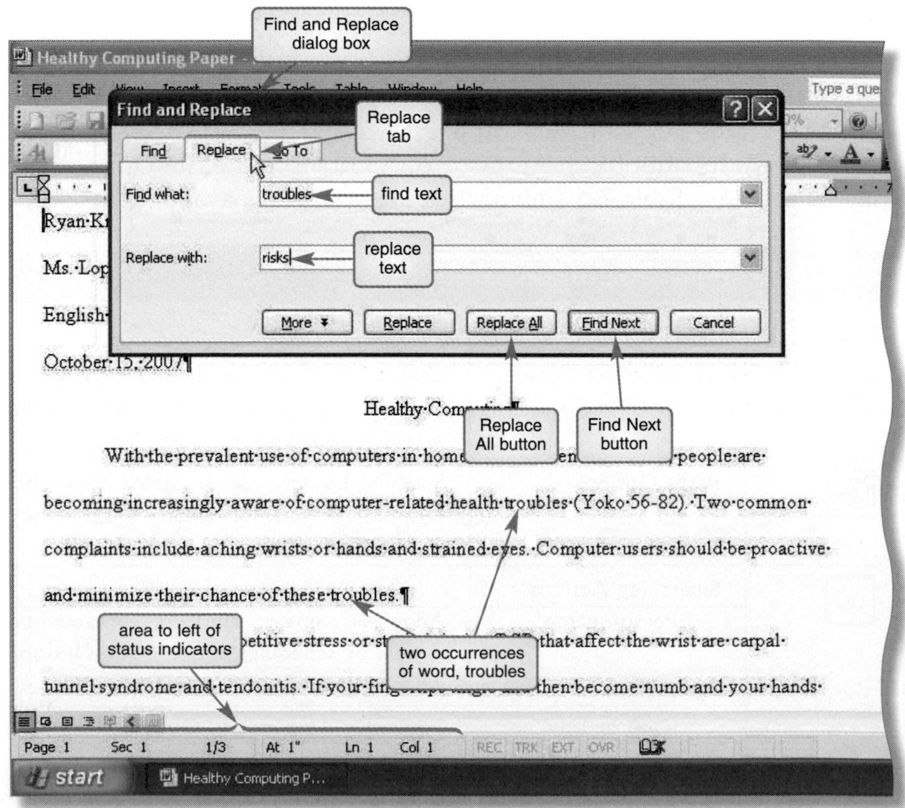

FIGURE 2-65

- **Click the Replace All button in the Find and Replace dialog box.**

A Microsoft Office Word dialog box displays indicating the total number of replacements made (Figure 2-66). The word, risks, displays in the document instead of the word, troubles.

3

- **Click the OK button in the Microsoft Office Word dialog box.**
- **Click the Close button in the Find and Replace dialog box.**

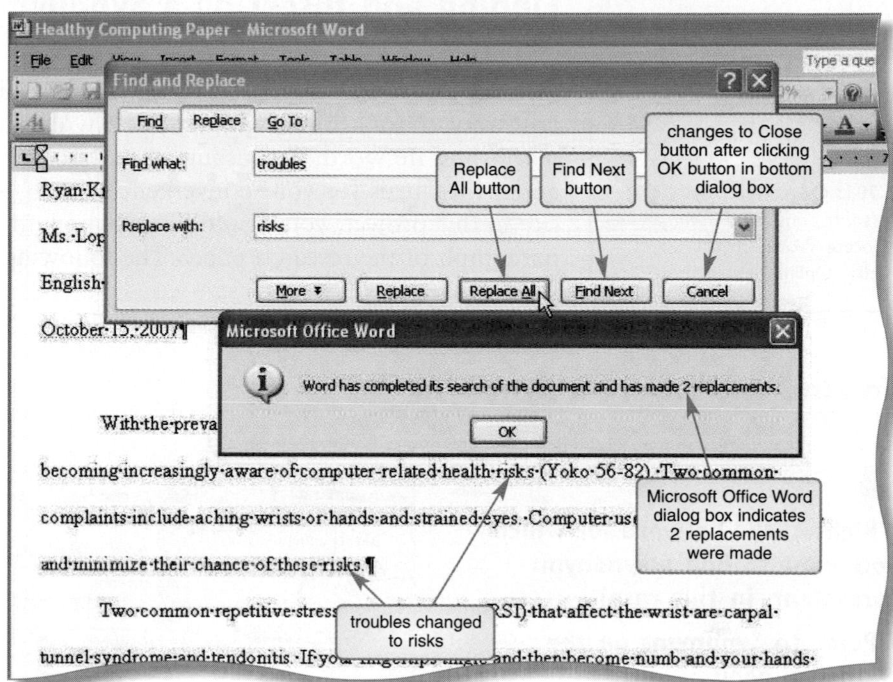

FIGURE 2-66

The Replace All button replaces all occurrences of the Find what text with the Replace with text. In some cases, you may want to replace only certain occurrences of a word or phrase, not all of them. To instruct Word to confirm each change, click the Find Next button in the Find and Replace dialog box (Figure 2-65), instead of the Replace All button. When Word locates an occurrence of the text, it pauses and waits for you to click either the Replace button or the Find Next button. Clicking the Replace button changes the text; clicking the Find Next button instructs Word to disregard the replacement and look for the next occurrence of the Find what text.

If you accidentally replace the wrong text, you can undo a replacement by clicking the Undo button on the Standard toolbar. If you used the Replace All button, Word undoes all replacements. If you used the Replace button, Word undoes only the most recent replacement.

Finding Text

Sometimes, you may want only to find text, instead of finding *and* replacing text. To search for just a single occurrence of text, you would follow these steps.

To Find Text

1. Click the Select Browse Object button on the vertical scroll bar and then click the Find icon on the Select Browse Object menu; or click Edit on the menu bar and then click Find; or press CTRL+F.
2. Type the text to locate in the Find what text box and then click the Find Next button. To edit the text, click the Cancel button in the Find and Replace dialog box; to find the next occurrence of the text, click the Find Next button.

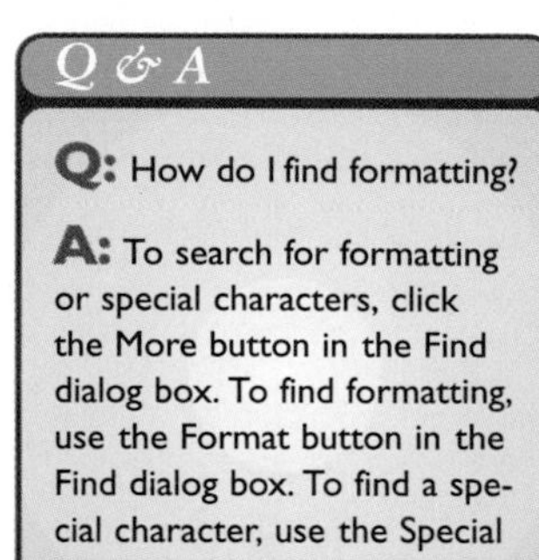

Q & A

Q: How do I find formatting?

A: To search for formatting or special characters, click the More button in the Find dialog box. To find formatting, use the Format button in the Find dialog box. To find a special character, use the Special button.

> *Q & A*
>
> **Q:** Does the Web have an online thesaurus?
>
> **A:** For access to an online thesaurus, visit the Office 2003 Q&A Web page (scsite.com/off2003sch/qa), locate Word Project 2, and click Online Thesaurus.

Finding and Inserting a Synonym

When writing, you may discover that you used the same word in multiple locations or that a word you used was not quite appropriate. In these instances, you will want to look up a **synonym**, or a word similar in meaning, to the duplicate or inappropriate word. A **thesaurus** is a book of synonyms. Word provides synonyms and a thesaurus for your convenience.

In this project, you would like a synonym for the word, prevalent, in the first paragraph of the research paper. The following steps show how to find an appropriate synonym.

To Find and Insert a Synonym

1

- **Right-click the word for which you want to find a synonym (prevalent, in this case).**
- **Point to Synonyms on the shortcut menu.**

Word displays a list of synonyms for the word that you right-clicked (Figure 2-67).

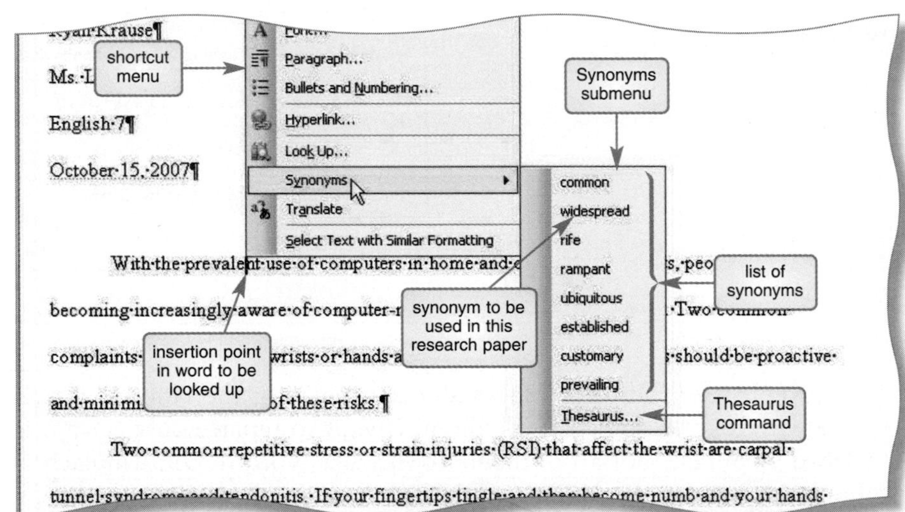

FIGURE 2-67

2

- **Click the synonym you want (widespread) on the Synonyms submenu.**

Word replaces the word, prevalent, in the document with the word, widespread (Figure 2-68).

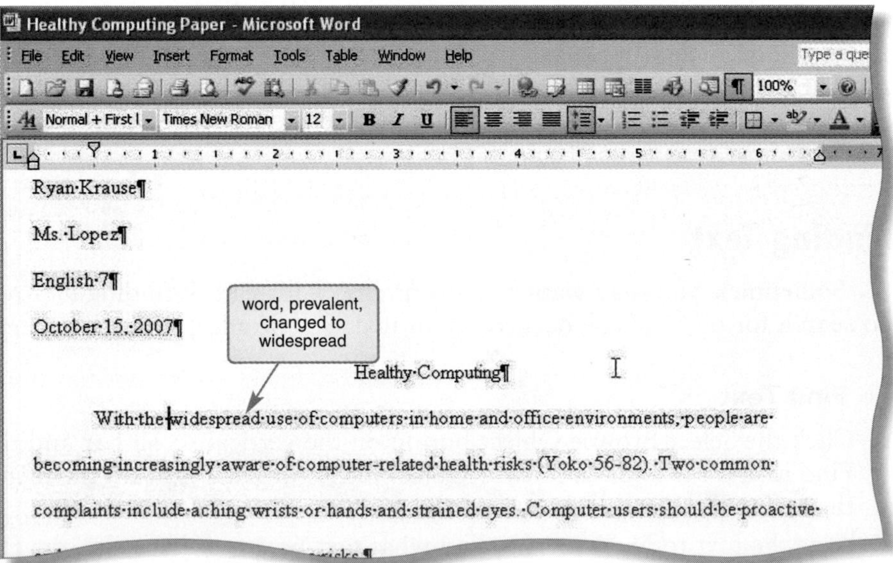

FIGURE 2-68

If the synonyms list on the shortcut menu does not display an appropriate word, you can display the thesaurus in the Research task pane by clicking Thesaurus on the Synonyms submenu (Figure 2-67). The Research task pane displays a complete thesaurus, in which you can look up synonyms for various meanings of a word. You also can look up an **antonym**, or word with an opposite meaning. The Research task pane is discussed later in this project.

Checking Spelling and Grammar at Once

As discussed in Project 1, Word checks spelling and grammar as you type and places a wavy underline below possible spelling or grammar errors. Project 1 illustrated how to check these flagged words immediately. As an alternative, you can wait and check the entire document for spelling and grammar errors at once.

The following steps illustrate how to check spelling and grammar in the Healthy Computing Paper at once. In the following example the word, hands, has been misspelled intentionally as hans to illustrate the use of Word's check spelling and grammar at once feature. If you are completing this project on a personal computer, your research paper may contain different misspelled words, depending on the accuracy of your typing.

To Check Spelling and Grammar at Once

1

- **Press CTRL+HOME to move the insertion point to the beginning of the document.**
- **Click the Spelling and Grammar button on the Standard toolbar.**

Word displays the Spelling and Grammar dialog box (Figure 2-69). The spelling and grammar check begins at the location of the insertion point, which, in this case, is at the beginning of the document. Word did not find the misspelled word, hans, in its dictionary. The Suggestions list displays suggested corrections for the flagged word.

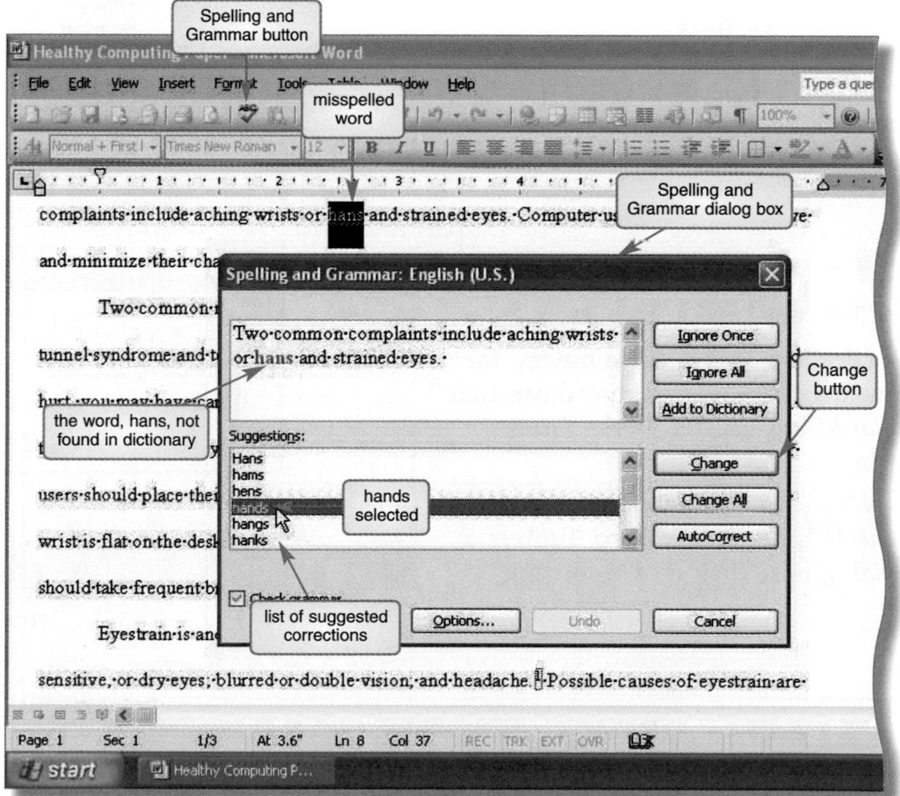

FIGURE 2-69

2

• Click the Change button in the Spelling and Grammar dialog box.

Word corrects the misspelled word and then continues the spelling and grammar check until it finds the next error or reaches the end of the document. In this case, it flags an error on the Works Cited page (Figure 2-70). The entry is correct, so you instruct Word to ignore it.

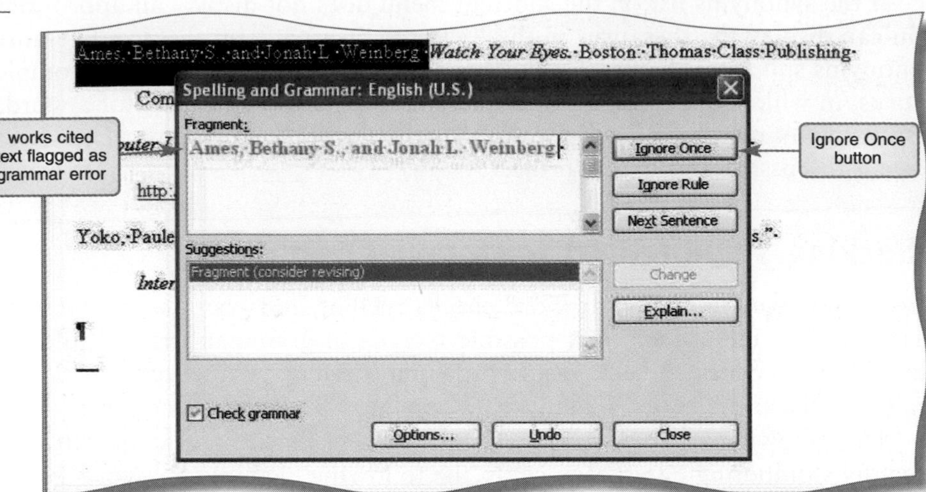

FIGURE 2-70

3

• Click the Ignore Once button.

• If necessary, click the Ignore Once button for the next grammar error that Word flags on the Works Cited page.

Word continues the spelling and grammar check and does not find Cashman in its dictionary (Figure 2-71). Cashman is a proper name and is spelled correctly.

4

• Click the Ignore All button.

• Click the Ignore Once button for each remaining grammar error that Word flags on the Works Cited page.

• When the spelling and grammar check is done and Word displays a dialog box, click its OK button.

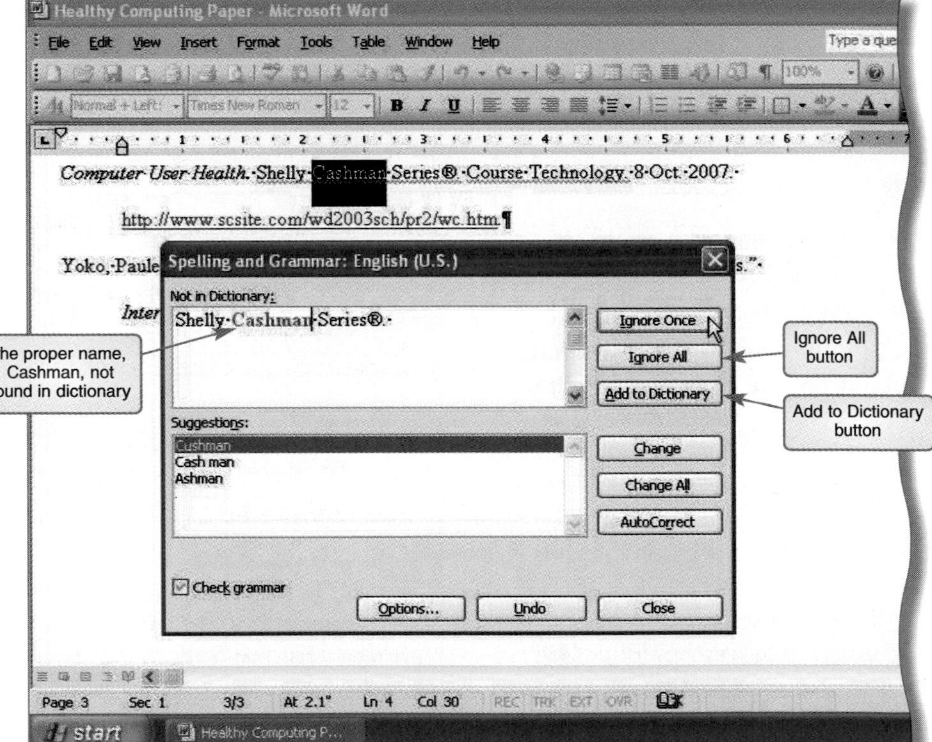

FIGURE 2-71

Your document no longer displays red and green wavy underlines below words and phrases. In addition, the red X on the Spelling and Grammar Status icon has returned to a red check mark.

Saving Again and Printing the Document

The document now is complete. You should save the research paper again and print it, as described in the following steps.

To Save a Document Again and Print It

1 **Click the Save button on the Standard toolbar.**

2 **Click the Print button on the Standard toolbar.**

Word saves the research paper with the same file name, Healthy Computing Paper. The completed research paper prints as shown in Figure 2-1 on page WD 75.

Skill Builder 2-3

To practice the following tasks, visit scsite.com/off2003sch/skill, locate Word Project 2, and then click Skill Builder 2-3.
- ❑ Sort paragraphs
- ❑ Move text
- ❑ Check spelling at once

Working with Main and Custom Dictionaries

As shown in the previous steps, Word often flags proper names as errors because these names are not in its main dictionary. To prevent Word from flagging proper names as errors, you can add the names to the custom dictionary. To add a correctly spelled word to the custom dictionary, click the Add to Dictionary button in the Spelling and Grammar dialog box (Figure 2-71) or right-click the flagged word and then click Add to Dictionary on the shortcut menu. Once you have added a word to the custom dictionary, Word no longer will flag it as an error. To view or modify the list of words in a custom dictionary, you would follow these steps.

To View or Modify Entries in a Custom Dictionary

1. Click Tools on the menu bar and then click Options.
2. Click the Spelling & Grammar tab in the Options dialog box.
3. Click the Custom Dictionaries button.
4. When Word displays the Custom Dictionaries dialog box, place a check mark next to the dictionary name to view or modify. Click the Modify button. (In this dialog box, you can add or delete entries to and from the selected custom dictionary.)
5. When finished viewing and/or modifying the list, click the OK button in the dialog box.
6. Click the OK button in the Custom Dictionaries dialog box.
7. If the Suggest from main dictionary only check box is selected in the Spelling & Grammar sheet in the Options dialog box, remove the check mark. Click the OK button in the Options dialog box.

If you have multiple custom dictionaries, you can specify which one Word should use when checking spelling. The following steps describe how to set the default custom dictionary.

To Set the Default Custom Dictionary

1. Click Tools on the menu bar and then click Options.
2. Click the Spelling & Grammar tab in the Options dialog box.
3. Click the Custom Dictionaries button.
4. When the Custom Dictionaries dialog box is displayed, place a check mark next to the desired dictionary name. Click the Change Default button.
5. Click the OK button in the Custom Dictionaries dialog box.
6. If the Suggest from main dictionary only check box is selected in the Spelling & Grammar dialog box, remove the check mark. Click the OK button in the Spelling & Grammar dialog box.

Q & A

Q: What is The Microsoft Office Certification program?

A: The Microsoft Office Specialist Certification program provides an opportunity for you to obtain a valuable industry credential — proof that you have the Word 2003 skills required by employers. For more information, see Appendix E or visit the Office 2003 Certification Web page (scsite.com/off2003sch/cert).

Navigating to a Hyperlink

Recall that a requirement of this research paper is that one of the works be a Web page and be formatted as a hyperlink. The following steps show how to check the hyperlink in the document.

To Navigate to a Hyperlink

• **Display the third page of the research paper in the document window and then position the mouse pointer in the hyperlink.**

When you position the mouse pointer in a hyperlink in a Word document, a ScreenTip is displayed above the hyperlink (Figure 2-72).

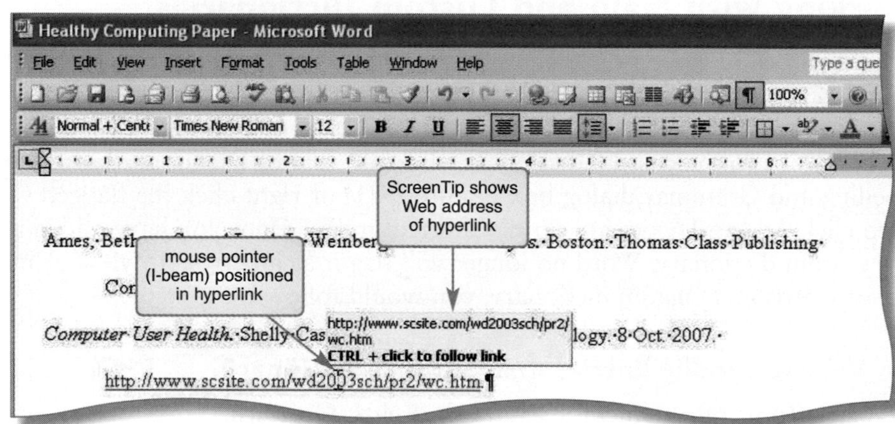

FIGURE 2-72

2

• **While holding down the CTRL key, click the hyperlink. Release the CTRL key.**

If you currently are not connected to the Web, Word connects you using your default browser. The www.scsite.com/wd2003sch/pr2/wc.htm Web page is displayed in a browser window (Figure 2-73).

• **Close the browser window.**

• **If necessary, click the Microsoft Word program button on the taskbar to redisplay the Word window.**

• **Press CTRL+HOME.**

Word displays the first page of the research paper on the screen.

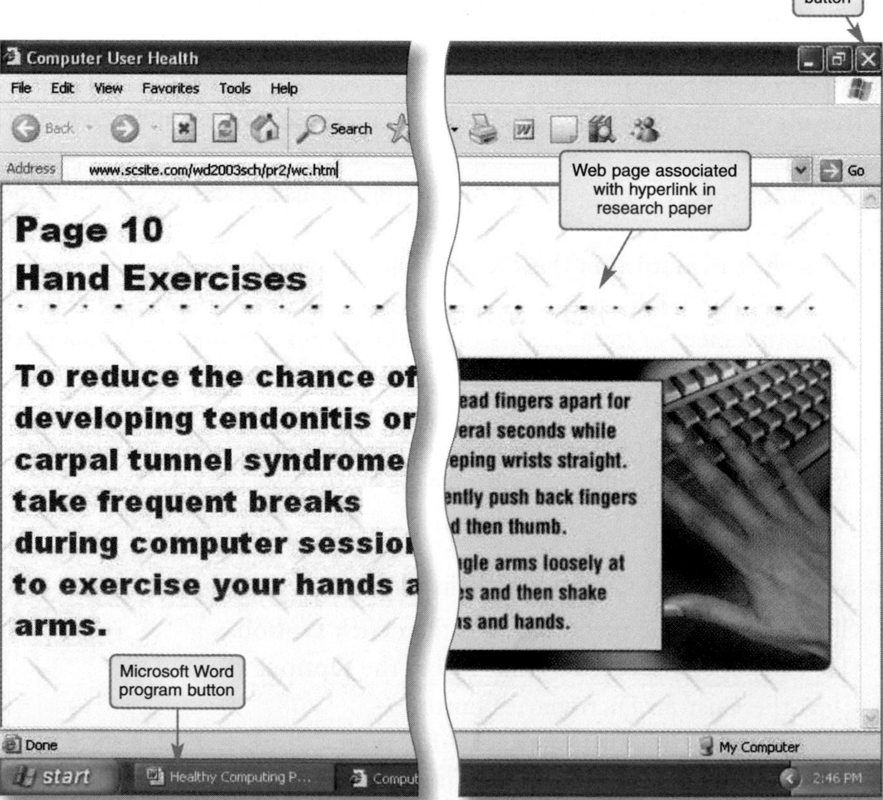

FIGURE 2-73

The hyperlink in the document changes color, which indicates you CTRL+clicked the hyperlink to display its associated Web page.

E-Mailing a Copy of the Research Paper

Your instructor, Ms. Lopez, has requested you e-mail her a copy of your research paper so she can verify your hyperlink. The following steps show how to e-mail the document from within Word if you use Outlook as your e-mail program.

To E-Mail a Document

1

- **Click the E-mail button on the Standard toolbar.**
- **Fill in the To text box with Ms. Lopez's e-mail address and the Introduction text box as shown in Figure 2-74.**

Word displays certain buttons and boxes from the e-mail editor inside the Word window. The file name is displayed automatically in the Subject text box.

2

- **Click the Send a Copy button.**

The document is e-mailed to the recipient named in the To text box.

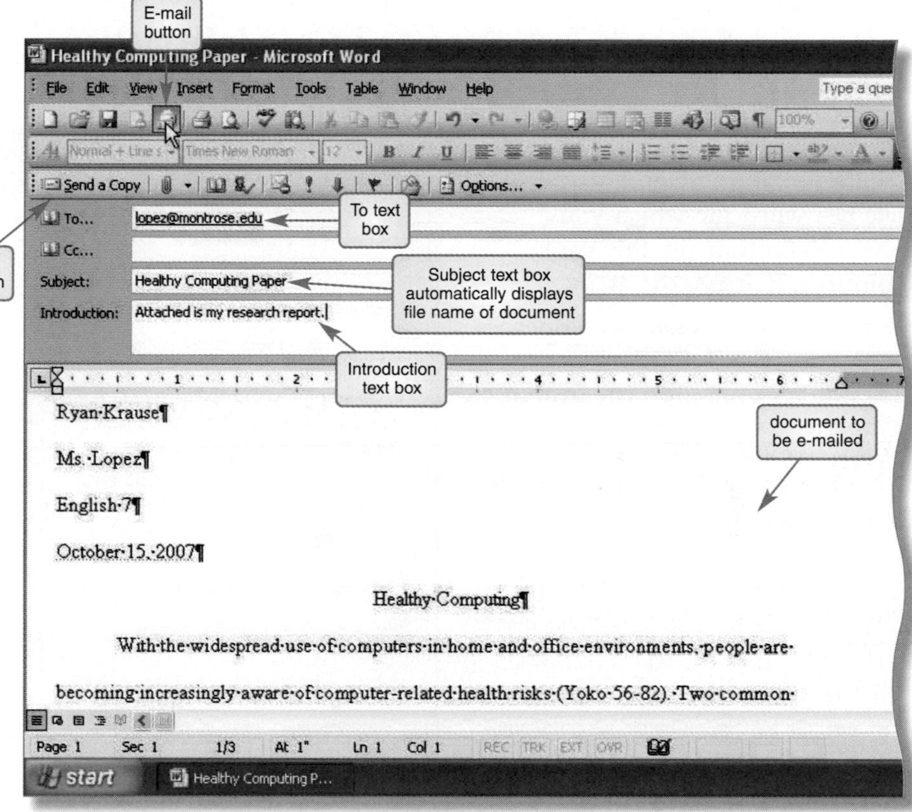

FIGURE 2-74

If you want to cancel the e-mail operation, click the E-mail button again.

In the steps above, the Word document becomes part of the e-mail message. If you wanted to send the Word document as an attachment to the e-mail message instead, do the following.

To E-Mail a Document as an Attachment

1. Click File on the menu bar, point to Send To, and then click Mail Recipient (as Attachment).
2. Fill in the text boxes.
3. Click the Send button.

Using the Research Task Pane

From within Word, you can search through various forms of online reference information. Earlier, this project discussed the Research task pane with respect to looking up a synonym in a thesaurus. Other services available in the Research task pane include the Microsoft Encarta English dictionary, bilingual dictionaries, the Microsoft Encarta Encyclopedia (with a Web connection), and Web sites that provide information such as stock quotes, news articles, and company profiles.

After reading a document you create, you might want to know the meaning of a certain word. For example, in the research paper, you might want to look up the definition of the word, minimize. The following step shows how to use the Research task pane to look up the definition of a word.

To Use the Research Task Pane to Locate Information

1

- **While holding down the ALT key, click the word for which you want a definition (in this case, minimize). Release the ALT key.**
- **If the Research task pane does not display the definition of the ALT+CLICKED word, click the Search for box arrow and then click All Reference Books.**

Word displays the Research task pane with the ALT+CLICKED word in the Search for text box (Figure 2-75). The Research button on the Standard toolbar is selected and the insertion point is in the ALT+CLICKED word. The contents of your reference book entry in the Research task pane may be different.

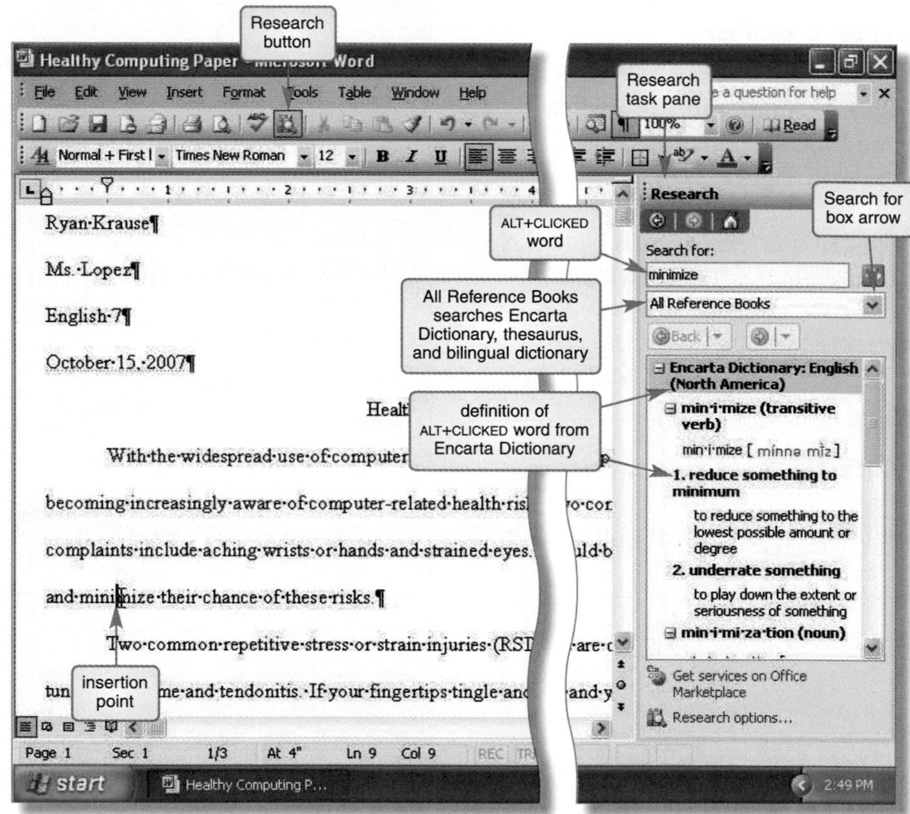

FIGURE 2-75

After you have looked up information in the Research task pane, you either can close the task pane or you can insert certain pieces of the information into the document. The next steps illustrate the procedure of copying information displayed in the Research task pane and inserting the copied text in a Word document.

To Insert Text from the Research Task Pane in a Word Document

1

- **In the Research task pane, double-click the word, reduce.**
- **Right-click the selected word.**

The word, reduce, is selected in the Research task pane and a shortcut menu is displayed (Figure 2-76).

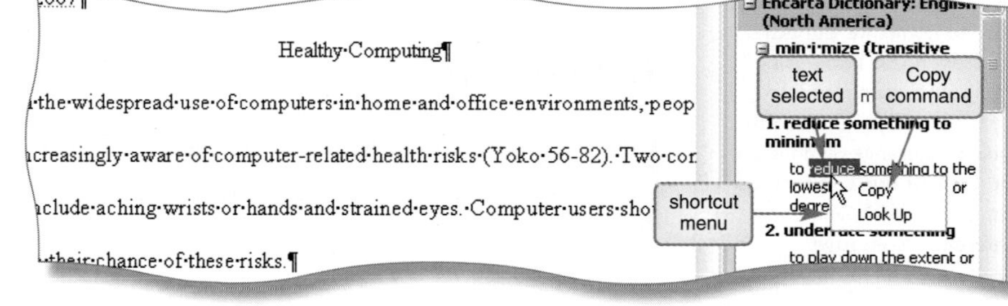

FIGURE 2-76

2

- **Click Copy on the shortcut menu to copy the selected text to the Clipboard.**
- **Drag through the word, minimize, in the research paper.**
- **Right-click the selected text in the document (Figure 2-77).**

The word, minimize, is selected in the document and a shortcut menu is displayed.

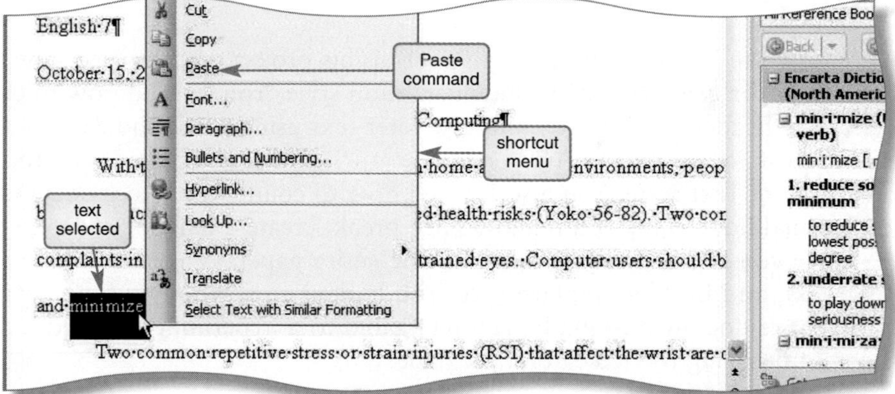

FIGURE 2-77

3

- **Click Paste on the shortcut menu.**
- **If necessary, press the SPACEBAR to insert a space after the inserted word.**
- **Click the Close button in the Research task pane.**

Word removes the selected word, minimize, and inserts the word, reduce, in its place (Figure 2-78).

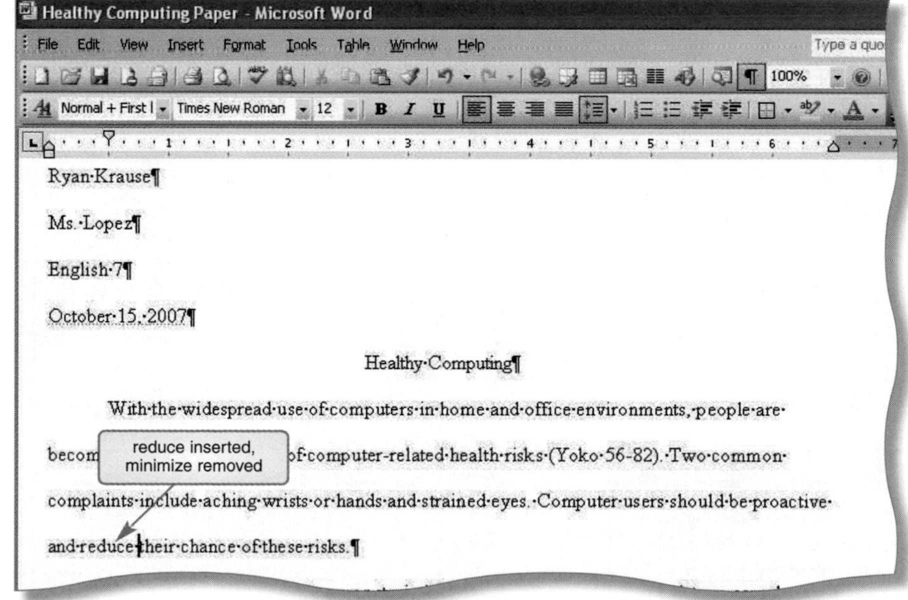

FIGURE 2-78

Q & A

Q: Is there more than one way to invoke a command in Word?

A: Yes. For a table that lists how to complete the tasks covered in this book using the mouse, menu, shortcut menu, and keyboard, see the Quick Reference Summary at the back of this book, or visit the Office 2003 Quick Reference Web page (scsite.com/off2003sch/qr).

When using Word to insert material from the Research task pane or any other online reference, be very careful not to plagiarize, or copy other's work and use it as your own. Not only is plagiarism unethical, but it is considered an academic crime that can have severe punishments such as failing a course or being expelled from school.

The final step in this project is to quit Word, as described below.

To Quit Word

1. **Click the Close button in the Word window.**
2. **If Word displays a dialog box, click the No button.**

The Word window closes.

Project Summary

In creating the Healthy Computing Paper in this project, you learned how to use Word to enter and format a research paper using the MLA documentation style. You learned how to change margin settings, adjust line spacing, create headers with page numbers, enter text using Click and Type, and first-line indent paragraphs. You learned how to use Word's AutoCorrect feature. Then, you added a footnote in the research paper and modified the Footnote Text style. You also learned how to count words in a document. In creating the Works Cited page, you learned how to insert a manual page break, create a hanging indent, create a hyperlink, and sort paragraphs.

Once you finished typing text into the entire paper, you learned how to browse through a Word document, move text, and find and replace text. You looked up a synonym for a word and checked spelling and grammar in the entire document. Finally, you navigated to a hyperlink, e-mailed a copy of a document, and looked up information using the Research task pane.

If you have a SAM user profile, you may have access to hands-on instruction, practice, and assessment of the skills covered in this project. Log in to your SAM account and go to your assignments page to see what your instructor has assigned.

Skill Builder 2-4

To practice the following tasks, visit scsite.com/off2003sch/skill, locate Word Project 2, and then click Skill Builder 2-4.

- ❑ Navigate to a hyperlink
- ❑ Use the Research task pane to look up information
- ❑ Copy and paste text from the Research task pane

What You Should Know

Having completed this project, you should be able to perform the tasks below. The tasks are listed in the same order they were presented in this project. For a list of the buttons, menus, toolbars, and commands introduced in this project, see the Quick Reference Summary at the back of this book and refer to the Page Number column.

1. Start and Customize Word (WD 77)
2. Display Formatting Marks (WD 77)
3. Change the Margin Settings (WD 78)
4. Double-Space Text (WD 80)
5. Display the Header Area (WD 81)
6. Click and Type (WD 83)
7. Enter a Page Number (WD 83)
8. Enter Name and Course Information (WD 85)
9. Format Text Using Shortcut Keys (WD 86)
10. Save a Document (WD 87)
11. First-Line Indent Paragraphs (WD 88)
12. AutoCorrect as You Type (WD 89)
13. Use the AutoCorrect Options Button (WD 90)
14. Create an AutoCorrect Entry (WD 91)
15. Enter More Text (WD 93)
16. Add a Footnote (WD 94)
17. Modify a Style (WD 96)
18. Close the Note Pane (WD 99)
19. Count Words (WD 100)
20. Page Break Automatically (WD 101)
21. Recount Words (WD 102)
22. Page Break Manually (WD 103)
23. Center the Title of the Works Cited Page (WD 104)
24. Create a Hanging Indent (WD 105)
25. Enter Works Cited Paragraphs (WD 105)
26. Insert a Symbol Automatically (WD 107)
27. Create a Hyperlink (WD 108)
28. Sort Paragraphs (WD 109)
29. Browse by Page (WD 111)
30. Select a Sentence (WD 112)
31. Move Selected Text (WD 113)
32. Display the Paste Options Menu (WD 115)
33. Find and Replace Text (WD 116)
34. Find Text (WD 117)
35. Find and Insert a Synonym (WD 118)
36. Check Spelling and Grammar at Once (WD 119)
37. Save a Document Again and Print It (WD 121)
38. View or Modify Entries in a Custom Dictionary (WD 121)
39. Set the Default Custom Dictionary (WD 121)
40. Navigate to a Hyperlink (WD 122)
41. E-Mail a Document (WD 123)
42. E-Mail a Document as an Attachment (WD 123)
43. Use the Research Task Pane to Locate Information (WD 124)
44. Insert Text from the Research Task Pane in a Word Document (WD 125)
45. Quit Word (WD 126)

Career Corner

Computer Technician

The demand for computer technicians is growing in every organization and industry. For many, this is the entry point for a career in the computer/information technology field. The responsibilities of a computer technician, also called a computer service technician, include a variety of duties. Most companies that employ someone with this title expect the technician to have basic across-the-board knowledge of concepts in the computer electronics field. Some of the tasks are hardware repair and installation; software installation, upgrade, and configuration; and troubleshooting client and/or server problems. Because the computer field is changing rapidly, technicians must work to remain abreast of current technology and become aware of future developments. Computer technicians generally work with a variety of users, which requires expert people skills, especially the ability to work with groups of nontechnical users.

Most entry-level computer technicians possess the *A+ certification*. This certification attests that a computer technician has demonstrated knowledge of core hardware and operating system technology, including installation, configuration, diagnosing, preventive maintenance, and basic networking that meets industry standards and has at least six months of experience in the field. The Electronics Technicians Association also provides a Computer Service Technician (CST) certification program.

Because this is an entry-level position, the pay scale is not as high as other more demanding and skilled positions. Individuals can expect an average annual starting salary of around $28,000 to $42,000. Companies pay more for computer technicians with experience and certification. For more information, visit scsite.com/off2003sch/careers and then click Computer Technician.

Learn It Online

Instructions: To complete the Learn It Online exercises, start your browser, click the Address bar, and then enter the Web address `scsite.com/off2003sch/learn`. When the Office 2003 Learn It Online page is displayed, follow the instructions in the exercises below. Each exercise has instructions for printing your results, either for your own records or for submission to your instructor.

1 Project Reinforcement TF, MC, and SA

Below Word Project 2, click the Project Reinforcement link. Print the quiz by clicking Print on the File menu for each page. Answer each question.

2 Flash Cards

Below Word Project 2, click the Flash Cards link and read the instructions. Type 20 (or a number specified by your instructor) in the Number of playing cards text box, type your name in the Enter your Name text box, and then click the Flip Card button. When the flash card is displayed, read the question and then click the ANSWER box arrow to select an answer. Flip through Flash Cards. If your score is 15 (75%) correct or greater, click Print on the File menu to print your results. If your score is less than 15 (75%) correct, then redo this exercise by clicking the Replay button.

3 Practice Test

Below Word Project 2, click the Practice Test link. Answer each question, enter your first and last name at the bottom of the page, and then click the Grade Test button. When the graded practice test is displayed on your screen, click Print on the File menu to print a hard copy. Continue to take practice tests until you score 80% or better.

4 Who Wants To Be a Computer Genius?

Below Word Project 2, click the Computer Genius link. Read the instructions, enter your first and last name at the bottom of the page, and then click the PLAY button. When your score is displayed, click the PRINT RESULTS link to print a hard copy.

5 Wheel of Terms

Below Word Project 2, click the Wheel of Terms link. Read the instructions, and then enter your first and last name and your school name. Click the PLAY button. When your score is displayed, right-click the score and then click Print on the shortcut menu to print a hard copy.

6 Crossword Puzzle Challenge

Below Word Project 2, click the Crossword Puzzle Challenge link. Read the instructions, and then enter your first and last name. Click the SUBMIT button. Work the crossword puzzle. When you are finished, click the Submit button. When the crossword puzzle is redisplayed, click the Print Puzzle button to print a hard copy.

7 Tips and Tricks

Below Word Project 2, click the Tips and Tricks link. Click a topic that pertains to Project 2. Right-click the information and then click Print on the shortcut menu. Construct a brief example of what the information relates to in Word to confirm you understand how to use the tip or trick.

8 Newsgroups

Below Word Project 2, click the Newsgroups link. Click a topic that pertains to Project 2. Print three comments.

9 Expanding Your Horizons

Below Word Project 2, click the Expanding Your Horizons link. Click a topic that pertains to Project 2. Print the information. Construct a brief example of what the information relates to in Word to confirm you understand the contents of the article.

10 Search Sleuth

Below Word Project 2, click the Search Sleuth link. To search for a term that pertains to this project, select a term below the Project 2 title and then use the Google search engine at google.com (or any major search engine) to display and print two Web pages that present information on the term.

11 Word Online Training

Below Word Project 2, click the Word Online Training link. When your browser displays the Microsoft Office Online Web page, click the Word link. Click one of the Word courses that covers one or more of the objectives listed at the beginning of the project on page WD 74. Print the first page of the course before stepping through it.

12 Office Marketplace

Below Word Project 2, click the Office Marketplace link. When your browser displays the Microsoft Office Online Web page, click the Office Marketplace link. Click a topic that relates to Word. Print the first page.

13 You're Hired!

Below Word Project 2, click the You're Hired! link to embark on the path to a career in computers. Directions about how to play the game will be displayed. When you are ready to play, click the begin the game button. If required, submit your score to your instructor.

Apply Your Knowledge

1 Revising a Document

Instructions: Start Word. Open the document, Apply 2-1 Home Networks Paragraph. See page xxiv at the front of this book for instructions for downloading the Data Files for Students or see your instructor for information about accessing the files required in this book.

The document you open is a paragraph of text. You are to revise the paragraph as follows: move a sentence; change the format of the moved sentence; change paragraph indentation, change line spacing, change margin settings, replace all occurrences of the word, programs, with the word, software; add a sentence; remove an automatic hyperlink format, and modify the header. The revised paragraph is shown in Figure 2-79.

Perform the following tasks:

Revised Home Networks Paragraph
10/20/2007 12:38:42 PM

An estimated 39 million homes have more than one computer. Thus, many home users are connecting multiple computers and devices together in a wired or wireless home network. Home networking provides many conveniences and saves the home user money. Each user on a networked computer in the house can connect to the Internet at the same time, share a single high-speed Internet connection, access files and software on the other computers in the house, share peripherals such as printers and scanners, and play multiplayer games with players on other computers in the house. Home networking packages that include all necessary hardware and software are available at a reasonable cost. For more information about home networks, visit www.scsite.com/dcfund/weblink and click Home Networks below Chapter 8.

FIGURE 2-79

1. Select the first sentence of the paragraph. Use drag-and-drop editing to move this sentence to the end of the paragraph, so it is the last sentence in the paragraph.
2. Click the Paste Options button that displays to the right of the moved sentence. Remove the italic format from the moved sentence by clicking Keep Text Only on the shortcut menu.
3. Use first-line indent to indent the first line of the paragraph.
4. Change the line spacing of the paragraph from single to double.
5. Change the left and right margins of the document to .75".
6. Use the Find and Replace dialog box to replace all occurrences of the word, programs, with the word, software.
7. Use Word's thesaurus to change the word, essential, to the word, necessary, in the last sentence of the paragraph.
8. At the end of the paragraph, press the SPACEBAR and then type this sentence: `For more information about home networks, visit www.scsite.com/dcfund/weblink and click Home Networks below Chapter 8.`
9. Remove the hyperlink automatic format from the Web address by positioning the mouse pointer at the beginning of the Web address (that is, the w in www), pointing to the small blue box below the w, clicking the AutoCorrect Options button, and then clicking Undo Hyperlink on the shortcut menu.
10. Display the header on the screen. Change the alignment of the text in the header from left to centered. Insert the word, Revised, in the text so it reads: Revised Home Networks Paragraph. On the second line of the header, insert and center the current date and the current time using buttons on the Header and Footer toolbar. Place one space between the current date and current time.
11. Click File on the menu bar and then click Save As. Save the document using the file name, Apply 2-1 Revised Home Networks Paragraph.
12. Print the revised paragraph, as shown in Figure 2-79.
13. Use the Research task pane to look up the computing definition of the word, peripherals, in the fourth sentence of the paragraph. Handwrite the definition on your printout.

1 Preparing a Short Research Paper

Problem: You are a high-school senior currently enrolled in an advanced business class. Your assignment is to prepare a short research paper (300–350 words) about the environmental impact of computers or computing. The requirements are that the paper be presented according to the MLA documentation style and have three references. One of the three references must be from the Web and formatted as a hyperlink on the Works Cited page. You prepare the paper shown in Figure 2-80, which discusses green computing.

Santoni 1

Louie Santoni

Ms. Mulroney

Business II

October 3, 2007

Green Computing

Green computing involves reducing the electricity and environmental waste during computer usage. People use, and often waste, resources such as electricity and paper while using a computer. Society has become aware of this waste and is taking measures to combat it (Mobley 24-30).

Personal computers, monitors, and printers should comply with guidelines of the ENERGY STAR program. This program, which was developed by the United States Department of Energy (DOE) and the United States Environmental Protection Agency (EPA), encourages manufacturers to create energy-efficient devices that require little power when they are not in use. For example, many devices switch to standby mode after a specified number of inactive minutes. Computers and devices that meet ENERGY STAR guidelines display an ENERGY STAR label.

Computer users should not store obsolete computers and devices in their basement, storage room, attic, warehouse, or any other location (Holmes and Marsden 78-84). Computers, monitors, and other equipment contain toxic materials and potentially dangerous elements including lead, mercury, and flame retardants. In a landfill, these materials release into the environment. Experts recommend refurbishing or recycling the equipment, which are much safer alternatives for the environment. Manufacturers can use the millions of pounds of recycled raw material in products such as outdoor furniture and automotive parts. Many computer

FIGURE 2-80a

In the Lab

Santoni 2

manufacturers, office supply stores, and other agencies offer free recycling to consumers and businesses.

To reduce further the environmental impact of computing, users simply can alter a few habits, such as using devices that comply with the ENERGY STAR program, recycling, and using paperless methods to communicate (*Green Computing Suggestions*). By following green computing suggestions, users can help to reduce electrical and environmental waste.

FIGURE 2-80b

Santoni 3

Works Cited

Green Computing Suggestions. Shelly Cashman Series® Course Technology. 2 Oct. 2007. http://www.scsite.com/wd2003sch/pr2/wc1.htm.

Holmes, James D., and Katie A. Marsden. *Computer Techniques for the New User*. Orlando: Park Publishing Company, 2007.

Mobley, Roger R. "Green Computing: Protecting Our Environment." *Simple Computer Talk* Aug. 2007: 9-34.

FIGURE 2-80c

Instructions:

1. If necessary, display formatting marks on the screen.
2. Change all margins to one inch.
3. Adjust line spacing to double.
4. Create a header to number pages.
5. Type the name and course information at the left margin. Center and type the title.
6. Set first-line indent for paragraphs in the body of the research paper.
7. Type the body of the paper as shown in Figures 2-80a and 2-80b. At the end of the body of the research paper, press the ENTER key and then insert a manual page break.
8. Create the works cited page (Figure 2-80c).
9. Check the spelling of the paper at once.
10. Save the document on a USB flash drive using Lab 2-1 Green Computing Paper as the file name.
11. Use the Select Browse Object button to go to page 3. If you have access to the Web, CTRL+click the hyperlink to test it.
12. Print the research paper. Handwrite the number of words, paragraphs, and characters in the research paper above the title of your printed research paper.

2 Preparing a Research Report with a Footnote(s)

Problem: You are a high-school student enrolled in a senior English class. Your assignment is to prepare a short research paper in any area of interest to you. The requirements are that the paper be presented according to the MLA documentation style, contain at least one explanatory note positioned as a footnote, and have three references. One of the three references must be from the Internet and formatted as a hyperlink on the works cited page. You prepare a paper about protecting computers from electrical power disturbances (Figure 2-81).

O'Malley 1

Kaden O'Malley

Mr. Dyrez

English 8

October 25, 2007

Is Your Computer Protected?

Electrical power variations can cause damage to computers and peripherals, often in the form of loss of data or loss of equipment. If a computer is linked to a network, a single power disturbance negatively can affect many computers and devices. Electrical disturbances include overvoltages and undervoltages. Is your computer protected from these types of disturbances?

Overvoltages, or power surges, occur when the incoming electrical power increases significantly above the normal 120 volts. Overvoltages can cause immediate and permanent damage to hardware. One type of overvoltage, called a spike, occurs when the increase in power lasts for less than one millisecond. Many sources cause spikes, ranging from uncontrollable disturbances, such as lightning bolts, to controllable disturbances, such as turning on a printer (Goldman 57-58). Surge protectors help to guard a computer and peripherals from spikes (*Preventing Damage from Electrical Power Variations*). Often resembling a power strip, a computer and other devices plug in the surge protector, which plugs in the power source.[1]

An undervoltage occurs when the electrical supply drops. In North America, a wall plug supplies electricity at approximately 120 volts. Any significant drop below 120 volts is an undervoltage. Brownouts and blackouts are two types of undervoltages. These types of electrical disturbances will not harm a computer or the equipment but can cause loss of data (Balitevich

[1] Goldman rates the top surge protectors. The personal computer surge protectors rated range in price from $29 to $139 (52-55).

FIGURE 2-81a

O'Malley 2

and Green 45-62). To protect against loss of data from an undervoltage, computer users often connect an uninterruptible power supply (UPS) to their computer.

Power disturbances can damage both hardware and software. Replacing either can be costly. Thus, all computers should be protected from overvoltages and undervoltages. Protecting your computer now before damage occurs can result in savings of time, money, and frustration.

FIGURE 2-81b

Instructions Part 1: Perform the following tasks to create the research paper:

1. If necessary, display formatting marks on the screen. Change all margin settings to one inch. Adjust line spacing to double. Create a header to number pages. Type the name and course information at the left margin. Center and type the title. Set first-line indent for paragraphs in the body of the research paper.
2. Type the body of the paper as shown in Figures 2-81a and 2-81b. Add the footnote as shown in Figure 2-81a. Change the Footnote Text style to the format specified in the MLA style. At the end of the body of the research paper, press the ENTER key once and insert a manual page break.
3. Create the works cited page. Enter the works cited shown below as separate paragraphs. Format the works according to the MLA documentation style and then sort the works cited paragraphs.
   (a) Goldman, Paul C. "Power Disturbances Can Be Dangerous to Your Hardware." Information Systems Technology Journal Oct. 2007: 47–65.
   (b) Preventing Damage from Electrical Power Variations. Shelly Cashman Series®. Course Technology. 15 Oct. 2007. http://www.scsite.com/wd2003sch/pr2/wc2.htm.
   (c) Balitevich, Doris S., and Marcus L. Green. Computers and Undervoltages. Chicago: West Davis Jones Publishing Company, 2007.
4. Check the spelling of the paper.
5. Save the document on a USB flash drive using Lab 2-2 Power Disturbances Paper as the file name.
6. If you have access to the Web, CTRL+click the hyperlink to test it.
7. Print the research paper. Handwrite the number of words, including the footnotes, in the research paper above the title of your printed research paper.

Instructions Part 2: Perform the following tasks to modify the research paper:

1. Use Word to find a synonym of your choice for the word, significantly, in the first sentence of the second paragraph.
2. Change all occurrences of the words, surge protector, to the words, surge suppressor.
3. Insert a second footnote at the end of the last sentence in the third paragraph of the research paper. Use the following footnote text: Goldman lists several models of uninterruptible power supplies with features and costs. In general, a basic UPS costs between $95 and $225 (72–75).
4. In the first footnote, find the word, top, and change it to the word, best.
5. Save the document on a USB flash drive using Lab 2-2 Power Disturbances Paper - Part 2 as the file name.
6. Print this revised research paper that has notes positioned as footnotes. Handwrite the number of words, including the footnotes, in the research paper above the title of the printed research paper.

Instructions Part 3: Perform the following tasks to modify the research paper created in Part 2:

1. Convert the footnotes to endnotes. Recall that endnotes display at the end of a document. Switch to print layout view to see the endnotes. ***Hint:*** Use Help to learn about print layout view and converting footnotes to endnotes.
2. Modify the Endnote text style to 12-point font, double-spaced text with a first-line indent. Insert a page break so the endnotes are placed on a separate, numbered page. Center the title, Endnotes, double-spaced above the notes.
3. Change the format of the note reference marks to capital letters (A, B, etc.). ***Hint:*** Use Help to learn about changing the number format of note reference marks.
4. Save the document on a USB flash drive using Lab 2-2 Power Disturbances Paper - Part 3 as the file name.
5. Print the revised research paper with notes positioned as endnotes. Handwrite the number of words, including the endnotes, in the research paper above the title of the printed research paper.

3 Composing a Research Paper from Notes

Problem: You have drafted the notes shown in Figure 2-82. Your assignment is to prepare a short research paper from these notes.

Instructions: Perform the following tasks:

1. Review the notes in Figure 2-82 and then rearrange and reword them. Embellish the paper as you deem necessary. Present the paper according to the MLA documentation style. Create an AutoCorrect entry that automatically corrects the spelling of the misspelled word, pasword, to the correct spelling, password. Add a footnote that refers the reader to the Web for more information. Create the works cited page from the listed sources. Be sure to sort the works.
2. Check the spelling and grammar of the paper. Save the document on a USB flash drive using Lab 2-3 Authenticating Users Paper as the file name.
3. Use the Research task pane to look up a definition. Copy and insert the definition into the document as a footnote. Be sure to quote the definition and cite the source.
4. Print the research paper. Handwrite the number of words, including the footnotes, in the research paper above the title of the printed research paper. Circle the definition inserted into the document from the Research task pane.
5. Use Word to e-mail the research paper to your instructor, if your instructor gives you permission to do so.

Commercial application programs often include computer security features that control who can access a computer, what actions they can perform while accessing the computer, and when they can access it. These types of access controls use a process called identification and authentication. Identification verifies that the user is a valid user. Authentication verifies that the user is who he or she claims to be. Three authentication methods are user names and passwords, possessed objects, and biometric devices.

User Names and Passwords
(Source: a Web site titled Selecting a Good Password sponsored by the Shelly Cashman Series® at Course Technology, site visited on October 8, 2007, Web address is http://www.scsite.com/wd2003sch/pr2/wc3.htm.)

- A user name is a unique combination of characters that identifies one specific user. A password is a private combination of characters associated with the user name.
- If the user name and password do not match entries in the authorization file, the user is denied access to the network.
- On many computers and networks, users are required to enter a user name and password before they can access the data, information, and programs stored on a computer or network.

Possessed Objects
(Source: "Security, Ethics, and Privacy", an article on pages 29-47 in the November 2007 issue of Computers and Society Journal, authors James R. Baker and Cynthia L. Ruiz.)

- Badges, cards, and keys are examples of possessed objects.
- A possessed object is any item that a user must carry to gain access to the computer or computer facility.
- Possessed objects often are used in conjunction with a personal identification number (PIN), which is a numeric password.

Biometric Devices
(Source: Information System Auditing and Control Techniques, a book published by Green Valley Publishing Company in St. Louis, 2007, written by Mae Li.)

- A biometric device translates a user's personal characteristics into a digital code that is compared to a digital code stored in the computer.
- If the digital code in the computer does not match the user's code, the computer denies access to the individual.
- A biometric device is one that verifies personal characteristics to authenticate a user. Examples of personal characteristics include fingerprints, voice patterns, facial features, signatures, hand geometry, and eye patterns.

A computer should implement one or more of these authentication techniques to secure it from accidental or intentional misuse. The authentication technique selected should match the degree of risk associated with the unauthorized access. The organization also regularly should review the techniques in place to determine if they still are appropriate.

FIGURE 2-82

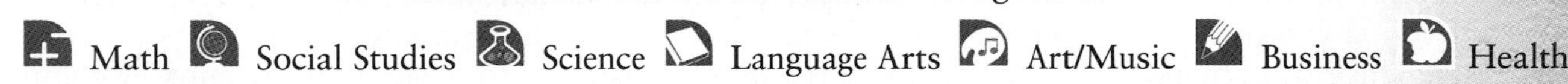

Cases and Places

The difficulty of these case studies varies:
are the least difficult and are more difficult.
Each exercise has a cross-curricular designation:

Math Social Studies Science Language Arts Art/Music Business Health

1 Your English teacher has assigned each student the task of writing a brief paper about the MLA documentation style. This Microsoft Word project presented the requirements of the MLA documentation style for writing research papers on page WD 76 and in several Q&A boxes dispersed throughout the project. Using the material presented in this project, write a short research paper (450–500 words) that describes the requirements of the MLA documentation style. Include at least two references and one explanatory note positioned as a footnote. Add an AutoCorrect entry to correct a word you commonly mistype. Use the concepts and techniques presented in this project to format the paper. Type the paper with the Word screen in normal view. Switch to print layout view to proofread the paper.

2 This week's assignment in environmental science is to research and write a brief paper about some aspect of a global positioning system (GPS). A GPS is a navigation system that consists of one or more earth-based receivers that accept and analyze signals sent by satellites in order to determine the receiver's geographic location. GPSs help scientists, farmers, pilots, dispatchers, and rescue workers operate more productively and safely. Using Word's Research task pane, the school library, other textbooks, magazines, the Internet, friends and family, or other resources, research GPSs. Then, prepare a brief research paper (450–500 words) that discusses your findings. Include at least one explanatory note and two references, one of which must be a Web site on the Internet. Use the concepts and techniques presented in this project to format the paper.

3 Today's assignment in health class was to research and write a brief paper about respiratory infections. Common names used to identify these infections include influenza, pneumonia, and the common cold. Some of these infections have similar symptoms, such as coughing. Each, however, has unique symptoms to differentiate it from the others. Using Word's Research task pane, the school library, other textbooks, the Internet, magazines, or other resources, research the symptoms and treatment of various respiratory infections. Then, prepare a brief research paper (450–500 words) that discusses your findings. Include at least one explanatory note and two references, one of which must be a Web site on the Internet. Use the concepts and techniques presented in this project to format the paper.

Cases and Places

4 This week's assignment in your business class is to research and write a brief paper about computer viruses. A computer virus is a potentially damaging computer program that affects, or infects, a computer negatively by altering the way the computer works without the user's knowledge or permission. If the infected software is transferred to or accessed by another computer or network, the virus spreads. Viruses have become a serious problem in recent years, and currently, thousands of known virus programs exist. Using Word's Research task pane, the school library, other textbooks, the Internet, magazines, interviews with programmers, or other resources, research the types of computer viruses and how to protect your computer against them. Then, prepare a brief research paper (450–500 words) that discusses your findings. Include at least one explanatory note and two references, one of which must be a Web site on the Internet. Use the concepts and techniques presented in this project to format the paper.

5 **Working Together** With spring break just two months away, your social studies teacher thought it would be interesting and informative for teams of students to research various spring break destinations and write a combined report presenting the team members' findings. The researched areas for spring break destinations could be at nearby locations or at spots across the country. Some may involve camping; others may involve hotel or condominium accommodations. Travel methods could include car, train, or airplane. Packages could be booked directly, through a travel agent, or on the Web.

Each team member is to research the attractions, accommodations, required transportation, and total cost of one spring break destination by looking through newspapers, magazines, searching the Web, and/or visiting a travel agency. Each team member is to write a minimum of 200 words summarizing his or her findings. Each team member also is to write at least one explanatory note and supply his or her reference for the works cited page. Then, the team should meet as a group to compose a research paper that includes all team members' write-ups. Start by copying and pasting the text into a single document and then write an introduction and conclusion as a group. Use the concepts and techniques presented in this project to format the paper according to the MLA documentation style. Set the default dictionary. If Word flags any of your last names as an error, add the name(s) to the custom dictionary. Hand in printouts of each team member's original write-up, as well as the final research paper.

MICROSOFT OFFICE
Word 2003

Creating a Resume Using a Wizard and a Cover Letter with a Table

PROJECT 3

CASE PERSPECTIVE

As a senior at Lincoln High School, Jasmine Baskerville is looking toward her upcoming post-secondary education at Hillside College, where she plans to major in accounting. During her college years, she plans to obtain a part-time job to help pay for expenses. Ideally, she would like to land a job in an accounting office to continue supplementing her education with real world experience. With graduation just six weeks away, Jasmine discussed her plans with you, one of her closest friends, during lunch today.

As soon as she graduates, Jasmine would like to obtain a part-time accounting clerk position with a major accounting firm in the Chicagoland area. She buys several local newspapers to begin her job hunt. While reading through the classified section of the *Herald Times*, Jasmine notices an accounting clerk position available at Triangle Accounting that seems perfect. The ad requests that all applicants send a resume and a cover letter to the managing partner, Mr. Joel Martello.

Jasmine asks you to help her create a professional resume and cover letter — because you are an expert in Microsoft Word and business writing rules. You immediately agree to help your friend. You suggest she use Word's Resume Wizard to create the resume, because the wizard saves time by formatting much of the document. You also advise Jasmine to include all essential business letter components in the cover letter. Then, you mention she can use Word to prepare and print an envelope, so the entire presentation looks professional.

As you read through this project, you will learn how to use Word to create a resume, a cover letter, and an addressed envelope.

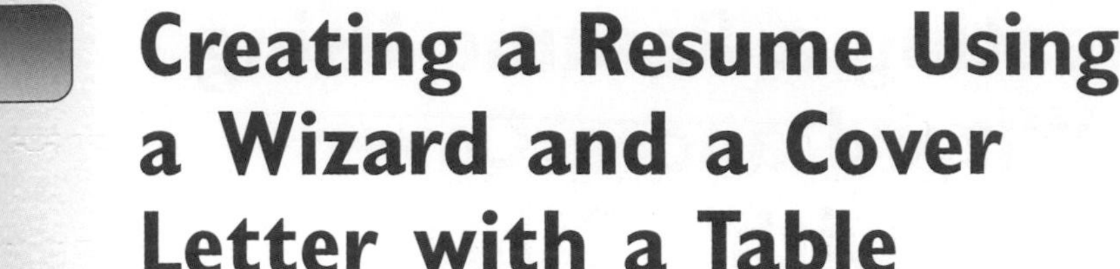

Creating a Resume Using a Wizard and a Cover Letter with a Table

PROJECT

Objectives

You will have mastered the material in this project when you can:

- Create a resume using Word's Resume Wizard
- Fill in a document template
- Use print preview to view and print a document
- Set and use tab stops
- Collect and paste using the Clipboard task pane
- Format paragraphs and characters
- Remove formatting from text
- Identify the components of a business letter
- Insert the current date
- Create and insert an AutoText entry
- Insert a Word table, enter data into the table, and format the table
- Address and print an envelope
- Work with smart tags
- Modify file properties

Introduction

At some time in your professional life, you will prepare a resume along with a personalized cover letter to send to a prospective employer(s). In addition to some personal information, a **resume** usually contains the applicant's educational background and job experience. Employers review many resumes for each vacant position. Thus, you should design your resume carefully so it presents you as the best candidate for the job. You also should attach a personalized cover letter to each resume you send. A **cover letter** enables you to elaborate on positive points in your resume; it also provides you with an opportunity to show a potential employer your written communications skills. Accordingly, it is important that your cover letter is written well and follows proper business letter rules.

Composing documents from scratch can be a difficult process for many people. To assist with this task, Word provides wizards and templates. A **wizard** asks you several basic questions and then, based on your responses, uses a template to prepare and format a document for you. A **template** is similar to a form with prewritten text; that is, Word prepares the requested document with text and/or formatting common to all documents of this nature. After Word creates a document from a template, you fill in the blanks or replace prewritten words in the document. In addition to templates used by wizards, Word provides other templates you can use to create documents.

Project Three — Resume and Cover Letter

Jasmine Leila Baskerville, a high-school senior, is seeking a part-time position in an accounting office upon graduation in six weeks. Project 3 uses Word to produce her resume, shown in Figure 3-1, and a personalized cover letter and an envelope, shown in Figure 3-2 on the next page.

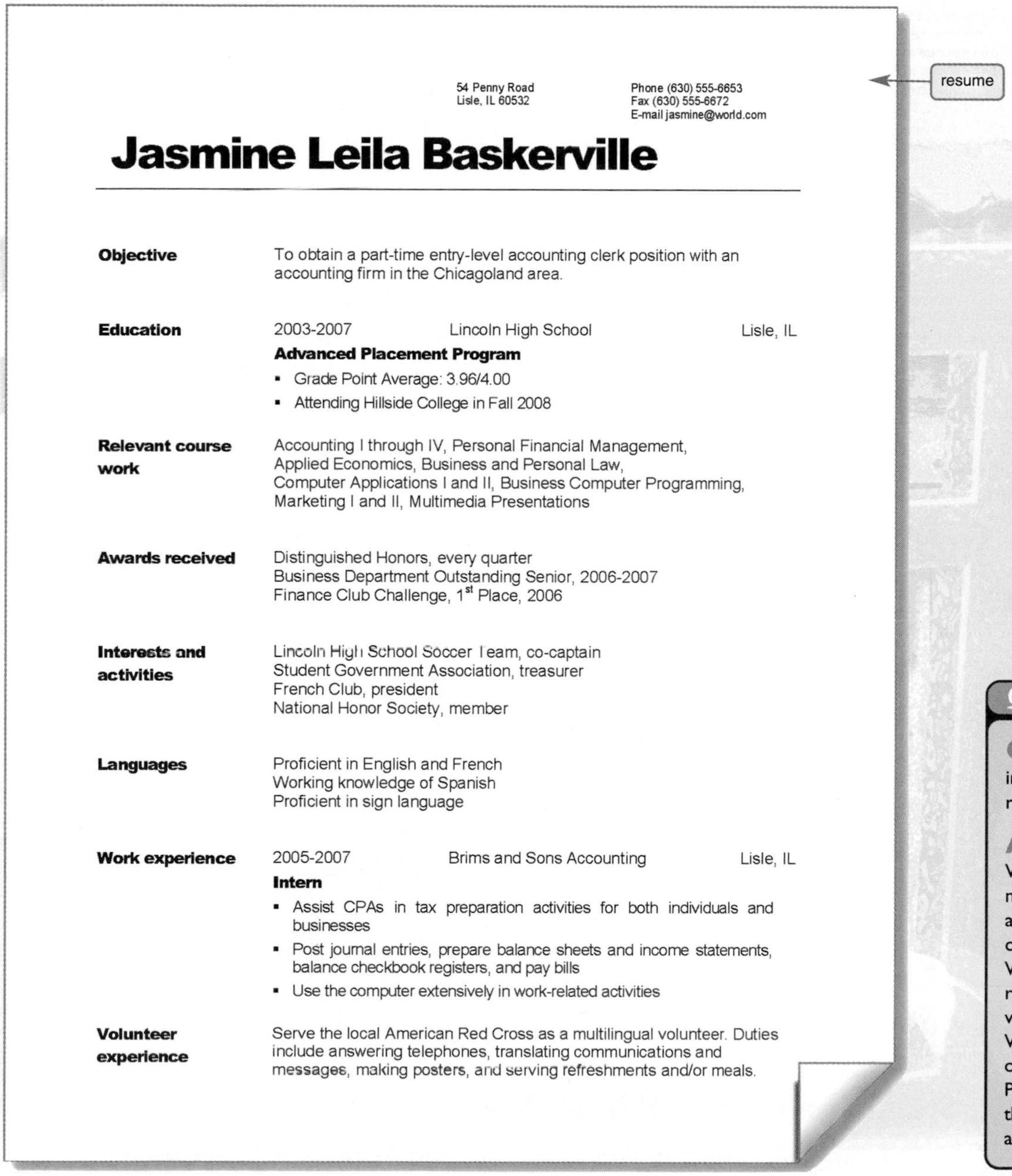

54 Penny Road
Lisle, IL 60532

Phone (630) 555-6653
Fax (630) 555-6672
E-mail jasmine@world.com

Jasmine Leila Baskerville

resume

Objective To obtain a part-time entry-level accounting clerk position with an accounting firm in the Chicagoland area.

Education 2003-2007 Lincoln High School Lisle, IL

Advanced Placement Program

- Grade Point Average: 3.96/4.00
- Attending Hillside College in Fall 2008

Relevant course work Accounting I through IV, Personal Financial Management, Applied Economics, Business and Personal Law, Computer Applications I and II, Business Computer Programming, Marketing I and II, Multimedia Presentations

Awards received Distinguished Honors, every quarter
Business Department Outstanding Senior, 2006-2007
Finance Club Challenge, 1st Place, 2006

Interests and activities Lincoln High School Soccer Team, co-captain
Student Government Association, treasurer
French Club, president
National Honor Society, member

Languages Proficient in English and French
Working knowledge of Spanish
Proficient in sign language

Work experience 2005-2007 Brims and Sons Accounting Lisle, IL

Intern

- Assist CPAs in tax preparation activities for both individuals and businesses
- Post journal entries, prepare balance sheets and income statements, balance checkbook registers, and pay bills
- Use the computer extensively in work-related activities

Volunteer experience Serve the local American Red Cross as a multilingual volunteer. Duties include answering telephones, translating communications and messages, making posters, and serving refreshments and/or meals.

FIGURE 3-1

Q & A

Q: Does the Web have information about writing resumes and cover letters?

A: Yes. The World Wide Web contains a host of information, tips, and suggestions about writing resumes and cover letters. For links to Web sites about writing resumes and cover letters, visit the Office 2003 Q&A Web page (scsite.com/off2003sch/qa), locate Word Project 3, and then click one of the Writing Research Papers and Cover Letters links.

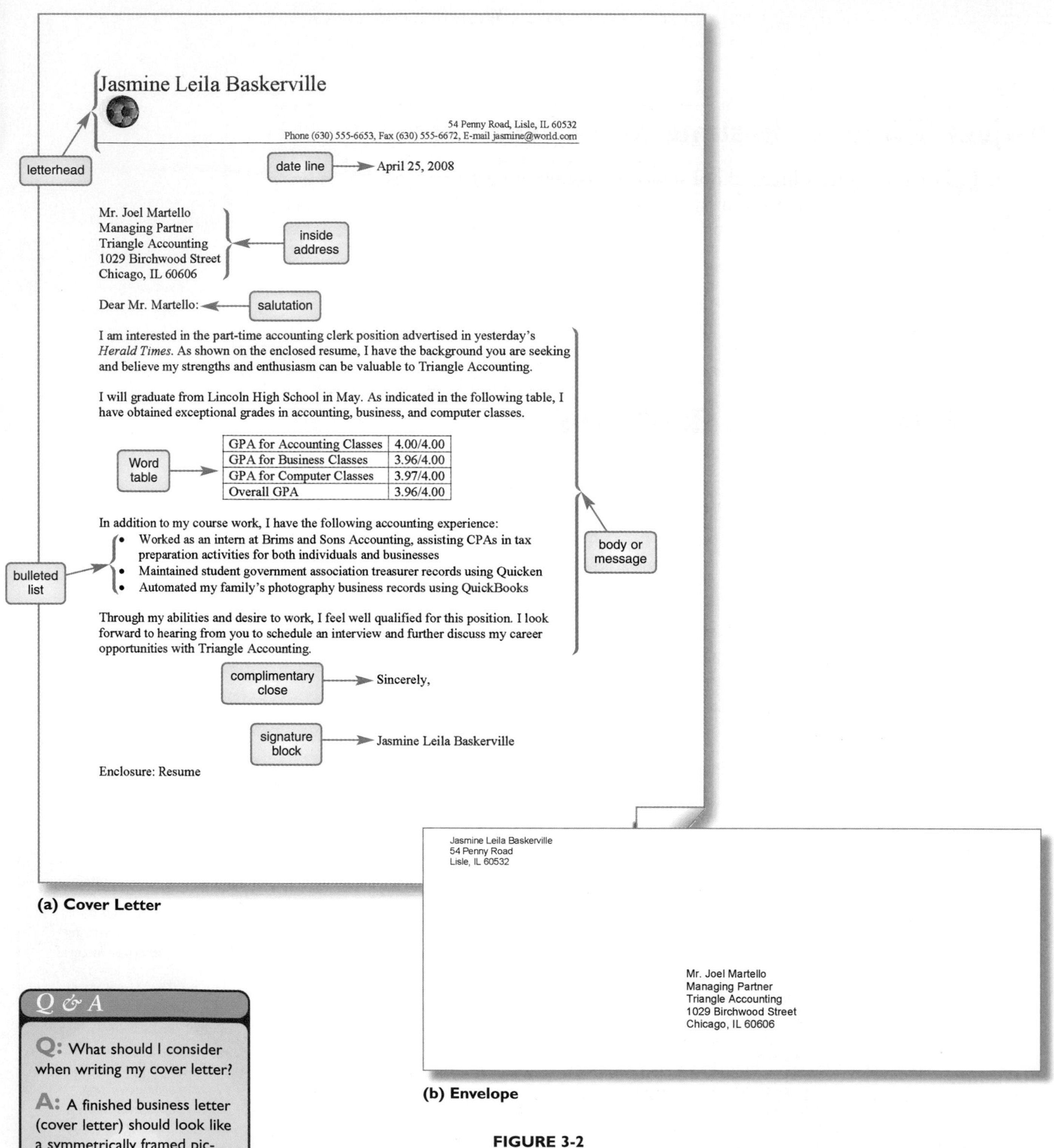

Jasmine Leila Baskerville

54 Penny Road, Lisle, IL 60532
Phone (630) 555-6653, Fax (630) 555-6672, E-mail jasmine@world.com

April 25, 2008

Mr. Joel Martello
Managing Partner
Triangle Accounting
1029 Birchwood Street
Chicago, IL 60606

Dear Mr. Martello:

I am interested in the part-time accounting clerk position advertised in yesterday's *Herald Times*. As shown on the enclosed resume, I have the background you are seeking and believe my strengths and enthusiasm can be valuable to Triangle Accounting.

I will graduate from Lincoln High School in May. As indicated in the following table, I have obtained exceptional grades in accounting, business, and computer classes.

GPA for Accounting Classes	4.00/4.00
GPA for Business Classes	3.96/4.00
GPA for Computer Classes	3.97/4.00
Overall GPA	3.96/4.00

In addition to my course work, I have the following accounting experience:

- Worked as an intern at Brims and Sons Accounting, assisting CPAs in tax preparation activities for both individuals and businesses
- Maintained student government association treasurer records using Quicken
- Automated my family's photography business records using QuickBooks

Through my abilities and desire to work, I feel well qualified for this position. I look forward to hearing from you to schedule an interview and further discuss my career opportunities with Triangle Accounting.

Sincerely,

Jasmine Leila Baskerville

Enclosure: Resume

Jasmine Leila Baskerville
54 Penny Road
Lisle, IL 60532

Mr. Joel Martello
Managing Partner
Triangle Accounting
1029 Birchwood Street
Chicago, IL 60606

(a) Cover Letter

(b) Envelope

FIGURE 3-2

Q & A

Q: What should I consider when writing my cover letter?

A: A finished business letter (cover letter) should look like a symmetrically framed picture with evenly spaced margins, all balanced below an attractive letterhead. In addition, the contents of the letter should contain proper grammar, correct spelling, logically constructed sentences, flowing paragraphs, and sound ideas.

Starting and Customizing Word

To start and customize Word, Windows must be running. If you are stepping through this project on a computer and you want your screen to match the figures in this book, then you should change your computer's resolution to 800 × 600 and reset the toolbars and menus. For information about changing the resolution and resetting toolbars and menus, read Appendix D.

The following steps describe how to start Word and customize the Word window. You may need to ask your instructor how to start Word for your system.

To Start and Customize Word

1. **Click the Start button on the Windows taskbar, point to All Programs on the Start menu, point to Microsoft Office on the All Programs submenu, and then click Microsoft Office Word 2003 on the Microsoft Office submenu.**
2. **If the Word window is not maximized, double-click its title bar to maximize it.**
3. **If the Language bar appears, right-click it and then click Close the Language bar on the shortcut menu.**
4. **If the Getting Started task pane is displayed in the Word window, click its Close button.**
5. **If the Standard and Formatting toolbar buttons are displayed on one row, click the Toolbar Options button and then click Show Buttons on Two Rows in the Toolbar Options list.**
6. **If your screen differs from Figure 3-3 on the next page, click View on the menu bar and then click Normal.**

Word starts and, after a few moments, displays an empty document in the Word window (shown in Figure 3-3).

Displaying Formatting Marks

As discussed in Project 1, it is helpful to display formatting marks that indicate where in the document you pressed the ENTER key, SPACEBAR, and other keys. The following step describes how to display formatting marks.

To Display Formatting Marks

1. **If the Show/Hide ¶ button on the Standard toolbar is not selected already, click it.**

Word displays formatting marks in the document window, and the Show/Hide ¶ button on the Standard toolbar is selected (shown in Figure 3-3).

Using Word's Resume Wizard to Create a Resume

You can type a resume from scratch into a blank document window, or you can use the **Resume Wizard** and let Word format the resume with appropriate headings and spacing. After answering several questions, you customize the resume created by the Resume Wizard by filling in blanks or selecting and replacing text.

When you use a wizard, Word displays a dialog box with the wizard's name on its title bar. A wizard's dialog box displays a list of **panel names** along its left side with the currently selected panel displaying on the right side of the dialog box (shown in Figure 3-6 on page WD 143). Each panel presents a different set of options, in which you select preferences or enter text. To move from one panel to the next within the wizard's dialog box, click the Next button or click the panel name on the left side of the dialog box.

Q & A

Q: Are additional templates and wizards available?

A: Yes. In addition to those installed on your hard disk, Microsoft has more wizards and templates available on the Web that you can download. To access these templates, click the Templates on Office Online link in the Template area in the New Document task pane.

The following steps show how to create a resume using the Resume Wizard. A wizard retains the settings selected by the last person who used the wizard. Thus, the wizard initially may display some text and selections different from the figures shown here. If you are stepping through this project on a computer, be sure to verify that your settings match the screens shown in the following steps before clicking the Next button in each dialog box.

To Create a Resume Using Word's Resume Wizard

1

• **Click File on the menu bar (Figure 3-3).**

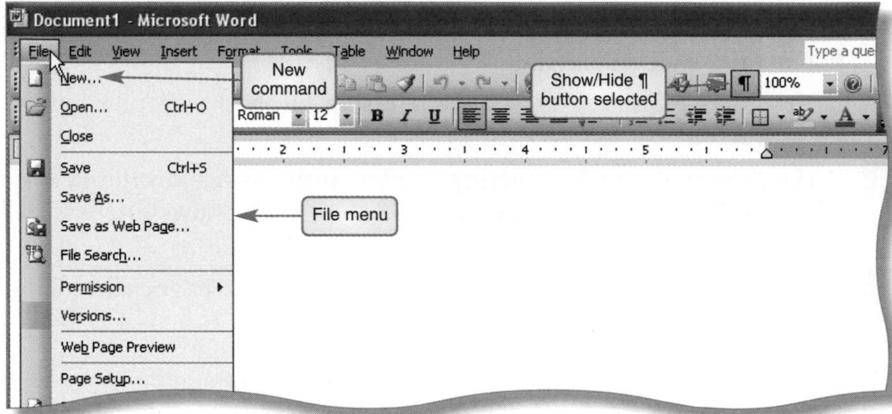

FIGURE 3-3

2

• **Click New on the File menu.**

Word displays the New Document task pane (Figure 3-4). You access wizards through the Templates area in the task pane.

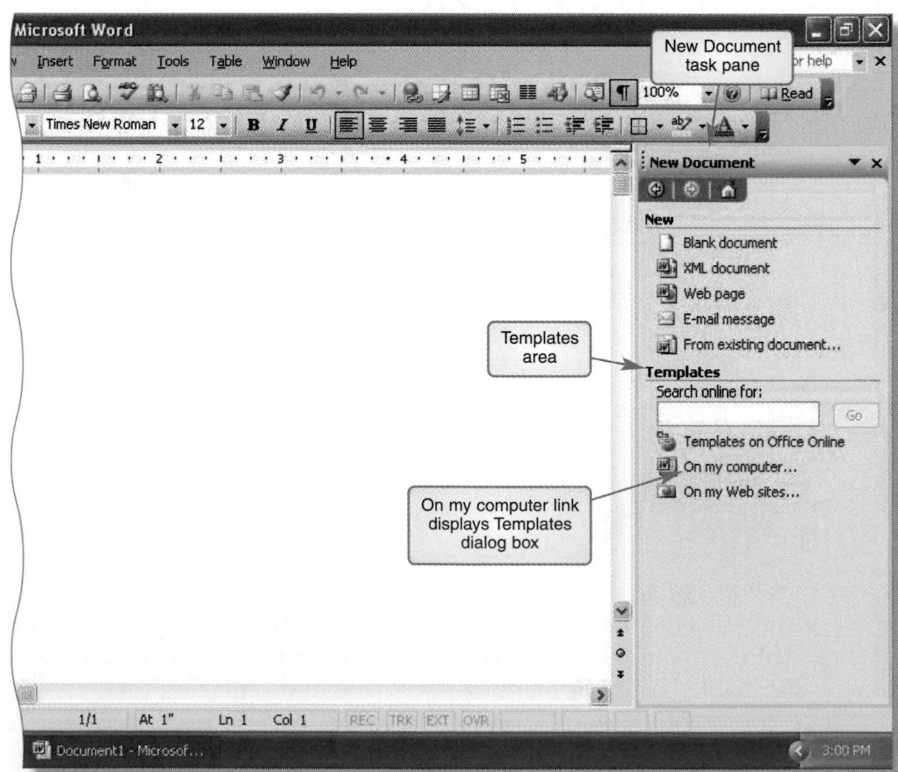

FIGURE 3-4

3

- **Click the On my computer link in the Templates area in the New Document task pane.**
- **When Word displays the Templates dialog box, click the Other Documents tab.**
- **Click the Resume Wizard icon.**

Word displays several wizard and template icons in the Other Documents sheet in the Templates dialog box (Figure 3-5). Icons without the word, wizard, are templates. If you click an icon, the Preview area shows a sample of the resulting document.

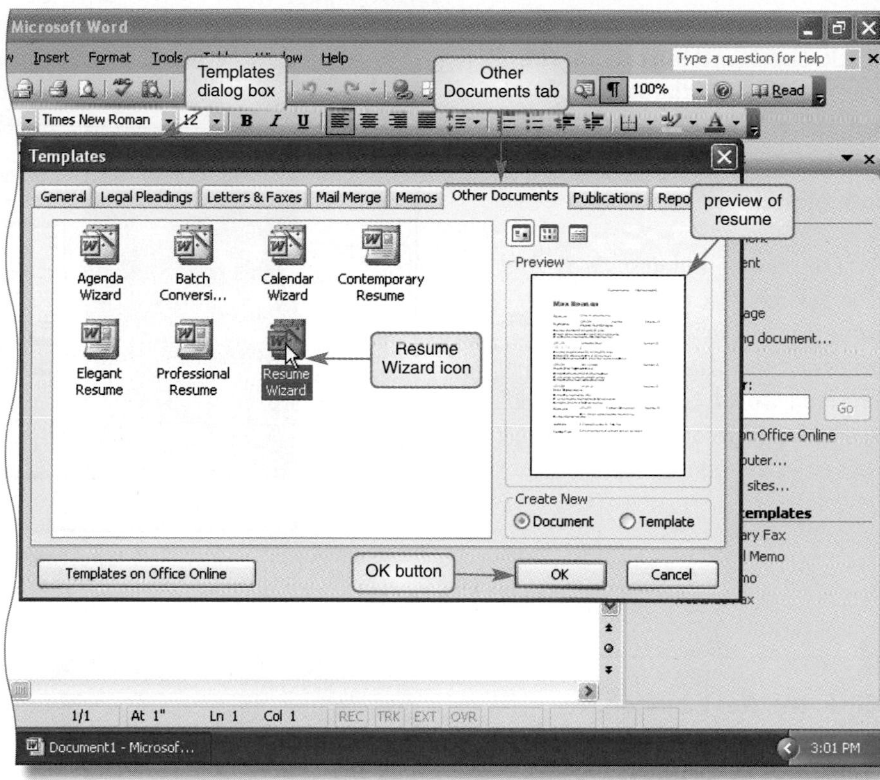

FIGURE 3-5

- **Click the OK button.**

After a few seconds, Word displays the Start panel in the Resume Wizard dialog box, informing you the Resume Wizard has started (Figure 3-6). This dialog box has a Microsoft Word Help button you can click to obtain help while using the wizard. When you create a document based on a wizard, Word creates a new document window, which is called Document2 in this figure.

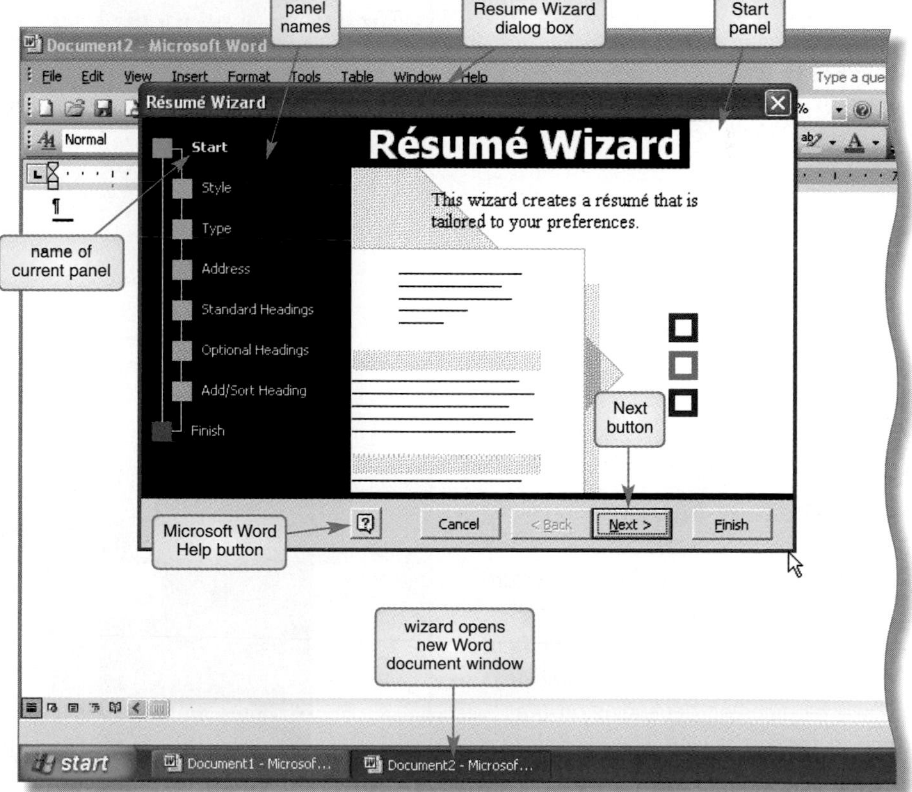

FIGURE 3-6

5

- **Click the Next button in the Resume Wizard dialog box.**
- **When the wizard displays the Style panel, if necessary, click Professional.**

The Style panel in the Resume Wizard dialog box requests the style of your resume (Figure 3-7). Three styles of wizards and templates are available in Word: Professional, Contemporary, and Elegant. A sample of each resume style is displayed in this panel.

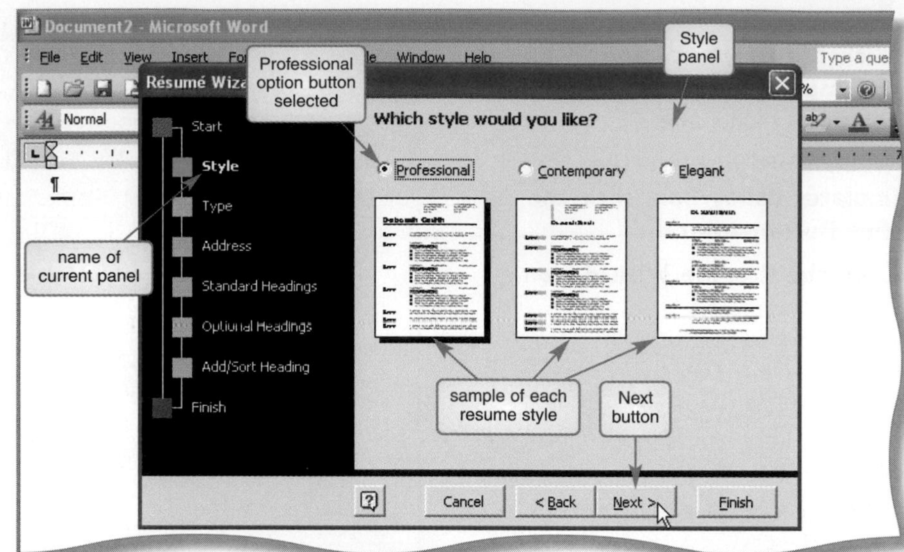

FIGURE 3-7

6

- **Click the Next button.**
- **When the wizard displays the Type panel, if necessary, click Entry-level resume.**

The Type panel in the Resume Wizard dialog box asks for the type of resume that you want to create (Figure 3-8).

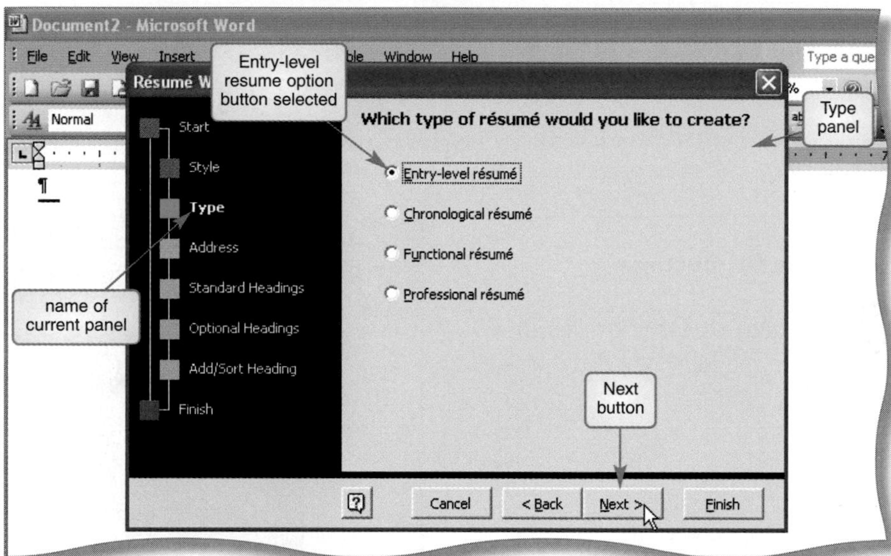

FIGURE 3-8

7

- **Click the Next button.**

The Address panel in the Resume Wizard dialog box requests name and mailing address information (Figure 3-9). The name displayed and selected in your Name text box will be different, depending on the name of the last person who used the Resume Wizard.

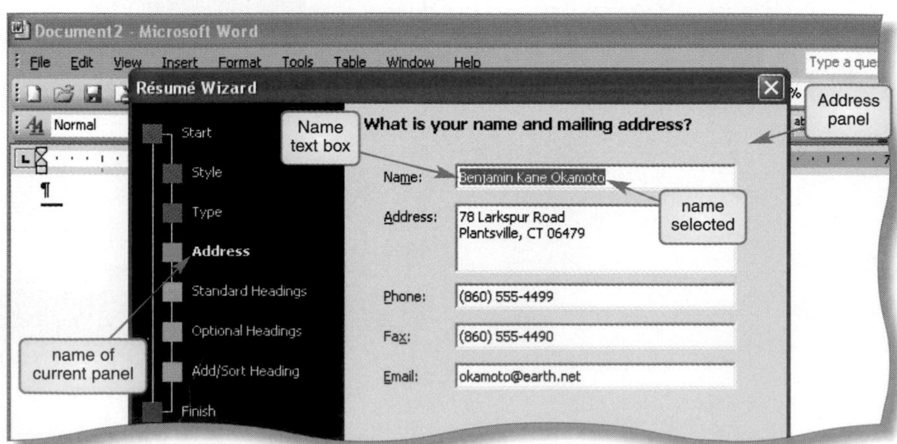

FIGURE 3-9

8

- **With the name in the Name text box selected, type** `Jasmine Leila Baskerville` **and then press the TAB key.**
- **Type** `54 Penny Road` **and then press the ENTER key.**
- **Type** `Lisle, IL 60532` **and then press the TAB key.**
- **Type** `(630) 555-6653` **and then press the TAB key.**
- **Type** `(630) 555-6672` **and then press the TAB key.**
- **Type** `jasmine@world.com` **as the e-mail address.**

As you type the new text, it automatically replaces any selected text (Figure 3-10).

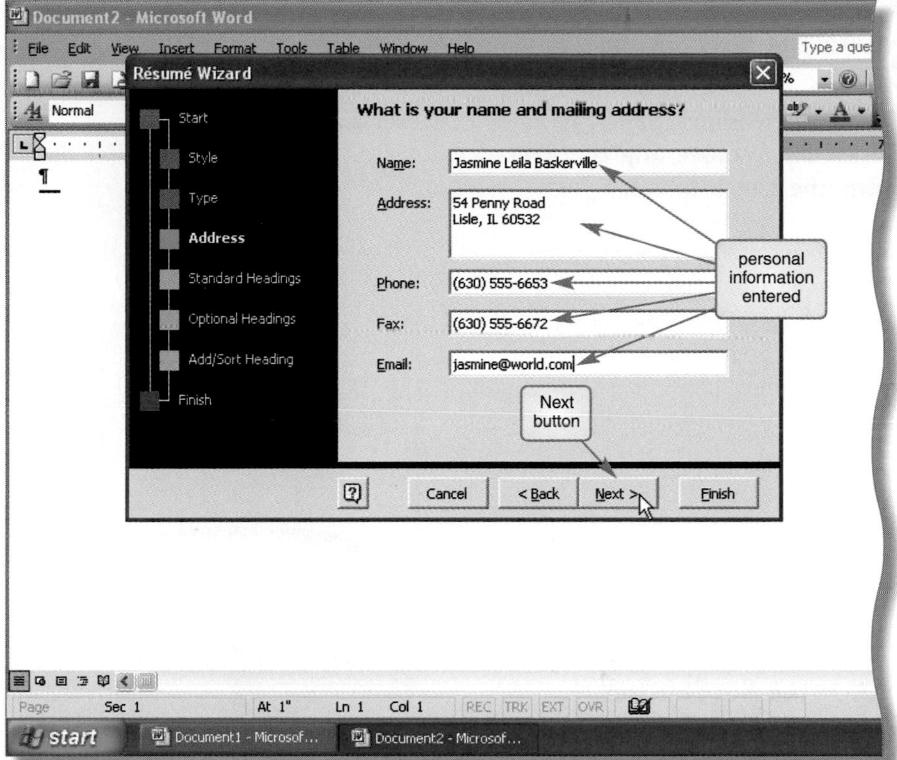

FIGURE 3-10

9

- **Click the Next button.**
- **When the wizard displays the Standard Headings panel, if necessary, click Hobbies and References to remove the check marks. All other check boxes should have check marks. If any do not, place a check mark in the check box by clicking it.**

The Standard Headings panel in the Resume Wizard dialog box requests the headings you want on your resume (Figure 3-11). You want all headings, except for these two: Hobbies and References.

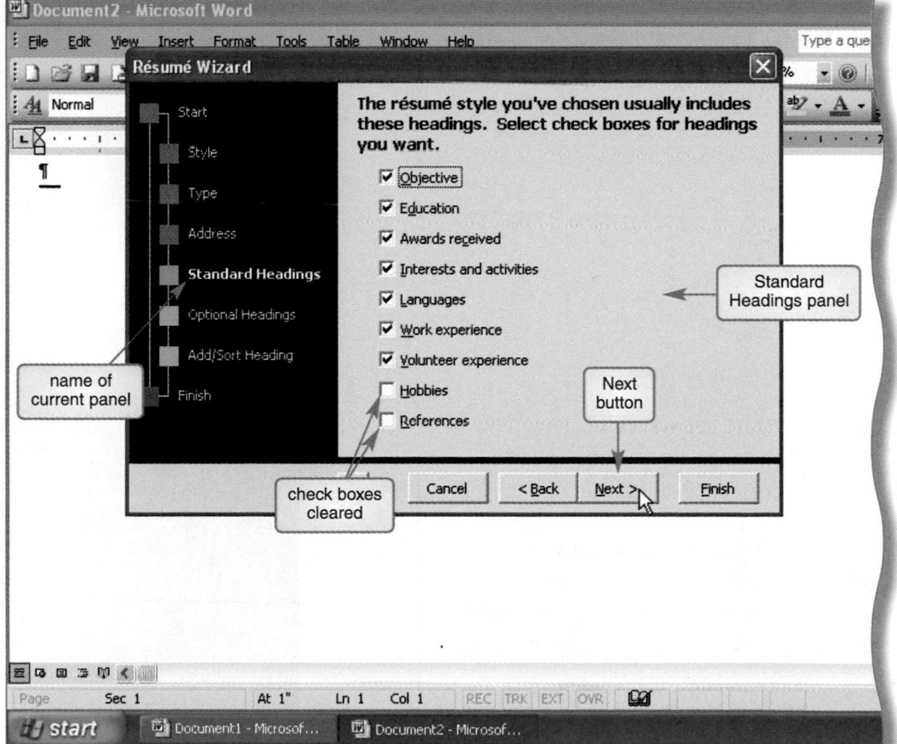

FIGURE 3-11

10

• **Click the Next button.**

• **When the wizard displays the Optional Headings panel, if necessary, remove any check marks from the check boxes.**

The Optional Headings panel in the Resume Wizard dialog box allows you to choose additional headings for your resume (Figure 3-12). All of these check boxes should be empty because none of these headings is on the resume in this project.

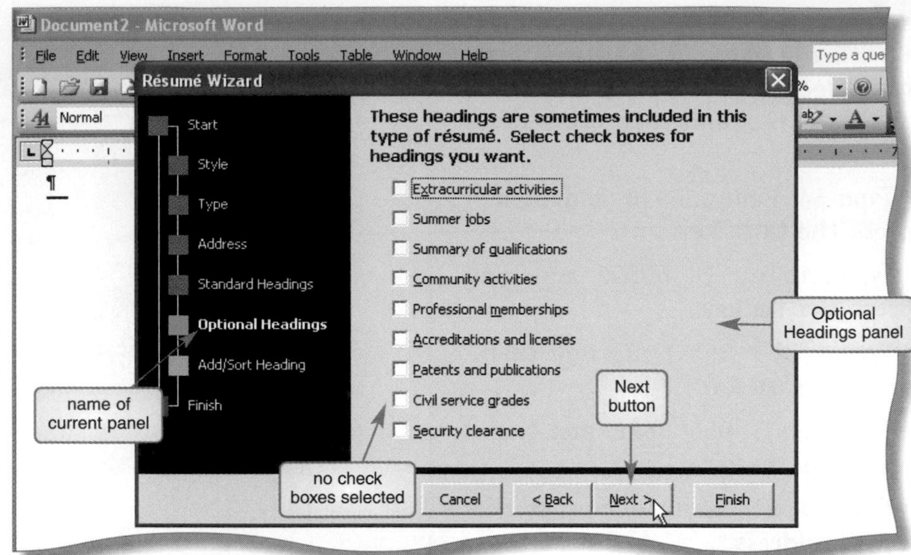

FIGURE 3-12

11

• **Click the Next button.**

• **When the wizard displays the Add/Sort Heading panel, type** `Relevant course work` **in the additional headings text box.**

The Add/Sort Heading panel in the Resume Wizard dialog box allows you to enter any additional headings you want on the resume (Figure 3-13).

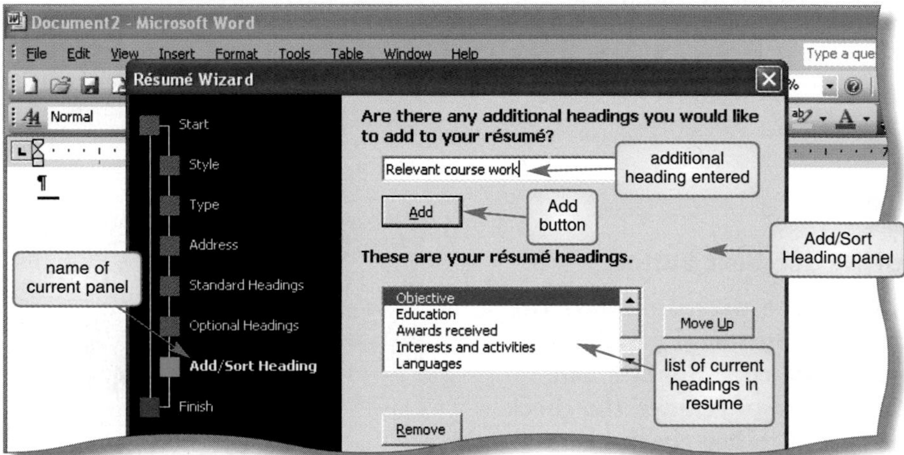

FIGURE 3-13

12

• **Click the Add button.**

• **Scroll to the bottom of the list of resume headings and then click Relevant course work.**

The Relevant course work heading is selected (Figure 3-14). You can rearrange the order of the headings on your resume by selecting a heading and then clicking the appropriate button (Move Up button or Move Down button).

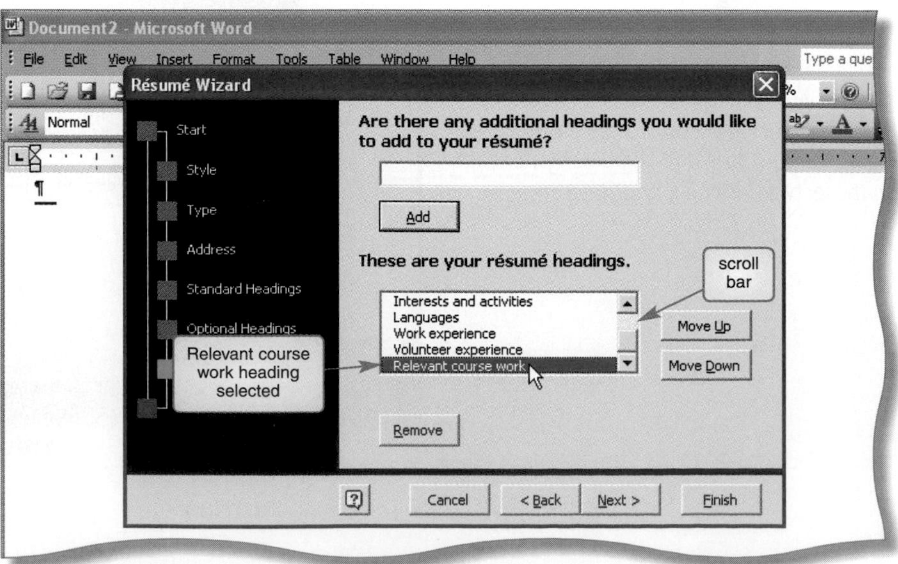

FIGURE 3-14

13

• **Click the Move Up button five times.**

The wizard moves the heading, Relevant course work, above the Awards received heading (Figure 3-15).

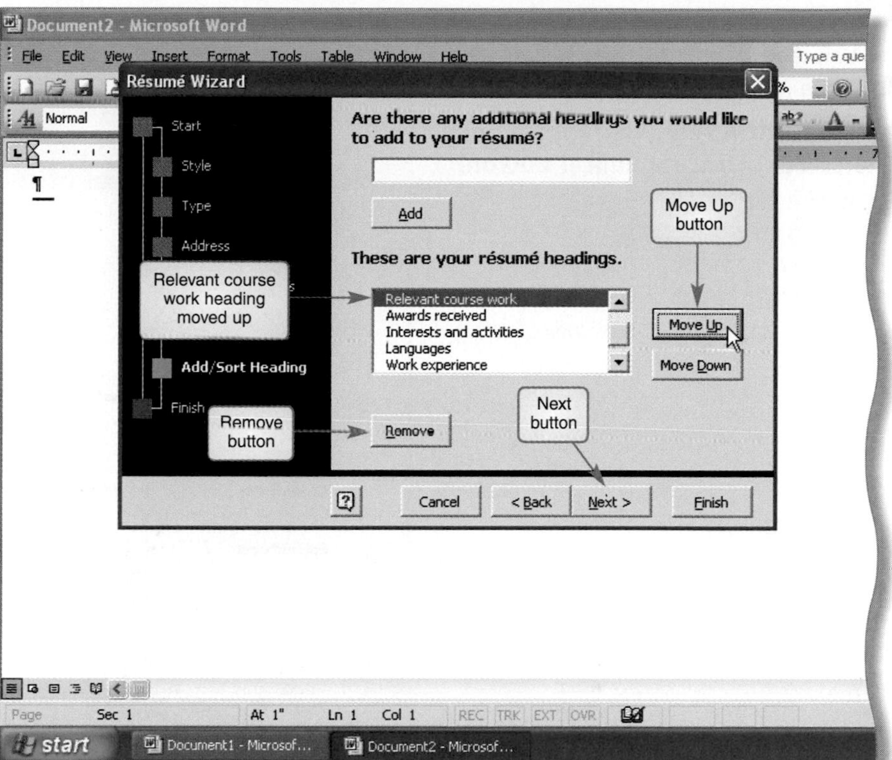

FIGURE 3-15

14

• **If the last person using the Resume Wizard included additional headings, you may have some unwanted headings. Your heading list should be as follows: Objective, Education, Relevant course work, Awards received, Interests and activities, Languages, Work experience, and Volunteer experience. If you have an additional heading(s), click the unwanted heading and then click the Remove button.**

15

• **Click the Next button.**

The Finish panel in the Resume Wizard dialog box indicates the wizard is ready to create your document (Figure 3-16).

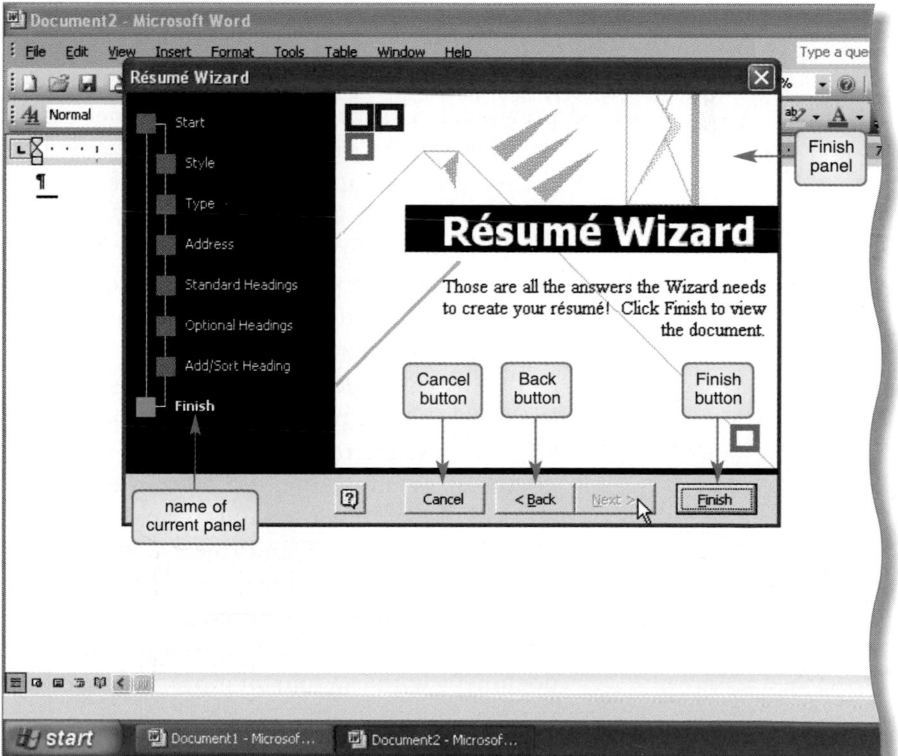

FIGURE 3-16

16

- **Click the Finish button in the Resume Wizard dialog box.**
- **If the Office Assistant appears on the screen, click its Cancel button.**

Word uses a template of an entry-level professional style resume to format a resume on the screen (Figure 3-17). You are to personalize the resume as indicated.

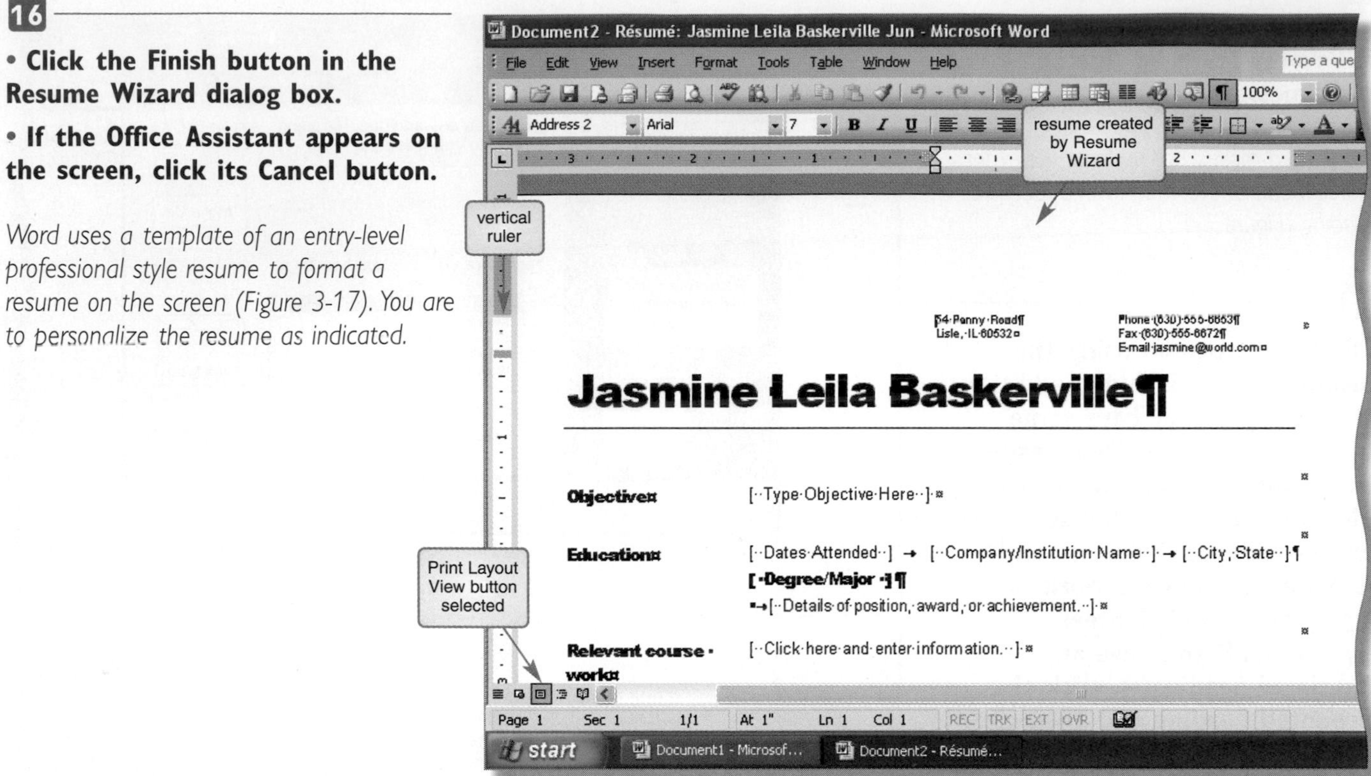

FIGURE 3-17

When you create a resume using the Resume Wizard (Figure 3-16 on the previous page), you can click the panel name or the Back button in any panel of the Resume Wizard dialog box to change the previously selected options. To exit from the Resume Wizard and return to the document window without creating the resume, click the Cancel button in any panel of the Resume Wizard dialog box.

In addition to the Resume Wizard, Word provides many other wizards to assist you in creating documents: agenda for a meeting, calendar, envelope, fax cover sheet, legal pleading, letter, mailing label, and memorandum.

Word displays the resume in the document window in print layout view. You can tell that the document window is in print layout view by looking at the screen (Figure 3-17). In print layout view, the Print Layout View button on the horizontal scroll bar is selected. Also, a vertical ruler is displayed at the left edge of the document window, in addition to the horizontal ruler at the top of the window.

The Word screen was in normal view while creating documents in Project 1 and for most of Project 2. In Project 2, the Word window switched to print layout view when the header was created. In both normal view and print layout view, you can type and edit text. The difference is that **print layout view** shows you an exact view of the printed page. That is, in print layout view, Word places a piece of paper in the document window, showing precisely the positioning of the text, margins, headers, footers, and footnotes.

To display more of the document on the screen in print layout view, you can hide the white space at the top and bottom of the pages and the gray space between pages. The next steps show how to hide the white space, if your screen displays it.

To Hide White Space

1

- **Point to the top of the page in the document window until the Hide White Space button appears.**

The mouse pointer changes to the Hide White Space button when positioned at the top of the page (Figure 3-18).

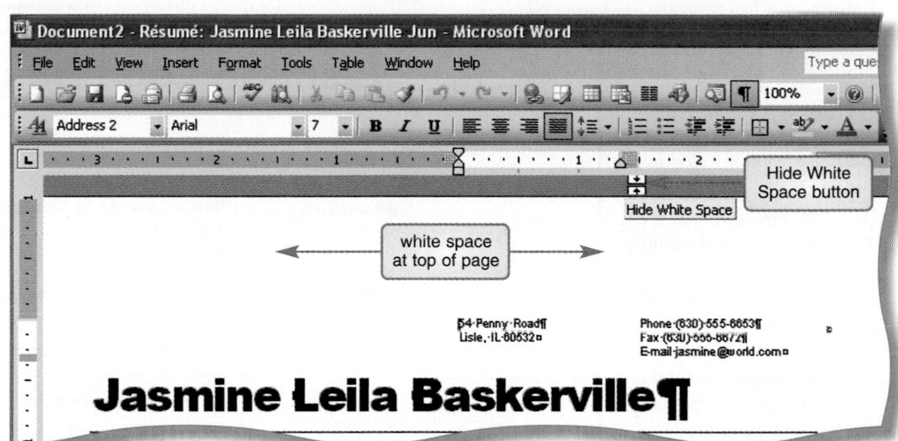

FIGURE 3-18

2

- **Click the Hide White Space button.**

Word removes white space, which causes the page to move up in the document window (Figure 3-19).

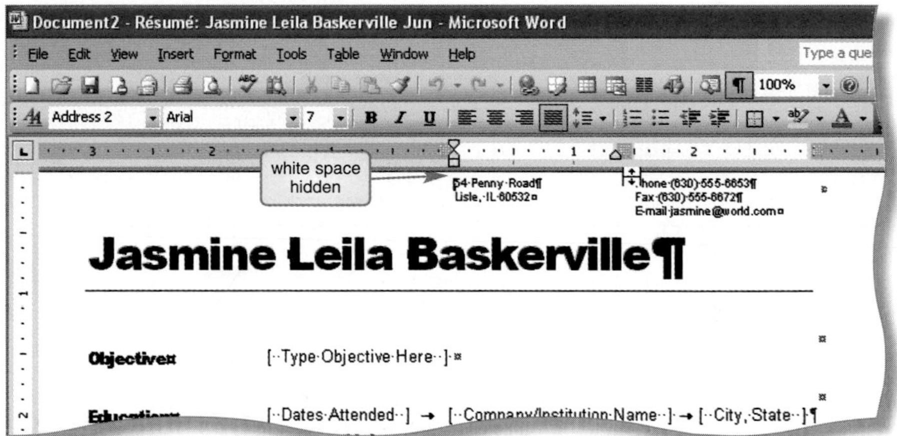

FIGURE 3-19

If you wanted to show the white space again, you would point between two pages and click when the mouse pointer changes to a Show White Space button.

To see the entire resume created by the Resume Wizard, print the document shown in the Word window, as described in the following steps.

To Print the Resume Created by the Resume Wizard

1. **Ready the printer and then click the Print button on the Standard toolbar.**
2. **When the printer stops, retrieve the hard copy resume from the printer.**

The printed resume is shown in Figure 3-20 on the next page.

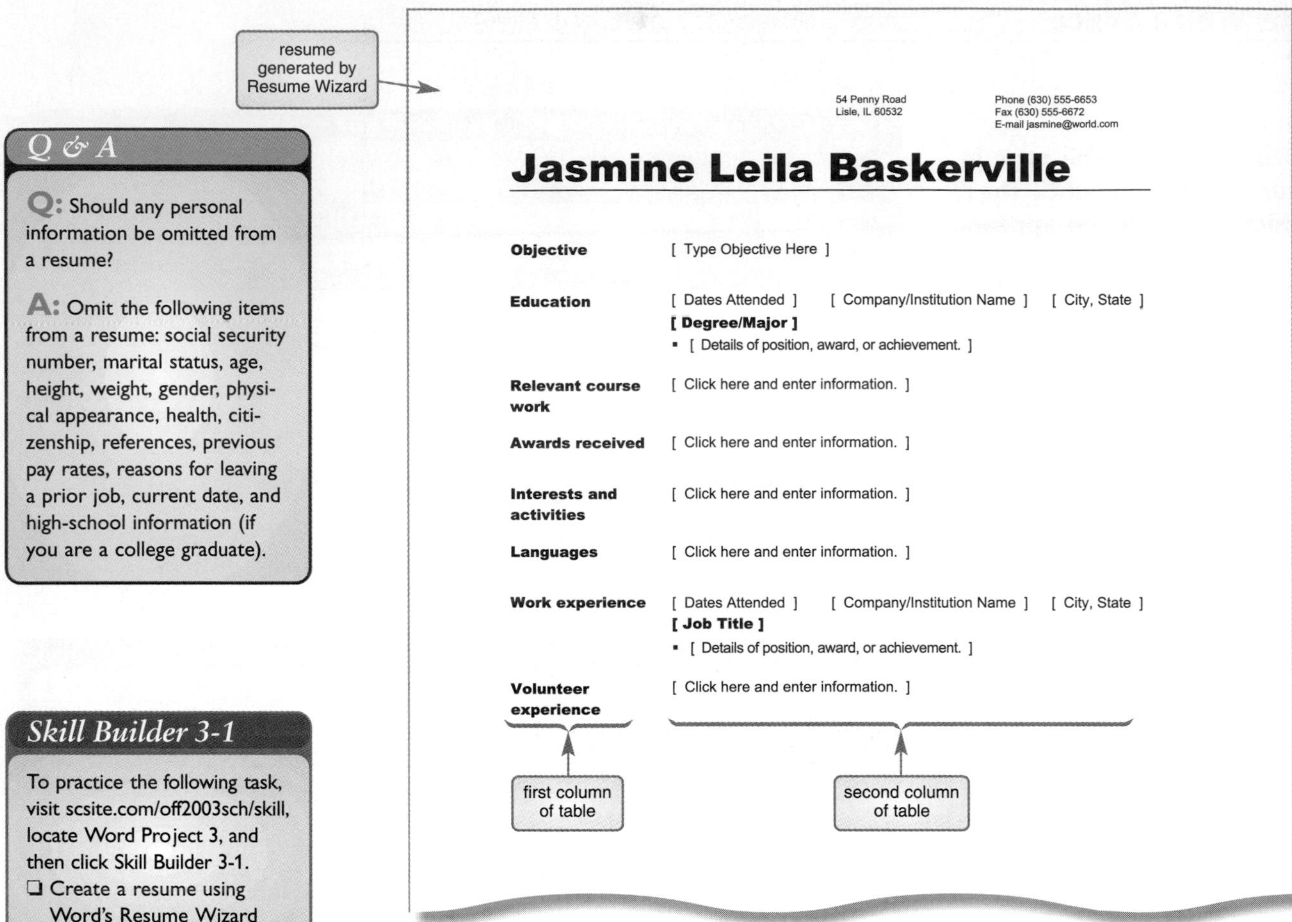

FIGURE 3-20

> *Q & A*
>
> **Q:** Should any personal information be omitted from a resume?
>
> **A:** Omit the following items from a resume: social security number, marital status, age, height, weight, gender, physical appearance, health, citizenship, references, previous pay rates, reasons for leaving a prior job, current date, and high-school information (if you are a college graduate).

> *Skill Builder 3-1*
>
> To practice the following task, visit scsite.com/off2003sch/skill, locate Word Project 3, and then click Skill Builder 3-1.
>
> ❑ Create a resume using Word's Resume Wizard

Personalizing the Resume

The next step is to personalize the resume. Where Word has indicated, you type the objective, education, relevant course work, awards received, interests and activities, languages, work experience, and volunteer experience next to the respective headings. The following pages show how to personalize the resume generated by the Resume Wizard.

Tables

When the Resume Wizard prepares a resume, it arranges the body of the resume as a table. A Word **table** is a collection of rows and columns. As shown in Figure 3-21, the first column of the table in the resume contains the section headings (Objective, Education, Relevant course work, Awards received, Interests and activities, Languages, Work experience, and Volunteer experience). The second column of the table contains the details for each of these sections. Thus, this table contains two columns. It also contains eight rows — one row for each section of the resume.

> *Q & A*
>
> **Q:** How do I select elements of a table?
>
> **A:** To select a single cell in a table, click to the left of the cell. To select an entire row, click to the left of the row. To select an entire column, click the column's top border. To add a row or column to the middle of a table, click where you want to insert the row or column, click Table on the menu bar, point to Insert, and then click the appropriate command.

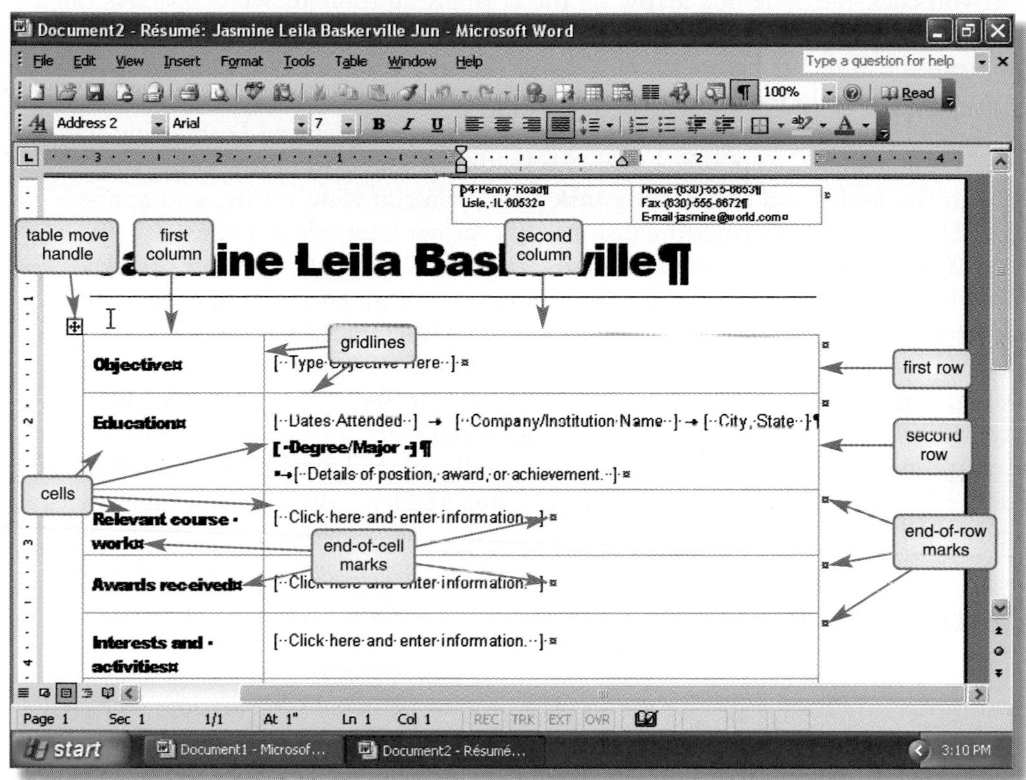

FIGURE 3-21

Q & A

Q: Why does the ruler look different when the insertion point is in a table?

A: When the insertion point is in a table, the ruler shows the boundaries of each column in the table. For example, in Figure 3-21, the address information at the top of the resume is a separate table of one row and two columns. The ruler show the width of each column.

The intersection of a row and a column is called a **cell**, and cells are filled with text. Each cell has an **end-of-cell mark**, which is a formatting mark that assists you with selecting and formatting cells. Recall that formatting marks do not print on a hard copy.

To see the rows, columns, and cells clearly in a Word table, some users prefer to show gridlines. As illustrated in Figure 3-21, **gridlines** help identify the rows and columns in a table. If you want to display gridlines in a table, position the insertion point somewhere in the table, click Table on the menu bar, and then click Show Gridlines. If you want to hide the gridlines, click somewhere in the table, click Table on the menu bar, and then click Hide Gridlines.

You can resize a table, add or delete rows or columns in a table, and format a table. When you point to the upper-left corner of the table, the table move handle appears. Using the table move handle, you can select or move a table. To select a table, click the table move handle; to move the table to a new location, drag the table move handle. These and other features of tables are discussed in more depth later in this project.

Styles

When you use a wizard to create a document, Word formats the document using styles. As discussed in Project 2, a **style** is a named group of formatting characteristics that you can apply to text. The Style box on the Formatting toolbar displays the name of the style associated with the location of the insertion point or selection. You can identify many of the characteristics assigned to a style by looking at the Formatting toolbar. For example, in Figure 3-22 on the next page, the characters in the selected paragraph are formatted with the Objective style, which uses 10-point Arial font.

Q: How can I apply a different style to text at the location of the insertion point?

A: The Styles and Formatting task pane displays the formats applied to text at the location of the insertion point. To apply a different style, click the desired style in the Pick formatting to apply list in the Styles and Formatting task pane. Or, click the Style box arrow on the Formatting toolbar and then click the desired style.

If you click the Style box arrow on the Formatting toolbar, Word displays the list of styles associated with the current document. You also can select the appropriate style from the Style list before typing text so that the text you type will be formatted according to the selected style.

Another way to work with styles is by clicking the Styles and Formatting button on the Formatting toolbar, which displays the Styles and Formatting task pane. Through the **Styles and Formatting task pane**, you can view, create, and apply styles. The Styles and Formatting task pane is shown later when it is used.

In Word, four basic styles exist: paragraph styles, character styles, list styles, and table styles. **Paragraph styles** affect formatting of an entire paragraph, whereas **character styles** affect formats of only selected characters. **List styles** affect alignment and fonts in a numbered or bulleted list, and **table styles** affect the borders, shading, alignment, and fonts in a Word table. In the Style list and Styles and Formatting task pane, paragraph style names usually are followed by a proofreader's paragraph mark (¶); character style names usually are followed by an underlined letter a (a); list styles usually are followed by a bulleted list icon (☰); and table styles usually are followed by a table icon (⊞).

Selecting and Replacing Text

The next step in personalizing the resume is to select text that the Resume Wizard inserted into the resume and replace it with personal information. The first heading on the resume is the objective. You enter the objective where the Resume Wizard inserted the words, Type Objective Here, which is called **placeholder text.**

To replace text in Word, select the text to be removed and then type the desired text. To select the placeholder text, Type Objective Here, you click it. Then, type the objective. As soon as you begin typing, Word deletes the selected placeholder text. Thus, you do not need to delete the selection before you begin typing.

The following steps show how to enter the objective into the resume.

To Select and Replace Placeholder Text

1

- **Click the placeholder text, Type Objective Here.**

Word selects the placeholder text in the resume (Figure 3-22). Notice the style is Objective in the Style box on the Formatting toolbar.

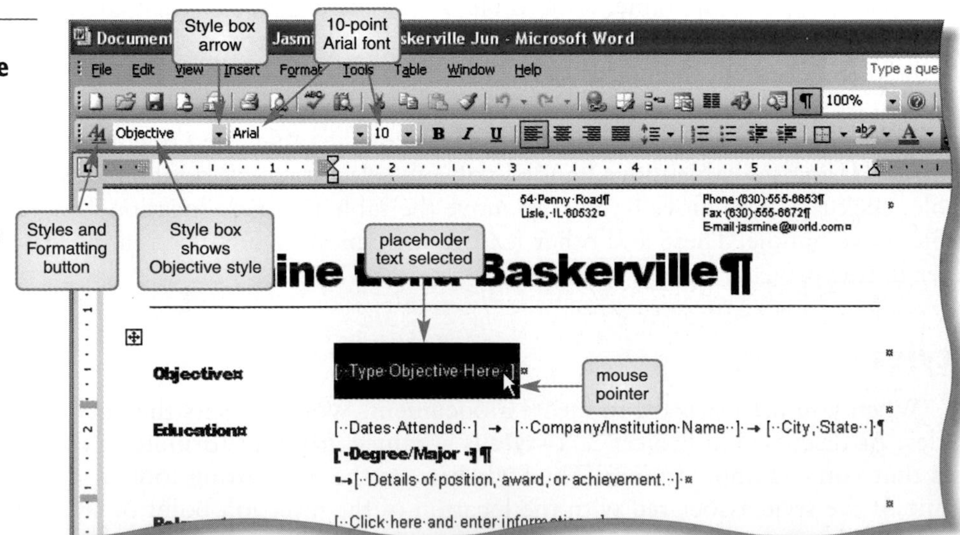

FIGURE 3-22

2

- **Type** `To obtain a part-time entry-level accounting clerk position with an accounting firm in the Chicagoland area.`

Word replaces the selected placeholder text, Type Objective Here, with the typed objective (Figure 3-23). Your document may wordwrap differently depending on the type of printer you are using.

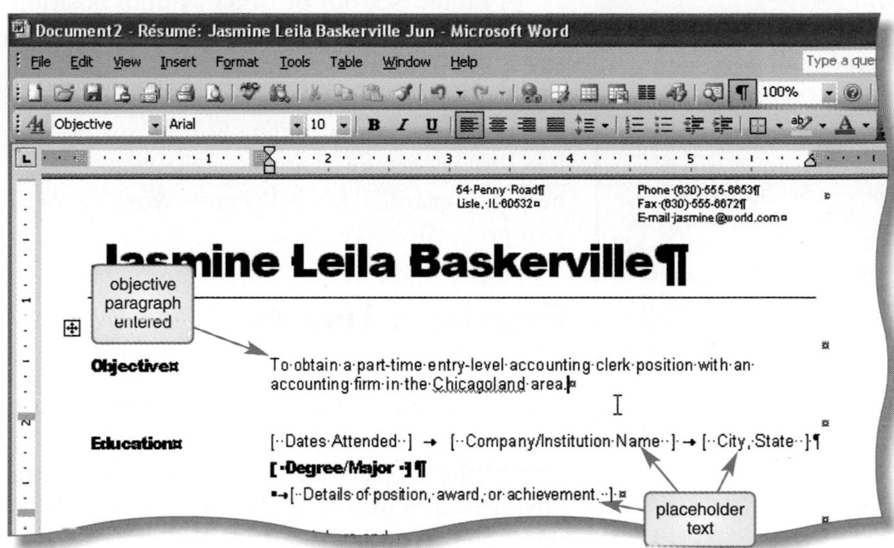

FIGURE 3-23

The next step in personalizing the resume is to replace the placeholder text in the education section of the resume with your own words and phrases, as described in the following steps.

To Select and Replace More Placeholder Text

1 **If necessary, scroll down to display the entire education section of the resume. Click, or if necessary drag through, the placeholder text, Dates Attended. Type** `2003-2007` **and then click the placeholder text, Company/Institution Name.**

2 **Type** `Lincoln High School` **and then click the placeholder text, City, State. Type** `Lisle, IL` **and then click the placeholder text, Degree/Major. Type** `Advanced Placement Program` **and then click the placeholder text, Details of position, award, or achievement.**

3 **Type** `Grade Point Average, 3.96/4.00` **and then press the ENTER key. Type** `Attending Hillside College in Fall 2008` **as the last item in the list.**

The education section is entered (Figure 3-24).

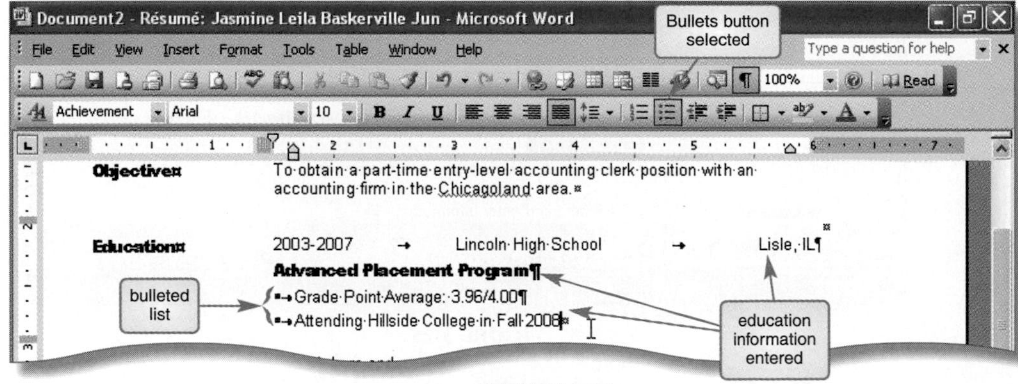

FIGURE 3-24

Q & A

Q: Can I change the look of a bullet character?

A: Yes. To apply a different bullet character to selected paragraphs, click Format on the menu bar, click Bullets and Numbering, click the Bulleted tab, click the desired bullet style, and then click the OK button. For additional bullet styles, click the Customize button in the Bullets and Numbering dialog box.

A **bullet** is a dot or other symbol positioned at the beginning of a paragraph. A **bulleted list** is a list of paragraphs that each begin with a bullet character. For example, the list of degrees in the education section of the resume is a bulleted list (Figure 3-24 on the previous page). When the insertion point is in a paragraph containing a bullet, the Bullets button on the Formatting toolbar is selected. In a bulleted list, each time you press the ENTER key, a bullet displays at the beginning of the new paragraph. This is because Word carries forward paragraph formatting when you press the ENTER key.

Entering a Line Break

The next step in personalizing the resume is to enter four lines of text in the relevant course work section. The style used for the characters in the relevant course work section of the resume is the Objective style. A paragraph formatting characteristic of the Objective style is that when you press the ENTER key, the insertion point advances downward at least 11 points, which leaves nearly an entire blank line between each paragraph.

You want the lines within the relevant course work section to be close to each other, as shown in Figure 3-1 on page WD 139. Thus, you will not press the ENTER key between each line. Instead, you press SHIFT+ENTER to create a **line break**, which advances the insertion point to the beginning of the next physical line.

The following steps show how to enter text in the relevant course work section using a line break, instead of a paragraph break, between each line.

To Enter a Line Break

1

- **If necessary, scroll down to display the relevant course work section of the resume.**
- **In the relevant course work section, click the placeholder text, Click here and enter information.**
- **Type** `Accounting I through IV, Personal Financial Management,` **and then press SHIFT+ENTER.**

*Word inserts a **line break character**, which is a formatting mark for a line break at the end of a line, and moves the insertion point to the beginning of the next physical line (Figure 3-25).*

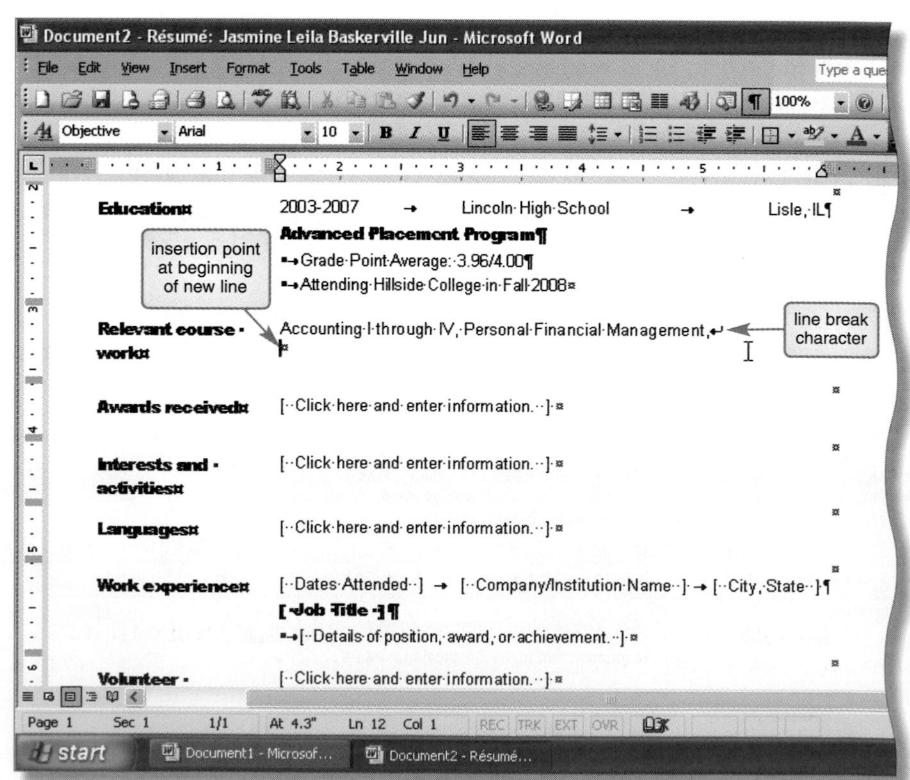

FIGURE 3-25

2

- **Type** Applied Economics, Business and Personal Law, **and then press SHIFT+ENTER.**
- **Type** Computer Applications I and II, Business Computer Programming, **and then press SHIFT+ENTER.**
- **Type** Marketing I and II, Multimedia Presentations **as the last entry. Do not press SHIFT+ENTER at the end of this line.**

The relevant course work section is entered (Figure 3-26).

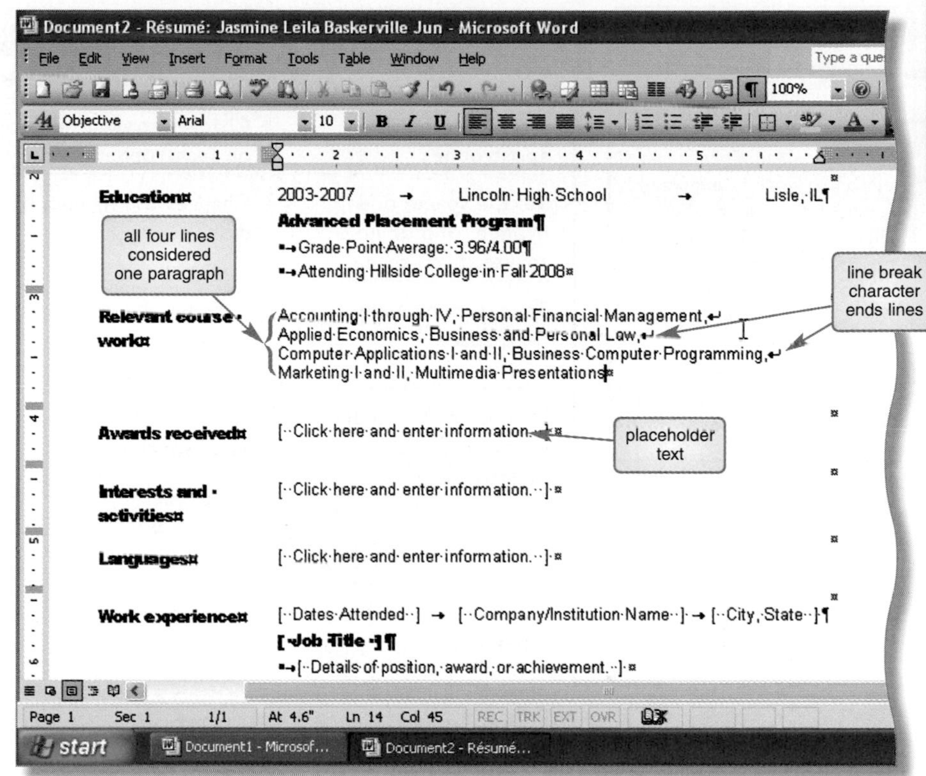

FIGURE 3-26

The next step is to enter the first two awards in the awards received section of the resume.

To Enter More Text with Line Breaks

1 **If necessary, scroll down to display the awards received section of the resume. In the awards received section, click the placeholder text, Click here and enter information. Type** Distinguished Honors, every quarter **and then press SHIFT+ENTER.**

2 **Type** Business Department Outstanding Senior, 2006-2007 **and then press SHIFT+ENTER.**

The first two awards are entered in the awards received section (shown in Figure 3-27 on the next page).

AutoFormat As You Type

As you type text in a document, Word automatically formats it for you. Table 3-1 on the next page outlines commonly used AutoFormat As You Type options and their results.

Q & A

Q: What if an AutoFormat option does not work?

A: For an AutoFormat option to work as expected, it must be turned on. To check if an AutoFormat option is enabled, click Tools on the menu bar, click AutoCorrect Options, click the AutoFormat As You Type tab, select the appropriate check boxes, and then click the OK button.

Table 3-1 Commonly Used AutoFormat As You Type Options

TYPED TEXT	AUTOFORMAT FEATURE	EXAMPLE
Quotation marks or apostrophes	Changes straight quotation marks or apostrophes to curly ones	"the" becomes “the”
Text, a space, one hyphen, one or no spaces, text, space	Changes the hyphen to an en dash	ages 20 - 45 becomes ages 20 – 45
Text, two hyphens, text, space	Changes the two hyphens to an em dash	Two types--yellow and red becomes Two types—yellow and red
Web or e-mail address followed by space or ENTER key	Formats Web or e-mail address as a hyperlink	www.scsite.com becomes www.scsite.com
Three hyphens, underscores, equal signs, asterisks, tildes, or number signs and then ENTER key	Places a border above a paragraph	--- This line becomes ——— This line
Number followed by a period, hyphen, right parenthesis, or greater than sign and then a space or tab followed by text	Creates a numbered list when you press the ENTER key	1. Word 2. Excel becomes 1. Word 2. Excel
Asterisk, hyphen, or greater than sign and then a space or tab followed by text	Creates a bulleted list when you press the ENTER key	* Standard toolbar * Formatting toolbar becomes • Standard toolbar • Formatting toolbar
Fraction and then a space or hyphen	Converts the entry to a fraction-like notation	1/2 becomes ½
Ordinal and then a space or hyphen	Makes the ordinal a superscript	3rd becomes 3rd

The next step in this project is to enter an ordinal (1st) and see how Word automatically makes the ordinal a superscript.

To AutoFormat As You Type

1

- **Type** `Finance Club Challenge, 1st` **(Figure 3-27).**

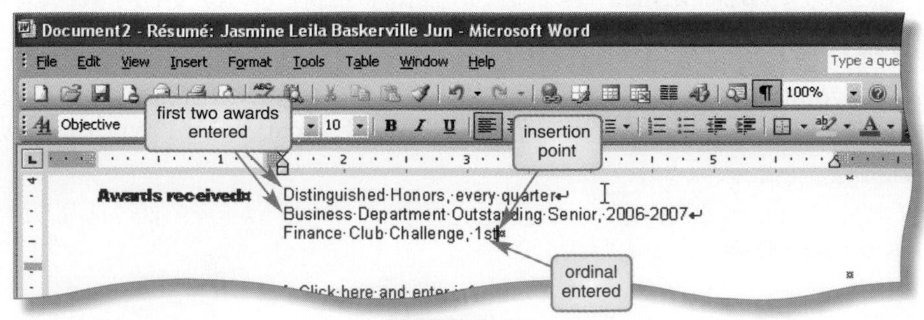

FIGURE 3-27

2

• **Press the SPACEBAR.**

• **Type** `Place, 2006` **as the end of the award.**

Word automatically converts the st in 1st to a superscript (Figure 3-28).

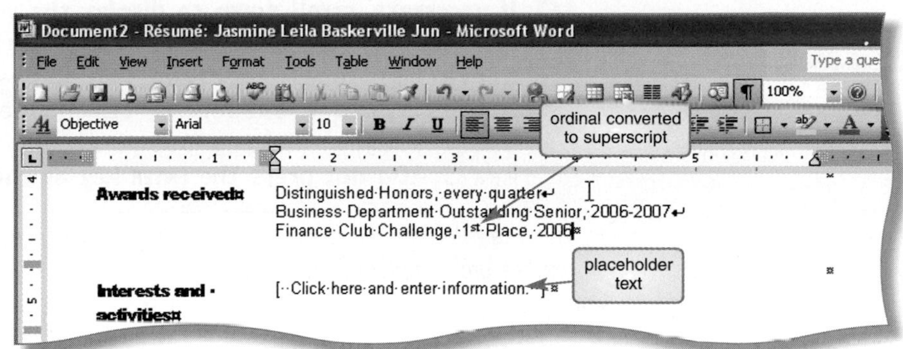

FIGURE 3-28

The next step is to enter the remaining text for the resume, as described below.

To Enter the Remaining Sections of the Resume

1. **If necessary, scroll down to display the interests and activities section of the resume. Click the placeholder text, Click here and enter information. Type** `Lincoln High School Soccer Team, co-captain` **and then press SHIFT+ENTER.**
2. **Type** `Student Government Association, treasurer` **and then press SHIFT+ENTER.**
3. **Type** `French Club, president` **and then press SHIFT+ENTER.**
4. **Type** `National Honor Society, member` **as the last activity. Do not press SHIFT+ENTER at the end of this line.**
5. **If necessary, scroll down to display the languages section of the resume. Click the placeholder text, Click here and enter information. Type** `Proficient in English and French` **and then press SHIFT+ENTER.**
6. **Type** `Working knowledge of Spanish` **and then press SHIFT+ENTER.**
7. **Type** `Proficient in sign language` **as the last language. Do not press SHIFT+ENTER at the end of this line.**
8. **If necessary, scroll down to display the work experience section of the resume. Click, or if necessary drag through, the placeholder text, Dates Attended. Type** `2005-2007` **as the years.**
9. **Click the placeholder text, Company/Institution Name. Type** `Brims and Sons Accounting` **and then click the placeholder text, City, State. Type** `Lisle, IL` **and then click the placeholder text, Job Title. Type** `Intern` **as the title.**
10. **Click the placeholder text, Details of position, award, or achievement. Type** `Assist CPAs in tax preparation activities for both individuals and businesses` **and then press the ENTER key.**
11. **Type** `Post journal entries, prepare balance sheets and income statements, balance checkbook registers, and pay bills` **and then press the ENTER key.**
12. **Type** `Use the computer extensively in work-related activities` **as the last item in the list.**

Q & A

Q: Should my resume contain references?

A: Do not list references on your resume, and do not state "References Available Upon Request." Employers assume you will give references, if asked, and this information simply clutters a resume. Often you are asked to list references on your application. Be sure to give your references a copy of your resume.

13 **If necessary, scroll down to display the volunteer experience section of the resume. Click the placeholder text, Click here and enter information. Type** `Serve the local American Red Cross as a multilingual volunteer. Duties include answering telephones, translating communications and messages, making posters, and serving refreshments and/or meals.` **Do not press the ENTER key at the end of this line.**

The interests and activities, languages, work experience, and volunteer experience sections of the resume are complete (Figure 3-29).

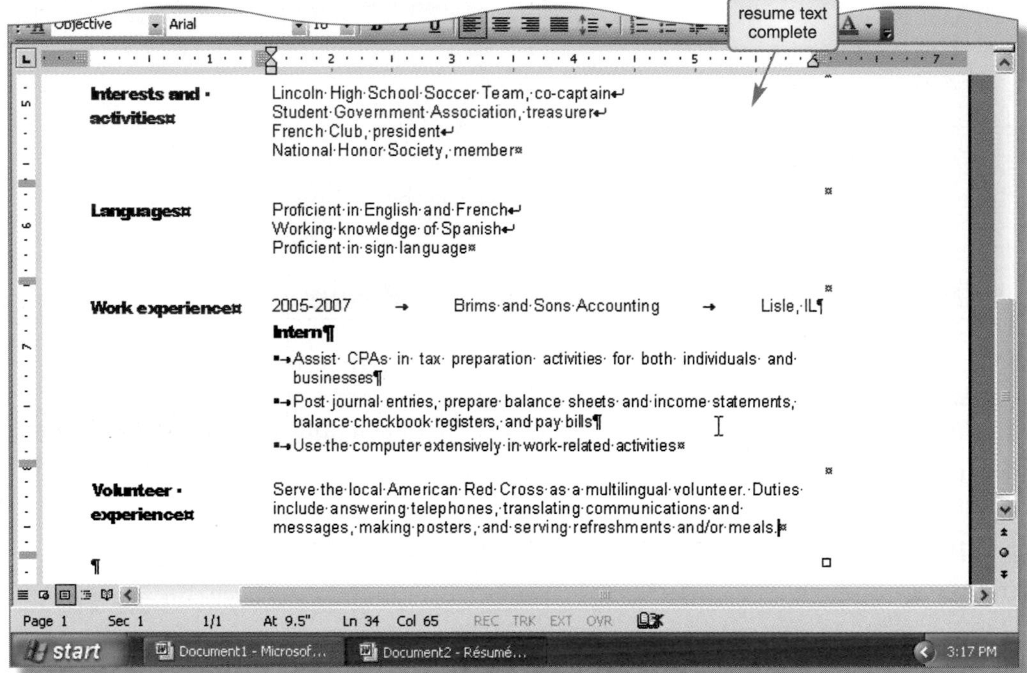

FIGURE 3-29

Viewing and Printing the Resume in Print Preview

To see exactly how a document will look when you print it, you could display it in print preview. **Print preview** displays the entire document in reduced size on the Word screen. In print preview, you can edit and format text, adjust margins, view multiple pages, reduce the document to fit on a single page, and print the document.

The following steps show how to view and print the resume in print preview.

To Print Preview a Document

1

• **Point to the Print Preview button on the Standard toolbar (Figure 3-30).**

FIGURE 3-30

2

• **Click the Print Preview button.**

Word displays the document in print preview (Figure 3-31). The Print Preview toolbar is displayed below the menu bar; the Standard and Formatting toolbars disappear from the screen.

3

• **Click the Print button on the Print Preview toolbar.**

• **Click the Close Preview button on the Print Preview toolbar.**

Word prints the resume, as shown in Figure 3-1 on page WD 139. When you close print preview, Word redisplays the resume in the document window.

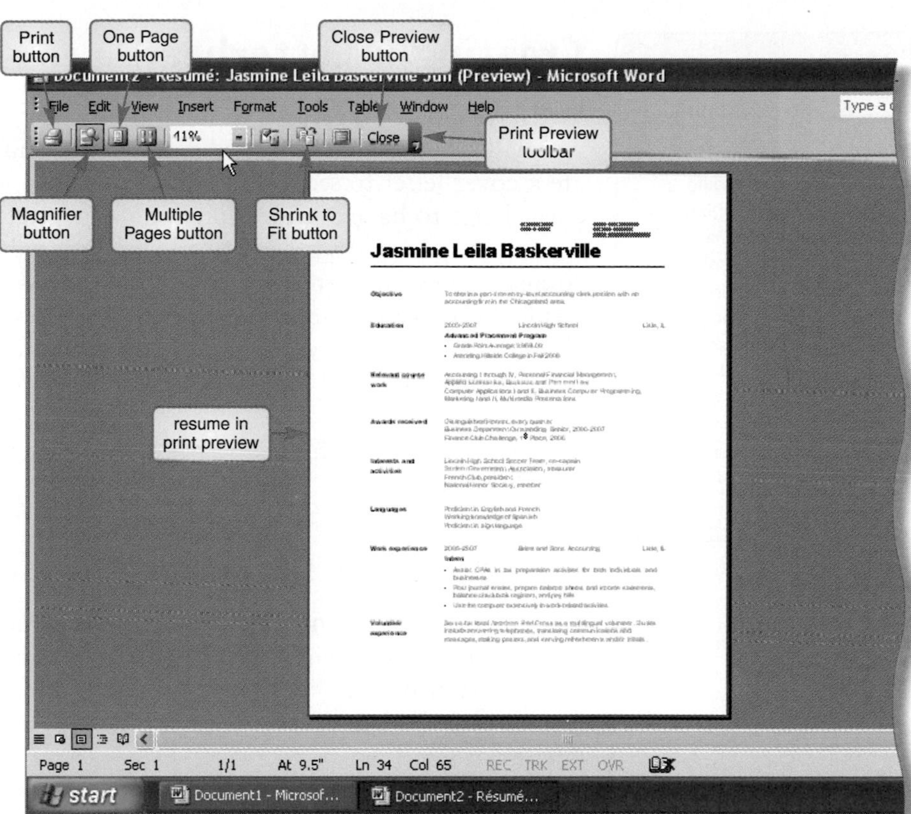

FIGURE 3-31

Saving the Resume

The resume now is complete. Thus, you should save it. For a detailed example of the procedure summarized below, refer to pages WD 28 through WD 30 in Project 1.

To Save a Document

1. **Connect a USB flash drive to one of the computer's USB ports.**
2. **Click the Save button on the Standard toolbar.**
3. **Type** `Baskerville Resume` **in the File name text box. Do not press the ENTER key.**
4. **Click the Save in box arrow and then click UDISK 2.0 (E:). (Your USB flash drive may have a different name and letter.)**
5. **Click the Save button in the Save As dialog box.**

Word saves the document on a USB flash drive with the file name, Baskerville Resume.

Do not close the Baskerville Resume. You will use it again later in this project to copy the address, telephone, fax, and e-mail information.

Q & A

Q: What is the purpose of the buttons identified on the Print Preview toolbar in Figure 3-31?

A: If the page is not centered in the Print Preview window, click the One Page button on the Print Preview toolbar. With the Magnifier button on the Print Preview toolbar selected, you can click in the document to zoom in or out. Magnifying a page does not affect the printed document. To edit a document, click the Magnifier button to deselect it and then edit the text. If a document spills onto a second page by a line or two, click the Shrink to Fit button and Word will try to fit it all on a single page.

Skill Builder 3-2

To practice the following tasks, visit scsite.com/off2003sch/skill, locate Word Project 3, and then click Skill Builder 3-2.

- ❑ Select and replace placeholder text
- ❑ Enter a line break
- ❑ Use print preview

Q & A

Q: What information should a letterhead contain?

A: A letterhead should contain the following information: complete legal name of the company, group, or individual; full street address including building, room, suite number, or post office box; city; state; and postal code. Some letterheads also include a logo, department name, telephone and fax number, Web address, and e-mail address.

Creating a Letterhead

You have created a resume to send to prospective employers. Along with the resume, you will enclose a personalized cover letter. Thus, the next step in Project 3 is to create a cover letter to send with the resume to a potential employer. You would like the cover letter to have a professional looking letterhead (Figure 3-2a on page WD 140).

In many businesses, letterhead is preprinted on stationery that everyone in a company uses for correspondence. For personal letters, the cost of preprinted letterhead can be high. An alternative is to create your own letterhead and save it in a file. At a later time, when you want to create a letter using the letterhead, simply open the letterhead file and then save the file with a new name — to preserve the original letterhead file.

The steps on the following pages illustrate how to use Word to create a personal letterhead file.

Opening a New Document Window

The resume currently is displayed in the document window. The resume document should remain open because you intend to use it again during this Word session. That is, you will be working with two documents at the same time: the resume and the letterhead. Word will display each of these documents in a separate document window.

The following step opens a new document window for the letterhead file.

To Open a New Document Window

1

• **Click the New Blank Document button on the Standard toolbar.**

Word opens a new document window (Figure 3-32).

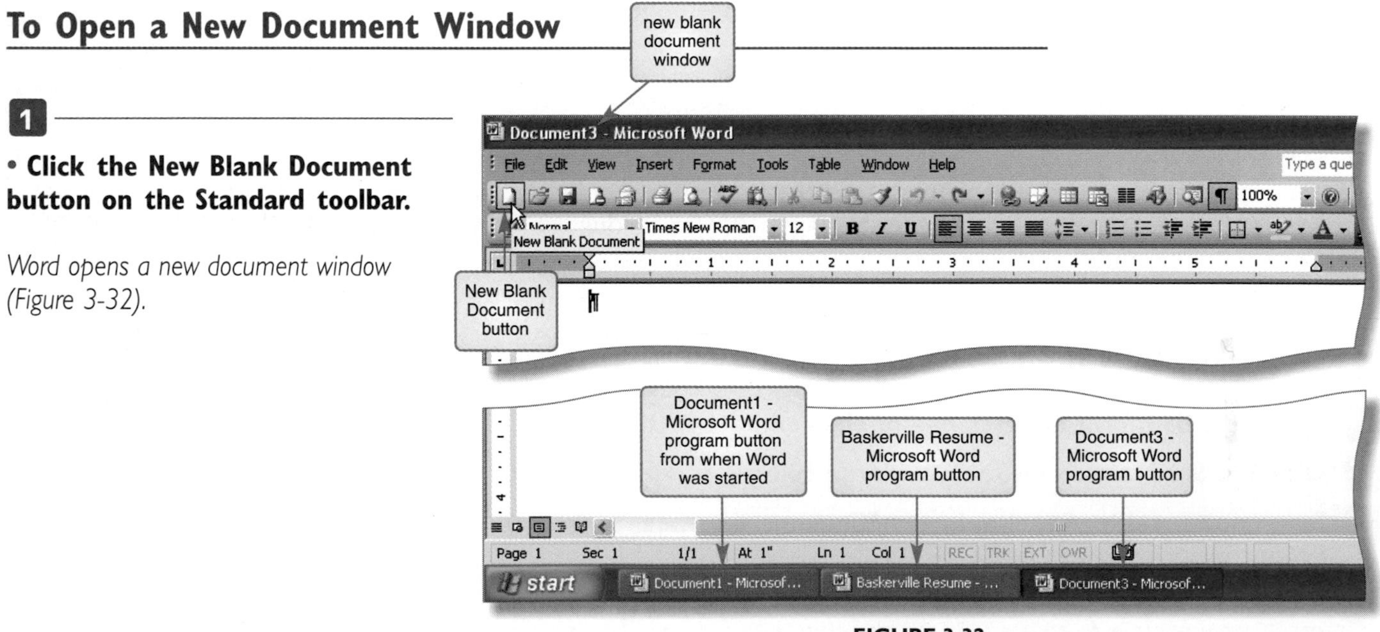

FIGURE 3-32

The Baskerville Resume document still is open. The program buttons on the taskbar display the names of the open Word document windows. The Document3 button on the taskbar is selected, indicating that it is the active document currently displayed in the Word document window.

The next step is to change the font size to 20 because you want the name in the letterhead to be a larger font size than the body of the letter. The next steps describe how to change the font size.

To Change the Font Size

1 **Click the Font Size box arrow on the Formatting toolbar.**

2 **Click 20 in the Font Size list.**

Word changes the font size to 20 (shown in Figure 3-33).

Changing Color of Text

The text in the letterhead is to be dark red. The following steps show how to change the color of the text before you type.

> **Q & A**
>
> **Q:** What if my Windows taskbar does not display a separate program button for each open Word document?
>
> **A:** If the Windows taskbar does not display a separate program button for each open Word document (Figure 3-32), click Tools on the menu bar, click Options, click the View tab, place a check mark in the Windows in Taskbar check box, and then click the OK button.

To Color Text

1

- **Click the Font Color button arrow on the Formatting toolbar.**

Word displays a list of available colors on the color palette (Figure 3-33). The color that displays below the letter A on the Font Color button is the most recently used text color. Your button may show a different color.

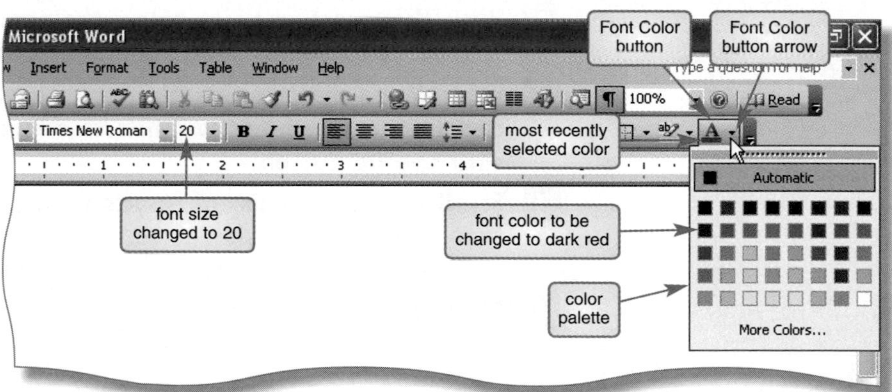

FIGURE 3-33

2

- **Click Dark Red, which is the first color on the second row of the color palette.**
- **Type** `Jasmine Leila Baskerville` **and then press the ENTER key.**

Word displays the first line of the letterhead in dark red (Figure 3-34).

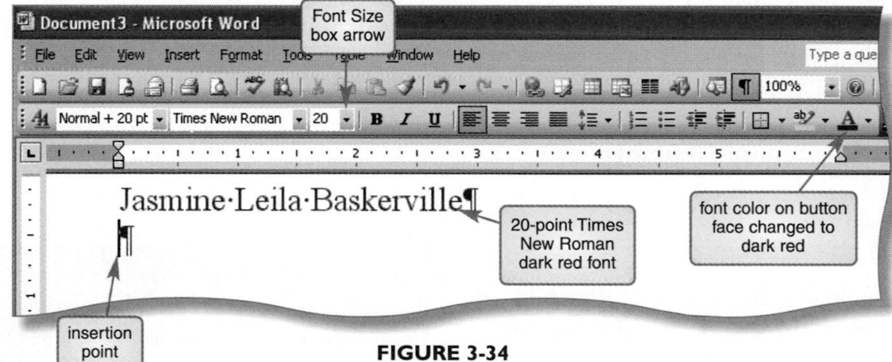

FIGURE 3-34

Notice the paragraph mark on line 2 is dark red. Recall that each time you press the ENTER key, Word carries forward formatting to the next paragraph. If, for some reason, you wanted to change the text back to black at this point, you would click the Font Color button arrow on the Formatting toolbar and then click Automatic on the color palette. Automatic is the default color, which usually is black.

The next step is to reduce the font size of text entered into the second line in the letterhead. The address, telephone, fax, and e-mail information is to be a font size of 9. The steps on the next page describe how to change the font size.

To Change the Font Size

1 **With the insertion point on line 2 as shown in Figure 3-34 on the previous page, click the Font Size box arrow on the Formatting toolbar.**

2 **Click 9 in the Font Size list.**

At the location of the insertion point, Word changes the font size to 9 (shown in Figure 3-37).

Inserting and Resizing a Graphic

The letterhead has a graphic of a soccer ball on line 2 below the job seeker's name. The following steps describe how to insert this graphic.

To Insert a Graphic

1 **With the insertion point below the name on line 2, click Insert on the menu bar, point to Picture, and then click Clip Art on the Picture submenu.**

2 **When Word displays the Clip Art task pane, if necessary, drag through any text in the Search for text box to select the text. Type** `soccer` **and then click the Go button.**

3 **Scroll through the list of results until you locate the graphic of a soccer ball that matches, or is similar to, the one shown in Figure 3-35. Click the graphic of the soccer ball to insert it in the document.**

4 **Click the Close button on the Clip Art task pane title bar.**

Word inserts the graphic of the soccer ball at the location of the insertion point (shown in Figure 3-35).

The next step is to reduce the size of the graphic to 25 percent of its current size. Instead of dragging the sizing handle, you can use the Format Picture dialog box to set exact size measurements. The following steps show how to resize a graphic using the Format Picture dialog box.

To Resize a Graphic

1

- **Position the mouse pointer in the graphic (in this case, the soccer ball) and then double-click.**
- **When Word displays the Format Picture dialog box, click the Size tab.**

The Size sheet allows you to specify exact measurements of the selected graphic (Figure 3-35).

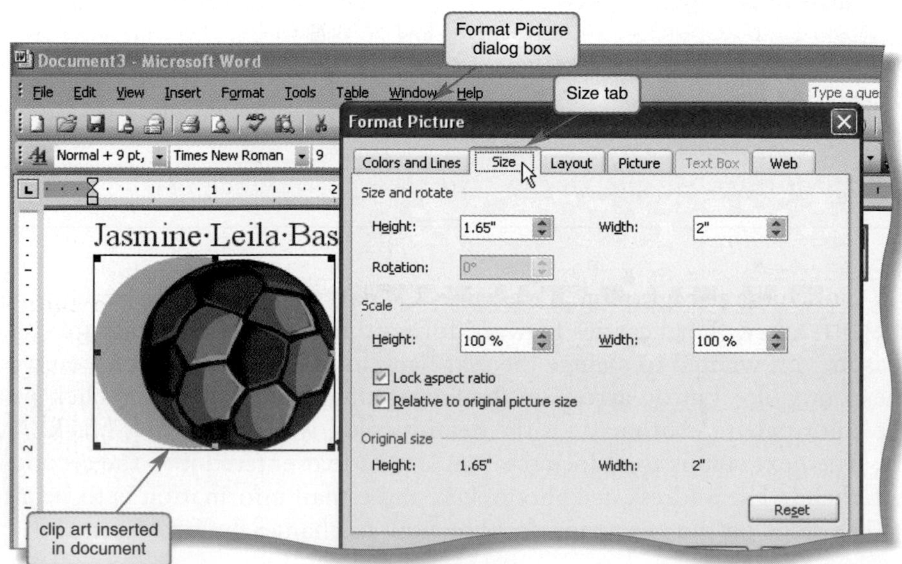

FIGURE 3-35

2

• **In the Scale area, double-click the Height box to select it.**

• **Type** 25 **and then press the TAB key.**

Word displays 25 % in the Height and Width boxes (Figure 3-36). When you press the TAB key from the Height box, the insertion point moves to the Width box and automatically changes the width to 25 % — to match the height proportionately.

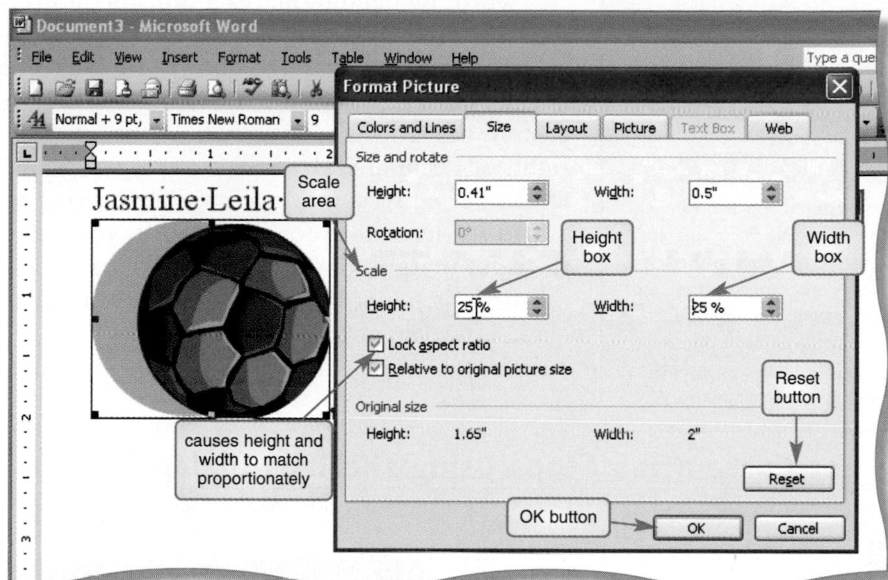

FIGURE 3-36

3

• **Click the OK button in the Format Picture dialog box.**

• **Press the END key to move the insertion point to the paragraph mark to the right of the graphic.**

Word resizes the graphic to 25 percent of its original size (Figure 3-37).

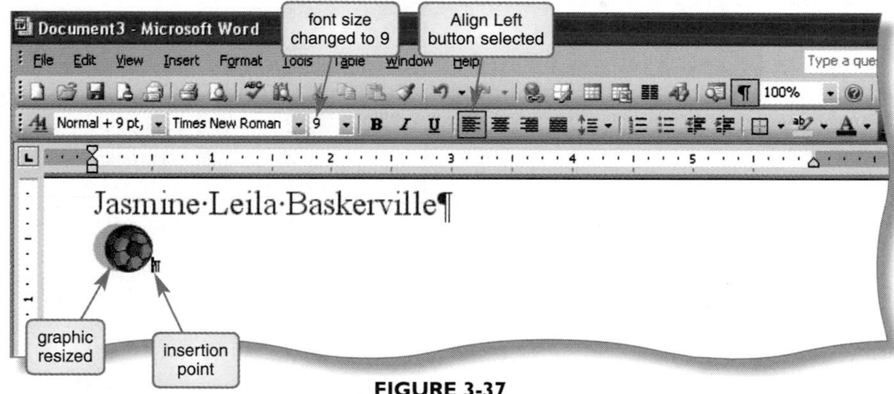

FIGURE 3-37

Sometimes, you might resize a graphic and realize it is the wrong size. In this case, you may want to return the graphic to its original size and start again. To restore a resized graphic to its exact original size, click the Reset button in the Format Picture dialog box (Figure 3-36).

Setting Tab Stops Using the Tabs Dialog Box

The graphic of the soccer ball is left-aligned (Figure 3-37). The address information in the letterhead is to be positioned at the right margin of the same line. If you click the Align Right button, the graphic will be right-aligned. In Word, a paragraph cannot be both left-aligned and right-aligned. To place text at the right margin of a left-aligned paragraph, you set a tab stop at the right margin.

A **tab stop** is a location on the horizontal ruler that tells Word where to position the insertion point when you press the TAB key on the keyboard. A tab stop is useful for indenting and aligning text.

Q & A

Q: Why would I use the Tabs dialog box?

A: You can use the Tabs dialog box to change an existing tab stop's alignment or position. You also can use the Tabs dialog box to place leader characters in the empty space occupied by the tab. Leader characters, such as a series of dots, often are used in a table of contents to precede the page number.

Word, by default, places a tab stop at every .5" mark on the ruler (shown in Figure 3-39). These default tab stops are indicated at the bottom of the horizontal ruler by small vertical tick marks. You also can set your own custom tab stops. When you set a **custom tab stop**, Word clears all default tab stops to the left of the custom tab stop. You specify how the text will align at a tab stop: left, centered, right, or decimal. Tab settings are a paragraph format. Thus, each time you press the ENTER key, any custom tab stops are carried forward to the next paragraph.

In the letterhead for this project, you want the tab stop to be right-aligned with the right margin, that is, at the 6" mark on the ruler. One method of setting custom tab stops is to click the ruler at the desired location of the tab stop. You cannot click, however, at the right margin location. Thus, use the Tabs dialog box to set a custom tab stop at the 6" mark, as shown in the following steps.

To Set Custom Tab Stops Using the Tabs Dialog Box

1

- **With the insertion point positioned between the paragraph mark and the graphic, click Format on the menu bar (Figure 3-38).**

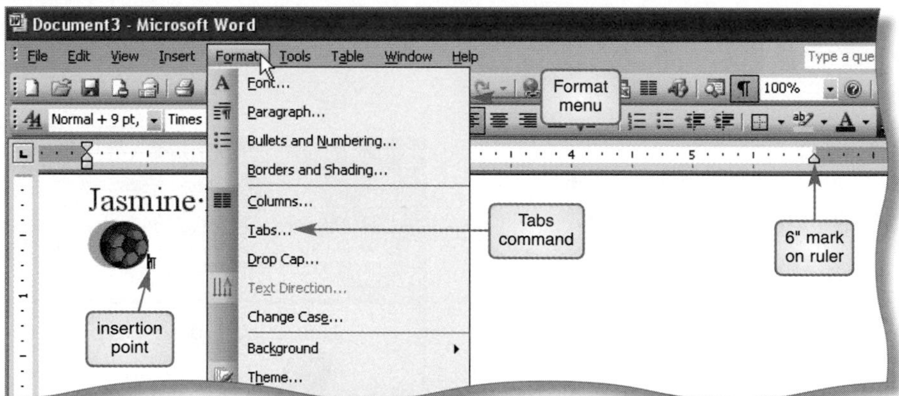

FIGURE 3-38

2

- **Click Tabs on the Format menu.**
- **When Word displays the Tabs dialog box, type** 6 **in the Tab stop position text box.**
- **Click Right in the Alignment area.**

The Tabs dialog box allows you to set and clear custom tabs (Figure 3-39).

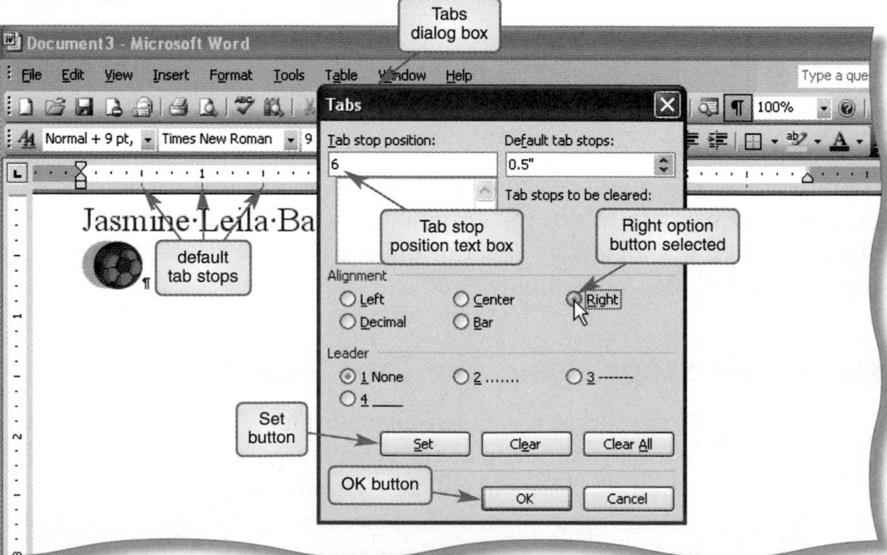

FIGURE 3-39

3

- **Click the Set button in the Tabs dialog box.**
- **Click the OK button.**

Word places a right tab marker at the 6" mark on the ruler and removes all default tab stops to the left of the tab marker on the ruler (Figure 3-40).

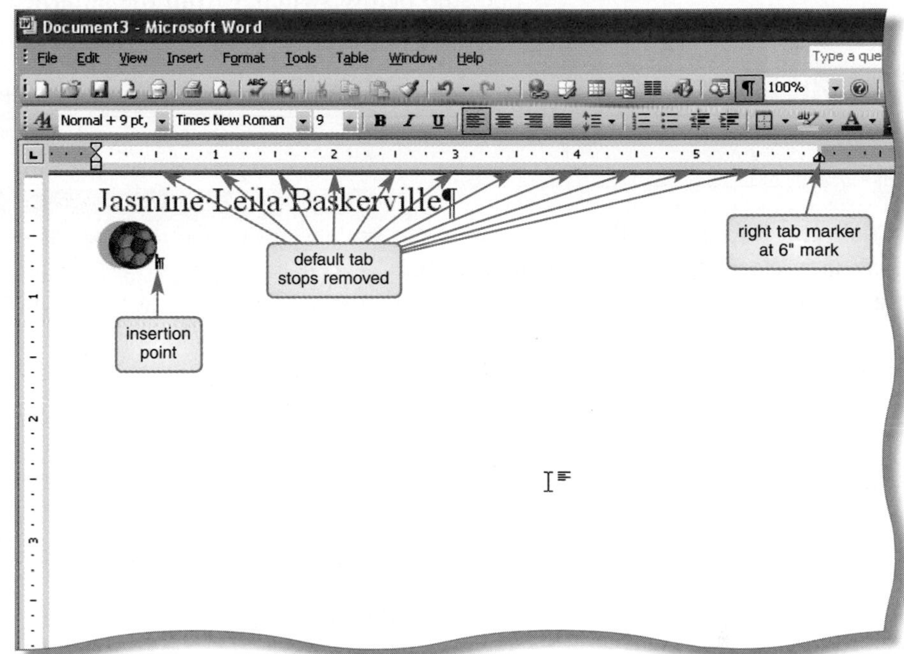

FIGURE 3-40

When you set a custom tab stop, the tab marker on the ruler reflects the alignment of the characters at the location of the tab stop. A capital letter L (L) indicates a left-aligned tab stop. A mirror image of a capital letter L (⅃) indicates a right-aligned tab stop. An upside down T (⊥) indicates a centered tab stop. An upside down T with a dot next to it (⊥) indicates a decimal-aligned tab stop. Specific tab markers are discussed as they are presented in these projects. The tab marker on the ruler in Figure 3-40 indicates text entered at that tab stop will be right-aligned.

To move the insertion point from one tab stop to another, press the TAB key on the keyboard. When you press the TAB key, a **tab character** formatting mark appears in the empty space between the tab stops.

> *Q & A*
>
> **Q:** When would I use a decimal-aligned tab stop?
>
> **A:** If you have a series of numbers that you want aligned on the decimal point, such as dollar amounts, use a decimal-aligned tab stop for the data.

Collecting and Pasting

The next step in creating the letterhead is to copy the address, telephone, fax, and e-mail information from the resume to the letterhead. To copy multiple items from one Office document to another, you use the Office Clipboard. The **Office Clipboard** is a temporary storage area that holds up to 24 items (text or graphics) copied from any Office application. You copy, or **collect**, items and then paste them in a new location. **Pasting** is the process of copying an item from the Office Clipboard into the document at the location of the insertion point. When you paste an item into a document, the contents of the Office Clipboard are not erased.

To copy the address, telephone, fax, and e-mail information from the resume to the letterhead, you first switch to the resume document, copy the items from the resume to the Office Clipboard, switch back to the letterhead document, and then paste the information from the Office Clipboard into the letterhead. The following pages illustrate this process.

> *Q & A*
>
> **Q:** Is the Windows Clipboard the same as the Office Clipboard?
>
> **A:** The Windows Clipboard, which can hold only one item at a time, is separate from the Office Clipboard. When you collect multiple items on the Office Clipboard, the last copied item also is copied to the Windows Clipboard. When you clear the Office Clipboard, the Windows Clipboard also is cleared.

The step below switches from the letterhead document to the resume document.

To Switch from One Open Document to Another

1

- **Click the Baskerville Resume - Microsoft Word program button on the Windows taskbar.**

Word switches from the letterhead document to the resume document (Figure 3-41). The letterhead document (Document3) still is open.

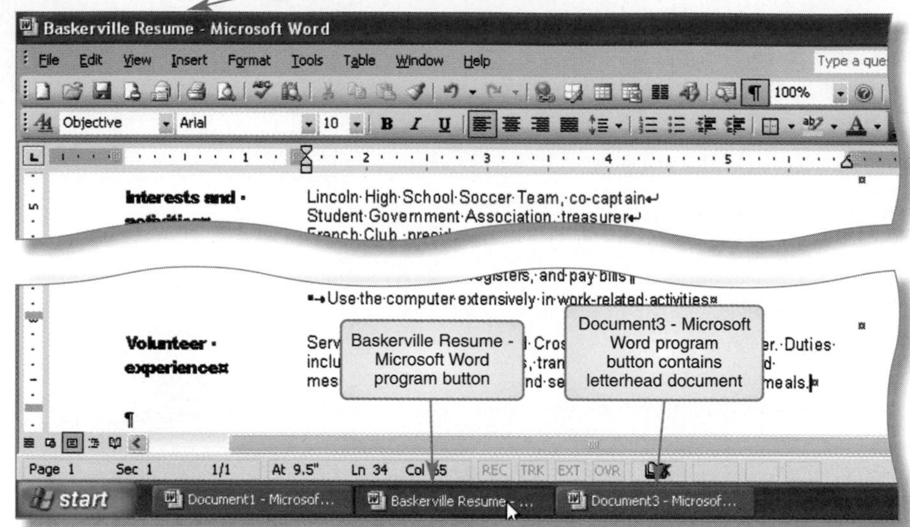

FIGURE 3-41

You can copy multiple items to the Office Clipboard and then can paste them later. Each copied item appears as an entry in the Office Clipboard gallery in the Clipboard task pane. The entry displays an icon that indicates the Office program from which the item was copied. The entry also displays a portion of text that was copied or a thumbnail of a graphic that was copied. The most recently copied item is displayed at the top of the gallery.

The following steps show how to copy five items to the Office Clipboard.

To Copy Items to the Office Clipboard

1

- **Press CTRL+HOME to display the top of the resume in the document window.**
- **Click Edit on the menu bar (Figure 3-42).**

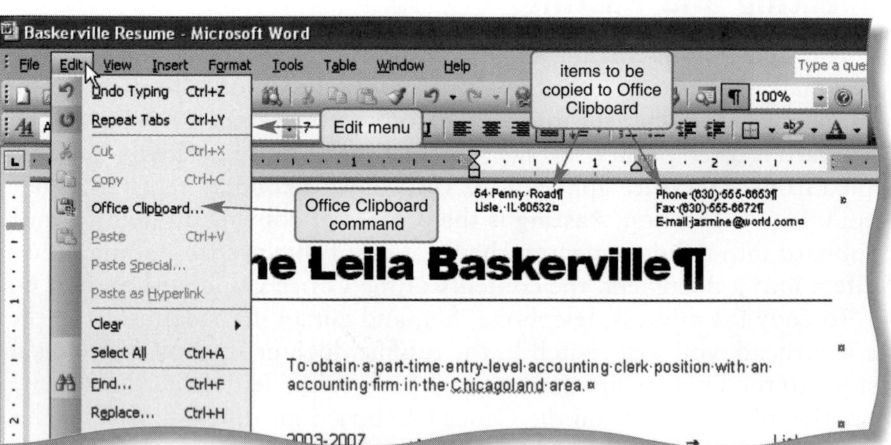

FIGURE 3-42

2

- **Click Office Clipboard on the Edit menu.**
- **If the Office Clipboard gallery in the Clipboard task pane is not empty, click the Clear All button in the Clipboard task pane.**
- **Scroll to the right to display all of the telephone, fax, and e-mail information in the resume.**
- **In the resume, drag through the street address, 54 Penny Road.**

Word displays the Clipboard task pane on the screen (Figure 3-43). The Office Clipboard icon appears in the notification area on the Windows taskbar, indicating the Office Clipboard is displayed in at least one open Office program.

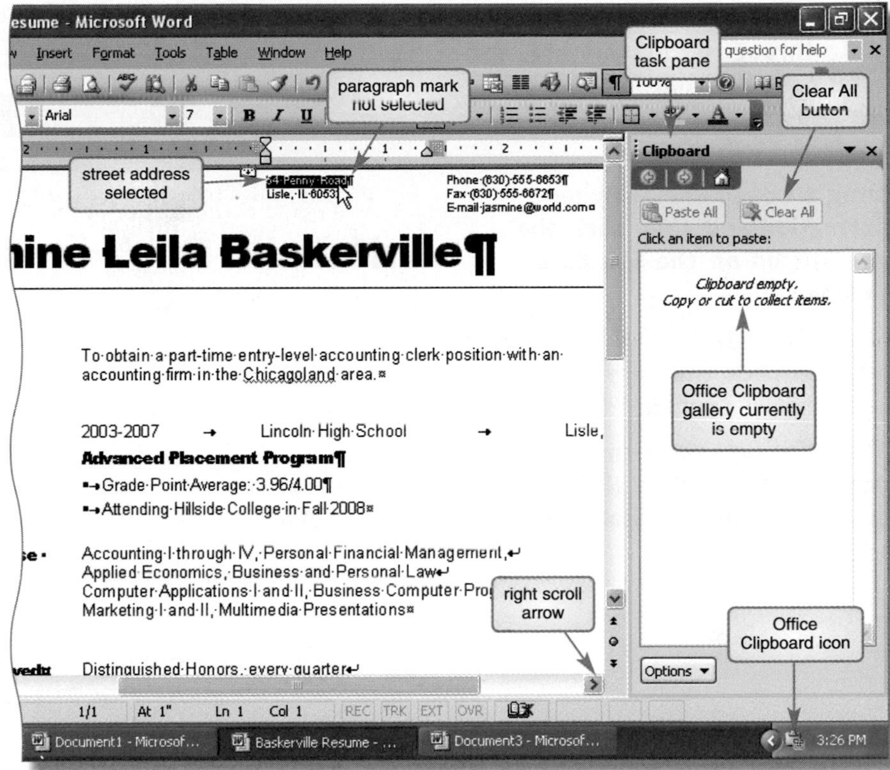

FIGURE 3-43

3

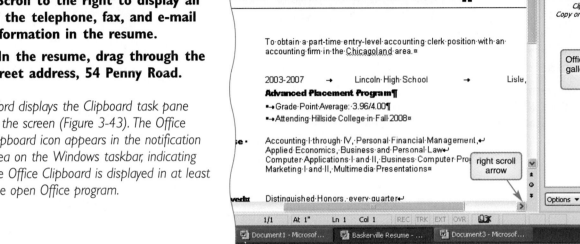

- **Click the Copy button on the Standard toolbar.**

Word copies the selection to the Office Clipboard and places an entry in the Office Clipboard gallery in the Clipboard task pane (Figure 3-44).

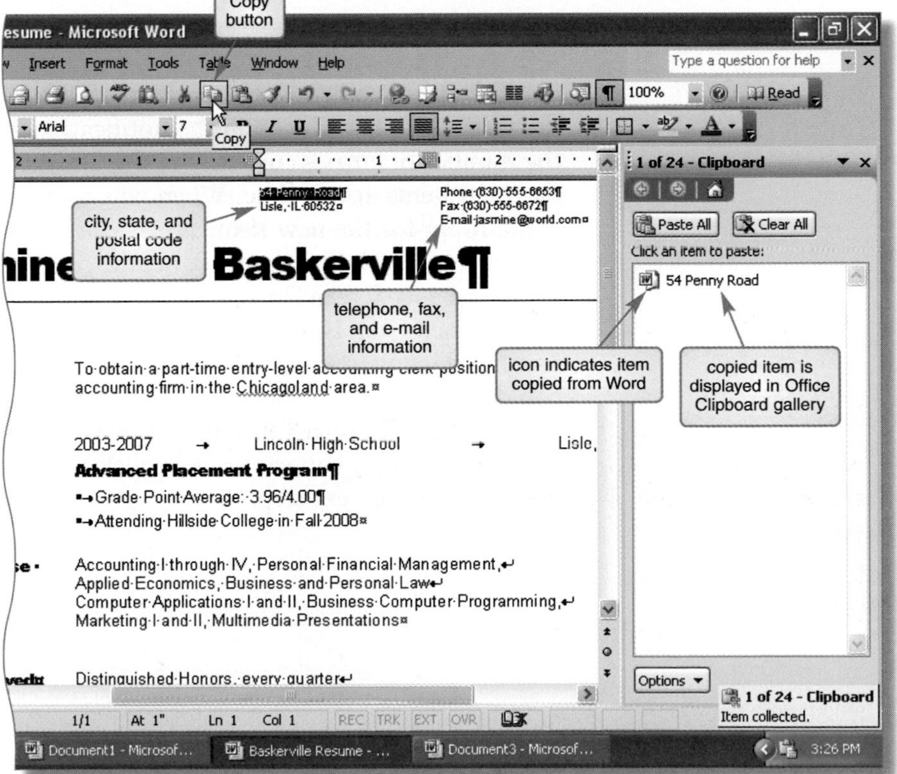

FIGURE 3-44

4

• **Drag through the city, state, and postal code information and then click the Copy button on the Standard toolbar.**

• **Drag through the telephone information and then click the Copy button on the Standard toolbar.**

• **Drag through the fax information and then click the Copy button on the Standard toolbar.**

• **Drag through the e-mail information and then click the Copy button on the Standard toolbar (Figure 3-45).**

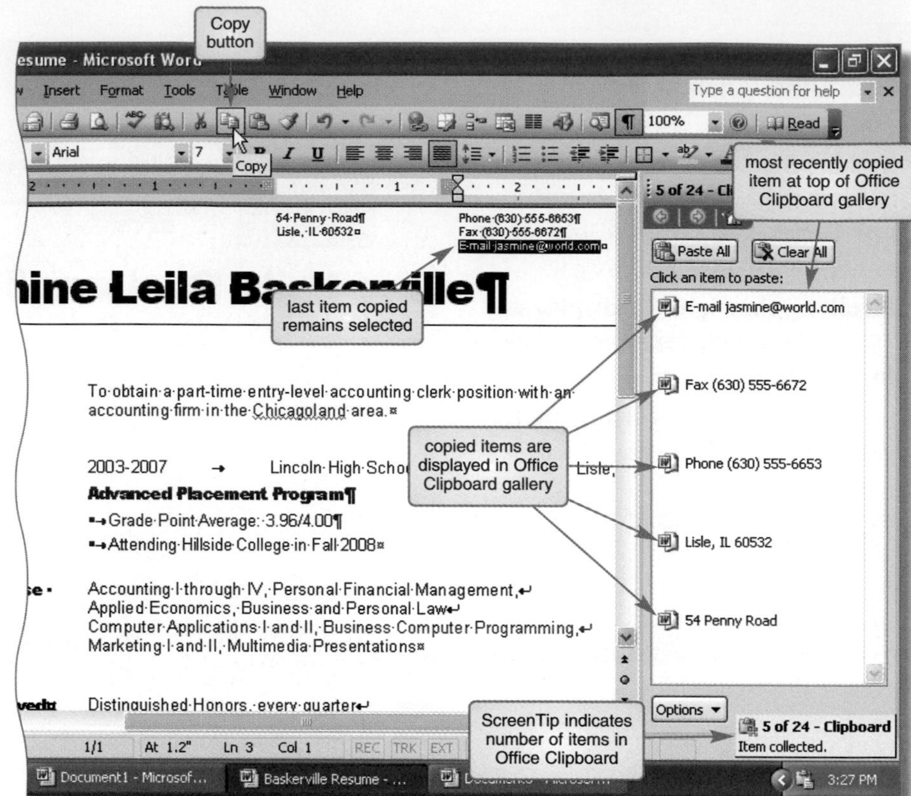

FIGURE 3-45

Each time you copy an item to the Office Clipboard, a ScreenTip appears above the Office Clipboard icon in the notification area on the Windows taskbar, indicating the number of entries currently in the Office Clipboard. The Office Clipboard stores up to 24 items at one time. When you copy a 25th item, Word deletes the first item to make room for the new item. When you point to a text entry in the Office Clipboard gallery in the Clipboard task pane, the first several characters of text in the item are displayed as a ScreenTip.

The next step is to paste the copied items into the letterhead. When you switch to another document, the Clipboard task pane might not be displayed on the screen. You could display it by clicking Edit on the menu bar and then clicking Office Clipboard. If the Office Clipboard icon is displayed in the notification area on the Windows taskbar, however, you can double-click the icon to display the Clipboard task pane, as described in the next step.

To Display the Clipboard Task Pane

1

- **Click the Document3 - Microsoft Word button on the Windows taskbar to display the letterhead.**
- **Double-click the Office Clipboard icon in the notification area on the Windows taskbar.**

Word displays the Clipboard task pane on the screen (Figure 3-46). The Office Clipboard gallery shows the items contained on the Clipboard.

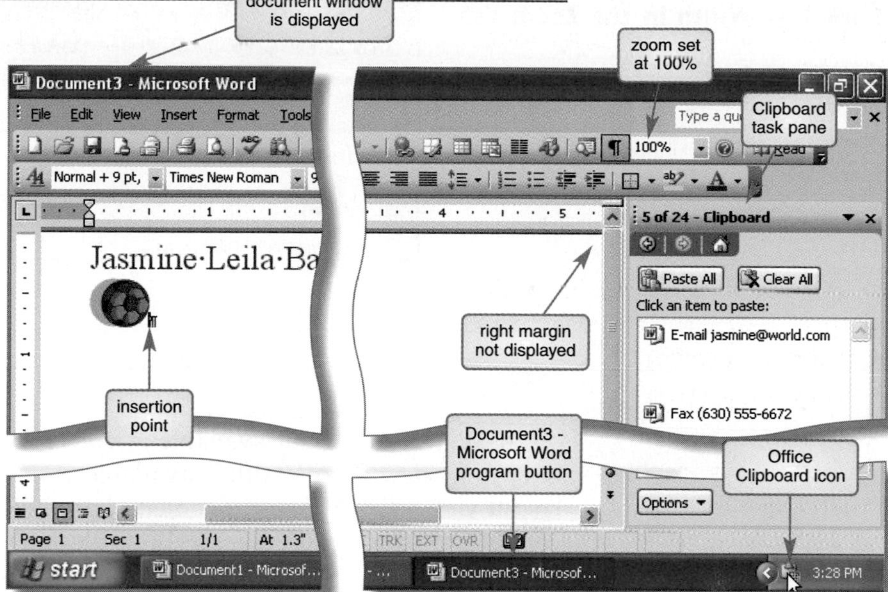

FIGURE 3-46

Q & A

Q: What if the Office Clipboard icon does not appear on the taskbar?

A: If the Office Clipboard icon does not appear on the Windows taskbar, click the Options button at the bottom of the Clipboard task pane and then click Show Office Clipboard icon on Taskbar.

The next step is to press the TAB key to position the insertion point at the location where the text will be copied. Recall that the address information is to be located at the right margin of the document window. Notice in Figure 3-46 that the right margin is not displayed on the screen when the task pane also is on the screen.

Depending on your Windows and Word settings, the horizontal ruler at the top of the document window may show more inches or fewer inches than the ruler shown in Figure 3-46. Two factors that affect how much of the ruler displays in the document window are the Windows screen resolution and the Word zoom percentage. The more inches of ruler that display, the smaller the text will be on the screen. The fewer inches of ruler that display, the larger the text will be on the screen.

To view both the right and left margins on the screen beside the Clipboard task pane, you need to change the zoom percent, which in this project is set at 100 percent. The following steps show how to let Word determine the best percentage to zoom when showing both the left and right margins at the same time.

To Zoom Text Width

- **Click the Zoom box arrow on the Standard toolbar (Figure 3-47).**

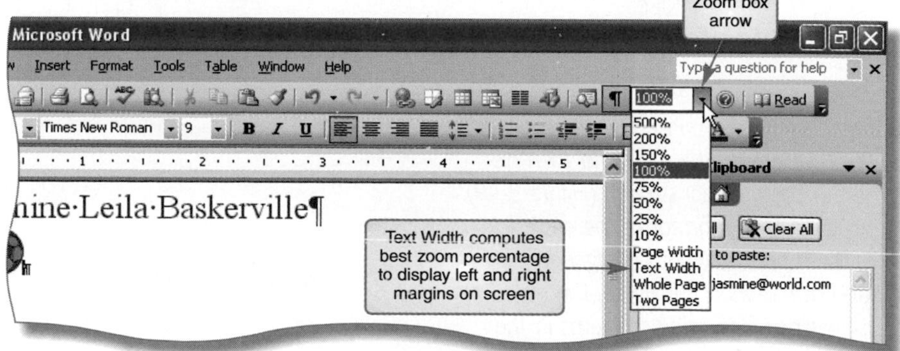

FIGURE 3-47

2

• **Click Text Width in the Zoom list.**

Word places the margins of the document in the window (Figure 3-48).

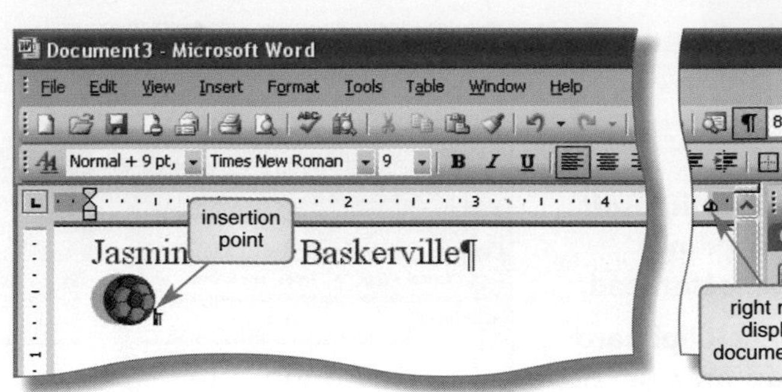

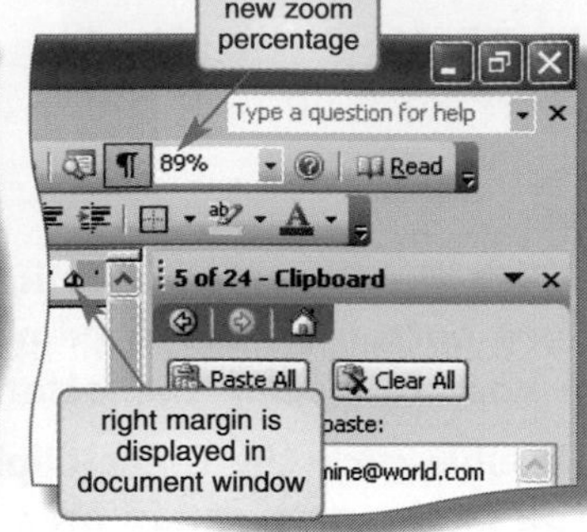

FIGURE 3-48

If Text Width is not available in your Zoom list, then your document window is in normal view. Text Width is available only in print layout view. To switch to print layout view, click View on the menu bar and then click Print Layout.

The Zoom box in Figure 3-48 displays 89%, which Word computes based on a variety of settings. Your percentage may be different, depending on your computer configuration.

When you paste items into a document, Word displays the Paste Options button on the screen. The Paste Options button allows you to change the format of pasted items. For example, you can instruct Word to format the pasted text the same as the text from where it was copied or format it the same as the text to where it was pasted. You also can have Word remove all extra non-text characters that were pasted. For example, if you included a paragraph mark when copying at the end of a line in the address of the resume, the Paste Options button allows you to remove the paragraph marks from the pasted text.

The following steps show how to paste the address information from the Office Clipboard into the letterhead — removing any extraneous paragraph marks after pasting.

To Paste from the Office Clipboard

1

• **With the insertion point between the paragraph mark and the soccer ball graphic (shown in Figure 3-48), press the TAB key.**

• **Click the bottom (first) entry in the Office Clipboard gallery.**

• **Click the Paste Options button.**

Word pastes the contents of the clicked item at the location of the insertion point, which is at the 6" mark on the ruler, and then displays the Paste Options menu (Figure 3-49). Depending on the format of the copied text, the pasted text may not be aligned or formatted as shown in this figure. The next step fixes any formatting problems in the pasted text.

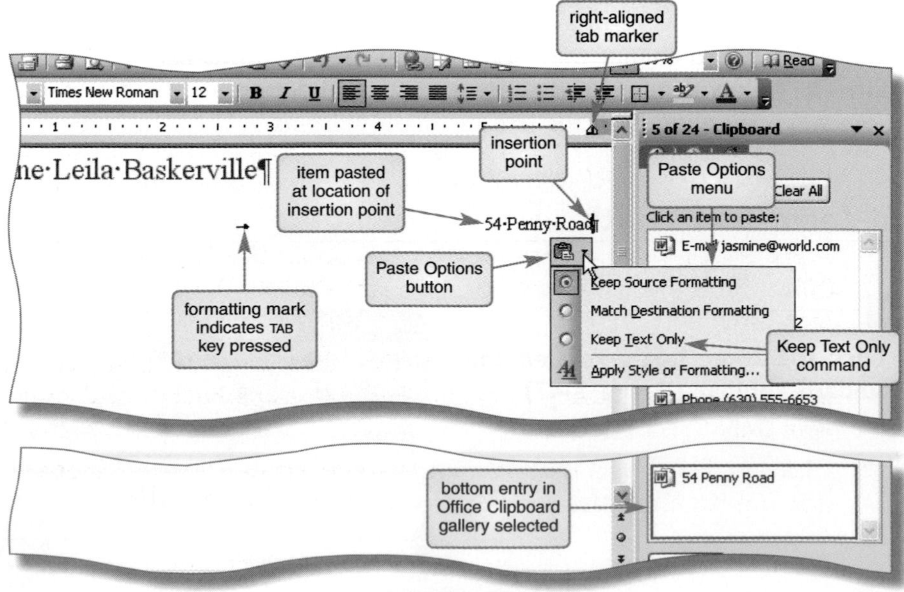

FIGURE 3-49

2

• **Click Keep Text Only on the Paste Options menu.**

• **Press the COMMA key. Press the SPACEBAR.**

• **Click the second entry (city, state, postal code) in the Office Clipboard gallery.**

• **Click the Paste Options button and then click Keep Text Only.**

The city, state, and postal code from the Office Clipboard are pasted into the letterhead (Figure 3-50). The Keep Text Only command removes any extraneous paragraph marks from the pasted text.

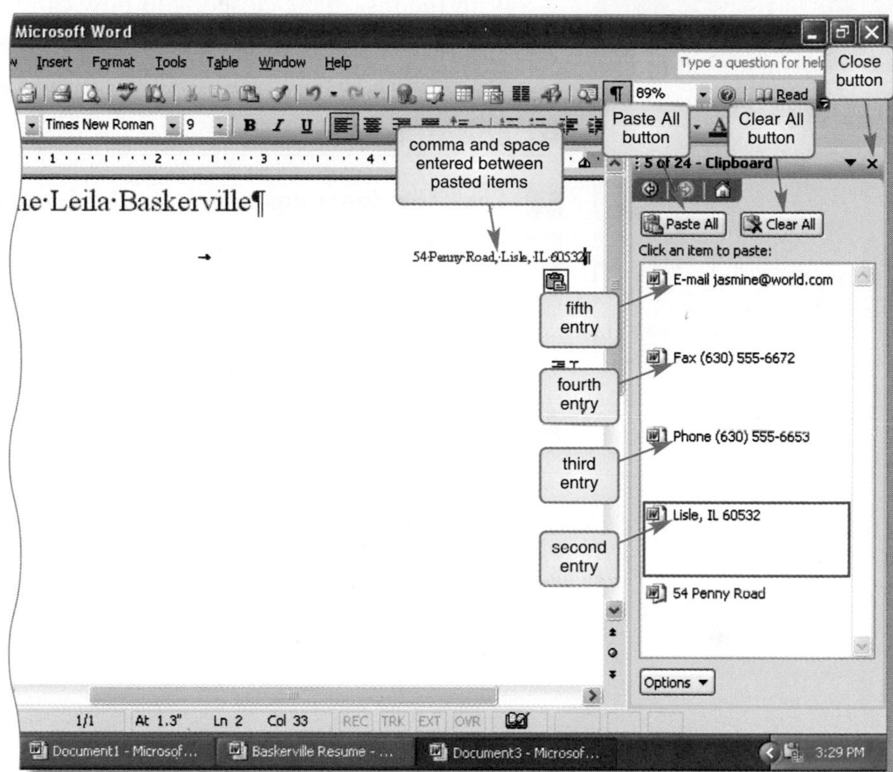

FIGURE 3-50

If you wanted to paste all items in a row without any characters in between them, you would click the Paste All button in the Clipboard task pane. If you wanted to erase all items on the Office Clipboard, you would click the Clear All button in the Clipboard task pane.

The following steps discuss how to paste the telephone, fax, and e-mail information into the letterhead from the resume.

To Paste More Information from the Office Clipboard

1. **Press the ENTER key. Press the TAB key. Click the third entry (telephone) in the Office Clipboard gallery. Click the Paste Options button and then click Keep Text Only.**
2. **Press the COMMA key. Press the SPACEBAR. Click the fourth entry (fax) in the Office Clipboard gallery. Click the Paste Options button and then click Keep Text Only.**
3. **Press the COMMA key. Press the SPACEBAR. Click the fifth entry (e-mail) in the Office Clipboard gallery. Click the Paste Options button and then click Keep Text Only.**
4. **Click the Close button in the upper-right corner of the Clipboard task pane title bar to close the task pane.**

All items are pasted from the Office Clipboard into the letterhead (shown in Figure 3-51 on the next page). The Clipboard task pane is closed.

Skill Builder 3-3

To practice the following tasks, visit scsite.com/off2003sch/skill, locate Word Project 3, and then click Skill Builder 3-3.

- ❑ Open a new document window
- ❑ Set tab stops using the Tabs dialog box
- ❑ Collect and paste using the Clipboard task pane

With the task pane closed, you now can return the zoom percentage of the document window to 100 percent, as described in the following steps.

To Zoom to 100%

1. **Click the Zoom box arrow on the Standard toolbar.**
2. **Click 100% in the Zoom list.**

Word changes the zoom to 100% (shown in Figure 3-51).

Adding a Bottom Border to a Paragraph

To add professionalism to the letterhead, you can draw a horizontal line from the left margin to the right margin immediately below the telephone, fax, and e-mail information. In Word, you draw a solid line, called a **border**, at any edge of a paragraph. That is, borders may be added above or below a paragraph, to the left or right of a paragraph, or any combination of these sides.

The following steps show how to add a bottom border to the paragraph containing telephone, fax, and e-mail information.

To Bottom Border a Paragraph

1

- **With the insertion point in the paragraph to border, click the Border button arrow on the Formatting toolbar.**

Word displays the border palette either horizontally or vertically below the Border button (Figure 3-51). Using the border palette, you can add a border to any edge of a paragraph.

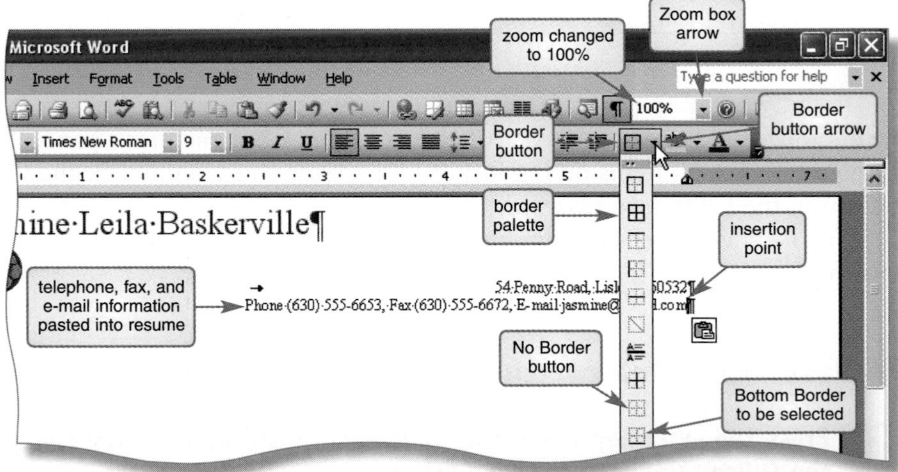

FIGURE 3-51

2

- **Click Bottom Border on the border palette.**

Word places a border below the paragraph containing the insertion point (Figure 3-52). The Border button on the Formatting toolbar now displays the icon for a bottom border.

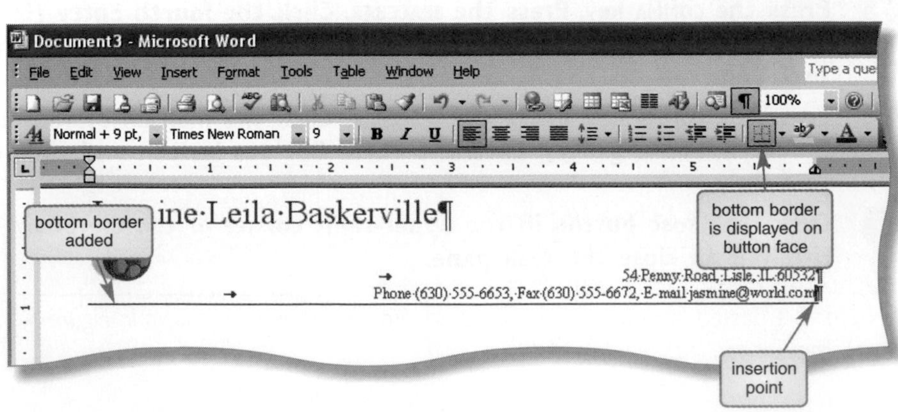

If, for some reason, you wanted to remove a border from a paragraph, you would position the insertion point in the paragraph, click the Border button arrow on the Formatting toolbar, and then click the No Border button (Figure 3-51) on the border palette.

Clearing Formatting

The next step is to position the insertion point below the letterhead, so that you can type the content of the letter. When you press the ENTER key at the end of a paragraph containing a border, Word moves the border forward to the next paragraph. It also retains all current settings. That is, the paragraph text will be dark red and will have a bottom border. Instead, you want the paragraph and characters on the new line to use the Normal style: black font with no border. In Word the term, **clear formatting**, refers to returning the formatting to the Normal style.

The following steps show how to clear formatting at the location of the insertion point.

To Clear Formatting

1

- **With the insertion point at the end of line 3 (Figure 3-52), press the ENTER key.**
- **Click the Styles and Formatting button on the Formatting toolbar.**

Word displays the Styles and Formatting task pane (Figure 3-53). The insertion point is on line 4. Formatting at the insertion point consists of a bottom border and a dark red font. You want to clear this formatting.

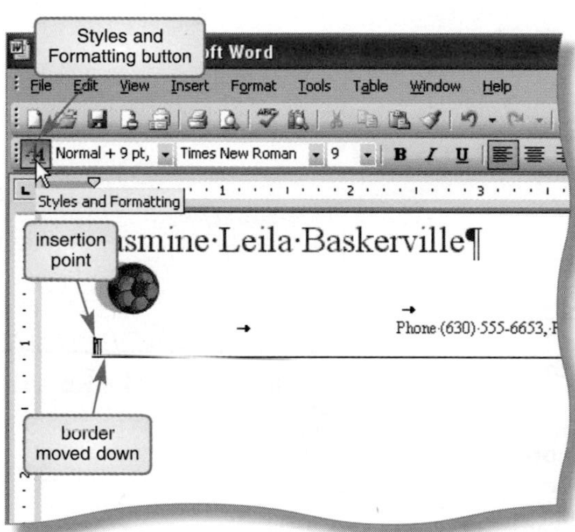

FIGURE 3-53

2

- **Click Clear Formatting in the Pick formatting to apply area in the Styles and Formatting task pane.**

Word applies the Normal style to the location of the insertion point (Figure 3-54).

3

- **Click the Close button in the upper-right corner of the Styles and Formatting task pane title bar.**

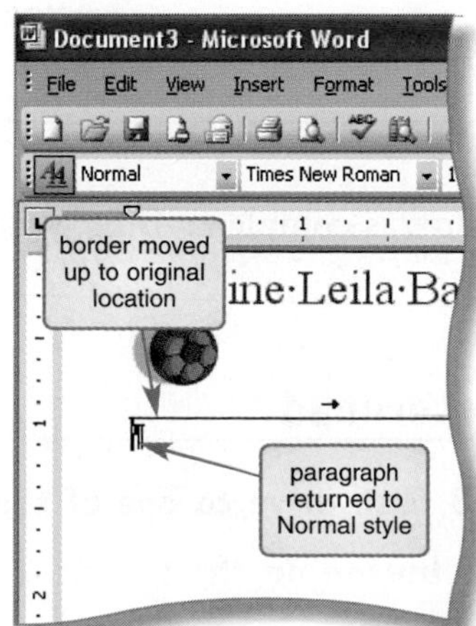

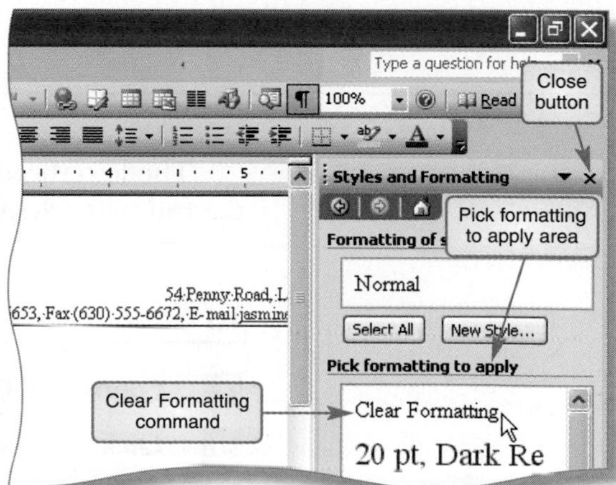

FIGURE 3-54

The next step is to remove the hyperlink autoformat from the e-mail address in the letterhead. As discussed earlier in this project, Word automatically formats text as you type. When you press the ENTER key or SPACEBAR after entering an e-mail address or Web address, Word automatically formats the address as a hyperlink, that is, colored blue and underlined. In Step 1 on the previous page, Word formatted the e-mail address as a hyperlink because you pressed the ENTER key at the end of the line. You want to remove the hyperlink format from the e-mail address.

The following steps show how to convert the e-mail address from a hyperlink to regular text.

To Convert a Hyperlink to Regular Text

1

- **Right-click the hyperlink, in this case, the e-mail address (Figure 3-55).**

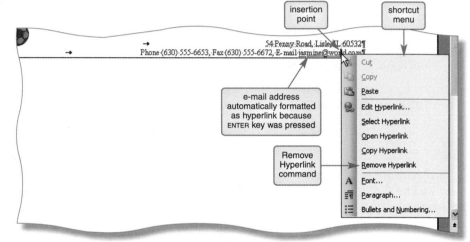

FIGURE 3-55

2

- **Click Remove Hyperlink on the shortcut menu.**
- **Position the insertion point on the paragraph mark below the border.**

Word removes the hyperlink format from the e-mail address (Figure 3-56).

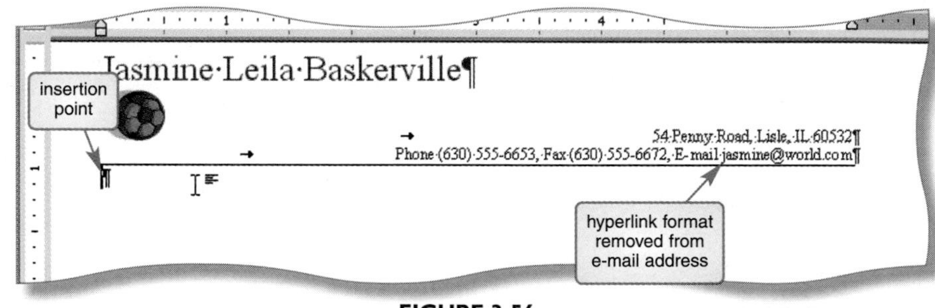

FIGURE 3-56

The letterhead now is complete. Thus, you should save it in a file, as described in the following steps.

To Save the Letterhead

1. **Connect a USB flash drive to one of the computer's USB ports.**
2. **Click the Save button on the Standard toolbar.**
3. **Type the file name** `Baskerville Letterhead` **in the File name text box.**
4. **If necessary, click the Save in box arrow and then click UDISK 2.0 (E:). (Your USB flash drive may have a different name and letter.)**

5 Click the Save button in the Save As dialog box.

Word saves the document on a USB flash drive with the file name, Baskerville Letterhead.

Each time you wish to create a letter, you would open the letterhead file (Baskerville Letterhead) and then immediately save it with a new file name. By doing this, the letterhead file will remain unchanged for future use.

Q & A

Q: Can I save a document as a template?

A: Yes. As an alternative to saving the letterhead as a Word document, you could save it as a template by clicking the Save as type box arrow in the Save As dialog box and then clicking Document Template. To use the template, click File on the menu bar, click New, click On my computer in the New Document task pane, and then double-click the template icon or name.

Creating a Cover Letter

You have created a letterhead for the cover letter. The next step is to compose the cover letter. The following pages outline how to use Word to compose a cover letter that contains a table and a bulleted list.

Components of a Business Letter

During your professional career, you most likely will create many business letters. A cover letter is one type of business letter. All business letters contain the same basic components.

When preparing business letters, you should include all essential elements. Essential business letter elements include the date line, inside address, message, and signature block (Figure 3-2a on page WD 140). The **date line**, which consists of the month, day, and year, is positioned two to six lines below the letterhead. The **inside address**, placed three to eight lines below the date line, usually contains the addressee's courtesy title plus full name, business affiliation, and full geographical address. The **salutation**, if present, begins two lines below the last line of the inside address. The body of the letter, the message, begins two lines below the salutation. Within the **message**, paragraphs are single-spaced with double-spacing between paragraphs. Two lines below the last line of the message, the **complimentary close** is displayed. Capitalize only the first word in a complimentary close. Type the **signature block** at least four lines below the complimentary close, allowing room for the author to sign his or her name.

You can follow many different styles when you create business letters. The cover letter in this project follows the modified block style. Table 3-2 outlines the differences among three common styles of business letters.

Q & A

Q: Do I have to send a cover letter with my resume?

A: You always should send a personalized cover letter with a resume. The cover letter should highlight aspects of your background relevant to the position. To help you recall past achievements and activities, keep a personal file containing documents that outline your accomplishments.

Table 3-2 Common Business Letter Styles

LETTER STYLES	FEATURES
Block	All components of the letter begin flush with the left margin.
Modified Block	The date, complimentary close, and signature block are positioned approximately ½" to the right of center, or at the right margin. All other components of the letter begin flush with the left margin.
Modified Semi-Block	The date, complimentary close, and signature block are centered, positioned approximately ½" to the right of center, or at the right margin. The first line of each paragraph in the body of the letter is indented ½" to 1" from the left margin. All other components of the letter begin flush with the left margin.

Saving the Cover Letter with a New File Name

The document in the document window currently has the name Baskerville Letterhead, the name of the personal letterhead. You want the letterhead to remain intact. Thus, you should save the document with a new file name, as described in the steps on the next page.

To Save the Document with a New File Name

1. **If necessary, connect a USB flash drive to one of the computer's USB ports.**
2. **Click File on the menu bar and then click Save As.**
3. **Type the file name** `Baskerville Cover Letter` **in the File name text box.**
4. **If necessary, click the Save in box arrow and then click UDISK 2.0 (E:). (Your USB flash drive may have a different name and letter.)**
5. **Click the Save button in the Save As dialog box.**

Word saves the document on a USB flash drive with the file name, Baskerville Cover Letter (shown in Figure 3-57).

Setting Tab Stops Using the Ruler

The first required element of the cover letter is the date line, which in this letter is to be positioned two lines below the letterhead. The date line contains the month, day, and year, and begins 3.5 inches from the left margin, or one-half inch to the right of center. Thus, you should set a custom tab stop at the 3.5" mark on the ruler. Earlier you used the Tabs dialog box to set a tab stop because you could not use the ruler to set a tab stop at the right margin. The following steps show how to set a left-aligned tab stop using the ruler.

To Set Custom Tab Stops Using the Ruler

1

- **With the insertion point on the paragraph mark below the border, press the ENTER key.**
- **If necessary, click the button at the left edge of the horizontal ruler until it displays the Left Tab icon.**
- **Position the mouse pointer on the 3.5" mark on the ruler.**

Each time you click the button at the left of the horizontal ruler, its icon changes (Figure 3-57). The left tab icon looks like a capital letter L (L).

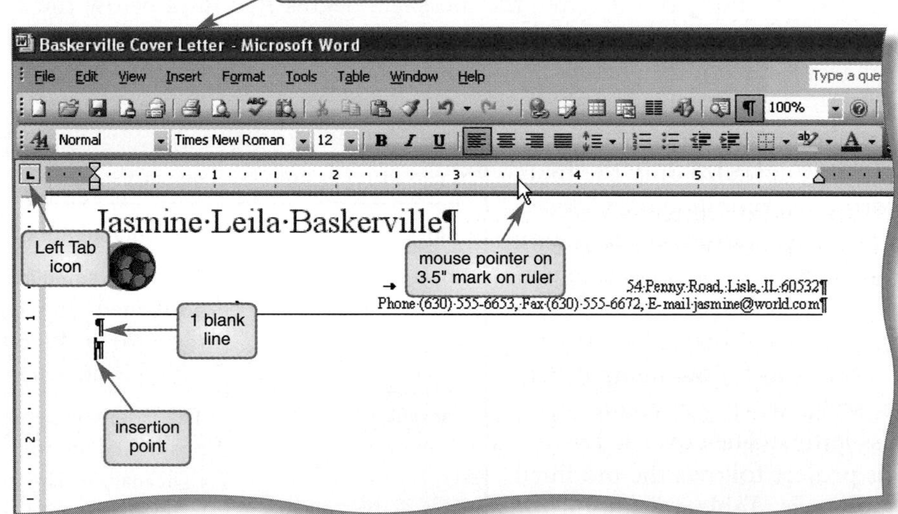

FIGURE 3-57

2

- **Click the 3.5" mark on the ruler.**

Word places a left tab marker at the 3.5" mark on the ruler (Figure 3-58). The text you type at this tab stop will be left-aligned.

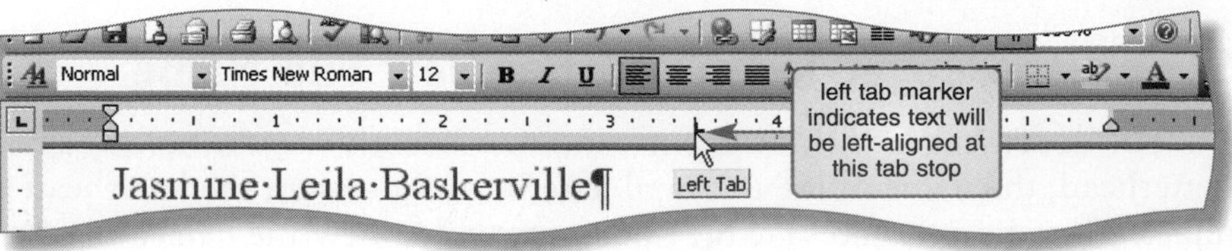

FIGURE 3-58

If, for some reason, you wanted to move a custom tab stop, you would drag the tab marker to the desired location on the ruler.

If you wanted to change the alignment of a custom tab stop, you could remove the existing tab stop and then insert a new one, as described in the previous steps. To remove a custom tab stop, point to the tab marker on the ruler and then drag the tab marker down and out of the ruler. You also could use the Tabs dialog box to change an existing tab stop's alignment or position. As discussed earlier in this project, you click Format on the menu bar and then click Tabs to display the Tabs dialog box. To remove all tab stops, click the Clear All button in the Tabs dialog box.

Inserting the Current Date in a Document

The next step is to enter the current date at the 3.5" tab stop in the document. Word provides a method of inserting a computer's system date in a document. The following steps show how to insert the current date in the cover letter.

To Insert the Current Date in a Document

1

- **Press the TAB key.**
- **Click Insert on the menu bar (Figure 3-59).**

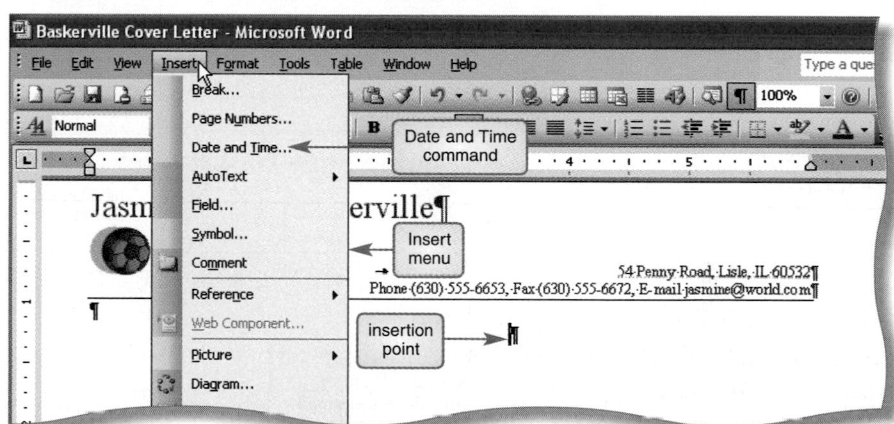

FIGURE 3-59

2

- **Click Date and Time on the Insert menu.**
- **When Word displays the Date and Time dialog box, click the desired format (in this case, April 25, 2008).**
- **If the Update automatically check box is selected, click the check box to remove the check mark.**

The Date and Time dialog box lists a variety of date and time formats (Figure 3-60). Your dialog box will differ, showing the current system date stored in your computer.

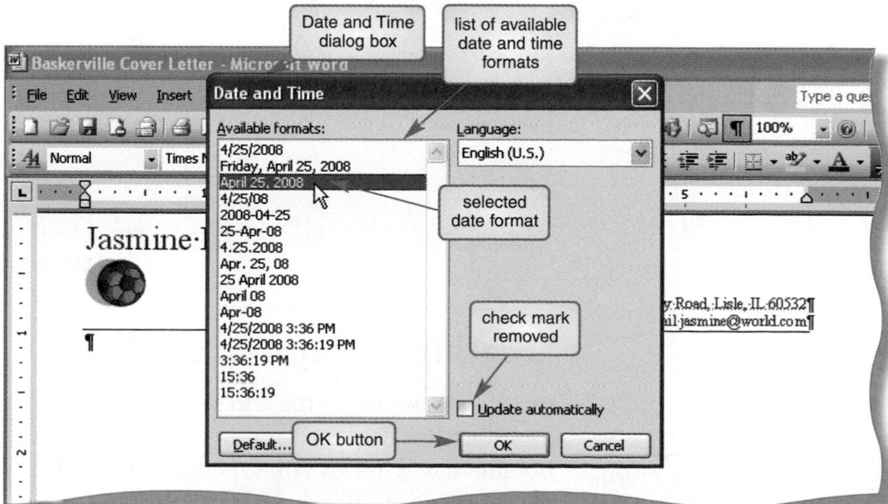

FIGURE 3-60

3

- **Click the OK button.**

Word inserts the current date at the location of the insertion point (shown in Figure 3-61 on the next page).

> **Q & A**
>
> **Q:** What is a date field?
>
> **A:** A field is a set of codes that instructs Word to perform a certain action. If you want Word to display the current date or time when you print a document, make it a field. That is, place a check mark in the Update automatically check box in the Date and Time dialog box (Figure 3-60 on the previous page) when you insert the current date or time.

The next step is to type the inside address and salutation in the cover letter, as described in the following steps.

To Enter the Inside Address and Salutation

1. **With the insertion point at the end of the date, press the ENTER key three times.**
2. **Type** `Mr. Joel Martello` **and then press the ENTER key.**
3. **Type** `Managing Partner` **and then press the ENTER key.**
4. **Type** `Triangle Accounting` **and then press the ENTER key.**
5. **Type** `1029 Birchwood Street` **and then press the ENTER key.**
6. **Type** `Chicago, IL 60606` **and then press the ENTER key twice.**
7. **Type** `Dear Mr. Martello` **and then press the COLON key (:).**

The inside address and salutation are entered (Figure 3-61).

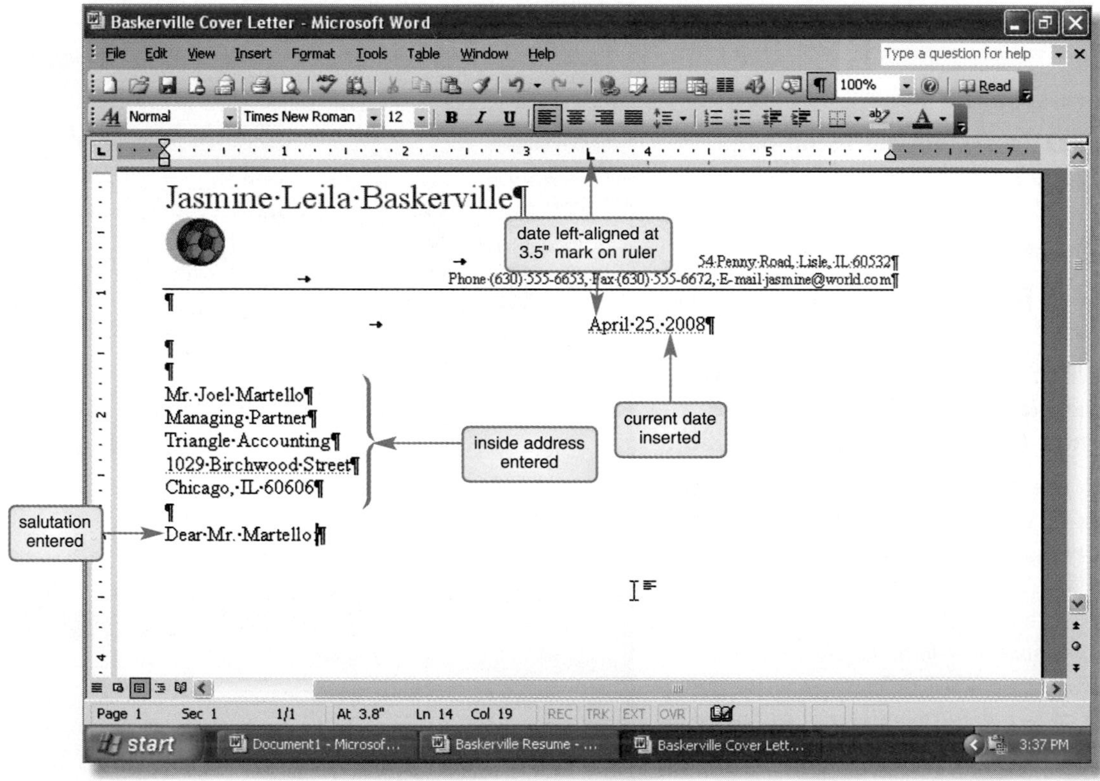

FIGURE 3-61

Creating an AutoText Entry

If you use the same text frequently, you can store the text in an **AutoText entry** and then use the stored entry throughout the open document, as well as future documents. That is, you type the entry only once, and for all future occurrences of the text, you access the stored entry as you need it. In this way, you avoid entering the text inconsistently or incorrectly in different locations throughout the same document.

The next steps show how to create an AutoText entry for the prospective employer's name.

To Create an AutoText Entry

1

- **Drag through the text to be stored, in this case, Triangle Accounting. Do not select the paragraph mark at the end of the text.**
- **Click Insert on the menu bar and then point to AutoText.**

The employer name, Triangle Accounting, in the inside address is selected (Figure 3-62). Notice the paragraph mark is not part of the selection.

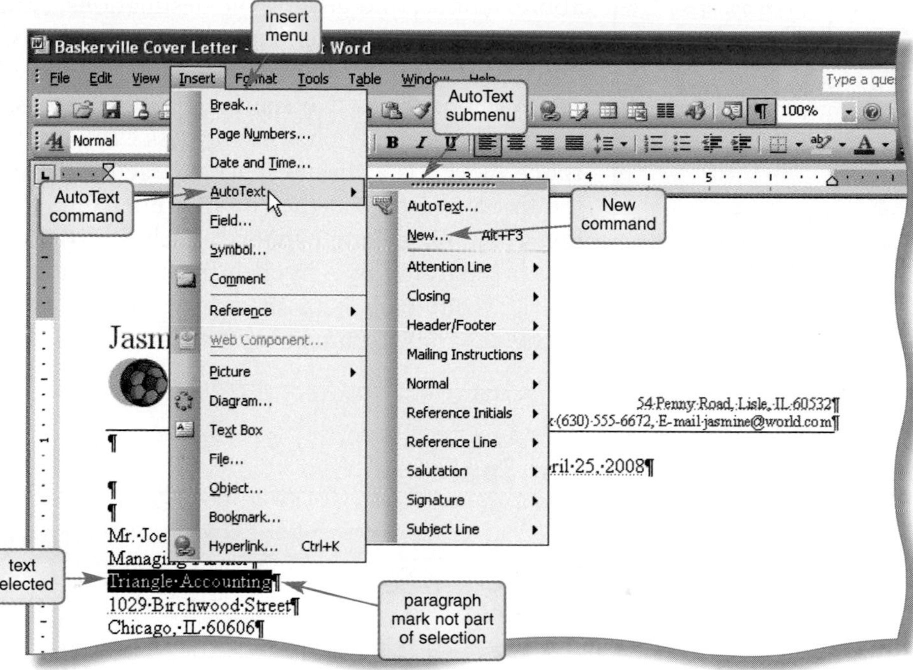

FIGURE 3-62

2

- **Click New on the AutoText submenu.**
- **When Word displays the Create AutoText dialog box, type** `ta` **as the AutoText entry name.**

When the Create AutoText dialog box first appears, Word proposes a name for the AutoText entry. You change Word's suggestion to ta (Figure 3-63).

3

- **Click the OK button.**
- **If Word displays another dialog box, click the Yes button.**

Word stores the AutoText entry and closes the AutoText dialog box.

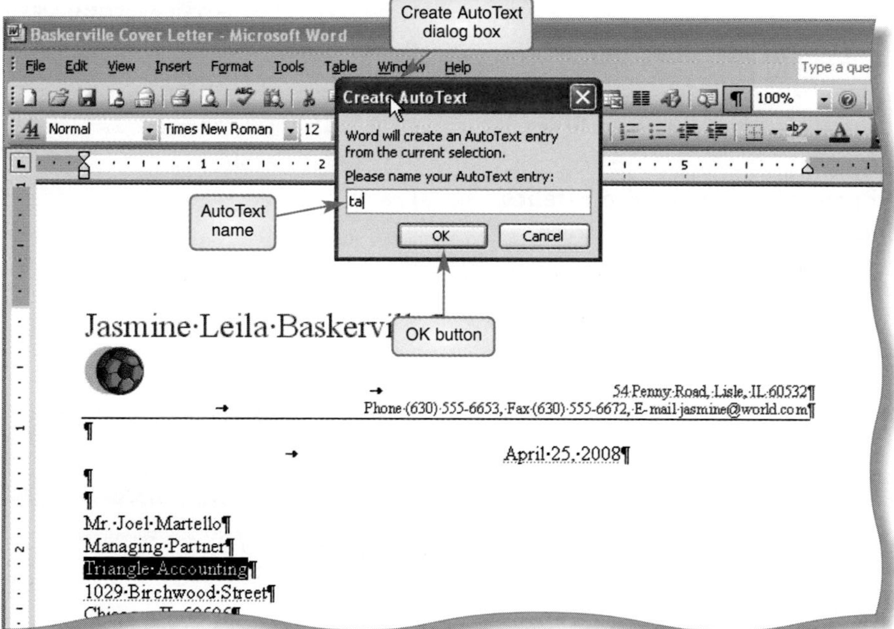

FIGURE 3-63

The name, ta, has been stored as an AutoText entry. Later in the project, you will use the AutoText entry, ta, instead of typing the employer name, Triangle Accounting.

Entering a Nonbreaking Space

Some compound words, such as proper names, dates, units of time and measure, abbreviations, and geographic destinations, should not be divided at the end of a line. These words either should fit as a unit at the end of a line or be wrapped together to the next line.

Word provides two special characters to assist with this task: nonbreaking space and nonbreaking hyphen. You press CTRL+SHIFT+SPACEBAR to insert a **nonbreaking space**, which is a special space character that prevents two words from splitting if the first word falls at the end of a line. Similarly, you press CTRL+SHIFT+HYPHEN to insert a **nonbreaking hyphen**, which is a special type of hyphen that prevents two words separated by a hyphen from splitting at the end of a line.

The following steps show how to enter a nonbreaking space between the words in the newspaper name.

Q & A

Q: What is an appropriate salutation if I do not know the recipient's name?

A: Avoid using the salutation "To whom it may concern" — it is extremely impersonal. If you cannot obtain the name and gender of the company officer to whom you are addressing the letter, then use the recipient's title in the salutation, e.g., Dear Personnel Supervisor.

To Insert a Nonbreaking Space

1

- **Scroll the salutation to the top of the document window. Click after the colon in the salutation and then press the ENTER key twice.**
- **Type** `I am interested in the part-time accounting clerk position advertised in yesterday's` **and then press the SPACEBAR.**
- **Press CTRL+I to turn on italics. Type** `Herald` **and then press CTRL+SHIFT+SPACEBAR.**

Word inserts a nonbreaking space after the word, Herald (Figure 3-64). The beginning of the newspaper title wraps to the next line.

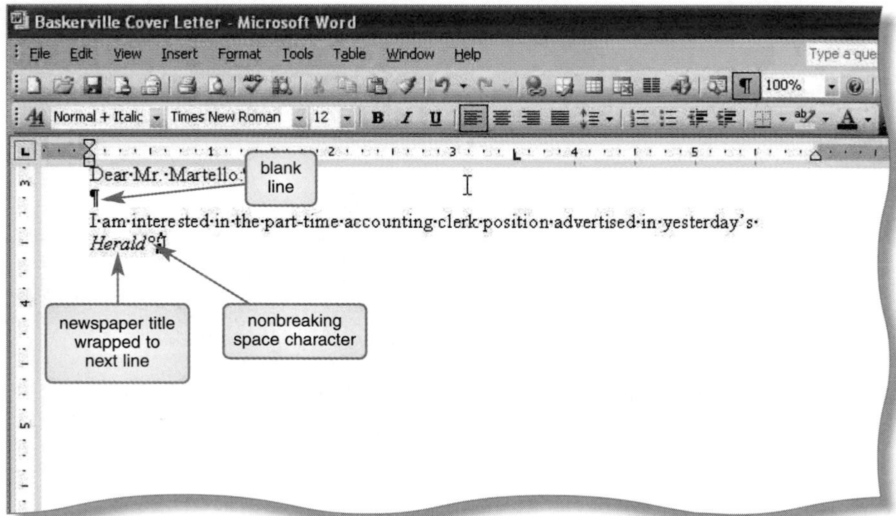

FIGURE 3-64

2

- **Type** `Times` **and then press CTRL+I to turn off italics. Press the PERIOD key.**

The entire newspaper title, Herald Times, is displayed on a single line (Figure 3-65).

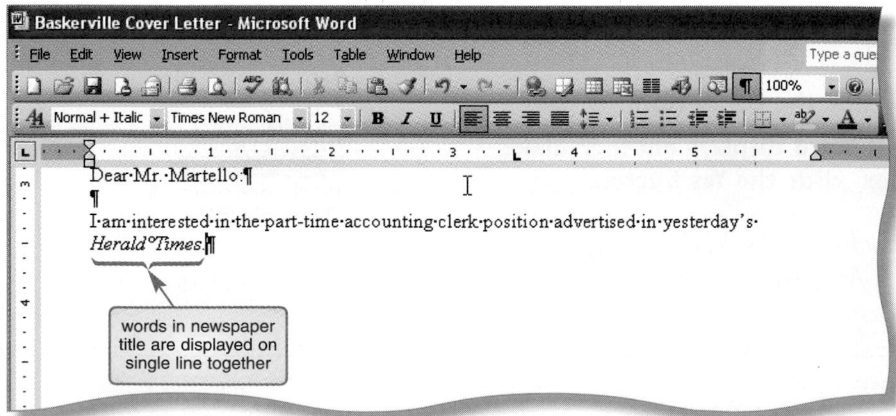

FIGURE 3-65

Inserting an AutoText Entry

At the end of the next sentence in the body of the cover letter, you want the prospective employer name, Triangle Accounting, to be displayed. Recall that earlier in this project, you created an AutoText entry name of ta for Triangle Accounting. Thus, you will type the AutoText entry's name and then instruct Word to replace the AutoText entry's name with the stored entry of Triangle Accounting.

The following steps show how to insert an AutoText entry.

To Insert an AutoText Entry

1

- **Press the SPACEBAR. Type** `As shown on the enclosed resume, I have the background you are seeking and believe my strengths and enthusiasm can be valuable to ta` **as shown in Figure 3-66.**

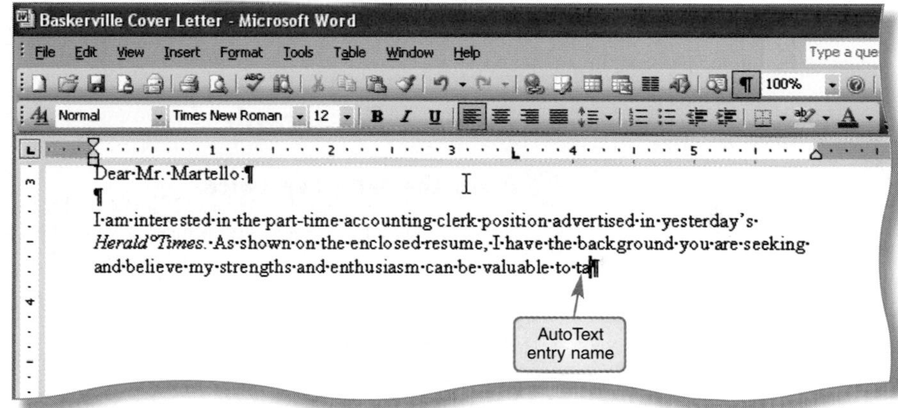

FIGURE 3-66

2

- **Press the F3 key.**
- **Press the PERIOD key.**

Word replaces the characters, ta, with the stored AutoText entry, Triangle Accounting, when you press the F3 key (Figure 3-67).

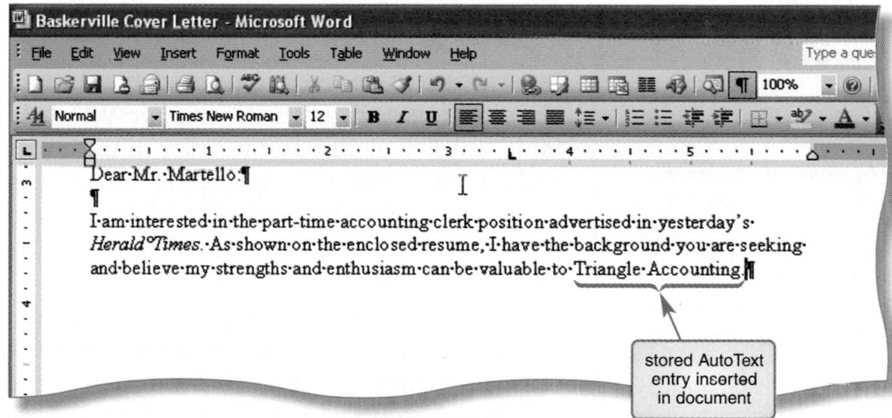

FIGURE 3-67

Pressing the **F3** key instructs Word to replace the AutoText entry name with the stored AutoText entry. In Project 2, you learned how to use the AutoCorrect feature, which enables you to insert and also create AutoCorrect entries (just as you did for this AutoText entry). The difference between an AutoCorrect entry and an AutoText entry is that the AutoCorrect feature makes corrections for you automatically as soon as you press the SPACEBAR or type a punctuation mark, whereas you must press the F3 key or click the AutoText command to instruct Word to make an AutoText correction.

If you watch the screen as you type, you may discover that AutoComplete tips appear on the screen. As you type, Word searches the list of AutoText entry names, and if one matches your typing, Word displays its complete name above your typing as an **AutoComplete tip**. If you press the ENTER key while an AutoComplete tip is displayed on the screen, Word places the text in the AutoComplete tip at the location of your typing. To ignore an AutoComplete tip proposed by Word, simply continue typing to remove the AutoComplete tip from the screen.

In addition to AutoText entries, Word proposes AutoComplete tips for the current date, days of the week, months, and so on. If your screen does not display AutoComplete tips, click Tools on the menu bar, click AutoCorrect Options, click the AutoText tab, click Show AutoComplete suggestions, and then click the OK button. To view the complete list of entries, click Tools on the menu bar, click AutoCorrect Options, click the AutoText tab, and then scroll through the list of entries.

The next step is to enter a paragraph of text into the cover letter, as described below.

To Enter a Paragraph

1 **Press the ENTER key twice.**

2 **Type** `I will graduate from Lincoln High School in May. As indicated in the following table, I have obtained exceptional grades in accounting, business, and computer classes.`

3 **Press the ENTER key twice.**

The paragraph is entered (shown in Figure 3-68).

Creating a Table with the Insert Table Button

The next step in composing the cover letter is to place a table listing your grade point averages (Figure 3-2a on page WD 140). You create this table using Word's table feature. As discussed earlier in this project, a Word table is a collection of rows and columns, and the intersection of a row and a column is called a cell.

Within a Word table, you easily can rearrange rows and columns, change column widths, sort rows and columns, and sum the contents of rows and columns. You also can format and chart table data.

The first step in creating a table is to insert an empty table into the document. When inserting a table, you must specify the total number of rows and columns required, which is called the **dimension** of the table. The table in this project has two columns. You often do not know the total number of rows in a table. Thus, many Word users create one row initially and then add more rows as needed. The first number in a dimension is the number of rows, and the second is the number of columns.

The following steps show how to insert a 1 × 2 (pronounced one by two) table; that is, a table with one row and two columns.

Q & A

Q: Can I create a table using the TAB key?

A: Although you can use the TAB key to align data in a table, many Word users prefer to use a table. With a Word table, you can arrange numbers and text in columns. For emphasis, tables can be shaded and have borders. The contents of Word tables can be sorted, and you can have Word sum the contents of an entire row or column.

To Insert an Empty Table

1

- **Click the Insert Table button on the Standard toolbar.**
- **Position the mouse pointer on the cell in the first row and second column of the grid.**

Word displays a grid so you can select the desired table dimension (Figure 3-68). Word will insert the table immediately above the insertion point.

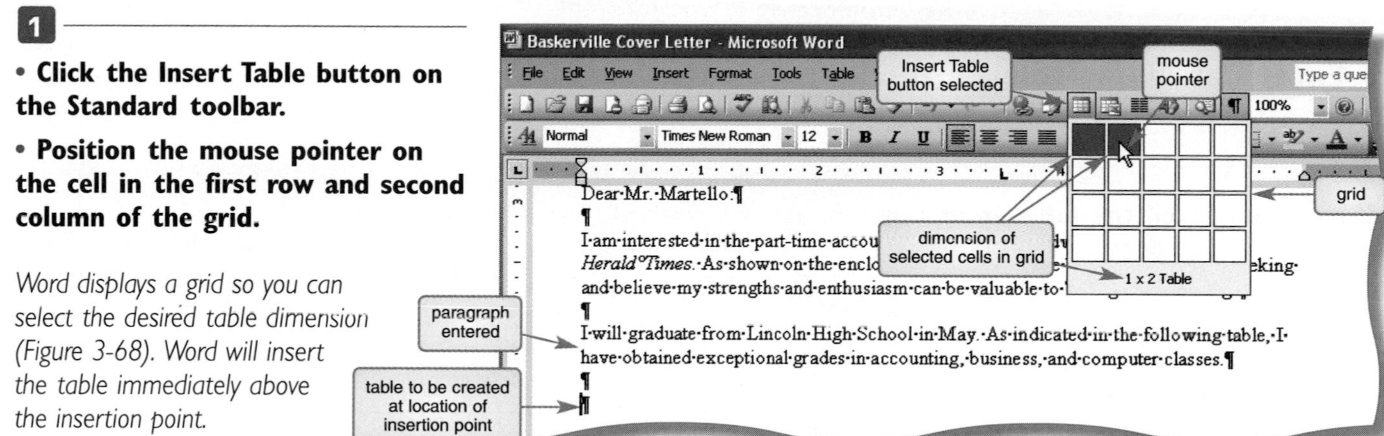

FIGURE 3-68

2

- **Click the cell in the first row and second column of the grid.**

Word inserts an empty 1 × 2 table in the document (Figure 3-69). The insertion point is in the first cell (row 1 and column 1) of the table.

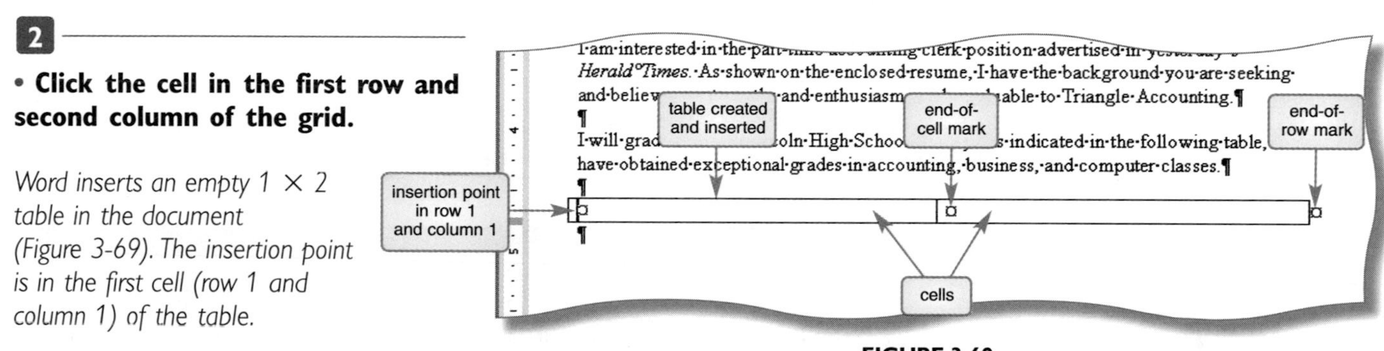

FIGURE 3-69

As discussed earlier in this project, each row of a table has an end-of-row mark, which you can use to add columns to the right of a table. Each cell has an end-of-cell mark, which you can use to select a cell. The end-of-cell mark currently is left-aligned; thus, it is positioned at the left edge of each cell. You can use any of the paragraph formatting buttons on the Formatting toolbar to change the alignment of the text within the cells. For example, if you click the Align Right button on the Formatting toolbar, the end-of-cell mark and any entered text will be displayed at the right edge of the cell.

For simple tables, such as the one just created, Word users click the Insert Table button to create a table. For more complex tables, such as one with a varying number of columns per row, Word has a Draw Table feature that allows you to use a pencil pointer to draw a table on the screen.

Entering Data in a Word Table

The next step is to enter data into the cells of the empty table. The data you enter within a cell wordwraps just as text does between the margins of a document. To place data in a cell, you click the cell and then type. To advance rightward from one cell to the next, press the TAB key. When you are at the rightmost cell in a row, also press the TAB key to move to the first cell in the next row; do not press the ENTER key. The ENTER key is used to begin a new paragraph within a cell.

To add new rows to a table, press the TAB key with the insertion point positioned in the bottom-right corner cell of the table.

The following steps show how to enter data in the table.

To Enter Data in a Table

1

- **If necessary, scroll the table up in the document window.**
- **With the insertion point in the left cell of the table, type** `GPA for Accounting Classes` **and then press the TAB key.**
- **Type** `4.00/4.00` **and then press the TAB key.**

Word enters the table data in the first row of the table and adds a second row to the table (Figure 3-70). The insertion point is positioned in the first cell of the second row.

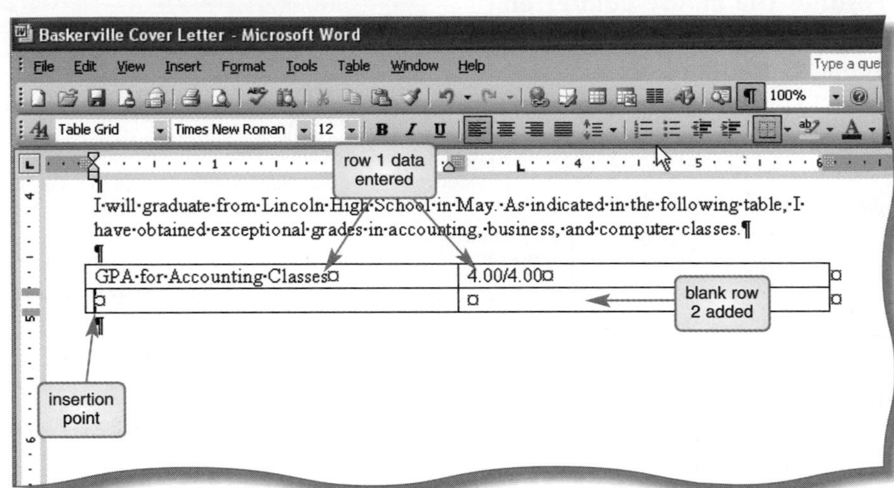

FIGURE 3-70

2

- **Type** `GPA for Business Classes` **and then press the TAB key. Type** `3.96/4.00` **and then press the TAB key.**
- **Type** `GPA for Computer Classes` **and then press the TAB key. Type** `3.97/4.00` **and then press the TAB key.**
- **Type** `Overall GPA` **and then press the TAB key. Type** `3.96/4.00` **as shown in Figure 3-71.**

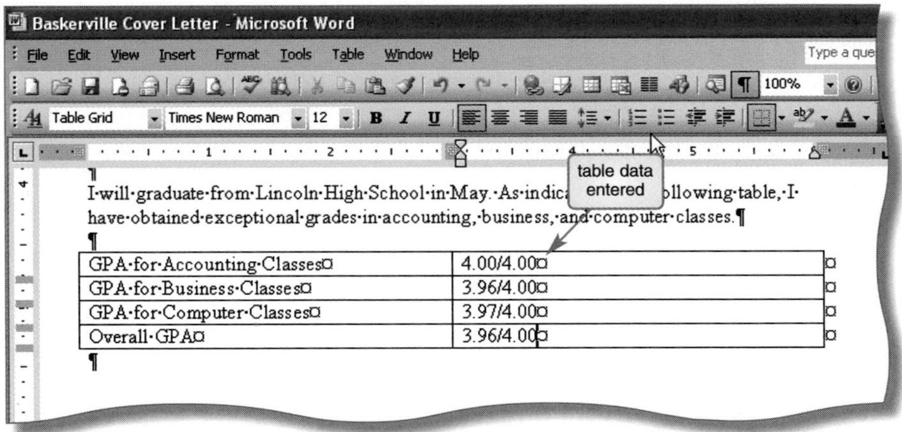

FIGURE 3-71

You modify the contents of cells just as you modify text in a document. To delete the contents of a cell, select the cell contents by pointing to the left edge of a cell and clicking when the mouse pointer changes direction, and then press the DELETE key. To modify text in a cell, click in the cell and then correct the entry. You can double-click the OVR indicator on the status bar to toggle between insert and overtype modes. You also can drag and drop or cut and paste the contents of cells.

As discussed in the previous steps, you add a row to the end of a table by positioning the insertion point in the bottom-right corner cell and then pressing the TAB key. To add a row in the middle of a table, select the row below where the new row is to be inserted, then click the Insert Rows button on the Standard toolbar (the same button location you clicked to insert a table); or click Insert Rows on the shortcut menu; or click Table on the menu bar, point to Insert, and then click Rows Above.

Q & A

Q: How do I insert a tab character into a cell?

A: The TAB key advances the insertion point from one cell to the next in a table. Thus, press CTRL+TAB to insert a tab character into a cell.

To add a column in the middle of a table, select the column to the right of where the new column is to be inserted and then click the Insert Columns button on the Standard toolbar (the same button location you clicked to insert a table); or click Insert Columns on the shortcut menu; or click Table on the menu bar, point to Insert, and then click Columns to the Left. To add a column to the right of a table, select the end-of-row marks at the right edge of the table, then click the Insert Columns button; or click Insert Columns on the shortcut menu; or click Table on the menu bar, point to Insert, and then click Columns to the Right.

If you want to delete row(s) or delete column(s) from a table, select the row(s) or column(s) to delete and then click Delete Rows or Delete Columns on the shortcut menu, or click Table on the menu bar, click Delete, and then click the appropriate item to delete.

> *Q & A*
>
> **Q:** Why is the Table command dimmed?
>
> **A:** If a Table command is dimmed on the Table menu, the insertion point might not be positioned in the table.

> *Q & A*
>
> **Q:** How do I change column and row measurements?
>
> **A:** To change the width of a column to an exact measurement. Hold down the ALT key while dragging markers on the ruler. Or, click Table on the menu bar, click Table Properties, click the Column tab, enter desired measurements, and then click the OK button. Similarly, to change the row height to an exact measurement, click the Row tab in the Table Properties dialog box, enter desired measurements, and then click the OK button.

Resizing Table Columns

The table in this project currently extends from the left margin to the right margin of the document. You want each column only to be as wide as the longest entry in the table. That is, the first column must be wide enough to accommodate the words, GPA for Accounting Classes; and the second column must be wide enough for the phrase, 4.00/4.00.

The following steps show how to instruct Word to fit the width of the columns to the contents of the table automatically.

To Fit Columns to Table Contents

1

- **Right-click the table and then point to AutoFit on the shortcut menu (Figure 3-72).**

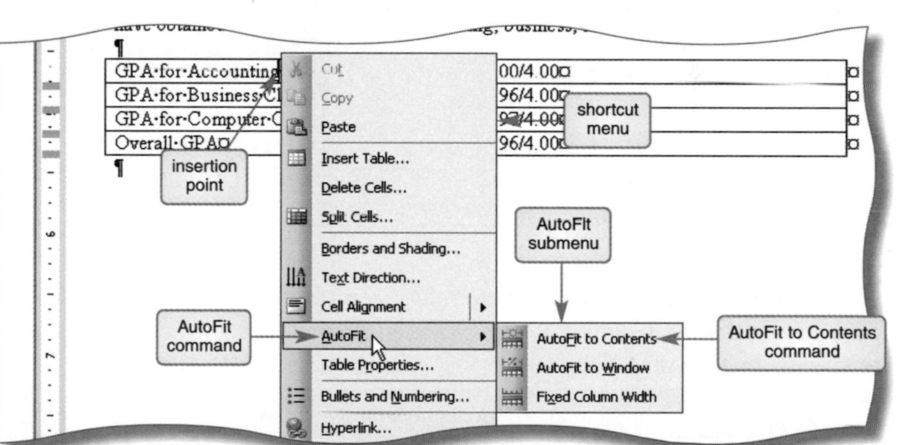

FIGURE 3-72

2

- **Click AutoFit to Contents on the AutoFit submenu.**

Word automatically adjusts the widths of the columns based on the text in the table (Figure 3-73). In this case, Word reduces the widths of the columns.

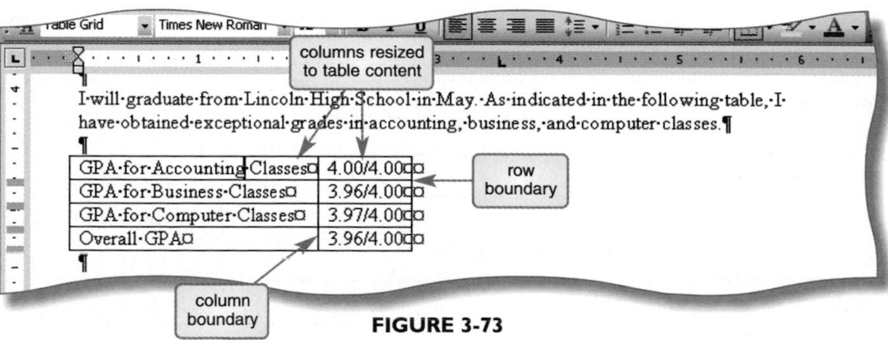

FIGURE 3-73

If you do not want to resize the columns to the table widths, Word provides other options. You can drag a **column boundary**, the border to the right of a column (Figure 3-73 on the previous page), until the column is the desired width. Similarly, you can resize a row by dragging the **row boundary**, the border at the bottom of a row, until the row is the desired height. You also can resize the entire table by dragging the **table resize handle**, which is a small square that appears when you point to the bottom-right corner of the table (shown in Figure 3-74).

Changing the Table Alignment

When you first create a table, it is left-aligned; that is, flush with the left margin. In this cover letter, the table should be centered. To center a table, select the entire table and then center it using the Center button on the Formatting toolbar, as shown in the following series of steps.

To Select a Table

1

- **Position the mouse pointer in the table so the table move handle appears.**
- **Click the table move handle.**

Word selects the entire table (Figure 3-74).

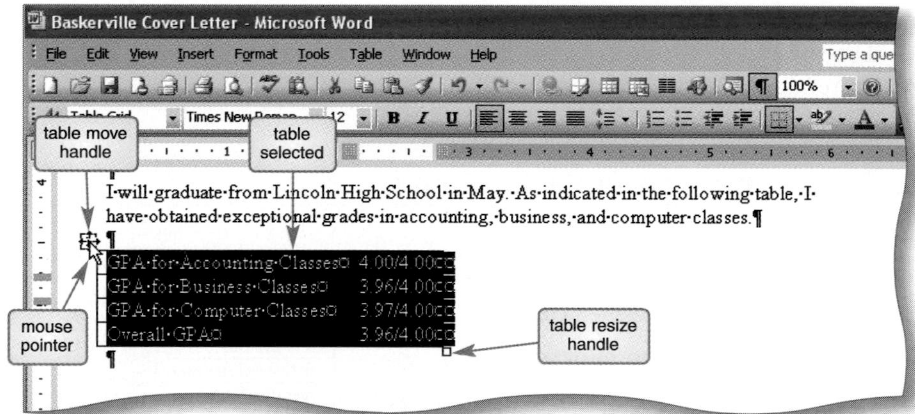

FIGURE 3-74

When working with tables, you may need to select the contents of cells, rows, columns, or the entire table. Table 3-3 identifies ways to select various items in a table.

Table 3-3 Selecting Items in a Table

ITEM TO SELECT	ACTION
Cell	Click left edge of cell
Column	Click border at top of column
Multiple cells, rows, or columns adjacent to one another	Drag through cells, rows, or columns
Multiple cells, rows, or columns not adjacent to one another	Select first cell, row, or column and then hold down CTRL key while selecting next cell, row, or column
Next cell	Press TAB key
Previous cell	Press SHIFT+TAB
Row	Click to left of row
Table	Click table move handle

The following step centers the selected table between the margins.

To Center a Selected Table

1 **Click the Center button on the Formatting toolbar.**

Word centers the selected table between the left and right margins (shown in Figure 3-75).

When an entire table is selected and you click the Center button on the Formatting toolbar, Word centers the entire table. If you wanted to center the contents of the cells, you would select the cells by dragging through them and then click the Center button.

The next step is to add more text below the table, as described here.

To Add More Text

1 **If necessary, scroll up. Click the paragraph mark below the table.**

2 **Press the ENTER key.**

3 **Type** `In addition to my course work, I have the following accounting experience` **and then press the COLON key. Press the ENTER key.**

The text is entered (shown in Figure 3-75).

Bulleting a List

You can type a list and then add bullets to the paragraphs at a later time, or you can use Word's AutoFormat As You Type feature to bullet the paragraphs as you type them (Table 3-1 on page WD 156).

The following steps show how to add bullets automatically to a list as you type.

To Bullet a List as You Type

1

- **Press the ASTERISK key (*).**
- **Press the SPACEBAR.**
- **Type** `Worked as an intern at Brims and Sons Accounting, assisting CPAs in tax preparation activities for both individuals and businesses` **(Figure 3-75).**

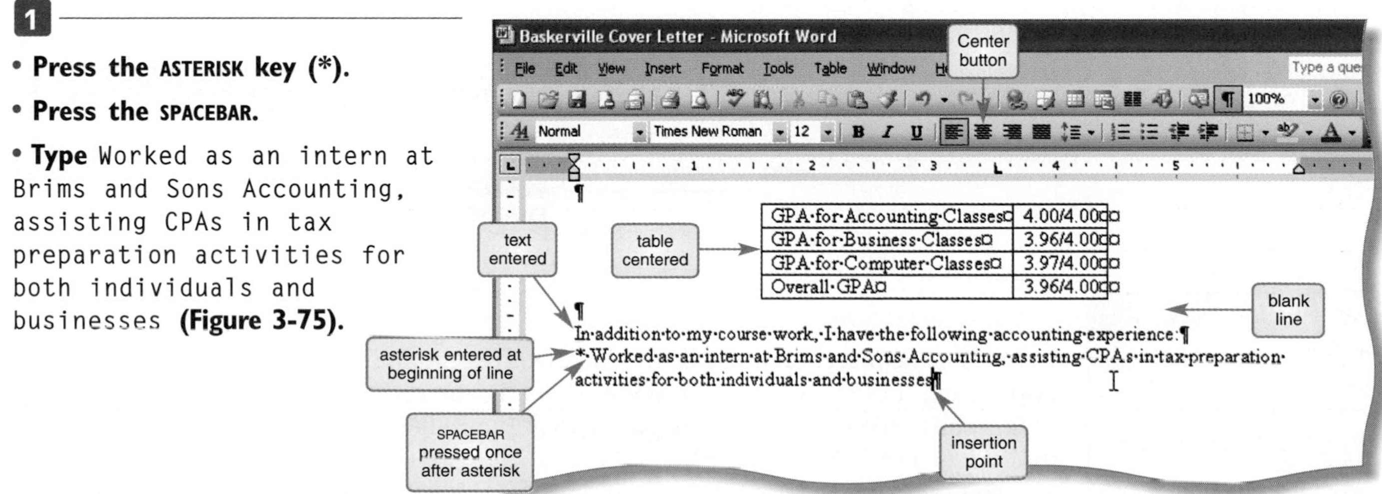

FIGURE 3-75

2

• **Press the ENTER key.**

Word converts the asterisk to a bullet character, places another bullet on the second list item, and indents the two bulleted paragraphs.

3

• **Type** `Maintaining student government association treasurer records using Quicken` **and then press the ENTER key.**

• **Type** `Automated my family's photography business records using QuickBooks` **and then press the ENTER key.**

Word places a bullet on the next line (Figure 3-76).

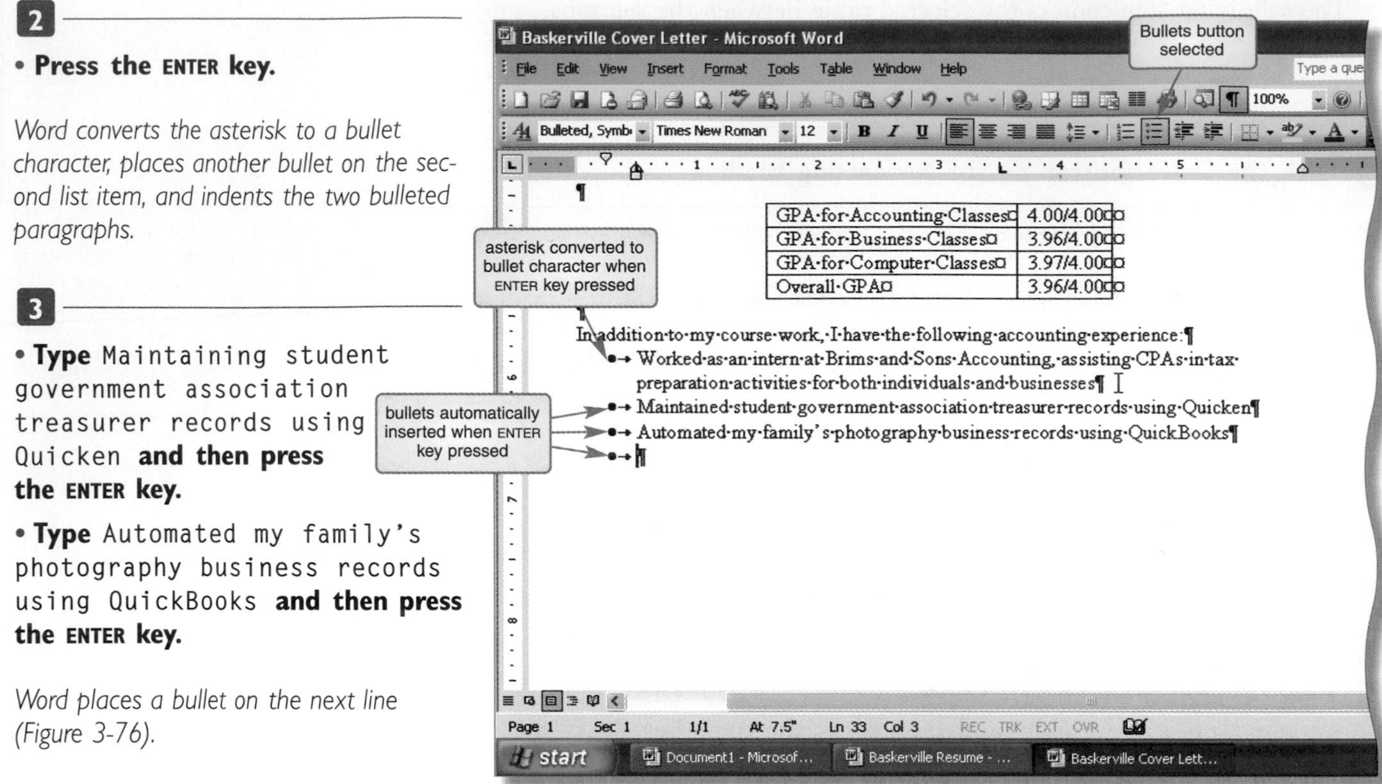

FIGURE 3-76

4

• **Press the ENTER key.**

Word removes the lone bullet because you pressed the ENTER key twice (Figure 3-77). The Bullets button no longer is selected.

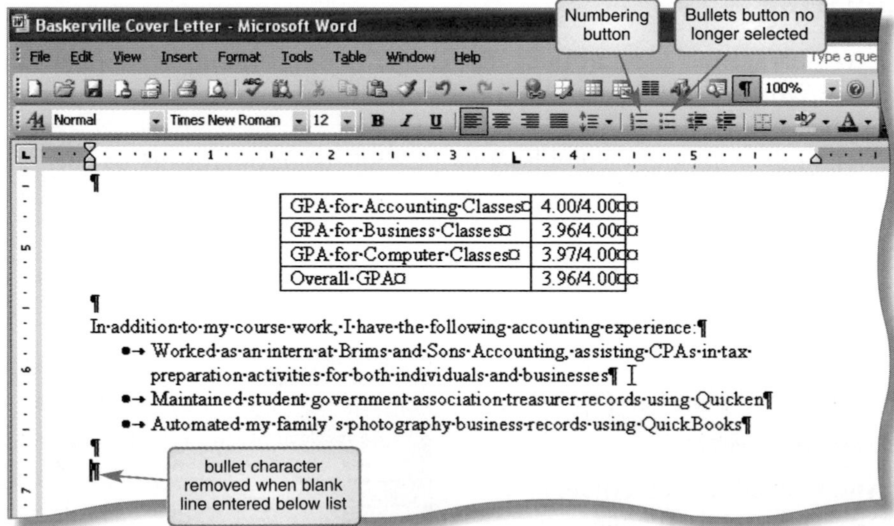

FIGURE 3-77

Skill Builder 3-4

To practice the following tasks, visit scsite.com/off2003sch/skill, locate Word Project 3, and then click Skill Builder 3-4.

- ❑ Set tab stops using the ruler
- ❑ Create a table and enter data into it
- ❑ Bullet a list

When the insertion point is in a bulleted list, the Bullets button on the Formatting toolbar is selected (Figure 3-76). To instruct Word to stop bulleting paragraphs, press the ENTER key twice, click the Bullets button on the Formatting toolbar, or press the BACKSPACE key to remove the bullet.

You may have noticed that Word displayed the AutoCorrect Options button when it formatted the list automatically as a bulleted list. If you did not want the list to be a bulleted list, you could click the AutoCorrect Options button and then click Undo Automatic Bullets on the shortcut menu.

You can add numbers as you type, just as you can add bullets as you type. To number a list, type the number one followed by a period and then a space (1.) at the beginning of the first item and then type your text. When you press the ENTER key, Word places the number two (2.) at the beginning of the next line automatically. As with bullets, press the ENTER key twice at the end of the list or click the Numbering button (Figure 3-77) on the Formatting toolbar to stop numbering.

The next step is to enter the remainder of the cover letter, as described below.

> **Q & A**
>
> **Q:** How do I create an outline numbered list?
>
> **A:** To create an outline numbered list, click Format on the menu bar, click Bullets and Numbering, click the Outline Numbered tab, and then click a style that does not contain the word, Heading. To promote or demote a list item to the next or previous levels, click the Increase Indent and Decrease Indent buttons on the Formatting toolbar.

To Enter the Remainder of the Cover Letter

1. **Type the paragraph shown in Figure 3-78, making certain you use the AutoText entry, ta, to insert the employer name.**
2. **Press the ENTER key twice. Press the TAB key. Type** `Sincerely` **and then press the COMMA key.**
3. **Press the ENTER key four times. Press the TAB key. Type** `Jasmine Leila Baskerville` **and then press the ENTER key twice.**
4. **Type** `Enclosure: Resume` **as the final text.**

The cover letter text is complete (Figure 3-78).

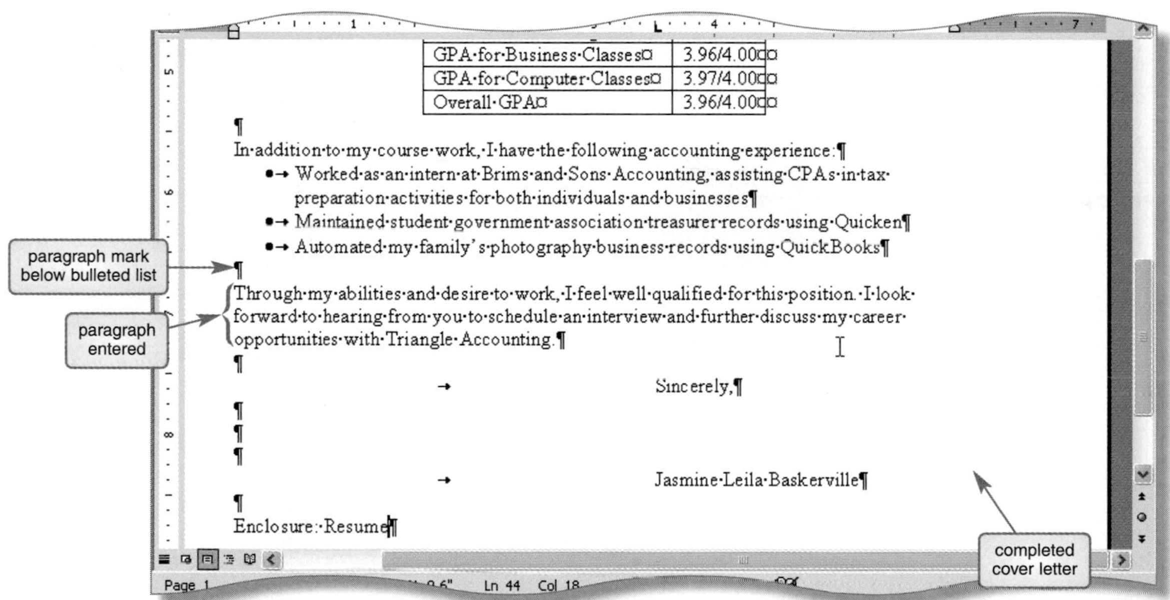

FIGURE 3-78

Saving Again and Printing the Cover Letter

The cover letter for the resume now is complete. You should save the cover letter again and then print it, as described in the following steps.

> **Q & A**
>
> **Q:** Should I proofread the resume and cover letter?
>
> **A:** You should be absolutely certain that your resume and cover letter are error free. Check spelling and grammar using Word. Proofread for errors. Set the resume and cover letter aside for a couple of days and then proofread them again. Ask others, such as a friend or teacher, to proofread them also.

To Save a Document Again

1. **Click the Save button on the Standard toolbar.**

Word saves the cover letter with the same file name, Baskerville Cover Letter.

> **Q & A**
>
> **Q:** How should I print the resume and cover letter?
>
> **A:** Use a laser printer to print the resume and cover letter on standard letter-size white or ivory paper. Be sure to print a copy for yourself, and read it — especially before the interview. Most likely, the interviewer will have copies in hand, ready to ask you questions about the contents of both the resume and cover letter.

To Print a Document

1 Click the Print button on the Standard toolbar.

The completed cover letter prints as shown in Figure 3-2a on page WD 140.

Addressing and Printing Envelopes and Mailing Labels

With Word, you can print address information on an envelope or on a mailing label. Computer-printed addresses look more professional than handwritten ones. Thus, the following steps show how to address and print an envelope.

To Address and Print an Envelope

1

- **Scroll through the cover letter to display the inside address in the document window.**
- **Drag through the inside address to select it.**
- **Click Tools on the menu bar and then point to Letters and Mailings (Figure 3-79).**

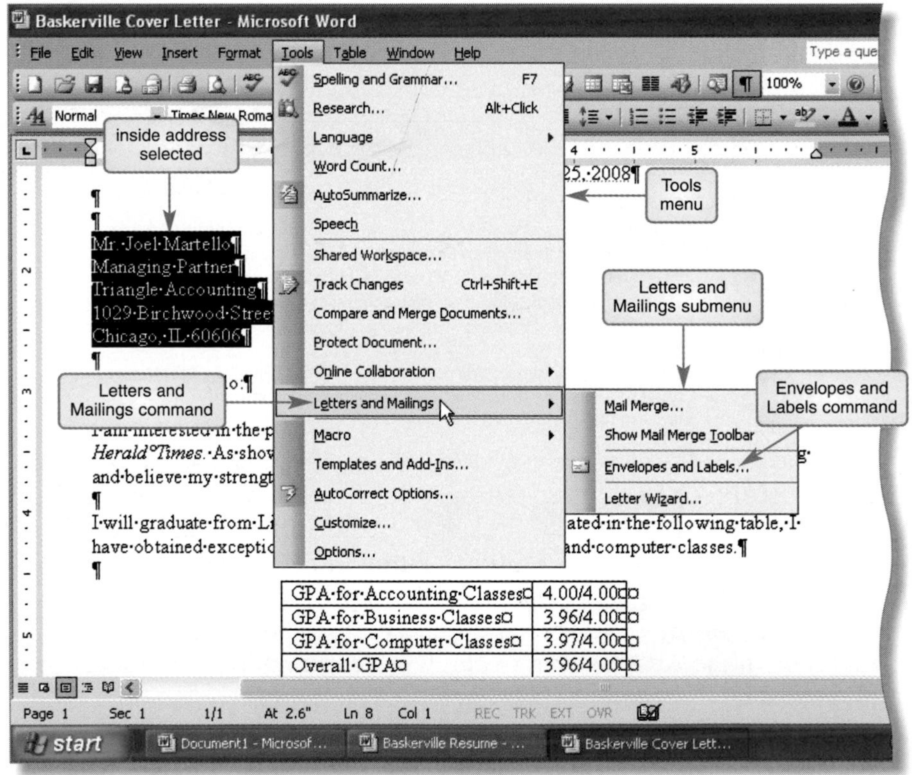

FIGURE 3-79

2

- **Click Envelopes and Labels on the Letters and Mailings submenu.**
- **When Word displays the Envelopes and Labels dialog box, if necessary, click the Envelopes tab.**
- **Click the Return address text box.**
- **Type** `Jasmine Leila Baskerville` **and then press the ENTER key.**
- **Type** `54 Penny Road` **and then press the ENTER key.**
- **Type** `Lisle, IL 60532` **(Figure 3-80).**

3

- **Insert an envelope into your printer, as shown in the Feed area of the dialog box (your Feed area may be different depending on your printer).**
- **Click the Print button in the Envelopes and Labels dialog box.**
- **If a dialog box is displayed, click the No button.**

FIGURE 3-80

Word prints the envelope (shown in Figure 3-2b on page WD 140).

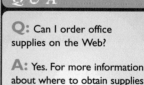

Instead of printing the envelope immediately, you can add it to the document by clicking the Add to Document button in the Envelopes and Labels dialog box. To specify a different envelope or label type (identified by a number on the box of envelopes or labels), click the Options button in the Envelopes and Labels dialog box.

Instead of printing an envelope, you can print a mailing label. To do this, click the Labels tab in the Envelopes and Labels dialog box (Figure 3-80). Type the delivery address in the Address box. To print the same address on all labels on the page, click Full page of the same label. Click the Print button in the dialog box.

Q & A

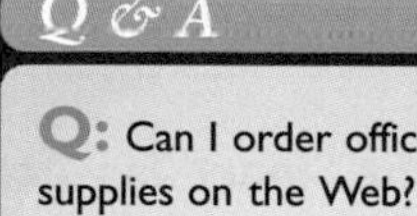

Q: Can I order office supplies on the Web?

A: Yes. For more information about where to obtain supplies for printing documents, visit the Office 2003 Q&A Web page (scsite.com/off2003sch/qa), locate Word Project 3, and then click Online Office Supplies.

Smart Tags

A **smart tag** is a button that automatically appears on the screen when Word performs a certain action. In this and previous projects, you worked with the AutoCorrect Options and Paste Options smart tags. This section discusses the third type of smart tag, called Smart Tag Actions, which performs various functions depending on the object identified by the smart tag indicator.

The smart tag indicator for Smart Tag Actions is a purple dotted underline. As shown throughout this project, a smart tag indicator appears below addresses and dates. A smart tag indicator also may appear below names, places, times, and financial symbols. To view or change the list of objects recognized as smart tags, click Tools on the menu bar, click AutoCorrect Options, and then click the Smart Tags tab.

When you point to a smart tag indicator, the Smart Tag Actions button appears on the screen. Clicking the Smart Tag Actions button displays a Smart Tag Actions menu. The commands in the Smart Tag Actions menu vary depending on the smart tag. For example, the Smart Tag Actions menu for a date includes commands that allow you to schedule a meeting in Outlook Calendar or display your Outlook Calendar. The Smart Tag Actions menu for an address includes commands for adding the address to your Outlook contacts list.

The following steps illustrate using a smart tag to display your Outlook Calendar. If you are stepping through this project on a computer and you want your screen to match the figures in the following steps, then your computer must have Outlook installed.

To Use the Smart Tag Actions Button

1

- **Click anywhere to remove the highlight from the inside address.**
- **Position the mouse pointer on the smart tag indicator below the date line, April 25, 2008, in the cover letter. (If the smart tag indicator is not displayed, click Tools on the menu bar, click AutoCorrect Options, click the Smart Tags tab, select the Date check box, click the Recheck Document button, and then click the OK button.)**

Word displays the Smart Tag Actions button (Figure 3-81).

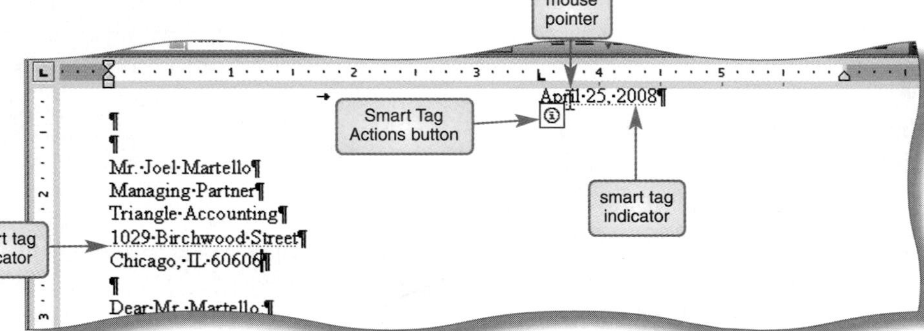

FIGURE 3-81

2

- **Click the Smart Tag Actions button.**

Word displays the Smart Tag Actions menu (Figure 3-82).

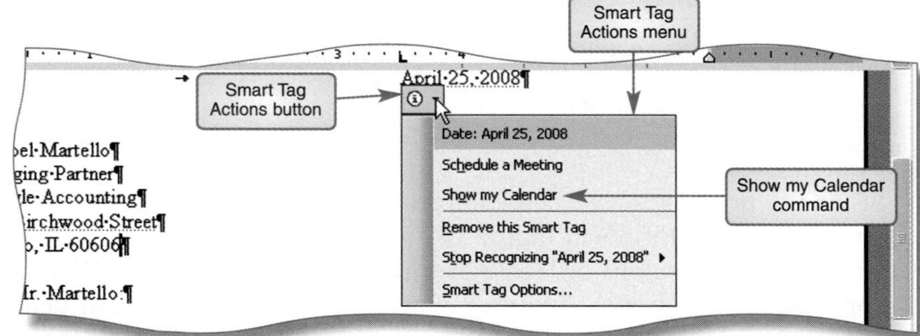

FIGURE 3-82

3

- **Click Show my Calendar on the Smart Tag Actions menu.**

Outlook starts and displays your calendar for today's date (Figure 3-83). Your date will differ, depending on the computer's system date.

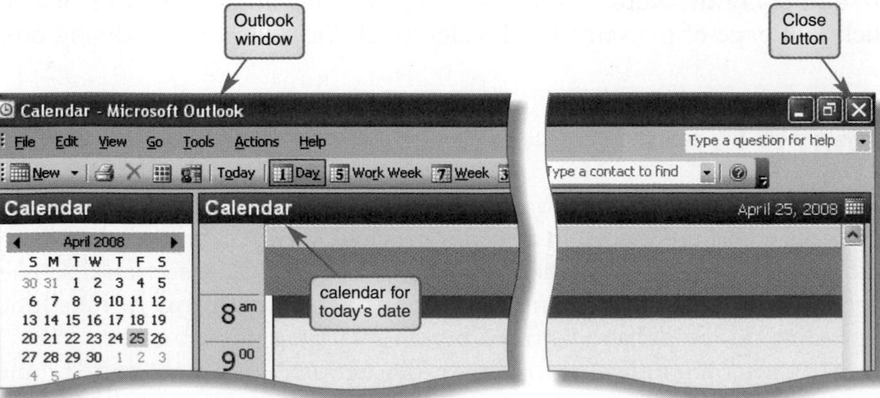

FIGURE 3-83

4

- **Click the Close button on the Outlook title bar to close Outlook.**

Document Summary

When you create and save many documents on a computer, you may not remember the name of each individual document. To help locate documents at a later time, you can store additional information about the document, called **file properties** or the **document summary**, when you save it. For example, you can specify items such as a title, subject, category, keyword(s), and comment(s).

The following steps show how to modify and view the document summary for the cover letter.

To Modify the Document Summary

1

- **Click File on the menu bar (Figure 3-84).**

2

- **Click Properties on the File menu.**
- **When Word displays the Baskerville Cover Letter Properties dialog box, if necessary, click the Summary tab.**
- **Type** `Triangle Accounting` **in the Title text box.**
- **Type** `Cover Letter` **in the Subject text box.**
- **Type** `Cover Letter` **in the Category text box.**
- **Type** `cover letter, Triangle Accounting` **in the Keywords text box.**
- **Type** `Cover letter to Mr. Joel Martello at Triangle Accounting` **in the Comments text box (Figure 3-85).**

3

- **Click the OK button to close the dialog box.**
- **Click the Save button on the Standard toolbar.**
- **Click File on the menu bar and then click Close to close the cover letter document window.**

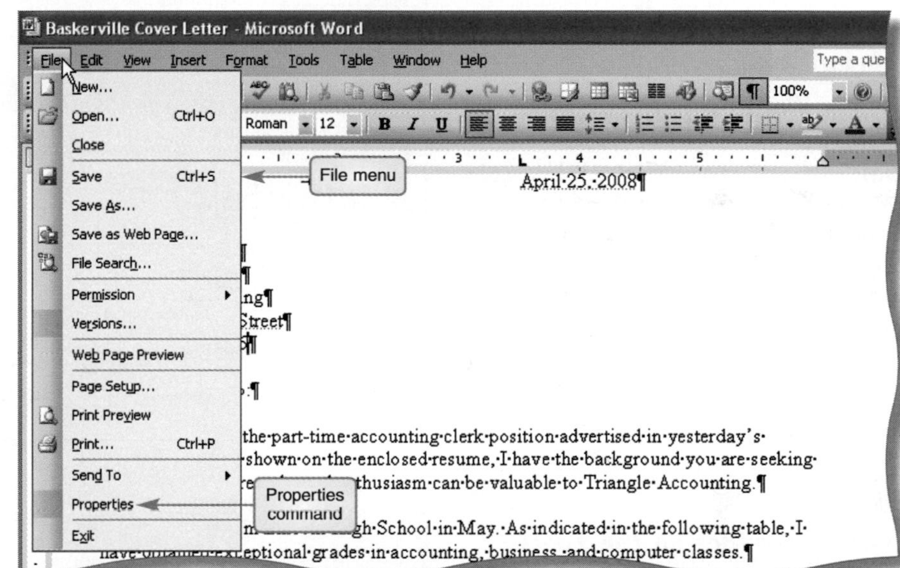

FIGURE 3-84

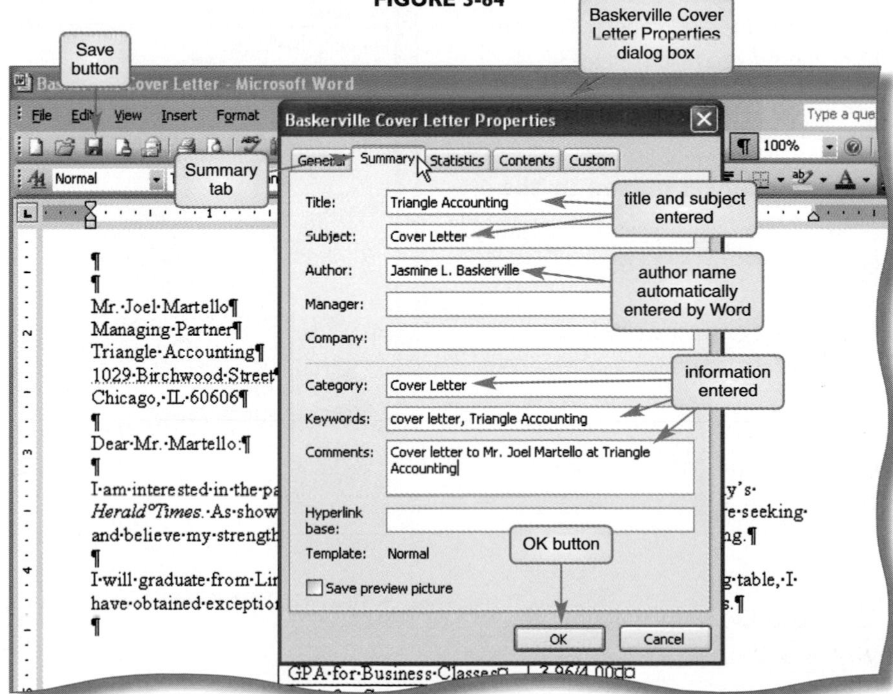

FIGURE 3-85

The updated file properties become part of the document when you save the document.

Word automatically pulls the author information from the user information stored on the computer. To change the user information, click Tools on the menu bar, click Options, click the User Information tab, enter the new information in the text boxes, and then click the OK button.

When opening a document at a later time, you can display the document properties to help you locate a particular file, as shown in the following steps.

To Display File Properties in the Open Dialog Box

1

- **Click the Open button on the Standard toolbar.**
- **When Word displays the Open dialog box, if necessary, click the Look in box arrow, click UDISK 2.0 (E:), and then click Baskerville Cover Letter.**
- **Click the Views button arrow in the Open dialog box.**

Word displays the Views menu in the Open dialog box (Figure 3-86).

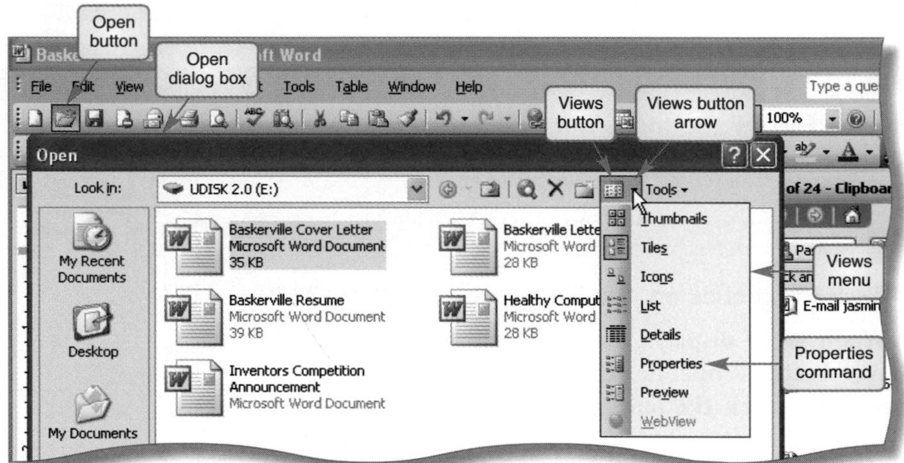

FIGURE 3-86

2

- **Click Properties on the Views menu.**

Word displays the file properties to the right of the selected file (Figure 3-87).

3

- **Click the Cancel button in the dialog box.**

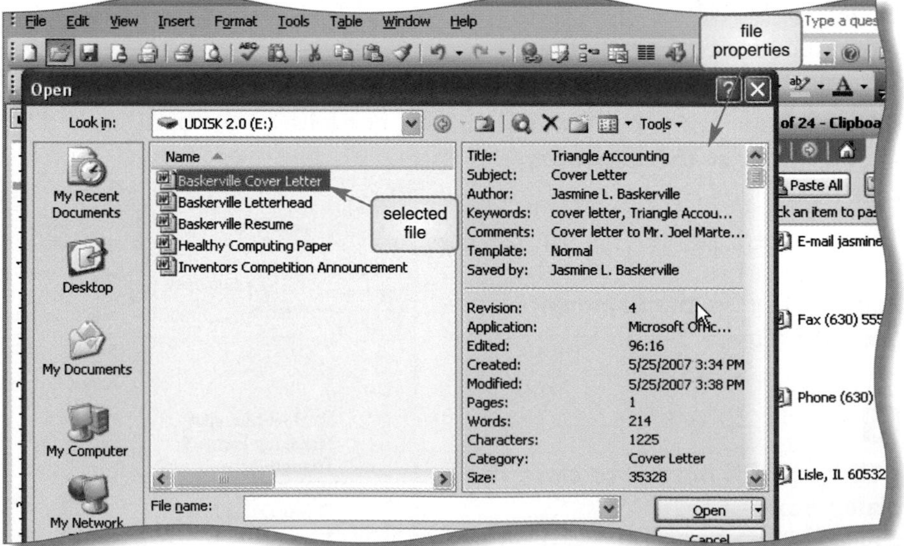

FIGURE 3-87

The final step in this project is to quit Word, as described in the next step.

To Quit Word

1 Click File on the menu bar and then click Exit. (If Word displays a dialog box about saving changes, click the No button.)

Word closes any open documents (in this case, the resume) and then the Word window closes.

> **Q & A**
>
> **Q:** Can I use the Web to search for job postings?
>
> **A:** Yes. For links to Web sites about job searches, visit the Office 2003 Q&A Web page (scsite.com/off2003sch/qa), locate Word Project 3, and then click one of the Job Searches links.

Project Summary

In creating the Baskerville Resume and Baskerville Cover Letter in this project, you learned how to use Word to enter and format a resume and cover letter. You learned how to use the Resume Wizard to create a resume. Then, you selected and replaced placeholder text in the document created by the resume. In personalizing the resume, you learned how to hide white space, enter a line break, and use Word's AutoFormat As You Type feature. This project also discussed how to view and print the resume in print preview.

Next, this project showed how to create a letterhead and then the cover letter. While creating the letterhead, you learned how to add color to characters, set custom tab stops, collect and paste between documents, add a border to a paragraph, and clear formatting. In the cover letter, this project showed how to insert a date, create and insert an AutoText entry, create and format a table, and enter a bulleted list. Finally, the project showed how to address and print an envelope, use smart tags, and modify the document summary.

If you have a SAM user profile, you may have access to hands-on instruction, practice, and assessment of the skills covered in this project. Log in to your SAM account and go to your assignments page to see what your instructor has assigned.

What You Should Know

Having completed this project, you should be able to perform the tasks below. The tasks are listed in the same order they were presented in this project. For a list of the buttons, menus, toolbars, and commands introduced in this project, see the Quick Reference Summary at the back of this book and refer to the Page Number column.

1. Start and Customize Word (WD 141)
2. Display Formatting Marks (WD 141)
3. Create a Resume Using Word's Resume Wizard (WD 142)
4. Hide White Space (WD 149)
5. Print the Resume Created by the Resume Wizard (WD 149)
6. Select and Replace Placeholder Text (WD 152)
7. Select and Replace More Placeholder Text (WD 153)
8. Enter a Line Break (WD 154)
9. Enter More Text with Line Breaks (WD 155)
10. AutoFormat As You Type (WD 156)
11. Enter the Remaining Sections of the Resume (WD 157)
12. Print Preview a Document (WD 158)
13. Save a Document (WD 159)
14. Open a New Document Window (WD 160)
15. Change the Font Size (WD 161, WD 162)
16. Color Text (WD 161)
17. Insert a Graphic (WD 162)
18. Resize a Graphic (WD 162)
19. Set Custom Tab Stops Using the Tabs Dialog Box (WD 164)
20. Switch from One Open Document to Another (WD 166)
21. Copy Items to the Office Clipboard (WD 166)
22. Display the Clipboard Task Pane (WD 169)
23. Zoom Text Width (WD 169)
24. Paste from the Office Clipboard (WD 170)
25. Paste More Information from the Office Clipboard (WD 171)

26. Zoom to 100% (WD 172)
27. Bottom Border a Paragraph (WD 172)
28. Clear Formatting (WD 173)
29. Convert a Hyperlink to Regular Text (WD 174)
30. Save the Letterhead (WD 174)
31. Save the Document with a New File Name (WD 176)
32. Set Custom Tab Stops Using the Ruler (WD 176)
33. Insert the Current Date in a Document (WD 177)
34. Enter the Inside Address and Salutation (WD 178)
35. Create an AutoText Entry (WD 179)
36. Insert a Nonbreaking Space (WD 180)
37. Insert an AutoText Entry (WD 181)
38. Enter a Paragraph (WD 182)
39. Insert an Empty Table (WD 183)
40. Enter Data in a Table (WD 184)
41. Fit Columns to Table Contents (WD 185)
42. Select a Table (WD 186)
43. Center a Selected Table (WD 187)
44. Add More Text (WD 187)
45. Bullet a List as You Type (WD 187)
46. Enter the Remainder of the Cover Letter (WD 189)
47. Save a Document Again (WD 189)
48. Print a Document (WD 190)
49. Address and Print an Envelope (WD 190)
50. Use the Smart Tag Actions Button (WD 192)
51. Modify the Document Summary (WD 193)
52. Display File Properties in the Open Dialog Box (WD 194)
53. Quit Word (WD 195)

Career Corner

Personal Computer Salesperson

When you decide to buy or upgrade a personal computer, the most important person with whom you interact probably will be a personal computer salesperson. This individual will be a valuable resource to you in providing the information and expertise you need to select a computer that meets your requirements.

Computer manufacturers and retailers that sell several types of personal computers need competent salespeople. A personal computer salesperson must be computer literate and have a specific knowledge of the computers he or she sells. In addition, a successful salesperson has a friendly, outgoing personality that helps customers feel comfortable. Through open-ended questions, the salesperson can determine a customer's needs and level of experience. With this information, the salesperson can choose the best computer for the customer and explain the features of the computer in language the customer will understand.

Most computer salespeople have at least a high school diploma. Before reaching the sales floor, however, salespeople usually complete extensive company training programs. These programs often consist of self-directed, self-paced Web-training classes. Most salespeople also participate in training updates, often on a monthly basis.

Personal computer salespeople generally earn a guaranteed amount plus a commission for each sale. A computer salesperson can earn about $40,000 a year. Top salespeople can be among a company's more highly compensated employees, earning in excess of $70,000. For more information, visit scsite.com/off2003sch/careers and then click Personal Computer Salesperson.

Q & A

Q: Is there more than one way to invoke a command in Word?

A: Yes. For a table that lists how to complete the tasks covered in this book using the mouse, menu, shortcut menu, and keyboard, see the Quick Reference Summary at the back of this book, or visit the Office 2003 Quick Reference Web page (scsite.com/ off2003sch/qr).

Q & A

Q: What is the Microsoft Office Certification program?

A: The Microsoft Office Specialist Certification program provides an opportunity for you to obtain a valuable industry credential — proof that you have the Word 2003 skills required by employers. For more information, see Appendix E or visit the Office 2003 Certification Web page (scsite.com/off2003sch/cert).

Learn It Online

Instructions: To complete the Learn It Online exercises, start your browser, click the Address bar, and then enter the Web address `scsite.com/off2003sch/learn`. When the Office 2003 Learn It Online page is displayed, follow the instructions in the exercises below. Each exercise has instructions for printing your results, either for your own records or for submission to your instructor.

1 Project Reinforcement TF, MC, and SA

Below Word Project 3, click the Project Reinforcement link. Print the quiz by clicking Print on the File menu for each page. Answer each question.

2 Flash Cards

Below Word Project 3, click the Flash Cards link and read the instructions. Type 20 (or a number specified by your instructor) in the Number of playing cards text box, type your name in the Enter your Name text box, and then click the Flip Card button. When the flash card is displayed, read the question and then click the ANSWER box arrow to select an answer. Flip through Flash Cards. If your score is 15 (75%) correct or greater, click Print on the File menu to print your results. If your score is less than 15 (75%) correct, then redo this exercise by clicking the Replay button.

3 Practice Test

Below Word Project 3, click the Practice Test link. Answer each question, enter your first and last name at the bottom of the page, and then click the Grade Test button. When the graded practice test is displayed on your screen, click Print on the File menu to print a hard copy. Continue to take practice tests until you score 80% or better.

4 Who Wants To Be a Computer Genius?

Below Word Project 3, click the Computer Genius link. Read the instructions, enter your first and last name at the bottom of the page, and then click the PLAY button. When your score is displayed, click the PRINT RESULTS link to print a hard copy.

5 Wheel of Terms

Below Word Project 3, click the Wheel of Terms link. Read the instructions, and then enter your first and last name and your school name. Click the PLAY button. When your score is displayed, right-click the score and then click Print on the shortcut menu to print a hard copy.

6 Crossword Puzzle Challenge

Below Word Project 3, click the Crossword Puzzle Challenge link. Read the instructions, and then enter your first and last name. Click the SUBMIT button. Work the crossword puzzle. When you are finished, click the Submit button. When the crossword puzzle is redisplayed, click the Print Puzzle button to print a hard copy.

7 Tips and Tricks

Below Word Project 3, click the Tips and Tricks link. Click a topic that pertains to Project 3. Right-click the information and then click Print on the shortcut menu. Construct a brief example of what the information relates to in Word to confirm you understand how to use the tip or trick.

8 Newsgroups

Below Word Project 3, click the Newsgroups link. Click a topic that pertains to Project 3. Print three comments.

9 Expanding Your Horizons

Below Word Project 3, click the Expanding Your Horizons link. Click a topic that pertains to Project 3. Print the information. Construct a brief example of what the information relates to in Word to confirm you understand the contents of the article.

10 Search Sleuth

Below Word Project 3, click the Search Sleuth link. To search for a term that pertains to this project, select a term below the Project 3 title and then use the Google search engine at google.com (or any major search engine) to display and print two Web pages that present information on the term.

11 Word Online Training

Below Word Project 3, click the Word Online Training link. When your browser displays the Microsoft Office Online Web page, click the Word link. Click one of the Word courses that covers one or more of the objectives listed at the beginning of the project on page WD 138. Print the first page of the course before stepping through it.

12 Office Marketplace

Below Word Project 3, click the Office Marketplace link. When your browser displays the Microsoft Office Online Web page, click the Office Marketplace link. Click a topic that relates to Word. Print the first page.

13 You're Hired!

Below Word Project 3, click the You're Hired! link to embark on the path to a career in computers. Directions about how to play the game will be displayed. When you are ready to play, click the begin the game button. If required, submit your score to your instructor.

1 Working with Tabs and a Table

Instructions: Start Word. Open the document, Apply 3-1 Projected College Expenses Table. See page xxiv at the front of this book for instructions for downloading the Data Files for Students or see your instructor for information about accessing the files required in this book.

The document is a Word table that you are to edit and format. The revised table is shown in Figure 3-88.

Perform the following tasks:

Projected College Expenses Table

	FRESHMAN	SOPHOMORE	JUNIOR	SENIOR
Room & Board	3390.00	3627.30	3881.21	4152.90
Tuition & Books	4850.50	5189.50	5552.72	5941.46
Entertainment	635.00	679.45	727.01	777.90
Cell Phone	359.88	365.78	372.81	385.95
Miscellaneous	325.00	347.75	372.09	398.14
Clothing	540.25	577.80	618.29	661.52
Total	*10100.63*	*10787.58*	*11524.13*	*12317.87*

FIGURE 3-88

1. In the line containing the table title, Projected College Expenses Table, remove the tab stop at the 1" mark on the ruler.
2. Set a centered tab at the 3" mark on the ruler.
3. Bold the characters in the title. Change their color to olive green.
4. Add a new row to the bottom of the table. In the first cell of the new row, type `Total` as the entry.
5. Delete the row containing the Food expenses.
6. Insert a column between the Sophomore and Senior columns. Fill in the column as follows: Column Title – Junior; Room & Board – 3881.21; Tuition & Books – 5552.72; Entertainment – 727.01; Cell Phone – 372.81; Miscellaneous – 372.09; Clothing – 618.29.
7. If necessary, click the Tables and Borders button on the Standard toolbar to display the Tables and Borders toolbar. If necessary, click the Draw Table button on the Tables and Borders toolbar to deselect the button. Position the insertion point in the Freshman Total cell (second column, last row). Click the AutoSum button on the Tables and Borders toolbar to sum the contents of the column. Repeat for Sophomore, Junior, and Senior totals. Click the Tables and Borders button on the Standard toolbar to remove the Tables and Borders toolbar from the screen. Leave the screen in print layout view.
8. Right-align all cells containing numbers.
9. Apply the Table Elegant style to the table. ***Hint:*** You may need to click the Show box arrow in the Styles and Formatting task pane and then click All styles to display all available styles.
10. Make all columns as wide as their contents (AutoFit to Contents).
11. Center the table between the left and right margins of the page.
12. Change the color of the table contents to brown. Bold the contents of the table.
13. Italicize the last row of the table, which contains the totals.
14. Click File on the menu bar and then click Save As. Save the document using the file name, Apply 3-1 Modified Projected College Expenses Table.
15. Print the revised table.

In the Lab

1 Using Word's Resume Wizard to Create a Resume

Problem: You are a student at Montgomery High School expecting to graduate this May. Graduation is approaching quickly and you would like a part-time job while attending college. Thus, you prepare the resume shown in Figure 3-89 using Word's Resume Wizard.

Instructions:

1. Use the Resume Wizard to create a Professional style resume. Use your own name and address information when the Resume Wizard requests it.
2. Hide white space on the screen. Personalize the resume as shown in Figure 3-89. When entering multiple lines in the software experience, awards received, interests and activities, and languages sections, be sure to enter a line break at the end of each line, instead of a paragraph break.
3. Check the spelling of the resume.
4. Save the resume with Lab 3-1 Kasoulos Resume as the file name.
5. View and print the resume from within print preview.

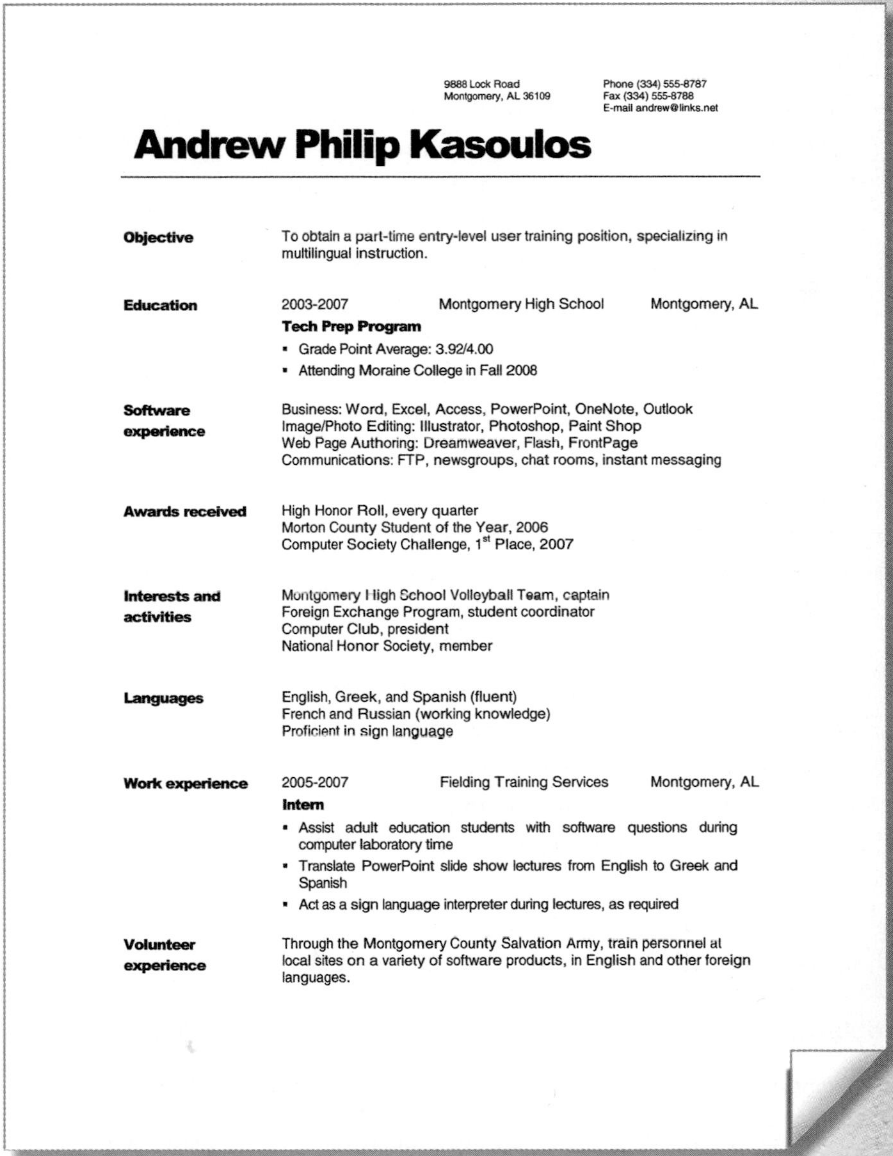

9888 Lock Road
Montgomery, AL 36109

Phone (334) 555-8787
Fax (334) 555-8788
E-mail andrew@links.net

Andrew Philip Kasoulos

Objective To obtain a part-time entry-level user training position, specializing in multilingual instruction.

Education 2003-2007 Montgomery High School Montgomery, AL
Tech Prep Program
- Grade Point Average: 3.92/4.00
- Attending Moraine College in Fall 2008

Software experience
Business: Word, Excel, Access, PowerPoint, OneNote, Outlook
Image/Photo Editing: Illustrator, Photoshop, Paint Shop
Web Page Authoring: Dreamweaver, Flash, FrontPage
Communications: FTP, newsgroups, chat rooms, instant messaging

Awards received
High Honor Roll, every quarter
Morton County Student of the Year, 2006
Computer Society Challenge, 1st Place, 2007

Interests and activities
Montgomery High School Volleyball Team, captain
Foreign Exchange Program, student coordinator
Computer Club, president
National Honor Society, member

Languages
English, Greek, and Spanish (fluent)
French and Russian (working knowledge)
Proficient in sign language

Work experience 2005-2007 Fielding Training Services Montgomery, AL
Intern
- Assist adult education students with software questions during computer laboratory time
- Translate PowerPoint slide show lectures from English to Greek and Spanish
- Act as a sign language interpreter during lectures, as required

Volunteer experience Through the Montgomery County Salvation Army, train personnel at local sites on a variety of software products, in English and other foreign languages.

FIGURE 3-89

2 Creating a Cover Letter with a Table

Problem: You prepared the resume shown in Figure 3-89 and now are ready to create a cover letter to send to a prospective employer (Figure 3-90 on the next page).

Instructions:

1. Create the letterhead shown at the top of Figure 3-90. If you completed In the Lab 1, use the Office Clipboard to copy and paste the address information from the resume to the letterhead. Save the letterhead with the file name, Lab 3-2 Kasoulos Letterhead.

(continued)

Creating a Cover Letter with a Table *(continued)*

2. Create the letter shown in Figure 3-90. Set a tab stop at the 3.5" mark on the ruler for the date line, complimentary close, and signature block. Insert the current date. After entering the inside address, create an AutoText entry for Worldwide Software and insert the AutoText entry whenever you have to enter the company name. Remove the hyperlink format from the e-mail address. Insert and center the table.
3. Modify the document summary as follows: Title – Worldwide Software; Subject – Cover Letter; Category – Cover Letter; Keywords – cover letter, Worldwide Software; Comments – Cover letter to Ms. Vidya Garlapati.
4. Check the spelling. Save the letter with Lab 3-2 Kasoulos Cover Letter as the file name.
5. View and print the cover letter from within print preview.
6. View the document summary. On the printout, write down the edited time.
7. Address and print an envelope and a mailing label using the inside and return addresses in the cover letter.

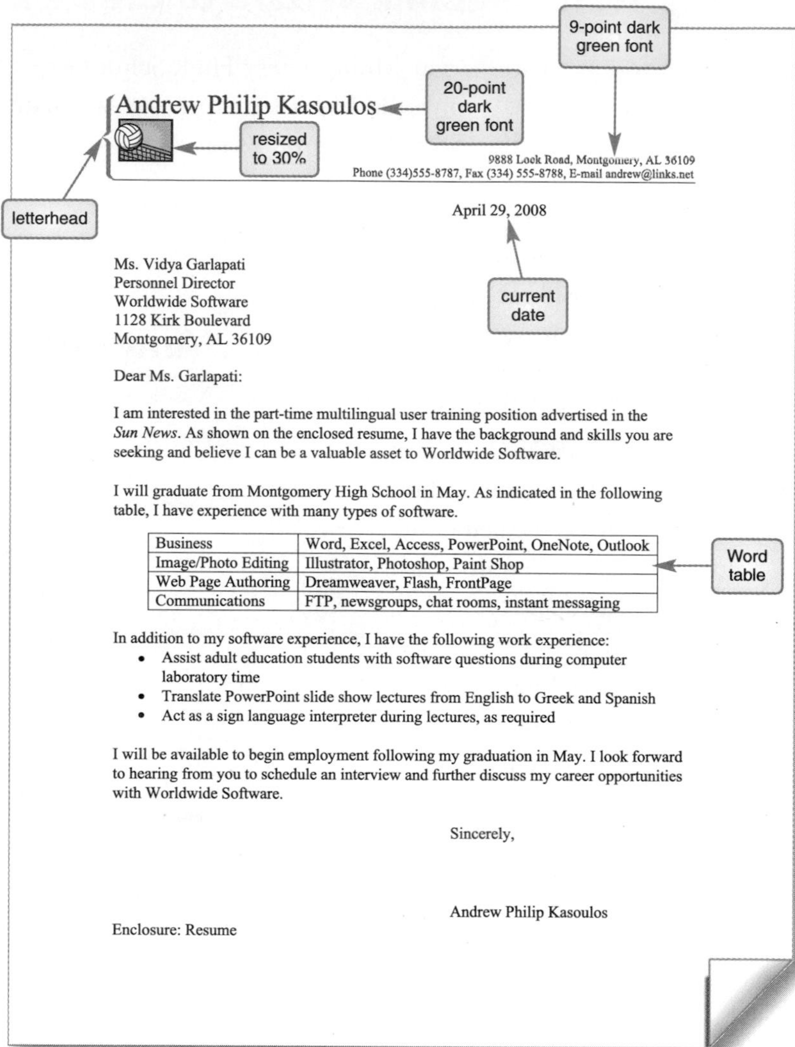

Andrew Philip Kasoulos

9888 Lock Road, Montgomery, AL 36109
Phone (334)555-8787, Fax (334) 555-8788, E-mail andrew@links.net

April 29, 2008

Ms. Vidya Garlapati
Personnel Director
Worldwide Software
1128 Kirk Boulevard
Montgomery, AL 36109

Dear Ms. Garlapati:

I am interested in the part-time multilingual user training position advertised in the *Sun News*. As shown on the enclosed resume, I have the background and skills you are seeking and believe I can be a valuable asset to Worldwide Software.

I will graduate from Montgomery High School in May. As indicated in the following table, I have experience with many types of software.

Business	Word, Excel, Access, PowerPoint, OneNote, Outlook
Image/Photo Editing	Illustrator, Photoshop, Paint Shop
Web Page Authoring	Dreamweaver, Flash, FrontPage
Communications	FTP, newsgroups, chat rooms, instant messaging

In addition to my software experience, I have the following work experience:

- Assist adult education students with software questions during computer laboratory time
- Translate PowerPoint slide show lectures from English to Greek and Spanish
- Act as a sign language interpreter during lectures, as required

I will be available to begin employment following my graduation in May. I look forward to hearing from you to schedule an interview and further discuss my career opportunities with Worldwide Software.

Sincerely,

Andrew Philip Kasoulos

Enclosure: Resume

FIGURE 3-90

3 Creating a Resume and Cover Letter

Problem: You are to create a personal resume and cover letter. Assume you are graduating this year.

Instructions:

1. Use the Resume Wizard to create a personal resume using whichever style you desire. Try to be as accurate as possible when personalizing the resume. Check spelling and grammar in the resume.
2. Obtain a copy of last Sunday's newspaper. Look through the classified section and cut out a want ad in an area that interests you. Create a cover letter for your resume, gearing the letter to the job advertised in the newspaper. Use the job advertisement information for the inside address and your personal information for the return address. After setting tabs at the 3.5" mark, change them to the 3" mark. Include a table and a numbered list in the cover letter. ***Hint:*** Use Help to learn how to create a numbered list.
3. Address and print an envelope. Then, print an entire page of mailing labels using your home address. Submit the want ad with your cover letter, resume, envelope, and mailing labels.

Cases and Places

The difficulty of these case studies varies:
are the least difficult and are more difficult.
Each exercise has a cross-curricular designation:

Math Social Studies Science Language Arts Art/Music Business Health

1 Your science teacher asked each student to create a calendar for October. The student with the best calendar will receive five extra credit points, and the calendar will be posted on the classroom bulletin board. Use the Calendar Wizard in the Other Documents sheet in the Templates dialog box. Use the following settings in the wizard: Banner style, landscape print direction, leave room for a picture, and October 2007 for both the start and end date. With the calendar on the screen, click the current graphic and delete it. Insert a clip art image related to science and then resize the image so it fits in the entire space for the graphic.

2 As secretary for the Math Club, you prepare the agenda for the monthly meetings and place one in each club member's locker. Use the Agenda Wizard in the Other Documents sheet in the Templates dialog box. Use the following settings in the wizard: style – boxes; meeting date – October 15, 2007; meeting time – 4:15 p.m. to 5:45 p.m.; title – Math Club October Meeting; meeting location – Room 10B; include Type of meeting and Please bring headings; include these names on agenda – Meeting called by, Note taker, Attendees, and Resource persons; Topics, People, and Minutes – Welcome and Roll Call, Mrs. Weaver, 10; Math Pros Competition, Crystal Walters, 30; Guest Speaker, Mr. VanWijk, 30; Refreshments, 20; do not add a form for recording the minutes. On the agenda created by the wizard, add the following names in the appropriate spaces: Mrs. Weaver, Algebra teacher, called the meeting. Math Club members are the attendees. The meeting is a monthly meeting. You are the note taker. Attendees should bring pencil, paper, and calculator to the meeting. Resource persons are Mrs. Weaver, Mrs. Ramos, or Mr. Spelbring.

3 A local college has asked all business students at your high school to fax their top six career choices. Use the Fax Wizard and the following settings: create the fax cover sheet with a note and print the fax so you can send it on a separate fax machine. It must be faxed to Ms. Dawn Metzger. Her fax number is (317) 555-5542 and her telephone number is (317) 555-5541. You will fax her just a cover sheet — one page. In the fax notes, write a message informing Ms. Metzger of your top six career choices. Use your own name, address, and telephone information in the fax and use whichever fax style you like best.

4 Your English teacher has assigned each student in her class to read a book and write her a memo that evaluates the book. The memo should identify the book's title, author, setting, main characters, and describe the book as fiction or nonfiction. It also should describe whether you liked the book or not and whether you would recommend the book. You prepare a memorandum according to your teacher's instructions. Use the Memo Wizard or a memo template, together with the concepts and techniques presented in this project, to create and format the interoffice memorandum.

Cases and Places

5 **Working Together** Your computer teacher explains that the guidance counselors at your school are looking for a sample resume to be used as a reference for other students in your school. They also would like a list of resume-writing tips they could share with other students. Your assignment is to form a three-member team. Each team member is to identify a minimum of five resume-writing tips by searching the Web, visiting a library, and/or talking to an expert in the area of resume writing. Then, the team should meet as a group to create a numbered list of resume-writing tips. Next, all team members are to look through the headings available in the Resume Wizard and select the ones best suited to high-school students, adding any not included in the wizard. Then, the members should divide up the headings among the team. After each team member writes his or her section(s) of the resume, the group should meet to copy and paste the individual sections into a single resume. Finally, write a memo indicating the work the team has completed. Use the concepts and techniques presented in this project to format the memo, resume-writing tips, and resume.

MICROSOFT OFFICE

Word 2003

Creating Web Pages Using Word

CASE PERSPECTIVE

In Project 3, Jasmine Leila Baskerville created her resume with your assistance (Figure 3-1 on page WD 139). Recently, Jasmine has been surfing the Internet and has discovered that many people have their own personal Web pages. Their Web pages contain links to other Web sites and also to personal Web pages such as resumes and favorite links. These personal Web pages are very impressive.

To make herself more marketable to a potential employer, Jasmine has asked you to help her create a personal Web page. She wants her Web page to contain a hyperlink to her resume — with the hyperlink on the left side of the page and her resume on the right side of the page. On the left side of the Web page, Jasmine would like another hyperlink called My Favorite Site. When a Web site visitor clicks this link, Jasmine's favorite Web site (www.scsite.com) will be displayed on the right side of her personal Web page. Finally, Jasmine wants the e-mail address on her resume Web page to be a hyperlink to an e-mail program. This way, potential employers easily can send her an e-mail message to schedule an interview or request additional information. You show Jasmine how to save her resume as a Web page and incorporate frames and hyperlinks into a Web page.

As you read through this Web Feature, you will learn how to use Word to create a Web page. If you are stepping through this feature on a computer, you will need the resume document named Baskerville Resume that was created in Project 3. (If you did not create the resume, see your instructor for a copy of it.)

Objectives

You will have mastered the material in this feature when you can:

- Save a Word document as a Web page
- Format and preview a Web page
- Create and modify a frames page
- Insert and modify hyperlinks

Introduction

Word provides two techniques for creating Web pages. If you have an existing Word document, you can save it as a Web page. If you do not have an existing Word document, you can use Word to create a Web page from scratch. Word has many Web page authoring tools that allow you to incorporate objects such as frames, hyperlinks, sounds, videos, pictures, scrolling text, bullets, horizontal lines, check boxes, option buttons, list boxes, text boxes, and scripts on Web pages.

This Web Feature illustrates how to save the resume created in Project 3 as a Web page. Then, it uses Word to create another Web page that contains two frames (Figure 1a on the next page). A **frame** is a rectangular section of a Web page that can display another separate Web page. Thus, a Web page with multiple frames can display multiple Web pages simultaneously. Word stores all frames associated with a Web page in a single file called the **frames page**. When you open the frames page in Word or a Web browser, all frames associated with the Web page are displayed on the screen.

In this Web Feature, the file name of the frames page is Baskerville Personal Web Page. When you initially open this frames page, the left frame contains the title, Jasmine Baskerville, and two hyperlinks — My Resume and My Favorite Site; the right frame displays Jasmine's resume (Figure 1a). As discussed in Project 3, a hyperlink is a shortcut that allows a user to jump easily and quickly to another location in the same document or to other documents or Web pages. In the left frame, the My Resume hyperlink is a link to the resume Web page, and the My Favorite Site hyperlink is a link to www.scsite.com.

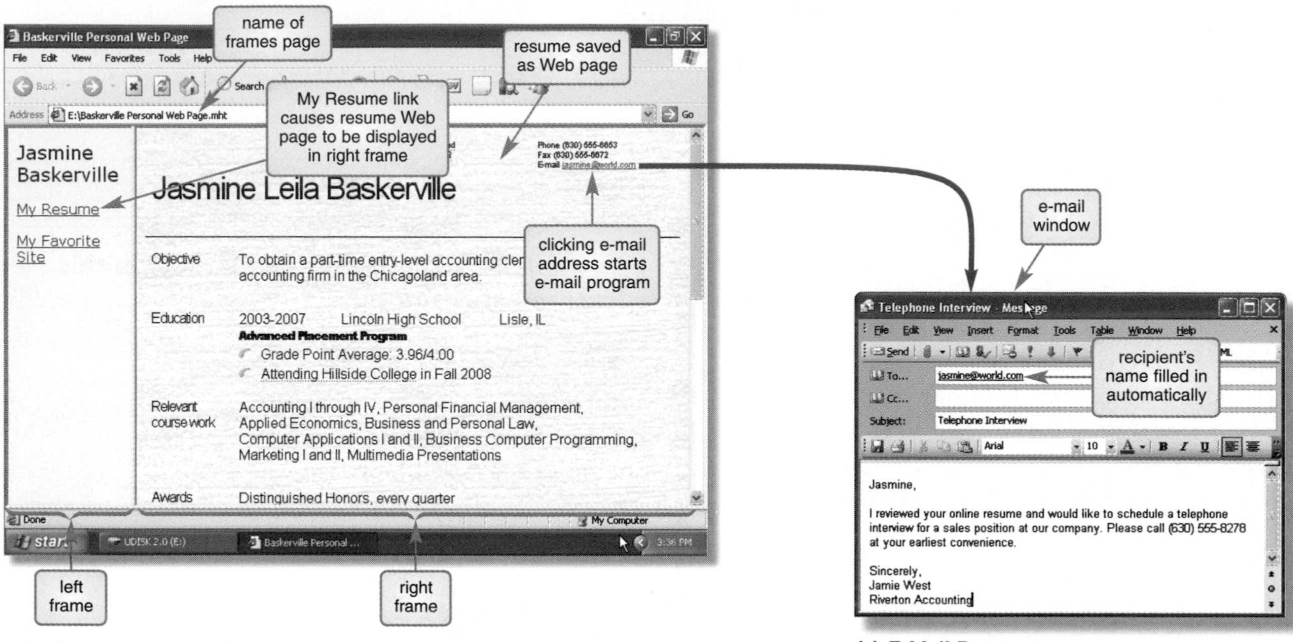

(a) Web Page Displaying Resume

(c) E-Mail Program

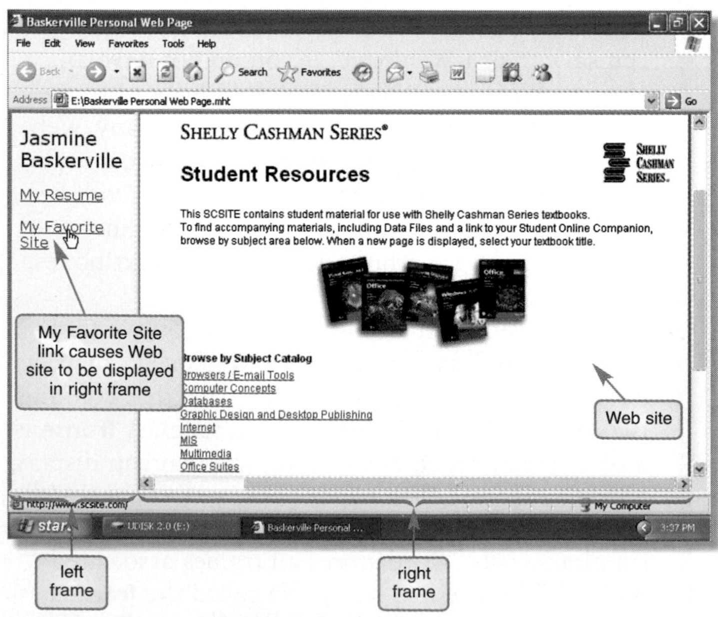

(b) Web Page Displaying Web Site

FIGURE 1

When you click the My Favorite Site hyperlink in the left frame, the www.scsite.com Web site is displayed in the right frame (Figure 1b). When you click the My Resume hyperlink in the left frame, the resume Web page is displayed in the right frame. The resume itself contains a hyperlink to an e-mail address. When you click the e-mail address, Word starts your e-mail program automatically with the recipient's address (jasmine@world.com) already filled in (Figure 1c). You simply type a subject and message and then click the Send button, which places the message in the Outbox or sends it if you are connected to an e-mail server.

Once you have created Web pages, you can publish them. **Publishing** is the process of making Web pages available to others, for example on the World Wide Web or on a company's intranet. In Word, you can publish Web pages by saving them to a Web folder or to an FTP location. The procedures for publishing Web pages in Microsoft Office are discussed in Appendix C.

This Web Feature is for instructional purposes. Thus, you create and save your frames page and associated Web pages to a USB flash drive rather than to the Web.

Saving a Word Document as a Web Page

Once you have created a Word document, you can save it as a Web page so that it can be published and then viewed by a Web browser, such as Internet Explorer. The following steps show how to save the resume created in Project 3 as a Web page.

To Save a Word Document as a Web Page

1

- **Start Word and then open the file named Baskerville Resume created in Project 3. Click File on the menu bar (Figure 2).**

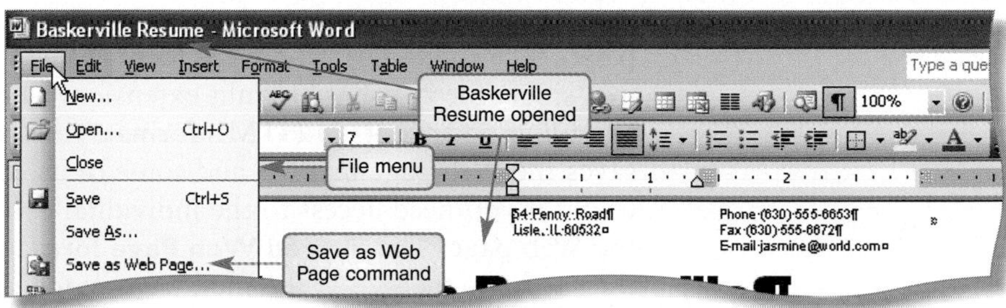

FIGURE 2

2

- **Click Save as Web Page on the File menu.**
- **When Word displays the Save As dialog box, type** `Baskerville Resume Web Page` **in the File name text box and then, if necessary, change the Save in location to UDISK 2.0 (E:). (Your USB flash drive may have a different name and letter.)**
- **Click the Change Title button.**
- **When Word displays the Set Page Title dialog box, type** `Baskerville Resume Web Page` **in the Page title text box (Figure 3).**

When the Web page is displayed in a browser, it will show the text, Baskerville Resume Web Page, on the title bar.

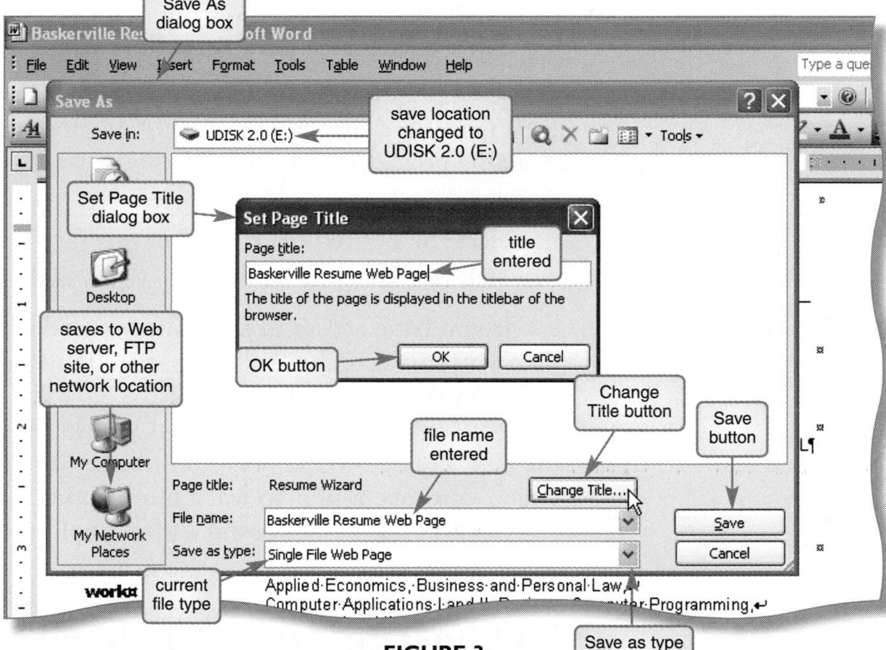

FIGURE 3

3

- **Click the OK button in the Set Page Title dialog box.**
- **Click the Save button in the Save As dialog box.**

Word saves the resume as a Web page and displays it in the Word window (Figure 4).

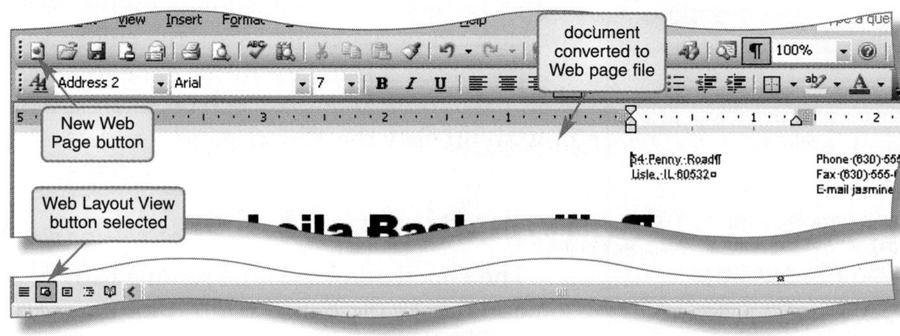

FIGURE 4

Word switches to Web layout view and also changes some of the toolbar buttons and menu commands to provide Web page authoring features. For example, the Standard toolbar now displays a New Web Page button (Figure 4 on the previous page). The Web Layout View button on the horizontal scroll bar is selected.

The resume is displayed in the Word window much like it will be displayed in a Web browser. Some of Word's formatting features are not supported by Web pages. Thus, your Web page may look slightly different from the original Word document.

When you save a file as a Web page, Word converts the contents of the document into **HTML** (hypertext markup language), which is a language that browsers can interpret. The Save as Web Page command, by default, saves the document in a format called single file Web page (shown in Figure 3 on the previous page). The **single file Web page format** saves all of the components of the Web page in a single file that has an .mht extension. This format is particularly useful for e-mailing documents in HTML format. Another format, called **Web Page format**, saves the Web page in a file and some of its components in a folder. This format is useful if you need access to the individual components, such as images, that make up the Web page. The **filtered Web Page format** saves the file in Web page format and then reduces the size of the file by removing specific Microsoft Office formats.

If you wanted to save a file using the Web Page format or the filtered Web page format, or any other type of format, you would follow these steps.

To Save a File in a Different Format

1. Click File on the menu bar and then click Save As.
2. When Word displays the Save As dialog box, type the desired file name in the File name box.
3. Click the Save as type box arrow.
4. Select the desired file format in the Save as type list.
5. Click the Save button in the Save As dialog box.

If you have access to a Web server and it allows you to save files to a Web folder, then you can save the Web page directly to the Web server by clicking My Network Places in the lower-left corner of the Save As dialog box (Figure 3). If you have access to a Web server that allows you to save to an FTP site, then you can select the FTP site below FTP locations in the Save in box just as you select any folder to which you save a file. To learn more about publishing Web pages to a Web folder or FTP location using Microsoft Office applications, refer to Appendix C.

Formatting and Previewing a Web Page

In this feature, the e-mail address on the Baskerville Resume Web page is to be formatted as a hyperlink. Also, the colors and formats of elements on the Web page should follow a standard theme. The following sections describe how to modify the Web page to include these enhancements. After modifying the Web page, you will see how to preview the Web page in Word.

Q & A

Q: Does the Web have information about Web page design guidelines?

A: Yes. For information on guidelines for designing Web pages, visit the Office 2003 Q&A Web page (scsite.com/off2003sch/qa), locate Word Web Feature, and click Web Page Design.

Formatting the E-Mail Address as a Hyperlink

The e-mail address in the resume is to be formatted as a hyperlink so that when someone clicks the e-mail address on the Web page, his or her e-mail program starts automatically and displays an e-mail window with the e-mail address already filled in.

The next steps show how to format the e-mail address as a hyperlink.

To Format Text as a Hyperlink

1

• **Select the e-mail address (jasmine@world.com) and then right-click the selected text (Figure 5).**

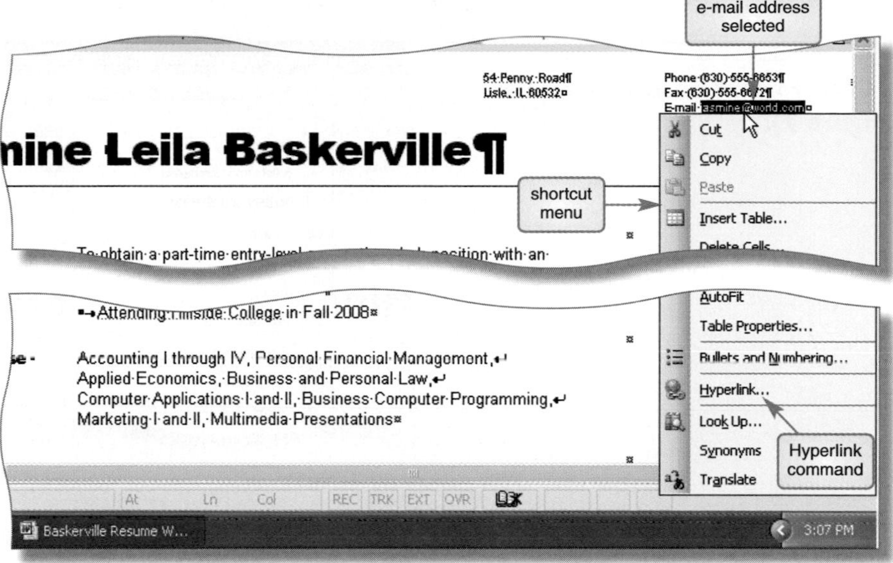

FIGURE 5

2

• **Click Hyperlink on the shortcut menu.**

• **When Word displays the Insert Hyperlink dialog box, click E-mail Address in the Link to bar.**

• **In the Text to display text box, type** `jasmine@world.com` **and then click the E-mail address text box.**

• **Type** `jasmine@world.com` **in the E-mail address text box.**

As soon as you begin typing the e-mail address, Word inserts mailto: in front of the address, which connects the hyperlink to your e-mail program (Figure 6). The text in the Text to display text box will be displayed as the hyperlink text on the screen.

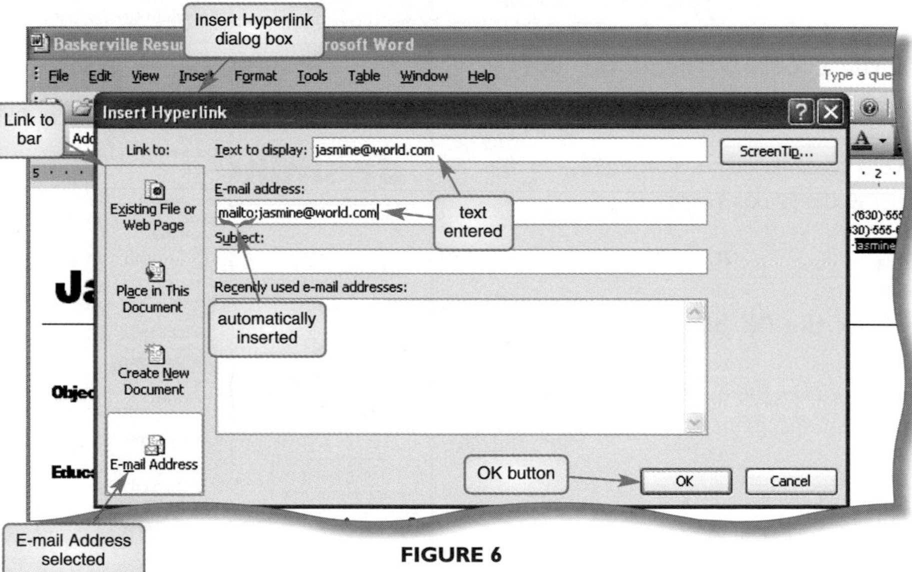

FIGURE 6

• **Click the OK button.**

Word formats the e-mail address as a hyperlink; that is, it is colored blue and underlined (shown in Figure 7 on the next page).

If you want to test the e-mail address hyperlink, CTRL+click the mouse while pointing to the hyperlink. This should open an e-mail window.

To edit a hyperlink, right-click the hyperlink and then click Edit Hyperlink on the shortcut menu.

Applying a Theme to the Web Page

The next step is to apply a theme to the Web page. A **theme** is a predefined set of colors, fonts, and other design elements for backgrounds, graphics, headings, lists, lines, hyperlinks, and tables. By using themes, you easily can make Web pages and other online documents consistent with one another.

The steps on the next page show how to apply a theme to the Baskerville Resume Web Page document.

To Apply a Theme

1

- **Click Format on the menu bar (Figure 7).**

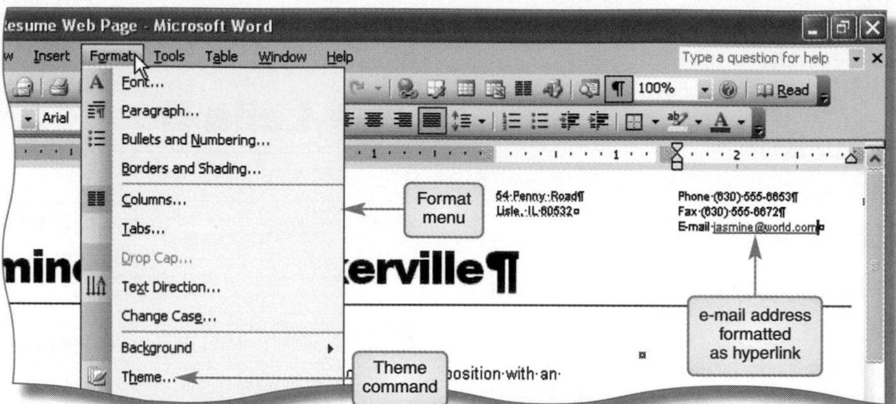

FIGURE 7

2

- **Click Theme on the Format menu.**
- **When Word displays the Theme dialog box, scroll to Sumi Painting in the Choose a Theme list and then click Sumi Painting.**

Word presents a variety of themes in the Theme dialog box (Figure 8).

3

- **Click the OK button.**

Word applies the Sumi Painting theme to the open document (shown in Figure 9).

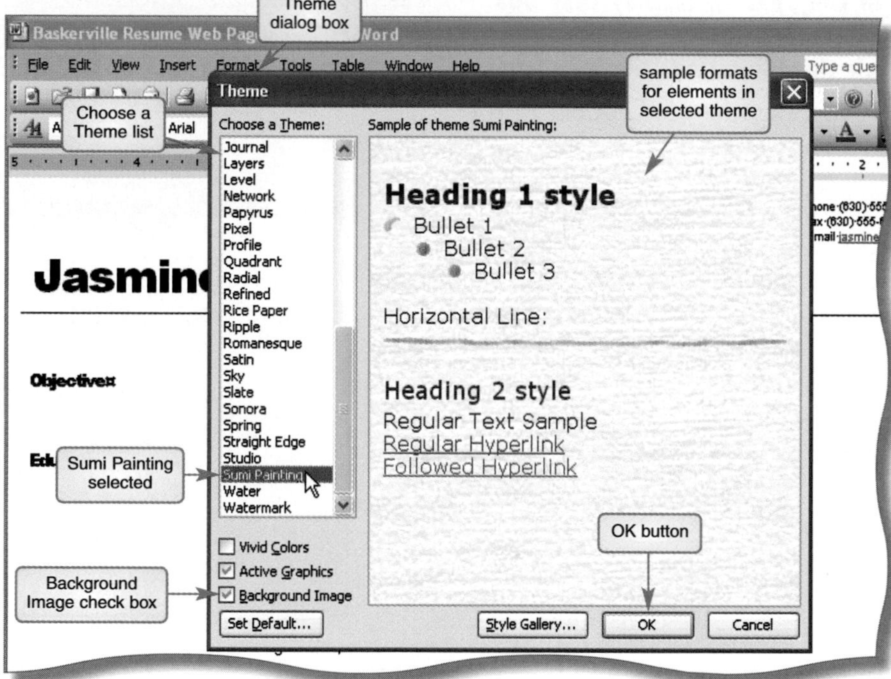

FIGURE 8

If you like all elements except for the background in a theme, remove the check mark from the Background Image check box in the Theme dialog box (Figure 8) before clicking the OK button.

Viewing the Web Page in Your Default Browser

In Word, you can see how a Web page looks in your default browser — before publishing it and without actually connecting to the Internet. To do this, use the Web Page Preview command, which appears on the File menu when Word is in Web layout view. The next steps show how to preview a Web page in Word.

To Preview a Web Page

1

- **Click File on the menu bar (Figure 9).**

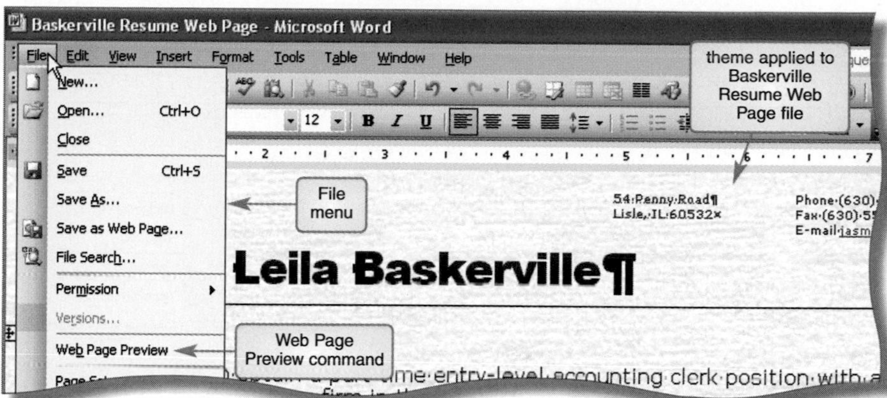

FIGURE 9

2

- **Click Web Page Preview on the File menu.**
- **If necessary, maximize the browser window.**

Word opens the Web browser in a separate window and displays the open Web page file in the browser window (Figure 10).

3

- **Click the Close button on the browser title bar to close the browser window.**

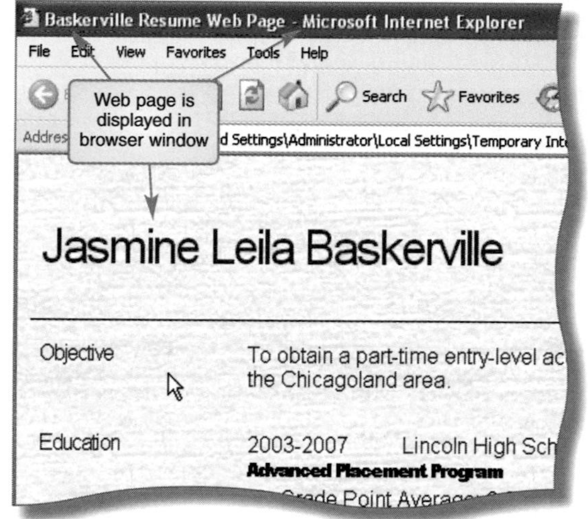

FIGURE 10

You now are finished modifying the Baskerville Resume Web Page file. The following step describes saving the file again.

To Save a Web Page

1 Click the Save button on the Standard toolbar.

Word saves the file.

> ***Skill Builder WF-1***
>
> To practice the following tasks, visit scsite.com/off2003sch/skill, locate Word Web Feature, and then click Skill Builder WF-1.
>
> ❑ Save a Word document as a Web page
> ❑ Apply a theme to a Web page
> ❑ Preview a Web page

Creating and Modifying a Frames Page

In the previous section, you saved an existing Word document as a Web page. Next, you want to create the frames page that will be divided into two separate frames. The left frame is to contain two links: one to the Baskerville Resume Web Page file just created and one to www.scsite.com.

The following steps show how to create a frames page and then add a frame so the frames page contains two frames side-by-side.

To Create a Frames Page

1

• **Click Format on the menu bar and then point to Frames (Figure 11).**

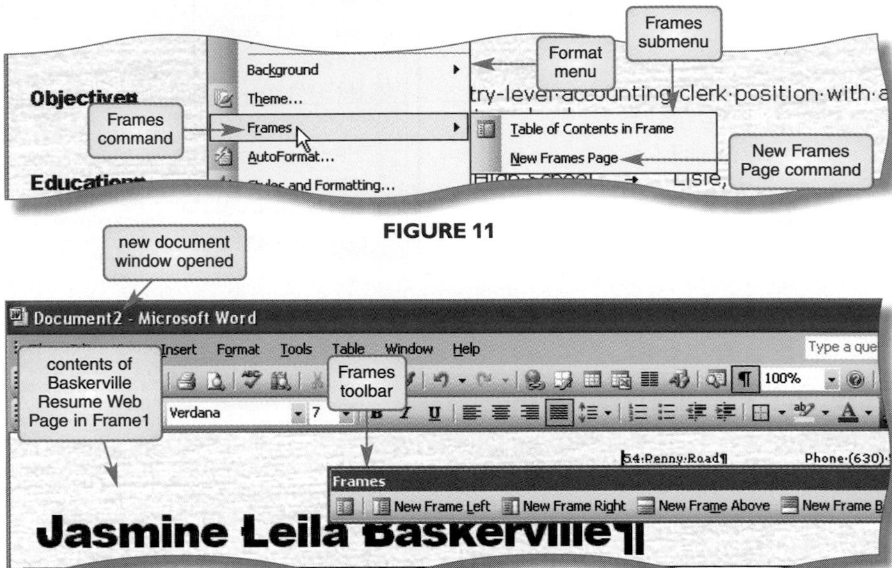

FIGURE 11

2

• **Click New Frames Page on the Frames submenu.**

Word opens a new document window that contains the Baskerville Resume Web Page in the current frame (called Frame1) and displays the Frames toolbar on the screen (Figure 12).

FIGURE 12

3

• **Click the New Frame Left button on the Frames toolbar.**

Word opens a new frame to the left of the current frame (Figure 13). The new frame is called Frame2.

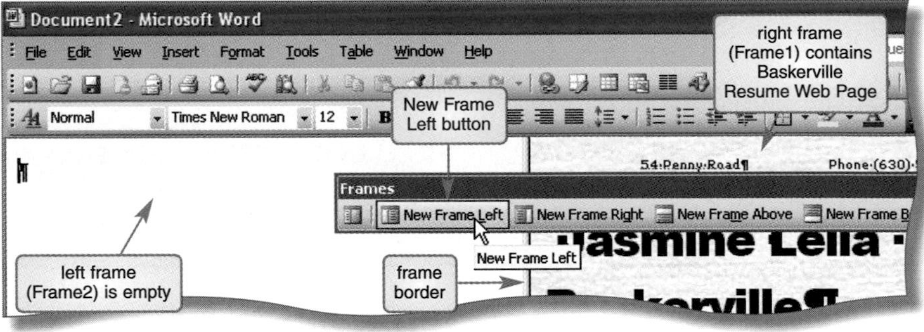

FIGURE 13

The frames page is divided into two frames, one on the left and one on the right. A **frame border** separates the frames. The next step is to add text to the left frame, as described below.

> **Q & A**
>
> **Q:** How can I separate sections of a Web page?
>
> **A:** You can use horizontal lines to separate sections of a Web page. To add a horizontal line at the location of the insertion point, click Format on the menu bar, click Borders and Shading, click the Horizontal Line button, click the desired line type in the Horizontal Line dialog box, and then click the OK button.

To Add Text to a Frame

1. **With the insertion point in the left frame (Frame2), click the Font Size box arrow. Click 16 in the Font Size list. Type** `Jasmine Baskerville` **and then click the Font Size box arrow. Click 12 in the Font Size list. Press the ENTER key twice.**
2. **Type** `My Resume` **and then press the ENTER key twice.**
3. **Type** `My Favorite Site` **as the last entry in the left frame.**

Word displays the text in the left frame (shown in Figure 14).

The next step is to make the left frame narrower. To do this, you drag the frame border. When you point to and drag the frame border, the mouse pointer shape changes to a double-headed arrow. The following step shows how to resize a Web page frame.

To Resize a Web Page Frame

1

- **Drag the frame border to the left until it is positioned on the letter v in Baskerville in the left frame (Figure 14).**

Word narrows the left frame and widens the right frame (shown in Figure 15). Although the text in the resume may wrap incorrectly after this step, it may be displayed properly as a Web page. You can fix any wrapping problems after viewing the resume at the end of this feature.

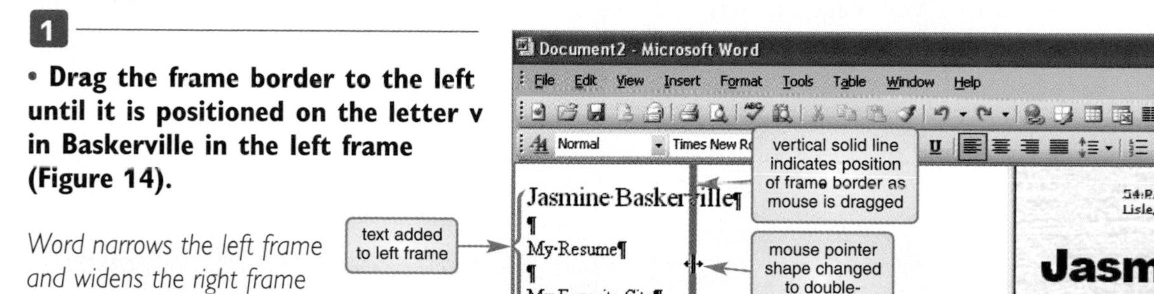

FIGURE 14

In this feature, the left frame uses the Sumi Painting theme, except it does not contain a background image. The following steps describe how to apply a theme, without a background image.

To Apply a Theme

1. **With the insertion point in the left frame, click Format on the menu bar and then click Theme.**
2. **When the Theme dialog box is displayed, scroll to and then click Sumi Painting in the Choose a Theme list.**
3. **Place a check mark in the Vivid Colors check box.**
4. **Remove the check mark from the Background Image check box (Figure 15).**
5. **Click the OK button.**

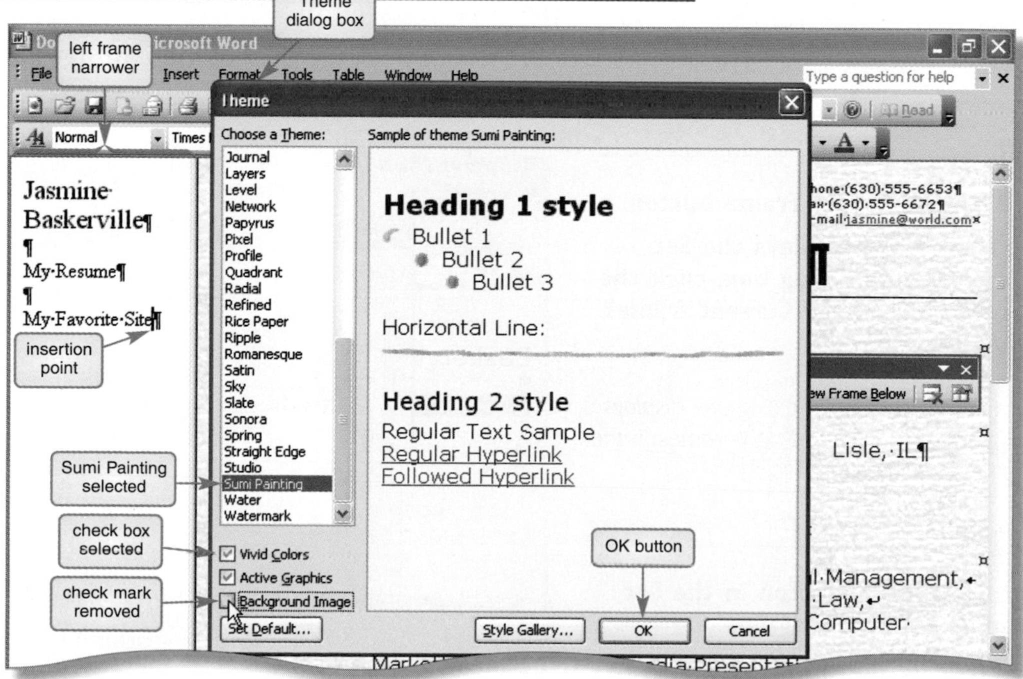

FIGURE 15

Word applies the Sumi Painting theme, without a background image (shown in Figure 16 on the next page).

In the left frame, you want the text, My Resume, to be a hyperlink to the Baskerville Resume Web Page document. This means when you click the My Resume link in the left frame, the Baskerville Resume Web Page file will be displayed in the right frame. Similarly, you want the My Favorite site text to be a hyperlink. That is, when you click the hyperlink in the left frame, the www.scsite.com Web site should be displayed in the right frame.

The following steps describe how to link the My Resume text in the left frame to an existing Web Page file that will be displayed in the right frame (Frame1) when the user clicks the My Resume link in the left frame (Frame2).

To Insert and Modify a Hyperlink

1

- **Drag through the text, My Resume, in the left frame to select it.**
- **Click the Insert Hyperlink button on the Standard toolbar.**
- **When Word displays the Insert Hyperlink dialog box, if necessary, click Existing File or Web Page in the Link to bar.**
- **If necessary, click the Look in box arrow and then click UDISK 2.0 (E:). (Your USB flash drive may have a different name and letter.)**
- **Click Baskerville Resume Web Page.**

Word displays the Baskerville Resume Web Page file name in the Address box (Figure 16).

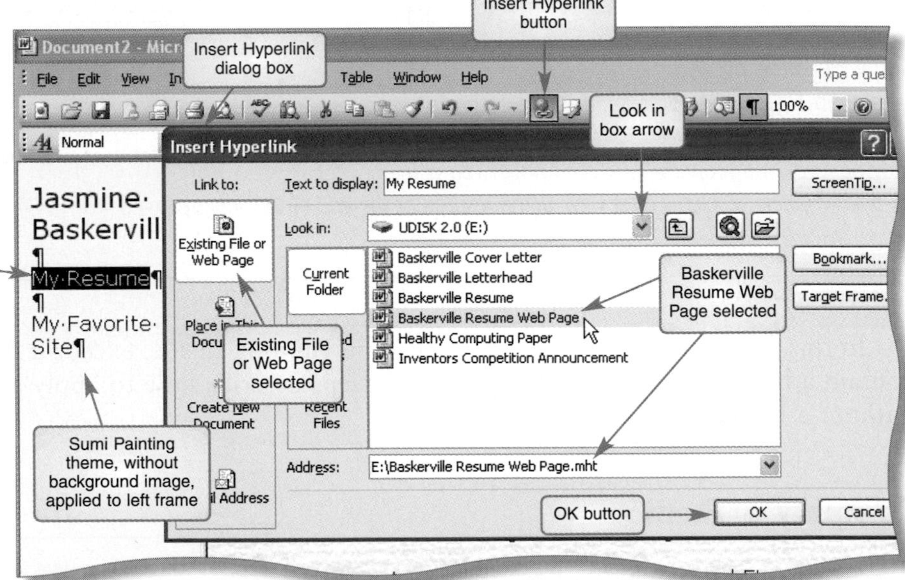

FIGURE 16

2

- **Click the Target Frame button.**
- **When Word displays the Set Target Frame dialog box, click the right frame in the Current frames page diagram.**

The Set Target Frame dialog box displays a diagram of the left and right frames in the frames page (Figure 17).

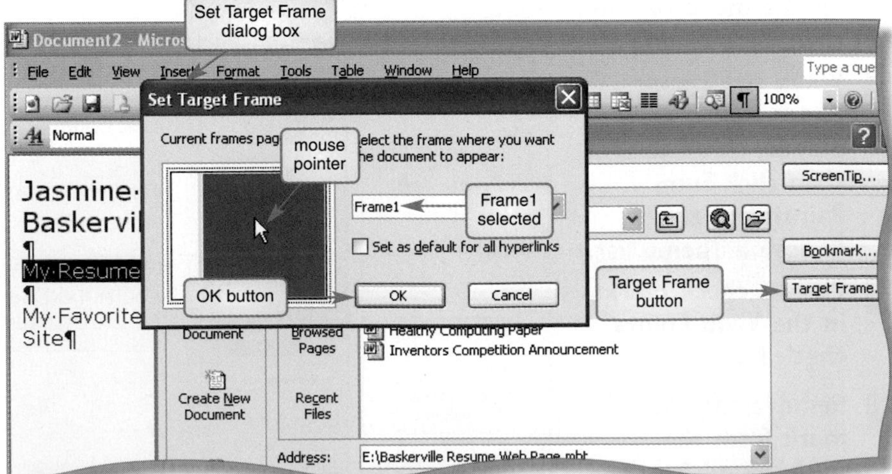

FIGURE 17

3

- **Click the OK button in the Set Target Frame dialog box.**
- **Click the OK button in the Insert Hyperlink dialog box.**

Word formats the selected text as a hyperlink (shown in Figure 18). When you click the My Resume link in the left frame, the Baskerville Resume Web Page file will be displayed in the right frame.

The following steps describe how to link the My Favorite Site text in the left frame to a Web site that will be displayed in the right frame.

To Insert and Modify a Hyperlink

1. **Drag through the text, My Favorite Site, in the left frame to select it.**
2. **Click the Insert Hyperlink button on the Standard toolbar.**
3. **When Word displays the Insert Hyperlink dialog box, if necessary, click Existing File or Web Page in the Link to bar. Type** `www.scsite.com` **in the Address text box.**
4. **Click the Target Frame button. When Word displays the Set Target Frame dialog box, click the right frame in the diagram (Figure 18).**
5. **Click the OK button in each dialog box.**

Word formats the text, My Favorite Site, as a hyperlink that, when clicked, displays the associated Web site in the right frame (shown in Figure 1b on page WD 204).

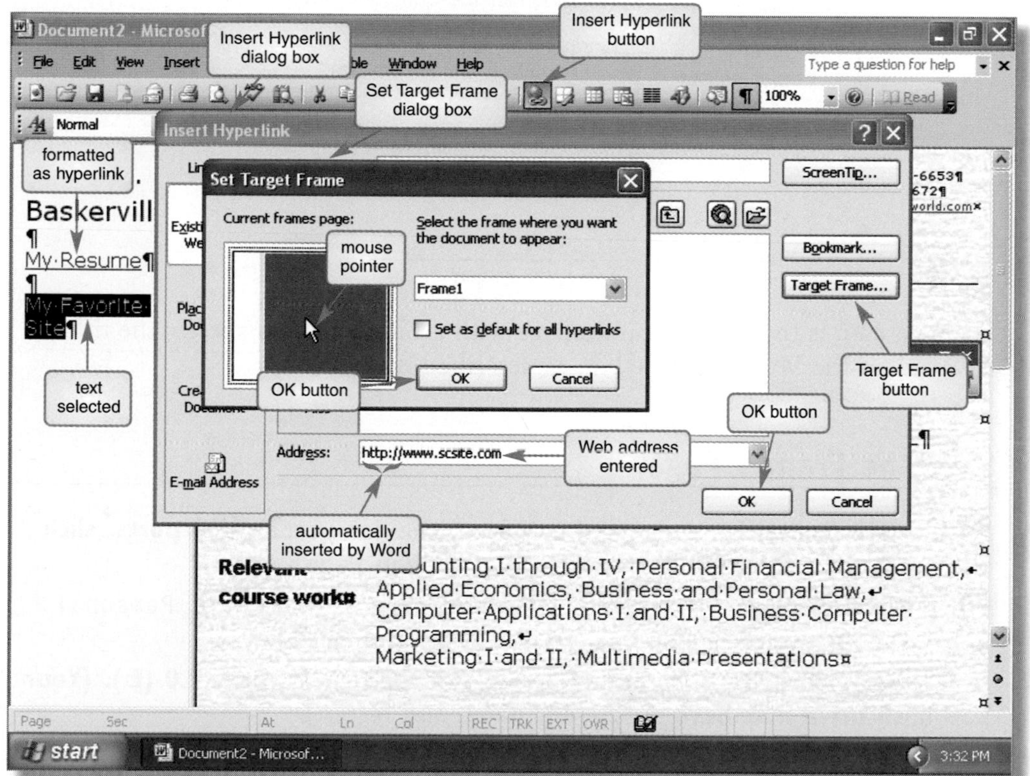

FIGURE 18

If you wanted to edit an existing hyperlink, you right-click the hyperlink text and then click Edit Hyperlink on the shortcut menu. Word will display the Edit Hyperlink dialog box instead of the Insert Hyperlink dialog box. Other than the title bar, these two dialog boxes are the same.

The next task is to modify the frame properties of the left frame so it does not display a scroll bar between the left and right frames, as shown on the next page.

Q & A

Q: Is there more than one way to invoke a command in Word?

A: Yes. For a table that lists how to complete the tasks covered in this book using the mouse, menu, shortcut menu, and keyboard, see the Quick Reference Summary at the back of this book, or visit the Office 2003 Quick Reference Web page (scsite.com/off2003sch/qr).

Skill Builder WF-2

To practice the following tasks, visit scsite.com/off2003sch/skill, locate Word Web Feature, and then click Skill Builder WF-2.

- ❑ Create and edit a frames page
- ❑ Insert and modify a hyperlink

To Modify Frame Properties

• **With the insertion point in the left frame, click the Frame Properties button on the Frames toolbar.**

• **When Word displays the Frame Properties dialog box, if necessary, click the Borders tab.**

• **Click the Show scrollbars in browser box arrow and then click Never.**

The Borders sheet in the Frame Properties dialog box allows you to set options related to the frame borders (Figure 19).

2

• **Click the OK button.**

Word formats the border to no scroll bars.

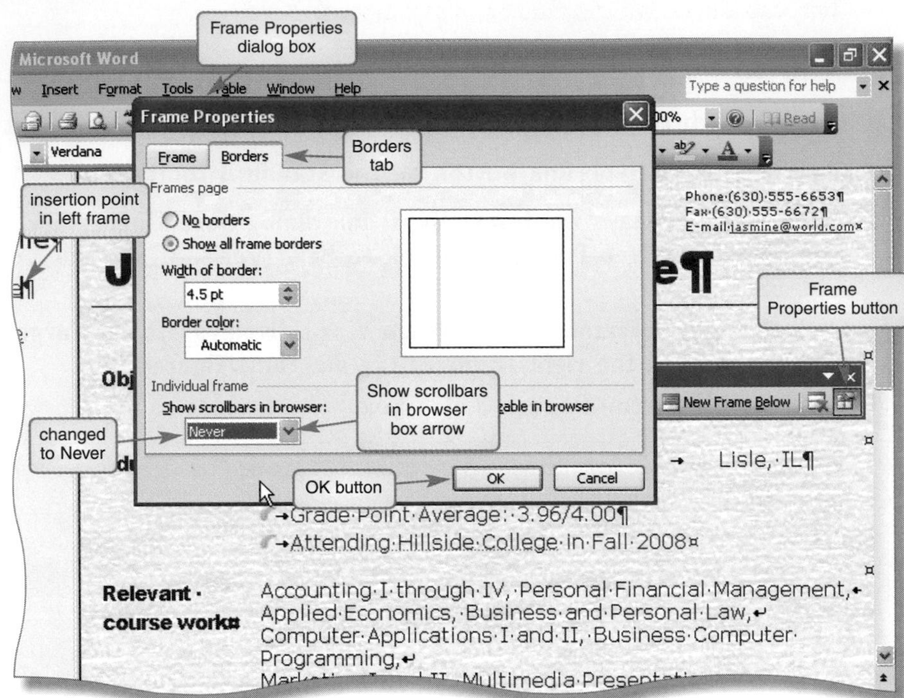

FIGURE 19

The next step is to save the frames page with a file name and specify the title to be displayed on the Web page title bar, as described below.

To Save the Frames Page

1. **With a USB flash drive connected to one of the computer's USB ports, click File on the menu bar and then click Save as Web Page.**
2. **When Word displays the Save As dialog box, type** `Baskerville Personal Web Page` **in the File name box. Do not press the ENTER key.**
3. **If necessary, click the Save in box arrow and then click UDISK 2.0 (E:). (Your USB flash drive may have a different name and letter.)**
4. **Click the Change Title button. When Word displays the Set Page Title dialog box, type** `Baskerville Personal Web Page` **in the Page title text box.**
5. **Click the OK button in the Set Page Title dialog box. Click the Save button in the Save As dialog box.**

Word saves the frames page on a USB flash drive with the file name, Baskerville Personal Web Page. When a user displays the Web page in a browser, the title bar also will show this same name.

The final step is to quit Word, as described next.

Q & A

Q: What is the Microsoft Office Certification program?

A: The Microsoft Office Specialist Certification program provides an opportunity for you to obtain a valuable industry credential — proof that you have the Word 2003 skills required by employers. For more information, see Appendix E or visit the Office 2003 Certification Web page (scsite.com/off2003sch/cert).

To Quit Word

1 Click the Close button on the Word title bar.

The Word window closes.

You can start Windows Explorer and double-click the file name, Baskerville Personal Web Page, to display the Web page in your browser. From the browser window (Figure 1a on page WD 204), you can test your hyperlinks to be sure they work — before publishing them to the Web. For example, in the left frame, click the My Favorite Site link to display the Web site www.scsite.com in the right frame. (If you are not connected to the Internet, your browser will connect you and then display the Web site.) Click the My Resume link to display the Baskerville Resume Web Page in the right frame. Click the e-mail address to start your e-mail program with the address, jasmine@world.com, entered in the recipient's address box.

The final step is to make your Web pages and associated files available to others on a network, on an intranet, or on the World Wide Web. Read Appendix C for instructions about publishing Web pages and then talk to your instructor about how you should do this for your system.

Q & A

Q: Can I edit Web pages?

A: Yes. You can edit a Web page directly from Internet Explorer. With the Internet Explorer window open and the Web page to edit displaying in the browser window, click the Edit with Microsoft Word button on the toolbar. Internet Explorer starts Word and displays the Web page in the Word window — ready for editing. Or, you can start Word and open the Web page directly in Word by clicking the Open button on the Standard toolbar, clicking the Files of type box arrow, clicking All Web Pages, selecting the Web page document, and then clicking the Open button in the dialog box.

Web Feature Summary

This Web Feature introduced you to creating a Web page by illustrating how to save an existing Word document as a Web page file. The feature then showed how to modify and format the Web page file. Next, you learned how to create a new Web page with frames and then modify the frames page. Finally, the project showed how to create one hyperlink to an e-mail address, one to a Web page file, and another to a Web site.

If you have a SAM user profile, you may have access to hands-on instruction, practice, and assessment of the skills covered in this project. Log in to your SAM account and go to your assignments page to see what your instructor has assigned.

What You Should Know

Having completed this feature, you should be able to perform the tasks below. The tasks are listed in the same order they were presented in this project. For a list of the buttons, menus, toolbars, and commands introduced in this feature, see the Quick Reference Summary at the back of this book and refer to the Page Number column.

1. Save a Word Document as a Web Page (WD 205)
2. Save a File in a Different Format (WD 206)
3. Format Text as a Hyperlink (WD 207)
4. Apply a Theme (WD 208, WD 211)
5. Preview a Web Page (WD 209)
6. Save a Web Page (WD 209)
7. Create a Frames Page (WD 210)
8. Add Text to a Frame (WD 210)
9. Resize a Web Page Frame (WD 211)
10. Insert and Modify a Hyperlink (WD 212, WD 213)
11. Modify Frame Properties (WD 214)
12. Save the Frames Page (WD 214)
13. Quit Word (WD 215)

1 Saving a Word Document as a Web Page and in Other Formats

Problem: You created the research paper shown in Figure 2-80 on pages WD 130 and WD 131 in Project 2. You decide to save this research paper in a variety of formats.

Instructions:

1. Open the Lab 2-1 Green Computing Paper shown in Figure 2-80. (If you did not create the research paper, see your instructor for a copy.)
2. Save the research paper as a single file Web page using the file name, Lab WF-1 Green Computing Paper Web Page A. Print the Web page.
3. Use the Web Page Preview command to view the Web page.
4. If you have access to a Web server or FTP site, save the Web page to the server or site (see Appendix C for instructions).
5. Using Windows Explorer, look at the contents of the storage medium containing the Web page. Write down the names of the files. Open the original Lab 2-1 Green Computing Paper. Save it as a Web page (not single file) using the file name, Lab WF-1 Green Computing Paper Web Page B. That is, change the file type in the Save as type box to Web Page. Again, look at the contents of the storage medium using Windows Explorer. Write down any additional file names. How many more files and folders are created by the Web Page format?
6. Open the original Lab 2-1 Green Computing Paper. Save it as plain text using the file name, Lab WF-1 Green Computing Paper Plain Text. That is, change the file type in the Save as type box to Plain Text. Click the OK button when Word displays the File Conversion dialog box. Open the plain text file. ***Hint:*** In the Open dialog box, click the Files of type box arrow and then click All Files. Write down the difference between the plain text file and the original file.

2 Creating a Web Page with Frames and Hyperlinks

Problem: You created the resume shown in Figure 3-89 on page WD 199 in Project 3. You decide to create a personal Web page with a link to this resume. Thus, you also must save the resume as a Web page.

Instructions:

1. Open the Lab 3-1 Kasoulos Resume shown in Figure 3-89. (If you did not create the resume, see your instructor for a copy.)
2. Save the resume as a single file Web page using the file name, Lab WF-2 Kasoulos Resume Web Page. Convert the e-mail address to a hyperlink. Apply the Rice Paper theme to the Web page. Preview the Web page using the Web Page Preview command. Save the Web page again.
3. Create a frames page. Insert a left frame. Add the following text to the left frame on three separate lines: Andrew Kasoulos, My Resume, My Favorite Site. Apply the Rice Paper theme to the left frame. Resize the left frame to the width of its text.
4. In the left frame of the frames page, format the text, My Resume and My Favorite Site, as hyperlinks. When clicked, the My Resume hyperlink should display the Lab WF-2 Kasoulos Resume Web Page in the right frame. The My Favorite Site hyperlink, when clicked, should display your favorite Web site in the right frame.
5. Modify the properties of the left frame to never display a scroll bar. Save the frames page using the file name, Lab WF-2 Kasoulos Personal Web Page and change the title of the Web page. Use the Web Page Preview command to view the Web page in your browser.
6. In Windows Explorer, double-click the name of the frames page. Test your Web page links. Print the Web page.
7. If you have access to a Web server or FTP site, save the Web page to the server or site (see Appendix C).

MICROSOFT OFFICE EXCEL

MICROSOFT OFFICE

Excel 2003

MICROSOFT OFFICE
Excel 2003

Creating a Worksheet and an Embedded Chart

PROJECT 1

CASE PERSPECTIVE

Three years ago while in high school, Amber Gordon and three of her friends came up with the idea of starting a fitness center that catered to young adults interested in their health. After graduating from high school, they invested $5,000 each and started their dream fitness center, A Better Body Shop.

The four friends opened their first fitness center in Las Vegas. Initially, they offered cardiovascular exercise and weight training. Members also were enrolled free of charge in their nutrition and jogging seminars. As business grew, they opened additional centers in Boston, Chicago, and Miami. Last year, they added aquatics, and yoga and stretching to their offerings. They also created an educational Web site that offers their customers information on fitness, jogging, and nutrition. Thanks to their market savvy and the popularity of their Web site, their company has become the premier fitness provider for young adults in the cities where they have centers.

As business continued to grow, senior management asked their financial analyst, Pedro Martinez, to develop a more effective way to show where the revenue comes from. As a first step, Pedro has asked you to prepare an easy-to-read worksheet that shows annual revenue by center and by offering (Figure 1-1 on page EX 5). In addition, Pedro has asked you to create a chart showing annual revenue because Amber, the president of the company, prefers to have a graphical representation of the breakdown of the revenue that allows her to identify quickly the stronger and weaker offerings at the four centers.

As you read through this project, you will learn how to use Excel to create, save, and print a financial report that includes a 3-D Clustered column chart.

MICROSOFT OFFICE

Excel 2003

Creating a Worksheet and an Embedded Chart

PROJECT

Objectives

You will have mastered the material in this project when you can:

- Start and quit Excel
- Describe the Excel worksheet
- Enter text and numbers
- Use the AutoSum button to sum a range of cells
- Copy a cell to a range of cells using the fill handle
- Format a worksheet
- Create a 3-D Clustered column chart
- Save a workbook and print a worksheet
- Open a workbook
- Use the AutoCalculate area to determine statistics
- Correct errors on a worksheet
- Use the Excel Help system to answer questions

What Is Microsoft Office Excel 2003?

Microsoft Office Excel 2003 is a powerful spreadsheet program that allows users to organize data, complete calculations, make decisions, graph data, develop professional-looking reports (Figure 1-1), publish organized data to the Web, and access real-time data from Web sites. The four major parts of Excel are:

- **Worksheets** Worksheets allow users to enter, calculate, manipulate, and analyze data, such as numbers and text. The term worksheet means the same as spreadsheet.
- **Charts** Excel can draw a variety of charts.
- **Lists** Lists organize and store data. For example, once a user enters data into a worksheet, Excel can sort the data, search for specific data, and select data that satisfies defined criteria.
- **Web Support** Web support allows users to save Excel worksheets or parts of a worksheet in HTML format, so a user can view and manipulate the worksheet using a browser. Excel Web support also provides access to real-time data, such as stock quotes, using Web queries.

This latest version of Excel makes it much easier to create and manipulate lists of data. It also offers industry-standard XML support that simplifies the sharing of data within and outside an organization; improved statistical functions; smart documents that automatically fill with data; information rights management; allows two workbooks to be compared side by side; and includes the capability of searching a variety of reference information.

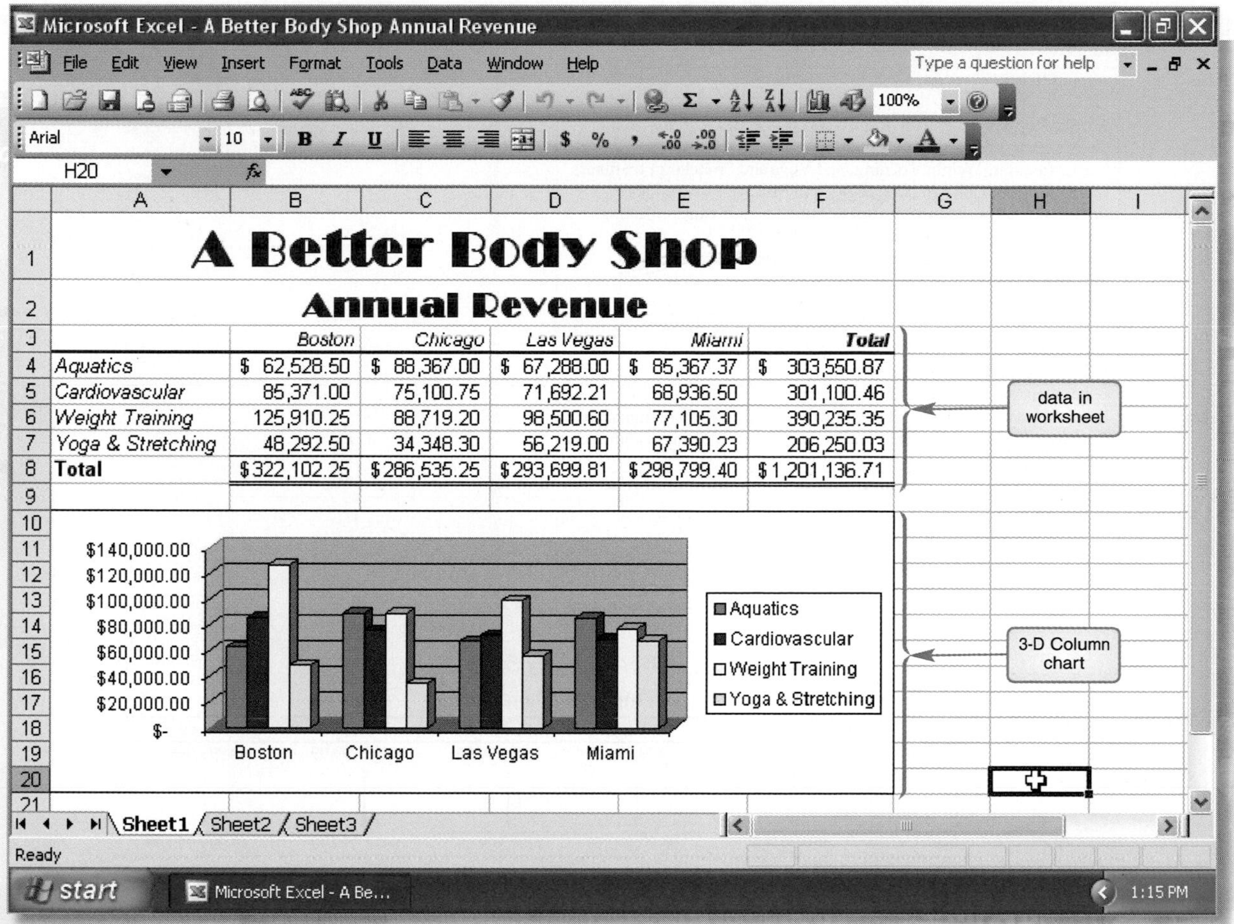

Microsoft Excel - A Better Body Shop Annual Revenue

A Better Body Shop

Annual Revenue

	Boston	*Chicago*	*Las Vegas*	*Miami*	***Total***
Aquatics	$ 62,528.50	$ 88,367.00	$ 67,288.00	$ 85,367.37	$ 303,550.87
Cardiovascular	85,371.00	75,100.75	71,692.21	68,936.50	301,100.46
Weight Training	125,910.25	88,719.20	98,500.60	77,105.30	390,235.35
Yoga & Stretching	48,292.50	34,348.30	56,219.00	67,390.23	206,250.03
Total	$322,102.25	$286,535.25	$293,699.81	$298,799.40	$1,201,136.71

FIGURE 1-1

Project One — A Better Body Shop Annual Revenue Worksheet

The first step in creating an effective worksheet is to make sure you understand what is required. The person or persons requesting the worksheet should supply their requirements in a requirements document. A **requirements document** includes a needs statement, source of data, summary of calculations, and any other special requirements for the worksheet, such as charting and Web support. Figure 1-2 on the next page shows the requirements document for the new worksheet to be created in this project.

After carefully reviewing the requirements document, the next step is to design a solution or draw a sketch of the worksheet based on the requirements, including titles, column and row headings, location of data values, and the 3-D Column chart, as shown in Figure 1-3 on the next page. The dollar signs, 9s, and commas that you see in the sketch of the worksheet indicate formatted numeric values.

Q & A

Q: How do spreadsheet specialists solve problems using Excel?

A: Spreadsheet specialists do not sit down and start entering text, formulas, and data into a blank Excel worksheet as soon as they have a spreadsheet assignment. Instead, they follow an organized plan, or methodology, that breaks the development cycle into a series of tasks. The recommended methodology for creating worksheets includes: (1) analyze requirements (supplied in a requirements document); (2) design solution; (3) validate design; (4) implement design; (5) test solution; and (6) document solution.

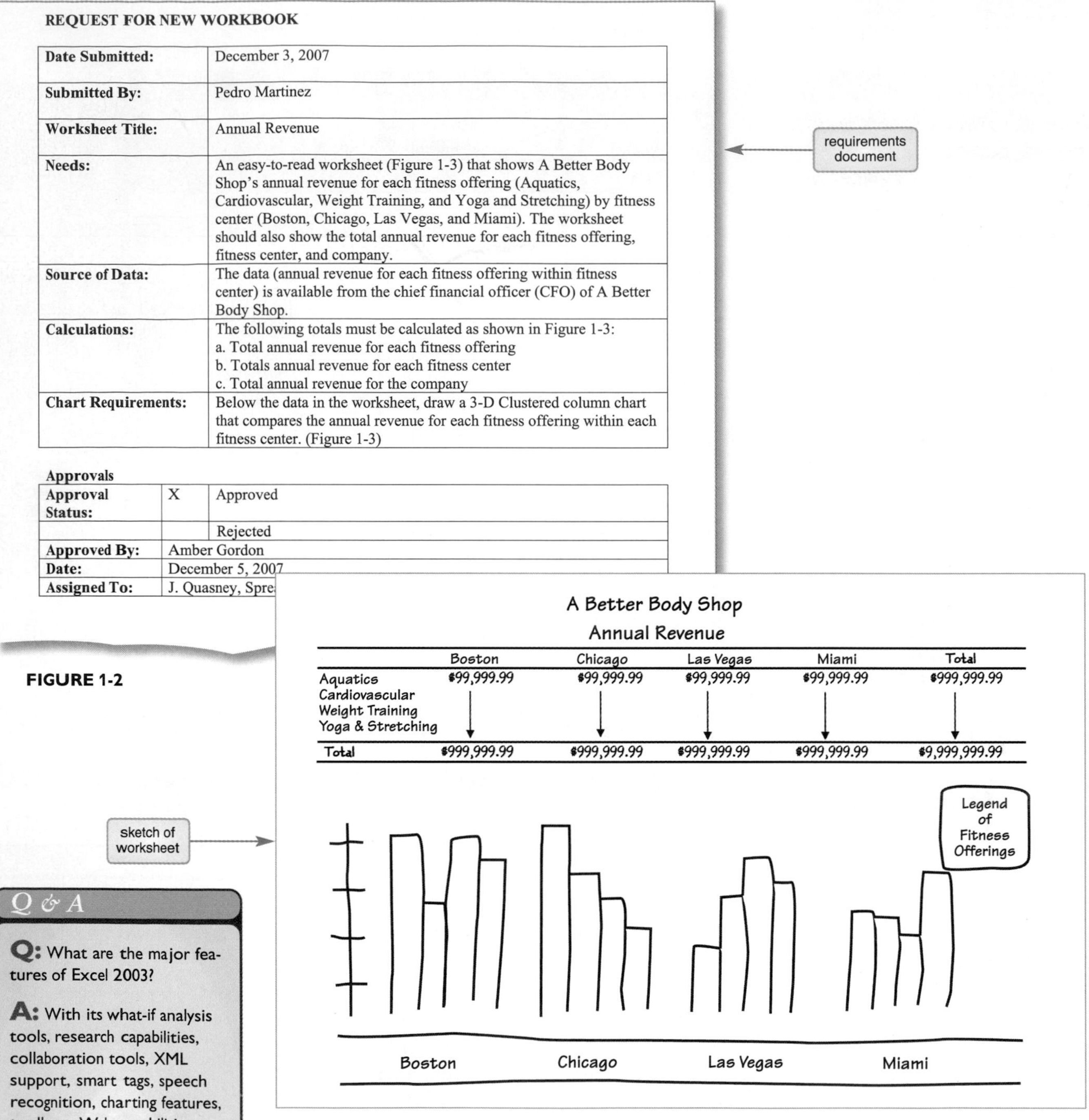

REQUEST FOR NEW WORKBOOK

Date Submitted:	December 3, 2007
Submitted By:	Pedro Martinez
Worksheet Title:	Annual Revenue
Needs:	An easy-to-read worksheet (Figure 1-3) that shows A Better Body Shop's annual revenue for each fitness offering (Aquatics, Cardiovascular, Weight Training, and Yoga and Stretching) by fitness center (Boston, Chicago, Las Vegas, and Miami). The worksheet should also show the total annual revenue for each fitness offering, fitness center, and company.
Source of Data:	The data (annual revenue for each fitness offering within fitness center) is available from the chief financial officer (CFO) of A Better Body Shop.
Calculations:	The following totals must be calculated as shown in Figure 1-3: a. Total annual revenue for each fitness offering b. Totals annual revenue for each fitness center c. Total annual revenue for the company
Chart Requirements:	Below the data in the worksheet, draw a 3-D Clustered column chart that compares the annual revenue for each fitness offering within each fitness center. (Figure 1-3)

Approvals

Approval Status:	X	Approved
		Rejected
Approved By:	Amber Gordon	
Date:	December 5, 2007	
Assigned To:	J. Quasney, Spre	

FIGURE 1-2

FIGURE 1-3

Q & A

Q: What are the major features of Excel 2003?

A: With its what-if analysis tools, research capabilities, collaboration tools, XML support, smart tags, speech recognition, charting features, toolbars, Web capabilities, hundreds of functions, and speech playback, Excel 2003 is one of the easier and more powerful spreadsheet packages available. Its dynamic analytical features make it possible to answer complicated what-if questions. Its Web capabilities allow you to create, publish, view, and analyze data on an intranet or the World Wide Web.

With a good understanding of the requirements document and a sketch of the worksheet, the next step is to use Excel to create the worksheet and chart.

Starting and Customizing Excel

If you are stepping through this project on a computer and you want your screen to match the figures in this book, then you should change your computer's resolution to 800 × 600. For more information on how to change the resolution on your computer, see Appendix D. The following steps show how to start Excel.

To Start Excel

1

• **Click the Start button on the Windows taskbar, point to All Programs on the Start menu, point to Microsoft Office on the All Programs submenu, and then point to Microsoft Office Excel 2003 on the Microsoft Office submenu.**

Windows displays the Start menu, the All Programs submenu, and the Microsoft Office submenu (Figure 1-4).

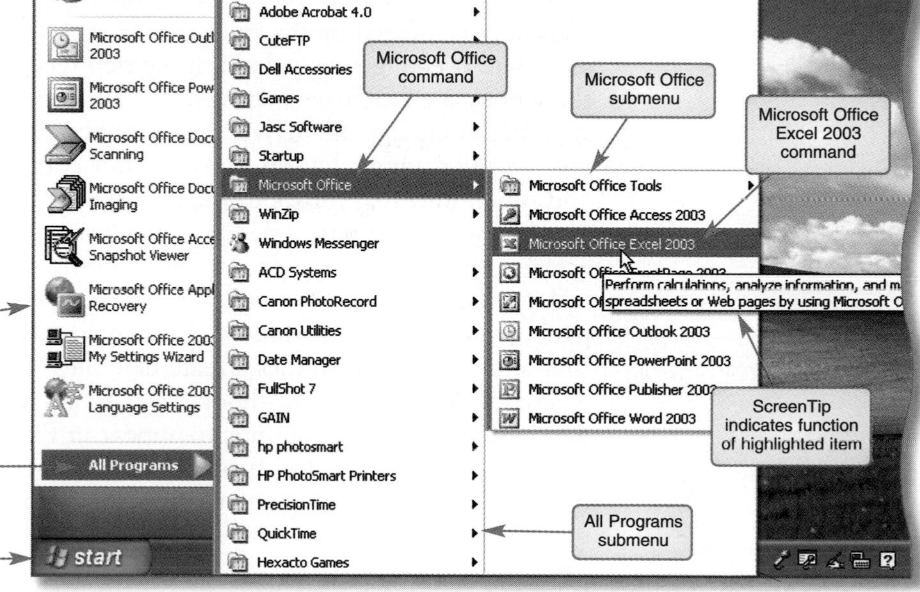

FIGURE 1-4

2

• **Click Microsoft Office Excel 2003.**

Excel starts. After several seconds, Excel displays a blank workbook titled Book1 in the Excel window (Figure 1-5).

3

• **If the Excel window is not maximized, double-click its title bar to maximize it.**

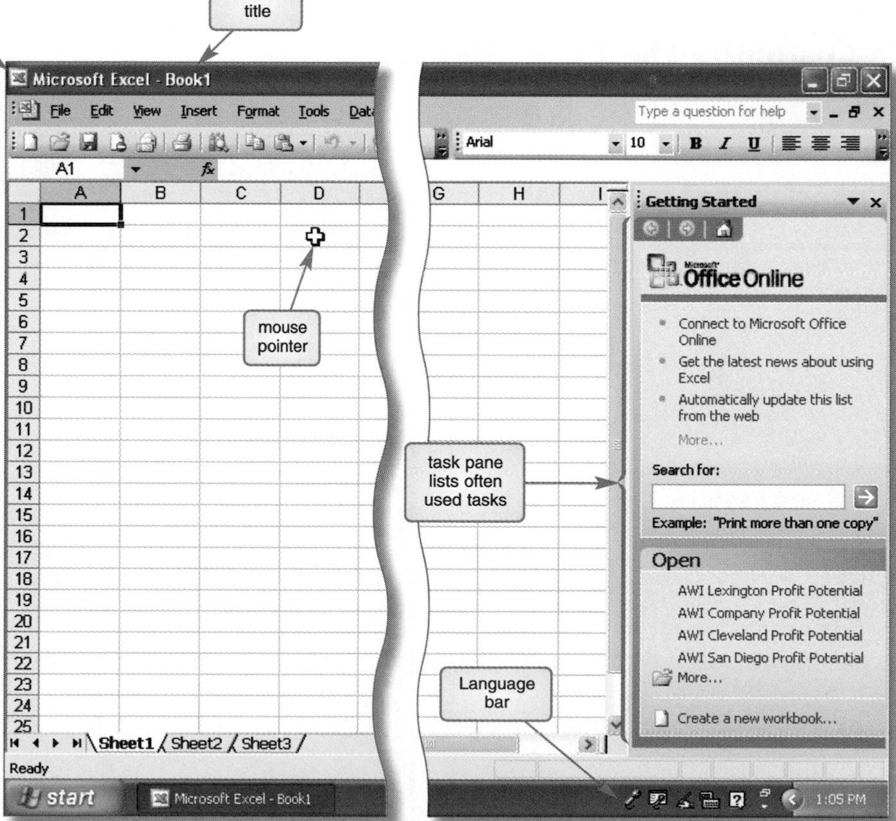

FIGURE 1-5

The screen shown in Figure 1-5 on the previous page illustrates how the Excel window looks the first time you start Excel after installation on most computers. If the Office Speech Recognition software is installed and active on your computer, then when you start Excel, the Language bar is displayed on the screen. The **Language bar** contains buttons that allow you to speak commands and dictate text. It usually is located on the right side of the Windows taskbar next to the notification area, and it changes to include the speech recognition functions available in Excel. In this book, the Language bar is closed because it takes up computer resources and with the Language bar active, the microphone can be turned on accidentally by clicking the Microphone button, causing your computer to act in an unstable manner. For additional information about the Language bar, see page EX 15 and Appendix B.

As shown in Figure 1-5, Excel displays a task pane on the right side of the screen. A **task pane** is a separate window that enables users to carry out some Excel tasks more efficiently. When you start Excel, it displays the Getting Started task pane, which is a small window that provides commonly used links and commands that allow you to open files, create new files, or search Office-related topics on the Microsoft Web site. In this book, the Getting Started task pane is hidden to allow the maximum number of columns to appear in Excel.

At startup, Excel also displays two toolbars on a single row. A **toolbar** contains buttons, boxes, and menus that allow you to perform tasks quickly. To allow for more efficient use of the buttons, the toolbars should appear on two separate rows, instead of sharing a single row. The following steps show how to close the Language bar, close the Getting Started task pane, and instruct Excel to display the toolbars on two separate rows.

To Customize the Excel Window

1

• **Right-click the Language bar.**

The Language bar shortcut menu appears (Figure 1-6).

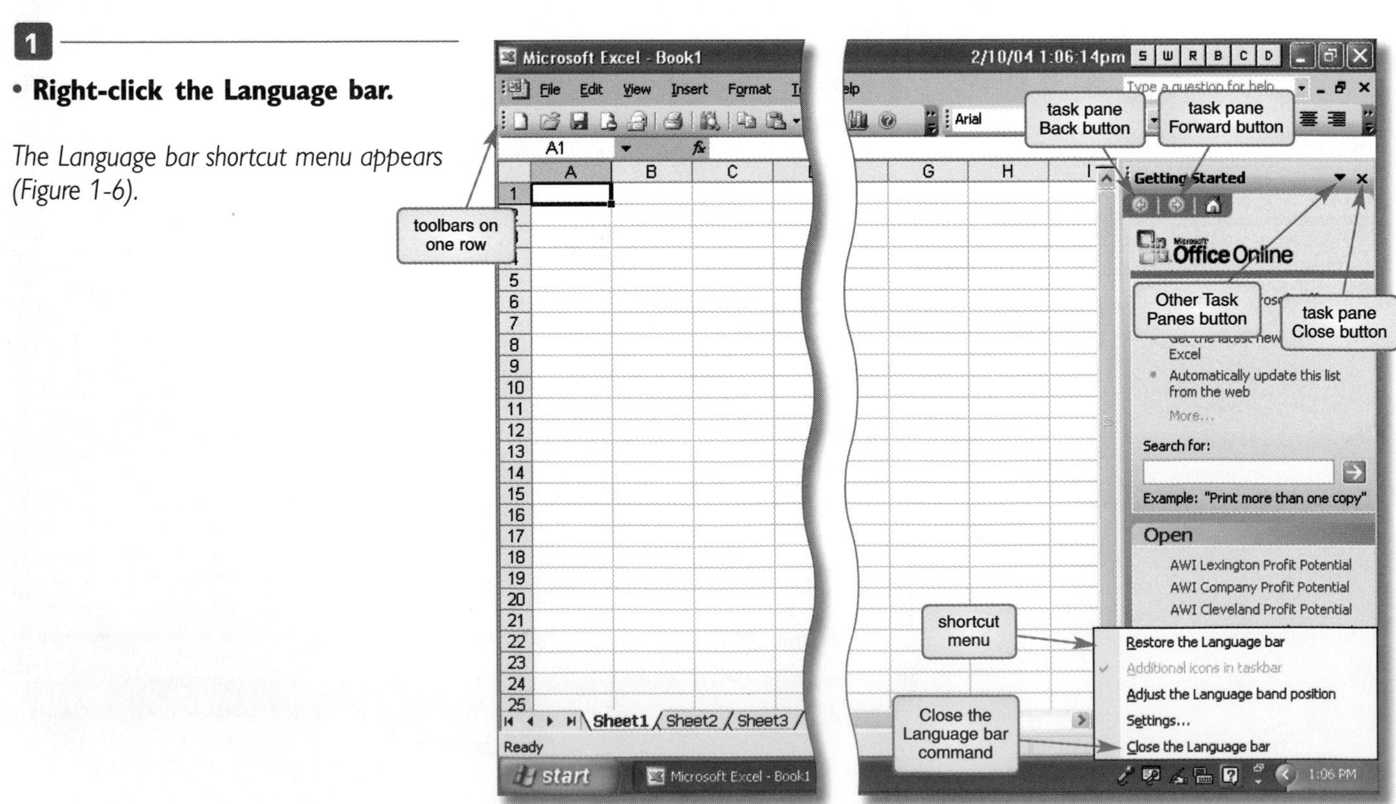

FIGURE 1-6

2

- **Click Close the Language bar.**
- **Click the Getting Started task pane Close button in the upper-right corner of the task pane.**
- **If the toolbars are positioned on the same row, click the Toolbar Options button.**

The Language bar disappears. Excel closes the Getting Started task pane and displays additional columns. Excel also displays the Toolbar Options list showing the buttons that do not fit on the toolbars when toolbars appear on one row (Figure 1-7).

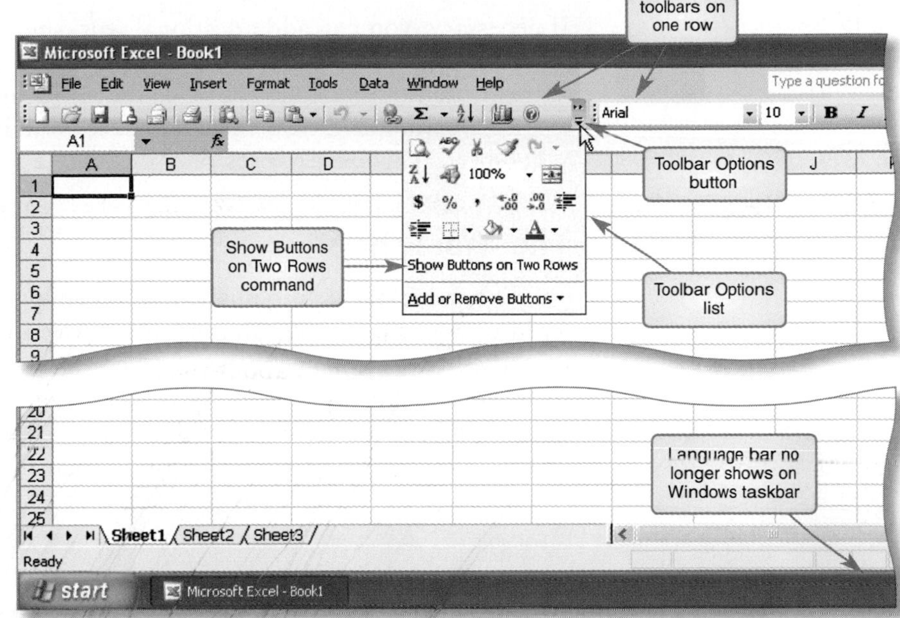

FIGURE 1-7

3

- **Click Show Buttons on Two Rows.**

Excel displays the toolbars on two separate rows (Figure 1-8). With the toolbars on two separate rows, all of the buttons fit on the two toolbars.

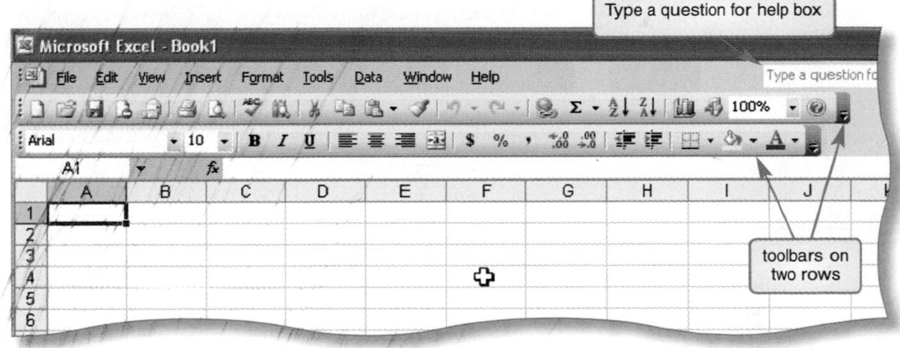

FIGURE 1-8

As you work through creating a worksheet, you will find that certain Excel operations cause Excel to display a task pane. Excel provides 11 task panes, in addition to the Getting Started task pane shown in Figure 1-6. Some of the more important ones are the Clipboard task pane, the Excel Help task pane, and the Clip Art task pane. Throughout the book, these task panes are discussed when they are used.

At any point while working with an Excel worksheet, you can open or close a task pane by clicking the Task Pane command on the View menu. You can activate additional task panes by clicking the Other Task Panes button to the left of the Close button on the task pane title bar (Figure 1-6) and then selecting a task pane in the Other Task Panes list. The Back and Forward buttons below the task pane title bar allow you to switch between task panes that you opened during a session.

Q & A

Q: Need help with Excel?

A: Help with Excel is no further away than the Type a question for help box on the menu bar in the upper-right corner of the window. Click the box that contains the text, Type a question for help (Figure 1-8), type `help`, and then press the ENTER key. Excel responds with a list of topics you can click to learn about obtaining help on any Excel-related topic. To find out what is new in Excel 2003, type `what is new in Excel` in the Type a question for help box.

The Excel Worksheet

When Excel starts, it creates a new blank workbook, called Book1. The **workbook** (Figure 1-9 on the next page) is like a notebook. Inside the workbook are sheets, each of which is called a **worksheet**. Excel opens a new workbook with three worksheets.

If necessary, you can add additional worksheets to a maximum of 255. Each worksheet has a sheet name that appears on a **sheet tab** at the bottom of the workbook. For example, Sheet1 is the name of the active worksheet displayed in the Book1 workbook. If you click the sheet tab labeled Sheet2, Excel displays the Sheet2 worksheet. This project uses only the Sheet1 worksheet.

The Worksheet

The worksheet is organized into a rectangular grid containing vertical columns and horizontal rows. A column letter above the grid, also called the **column heading**, identifies each column. A row number on the left side of the grid, also called the **row heading**, identifies each row. With the screen resolution set to 800 × 600 and the Excel window maximized, Excel displays 12 columns (A through L) and 23 rows (1 through 23) of the worksheet on the screen, as shown in Figure 1-9.

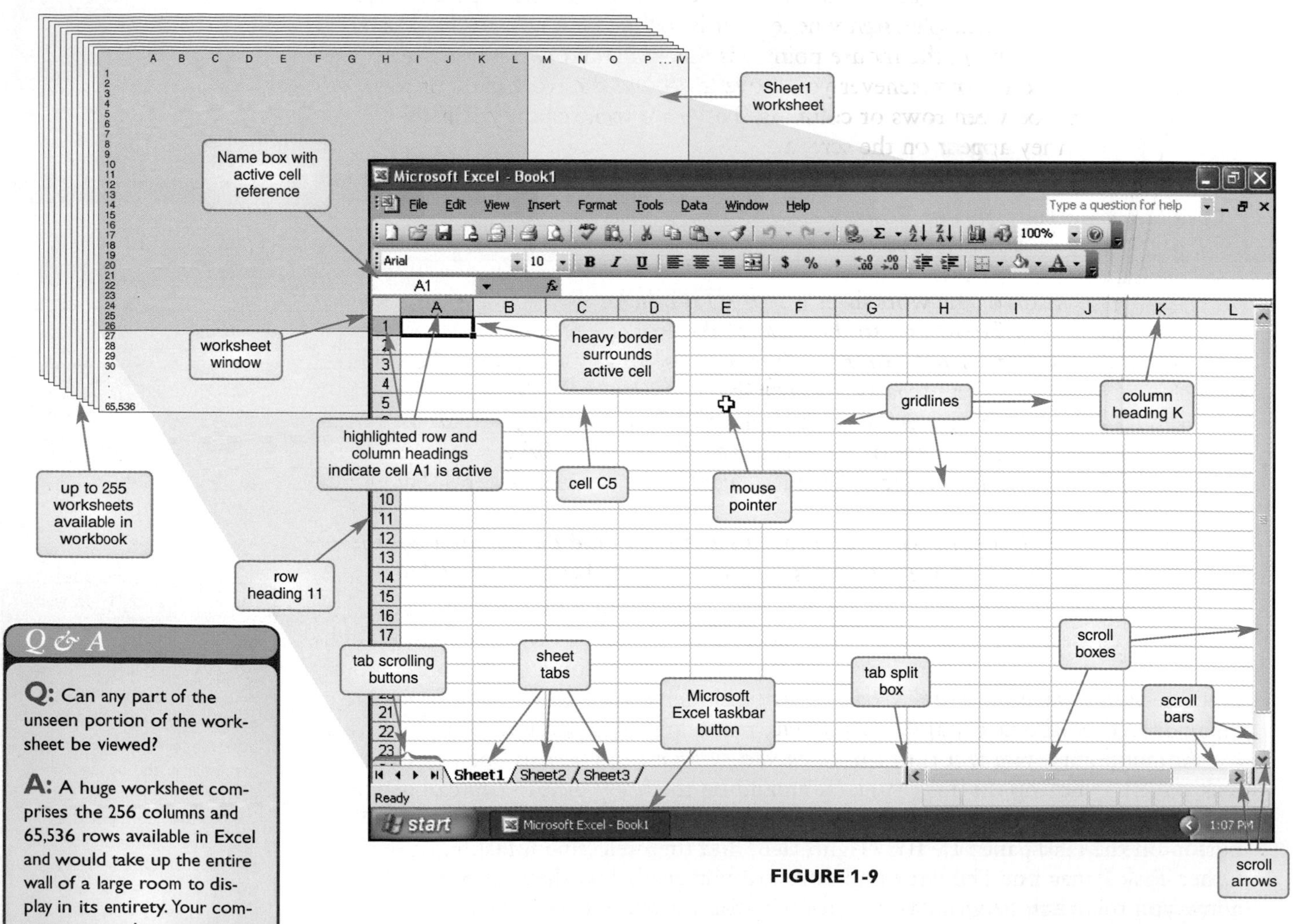

FIGURE 1-9

> **Q & A**
>
> **Q:** Can any part of the unseen portion of the worksheet be viewed?
>
> **A:** A huge worksheet comprises the 256 columns and 65,536 rows available in Excel and would take up the entire wall of a large room to display in its entirety. Your computer screen, by comparison, is a small window that allows you to view only a minute area of the worksheet at one time. While you cannot see the entire worksheet, you can move the window over the worksheet to view any part of it.

The intersection of each column and row is a cell. A **cell** is the basic unit of a worksheet into which you enter data. Each worksheet in a workbook has 256 columns and 65,536 rows for a total of 16,777,216 cells. The column headings begin with A and end with IV. The row headings begin with 1 and end with 65,536. Only a small fraction of the active worksheet appears on the screen at one time.

A cell is referred to by its unique address, or **cell reference**, which is the coordinates of the intersection of a column and a row. To identify a cell, specify the column letter first, followed by the row number. For example, cell reference C5 refers to the cell located at the intersection of column C and row 5 (Figure 1-9).

One cell on the worksheet, designated the **active cell**, is the one into which you can enter data. The active cell in Figure 1-9 is A1. The active cell is identified in three ways. First, a heavy border surrounds the cell; second, the active cell reference shows immediately above column A in the Name box; and third, the column heading A and row heading 1 are highlighted so it is easy to see which cell is active (Figure 1-9).

The horizontal and vertical lines on the worksheet itself are called **gridlines**. Gridlines make it easier to see and identify each cell in the worksheet. If desired, you can turn the gridlines off so they do not show on the worksheet, but it is recommended that you leave them on for now.

The mouse pointer in Figure 1-9 has the shape of a block plus sign. The mouse pointer appears as a block plus sign whenever it is located in a cell on the worksheet. Another common shape of the mouse pointer is the block arrow. The mouse pointer turns into the block arrow whenever you move it outside the worksheet or when you drag cell contents between rows or columns. The other mouse pointer shapes are described when they appear on the screen.

Q & A

Q: Does the mouse pointer always appear as a block plus sign in Excel?

A: The mouse pointer can change to one of more than 15 different shapes, such as a block arrow, cross hair, or chart symbol, depending on the task you are performing in Excel and the mouse pointer's location on the screen.

Worksheet Window

You view the portion of the worksheet displayed on the screen through a **worksheet window** (Figure 1-9). Below and to the right of the worksheet window are **scroll bars**, **scroll arrows**, and **scroll boxes** that you can use to move the worksheet window around to view different parts of the active worksheet. To the right of the sheet tabs at the bottom of the screen is the tab split box. You can drag the **tab split box** to increase or decrease the view of the sheet tabs (Figure 1-9). When you decrease the view of the sheet tabs, you increase the length of the horizontal scroll bar, and vice versa.

The menu bar, Standard toolbar, Formatting toolbar, and formula bar appear at the top of the screen, above the worksheet window and below the title bar.

Q & A

Q: Can the Excel window or viewing area be increased to show more of the worksheet?

A: Yes. Two ways exist to increase what you can see in the viewing area: (1) on the View menu, click Full Screen; and (2) change to a higher resolution. See Appendix D for information about how to change to a higher resolution.

Menu Bar

The **menu bar** is a special toolbar that includes the menu names, as shown in Figure 1-10a on the next page. Each **menu name** represents a menu. A **menu** is a list of commands that you can use to retrieve, store, print, and manipulate data on the worksheet. When you point to a menu name on the menu bar, the area of the menu bar containing the name changes to a button. To display a menu, such as the Edit menu, click the Edit menu name on the menu bar (Figures 1-10b and 1-10c on the next page). If you point to a menu command with an arrow to its right, Excel displays a **submenu** from which you can choose a command.

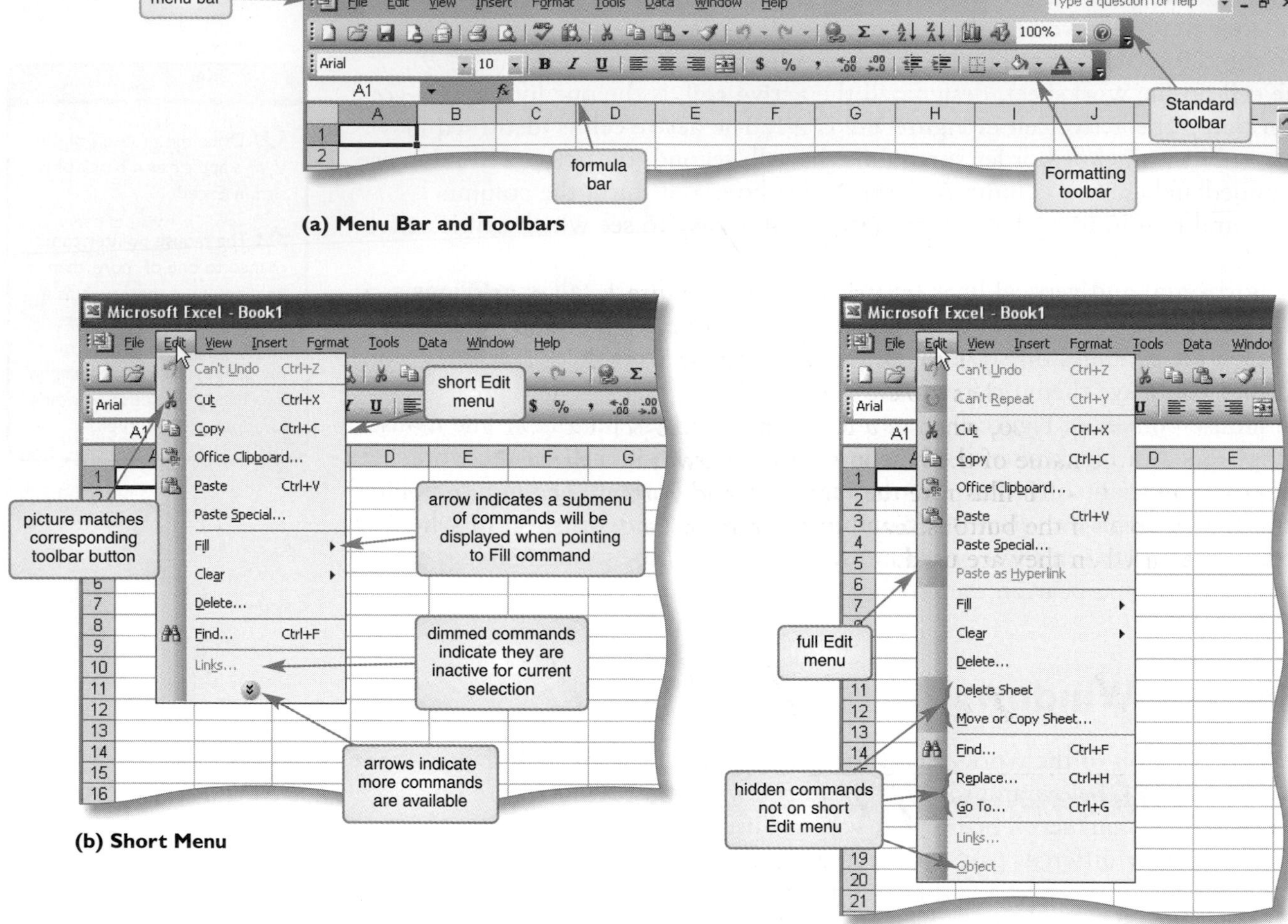

FIGURE 1-10

When you click a menu name on the menu bar, Excel displays a **short menu** listing the most recently used commands (Figure 1-10b). If you wait a few seconds or click the arrows at the bottom of the short menu, Excel displays the full menu. The **full menu** lists all of the commands associated with a menu (Figure 1-10c). You also can display a full menu immediately by double-clicking the menu name on the menu bar. In this book, use one of the following techniques to ensure that Excel always displays the full menu.

1. Click the menu name on the menu bar and then wait a few seconds.
2. Click the menu name on the menu bar and then click the arrows at the bottom of the short menu.
3. Click the menu name on the menu bar and then point to the arrows at the bottom of the short menu.
4. Double-click the menu name on the menu bar.

Both short and full menus display some dimmed commands. A **dimmed command** appears gray, or dimmed, instead of black, which indicates it is not available for the current selection. A command with medium-blue shading to the left of it on a full menu is called a **hidden command** because it does not appear on a short menu. As you use Excel, it automatically personalizes the short menus for you based on how often you use commands. That is, as you use hidden commands, Excel *unhides* them and places them on the short menu.

The menu bar can change to include other menu names, depending on the type of work you are doing in Excel. For example, if you are working with a chart sheet rather than a worksheet, Excel displays the Chart menu bar with menu names that reflect charting commands.

Q & A

Q: Can toolbars be moved to other locations on the screen?

A: You can move a toolbar to any location on the screen. Drag the move handle (Figure 1-12a on the next page) to the desired location. Once the toolbar is in the window area, drag the title bar to move it. Each side of the screen is called a dock. You can drag a toolbar to a dock so it does not clutter the window.

Standard Toolbar and Formatting Toolbar

The Standard toolbar and the Formatting toolbar (Figure 1-11) contain buttons and boxes that allow you to perform frequent tasks more quickly than when using the menu bar. For example, to print a worksheet, you click the Print button on the Standard toolbar. Each button has a picture on the button face to help you remember the button's function. Also, when you move the mouse pointer over a button or box, Excel displays the name of the button or box below it in a **ScreenTip**.

Figures 1-11a and 1-11b illustrate the Standard and Formatting toolbars and describe the functions of the buttons. Each of the buttons and boxes will be explained in detail when they are used.

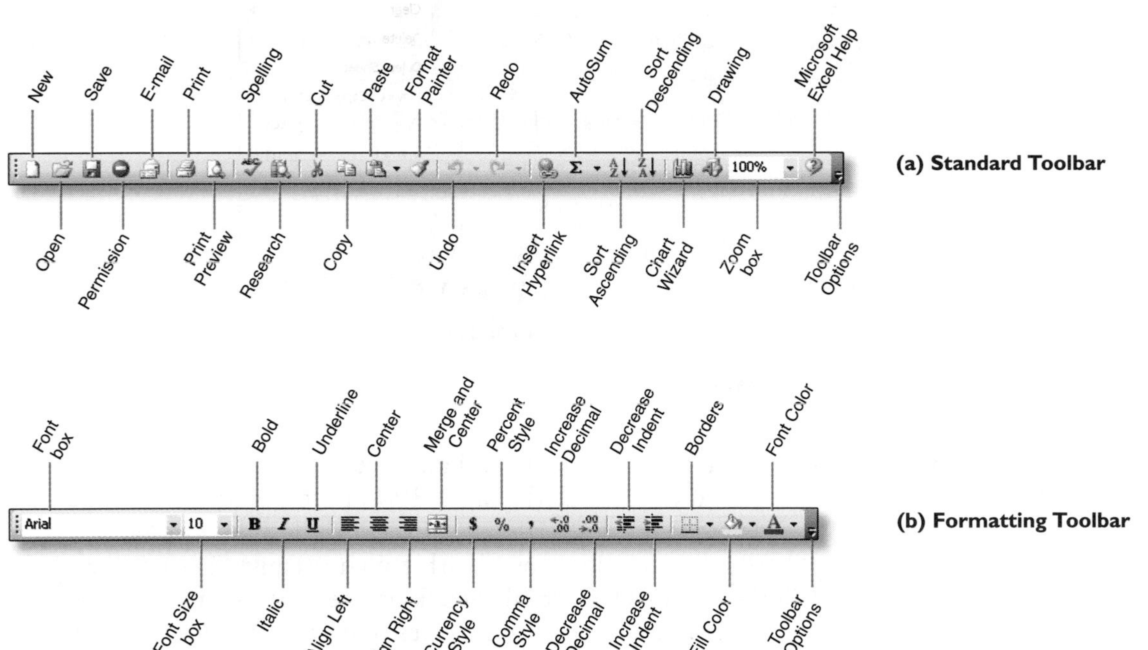

FIGURE 1-11

When you first install Excel, both the Standard and Formatting toolbars are preset to display on the same row (Figure 1-12a on the next page), immediately below the menu bar. Unless the resolution of your display device is greater than 800 × 600, many of the buttons that belong on these toolbars are hidden. Hidden buttons appear in the Toolbar Options list (Figure 1-12b on the next page). In this mode, you also can display all the buttons on either toolbar by double-clicking the **move handle** on the left of each toolbar (Figure 1-12a).

Q & A

Q: Can toolbars with a different set of buttons than shown in the book be reset so they appear the same as in the book?

A: If your toolbars have a different set of buttons than shown in Figure 1-11, it probably means that a previous user added or deleted buttons. To reset the toolbars to their default, see Appendix D.

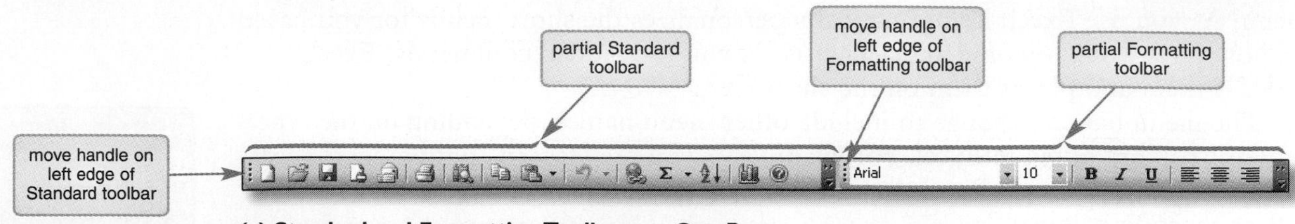

(a) Standard and Formatting Toolbars on One Row

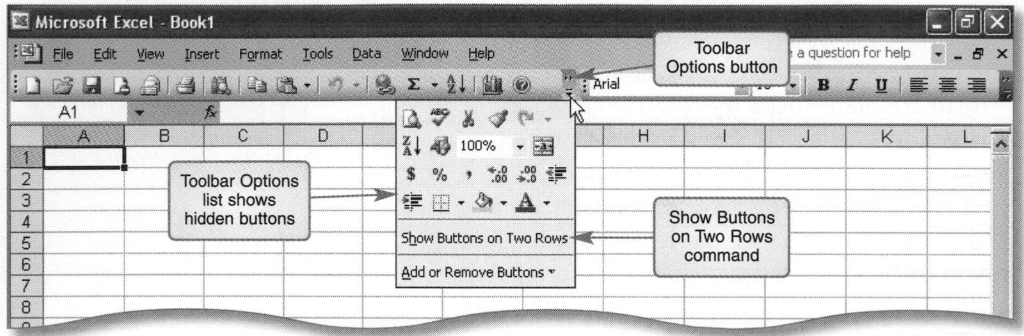

(b) Toolbar Options List

(c) Standard and Formatting Toolbars on Two Rows

FIGURE 1-12

In this book, the Standard and Formatting toolbars are shown on two rows, one below the other, so that all buttons appear on a screen with the resolution set to 800 × 600 (Figure 1-12c). You can show the two toolbars on two rows by clicking the Show Buttons on Two Rows command in the Toolbar Options list (Figure 1-12b).

Formula Bar

The formula bar appears below the Standard and Formatting toolbars (Figure 1-13). As you type, Excel displays the entry in the **formula bar**. Excel also displays the active cell reference in the Name box on the left side of the formula bar.

Status Bar

The status bar is located immediately above the Windows taskbar at the bottom of the screen (Figure 1-13). The **status bar** displays a brief description of the command selected (highlighted) on a menu, the function of the button the mouse pointer is pointing to, or the mode of Excel. **Mode indicators**, such as Enter and Ready, appear on the status bar and specify the current mode of Excel. When the mode is **Ready**, Excel is ready to accept the next command or data entry. When the mode indicator reads **Enter**, Excel is in the process of accepting data through the keyboard into the active cell.

In the middle of the status bar is the AutoCalculate area. The **AutoCalculate area** can be used in place of a calculator or formula to view the sum, average, or other types of totals of a group of numbers on the worksheet. The AutoCalculate area is discussed in detail later in this project.

Keyboard indicators, such as CAPS (Caps Lock), NUM (Num Lock), and SCRL (Scroll), show which keys are engaged. Keyboard indicators appear in the small rectangular boxes on the right side of the status bar (Figure 1-13).

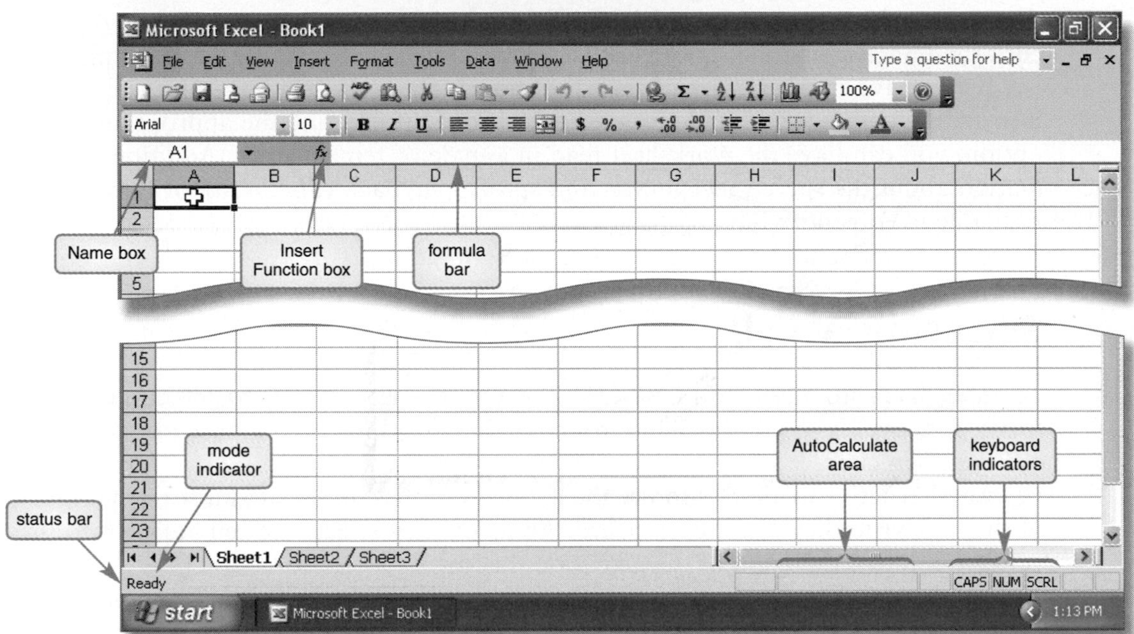

FIGURE 1-13

Speech Recognition and Speech Playback

With the **Office Speech Recognition software** installed and a microphone, you can speak the names of toolbar buttons, menus, menu commands, list items, alerts, and dialog box controls, such as OK and Cancel. You also can dictate cell entries, such as text and numbers. To indicate whether you want to speak commands or dictate cell entries, you use the Language bar. The Language bar can be in one of four states: (1) **restored**, which means it is displayed somewhere in the Excel window (Figure 1-14a); (2) **minimized**, which means it is displayed on the Windows taskbar (Figure 1-14b); (3) **hidden**, which means you do not see it on the screen, but it will be displayed the next time you start your computer; (4) **closed**, which means it is hidden permanently until you enable it. If the Language bar is hidden or closed and you want it to display, then do the following:

1. Right-click an open area on the Windows taskbar at the bottom of the screen.
2. Point to Toolbars on the shortcut menu and then click Language bar on the Toolbars submenu.

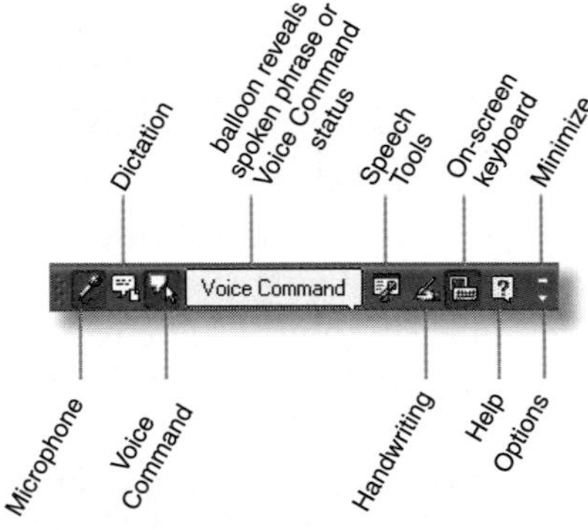

(a) Language Bar in Excel Window with Microphone Enabled

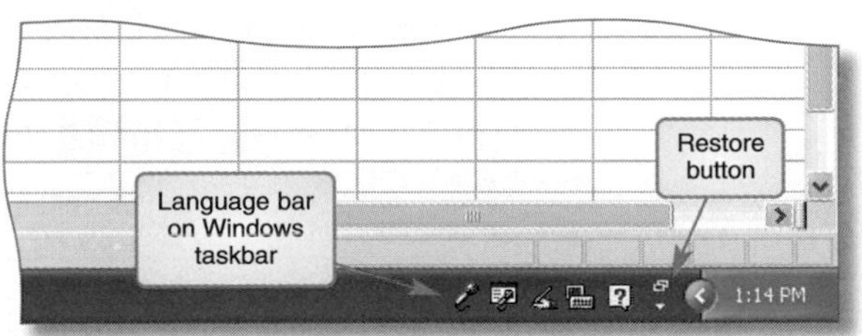

(b) Language Bar Minimized on Windows Taskbar

FIGURE 1-14

If the Language bar command is dimmed on the Toolbars submenu or if the Speech command is dimmed on the Tools menu, the Office Speech Recognition software is not installed.

In this book, the Language bar does not appear in the figures. If you want to close the Language bar so that your screen is identical to what you see in the book, right-click the Language bar and then click Close the Language bar on the shortcut menu.

If you have speakers, you can use the **speech playback** functions of Excel to instruct the computer to read a worksheet to you. By selecting the appropriate option, you can have the worksheet read in a male or female voice. Additional information about the speech recognition and speech playback capabilities of Excel is available in Appendix B.

Selecting a Cell

To enter data into a cell, you first must select it. The easiest way **to select a cell** (make it active) is to use the mouse to move the block plus sign mouse pointer to the cell and then click.

An alternative method is to use the arrow keys that are located just to the right of the typewriter keys on the keyboard. An arrow key selects the cell adjacent to the active cell in the direction of the arrow on the key.

You know a cell is selected, or active, when a heavy border surrounds the cell and the active cell reference appears in the Name box on the left side of the formula bar. Excel also changes the active cell's column heading and row heading to a gold color.

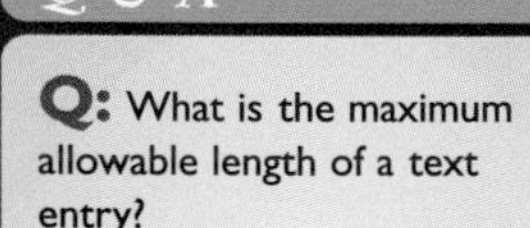

Q: What is the maximum allowable length of a text entry?

A: A text entry in a cell can contain from 1 to 32,767 characters. Although text entries primarily are used to identify parts of a worksheet, some worksheet applications use text entries as data that you dissect, string together, and manipulate using text functions.

Entering Text

In Excel, any set of characters containing a letter, hyphen (as in a telephone number), or space is considered text. **Text** is used to place titles, such as worksheet titles, column titles, and row titles, on the worksheet. For example, as shown in Figure 1-15, the worksheet title, A Better Body Shop, identifies the worksheet created in Project 1. The worksheet subtitle, Annual Revenue, identifies the type of report. The column titles in row 3 (Boston, Chicago, Las Vegas, Miami, and Total) identify the numbers in each column. The row titles in column A (Aquatics, Cardiovascular, Weight Training, Yoga & Stretching, and Total) identify the numbers in each row.

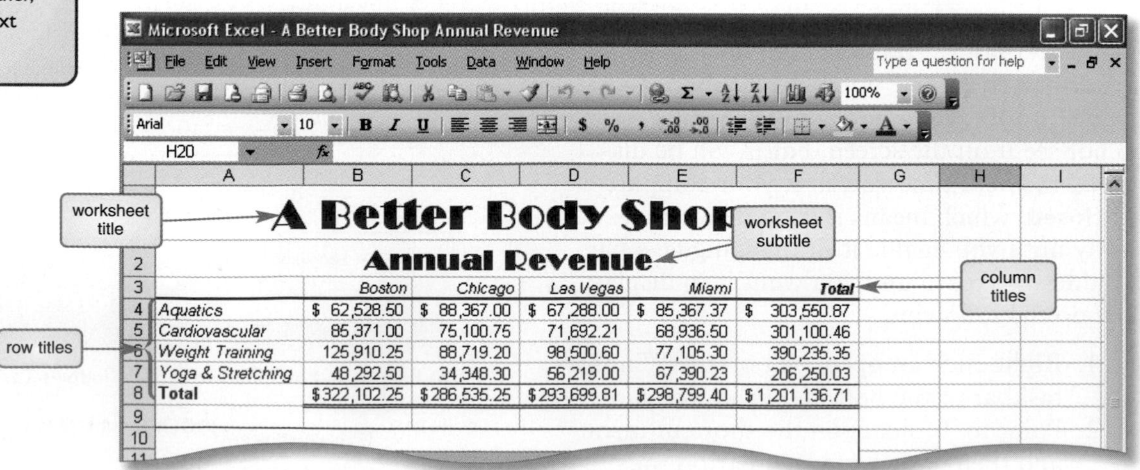

FIGURE 1-15

Entering the Worksheet Titles

The following steps show how to enter the worksheet titles in cells A1 and A2. Later in this project, the worksheet titles will be formatted so they appear as shown in Figure 1-15.

To Enter the Worksheet Titles

- **Click cell A1.**

Cell A1 becomes the active cell and a heavy border surrounds it (Figure 1-16).

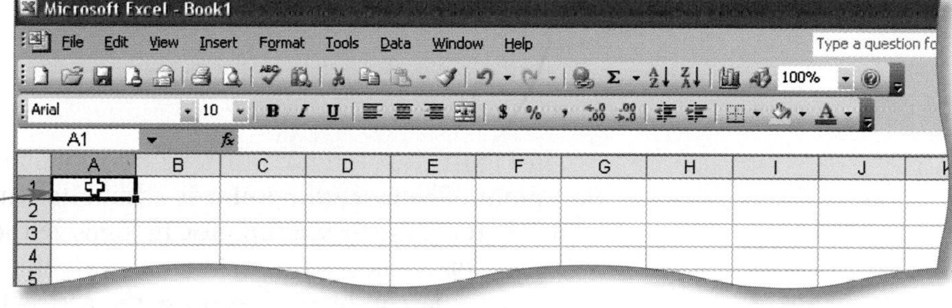

FIGURE 1-16

2

- **Type** `A Better Body Shop` **in cell A1, and then point to the Enter box in the formula bar.**

Excel displays the title in the formula bar and in cell A1 (Figure 1-17). When you begin typing a cell entry, Excel displays two additional boxes in the formula bar: the Cancel box and the Enter box.

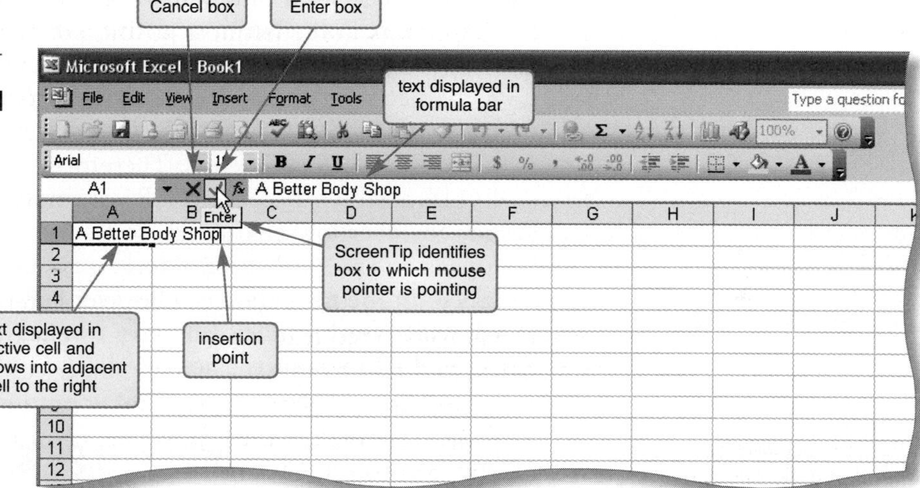

FIGURE 1-17

3

- **Click the Enter box to complete the entry.**

Excel enters the worksheet title in cell A1 (Figure 1-18).

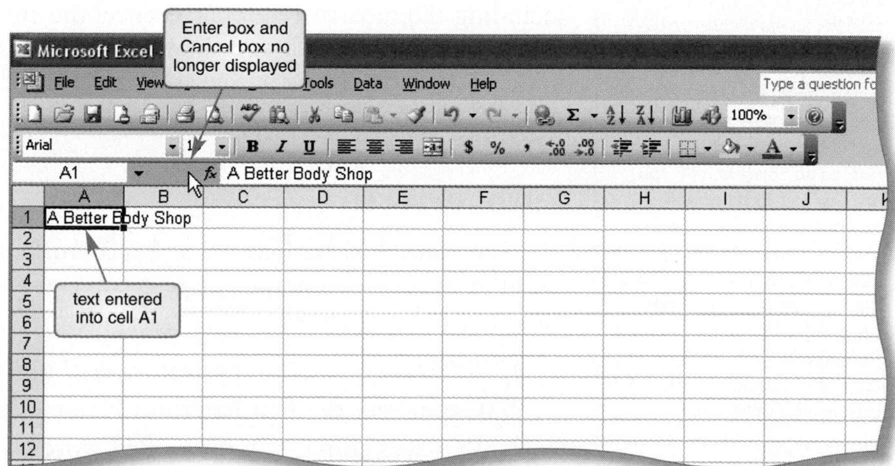

FIGURE 1-18

4

• **Click cell A2 to select it. Type** `Annual Revenue` **as the cell entry. Click the Enter box to complete the entry.**

Excel enters the worksheet subtitle in cell A2 (Figure 1-19).

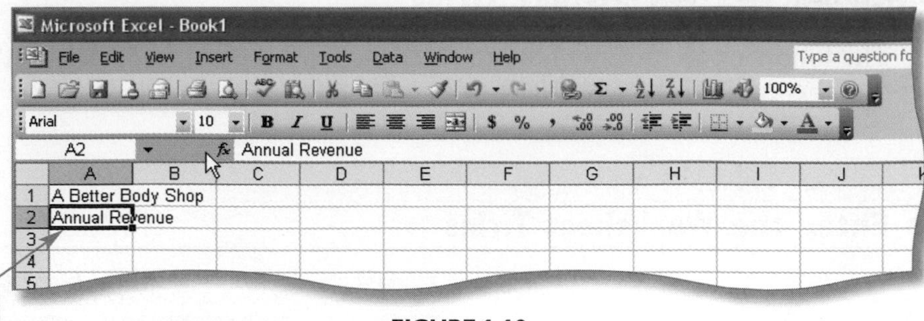

FIGURE 1-19

In Figure 1-17 on the previous page, the text in cell A1 is followed by the insertion point. The **insertion point** is a blinking vertical line that indicates where the next typed character will appear. In Steps 3 and 4, clicking the **Enter box** completes the entry. Clicking the **Cancel box** cancels the entry.

When you complete a text entry into a cell, a series of events occurs. First, Excel positions the text left-aligned in the cell. **Left-aligned** means the cell entry is positioned at the far left in the cell. Therefore, the A in the worksheet title, A Better Body Shop, begins in the leftmost position of cell A1.

Second, when the text is longer than the width of a column, Excel displays the overflow characters in adjacent cells to the right as long as these adjacent cells contain no data. In Figure 1-19, the width of cell A1 is approximately nine characters. The text consists of 18 characters. Therefore, Excel displays the overflow characters from cell A1 in cell B1, because cell B1 is empty. If cell B1 contained data, Excel would hide the overflow characters, so that only the first nine characters in cell A1 would appear on the worksheet. Excel stores the overflow characters in cell A1 and displays them in the formula bar whenever cell A1 is the active cell.

Third, when you complete an entry by clicking the Enter box, the cell in which the text is entered remains the active cell.

Q & A

Q: Can Excel be instructed to maintain the current active cell when the ENTER key is pressed?

A: Yes. When you first install Excel, the ENTER key not only completes the entry, but it also moves the selection to an adjacent cell. You can instruct Excel not to move the selection after pressing the ENTER key by clicking Options on the Tools menu, clicking the Edit tab, removing the check mark from the Move Selection after Enter check box, and then clicking the OK button.

Correcting a Mistake while Typing

If you type the wrong letter and notice the error before clicking the Enter box or pressing the ENTER key, use the BACKSPACE key to delete all the characters back to and including the incorrect letter. To cancel the entire entry before entering it into the cell, click the Cancel box in the formula bar or press the ESC key. If you see an error in a cell after entering the text, select the cell and retype the entry. Later in this project, additional error-correction techniques are discussed.

AutoCorrect

The **AutoCorrect feature** of Excel works behind the scenes, correcting common mistakes when you complete a text entry in a cell. AutoCorrect makes three types of corrections for you:

1. Corrects two initial capital letters by changing the second letter to lowercase.
2. Capitalizes the first letter in the names of days.
3. Replaces commonly misspelled words with their correct spelling. For example, it will change the misspelled word *recieve* to *receive* when you complete the entry. AutoCorrect will correct the spelling of hundreds of commonly misspelled words automatically.

Entering Column Titles

To enter the column titles in row 3, select the appropriate cell and then enter the text, as described in the following steps.

To Enter Column Titles

1

- **Click cell B3.**

Cell B3 becomes the active cell. The active cell reference in the Name box changes from A2 to B3 (Figure 1-20).

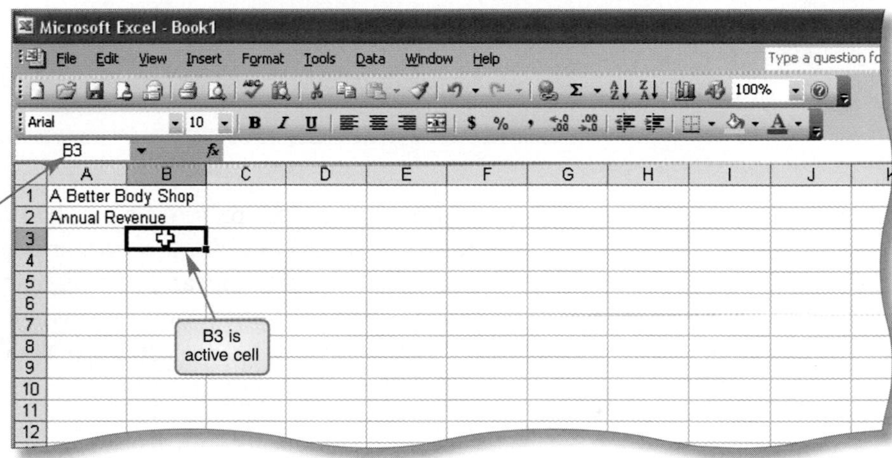

FIGURE 1-20

2

- **Type** `Boston` **in cell B3.**

Excel displays Boston in the formula bar and in cell B3 (Figure 1-21).

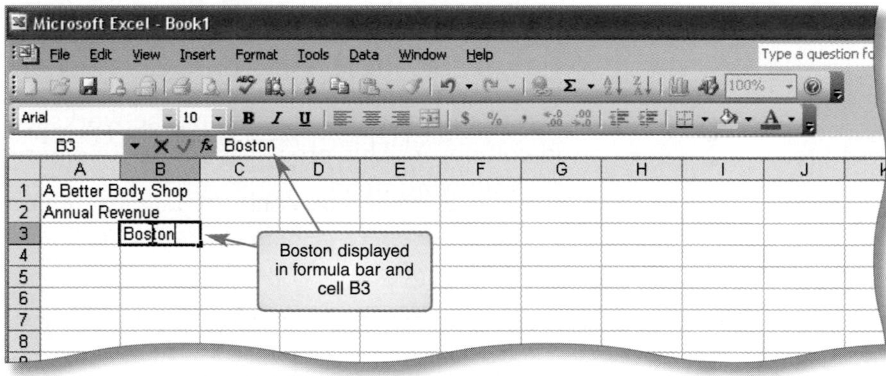

FIGURE 1-21

3

- **Press the RIGHT ARROW key.**

Excel enters the column title, Boston, in cell B3 and makes cell C3 the active cell (Figure 1-22).

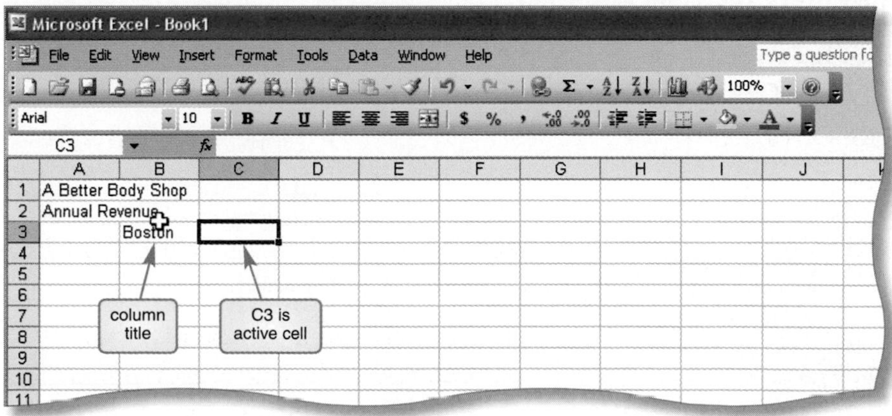

FIGURE 1-22

4

• **Repeat Steps 2 and 3 for the remaining column titles in row 3; that is, enter** `Chicago` **in cell C3,** `Las Vegas` **in cell D3,** `Miami` **in cell E3, and** `Total` **in cell F3 (complete the last entry in cell F3 by clicking the Enter box in the formula bar).**

Excel displays the column titles left aligned, as shown in Figure 1-23.

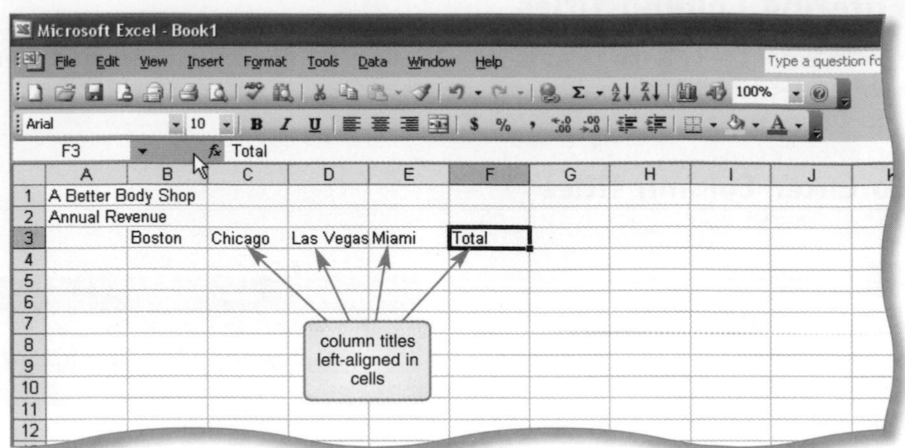

FIGURE 1-23

If the next entry is in an adjacent cell, use the arrow keys to complete the entry in a cell. When you press an arrow key to complete an entry, the adjacent cell in the direction of the arrow (up, down, left, or right) becomes the active cell. If the next entry is in a nonadjacent cell, complete an entry by clicking the next cell in which you plan to enter data. You also can click the Enter box or press the ENTER key and then click the appropriate cell for the next entry.

Entering Row Titles

The next step in developing the worksheet in Project 1 is to enter the row titles in column A. This process is similar to entering the column titles and is described in the following steps.

To Enter Row Titles

1

• **Click cell A4. Type** `Aquatics` **and then press the DOWN ARROW key.**

Excel enters the row title, Aquatics, in cell A4, and cell A5 becomes the active cell (Figure 1-24).

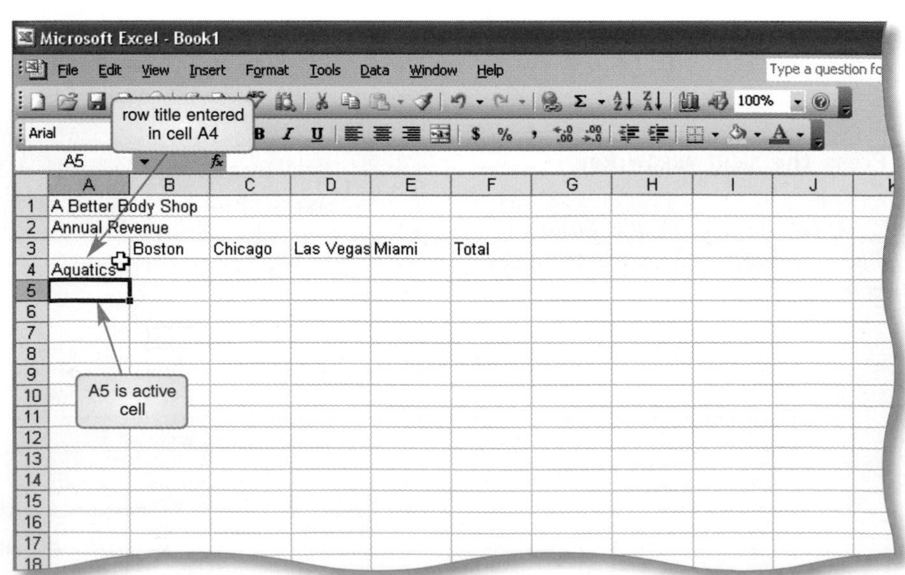

FIGURE 1-24

2

• **Repeat Step 1 for the remaining row titles in column A; that is, enter** `Cardiovascular` **in cell A5,** `Weight Training` **in cell A6,** `Yoga & Stretching` **in cell A7, and** `Total` **in cell A8.**

Excel displays the row titles, as shown in Figure 1-25.

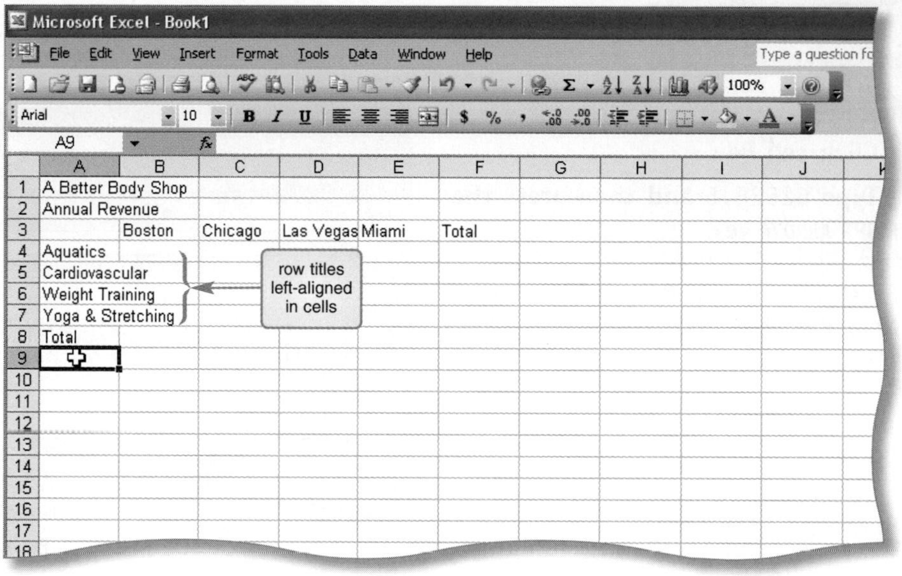

	A	B	C	D	E	F
1	A Better Body Shop					
2	Annual Revenue					
3		Boston	Chicago	Las Vegas	Miami	Total
4	Aquatics					
5	Cardiovascular					
6	Weight Training					
7	Yoga & Stretching					
8	Total					

row titles left-aligned in cells

FIGURE 1-25

When you enter text, Excel automatically left-aligns the text in the cell. Excel treats any combination of numbers, spaces, and nonnumeric characters as text. For example, the following entries are text:

401AX21, 921-231, 619 321, 883XTY

You can change the text alignment in a cell by realigning it. Several alignment techniques are discussed later in the project.

Q & A

Q: Can numbers be entered as text?

A: Yes. Sometimes, you will want Excel to treat numbers, such as Zip codes and telephone numbers, as text. To enter a number as text, start the entry with an apostrophe (').

Entering Numbers

In Excel, you can enter numbers into cells to represent amounts. A **number** can contain only the following characters:

0 1 2 3 4 5 6 7 8 9 + - ( ) , / . $ % E e

If a cell entry contains any other keyboard character (including spaces), Excel interprets the entry as text and treats it accordingly. The use of the special characters is explained when they are used in the project.

The A Better Body Shop Annual Revenue numbers used in Project 1 are summarized in Table 1-1. These numbers, which represent annual revenue for each of the fitness offerings and fitness centers, must be entered in rows 4, 5, 6, and 7. The steps on the next page enter the numbers in Table 1-1 one row at a time.

Table 1-1 A Better Body Shop Annual Revenue Numbers

	Boston	Chicago	Las Vegas	Miami
Aquatics	62528.50	88367.00	67288.00	85367.37
Cardiovascular	85371.00	75100.75	71692.21	68936.50
Weight Training	125910.25	88719.20	98500.60	77105.30
Yoga & Stretching	48292.50	34348.30	56219.00	67390.23

To Enter Numbers

1

- **Click cell B4.**
- **Type** 62528.5 **and then press the RIGHT ARROW key.**

Excel enters the number 62528.5 in cell B4 and changes the active cell to cell C4 (Figure 1-26).

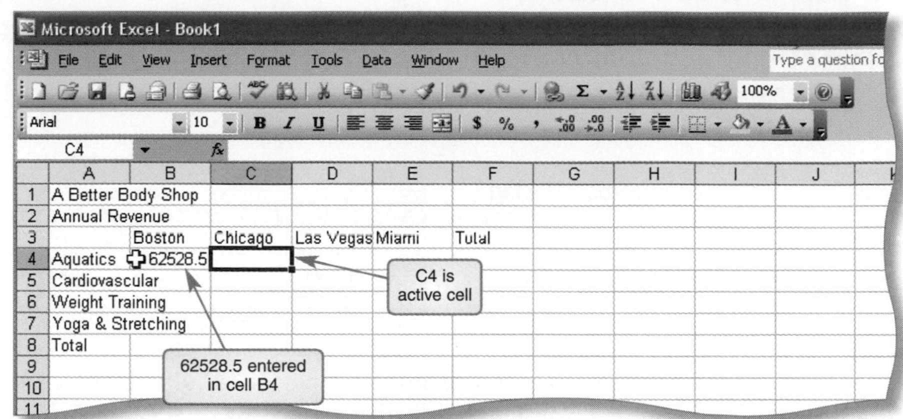

FIGURE 1-26

2

- **Enter** 88367 **in cell C4,** 67288 **in cell D4, and** 85367.37 **in cell E4.**

Row 4 now contains the annual revenue by fitness center for the Aquatics offering (Figure 1-27). The numbers in row 4 are right-aligned, which means Excel displays the cell entry to the far right in the cell.

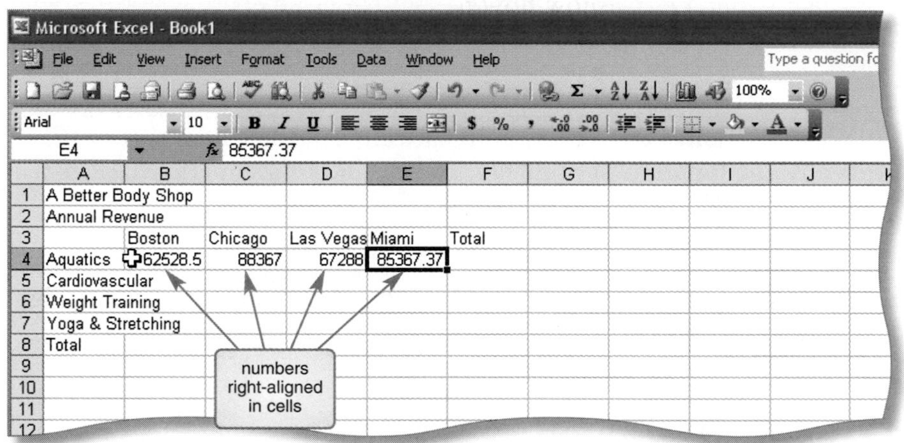

FIGURE 1-27

3

- **Click cell B5.**
- **Enter the remaining annual revenue numbers provided in Table 1-1 on the previous page for each of the three remaining offerings in rows 5, 6, and 7.**

Excel displays the annual revenue, as shown in Figure 1-28.

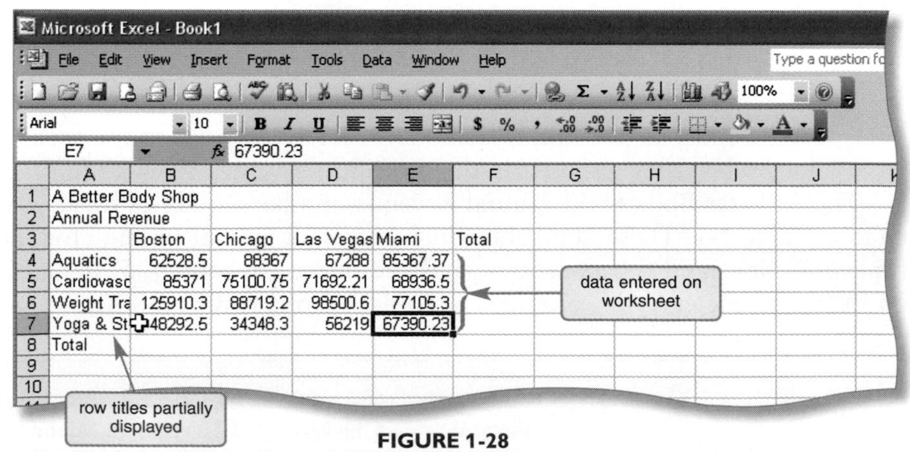

FIGURE 1-28

When the numbers are entered into the cells in column B, Excel only partially displays the row titles in column A. When the worksheet is formatted later in the project, the row titles will appear in their entirety.

Steps 1 through 3 complete the numeric entries. You are not required to type dollar signs, commas, or trailing zeros. When you enter a dollar value that has cents, however, you must add the decimal point and the numbers representing the cents. Later in this project, the numbers will be formatted to use dollar signs, commas, and trailing zeros to improve the appearance and readability of the numbers.

Q & A

Q: What are the limits on numeric entries in Excel?

A: In Excel, a number can be between approximately -1×10^{308} and 1×10^{308} that is, between a negative 1 followed by 308 zeros and a positive 1 followed by 308 zeros. To enter a number such as 6,000,000,000,000,000, you can type 6,000,000,000,000,000, or you can type 6E15, which stands for 6×10^{15}.

Calculating a Sum

The next step in creating the worksheet is to determine the total annual revenue for the fitness center in Boston in column B. To calculate this value in cell B8, Excel must add, or sum, the numbers in cells B4, B5, B6, and B7. Excel's **SUM function**, which adds all of the numbers in a range of cells, provides a convenient means to accomplish this task.

A **range** is a series of two or more adjacent cells in a column or row or a rectangular group of cells. For example, the group of adjacent cells B4, B5, B6, and B7 is called a range. Many Excel operations, such as summing numbers, take place on a range of cells.

The following steps show how to sum the numbers in column B.

To Sum a Column of Numbers

1

• **Click cell B8.**

Cell B8 becomes the active cell (Figure 1-29).

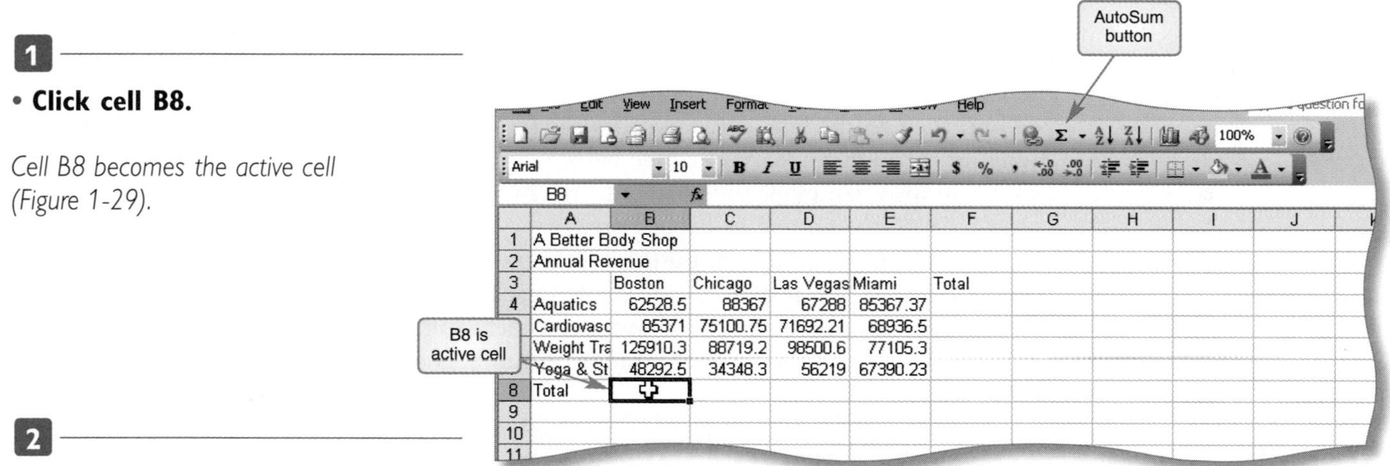

FIGURE 1-29

2

• **Click the AutoSum button on the Standard toolbar.**

Excel responds by displaying =SUM(B4:B7) in the formula bar and in the active cell B8 (Figure 1-30). Excel displays a ScreenTip below the active cell. The B4:B7 within parentheses following the function name, SUM, is Excel's way of identifying that the SUM function will add the numbers in the range B4 through B7. Excel also surrounds the proposed cells to sum with a moving border, called a ***marquee****.*

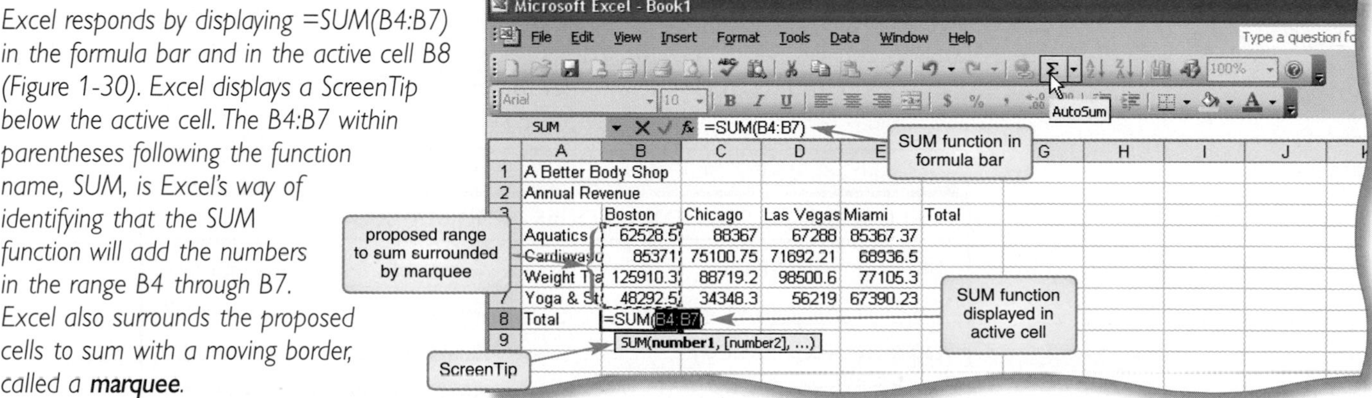

FIGURE 1-30

3

• Click the AutoSum button a second time.

Excel enters the sum of the annual revenues for the four fitness offerings for Boston in cell B8 (Figure 1-31). The SUM function assigned to cell B8 appears in the formula bar when cell B8 is the active cell.

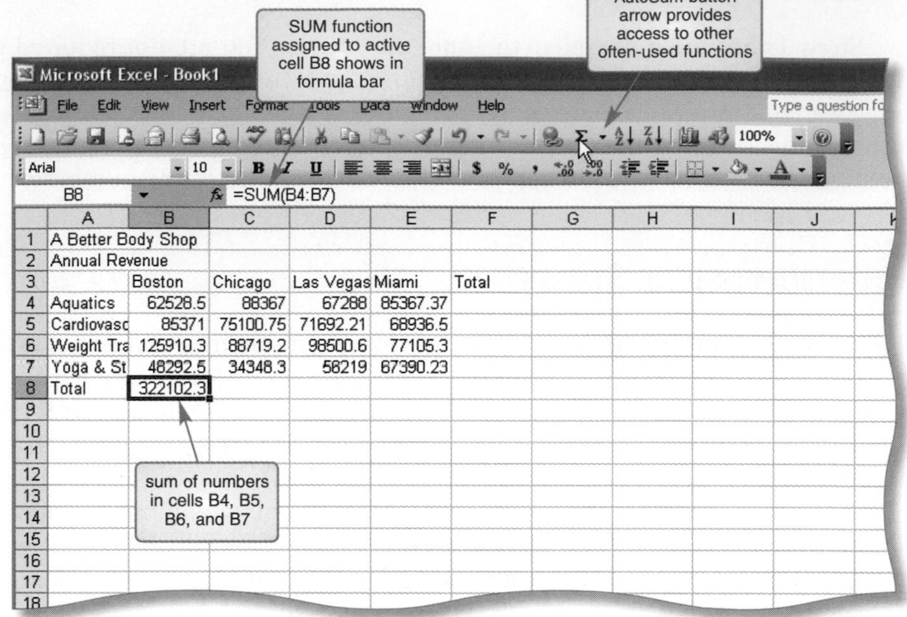

FIGURE 1-31

When you enter the SUM function using the AutoSum button, Excel automatically selects what it considers to be your choice of the range to sum. When proposing the range to sum, Excel first looks for a range of cells with numbers above the active cell and then to the left. If Excel proposes the wrong range, you can correct it by dragging through the correct range before clicking the AutoSum button a second time. You also can enter the correct range by typing the beginning cell reference, a colon (:), and the ending cell reference.

If you click the AutoSum button arrow on the right side of the AutoSum button (Figure 1-31), Excel displays a list of often used functions from which you can choose. The list includes functions that allow you to determine the average, the minimum value, or the maximum value of a range of numbers.

Using the Fill Handle to Copy a Cell to Adjacent Cells

Excel also must calculate the totals for Chicago in cell C8, Las Vegas in cell D8, and for Miami in cell E8. Table 1-2 illustrates the similarities between the entry in cell B8 and the entries required to sum the totals in cells C8, D8, and E8.

Table 1-2 Sum Function Entries in Row 8

CELL	SUM FUNCTION ENTRIES	REMARK
B8	=SUM(B4:B7)	Sums cells B4, B5, B6, and B7
C8	=SUM(C4:C7)	Sums cells C4, C5, C6, and C7
D8	=SUM(D4:D7)	Sums cells D4, D5, D6, and D7
E8	=SUM(E4:E7)	Sums cells E4, E5, E6, and E7

To place the SUM functions in cells C8, D8, and E8, follow the same steps shown previously in Figures 1-29 through 1-31. A second, more efficient method is to copy the SUM function from cell B8 to the range C8:E8. The cell being copied is called the **source area** or **copy area**. The range of cells receiving the copy is called the **destination area** or **paste area**.

Although the SUM function entries in Table 1-2 are similar, they are not exact copies. The range in each SUM function entry uses cell references that are one column to the right of the previous column. When you copy cell references, Excel automatically adjusts them for each new position, resulting in the SUM function entries illustrated in Table 1-2. Each adjusted cell reference is called a **relative reference.**

The easiest way to copy the SUM formula from cell B8 to cells C8, D8, and E8 is to use the fill handle. The **fill handle** is the small black square located in the lower-right corner of the heavy border around the active cell. The following steps show how to use the fill handle to copy cell B8 to the adjacent cells C8:E8.

To Copy a Cell to Adjacent Cells in a Row

1

• **With cell B8 active, point to the fill handle.**

The mouse pointer changes to a cross hair (Figure 1-32).

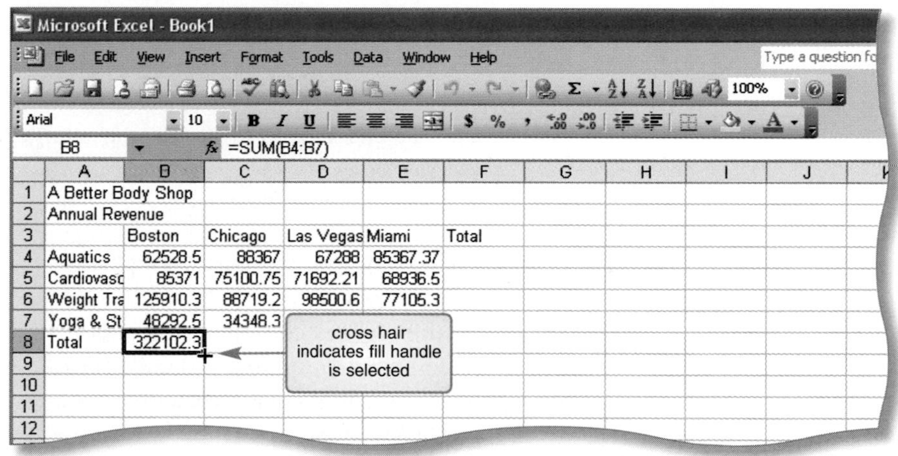

FIGURE 1-32

2

• **Drag the fill handle to select the destination area, range C8:E8. Do not release the mouse button.**

Excel displays a shaded border around the destination area, range C8:E8, and the source area, cell B8 (Figure 1-33).

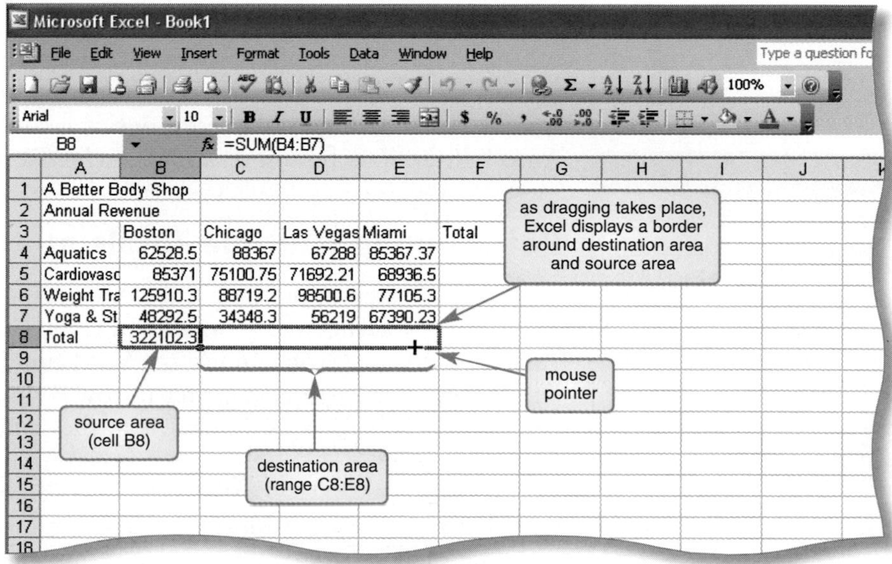

FIGURE 1-33

3

• **Release the mouse button.**

Excel copies the SUM function in cell B8 to the range C8:E8 (Figure 1-34). In addition, Excel calculates the sums and enters the results in cells C8, D8, and E8. The Auto Fill Options button appears to the right and below the destination area.

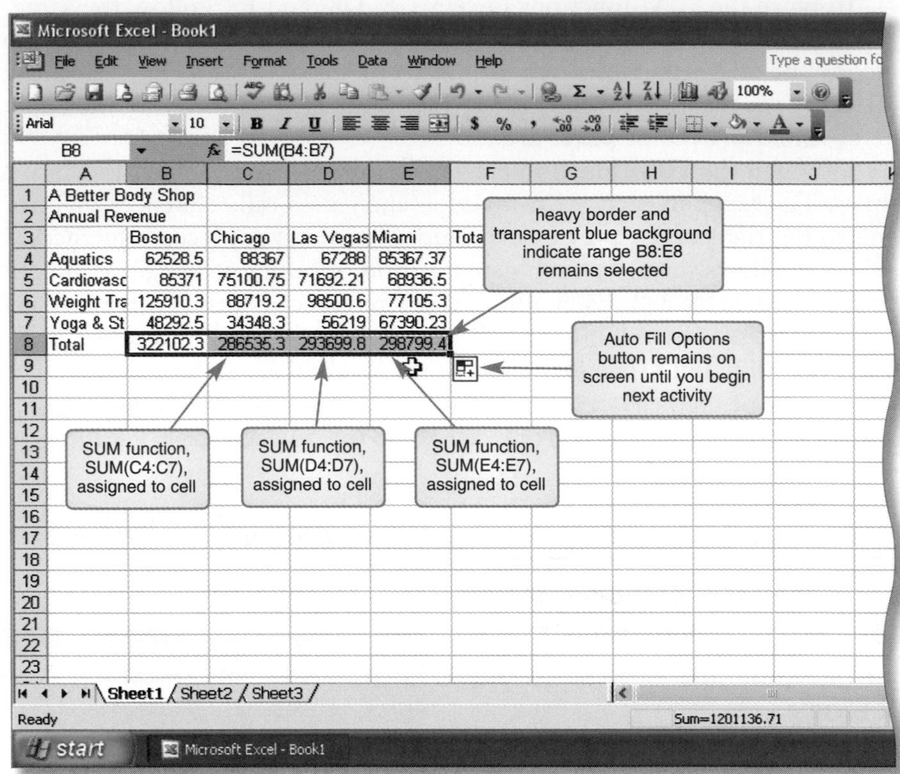

FIGURE 1-34

Once the copy is complete, Excel continues to display a heavy border and transparent blue background around cells B8:E8. The heavy border and transparent blue background are called **see-through view** and indicates a selected range. Excel does not display the transparent blue background around cell B8, the first cell in the range, because it is the active cell. If you click any cell, Excel will remove the heavy border and transparent blue background of the see-through view.

When you copy one range to another, Excel displays an Auto Fill Options button to the right and below the destination area (Figure 1-34). The Auto Fill Options button allows you to choose whether you want to copy the values from the source area to the destination area with formatting, without formatting, or only copy the format. To view the available fill options, click the Auto Fill Options button. The Auto Fill Options button disappears when you begin another activity.

Skill Builder 1-1

To practice the following tasks, visit scsite.com/off2003/sch/skill, locate Excel Project 1, and then and click Skill Builder 1-1.

- ❑ Start Excel
- ❑ Select a cell
- ❑ Enter text and numbers
- ❑ Calculate a sum
- ❑ Use the fill Handle to copy

Determining Multiple Totals at the Same Time

The next step in building the worksheet is to determine the annual revenue for each fitness offering and total annual revenue for the company in column F. To calculate these totals, you can use the SUM function much as you used it to total the annual revenues by fitness center in row 8. In this example, however, Excel will determine totals for all of the rows at the same time. The following steps illustrate this process.

To Determine Multiple Totals at the Same Time

1

• **Click cell F4.**

Cell F4 becomes the active cell (Figure 1-35).

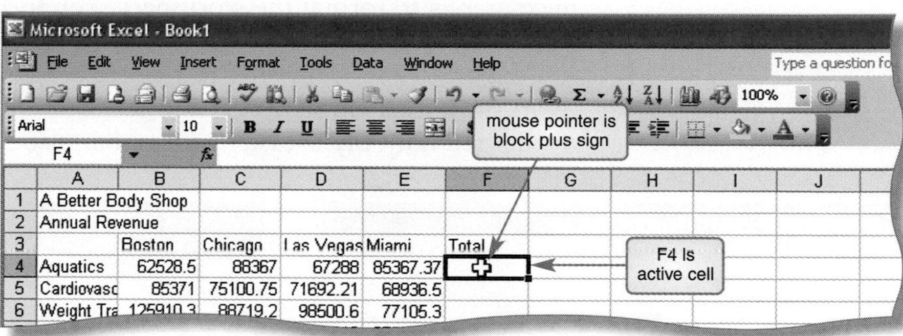

FIGURE 1-35

2

• **With the mouse pointer in cell F4 and in the shape of a block plus sign, drag the mouse pointer down to cell F8.**

Excel highlights the range F4:F8 with a see-through view (Figure 1-36).

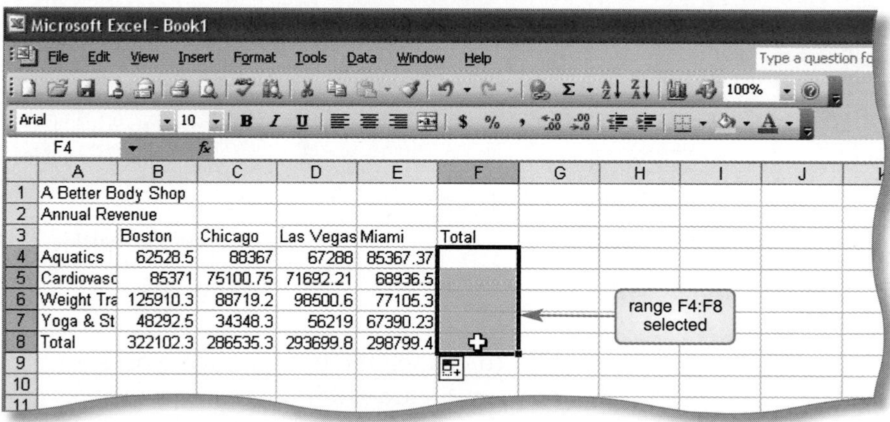

FIGURE 1-36

3

• **Click the AutoSum button on the Standard toolbar.**

Excel assigns the appropriate SUM functions to cells F4, F5, F6, F7, and F8 and then calculates and displays the sums in the respective cells (Figure 1-37).

4

• **Select cell A9 to deselect the range F4:F8.**

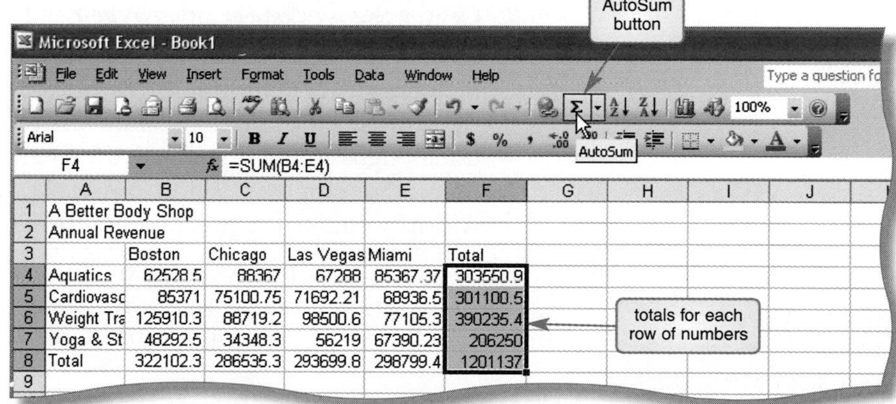

FIGURE 1-37

If each cell in a selected range is next to a row of numbers, Excel assigns the SUM function to each cell when you click the AutoSum button. Thus, as shown in the previous steps, each of the five cells in the selected range is assigned a SUM function with a different range, based on its row. This same procedure could have been used earlier to sum the columns. That is, instead of clicking cell B8, clicking the AutoSum button twice, and then copying the SUM function to the range C8:E8, the range B8:E8 could have been selected and then the AutoSum button clicked once, which would have assigned the SUM function to the entire range.

Q & A

Q: Can the rows and columns be summed at the same time?

A: Yes. A more efficient way to determine the totals in row 8 and column F in Figure 1-37 is to select the range (B4:F8) and then click the AutoSum button on the Standard toolbar.

Formatting the Worksheet

The text, numeric entries, and functions for the worksheet now are complete. The next step is to format the worksheet. You **format** a worksheet to emphasize certain entries and make the worksheet easier to read and understand.

Figure 1-38a shows the worksheet before formatting. Figure 1-38b shows the worksheet after formatting. As you can see from the two figures, a worksheet that is formatted not only is easier to read but also looks more professional.

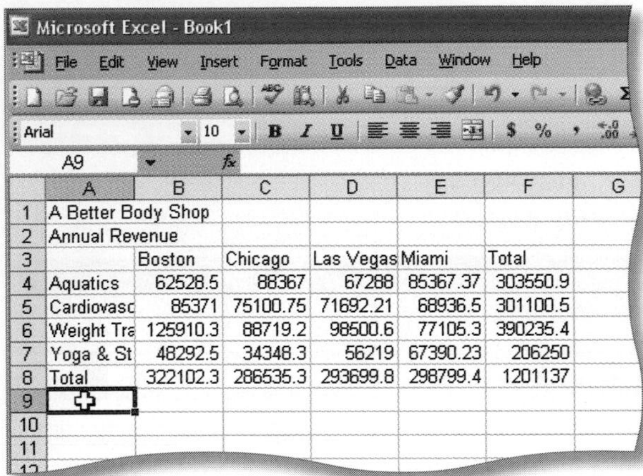

(a) Before Formatting

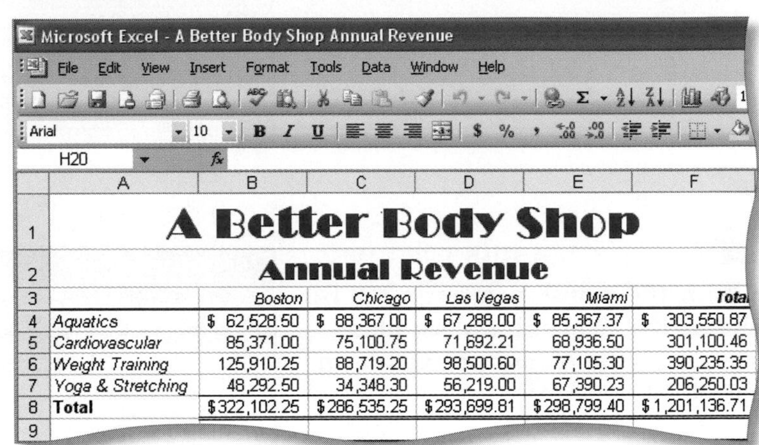

(b) After Formatting

FIGURE 1-38

To change the unformatted worksheet in Figure 1-38a to the formatted worksheet in Figure 1-38b, the following tasks must be completed:

1. Change the font type, change the font style to bold, increase the font size, and change the font color of the worksheet titles in cells A1 and A2.
2. Center the worksheet titles in cells A1 and A2 across columns A through F.
3. Format the body of the worksheet. The body of the worksheet, range A3:F8, includes the column titles, row titles, and numbers. Formatting the body of the worksheet changes the numbers to use a dollars-and-cents format, with dollar signs in the first row (row 4) and the total row (row 8); adds underlining that emphasizes portions of the worksheet; and modifies the column widths to make the text and numbers readable.

The remainder of this section explains the process required to format the worksheet. Although the format procedures are explained in the order described above, you should be aware that you can make these format changes in any order.

Font Type, Style, Size, and Color

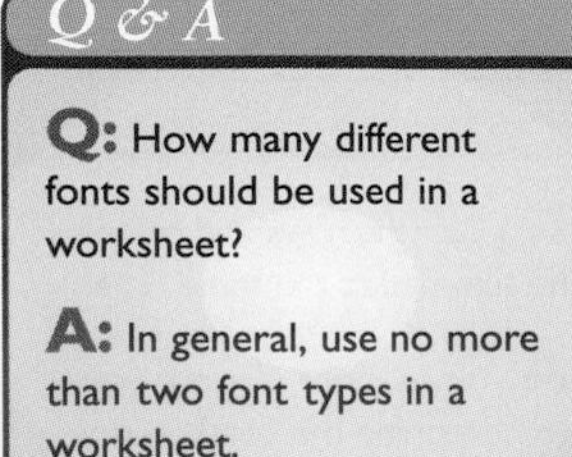
Q & A

Q: How many different fonts should be used in a worksheet?

A: In general, use no more than two font types in a worksheet.

The characters that Excel displays on the screen are a specific font type, style, size, and color. The **font type**, or font face, defines the appearance and shape of the letters, numbers, and special characters. Examples of font types include Times New Roman, Arial, and Courier. **Font style** indicates how the characters are formatted. Common font styles include regular, bold, underline, or italic. The **font size** specifies the size of the characters on the screen. Font size is gauged by a measurement system called points. A single point is about 1/72 of one inch in height. Thus, a character with a **point size** of 10 is about 10/72 of one inch in height. The **font color** defines the color of the characters. Excel can display characters in a wide variety of colors, including black, red, orange, and blue.

When Excel begins, the preset font type for the entire workbook is Arial, with a font size and font style of 10-point regular black. Excel allows you to change the font characteristics in a single cell, a range of cells, the entire worksheet, or the entire workbook.

Changing the Font Type

Different font types often are used in a worksheet to make it more appealing to the reader. The following steps show how to change the worksheet title font type from Arial to Broadway.

To Change the Font Type

1

- **Click cell A1 and then point to the Font box arrow on the Formatting toolbar.**

Cell A1 is the active cell (Figure 1-39).

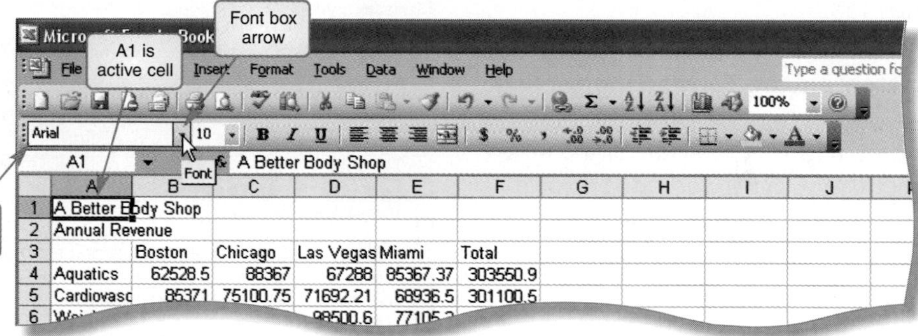

FIGURE 1-39

2

- **Click the Font box arrow, scroll down, and then point to Broadway (or a similar font).**

Excel displays the Font list with Broadway (or a similar font) highlighted (Figure 1-40).

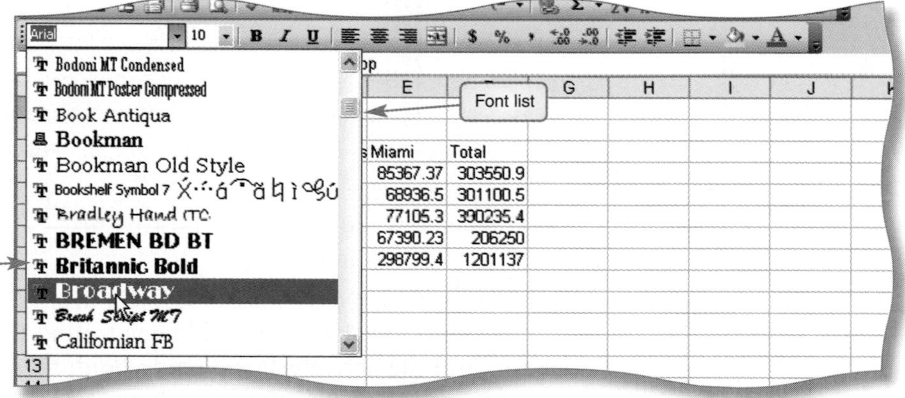

FIGURE 1-40

3

- **Click Broadway (or a similar font).**

Excel changes the font type of cell A1 from Arial to Broadway or a similar font (Figure 1-41).

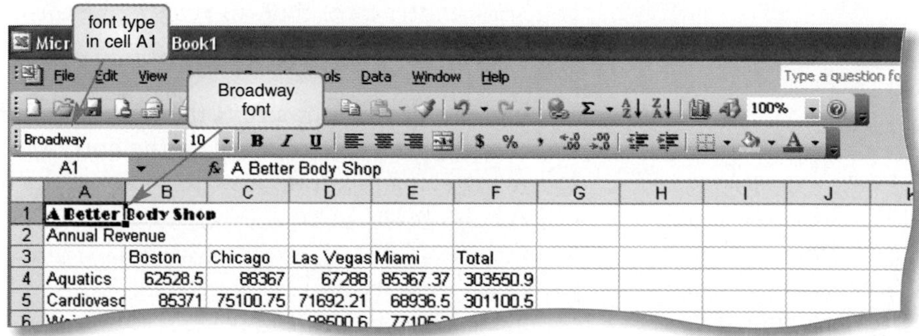

FIGURE 1-41

Because many applications supply additional font types beyond what comes with the Windows operating system, the number of font types available on your computer will depend on the applications installed. This book only uses font types that come with the Windows operating system.

Bolding a Cell

You **bold** an entry in a cell to emphasize it or make it stand out from the rest of the worksheet. The following step shows how to bold the worksheet title in cell A1.

To Bold a Cell

1

• With cell A1 active, click the Bold button on the Formatting toolbar.

Excel changes the font style of the worksheet title, A Better Body Shop, to bold. With the mouse pointer pointing to the Bold button, Excel displays a ScreenTip immediately below the Bold button to identify the function of the button (Figure 1-42).

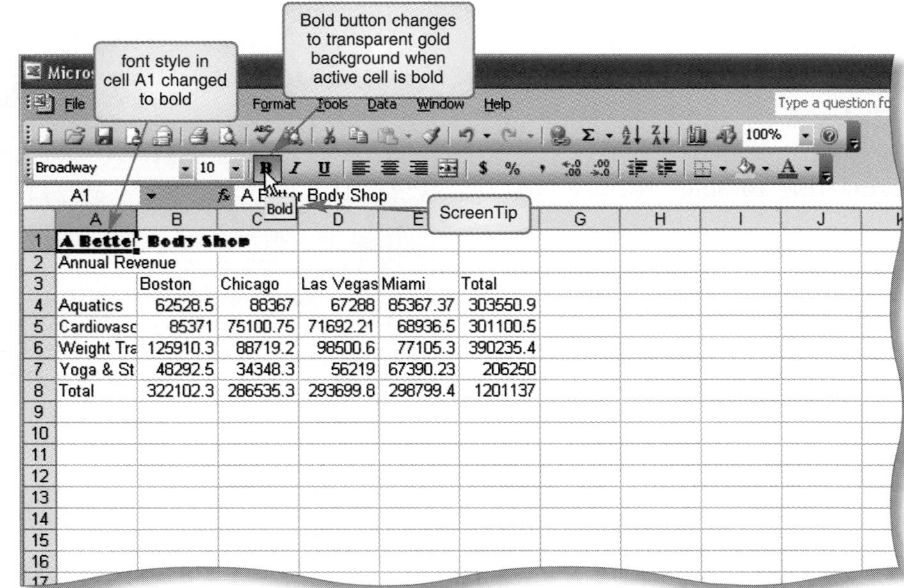

FIGURE 1-42

When the active cell is bold, Excel displays the Bold button on the Formatting toolbar with a transparent gold background (Figure 1-42). If you point to the Bold button and the active cell is already bold, then Excel displays the button with a transparent red background. Clicking the Bold button a second time removes the bold font style.

Increasing the Font Size

Increasing the font size is the next step in formatting the worksheet title. You increase the font size of a cell so the entry stands out and is easier to read. The following steps illustrate how to increase the font size of the worksheet title in cell A1.

To Increase the Font Size of a Cell Entry

1

- **With cell A1 selected, click the Font Size box arrow on the Formatting toolbar.**

Excel displays the Font Size list, as shown in Figure 1-43.

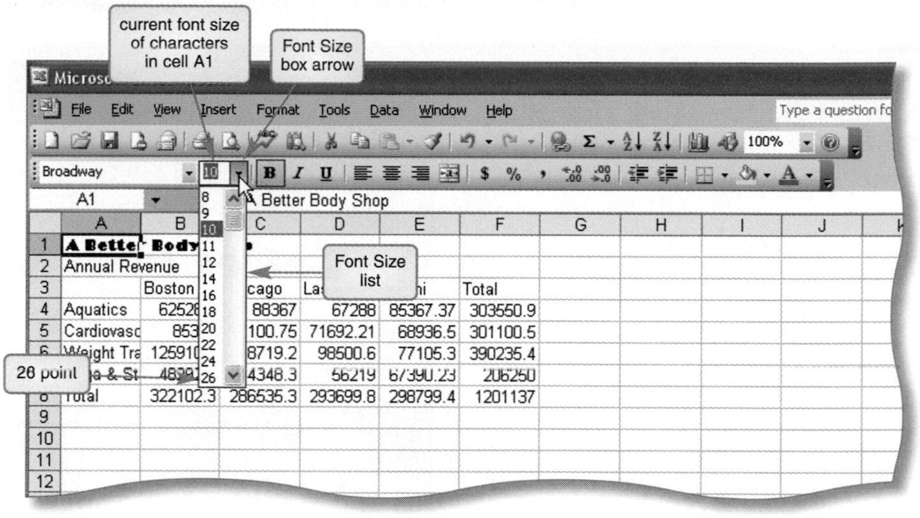

FIGURE 1-43

2

- **Click 26 in the Font Size list.**

The font size of the characters in cell A1 increase from 10 point to 26 point (Figure 1-44). The increased font size makes the worksheet title easier to read.

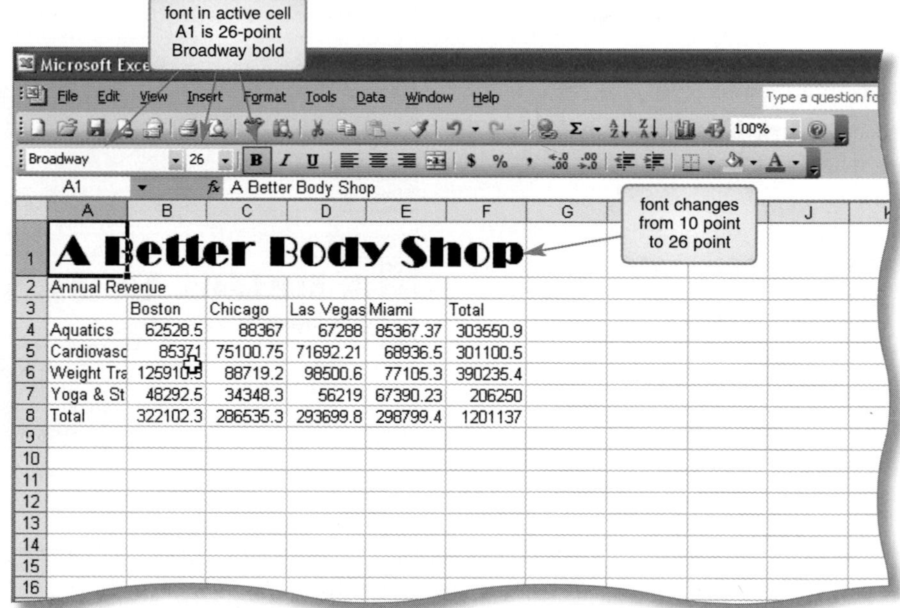

FIGURE 1-44

An alternative to clicking a font size in the Font Size list is to click the Font Size box, type the font size, and then press the ENTER key. This procedure allows you to assign a font size not available in the Font Size list to a selected cell entry. With cell A1 selected (Figure 1-44), the Font Size box shows that the new font size is 26 and the transparent gold Bold button shows that the font style is bold.

Changing the Font Color of a Cell Entry

The next step is to change the color of the font in cell A1 from black to dark blue. The steps on the next page show how to change the font color of a cell entry.

To Change the Font Color of a Cell Entry

1

• **With cell A1 selected, click the Font Color button arrow on the Formatting toolbar.**

Excel displays the Font Color palette (Figure 1-45).

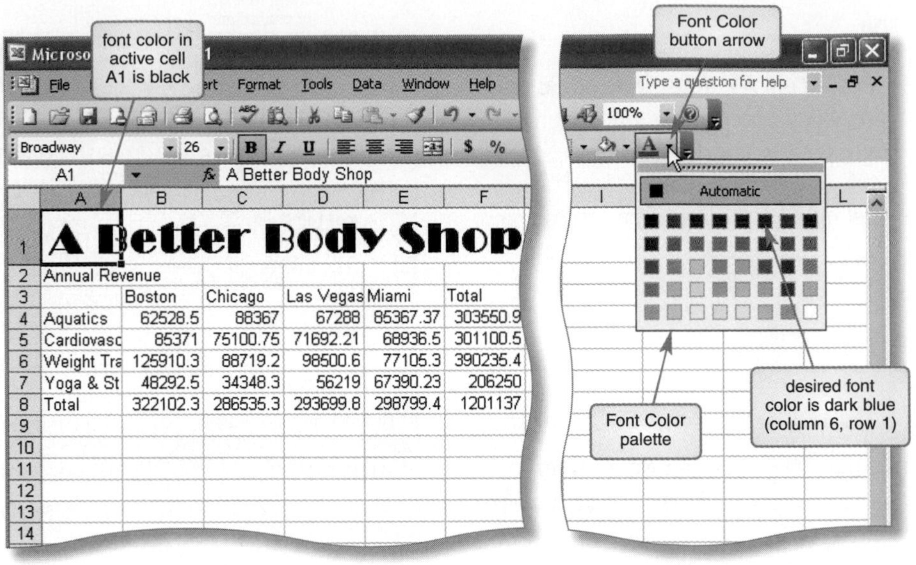

FIGURE 1-45

2

• **Click Dark Blue (column 6, row 1) on the Font Color palette.**

The font in the worksheet title in cell A1 changes from black to dark blue (Figure 1-46).

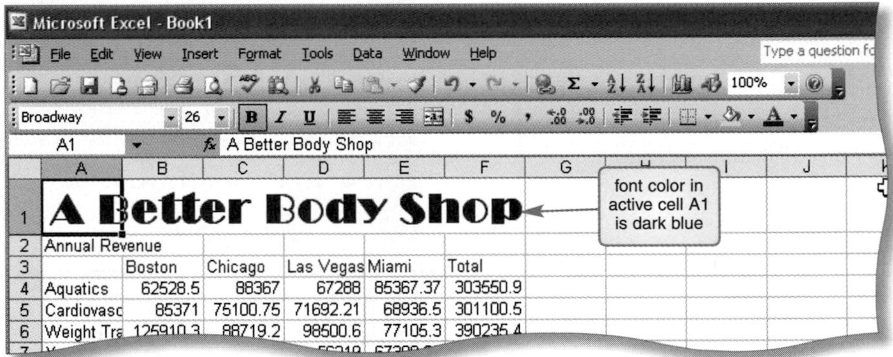

FIGURE 1-46

As shown in Figure 1-45, you can choose from 40 different font colors on the Font Color palette. Your Font Color palette may have more or fewer colors, depending on color settings of your operating system. When you choose a color on the Font Color palette, Excel changes the Font Color button on the Formatting toolbar to the chosen color. Thus, to change the font color of the cell entry in another cell to the same color, you need only to select the cell and then click the Font Color button.

Centering a Cell Entry across Columns by Merging Cells

The final step in formatting the worksheet title is to center it across columns A through F. Centering a worksheet title across the columns used in the body of the worksheet improves the worksheet's appearance. To do this, the six cells in the range A1:F1 are combined, or merged, into a single cell that is the width of the columns in the body of the worksheet. **Merging cells** involves creating a single cell by combining two or more selected cells. The following steps illustrate how to center the worksheet title across columns by merging cells.

To Center a Cell Entry across Columns by Merging Cells

1

- **With cell A1 selected, drag to cell F1.**

Excel highlights the selected cells (Figure 1-47).

FIGURE 1-47

2

- **Click the Merge and Center button on the Formatting toolbar.**

Excel merges the cells A1 through F1 to create a new cell A1 and centers the contents of cell A1 across columns A through F (Figure 1-48). After the merge, cells B1 through F1 no longer exist on the worksheet.

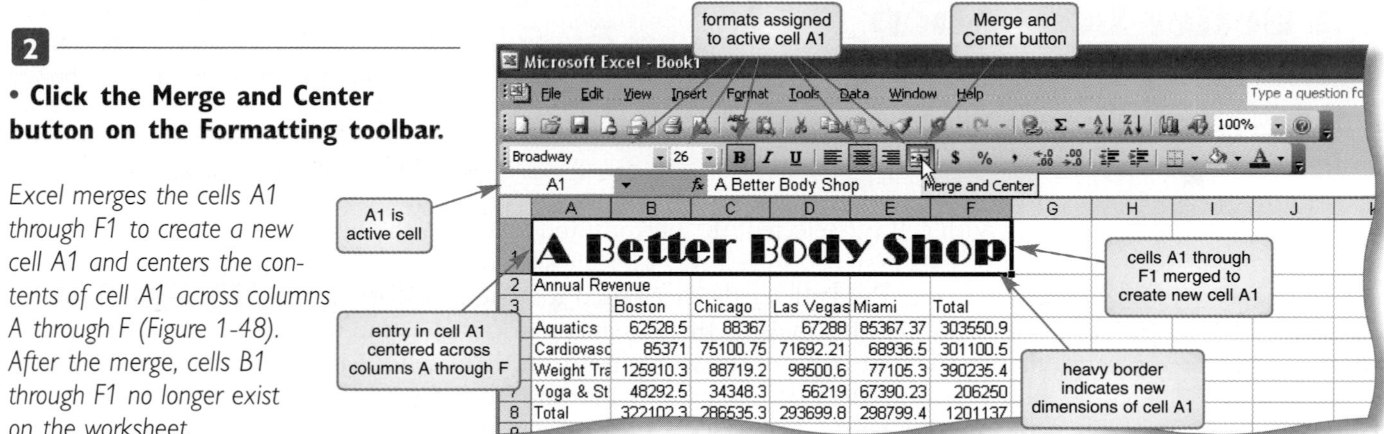

FIGURE 1-48

Excel not only centers the worksheet title across the range A1:F1, but it also merges cells A1 through F1 into one merged cell, cell A1. For the Merge and Center button to work properly, all the cells except the leftmost cell in the selected range must be empty.

The opposite of merging cells is **splitting a merged cell**. After you have merged multiple cells to create one merged cell, you can unmerge, or split, the merged cell to display the original cells on the worksheet. You split a merged cell by selecting it and clicking the Merge and Center button. For example, if you click the Merge and Center button a second time in Step 2, it will split the merged cell A1 to cells A1, B1, C1, D1, E1, and F1.

Most formats assigned to a cell will appear on the Formatting toolbar when the cell is selected. For example, with cell A1 selected in Figure 1-48, Excel displays the font type and font size of the active cell in their appropriate boxes. Transparent gold buttons on the Formatting toolbar indicate other assigned formatting. To determine if less frequently used formats are assigned to a cell, right-click the cell, click Format Cells on the shortcut menu, and then click each of the tabs in the Format Cells dialog box.

Formatting the Worksheet Subtitle

The worksheet subtitle in cell A2 is to be formatted the same as the worksheet title in cell A1, except that the font size should be 18 rather than 26. The steps on the next page show how to format the worksheet subtitle in cell A2.

To Format the Worksheet Subtitle

1. Select cell A2.
2. Click the Font box arrow on the Formatting toolbar, scroll down the font list, and then click Broadway (or a font of your choice).
3. Click the Bold button on the Formatting toolbar.
4. Click the Font Size box arrow on the Formatting toolbar and then click 18.
5. Click the Font Color button on the Formatting toolbar.
6. Select the range A2:F2 and then click the Merge and Center button on the Formatting toolbar.

Excel displays the worksheet subtitle in cell A2, as shown in Figure 1-49.

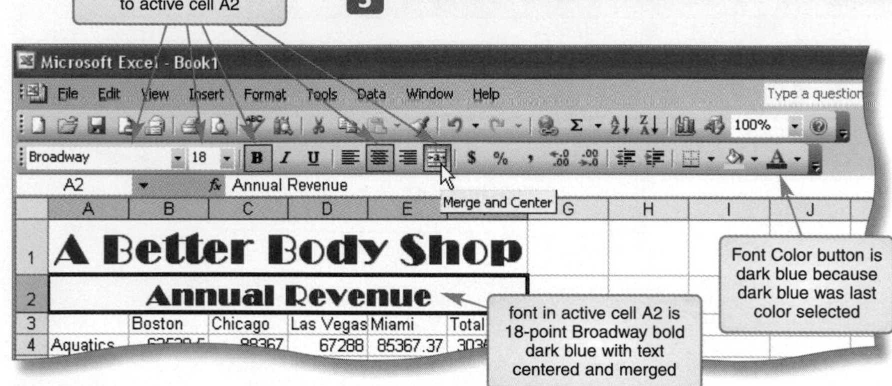

FIGURE 1-49

With cell A2 selected, the buttons and boxes on the Formatting toolbar describe the formats assigned to cell A2. The steps used to format the worksheet subtitle in cell A2 were the same as the steps used to assign the formats to the worksheet title in cell A1, except for the step that assigned dark blue as the font color. The step to change the font color of the worksheet subtitle in cell A2 used only the Font Color button, rather than the Font Color button arrow. Recall that, when you choose a color on the Font Color palette, Excel assigns the last font color used (in this case, dark blue) to the Font Color button.

Using AutoFormat to Format the Body of a Worksheet

Excel has customized autoformats that allow you to format the body of the worksheet to give it a professional look. An **autoformat** is a built-in collection of formats, such as font style, font color, borders, and alignment, which you can apply to a range of cells. The following steps format the range A3:F8 using the AutoFormat command on the Format menu.

To Use AutoFormat to Format the Body of a Worksheet

1

- **Select cell A3, the upper-left corner cell of the rectangular range to format.**
- **Drag the mouse pointer to cell F8, the lower-right corner cell of the range to format.**

Excel highlights the range to format with a heavy border and transparent blue background (Figure 1-50).

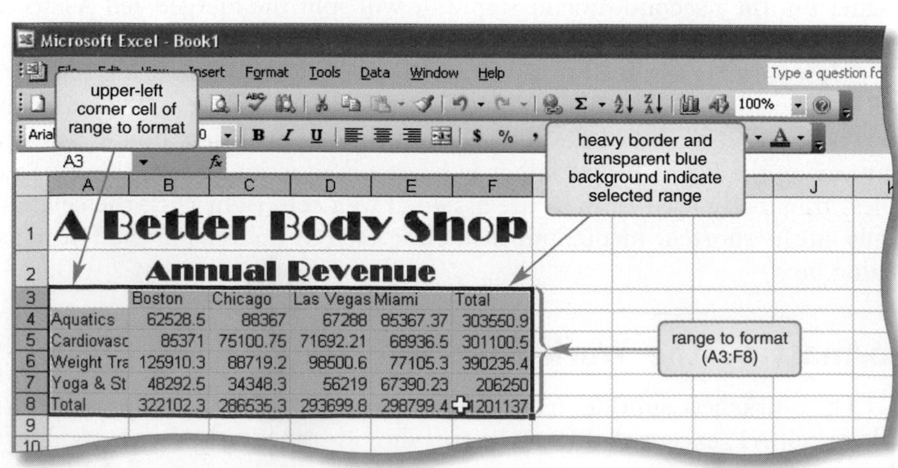

FIGURE 1-50

2

- **Click Format on the menu bar.**

Excel displays the Format menu (Figure 1-51).

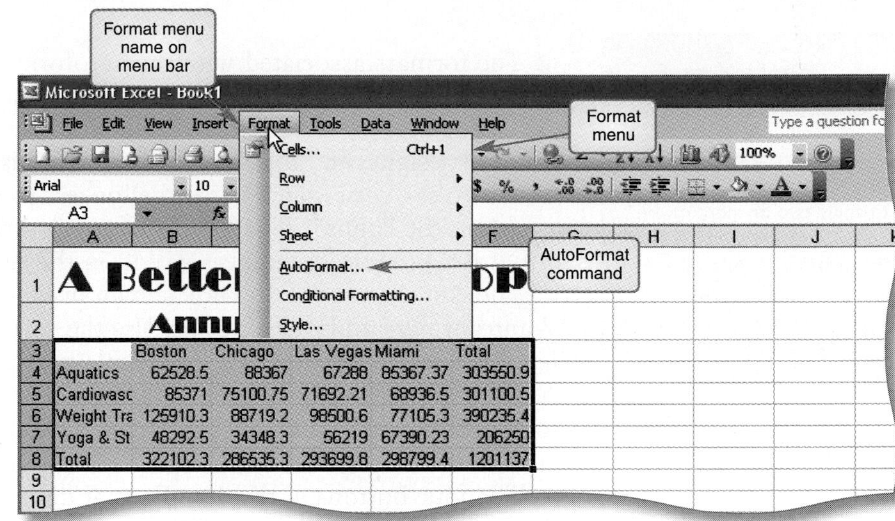

FIGURE 1-51

3

- **Click AutoFormat on the Format menu.**
- **When Excel displays the AutoFormat dialog box, scroll down, and then click the Accounting 3 format.**

Excel displays the AutoFormat dialog box with a list of available autoformats (Figure 1-52). For each autoformat, Excel provides a sample to illustrate how the body of the worksheet will appear if that autoformat is chosen.

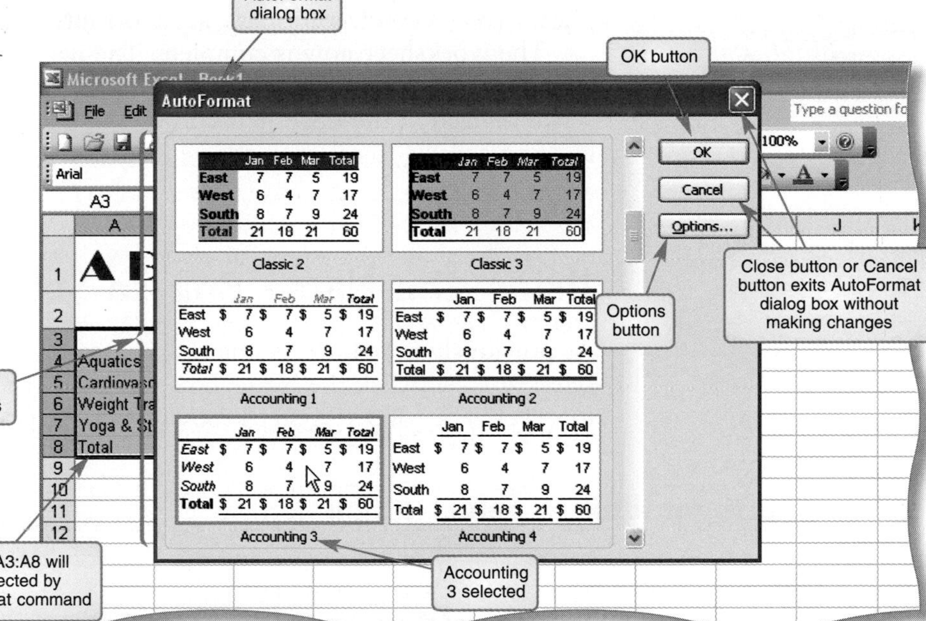

FIGURE 1-52

4

- **Click the OK button.**
- **Select cell A10 to deselect the range A3:F8.**

Excel displays the worksheet with the range A3:F8 formatted using the autoformat, Accounting 3 (Figure 1-53).

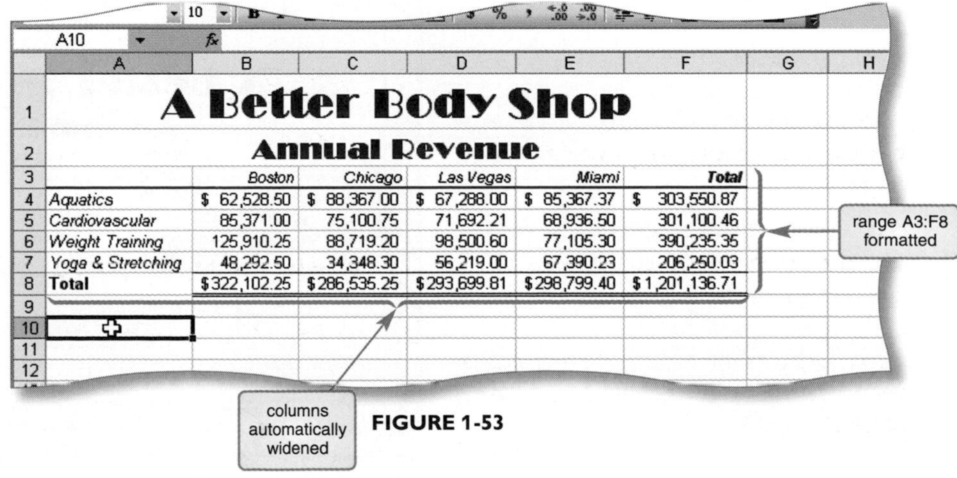

FIGURE 1-53

Q & A

Q: Can more than one autoformat be assigned to a range?

A: Yes. It is not uncommon to apply two or more of the table formats (Figure 1-52 on the previous page) to the same range. If you assign two table formats to a range, Excel merges the formats.

The formats associated with the autoformat Accounting 3 include right-aligned column titles; numbers displayed as dollars and cents with comma separators; numbers aligned on the decimal point; the first row and total row of numbers displayed with dollar signs; and top and bottom rows displayed with borders. The width of column A has been increased so the longest row title in cell A7, Yoga & Stretching, just fits in the column. The widths of columns B through F also have been increased so that the formatted numbers will fit in the cells.

The AutoFormat dialog box shown in Figure 1-52 on the previous page includes 17 autoformats and four buttons. Use the vertical scroll bar in the dialog box to view the autoformats that are not displayed when the dialog box first opens. Each one of these autoformats offers a different look. The one you choose depends on the worksheet you are creating. The last autoformat in the list, called None, removes all formats.

The four buttons in the AutoFormat dialog box allow you to complete the entries, modify an autoformat, or cancel changes and close the dialog box. The Close button on the title bar and the Cancel button both terminate the current activity and close the AutoFormat dialog box without making changes. The Options button allows you to deselect formats, such as fonts or borders, within an autoformat.

The worksheet now is complete. The next step is to chart the annual revenue for the four fitness offerings by the fitness centers. To create the chart, you must select the cell in the upper-left corner of the range to chart (cell A3). Rather than clicking cell A3 to select it, the next section describes how to use the Name box to select the cell.

Skill Builder 1-2

To practice the following tasks, visit scsite.com/off2003sch/skill, locate Excel Project 1, and click SkillBuilder 1-2.

- ❑ Change font style, size, and color
- ❑ Bold and merge and center
- ❑ Apply an autoformat

Using the Name Box to Select a Cell

As previously noted, the Name box is located on the left side of the formula bar. To select any cell, click the Name box and enter the cell reference of the cell you want to select. The following steps show how to select cell A3.

To Use the Name Box to Select a Cell

1

- **Click the Name box in the formula bar and then type** a3 **as the cell to select.**

Even though cell A10 is the active cell, Excel displays the typed cell reference a3 in the Name box (Figure 1-54).

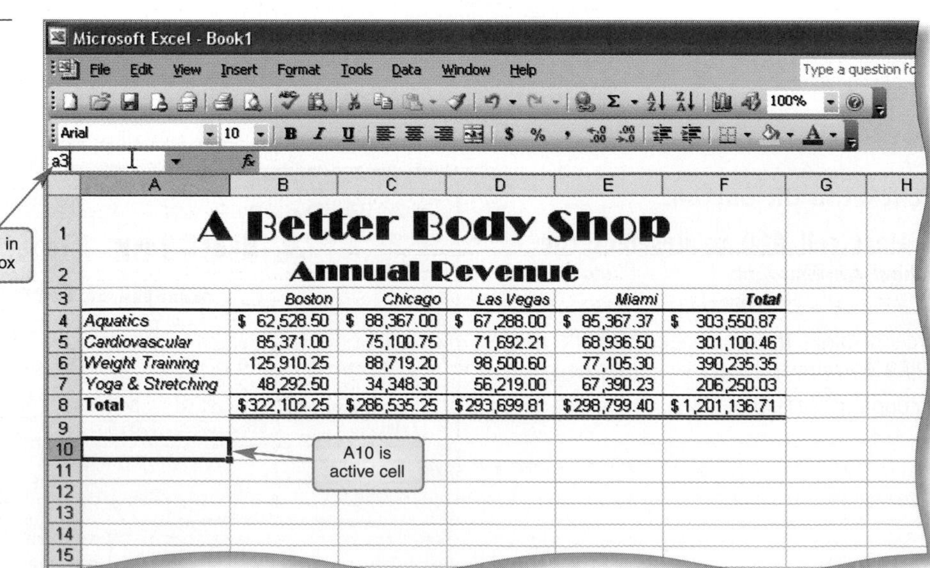

	Boston	Chicago	Las Vegas	Miami	Total
Aquatics	$ 62,528.50	$ 88,367.00	$ 67,288.00	$ 85,367.37	$ 303,550.87
Cardiovascular	85,371.00	75,100.75	71,692.21	68,936.50	301,100.46
Weight Training	125,910.25	88,719.20	98,500.60	77,105.30	390,235.35
Yoga & Stretching	48,292.50	34,348.30	56,219.00	67,390.23	206,250.03
Total	$322,102.25	$286,535.25	$293,699.81	$298,799.40	$1,201,136.71

FIGURE 1-54

2

• **Press the ENTER key.**

Excel changes the active cell from cell A10 to cell A3 (Figure 1-55).

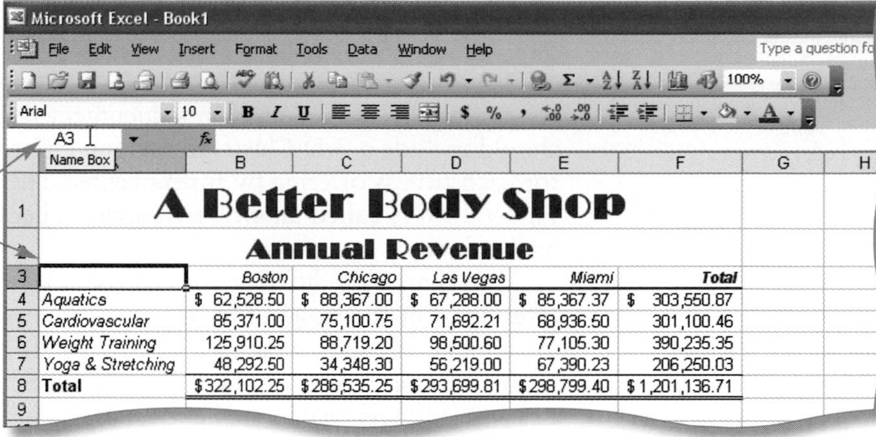

FIGURE 1-55

As you will see in later projects, in addition to using the Name box to select any cell in a worksheet, you also can use it to assign names to a cell or range of cells. Excel supports several additional ways to select a cell, as summarized in Table 1-3.

Q & A

Q: Can a cell be selected on the basis of its contents?

A: Yes. For more information about selecting cells that contain certain entries, such as constants or formulas, visit the Office 2003 Q&A Web page (scsite.com/off2003sch/qa), locate Excel Project 1, and click Using Go To Special.

Table 1-3 Selecting Cells in Excel

KEY, BOX, OR COMMAND	FUNCTION
ALT+PAGE DOWN	Selects the cell one worksheet window to the right and moves the worksheet window accordingly.
ALT+PAGE UP	Selects the cell one worksheet window to the left and moves the worksheet window accordingly.
ARROW	Selects the adjacent cell in the direction of the arrow on the key.
CTRL+ARROW	Selects the border cell of the worksheet in combination with the arrow keys and moves the worksheet window accordingly. For example, to select the rightmost cell in the row that contains the active cell, press CTRL+RIGHT ARROW. You also can press the END key, release it, and then press the appropriate arrow key to accomplish the same task.
CTRL+HOME	Selects cell A1 or the cell one column and one row below and to the right of frozen titles and moves the worksheet window accordingly.
Find command on Edit menu or SHIFT+F5	Finds and selects a cell that contains specific contents that you enter in the Find dialog box. If necessary, Excel moves the worksheet window to display the cell. You also can press CTRL+F to display the Find dialog box.
Go To command on Edit menu or F5	Selects the cell that corresponds to the cell reference you enter in the Go To dialog box and moves the worksheet window accordingly. You also can press CTRL+G to display the Go To dialog box.
HOME	Selects the cell at the beginning of the row that contains the active cell and moves the worksheet window accordingly.
Name box	Selects the cell in the workbook that corresponds to the cell reference you enter in the Name box.
PAGE DOWN	Selects the cell down one worksheet window from the active cell and moves the worksheet window accordingly.
PAGE UP	Selects the cell up one worksheet window from the active cell and moves the worksheet window accordingly.

Adding a 3-D Clustered Column Chart to the Worksheet

As outlined in the requirements document in Figure 1-2 on page EX 6, the worksheet should include a 3-D Clustered column chart to graphically represent annual revenue for each fitness offering by fitness center. The 3-D Clustered column chart shown in Figure 1-56 is called an **embedded chart** because it is drawn on the same worksheet as the data.

The chart uses different colored columns to represent sales for different fitness offerings. For the Boston fitness center, for example, the light blue column represents the annual revenue for Aquatics ($62,528.50); for the Chicago fitness center, the purple column represents the annual revenue for Cardiovascular ($75,100.75); for the Las Vegas fitness center, the light yellow column represents the annual revenue for Weight Training ($98,500.60); and for the Miami fitness center, the turquoise column represents the annual revenue for Yoga & Stretching ($67,390.23). Because the same color scheme is used to represent the four fitness offerings, you can easily compare the fitness offerings among the fitness centers. The totals from the worksheet are not represented, because the totals are not in the range specified for charting.

Excel derives the chart scale based on the values in the worksheet and then displays the scale along the vertical axis (also called the **y-axis** or **value axis**) of the chart. For example, no value in the range B4:E7 is less than 0 or greater than $140,000.00, so the scale ranges from 0 to $140,000.00. Excel also determines the $20,000.00 increments of the scale automatically. For the numbers along the y-axis, Excel uses a format that includes representing the 0 value with a dash (Figure 1-56).

> *Q & A*
>
> **Q:** If a user changes a cell value on which the chart is dependent, will Excel redraw the chart?
>
> **A:** Yes. Excel redraws the chart instantaneously, unless automatic recalculation is disabled. If automatic recalculation is disabled, then you must press function key F9 to redraw the chart. To enable or disable automatic recalculation, invoke the Options command on the Tools menu and click the Calculation tab.

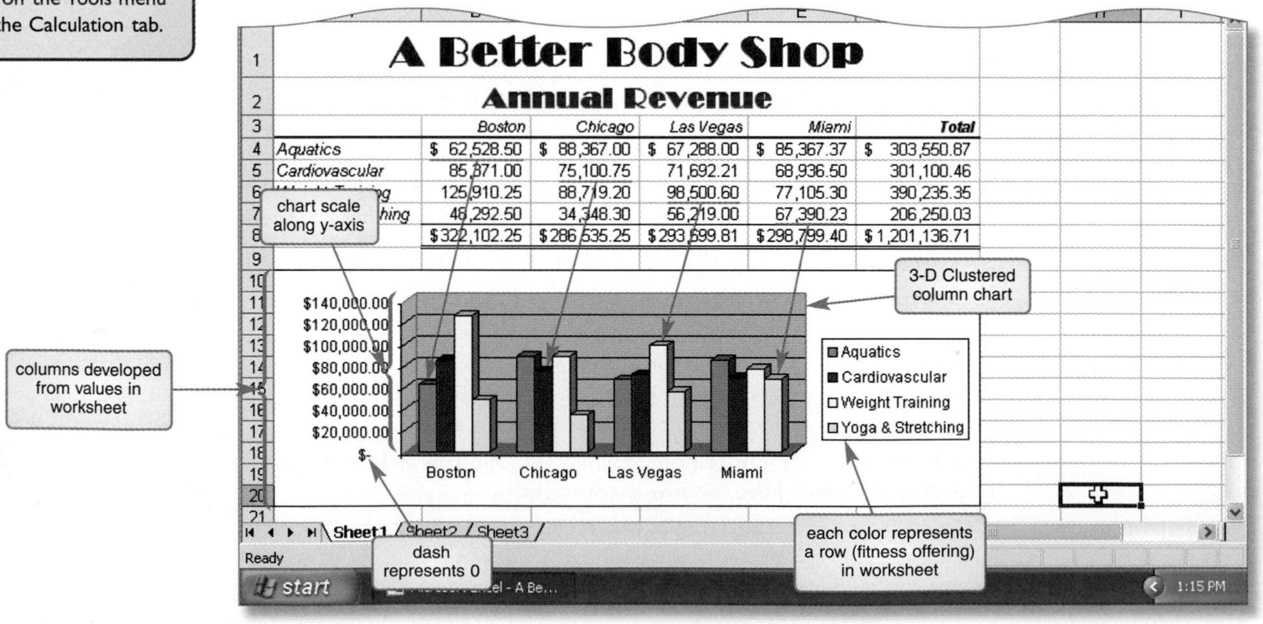

A Better Body Shop

Annual Revenue

	Boston	Chicago	Las Vegas	Miami	Total
Aquatics	$ 62,528.50	$ 88,367.00	$ 67,288.00	$ 85,367.37	$ 303,550.87
Cardiovascular	85,871.00	75,100.75	71,692.21	68,936.50	301,100.46
[illegible]g	125,910.25	88,719.20	98,500.60	77,105.30	390,235.35
[illegible]hing	48,292.50	34,348.30	56,219.00	67,390.23	206,250.03
	$322,102.25	$286,535.25	$293,699.81	$298,799.40	$1,201,136.71

FIGURE 1-56

With the range to chart selected, you click the Chart Wizard button on the Standard toolbar to initiate drawing the chart. The area on the worksheet where the chart appears is called the **chart location**. As shown in Figure 1-56, the chart location in this worksheet is the range A10:F20, immediately below the worksheet data.

The following steps show how to draw a 3-D Clustered column chart that compares the annual revenue by fitness offering for the four fitness centers.

To Add a 3-D Clustered Column Chart to the Worksheet

1

- **With cell A3 selected, position the block plus sign mouse pointer within the cell's border and drag the mouse pointer to the lower-right corner cell (cell E7) of the range to chart (A3:E7).**

Excel highlights the range to chart (Figure 1-57).

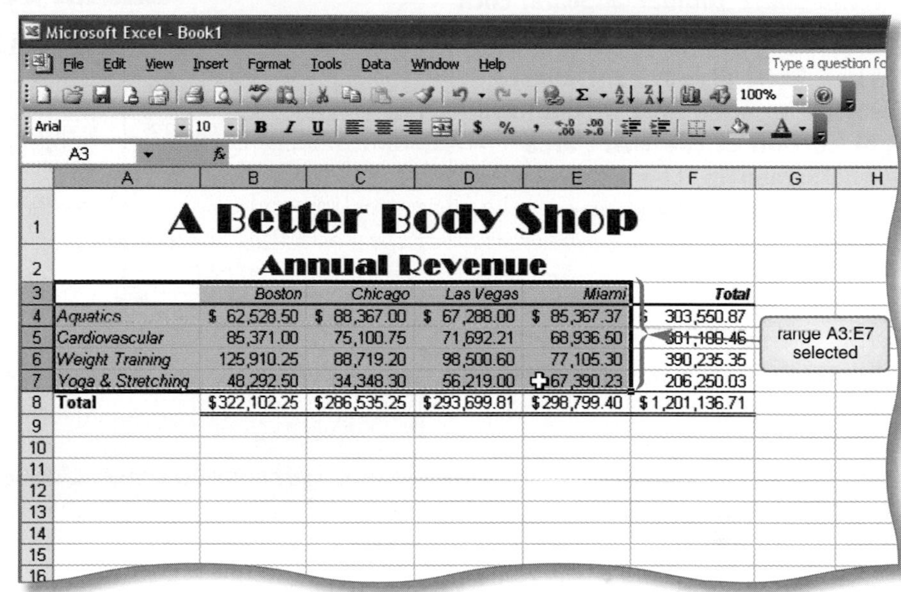

FIGURE 1-57

2

- **Click the Chart Wizard button on the Standard toolbar.**
- **When Excel displays the Chart Wizard - Step 1 of 4 - Chart Type dialog box, and with Column selected in the Chart type list, click Clustered column with a 3-D visual effect (column 1, row 2) in the Chart sub-type area.**

Excel displays the Chart Wizard - Step 1 of 4 - Chart Type dialog box as shown in Figure 1-58.

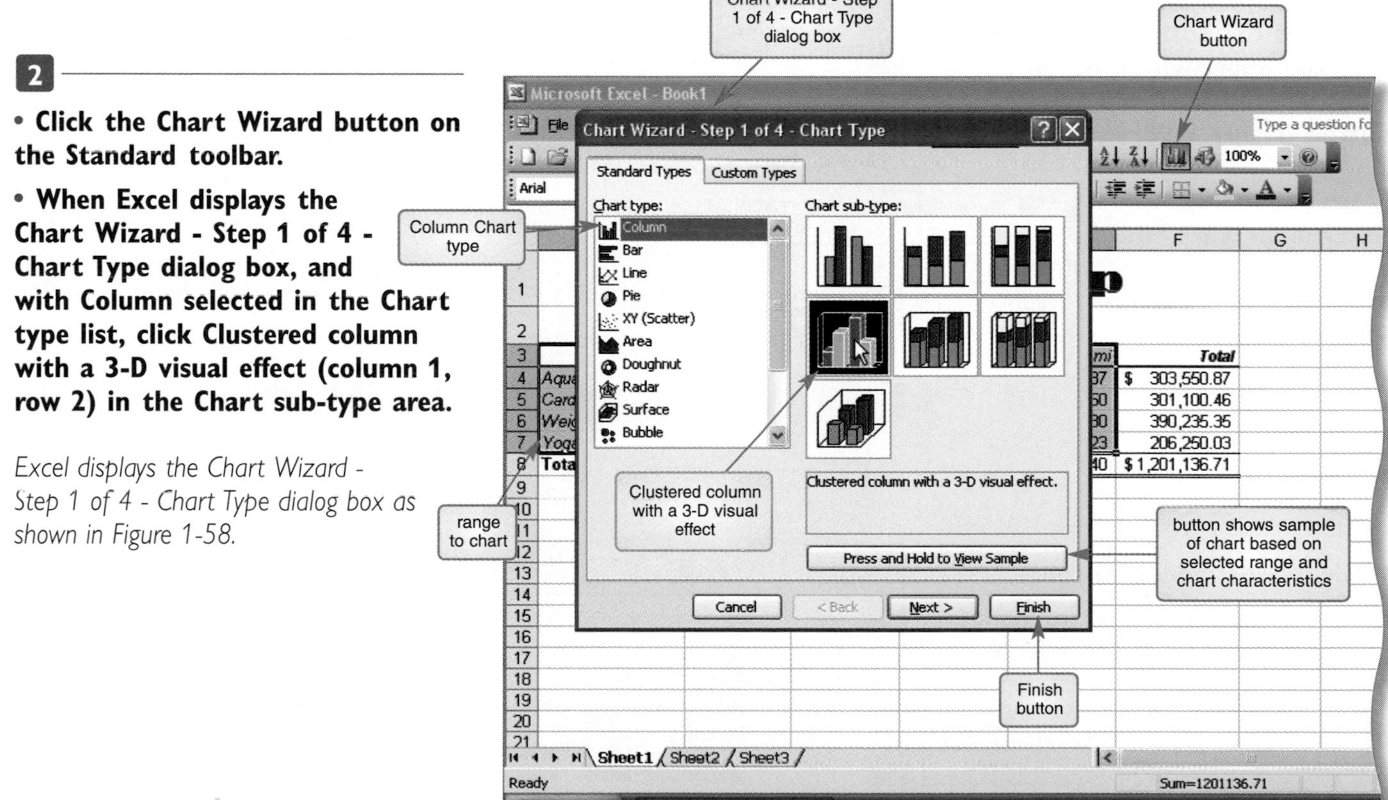

FIGURE 1-58

3

- **Click the Finish button.**
- **If the Chart toolbar appears, click its Close button.**
- **When Excel displays the chart, point to an open area in the lower-right section of the chart area so the ScreenTip, Chart Area, appears next to the mouse pointer.**

Excel draws the 3-D Clustered column chart (Figure 1-59). The chart appears in the middle of the worksheet window in a selection rectangle. The small sizing handles at the corners and along the sides of the selection rectangle indicate the chart is selected.

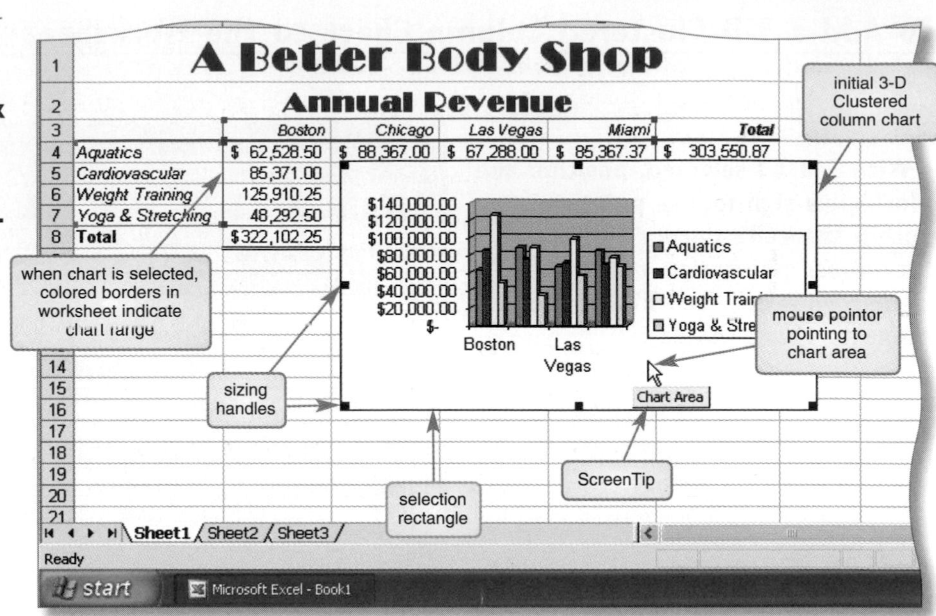

FIGURE 1-59

4

- **Drag the chart down and to the left to position the upper-left corner of the dotted line rectangle over the upper-left corner of cell A10. Do not release the mouse button (Figure 1-60).**

As you drag the selected chart, Excel displays a dotted line rectangle showing the new chart location and the mouse pointer changes to a cross hair with four arrowheads.

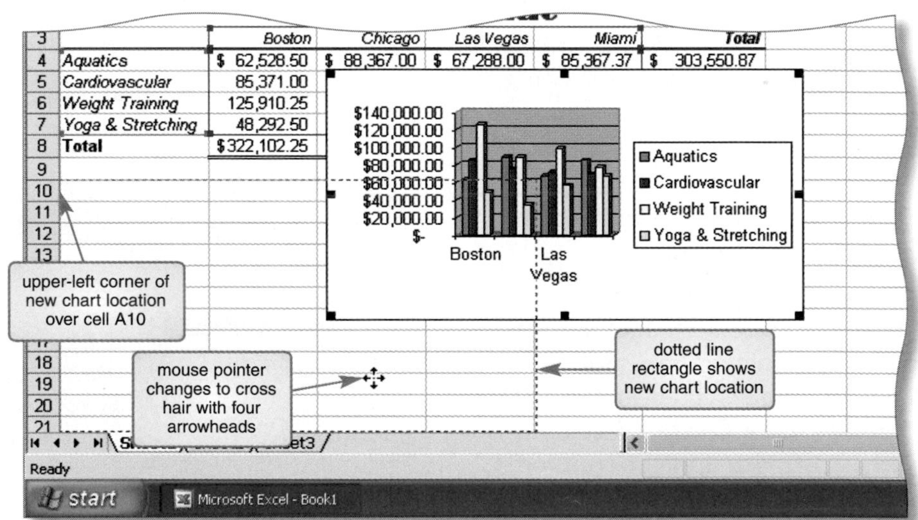

FIGURE 1-60

5

- **Release the mouse button.**
- **Point to the middle sizing handle on the right edge of the selection rectangle.**

The chart appears in a new location (Figure 1-61). The mouse pointer changes to a horizontal line with two arrowheads when it points to a sizing handle.

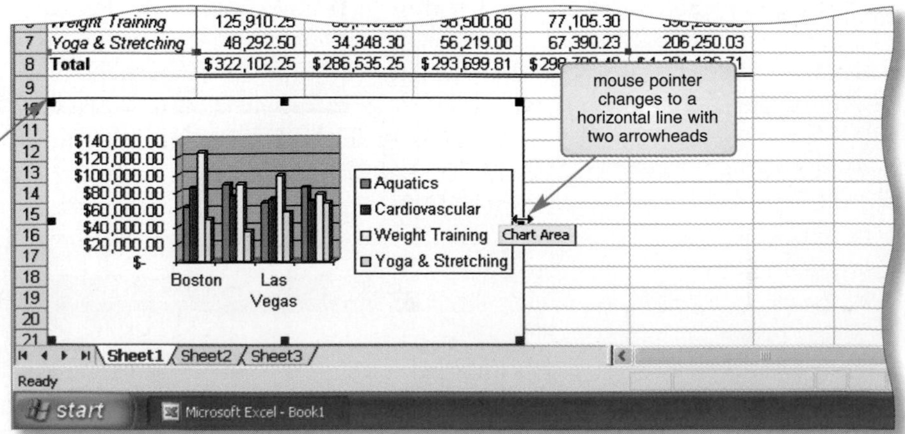

FIGURE 1-61

6

• **While holding down the ALT key, drag the sizing handle to the right edge of column F.**

*While you drag, the dotted line rectangle shows the new chart location (Figure 1-62). Holding down the ALT key while you drag a chart **snaps** (aligns) the edge of the chart area to the worksheet gridlines.*

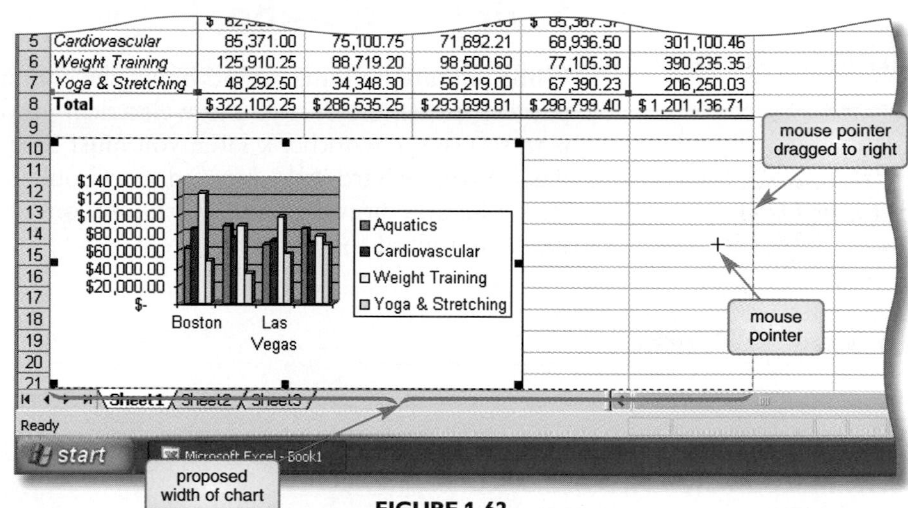

FIGURE 1-62

7

• **If necessary, hold down the ALT key and drag the lower-middle sizing handle up to the bottom border of row 20.**

• **Click cell H20 to deselect the chart.**

The new chart location extends from the top of cell A10 to the bottom of cell F20 (Figure 1-63).

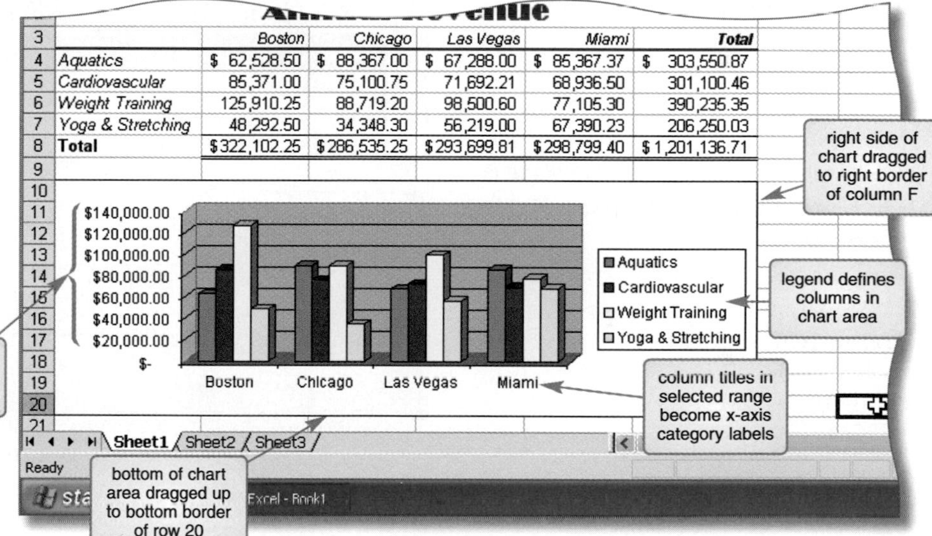

FIGURE 1-63

The embedded 3-D Clustered column chart in Figure 1-63 compares the annual revenue for the four fitness offerings within each fitness center. It also allows you to compare the annual revenue for the four fitness offerings between the fitness centers.

Excel automatically selects the entries in the topmost row of the chart range (row 3) as the titles for the horizontal axis (also called the **x-axis** or **category axis**) and draws a column for each of the 16 cells in the range containing numbers. The small box to the right of the column chart in Figure 1-63 contains the **legend**, which identifies the colors assigned to each bar in the chart. Excel automatically selects the entries in the leftmost column of the chart range (column A) as titles within the legend. As indicated earlier, Excel also automatically derives the chart scale on the y-axis based on the highest and lowest numbers in the chart range.

Excel offers 14 different chart types (Figure 1-58 on page EX 39). The **default chart type** is the chart Excel draws if you click the Finish button in the first Chart Wizard dialog box. When you install Excel on a computer, the default chart type is the 2-D (two-dimensional) Column chart.

Q & A

Q: Can the chart be printed without printing the worksheet?

A: Yes. To print the embedded chart without printing the worksheet, select the chart, click File on the menu bar, click Page Setup, click the Chart tab, click the Scale to fit page in the Printed chart size area, click the Print button, and then click the OK button.

Saving a Workbook

While you are building a workbook, the computer stores it in memory. If the computer is turned off or if you lose electrical power, the workbook is lost. Hence, if you plan to use the workbook later, you must save the workbook on a floppy disk, USB flash drive, or hard disk. A saved workbook is referred to as a **file**. The following steps illustrate how to save a workbook on a USB flash drive using the Save button on the Standard toolbar.

To Save a Workbook

1

- **With a USB flash drive connected to one of the computer's USB ports, click the Save button on the Standard toolbar.**

Excel displays the Save As dialog box (Figure 1-64). The default Save in folder is Documents and Settings (your Save in folder may be different), the default file name is Book1, and the default file type is Microsoft Office Excel Workbook.

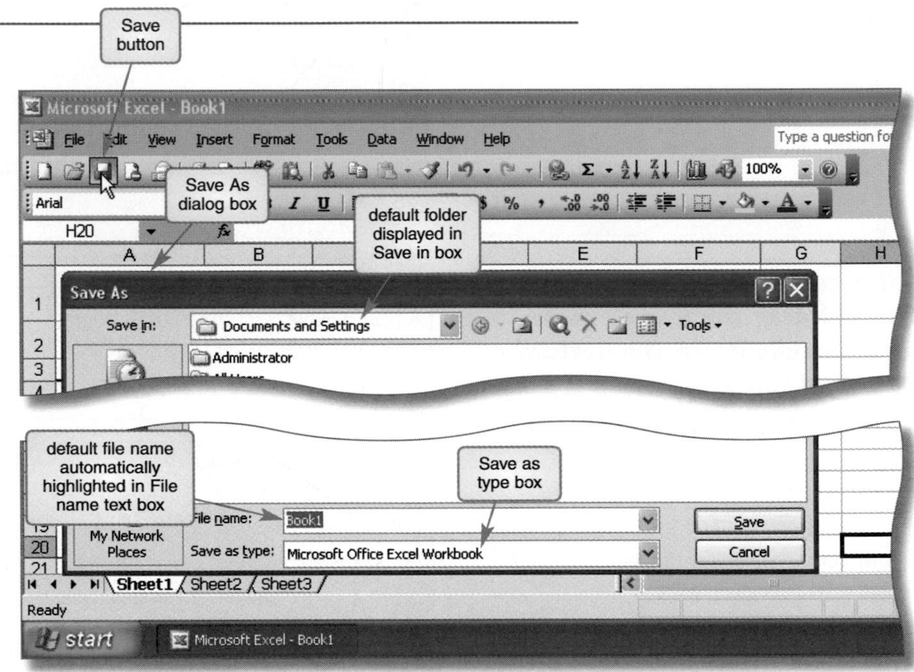

FIGURE 1-64

2

- **Type** `A Better Body Shop Annual Revenue` **in the File name text box.**
- **Click the Save in box arrow.**

The new file name replaces Book1 in the File name text box (Figure 1-65). A file name can be up to 255 characters and can include spaces. Excel displays a list of available drives and folders.

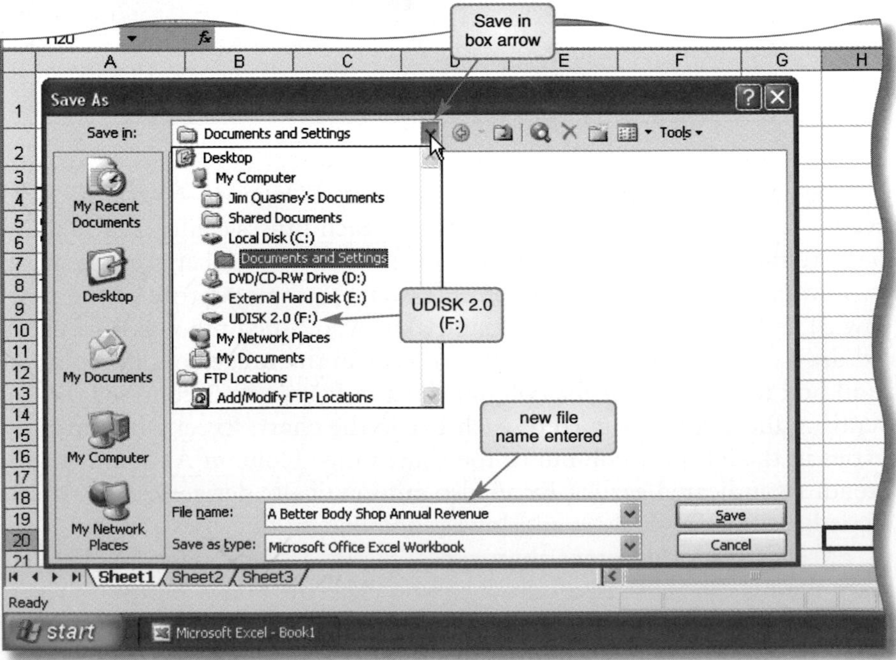

FIGURE 1-65

3

• **Click UDISK 2.0 (F:) in the Save in list. (Your USB flash drive may have a different name and letter.)**

The USB flash drive becomes the selected drive (Figure 1-66). The buttons on the top and on the side of the dialog box are used to select folders, change the appearance of file names, and complete other tasks.

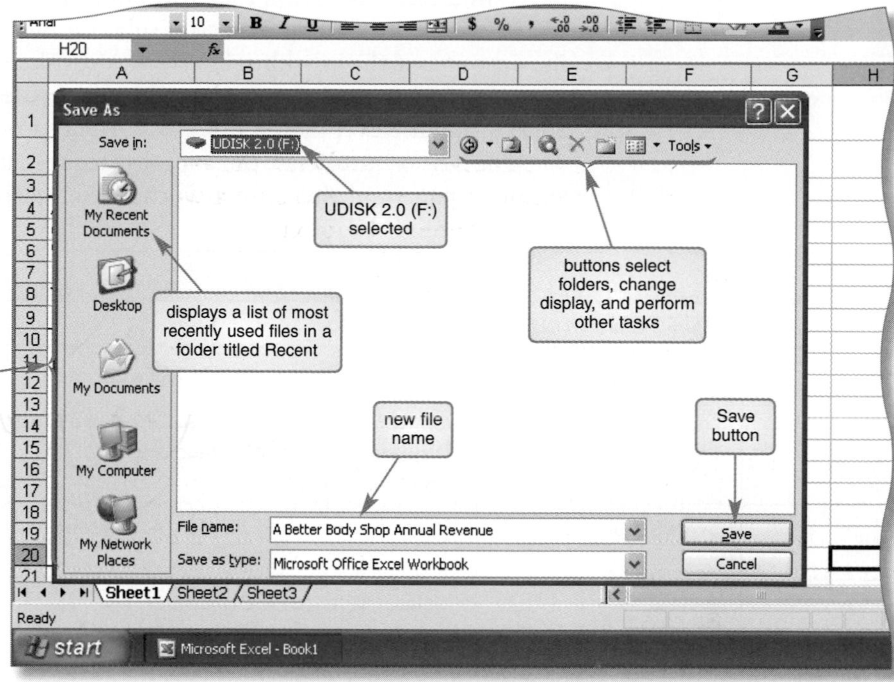

FIGURE 1-66

4

• **Click the Save button in the Save As dialog box.**

Excel saves the workbook on the USB flash drive using the file name, A Better Body Shop Annual Revenue. Excel automatically appends the extension ***.xls*** *to the file name you entered in Step 2, which stands for Excel workbook. Although the workbook is saved on a USB flash drive, it also remains in memory and is displayed on the screen (Figure 1-67). Excel displays the new file name on the title bar.*

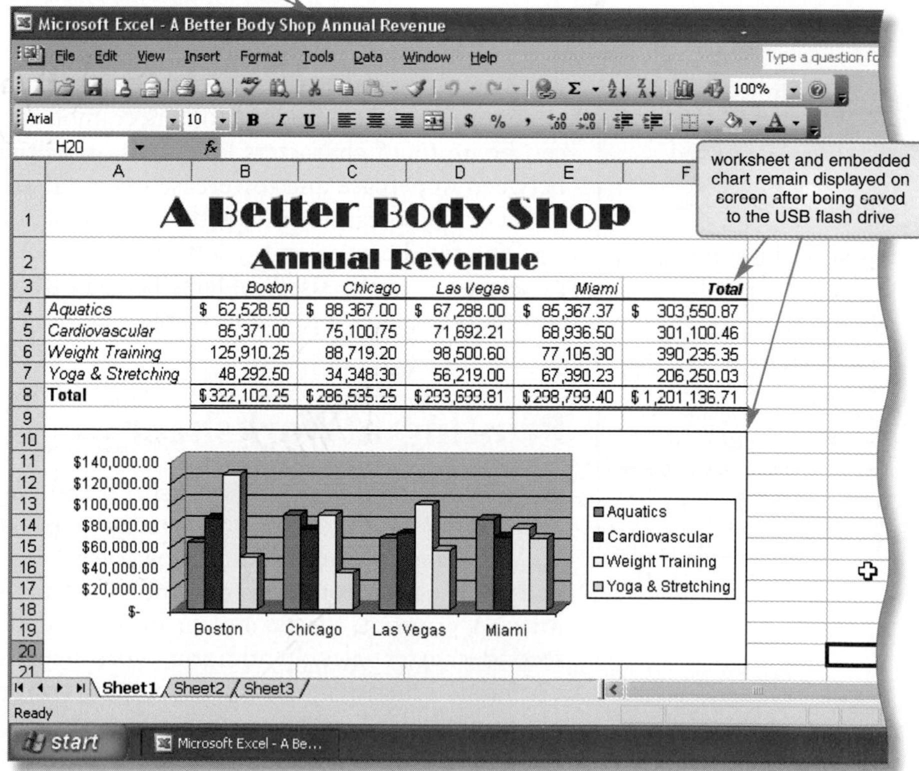

FIGURE 1-67

While Excel is saving the workbook, it momentarily changes the word Ready on the status bar to Saving. It also displays a horizontal bar on the status bar indicating the amount of the workbook saved. After the save operation is complete, Excel changes the name of the workbook on the title bar from Book1 to A Better Body Shop Annual Revenue (Figure 1-67 on the previous page).

The seven buttons at the top of the Save As dialog box in Figure 1-66 on the previous page and their functions are summarized in Table 1-4.

Table 1-4 Save As Dialog Box Toolbar Buttons

BUTTON	BUTTON NAME	FUNCTION
	Default File Location	Displays contents of default file location
	Up One Level	Displays contents of folder one level up from current folder
	Search the Web	Starts browser and displays search engine
	Delete	Deletes selected file or folder
	Create New Folder	Creates new folder
	Views	Changes view of files and folders
Tools	Tools	Lists commands to print or modify file names and folders

When you click the Tools button in the Save As dialog box, Excel displays the Tools menu. The General Options command on the menu allows you to save a backup copy of the workbook, create a password to limit access to the workbook, and carry out other functions that are discussed later. Saving a **backup copy** of the workbook means that each time you save a workbook, Excel copies the current version of the workbook to a file with the same name, but with the words, Backup of, appended to the front of the file name. In the case of a power failure or some other problem, you can use the backup copy to restore your work.

You also can use the General Options command on the Tools menu to assign a password to a workbook so others cannot open it. A password is case-sensitive and can be up to 15 characters long. **Case-sensitive** means Excel can differentiate between uppercase and lowercase letters. If you assign a password and forget the password, you cannot access the workbook.

The five buttons on the left of the Save As dialog box in Figure 1-66 allow you to select frequently used folders. The My Recent Documents button displays a list of shortcuts (pointers) to the most recently used files in a folder titled Recent.

Q & A

Q: Can an Excel workbook be saved in an alternative file format so it can be opened by other applications?

A: Yes. Excel allows you to save a workbook in more than 30 different file formats. Choose the file format by clicking the Save as type box arrow at the bottom of the Save As dialog box (Figure 1-66). Microsoft Office Excel Workbook is the default file format.

Printing a Worksheet

Once you have created the worksheet, you might want to print it. A printed version of the worksheet is called a **hard copy** or **printout**.

You might want a printout for several reasons. First, to present the worksheet and chart to someone who does not have access to a computer, it must be in printed form. A printout, for example, can be handed out in a management meeting about second quarter sales. In addition, worksheets and charts often are kept for reference by people other than those who prepare them. In many cases, worksheets and charts are printed and kept in binders for use by others. The following steps illustrate how to print the worksheet.

To Print a Worksheet

1

• **Ready the printer according to the printer instructions and then click the Print button on the Standard toolbar (Figure 1-68).**

Print button

Microsoft Excel - A Better Body Shop Annual Revenue

File Edit View Insert Format Tools Data Window Help

Print (HP LaserJet 4P/4MP PS)

	A	B	C	D	E	F
1	A Better Body Shop					
2	Annual Revenue					
3		Boston	Chicago	Las Vegas	Miami	Total
4	Aquatics	$ 62,528.50	$ 88,367.00	$ 67,288.00	$ 85,367.37	$ 303,550.87
5	Cardiovascular	85,371.00	75,100.75	71,692.21	68,936.50	301,100.46
6	Weight Training	125,910.25	88,719.20	98,500.60	77,105.30	390,235.35
7	Yoga & Stretching	48,292.50	34,348.30	56,219.00	67,390.23	206,250.03
8	Total	$322,102.25	$286,535.25	$293,699.81	$298,799.40	$1,201,136.71

FIGURE 1-68

2

• **When the printer stops printing the worksheet and the chart, retrieve the printout.**

Excel sends the worksheet to the printer, which prints it (Figure 1-69).

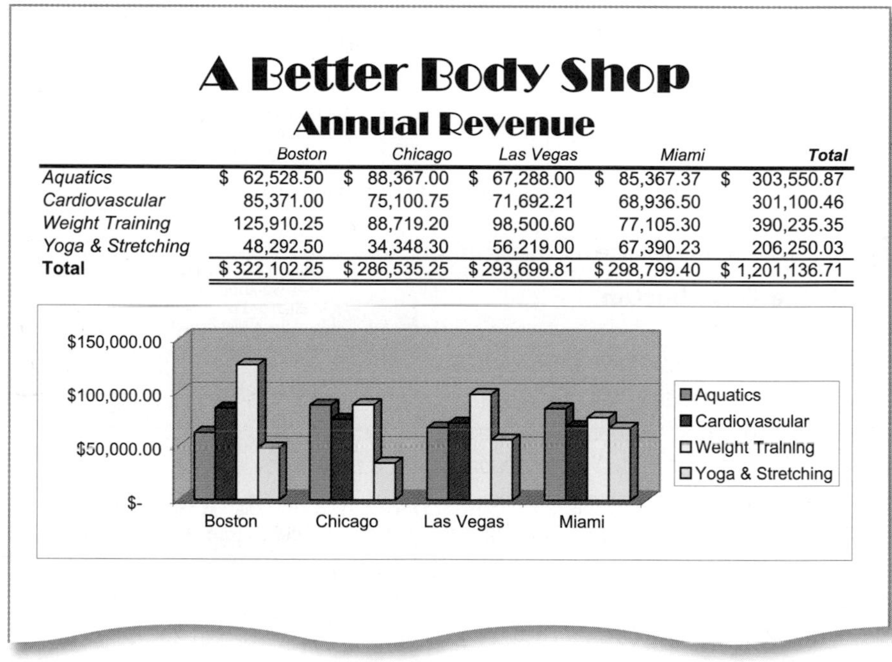

A Better Body Shop

Annual Revenue

	Boston	Chicago	Las Vegas	Miami	Total
Aquatics	$ 62,528.50	$ 88,367.00	$ 67,288.00	$ 85,367.37	$ 303,550.87
Cardiovascular	85,371.00	75,100.75	71,692.21	68,936.50	301,100.46
Weight Training	125,910.25	88,719.20	98,500.60	77,105.30	390,235.35
Yoga & Stretching	48,292.50	34,348.30	56,219.00	67,390.23	206,250.03
Total	$ 322,102.25	$ 286,535.25	$ 293,699.81	$ 298,799.40	$ 1,201,136.71

FIGURE 1-69

Prior to clicking the Print button, you can select which columns and rows in the worksheet to print. The range of cells you choose to print is called the **print area**. If you do not select a print area, as was the case in the previous set of steps, Excel automatically selects a print area on the basis of used cells. As you will see in future projects, Excel has many different print options, such as allowing you to preview the printout on the screen to see if the printout is satisfactory before sending it to the printer.

Skill Builder 1-3

To practice the following tasks, visit scsite.com/off2003sch/skill, locate Excel Project 1, and then click Skill Builder 1-3.

- ❑ Create an embeded chart
- ❑ Save a workbook
- ❑ Print a worksheet

Quitting Excel

The Project 1 worksheet and embedded chart are complete. The following steps show how to quit Excel.

To Quit Excel

1

• **Point to the Close button on the right side of the title bar (Figure 1-70).**

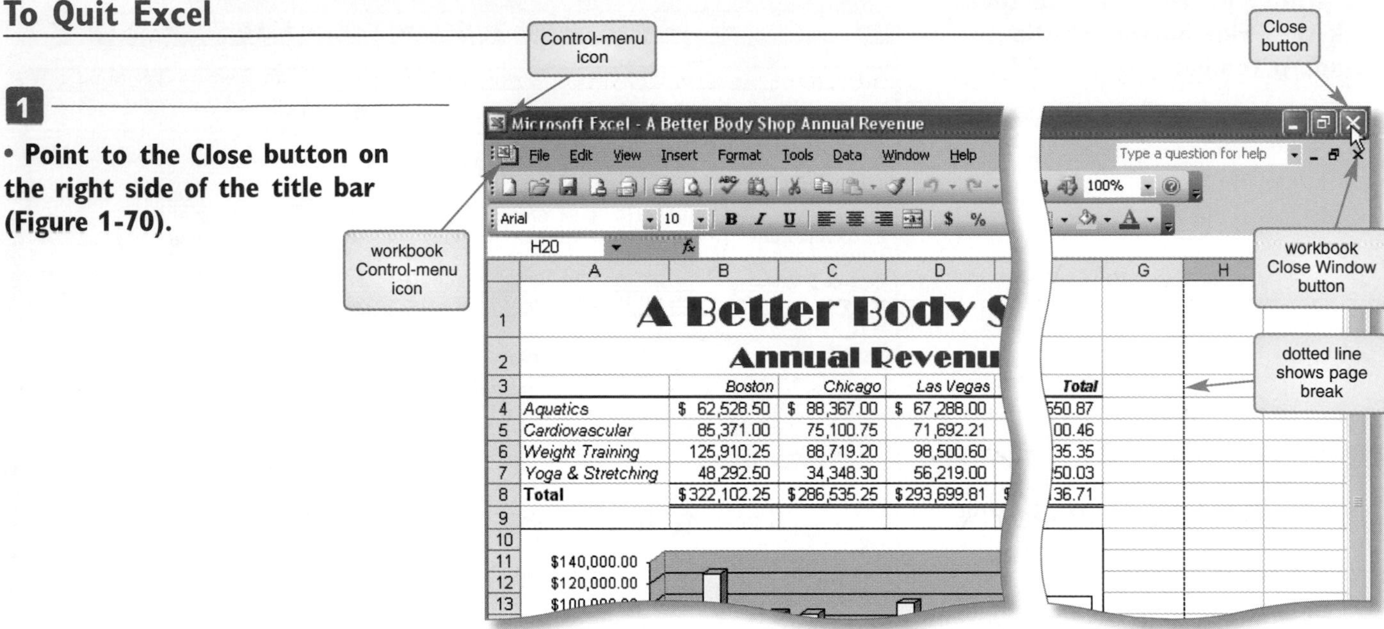

FIGURE 1-70

2

• **Click the Close button.**

If the worksheet was changed or printed, the Microsoft Excel dialog box displays the question, Do you want to save the changes you made to 'A Better Body Shop Annual Revenue'? (Figure 1-71). Clicking the Yes button saves the changes before quitting Excel. Clicking the No button quits Excel without saving the changes. Clicking the Cancel button closes the dialog box and returns control to the worksheet without saving the changes.

3

• **Click the No button.**

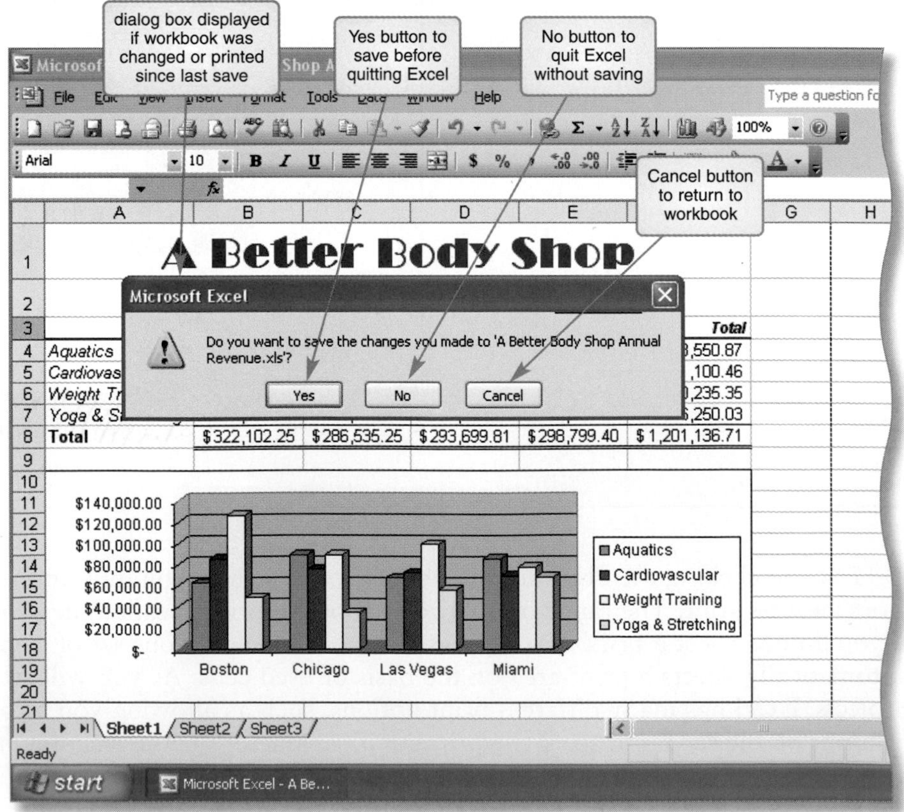

FIGURE 1-71

In Figure 1-70, you can see that the Excel window includes two Close buttons and two Control-menu icons. The Close button and Control-menu icon on the title bar can be used to quit Excel. The Close Window button and Control-menu icon on the menu bar can be used to close the workbook but not to quit Excel.

Q & A

Q: Does a way exist to circumvent the heavy use of paper and ink with computers?

A: Yes. You can preview the printout on your screen using the Print Preview button on the Standard toolbar, make adjustments to the worksheet, and then print it only when it appears exactly as you want. Each time you preview rather than print, you save both ink and paper.

Starting Excel and Opening a Workbook

After creating and saving a workbook, you often will have reason to retrieve it from a USB flash drive. For example, you might want to review the calculations on the worksheet and enter additional or revised data. The following steps assume Excel is not running.

To Start Excel and Open a Workbook

1

- **With your USB flash drive connected to one of the computer's USB ports, click the Start button on the Windows taskbar, point to All Programs on the Start menu, point to Microsoft Office on the All Programs submenu, and then click Microsoft Office Excel 2003 on the Microsoft Office submenu.**

Excel starts. The Getting Started task pane lists the four most recently used files in the Open area (Figure 1-72).

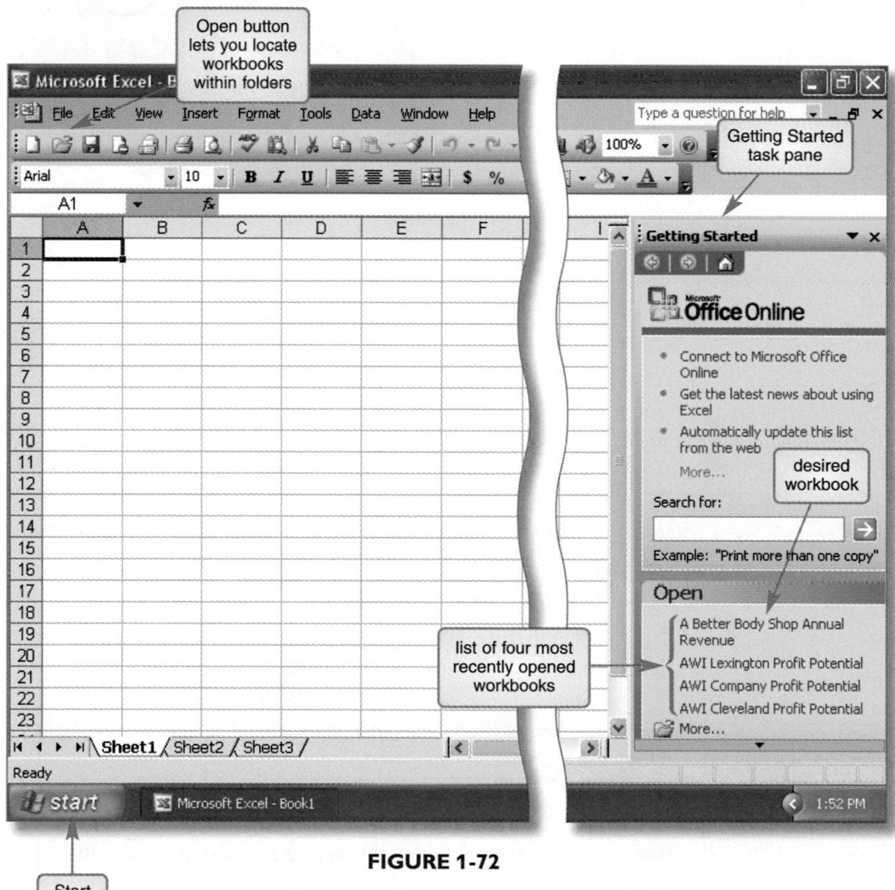

FIGURE 1-72

2

• Click A Better Body Shop Annual Revenue in the Open area in the Getting Started task pane.

Excel opens the workbook A Better Body Shop Annual Revenue (Figure 1-73). The Getting Started task pane closes.

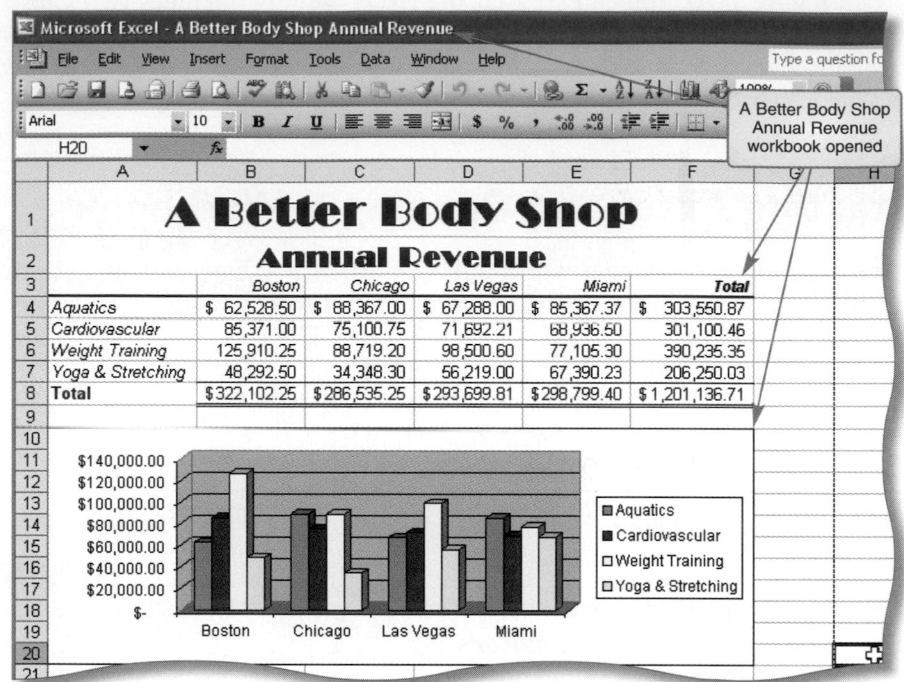

FIGURE 1-73

If you want to open a workbook other than one of the four most recently opened ones, click the Open button on the Standard toolbar or the More link in the Getting Started task pane. Clicking the Open button or the More link displays the Open dialog box, which allows you to navigate to a workbook stored on disk.

AutoCalculate

You easily can obtain a total, an average, or other information about the numbers in a range by using the **AutoCalculate area** on the status bar. First, select the range of cells containing the numbers you want to check. Next, right-click the AutoCalculate area to display the shortcut menu (Figure 1-74). The check mark to the left of the active function (Sum) indicates that the sum of the selected range is displayed in the AutoCalculate area on the status bar. The function of the commands on the AutoCalculate shortcut menu are described in Table 1-5.

The following steps show how to display the average annual revenue for the Weight Training offering.

Table 1-5 AutoCalculate Shortcut Menu Commands

COMMAND	FUNCTION
None	No value is displayed in the AutoCalculate area
Average	AutoCalculate area displays the average of the numbers in the selected range
Count	AutoCalculate area displays the number of nonblank cells in the selected range
Count Nums	AutoCalculate area displays the number of cells containing numbers in the selected range
Max	AutoCalculate area displays the highest value in the selected range
Min	AutoCalculate area displays the lowest value in the selected range
Sum	AutoCalculate area displays the sum of the numbers in the selected range

To Use the AutoCalculate Area to Determine an Average

1

- **Select the range B6:E6 and then right-click the AutoCalculate area on the status bar.**

The sum of the numbers in the range B6:E6 is displayed (390,235.35) in the AutoCalculate area, because Sum is the active function (Figure 1-74). Excel displays a shortcut menu listing the other available functions above the AutoCalculate area. If another function is active on your shortcut menu, you may see a different value in the AutoCalculate area.

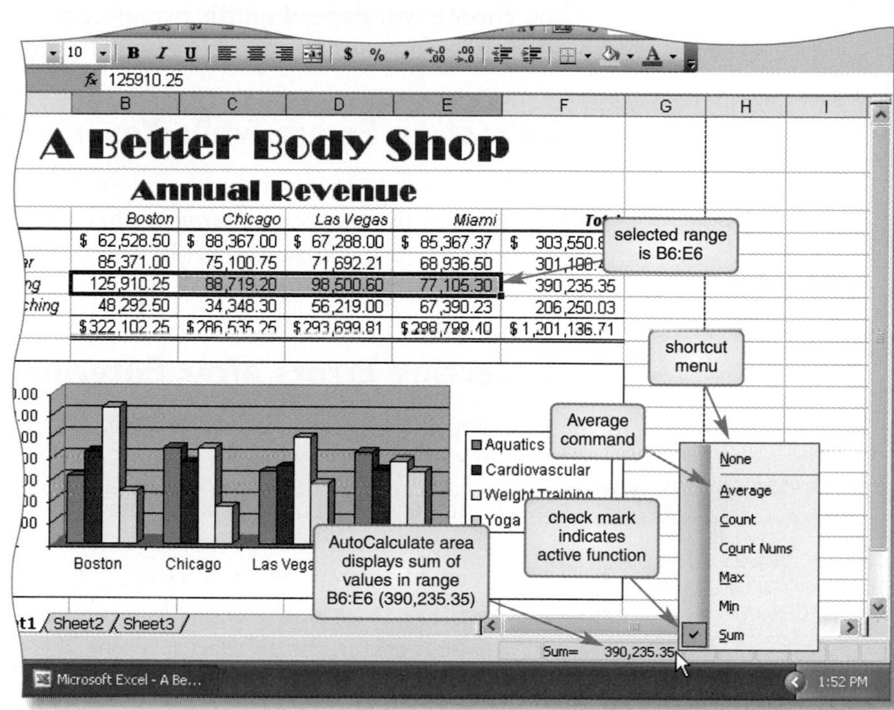

FIGURE 1-74

2

- **Click Average on the shortcut menu.**

Excel displays the average of the numbers in the range B6:E6 (97,558.84) in the AutoCalculate area (Figure 1-75).

3

- **Right-click the AutoCalculate area and then click Sum on the shortcut menu.**

The AutoCalculate area displays the sum, as shown earlier in Figure 1-74.

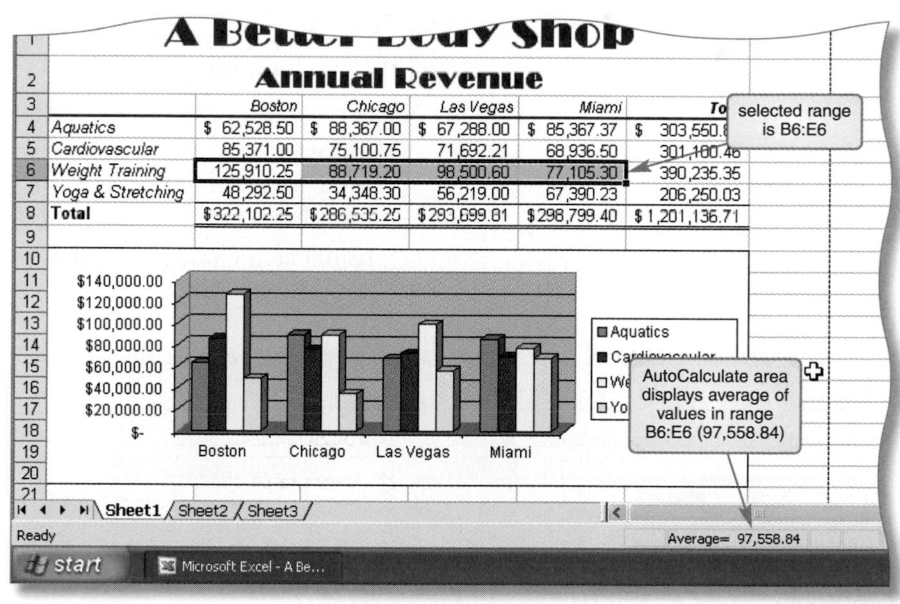

FIGURE 1-75

To change to any one of the other five functions for the range B6:E6, right-click the AutoCalculate area and then click the desired function. Clicking None at the top of the AutoCalculate shortcut menu in Figure 1-74 turns off the AutoCalculate area. Thus, if you select None, then no value will be displayed in the AutoCalculate area when you select a range.

Correcting Errors

You can correct errors on a worksheet using one of several methods. The method you choose will depend on the extent of the error and whether you notice it while typing the data or after you have entered the incorrect data into the cell.

Correcting Errors while You Are Typing Data into a Cell

If you notice an error while you are typing data into a cell, press the BACKSPACE key to erase the incorrect characters and then type the correct characters. If the error is a major one, click the Cancel box in the formula bar or press the ESC key to erase the entire entry and then reenter the data from the beginning.

Correcting Errors after Entering Data into a Cell

If you find an error in the worksheet after entering the data, you can correct the error in one of two ways:

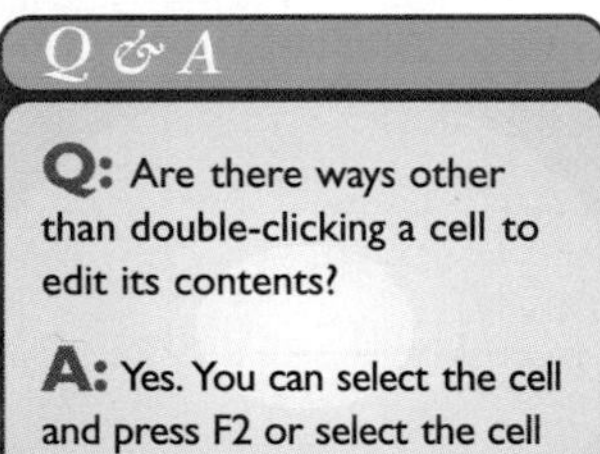

Q & A

Q: Are there ways other than double-clicking a cell to edit its contents?

A: Yes. You can select the cell and press F2 or select the cell and click in the formula bar.

1. If the entry is short, select the cell, retype the entry correctly, and then click the Enter box or press the ENTER key. The new entry will replace the old entry.
2. If the entry in the cell is long and the errors are minor, using Edit mode may be a better choice than retyping the cell entry. Use the Edit mode as described below.
   a. Double-click the cell containing the error to switch Excel to Edit mode. In **Edit mode**, Excel displays the active cell entry in the formula bar and a flashing insertion point in the active cell (Figure 1-76). With Excel in Edit mode, you can edit the contents directly in the cell — a procedure called **in-cell editing**.
   b. Make changes using in-cell editing, as indicated below.
      (1) To insert new characters between two characters, place the insertion point between the two characters and begin typing. Excel inserts the new characters at the location of the insertion point.
      (2) To delete a character in the cell, move the insertion point to the left of the character you want to delete and then press the DELETE key or place the insertion point to the right of the character you want to delete and then press the BACKSPACE key. You also can use the mouse to drag through the character or adjacent characters you want to delete and then press the DELETE key or click the Cut button on the Standard toolbar.
      (3) When you are finished editing an entry, click the Enter box or press the ENTER key.

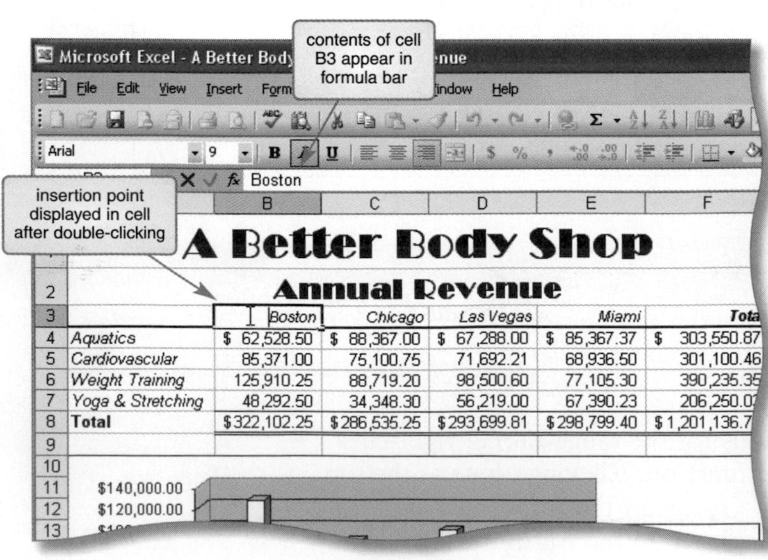

FIGURE 1-76

When Excel enters the Edit mode, the keyboard usually is in Insert mode. In **Insert mode**, as you type a character, Excel inserts the character and moves all characters to the right of the typed character one position to the right. You can change to Overtype mode by pressing the INSERT key. In **Overtype mode**, Excel overtypes, or replaces, the character to the right of the insertion point. The INSERT key toggles the keyboard between Insert mode and Overtype mode.

While in Edit mode, you may have reason to move the insertion point to various points in the cell, select portions of the data in the cell, or switch from inserting characters to overtyping characters. Table 1-6 summarizes the more common tasks used during in-cell editing.

Table 1-6 Summary of In-Cell Editing Tasks

	TASK	MOUSE	KEYBOARD
1	Move the insertion point to the beginning of data in a cell.	Point to the left of the first character and click.	Press HOME
2	Move the insertion point to the end of data in a cell.	Point to the right of the last character and click.	Press END
3	Move the insertion point anywhere in a cell.	Point to the appropriate position and click the character.	Press RIGHT ARROW or LEFT ARROW
4	Highlight one or more adjacent characters.	Drag the mouse pointer through adjacent characters.	Press SHIFT+RIGHT ARROW or SHIFT+LEFT ARROW
5	Select all data in a cell.	Double-click the cell with the insertion point in the cell.	
6	Delete selected characters.	Click the Cut button on the Standard toolbar.	Press DELETE
7	Delete characters to the left of the insertion point.		Press BACKSPACE
8	Toggle between Insert and Overtype modes.		Press INSERT

Undoing the Last Cell Entry

Excel provides the Undo command on the Edit menu and the Undo button on the Standard toolbar (Figure 1-77), both of which allow you to erase recent cell entries. Thus, if you enter incorrect data in a cell and notice it immediately, click the Undo command or Undo button and Excel changes the cell entry to what it was prior to the incorrect data entry.

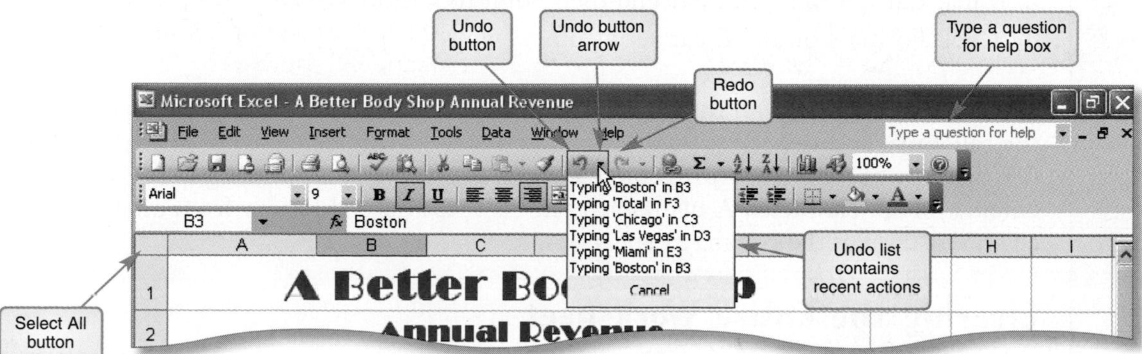

FIGURE 1-77

Q & A

Q: Does the Undo command have limits as to what it can undo?

A: Yes, but the Undo button can undo far more complicated worksheet activities than just removing the latest entry from a cell. In fact, most commands can be undone if you click the Undo button before you make another entry or issue another command. You cannot undo a save or print, but, as a rule, the Undo button can restore the worksheet data and settings to what they were the last time Excel was in Ready mode. With Excel, you have multiple-level undo and redo capabilities.

Excel remembers the last 16 actions you have completed. Thus, you can undo up to 16 previous actions by clicking the Undo button arrow to display the Undo list and then clicking the action to be undone (Figure 1-77 on the previous page). You can drag through several actions in the Undo list to undo all of them at once. If no actions are available for Excel to undo, then the Undo button is dimmed and inoperative.

The Redo button, next to the Undo button on the Standard toolbar, allows you to repeat previous actions. You also can click Redo on the Edit menu, instead of using the Redo button.

Clearing a Cell or Range of Cells

If you enter data into the wrong cell or range of cells, you can erase, or **clear**, the data using one of the first four methods listed below. The fifth method clears the formatting from the selected cells.

To Clear Cell Entries Using the Fill Handle

1. Select the cell or range of cells and then point to the fill handle so the mouse pointer changes to a cross hair.
2. Drag the fill handle back into the selected cell or range until a shadow covers the cell or cells you want to erase. Release the mouse button.

To Clear Cell Entries Using the Shortcut Menu

1. Select the cell or range of cells to be cleared.
2. Right-click the selection.
3. Click Clear Contents on the shortcut menu.

To Clear Cell Entries Using the DELETE Key

1. Select the cell or range of cells to be cleared.
2. Press the DELETE key.

To Clear Cell Entries Using the Clear Command

1. Select the cell or range of cells to be cleared.
2. Click Edit on the menu bar and then point to Clear.
3. Click All on the Clear submenu.

To Clear Formatting Using the Clear Command

1. Select the cell or range of cells that you want to remove the formatting from.
2. Click Edit on the menu bar and then point to Clear.
3. Click Formats on the Clear submenu.

Q & A

Q: Is there more than one way to invoke a command in Excel?

A: Yes. For a table that lists how to complete the tasks covered in this book using the mouse, menu, shortcut menu, and keyboard, see the Quick Reference Summary at the back of this book, or visit the Office 2003 Quick Reference Web page (scsite.com/off2003sch/qr).

The All command on the Clear submenu is the only command that clears both the cell entry and the cell formatting. As you are clearing cell entries, always remember that you should ***never press the* SPACEBAR *to clear a cell.*** Pressing the SPACEBAR enters a blank character. A blank character is text and is different from an empty cell, even though the cell may appear empty.

Clearing the Entire Worksheet

If required worksheet edits are extremely extensive, you may want to clear the entire worksheet and start over. To clear the worksheet or delete an embedded chart, use the following steps.

To Clear the Entire Worksheet

1. Click the Select All button on the worksheet (Figure 1-77 on page EX 51).
2. Press the DELETE key to delete all the entries. Click Edit on the menu bar, point to Clear, and then click All on the Clear submenu to delete both the entries and formats.

The Select All button selects the entire worksheet. Instead of clicking the Select All button, you also can press CTRL+A. To clear an unsaved workbook, click the workbook's Close Window button or click the Close command on the File menu. Click the No button if the Microsoft Excel dialog box asks if you want to save changes. To start a new, blank workbook, click the New button on the Standard toolbar or click the New command on the File menu and begin working on a new workbook.

To delete an embedded chart, complete the following steps.

To Delete an Embedded Chart

1. Click the chart to select it.
2. Press the DELETE key.

Q & A

Q: What is the Microsoft Office Specialist Certification program?

A: The Microsoft Office Specialist Certification program provides an opportunity for you to obtain a valuable industry credential — proof that you have the Excel 2003 skills required by employers. For more information, see Appendix E, or visit the Office 2003 Certification Web page (scsite.com/off2003sch/cert).

Excel Help System

At any time while you are using Excel, you can get answers to questions using the **Excel Help** system. You can activate the Excel Help system by using the Type a question for help box on the menu bar, the Microsoft Excel Help button on the Standard toolbar, or by clicking Help on the menu bar (Figure 1-78). Used properly, this form of online assistance can increase your productivity and reduce your frustrations by minimizing the time you spend learning how to use Excel.

The following section shows how to get answers to your questions using the Type a question for help box. Additional information on using the Excel Help system is available in Appendix A.

Q & A

Q: What is the best way to become familiar with the Excel Help system?

A: The best way to become familiar with the Excel Help system is to use it. Appendix A includes detailed information on the Excel Help system and exercises that will help you gain confidence in using it.

Obtaining Help Using the Type a Question for Help Box on the Menu Bar

The Type a question for help box on the right side of the menu bar (see Figure 1-77 on page EX 51) lets you type free-form questions such as, how do I save or how do I create a Web page, phrases such as save a workbook or print a worksheet, or key terms such as, copy, save, or formatting. Excel responds by displaying a list of topics related to the question or terms you entered in the Search Results task pane. The following steps show how to use the Type a question for help box to obtain information on saving a workbook.

Q & A

Q: Are there Web sites that offer tips on using Excel?

A: To receive a free newsletter titled ExcelTips regularly via e-mail, visit the Office 2003 Q&A Web page (scsite.com/off2003sch/qa), locate Excel Project 1, and click ExcelTips.

To Obtain Help Using the Type a Question for Help Box

1

- **Type** save a workbook **in the Type a question for help box on the right side of the menu bar (Figure 1-78).**

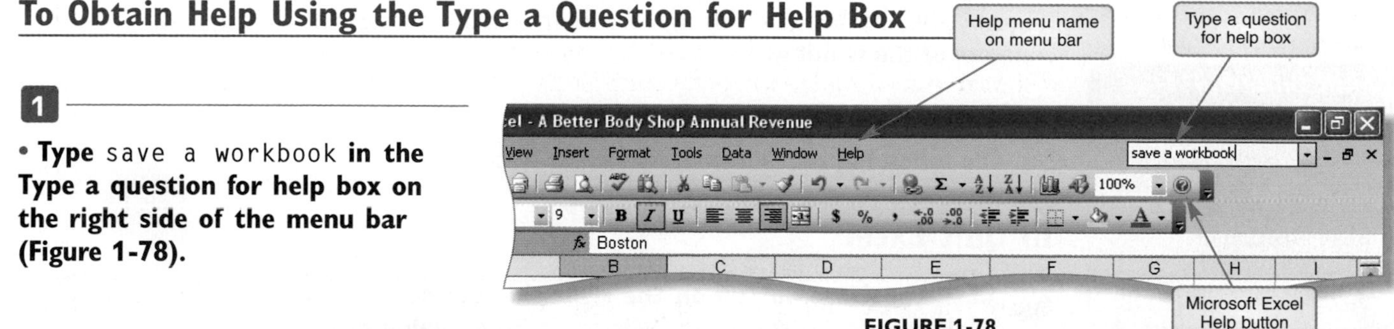

FIGURE 1-78

2

- **Press the ENTER key.**
- **When Excel displays the Search Results task pane, scroll down and then click the link Save a file.**
- **If necessary, click the AutoTile button (see Figure 1-80) to tile the windows.**

Excel displays the Search Results task pane with a list of topics related to the term, save. Excel found 30 search results (Figure 1-79). When the Save a file link is clicked, Excel opens the Microsoft Excel Help window on the left side of the screen.

3

- **Click the Show All link on the right side of the Microsoft Excel Help window to expand the links in the window.**
- **Double-click the Microsoft Excel Help title bar to maximize it.**

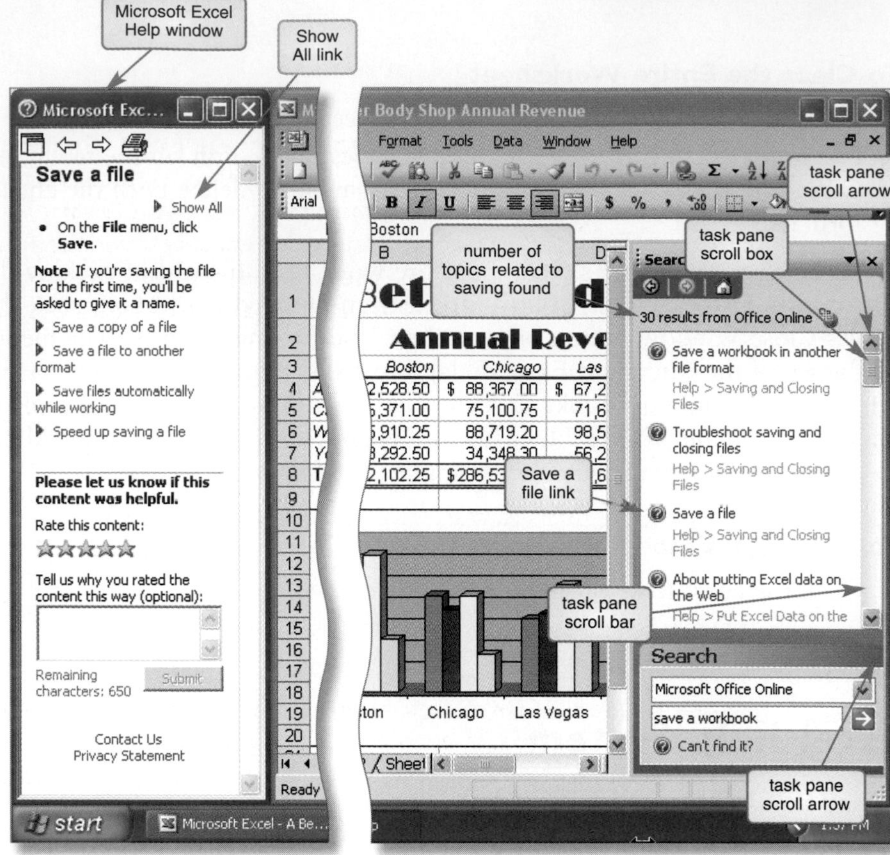

FIGURE 1-79

The links in the Microsoft Excel Help window are expanded. Excel maximizes the window that provides Help information about saving a file (Figure 1-80).

4

- **Click the Close button on the Microsoft Excel Help window title bar.**

The Microsoft Excel Help window closes and the worksheet is active.

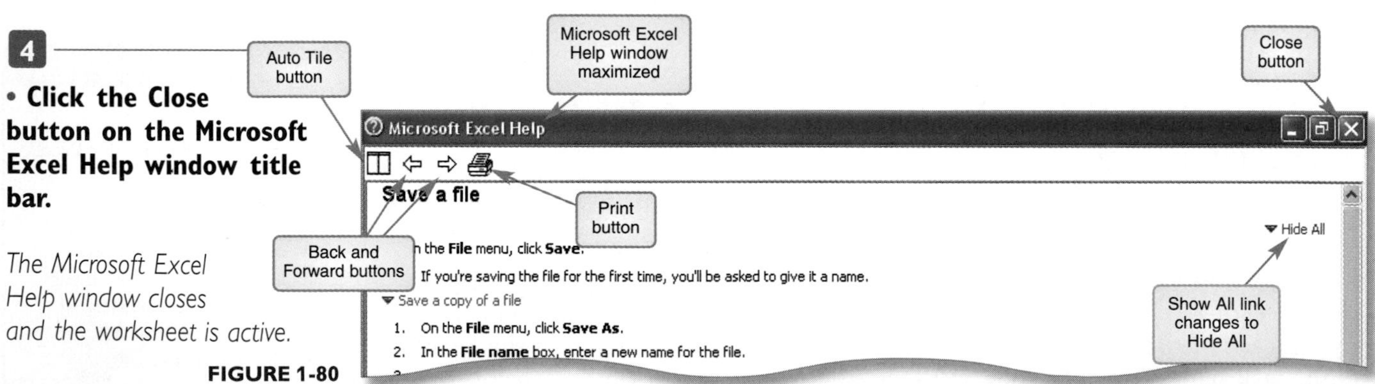

FIGURE 1-80

Use the buttons in the upper-left corner of the Microsoft Excel Help window (Figure 1-80) to navigate through the Help system, change the display, and print the contents of the window.

> ***Skill Builder 1-4***
>
> To practice the following tasks, visit scsite.com/off2003sch/skill, locate Excel Project 1, and then click Excel Skill Builder 1-4.
> - ❑ Use AutoCalculate
> - ❑ Edit worksheets
> - ❑ Use the Excel Help system

Quitting Excel

The following step shows how to quit Excel.

To Quit Excel

1 **Click the Close button on the right side of the title bar, and, if necessary, click the No button in the Microsoft Excel dialog box.**

Project Summary

This project presented Excel basics. You learned about the Excel window and how to enter text and numbers to create a worksheet. You learned how to select a range and how to use the AutoSum button. You learned how to copy a cell to adjacent cells. Once the worksheet was built, you learned how to format cells. You then learned how to use the Chart Wizard. After completing the worksheet, you learned how to save the workbook, print the worksheet and chart, and then quit Excel. You also learned how to start Excel by opening an Excel document, use the AutoCalculate area, and edit data in cells. Finally, you learned how to use the Excel Help system to answer your questions.

If you have a SAM user profile, you may have access to hands-on instruction, practice, and assessment of the skills covered in this project. Log in to your SAM account and go to your assignments page to see what your instructor has assigned.

What You Should Know

Having completed this project, you should be able to perform the tasks below. The tasks are listed in the same order they were presented in this project. For a list of the buttons, menus, toolbars, and commands introduced in this project, see the Quick Reference Summary at the back of this book and refer to the Page Number column.

1. Start Excel (EX 7)
2. Customize the Excel Window (EX 8)
3. Enter the Worksheet Titles (EX 17)
4. Enter Column Titles (EX 19)
5. Enter Row Titles (EX 20)
6. Enter Numbers (EX 22)
7. Sum a Column of Numbers (EX 23)
8. Copy a Cell to Adjacent Cells in a Row (EX 25)
9. Determine Multiple Totals at the Same Time (EX 27)
10. Change the Font Type (EX 29)
11. Bold a Cell (EX 30)
12. Increase the Font Size of a Cell Entry (EX 31)
13. Change the Font Color of a Cell Entry (EX 32)
14. Center a Cell Entry across Columns by Merging Cells (EX 33)
15. Format the Worksheet Subtitle (EX 34)
16. Use AutoFormat to Format the Body of a Worksheet (EX 34)
17. Use the Name Box to Select a Cell (EX 36)
18. Add a 3-D Clustered Column Chart to the Worksheet (EX 39)
19. Save a Workbook (EX 42)
20. Print a Worksheet (EX 45)
21. Quit Excel (EX 46)
22. Start Excel and Open a Workbook (EX 47)
23. Use the AutoCalculate Area to Determine an Average (EX 49)
24. Clear Cell Entries Using the Fill Handle (EX 52)
25. Clear Cell Entries Using the Shortcut Menu (EX 52)
26. Clear Cell Entries Using the DELETE Key (EX 52)
27. Clear Cell Entries Using the Clear Command (EX 52)
28. Clear the Entire Worksheet (EX 53)
29. Delete an Embedded Chart (EX 53)
30. Obtain Help Using the Type a Question for Help Box (EX 53)
31. Quit Excel (EX 54)

Career Corner

Programmer

If you are the curious, creative type, enjoy solving puzzles, and gain satisfaction in making things work, you may want to consider a career in programming. A programmer designs, writes, and tests the code that tells computers what to do. Most programmers specialize in one of three fields: system programming, application programming, or Web development programming.

Some jobs may require that the programmer develop an entire program, while other jobs require program maintenance. Likewise, programmers can work for a small company in which they are responsible for the entire system development cycle, or for a larger company in which they are part of a team and individual duties are specialized. Projects can range from computer games to essential business applications. Programmers enjoy the achievements of working with computers to accomplish objectives as well as developing efficient instructions that tell computers how to perform specific tasks.

Academic credentials are essential for success in this career. A bachelor's degree in Computer Science or Information Technology usually is required. The key to success is familiarity with programming languages and a good foundation in programming logic. Surveys indicate that average salaries for entry level programmers are about $45,500 and can exceed $95,000 for senior programmers. For more information, visit scsite.com/off2003sch/careers and then click Programmer.

Learn It Online

Instructions: To complete the Learn It Online exercises, start your browser, click the Address bar, and then enter the Web address scsite.com/off2003sch/learn. When the Office 2003 Learn It Online page is displayed, follow the instructions in the exercises below. Each exercise has instructions for printing your results, either for your own records or for submission to your instructor.

1 Project Reinforcement TF, MC, and SA

Below Excel Project 1, click the Project Reinforcement link. Print the quiz by clicking Print on the File menu for each page. Answer each question.

2 Flash Cards

Below Excel Project 1, click the Flash Cards link and read the instructions. Type 20 (or a number specified by your instructor) in the Number of playing cards text box, type your name in the Enter your Name text box, and then click the Flip Card button. When the flash card is displayed, read the question and then click the ANSWER box arrow to select an answer. Flip through Flash Cards. If your score is 15 (75%) correct or greater, click Print on the File menu to print your results. If your score is less than 15 (75%) correct, then redo this exercise by clicking the Replay button.

3 Practice Test

Below Excel Project 1, click the Practice Test link. Answer each question, enter your first and last name at the bottom of the page, and then click the Grade Test button. When the graded practice test is displayed on your screen, click Print on the File menu to print a hard copy. Continue to take practice tests until you score 80% or better.

4 Who Wants To Be a Computer Genius?

Below Excel Project 1, click the Computer Genius link. Read the instructions, enter your first and last name at the bottom of the page, and then click the PLAY button. When your score is displayed, click the PRINT RESULTS link to print a hard copy.

5 Wheel of Terms

Below Excel Project 1, click the Wheel of Terms link. Read the instructions, and then enter your first and last name and your school name. Click the PLAY button. When your score is displayed, right-click the score and then click Print on the shortcut menu to print a hard copy.

6 Crossword Puzzle Challenge

Below Excel Project 1, click the Crossword Puzzle Challenge link. Read the instructions, and then enter your first and last name. Click the SUBMIT button. Work the crossword puzzle. When you are finished, click the Submit button. When the crossword puzzle is redisplayed, click the Print Puzzle button to print a hard copy.

7 Tips and Tricks

Below Excel Project 1, click the Tips and Tricks link. Click a topic that pertains to Project 1. Right-click the information and then click Print on the shortcut menu. Construct a brief example of what the information relates to in Excel to confirm you understand how to use the tip or trick.

8 Newsgroups

Below Excel Project 1, click the Newsgroups link. Click a topic that pertains to Project 1. Print three comments.

9 Expanding Your Horizons

Below Excel Project 1, click the Expanding Your Horizons link. Click a topic that pertains to Project 1. Print the information. Construct a brief example of what the information relates to in Excel to confirm you understand the contents of the article.

10 Search Sleuth

Below Excel Project 1, click the Search Sleuth link. To search for a term that pertains to this project, select a term below the Project 1 title and then use the Google search engine at google.com (or any major search engine) to display and print two Web pages that present information on the term.

11 Excel Online Training

Below Excel Project 1, click the Excel Online Training link. When your browser displays the Microsoft Office Online Web page, click the Excel link. Click one of the Excel courses that covers one or more of the objectives listed at the beginning of the project on page EX 4. Print the first page of the course before stepping through it.

12 Office Marketplace

Below Excel Project 1, click the Office Marketplace link. When your browser displays the Microsoft Office Online Web page, click the Office Marketplace link. Click a topic that relates to Excel. Print the first page.

13 You're Hired!

Below Excel Project 1, click the You're Hired! link to embark on the path to a career in computers. Directions about how to play the game will be displayed. When you are ready to play, click the begin the game button. If required, submit your score to your instructor.

Apply Your Knowledge

1 Changing the Values in a Worksheet

Instructions: Start Excel. Open the workbook Apply 1-1 Youth Clothier Fourth Quarter Expenses (Figure 1-81a). See page xxiv at the front of this book for instructions for downloading the Data Files for Students, or see your instructor for information on accessing the files required in this book.

Make the changes to the worksheet described in Table 1-7 so that the worksheet appears as shown in Figure 1-81b. As you edit the values in the cells containing numeric data, watch the totals in row 7, the totals in column F, and the chart change.

Change the worksheet title in cell A1 to 28-point Arial Rounded MT Bold (or a similar font) violet, bold font, and then center it across columns A through F. Change the worksheet subtitle in cell A2 to 20-point Arial Rounded MT Bold (or a similar font) violet, bold font, and then center it across columns A through F.

Enter your name, course, laboratory assignment number, date, and instructor name in cells A21 through A25. Save the workbook using the file name, Apply 1-1 Just For Teens Clothier Fourth Quarter Expenses. Print the revised worksheet and hand in the printout to your instructor.

Table 1-7 New Worksheet Data

CELL	CHANGE CELL CONTENTS TO
A1	Just For Teens Clothier
B4	33829.33
C4	22613.45
D5	26771.84
E5	19010.68
E6	38102.75

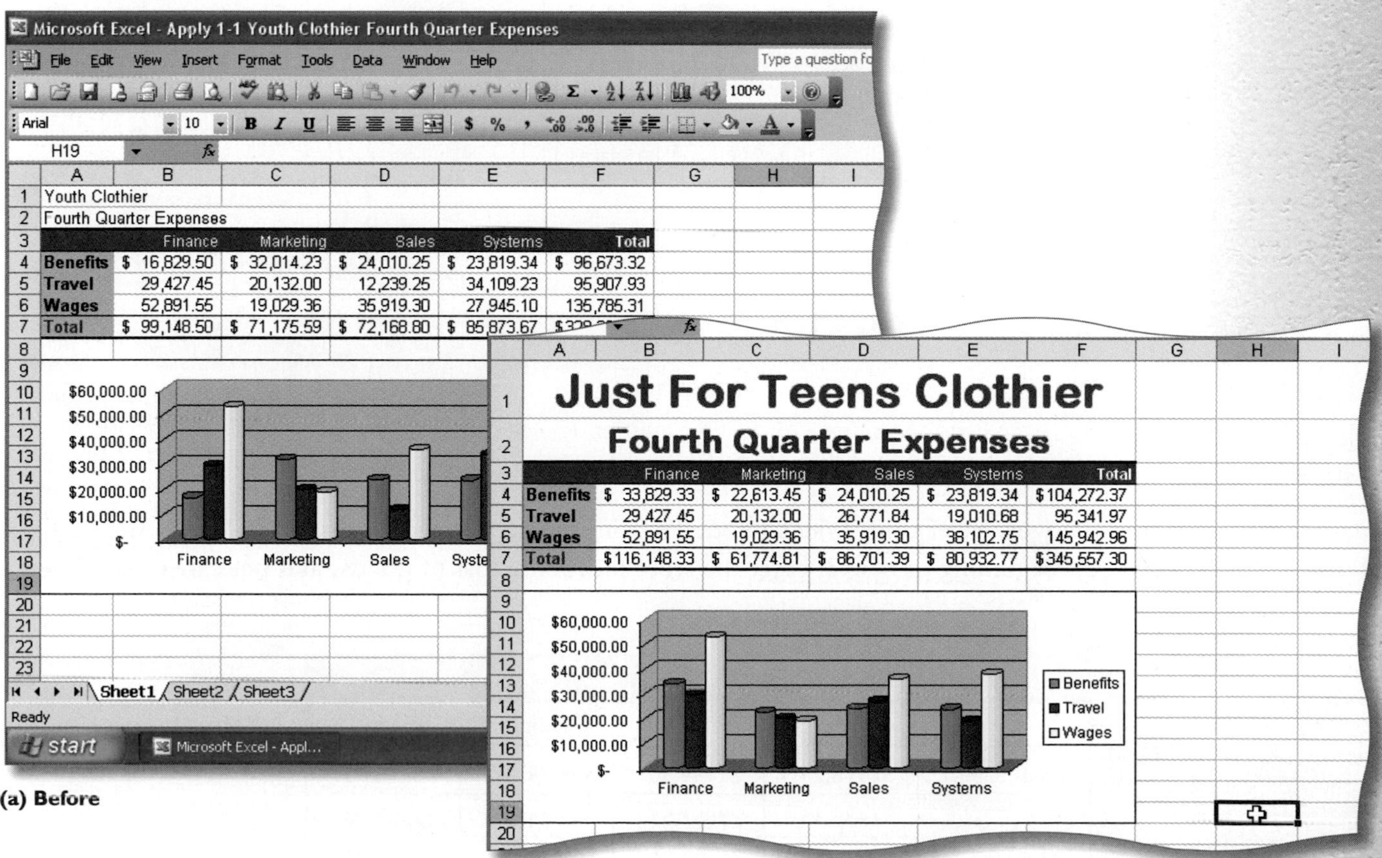

(a) Before

FIGURE 1-81 (b) After

1 Annual Cost of Goods Analysis Worksheet

Problem: You work part-time as a spreadsheet specialist for Tyler's Exotic Pets, one of the larger exotic pet companies in the United States. Your manager has asked you to develop an annual cost of goods analysis worksheet similar to the one shown in Figure 1-82.

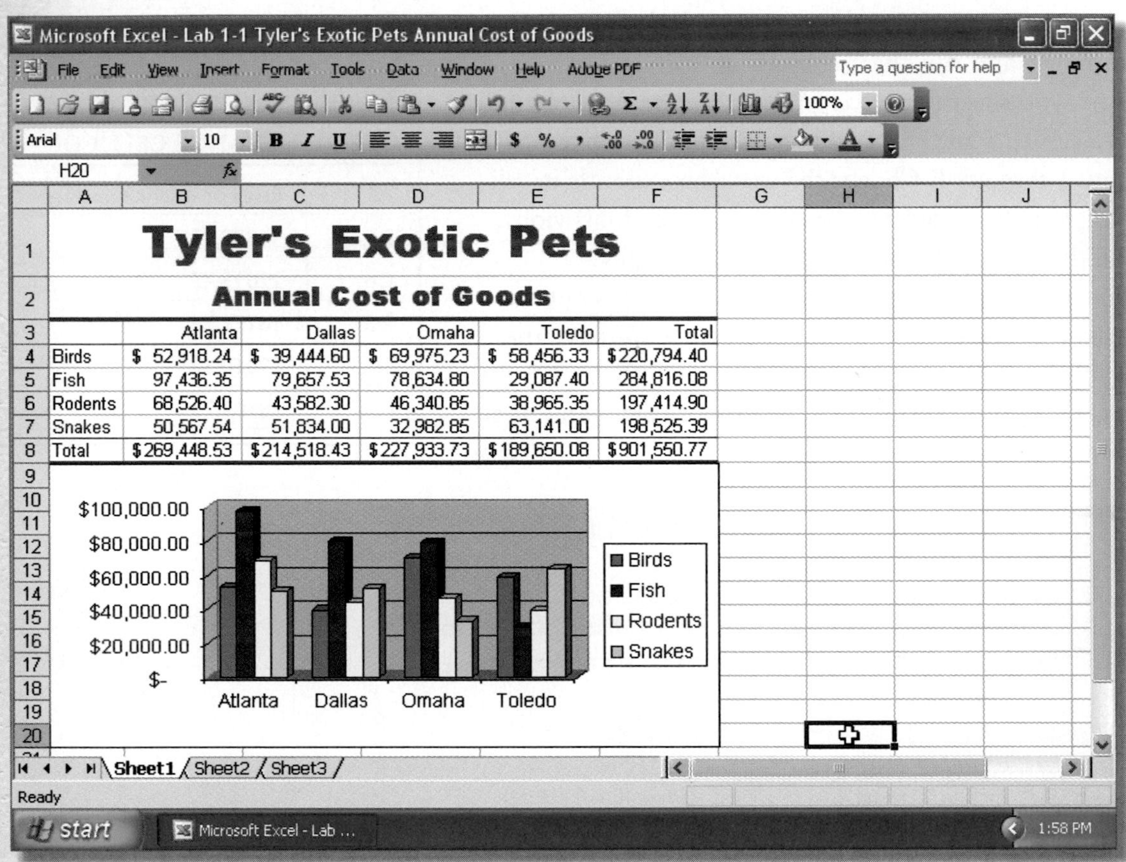

FIGURE 1-82

Instructions: Perform the following tasks.

1. Start Excel. Enter the worksheet title, Tyler's Exotic Pets, in cell A1 and the worksheet subtitle, Annual Cost of Goods, in cell A2. Beginning in row 3, enter the store locations, cost of goods, and pet categories shown in Table 1-8.

Table 1-8 Tyler's Exotic Pet Shop Annual Cost of Goods

	Atlanta	Dallas	Omaha	Toledo
Birds	52918.24	39444.60	69975.23	58456.33
Fish	97436.35	79657.53	78634.80	29087.40
Rodents	68526.40	43582.30	46340.85	38965.35
Snakes	50567.54	51834.00	32982.85	63141.00

In the Lab

2. Use the SUM function to determine the totals for the store locations, exotic pet categories, and company totals.
3. Format the worksheet title to 24-point Arial Black (or a similar font) plum, bold font, and center it across columns A through F.
4. Format the worksheet subtitle to 14-point Arial Black (or a similar font) plum, bold font, and center it across columns A through F.
5. Format the range A3:F8 using the AutoFormat command. Select the Accounting 2 autoformat.
6. Select the range A3:E7, and then use the Chart Wizard button on the Standard toolbar to draw a Clustered column with a 3-D visual effect chart (column 1, row 2 in the Chart sub-type list). Move and resize the chart so that it appears in the range A9:F20. If the labels along the horizontal axis (x-axis) do not appear as shown in Figure 1-82, then drag the right side of the chart so that the chart is displayed in the range A9:H20.
7. Enter your name, course, laboratory assignment number, date, and instructor name in cells A23 through A27.
8. Save the workbook using the file name, Lab 1-1 Tyler's Exotic Pets Annual Cost of Goods.
9. Print the worksheet.
10. Make the following two corrections to the cost: 72,545.60 for Dallas Rodents (cell C6), 110,235.25 for Toledo Birds (cell E4). After you enter the corrections, the company totals in cell F8 should equal $982,292.99.
11. Print the revised worksheet. Close the workbook without saving the changes.

2 Semiannual Revenue Analysis Worksheet

Problem: As the chief accountant for Play 'em Again, a reseller of cell phones, CDs, DVDs, electronic games, and iPods, you have been asked by the vice president to create a worksheet to analyze the semiannual revenue for the company by product across sales channels (Figure 1-83 on the next page). The sales channels and corresponding revenue by product are shown in Table 1-9.

Instructions: Perform the following tasks.

1. Enter the worksheet title, Play 'em Again, in cell A1 and the worksheet subtitle, Semiannual Revenue, in cell A2. Beginning in row 3, enter the sales channels, products, and revenues shown in Table 1-9. Enter the word, Total, in cells A16 and E3.
2. Use the SUM function to determine total expenses for the three sales channels, the totals for each product, and the company total.
3. Change the worksheet title to 26-point Arial Rounded MT Bold (or a similar font) green, bold font, and center it across columns A through E. Format the worksheet subtitle to 16-point Arial Rounded MT Bold (or a similar font) green, bold font, and center it across columns A through E.

Table 1-9 Play 'em Again Semiannual Revenue

	Mail	Store	Web
Accessories	12910.50	15320.10	18329.19
Cell Phone	58349.25	45015.35	96156.37
CD	89215.45	85019.00	105217.21
Controller	6819.45	8225.65	12230.00
DVD	96013.80	105672.05	215718.50
Games	35812.13	27210.60	175001.20
Gameboy	34910.55	56103.65	25100.45
iPod	89371.75	92818.30	105145.20
Other	10273.25	15444.23	18200.10
PlayStation 2	51837.95	167320.69	417025.80
PSP	75919.20	36193.25	87218.50
Xbox	56392.10	41341.90	153014.78

(continued)

Annual Business Expense Analysis Worksheet *(continued)*

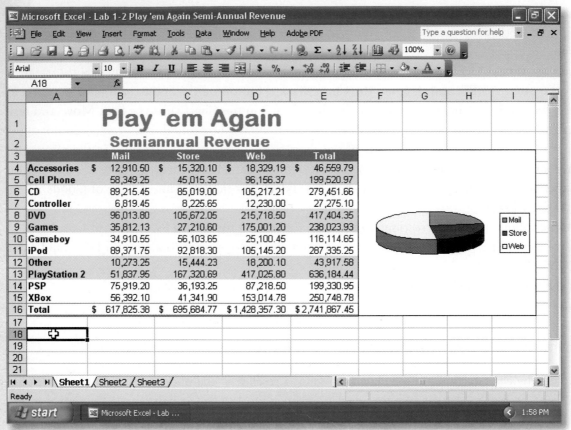

Microsoft Excel - Lab 1-2 Play 'em Again Semi-Annual Revenue

Play 'em Again

Semiannual Revenue

	Mail	Store	Web	Total
Accessories	$ 12,910.50	$ 15,320.10	$ 18,329.19	$ 46,559.79
Cell Phone	58,349.25	45,015.35	96,156.37	199,520.97
CD	89,215.45	85,019.00	105,217.21	279,451.66
Controller	6,819.45	8,225.65	12,230.00	27,275.10
DVD	96,013.80	105,672.05	215,718.50	417,404.35
Games	35,812.13	27,210.60	175,001.20	238,023.93
Gameboy	34,910.55	56,103.65	25,100.45	116,114.65
iPod	89,371.75	92,818.30	105,145.20	287,335.25
Other	10,273.25	15,444.23	18,200.10	43,917.58
PlayStation 2	51,837.95	167,320.69	417,025.80	636,184.44
PSP	75,919.20	36,193.25	87,218.50	199,330.95
XBox	56,392.10	41,341.90	153,014.78	250,748.78
Total	$ 617,825.38	$ 695,684.77	$ 1,428,357.30	$ 2,741,867.45

Mail, Store, Web

FIGURE 1-83

4. Format the range A3:E16 using the AutoFormat command on the Format menu as follows: (a) apply the autoformat Accounting 3; and (b) with the range A3:E16 still selected, apply the autoformat List 2. If you make a mistake, apply the autoformat None and then apply the autoformats again. Select the range A4:A15, and click the Bold button to bold the product names.
5. Create a pie chart that shows the revenue contributions of each sales channel. Chart the sales channel names (B3:D3) and corresponding totals (B16:D16). That is, select the range B3:D3, and then while holding down the CTRL key, select the range B16:D16. Draw the 3-D Pie Chart, as shown in Figure 1-83, by clicking the Chart Wizard button on the Standard toolbar. When Excel displays the Chart Wizard dialog box, select Pie in the Chart type list, and then select column 2, row 1 in the Chart sub-type list. Use the chart location F3:I16.
6. Enter your name, course, laboratory assignment number, date, and instructor name in cells A23 through A27.
7. Save the workbook using the file name, Lab 1-2 Play 'em Again Semiannual Revenue. Print the worksheet in landscape orientation. You print in landscape orientation by invoking the Page Setup command on the File menu and then clicking Landscape on the Page sheet in the Page Setup dialog box.
8. Two corrections to the product revenues were sent in from the accounting department. The correct product revenues are $65,450.25 for the Store Cell Phone revenue (cell C5) and $212,382.60 for the Web Games revenue (cell D9). After you enter the two corrections, the company total in cell E16 should equal $2,799,683.75. Print the revised worksheet.
9. Use the Undo button to change the worksheet back to the original numbers in Table 1-9. Use the Redo button to change the worksheet back to the revised state.

In the Lab

10. Quit Excel without saving the latest changes. Start Excel and open the workbook saved in Step 7. Double-click cell D6 and use in-cell editing to change the CD sales on the Web to $363,349.76. Write the company total in cell E16 at the top of the first printout. Click the Undo button.
11. Click cell A1 and then click the Merge and Center button to split cell A1 into cells A1, B1, C1, D1, and E1. To re-merge the cells into one, select the range A1:E1 and then click the Merge and Center button.
12. Hand in the two printouts to your instructor. Close the workbook without saving the changes.

3 College Cost and Financial Support Worksheet

Problem: Attending college is an expensive proposition, and your resources are limited. To plan for your four-year college career, you have decided to organize your anticipated resources and expenses in a worksheet. The data required to prepare your worksheet is shown in Table 1-10.

Table 1-10 College Cost and Financial Support

Cost	Freshman	Sophomore	Junior	Senior
Clothes	600.00	648.00	699.84	755.83
Entertainment	1030.00	1112.40	1201.39	1297.50
Books	900.00	972.00	1049.76	1133.74
Room & Board	6350.00	6858.00	7406.64	7999.17
Tuition	6100.00	6588.00	7115.04	7684.24
Financial Support				
Financial Aid	4550.00	4914.00	5307.12	5731.69
Job	2400.00	2592.00	2799.36	3023.30
Parents	3550.00	3834.00	4140.72	4471.98
Savings	3800.00	4104.00	4432.32	4786.91
Other	680.00	734.40	793.15	856.60

Instructions Part 1: Start Excel. Using the numbers in Table 1-10, create the worksheet shown in columns A through F in Figure 1-84 on the next page. Format the worksheet title in cell A1 to 26-point Bernard MT Condensed (or a similar font) red, bold font. Merge and center the worksheet title in cell A1 across columns A through F. Format the worksheet subtitles in cells A2 and A10 to 16-point Bernard MT Condensed (or a similar font) green (for cell A2) and blue (for cell A10) bold font. Format the range A3:F9 using the AutoFormat command on the Format menu as follows: (a) select the range A3:F9 and then apply the autoformat Accounting 3; and (b) with the range A3:F9 still selected, apply the autoformat Colorful 2. Use the same autoformats for the range A11:F17. Use the Fill Color button on the Formatting toolbar to change the background colors of the range A3:F3 to green and the range A11:F11 to blue.

Enter your identification on the worksheet and save the workbook using the file name, Lab 1-3 Part 1 College Cost and Financial Support. Print the worksheet in landscape orientation. You print in landscape orientation by invoking the Page Setup command on the File menu and then clicking Landscape on the Page sheet in the Page Setup dialog box. Click the Save button on the Standard toolbar to save the workbook with the new print settings.

(continued)

College Cost and Financial Support Worksheet *(continued)*

After reviewing the numbers, you realize you need to increase manually each of the Junior-year expenses in column D by $500. Manually change the Junior-year expenses to reflect this change. Manually change the financial aid for the Junior year by the amount required to cover the increase in expenses. The totals in cells F9 and F17 should equal $70,001.55. Print the worksheet. Close the workbook without saving changes. Hand in the two printouts to your instructor.

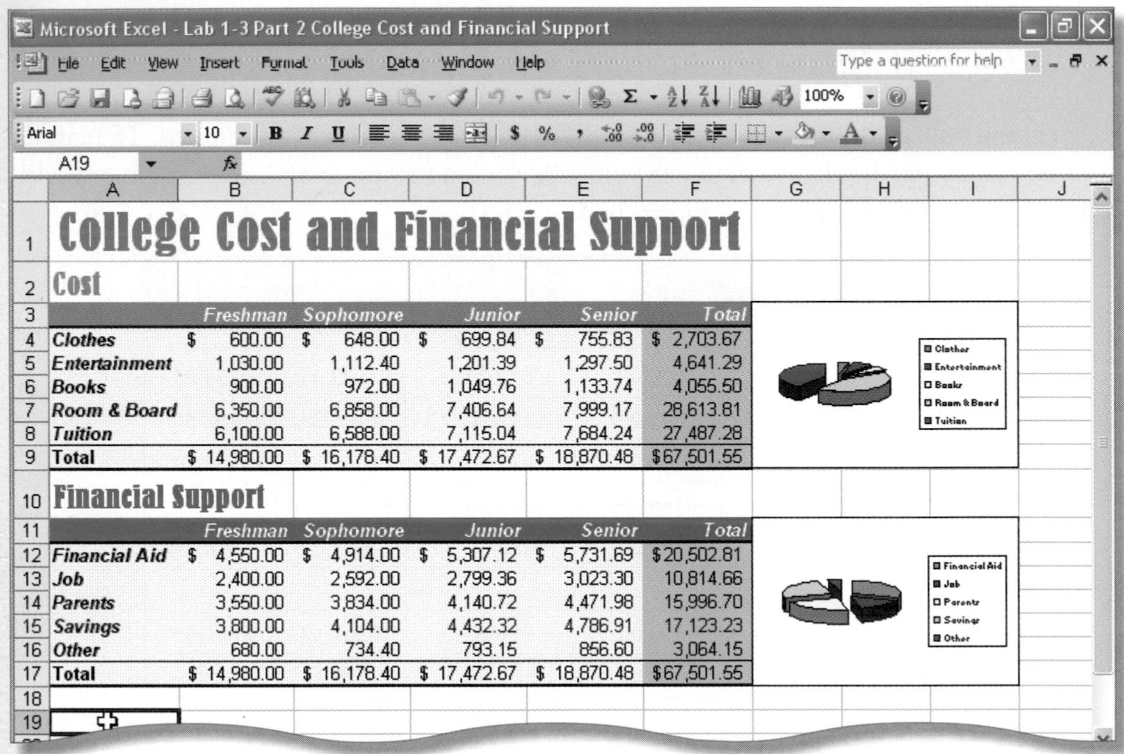

	A	B	C	D	E	F
1	**College Cost and Financial Support**					
2	**Cost**					
3		Freshman	Sophomore	Junior	Senior	Total
4	Clothes	$ 600.00	$ 648.00	$ 699.84	$ 755.83	$ 2,703.67
5	Entertainment	1,030.00	1,112.40	1,201.39	1,297.50	4,641.29
6	Books	900.00	972.00	1,049.76	1,133.74	4,055.50
7	Room & Board	6,350.00	6,858.00	7,406.64	7,999.17	28,613.81
8	Tuition	6,100.00	6,588.00	7,115.04	7,684.24	27,487.28
9	Total	$ 14,980.00	$ 16,178.40	$ 17,472.67	$ 18,870.48	$67,501.55
10	**Financial Support**					
11		Freshman	Sophomore	Junior	Senior	Total
12	Financial Aid	$ 4,550.00	$ 4,914.00	$ 5,307.12	$ 5,731.69	$20,502.81
13	Job	2,400.00	2,592.00	2,799.36	3,023.30	10,814.66
14	Parents	3,550.00	3,834.00	4,140.72	4,471.98	15,996.70
15	Savings	3,800.00	4,104.00	4,432.32	4,786.91	17,123.23
16	Other	680.00	734.40	793.15	856.60	3,064.15
17	Total	$ 14,980.00	$ 16,178.40	$ 17,472.67	$ 18,870.48	$67,501.55

FIGURE 1-84

Instructions Part 2: Open the workbook, Lab 1-3 Part 1 College Cost and Financial Support, and draw the two charts shown in Figure 1-84. Draw an exploded pie with a 3-D visual effect in the range G3:I9 to show the contribution of each category of cost for the four years. Chart the range A4:A8 and F4:F8. That is, select the range A4:A8, and then, while holding down the CTRL key, select the range F4:F8. Draw an exploded pie with a 3-D visual effect in the range G11:I17 to show the contribution of each category of financial support for the four years. Chart the range A12:A16 and F12:F16. Save the workbook using the file name, Lab 1-3 Part 2 College Cost and Financial Support. Print the worksheet. Hand in the printout to your instructor.

Instructions Part 3: Open the workbook, Lab 1-3 Part 2 College Cost and Financial Support. A close inspection of Table 1-10 on the previous page shows that both the cost and the financial support increase 8% each year. Use the Type a question for help box on the menu bar to learn how to enter the data for the last three years using a formula and the Copy command. For example, the formula to enter in cell C4 is =B4 * 1.08. Enter formulas to replace all the numbers in the range C4:E8 and C12:E16. If necessary, reformat the tables using the autoformats, as described in Part 1. The worksheet should appear as shown in Figure 1-84. Save the worksheet using the file name, Lab 1-3 Part 3 College Cost and Financial Support. Print the worksheet. Press CTRL+ACCENT MARK (`) to display the formulas. Print the formulas version. Close the workbook without saving changes. Hand in both printouts to your instructor.

Cases and Places

The difficulty of these case studies varies: ■ are the least difficult and ■■ are more difficult. Each exercise has a cross-curricular designation:

Math Social Studies Science Language Arts Art/Music Business Health

1 You work part-time for a credit and debt counseling service. To estimate the funds a family needs to make it through the upcoming year, you decide to create a personal budget worksheet that itemizes expected quarterly expenses. The anticipated expenses are listed in Table 1-11. Use the concepts and techniques presented in this project to create the worksheet and an embedded 100% stacked column with a 3-D visual effect (column 3, row 2) that shows the quarterly contribution of each expense. If necessary, reduce the size of the font in the chart so that each expense category name appears on the horizontal axis (x-axis). Use the AutoCalculate area to determine the average amount spent per quarter on each expense. Manually insert the averages with appropriate titles in an empty area on the worksheet. Print the worksheet in landscape orientation. You print in landscape orientation by invoking the Page Setup command on the File menu and then clicking Landscape in the Page sheet in the Page Setup dialog box.

Table 1-11 Quarterly Personal Budget

	Jan – Mar	April – June	July – Sept	Oct – Dec
Car & Insurance	350	350	350	350
Clothes	275	330	300	350
Food	550	600	650	700
Misc.	257	147	185	234
Rent	400	400	400	400
Utilities	100	90	150	125

2 You are employed by the Jazz Music Company. The president of the company has asked you to prepare a worksheet to help her analyze monthly sales by store and by type of jazz music (Table 1-12). Use the concepts and techniques presented in this project to create the worksheet and an embedded Clustered bar chart with a 3-D visual effect. If necessary, reduce the size of the font in the chart so that each category name appears on the horizontal axis (x-axis).

Table 1-12 Jazz Music Company Monthly Sales

	Chicago	Kansas City	New Orleans	San Fransisco
Bebop	8234	9221	6201	8343
Chicago Style	6223	3213	7291	7182
Cool	4295	9261	8102	6109
Fusion	7989	6271	10237	8210
New Orleans Style	9120	8106	7182	4510
Swing	3134	3409	4520	3250
Work Song	3562	2501	7810	8193

Cases and Places

3 Arnold's Five Star Health Club on State Street in Chicago offers membership to an exclusive clientele. The company is trying to decide whether it is feasible to open another health club in the Chicago area. You have been asked to develop a worksheet totaling all the revenue received last year from customers living in the Chicago area. The revenue from customers living in the Chicago area by quarter is: Quarter 1, $550,400.25; Quarter 2, $391,503.77; Quarter 3, $456,333.43; and Quarter 4, $562,561.75. Create a pie chart with a 3-D visual effect to illustrate Chicago-area revenue contribution by quarter. Use the AutoCalculate area to find the average, maximum, and minimum quarterly revenue and manually enter them and their corresponding identifiers in an empty area on the worksheet.

4 The Central High School Drama Club is planning its annual play, which runs for seven days. This year, they plan to produce *It's a Wonderful Life*. The play runs weekday evenings, weekend matinees, and weekend evenings. Three types of tickets are sold at each presentation: general admission, senior citizen, and children. The Drama Club advisor has asked you to prepare a worksheet, based on the revenue from last year's run that can be used to reevaluate its ticket structure. Last year, weekday evening showings generated $1,225 from general admission ticket sales, $1,315 from senior citizen ticket sales, and $1,575 from children ticket sales. Weekend matinee showings made $3,223 from general admission ticket sales, $1,850 from senior citizen ticket sales, and $1,250 from children ticket sales. Weekend evening shows earned $3,215 from general admission ticket sales, $2,723 from senior citizen ticket sales, and $1,546 from children ticket sales. Use the concepts and techniques presented in this project to prepare a worksheet that includes total revenues for each type of ticket and for each presentation time, and a 3-D pie chart that shows the revenue contributions for general admissions, senior citizens, and children.

5 **Working Together** Visit the registrar's office at your local community college and obtain data, such as age, gender, and resident status, for the students majoring in at least five different academic departments this semester. Have each member of your team divide the data into different categories. For example, separate the data by:

1. Age, divided into four different age groups
2. Gender, divided into male and female
3. Resident status, divided into resident and nonresident

After coordinating the data as a group, have each member independently use the concepts and techniques presented in this project to create a worksheet and appropriate chart to show the total students by characteristics by academic department. As a group, critique each worksheet and have each member modify his or her worksheet based on the group recommendations. Hand in printouts of your original worksheet and final worksheet.

MICROSOFT OFFICE

Excel 2003

Formulas, Functions, Formatting, and Web Queries

PROJECT

2

CASE PERSPECTIVE

Tom and Emma Smith own and operate The Awesome Music Store where your friend Carlos Blanco works part time after school. The store, located near the town's high school, sells CDs, DVDs, players, electronic games, and audio accessories. The in-store café with hotspot service has been especially popular with younger customers.

Because of the Smiths' success, they have decided to expand their business by adding a second store in a neighboring town. At the same time, they plan to begin selling their products on the Web.

Tom and Emma recently visited the loan department of the local savings and loan association. The loan officer recommended that the Smiths computerize their payroll before proceeding with their expansion plans. They learned through Carlos that you are taking a Microsoft Office class and have asked if you would be interested in creating a payroll worksheet similar to the one shown in Figure 2-1a. After meeting with Tom and Emma you decide to take on the project.

Tom also invests in the stock market and recently learned that you can use Excel to access real-time stock quotes over the Internet (Figure 2-1b). As a sideline to the payroll project, he wants you to show him how to e-mail attachments from within Excel and how to use Excel to access the real-time stock quotes for General Electric, Intel, Kimberly Clark, Merck, Microsoft, and United Parcel Service.

As you read through this project, you will learn how to enter formulas and functions, how to improve the appearance of a worksheet, how to perform Web queries, and how to e-mail from within Excel.

Formulas, Functions, Formatting, and Web Queries

PROJECT

Objectives

You will have mastered the material in this project when you can:

- Enter formulas using the keyboard and Point mode
- Recognize smart tags and option buttons
- Apply the AVERAGE, MAX, and MIN functions
- Verify a formula using Range Finder
- Format a worksheet using buttons and commands
- Add conditional formatting to a range of cells
- Change the width of a column and height of a row
- Check the spelling of a worksheet
- Preview how a printed copy of the worksheet will look
- Print a partial or complete worksheet
- Display and print the formulas version of a worksheet
- Use a Web query to get real-time data from a Web site
- Rename sheets in a workbook
- E-mail the active workbook from within Excel

Introduction

In Project 1, you learned how to enter data, sum values, format the worksheet to make it easier to read, and draw a chart. You also learned about online Help and saving, printing, and opening a workbook. This project continues to emphasize these topics and presents some new ones.

The new topics covered in this project include using formulas and functions to create the worksheet shown in Figure 2-1a. Other new topics include smart tags and option buttons, verifying formulas, adding borders, formatting numbers and text, using conditional formatting, changing the widths of columns and heights of rows, spell checking, e-mailing from within an application, renaming worksheets, and using alternative types of worksheet displays and printouts. One alternative worksheet display and printout shows the formulas in the worksheet, instead of the values. When you display the formulas in the worksheet, you see exactly what text, data, formulas, and functions you have entered into it. Finally, this project covers Web queries to obtain real-time data from a Web site (Figure 2-1b).

(a) Worksheet

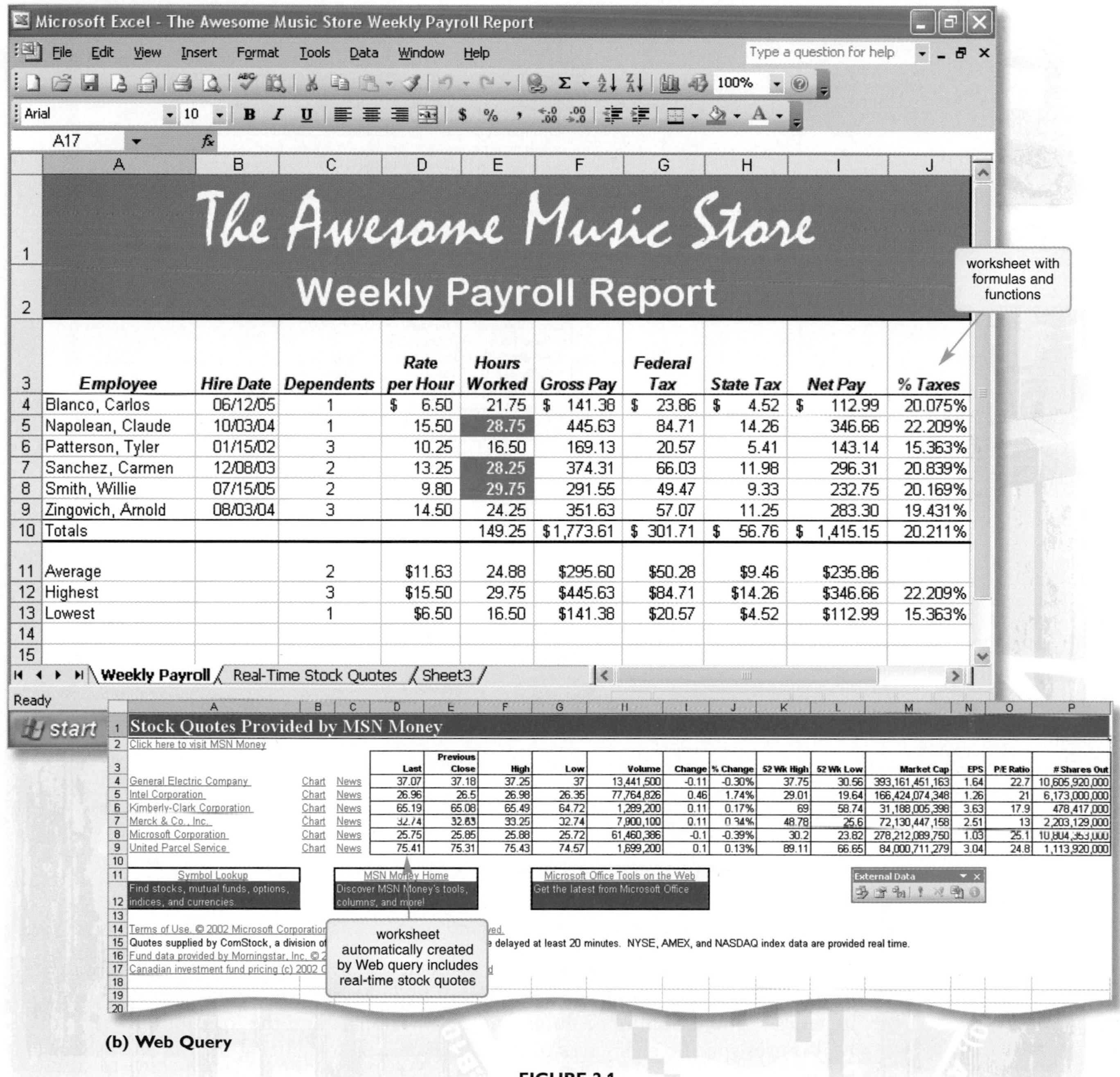

	Employee	Hire Date	Dependents	Rate per Hour	Hours Worked	Gross Pay	Federal Tax	State Tax	Net Pay	% Taxes
4	Blanco, Carlos	06/12/05	1	$ 6.50	21.75	$ 141.38	$ 23.86	$ 4.52	$ 112.99	20.075%
5	Napolean, Claude	10/03/04	1	15.50	28.75	445.63	84.71	14.26	346.66	22.209%
6	Patterson, Tyler	01/15/02	3	10.25	16.50	169.13	20.57	5.41	143.14	15.363%
7	Sanchez, Carmen	12/08/03	2	13.25	28.25	374.31	66.03	11.98	296.31	20.839%
8	Smith, Willie	07/15/05	2	9.80	29.75	291.55	49.47	9.33	232.75	20.169%
9	Zingovich, Arnold	08/03/04	3	14.50	24.25	351.63	57.07	11.25	283.30	19.431%
10	Totals				149.25	$1,773.61	$ 301.71	$ 56.76	$ 1,415.15	20.211%
11	Average		2	$11.63	24.88	$295.60	$50.28	$9.46	$235.86	
12	Highest		3	$15.50	29.75	$445.63	$84.71	$14.26	$346.66	22.209%
13	Lowest		1	$6.50	16.50	$141.38	$20.57	$4.52	$112.99	15.363%

	Company			Last	Previous Close	High	Low	Volume	Change	% Change	52 Wk High	52 Wk Low	Market Cap	EPS	P/E Ratio	# Shares Out
4	General Electric Company	Chart	News	37.07	37.18	37.25	37	13,441,500	-0.11	-0.30%	37.75	30.56	393,161,451,163	1.64	22.7	10,605,920,000
5	Intel Corporation	Chart	News	26.96	26.5	26.98	26.35	77,764,826	0.46	1.74%	29.01	19.64	166,424,074,348	1.26	21	6,173,000,000
6	Kimberly-Clark Corporation	Chart	News	65.19	65.08	65.49	64.72	1,289,200	0.11	0.17%	69	58.74	31,188,005,398	3.63	17.9	478,417,000
7	Merck & Co., Inc.	Chart	News	32.74	32.83	33.25	32.74	7,900,100	0.11	0.34%	48.78	25.6	72,130,447,158	2.51	13	2,203,129,000
8	Microsoft Corporation	Chart	News	25.75	25.85	25.88	25.72	61,460,386	-0.1	-0.39%	30.2	23.82	278,212,089,750	1.03	25.1	10,804,353,000
9	United Parcel Service	Chart	News	75.41	75.31	75.43	74.57	1,699,200	0.1	0.13%	89.11	66.65	84,000,711,279	3.04	24.8	1,113,920,000

(b) Web Query

FIGURE 2-1

Project Two — The Awesome Music Store Weekly Payroll Report

Recall that the first step in creating an effective worksheet is to make sure you understand what is required. Requirements usually are provided by the people who will use the worksheet. The requirements document for The Awesome Music Store Weekly Payroll Report worksheet includes the following: needs, source of data, summary of calculations, Web requirements, and other facts about its development (Figure 2-2 on the next page).

REQUEST FOR NEW WORKSHEET

Date Submitted:	November 28, 2007
Submitted By:	Tom and Emma Smith
Worksheet Title:	The Awesome Music Music Store Weekly Payroll Report
Needs:	An easy-to-read worksheet that summarizes the weekly payroll investments (Figure 2-3). For each employee, the worksheet is to include the employee name, hire date, dependents, hourly rate of pay, hours worked, gross pay, federal tax, state tax, net pay, and percent of gross pay that went to taxes. Also include totals and the average, highest value, and lowest value for each column of numbers. Use the import data capabilities of Excel to access real-time stock quotes using Web queries.
Source of Data:	The data supplied by Emma includes the employee name, hire date, dependents, hourly rate of pay, and hours worked. This data is shown in Table 2-1 on page EX 71.
Calculations:	The following calculations must be made for each of the stocks: 1. Gross Pay = Rate per Hour *Hours Worked 2. Fed. Tax = 20% * (Gross Pay – Dep. * 22.09) 3. State Tax = 3.2% * Gross Pay 4. Net Pay = Gross Pay – (Fed. Tax + State Tax) 5. % Taxes = (Fed. Tax + State Tax) / Gross Pay 6. Compute the totals for hours worked, gross pay, federal tax, state tax, net pay, percent of gross pay that went to taxes. 7. Use the AVERAGE function to determine the average for the dependents, hourly rate of pay, hours worked, gross pay, federal tax, state tax, and net pay. 8. Use the MAX and MIN functions to determine the highest and lowest values for the dependents, hourly rate of pay, hours worked, gross pay, federal tax, state tax, net pay, and percent of gross pay that went to taxes.
Special Requirements:	Highlight an employee's hours worked if the hours worked exceeds 25.
Web Requirements:	Use the Web query feature of Excel to get real-time stock quotes for General Electric, Intel, Kimberly Clark, Merck, Microsoft, and United Parcel Service.

Approvals

Approval Status:	X	Approved
		Rejected
Approved By:	J. Quasney	
Date:	December 3, 2007	
Assigned To:	J. Quasney, Spreadsheet Specialist	

FIGURE 2-2

Q & A

Q: Which comes first in designing a worksheet, functional considerations or aesthetics?

A: In designing a worksheet, functional considerations should come first, before visual aesthetics. The function, or purpose, of a worksheet is to provide a user with direct ways to accomplish tasks. Avoid the temptation to use flashy or confusing visual elements within the worksheet, unless they will help the user more easily complete a task.

In addition, using a sketch of the worksheet can help you visualize its design. The sketch for The Awesome Music Store Weekly Payroll Report worksheet (Figure 2-3) includes a title, a subtitle, column and row headings, and the location of data values. It also uses specific characters to define the desired formatting for the worksheet as follows:

1. The row of Xs below the leftmost column defines the cell entries as text, such as employee names.
2. The rows of Zs and 9s with slashes, dollar signs, decimal points, commas, and percent signs in the remaining columns define the cell entries as numbers. The Zs indicate that the selected format should instruct Excel to suppress leading 0s. The 9s indicate that the selected format should instruct Excel to display any digits, including 0s.

3. The decimal point means that a decimal point should appear in the cell entry and indicates the number of decimal places to use.
4. The commas indicate that the selected format should instruct Excel to display a comma separator only if the number has enough digits to the left of the decimal point.
5. The slashes in the second column identify the cell entry as a date.
6. The dollar signs that are not adjacent to the Zs in the first row below the column headings and in the total row signify a fixed dollar sign. The dollar signs that are adjacent to the Zs below the total row signify a floating dollar sign, or one that appears next to the first significant digit.
7. The percent sign (%) in the far right column indicates a percent sign should appear after the number.

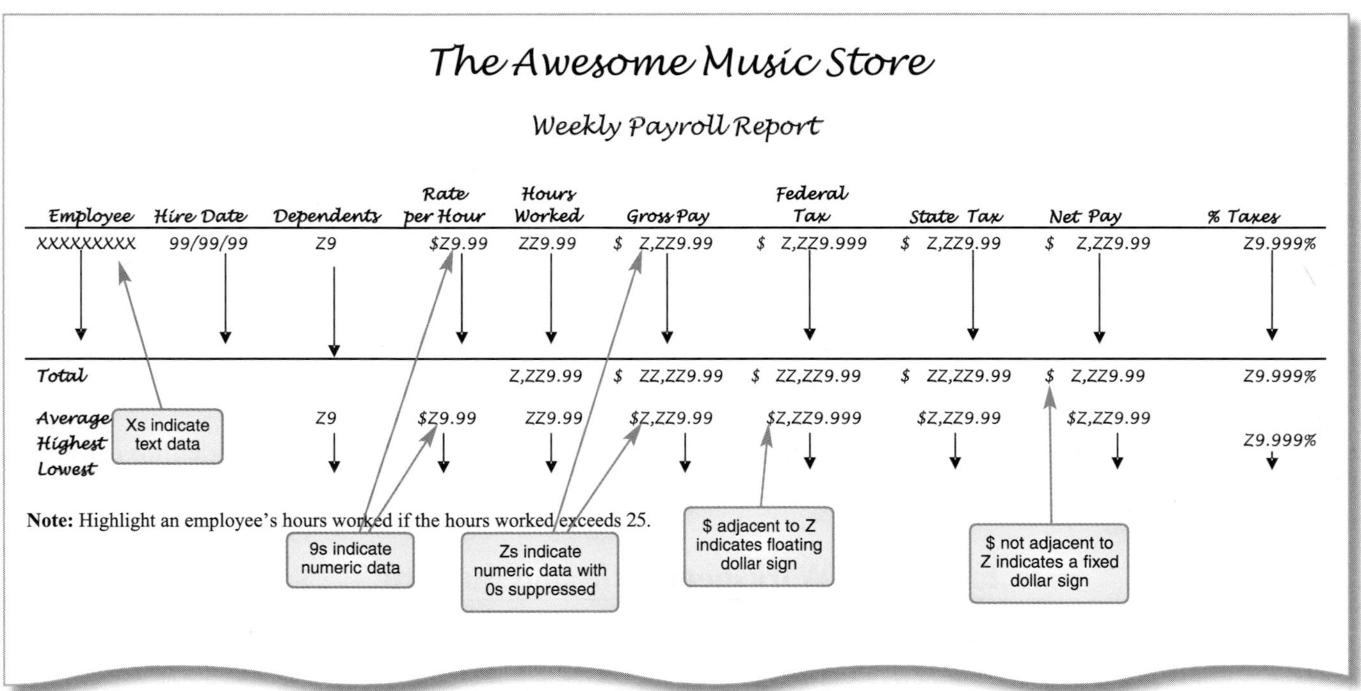

FIGURE 2-3

The real-time stock quotes (shown in Figure 2-1b on page EX 67) will be accessed via a Web query. The stock quotes will be returned to the active workbook on a separate worksheet. Microsoft determines the content and format of the Real-Time Stock Quotes worksheet.

Starting and Customizing Excel

With the requirements document and sketch of the worksheet complete, the next step is to use Excel to create the worksheet. To start and customize Excel, Windows must be running. If you are stepping through this project on a computer and you want your screen to match the figures in this book, then you should change your computer's resolution to 800 × 600. For more information on how to change the resolution on your computer, see Appendix B. The steps on the next page start Excel and customize the Excel window.

To Start and Customize Excel

1. **Click the Start button on the Windows taskbar, point to All Programs on the Start menu, point to Microsoft Office on the All Programs submenu, and then click Microsoft Office Excel 2003 on the Microsoft Office submenu.**
2. **If the Excel window is not maximized, double-click its title bar to maximize it.**
3. **If the Language bar appears, right-click it and then click Close the Language bar on the shortcut menu.**
4. **If the Getting Started task pane appears in the Excel window, click its Close button in the upper-right corner.**
5. **If the Standard and Formatting toolbars are positioned on the same row, click the Toolbar Options button and then click Show Buttons on Two Rows.**

The Excel window with the Standard and Formatting toolbars on two rows appears as shown in Figure 2-1a on page EX 67.

After the Excel window is opened, Steps 3 through 5 close the Getting Started task pane, close the Language bar, and ensure that the Standard and Formatting toolbars appear on two rows.

Entering the Titles and Numbers into the Worksheet

The following steps show how to enter the worksheet title and subtitle into cells A1 and A2.

To Enter the Worksheet Title and Subtitle

1. **Select cell A1. Type** `The Awesome Music Store` **in the cell and then press the DOWN ARROW key.**
2. **Type** `Weekly Payroll Report` **in cell A2 and then press the DOWN ARROW key.**

Excel displays the worksheet title in cell A1 and the worksheet subtitle in cell A2, as shown in Figure 2-4 on page EX 73.

The column titles in row 3 begin in cell A3 and extend through cell J3. The column titles in Figure 2-3 include multiple lines of text. To start a new line in a cell, press ALT+ENTER after each line, except for the last line, which is completed by clicking the Enter box, pressing the ENTER key, or pressing one of the arrow keys. When you see ALT+ENTER in a step, press the ENTER key while holding down the ALT key and then release both keys.

The employee names and the row titles Totals, Average, Highest, and Lowest in the leftmost column begin in cell A4 and continue down to cell A13.

The payroll data is summarized in Table 2-1. This data is entered into rows 4 through 9 of the worksheet. The remainder of this section explains the steps required to enter the column titles, payroll data, and row titles as shown in Figure 2-4 and then save the workbook.

Table 2-1 The Awesome Music Store Weekly Payroll Data

Employee	Hire Date	Dependents	Rate Per Hour	Hours Worked
Blanco, Carlos	6/12/05	1	6.50	21.75
Napolean, Claude	10/3/04	1	15.50	28.75
Patterson, Tyler	1/15/02	3	10.25	16.50
Sanchez, Carmen	12/8/03	2	13.25	28.25
Smith, Willie	7/15/05	2	9.80	29.75
Zingovich, Arnold	8/3/04	3	14.50	24.25

To Enter the Column Titles

1. **With cell A3 selected, type** `Employee` **and then press the RIGHT ARROW key.**
2. **Type** `Hire Date` **in cell B3 and then press the RIGHT ARROW key.**
3. **In cell C3, type** `Dependents` **and then press the RIGHT ARROW key.**
4. **In cell D3, type** `Rate` **and then press ALT+ENTER. Type** `per Hour` **and then press the RIGHT ARROW key.**
5. **In cell E3, type** `Hours` **and then press ALT+ENTER. Type** `Worked` **and then press the RIGHT ARROW key.**
6. **Type** `Gross Pay` **in cell F3 and then press the RIGHT ARROW key.**
7. **In cell G3, type** `Federal` **and then press ALT+ENTER. Type** `Tax` **and then press the RIGHT ARROW key.**
8. **Type** `State Tax` **in cell H3 and then press the RIGHT ARROW key.**
9. **In cell I3, type** `Net Pay` **and then press the RIGHT ARROW key.**
10. **In cell J3, type** `% Taxes` **and then click cell A4.**

The column titles appear as shown in row 3 of Figure 2-4 on page EX 73. When you press ALT+ENTER to add more lines to a cell, Excel automatically increases the height of the entire row.

The payroll data in Table 2-1 includes a date on which each employee was hired. Excel considers a date to be a number and, therefore, it displays the date right-aligned in the cell. The steps on the next page describe how to enter the payroll data shown in Table 2-1.

Q & A

Q: Can text be wrapped in a cell in the same way it can be wrapped in Word?

A: Yes. If you have a long text entry, such as a paragraph, you can instruct Excel to wrap the text in a cell, rather than pressing ALT+ENTER to end a line. To wrap text, right-click in the cell, click Format Cells on the shortcut menu, click the Alignment tab, and then click Wrap text. Excel will increase the height of the cell automatically so the additional lines will fit. If you want to control where each line ends in the cell, rather than letting Excel wrap based on the cell width, however, then you must end each line with ALT+ENTER.

Q & A

Q: What rule does Excel use to determine the century from a two-digit year entry in a cell?

A: When you enter a two-digit year value, Excel changes a two-digit year less than 30 to 20xx and a two-digit year of 30 and greater to 19xx. Use four-digit years to ensure that Excel interprets year values the way you intend, if necessary.

To Enter the Payroll Data

1. **With cell A4 selected, type** `Blanco, Carlos` **and then press the RIGHT ARROW key.**
2. **Type** `6/12/05` **in cell B4 and then press the RIGHT ARROW key.**
3. **Type** `1` **in cell C4 and then press the RIGHT ARROW key.**
4. **Type** `6.50` **in cell D4 and then press the RIGHT ARROW key.**
5. **Type** `21.75` **in cell E4 and then click cell A5.**
6. **Enter the payroll data in Table 2-1 for the five remaining employees in rows 5 through 9.**

The payroll data appears in rows 4 through 9 as shown in Figure 2-4.

Q & A

Q: Should rows be skipped in a worksheet to add white space to improve readability?

A: No. With early worksheet programs, users often skipped rows to improve the appearance of the worksheet. With Excel it is not necessary to skip rows because you can increase row heights to add white space between information.

To Enter the Row Titles

1. **Click cell A10. Type** `Totals` **and then press the DOWN ARROW key. Type** `Average` **in cell A11 and then press the DOWN ARROW key.**
2. **Type** `Highest` **in cell A12 and then press the DOWN ARROW key. Type** `Lowest` **in cell A13 and then press the ENTER key. Click cell F4.**

The row titles appear in rows 10 through 13 as shown in Figure 2-4.

With the data entered into the worksheet, the next step is to save the workbook using the file name, The Awesome Music Store Weekly Payroll Report. As you are building a workbook, it is a good idea to save it often so that you do not lose your work if the computer is turned off or if you lose electrical power.

To Save the Workbook

1. **With a USB flash drive connected to one of the computer's USB ports, click the Save button on the Standard toolbar.**
2. **When Excel displays the Save As dialog box, type** `The Awesome Music Store Weekly Payroll Report` **in the File name text box.**
3. **If necessary, click UDISK 2.0 (F:) in the Save in list (your USB flash drive may have a different name and letter). Click the Save button in the Save As dialog box.**

Excel saves the workbook on the USB flash drive using the file name, The Awesome Music Store Weekly Payroll Report.

This concludes entering the data into the worksheet. After saving the file, the worksheet remains on the screen with the file name, The Awesome Music Store Weekly Payroll Report, on the title bar.

Entering Formulas

The gross pay for each employee, which appears in column F, is equal to the rate per hour in column D times the hours worked in column E. Thus, the gross pay for Carlos Blanco in cell F4 is obtained by multiplying 6.5 (cell D4) by 21.75 (cell E4).

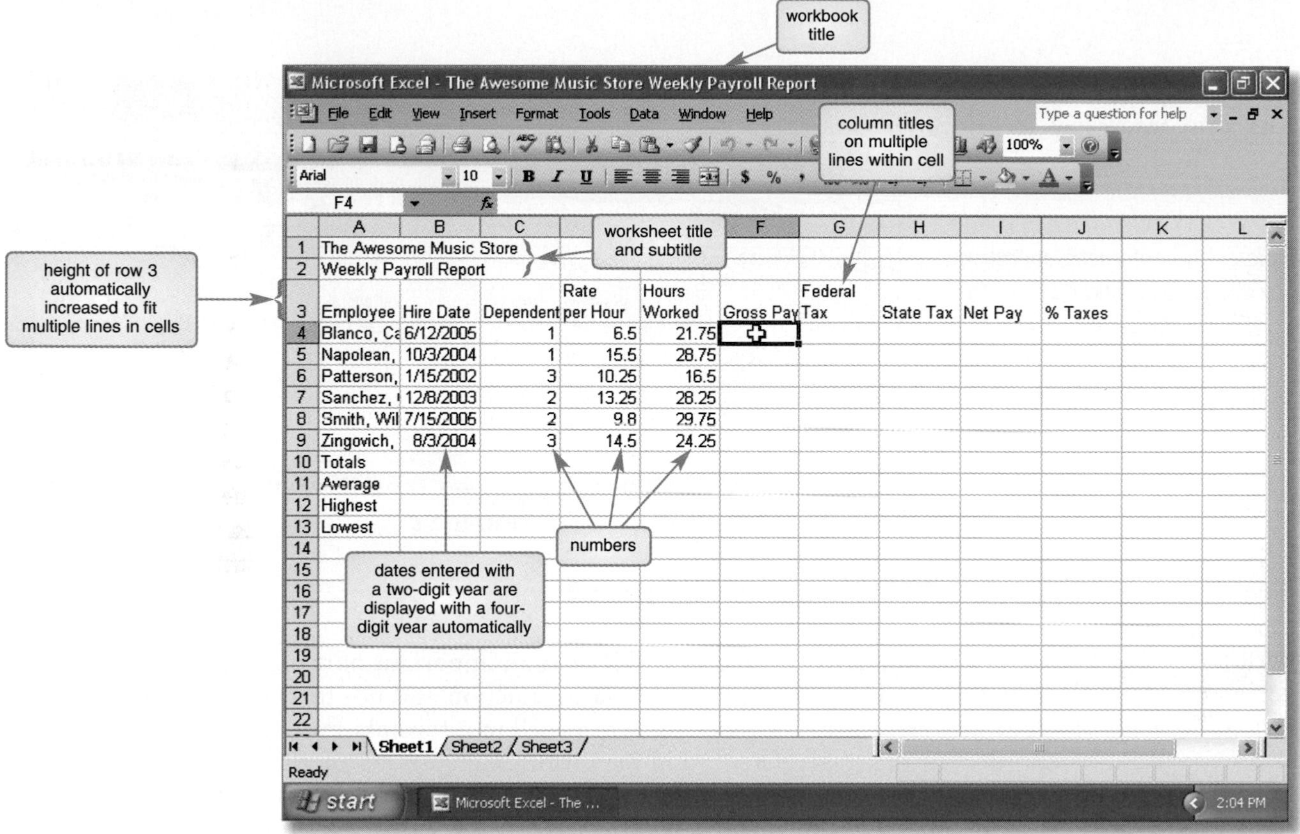

FIGURE 2-4

One of the reasons Excel is such a valuable tool is that you can assign a **formula** to a cell and Excel will calculate the result. Consider, for example, what would happen if you had to multiply 6.5 × 21.75 and then manually enter the product, 141.375, in cell F4. Every time the values in cells D4 or E4 changed, you would have to recalculate the product and enter the new value in cell F4. By contrast, if you enter a formula in cell F4 to multiply the values in cells D4 and E4, Excel recalculates the product whenever new values are entered into those cells and displays the result in cell F4. The following steps enter the gross pay formula in cell F4 using the keyboard.

To Enter a Formula Using the Keyboard

1

- **With cell F4 selected, type** `=d4*e4` **in the cell.**

Excel displays the formula in the formula bar and in cell F4 (Figure 2-5). Excel also displays colored borders around the cells referenced in the formula.

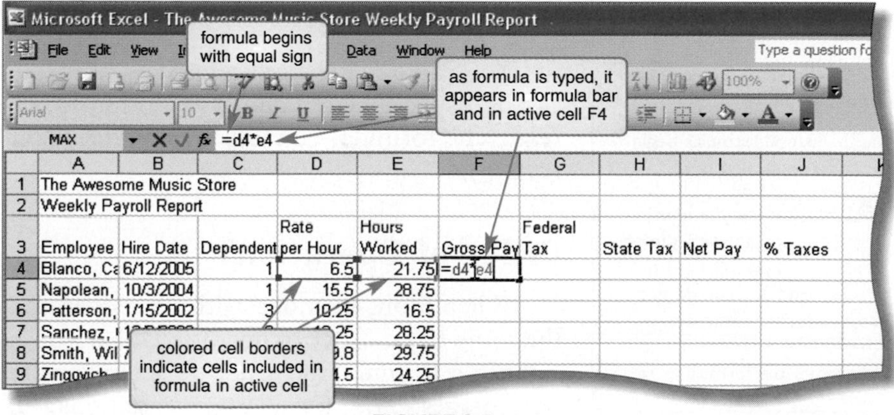

FIGURE 2-5

2

• **Press the RIGHT ARROW key to select cell G4.**

Instead of displaying the formula in cell F4, Excel completes the arithmetic operation indicated by the formula and displays the result, 141.375 (Figure 2-6).

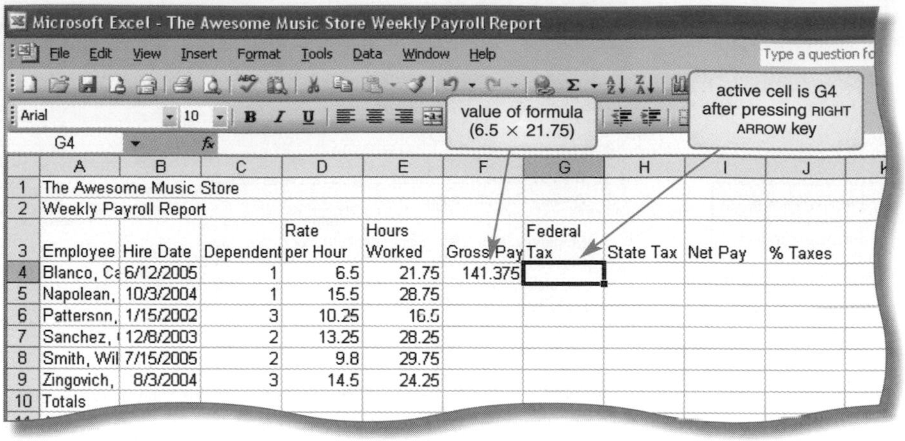

FIGURE 2-6

Q & A

Q: What is the difference between automatic and manual recalculation?

A: Every time you enter a value into a cell in the worksheet, Excel automatically recalculates all formulas. You can change to manual recalculation by clicking Options on the Tools menu and then clicking Manual on the Calculation sheet. In manual calculation mode, press F9 to instruct Excel to recalculate all formulas.

The **equal sign** (=) preceding d4*e4 is an important part of the formula: it alerts Excel that you are entering a formula or function and not text. Because the most common error is to reference the wrong cell in a formula mistakenly, Excel colors the borders of the cells referenced in the formula (Figure 2-5 on the previous page). The coloring helps in the reviewing process to ensure the cell references are correct. The **asterisk** (*) following d4 is the arithmetic operator that directs Excel to perform the multiplication operation. Table 2-2 describes multiplication and other valid Excel arithmetic operators.

Table 2-2 Summary of Arithmetic Operators

ARITHMETIC OPERATOR	MEANING	EXAMPLE OF USAGE	MEANING
–	Negation	–63	Negative 63
%	Percentage	=13%	Multiplies 13 by 0.01
^	Exponentiation	=5 ^ 2	Raises 5 to the second power
*	Multiplication	=17.5 * E4	Multiplies the contents of cell E4 by 17.5
/	Division	=A2 / A4	Divides the contents of cell A2 by the contents of cell A4
+	Addition	=4 + 8	Adds 4 and 8
–	Subtraction	=K15 – 13	Subtracts 13 from the contents of cell K15

Q & A

Q: Must all formulas begin with an equal sign?

A: No. Besides the equal sign (=), you can start a formula with a plus sign (+) or a minus sign (-). If you do not begin a formula with one of these three characters, Excel interprets the formula as text.

You can enter the cell references in formulas in uppercase or lowercase, and you can add spaces before and after arithmetic operators to make the formulas easier to read. The formula, =d4*e4, is the same as the formulas, =d4 * e4, =D4 * e4, or =D4 * E4.

Order of Operations

When more than one arithmetic operator is involved in a formula, Excel follows the same basic order of operations that you use in algebra. Moving from left to right in a formula, the **order of operations** is as follows: first negation (–), then all percentages (%), then all exponentiations (^), then all multiplications (*) and divisions (/), and finally, all additions (+) and subtractions (–).

You can use parentheses to override the order of operations. For example, if Excel follows the order of operations, 8 * 3 + 2 equals 26. If you use parentheses, however, to change the formula to 8 * (3 + 2), the result is 40, because the parentheses instruct Excel to add 3 and 2 before multiplying by 8. Table 2-3 illustrates several examples of valid Excel formulas and explains the order of operations.

Table 2-3 Examples of Excel Formulas

FORMULA	MEANING
=M5	Assigns the value in cell M5 to the active cell.
=12 + – 3^2	Assigns the sum of 12 + 9 (or 21) to the active cell.
=6 * E22 or =E22 * 6 or =(6 * E22)	Assigns six times the contents of cell E22 to the active cell.
=70% * 6	Assigns the product of 0.70 times 6 (or 4.2) to the active cell.
– (G7 * V67)	Assigns the negative value of the product of the values contained in cells G7 and V67 to the active cell.
=5 * (P4 – G4)	Assigns the product of five times the difference between the values contained in cells P4 and G4 to the active cell.
=K5 / Y7 – D6 * L9 + W4 ^ V10	Instructs Excel to complete the following arithmetic operations, from left to right: first exponentiation (W4 ^ V10), then division (K5 / Y7), then multiplication (D6 * L9), then subtraction (K5 / Y7) – (D6 * L9), and finally addition (K5 / Y7 – D6 * L9) + (W4 ^ V10). If cells K5 = 10, D6 = 6, L9 = 2, W4 = 5, V10 = 2, and Y7 = 2, then Excel assigns the active cell the value 18; that is, 10 / 2 – 6 * 2 + 5 ^ 2 = 18.

Entering Formulas Using Point Mode

The sketch of the worksheet in Figure 2-3 on page EX 69 calls for the federal tax, state tax, net pay, and % taxes for each employee to appear in columns G, H, I, and J, respectively. All four of these values are calculated using the following formulas in row 4:

Federal tax (cell G4) = 20% × (Gross Pay – Dependents × 22.09) or =20%*(F4-C4*22.09)

State Tax (cell H4) = 3.2% × Gross Pay or =3.2% * F4

Net Pay (cell I4) = Gross Pay – (Federal Tax + State Tax) or =F4 – (G4 + H4)

% Taxes (cell J4) = (Federal Tax + State Tax) / Gross Pay or =(G4 + H4) / F4

An alternative to entering the formulas in cells G4, H4, I4, and J4 using the keyboard is to enter the formulas using the mouse and Point mode. **Point mode** allows you to select cells for use in a formula by using the mouse. The following steps illustrate how to enter formulas using Point mode.

Q & A

Q: Can entire formulas, including arithmetic operators, be entered using Point mode?

A: You can enter arithmetic operators using the mouse and on-screen keyboard that is available through the Language bar (see Appendix B). Thus, with Excel, you can enter entire formulas without ever touching the keyboard.

To Enter Formulas Using Point Mode

1

- **With cell G4 selected, type** =20%*(**to begin the formula and then click cell F4.**

Excel surrounds cell F4 with a marquee and appends F4 to 20%(in cell G4 (Figure 2-7).*

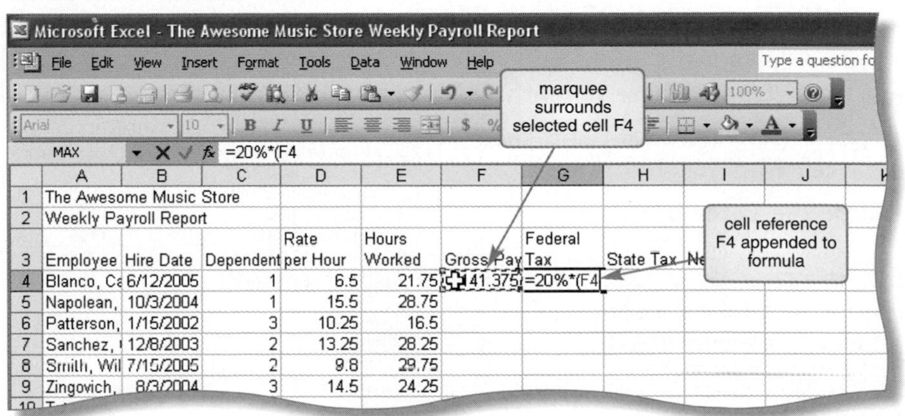

FIGURE 2-7

2

- **Type – (minus sign), click cell C4, and then type `*22.09)`.**

Excel surrounds C4 with a marquee and appends C4 to =20%(F4- followed by the *22.09).*

FIGURE 2-8

- **Click the Enter box and then click cell H4.**
- **Type `=3.2%*`, click cell F4, and then click the Enter box.**
- **Click cell I4, type = (equal sign), click cell F4, type `-(` (minus sign followed by left parenthesis), click cell G4, type + (plus sign), click cell H4, and then type) (close parenthesis).**

*Excel determines the result of the formula =3.2%*F4 and displays the result, 4.524, in cell H4. The formula =F4-(G4+H4) appears in cell I4 and in the formula bar (Figure 2-9).*

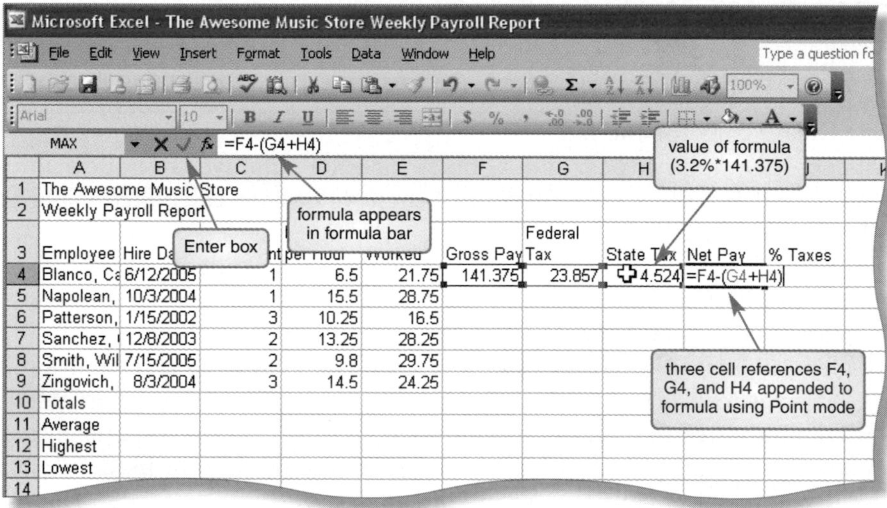

FIGURE 2-9

- **Click the Enter box, click cell J4, type `=(` (equal sign followed by left parenthesis), and then click cell G4.**
- **Type + (plus sign), click cell H4, and then type) (close parenthesis).**
- **Type / (forward slash) and then click cell F4.**
- **Click the Enter box.**

Excel calculates and then displays the net pay (112.994) in cell I4 and the percent of the gross pay paid to taxes (0.20075) for Carlos Blanco (Figure 2-10). The 0.20075 represents 20.075%.

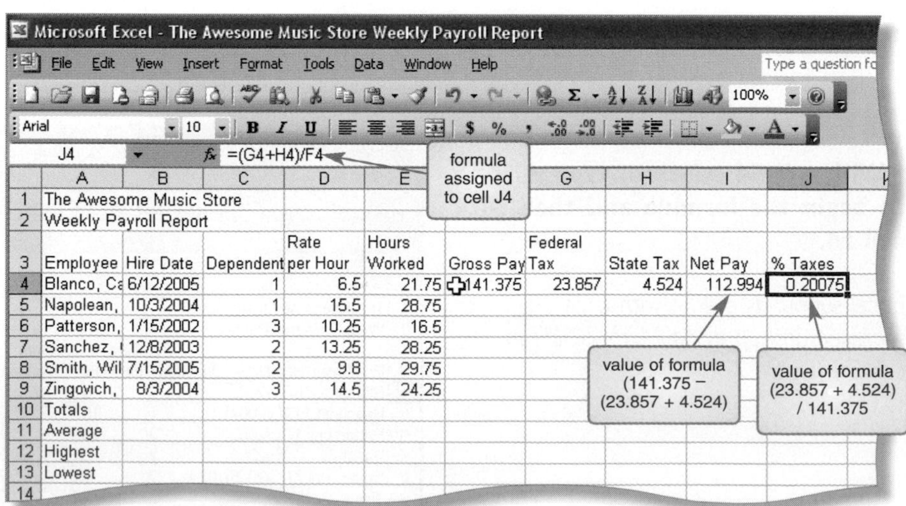

FIGURE 2-10

Depending on the length and complexity of the formula, using Point mode to enter formulas often is faster and more accurate than using the keyboard to type the entire formula. In many instances, as in the previous steps, you may want to use both the keyboard and mouse when entering a formula in a cell. You can use the keyboard to begin the formula, for example, and then use the mouse to select a range of cells.

The actual value assigned by Excel to cell J4 from the division operation in Step 4 is 0.200749779. While all the decimal places do not appear in Figure 2-10, Excel maintains all of them for computational purposes. Thus, if cell J4 is referenced in a formula, the value used for computational purposes is 0.200749779, not 0.20075. Excel displays the value in cell J4 as 0.20075 because the cell formatting is set to display only 6 digits after the decimal point. If you change the cell formatting of column J to display 15 digits after the decimal point, then Excel displays the true value 0.200749779. It is important to recognize this difference between the value Excel displays in a cell and the actual value to understand why the sum of data in a column sometimes is a tenth or hundredth off from the expected value.

Copying Formulas Using the Fill Handle

The five formulas for Carlos Blanco in cells F4, G4, H4, I4, and J4 now are complete. You could enter the same five formulas one at a time for the five remaining employees. A much easier method of entering the formulas, however, is to select the formulas in row 4 and then use the fill handle to copy them through row 9. Recall from Project 1 that the fill handle is a small rectangle in the lower-right corner of the active cell or active range. The following steps show how to copy the formulas using the fill handle.

To Copy Formulas Using the Fill Handle

1

- **Select the range F4:J4 and then point to the fill handle.**

A border surrounds the source area F4:J4 and the mouse pointer changes to a cross hair (Figure 2-11).

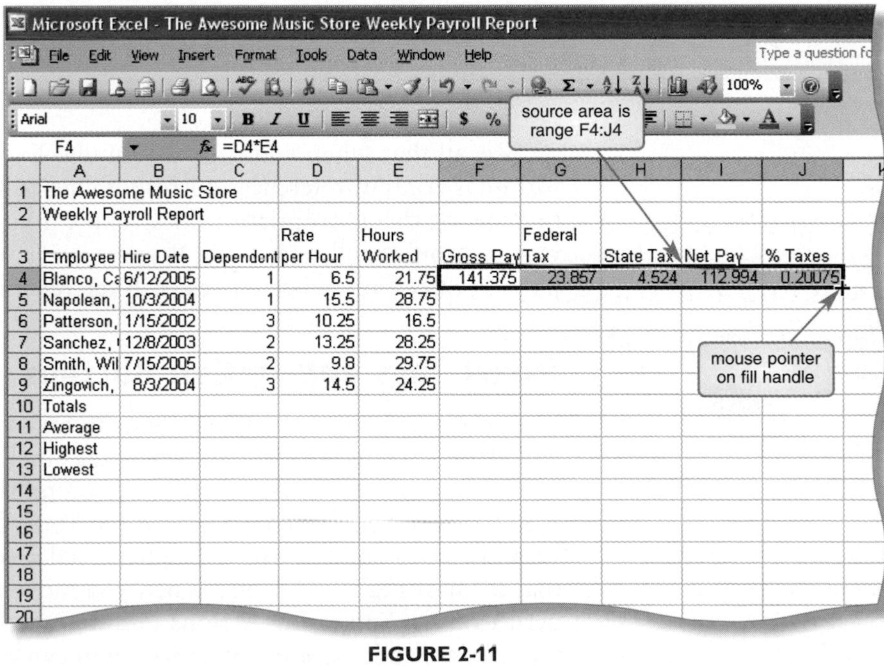

FIGURE 2-11

2

• **Drag the fill handle down through the range F5:J9.**

A border surrounds the source and destination areas (Figure 2-12).

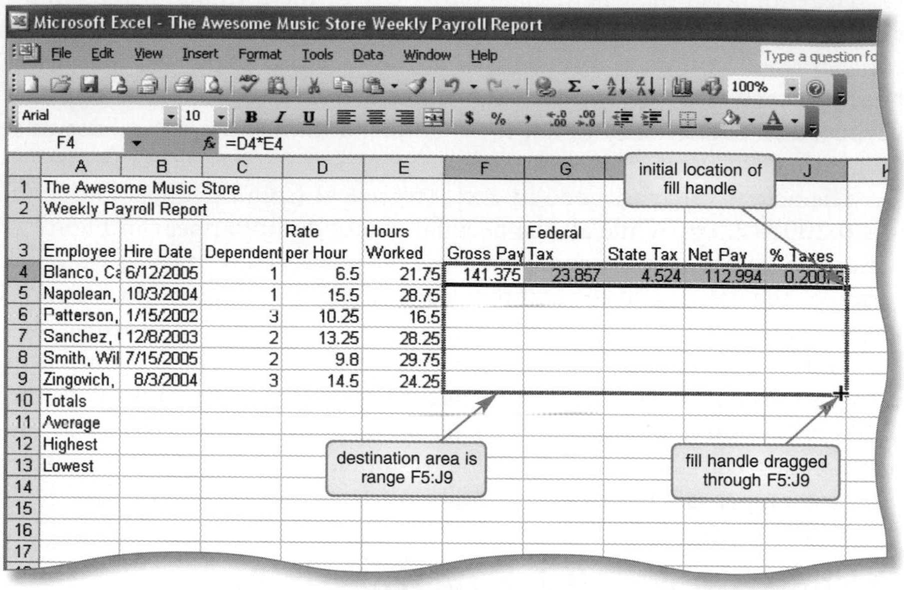

FIGURE 2-12

3

• **Release the mouse button.**

Excel copies the five formulas in the range F4:J4 to the range F5:J9 (Figure 2-13). The worksheet displays the payroll information for the six employees.

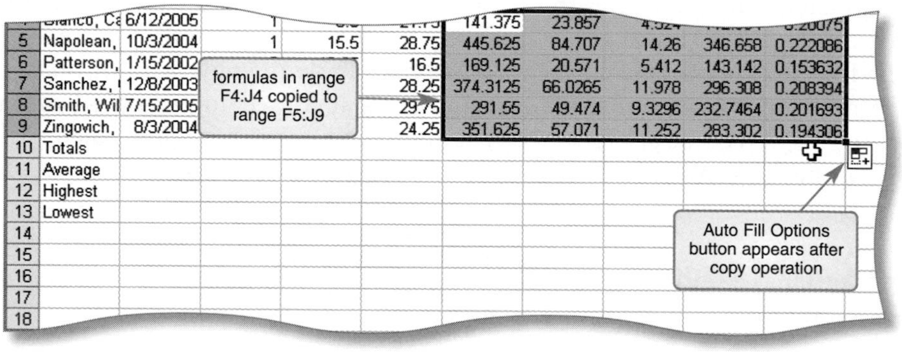

FIGURE 2-13

Recall that when you copy a formula, Excel adjusts the cell references so the new formulas contain references corresponding to the new location and performs calculations using the appropriate values. Thus, if you copy downward, Excel adjusts the row portion of cell references. If you copy across, then Excel adjusts the column portion of cell references. These cell references are called **relative references.**

Smart Tags and Option Buttons

Excel can identify certain actions to take on specific data in workbooks using **smart tags**. Data labeled with smart tags includes dates, financial symbols, people's names, and more. To use smart tags, you must turn on smart tags using the AutoCorrect Options command on the Tools menu. Once smart tags are turned on, Excel places a small purple triangle, called a **smart tag indicator**, in a cell to indicate that a smart tag is available. When you move the insertion point over the smart tag indicator, the Smart Tag Actions button appears. Clicking the Smart Tag Actions button arrow produces a list of actions you can perform on the data in that specific cell.

In addition to smart tags, Excel also displays Options buttons in a workbook while you are working on it to indicate that you can complete an operation using automatic features such as AutoCorrect, Auto Fill, error checking, and others. For example, the Auto Fill Options button shown in Figure 2-13 appears after a fill operation, such as dragging the fill handle. When an error occurs in a formula in a cell, Excel displays the Trace Error button next to the cell and identifies the cell with the error by placing a green triangle in the upper left of the cell.

Table 2-4 summarizes the smart tag and Options buttons available in Excel. When one of these buttons appears on your worksheet, click the button arrow to produce the list of options for modifying the operation or to obtain additional information.

Table 2-4 Smart Tag and Options Buttons in Excel

BUTTON	NAME	MENU FUNCTION
	Auto Fill Options	Gives options for how to fill cells following a fill operation, such as dragging the fill handle
	AutoCorrect Options	Undoes an automatic correction, stops future automatic corrections of this type, or causes Excel to display the AutoCorrect Options dialog box
	Insert Options	Lists formatting options following an insert of cells, rows, or columns
	Paste Options	Specifies how moved or pasted items should appear (for example, with original formatting, without formatting, or with different formatting)
	Smart Tag Actions	Lists information options for a cell containing data recognized by Excel, such as a stock symbol
	Trace Error	Lists error checking options following the assignment of an invalid formula to a cell

Determining Totals Using the AutoSum Button

The next step is to determine the totals in row 10 for the hours worked in column E, the gross pay in column F, the federal tax in column G, the state tax in column H, and the net pay in column I. To determine the total hours worked in column E, the values in the range E4 through E9 must be summed. To do so, enter the function =sum(e4:e9) in cell E10 or select cell E10 and then use the AutoSum button on the Standard toolbar. Similar SUM functions or the AutoSum button can be used in cells F10, G10, H13, and I10, respectively. Recall from Project 1 that when you select one cell and use the AutoSum button, you must click the AutoSum button twice. If you select a range, then you need to click the AutoSum button only once.

To Determine Totals Using the AutoSum Button

1 Select the range E10:I10 and then click the AutoSum button.

Excel displays the five totals in row 10 as shown in Figure 2-14.

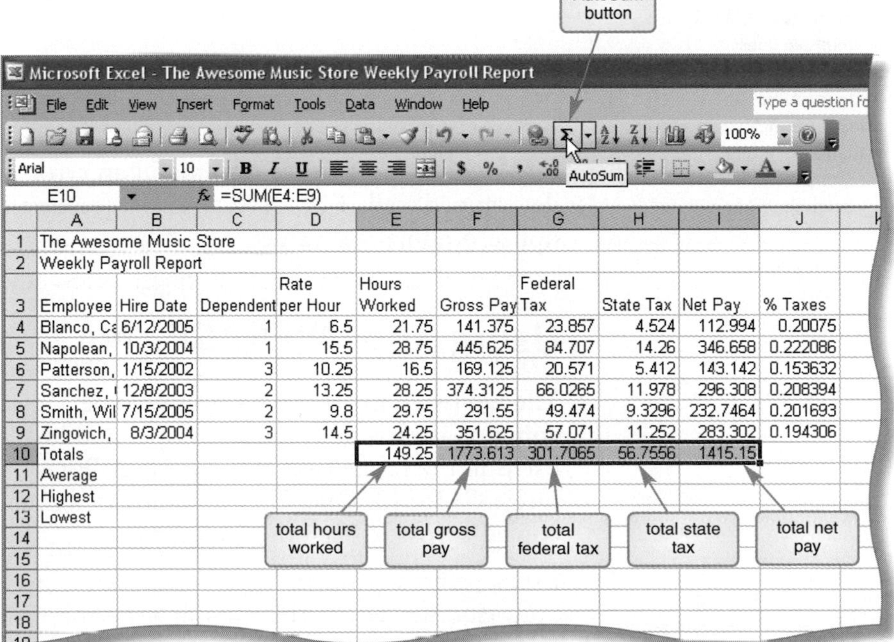

FIGURE 2-14

Determining the Total Percent Taxes

With the totals in row 10 determined, the next step is to copy the percent taxes formula in cell J9 to cell J10 as shown in the following steps.

To Determine the Total Percent Taxes

1 **Select cell J9 and then point to the fill handle.**

2 **Drag the fill handle down through cell J10.**

Excel copies the formula =(G9+H9)/F9 in cell J9 to cell J10 and then adjusts the row references. The resulting formula in cell J10 is =(G10+H10)/F10, which shows the percent of the total gross pay paid to taxes (Figure 2-15).

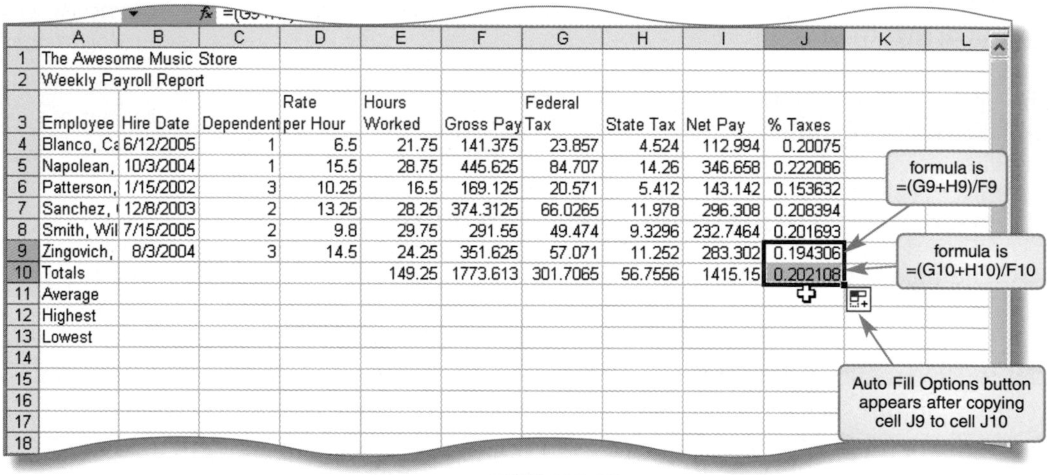

fx =(G9+H...

	A	B	C	D	E	F	G	H	I	J	K	L
1	The Awesome Music Store											
2	Weekly Payroll Report											
3	Employee	Hire Date	Dependent	Rate per Hour	Hours Worked	Gross Pay	Federal Tax	State Tax	Net Pay	% Taxes		
4	Blanco, Ca	6/12/2005	1	6.5	21.75	141.375	23.857	4.524	112.994	0.20075		
5	Napolean,	10/3/2004	1	15.5	28.75	445.625	84.707	14.26	346.658	0.222086		
6	Patterson,	1/15/2002	3	10.25	16.5	169.125	20.571	5.412	143.142	0.153632		
7	Sanchez,	12/8/2003	2	13.25	28.25	374.3125	66.0265	11.978	296.308	0.208394		
8	Smith, Wil	7/15/2005	2	9.8	29.75	291.55	49.474	9.3296	232.7464	0.201693		
9	Zingovich,	8/3/2004	3	14.5	24.25	351.625	57.071	11.252	283.302	0.194306		
10	Totals				149.25	1773.613	301.7065	56.7556	1415.15	0.202108		
11	Average											
12	Highest											
13	Lowest											
14												
15												
16												
17												
18												

formula is =(G9+H9)/F9

formula is =(G10+H10)/F10

Auto Fill Options button appears after copying cell J9 to cell J10

FIGURE 2-15

The formula, (G4+H4)/F4, was not copied to cell J10 when cell J4 was copied to the range J5:J10 because the three cells involved in the computation (F10, H10, and I10) were blank, or zero, at the time. A **blank cell** in Excel has a numerical value of zero, which would have resulted in an error message in cell J10. Once the totals were determined, cells F10, H10, and I10 (especially F10, because it is the divisor) had nonzero numerical values.

Using the AVERAGE, MAX, and MIN Functions

The next step in creating The Awesome Music Store Weekly Payroll Report is to compute the average, highest value, and lowest value for the number of dependents listed in the range C4:C9 using the AVERAGE, MAX, and MIN functions in the range C11:C13. Once the values are determined for column C, the entries can be copied across to the other columns.

Q & A

Q: Can a range be selected using the keyboard?

A: Yes. Press F8 and then use the arrow keys to select the desired range. After you are finished, make sure to press F8 to turn the selection off or you will continue to select ranges.

Q & A

Q: Is additional information available on entering formulas and functions?

A: For more information on entering formulas and functions, visit the Office 2003 Q&A Web page (scsite.com/off2003sch/qa), locate Excel Project 2, and click Formulas and Functions.

Skill Builder 2-1

To practice the following tasks, visit scsite.com/off2003sch/skill, locate Excel Project 2, and then click Skill Builder 2-1.

- ❑ Enter text in a cell on multiple lines
- ❑ Use arithmetic operators in formulas
- ❑ Use parentheses in a formula
- ❑ Enter formulas
- ❑ Copy multiple formulas using the fill handle

Excel includes prewritten formulas called functions to help you compute these statistics. A **function** takes a value or values, performs an operation, and returns a result to the cell. The values that you use with a function are called **arguments**. All functions begin with an equal sign and include the arguments in parentheses after the function name. For example, in the function =AVERAGE(C4:C9), the function name is AVERAGE, and the argument is the range C4:C9.

With Excel, you can enter functions using one of six methods: (1) the keyboard or mouse; (2) the Insert Function box in the formula bar; (3) the AutoSum button menu; (4) the Function command on the Insert menu; (5) the Name box area in the formula bar (Figure 2-16); and (6) Voice Command mode. The method you choose will depend on your typing skills and whether you can recall the function name and required arguments.

The following pages uses each of the first three methods. The keyboard and mouse method will be used to determine the average number of dependents (cell C11). The Insert Function button in the formula bar method will be used to determine the highest number of dependents (cell C12). The AutoSum button menu method will be used to determine the lowest number of dependents (cell C13).

Q & A

Q: How do the statistical functions handle a blank cell?

A: Excel usually considers a blank cell to be equal to 0. The statistical functions, however, ignore blank cells. Excel thus calculates the average of 3 cells with values of 7, blank, and 5 to be 6 or (7 + 5) / 2 and not 4 or (7 + 0 + 5) /3.

Determining the Average of a Range of Numbers

The **AVERAGE function** sums the numbers in the specified range and then divides the sum by the number of nonzero cells in the range. To determine the average of the numbers in the range C4:C9, use the AVERAGE function, as shown in the following steps.

To Determine the Average of a Range of Numbers Using the Keyboard and Mouse

- **Select cell C11.**
- **Type** =average(**in the cell.**
- **Click cell C4, the first endpoint of the range to average and drag through cell C9, the second endpoint of the range to average. Do not release the mouse button.**

A marquee surrounds the range C4:C9. When you click cell C4, Excel appends cell C4 to the left parenthesis in the formula bar and surrounds cell C4 with a marquee. When you begin dragging, Excel appends to the argument a colon (:) and the cell reference of the cell where the mouse pointer is located (Figure 2-16).

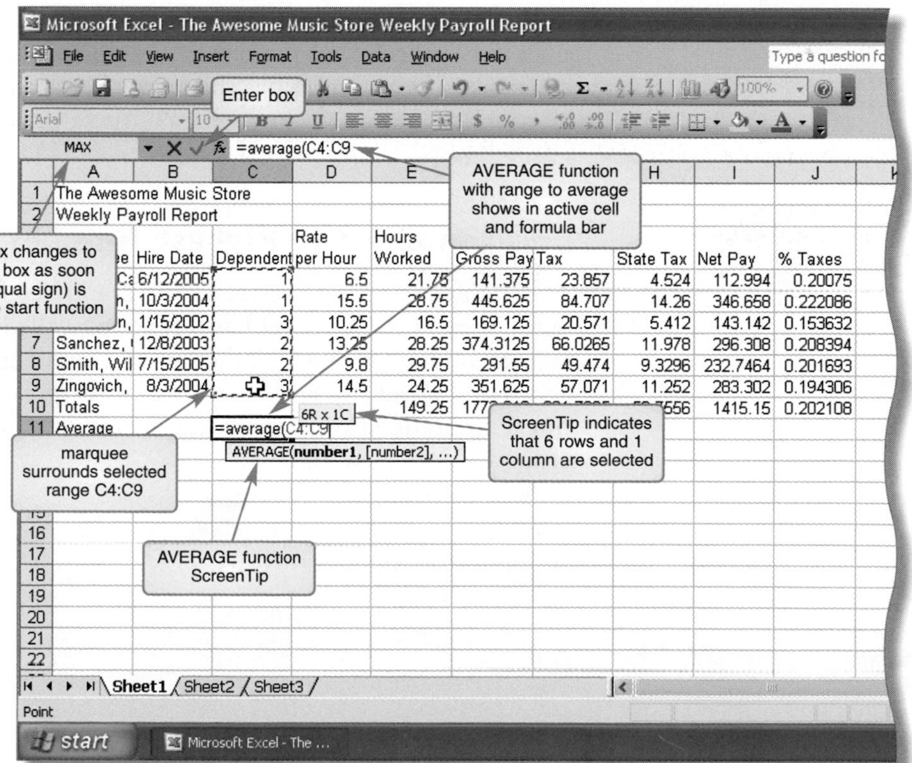

FIGURE 2-16

2

• **Release the mouse button and then click the Enter box.**

Excel computes the average of the six numbers in the range C4:C9 and displays the result, 2, in cell C11 (Figure 2-17). Thus, the average number of dependents for the six employees is 2.

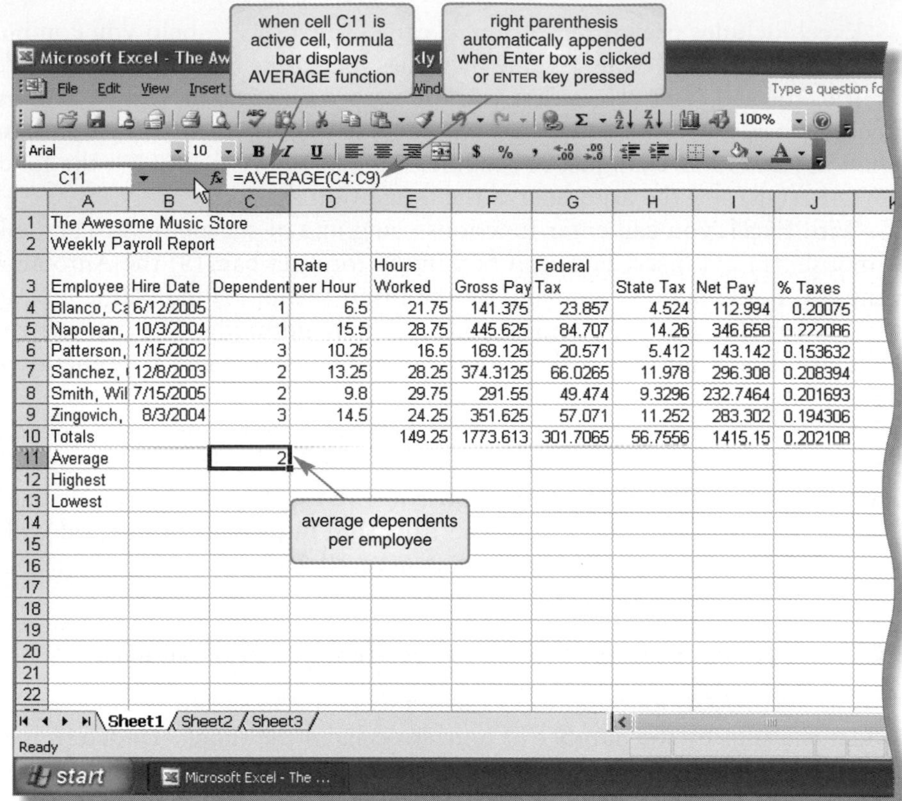

FIGURE 2-17

The AVERAGE function requires that the argument (in this case, the range C4:C9) be included within parentheses following the function name. Excel automatically appends the right parenthesis to complete the AVERAGE function when you click the Enter box or press the ENTER key. When you use Point mode, as in the previous steps, you cannot use the arrow keys to complete the entry. While in Point mode, the arrow keys change the selected cell reference in the range you are selecting.

Determining the Highest Number in a Range of Numbers

The next step is to select cell C12 and determine the highest (maximum) number in the range C4:C9. Excel has a function called the **MAX function** that displays the highest value in a range. Although you could enter the MAX function using the keyboard and Point mode as described in the previous steps, an alternative method to entering the function is to use the Insert Function box in the formula bar, as shown in the following steps.

To Determine the Highest Number in a Range of Numbers Using the Insert Function Box

1

- **Select cell C12.**
- **Click the Insert Function box in the formula bar.**
- **When Excel displays the Insert Function dialog box, click MAX in the Select a function list.**

Excel displays the Insert Function dialog box (Figure 2-18).

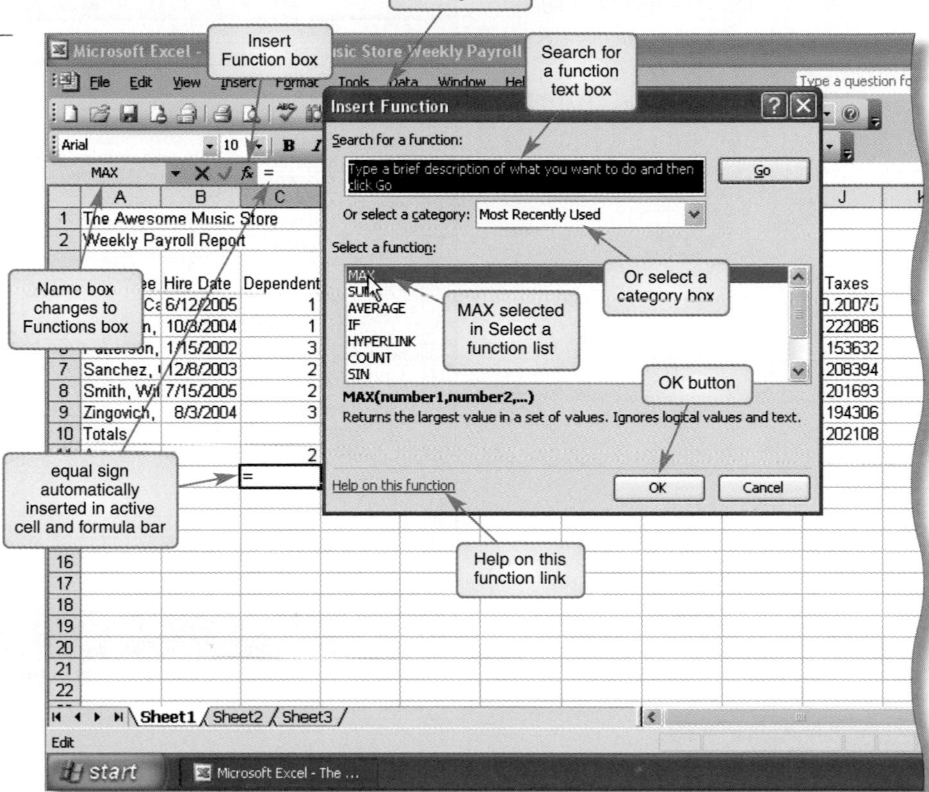

FIGURE 2-18

2

- **Click the OK button.**
- **When Excel displays the Function Arguments dialog box, type** `c4:c9` **in the Number 1 box.**

Excel displays the Function Arguments dialog box with the range c4:c9 entered in the Number 1 box (Figure 2-19). The completed MAX function appears in the formula bar, and the last part of the function appears in the active cell, C12.

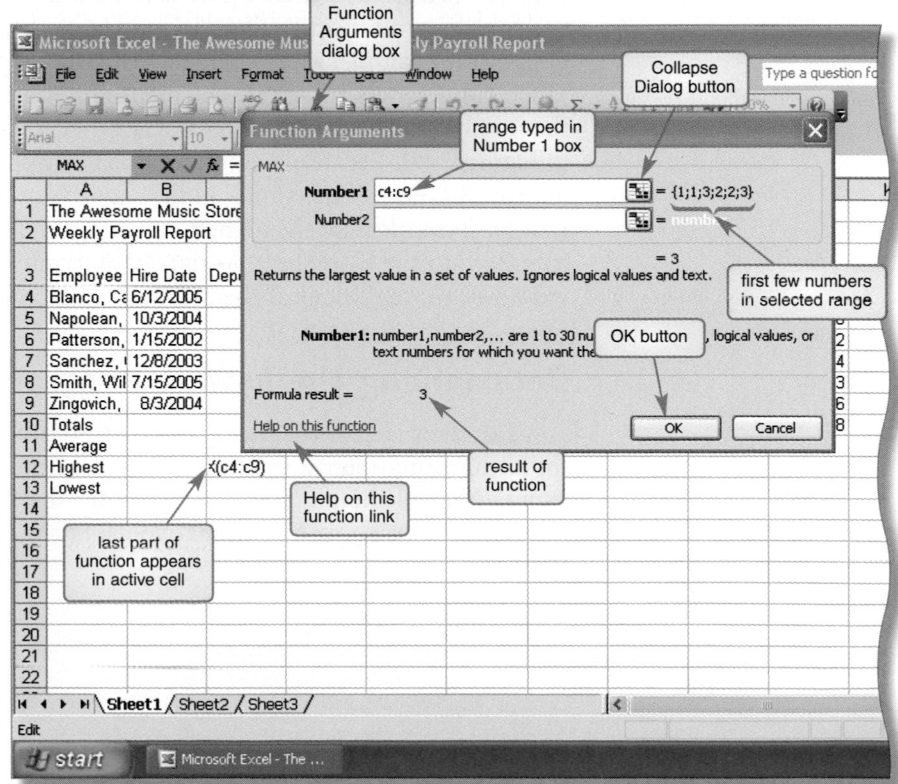

FIGURE 2-19

3

- **Click the OK button.**

Excel determines that the highest value in the range C4:C9 is 3 (value in cells C6 and C9) and displays it in cell C12 (Figure 2-20).

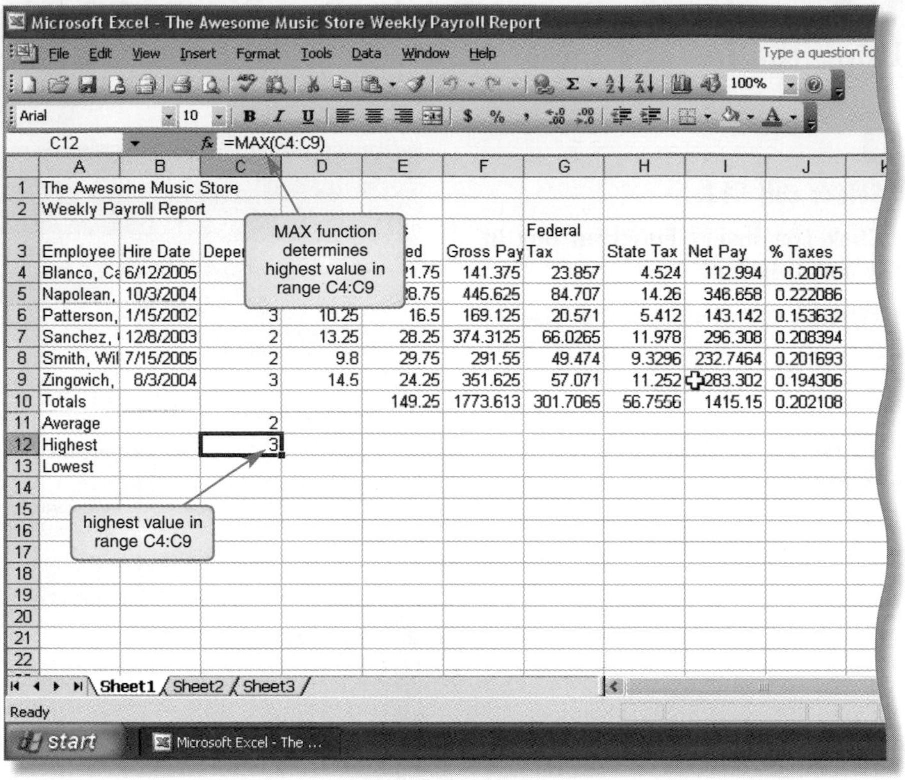

FIGURE 2-20

As shown in Figure 2-19 on the previous page, Excel displays the value the MAX function will return to cell C12 in the Function Arguments dialog box. It also lists the first few numbers in the selected range, next to the Number 1 box.

In this example, rather than entering the MAX function, you easily could scan the range C4:C9, determine that the highest number of dependents is 3, and manually enter the number 3 as a constant in cell C12. Excel would display the number the same as in Figure 2-20. Because it contains a constant, however, Excel will continue to display 3 in cell C12, even if the values in the range C4:C9 change. If you use the MAX function, Excel will recalculate the highest value in the range C4:C9 each time a new value is entered into the worksheet. Manually determining the highest value in the range also would be more difficult if the company had more employees.

Determining the Lowest Number in a Range of Numbers

The next step is to enter the **MIN function** in cell C13 to determine the lowest (minimum) number in the range C4:C9. Although you can enter the MIN function using either of the methods used to enter the AVERAGE and MAX functions, the following steps show an alternative using the AutoSum button menu on the Standard toolbar.

To Determine the Lowest Number in a Range of Numbers Using the AutoSum Button Menu

1

- **Select cell C13.**
- **Click the AutoSum button arrow on the Standard toolbar.**

Excel displays the AutoSum button menu (Figure 2-21).

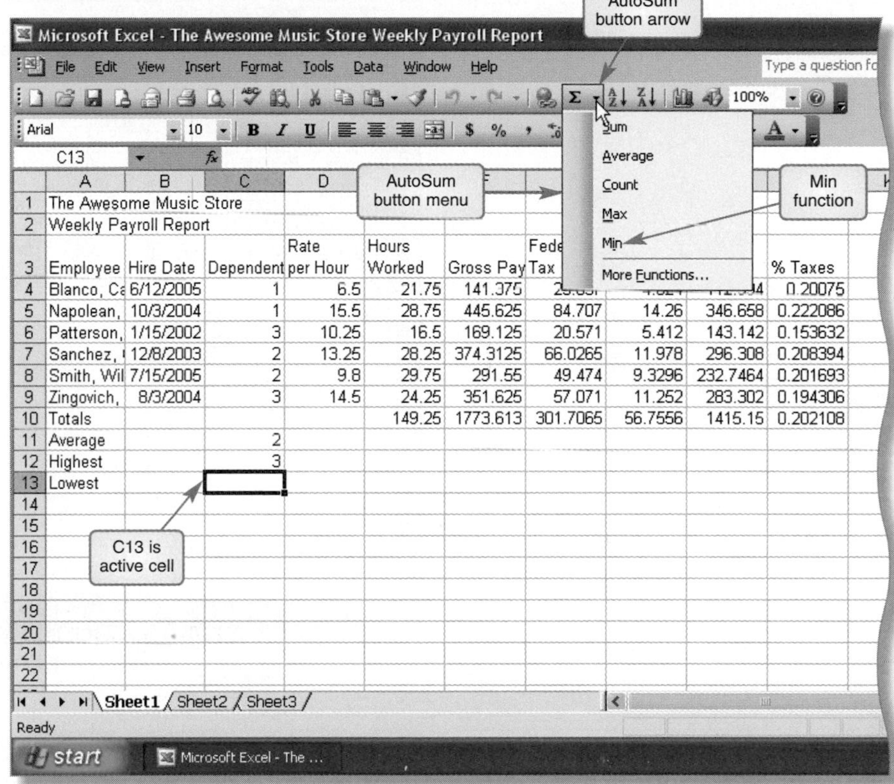

FIGURE 2-21

2

- **Click Min.**

The function =MIN(C11:C12) appears in the formula bar and in cell C13. A marquee surrounds the range C11:C12 (Figure 2-22). The range C11:C12 automatically selected by Excel is not correct.

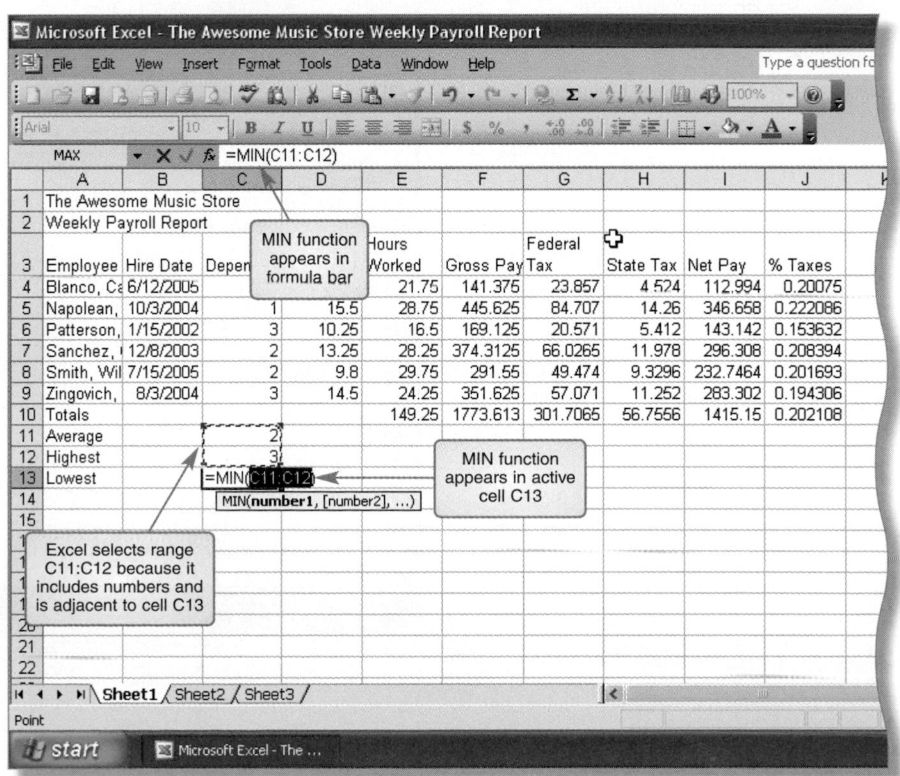

FIGURE 2-22

3

• **Click cell C4 and then drag through cell C9.**

Excel displays the function in the formula bar and in cell C13 with the new range C4:C9 (Figure 2-23).

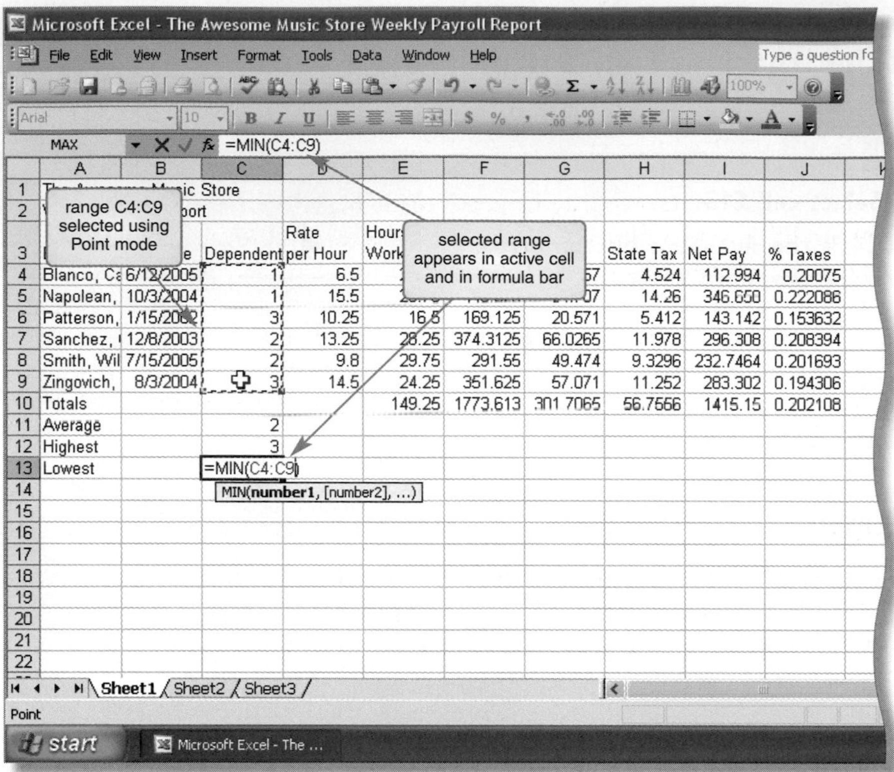

FIGURE 2-23

4

• **Click the Enter box.**

Excel determines that the lowest value in the range C4:C9 is 1 and displays it in cell C13 (Figure 2-24).

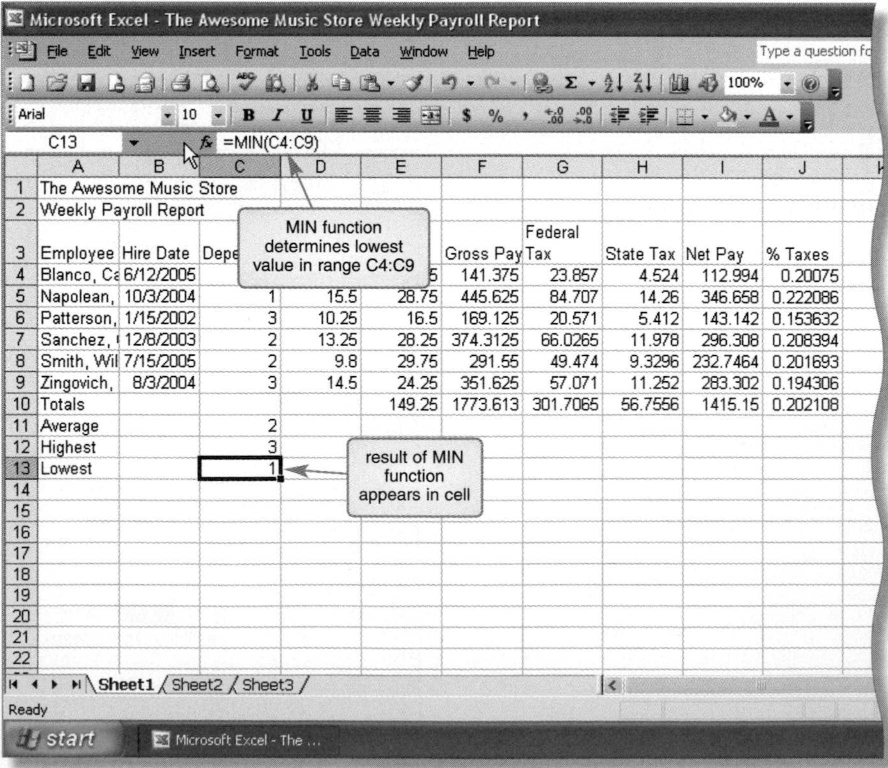

FIGURE 2-24

You can see from the previous example that using the AutoSum button menu allows you to enter one of five often-used functions easily into a cell, without having to memorize its name or the required arguments. If you need to enter a function not available on the AutoSum button menu and cannot remember its name, then click More Functions on the AutoSum button menu or click the Insert Function box in the formula bar.

Thus far, you have learned to use the SUM, AVERAGE, MAX, and MIN functions. In addition to these four functions, Excel has more than 400 additional functions that perform just about every type of calculation you can imagine. These functions are categorized in the Insert Function dialog box shown in Figure 2-18 on page EX 83. To view the categories, click the Or select a category box arrow. To obtain a description of a selected function, select its name in the Insert Function dialog box. Excel displays the description of the function below the Select a function list in the dialog box.

Copying the AVERAGE, MAX, and MIN Functions

The next step is to copy the AVERAGE, MAX, and MIN functions in the range C11:C13 to the adjacent range D11:J13. The fill handle again will be used to complete the copy. The following steps illustrate this procedure.

To Copy a Range of Cells across Columns to an Adjacent Range Using the Fill Handle

1

- **Select the range C11:C13.**
- **Drag the fill handle in the lower-right corner of the selected range through cell J13 and continue to hold down the mouse button.**

Excel displays an outline around the source and destination areas (range C11:J13) as shown in Figure 2-25.

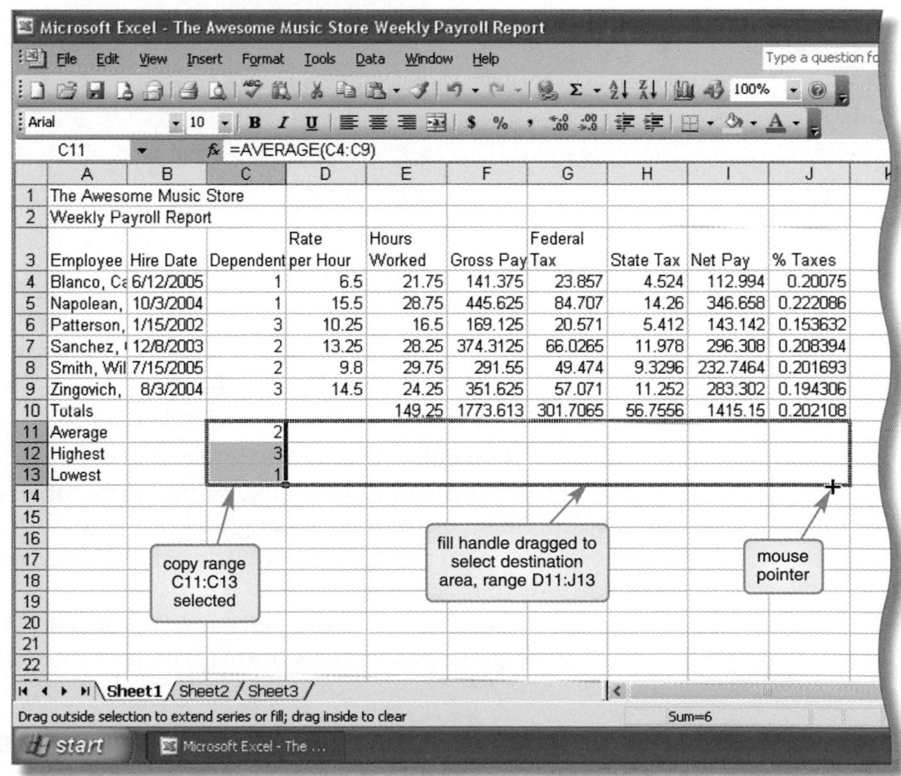

FIGURE 2-25

2

• **Release the mouse button.**

Excel copies the three functions to the range D11:J13 (Figure 2-26). The Auto Fill Options button appears to allow you to refine the copy.

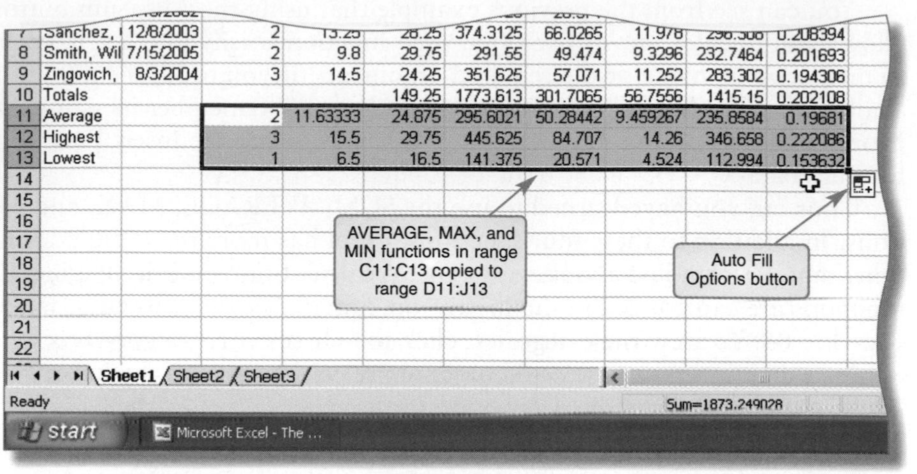

FIGURE 2-26

3

• **Select cell J11 and press the DELETE key to delete the average of the percent taxes.**

Cell J11 is blank (Figure 2-27).

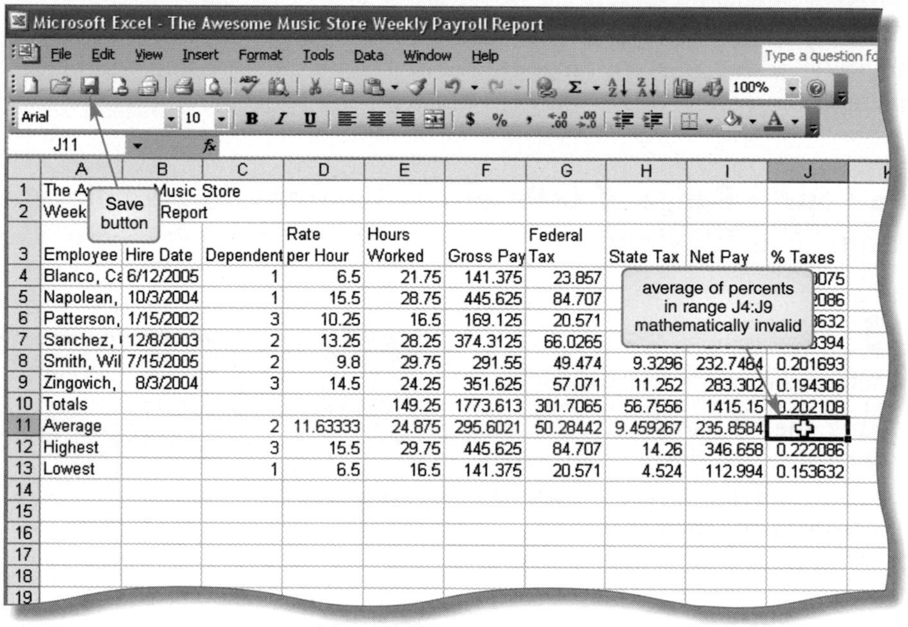

FIGURE 2-27

Remember that Excel adjusts the cell references in the copied functions so each function refers to the range of numbers above it in the same column. Review the numbers in rows 11 through 13 in Figure 2-26. You should see that the functions in each column return the appropriate values, based on the numbers in rows 4 through 9 of that column.

The average of the percent taxes in cell J11 was deleted in Step 3 because an average of percentages of this type is mathematically invalid.

Saving a Workbook Using the Same File Name

Earlier in this project, an intermediate version of the workbook was saved using the file name, The Awesome Music Store Weekly Payroll Report. The following step saves the workbook a second time using the same file name.

To Save a Workbook Using the Same File Name

1 Click the Save button on the Standard toolbar.

Excel saves the workbook on the on the USB flash drive using the file name, The Awesome Music Store Weekly Payroll Report.

Excel automatically stores the latest version of the workbook using the same file name, The Awesome Music Store Weekly Payroll Report. When you save a workbook a second time using the same file name, Excel will not display the Save As dialog box as it does the first time you save the workbook. You also can click Save on the File menu or press SHIFT+F12 or CTRL+S to save a workbook again.

If you want to save the workbook using a new name or on a different drive, click Save As on the File menu. Some Excel users, for example, use the Save button to save the latest version of the workbook on the default drive. Then, they use the Save As command to save a copy of the workbook on another drive.

Verifying Formulas Using Range Finder

One of the more common mistakes made with Excel is to include a wrong cell reference in a formula. An easy way to verify that a formula references the cells you want it to reference is to use Excel's Range Finder. **Range Finder** can be used to check which cells are referenced in the formula assigned to the active cell. Range Finder allows you to make immediate changes to the cells referenced in a formula.

To use Range Finder to verify that a formula contains the intended cell references, double-click the cell with the formula you want to check. Excel responds by highlighting the cells referenced in the formula so you can check that the cell references are correct. The following steps use Range Finder to check the formula in cell J4.

To Verify a Formula Using Range Finder

1

- **Double-click cell J4.**

Excel responds by displaying different colored borders around the cells referenced by the formula in cell J4 (Figure 2-28). The different colors allow you to see easily which cells are referenced by the formula in cell J4.

- **Press the ESC key to quit Range Finder.**
- **Select cell A15.**

Microsoft Excel - The Awesome Music Store Weekly Payroll Report

cells referenced in formula in active cell are highlighted with corresponding colors

color of cell references corresponds to color of highlighted cells

MAX =(G4+H4)/F4

	A	B	C	D	E	F	G	H	I	J
1	The Awesome Music Store									
2	Weekly Payroll Report									
3	Employee	Hire Date	Dependent	Rate per Hour	Hours Worked	Gross Pay	Federal Tax	State Tax	Net Pay	% Taxes
4	Blanco, Ca	6/12/2005	1	6.5	21.75	141.375	23.857	4.524	112.994	=(G4+H4)/F4
5	Napolean,	10/3/2004	1	15.5	28.75	445.625	84.707	14.26	346.658	0.222086
6	Patterson,	1/15/2002	3	10.25	16.5	169.125	20.571	5.412	143.142	0.153632
7	Sanchez,	12/8/2003	2	13.25	28.25	374.3125	66.0265	11.978	296.308	0.208394
8	Smith, Wil	7/15/2005	2	9.8	29.75	291.55	49.474	9.3296	232.7464	0.201693
9	Zingovich,	8/3/2004	3	14.5	24.25	351.625	57.071	11.252	283.302	0.194306
10	Totals				149.25	1773.613	301.7065	56.7556	1415.15	0.202108
11	Average		2	11.63333	24.875	295.6021	50.28442	9.459267	235.8584	
12	Highest		3	15.5	29.75	445.625	84.707	14.26	346.658	0.222086
13	Lowest		1	6.5	16.5	141.375	20.571	4.524	112.994	0.153632

FIGURE 2-28

> **Skill Builder 2-2**
>
> To practice the following tasks, visit scsite.com/off2003sch/skill, locate Excel Project 2, and then click Skill Builder 2-2.
> - ❑ Enter functions using the keyboard
> - ❑ Enter functions using the Insert Function box
> - ❑ Enter functions using the AutoSum Button menu
> - ❑ Verify formulas using Range Finder

Not only does Range Finder show you the cells referenced in the formula in cell J4, but it also allows you to drag the colored borders to other cells to instruct Excel to change the cell references in the formula to the newly selected cells. If you use Range Finder to change the cells referenced in a formula, press the ENTER key to complete the edit.

Formatting the Worksheet

Although the worksheet contains the appropriate data, formulas, and functions, the text and numbers need to be formatted to improve their appearance and readability.

In Project 1, the AutoFormat command was used to format the majority of the worksheet. This section describes how to change the unformatted worksheet in Figure 2-29a to the formatted worksheet in Figure 2-29b using the Formatting toolbar and Format Cells command.

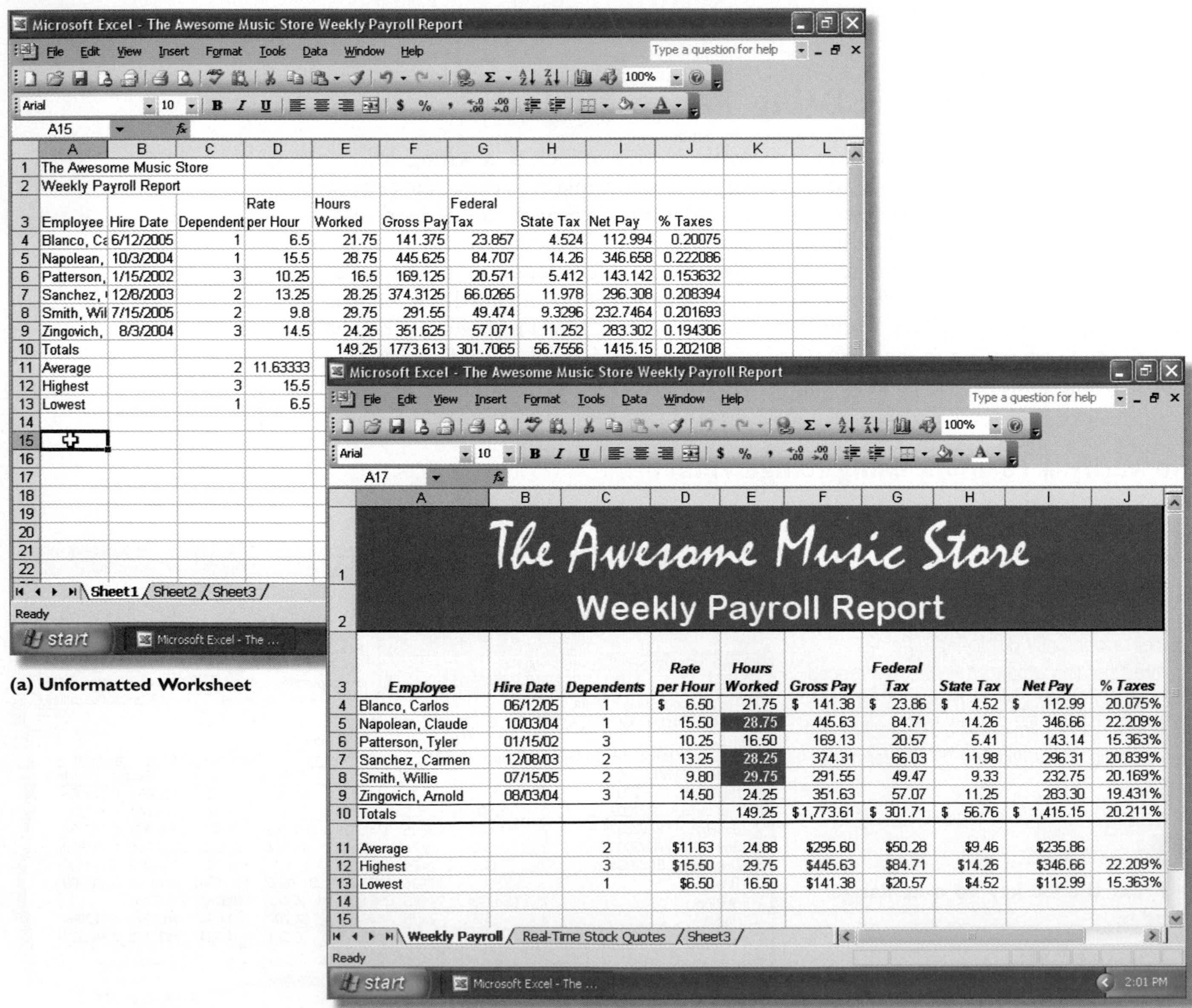

(a) Unformatted Worksheet

(b) Formatted Worksheet

FIGURE 2-29

The following outlines the formatting suggested in the sketch of the worksheet in Figure 2-3 on page EX 69:

1. Worksheet title and subtitle
   a. Font type — title Mistral; subtitle Arial Rounded MT Bold
   b. Font size — title 48; subtitle 24
   c. Alignment — center across columns A through J and center vertically
   d. Background color (range A1:J2) — light blue
   e. Font color — white
   f. Border — thick box border around range A1:J2
2. Column titles
   a. Font style — bold, italic
   b. Alignment — center
   c. Border — bottom border
3. Data
   a. Dates in column B — mm/dd/yy format
   b. Alignment — center data in column C
   c. Numbers in top row (range D4 and F4:I4) — Currency style; cell E4 — Comma style
   d. Numbers below top row (range D5:I9) — Comma style
   e. If value of cell in range E4:E9 greater than 25, then cell appears with bold white font and background color of red.
4. Totals line
   a. Numbers (cell E10) — Comma style; (range F10:I10) — Currency style
   b. Border — top and thick bottom border on row 10
5. Average, Highest, and Lowest lines
   a. Numbers (range D11:D13 and range F11:I13) — Currency style with floating dollar sign; (range E11:E13) — Comma style
6. Percentages in column J
   a. Numbers — Percent style with three decimal places
7. Column widths
   a. Column A — 17.00 characters
   b. Columns B through F — best fit
   c. Columns G, H, and J — 8.86 characters
   d. Columns I — 10.86 characters
8. Row heights
   a. Row 1 — 54.00 points; row 2 — 33.00 points; row 3 — 45.00 points; row 11 — 24.00 points
   b. Remaining rows — default

Except for vertically centering the worksheet titles in rows 1 and 2, the Date format assigned to the dates in column B, the Currency style assigned to the functions in rows 11 through 13, and the conditional formatting in column E, all of the listed formats can be assigned to cells using the Formatting toolbar and mouse.

> *Q & A*
>
> **Q:** Do colors have meaning?
>
> **A:** Knowing how people perceive colors helps you emphasize parts of your worksheet. Warmer colors (red and orange) tend to reach toward the reader. Cooler colors (blue, green, and violet) tend to pull away from the reader. Bright colors jump out of a dark background and are easiest to see. White or yellow text on a dark blue, green, purple, or black background is ideal.

Changing the Font and Centering the Worksheet Title and Subtitle

When developing presentation-quality worksheets, different fonts often are used in the same worksheet. Excel allows you to change the font of individual characters in a cell or all the characters in a cell, in a range of cells, or in the entire worksheet. To emphasize the worksheet title and subtitle in cells A1 and A2, the font type, size, and style are changed and the title and subtitle are centered as described in the following two sets of steps.

To Change the Font and Center the Worksheet Title

1

- **Click cell A1.**
- **Click the Font box arrow on the Formatting toolbar, scroll down and point to Mistral (or a similar font).**

Excel displays the Font list with Mistral highlighted (Figure 2-30).

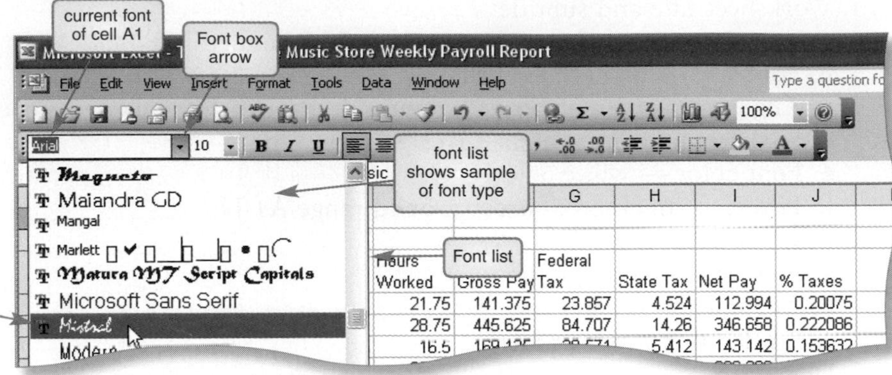

FIGURE 2-30

2

- **Click Mistral (or a similar font).**
- **Click the Font Size box arrow on the Formatting toolbar and then click 48 in the Font Size list.**
- **Select the range A1:J1. Right-click the selection.**

Excel displays the text in cell A1 in 48-point Mistral font. Excel automatically increases the height of row 1 so that the taller characters fit in the cell. Excel displays the shortcut menu for the selected range A1:J1 (Figure 2-31).

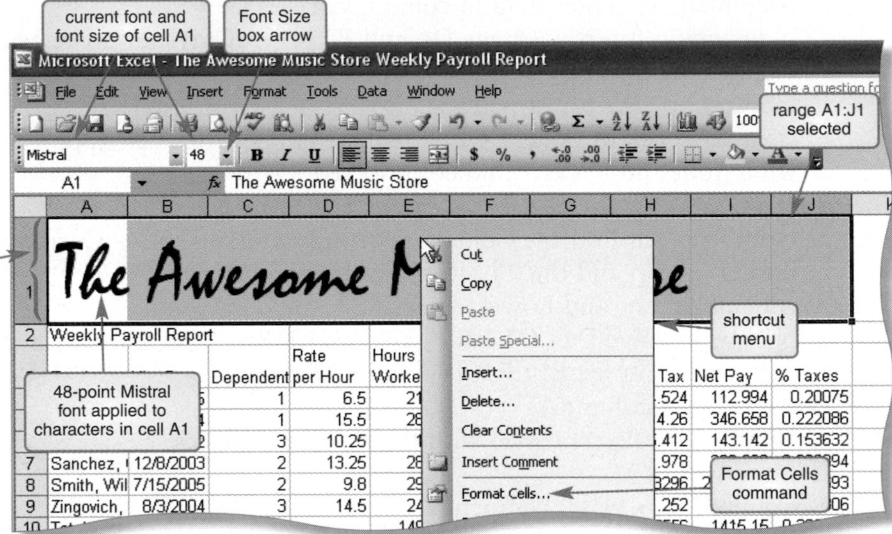

FIGURE 2-31

3

- **Click Format Cells on the shortcut menu.**
- **When Excel displays the Format Cells dialog box, click the Alignment tab.**
- **Click the Horizontal box arrow and select Center in the Horizontal list.**
- **Click the Vertical box arrow and select Center in the Vertical list.**
- **Click Merge cells in the Text control area.**

Excel displays the Format Cells dialog box as shown in Figure 2-32.

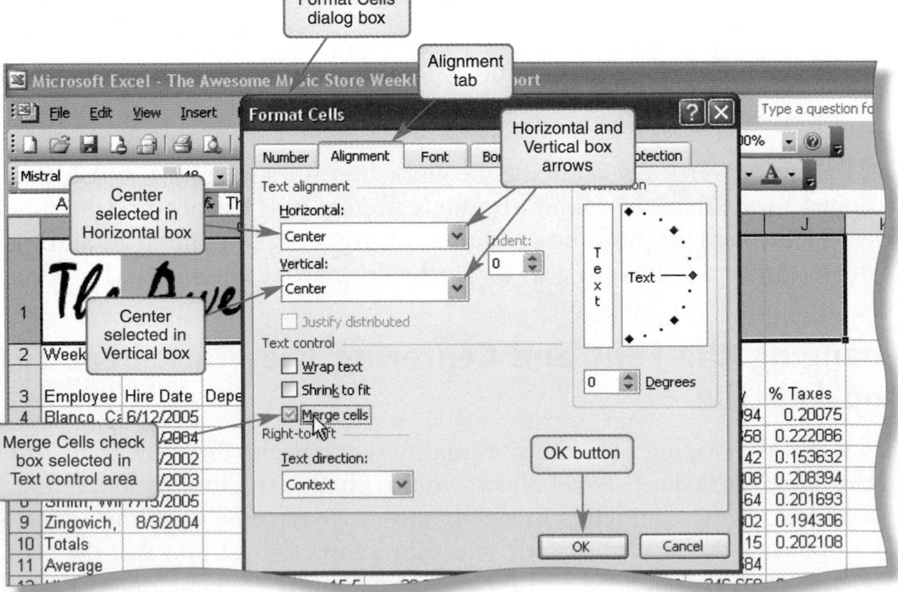

FIGURE 2-32

4

- **Click the OK button.**

Excel merges the cells A1 through J1 to create a new cell A1 and then centers the worksheet title horizontally across columns A through J and centers it vertically in row 1 (Figure 2-33).

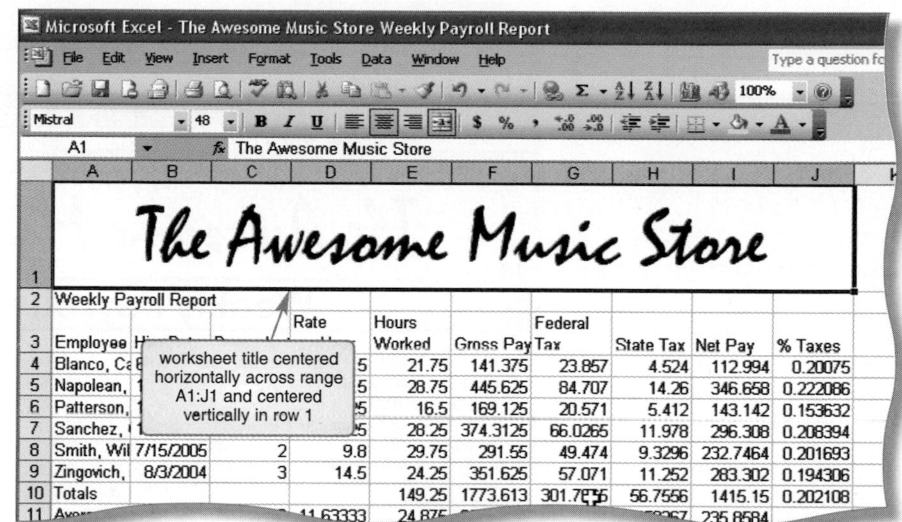

FIGURE 2-33

You can change a font type, size, or style at any time while the worksheet is active. Some Excel users prefer to change fonts before they enter any data. Others change the font while they are building the worksheet or after they have entered all the data.

In Project 1, the Merge and Center button on the Formatting toolbar was used to center the worksheet title across columns. In Step 3 of the previous steps, the Alignment tab in the Format Cells dialog box is used to center the worksheet title across columns, because the project also called for vertically centering the worksheet title in row 1.

The next step is to format the worksheet subtitle in the same fashion as the worksheet title, except that the font size will be changed to 24 rather than 48.

To Change the Font and Center the Worksheet Subtitle

1. **Click cell A2. Click the Font box arrow on the Formatting toolbar.**
2. **Click Arial Rounded MT Bold (or a similar font).**
3. **Click the Font Size box arrow on the Formatting toolbar and then click 24 in the Font Size list.**
4. **Select the range A2:J2. Right-click the selection. Click Format Cells on the shortcut menu. When Excel displays the Format Cells dialog box, click the Alignment tab. Click the Horizontal box arrow and select Center in the Horizontal list. Click the Vertical box arrow and select Center in the Vertical list. Click Merge cells in the Text control area. Click the OK button.**

Excel changes the font in cell A2 to Arial Rounded MT Bold, increases the font size to 24, centers it horizontally across columns A through J, centers it vertically in row 2, and merges the cells A2 through J2 to create a new cell A2 (Figure 2-34 on the next page).

Q & A

Q: What is the most popular background color?

A: Blue. Research shows that the color blue is used most often because this color connotes serenity, reflection, and proficiency.

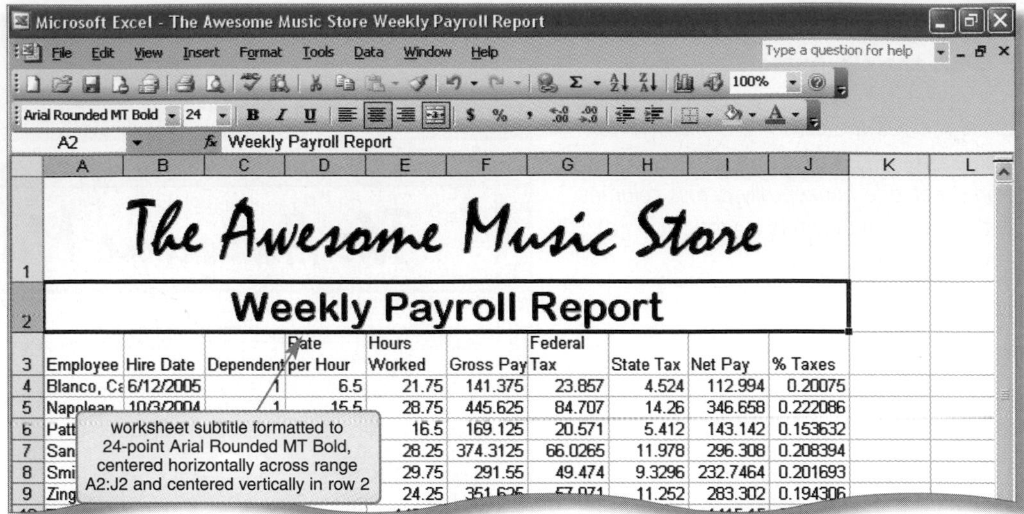

FIGURE 2-34

Some of the formatting, such as the font type, font style, and alignment, could have been done to both titles at the same time by selecting the range A1:A2 before assigning the formats. The font size, which is different, and the merging of cells, however, cannot be done to both titles at the same time.

Changing the Background and Font Colors and Applying a Box Border to the Worksheet Title and Subtitle

The final formats to be assigned to the worksheet title and subtitle are the blue background color, white font color, and thick box border (Figure 2-29b on page EX 90). The following steps complete the formatting of the worksheet titles.

To Change the Background and Font Colors and Apply a Box Border to the Worksheet Title and Subtitle

1

- **Select the range A1:A2, and then click the Fill Color button arrow on the Formatting toolbar.**

Excel displays the Fill Color palette (Figure 2-35).

FIGURE 2-35

2

- **Click Light Blue (column 6, row 3) on the Fill Color palette.**
- **Click the Font Color button arrow on the Formatting toolbar.**

Excel changes the background color of cells A1 and A2 from white to light blue and displays the Font Color palette (Figure 2-36).

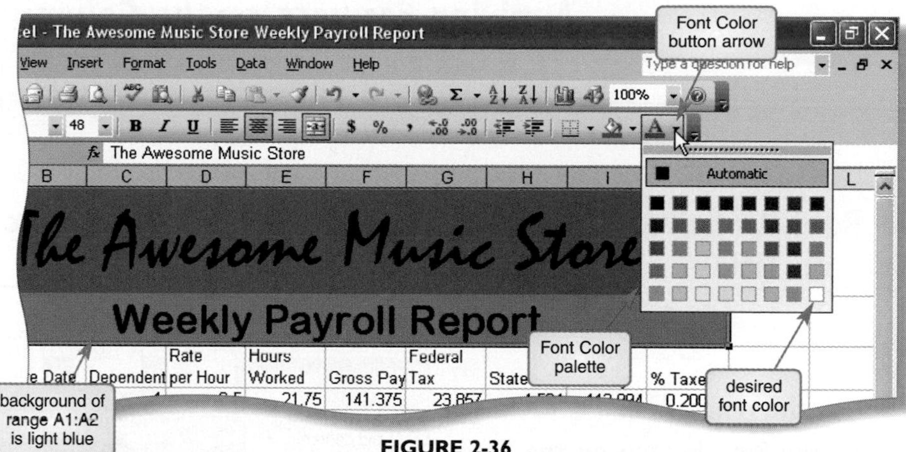

FIGURE 2-36

3

- **Click White (column 8, row 5) on the Font Color palette.**
- **Click the Borders button arrow on the Formatting toolbar.**

Excel changes the font in the worksheet titles from black to white and displays the Borders palette (Figure 2-37).

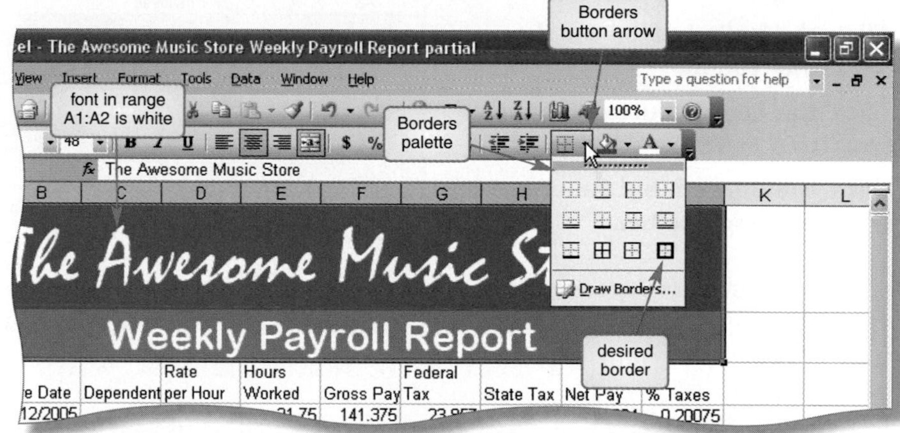

FIGURE 2-37

4

- **Click the Thick Box Border button (column 4, row 3) on the Borders palette.**
- **Click cell A15 to deselect the range A1:A2.**

Excel displays a thick box border around the range A1:A2 (Figure 2-38).

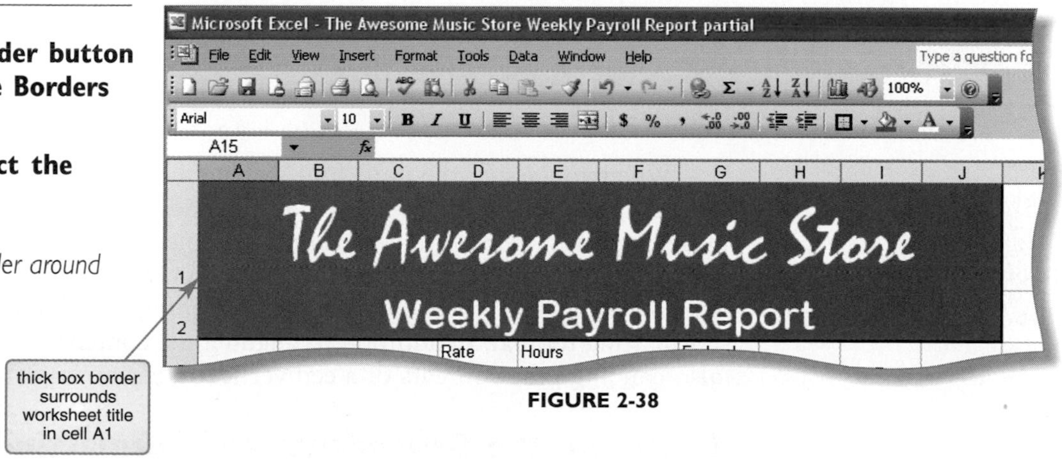

thick box border surrounds worksheet title in cell A1

FIGURE 2-38

You can remove borders, such as the thick box border around the range A1:A2, by selecting the range and clicking the No Border button on the Borders palette. You can remove a background color by selecting the range, clicking the Fill Color button arrow on the Formatting toolbar, and then clicking the No Fill button on the Fill Color palette. The same technique allows you to change the font color back to Excel's default color, except you use the Font Color button arrow and click the Automatic button on the Font Color palette.

Applying Formats to the Column Titles

As shown in Figure 2-29b on page EX 90, the column titles are bold, italicized, centered, and have a bottom border (underline). The following steps assign these formats to the column titles.

To Bold, Italicize, Center, and Apply a Bottom Border to the Column Titles

1

- **Select the range A3:J3.**
- **Click the Bold button on the Formatting toolbar.**
- **Click the Italic button on the Formatting toolbar.**
- **Click the Center button on the Formatting toolbar.**
- **Click the Borders button arrow on the Formatting toolbar.**

The column titles in row 3 are bold, italic, and centered (Figure 2-39). Excel displays the Borders palette.

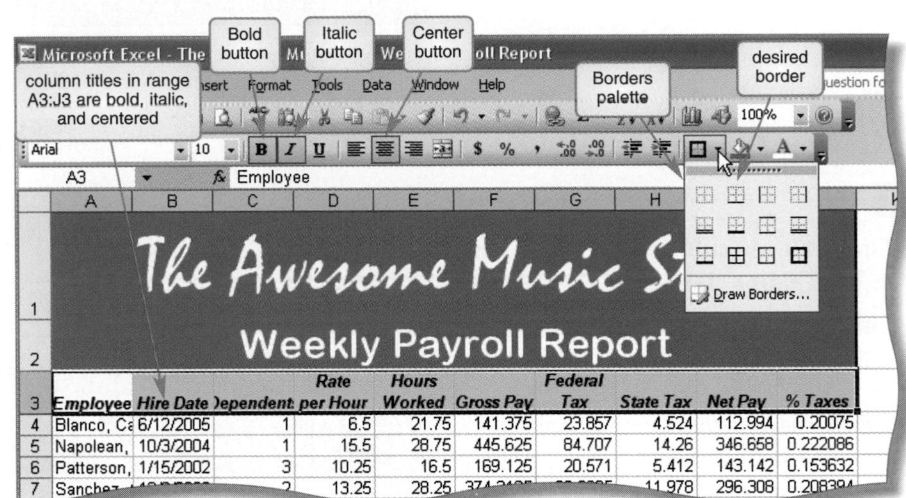

FIGURE 2-39

2

- **Click the Bottom Border button (column 2, row 1) on the Borders palette.**

Excel adds a bottom border to the range A3:J3.

When you assign the italic font style to a cell, Excel slants the characters slightly to the right as shown in Figure 2-39. You can align the contents of cells in several different ways. Left alignment, center alignment, and right alignment are the more frequently used horizontal alignments. In fact, these three horizontal alignments are used so often that Excel has Align Left, Center, and Align Right buttons on the Formatting toolbar. In addition to aligning the contents of a cell horizontally, you also can align the contents of a cell vertically, as shown earlier.

Centering the Dependents and Formatting the Dates in the Worksheet

With the column titles formatted, the next step is to format the dates in column B and center the dependents in column C. If a cell entry is short, such as the dependents in column C, centering the entries within their respective columns improves the appearance of the worksheet. The following steps format the dates in the range B4:B9 and center the data in the range C4:C13.

To Format Dates and Center Data in Cells

1

- **Select the range B4:B9.**
- **Right-click the selected range and then click Format Cells on the shortcut menu.**
- **When Excel displays the Format Cells dialog box, click the Number tab, click Date in the Category list, and then click 03/14/01 in the Type list.**

Excel displays the Format Cells dialog box as shown in Figure 2-40.

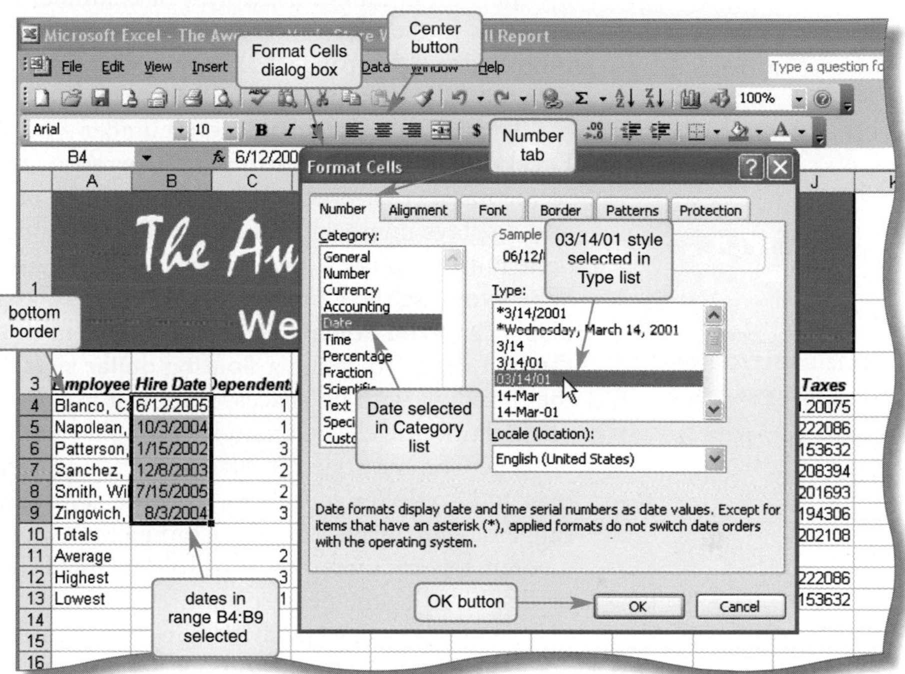

FIGURE 2-40

2

- **Click the OK button.**
- **Select the range C4:C13 and then click the Center button on the Formatting toolbar.**
- **Select cell D4 to deselect the range C4:C13.**

Excel displays the dates in column B using the date format style, mm/dd/yy, and centers the dependents in the range C4:C9 (Figure 2-41).

Weekly Payroll Report

	Employee	Hire Date	)ependent	Rate per Hour	Hours Worked	Gross Pay	Federal Tax	State Tax	Net Pay	% Taxes
4	Blanco, C	06/12/05	1	6.5	21.75	141.375	23.857	4.524	112.994	0.20075
5	Napolean,	10/03/04	1	15.5	28.75	445.625	84.707	14.26	346.658	0.222086
6	Patterson,	01/15/02	3	10.25	16.5	169.125	20.571	5.412	143.142	0.153632
7	Sanchez,	12/08/03	2	13.25	28.25	374.3125	66.0265	11.978	296.308	0.208394
8	Smith, Wil	07/15/05	2	9.8	29.75	291.55	49.474	9.3296	232.7464	0.201693
9	Zingovich,	08/03/04	3	14.5	24.25	351.625	57.071	11.252	283.302	0.194306
10	Totals				149.25	1773.613	301.7065	56.7556	1415.15	0.202108
11	Average		2	11.63333	24.875	295.6021	50.28442	9.459267	235.8584	
12	Highest		3	15.5	29.75	445.625	84.707	14.26	346.658	0.222086
13	Lowest		1	6.5	16.5	141.375	20.571	4.524	112.994	0.153632

Excel displays dates in range B4:B9 using the date style, mm/dd/yy

dependants in range C4:C13 centered

FIGURE 2-41

Rather than selecting the range C4:C13 in Step 2, you could have clicked the column C heading immediately above cell C1, and then clicked the Center button on the Formatting toolbar. In this case, all cells in column C down to cell C65536 would have been formatted to use center alignment. This same procedure could have been used to format the dates in column B.

Formatting Numbers Using the Formatting Toolbar

As shown in Figure 2-29b on page EX 90, the worksheet is formatted to resemble an accounting report. For example, in columns D and F through I, the numbers in the first row (row 4), the totals row (row 10), and the rows below the totals (rows 11 through 13) have dollar signs, while the remaining numbers (rows 5 through 9) in columns D and F through I do not.

To append a dollar sign to a number, you should use the Currency style format. Excel displays numbers using the **Currency style format** with a dollar sign to the left of the number, inserts a comma every three positions to the left of the decimal point, and displays numbers to the nearest cent (hundredths place). Clicking the Currency Style button on the Formatting toolbar assigns the desired Currency style format. When you use the Currency Style button to assign the Currency style format, Excel displays a **fixed dollar sign** to the far left in the cell, often with spaces between it and the first digit. To assign a **floating dollar sign** that appears immediately to the left of the first digit with no spaces, you must use the Cells command on the Format menu or the Format Cells command on the shortcut menu.

The Comma style format is used to instruct Excel to display numbers with commas and no dollar signs. The **Comma style format**, which can be assigned to a range of cells by clicking the Comma Style button on the Formatting toolbar, inserts a comma every three positions to the left of the decimal point and causes numbers to be displayed to the nearest hundredths.

The following steps show how to assign formats using the Currency Style button and the Comma Style button on the Formatting toolbar.

To Apply a Currency Style Format and Comma Style Format Using the Formatting Toolbar

1

- **Select cell D4.**
- **While holding down the CTRL key, select the ranges F4:I4 and F10:I10.**
- **Click the Currency Style button on the Formatting toolbar.**

Excel applies the Currency style format with fixed dollar signs to cell D4 and the nonadjacent ranges F4:I4 and F10:I10 as shown in Figure 2-42. Excel automatically increases the width of column I to best fit, so the formatted numbers fit in the cells.

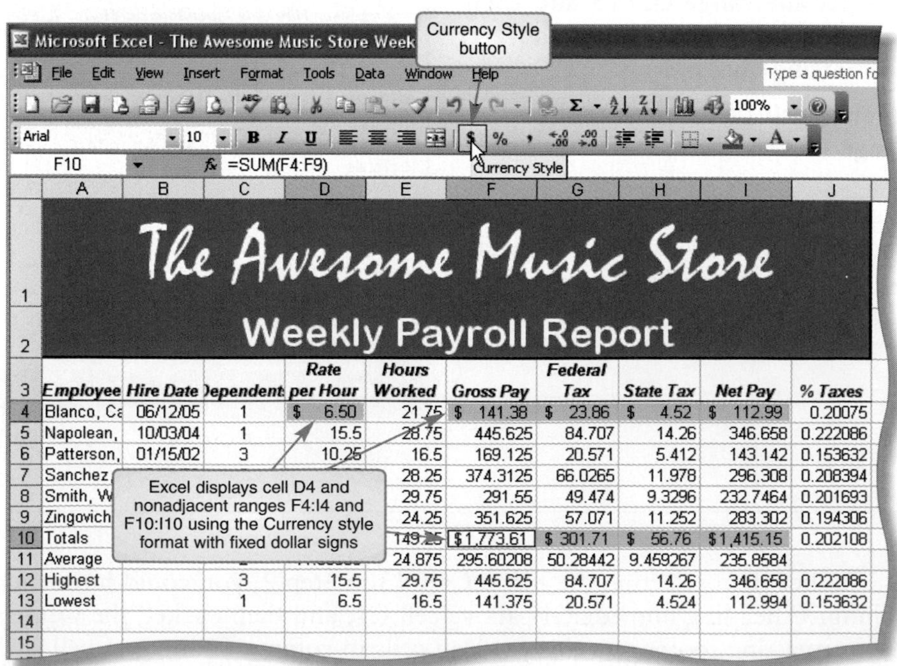

FIGURE 2-42

2

- **Select the ranges D5:D9 and E4:E13.**
- **Click the Comma Style button on the Formatting toolbar.**

Excel assigns the Comma style format to the ranges D5:D9 and E4:E13 (Figure 2-43).

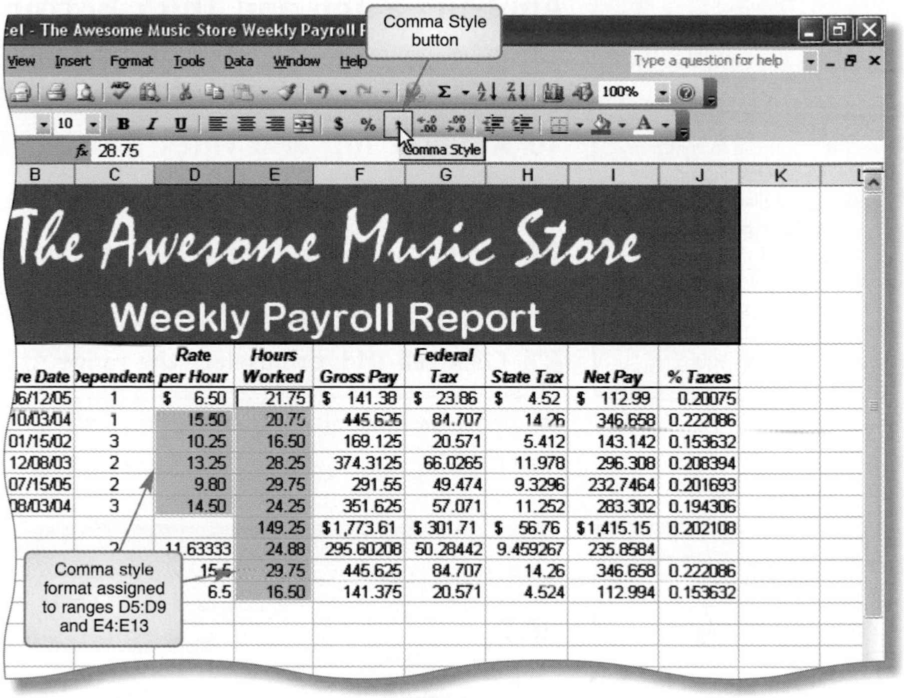

FIGURE 2-43

3

- **Select the range F5:I9 and then click the Comma Style button on the Formatting toolbar.**

Excel assigns the Comma style to the range F5:I9 (Figure 2-44).

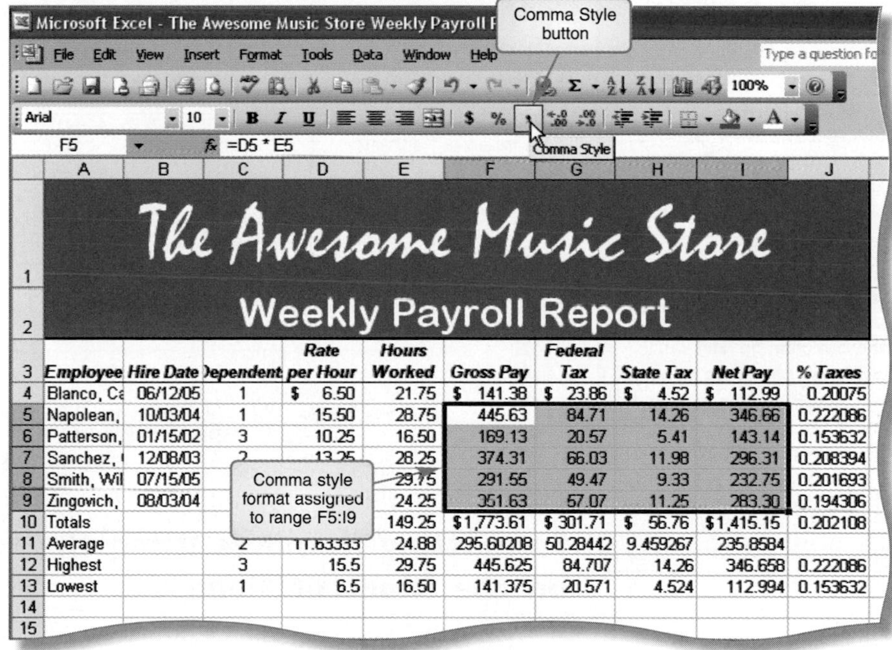

FIGURE 2-44

The Currency Style button assigns a fixed dollar sign to the numbers in cell D4 and the ranges F4:I4 and F10:I10. In each cell in these ranges, Excel displays the dollar sign to the far left with spaces between it and the first digit in the cell. Excel automatically rounds a number to fit the selected format.

Q & A

Q: Can numbers be formatted as they are entered?

A: Yes. You can format numbers as you enter them by entering a dollar sign ($), comma (,), or percent sign (%) as part of the number. For example, if you enter 1500, Excel displays 1500. If you enter $1500, however, Excel displays $1,500.

Applying a Top and Thick Bottom Border to the Totals Row

The following steps add a top and thick bottom border to the totals in row 10.

To Apply a Top and Thick Bottom Border to the Row above the Totals Row

1. **Select the range A10:J10, click the Borders button arrow on the Formatting toolbar, and then click the Top and Thick Bottom Border button (column 1, row 3) on the Borders palette.**
2. **Click cell D11 to deselect the range A10:J10.**

The totals row (row 10) has a top and thick bottom border, signifying the row contains totals (Figure 2-45).

Q & A

Q: What causes the sum of a group of numbers to be a penny or two off from an expected result?

A: If the numbers being summed are the result of multiplication or division of decimal fraction numbers, or the sum or difference of numbers with different numbers of decimal places, then the numbers you see on your screen may not be the same as the numbers used in calculations. When a number has more decimal places than Excel displays on the screen, the actual number (not the displayed number) is used in the computation. This can cause the sum to be a penny or two off from an expected result. You can eliminate this problem by using the ROUND function in formulas involving decimal fraction numbers.

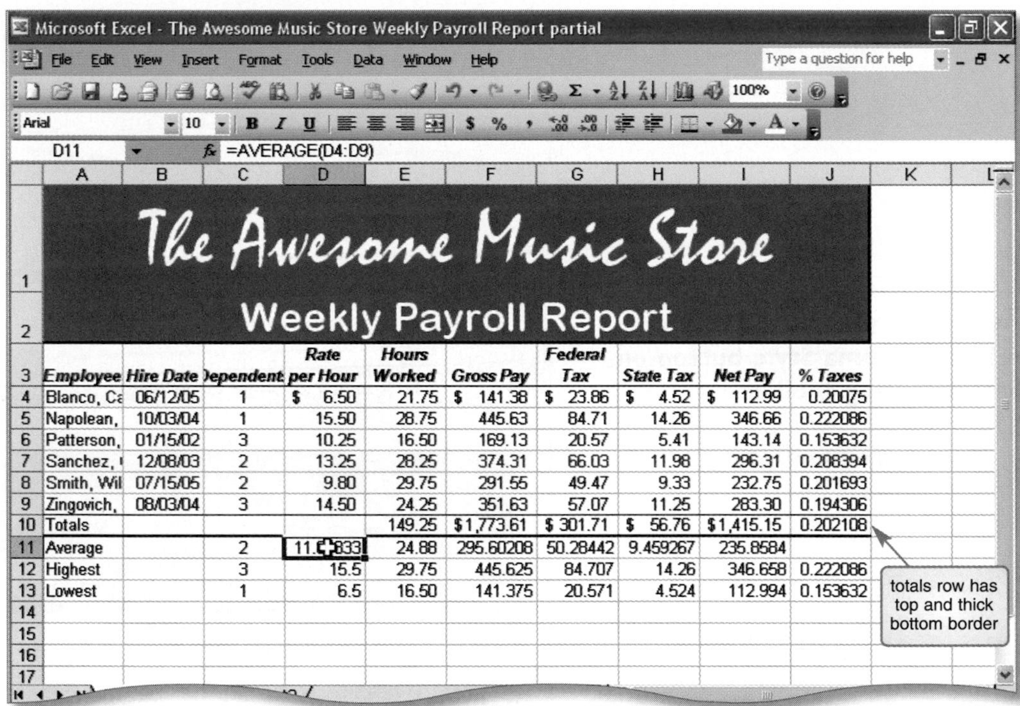

FIGURE 2-45

Formatting Numbers Using the Format Cells Command on the Shortcut Menu

The following steps show you how to use the Format Cells command on the shortcut menu to apply the Currency style format with a floating dollar sign to the numbers in the ranges D11:D13 and F11:I13.

To Apply a Currency Style Format with a Floating Dollar Sign Using the Format Cells Command

1

- **Select the range D11:D13 and then while holding down the CTRL key select the range F11:I13. Right-click the selected range.**

Excel highlights the two nonadjacent ranges D11:D13 and F11:I13, and displays the shortcut menu (Figure 2-46).

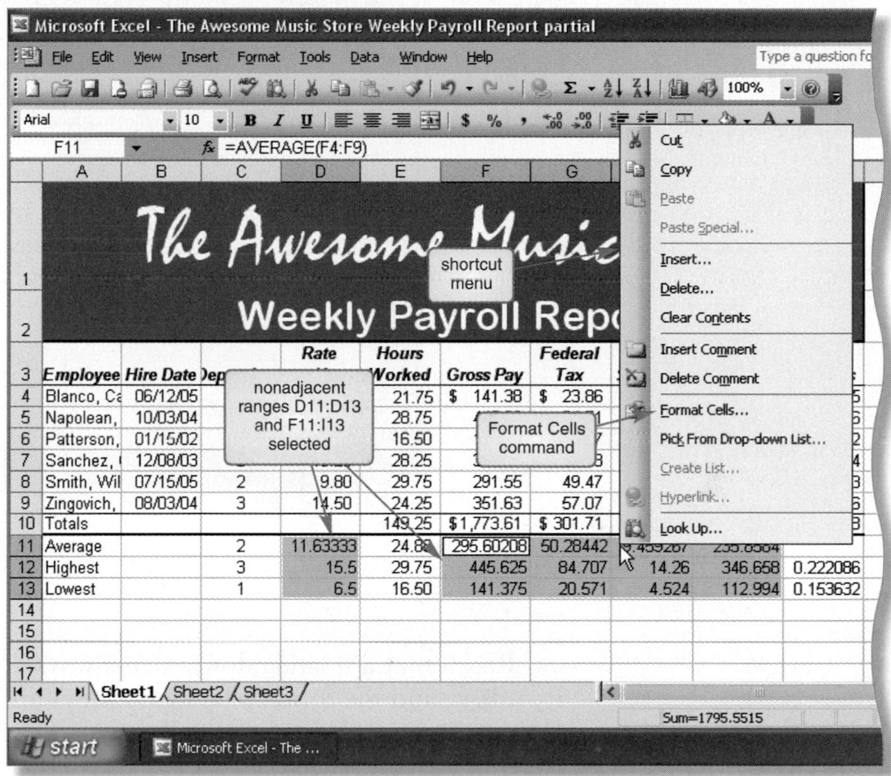

FIGURE 2-46

2

- **Click Format Cells on the shortcut menu.**
- **Click the Number tab in the Format Cells dialog box.**
- **Click Currency in the Category list and then click the third style ($1,234.10) in the Negative numbers list.**

Excel displays the Format Cells dialog box as shown in Figure 2-47.

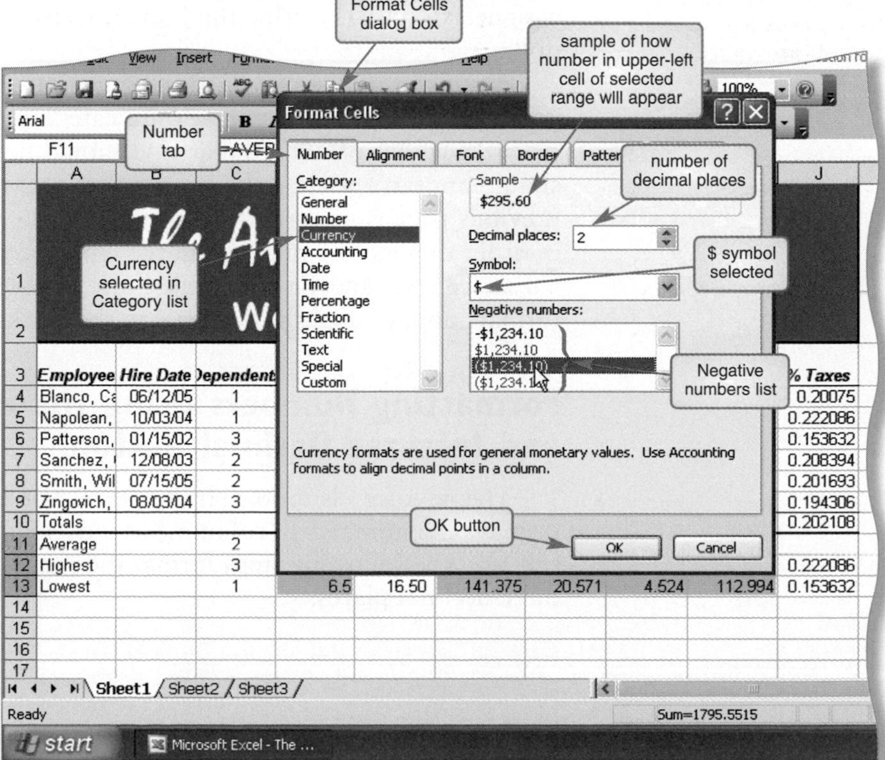

FIGURE 2-47

• **Click the OK button.**

Excel displays the worksheet with the numbers in the ranges D11:D13 and F11:I13 assigned the Currency style format with a floating dollar sign (Figure 2-48).

The Awesome Music Store

Weekly Payroll Report

	A	B	C	D	E	F	G	H	I	J
3	Employee	Hire Date	Depe			ss Pay	Federal Tax	State Tax	Net Pay	% Taxes
4	Blanco, Ca	06/12/05				141.38	$ 23.86	$ 4.52	$ 112.99	0.20075
5	Napolean,	10/03/04				445.63	84.71	14.26	346.66	0.222086
6	Patterson,	01/15/02	3	10.25	16.50	169.13	20.57	5.41	143.14	0.153632
7	Sanchez,	12/08/03	2	13.25	28.25	374.31	66.03	11.98	296.31	0.208394
8	Smith, Wil	07/15/05	2	9.80	29.75	291.55	49.47	9.33	232.75	0.201693
9	Zingovich,	08/03/04	3	14.50	24.25	351.63	57.07	11.25	283.30	0.194306
10	Totals				149.25	$1,773.61	$ 301.71	$ 56.76	$1,415.15	0.202108
11	Average		2	$11.63	24.88	$295.60	$50.28	$9.46	$235.86	
12	Highest		3	$15.50	29.75	$445.63	$84.71	$14.26	$346.66	0.222086
13	Lowest		1	$6.50	16.50	$141.38	$20.57	$4.52	$112.99	0.153632

Excel displays the ranges D11:D13 and F11:I13 using Currency style format with floating dollar signs

Sheet1 / Sheet2 / Sheet3

Ready

Sum=$1,795.55

start

Microsoft Excel - The ...

FIGURE 2-48

Recall that a floating dollar sign always appears immediately to the left of the first digit, and the fixed dollar sign always appears on the left side of the cell. Cell D4, for example, has a fixed dollar sign, while cell D11 has a floating dollar sign. Also recall that, while cells D4 and D11 both were assigned a Currency style format, the Currency style was assigned to cell D4 using the Currency Style button on the Formatting toolbar and the result is a fixed dollar sign. The Currency style was assigned to cell D11 using the Format Cells dialog box and the result is a floating dollar sign.

As shown in Figure 2-47 on the previous page, you can choose from 12 categories of formats. Once you select a category, you can select the number of decimal places, whether or not a dollar sign should be displayed, and how negative numbers should appear. Selecting the appropriate negative numbers format in Step 2 on the previous page is important, because doing so adds a space to the right of the number in order to align the numbers in the worksheet on the decimal points (as do the Currency Style and Comma Style buttons). Some of the available negative number formats do not align the numbers in the worksheet on the decimal points.

Formatting Numbers Using the Percent Style Button and Increase Decimal Button

The next step is to format the percent of taxes paid in column J. Currently, Excel displays the numbers in column J as a decimal fraction (for example, 0.20075 in cell J4). The following steps format the range J4:J13 to the Percent style format with three decimal places.

To Apply a Percent Style Format

1

- **Select the range J4:J13.**
- **Click the Percent Style button on the Formatting toolbar.**

Excel displays the numbers in column J as a rounded whole percent.

2

- **Click the Increase Decimal button on the Formatting toolbar three times.**

Excel displays the numbers in column J with the Percent style format with three decimal places (Figure 2-49).

Percent Style button

Increase Decimal button

Decrease Decimal button

Excel displays range J4:J13 using Percent style format with three decimal places

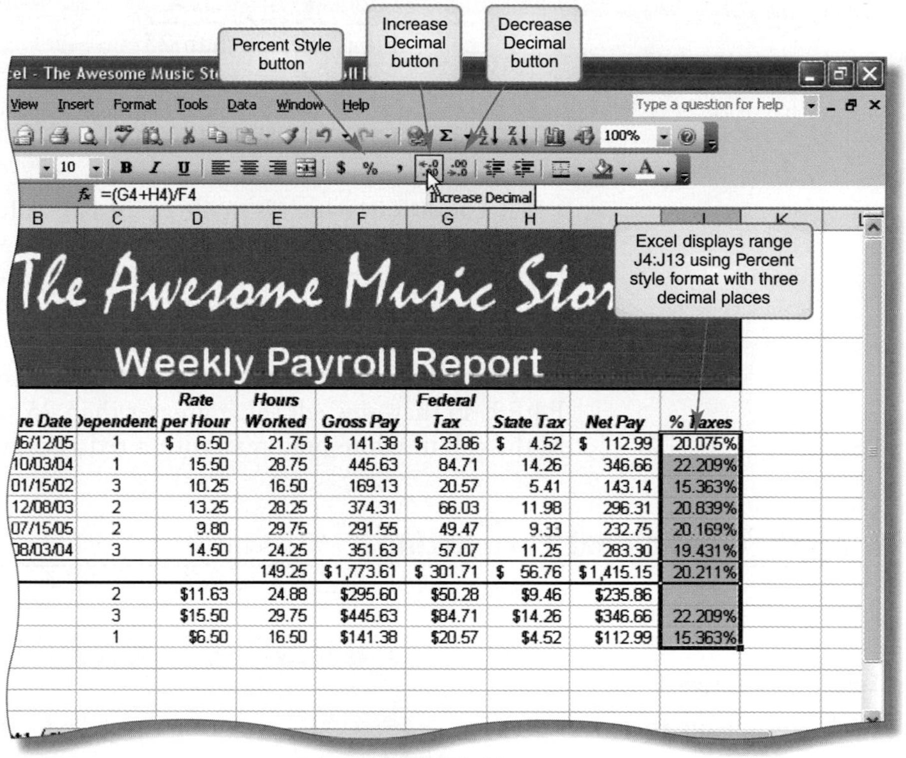

FIGURE 2-49

The Percent Style button on the Formatting toolbar is used to instruct Excel to display a value as a percentage, determined by multiplying the cell entry by 100, rounding the result to the nearest percent, and adding a percent sign. For example, when cell J4 is formatted using the Percent Style and Increase Decimal buttons, Excel displays the actual value 0.200749779 as 20.075%.

Using the Increase Decimal button on the Formatting toolbar instructs Excel to display additional decimal places in a cell. Each time you click the Increase Decimal button, Excel adds a decimal place to the selected cell. Using the Decrease Decimal button on the Formatting toolbar instructs Excel to display fewer decimal places in a cell. Each time you click the Decrease Decimal button, Excel removes a decimal place from the selected cell.

Conditional Formatting

The next step is to emphasize hours worked greater than 25 in column E by formatting them to appear with white bold text on a red background. The Conditional Formatting command on the Format menu will be used to complete this task.

Excel lets you apply formatting that appears only when the value in a cell meets conditions that you specify. This type of formatting is called **conditional formatting**. You can apply conditional formatting to a cell, a range of cells, the entire worksheet, or the entire workbook. Usually, you apply conditional formatting to a range of cells that contains values you want to highlight, if conditions warrant. For example, you can instruct Excel to use the bold font style and change the color of the background of a cell if the value in the cell meets a condition, such as being greater than 25 as shown below.

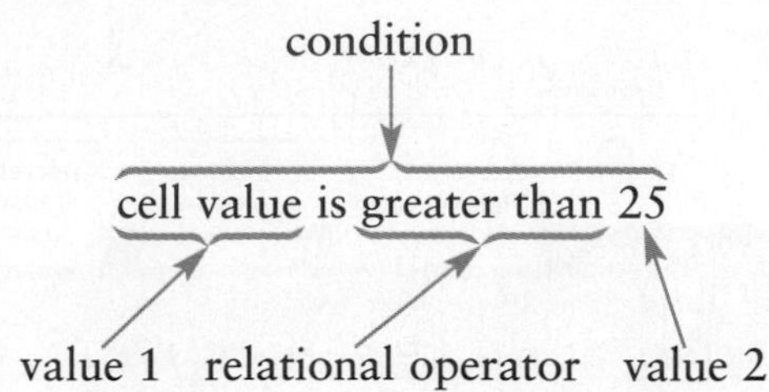

A **condition**, which is made up of two values and a relational operator, is true or false for each cell in the range. If the condition is true, then Excel applies the formatting. If the condition is false, then Excel suppresses the formatting. What makes conditional formatting so powerful is that the cell's appearance can change as you enter new values in the worksheet.

The following steps show how to assign conditional formatting to the range E4:E9, so that any cell value greater than 25 will cause Excel to display the number in the cell in white bold text with a red background.

To Apply Conditional Formatting

1

- **Select the range E4:E9.**
- **Click Format on the menu bar.**

Excel displays the Format menu (Figure 2-50).

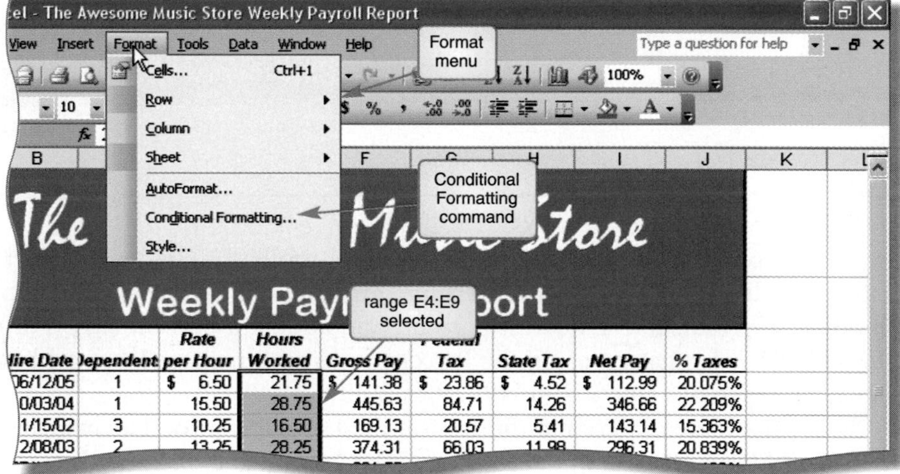

FIGURE 2-50

2

- **Click Conditional Formatting.**
- **When the Conditional Formatting dialog box appears, if necessary, click the leftmost text box arrow and then click Cell Value Is.**
- **Click the middle text box arrow and then click greater than.**
- **Type** 25 **in the rightmost text box.**

Excel displays the Conditional Formatting dialog box as shown in Figure 2-51.

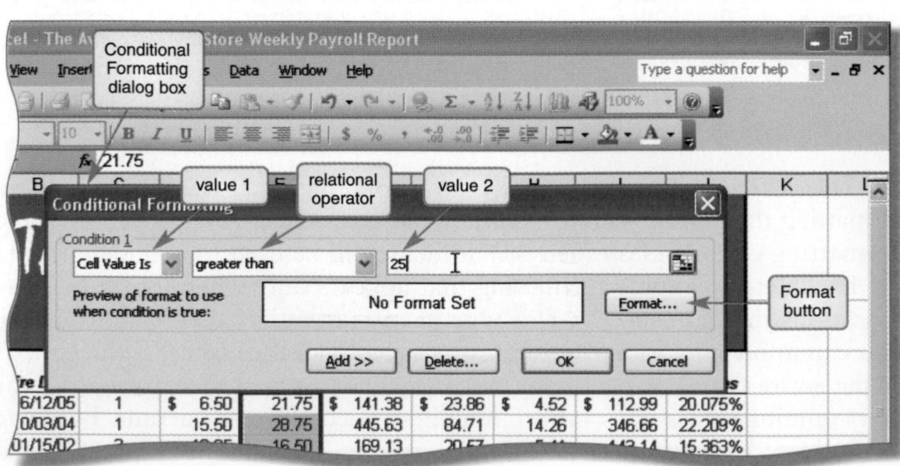

FIGURE 2-51

3

- **Click the Format button.**
- **When Excel displays the Format Cells dialog box, click the Patterns tab and then click Red (column 1, row 3).**
- **Click the Font tab and then click Bold in the Font style list.**
- **Click the Color box arrow.**

Excel displays the Format Cells dialog box as shown in Figure 2-52.

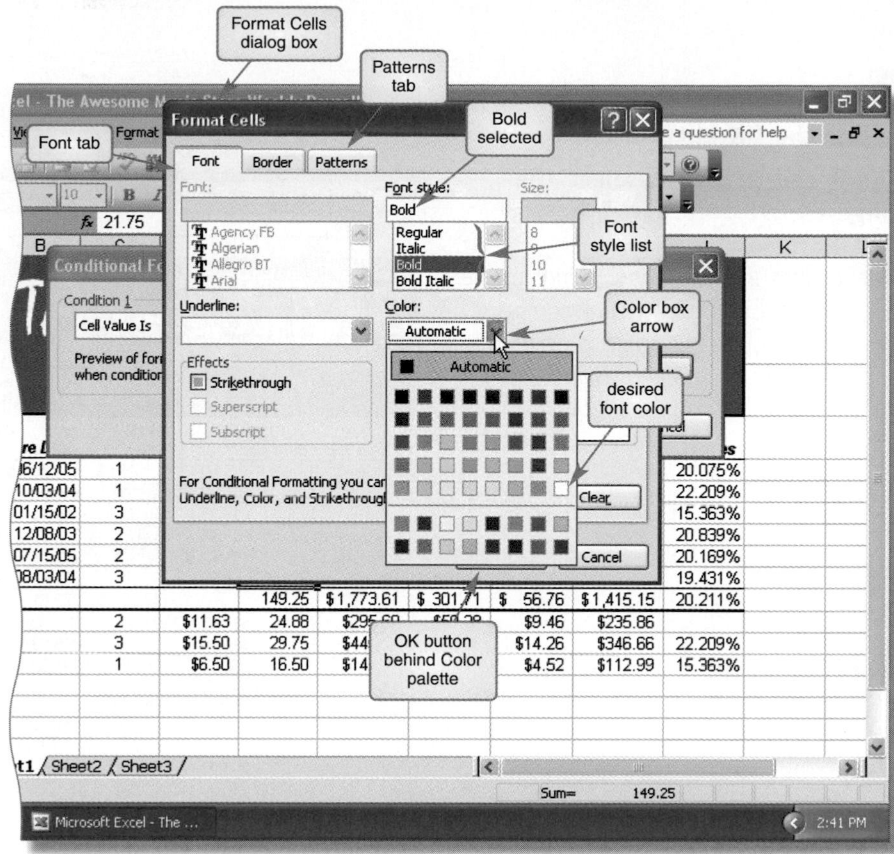

FIGURE 2-52

4

- **Click White (column 8, row 5) and then click the OK button.**

Excel displays the Conditional Formatting dialog box as shown in Figure 2-53. In the middle of the dialog box, Excel displays a preview of the format that Excel will use when the condition is true.

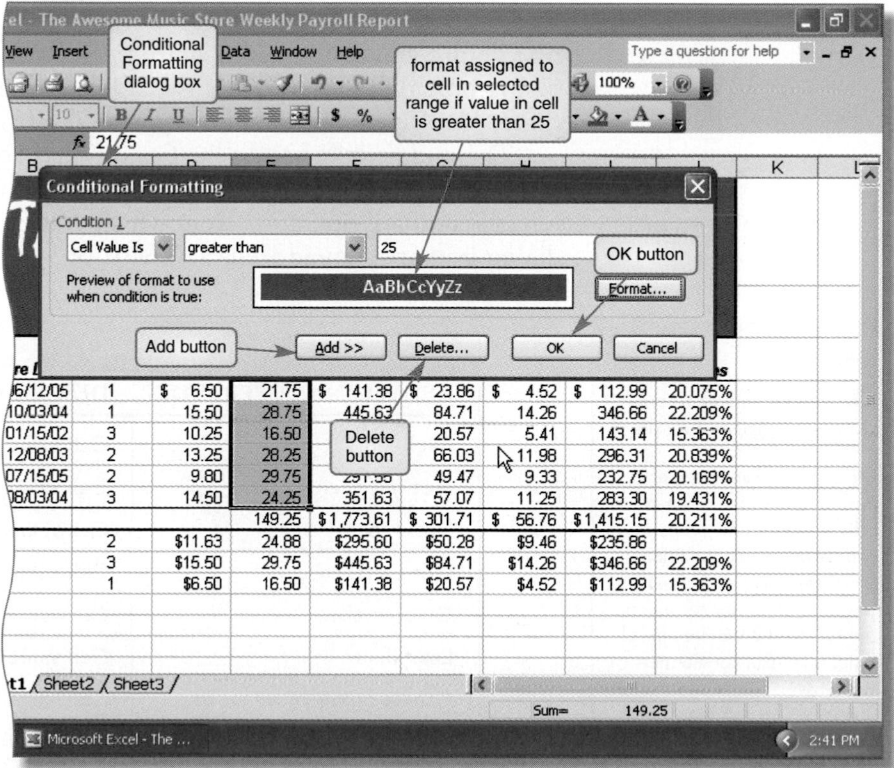

FIGURE 2-53

5

- **Click the OK button.**
- **Click cell A15 to deselect the range E4:E9.**

Excel assigns the conditional format to the range E4:E9. Excel displays any number greater than 25 in this range in white bold font with a red background (Figure 2-54).

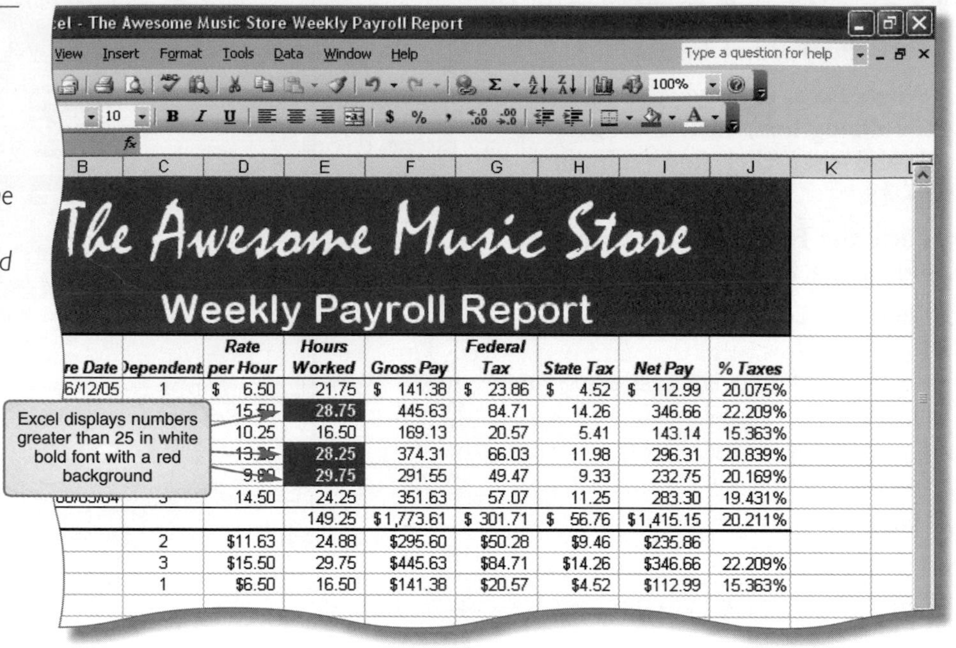

FIGURE 2-54

In Figure 2-53 on the previous page, the preview box in the Conditional Formatting dialog box shows the format that will be assigned to all cells in the range E4:E9 that have a value greater than 25. This preview allows you to review the format before you click the OK button. The Add button in the Conditional Formatting dialog box allows you to add two additional conditions for a total of three conditions. The Delete button allows you to delete one or more active conditions.

The middle text box in the Conditional Formatting dialog box allows you to select a relational operator, such as less than, to use in the condition. The eight different relational operators from which you can choose in the Conditional Formatting dialog box are summarized in Table 2-5.

Q & A

Q: Can any format be conditionally assigned to a cell?

A: Yes. You can assign any format to a cell, a range of cells, a worksheet, or an entire workbook conditionally. If the value of the cell changes and no longer meets the specified condition, Excel suppresses the conditional formatting.

Table 2-5 Summary of Conditional Formatting Relational Operators

RELATIONAL OPERATOR	DESCRIPTION
Between	Cell value is between two numbers
Not between	Cell value is not between two numbers
Equal to	Cell value is equal to a number
Not equal to	Cell value is not equal to a number
Greater than	Cell value is greater than a number
Less than	Cell value is less than a number
Greater than or equal to	Cell value is greater than or equal to a number
Less than or equal to	Cell value is less than or equal to a number

With the conditional formatting complete, the next step is to change the column widths and row heights to make the worksheet easier to read.

Changing the Widths of Columns and Heights of Rows

When Excel starts and displays a blank worksheet on the screen, all of the columns have a default width of 8.43 characters, or 64 pixels. A **character** is defined as a letter, number, symbol, or punctuation mark in 10-point Arial font, the default font used by Excel. An average of 8.43 characters in 10-point Arial font will fit in a cell.

Another measure is pixels, which is short for picture element. A **pixel** is a dot on the screen that contains a color. The size of the dot is based on your screen's resolution. At a common resolution of 800 × 600, 800 pixels appear across the screen and 600 pixels appear down the screen for a total of 480,000 pixels. It is these 480,000 pixels that form the font and other items you see on the screen.

The default row height in a blank worksheet is 12.75 points (or 17 pixels). Recall from Project 1 that a point is equal to 1/72 of an inch. Thus, 12.75 points is equal to about 1/6 of an inch. You can change the width of the columns or height of the rows at any time to make the worksheet easier to read or to ensure that Excel displays an entry properly in a cell.

Q: Can a format assigned to one cell be copied to another cell?

A: Yes. If one cell has a format that you want to assign to another cell or range of cells, click the cell with the desired format, click the Format Painter button on the Standard toolbar, and then select the cell or range of cells to paint with the desired format.

Changing the Widths of Columns

When changing the column width, you can set the width manually or you can instruct Excel to size the column to best fit. **Best fit** means that the width of the column will be increased or decreased so the widest entry will fit in the column. Sometimes, you may prefer more or less white space in a column than best fit provides. Excel thus allows you to change column widths manually.

When the format you assign to a cell causes the entry to exceed the width of a column, Excel automatically changes the column width to best fit. If you do not assign a format to a cell or cells in a column, the column width will remain 8.43 characters. To set a column width to best fit, double-click the right boundary of the column heading above row 1.

The following steps change the column widths: column A to 17.00 characters; columns B through F to best fit; columns G, H, and J to 8.86 characters; and column I to 10.86 characters.

To Change the Widths of Columns

1

- **Point to the boundary on the right side of the column A heading above row 1.**
- **When the mouse pointer changes to a split double arrow, drag to the right until the ScreenTip indicates Width: 17.00 (124 pixels). Do not release the mouse button.**

A dotted line shows the proposed right border of column A (Figure 2-55).

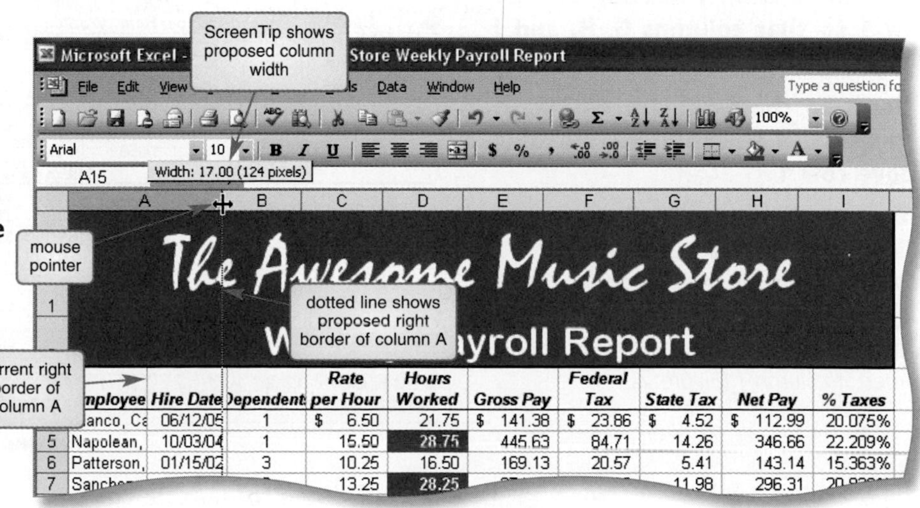

FIGURE 2-55

2

- **Release the mouse button.**
- **Drag through column headings B through F above row 1.**
- **Point to the boundary on the right side of column heading F.**

The mouse pointer becomes a split double arrow (Figure 2-56).

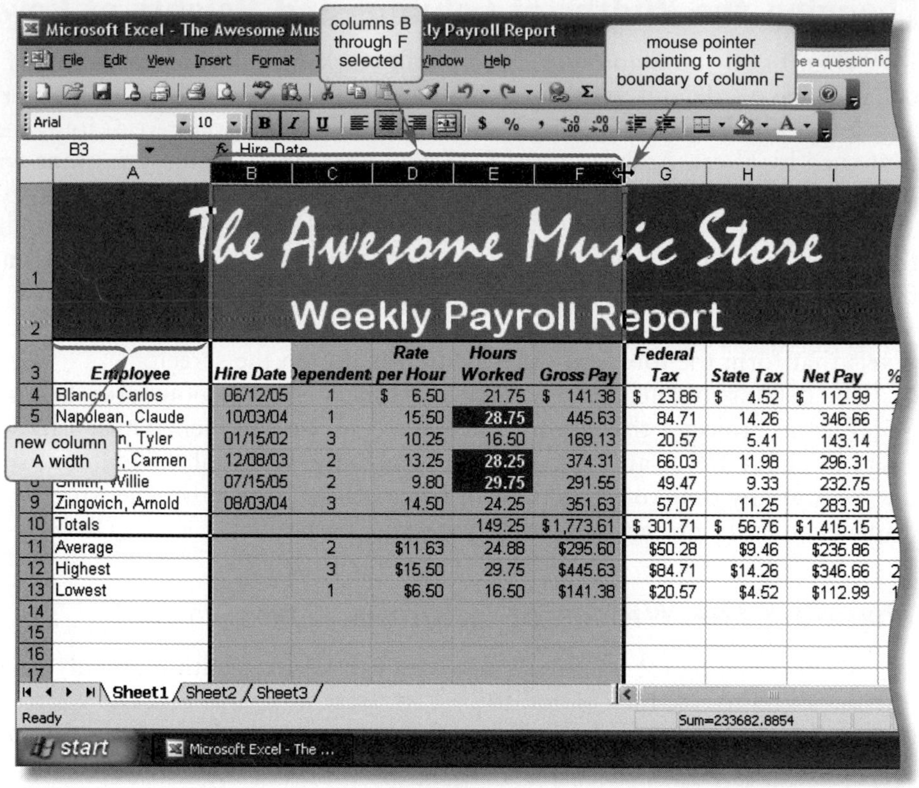

FIGURE 2-56

3

- **Double-click the right boundary of column heading F to change the width of columns B, C, D, E, and F to best fit.**
- **Click the column heading G above row 1 and drag through the column heading H above row 1.**
- **While holding down the CTRL key, click the column J heading above row 1 so that columns G, H, and J are selected.**
- **Point to the boundary on the right side of the column J heading above row 1.**
- **Drag until the ScreenTip indicates Width: 8.86 (67 pixels). Do not release the mouse button.**

A dotted line shows the proposed right border of column J (Figure 2-57).

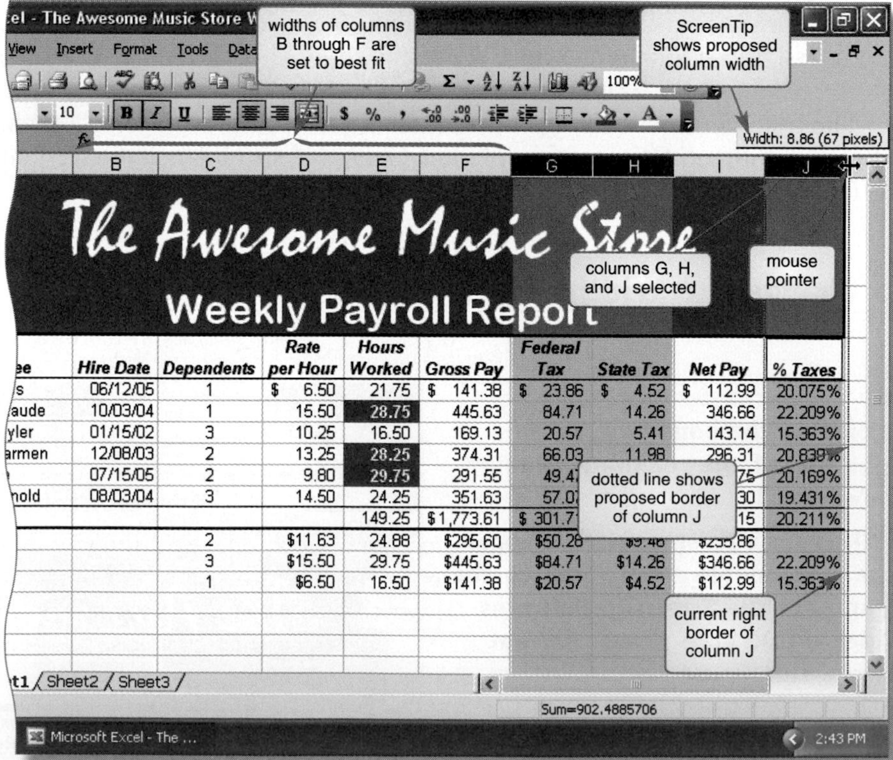

FIGURE 2-57

4

• **Release the mouse button and select cell A15.**

• **Point to the boundary on the right side of the column I heading above row 1.**

• **Drag to the right until the ScreenTip indicates Width: 10.86 (81 pixels). Do not release the mouse button.**

A dotted line shows the proposed right border of column I (Figure 2-58).

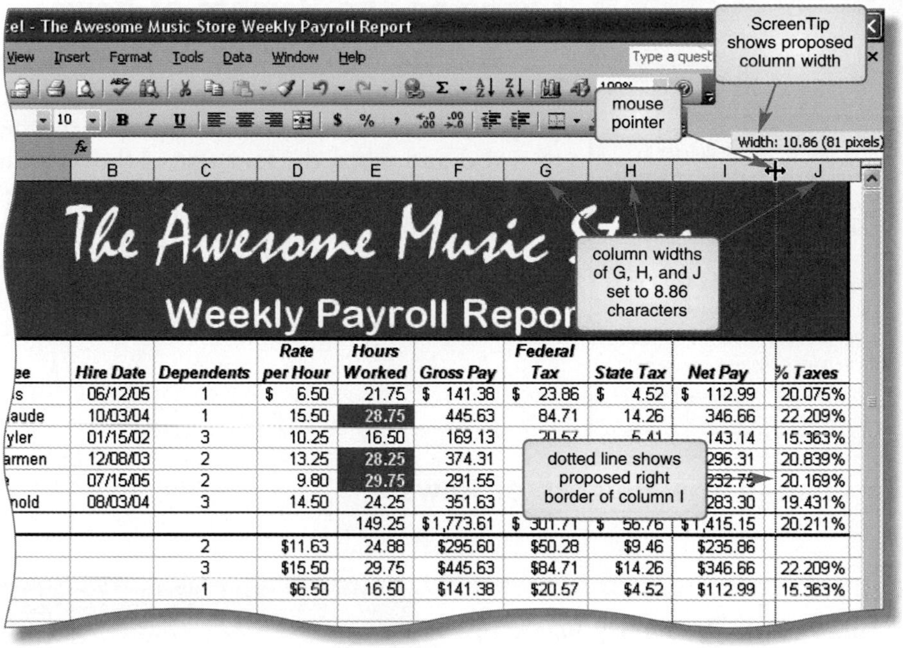

FIGURE 2-58

5

• **Release the mouse button.**

Excel displays the worksheet with the new column widths (Figure 2-59).

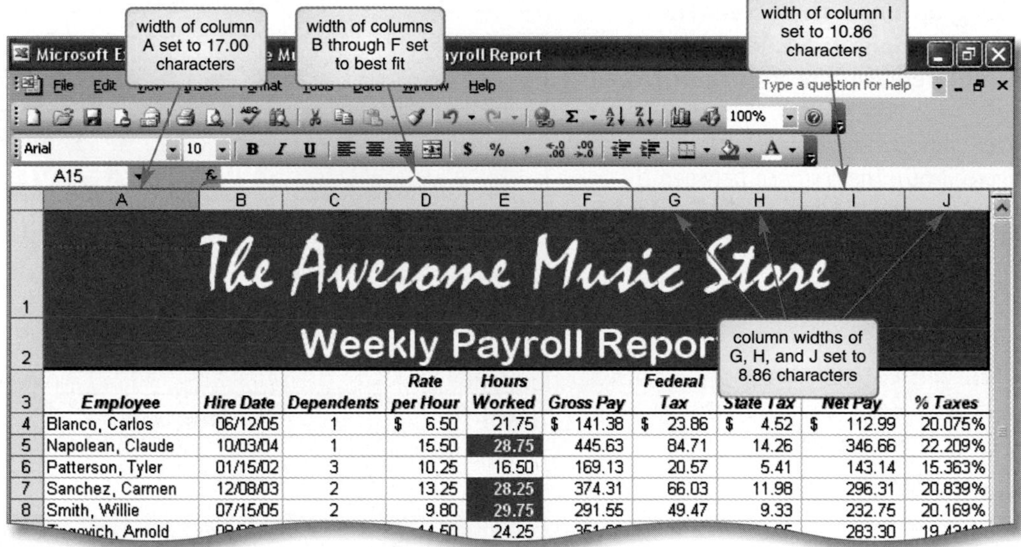

FIGURE 2-59

If you want to increase or decrease column width significantly, you can right-click a column heading and then use the Column Width command on the shortcut menu to change the column's width. To use this command, however, you must select one or more entire columns. As shown in the previous set of steps, you select entire columns by dragging through the column headings above row 1.

A column width can vary from zero (0) to 255 characters. If you decrease the column width to 0, the column is hidden. **Hiding cells** is a technique you can use to hide data that might not be relevant to a particular report or sensitive data that you do not want others to see. When you print a worksheet, hidden columns do not print. To instruct Excel to display a hidden column, position the mouse pointer to the right of the column heading boundary where the hidden column is located and then drag to the right.

> **Q & A**
>
> **Q:** Can the keyboard be used to unhide a range of columns?
>
> **A:** Yes. Trying to unhide a range of columns using the mouse can be frustrating. An alternative is to use the keyboard, by selecting the columns to the right and left of the hidden columns and then pressing CTRL+SHIFT+RIGHT PARENTHESIS. To use the keyboard to hide a range of columns, press CTRL+0.

Changing the Heights of Rows

When you increase the font size of a cell entry, such as the title in cell A1, Excel automatically increases the row height to best fit so it can display the characters properly. Recall that Excel did this earlier when multiple lines were entered in a cell in row 3 and when the font size of the worksheet title and subtitle were increased.

You also can increase or decrease the height of a row manually to improve the appearance of the worksheet. The following steps show how to improve the appearance of the worksheet by decreasing the height of row 1 to 54.00 points, increasing the height of row 2 to 33.00 points, increasing the height of row 3 to 45.00 points, and increasing the height of row 11 to 24.00 points.

To Change the Heights of Rows

1

- **Point to the boundary below row heading 1.**
- **Drag up until the ScreenTip indicates Height: 54.00 (72 pixels). Do not release the mouse button.**

Excel displays a horizontal dotted line (Figure 2-60). The distance between the dotted line and the top of row 1 indicates the proposed height for row 1.

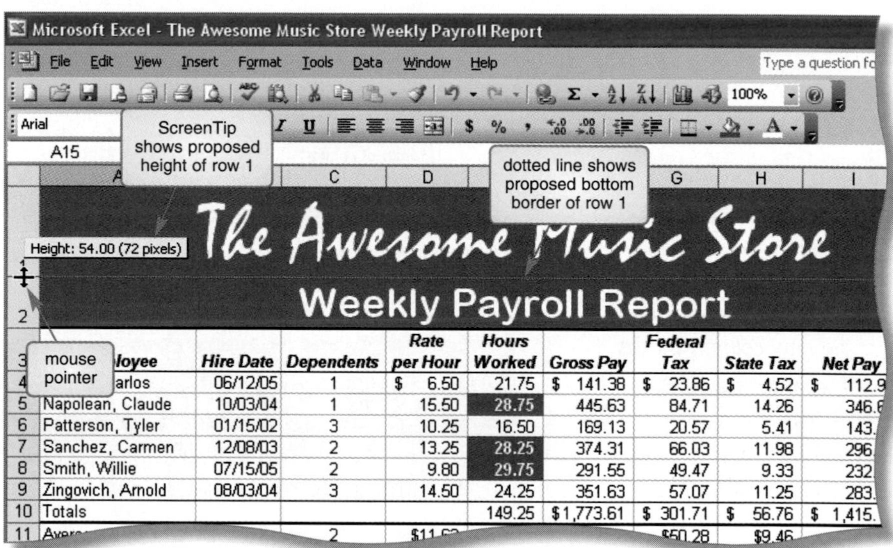

FIGURE 2-60

2

- **Release the mouse button.**
- **Point to the boundary below row heading 2.**
- **Drag down until the ScreenTip indicates Height: 33.00 (44 pixels). Do not release the mouse button.**

Excel displays a horizontal dotted line (Figure 2-61). The distance between the dotted line and the top of row 2 indicates the proposed height for row 2.

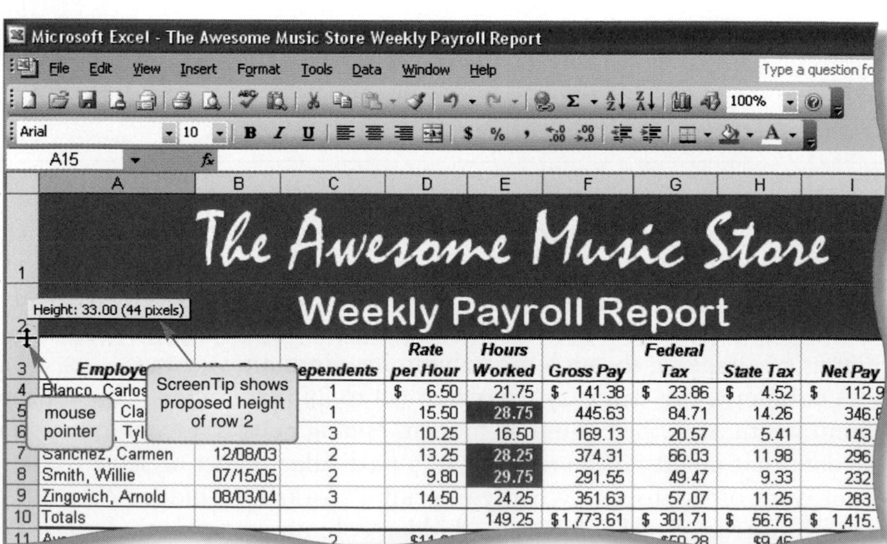

FIGURE 2-61

3

- **Release the mouse button.**
- **Drag the boundary below row heading 3 until the ScreenTip indicates Height 45.00 (60 pixels).**
- **Drag the boundary below row heading 11 until the ScreenTip indicates Height 24.00 (32 pixels).**

Rows 3 and 11 have additional white space, which improves the appearance of the worksheet (Figure 2-62). The formatting of the worksheet is complete.

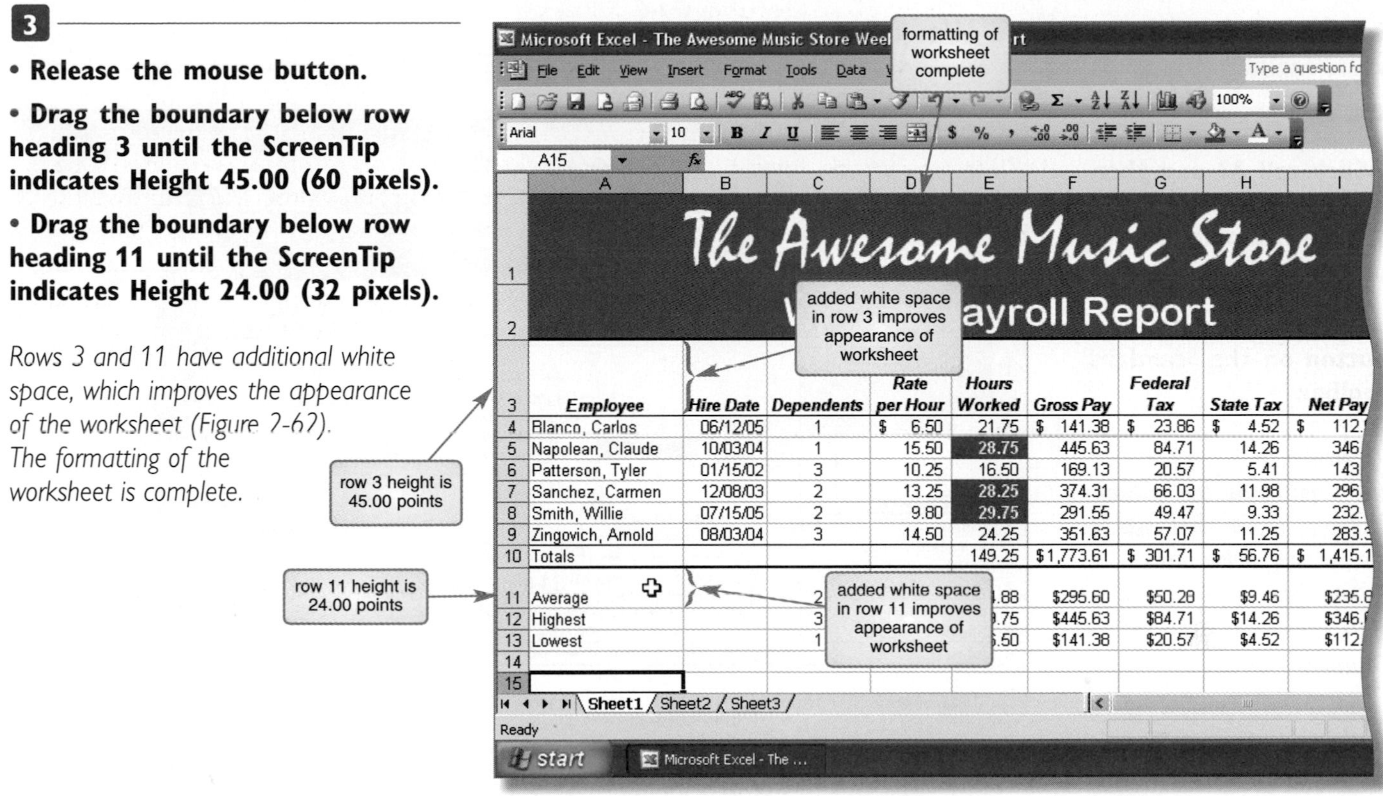

FIGURE 2-62

The row height can vary between 0 and 409 points. As with column widths, when you decrease the row height to 0, the row is hidden. To instruct Excel to display a hidden row, position the mouse pointer just below the row heading boundary where the row is hidden and then drag down. To set a row height to best fit, double-click the bottom boundary of the row heading.

The task of formatting the worksheet is complete. The next step is to check the spelling of the worksheet.

Checking Spelling

Excel has a **spell checker** you can use to check the worksheet for spelling errors. The spell checker looks for spelling errors by comparing words on the worksheet against words contained in its standard dictionary. If you often use specialized terms that are not in the standard dictionary, you may want to add them to a custom dictionary using the Spelling dialog box.

When the spell checker finds a word that is not in either dictionary, it displays the word in the Spelling dialog box. You then can correct it if it is misspelled.

To illustrate how Excel responds to a misspelled word, the word, Employee, in cell A3 is misspelled purposely as the word, Emloyee, as shown in Figure 2-63 on the next page.

Skill Builder 2-3

To practice the following tasks, visit scsite.com/off2003sch/skill, locate Excel Project 2, and then click Skill Builder 2-3.

- ❑ Format worksheet titles and column titles
- ❑ Format numbers using Currency and Comma styles
- ❑ Center, bold, and italicize cell entries
- ❑ Assign conditional formatting
- ❑ Change column widths and row heights

Q & A

Q: Can the keyboard be used to unhide a range of rows?

A: Yes. You can use the keyboard to unhide a range of rows by selecting the rows immediately above and below the hidden rows and then pressing CTRL+SHIFT+LEFT PARENTHESIS. To use the keyboard to hide a range of rows, press CTRL+9.

To Check Spelling on the Worksheet

1

- **Click cell A3 and then type** `Emloyee` **to misspell the word Employee.**
- **Click cell A1.**
- **Click the Spelling button on the Standard toolbar.**

When the spell checker identifies the misspelled word, Emloyee, in cell A3 it displays the Spelling dialog box (Figure 2-63).

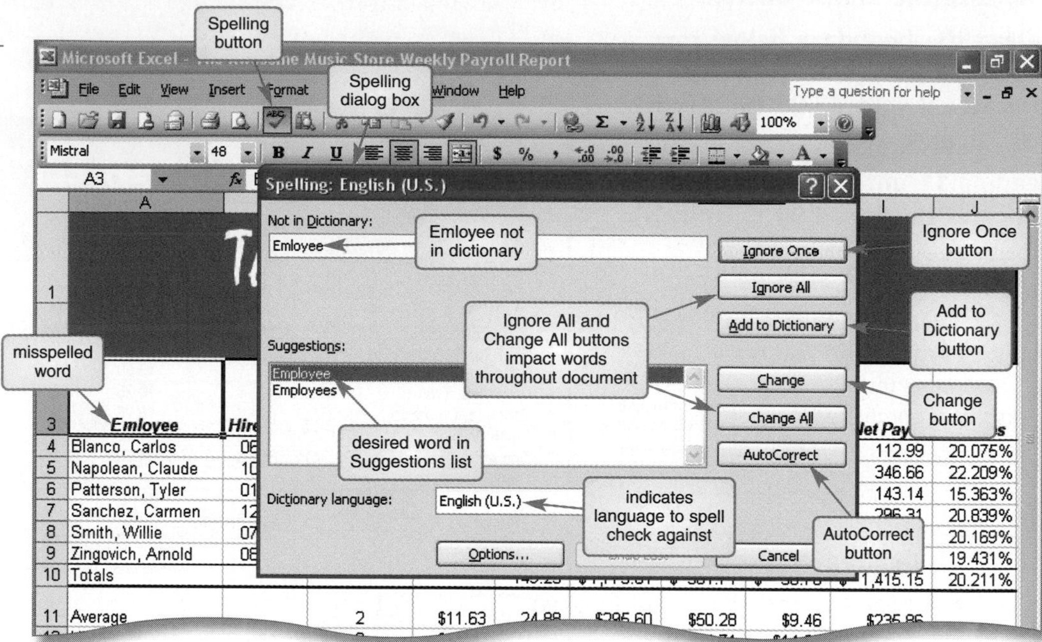

FIGURE 2-63

2

- **With the word Employee highlighted in the Suggestions list, click the Change button.**
- **As the spell checker checks the remainder of the worksheet, click the Ignore All and Change buttons as needed.**

The spell checker changes the misspelled word, Emloyee, to the correct word, Employee, and continues spell checking the worksheet. When the spell checker is finished, it displays the Microsoft Office Excel dialog box with a message indicating that the spell check is complete (Figure 2-64).

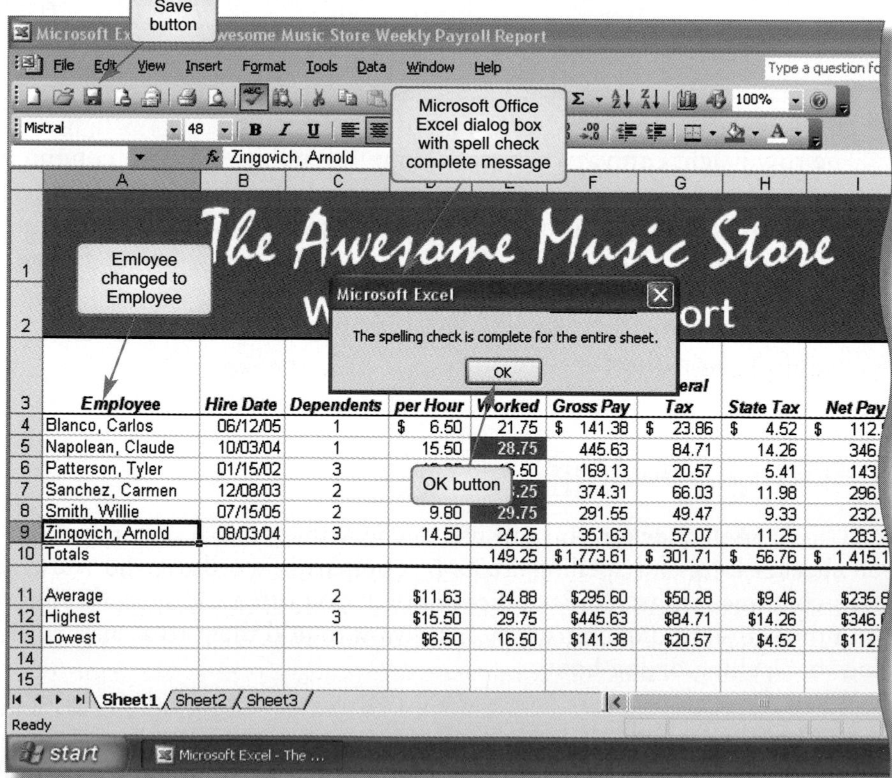

FIGURE 2-64

3

- **Click the OK button.**
- **Click the Save button on the Standard toolbar to save the workbook.**

When the spell checker identifies that a cell contains a word not in its standard or custom dictionary, it selects that cell as the active cell and displays the Spelling dialog box. The Spelling dialog box (Figure 2-63) lists the word not found in the dictionary, a suggested correction, and a list of alternative suggestions. If one of the words in the Suggestions list is correct, click it and then click the Change button. If none of the suggestions is correct, type the correct word in the Not in Dictionary text box and then click the Change button. To change the word throughout the worksheet, click the Change All button instead of the Change button. To skip correcting the word, click the Ignore Once button. To have Excel ignore the word for the remainder of the worksheet, click the Ignore All button.

Consider these additional guidelines when using the spell checker:

- To check the spelling of the text in a single cell, double-click the cell to make the formula bar active and then click the Spelling button on the Standard toolbar.
- If you select a single cell so that the formula bar is not active and then start the spell checker, Excel checks the remainder of the worksheet, including notes and embedded charts.
- If you select a range of cells before starting the spell checker, Excel checks the spelling of the words only in the selected range.
- To check the spelling of all the sheets in a workbook, click Select All Sheets on the sheet tab shortcut menu and then start the spell checker. To instruct Excel to display the sheet tab shortcut menu, right-click any sheet tab.
- If you select a cell other than cell A1 before you start the spell checker, Excel will display a dialog box when the spell checker reaches the end of the worksheet, asking if you want to continue checking at the beginning.
- To add words to the dictionary such as your last name, click the Add to Dictionary button in the Spelling dialog box (Figure 2-63) when Excel identifies the word as not in the dictionary.
- Click the AutoCorrect button (Figure 2-63) to add the misspelled word and the correct version of the word to the AutoCorrect list. For example, suppose you misspell the word, do, as the word, dox. When the spell checker displays the Spelling dialog box with the correct word, do, in the Change to box, click the AutoCorrect button. Then, anytime in the future that you type the word, dox, Excel automatically will change it to the word, do.

Q & A

Q: Can I rely on the spell checker to find every misspelling?

A: While Excel's spell checker is a valuable tool, it is not infallible. You should proofread your workbook carefully by pointing to each word and saying it aloud as you point to it. Be mindful of misused words such as its and it's, through and though, and to and too. Nothing undermines a good impression more than a professional looking report with misspelled words.

Previewing and Printing the Worksheet

In Project 1, the worksheet was printed without first previewing it on the screen. By **previewing the worksheet**, however, you see exactly how it will look without generating a printout. Previewing allows you to see if the worksheet will print on one page in portrait orientation. **Portrait orientation** means the printout is printed across the width of the page. **Landscape orientation** means the printout is printed across the length of the page. Previewing a worksheet using the Print Preview command on the File menu or Print Preview button on the Standard toolbar can save time, paper, and the frustration of waiting for a printout only to discover it is not what you want.

The steps on the next page preview and then print the worksheet.

To Preview and Print a Worksheet

1

- **Point to the Print Preview button on the Standard toolbar (Figure 2-65).**

FIGURE 2-65

2

- **Click the Print Preview button.**

Excel displays a preview of the worksheet in portrait orientation, because portrait is the default orientation. In portrait orientation, the worksheet does not fit on one page (Figure 2-66).

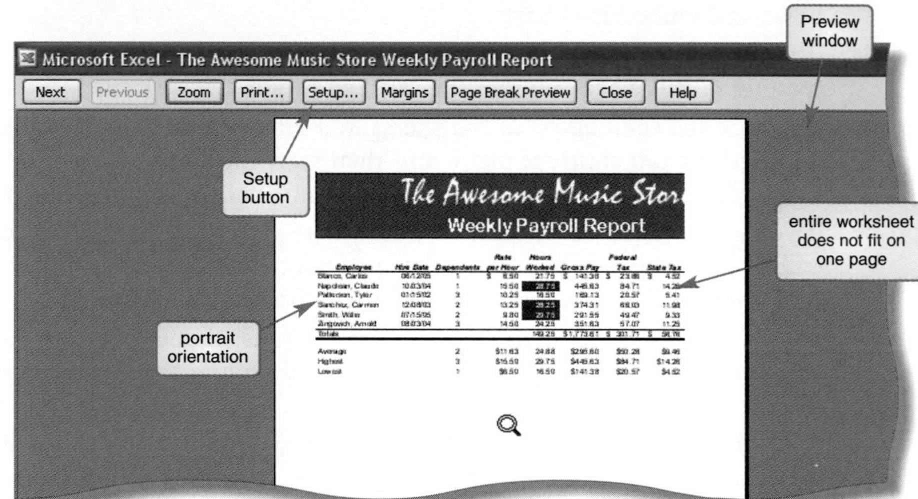

FIGURE 2-66

3

- **Click the Setup button.**
- **When Excel displays the Page Setup dialog box, click the Page tab and then click Landscape in the Orientation area.**

Excel displays the Page Setup dialog box. The Orientation area contains two option buttons, Portrait and Landscape. The Landscape option button is selected (Figure 2-67).

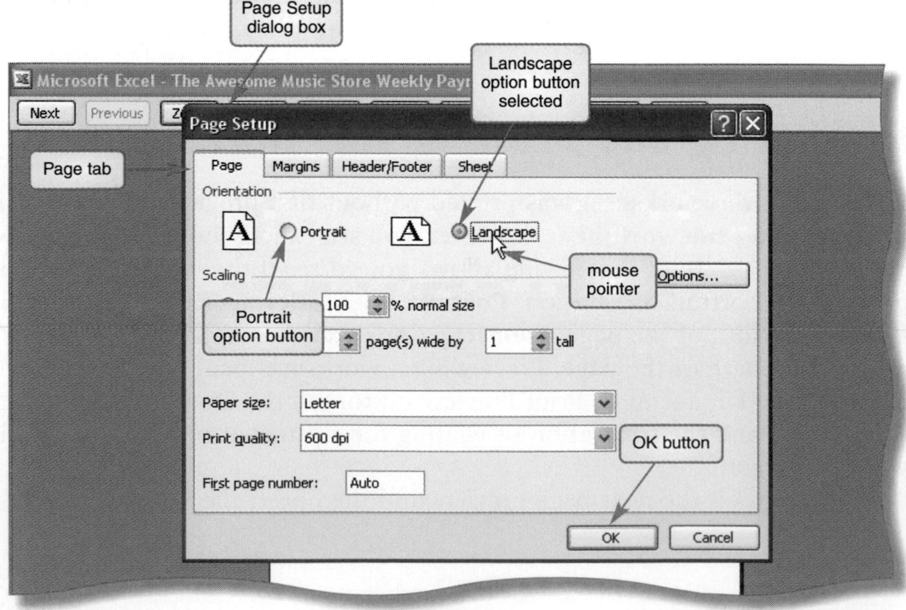

FIGURE 2-67

4

- **Click the OK button.**

Excel displays the worksheet in the Preview window. In landscape orientation, the entire worksheet fits on one page (Figure 2-68).

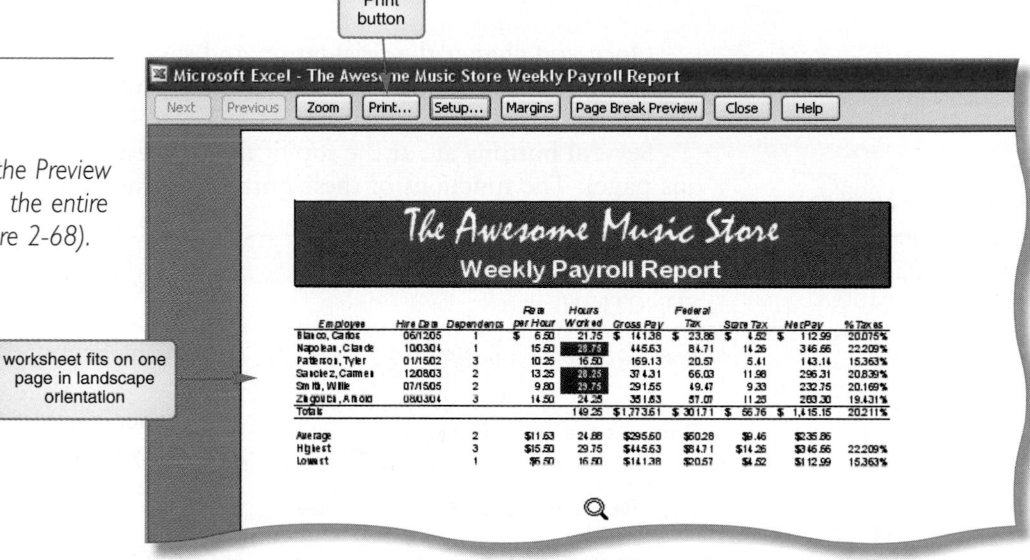

FIGURE 2-68

5

- **Click the Print button.**

Excel displays the Print dialog box as shown in Figure 2-69.

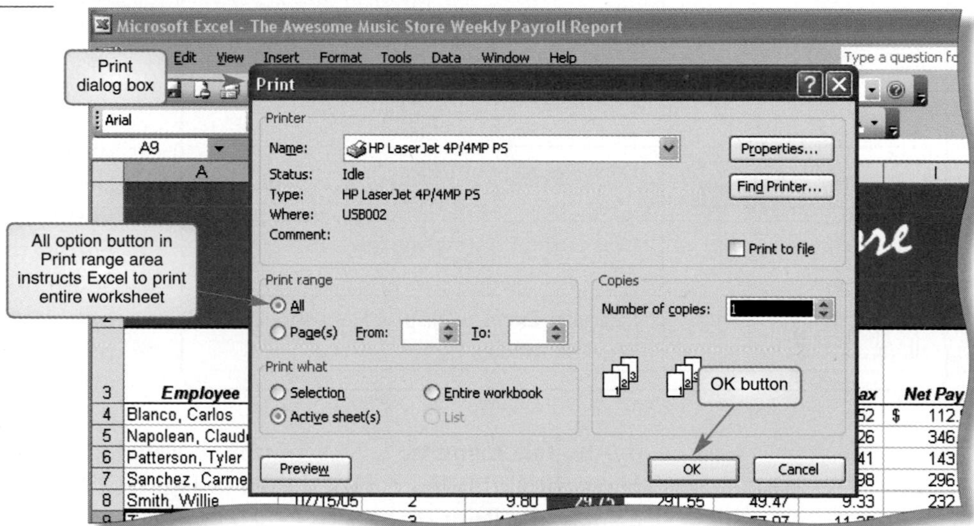

FIGURE 2-69

6

- **Click the OK button.**
- **Click the Save button on the Standard toolbar.**

Excel prints the worksheet (Figure 2-70). Excel saves the workbook with the landscape orientation print setting.

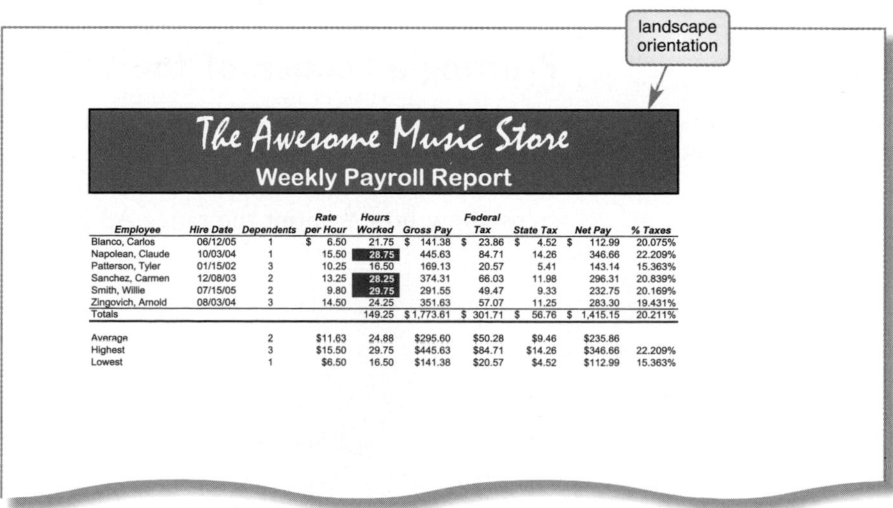

Employee	Hire Date	Dependents	Rate per Hour	Hours Worked	Gross Pay	Federal Tax	State Tax	Net Pay	% Taxes
Blanco, Carlos	06/12/05	1	$ 6.50	21.75	$ 141.38	$ 23.86	$ 4.52	$ 112.99	20.075%
Napolean, Claude	10/03/04	1	15.50	28.75	445.63	84.71	14.26	346.66	22.209%
Patterson, Tyler	01/15/02	3	10.25	16.50	169.13	20.57	5.41	143.14	15.363%
Sanchez, Carmen	12/08/03	2	13.25	28.25	374.31	66.03	11.98	296.31	20.839%
Smith, Willie	07/15/05	2	9.80	29.75	291.55	49.47	9.33	232.75	20.169%
Zingovich, Arnold	08/03/04	3	14.50	24.25	351.63	57.07	11.25	283.30	19.431%
Totals				149.25	$ 1,773.61	$ 301.71	$ 56.76	$ 1,415.15	20.211%
Average		2	$11.63	24.88	$295.60	$50.28	$9.46	$235.86	
Highest		3	$15.50	29.75	$445.63	$84.71	$14.26	$346.66	22.209%
Lowest		1	$6.50	16.50	$141.38	$20.57	$4.52	$112.99	15.363%

FIGURE 2-70

Once you change the orientation and save the workbook, Excel will save the orientation setting for that workbook until you change it. When you open a new workbook, Excel sets the orientation to portrait.

Several buttons are at the top of the Preview window (Figure 2-68 on the previous page). The functions of these buttons are summarized in Table 2-6.

Table 2-6 Print Preview Buttons

BUTTON	FUNCTION
Next	Previews the next page
Previous	Previews the previous page
Zoom	Magnifies or reduces the print preview
Print...	Prints the worksheet
Setup...	Instructs Excel to display the Print Setup dialog box
Margins	Changes the print margins
Page Break Preview	Previews page breaks
Close	Closes the Preview window
Help	Instructs Excel to display Help about the Preview window

Rather than click the Next and Previous buttons to move from page to page as described in Table 2-6, you can press the PAGE UP and PAGE DOWN keys on your keyboard. You also can click the previewed page in the Preview window when the mouse pointer shape is a magnifying glass to carry out the function of the Zoom button.

The Page Setup dialog box shown in Figure 2-67 on page EX 114 allows you to make changes to the default settings for a printout. For example, on the Page tab, you can set the page orientation, as shown in the previous set of steps; scale the printout so it fits on one page; and set the page size and print quality. Scaling, which can be used to fit a wide worksheet on one page, will be discussed later in the project. The Margins tab, Header/Footer tab, and Sheet tab in the Page Setup dialog box provide additional options that allow for even more control of the way the printout will appear. These tabs will be discussed when they are used.

When you click the Print command on the File menu or a Print button in a dialog box or Preview window, Excel displays the Print dialog box shown in Figure 2-69 on the previous page. Excel does not display the Print dialog box when you use the Print button on the Standard toolbar, as was the case in Project 1. The Print dialog box allows you to select a printer, instruct Excel what to print, and indicate how many copies of the printout you want.

Printing a Section of the Worksheet

You might not always want to print the entire worksheet. You can print portions of the worksheet by selecting the range of cells to print and then clicking the Selection option button in the Print what area in the Print dialog box. The following steps show how to print the range A3:F13.

To Print a Section of the Worksheet

1

- **Select the range A3:F13.**
- **Click File on the menu bar and then click Print.**
- **Click Selection in the Print what area.**

Excel displays the Print dialog box (Figure 2-71). Because the Selection option button is selected, Excel will print only the selected range.

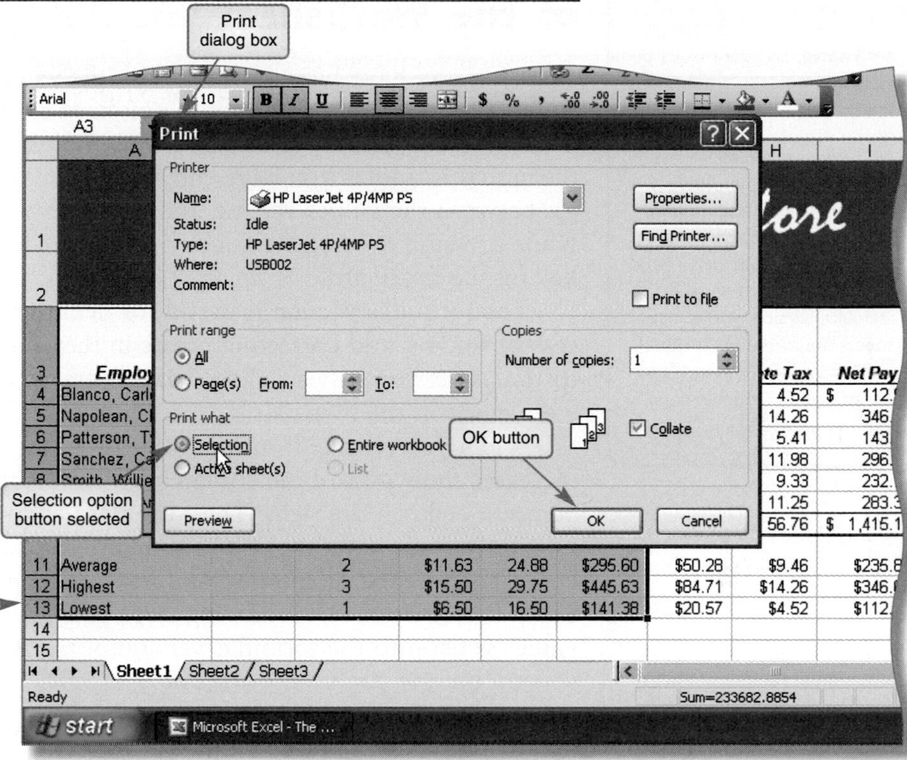

FIGURE 2-71

2

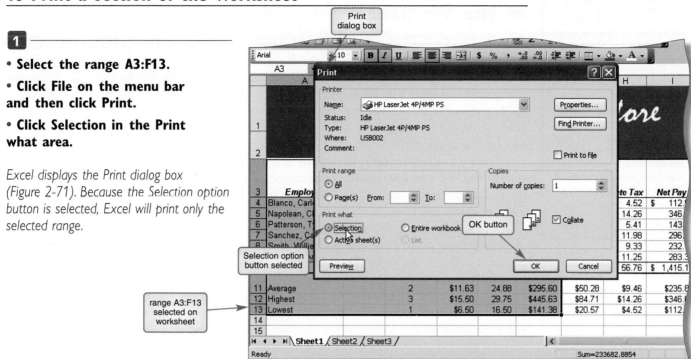

- **Click the OK button.**
- **Click cell A15 to deselect the range A3:F13.**

Excel prints the selected range of the worksheet on the printer (Figure 2-72).

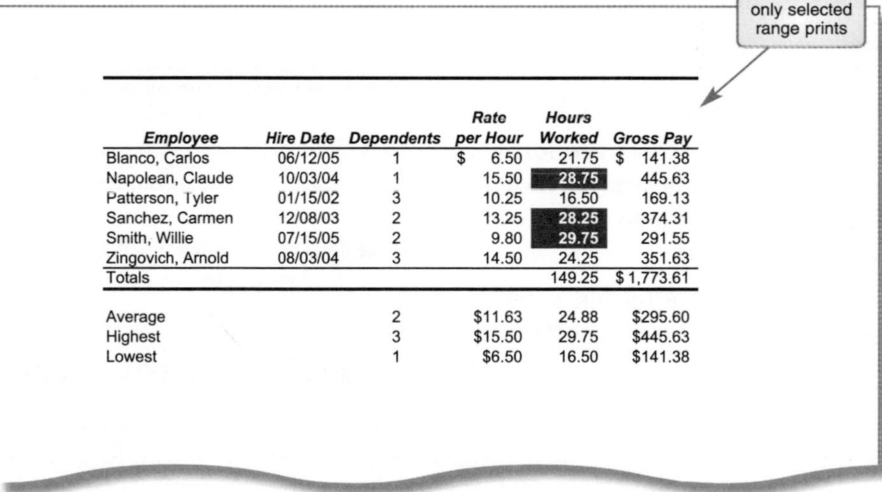

Employee	Hire Date	Dependents	Rate per Hour	Hours Worked	Gross Pay
Blanco, Carlos	06/12/05	1	$ 6.50	21.75	$ 141.38
Napolean, Claude	10/03/04	1	15.50	28.75	445.63
Patterson, Tyler	01/15/02	3	10.25	16.50	169.13
Sanchez, Carmen	12/08/03	2	13.25	28.25	374.31
Smith, Willie	07/15/05	2	9.80	29.75	291.55
Zingovich, Arnold	08/03/04	3	14.50	24.25	351.63
Totals				149.25	$ 1,773.61
Average		2	$11.63	24.88	$295.60
Highest		3	$15.50	29.75	$445.63
Lowest		1	$6.50	16.50	$141.38

FIGURE 2-72

The Print what area of the Print dialog box includes three option buttons (Figure 2-71). As shown in the previous steps, the Selection option button instructs Excel to print the selected range. The Active sheet(s) option button instructs Excel to print the active worksheet (the worksheet currently on the screen) or the selected worksheets. Finally, the Entire workbook option button instructs Excel to print all of the worksheets in the workbook.

Displaying and Printing the Formulas Version of the Worksheet

> *Q & A*
>
> **Q:** If the results of formulas are known, can the results be entered into cells instead of the formulas?
>
> **A:** When completing class assignments, do not enter numbers in cells that require formulas. Most instructors require their students to hand in both the values version and formulas version of the worksheet. The formulas version verifies that you entered formulas, rather than numbers, in formula-based cells.

Thus far, you have been working with the **values version** of the worksheet, which shows the results of the formulas you have entered, rather than the actual formulas. Excel also can display and print the **formulas version** of the worksheet, which shows the actual formulas you have entered, rather than the resulting values. You can toggle between the values version and formulas version by holding down the CTRL key while pressing the ACCENT MARK (`) key, which is located to the left of the number 1 key on the keyboard.

The formulas version is useful for debugging a worksheet. **Debugging** is the process of finding and correcting errors in the worksheet. Viewing and printing the formulas version instead of the values version makes it easier to see if any mistakes were made in the formulas.

When you change from the values version to the formulas version, Excel increases the width of the columns so the formulas and text do not overflow into adjacent cells on the right. The formulas version of the worksheet thus usually is significantly wider than the values version. To fit the wide printout on one page, you can use landscape orientation and the Fit to option in the Page sheet in the Page Setup dialog box. The following steps change the view of the worksheet from the values version to the formulas version of the worksheet and then print the formulas version on one page.

To Display the Formulas in the Worksheet and Fit the Printout on One Page

1

- **Press CTRL+ACCENT MARK (`).**
- **When Excel displays the formulas version of the worksheet, click the right horizontal scroll arrow until column J appears.**
- **If the Formula Auditing toolbar appears, click its Close button.**

Excel changes the display of the worksheet from values to formulas (Figure 2-73). It displays the formulas in the worksheet showing unformatted numbers, formulas, and functions that were assigned to the cells. Excel automatically increases the column widths.

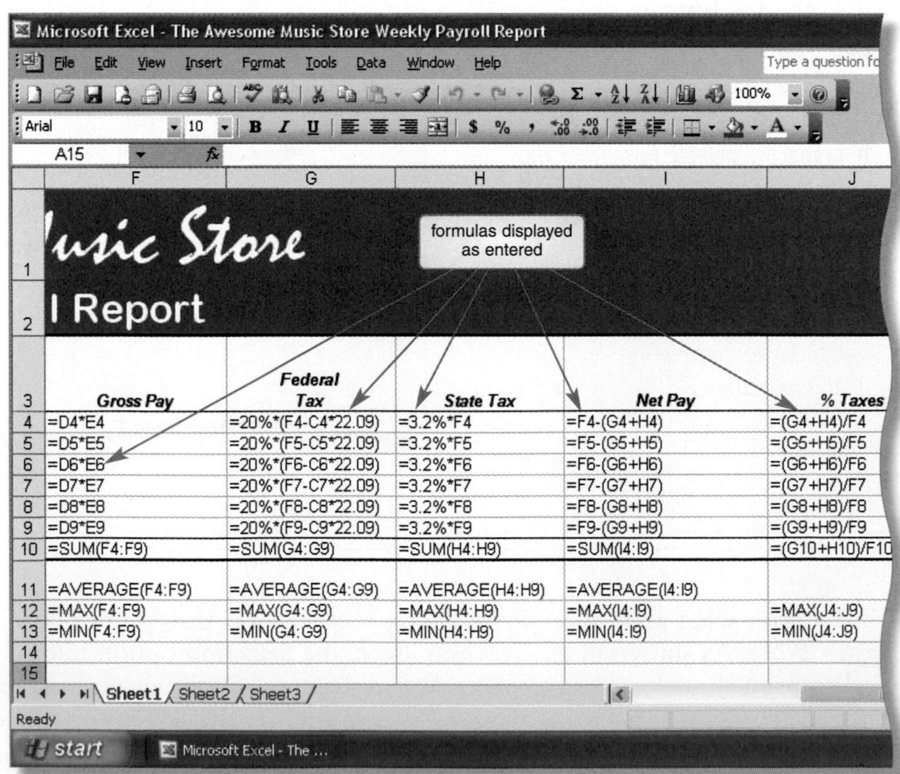

FIGURE 2-73

2

- **Click File on the menu bar and then click Page Setup.**
- **When Excel displays the Page Setup dialog box, click the Page tab.**
- **If necessary, click Landscape to select it and then click Fit to in the Scaling area.**

Excel displays the Page Setup dialog box with the Landscape and Fit to option buttons selected (Figure 2-74).

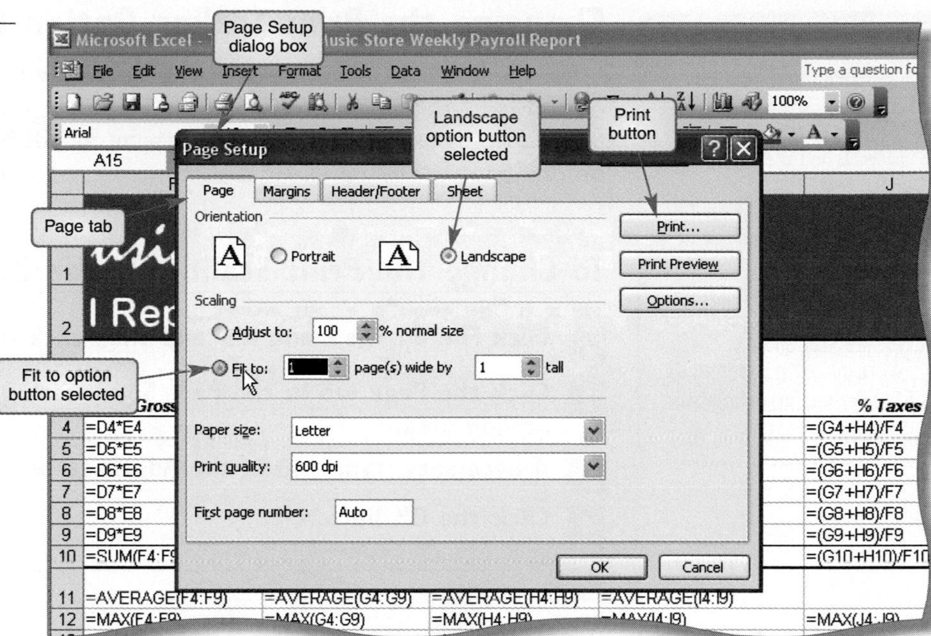

FIGURE 2-74

3

- **Click the Print button in the Page Setup dialog box.**
- **When Excel displays the Print dialog box, click the OK button.**
- **After viewing and printing the formulas version, press CTRL+ACCENT mark (`) to instruct Excel to display the values version.**

Excel prints the formulas in the worksheet on one page in landscape orientation (Figure 2-75). Excel displays the values version of the worksheet.

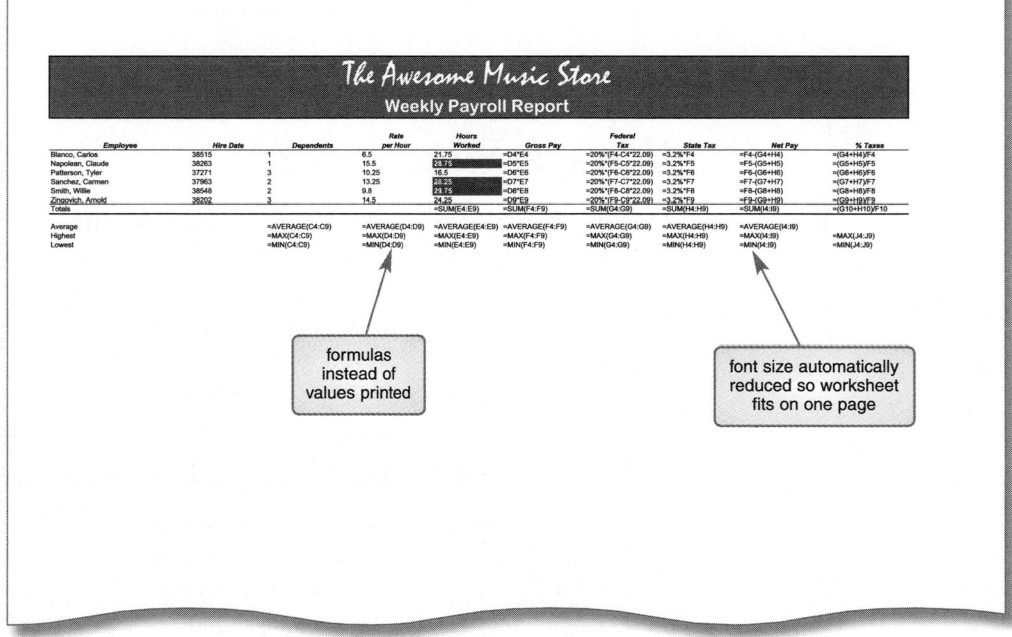

FIGURE 2-75

Although the formulas version of the worksheet was printed in the previous example, you can see from Figure 2-73 that you can review the formulas on the screen.

Skill Builder 2-4

To practice the following tasks, visit scsite.com/off2003sch/skill, locate Excel Project 2, and then click Skill Builder 2-4.

- ❑ Check spelling
- ❑ Preview and print worksheet
- ❑ Change orientation of printout
- ❑ Print a section of a worksheet
- ❑ Display and print formulas version

Changing the Print Scaling Option Back to 100%

Depending on your printer driver, you may have to change the Print Scaling option back to 100% after using the Fit to option. The following steps reset the Print Scaling option so future worksheets print at 100%, instead of being resized to print on one page.

To Change the Print Scaling Option Back to 100%

1. **Click File on the menu bar and then click Page Setup.**
2. **Click the Page tab in the Page Setup dialog box. Click Adjust to in the Scaling area.**
3. **If necessary, type** 100 **in the Adjust to box.**
4. **Click the OK button.**

The print scaling is set to normal.

The Adjust to box allows you to specify the percentage of reduction or enlargement in the printout of a worksheet. The default percentage is 100%. When you click the Fit to option, this percentage automatically changes to the percentage required to fit the printout on one page.

Importing External Data from a Web Source Using a Web Query

One of the major features of Excel is its capability of importing external data from Web sites. To import external data from a Web site, you must have access to the Internet. You then can import data stored on a Web site using a **Web query**. When you run a Web query, Excel imports the external data in the form of a worksheet. As described in Table 2-7, three Web queries are available when you first install Excel. All three Web queries relate to investment and stock market activities.

Table 2-7 Excel Web Queries

QUERY	EXTERNAL DATA RETURNED
MSN MoneyCentral Investor Currency Rates	Currency rates
MSN MoneyCentral Investor Major Indices	Major indices
MSN MoneyCentral Investor Stock Quotes	Up to 20 stocks of your choice

The data returned by the stock-related Web queries is real time in the sense that it is no more than 20 minutes old during the business day. The following steps show how to get the most recent stock quotes for the following stocks: General Electric (GE), Intel (INTC), Kimberly Clark (KMB), Merck (MRK), Microsoft (MSFT), and United Parcel Service (UPS). The stock symbols that follow each company name in parentheses will be used in the Web query to identify the companies. Although you can have a Web query return data to a blank workbook, the following steps have the data returned to a blank worksheet in The Awesome Music Store Weekly Payroll Report workbook.

To Import Data from a Web Source Using a Web Query

1

- **With The Awesome Music Store Weekly Payroll Report workbook open, click the Sheet2 tab at the bottom of the window.**
- **With cell A1 active, click Data on the menu bar, and then point to Import External Data on the Data menu.**

Excel displays the Data menu and Import External Data submenu as shown in Figure 2-76.

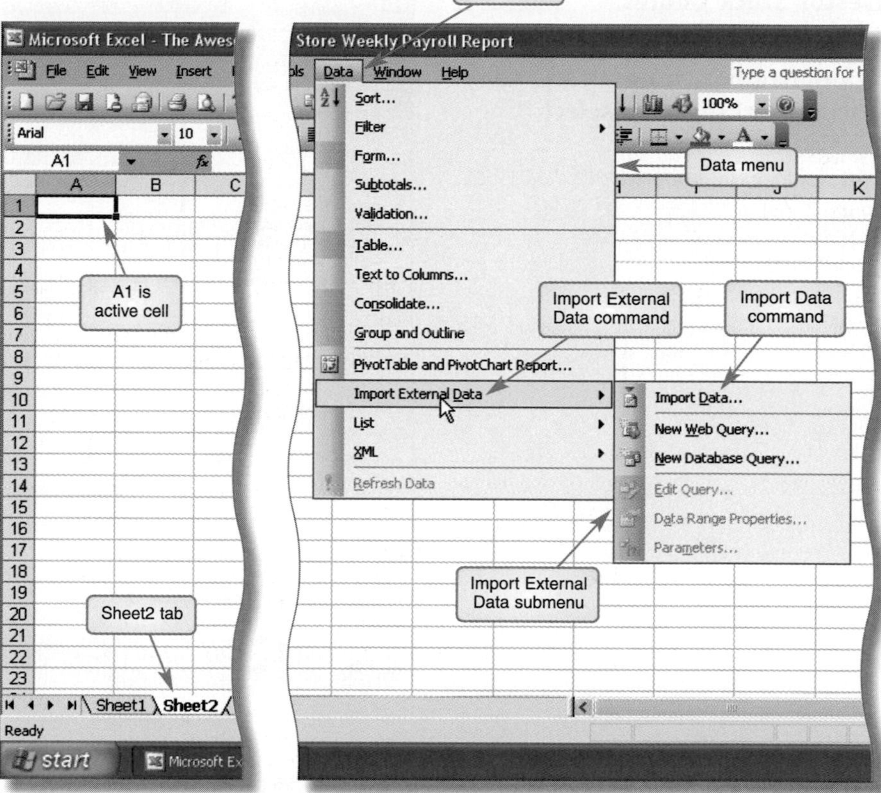

FIGURE 2-76

2

- **Click Import Data on the Import External Data submenu.**

Excel displays the Select Data Source dialog box (Figure 2-77). If your screen is different, ask your instructor for the folder location of the Web queries.

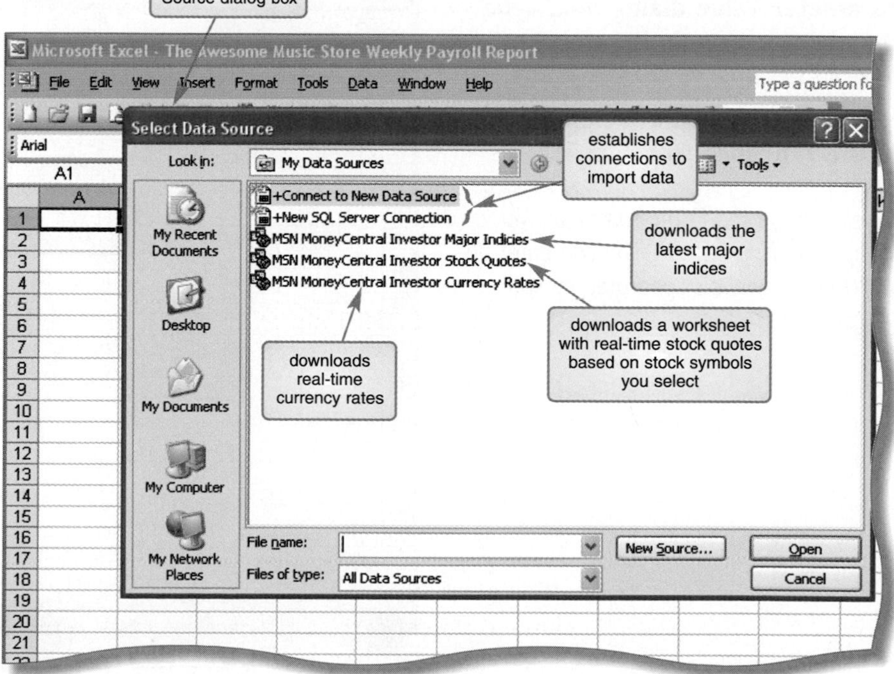

FIGURE 2-77

3

- **Double-click MSN MoneyCentral Investor Stock Quotes.**
- **When Excel displays the Import Data dialog box, if necessary, click Existing worksheet to select it.**

Excel displays the Import Data dialog box (Figure 2-78).

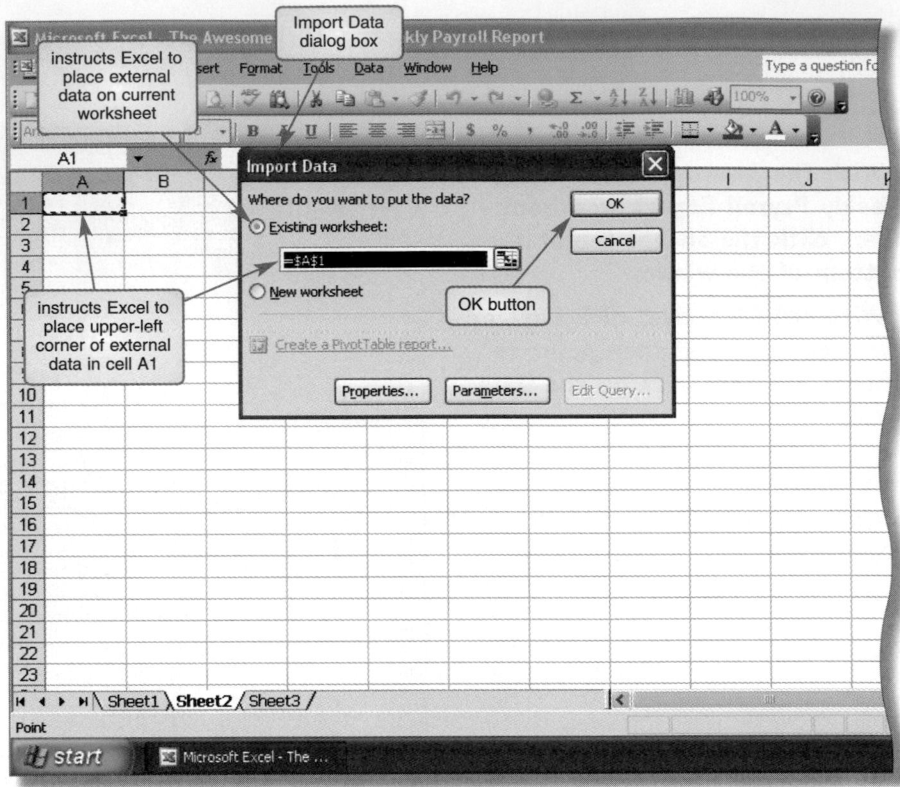

FIGURE 2-78

4

- **Click the OK button.**
- **When Excel displays the Enter Parameter Value dialog box, type the six stock symbols** `ge intc kmb mrk msft ups` **in the text box.**
- **Click Use this value/reference for future refreshes to select it.**

Excel displays the Enter Parameter Value dialog box (Figure 2-79). You can enter up to 20 stock symbols separated by spaces (or commas).

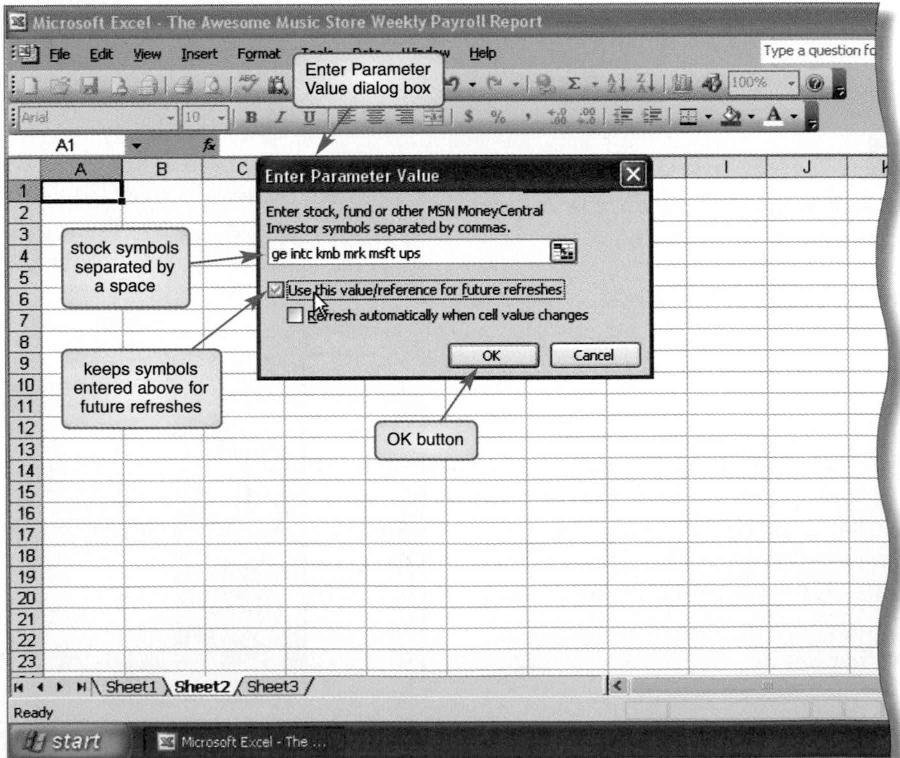

FIGURE 2-79

5

• **Click the OK button.**

Once your computer connects to the Internet, a message appears informing you that Excel is getting external data. After a short period, Excel displays a new worksheet with the desired data (Figure 2-80). The complete worksheet is shown in Figure 2-1b on page EX 67.

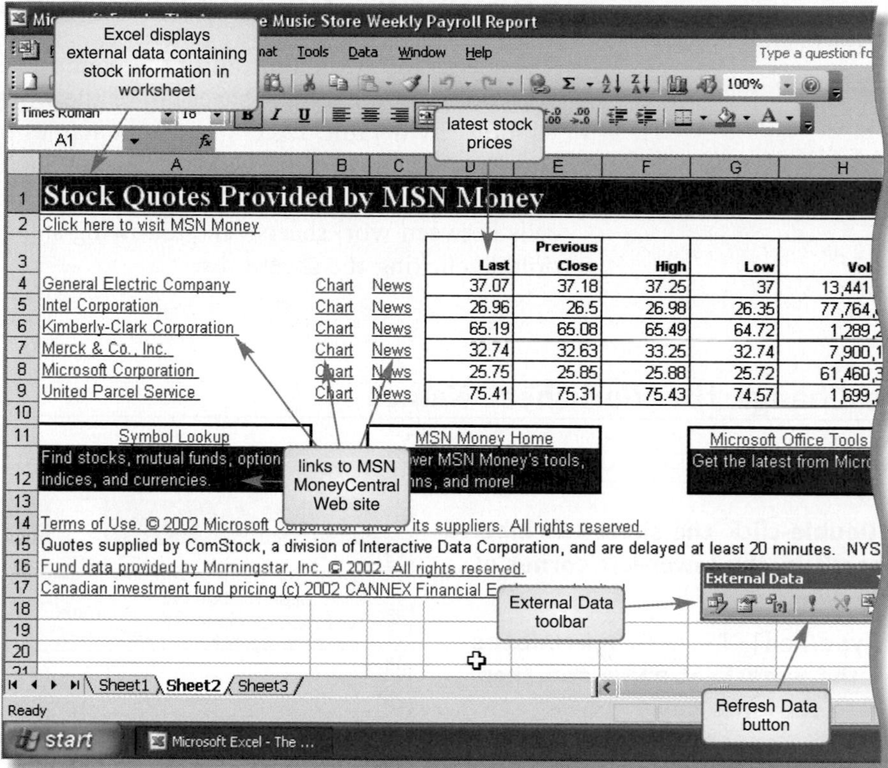

FIGURE 2-80

As shown in Figure 2-80, Excel displays the data returned from the Web query in an organized, formatted worksheet, which has a worksheet title, column titles, and a row of data for each stock symbol entered. Other than the first column, which contains the stock name and stock symbol, you have no control over the remaining columns of data returned. The latest price of each stock appears in column D.

Once Excel displays the worksheet, you can refresh the data as often as you want. To refresh the data for all the stocks, click the Refresh All button on the External Data toolbar (Figure 2-81). Because the Use this value/reference for future refreshes check box was selected in Step 4 of the previous steps (Figure 2-79), Excel will continue to use the same stock symbols each time it refreshes. You can change the symbols by clicking the Query Parameters button on the External Data toolbar.

If the External Data toolbar does not appear, right-click any toolbar and then click External Data. Instead of using the External Data toolbar, you also can invoke any Web query command by right-clicking any cell in the returned worksheet to display a shortcut menu with several of the same commands as the External Data toolbar.

This section gives you an idea of the potential of Web queries by having you use just one of Excel's Web queries. To reinforce the topics covered here, work through In the Lab 3 on page EX 136.

The workbook is nearly complete. The final step is to change the names of the sheets located on the sheet tabs at the bottom of the Excel window.

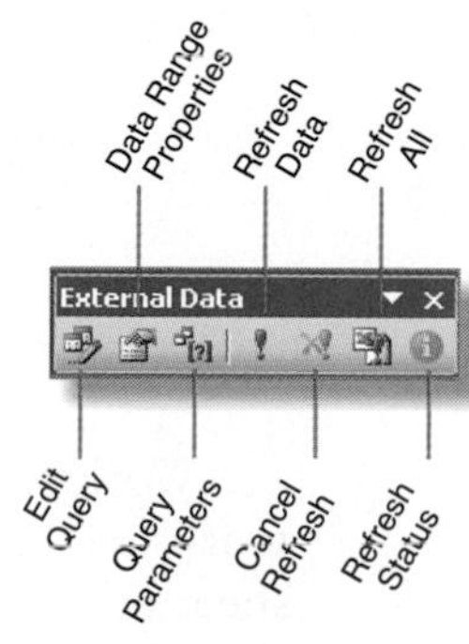

FIGURE 2-81

Changing the Worksheet Names

The sheet tabs at the bottom of the window allow you to view any worksheet in the workbook. You click the sheet tab of the worksheet you want to view in the Excel window. By default, Excel presets the names of the worksheets to Sheet1, Sheet2, and so on. The worksheet names become increasingly important as you move towards more sophisticated workbooks, especially those in which you reference cells between worksheets. The following steps show how to rename worksheets by double-clicking the sheet tabs.

To Change the Worksheet Names

1

- **Double-click the sheet tab labeled Sheet2 in the lower-left corner of the window.**
- **Type** `Real-Time Stock Quotes` **as the worksheet name and then press the ENTER key.**

The new worksheet name appears on the sheet tab (Figure 2-82).

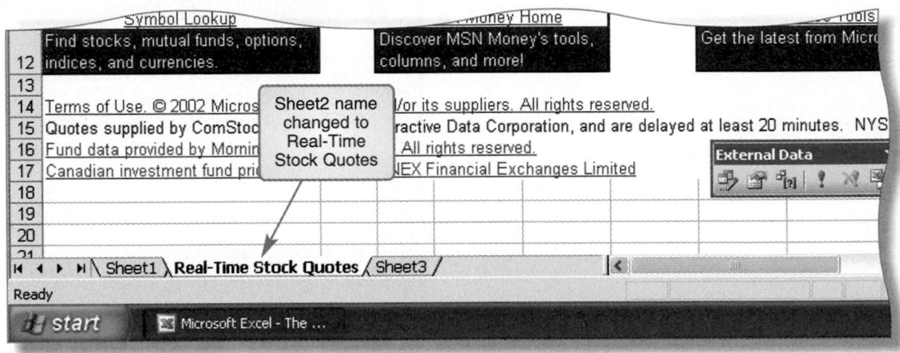

FIGURE 2-82

2

- **Double-click the sheet tab labeled Sheet1 in the lower-left corner of the window.**
- **Type** `Weekly Payroll` **as the worksheet name and then press the ENTER key.**

Excel changes the worksheet name from Sheet1 to Weekly Payroll (Figure 2-83).

	Employee	Hire Date	Dependents	per Hour	Hours Worked	Gross Pay	Tax	State Tax	Net Pay
4	Blanco, Carlos	06/12/05	1	$ 6.50	21.75	$ 141.38	$ 23.86	$ 4.52	$ 112.
5	Napolean, Claude	10/03/04	1	15.50	28.75	445.63	84.71	14.26	346.
6	Patterson, Tyler	01/15/02	3	10.25	16.50	169.13	20.57	5.41	143.
7	Sanchez, Carmen	12/08/03	2	13.25	28.25	374.31	66.03	11.98	296.
8	Smith, Willie	07/15/05	2	9.80	29.75	291.55	49.47	9.33	232.
9		08/03/04	3	14.50	24.25	351.63	57.07	11.25	283.3
10					149.25	$1,773.61	$ 301.71	$ 56.76	$ 1,415.1
11			2	$11.63	24.	.60	$50.28	$9.46	$235.8
12	Highest		3	$15.50	29.	.63	$84.71	$14.26	$346.
13	Lowest		1	$6.50	16.50	$141.38	$20.57	$4.52	$112.
14									
15									

Sheet1 name changed to Weekly Payroll

tab split box

Weekly Payroll / Real-Time Stock Quotes / Sheet3

Ready

start | Microsoft Excel - The ...

tab scrolling buttons

FIGURE 2-83

Worksheet names can be up to 31 characters (including spaces) in length. Longer worksheet names, however, mean that fewer sheet tabs will show. To view more sheet tabs, you can drag the tab split box (Figure 2-83) to the right. This will reduce the size of the scroll bar at the bottom of the screen. Double-click the tab split box to reset it to its normal position.

You also can use the tab scrolling buttons to the left of the sheet tabs (Figure 2-83) to move between worksheets. The leftmost and rightmost scroll buttons move to the first or last worksheet in the workbook. The two middle scroll buttons move one worksheet to the left or right.

E-Mailing a Workbook from within Excel

The most popular service on the Internet is electronic mail, or **e-mail**, which is the electronic transmission of messages and files to and from other computers using the Internet. Using e-mail, you can converse with friends across the room or on another continent. One of the features of e-mail is the ability to attach Office files, such as Word documents or Excel workbooks, to an e-mail message and send it to a coworker. In the past, if you wanted to e-mail a workbook, you saved the workbook, closed the file, started your e-mail program, and then attached the workbook to the e-mail message before sending it. With Excel you have the capability of e-mailing a worksheet or workbook directly from within Excel. For these steps to work properly, you must have an e-mail address and one of the following as your e-mail program: Microsoft Outlook, Microsoft Outlook Express, Microsoft Exchange Client, or another 32-bit e-mail program compatible with Messaging Application Programming Interface. The following steps show how to e-mail The Awesome Music Store Weekly Payroll Report workbook from within Excel to Tom Smith at the e-mail address tom_smith55475xd@hotmail.com.

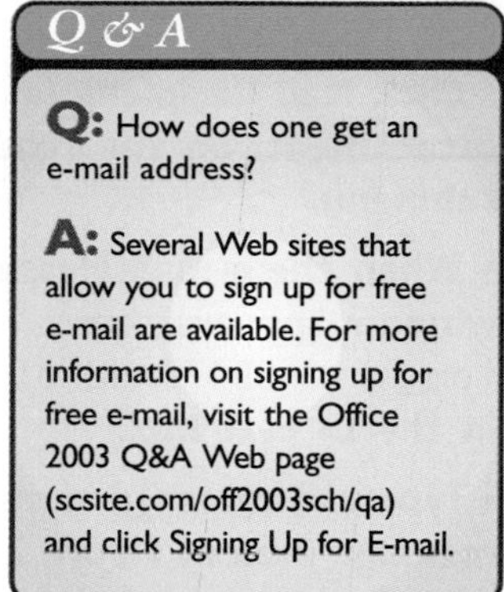

To E-Mail a Workbook from within Excel

1

- **With The Awesome Music Store Weekly Payroll Report workbook open, click File on the menu bar and then point to Send To.**

Excel displays the File menu and Send To submenu as shown in Figure 2-84.

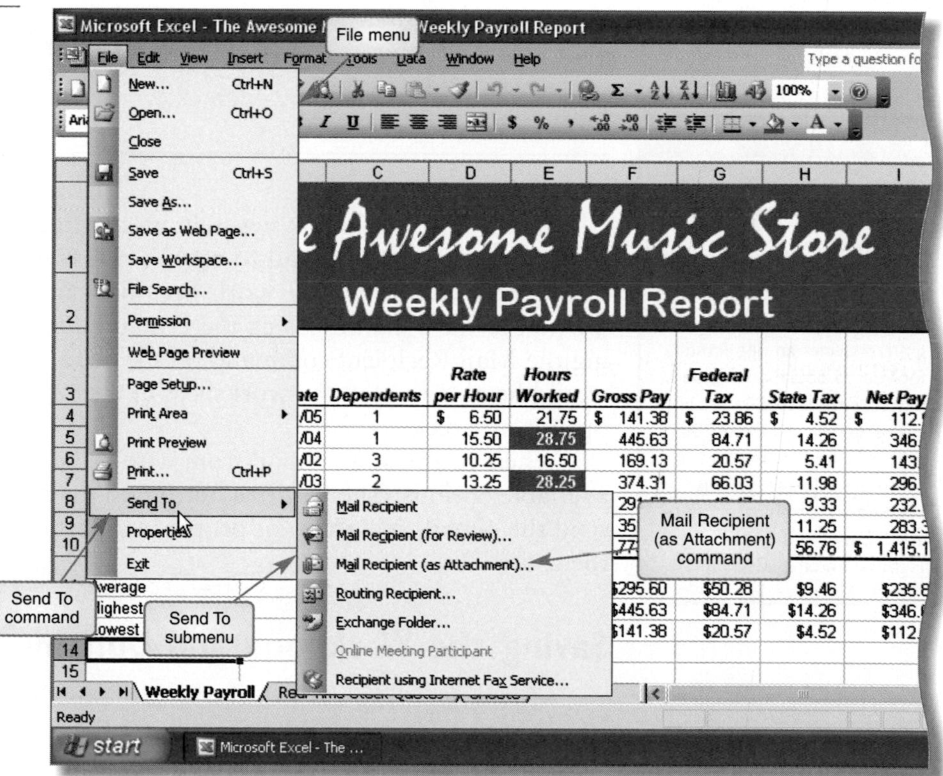

FIGURE 2-84

2

- **Click Mail Recipient (as Attachment) on the Send To submenu.**
- **When the e-mail Message window appears, type** tom_smith55475xd@hotmail.com **in the To text box.**
- **Type the message shown in the message area in Figure 2-85.**

Excel displays the e-mail Message window. The workbook is included as an attachment (Figure 2-85).

3

- **Click the Send button.**

The e-mail with the attached workbook is sent to tom_smith55475xd@hotmail.com.

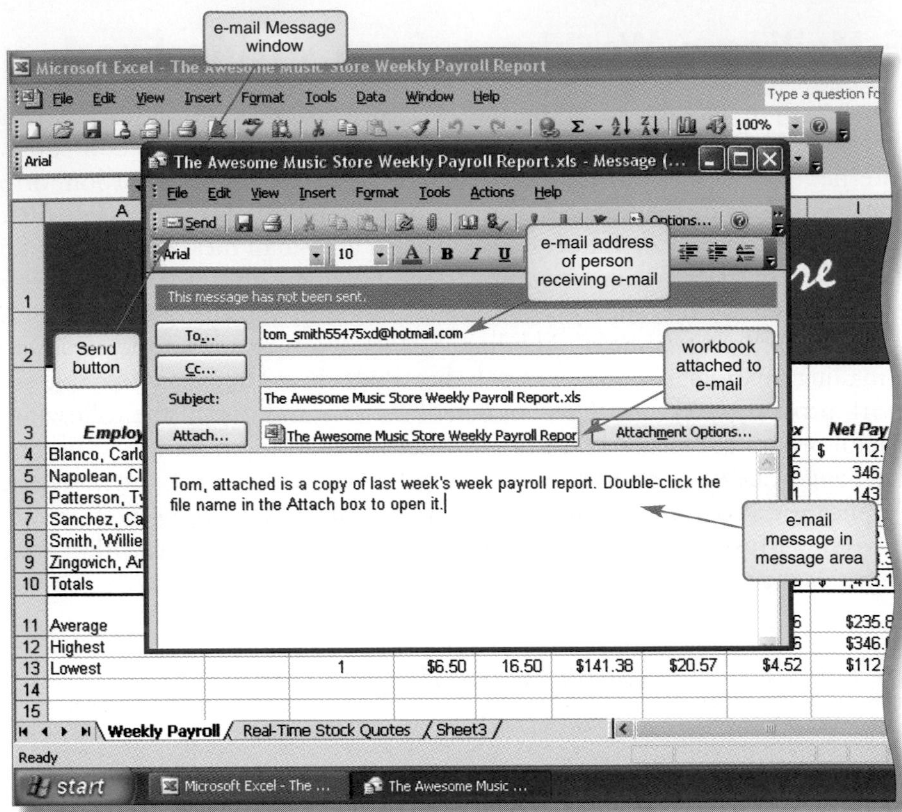

FIGURE 2-85

> **Q & A**
>
> **Q:** What is the Microsoft Office Specialist Certification program?
>
> **A:** The Microsoft Office Specialist Certification program provides an opportunity for you to obtain a valuable industry credential — proof that you have the Excel 2003 skills required by employers. For more information, see Appendix E or visit the Office 2003 Certification Web page (scsite.com/off2003sch/cert).

Because the workbook was sent as an attachment, Tom Smith can double-click the attachment in the e-mail to open it in Excel, or he can save it on disk and then open it at a later time. The worksheet also could have been sent as part of the text portion of the e-mail by using the E-mail button on the Standard toolbar or by clicking the Mail Recipient command on the Send To submenu. In this case, the recepient would be able to read the worksheet in the e-mail message, but would not be able to open it in Excel.

When you send an e-mail from within Excel, you can choose from many other available options. The Options button on the toolbar, for example, allows you to send the e-mail to a group of people in a particular sequence and get responses along the route.

Saving the Workbook and Quitting Excel

After completing the workbook and e-mailing a copy of the workbook, the final steps are to save the workbook and quit Excel.

> **Skill Builder 2-5**
>
> To practice the following tasks, visit scsite.com/off2003sch/skill, locate Excel Project 2, and then click Skill Builder 2-5.
> - ❑ Import external data using a Web Query
> - ❑ Change worksheet names
> - ❑ E-mail a workbook

To Save the Workbook and Quit Excel

1. **Click the Save button on the Standard toolbar.**
2. **Click the Close button on the upper-right corner of the title bar.**

Project Summary

In creating The Awesome Music Store Weekly Payroll Report workbook, you learned how to enter formulas, calculate an average, find the highest and lowest numbers in a range, verify formulas using Range Finder, change fonts, draw borders, align text, format numbers, change column widths and row heights, and add conditional formatting to a range of numbers. You learned how to spell check a worksheet, preview a worksheet, print a worksheet, print a section of a worksheet, and display and print the formulas version of the worksheet using the Fit to option. You also learned how to complete a Web query to generate a worksheet using external data obtained from the Web and rename sheet tabs. Finally, you learned how to send an e-mail directly from within Excel with the opened workbook as an attachment.

If you have a SAM user profile, you may have access to hands-on instruction, practice, and assessment of the skills covered in this project. Log in to your SAM account and go to your assignments page to see what your instructor has assigned.

What You Should Know

Having completed this project, you should be able to perform the tasks below. The tasks are listed in the same order they were presented in this project. For a list of the buttons, menus, toolbars, and commands introduced in this project, see the Quick Reference Summary at the back of this book and refer to the Page Number column.

(continued)

What You Should Know *(continued)*

28. Change the Widths of Columns (EX 107)
29. Change the Heights of Rows (EX 110)
30. Check Spelling on the Worksheet (EX 112)
31. Preview and Print a Worksheet (EX 114)
32. Print a Section of the Worksheet (EX 117)
33. Display the Formulas in the Worksheet and Fit the Printout on One Page (EX 118)
34. Change the Print Scaling Option Back to 100% (EX 120)
35. Import Data from a Web Source Using a Web Query (EX 121)
36. Change the Worksheet Names (EX 124)
37. E-Mail a Workbook from within Excel (EX 125)
38. Save the Workbook and Quit Excel (EX 126)

Q & A

Q: Is there more than one way to invoke a command in Excel?

A: Yes. For a table that lists how to complete the tasks covered in this book using the mouse, menu, shortcut menu, and keyboard, see the Quick Reference Summary at the back of this book or visit the Office 2003 Quick Reference Web page (scsite.com/off2003sch/qr).

Career Corner

Systems Analyst

One of the fastest growing IT (information technology) positions in the country is that of *systems analyst*. The primary focus of this type of work is to design systems and to incorporate new technologies.

Typically, systems analysts are more involved in design issues than in day-to-day programming. The specific duties of a systems analyst vary from company to company. Systems analysts work closely with users to identify operating procedures and clarify system objectives. They must be familiar with concepts and practices within a specific field. A successful systems analyst is willing to embrace new technologies and is open to continued learning. Good communications skills are important. Systems analysts may be expected to write program documentation and operating manuals. Growing in demand are skills for the systems analyst that include e-commerce, enterprisewide networking, and intranet technologies. Given the technology available today, telecommuting is common for computer professionals, including the systems analyst. Many analysts work as consultants.

The minimum educational requirement is a bachelor's degree, but many people opt for a master's degree. Salaries are excellent in this fast-growing occupation in the IT field. They range from $40,000 to $80,000 and up. Graduates with a master's degree can expect to earn in excess of $90,000 per year. For more information, visit scsite.com/off2003sch/careers and then click Systems Analyst.

Learn It Online

Instructions: To complete the Learn It Online exercises, start your browser, click the Address bar, and then enter the Web address `scsite.com/off2003sch/learn`. When the Office 2003 Learn It Online page is displayed, follow the instructions in the exercises below. Each exercise has instructions for printing your results, either for your own records or for submission to your instructor.

1 Project Reinforcement TF, MC, and SA

Below Excel Project 2, click the Project Reinforcement link. Print the quiz by clicking Print on the File menu for each page. Answer each question.

2 Flash Cards

Below Excel Project 2, click the Flash Cards link and read the instructions. Type 20 (or a number specified by your instructor) in the Number of playing cards text box, type your name in the Enter your Name text box, and then click the Flip Card button. When the flash card is displayed, read the question and then click the ANSWER box arrow to select an answer. Flip through Flash Cards. If your score is 15 (75%) correct or greater, click Print on the File menu to print your results. If your score is less than 15 (75%) correct, then redo this exercise by clicking the Replay button.

3 Practice Test

Below Excel Project 2, click the Practice Test link. Answer each question, enter your first and last name at the bottom of the page, and then click the Grade Test button. When the graded practice test is displayed on your screen, click Print on the File menu to print a hard copy. Continue to take practice tests until you score 80% or better.

4 Who Wants To Be a Computer Genius?

Below Excel Project 2, click the Computer Genius link. Read the instructions, enter your first and last name at the bottom of the page, and then click the PLAY button. When your score is displayed, click the PRINT RESULTS link to print a hard copy.

5 Wheel of Terms

Below Excel Project 2, click the Wheel of Terms link. Read the instructions, and then enter your first and last name and your school name. Click the PLAY button. When your score is displayed, right-click the score and then click Print on the shortcut menu to print a hard copy.

6 Crossword Puzzle Challenge

Below Excel Project 2, click the Crossword Puzzle Challenge link. Read the instructions, and then enter your first and last name. Click the SUBMIT button. Work the crossword puzzle. When you are finished, click the Submit button. When the crossword puzzle is redisplayed, click the Print Puzzle button to print a hard copy.

7 Tips and Tricks

Below Excel Project 2, click the Tips and Tricks link. Click a topic that pertains to Project 2. Right-click the information and then click Print on the shortcut menu. Construct a brief example of what the information relates to in Excel to confirm you understand how to use the tip or trick.

8 Newsgroups

Below Excel Project 2, click the Newsgroups link. Click a topic that pertains to Project 2. Print three comments.

9 Expanding Your Horizons

Below Excel Project 2, click the Expanding Your Horizons link. Click a topic that pertains to Project 2. Print the information. Construct a brief example of what the information relates to in Excel to confirm you understand the contents of the article.

10 Search Sleuth

Below Excel Project 2, click the Search Sleuth link. To search for a term that pertains to this project, select a term below the Project 2 title and then use the Google search engine at google.com (or any major search engine) to display and print two Web pages that present information on the term.

11 Excel Online Training

Below Excel Project 2, click the Excel Online Training link. When your browser displays the Microsoft Office Online Web page, click the Excel link. Click one of the Excel courses that covers one or more of the objectives listed at the beginning of the project on page EX 66. Print the first page of the course before stepping through it.

12 Office Marketplace

Below Excel Project 2, click the Office Marketplace link. When your browser displays the Microsoft Office Online Web page, click the Office Marketplace link. Click a topic that relates to Excel. Print the first page.

13 You're Hired

Below Excel Project 2, click the You're Hired! link to embark on the path to a career in computers. Directions about how to play the game will be displayed. When you are ready to play, click the begin the game button. If required, submit your score to your instructor.

Apply Your Knowledge

1 Profit Analysis Worksheet

Instructions Part 1: Start Excel. Open the workbook Apply 2-1 Early Bird Mart Return on Investment. See page xxiv at the front of this book for instructions for downloading the Data Files for Students or see your instructor for information on accessing the files required in this book. The purpose of this exercise is to open a partially completed workbook, enter formulas and functions, copy the formulas and functions, and then format the worksheet titles and numbers. As shown in Figure 2-86, the completed worksheet analyzes the return on investment by item. Use the following formulas in cells E3, F3, and G3:

Gross Sales (cell E3) = Units Sold * (Unit Cost + Unit Profit) or =D3 * (B3 + C3)
Return on Investment (cell F3) = Units Sold * Unit Profit or = D3 * C3
% Return on Investment (cell G3) = Return on Investment / Gross Sales or = F3 / E3

Microsoft Excel - Apply 2-1 Early Bird Mart Return on Investment Complete

Early Bird Mart
Return on Investment

Item	Unit Cost	Unit Profit	Units Sold	Gross Sales	Return on Investment	% Return on Investment
Calculator	$ 71.25	$ 15.27	34,723	$ 3,004,233.96	$ 530,220.21	17.649%
Color Printer	123.58	41.80	52,438	8,672,196.44	2,191,908.40	25.275%
External Drive	231.56	93.27	22,019	7,152,431.77	2,053,712.13	28.713%
Firewall Plus	56.24	15.21	83,375	5,957,143.75	1,268,133.75	21.288%
Hard Disk	210.60	75.30	38,102	10,893,361.80	2,869,080.60	26.338%
Monitor	108.35	22.28	41,562	5,429,244.06	926,001.36	17.056%
Speakers	23.15	13.67	75,815	2,791,508.30	1,036,391.05	37.127%
System Unit	451.45	125.85	65,100	37,582,230.00	8,192,835.00	21.800%
Wireless Hub	178.23	35.17	23,019	4,912,254.60	809,578.23	16.481%
Totals			436,153	$ 86,394,604.68	$ 19,877,860.73	23.008%
Lowest	$23.15	$13.67	22,019	$2,791,508.30	$530,220.21	16.481%
Highest	$451.45	$125.85	83,375	$37,582,230.00	$8,192,835.00	37.127%
Average	$161.60	$48.65	48,461	$9,599,400.52	$2,208,651.19	

FIGURE 2-86

Use the fill handle to copy the three formulas in the range E3:G3 to the range E4:G11. After the copy is complete, click the Auto Fill Options button and then click the Fill Without Formatting option to maintain the bottom border in the range E11:G11. Determine totals for the units sold, gross sales, and return on investment in row 12. Copy cell G11 to G12 to assign the formula in cell G11 to G12 in the total line and again use the Auto Fill Options button to maintain the top and bottom border in cell G12. In the range B13:B15, determine the lowest value, highest value, and average value, respectively, for the values in the range B3:B11. Use the fill handle to copy the three functions to the range C13:G15. Delete the average from cell G15, because an average of percentages of this type is mathematically invalid.

Apply Your Knowledge

Format the worksheet as follows:

(1) cell A1 — change to Bookman Old Style (or a similar font) italics with a red (column 1, row 3) background
(2) cells B3:C3, E3:F3, and E12:F12 — Currency style format with two decimal places and fixed dollar signs (use the Currency Style button on the Formatting toolbar)
(3) cells B4:C11 and E4:F11 — Comma style format with two decimal places (use the Comma Style button on the Formatting toolbar)
(4) cells D3:D15 — Comma style format with no decimal places
(5) cells G3:G14 — Percent style format with three decimal places
(6) cells B13:C15 and E13:F15 — Currency style format with floating dollar signs (use the Format Cells command on the shortcut menu)

Enter your name, course, laboratory assignment number (Apply 2-1), date, and instructor name in the range A20:A24. Preview and print the worksheet in landscape orientation. Save the workbook using the file name, Apply 2-1 Early Bird Mart Return on Investment Complete.

Use Range Finder to verify the formula in cell F3. Print the range A2:E15. Press CTRL+ACCENT MARK (`) to change the display from the values version of the worksheet to the formulas version. Print the formulas version in landscape orientation on one page with gridlines showing (Figure 2-87) by: (1) using the Fit to option in the Page sheet in the Page Setup dialog box; and (2) clicking Gridlines on the Sheet sheet in the Page Setup dialog box. Press CTRL+ACCENT MARK (`) to change the display of the worksheet back to the values version. Do not save the workbook. Hand in the three printouts to your instructor.

Instructions Part 2: In column C, use the keyboard to add manually $5.00 to the profit of each product with a unit profit less than $40.00 and $7.00 to the profits of all other products. You should end up with $22,413,943.73 in cell F12. Print the worksheet. Do not save the workbook. Hand in the printout to your instructor.

Report

Early Bird Mart
Return on Investment

Item	Unit Cost	Unit Profit	Units Sold	Gross Sales	Return on Investment	% Return on Investment
Calculator	71.25	15.27	34723	=D3*(B3+C3)	=C3*D3	=F3/E3
Color Printer	123.58	41.8	52438	=D4*(B4+C4)	=C4*D4	=F4/E4
External Drive	231.56	93.27	22019	=D5*(B5+C5)	=C5*D5	=F5/E5
Firewall Plus	56.24	15.21	83375	=D6*(B6+C6)	=C6*D6	=F6/E6
Hard Disk	210.6	75.3	38102	=D7*(B7+C7)	=C7*D7	=F7/E7
Monitor	108.35	22.28	41562	=D8*(B8+C8)	=C8*D8	=F8/E8
Speakers	23.15	13.67	75815	=D9*(B9+C9)	=C9*D9	=F9/E9
System Unit	451.45	125.85	65100	=D10*(B10+C10)	=C10*D10	=F10/E10
Wireless Hub	178.23	35.17	23019	=D11*(B11+C11)	=C11*D11	=F11/E11
Totals			=SUM(D3:D11)	=SUM(E3:E11)	=SUM(F3:F11)	=F12/E12
Lowest	=MIN(B3:B11)	=MIN(C3:C11)	=MIN(D3:D11)	=MIN(E3:E11)	=MIN(F3:F11)	=MIN(G3:G11)
Highest	=MAX(B3:B11)	=MAX(C3:C11)	=MAX(D3:D11)	=MAX(E3:E11)	=MAX(F3:F11)	=MAX(G3:G11)
Average	=AVERAGE(B3:B11)	=AVERAGE(C3:C11)	=AVERAGE(D3:D11)	=AVERAGE(E3:E11)	=AVERAGE(F3:F11)	

FIGURE 2-87

In the Lab

1 Sales Analysis Worksheet

Problem: The computer consulting firm you and a friend work part-time for has received its first major contract. The client, Pacific Rim Garments, has specified in the contract that you are to build a sales analysis worksheet that determines the sales quota and percentage of quota met for the sales representatives in Table 2-8. The desired worksheet is shown in Figure 2-88.

Table 2-8 Pacific Rim Garment Sales Data

SALES REPRESENTATIVE	SALES AMOUNT	SALES RETURN	SALES QUOTA
Santori, Manual	746923	24500	645000
Johnson, Lee	456378	34258	475000
Freundski, Sarah	812736	35217	750000
Chang, Ti	912016	89156	695000
Andrews, Philip	563728	95019	475000
Seth, Amy	301982	20500	275000

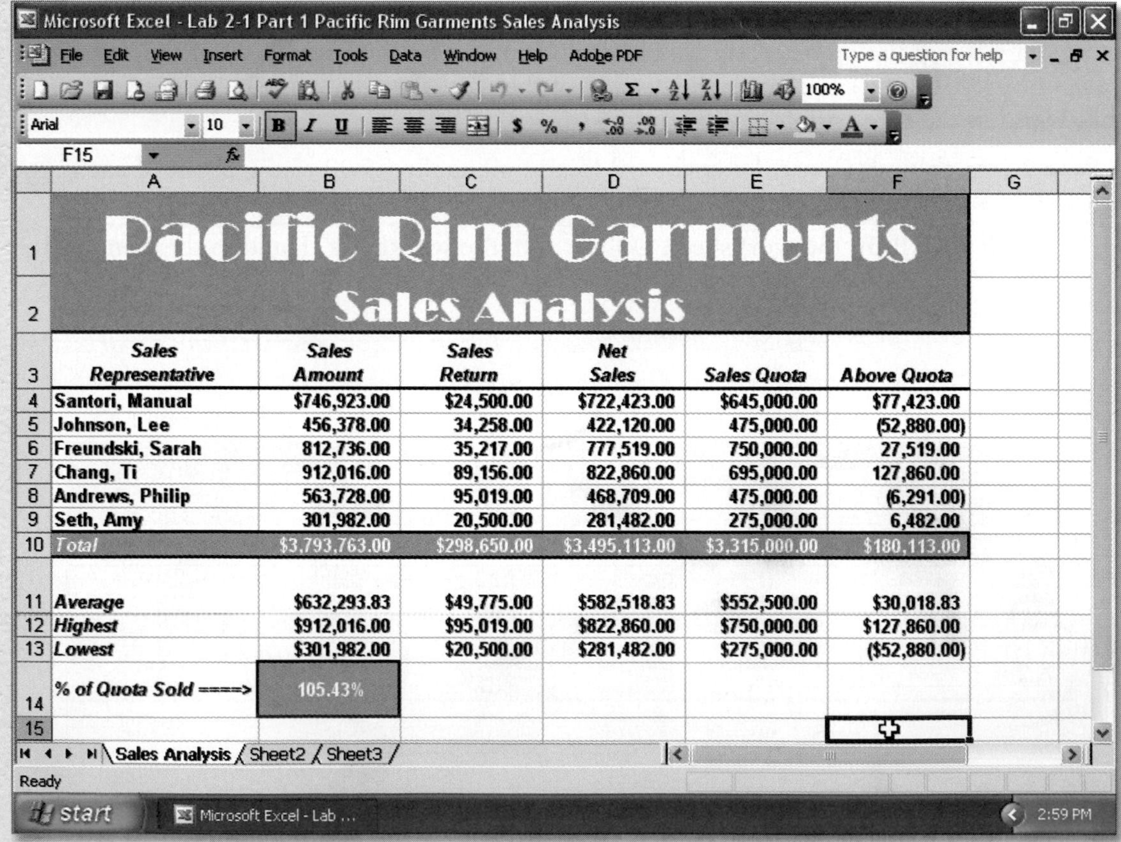

	A	B	C	D	E	F
3	Sales Representative	Sales Amount	Sales Return	Net Sales	Sales Quota	Above Quota
4	Santori, Manual	$746,923.00	$24,500.00	$722,423.00	$645,000.00	$77,423.00
5	Johnson, Lee	456,378.00	34,258.00	422,120.00	475,000.00	(52,880.00)
6	Freundski, Sarah	812,736.00	35,217.00	777,519.00	750,000.00	27,519.00
7	Chang, Ti	912,016.00	89,156.00	822,860.00	695,000.00	127,860.00
8	Andrews, Philip	563,728.00	95,019.00	468,709.00	475,000.00	(6,291.00)
9	Seth, Amy	301,982.00	20,500.00	281,482.00	275,000.00	6,482.00
10	Total	$3,793,763.00	$298,650.00	$3,495,113.00	$3,315,000.00	$180,113.00
11	Average	$632,293.83	$49,775.00	$582,518.83	$552,500.00	$30,018.83
12	Highest	$912,016.00	$95,019.00	$822,860.00	$750,000.00	$127,860.00
13	Lowest	$301,982.00	$20,500.00	$281,482.00	$275,000.00	($52,880.00)
14	% of Quota Sold ====>	105.43%				

FIGURE 2-88

Instructions Part 1: Perform the following tasks to build the worksheet shown in Figure 2-88.

1. Use the Select All button and the Bold button to bold the entire worksheet.
2. Increase the width of column A to 21.00 points and the width of columns B through F to 14.00 points.
3. Enter the worksheet title `Pacific Rim Garments` in cell A1 and the worksheet subtitle in cell A2. Enter the column titles in row 3 as shown in Figure 2-88. In row 3, use ALT+ENTER to start a new line in a cell.

In the Lab

4. Enter the sales data described in Table 2-8 in columns A, B, C, and E in rows 4 through 9. Enter the row titles in the range A10:A14 as shown in Figure 2-88.
5. Obtain the net sales in column D by subtracting the sales returns in column C from the sales amount in column B. Enter the formula in cell D4 and copy it to the range D5:D9.
6. Obtain the above quota amounts in column F by subtracting the sales quota in column E from the net sales in column D. Enter the formula in cell F4 and copy it to the range F5:F9.
7. Obtain the totals in row 10 by adding the column values for each salesperson. In the range B11:B13, use the AVERAGE, MAX, and MIN functions to determine the average, highest value, and lowest value in the range B4:B9. Copy the range B11:B13 to the range C11:F13.
8. Determine the percent of quota sold in cell B14 by dividing the total net sales amount in cell D10 by the total sales quota amount in cell E10.
9. One at a time, merge and center the worksheet title and subtitle across columns A through F. Select cells A1 and A2 and change the background color to rose (column 1, row 5 on the Fill Color palette). Change the worksheet title in cell A1 to 36-point Broadway font (or a similar font) white (column 8, row 5 on the Font Color palette). Change the worksheet subtitle to the same font type and color and apply a 24-point font size. Assign a thick box border (column 4, row 3 on the Borders palette) to the range A1:A2.
10. Center the titles in row 3, columns A through F. Use the Italicize button on the Formatting toolbar to italicize the column titles in row 3 and the row titles in the range A10:A14. Draw a thick bottom border (column 2, row 2 on the Borders palette) in the range A3:F3.
11. Change the background and font colors in the range A10:F10 and cell B14 to the same colors applied to the worksheet title in Step 9. Assign a thick box border (column 4, row 3 on the Borders palette) to the range A10:F10 and cell B14.
12. Change the row heights of rows 3, 11, and 14 to 30.00 points.
13. Select the range A14:B14. Use the Format Cells command on the shortcut to horizontally and vertically center the contents of the cells. That is, when the Format Cells dialog box is displayed, click the Alignment tab and select Center in the Horizontal box and Vertical box. Select cell B14. Click the Percent Style button on the Standard toolbar. Click the Increase Decimal button on the Standard toolbar twice to display the percent in cell B14 to hundredths.
14. Use the CTRL key to select the ranges B4:F4 and B10:F13. That is, select the range B4:F4 and then while holding down the CTRL key, select the range B10:F13. Use the Format Cells command on the shortcut to assign the selected ranges a Floating Dollar Sign style format with two decimal places and parentheses to represent negative numbers. Select the range B5:F9 and click the Comma Style button on the standard toolbar.
15. Enter your name, course, computer laboratory assignment number (Lab 2-1), date, and instructor name below the entries in the range A16:A20.
16. Save the workbook using the file name Lab 2-1 Part 1 Pacific Rim Garments Sales Analysis. Print the entire worksheet in landscape orientation. Print only the range A3:B10.
17. Display the formulas version by pressing CTRL + ACCENT MARK (`). Print the formulas version using the Fit to option button in the Scaling box on the Page tab in the Page Setup dialog box. After printing the worksheet, reset the Scaling option by selecting the Adjust to option button on the Page tab in the Page Setup dialog box and changing the percent value to 100%. Change the display from the formulas version to the values version by pressing CTRL + ACCENT MARK (`). Do not save the worksbook.

Instructions Part 2: With the workbook created in Part 1, manually increment each of the six values in the sales quota column by $15,000.00 until the percent of quota sold in cell B14 is below, yet as close as possible to, 100%.

(continued)

Sales Analysis Worksheet *(continued)*

All six values in column E must be incremented the same number of times. The percent of quota sold in B14 should equal 97.49%. Save the workbook as Lab 2-1 Part 2 Pacific Rim Garments Sales Analysis. Print the worksheet.

Instructions Part 3: With the percent of quota sold in cell B14 equal to 97.49% from Part 2, manually decrement each of the six values in the sales return column by $8,000.00 until the percent of quota sold in cell B14 is above, yet as close as possible to, 100%. Decrement all six values in column C the same number of times. Your worksheet is correct when the percent of quota sold in cell B14 is equal to 100.17%. Save the workbook as Lab 2-1 Part 3 Pacific Rim Garments Sales Analysis 3. Print the worksheet.

2 Balance Due Worksheet

Problem: You are a spreadsheet intern for Emily's Music Emporium, a popular Chicago-based music store with outlets in major cities across the United States. You have been asked to use Excel to generate a report (Figure 2-89) that summarizes the monthly balance due. A graphic breakdown of the data also is desired. The customer data in Table 2-9 is available for test purposes.

Table 2-9 Emily's Music Emporium Monthly Balance Due Data

CUSTOMER	BEGINNING BALANCE	CREDITS	PAYMENTS	PURCHASES
Aaronoli, Lester	356.12	123.30	15.00	17.50
Calibratski, Hans	126.50	12.55	22.00	23.75
Sanchez, Juanita	619.45	63.50	30.75	12.99
Perez, Carlos	89.21	32.10	10.00	81.05
Pital, Nalin	201.75	0.00	28.00	69.26
Eagelton, LaTroy	915.25	2.15	75.00	18.00
Dae-Song, Melinda	731.28	35.00	100.00	34.00

Instructions Part 1: Create a worksheet similar to the one shown in Figure 2-89. Include the five columns of customer data in Table 2-9 in the report, plus two additional columns to compute a service charge and a new balance for each customer. Assume no negative unpaid monthly balances. Perform the following tasks.

1. Enter and format the worksheet title `Emily's Music Emporium` and worksheet subtitle `Monthly Balance Due Report` in cells A1 and A2. Change the font in cell A1 to 28-point Arial Black (or a similar font) bold and the font in cell A2 to 20-point Arial Black (or a similar font) bold. One at a time, merge and center the worksheet title and subtitle across columns A through G. Change the background color of cells A1 and A2 to light yellow (column 3, row 5). Draw a thick box border around the range A1:A2.
2. Change the width of column A to 18.00 characters. Change the widths of columns B through G to 12.00. Change the heights of row 3 to 30.00 and row 12 to 33.00 points.
3. Enter the column titles in row 3 and row titles in the range A11:A14 as shown in Figure 2-89. Bold the column titles, add a bottom border to the column titles, and center the column titles in the range A3:G3. Bold the titles in the range A11:A14. Add a top and bottom border to the range A11:G11.
4. Enter the data in Table 2-9 in the range A4:E10.

5. Use the following formulas to determine the service charge in column F and the new balance in column G for the first customer. Copy the two formulas down through the remaining customers.
   a. Service Charge (cell F4) = 2.15% * (Beginning Balance – Payments – Credits) or = 0.0215 * (B4 – C4 – D4)
   b. New Balance (G4) = Beginning Balance + Purchases – Payments – Credits + Service Charge or =B4 + E4 – C4 – D4 + F4

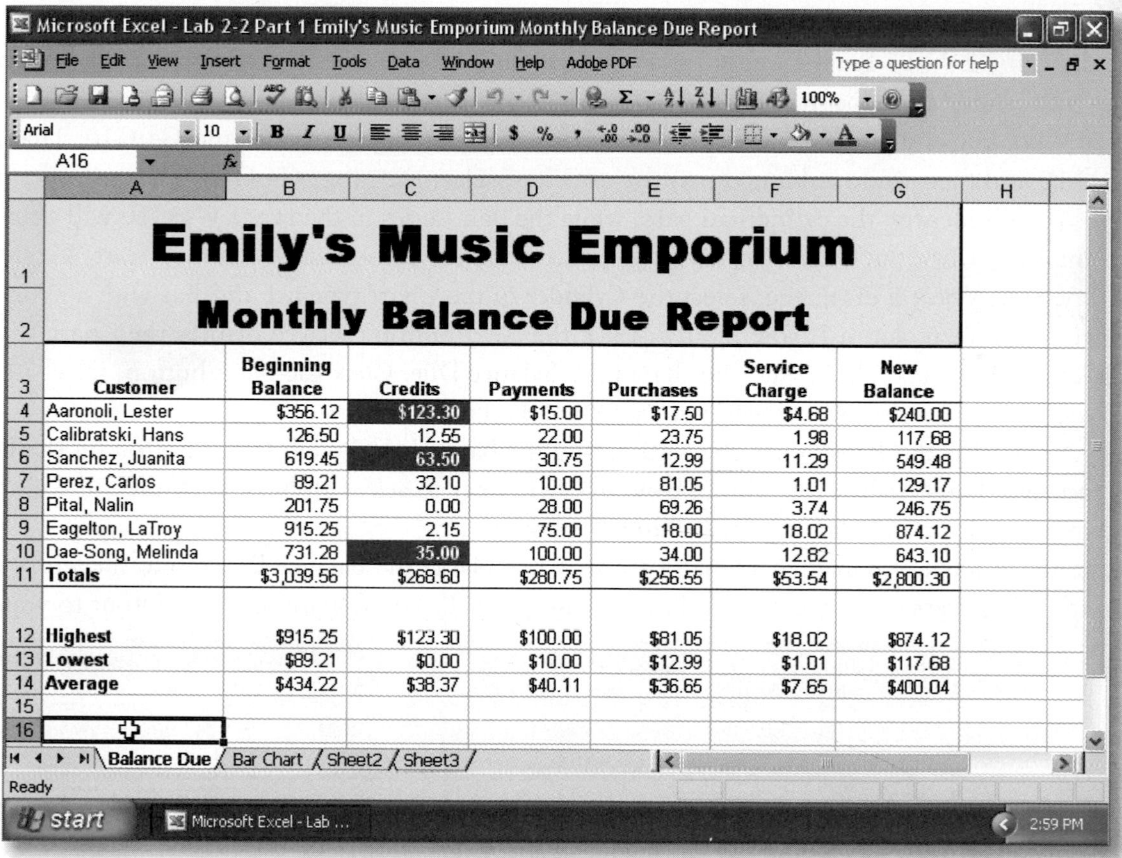

Emily's Music Emporium

Monthly Balance Due Report

Customer	Beginning Balance	Credits	Payments	Purchases	Service Charge	New Balance
Aaronoli, Lester	$356.12	$123.30	$15.00	$17.50	$4.68	$240.00
Calibratski, Hans	126.50	12.55	22.00	23.75	1.98	117.68
Sanchez, Juanita	619.45	63.50	30.75	12.99	11.29	549.48
Perez, Carlos	89.21	32.10	10.00	81.05	1.01	129.17
Pital, Nalin	201.75	0.00	28.00	69.26	3.74	246.75
Eagelton, LaTroy	915.25	2.15	75.00	18.00	18.02	874.12
Dae-Song, Melinda	731.28	35.00	100.00	34.00	12.82	643.10
Totals	$3,039.56	$268.60	$280.75	$256.55	$53.54	$2,800.30
Highest	$915.25	$123.30	$100.00	$81.05	$18.02	$874.12
Lowest	$89.21	$0.00	$10.00	$12.99	$1.01	$117.68
Average	$434.22	$38.37	$40.11	$36.65	$7.65	$400.04

FIGURE 2-89

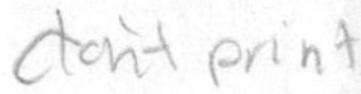

6. Determine the totals in row 11.
7. Determine the maximum, minimum, and average values in cells B12:B14 for the range B4:B10 and then copy the range B12:B14 to C12:G14.
8. Use the Format Cells command on the shortcut menu to format the numbers as follows: (a) assign the Currency style with a floating dollar sign to the cells containing numeric data in the ranges B4:G4 and B11:G14; and (b) assign the Comma style (currency with no dollar sign) to the range B5:G10.
9. Use conditional formatting to change the formatting to white bold font on a red background in any cell in the range C4:C10 that contains a value greater than or equal to 33.
10. Change the worksheet name from Sheet1 to Balance Due.
11. Enter your name, course, laboratory assignment number (Lab 2-2), date, and instructor name in the range A16:A20.
12. Spell check the worksheet. Preview and then print the worksheet in landscape orientation. Save the workbook using the file name, Lab 2-2 Part 1 Emily's Music Emporium Monthly Balance Due Report.

(continued)

Balance Due Worksheet *(continued)*

13. Print the range A3:D14. Print the formulas version on one page. Close the workbook without saving the changes. Hand in the three printouts to your instructor.

Instructions Part 2: This part requires that you use the Chart Wizard button on the Standard toolbar to draw a 3-D Bar Chart with a cylindrical shape. If necessary, use the Type a question for help box on the menu bar to obtain information on drawing a chart on a separate sheet in the workbook.

With the Lab 2-2 Part 1 Emily's Music Emporium Monthly Balance Due Report workbook open, draw the 3-D Bar Chart with cylindrical shape showing each customer's total new balance as shown in Figure 2-90.

Use the CTRL key and mouse to select the nonadjacent chart ranges A4:A10 and G4:G10. That is, select the range A4:A10 and then while holding down the CTRL key, select the range G4:G10. The customer names in the range A4:A10 will identify the cylindrical bars, while the data series in the range G4:G10 will determine the length of the bars. Click the Chart Wizard button on the Standard toolbar. When the Chart Wizard - Step 1 of 4 - Chart Type dialog box is displayed, select the Cylinder in the Chart type list and Bar with a cylindrical shape in the Chart sub-type (column 1, row 2) area. Click the Next button twice to display the Chart Wizard - Step 3 of 4 - Chart Options dialog box. Add the chart title, Balance Due. Click the Next button, select As new sheet to draw the bar chart on a new worksheet and then click the Finish button.

When the chart is displayed, click the wall behind the bars, click the Fill Color button on the Formatting toolbar, and click Light Yellow (column 3, row 5). Click a bar to select all bars, click the Fill Color button on the Formatting toolbar, and click Green (column 4, row 2).

Change the worksheet name from Chart1 to Bar Chart. Drag the Balance Due tab to the left of the Bar Chart tab to reorder the sheets in the workbook. Preview and print the chart. Hand in the printout to your instructor.

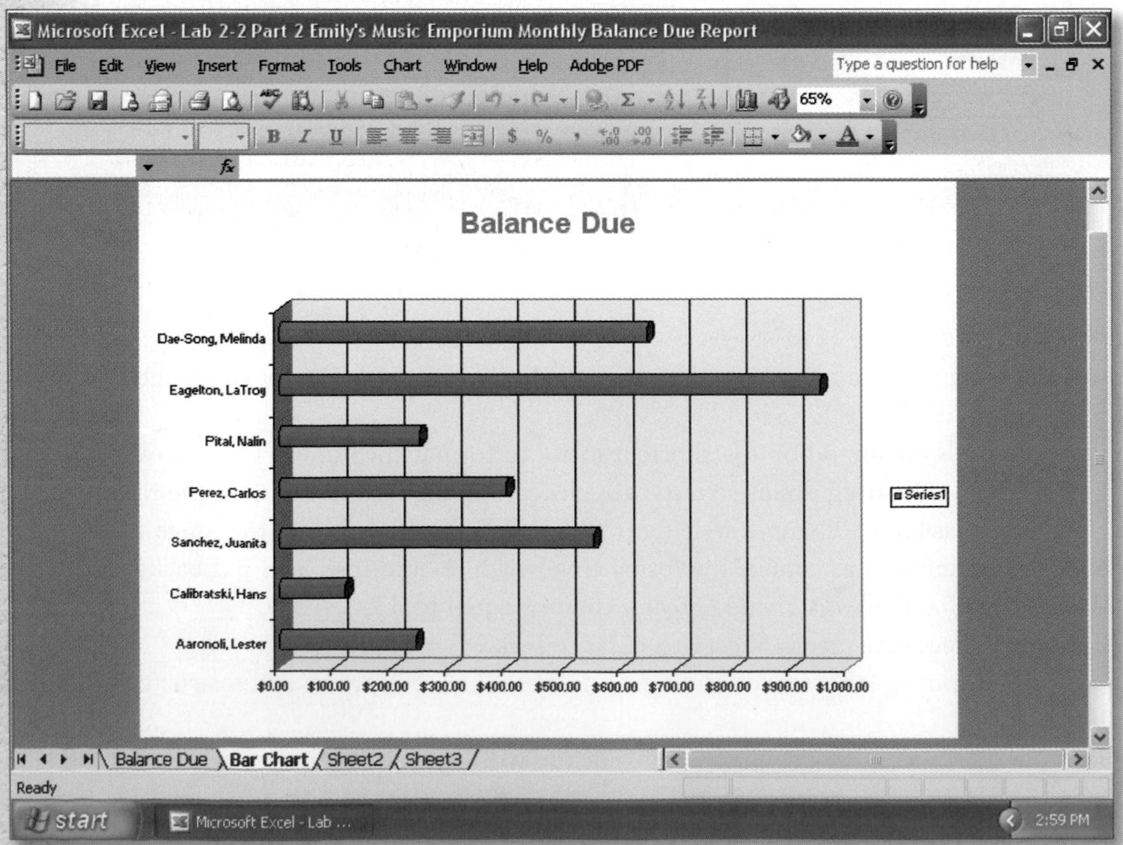

FIGURE 2-90

In the Lab

Click the Balance Due tab. Change the following purchases: customer Carlos Perez to $352.00; customer LaTroy Eagelton to $89.25. The company also decided to change the service charge to from 2.15% to 2.75% for all customers. The total new balance in cell G11 should equal $3,157.44. Select both sheets by holding down the SHIFT key and then clicking the Bar Chart tab. Preview and print the selected sheets. Hand in the printouts to your instructor. Save the worksheet using the file name, Lab 2-2 Part 2 Emily's Music Emporium Monthly Balance Due Report.

Instructions Part 3: With your instructor's permission, e-mail the workbook created in this exercise with the changes indicated in Part 2 as an attachment to your instructor. Close the workbook without saving the changes.

Print

3 Stock Club Investment Analysis and Equity Web Queries

Problem: Several years ago while a junior in high school, your brother and a group of his friends started a stock club. Each member contributed $10 per month. Now, the club members are out of college, married, and have taken jobs around the country. They continue to invest in the stock market as a group, however, using e-mail, chat rooms, and Web cams to communicate and conduct their monthly meetings via the Internet. A few years ago, the members increased their monthly contribution to $100. A budding stock enthusiast yourself, each month you help your brother by summarizing the club's financial status. With your recent introduction to Excel, you have decided to create a portfolio worksheet (Figure 2-91 on the next page) that you can e-mail to the members. The club's portfolio is summarized in Table 2-10. Table 2-10 also shows the general layout of the worksheet to be created.

Table 2-10 Learn 'N Earn Stock Club Portfolio

COMPANY	STOCK SYMBOL	PURCHASE DATE	SHARES	INITIAL PRICE PER SHARE	INITIAL COST	CURRENT PRICE PER SHARE	CURRENT VALUE	GAIN/ LOSS	PERCENT GAIN/ LOSS
Boeing	BA	03/03/03	600	25.46	Formula A	60.65	Formula B	Formula C	Formula D
Coca-Cola	KO	06/14/04	1200	50.25	↓	43.32	↓	↓	↓
Disney	DIS	10/11/02	400	16.25	↓	26.74	↓	↓	↓
General Electric	GE	03/04/05	350	36.75	↓	35.80	↓	↓	↓
McDonalds	MCD	01/15/04	500	25.24	↓	29.89	↓	↓	↓
MGM Mirage	MGM	11/15/02	263	37.38	↓	66.80	↓	↓	↓
Southwest	LUV	02/15/02	450	22.25	↓	14.91	↓	↓	↓
Walgreens	WAG	05/11/00	650	23.25	↓	43.75	↓	↓	↓
Wal-Mart	WMT	04/14/05	600	45.35	↓	47.50	↓	↓	↓
Total					--		--	--	--
Average			Formula E →						
Highest			Formula F →						
Lowest			Formula G →						

(continued)

Stock Club Investment Analysis and Equity Web Queries *(continued)*

Instructions Part 1: Perform the following tasks to create a worksheet similar to the one in Figure 2-91.

1. Change the column widths and row heights as follows: column widths: column A — 13.00; columns F, H, and I — 12.00 characters; column G and J — 10.00; row heights: row 3 — 45.00 points; row 14 — 22.50 points; remaining rows — default
2. Enter the worksheet titles `Learn 'n Earn Stock Club` in cell A1 and `Summary of Investments` in cell A2.
3. Enter the column titles and data in Table 2-10 in the appropriate columns beginning in row 3. When entering the column titles, use ALT+ENTER to continue the text in a cell on the next line as shown in Figure 2-91.
4. As shown in Table 2-10, enter the following formulas in row 4 and then copy them down through row 12:
   a. Enter Formula A in cell F4: Initial Cost = Shares x Initial Price per Share (or =D4 * E4)
   b. Enter Formula B in cell H4: Current Value = Shares – Current Price per Share (or =D4 * G4)
   c. Enter Formula C in cell I4: Gain/Loss = Current Value – Initial Cost (=H4 - F4)
   d. Enter Formula D in cell J4: Percent Gain/Loss = Gain/Loss / Initial Cost (=I4 / F4)
5. Compute the totals for initial cost, current value, and gain/loss in cells F13, H13, I13, and J13. For the percent gain/loss in cell J13, copy cell J12.
6. In cells D14, D15, and D16, enter Formula E, F, and G: Use the AVERAGE, MAX, and MIN functions to determine the average, highest, and lowest values for the number of shares. Copy the three functions across columns E through J. Delete the value in cell J14, because an average of percentages of this type is mathematically invalid.

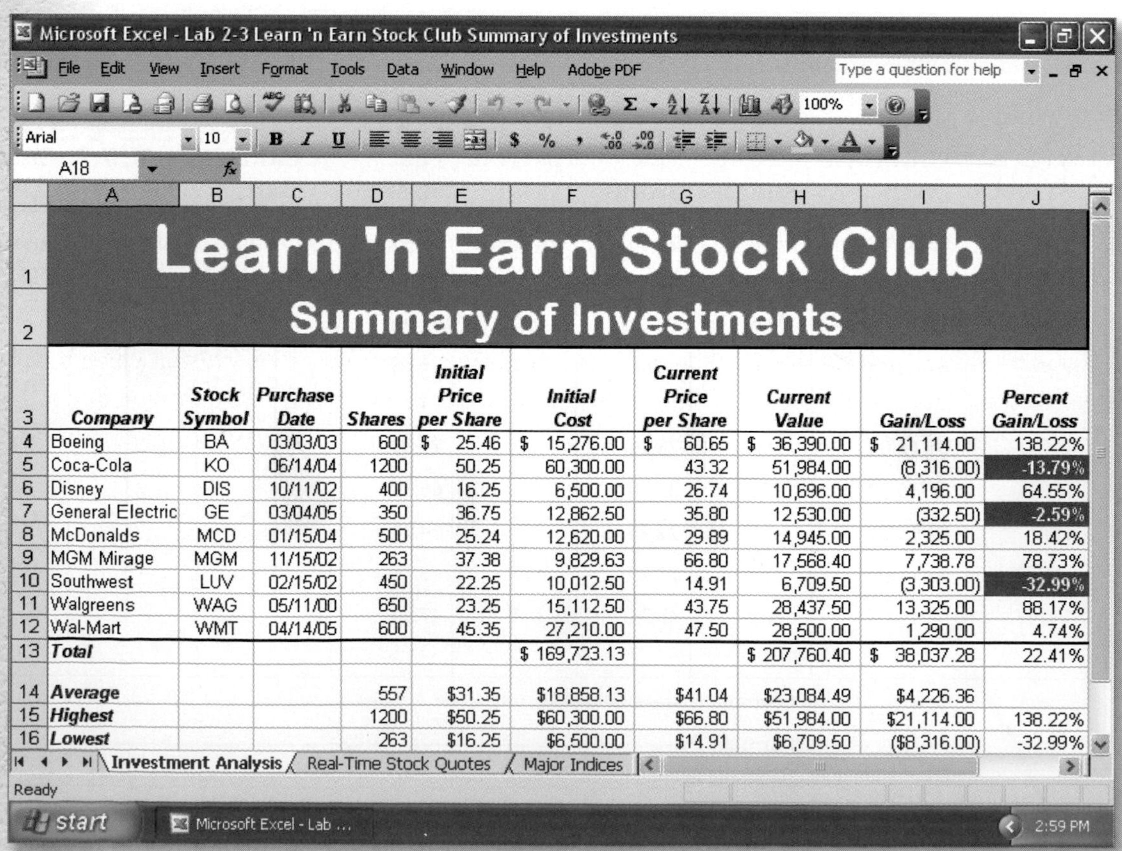

Microsoft Excel - Lab 2-3 Learn 'n Earn Stock Club Summary of Investments

Learn 'n Earn Stock Club

Summary of Investments

	A	B	C	D	E	F	G	H	I	J
3	Company	Stock Symbol	Purchase Date	Shares	Initial Price per Share	Initial Cost	Current Price per Share	Current Value	Gain/Loss	Percent Gain/Loss
4	Boeing	BA	03/03/03	600	$ 25.46	$ 15,276.00	$ 60.65	$ 36,390.00	$ 21,114.00	138.22%
5	Coca-Cola	KO	06/14/04	1200	50.25	60,300.00	43.32	51,984.00	(8,316.00)	-13.79%
6	Disney	DIS	10/11/02	400	16.25	6,500.00	26.74	10,696.00	4,196.00	64.55%
7	General Electric	GE	03/04/05	350	36.75	12,862.50	35.80	12,530.00	(332.50)	-2.59%
8	McDonalds	MCD	01/15/04	500	25.24	12,620.00	29.89	14,945.00	2,325.00	18.42%
9	MGM Mirage	MGM	11/15/02	263	37.38	9,829.63	66.80	17,568.40	7,738.78	78.73%
10	Southwest	LUV	02/15/02	450	22.25	10,012.50	14.91	6,709.50	(3,303.00)	-32.99%
11	Walgreens	WAG	05/11/00	650	23.25	15,112.50	43.75	28,437.50	13,325.00	88.17%
12	Wal-Mart	WMT	04/14/05	600	45.35	27,210.00	47.50	28,500.00	1,290.00	4.74%
13	*Total*					$ 169,723.13		$ 207,760.40	$ 38,037.28	22.41%
14	*Average*			557	$31.35	$18,858.13	$41.04	$23,084.49	$4,226.36	
15	*Highest*			1200	$50.25	$60,300.00	$66.80	$51,984.00	$21,114.00	138.22%
16	*Lowest*			263	$16.25	$6,500.00	$14.91	$6,709.50	($8,316.00)	-32.99%

Investment Analysis / Real-Time Stock Quotes / Major Indices

FIGURE 2-91

In the Lab

7. Format the worksheet as follows:
   a. Worksheet title in cell A1: 36 point Arial Rounded MT Bold bold aligned across columns A through J; background color green (column 4, row 2); font color white (column 8, row 5)
   b. Worksheet subtitle in cell A2: same as worksheet title, except font size 24
   c. Worksheet title and subtitle border (A1:J2): thick box border
   d. Column titles in row 3: bold, italicized, centered, and a bottom border on row 3
   e. Data in rows 4 through 12: center data in column B; format dates in column C to the mm/dd/yy format; range E4:I4 — Currency style with fixed dollar sign; numbers in range E5:I12 — Comma style; range J4:J12 — Percent style with two decimal places; border — thick bottom border on row 12
   f. Total line: Font style of row title in cell A13 — bold and italicized; numbers in F13, H13, and I13— Currency style with floating dollar sign, negative numbers in parentheses; cell J13 — Percent style with two decimal places; set the width of columns B through E to best fit
   g. Average, Highest, and Lowest lines: Font style of row titles in range A14:A16 — bold and italicized; range E14: I16 — Currency style with floating dollar sign; cells J15 and J16 — Percent style with two decimal places
   h. Range J4:J12 — apply conditional formatting so that if a cell in range is less than 0, then cell appears with bold white font and background color of red
8. Change the worksheet name from Sheet1 to Investment Analysis.
9. Enter your name, course, laboratory assignment number (Lab 2-2), date, and instructor name in the range A20:A24.
10. Spell check the worksheet. Preview and then print the worksheet in landscape orientation. Save the workbook using the file name, Lab 2-3 Learn 'n Earn Stock Club Summary of Investments.
11. Print the range A3:B12. Print the formulas version on one page. Close the workbook without saving the changes. Hand in the three printouts to your instructor.

Instructions Part 2: If necessary, connect to the Internet. Open Lab 2-3 Learn 'n Earn Stock Club Summary of Investments. Perform a Web query to obtain multiple stock quotes (Figure 2-92), using the stock symbols in the second column of Table 2-10. Place the results of the Web query on a new worksheet. Rename the worksheet Real-Time Stock Quotes, and drag its tab to the right of the Investment Analysis tab. Save the workbook using the same file name as in Part 1. Preview and then print the worksheet in landscape orientation using the Fit to option.

Click the following links and print the Web page that appears in the browser window: Click here to visit MSN Money; Walgreen Company; Chart to the right of Boeing Company; and News to the right of McDonald's Corporation. Hand in the printouts to your instructor.

(continued)

Stock Club Investment Analysis and Equity Web Queries *(continued)*

Microsoft Excel - Lab 2-3 Learn 'n Earn Stock Club Summary of Investments

A1 | Stock Quotes Provided by MSN Money

	A	B	C	D	E	F	G	H	I
1	Stock Quotes Provided by MSN Money								
2	Click here to visit MSN Money								
3				Last	Previous Close	High	Low	Volume	Change
4	Boeing Company, The	Chart	News	61.82	60.91	62.51	60.43	3,649,800	0.91
5	The Coca-Cola Company	Chart	News	44.85	44.4	44.89	44.35	4,663,600	0.45
6	Walt Disney Company, The	Chart	News	27.55	27.28	27.6	27.16	5,387,200	0.27
7	General Electric Company	Chart	News	36.98	36.46	37	36.48	17,293,200	0.52
8	McDonald's Corporation	Chart	News	30.61	29.97	30.66	30.08	4,292,300	0.64
9	MGM MIRAGE	Chart	News	72.33	70.62	73.49	70.4	1,130,300	1.71
10	Southwest Airlines Co.	Chart	News	14.98	15	15.27	14.93	5,229,400	-0.02
11	Walgreen Company	Chart	News	45.99	45.46	46.2	45.51	2,276,500	0.53
12	Wal-M	Chart	N			47.67			0.74

FIGURE 2-92

Instructions Part 3: While connected to the Internet and with Lab 2-3 Learn 'n Earn Stock Club Summary of Investments open, create a worksheet listing the major indices and their current values on Sheet 2 of the workbook (Figure 2-93). After clicking the Sheet2 tab, create the worksheet by double-clicking MSN MoneyCentral Investor Major Indices in the Select Data Source dialog box. The dialog box is displayed when you invoke the Import Data on the Import External Data submenu. Rename the worksheet Major Indices. Preview and then print the Major Indices worksheet in landscape orientation using the Fit to option. Save the workbook using the same file name as in Part 1. Hand in the printout to your instructor.

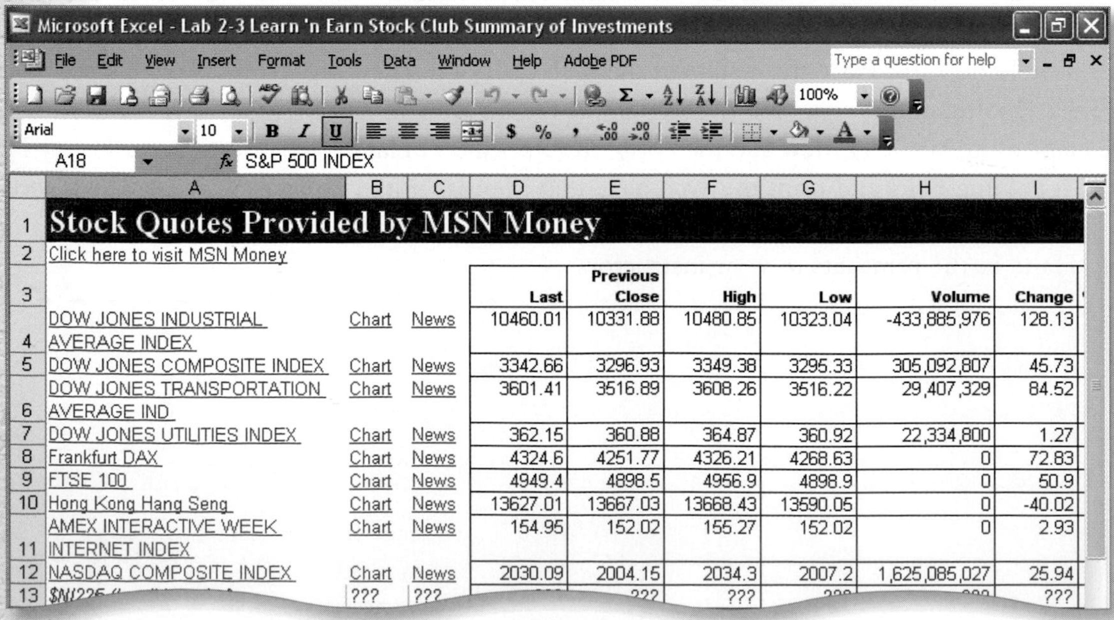

Microsoft Excel - Lab 2-3 Learn 'n Earn Stock Club Summary of Investments

A18 | S&P 500 INDEX

	A	B	C	D	E	F	G	H	I
1	Stock Quotes Provided by MSN Money								
2	Click here to visit MSN Money								
3				Last	Previous Close	High	Low	Volume	Change
4	DOW JONES INDUSTRIAL AVERAGE INDEX	Chart	News	10460.01	10331.88	10480.85	10323.04	-433,885,976	128.13
5	DOW JONES COMPOSITE INDEX	Chart	News	3342.66	3296.93	3349.38	3295.33	305,092,807	45.73
6	DOW JONES TRANSPORTATION AVERAGE IND	Chart	News	3601.41	3516.89	3608.26	3516.22	29,407,329	84.52
7	DOW JONES UTILITIES INDEX	Chart	News	362.15	360.88	364.87	360.92	22,334,800	1.27
8	Frankfurt DAX	Chart	News	4324.6	4251.77	4326.21	4268.63	0	72.83
9	FTSE 100	Chart	News	4949.4	4898.5	4956.9	4898.9	0	50.9
10	Hong Kong Hang Seng	Chart	News	13627.01	13667.03	13668.43	13590.05	0	-40.02
11	AMEX INTERACTIVE WEEK INTERNET INDEX	Chart	News	154.95	152.02	155.27	152.02	0	2.93
12	NASDAQ COMPOSITE INDEX	Chart	News	2030.09	2004.15	2034.3	2007.2	1,625,085,027	25.94
13	$NI225	???	???			???			???

FIGURE 2-93

Cases and Places

The difficulty of these cases studies varies: ■ are the least difficult and ■■ are more difficult. Each exercise has a cross-curricular designation:

Math Social Studies Science Language Arts Art/Music Business Health

1 As a summer intern working for the Gaselec Company, a supplier of gas and electric to upper New York, you have been asked to create a worksheet that estimates the monthly electric bill for a one-bedroom apartment. You have been given the company's typical operating costs of appliances based on average sizes and local electricity rates (Table 2-11). Use the following formulas:

Formula A: Total Cost per Day = Cost per Hour x Average Hours Used Daily

Formula B: Total Cost per Month (30 days) = 30 * Total Cost per Day

Formula C: Average function

Formula D: Max function

Formula E: Min function

Use the concepts and techniques presented in this project to create and format the worksheet. Include an embedded 3-D Pie Chart that shows the contribution of each appliance to the total cost per day.

Table 2-11 Appliances with Corresponding Electrical Cost per Hour and Worksheet Layout

APPLIANCE	COST PER HOUR	AVERAGE HOURS USED DAILY	TOTAL COST PER DAY	TOTAL COST PER MONTH (30 DAYS)
Clothes dryer	$0.6332	1.5	Formula A	Formula B
Iron	$0.1373	0.75	↓	↓
Laptop	$0.0345	5.5	↓	↓
Light bulb (150 watt)	$0.0250	6	↓	↓
Radio	$0.0125	2.5	↓	↓
Refrigerator	$0.0157	24	↓	↓
Stereo	$0.0078	4	↓	↓
Television	$0.0234	5.75	↓	↓
DVD/VCR	$0.0043	1.5	↓	↓
Totals		--	--	--
Average		Formula C	→	→
Highest		Formula D	→	→
Lowest		Formula E	→	→

Cases and Places

2 You work part-time for Computer Depot, a major computer retail outlet. Your manager wants to know the profit potential of their inventory. The data and the format of the desired report are shown in Table 2-12. The required formulas are shown in Table 2-13.

Use the concepts and techniques developed in this project to create and format the worksheet. Hand in a printout of the values version and formulas version of the worksheet. The company just received a shipment of 250 additional desktops and 200 laptops. Update the appropriate cells in the Units on Hand column. The additional inventory yields a total profit potential of $3,959,200.21.

Table 2-12 Computer Depot Profit Potential Data and Worksheet Layout

ITEM	UNITS ONHAND	UNIT COST	TOTAL COST	AVERAGE UNIT PRICE	TOTAL VALUE	POTENTIAL PROFIT
Desktops	1,675	577.25	Formula A	Formula B	Formula C	Formula D
External Drives	3,587	81.85				
Laptops	1,398	696.00				
Monitors	2,813	78.45				
Printers	1,453	$89.00				
Total						
Average	Formula E					
Lowest	Formula F					
Highest	Formula G					

Table 2-13 Computer Depot Profit Potential Formulas

Formula A = Units on Hand * Unit Cost

Formula B = Unit Cost * (1 / (1 – .58))

Formula C = Units on Hand * Average Unit Price

Formula D = Total Value – Total Cost

Formula E = AVERAGE function

Formula F = MIN function

Formula G = MAX function

Cases and Places

3 You are the chairman of the fund-raising committee for the school's band. You want to compare various fund-raising ideas to determine which will give you the best profit. The data obtained from six businesses about their products and the format of the desired report are shown in Table 2-14. The required formulas are shown in Table 2-15. Use the concepts and techniques presented in this project to create and format the worksheet.

Table 2-14 Band Fund-Raising Data and Worksheet Layout

PRODUCT	COMPANY	COST PER UNIT	MARGIN	SELLING PRICE	PROFIT PER 3000 SALES	PROFIT PER 5000 SALES
Candy	Ti Chi	$1.75	65%	Formula A	Formula B	Formula C
Coffee	Julio's Java	2.00	55%	↓	↓	↓
Flashlights	Night Riders	3.50	60%	↓	↓	↓
Hats	J&B	2.60	45%	↓	↓	↓
Pens	Pete's Pens	1.60	50%	↓	↓	↓
T-shirts	Freddies	3.75	53%	↓	↓	↓
Minimum		Formula D →	→	→	→	→
Maximum		Formula E →	→	→	→	→

Table 2-15 Band Fund-Raising Formulas

Formula A = Cost per Unit / (1 – Margin)

Formula B = 3000 * (Selling Price – Cost per Unit)

Formula C = 5000 *110% * (Selling Price – Cost per Unit)

Formula D = MIN function

Formula E = MAX function

Cases and Places

4 Seagram Pharmaceutical pays a 5.75% commission to its salespeople to stimulate drug sales. The company also pays each salesperson a base salary. The management has projected each salesperson's sales for the next year. The salespersons' name, base salary, and projected sales is as follows: Bates, Sidney, $19,325.00, $1,375,850.00; Horne, Roger, $22,000.00, $1,754,218.00; Patterson, Lee, $18,550.00, $1,827,932.00; Sachowicz, Stanley, $16,870.00, $1,653,365.00; Smith, Odessa $19,250.00, $1,767,325.00.

With this data, you have been asked to develop a worksheet calculating the amount of commission and the projected annual salary for each employee. The following formulas can be used to obtain this information:

Commission Amount = 5.75% x Projected Sales

Annual Salary = Base Salary + Commission Amount

Include a total, average value, highest value, and lowest value for employee base salary, projected sales, commission amount, and annual salary. Use the concepts and techniques presented in this project to create and format the worksheet.

Create a 3-D Pie Chart on a separate sheet illustrating the portion each employee's annual salary contributes to the total annual salary. Use the Microsoft Excel Help system to create a professional looking 3-D Pie Chart with title and data labels.

5 **Working Together** Have each member of your team select six stocks — two transportation stocks, two health stocks, and two Internet stocks. Each member should submit the stock names, stock symbols, and an approximate six-month-old price. Create a worksheet that lists the stock names, symbols, price, and number of shares for each stock (use 250 shares as the number of shares for all stocks). Format the worksheet so that it has a professional appearance and is as informative as possible.

Have the group do research on the use of 3-D references, which is a reference to a range that spans two or more worksheets in a workbook (use Microsoft Excel Help). Use what the group learns to create a Web query on the Sheet2 worksheet by referencing the stock symbols on the Sheet1 worksheet. Change the cells that list current price per share numbers on the Sheet1 worksheet to use 3-D cell references that refer to the worksheet created by the Web query on the Sheet2 worksheet. Present your workbook and findings to the class.

MICROSOFT OFFICE

Excel 2003

What-If Analysis, Charting, and Working with Large Worksheets

PROJECT 3

CASE PERSPECTIVE

Each day millions of people connect to the Internet to browse and search the World Wide Web using service providers that charge a small monthly fee. Quick Connect, a major supplier of cable television for many years, has recently become the premier Internet service provider in the Northeast.

Each June and December, the director of finance and accounting of Quick Connect, Aretha Jenkins, submits a plan to the management team to show projected monthly revenues, cost of goods, margin, expenses, and operating income for the next six months.

Last June, Aretha used pencil, paper, and a calculator to complete the report and draw a Pie chart. When she presented her report, members of the management team asked for the effect on the projected operating income if the percentage of expenses allocated to marketing was changed. While the management team impatiently waited, it took a flustered Aretha several minutes to calculate the answers by hand. Once she changed the percentage of expenses allocated to marketing, the Pie chart no longer matched the projections and thus was meaningless. Aretha now wants to use a computer and spreadsheet software to address what-if questions so she can take advantage of its instantaneous recalculation feature.

Aretha has asked you to assist her in preparing an easy-to-read worksheet that shows financial projections for the next six months (Figure 3-1a). In addition, she wants a 3-D Pie chart (Figure 3-1b) that shows the projected operating income contribution for each of the six months, because the management team prefers a graphical representation to numbers.

As you read through this project, you will learn how to create large worksheets, develop professional-looking charts, and complete what-if analyses.

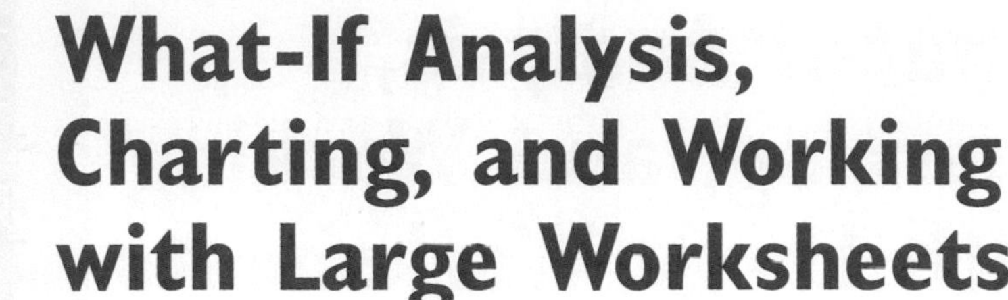

What-If Analysis, Charting, and Working with Large Worksheets

PROJECT 3

Objectives

You will have mastered the material in this project when you can:

- Rotate text in a cell
- Create a series of month names
- Use the Format Painter button to format cells
- Copy, paste, insert, and delete cells
- Format numbers using format symbols
- Freeze and unfreeze titles
- Show and format the system date
- Use absolute cell references in a formula
- Use the IF function to perform a logical test
- Show and dock toolbars
- Create a 3-D Pie chart on a separate chart sheet
- Color and rearrange worksheet tabs
- Change the worksheet view
- Answer what-if questions
- Goal seek to answer what-if questions

Introduction

Worksheets normally are much larger than those created in the previous projects, often extending beyond the size of the window (Figure 3-1a). Because you cannot see the entire worksheet on the screen at one time, working with a large worksheet sometimes can be frustrating. This project introduces several Excel commands that allow you to control what displays on the screen so you can view critical parts of a large worksheet at one time. One command lets you freeze the row and column titles so Excel always displays them on the screen. Another command splits the worksheet into separate window panes so you can view different parts of a worksheet on the screen at one time.

When you set up a worksheet, you should use as many cell references in formulas as possible, rather than constant values. The cell references in a formula are called assumptions. **Assumptions** are values in cells that you can change to determine new values for formulas. This project emphasizes the use of assumptions and shows how to use Excel to answer what-if questions such as, what happens to the semiannual operating income (cell H16 in Figure 3-1a) if you decrease the marketing expenses assumption (cell B22 in Figure 3-1a) by 2%? Being able to analyze quickly the effect of changing values in a worksheet is an important skill in making business decisions.

This project also introduces you to techniques that will enhance your ability to create worksheets and draw charts. From your work in Project 1, you are aware of how easily charts can be created. This project covers additional charting techniques that allow you to convey your message in a dramatic pictorial fashion (Figure 3-1b). This project also covers other methods for entering values in cells and formatting these values. In addition, you will learn how to use absolute cell references and how to use the IF function to assign a value to a cell based on a logical test.

In the previous projects, you learned how to use the Standard and Formatting toolbars. Excel has several other toolbars that can make your work easier. One such toolbar is the Drawing toolbar, which allows you to draw shapes and arrows and add drop shadows to cells you want to emphasize.

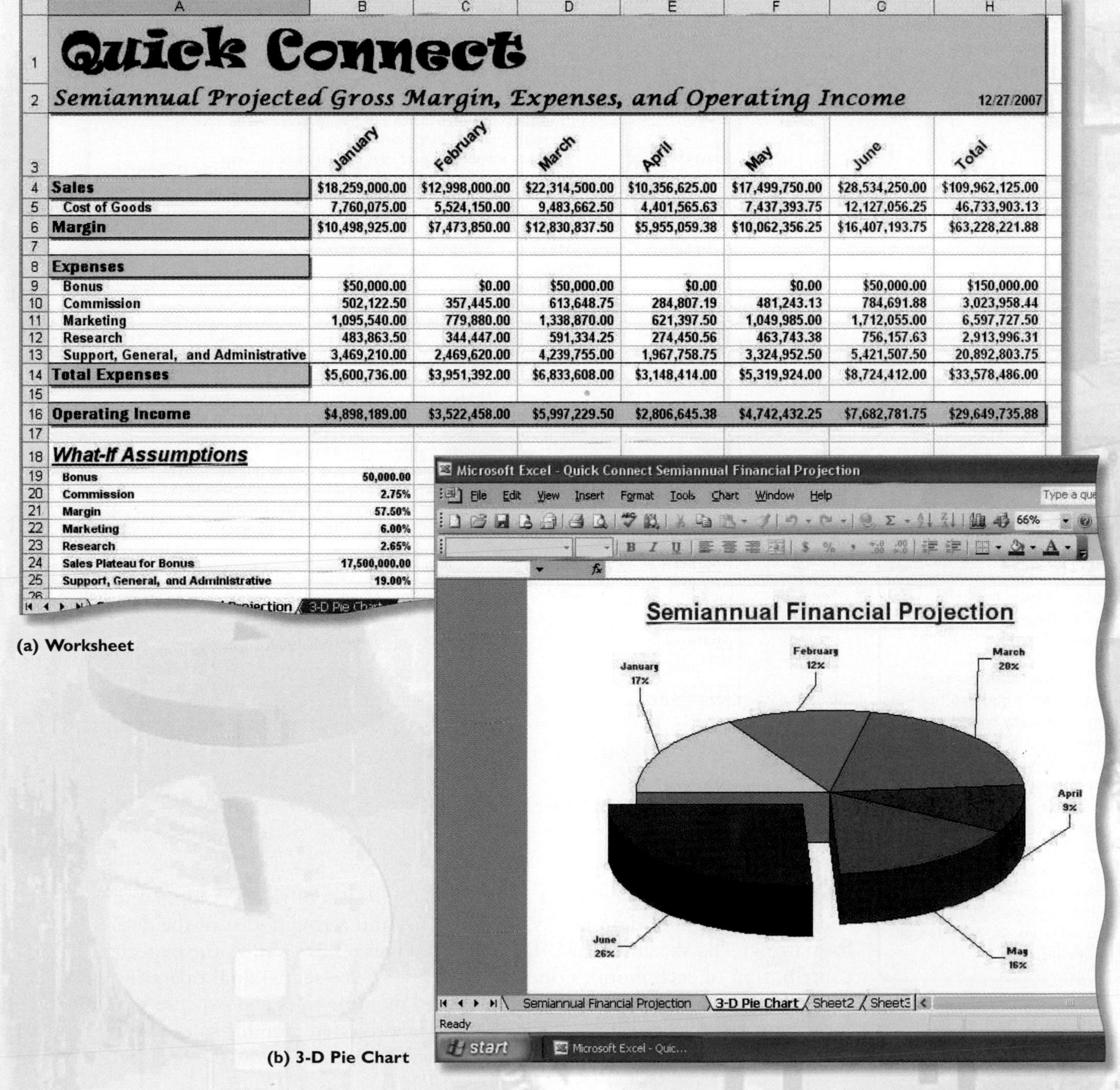

	A	B	C	D	E	F	G	H
1	Quick Connect							
2	Semiannual Projected Gross Margin, Expenses, and Operating Income							12/27/2007
3		January	February	March	April	May	June	Total
4	Sales	$18,259,000.00	$12,998,000.00	$22,314,500.00	$10,356,625.00	$17,499,750.00	$28,534,250.00	$109,962,125.00
5	Cost of Goods	7,760,075.00	5,524,150.00	9,483,662.50	4,401,565.63	7,437,393.75	12,127,056.25	46,733,903.13
6	Margin	$10,498,925.00	$7,473,850.00	$12,830,837.50	$5,955,059.38	$10,062,356.25	$16,407,193.75	$63,228,221.88
7								
8	Expenses							
9	Bonus	$50,000.00	$0.00	$50,000.00	$0.00	$0.00	$50,000.00	$150,000.00
10	Commission	502,122.50	357,445.00	613,648.75	284,807.19	481,243.13	784,691.88	3,023,958.44
11	Marketing	1,095,540.00	779,880.00	1,338,870.00	621,397.50	1,049,985.00	1,712,055.00	6,597,727.50
12	Research	483,863.50	344,447.00	591,334.25	274,450.56	463,743.38	756,157.63	2,913,996.31
13	Support, General, and Administrative	3,469,210.00	2,469,620.00	4,239,755.00	1,967,758.75	3,324,952.50	5,421,507.50	20,892,803.75
14	Total Expenses	$5,600,736.00	$3,951,392.00	$6,833,608.00	$3,148,414.00	$5,319,924.00	$8,724,412.00	$33,578,486.00
15								
16	Operating Income	$4,898,189.00	$3,522,458.00	$5,997,229.50	$2,806,645.38	$4,742,432.25	$7,682,781.75	$29,649,735.88
17								
18	What-If Assumptions							
19	Bonus	50,000.00						
20	Commission	2.75%						
21	Margin	57.50%						
22	Marketing	6.00%						
23	Research	2.65%						
24	Sales Plateau for Bonus	17,500,000.00						
25	Support, General, and Administrative	19.00%						

(a) Worksheet

(b) 3-D Pie Chart

FIGURE 3-1

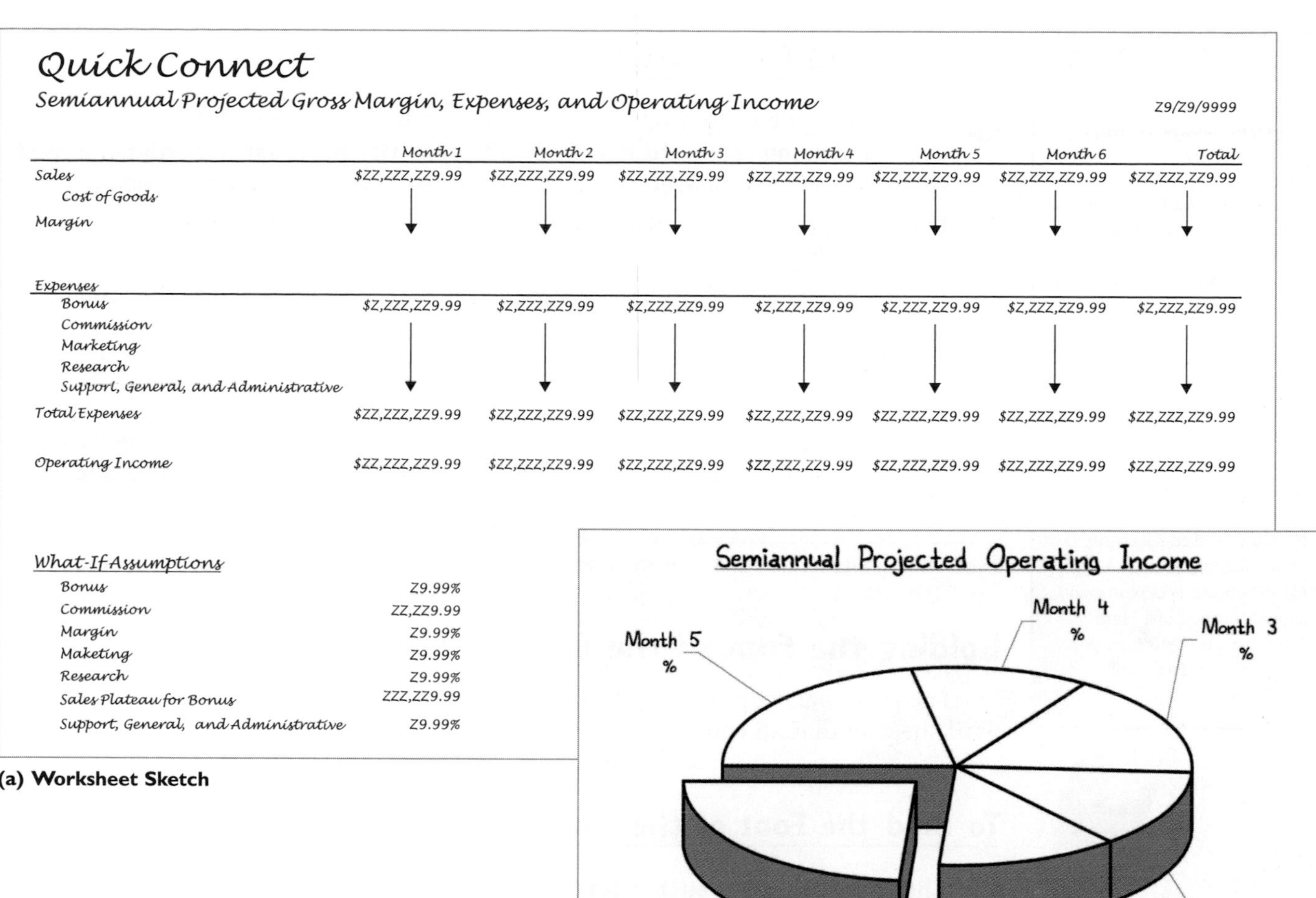

Quick Connect
Semiannual Projected Gross Margin, Expenses, and Operating Income
Z9/Z9/9999
Month 1
Month 2
Month 3
Month 4
Month 5
Month 6
Total
Sales
Cost of Goods
Margin
Expenses
Bonus
Commission
Marketing
Research
Support, General, and Administrative
Total Expenses
Operating Income
What-If Assumptions
Bonus
Commission
Margin
Maketing
Research
Sales Plateau for Bonus
Support, General, and Administrative
Semiannual Projected Operating Income
Month 1
Month 2
Month 3
Month 4
Month 5
Month 6
%

(a) Worksheet Sketch

(b) 3-D Pie Chart Sketch

FIGURE 3-3

(Figure 3-3a). The projected monthly sales and the assumptions will be used to calculate the remaining numbers in the worksheet.

Starting and Customizing Excel

With the requirements document and sketch of the worksheet and chart complete, the next step is to start and customize Excel. If you are stepping through this project on a computer and you want your screen to agree with the figures in this book, then you should change your computer's resolution to 800 × 600. For information on changing the resolution on your computer, see Appendix B. The steps on the next page start Excel and customize the Excel window.

Table 3-1 Quick Connect Semiannual Financial Projections Data and What-If Assumptions

PROJECTED MONTHLY TOTAL NET REVENUES	
January	$18,259,000
February	12,998,000
March	22,314,500
April	10,356,625
May	17,499,750
June	28,534,250
WHAT-IF ASSUMPTIONS	
Bonus	$50,000.00
Commission	2.75%
Margin	57.50%
Marketing	6.00%
Research	2.65%
Sales Plateau for Bonus	$17,500,000.00
Support, General, and Administrative	19.00%

Q & A

Q: Can Excel be started automatically when a computer is turned on?

A: Any application on the Startup submenu starts automatically when you turn your computer on. To add Excel to the Startup submenu, do the following: (1) Click the Start button on the Windows taskbar, point to All Programs on the Start menu, and then point to Microsoft Office on the All Programs submenu; (2) Right-drag Microsoft Office Excel 2003 from the Microsoft Office submenu to the Startup submenu; and (3) When the shortcut menu appears, click Copy Here. The next time you turn your computer on, Excel will start automatically.

To Start and Customize Excel

1. **Click the Start button on the Windows taskbar, point to All Programs on the Start menu, point to Microsoft Office on the All Programs submenu, and then click Microsoft Office Excel 2003 on the Microsoft Office submenu.**
2. **If the Excel window is not maximized, double-click its title bar to maximize it.**
3. **If the Language bar appears, right-click it and then click Close the Language bar on the shortcut menu.**
4. **If the Getting Started task pane appears in your Excel window, click its Close button in the upper-right corner.**
5. **If the Standard and Formatting toolbars are positioned on the same row, click the Toolbar Options button on the right side of either toolbar and then click Show Buttons on Two Rows.**

Excel displays its window with the Standard and Formatting toolbars on two rows.

Bolding the Font of the Entire Worksheet

The following steps show how to assign a bold format to the font for the entire worksheet so that all entries will be emphasized.

To Bold the Font of the Entire Worksheet

1. **Click the Select All button immediately above row heading 1 and to the left of column heading A (Figure 3-4).**
2. **Click the Bold button on the Formatting toolbar.**

No immediate change takes place on the screen. As you enter text and numbers into the worksheet, however, Excel will display them in bold.

Entering the Worksheet Titles and Saving the Workbook

Q & A

Q: What are three alternatives to bolding to make it easier for users to read a worksheet on the screen?

A: Select easy-to-read font styles, increase the font size, or increase the percentage in the Zoom box. The latter is particularly useful if users have less-than-average eyesight.

The worksheet contains two titles, one in cell A1 and another in cell A2. In the previous projects, titles were centered across the worksheet. With large worksheets that extend beyond the size of a window, it is best to enter titles in the upper-left corner as shown in the sketch of the worksheet in Figure 3-3a on the previous page. The following steps enter the worksheet titles and save the workbook.

To Enter the Worksheet Titles and Save the Workbook

1. **Click cell A1 and then enter** `Quick Connect` **as the worksheet title.**
2. **Click cell A2 and then enter** `Semiannual Projected Gross Margin, Expenses, and Operating Income` **as the worksheet subtitle.**
3. **With a USB flash drive connected to one of the computer's USB ports, click the Save button on the Standard toolbar.**

4 **When Excel displays the Save As dialog box, type** `Quick Connect Semiannual Financial Projection` **in the File name text box.**

5 **If necessary, click UDISK 2.0 (F:) in the Save in list (your USB flash drive may have a different name and letter). Click the Save button in the Save As dialog box.**

Excel responds by displaying the worksheet titles in cells A1 and A2 in bold as shown in Figure 3-4. Excel saves the workbook on the USB flash drive using the file name Aquatics Wear Six-Month Financial Projection.

Q & A

Q: What are the alignment options for entries in a cell?

A: In Excel, you use the Alignment sheet on the Format Cells dialog box, as shown in Figure 3-5 on the next page, to position data in a cell by centering, left-aligning, or right-aligning; indenting; aligning at the top, bottom, or center; and rotating. If you enter 90 in the Degrees box in the Orientation area, the text will appear vertically and read from bottom to top in the cell.

Rotating Text and Using the Fill Handle to Create a Series

When you first enter text, its angle is zero degrees (0°), and it reads from left to right in a cell. Text in a cell can be rotated counterclockwise by entering a number between 1° and 90° on the Alignment sheet in the Format Cells dialog box.

Projects 1 and 2 used the fill handle to copy a cell or a range of cells to adjacent cells. The fill handle also can be used to create a series of numbers, dates, or month names automatically. The following steps illustrate how to enter the month name, January, in cell B3; format cell B3 (including rotating the text); and then use the fill handle to enter the remaining month names in the range C3:G3.

To Rotate Text and Use the Fill Handle to Create a Series of Month Names

1

- **Select cell B3.**
- **Type** `January` **as the cell entry and then click the Enter box.**
- **Click the Font Size box arrow on the Formatting toolbar and then click 11 in the Font Size list.**
- **Click the Borders button arrow on the Formatting toolbar and then click the Bottom Border button (column 2, row 1) on the Borders palette.**
- **Right-click cell B3.**

Excel displays the text, January, in cell B3 using the assigned formats and it displays the shortcut menu (Figure 3-4).

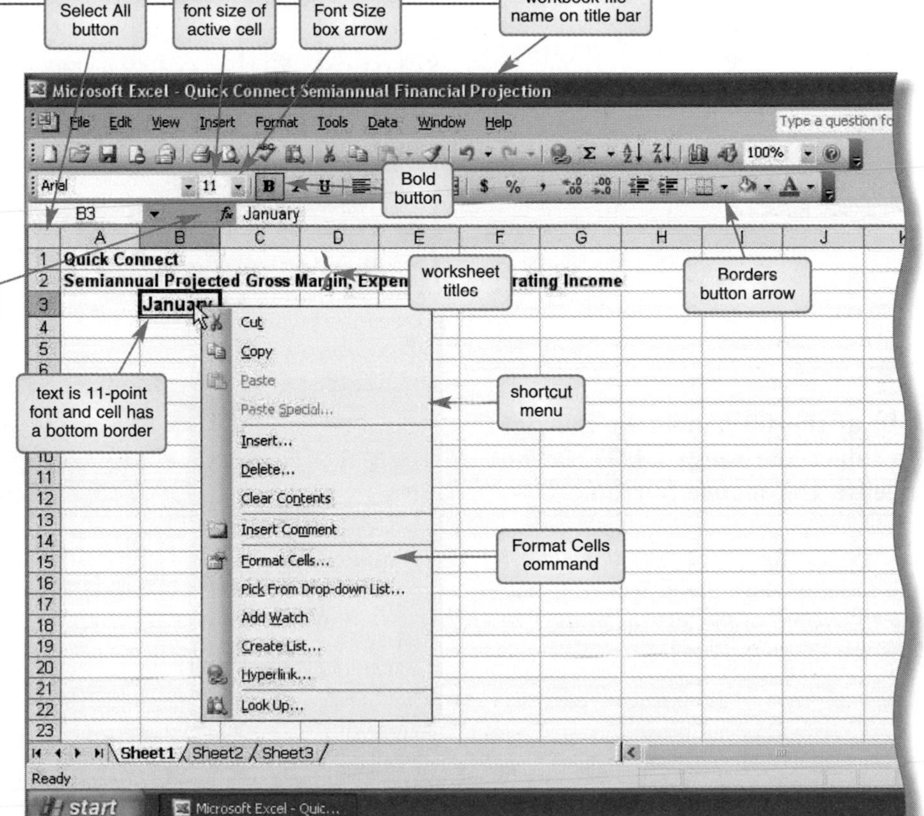

FIGURE 3-4

2

- **Click Format Cells on the shortcut menu.**
- **When the Format Cells dialog box is displayed, click the Alignment tab.**
- **Click the 45° point in the Orientation area.**

Excel displays the Alignment sheet in the Format Cells dialog box. The Text hand in the Orientation area points to the 45° point and 45 appears in the Degrees box (Figure 3-5).

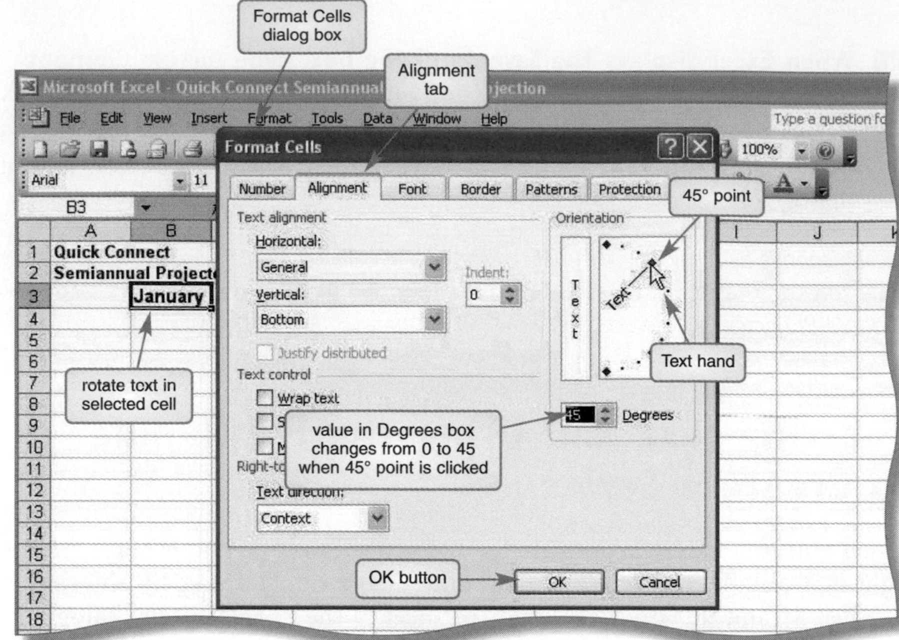

FIGURE 3-5

3

- **Click the OK button.**
- **Point to the fill handle on the lower-right corner of cell B3.**

Excel displays the text, January, in cell B3 at a 45° angle and automatically increases the height of row 3 to best fit the rotated text (Figure 3-6). The mouse pointer changes to a cross hair.

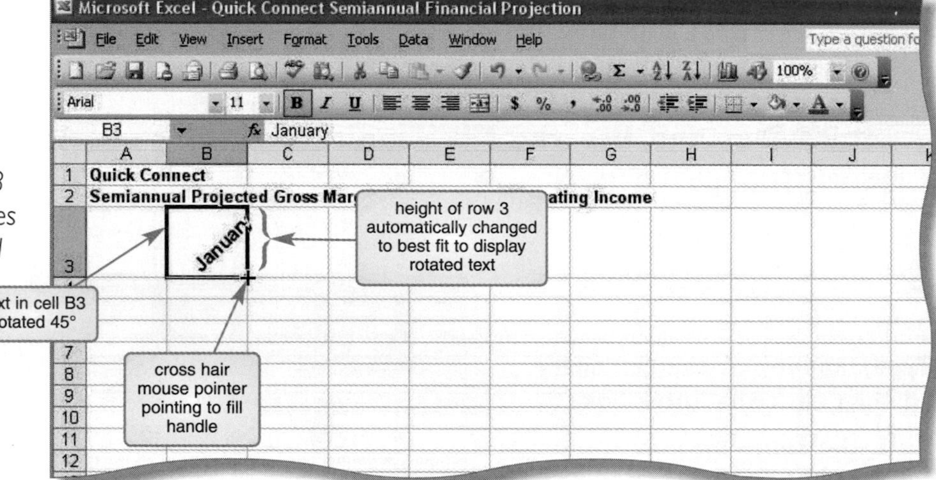

FIGURE 3-6

4

- **Drag the fill handle to the right to select the range C3:G3. Do not release the mouse button.**

Excel displays a light border that surrounds the selected range and a ScreenTip indicating the month of the last cell in the selected range (Figure 3-7).

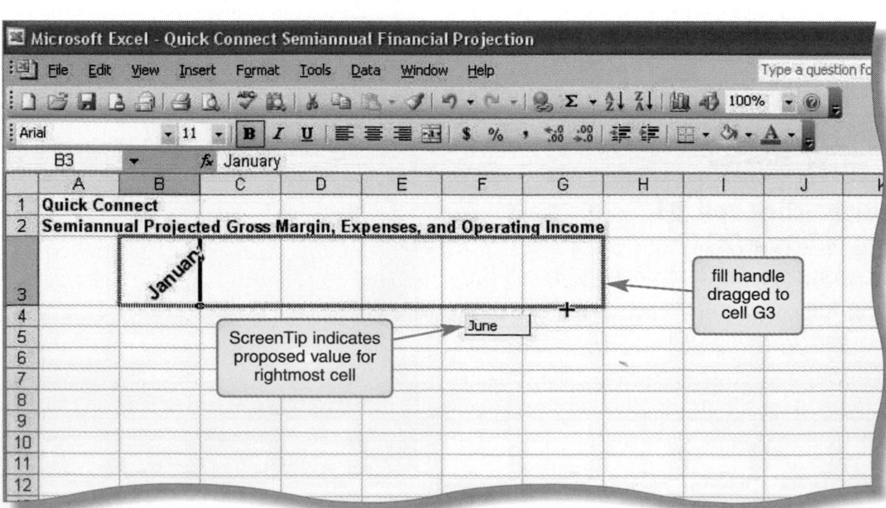

FIGURE 3-7

5

- **Release the mouse button.**
- **Click the Auto Fill Options button below the lower-right corner of the fill area.**

Using January in cell B3 as the basis, Excel creates the month name series January through June in the range B3:G3 (Figure 3-8). The formats assigned to cell B3 earlier in the previous steps (11-point font, bottom border, and text rotated 45°) also are copied to the range C3:G3. The Auto Fill Options menu shows the available fill options.

6

- **Click the Auto Fill Options button to hide the Auto Fill Options menu.**

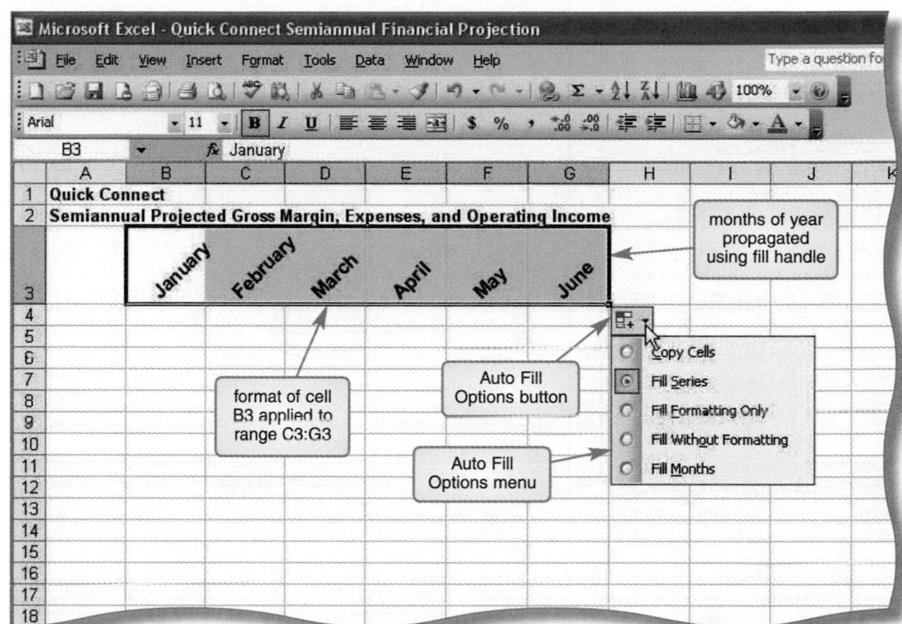

FIGURE 3-8

In addition to creating a series of values, dragging the fill handle instructs Excel to copy the format of cell B3 to the range C3:G3. With some fill operations, you may not want to copy the formats of the source cell or range to the destination cell or range. If this is the case, click the Auto Fill Options button after the range fills (Figure 3-8) and then select the option you desire on the Auto Fill Options menu. As shown in Figure 3-8, Fill Series is the default option that Excel uses to fill the area, which means it fills the destination area with a series, using the same formatting as the source area. If you choose another option on the Auto Fill Options menu, then Excel immediately changes the contents of the destination range. Following the use of the fill handle, the Auto Fill Options button remains active until you begin the next Excel operation. Table 3-2 summarizes the options on the Auto Fill Options menu.

You can use the fill handle to create a series longer than the one shown in Figure 3-8. If you drag the fill handle past cell G3 in Step 4, Excel continues to increment the months and logically will repeat January, February, and so on, if you extend the range far enough to the right.

You can create several different types of series using the fill handle. Table 3-3 on the next page illustrates several examples. Notice in examples 4 through 7 that, if you use the fill handle to create a series of numbers or non-sequential months, you must enter the first item in the series in one cell and the second item in the series in an adjacent cell. Next, select both cells and drag the fill handle through the destination area.

Table 3-2 Options Available on the Auto Fill Options Menu

AUTO FILL OPTION	DESCRIPTION
Copy Cells	Fill destination area with contents using format of source area. Do not create a series.
Fill Series	Fill destination area with series using format of source area. This option is the default.
Fill Formatting Only	Fill destination area using format of source area. No content is copied unless fill is series.
Fill Without Formatting	Fill destination area with contents, without the formatting of source area.
Fill Months	Fill destination area with series of months using format of source area. Same as Fill Series and shows as an option only if source area contains a month.

Q & A

Q: Can the fill handle be used to copy to the left or upward?

A: If you drag the fill handle to the left or up, Excel will decrement the series rather than increment the series. To copy a word, such as January or Monday, which Excel might interpret as the start of a series, hold down the CTRL key while you drag the fill handle to a destination area. If you drag the fill handle back into the middle of a cell, Excel erases the contents.

Table 3-3 Examples of Series Using the Fill Handle

EXAMPLE	CONTENTS OF CELL(S) COPIED USING THE FILL HANDLE	NEXT THREE VALUES OF EXTENDED SERIES
1	2:00	3:00, 4:00, 5:00
2	Qtr3	Qtr4, Qtr1, Qtr2
3	Quarter 1	Quarter 2, Quarter 3, Quarter 4
4	5-Jan, 5-Mar	5-May, 5-Jul, 5-Sep
5	2005, 2006	2007, 2008, 2009
6	1, 2	3, 4, 5
7	430, 410	390, 370, 350
8	Sun	Mon, Tue, Wed
9	Sunday, Tuesday	Thursday, Saturday, Monday
10	4th Section	5th Section, 6th Section, 7th Section
11	-205, -208	-211, -214, -217

Copying a Cell's Format Using the Format Painter Button

Because the last column title, Total, is not part of the series, it must be entered separately in cell H3 and formatted to match the other column titles. Imagine how many steps it would take, however, to assign the formatting of the other column titles to this cell — first, you have to change the font to 11 point, and then add a bottom border, and finally, rotate the text 45°. Using the Format Painter button on the Standard toolbar, however, you can format a cell quickly by copying a cell's format to another cell. The following steps enter the column title, Total, in cell H3 and format the cell using the Format Painter button.

To Copy a Cell's Format Using the Format Painter Button

1

- **Click cell H3.**
- **Type** `Total` **and then press the LEFT ARROW key.**
- **With cell G3 selected, click the Format Painter button on the Standard toolbar.**
- **Point to cell H3.**

The mouse pointer changes to a block plus sign with a paint brush (Figure 3-9).

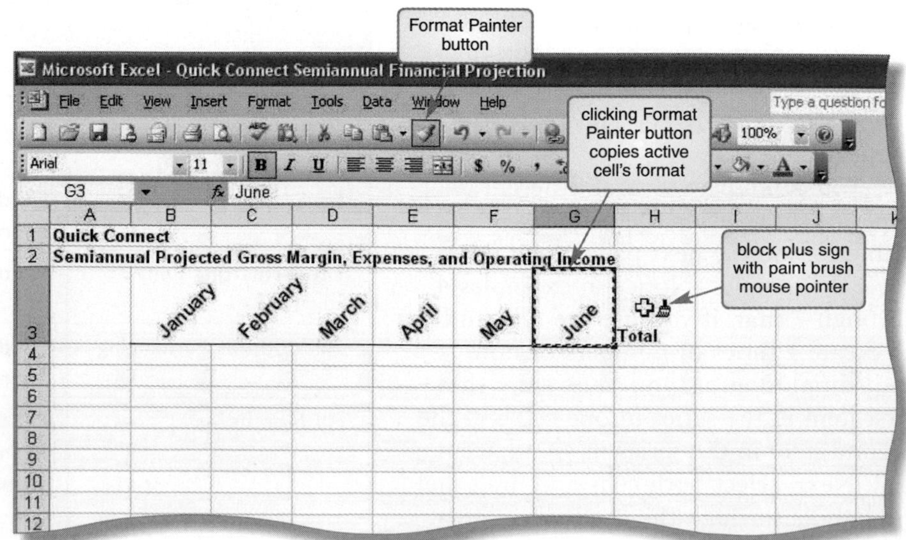

FIGURE 3-9

2

- **Click cell H3 to assign the format of cell G3 to cell H3.**
- **Click cell A4.**

Excel copies the format of cell G3 (11-point font, bottom border, text rotated 45°) to cell H3 (Figure 3-10). Cell A4 is now the active cell.

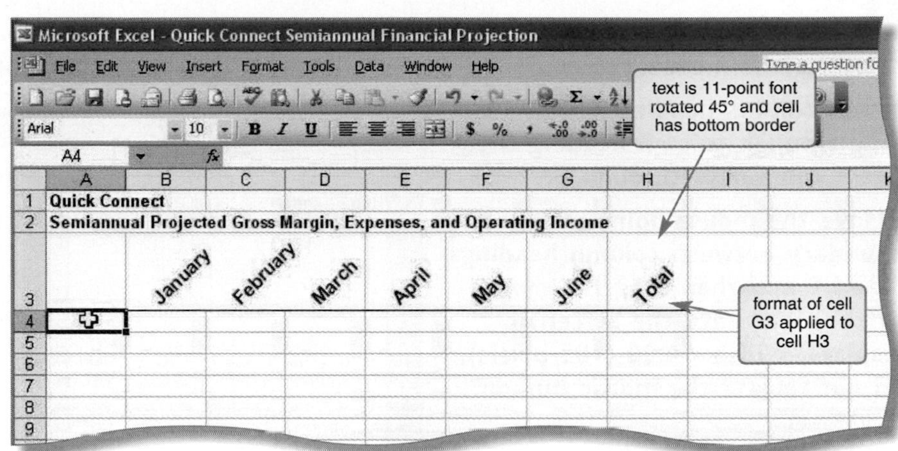

FIGURE 3-10

> **Q & A**
>
> **Q:** Can the Format Painter button be used to assign formats to nonadjacent ranges?
>
> **A:** Yes. Double-click the Format Painter button on the Standard toolbar and then drag through the nonadjacent ranges to paint the formats to the ranges. Click the Format Painter button to deactivate it.

The Format Painter button also can be used to copy the formats of a cell to a range of cells. To copy formats to a range of cells, select the cell or range with the desired format, click the Format Painter button on the Standard toolbar, and then drag through the range to which you want to paste the formats.

Increasing the Column Widths and Indenting Row Titles

In Project 2, the column widths were increased after the values were entered into the worksheet. Sometimes, you may want to increase the column widths before you enter the values and, if necessary, adjust them later. The following steps increase the column widths and then enter the row titles in column A down to What-If Assumptions in cell A18.

To Increase Column Widths and Enter Row Titles

1

- **Move the mouse pointer to the boundary between column heading A and column heading B so that the mouse pointer changes to a split double arrow.**
- **Drag the mouse pointer to the right until the ScreenTip displays, Width: 36.00 (257 pixels). Do not release the mouse button.**

The distance between the left edge of column A and the vertical dotted line below the mouse pointer shows the proposed column width (Figure 3-11). The ScreenTip displays the proposed width in points and pixels.

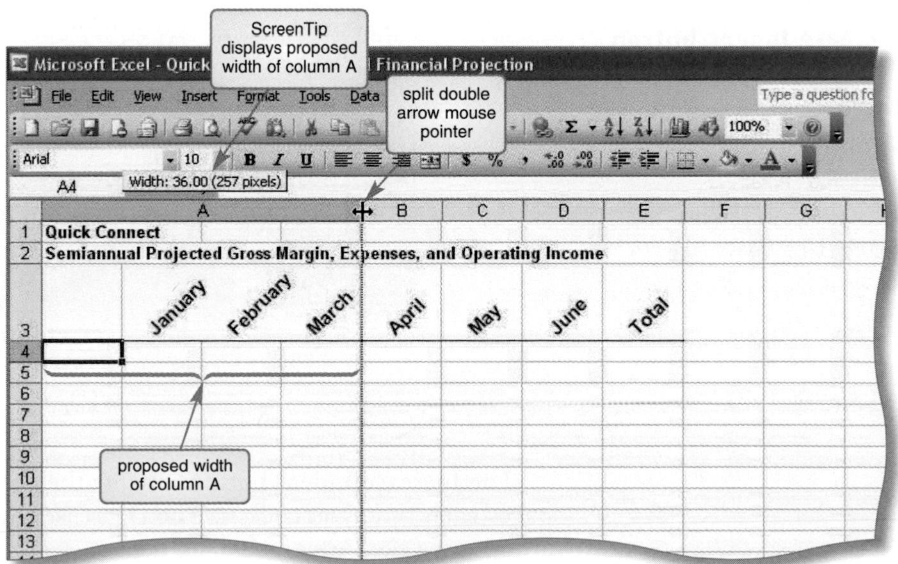

FIGURE 3-11

2

- **Release the mouse button.**
- **Click column heading B and then drag through column heading G to select columns B through G.**
- **Move the mouse pointer to the boundary between column headings B and C and then drag the mouse to the right until the ScreenTip displays, Width: 14.00 (103 pixels). Do not release the mouse button.**

The distance between the left edge of column B and the vertical line below the mouse pointer shows the proposed width of columns B through G (Figure 3-12). The ScreenTip displays the proposed width in points and pixels.

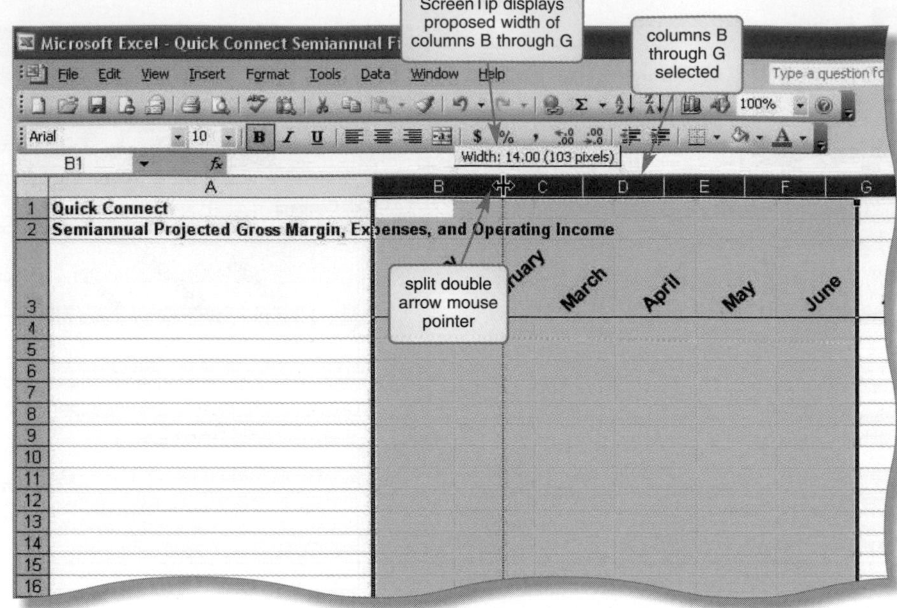

FIGURE 3-12

3

- **Release the mouse button.**
- **Use the technique described in Step 1 to increase the width of column H to 15.00.**
- **Enter the row titles in the range A4:A18 as shown in Figure 3-13, but without the indents.**
- **Click cell A5 and then click the Increase Indent button on the Formatting toolbar.**
- **Select the range A9:A13 and then click the Increase Indent button on the Formatting toolbar.**
- **Click cell A19.**

Excel displays the row titles as shown in Figure 3-13.

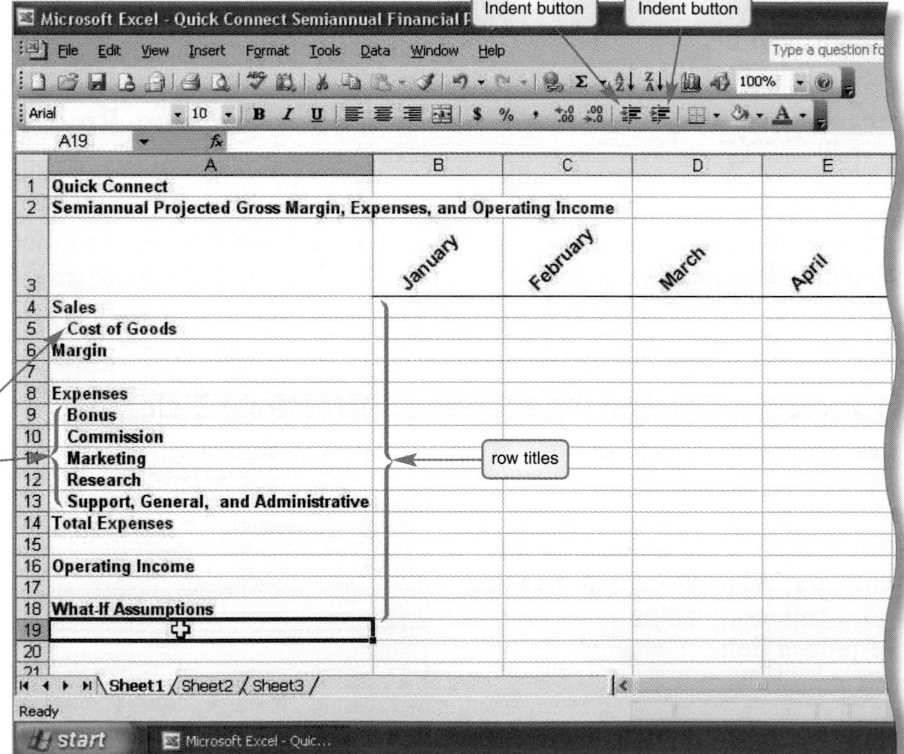

FIGURE 3-13

The Increase Indent button indents the contents of a cell to the right by three spaces each time you click it. The Decrease Indent button decreases the indent by three spaces each time you click it.

Copying a Range of Cells to a Nonadjacent Destination Area

As shown in the sketch of the worksheet (Figure 3-3a on page EX 149), the row titles in the range A9:A13 are the same as the row titles in the What-If Assumptions table in the range A19:A25, with the exception of the two additional entries in cells A21 (Margin) and A24 (Sales Plateau for Bonus). Hence, the What-If Assumptions table row titles can be created by copying the range A9:A13 to the range A19:A23 and then inserting two rows for the additional entries in cells A21 and A24. The source area (range A9:A13) is not adjacent to the destination area (range A19:A23). The first two projects used the fill handle to copy a source area to an adjacent destination area. To copy a source area to a nonadjacent destination area, however, you cannot use the fill handle.

A more versatile method of copying a source area is to use the Copy button and Paste button on the Standard toolbar. You can use these two buttons to copy a source area to an adjacent or nonadjacent destination area.

The Copy button copies the contents and format of the source area to the **Office Clipboard**, a special place in the computer's memory that allows you to collect text and graphic items from an Office document and then paste them into any Office document. The Copy command on the Edit menu or shortcut menu works the same as the Copy button. The Paste button copies the item from the Office Clipboard to the destination area. The Paste command on the Edit menu or shortcut menu works the same as the Paste button.

The following steps use the Copy and Paste buttons to copy the range A9:A13 to the nonadjacent range A19:A23.

> **Q & A**
>
> **Q:** Can cell entries be shrunk to fit in a cell?
>
> **A:** Yes. An alternative to increasing the column widths or row heights is to shrink the characters in the cell to fit the current width of the column. To shrink to fit, click Format on the menu bar, click Cells on the Format menu, click the Alignment tab, and click Shrink to fit in the Text control area. After shrinking entries to fit in a cell, con sider using the Zoom box on the Standard toolbar to make the entries more readable.

To Copy a Range of Cells to a Nonadjacent Destination Area

1

- **Select the range A9:A13 and then click the Copy button on the Standard toolbar.**
- **Click cell A19, the top cell in the destination area.**

Excel surrounds the source area A9:A13 with a marquee (Figure 3-14). Excel also copies the values and formats of the range A9:A13 to the Office Clipboard.

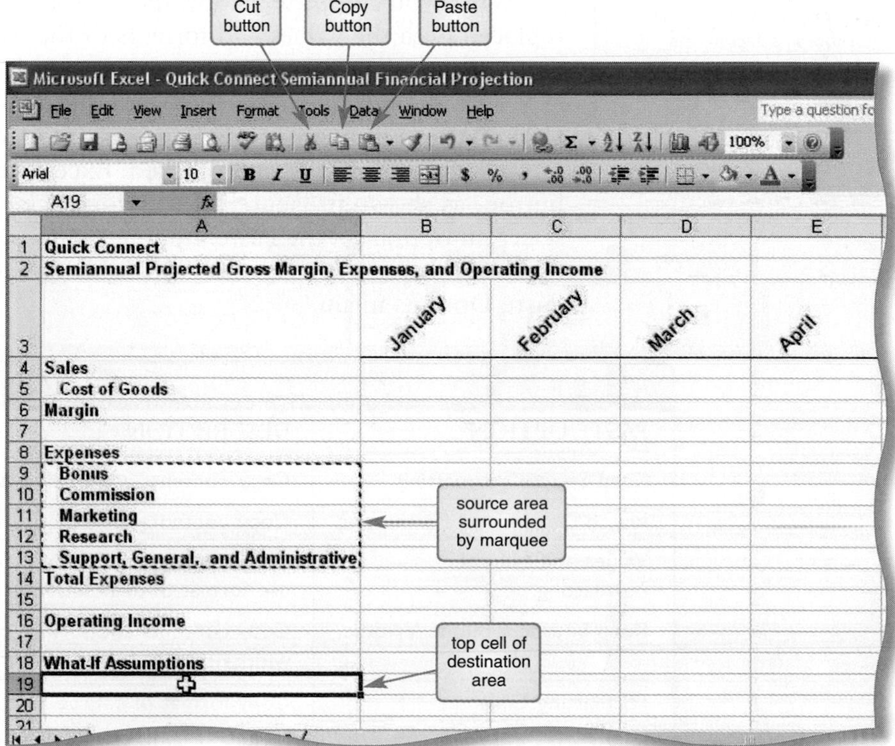

FIGURE 3-14

2

- **Click the Paste button on the Standard toolbar.**
- **Scroll down so row 5 appears at the top of the window.**

Excel copies the values and formats of the last item placed on the Office Clipboard (range A9:A13) to the destination area A19:A23 (Figure 3-15). The Paste Options button appears.

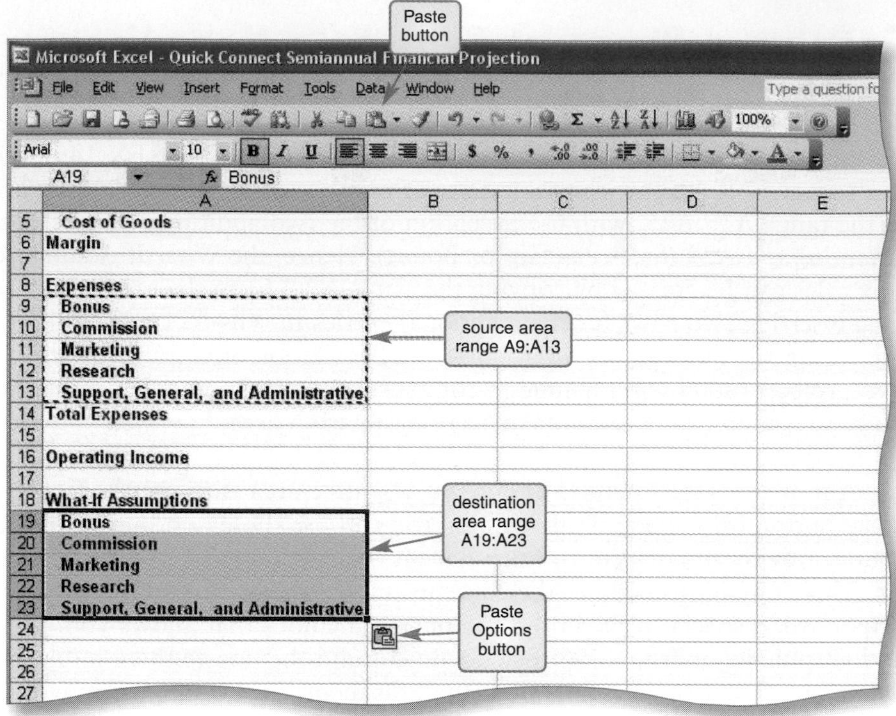

FIGURE 3-15

3

- **Press the ESC key.**

Excel removes the marquee from the source area and disables the Paste button on the Standard toolbar.

Q: Can you copy a range of cells from one workbook to another workbook?

A: Yes. You can copy a range of cells from one workbook to another by opening the source workbook, selecting the range, clicking the Copy button to place the range of cells on the Office Clipboard, activating the destination workbook, selecting the destination area, and then clicking the Paste button.

As shown in Step 1 and Figure 3-14 on the previous page, you are not required to select the entire destination area (range A19:A23) before clicking the Paste button. Excel only needs to know the upper-left cell of the destination area. In the case of a single column range, such as A19:A23, the top cell of the destination area (cell A19) also is the upper-left cell of the destination area.

When you complete a copy, the values and formats in the destination area are replaced with the values and formats of the source area. Any data contained in the destination area prior to the copy and paste is lost. If you accidentally delete valuable data, immediately click the Undo button on the Standard toolbar or click the Undo Paste command on the Edit menu to undo the paste.

After the Paste button is clicked, Excel immediately displays the Paste Options button, as shown in Figure 3-15. If you click the Paste Options button arrow and select an option on the Paste Options menu, Excel modifies the most recent paste operation based on your selection. Table 3-4 summarizes the options available on the Paste Options menu.

Table 3-4 Options Available on the Paste Options Menu

PASTE OPTION	DESCRIPTION
Keep Source Formatting	Copy contents and format of source area. This option is the default.
Match Destination Formatting	Copy contents of source area, but not the format.
Values and Number Formatting	Copy contents and format of source area for numbers or formulas, but use format of destination area for text.
Keep Source Column Widths	Copy contents and format of source area. Change destination column widths to source column widths.
Formatting Only	Copy format of source area, but not the contents.
Link Cells	Copy contents and format and link cells so that a change to the cells in source area updates the corresponding cells in destination area.

The Paste button on the Standard toolbar (Figure 3-15) includes an arrow, which displays a list of advanced paste options (Formulas, Values, No Borders, Transpose, Paste Link, and Paste Special). These options will be discussed when they are used.

An alternative to clicking the Paste button is to press the ENTER key. The ENTER key completes the paste operation, removes the marquee from the source area, and disables the Paste button so that you cannot paste the copied source area to other destination areas. The ENTER key was not used in the previous set of steps so that the capabilities of the Paste Options button could be discussed. The Paste Options button does not appear on the screen when you use the ENTER key to complete the paste operation.

As previously indicated, the Office Clipboard allows you to collect text and graphic items from an Office document and then paste them into any Office document. You can use the Office Clipboard to collect up to 24 different items. To collect multiple items, you first must display the Clipboard task pane by clicking Office Clipboard on the Edit menu. If you want to paste an item on the Office Clipboard into a document, such as a workbook, click the icon representing the item in the Clipboard task pane.

Q & A

Q: Is moving a range the same as copying a range?

A: No. You may hear someone say, "move it or copy it, it's all the same." No, it's is not the same! When you move a cell, the data in the original location is cleared and the format is reset to the default. When you copy a cell, the data and format of the copy area remains intact. In short, you should copy cells to duplicate entries and move cells to rearrange entries.

Using Drag and Drop to Move or Copy Cells

You also can use the mouse to move or copy cells. First, you select the source area and point to the border of the cell or range. You know you are pointing to the border of the cell or range when the mouse pointer changes to a block arrow. To move the selected cell or cells, drag the selection to the destination area. To copy a selection, hold down the CTRL key while dragging the selection to the destination area. You know Excel is in copy mode when a small plus sign appears next to the block arrow mouse pointer. Be sure to release the mouse button before you release the CTRL key. Using the mouse to move or copy cells is called **drag and drop**.

Skill Builder 3-1

To practice the following tasks, visit scsite.com/off2003sch/skill, locate Excel Project 3, and then click Skill Builder 3-1.

- ❑ Rotate text
- ❑ Use the fill handle to create a series
- ❑ Use the Format Painter button
- ❑ Copying a range of cells to a nonadjacent range

Using Cut and Paste to Move or Copy Cells

Another way to move cells is to select them, click the Cut button on the Standard toolbar (Figure 3-14 on page EX 157) to remove them from the worksheet and copy them to the Office Clipboard, select the destination area, and then click the Paste button on the Standard toolbar or press the ENTER key. You also can use the Cut command on the Edit menu or shortcut menu, instead of the Cut button.

Inserting and Deleting Cells in a Worksheet

At anytime while the worksheet is on the screen, you can insert cells to enter new data or delete cells to remove unwanted data. You can insert or delete individual cells, a range of cells, rows, columns, or entire worksheets.

Inserting Rows

The Rows command on the Insert menu or the Insert command on the shortcut menu allows you to insert rows between rows that already contain data. According to the sketch of the worksheet in Figure 3-3a on page EX 149, two rows must be inserted in the What-If Assumptions table, one between Commission and Marketing for the Margin assumption and another between Research and Support, General, and Administrative for the Sales Plateau for Bonus assumption. The steps on the next page show how to accomplish the task of inserting the new rows into the worksheet.

To Insert a Row

1

- **Right-click row heading 21, the row below where you want to insert a row.**

Excel highlights row 21 and displays the shortcut menu (Figure 3-16).

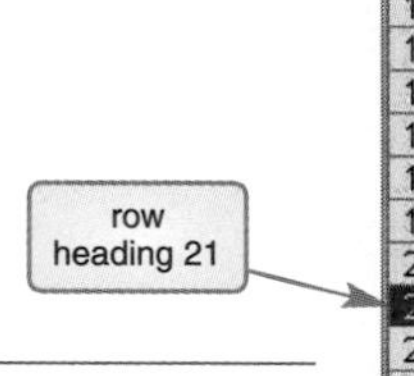

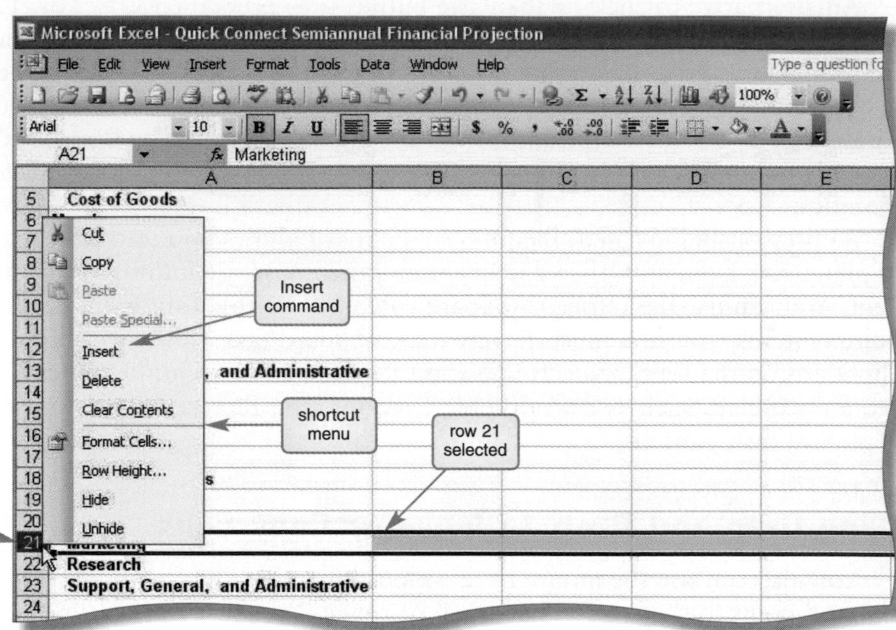

FIGURE 3-16

2

- **Click Insert on the shortcut menu.**
- **Click cell A21 in the new row and then enter** `Margin` **as the row title.**

Excel inserts a new row in the worksheet by shifting the selected row 21 and all rows below it down one row (Figure 3-17). Excel displays the new row title in cell A21. The cells in the new row inherit the formats of the cells in the row above them.

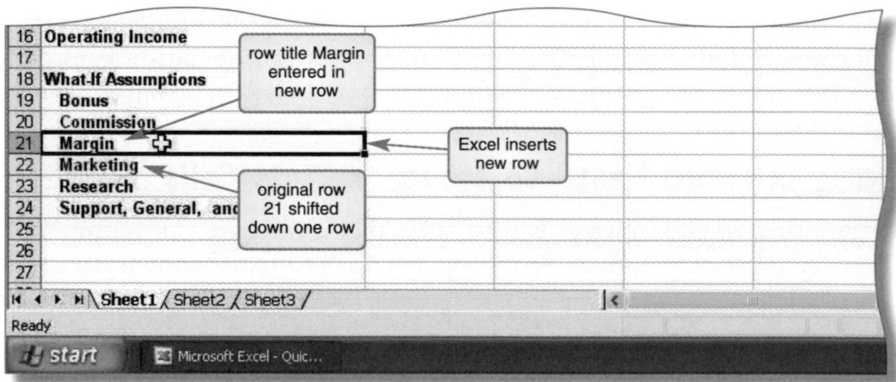

FIGURE 3-17

3

- **Right-click row heading 24 and then click Insert on the shortcut menu.**
- **Click cell A24 in the new row and then enter** `Sales Plateau for Bonus` **as the row title.**

Excel inserts a new row in the worksheet and displays the new row title in cell A24 (Figure 3-18).

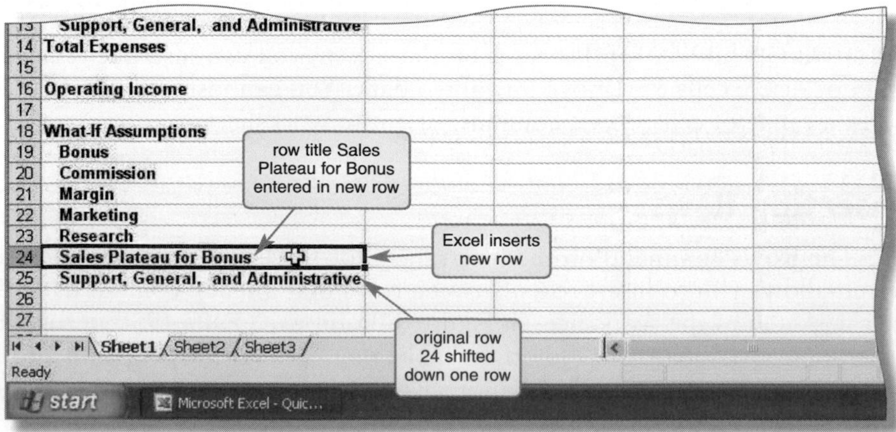

FIGURE 3-18

When you insert a row, it inherits the format of the row above it. You can change this by clicking the Insert Options button that appears immediately above the inserted row. Following the insertion of a row, the Insert Options button lets you select from the following options: (1) Format Same As Above; (2) Format Same As Below; and (3) Clear Formatting. The Format Same as Above option is the default. The Insert Options button remains active until you begin the next Excel operation.

If the rows that are shifted down include cell references in formulas located in the worksheet, Excel automatically adjusts the cell references in the formulas to their new locations. Thus, in Step 2 in the previous steps, if a formula in the worksheet references a cell in row 21 before the insert, then the cell reference in the formula is adjusted to row 22 after the insert.

The primary difference between the Insert command on the shortcut menu and the Rows command on the Insert menu is that the Insert command on the shortcut menu requires that you select an entire row (or rows) in order to insert a row (or rows). The Rows command on the Insert menu requires that you select a single cell in a row to insert one row or a range of cells to insert multiple rows.

Q & A

Q: Can multiple adjacent rows or columns be inserted at one time?

A: Yes. If you want to insert multiple rows, you have two choices. First, you can insert a single row by using the Insert command on the shortcut menu and then repeatedly press F4 to keep inserting rows. Alternatively, you can select any number of existing rows before inserting new rows. For instance, if you want to insert five rows, select five existing rows in the worksheet, right-click the rows, and then click Insert on the shortcut menu.

Inserting Columns

You insert columns into a worksheet in the same way you insert rows. To insert columns, select one or more columns immediately to the right of where you want Excel to insert the new column or columns. Select the number of columns you want to insert. Next, click Columns on the Insert menu or click Insert on the shortcut menu. The primary difference between these two commands is this: the Columns command on the Insert menu requires that you select a single cell in a column to insert one column or a range of cells to insert multiple columns. The Insert command on the shortcut menu, however, requires that you select an entire column (or columns) to insert a column (or columns). Following the insertion of a column, Excel displays the Insert Options button, which allows you to modify the insertion in a fashion similar to that discussed earlier when inserting rows.

Inserting Single Cells or a Range of Cells

The Insert command on the shortcut menu or the Cells command on the Insert menu allows you to insert a single cell or a range of cells. You should be aware that if you shift a single cell or a range of cells, however, it no longer may be lined up with its associated cells. To ensure that the values in the worksheet do not get out of order, it is recommended that you insert only entire rows or entire columns. When you insert a single cell or a range of cells, Excel displays the Insert Options button so that you can change the format of the inserted cell, using options similar to those for inserting rows and columns.

Q & A

Q: Can a range of cells be inserted between two adjacent cells with entries?

A: Yes. You can move and insert a selected cell or range between two adjacent cells with entries by holding down the SHIFT key while you drag the selection to the gridline where you want to insert. You also can copy and insert by holding down the CTRL+SHIFT keys while you drag the selection to the desired gridline.

Deleting Columns and Rows

The Delete command on the Edit menu or shortcut menu removes cells (including the data and format) from the worksheet. Deleting cells is not the same as clearing cells. The Clear command, which was described earlier in Project 1 on page EX 52, clears the data from the cells, but the cells remain in the worksheet. The Delete command removes the cells from the worksheet and shifts the remaining

Q & A

Q: Are the worksheets used in business error free?

A: No. Studies have shown that more than 25 percent of all business worksheets have errors. If you are not careful entering data and formulas, then your worksheet is prone to errors. You can ensure correctness in your formulas by carefully checking them using Range Finder and the Error Checking command on the Tools menu. The Formula Auditing command on the Tools menu also can be helpful when verifying formulas.

Project Three — Quick Connect Semiannual Financial Projection

The requirements document for the Quick Connect Semiannual Financial Projection worksheet is shown in Figure 3-2. It includes the needs, source of data, summary of calculations, chart requirements, and other facts about its development.

REQUEST FOR NEW WORKSHEET

Date Submitted:	December 17, 2007
Submitted By:	Aretha Jenkins
Worksheet Title:	Quick Connect Semiannual Financial Projections
Needs:	The needs are: (1) a worksheet (Figure 3-3a) that shows Quick Connect's projected monthly sales, cost of goods, margin, expenses, and operating income for a six-month period; and (2) a 3-D Pie chart (Figure 3-3b) that shows the projected contribution of each month's operating income to the six-month period operating income.
Source of Data:	The data supplied by the Finance department includes projections of the monthly sales and expenses (Table 3-1) that are based on prior years. All the remianing numbers in the worksheet are determined from these 13 numbers using formulas.
Calculations:	The following calculations must be made for each month: 1. Cost of Goods = Sales – Sales * Margin 2. Margin = Sales – Cost of Goods 3. Advertising Expense = Advertising Assumption * Sales 4. Bonus Expense = $50,000.00 if the Sales exceeds the Sales Plateau for Bonus; otherwise Bonus Expense = 0 5. Commission Expense = Commission Assumption * Sales 6. Research Expense = Research Assumption * Sales 7. Support, General, and Administrative Expense = Support, General, and Administrative Assumption * Sales 8. Total Expenses = Sum of Expenses 9. Operating Income = Margin – Total Expenses
Chart Requirements:	A 3-D Pie chart is required on a separate sheet (Figure 3-3b) to show the contribution of each month's operating income to the six-month period operating income. The chart should also emphasize the month with the greatest operating income.

Approvals

Approval Status:	X	Approved
		Rejected
Approved By:	Jack Hartley, CFO	
Date:	December 21, 2007	
Assigned To:	J. Quasney, Spreadsheet Specialist	

FIGURE 3-2

Q & A

Q: How did businesses answer what-if questions before the advent of spreadsheet software?

A: Just a few short years ago, a what-if question of any complexity could be answered only by using a large, expensive computer programmed by highly paid computer professionals. Generating a result could take days. Excel gives the noncomputer professional the ability to get complex business-related questions answered instantaneously and economically.

The sketch of the worksheet (Figure 3-3a) consists of titles, column and row headings, location of data values, calculations, and a rough idea of the desired formatting. The sketch of the 3-D Pie chart (Figure 3-3b) shows the expected contribution of each month's operating income to the semiannual operating income.

Table 3-1 includes the company's projected monthly sales and expense assumptions for the six months based on historical sales. The projected monthly sales will be entered in row 4 of the worksheet. The assumptions will be entered below the operating income

rows up (when you delete rows) or shifts the remaining columns to the left (when you delete columns). If formulas located in other cells reference cells in the deleted row or column, Excel does not adjust these cell references. Excel displays the error message **#REF!** in those cells to indicate a cell reference error. For example, if cell A7 contains the formula =A4+A5 and you delete row 5, Excel assigns the formula =A4+#REF! to cell A6 (originally cell A7) and displays the error message #REF! in cell A6. It also displays an Error Options button when you select the cell containing the error message #REF!, which allows you to select options to determine the nature of the problem.

Q & A

Q: Can you undo copying, deleting, inserting, and moving ranges of cells?

A: Yes. Copying, deleting, inserting, and moving ranges of cells have the potential to render a worksheet useless. Carefully review these actions before continuing on to the next task. If you are not sure the action is correct, click the Undo button on the Standard toolbar.

Deleting Individual Cells or a Range of Cells

Although Excel allows you to delete an individual cell or range of cells, you should be aware that if you shift a cell or range of cells on the worksheet, it no longer may be lined up with its associated cells. For this reason, it is recommended that you delete only entire rows or entire columns.

Entering Numbers with Format Symbols

The next step in creating the Semiannual Financial Projection worksheet is to enter the what-if assumptions values in the range B19:B25. The numbers in the table can be entered and then formatted as in Projects 1 and 2, or each one can be entered with format symbols. When a number is entered with a **format symbol**, Excel immediately displays it with the assigned format. Valid format symbols include the dollar sign ($), comma (,), and percent sign (%).

If you enter a whole number, it appears without any decimal places. If you enter a number with one or more decimal places and a format symbol, Excel displays the number with two decimal places. Table 3-5 illustrates several examples of numbers entered with format symbols. The number in parentheses in column 4 indicates the number of decimal places.

Table 3-5 Numbers Entered with Format Symbols

FORMAT SYMBOL	TYPED IN FORMULA BAR	DISPLAYS IN CELL	COMPARABLE FORMAT
,	83,341	83,341	Comma (0)
	1,675.8	1,675.80	Comma (2)
$	$278	$278	Currency (0)
	$3818.54	$3,818.54	Currency (2)
	$45,612.3	$45,612.30	Currency (2)
%	23%	23%	Percent (0)
	97.5%	97.50%	Percent (2)
	39.833%	39.83%	Percent (2)

The following step enters the numbers in the What-If Assumptions table with format symbols.

To Enter Numbers with Format Symbols

1

- **Enter** 50,000.00 **in cell B19,** 2.75% **in cell B20,** 57.50% **in cell B21,** 6.00% **in cell B22,** 2.65% **in cell B23,** 17,500,000.00 **in cell B24, and** 19.00% **in cell B25.**

Excel displays the entries using a format based on the format symbols entered with the numbers (Figure 3-19).

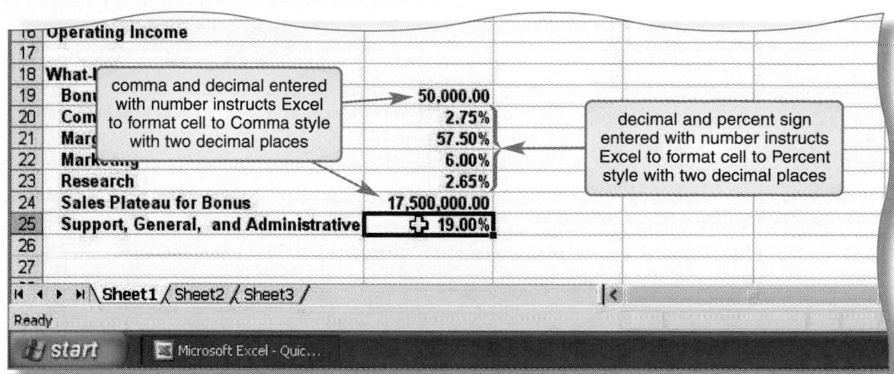

FIGURE 3-19

Freezing Worksheet Titles

Freezing worksheet titles is a useful technique for viewing large worksheets that extend beyond the window. Normally, when you scroll down or to the right, the column titles in row 3 and the row titles in column A that define the numbers no longer appear on the screen. This makes it difficult to remember what the numbers in these rows and columns represent. To alleviate this problem, Excel allows you to **freeze the titles**, so that Excel displays the titles on the screen, no matter how far down or to the right you scroll.

The following steps show how to use the Freeze Panes command on the Window menu to freeze the worksheet title and column titles in rows 1, 2, and 3, and the row titles in column A.

To Freeze Column and Row Titles

1

- **Press CTRL+HOME to select cell A1 and ensure that Excel displays row 1 and column A on the screen.**
- **Select cell B4.**
- **Click Window on the menu bar.**

Excel displays the Window menu (Figure 3-20).

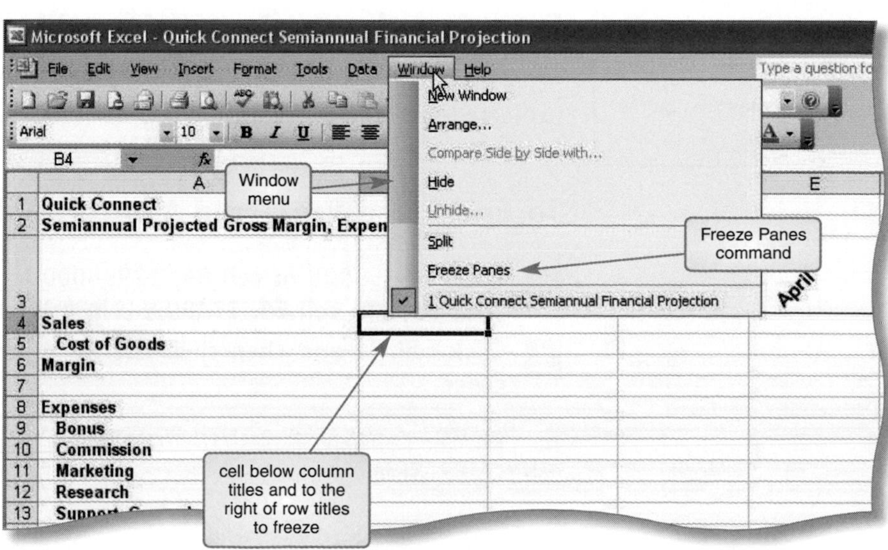

FIGURE 3-20

• Click Freeze Panes on the Window menu.

Excel displays a thin black line on the right side of column A, indicating the split between the frozen row titles in column A and the rest of the worksheet. It also displays a thin black line below row 3, indicating the split between the frozen column titles in rows 1 through 3 and the rest of the worksheet (Figure 3-21).

FIGURE 3-21

Q & A

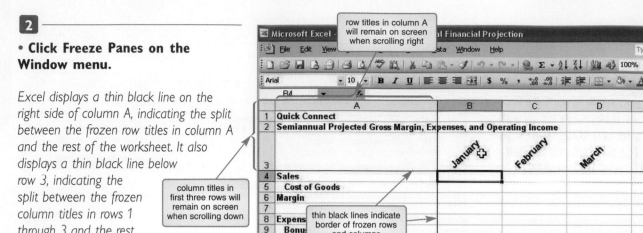

Q: Can only column titles or row titles be frozen?

A: Yes. If you want to freeze only column titles, select the appropriate cell in column A before you click Freeze Panes on the Window menu. If you want to freeze only row titles, then select the appropriate cell in row 1. To freeze both column headings and row titles, select the cell that is the intersection of the column and row titles before you click Freeze Panes on the Window menu.

Once frozen, the column titles in rows 1 through 3 and the row titles in column A will remain on the screen even when you scroll to the right. The titles remain frozen until you unfreeze them. You unfreeze the titles by clicking the Unfreeze Panes command on the Window menu. You will learn how to use the Unfreeze Panes command later in this project.

Before freezing the titles, it is important that Excel displays cell A1 in the upper-left corner of the screen. For example, if in Step 1 on the previous page, cell B4 was selected without first selecting cell A1 to ensure Excel displays the upper-left corner of the screen, then Excel would have frozen the titles and also hidden rows 1 and 2. Excel thus would not be able to display rows 1 and 2 until they are unfrozen.

Entering the Projected Monthly Sales

The next step is to enter the projected monthly sales in row 4 and compute the projected semiannual sales in cell H4.

To Enter the Projected Monthly Sales

1. **Enter** `18259000` **in cell B4,** `12998000` **in cell C4,** `22314500` **in cell D4,** `10356625` **in cell E4,** `17499750` **in cell F4, and** `28534250` **in cell G4.**
2. **Click cell H4 and then click the AutoSum button on the Standard toolbar twice.**

The projected semiannual sales (109962125) appears in cell H4 (Figure 3-22). Columns B, C, and D have scrolled off the screen, but column A remains because it was frozen earlier.

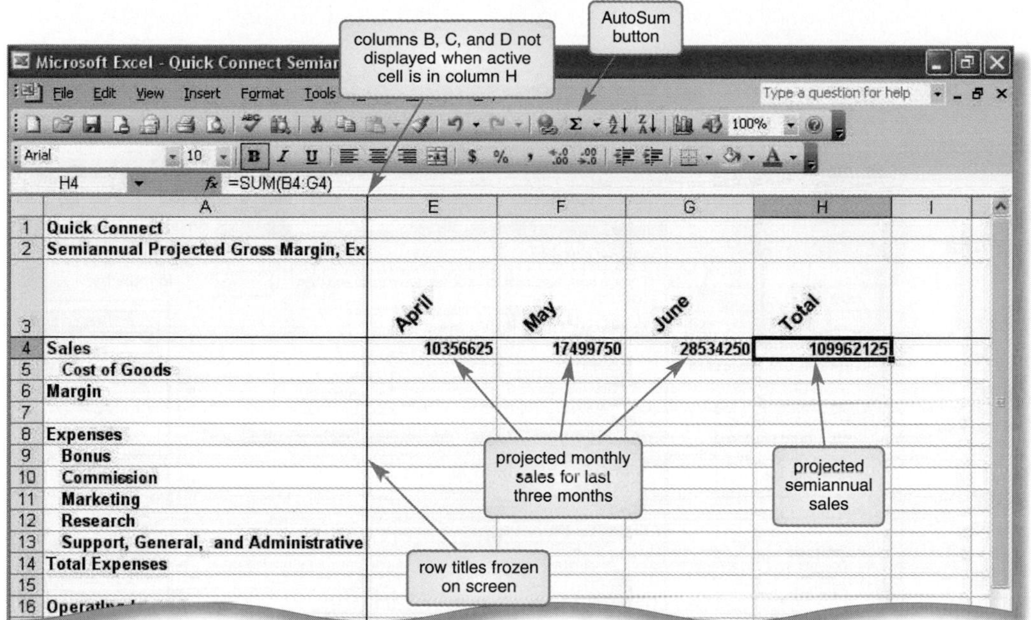

FIGURE 3-22

Recall from Projects 1 and 2 that if you select a single cell below or to the right of a range of numbers, you must click the AutoSum button twice to instruct Excel to display the sum. If you select a range of cells below or to the right of a range of numbers, you only need to click the AutoSum button once to instruct Excel to display the sums.

Displaying a System Date

The sketch of the worksheet in Figure 3-3a on page EX 149 includes a date stamp on the right side of the heading section. A **date stamp** shows the date a workbook, report, or other document was created or the period it represents. In business, a report often is meaningless without a date stamp. For example, if a printout of the worksheet in this project were distributed to the company's analysts, the date stamp would show when the six-month projections were made, as well as what period the report represents.

A simple way to create a date stamp is to use the NOW function to enter the system date tracked by your computer in a cell in the worksheet. The **NOW function** is one of 14 date and time functions available in Excel. When assigned to a cell, the NOW function returns a number that corresponds to the system date and time beginning with December 31, 1899. For example, January 1, 1900 equals 1, January 2, 1900 equals 2, and so on. Noon equals .5. Thus, noon on January 1, 1900 equals 1.5 and 6 P.M. on January 1, 1900 equals 1.75. If the computer's system date is set to the current date, which normally it is, then the date stamp is equivalent to the current date.

Excel automatically formats this number as a date, using the date and time format, mm/dd/yyyy hh:mm, where the first mm is the month, dd is the day of the month, yyyy is the year, hh is the hour of the day, and mm is the minutes past the hour.

The steps on the next page show how to enter the NOW function and change the format from mm/dd/yyyy hh:mm to mm/dd/yyyy.

Q & A

Q: How many days have you been alive?

A: Enter today's date (e.g., 12/5/2007) in cell A1. Next, enter your birth date (e.g., 6/22/1990) in cell A2. Select cell A3 and enter the formula =A1 – A2. Format cell A3 to the General style using the Cells command on the Format menu. Cell A3 will display your age in days.

To Enter and Format the System Date

1

- **Click cell H2 and then click the Insert Function box in the formula bar.**
- **When Excel displays the Insert Function dialog box, click the Or select a category box arrow, and then select Date & Time in the list.**
- **Scroll down in the Select a function list and then click NOW.**

An equal sign appears in the active cell and in the formula bar. Excel displays the Insert Function dialog box as shown in Figure 3-23.

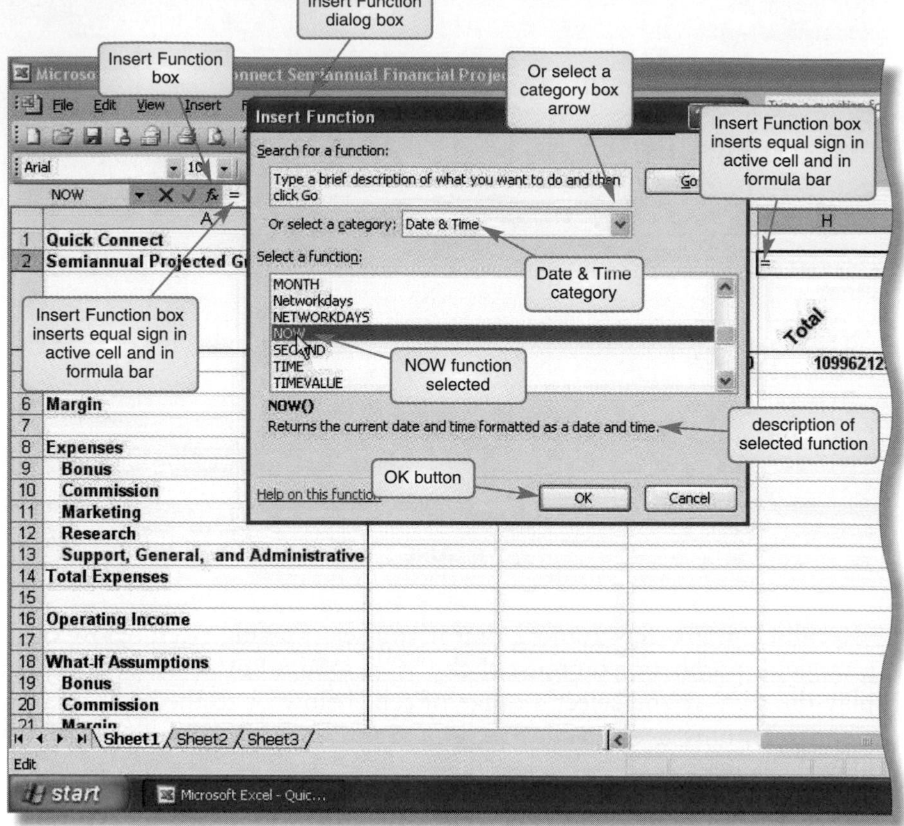

FIGURE 3-23

2

- **Click the OK button.**
- **When Excel displays the Function Arguments dialog box, click the OK button.**
- **Right-click cell H2.**

Excel displays the system date and time in cell H2, using the default date and time format mm/dd/yyyy hh:mm. It also displays the shortcut menu (Figure 3-24). The system date on your computer may be different.

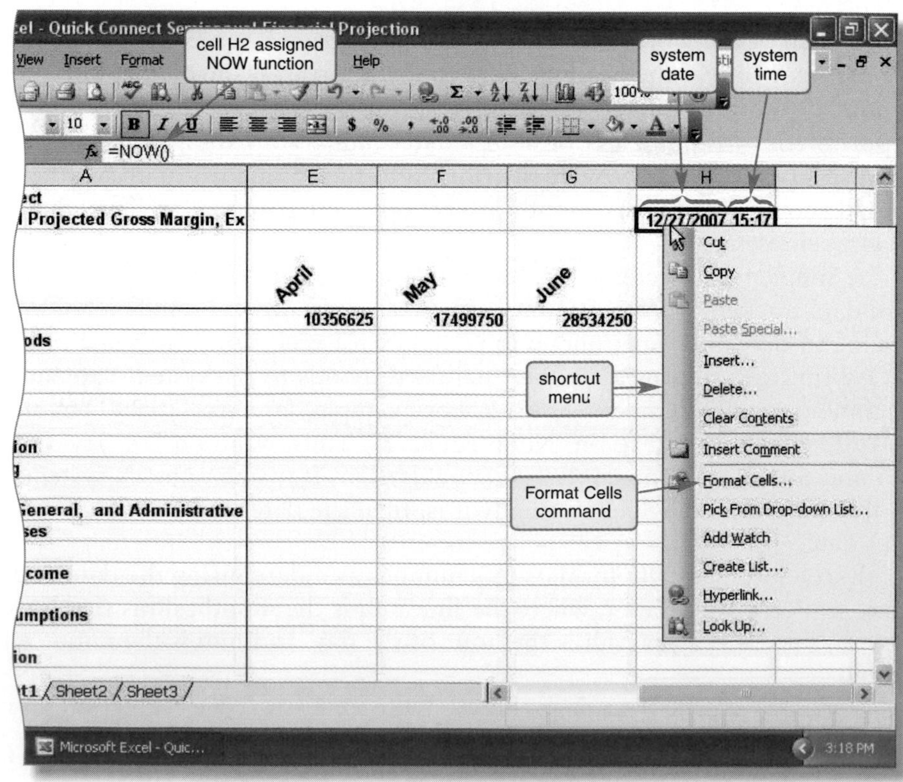

FIGURE 3-24

3

- **Click Format Cells on the shortcut menu.**
- **When Excel displays the Format Cells dialog box, if necessary, click the Number tab.**
- **Click Date in the Category list. Scroll down in the Type list and then click 3/14/2001.**

Excel displays the Format Cells dialog box with Date selected in the Category list and 3/14/2001 (mm/dd/yyyy) selected in the Type list (Figure 3-25). A sample of the data in the active cell (H2) using the selected format appears in the Sample area.

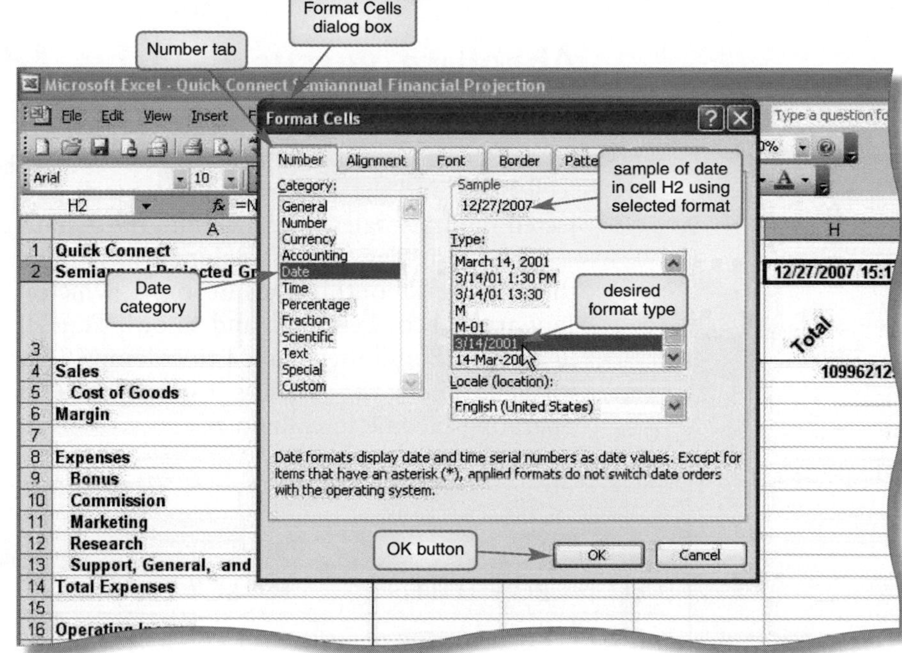

FIGURE 3-25

4

- **Click the OK button.**

Excel displays the system date in the form mm/dd/yyyy (Figure 3-26).

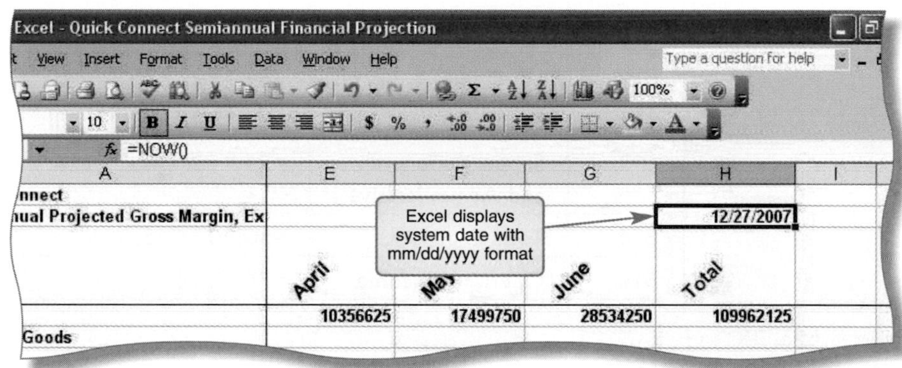

FIGURE 3-26

Skill Builder 3-2

To practice the following tasks, visit scsite.com/off2003sch/skill, locate Excel Project 3, and then click Skill Builder 3-2.

- ❑ Insert and delete cells
- ❑ Enter numbers with format symbols
- ❑ Freeze worksheet titles
- ❑ Display a system date

In Figure 3-26, the date is displayed right-aligned in the cell because Excel treats a date as a number formatted to display as a date. If you assign the General format (Excel's default format for numbers) to a date in a cell, the date is displayed as a number with two decimal places. For example, if the system time and date is 6:00 PM on December 28, 2007 and the cell containing the NOW function is assigned the General format, then Excel displays the following number in the cell:

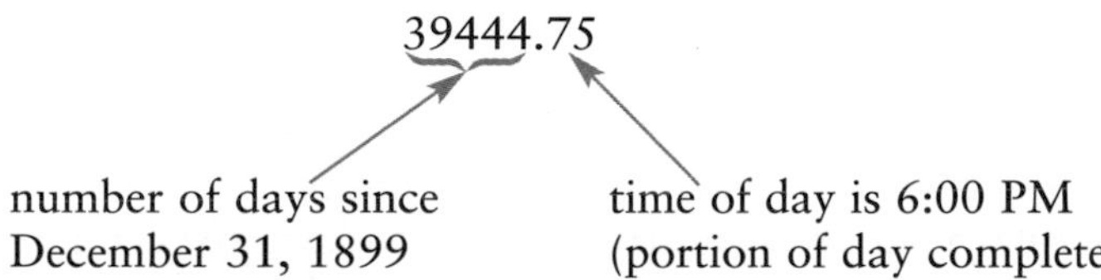

The whole number portion of the number (39444) represents the number of days since December 31, 1899. The decimal portion of the number (.75) represents 6:00 PM as the time of day, at which point ¾ of the day is complete. To assignthe General format to a cell, click General in the Category list in the Format Cells dialog box (Figure 3-25).

Absolute versus Relative Addressing

The next step is to enter the formulas that calculate the following values for January: cost of goods (cell B5), margin (cell B6), expenses (range B9:B13), total expenses (cell B14), and the operating income (cell B16). The formulas are based on the projected monthly sales in cell B4 and the assumptions in the range B19:B25.

The formulas for each column (month) are the same, except for the reference to the projected monthly sales in row 4, which varies according to the month (B4 for January, C4 for February, and so on). Thus, the formulas for January can be entered in column B and then copied to columns C through G. Table 3-6 shows the formulas for determining the January costs of goods, margin, expenses, total expenses, and operating income in column B.

Table 3-6 Formulas for Determining Cost of Goods, Margin, Expenses, Total Expenses, and Operating Income for January

CELL	ROW TITLE	FORMULA	COMMENT
B5	Cost of Goods	=B4 * (1 – B21)	Sales * (1 – Margin %)
B6	Margin	= B4 – B5	Sales minus Cost of Goods
B9	Bonus	=IF(B4 >= B24, B19, 0)	Bonus equals value in B19 or 0
B10	Commission	=B4 * B20	Sales times Equipment %
B11	Marketing	=B4 * B22	Sales times Marketing %
B12	Research	=B4 * B23	Sales times Research %
B13	Support, General, and Administrative	=B4 * B25	Sales times Support, General, and Administrative %
B14	Total Expenses	=SUM(B9:B13)	Sum of January Expenses
B16	Operating Income	=B6 – B14	Margin minus Total Expenses

If the formulas are entered as shown in Table 3-6 in column B for January and then copied to columns C through G (February through June) in the worksheet, Excel will adjust the cell references for each column automatically. Thus, after the copy, the February Commission expense in cell C10 would be =C4 * C20. While the cell reference C4 (February Sales) is correct, the cell reference C20 references an empty cell. The formula for cell C7 should read =C4 * B20, rather than =C4 * C20, because B20 references the Commission % value in the What-If Assumptions table. In this instance, a way is needed to keep a cell reference in a formula the same, or constant, when it is copied.

To keep a cell reference constant when copying a formula or function, Excel uses a technique called absolute cell referencing. To specify an absolute cell reference in a formula, enter a dollar sign ($) before any column letters or row numbers you want to keep constant in formulas you plan to copy. For example, $B$20 is an absolute cell reference, while B20 is a relative cell reference. Both reference the same cell. The difference becomes apparent when they are copied to a destination area. A formula using the **absolute cell reference** $B$20 instructs Excel to keep the cell reference B20 constant (absolute) in the formula as it copies it to the destination area. A formula using the **relative cell reference** B20 instructs Excel to adjust the cell reference as it copies it to the destination area. A cell reference with only one dollar sign before either the column or the row is called a **mixed cell reference**. Table 3-7 gives some additional examples of absolute, relative, and mixed cell references.

Table 3-7 Examples of Absolute, Relative, and Mixed Cell References

CELL REFERENCE	TYPE OF REFERENCE	MEANING
$B$20	Absolute cell reference	Both column and row references remain the same when you copy this cell, because the cell references are absolute.
B$20	Mixed reference	This cell reference is mixed. The column reference changes when you copy this cell to another column because it is relative. The row reference does not change because it is absolute.
$B20	Mixed reference	This cell reference is mixed. The column reference does not change because it is absolute. The row reference changes when you copy this cell reference to another row because it is relative.
B20	Relative cell reference	Both column and row references are relative. When copied to another cell, both the column and row in the cell reference are adjusted to reflect the new location.

Entering a Formula Containing Absolute Cell References

The following steps show how to enter the cost of goods formula = B4*(1 – $B$21) in cell B5 using Point mode. To enter an absolute cell reference, you can type the dollar sign ($) as part of the cell reference or enter it by pressing F4 with the insertion point in or to the right of the cell reference to change to absolute.

To Enter a Formula Containing Absolute Cell References

1

- **Press CTRL+HOME and then click cell B5.**
- **Type = (equal sign), click cell B4, type `*(1-b21` and then press F4 to change b21 from a relative cell reference to an absolute cell reference.**
- **Type) to complete the formula.**

Excel displays the formula =B4(1–$B$21) in cell B5 and in the formula bar (Figure 3-27). The formula always will reference the Margin percent in cell B21, even if it is copied.*

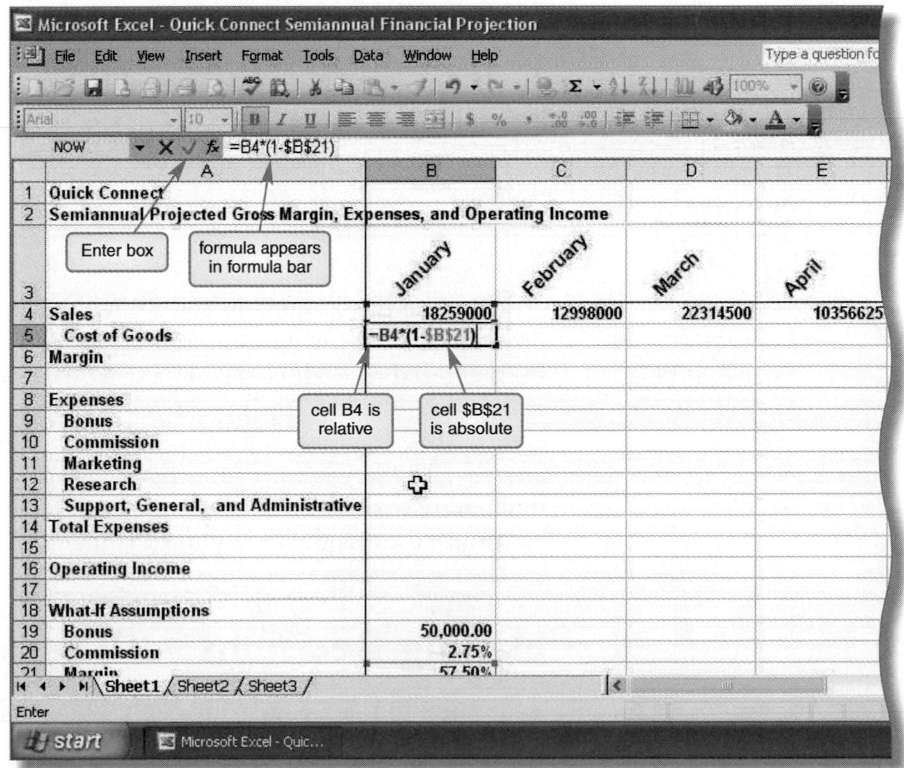

FIGURE 3-27

2

- **Click the Enter box in the formula bar.**

Excel displays the result, 7760075, in cell B5, instead of the formula (Figure 3-28). With cell B5 selected, the formula assigned to it appears in the formula bar.

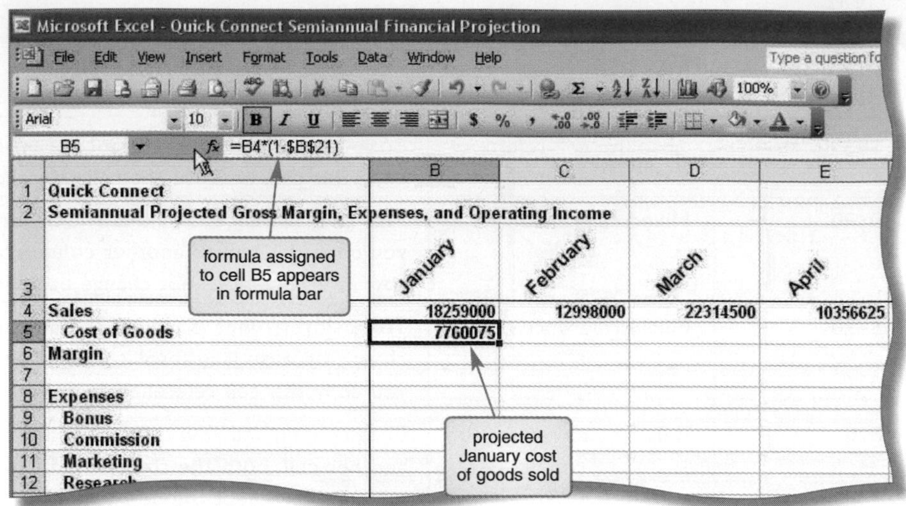

FIGURE 3-28

3

- **Click cell B6, type = (equal sign), click cell B4, type – and then click cell B5.**
- **Click the Enter box in the formula bar.**

Excel displays the margin for January, 10498925, in cell B6.

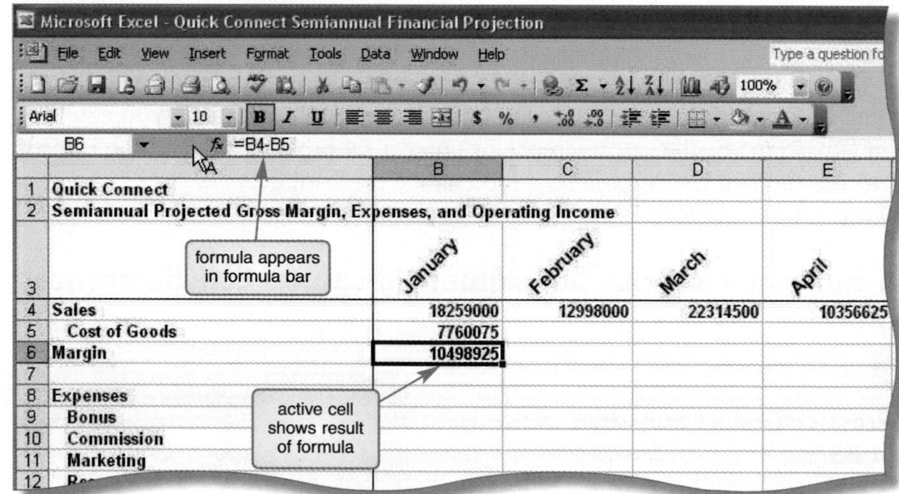

FIGURE 3-29

Because the formula in cell B4 will be copied across columns, rather than down rows, the formula entered in cell B4 in Step 1 on the previous page could have been entered as =B4*(1–$B21), rather than =B4*(1–$B$21). That is, the formula could have included the mixed cell reference $B21, rather than the absolute cell reference $B$21. When you copy a formula across columns, the row does not change anyway. The key is to ensure that column B remains constant as you copy the formula across rows. To change the absolute cell reference to a mixed cell reference, continue to press the F4 key until you get the desired cell reference.

Making Decisions — The IF Function

According to the Request for New Workbook in Figure 3-2 on page EX 148, if the projected January sales in cell B4 is greater than or equal to the sales plateau for bonus in cell B24 (17,500,000.00), then the January bonus value in cell B9 is equal to the bonus value in cell B19 (50,000.00); otherwise, cell B9 is equal to 0. One way to assign the January bonus value in cell B9 is to check to see if the sales in cell B4 equal or exceed the sales plateau for bonus amount in cell B24 and, if so, then to enter 50,000.00 in cell B9. You can use this manual process for all six months by checking the values for the corresponding month.

Because the data in the worksheet changes each time a report is prepared or the figures are adjusted, however, it is preferable to have Excel assign the monthly bonus to the entries in the appropriate cells automatically. To do so, cell B9 must include a formula or function that displays 50,000.00 or 0.00 (zero), depending on whether the projected January sales in cell B4 is greater than or equal to or less than the sales plateau for bonus value in cell B24.

The **IF function** is useful when you want to assign a value to a cell based on a logical test. For example, using the IF function, cell B9 can be assigned the following IF function:

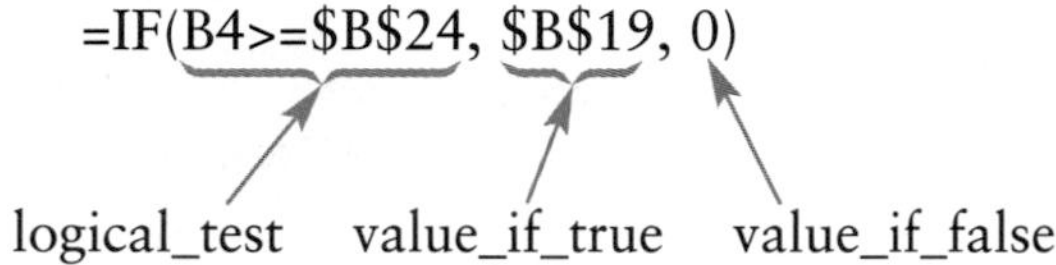

The IF function instructs Excel that, if the projected January sales in cell B4 is greater than or equal to the sales plateau for bonus value in cell B24, then Excel should display the value 50000 in cell B19, in cell B9. If the projected January sales in cell B4 is less than the sales plateau for bonus value in cell B24, then Excel displays a 0 (zero) in cell B9.

The general form of the IF function is:

=IF(logical_test, value_if_true, value_if_false)

The argument, logical_test, is made up of two expressions and a comparison operator. Each expression can be a cell reference, a number, text, a function, or a formula. Valid comparison operators, their meaning, and examples of their use in IF functions are shown in Table 3-8. The argument, value_if_true, is the value you want Excel to display in the cell when the logical test is true. The argument, value_if_false, is the value you want Excel to display in the cell when the logical test is false.

Table 3-8 Comparison Operators

COMPARISON OPERATOR	MEANING	EXAMPLE
=	Equal to	=IF(H7 = 0, J6 ^ H4, L9 + D3)
<	Less than	=IF(C34 * W3 < K7, $K$6, L33 – 5)
>	Greater than	=IF(MIN(K8:K12) > 75, 1, 0)
>=	Greater than or equal to	=IF(P8 >= $H$6, J7 / V4, 7.5)
<=	Less than or equal to	=IF(G7 – G2 <= 23, L$9, 35 / Q2)
<>	Not equal to	=IF(B1 <> 0, "No","Yes")

The steps on the next page assign the IF function =IF(B4>=$B$24,$B$19,0) to cell B9. This IF function determines whether or not the worksheet assigns a bonus for January.

Q & A

Q: Does Excel have logical operators?

A: Yes. IF functions can use logical operators, such as AND, OR, and NOT. For example, the three IF functions =IF(AND(B3>C3, D3<C5), "OK", "Not OK") and =IF(OR(C3>G5, D2<X3), "OK", "Not OK") and =IF(NOT(A6<H7), "OK", "Not OK") use logical operators. In the first example, both logical tests must be true for the value_if_true OK to be assigned to the cell. In the second example, one or the other logical tests must be true for the value_if_true OK to be assigned to the cell. In the third example, the logical test A6<H7 must be false for the value_if_true OK to be assigned to the cell.

To Enter an IF Function

1

- **Click cell B9. Type `=if(b4>=$b$24,$b$19,0)` in the cell.**

Excel displays the IF function in the formula bar and in the active cell B9. Excel also displays a ScreenTip showing the general form of the IF function (Figure 3-30).

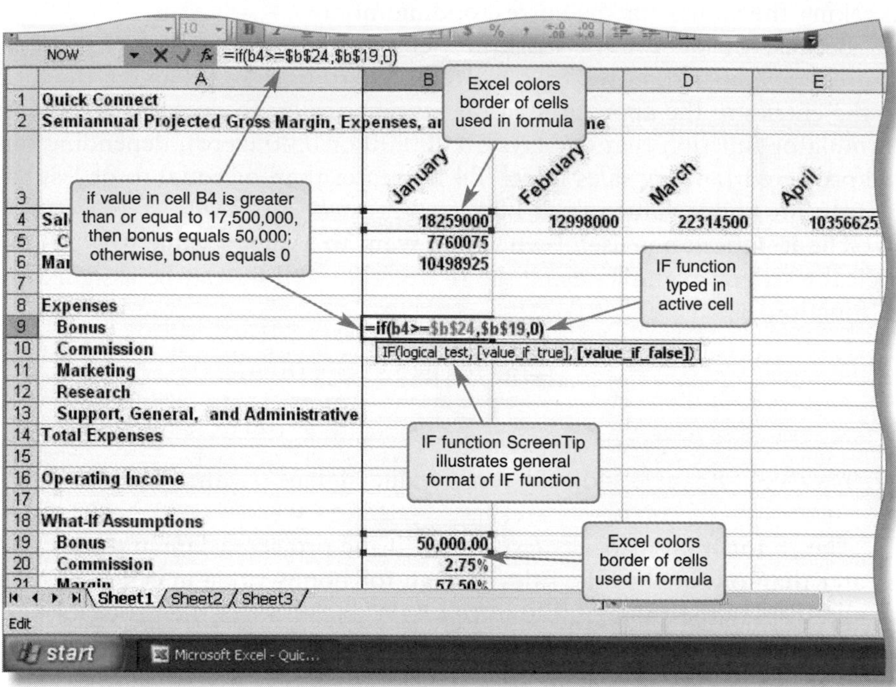

FIGURE 3-30

2

- **Click the Enter box in the formula bar.**

Excel displays 50000 in cell B9 (Figure 3-31), because the value in cell B4 (18259000) is greater than or equal to the value in cell B24 (17,500,000.00).

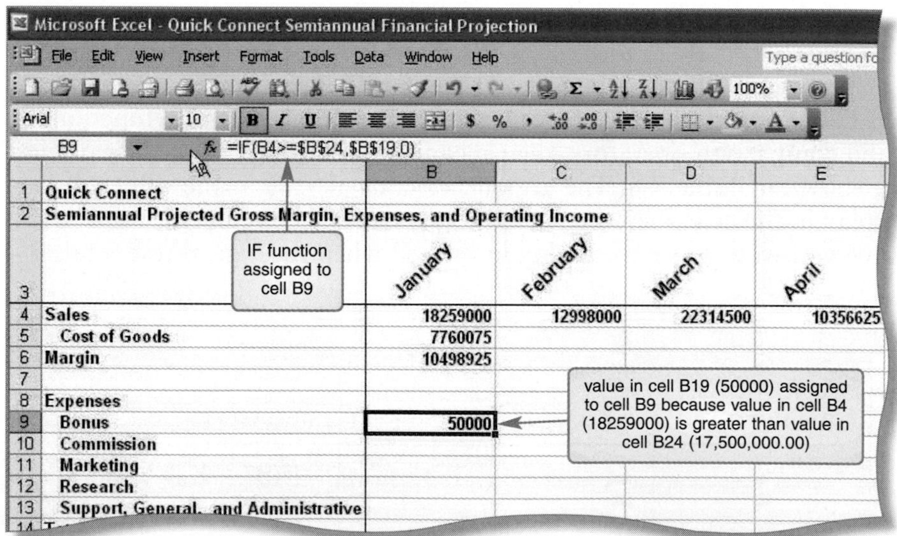

FIGURE 3-31

The value that Excel displays in cell B9 depends on the values assigned to cells B4, B19, and B24. For example, if the value for January sales in cell B4 is reduced below 17,500,000.00, then the IF function in cell B9 will cause Excel to display a 0. If you change the bonus in cell B19 from 50,000.00 to another number and the value in cell B4 greater than or equal to the value in cell B24, it will change the results in cell B9 as well. Finally, increasing the sales plateau for bonus in cell B24 so that it is greater than the value in cell B4 will change the result in cell B9.

Entering the Remaining Formulas

The January commission expense in cell B10 is equal to the sales in cell B4 times the commission assumption in cell B20 (2.75%). The January marketing expense in cell B11 is equal to the projected January sales in cell B4 times the marketing assumption in cell B22 (6.00%). Similar formulas determine the remaining January expenses in cells B12 and B13.

The total expenses value in cell B14 is equal to the sum of the expenses in the range B9:B13. The operating income in cell B16 is equal to the margin in cell B6 minus the total expenses in cell B14. The formulas are short, and therefore, they are typed in the following steps, rather than entered using Point mode.

To Enter the Remaining January Formulas

1. **Click cell B10. Type** `=b4*$b$20` **and then press the DOWN ARROW key. Type** `=b4*$b$22` **and then press the down arrow key. Type** `=b4*$b$23` **and then press the DOWN ARROW key. Type** `=b4*$b$25` **and then press the DOWN ARROW key.**
2. **With cell B14 selected, click the AutoSum button on the Standard toolbar twice. Click cell B16. Type** `=b6-b14` **and then press the ENTER key.**
3. **Press CTRL+ACCENT MARK (`) to instruct Excel to display the formulas version of the worksheet.**
4. **When you are finished viewing the formulas version, press CTRL+ACCENT MARK (`) to instruct Excel to display the values version of the worksheet.**

Following Step 2 and Step 4, Excel displays the results of the remaining January formulas (Figure 3-32a). Following Step 3, Excel displays the formulas version of the worksheet (Figure 3-32b).

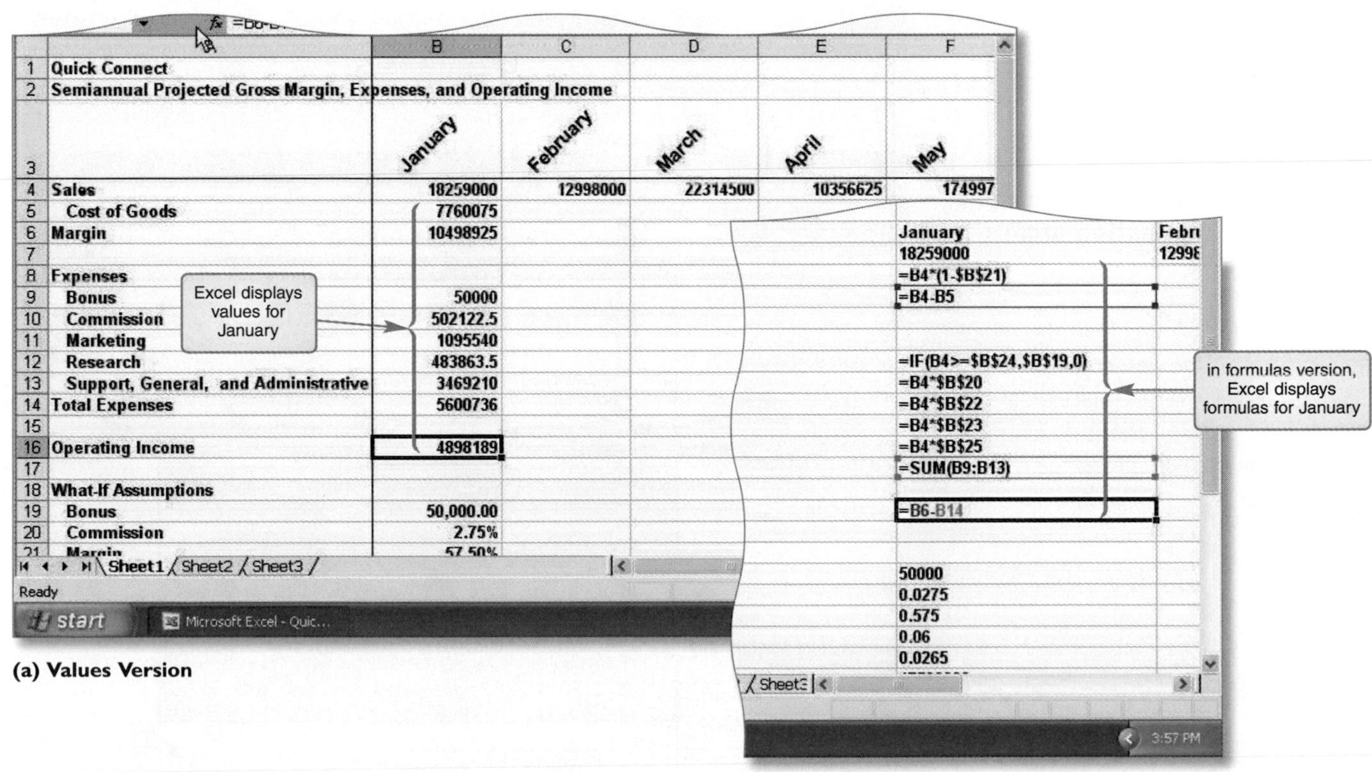

(a) Values Version

(b) Formulas Version

FIGURE 3-32

Viewing the formulas version (Figure 3-32b on the previous page) of the worksheet allows you to check the formulas assigned to the range B5:B16. You can see that Excel converts all the formulas from lowercase to uppercase.

Copying Formulas with Absolute Cell References

The following steps show how to use the fill handle to copy the January formulas in column B to the other five months in columns C through G.

To Copy Formulas with Absolute Cell References Using the Fill Handle

1

- **Select the range B5:B16 and then point to the fill handle in the lower-right corner of cell B16.**

Excel highlights the range B5:B16 and the mouse pointer changes to a cross hair (Figure 3-33).

		January	February	March	April
3					
4	Sales	18259000	12998000	22314500	10356625
5	Cost of Goods	7760075			
6	Margin	10498925			
7					
8	Expenses				
9	Bonus	50000			
10	Commission	502122.5			
11	Marketing	1095540			
12	Research	483863.5			
13	Support, General, and Administrative	3469210			
14	Total Expenses	5600736			
15					
16	Operating Income	4898189			
17					
18	What-If Assumptions				
19	Bonus	50,000.00			
20	Commission	2.75%			
21	Margin	57.50%			

source area is B5:B16

mouse pointer changes to a cross hair

Sheet1 / Sheet2 / Sheet3 /

Ready Sum=34358661 CAPS

start Microsoft Excel - Quic...

FIGURE 3-33

2

- **Drag the fill handle to the right to select the destination area C5:G16.**

Excel copies the formulas from the source area (B5:B16) to the destination area (C5:G16) and displays the calculated amounts (Figure 3-34). The Auto Fill Options button appears below the fill area.

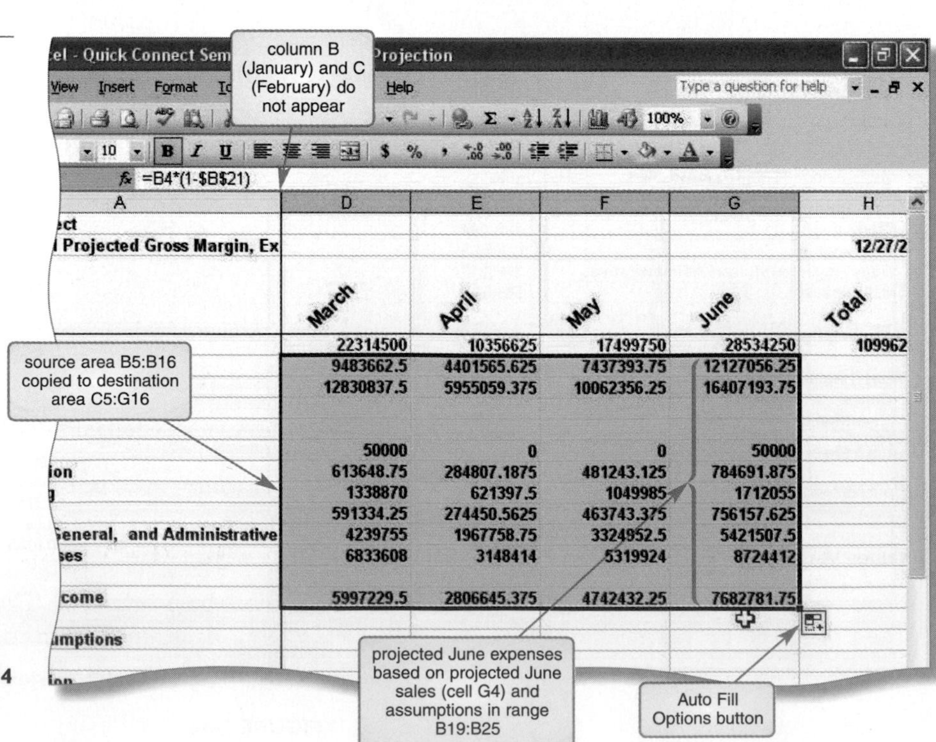

FIGURE 3-34

Because the formulas in the range B5:B16 use absolute cell references, the formulas still refer to the current values in the Assumptions table when the formulas are copied to the range C5:G16.

As shown in Figure 3-34, as the fill handle is dragged to the right, columns B and C no longer appear on the screen. Column A, however, remains on the screen, because the row titles were frozen earlier in this project.

Q: What types of error messages does Excel display when it can close as one word not calculate a formula?

A: When Excel cannot calculate a formula, it displays an error message in a cell. These error messages always begin with a number sign (#). The more commonly occurring error messages are: #DIV/0! (tries to divide by zero); #NAME? (uses a name Excel does not recognize); #N/A (refers to a value not available); #NULL! (specifies an invalid intersection of two areas); #NUM! (uses a number incorrectly); #REF (refers to a cell that is not valid); #VALUE! (uses an incorrect argument or operand); and ###### (cell not wide enough to display entire entry).

Determining Row Totals in Nonadjacent Cells

The following steps determine the row totals in column H. To determine the row totals using the AutoSum button, select only the cells in column H containing numbers in adjacent cells to the left. If, for example, you select the range H5:H16, Excel will display 0s as the sum of empty rows in cells H7, H8, and H15.

To Determine Row Totals in Nonadjacent Cells

1. **Select the range H5:H6. Hold down the CTRL key and select the range H9:H14 and cell H16 as shown in Figure 3-35.**
2. **Click the AutoSum button on the Standard toolbar.**

Excel displays the row totals in column H (Figure 3-35).

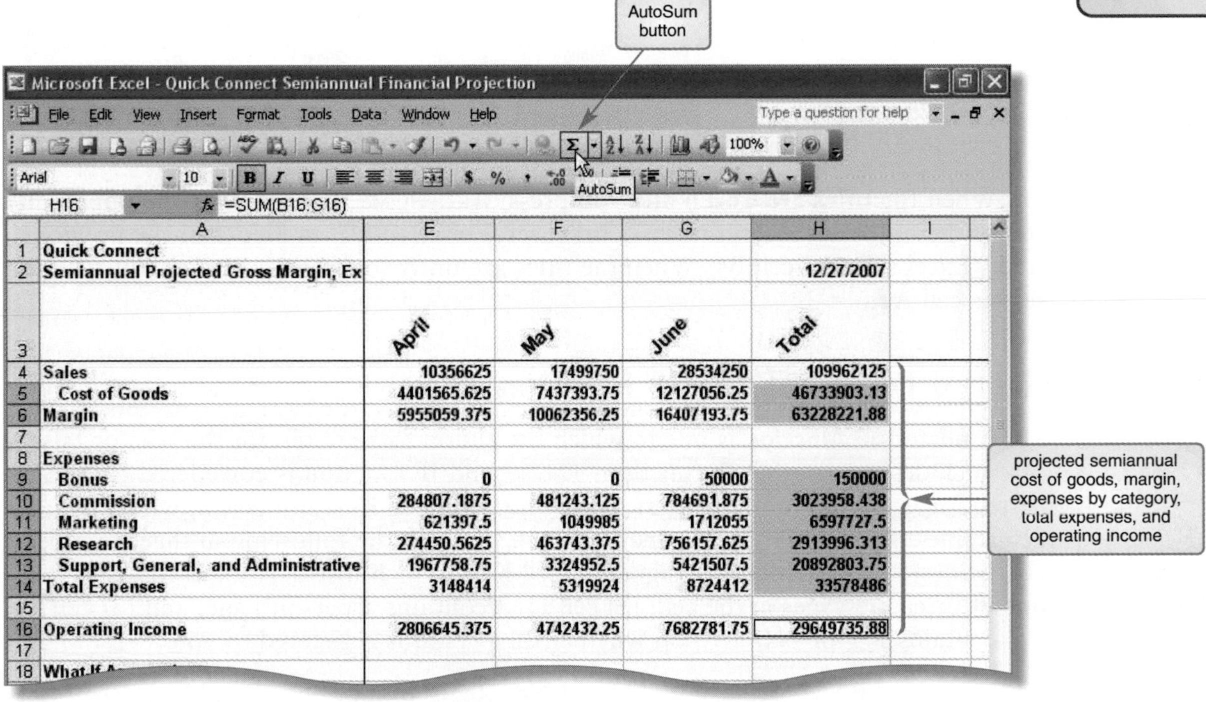

FIGURE 3-35

Unfreezing Worksheet Titles and Saving the Workbook

All the text, data, and formulas have been entered into the worksheet. The steps on the next page unfreeze the titles and save the workbook using its current file name, Quick Connect Semiannual Financial Projection.

Q & A

Q: Can Excel calculate the number of workdays between two dates?

A: Yes. Assume that you have two dates: one in cell F3 and the other in cell F4. The date in cell F3 is your starting date and the date in cell F4 is the ending date. To calculate the workdays between the two dates (excludes weekends), use the following formula: =NETWORKDAYS(F3, F4). For this function to work, make sure the Analysis ToolPak add-in is installed. You can install it by clicking Add-Ins on the Tools menu.

To Unfreeze the Worksheet Titles and Save the Workbook

1. **Press CTRL+HOME to select cell B4 and view the upper-left corner of the screen.**
2. **Click Window on the menu bar (Figure 3-36) and then click Unfreeze Panes.**
3. **Click the Save button on the Standard toolbar.**

Excel unfreezes the titles so that column A scrolls off the screen when you scroll to the right and the first three rows scroll off the screen when you scroll down. The latest changes to the workbook are saved on the USB flash drive using the file name, Quick Connect Semiannual Financial Projection.

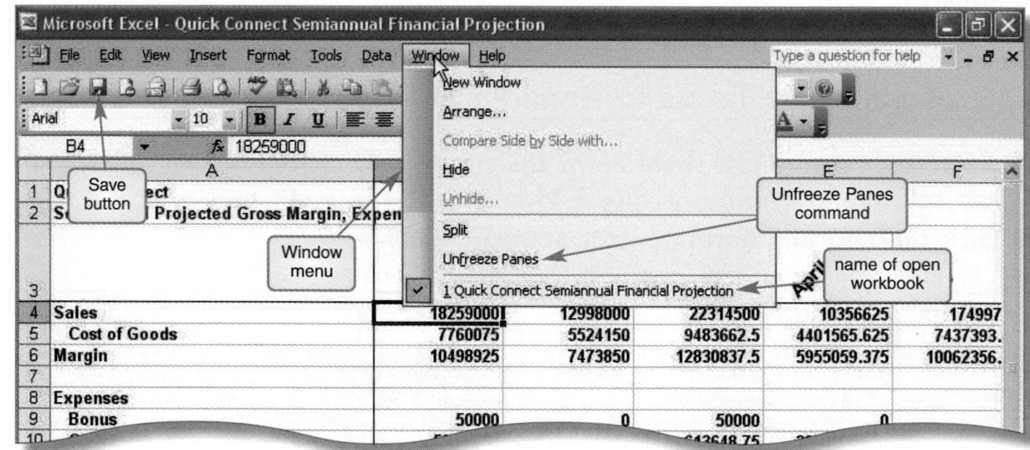

FIGURE 3-36

When the titles are frozen and you press CTRL+HOME, Excel selects the upper-left cell of the unfrozen section of the worksheet. For example, in Step 1 of the previous steps, Excel selected cell B4. When the titles are unfrozen, then pressing CTRL+HOME selects cell A1.

Skill Builder 3-3

To practice the following tasks, visit scsite.com/off2003sch/skill, locate Excel Project 3, and then click Skill Builder 3-3.

- Write formulas with absolute cell references
- Write IF functions
- Unfreeze worksheet titles

Nested Forms of the IF function

A **nested IF function** is one in which the action to be taken for the true or false case includes yet another IF function. The second IF function is considered to be nested, or layered, within the first. Study the nested IF function below, which determines the eligibility of a person to vote. Assume the following in this example: (1) the nested IF function is assigned to cell K12, which instructs Excel to display one of three messages in the cell; (2) cell H12 contains a person's age; and (3) cell I12 contains a Y or N, based on whether the person is registered to vote.

=IF(H12>=18, IF(I12="Y","Registered","Eligible and Not Registered"),"Not Eligible to Register")

The nested IF function instructs Excel to display one, and only one, of the following three messages in cell K12: (1) Registered; or (2) Eligible and Not Registered; or (3) Not Eligible to Register.

You can nest IF functions as deep as you want, but after you get beyond a nest of three IF functions, the logic becomes difficult to follow and alternative solutions, such as the use of multiple cells and simple IF functions, should be considered.

Formatting the Worksheet

The worksheet created thus far shows the financial projections for the six-month period, from January to June. Its appearance is uninteresting, however, even though some minimal formatting (bolding the worksheet, formatting assumptions numbers, changing the column widths, and formatting the date) was performed earlier. This section will complete the formatting of the worksheet to make the numbers easier to read and to emphasize the titles, assumptions, categories, and totals. The worksheet will be formatted in the following manner so it appears as shown in Figure 3-37: (1) format the numbers; (2) format the worksheet title, column titles, row titles, and operating income row; and (3) format the assumptions table.

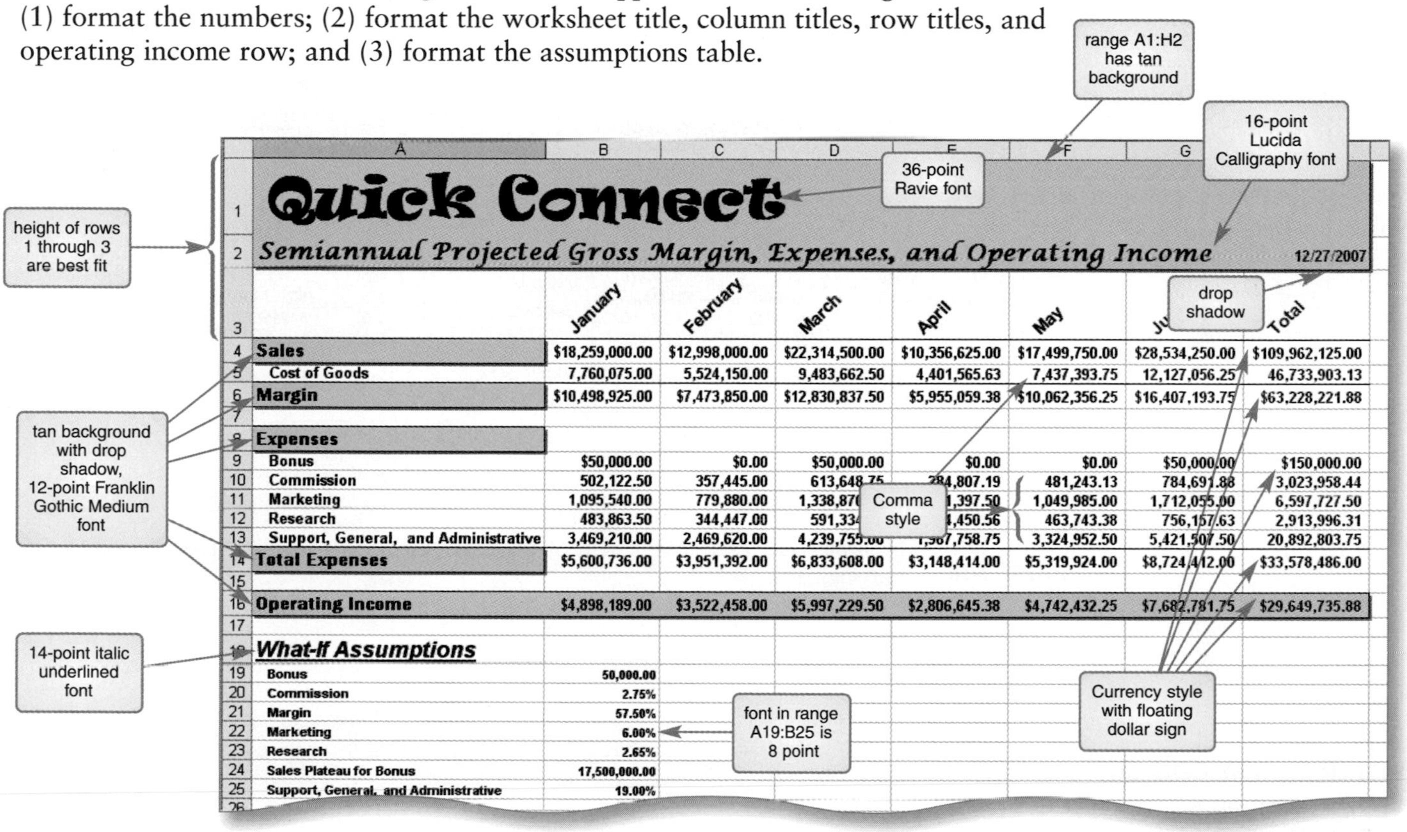

	A	B	C	D	E	F	G	H
1	Quick Connect							
2	Semiannual Projected Gross Margin, Expenses, and Operating Income							12/27/2007
3		January	February	March	April	May	Ju	Total
4	Sales	$18,259,000.00	$12,998,000.00	$22,314,500.00	$10,356,625.00	$17,499,750.00	$28,534,250.00	$109,962,125.00
5	Cost of Goods	7,760,075.00	5,524,150.00	9,483,662.50	4,401,565.63	7,437,393.75	12,127,056.25	46,733,903.13
6	Margin	$10,498,925.00	$7,473,850.00	$12,830,837.50	$5,955,059.38	$10,062,356.25	$16,407,193.75	$63,228,221.88
7								
8	Expenses							
9	Bonus	$50,000.00	$0.00	$50,000.00	$0.00	$0.00	$50,000.00	$150,000.00
10	Commission	502,122.50	357,445.00	613,648.75	384,807.19	481,243.13	784,691.88	3,023,958.44
11	Marketing	1,095,540.00	779,880.00	1,338,87	1,397.50	1,049,985.00	1,712,055.00	6,597,727.50
12	Research	483,863.50	344,447.00	591,33	4,450.56	463,743.38	756,157.63	2,913,996.31
13	Support, General, and Administrative	3,469,210.00	2,469,620.00	4,239,755.00	7,758.75	3,324,952.50	5,421,507.50	20,892,803.75
14	Total Expenses	$5,600,736.00	$3,951,392.00	$6,833,608.00	$3,148,414.00	$5,319,924.00	$8,724,412.00	$33,578,486.00
15								
16	Operating Income	$4,898,189.00	$3,522,458.00	$5,997,229.50	$2,806,645.38	$4,742,432.25	$7,682,781.75	$29,649,735.88
17								
18	What-If Assumptions							
19	Bonus	50,000.00						
20	Commission	2.75%						
21	Margin	57.50%						
22	Marketing	6.00%						
23	Research	2.65%						
24	Sales Plateau for Bonus	17,500,000.00						
25	Support, General, and Administrative	19.00%						

FIGURE 3-37

Formatting the Numbers

The numbers in the range B4:H16 are to be formatted as follows:

1. Assign the Currency style with a floating dollar sign to rows 4, 6, 9, 14, and 16.
2. Assign a Comma style to rows 5 and 10 through 13.

To assign a Currency style with a floating dollar sign, the Format Cells command will be used, rather than the Currency Style button on the Formatting toolbar, which assigns a fixed dollar sign. The Comma style also must be assigned using the Format Cells command, because the Comma Style button on the Formatting toolbar assigns a format that displays a dash (-) when a cell has a value of 0. The specifications for this worksheet call for displaying a value of 0 as 0.00 (see cell C9 in Figure 3-37), rather than as a dash. To create a Comma style using the Format Cells command, you can assign a Currency style with no dollar sign. The steps on the next page show how to assign formats to the numbers in rows 4 through 16.

Q & A

Q: How do you select nonadjacent ranges?

A: One of the more difficult tasks to learn is selecting nonadjacent ranges. To complete this task, do not hold down the CTRL key when you select the first range because Excel will consider the current active cell to be the first selection. Once the first range is selected, hold down the CTRL key and drag through the nonadjacent ranges. If a desired range is not visible in the window, use the scroll arrows to view the range. It is not necessary to hold down the CTRL key while you scroll.

To Assign Formats to Nonadjacent Ranges

1

- **Select the range B4:H4.**
- **While holding down the CTRL key, select the nonadjacent ranges B6:H6, B9:H9, B14:H14, and B16:H16, and then release the CTRL key.**
- **Right-click the selected range.**

Excel highlights the selected nonadjacent ranges and displays the shortcut menu as shown in Figure 3-38.

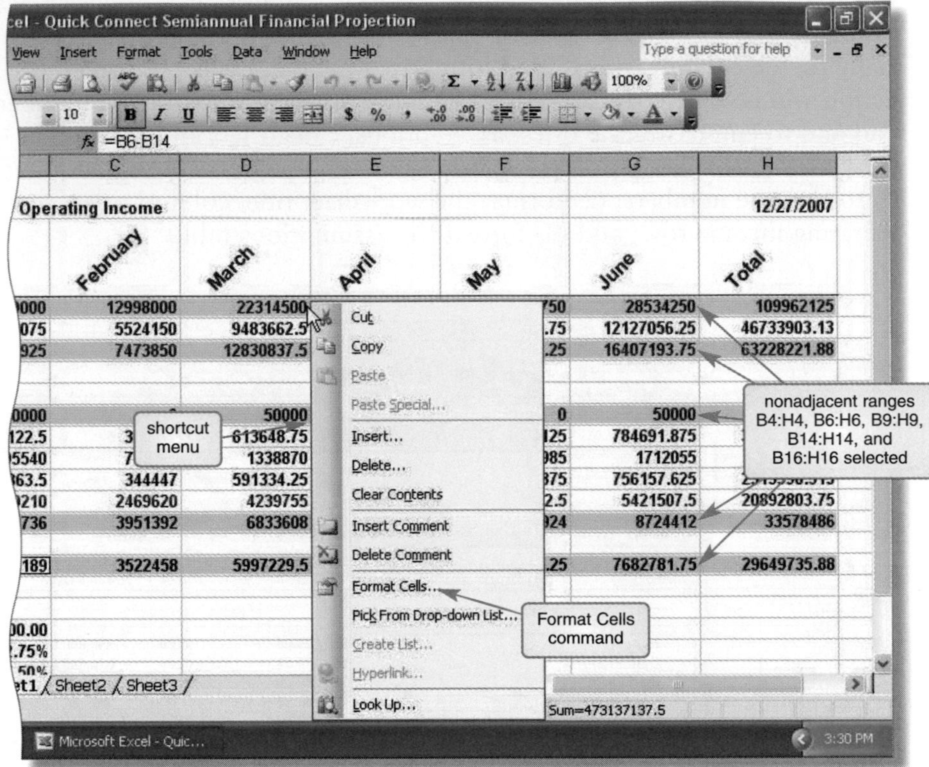

FIGURE 3-38

2

- **Click Format Cells on the shortcut menu.**
- **When Excel displays the Format Cells dialog box, click the Number tab, click Currency in the Category list, select 2 in the Decimal places box, click $ in the Symbol list to ensure a dollar sign shows, and click the black font color ($1,234.10) in the Negative numbers list.**

Excel displays the cell format settings in the Number sheet in the Format Cells dialog box as shown in Figure 3-39.

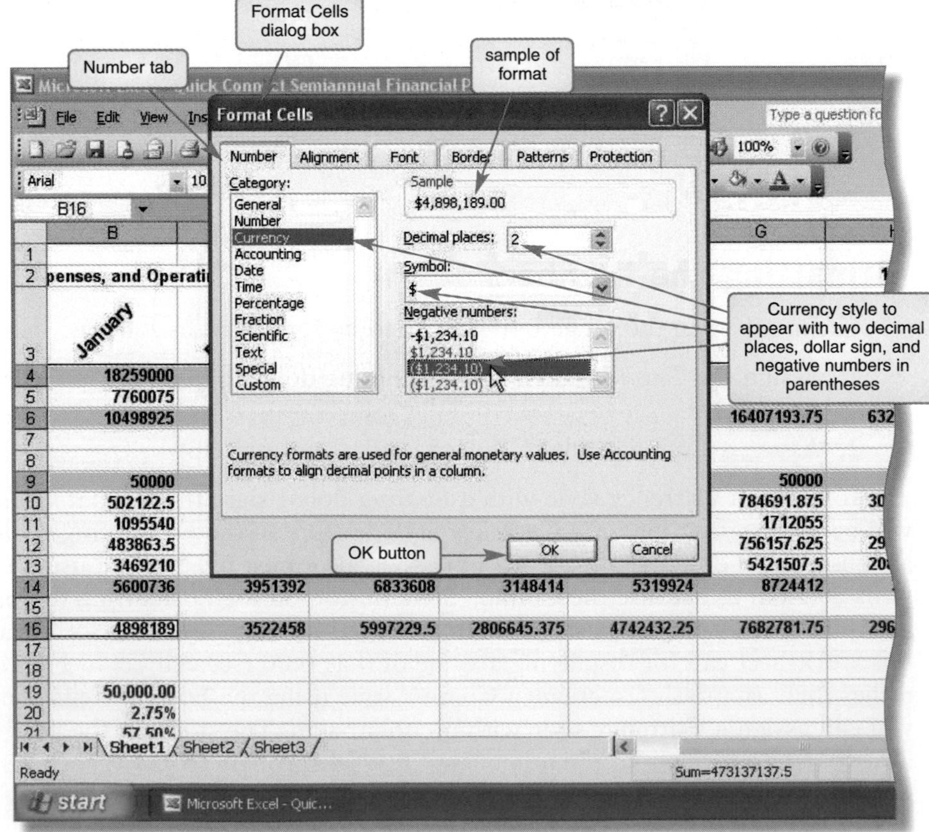

FIGURE 3-39

3

- **Click the OK button.**
- **Select the range B5:H5.**
- **While holding down the CTRL key, select the range B10:H13, and then release the CTRL key.**
- **Right-click the selected range.**
- **Click Format Cells on the shortcut menu.**

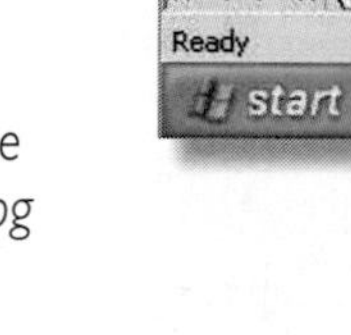

4

- **When Excel displays the Format Cells dialog box, click Currency in the Category list, select 2 in the Decimal places box, click None in the Symbol list so a dollar sign does not show, click the black font color (1,234.10) in the Negative numbers list.**

Excel displays the format settings in the Number sheet in the Format Cells dialog box as shown in Figure 3-40.

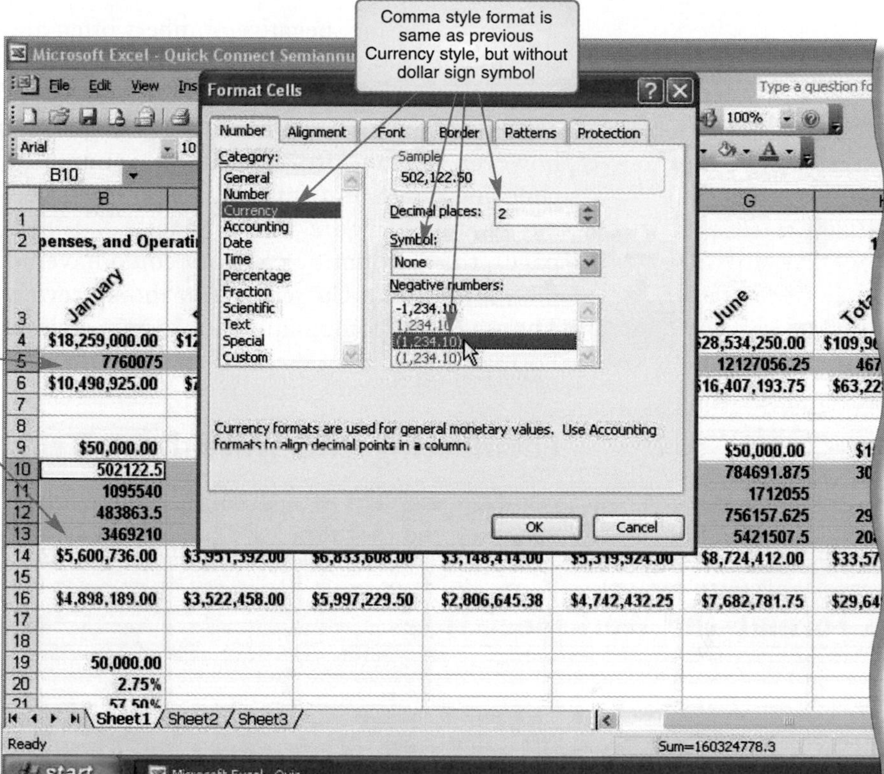

FIGURE 3-40

5

- **Click the OK button.**
- **Press CTRL+HOME to select cell A1.**

Excel displays the formatted numbers as shown in Figure 3-41.

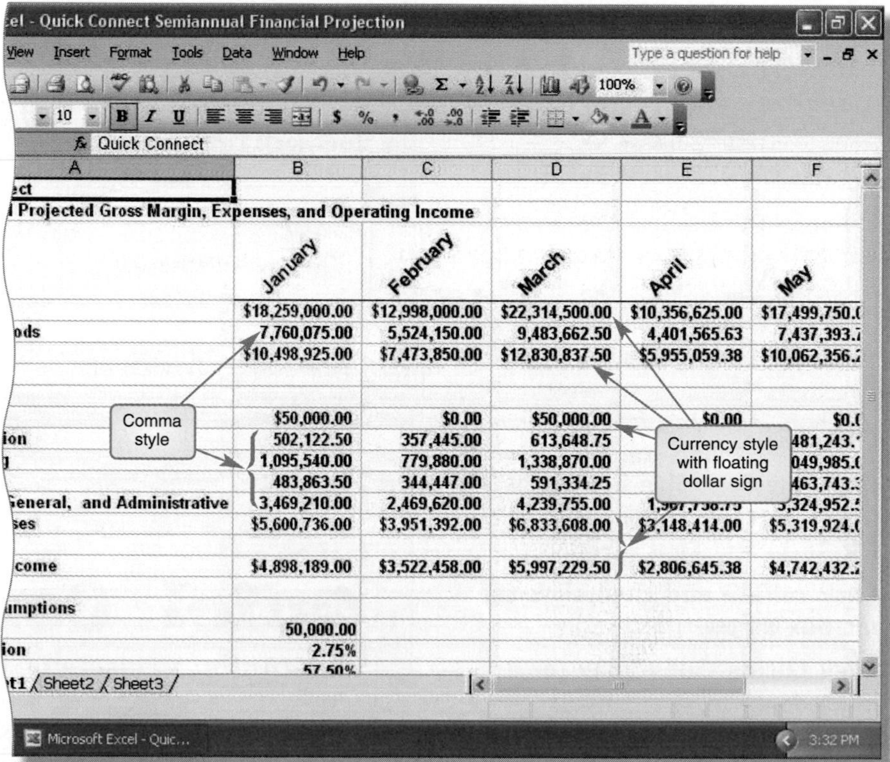

FIGURE 3-41

In accounting, negative numbers often are shown with parentheses surrounding the value rather than with a negative sign preceding the value. Thus, in Step 2 and Step 4 of the previous steps, the format (1,234.10) in the Negative numbers list was clicked. The data being used in this project contains no negative numbers. You must, however, select a format for negative numbers, and you must be consistent if you are choosing different formats in a column, otherwise the decimal points may not line up.

In Step 2 (Figure 3-39 on page EX 178) and Step 4 (Figure 3-40 on the previous page), the Accounting category could have been selected to generate the same format, rather than Currency. You should review the formats available in each category. Thousands of combinations of format styles can be created using the options in the Format Cells dialog box.

Formatting the Worksheet Titles

The next step is to emphasize the worksheet titles in cells A1 and A2 by changing the font type, size, and color as described in the following steps.

To Format the Worksheet Titles

1

- **With cell A1 selected, click the Font box arrow on the Formatting toolbar.**
- **Scroll down and point to Ravie (or a similar font) in the Font list.**

Excel displays the Font list as shown in Figure 3-42. The names in the Font list are displayed in the font type they represent, allowing you to view the font type before you assign it to a cell or range of cells.

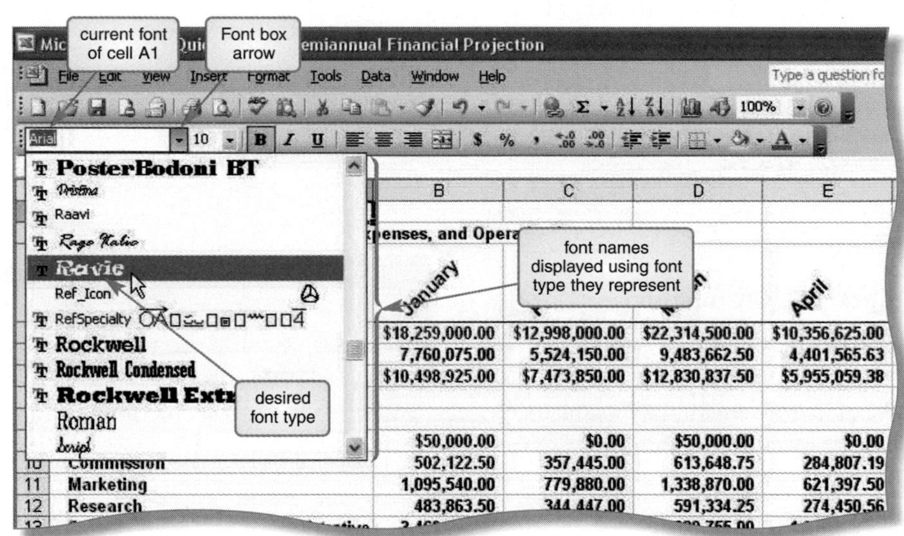

FIGURE 3-42

2

- **Click Ravie.**
- **Click the Font Size box arrow on the Formatting toolbar, and then click 36 in the Font Size list.**
- **Click cell A2 and then click the Font box arrow.**
- **Click Lucida Calligraphy (or a similar font) in the Font list.**
- **Click the Font Size box arrow and then click 16 in the Font Size list.**

Excel displays the worksheet titles in cells A1 and A2 as shown in Figure 3-43.

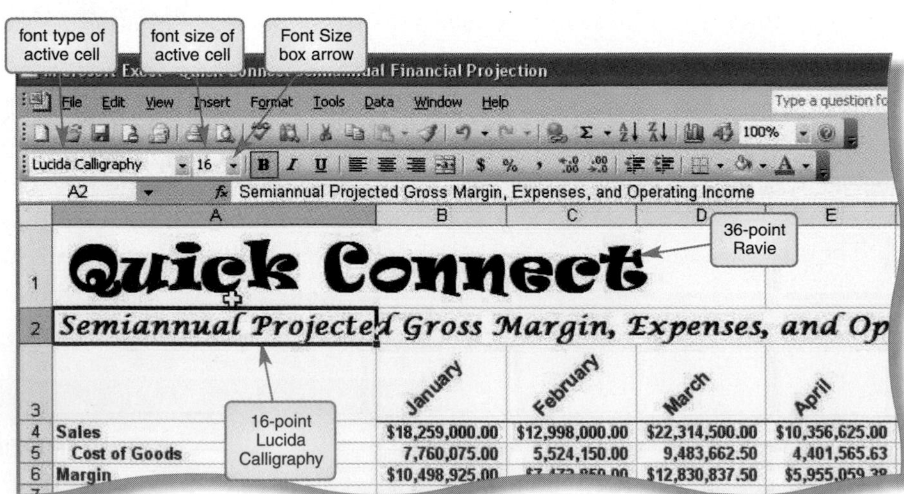

FIGURE 3-43

3

- **Select the range A1:H2 and then click the Fill Color button arrow on the Formatting toolbar.**
- **Click Tan (column 2, row 5) on the Fill Color palette.**

Excel assigns a tan background to the selected range (Figure 3-44).

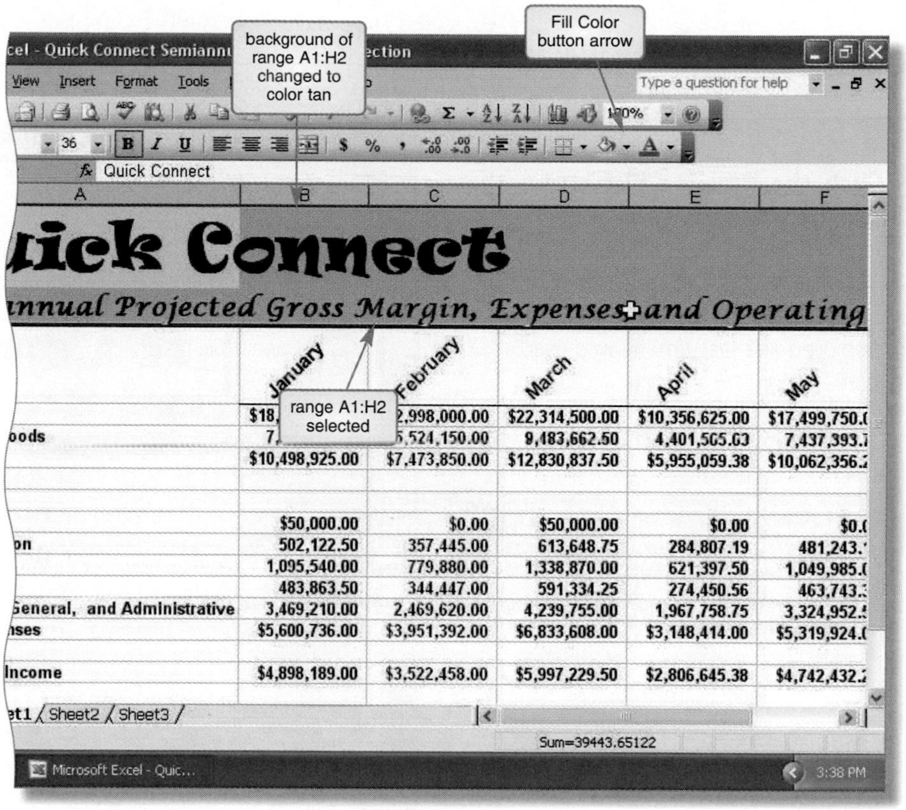

FIGURE 3-44

Showing the Drawing Toolbar

The next step is to add a drop shadow to the selected range A1:H2 using the Shadow button on the Drawing toolbar. The Drawing toolbar currently is hidden. Before using the Drawing toolbar, Excel must be instructed to display the Drawing toolbar on the screen. This section describes how to show an inactive (hidden) toolbar and then dock it.

Excel has hundreds of toolbar buttons, most of which it displays on 22 built-in toolbars. Two of these 22 built-in toolbars are the Standard toolbar and Formatting toolbar, which usually appear at the top of the screen. Another built-in toolbar is the Drawing toolbar. The **Drawing toolbar** provides tools that can simplify adding lines, boxes, and other geometric figures to a worksheet. You also can create customized toolbars containing the buttons that you use often.

To show or hide any Excel toolbar, you can use the shortcut menu that Excel displays when you right-click a toolbar, or you can use the Toolbars command on the View menu. The Drawing toolbar also can be displayed or hidden by clicking the Drawing button on the Standard toolbar.

The step on the next page illustrates how to show the Drawing toolbar.

To Show the Drawing Toolbar

1

• **Click the Drawing button on the Standard toolbar.**

Excel displays the Drawing toolbar in the same location and with the same shape as it displayed the last time it was used (Figure 3-45).

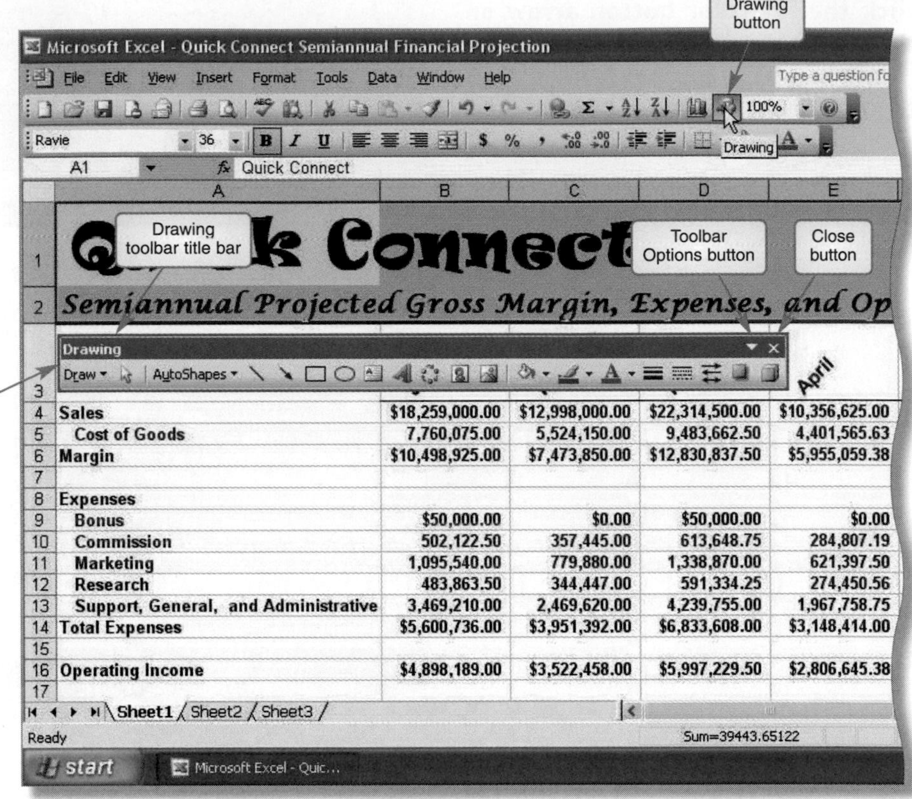

FIGURE 3-45

When a toolbar is displayed in the middle of the screen as shown in Figure 3-45, the toolbar includes a title bar. The Toolbar Options button and Close button are on the right side of the title bar.

Moving and Docking a Toolbar

The Drawing toolbar in Figure 3-45 is called a **floating toolbar** because it is displayed in its own window and can be moved anywhere in the Excel window. You move the toolbar by pointing to the toolbar title bar or to a blank area within the toolbar window (not a button) and then dragging the toolbar to its new location. As with any window, you also can resize the toolbar by dragging the toolbar window borders.

Sometimes a floating toolbar gets in the way no matter where you move it or how you resize it. You can hide the floating toolbar by clicking the Close button on the toolbar title bar. At times, however, you will want to keep the toolbar available for use. For this reason, Excel allows you to position toolbars on the edge of its window. If you drag the toolbar close to the edge of the window, Excel positions the toolbar in a **toolbar dock**.

Excel has four toolbar docks, one on each of the four sides of the window. You can add as many toolbars to a toolbar dock as you want. Each time you dock a toolbar, however, the Excel window slightly decreases in size to compensate for the room occupied by the toolbar. The following step shows how to dock the Drawing toolbar at the bottom of the screen below the scroll bar.

Q: What happens when you dock a toolbar with a box or a button with a list on the left or right edge of the window?

A: If you dock a toolbar that includes a box or a button with a list on the left or right edge of the window, the box and its list will not appear on the toolbar and will not be available.

To Move and Dock a Toolbar

1

- **Point to the Drawing toolbar title bar or to a blank area in the Drawing toolbar.**
- **Drag the Drawing toolbar over the status bar at the bottom of the screen.**

Excel docks the Drawing toolbar at the bottom of the screen (Figure 3-46).

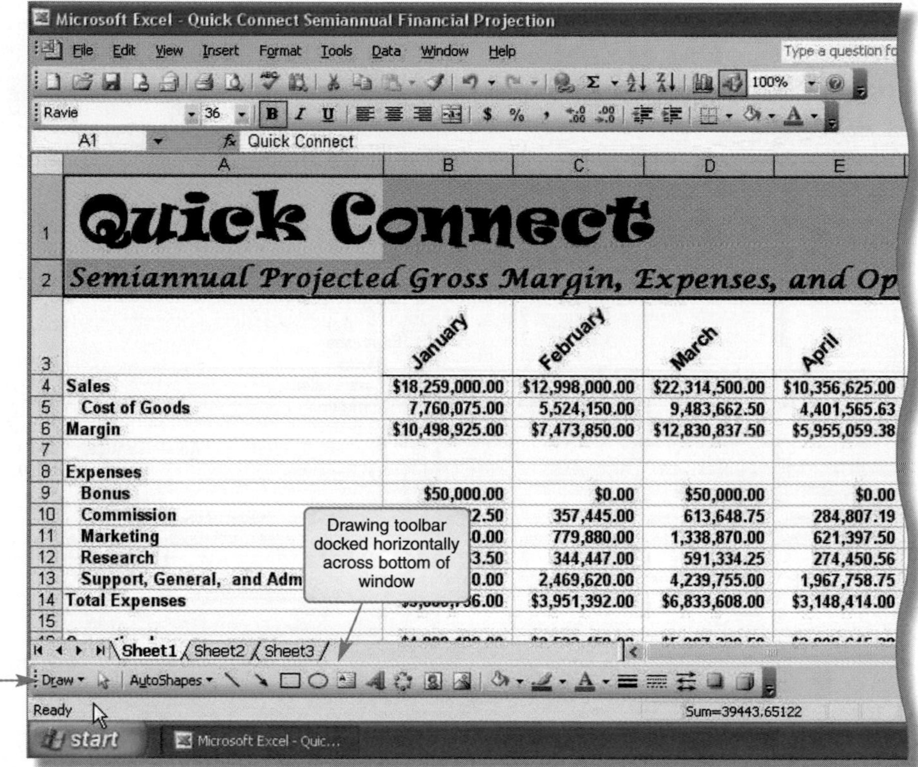

FIGURE 3-46

Compare Figure 3-46 with Figure 3-45. The heavy window border that surrounded the floating toolbar has changed to a light border and the title bar no longer appears.

To move a toolbar to any of the other three toolbar docks, drag the toolbar from its current position to the desired side of the window. To move a docked toolbar, it is easiest to point to the move handle and, when the mouse pointer changes to a cross with four arrowheads, drag it to the desired location.

> **Q & A**
>
> **Q:** How are custom toolbars created?
>
> **A:** You can create and add buttons to your own toolbar by clicking the Customize command on the shortcut menu that appears when you right-click a toolbar. When Excel displays the Customize dialog box, click the Toolbars tab, click the New button, name the toolbar, click the Commands tab, and then drag buttons to the new toolbar.

Adding a Drop Shadow

With the Drawing toolbar docked at the bottom of the screen, the next step is to add the drop shadow to the range A1:H2, as shown in the steps on the next page.

To Add a Drop Shadow

1

• **With the range A1:H2 selected, click the Shadow Style button on the Drawing toolbar.**

Excel displays the Shadow Style palette of drop shadows with varying shadow depths (Figure 3-47).

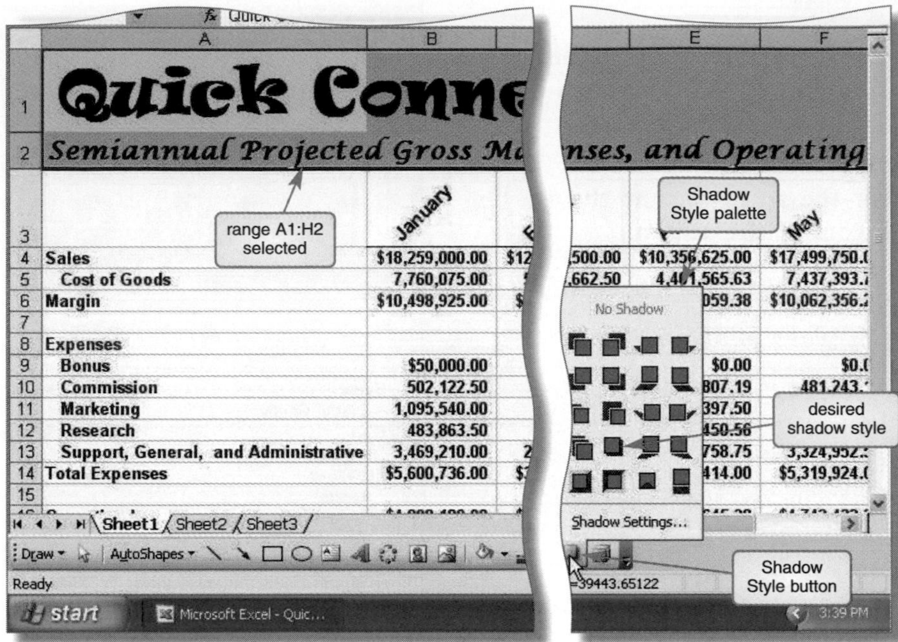

FIGURE 3-47

2

• **Click Shadow Style 14 (column 2, row 4) on the Shadow Style palette.**

• **Click cell A4 to deselect the range A1:H2.**

Excel adds a drop shadow to the range A1:H2 (Figure 3-48).

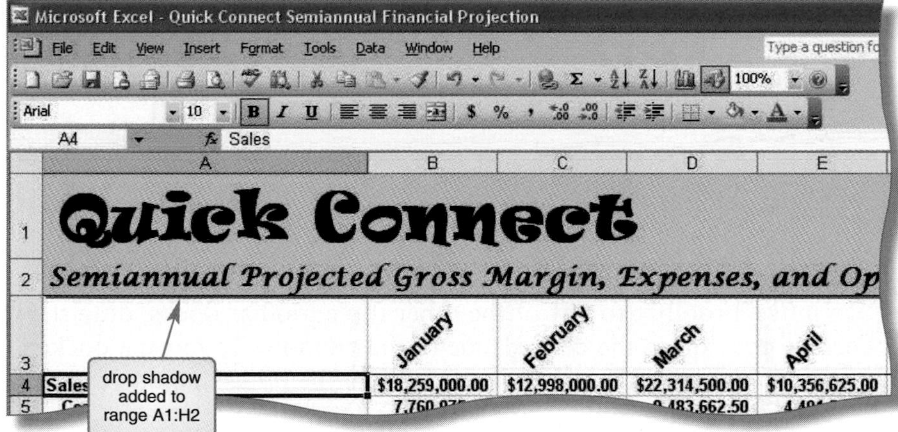

FIGURE 3-48

When you add a drop shadow to a range of cells, Excel selects the drop shadow and surrounds it with handles. To deselect the drop shadow, click any cell, as described in Step 2 above.

Formatting Nonadjacent Cells

The following steps change the font type and font size of the nonadjacent cells A4, A6, A8, A14, and A16 to 12-point Franklin Gothic Medium. The steps then add the tan background color and drop shadows to the nonadjacent cells A4, A6, A8, A14, and the range A16:H16.

To Change Font, Add Underlines, Add Background Colors, and Add Drop Shadows to Nonadjacent Cells

1

- **With cell A4 selected, hold down the CTRL key, and click cells A6, A8, A14, and A16.**
- **Click the Font box arrow on the Formatting toolbar, scroll down and click Franklin Gothic Medium (or a similar font) in the Font list. Select cell B5.**
- **Click the Font Size box arrow on the Formatting toolbar and then click 12 in the Font Size list.**
- **Use the CTRL key to select the nonadjacent ranges B5:H5 and B13:H13 and then click the Borders button on the Formatting toolbar.**
- **Click cell A4 and then while holding down the CTRL key, click cells A6, A8, A14, and select the range A16:H16.**
- **Click the Fill Color button arrow on the Formatting toolbar and then click Tan (column 2, row 5).**
- **Click the Shadow Style button on the Drawing toolbar.**

Excel displays the worksheet with the new formats (Figure 3-49). The Shadow Style palette appears at the bottom of the window.

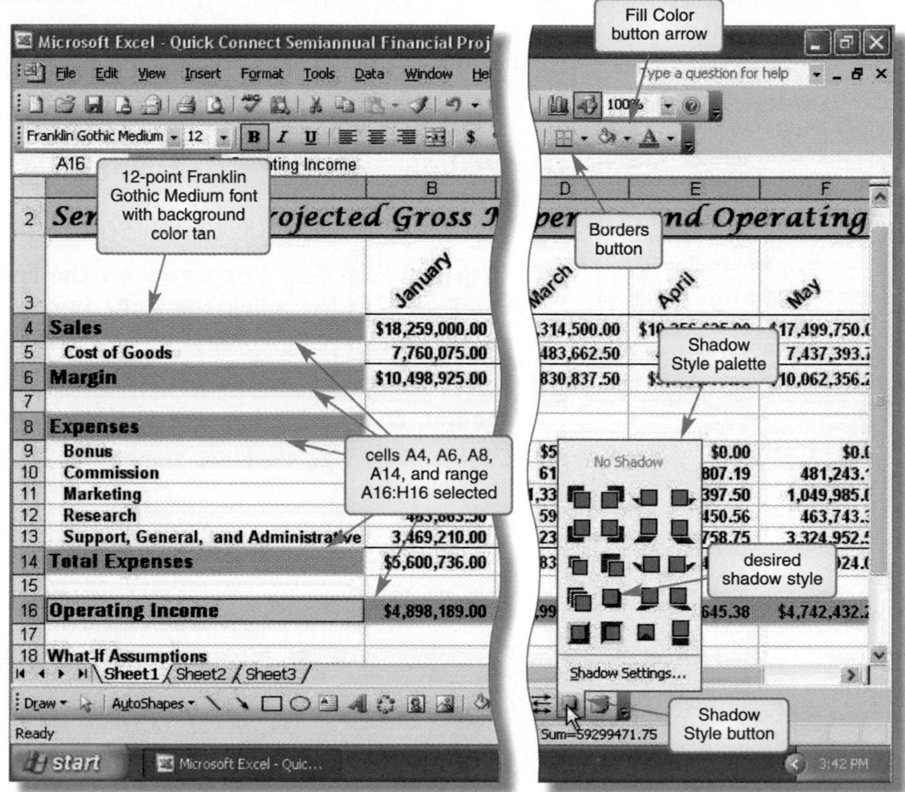

FIGURE 3-49

2

- **Click Shadow Style 14 (column 2, row 4) on the Shadow palette.**

Excel adds a drop shadow to cells A4, A6, A8, A14, and the range A16:H16 (Figure 3-50).

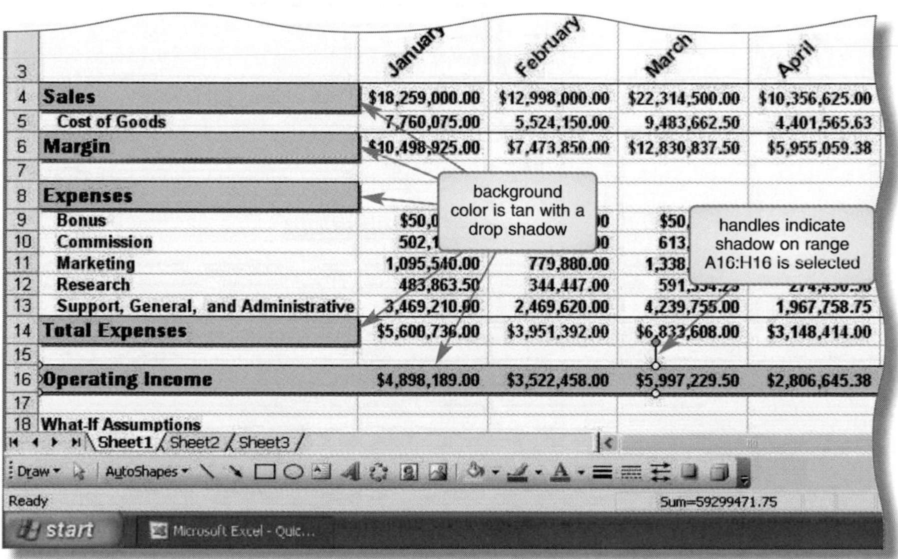

FIGURE 3-50

An alternative to formatting the nonadjacent ranges at once is to select each range separately and then apply the formats.

Formatting the What-If Assumptions Table

Q & A

Q: How can unwanted drop shadows be deleted?

A: To remove an unwanted drop shadow, click the drop shadow so its handles appear and then press the DELETE key. A drop shadow is a shape and not a format. Thus, if you used the Format Painter button to apply formats from a range with a drop shadow, then the drop shadow will not be copied.

The last step to improving the appearance of the worksheet is to format the What-If Assumptions table in the range A18:B25. The specifications in Figure 3-37 on page EX 177 require a 14-point italic underlined font for the title in cell A18 and 8-point font in the range A19:B25. The following steps format the What-If Assumptions table.

To Format the What-If Assumptions Table

1. **Scroll down to view rows 18 through 25 and then click cell A18.**
2. **Click the Font Size box arrow on the Formatting toolbar and then click 14 in the Font Size list. Click the Italic button and then click the Underline button on the Formatting toolbar.**
3. **Select the range A19:B25, click the Font Size button on the Formatting toolbar, and then click 8 in the Font Size list.**
4. **Click cell D25 to deselect the range A19:B25.**

Excel displays the What-If Assumptions table as shown in Figure 3-51.

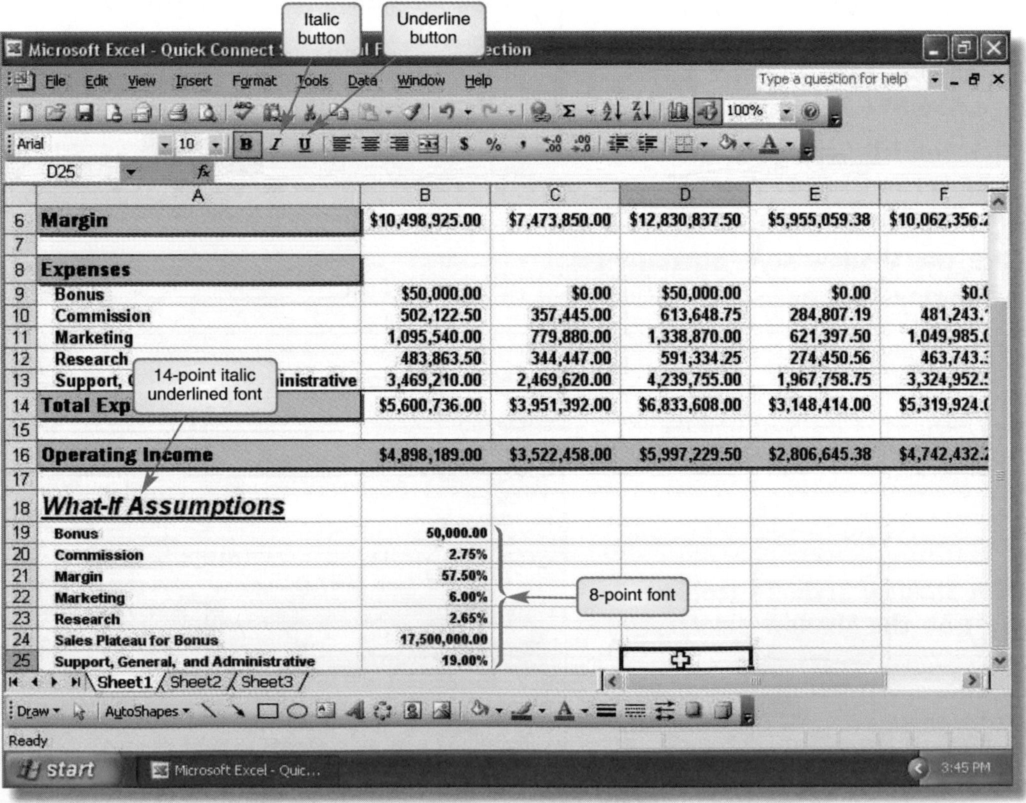

FIGURE 3-51

Recall that when you assign the italic font style to a cell, Excel slants the characters slightly to the right as shown in cell A18 in Figure 3-51. The **underline** format underlines only the characters in the cell, rather than the entire cell, as is the case when you assign a cell a bottom border.

Skill Builder 3-4

To practice the following tasks, visit scsite.com/off2003sch/skill, locate Excel Project 3, and then click Skill Builder 3-4.

- ❑ Show and hide Drawing toolbar
- ❑ Dock a toolbar
- ❑ Add a drop shadow to a range

Hiding the Drawing Toolbar and Saving the Workbook

The formatting of the worksheet is complete. The following steps hide the Drawing toolbar and save the workbook.

To Hide the Drawing Toolbar and Save the Workbook

1. **Click the Drawing button on the Standard toolbar.**
2. **Click the Save button on the Standard toolbar.**

Excel hides the Drawing toolbar (Figure 3-52) and saves the workbook using the file name Quick Connect Semiannual Financial Projection.

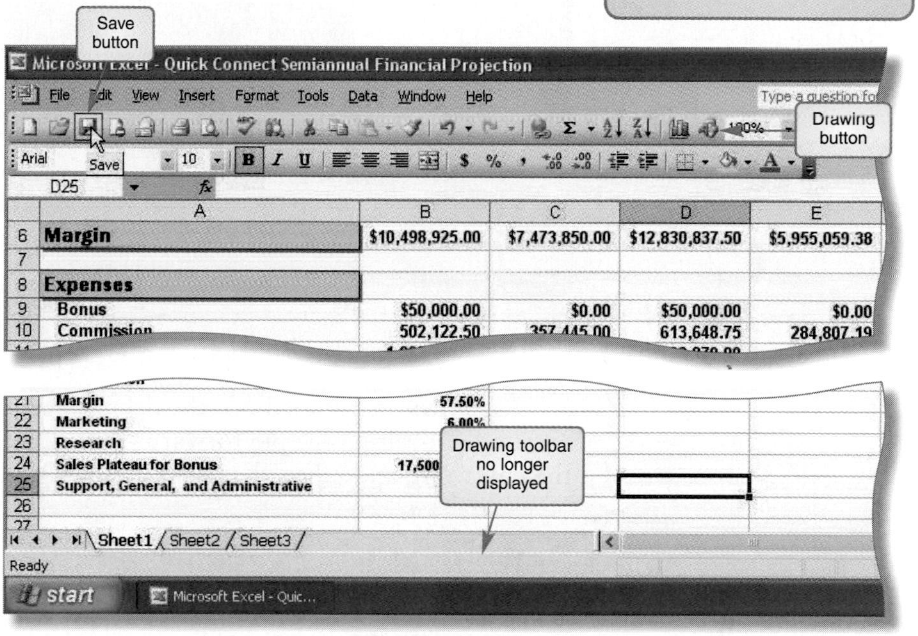

FIGURE 3-52

Adding a 3-D Pie Chart to the Workbook

The next step in the project is to draw the 3-D Pie chart on a separate sheet in the workbook, as shown in Figure 3-53 on the next page. A **Pie chart** is used to show the relationship or proportion of parts to a whole. Each slice (or wedge) of the pie shows what percent that slice contributes to the total (100%). The 3-D Pie chart in Figure 3-53 shows the contribution of each month's projected operating income to the six-month projected operating income. The 3-D Pie chart makes it easy to evaluate the contribution of one month to the six-month projected operating income in comparison to the other months.

Unlike the 3-D Column chart created in Project 1, the 3-D Pie chart shown in Figure 3-53 is not embedded in the worksheet. Instead, the Pie chart resides on a separate sheet, called a **chart sheet**, which contains only the chart.

In this worksheet, the ranges to chart are the nonadjacent ranges B3:G3 (month names) and B16:G16 (monthly operating incomes). The month names in the range B3:G3 will identify the slices of the Pie chart; these entries are called **category names**. The range B16:G16 contains the data that determines the size of the slices in the pie; these entries are called the **data series**. Because six months are being charted, the 3-D Pie chart contains six slices.

The sketch of the 3-D Pie chart in Figure 3-3b on page EX 149 also calls for emphasizing the month with the greatest contribution to the six-month projected operating income (in this case, June) by offsetting its slice from the main portion. A Pie chart with one or more slices offset is called an **exploded Pie chart**.

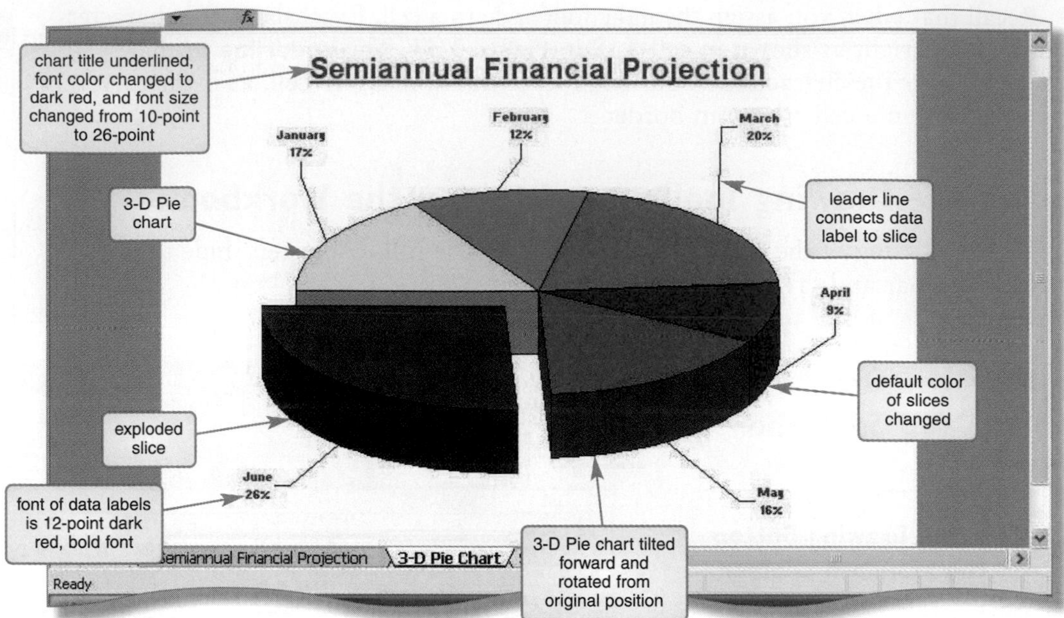

FIGURE 3-53

As shown in Figure 3-53, the default 3-D Pie chart also has been enhanced by rotating and tilting the pie forward, changing the colors of the slices, and modifying the chart title and labels that identify the slices.

Drawing a 3-D Pie Chart on a Separate Chart Sheet

The following steps show how to draw the 3-D Pie chart on a separate chart sheet using the Chart Wizard button on the Standard toolbar.

To Draw a 3-D Pie Chart on a Separate Chart Sheet

1

- **Select the range B3:G3.**
- **While holding down the CTRL key, select the range B16:G16.**
- **Click the Chart Wizard button on the Standard toolbar.**
- **When Excel displays the Chart Wizard - Step 1 of 4 - Chart Type dialog box, click Pie in the Chart type list and then click the 3-D Pie chart (column 2, row 1) in the Chart sub-type box.**

Excel displays the Chart Wizard - Step 1 of 4 - Chart Type dialog box, which allows you to select one of the 14 types of charts available in Excel (Figure 3-54).

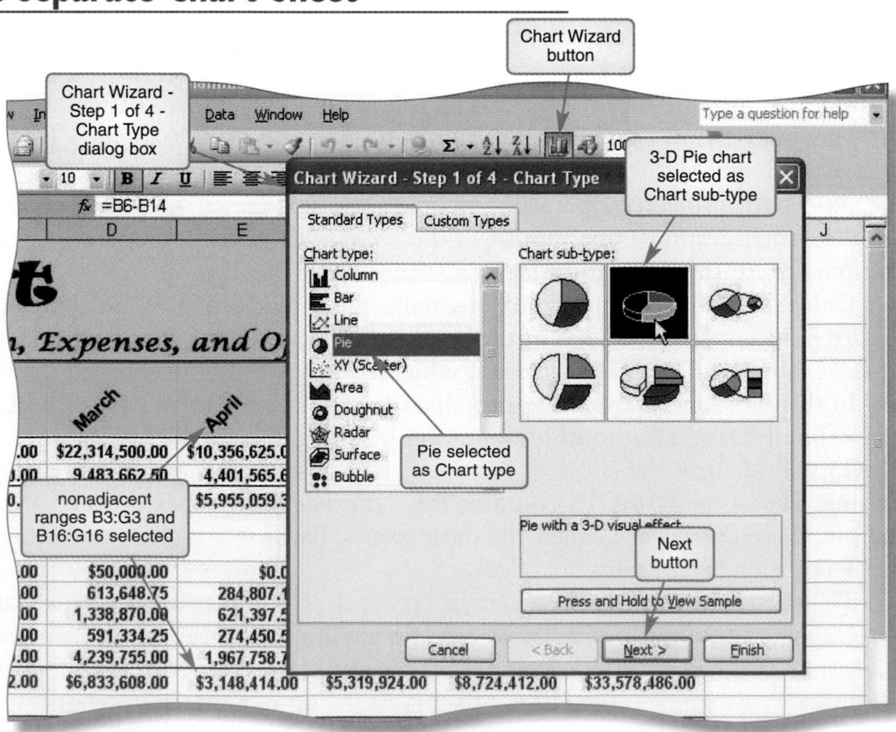

FIGURE 3-54

2

• **Click the Next button.**

Excel displays the Chart Wizard - Step 2 of 4 - Chart Source Data dialog box showing a sample of the 3-D Pie chart and the chart data range. A marquee surrounds the selected nonadjacent ranges on the worksheet (Figure 3-55).

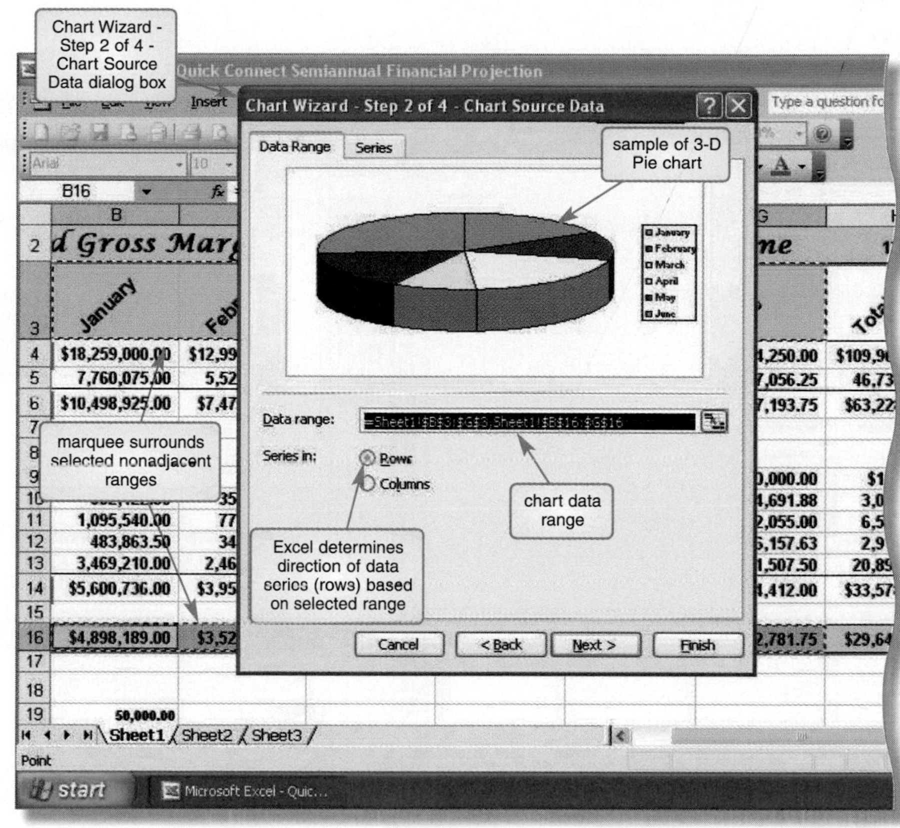

FIGURE 3-55

3

• **Click the Next button.**

• **When Excel displays the Chart Wizard - Step 3 of 4 - Chart Options dialog box, click the Titles tab, and then type** `Semiannual Financial Projection` **in the Chart title text box.**

Excel redraws the sample 3-D Pie chart with the chart title, Semiannunal Financial Projection (Figure 3-56). Excel automatically bolds the chart title.

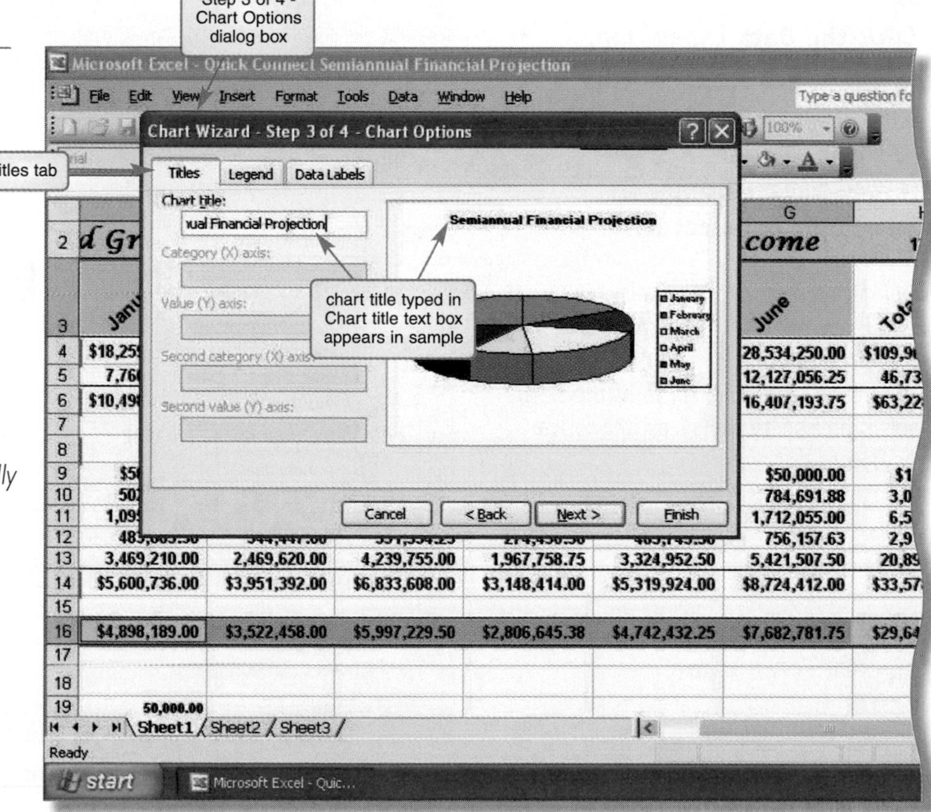

FIGURE 3-56

4

• **Click the Legend tab and then click Show legend to remove the check mark.**

Excel displays the Legend sheet. Excel redraws the sample 3-D Pie chart without the legend (Figure 3-57).

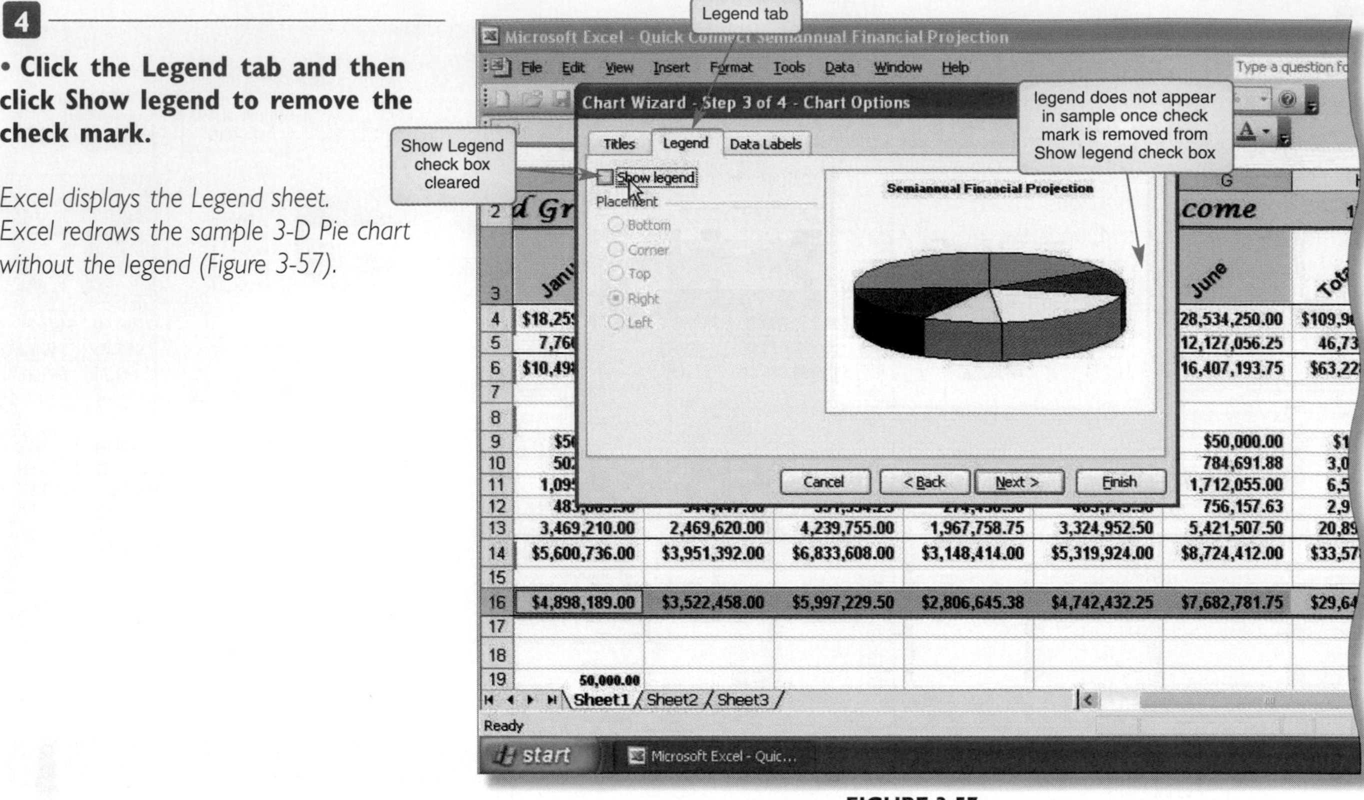

FIGURE 3-57

5

• **Click the Data Labels tab.**

• **In the Label Contains area, click Category name and click Percentage to select them.**

• **If necessary, click Show leader lines to select it.**

Excel displays the Data Labels sheet. Excel redraws the sample 3-D Pie chart with data labels and percentages (Figure 3-58). Because some of the data labels are close to the slices, the leader lines do not appear.

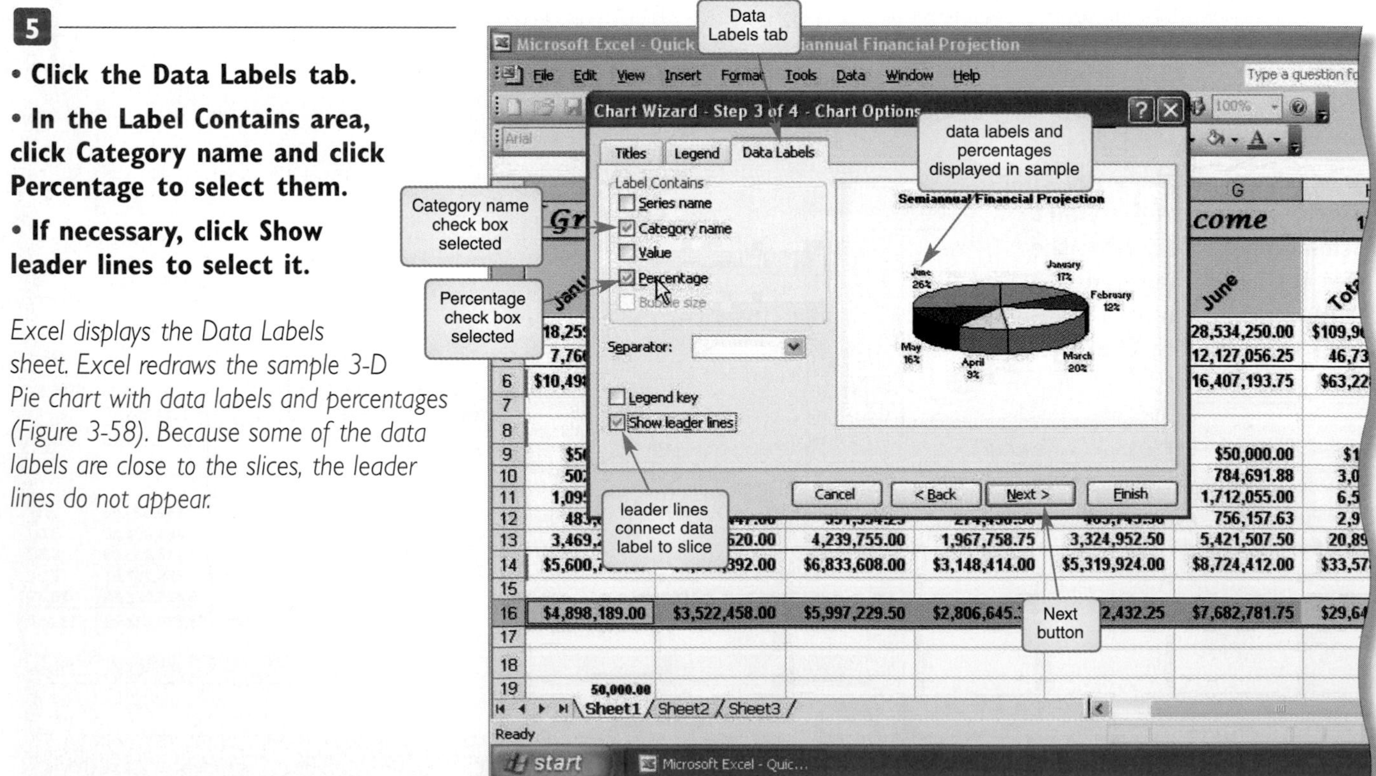

FIGURE 3-58

6

- **Click the Next button.**
- **When Excel displays the Chart Wizard - Step 4 of 4 - Chart Location dialog box, click As new sheet.**

Excel displays the Chart Wizard - Step 4 of 4 - Chart Location dialog box (Figure 3-59). It offers two chart location options: to draw the chart on a new sheet in the workbook or to draw it as an object in an existing worksheet.

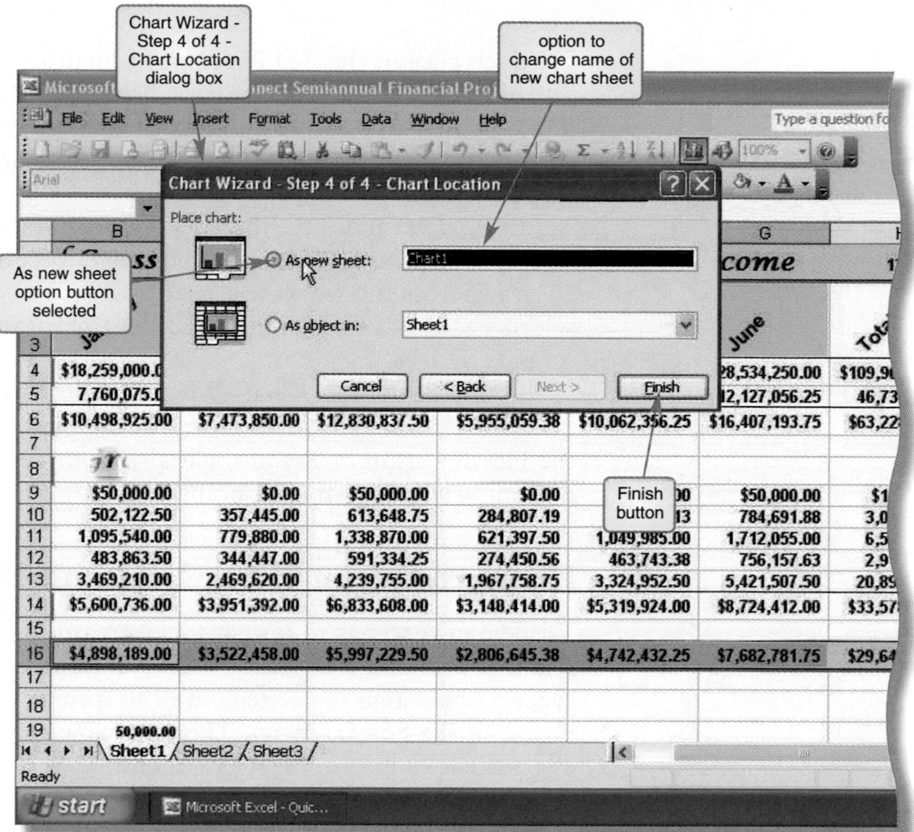

FIGURE 3-59

7

- **Click the Finish button.**
- **If the Chart toolbar appears, click its Close button.**

Excel draws the 3-D Pie chart on a separate chart sheet (Chart1) in the Quick Connect Semiannual Financial Projection workbook (Figure 3-60).

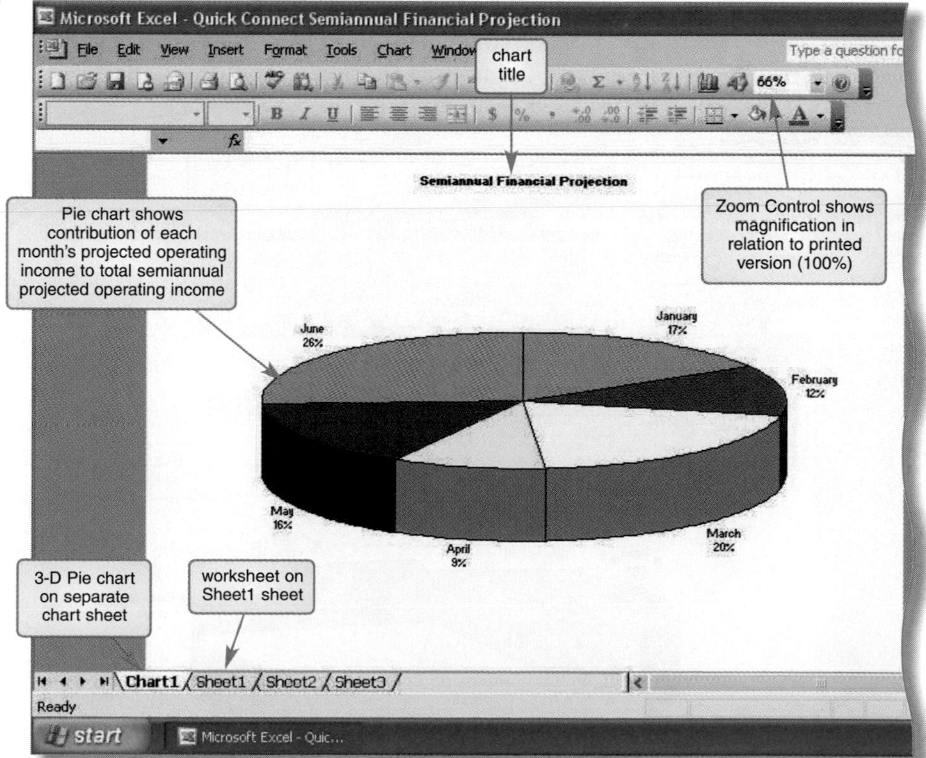

FIGURE 3-60

Each slice of the 3-D Pie chart in Figure 3-60 on the previous page represents one of the six months — January, February, March, April, May, and June. Excel displays the names of the months and the percent contribution outside the slices. The chart title, Semiannual Financial Projection, appears immediately above the 3-D Pie chart.

Excel determines the direction of the data series range (down a column or across a row) on the basis of the selected range. Because the range selected for the 3-D Pie chart is across the worksheet (ranges B3:G3 and B16:G16), Excel automatically selects the Rows option button in the Data Range sheet as shown in Figure 3-55 on page EX 189.

In any of the four Chart Wizard dialog boxes (Figures 3-54 through 3-59), a Back button is available to return to the previous Chart Wizard dialog box. Clicking the Finish button in any of the dialog boxes creates the 3-D Pie chart with the options selected up to that point.

Formatting the Chart Title and Data Labels

The next step is to format the chart title and labels that identify the slices. Before you can format a chart item, such as the chart title or data labels, you must select it. Once a chart item is selected, you can format it using the Formatting toolbar, shortcut menu, or the Format menu. The following steps use the Formatting toolbar to format chart items similar to the way cell entries were formatted earlier in this project.

To Format the Chart Title and Data Labels

1 Click the chart title. On the Formatting toolbar, click the Font Size box arrow, click 26 in the Font Size list, click the Underline button, click the Font Color button arrow, and then click Dark Red (column 1, row 2) on the Font Color palette.

2 Click one of the six data labels that identify the slices. On the Formatting toolbar, click the Font Size box arrow, click 12 in the Font Size list, click the Bold button, and then click the Font Color button to change the font to the color dark red.

Excel increases the font size of the chart title, underlines the chart title, and displays the chart title and data labels in dark red as shown in Figure 3-61. The data labels are selected.

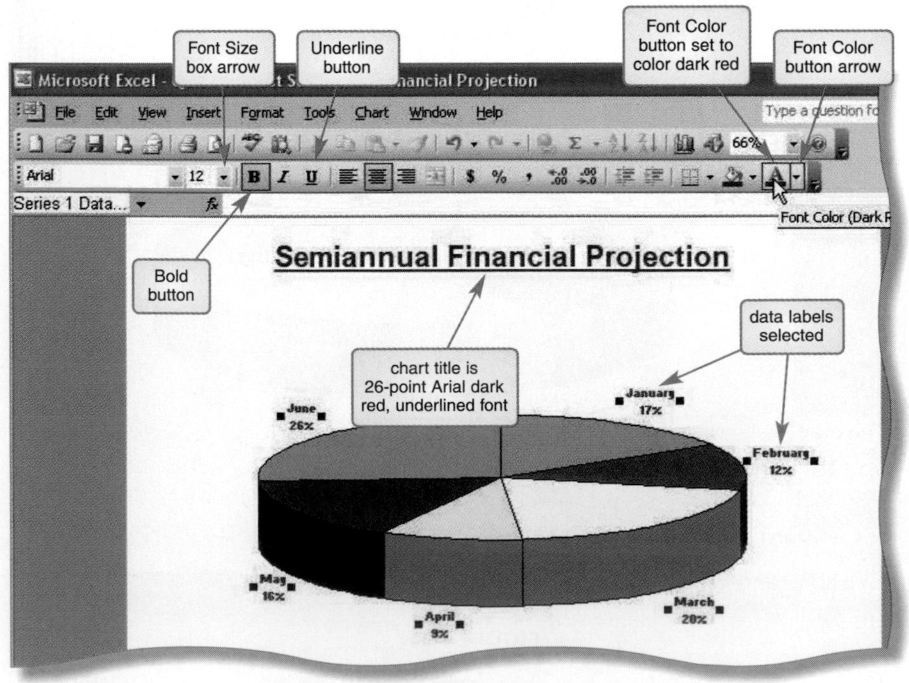

FIGURE 3-61

If you compare Figure 3-61 with Figure 3-60 on EX 191, you can see that the labels and chart title are easier to read and make the chart sheet look more professional.

Changing the Colors of Slices in a Pie Chart

The next step is to change the colors of the slices of the pie. The colors shown in Figure 3-61 are the default colors Excel uses when you first create a 3-D Pie chart. Project 3 requires that the colors be changed to those shown in Figure 3-53 on page EX 188. The following steps show how to change the colors of the slice by selecting them one at a time and using the Fill Color button arrow on the Formatting toolbar.

To Change the Colors of Slices in a Pie Chart

1

- **Click the January slice twice (do not double-click). Click the Fill Color button arrow on the Formatting toolbar.**

Excel displays sizing handles around the January slice. Excel also displays the Fill Color palette (Figure 3-62).

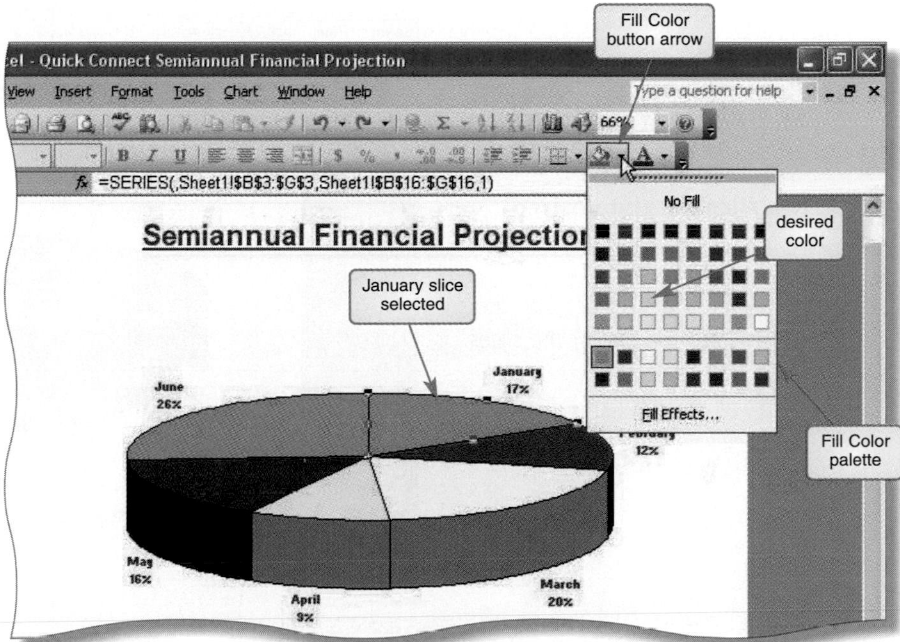

FIGURE 3-62

2

- **Click Yellow (column 3, row 4). One at a time, click the remaining slices and then use the Fill Color button arrow on the Formatting toolbar to change each slice to the following colors: February – Green (column 4, row 2); March – Orange (column 2, row 2); April – Blue (column 6, row 2); May – Red (column 1, row 3); and June – Dark Red (column 1, row 2).**

Excel displays the 3-D Pie chart as shown in Figure 3-63.

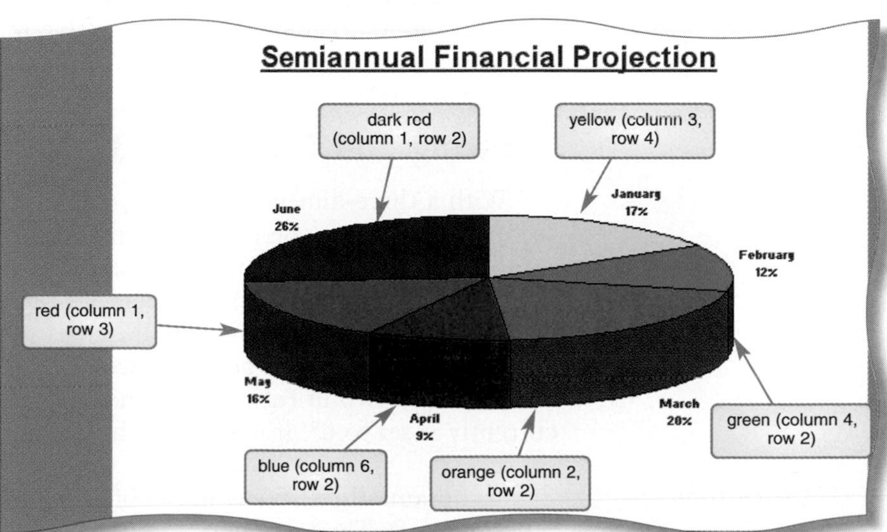

FIGURE 3-63

Exploding the 3-D Pie Chart

The next step is to emphasize the slice representing June, the month with the greatest contribution to the operating income, by **offsetting**, or exploding, it from the rest of the slices so that it stands out. The following steps show how to explode a slice of the 3-D Pie chart.

To Explode the 3-D Pie Chart

1

- **Click the slice labeled June twice (do not double-click).**

Excel displays sizing handles around the June slice.

2

- **Drag the slice to the desired position.**

Excel redraws the 3-D Pie chart with the June slice offset from the rest of the slices (Figure 3-64).

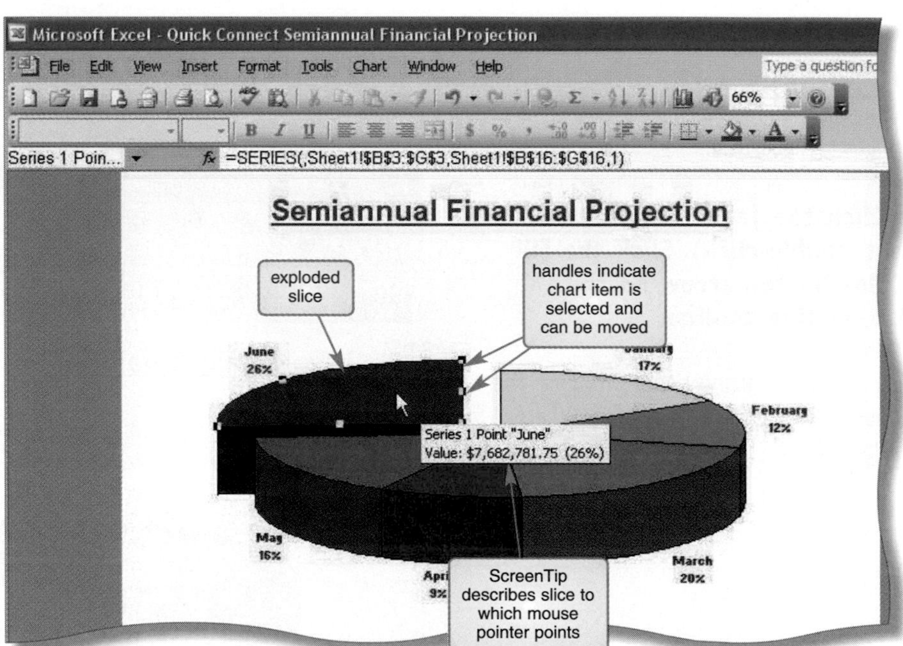

FIGURE 3-64

You can offset as many slices as you want, but remember that the reason for offsetting a slice is to emphasize it. Offsetting multiple slices tends to reduce the impact on the reader and reduces the overall size of the Pie chart.

Rotating and Tilting the 3-D Pie Chart

With a three-dimensional chart, you can change the view to better show the section of the chart you are trying to emphasize. Excel allows you to control the rotation angle, elevation, perspective, height, and angle of the axes by using the 3-D View command on the Chart menu.

When Excel initially draws a Pie chart, it always positions the chart so that one of the dividing lines between two slices is a straight line pointing to 12 o'clock (or 0°). As shown in Figure 3-64, the line that divides the January and June slices currently is set to 0°. It is this line that defines the rotation angle of the 3-D Pie chart.

To obtain a better view of the offset June slice, the 3-D Pie chart can be rotated 90° to the left. The following steps show how to rotate the 3-D Pie chart and change, or tilt, the elevation so the 3-D Pie chart is at less of an angle to the viewer.

To Rotate and Tilt the 3-D Pie Chart

1

• **With the June slice selected, click Chart on the menu bar.**

Excel displays the Chart menu (Figure 3-65).

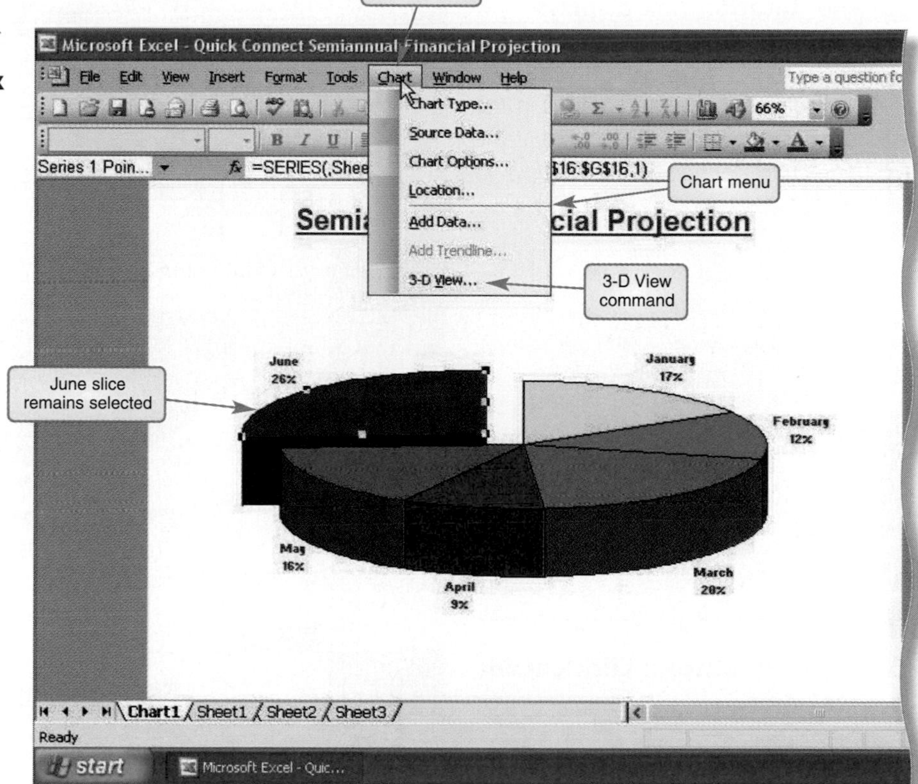

FIGURE 3-65

2

• **Click 3-D View.**

• **When Excel displays the 3-D View dialog box, click the Up Arrow button until 25 shows in the Elevation box.**

Excel displays the 3-D View dialog box, which includes a sample of the 3-D Pie chart (Figure 3-66). Increasing the elevation of the 3-D Pie chart causes it to tilt forward.

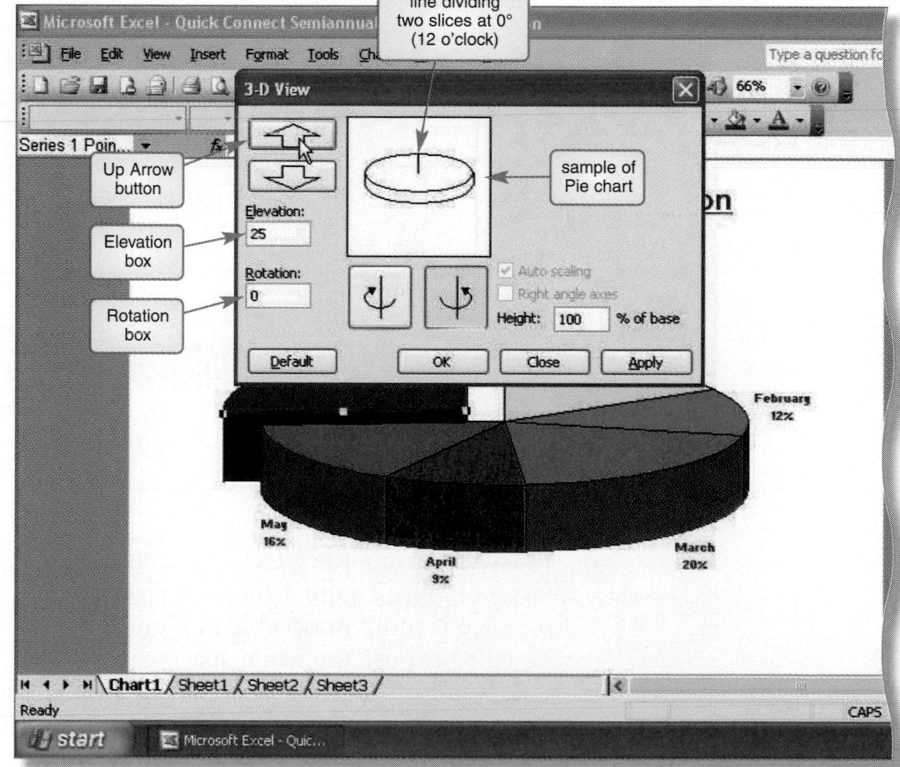

FIGURE 3-66

3

• Click the Left Rotation button until the Rotation box displays 270.

The new rotation setting (270) shows in the Rotation box (Figure 3-67). A sample of the rotated Pie chart appears in the dialog box.

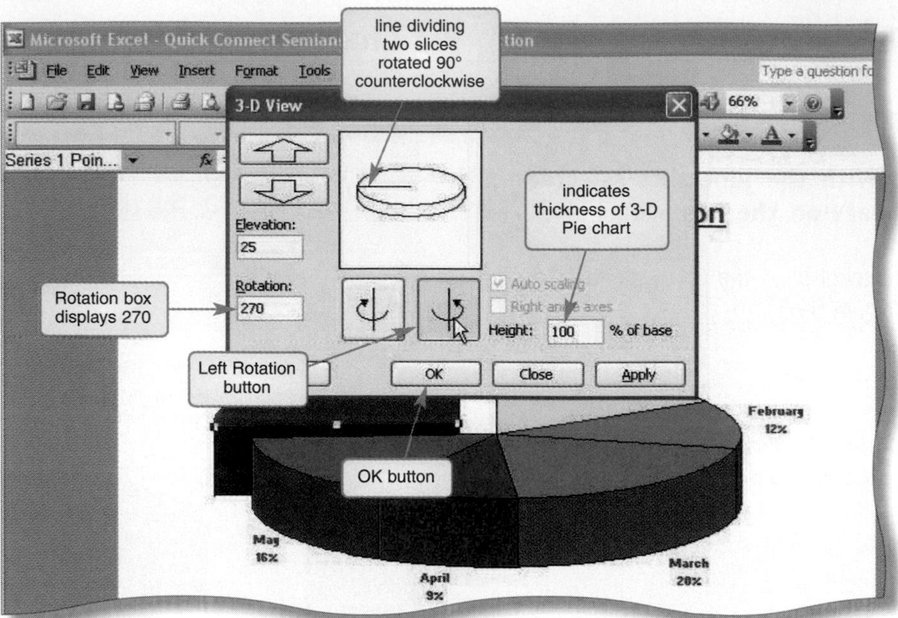

FIGURE 3-67

4

• Click the OK button. Click outside the chart area.

Excel displays the 3-D Pie chart tilted forward and rotated to the left, which makes the space between the June slice and the main portion of the pie more prominent (Figure 3-68).

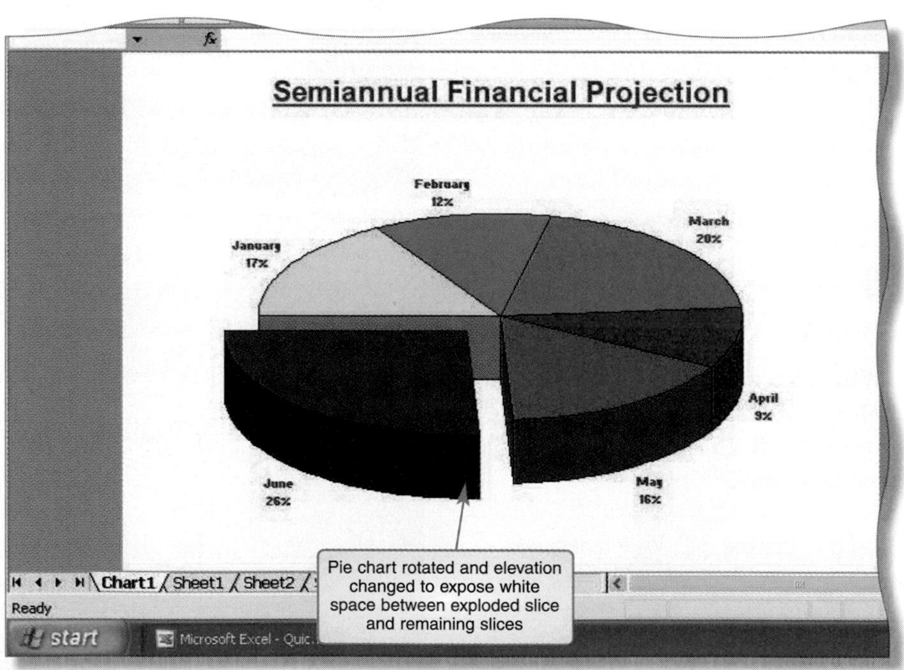

FIGURE 3-68

To appreciate the effect of changing the elevation and rotation of the 3-D Pie chart, compare Figure 3-68 with Figure 3-65 on the previous page. The offset of the June slice is more noticeable in Figure 3-68, because the Pie chart has been tilted and rotated to expose the white space between the June slice and the rest of the Pie chart.

In addition to controlling the rotation angle and elevation, you also can control the thickness of the 3-D Pie chart by entering a percent smaller or larger than the default 100% in the Height box (Figure 3-67).

Showing Leader Lines with the Data Labels

In Step 5 on page EX 190 in the Data Labels sheet of the Chart Wizard - Step 3 of 4 - Chart Options dialog box, the Show leader lines option was selected to instruct Excel to display leader lines. As the data labels are dragged away from each slice, Excel draws thin leader lines that connect each data label to its corresponding slice. The following steps show how to add leader lines to the data labels.

> *Skill Builder 3-5*
>
> To practice the following tasks, visit scsite.com/off2003sch/skill, locate Excel Project 3, and then click Skill Builder 3-5.
> - ❑ Draw a 3-D Pie chart
> - ❑ Change colors of slices
> - ❑ Explode a 3-D Pie chart
> - ❑ Change the view of a 3-D Pie Chart

To Show Leader Lines with the Data Labels

1

- **Click the June data label twice (do not double-click).**

Excel displays a box with handles around the June data label.

2

- **Point to the upper-left sizing handle on the box border and drag the June data label away from the June slice.**
- **Select and drag the remaining data labels away from their corresponding slices as shown in Figure 3-69.**
- **Click outside the chart area.**

Excel displays the data labels with leader lines as shown in Figure 3-69.

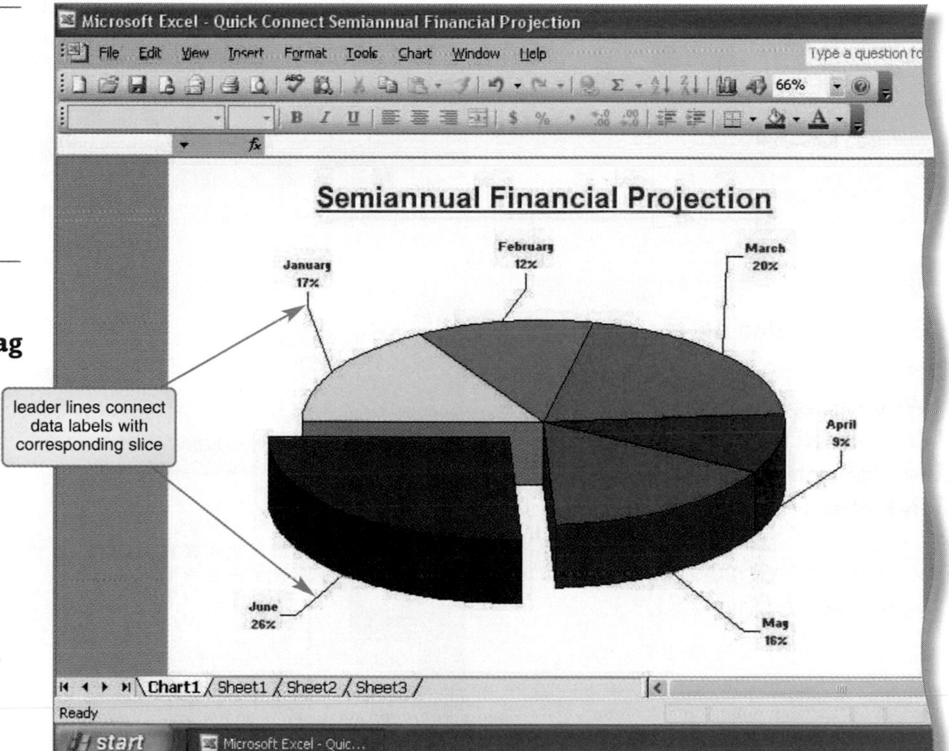

FIGURE 3-69

You also can select and format individual labels by clicking a specific data label after all the data labels have been selected. Making an individual data label larger or a different color, for example, helps emphasize a small or large slice in a Pie chart.

Renaming and Reordering the Sheets and Coloring Their Tabs

The final step in creating the workbook is to reorder the sheets and modify the tabs at the bottom of the screen. The steps on the next page show how to rename the sheets, color the tabs, and reorder the sheets so the worksheet precedes the chart sheet in the workbook.

To Rename and Reorder the Sheets and Color Their Tabs

1

- **Double-click the tab labeled Chart1 at the bottom of the screen.**
- **Type** `3-D Pie Chart` **and then press the ENTER key.**
- **Right-click the tab.**

The label on the Chart1 tab changes to 3-D Pie Chart (Figure 3-70). Excel displays the tab's shortcut menu.

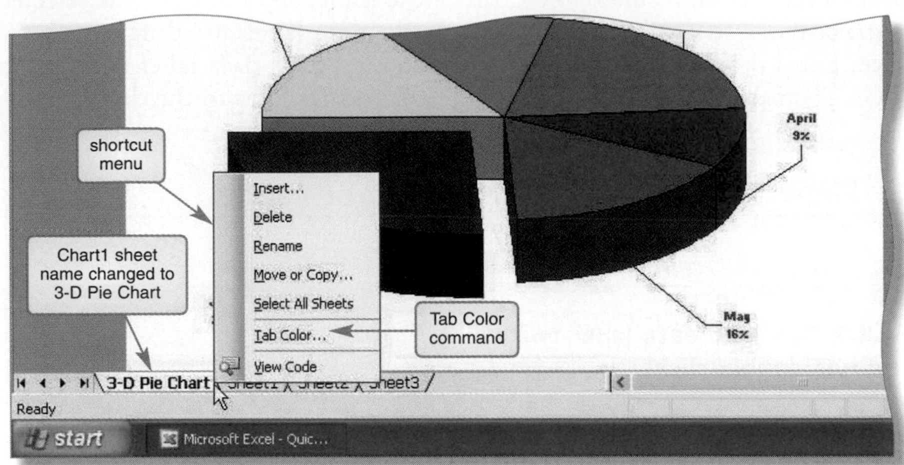

FIGURE 3-70

2

- **Click Tab Color on the shortcut menu.**
- **When Excel displays the Format Tab Color dialog box, click Dark Red (column 1, row 2) in the Tab Color area.**

Excel displays the Format Tab Color dialog box as shown in Figure 3-71.

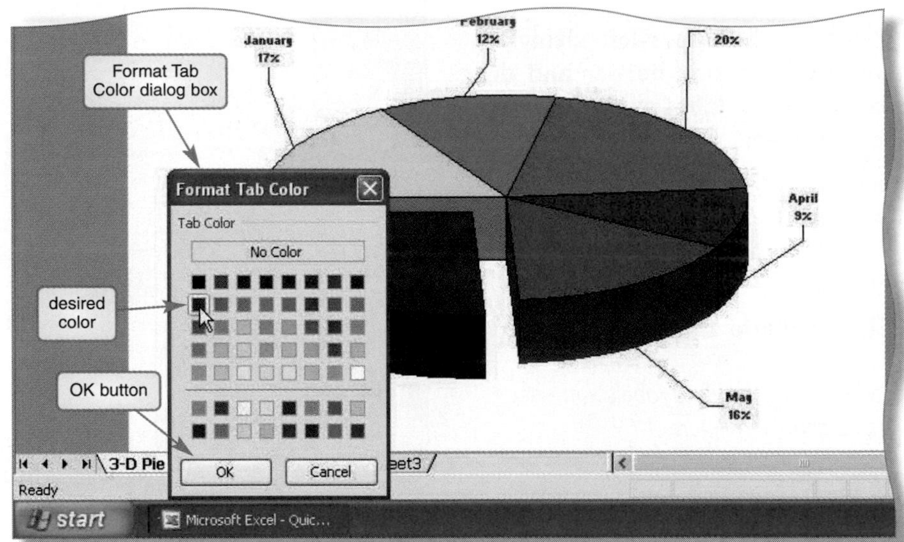

FIGURE 3-71

3

- **Click the OK button.**

Excel displays the name on the tab with a dark red underline (Figure 3-72). The dark red underline indicates the sheet is active. When the sheet is inactive, Excel displays the tab with a dark red background.

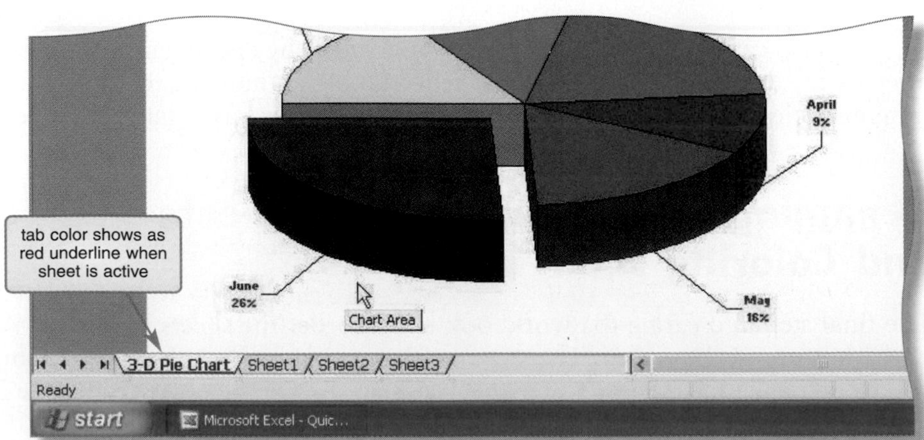

FIGURE 3-72

4

- **Double-click the tab labeled Sheet1 at the bottom of the screen.**
- **Type** `Semiannual Financial Projection` **as the new sheet name and then press the ENTER key.**
- **Right-click the tab and then click Tab Color on the shortcut menu.**
- **When Excel displays the Format Tab Color dialog box, click Tan (column 2, row 5) in the Tab Color area, and then click the OK button.**
- **Drag the Semiannual Financial Projection tab to the left in front of the 3-D Pie Chart tab and then click cell E18.**

Excel rearranges the sequence of the sheets and displays the Semiannual Financial Projection worksheet (Figure 3-73). The tan underline indicates the sheet is active.

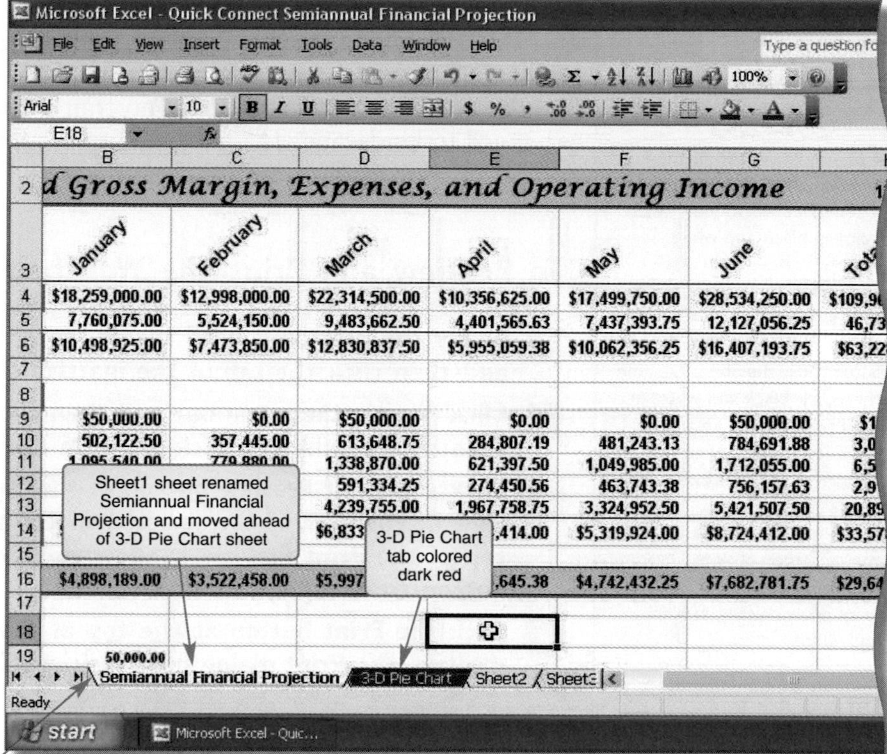

FIGURE 3-73

Checking Spelling, Saving, Previewing, and Printing the Workbook

With the workbook complete, this section checks spelling, saves, previews, and then prints the workbook. Each set of steps concludes with saving the workbook to ensure that the latest changes are saved.

Checking Spelling in Multiple Sheets

By default, the spell checker checks the spelling only in the selected sheets. It will check all the cells in the selected sheets, unless you select a range of two or more cells. Before checking the spelling, the following steps select the 3-D Pie Chart sheet so that the entire workbook is checked for spelling errors.

Q & A

Q: How does Excel determine which part of the worksheet to spell check?

A: Unless you first select a range of cells or an object before starting the spell checker, Excel checks the selected worksheet, including all cell values, cell comments, embedded charts, text boxes, buttons, and headers and footers.

To Check Spelling in Multiple Sheets

1. **With the Semiannual Financial Projection sheet active, press CTRL+HOME to select cell A1. Hold down the CTRL key and then click the 3-D Pie Chart tab.**
2. **Click the Spelling button on the Standard toolbar.**
3. **Correct any errors and then click the OK button when the spell check is complete.**
4. **Click the Save button on the Standard toolbar.**

Previewing and Printing the Workbook

After checking the spelling, the next step is to preview and print the sheets. As with spelling, Excel previews and prints only the selected sheets. Also, because the worksheet is too wide to print in portrait orientation, the orientation must be changed to landscape. The following steps adjust the orientation and scale, preview the workbook, and then print the workbook.

To Preview and Print the Workbook

1. **Ready the printer. If both sheets are not selected, hold down the CTRL key and then click the tab of the inactive sheet.**
2. **Click File on the menu bar and then click Page Setup. Click the Page tab and then click Landscape. Click Fit to in the Scaling area.**
3. **Click the Print Preview button in the Page Setup dialog box. When the preview of the first of the selected sheets appears, click the Next button at the top of the Print Preview window to view the next sheet. Click the Previous button to redisplay the first sheet.**
4. **Click the Print button at the top of the Print Preview window. When Excel displays the Print dialog box, click the OK button.**
5. **Right-click the Semiannual Financial Projection tab. Click Ungroup Sheets on the shortcut menu to deselect the 3-D Pie Chart tab.**
6. **Click the Save button on the Standard toolbar.**

The worksheet and 3-D Pie chart print as shown in Figures 3-74a and 3-74b. Excel saves the print settings with the workbook.

Q & A

Q: Is there a way to speed up the printing of colorful worksheets?

A: You can speed up the printing process and save ink if you print worksheets with color in black and white. To print a worksheet in black and white on a color printer, do the following: (1) Click File on the menu bar, click Page Setup, click the Sheet tab, and then click Black and white in the Print Preview area; and (2) Click the Print Preview button to see that Excel has removed the colored backgrounds, click the Close button, and then click the OK button. You now are ready to print economically, in black and white.

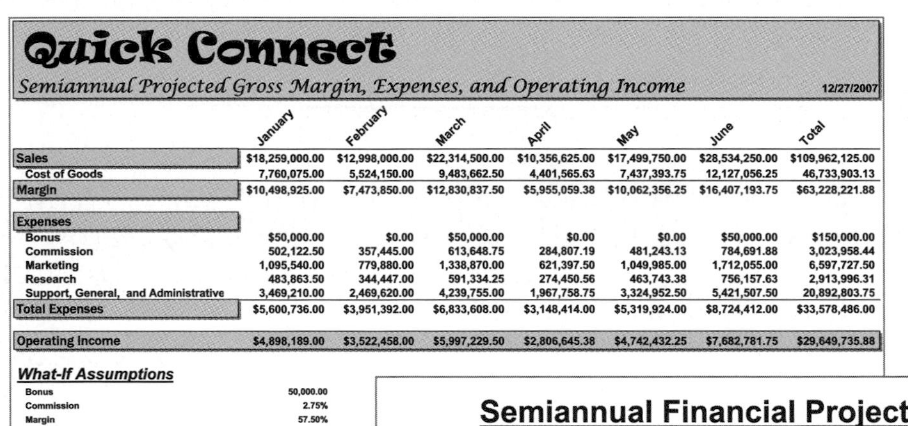

Quick Connect

Semiannual Projected Gross Margin, Expenses, and Operating Income — 12/27/2007

	January	February	March	April	May	June	Total
Sales	$18,259,000.00	$12,998,000.00	$22,314,500.00	$10,356,625.00	$17,499,750.00	$28,534,250.00	$109,962,125.00
Cost of Goods	7,760,075.00	5,524,150.00	9,483,662.50	4,401,565.63	7,437,393.75	12,127,056.25	46,733,903.13
Margin	$10,498,925.00	$7,473,850.00	$12,830,837.50	$5,955,059.38	$10,062,356.25	$16,407,193.75	$63,228,221.88
Expenses							
Bonus	$50,000.00	$0.00	$50,000.00	$0.00	$0.00	$50,000.00	$150,000.00
Commission	502,122.50	357,445.00	613,648.75	284,807.19	481,243.13	784,691.88	3,023,958.44
Marketing	1,095,540.00	779,880.00	1,338,870.00	621,397.50	1,049,985.00	1,712,055.00	6,597,727.50
Research	483,863.50	344,447.00	591,334.25	274,450.56	463,743.38	756,157.63	2,913,996.31
Support, General, and Administrative	3,469,210.00	2,469,620.00	4,239,755.00	1,967,758.75	3,324,952.50	5,421,507.50	20,892,803.75
Total Expenses	$5,600,736.00	$3,951,392.00	$6,833,608.00	$3,148,414.00	$5,319,924.00	$8,724,412.00	$33,578,486.00
Operating Income	$4,898,189.00	$3,522,458.00	$5,997,229.50	$2,806,645.38	$4,742,432.25	$7,682,781.75	$29,649,735.88

What-If Assumptions

Bonus	50,000.00
Commission	2.75%
Margin	57.50%
Marketing	6.00%
Research	2.65%
Sales Plateau for Bonus	17,500,000.00
Support, General, and Administrative	19.00%

(a) Worksheet

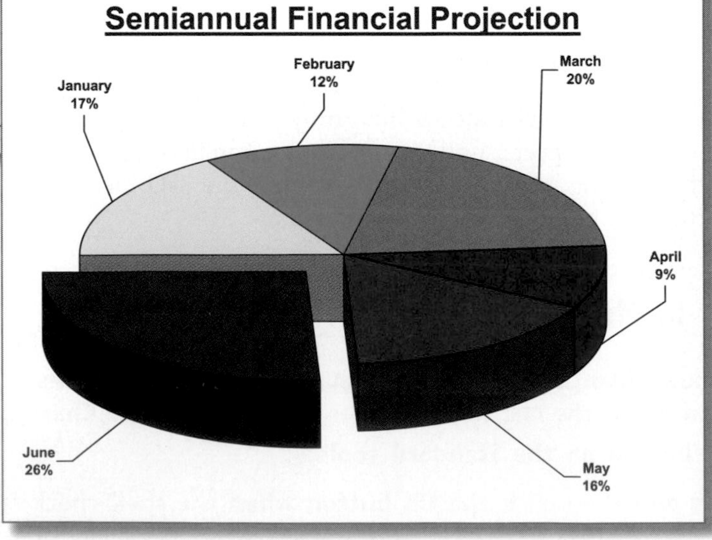

(b) 3-D Pie Chart

FIGURE 3-74

Changing the View of the Worksheet

With Excel, you easily can change the view of the worksheet. For example, you can magnify or shrink the worksheet on the screen. You also can view different parts of the worksheet through window panes.

Shrinking and Magnifying the View of a Worksheet or Chart

You can magnify (zoom in) or shrink (zoom out) the appearance of a worksheet or chart by using the Zoom box on the Standard toolbar. When you magnify a worksheet, Excel enlarges the view of the characters on the screen, but displays fewer columns and rows. Alternatively, when you shrink a worksheet, Excel is able to display more columns and rows. Magnifying or shrinking a worksheet affects only the view; it does not change the window size or printout of the worksheet or chart. The following steps shrink and magnify the view of the worksheet.

To Shrink and Magnify the View of a Worksheet or Chart

1

- **If cell A1 is not active, press CTRL+HOME.**
- **Click the Zoom box arrow on the Standard toolbar.**

Excel displays a list of percentages in the Zoom list (Figure 3-75).

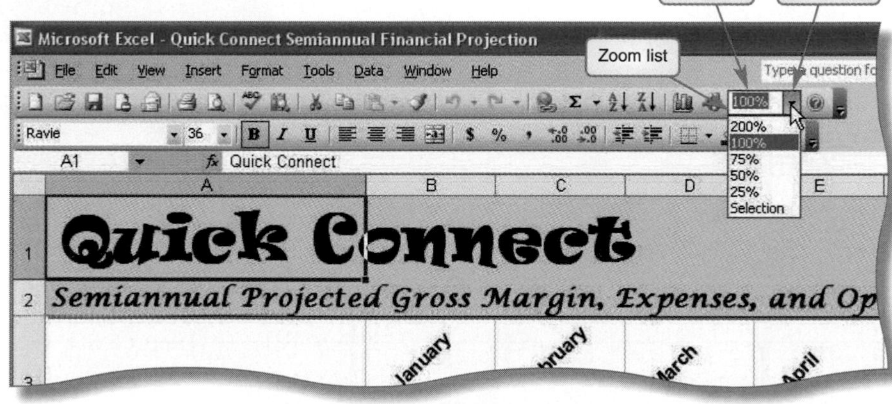

FIGURE 3-75

2

- **Click 75%.**

Excel shrinks the display of the worksheet to 75% of its normal display (Figure 3-76). With the worksheet zoomed out to 75%, you can see more rows and columns than you did at 100% magnification. Some of the numbers, however, appear as a series of number signs (#), because the columns are not wide enough to show the formatted numbers.

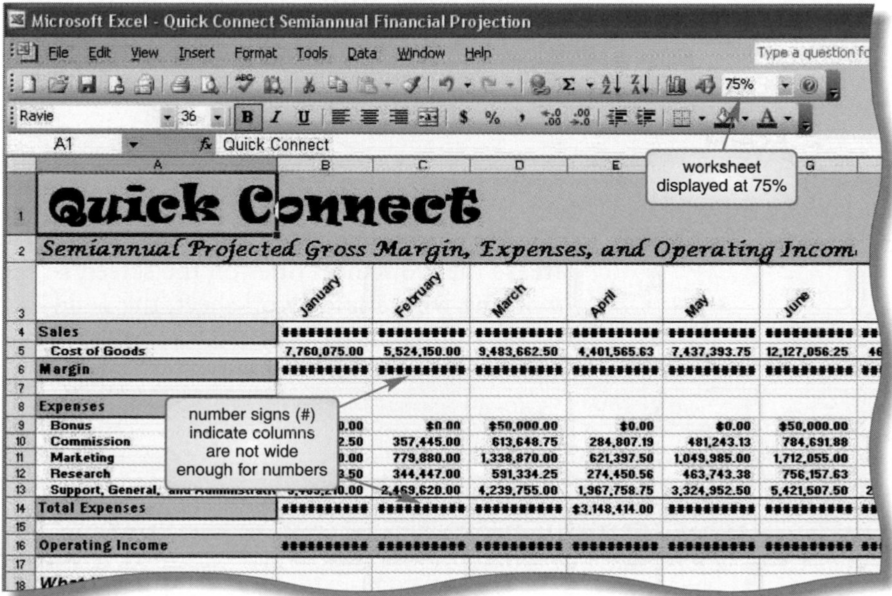

FIGURE 3-76

3

• **Click the Zoom box arrow on the Standard toolbar and then click 100%.**

Excel displays the worksheet at 100%.

4

• **Click the 3-D Pie Chart tab at the bottom of the screen. Click the Zoom box arrow on the Standard toolbar and then click 100%.**

Excel changes the magnification of the chart from 66% (shown in Figure 3-69 on page EX 197) to 100% (Figure 3-77). Excel displays the chart at the same size as the printout of the chart.

• **Enter** 66 **in the Zoom box to return the chart to its original magnification.**

Excel changes the magnification of the chart back to 66%.

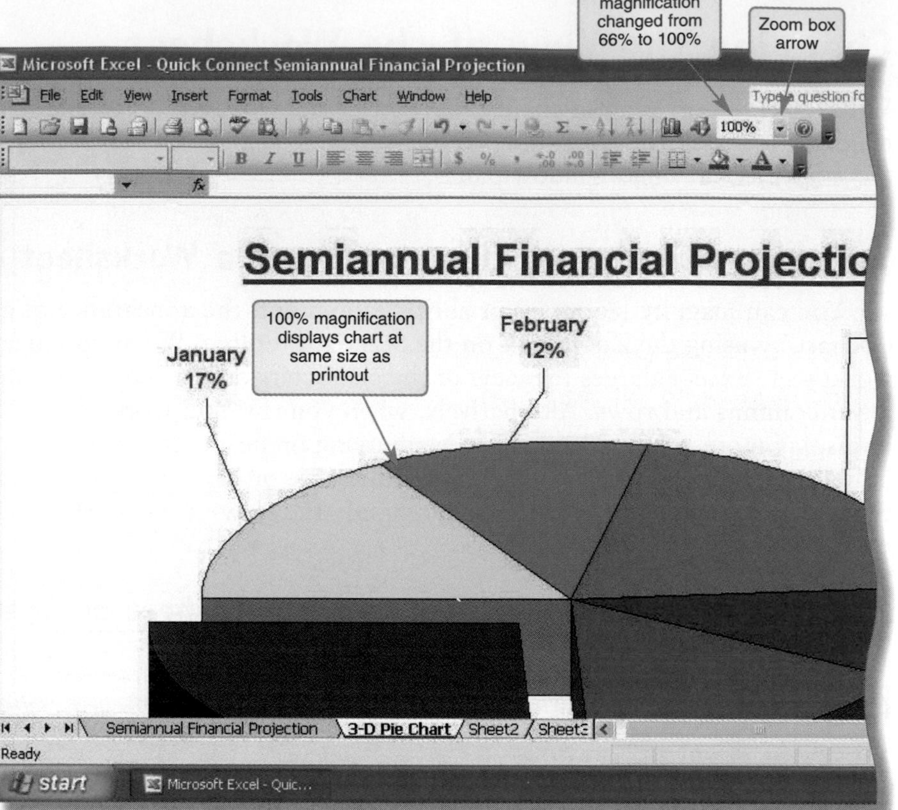

FIGURE 3-77

At 800 × 600 resolution, Excel normally displays a chart in the range of 65% to 70% magnification, so that the entire chart appears on the screen. By changing the magnification to 100%, you can see only a part of the chart, but at a magnification that corresponds with the chart's size on a printout. Excel allows you to enter a percent magnification between 10 and 400 in the Zoom box for worksheets and chart sheets.

Splitting the Window into Panes

This project previously used the Freeze Panes command to instruct Excel to freeze the worksheet titles on the screen so they always show when you scroll. When working with a large worksheet, the window also can be split into two or four panes to view different parts of the worksheet at the same time. The following steps show how to split the Excel window into four panes.

To Split a Window into Panes

1

- **Click the Semiannual Financial Projection tab at the bottom of the screen.**
- **Select cell D7, the intersection of the four proposed panes.**
- **Click Window on the menu bar.**

Excel displays the Window menu (Figure 3-78). Cell D7 is the active cell.

Window menu
Split command
panes will be divided above and to the left of active cell

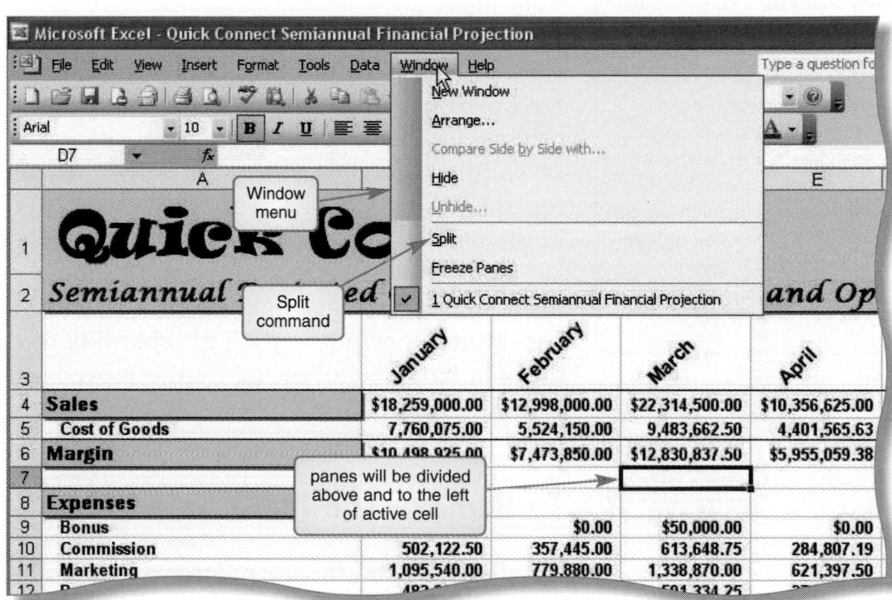

FIGURE 3-78

2

- **Click Split on the Window menu.**
- **Use the scroll arrows to show the four corners of the worksheet at the same time.**

Excel divides the window into four panes and displays the four corners of the worksheet (Figure 3-79).

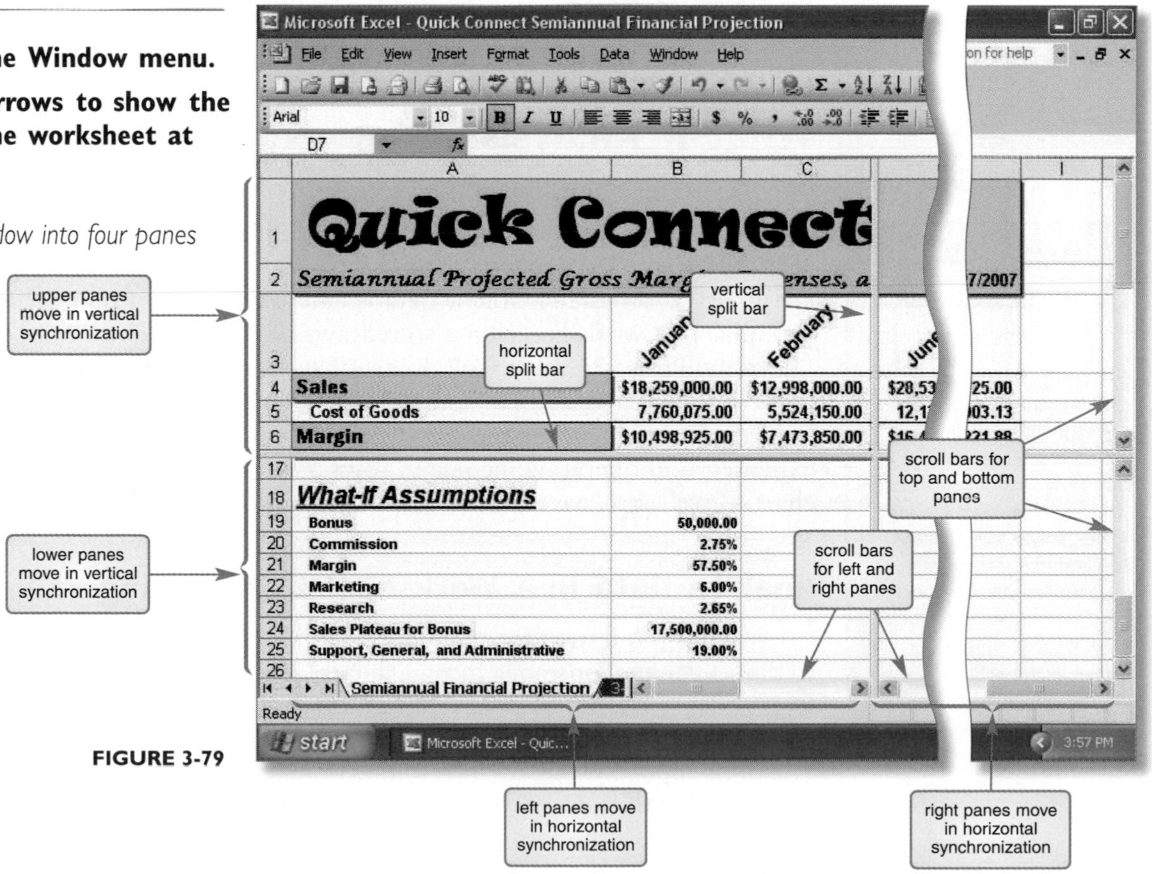

upper panes move in vertical synchronization
lower panes move in vertical synchronization
vertical split bar
horizontal split bar
scroll bars for top and bottom panes
scroll bars for left and right panes
left panes move in horizontal synchronization
right panes move in horizontal synchronization

FIGURE 3-79

Q & A

Q: Is there more than one way to invoke a command in Excel?

A: Yes. For a table that lists how to complete the tasks covered in this book using the mouse, menu, shortcut menu, and keyboard, see the Quick Reference Summary at the back of this book or visit the Office 2003 Quick Reference Web page (scsite.com/off2003sch/qr).

The four panes in Figure 3-79 on the previous page are used to show the following: (1) range A1:C6 in the upper-left pane; (2) range G1:I6 in the upper-right pane; (3) range A17:C26 in the lower-left pane; and (4) range G17:I26 in the lower-right pane.

The vertical bar going up and down the middle of the window is called the **vertical split bar**. The horizontal bar going across the middle of the window is called the **horizontal split bar**. If you use the scroll bars below the window and to the right of the window to scroll the window, you will see that the panes split by the horizontal split bar scroll together vertically. The panes split by the vertical split bar scroll together horizontally. To resize the panes, drag either split bar to the desired location in the window.

You can change the values of cells in any of the four panes. Any change you make in one pane also takes effect in the other panes. To remove one of the split bars from the window, drag the split box to the edge of the window or double-click the split bar. The following steps remove both split bars to remove the four panes from the window.

To Remove the Panes from the Window

1. **Position the mouse pointer at the intersection of the horizontal and vertical split bars.**
2. **When the mouse pointer changes to a four-headed arrow, double-click.**

Excel removes the four panes from the window.

What-If Analysis

The automatic recalculation feature of Excel is a powerful tool that can be used to analyze worksheet data. Using Excel to scrutinize the impact of changing values in cells that are referenced by a formula in another cell is called **what-if analysis** or **sensitivity analysis**. When new data is entered, Excel not only recalculates all formulas in a worksheet, but also redraws any associated charts.

In the Project 3 workbook, many of the formulas are dependent on the assumptions in the range B19:B25. Thus, if you change any of the assumption values, Excel immediately recalculates the cost of goods, margin, monthly expenses, total expenses, and operating income in rows 5 through 16. Excel redraws the 3-D Pie chart as well, because it is based on these numbers.

Q & A

Q: Does Excel have what-if analysis tools?

A: Yes. Instead of requiring you to change assumptions in a worksheet manually, Excel has additional methods for answering what-if questions, including Goal Seek, Data Tables, Solver, PivotTables, Scenario Manager, and the Analysis ToolPak. For more information, enter each of these what-if tools in the Type a question for help box on the menu bar.

Analyze Data in a Worksheet by Changing Values

A what-if question for the worksheet in Project 3 might be *what* would happen to the semiannual operating income in cell H16 *if* the Bonus, Commission, Support, General, and Administrative assumptions in the What-If Assumptions table are changed as follows: Bonus $50,000.00 to $35,000.00; Commission 2.75% to 1.25%; Support, General, and Administrative 19.00% to 16.50%? To answer a question like this, you need to change only the first, second, and seventh values in the What-If Assumptions table. Excel instantaneously recalculates the formulas in the worksheet and redraws the 3-D Pie chart to answer the question.

The following steps change the three assumptions as indicated in the previous paragraph to determine the new semiannual operating income in cell H16. To ensure that the What-If Assumtions table and the semiannual operating income in cell H16 show on the screen at the same time, the steps also divide the window into two vertical panes.

To Analyze Data in a Worksheet by Changing Values

1

- **Use the vertical scroll bar to move the window so cell A6 is in the upper-left corner of the screen.**
- **Drag the vertical split box from the lower-right corner of the screen to the left so that the vertical split bar is positioned as shown in Figure 3-80.**
- **Use the right scroll arrow to view the totals in column H in the right pane.**
- **Click cell B19 in the left pane.**

Excel divides the window into two vertical panes and shows the totals in column H in the pane on the right side of the window (Figure 3-80).

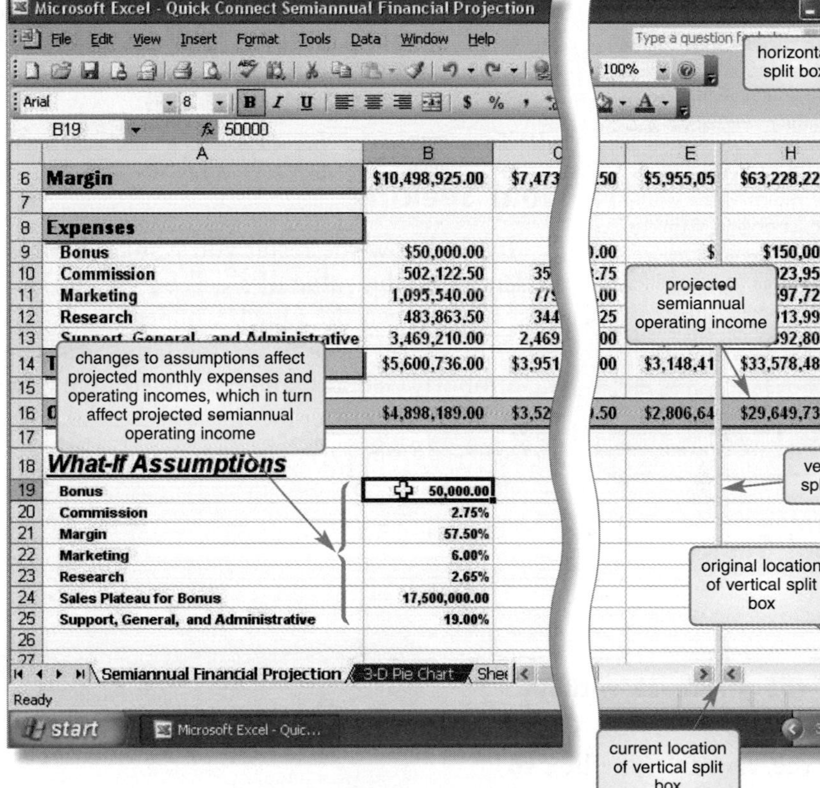
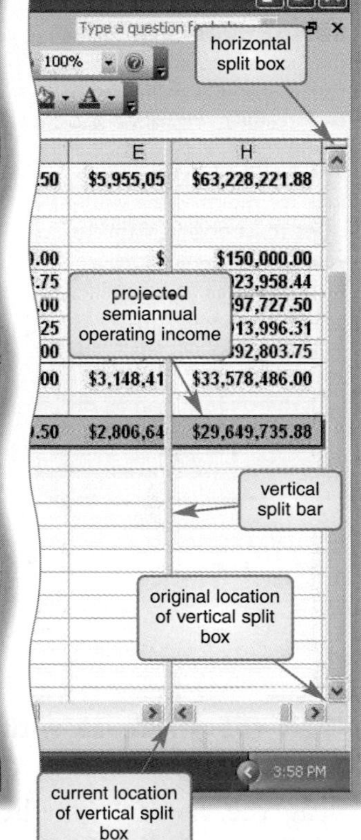

FIGURE 3-80

2

- **Enter** 35000 **in cell B19,** 1.25 **in cell B20, and** 16.50 **in cell B25.**

Excel immediately recalculates all the formulas in the worksheet (Figure 3-81).

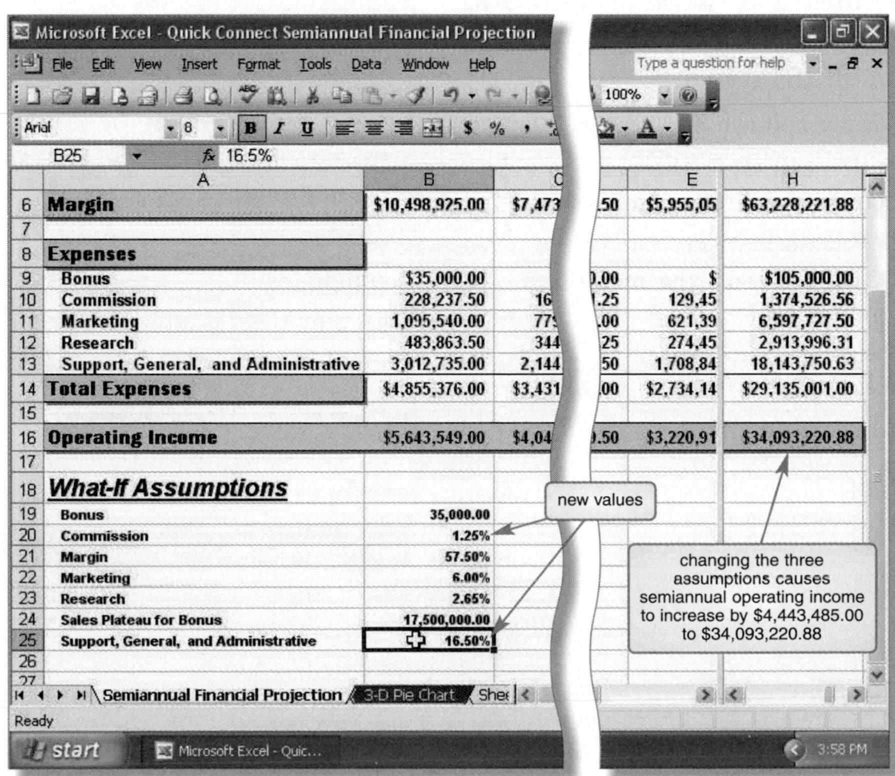

FIGURE 3-81

Each time you enter a new assumption, Excel recalculates the worksheet and redraws the 3-D Pie chart. This process usually takes less than one second, depending on how many calculations must be performed and the speed of your computer. Compare the semiannual operating income in cell H16 in Figures 3-80 and 3-81 on the previous page. By changing the values of the three assumptions (Figure 3-81), the semiannual operating income in cell H16 increases from $29,649,735.88 to $34,093,220.88. This translates into an increase of $4,443,485.00 for the semiannual operating income.

Q & A

Q: Can the Undo button on the Standard toolbar be used to change the assumptions back to their original values?

A: Yes. The Undo button is ideal for returning the worksheet to its original state after you have changed the values in a worksheet to answer a what-if question. To view the original worksheet after answering a what-if question, click the Undo button on the Standard toolbar for each value you changed.

Goal Seeking

If you know the result you want a formula to produce, you can use **goal seeking** to determine the value of a cell on which the formula depends. The following steps close and reopen the Quick Connect Semiannual Financial Projection workbook. They then show how to use the Goal Seek command on the Tools menu to determine the Support, General, and Administrative percentage in cell B25 that will yield a semiannual operating income of $34,000,000 in cell H16, rather than the original $29,649,735.88.

To Goal Seek

1

- **Close the workbook without saving changes and then reopen it.**
- **Drag the vertical split box so that the vertical split bar is positioned as shown in Figure 3-82.**
- **Scroll down so row 6 is at the top of the screen.**
- **Show column H in the right pane.**
- **Click cell H16, the cell that contains the semiannual operating income.**
- **Click Tools on the menu bar.**

Excel displays the Tools menu and the vertical split bar as shown in Figure 3-82.

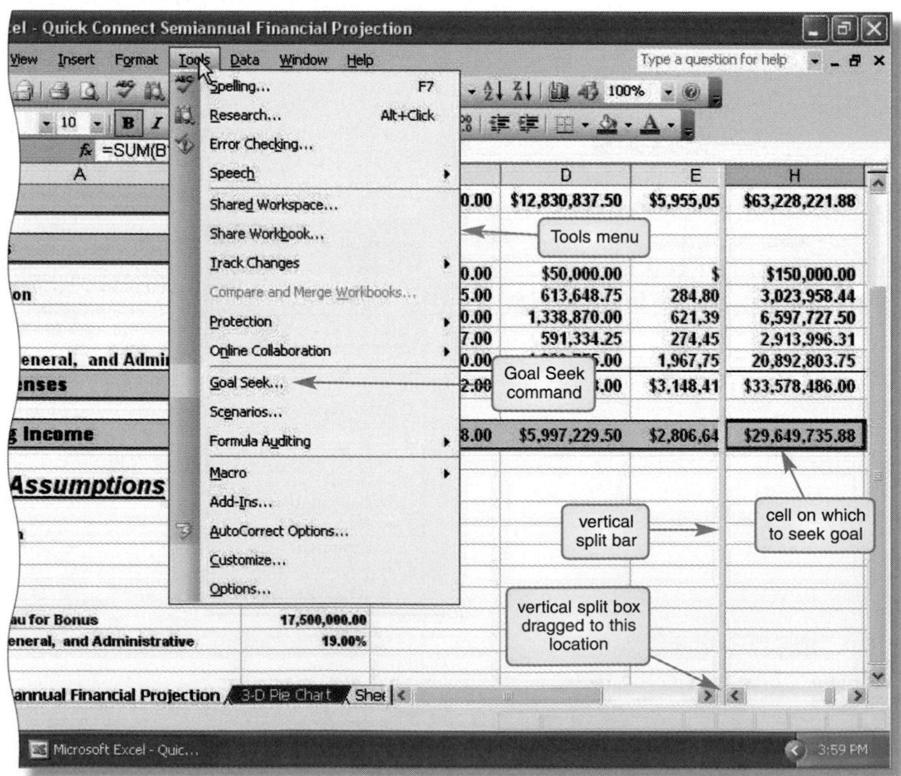

FIGURE 3-82

2

- **Click Goal Seek.**
- **When Excel displays the Goal Seek dialog box, click the To value text box, type** 34,000,000 **and then click the By changing cell box.**
- **Click cell B25 on the worksheet.**

Excel displays the Goal Seek dialog box as shown in Figure 3-83. Excel automatically assigns the Set cell box the cell reference of the active cell in the worksheet (cell H16). A marquee surrounds cell B25, which is set as the cell reference in the By changing cell box.

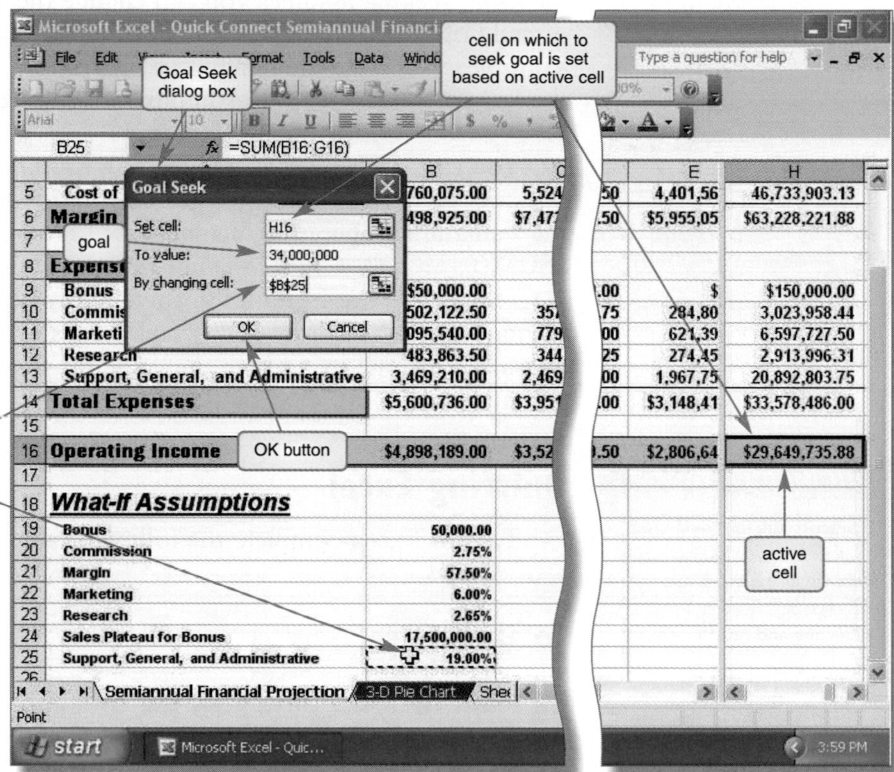

FIGURE 3-83

3

- **Click the OK button.**

Excel immediately changes cell H16 from $29,649,735.88 to the desired value of $34,000,000.00. More importantly, Excel changes the Support, General, and Administrative assumption in cell B25 from 19.00% to 15.04% (Figure 3-84). Excel also displays the Goal Seek Status dialog box. If you click the OK button, Excel keeps the new values in the worksheet. If you click the Cancel button, Excel redisplays the original values.

4

- **Click the Cancel button in the Goal Seek Status dialog box.**

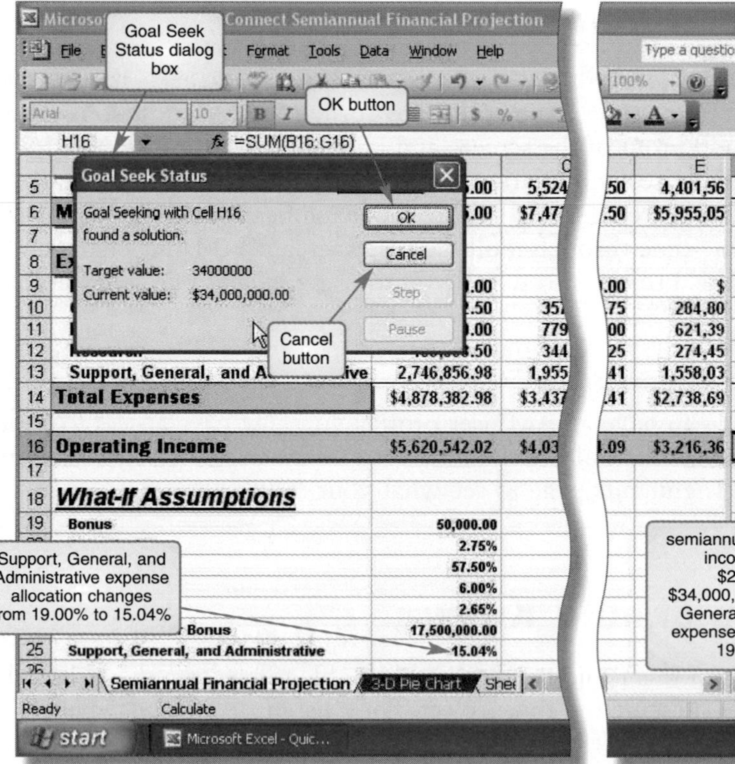

FIGURE 3-84

Goal seeking assumes you can change the value of only one cell referenced directly or indirectly to reach a specific goal for a value in another cell. In this example, to change the semiannual operating income in cell H16 to $34,000,000.00, the Support, General, and Administrative percentage in cell B25 must decrease by 3.96% from 19.00% to 15.04%.

You can see from this goal seeking example that the cell to change (cell B25) does not have to be referenced directly in the formula or function. For example, the semiannual operating income in cell H16 is calculated by the function =SUM(B16:G16). Cell B25 is not referenced in this function. Instead, cell B25 is referenced in the formulas in rows 9 through 13, on which the monthly operating incomes in row 16 are based. Excel thus is capable of goal seeking on the semiannual operating income by varying the value for the Support, General, and Administrative assumption.

Skill Builder 3-6

To practice the following tasks, visit scsite.com/off2003sch/skill, locate Excel Project 3, and then click Skill Builder 3-6.

- ❑ Rename and reorder sheets
- ❑ Color tabs
- ❑ Shrink and magnify the view of a worksheet
- ❑ Split a window into panes
- ❑ Do simple what-if analysis
- ❑ Goal seek

Quitting Excel

To quit Excel, complete the following steps.

To Quit Excel

1. **Click the Close button on the title bar.**
2. **If the Microsoft Excel dialog box is displayed, click the No button.**

Project Summary

In this project, you learned how to work with large worksheets that extend beyond the window, how to use the fill handle to create a series, and some new formatting techniques. You learned to show hidden toolbars, dock a toolbar at the bottom of the screen, and hide an active toolbar. You learned about the difference between absolute cell references and relative cell references and how to use the IF function. You also learned how to rotate text in a cell, freeze titles, change the magnification of the worksheet, show different parts of the worksheet at the same time through multiple panes, create a 3-D Pie chart, and improve the appearance of a 3-D Pie chart. Finally, this project introduced you to using Excel to do what-if analysis by changing values in cells and goal seeking.

If you have a SAM user profile, you may have access to hands-on instruction, practice, and assessment of the skills covered in this project. Log in to your SAM account and go to your assignments page to see what your instructor has assigned.

What You Should Know

Having completed this project, you should be able to perform the tasks below. The tasks are listed in the same order they were presented in this project. For a list of the buttons, menus, toolbars, and commands introduced in this project, see the Quick Reference Summary at the back of this book and refer to the Page Number column.

1. Start and Customize Excel (EX 150)
2. Bold the Font of the Entire Worksheet (EX 150)
3. Enter the Worksheet Titles and Save the Workbook (EX 150)
4. Rotate Text and Use the Fill Handle to Create a Series of Month Names (EX 151)
5. Copy a Cell's Format Using the Format Painter Button (EX 154)

6. Increase Column Widths and Enter Row Titles (EX 155)
7. Copy a Range of Cells to a Nonadjacent Destination Area (EX 157)
8. Insert a Row (EX 160)
9. Enter Numbers with Format Symbols (EX 163)
10. Freeze Column and Row Titles (EX 163)
11. Enter the Projected Monthly Sales (EX 164)
12. Enter and Format the System Date (EX 166)
13. Enter a Formula Containing Absolute Cell References (EX 169)
14. Enter an IF Function (EX 172)
15. Enter the Remaining January Formulas (EX 173)
16. Copy Formulas with Absolute Cell References Using the Fill Handle (EX 174)
17. Determine Row Totals in Nonadjacent Cells (EX 175)
18. Unfreeze the Worksheet Titles and Save the Workbook (EX 176)
19. Assign Formats to Nonadjacent Ranges (EX 178)
20. Format the Worksheet Titles (EX 180)
21. Show the Drawing Toolbar (EX 182)
22. Move and Dock a Toolbar (EX 183)
23. Add a Drop Shadow (EX 184)
24. Change Font, Add Underlines, Add Background Colors, and Add Drop Shadows to Nonadjacent Cells (EX 185)
25. Format the What-If Assumptions Table (EX 186)
26. Hide the Drawing Toolbar and Save the Workbook (EX 187)
27. Draw a 3-D Pie Chart on a Separate Chart Sheet (EX 188)
28. Format the Chart Title and Data Labels (EX 192)
29. Change the Colors of the Slices in a Pie Chart (EX 193)
30. Explode the 3-D Pie Chart (EX 194)
31. Rotate and Tilt the 3-D Pie Chart (EX 195)
32. Show Leader Lines with the Data Labels (EX 197)
33. Rename and Reorder the Sheets and Color Their Tabs (EX 198)
34. Check Spelling in Multiple Sheets (EX 199)
35. Preview and Print the Workbook (EX 200)
36. Shrink and Magnify the View of a Worksheet or Chart (EX 201)
37. Split a Window into Panes (EX 203)
38. Remove the Panes from the Window (EX 204)
39. Analyze Data in a Worksheet by Changing Values (EX 205)
40. Goal Seek (EX 206)
41. Quit Excel (EX 208)

Career Corner

Systems Programmer

System software is a key component in any computer. A *systems programmer* evaluates, installs, and maintains system software and provides technical support to the programming staff.

Systems programmers work with the programs that control computers, such as operating systems, network operating systems, and database systems. They identify current and future processing needs and then recommend the software and hardware necessary to meet those needs. In addition to selecting and installing system software, systems programmers must be able to adapt system software to the requirements of an organization, provide regular maintenance, measure system performance, determine the impact of new or updated software on the system, design and implement special software, and provide documentation. Because they are familiar with the entire system, systems programmers often help application programmers to diagnose technical problems.

Systems programmers must be acquainted thoroughly with a variety of operating systems. They must be able to think logically, pay attention to detail, work with abstract concepts, and devise solutions to complex problems. Systems programmers often work in teams and interact with programmers and nontechnical users, so communications skills are important.

Most systems programmers have a four-year B.S. degree in Computer Science or Information Technology. Depending on responsibilities and experience, salaries range from $53,000 to more than $100,000. For more information, visit scsite.com/off2003sch/careers and then click Systems Programmer.

Learn It Online

Instructions: To complete the Learn It Online exercises, start your browser, click the Address bar, and then enter the Web address scsite.com/off2003sch/learn. When the Office 2003 Learn It Online page is displayed, follow the instructions in the exercises below. Each exercise has instructions for printing your results, either for your own records or for submission to your instructor.

1 Project Reinforcement TF, MC, and SA

Below Excel Project 3, click the Project Reinforcement link. Print the quiz by clicking Print on the File menu for each page. Answer each question.

2 Flash Cards

Below Excel Project 3, click the Flash Cards link and read the instructions. Type 20 (or a number specified by your instructor) in the Number of playing cards text box, type your name in the Enter your Name text box, and then click the Flip Card button. When the flash card is displayed, read the question and then click the ANSWER box arrow to select an answer. Flip through Flash Cards. If your score is 15 (75%) correct or greater, click Print on the File menu to print your results. If your score is less than 15 (75%) correct, then redo this exercise by clicking the Replay button.

3 Practice Test

Below Excel Project 3, click the Practice Test link. Answer each question, enter your first and last name at the bottom of the page, and then click the Grade Test button. When the graded practice test is displayed on your screen, click Print on the File menu to print a hard copy. Continue to take practice tests until you score 80% or better.

4 Who Wants To Be a Computer Genius?

Below Excel Project 3, click the Computer Genius link. Read the instructions, enter your first and last name at the bottom of the page, and then click the PLAY button. When your score is displayed, click the PRINT RESULTS link to print a hard copy.

5 Wheel of Terms

Below Excel Project 3, click the Wheel of Terms link. Read the instructions, and then enter your first and last name and your school name. Click the PLAY button. When your score is displayed, right-click the score and then click Print on the shortcut menu to print a hard copy.

6 Crossword Puzzle Challenge

Below Excel Project 3, click the Crossword Puzzle Challenge link. Read the instructions, and then enter your first and last name. Click the SUBMIT button. Work the crossword puzzle. When you are finished, click the Submit button. When the crossword puzzle is redisplayed, click the Print Puzzle button to print a hard copy.

7 Tips and Tricks

Below Excel Project 3, click the Tips and Tricks link. Click a topic that pertains to Project 3. Right-click the information and then click Print on the shortcut menu. Construct a brief example of what the information relates to in Excel to confirm you understand how to use the tip or trick.

8 Newsgroups

Below Excel Project 3, click the Newsgroups link. Click a topic that pertains to Project 3. Print three comments.

9 Expanding Your Horizons

Below Excel Project 3, click the Expanding Your Horizons link. Click a topic that pertains to Project 3. Print the information. Construct a brief example of what the information relates to in Excel to confirm you understand the contents of the article.

10 Search Sleuth

Below Excel Project 3, click the Search Sleuth link. To search for a term that pertains to this project, select a term below the Project 3 title and then use the Google search engine at google.com (or any major search engine) to display and print two Web pages that present information on the term.

11 Excel Online Training

Below Excel Project 3, click the Excel Online Training link. When your browser displays the Microsoft Office Online Web page, click the Excel link. Click one of the Excel courses that covers one or more of the objectives listed at the beginning of the project on page EX 146. Print the first page of the course before stepping through it.

12 Office Marketplace

Below Excel Project 3, click the Office Marketplace link. When your browser displays the Microsoft Office Online Web page, click the Office Marketplace link. Click a topic that relates to Excel. Print the first page.

13 You're Hired!

Below Excel Project 3, click the You're Hired! link to embark on the path to a career in computers. Directions about how to play the game will be displayed. When you are ready to play, click the begin the game button. If required, submit your score to your instructor.

Apply Your Knowledge

1 Understanding the IF Function and Absolute Cell Referencing

Instructions: Fill in the correct answers.

1. Determine the truth value of the logical tests, given the following cell values: E1 = 500; F1 = 500; G1 = 2; H1 = 50; and I1 = 40. Enter true or false.
   a. E1 < 400 Truth value: ____________________
   b. F1 = E1 Truth value: ____________________
   c. 10 * H1 + I1 <> E1 Truth value: ____________________
   d. E1 + F1 >= 1000 Truth value: ____________________
   e. E1/H1 > G1 * 6 Truth value: ____________________
   f. 5 * G1 + I1 = H1 Truth value: ____________________
   g. 10 * I1 + 2 <= F1 + 2 Truth value: ____________________
   h. H1 – 10 < I1 Truth value: ____________________
2. The active cell is cell F15. Write an IF function that assigns the value zero (0) or 1 to cell F15. Assign zero to cell F15 if the value in cell B3 is greater than the value in cell C12; otherwise assign 1 to cell F15.
   Function: ____________________
3. Write an IF function for cell J5 that assigns the value Credit OK or Credit Not OK. Assign the label Credit OK if the value in cell A1 is not equal to the value in cell B1; otherwise assign the label Credit Not OK.
   Function: ____________________
4. Write cell D15 as a relative reference, absolute reference, mixed reference with the row varying, and mixed reference with the column varying.

   ______________ ______________ ______________ ______________
5. Write the formula for cell B8 that multiplies cell B1 times the sum of cells B4, B5, and B6. Write the formula so that when it is copied to cells C8 and D8, cell B1 remains absolute.
   Function: ____________________
6. Write the formula for cell B8 that divides cell D5 by the sum of cells N10 through N13. Write the formula so that when it is copied to cells C8 and D8, cell N10 through N13 remains absolute.
   Formula: ____________________
7. Write the formula for cell H6 that multiplies cell L6 by the sum of cells G4, H4, and I4. Write the formula so that when it is copied to cells H7, H8, and H9, cell H4 remains absolute.
   Formula: ____________________
8. Write the formula for cell K2 that multiplies cell W4 by the sum of cells C4 through C8. Write the formula so that when it is copied to cells K3 and K4, Excel adjusts all the cell references according to the new locations.
   Formula: ____________________
9. A nested IF function is an IF function that contains another IF function in the value_if_true or value_if_false arguments. For example, =IF(C1 <= 500,5%, IF(C1 <=1000, 6%, 7%)) is a valid nested IF function. Start Excel and enter this IF function in cell D11, and then use the fill handle to copy the function down through cell D17. Enter the following data in the cells in the range C1:C7, and then write down the results found in cells D11 through D17 for each set. Set 1: C1 = 750; C2 = 2000; C3 = 501; C4 = 500; C5 = 1000; C6 = 250; C7 = 1001. Set 2: C1= 525; C2 = 0; C3 = –50; C4 = 3000; C5 = 987; C6 = 3400; C7 = 800.
   Set 1 Results: ____________________
   Set 2 Results: ____________________

1 Projected Quarterly Report

Problem: You work part-time after school and on weekends at Encrypt-It Inc., a leader in the field of keeping secret information safe and secure from outsiders. The company utilizes assumptions, based on past business practice, to plan for the next six-month period. Your manager recently learned that you have experience with Excel. She has asked you to create a worksheet similar to the one shown in Figure 3-85.

Table 3-9 Encrypt-It Inc. Six-Month Assumptions

Advertising	2.50%
Bonuses	50,000.00
Commissions	2.25%
Manufacturing	21.65%
Margin	62.00%
Sales for Bonuses	3,000,000.00
Technical Support	21.50%

Instructions Part 1: Start Excel. Do the following to create the worksheet shown in Figure 3-85.

1. Bold the entire worksheet. Enter the worksheet titles `Encrypt-It Inc.` and `Six-Month Plan` in cells A1 and A2.
2. Change the width of the columns as follows: column A = 25.00 characters; columns B through G = 13.00 characters; and column H = 15.00 characters.
3. Enter the month name `July` in cell B3. Format cell B3 as follows: italicize, rotate its contents 45°, change the font size to 11, and add a thick bottom border. Enter the month names August through December in the range C3:G3 by dragging cell B3's fill handle through the range C3:G3. Enter Total in cell H3 and use the Format Painter button on the Standard toolbar to format it the same as cell G3.
4. Enter the row titles down through Assumptions in cell A17. Copy the row titles in the range A9:A13 to A18:A22.
5. Insert two rows between rows 21 and 22. Add the row titles in cells 22 and 23 as shown in Figure 3-85.
6. Enter the assumptions in Table 3-9 in the range B18:B24 with the format symbols shown.
7. Enter the sales revenue in Table 3-10 in row 4.

Table 3-10 Encrypt-It Inc. Planned Sales for July through December

July	August	September	October	November	December
3542126	2497214	4613823	1987981	2671015	3281395

8. Enter the following formulas in column B:
   a. Cost of Goods Sold (cell B5) = Sales – Sales * Margin assumption or =B4 – B4 * $B$22
   b. Gross Margin (cell B6) = Sales – Cost of Goods Sold or =B4 – B5
   c. Advertising (cell B9) = Advertising assumption * Sales or =$B$18 * B4
   d. Bonuses (cell B10): If Sales is greater than Sales for Bonuses (cell B23), then Bonuses = B19, otherwise Bonuses = 0 or =IF(B4>$B$23,$B$19,0)
   e. Commissions (cell B11) = Commissions assumption * Sales or =$B$20 * B4
   f. Manufacturing (cell B12) = Manufacturing assumption * Sales or =$B$21 * B4
   g. Technical Support (cell B13) = Technical Support assumption * Sales or =$B$24 * B4
   h. Total Expenses (cell B14) = Sum of expenses or =SUM(B9:B13)
   i. Operating Income (cell B15) = Gross Margin – Total Expenses or =B6 – B14
9. Copy the range B5:B15 to the range C5:G15.

In the Lab

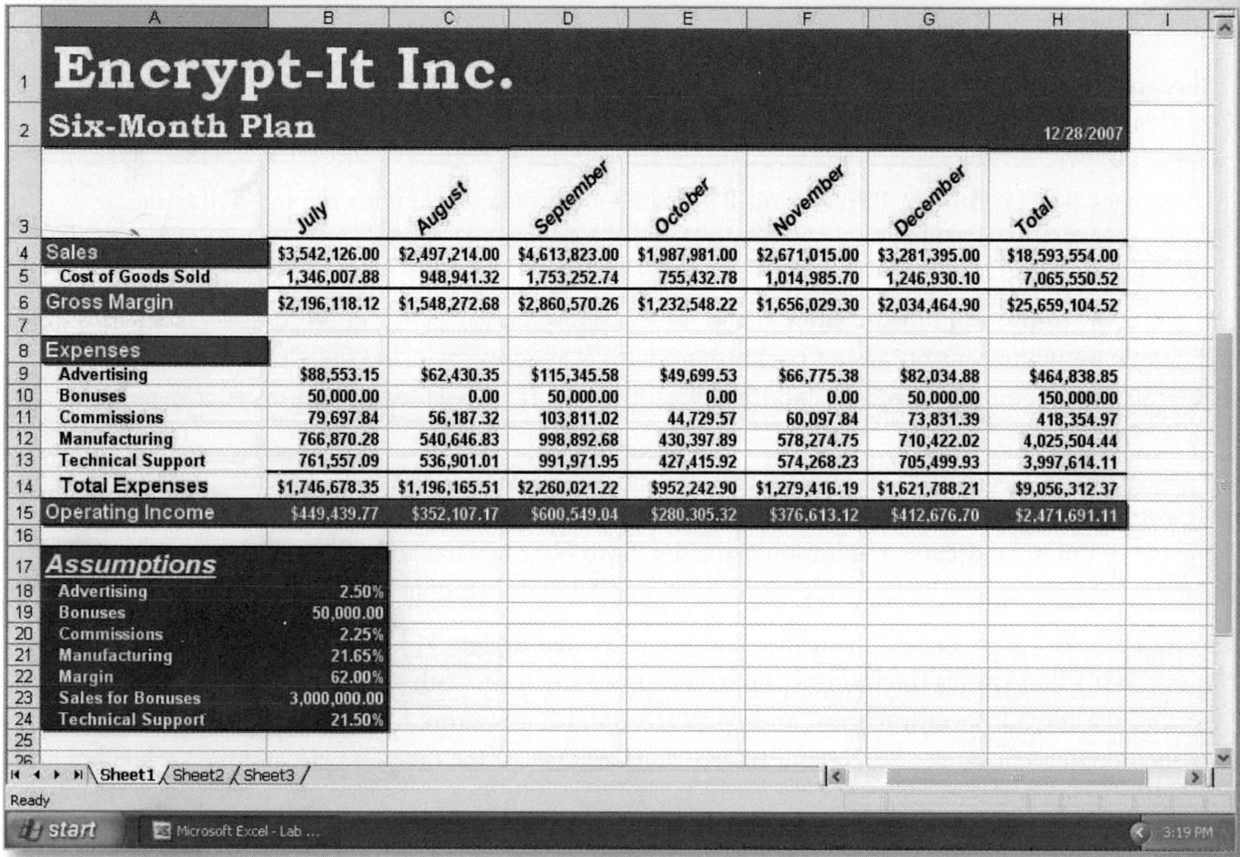

	A	B	C	D	E	F	G	H
1	Encrypt-It Inc.							
2	Six-Month Plan							12/28/2007
3		July	August	September	October	November	December	Total
4	Sales	$3,542,126.00	$2,497,214.00	$4,613,823.00	$1,987,981.00	$2,671,015.00	$3,281,395.00	$18,593,554.00
5	Cost of Goods Sold	1,346,007.88	948,941.32	1,753,252.74	755,432.78	1,014,985.70	1,246,930.10	7,065,550.52
6	Gross Margin	$2,196,118.12	$1,548,272.68	$2,860,570.26	$1,232,548.22	$1,656,029.30	$2,034,464.90	$25,659,104.52
7								
8	Expenses							
9	Advertising	$88,553.15	$62,430.35	$115,345.58	$49,699.53	$66,775.38	$82,034.88	$464,838.85
10	Bonuses	50,000.00	0.00	50,000.00	0.00	0.00	50,000.00	150,000.00
11	Commissions	79,697.84	56,187.32	103,811.02	44,729.57	60,097.84	73,831.39	418,354.97
12	Manufacturing	766,870.28	540,646.83	998,892.68	430,397.89	578,274.75	710,422.02	4,025,504.44
13	Technical Support	761,557.09	536,901.01	991,971.95	427,415.92	574,268.23	705,499.93	3,997,614.11
14	Total Expenses	$1,746,678.35	$1,196,165.51	$2,260,021.22	$952,242.90	$1,279,416.19	$1,621,788.21	$9,056,312.37
15	Operating Income	$449,439.77	$352,107.17	$600,549.04	$280,305.32	$376,613.12	$412,676.70	$2,471,691.11

	A	B
17	Assumptions	
18	Advertising	2.50%
19	Bonuses	50,000.00
20	Commissions	2.25%
21	Manufacturing	21.65%
22	Margin	62.00%
23	Sales for Bonuses	3,000,000.00
24	Technical Support	21.50%

Sheet1 / Sheet2 / Sheet3

FIGURE 3-85

10. Determine the row totals in the range H4:H15.
11. Format the worksheet as follows so that it resembles Figure 3-85:
    a. Worksheet title and subtitle
        1. Font type — Bookman Old Style
        2. Font size — title 36; subtitle 20
        3. Background color (range A1:J2) — red
        4. Font color — white
        5. Border — Shadow style 14
    b. Row titles
        1. Cells A4, A6, and A8 — 12-point white font on a red background with a Shadow style 14
        2. Cell A14 — 12-point
        3. Cell A15 — 12-point white font on a red background
        4. Indent text in cell A5, range A9:A14, and range A18:A24
    c. Operating Income row — white font on a red background with a Shadow style 14

(continued)

Projected Quarterly Report *(continued)*

d. Borders
   1. Draw a thick bottom border across ranges B5:H5 and B13:H13

e. Data
   1. Ranges B4:H4, B6:H6, B9:H9, and B14:H15 — Currency style with a fixed dollar sign
   2. Ranges B5:H5, B10:H13 — Comma style with two decimal places

f. Assumptions Table
   1. Title — 16-point italic and underlined
   2. Table — white font on a blue background with a Shadow style 14

12. Enter your name, course, computer laboratory assignment (Lab 3-1), date, and instructor name in the range A28:A32.
13. Save the workbook using the file name Lab 3-1 Part 1 Encrypt-It Six-Month Plan.
14. Preview and print the worksheet in landscape orientation using the Fit to option. Preview and print the formulas version in landscape orientation using the Fit to option. Change the display back to the values version.
15. Save the workbook using the same file name as in Step 13 and then quit Excel.

Instructions Part 2: Start Excel. Open the workbook created in Part 1. Draw a Pie chart with a 3-D visual effect (Figure 3-86) that shows the monthly contribution to the six-month operating income. That is, chart the nonadjacent range B3:G3 (month names) and B15:G15 (month operating incomes). Do the following:

1. Select the nonadjacent ranges B3:G3 and B15:G15. That is, select the range B3:G3 and then while holding down the CTRL key select the range B15:G15.
2. Click the Chart Wizard button on the Standard toolbar and select Pie in the Chart type list and Pie with a 3-D visual effect (column 2, row 1) in the Chart sub-type area.
3. Add the chart title `Monthly Contribution to Six-Month Operating Income`. Do not show a legend. Show the percentage and category names in the labels. Show leader lines.
4. Create the chart on a separate sheet.

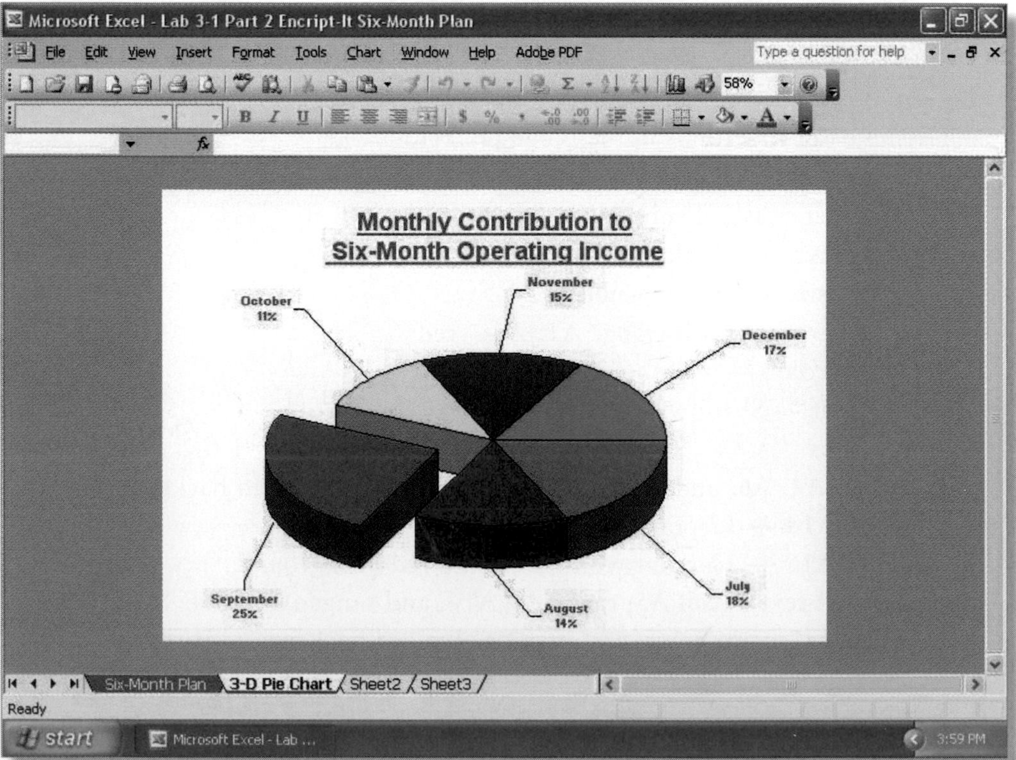

FIGURE 3-86

In the Lab

5. Format the chart title to 24-point bold red font with an underline. Use the ENTER key to place the chart title on separate lines.
6. Change the pie slice colors as shown in Figure 3-86. Explode the month slice with the greatest contribution to the six-month operating income. Change the pie chart elevation to 30 and the rotation to 90.
7. Change the data labels to 12-point bold red font. Drag the data labels away from each slice as shown in Figure 3-86.
8. Rename the tabs as follows: Chart1 to `3-D Pie Chart`; Sheet1 to `Six-Month Plan`. Rearrange the tabs so the Six-Month Plan tab is to the left of the 3-D Pie Chart tab. Color the tabs red and dark red as shown in Figure 3-86.
9. Save the workbook using the file name Lab 3-1 Part 2 Encrypt-It Six-Month Plan.
10. Print both sheets and quit Excel.

Table 3-11 Encrypt-It Inc. What-If Analyses Data

	Case 1	Case 2	Case 3
Advertising	3.50%	3.75%	1.25%
Commissions	5.25%	3.25%	2.75%
Manufacturing	20.00%	19.50%	18.50%
Margin	58.00%	65.00%	61.00%
Technical Support	11.50%	18.75%	20.00%

Instructions Part 3: Start Excel. Open the workbook created in Part 2. If the 3-D Column chart is on the screen, click the Six-Month Plan tab to display the worksheet shown in Figure 3-85 on page EX 213. Using the numbers in the Table 3-11, analyze the effect of changing the assumptions in rows 18 through 24 on the total operating income in cell H15. Print only the worksheet for each case.

The total operating incomes in cell H15 are:
Case 1 = $3,150,355.84; Case 2 = $3,522,226.92; Case 3 = $3,289,807.49.

Close the workbook Lab 3-1 Part 2 Encrypt-It Six-Month Plan without saving it, and then reopen it. Use the Goal Seek command to determine the margin percentage (cell B22) that would result in a total operating income of $3,000,000 in cell H15. You should end up with a margin percentage of 64.84%. Print only the worksheet. Save the workbook using the file name, Lab 3-1 Part 3 Encrypt-It Six-Month Plan.

2 Modifying the Weekly Payroll Worksheet

Problem: You have been asked to modify the payroll workbook developed in Project 2 (see Figure 2-1 on page EX 67), so that it appears as shown in Figure 3-87 on the next page. If you did not complete Project 2, ask your instructor for a copy of The Awesome Music Store Weekly Payroll Report or complete Project 2 before you begin this exercise.

The major modifications to the payroll report to be made in this exercise include: (1) reformatting the worksheet; (2) adding computations of time-and-a-half for hours worked greater than 40; (3) removing the conditional formatting assigned to the range E4:E9; (4) adding calculations to charge no federal tax in certain situations; (5) adding Social Security and Medicare deductions; (6) adding and deleting employees; and (7) changing employee information.

Instructions Part 1: Start Excel. Open the workbook, The Awesome Music Store Weekly Payroll Report, created in Project 2 (Figure 2-88 on page EX 132). Perform the following tasks.

1. Delete rows 11 through 13 to remove the statistics below the Totals row. Delete column B. Change all the row heights back to the default height (12.75). Select the entire sheet using the Select All button and then

(continued)

Modifying the Weekly Payroll Worksheet *(continued)*

	A	B	C	D	E	F	G	H	I	J	K	L
1	Social Security Tax	6.20%										
2	Medicare Tax	1.45%										
3	Maximum Social Security	$5,580										
4												
5	The Awesome Music Store											
6	Weekly Payroll Report	27-Dec-07										
7	Employee	Dependents	Rate per Hour	YTD Soc. Sec.	Hours Worked	Gross Pay	Soc. Sec.	Medicare	Federal Tax	State Tax	Net Pay	% Taxes
8	Blanco, Carlos	1	6.50	567.00	3.00	19.50	1.21	0.28	0.00	0.62	17.38	12.17%
9	Napolean, Claude	8	7.75	1,206.25	28.75	222.81	13.81	3.23	9.22	7.13	189.42	17.63%
10	Patterson, Tyler	3	10.25	812.34	16.50	169.13	10.49	2.45	20.57	5.41	130.20	29.89%
11	Sanchez, Carmen	2	13.25	5,580.00	46.50	659.19	0.00	9.56	123.00	21.09	505.53	30.39%
12	Zingovich, Arnold	3	14.50	5,579.00	55.00	906.25	1.00	13.14	168.00	29.00	695.11	30.37%
13	Tough, John	4	12.75	3,812.68	38.00	484.50	30.04	7.03	79.23	15.50	352.70	37.37%
14	Small, Richard	6	22.75	5,565.00	42.25	986.78	15.00	14.31	170.85	31.58	755.05	30.69%
15	Totals		87.75	23,122.27	230.00	3,448.16	71.55	50.00	570.86	110.34	2,645.41	30.35%
16												
17												
18												
19												

FIGURE 3-87

clear all remaining formats using the Formats command on the Clear submenu of the Edit menu. Bold the entire worksheet.

2. Insert four rows above row 1 by selecting rows 1 through 4, right-clicking the selection, and clicking Insert on the shortcut menu.
3. Change the row heights as follows: row 5 = 48.00; rows 6 and 7 = 24.00. One at a time, select cells C7, D7, and F7. For each cell, press the F2 key and then the ENTER key to display the column headings on multiple rows.
4. Enhance the worksheet title in cell A5 by using a 28-point green Arial Rounded MT Bold (or a similar font) font style as shown in Figure 3-87.
5. Insert a new column between columns C and D. Enter the new column D title `YTD Soc. Sec.` in cell D7. Insert two new columns between columns F and G. Enter the new column G title `Soc. Sec.` in cell G7. Enter the new column H title `Medicare` in cell H7.
6. Assign the NOW function to cell B6 and format it to the 14-Mar-01 style.
7. Change the column widths as follows: A = 25.00; D = 13.00; F through K = 9.71; and L = 8.43.
8. Delete row 12 (Smith, Willie). Change Carlos Blanco's (row 8) hours worked to 3. Change Claude Napolean's (row 9) number of dependents to 8 and rate per hour to $7.75. Change Carmen Sanchez's (row 11) hours worked to 46.5 and Arnold Zingovich's (row 12) hours worked to 55.
9. Freeze column A and rows 1 through 7. In column D, enter the YTD Soc. Sec. values listed in Table 3-12.
10. Insert two new rows immediately above the Totals row. Add the new employee data as listed in Table 3-13.

Table 3-12 The Awesome Music Store YTD Social Security Values

Employee	YTD Soc. Sec.
Blanco, Carlos	567.00
Napolean, Claude	1206.25
Patterson, Tyler	812.34
Sanchez, Carmen	5580.00
Zingovich, Arnold	5579.00

In the Lab

Table 3-13 New Employee Data

Employee	Dependents	Rate Per Hour	YTD Soc. Sec.	Hours Worked
Tough, John	4	12.75	3,812.68	38.00
Small, Richard	6	22.75	5,565.00	42.25

11. Center the range B6:B14. Use the Currency category in the Format Cells dialog box to assign a Comma style (no dollar signs) with two decimal places to the ranges C8:K15. Assign a Percent style and two decimal places to the range L8:L15. Draw a bottom border in the ranges A7:L7 and A14:L14.
12. As shown in Figure 3-87, enter and format the Social Security and Medicare tax information in the range A1:B3. Use format symbols where applicable.
13. Change the formulas to determine the gross pay in column F and the federal tax in column I as follows:
    a. In cell F8, enter an IF function that applies the following logic and then copy it to the range F9:F14.
    If Hours Worked <= 40, then Rate per Hour * Hours Worked, otherwise Rate per Hour * Hours Worked + 0.5 * Rate per Hour * (Hours Worked – 40) or =IF(E8 <= 40, C8 * E8, C8 * E8 + 0.5 * C8 *(E8 – 40))
    b. In cell I8, enter the IF function that applies the following logic and then copy it to the range I9:I14.
    If (Gross Pay – Dependents * 22.09 > 0, then 20% * (Gross Pay – Dependents * 22.09), otherwise 0 or +IF(F8 – B8 * 22.09 > 0, 20% * (F8 – B8 * 22.09), 0)
14. An employee pays Social Security tax only if his or her YTD Soc. Sec. in column D is less than the Maximum Social Security value in cell B3. Use the following logic to determine the Social Security tax for Carlos Blanco in cell G8 and then copy it to the range G9:G14.
    Soc. Sec. (cell G8): If Social Security Tax * Gross Pay + YTD Soc. Sec. > Maximum Social Security, then Maximum Social Security – YTD Soc. Sec., otherwise Social Security Tax * Gross Pay or =IF($B$1 * F8 + D8 >= $B$3, $B$3 – D8, $B$1 * F8)
    Use absolute cell references for the Social Security Tax and Maximum Social Security values.
15. In cell H8, enter the following formula and then copy it to the range H9:H14:
    Medicare (cell H8) = Medicare Tax * Gross Pay or =$B$2 * F8
    Use an absolute cell reference for the Medicare Tax value.
16. In cell K8, enter the following formula and copy it to the range K9:K14:
    Net Pay (K8) = Gross Pay – (Soc. Sec. + Medicare + Federal Tax + State Tax) or =F8 – (G8 + H8 + I8 + J8)
17. In cell L8, enter the following formula and copy it to the range L9:L14:
    % Taxes (cell L8) = (Soc. Sec. + Medicare + Federal Tax + State Tax) / Gross Pay or = (G8 + H8 + I8 + J8) / F8
18. Determine any new totals as shown in row 15 in Figure 3-87. Unfreeze the worksheet.
19. Use alignment, borders, and drop shadows to format the worksheet as shown in Figure 3-87.
20. Enter your name, course, laboratory assignment (Lab 3-2), date, and instructor name in the range A17:A21.
21. Save the workbook using the file name, Lab 3-2 The Awesome Music Store Weekly Payroll Report.
22. Use the Zoom box on the Standard toolbar to change the view of the worksheet. One by one, select all the percents in the Zoom list. When you are done, return the worksheet to 100% magnification.
23. Use the Page Setup command on the File menu to change the orientation to landscape. Preview the worksheet. If number signs appear in place of numbers in any columns, adjust the column widths. Print the worksheet. Save the worksheet using the same file name.
24. Preview and print the formulas version (CTRL+`) in landscape orientation using the Fit to option button in the Page Setup dialog box. Close the worksheet without saving the latest changes.

(continued)

Modifying the Weekly Payroll Worksheet *(continued)*

Instructions Part 2: Start Excel. Open Lab 3-2 The Awesome Music Store Weekly Payroll Report. Using the numbers in Table 3-14, analyze the effect of changing the Medicare tax in cell B2. Print the worksheet for each case. The first case should result in a total Medicare tax in cell H15 of $129.31. The second case should result in a total Medicare tax of $184.48. Close the workbook without saving changes.

Table 3-14 The Awesome Music Store Medicare Tax Cases

Case	Medicare Tax
1	3.75%
2	5.35%

Instructions Part 3: Hand in your handwritten results for this part to your instructor.

1. Start Excel. Open Lab 3-2 The Awesome Music Store Weekly Payroll Report. Select cell F8. Write down the formula that Excel displays in the formula bar. Select the range C8:C14. Point to the border surrounding the range and drag the selection to the range D17:D23. Click cell F8, and write down the formula that Excel displays in the formula bar below the one you wrote down earlier. Compare the two formulas. What can you conclude about how Excel responds when you move cells involved in a formula? Click the Undo button on the Standard toolbar.
2. Right-click the range C8:C14 and then click Delete on the shortcut menu. When Excel displays the Delete dialog box, click Shift cells left and then click the OK button. What does Excel display in cell F8? Use the Type a question for help box on the menu bar to find a definition of the result in cell F8. Write down the definition. Click the Undo button on the Standard toolbar.
3. Right-click the range C8:C14 and then click Insert on the shortcut menu. When Excel displays the Insert dialog box, click Shift cells right and then click the OK button. What does Excel display in the formula bar when you click cell F8? What does Excel display in the formula bar when you click cell G8? What can you conclude about how Excel responds when you insert cells next to cells involved in a formula? Close the workbook without saving the changes.

3 Five-Year Financial Projection

Problem: As a summer intern at E-Book.com, you have been asked to create a worksheet that will project the annual gross margin, expenses, operating income, income taxes, and net income for the next five years based on the assumptions in Table 3-15. The desired worksheet is shown in Figure 3-88 on page EX 220.

Table 3-15 E-Book.com Assumptions

Units Sold in Previous Year	14,231,981
Unit Cost	$15.10
Annual Sales Growth	2.70%
Annual Price Decrease	1.15%
Margin	40.40%

Instructions Part 1: Start Excel and complete the following steps to create the worksheet shown in Figure 3-88.

1. Bold the entire worksheet. Enter the worksheet titles in cells A8 and A9. Format the worksheet title in cell A8 to 28-point Ravie (or a similar font). Format the worksheet subtitle in cell A9 to 20-point Rockwell (or a similar font). Enter the system date in cell F9 using the NOW function. Format the date to the 14-Mar 2001 style.
2. Enter the five column titles Year 1 through Year 5 in the range B10:F10 by entering Year 1 in cell B10 and then dragging cell B10's fill handle through the range C10:F10. Next, format cell B10 as follows: (a) center and italicize cell B10; and (b) rotate its contents 45°. Use the Format Painter button to copy the format assigned to cell B10 to the range C10:F10.

In the Lab

3. Change the following column widths: A = 25.00 characters; B through F = 15.00 characters. Change the heights of rows 7, 10, and 21 to 36.00 points.
4. Enter the row titles in the range A11:A24. Change the font in cells A14, A20, A22, and A24 to 14-point Rockwell (or a similar font). Add thick bottom borders to the ranges A10:F10 and B12:F12.
5. Enter the table title `Assumptions` in cell A1. Enter the assumptions in Table 3-15 in the range A2:B6. Use format symbols when entering the numbers. Change the font size of the table title to 14-point and underline it.
6. Use the Number category in the Format Cells dialog box to assign the Comma style with no decimal places and negative numbers enclosed in parentheses to the range B11:F24.
7. Complete the following entries:
   a. Year 1 Sales (cell B11) = Units Sold in Previous Year * (Unit Cost / (1 – Margin)) or =B2 * (B3 / (1 – B6))
   b. Year 2 Sales (cell C11) = Year 1 Sales * (1 + Annual Sales Growth) * (1 – Annual Price Decrease) or =B11 * (1 + $B$4) * (1 – $B$5)
   c. Copy cell C11 to the range D11:F11.
   d. Year 1 Cost of Goods Sold (cell B12) = Year 1 Sales – (Year 1 Sales * Margin) or =B11 * (1 – $B$6)
   e. Copy cell B12 to the range C12:F12.
   f. Gross Margin (cell B13) = Year 1 Sales – Year 1 Cost of Goods Sold or =B11 – B12
   g. Copy cell B13 to the range C13:F13.
   h. Year 1 Administrative (cell B15) = 500 + 11% * Year 1 Sales or =500 + 11% * B11
   i. Copy cell B15 to the range C15:F15.
   j. Commissions (row 16): Year 1 = 6,325,000; Year 2 = 5,600,000; Year 3 = 4,550,000; Year 4 = 4,000,000; Year 5 = 4,250,000
   k. Year 1 Marketing (cell B17) = 4,250,000
   l. Year 2 Marketing (cell C17) = Year 1 Marketing + 10% * Year 1 Marketing or =B17 * (1 + 10%)
   m. Copy cell C17 to the range D17:F17.
   n. Year 1 Miscellaneous (cell B18) = 5% * Year 1 Sales or =5% * B11
   o. Copy cell B18 to the range C18:F18.
   p. Year 1 Technical Support (cell B19) = 21.5% * Year 1 Sales or =21.5% * B11
   q. Copy cell B19 to the range C19:F19.
   r. Year 1 Total Expenses (cell B20) or =SUM(B15:B19)
   s. Copy cell B20 to the range C20:F20.
   t. Year 1 Operating Income (cell B22) = Year 1 Gross Margin – Year 1 Total Expenses or =B13 – B20
   u. Copy cell B22 to the range C22:F22.
   v. Year 1 Income Taxes (cell B23): If Year 1 Operating Income is less than 0, then Year 1 Income Taxes equal 0; otherwise Year 1 Income Taxes equal 35% * Year 1 Operating Income or =IF(B22 < 0, 0, 35% * B22)
   w. Copy cell B23 to the range C23:F23.
   x. Year 1 Net Income (cell B24) = Year 1 Operating Income – Year 1 Income Taxes or =B22 – B23
   y. Copy cell B24 to the range C24:F24.
8. Change the background colors and add drop shadows as shown in Figure 3-88. Use light green (column 4, row 5) for the background colors.
9. Enter your name, course, laboratory assignment (Lab 3-3), date, and instructor name in the range A27:A31. Save the workbook using the file name, Lab 3-3 E-Book Five-Year Financial Projection.

(continued)

Five-Year Financial Projection *(continued)*

10. Use the Page Setup command on the File menu to fit the printout on one page in portrait orientation. Preview and print the worksheet. Preview and print the formulas version (CTRL+`) of the worksheet in landscape orientation using the Fit to option button in the Page Setup dialog box. After printing the formulas version, reset the print scaling to 100%. Press CTRL+` to instruct Excel to display the values version of the worksheet. Save the workbook again.
11. Zoom to: (a) 200%; (b) 75%; (c) 25%; and (d) 100%.

	A	B	C	D	E	F
1	Assumptions					
2	Units Sold in Previous Year	14,231,981				
3	Unit Cost	$15.10				
4	Annual Sales Growth	2.70%				
5	Annual Price Decrease	1.15%				
6	Margin	40.40%				
7						
8	E-Book.com					
9	Five-Year Financial Projection					27-Dec-2007
10		Year 1	Year 2	Year 3	Year 4	Year 5
11	Sales	360,575,358	366,052,317	371,612,469	377,257,076	382,987,423
12	Cost of Goods Sold	214,902,913	218,167,181	221,481,031	224,845,217	228,260,504
13	Gross Margin	145,672,444	147,885,136	150,131,437	152,411,859	154,726,919
14	Expenses					
15	Administrative	39,663,789	40,266,255	40,877,872	41,498,778	42,129,116
16	Commissions	6,325,000	5,600,000	4,550,000	4,000,000	4,250,000
17	Marketing	4,250,000	4,675,000	5,142,500	5,656,750	6,222,425
18	Miscellaneous	18,028,768	18,302,616	18,580,623	18,862,854	19,149,371
19	Technical Support	77,523,702	78,701,248	79,896,681	81,110,271	82,342,296
20	Total Expenses	145,791,259	147,545,119	149,047,676	151,128,654	154,093,208
21						
22	Operating Income	(118,815)	340,017	1,083,762	1,283,205	633,710
23	Income Taxes	0	119,006	379,317	449,122	221,799
24	Net Income	(118,815)	221,011	704,445	834,083	411,912

Five-Year Financial Projection / 3-D Column Chart / Sheet2 / Shee

Ready

FIGURE 3-88

Instructions Part 2: Start Excel. Open the workbook created in Part 1. Draw a 3-D Column chart (Figure 3-89) that compares the projected net incomes for each of the five years. Use the nonadjacent ranges B10:F10 and B24:F24 to create the 3-D Column chart on a new sheet. Do not show a legend, add the chart title, and format it as shown in Figure 3-89. To change the color of the wall, right-click the wall behind the columns and then click Format Walls on the shortcut menu. To change the color of the columns, right-click a column and then click Format Data Series on the shortcut menu. Rename and rearrange the sheets, and color their tabs as shown in Figure 3-89. Save the workbook using the same file name (Lab 3-3 E-Book Five-Year Financial Projection) as defined in Part 1. Print both sheets.

Instructions Part 3: Start Excel. Open the workbook created in Part 2. If the 3-D Column chart is on the screen, click the Five-Year Financial Projection tab to view the worksheet. Divide the window into two panes by dragging the horizontal split box between rows 6 and 7. Use the scroll bars to show both the top and bottom of the worksheet.

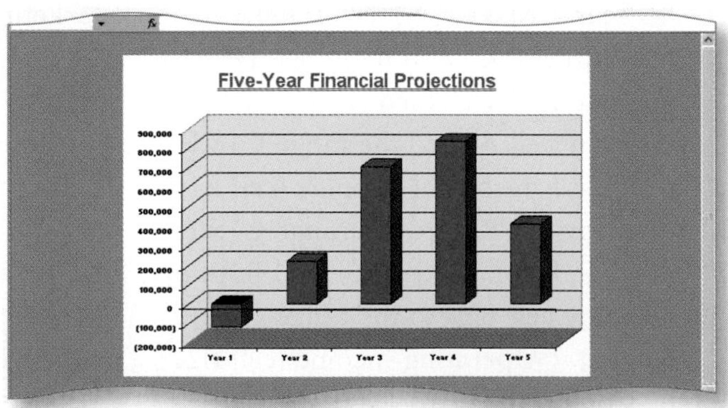

FIGURE 3-89

Using the numbers in columns 2 and 3 of Table 3-16, analyze the effect of changing the annual sales growth (cell B4) and annual price decrease (cell B5) on the net incomes in row 24. The resulting answers are in column 4 of Table 3-16. Print both the worksheet and chart for each case.

Close the workbook without saving it, and then reopen it. Use the Goal Seek command to determine a margin (cell B6) that would result in a Year 5 net income of $4,000,000 (cell F24). You should end up with a margin of 41.74% in cell B6. After you complete the goal seeking, print only the worksheet. Do not save the workbook with the latest changes.

Table 3-16 E-Book.com Data to Analyze and Results

Case	Annual Sales Growth	Annual Price Decrease	Year 5 Resulting Net Income In Cell F24
1	8.35%	4.25%	1,066,287
2	11.25%	-5.00%	5,847,672
3	27.25%	11.65%	4,050,972

Cases and Places

The difficulty of the case studies varies:

■ are the least difficult and ■■ are more difficult. Each exercise has a cross-curricular designation:

Math Social Studies Science Language Arts Art/Music Business Health

1 The Johannesburg Daily is a small newspaper that publishes stories of local interest. Revenues are earned from subscriptions and the sale of advertising space. A fixed percentage of the proceeds are spent on marketing, payroll, commissions (advertising sales only), production costs, and reportorial expenses. The Daily's editor has summarized the paper's expenditures over the past year and the anticipated income from subscriptions and advertising on a bimonthly basis as shown in Table 3-17.

With the data, you have been asked to prepare a worksheet for the next shareholder's meeting showing total revenues, total expenditures, and operating incomes for each bimonthly period. Include a 3-D Pie chart that illustrates each bimonthly operating income contribution to the total operating income. Use the concepts and techniques presented in this project to create and format the worksheet and chart.

Table 3-17 Johannesburg Daily Bimonthly Projected Earnings and Expenditures

	February	April	June	August	October	December
Revenue						
Subscriptions	9526.34	7856.25	12908.60	14786.50	10987.45	11900.35
Advertising	3478.12	4525.00	5689.12	4067.36	6012.78	8163.20
Assumptions						
Marketing	12.60%					
Payroll	24.90%					
Commissions on Advertising	2.75%					
Production Costs	9.75%					
Reportorial Expenses	3.00%					

One shareholder lobbied to reduce marketing expenditures by 3% and payroll costs by 5%. Perform a what-if-analysis reflecting the proposed changes in expenditure assumptions. The reduction in expenditures should result in a total operating income of $56,814.64 or an increase of $7,992.09.

Cases and Places

2 A government agency plans to conduct experiments that will result in some radioactive waste. Although the isotopes will break apart into atoms of other elements over time, agency watchdogs are concerned about containment costs while the material still is radioactive. The agency director has asked you to prepare a worksheet showing the amount of radioactive material remaining, containment costs, estimated agency appropriations, and the percentage of appropriations that will be spent on containment every year for the next decade. The director has outlined the desired worksheet as shown in Table 3-18.

These formulas have been supplied:

Formula A: Amount Remaining = Original Amount x $0.5^{(\text{Number of Years Stored / Half-Life})}$

Formula B: Containment Costs = Containment Cost Per Kilogram x Total Amount Remaining

Formula C: Estimated Appropriations = Appropriations x $(1 + \text{Estimated Yearly Increase})^{\text{Number of Years Stored}}$

Formula D: Percentage Spent on Containment = Containment Costs / Estimated Appropriations

The director has asked you to include a function that prints "Acceptable" below the percentage spent on containment whenever the percentage is less than 1%, otherwise print "Not Acceptable." Use the concepts and techniques presented in this project to create and format the worksheets.

Table 3-18 Cost of Storing Radioactive Isotopes

	Number of Years Stored				
Number of Years Stored	1	2	3	...	10
Amount of Isotope X Remaining (in kg)	Formula A	→	→	→	→
Amount of Isotope Y Remaining (in kg)	Formula A	→	→	→	→
Total Remaining (in kg)	—	—	—	—	—
Containment Costs	Formula B	→	→	→	→
Estimated Appropriations	Formula C	→	→	→	→
Percentage Spent on Containment	Formula D	→	→	→	→
	Message	→	→	→	→
Assumptions					
Original Amount of Isotope X Remaining (in kg)		700			
Half-Life of Isotope X (in years)		1			
Containment Cost per Kilogram		$1,000.00			
Estimated Yearly Increase		8%			
Original Amount of Isotope Y Remaining (in kg)		2,500			
Half-Life of Isotope Y (in years)		0.5			
Appropriations		$5,000,000.00			

Cases and Places

3 Sweet Notes is one of the largest musical instrument and services company in the Northwest. The company generates revenue from the sale of musical instruments and services. A fixed percentage of the total net revenue is spent on administrative, quarterly bonus if the total net revenue for the quarter exceeds $12,000,000, equipment, marketing, payroll, and production expenses. The company's projected receipts and expenditures for the next four quarters are shown in Table 3-19.

With this data, you have been asked to prepare a worksheet and chart similar to Figure 3-1 on page EX 147 for the next management team meeting. The worksheet should show total net revenues, total expenditures, and operating income for each quarterly period. Include a 3-D Pie chart on a separate sheet that shows the quarterly income contributions to the annual operating income. Use the concepts and techniques presented in this project to create and format the worksheet and chart.

During the meeting, one manager lobbied to reduce marketing expenditures by 1.75% and payroll costs by 2.25%. Perform a what-if analysis reflecting the proposed changes in expenditures. The changes should result in an operating income of $13,599,890 for the year. Using the original assumptions shown in Table 3-19, another manager asked to what extent marketing would have to be reduced to generate an annual operating income of $15,000,000. Marketing would need to be reduced by 6.62%, from 15.50% to 8.88%.

Table 3-19 Sweet Notes Musical Instruments and Services Projected Annual Revenues and Expenses by Quarter

Revenues	Quarter 1	Quarter 2	Quarter 3	Quarter 4
Sales	9,247,999	11,234,813	14,567,102	8,619,201
Consulting	1,678,153	2,901,988	3,718,231	1,569,378
Expenditures				
Administrative	11.50%			
Bonus	$200,000.00			
Equipment	18.75%			
Marketing	15.50%			
Payroll	24.85%			
Production	7.25%			
Revenue for Bonus	$12,000,000.00			

Cases and Places

4 **Working Together** Your group has been asked to develop a worksheet for Outland Aluminum that shows annual growth for the next three years based on the previous year's sales and growth data. The data and general layout of the worksheet, including the totals, are shown in Table 3-20.

Table 3-20 Outland Aluminum Sales Data and General Layout

	Previous Year	Year 1	Year 2	Year 3	Total
Revenue	Formula A	Formula D →		→	—
Cost of Goods Sold	Formula B →			→	—
Gross Margin	Formula C →			→	—
Assumptions					
Previous Year Revenue	$22,235,560.00				
Annual Growth Rate	0.00%	7.75%	4.00%	4.35%	
Annual Cost Rate	41.25%	44.00%	41.00%	40.00%	
Extra	2.75%	2.15%	5.15%	3.50%	

Enter the formulas shown in Table 3-21 in the locations shown in Table 3-20. Copy Formula B, C, and D to the remaining years.

Table 3-21 Outland Aluminum Formulas

Formula A = Previous Year Revenue
Formula B = IF(Annual Growth Rate < 0, Annual Revenue * (Annual Cost Rate + Extra), Annual Revenue * Annual Cost Rate)
Formula C = Annual Revenue – Cost of Goods Sold
Formula D = Annual Revenue * (1 + Annual Growth Rate)

Have each member of your team submit a sketch of the proposed worksheet and then implement the best one. The gross margin for the previous year and next three years should equal $56,782,097.06. Include an embedded exploded 3-D Pie chart that shows the contribution of each year to the total gross margin. Use the concepts and techniques developed in the first three projects to create and format the worksheet and embedded 3-D Pie chart.

Use the Goal Seek command to determine the Year 1 annual growth rate that will generate a total gross margin of $60,000,000.00. Your team should end up with a Year 1 annual growth rate of 15.68%. Hand in the sketches submitted by each team member and a printout of the modified worksheet and embedded 3-D Pie chart.

Creating Static and Dynamic Web Pages Using Excel

CASE PERSPECTIVE

Angelo's Pizzeria, a domestic restaurant chain with four Midwest locations, has experienced significant growth since it began marketing its healthy-food menu. In three years, the company's annual sales have skyrocketed from less than $1 million to over $10 million.

Denise Waters is a spreadsheet specialist at the national headquarters for Angelo's Pizzeria. One of Denise's responsibilities is a workbook that summarizes quarterly sales (Figure 1a on the next page). In the past, Denise printed the worksheet and chart, sent it out to make copies of it, and then mailed it to her distribution list.

Angelo's Pizzeria recently upgraded to Office 2003 because of its Web and collaboration capabilities. After attending an Office 2003 training session, Denise had a great idea and called you for help. She would like to save the Excel worksheet and 3-D Bar chart (Figure 1a) on the company's intranet as a static Web page (Figure 1b), so that lower-level management on the distribution list can display it using a browser. She also suggested publishing the same workbook on the company's intranet as a dynamic (interactive) Web page (Figure 1c), so the higher-level management could use its browser to manipulate the data in the worksheet without requiring Excel.

Finally, Denise wants both the static and dynamic Web pages saved as single files, also called Single File Web Page format, rather than in the traditional file and folder format, called Web Page format.

As you read through this Web feature, you will learn how to create static and dynamic Web pages from workbooks in Excel and then display the results using a browser.

Objectives

You will have mastered the material in this Web feature when you can:

- Publish a worksheet and chart as a static or a dynamic Web page
- Display Web pages published in Excel in a browser
- Manipulate the data in a published Web page using a browser
- Complete file management tasks within Excel

Introduction

Excel provides fast, easy methods for saving workbooks as Web pages that can be stored on the World Wide Web, a company's intranet, or a local hard disk. A user then can display the workbook using a browser, rather than Excel.

You can save a workbook, or a portion of a workbook, as a static Web page or a dynamic Web page. A **static Web page**, also called a **noninteractive Web page** or **view-only Web page**, is a snapshot of the workbook. It is similar to a printed report in that you can view it through your browser, but you cannot modify it. In the browser window, the workbook appears as it would in Microsoft Excel, including sheet tabs that you can click to switch between worksheets. A **dynamic Web page**, also called an **interactive Web page**, includes the interactivity and functionality of the workbook. For example, with a dynamic Web page, you can view a copy of the worksheet in your browser and then enter formulas, reformat cells, and change values in the worksheet to perform a what-if analysis. A user does not need Excel on his or her computer to complete these tasks.

As illustrated in Figure 1, this Web feature shows you how to save a workbook (Figure 1a) as a static Web page (Figure 1b) and view it using your browser. Then, using the same workbook, the steps show how to save it as a dynamic Web page (Figure 1c), view it using your browser, and then change values to test the Web page's interactivity and functionality.

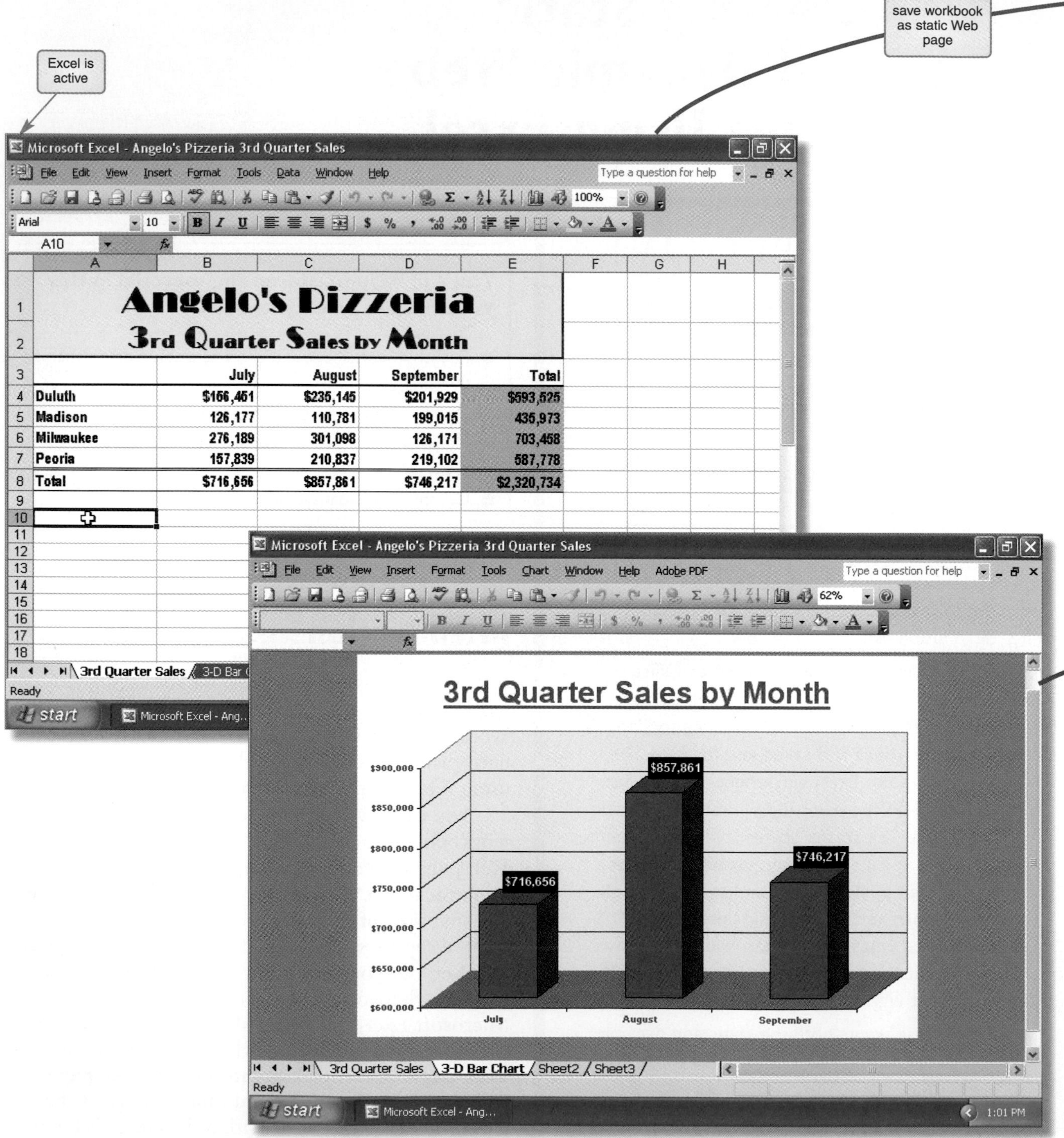

(a) Workbook Viewed in Excel

FIGURE 1

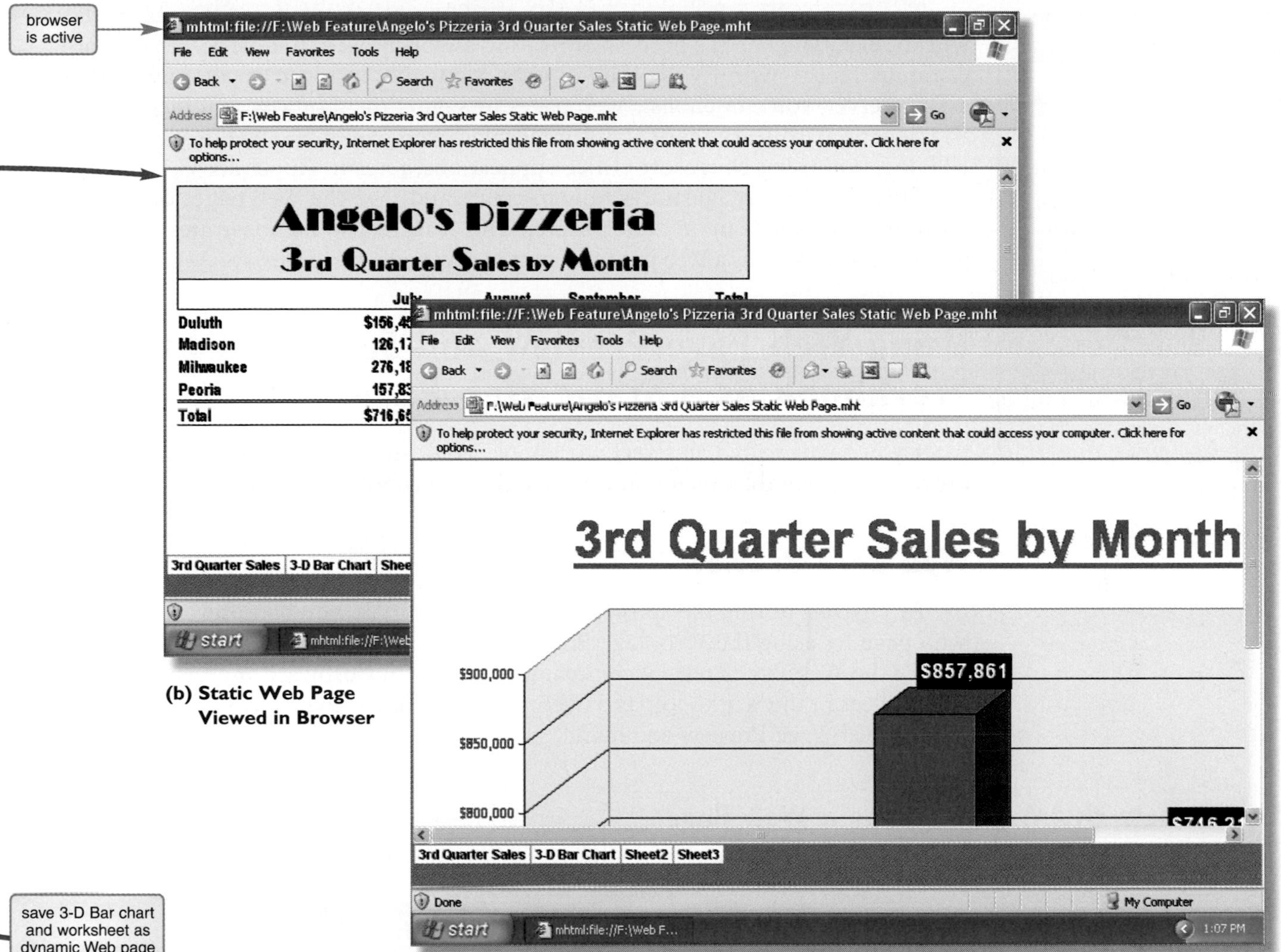

browser is active

mhtml:file://F:\Web Feature\Angelo's Pizzeria 3rd Quarter Sales Static Web Page.mht

File Edit View Favorites Tools Help

Back Search Favorites

Address F:\Web Feature\Angelo's Pizzeria 3rd Quarter Sales Static Web Page.mht Go

To help protect your security, Internet Explorer has restricted this file from showing active content that could access your computer. Click here for options...

Angelo's Pizzeria

3rd Quarter Sales by Month

Duluth $156,45
Madison 126,17
Milwaukee 276,18
Peoria 157,83
Total $716,65

3rd Quarter Sales | 3-D Bar Chart | Shee

start mhtml:file://F:\Web

mhtml:file://F:\Web Feature\Angelo's Pizzeria 3rd Quarter Sales Static Web Page.mht

File Edit View Favorites Tools Help

Back Search Favorites

Address F:\Web Feature\Angelo's Pizzeria 3rd Quarter Sales Static Web Page.mht Go

To help protect your security, Internet Explorer has restricted this file from showing active content that could access your computer. Click here for options...

3rd Quarter Sales by Month

$900,000
$850,000
$800,000
$857,861

3rd Quarter Sales | 3-D Bar Chart | Sheet2 | Sheet3

Done My Computer

start mhtml:file://F:\Web F... 1:07 PM

(b) Static Web Page Viewed in Browser

save 3-D Bar chart and worksheet as dynamic Web page

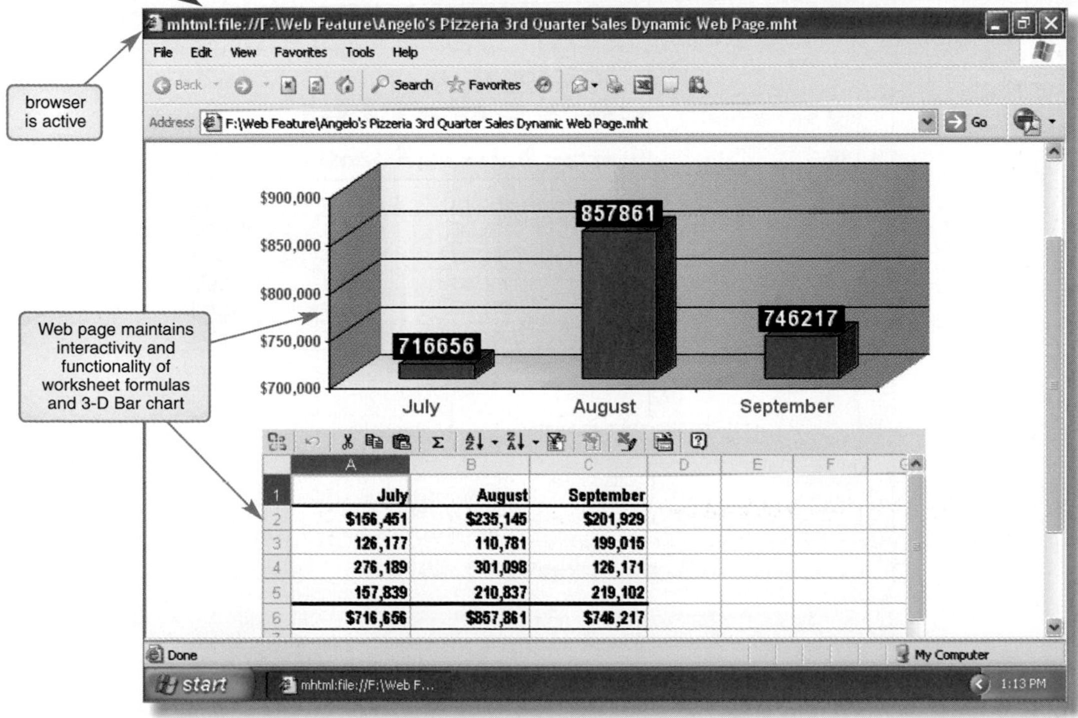

(c) Dynamic Web Page Viewed in Browser

Q & A

Q: Can any type of file be saved to a Web folder or FTP location?

A: You can save any type of file to a Web folder or on an FTP location, just as you would save to a folder on your hard disk. Web folders and FTP locations are particularly useful because they appear as standard folders in Windows Explorer or in the Save in list. For additional information, see Appendix C.

The Save as Web Page command on the File menu allows you to **publish workbooks**, which is the process of making a workbook available to others; for example, on the World Wide Web or on a company's intranet. If you have access to a Web server, you can publish Web pages by saving them in a Web folder or on an FTP location. To learn more about publishing Web pages in a Web folder or on an FTP location using Microsoft Office applications, refer to Appendix C.

This Web feature illustrates how to create and save the Web pages on a USB flash drive, rather than on a Web server. This feature also demonstrates how to preview a workbook as a Web page and create a new folder using the Save As dialog box.

Using Web Page Preview and Saving an Excel Workbook as a Static Web Page

After you have created an Excel workbook, you can preview it as a Web page. If the preview is acceptable, then you can save the workbook as a Web page.

Web Page Preview

At anytime during the construction of a workbook, you can preview it as a Web page by using the Web Page Preview command on the File menu. When you invoke the Web Page Preview command, it starts your browser and displays the active sheet in the workbook as a Web page. The following steps show how to use the Web Page Preview command.

To Preview the Workbook as a Web Page

1

- **Connect a USB flash drive to one of the computer's USB ports.**
- **Start Excel and then open the workbook, Angelo's Pizzeria 3rd Quarter Sales from the Data Files for students.**
- **Click File on the menu bar.**

Excel starts and opens the workbook, Angelo's Pizzeria 3rd Quarter Sales. The workbook is made up of two sheets: a worksheet and a chart. (If your system does not have Broadway font, the worksheet titles will display in a different font.) Excel displays the File menu (Figure 2).

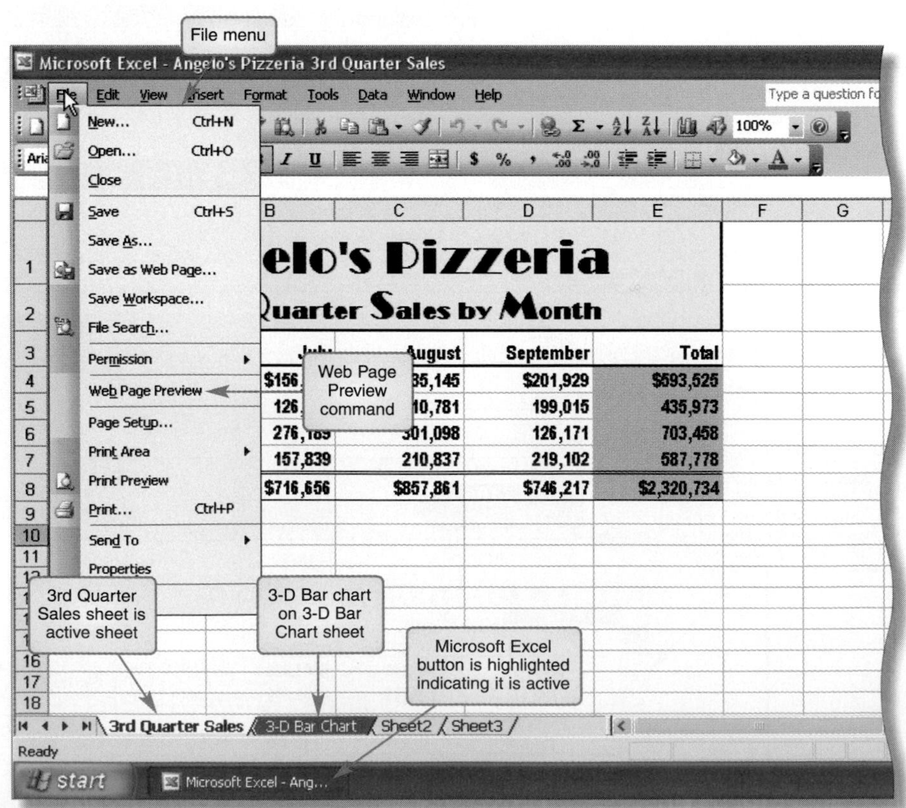

FIGURE 2

2

• **Click Web Page Preview.**

Excel starts your browser. The browser displays a preview of how the 3rd Quarter Sales sheet will appear as a Web page (Figure 3). The Web page preview in the browser is nearly identical to the display of the worksheet in Excel. A highlighted browser button appears on the Windows taskbar indicating it is active. The Excel button on the Windows taskbar no longer is highlighted.

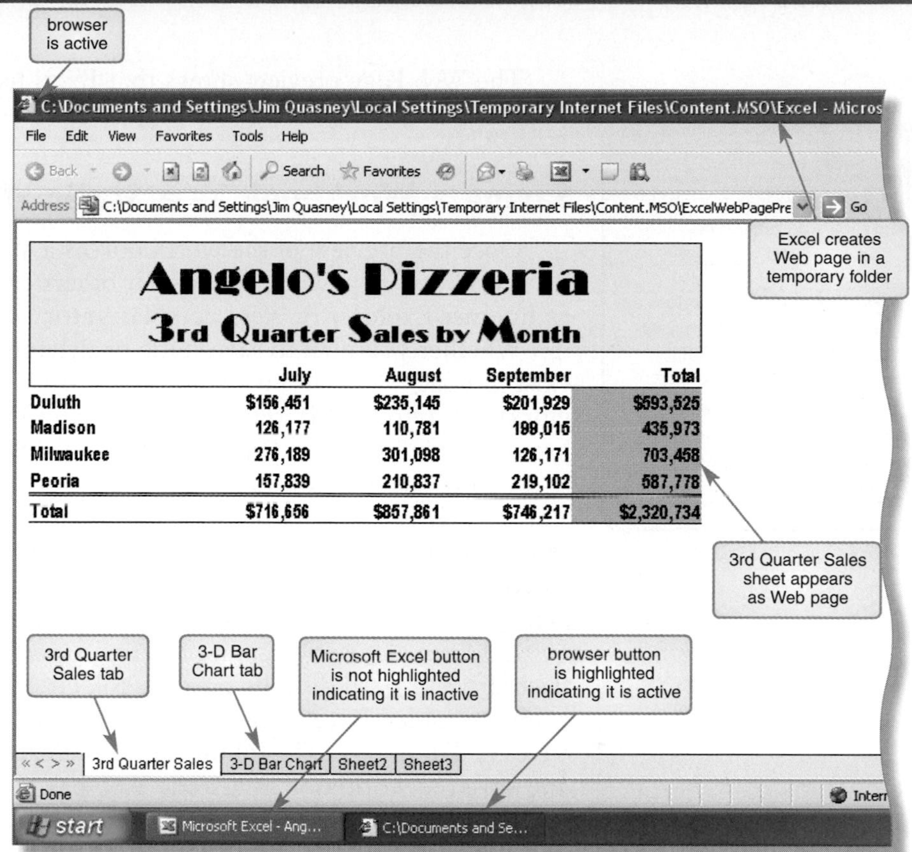

FIGURE 3

3

• **Click the 3-D Bar Chart tab at the bottom of the Web page.**

The browser displays the 3-D Bar chart (Figure 4).

4

• **After viewing the Web page preview of the Angelo's Pizzeria 3rd Quarter Sales workbook, click the Close button on the right side of the browser title bar.**

The browser closes. Excel becomes active and again displays the Angelo's Pizzeria 3rd Quarter Sales worksheet.

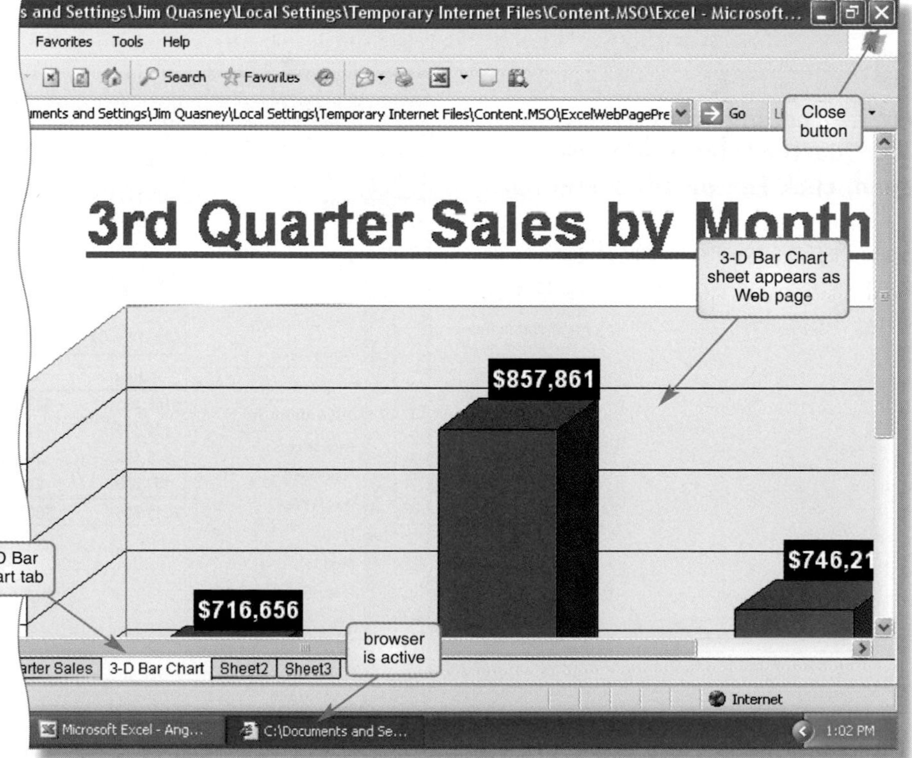

FIGURE 4

The Web Page preview shows that Excel has the capability of producing professional looking Web pages from workbooks.

Q & A

Q: Is more information available on publishing Web pages in Excel?

A: For more information about publishing Web pages using Excel, visit the Office 2003 Q&A Web page (scsite.com/off2003sch/qa), locate Excel Web Feature, and click Publishing Web Pages Using Excel.

Saving a Workbook as a Static Web Page in a New Folder

Once the preview of the workbook as a Web page is acceptable, you can save the workbook as a Web page so that others can view it using a Web browser, such as Internet Explorer or Netscape Navigator.

Whether you plan to save static or dynamic Web pages, two Web page formats exist in which you can save workbooks. Both formats convert the contents of the workbook into HTML (HyperText Markup Language), which is a language browsers can interpret. One format is called **Single File Web Page format**, which saves all of the components of the Web page in a single file with an .mht extension. This format is useful particularly for e-mailing workbooks in HTML format. The second format, called **Web Page format,** saves the Web page in a file and some of its components in a folder. This format is useful if you need access to the components, such as images, that make up the Web page.

Experienced users organize the files saved on a storage medium, such as a USB flash drive or hard disk, by creating folders. They then save related files in a common folder. Excel allows you to create folders before saving a file using the Save As dialog box. The following steps create a new folder on the USB flash drive and save the workbook as a static Web page in the new folder.

To Save an Excel Workbook as a Static Web Page in a Newly Created Folder

1

- **With the Angelo's Pizzeria 3rd Quarter Sales workbook open, click File on the menu bar.**

Excel displays the File menu (Figure 5).

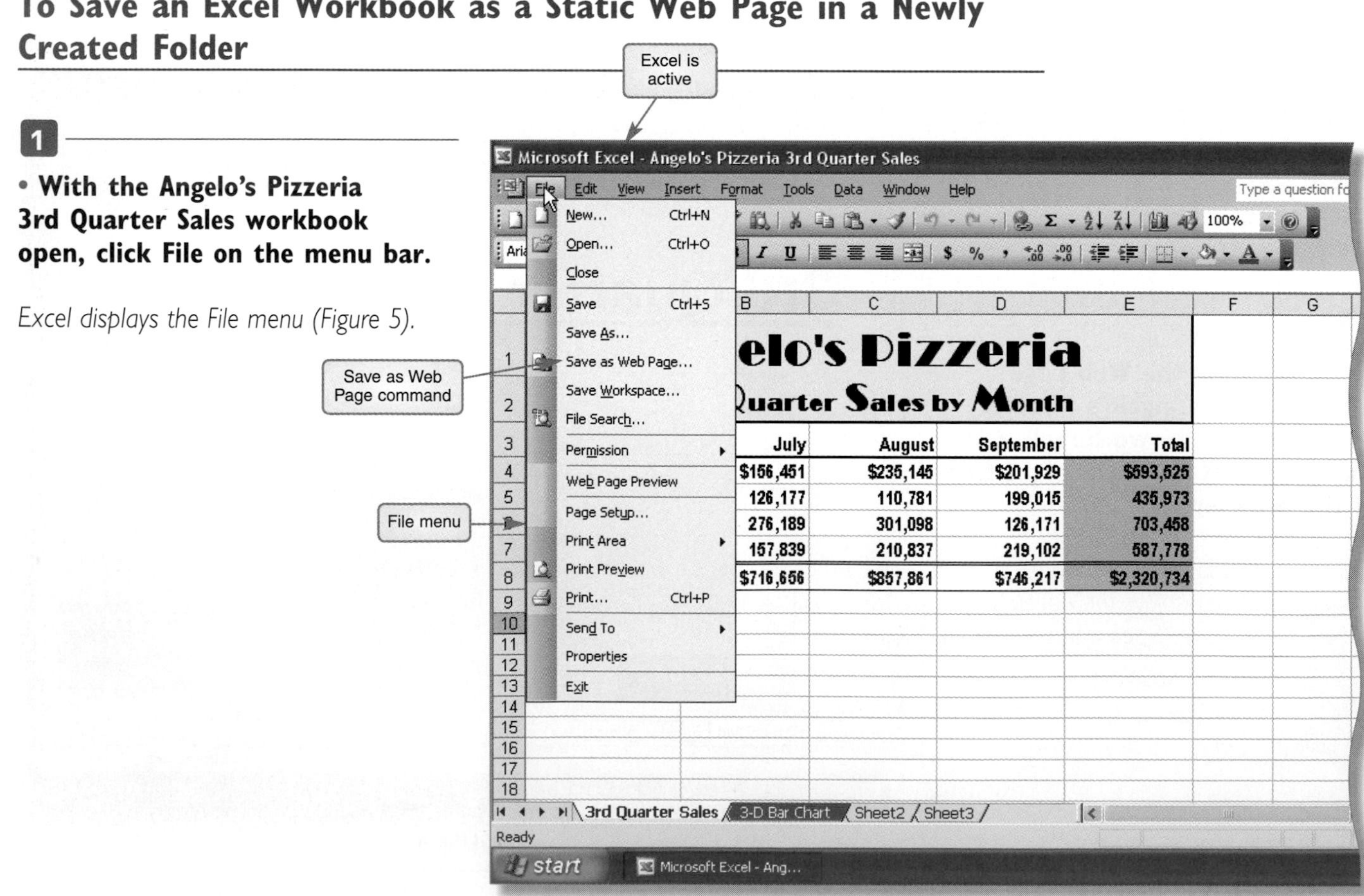

FIGURE 5

- **Click Save as Web Page.**
- **When Excel displays the Save As dialog box, type** `Angelo's Pizzeria 3rd Quarter Sales Static Web Page` **in the File name text box.**
- **Click the Save as type box arrow and then click Single File Web Page.**
- **Click the Save in box arrow, select UDISK 2.0 (F:) (your USB flash drive name and letter may be different), and then click the Create New Folder button.**
- **When Excel displays the New Folder dialog box, type** `Web Feature` **in the Name text box.**

Excel displays the Save As dialog box and New Folder dialog box as shown in Figure 6.

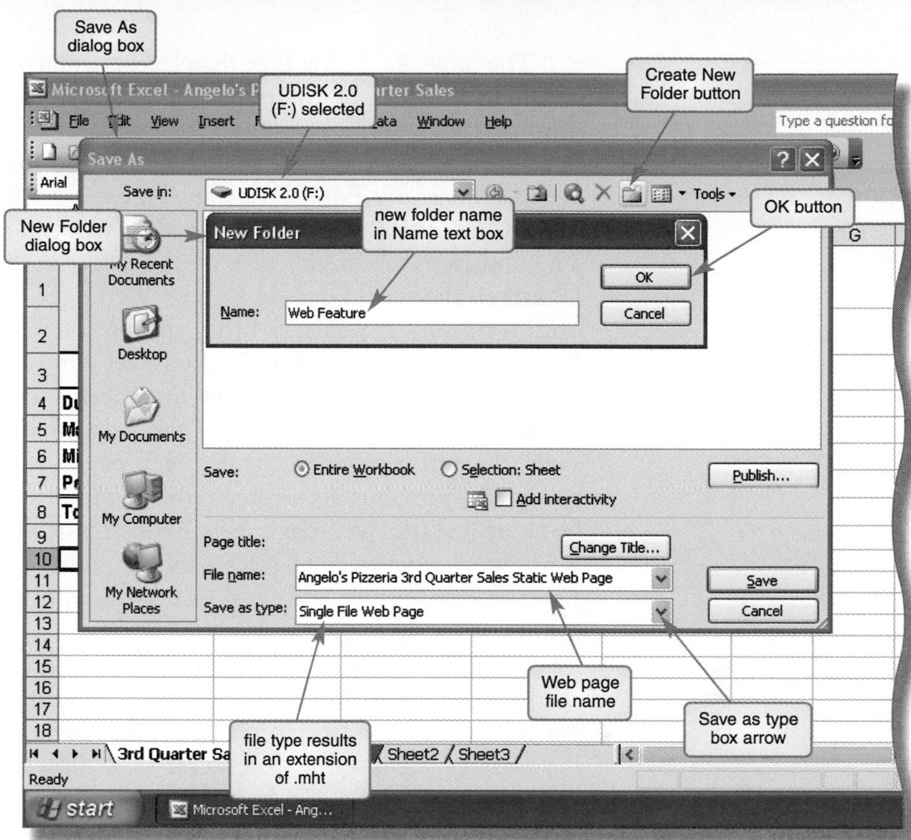

FIGURE 6

- **Click the OK button in the New Folder dialog box.**

Excel automatically selects the new folder Web Feature in the Save in box (Figure 7). The Entire Workbook option in the Save area instructs Excel to save all sheets in the workbook as static Web pages.

4

- **Click the Save button in the Save As dialog box.**
- **Click the Close button on the right side of the Excel title bar to quit Excel.**

Excel saves the workbook in a single file in HTML format in the Web Feature folder on the USB flash drive.

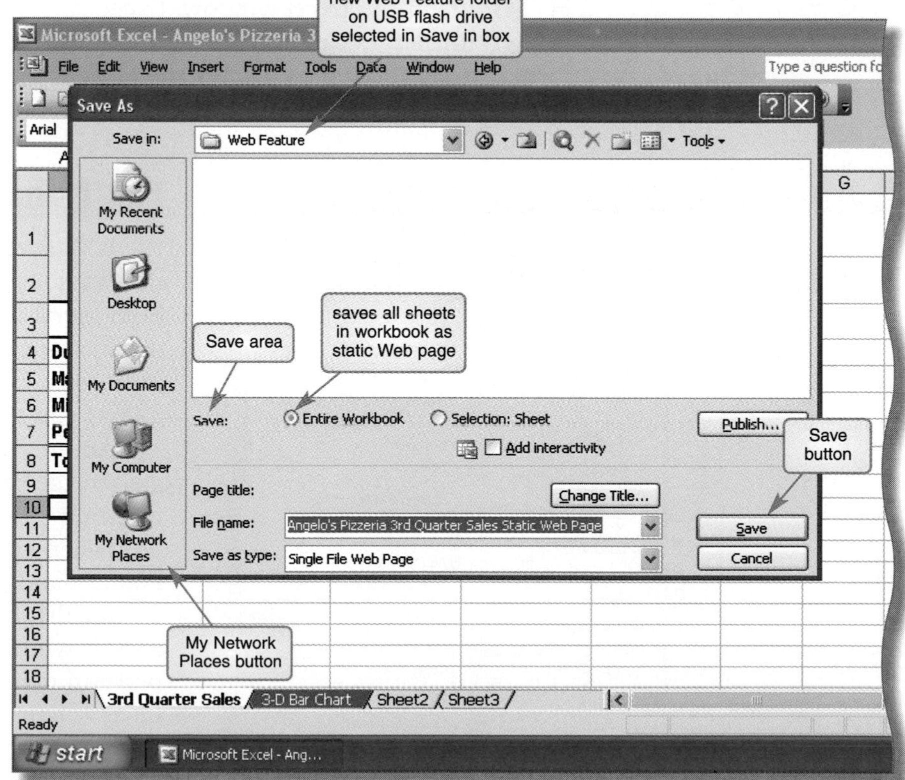

FIGURE 7

The Save As dialog box that Excel displays when you use the Save as Web Page command is slightly different from the Save As dialog box that Excel displays when you use the Save As command. When you use the Save as Web Page command, a Save area appears in the dialog box. Within the Save area are two option buttons, a check box, and a Publish button (Figure 7 on the previous page). You can select only one of the option buttons. The Entire Workbook option button is selected by default. This indicates Excel will save all the active sheets (3rd Quarter Sales and 3-D Bar Chart) in the workbook as a static Web page. The alternative is the Selection: Sheet option button. If you select this option, Excel will save only the active sheet (the one that currently is displaying in the Excel window) in the workbook. If you add a check mark to the Add interactivity check box, then Excel saves the active sheet as a dynamic Web page. If you leave the Add interactivity check box unchecked, Excel saves the active sheet as a static Web page.

In the previous set of steps, the Save button was used to save the Excel workbook as a static Web page. The Publish button in the Save As dialog box in Figure 7 is an alternative to the Save button. It allows you to customize the Web page further. Later in this feature, the Publish button will be used to explain how you can customize a Web page further.

If you have access to a Web server and it allows you to save files in a Web folder, then you can save the Web page directly on the Web server by clicking the My Network Places button in the lower-left corner of the Save As dialog box (Figure 7). If you have access to a Web server that allows you to save on an FTP site, then you can select the FTP site below FTP locations in the Save in box just as you select any folder on which to save a file. To learn more about publishing Web pages in a Web folder or on an FTP location using Office applications, refer to Appendix C.

After Excel saves the workbook in Step 4 on the previous page, it displays the HTML file in the Excel window. Excel can continue to display the workbook in HTML format, because, within the HTML file that it created, it also saved the Excel formats that allow it to display the HTML file in Excel. This is referred to as **round tripping** the HTML file back to the application in which it was created.

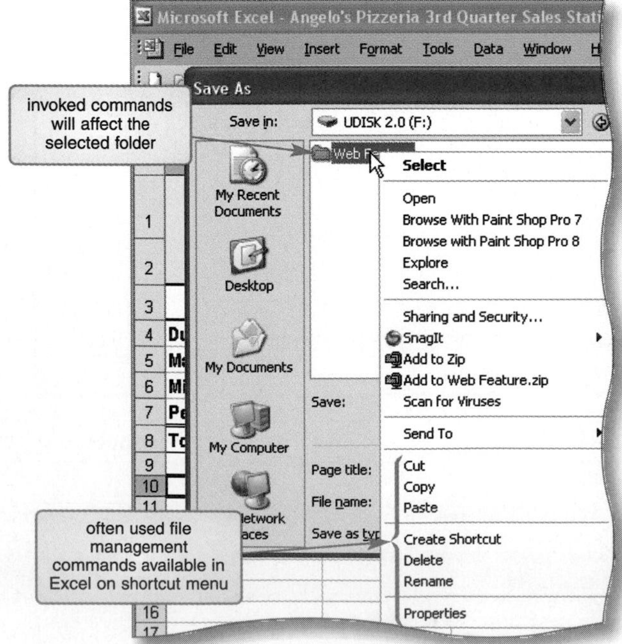

FIGURE 8

File Management Tools in Excel

It was not necessary to create a new folder in the previous set of steps. The Web page could have been saved on the USB flash drive in the same manner files were saved on the USB flash drive in the previous projects. Creating a new folder, however, allows you to organize your work.

Another point concerning the new folder created in the previous set of steps is that Excel automatically inserts the new folder name in the Save in box when you click the OK button in the New Folder dialog box (Figure 7).

Finally, once you create a folder, you can right-click it while the Save As dialog box is active and perform many file management tasks directly in Excel (Figure 8). For example, once the shortcut menu appears, you can rename the selected folder, delete it, copy it, display its properties, and perform other file management functions.

Viewing the Static Web Page Using a Browser

With the static Web page saved in the Web Feature folder on the USB flash drive, the next step is to view it using a browser, as shown in the following steps.

To View and Manipulate the Static Web Page Using a Browser

1

- **If necessary, connect the USB flash drive to one of the computer's USB ports.**
- **Click the Start button on the Windows taskbar, point to All Programs on the Start menu, and then click Internet Explorer on the All Programs submenu.**
- **When the Internet Explorer window appears, type** `f:\web feature\angelo's pizzeria 3rd quarter sales static web page.mht` **in the Address box and then press the ENTER key. (Your USB flash drive may have a different name and letter).**
- **If the Information Bar dialog box appears, click the OK button.**

The browser displays the Web page, Angelo's Pizzeria 3rd Quarter Sales Static Web Page.mht, with the 3rd Quarter Sales sheet active (Figure 9).

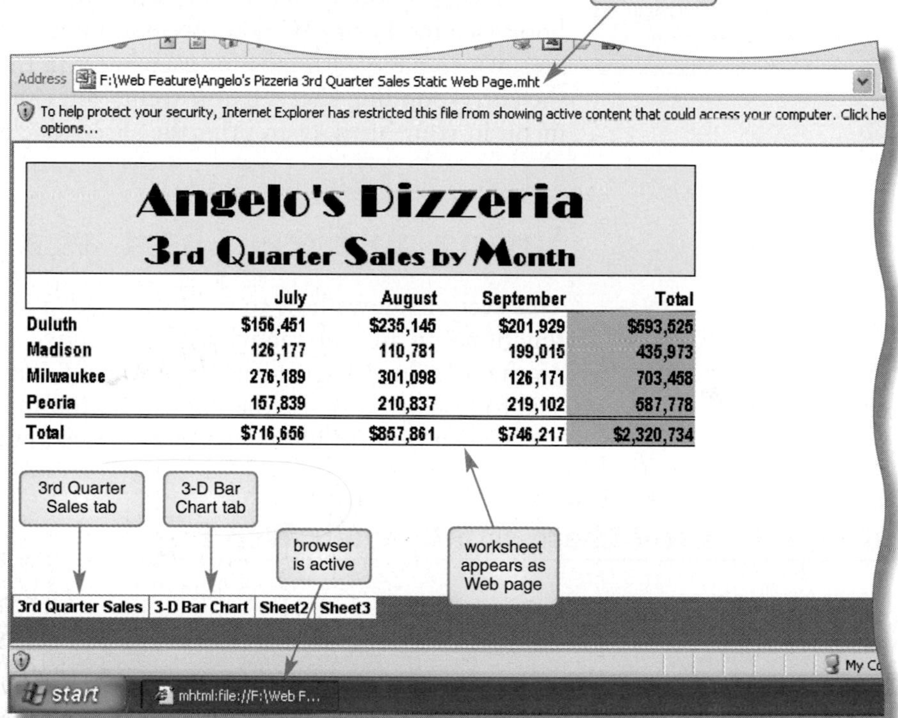

FIGURE 9

2

- **Click the 3-D Bar Chart tab at the bottom of the window.**
- **Use the scroll arrows to display the lower portion of the chart.**

The browser displays the 3-D Bar chart as shown in Figure 10.

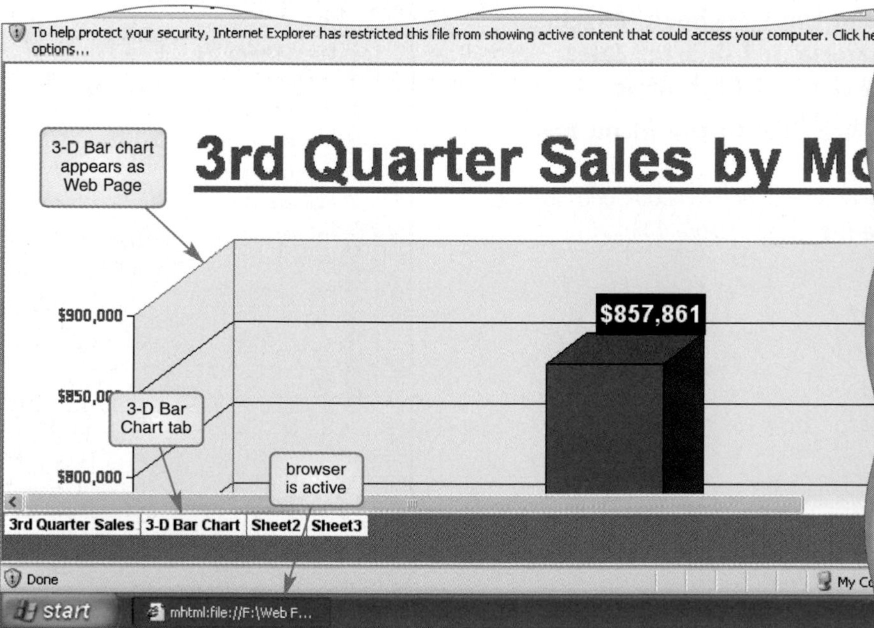

FIGURE 10

3

- **Click the Close button on the right side of the browser title bar to close the browser.**

> *Skill Builder WF-1*
>
> To practice the following tasks, visit scsite.com/off2003sch/skill, locate Excel Web Feature, and then click Skill Builder WF-1.
> - ❑ Preview a workbook as a Web page in Excel
> - ❑ Create a folder
> - ❑ Create a static Web page
> - ❑ View a static Web page

You can see from Figures 9 and 10 on the previous page that a static Web page is an ideal way to distribute information to a large group of people. For example, the static Web page could be published on a Web server connected to the Internet and made available to anyone with a computer, browser, and the address of the Web page. It also can be e-mailed easily, because the Web page resides in a single file, rather than in a file and folder. Publishing a static Web page of a workbook thus is an excellent alternative to distributing printed copies of the workbook.

Figures 9 and 10 show that, when you instruct Excel to save the entire workbook (see the Entire Workbook option button in Figure 7 on page EX 231), it creates a Web page with tabs for each sheet in the workbook. Clicking a tab displays the corresponding sheet. If you want, you can use the Print command on the File menu in your browser to print the sheets one at a time.

Saving an Excel Chart as a Dynamic Web Page

This section shows how to publish a dynamic Web page that includes Excel functionality and interactivity. The objective is to publish the 3-D Bar chart that is on the 3-D Bar Chart sheet in the Angelo's Pizzeria 3rd Quarter Sales workbook. The following steps use the Publish button in the Save As dialog box, rather than the Save button, to illustrate the additional publishing capabilities of Excel.

To Save an Excel Chart as a Dynamic Web Page

1

- **If necessary, connect the USB flash drive to one of the computer's USB ports.**
- **Start Excel and then open the workbook, Angelo's Pizzeria 3rd Quarter Sales, on the USB flash drive.**
- **Click File on the menu bar.**

Excel opens the workbook and displays the File menu (Figure 11).

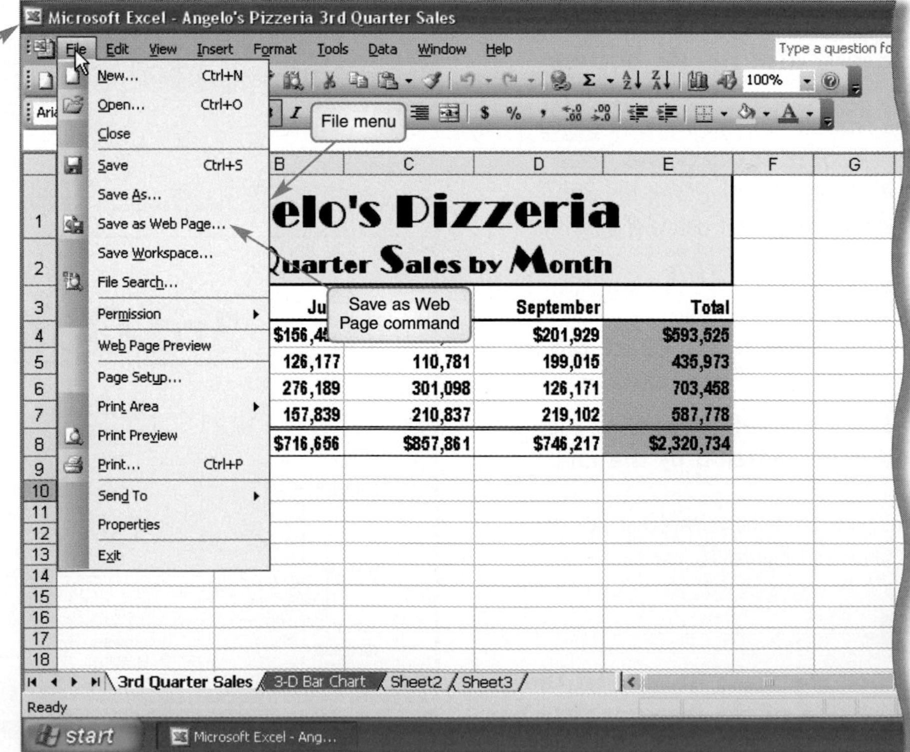

FIGURE 11

2

- **Click Save as Web Page.**
- **When Excel displays the Save As dialog box, type** `Angelo's Pizzeria 3rd Quarter Sales Dynamic Web Page` **in the File name text box.**
- **Click the Save as type box arrow and then click Single File Web Page.**
- **If necessary, click the Save in box arrow, select UDISK 2.0 (F:) (your USB flash drive name and letter may be different) in the Save in list, and then select the Web Feature folder.**

Excel displays the Save As dialog box as shown in Figure 12.

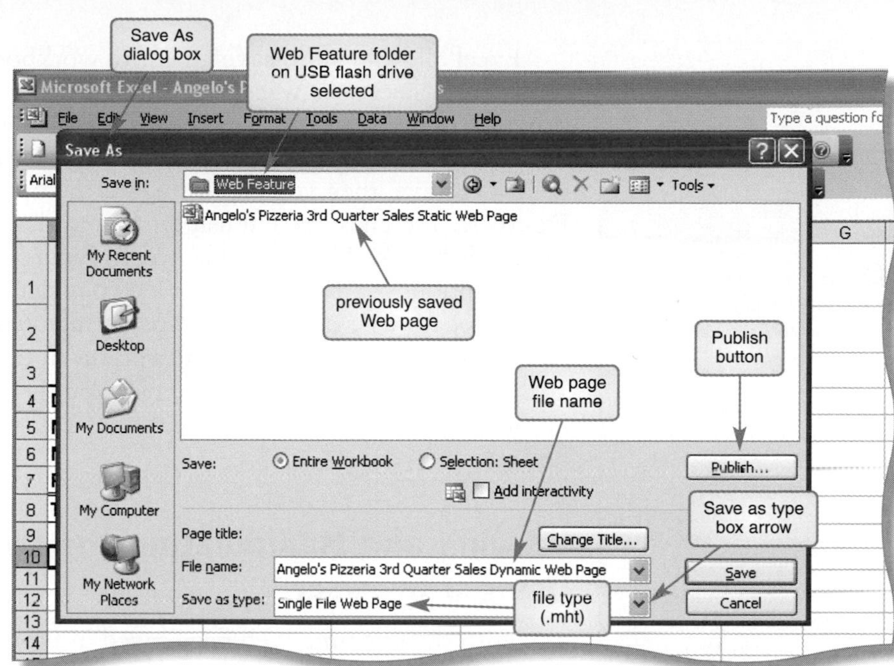

FIGURE 12

3

- **Click the Publish button.**
- **When Excel displays the Publish as Web Page dialog box, click the Choose box arrow and then click Items on 3-D Bar Chart.**
- **Click the Add interactivity with check box in the Viewing options area.**
- **If necessary, click the Add interactivity with box arrow, click Chart functionality, and then click the Open published web page in browser check box to deselect it.**

Excel displays the Publish as Web Page dialog box as shown in Figure 13.

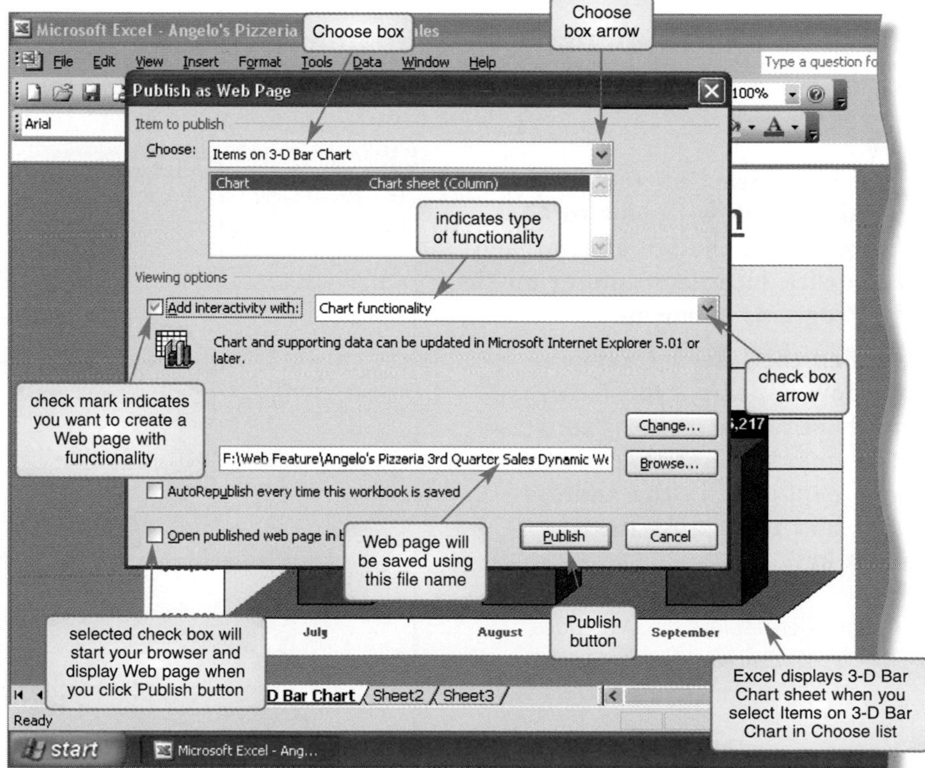

FIGURE 13

4

- **Click the Publish button, click the Close button on the right side of the Excel title bar, and if necessary, click the No button in the Microsoft Excel dialog box.**

Excel saves the dynamic Web page in the Web Feature folder on the USB flash drive. The Excel window is closed.

Excel allows you to save an entire workbook, a sheet in the workbook, or a range on a sheet as a Web page. In Figure 12 on the previous page, the Save area provides options that allow you to save the entire workbook or only a sheet. These option buttons are used with the Save button. If you want to be more selective in what you save, then you can disregard the option buttons in the Save area in Figure 12 and click the Publish button, as described in Step 3. The Choose box in the Publish as Web Page dialog box in Figure 13 on the previous page provides additional options for you to select what to include on the Web page. You also may save the Web page as a dynamic Web page (interactive) or a static Web page (noninteractive) by selecting the appropriate options in the Viewing options area. The check box at the bottom of the dialog box gives you the opportunity to start your browser automatically and display the newly created Web page when you click the Publish button.

Q & A

Q: How can a user display a dynamic Web page if Internet Explorer blocks its display for security purposes?

A: Dynamic Web pages contain ActiveX controls. If Internet Explorer blocks the display of a dynamic Web page, then click the Information Bar below the Address bar, click Allow blocked content on the shortcut menu, and then click the Yes button when the Security Warning dialog box appears.

Viewing and Manipulating the Dynamic Web Page Using a Browser

With the dynamic Web page saved in the Web Feature folder on the USB flash, the next step is to view and manipulate the dynamic Web page using a browser, as shown in the following steps.

To View and Manipulate the Dynamic Web Page Using a Browser

1

- **Click the Start button on the Windows taskbar, point to All Programs on the Start menu, and then click Internet Explorer on the All Programs submenu.**
- **When the Internet Explorer window appears, type** `f:\web feature\angelo's pizzeria 3rd quarter sales dynamic web page.mht` **in the Address box, and then press the ENTER key.**

The browser displays the Web page, Angelo's Pizzeria 3rd Quarter Sales Dynamic Web Page.mht, as shown in Figure 14. The 3-D Bar chart appears at the top of the Web page. The rows and columns of the worksheet that determine the size of the bars appear immediately below the 3-D Bar chart.

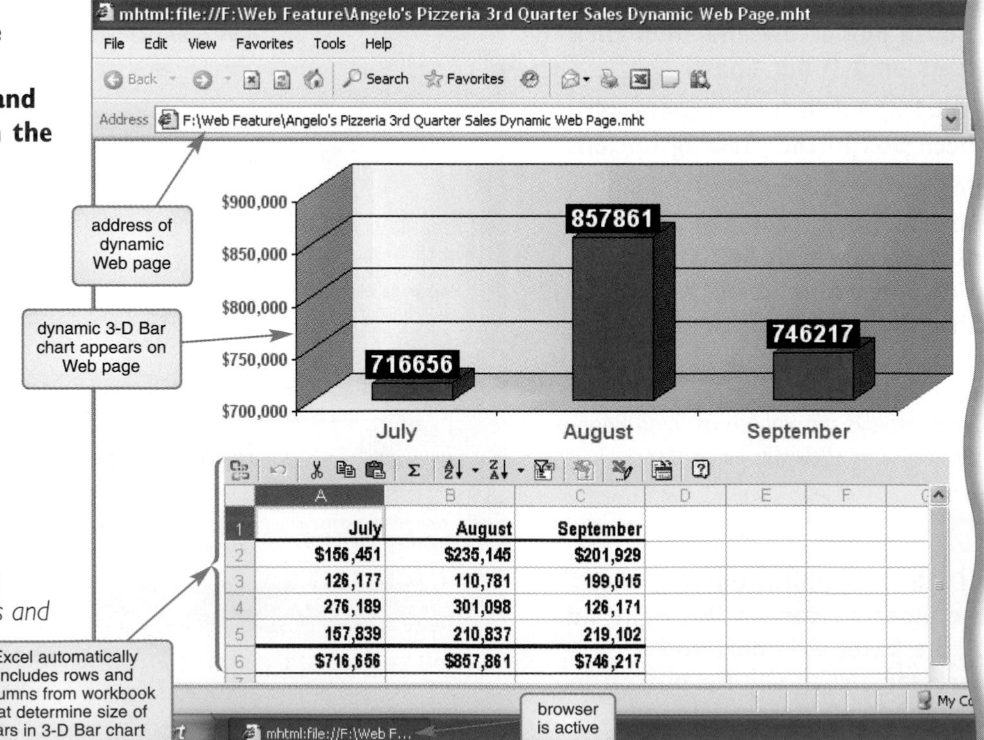

	A	B	C
1	July	August	September
2	$156,451	$235,145	$201,929
3	126,177	110,781	199,015
4	276,189	301,098	126,171
5	157,839	210,837	219,102
6	$716,656	$857,861	$746,217

FIGURE 14

2

• **Click cell A3 and then enter** 250000 **as the new value.**

The number 250,000 replaces the number 126,177 in cell A3. The formulas in the worksheet portion recalculate the totals in row 6 and the bars in the 3-D Bar chart change to agree with the new totals (Figure 15).

3

• **Click the Close button on the right side of the browser title bar to close the browser.**

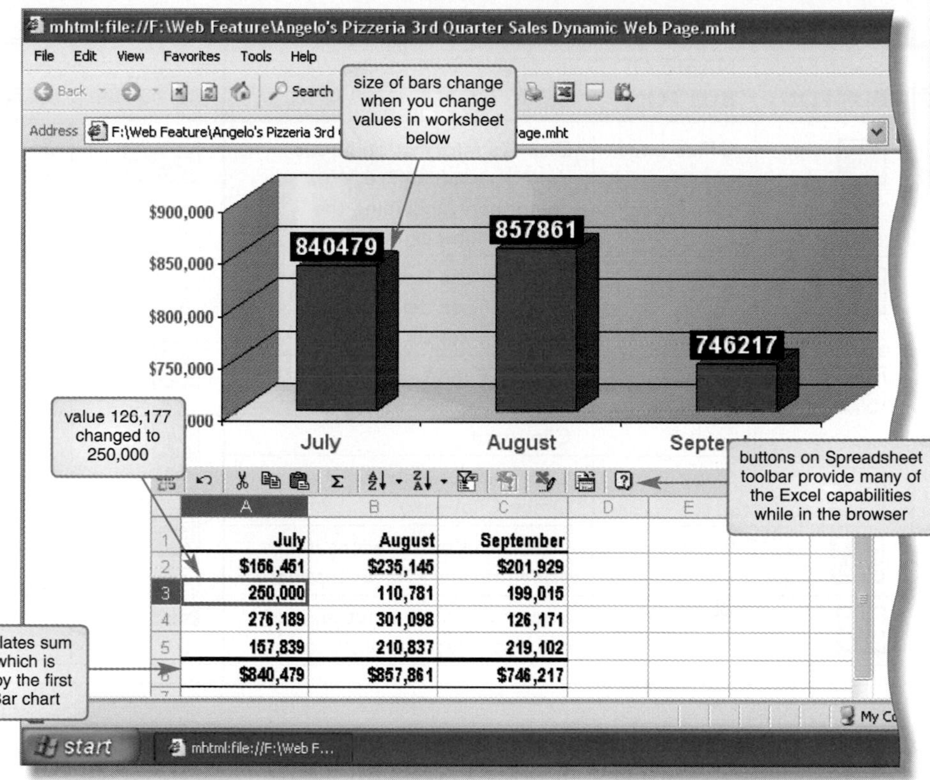

FIGURE 15

Q & A

Q: When you change a value in a dynamic Web page, does it affect the original wookbook?

A: If you change a value on a dynamic Web page and then save the Web page using the Save As command on the browser's File menu, Excel will save the original version, not the modified one that appears on the screen.

Figure 14 shows the result of saving the 3-D Bar chart as a dynamic Web page. Excel displays a slightly skewed version of the 3-D Bar chart and automatically adds the columns and rows from the worksheet that affect the chart directly below the chart. As shown in Figure 15, when a number in the worksheet that determines the size of a bar in the 3-D Bar chart is changed, the Web page instantaneously recalculates all formulas and redraws the 3-D Bar chart. For example, when cell A3 is changed from 126,177 to 250,000, the Web page recalculates the totals in row 6. The bar representing July sales is based on the number in cell A6. Thus, when the number in cell A6 changes from $716,656 to $840,479 because of the change made in cell A3, the bar representing July sales changes to a taller bar in relation to the others. The interactivity and functionality allow you to share a workbook's formulas and charts with others who may not have access to Excel, but do have access to a browser.

Modifying the Worksheet on a Dynamic Web Page

As shown in Figure 15, the Web page displays a toolbar immediately above the rows and columns in the worksheet. This toolbar, called the Spreadsheet toolbar, allows you to invoke the most commonly used worksheet commands. For example, you can select a cell immediately below a column of numbers and click the AutoSum button to sum the numbers in the column. Cut, copy, and paste capabilities also are available. Table 1 on the next page summarizes the functions of the buttons on the Spreadsheet toolbar shown in Figure 15.

Q & A

Q: Can hyperlinks be added to Web pages created in Excel?

A: Yes. You can add hyperlinks to an Excel workbook before you save it as a Web page. The hyperlinks in the Excel workbook can link to a Web page, a location in a Web page, or an e-mail address that automatically starts the viewer's e-mail program.

Table 1 Spreadsheet Toolbar Buttons

BUTTON	NAME OF BUTTON	FUNCTION
	Office Logo	Displays information about the Microsoft Office Web component, including the version number installed
	Undo	Reverses the last command or action, or deletes the last entry typed
	Cut	Removes the selection and places it on the Office Clipboard
	Copy	Copy the selection to the Office Clipboard
	Paste	Inserts the most recent item placed on the Office Clipboard
	AutoSum	Inserts the SUM function in a cell and selects a range to sum
	Sort Ascending	Sorts the selected items in ascending sequence
	Sort Descending	Sorts the selected items in descending sequence
	AutoFilter	Selects specific items you want to display in a list
	Refresh All	Refreshes data when connected to the Web
	Export to Microsoft Office Excel	Opens the Web page as a workbook in Excel
	Commands and Options	Displays the Commands and Options dialog box
	Help	Displays Microsoft Office 2003 Spreadsheet Components Help

Skill Builder WF-2

To practice the following tasks, visit scsite.com/off2003sch/skill, locate Excel Web Feature, and then click Skill Builder WF-2.
- ❑ Create a dynamic Web page
- ❑ View dynamic Web page
- ❑ Change values in a dynamic Web page
- ❑ Use the speadsheet toolbar

In general, the Spreadsheet toolbar allows you to add formulas, format, sort, and export the Web page to Excel. Many additional Excel capabilities are available through the Commands and Options dialog box. You display the Commands and Options dialog box by clicking the Commands and Options button on the Spreadsheet toolbar. When Excel displays the Command and Options dialog box, click the Format tab. The Format sheet makes formatting options, such as bold, italic, underline, font color, font style, and font size, available through your browser for the purpose of formatting cells in the worksheet below the 3-D Bar chart on the Web page.

Modifying the dynamic Web page does not change the makeup of the original workbook or the Web page stored on the USB flash drive, even if you use the Save As command on the browser's File menu. If you do use the Save As command in your browser, it will save the original mht file without any changes you might have made. You can, however, use the Export to Excel button on the Spreadsheet toolbar to create a workbook that will include any changes you made in your browser. The Export to Excel button saves only the worksheet and not the chart.

Web Feature Summary

This Web feature introduced you to previewing a workbook as a Web page, creating a new folder on a USB flash drive, and publishing and viewing two types of Web pages: static and dynamic. Whereas the static Web page is a snapshot of the workbook, a dynamic Web page adds functionality and interactivity to the Web page. Besides changing the data and generating new results with a dynamic Web page, you also learned how to use your browser to add formulas and change the formats to improve the appearance of the Web page.

If you have a SAM user profile, you may have access to hands-on instruction, practice, and assessment of the skills covered in this project. Log in to your SAM account and go to your assignments page to see what your instructor has assigned.

What You Should Know

Having completed this Web feature, you should be able to perform the tasks listed below. The tasks are listed in the same order they were presented in this Web feature. For a list of the buttons, menus, toolbars, and commands introduced in this Web feature, see the Quick Reference Summary at the back of this book and refer to the Page Number column.

1. Preview the Workbook as a Web Page (EX 228)
2. Save an Excel Workbook as a Static Web Page in a Newly Created Folder (EX 230)
3. View and Manipulate the Static Web Page Using a Browser (EX 233)
4. Save an Excel Chart as a Dynamic Web Page (EX 234)
5. View and Manipulate the Dynamic Web Page Using a Browser (EX 236)

1 Creating Static and Dynamic Web Pages I

Problem: You are a summer intern working as a spreadsheet specialist for Scholastic Fund Raising. Your mentor has asked you to create a static Web page and dynamic Web page from the company's annual sales workbook.

Instructions Part 1: Start Excel and open the Lab WF-1 Scholastic Fund Raising Annual Sales workbook from the Data Files for Students. Perform the following tasks:

1. Review the worksheet and chart so you have an idea of what the workbook contains. Preview the workbook as a Web page. Close the browser.
2. Save the workbook as a single file Web page in a new folder titled Web Feature Exercises using the file name, Lab WF-1 Scholastic Fund Raising Annual Sales Static Web Page. Make sure you select Entire Workbook in the Save area before you click the Save button. Quit Excel.
3. Start your browser. With the Web page located on the USB flash drive, type `f:\web feature exercises\lab wf-1 scholastic fund raising annual sales static web page.mht` in the Address box (your USB flash drive may have a different name and letter). When the browser displays the Web page, click the tabs at the bottom of the window to view the sheets. As you view each sheet, print it in landscape orientation. Close the browser.

Instructions Part 2: Start Excel and open the Lab WF-1 Scholastic Fund Raising Annual Sales workbook from the Data Files for Students. Perform the following tasks:

1. Click File on the menu bar and then click Save as Web Page. Use the Publish button to save the workbook as a single file Web page in the Web Feature Exercises folder using the file name, Lab WF-1 Scholastic Fund Raising Annual Sales Dynamic Web Page. In the Publish as Web Page dialog box, select Items on Bar Chart in the Choose list and click the Add interactivity with check box to add chart functionality. Click the Publish button. Quit Excel without saving changes.
2. Start your browser. With the Web page located on the USB drive, type `f:\web feature exercises\lab wf-1 scholastic fund raising annual sales dynamic web page.mht` in the Address box (your USB flash drive may have a different name and letter). When the browser displays the Web page, click cell B6 and then click the AutoSum button on the Spreadsheet toolbar twice. Cell B6 should equal $12,060,255. Print the Web page.
3. If necessary, drag the lower-right corner of the worksheet to make it larger. Update the range B1:B5 on the dynamic Web page by entering the following gross sales: East = 2,100,000; North = 1,310,100; South = 1,300,250; West = 1,225,000; and International = 1,375,000. Cell B6 should equal $7,310,350. Print the Web page. Close the browser.

2 Creating Static and Dynamic Web Pages II

Problem: You work part-time as a spreadsheet analyst for Band Uniforms of America. You have been asked to create a static Web page and dynamic Web page from the workbook that the company uses to project sales and payroll expenses.

Instructions Part 1: Start Excel and open the Lab WF-2 Band Uniforms of America Projections workbook from the Data Files for Students. Perform the following tasks:

1. Display the 3-D Pie Chart sheet. Redisplay the Projected Expenses sheet. Preview the workbook as a Web page. Close the browser.
2. Save the workbook as a Web page (select Web Page in the Save as type box) in the Web Feature Exercises folder using the file name, Lab WF-2 Band Uniforms of America Projections Static Web Page. Make sure you select Entire Workbook in the Save area before you click the Save button. Quit Excel. Saving the workbook as a Web page, rather than a single file Web page, will result in an additional folder being added to the Web Feature Exercises folder.
3. Start your browser. Type `f:\web feature exercises\lab wf-2 band uniforms of america projections static web page.htm` in the Address box (your USB flash drive may have a different name and letter). When the browser displays the Web page, click the tabs at the bottom of the window to view the sheets. Print each sheet in landscape orientation. Close the browser.

Instructions Part 2: Start Excel and open the Lab WF-2 Band Uniforms of America Projections workbook from the Data Disk. Perform the following tasks:

1. Click File on the menu bar and then click Save as Web Page. Use the Publish button to save the workbook as a single file Web page in the Web Feature Exercises folder using the file name, Lab WF-2 Band Uniforms of America Projections Dynamic Web Page. In the Publish as Web Page dialog box, select Items on 3-D Pie Chart in the Choose list and click the Add interactivity with check box to add chart functionality. Click the Publish button. Quit Excel without saving changes.
2. Start your browser. Type `f:\web feature exercises\lab wf-2 band uniforms of america projections dynamic web page.mht` in the Address box (your USB flash drive may have a different name and letter). When the browser displays the Web page, print it in landscape orientation.
3. If necessary, drag the lower-right corner of the worksheet to make it larger. Scroll down and change the values of the following cells on the dynamic Web page: cell B15 = 18.00%; cell B16 = 7.50%; cell B17 = 50,000; cell B19 = 21.50%; and cell B20 = 9.50%. Cell H12 should equal $7,161,238.21. The 3-D Pie chart should change to show the new contributions to the projected payroll expenses. Close the browser.

3 File Management within Excel

Problem: Your manager at Band Uniforms of America as asked you to teach him to complete basic file management tasks from within Excel.

Instructions: Start Excel and click the Open button on the Standard toolbar. When Excel displays the Open dialog box, create a new folder called In the Lab 3. Click the Up One Level button to reselect the drive in the Look in box. Use the shortcut menu to complete the following tasks: (1) rename the In the Lab 3 folder to In the Lab 3A; (2) show the properties of the In the Lab 3A folder; and (3) delete the In the Lab 3A folder.

MICROSOFT OFFICE

Access 2003

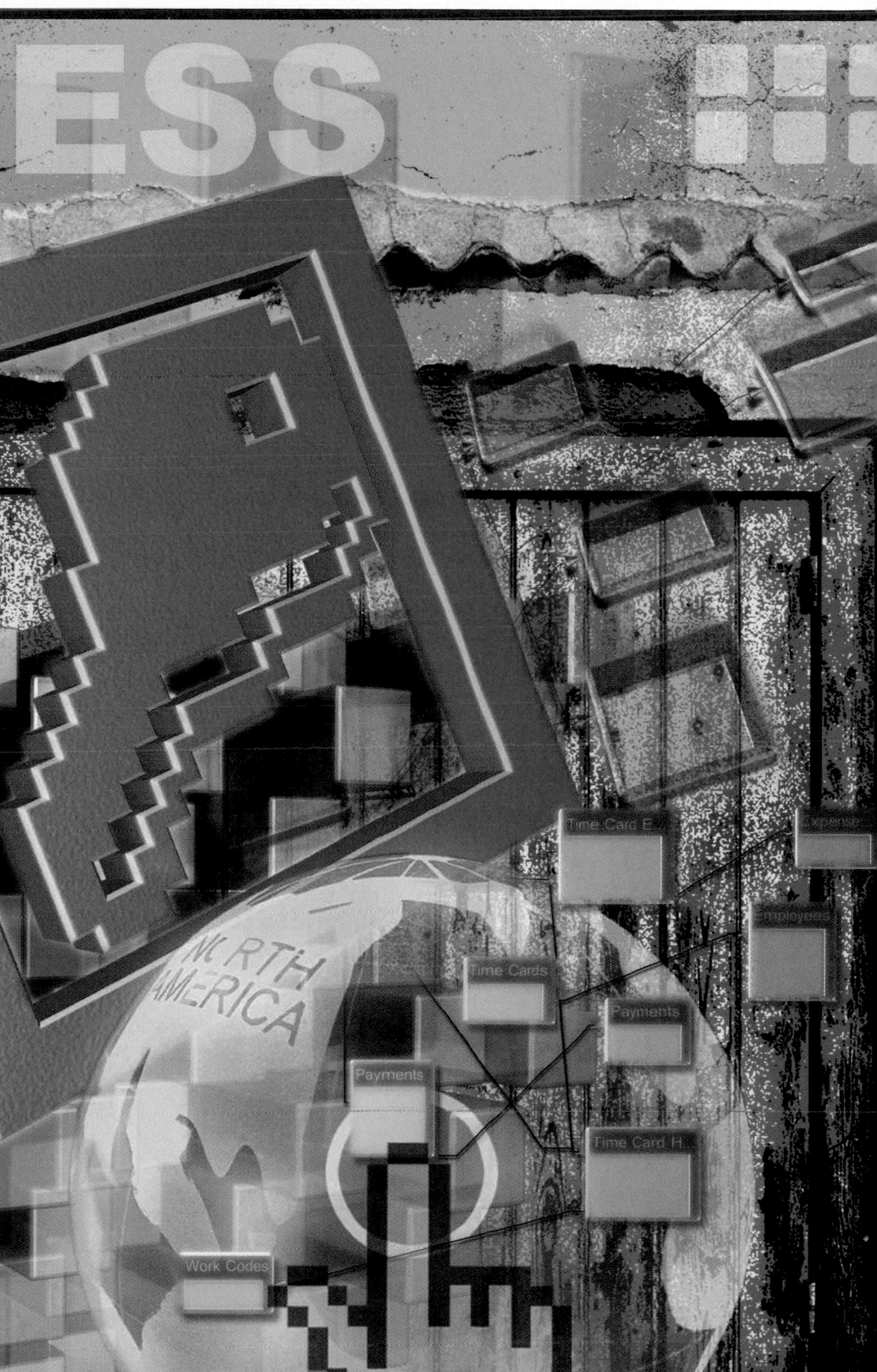

MICROSOFT OFFICE ACCESS

MICROSOFT OFFICE

Access 2003

Creating and Using a Database

PROJECT

1

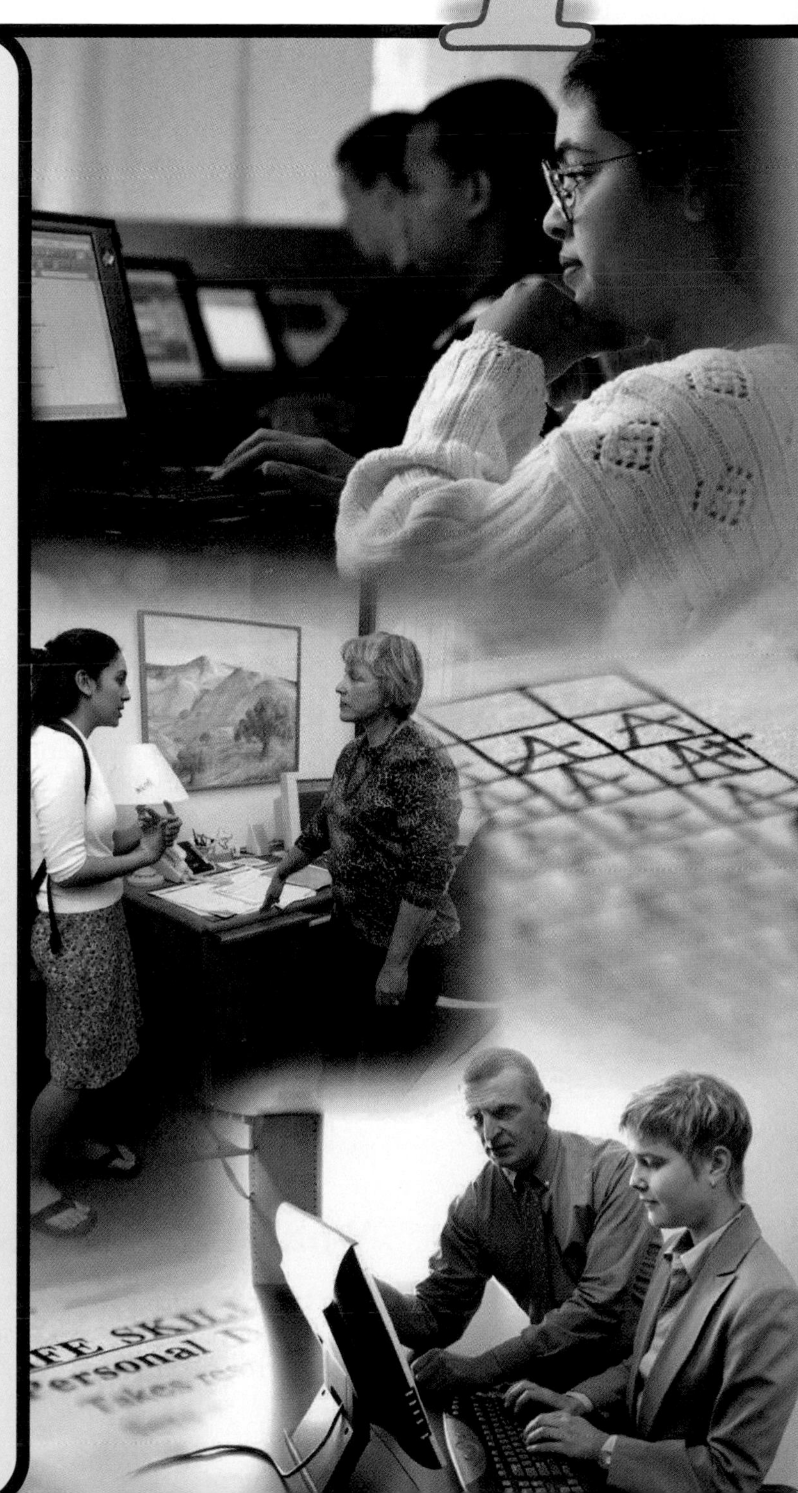

CASE PERSPECTIVE

Alyssa High School of Information Technology is a magnet high school that specializes in providing learning opportunities for students in information technology (IT). One of the school's goals is to encourage students to pursue further education in IT-related disciplines, such as computer science, computer engineering, and information systems. As part of their high school education, juniors and seniors can participate in corporate internships. These internships provide participants with practical experience working with professionals in computer-related fields. To participate in the internship program, students must meet a minimum GPA requirement. Students also must keep a journal of their experiences and are evaluated by the corporate clients for whom they work.

To manage the corporate internships, the school district has created a Corporate Partnership department. The department recruits corporate clients, matches students with clients, and handles administrative duties related to the program. To provide the interns with a variety of experiences, each student is assigned to one or more clients.

To ensure that operations run smoothly, the Corporate Partnership department needs to maintain data on the student interns and their clients. The school district administration wants to organize the data in a database, managed by a database management system such as Access. In this way, the school district can keep its data current and accurate while program administrators analyze the data for trends and produce a variety of useful reports. Your task is to help the director of corporate partnerships, Dr. Marisa Gervase, create and use the database.

As you read through this project, you will learn how to use Access to create a database.

Creating and Using a Database

PROJECT

Objectives

You will have mastered the material in this project when you can:

- Describe databases and database management systems
- Start Access
- Describe the features of the Access desktop
- Create a database
- Create a table and add records
- Close a table
- Close a database and quit Access
- Open a database
- Print the contents of a table
- Create and use a simple query
- Create and use a simple form
- Create and print a custom report
- Design a database to eliminate redundancy

What Is Microsoft Office Access 2003?

Microsoft Office Access 2003 is a powerful database management system (DBMS) that functions in the Windows environment and allows you to create and process data in a database. Some of the key features are:

- **Data entry and update** Access provides easy mechanisms for adding, changing, and deleting data, including the capability of making mass changes in a single operation.
- **Queries (questions)** Access makes it possible to ask complex questions concerning the data in the database and then receive instant answers.
- **Forms** Access allows the user to produce attractive and useful forms for viewing and updating data.
- **Reports** Access report creation tools make it easy to produce sophisticated reports for presenting data.
- **Web support** Access allows you to save objects, reports, and tables in HTML format so they can be viewed using a browser. You also can import and export documents in XML format. Access' capability of creating data access pages allows real-time access to data in the database via the Internet.

What Is New in Access?

This latest version of Access has many new features to make you more productive. You can view information on dependencies between various database objects. You can enable error checking for many common errors in forms and reports. You can add smart tags to fields in tables, queries, forms, or data access pages. Access now has a command to backup a database. Many wizards provide more options for sorting data. You can export to, import from, or link to a Windows SharePoint Services list. Access now offers enhanced XML support.

Project One — AHSIT Internships Database

Creating, storing, sorting, and retrieving data are important tasks. In their personal lives, many people keep a variety of records, such as names, addresses, and telephone numbers of friends and business associates, records of investments, records of expenses for tax purposes, and so on. For effective use of this data, users must have quick access to it. Businesses also must be able to store and access information quickly and easily.

The term **database** describes a collection of data organized in a manner that allows access, retrieval, and use of that data. A **database management system**, such as Access, is a software tool that allows you to use a computer to create a database; add, change, and delete data in the database; sort the data in the database; retrieve data in the database; and create forms and reports using the data in the database.

In Access, a database consists of a collection of tables. Figure 1-1 shows a sample database for Alyssa High School of Information Technology (AHSIT), which consists of two tables. The Client table contains information about the clients to which interns at AHSIT provide services. The school assigns each client to a specific intern. The Intern table contains information about the interns to whom these clients are assigned.

Client table

CLIENT NUMBER	NAME	ADDRESS	CITY	STATE	ZIP CODE	AMOUNT PAID	CURRENT DUE	INTERN NUMBER
A54	Afton Mills	612 Revere	Grant City	ND	58120	$892.50	$315.50	22
A62	Atlas Suppliers	227 Dandelion	Empeer	ND	58216	$2,672.00	$525.00	24
B26	Blake-Scripps	557 Maum	Grant City	ND	58120	$0.00	$229.50	24
D76	Dege Grocery	446 Linton	Portage	MN	59130	$1,202.00	$485.75	34
G56	Grand Cleaners	337 Abelard	Portage	MN	59131	$925.50	$265.00	22
H21	Hill Shoes	247 Fulton	Grant City	ND	58121	$228.50	$0.00	24
J77	Jones Plumbing	75 Getty	E. Portage	MN	59135	$0.00	$0.00	34
M26	Mohr Crafts	665 Market	Empeer	ND	58216	$1,572.00	$312.50	22
S56	SeeSaw Ind.	31 Liatris	Portage	MN	59130	$2,827.50	$362.50	34
T45	Tate Repair	824 Revere	Grant City	ND	58120	$254.00	$0.00	24

Intern table

INTERN NUMBER	LAST NAME	FIRST NAME	ADDRESS	CITY	STATE	ZIP CODE	HOURLY RATE	YTD EARNINGS
22	Lewen	Joann	26 Cotton	Portage	MN	59130	$5.50	$1,320.00
24	Rodriguez	Mario	79 Marsden	E. Portage	MN	59135	$5.40	$1,280.50
34	Wong	Shawn	263 Topper	Portage	MN	59130	$5.75	$1,500.25
42	Trent	Roberta	45 Magee	W. Portage	MN	59136	$5.60	$0.00

FIGURE 1-1

The rows in the tables are called records. A **record** contains information about a given person, product, or event. A row in the Client table, for example, contains information about a specific client.

The columns in the tables are called fields. A **field** contains a specific piece of information within a record. In the Client table, for example, the fourth field, City, contains the city where the client is located.

The first field in the Client table is the Client Number. Alyssa High School assigns a number to each client. As is common to the way in which many organizations format client numbers, Alyssa High School calls it a *number*, although it actually contains letters. The AHSIT client numbers consist of an uppercase letter followed by a two-digit number.

These numbers are unique; that is, no two clients are assigned the same number. Such a field can be used as a **unique identifier**. This simply means that a given client number will appear only in a single record in the table. Only one record exists, for example, in which the client number is A62. A unique identifier also is called a **primary key**. Thus, the Client Number field is the primary key for the Client table.

The next seven fields in the Client table are Name, Address, City, State, Zip Code, Amount Paid, and Current Due. The Amount Paid field contains the amount that the client has paid Alyssa High School year-to-date (YTD), but before the current period. The Current Due field contains the amount due to AHSIT for the current period.

For example, client A62 is Atlas Suppliers. The address is 227 Dandelion in Empeer, North Dakota. The Zip code is 58216. The client has paid $2,672.00 for services so far this year. The amount due for the current period is $525.00.

AHSIT assigns each client a single intern. The last field in the Client table, Intern Number, gives the number of the client's intern.

The first field in the Intern table, Intern Number, is the number Alyssa High School assigns to the intern. These numbers are unique, so Intern Number is the primary key of the Intern table.

The other fields in the Intern table are Last Name, First Name, Address, City, State, Zip Code, Hourly Rate, and YTD Earnings. The Hourly Rate field gives the intern's hourly billing rate, and the YTD Earnings field contains the total amount that AHSIT has paid the intern for services so far this year.

For example, Intern 22 is Joann Lewen. Her address is 26 Cotton in Portage, Minnesota. The Zip code is 59130. Her hourly billing rate is $5.50, and her YTD earnings are $1,320.00.

The intern number appears in both the Client table and the Intern table. It relates clients and interns. For example, in the Client table, you see that the intern number for client A54 is 22. To find the name of this intern, look for the row in the Intern table that contains 22 in the Intern Number field. After you have found it, you know the client is assigned to Joann Lewen. To find all the clients assigned to Joann Lewen, look through the Client table for all the clients that contain 22 in the Intern Number field. Her clients are A54 (Afton Mills), G56 (Grand Cleaners), and M26 (Mohr Crafts).

The last intern in the Intern table, Roberta Trent, has not been assigned any clients yet; therefore, her intern number, 42, does not currently appear on any row in the Client table.

Figure 1-1 on page AC 5 shows the data that must be maintained in the database. The first step is to create the database and the tables it contains. In the process, you must define the fields included in the two tables, as well as the type of data each field will contain. Then, you must add the appropriate records to the tables. Finally, you will print the contents of the tables. After you have completed these tasks, you will create a query, a form, and a report.

> *Q & A*
>
> **Q:** Need help with Access?
>
> **A:** Help with Access is no further than the Type a question for help box on the menu bar in the upper-right corner of the window. Click the box that contains the text, Type a question for help (Figure 1-3 on the next page), type `help`, and then press the ENTER key. Access responds with a list of topics you can click to learn about obtaining help on any Access-related topic. To find out what is new in Access 2003, type `what is new in Access` in the Type a question for help box.

Starting Access

If you are stepping through this project on a computer, and you want your screen to agree with the figures in this book, then you should change your computer's resolution to 800 × 600. For more information on how to change the resolution on your computer, see Appendix D. To start Access, Windows must be running. The following steps show how to start Access.

To Start Access

1

- **Click the Start button on the Windows taskbar, point to All Programs on the Start menu, and then point to Microsoft Office on the All Programs submenu.**

Windows displays the Start menu, the All Programs submenu, and the Microsoft Office submenu (Figure 1-2).

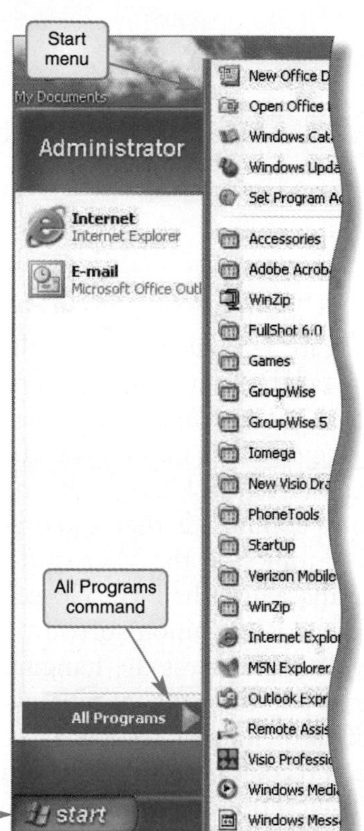

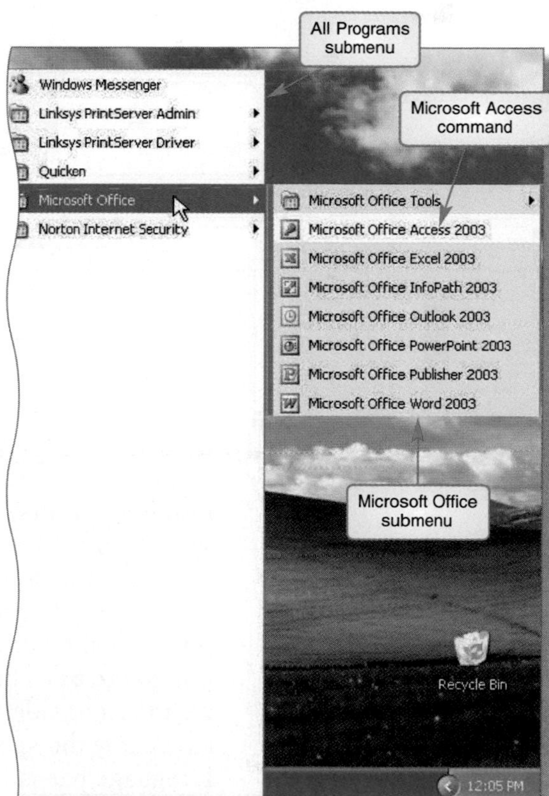

FIGURE 1-2

2

• **Click Microsoft Office Access 2003.**

Access starts. After several seconds, the Access window appears (Figure 1-3).

3

• **If the Access window is not maximized, double-click its title bar to maximize it.**

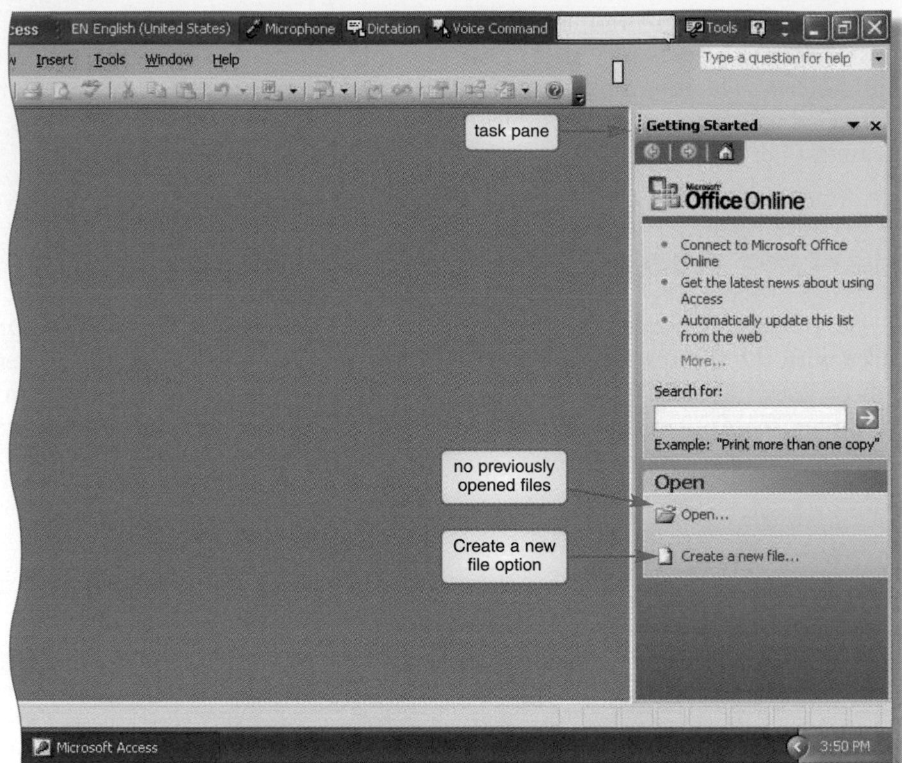

FIGURE 1-3

The screen in Figure 1-3 illustrates how the Access window looks the first time you start Access after installation on most computers. Access displays a task pane on the right side of the screen at startup. A **task pane** is a separate window that enables users to carry out some Access tasks more efficiently. When you start Access, it displays the Getting Started task pane, which is a small window that provides commonly used links and commands that allow you to open files, create new files, or search Office-related topics on the Microsoft Web site. The task pane is used only to create a new database and then it is closed.

If the Office Speech Recognition software is installed and active on your computer, then when you start Access the Language bar is displayed on the screen. The **Language bar** allows you to speak commands and dictate text. It usually is located on the right side of the Windows taskbar next to the notification area and changes to include the speech recognition functions available in Access. In this book, the Language bar is closed. For additional information about the Language bar, see the next page and Appendix B. The following steps show how to close the Language bar if it appears on the screen.

To Close the Language Bar

1

• **Right-click the Language bar to display a list of commands.**

The Language bar shortcut menu appears (Figure 1-4).

2

• **Click Close the Language bar.**

• **Click the OK button.**

The Language bar disappears.

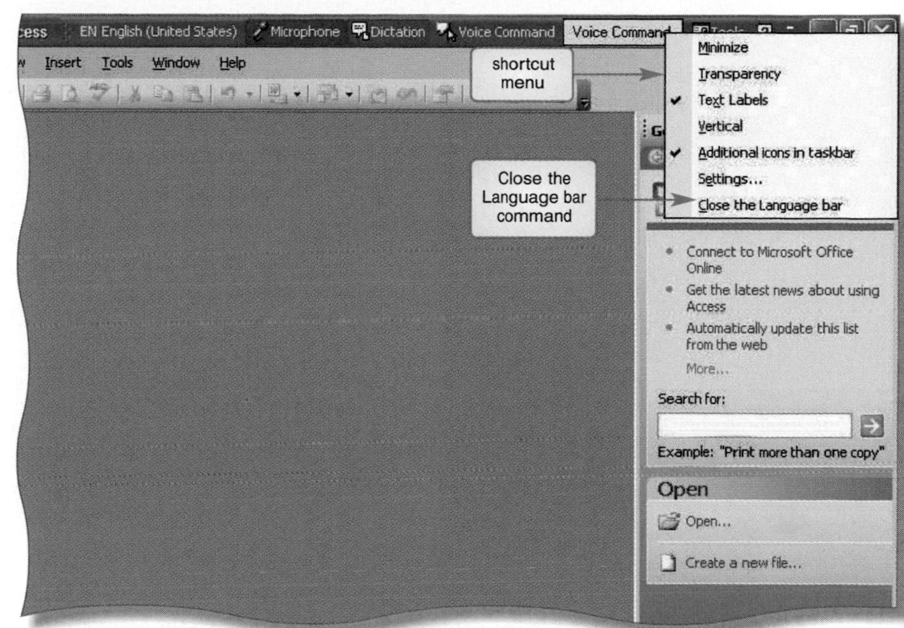

FIGURE 1-4

Speech Recognition

With the **Office Speech Recognition software** installed and a microphone, you can speak the names of toolbar buttons, menus, menu commands, list items, alerts, and dialog box controls, such as OK and Cancel. You also can dictate field entries, such as text and numbers. To indicate whether you want to speak commands or dictate cell entries, you use the Language bar. The Language bar can be in one of three states: (1) **restored**, which means it is displayed somewhere in the Access window (Figure 1-5a); (2) **minimized**, which means it is displayed on the Windows taskbar (Figure 1-5b); or (3) **hidden**, which means you do not see it on the screen. If the Language bar is hidden and you want it to display, then do the following:

1. Right-click an open area on the Windows taskbar at the bottom of the screen.
2. Point to Toolbars and then click Language bar on the Toolbars submenu.

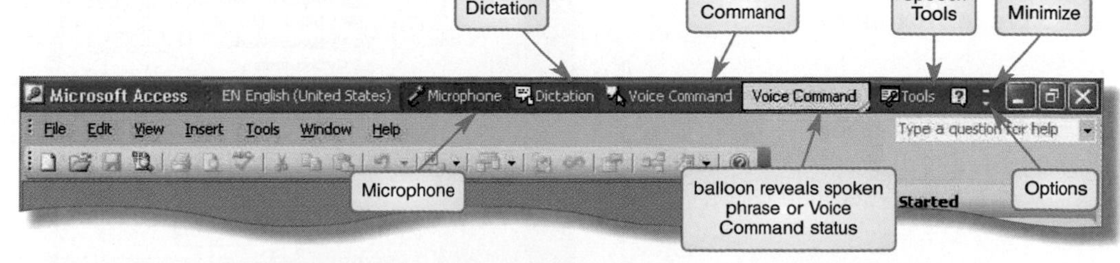

(a) Language Bar in Access Window with Microphone Enabled

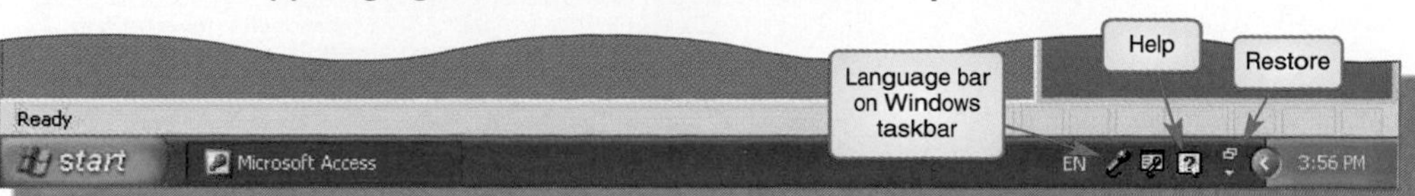

(b) Language Bar Minimized on Windows Taskbar

FIGURE 1-5

If the Language bar command is dimmed on the Toolbars submenu or if the Speech command is dimmed on the Tools menu, the Office Speech Recognition software is not installed.

Creating a New Database

In Access, all the tables, reports, forms, and queries that you create are stored in a single file called a database. Thus, before creating any of these objects, you first must create the database that will hold them. You can use either the Database Wizard or the Blank database option in the task pane to create a new database. The Database Wizard can guide you by suggesting some commonly used databases. If you choose to create a database using the Database Wizard, you would use the following steps.

To Create a Database Using the Database Wizard

1. Click the New button on the Database toolbar and then click the On my computer link in the New File task pane.
2. When Access displays the Templates dialog box, click the Databases tab, and then click the database that is most appropriate for your needs.
3. Follow the instructions in the Database Wizard dialog box to create the database.

Because you already know the tables and fields you want in the Alyssa High School database, you would use the Blank database option in the task pane rather than the Database Wizard. The following steps illustrate how to use the Blank database option to create a database on a USB flash drive.

To Create a New Database

1

- **With a USB flash drive connected to one of the computer's USB ports, click the New button on the Database toolbar to display the task pane.**
- **Click the Blank database option in the task pane, and then click the Save in box arrow.**

Access displays the File New Database dialog box and the Save in list appears (Figure 1-6a). Your File name text box may display db1.mdb, rather than db1.

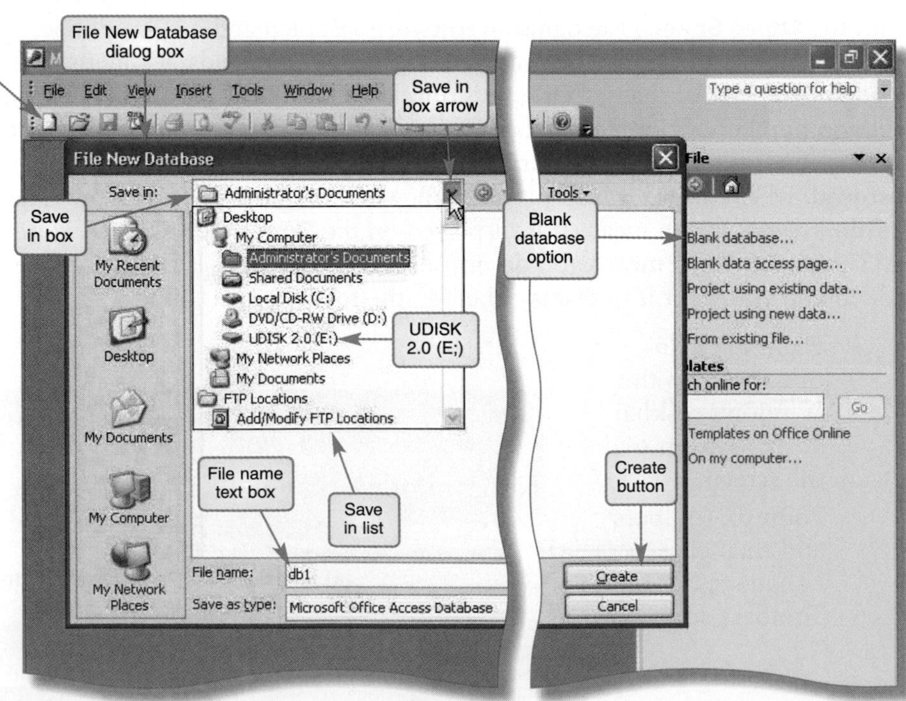

FIGURE 1-6a

2

- **Click UDISK 2.0 (E:). (Your USB flash drive may have a different name and letter.)**
- **Click the File name text box.**
- **Use the BACKSPACE key or the DELETE key to delete db1 and then type** `AHSIT Internships` **as the file name.**

The file name is changed to AHSIT Internships (Figure 1-6b).

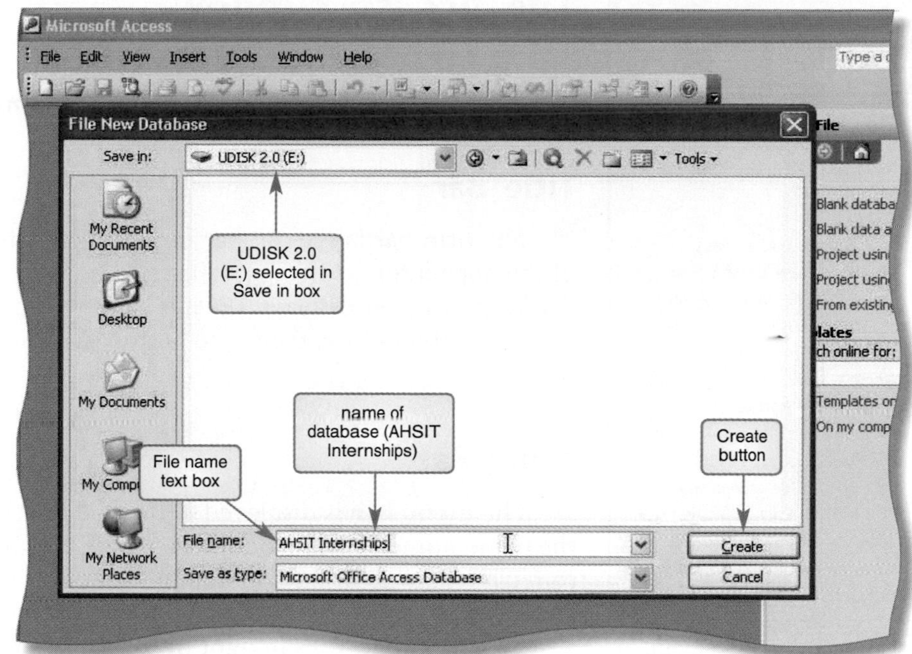

FIGURE 1-6b

3

- **Click the Create button to create the database.**

The AHSIT Internships database is created. The AHSIT Internships : Database window appears in the Microsoft Access window (Figure 1-7). The task pane does not appear.

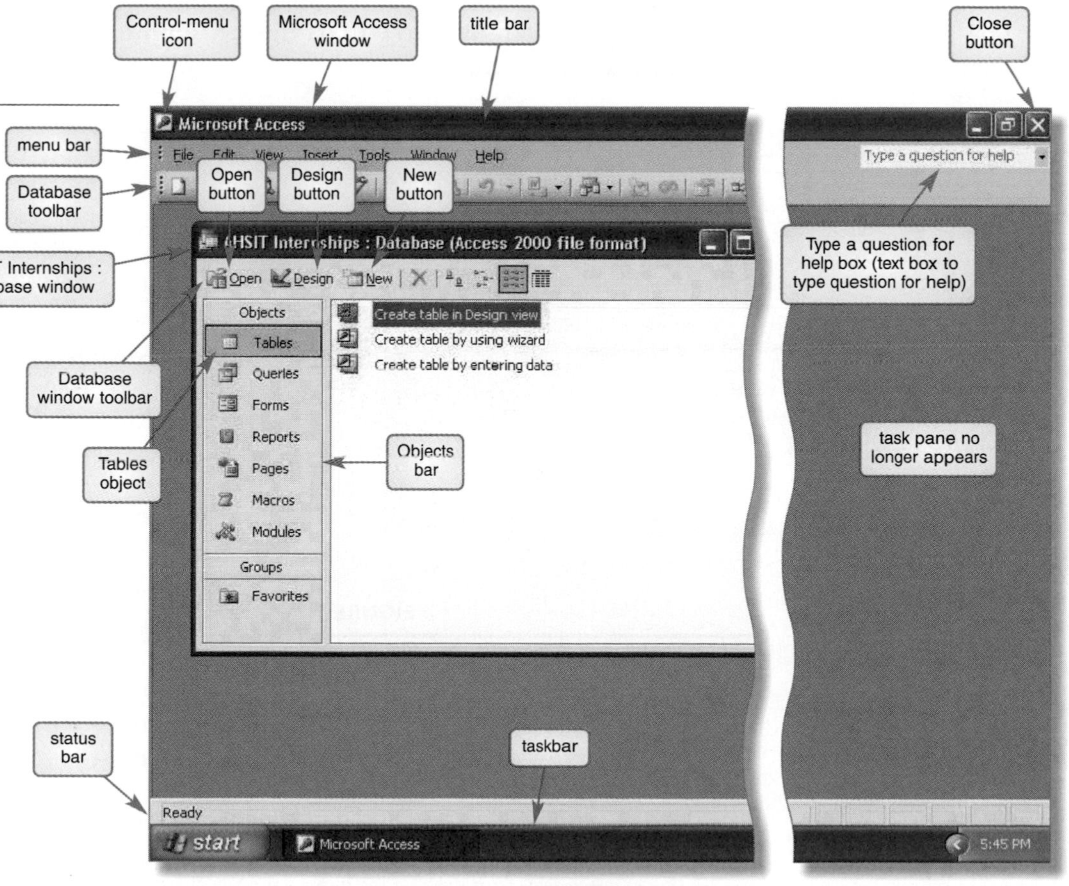

FIGURE 1-7

> *Q & A*
>
> **Q:** Why does the AHSIT Internships : Database window in Figure 1-7 on the previous page display the words, Access 2000 file format?
>
> **A:** By default, Access creates a new database in Access 2000 format. A file in Access 2000 format can be opened in Access 2000, Access 2002, or Access 2003. This allows you to share your database with users who do not have Access 2003. You can open a file in Access 2002-2003 only in Access 2002 or later. Certain features of Access 2003 are not available if the database is in Access 2000 file format.

The Access Window

The Access window (Figure 1-7 on the previous page) contains a variety of features that play important roles when you are working with a database.

Title Bar

The **title bar** is the top bar in the Microsoft Access window. It includes the title of the application, Microsoft Access. The icon on the left is the Control-menu icon. Clicking this icon displays a menu from which you can close the Access window. The button on the right is the Close button. Clicking the Close button closes the Access window.

Menu Bar

The **menu bar** is displayed below the title bar. It is a special toolbar that displays the menu names. Each menu name represents a menu of commands that you can use to retrieve, store, print, and manipulate data. When you point to a menu name on the menu bar, the area of the menu bar is displayed as a selected button. Access shades selected buttons in light orange and surrounds them with a blue outline. To display a menu, such as the Edit menu, click the Edit menu name on the menu bar (Figures 1-8a and 1-8b). A **menu** is a list of commands. If you point to a command on the menu with an arrow to its right, a **submenu** is displayed from which you can choose a command.

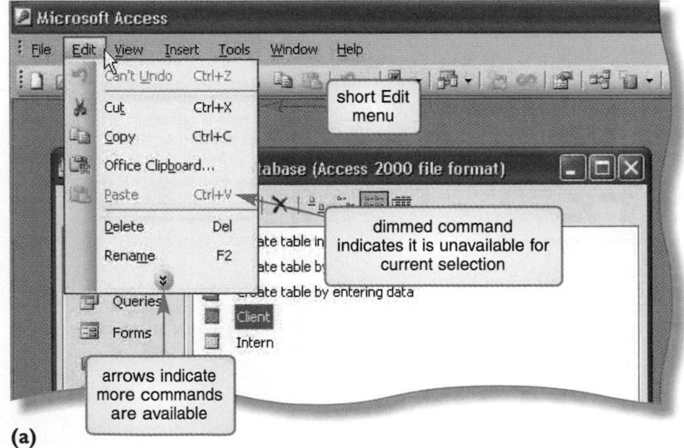

(a)

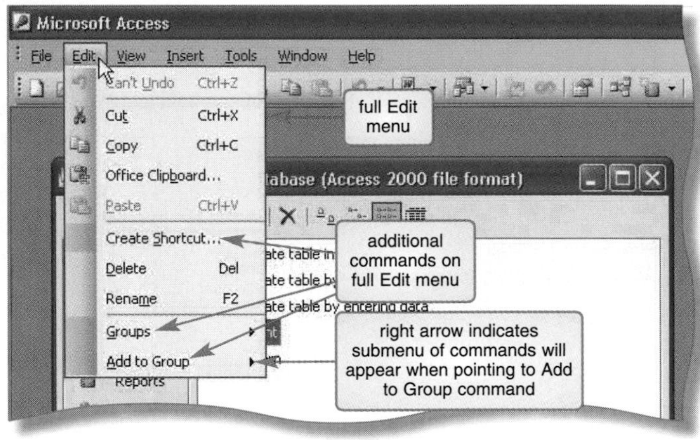

(b)

FIGURE 1-8

When you click a menu name on the menu bar, Access displays a **short menu** listing the most recently used commands (Figure 1-8a). If you wait a few seconds or click the arrows at the bottom of the short menu, the full menu appears. The **full menu** lists all the commands associated with a menu (Figure 1-8b). You also can display a full menu immediately by double-clicking the menu name on the menu bar. In this book, always have Access display the full menu using one of the following techniques:

1. Click the menu name on the menu bar and then wait a few seconds.
2. Click the menu name and then click the arrows at the bottom of the short menu.

3. Click the menu name and then point to the arrows at the bottom of the short menu.
4. Double-click the menu name.

Both short and full menus display some **dimmed commands** that appear gray, or dimmed, instead of black, which indicates they are not available for the current selection. A command with a medium-blue shading to the left of it on a full menu is called a **hidden command** because it does not display on a short menu. As you use Access, it automatically personalizes the short menus for you based on how often you use commands. That is, as you use hidden commands, Access *unhides* them and places them on the short menu.

Q & A

Q: Will Access automatically display the correct toolbar for the task on which I am working?

A: Normally, Access will display the correct toolbar. If it does not, click View on the menu bar, and then click Toolbars. On the Toolbars submenu, select the toolbar for the activity in which you are engaged. See Appendix D for additional details.

Toolbars

Below the menu bar is a toolbar. A **toolbar** contains buttons that allow you to perform certain tasks more quickly than using the menu bar. Each button contains a picture, or **icon**, depicting its function. When you move the mouse pointer over a button, the name of the button appears below it in a **ScreenTip**. The toolbar shown in Figure 1-7 on page AC 11 is the Database toolbar. The specific toolbar or toolbars that appear will vary, depending on the task on which you are working. Access routinely displays the toolbar or toolbars you will need for the task. If you want to change these or simply to determine what toolbars are available for the given task, consult Appendix D.

Taskbar

The Windows **taskbar** at the bottom of the screen displays the Start button, any active windows, and the current time.

Status Bar

Immediately above the Windows taskbar is the **status bar**. It contains special information that is appropriate for the task on which you are working. Currently, it contains the word, Ready, which means Access is ready to accept commands.

Database Window

The **Database window**, referred to in Figure 1-7 as the AHSIT Internships : Database window, is a special window that allows you to access easily and rapidly a variety of objects, such as tables, queries, forms, and reports. To do so, you will use the various components of the window.

Shortcut Menus

Rather than use toolbars to accomplish a given task, you also can use **shortcut menus**, which are menus that display the actions available for a particular item. To display the shortcut menu for an item, right-click the item; that is, point to the item and then click the right mouse button. Figures 1-9a and 1-9b on the next page illustrate the use of toolbars and shortcut menus to perform the same task, namely to print the contents of the Client table. In the figure, the tables you will create in this project already have been created.

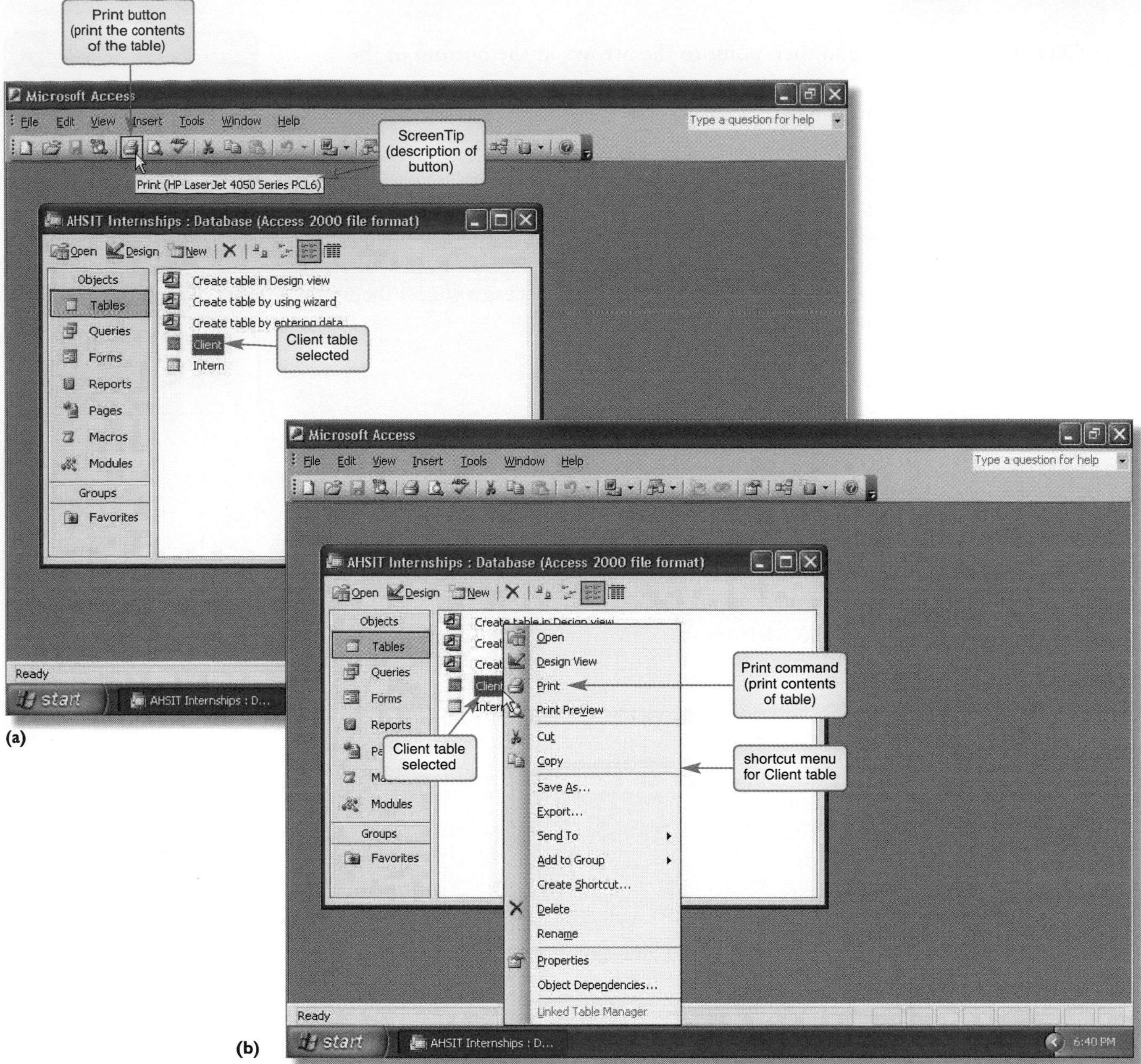

FIGURE 1-9

> **Q & A**
>
> **Q:** Is there more than one way to invoke a command in Access?
>
> **A:** Yes. For a table that lists how to complete tasks covered in this book using the mouse, menu, shortcut menu, and keyboard, see the Quick Reference Summary at the back of this book, or visit the Office 2003 Quick Reference Web page (scsite.com/off2003sch/qr).

Before the action illustrated in Figure 1-9a, you would have to select the Client table by clicking it. Then, you would point to the Print button on the toolbar, as shown in the figure. When you point to a button on a toolbar, the ScreenTip appears, indicating the purpose of the button, in this case Print. When you click the button, the corresponding action takes place. In this case, Access will print the contents of the Client table.

To use a shortcut menu to perform the same task, you would right-click the Client table, which produces the shortcut menu shown in Figure 1-9b. You then would click the desired command, in this case the Print command, on the shortcut menu. The corresponding action then takes place.

You can use whichever option you prefer. Many professionals who use Access will use a combination. If it is simplest to use the shortcut menu, which often is the case, they will use the shortcut menu. If it is simpler just to click a toolbar button, they will do that. The steps in this text follow this approach; that is, using a combination of both options.

AutoCorrect

Not visible in the Access window, the **AutoCorrect** feature of Access works behind the scenes, correcting common mistakes when you complete a text entry in a cell. AutoCorrect makes three types of corrections for you:

1. Corrects two initial capital letters by changing the second letter to lowercase
2. Capitalizes the first letter in the names of days
3. Replaces commonly misspelled words with their correct spelling. For example, it will change the misspelled word *recieve* to *receive* when you complete the entry. AutoCorrect will correct the spelling automatically of more than 400 commonly misspelled words.

Creating a Table

An Access database consists of a collection of tables. After you have created the database, you must create each of the tables within it. In this project, for example, you must create both the Client and Intern tables shown in Figure 1-1 on page AC 5.

To create a table, you describe the structure of the table to Access by describing the fields within the table. For each field, you indicate the following:

1. **Field name** — Each field in the table must have a unique name. In the Client table (Figure 1-10a below and 1-10b on the next page), for example, the field names are Client Number, Name, Address, City, State, Zip Code, Amount Paid, Current Due, and Intern Number.

Q & A

Q: Does Access include a wizard for creating a table:

A: Access includes a Table Wizard that guides you by suggesting some commonly used tables and fields. To use the Table Wizard, click Tables on the Objects bar, click New on the Database window toolbar, click Table Wizard and then click OK. Follow the directions in the Table Wizard dialog boxes. After you create the table, you can modify it at any time by opening the table in Design view.

Structure of Client table

FIELD NAME	DATA TYPE	FIELD SIZE	PRIMARY KEY?	DESCRIPTION
Client Number	Text	4	Yes	Client Number (Primary Key)
Name	Text	20		Client Name
Address	Text	15		Street Address
City	Text	15		City
State	Text	2		State (Two-Character Abbreviation)
Zip Code	Text	5		Zip Code (Five-Character Version)
Amount Paid	Currency			Amount Paid by Client This Year
Current Due	Currency			Current Due from Client This Period
Intern Number	Text	2		Number of Client's Intern

FIGURE 1-10a

Client table

CLIENT NUMBER	NAME	ADDRESS	CITY	STATE	ZIP CODE	AMOUNT PAID	CURRENT DUE	INTERN NUMBER
A54	Afton Mills	612 Revere	Grant City	ND	58120	$892.50	$315.50	22
A62	Atlas Suppliers	227 Dandelion	Empeer	ND	58216	$2,672.00	$525.00	24
B26	Blake-Scripps	557 Maum	Grant City	ND	58120	$0.00	$229.50	24
D76	Dege Grocery	446 Linton	Portage	MN	59130	$1,202.00	$485.75	34
G56	Grand Cleaners	337 Abelard	Portage	MN	59131	$925.50	$265.00	22
H21	Hill Shoes	247 Fulton	Grant City	ND	58121	$228.50	$0.00	24
J77	Jones Plumbing	75 Getty	E. Portage	MN	59135	$0.00	$0.00	34
M26	Mohr Crafts	665 Market	Empeer	ND	58216	$1,572.00	$312.50	22
S56	SeeSaw Ind.	31 Liatris	Portage	MN	59130	$2,827.50	$362.50	34
T45	Tate Repair	824 Revere	Grant City	ND	58120	$254.00	$0.00	24

FIGURE 1-10b

2. **Data type** — Data type indicates to Access the type of data the field will contain. Some fields can contain only numbers. Others, such as Amount Paid and Current Due, can contain numbers and dollar signs. Still others, such as Name and Address, can contain letters.
3. **Description** — Access allows you to enter a detailed description of the field.

You also can assign field widths to text fields (fields whose data type is Text). This indicates the maximum number of characters that can be stored in the field. If you do not assign a width to such a field, Access assumes the width is 50.

You also must indicate which field or fields make up the primary key; that is, the unique identifier, for the table. In the Alyssa High School database, the Client Number field is the primary key of the Client table and the Intern Number field is the primary key of the Intern table.

The rules for field names are:

1. Names can be up to 64 characters in length.
2. Names can contain letters, digits, and spaces, as well as most of the punctuation symbols.
3. Names cannot contain periods, exclamation points (!), accent graves (`), or square brackets ([ ]).
4. The same name cannot be used for two different fields in the same table.

Each field has a **data type.** This indicates the type of data that can be stored in the field. The data types you will use in this project are:

1. **Text** — The field can contain any characters. A maximum number of 255 characters is allowed in a field whose data type is Text.
2. **Number** — The field can contain only numbers. The numbers either can be positive or negative. Fields are assigned this type so they can be used in arithmetic operations. Fields that contain numbers but will not be used for arithmetic operations usually are assigned a data type of Text. The Intern Number field, for example, is a text field because the intern numbers will not be involved in any arithmetic.

Q & A

Q: Do all database management systems use the same data types?

A: No. Different database management systems have different available data types. Even data types that are essentially the same can have different names. The Access 2003 Text data type, for example, is referred to as Character in some systems and Alpha in others.

Q & A

Q: Must the primary key be a single field?

A: In some cases, the primary key consists of a combination of fields rather than a single field. For more information about determining primary keys in such situations, visit the Office 2003 Q&A Web page (scsite.com/off2003sch/qa), locate Access Project 1, and click Primary Keys.

3. **Currency** — The field can contain only monetary data. The values will appear with currency symbols, such as dollar signs, commas, decimal points, and with two digits following the decimal point. Like numeric fields, you can use currency fields in arithmetic operations. Access assigns a size to currency fields automatically.

Table 1-1 shows the other data types that are available.

Table 1-1 Additional Data Types

DATA TYPE	DESCRIPTION
Memo	Field can store a variable amount of text or combinations of text and numbers where the total number of characters may exceed 255.
Date/Time	Field can store dates and times.
AutoNumber	Field can store a unique sequential number that Access assigns to a record. Access will increment the number by 1 as each new record is added.
Yes/No	Field can store only one of two values. The choices are Yes/No, True/False, or On/Off.
OLE Object	Field can store an OLE object, which is an object linked to or embedded in the table.
Hyperlink	Field can store text that can be used as a hyperlink address.
Lookup Wizard	Field can store a value from another table or from a list of values by using a list box or combo box. Choosing this data type starts the Lookup Wizard, which assists in the creation of the field. The field then is a Lookup field. The data type is set based on the values you selected in the wizard. If the values are text, for example, the field is assigned the Text data type.

The field names, data types, field sizes, primary key information, and descriptions for the Client table are shown in Figure 1-10a on page AC 15.

With the information in Figures 1-10a and 1-10b, you are ready to begin creating the table. The following steps illustrate how to create a table.

To Create a Table

1

- **Click the New button on the Database window toolbar.**

The New Table dialog box appears (Figure 1-11).

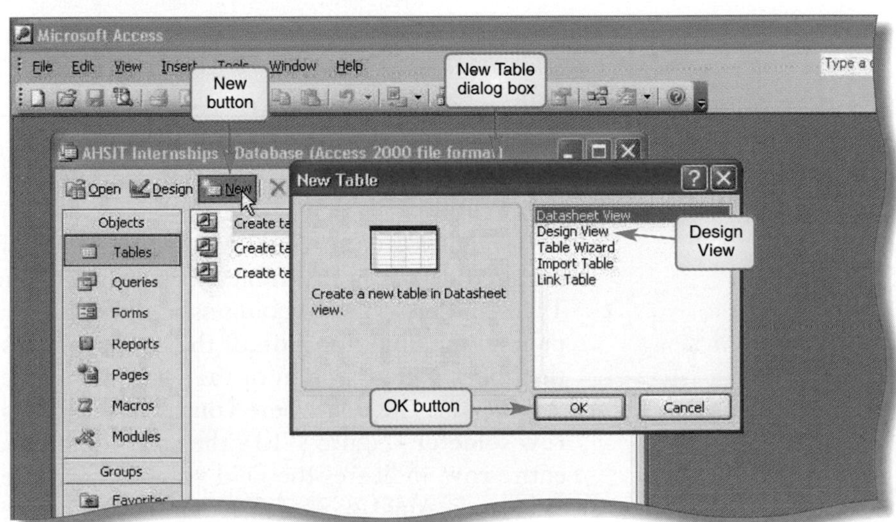

2

• **Click Design View and then click the OK button.**

The Table1 : Table window appears (Figure 1-12).

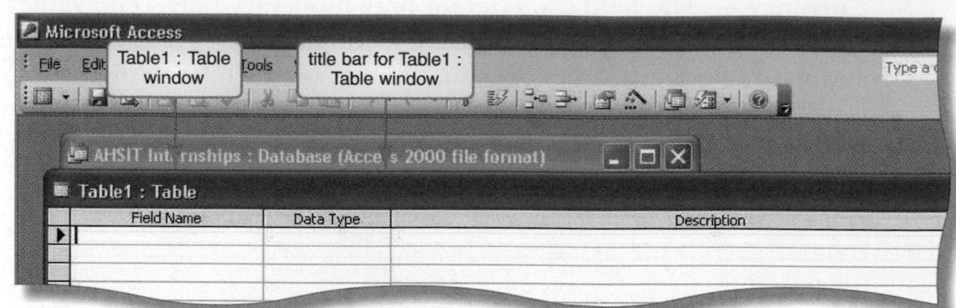

FIGURE 1-12

3

• **Double-click the title bar of the Table1 : Table window to maximize the window.**

Access displays the maximized Table1 : Table window (Figure 1-13).

maximized Table1 : Table window

Field Name column

Data Type column

Description column

row selector

Restore Down button

pane in which fields are created

pane in which field properties are specified

pressing F6 switches between panes

Field Properties

General

Lookup

Design view. F6 = Switch panes. F1 = Help.

FIGURE 1-13

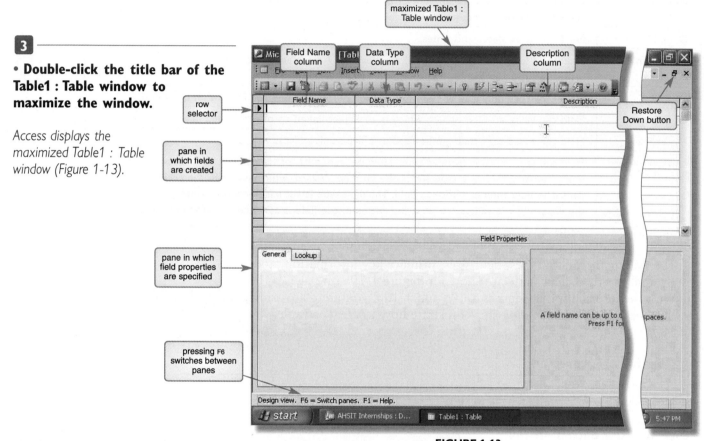

Defining the Fields

The next step in creating the table is to define the fields by specifying the required details in the Table window, which include entries in the Field Name, Data Type, and Description columns and additional information in the Field Properties pane in the lower portion of the Table window. You press the F6 key to move from the upper **pane** (portion of the screen), the one where you define the fields, to the lower pane, the one where you define field properties. As you define the fields, the **row selector** (Figure 1-13), the small box or bar that, when you click it, selects the entire row, indicates the field you currently are describing. It is positioned on the first field, indicating Access is ready for you to enter the name of the first field in the Field Name column.

The following steps show how to define the fields in the table.

To Define the Fields in a Table

1

• **Type** `Client Number` **(the name of the first field) in the Field Name column, and then press the TAB key.**

The words, Client Number, appear in the Field Name column and the insertion point advances to the Data Type column, indicating you can enter the data type (Figure 1-14). The word, Text, one of the possible data types, currently appears. The box arrow indicates a list of data types is available by clicking the arrow.

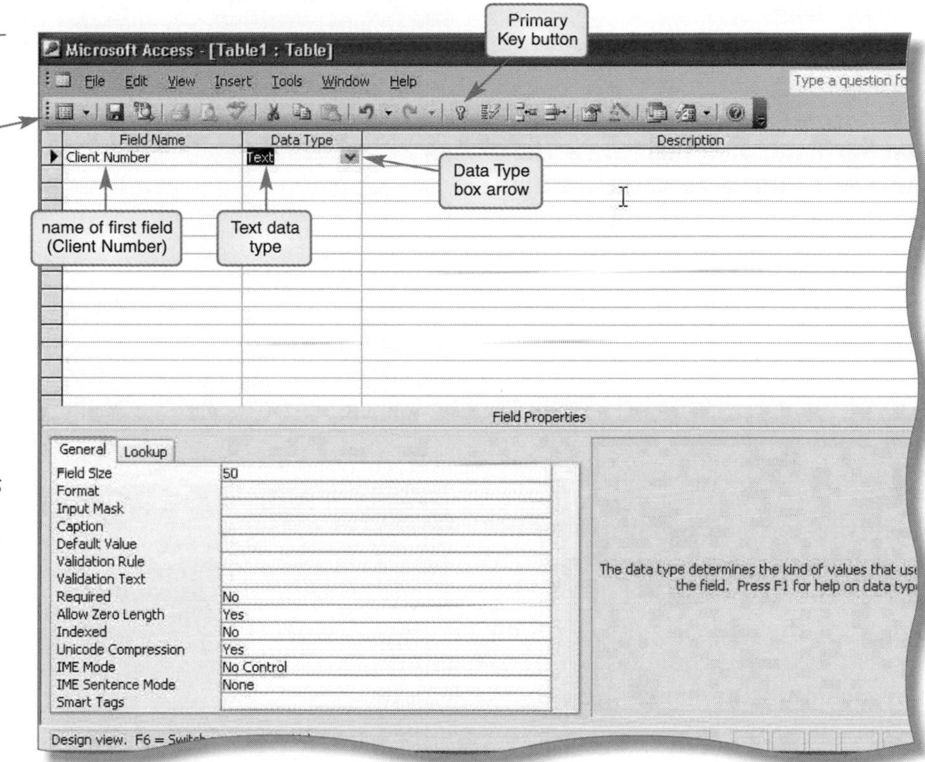

FIGURE 1-14

2

• **Because Text is the correct data type, press the TAB key to move the insertion point to the Description column, type** `Client Number (Primary Key)` **as the description, and then click the Primary Key button on the Table Design toolbar.**

The Client Number field is the primary key, as indicated by the key symbol that appears in the row selector (Figure 1-15). A ScreenTip, which is a description of the button, appears.

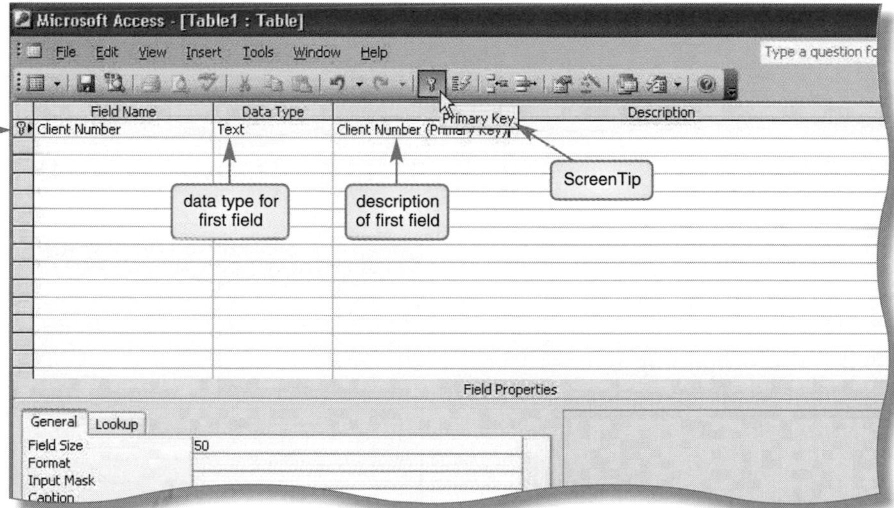

FIGURE 1-15

3

• **Press the F6 key.**

The current entry in the Field Size property box (50) is selected (Figure 1-16).

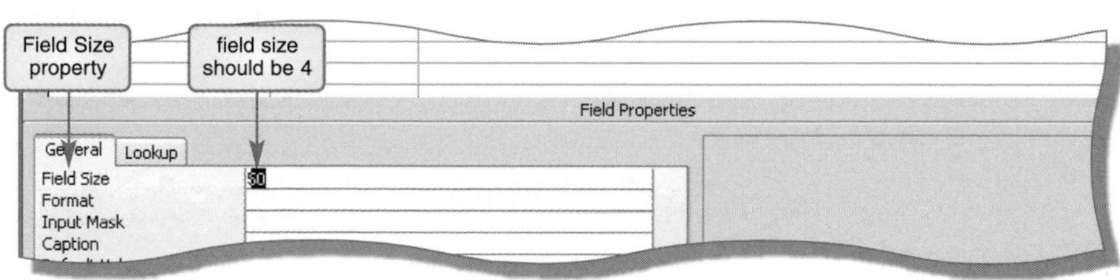

FIGURE 1-16

4

- **Type** 4 **as the size of the Client Number field.**
- **Press the F6 key to return to the Description column for the Client Number field, and then press the TAB key to move to the Field Name column in the second row.**

The insertion point moves to the second row just below the field name Client Number (Figure 1-17).

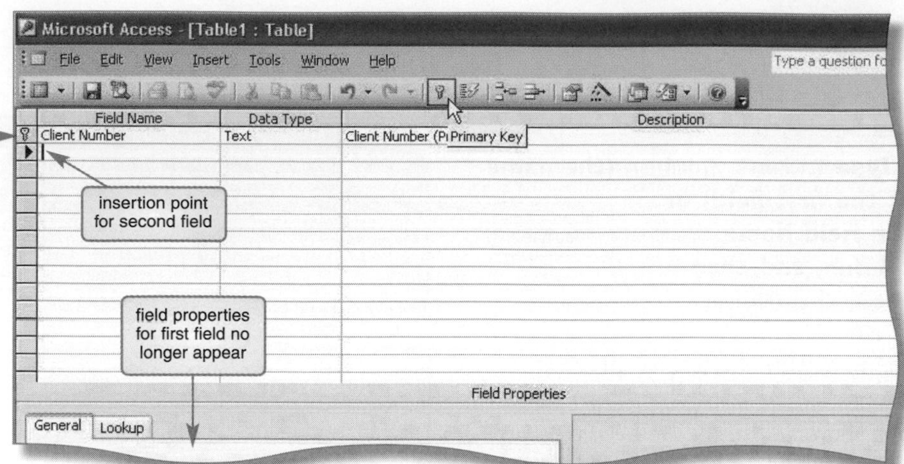

FIGURE 1-17

5

- **Use the techniques illustrated in Steps 1 through 4 to make the entries from the Client table structure shown in Figure 1-10a on page AC 15 up through and including the name of the Amount Paid field.**
- **Click the Data Type box arrow.**

The additional fields are entered (Figure 1-18). A list of available data types appears in the Data Type column for the Amount Paid field.

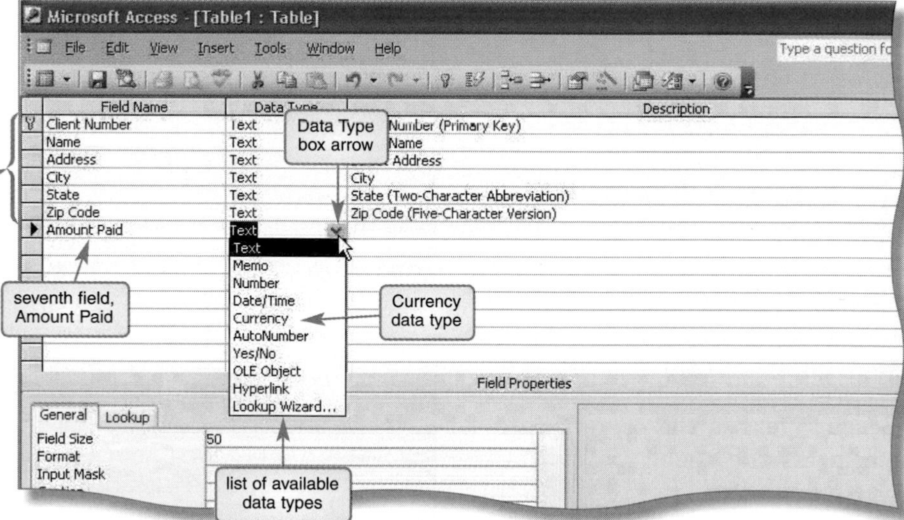

FIGURE 1-18

6

- **Click Currency and then press the TAB key.**
- **Make the remaining entries from the Client table structure shown in Figure 1-10a.**

All the fields are entered (Figure 1-19).

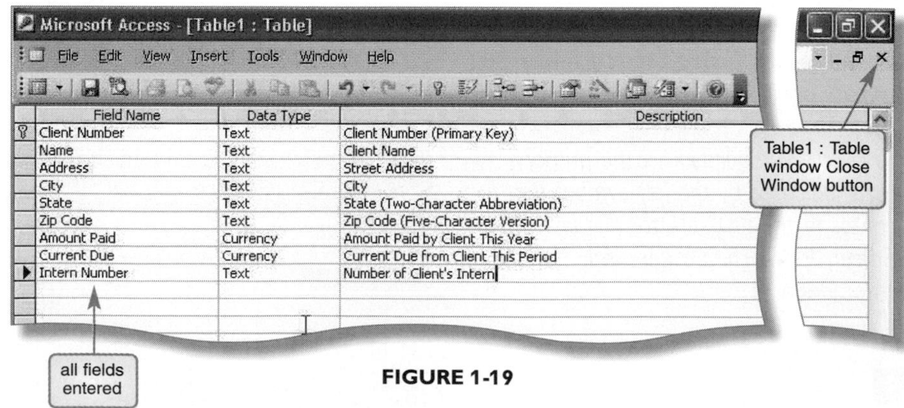

FIGURE 1-19

The description of the table is now complete.

Correcting Errors in the Structure

When creating a table, check the entries carefully to ensure they are correct. If you make a mistake and discover it before you press the TAB key, you can correct the error by repeatedly pressing the BACKSPACE key until the incorrect characters are removed. Then, type the correct characters. If you do not discover a mistake until later, you can click the entry, type the correct value, and then press the ENTER key.

If you accidentally add an extra field to the structure, select the field by clicking the row selector (the leftmost column on the row that contains the field to be deleted). After you have selected the field, press the DELETE key. This will remove the field from the structure.

If you forget a field, select the field that will follow the field you want to add by clicking the row selector, and then press the INSERT key. The remaining fields move down one row, making room for the missing field. Make the entries for the new field in the usual manner.

If you made the wrong field a primary key field, click the correct primary key entry for the field and then click the Primary Key button on the Table Design toolbar.

As an alternative to these steps, you may want to start over. To do so, click the Close Window button for the Table1 : Table window and then click the No button in the Microsoft Office Access dialog box. The initial Microsoft Access window is displayed, and you can repeat the process you used earlier.

Q & A

Q: Are there any other ways to correct errors?

A: You also can correct errors by using the Undo button on the Table Design toolbar. Access displays a list of the 20 most recent actions you can undo. When you undo an action, you also undo all actions above it in the list. If you later decide you did not want to undo an action, click Redo.

Q & A

Q: Why is the data type for Zip Code Text instead of Number?

A: Zip codes are not used in arithmetic operations. You do not add Zip codes or find an average Zip code, for example.

Closing and Saving a Table

The Client table structure now is complete. The final step is to close and save the table within the database. At this time, you should give the table a name.

Table names are from 1 to 64 characters in length and can contain letters, numbers, and spaces. The two table names in this project are Client and Intern.

The following steps close and save the table.

To Close and Save a Table

1

- **Click the Close Window button for the Table 1: Table window (see Figure 1-19). (Be sure not to click the Close button on the Microsoft Access title bar, because this would close Microsoft Access.)**

The Microsoft Office Access dialog box appears (Figure 1-20).

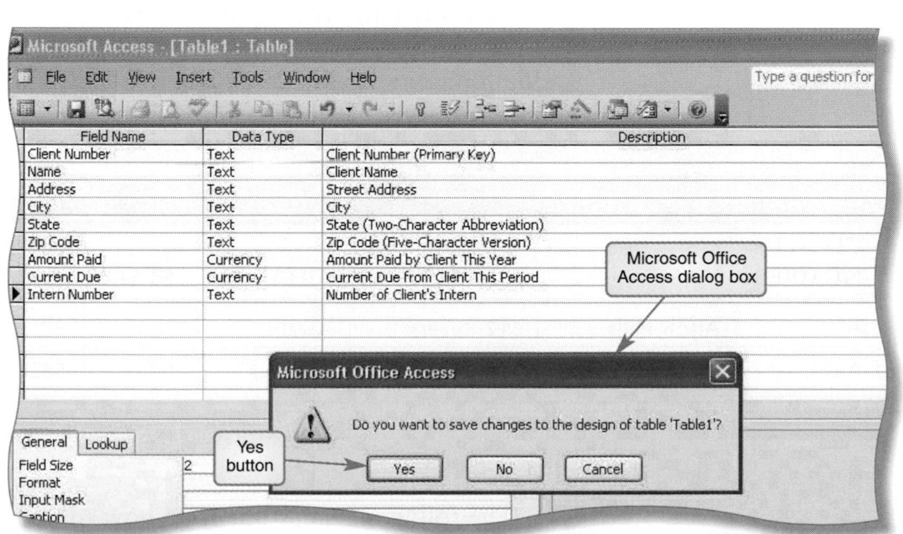

FIGURE 1-20

2

• **Click the Yes button in the Microsoft Office Access dialog box, and then type `Client` as the name of the table.**

The Save As dialog box appears (Figure 1-21). The table name is entered.

3

• **Click the OK button in the Save As dialog box.**

The table is saved. The window containing the table design no longer is displayed.

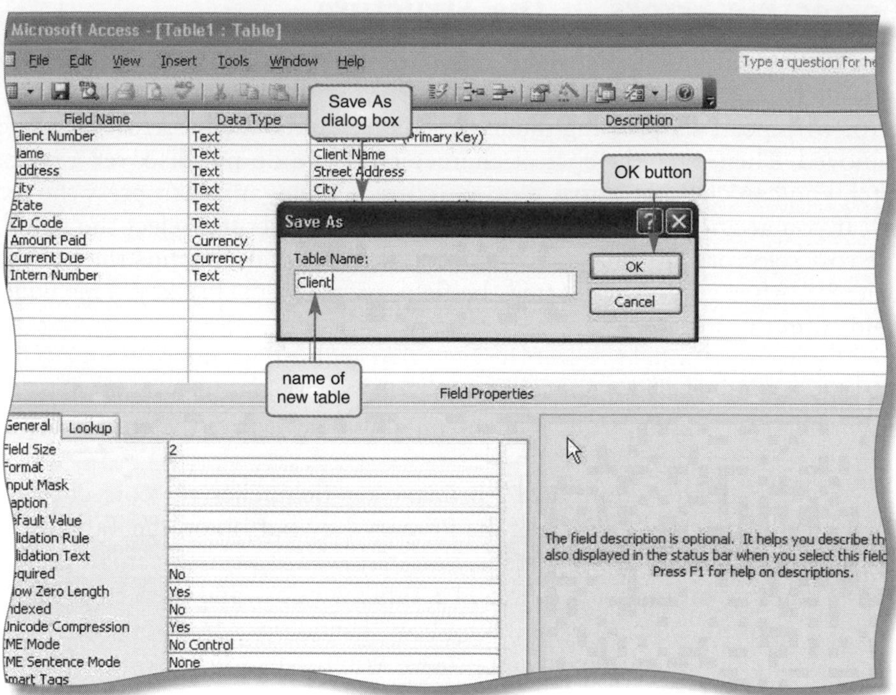

FIGURE 1-21

Skill Builder 1-1

To practice the following tasks, visit scsite.com/off2003sch/skill, locate Access Project 1, and then click Skill Builder 1-1.

- ❑ Create a table
- ❑ Define the fields
- ❑ Close and save the table

Adding Records to a Table

Creating a table by building the structure and saving the table is the first step in a two-step process. The second step is to add records to the table. To add records to a table, the table must be open. When making changes to tables, you work in Datasheet view. In **Datasheet view**, the table is represented as a collection of rows and columns called a **datasheet**. It looks very much like the tables shown in Figure 1-1 on page AC 5.

You often add records in phases. You may, for example, not have enough time to add all the records in one session. To illustrate this process, this project begins by adding the first two records in the Client table (Figure 1-22). The remaining records are added later.

Client table (first 2 records)

CLIENT NUMBER	NAME	ADDRESS	CITY	STATE	ZIP CODE	AMOUNT PAID	CURRENT DUE	INTERN NUMBER
A54	Afton Mills	612 Revere	Grant City	ND	58120	$892.50	$315.50	22
A62	Atlas Suppliers	227 Dandelion	Empeer	ND	58216	$2,672.00	$525.00	24

FIGURE 1-22

The following steps illustrate how to open the Client table and then add records.

To Add Records to a Table

1

• **Right-click the Client table in the AHSIT Internships : Database window.**

The shortcut menu for the Client table appears (Figure 1-23). The AHSIT Internships : Database window is maximized because the previous window, the Client : Table window, was maximized. (If you wanted to restore the Database window to its original size, you would click the Restore Window button.)

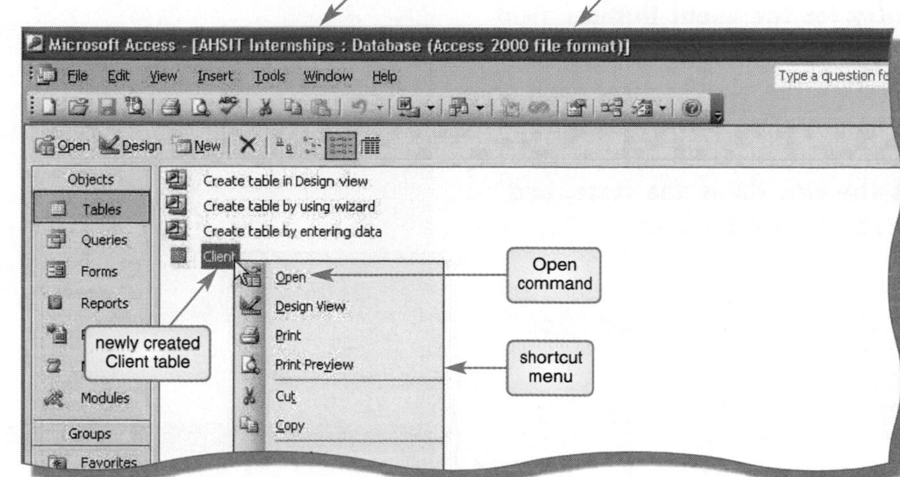

FIGURE 1-23

2

• **Click Open on the shortcut menu.**

Access displays the Client : Table window (Figure 1-24). The window contains the Datasheet view for the Client table. The ***record selector****, the small box or bar that, when clicked, selects the entire record, is positioned on the first record. The status bar at the bottom of the window also indicates that the record selector is positioned on record 1.*

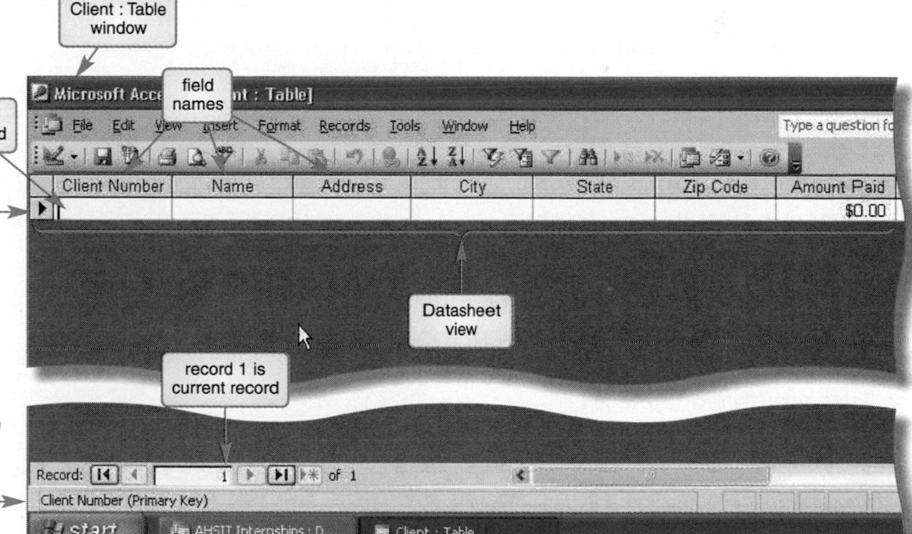

FIGURE 1-24

3

• **Type** A54 **as the first client number (see Figure 1-22). Be sure you type the letters in uppercase, as shown in the table in Figure 1-22, so they are entered in the database correctly.**

The client number is entered, but the insertion point is still in the Client Number field (Figure 1-25). The pencil icon in the record selector column indicates that the record is being edited, but changes to the record are not saved yet. Microsoft Access also creates a row for a new record.

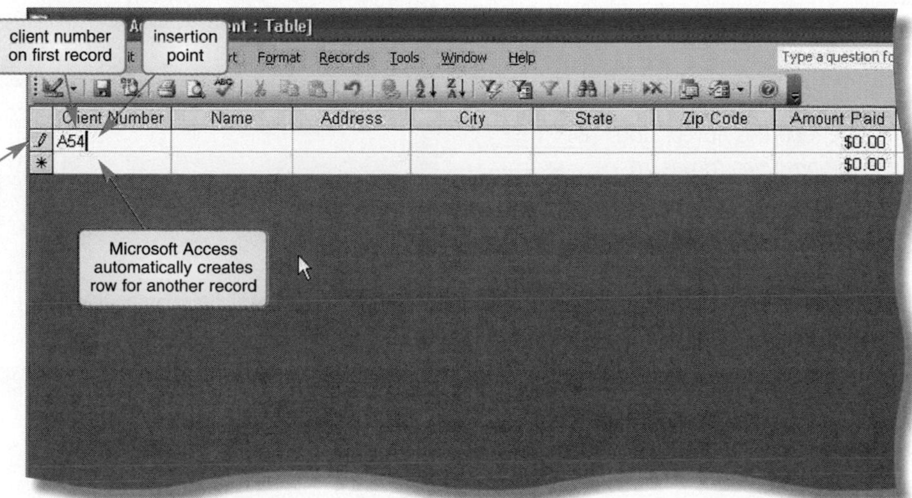

FIGURE 1-25

4

• **Press the TAB key to complete the entry for the Client Number field.**

• **Type the following entries, pressing the TAB key after each one:** `Afton Mills` **as the name,** `612 Revere` **as the address,** `Grant City` **as the city,** `ND` **as the state, and** `58120` **as the Zip code.**

The Name, Address, City, State, and Zip Code fields are entered (Figure 1-26).

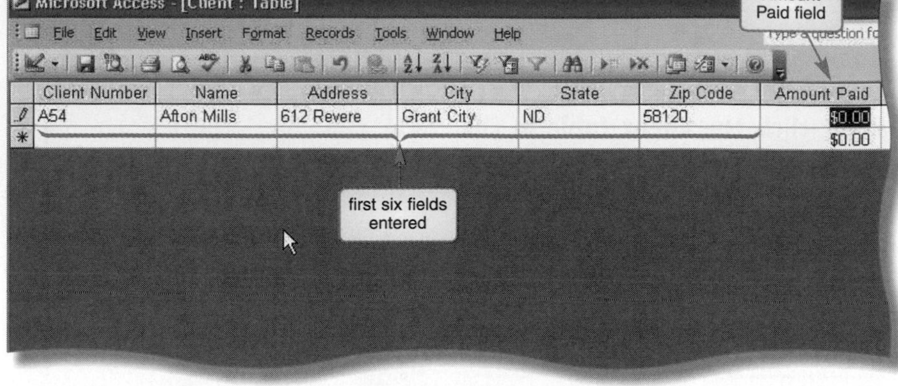

FIGURE 1-26

5

• **Type** `892.50` **as the Amount Paid amount and then press the TAB key. (You do not need to type dollar signs or commas. In addition, if the digits to the right of the decimal point were both zeros, you would not need to type either the decimal point or the zeros.)**

• **Type** `315.50` **as the current due amount and then press the TAB key.**

• **Type** `22` **as the intern number to complete data entry for the record.**

The fields have shifted to the left (Figure 1-27). The Amount Paid and Current Due values appear with dollar signs and decimal points. The insertion point is positioned in the Intern Number field.

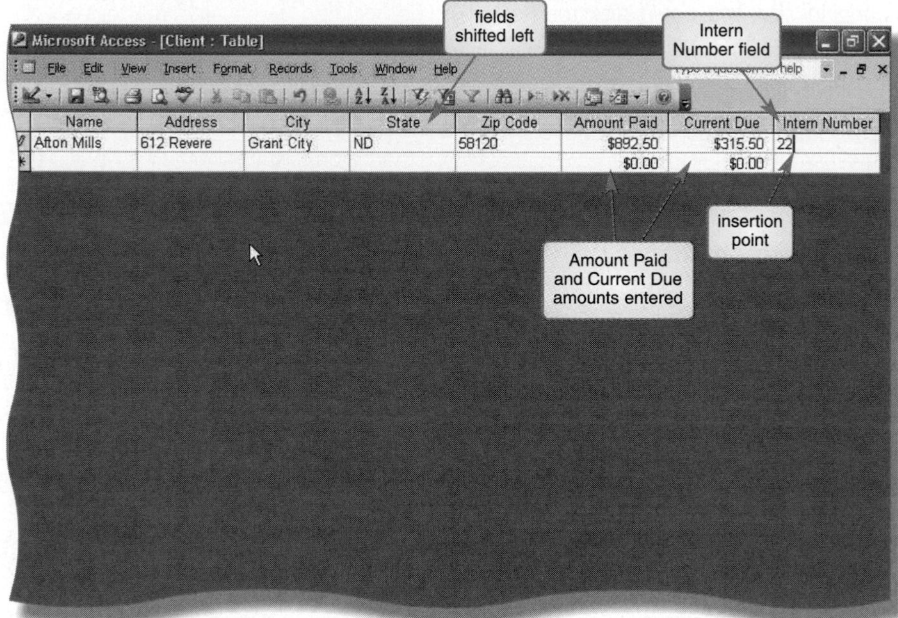

FIGURE 1-27

6

• **Press the TAB key.**

The fields shift back to the right, the record is saved, and the insertion point moves to the Client Number field on the second row (Figure 1-28).

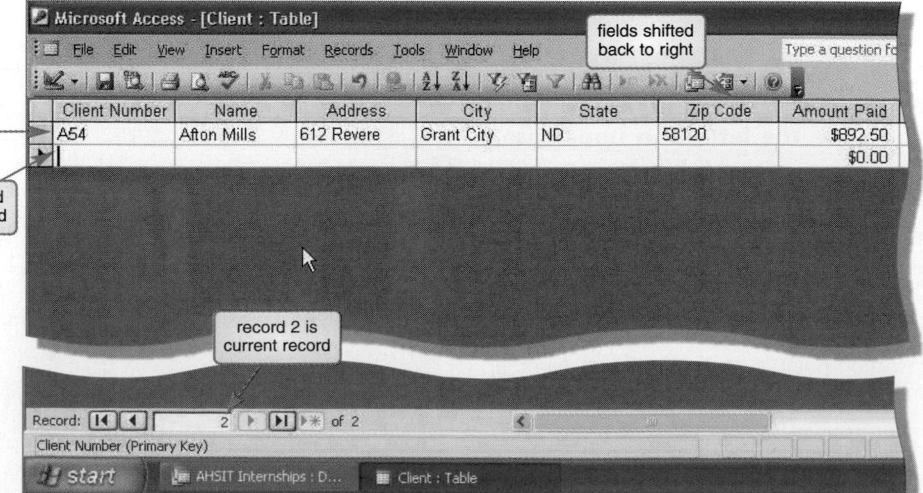

FIGURE 1-28

7

• **Use the techniques shown in Steps 3 through 6 to add the data for the second record shown in Figure 1-22 on page AC 22.**

The second record is added and the insertion point moves to the Client Number field on the third row (Figure 1-29).

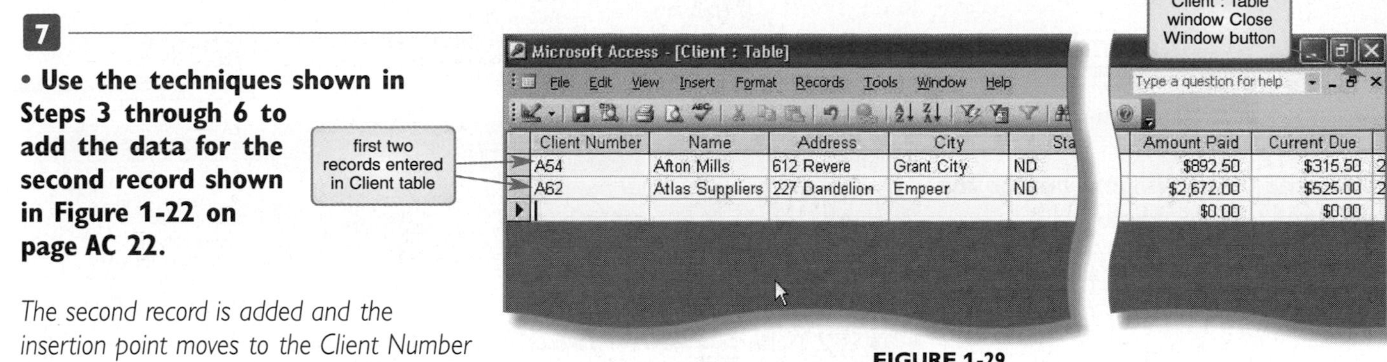

FIGURE 1-29

As soon as you have entered or modified a record and moved to another record, the original record is saved. This is different from other applications. The rows entered in a spreadsheet, for example, are not saved until the entire spreadsheet is saved.

Correcting Errors in the Data

Check your entries carefully to ensure they are correct. If you make a mistake and discover it before you press the TAB key, correct it by pressing the BACKSPACE key until the incorrect characters are removed and then typing the correct characters.

If you discover an incorrect entry later, correct the error by clicking the incorrect entry and then making the appropriate correction. If the record you must correct is not on the screen, use any technique, such as the UP ARROW and DOWN ARROW keys to move to it. If the field you want to correct is not visible on the screen, use the horizontal scroll bar along the bottom of the screen to shift all the fields until the one you want appears. Then make the correction.

If you add an extra record accidentally, select the record by clicking the record selector that immediately precedes the record. Then, press the DELETE key. This will remove the record from the table. If you forget a record, add it using the same procedure as for all the other records. Access will place it in the correct location in the table automatically.

If you cannot determine how to correct the data, you are, in effect, stuck on the record. Access neither allows you to move to any other record until you have made the correction nor allows you to close the table. If you encounter this situation, simply press the ESC key. Pressing the ESC key will remove from the screen the record you are trying to add. You then can move to any other record, close the table, or take any other action you desire.

Q & A

Q: Is there any other way to correct errors in the data?

A: You also can undo changes to a field by clicking the Undo typing button on the Table Datasheet toolbar. If you already have moved to another record and want to delete the record you just added, click Edit on the menu bar and then click Undo Saved Record.

Closing a Table and Database and Quitting Access

It is a good idea to close a table as soon as you have finished working with it. It keeps the screen from getting cluttered and prevents you from making accidental changes to the data in the table. If you no longer will work with the database, you should close the database as well. With the creation of the Client table complete, you also can quit Access at this point.

The steps on the next page close the table and the database and then quit Access.

To Close a Table and Database and Quit Access

1

- **Click the Close Window button for the Client : Table window.**

The datasheet for the Client table no longer appears (Figure 1-30).

2

- **Click the Close Window button for the AHSIT Internships : Database window.**

The AHSIT Internships : Database window no longer appears.

3

- **Click the Close button for the Microsoft Access window.**

The Microsoft Access window closes and the Windows desktop appears.

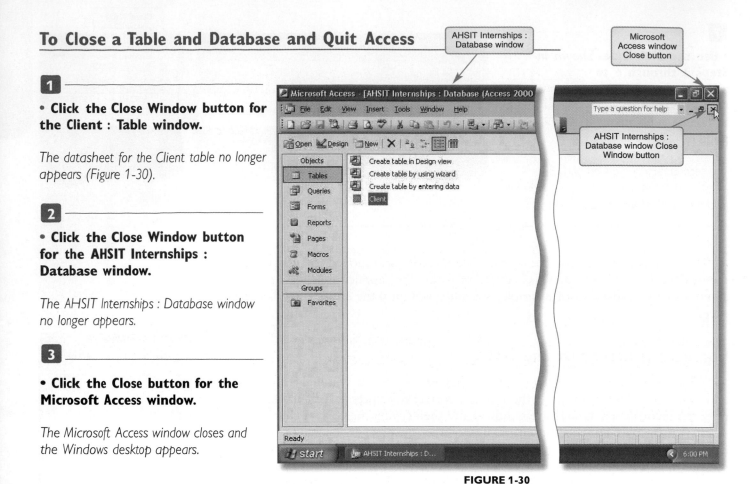

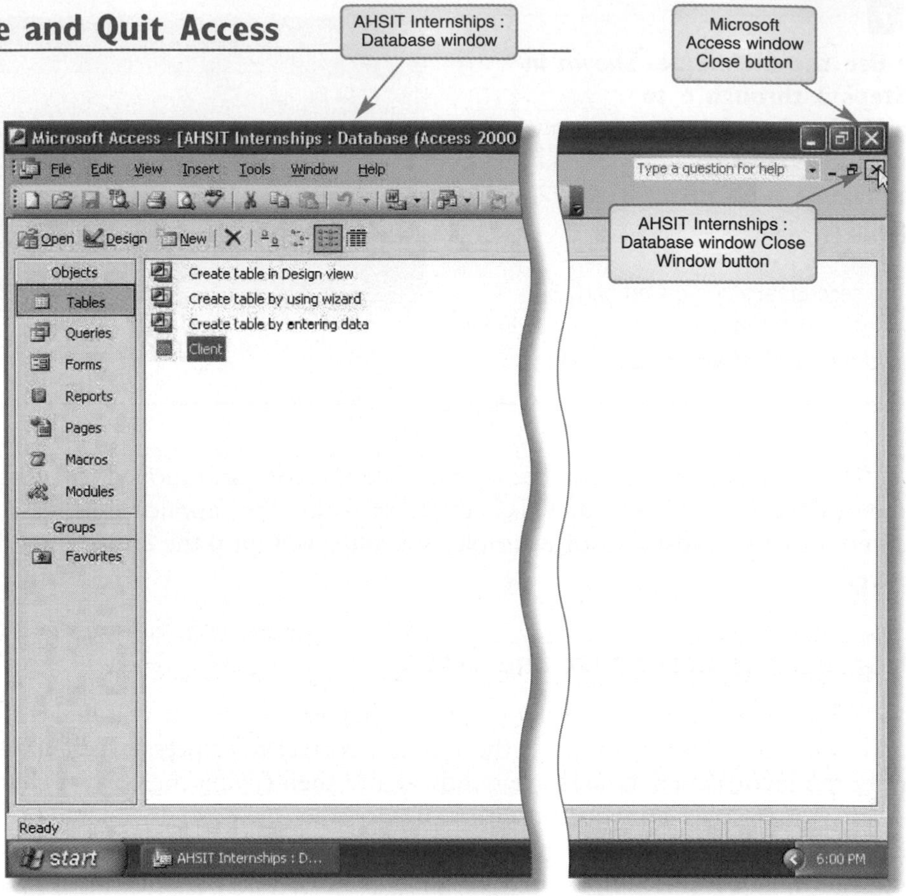

FIGURE 1-30

Opening a Database

To work with any of the tables, reports, or forms in a database, the database must be open. The following steps open the database from within Access.

To Open a Database

1

- **Start Access following the steps on pages AC 7 and AC 8.**
- **If the task pane appears, click its Close button.**
- **Click the Open button on the Database toolbar.**

The Open dialog box appears (Figure 1-31).

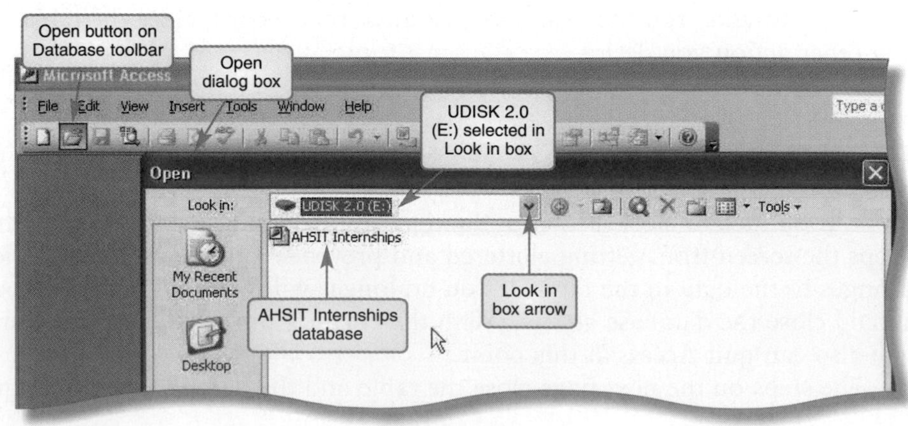

FIGURE 1-31

2

- **Be sure UDISK 2.0 (E:) appears in the Look in box. (You might have a different letter in parentheses.) If not, click the Look in box arrow and click UDISK 2.0 (E:). (Your letter might be different.)**
- **Click AHSIT Internships.**

Access displays the Open dialog box (Figure 1-32). UDISK 2.0 (E:) appears in the Look in box, and the databases on the USB flash drive are displayed. (Your list may be different.)

- **Click the Open button in the Open dialog box.**
- **If a Security Warning dialog box appears, click the Open button.**

The database opens and the AHSIT Internships : Database window appears.

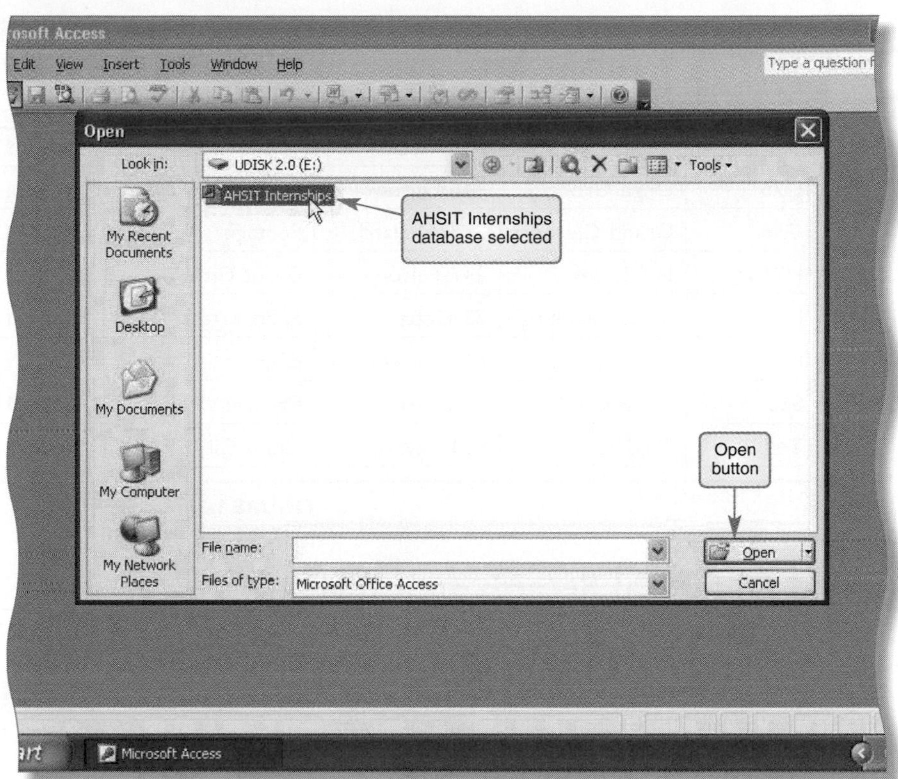

FIGURE 1-32

Adding Additional Records

You can add records to a table that already contains data using a process almost identical to that used to add records to an empty table. The only difference is that you place the insertion point after the last data record before you enter the additional data. To do so, use the **Navigation buttons**, which are buttons used to move within a table, found near the lower-left corner of the screen shown in Figure 1-34 on the next page. The purpose of each of the Navigation buttons is described in Table 1-2.

Q & A

Q: What should I do if I try to open a database and a Microsoft Office Access dialog box appears asking if I want to block unsafe expressions?

A: Click the No button when asked if you want to block unsafe expressions. If another dialog box appears with questions about the Microsoft Jet Engine, click Yes and then click Open.

Table 1-2 Navigation Buttons in Datasheet View

BUTTON	PURPOSE
First Record	Moves to the first record in the table
Previous Record	Moves to the previous record
Next Record	Moves to the next record
Last Record	Moves to the last record in the table
New Record	Moves to the end of the table to a position for entering a new record

The steps on the next page add the remaining records (Figure 1-33 on the next page) to the Client table.

Client table (last 8 records)

CLIENT NUMBER	NAME	ADDRESS	CITY	STATE	ZIP CODE	AMOUNT PAID	CURRENT DUE	INTERN NUMBER
B26	Blake-Scripps	557 Maum	Grant City	ND	58120	$0.00	$229.50	24
D76	Dege Grocery	446 Linton	Portage	MN	59130	$1,202.00	$485.75	34
G56	Grand Cleaners	337 Abelard	Portage	MN	59131	$925.50	$265.00	22
H21	Hill Shoes	247 Fulton	Grant City	ND	58121	$228.50	$0.00	24
J77	Jones Plumbing	75 Getty	E. Portage	MN	59135	$0.00	$0.00	34
M26	Mohr Crafts	665 Market	Empeer	ND	58216	$1,572.00	$312.50	22
S56	SeeSaw Ind.	31 Liatris	Portage	MN	59130	$2,827.50	$362.50	34
T45	Tate Repair	824 Revere	Grant City	ND	58120	$254.00	$0.00	24

FIGURE 1-33

To Add Additional Records to a Table

1

- **Right-click the Client table in the AHSIT Internships : Database window, and then click Open on the shortcut menu.**
- **When the Client table appears, maximize the window by double-clicking its title bar.**

The datasheet appears (Figure 1-34).

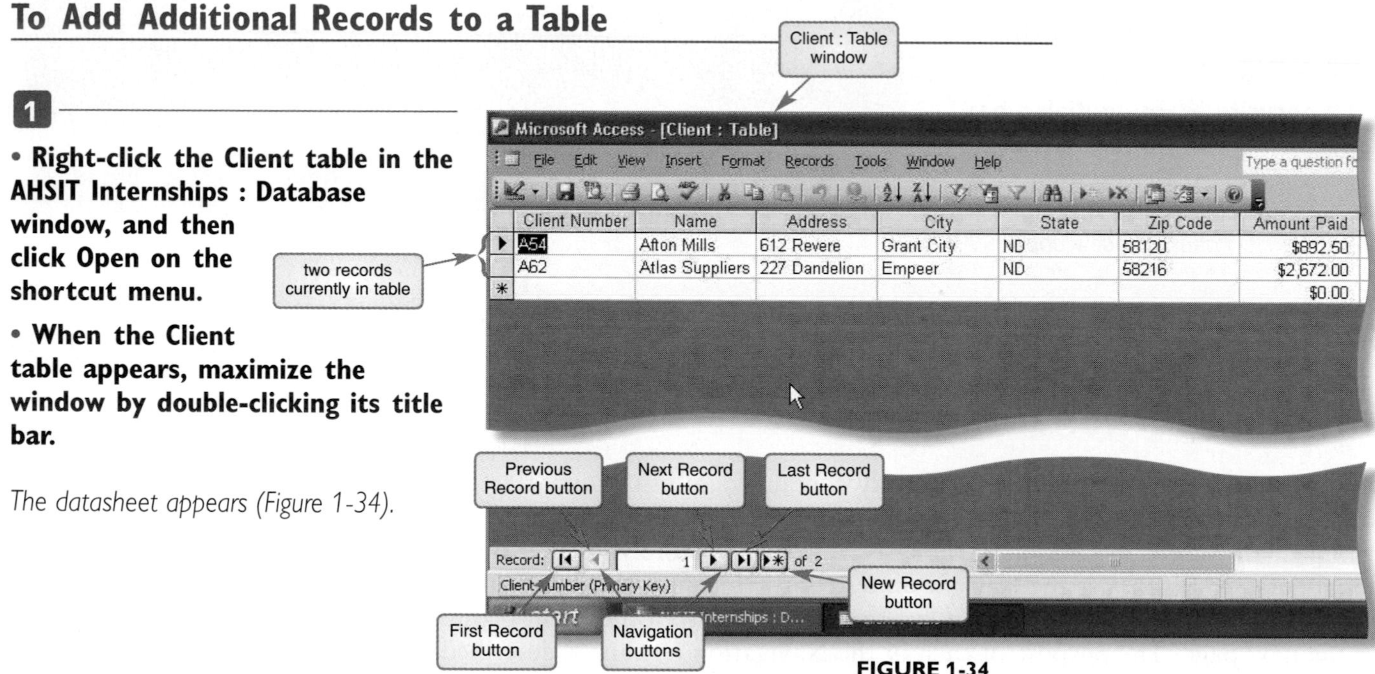

FIGURE 1-34

2

- **Click the New Record button.**

Access places the insertion point in position to enter a new record (Figure 1-35).

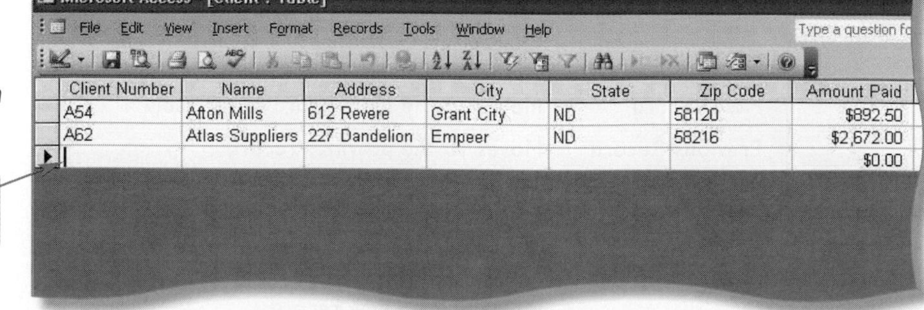

FIGURE 1-35

3

• **Add the records from Figure 1-33 using the same techniques you used to add the first two records.**

The additional records are added (Figure 1-36).

4

• **Click the Close Window button for the datasheet.**

The window containing the table closes and the AHSIT Internships : Database window appears.

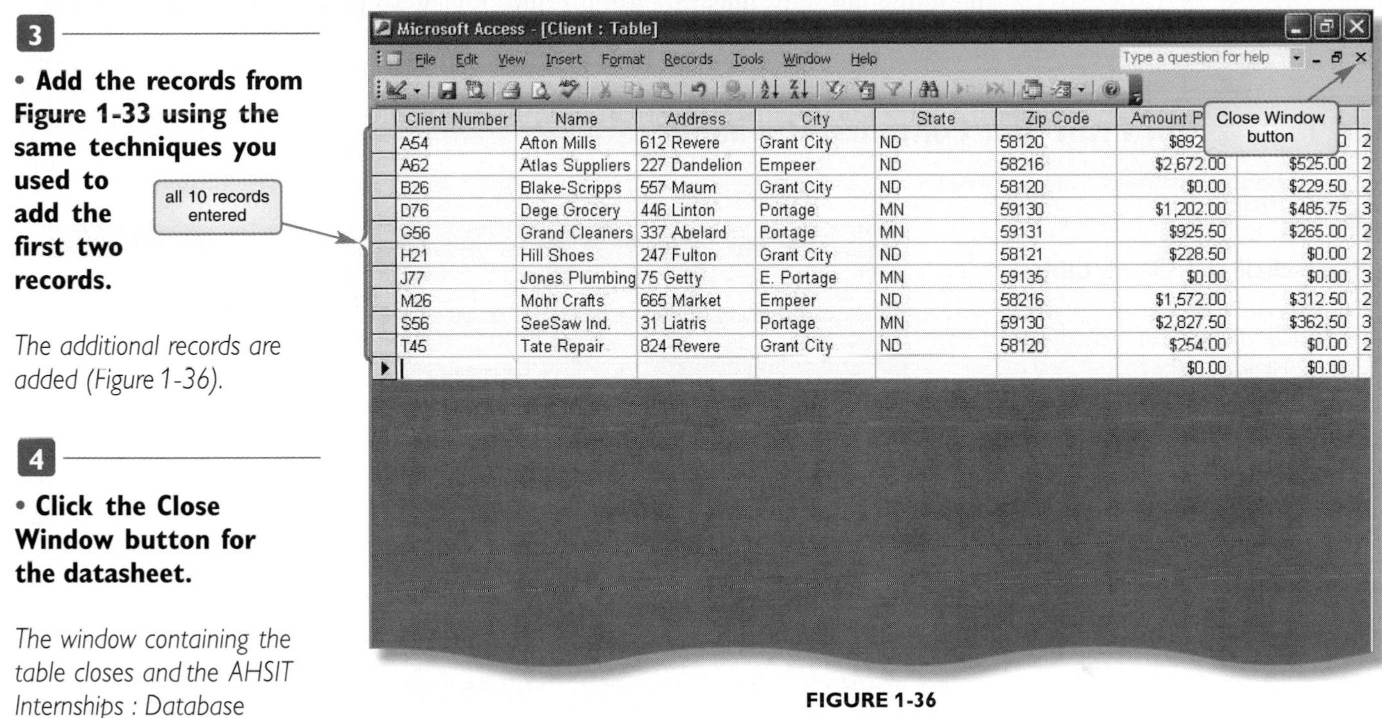

FIGURE 1-36

Previewing and Printing the Contents of a Table

When working with a database, you often will need to print a copy of the table contents. Figure 1-37 shows a printed copy of the contents of the Client table. (Yours may look slightly different, depending on your printer.) Because the Client table is substantially wider than the screen, it also will be wider than the normal printed page in portrait orientation. **Portrait orientation** means the printout is across the width of the page. **Landscape orientation** means the printout is across the length of the page. Thus, to print the wide database table, use landscape orientation. If you are printing the contents of a table that fit on the screen, you will not need landscape orientation. A convenient way to change to landscape orientation is to preview what the printed copy will look like by using Print Preview. This allows you to determine whether landscape orientation is necessary and, if it is, to change the orientation easily to landscape. In addition, you also can use Print Preview to determine whether any adjustments are necessary to the page margins.

Skill Builder 1-2

To practice the following tasks, visit scsite.com/off2003sch/skill, locate Access Project 1, and then click Skill Builder 1-2.

- ❑ Open a table in Datasheet view
- ❑ Add records
- ❑ Close the table

Client 9/17/2007

Client Number	Name	Address	City	State	Zip Code	Amount Paid	Current Due	Intern Number
A54	Afton Mills	612 Revere	Grant City	ND	58120	$892.50	$315.50	22
A62	Atlas Suppliers	227 Dandelion	Empeer	ND	58216	$2,672.00	$525.00	24
B26	Blake-Scripps	557 Maum	Grant City	ND	58120	$0.00	$229.50	24
D76	Dege Grocery	446 Linton	Portage	MN	59130	$1,202.00	$485.75	34
G56	Grand Cleaner	337 Abelard	Portage	MN	59131	$925.50	$265.00	22
H21	Hill Shoes	247 Fulton	Grant City	ND	58121	$228.50	$0.00	24
J77	Jones Plumbin	75 Getty	E. Portage	MN	59135	$0.00	$0.00	34
M26	Mohr Crafts	665 Market	Empeer	ND	58216	$1,572.00	$312.50	22
S56	SeeSaw Ind.	31 Liatris	Portage	MN	59130	$2,827.50	$362.50	34
T45	Tate Repair	824 Revere	Grant City	ND	58120	$254.00	$0.00	24

FIGURE 1-37

The following steps illustrate using Print Preview to preview and then print the Client table.

To Preview and Print the Contents of a Table

1

• **Right-click the Client table.**

The shortcut menu for the Client table appears (Figure 1-38).

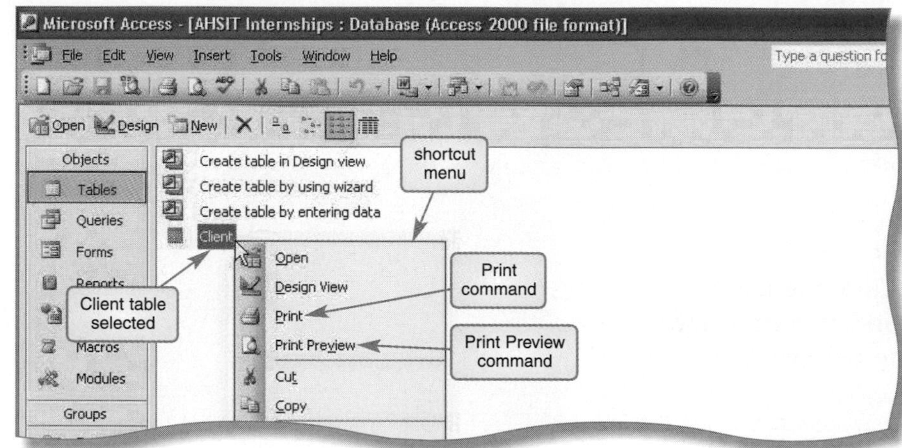

FIGURE 1-38

2

• **Click Print Preview on the shortcut menu.**

• **Point to the approximate position shown in Figure 1-39.**

The preview of the report appears. The mouse pointer shape changes to a magnifying glass, indicating you can magnify a portion of the report.

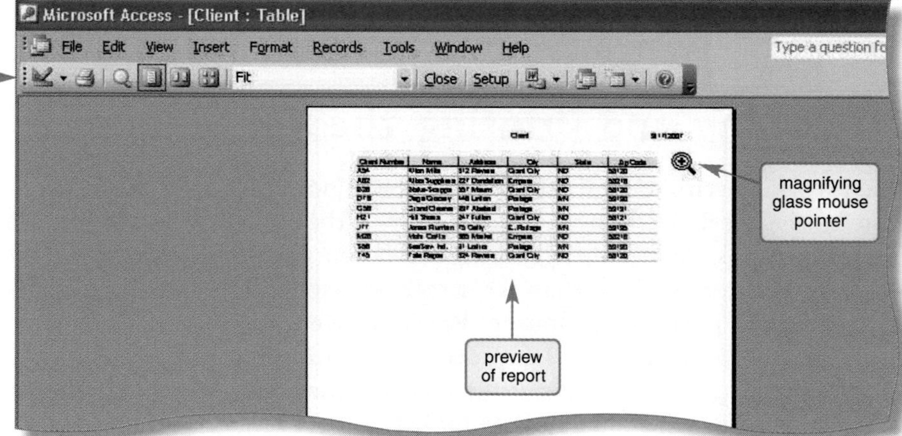

FIGURE 1-39

3

• **Click the magnifying glass mouse pointer in the approximate position shown in Figure 1-39.**

The portion surrounding the mouse pointer is magnified (Figure 1-40). The last field that appears is the Zip Code field. The Amount Paid, Current Due, and Intern Number fields do not appear. To display the additional fields, you will need to switch to landscape orientation.

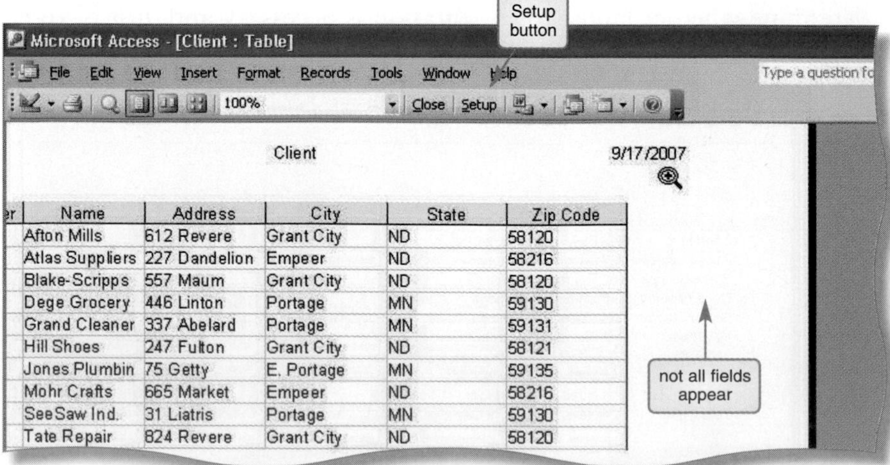

Name	Address	City	State	Zip Code
Afton Mills	612 Revere	Grant City	ND	58120
Atlas Suppliers	227 Dandelion	Empeer	ND	58216
Blake-Scripps	557 Maum	Grant City	ND	58120
Dege Grocery	446 Linton	Portage	MN	59130
Grand Cleaner	337 Abelard	Portage	MN	59131
Hill Shoes	247 Fulton	Grant City	ND	58121
Jones Plumbin	75 Getty	E. Portage	MN	59135
Mohr Crafts	665 Market	Empeer	ND	58216
SeeSaw Ind.	31 Liatris	Portage	MN	59130
Tate Repair	824 Revere	Grant City	ND	58120

FIGURE 1-40

4

• **Click the Setup button on the Print Preview toolbar.**

Access displays the Page Setup dialog box (Figure 1-41).

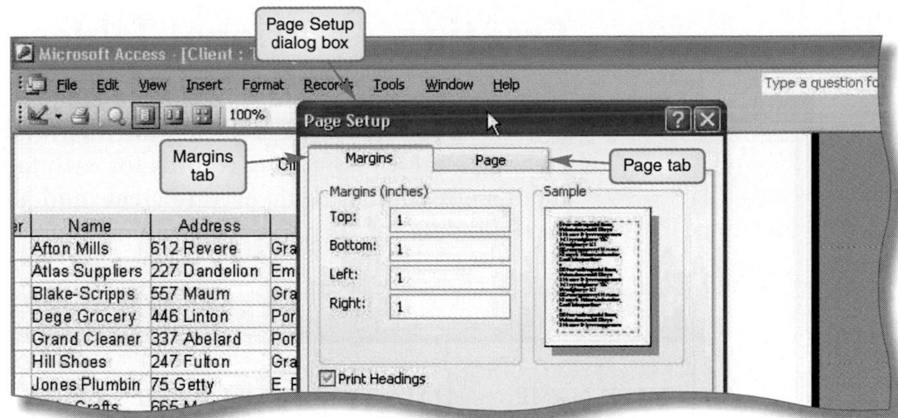

FIGURE 1-41

5

• **Click the Page tab.**

*The Page sheet appears (Figure 1-42). The Portrait option button currently is selected. (**Option button** refers to the round button that indicates choices in a dialog box. When the corresponding option is selected, the button contains within it a solid circle. Clicking an option button selects it, and deselects all others.)*

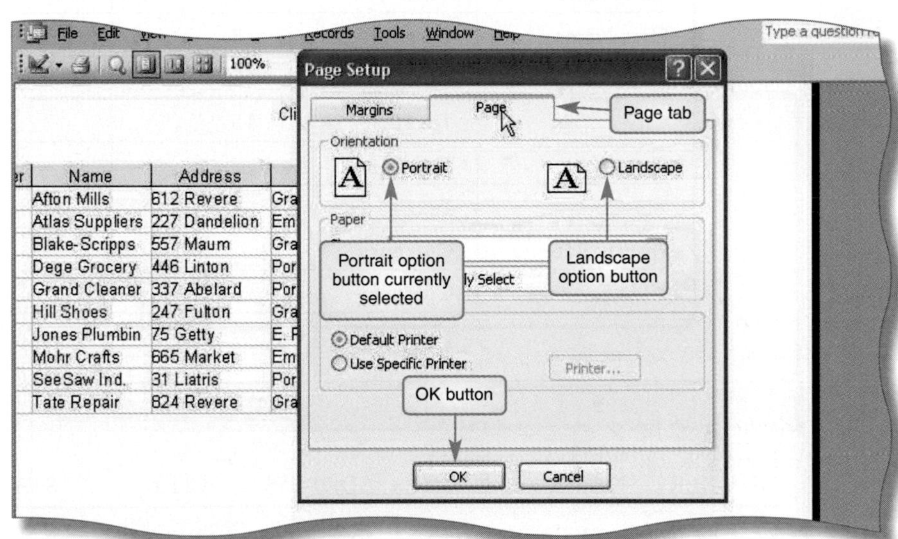

FIGURE 1-42

6

• **Click Landscape and then click the OK button.**

The orientation is changed to landscape, as shown by the report that appears on the screen (Figure 1-43). The last field that is displayed is the Intern Number field; so all fields currently appear. If they did not, you could decrease the left and right margins; that is, the amount of space left by Access on the left and right edges of the report.

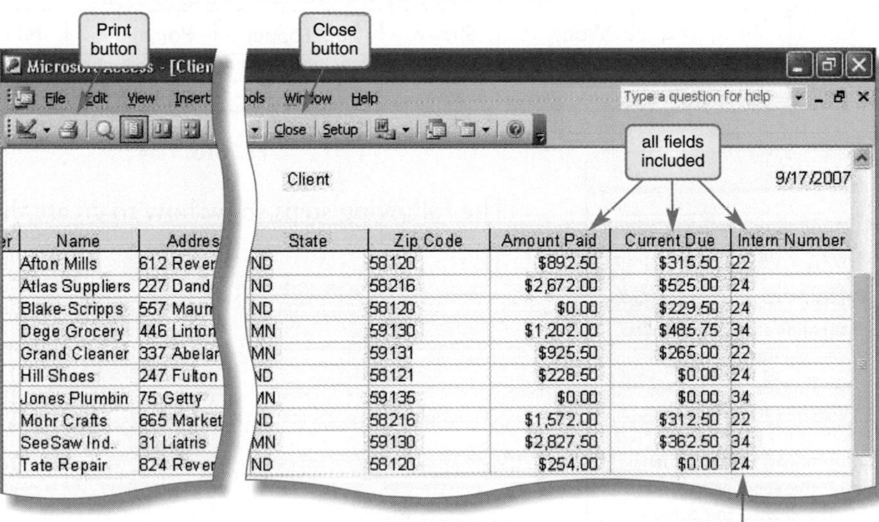

FIGURE 1-43

7

• **Click the Print button to print the report, and then click the Close button on the Print Preview toolbar.**

The report prints. It looks like the report shown in Figure 1-37 on page AC 29. The Print Preview window closes and the AHSIT Internships : Database window appears.

Creating Additional Tables

A database typically consists of more than one table. The AHSIT Internships database contains two, the Client table and the Intern table. You need to repeat the process of creating a table and adding records for each table in the database. In the AHSIT Internships database, you need to create and add records to the Intern table. The structure and data for the table are given in Figure 1-44.

Structure of Intern table

FIELD NAME	DATA TYPE	FIELD SIZE	PRIMARY KEY?	DESCRIPTION
Intern Number	Text	2	Yes	Intern Number (Primary Key)
Last Name	Text	10		Last Name of Intern
First Name	Text	8		First Name of Intern
Address	Text	15		Street Address
City	Text	15		City
State	Text	2		State (Two-Character Abbreviation)
Zip Code	Text	5		Zip Code (Five-Character Version)
Hourly Rate	Currency			Hourly Rate of Intern
YTD Earnings	Currency			YTD Earnings of Intern

Intern table

INTERN NUMBER	LAST NAME	FIRST NAME	ADDRESS	CITY	STATE	ZIP CODE	HOURLY RATE	YTD EARNINGS
22	Lewen	Joann	26 Cotton	Portage	MN	59130	$5.50	$1,320.00
24	Rodriguez	Mario	79 Marsden	E. Portage	MN	59135	$5.40	$1,280.50
34	Wong	Shawn	263 Topper	Portage	MN	59130	$5.75	$1,500.25
42	Trent	Roberta	45 Magee	W. Portage	MN	59136	$5.60	$0.00

FIGURE 1-44

The following steps show how to create the table.

Q & A

Q: What can I change when printing a report?

A: You can change the margins, paper size, paper source, or the printer that will be used to print the report. To change the margins, select the Margins sheet in the Page Setup dialog box and then enter the appropriate margin size. To change the paper size, paper source, or the printer, select the Page sheet in the Page Setup dialog box, click the appropriate down arrow, and then select the desired option.

To Create an Additional Table

1

- **Make sure the AHSIT Internships database is open.**
- **Click the New button on the Database window toolbar, click Design View, and then click the OK button.**
- **Enter the data for the fields for the Intern table from Figure 1-44. Be sure to click the Primary Key button when you enter the Intern Number field.**

The entries appear (Figure 1-45).

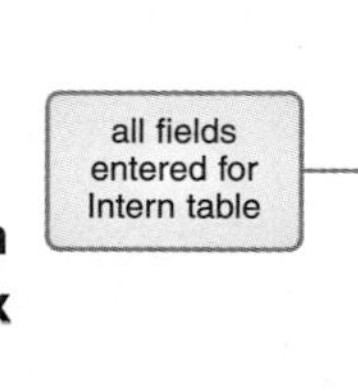

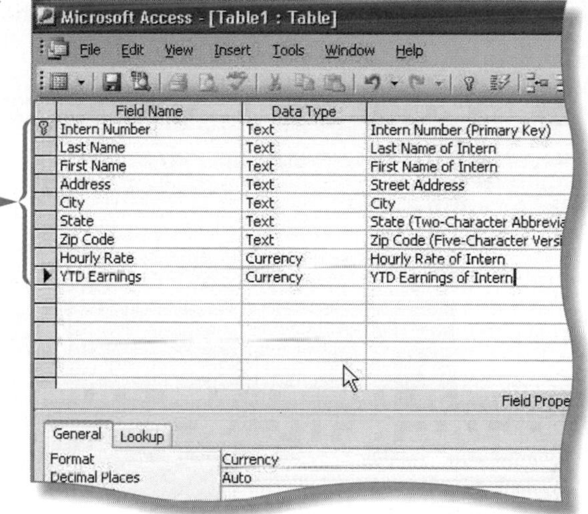

FIGURE 1-45

2

- **Click the Close Window button, click the Yes button in the Microsoft Office Access dialog box when asked if you want to save the changes, and then type** `Intern` **as the name of the table.**

The Save As dialog box appears (Figure 1-46). The table name is entered.

3

- **Click the OK button.**

The table is saved in the AHSIT Internships database. The window containing the table structure no longer appears.

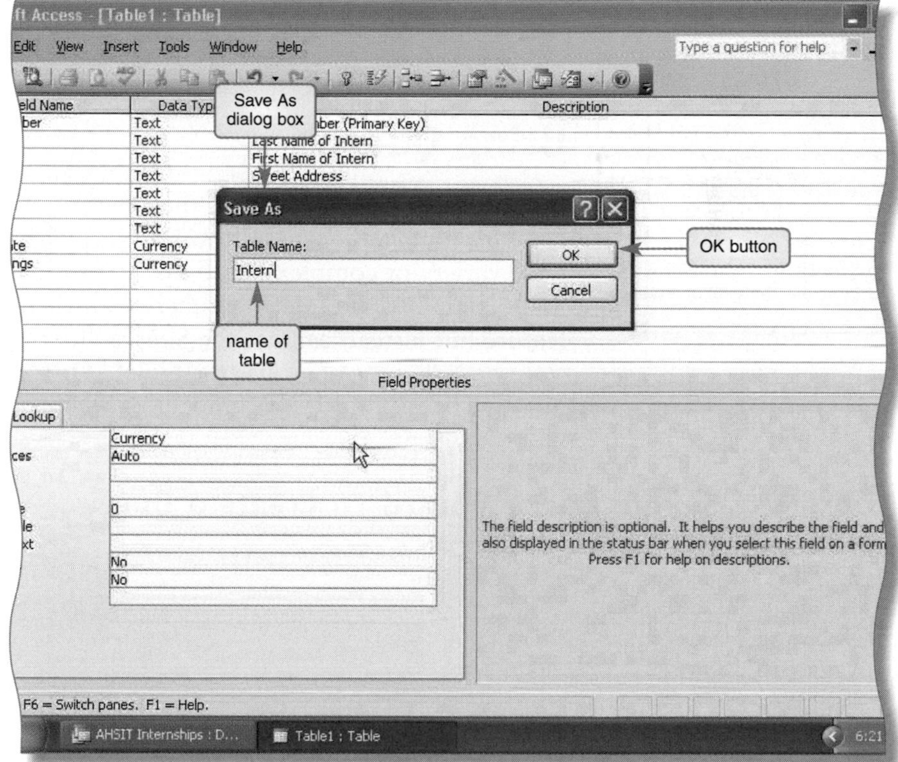

FIGURE 1-46

Adding Records to the Additional Table

Now that you have created the Intern table, use the steps on the next page to add records to it.

To Add Records to an Additional Table

1

• **Right-click the Intern table, and then click Open on the shortcut menu. Enter the Intern data from Figure 1-44 on page AC 32 into the Intern table.**

The datasheet displays the entered records (Figure 1-47).

2

• **Click the Close Window button for the Intern : Table window.**

Access closes the table and removes the datasheet from the screen.

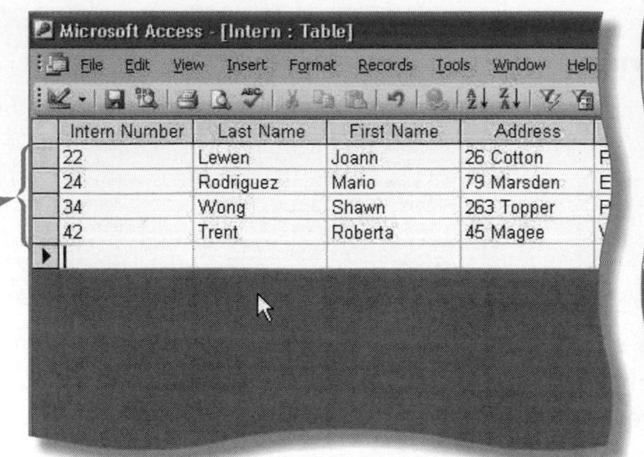

FIGURE 1-47

Skill Builder 1-3

To practice the following tasks, visit scsite.com/off2003sch/skill, locate Access Project 1, and then click Skill Builder 1-3.
- ❑ Preview the contents of a table
- ❑ Change the orientation
- ❑ Print the contents of a table

The records are now in the table.

Using Queries

Queries are simply questions, the answers to which are in the database. Access contains a powerful query feature. Through the use of this feature, you can ask a wide variety of complex questions. For simple requests, however, such as listing the number, name, and intern number of all clients, you do not need to use the query feature but instead can use the Simple Query wizard.

The following steps use the Simple Query wizard to create a query to display the number, name, and intern number of all clients.

To Use the Simple Query Wizard to Create a Query

1

• **With the Tables object selected and the Client table selected, click the New Object button arrow on the Database toolbar.**

A list of objects that can be created is displayed (Figure 1-48).

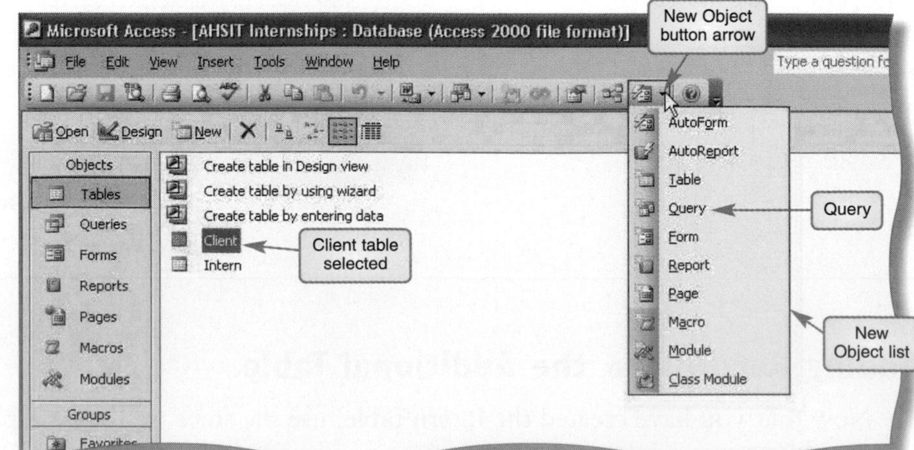

FIGURE 1-48

2

• Click Query in the New Object list.

The New Query dialog box appears (Figure 1-49).

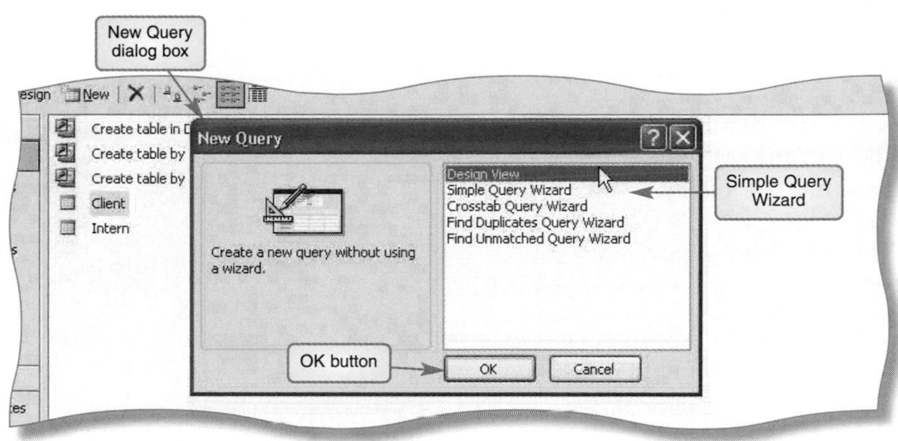

FIGURE 1-49

3

• Click Simple Query Wizard, and then click the OK button.

Access displays the Simple Query Wizard dialog box (Figure 1-50). It contains a list of available fields and a list of selected fields. Currently, no fields are selected for the query.

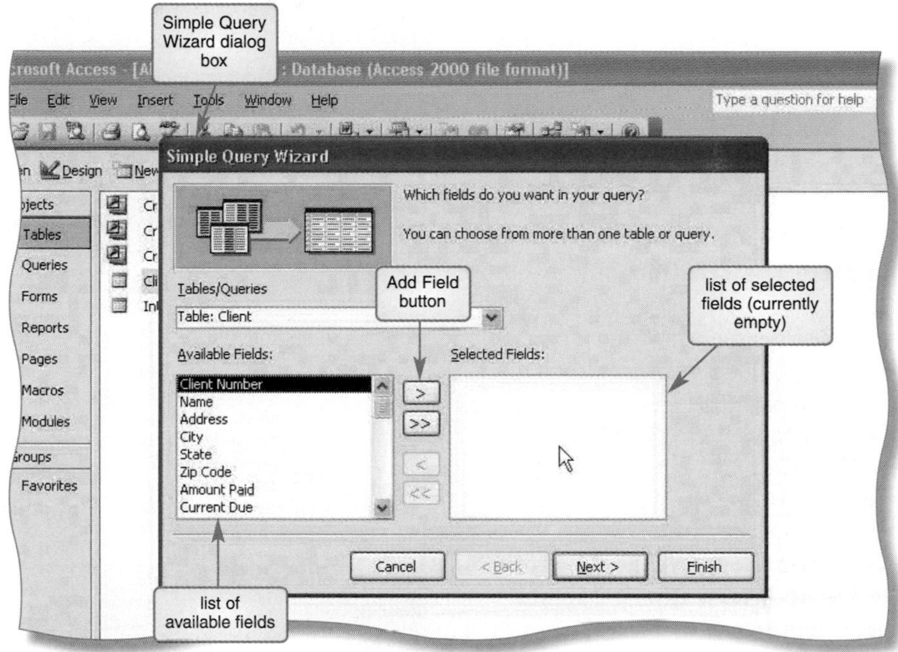

FIGURE 1-50

4

• Click the Add Field button to add the Client Number field.

• Click the Add Field button a second time to add the Name field.

• Click the Intern Number field, and then click the Add Field button to add the Intern Number field.

The fields are selected (Figure 1-51).

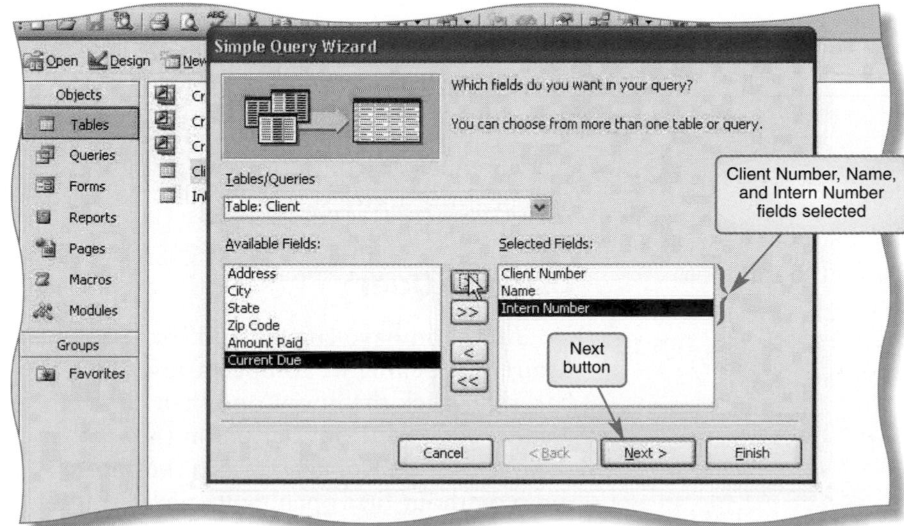

FIGURE 1-51

5

• **Click the Next button, and then type** `Client-Intern Query` **as the name for the query.**

The Simple Query Wizard dialog box displays the new query name (Figure 1-52).

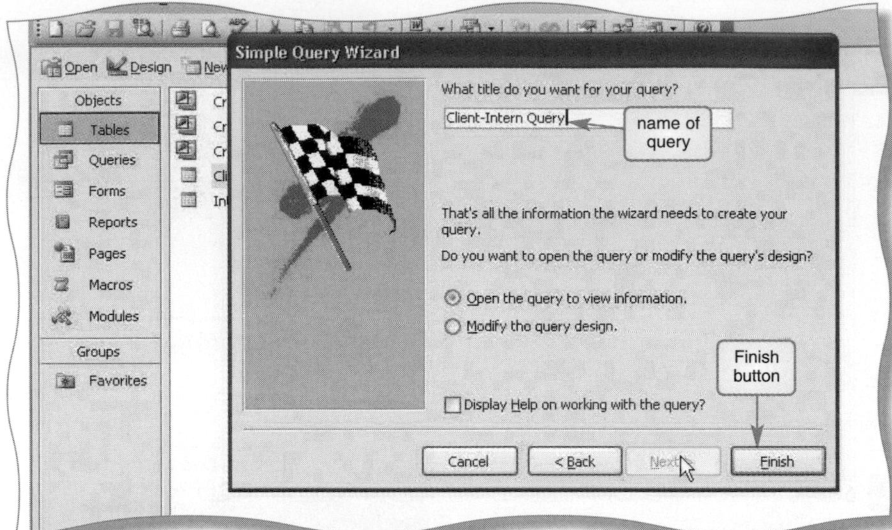

FIGURE 1-52

6

• **Click the Finish button to complete the creation of the query.**

Access displays the query results (Figure 1-53). The results contain all records but contain only the Client Number, Name, and Intern Number fields.

7

• **Click the Close Window button for the Client-Intern Query : Select Query window.**

Access closes the query and the AHSIT Internships : Database window appears.

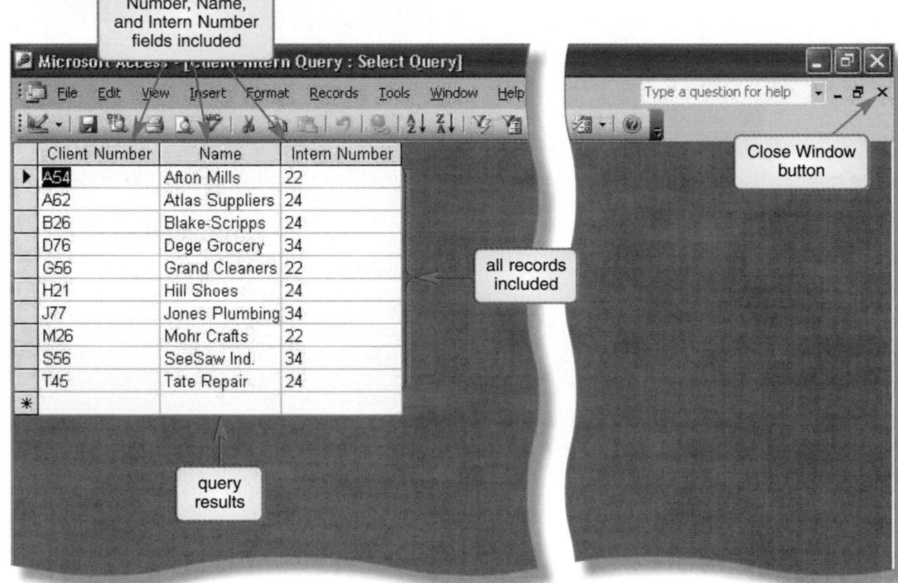

Client Number	Name	Intern Number
A54	Afton Mills	22
A62	Atlas Suppliers	24
B26	Blake-Scripps	24
D76	Dege Grocery	34
G56	Grand Cleaners	22
H21	Hill Shoes	24
J77	Jones Plumbing	34
M26	Mohr Crafts	22
S56	SeeSaw Ind.	34
T45	Tate Repair	24

FIGURE 1-53

The query is complete. You can use it at any time in the future without needing to repeat the above steps.

Using a Query

After you have created and saved a query, you can use it at any time in the future by opening it. To open a saved query, click the Queries object on the Objects bar, right-click the query, and then click Open on the shortcut menu. To print the results, click the Print button on the toolbar. If you want to change the design of the query, click Design View on the shortcut menu rather than Open. To print the query without first opening it, click Print on the shortcut menu.

You often want to restrict the records that are included. For example, you might want to include only those clients whose intern number is 24. In such a case, you need to enter the 24 as a **criterion**, which is a condition that the records to be included must satisfy. To do so, you will open the query in Design view, enter the criterion below the appropriate field, and then run the query. The following steps show how to enter a criterion to include only clients of intern 24 and then run the query.

To Use a Query

1

• **If necessary, click the Queries object. Right-click the Client-Intern Query.**

The shortcut menu for the Client-Intern Query is displayed (Figure 1-54).

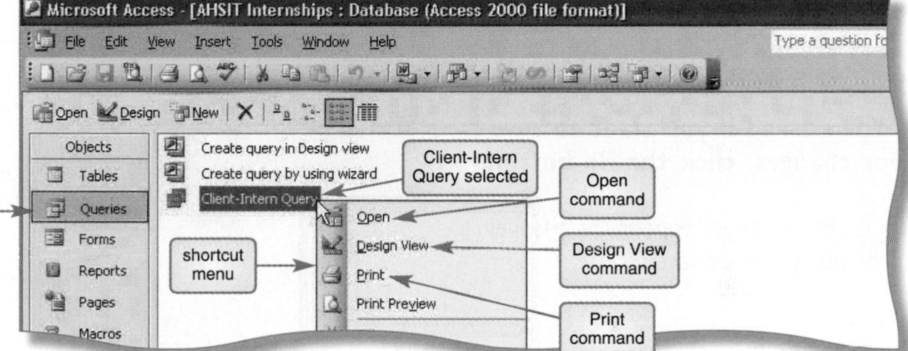

FIGURE 1-54

2

• **Click Design View on the shortcut menu.**

The query appears in Design view (Figure 1-55).

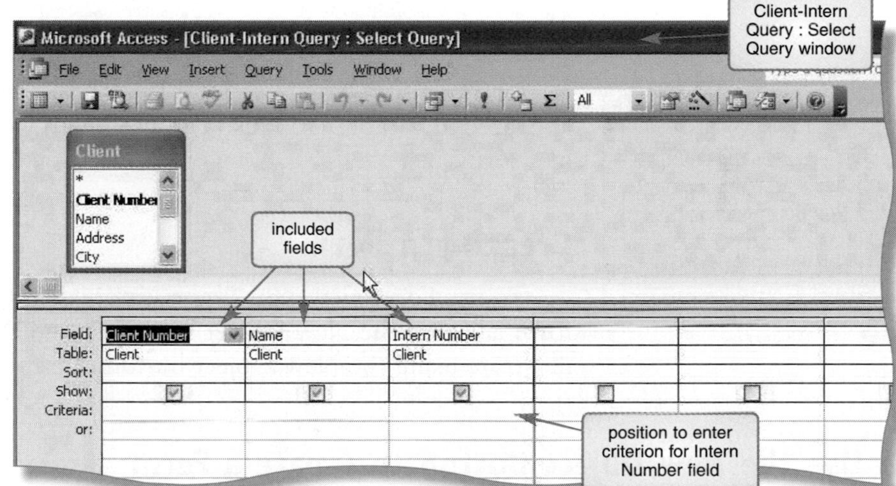

FIGURE 1-55

3

• **Click the Criteria row in the Intern Number column of the grid, and then type** 24 **as the criterion.**

The criterion is typed (Figure 1-56).

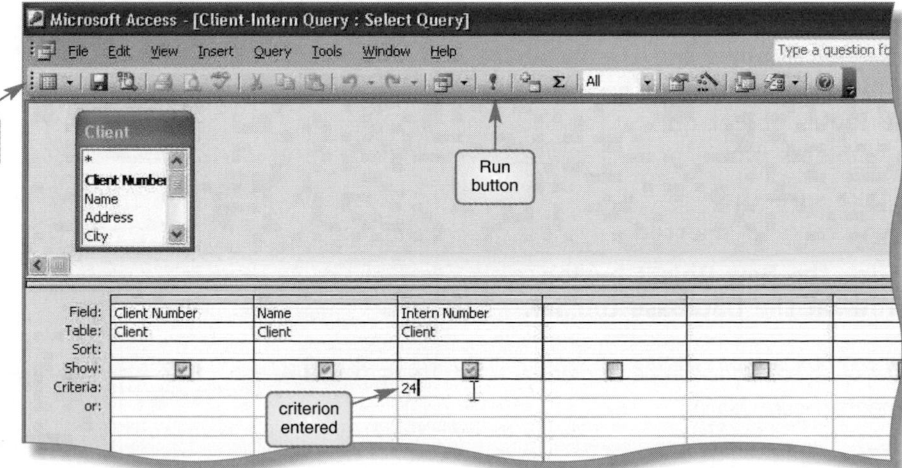

FIGURE 1-56

4

• **Click the Run button on the Query Design toolbar.**

Access displays the results (Figure 1-57). Only the clients of intern 24 are included (Your results may appear in a different order.)

5

• **Close the window containing the query results by clicking its Close Window button.**

• **When asked if you want to save your changes, click the No button.**

The results no longer appear. The changes to the query are not saved.

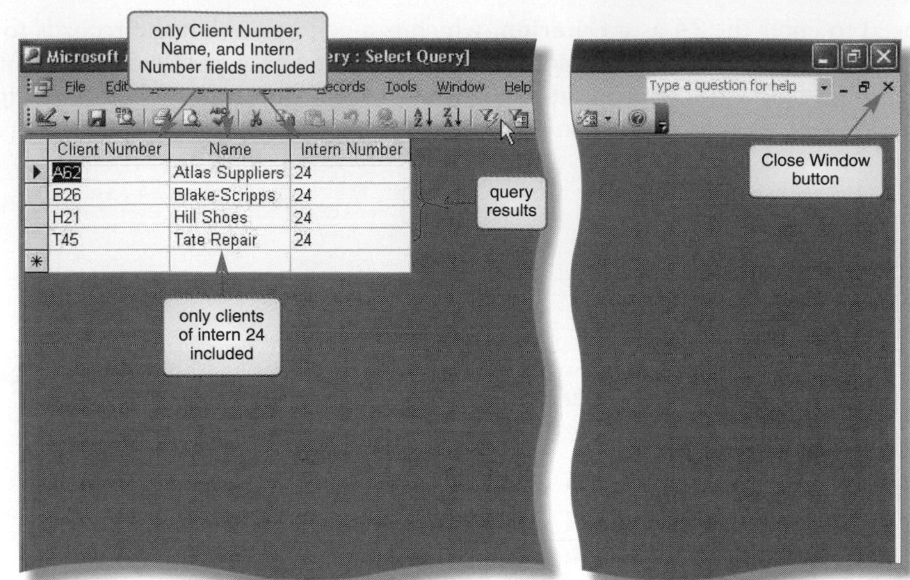

FIGURE 1-57

Using a Form to View Data

> **Q & A**
>
> **Q:** If you saved the query, what would happen the next time you ran the query?
>
> **A:** You would see only clients of intern 24.

In creating tables, you have used Datasheet view; that is, the data on the screen appeared as a table. You also can use **Form view**, in which you see data contained in a form.

Creating a Form

To use Form view, you first must create a form. The simplest way to create a form is to use the New Object button on the Database toolbar. The following steps illustrate using the New Object button to create a form for the Client table.

To Use the New Object Button to Create a Form

1

• **Make sure the AHSIT Internships database is open and the Database window appears. Click the Tables object on the Objects bar.**

• **Make sure the Client table is selected.**

• **Click the New Object button arrow on the Database toolbar.**

A list of objects that can be created appears (Figure 1-58).

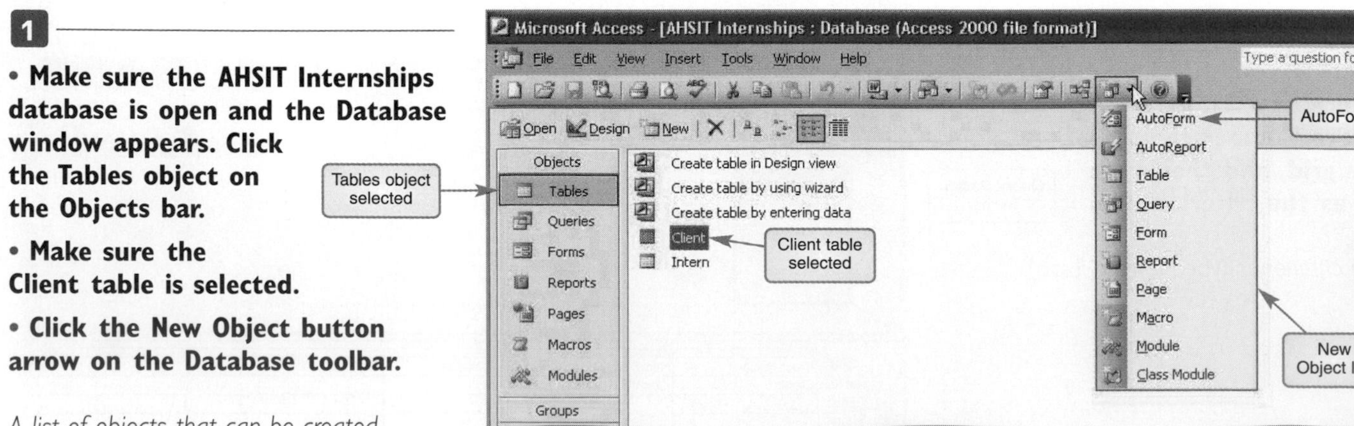

FIGURE 1-58

2

• **Click AutoForm in the New Object list.**

After a brief delay, the form appears (Figure 1-59). If you do not move the mouse pointer after clicking the New Object button, the ScreenTip for the Properties button may appear when the form opens. Access displays the Formatting toolbar when a form is created. (When you close the form, this toolbar no longer appears.)

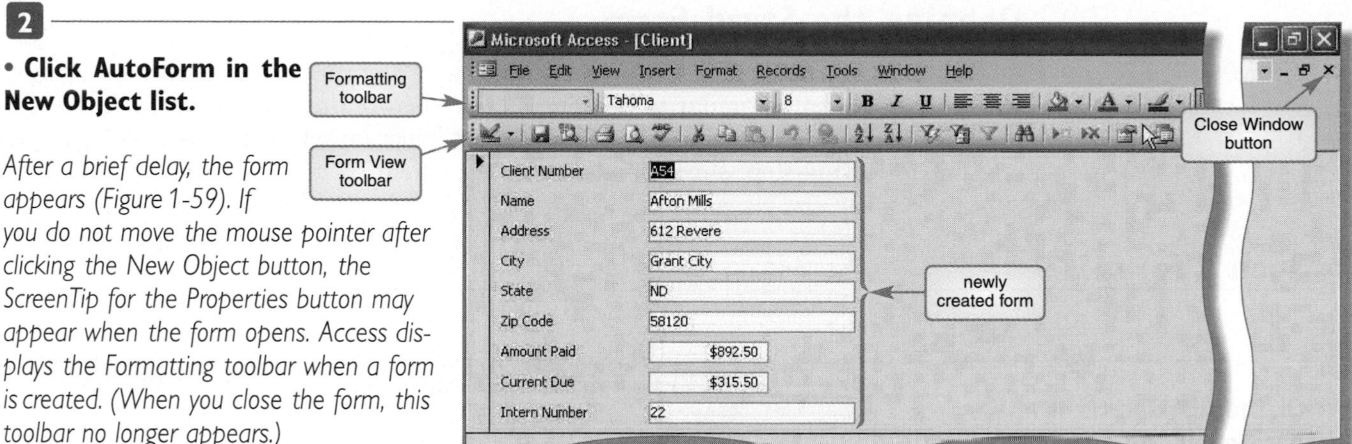

FIGURE 1-59

Closing and Saving the Form

Closing a form is similar to closing a table. The only difference is that you will be asked if you want to save the form unless you previously have saved it. The following steps close the form and save it as Client.

Skill Builder 1-4

To practice the following tasks, visit scsite.com/off2003sch/skill, locate Access Project 1, and then click Skill Builder 1-4.
- ❑ Create a query using the Simple Query wizard
- ❑ Modify the query
- ❑ Run the query

To Close and Save a Form

1

• **Click the Close Window button for the Client window (see Figure 1-59).**

Access displays the Microsoft Office Access dialog box (Figure 1-60).

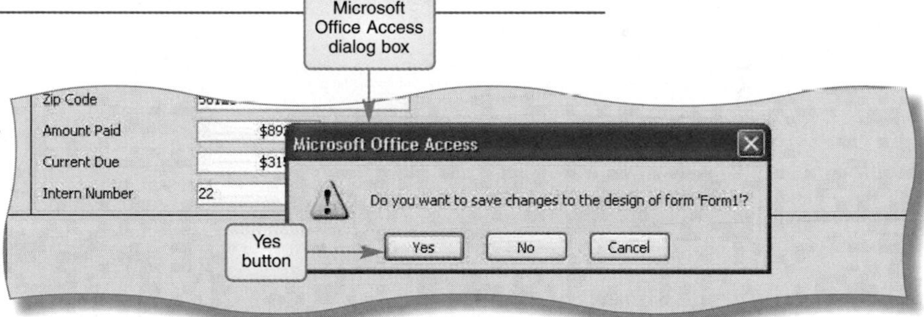

FIGURE 1-60

2

• **Click the Yes button.**

The Save As dialog box appears (Figure 1-61). The name of the table (Client) becomes the name of the form automatically. This name could be changed, if desired.

3

• **Click the OK button.**

The form is saved as part of the database and the form closes. The AHSIT Internships : Database window is redisplayed.

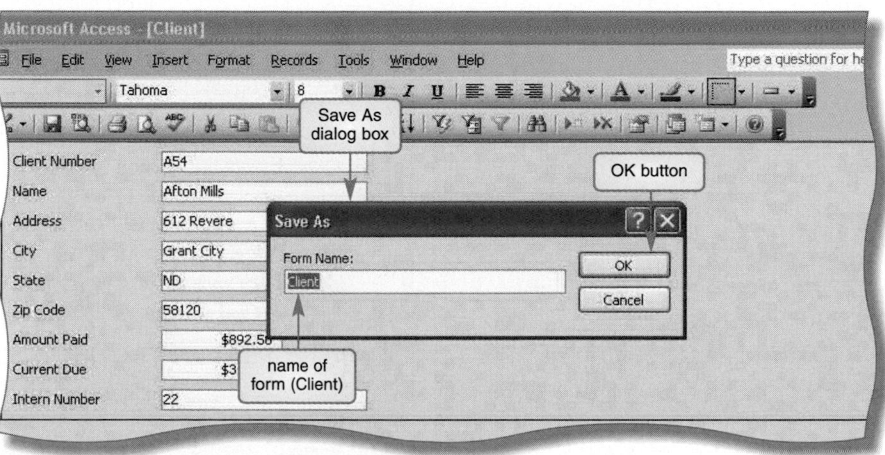

FIGURE 1-61

Opening the Saved Form

After you have saved a form, you can use it at any time in the future by opening it. Opening a form is similar to opening a table. Before opening the form, however, the Forms object, rather than the Tables object, must be selected.

The following steps show how to open the Client form.

To Open a Form

1

- **With the AHSIT Internships database open and the Database window on the screen, click Forms on the Objects bar, and then right-click the Client form.**

The list of forms appears (Figure 1-62). The shortcut menu for the Client form appears.

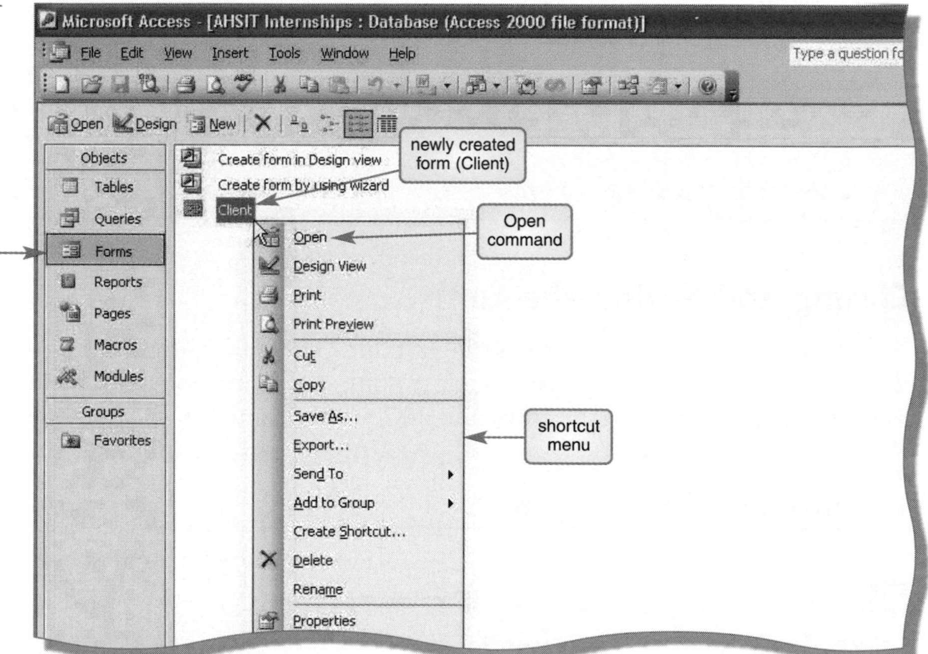

FIGURE 1-62

2

- **Click Open on the shortcut menu.**

The Client form appears (Figure 1-63).

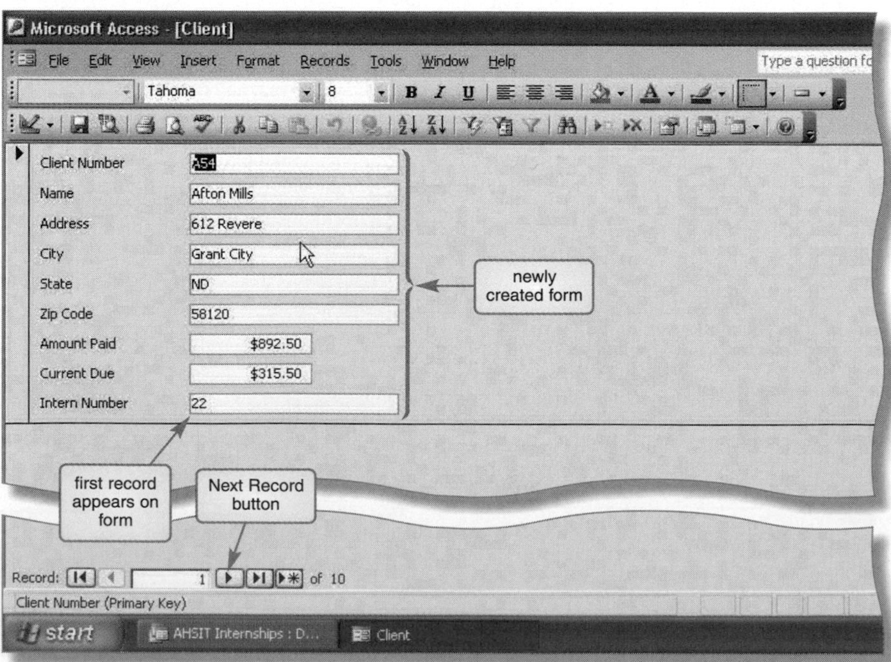

FIGURE 1-63

Using the Form

You can use the form just as you used Datasheet view. You use the Navigation buttons to move between records. You can add new records or change existing ones. To delete the record appearing on the screen, after selecting the record by clicking its record selector, press the DELETE key. Thus, you can perform database operations using either Form view or Datasheet view.

Because you can see only one record at a time in Form view, to see a different record, such as the fifth record, you must use the Navigation buttons to move to it. The following step illustrates moving from record to record in Form view.

To Use a Form

1

- **Click the Next Record button four times.**

Access displays the fifth record on the form (Figure 1-64).

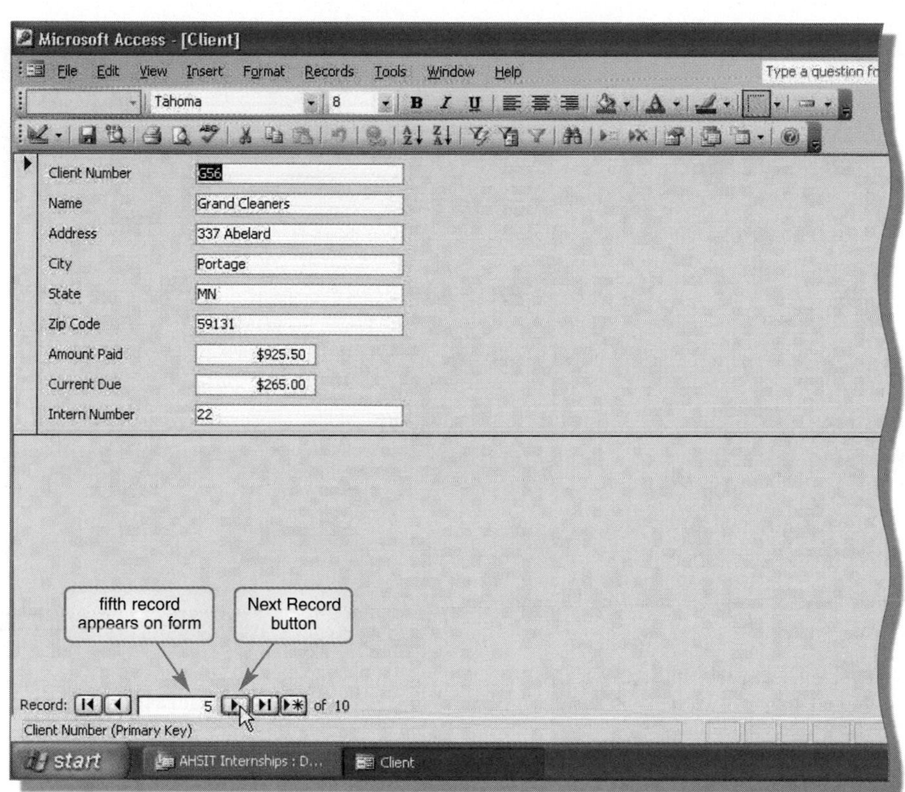

FIGURE 1-64

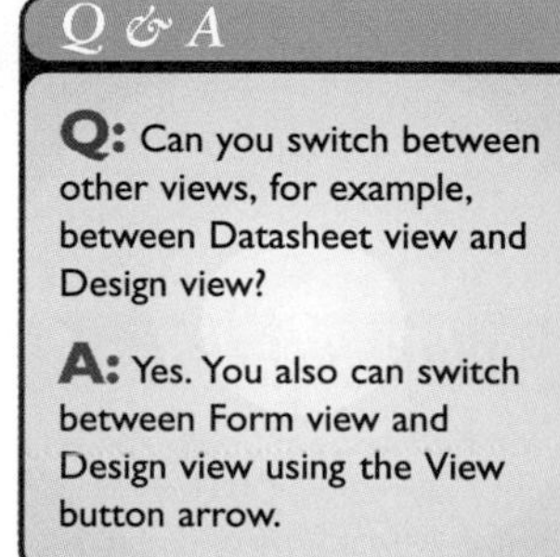

Q & A

Q: Can you switch between other views, for example, between Datasheet view and Design view?

A: Yes. You also can switch between Form view and Design view using the View button arrow.

Switching Between Form View and Datasheet View

In some cases, after you have seen a record in Form view, you will want to switch to Datasheet view to see the collection of records. The steps on the next page show how to switch from Form view to Datasheet view.

To Switch from Form View to Datasheet View

1

• **Click the View button arrow on the Form View toolbar.**

The list of available views appears (Figure 1-65).

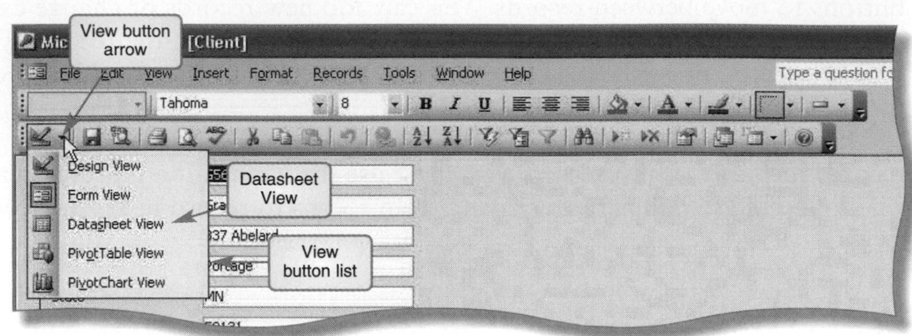

FIGURE 1-65

2

• **Click Datasheet View.**

The table appears in Datasheet view (Figure 1-66). The record selector is positioned on the fifth record.

3

• **Click the Close Window button.**

The Client window closes and the datasheet no longer appears.

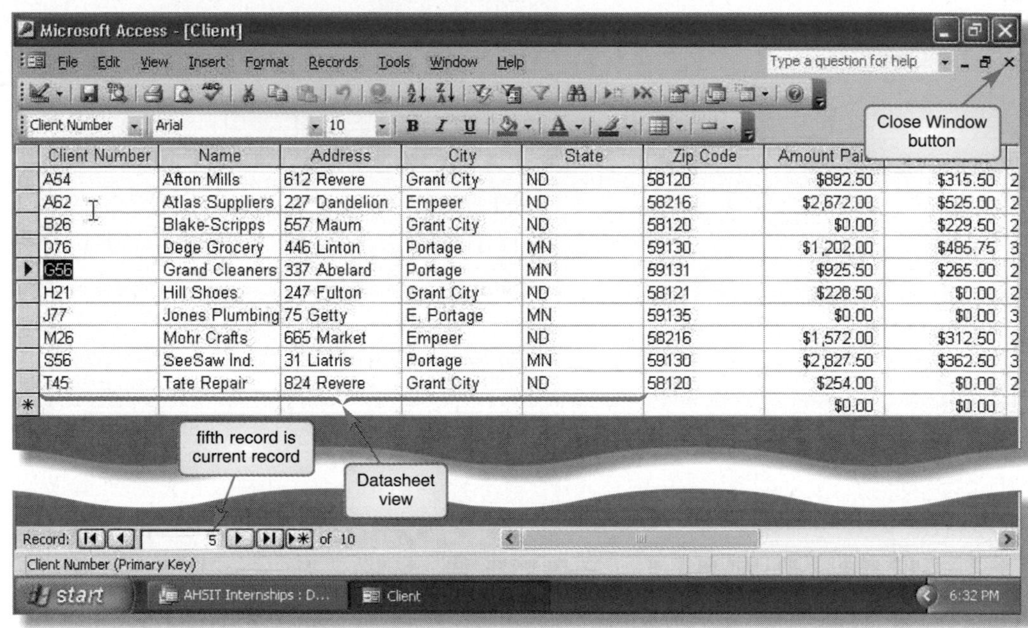

FIGURE 1-66

Creating a Report

Earlier in this project, you printed a table using the Print button. The report you produced was shown in Figure 1-37 on page AC 29. While this type of report presented the data in an organized manner, the format is very rigid. You cannot select the fields to appear, for example; the report automatically includes all the fields and they appear in precisely the same order as in the table. A way to change the title of the table is not available. Therefore, it will be the same as the name of the table.

In this section, you will create the report shown in Figure 1-67. This report features significant differences from the one in Figure 1-37. The portion at the top of the report in Figure 1-67, called a **page header**, contains a custom title. The contents of this page header appear at the top of each page. The **detail lines**, which are the lines that are printed for each record, contain only those fields you specify and in the order you specify.

Skill Builder 1-5

To practice the following tasks, visit scsite.com/off2003sch/skill, locate Access Project 1, and then click Skill Builder 1-5.

- ❑ Create a form
- ❑ Open the form
- ❑ Navigate to a different record
- ❑ Switch to Datasheet view

Client Amount Report

Client Number	Name	Amount Paid	Current Due
A54	Afton Mills	$892.50	$315.50
A62	Atlas Suppliers	$2,672.00	$525.00
B26	Blake-Scripps	$0.00	$229.50
D76	Dege Grocery	$1,202.00	$485.75
G56	Grand Cleaners	$925.50	$265.00
H21	Hill Shoes	$228.50	$0.00
J77	Jones Plumbing	$0.00	$0.00
M26	Mohr Crafts	$1,572.00	$312.50
S56	SeeSaw Ind.	$2,827.50	$362.50
T45	Tate Repair	$254.00	$0.00

FIGURE 1-67

The following steps show how to create the report shown in Figure 1-67.

To Create a Report

1

- **Click Tables on the Objects bar, and then make sure the Client table is selected.**
- **Click the New Object button arrow on the Database toolbar.**

The list of available objects appears (Figure 1-68).

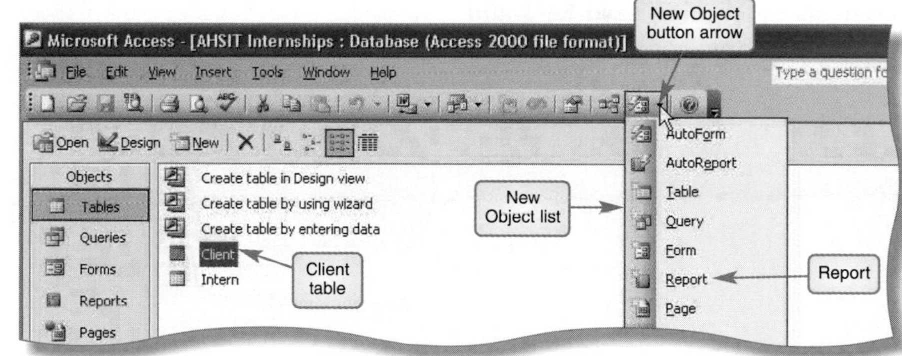

FIGURE 1-68

2

- **Click Report.**

Access displays the New Report dialog box (Figure 1-69).

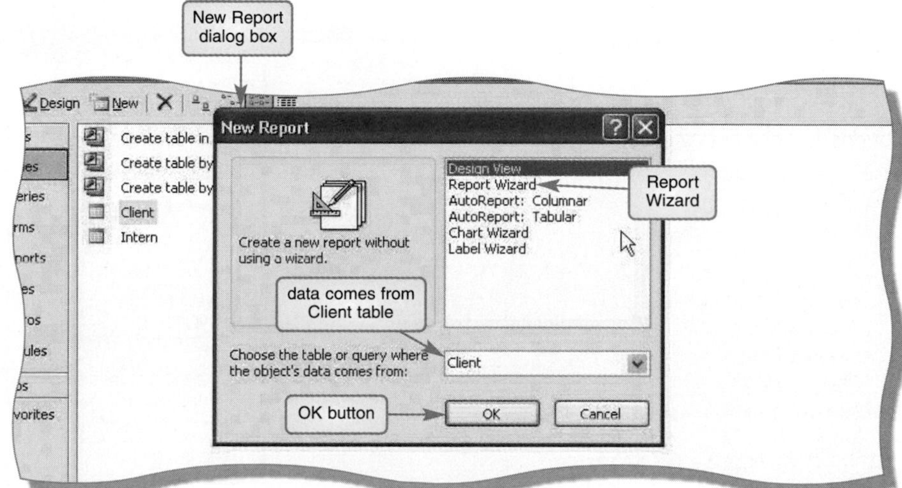

FIGURE 1-69

3

- **Click Report Wizard, and then click the OK button.**

Access displays the Report Wizard dialog box (Figure 1-70). As you click the Next button in this dialog box, a series of options helps you create the report.

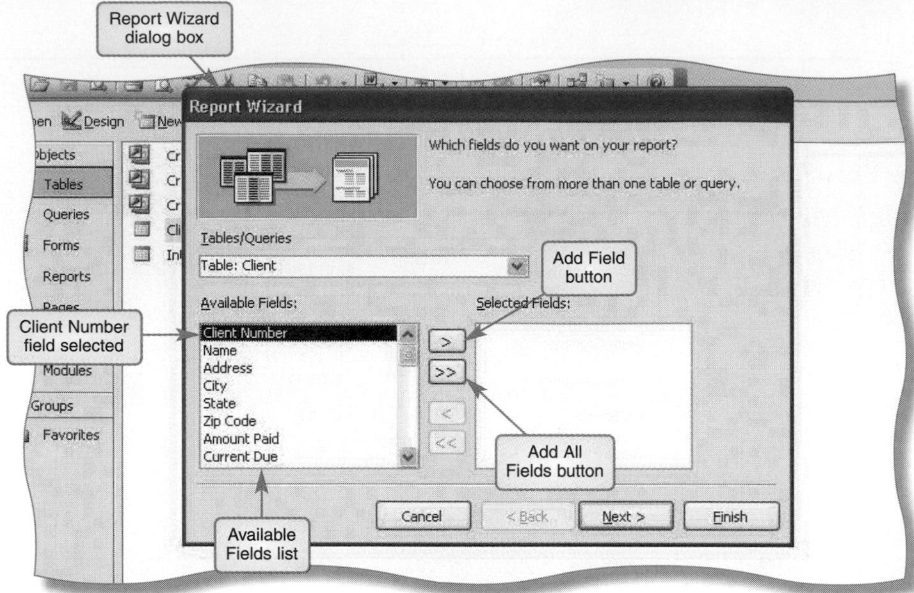

FIGURE 1-70

- **Click the Add Field button to add the Client Number field.**
- **Click the Add Field button to add the Name field.**
- **Add the Amount Paid and Current Due fields by clicking each field and then clicking the Add Field button.**

The fields for the report appear in the Selected Fields box (Figure 1-71).

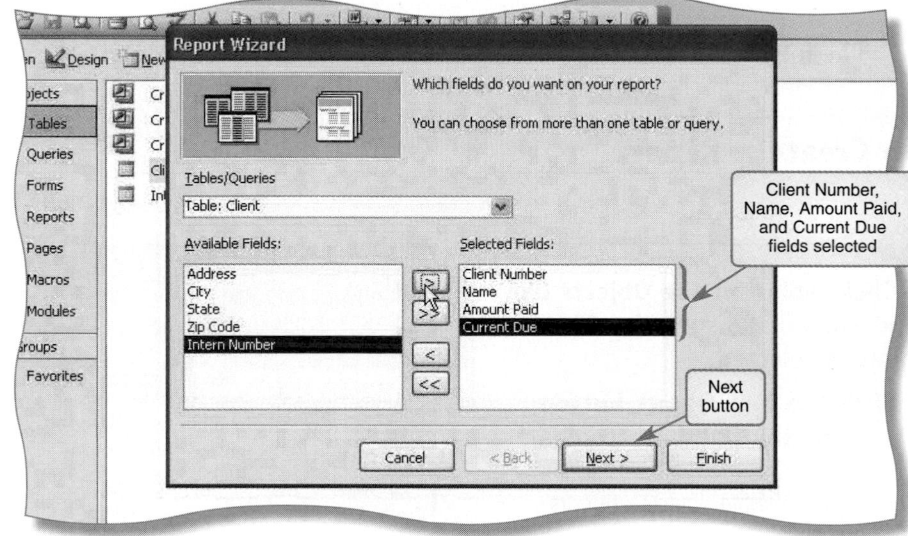

FIGURE 1-71

5

- **Click the Next button.**

The Report Wizard dialog box displays options to specify any grouping that is to take place (Figure 1-72).

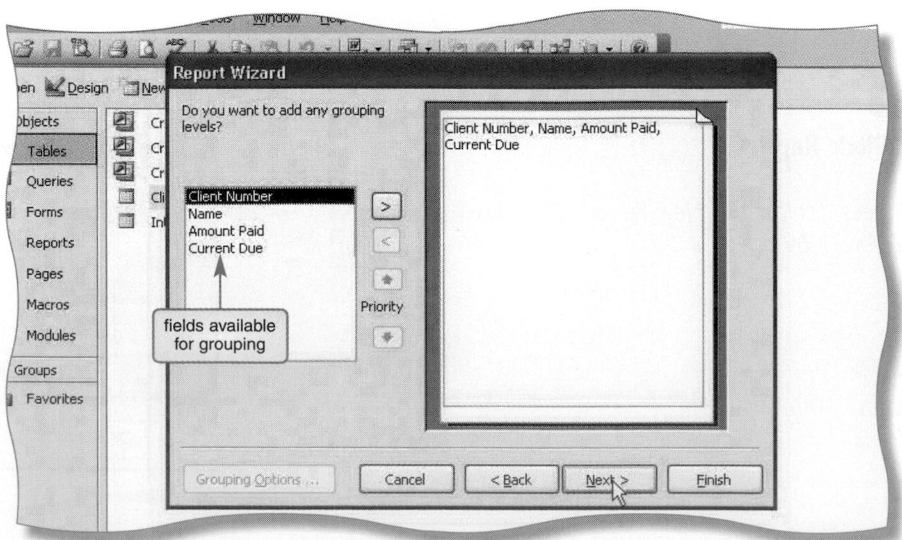

FIGURE 1-72

6

- **Because you will not specify any grouping, click the Next button in the Report Wizard dialog box.**
- **Click the Next button a second time because you will not need to change the sort order for the records.**

The Report Wizard dialog box displays options for changing the layout and orientation of the report (Figure 1-73).

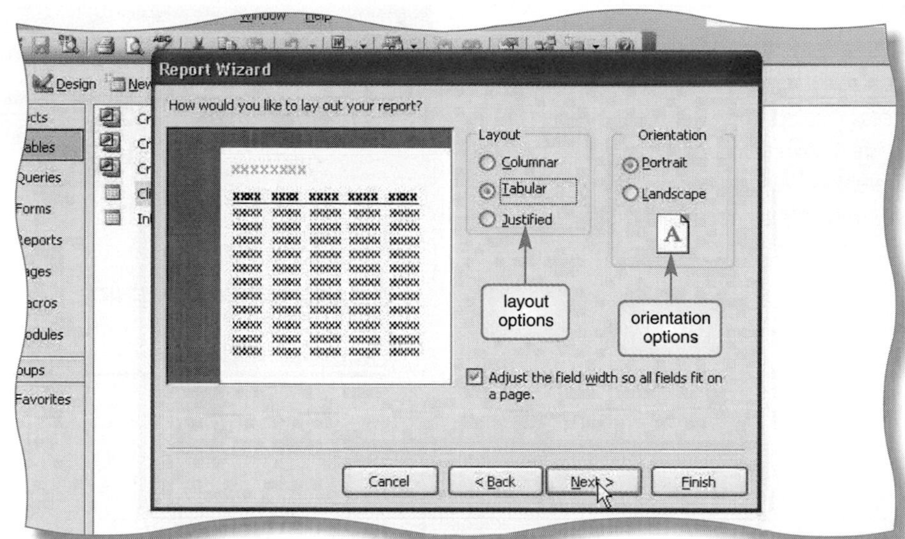

FIGURE 1-73

7

- **Make sure that Tabular is selected as the Layout and Portrait is selected as the Orientation, and then click the Next button.**

The Report Wizard dialog box displays options you can select for the style of the report (Figure 1-74).

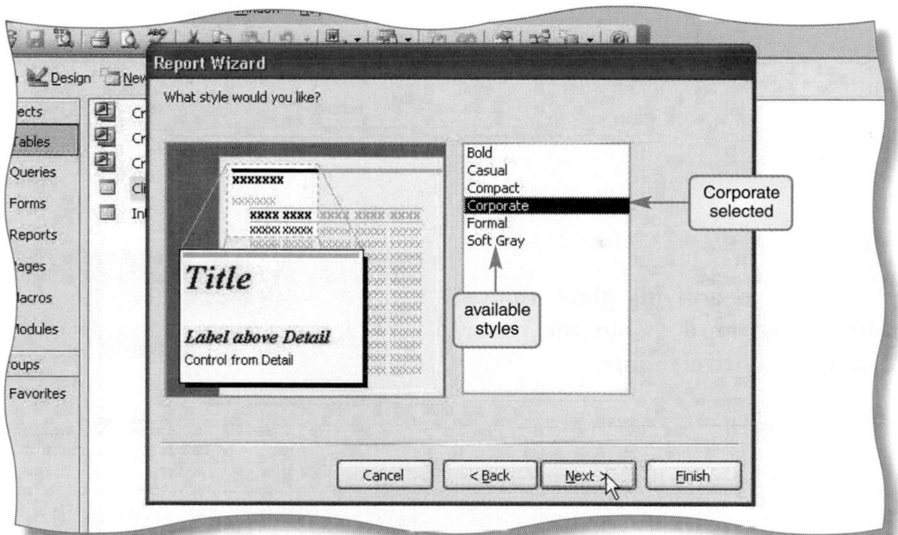

FIGURE 1-74

8

- **Be sure the Corporate style is selected, click the Next button, and then type** `Client Amount Report` **as the new title.**

The Report Wizard dialog box displays the new title of the report (Figure 1-75).

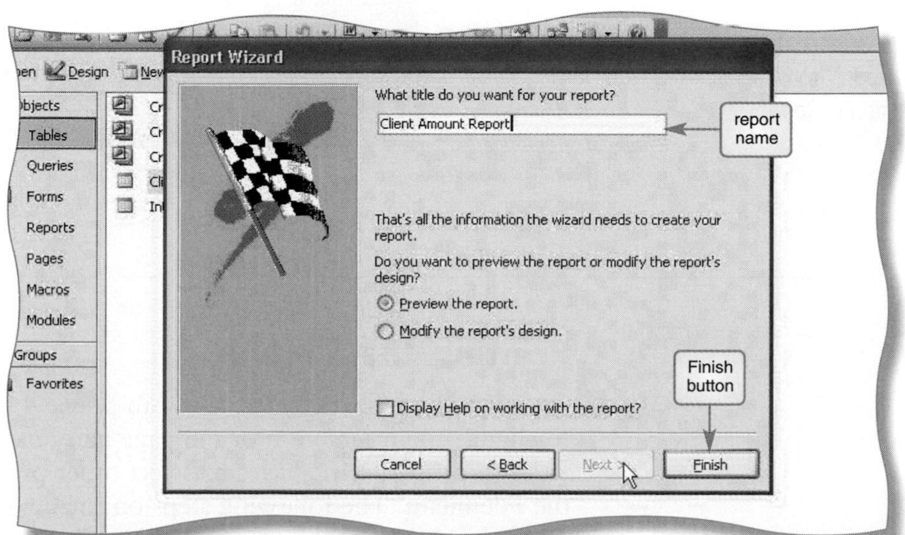

FIGURE 1-75

• **Click the Finish button.**

Access displays a preview of the report (Figure 1-76). Your report may look slightly different, depending on your printer. (Your report may appear in a different order.)

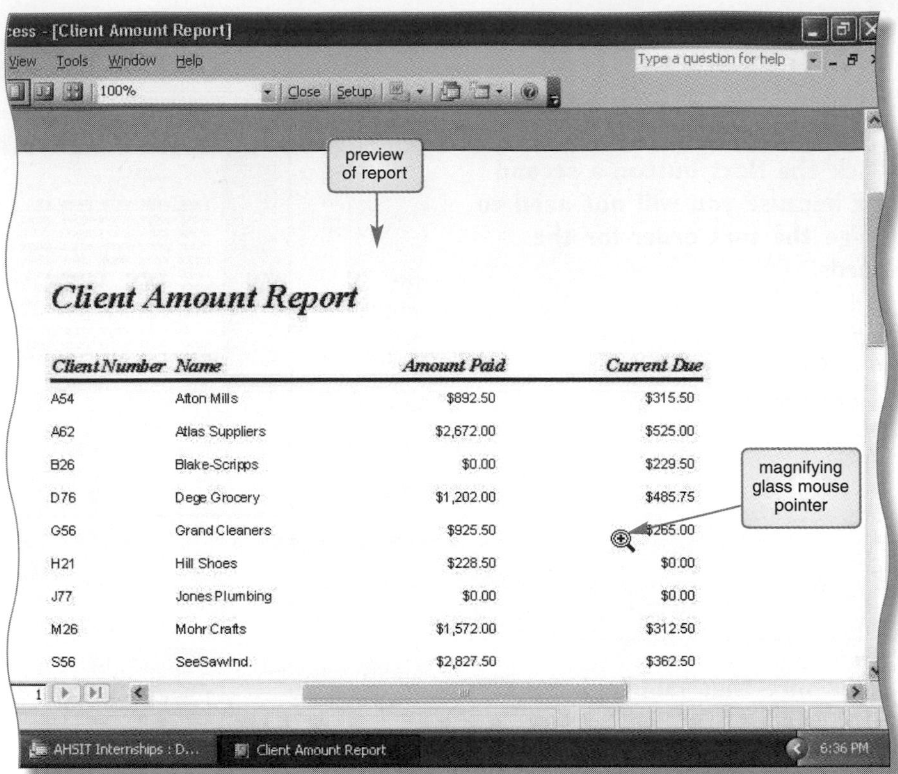

FIGURE 1-76

• **Click the magnifying glass mouse pointer anywhere within the report to see the entire report.**

The entire report appears (Figure 1-77).

• **Click the Close Window button in the Client Amount Report window.**

The report no longer appears. It has been saved automatically using the name Client Amount Report.

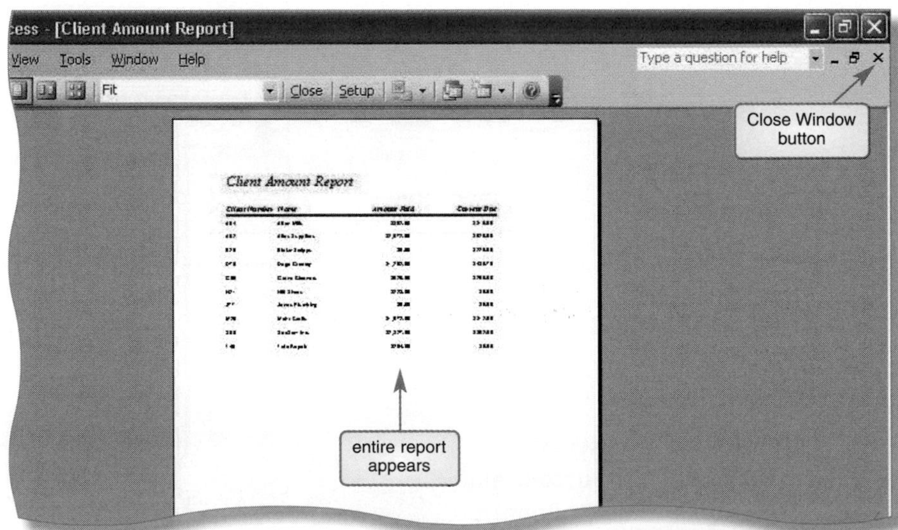

FIGURE 1-77

Printing the Report

With the report created, you can preview the report to determine if you need to change the orientation or the page margins. You also can print the report. If you want to print specific pages or select other print options, use the Print command on the File menu. The following steps on the next page show how to print a report using the shortcut menu.

To Print a Report

1

- **If necessary, click Reports on the Objects bar in the Database window.**
- **Right-click the Client Amount Report.**

The Client Amount Report is selected and the shortcut menu appears (Figure 1-78).

2

- **Click Print on the shortcut menu.**

The report prints. It should look similar to the one shown in Figure 1-67 on page AC 43.

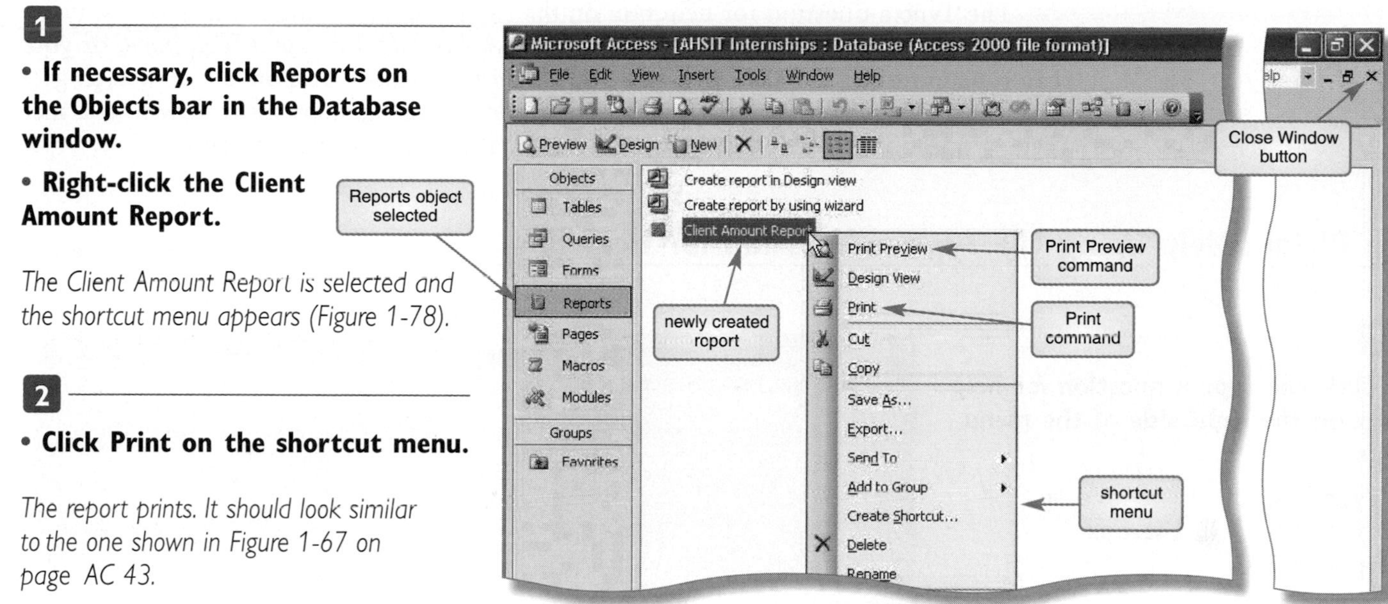

FIGURE 1-78

Closing the Database

After you have finished working with a database, you should close it. The following step closes the database by closing its Database window.

To Close a Database

1 **Click the Close Window button for the AHSIT Internships : Database window.**

Access Help System

At any time while you are using Access, you can get answers to questions by using the Access Help system. You can activate the Access Help system by using the Type a question for help box on the menu bar, by clicking the Microsoft Office Access Help button on the toolbar, or by clicking Help on the menu bar (Figure 1-79 on the next page). Used properly, this form of online assistance can increase your productivity and reduce your frustrations by minimizing the time you spend learning how to use Access.

The section on the next page shows how to get answers to your questions using the Type a question for help box. Additional information about using the Access Help system is available in Appendix A.

Skill Builder 1-6

To practice the following tasks, visit scsite.com/off2003sch/skill, locate Access Project 1, and then click Skill Builder 1-6.

- ❑ Create a report using the Report Wizard.
- ❑ Print the report.

Obtaining Help Using the Type a Question for Help Box on the Menu Bar

The Type a question for help box on the right side of the menu bar lets you type in free-form questions, such as *how do I save* or *how do I create a Web page,* or you can type in terms, such as *copy*, *save*, or *formatting*. Access responds by displaying a list of topics related to what you entered. The following steps show how to use the Type a question for help box to obtain information on removing a primary key.

To Obtain Help Using the Type a Question for Help Box

1

- **Click the Type a question for help box on the right side of the menu bar.**
- **Type** `how do I remove a primary key` **in the box (Figure 1-79).**

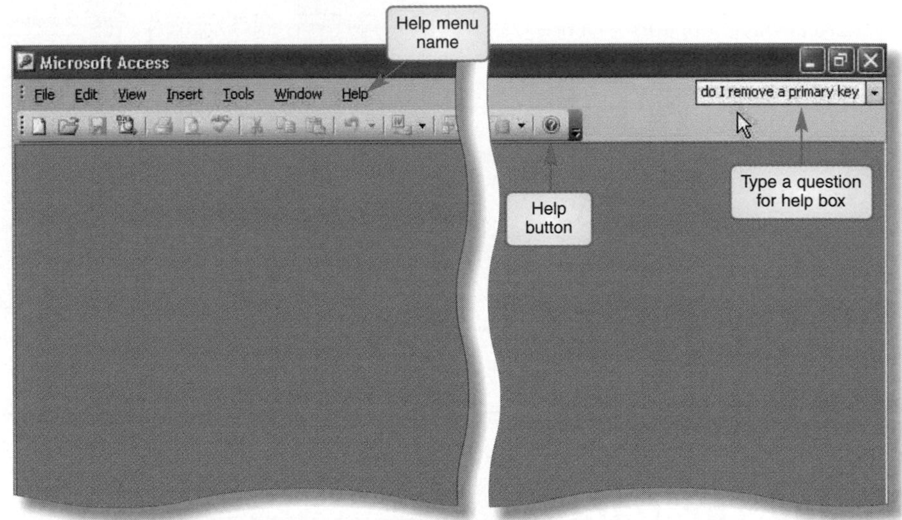

FIGURE 1-79

2

- **Press the ENTER key.**

Access displays the Search Results task pane, which includes a list of topics relating to the question, how do I remove a primary key (Figure 1-80). Your list may be different.

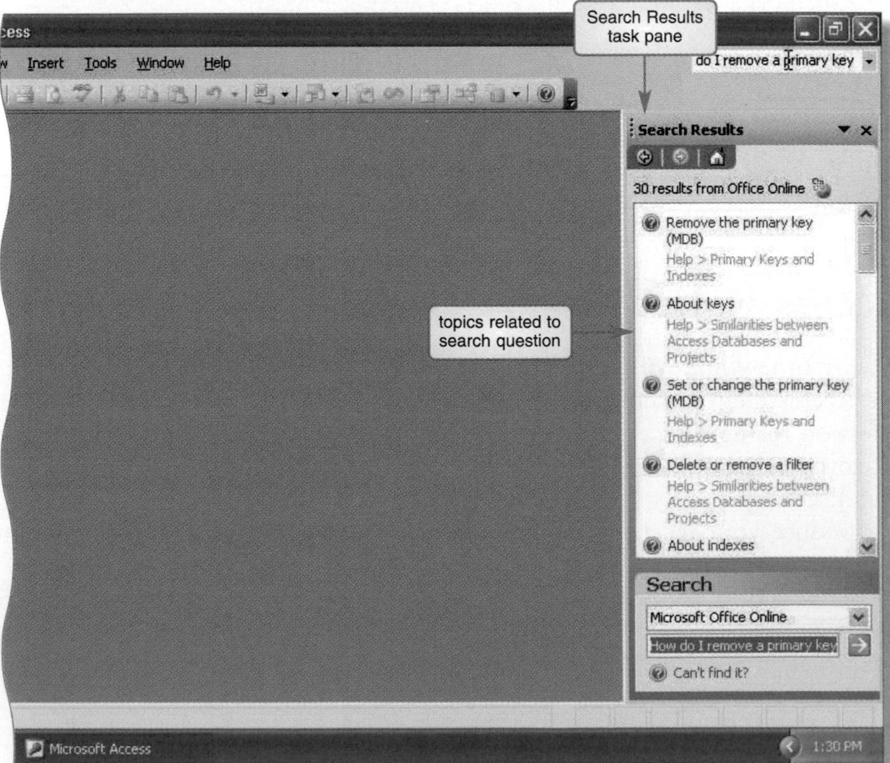

FIGURE 1-80

3

• Point to the Remove the primary key (MDB) topic.

The mouse pointer changes to a hand, indicating it is pointing to a link (Figure 1-81).

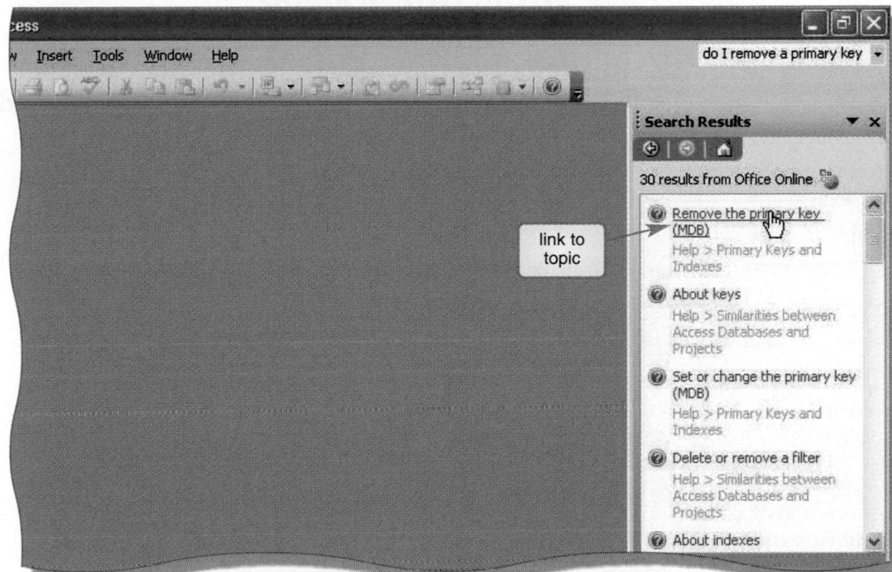

FIGURE 1-81

4

• Click Remove the primary key (MDB).

Access displays a Microsoft Office Access Help window that provides Help information about removing the primary key (Figure 1-82). Your window may be in a different position.

5

• Click the Close button on the Microsoft Office Access Help window title bar.

The Microsoft Access Help window closes.

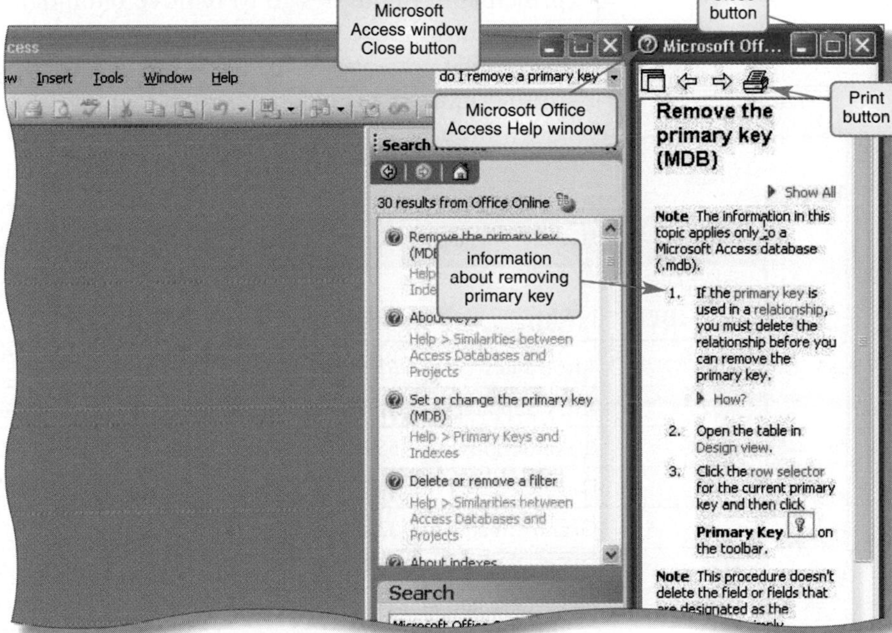

FIGURE 1-82

Use the buttons in the upper-left corner of the Microsoft Office Access Help window (Figure 1-82) to navigate through the Help system, and change the appearance and print the contents of the window.

As you enter questions and terms in the Type a question for help box, Access adds them to its list. Thus, if you click the Type a question for help box arrow, a list of previously asked questions and terms will appear.

Quitting Access

After you close a database, you can open another database, create a new database, or simply quit Access and return to the Windows desktop. The following step quits Access.

To Quit Access

1. **Click the Close button in the Microsoft Access window (see Figure 1-82 on the previous page).**

Q & A

Q: Is there a specific method for designing a database?

A: A variety of methods have been developed for designing complex databases given a set of input and output requirements. For more information about database design methods, visit the Office 2003 Q&A Web page (scsite.com/off2003sch/qa), locate Access Project 1, and click Database Design.

Designing a Database

Database design refers to the arrangement of data into tables and fields. In the example in this project, the design is specified, but in many cases, you will have to determine the design based on what you want the system to accomplish.

With large, complex databases, the database design process can be extensive. Major sections of advanced database textbooks are devoted to this topic. Often, however, you should be able to design a database effectively by keeping one simple principle in mind: design to remove redundancy. **Redundancy** means storing the same fact in more than one place.

To illustrate, you need to maintain the following information shown in Figure 1-83. In the figure, all the data is contained in a single table. Notice that the data for a given intern (number, name, address, and so on) occurs on more than one record.

Client table

duplicate intern names

CLIENT NUMBER	NAME	ADDRESS	...	CURRENT DUE	INTERN NUMBER	LAST NAME	FIRST NAME	...
A54	Afton Mills	612 Revere	...	$315.50	22	Lewen	Joann	...
A62	Atlas Suppliers	227 Dandelion	...	$525.00	24	Rodriguez	Mario	...
B26	Blake-Scripps	557 Maum	...	$229.50	24	Rodriguez	Mario	...
D76	Dege Grocery	446 Linton	...	$485.75	34	Wong	Shawn	...
G56	Grand Cleaners	337 Abelard	...	$265.00	22	Lewen	Joann	...
H21	Hill Shoes	247 Fulton	...	$0.00	24	Rodriguez	Mario	...
J77	Jones Plumbing	75 Getty	...	$0.00	34	Wong	Shawn	...
M26	Mohr Crafts	665 Market	...	$312.50	22	Lewen	Joann	...
S56	SeeSaw Ind.	31 Liatris	...	$362.50	34	Wong	Shawn	...
T45	Tate Repair	824 Revere	...	$0.00	24	Rodriguez	Mario	...

FIGURE 1-83

Storing this data on multiple records is an example of redundancy, which causes several problems, including:

1. Redundancy wastes space on the disk. The name of intern 22 (Joann Lewen), for example, should be stored only once. Storing this fact several times is wasteful.
2. Redundancy makes updating the database more difficult. If, for example, Joann Lewen's name changes, her name would need to be changed in several different places.

3. A possibility of inconsistent data exists. If, for example, you change the name of Joann Lewen on client A54's record to Joann Webb, but do not change it on client G56's record, the data is inconsistent. In both cases, the intern number is 22, but the intern's names are different.

The solution to the problem is to place the redundant data in a separate table, one in which the data no longer will be redundant. If, for example, you place the data for interns in a separate table (Figure 1-84), the data for each intern will appear only once.

Q & A

Q: Is there a technique for identifying redundancy in a database design?

A: A special technique, called normalization, identifies and eliminates redundancy. For more information about normalization, visit the Office 2003 Q&A Web page (scsite.com/off2003sch/qa), locate Access Project 1, and click Normalization.

intern data is in separate table

Intern table

INTERN NUMBER	LAST NAME	FIRST NAME	ADDRESS	CITY	STATE	ZIP CODE	HOURLY RATE	YTD EARNINGS
22	Lewen	Joann	26 Cotton	Portage	MN	59130	$5.50	$1,320.00
24	Rodriguez	Mario	79 Marsden	E. Portage	MN	59135	$5.40	$1,280.50
34	Wong	Shawn	263 Topper	Portage	MN	59130	$5.75	$1,500.25
42	Trent	Roberta	45 Magee	W. Portage	MN	59136	$5.60	$0.00

Client table

CLIENT NUMBER	NAME	ADDRESS	CITY	STATE	ZIP CODE	AMOUNT PAID	CURRENT DUE	INTERN NUMBER
A54	Afton Mills	612 Revere	Grant City	ND	58120	$892.50	$315.50	22
A62	Atlas Suppliers	227 Dandelion	Empeer	ND	58216	$2,672.00	$525.00	24
B26	Blake-Scripps	557 Maum	Grant City	ND	58120	$0.00	$229.50	24
D76	Dege Grocery	446 Linton	Portage	MN	59130	$1,202.00	$485.75	34
G56	Grand Cleaners	337 Abelard	Portage	MN	59131	$925.50	$265.00	22
H21	Hill Shoes	247 Fulton	Grant City	ND	58121	$228.50	$0.00	24
J77	Jones Plumbing	75 Getty	E. Portage	MN	59135	$0.00	$0.00	34
M26	Mohr Crafts	665 Market	Empeer	ND	58216	$1,572.00	$312.50	22
S56	SeeSaw Ind.	31 Liatris	Portage	MN	59130	$2,827.50	$362.50	34
T45	Tate Repair	824 Revere	Grant City	ND	58120	$254.00	$0.00	24

FIGURE 1-84

Notice that you need to have the intern number in both tables. Without it, no way exists to tell which intern is associated with which client. The remaining intern data, however, was removed from the Client table and placed in the Intern table. This new arrangement corrects the problems of redundancy in the following ways:

1. Because the data for each intern is stored only once, space is not wasted.
2. Changing the name of an intern is easy. You have to change only one row in the Intern table.
3. Because the data for an intern is stored only once, inconsistent data cannot occur.

Designing to omit redundancy will help you to produce good and valid database designs.

Q & A

Q: What is the Microsoft Office Certification program?

A: The Microsoft Office Specialist Certification program provides an opportunity for you to obtain a valuable industry credential — proof that you have the Access 2003 skills required by employers. For more information, see Appendix E, or visit the Office 2003 Certification Web page (scsite.com/off2003sch/cert).

Project Summary

In Project 1, you learned about databases and database management systems. You learned how to create a database and how to create the tables within a database. You saw how to define the fields in a table by specifying the characteristics of the fields. You learned how to open a table, how to add records to it, and how to close it. You also printed the contents of a table. You learned how to use the Simple Query wizard to create a query that included columns from a table, as well as how to enter a criterion to restrict the rows that were included. You created a form to view data on the screen and also created a custom report. You learned how to use Microsoft Access Help. Finally, you learned how to design a database to eliminate redundancy.

If you have a SAM user profile, you may have access to hands-on instruction, practice, and assessment of the skills covered in this project. Log in to your SAM account and go to your assignments page to see what your instructor has assigned.

What You Should Know

Having completed this project, you should be able to perform the tasks below. The tasks are listed in the same order they were presented in this project. For a list of the buttons, menus, toolbars, and commands introduced in this project, see the Quick Reference Summary at the back of this book and refer to the Page Number column.

1. Start Access (AC 7)
2. Close the Language Bar (AC 9)
3. Create a New Database (AC 10)
4. Create a Table (AC 17)
5. Define the Fields in a Table (AC 19)
6. Close and Save a Table (AC 21)
7. Add Records to a Table (AC 23)
8. Close a Table and Database and Quit Access (AC 26)
9. Open a Database (AC 26)
10. Add Additional Records to a Table (AC 28)
11. Preview and Print the Contents of a Table (AC 30)
12. Create an Additional Table (AC 33)
13. Add Records to an Additional Table (AC 34)
14. Use the Simple Query Wizard to Create a Query (AC 34)
15. Use a Query (AC 37)
16. Use the New Object Button to Create a Form (AC 38)
17. Close and Save a Form (AC 39)
18. Open a Form (AC 40)
19. Use a Form (AC 41)
20. Switch from Form View to Datasheet View (AC 42)
21. Create a Report (AC 43)
22. Print a Report (AC 47)
23. Close a Database (AC 47)
24. Obtain Help Using the Type a Question for Help Box (AC 48)
25. Quit Access (AC 50)

Career Corner

Database Administrator

Most businesses and organizations are built around databases. Access to timely, accurate, and relevant information is a company's lifeline. A database administrator (DBA) creates, applies, supports, and administers the policies and procedures for maintaining a company's database. Database administrators construct logical and physical descriptions of the database, establish database parameters, develop data models characterizing data elements, ensure database integrity, and coordinate database security measures including developing and implementing disaster recovery and archiving procedures. They also use query languages to obtain reports of the information in the database. With the large amounts of sensitive data generated, data integrity, backup, and security have become increasingly important aspects of the administrator's responsibilities.

Administering a database requires a great deal of mental work and the ability to focus on finite details. Database administrators must be able to read and comprehend business related information, organize data in a logical manner, apply general rules to specific problems, identify business principles and practices, and communicate clearly with database users. Being proficient with a particular database such as Oracle, Informix, or SQL Server is an added advantage. The real key, however, is learning, understanding, and becoming an expert in database design.

Database administrators usually have a bachelor or associate degree and experience with computer programming, relational databases, query languages, and online analytical processing. Typical salaries for database administrators are between $69,000 and $95,000, depending on experience. For more information, visit scsite.com/off2003sch/careers and then click Database Administrator.

Learn It Online

Instructions: To complete the Learn It Online exercises, start your browser, click the Address bar, and then enter the Web address `scsite.com/off2003sch/learn`. When the Office 2003 Learn It Online page is displayed, follow the instructions in the exercises below. Each exercise has instructions for printing your results, either for your own records or for submission to your instructor.

1 Project Reinforcement TF, MC, and SA

Below Access Project 1, click the Project Reinforcement link. Print the quiz by clicking Print on the File menu for each page. Answer each question.

2 Flash Cards

Below Access Project 1, click the Flash Cards link and read the instructions. Type 20 (or a number specified by your instructor) in the Number of playing cards text box, type your name in the Enter your Name text box, and then click the Flip Card button. When the flash card is displayed, read the question and then click the ANSWER box arrow to select an answer. Flip through Flash Cards. If your score is 15 (75%) correct or greater, click Print on the File menu to print your results. If your score is less than 15 (75%) correct, then redo this exercise by clicking the Replay button.

3 Practice Test

Below Access Project 1, click the Practice Test link. Answer each question, enter your first and last name at the bottom of the page, and then click the Grade Test button. When the graded practice test is displayed on your screen, click Print on the File menu to print a hard copy. Continue to take practice tests until you score 80% or better.

4 Who Wants To Be a Computer Genius?

Below Access Project 1, click the Computer Genius link. Read the instructions, enter your first and last name at the bottom of the page, and then click the PLAY button. When your score is displayed, click the PRINT RESULTS link to print a hard copy.

5 Wheel of Terms

Below Access Project 1, click the Wheel of Terms link. Read the instructions, and then enter your first and last name and your school name. Click the PLAY button. When your score is displayed, right-click the score and then click Print on the shortcut menu to print a hard copy.

6 Crossword Puzzle Challenge

Below Access Project 1, click the Crossword Puzzle Challenge link. Read the instructions, and then enter your first and last name. Click the SUBMIT button. Work the crossword puzzle. When you are finished, click the Submit button. When the crossword puzzle is redisplayed, click the Print Puzzle button to print a hard copy.

7 Tips and Tricks

Below Access Project 1, click the Tips and Tricks link. Click a topic that pertains to Project 1. Right-click the information and then click Print on the shortcut menu. Construct a brief example of what the information relates to in Access to confirm you understand how to use the tip or trick.

8 Newsgroups

Below Access Project 1, click the Newsgroups link. Click a topic that pertains to Project 1. Print three comments.

9 Expanding Your Horizons

Below Access Project 1, click the Expanding Your Horizons link. Click a topic that pertains to Project 1. Print the information. Construct a brief example of what the information relates to in Access to confirm you understand the contents of the article.

10 Search Sleuth

Below Access Project 1, click the Search Sleuth link. To search for a term that pertains to this project, select a term below the Project 1 title and then use the Google search engine at google.com (or any major search engine) to display and print two Web pages that present information on the term.

11 Access Online Training

Below Access Project 1, click the Access Online Training link. When your browser displays the Microsoft Office Online Web page, click the Access link. Click one of the Access courses that covers one or more of the objectives listed at the beginning of the project on page AC 4. Print the first page of the course before stepping through it.

12 Office Marketplace

Below Access Project 1, click the Office Marketplace link. When your browser displays the Microsoft Office Online Web page, click the Office Marketplace link. Click a topic that relates to Access. Print the first page.

13 You're Hired!

Below Access Project 1, click the You're Hired! link to embark on the path to a career in computers. Directions about how to play the game will be displayed. When you are ready to play, click the begin the game button. If required, submit your score to your instructor.

Apply Your Knowledge

1 Changing Data, Creating Queries, and Creating Reports

Instructions: Start Access. Open the Keep It Green database. See page xxiv at the front of this book for instructions for downloading the Data Files for Students, or see your instructor for information on accessing the files required in this book.

Keep It Green provides plants and plant care to local businesses. It was started by two horticultural students at the local community college. Keep It Green has a database that keeps track of its workers and customers. The database has two tables. The Customer table contains data on the customers who use the services of Keep It Green. The Worker table contains data on the individuals employed by Keep It Green. The structure and data are shown for the Customer table in Figure 1-85 and for the Worker table in Figure 1-86.

Structure of Customer table

FIELD NAME	DATA TYPE	FIELD SIZE	PRIMARY KEY?	DESCRIPTION
Customer Number	Text	4	Yes	Customer Number (Primary Key)
Name	Text	20		Customer Name
Address	Text	15		Street Address
City	Text	15		City
State	Text	2		State (Two-Character Abbreviation)
Zip Code	Text	5		Zip Code (Five-Character Version)
Balance	Currency			Amount Owed by Customer
Worker Number	Text	3		Number of Customer's Worker

Customer table

CUSTOMER NUMBER	NAME	ADDRESS	CITY	STATE	ZIP CODE	BALANCE	WORKER NUMBER
AS36	Aster Shoes	22 Bard	Kordy	OK	42514	$185.00	102
AU54	Author Books	41 Birchwood	Conner	OK	42547	$150.00	109
BI92	Bike Shop	43 Chelton	Kordy	OK	42514	$140.00	109
CC76	Coffee House	87 Fletcher	Cary	TX	52764	$0.00	113
CJ16	CJ's Music	23 Fairhaven	Conner	OK	42546	$105.00	102
JO62	Jordan Cafe	24 Bard	Kordy	OK	42514	$174.00	109
KL55	Klean n Dri	37 Strand	Cary	TX	52764	$215.00	109
ME71	Mel's Carpet	10 Main	Cary	TX	52764	$238.00	102
MO13	M&M Games	73 Lawton	Conner	OK	42547	$0.00	113
RO32	Royal Mfg Co.	87 Redwood	Kordy	OK	42515	$193.00	109

FIGURE 1-85

Apply Your Knowledge

Structure of Worker Table

FIELD NAME	DATA TYPE	FIELD SIZE	PRIMARY KEY?	DESCRIPTION
Worker Number	Text	3	Yes	Worker Number (Primary Key)
Last Name	Text	10		Last Name of Worker
First Name	Text	8		First Name of Worker
Address	Text	15		Street Address
City	Text	15		City
State	Text	2		State (Two-Character Abbreviation)
Zip Code	Text	5		Zip Code (Five-Character Version)
Hourly Rate	Currency			Hourly Pay Rate

Worker table

WORKER NUMBER	LAST NAME	FIRST NAME	ADDRESS	CITY	STATE	ZIP CODE	HOURLY RATE
102	Estevez	Manuel	467 Clay	Kordy	OK	42517	$7.50
109	Hilldon	Rita	78 Parkton	Conner	OK	42547	$7.75
113	Lee	Chou	897 North	Cary	TX	52764	$7.65
119	Shorter	Tracy	111 Maple	Conner	OK	42547	$7.50

FIGURE 1-86

Instructions: Perform the following tasks:

1. Open the Customer table and change the Worker Number for customer KL55 to 113.
2. Print the Customer table.
3. Use the Simple Query Wizard to create a new query to display and print the customer number, name, and worker number for records in the Customer table, as shown in Figure 1-87 on the next page.
4. Save the query as Customer-Worker Query and then close the query.
5. Open the Customer-Worker Query in Design View and restrict the query results to only those customers whose worker number is 109.
6. Print the query but do not save the changes.
7. Create the report shown in Figure 1-88 on the next page for the Customer table.
8. Print the report.

(continued)

Changing Data, Creating Queries, and Creating Reports *(continued)*

Microsoft Access - [Customer-Worker Query : Sel

Customer Numb	Name	Worker Number
AS36	Aster Shoes	102
AU54	Author Books	109
BI92	Bike Shop	109
CC76	Coffee House	113
CJ16	CJ's Music	102
JO62	Jordan Cafe	109
KL55	Klean n Dri	113
ME71	Mel's Carpet	102
MO13	M&M Games	113
RO32	Royal Mfg Co.	109

FIGURE 1-87

Customer Amount Report

Customer Number	*Name*	*Balance*
AS36	Aster Shoes	$185.00
AU54	Author Books	$150.00
BI92	Bike Shop	$140.00
CC76	Coffee House	$0.00
CJ16	CJ's Music	$105.00
JO62	Jordan Cafe	$174.00
KL55	Klean n Dri	$215.00
ME71	Mel's Carpet	$238.00
MO13	M&M Games	$0.00
RO32	Royal Mfg Co.	$193.00

FIGURE 1-88

1 Creating the Alumni Connection Database

Problem: The Alumni Association raises money by selling via the World Wide Web merchandise imprinted with the school logo. The database consists of two tables. The Item table contains information on items available for sale. The Vendor table contains information on the vendors.

Instructions: Perform the following tasks:

1. Create a new database in which to store all the objects related to the items for sale. Call the database Alumni Connection.
2. Create the Item table using the structure shown in Figure 1-89. Use the name Item for the table.
3. Add the data shown in Figure 1-89 to the Item table.
4. Print the Item table.

Structure of Item table

FIELD NAME	DATA TYPE	FIELD SIZE	PRIMARY KEY?	DESCRIPTION
Item Code	Text	4	Yes	Item Code (Primary Key)
Description	Text	25		Description of Item
On Hand	Number			Number of Units On Hand
Cost	Currency			Cost of Item
Selling Price	Currency			Selling Price of Item
Vendor Code	Text	2		Code of Item's Vendor

Item table

ITEM CODE	DESCRIPTION	ON HAND	COST	SELLING PRICE	VENDOR CODE
BA35	Baseball Cap	14	$10.50	$13.50	AL
CM02	Coffee Mug	20	$3.10	$5.00	GG
DS19	Desk Set	7	$9.80	$12.50	GG
KE06	Keychain	25	$1.25	$1.99	TM
OR24	Ornament	30	$3.25	$4.75	GG
PE12	Pennant	12	$5.65	$7.00	TM
PL01	Pillow	5	$11.35	$14.25	TM
SP05	Sports Bottle	18	$2.10	$2.95	GG
TW03	Towel	7	$8.05	$9.95	AL
WA34	Wastebasket	3	$14.25	$15.95	AL

FIGURE 1-89

5. Create the Vendor table using the structure shown in Figure 1-90 on the next page. Use the name Vendor for the table.
6. Add the data shown in Figure 1-90 to the Vendor table.
7. Print the Vendor table.
8. Create a form for the Vendor table. Use the name Vendor for the form.
9. Open the form you created and change the address for Vendor Code TM to 54 Maplewood.
10. Create and print the report shown in Figure 1-91 on the next page for the Item table.

(continued)

Creating the Alumni Connection Database *(continued)*

Structure of Vendor table

FIELD NAME	DATA TYPE	FIELD SIZE	PRIMARY KEY?	DESCRIPTION
Vendor Code	Text	2	Yes	Vendor Code (Primary Key)
Name	Text	20		Vendor Name
Address	Text	15		Street Address
City	Text	15		City
State	Text	2		State (Two-Character Abbreviation)
Zip Code	Text	5		Zip Code (Five-Character Version)
Telephone Number	Text	12		Telephone Number (999-999-9999 Version)

Vendor table

VENDOR CODE	NAME	ADDRESS	CITY	STATE	ZIP CODE	TELEPHONE NUMBER
AL	All Logo Inc.	234 South	Elgin	AZ	85165	602-555-6756
GG	GG Gifts	38 Stream	Grand	TX	78628	512-555-3402
SS	Sports Stuff	67 Main	Ghost	MI	49301	610-555-3333
TM	Trinkets 'n More	56 Maple	Holly	CA	95418	707-555-4545

FIGURE 1-90

Inventory Report

Item Code	*Description*	*On Hand*	*Cost*
BA35	Baseball Cap	14	$10.50
CM02	Coffee Mug	20	$3.10
DS19	Desk Set	7	$9.80
KE06	Keychain	25	$1.25
OR24	Ornament	30	$3.25
PE12	Pennant	12	$5.65
PL01	Pillow	5	$11.35
SP05	Sports Bottle	18	$2.10
TW03	Towel	7	$8.05
WA34	Wastebasket	3	$14.25

FIGURE 1-91

In the Lab

2 Creating the Clean n Neat Database

Problem: Clean n Neat is a local company that provides cleaning services to several small businesses in the area. The company employs high school and college students on a part-time basis. The database consists of two tables. The Client table contains information on the businesses that use Clean n Neat's services. The Custodian table contains information on the custodian assigned to the business.

Instructions: Perform the following tasks:

1. Create a new database in which to store all the objects related to the bookkeeping data. Call the database Clean n Neat.
2. Create and print the Client table using the structure and data shown in Figure 1-92. Then, create and print the Custodian table using the structure and data shown in Figure 1-93 on the next page.

Structure of Client table

FIELD NAME	DATA TYPE	FIELD SIZE	PRIMARY KEY?	DESCRIPTION
Client Number	Text	4	Yes	Client Number (Primary Key)
Name	Text	20		Name of Client
Address	Text	15		Street Address
City	Text	15		City
State	Text	2		State (Two-Character Abbreviation)
Zip Code	Text	5		Zip Code (Five-Character Version)
Balance	Currency			Amount Currently Owed for Services
Custodian Id	Text	2		Id of Client's Custodian

Client table

CLIENT NUMBER	NAME	ADDRESS	CITY	STATE	ZIP CODE	BALANCE	CUSTODIAN ID
AD03	Adly Cleaners	47 Mallory	Andice	GA	31501	$105.00	02
AR56	Art's Flowers	20 Wymberly	Liberty	GA	31499	$90.00	09
BE09	Beach Cafe	24 Harbor Oak	Liberty	GA	31499	$70.00	09
CR47	Casa Designs	50 Mallory	Andice	GA	31501	$0.00	02
DL41	Dos Salsos	123 Village	Kingston	GA	31534	$135.00	13
GR16	Great Movies	134 Main	Kingston	GA	31534	$104.00	13
HA09	Hal's Games	75 Demere	Andice	GA	31501	$145.00	09
ME16	Merry Music	13 Wild Heron	Kingston	GA	31534	$168.00	13
RO25	Royal Rentals	31 Red Poppy	Andice	GA	31501	$0.00	02
ST21	Steen's	82 Thistle	Liberty	GA	31499	$125.00	09

FIGURE 1-92

(continued)

Creating the Clean n Neat Database *(continued)*

Structure of Custodian table

FIELD NAME	DATA TYPE	FIELD SIZE	PRIMARY KEY?	DESCRIPTION
Custodian Id	Text	2	Yes	Custodian Id (Primary Key)
Last Name	Text	12		Last Name of Custodian
First Name	Text	8		First Name of Custodian
Address	Text	15		Street Address
City	Text	15		City
State	Text	2		State (Two-Character Abbreviation)
Zip Code	Text	5		Zip Code (Five-Character Version)
Hourly Rate	Currency			Hourly Rate
YTD Earnings	Currency			Year-to-Date Earnings

Custodian table

CUSTODIAN ID	LAST NAME	FIRST NAME	ADDRESS	CITY	STATE	ZIP CODE	HOURLY RATE	YTD EARNINGS
02	Dench	Terry	76 Hubbard	Andice	GA	31501	$9.50	$11,145.25
09	Lee	Marie	79 Dunlop	Liberty	GA	31499	$9.75	$9,893.50
13	Torres	Jorge	34 Liatris	Andice	GA	31501	$9.65	$13,417.00

FIGURE 1-93

3. Change the Custodian Id for client HA09 to 02.
4. Use the Simple Query Wizard to create a new query to display and print the Client Number, Name, and Custodian Id for all clients where the custodian id is 09.
5. Create and print the report shown in Figure 1-94 for the Client table.

Balance Due Report

Client Number	*Name*	*Balance*
AD03	Adly Cleaners	$105.00
AR56	Art's Flowers	$90.00
BE09	Beach Café	$70.00
CR47	Case Designs	$0.00
DL41	Dos Salsos	$135.00
GR16	Great Movies	$104.00
HA09	Hal's Games	$145.00
ME16	Merry Music	$168.00
RO25	Royal Rentals	$0.00
ST21	Steen's	$125.00

FIGURE 1-94

3 Creating the Centinel Database

Problem: *The Centinel* is a weekly newspaper that focuses on local news and includes a section on school news written by high school students. One of the main sources of revenue for any newspaper is advertising. Advertising representatives receive a commission based on the advertising revenues they generate. The database consists of two tables. The Advertiser table contains information on the businesses that advertise in the newspaper. The Ad Rep table contains information on the advertising representative assigned to the account.

Instructions Part 1: Using the data shown in Figures 1-95 below and 1-96 on the next page, create the Centinel database, the Advertiser table, and the Ad Rep table. Note that the Ad Rep table uses the number data type. Print the tables. Then, create a form for the Advertiser table.

Structure of Advertiser table

FIELD NAME	DATA TYPE	FIELD SIZE	PRIMARY KEY?	DESCRIPTION
Advertiser Number	Text	3	Yes	Advertiser Number (Primary Key)
Name	Text	20		Name of Advertiser
Address	Text	15		Street Address
Zip Code	Text	5		Zip Code (Five-Character Version)
Telephone Number	Text	8		Telephone Number (999-9999 Version)
Balance	Currency			Amount Currently Owed
Amount Paid	Currency			Amount Paid Year-to-Date
Ad Rep Number	Text	2		Number of Advertising Representative

Data for Advertiser table

ADVERTISER NUMBER	NAME	ADDRESS	ZIP CODE	TELEPHONE NUMBER	BALANCE	AMOUNT PAID	AD REP NUMBER
A28	Adam's Music	47 Cantor	19163	555-0909	$190.00	$465.00	36
B03	Barbecue Place	483 Barton	19163	555-8990	$285.00	$725.00	39
C48	Chloe's Salon	10 Jefferson	19162	555-2334	$0.00	$475.00	39
C75	Creative Toys	26 Main	19162	555-1357	$30.00	$965.00	42
D21	Dog Groomers	33 Beech	19162	555-2468	$190.00	$615.00	36
G34	GG's Pizza	196 Washington	19164	555-3579	$0.00	$705.00	39
M32	M&E Expresso	234 Oleander	19163	555-6802	$115.00	$945.00	42
P12	Paris Movies	22 Main	19164	555-8024	$165.00	$280.00	36
S11	Suds n Spuds	14 Jefferson	19165	555-5791	$365.00	$630.00	42
W45	Western Tack	345 Oakleigh	19163	555-7913	$205.00	$165.00	36

FIGURE 1-95

(continued)

Creating the Centinel Database *(continued)*

Structure for Ad Rep table

FIELD NAME	DATA TYPE	FIELD SIZE	PRIMARY KEY?	DESCRIPTION
Ad Rep Number	Text	2	Yes	Advertising Rep Number (Primary Key)
Last Name	Text	10		Last Name of Advertising Rep
First Name	Text	8		First Name of Advertising Rep
Address	Text	15		Street Address
City	Text	15		City
Zip Code	Text	5		Zip Code (Five-Character Version)
Comm Rate	Number	Double		Commission Rate on Advertising Sales
Commission	Currency			Year-to-Date Total Commissions

Data for Ad Rep table

AD REP NUMBER	LAST NAME	FIRST NAME	ADDRESS	CITY	ZIP CODE	COMM RATE	COMMISSION
36	Denton	Heather	57 Blaze	Chelton	19063	0.08	$4,500.00
39	Merton	Curran	87 Poppy	Newham	19054	0.07	$4,250.00
42	Tan	Elaine	45 Star	Sansor	19078	0.08	$5,000.00

FIGURE 1-96

Instructions Part 2: Correct the following error. The ad rep assigned to the Dog Groomers account should be Curran Merton. Use the form you created to make the correction, and then print the form showing the corrected record. To print the form, open the form, click File on the menu bar, and then click Print. Click Selected Records(s) as the Print Range. Click the OK button.

Instructions Part 3: Create a query to find which accounts Curran Merton represents. Print the results. Prepare an advertiser status report that lists the advertiser's number, name, balance currently owed, and amount paid to date.

Cases and Places

The difficulty of the case studies varies:

■ are the least difficult and ■■ are more difficult.

Each exercise has a cross-curricular designation:

Math Social Studies Science Language Arts Art/Music Business Health

1 To help finance your future college education, you formed a small business. You provide lawn services to local residents. The business has grown rapidly, and you now have several other students working for you. You realize that you need to computerize your business.

Design and create a database to store the data that College Lawn Services needs to manage its business. Then create the necessary tables, and enter the data from the Case 1-1 College Lawn Services Word document. Print the tables. See page xxiv at the front of this book for instructions for downloading the Data Files for Students, or see your instructor for information on accessing the files required in this book.

2 Your high school recently was renovated and now includes an indoor pool and fitness center. The pool and fitness center is open to the community during nonschool hours. Various types and levels of membership are available. Design and create a database to store the data that the fitness center needs to manage its memberships. Then create the necessary tables, and enter the data from the Case 1-2 Community Fitness Center Word document. Print the tables. See page xxiv at the front of this book for instructions for downloading the Data Files for Students, or see your instructor for information on accessing the files required in this book.

3 Student Government has decided to organize a used-book cooperative for books that are required reading in English classes. As a member of student government, you create a system whereby students can locate other students who have used a particular book in a previous semester and want to sell it to another student.

Design and create a database to store the book data. To create the Book table, use the Table Wizard and select the Books sample table. You do not need to select all the fields the Table Wizard provides, and you can rename the fields in the table. Enter the data from the Case 1-3 Book Cooperative Word document. Print the tables. Prepare a sample query and a sample report to illustrate to student government the types of tasks that can be done with a database management system. See page xxiv at the front of this book for instructions for downloading the Data Files for Students, or see your instructor for information on accessing the files required in this book.

Cases and Places

4. The Alyssa High School Math Club has started a tutoring program for freshman and sophomore students in all the high schools in the school district. Each Math Club member is assigned one or more students to tutor in subjects, such as factoring, quadratic formulas, side angle side (SAS) proofs, and similar triangles. Students who participate can earn points that can be redeemed for prizes donated by local merchants. Club members who participate keep track of the hours they spend tutoring. The hours are counted as part of the community service graduation requirement.

Design and create a database to meet the needs of the Math Club. Then create the necessary tables and enter the data from the Case 1-4 Math Club Tutors Word document. Print the tables. Prepare a sample form, sample query, and sample report to illustrate to the Math Club the types of tasks that can be done with a database management system. See page xxiv at the front of this book for instructions for downloading the Data Files for Students, or see your instructor for information on accessing the files required in this book.

Working Together Organizing special events, such as music recitals, proms, and art exhibits, requires careful preparation. In addition to deciding on the event logistics (dates, times, location) organizers also must create announcements and programs and keep track of expenses. Microsoft Access can help you manage special events. The Database Wizard includes an Event Management template that can create a database that will help you keep track of your special events.

Have each member of your team explore the features of the Database Wizard and determine individually which tables and fields should be included in an Event Management database. As a group, review your choices and decide on one common design. Prepare a short paper for your instructor that explains why your team chose the particular database design.

After agreeing on the database design, assign one member to create the database using the Database Wizard. Every other team member should contribute data and add the data to the database. Print at least one of each of the tables, reports, and forms that the Database Wizard creates. Turn in the short paper and the printouts to your instructor.

MICROSOFT OFFICE

Access 2003

Querying a Database Using the Select Query Window

PROJECT 2

CASE PERSPECTIVE

The corporate internship program at Alyssa High School of Information Technology (AHSIT) has proven popular with both student interns and corporate clients. As a result, Dr. Gervase finds that she must answer many questions about the program. She and her staff frequently are asked to give presentations to community groups and provide information to other school districts about the program. She also must answer questions and provide various statistics to school administration personnel. The AHSIT database allows Dr. Gervase easily and rapidly to get answers to questions such as the following concerning the data in the database:

1. Which clients are located in Grant City?
2. Which clients of intern 34 have paid more than $1,000?
3. What is the average amount paid for clients of each intern?

Alyssa High School frequently needs to ask the same question, each time with a different criterion. For example, Dr. Gervase needs to find information about clients located in a specific city but wants to use a different city each time she asks the question. A parameter query would enable her to do this. In addition, the corporate internship department also has a special way they want to summarize their data; a crosstab query will present the data in the desired form.

Your task is to assist Dr. Gervase and the corporate internship department in obtaining answers to these and other questions using Access query features.

As you read through this project, you will learn how to query a database using the Select Query window.

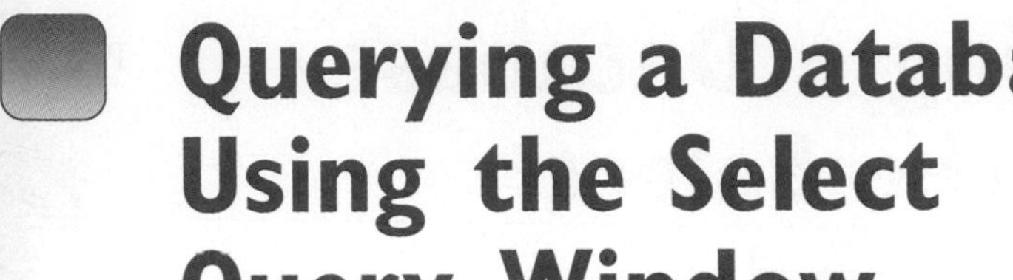

Querying a Database Using the Select Query Window

PROJECT

Objectives:

You will have mastered the material in this project when you can:

- Create and run queries
- Print query results
- Include fields in the design grid
- Use text and numeric data in criteria
- Create and use parameter queries
- Save a query and use the saved query
- Use compound criteria in queries
- Sort data in queries
- Join tables in queries
- Perform calculations in queries
- Use grouping in queries
- Create crosstab queries

Introduction

A database management system such as Access offers many useful features, among them the capability of answering questions such as those posed by the administration of Alyssa High School (Figure 2-1). The answers to these questions, and many more, are found in the database, and Access can find the answers quickly. When you pose a question to Access, or any other database management system, the question is called a query. A **query** is simply a question represented in a way that Access can understand.

Thus, to find the answer to a question, you first create a corresponding query using the techniques illustrated in this project. After you have created the query, you instruct Access to run the query; that is, to perform the steps necessary to obtain the answer. Access then will display the answer in Datasheet view.

Project Two — Querying the AHSIT Internships Database

The steps in this project obtain answers to the questions posed by the administration of Alyssa High School. These include the questions shown in Figure 2-1, as well as many other questions that may be deemed important.

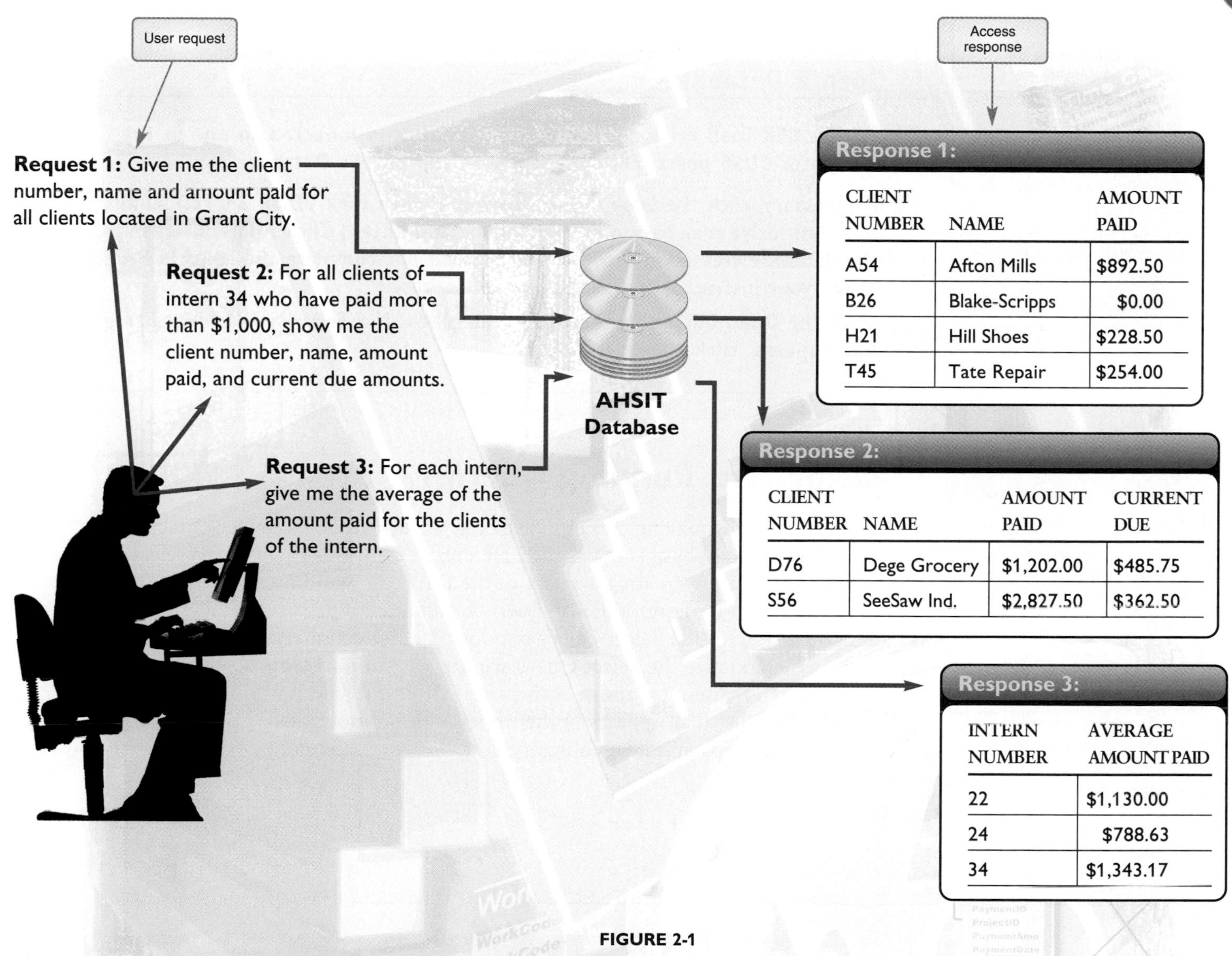
User request
Request 1: Give me the client number, name and amount paid for all clients located in Grant City.
Request 2: For all clients of intern 34 who have paid more than $1,000, show me the client number, name, amount paid, and current due amounts.
Request 3: For each intern, give me the average of the amount paid for the clients of the intern.
AHSIT Database
Access response
Response 1:
CLIENT NUMBER | NAME | AMOUNT PAID
A54 | Afton Mills | $892.50
B26 | Blake-Scripps | $0.00
H21 | Hill Shoes | $228.50
T45 | Tate Repair | $254.00
Response 2:
CLIENT NUMBER | NAME | AMOUNT PAID | CURRENT DUE
D76 | Dege Grocery | $1,202.00 | $485.75
S56 | SeeSaw Ind. | $2,827.50 | $362.50
Response 3:
INTERN NUMBER | AVERAGE AMOUNT PAID
22 | $1,130.00
24 | $788.63
34 | $1,343.17

FIGURE 2-1

> **Q & A**
>
> **Q:** Need help with Access?
>
> **A:** Help with Access is no further than the Type a question for help box on the menu bar in the upper-right corner of the window. Click the box that contains the text, Type a question for help (Figure 2-5), type `help`, and then press the ENTER key. Access responds with a list of topics you can click to learn about obtaining help on any Access-related topic. To find out what is new in Access 2003, type `what is new in Access` in the Type a question for help box.

Opening the Database

If you are stepping through this project on a computer, and you want your screen to agree with the figures in this book, then you should change your computer's resolution to 800 × 600. For more information on how to change the resolution on your computer, see Appendix D. Before creating queries, first you must open the database. The following steps summarize the procedure to complete this task, once you have started Access.

To Open a Database

1. **With a USB flash drive containing your database connected to one of the computer's USB ports, click the Open button on the Database toolbar.**
2. **If necessary, click the Look in box arrow and then click UDISK 2.0 (E:). (Your USB flash drive may have a different name and letter.) Click AHSIT Internships, the database created in Project 1. (If you did not complete the steps in Project 1, see your instructor for a copy of the database.)**
3. **Click the Open button in the Open dialog box. If a Security Warning dialog box appears, click the Open button.**

The database opens and the AHSIT Internships : Database window appears.

> **Q & A**
>
> **Q:** What should I do if I try to open a database and a Microsoft Office Access dialog box appears asking if I want to block unsafe expressions?
>
> **A:** Click the No button when asked if you want to block unsafe expressions. If another dialog box appears with questions about the Microsoft Jet Engine, click Yes and then click Open.

Creating and Running Queries

You create a query by making entries in a special window called a **Select Query window**. Once the database is open, the first step in creating a query is to select the table for which you are creating a query in the Database window. Then, you use the New Object button to design the new query in the Select Query window. It typically is easier to work with the Select Query window if it is maximized. Thus, as a standard practice, maximize the Select Query window as soon as you have created it. In addition, it often is useful to resize both panes within the window. This enables you to resize the field list that appears in the upper pane so more fields appear.

The following steps initiate creating a query.

To Create a Query

- **Be sure the AHSIT Internships database is open, the Tables object is selected, and the Client table is selected.**
- **Click the New Object button arrow on the Database toolbar.**

The list of available objects appears (Figure 2-2).

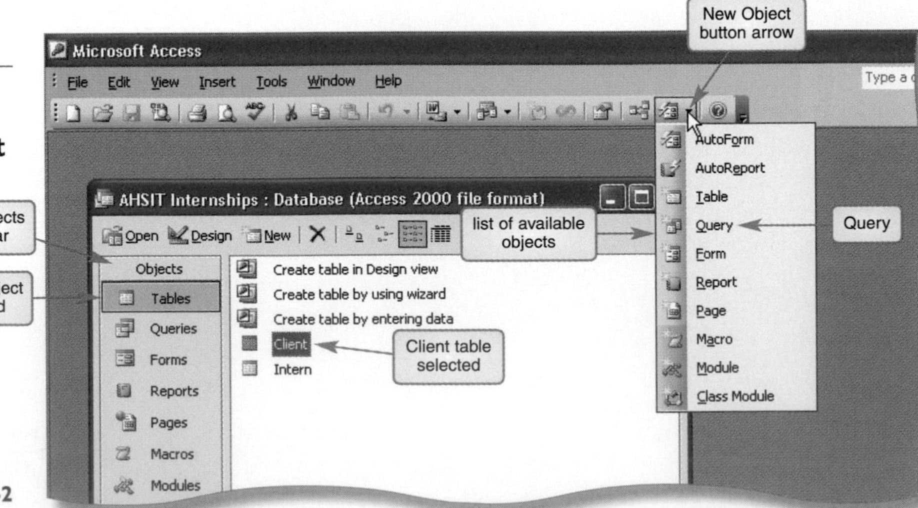

FIGURE 2-2

2

• **Click Query.**

Access displays the New Query dialog box (Figure 2-3).

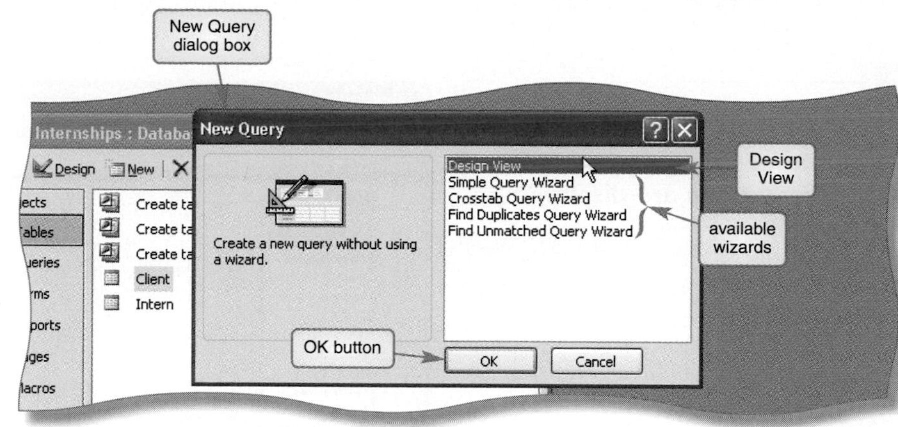

FIGURE 2-3

3

• **With Design View selected, click the OK button.**

The Query1 : Select Query window appears (Figure 2-4).

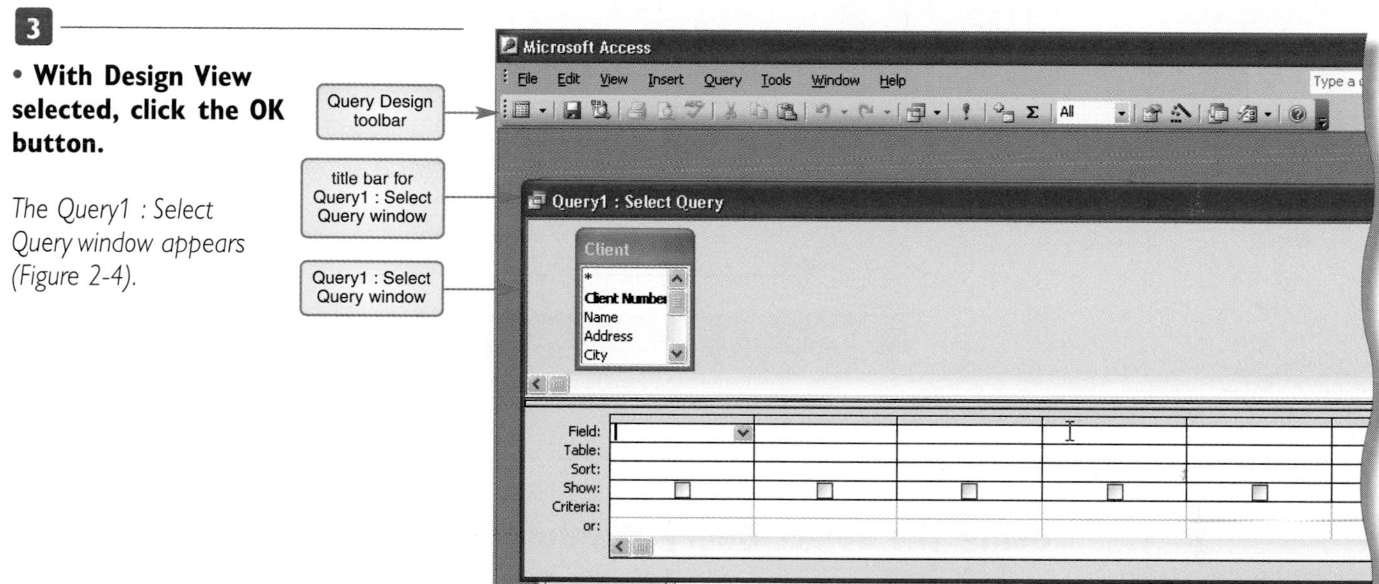

FIGURE 2-4

4

• **Maximize the Query1 : Select Query window by double-clicking its title bar, and then drag the line separating the two panes to the approximate position shown in Figure 2-5.**

The Query1 : Select Query window is maximized. The upper pane contains a field list for the Client table. The lower pane contains the ***design grid****, which is the area where you specify fields to be included, sort order, and the criteria the records you are looking for must satisfy. The mouse pointer shape indicates you can drag the line.*

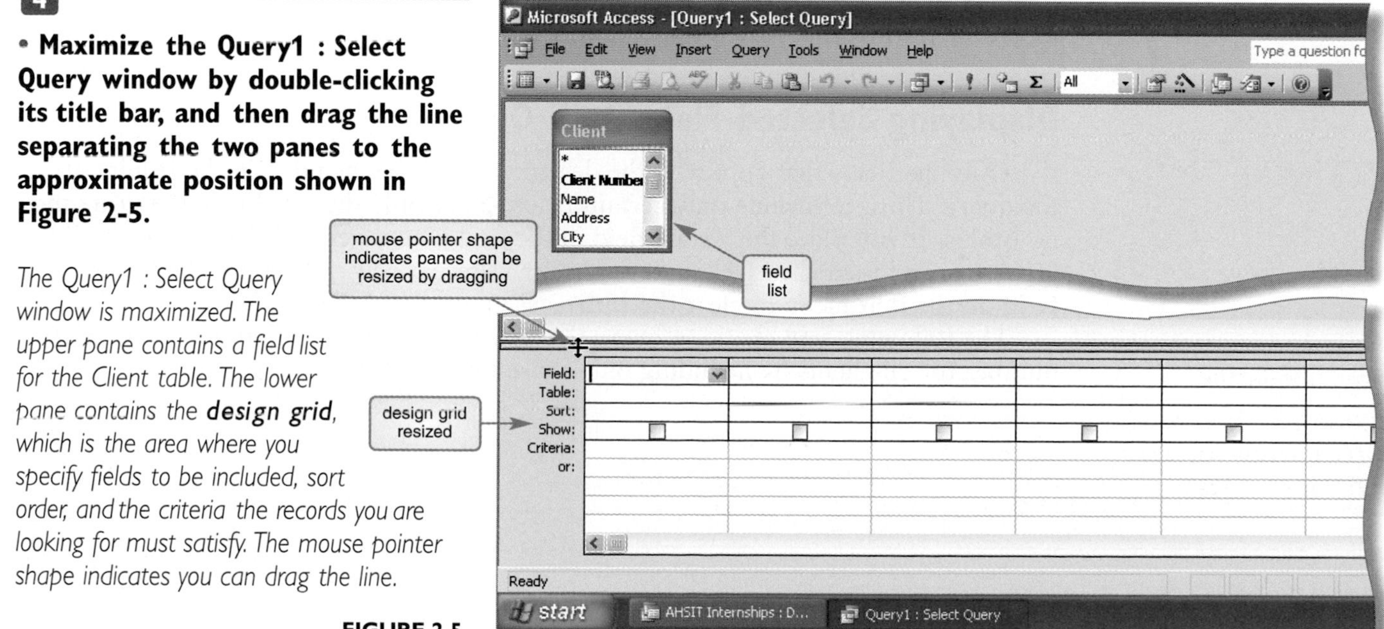

FIGURE 2-5

5

• **Drag the lower edge of the field box down far enough so all fields in the Client table are displayed (Figure 2-6).**

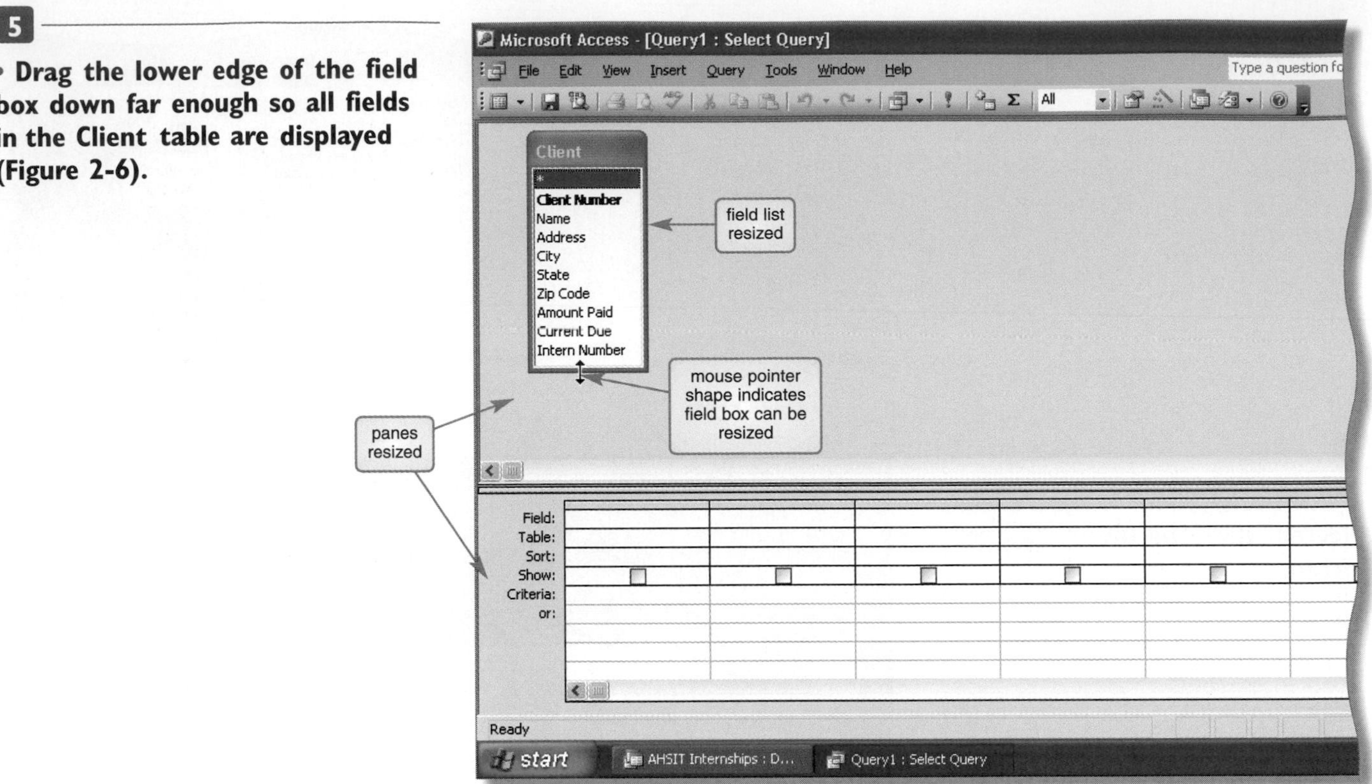

FIGURE 2-6

Using the Select Query Window

Once you have created a new Select Query window, you are ready to create the actual query by making entries in the design grid in the lower pane of the window. You enter the names of the fields you want included in the Field row in the grid. You also can enter criteria, such as the fact that the client number must be a specific number, such as G56, in the Criteria row of the grid. When you do so, only the record or records that match the criterion will be included in the answer.

Displaying Selected Fields in a Query

Only the fields that appear in the design grid will be included in the results of the query. Thus, to include only certain fields, place only these fields in the grid, and no others. If you place the wrong field in the grid inadvertently, click Edit on the menu bar and then click Delete to remove it. Alternatively, you could click Clear Grid on the Edit menu to clear the entire design grid and then start over.

The following step creates a query to show the client number, name, and intern number for all clients by including only those fields in the design grid.

To Include Fields in the Design Grid

1

- **If necessary, maximize the Query1 : Select Query window containing the field list for the Client table in the upper pane of the window and an empty design grid in the lower pane.**
- **Double-click the Client Number field in the field list to include it in the query.**
- **Double-click the Name field to include it in the query, and then double-click the Intern Number field to include it as well.**

The Client Number, Name, and Intern Number fields are included in the query (Figure 2-7).

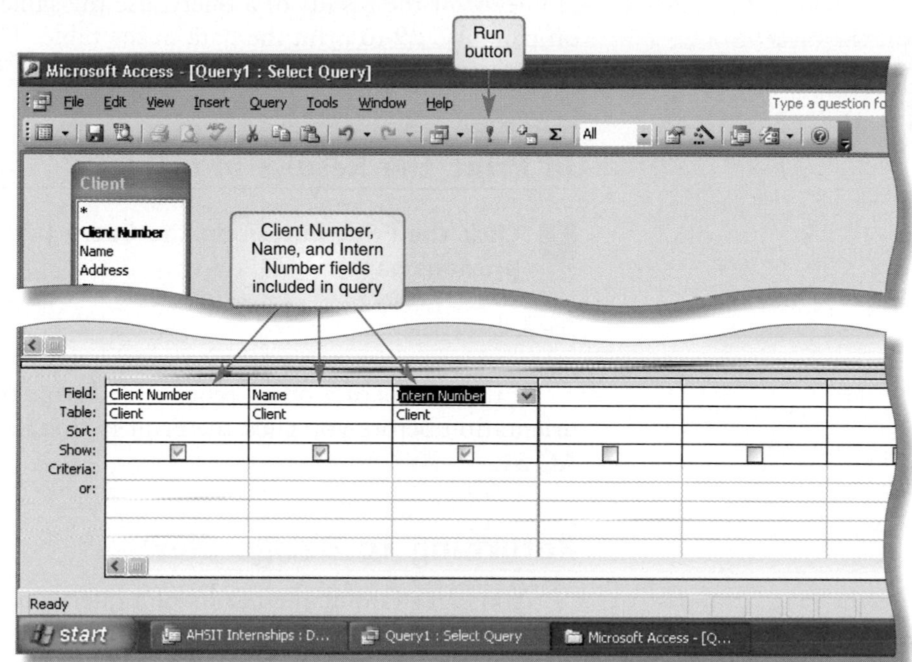

FIGURE 2-7

Running a Query

Once you have created the query, you run the query to produce the results using the Run button on the Query Design toolbar. Access performs the steps necessary to obtain and display the answer. The set of records that makes up the answer will be displayed in Datasheet view. Although it looks like a table that is stored on your disk, it really is not. The records are constructed from data in the existing Client table. If you were to change the data in the Client table and then rerun this same query, the results would reflect the changes. The following step runs the query.

To Run the Query

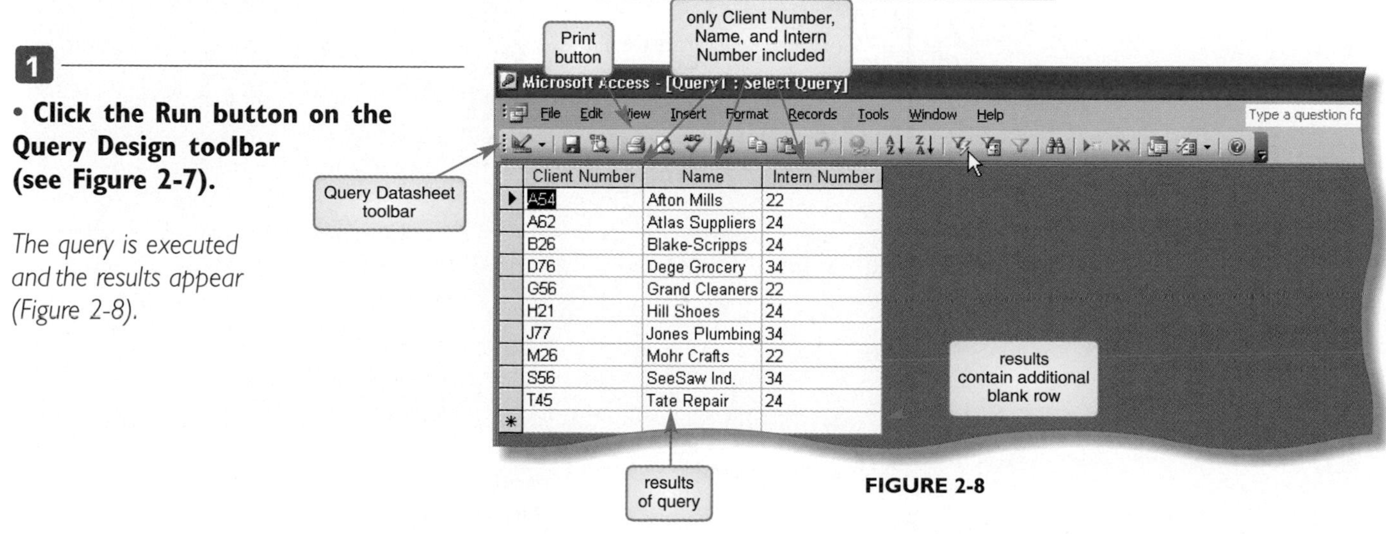

1

- **Click the Run button on the Query Design toolbar (see Figure 2-7).**

The query is executed and the results appear (Figure 2-8).

Client Number	Name	Intern Number
A54	Afton Mills	22
A62	Atlas Suppliers	24
B26	Blake-Scripps	24
D76	Dege Grocery	34
G56	Grand Cleaners	22
H21	Hill Shoes	24
J77	Jones Plumbing	34
M26	Mohr Crafts	22
S56	SeeSaw Ind.	34
T45	Tate Repair	24

FIGURE 2-8

Printing the Results of a Query

To print the results of a query, use the same techniques you learned in Project 1 on page AC 29 to print the data in the table. The following step prints the current query results.

To Print the Results of a Query

1 **Click the Print button on the Query Datasheet toolbar (see Figure 2-8 on the previous page).**

The results print.

If the results of a query require landscape orientation, switch to landscape orientation before you click the Print button as indicated in Project 1 on page AC 31.

Returning to Design View

You can examine the results of a query on your screen to see the answer to your question. You can scroll through the records, if necessary, just as you scroll through the records of any other table. You also can print a copy of the table. In any case, once you are finished working with the results, you can return to Design view to ask another question. The following steps illustrate how to return to the Select Query window in Design view.

To Return to Design View

1

- **Click the View button arrow on the Query Datasheet toolbar.**

The Query View list appears (Figure 2-9).

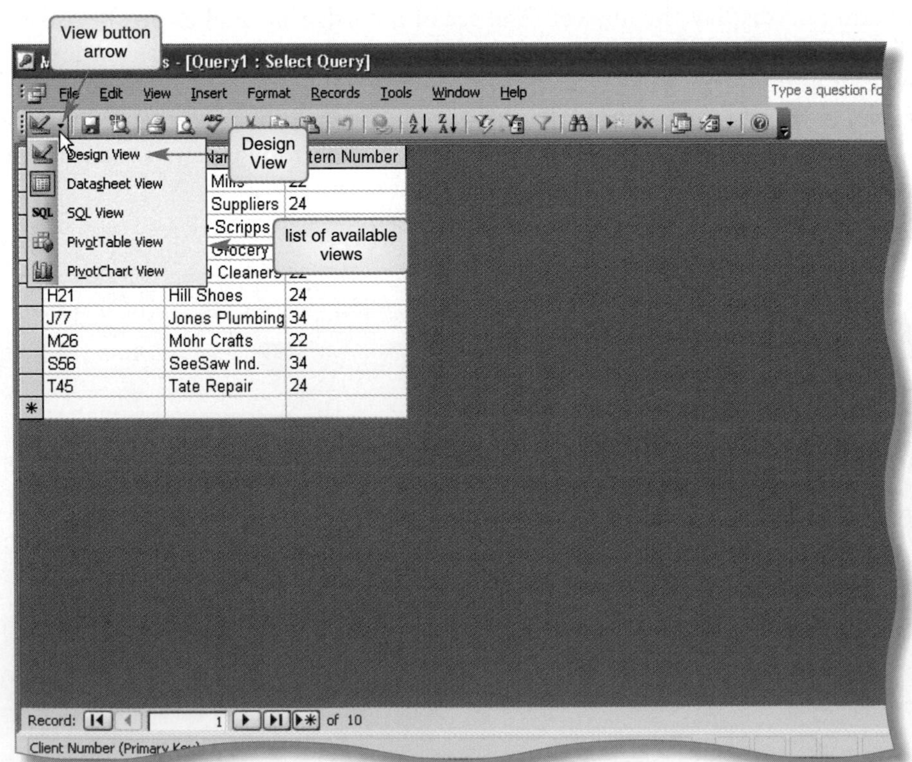

FIGURE 2-9

2

• **Click Design View.**

The query once again appears in Design view (Figure 2-10).

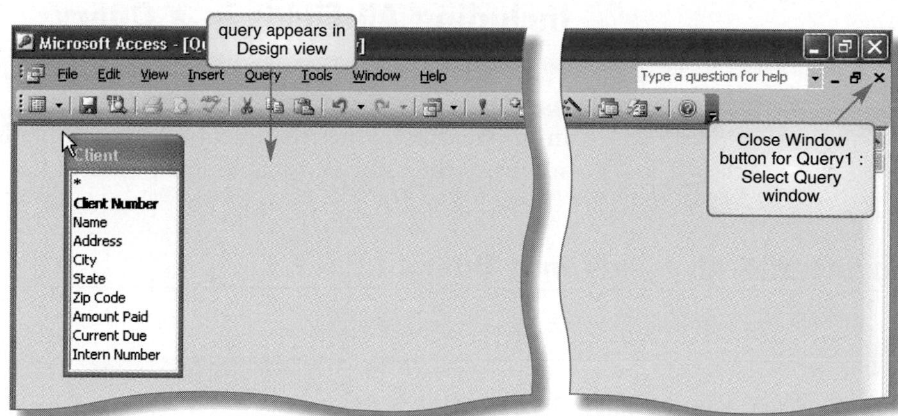

FIGURE 2-10

Notice that the icon on the View button is the Design View icon. This indicates that the next time you want to display the window in Design view, you need only click the View button.

Closing a Query

To close a query, close the Select Query window. When you do so, Access displays the Microsoft Office Access dialog box asking if you want to save your query for future use. If you think you will need to create the same exact query often, you should save the query. For now, you will not save any queries. You will see how to save them later in the project. The following steps close a query without saving it.

To Close the Query

1

• **Click the Close Window button for the Query1 : Select Query window (see Figure 2-10).**

Access displays the Microsoft Office Access dialog box (Figure 2-11). Clicking the Yes button saves the query and clicking the No button closes the query without saving.

2

• **Click the No button in the Microsoft Office Access dialog box.**

The Query1 : Select Query window closes. The query is not saved.

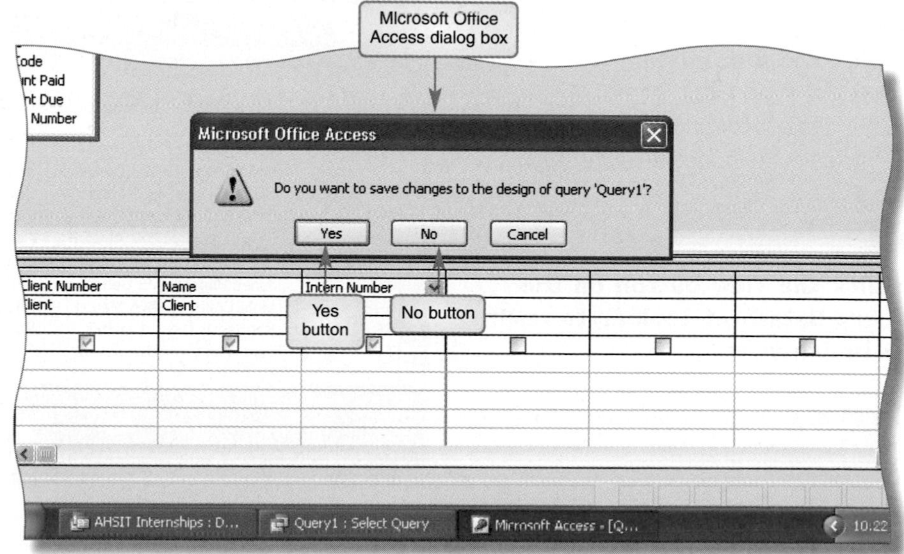

FIGURE 2-11

Including All Fields in a Query

If you want to include all fields in a query, you could select each field individually. A simpler way to include all fields is available, however. By selecting the asterisk (*) in the field list, you are indicating that all fields are to be included. The following steps use the asterisk to include all fields.

To Include All Fields in a Query

1

- **Be sure you have a maximized Query1 : Select Query window with resized upper and lower panes, an expanded field list for the Client table in the upper pane, and an empty design grid in the lower pane. (See Steps 1 through 5 on pages AC 68 through AC 70 to create the query and resize the panes and field list.)**
- **Double-click the asterisk at the top of the field list.**

The maximized Query1 : Select Query window displays two resized panes. The table name, Client, followed by a period and an asterisk is added to the design grid, indicating all fields are included (Figure 2-12).

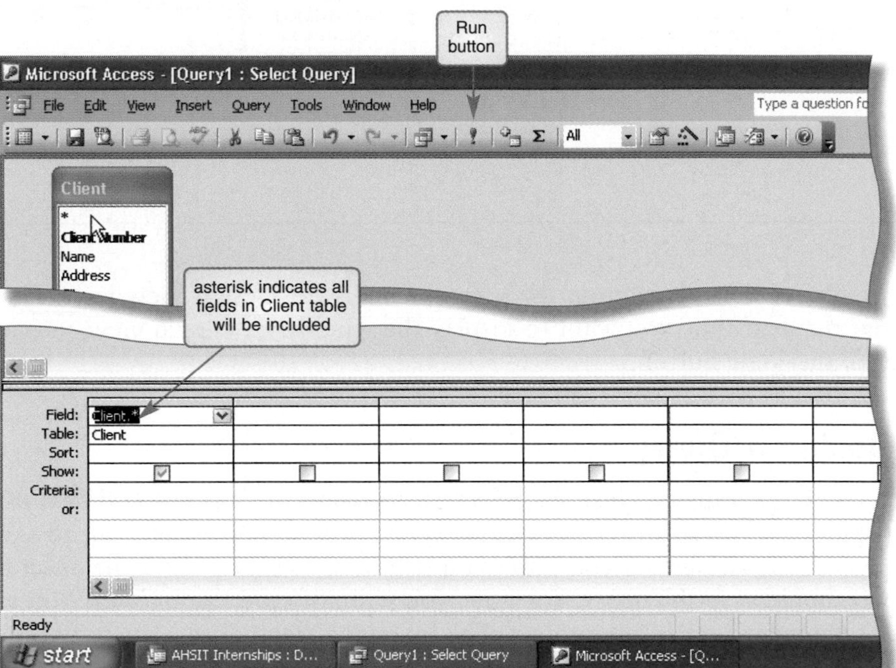

FIGURE 2-12

- **Click the Run button.**

The results appear and all fields in the Client table are included (Figure 2-13).

- **Click the View button on the Query Datasheet toolbar to return to Design view.**

Design view replaces Datasheet view.

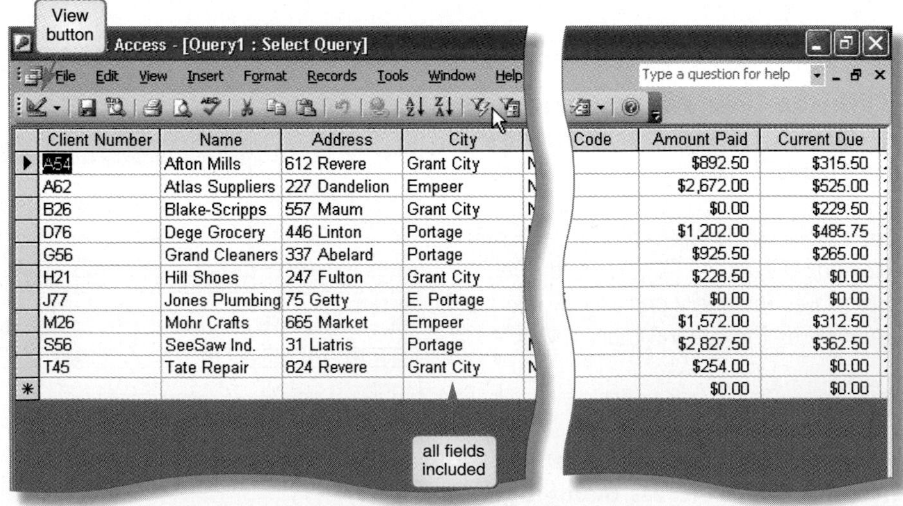

Client Number	Name	Address	City	Code	Amount Paid	Current Due
A54	Afton Mills	612 Revere	Grant City		$892.50	$315.50
A62	Atlas Suppliers	227 Dandelion	Empeer		$2,672.00	$525.00
B26	Blake-Scripps	557 Maum	Grant City		$0.00	$229.50
D76	Dege Grocery	446 Linton	Portage		$1,202.00	$485.75
G56	Grand Cleaners	337 Abelard	Portage		$925.50	$265.00
H21	Hill Shoes	247 Fulton	Grant City		$228.50	$0.00
J77	Jones Plumbing	75 Getty	E. Portage		$0.00	$0.00
M26	Mohr Crafts	665 Market	Empeer		$1,572.00	$312.50
S56	SeeSaw Ind.	31 Liatris	Portage		$2,827.50	$362.50
T45	Tate Repair	824 Revere	Grant City		$254.00	$0.00
*					$0.00	$0.00

FIGURE 2-13

Clearing the Design Grid

If you make mistakes as you are creating a query, you can fix each one individually. Alternatively, you simply may want to clear the query; that is, clear out the entries in the design grid and start over. One way to clear out the entries is to close the Select Query window and then start a new query just as you did earlier. A simpler approach, however, is to use the Clear Grid command on the Edit menu. The following steps clear the design grid.

Q & A

Q: Can you use the asterisk if you want to include all fields, but in a different order?

A: No. You will need to select the fields individually in the order you want.

To Clear the Design Grid

1

- **Click Edit on the menu bar.**

The Edit menu appears (Figure 2-14).

2

- **Click Clear Grid.**

Access clears the design grid so you can enter your next query.

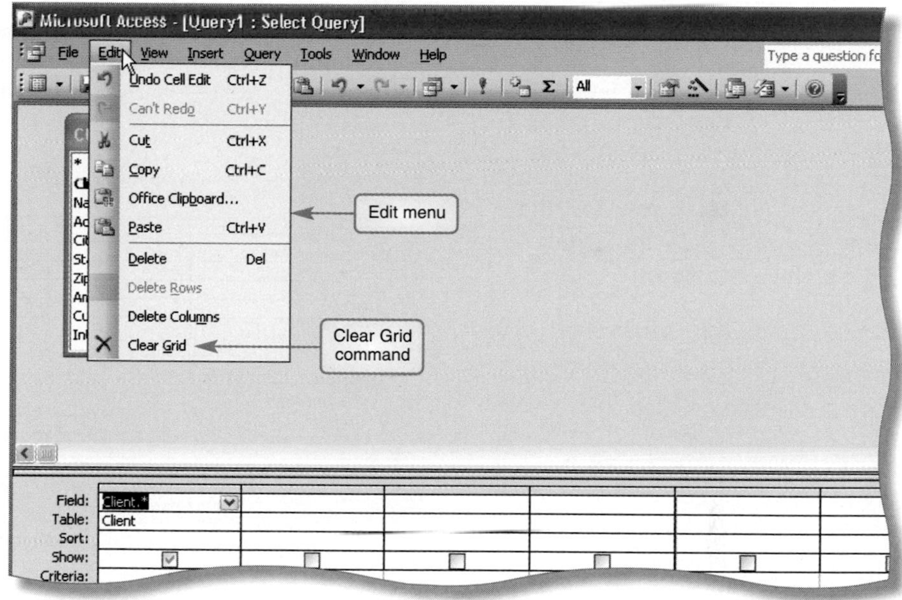

FIGURE 2-14

Entering Criteria

When you use queries, usually you are looking for those records that satisfy some criterion. You might want the name, amount paid, and current due amounts of the client whose number is G56, for example, or of those clients whose names start with the letter A. To enter criteria, enter them in the Criteria row in the design grid below the field name to which the criterion applies. For example, to indicate that the client number must be G56, you first must add the Client Number field to the design grid. You then would type G56 in the Criteria row below the Client Number field.

The next examples illustrate the types of criteria that are available.

Skill Builder 2-1

To practice the following tasks, visit scsite.com/off2003sch/skill, locate Access Project 2, and then click Skill Builder 2-1.

- ❑ Create a query
- ❑ Add fields to the design grid
- ❑ Run the query

Using Text Data in Criteria

To use **text data** (data in a field whose data type is Text) in criteria, simply type the text in the Criteria row below the corresponding field name. The steps on the next page query the Client table and display the client number, name, amount paid, and current due amount of client G56.

To Use Text Data in a Criterion

1

- **One by one, double-click the Client Number, Name, Amount Paid, and Current Due fields to add them to the query.**

The Client Number, Name, Amount Paid, and Current Due fields are added to the design grid (Figure 2-15).

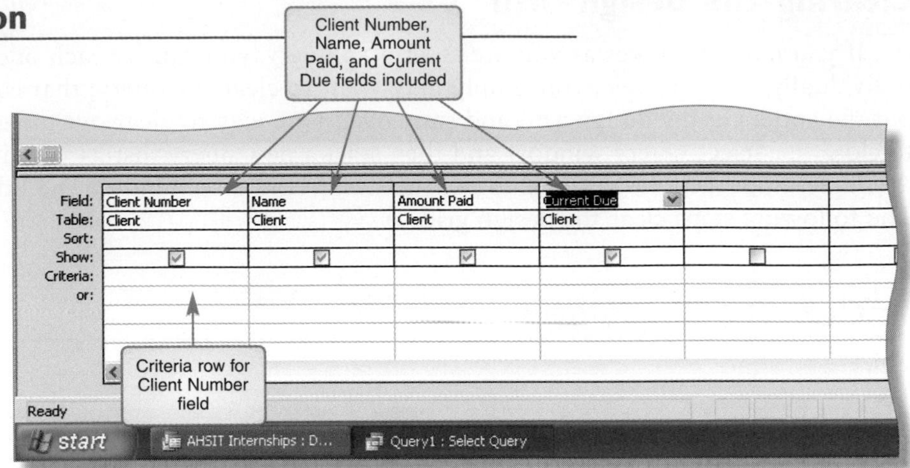

FIGURE 2-15

2

- **Click the Criteria row for the Client Number field and then type** G56 **as the criterion.**

The criterion is entered (Figure 2-16). When the mouse pointer is in the Criteria box, its shape changes to an I-beam.

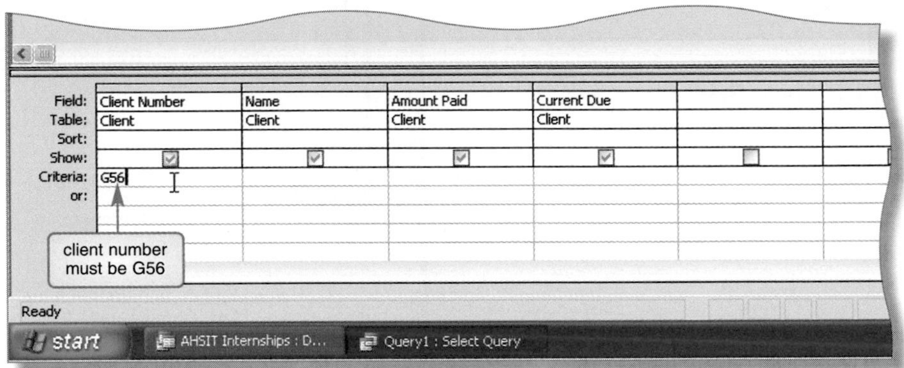

FIGURE 2-16

3

- **Click the Run button to run the query.**

The results appear (Figure 2-17). Only client G56 is included. (The extra blank row contains $0.00 in the Amount Paid and Current Due fields. Unlike text fields, which are left blank, number and currency fields in the extra row contain 0. Because the Amount Paid and Current Due fields are currency fields, the values are displayed as $0.00.)

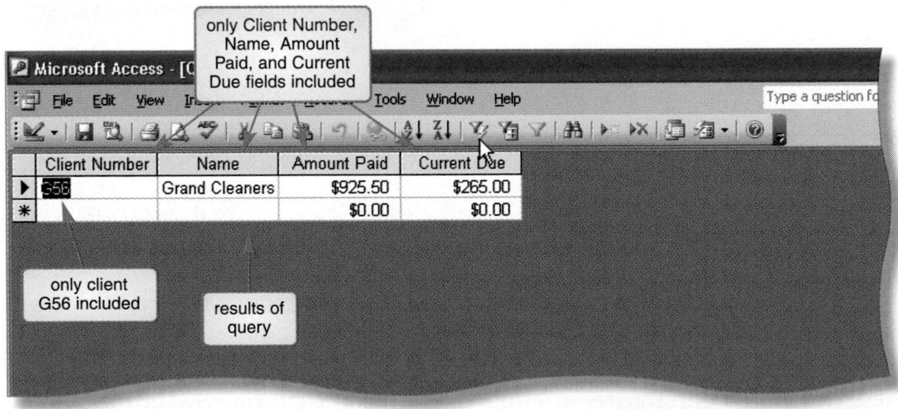

FIGURE 2-17

Using Wildcards

Two common wildcards are available in Microsoft Access. **Wildcards** are symbols that represent any character or combination of characters. The first of the two wildcards, the **asterisk** (*), represents any collection of characters. Thus A* represents the letter A, followed by any collection of characters. The other wildcard symbol is the **question mark** (?), which represents any individual character. Thus t?m represents the letter, T, followed by any single character followed by the letter, m, such as Tim or Tom.

The following steps use a wildcard to find the number, name, and address of those clients whose names begin with A. Because you do not know how many characters will follow the A, the asterisk is appropriate.

To Use a Wildcard

- **Click the View button on the Query Datasheet toolbar to return to Design view.**
- **If necessary, click the Criteria row below the Client Number field.**
- **Use the DELETE or BACKSPACE key as necessary to delete the current entry ("G56").**
- **Click the Criteria row below the Name field.**
- **Type A* as the criterion.**

The criterion is entered (Figure 2-18).

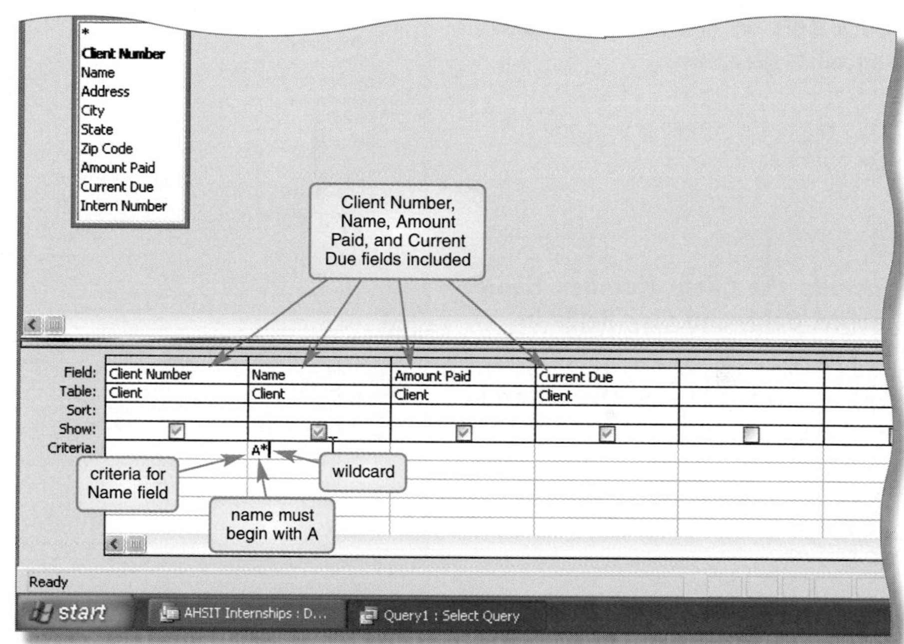

FIGURE 2-18

- **Click the Run button to run the query.**
- **If instructed to do so, print the results by clicking the Print button on the Query Datasheet toolbar.**

The results appear (Figure 2-19). Only the clients whose names start with A are included.

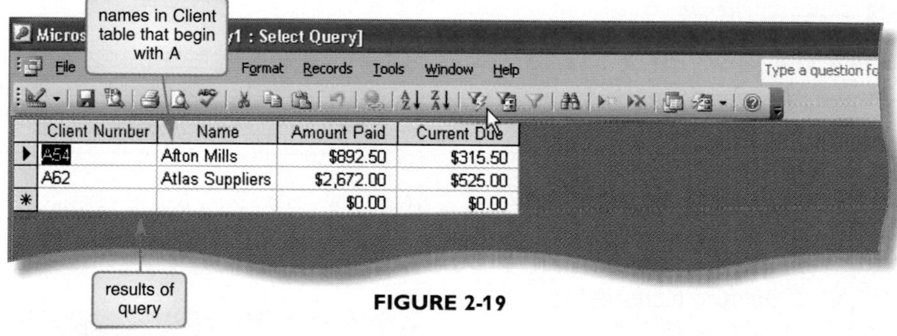

FIGURE 2-19

Criteria for a Field Not in the Result

In some cases, you may have criteria for a particular field that should not appear in the results of the query. For example, you may want to see the client number, name, and amount paid for all clients located in Grant City. The criteria involve the City field, which is not one of the fields to be included in the results.

To enter a criterion for the City field, it must be included in the design grid. Normally, this also would mean it would appear in the results. To prevent this from happening, remove the check mark from its Show check box in the Show row of the grid. The steps on the next page illustrate the process by displaying the client number, name, and amount paid for clients located in Grant City.

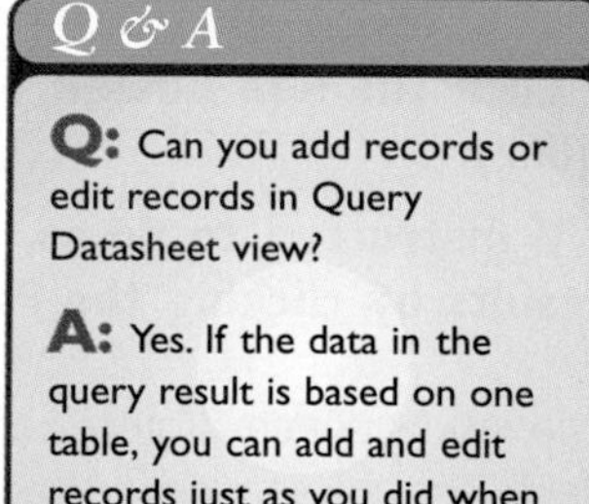

Q & A

Q: Can you add records or edit records in Query Datasheet view?

A: Yes. If the data in the query result is based on one table, you can add and edit records just as you did when the table was displayed in Table Datasheet view.

To Use Criteria for a Field Not Included in the Results

1

- **Click the View button on the Query Datasheet toolbar to return to Design view.**
- **Click Edit on the menu bar and then click Clear Grid.**

Access clears the design grid so you can enter the next query.

2

- **Include the Client Number, Name, Amount Paid, and City fields in the query.**
- **Type** `Grant City` **as the criterion for the City field.**

The fields are included in the grid, and the criterion for the City field is entered (Figure 2-20).

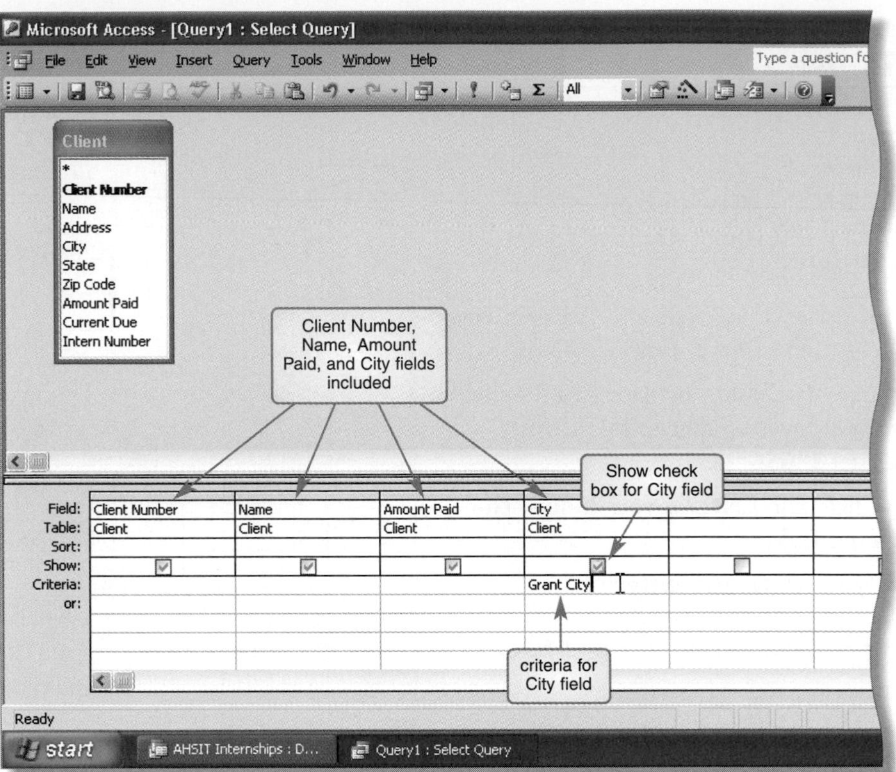

FIGURE 2-20

3

- **Click the Show check box to remove the check mark.**

The check mark is removed from the Show check box for the City field (Figure 2-21), indicating it will not show in the result. Because the City field is a text field, Access has added quotation marks before and after Grant City automatically.

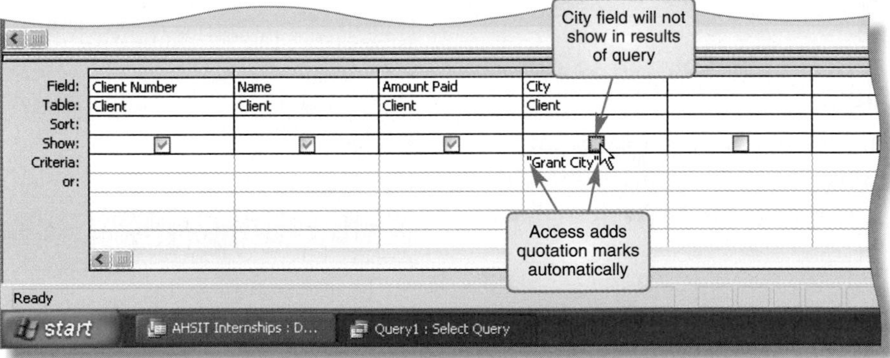

FIGURE 2-21

4

- **Click the Run button to run the query.**
- **If instructed to do so, print the results by clicking the Print button.**

The results appear (Figure 2-22). The City field does not appear. The only clients included are those located in Grant City.

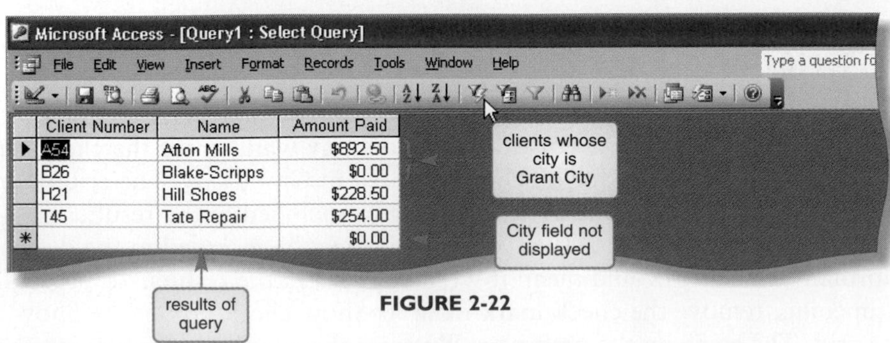

Client Number	Name	Amount Paid
A54	Afton Mills	$892.50
B26	Blake-Scripps	$0.00
H21	Hill Shoes	$228.50
T45	Tate Repair	$254.00
		$0.00

FIGURE 2-22

Creating a Parameter Query

Rather than giving a specific criterion when you first create the query, on occasion, you may want to be able to enter part of the criterion when you run the query and then have the appropriate results appear. For example, to include all the clients located in Portage, you could enter Portage as a criterion in the City field. From that point on, every time you ran the query, only the clients in Portage would appear.

A better way is to allow the user to enter the city at the time the query is run. Thus a user could run the query, enter Portage as the city and then see all the clients in Portage. Later, the user could run the same query, but enter Grant City as the city, and then see all the clients in Grant City. To do this, you create a **parameter query**, which is a query that prompts for input whenever it is run. You enter a parameter, rather than a specific value as the criterion. You create one by enclosing a value in a criterion in square brackets. It is important that the value in the brackets does not match the name of any field. If you enter a field name in square brackets, Access assumes you want that particular field and will not prompt the user for input. For example, you could place [Enter City] as the criterion in the City field.

The following steps create a parameter query that will prompt the user to enter a city, and then display the client number, name, address, and amount paid for all clients located in that city.

> **Q & A**
>
> **Q:** What actions could you take to find clients located in Grant City rather than Portage?
>
> **A:** Either create a new query or modify the existing query by replacing Portage with Grant City as the criterion.

> **Q & A**
>
> **Q:** When are parameter queries useful?
>
> **A:** Parameter queries are especially useful in cases where the same query is run frequently with slight changes to one or more of the query's criteria. By using parameters rather than specific values, you can enter the values for the criterion as the query is run, rather than having to change the query design.

To Create and Run a Parameter Query

1

- **Click the View button on the Query Datasheet toolbar to return to Design view.**
- **Erase the current criterion in the City column, and then type** `[Enter City]` **as the new criterion.**

The criterion is entered (Figure 2-23).

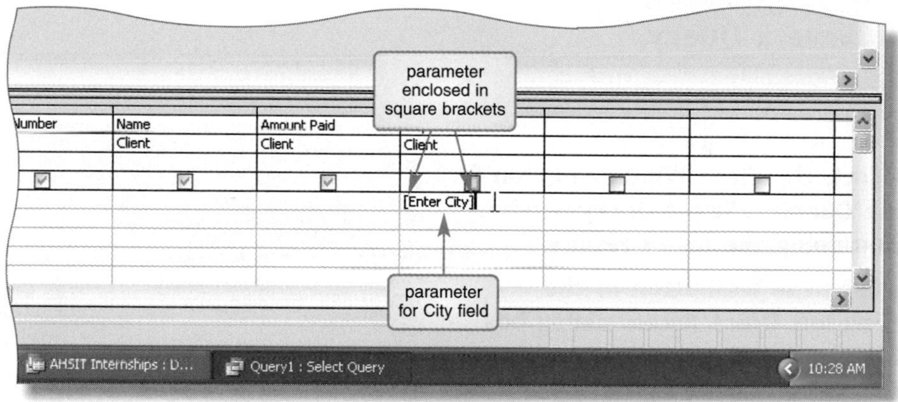

FIGURE 2-23

2

- **Click the Run button to run the query.**

Access displays the Enter Parameter Value dialog box (Figure 2-24). The value (Enter City) previously entered in brackets appears in the dialog box.

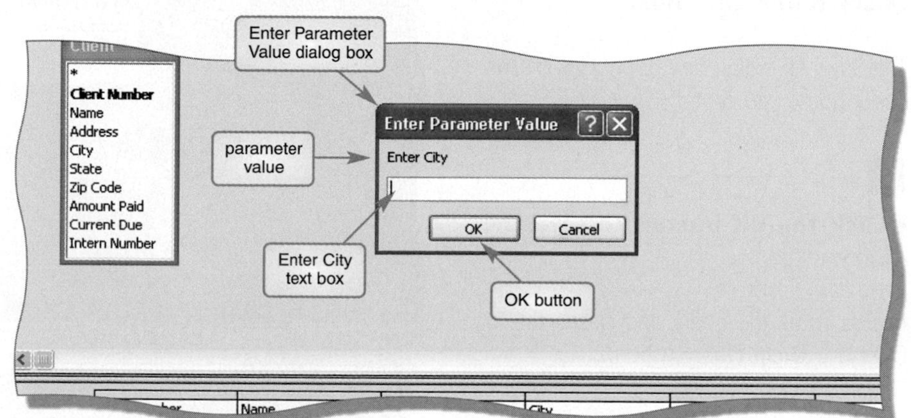

FIGURE 2-24

3

• **Type** Portage **in the Enter City text box and then click the OK button.**

The results appear (Figure 2-25). Only clients whose city is Portage are included. The city name is not displayed in the results.

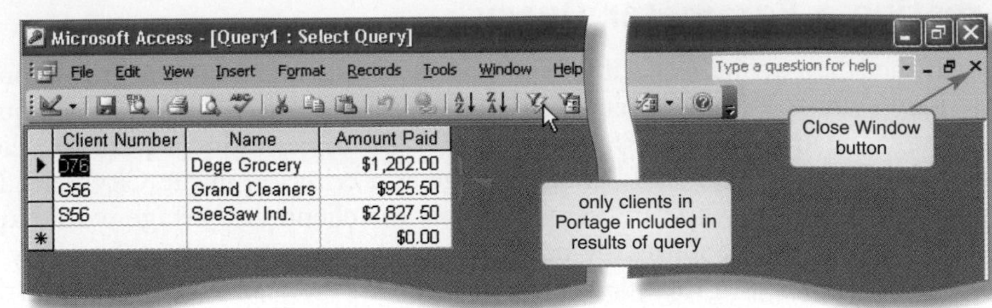

Client Number	Name	Amount Paid
D76	Dege Grocery	$1,202.00
G56	Grand Cleaners	$925.50
S56	SeeSaw Ind.	$2,827.50
		$0.00

FIGURE 2-25

Skill Builder 2-2

To practice the following tasks, visit scsite.com/off2003sch/skill, locate Access Project 2, and then click Skill Builder 2-2.

❑ Create a query
❑ Add fields to the design grid
❑ Add a criterion involving a wildcard
❑ Run the query

Each time you run this query, you will be asked to enter a city. Only clients in the city you enter will be included in the results.

Saving a Query

In many cases, you will construct a query you will want to use again. By saving the query, you will eliminate the need to repeat all your entries. The following steps illustrate the process by saving the query you just have created and assigning it the name Client-City Query. You can save with either the query design or the query results appearing on the screen.

To Save a Query

1

• **Click the Close Window button for the Query1 : Select Query window containing the query results.**

• **Click the Yes button in the Microsoft Office Access dialog box when asked if you want to save the changes to the design of the query.**

• **Type** Client-City Query **in the Query Name text box.**

The Save As dialog box appears with the query name you typed (Figure 2-26).

2

• **Click the OK button to save the query.**

Access saves the query and closes the Query1 : Select Query window.

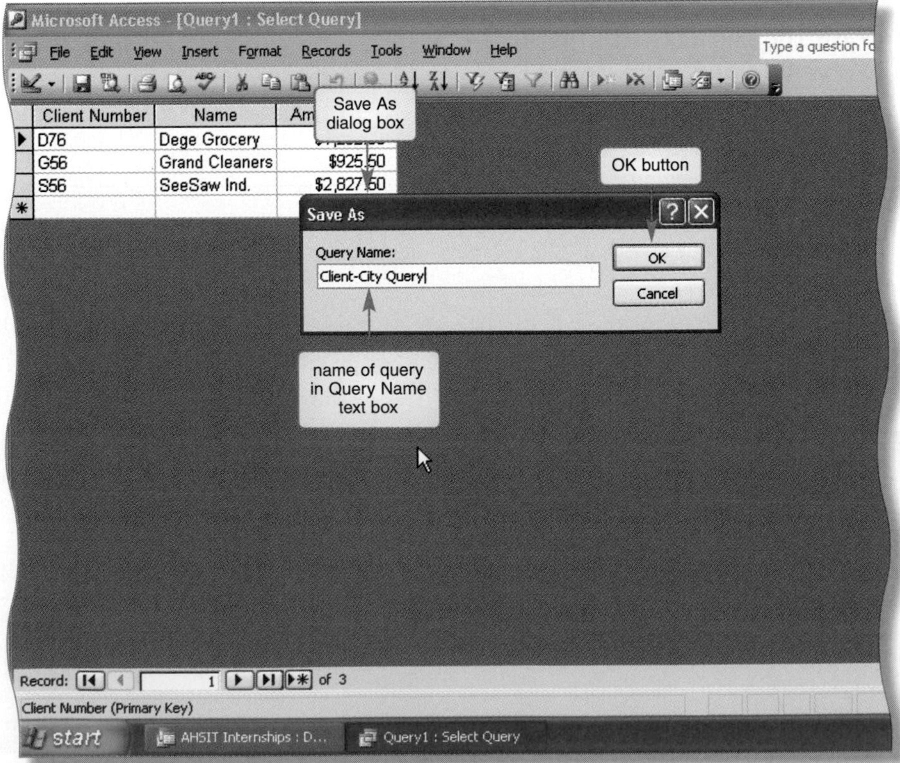

FIGURE 2-26

Using a Saved Query

Once you have saved a query, you can use and manipulate it at any time in the future by opening it. When you right-click the query in the Database window, Access displays a shortcut menu containing commands that allow you to open, print, and change the design of the query. You also can print the results by clicking the Print button on the toolbar. If you want to print the query results without first opening the query, you would click Print on the shortcut menu.

The query is run against the current database. Thus, if changes have been made to the data since the last time you ran it, the results of the query may be different. The following steps use the query named Client-City Query.

> *Q & A*
>
> **Q:** Can you use a saved query for forms or reports?
>
> **A:** Forms and reports can be based on either tables or saved queries. To create a report or form based on a query, click the Query tab, select the query, click the New Object button arrow, and then click the appropriate command (Report or Form). From that point on, the process is the same as for a table.

To Use a Saved Query

1

- **Click Queries on the Objects bar, and then right-click Client-City Query.**

The shortcut menu for Client-City Query appears (Figure 2-27).

2

- **Click Open on the shortcut menu, type** `Portage` **in the Enter City text box, and then click the OK button.**

The results appear. They look like the results shown in Figure 2-25.

3

- **Click the Close Window button for the Client-City Query : Select Query window containing the query results.**

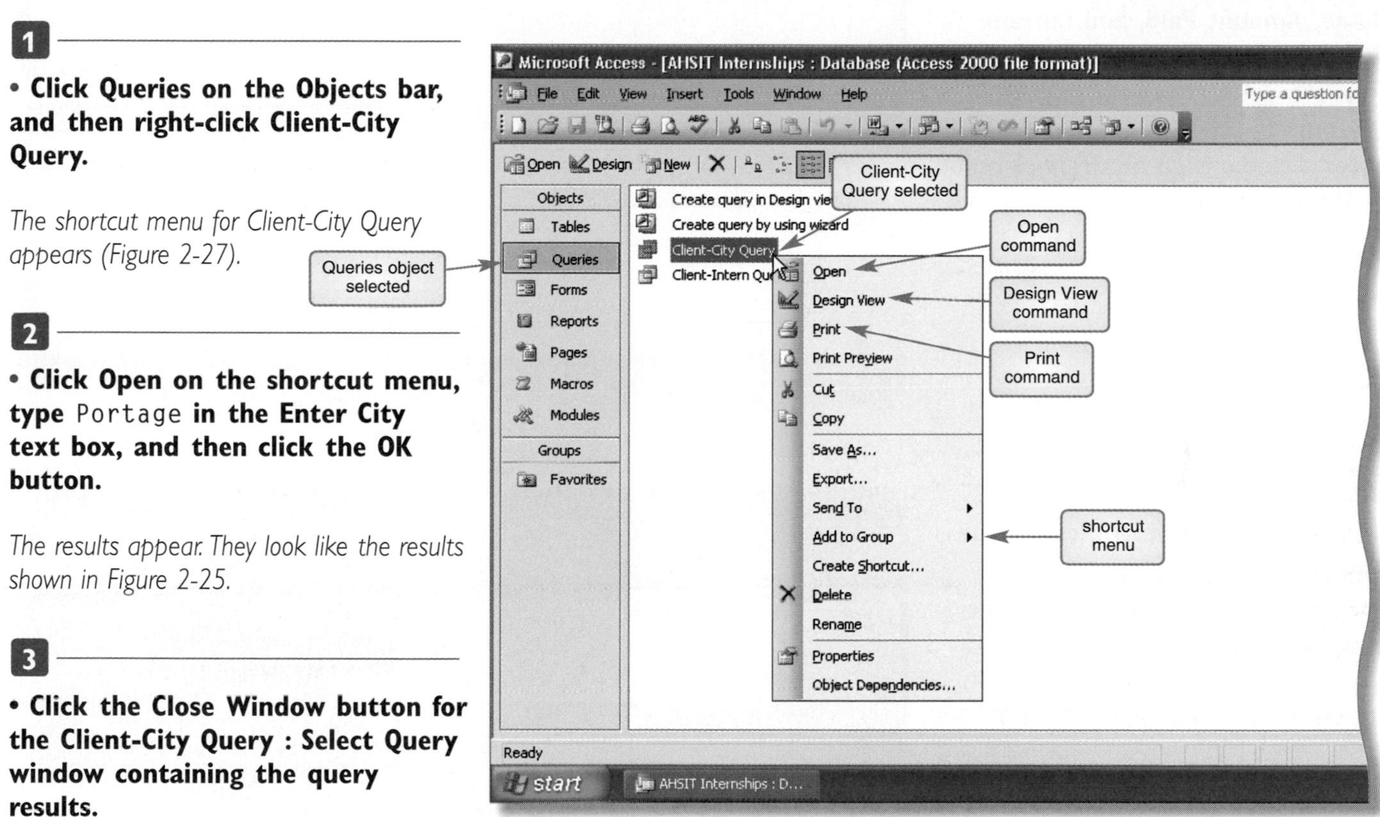

FIGURE 2-27

You can use the query at any time by following the above steps. Each time you do so, you will be prompted to enter a city. Only the clients in that city will be displayed in the results.

Using Numeric Data in Criteria

To enter a number in a criterion, type the number without any dollar signs or commas. The steps on the next page display all clients whose current due amount is $0.00.

To Use a Number in a Criterion

1

- **Be sure you have a maximized Query 1: Select Query window with resized upper and lower panes, an expanded field list for the Client table in the upper pane, and an empty design grid in the lower pane. (See Steps 1 through 5 on pages AC 68 through AC 70 to create the query and resize the panes and field list.) Include the Client Number, Name, Amount Paid, and Current Due fields in the query.**
- **Type** 0 **as the criterion for the Current Due field. You should not enter a dollar sign or decimal point in the criterion.**

The fields are selected and the criterion is entered (Figure 2-28).

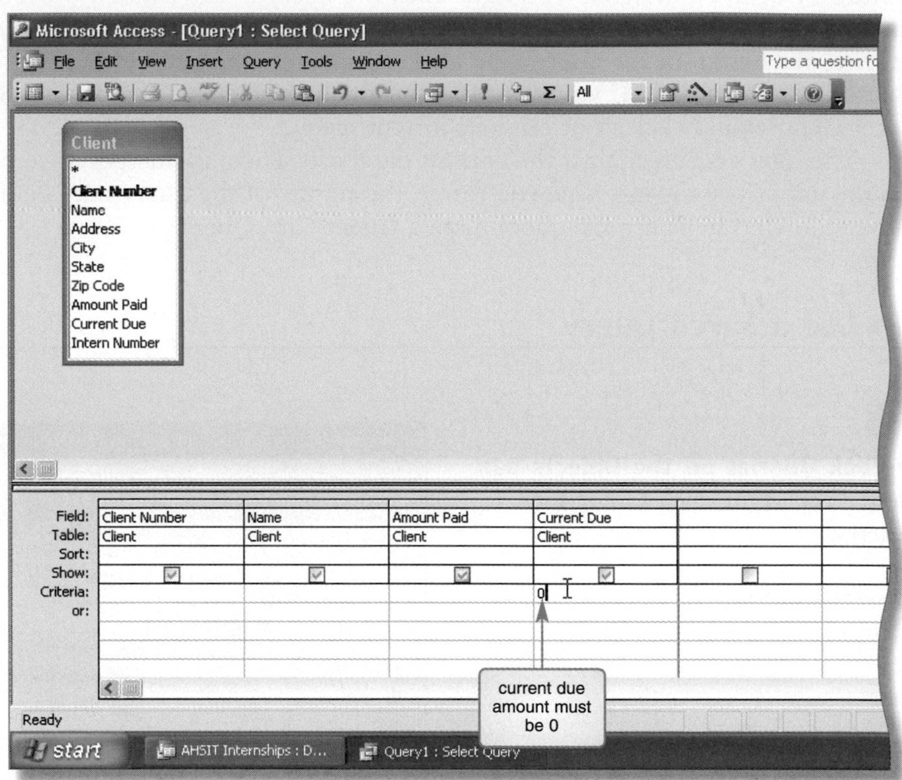

FIGURE 2-28

2

- **Click the Run button to run the query.**
- **If instructed to print the results, click the Print button.**

The results appear (Figure 2-29). Only those clients that have a current due amount of $0.00 are included.

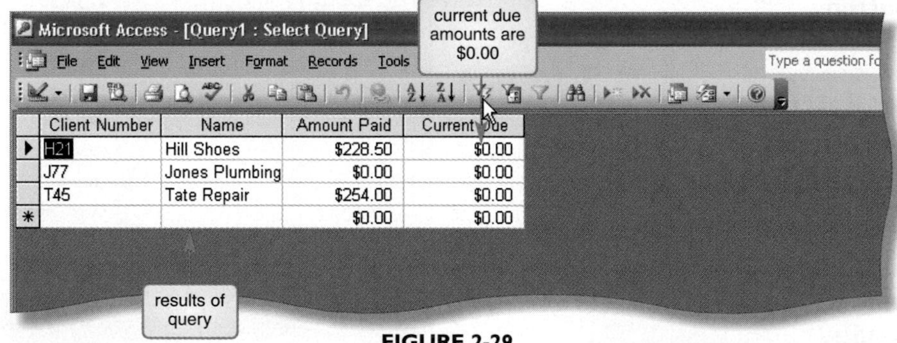

FIGURE 2-29

Using Comparison Operators

Unless you specify otherwise, Access assumes that the criteria you enter involve equality (exact matches). In the last query, for example, you were requesting those clients whose current due amount is equal to 0 (zero). If you want something other than an exact match, you must enter the appropriate **comparison operator**. The comparison operators are > (greater than), < (less than), >= (greater than or equal to), <= (less than or equal to), and NOT (not equal to).

The following steps use the > operator to find all clients whose amount paid is more than $1,000.00.

To Use a Comparison Operator in a Criterion

1

- **Click the View button on the Query Datasheet toolbar to return to Design view.**
- **Erase the 0 in the Current Due column.**
- **Type** `>1000` **as the criterion for the Amount Paid field. Remember that you should not enter a dollar sign, a comma, or decimal point in the criterion.**

The fields are selected and the criterion is entered (Figure 2-30).

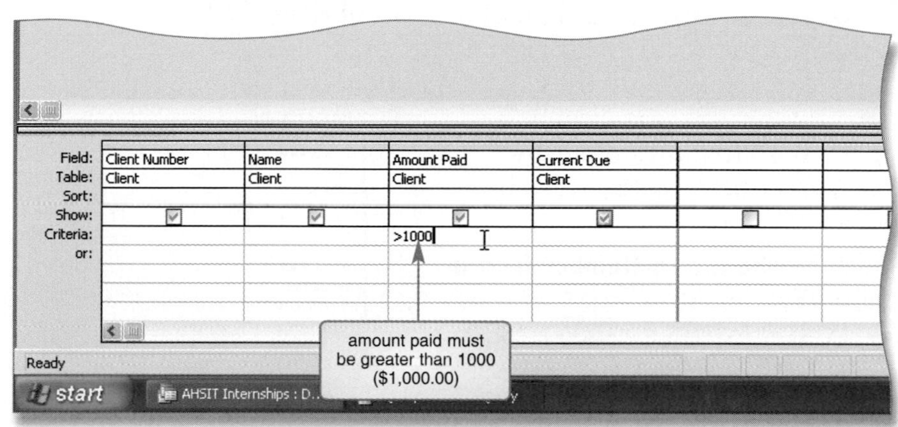

FIGURE 2-30

- **Click the Run button to run the query.**
- **If instructed to print the results, click the Print button.**

The results appear (Figure 2-31). Only those clients who have an amount paid greater than $1,000.00 are included.

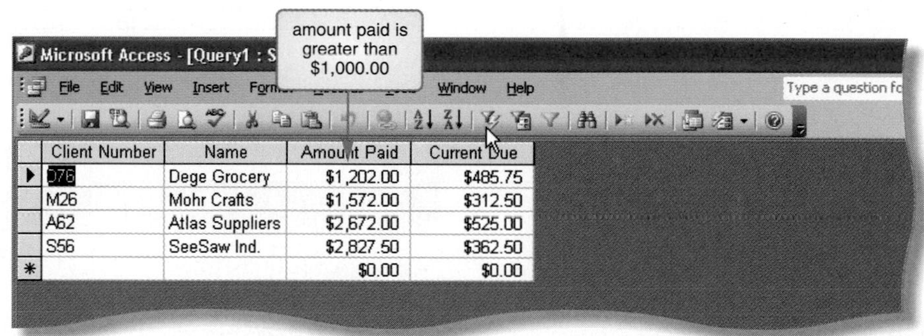

FIGURE 2-31

Using Compound Criteria

Often you will have more than one criterion that the data for which you are searching must satisfy. This type of criterion is called a **compound criterion**. Two types of compound criteria exist.

In an **AND criterion**, each individual criterion must be true in order for the compound criterion to be true. For example, an AND criterion would allow you to find those clients that have an amount paid greater than $1,000.00 and whose intern is intern 34.

Conversely, an **OR criterion** is true provided either individual criterion is true. An OR criterion would allow you to find those clients that have an amount paid greater than $1,000.00 or whose intern is intern 34. In this case, any client whose amount paid is greater than $1,000.00 would be included in the answer whether or not the client's intern is intern 34. Likewise, any client whose intern is intern 34 would be included whether or not the client had an amount paid greater than $1,000.00.

Q & A

Q: Does a simple way exist to test for those records whose value in a certain field falls within a specific range of values?

A: The BETWEEN operator allows you to search for a range of values in one field. For example, to find all clients whose amount paid amount is between $500 and $1,000 you would enter Between 500 and 1000 in the Criteria row for the Amount Paid field. It also is possible to create compound criteria involving both OR and AND operators. For more information, visit the Office 2003 Q&A Web page (off2003sch/qa), locate Access Project 2, and click Compound Criteria.

Using AND Criteria

To combine criteria with AND, place the criteria on the same line. The following steps use an AND criterion to find those clients whose amount paid is greater than $1,000.00 and whose intern is intern 34.

To Use a Compound Criterion Involving AND

1

- **Click the View button on the Query Datasheet toolbar to return to Design view.**
- **Include the Intern Number field in the query.**
- **Type** 34 **as the criterion for the Intern Number field.**

Criteria have been entered for the Amount Paid and Intern Number fields (Figure 2-32).

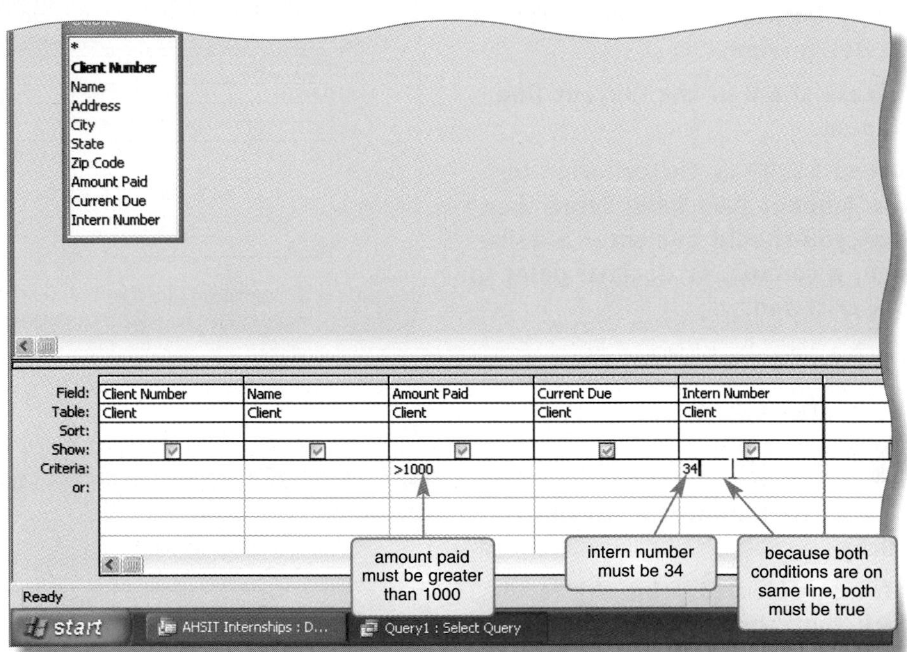

FIGURE 2-32

2

- **Click the Run button to run the query.**
- **If instructed to print the results, click the Print button.**

The results appear (Figure 2-33). Only the clients whose amount paid is greater than $1,000.00 and whose intern number is 34 are included.

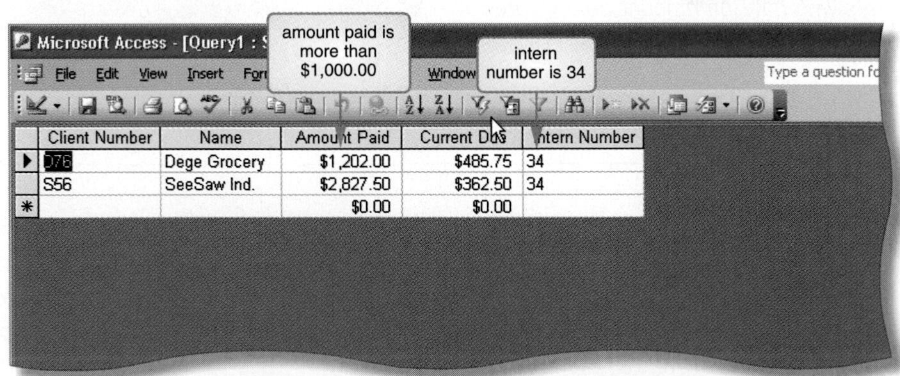

FIGURE 2-33

Using OR Criteria

To combine criteria with OR, the criteria must go on separate lines in the Criteria area of the grid. The following steps use an OR criterion to find those clients whose amount paid is greater than $1,000.00 or whose intern is intern 34 (or both).

To Use a Compound Criterion Involving OR

1

- **Click the View button on the Query Datasheet toolbar to return to Design view.**

2

- **If necessary, click the Criteria entry for the Intern Number field and then use the BACKSPACE key or the DELETE key to erase the entry ("34").**
- **Click the or row (below the Criteria row) for the Intern Number field and then type** 34 **as the entry.**

The criteria are entered for the Amount Paid and Intern Number fields on different lines (Figure 2-34).

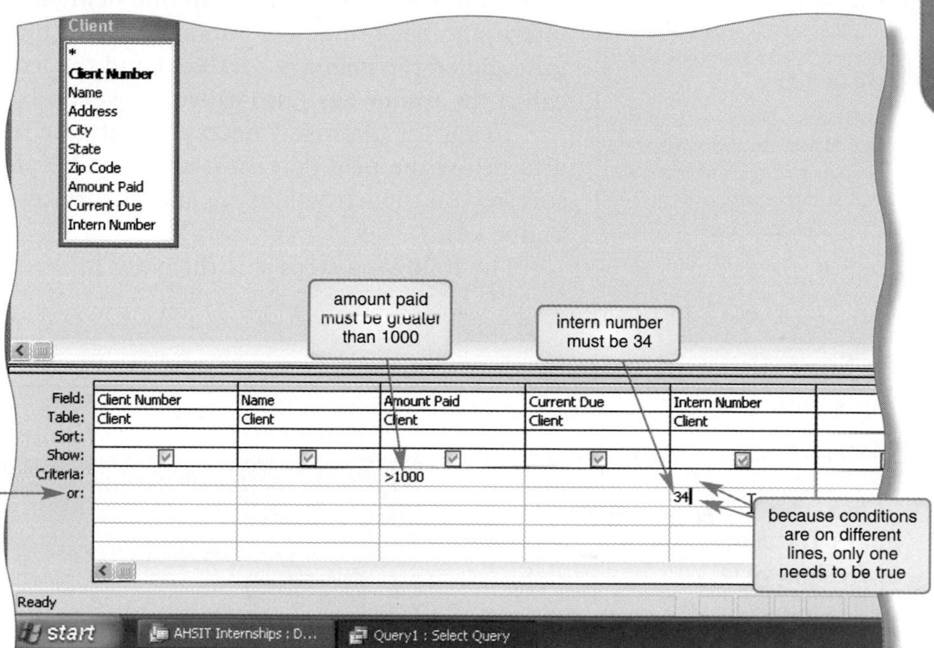

FIGURE 2-34

3

- **Click the Run button to run the query.**
- **If instructed to print the results, click the Print button.**

The results appear (Figure 2-35). Only those clients whose amount paid is greater than $1,000.00 or whose intern number is 34 are included.

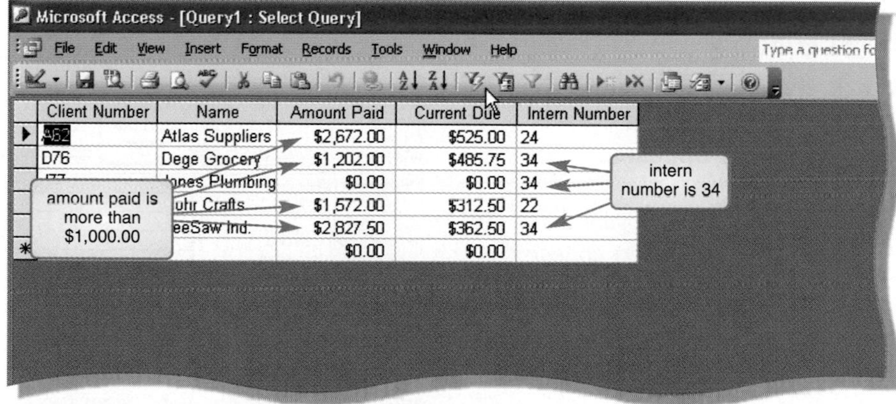

FIGURE 2-35

Sorting Data in a Query

In some queries, the order in which the records appear really does not matter. All you need be concerned about are the records that appear in the results. It does not matter which one is first or which one is last.

In other queries, however, the order can be very important. You may want to see the cities in which clients are located and would like them arranged alphabetically. Perhaps you want to see the clients listed by intern number. Further, within all the clients of any given intern, you might want them to be listed by amount paid.

Skill Builder 2-3

To practice the following tasks, visit scsite.com/off2003sch/skill, locate Access Project 2, and then click Skill Builder 2-3.

- ❑ Create a query
- ❑ Add fields to the design grid
- ❑ Enter a compound criterion
- ❑ Run the query

To order the records in the answer to a query in a particular way, you **sort** the records. The field or fields on which the records are sorted is called the **sort key**. If you are sorting on more than one field (such as sorting by amount paid within intern number), the more important field (Intern Number) is called the **major key** (also called the **primary sort key**) and the less important field (Amount Paid) is called the **minor key** (also called the **secondary sort key**).

To sort in Microsoft Access, specify the sort order in the Sort row of the design grid below the field that is the sort key. If you specify more than one sort key, the sort key on the left will be the major sort key and the one on the right will be the minor key.

The following steps sort the cities in the Client table.

To Sort Data in a Query

1

- **Click the View button on the Query Datasheet toolbar to return to Design view.**
- **Click Edit on the menu bar and then click Clear Grid.**

2

- **Include the City field in the design grid.**
- **Click the Sort box below the City field, and then click the Sort box arrow that appears.**

The City field is included (Figure 2-36). A list of available sort orders appears.

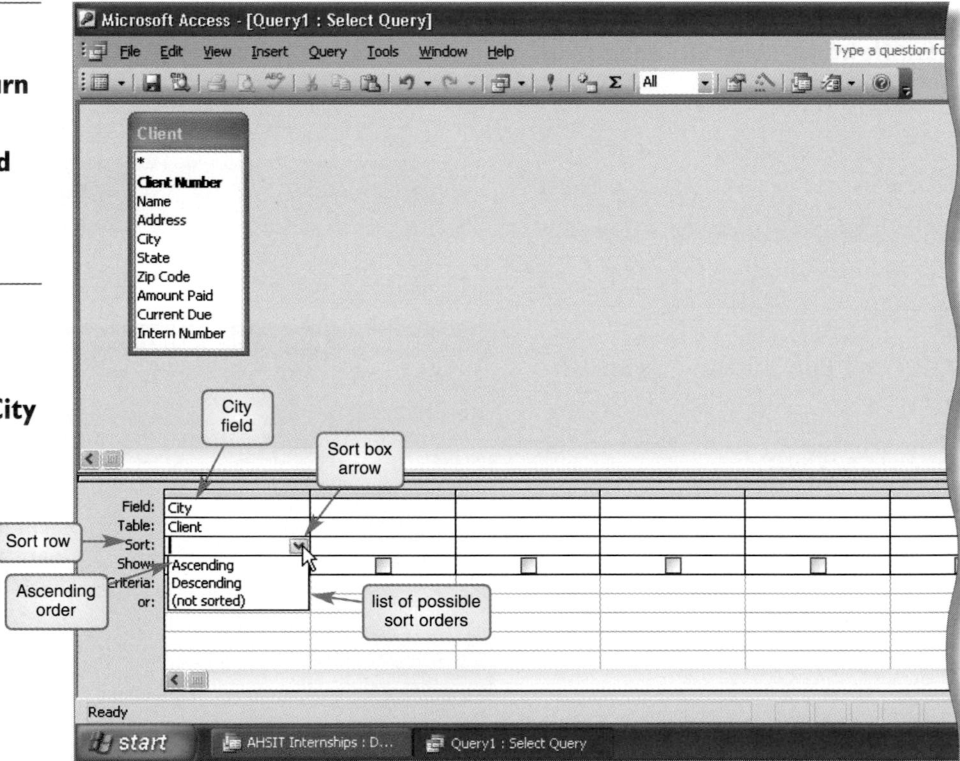

FIGURE 2-36

3

- **Click Ascending.**

Ascending is selected as the order (Figure 2-37).

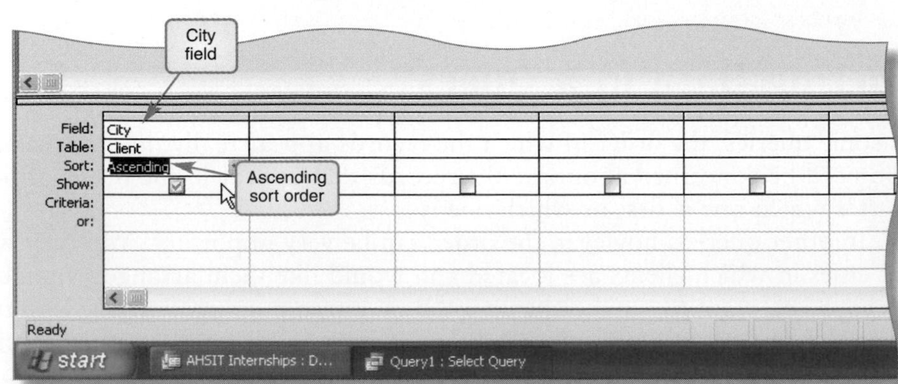

FIGURE 2-37

4

- **Click the Run button to run the query.**
- **If instructed to print the results, click the Print button.**

The results contain the cities from the Client table (Figure 2-38). The cities appear in alphabetical order. Duplicates are included.

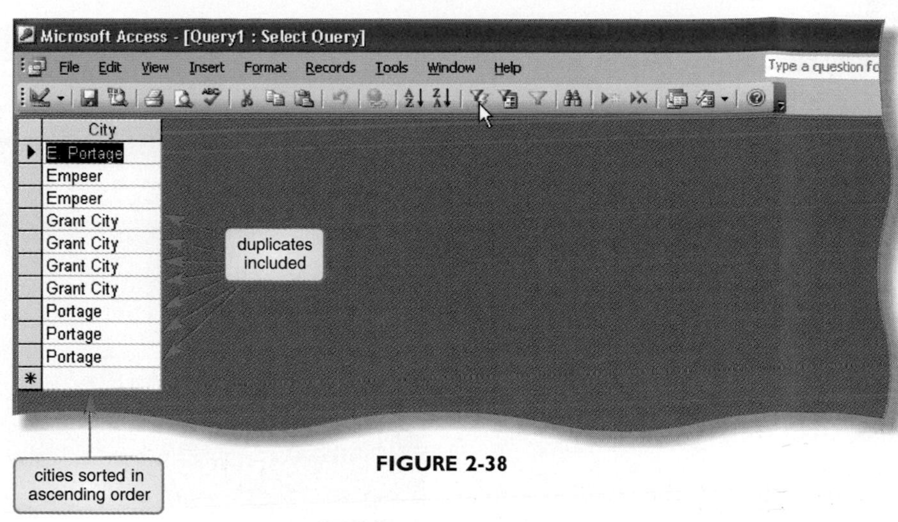

FIGURE 2-38

Omitting Duplicates

When you sort data, duplicates normally are included. In Figure 2-38, for example, Empeer appeared twice, Grant City appeared four times, and Portage appeared three times. To sort to eliminate duplicates, use the Properties button on the Query Design toolbar or the Properties command on the shortcut menu to display the query object's property sheet. A **property sheet** is a window containing the various properties of the object. To omit duplicates, you will use the property sheet to change the Unique Values property.

The following steps produce a sorted list of the cities in the Client table in which each city is listed only once.

To Omit Duplicates

1

- **Click the View button on the Query Datasheet toolbar to return to Design view.**
- **Click the second field in the design grid (the empty field following City). You must click the second field or you will not get the correct results and will have to repeat this step.**
- **Click the Properties button on the Query Design toolbar.**

Access displays the Query Properties sheet (Figure 2-39). (If your sheet looks different, you clicked the wrong place and will have to repeat the step.)

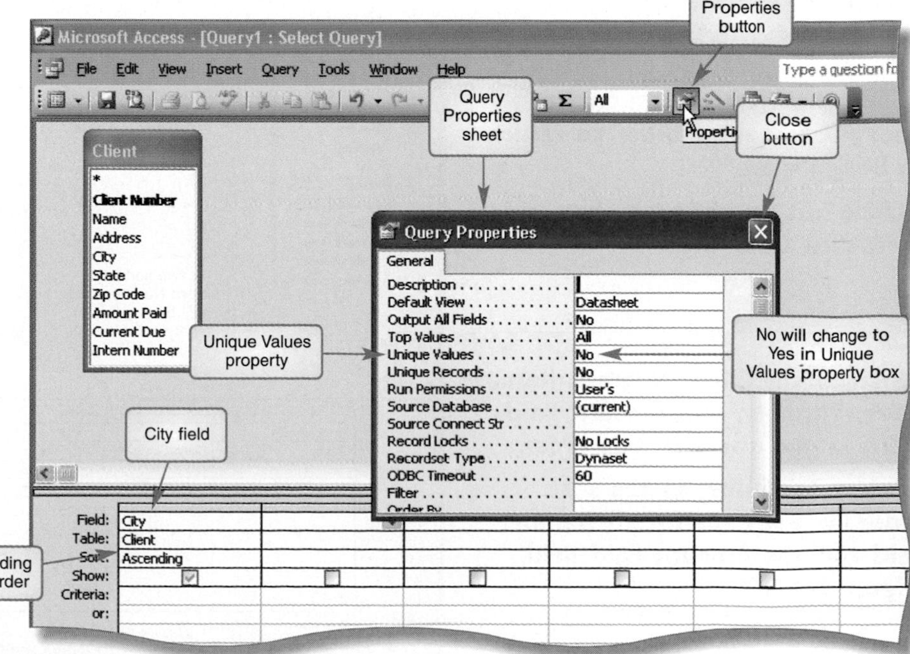

FIGURE 2-39

2

- **Click the Unique Values property box, and then click the box arrow that appears to produce a list of available choices for Unique Values.**
- **Click Yes and then close the Query Properties sheet by clicking its Close button.**
- **Click the Run button to run the query.**
- **If instructed to print the results, click the Print button.**

The results appear (Figure 2-40). The cities are sorted alphabetically. Each city is included only once.

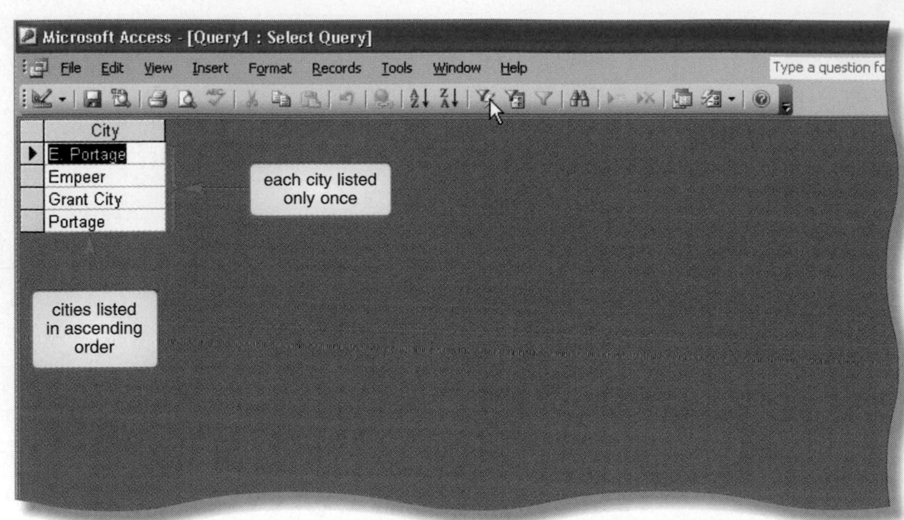

FIGURE 2-40

Sorting on Multiple Keys

The next example lists the number, name, intern number, and amount paid for all clients. The data is to be sorted by amount paid (low to high) within intern number, which means that the Intern Number field is the major key and the Amount Paid field is the minor key.

The following steps accomplish this sorting by specifying the Intern Number and Amount Paid fields as sort keys.

To Sort on Multiple Keys

1

- **Click the View button on the Query Datasheet toolbar to return to Design view.**
- **Click Edit on the menu bar and then click Clear Grid.**

2

- **Include the Client Number, Name, Intern Number, and Amount Paid fields in the query in this order.**
- **Select Ascending as the sort order for both the Intern Number field and the Amount Paid field (Figure 2-41).**

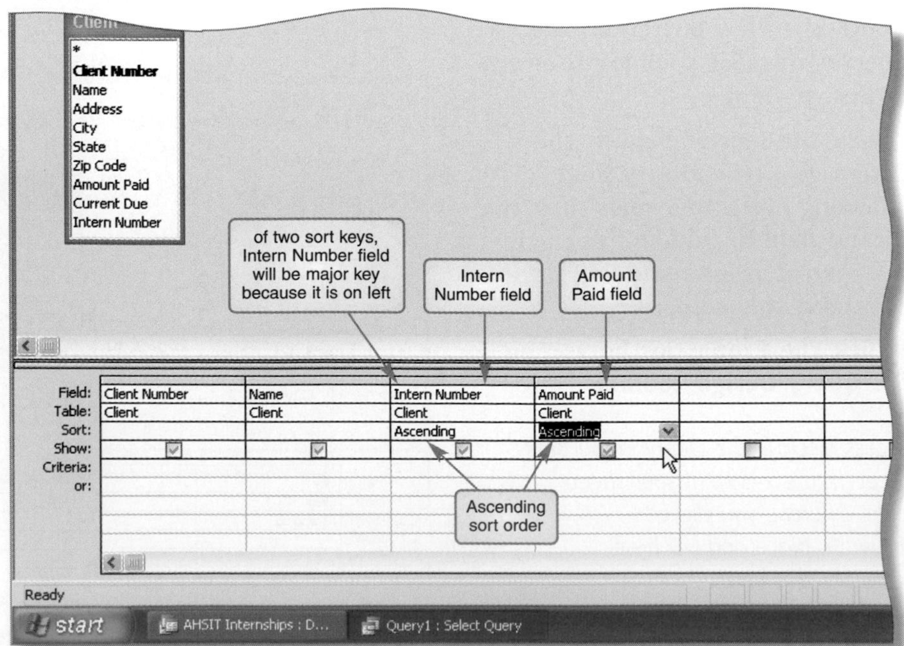

FIGURE 2-41

3

- **Click the Run button to run the query.**
- **If instructed to print the results, click the Print button.**

The results appear (Figure 2-42). The clients are sorted by intern number. Within the collection of clients having the same intern, the clients are sorted by amount paid.

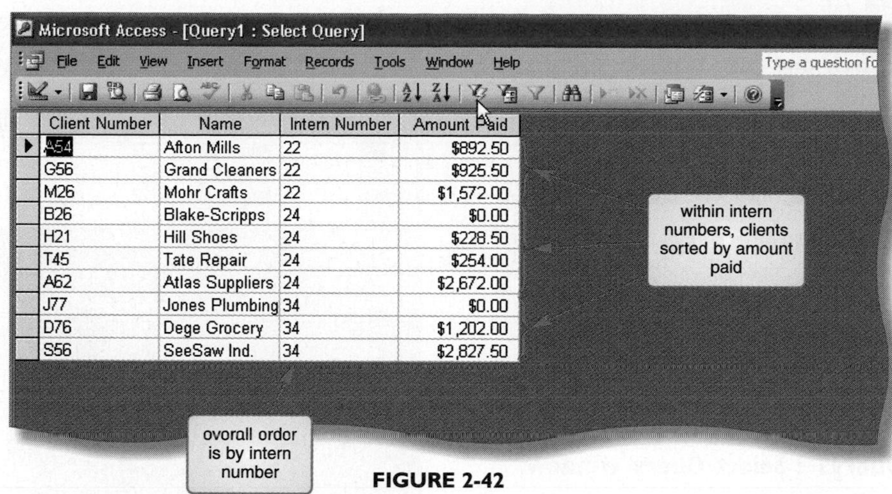

FIGURE 2-42

It is important to remember that the major sort key must appear to the left of the minor sort key in the design grid. If you attempted to sort by amount paid within intern number, but placed the Amount Paid field to the left of the Intern Number field, your results would be incorrect.

Creating a Top-Values Query

Rather than show all the results of a query, you may want to show only a specified number of records or a percentage of records. Creating a **top-values query** allows you to quantify the results. When you sort records, you can limit results to those records having the highest (descending sort) or lowest (ascending sort) values. To do so, first create a query that sorts the data in the desired order. Next, use the Top Values box on the Query Design toolbar to change the number of records to be included from All to the desired number. The following steps show the first four records that were included in the results of the previous query.

To Create a Top-Values Query

1

- **Click the View button on the Query Datasheet toolbar to return to Design view.**
- **Click the Top Values box on the Query Design toolbar, and then type** 4 **as the new value.**

The value in the Top Values box is changed from All to 4 (Figure 2-43).

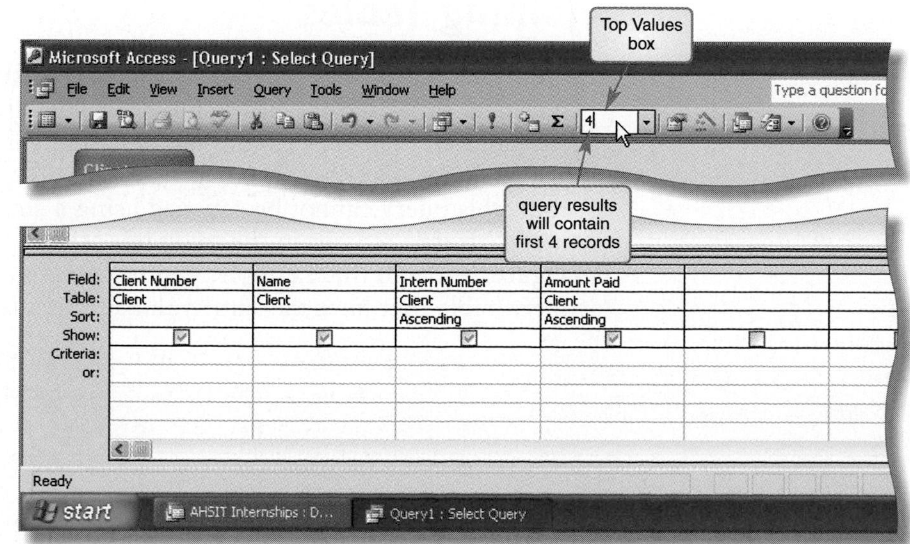

FIGURE 2-43

2

• **Click the Run button to run the query.**

• **If instructed to print the results, click the Print button.**

The results appear (Figure 2-44). Only the first four records are included.

3

• **Close the query by clicking the Close Window button for the Query1 : Select Query window.**

• **When asked if you want to save your changes, click the No button.**

The Query1 : Select Query window closes. The query is not saved.

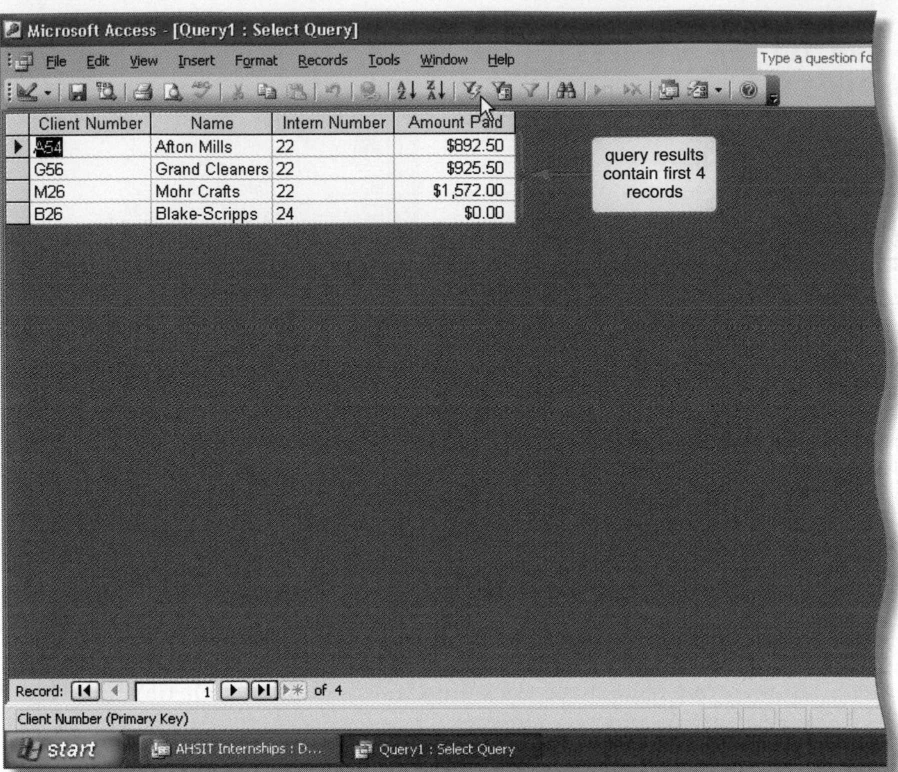

FIGURE 2-44

When you run a top-values query, it is important to change the value in the Top Values box back to All. If you do not change the Top Values value back to All, the previous value will remain in force. Consequently, you may very well not get all the records you should in the next query.

A good practice whenever you use a top-values query is to close the query as soon as you are done. That way, you will begin your next query from scratch, which guarantees that the value is set back to All.

Joining Tables

The AHSIT Internships database needs to satisfy a query that requires values from the Client table and the Intern table. Specifically, the query needs to list the number and name of each client along with the number and name of the client's intern. The client's name is in the Client table, whereas the intern's name is in the Intern table. Thus, this query cannot be satisfied using a single table. You need to **join** the tables; that is, to find records in the two tables that have identical values in matching fields (Figure 2-45). In this example, you need to find records in the Client table and the Intern table that have the same value in the Intern Number fields.

Give me the number and name of each client along with the number and name of each client's intern.

Client table

CLIENT NUMBER	NAME	...	INTERN NUMBER
A54	Afton Mills	...	22
A62	Atlas Suppliers	...	24
B26	Blake-Scripps	...	24
D76	Dege Grocery	...	34
G56	Grand Cleaners	...	22
H21	Hill Shoes	...	24
J77	Jones Plumbing	...	34
M26	Mohr Crafts	...	22
S56	SeeSaw Ind.	...	34
T45	Tate Repair	...	24

Intern table

INTERN NUMBER	LAST NAME	FIRST NAME	...
22	Lewen	Joann	...
24	Rodriguez	Mario	...
34	Wong	Shawn	...
42	Trent	Roberta	...

Join of Client and Intern table

CLIENT NUMBER	NAME	...	INTERN NUMBER	LAST NAME	FIRST NAME	...
A54	Afton Mills	...	22	Lewen	Joann	...
A62	Atlas Suppliers	...	24	Rodriguez	Mario	...
B26	Blake-Scripps	...	24	Rodriguez	Mario	...
D76	Dege Grocery	...	34	Wong	Shawn	...
G56	Grand Cleaners	...	22	Lewen	Joann	...
H21	Hill Shoes	...	24	Rodriguez	Mario	...
J77	Jones Plumbing	...	34	Wong	Shawn	...
M26	Mohr Crafts	...	22	Lewen	Joann	...
S56	SeeSaw Ind.	...	34	Wong	Shawn	...
T45	Tate Repair	...	24	Rodriguez	Mario	...

FIGURE 2-45

To join tables in Access, first you bring field lists for both tables to the upper pane of the Select Query window. Access will draw a line, called a **join line**, between matching fields in the two tables indicating that the tables are related. You then can select fields from either table. Access will join the tables automatically.

The first step is to select the Intern table in the Database window and create a new query. Then, add the Client table to the query. A join line will appear connecting the Intern Number fields in the two field lists. This join line indicates how the tables are related; that is, linked through these matching fields. (If you fail to give the matching fields the same name, Access will not insert the line. You can insert it manually, however, by clicking one of the two matching fields and dragging the mouse pointer to the other matching field.)

The steps on the next page create a new query, add the Client table and then select the appropriate fields.

Q & A

Q: Assuming you want the Intern Number field to be the major key and the Amount Paid field to be the minor key as in the previous steps, how could you display the Amount Paid field before the Intern Number field?

A: Include the Intern Number field, the Amount Paid field, and then the Intern Number field a second time. Select Ascending as the sort order for the first Intern Number field and for the Amount Paid field. Remove the check mark from the Show check box for the first Intern Number field. Thus, the first Intern Number field will be part of the sort key but will not appear in the results. The second Intern Number field will appear in the results after the Amount Paid field.

To Join Tables

1

- **With the Tables object selected and the Intern table selected, click the New Object button arrow on the Database toolbar.**
- **Click Query, and then click the OK button.**
- **Drag the line separating the two panes to the approximate position shown in Figure 2-46, and then drag the lower edge of the field list box down far enough so all fields in the Intern table appear.**
- **Click the Show Table button on the Query Design toolbar.**

Access displays the Show Table dialog box (Figure 2-46).

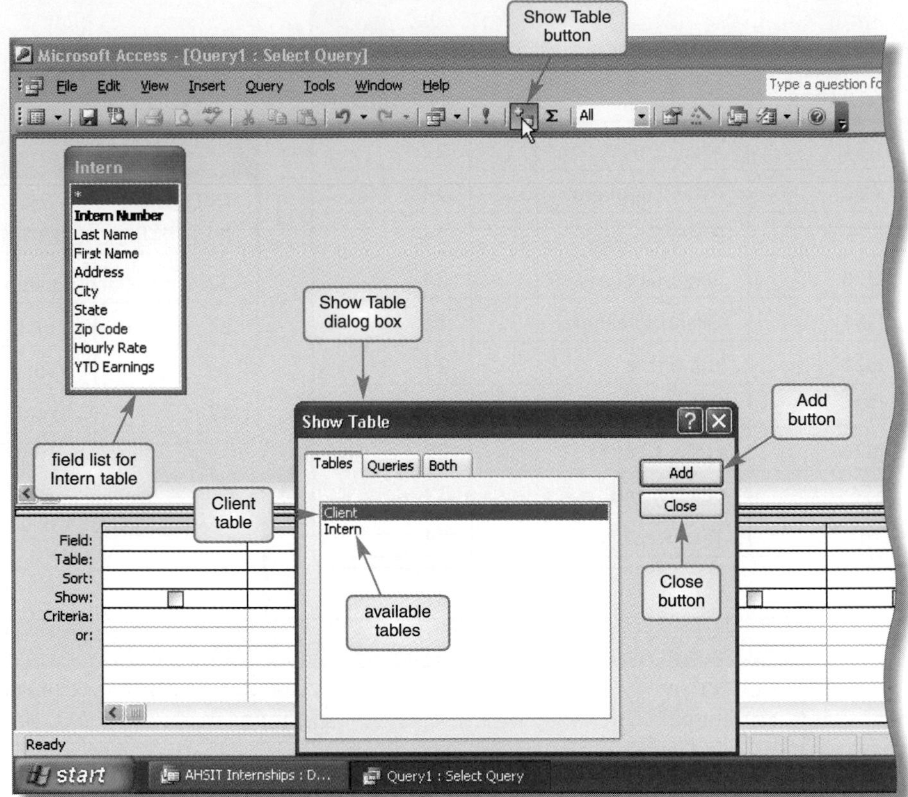

FIGURE 2-46

2

- **Be sure the Client table is selected, and then click the Add button.**
- **Close the Show Table dialog box by clicking the Close button.**
- **Expand the size of the field list so all the fields in the Client table appear.**

The field lists for both tables appear (Figure 2-47). A join line connects the two field lists.

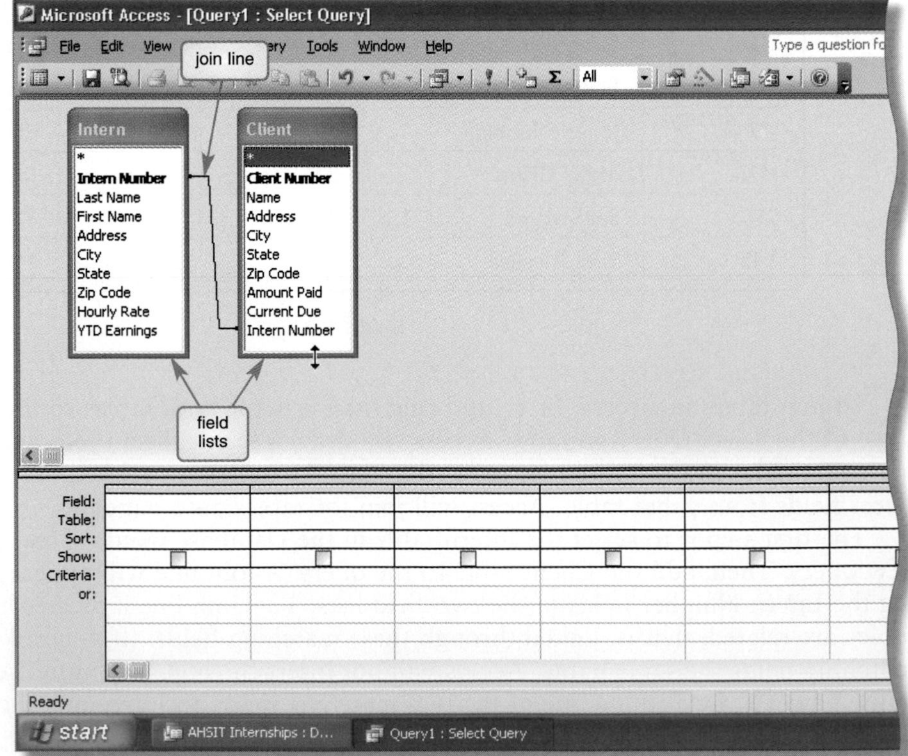

FIGURE 2-47

3

- **Include the Intern Number, Last Name, and First Name fields from the Intern table as well as the Client Number and Name fields from the Client table.**
- **Select Ascending as the sort order for both the Intern Number field and the Client Number field.**

The fields from both tables are selected (Figure 2-48).

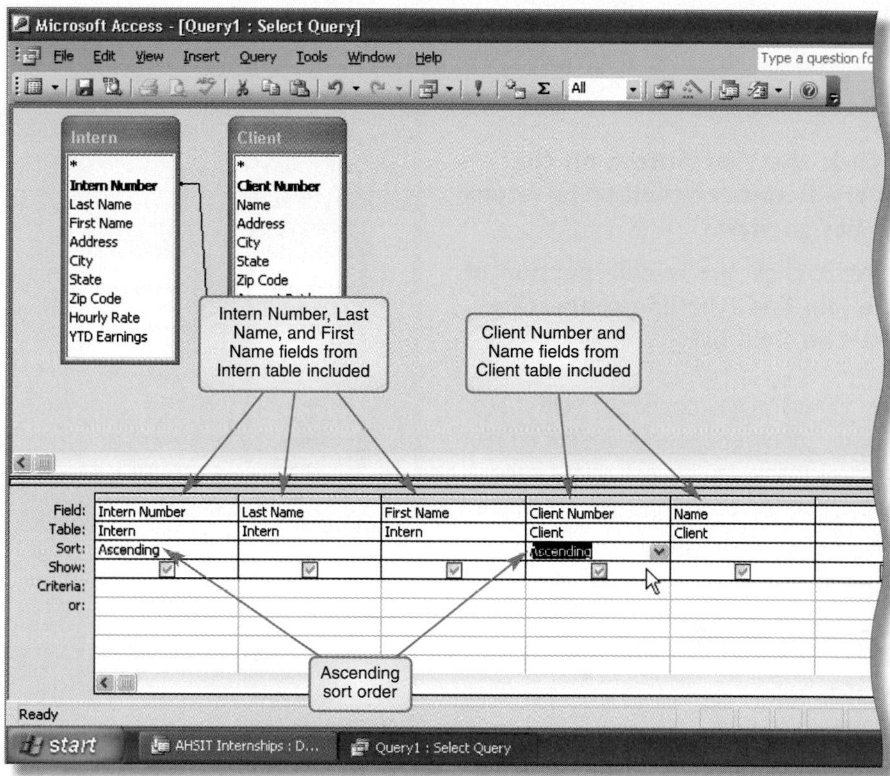

FIGURE 2-48

4

- **Click the Run button to run the query.**
- **If instructed to print the results, click the Print button.**

The results appear (Figure 2-49). They contain data from both the Intern and Client tables. The records are sorted by intern number and within intern number by client number.

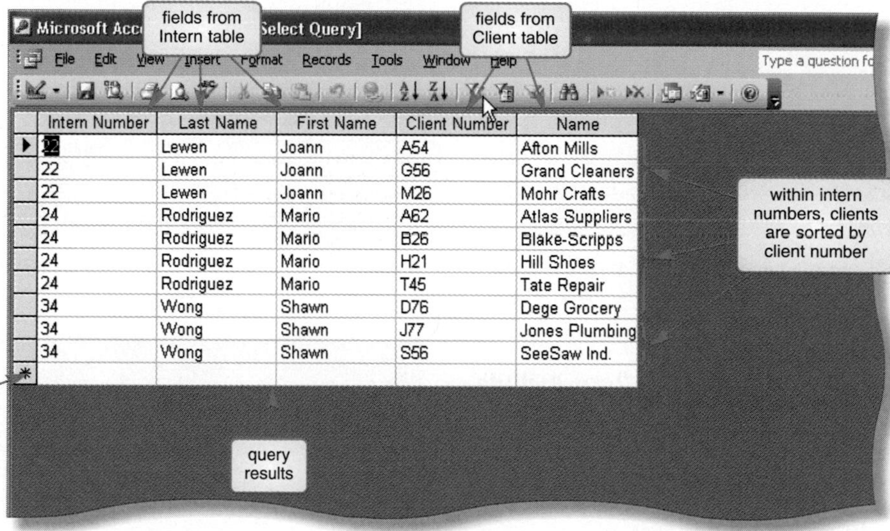

Intern Number	Last Name	First Name	Client Number	Name
22	Lewen	Joann	A54	Afton Mills
22	Lewen	Joann	G56	Grand Cleaners
22	Lewen	Joann	M26	Mohr Crafts
24	Rodriguez	Mario	A62	Atlas Suppliers
24	Rodriguez	Mario	B26	Blake-Scripps
24	Rodriguez	Mario	H21	Hill Shoes
24	Rodriguez	Mario	T45	Tate Repair
34	Wong	Shawn	D76	Dege Grocery
34	Wong	Shawn	J77	Jones Plumbing
34	Wong	Shawn	S56	SeeSaw Ind.

FIGURE 2-49

Changing Join Properties

Normally, records that do not match will not appear in the results of a join query. An intern such as Roberta Trent, for whom no clients currently exist, for example, would not appear. To cause such a record to be displayed, you need to change the **join properties**, which are the properties that indicate which records appear in a join of the query, as the steps on the next page illustrate.

To Change Join Properties

1

- **Click the View button on the Query Datasheet toolbar to return to Design view.**
- **Right-click the middle portion of the join line (the line connecting the two field lists).**

The shortcut menu appears (Figure 2-50). (If Join Properties does not appear on your shortcut menu, you did not point to the appropriate portion of the join line. You will need to right-click again.)

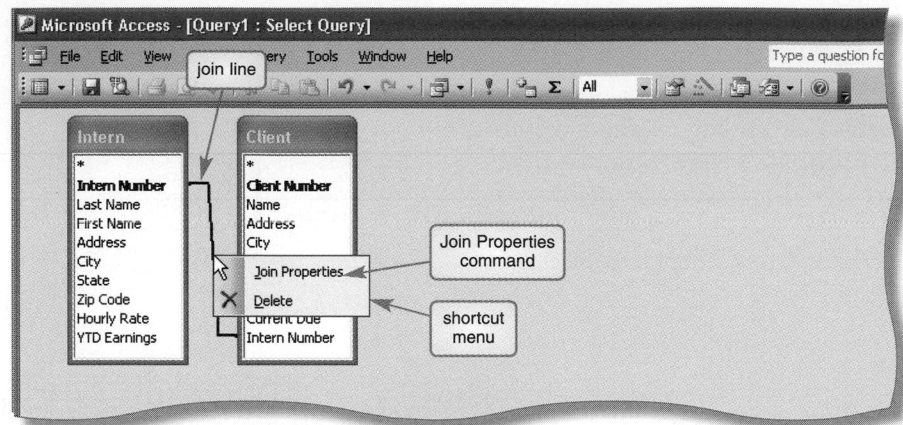

FIGURE 2-50

2

- **Click Join Properties on the shortcut menu.**

Access displays the Join Properties dialog box (Figure 2-51).

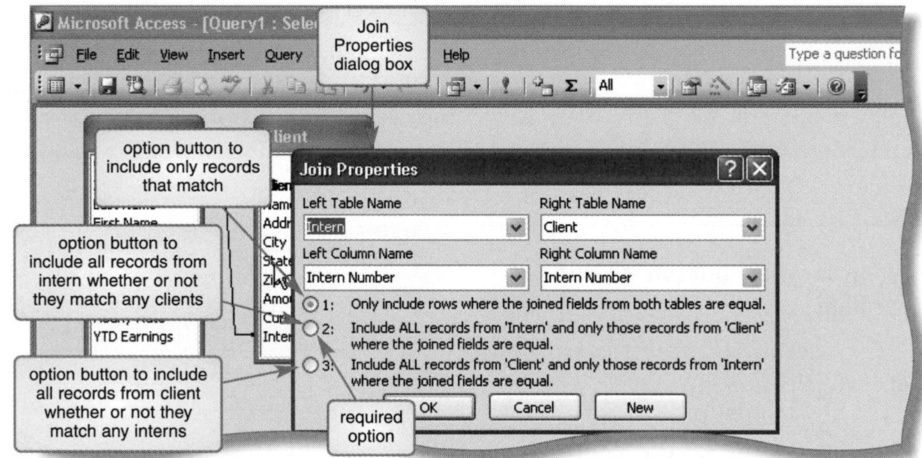

FIGURE 2-51

3

- **Click option button 2 to include all records from the Intern table regardless of whether or not they match any clients.**
- **Click the OK button.**
- **Run the query by clicking the Run button.**
- **If instructed to print the results, click the Print button.**

The results appear (Figure 2-52).

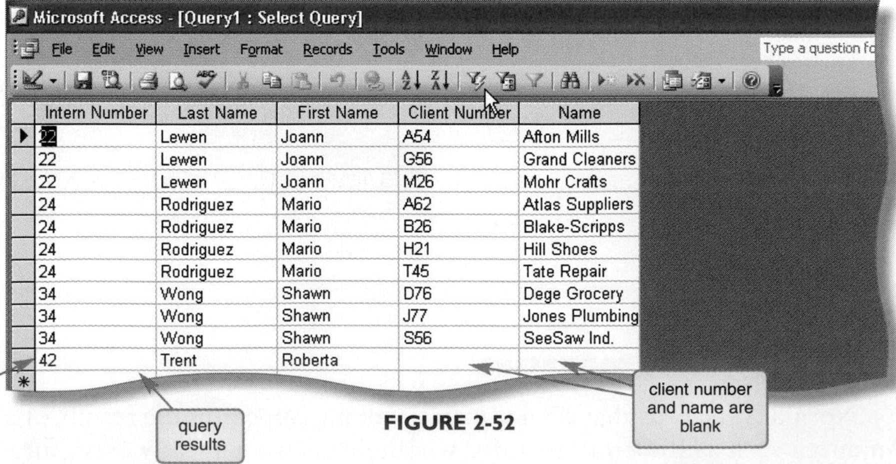

FIGURE 2-52

With the change to the join properties, intern 42 is included, even though the intern does not have any clients.

Restricting Records in a Join

Sometimes you will want to join tables, but you will not want to include all possible records. In such cases, you will relate the tables and include fields just as you did before. You also will include criteria. For example, to include the same fields as in the previous query, but only those clients whose amount paid is more than $1,000.00, you will make the same entries as before, but also include >1000 as a criterion for the Amount Paid field.

The following steps modify the query from the previous example to restrict the records that will be included in the join.

Skill Builder 2-4

To practice the following tasks, visit scsite.com/off2003sch/skill, locate Access Project 2, and then click Skill Builder 2-4.

- ❑ Create a query
- ❑ Add an additional table to the query
- ❑ Join the tables and change join properties
- ❑ Add fields and a criterion to the design grid
- ❑ Run the query

To Restrict the Records in a Join

1

- **Click the View button on the Query Datasheet toolbar to return to Design view.**
- **Add the Amount Paid field to the query.**
- **Type >1000 as the criterion for the Amount Paid field and then click the Show check box for the Amount Paid field to remove the check mark.**

The Amount Paid field appears in the design grid (Figure 2-53). A criterion is entered for the Amount Paid field, and the Show check box is empty, indicating that the field will not appear in the results of the query.

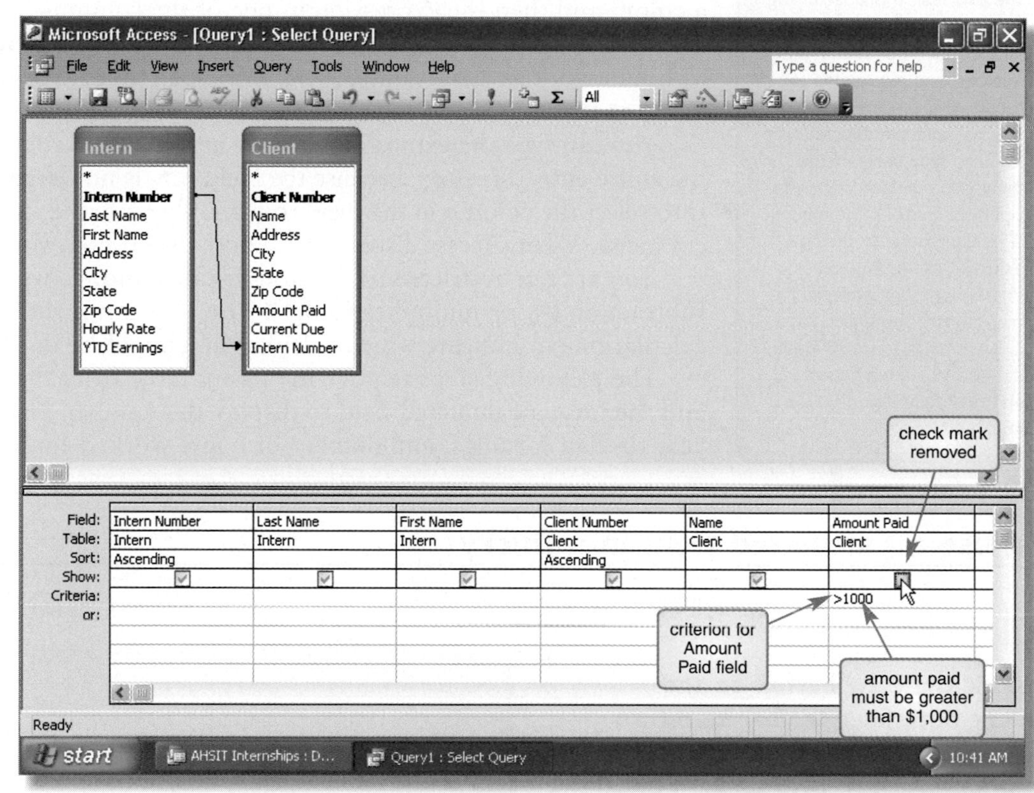

FIGURE 2-53

2

- **Click the Run button to run the query.**
- **If instructed to print the results, click the Print button.**

The results appear (Figure 2-54). Only those clients with an amount paid greater than $1,000.00 are displayed in the result. The Amount Paid field does not appear.

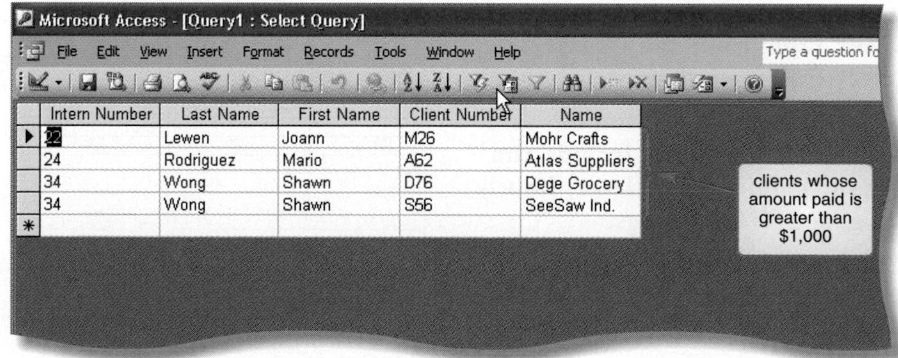

FIGURE 2-54

Calculations

Many types of calculations are available for use in queries. For example, you can add the values in two fields together, or you can calculate the sum or average of the values in one field.

> *Q & A*
>
> **Q:** Does Access have any tools that help create expressions?
>
> **A:** Access includes a tool to help you create complex expressions. If you click Build on the shortcut menu (see Figure 2-55), Access displays the Expression Builder dialog box. The dialog box includes an expression box, operator buttons, and expression elements. You use the expression box to build the expression. You can type parts of the expression directly and paste operator buttons and expression elements into the box. You also can use functions in expressions. For more information, visit the Office 2003 Q&A Web page (off2003sch/qa), locate Access Project 2, and click Expression Builder and Functions.

Using Calculated Fields

Suppose that Alyssa High School wants to know the number of hours worked by each intern. This poses a problem because the Intern table does not include a field for hours worked. You can calculate it, however, because the number of hours worked is equal to the YTD earnings divided by the hourly rate. A field that can be computed from other fields is called a **calculated field**.

To include calculated fields in queries, you enter a name for the calculated field, a colon, and then the expression in one of the columns in the Field row. Any fields included in the expression must be enclosed in square brackets ([ ]). For the number of hours worked, for example, you will type Hours Worked:[YTD Earnings]/[Hourly Rate] as the expression.

You can type the expression directly into the Field row. You will not be able to see the entire entry, however, because the Field row is not large enough. The preferred way is to select the column in the Field row and then use the Zoom command on its shortcut menu. When Access displays the Zoom dialog box, you can enter the expression.

You are not restricted to division in calculations. You can use addition (+), subtraction (-), or multiplication (*). You also can include parentheses in your calculations to indicate which calculations should be done first.

The following steps remove the Client table from the query (it is not needed) and then use a calculated field to display the number, last name, hourly rate, year-to-date earnings, and number of hours worked for all interns.

To Use a Calculated Field in a Query

- **Click the View button on the Query Datasheet toolbar to return to Design view.**
- **Right-click any field in the Client table field list.**
- **Click Remove Table on the shortcut menu to remove the Client table from the Query1 : Select Query window.**
- **Click Edit on the menu bar and then click Clear Grid. Include the Intern Number, Last Name, Hourly Rate, and YTD Earnings.**
- **Right-click the Field row in the first open column in the design grid.**

The shortcut menu appears (Figure 2-55).

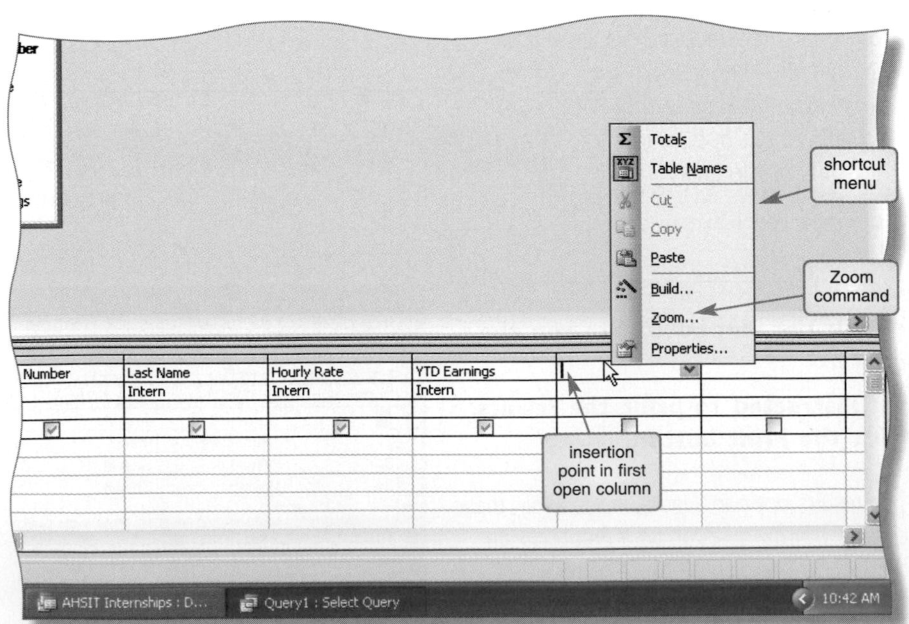

FIGURE 2-55

2

• **Click Zoom on the shortcut menu.**

• **Type** `Hours Worked:[YTD Earnings]/[Hourly Rate]` **in the Zoom dialog box that appears.**

Access displays the Zoom dialog box (Figure 2-56). The expression you typed appears within the dialog box.

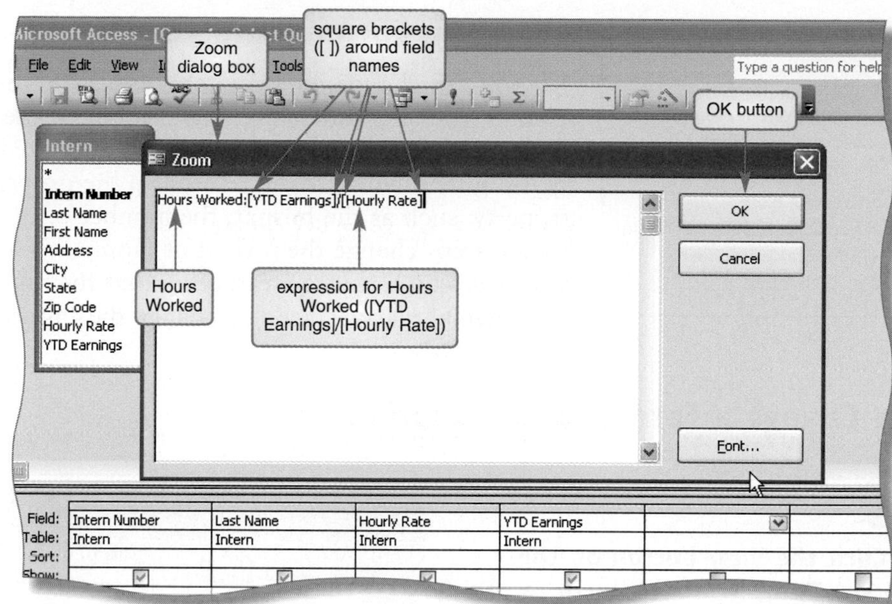

FIGURE 2-56

3

• **Click the OK button.**

A portion of the expression you entered appears in the fifth field in the design grid (Figure 2-57).

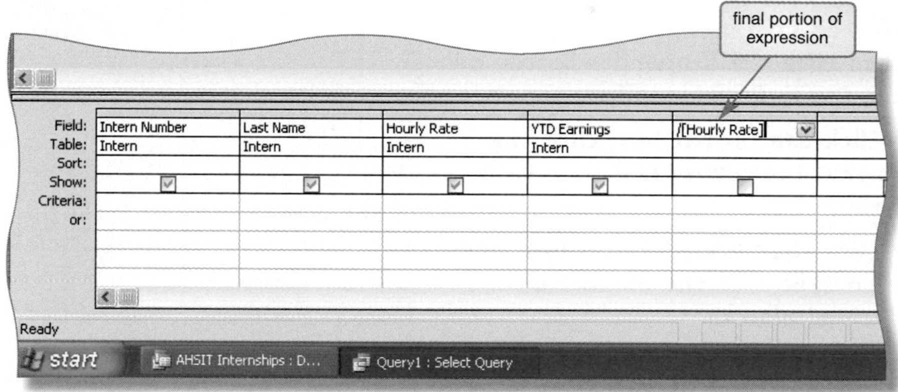

FIGURE 2-57

4

• **Click the Run button to run the query.**

• **If instructed to print the results, click the Print button.**

The results appear (Figure 2-58). Microsoft Access has calculated and displayed the number of hours worked for each intern.

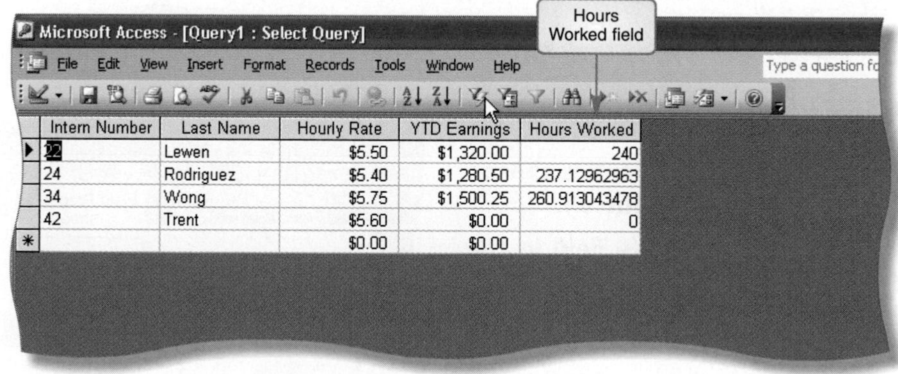

FIGURE 2-58

Instead of clicking Zoom on the shortcut menu, you can click Build. Access displays the Expression Builder dialog box that provides assistance in creating the expression. If you know the expression you will need, however, usually it is easier to enter it using the Zoom command.

Skill Builder 2-5

To practice the following tasks, visit scsite.com/off2003sch/skill, locate Access Project 2, and then click Skill Builder 2-5.

- ❑ Create a query
- ❑ Add fields to the design grid
- ❑ Add a calculated field
- ❑ Run the query

Changing Format and Caption

You can change the way items appear in the results of a query by changing their format. You also can change the heading at the top of a column in the results by changing the caption. Just as when you omitted duplicates, you will make this change by using the field's property sheet. In the property sheet, you can change the desired property, such as the format, the number of decimal places, or the caption. The following steps change the format of Hours Worked to Fixed and the number of decimal places to 1, thus guaranteeing that the number on each row will contain exactly one decimal place. They also change the caption of the Hourly Rate field to Rate.

To Change a Format and a Caption

1

- **Click the View button on the Query Datasheet toolbar to return to Design view.**
- **If necessary, click the Hours Worked field in the design grid, and then click the Properties button on the Query Design toolbar.**
- **Click the Format box, click the Format box arrow, and then click Fixed.**
- **Click the Decimal Places box, and then type 1 as the number of decimal places.**

Access displays the Field Properties sheet (Figure 2-59). The format is changed to Fixed and the number of decimal places is set to 1.

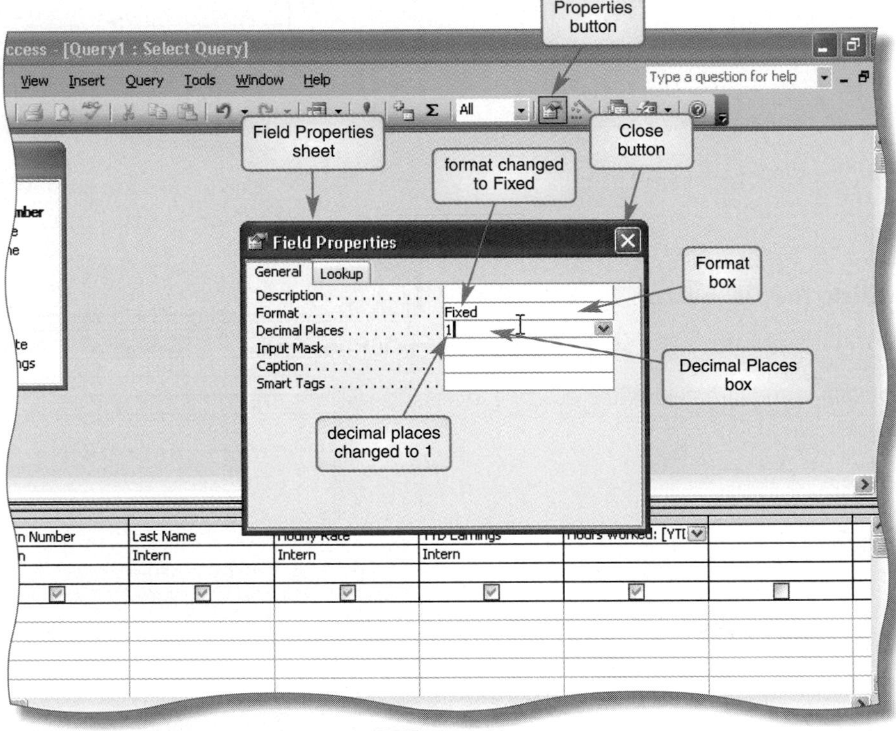

FIGURE 2-59

- **Close the Field Properties sheet by clicking its Close button.**
- **Click the Hourly Rate field in the design grid, and then click the Properties button on the Query Design toolbar.**
- **Click the Caption box, and then type Rate as the caption.**

Access displays the Field Properties sheet (Figure 2-60). The caption is changed to Rate.

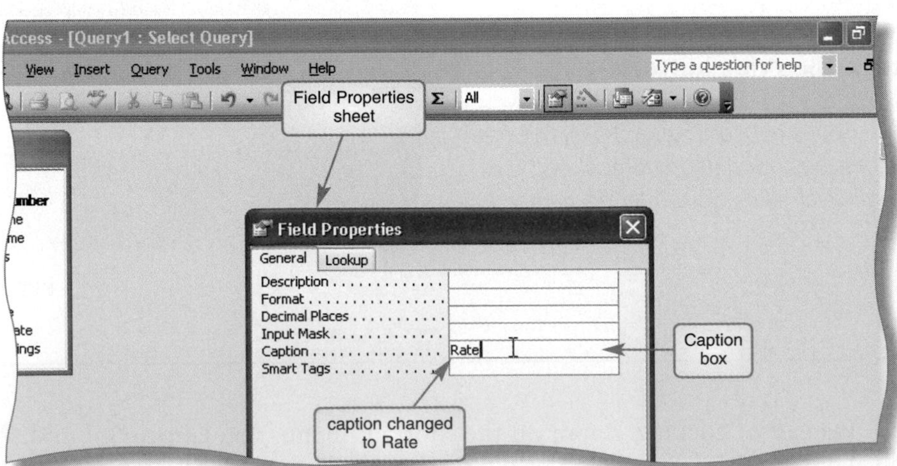

FIGURE 2-60

3

- **Close the Field Properties sheet by clicking its Close button.**
- **Click the Run button to run the query.**
- **If instructed to print the results, click the Print button.**

The results appear (Figure 2-61). The Hourly Rate caption is changed to Rate. The numbers in the Hours Worked column all contain exactly one decimal place.

4

- **Click the Close Window button for the Query1 : Select Query window.**
- **When asked if you want to save your changes, click the No button.**

The Query1 : Select Query window closes. The query is not saved.

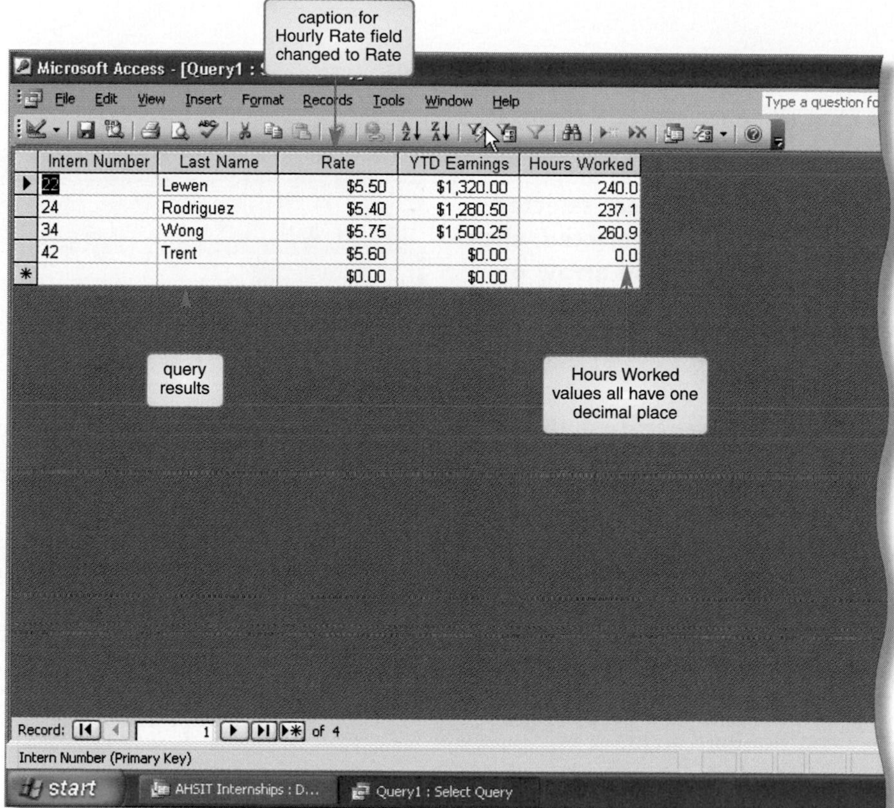

FIGURE 2-61

If you had saved the query, the changes you made to the properties would be saved along with the query.

Calculating Statistics

Microsoft Access supports the built-in statistics: COUNT, SUM, AVG (average), MAX (largest value), MIN (smallest value), STDEV (standard deviation), VAR (variance), FIRST, and LAST. These statistics are called aggregate functions. An **aggregate function** is a function that performs some mathematical function against a group of records. To use any of these aggregate functions in a query, you include it in the Total row in the design grid. The Total row routinely does not appear in the grid. To include it, click the Totals button on the Query Design toolbar.

The steps on the next page create a new query for the Client table and then calculate the average amount paid for all clients.

To Calculate Statistics

1

- **With the Tables object selected and the Client table selected, click the New Object button arrow on the Database toolbar.**
- **Click Query, and then click the OK button.**
- **Drag the line separating the two panes to the approximate position shown in Figure 2-62, and drag the lower edge of the field list box down far enough so all fields in the Client table appear.**
- **Click the Totals button on the Query Design toolbar, and then double-click the Amount Paid field.**

The Total row now is included in the design grid (Figure 2-62). The Amount Paid field is included, and the entry in the Total row is Group By.

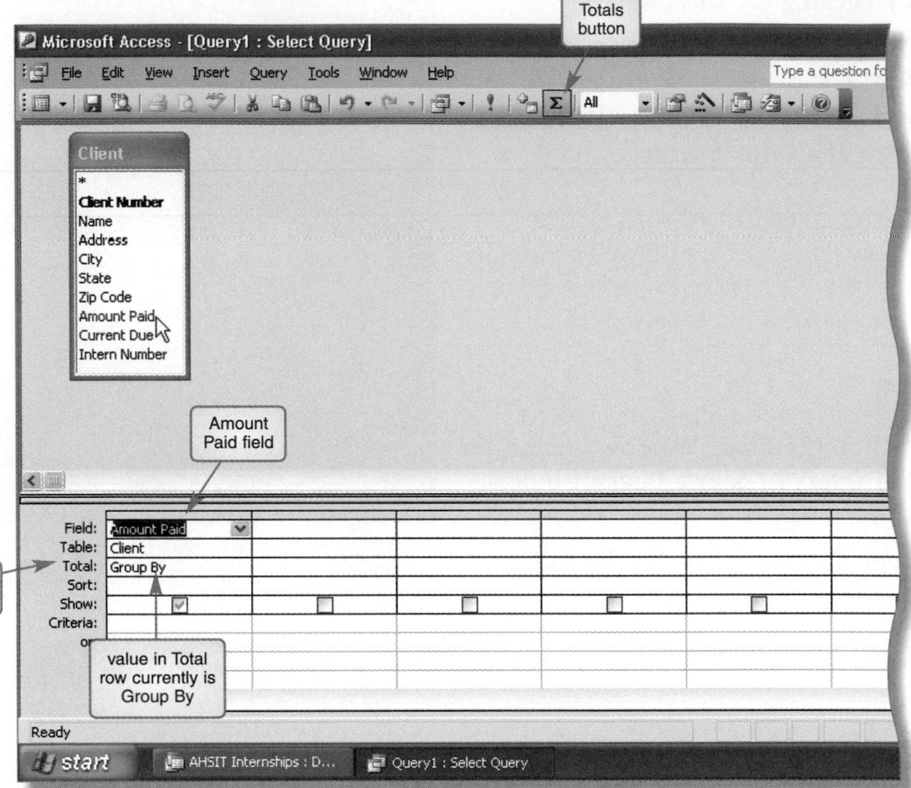

FIGURE 2-62

2

- **Click the Total row in the Amount Paid column, and then click the Total box arrow that appears.**

The list of available options appears (Figure 2-63).

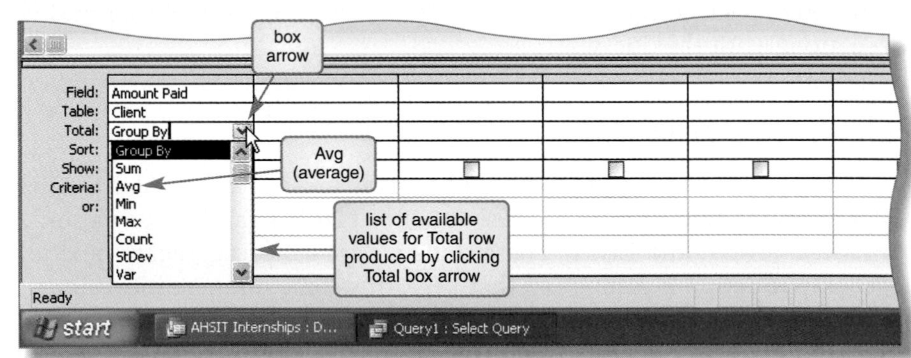

FIGURE 2-63

3

- **Click Avg.**

Avg is selected (Figure 2-64).

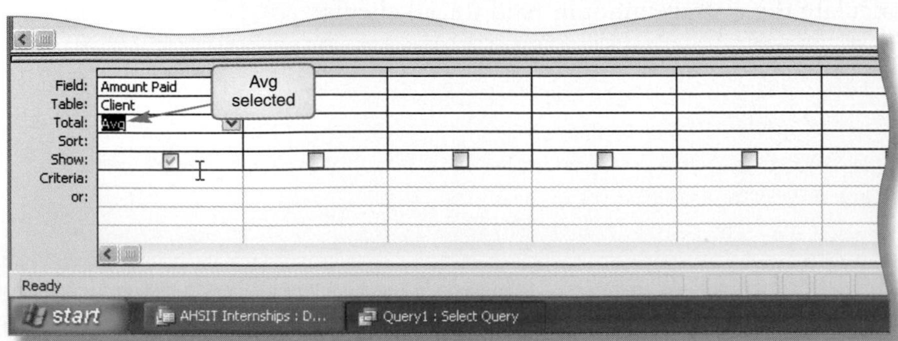

FIGURE 2-64

4

- **Click the Run button to run the query.**
- **If instructed to print the results, click the Print button.**

The result appears (Figure 2-65), showing the average amount paid for all clients.

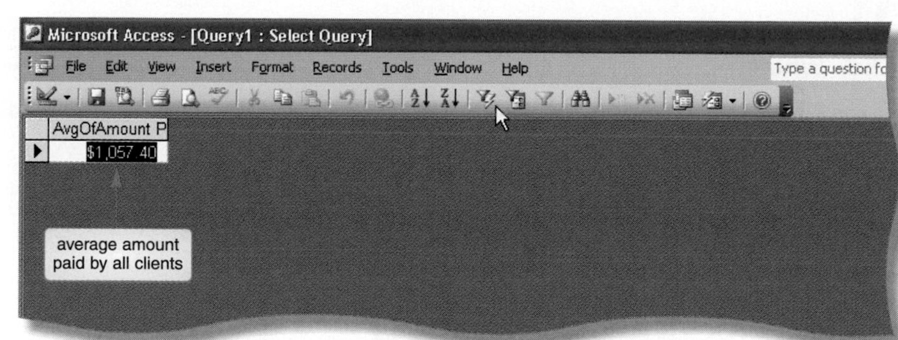

FIGURE 2-65

Using Criteria in Calculating Statistics

Sometimes calculating statistics for all the records in the table is appropriate. In other cases, however, you will need to calculate the statistics for only those records that satisfy certain criteria. To enter a criterion in a field, first you select Where as the entry in the Total row for the field and then enter the criterion in the Criteria row. The following steps use this technique to calculate the average amount paid for clients of intern 24.

To Use Criteria in Calculating Statistics

1

- **Click the View button on the Query Datasheet toolbar to return to Design view.**

2

- **Include the Intern Number field in the design grid.**
- **Produce the list of available options for the Total row entry just as you did when you selected Avg for the Amount Paid field.**
- **Use the vertical scroll bar to move through the options until the Where option appears.**

The list of available options appears (Figure 2-66). The Group By entry in the Intern Number field may not be highlighted on your screen depending on where you clicked in the Total row.

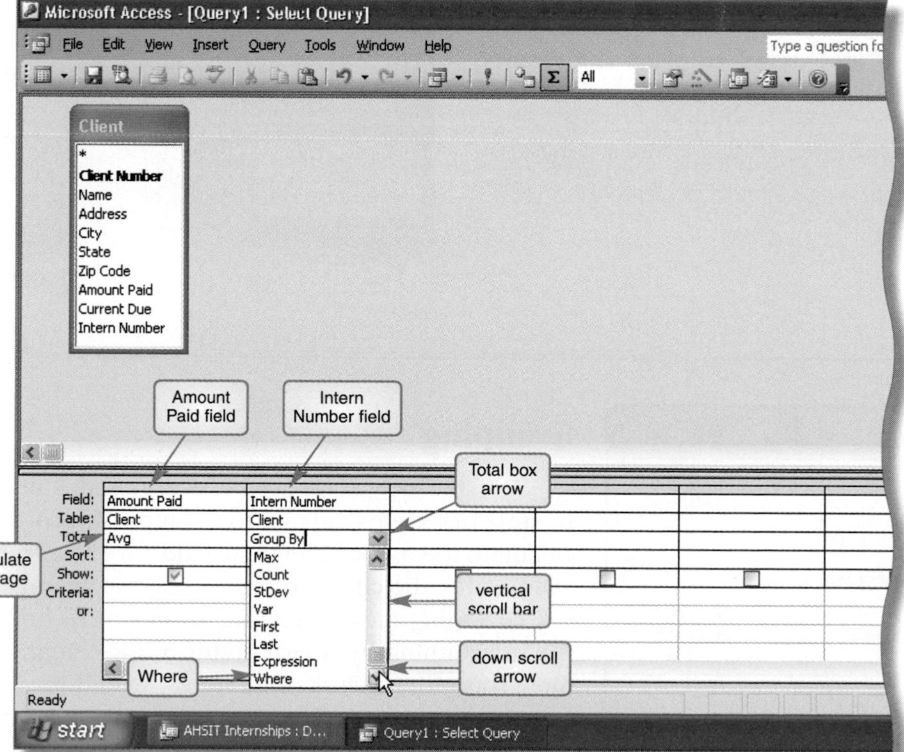

FIGURE 2-66

3

- **Click Where.**
- **Type** 24 **as the criterion for the Intern Number field.**

Where is selected as the entry in the Total row for the Intern Number field and 24 is entered in the Criteria row (Figure 2-67).

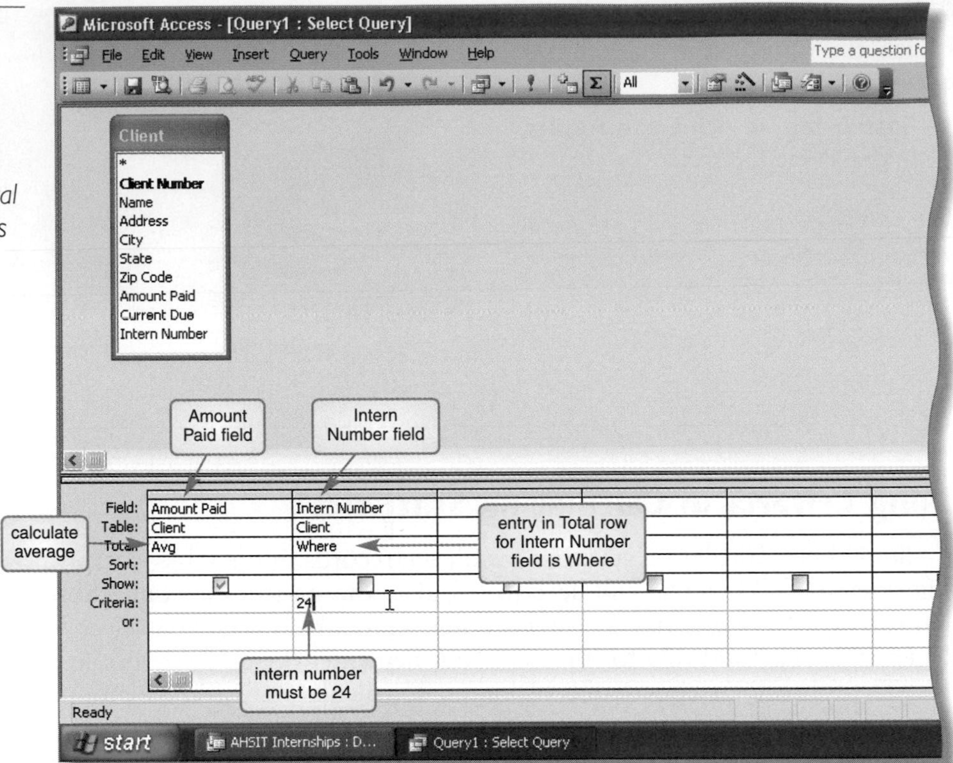

FIGURE 2-67

4

- **Click the Run button to run the query.**
- **If instructed to print the results, click the Print button.**

The results appear (Figure 2-68), giving the average amount paid for clients of intern 24.

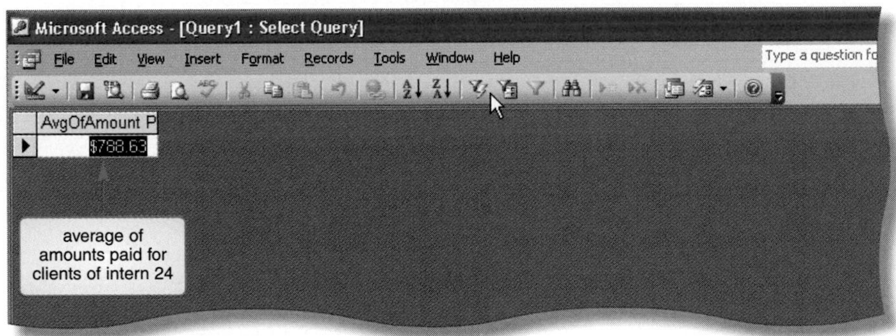

FIGURE 2-68

> *Q & A*
>
> **Q:** Is there more than one way to invoke a command in Access?
>
> **A:** Yes. For a table that lists how to complete tasks covered in this book using the mouse, menu, shortcut menu, and keyboard, see the Quick Reference Summary at the back of this book, or visit the Office 2003 Quick Reference Web page (scsite.com/off2003sch/qr).

Grouping

Another way statistics often are used is in combination with grouping; that is, statistics are calculated for groups of records. You may, for example, need to calculate the average amount paid for the clients of each intern. You will want the average for the clients of intern 22, the average for clients of intern 24, and so on.

Grouping means creating groups of records that share some common characteristic. In grouping by Intern Number, for example, the clients of intern 22 would form one group, the clients of intern 24 would be a second, and the clients of intern 34 form a third group. The calculations then are made for each group. To indicate grouping in Access, select Group By as the entry in the Total row for the field to be used for grouping.

The following steps calculate the average amount paid for clients of each intern.

To Use Grouping

1

- **Click the View button on the Query Datasheet toolbar to return to Design view.**
- **Click Edit on the menu bar and then click Clear Grid.**
- **Include the Intern Number field.**
- **Include the Amount Paid field, and then click Avg as the calculation in the Total row.**

The Intern Number and Amount Paid fields are included (Figure 2-69). Group By currently is the entry in the Total row for the Intern Number field, which is correct; thus, it was not changed.

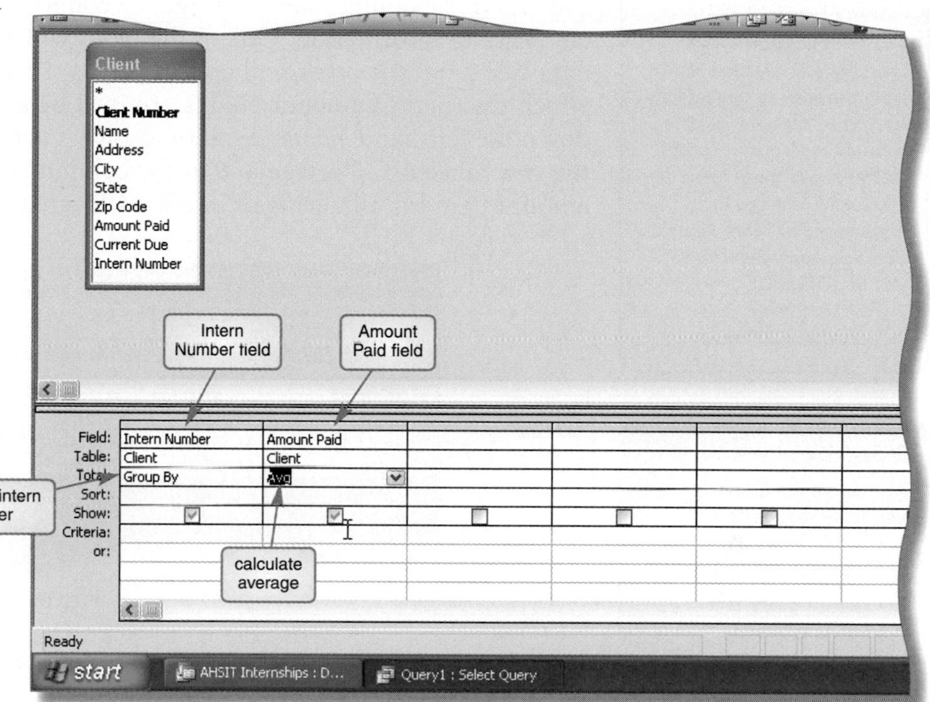

FIGURE 2-69

2

- **Click the Run button to run the query.**
- **If instructed to print the results, click the Print button.**

The results appear (Figure 2-70), showing each intern's number along with the average amount paid for the clients of that intern. Because the results are grouped by intern number, a single row exists for each intern summarizing all the clients of that intern.

3

- **Close the query by clicking the Close Window button for the Query1 : Select Query window.**
- **When asked if you want to save your changes, click the No button.**

The Query1 : Select Query window closes. The query is not saved.

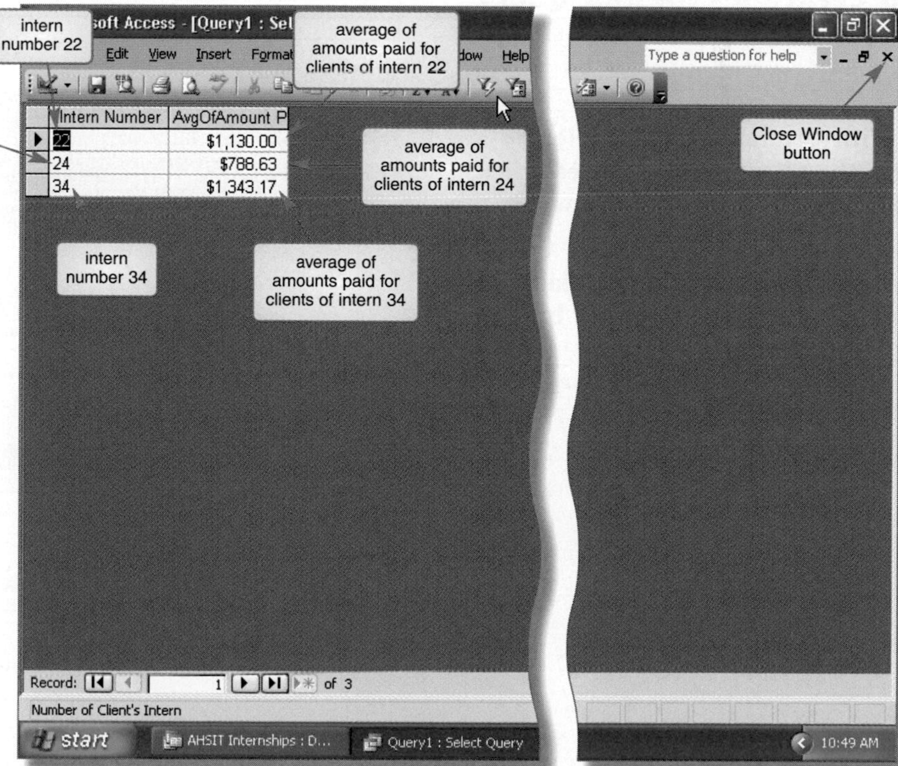

FIGURE 2-70

> **Q & A**
>
> **Q:** What is the Microsoft Office Certification program?
>
> **A:** The Microsoft Office Specialist Certification program provides an opportunity for you to obtain a valuable industry credential — proof that you have the Access 2003 skills required by employers. For more information, see Appendix E, or visit the Office 2003 Certification Web page (scsite.com/off2003sch/cert).

> **Skill Builder 2-6**
>
> To practice the following tasks, visit scsite.com/off2003sch/skill, locate Access Project 2, and then click Skill Builder 2-6.
>
> - ❑ Create a query that involves grouping
> - ❑ Run the query

Crosstab Queries

Crosstab queries are useful for summarizing data. A **crosstab query** calculates a statistic (for example, sum, average, or count) for data that is grouped by two different types of information. One of the types will appear down the side of the resulting datasheet, and the other will appear across the top. Figure 2-71 shows a crosstab in which the total of amount paid is grouped by both city and intern number with cities down the left-hand side and intern numbers across the top. For example, the entry in the row labeled E. Portage and in the column labeled 34 represents the total of the amount paid for all clients of intern 34 located in E. Portage.

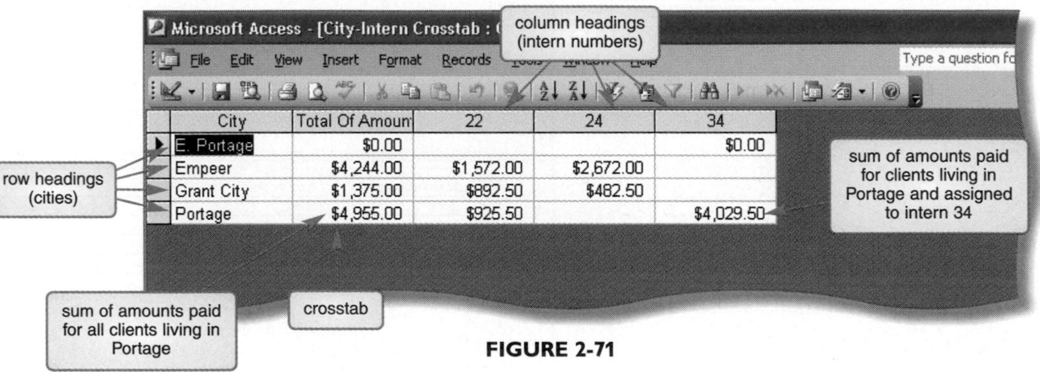

FIGURE 2-71

The following steps use the Crosstab Query wizard to create a crosstab query.

To Create a Crosstab Query

1

- **With the Tables object selected and the Client table selected, click the New Object button arrow.**
- **Click Query, click Crosstab Query Wizard in the New Query dialog box, and then click the OK button.**

Access displays the Crosstab Query Wizard dialog box (Figure 2-72).

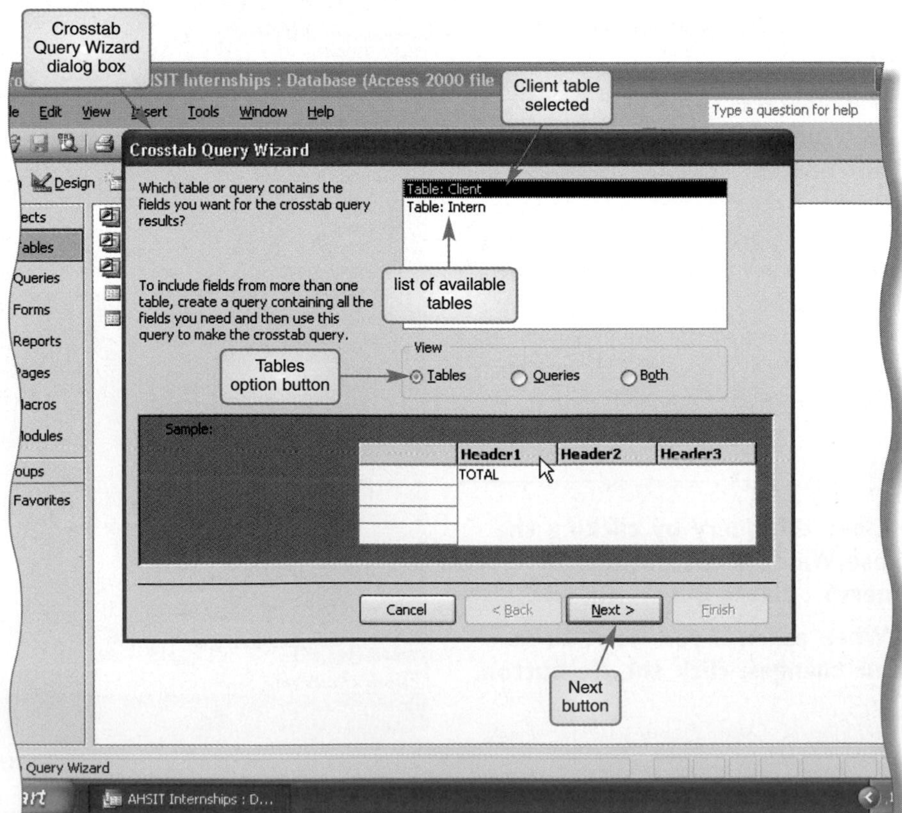

FIGURE 2-72

2

- **With the Tables option button selected and the Client table selected, click the Next button.**
- **Click the City field, and then click the Add Field button.**

The Crosstab Query Wizard dialog box displays options for selecting field values as row headings (Figure 2-73). The City field is selected as the field whose values will provide the row headings.

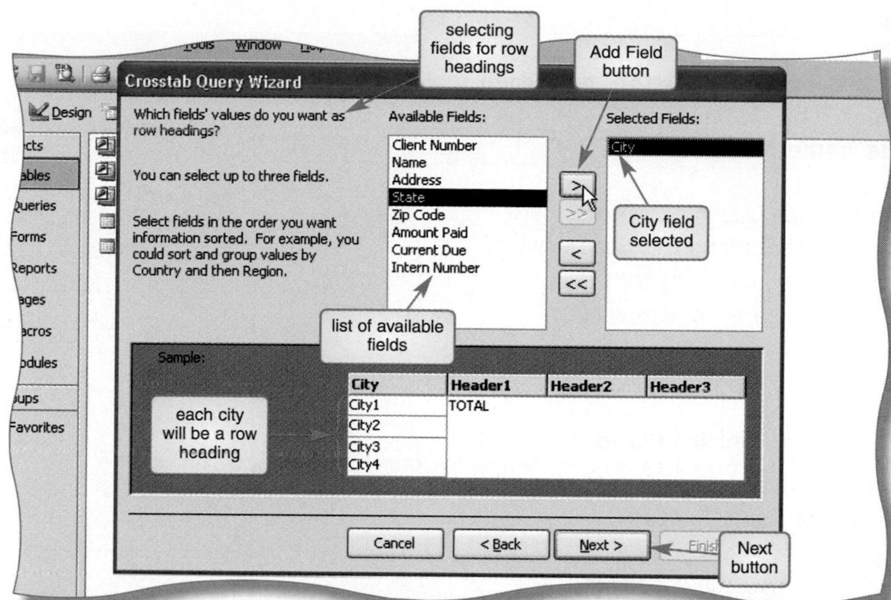

FIGURE 2-73

3

- **Click the Next button, and then click the Intern Number field.**

The Crosstab Query Wizard dialog box displays options for selecting field values as column headings (Figure 2-74). The Intern Number field is selected as the field whose values will provide the column headings.

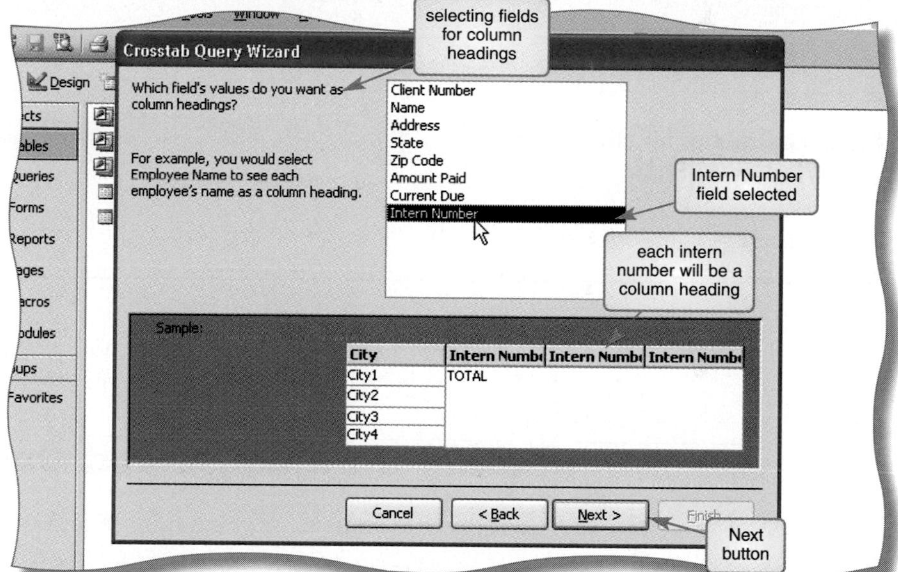

FIGURE 2-74

4

- **Click the Next button, click the Amount Paid field, and then click Sum.**

The Crosstab Query Wizard dialog box displays options for selecting fields for calculations for column and row intersections (Figure 2-75). The Amount Paid field is selected as the field whose value will be calculated for each row and column intersection. Because Sum is the selected function, the calculation will be the total amount paid.

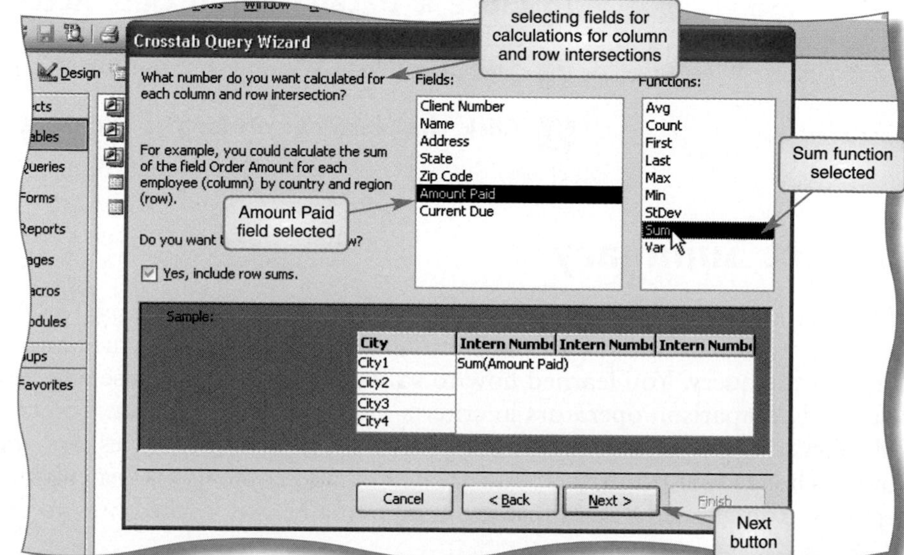

FIGURE 2-75

- **Click the Next button, and then type** `City-Intern Crosstab` **as the name of the query.**

The Crosstab Query Wizard dialog box displays options for naming and viewing the query and modifying the design (Figure 2-76). The name is entered.

- **Click the Finish button.**
- **If instructed to print the results, click the Print button.**

The results now can appear. They look like the results shown in Figure 2-71 on page AC 104.

7

- **Close the query by clicking its Close Window button.**

The query no longer appears.

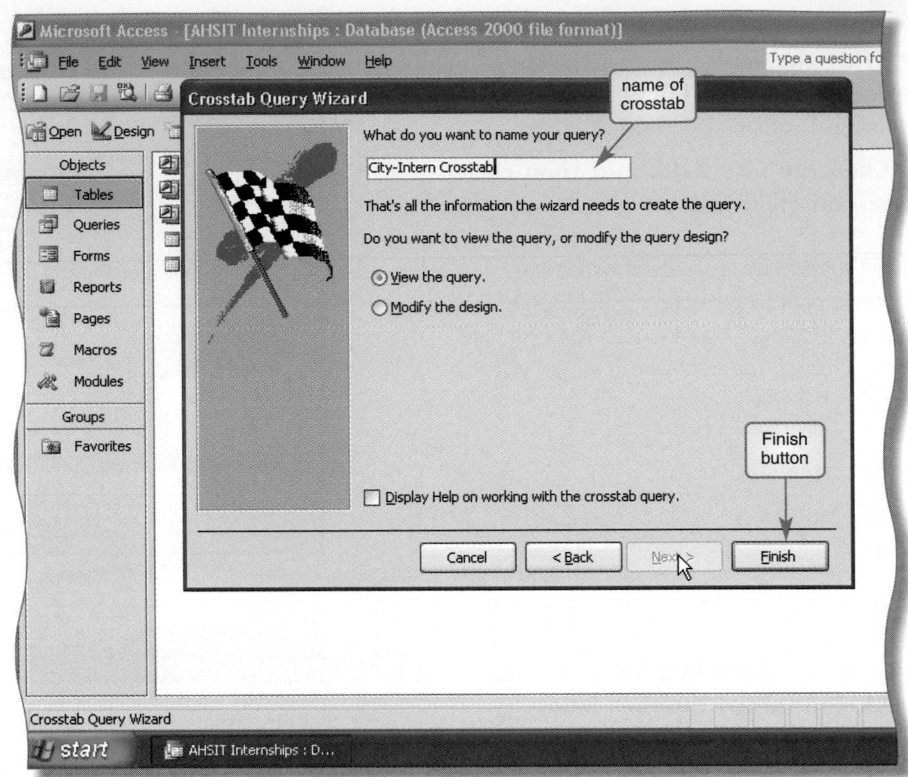

FIGURE 2-76

The query containing the crosstab now can be run just like any other query.

Closing a Database and Quitting Access

The following steps close the database and quit Access.

To Close a Database and Quit Access

1. **Click the Close Window button for the AHSIT Internships : Database window.**
2. **Click the Close button for the Microsoft Access window.**

Project Summary

In Project 2, you created and ran a variety of queries. You saw how to select fields in a query. You used text data and wildcards in criteria. You created a parameter query, which allowed users to enter a criterion when they run the query. You learned how to save a query for future use and how to use a query you have saved. You also used comparison operators in criteria involving numeric data. You combined criteria with both AND and OR. You saw how to sort the results of a query, how to join tables, how to restrict the records in a join, and how to change join properties. You created computed fields and calculated statistics. You changed formats and captions. You learned how to use grouping. Finally, you learned how to create a crosstab query.

If you have a SAM user profile, you may have access to hands-on instruction, practice, and assessment of the skills covered in this project. Log in to your SAM account and go to your assignments page to see what your instructor has assigned.

What You Should Know

Having completed this project, you should be able to perform the tasks below. The tasks are listed in the same order they were presented in this project. For a list of the buttons, menus, toolbars, and commands introduced in this project, see the Quick Reference Summary at the back of this book and refer to the Page Number column.

1. Open a Database (AC 68)
2. Create a Query (AC 68)
3. Include Fields in the Design Grid (AC 71)
4. Run the Query (AC 71)
5. Print the Results of a Query (AC 72)
6. Return to Design view (AC 72)
7. Close the Query (AC 73)
8. Include All Fields in a Query (AC 74)
9. Clear the Design Grid (AC 75)
10. Use Text Data in a Criterion (AC 76)
11. Use a Wildcard (AC 77)
12. Use Criteria for a Field Not Included in the Results (AC 78)
13. Create and Run a Parameter Query (AC 79)
14. Save a Query (AC 80)
15. Use a Saved Query (AC 81)
16. Use a Number in a Criterion (AC 82)
17. Use a Comparison Operator in a Criterion (AC 83)
18. Use a Compound Criterion Involving AND (AC 84)
19. Use a Compound Criterion Involving OR (AC 85)
20. Sort Data in a Query (AC 86)
21. Omit Duplicates (AC 87)
22. Sort on Multiple Keys (AC 88)
23. Create a Top-Values Query (AC 89)
24. Join Tables (AC 92)
25. Change Join Properties (AC 94)
26. Restrict the Records in a Join (AC 95)
27. Use a Calculated Field in a Query (AC 96)
28. Change a Format and a Caption (AC 98)
29. Calculate Statistics (AC 100)
30. Use Criteria in Calculating Statistics (AC 101)
31. Use Grouping (AC 103)
32. Create a Crosstab Query (AC 104)
33. Close a Database and Quit Access (AC 106)

Career Corner

Computer Forensics Specialist

Computer forensics is a rapidly growing field that involves gathering and analyzing evidence from computers and networks. It is the responsibility of the computer forensics specialist to carefully take several steps to identify and retrieve possible evidence that may exist on a suspect's computer. These steps include protecting the suspect's computer, discovering all files, recovering deleted files, revealing hidden files, accessing protected or encrypted files, analyzing all the data, and providing expert consultation and/or testimony as required. A computer forensics specialist must have knowledge of all aspects of the computer, from the operating system to computer architecture and hardware design.

In the past, many computer forensics specialists were self-taught computer users who may have attended computer forensics seminars, or they may have been trained in the use of one or more computer forensics tools by software vendors. The computer forensics specialist of today needs extensive training, usually from several different sources. A degree in Computer Science should be supplemented with graduate courses and university level professional development certificates.

Entry level salaries for computer forensics specialists range from $45,000 to $75,000. With experience and certifications, salaries can exceed $125,000. For more information, read the Computer Forensics Special Feature that follows this chapter or visit scsite.com/off2003sch/careers and then click Computer Forensics Specialist.

Learn It Online

Instructions: To complete the Learn It Online exercises, start your browser, click the Address bar, and then enter the Web address scsite.com/off2003sch/learn. When the Office 2003 Learn It Online page is displayed, follow the instructions in the exercises below. Each exercise has instructions for printing your results, either for your own records or for submission to your instructor.

1 Project Reinforcement TF, MC, and SA

Below Access Project 2, click the Project Reinforcement link. Print the quiz by clicking Print on the File menu for each page. Answer each question.

2 Flash Cards

Below Access Project 2, click the Flash Cards link and read the instructions. Type 20 (or a number specified by your instructor) in the Number of playing cards text box, type your name in the Enter your Name text box, and then click the Flip Card button. When the flash card is displayed, read the question and then click the ANSWER box arrow to select an answer. Flip through Flash Cards. If your score is 15 (75%) correct or greater, click Print on the File menu to print your results. If your score is less than 15 (75%) correct, then redo this exercise by clicking the Replay button.

3 Practice Test

Below Access Project 2, click the Practice Test link. Answer each question, enter your first and last name at the bottom of the page, and then click the Grade Test button. When the graded practice test is displayed on your screen, click Print on the File menu to print a hard copy. Continue to take practice tests until you score 80% or better.

4 Who Wants To Be a Computer Genius?

Below Access Project 2, click the Computer Genius link. Read the instructions, enter your first and last name at the bottom of the page, and then click the PLAY button. When your score is displayed, click the PRINT RESULTS link to print a hard copy.

5 Wheel of Terms

Below Access Project 2, click the Wheel of Terms link. Read the instructions, and then enter your first and last name and your school name. Click the PLAY button. When your score is displayed, right-click the score and then click Print on the shortcut menu to print a hard copy.

6 Crossword Puzzle Challenge

Below Access Project 2, click the Crossword Puzzle Challenge link. Read the instructions, and then enter your first and last name. Click the SUBMIT button. Work the crossword puzzle. When you are finished, click the Submit button. When the crossword puzzle is redisplayed, click the Print Puzzle button to print a hard copy.

7 Tips and Tricks

Below Access Project 2, click the Tips and Tricks link. Click a topic that pertains to Project 2. Right-click the information and then click Print on the shortcut menu. Construct a brief example of what the information relates to in Access to confirm you understand how to use the tip or trick.

8 Newsgroups

Below Access Project 2, click the Newsgroups link. Click a topic that pertains to Project 2. Print three comments.

9 Expanding Your Horizons

Below Access Project 2, click the Expanding Your Horizons link. Click a topic that pertains to Project 2. Print the information. Construct a brief example of what the information relates to in Access to confirm you understand the contents of the article.

10 Search Sleuth

Below Access Project 2, click the Search Sleuth link. To search for a term that pertains to this project, select a term below the Project 2 title and then use the Google search engine at google.com (or any major search engine) to display and print two Web pages that present information on the term.

11 Access Online Training

Below Access Project 2, click the Access Online Training link. When your browser displays the Microsoft Office Online Web page, click the Access link. Click one of the Access courses that covers one or more of the objectives listed at the beginning of the project on page AC 66. Print the first page of the course before stepping through it.

12 Office Marketplace

Below Access Project 2, click the Office Marketplace link. When your browser displays the Microsoft Office Online Web page, click the Office Marketplace link. Click a topic that relates to Access. Print the first page.

13 You're Hired!

Below Access Project 2, click the You're Hired! link to embark on the path to a career in computers. Directions about how to play the game will be displayed. When you are ready to play, click the begin the game button. If required, submit your score to your instructor.

Apply Your Knowledge

1 Querying the Keep It Green Database

Instructions: Start Access. Open the Keep It Green database that you modified in Apply Your Knowledge 1 in Project 1 on page AC 54. (If you did not complete this exercise, see your instructor for a copy of the modified database.) Perform the following tasks:

1. Create a query for the Customer table and add the Name and Address fields to the design grid.
2. Find only those records where the customer has an address on Bard. Run the query and change the address for the customer on 24 Bard to 27 Bard. Print the results. Return to Design view and clear the grid.
3. Add the Customer Number, Name, City, and Balance fields to the design grid. Sort the records in ascending order by City and descending by Balance. Run the query and print the results. Return to Design view.
4. Modify the query to allow the user to enter a different city each time the query is run. Run the query to find all customers who live in Kordy. Print the query results. Save the query as Customer-City Query.
5. Open the Customer-City Query in Design view. Run the query to find all customers who live in Conner but restrict retrieval to the top two records. Print the results. Close the query without saving it.
6. Create a new query for the Worker table and then join the Worker and Customer tables. Add the Worker Number, First Name, and Last Name fields from the Worker table and the Customer Number and Name fields from the Customer table. Sort the records in ascending order by Worker Number and Customer Number. All workers should appear in the result even if they currently have no customers. Run the query and print the results.
7. Restrict the records retrieved in Step 6 above to only those customers who have a balance greater than $200.00. Do not display the balance. Run the query and print the results. Close the query without saving it.
8. Create and print the crosstab shown in Figure 2-77. The crosstab groups total of customers' balances by city and worker number.

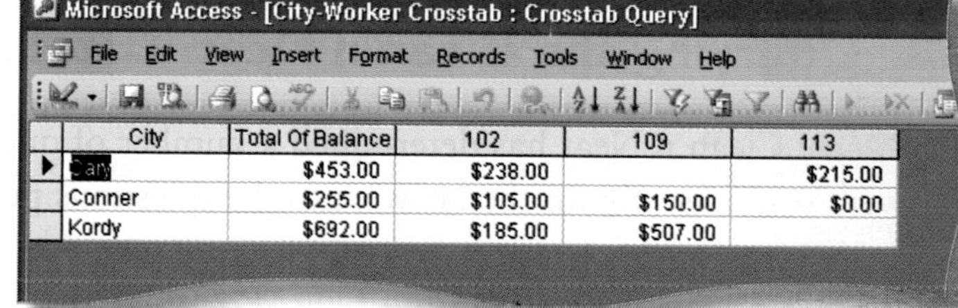

City	Total Of Balance	102	109	113
Cary	$453.00	$238.00		$215.00
Conner	$255.00	$105.00	$150.00	$0.00
Kordy	$692.00	$185.00	$507.00	

FIGURE 2-77

In the Lab

1 Querying Alumni Connection Database

Problem: The alumni association has determined a number of questions it wants the database management system to answer. You must obtain the answers to the questions posed by the association.

Instructions: Use the database created in the In the Lab 1 of Project 1 on page AC 57 for this assignment or see your instructor for information on accessing the files required for this book. Perform the following tasks:

1. Open the Alumni Connection database and create a new query to display and print the Item Code, Description, On Hand, and Selling Price for all records in the Item table.
2. Display and print the Item Code, Description, Cost, and Vendor Code fields for all products where the Vendor Code is GG.
3. Display and print the Item Code and Description fields for all items where the description starts with the letter P.
4. Display and print the Item Code and Description fields for all items with a cost less than $5.00.

(continued)

Cases and Places

The difficulty of the cases studies varies:

are the least difficult and are more difficult.

Each exercise has a cross-curricular designation.

Math Social Studies Science Language Arts Art/Music Business Health

1 Use the College Lawn Services database you created in Cases and Places 1 in Project 1 on page AC 63 for this assignment or see your instructor for information on accessing the files required for this book. Perform the following: (1) Display and print the number and name of all customers who live on Shue. (2) Display and print the number, name, telephone number, and balance for all customers who have a balance of at least $50.00. (3) Display and print the number, name, balance, worker first name, and worker last name for all customers. Sort the records in ascending order by worker last name. (4) Display and print the average balance of all customers. (5) Display and print the average balance of customers grouped by worker. (6) Display and print the total balance of all customers.

2 Use the Community Fitness Center database you created in Cases and Places 2 in Project 1 on page AC 63 for this assignment or see your instructor for information on accessing the files required for this book. Perform the following: (1) Display and print the number, member last name, and member first name for all members that have a particular type of membership. The fitness center should be able to enter a different membership type each time the query is run. (2) Display and print the member number, first name, last name and membership cost. (3) Display and print the sum of all memberships. (4) Display and print the member number, last name, first name, and membership description for all members. Sort the data ascending by membership description and last name. (5) Display and print the total membership cost grouped by membership type.

3 Use the Book Cooperative database you created in Cases and Places 3 in Project 1 on page AC 63 for this assignment or see your instructor for information on accessing the files required for this book. Perform the following: (1) List the book code, title, and seller of all books. (2) List the book code, title, and price of all books that are in excellent condition. (3) List the title of all books available for sale and the number of copies of each different title. (4) Display and print the book code, title, and author for all books. (5) Find the average price of all books and the average book price by seller.

4 Use the Math Club database you created in Cases and Places 4 in Project 1 on page AC 64 for this assignment or see your instructor for information on accessing the files required for this book. Display and print the following: (1) List all students requiring tutoring in a particular math subject. The Math Club should be able to enter a different subject each time the query is run. (2) List all students that are being tutored by Craig Anders. (3) List all students who have earned 30 or more points. (4) Find the tutor who has worked the most hours. (5) Find the student with the least number of points. (6) List the different math subjects in ascending order. Each subject should display only once.

5 **Working Together** Obtain a copy of the weather page of your local newspaper. As a team, choose 30 cities of interest. Create a database that contains one table and has three fields (City, High Temp, Low Temp). Create queries that do the following: (1) Convert all temperatures from one temperature scale to another (for example, if temperatures are given in Fahrenheit, convert to Celsius). (2) Display the five cities with the highest low temperatures. (3) Display the average high and low temperatures for all cities. Create an additional query determined by the team. Run the queries and print the results. Write a one-page paper that explains what you learned from querying the database and any conclusions you can draw about the data — for example, were the five cities with the highest lows in a particular region of the country?

MICROSOFT OFFICE

Access 2003

Maintaining a Database Using the Design and Update Features of Access

PROJECT 3

CASE PERSPECTIVE

Dr. Gervase and her staff at Alyssa High School of Information Technology (AHSIT) have received many benefits from the database they created for the corporate internship program that matches students with corporations. They now face the task of keeping the database up-to-date. Because of the growing popularity of the internship program, they are taking on new clients and interns and need to add new records and make changes to existing records.

Access offers many features for maintaining a database that Dr. Gervase and her staff want to utilize. For example, they must change the structure of the database to categorize the clients by type. This will allow Alyssa High School to ensure a diverse work experience for their students. They will do this by adding a Client Type field to the Client table. They discovered the Name field was too short to contain the name of one of the clients, so they will enlarge the size of the field. Along with these changes, they want to change the appearance of a datasheet when displaying data.

They would like the capability of making mass updates; that is, to update many records in a single operation. They want rules that make sure users can enter only valid data into the database, and they want to ensure that it is not possible for the database to contain a client who is not associated with a specific intern. Finally, they want to improve the efficiency of certain types of processing, specifically sorting and retrieving data. Your task is to help Dr. Gervase accomplish these goals.

As you read through this project, you will learn how to use the Access design and update features to maintain a database.

MICROSOFT OFFICE
Access 2003

Maintaining a Database Using the Design and Update Features of Access

PROJECT

Objectives

You will have mastered the material in this project when you can:

- Add, change, and delete records
- Search for records
- Filter records
- Update a table design
- Format a datasheet
- Use queries to update records
- Specify validation rules, default values, and formats
- Create and use a lookup field
- Specify referential integrity
- Use a subdatasheet
- Sort records
- Create indexes

Introduction

Once a database has been created and loaded with data, it must be maintained. **Maintaining the database** means modifying the data to keep it up-to-date, such as adding new records, changing the data for existing records, and deleting records. Updating can include mass updates or mass deletions; that is, updates to, or deletions of, many records at the same time.

In addition to adding, changing, and deleting records, maintenance of a database can involve the need to **restructure the database** periodically; that is, to change the database structure. This can include adding new fields to a table, changing the characteristics of existing fields, and removing existing fields. It also can involve the creation of indexes, which are similar to indexes found in the back of books. Indexes are used to improve the efficiency of certain operations.

Figure 3-1 summarizes some of the various types of activities involved in maintaining a database.

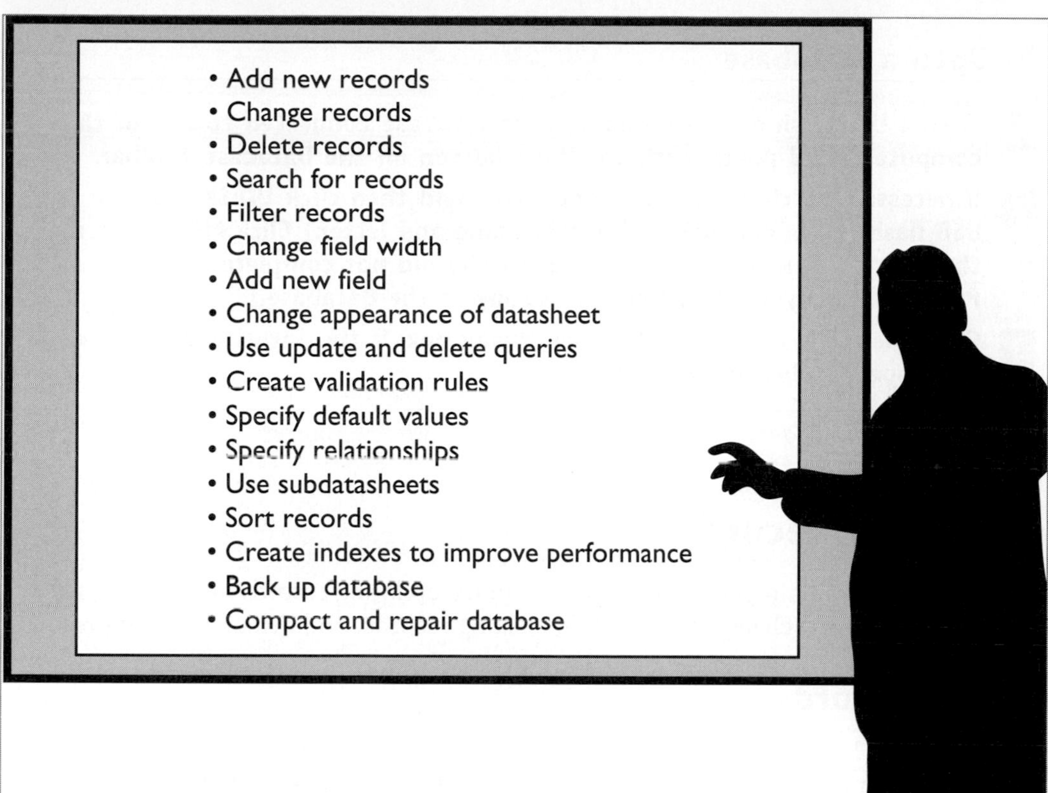
• Add new records
• Change records
• Delete records
• Search for records
• Filter records
• Change field width
• Add new field
• Change appearance of datasheet
• Use update and delete queries
• Create validation rules
• Specify default values
• Specify relationships
• Use subdatasheets
• Sort records
• Create indexes to improve performance
• Back up database
• Compact and repair database

FIGURE 3-1

Project Three — Maintaining the AHSIT Internships Database

The steps in this project show how to make changes to the data in the AHSIT Internships database. They also illustrate how to search for records as well as filter records. The steps restructure the database, that is, make changes that meet the needs of the user, in this case, Alyssa High School. This includes adding an additional field as well as increasing the width of one of the existing fields. Other changes modify the structure of the database in a way that prevents users from entering invalid data. Steps are presented to create indexes that reduce the time it takes for some operations, for example, those involving sorting the data.

Opening the Database

If you are stepping through this project on a computer and you want your screen to match the figures in this book, then you should change your computer's resolution to 800 × 600. For more information on how to change the resolution on your computer, see Appendix D. Before carrying out the steps in this project, first you must open the database. The steps on the next page assume that Access is started and that the AHSIT Internships database is located on a USB flash drive. If your database is located anywhere else, you will need to adjust the appropriate steps.

Q & A

Q: Need help with Access?

A: Help with Access is no further than the Type a question for help box on the menu bar in the upper-right corner of the window. Click the box that contains the text, Type a question for help (Figure 3-3), type `help`, and then press the ENTER key. Access responds with a list of topics you can click to learn about obtaining help on any Access-related topic. To find out what is new in Access 2003, type `what is new in Access` in the Type a question for help box.

Q & A

Q: What should I do if I try to open a database and a Microsoft Office Access dialog box appears asking if I want to block unsafe expressions?

A: Click the No button when asked if you want to block unsafe expressions. If another dialog box appears with questions about the Microsoft Jet Engine, click Yes and then click Open.

To Open a Database

1. **With a USB flash drive containing your database connected to one of the computer's USB ports, click the Open button on the Database toolbar.**
2. **If necessary, click the Look in box arrow and then click UDISK 2.0 (E:). (Your USB flash drive may have a different name and letter.) Click AHSIT Internships, the database modified in Project 2. (If you did not complete the steps in Project 2, see your instructor for a copy of the database.)**
3. **Click the Open button in the Open dialog box. If the Security Warning dialog box appears, click the Open button.**

The database opens and the AHSIT Internships : Database window appears.

Updating Records

Keeping the data in a database up-to-date requires updating records in three ways: adding new records, changing the data in existing records, and deleting existing records.

Adding Records

In Project 1, you added records to a database using Datasheet view; that is, as you were adding records, the records were appearing on the screen in the form of a datasheet, or table. When you need to add additional records, you can use the same techniques.

In Project 1, you used a form to view records. This is called Form view. You also can use **Form view** to update the data in a table. To add new records, change existing records, or delete records, you will use the same techniques you used in Datasheet view. The following steps add a record to the Client table with a form, for example. These steps use the Client form created in Project 1.

To Use a Form to Add Records

1

• **With the AHSIT Internships database open, click Forms on the Objects bar, and then right-click the Client form.**

The list of forms appears (Figure 3-2). The shortcut menu for the Client form also appears.

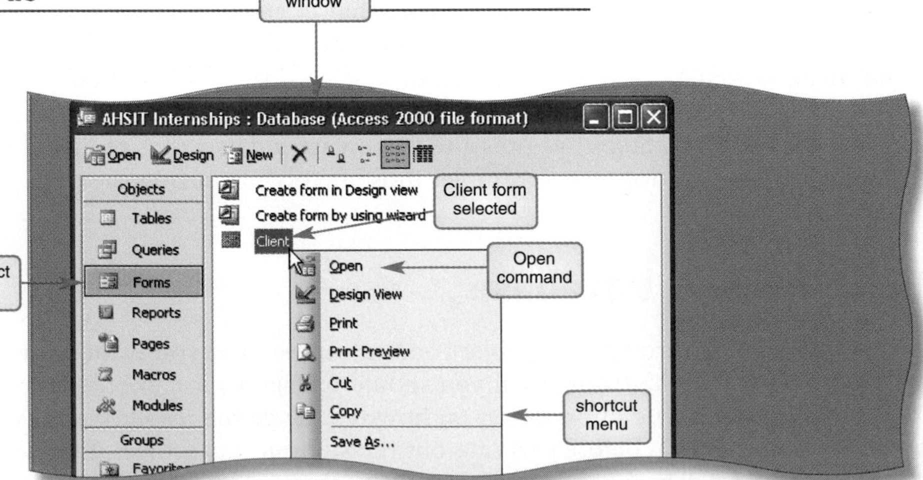

FIGURE 3-2

2

• **Click Open on the shortcut menu.**

The form for the Client table appears (Figure 3-3). Your toolbars may be arranged differently.

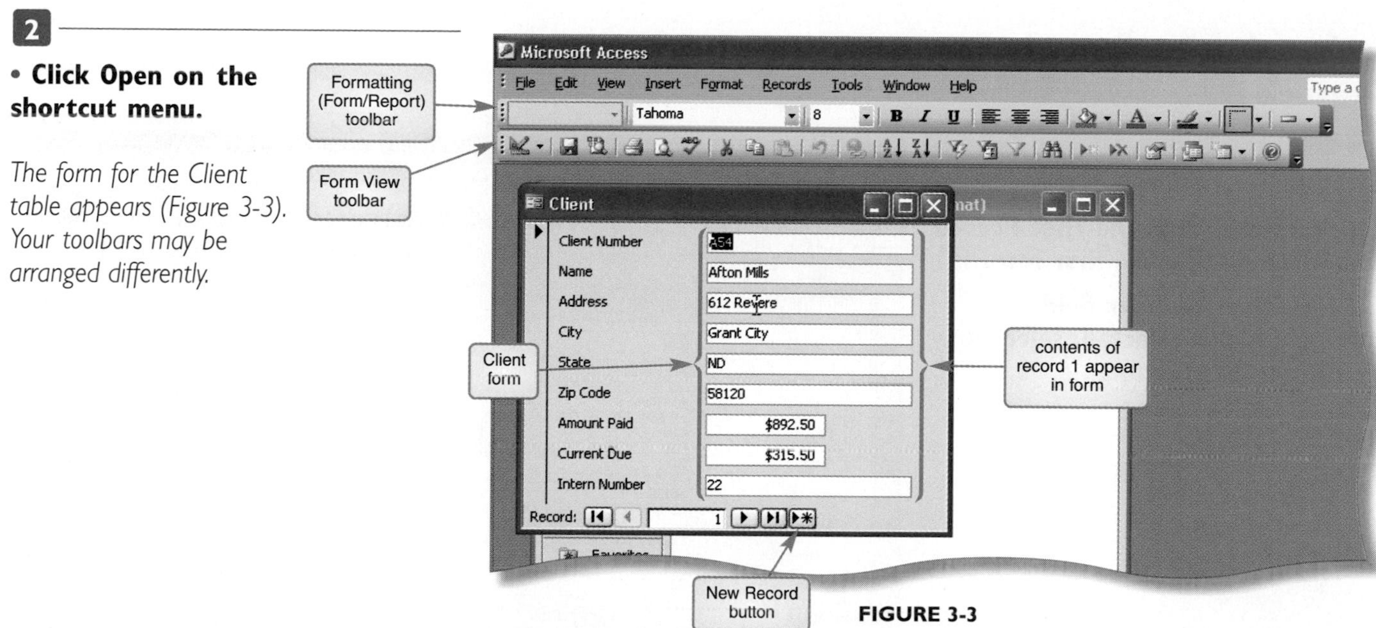

FIGURE 3-3

3

• **Click the New Record button on the Navigation bar, and then type the data for the new record as shown in Figure 3-4. Press the TAB key after typing the data in each field, except after typing the data for the final field (Intern Number).**

The record appears.

4

• **Press the TAB key.**

The record now is added to the Client table and the contents of the form are erased.

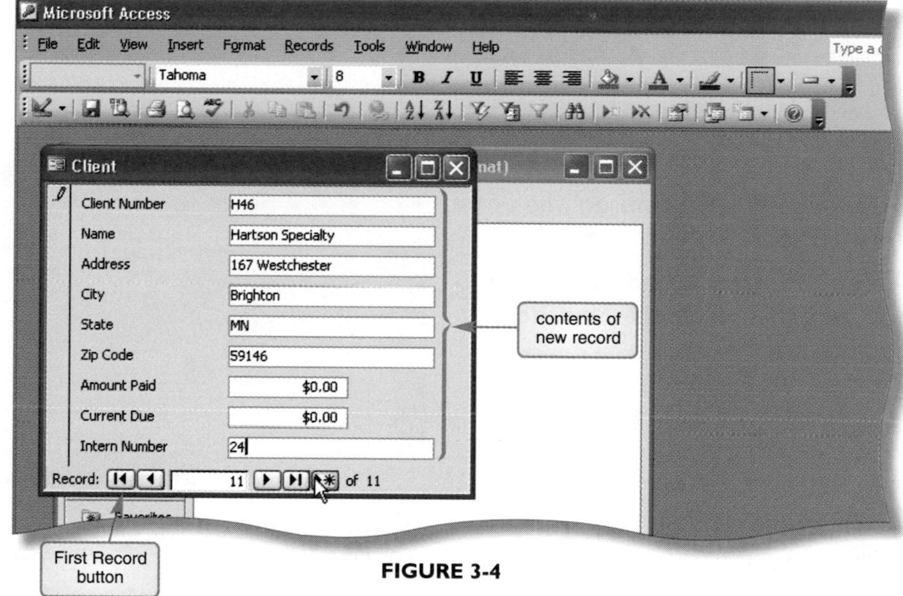

FIGURE 3-4

Searching for a Record

In the database environment, **searching** means looking for records that satisfy some criteria. Looking for the client whose number is H21 is an example of searching. The queries in Project 2 also were examples of searching. Access had to locate those records that satisfied the criteria.

A need for searching also exists when using Form view or Datasheet view. To update client H21, for example, first you need to find the client.

You need a way to be able to go directly to a record just by giving the value in some field. This is the function of the Find button. Before clicking the Find button, select the field for the search.

The steps on the next page show how to search for the client whose number is H21.

To Search for a Record

1

- **Make sure the Client form is open.**
- **If necessary, click the First Record button to display the first record.**
- **If the Client Number field currently is not selected, select it by clicking the field name.**

The first record appears on the form (Figure 3-5).

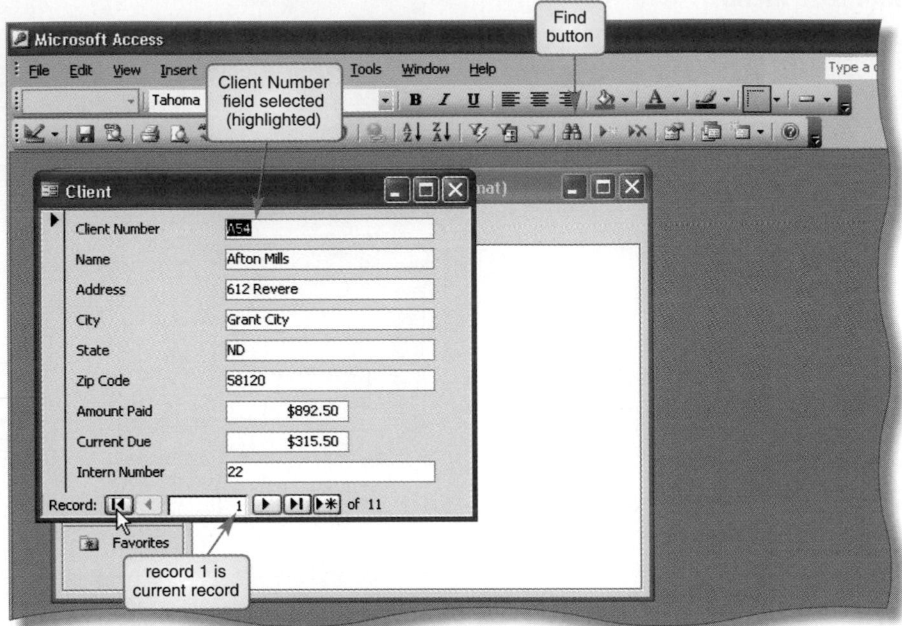

FIGURE 3-5

2

- **Click the Find button on the Form View toolbar.**
- **Type `H21` in the Find What text box and then click the Find Next button.**

Access displays the Find and Replace dialog box, locates the record for client H21, and displays it in the Client form (Figure 3-6). The Find What text box contains the entry, H21.

3

- **Click the Cancel button in the Find and Replace dialog box.**

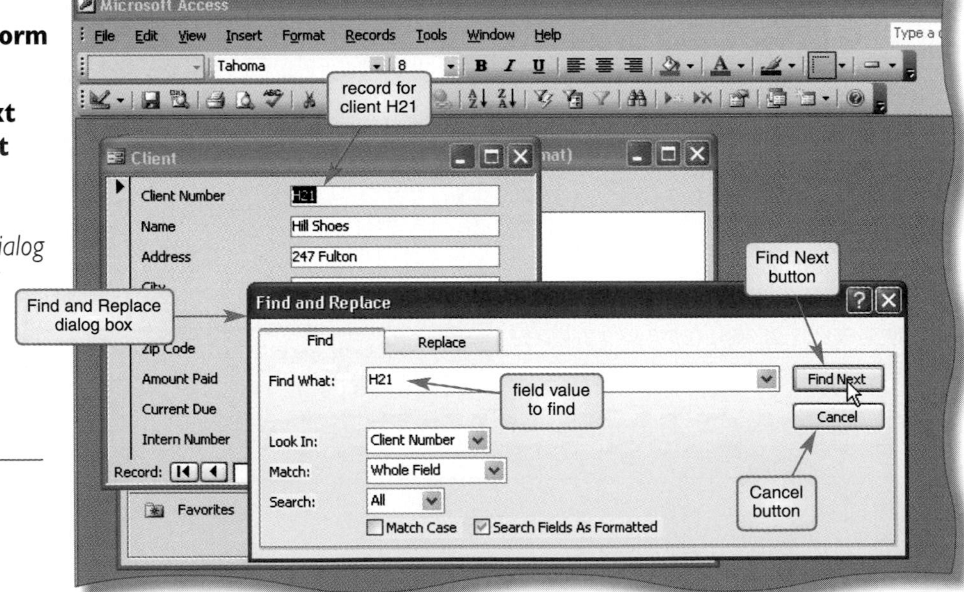

FIGURE 3-6

In some cases, after locating a record that satisfies a criterion, you might need to find the next record that satisfies the same criterion. For example, if you just found the first client whose intern number is 24, you then may want to find the second such client, then the third, and so on. To do so, repeat the same process. You will not need to retype the value each time, however.

Changing the Contents of a Record

After locating the record to be changed, select the field to be changed by clicking the field. You also can press the TAB key repeatedly. Then make the appropriate changes. (Clicking the field automatically produces an insertion point. If you use the TAB key, you will need to press F2 to produce an insertion point.)

Normally, Access is in **Insert mode**, so the characters typed will be inserted at the appropriate position. To change to **Overtype mode**, press the INSERT key. The letters, OVR, will appear near the bottom right edge of the status bar. To return to Insert mode, press the INSERT key. In Insert mode, if the data in the field completely fills the field, no additional characters can be inserted. In this case, you would need to increase the size of the field before inserting the characters. You will see how to do this later in the project.

The following step uses Form view to change the name of client H21 to Hill's Shoes by inserting an apostrophe (') and the letter s after Hill. Sufficient room exists in the field to make this change.

Q & A

Q: Why can you not use the Next Record button to find client H21?

A: In a small table, repeatedly clicking the Next Record button until client H21 is on the screen may not be particularly difficult. In a large table with many records, however, this would be extremely cumbersome.

To Update the Contents of a Field

1

- **Click in the Name field text box for client H21 after the word Hill, and then type 's (an apostrophe and the letter s) to change the name.**

The name is changed. The mouse pointer shape is an I-beam (Figure 3-7).

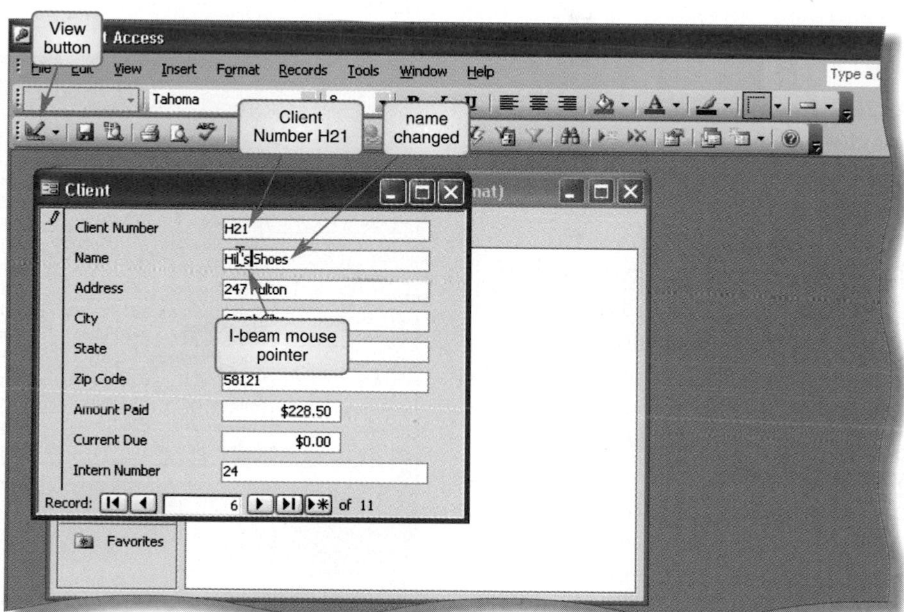

FIGURE 3-7

Once you move to another record or close this table, the change to the name will become permanent.

Q & A

Q: Do I have to use the View button arrow or could I simply click the View button?

A: You can use the View button to switch easily between viewing the form, called Form view, and viewing the design of the form, called Design view. To switch to Datasheet view, you *must* click the down arrow, and then click Datasheet view in the list that appears.

Switching Between Views

Sometimes, after working in Form view where you can see all fields, but only one record, it is helpful to see several records at a time. To do so, switch to Datasheet view. The steps on the next page switch from Form view to Datasheet view.

To Switch from Form View to Datasheet View

1

- **Click the View button arrow on the Form View toolbar.**

The View button list appears (Figure 3-8).

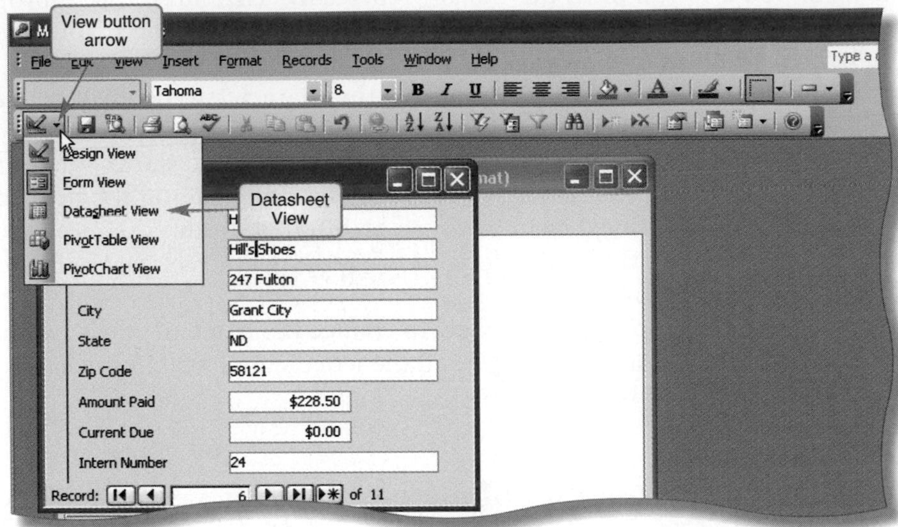

FIGURE 3-8

2

- **Click Datasheet View, and then maximize the window containing the datasheet by double-clicking its title bar.**

The datasheet appears (Figure 3-9). The position in the table is maintained. The current record selector points to client H21, the client that appeared on the screen in Form view. The Name field, the field in which the insertion point appears, is selected. The new record for client H46 currently is the last record in the table. When you close the table and open it later, client H46 will be in its appropriate location.

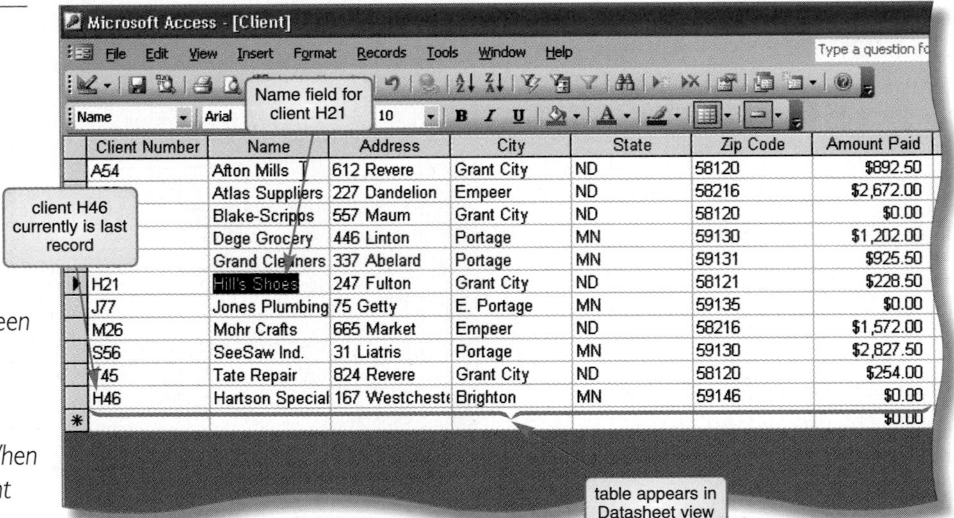

Client Number	Name	Address	City	State	Zip Code	Amount Paid
A54	Afton Mills	612 Revere	Grant City	ND	58120	$892.50
	Atlas Suppliers	227 Dandelion	Empeer	ND	58216	$2,672.00
	Blake-Scripps	557 Maum	Grant City	ND	58120	$0.00
	Dege Grocery	446 Linton	Portage	MN	59130	$1,202.00
	Grand Cleaners	337 Abelard	Portage	MN	59131	$925.50
H21	Hill's Shoes	247 Fulton	Grant City	ND	58121	$228.50
J77	Jones Plumbing	75 Getty	E. Portage	MN	59135	$0.00
M26	Mohr Crafts	665 Market	Empeer	ND	58216	$1,572.00
S56	SeeSaw Ind.	31 Liatris	Portage	MN	59130	$2,827.50
T45	Tate Repair	824 Revere	Grant City	ND	58120	$254.00
H46	Hartson Special	167 Westchest	Brighton	MN	59146	$0.00
*						$0.00

FIGURE 3-9

If you want to return to Form view, use the same process. The only difference is that you click Form View rather than Datasheet View.

Filtering Records

You can use the Find button in either Datasheet view or Form view to locate a record quickly that satisfies some criterion (for example, the client number is H21). All records appear, however, not just the record or records that satisfy the criterion. To have only the record or records that satisfy the criterion appear, use a **filter**. Three types of filters are available: Filter By Selection, Filter By Form, and Advanced Filter/Sort. You can use a filter in either Datasheet view or Form view.

Using Filter By Selection

The simplest type of filter is called **Filter By Selection.** To use Filter By Selection, you first must give Access an example of the data you want by selecting the data within the table. The following steps use Filter By Selection in Datasheet view to display only the records for clients in Empeer.

To Use Filter By Selection

1

- **Click the City field on the second record.**

The insertion point appears in the City field on the second record (Figure 3-10). The city on this record is Empeer.

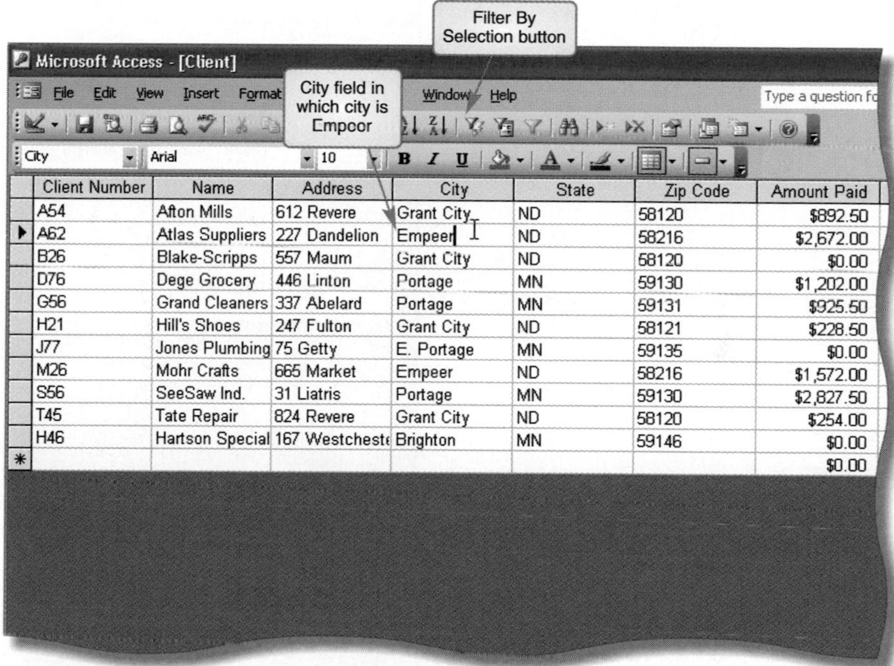

Client Number	Name	Address	City	State	Zip Code	Amount Paid
A54	Afton Mills	612 Revere	Grant City	ND	58120	$892.50
A62	Atlas Suppliers	227 Dandelion	Empeer	ND	58216	$2,672.00
B26	Blake-Scripps	557 Maum	Grant City	ND	58120	$0.00
D76	Dege Grocery	446 Linton	Portage	MN	59130	$1,202.00
G56	Grand Cleaners	337 Abelard	Portage	MN	59131	$925.50
H21	Hill's Shoes	247 Fulton	Grant City	ND	58121	$228.50
J77	Jones Plumbing	75 Getty	E. Portage	MN	59135	$0.00
M26	Mohr Crafts	665 Market	Empeer	ND	58216	$1,572.00
S56	SeeSaw Ind.	31 Liatris	Portage	MN	59130	$2,827.50
T45	Tate Repair	824 Revere	Grant City	ND	58120	$254.00
H46	Hartson Special	167 Westcheste	Brighton	MN	59146	$0.00
*						$0.00

FIGURE 3-10

2

- **Click the Filter By Selection button on the Table Datasheet toolbar (see Figure 3-10).**
- **If instructed to do so, print the results by clicking the Print button on the Table Datasheet toolbar.**

Only the clients located in Empeer appear (Figure 3-11).

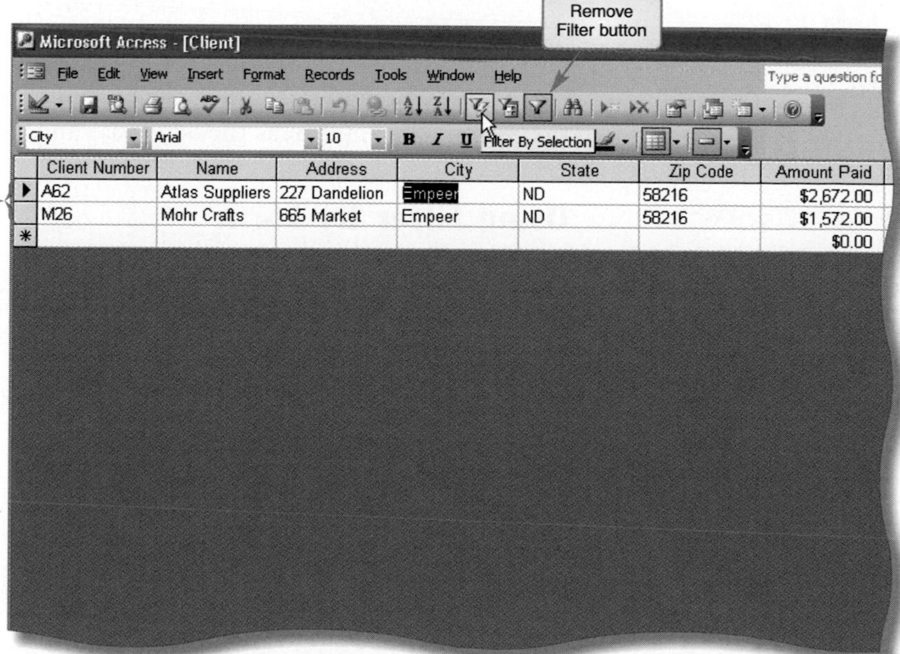

Client Number	Name	Address	City	State	Zip Code	Amount Paid
A62	Atlas Suppliers	227 Dandelion	Empeer	ND	58216	$2,672.00
M26	Mohr Crafts	665 Market	Empeer	ND	58216	$1,572.00
*						$0.00

FIGURE 3-11

To redisplay all the records, remove the filter as shown in the following step.

To Remove a Filter

1

- **Click the Remove Filter button on the Table Datasheet toolbar (see Figure 3-11 on the previous page).**

All records appear (Figure 3-12).

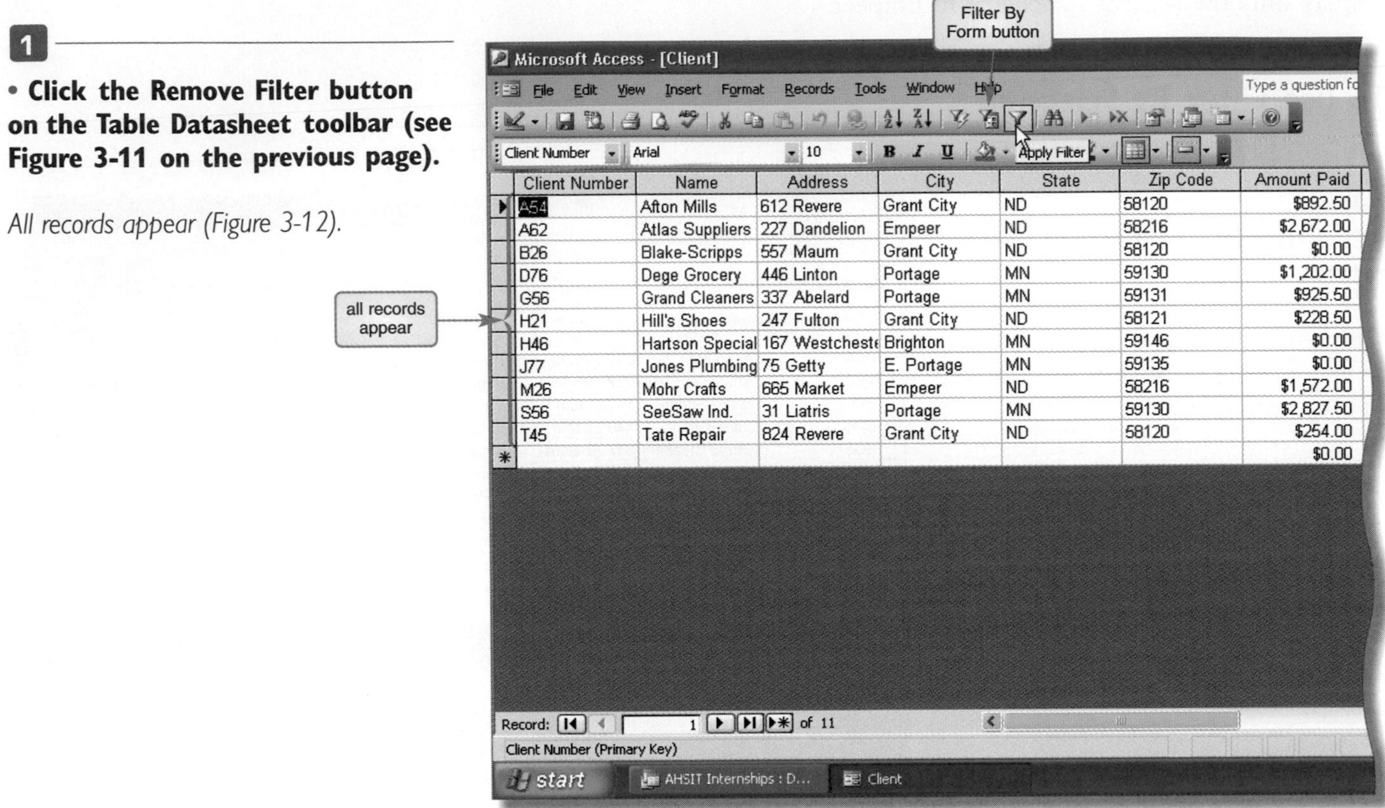

Client Number	Name	Address	City	State	Zip Code	Amount Paid
A54	Afton Mills	612 Revere	Grant City	ND	58120	$892.50
A62	Atlas Suppliers	227 Dandelion	Empeer	ND	58216	$2,672.00
B26	Blake-Scripps	557 Maum	Grant City	ND	58120	$0.00
D76	Dege Grocery	446 Linton	Portage	MN	59130	$1,202.00
G56	Grand Cleaners	337 Abelard	Portage	MN	59131	$925.50
H21	Hill's Shoes	247 Fulton	Grant City	ND	58121	$228.50
H46	Hartson Special	167 Westcheste	Brighton	MN	59146	$0.00
J77	Jones Plumbing	75 Getty	E. Portage	MN	59135	$0.00
M26	Mohr Crafts	665 Market	Empeer	ND	58216	$1,572.00
S56	SeeSaw Ind.	31 Liatris	Portage	MN	59130	$2,827.50
T45	Tate Repair	824 Revere	Grant City	ND	58120	$254.00
						$0.00

FIGURE 3-12

After you remove the filter, the button changes from the Remove Filter button to the Apply Filter button as the ScreenTip indicates.

Using Filter By Form

Filter By Selection is a quick and easy way to filter by the value in a single field. For more complex criteria, however, it is not appropriate. For example, you could not use Filter By Selection to restrict the records to those for which the city is Grant City and the intern number is 22. For this type of query, in which you want to specify multiple criteria, you can use **Filter By Form.** The following steps illustrate using this filtering method in Datasheet view.

To Use Filter By Form

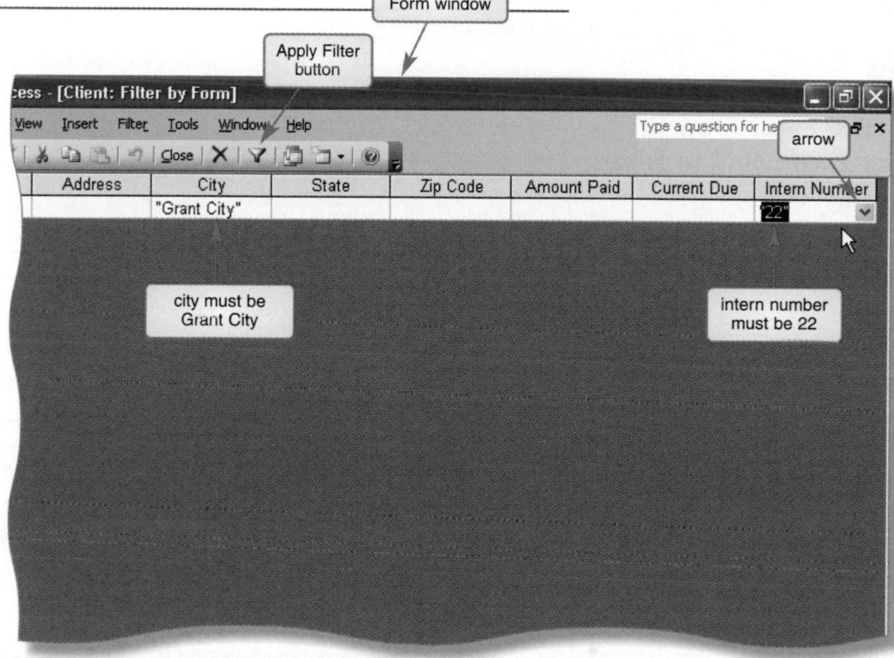

FIGURE 3-13

1

- **Click the Filter By Form button on the Table Datasheet toolbar (see Figure 3-12).**
- **Click the City field (Empeer may appear in the field), click the arrow that appears, and then click Grant City.**
- **Click the right scroll arrow so the Intern Number field is on the screen, click the Intern Number field, click the down arrow that appears, and then click 22.**

The form for filtering appears (Figure 3-13). Grant City is selected as the city, and 22 is selected as the intern number.

2

- **Click the Apply Filter button on the Filter/Sort toolbar.**
- **If instructed to do so, print the results by clicking the Print button on the Table Datasheet toolbar.**

The only record included is the record on which the city is Grant City and the intern number is 22 (Figure 3-14).

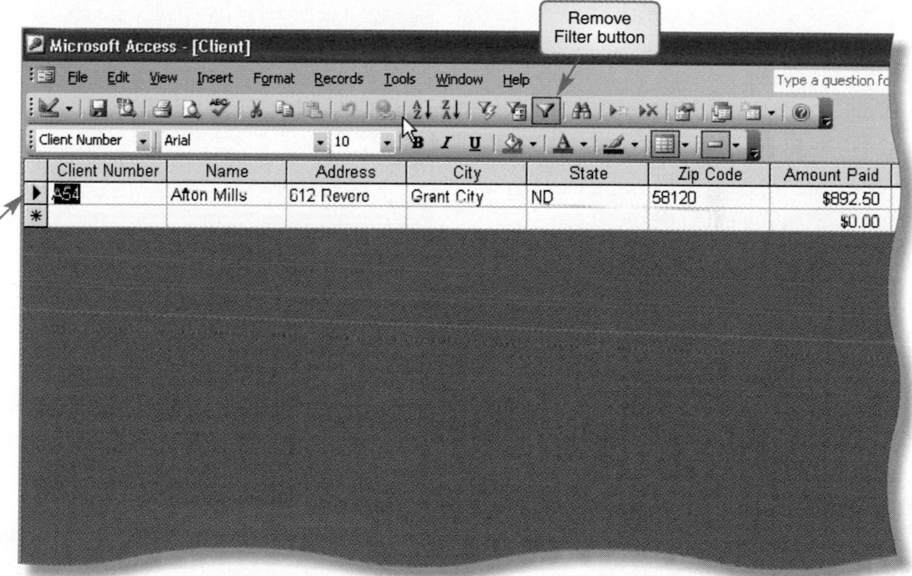

FIGURE 3-14

3

- **Click the Remove Filter button on the Table Datasheet toolbar.**

All records are shown.

Using Advanced Filter/Sort

In some cases, your criteria may be too complex even for Filter By Form. For example, you might want to include any client for which the city is Grant City and the intern is number 22. You also may want to include any client of intern 24, no matter where the client is located. Further, you might want to have the results sorted by name. To filter records using complex criteria, you need to use **Advanced Filter/Sort** as illustrated in the steps on the next page.

Skill Builder 3-1

To practice the following tasks, visit scsite.com/off2003sch/skill, locate Access Project 3, and then click Skill Builder 3-1.

- ❑ Filter records using Filter By Selection
- ❑ Remove the filter
- ❑ Filter records using Filter By Form
- ❑ Remove the filter

To Use Advanced Filter/Sort

1

• **Click Records on the menu bar, and then point to Filter.**

The Filter submenu appears (Figure 3-15).

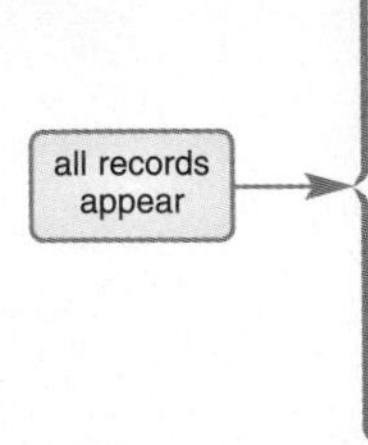

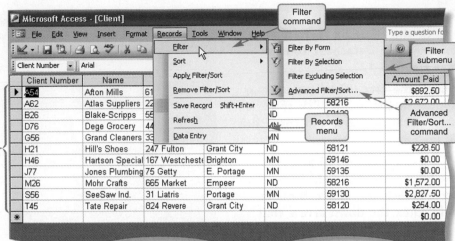

FIGURE 3-15

2

• **Click Advanced Filter/Sort.**

Access displays the ClientFilter1 : Filter window (Figure 3-16). The screen looks just like the screens you used to create queries. The city and intern number criteria from the previous filter appear. If you were creating a different filter, you could delete these.

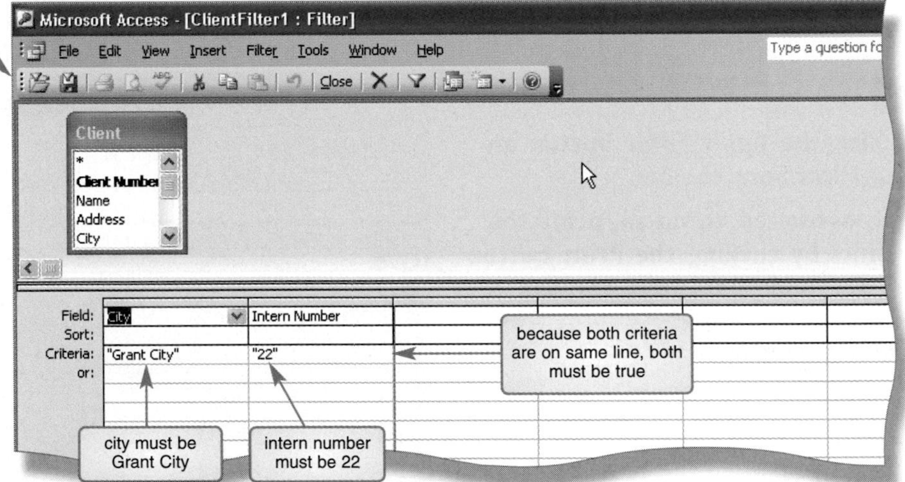

FIGURE 3-16

3

• **Type** 24 **as the criterion in the second Criteria row (the or row) of the Intern Number column, double-click the Name field to add the field to the filter, click the Sort row for the Name column, click the arrow that appears, and then click Ascending.**

The additional criteria for the Intern Number field are entered (Figure 3-17). The data will be sorted on Name in ascending order.

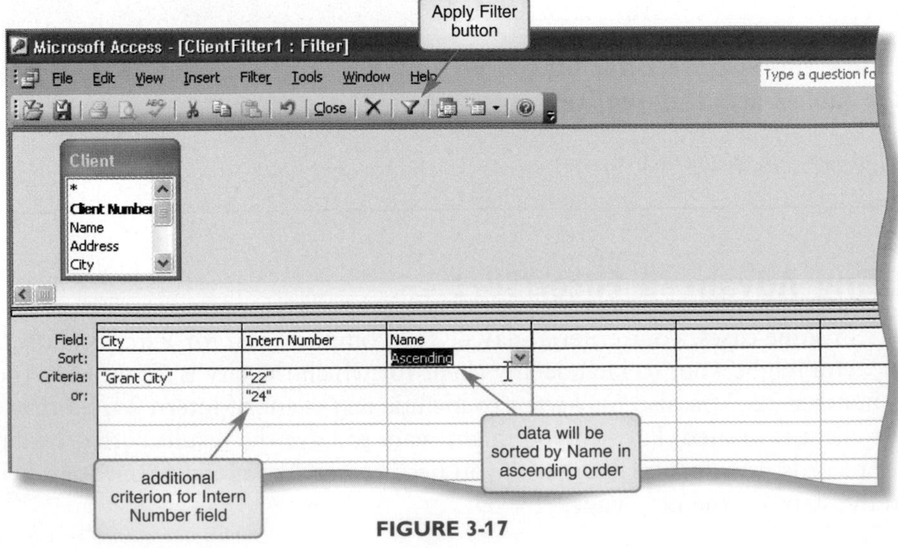

FIGURE 3-17

4

• **Click the Apply Filter button on the Filter/Sort toolbar.**

• **If instructed to do so, print the results by clicking the Print button on the Table Datasheet toolbar.**

The filtered data appears (Figure 3-18). Only the clients who satisfy the criteria in the filter are included. The clients are ordered by name.

5

• **Click the Remove Filter button on the Table Datasheet toolbar.**

All records are shown.

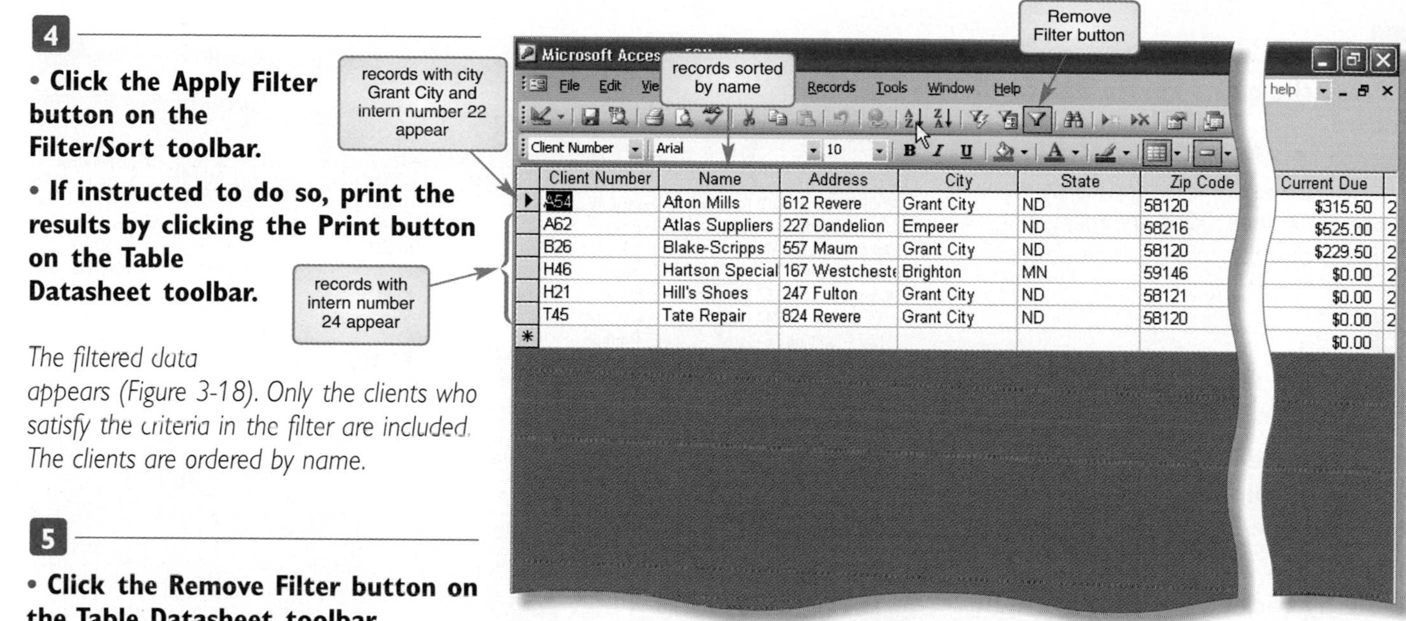

FIGURE 3-18

Deleting Records

When records no longer are needed, **delete the records** (remove them) from the table. For example, suppose client D76 no longer participates in the internship program at Alyssa High School and its final payment is made. The record for that client should be deleted. The following steps delete client D76.

Q & A

Q: Can you filter records that have been retrieved as the result of a query?

A: Yes. You can use Filter By Selection, Filter By Form, and Advanced Filter/Sort in the Query Datasheet window just as you did in the Table Datasheet window. You also can use the command in Form view.

To Delete a Record

1

• **With the datasheet for the Client table on the screen, click the record selector of the record in which the client number is D76.**

The record is selected (Figure 3-19).

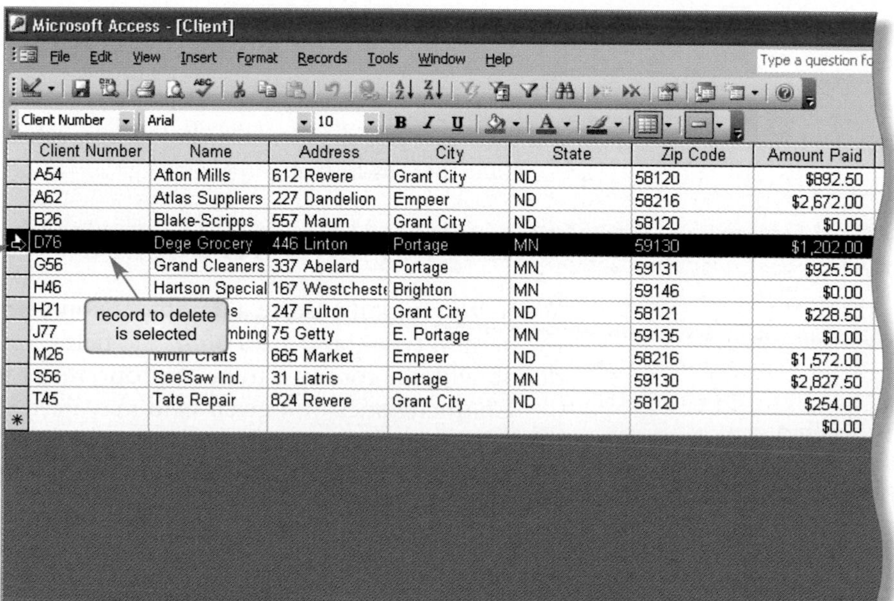

FIGURE 3-19

2

• **Press the DELETE key to delete the record.**

Access displays the Microsoft Office Access dialog box (Figure 3-20). The message indicates that one record will be deleted.

3

• **Click the Yes button to complete the deletion.**

• **If instructed to do so, print the results by clicking the Print button on the Table Datasheet toolbar.**

• **Close the window containing the table by clicking its Close Window button.**

The record is deleted and the table no longer appears.

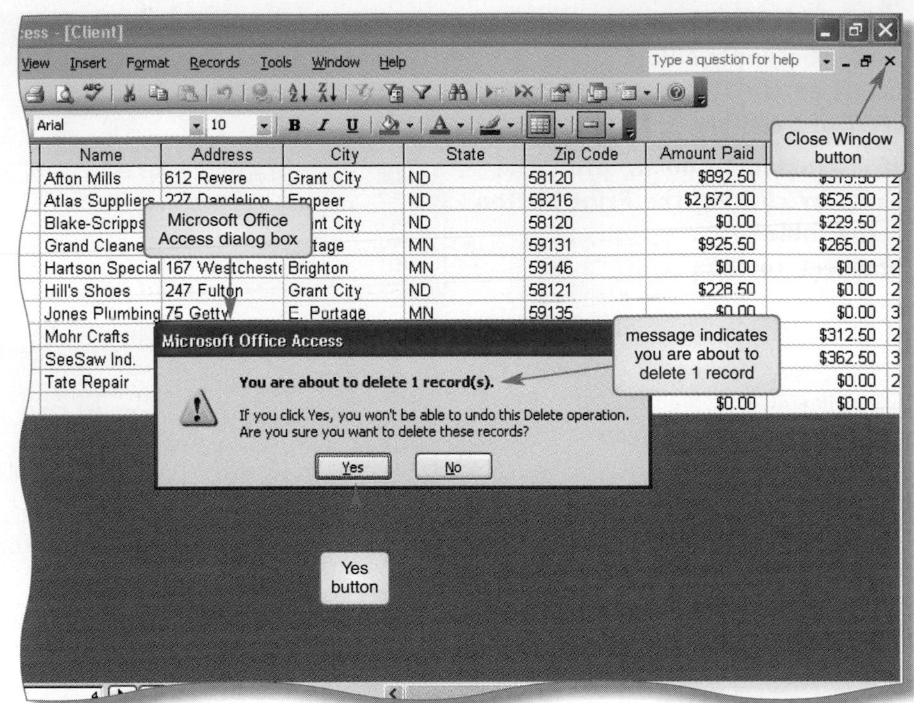

FIGURE 3-20

You can delete records using a form just as you delete records using a datasheet. To do so, first navigate to the record to be deleted. For example, you can use the Navigation buttons or you can locate the desired record using the Find button. The following steps illustrate how to delete a record in Form view after you have located the record to be deleted.

To Delete a Record in Form View

1. Click the Record Selector (the triangle in front of the record) to select the entire record.
2. Press the DELETE key.
3. When Access displays the dialog box asking if you want to delete the record, click the Yes button.

Changing the Structure

When you initially create a database, you define its **structure**; that is, you indicate the names, types, and sizes of all the fields. In many cases, the structure you first define will not continue to be appropriate as you use the database.

Characteristics of a given field may need to change. For example, a client name might be stored incorrectly in the database. In this example, the name of client H46 should be Hartson Specialty Shops. The Name field is not large enough, however, to hold the correct name. To accommodate this change, you need to restructure the database by increasing the width of the Name field.

It may be that a field currently in the table no longer is necessary. If no one ever uses a particular field, it is not needed in the table. Because it is occupying space and serving no useful purpose, it should be removed from the table. You also would need to delete the field from any forms, reports, or queries that include it.

To make any of these changes, you first must open the table in Design view.

Changing the Size of a Field

The following steps change the size of the Name field from 20 to 25 to accommodate the change of name for client H46 to Hartson Specialty Shops.

To Change the Size of a Field

1

• In the Database window, click Tables on the Objects bar, and then right-click Client.

The shortcut menu for the Client table appears (Figure 3-21).

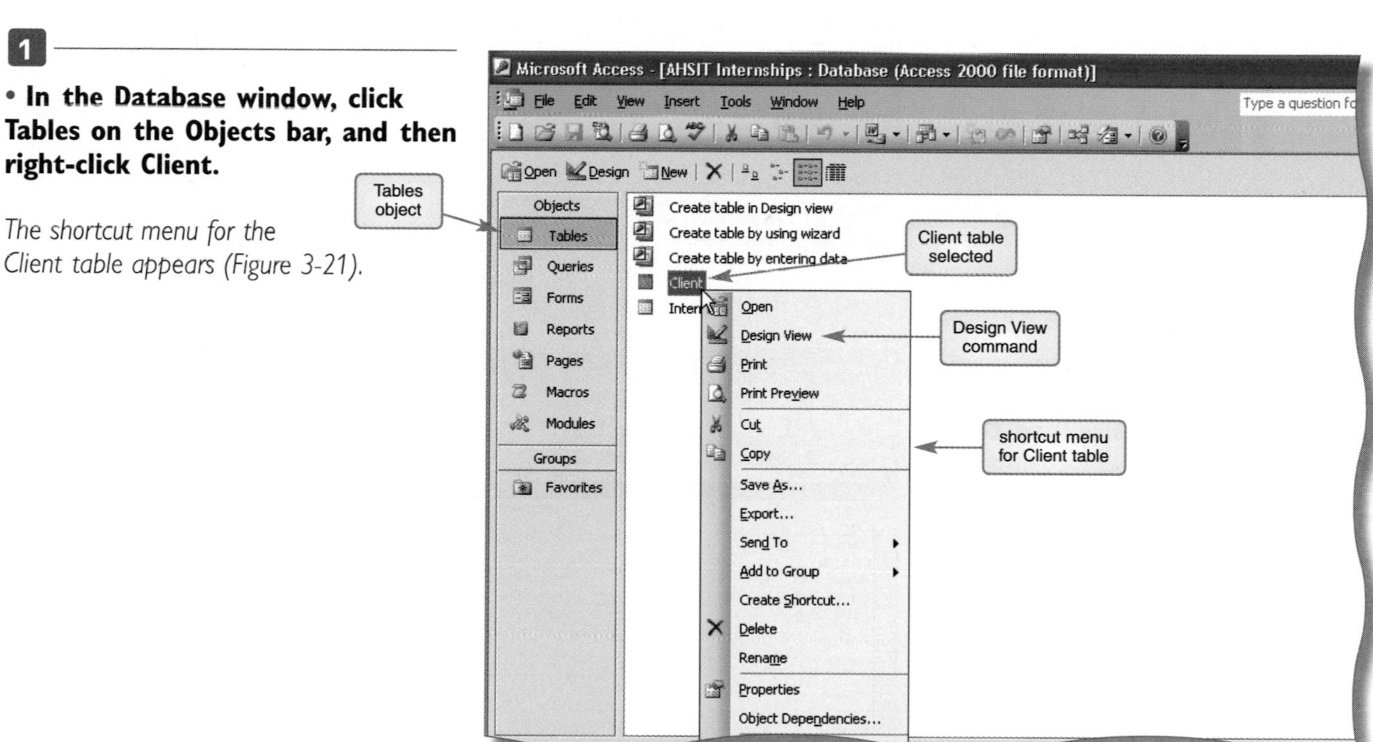

FIGURE 3-21

2

• Click Design View on the shortcut menu.

Access displays the Client : Table window (Figure 3-22).

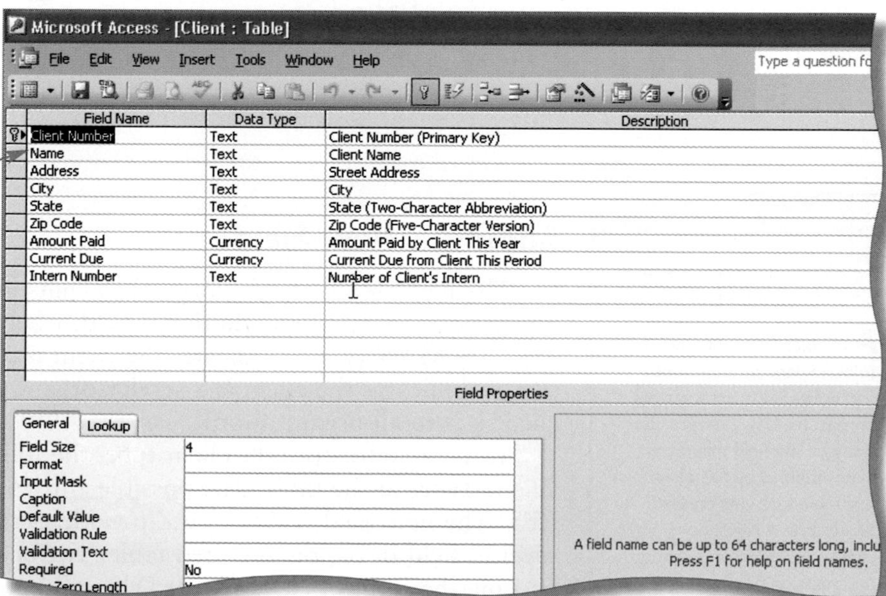

FIGURE 3-22

3

• **Click the row selector for the Name field.**

The Name field is selected (Figure 3-23).

Name field selected

current field size will be changed to 25

FIGURE 3-23

4

• **Press F6 to select the field size, type** 25 **as the new size, and then press F6 again.**

The field size is changed (Figure 3-24).

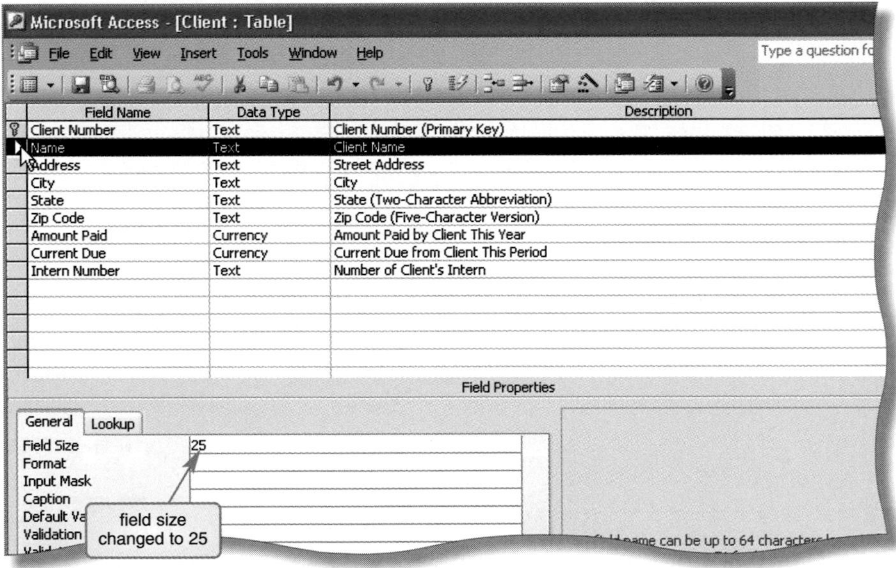

FIGURE 3-24

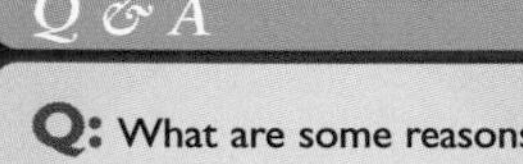

Q: What are some reasons for adding a field to a table?

A: Tables frequently need to be expanded to include additional fields for a variety of reasons. Users' needs can change. The field may have been omitted by mistake when the table first was created. Government regulations may change in such a way that an organization needs to maintain additional information.

Adding a New Field

The next step is to categorize the clients in the AHSIT Internships database. To do so, you must add an additional field, Client Type. The possible values for Client Type are MAN (which indicates the client is a manufacturing organization), or SER (which indicates the client is a service organization), or RET (which indicates the client is a retail organization).

To be able to store the client type, the following steps add a new field, called Client Type, to the table. The possible entries in this field are MAN, SER, and RET. The new field will follow Zip Code in the list of fields; that is, it will be the seventh field in the restructured table. The current seventh field (Amount Paid) will become the eighth field, Current Due will become the ninth field, and so on. The following steps add the field.

To Add a Field to a Table

1

• **Click the row selector for the Amount Paid field, and then press the INSERT key to insert a blank row.**

A blank row appears in the position for the new field (Figure 3-25).

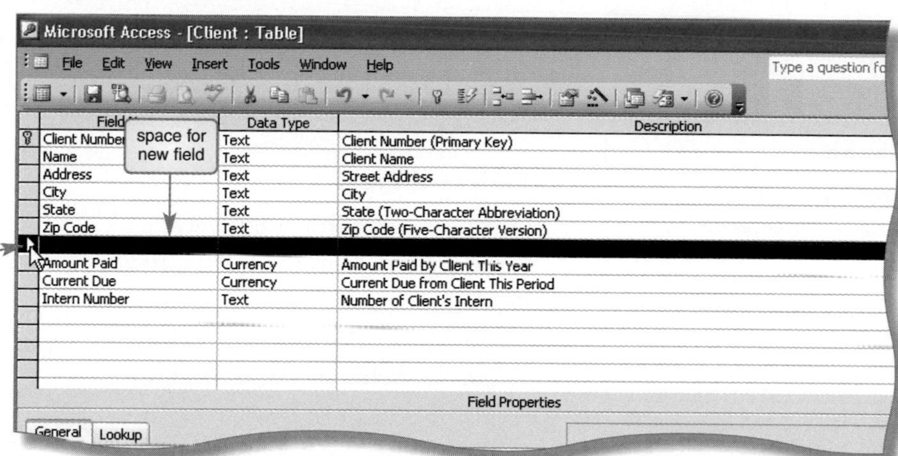

FIGURE 3-25

2

• **Click the Field Name column for the new field.**

• **Type** `Client Type` **as the field name and then press the TAB key. Select the Text data type by pressing the TAB key.**

• **Type** `Client Type (MAN - Manufacturing, SER - Service, RET - Retail)` **as the description.**

• **Press F6 to move to the Field Size text box, type** 3 **(the size of the Client Type field), and then press F6 again.**

The entries for the new field are complete (Figure 3-26).

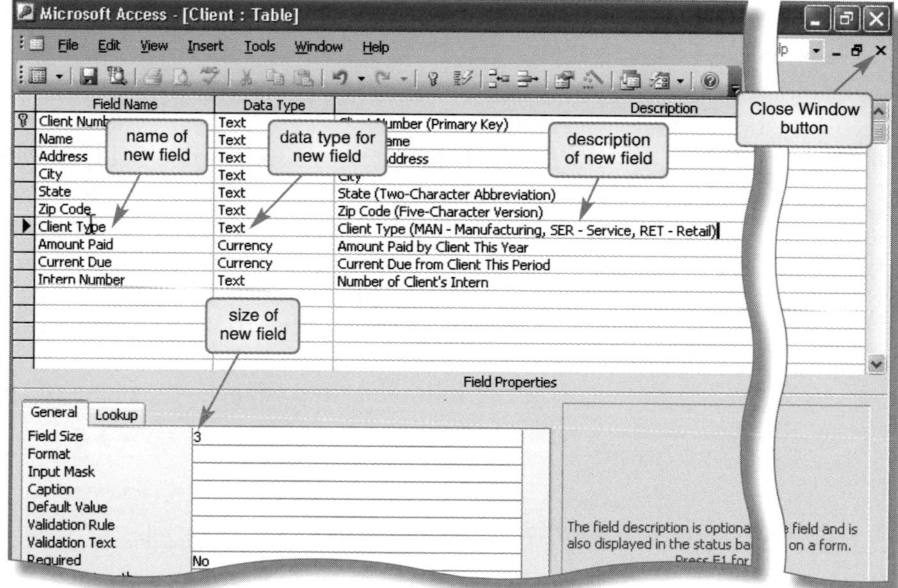

FIGURE 3-26

3

• **Close the Client : Table window by clicking its Close Window button.**

The Microsoft Office Access dialog box is displayed (Figure 3-27).

4

Click the Yes button to save the changes.

The changes are saved.

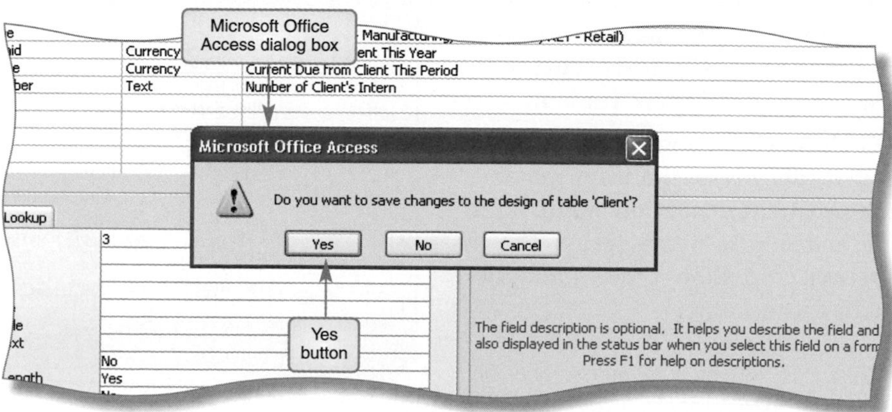

FIGURE 3-27

The Client Type field now is included in the table and available for use.

Q & A

Q: What if I find that I have a field at the wrong position in the table structure? Can I move it?

A: If you add a field to a table and later realize the field is in the wrong location, you can move the field. To do so, click the row selector for the field twice, and then drag the field to the new location.

Deleting a Field

If a field in one of your tables no longer is needed — for example, it serves no useful purpose or it may have been included by mistake — you should delete the field. The following steps illustrate how to delete a field.

To Delete a Field

1. Open the table in Design view.
2. Click the row selector for the field to be deleted.
3. Press the DELETE key.
4. When Access displays the dialog box requesting confirmation that you want to delete the field, click the Yes button.

When you save your changes to the table structure, the field will be removed from the table.

Q & A

Q: Can I change the data type for a field that already is in the table?

A: It is possible to change the data type for a field that already contains data. Before you change a data type, however, you should consider what effect the change will have on other database objects, such as forms, queries, and reports. For example, you could convert a Text field to a Memo field or to a Hyperlink field. You also could convert a Number field to a Currency field or vice versa.

Updating the Restructured Database

Changes to the structure are available immediately. The Name field is longer, although it does not appear that way on the screen, and the new Client Type field is included.

To make a change to a single field, such as changing the name of client H46 to Hartson Specialty Shops, click the field to be changed, and then make the necessary correction. If the record to be changed is not on the screen, use the Navigation buttons (Next Record, Previous Record) to move to it. If the field to be corrected simply is not visible on the screen, use the horizontal scroll bar along the bottom of the screen to shift all the fields until the correct one appears. Then make the change.

The following step changes the name of client H46 to Hartson Specialty Shops.

To Update the Contents of a Field

1

- **Be sure the Client table is selected in the Database window, and then click the Open button on the Database window toolbar.**
- **Click in the name of client H46, repeatedly press the RIGHT ARROW key until the insertion point is at the end of the name, press the SPACEBAR, and then type** Shops **to change the name.**

The name is changed from Hartson Specialty to Hartson Specialty Shops (Figure 3-28). Only the final portion of the name currently appears.

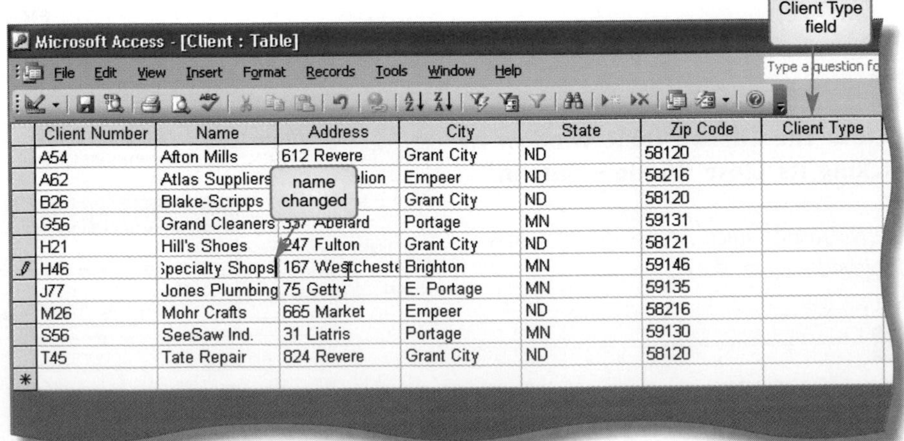

FIGURE 3-28

Changing the Appearance of a Datasheet

You can change the appearance of a datasheet in a variety of ways. You can resize columns and rows. You can change the font, the font size, the font style, and the color. You also can change the color of the gridlines in the datasheet as well as the cell effects.

> *Q & A*
>
> **Q:** Why would you need to change a data type?
>
> **A:** You may need to change a data type because you imported data from another tool and Access imported the data type incorrectly. Also, you may find that a data type no longer is appropriate for a field. For example, a Text field can contain a maximum of 255 characters. If the data stored in a Text field exceeds 255 characters, you could change the data type to Memo.

Resizing Columns

The Access default column sizes do not always allow all the data in the field to appear. You can correct this problem by **resizing** the column (changing its size) in the datasheet. In some instances, you actually may want to reduce the size of a column. The State field, for example, is short enough that it does not require all the space on the screen that is allotted to it.

Both types of changes are made the same way. Position the mouse pointer on the right boundary of the column's **field selector** (the line in the column heading immediately to the right of the name of the column to be resized). The mouse pointer will change to a two-headed arrow with a vertical bar. You then can drag the line to resize the column. In addition, you can double-click in the line, in which case Access will determine the **best fit** for the column.

The following steps illustrate the process for resizing the Name column to the size that best fits the data.

To Resize a Column

1

- **Point to the right boundary of the field selector for the Name field.**

The mouse pointer shape changes to a bar with a double-arrow, indicating that the column can be resized (Figure 3-29).

field selector for Name field

right boundary of field selector

mouse pointer shape indicates column can be resized

Client Number	Name	Address	City	State	Zip Code	Client Type
A54	Afton Mills	612 Revere	Grant City	ND	58120	
A62	Atlas Suppliers	227 Dandelion	Empeer	ND	58216	
B26	Blake-Scripps	557 Maum	Grant City	ND	58120	
G56	Grand Cleaners	337 Abelard	Portage	MN	59131	
H21	Hill's Shoes	247 Fulton	Grant City	ND	58121	
H46	;pecialty Shops	167 Westchest	Brighton	MN	59146	
J77	Jones Plumbing	75 Getty	E. Portage	MN	59135	
M26	Mohr Crafts	665 Market	Empeer	ND	58216	
S56	SeeSaw Ind.	31 Liatris	Portage	MN	59130	
T45	Tate Repair	824 Revere	Grant City	ND	58120	

FIGURE 3-29

2

- **Double-click the right boundary of the field selector for the Name field.**

The Name column has been resized (Figure 3-30).

FIGURE 3-30

3

• Use the same technique to resize the Client Number, Address, City, State, Zip Code, Client Type, and Amount Paid columns to best fit the data.

The columns have been resized (Figure 3-31).

Name	Address	City	State	Zip Code	Client Type	Amount Paid	Current Du
Afton Mills	612 Revere	Grant City	ND	58120		$892.50	$315.
Atlas Suppliers	227 Dandelion	Empeer	ND	58216		$2,672.00	$525.
Blake-Scripps	557 Maum	Grant City	ND	58120		$0.00	$229.
Grand Cleaners	337 Abelard	Portage	MN	59131		$925.50	$265.
Hill's Shoes	247 Fulton	Grant City	ND	58121		$228.50	$0.
Hartson Specialty Shops	167 Westchester	Brighton	MN	59146		$0.00	$0.
Jones Plumbing	75 Getty	E. Portage	MN	59135		$0.00	$0.
Mohr Crafts	665 Market	Empeer	ND	58216		$1,572.00	$312.
SeeSaw Ind.	31 Liatris	Portage	MN	59130		$2,827.50	$362.
Tate Repair	824 Revere	Grant City	ND	58120		$254.00	$0.
						$0.0	

FIGURE 3-31

4

• If necessary, click the right scroll arrow to display the Current Due and Intern Number columns, and then resize the columns to best fit the data.

All the columns have been resized (Figure 3-32).

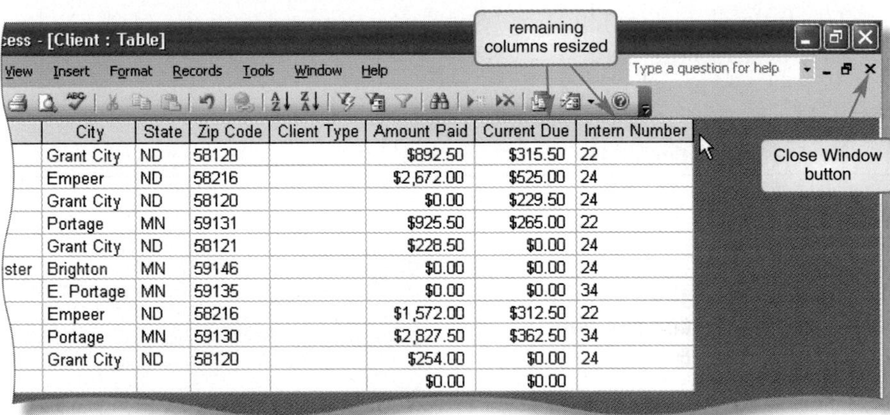

	City	State	Zip Code	Client Type	Amount Paid	Current Due	Intern Number
	Grant City	ND	58120		$892.50	$315.50	22
	Empeer	ND	58216		$2,672.00	$525.00	24
	Grant City	ND	58120		$0.00	$229.50	24
	Portage	MN	59131		$925.50	$265.00	22
	Grant City	ND	58121		$228.50	$0.00	24
ster	Brighton	MN	59146		$0.00	$0.00	24
	E. Portage	MN	59135		$0.00	$0.00	34
	Empeer	ND	58216		$1,572.00	$312.50	22
	Portage	MN	59130		$2,827.50	$362.50	34
	Grant City	ND	58120		$254.00	$0.00	24
					$0.00	$0.00	

FIGURE 3-32

5

• Close the Client : Table window by clicking its Close Window button.

The Microsoft Office Access dialog box is displayed (Figure 3-33). Changing a column width changes the layout, or design, of a table.

6

• Click the Yes button.

The next time the datasheet is displayed, the columns will have the new widths.

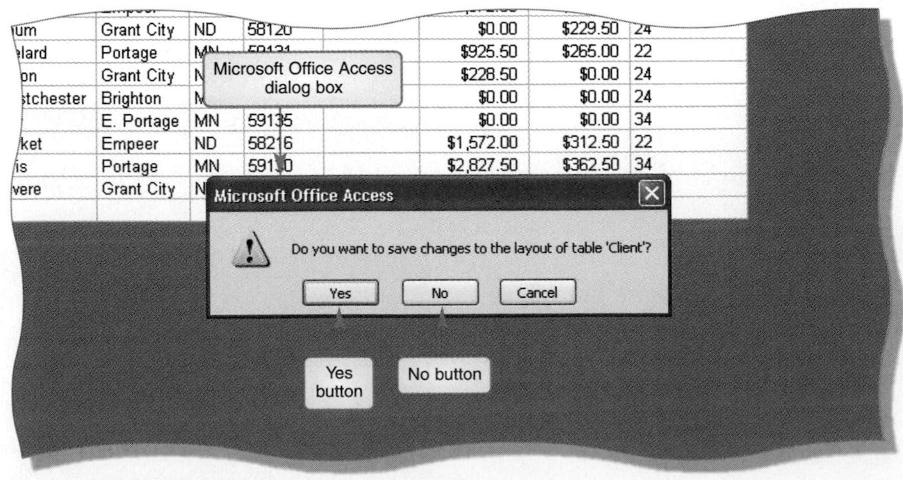

FIGURE 3-33

The change to the layout is saved.

Formatting a Datasheet

In addition to changing the column size, you can format a datasheet in other ways. You can change various aspects of the font, including the font itself, the font style, the size, and the color. You can change the cell effects to make the cells appear raised or sunken, and you can change the gridline color.

The changes to the datasheet will be reflected not only on the screen, but also when you print or preview the datasheet.

In this section, the following steps illustrate how to change the font in the datasheet and the format of the datasheet grid. You then will preview what the datasheet would look like when it is printed. At this point, you can print the datasheet if you so desire. Finally, you will close the datasheet without saving the changes. That way, the next time you view the datasheet, it will appear in its original format.

These steps show how to open the Intern table in Datasheet view and then change the font.

Skill Builder 3-2

To practice the following tasks, visit scsite.com/off2003sch/skill, locate Access Project 3, and then click Skill Builder 3-2.

- ❑ Open a table in Design view
- ❑ Change the size of a field
- ❑ Add a field

To Change the Font in a Datasheet

1

- **With the Tables object selected and the Intern table selected, click the Open button on the Database Window toolbar.**
- **Click Format on the menu bar.**

Access displays the Intern table in Datasheet view (Figure 3-34). The Format menu appears.

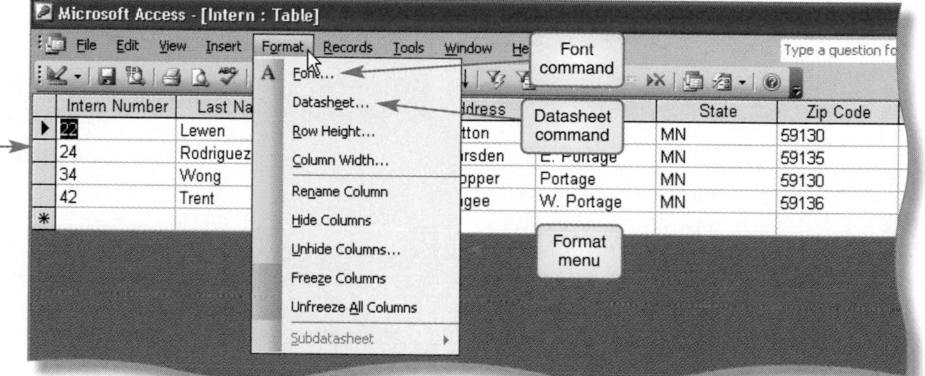

FIGURE 3-34

2

- **Click Font, click Arial Rounded MT Bold in the Font list, scroll to 9 in the Size list and then click 9 in the Size list. (If you do not have Arial Rounded MT Bold available, click another similar font.)**

Access displays the Font dialog box (Figure 3-35). Arial Rounded MT Bold is selected as the font style and 9 is selected as the font size.

3

- **Click the OK button.**

The font is changed.

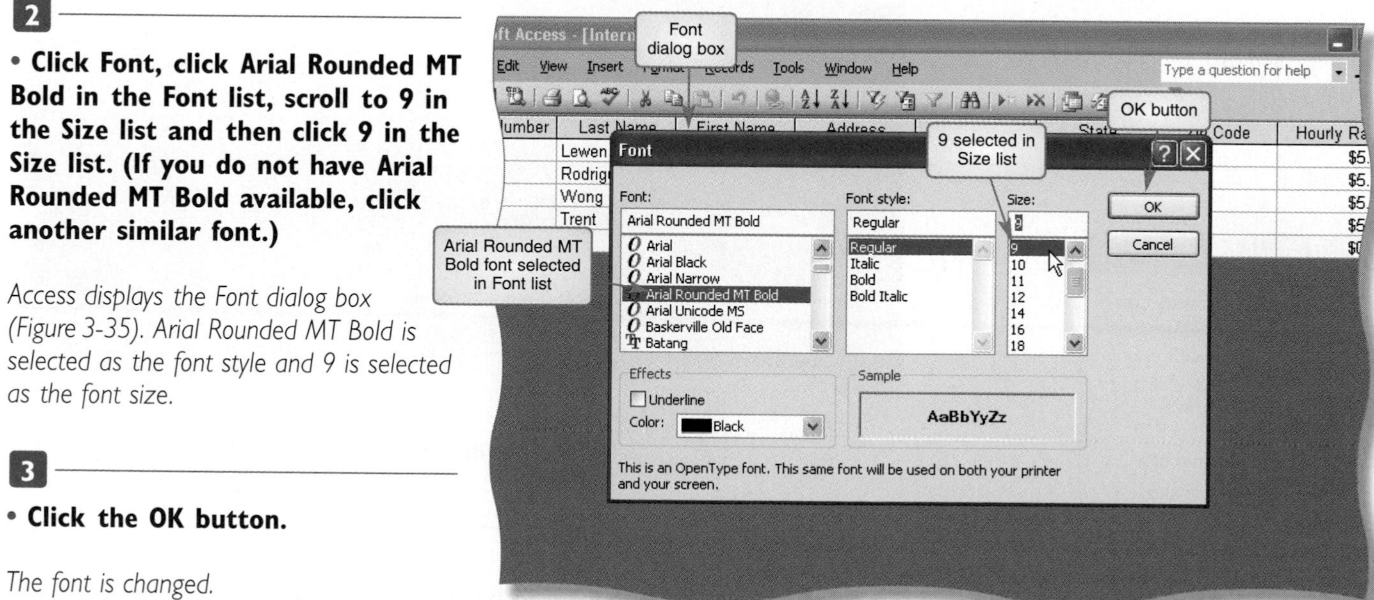

FIGURE 3-35

The following steps change the format of the grid.

To Change the Format of the Datasheet Grid

1

• **Click Format on the menu bar, and then click Datasheet.**

Access displays the Datasheet Formatting dialog box (Figure 3-36).

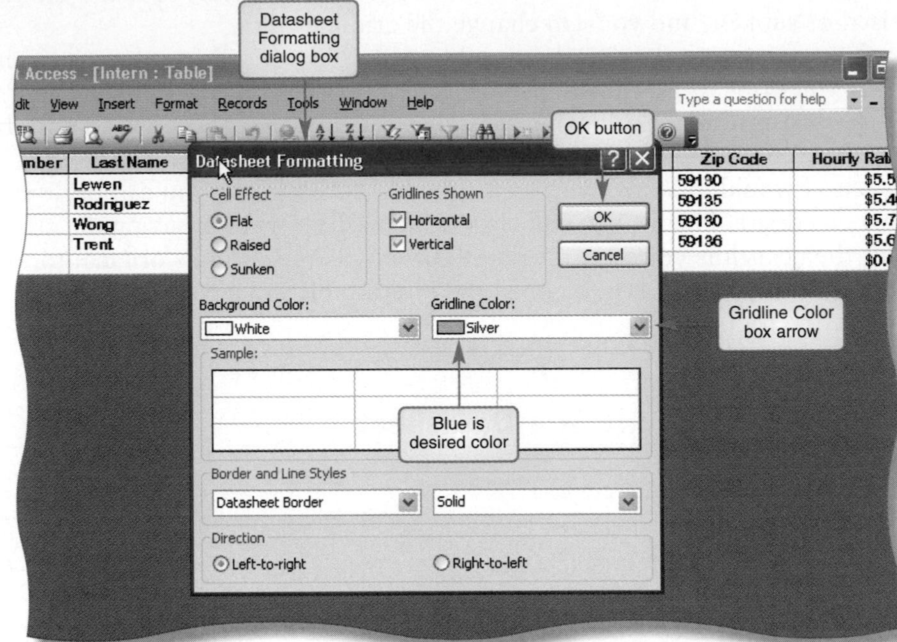

FIGURE 3-36

2

• **Click the Gridline Color box arrow, click Blue, and then click the OK button.**

• **Resize the columns to best fit the data.**

The gridline color is changed to blue and the columns have been resized (Figure 3-37).

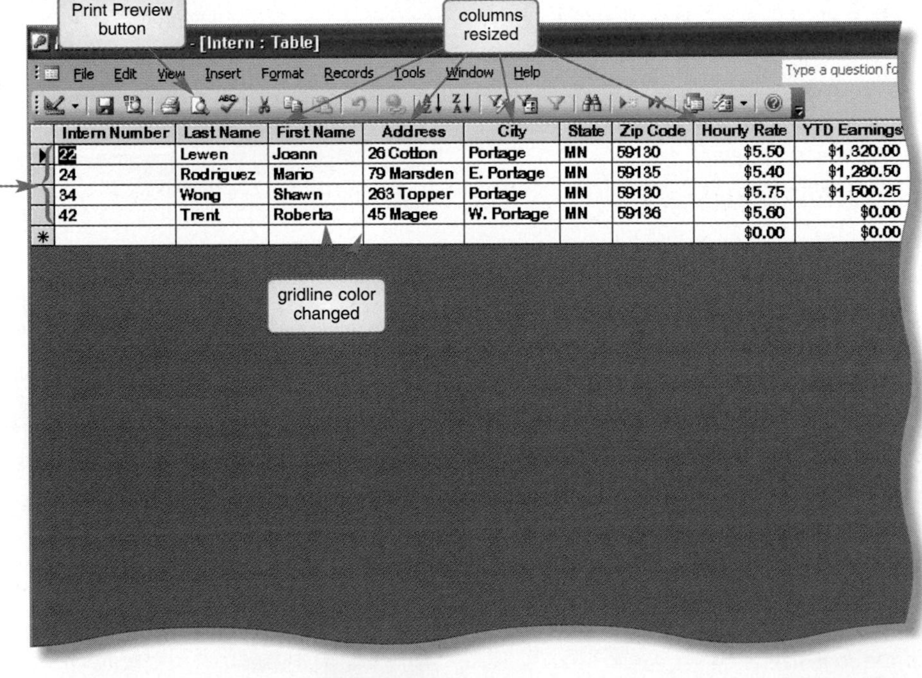

FIGURE 3-37

Skill Builder 3-3

To practice the following tasks, visit scsite.com/off2003sch/skill, locate Access Project 3, and then click Skill Builder 3-3.

- ❑ Change the font in a datasheet
- ❑ Change the format of a datasheet
- ❑ Resize the columns in a datasheet to best fit the data

The following steps use Print Preview to preview the changes to the datasheet.

To Use Print Preview

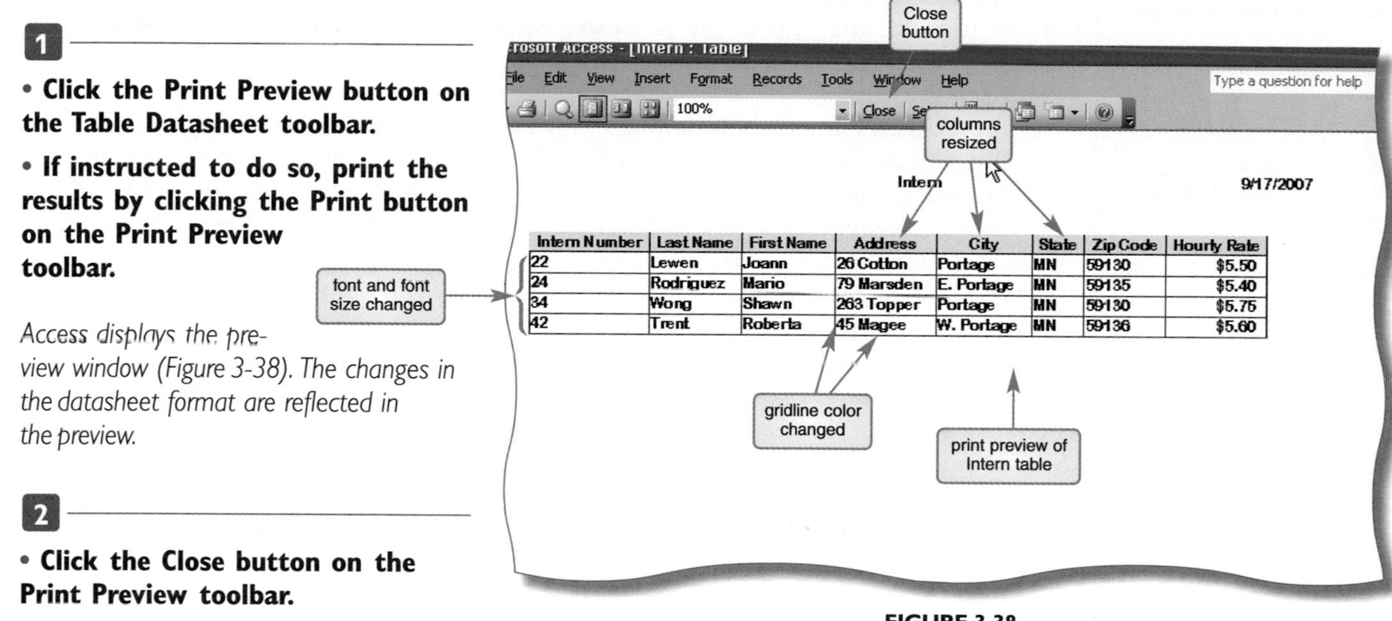

1

- **Click the Print Preview button on the Table Datasheet toolbar.**
- **If instructed to do so, print the results by clicking the Print button on the Print Preview toolbar.**

Access displays the preview window (Figure 3-38). The changes in the datasheet format are reflected in the preview.

2

- **Click the Close button on the Print Preview toolbar.**

The preview no longer appears.

FIGURE 3-38

To print the datasheet, click the Print button on either the Table Datasheet toolbar or the Print Preview toolbar. The changes to the format are reflected in the printout.

The following steps show how to close the datasheet without saving the changes to the format.

To Close the Datasheet Without Saving the Format Changes

1. **Click the Close Window button for the Intern : Table window.**
2. **Click the No button in the Microsoft Office Access dialog box when asked if you want to save your changes.**

Because the changes are not saved, the next time you open the Intern table it will appear in the original format (see Figure 3-34 on page AC 133). If you had saved the changes, the changes would be reflected in its appearance.

> *Q & A*
>
> **Q:** Can you format query results?
>
> **A:** Yes. You can format the results of a query in Query Datasheet view just as you can in Table Datasheet view. You can resize columns, change various aspects of the font, change cell effects, and change gridline colors.

Mass Changes

In some cases, rather than making individual changes, you will want to make mass changes. That is, you will want to add, change, or delete many records in a single operation. You can do this with queries. An update query allows you to make the same change to all records satisfying some criterion. If you omit the criterion, you will make the same changes to all records in the table. A delete query allows you to delete all the records satisfying some criterion. You can add the results of a query to an existing table by using an append query. You also can add the results to a new table by using a make-table query.

Q & A

Q: When I change the size of a field in my table structure, will the form I created earlier automatically reflect the new size?

A: After you have changed the size of a field, the forms you have created will not reflect your changes. If you used the AutoForm command, you can change the field sizes simply by recreating the form. To do so, right-click the form, click Delete on the shortcut menu, and then create the form as you did in Project 1.

Using an Update Query

The Client Type field is blank on every record. One approach to entering the information for the field would be to step through the entire table, assigning each record its appropriate value. If most of the clients have the same type, a simpler approach is available.

In the AHSIT Internships database, for example, most clients are type RET. Initially, you can set all the values to RET. To accomplish this quickly and easily, you can use an **update query**, which is a query that makes the same change to all the records satisfying a criterion. Later, you can change the type for service organizations and manufacturing organizations.

The process for creating an update query begins the same as the process for creating the queries in Project 2. You select the table for the query and then use the Query Type button to change to an update query. In the design grid, an extra row, Update To, appears. Use this additional row to indicate the way the data will be updated. If a criterion is entered, then only those records that satisfy the criterion will be updated.

The following steps change the value in the Client Type field to RET for all the records. Because all records are to be updated, criteria are not required.

To Use an Update Query to Update All Records

1

- **With the Client table selected, click the New Object button arrow on the Database toolbar and then click Query. With Design View selected in the New Query dialog box, click the OK button.**
- **Be sure the Query1 : Select Query window is maximized.**
- **Resize the upper and lower panes of the window as well as the Client field list so all fields in the Client table field list appear (see Figure 2-6 on page AC 70 in Project 2).**
- **Click the Query Type button arrow on the Query Design toolbar.**

The list of available query types appears (Figure 3-39).

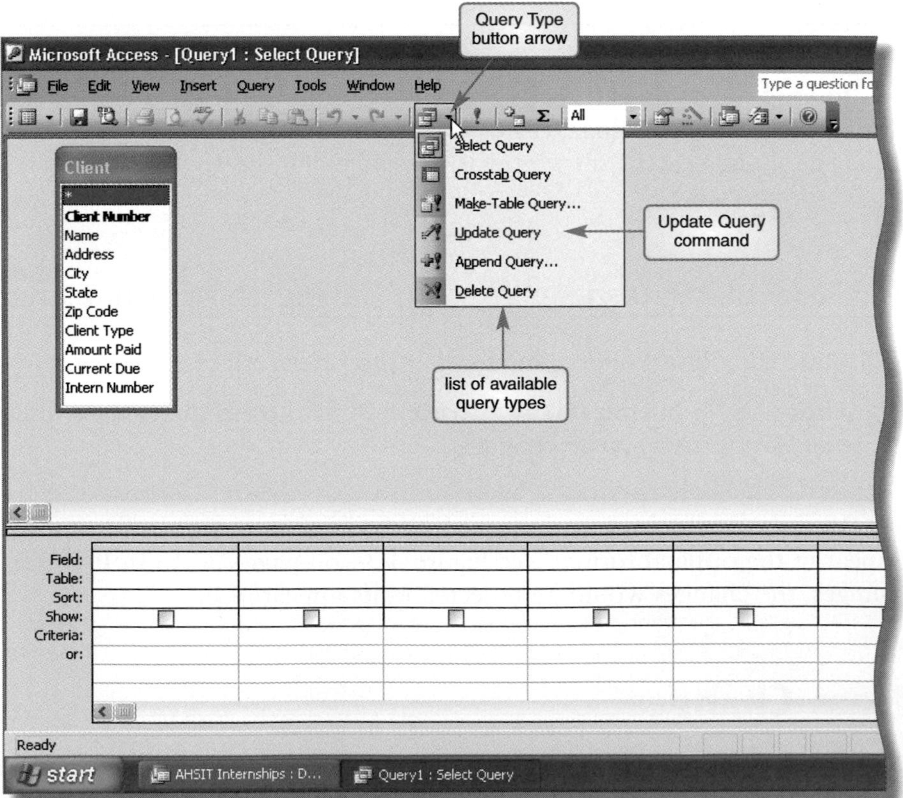

FIGURE 3-39

2

• **Click Update Query, double-click the Client Type field to select the field, click the Update To row in the first column of the design grid, and then type** RET **as the new value.**

The Client Type field is selected (Figure 3-40). In an update query, the Update To row appears in the design grid. The value to which the field is to be changed is entered as RET. Because no criteria are entered, the Client Type value on every row will be changed to RET.

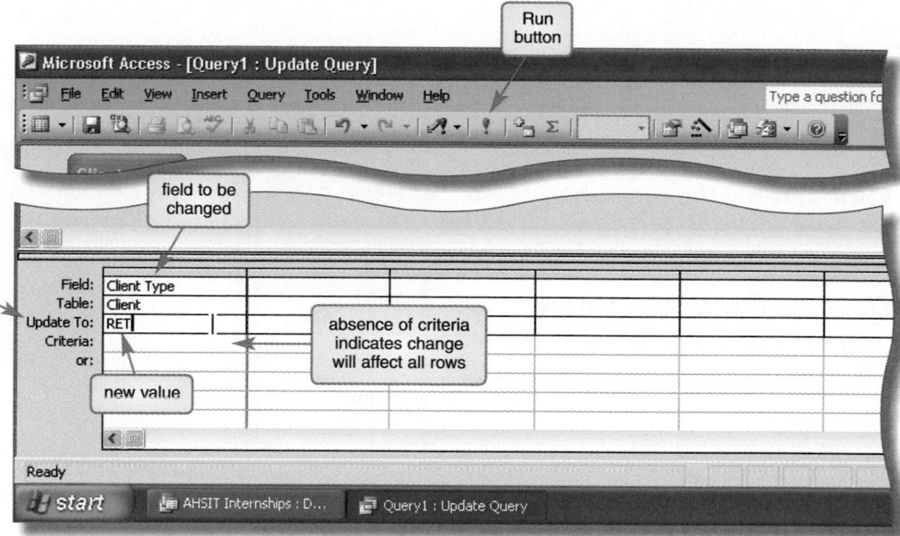

FIGURE 3-40

3

• **Click the Run button on the Query Design toolbar.**

The Microsoft Office Access dialog box is displayed (Figure 3-41). The message indicates that 10 rows (records) will be updated by the query.

4

• **Click the Yes button.**

The changes are made.

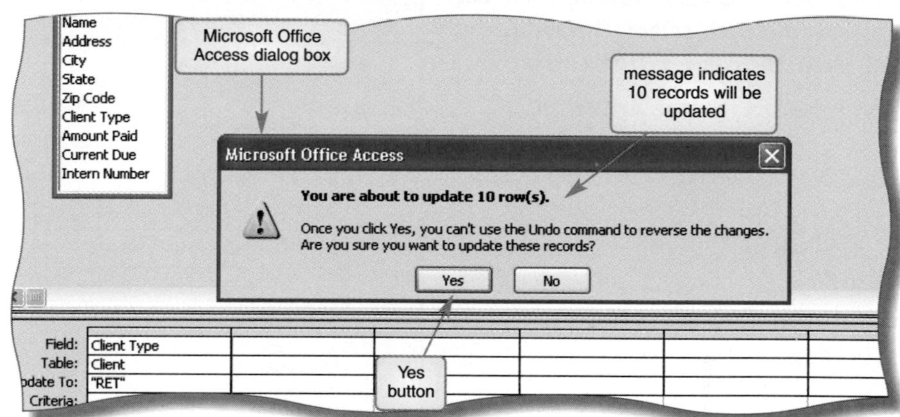

FIGURE 3-41

Using a Delete Query

In some cases, you may need to delete several records at a time. If, for example, all clients in a particular Zip code are to be serviced by another institution, the clients with this Zip code can be deleted from the AHSIT Internships database. Instead of deleting these clients individually, which could be very time-consuming in a large database, you can delete them in one operation by using a **delete query**, which is a query that will delete all the records satisfying the criteria entered in the query.

You can preview the data to be deleted in a delete query before actually performing the deletion. To do so, click the View button arrow on the Query Design toolbar and then click Datasheet View after you create the query but before you run it. The records to be deleted then would appear in Datasheet view. To delete the records, click the View button arrow on the Query Datasheet toolbar and then click Design View to return to Design view. Click the Run button on the Query Design toolbar, and then click the Yes button in the Microsoft Office Access dialog box when asked if you want to delete the records.

The steps on the next page use a delete query to delete any client whose Zip code is 58121 without first previewing the data to be deleted. (Only one such client currently exists in the database.)

Q & A

Q: Why should you preview the data before running a delete query?

A: If you inadvertently enter the wrong criterion and do not realize it before you click the Yes button, you will delete the incorrect set of records. Worse yet, you might not even realize that you have done so.

To Use a Delete Query to Delete a Group of Records

1

- **Click Edit on the menu bar and then click Clear Grid to clear the grid.**
- **Click the Query Type button arrow on the Query Design toolbar.**

The list of available query types appears (Figure 3-42).

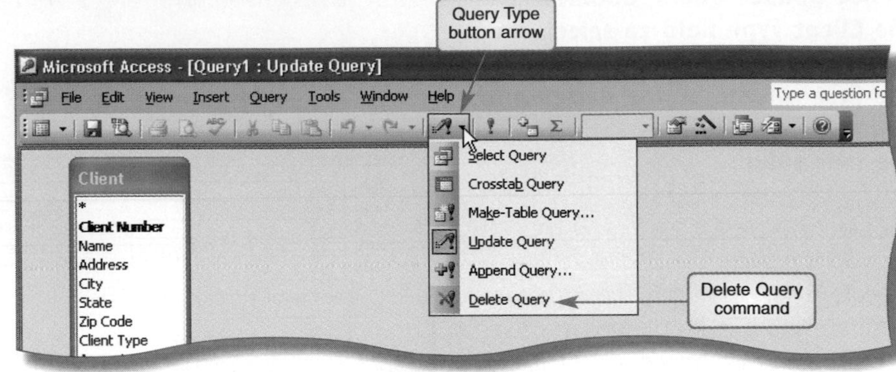

FIGURE 3-42

2

- **Click Delete Query, double-click the Zip Code field to select the field, and then click the Criteria row.**
- **Type** `58121` **as the criterion.**

The criterion is entered in the Zip Code column (Figure 3-43). In a delete query, the Delete row appears in the design grid.

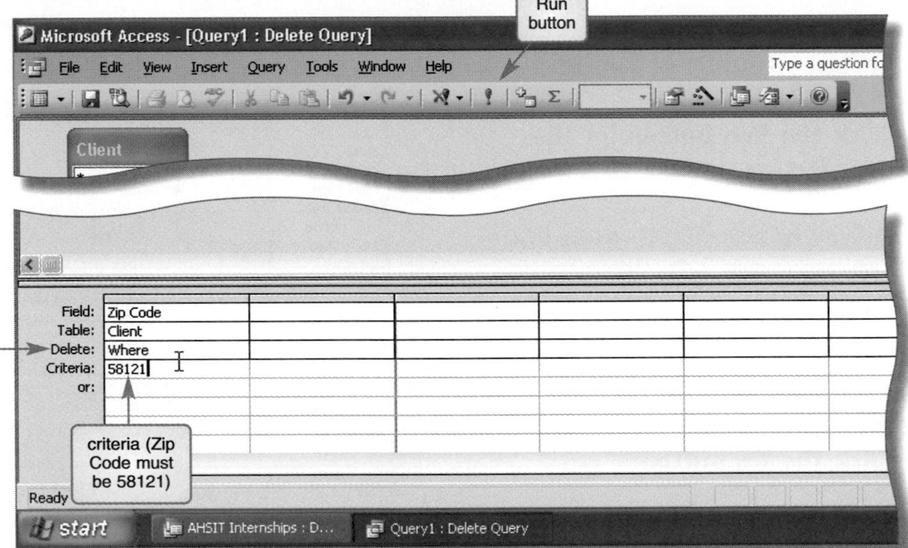

FIGURE 3-43

3

- **Click the Run button on the Query Design toolbar to run the query.**

The Microsoft Office Access dialog box is displayed (Figure 3-44). The message indicates the query will delete 1 row (record).

4

- **Click the Yes button.**
- **Close the Query window. Do not save the query.**

The client with Zip code 58121 has been removed from the table.

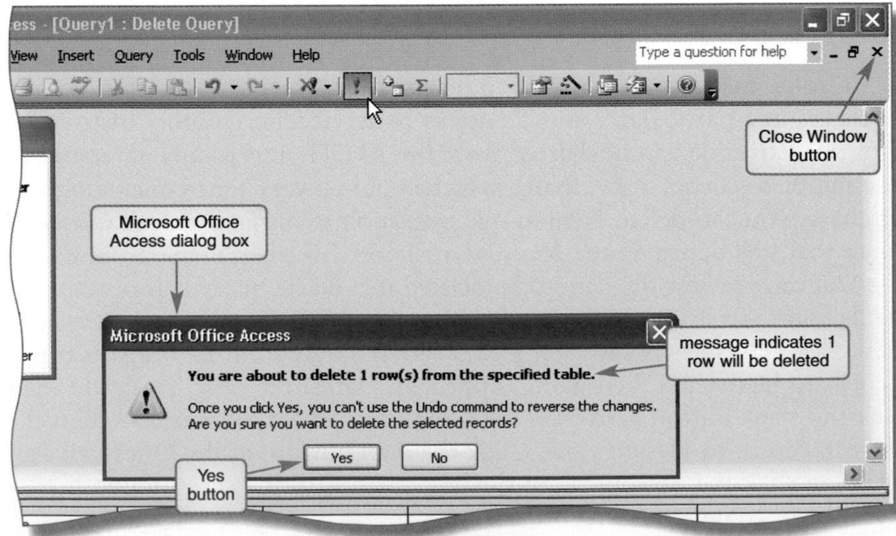

FIGURE 3-44

Using Append and Make-Table Queries

An **append query** adds a group of records from one table to the end of another table. For example, suppose that Alyssa High School acquires some new clients and a database containing a table with those clients. To avoid entering all this information manually, you can append it to the Client table in the AHSIT Internships database using the append query. The following steps illustrate how to create an append query.

Skill Builder 3-4

To practice the following tasks, visit scsite.com/off2003sch/skill, locate Access Project 3, and then click Skill Builder 3-4.
- ❑ Use an update query to change multiple records in a table
- ❑ Use a delete query to delete multiple records in a table

To Create an Append Query

1. Create a select query for the table containing the records to append.
2. In the design grid, indicate the fields to include, and then enter any necessary criteria.
3. Run the query to be sure you have specified the correct data, and then return to the design grid.
4. Click the Query Type button arrow on the Query Design toolbar, and then click Append Query.
5. When Access displays the Append Query dialog box, specify the name of the table to receive the new records and its location. Run the query by clicking the OK button.
6. When Access indicates the number of records to be appended, click the OK button.

The records then are added to the indicated table.

In some cases, you might want to add the records to a new table; that is, a table that has not yet been created. If so, use a **make-table query** to add the records to a new table. Access will create this table as part of the process and add the records to it.

Validation Rules

You now have created, loaded (that is, added the records), queried, and updated a database. Nothing you have done so far, however, makes sure that users enter only valid data. To ensure the entry of valid data, you create **validation rules**, which are rules that a user must follow when entering the data. As you will see, Access will prevent users from entering data that does not follow the rules. The steps also specify **validation text**, which is the message that will appear if a user violates the validation rule.

Validation rules can indicate a **required field**, a field in which the user actually must enter data. For example, by making the Name field a required field, a user actually must enter a name (that is, the field cannot be blank). Validation rules can make sure a user's entry lies within a certain **range of values**; for example that the values in the Amount Paid field are between $0.00 and $10,000.00. They can specify a **default value**; that is, a value that Access will display on the screen in a particular field before the user begins adding a record. To make data entry of client numbers more convenient, you also can have lowercase letters appear automatically as uppercase letters. Finally, validation rules can specify a collection of acceptable values; for example, that the only legitimate entries for the Client Type field are MAN, SER, and RET.

Specifying a Required Field

To specify that a field is to be required, change the value for the Required property from No to Yes. The steps on the next page specify that the Name field is to be a required field.

To Specify a Required Field

1

- **With the Database window open, the Tables object selected, and the Client table selected, click the Design button on the Database Window toolbar.**
- **Select the Name field by clicking its row selector.**

Access displays the Client : Table window (Figure 3-45). The Name field is selected.

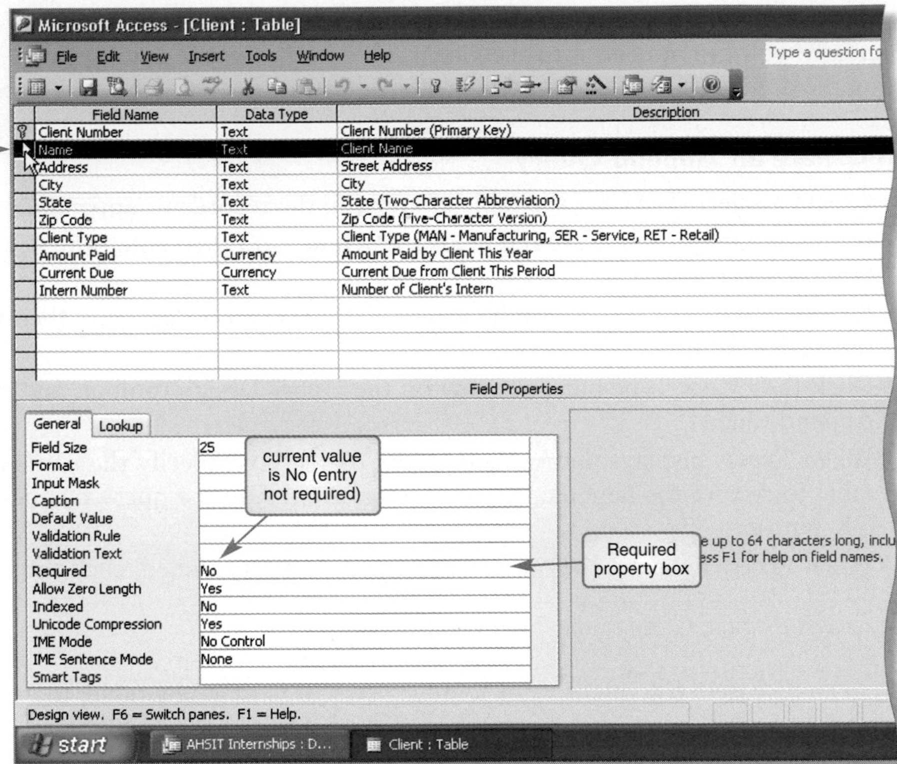

FIGURE 3-45

2

- **Click the Required property box in the Field Properties pane, and then click the box arrow that appears.**
- **Click Yes in the list.**

The value in the Required property box changes to Yes (Figure 3-46). It now is required that the user enter data into the Name field when adding a record.

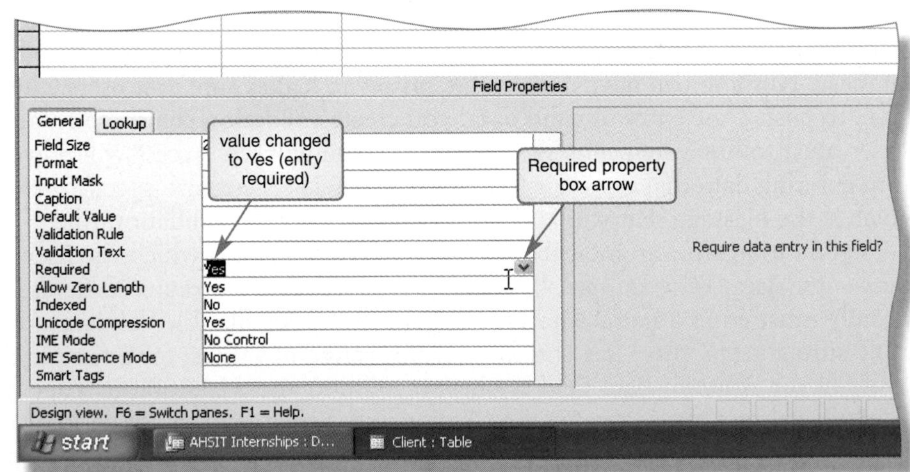

FIGURE 3-46

Specifying a Range

The following step specifies that entries in the Amount Paid field must be between $0.00 and $10,000.00. To indicate this range, the criterion specifies that the amount paid amount must be both >= 0 (greater than or equal to 0) and <= 10000 (less than or equal to 10000).

To Specify a Range

1

- **Select the Amount Paid field by clicking its row selector. Click the Validation Rule property box to produce an insertion point, and then type** `>=0 and <=10000` **as the rule.**
- **Click the Validation Text property box to produce an insertion point, and then type** `Must be between $0.00 and $10,000` **as the text.**

The validation rule and text are entered (Figure 3-47). In the Validation Rule property box, Access automatically changed the lowercase letter, a, to uppercase in the word, and. In the Validation Text property box, you should type all the text, including the dollar signs, decimal points, and comma.

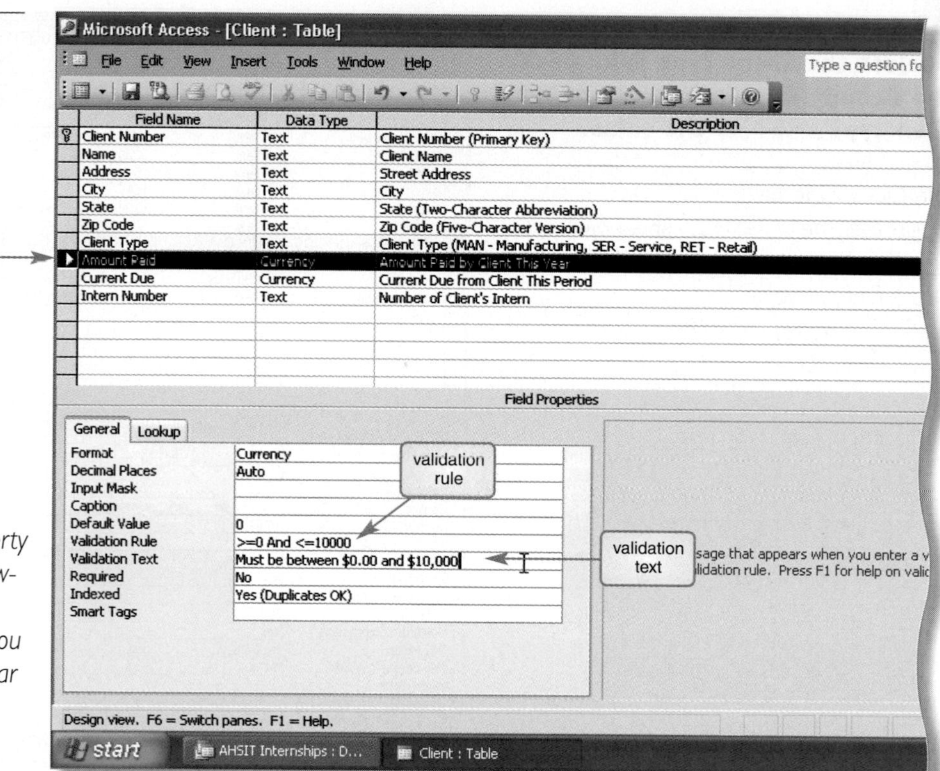

FIGURE 3-47

Users now will be prohibited from entering an amount paid amount that either is less than $0.00 or greater than $10,000.00 when they add records or change the value in the Amount Paid field.

Specifying a Default Value

To specify a default value, enter the value in the Default Value property box. The step on the next page specifies RET as the default value for the Client Type field. This simply means that if users do not enter a client type, the type will be RET.

To Specify a Default Value

1

• **Select the Client Type field. Click the Default Value property box, and then type =RET as the value.**

The Client Type field is selected. The default value is entered in the Default Value property box (Figure 3-48).

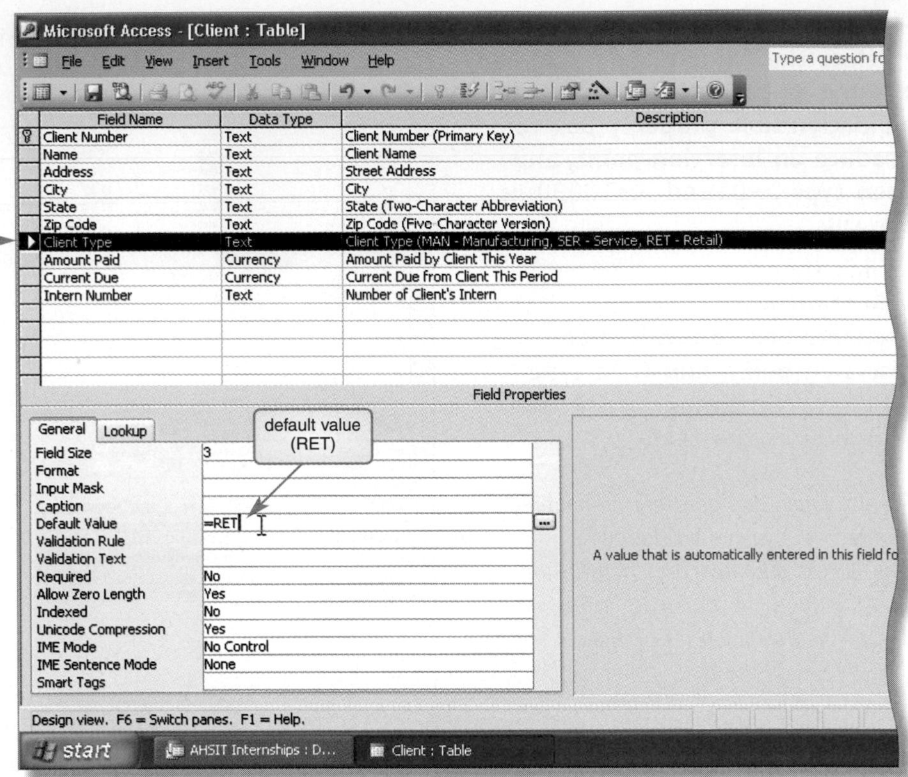

FIGURE 3-48

> *Q & A*
>
> **Q:** Can I include wildcards in validation rules?
>
> **A:** You can include wildcards in validation rules. For example, if you enter the expression, like T?, in the Validation Rule box for the State field, the only valid entries for the field will be TX and TN.

From this point on, if users do not make an entry in the Client Type field when adding records, Access will set the value equal to RET.

Specifying a Collection of Legal Values

The only **legal values** for the Client Type field are MAN, SER, and RET. An appropriate validation rule for this field can direct Access to reject any entry other than these three possibilities. The following step specifies the legal values for the Client Type field.

To Specify a Collection of Legal Values

1

- **Make sure the Client Type field is selected.**
- **Click the Validation Rule property box and then type** =MAN or =SER or =RET **as the validation rule.**
- **Click the Validation Text property box and then type** Must be MAN, SER, or RET **as the validation text.**

The Client Type field is selected. The validation rule and text have been entered (Figure 3-49). In the Validation Rule property box, Access automatically inserted quotation marks around the MAN, SER, and RET values and changed the lowercase letter, o, to uppercase in the word, or.

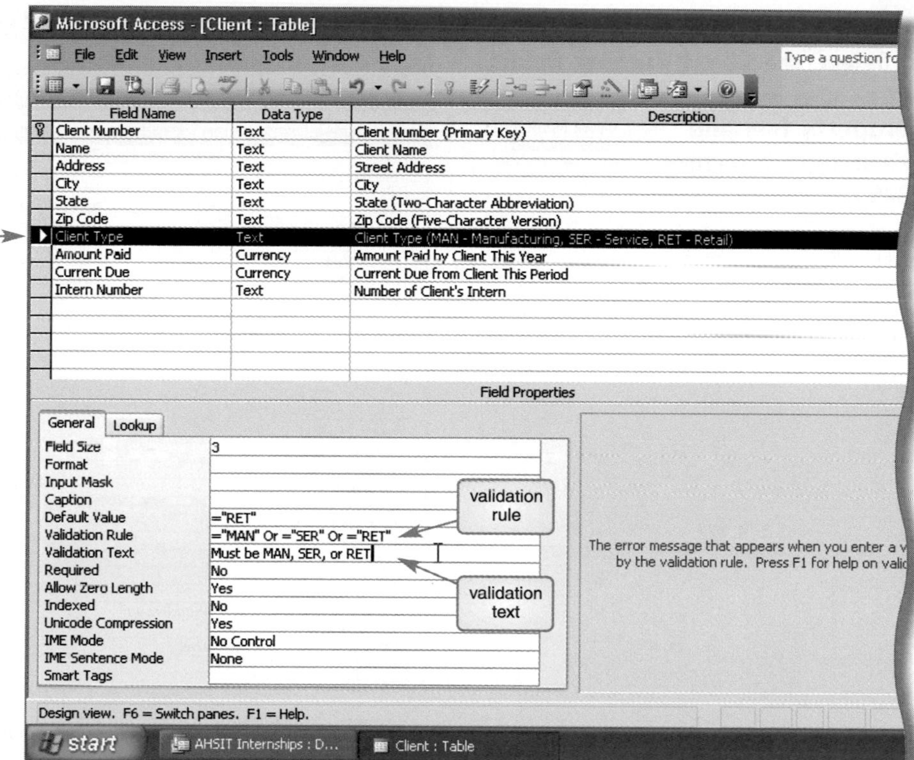

FIGURE 3-49

Users now will be allowed to enter only MAN, SER, or RET in the Client Type field when they add records or make changes to this field.

Using a Format

To affect the way data appears in a field, you can use a **format**. To use a format with a Text field, you enter a special symbol, called a **format symbol**, in the field's Format property box. The Format property uses different settings for different data types. The following step specifies a format for the Client Number field in the Client table and illustrates the way you enter a format. The format symbol used in the example is >, which causes Access to display lowercase letters automatically as uppercase letters. The format symbol < causes Access to display uppercase letters automatically as lowercase letters.

Q & A

Q: Are there any restrictions on using the Lookup Wizard?

A: You cannot change the data type for a field that participates in a relationship between two tables. For example, you cannot change the data type for the Intern Number field in the Client table to Lookup Wizard because a one-to-many relation exists between the Intern table and the Client table. If you want to change the data type for the Intern Number field, first you must delete the relationship in the Relationships window, change the data type to Lookup Wizard, and then recreate the relationship.

To Specify a Format

1

• Select the Client Number field. Click the Format property box and then type > (Figure 3-50).

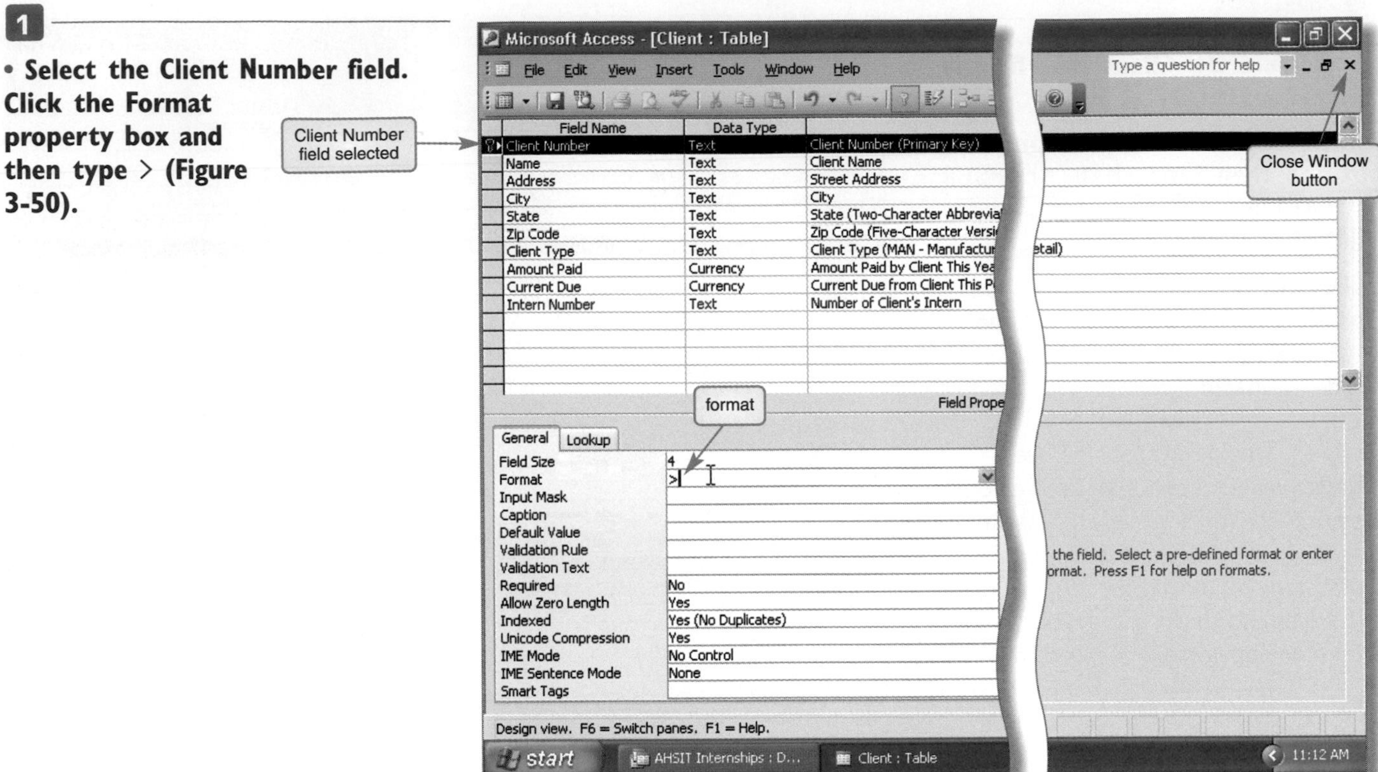

FIGURE 3-50

From this point on, any lowercase letters will appear automatically as uppercase when users add records or change the value in the Client Number field.

Saving Rules, Values, and Formats

The following steps save the validation rules, default values, and formats.

To Save the Validation Rules, Default Values, and Formats

1

• Click the Close Window button for the Client : Table window to close the window (see Figure 3-50).

The Microsoft Office Access dialog box is displayed, asking if you want to save your changes (Figure 3-51).

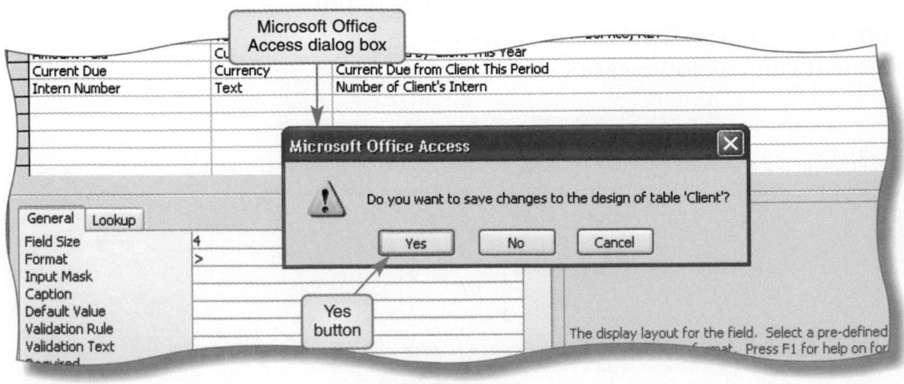

FIGURE 3-51

2

• **Click the Yes button to save the changes.**

The Microsoft Office Access dialog box is displayed (Figure 3-52). This message asks if you want the new rules applied to current records. If this were a database used to run a business or to solve some other critical need, you would click Yes. You would want to be sure that the data already in the database does not violate the rules.

3

• **Click the No button.**

The changes are saved. Existing data is not tested.

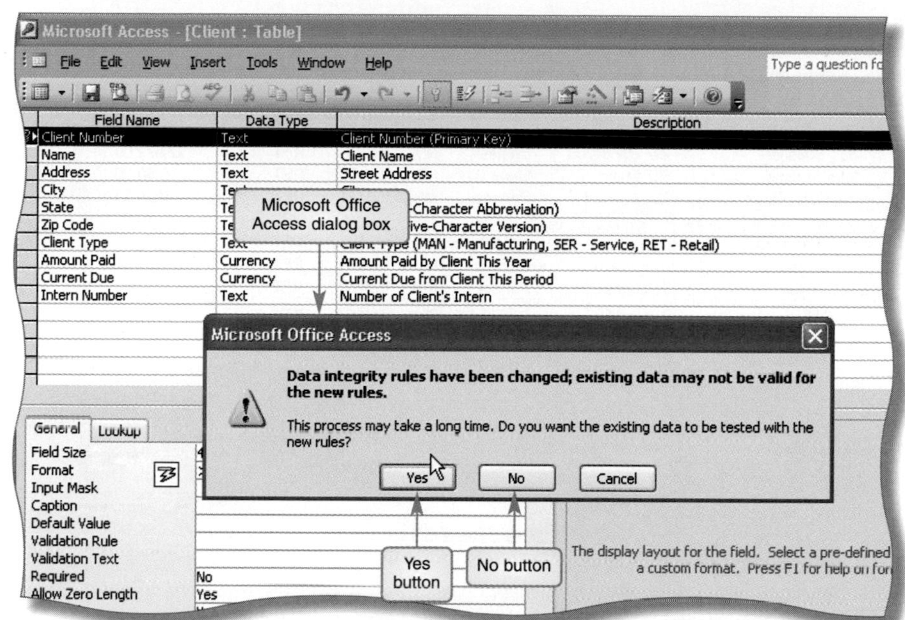

FIGURE 3-52

Updating a Table that Contains Validation Rules

When updating a table that contains validation rules, Access provides assistance in making sure the data entered is valid. It helps in making sure that data is formatted correctly. Access also will not accept invalid data. Entering a number that is out of the required range, for example, or entering a value that is not one of the possible choices, will produce an error message in the form of a dialog box. The database will not be updated until the error is corrected.

If the client number entered contains lowercase letters, such as r12 (Figure 3-53), Access will display the data automatically as R12 (Figure 3-54).

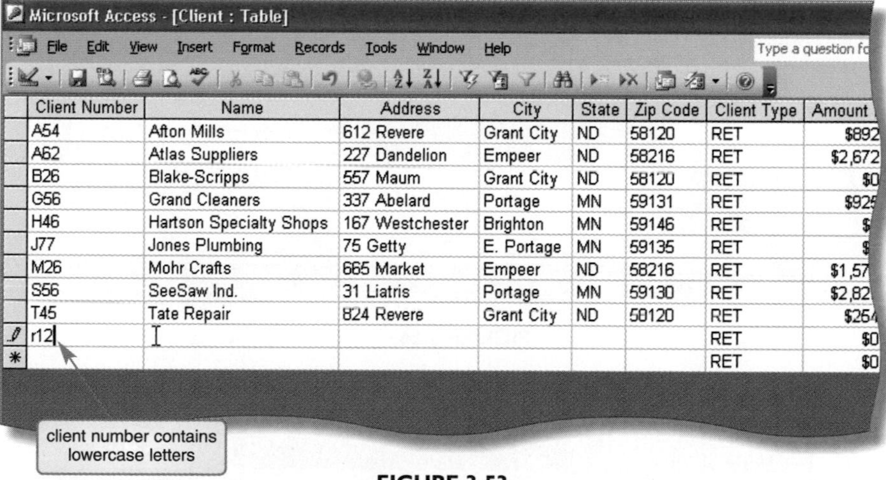

FIGURE 3-53

Client Number	Name	Address	City	State	Zip Code	Client Type	Amount
A54	Afton Mills	612 Revere	Grant City	ND	58120	RET	$892
A62	Atlas Suppliers	227 Dandelion	Empeer	ND	58216	RET	$2,672
B26	Blake-Scripps	557 Maum	Grant City	ND	58120	RET	$0
G56	Grand Cleaners	337 Abelard	Portage	MN	59131	RET	$925
H46	Hartson Specialty Shops	167 Westchester	Brighton	MN	59146	RET	$
J77	Jones Plumbing	75 Getty	E. Portage	MN	59135	RET	$
M26	Mohr Crafts	665 Market	Empeer	ND	58216	RET	$1,57
S56	SeeSaw Ind.	31 Liatris	Portage	MN	59130	RET	$2,82
T45	Tate Repair	824 Revere	Grant City	ND	58120	RET	$254
R12						RET	$0
						RET	$0

letters automatically appear as uppercase

FIGURE 3-54

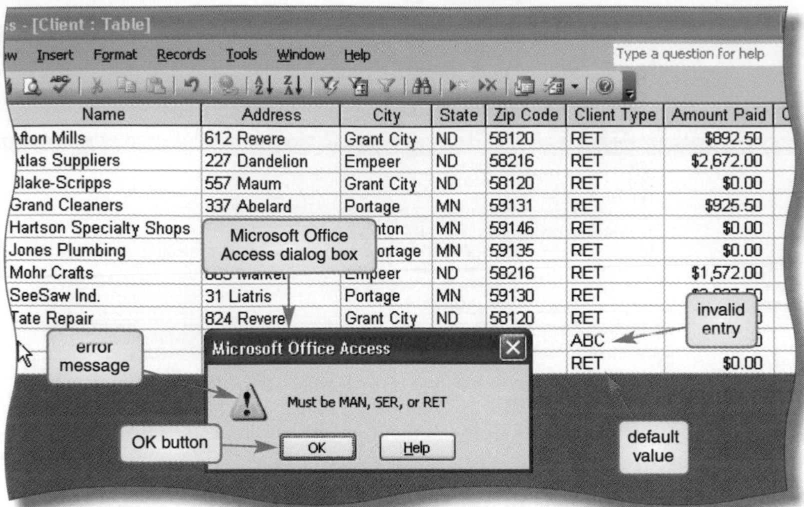

FIGURE 3-55

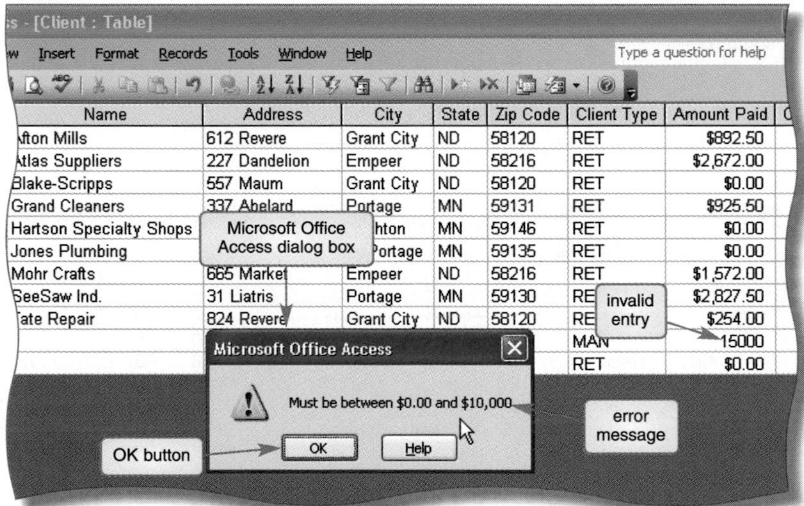

FIGURE 3-56

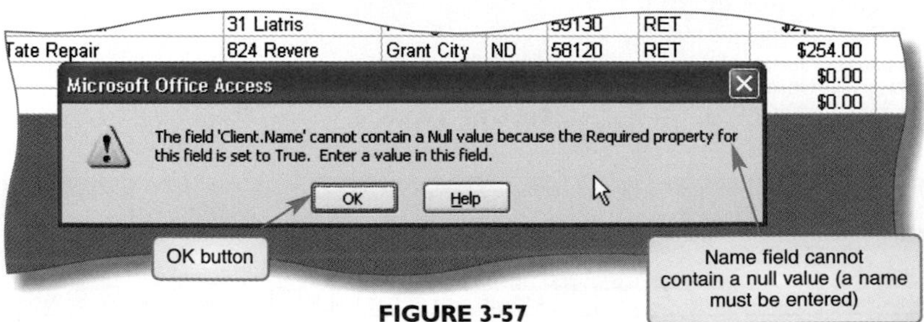

FIGURE 3-57

If the client type is not valid, such as ABC, Access will display the text message you specified (Figure 3-55) and not allow the data to enter the database.

If the amount paid value is not valid, such as 15000, which is too large, Access also displays the appropriate message (Figure 3-56) and refuses to accept the data.

If a required field contains no data, Access indicates this by displaying an error message as soon as you attempt to leave the record (Figure 3-57). The field must contain a valid entry before Access will move to a different record.

When entering data into a field with a validation rule, you may find that Access displays the error message and you are unable to make the necessary correction. It may be that you cannot remember the validation rule you created or it was created incorrectly. In such a case, you neither can leave the field nor close the table because you have entered data into a field that violates the validation rule.

If this happens, first try again to type an acceptable entry. If this does not work, repeatedly press the BACKSPACE key to erase the contents of the field and then try to leave the field. If you are unsuccessful using this procedure, press the ESC key until the record is removed from the screen. The record will not be added to the database.

Should the need arise to take this drastic action, you probably have a faulty validation rule. Use the techniques of the previous sections to correct the existing validation rules for the field.

Creating a Lookup Field

Currently, the data type for the Client Type field is text. Users must enter a type. The validation rules ensure that they can enter only a valid type, but they do not assist the users in making the entry. To assist them in the data-entry process, you can change the Client Type field to a lookup field (also called a lookup column). A **lookup field** (also called a lookup column) allows the user to select from a list of values.

To change a field to a lookup field that selects from a list of values, use the Lookup Wizard data type as shown in the following steps.

To Create a Lookup Field

1

- **If necessary, click the Tables object. Click Client and then click the Design button on the Database Window toolbar.**
- **Click the Data Type column for the Client Type field, and then click the box arrow.**

The list of available data types appears (Figure 3-58).

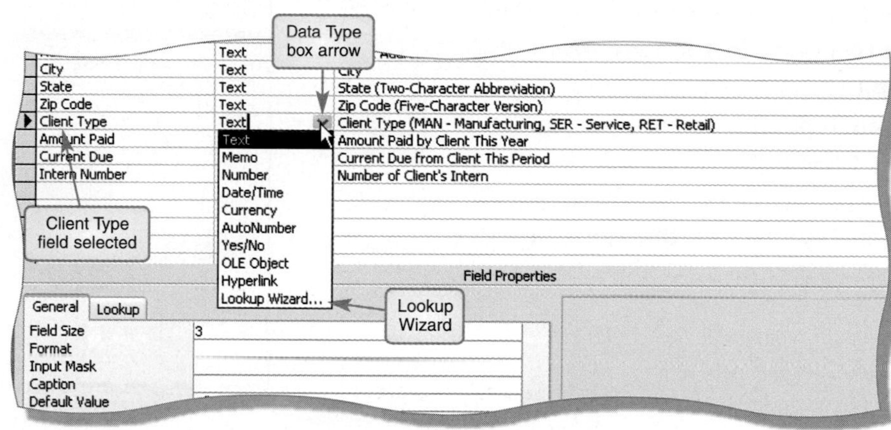

FIGURE 3-58

2

- **Click Lookup Wizard, and then click the I will type in the values that I want option button.**

Access displays the Lookup Wizard dialog box with options for creating a lookup column (Figure 3-59).

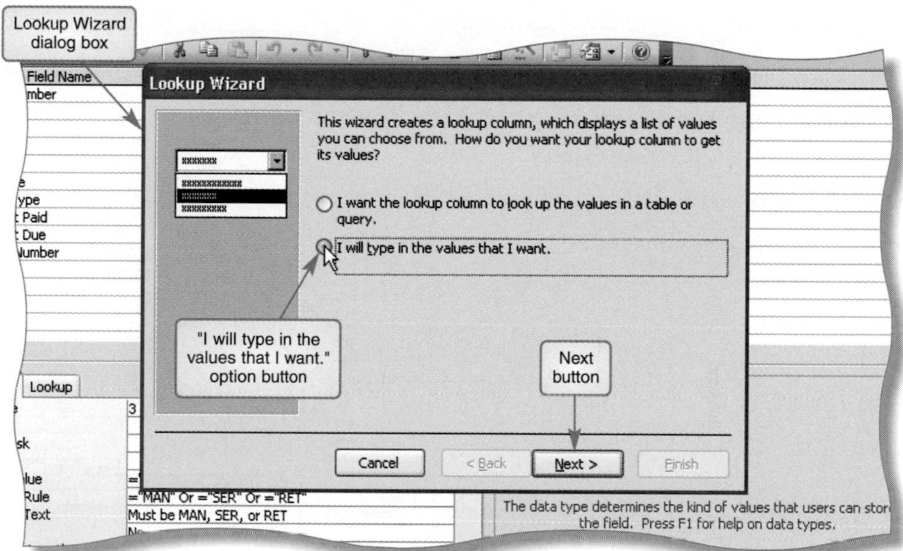

FIGURE 3-59

3

- **Click the Next button.**

The Lookup Wizard dialog box displays options for the number of columns and their values (Figure 3-60). In this screen, you enter the list of values.

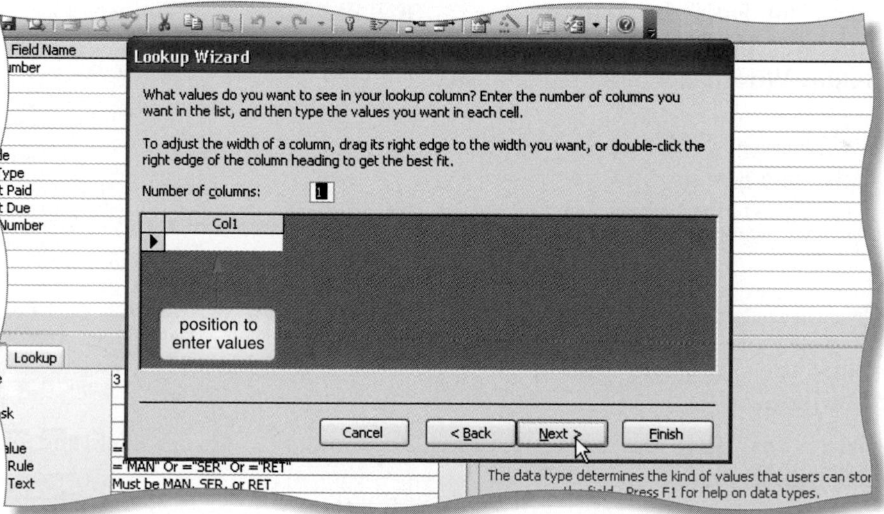

FIGURE 3-60

4

- **Click the first row of the table (below Col1), and then type** MAN **as the value in the first row.**
- **Press the DOWN ARROW key, and then type** SER **as the value in the second row.**
- **Press the DOWN ARROW key, and then type** RET **as the value in the third row.**

The list of values for the Lookup field is entered (Figure 3-61).

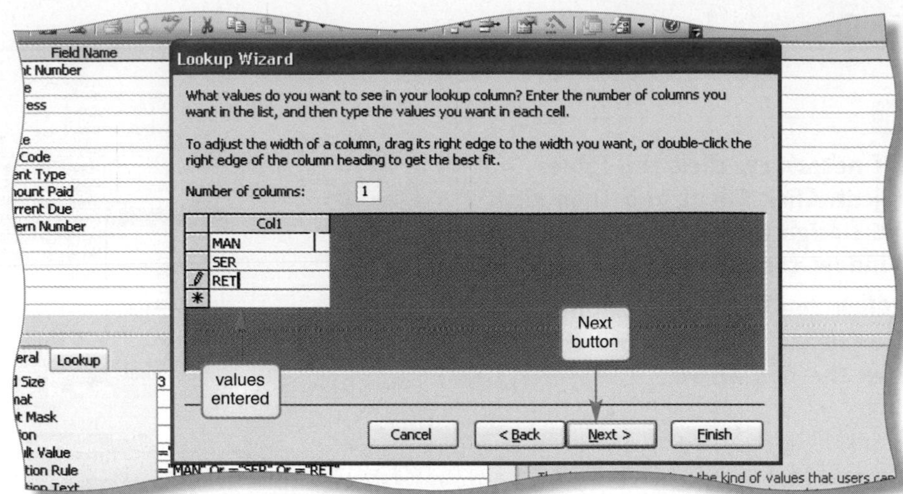

FIGURE 3-61

5

- **Click the Next button.**
- **Ensure Client Type is entered as the label for the Lookup field.**
- **The label is entered (Figure 3-62).**

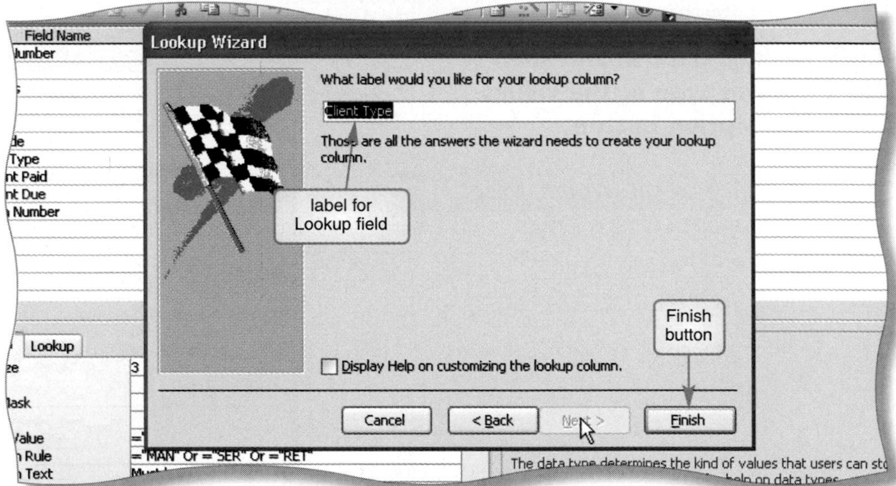

FIGURE 3-62

6

- **Click the Finish button to complete the definition of the Lookup Wizard field.**

Client Type is now a Lookup Wizard field, but the data type still is Text because the values entered in the wizard were entered as text (Figure 3-63).

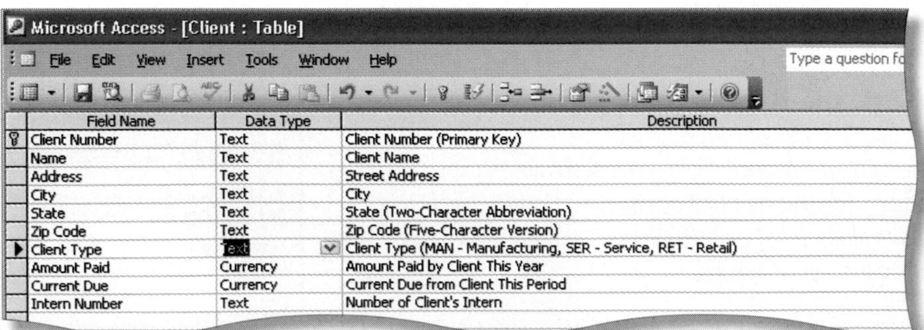

FIGURE 3-63

- **Click the Close Window button on the Client : Table window title bar to close the window.**
- **When the Microsoft Office Access dialog box is displayed, click the Yes button to save your changes.**

The Client Type field is now a lookup field and the changes are saved.

Using a Lookup Field

Earlier, you changed all the entries in the Client Type field to SER. Thus, you have created a rule that will ensure that only legitimate values (MAN, SER, or RET) can be entered in the field. You also made Client Type a lookup field. You can make changes to a lookup field by clicking the field to be changed, clicking the arrow that appears in the field, and then selecting the desired value from the list.

The following steps change the Client Type value on the second and sixth records to MAN and on the seventh and ninth records to SER.

Q & A

Q: Is it possible to create a lookup field that looks up values in a table or query?

A: Yes. To do so, click the "I want the lookup column to look up values in a table or query." option button (Figure 3-59 on AC 147) in the Lookup Wizard dialog box.

To Use a Lookup Field

1

- **Make sure the Client table is displayed in Datasheet view.**
- **Click to the right of the RET entry in the Client Type field on the second record.**

An insertion point and box arrow appear in the Client Type field on the second record (Figure 3-64).

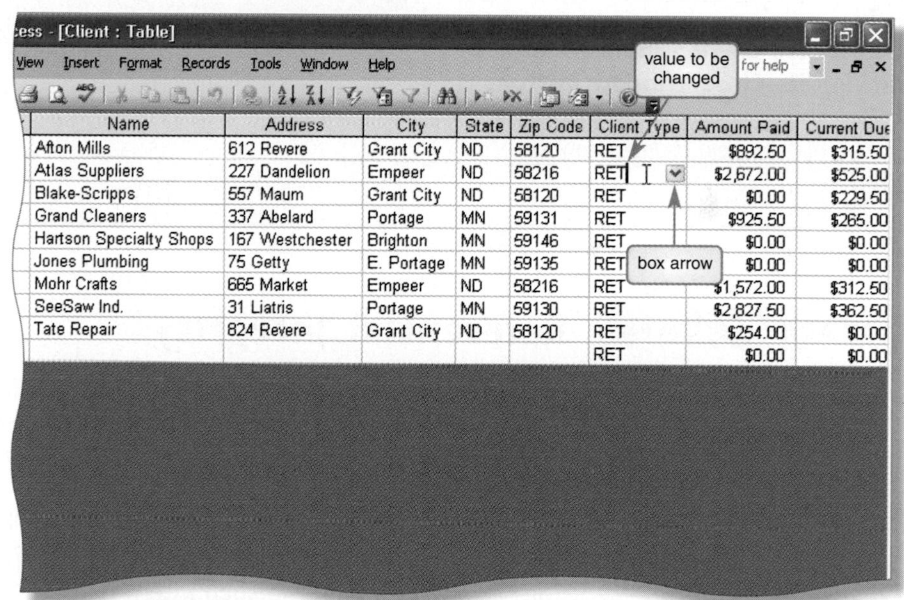

FIGURE 3-64

2

- **Click the box arrow.**

The list of values for the Client Type field appears (Figure 3-65).

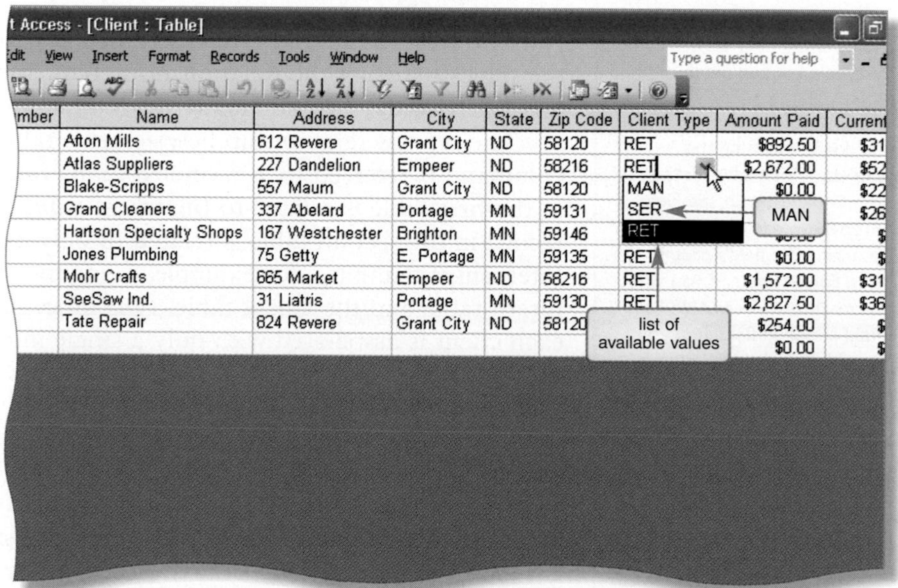

FIGURE 3-65

3

- **Click MAN to change the value.**
- **In a similar fashion, change the RET on the sixth record to MAN, on the seventh record to SER, and on the ninth record to SER (Figure 3-66).**
- **If instructed to do so, print the results by clicking the Print button on the Table Datasheet toolbar.**

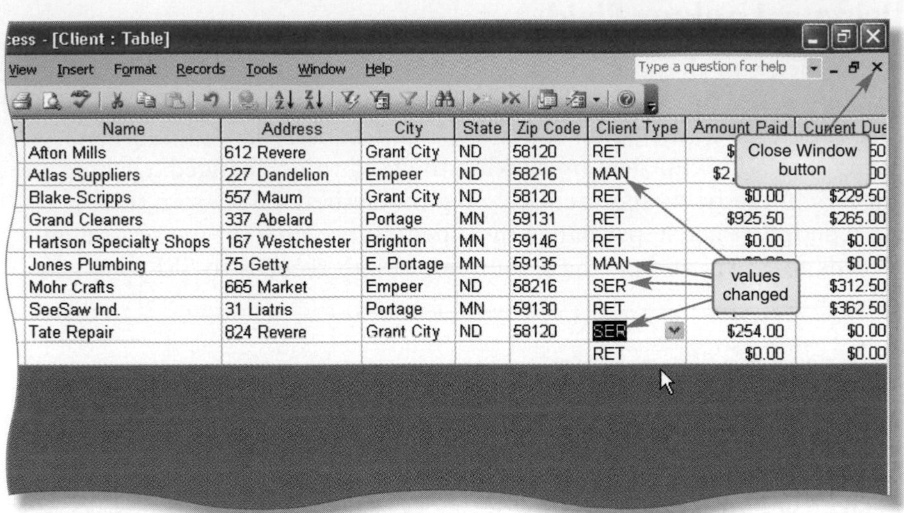

Name	Address	City	State	Zip Code	Client Type	Amount Paid	Current Due
Afton Mills	612 Revere	Grant City	ND	58120	RET	$	50
Atlas Suppliers	227 Dandelion	Empeer	ND	58216	MAN	$2	00
Blake-Scripps	557 Maum	Grant City	ND	58120	RET	$0.00	$229.50
Grand Cleaners	337 Abelard	Portage	MN	59131	RET	$925.50	$265.00
Hartson Specialty Shops	167 Westchester	Brighton	MN	59146	RET	$0.00	$0.00
Jones Plumbing	75 Getty	E. Portage	MN	59135	MAN		$0.00
Mohr Crafts	665 Market	Empeer	ND	58216	SER		$312.50
SeeSaw Ind.	31 Liatris	Portage	MN	59130	RET		$362.50
Tate Repair	824 Revere	Grant City	ND	58120	SER	$254.00	$0.00
					RET	$0.00	$0.00

FIGURE 3-66

4

- **Close the Client : Table window by clicking its Close Window button.**

The Client Type field changes now are complete.

Skill Builder 3-5

To practice the following tasks, visit scsite.com/off2003sch/skill, locate Access Project 3, and then click Skill Builder 3-5.

- ❑ Specify validation rules in a table
- ❑ Create a Lookup field in a table

Referential Integrity

The property that ensures that the value in a foreign key must match that of another table's primary key is called **referential integrity**. A **foreign key** is a field in one table whose values are required to match the *primary key* of another table. In the Client table, the Intern Number field is a foreign key that must match the primary key of the Intern table; that is, the intern number for any client must be a intern currently in the Intern table. A client whose intern number is 92, for example, should not be stored because no such intern exists.

Q & A

Q: Is using the Lookup Wizard the only way to create a Lookup field?

A: You can create a lookup field without using the Lookup Wizard by clicking the Lookup tab in the Field Properties pane and then changing the field's properties. For example, if you want to make the Intern Number field a lookup field, first you would click the Lookup tab, and then select Combo Box as the type in the Display Control property box. When the properties associated with the Combo Box control are displayed, you would select the Intern table as the Row Source and specify the number of columns to display in the combo box.

Specifying Referential Integrity

In Access, to specify referential integrity, you must define a relationship between the tables by using the Relationships command. Access then prohibits any updates to the database that would violate the referential integrity.

The type of relationship between two tables specified by the Relationships command is referred to as a **one-to-many relationship**. This means that *one* record in the first table is related to (matches) *many* records in the second table, but each record in the second table is related to only *one* record in the first. In the AHSIT Internships database, for example, a one-to-many relationship exists between the Intern table and the Client table. *One* intern is associated with *many* clients, but each client is associated with only a single intern. In general, the table containing the foreign key will be the *many* part of the relationship.

When specifying referential integrity, two ways exist to handle deletions. In the relationship between clients and interns, for example, deletion of an intern for whom clients exist, such as intern number 24, would violate referential integrity. Any clients for intern number 24 no longer would relate to any intern in the database. The normal way to avoid this problem is to prohibit such a deletion. The other option is to **cascade the delete**; that is, have Access allow the deletion but then automatically delete any clients related to the deleted intern.

Two ways also exist to handle the update of the primary key of the Intern table. In the relationship between interns and clients, for example, changing the intern number for intern 24 to 26 in the Intern table would cause a problem. Clients are in the Client table on which the intern number is 24. These clients no longer would relate to any intern. Again, the normal way of avoiding the problem is to prohibit this type of update. The other option is to **cascade the update**; that is, have Access allow the update but then automatically make the corresponding change for any client whose intern number was 24. It now will be 26.

The following steps use the Relationships command to specify referential integrity by specifying a relationship between the Intern and Client tables. The steps also ensure that update will cascade, but that delete will not.

Q & A

Q: Is it possible to print a copy of the relationship I created?

A: You can obtain a printed copy of your relationships after you have created them. To do so, first click the Relationships button to display the relationships. Next click File on the menu bar and then click Print Relationships. When Access displays the Print Preview window, click the Print button on the Print Preview toolbar.

To Specify Referential Integrity

1

- **With the Database window displaying, click the Relationships button on the Database toolbar.**

Access displays the Show Table dialog box (Figure 3-67).

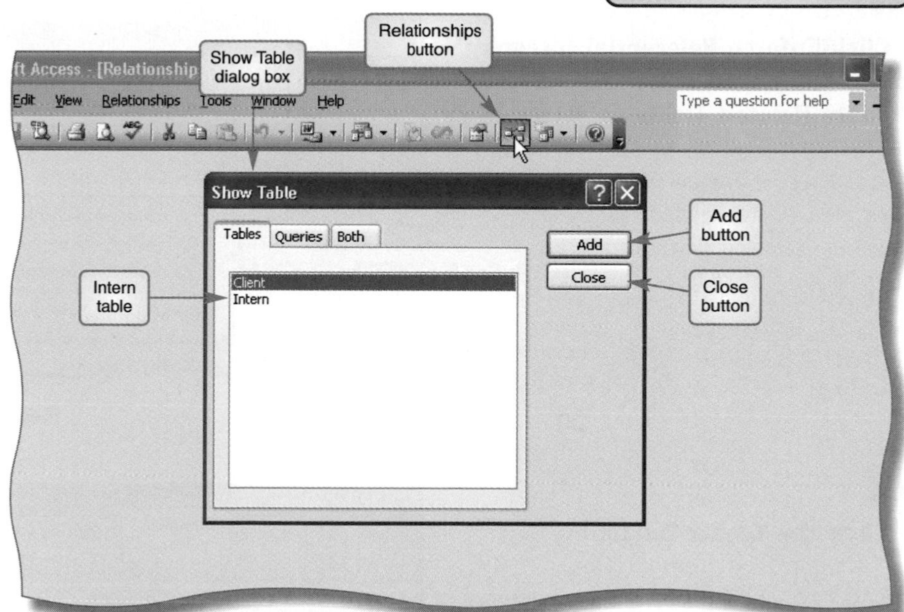

FIGURE 3-67

2

- **Click the Intern table and then click the Add button. Click the Client table, click the Add button again, and then click the Close button in the Show Table dialog box.**
- **Resize the field lists that appear so all fields are visible.**

Field lists for the Intern and Client tables appear (Figure 3-68). The lists have been resized so all fields are visible.

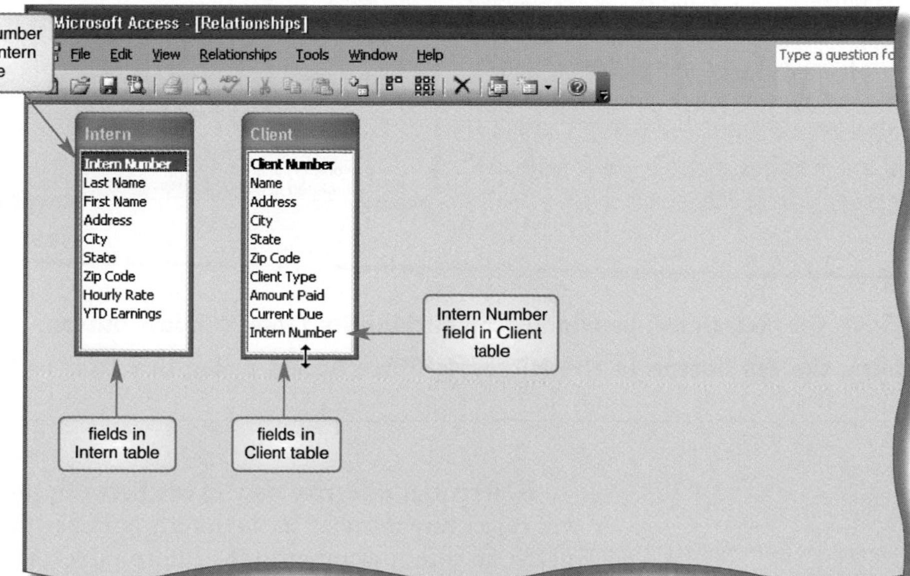

FIGURE 3-68

3

- **Drag the Intern Number field in the Intern table field list to the Intern Number field in the Client table field list.**

Access displays the Edit Relationships dialog box (Figure 3-69). The correct fields (the Intern Number fields) have been identified as the matching fields.

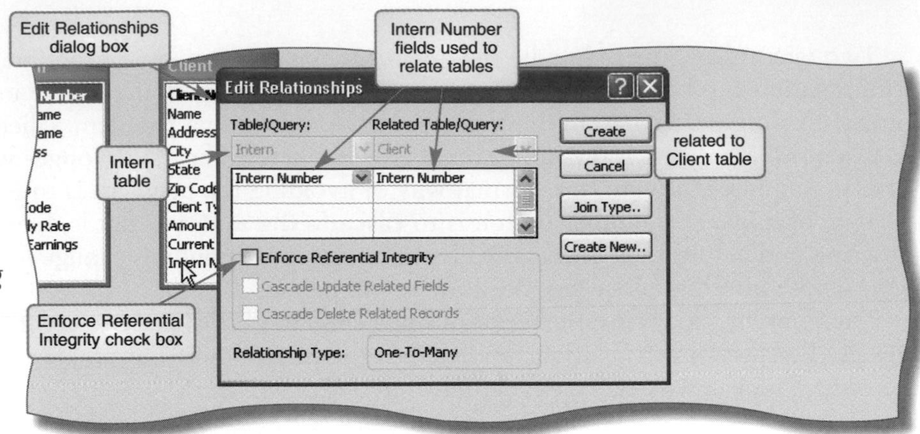

FIGURE 3-69

4

- **Click Enforce Referential Integrity to select it, and then click Cascade Update Related Fields to select it.**

The Enforce Referential Integrity and Cascade Update Related Fields check boxes are selected (Figure 3-70).

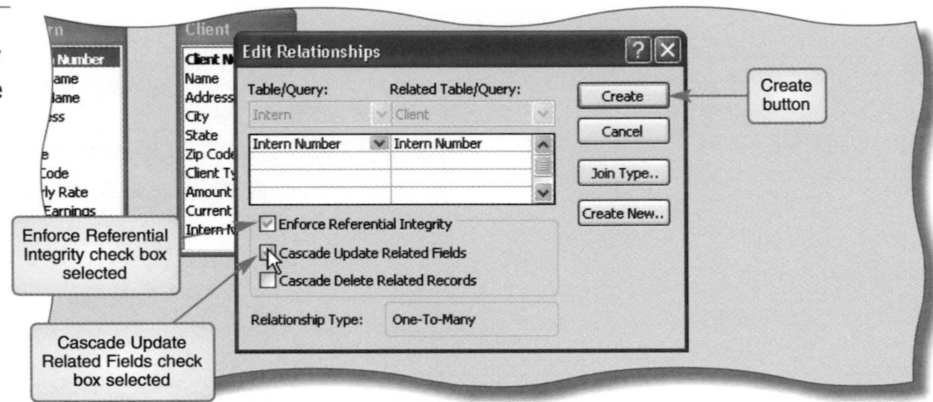

FIGURE 3-70

5

- **Click the Create button.**

Access creates the relationship and displays it visually with the ***relationship line*** *joining the two Intern Number fields (Figure 3-71). The number 1 at the top of the relationship line close to the Intern Number field in the Intern table indicates that the Intern table is the one part of the relationship. The infinity symbol at the other end of the relationship line indicates that the Client table is the many part of the relationship.*

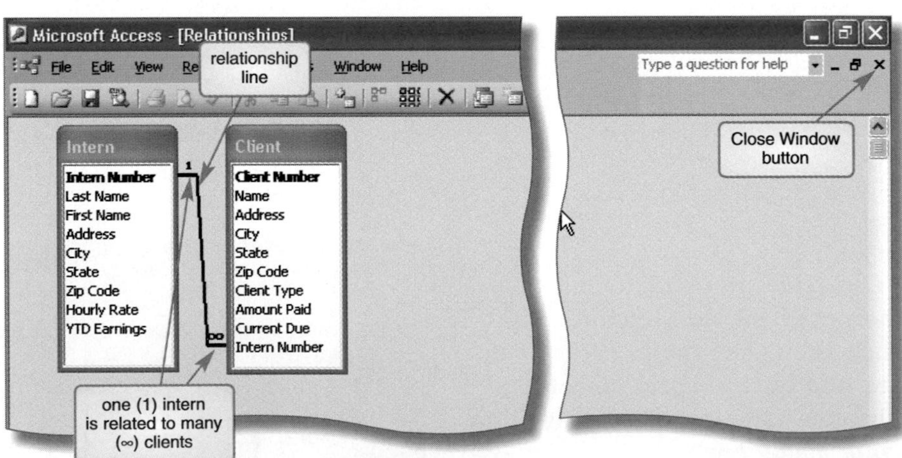

FIGURE 3-71

6

- **Close the Relationships window by clicking its Close Window button.**
- **Click the Yes button in the Microsoft Office Access dialog box to save the relationship you created.**

Referential integrity now exists between the Intern and Client tables. Access now will reject any number in the Intern Number field in the Client table that does not match an intern number in the Intern table. Attempting to add a client whose

Intern Number field does not match would result in the error message shown in Figure 3-72.

A deletion of an intern for whom related clients exist also would be rejected. Attempting to delete intern 24 from the Intern table, for example, would result in the message shown in Figure 3-73.

Access would, however, allow the change of an intern number in the Intern table. Then it automatically makes the corresponding change to the intern number for all the intern's clients. For example, if you changed the intern number of intern 24 to 26, the same 26 would appear in the intern number field for clients.

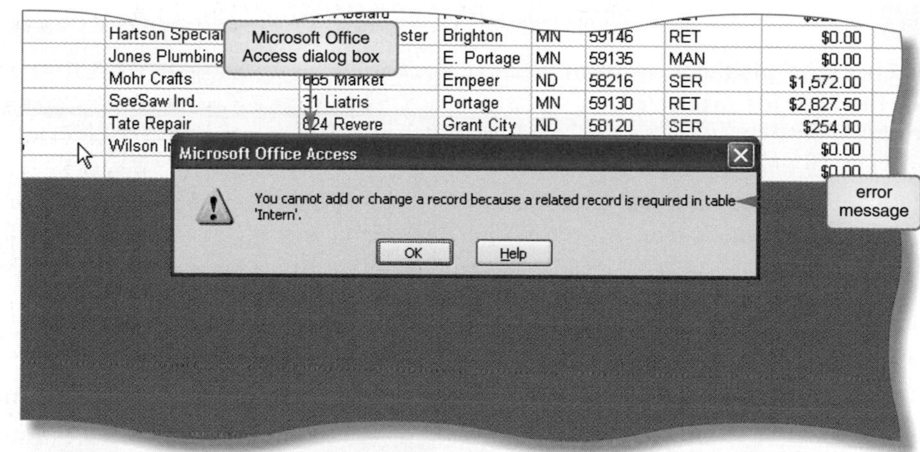

FIGURE 3-72

Using Subdatasheets

Now that the Intern table is related to the Client table, it is possible to view the clients of a given intern when you are viewing the datasheet for the Intern table. The clients for the intern will appear below the intern in a **subdatasheet**. The fact that such a subdatasheet is available is indicated by a plus sign that appears in front of the rows in the Intern table. The following steps display the subdatasheet for intern 24.

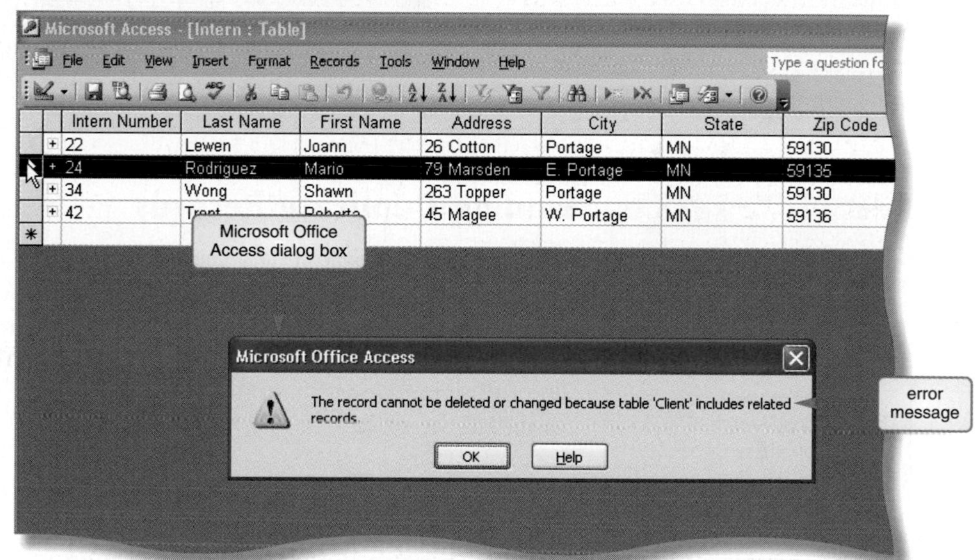

FIGURE 3-73

To Use a Subdatasheet

1

• **With the Database window on the screen, the Tables object selected, and the Intern table selected, click the Open button on the Database Window toolbar.**

The datasheet for the Intern table appears (Figure 3-74).

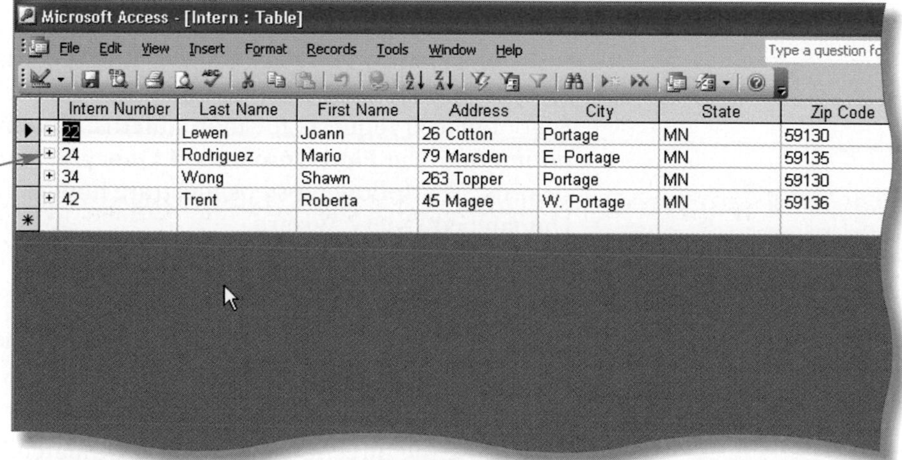

FIGURE 3-74

2

• **Click the plus sign in front of the row for intern 24.**

The subdatasheet appears (Figure 3-75). It contains only those clients that are assigned to intern 24.

3

• **Click the minus sign to remove the subdatasheet, and then close the datasheet for the Intern table by clicking its Close Window button.**

The datasheet no longer appears.

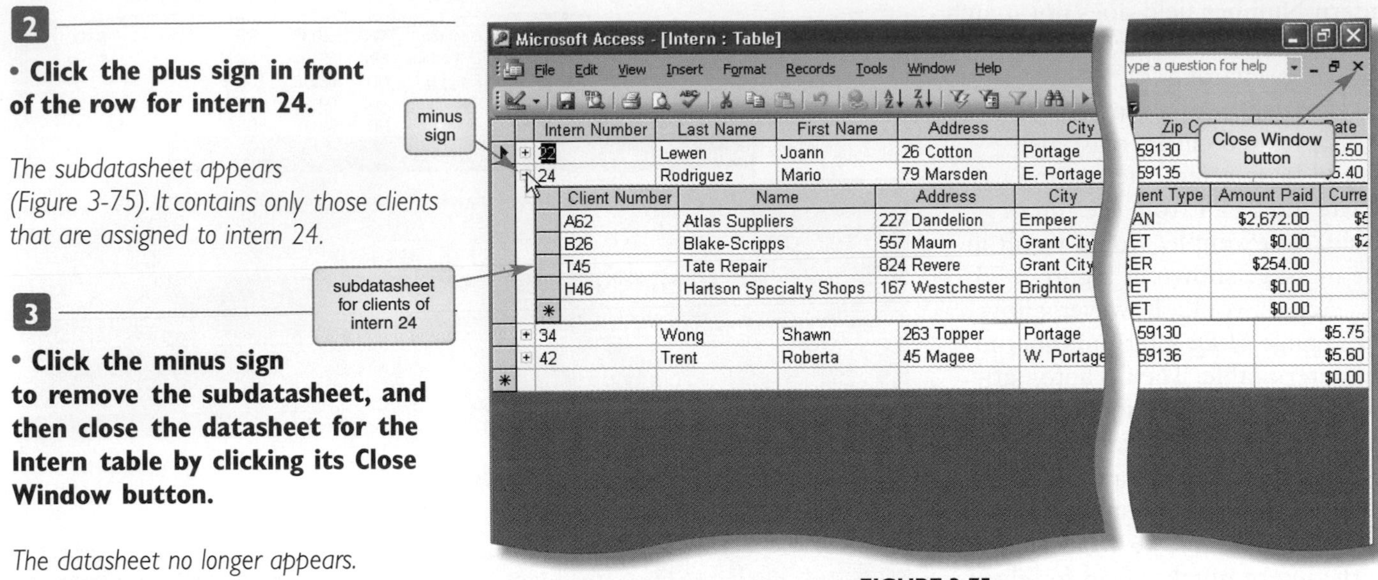

FIGURE 3-75

Skill Builder 3-6

To practice the following tasks, visit scsite.com/off2003sch/skill, locate Access Project 3, and then click Skill Builder 3-6.

- ❑ Create a relationship between tables and specify referential integrity
- ❑ Use a subdatasheet

Finding Duplicate Records

One reason to include a primary key for a table is to eliminate duplicate records. A possibility still exists, however, that duplicate records can get into your database. Perhaps, a client's name was misspelled and the data entry person assumed it was a new client. The **Find Duplicates Query Wizard** allows you to find duplicate records. The following steps illustrate how to use the Find Duplicates Query Wizard to find duplicate records.

To Find Duplicate Records

1. Select the table that you want to query.
2. Click the New Object button arrow, and then click Query.
3. When Access displays the New Query dialog box, click the Find Duplicates Query Wizard and then click the OK button.
4. Follow the directions in the Find Duplicates Query Wizard dialog boxes.

Finding Unmatched Records

Occasionally, you may want to find records in one table that have no matching records in another table. For example, suppose the clients of interns at Alyssa High School placed requests for more interns. You may want to know which clients have no interns. The **Find Unmatched Query Wizard** allows you to find unmatched records. The following steps illustrate how to find unmatched records using the Find Unmatched Query Wizard.

To Find Unmatched Records

1. Click the New Object button arrow, and then click Query.
2. When Access displays the New Query dialog box, click Find Unmatched Query Wizard and then click the OK button.
3. Follow the directions in the Find Unmatched Query Wizard dialog boxes.

Ordering Records

Normally, Access sequences the records in the Client table by client number whenever listing them because the Client Number field is the primary key. You can change this order, if desired.

Using the Sort Ascending Button to Order Records

To change the order in which records appear, use the Sort Ascending or Sort Descending buttons. Either button reorders the records based on the field in which the insertion point is located.

The following steps order the records by city using the Sort Ascending button.

To Use the Sort Ascending Button to Order Records

1

- **With the Database window on the screen, the Tables object selected, and the Client table selected, click the Open button on the Database Window toolbar.**
- **Click the City field on the first record (any other record would do as well).**

An insertion point appears in the City field (Figure 3-76).

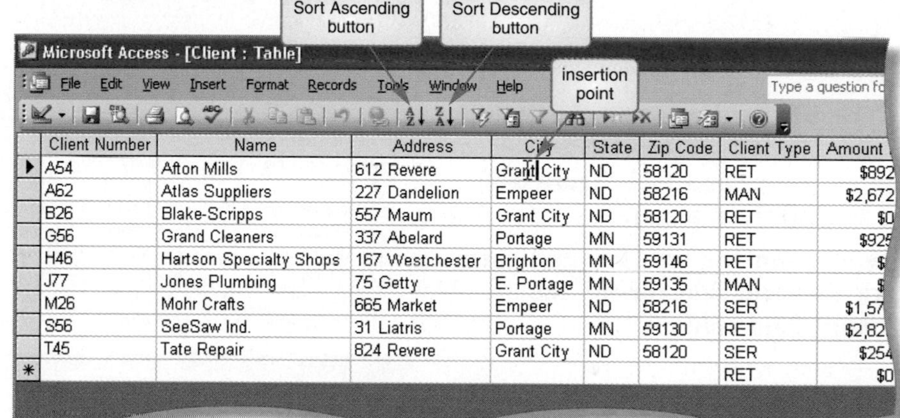

FIGURE 3-76

2

- **Click the Sort Ascending button on the Table Datasheet toolbar.**
- **If instructed to do so, print the table by clicking the Print button on the Table Datasheet toolbar.**

The rows now are ordered by city (Figure 3-77).

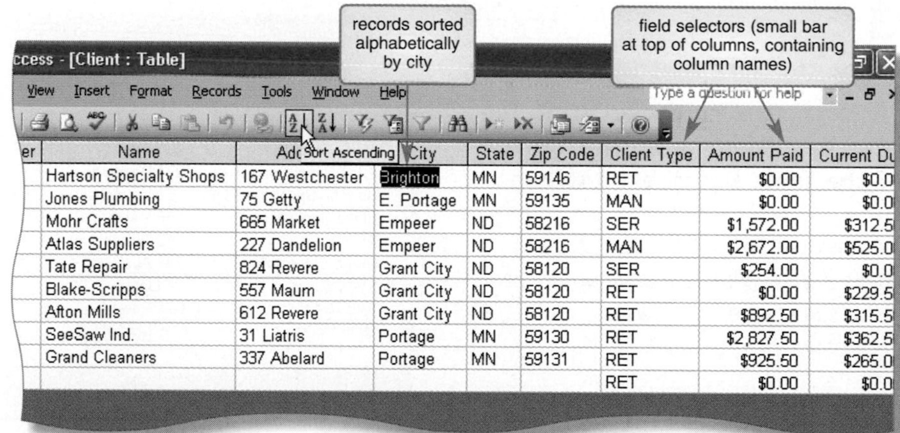

FIGURE 3-77

If you wanted to sort the data in reverse order, you would use the Sort Descending button instead of the Sort Ascending button.

Ordering Records on Multiple Fields

Just as you are able to sort the answer to a query on multiple fields, you also can sort the data that appears in a datasheet on multiple fields. To do so, the major and minor keys must be next to each other in the datasheet with the major key on the left. (If this is not the case, you can drag the columns into the correct position. Instead of dragging, however, usually it will be easier to use a query that has the data sorted in the desired order.)

The following steps order records that have the major and minor keys in the correct position on the combination of the Client Type and Amount Paid fields. To select the fields, use the field selector, which is the small bar at the top of the column that you click to select an entire field in a datasheet.

To Use the Sort Ascending Button to Order Records on Multiple Fields

1

- **Click the field selector at the top of the Client Type column to select the entire column (see Figure 3-77 on the previous page).**
- **Hold down the SHIFT key and then click the field selector for the Amount Paid column.**

The Client Type and Amount Paid columns both are selected (Figure 3-78).

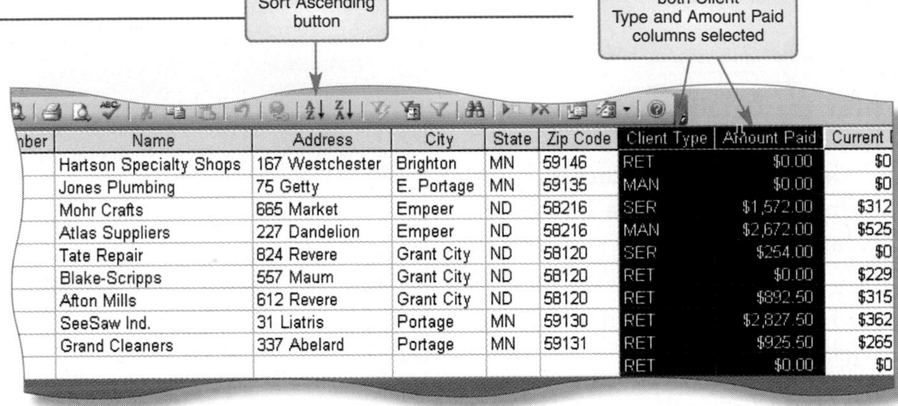

FIGURE 3-78

2

- **Click the Sort Ascending button.**
- **If instructed to do so, print the table by clicking the Print button on the Table Datasheet toolbar.**

The rows are ordered by client type (Figure 3-79). Within each group of clients of the same type, the rows are ordered by the amount paid amount.

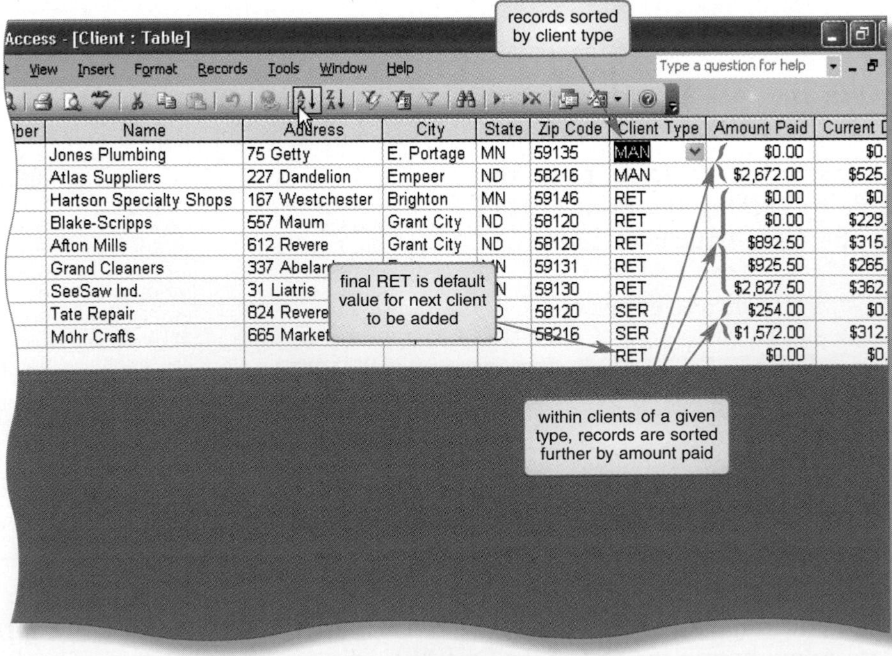

FIGURE 3-79

3

- **Close the Client : Table window by clicking its Close Window button.**
- **Click the No button in the Microsoft Office Access dialog box to abandon the changes.**

The next time the table is open, the records will appear in their original order.

Creating and Using Indexes

You already are familiar with the concept of an index. The index in the back of a book contains important words or phrases together with a list of pages on which the given words or phrases can be found. An **index** for a table is similar. Figure 3-80, for example, shows the Client table along with an index built on client numbers. In this case, the items of interest are client numbers instead of keywords or phrases, as is the case in the back of this book. The field or fields on which the index is built is called the **index key**. Thus, in Figure 3-80, the Client Number field is the index key. (The structure of an index actually is a little more complicated than the one shown in the figure and is beyond the scope of this book. The concept is the same, however, and the structure shown in the figure illustrates the important concepts.)

Index on Client Number

CLIENT NUMBER	RECORD NUMBER
A54	1
A62	2
B26	3
G56	4
H46	9
J77	5
M26	6
S56	7
T45	8

Client Table

RECORD NUMBER	CLIENT NUMBER	NAME	ADDRESS	CITY	STATE	ZIP CODE	CLIENT TYPE	...
1	A54	Afton Mills	612 Revere	Grant City	ND	58120	RET	
2	A62	Atlas Suppliers	227 Dandelion	Empeer	ND	58216	MAN	...
3	B26	Blake-Scripps	557 Maum	Grant City	ND	58120	RET	...
4	G56	Grand Cleaners	337 Abelard	Portage	MN	59131	RET	...
5	J77	Jones Plumbing	75 Getty	E. Portage	MN	59135	MAN	...
6	M26	Mohr Crafts	665 Market	Empeer	ND	58216	SER	...
7	S56	SeeSaw Ind.	31 Liatris	Portage	MN	59130	RET	...
8	T45	Tate Repair	824 Revere	Grant City	ND	58120	SER	...
9	H46	Hartson Specialty Shops	167 Westchester	Brighton	MN	59146	RET	...

FIGURE 3-80

Each client number occurs in the index along with the number of the record on which the corresponding client is located. Further, the client numbers appear in the index in alphabetical order. If Access were to use this index to find the record on which the client number is M26, for example, it could scan the client numbers in the index rapidly to find M26. Once it did, it would determine the corresponding record number (6) and then go immediately to record 6 in the Client table, thus finding this client more quickly than if it had to look through the entire Client table one record at a time. Indexes make the process of retrieving records very fast and efficient. With relatively small tables, the increased efficiency associated with indexes will not be as apparent as in larger tables. In practice, it is common to encounter tables with thousands, tens of thousands, or even hundreds of thousands of records. In such cases, the increase in efficiency is dramatic. In fact, without indexes, many operations in such databases simply would not be practical. They would take too long to complete.

Because no two clients happen to have the same number, the Record Number column contains only single values. This may not always be the case. Consider the index on the Zip Code field shown in Figure 3-81 on the next page. In this index, the Record Number column contains several values, namely all the records on which the corresponding Zip code appears. The first row, for example, indicates that Zip code 58120 is found on records 1, 3, and 8; the second row indicates that Zip code 58216 is found on records 2 and 6. If Access were to use this index to find all clients in Zip code 58216, it could scan the Zip codes in the index rapidly to find

Q & A

Q: What is the actual structure of an index?

A: The most common structure for high-performance indexes is called a B-tree. It is a highly efficient structure that supports very rapid access to records in the database as well as a rapid alternative to sorting records. Virtually all systems use some version of the B-tree structure. For more information about B-tree indexes, visit the Office 2003 Q&A Web page (off2003sch/qa), locate Access Project 3, and click B-tree.

58216. Once it did, it would determine the corresponding record numbers (2 and 6) and then go immediately to these records. It would not have to examine any other records in the Client table.

Index on Zip Code

ZIP CODE	RECORD NUMBER
58120	1, 3, 8
58216	2, 6
59130	7
59131	4
59135	5
59146	9

Client Table

RECORD NUMBER	CLIENT NUMBER	NAME	ADDRESS	CITY	STATE	ZIP CODE	CLIENT TYPE	...
1	A54	Afton Mills	612 Revere	Grant City	ND	58120	RET	...
2	A62	Atlas Suppliers	227 Dandelion	Empeer	ND	58216	MAN	...
3	B26	Blake-Scripps	557 Maum	Grant City	ND	58120	RET	...
4	G56	Grand Cleaners	337 Abelard	Portage	MN	59131	RET	...
5	J77	Jones Plumbing	75 Getty	E. Portage	MN	59135	MAN	...
6	M26	Mohr Crafts	665 Market	Empeer	ND	58216	SER	...
7	S56	SeeSaw Ind.	31 Liatris	Portage	MN	59130	RET	...
8	T45	Tate Repair	824 Revere	Grant City	ND	58120	SER	...
9	H46	Hartson Specialty Shops	167 Westchester	Brighton	MN	59146	RET	...

FIGURE 3-81

Another benefit of indexes is that they provide an efficient way to order records. That is, if the records are to appear in a certain order, Access can use an index instead of physically having to rearrange the records in the database. Physically rearranging the records in a different order can be a very time-consuming process.

To use the index to order records, use record numbers in the index; that is, simply follow down the Record Number column, listing the corresponding clients. If you used the index on Zip Code, for example, you would first list the clients on records 1, 3, and 8 (the clients whose Zip code is 58120), then the clients on records 2 and 6 (the clients whose Zip code is 58216), then the client on record 7 (the client whose Zip code is 59130), and so on. The clients would be listed by Zip code without actually sorting the table.

To gain the benefits from an index, you first must create one. Access automatically creates an index on the primary key, as well as some other special fields. If, as is the case with both the Client and Intern tables, a table contains a field called Zip Code, for example, Access will create an index for it automatically. You must create any other indexes you feel you need, indicating the field or fields on which the index is to be built.

Although the index key usually will be a single field, it can be a combination of fields. For example, you might want to sort records by amount paid within client type. In other words, the records are ordered by a combination of fields: Client Type and Amount Paid. An index can be used for this purpose by using a combination of fields for the index key. In this case, you must assign a name to the index. It is a good idea to assign a name that represents the combination of fields. For example, an index whose key is the combination of the Client Type and Amount Paid fields might be called TypePaid.

How Does Access Use an Index?

Access creates an index whenever you request that it do so. It takes care of all the work in setting up and maintaining the index. In addition, Access will use the index automatically.

If you request that data be sorted in a particular order and Access determines that an index is available that it can use to make the process efficient, it will do so. If no index is available, it still will sort the data in the order you requested; it just will take longer.

Similarly, if you request that Access locate a particular record that has a certain value in a particular field, Access will use an index if an appropriate one exists. If not, it will have to examine each record until it finds the one you want.

In both cases, the added efficiency provided by an index will not be apparent readily in tables that have only a few records. As you add more records to your tables, however, the difference can be dramatic. Even with only 50 to 100 records, you will notice a difference. You can imagine how dramatic the difference would be in a table with 50,000 records.

When Should You Create an Index?

An index improves efficiency for sorting and finding records. On the other hand, indexes occupy space on your disk. They also require Access to do extra work. Access must keep all the indexes that have been created up-to-date. Thus, both advantages and disadvantages exist to using indexes. Consequently, the decision as to which indexes to create is an important one. The following guidelines should help you in this process.

Create an index on a field (or combination of fields) if one or more of the following conditions are present:

1. The field is the primary key of the table (Access will create this index automatically).
2. The field is the foreign key in a relationship you have created.
3. You frequently will need your data to be sorted on the field.
4. You frequently will need to locate a record based on a value in this field.

Because Access handles 1 automatically, you need only to concern yourself about 2, 3, and 4. If you think you will need to see client data arranged in order of amount paid amounts, for example, you should create an index on the Amount Paid field. If you think you will need to see the data arranged by amount paid within intern number, you should create an index on the combination of the Intern Number field and the Amount Paid field. Similarly, if you think you will need to find a client given the client's name, you should create an index on the Name field.

Q & A

Q: Are any other methods available to change properties?

A: You can change the properties of a table by opening the table in Design view and then clicking the Properties button on the Table Design toolbar. Access will display the property sheet for the table. To display the records in a table in an order other than primary key order (the default sort order), use the Order By property. For example, to display the Client table automatically in Name order, click the Order By property box, type `Client.Name` in the property box, close the property sheet, and save the change to the table design. When you open the Client table in Datasheet view, the records will be sorted in Name order.

Creating Single-Field Indexes

A **single-field index** is an index whose key is a single field. In this case, the index key is to be the Name field. In creating an index, you need to indicate whether to allow duplicates in the index key; that is, two records that have the same value. For example, in the index for the Name field, if duplicates are not allowed, Access would not allow the addition of a client whose name is the same as the name of a client already in the database. In the index for the Name field, duplicates will be allowed. The steps on the next page create a single-field index.

To Create a Single-Field Index

1

- **With the Database window on the screen, the Tables object selected, and the Client table selected, click the Design button on the Database Window toolbar.**
- **Be sure the Client : Table window is maximized.**
- **Click the row selector to select the Name field.**
- **Click the Indexed property box in the Field Properties pane.**
- **Click the box arrow that appears.**

The Indexed list appears (Figure 3-82). The items in the list are No (no index), Yes (Duplicates OK) (create an index and allow duplicates), and Yes (No Duplicates) (create an index but reject (do not allow) duplicates).

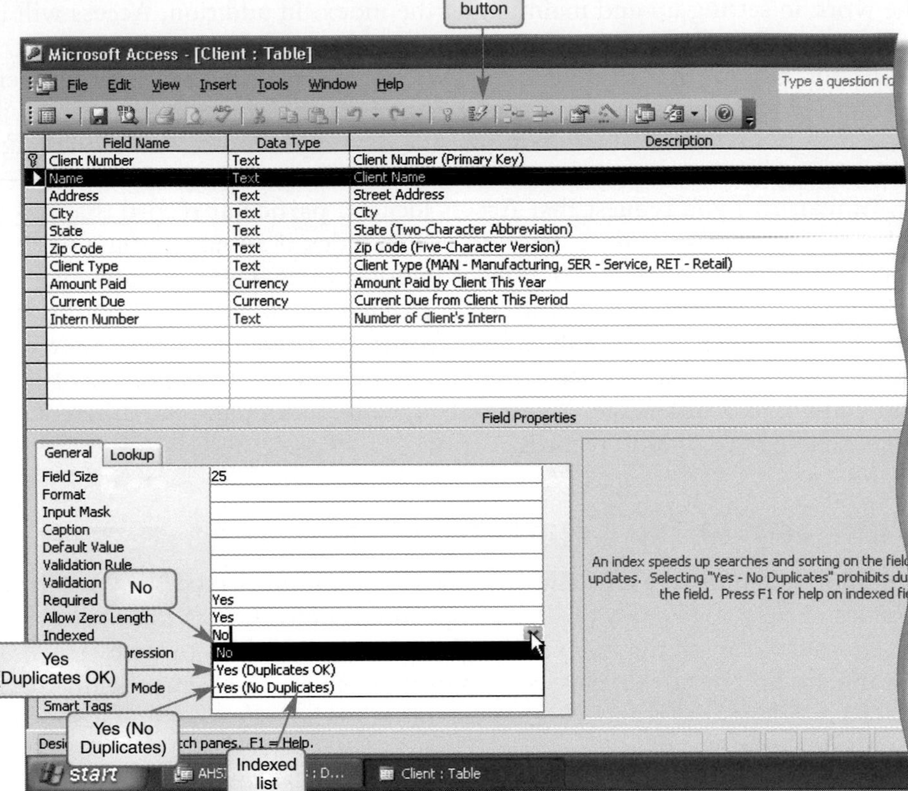

FIGURE 3-82

2

- **Click Yes (Duplicates OK) in the list.**

The index on the Name field now will be created and is ready for use as soon as you save your work.

Creating Multiple-Field Indexes

Creating **multiple-field indexes**, that is, indexes whose key is a combination of fields, involves a different process from creating single-field indexes. To create multiple-field indexes, you will use the Indexes button, enter a name for the index, and then enter the combination of fields that make up the index key. The following steps create a multiple-field index with the name TypePaid. The key will be the combination of the Client Type field and the Amount Paid field.

To Create a Multiple-Field Index

1

- **Click the Indexes button on the Table Design toolbar (see Figure 3-82).**
- **Click the blank row (the row following Name) in the Index Name column in the Indexes: Client dialog box.**
- **Type** `TypePaid` **as the index name, and then press the TAB key.**

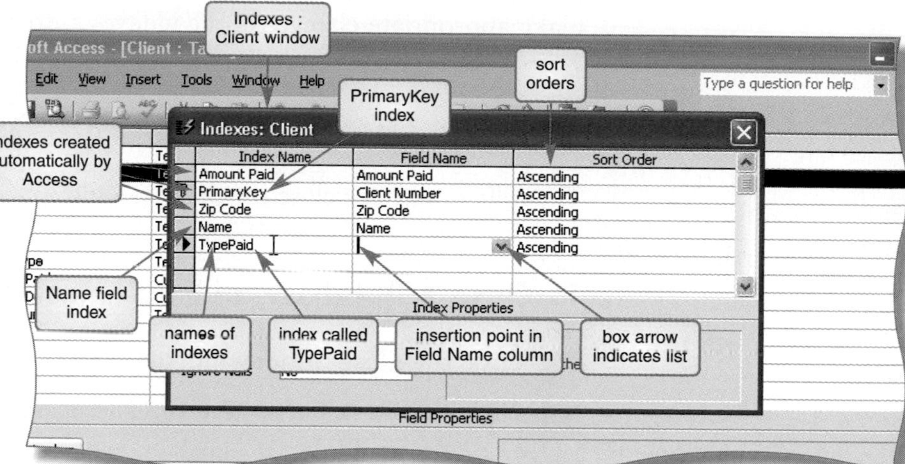

FIGURE 3-83

Access displays the Indexes: Client dialog box. It shows the indexes that already have been created and allows you to create additional indexes (Figure 3-83). The index name has been entered as TypePaid. An insertion point appears in the Field Name column. The index on the Client Number field is the primary index and was created automatically by Access. The index on the Name field is the one just created. Access created other indexes (for example, the Zip Code and Amount Paid fields) automatically. In this dialog box, you can create additional indexes.

2

- **Click the box arrow in the Field Name column to produce a list of fields in the Client table. Select Client Type.**
- **Press the TAB key three times to move to the Field Name column on the following row.**
- **Select the Amount Paid field in the same manner as the Client Type field.**

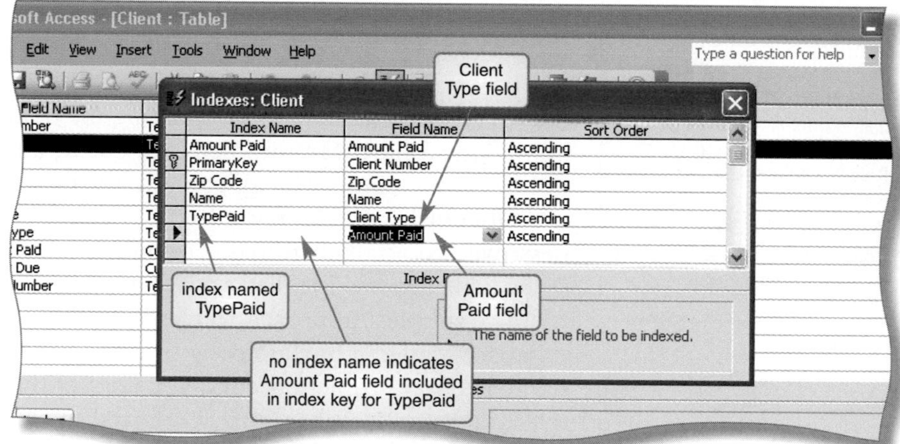

FIGURE 3-84

Client Type and Amount Paid are selected as the two fields for the TypePaid index (Figure 3-84). The absence of an index name on the row containing the Amount Paid field indicates that it is part of the previous index, TypePaid.

3

- **Close the Indexes: Client dialog box by clicking its Close button, and then close the Client : Table window by clicking its Close Window button.**
- **Click the Yes button in the Microsoft Office Access dialog box to save your changes.**

The indexes are created and Access displays the Database window.

The indexes are created. Access will use them automatically whenever possible to improve efficiency of ordering or finding records. Access also will maintain them automatically. That is, whenever the data in the Client table is changed, Access will make appropriate changes in the indexes automatically.

Closing the Database and Quitting Access

The following steps close the database and quit Access.

To Close a Database and Quit Access

1. **Click the Close Window button for the AHSIT Internships : Database window.**
2. **Click the Close button for the Microsoft Access window.**

The database and Access close.

Special Database Operations

The special operations involved in maintaining a database are backup, recovery, compacting a database, and repairing a database.

Backup and Recovery

It is possible to damage or destroy a database. Users can enter data that is incorrect; programs that are updating the database can end abnormally during an update; a hardware problem can occur; and so on. After any such event has occurred, the database may contain invalid data. It even may be totally destroyed.

Obviously, you cannot allow a situation in which data has been damaged or destroyed to go uncorrected. You must somehow return the database to a correct state. This process is called **recovery**; that is, you say that you **recover** the database.

The simplest approach to recovery involves periodically making a copy of the database (called a **backup copy** or a **save copy**). This is referred to as **backing up** the database. If a problem occurs, you correct the problem by copying this backup copy over the actual database, often referred to as the **live database**.

To back up the database that currently is open, you use the Back Up Database command on the File menu. In the process, Access suggests a name that is a combination of the database name and the current date. For example, if you back up the AHSIT Internships database on April 20, 2007, Access will suggest the name AHSIT Internships_2007-04-20. You can change this name if you desire, although it is a good idea to use this name. By doing so, it will be easy to distinguish between all the backup copies you have made to determine which is the most recent. In addition, if you discover that a critical problem occurred on April 18, 2007, you may want to go back to the most recent backup before April 18. If, for example, the database was not backed up on April 17 but was backed up on April 16, you would use AHSIT Internships_2007-04-16.

Q & A

Q: Is there more than one way to invoke a command in Access?

A: Yes. For a table that lists how to complete tasks covered in this book using the mouse, menu, shortcut menu, and keyboard, see the Quick Reference Summary at the back of this book, or visit the Office 2003 Quick Reference Web page (scsite.com/off2003sch/qr).

Q & A

Q: What is the Microsoft Office Certification program?

A: The Microsoft Office Specialist Certification program provides an opportunity for you to obtain a valuable industry credential — proof that you have the Access 2003 skills required by employers. For more information, see Appendix E, or visit the Office 2003 Certification Web page (scsite.com/off2003sch/cert).

The following steps back up a database to a file on a hard disk or high-capacity removable disk. You should check with your instructor before completing these steps.

To Back Up a Database

1. Open the database to be backed up.
2. Click File on the menu bar, and then click Back Up Database.
3. Selected the desired location in the Save in box. If you do not want the name Access has suggested, enter the desired name in the File name text box.
4. Click the Save button.

Access creates a backup copy with the desired name in the desired location. Should you ever need to recover the database using this backup copy, you simply can copy it over the live version.

Compacting and Repairing a Database

As you add more data to a database, it naturally grows larger. Pictures will increase the size significantly. When you delete objects (for example, records, tables, forms, or pictures), the space previously occupied by the object does not become available for additional objects. Instead, the additional objects are given new space; that is, space that was not already allocated. If you decide to change a picture, for example, the new picture will not occupy the same space as the previous picture, but instead it will be given space of its own.

To remove this wasted space from the database, you must **compact** the database. Compacting the database makes an additional copy of the database, one that contains the same data, but does not contain the wasted space that the original does. The original database will still exist in its unaltered form.

A typical three-step process for compacting a database is as follows:

1. Compact the original database (for example, AHSIT Internships) and give the compacted database a different name (for example, AHSIT Internships Compacted).
2. Assuming that the compacting operation completed successfully, delete the original database (AHSIT Internships).
3. Also assuming that the compacting operation completed successfully, rename the compacted database (AHSIT Internships Compacted) with the name of the original database (AHSIT Internships).

Of course, if a problem occurs in the compacting operation, you should continue to use the original database; that is, do not complete Steps 2 and 3.

The operation can be carried out on a USB flash drive, provided sufficient space is available. If the database to be compacted occupies more than half the USB flash drive, however, Access may not have enough room to create the compacted database. In such a case, you should first copy the database to a hard disk or network drive. (You can use whatever Windows technique you prefer for copying files to do so.) You then can complete the process on the hard disk or network drive.

In addition to compacting the database, the same operation is used to **repair** the database in case of problems. If Microsoft Access reports a problem with the database or if some aspect of the database seems to be behaving in an unpredictable fashion, you should run the Compact and Repair operation to attempt to correct the problem. If Access is unable to repair the database, you will need to revert to your most recent backup copy.

Q & A

Q: Is there any way to have Access compact a table automatically?

A: You can require Access to compact a database automatically whenever the database is closed. To do so, click Tools on the menu bar and then click Options. When Access displays the Options dialog box, click the General tab. Click the Compact on Close check box.

Q & A

Q: Is it possible to compact an open database?

A: Yes, to do so, click Tools on the menu bar, point to Database Utilities, and then click Compact and Repair Database on the Database Utilities submenu.

The following steps compact a database and repair any problems after you have copied the database to a hard disk. If you have not copied the database to a hard disk, check with your instructor before completing these steps.

To Compact and Repair a Database

1. Be sure the database is closed. Click Tools on the menu bar, point to Database Utilities, and then click Compact and Repair Database on the Database Utilities submenu.
2. In the Database to Compact From dialog box, select the database to be compacted and then click the Compact button.
3. In the Compact Database Into dialog box, enter a new name for the compacted database and then click the Save button.
4. Assuming the operation is completed successfully, delete the original database and rename the compacted database as the original name.

The database now is the compacted form of the original.

Project Summary

In Project 3, you learned how to maintain a database. You saw how to use Form view to add records to a table. You learned how to locate and filter records. You saw how to change the contents of records in a table and how to delete records from a table. You restructured a table, both by changing field characteristics and by adding a new field. You saw how to make a variety of changes to the appearance of a datasheet. You learned how to make changes to groups of records and delete a group of records. You created a variety of validation rules that specified a required field, a range, a default value, legal values, and a format. You examined the issues involved in updating a table with validation rules. You also saw how to specify referential integrity. You learned how to view related data by using subdatasheets. You learned how to order records. You saw how to improve performance by creating single-field and multiple-field indexes. You also saw backup and recover procedures as well as how to compact and repair a database.

If you have a SAM user profile, you may have access to hands-on instruction, practice, and assessment of the skills covered in this project. Log in to your SAM account and go to your assignments page to see what your instructor has assigned.

What You Should Know

Having completed this project, you should be able to perform the tasks below. The tasks are listed in the same order they were presented in this project. For a list of the buttons, menus, toolbars, and commands introduced in this project, see the Quick Reference Summary at the back of this book and refer to the Page Number column.

1. Open a Database (AC 116)
2. Use a Form to Add Records (AC 116)
3. Search for a Record (AC 118)
4. Update the Contents of a Field (AC 119)
5. Switch from Form View to Datasheet View (AC 120)
6. Use Filter By Selection (AC 121)
7. Remove a Filter (AC 122)
8. Use Filter By Form (AC 123)
9. Use Advanced Filter/Sort (AC 124)
10. Delete a Record (AC 125)
11. Delete a Record in Form View (AC 126)
12. Change the Size of a Field (AC 127)
13. Add a Field to a Table (AC 129)
14. Delete a Field (AC 130)
15. Update the Contents of a Field (AC 130)
16. Resize a Column (AC 131)
17. Change the Font in a Datasheet (AC 133)
18. Change the Format of the Datasheet Grid (AC 134)
19. Use Print Preview (AC 135)
20. Close the Datasheet Without Saving the Format Changes (AC 135)
21. Use an Update Query to Update All Records (AC 136)
22. Use a Delete Query to Delete a Group of Records (AC 138)
23. Create an Append Query (AC 139)
24. Specify a Required Field (AC 140)
25. Specify a Range (AC 141)
26. Specify a Default Value (AC 142)
27. Specify a Collection of Legal Values (AC 143)
28. Specify a Format (AC 144)
29. Save the Validation Rules, Default Values, and Formats (AC 144)
30. Create a Lookup Field (AC 147)
31. Use a Lookup Field (AC 149)
32. Specify Referential Integrity (AC 151)
33. Use a Subdatasheet (AC 153)
34. Find Duplicate Records (AC 154)
35. Find Unmatched Records (AC 154)
36. Use the Sort Ascending Button to Order Records (AC 155)
37. Use the Sort Ascending Button to Order Records on Multiple Fields (AC 156)
38. Create a Single-Field Index (AC 160)
39. Create a Multiple-Field Index (AC 161)
40. Close a Database and Quit Access (AC 162)
41. Back Up a Database (AC 163)
42. Compact and Repair a Database (AC 164)

Career Corner

Network Specialist

As more companies rely on networks, the demand for network specialists will continue to grow. A *network specialist* must have a working knowledge of local area networks and their application within wide area networks. A network specialist also must be familiar with the Internet, its connectivity to LANs and WANs, and Web server management. Responsibilities of a network specialist include installing, configuring, and troubleshooting network systems. Other responsibilities may include managing system and client software, Web page integration and creation, network security measures, user accounting, and monitoring network event logs for problem resolution. A network specialist must possess good problem-solving skills and the ability to work independently. They also must have the ability to concentrate on detailed projects for long periods of time. Good oral, written, and team-oriented interpersonal skills also are beneficial.

Many institutions offer two-year network specialist programs. In addition to a college degree, industry certifications are available for further career enhancement. Two of the more notable certifications are the Novell CNA (Certified Novell Administrator) and the Cisco CCNA (Certified Cisco Networking Associate). Network specialist salaries will vary depending on education, certifications, and experience. Individuals with certifications can expect an approximate starting salary between $43,000 and $55,000. For more information, visit scsite.com/off2003sch/careers and then click Network Specialist.

Learn It Online

Instructions: To complete the Learn It Online exercises, start your browser, click the Address bar, and then enter the Web address scsite.com/off2003sch/learn. When the Office 2003 Learn It Online page is displayed, follow the instructions in the exercises below. Each exercise has instructions for printing your results, either for your own records or for submission to your instructor.

1 Project Reinforcement TF, MC, and SA

Below Access Project 3, click the Project Reinforcement link. Print the quiz by clicking Print on the File menu for each page. Answer each question.

2 Flash Cards

Below Access Project 3, click the Flash Cards link and read the instructions. Type 20 (or a number specified by your instructor) in the Number of playing cards text box, type your name in the Enter your Name text box, and then click the Flip Card button. When the flash card is displayed, read the question and then click the ANSWER box arrow to select an answer. Flip through Flash Cards. If your score is 15 (75%) correct or greater, click Print on the File menu to print your results. If your score is less than 15 (75%) correct, then redo this exercise by clicking the Replay button.

3 Practice Test

Below Access Project 3, click the Practice Test link. Answer each question, enter your first and last name at the bottom of the page, and then click the Grade Test button. When the graded practice test is displayed on your screen, click Print on the File menu to print a hard copy. Continue to take practice tests until you score 80% or better.

4 Who Wants To Be a Computer Genius?

Below Access Project 3, click the Computer Genius link. Read the instructions, enter your first and last name at the bottom of the page, and then click the PLAY button. When your score is displayed, click the PRINT RESULTS link to print a hard copy.

5 Wheel of Terms

Below Access Project 3, click the Wheel of Terms link. Read the instructions, and then enter your first and last name and your school name. Click the PLAY button. When your score is displayed, right-click the score and then click Print on the shortcut menu to print a hard copy.

6 Crossword Puzzle Challenge

Below Access Project 3, click the Crossword Puzzle Challenge link. Read the instructions, and then enter your first and last name. Click the SUBMIT button. Work the crossword puzzle. When you are finished, click the Submit button. When the crossword puzzle is redisplayed, click the Print Puzzle button to print a hard copy.

7 Tips and Tricks

Below Access Project 3, click the Tips and Tricks link. Click a topic that pertains to Project 3. Right-click the information and then click Print on the shortcut menu. Construct a brief example of what the information relates to in Access to confirm you understand how to use the tip or trick.

8 Newsgroups

Below Access Project 3, click the Newsgroups link. Click a topic that pertains to Project 3. Print three comments.

9 Expanding Your Horizons

Below Access Project 3, click the Expanding Your Horizons link. Click a topic that pertains to Project 3. Print the information. Construct a brief example of what the information relates to in Access to confirm you understand the contents of the article.

10 Search Sleuth

Below Access Project 3, click the Search Sleuth link. To search for a term that pertains to this project, select a term below the Project 3 title and then use the Google search engine at google.com (or any major search engine) to display and print two Web pages that present information on the term.

11 Access Online Training

Below Access Project 3, click the Access Online Training link. When your browser displays the Microsoft Office Online Web page, click the Access link. Click one of the Access courses that covers one or more of the objectives listed at the beginning of the project on page AC 114. Print the first page of the course before stepping through it.

12 Office Marketplace

Below Access Project 3, click the Office Marketplace link. When your browser displays the Microsoft Office Online Web page, click the Office Marketplace link. Click a topic that relates to Access. Print the first page.

13 You're Hired!

Below Access Project 3, click the You're Hired! link to embark on the path to a career in computers. Directions about how to play the game will be displayed. When you are ready to play, click the begin the game button. If required, submit your score to your instructor.

Apply Your Knowledge

1 Maintaining the Keep It Green Database

Instructions: Start Access. Open the Keep It Green database that you modified in Apply Your Knowledge 1 in Project 2 on page AC 109. (If you did not complete this exercise, see your instructor for a copy of the modified database.) Perform the following tasks:

1. Open the Customer table in Design view as shown in Figure 3-85.

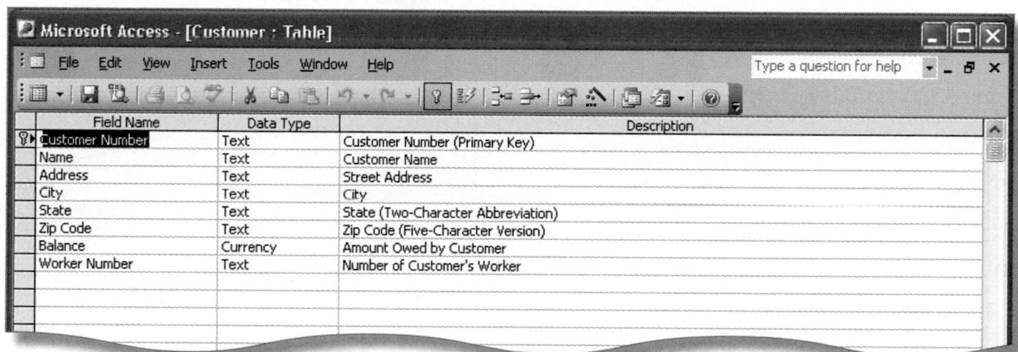

FIGURE 3-85

2. Increase the size of the Name field to 25.
3. Format the Customer Number and State fields so any lowercase letters appear in uppercase.
4. Make the Name field a required field.
5. Specify that balance amounts must be less than or equal to $500.00. Include validation text.
6. Create an index that allows duplicates for the Name field.
7. Save the changes to the structure.
8. Open the Customer table in Datasheet view.
9. Change the name of customer RO32 to Royal Manufacturing Ltd and the address of customer CC76 to 109 Fletcher.
10. Resize the Name column so the complete name for customer RO32 appears. Resize the remaining columns to the best fit.
11. Close the table and click the Yes button to save the changes to the layout of the table.
12. Print the table. If necessary, change the margins so the table prints on one page in landscape orientation.
13. Open the Customer table and use Filter By Selection to find the record for client MO13. Delete the record.
14. Remove the filter and then print the table.
15. Sort the data in descending order by balance.
16. Print the table in landscape orientation. Close the table. If you are asked to save changes to the design of the table, click the No button.
17. Establish referential integrity between the Worker table (the one table) and the Customer table (the many table). Cascade the update but do not cascade the delete. Print the Relationships window by making sure the Relationships window is open, clicking File on the menu bar, and then clicking Print Relationships. When Access displays the Print Preview window, click the Print button on the Print Preview toolbar. Do not save the report.
18. Back up the database.

1 Maintaining the Alumni Connection Database

Problem: The Athletic Department recently asked the alumni association to take over the selling of school athletic items to students. Because the Athletic Department had its own database of items, you now need to append these new items to the current Item table. You also need to change the database structure and add some validation rules to the database.

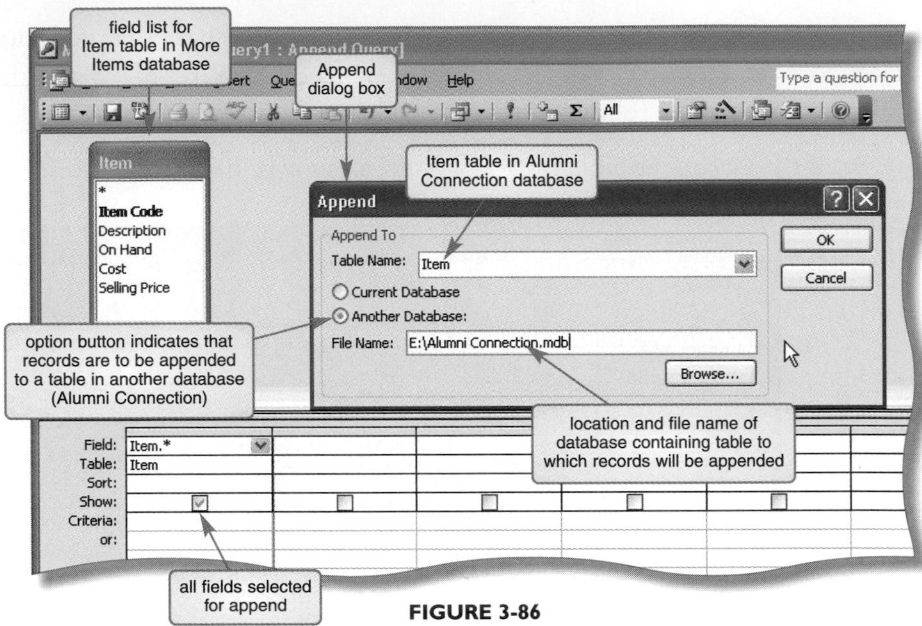

FIGURE 3-86

Instructions: Use both the Alumni Connection database created in the In the Lab 1 of Project 1 on page AC 56 and the More Items database for this assignment. Perform the following tasks:

1. Open the More Items database. See page xxiv at the front of this book for instructions for downloading the Data Files for Students or see your instructor for information on accessing the files required in this book.
2. Create a new query for the Item table and double-click the asterisk in the field list to add all fields to the query.
3. Change the query type to an Append Query. When Access displays the Append dialog box, make the entries shown in Figure 3-86 and then click the OK button. Be sure to insert the correct drive letter for your USB device in the File name text box.
4. Click the Run button on the Query Design toolbar to run the append query. Click the Yes button in the Microsoft Office Access dialog box that displays the message that you are about to append 4 rows.
5. Close the append query without saving it, and then close the More Items database. Open the Alumni Connection database, and then open the Item table in Datasheet view. The table should contain 14 records.
6. The items added from the More Items database do not have a vendor assigned to them. Assign these four records to vendor SS.
7. Resize the columns to best fit the data and print the Item table. Save the changes to the layout.
8. Using a query, delete all records in the Item table where the description starts with the letter K. (*Hint*: Use Help to solve this problem.) Close the query without saving it. Print the Item table.
9. Open the Vendor table in Design view and add a new field to the end of the table. Name the field, Fax Number. This new field has the same data type and field size as Telephone Number. Enter the same description as Telephone Number but replace Telephone with Fax. Save the change to the table design.
10. Add the data shown at the right to the Fax Number field.
11. Resize all columns in the Vendor table to the best fit.
12. Print the table on one page in landscape orientation. Save the change to the layout.
13. Specify referential integrity between the Vendor table (the one table) and the Item table (the many table). Cascade the update but not the delete. Print the Relationships window.
14. Compact the database.

AL	602-555-6574
GG	512-555-8967
SS	610-555-3344
TM	707-555-9991

2 Maintaining the Clean n Neat Database

Problem: Clean n Neat is expanding rapidly and needs to make some database changes to handle the expansion. The company needs to know more about its clients, such as its type of business, and it needs to ensure that data that is entered in the database is valid. It also needs to add some new clients to the database.

Instructions: Use the Clean n Neat database created in the In the Lab 2 of Project 1 on page AC 59 or see your instructor for information about accessing the files required for this book. Perform the following tasks:

1. Open the Clean n Neat database and then open the Client table in Design view.
2. Add the field, Client Type, to the Client table. The field should appear after the Zip Code field. Define the field as text with a width of 3. This field will contain data on the type of client. The client types are MAN (Manufacturing), RET (Retail), and SER (Service). Save these changes to the structure.
3. Using a query, change all the entries in the Client Type column to RET. This will be the type of most clients. Do not save the query.
4. Open the Client table and resize all columns to best fit the data. Print the table in landscape orientation. Save the changes to the layout of the table.
5. Create the following validation rules for the Client table and save the changes to the table. List the steps involved on your own paper.
   a. Increase the size of the Name field to 25 and make the Name field a required field.
   b. Specify the legal values MAN, RET, and SER for the Client Type field. Include validation text.
   c. Assign a default value of RET to the Client Type field.
   d. Ensure that any letters entered in the Client Number field appear as uppercase.
   e. Specify that Balance must be less than or equal to $500.00. Include validation text.
   f. Make the Client Type field a lookup field.
6. Make the following changes to the Client table. You can use either the Find button or Filter By Selection to locate the records to change:
   a. Change the client type for clients AD03, BE09, DL41, and HA09 to SER.
   b. Change the client type for clients CR47 and ST21 to MAN.
   c. Change the name of client BE09 to Beachside Restaurant.
7. Add the following clients to the Client table:

CT12	Cary's Beach Togs	56 Mallory	Andice	GA	31501	RET	$0.00	02
LC20	Larry's Fitness Center	25 Wymberly	Liberty	GA	31499	SER	$0.00	13

8. Resize the Name column to best fit the new data, and save the changes to the layout of the table.
9. Open the Client table and use Filter By Form to find all records where the client has a balance of $0.00 and has the Client Type of MAN. Delete these records.
10. Remove the filter, change the font to Courier New and the font size to 9. Change the gridline color to blue. Print the table in landscape orientation. Close the Client table and do not save any changes.
11. Specify referential integrity between the Custodian table (the one table) and the Client table (the many table). Cascade the update but not the delete. Print the Relationships window. Do not save the report.
12. Compact the database and then back up the database.

3 Maintaining the Centinel Database

Problem: The newspaper has determined that some changes must be made to the advertising database structure. Another field must be added. Because student interns update the data, the newspaper also would like to add some validation rules to the database. Finally, some additions and deletions are required to the database.

Instructions: Use the database created in the In the Lab 3 of Project 1 on page AC 61 for this exercise or see your instructor for information about accessing the files required for this book.

Instructions Part 1: Several changes must be made to the database structure. For example, the newspaper would like to categorize the businesses that advertise in the paper. It has determined that the businesses should be categorized as Retail, Dining, or Service establishments and suggest you use the advertiser types RET, DIN, and SER, respectively. Further, the newspaper has identified advertisers A28, C75, and W45 as retail businesses. Advertisers C48, D21, P12, and S11 are service establishments and advertisers B03, G34, and M32 are restaurants. The newspaper wants to ensure that only those types are entered, and it wants to provide some type of lookup to help the interns that do the data entry. It also wants to ensure that an entry always appears in the Name field and that any letters entered in the Advertiser Number field appear in uppercase. Because it often sorts the data by advertiser name, it wants to make the sorting process more efficient. Make the changes to the database structure and then print the Advertiser table. Place the Advertiser Type field after the Telephone Number field. To ensure that the table prints on one page, adjust the column widths to best fit the data and print the table in landscape orientation.

Instructions Part 2: The newspaper has acquired two new advertisers. These advertisers are:

E04	Effel's Nails	14 Barton	19163	555-7788	SER	$0.00	$0.00	42
R11	Roundtop Grille	20 Main	19164	555-4455	DIN	$50.00	$0.00	36

Also, the owner of M&E Expresso has sold the business and the new owner now wants to advertise under the name, Oleander Coffee. Another advertiser, Creative Toys, has gone out of business. You can use either Datasheet view or Form view to make these changes. To show the newspaper that you have made the appropriate changes, adjust column widths and print the Advertiser table. Be sure the table prints on one page.

Instructions Part 3: Because the ad reps work on commission, the newspaper wants to make sure that advertisers are not assigned to an ad rep that is not in the database. It also wants the ability to change an ad rep number in the Ad Rep table and have the change applied to the Advertiser table. Create the appropriate relationship that would satisfy the newspaper's needs and print the relationship. Then, change the ad rep number for ad rep 39 to 41. Print the Advertiser table. Be sure the table prints on one page.

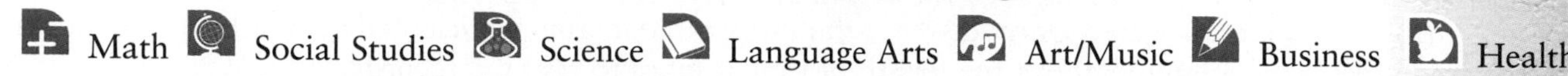

Cases and Places

The difficulty of the case studies varies:
■ are the least difficult and ■■ are more difficult.
Each exercise has a cross-curricular designation:

Math Social Studies Science Language Arts Art/Music Business Health

1 Use the College Lawn Services database you created in Case Study 1 of Project 1 on page AC 63 for this assignment or see your instructor for information about accessing the files required for this book. Perform each of the following tasks and then print the results:

(a) Barbara TerHorst recently married. Her new name is Barbara Wickenberger.
(b) Dave Grangas's new balance is $75.00. Also, no customer should be allowed to have a balance greater than $150.00.
(c) Johan Croeger received a raise and now makes $7.50 an hour.
(d) Specify referential integrity. Cascade the update but not the delete.
(e) Compact and then back up the database.

2 Use the Community Fitness Center database you created in Case Study 2 of Project 1 on page AC 63 for this assignment or see your instructor for information about accessing the files required for this book. Perform each of these tasks and then print the results:

(a) Create an index on the Last Name and First Name fields in the Member table. Sort the records in the table in descending order by last name and first name.
(b) Add a City field to the Member table. The field should appear after the Address field. The field is a text field, and the data length is determined by the length of the specific city that you choose to enter. For example, if your city is Philadelphia, the data length should be 12. Use an update query to add your own city.
(c) Resize the columns in both tables to best fit the data.
(d) Change the cell effect for the Rate table to Sunken.
(e) Specify referential integrity. Cascade the update but not the delete.
(f) Compact and then back up the database.

Cases and Places

3 Use the Book Cooperative database you created in Case Study 3 of Project 1 on page AC 63 for this assignment or see your instructor for information about accessing the files required for this book:

(a) The cooperative frequently displays the Book table in alphabetical order by title. The cooperative is complaining about the length of time it takes to sort the records.

(b) All books must have a title, and the price should be greater than $0.00 and less than $15.00.

(c) The title for the book 4365 actually is Molly's Trials and Tribulations.

(d) John Mott wants to sell another book. The book is County Politics by Estelle Dearling. John is selling the book for $8.50 and claims it is in good condition. The cooperative would like to assign the code 9867 to the book.

(e) Joe Van sold his copy of Hill Country Blues.

(f) Determine whether any records are in one table that do not have related records in another table.

(g) Analyze the database and determine if you have a one-to-many relationship between any tables. If so, specify referential integrity between the tables. Cascade the update but not the delete.

4 Use the Math Club database you created in Case Study 4 of Project 1 on page AC 64 for this assignment or see your instructor for information about accessing the files required for this book:

(a) Marcia Patterson's twin brother Mark recently asked to be tutored in Algebra. He hasn't earned any points yet, and his tutor is Della Hanley.

(b) The Math Club would like to sort records quickly by last name within high school.

(c) Currently, the only valid tutoring subjects are Algebra and Geometry. More students seem to need help in Geometry.

(d) All the students from Brynn High School have earned 10 additional points.

(e) John Shoppers has dropped out of the tutoring program.

(f) Ron Rodell is a new tutor. He has not worked any hours yet. The Math Club has designated him as tutor number 80.

(g) Determine whether your database contains any duplicate records.

(h) Analyze the database and determine if you have a one-to-many relationship between any tables. If so, specify referential integrity. Cascade the update but not the delete.

5 **Working Together** Open the Event Management database that you created in Project 1. As a team, review the data types for each of the fields in the database. Do any of these data types need to be changed? For example, is there a Text field that is storing notes about an event? Change the data types as necessary and write a one-page paper that explains your reasons for changing (or not changing) the data types in the Event Management database.

Make a copy of the College Lawn Services database and name it College Bound Lawn Services. Research the purpose of the Find Unmatched Query Wizard and the Find Duplicates Query Wizard. Create queries using each of these wizards. Did the queries perform as expected? Open each query in Design view and modify it. For example, add another field to the query. What happened to the query results? Write a one-page paper that explains the purpose of each query wizard and describes your experiences with creating and modifying the queries.

MICROSOFT OFFICE
Access 2003

Sharing Data among Applications

CASE PERSPECTIVE

Alyssa High School of Information Technology (AHSIT) has an active alumni association. Association members have been using Microsoft Excel to automate a variety of tasks for several years. Currently, they are seeking to raise enough money to install a wireless network on campus and provide computer training for the community. A group of alumni has been responsible for contacting other alumni and friends of the school to raise the necessary funds. Fund-raising data has been stored in an Excel worksheet. After noticing how efficiently the Corporate Internship department maintains its data, the alumni association has decided they need to maintain the fund-raising data in an Access database. They need an easy way to copy the data to Access.

Additionally, the corporate internship program has determined that it needs to export (copy) some of the data in its database to other formats. Some school district personnel need the data in Excel, others want it placed in a Microsoft Word document, and still others want the ability to send a report via e-mail.

Dr. Gervase would like to export the Client and Intern tables in such a way that they can be imported easily to a database maintained by the school district, which handles various accounting functions for AHSIT. The users have learned that the easiest way to do this is to use XML (Extensible Markup Language).

As you read through this Integration Feature, you will learn how to use Access to both import and export data for use with other applications desired by the alumni association and by the corporate partnership program at Alyssa High School of Information Technology.

Objectives

You will have mastered the material in this Integration Feature when you can:

- Import or link an Excel worksheet
- Export data to Excel and Word
- Create report snapshots
- Export and import XML data

Introduction

It is not uncommon for people to use an application for some specific purpose, only to find later that another application may be better suited. For example, an organization such as the alumni association for Alyssa High School initially might keep data in an Excel worksheet, only to discover later that the data would be better maintained in an Access database. The following are some common reasons for using a database instead of a worksheet:

1. The worksheet contains a great deal of redundant data. As discussed in Project 1 on pages AC 50 and AC 51, databases can be designed to eliminate redundant data.
2. The worksheet would need to be larger than Excel can handle. Excel has a limit of 16,384 rows. In Access, no such limit exists.
3. The data to be maintained consists of multiple interrelated items. For example, the AHSIT Internships database maintains data on two items, clients and interns, and these items are interrelated. A client has a single intern, and each intern works for several clients. The AHSIT Internships database is a very simple one. Databases easily can contain thirty or more interrelated items.

4. You want to use the extremely powerful query and report capabilities of Microsoft Access.

Regardless of the reasons for making the change from a worksheet to a database, it is important to be able to make the change easily. In the not-too-distant past, converting data from one tool to another often could be a very difficult, time-consuming task. Fortunately, an easy way of converting data from Excel to Access is available.

Figures 1a and 1b illustrate the conversion process. The type of worksheet that can be converted is one in which the data is stored as a **list**; that is, a labeled series of rows in which each row contains the same type of data. For example, in the worksheet in Figure 1a, the first row contains the labels, which are entries indicating the type of data found in the column. The entry in the first column, for example, is Donor Number, indicating that all the other values in the column are donor numbers. The entry in the second column is Last Name, indicating that all the other values in the column are last names. Other than the first row, which contains the labels, all the rows contain precisely the same type of data shown in the Access database in Figure 1b: a donor number in the first column, a last name in the second column, a first name in the third column, and so on.

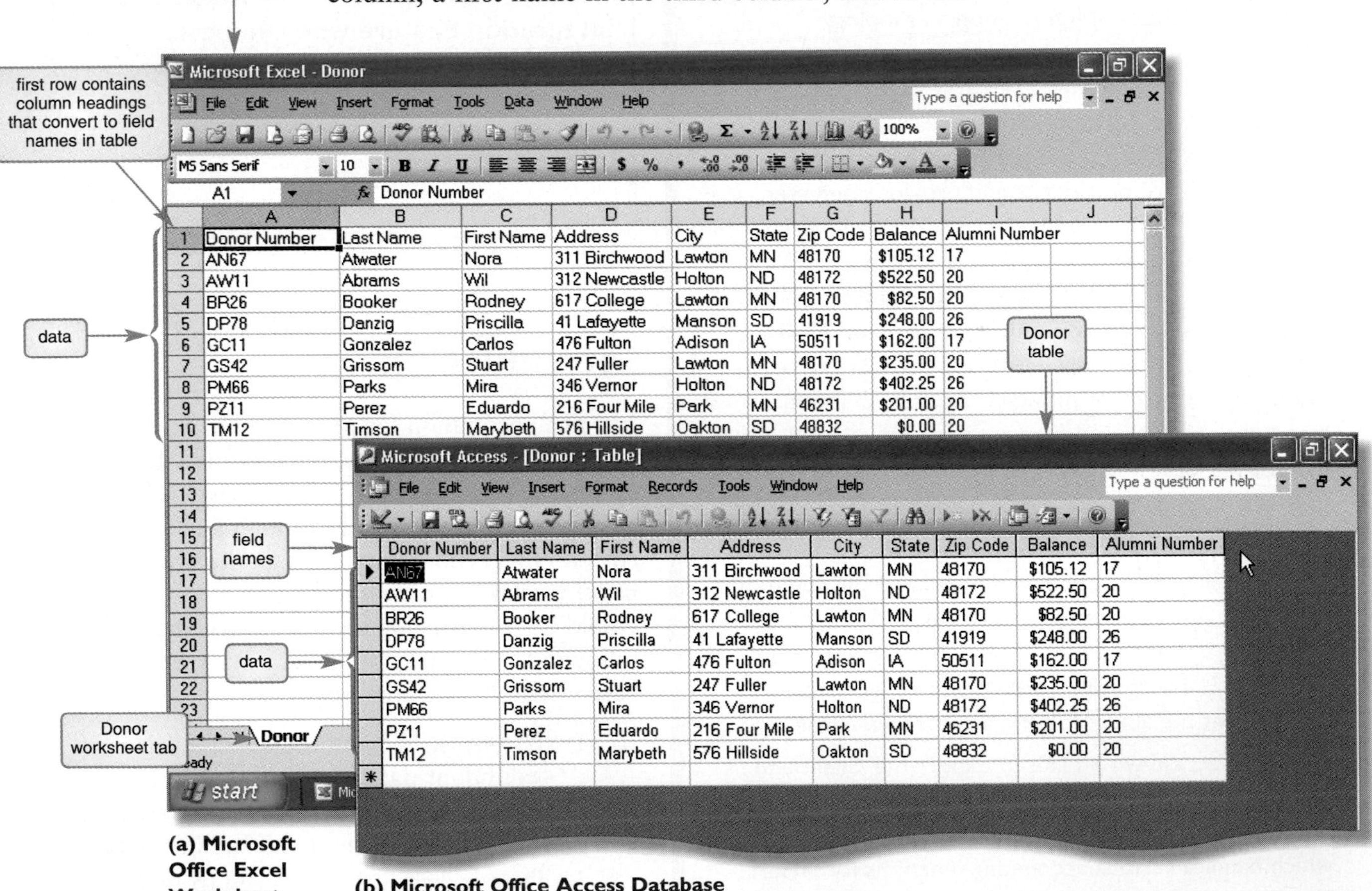

(a) Microsoft Office Excel Worksheet

(b) Microsoft Office Access Database

FIGURE 1

As the figures illustrate, the worksheet, shown in Figure 1a, is copied to a database table, shown in Figure 1b. The columns in the worksheet become the fields. The column headings in the first row of the worksheet become the field names. The rows of the worksheet, other than the first row, which contains the labels, become the records in the table. In the process, each field will be assigned the data type that seems the most reasonable, given the data currently in the worksheet.

Conversely, you can copy data from an Access database so that another application (for example, Excel) can use the data. Several different ways exist to export data. The two most common are to use the Export command on the File menu, which you will use to export a query to an Excel worksheet (Figure 2a), and to use drag-and-drop, which you will use to export a query to a Word document (Figure 2b).

At times you may want to send a report to a user via e-mail. It would be prohibitive to send the whole database to the other user, just so the user could print or view the report. In addition, doing so would require the other user to have Microsoft Access installed. A better way is to create a snapshot of the report. A **snapshot** is a special file that contains the report exactly as it appears when printed (Figure 2c). The other user then can use the Snapshot Viewer, which is a Microsoft Office tool, to view or print the report.

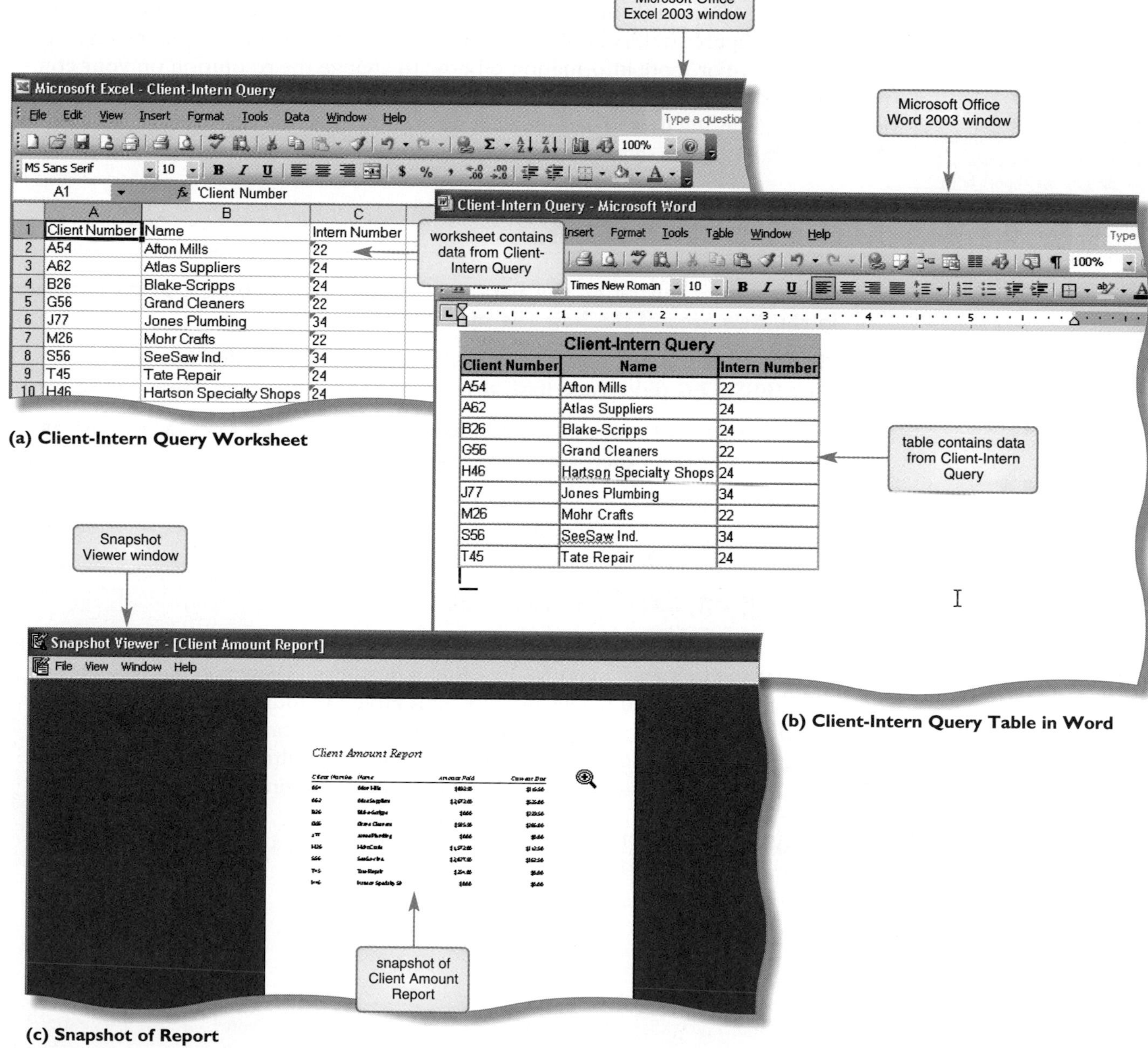

(a) Client-Intern Query Worksheet

(b) Client-Intern Query Table in Word

(c) Snapshot of Report

FIGURE 2

You also can export and import data using XML, which is a format for exchanging data between dissimilar applications. The XML format allows you to export and import both data and structure of multiple related tables in a single operation.

Q & A

Q: What kind of database objects can I import using the Import command?

A: You can use the Import command to import objects, such as tables, queries, reports, and forms, from other databases. When you select a database in the Import dialog box, Access displays the Import Objects dialog box. You then can select the type of object to import. Click the Options button in the Import Objects dialog box to display a list of options. For example, you can import only the structure of a table or you can import both the structure and the data.

Convert Data from Other Applications to Access

The process of converting data to an Access database, referred to as **importing**, uses an Import wizard. Specifically, if the data is copied from an Excel worksheet, the process will use the **Import Spreadsheet Wizard**. The wizard takes you through some basic steps, asking a few simple questions. After you have answered the questions, the wizard will perform the conversion, creating an appropriate table in the database and filling it with the data from the worksheet.

Creating an Access Database

If you are stepping through this project on a computer and you want your screen to match the figures in this book, then you should change your computer's resolution to 800 × 600. For more information on how to change the resolution on your computer, see Appendix D. Before converting the data, you need to create the database that will contain the data. The following steps show how to create the Alyssa Alumni database. The steps assume that you already have started Access.

To Create a New Database

1. **Click the New button on the Database toolbar, and then click Blank database in the New area of the New File task pane.**
2. **Click the Save in box arrow in the File New Database dialog box and then click UDISK 2.0 (E:). (Your flash drive may have a different name and letter.)**
3. **Erase the current entry in the File name text box, type** `Alyssa Alumni` **as the file name, and then click the Create button.**

Access creates the database. It is open and ready for use.

Importing an Excel Worksheet

To convert the data, use the Import Spreadsheet Wizard. In the process, you will indicate that the first row contains the column headings. These column headings then will become the field names in the Access table. In addition, you will indicate the primary key for the table. As part of the process, you can, if you desire, choose not to include all the fields from the worksheet in the resulting table. You should be aware that some of the steps might take a significant amount of time for Access to execute.

The following steps illustrate the process of importing an Excel worksheet.

To Import an Excel Worksheet

1

- **With the Alyssa Alumni database open, right-click in the open area of the Database window.**

The shortcut menu appears (Figure 3).

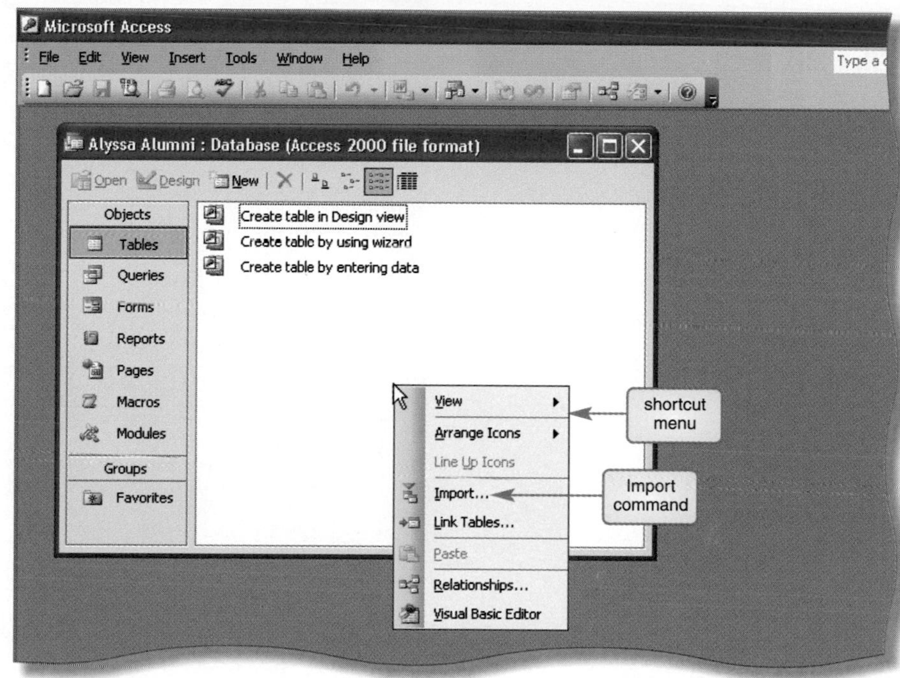

FIGURE 3

2

- **Click Import.**
- **When Access displays the Import dialog box, click the Files of type box arrow and then click Microsoft Excel.**
- **If necessary, select UDISK 2.0 (E:) (your USB flash drive may have a different name and letter) in the Look in list.**
- **Make sure the Donor workbook is selected, and then click the Import button.**
- **When Access displays the Import Spreadsheet Wizard dialog box, if necessary, click Show Worksheets.**
- **Be sure the Donor worksheet is selected, and then click the Next button.**

Access displays the Import Spreadsheet Wizard dialog box requesting you to indicate whether the first row contains column headings (Figure 4).

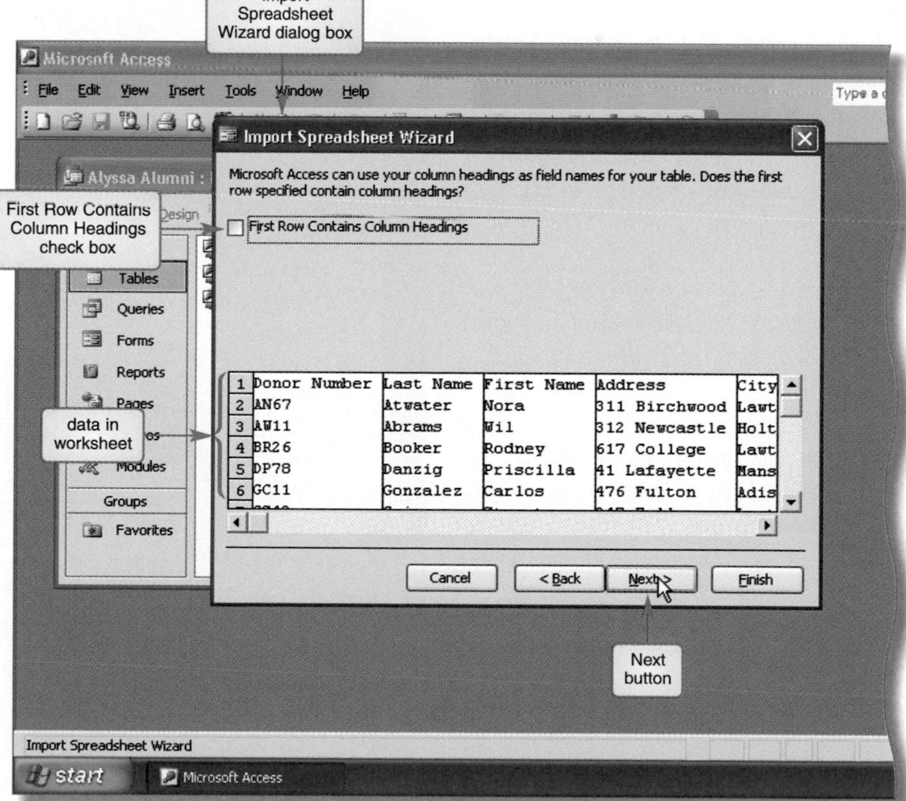

FIGURE 4

3

- **If necessary, click First Row Contains Column Headings to select it.**
- **Click the Next button.**

The Import Spreadsheet Wizard dialog box displays options for storing data in a new table or in an existing table (Figure 5).

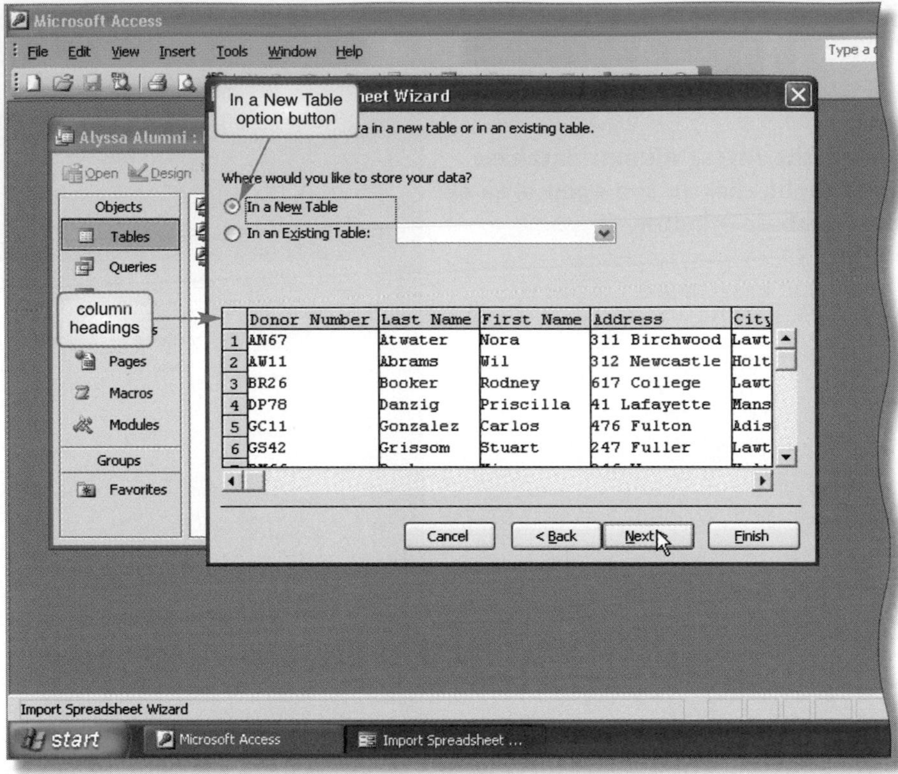

FIGURE 5

4

- **If necessary, click In a New Table to select it and then click the Next button.**
- **Because the Field Options need not be specified, click the Next button.**

The Import Spreadsheet Wizard dialog box displays options for defining a primary key for the new Access table (Figure 6). Options allow Access to add a special field to serve as the primary key, allow the user to choose an existing field to serve as the primary key, or allow the user to indicate no primary key. Most of the time, one of the existing fields will serve as the primary key. In this worksheet, for example, the Donor Number serves as the primary key.

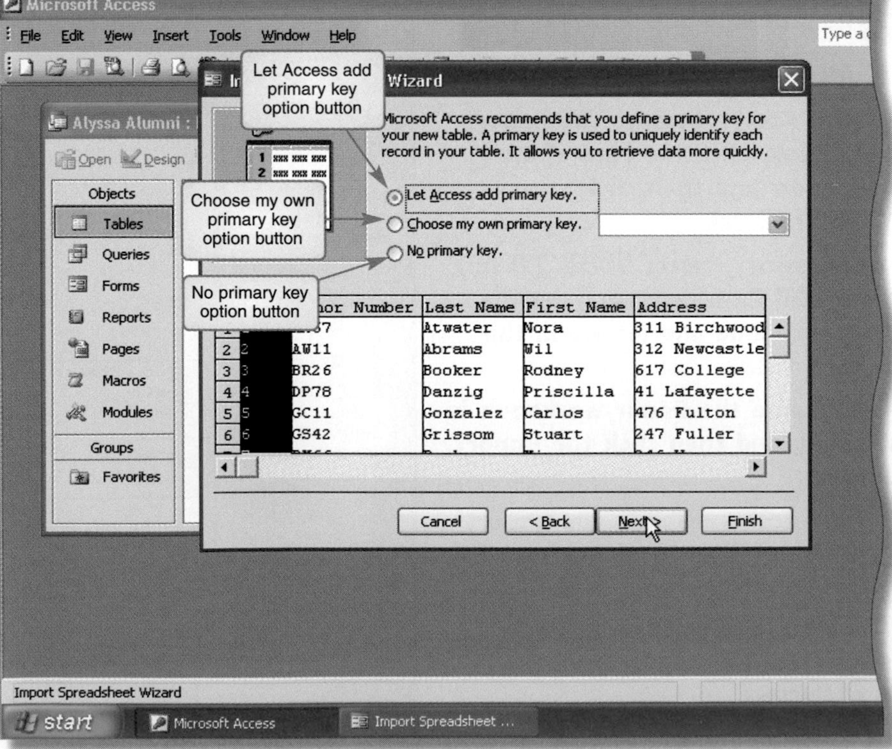

FIGURE 6

5

- **Click Choose my own primary key.**
- **Because the Donor Number field, which is the correct field, already is selected as the primary key, click the Next button. (If some other field were to be the primary key, you could click the down arrow and select the other field from the list of available fields.)**
- **Be sure Donor appears in the Import to Table text box.**
- **Click the Finish button.**

The worksheet is converted into an Access table named Donor. When the process is completed, Access displays the Import Spreadsheet Wizard dialog box (Figure 7).

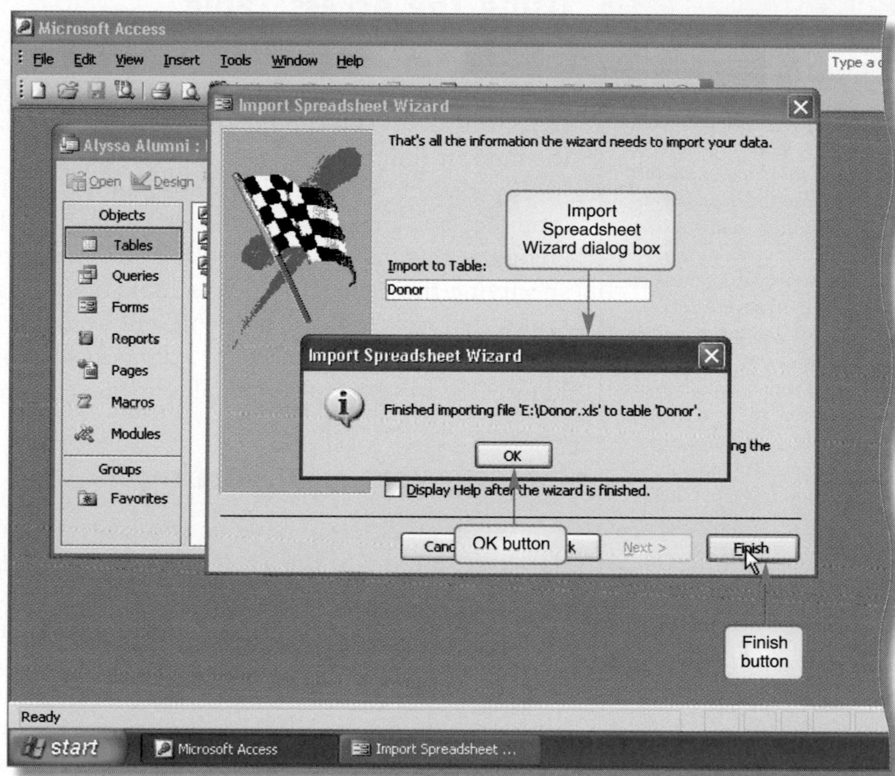

FIGURE 7

6

- **Click the OK button.**

Access has created the table (Figure 8). The table name appears in the Database window.

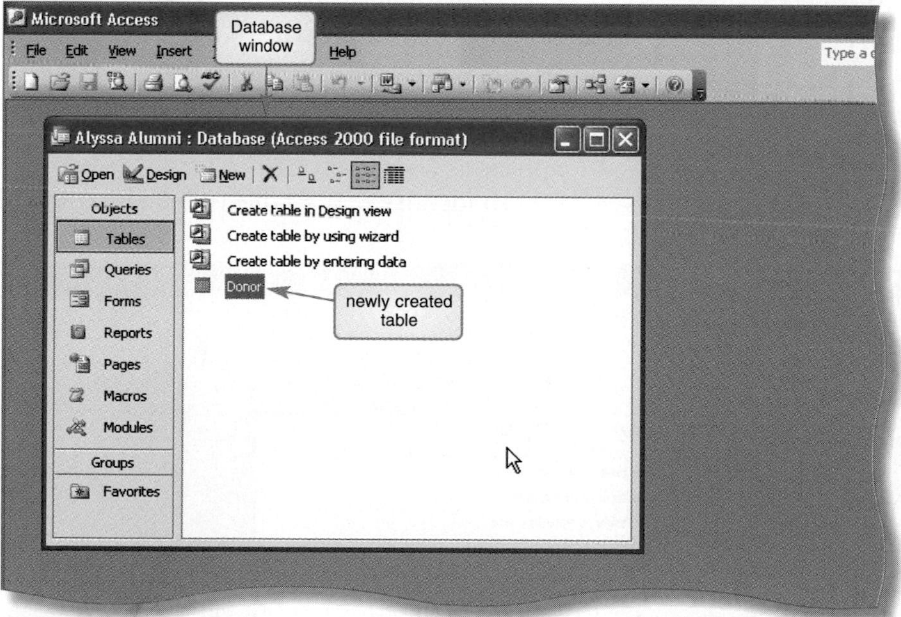

FIGURE 8

Q & A

Q: Need help with Access?

A: Help with Access is no further than the Type a question for help box on the menu bar in the upper-right corner of the window. Click the box that contains the text, Type a question for help (Figure 1b on page AC 174), type `help`, and then press the ENTER key. Access responds with a list of topics you can click to learn about obtaining help on any Access-related topic. To find out what is new in Access 2003, type `what is new in Access` in the Type a question for help box.

Using the Access Table

After the Access version of the table has been created, you can treat it as you would any other table. You can open the table in Datasheet view (Figure 1b on page AC 174). You can make changes to the data. You can create queries that use the data in the table.

By clicking Design View on the table's shortcut menu, you can view the table's structure and make any necessary changes to the structure. The changes may include changing field sizes and types (for those that may not be correct), creating indexes, specifying the primary key, or adding additional fields. If you have imported multiple tables that are to be related, you will need to relate the tables. To accomplish any of these tasks, use the same steps you used in Project 3. In the Donor table shown in Figure 1b, for example, the columns have been resized to best fit the data.

Linking versus Importing

When an external table or worksheet is imported, or converted, into an Access database, a copy of the data is placed as a table in the database. The original data still exists, just as it did before, but no further connection exists between it and the data in the database. Changes to the original data do not affect the data in the database. Likewise, changes in the database do not affect the original data.

It also is possible to **link** data stored in a variety of formats to Access databases by selecting Link instead of Import on the shortcut menu. (The available formats include several other database management systems as well as a variety of nondatabase formats, including Excel worksheets.) With linking, the connection is maintained.

When an Excel worksheet is linked, for example, the worksheet is not stored in the database. Instead, Access simply establishes a connection to the worksheet so you can view or edit the data in either Access or Excel. Any change made in either one will be immediately visible in the other. For example, if you would change an address in Access and then view the worksheet in Excel, you would see the new address. If you add a new row in Excel and then view the table in Access, the row would appear as a new record.

To identify that a table is linked to other data, Access places an arrow in front of the table (Figure 9). In addition, the Excel icon in front of the name identifies the fact that the data is linked to an Excel worksheet.

After you link tables between a worksheet and a database or between two databases, you can modify many of the linked table's features. For example, you can rename the linked table, set view properties, and set links between tables in queries. If you move, rename, or modify linked tables, you can use the **Linked Table Manager** to update the links. To do so, use the Tools menu, click Database Utilities, and then click Linked Table Manager. The Linked Table Manager dialog box that appears includes instructions on how to update the links.

Skill Builder IF-1

To practice the following tasks, visit scsite.com/off2003sch/skill, locate Access Integration Feature, and then click Skill Builder IF-1.

- ❑ Create a database
- ❑ Import an Excel worksheet

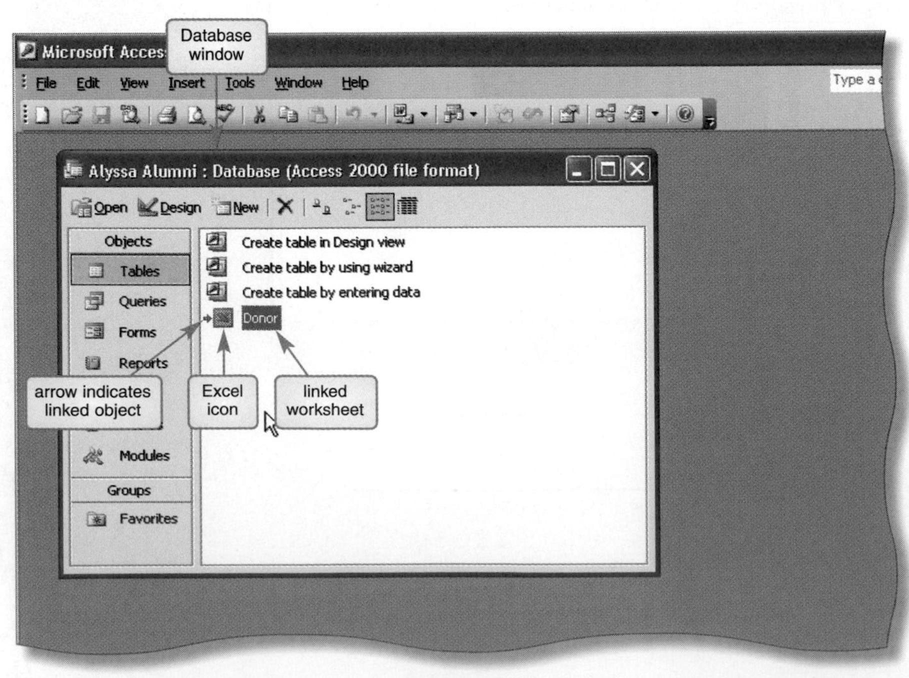

FIGURE 9

Closing the Database

The following step shows how to close the database by closing its Database window.

To Close a Database

1 **Click the Close button for the Alyssa Alumni : Database window.**

> *Q & A*
>
> **Q:** What should I do if I try to open a database and a Microsoft Office Access dialog box appears asking if I want to block unsafe expressions?
>
> **A:** Click the No button when asked if you want to block unsafe expressions. If another dialog box appears with questions about the Microsoft Jet Engine, click Yes and then click Open.

Copy Data from Access to Other Applications

Exporting is the process of copying database objects to another database, to a worksheet, or to some other format so another application (for example, Excel) can use the data. Several ways exist for exporting data. The two most common are to use the Export command, which you will use to export a query to Excel, and to use drag-and-drop, which you will use to export a query to a Word document. You also will use the Export command to export a report as a snapshot.

Opening the Database

Before exporting the AHSIT Internships data, you first must open the database. The following steps show how to open a database.

To Open a Database

1 **Click the Open button on the Database toolbar.**

2 **If necessary, click the Look in box arrow and then click UDISK 2.0 (E:). (Your USB flash drive may have a different name and letter.) Click AHSIT Internships, the database modified in Project 3. (If you did not complete the steps in Project 3, see your instructor for a copy of the database.)**

3 **Click the Open button in the Open dialog box. If a Security Warning dialog box appears, click the Open button.**

Access opens the AHSIT Internships database in the Database window.

Using the Export Command to Export Data to Excel

One way to export data to Excel, as well as to a variety of other formats, is to select the database object to be exported and then select the Export command on the shortcut menu. After you have selected the command, indicate the file type (for example, Microsoft Excel 97-2003) and then click the Save button. For some of the formats, including Excel, you can select Save formatted, in which case the export process will attempt to preserve as much of the Access formatting of the data as possible. You also can select Autostart, in which case the application receiving the data will start automatically once the data is exported. The resulting data then will appear in the application.

The steps on the next page show how to use the Export command to export the Client-Intern Query to Excel.

> *Q & A*
>
> **Q:** How could you export records from a table?
>
> **A:** The process of exporting records from a table is identical to that of exporting records from a query. Simply select the Tables object and then the table containing the records to be exported before selecting the Export command. All records and fields from the table then will be exported.

To Use the Export Command to Export Data to Excel

1

• **Click Queries on the Objects bar, and then right-click Client-Intern Query.**

The shortcut menu appears (Figure 10).

2

• **Click Export.**

• **If necessary, click the Save in box arrow and then click UDISK 2.0 (E:). (Your USB flash drive may have a different name and letter.)**

• **Click the Save as type box arrow, and then click Microsoft Excel 97-2003 in the Save as type list.**

• **Be sure the file name is Client-Intern Query, and then click the Export button.**

The worksheet is created.

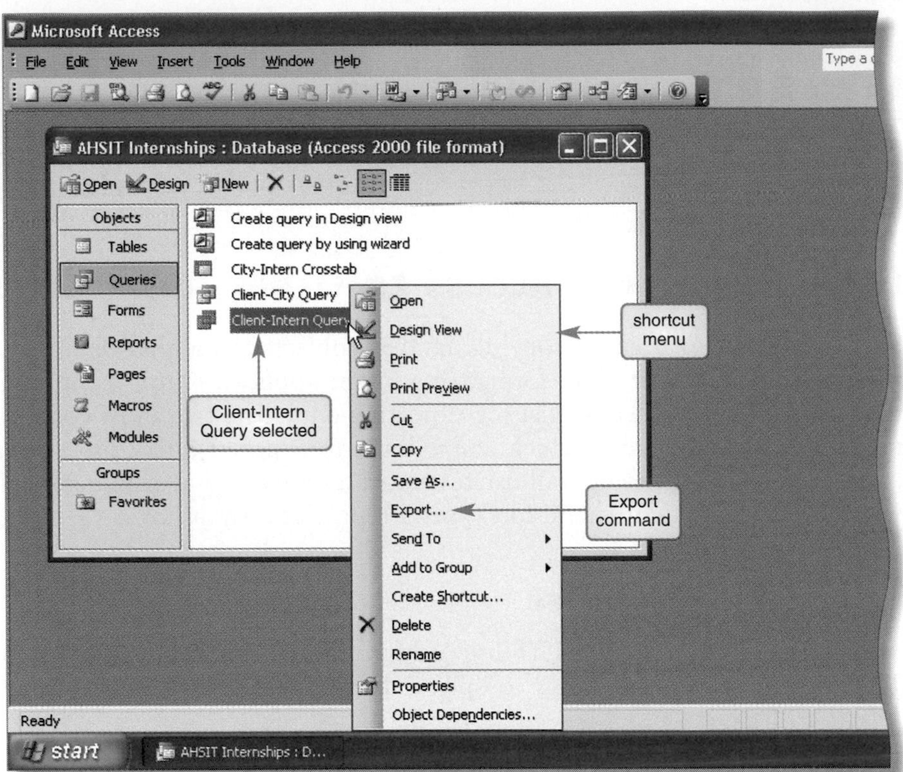

FIGURE 10

To view the worksheet, you could open it in Excel. You then could make any changes to it. For example, you could resize the columns to best fit the data by double-clicking the right edge of the column heading. Figure 2a on page AC 175 shows the worksheet displayed in Excel with the columns resized.

Q & A

Q: Can you use drag-and-drop to export data to Excel?

A: Yes. You can use drag-and-drop to export data to Excel just as you can to export data to Word. Be sure that Excel is running instead of Word. Drag the table or query from the Database window in Access to the Excel worksheet. The records will be converted to rows in the worksheet, and the fields will be converted to columns.

Using Drag-and-Drop to Export Data to Word

When using the Export command, Microsoft Word is not one of the available file types. You would need to select one of the file types that can be imported into Word, export from Access to the selected file type, and then import the file that is created into Word. A simpler way to export to Word is to use the drag-and-drop method. In this method, both Access and Word must be open simultaneously. You then drag the object to be imported from Access to the Word document. The following steps show how to export the Client-Intern Query to Word using the drag-and-drop method.

To Use Drag-and-Drop to Export Data to Word

1

- **Click the Start button on the Windows taskbar, point to All Programs on the Start menu, point to Microsoft Office on the All Programs submenu, and then click Microsoft Office Word 2003 on the Microsoft Office submenu.**
- **Close the Getting Started task pane.**
- **Click the Microsoft Access button on the taskbar to return to Microsoft Access.**
- **Click the Restore Down button or resize the Access window so the Access window does not occupy the full screen.**
- **Be sure the Queries object is selected.**
- **Drag the Client-Intern Query icon to the upper-left corner of the Word document. Do not release the mouse button.**

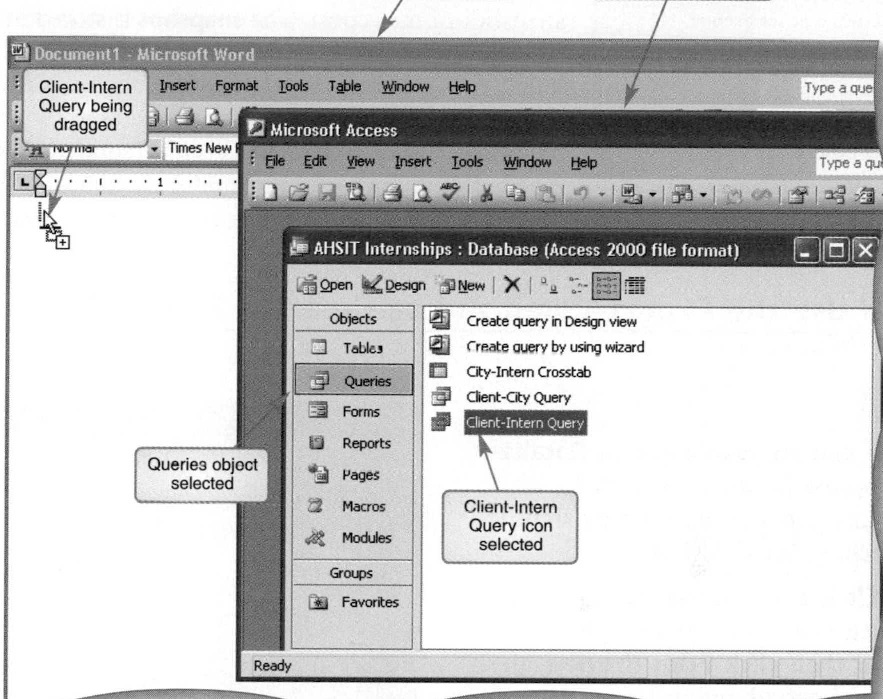

FIGURE 11

Microsoft Office Word is displayed in a maximized window (Figure 11). Microsoft Office Access is displayed in a resized, smaller window. The Queries object is selected and the Client-Intern Query is selected. The mouse pointer indicates that the Client-Intern Query is being dragged to Word.

2

- **Release the mouse button and then click the Save button on the Standard toolbar in Microsoft Word.**
- **If necessary, click the Save in box arrow and then click UDISK 2.0 (E:). (Your USB flash drive may have a different name and letter.)**
- **Type** `Client-Intern Query` **in the File name text box, and then click the Save button in the Save As dialog box.**
- **Click in the Word window to deselect the table.**

The data from the query is inserted in the Word document. The title of the query appears in bold at the top of the document. The data is inserted as a Word table. The document is saved. It looks like the one shown in Figure 2b on page AC 175.

3

- **Quit Word by clicking its Close button.**
- **Maximize the Microsoft Office Access window by double-clicking its title bar.**

The Microsoft Word window closes. The file is saved and available for use.

Skill Builder IF-2

To practice the following tasks, visit scsite.com/off2003sch/skill, locate Access Integration Feature, and then click Skill Builder IF-2.
- ❑ Export data to Word
- ❑ Export data to Excel

Using the Export Command to Create a Snapshot

If you want to send a report to someone via e-mail, the simplest way is to create a snapshot of the report. The **snapshot** is stored in a separate file with an extension of snp. This file contains all the details of the report, including fonts, effects (for example, bold or italic), and graphics. In other words, the contents of the snapshot file look precisely like the report. The snapshot file can be viewed by anyone having the Snapshot Viewer; Microsoft Office Access 2003 is *not* required. You can use the **Snapshot Viewer** to e-mail the snapshot; the recipient can use the Snapshot Viewer to view or print the snapshot.

The following steps illustrate how to create a snapshot.

To Use the Export Command to Create a Snapshot

1

- **If the Microsoft Access Database window is not maximized, maximize the window by double-clicking its title bar.**
- **Click the Reports object, right-click the Client Amount Report, and then click Print Preview on the shortcut menu.**
- **Right-click the preview of the report.**

Access displays the Client Amount Report window with a preview of the report (Figure 12). The shortcut menu appears.

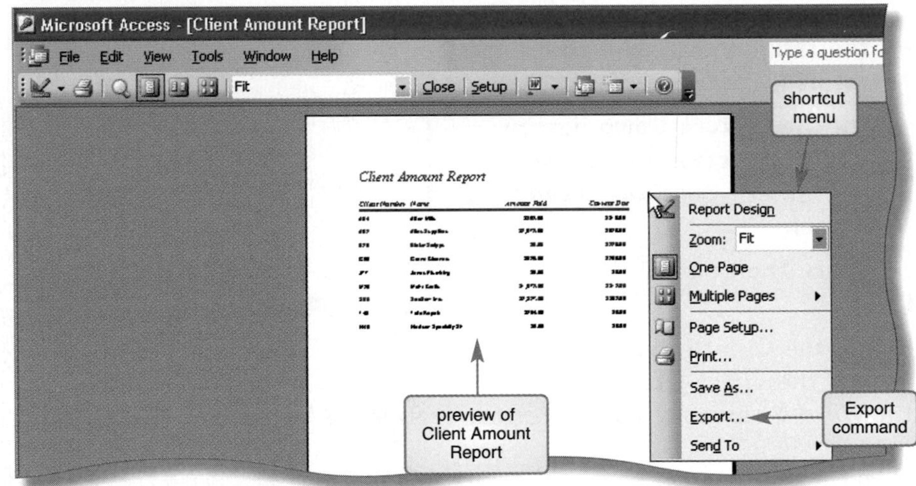

FIGURE 12

2

- **Click Export.**
- **If necessary, click the Save in box arrow and then click UDISK 2.0 (E:). (Your USB flash drive may have a different name and letter.)**
- **Click the Save as type box arrow, select Snapshot Format, be sure the Autostart check box is checked, and then click the Export button.**
- **If a Microsoft Office Access dialog box is displayed asking if you want to install Snapshot Viewer, click the No button and see your instructor.**

The snapshot of the report is created. It looks similar to the one in Figure 2c on page AC 175.

3

- **Click the Close button for the Snapshot Viewer - [Client Amount Report] window.**
- **Click the Close button on the Print Preview toolbar.**

The Snapshot Viewer and Print Preview windows close. Access displays the Database window.

You can e-mail the snapshot to other users. The other users can use the Snapshot Viewer to view the report online or to print the report.

XML

Just as Hypertext Markup Language (HTML) is the standard language for creating and displaying Web pages, **Extensible Markup Language** (**XML**) is the standard language for describing and delivering data on the Web. XML is a data interchange format that allows you to exchange data between dissimilar systems or applications. With XML, you can describe both the data and the structure (**schema**) of the data. You can export tables, queries, forms, or reports.

When exporting XML data, you can choose to export multiple related tables in a single operation to a single XML file. If you later import this XML data to another database, you will import all the tables in a single operation. Thus, the new database would contain each of the tables. All the fields would have all the correct data types and sizes. The primary keys would be correct, and the tables would be related exactly as they were in the original database.

Q & A

Q: Is there more than one way to invoke a command in Access?

A: Yes. For a table that lists how to complete tasks covered in this book using the mouse, menu, shortcut menu, and keyboard, see the Quick Reference Summary at the back of this book, or visit the Office 2003 Quick Reference Web page (scsite.com/off2003sch/qr).

Exporting XML Data

To export XML data, you use the same Export command you used to export to other formats. You then select XML as the Save as type. You indicate whether to save only the data or to save both the data and the schema (that is, the structure). If you have made changes to the appearance of the data, such as changing the font, and want these changes saved as well, you save what is termed the **presentation**. The data is saved in a file with the XML extension, the schema is saved in a file with the XSD extension, and the presentation is saved in a file with the XSL extension. The default choice, which usually is appropriate, is to save both the data and schema, but not the presentation. If multiple tables are related, such as the Client and Intern tables in the AHSIT Internships data, you can export both tables to a single file.

The following steps export both the Client and Intern tables to a single XML file called Client. The steps save the data and the schema, but do not save the presentation.

Q & A

Q: What are some advantages of report snapshots?

A: When you use Access to create a report snapshot, you can distribute reports electronically to users both inside and outside your organization. You do not need to photocopy or mail printed reports. Instead, users can view the reports online and print only the reports they need.

To Export XML Data

1

• **Click the Tables object, and then right-click Client.**

The shortcut menu for the Client table appears (Figure 13).

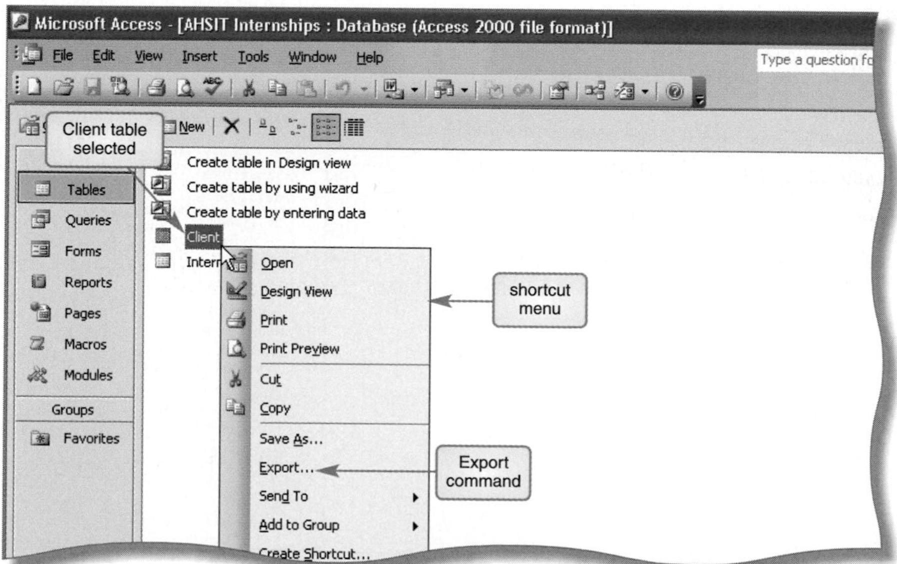

FIGURE 13

2

• **Click Export on the shortcut menu.**

• **Click the Save as type box arrow, scroll down, and then click XML in the list.**

• **If necessary, select UDISK 2.0 (E:) (your USB flash drive may have a different name and letter) in the Save in list.**

Access displays the Export Table 'Client' As dialog box (Figure 14). The file name is Client and the Save as type is XML.

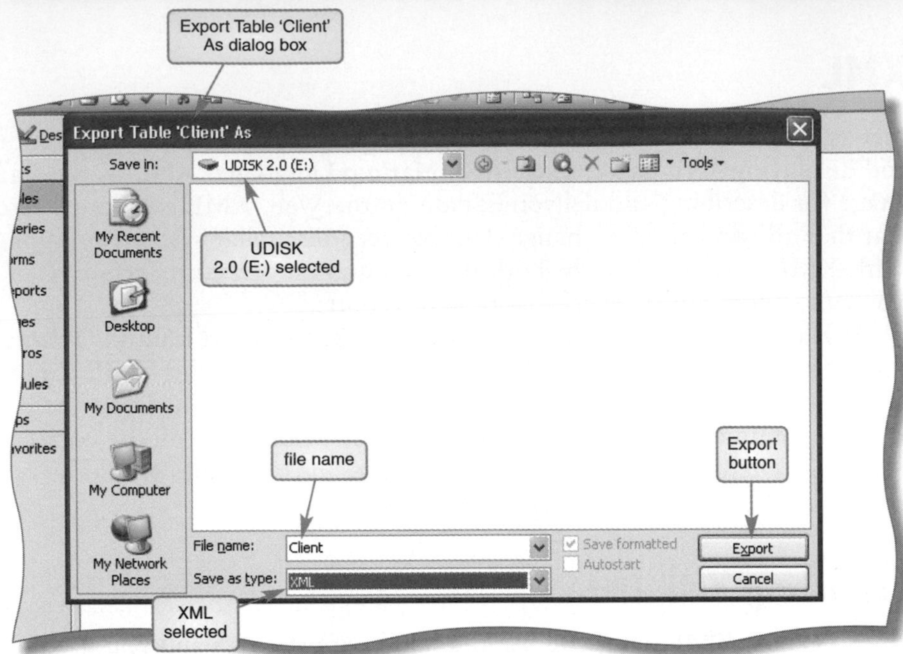

FIGURE 14

3

• **Click the Export button.**

Access displays the Export XML dialog box (Figure 15). The current selections call for the data and schema to be exported. The presentation will not be exported.

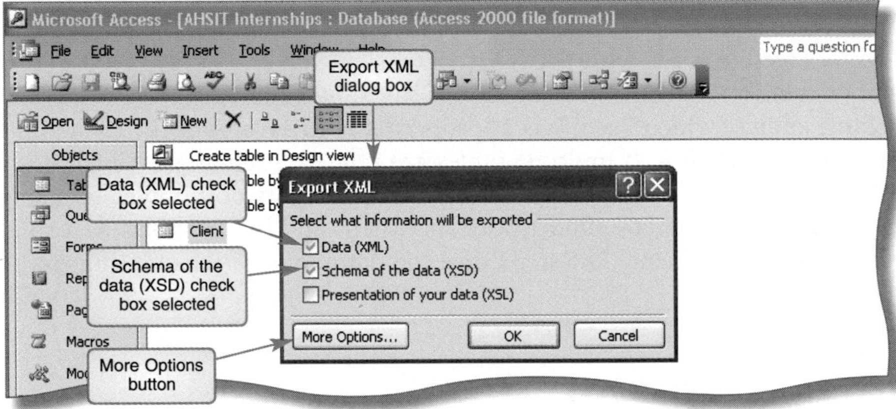

FIGURE 15

4

• **Click the More Options button.**

Access displays the Export XML dialog box (Figure 16). The Data tab is selected.

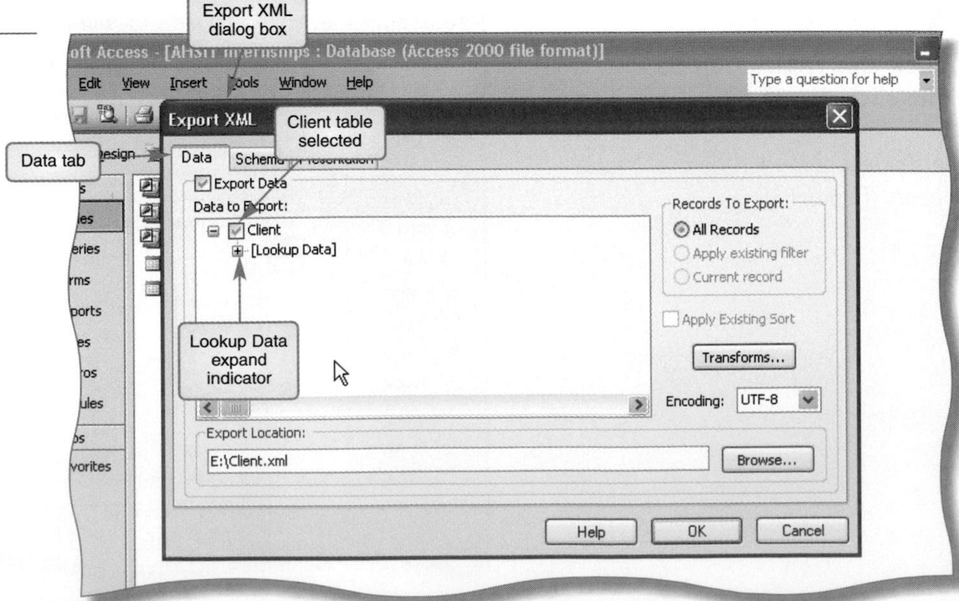

FIGURE 16

5

• **Click the expand indicator (the plus sign) to the left of [Lookup Data], and then click the Intern check box to select the Intern table.**

Both the Client table and the Intern table are selected (Figure 17). The export location is E:\Client.xml.

6

• **Click the OK button.**

• **Click the Close button for the Microsoft Access [AHSIT Internships : Database (Access 2000 file format)] window.**

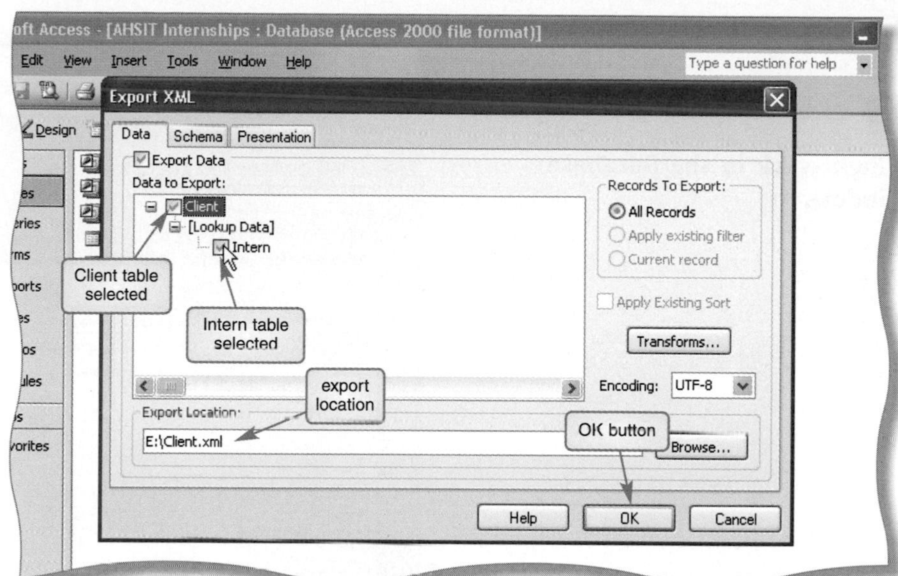

FIGURE 17

The data and structure for both the Client table and the Intern table are exported to the file named Client. The file also contains the relationship between the two tables. The AHSIT Internships database is closed.

Creating an Access Database

Before importing the data, you need to create the database that will contain the data. The following steps create the AD Internships database.

To Create a New Database

1 **Click the New button on the Database toolbar, and then click Blank database in the New area of the New File task pane.**

2 **If necessary, click the Save in box arrow in the File New Database dialog box and then click UDISK 2.0 (E:). (Your USB flash drive may have a different name and letter.)**

3 **Type** `AD Internships` **in the File name text box and then click the Create button.**

Access creates the database. It is open and ready for use.

Importing XML Data

To import XML data, use the Import command and select XML as the type. You then select the XML file that contains the data to be imported. The steps on the next page import the Client and Intern tables stored in the XML file called Client.

To Import XML Data

1

• **Right-click in the Database window.**

The shortcut menu for the Database window appears (Figure 18).

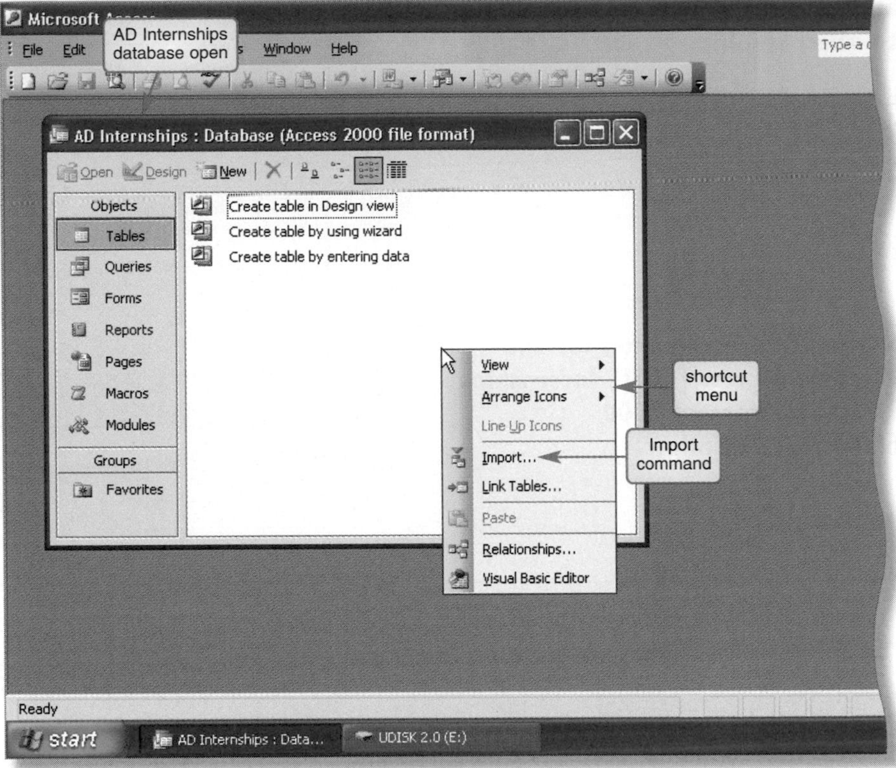

FIGURE 18

2

• **Click Import on the shortcut menu.**

• **When the Import dialog box is displayed, click the Files of type box arrow, scroll down, and then click XML in the list.**

• **If necessary, select UDISK 2.0 (E:) (your USB flash drive may have a different name and letter) in the Look in list.**

• **Click the Client file. (Do not click the xsd version. If you do, you will import both tables, but none of the data. That is, the tables will be empty.)**

Access displays the Import dialog box (Figure 19). The Client file is selected. XML is the file type.

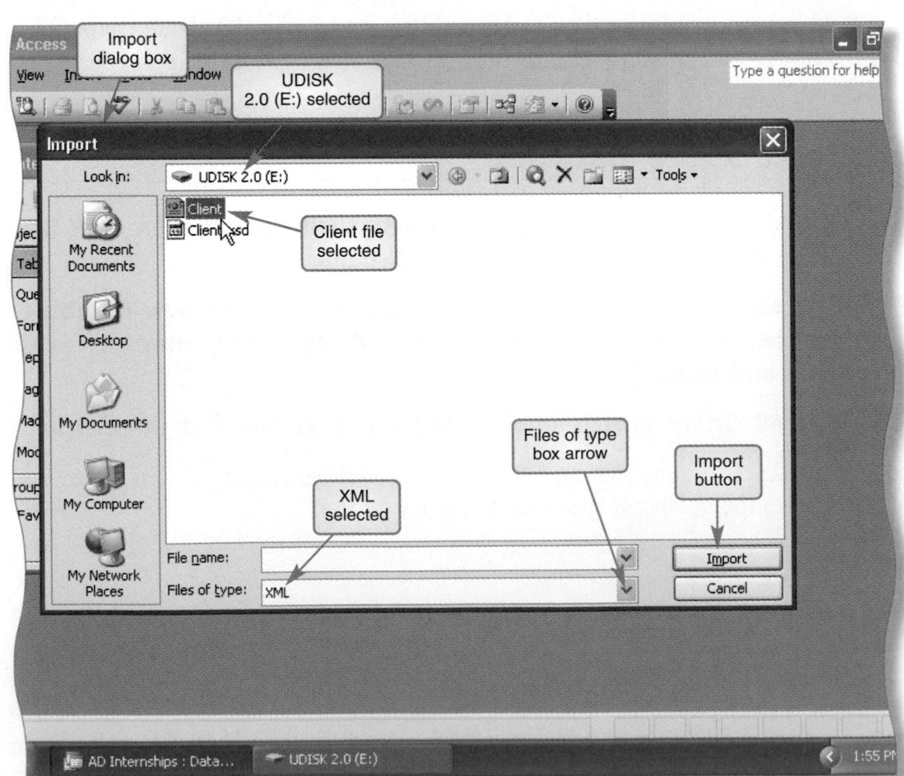

FIGURE 19

3

• **Click the Import button.**

Access displays the Import XML dialog box (Figure 20). Both the Client and Intern tables will be imported. Clicking the expand indicator to the left of either table will display a list of fields in the table.

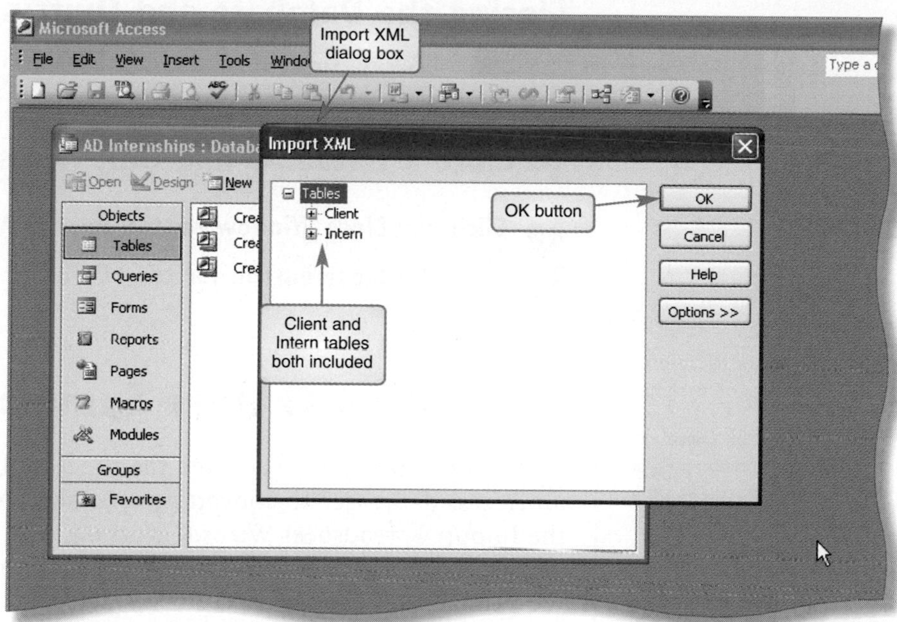

FIGURE 20

4

• **Click the OK button.**

The data is imported and the Microsoft Office Access dialog box is displayed (Figure 21).

5

• **Click the OK button.**

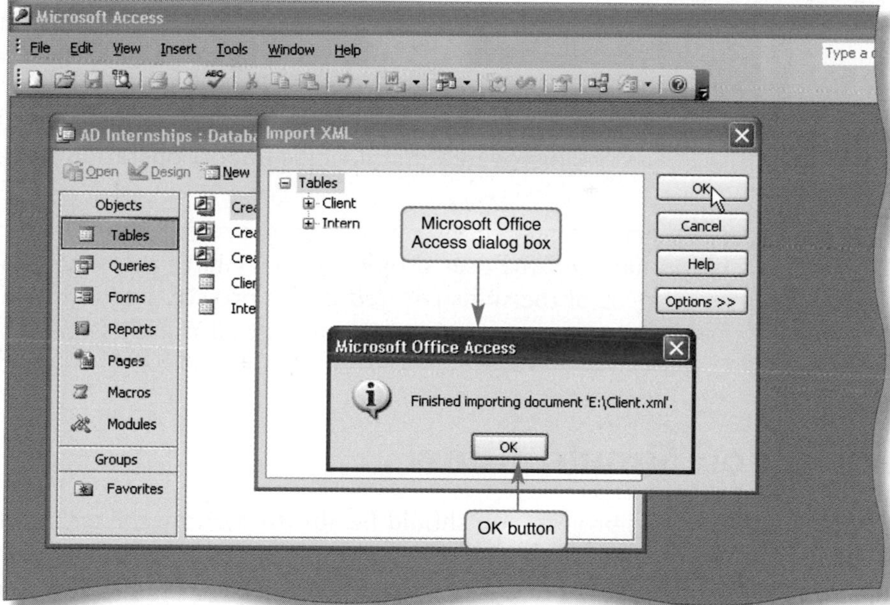

FIGURE 21

Both tables have been imported as part of this single Import operation. In addition to having the same data, the fields in both tables have precisely the same data types and sizes as in the original database. Also, the same fields have been designated primary keys.

Skill Builder IF-3

To practice the following tasks, visit scsite.com/off2003sch/skill, locate Access Integration Feature, and then click Skill Builder IF-3.

❑ Export XML data from a database
❑ Import the XML data to a different database

Closing the Database and Quitting Access

The following steps close the database and quit Access.

To Close a Database and Quit Access

1. **Click the Close Window button for the AD Internships : Database window.**
2. **Click the Close button for the Microsoft Access window.**

Q & A

Q: What is the Microsoft Office Certification program?

A: The Microsoft Office Specialist Certification program provides an opportunity for you to obtain a valuable industry credential — proof that you have the Access 2003 skills required by employers. For more information, see Appendix E, or visit the Office 2003 Certification Web page (scsite.com/off2003sch/cert).

Integration Feature Summary

The Integration Feature covered the process of integrating an Excel worksheet into an Access database. To convert a worksheet to an Access table, you learned to use the Import Spreadsheet Wizard. Working with the wizard, you identified the first row of the worksheet as the row containing the column headings and you indicated the primary key. The wizard then created the table for you and placed it in a new database. You also saw how you could link data instead of importing it.

You learned to use the Export command and used it to export data to an Excel worksheet. You also learned to use the drag-and-drop feature and used it to export data to a Word document. The project illustrated how to use the Export command to create a snapshot of a report. You learned how to export XML data. You exported both structure and data for multiple related tables in a single operation. Finally, you learned how to import the XML data to a separate database and discovered that a single import operation imported both tables and their structures.

If you have a SAM user profile, you may have access to hands-on instruction, practice, and assessment of the skills covered in this project. Log in to your SAM account and go to your assignments page to see what your instructor has assigned.

What You Should Know

Having completed this project, you should be able to perform the tasks below. The tasks are listed in the same order they were presented in this project. For a list of the buttons, menus, toolbars, and commands introduced in this project, see the Quick Reference Summary at the back of this book and refer to the Page Number column.

1. Create a New Database (AC 176)
2. Import an Excel Worksheet (AC 177)
3. Close a Database (AC 181)
4. Open a Database (AC 181)
5. Use the Export Command to Export Data to Excel (AC 182)
6. Use Drag-and-Drop to Export Data to Word (AC 183)
7. Use the Export Command to Create a Snapshot (AC 184)
8. Export XML Data (AC 185)
9. Create a New Database (AC 187)
10. Import XML Data (AC 188)
11. Close a Database and Quit Access (AC 190)

In the Lab

1 Importing Data to an Access Database

Problem: Atlas Suppliers is one of the partners in the corporate partnership program. The company is a wholesale distributor of computer accessories. Atlas uses several worksheets to keep track of inventory and customers. Mario Rodriguez, the intern at Atlas, has convinced the company that the customer data would be better handled if maintained in an Access database. The company wants to maintain the inventory data in Excel worksheets but also would like to be able to use the query and report features of Access.

Instructions: For this assignment, you will need the data files Customer.xls and Inventory.xls. See page xxiv at the front of this book for instructions for downloading the Data Files for Students or see your instructor for information on accessing the files required in this book. Perform the following tasks:

1. Start Access and create a new database in which to store all the objects for Atlas Suppliers. Call the database Atlas Suppliers.
2. Import the Customer worksheet shown in Figure 22 into Access. The worksheet is in the Customer workbook.
3. Use Customer as the name of the Access table and Customer Number as the primary key.
4. Open the Customer table in Datasheet view and resize the columns to best fit the data. Print the table.
5. Link the Inventory worksheet shown in Figure 23 to the database. The worksheet is in the Inventory workbook.
6. Open the linked Inventory table in Datasheet view and resize the columns to best fit the data. Print the table.
7. Rename the linked Inventory table as Computer Items. Then, use the Linked Table Manager to update the link between the Excel worksheet and the Access table. (If the Linked Table Manager wizard is not installed on your computer, see your instructor before continuing.)
8. Print the Computer Items table.
9. Link the Intern table in the AD Internships database to the Atlas Suppliers database. Atlas may hire more interns to help with data entry.

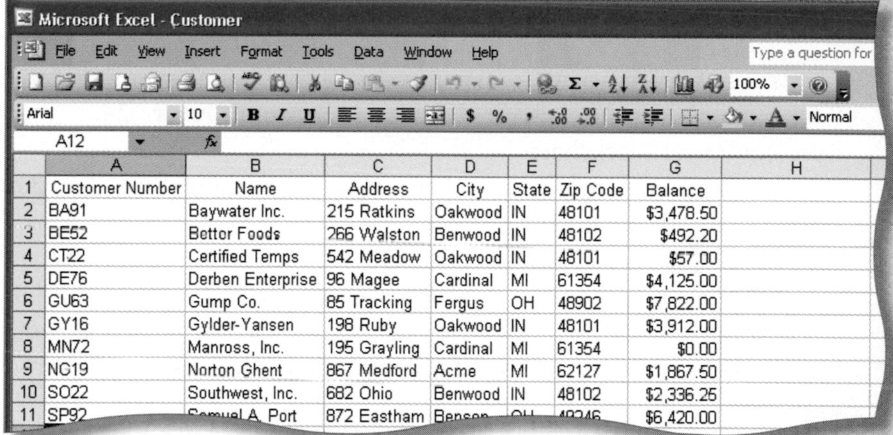

Microsoft Excel - Customer

	A	B	C	D	E	F	G
1	Customer Number	Name	Address	City	State	Zip Code	Balance
2	BA91	Baywater Inc.	215 Ratkins	Oakwood	IN	48101	$3,478.50
3	BE52	Bettor Foods	266 Walston	Benwood	IN	48102	$492.20
4	CT22	Certified Temps	542 Meadow	Oakwood	IN	48101	$57.00
5	DE76	Derben Enterprise	96 Magee	Cardinal	MI	61354	$4,125.00
6	GU63	Gump Co.	85 Tracking	Fergus	OH	48902	$7,822.00
7	GY16	Gylder-Yansen	198 Ruby	Oakwood	IN	48101	$3,912.00
8	MN72	Manross, Inc.	195 Grayling	Cardinal	MI	61354	$0.00
9	NC19	Norton Ghent	867 Medford	Acme	MI	62127	$1,867.50
10	SO22	Southwest, Inc.	682 Ohio	Benwood	IN	48102	$2,336.25
11	SP92	Samuel A. Port	872 Eastham	Benson	[illegible]	[illegible]	$6,420.00

FIGURE 22

Microsoft Excel - Inventory

	A	B	C	D	E	F
1	Item Id	Description	Units On Hand	Cost	Selling Price	Supplier Code
2	1663	16 Port Hub	30	$20.00	$25.00	ER
3	1683	Optical USB Mouse	25	$4.25	$6.50	HI
4	2563	PC Microphone	4	$1.95	$3.00	ER
5	2593	Game Pad	50	$6.30	$8.50	HI
6	3923	Laptop Keyboard	12	$22.00	$27.00	HI
7	3953	CD/RW Drive	10	$16.00	$19.00	MT
8	4343	20G Hard Drive	16	$19.00	$23.00	MT
9	5810	15" Monitor	25	$21.00	$27.25	MT
10	6140	Remote Control UFO	3	$24.00	$28.25	HI
11						

FIGURE 23

(continued)

Importing Data to an Access Database *(continued)*

10. Rename the Intern table as Potential Interns. Then, use the Linked Table Manager to update the link between the two tables.
11. Print the Potential Interns table.

2 Exporting Data to Other Applications

Problem: Keep It Green wants to be able to export some of the data in the Access database to other applications. The company wants to export the City-Worker Crosstab query for further processing in Excel. It also wants to use the Customer-Worker query in a Word document, as well as e-mail the Customer Amount Report to the company's accounting firm. The company has decided to branch out and offer gardening services. It wants to export the Customer and Worker tables as a single XML file and then import it to a new database.

Instructions: Start Access. Open the Keep It Green database that you modified in Apply Your Knowledge 1 in Project 3 on page AC 167. (If you did not complete this exercise, see your instructor for a copy of the modified database.) Perform the following tasks:

1. Export the City-Worker Crosstab query to Excel as shown in Figure 24.
2. Resize the columns to best fit the data as shown in Figure 24.
3. Print the Excel worksheet.
4. Use drag-and-drop to place the Customer-Worker query in a Word document.
5. Print the Word document.
6. Preview the Customer Amount Report and then export the report as a snapshot.
7. Open the report in the Snapshot Viewer and print it. (If a Microsoft Office Access dialog box is displayed asking if you want to install Snapshot Viewer, click the No button and see your instructor.)
8. Export both the Customer and Worker tables in XML format. Be sure that both tables are exported to the same file.
9. Create a new database called Keep It Green Outdoors.
10. Import the Customer file containing both the Customer and Worker tables to the Keep It Green Outdoors database.
11. Change the name of customer BI92 to Cycle Shop.
12. Change the last name of worker 119 to Martin.
13. Print the Customer and Worker tables.

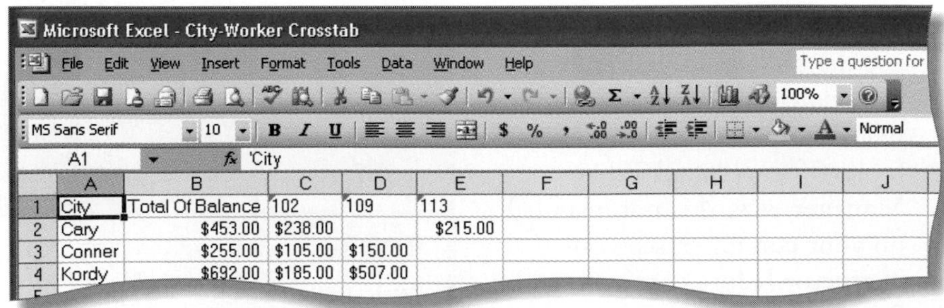

FIGURE 24

MICROSOFT OFFICE

PowerPoint 2003

MICROSOFT OFFICE POWERPOINT

MICROSOFT OFFICE
PowerPoint 2003

Using a Design Template and Text Slide Layout to Create a Presentation

PROJECT 1

CASE PERSPECTIVE

As director of the Career Center at Calumet High School, John Wendt has realized that choosing a career is one of the more difficult decisions students make in life. He believes that, while others can offer advice and guidance, ultimately each person must decide which career best fits his talents and personality. He is convinced that job shadowing, interning, and volunteering give experience and glimpses of work world realities, and career and personality tests may provide students with insights about which paths they should pursue.

Advisers in the Career Center at Calumet High School also are aware that students often need help making a plan on how to achieve success. Teaching is a top career choice in a recent Gallup Youth Survey of teenagers about their career goals. Other popular dream jobs are doctor, lawyer, and architect.

To assist students in making decisions about their future careers, the advisers have scheduled a series of presentations about career planning, with their first seminar focusing on developing the right mind-set toward setting career goals.

John Wendt has asked you to help him create a PowerPoint slide show to use at next week's after-school session (Figure 1-1 on page PPT 5). In addition, he would like handouts of the slides to distribute to students in attendance.

As you read through this project, you will learn how to use PowerPoint to create, save, and print a slide show that is composed of single- and multi-level bulleted lists.

MICROSOFT OFFICE
PowerPoint 2003

Using a Design Template and Text Slide Layout to Create a Presentation

PROJECT

1

Objectives

You will have mastered the material in this project when you can:

- Start and customize PowerPoint
- Describe the PowerPoint window
- Select a design template
- Create a title slide and text slides with single- and multi-level bulleted lists
- Change the font size and font style
- Save a presentation
- End a slide show with a black slide
- View a presentation in slide show view
- Quit PowerPoint and then open a presentation
- Display and print a presentation in black and white
- Use the PowerPoint Help system

What Is Microsoft Office PowerPoint 2003?

Microsoft Office PowerPoint 2003 is a complete presentation graphics program that allows you to produce professional-looking presentations (Figure 1-1). A PowerPoint **presentation** also is called a **slide show**.

PowerPoint contains several features to simplify creating a slide show. For example, you can instruct PowerPoint to create a predesigned presentation, and then you can modify the presentation to fulfill your requirements. You quickly can format a slide show using one of the professionally designed presentation design templates. To make your presentation more impressive, you can add tables, charts, pictures, video, sound, and animation effects. Additional PowerPoint features include the following:

- **Word processing** create bulleted lists, combine words and images, find and replace text, and use multiple fonts and type sizes.
- **Outlining** develop your presentation using an outline format. You also can import outlines from Microsoft Word or other word processing programs.
- **Charting** create and insert charts into your presentations. The two chart types are: standard, which includes bar, line, pie, and xy (scatter) charts; and custom, which shows such objects as floating bars and colored lines.
- **Drawing** form and modify diagrams using shapes such as arcs, arrows, cubes, rectangles, stars, and triangles.
- **Inserting multimedia** insert artwork and multimedia effects into your slide show. The Microsoft Clip Organizer contains hundreds of media files, including pictures, photos, sounds, and movies.

(a) Slide 1 (Title Slide)

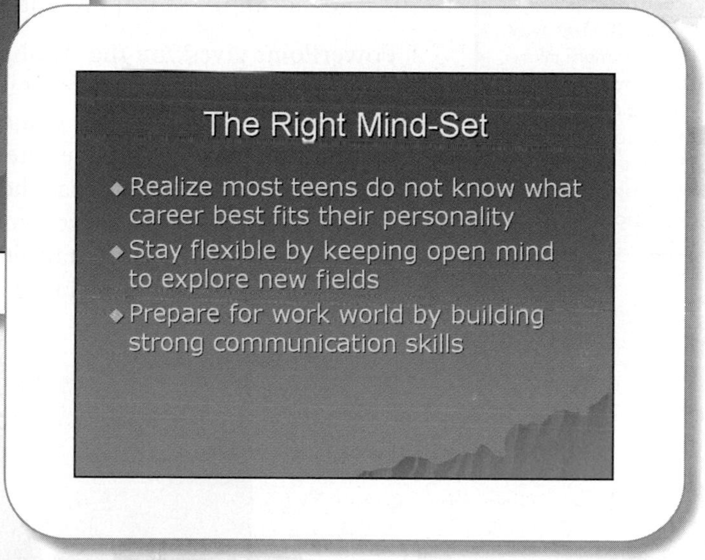

(b) Slide 2 (Single-Level Bulleted List)

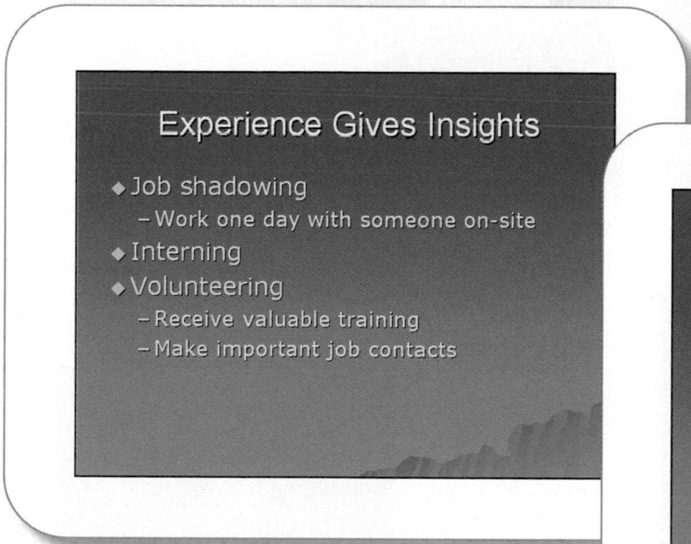

(c) Slide 3 (Multi-Level Bulleted List)

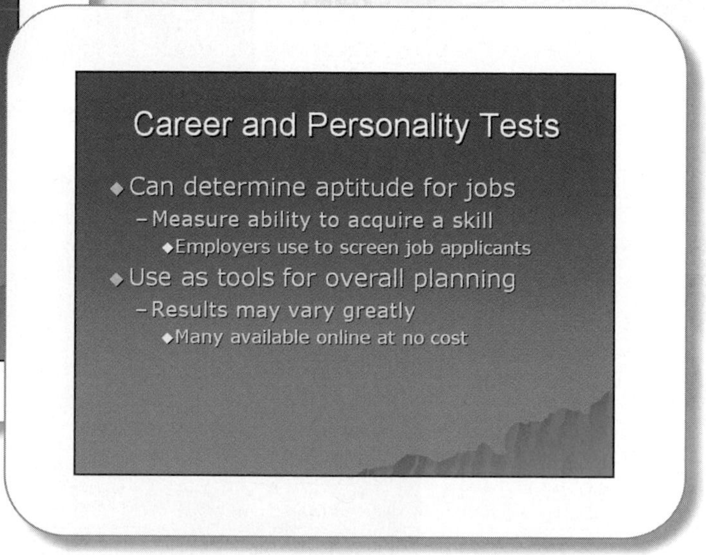

(d) Slide 4 (Multi-Level Bulleted List)

FIGURE 1-1

Q & A

Q: What types of new portable projection devices are available?

A: New multimedia projectors weigh less than three pounds and can be held in one hand. Some projectors allow users to control the projector wirelessly from 300 feet away using a PDA. For more information about projectors, visit the Office 2003 Q&A Web page (`scsite.com/off2003sch/qa`), locate PowerPoint Project 1, and then click Projectors.

- **Web support** save presentations or parts of a presentation in HTML format so they can be viewed and manipulated using a browser. You can publish your slide show to the Internet or to an intranet.
- **E-mailing** send your entire slide show as an attachment to an e-mail message.
- **Using Wizards** create a presentation quickly and efficiently by answering prompts for specific content criteria. For example, the **AutoContent Wizard** gives prompts for the type of slide show you are planning, such as communicating serious news or motivating a team, and the type of output, such as an on-screen presentation or black and white overheads.

PowerPoint gives you the flexibility to make presentations using a projection device attached to a personal computer (Figure 1-2a) and using overhead transparencies (Figure 1-2b). In addition, you can take advantage of the World Wide Web and run virtual presentations on the Internet (Figure 1-2c). PowerPoint also can create paper printouts of the individual slides, outlines, and speaker notes.

This latest version of PowerPoint has many new features to make you more productive. It saves the presentation to a CD; uses pens, highlighters, arrows, and pointers for emphasis; and includes a thesaurus and other research tools.

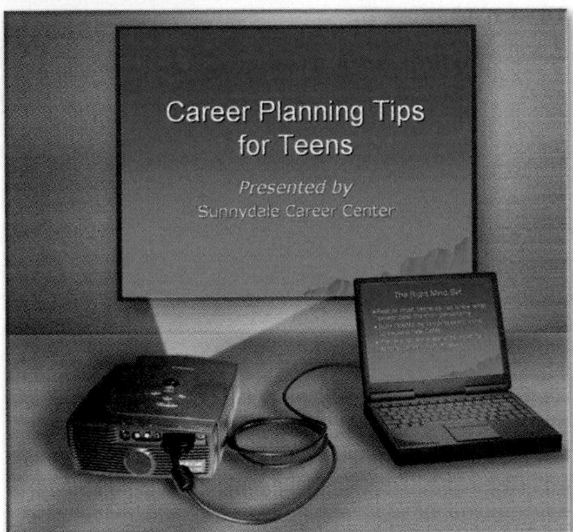

(a) Projection Device Connected to a Personal Computer

(b) Overhead Transparencies

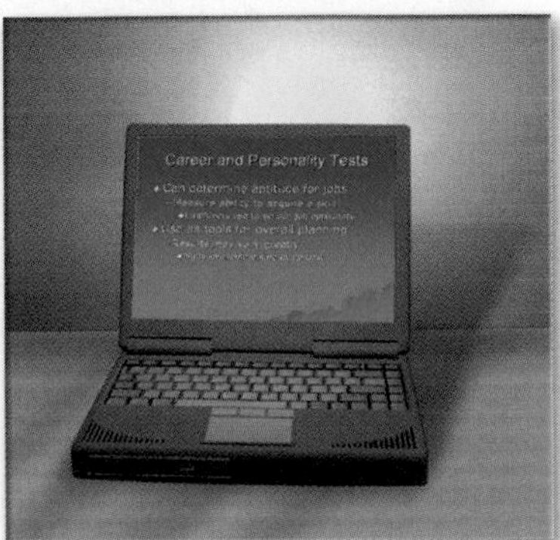

(c) PowerPoint Presentation on the World Wide Web

FIGURE 1-2

Project One — Career Planning Tips for Teens

PowerPoint allows you to produce slides to use in an academic, business, or other environment. In Project 1, you create the presentation shown in Figures 1-1a through 1-1d on page PPT 5. The objective is to produce a presentation, called Career Planning Tips for Teens, to be displayed using a projection device. As an introduction to PowerPoint, this project steps you through the most common type of presentation, which is a **text slide** consisting of a bulleted list. A **bulleted list** is a list of paragraphs, each preceded by a bullet. A **bullet** is a symbol such as a heavy dot (•) or other character that precedes text when the text warrants special emphasis.

Q & A

Q: Can I change the bullet characters?

A: Yes. While default bullets are part of the design templates, they can be modified or deleted. You can use symbols, numbers, and picture files as revised bullets. You also can change their size and color.

Starting and Customizing PowerPoint

If you are stepping through this project on a computer and you want your screen to agree with the figures in this book, then you should change your computer's resolution to 800 × 600. To change the resolution on your computer, see Appendix D.

To start PowerPoint, Windows must be running. The quickest way to begin a new presentation is to use the Start button on the **Windows taskbar** at the bottom of the screen. The following steps show how to start PowerPoint and a new presentation.

To Start PowerPoint

1

- **Click the Start button on the Windows taskbar, point to All Programs on the Start menu, point to Microsoft Office on the All Programs submenu, and then point to Microsoft Office PowerPoint 2003 on the Microsoft Office submenu.**

Windows displays the commands on the Start menu above the Start button, the All Programs submenu, and the Microsoft Office submenu (Figure 1-3).

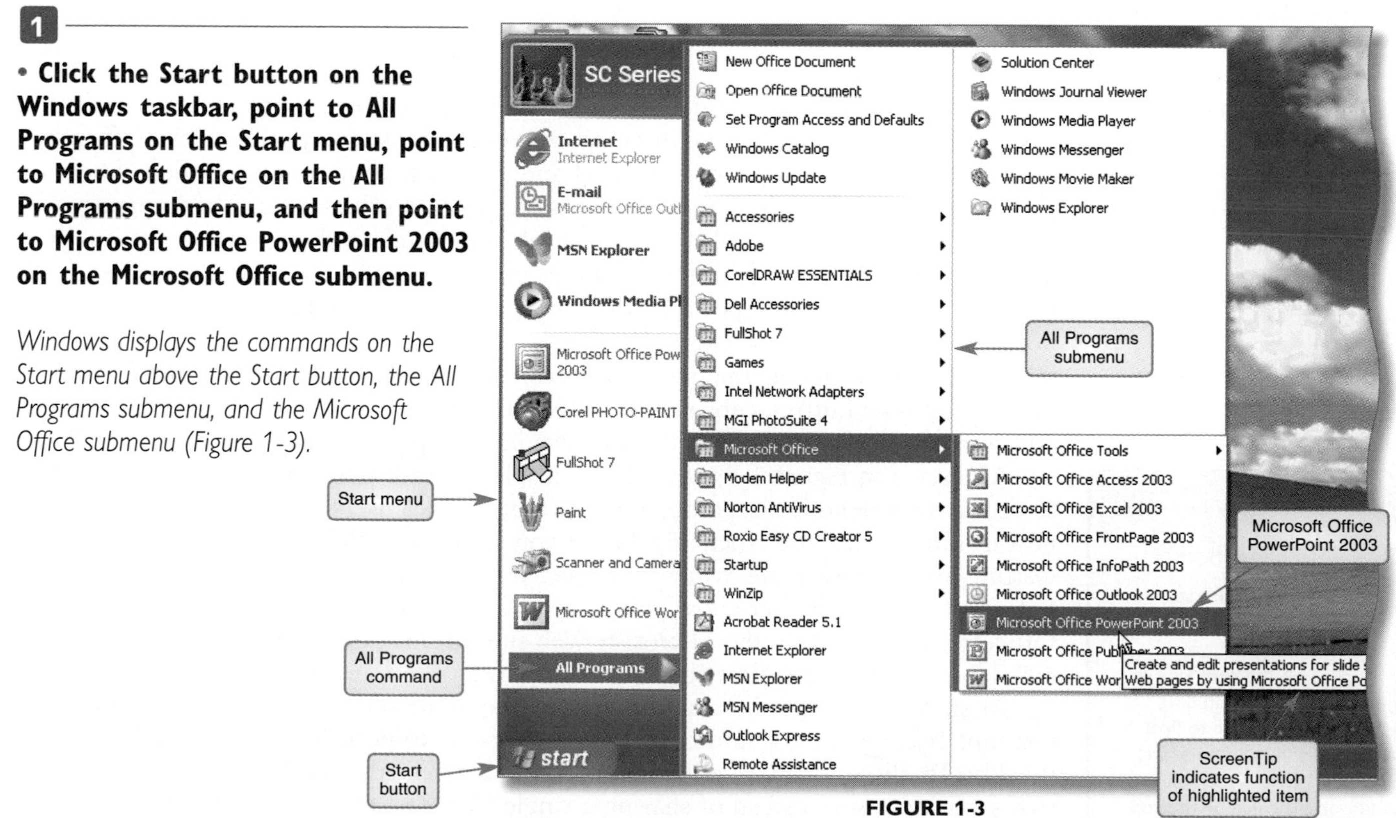

FIGURE 1-3

2

• Click Microsoft Office PowerPoint 2003.

PowerPoint starts. While PowerPoint is starting, the mouse pointer changes to the shape of an hourglass. After several seconds, PowerPoint displays a blank presentation titled Presentation1 in the PowerPoint window (Figure 1-4).

3

• If the PowerPoint window is not maximized, double-click its title bar to maximize it.

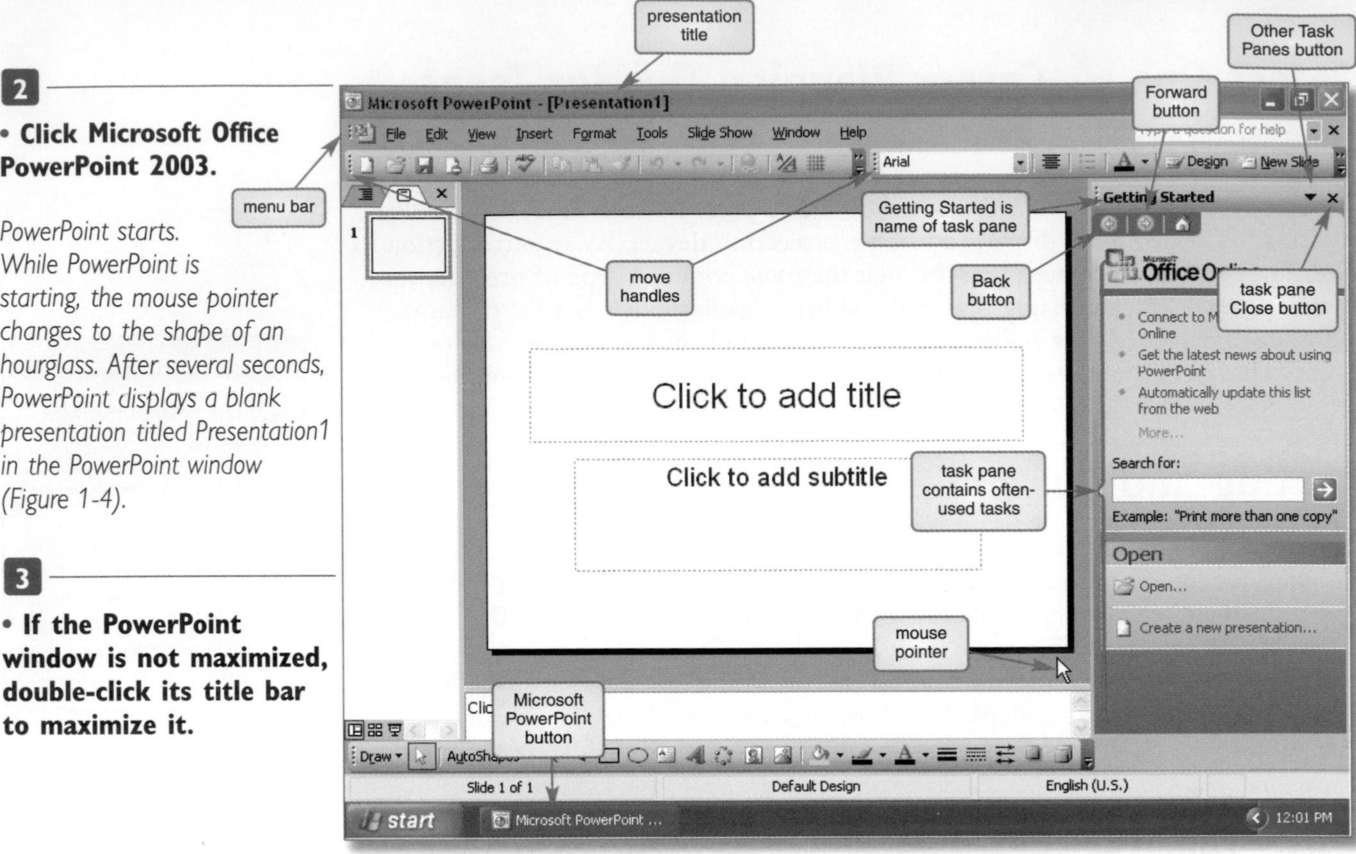

FIGURE 1-4

The screen shown in Figure 1-4 illustrates how the PowerPoint window looks the first time you start PowerPoint after installation on most computers. If the Office Speech Recognition software is installed and active on your computer, then, when you start PowerPoint, the Language bar is displayed on the screen. The **Language bar** contains buttons that allow you to speak commands and dictate text. It usually is located on the right side of the Windows taskbar next to the notification area, and it changes to include the speech recognition functions available in PowerPoint. In this book, the Language bar is closed because it takes up computer resources, and with the Language bar active, the microphone can be turned on accidentally by clicking the Microphone button, causing your computer to act in an unstable manner. For additional information about the Language bar, see page PPT 16 and Appendix B.

As shown in Figure 1-4, PowerPoint displays a task pane on the right side of the screen. A **task pane** is a separate window that enables users to carry out some PowerPoint tasks more efficiently. When you start PowerPoint, it displays the Getting Started task pane, which is a small window that provides commonly used links and commands that allow you to open files, create new files, or search Office-related topics on the Microsoft Web site. In this book, the Getting Started task pane is hidden to allow the maximum screen size to appear in PowerPoint.

At startup, PowerPoint also displays two toolbars on a single row. A **toolbar** contains buttons, boxes, and menus that allow you to perform frequent tasks quickly. To allow for more efficient use of the buttons, the toolbars should appear on two separate rows, instead of sharing a single row. The following steps show how to close the Language bar, close the Getting Started task pane, and instruct PowerPoint to display the toolbars on two separate rows.

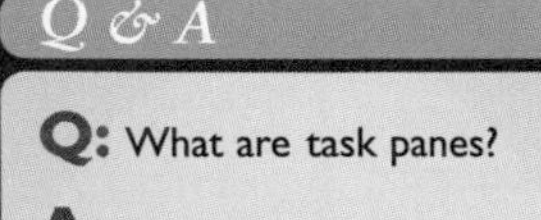
Q & A

Q: What are task panes?

A: When you first start PowerPoint, a small window called a task pane may be docked on the right side of the screen. You can drag a task pane title bar to float the pane in your work area or dock it on either the left or right side or the top or bottom of a screen, depending on your personal preference.

To Customize the PowerPoint Window

1

- **If the Language bar appears, right-click it to display a list of commands.**

The Language bar shortcut menu appears (Figure 1-5).

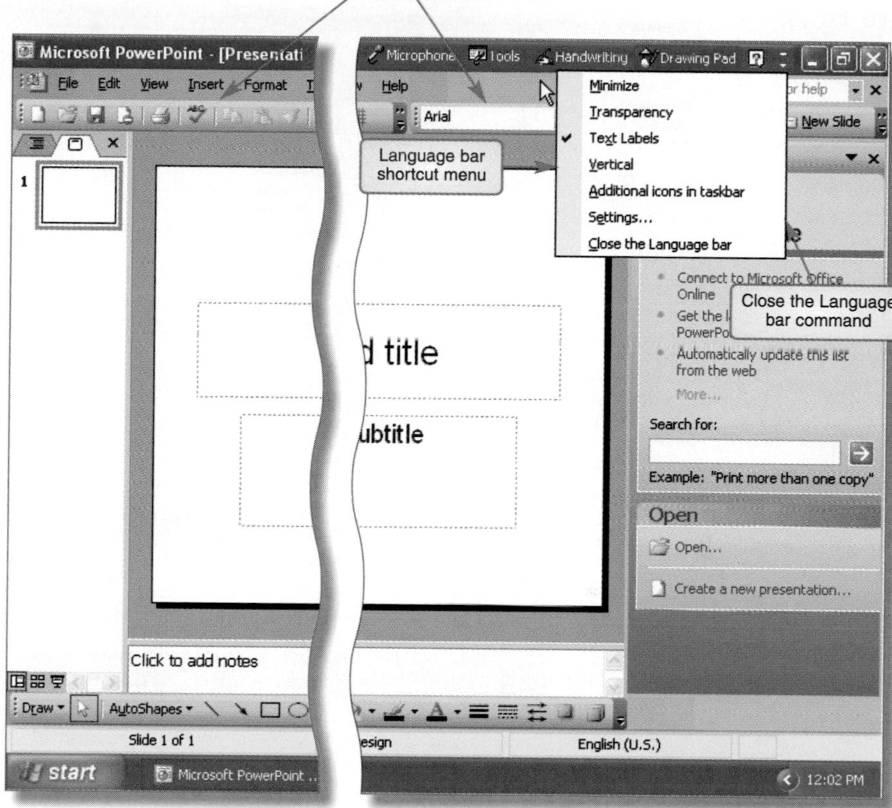

FIGURE 1-5

2

- **Click the Close the Language bar command.**
- **If necessary, click the OK button in the Language Bar dialog box.**
- **Click the Getting Started task pane Close button in the upper-right corner of the task pane.**
- **If the Standard and Formatting toolbars are positioned on the same row, click the Toolbar Options button on the Standard toolbar.**

The Language bar disappears. PowerPoint closes the Getting Started task pane and increases the size of the PowerPoint window. PowerPoint also displays the Toolbar Options list showing the buttons that do not fit on the toolbars when the toolbars are displayed on one row (Figure 1-6).

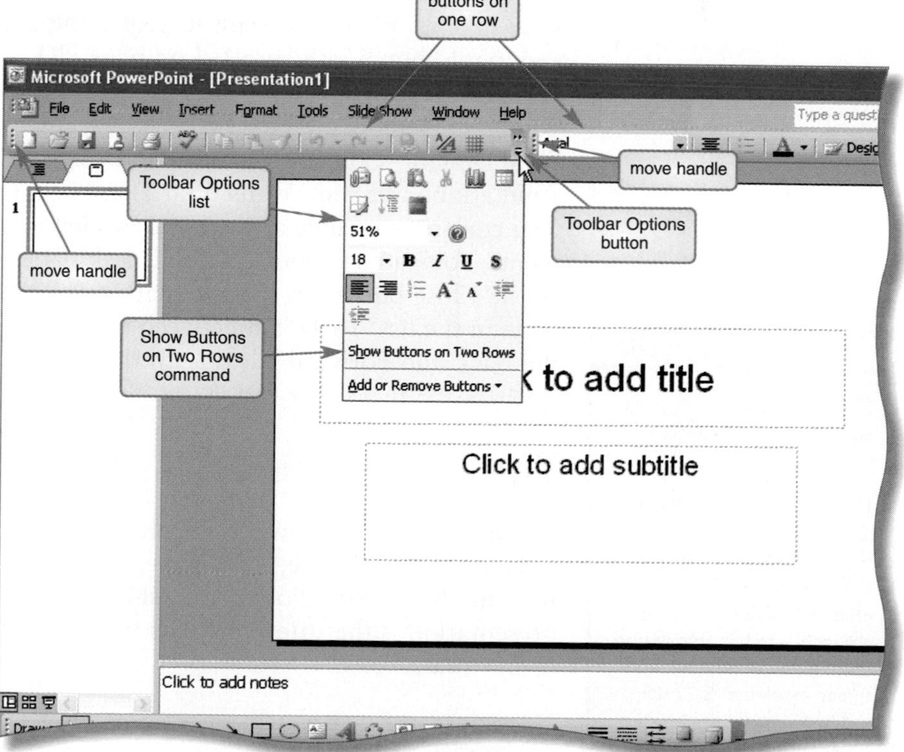

FIGURE 1-6

3

- **Click Show Buttons on Two Rows.**

PowerPoint displays the buttons on two separate rows (Figure 1-7). The Toolbar Options list shown in Figure 1-6 on the previous page is empty because all the buttons are displayed on two rows.

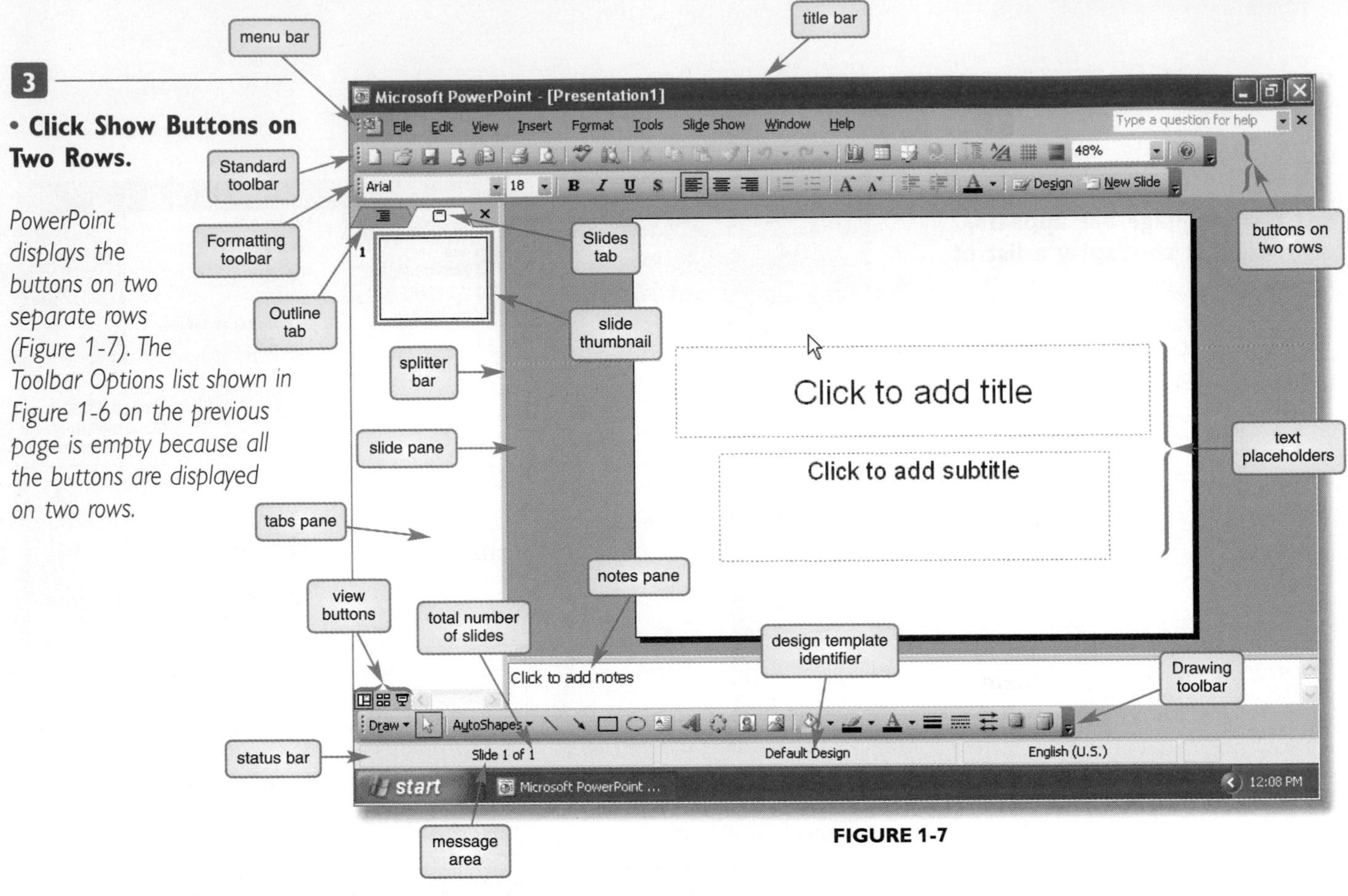

FIGURE 1-7

As you work through creating a presentation, you will find that certain PowerPoint operations result in displaying a task pane. Besides the Getting Started task pane shown in Figure 1-4 on page PPT 8, PowerPoint provides 15 additional task panes: Help, Search Results, Clip Art, Research, Clipboard, New Presentation, Template Help, Shared Workspace, Document Updates, Slide Layout, Slide Design, Slide Design - Color Schemes, Slide Design - Animation Schemes, Custom Animation, and Slide Transition. These task panes are discussed when they are used. You can show or hide a task pane by clicking the Task Pane command on the View menu. You can activate additional task panes by clicking the down arrow to the left of the Close button on the task pane title bar (Figure 1-4) and then selecting a task pane in the list. To switch between task panes that you opened during a session, use the Back and Forward buttons on the left side of the task pane title bar.

Q & A

Q: What resolution should I set for my slide show and printouts?

A: Resolution refers to the number of pixels, or dots, that can fit into one square inch of a monitor. It is measured, consequently, in dots per inch, which is abbreviated, dpi. PowerPoint's default screen resolution is 72 dpi, and it can be set as high as 1,200 dpi. Use a resolution of 150 dpi if you are going to print handouts of your slides.

The PowerPoint Window

The basic unit of a PowerPoint presentation is a **slide.** A slide contains one or many **objects**, such as a title, text, graphics, tables, charts, and drawings. An object is the building block for a PowerPoint slide. PowerPoint assumes the first slide in a new presentation is the **title slide**. The title slide's purpose is to introduce the presentation to the audience.

In PowerPoint, you have the option of using the PowerPoint default settings or establishing your own. A **default setting** is a particular value for a variable that PowerPoint assigns initially. It controls the placement of objects, the color scheme, the transition between slides, and other slide attributes, and it remains in effect unless you cancel or override it. **Attributes** are the properties or characteristics of an object. For example, if you underline the title of a slide, the title is the object, and the underline is the attribute. When you start PowerPoint, the default **slide layout** is **landscape orientation**, where the slide width is greater than its height. In landscape orientation, the slide size is preset to 10 inches wide and 7.5 inches high. You can change the slide layout to **portrait orientation**, so the slide height is greater than its width, by clicking Page Setup on the File menu. In portrait orientation, the slide width is 7.5 inches, and the height is 10 inches.

When a PowerPoint window is open, its name appears in an icon on the Windows taskbar. The **active application** is the one displaying in the foreground of the desktop. That application's corresponding icon on the Windows taskbar is displayed recessed.

PowerPoint Views

PowerPoint has three main views: normal view, slide sorter view, and slide show view. A **view** is the mode in which the presentation appears on the screen. You may use any or all views when creating a presentation, but you can use only one at a time. You also can select one of these views to be the default view. Change views by clicking one of the view buttons located at the lower-left of the PowerPoint window above the Drawing toolbar (Figure 1-7). The PowerPoint window display varies depending on the view. Some views are graphical while others are textual.

You generally will use normal view and slide sorter view when you are creating a presentation. **Normal view** is composed of three working areas that allow you to work on various aspects of a presentation simultaneously (Figure 1-7). The left side of the screen has a tabs pane that consists of an **Outline tab** and a **Slides tab** that alternate between views of the presentation in an outline of the slide text and a thumbnail, or miniature, view of the slides. You can type the text of the presentation on the Outline tab and easily rearrange bulleted lists, paragraphs, and individual slides. As you type, you can view this text in the **slide pane**, which shows a large view of the current slide on the right side of the window. You also can enter text, graphics, animations, and hyperlinks directly in the slide pane. The **notes pane** at the bottom of the window is an area where you can type notes and additional information. This text can consist of notes to yourself or remarks to share with your audience.

Q & A

Q: Can I size the panes?

A: Yes. The three panes in normal view allow you to work on all aspects of your presentation simultaneously. You can drag the splitter bar and the pane borders to make each area larger or smaller.

In normal view, you can adjust the width of the slide pane by dragging the **splitter bar** and the height of the notes pane by dragging the pane borders. After you have created at least two slides, **scroll bars**, **scroll arrows**, and **scroll boxes** will be displayed below and to the right of the windows, and you can use them to view different parts of the panes.

Slide sorter view is helpful when you want to see all the slides in the presentation simultaneously. A thumbnail version of each slide is displayed, and you can rearrange their order, add transitions and timings to switch from one slide to the next in a presentation, add and delete slides, and preview animations.

Slide show view fills the entire screen and allows you to see the slide show just as your audience will view it. Transition effects, animation, graphics, movies, and timings are shown as they will appear during an actual presentation.

Table 1-1 identifies the view buttons and provides an explanation of each view.

Table 1-1 View Buttons and Functions

BUTTON	BUTTON NAME	FUNCTION
	Normal View	Shows three panes: the tabs pane with either the Outline tab or the Slides tab, the slide pane, and the notes pane.
	Slide Sorter View	Shows thumbnail versions of all slides in a presentation. You then can copy, cut, paste, or otherwise change the slide position to modify the presentation. Slide sorter view also is used to add timings, to select animated transitions, and to preview animations.
	Slide Show View	Shows the slides as an electronic presentation on the full screen of your computer's monitor. Looking much like a slide projector display, this view can show you the effect of transitions, build effects, slide timings, and animations.

Q & A

Q: How is the 7 x 7 rule applied to slide design?

A: All slide shows in the projects and exercises in this textbook follow the 7 x 7 rule. This guideline states that each slide should have a maximum of seven lines, and each of these lines should have a maximum of seven words. This rule requires PowerPoint designers to choose their words carefully and, in turn, helps viewers read the slides easily.

Placeholders, Text Areas, Mouse Pointer, and Scroll Bars

The PowerPoint window contains elements similar to the document windows in other Microsoft Office applications. Other features are unique to PowerPoint. The main elements are the placeholders, text areas, mouse pointer, and scroll bars.

PLACEHOLDERS **Placeholders** are boxes that are displayed when you create a new slide. All layouts except the Blank slide layout contain placeholders. Depending on the particular slide layout selected, placeholders are displayed for the slide title, body text, charts, tables, organization charts, media clips, and clip art. You type titles, body text, and bulleted lists in **text placeholders**; you place graphic elements in chart placeholders, table placeholders, organizational chart placeholders, and clip art placeholders. A placeholder is considered an **object**, which is a single element of a slide.

TEXT AREAS **Text areas** are surrounded by a dotted outline. The title slide in Figure 1-7 on page PPT 10 has two text areas that contain the text placeholders where you will type the main heading, or title, of a new slide and the subtitle, or other object. Other slides in a presentation may use a layout that contains text areas for a title and bulleted lists.

MOUSE POINTER The **mouse pointer** can become one of several different shapes depending on the task you are performing in PowerPoint and the pointer's location on the screen. The different shapes are discussed when they appear.

SCROLL BARS When you add a second slide to a presentation, a **vertical scroll bar** appears on the right side of the slide pane. PowerPoint allows you to use the scroll bar to move forward or backward through the presentation.

The **horizontal scroll bar** also may be displayed. It is located on the bottom of the slide pane and allows you to display a portion of the slide when the entire slide does not fit on the screen.

Status Bar, Menu Bar, Standard Toolbar, Formatting Toolbar, and Drawing Toolbar

The status bar is displayed at the bottom of the screen above the Windows taskbar (Figure 1-7 on page PPT 10). The menu bar, Standard toolbar, and Formatting toolbar are displayed at the top of the screen just below the title bar. The Drawing toolbar is displayed above the status bar.

STATUS BAR Immediately above the Windows taskbar at the bottom of the screen is the status bar. The **status bar** consists of a message area and a presentation design template identifier (Figure 1-7). Generally, the message area shows the current slide number and the total number of slides in the slide show. For example, in Figure 1-7 the message area shows Slide 1 of 1. Slide 1 is the current slide, and of 1 indicates the slide show contains only one slide. The template identifier shows Default Design, which is the template PowerPoint uses initially.

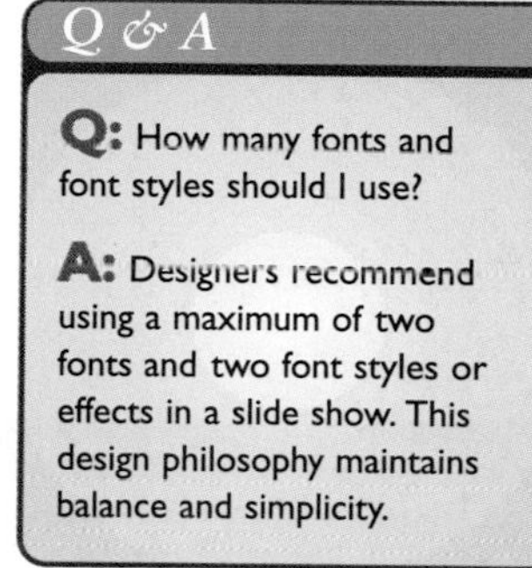

Q & A

Q: How many fonts and font styles should I use?

A: Designers recommend using a maximum of two fonts and two font styles or effects in a slide show. This design philosophy maintains balance and simplicity.

MENU BAR The **menu bar** is a special toolbar that includes the PowerPoint menu names (Figure 1-8a). Each **menu name** represents a menu of commands that you can use to perform tasks such as retrieving, storing, printing, and manipulating objects in a presentation. When you point to a menu name on the menu bar, the area of the menu bar containing the name changes to a button. To display a menu, such as the Edit menu, click the Edit menu name on the menu bar. A **menu** is a list of commands. If you point to a command on a menu that has an arrow to its right edge, a **submenu** shows another list of commands.

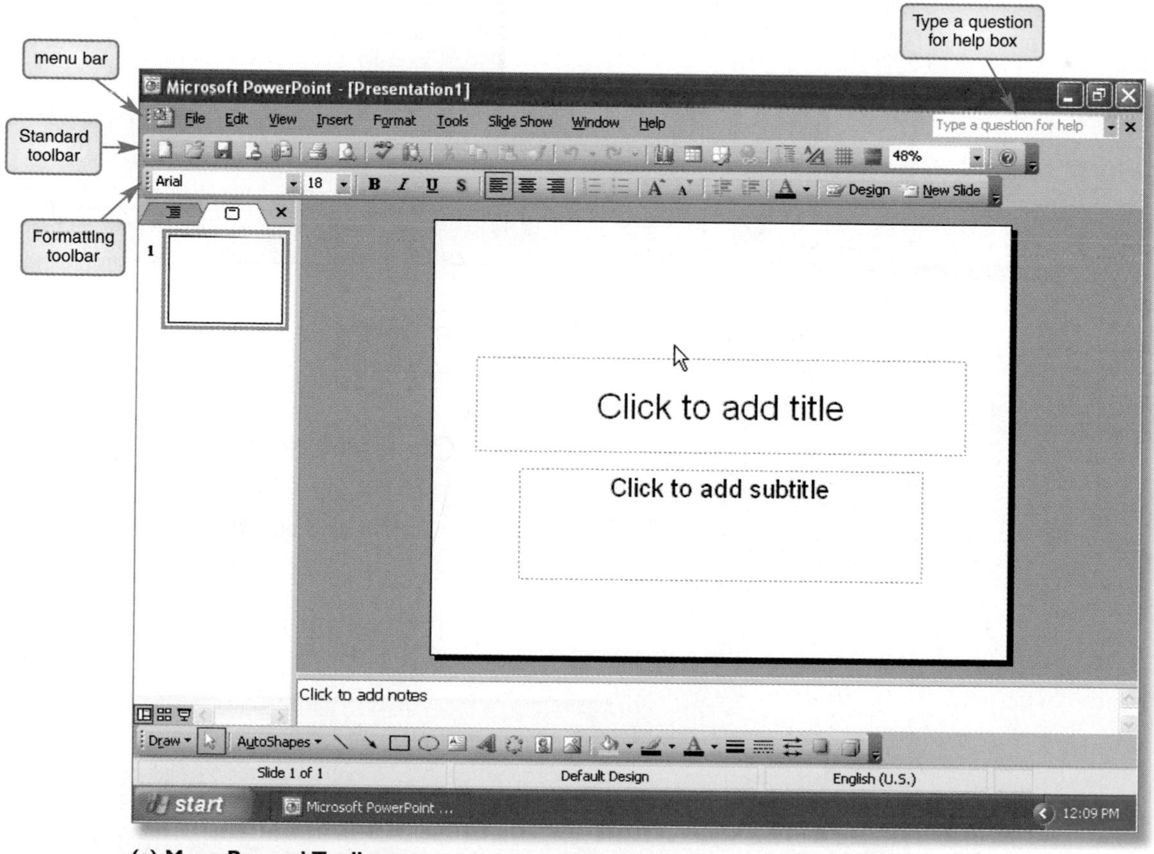

(a) Menu Bar and Toolbars

FIGURE 1-8

When you click a menu name on the menu bar, PowerPoint displays a **short menu** listing the most recently used commands (Figure 1-8b). If you wait a few seconds or click the arrows at the bottom of the short menu, it expands into a full menu. A **full menu** lists all the commands associated with a menu (Figure 1-8c). You also can display a full menu immediately by double-clicking the menu name on the menu bar. In this book, always have PowerPoint show the full menu by using one of the following techniques:

1. Click the menu name on the menu bar and then wait a few seconds.
2. Click the menu name on the menu bar and then click the arrows at the bottom of the short menu.
3. Click the menu name on the menu bar and then point to the arrows at the bottom of the short menu.
4. Double-click the menu name on the menu bar.

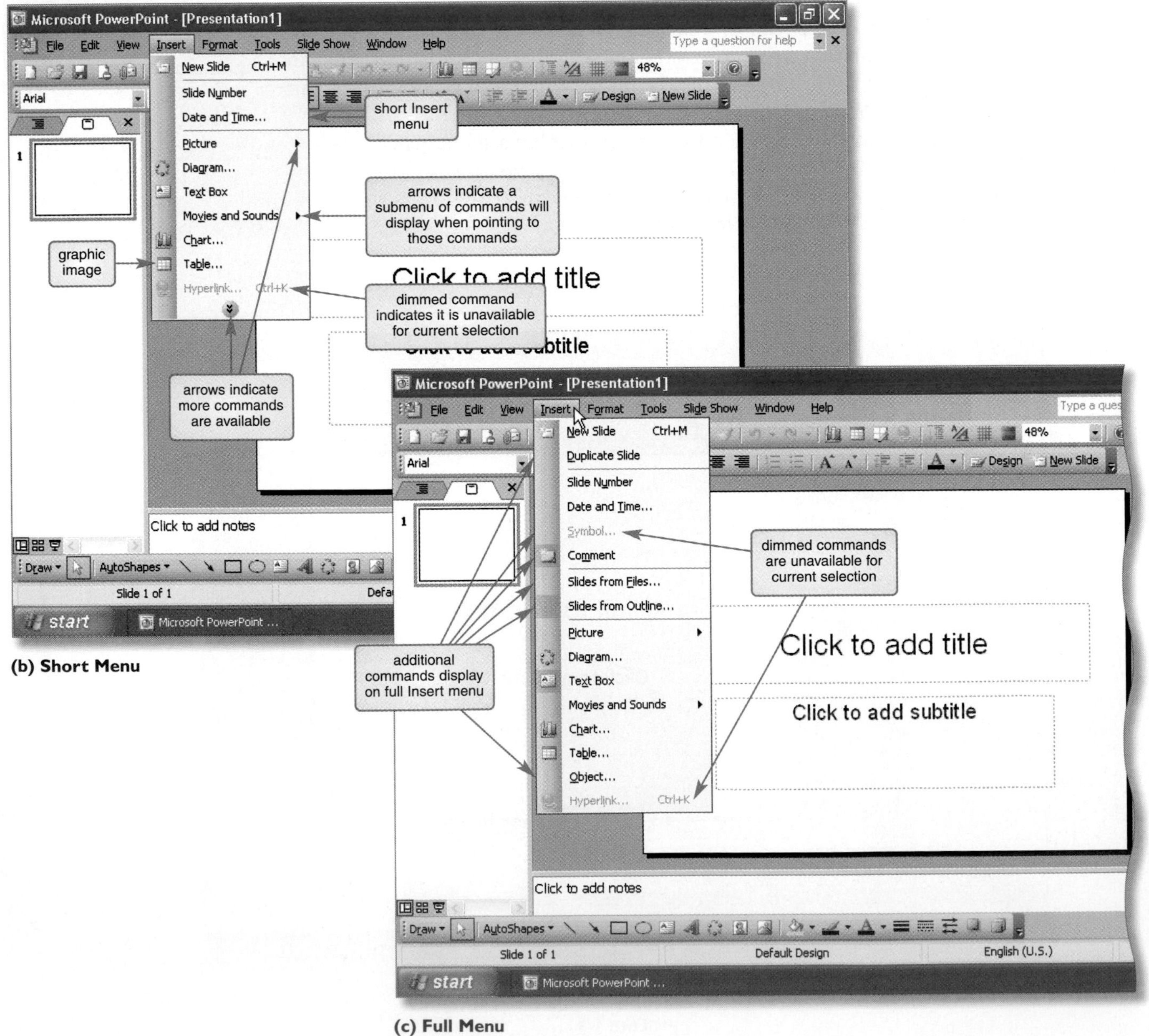

(b) Short Menu

(c) Full Menu

FIGURE 1-8 ***(continued)***

Both short and full menus display some **dimmed commands** that appear gray, or dimmed, instead of black, which indicates they are not available for the current selection. A command with a dark gray shading to the left of it on a full menu is a **hidden command** because it does not appear on a short menu. As you use PowerPoint, it automatically personalizes the short menus for you based on how often you use commands. That is, as you use hidden commands, PowerPoint *unhides* them and places them on the short menu.

The menu bar can change to include other menu names depending on the type of work you are doing in PowerPoint. For example, if you are adding a chart to a slide, Data and Chart menu names are added to the menu bar with commands that reflect charting options.

STANDARD, FORMATTING, AND DRAWING TOOLBARS The **Standard toolbar** (Figure 1-9a), **Formatting toolbar** (Figure 1-9b), and **Drawing toolbar** (Figure 1-9c on the next page) contain buttons and boxes that allow you to perform frequent tasks more quickly than when using the menu bar. For example, to print a slide show, you click the Print button on the Standard toolbar. Each button has an image on the button face that helps you remember the button's function. Also, when you move the mouse pointer over a button or box, the name of the button or box appears below it in a ScreenTip. A **ScreenTip** is a short on-screen note associated with the object to which you are pointing. For examples of ScreenTips, see Figures 1-3 and 1-13 on pages PPT 7 and PPT 19.

Figure 1-9 illustrates the Standard, Formatting, and Drawing toolbars and describes the functions of the buttons. Each of the buttons and boxes will be explained in detail when they are used.

Q: Can I hide a toolbar?

A: Yes. To display more of the PowerPoint window, you can hide a toolbar you no longer need. To hide a toolbar, right-click any toolbar and then click the check mark next to the toolbar you want to hide on the shortcut menu.

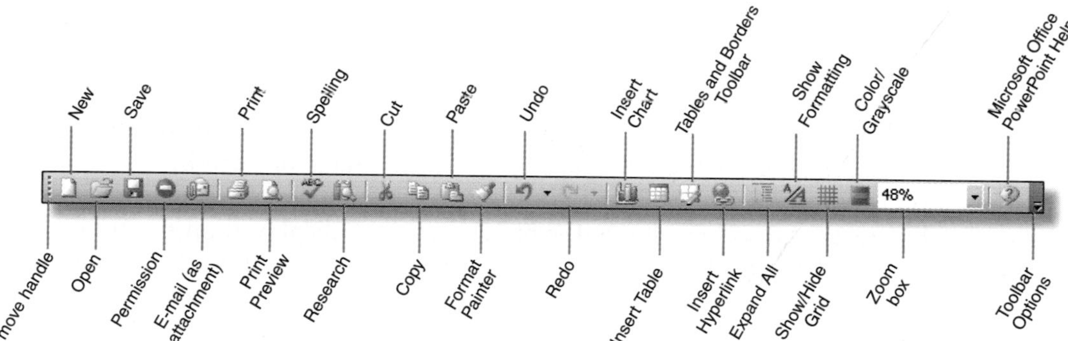

(a) Standard Toolbar

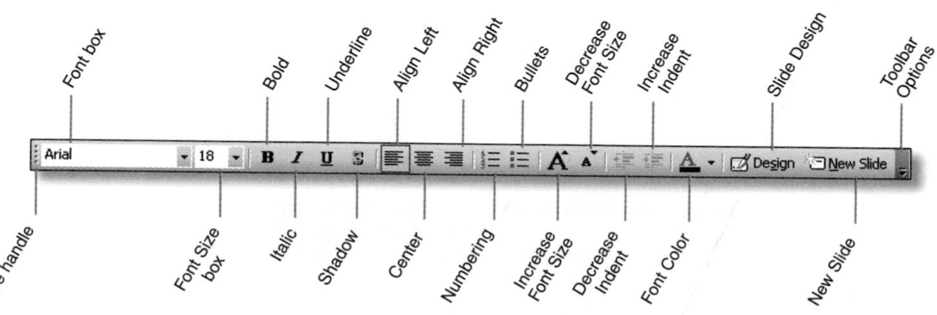

(b) Formatting Toolbar

FIGURE 1-9

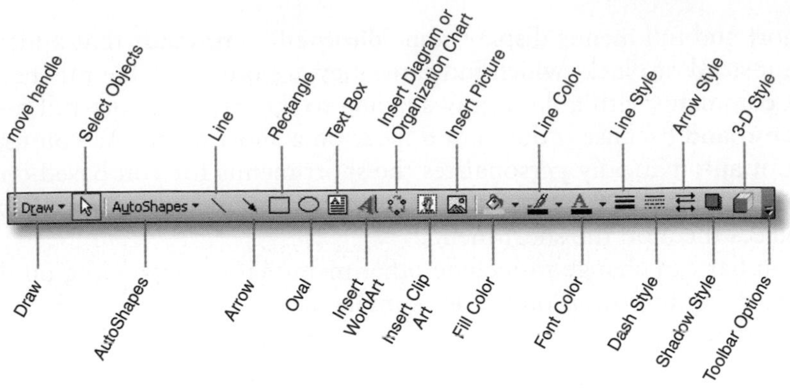

(c) Drawing Toolbar

FIGURE 1-9 *(continued)*

> *Q & A*
>
> **Q:** What is a shortcut menu?
>
> **A:** When you point to or select an item and right-click, a shortcut menu usually displays. This special menu contains frequently used commands related to that object. In some cases, you also can display the shortcut menu by selecting an object, such as a paragraph, and then pressing SHIFT+F10. To hide a shortcut menu, click outside the shortcut menu or press the ESC key.

PowerPoint has several additional toolbars you can display by pointing to Toolbars on the View menu and then clicking the respective name on the Toolbars submenu. You also may display a toolbar by pointing to a toolbar and right-clicking to display a shortcut menu, which lists the available toolbars. A **shortcut menu** contains a list of commands or items that relate to the item to which you are pointing when you right-click.

Speech Recognition

With the **Office Speech Recognition software** installed and a microphone, you can speak the names of toolbar buttons, menus, menu commands, list items, alerts, and dialog box controls, such as OK and Cancel. You also can dictate words to fill the placeholders. To indicate whether you want to speak commands or dictate placeholder entries, you use the Language bar. The Language bar can be in one of four states: (1) **restored**, which means it is displayed somewhere in the PowerPoint window (Figure 1-10a); (2) **minimized**, which means it is displayed on the Windows taskbar (Figure 1-10b); (3) **hidden**, which means you do not see it on the screen but it will be displayed the next time you start your computer; and (4) **closed**, which means it is hidden permanently until you enable it. If the Language bar is hidden or closed and you want it to display, then do the following:

1. Right-click an open area on the Windows taskbar at the bottom of the screen.
2. Point to Toolbars and then click Language bar on the Toolbars submenu.

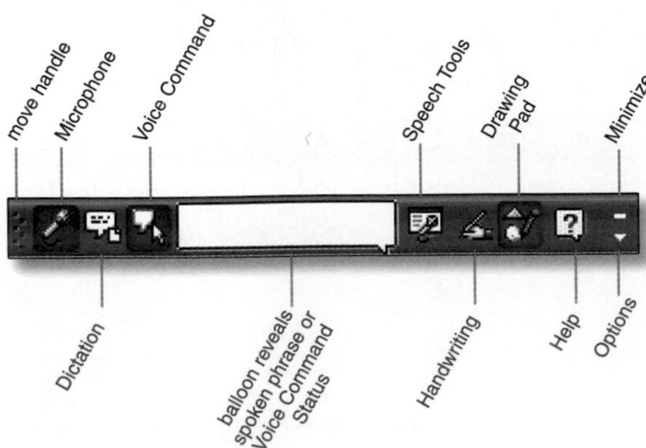

(a) Language Bar Restored

FIGURE 1-10

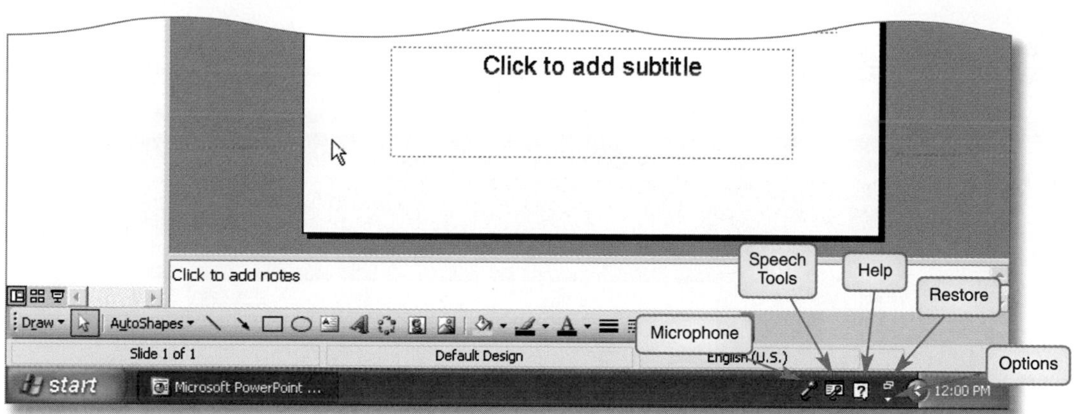

(b) Language Bar Minimized on Windows Taskbar

FIGURE 1-10 ***(continued)***

If the Language bar command is dimmed on the Toolbars submenu or if the Speech command is dimmed on the Tools menu, the Office Speech Recognition software is not installed.

In this book, the Language bar does not appear in the figures. If you want to close the Language bar so that your screen is identical to what you see in the book, right-click the Language bar and then click Close the Language bar on the shortcut menu.

Additional information about the speech recognition capabilities of PowerPoint is available in Appendix B.

Choosing a Design Template

A **design template** provides consistency in design and color throughout the entire presentation. It determines the color scheme, font and font size, and layout of a presentation. PowerPoint has three Slide Design task panes that allow you to choose and change the appearance of slides in your presentation. The **Slide Design task pane** shows a variety of styles. You can alter the colors used in the design templates by using the **Slide Design – Color Schemes task pane.** In addition, you can animate elements of your presentation by using the **Slide Design – Animation Schemes task pane.**

In this project, you will select a particular design template by using the Slide Design task pane. The top section of the task pane, labeled Used in This Presentation, shows the template currently used in the slide show. PowerPoint uses the **Default Design** template until you select a different style. When you place your mouse over a template, the name of the template appears. Once a PowerPoint slide show has been created on the computer, the next section of the task pane displayed is the Recently Used templates. This area shows the four templates you have used in your newest slide shows. The Available For Use area shows additional templates. The templates are displayed in alphabetical order in the two columns.

You want to change the template for this presentation from the Default Design to Cliff. The steps on the next page apply the Cliff design template.

Q & A

Q: When is the default design template used?

A: Some PowerPoint slide show designers create presentations using the Default Design template. This blank design allows them to concentrate on the words being used to convey the message and does not distract them with colors and various text attributes. Once the text is entered, the designers then select an appropriate design template.

To Choose a Design Template

1

- **Point to the Slide Design button on the Formatting toolbar (Figure 1-11).**

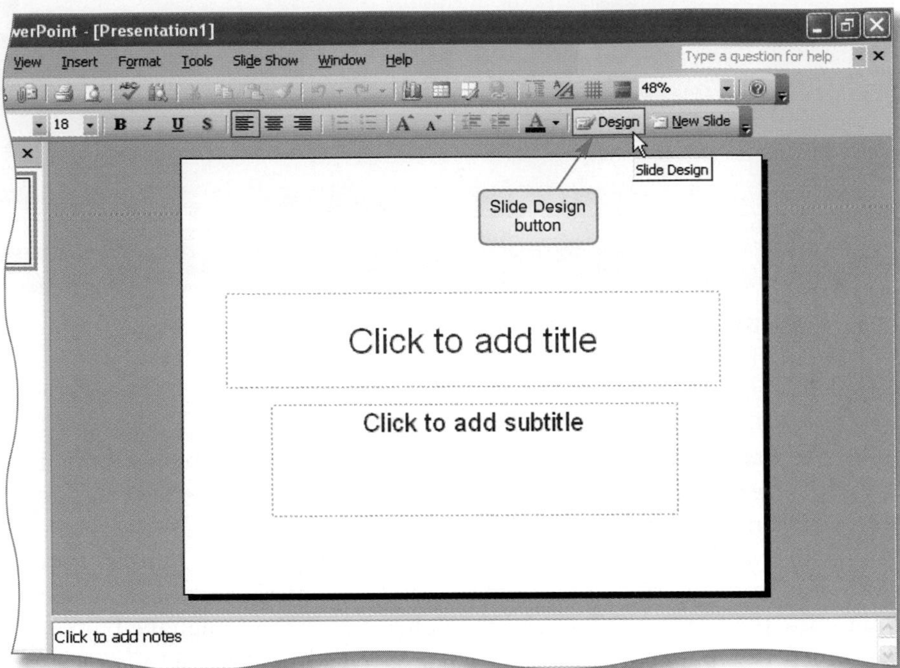

FIGURE 1-11

2

- **Click the Slide Design button and then point to the down scroll arrow in the Apply a design template list.**

The Slide Design task pane appears (Figure 1-12). The Apply a design template list shows thumbnail views of numerous design templates. Your list may look different depending on your computer. The Default Design template is highlighted in the Used in This Presentation area. Other templates display in the Available For Use area and possibly in the Recently Used area. The Close button in the Slide Design task pane can be used to close the task pane if you do not want to apply a new template.

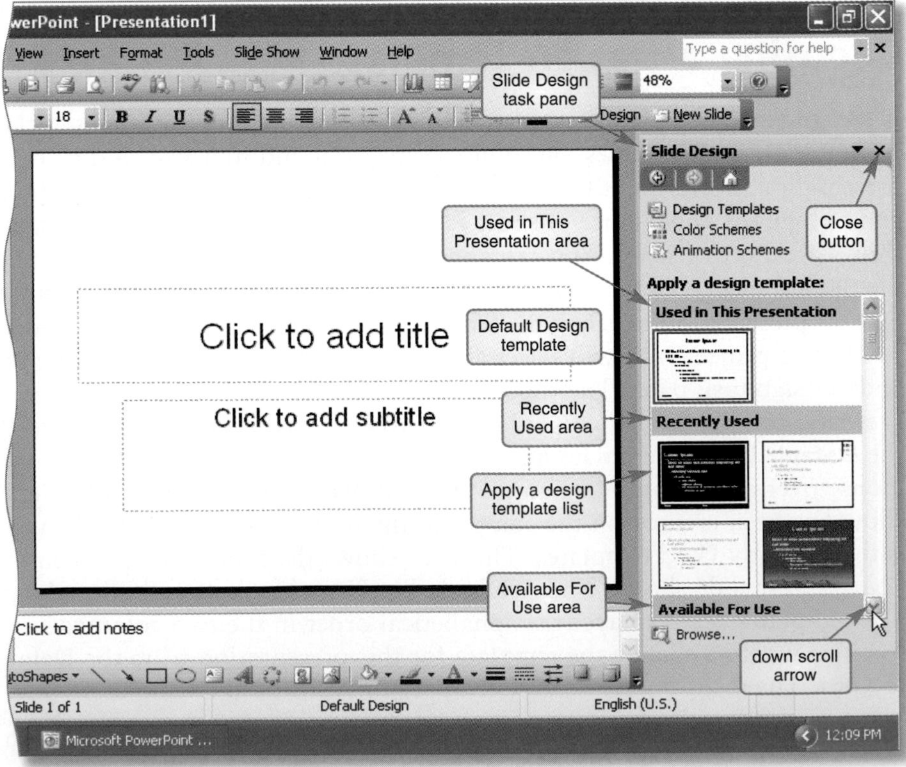

FIGURE 1-12

3

- **Click the down scroll arrow to scroll through the list of design templates until Cliff appears in the Available For Use area. Point to the Cliff template.**

The Cliff template is selected, as indicated by the blue box around the template and the arrow button on the right side (Figure 1-13). PowerPoint provides 15 templates in the Available For Use area. Additional templates are available on the Microsoft Office Online Web site. A ScreenTip shows the template's name. Your system may display the ScreenTip, Cliff.pot, which indicates the design template's file extension (.pot).

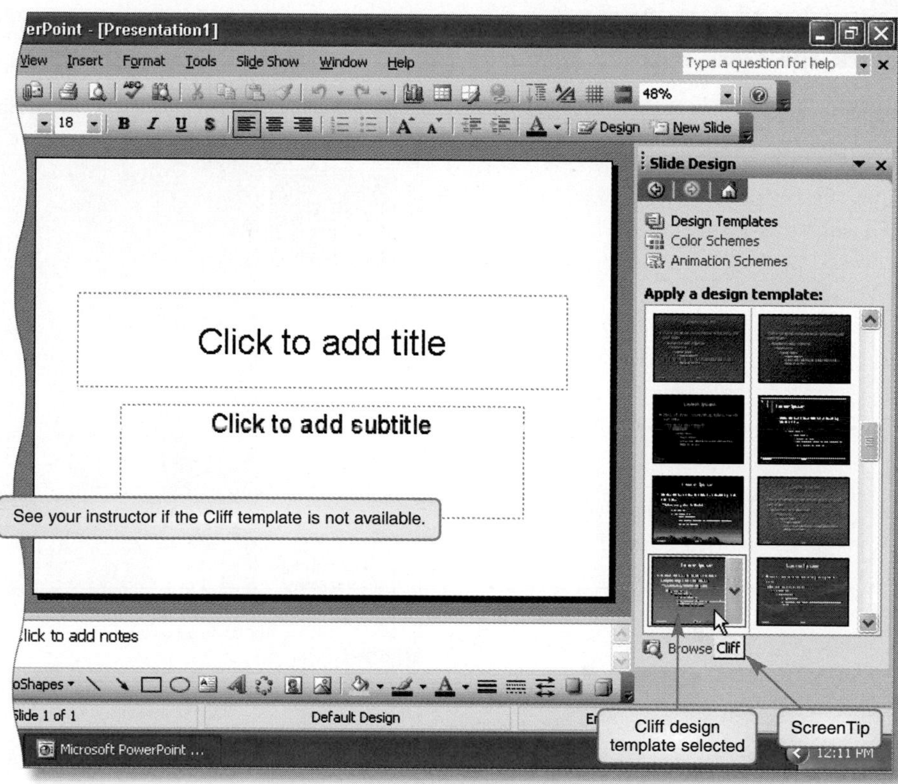

FIGURE 1-13

4

- **Click Cliff.**
- **Point to the Close button in the Slide Design task pane.**

The template is applied to Slide 1, as shown in the slide pane and Slides tab (Figure 1-14).

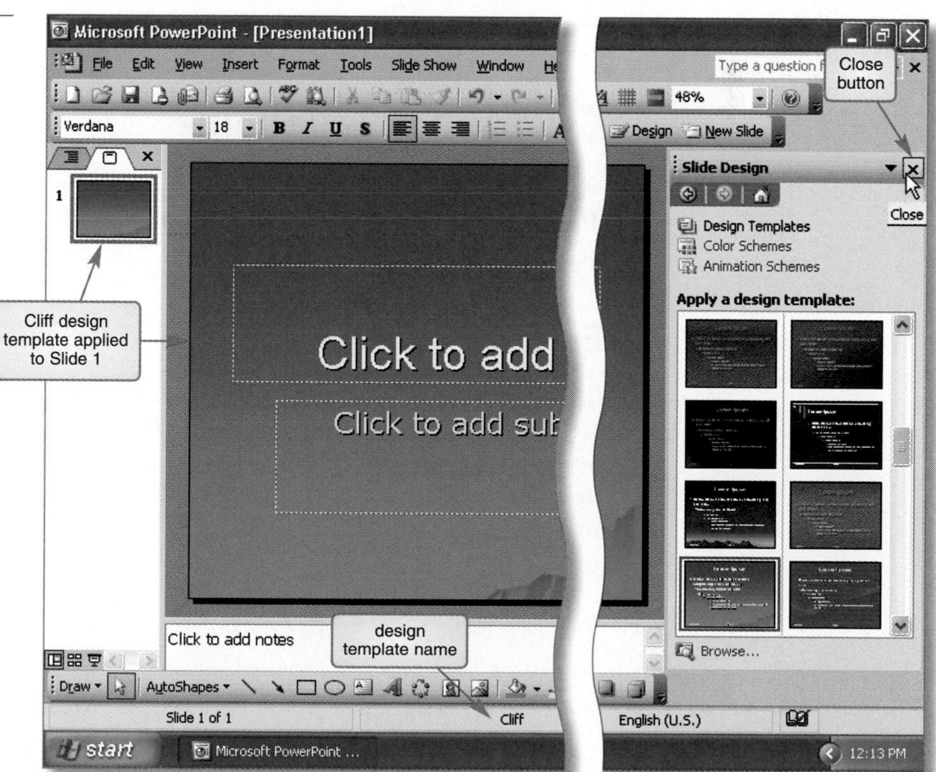

FIGURE 1-14

5

- **Click the Close button.**

Slide 1 is displayed in normal view with the Cliff design template (Figure 1-15).

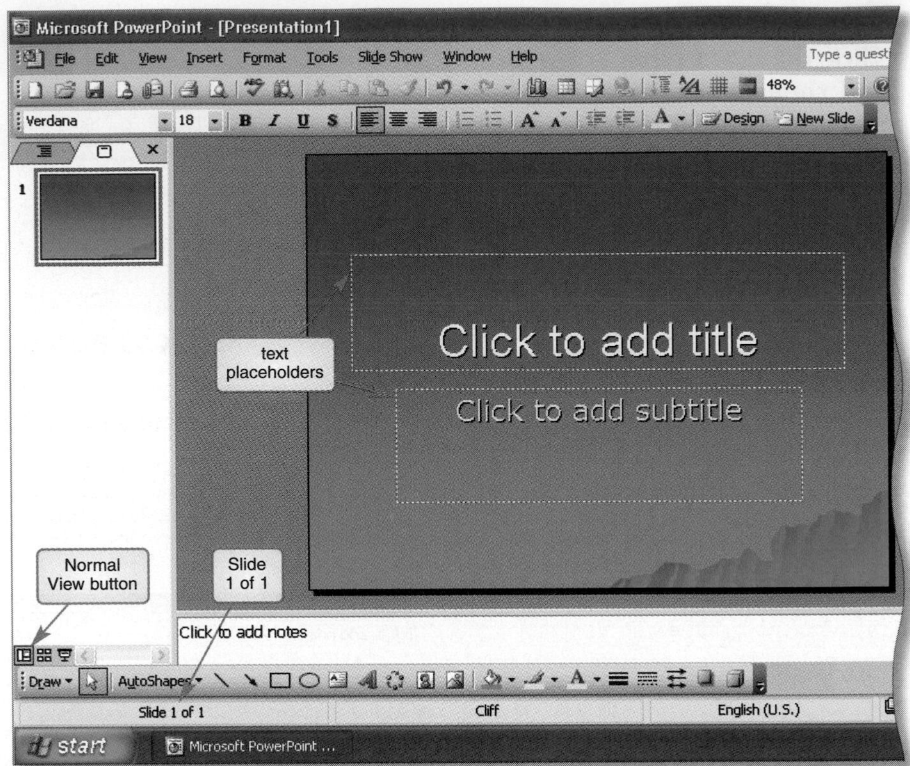

FIGURE 1-15

Creating a Title Slide

With the exception of a blank slide, PowerPoint assumes every new slide has a title. To make creating a presentation easier, any text you type after a new slide appears becomes title text in the title text placeholder.

Entering the Presentation Title

The presentation title for Project 1 is Career Planning Tips for Teens. To enter text in your slide, you type on the keyboard or speak into the microphone. As you begin entering text in the title text placeholder, the title text is displayed immediately in the Slide 1 thumbnail in the Slides tab. The following steps create the title slide for this presentation.

To Enter the Presentation Title

1

• **Click the label, Click to add title, located inside the title text placeholder.**

The insertion point is in the title text placeholder (Figure 1-16). The ***insertion point*** *is a blinking vertical line (|), which indicates where the next character will be displayed. The mouse pointer changes to an I-beam. A* ***selection rectangle*** *appears around the title text placeholder. The placeholder is selected as indicated by the border and sizing handles displaying on the edges.*

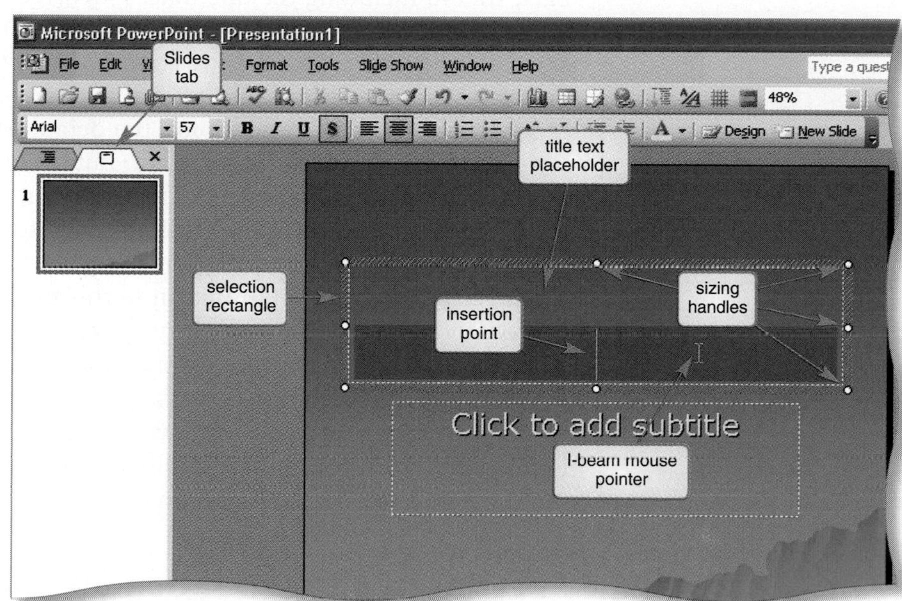

FIGURE 1-16

2

• **Type** `Career Planning Tips for Teens` **in the title text placeholder. Do not press the ENTER key. Click the Center button on the Formatting toolbar.**

The title text, Career Planning Tips for Teens, appears on two lines in the title text placeholder and in the Slides tab (Figure 1-17). The insertion point appears after the letter s in Teens. The title text is displayed centered in the placeholder with the default text attributes of the Arial font and font size 57.

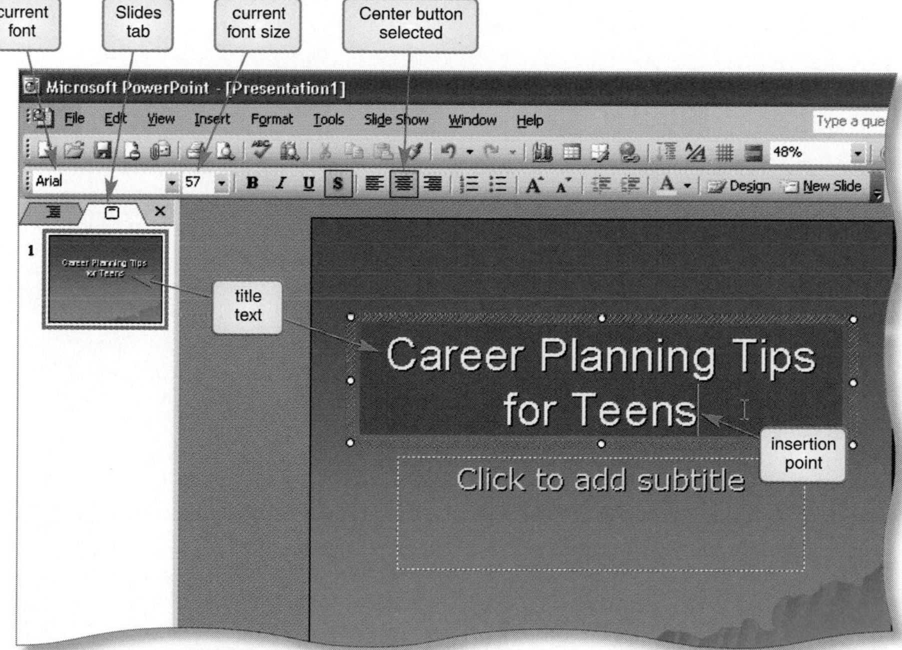

FIGURE 1-17

PowerPoint **line wraps** text that exceeds the width of the placeholder. One of PowerPoint's features is **text AutoFit.** If you are creating a slide and need to squeeze an extra line in the text placeholder, PowerPoint will prompt you to resize the existing text in the placeholder so the spillover text will fit on the slide.

Correcting a Mistake When Typing

If you type the wrong letter, press the BACKSPACE key to erase all the characters back to and including the one that is incorrect. If you mistakenly press the ENTER key after typing the title and the insertion point is on the new line, simply press the BACKSPACE key to return the insertion point to the right of the letter s in the word Teens.

When you install PowerPoint, the default setting allows you to reverse up to the last 20 changes by clicking the Undo button on the Standard toolbar. The ScreenTip that appears when you point to the Undo button changes to indicate the type of change just madc. For example, if you type text in the title text placeholder and then point to the Undo button, the ScreenTip that appears is Undo Typing. For clarity, when referencing the Undo button in this project, the name displaying in the ScreenTip is referenced. Another way to reverse changes is to click the Undo command on the Edit menu. As with the Undo button, the Undo command reflects the last type of change made to the presentation.

You can reapply a change that you reversed with the Undo button by clicking the Redo button on the Standard toolbar. Clicking the Redo button reverses the last undo action. The ScreenTip name reflects the type of reversal last performed.

Q & A

Q: Can I change the capitalization of letters and words?

A: Yes. Simply select the text you want to change, click Change Case on the Format menu, and then click the desired option. For example, you can change all uppercase letters to lowercase letters or capitalize the first letter in each word.

Entering the Presentation Subtitle

The next step in creating the title slide is to enter the subtitle text into the subtitle text placeholder. Complete the following steps to enter the presentation subtitle.

To Enter the Presentation Subtitle

1

- **Click the label, Click to add subtitle, located inside the subtitle text placeholder.**

The insertion point appears in the subtitle text placeholder (Figure 1-18). The mouse pointer changes to an I-beam, indicating the mouse is in a text placeholder. The selection rectangle indicates the placeholder is selected.

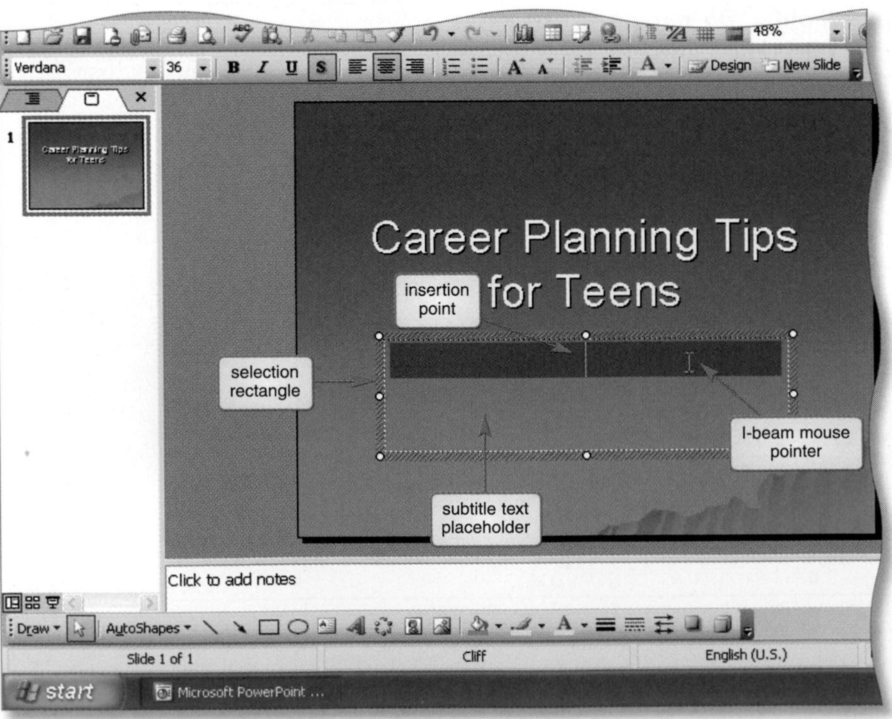

FIGURE 1-18

2

• **Type** `Presented by` **and then press the ENTER key.**

• **Type** `Sunnydale Career Center` **but do not press the ENTER key.**

The subtitle text appears in the subtitle text placeholder and the Slides tab (Figure 1-19). The insertion point appears after the letter r in Center. A red wavy line appears below the word, Sunnydale, to indicate a possible spelling error.

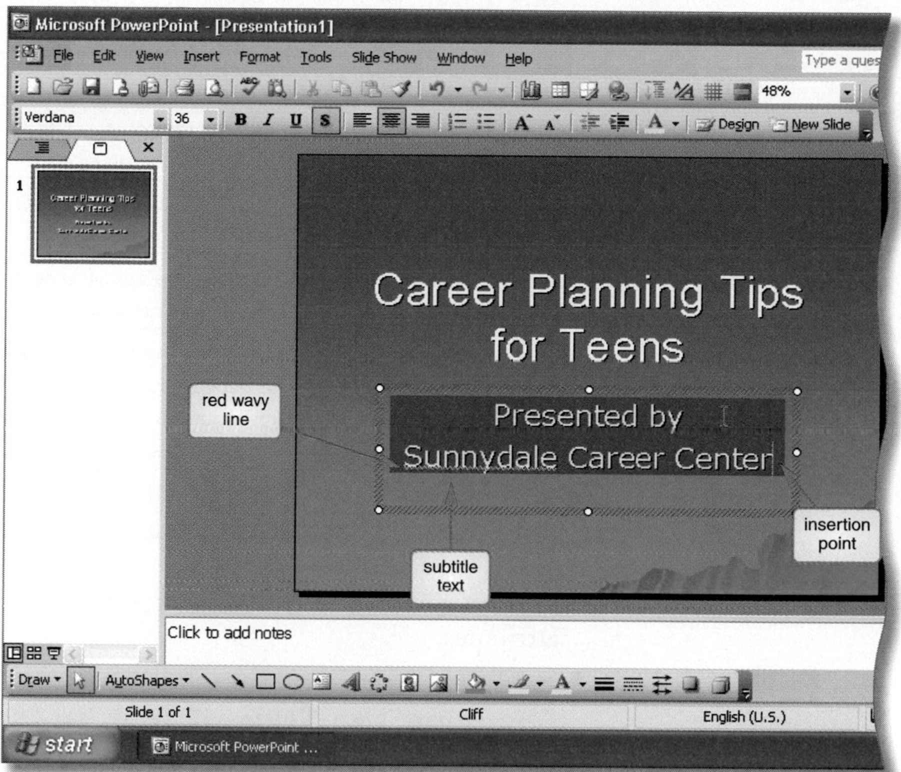

FIGURE 1-19

After pressing the ENTER key in Step 2, PowerPoint created a new line, which is the second paragraph in the placeholder. A **paragraph** is a segment of text with the same format that begins when you press the ENTER key and ends when you press the ENTER key again.

Text Attributes

This presentation uses the Cliff design template. Each design template has its own text attributes. A **text attribute** is a characteristic of the text, such as font, font size, font style, or text color. You can adjust text attributes any time before, during, or after you type the text. Recall that a design template determines the color scheme, font and font size, and layout of a presentation. Most of the time, you use the design template's text attributes and color scheme. Occasionally, you may want to change the way a presentation looks, however, and still keep a particular design template. PowerPoint gives you that flexibility. You can use the design template and change the font and the font's color, effects, size, and style. Text may have one or more font styles and effects simultaneously. Table 1-2 on the next page explains the different text attributes available in PowerPoint.

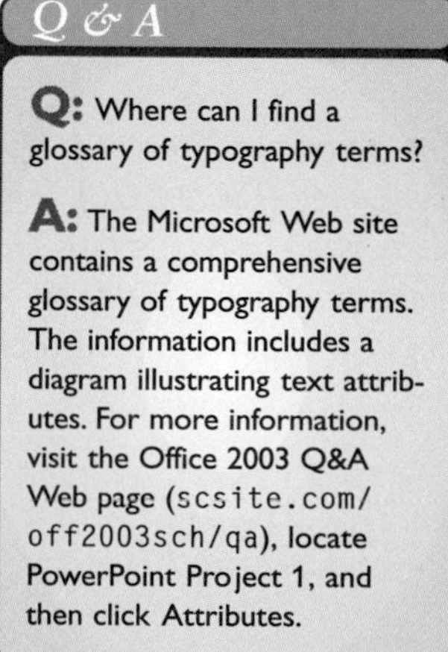

Q & A

Q: Where can I find a glossary of typography terms?

A: The Microsoft Web site contains a comprehensive glossary of typography terms. The information includes a diagram illustrating text attributes. For more information, visit the Office 2003 Q&A Web page (`scsite.com/off2003sch/qa`), locate PowerPoint Project 1, and then click Attributes.

Table 1-2 Design Template Text Attributes

ATTRIBUTE	DESCRIPTION
Color	Defines the color of text. Printing text in color requires a color printer or plotter.
Effects	Effects include underline, shadow, emboss, superscript, and subscript. Effects can be applied to most fonts.
Font	Defines the appearance and shape of letters, numbers, and special characters.
Size	Specifies the height of characters on the screen. Character size is gauged by a measurement system called points. A single point is about 1/72 of an inch in height. Thus, a character with a point size of 18 is about 18/72 (or 1/4) of an inch in height.
Style	Font styles include regular, bold, italic, and bold italic.

The next two sections explain how to change the font size and font style attributes.

Changing the Style of Text to Italic

Text font styles include plain, italic, bold, shadowed, and underlined. PowerPoint allows you to use one or more text font styles in a presentation. The following steps add emphasis to the first line of the subtitle text by changing regular text to italic text.

To Change the Text Font Style to Italic

1

• **Triple-click the paragraph, Presented by, in the subtitle text placeholder, and then point to the Italic button on the Formatting toolbar.**

The paragraph, Presented by, is highlighted (Figure 1-20). The Italic button is surrounded by a blue box. You select an entire paragraph quickly by triple-clicking any text within the paragraph.

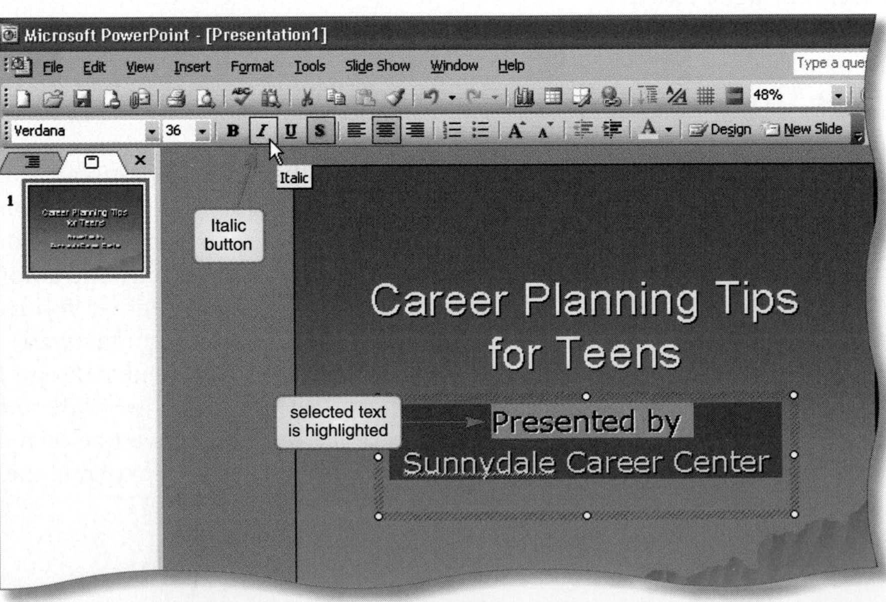

FIGURE 1-20

2

• **Click the Italic button.**

The text is italicized on the slide and the slide thumbnail (Figure 1-21).

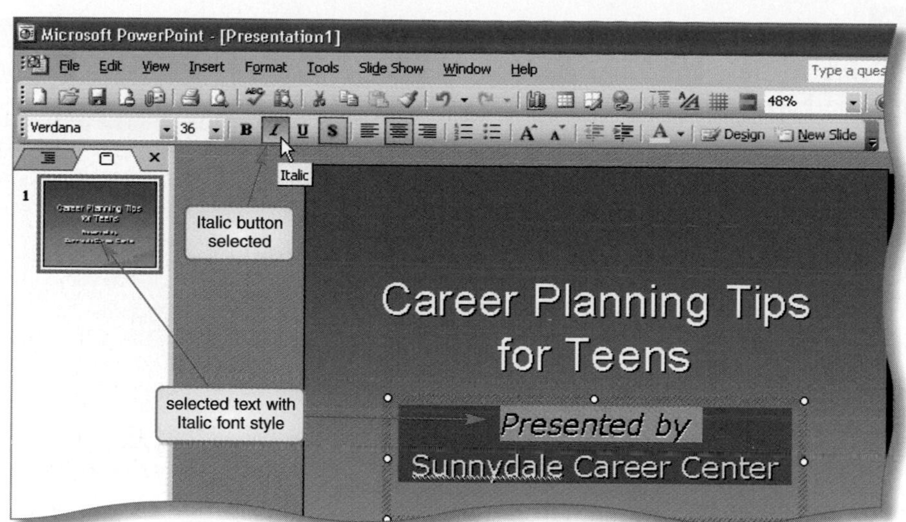

FIGURE 1-21

To remove the italic style from text, select the italicized text and then click the Italic button. As a result, the Italic button is not selected, and the text does not have the italic font style.

Changing the Font Size

The Cliff design template default font size is 57 point for title text and 36 point for body text. A point is 1/72 of an inch in height. Thus, a character with a point size of 36 is 36/72 (or 1/2) of an inch in height. Slide 1 requires you to increase the font size for the paragraph, Sunnydale Career Center. The following steps illustrate how to increase the font size.

To Increase Font Size

1

• **Position the mouse pointer in the paragraph, Sunnydale Career Center, and then triple-click.**

PowerPoint selects the entire paragraph (Figure 1-22).

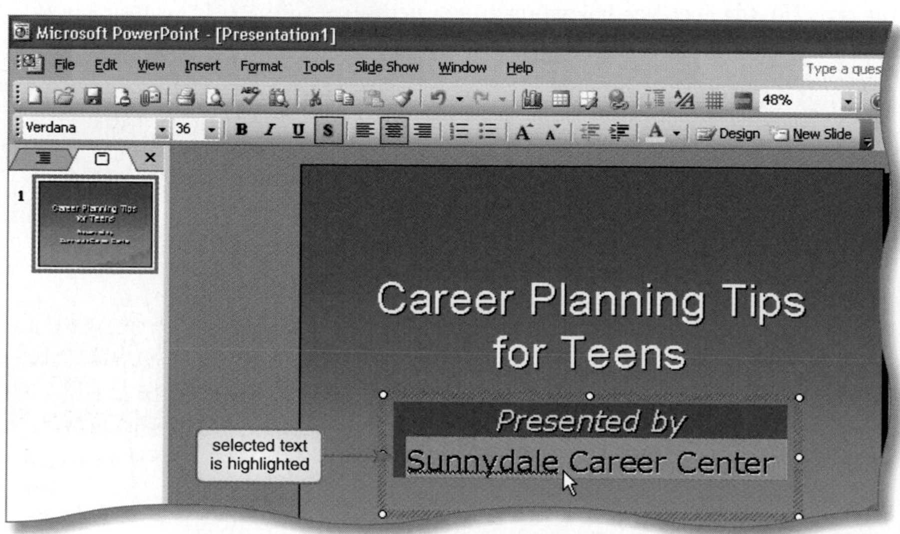

FIGURE 1-22

2

- **Point to the Font Size box arrow on the Formatting toolbar.**

The ScreenTip shows the words, Font Size (Figure 1-23). The ***Font Size box*** *is surrounded by a box and indicates that the subtitle text is 36 point.*

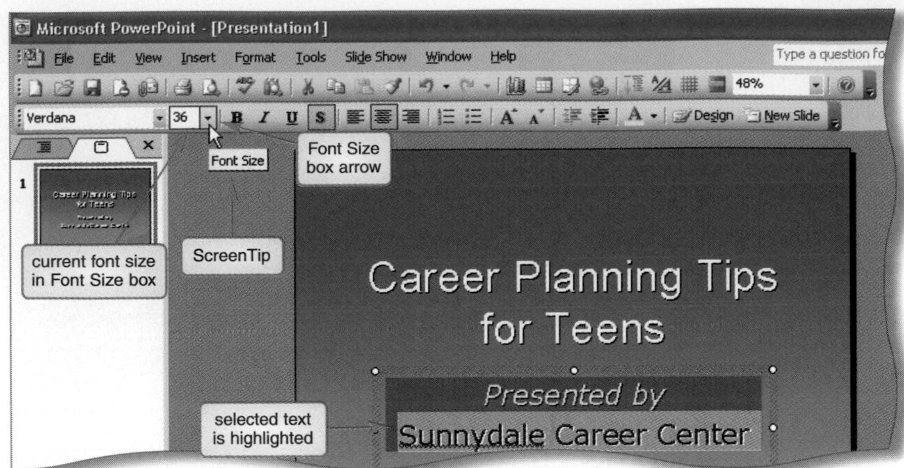

FIGURE 1-23

3

- **Click the Font Size box arrow and then point to 32 in the Font Size list.**

When you click the Font Size box, a list of available font sizes is displayed in the Font Size list (Figure 1-24). The font sizes displayed depend on the current font, which is Verdana. Font size 32 is highlighted.

FIGURE 1-24

4

- **Click 32.**

The font size of the subtitle text, Sunnydale Career Center, decreases to 32 point (Figure 1-25). The Font Size box on the Formatting toolbar shows 32, indicating the selected text has a font size of 32.

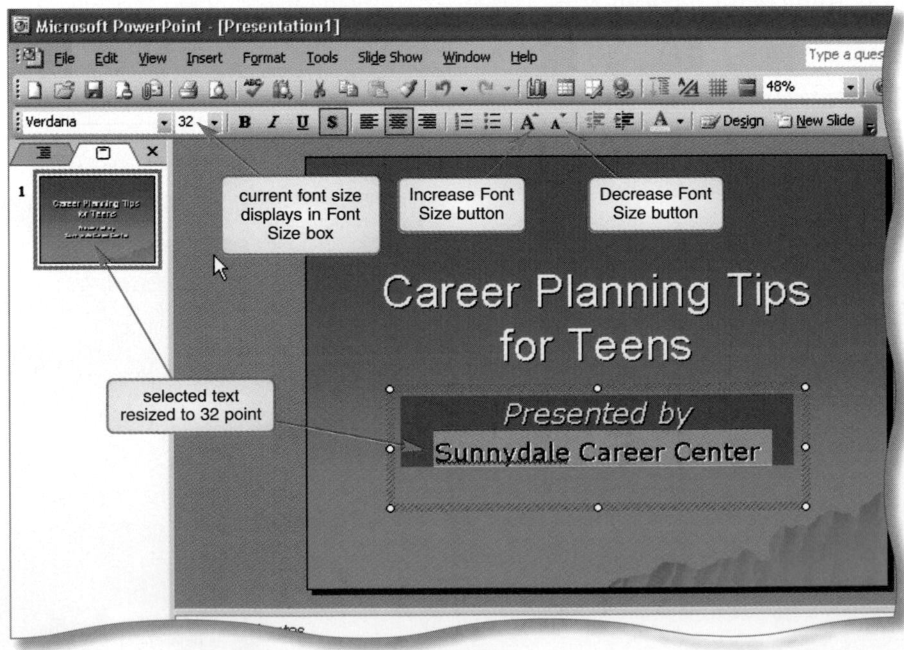

FIGURE 1-25

Skill Builder 1-1

To practice the following tasks, visit scsite.com/off2003sch/skill, locate PowerPoint Project 1, and then click Skill Builder 1-1.

- ❑ Start PowerPoint
- ❑ Enter a presentation title
- ❑ Enter a presentation subtitle
- ❑ Change text attributes

The Increase Font Size button on the Formatting toolbar (Figure 1-25) increases the font size in preset increments each time you click the button. If you need to decrease the font size, click the Font Size box arrow and then select a size smaller than 32. The Decrease Font Size button on the Formatting toolbar (Figure 1-25) also decreases the font size in preset increments each time you click the button.

Saving the Presentation

While you are building a presentation, the computer stores it in memory. It is important to save the presentation frequently because the presentation will be lost if the computer is turned off or you lose electrical power. Another reason to save your work is that if you run out of lab time before completing your project, you may finish the project later without starting over. Therefore, always save any presentation you will use later on a floppy disk, USB flash drive, or hard disk. A saved presentation is referred to as a **file**. Before you continue with Project 1, save the work completed thus far. The following steps illustrate how to save a presentation on a USB flash drive using the Save button on the Standard toolbar.

Q & A

Q: Does PowerPoint save files automatically?

A: Yes. Every 10 minutes PowerPoint saves a copy of your presentation. To check or change the save interval, click Options on the Tools menu and then click the Save tab. Click the Save AutoRe cover info every check box and then type the specific time in the minutes box.

To Save a Presentation

1

- **With a USB flash drive connected to one of the computer's USB ports, click the Save button on the Standard toolbar.**

The Save As dialog box is displayed (Figure 1-26). The default folder, My Documents, appears in the Save in box. Career Planning Tips for Teens appears highlighted in the File name text box because PowerPoint uses the words in the title text placeholder as the default file name. Presentation appears in the Save as type box. The buttons on the top and on the side are used to select folders and change the appearance of file names and other information.

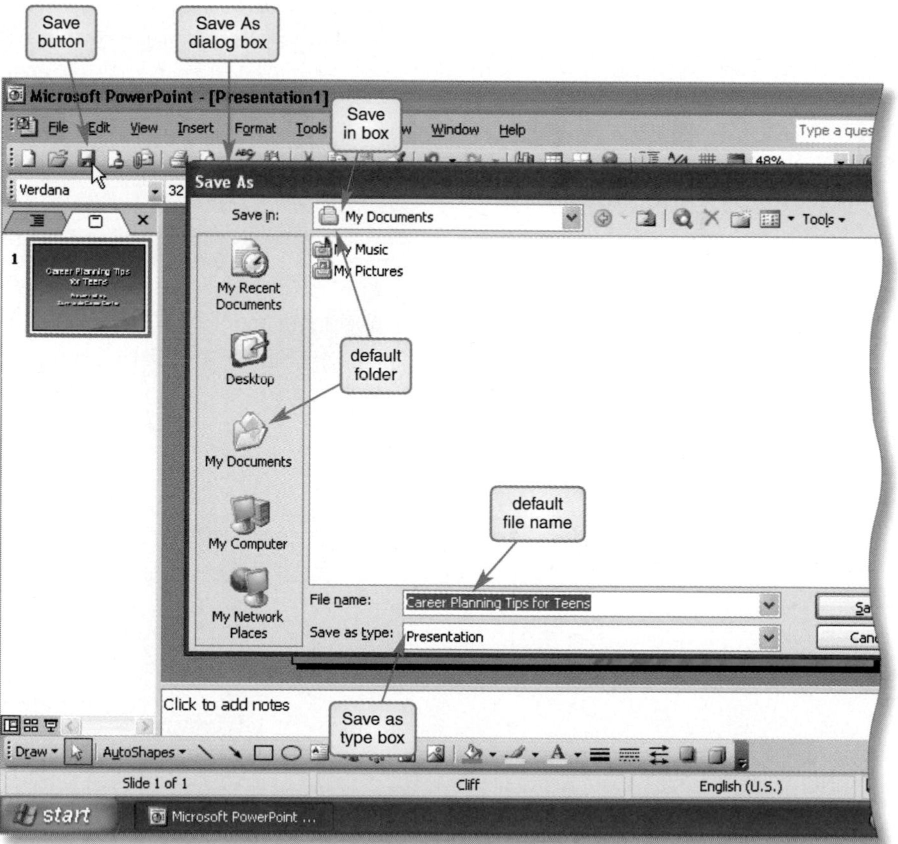

FIGURE 1-26

2

- **Type** `Career Planning` **in the File name text box. Do not press the ENTER key after typing the file name.**
- **Click the Save in box arrow.**

The name, Career Planning, appears in the File name text box (Figure 1-27). A file name can be up to 255 characters and can include spaces. The Save in list shows a list of locations in which to save a presentation. Your list may look different depending on the configuration of your system. Clicking the Cancel button closes the Save As dialog box.

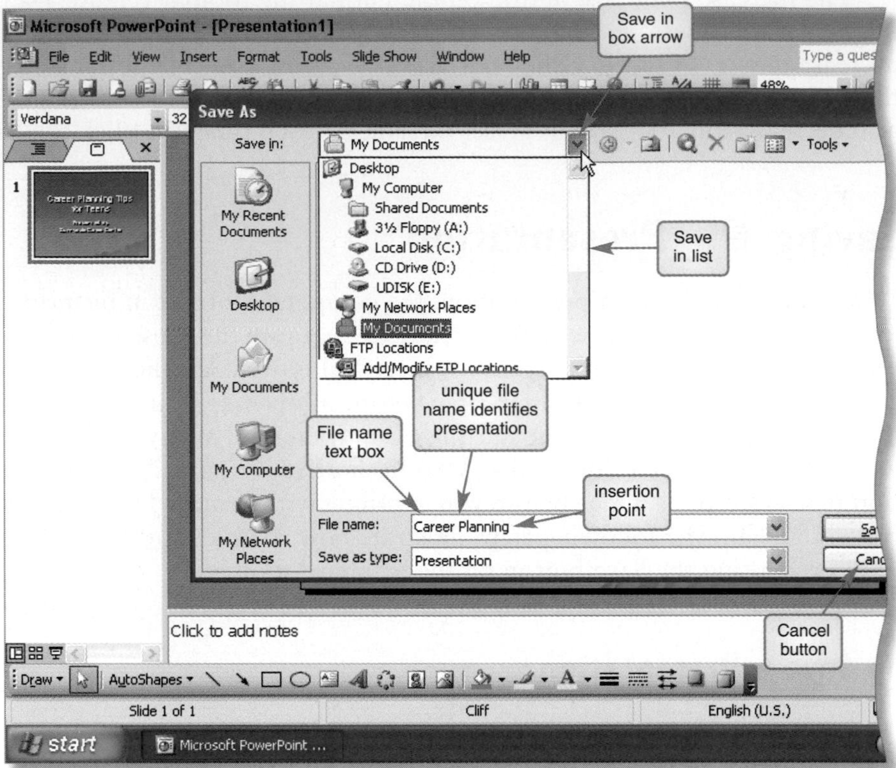

FIGURE 1-27

3

- **Click UDISK (E:) in the Save in list.**

Drive E becomes the selected drive (Figure 1-28). The drive on your computer may be different.

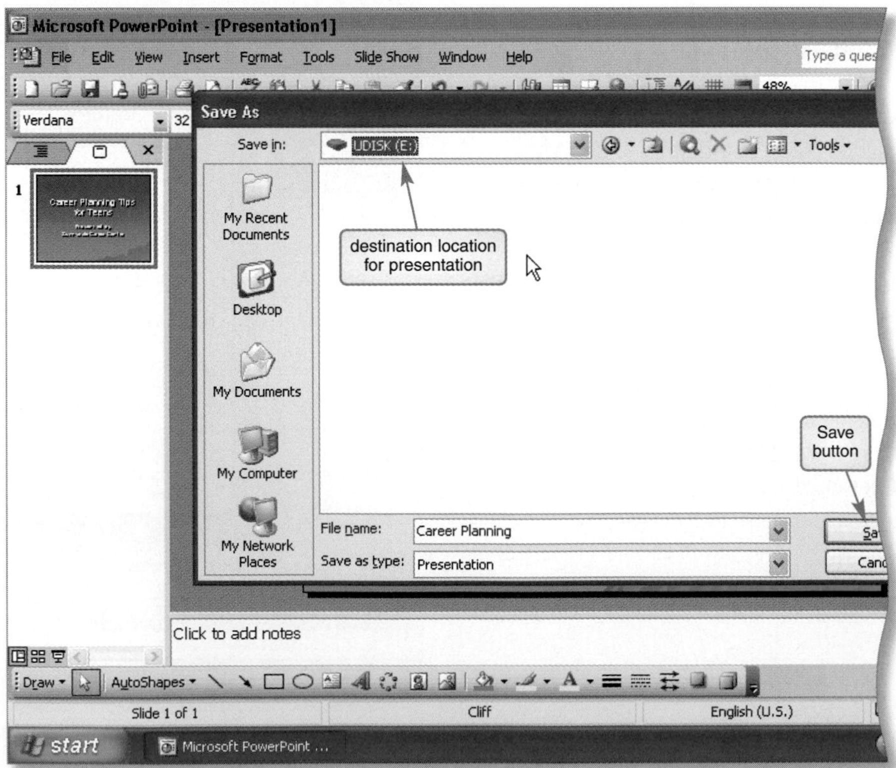

FIGURE 1-28

4

• **Click the Save button in the Save As dialog box.**

PowerPoint saves the presentation on the USB flash drive. The title bar shows the file name used to save the presentation, Career Planning (Figure 1-29).

FIGURE 1-29

PowerPoint automatically appends the extension .ppt to the file name, Career Planning. The **.ppt** extension stands for **P**ower**P**oin**t**. Although the slide show, Career Planning, is saved on a USB flash drive, it also remains in memory and is displayed on the screen.

It is a good practice to save periodically while you are working on a project. By doing so, you protect yourself from losing all the work you have done since the last time you saved.

The seven buttons at the top and to the right in the Save As dialog box in Figure 1-28 and their functions are summarized in Table 1-3.

Table 1-3 Save As Dialog Box Toolbar Buttons

BUTTON	BUTTON NAME	FUNCTION
	Default File Location	Displays contents of default file location
	Up One Level	Displays contents of folder one level up from current folder
	Search the Web	Starts browser and displays search engine
	Delete	Deletes selected file or folder
	Create New Folder	Creates new folder
	Views	Changes view of files and folders
Tools	Tools	Lists commands to print or modify file names and folders

When you click the Tools button in the Save As dialog box, PowerPoint displays a list. The Save Options command in the list allows you to save the presentation automatically at a specified time interval and to reduce the file size. The Security Options command allows you to modify the security level for opening files that may contain harmful computer viruses and to assign a password to limit access to the file. A password is case-sensitive and can be up to 15 characters long. **Case-sensitive** means PowerPoint can differentiate between uppercase and lowercase letters. If you assign a password and then forget the password, you cannot access the file.

The file buttons on the left of the Save As dialog box in Figure 1-28 on page PPT 28 allow you to select frequently used folders. The My Recent Documents button displays a list of shortcuts (pointers) to the most recently used files in a folder titled Recent. You cannot save presentations to the Recent folder.

Q & A

Q: What are some guidelines for choosing a password?

A: The most common word used for a password is the word, password. When choosing a password for your files, experts recommend using a combination of letters and numbers and making the word at least eight characters. Avoid using your name and the names of family members or pets.

Adding a New Slide to a Presentation

With the title slide for the presentation created, the next step is to add the first text slide immediately after the title slide. Usually, when you create a presentation, you add slides with text, graphics, or charts. When you add a new slide, PowerPoint uses the Title and Text slide layout. Some placeholders allow you to double-click the placeholder and then access other objects, such as media clips, charts, diagrams, and organization charts.

The following steps add a new Text slide layout with a bulleted list. The default PowerPoint setting will display the Slide Layout task pane each time a new slide is added. Your system may not display this task pane if the setting has been changed.

To Add a New Text Slide with a Bulleted List

• **Click the New Slide button on the Formatting toolbar.**

The Slide Layout task pane opens. The Title and Text slide layout is selected. Slide 2 of 2 appears on the status bar (Figure 1-30).

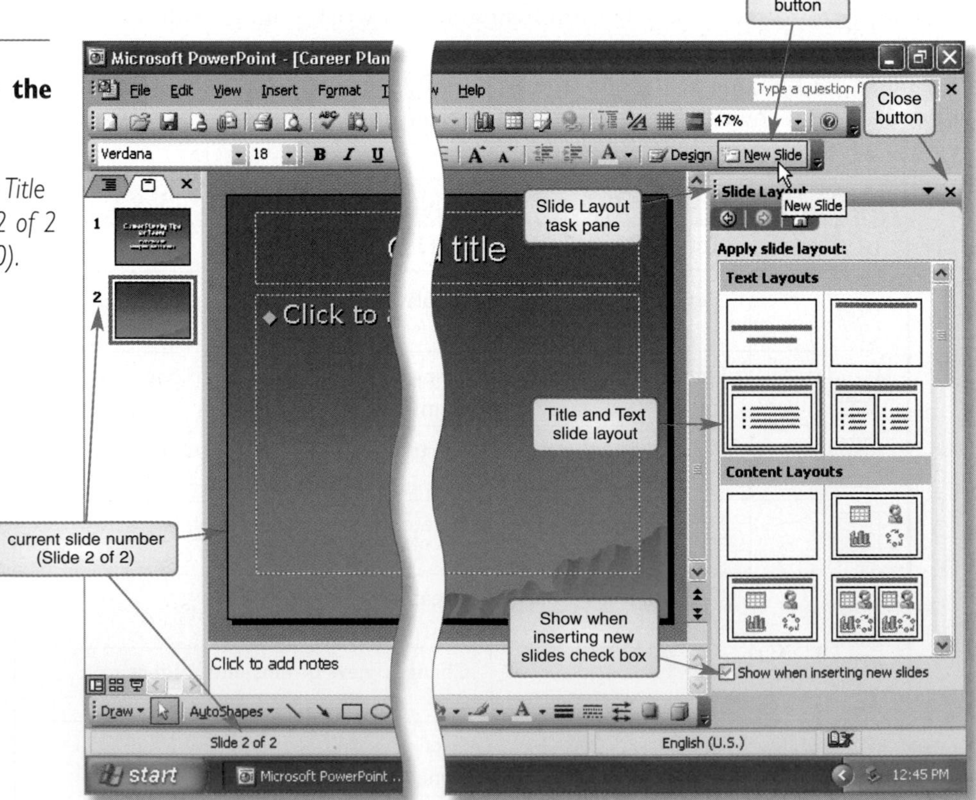

FIGURE 1-30

2

• If necessary, click the Show when inserting new slides check box to remove the check mark, and then click the Close button on the Slide Layout task pane.

Slide 2 appears in both the slide pane and Slides tab retaining the attributes of the Cliff design template (Figure 1-31). The vertical scroll bar appears in the slide pane. The bullet appears as an outline square.

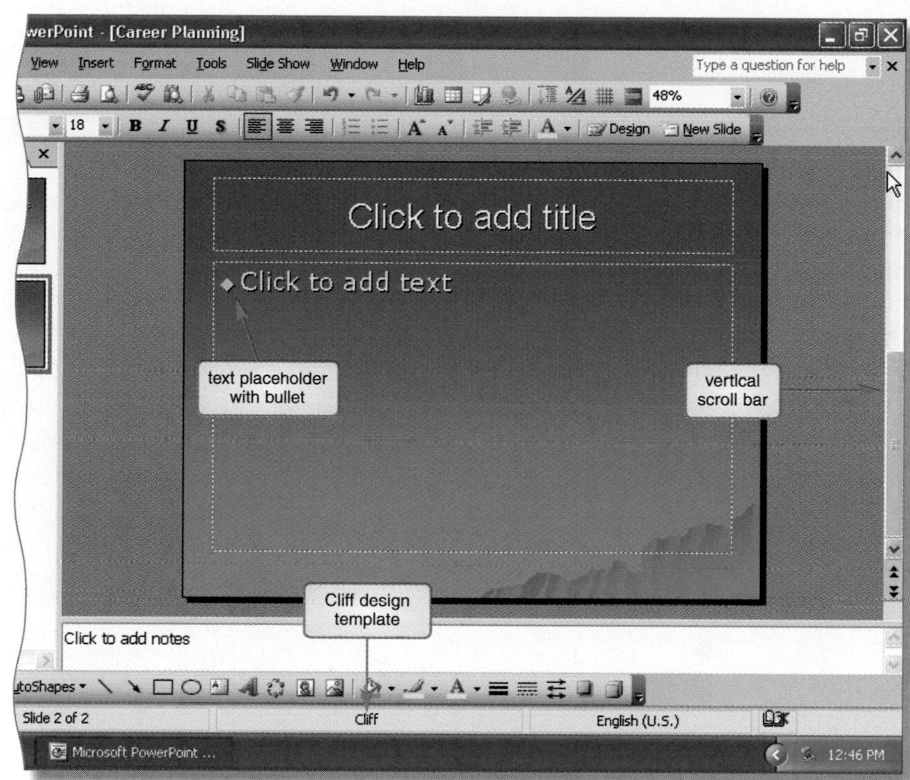

FIGURE 1-31

Slide 2 appears with a title text placeholder and a text placeholder with a bullet. You can change the layout for a slide at any time during the creation of a presentation by clicking Format on the menu bar and then clicking Slide Layout. You also can click View on the menu bar and then click Task Pane. You then can double-click the slide layout of your choice from the Slide Layout task pane.

Creating a Text Slide with a Single-Level Bulleted List

The information in the Slide 2 text placeholder is presented in a bulleted list. All the bullets appear on one level. A **level** is a position within a structure, such as an outline, that indicates the magnitude of importance. PowerPoint allows for five paragraph levels. Each paragraph level has an associated bullet. The bullet font is dependent on the design template.

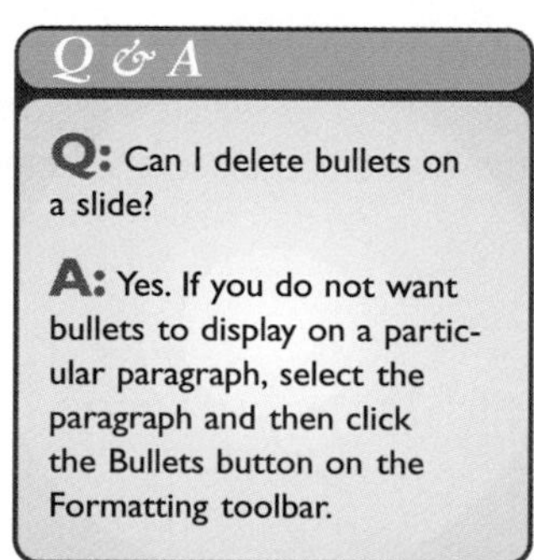

Q & A

Q: Can I delete bullets on a slide?

A: Yes. If you do not want bullets to display on a particular paragraph, select the paragraph and then click the Bullets button on the Formatting toolbar.

Entering a Slide Title

PowerPoint assumes every new slide has a title. The title for Slide 2 is The Right Mind-Set. The step on the next page shows how to enter this title.

To Enter a Slide Title

1

- **Click the title text placeholder and then type** `The Right Mind-Set` **in the placeholder. Do not press the ENTER key.**

The title, The Right Mind-Set, appears in the title text placeholder and in the Slides tab (Figure 1-32). The insertion point appears after the t in Mind-Set. The selection rectangle indicates the title text placeholder is selected.

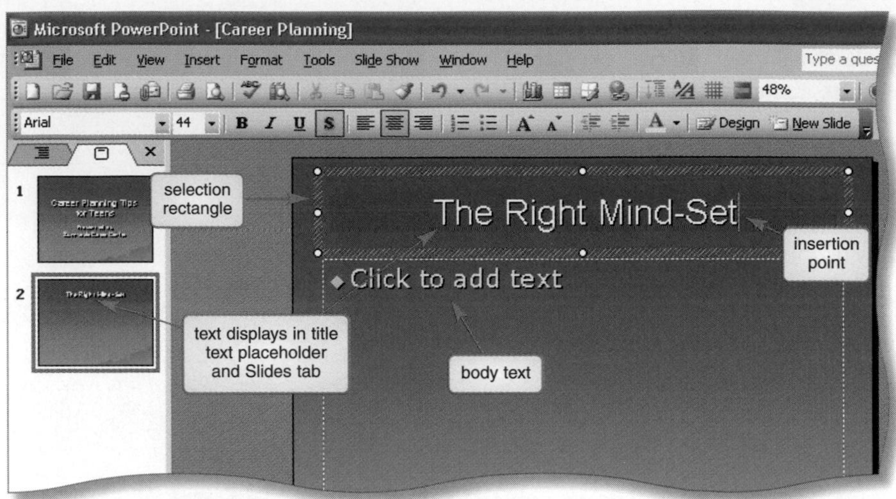

FIGURE 1-32

Selecting a Text Placeholder

Before you can type text into the text placeholder, you first must select it. The following step selects the text placeholder on Slide 2.

To Select a Text Placeholder

1

- **Click the bulleted paragraph labeled, Click to add text.**

The insertion point appears immediately to the right of the bullet on Slide 2 (Figure 1-33). The mouse pointer may change shape if you move it away from the bullet. The selection rectangle indicates the text placeholder is selected.

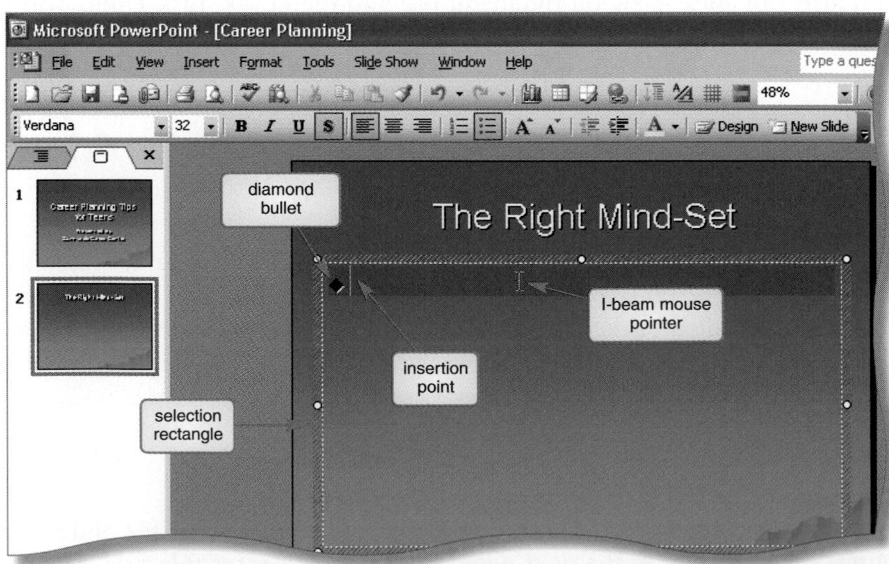

FIGURE 1-33

Typing a Single-Level Bulleted List

As discussed previously, a bulleted list is a list of paragraphs, each of which is preceded by a bullet. A paragraph is a segment of text ended by pressing the ENTER key. The next step is to type the single-level bulleted list, which consists of three entries (Figure 1-1b on page PPT 5). The following steps illustrate how to type a single-level bulleted list.

To Type a Single-Level Bulleted List

1

• **Type** `Realize most teens do not know what career best fits their personality` **and then press the ENTER key.**

The paragraph, Realize most teens do not know what career best fits their personality, appears (Figure 1-34). The font size is 32. The insertion point appears after the second bullet. When you press the ENTER key, PowerPoint ends one paragraph and begins a new paragraph. With the Title and Text slide layout, PowerPoint places a diamond bullet in front of the new paragraph.

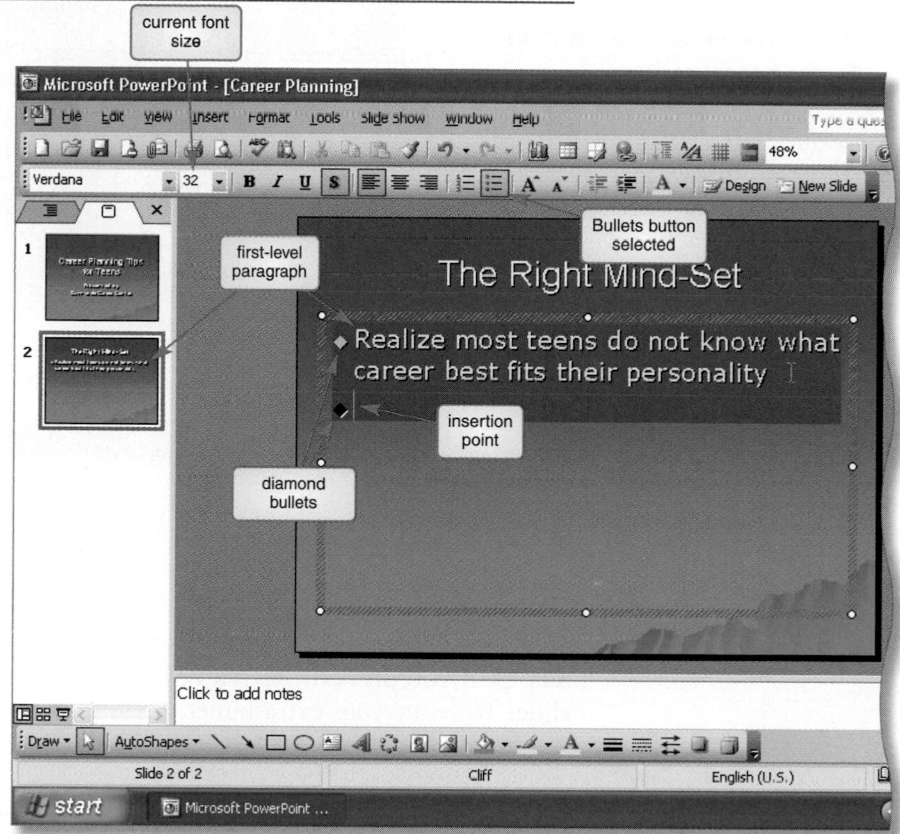

FIGURE 1-34

2

- **Type** Stay flexible by keeping open mind to explore new fields **and then press the ENTER key.**
- **Type** Prepare for work world by building strong communication skills **but do not press the ENTER key.**
- **Point to the New Slide button on the Formatting toolbar.**

The insertion point is displayed after the second s in skills (Figure 1-35). Three new first-level paragraphs are displayed with diamond bullets in both the text placeholder and the Slides tab. When you press the ENTER key, PowerPoint adds a new paragraph at the same level as the previous paragraph.

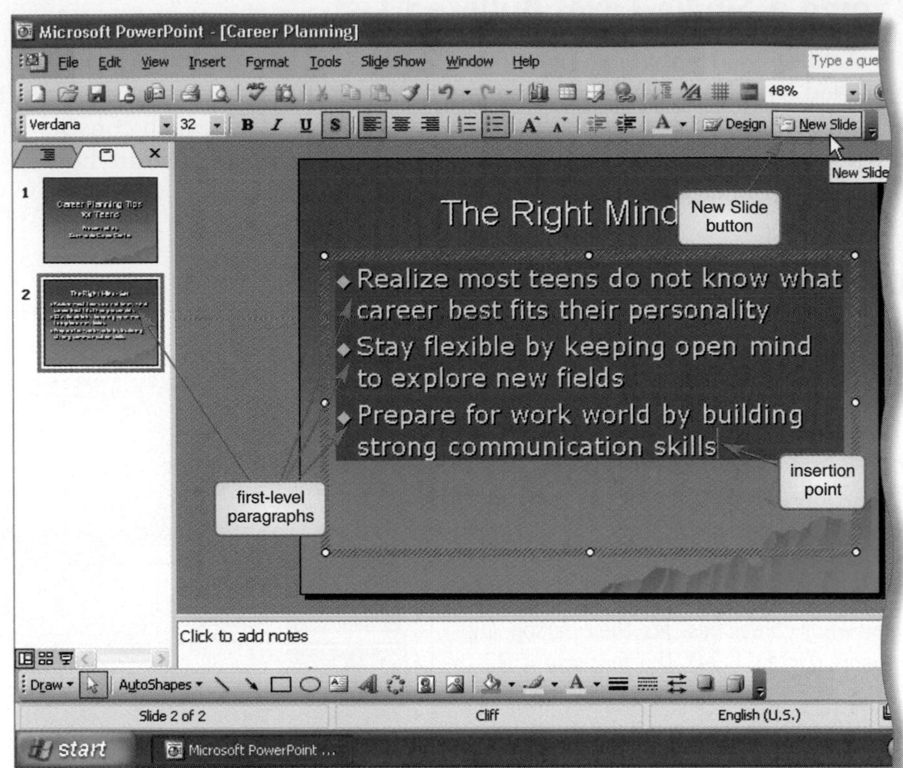

FIGURE 1-35

Notice that you did not press the ENTER key after typing the last paragraph in Step 2. If you press the ENTER key, a new bullet appears after the last entry on this slide. To remove an extra bullet, press the BACKSPACE key.

Creating a Text Slide with a Multi-Level Bulleted List

Slides 3 and 4 in Figure 1-1 on page PPT 5 contain more than one level of bulleted text. A slide that consists of more than one level of bulleted text is called a **multi-level bulleted list slide**. Beginning with the second level, each paragraph indents to the right of the preceding level and is pushed down to a lower level. For example, if you increase the indent of a first-level paragraph, it becomes a second-level paragraph. This lower-level paragraph is a subset of the higher-level paragraph. It usually contains information that supports the topic in the paragraph immediately above it. You increase the indent of a paragraph by clicking the Increase Indent button on the Formatting toolbar.

When you want to raise a paragraph from a lower level to a higher level, you click the Decrease Indent button on the Formatting toolbar.

Creating a text slide with a multi-level bulleted list requires several steps. Initially, you enter a slide title in the title text placeholder. Next, you select the body text placeholder. Then, you type the text for the multi-level bulleted list, increasing and decreasing the indents as needed. The next several sections explain how to add a slide with a multi-level bulleted list.

Adding New Slides and Entering Slide Titles

When you add a new slide to a presentation, PowerPoint keeps the same layout used on the previous slide. PowerPoint assumes every new slide has a title. The title for Slide 3 is Experience Gives Insights. The following steps show how to add a new slide (Slide 3) and enter a title.

To Add a New Slide and Enter a Slide Title

1

- **Click the New Slide button.**

Slide 3 of 3 appears in the slide pane and Slides tab (Figure 1-36).

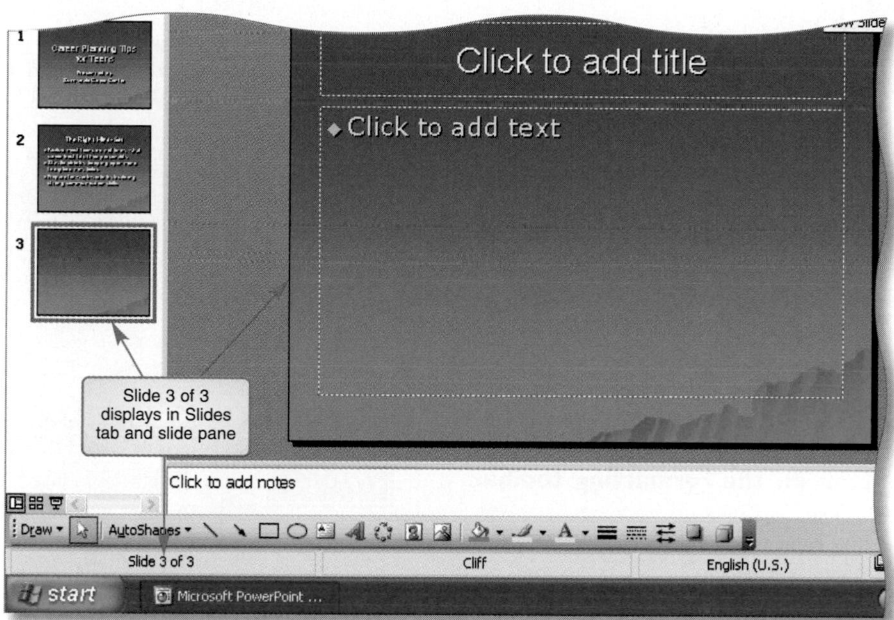

FIGURE 1-36

2

- **Type** `Experience Gives Insights` **in the title text placeholder. Do not press the ENTER key.**

Slide 3 shows the Title and Text slide layout with the title, Experience Gives Insights, in the title text placeholder and in the Slides tab (Figure 1-37). The insertion point appears after the second s in Insights.

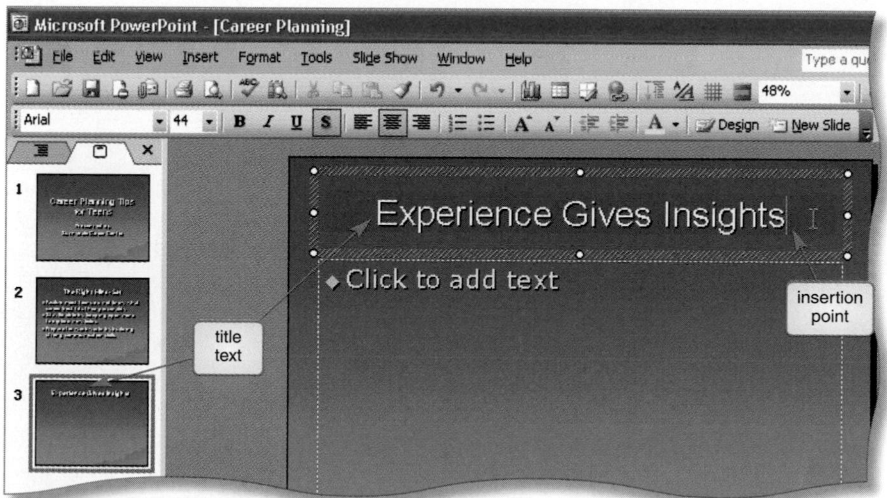

FIGURE 1-37

Slide 3 is added to the presentation with the desired title.

Typing a Multi-Level Bulleted List

The next step is to select the body text placeholder and then type the multi-level bulleted list, which consists of six entries (Figure 1-1c on page PPT 5). The following steps show how to create a list consisting of three levels.

To Type a Multi-Level Bulleted List

- **Click the bulleted paragraph labeled, Click to add text.**

The insertion point appears immediately to the right of the bullet on Slide 3. The mouse pointer may change shape if you move it away from the bullet.

2

- **Type** `Job shadowing` **and then press the ENTER key.**
- **Point to the Increase Indent button on the Formatting toolbar.**

The paragraph, Job shadowing, appears (Figure 1-38). The font size is 32. The insertion point appears to the right of the second bullet.

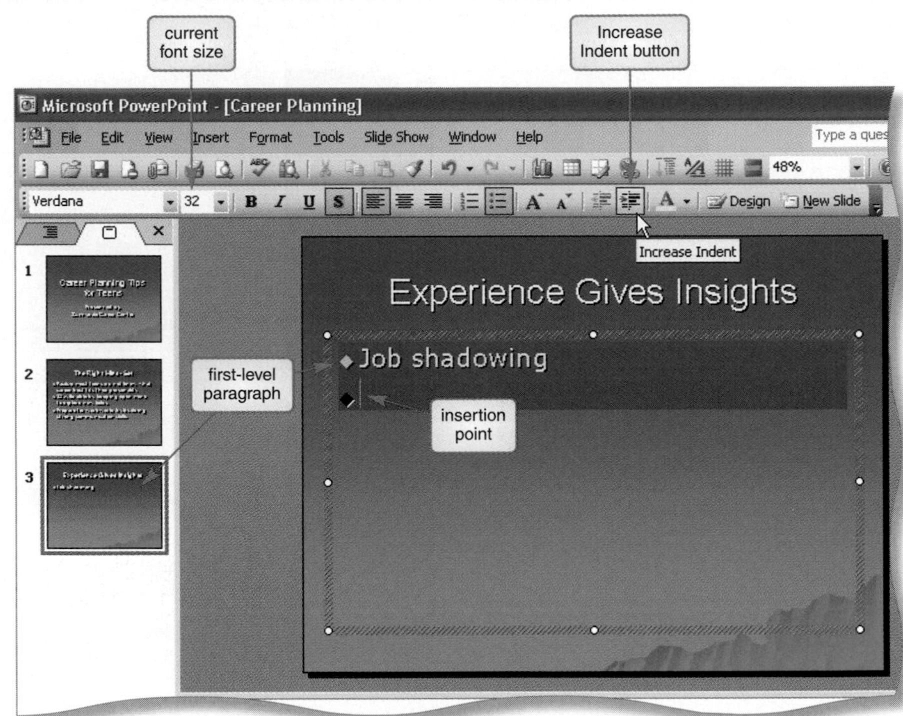

FIGURE 1-38

- **Click the Increase Indent button.**

The second paragraph indents below the first and becomes a second-level paragraph (Figure 1-39). The bullet to the left of the second paragraph changes from a diamond to a dash, and the font size for the paragraph now is 28. The insertion point appears to the right of the dash.

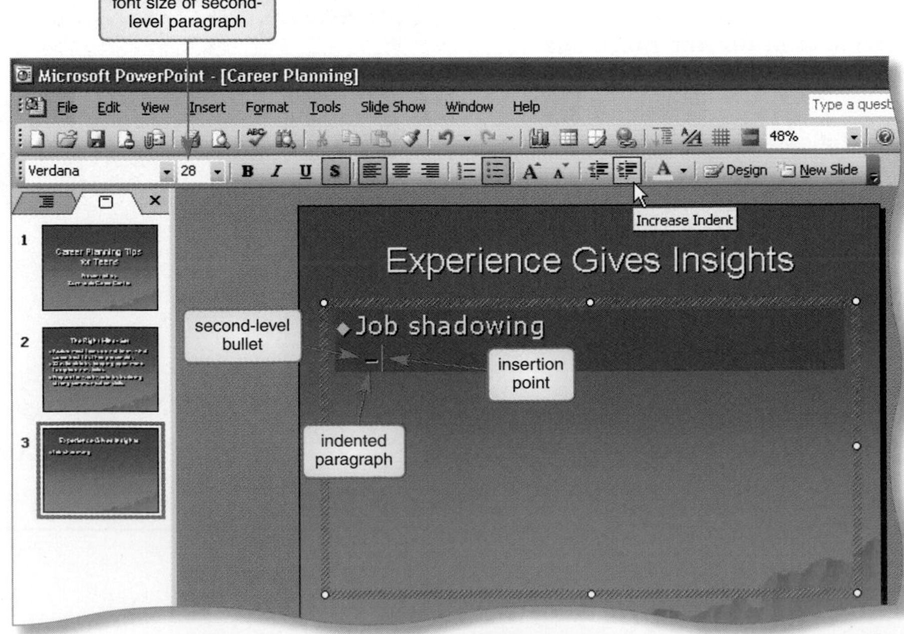

FIGURE 1-39

4

- **Type** `Work one day with someone on-site` **and then press the ENTER key.**
- **Point to the Decrease Indent button on the Formatting toolbar.**

The first second-level paragraph appears with a dash bullet in both the slide pane and the Slides tab (Figure 1-40). When you press the ENTER key, PowerPoint adds a new paragraph at the same level as the previous paragraph.

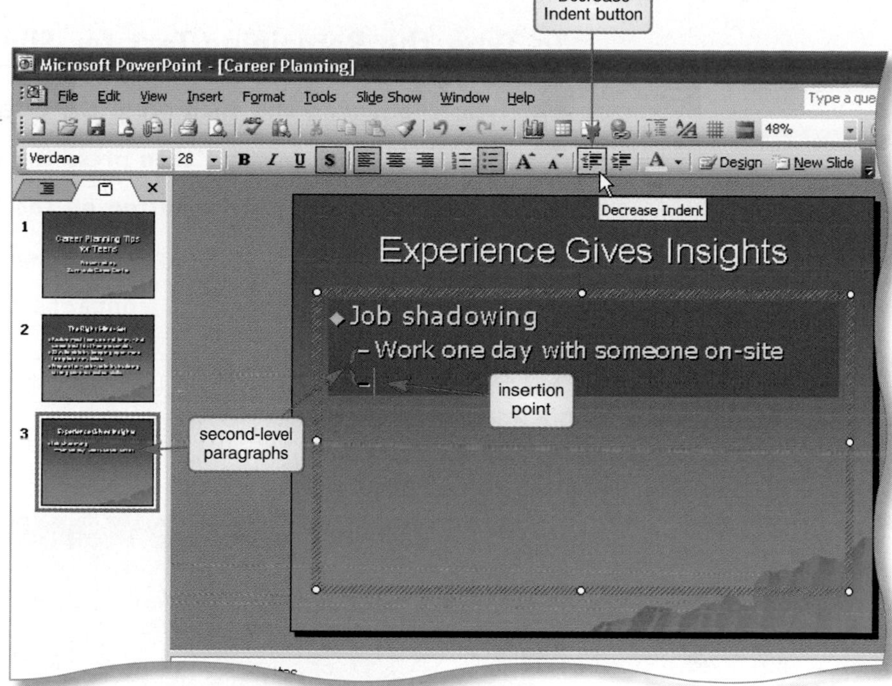

FIGURE 1-40

5

- **Click the Decrease Indent button.**

The second-level paragraph becomes a first-level paragraph (Figure 1-41). The bullet of the new paragraph changes from a dash to a diamond, and the font size for the paragraph is 32. The insertion point appears to the right of the diamond bullet.

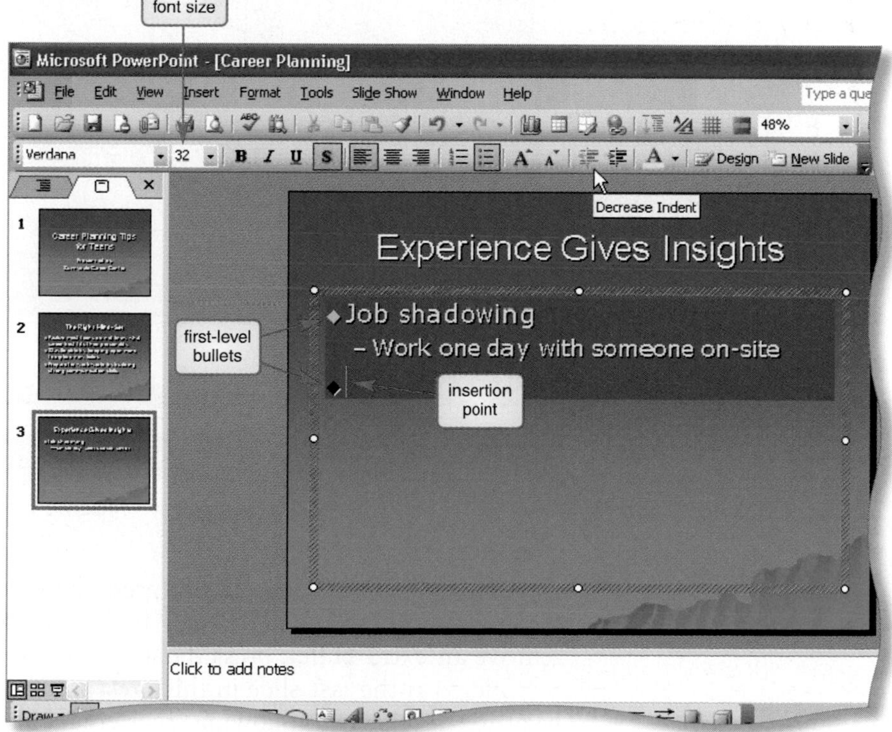

FIGURE 1-41

The steps on the next page complete the text for Slide 3.

To Type the Remaining Text for Slide 3

1. **Type** `Interning` **and then press the ENTER key.**
2. **Type** `Volunteering` **and then press the ENTER key.**
3. **Click the Increase Indent button on the Formatting toolbar.**
4. **Type** `Receive valuable training` **and then press the ENTER key.**
5. **Type** `Make important job contacts` **but do not press the ENTER key.**

Slide 3 is displayed as shown in Figure 1-42. The insertion point appears after the s in contacts.

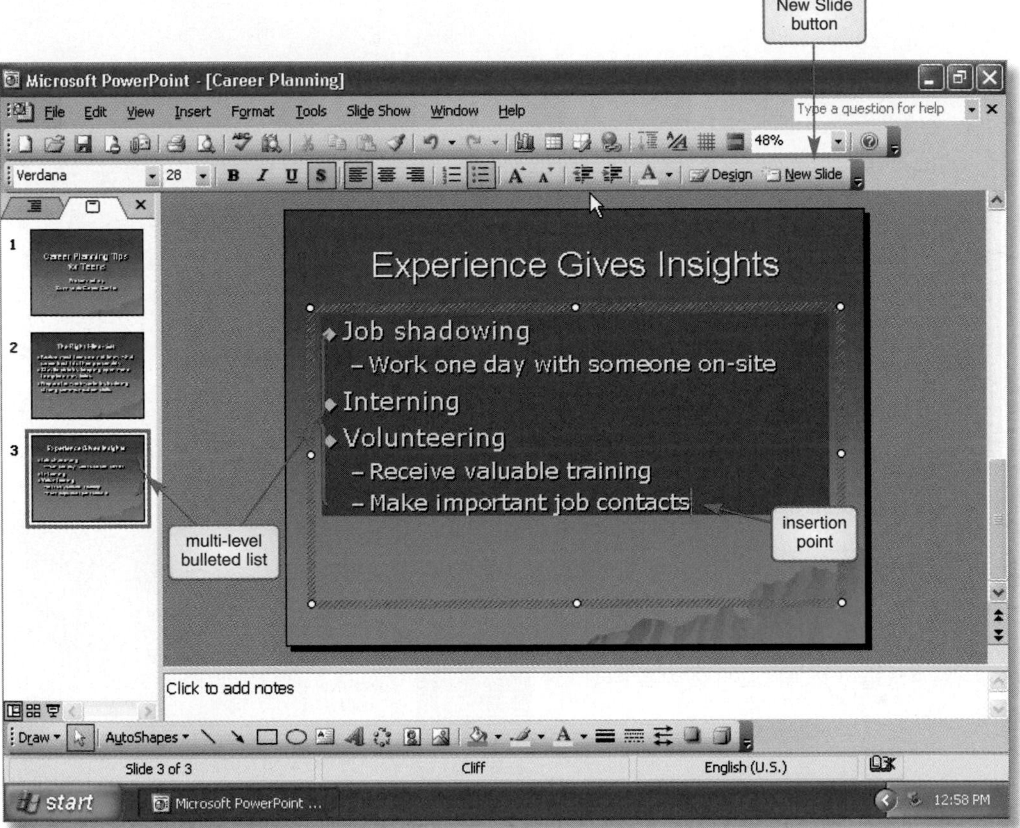

FIGURE 1-42

In Step 4 above, you did not press the ENTER key after typing the last paragraph. If you press the ENTER key, a new bullet appears after the last entry on this slide. To remove an extra bullet, press the BACKSPACE key.

Slide 4 is the last slide in this presentation. It also is a multi-level bulleted list and has three levels. The following steps create Slide 4.

To Create Slide 4

1. **Click the New Slide button on the Formatting toolbar.**
2. **Type** `Career and Personality Tests` **in the title text placeholder.**
3. **Press CTRL+ENTER to move the insertion point to the body text placeholder.**
4. **Type** `Can determine aptitude for jobs` **and then press the ENTER key.**
5. **Click the Increase Indent button on the Formatting toolbar. Type** `Measure ability to acquire a skill` **and then press the ENTER key.**

The title and first two levels of bullets are added to Slide 4 (Figure 1-43).

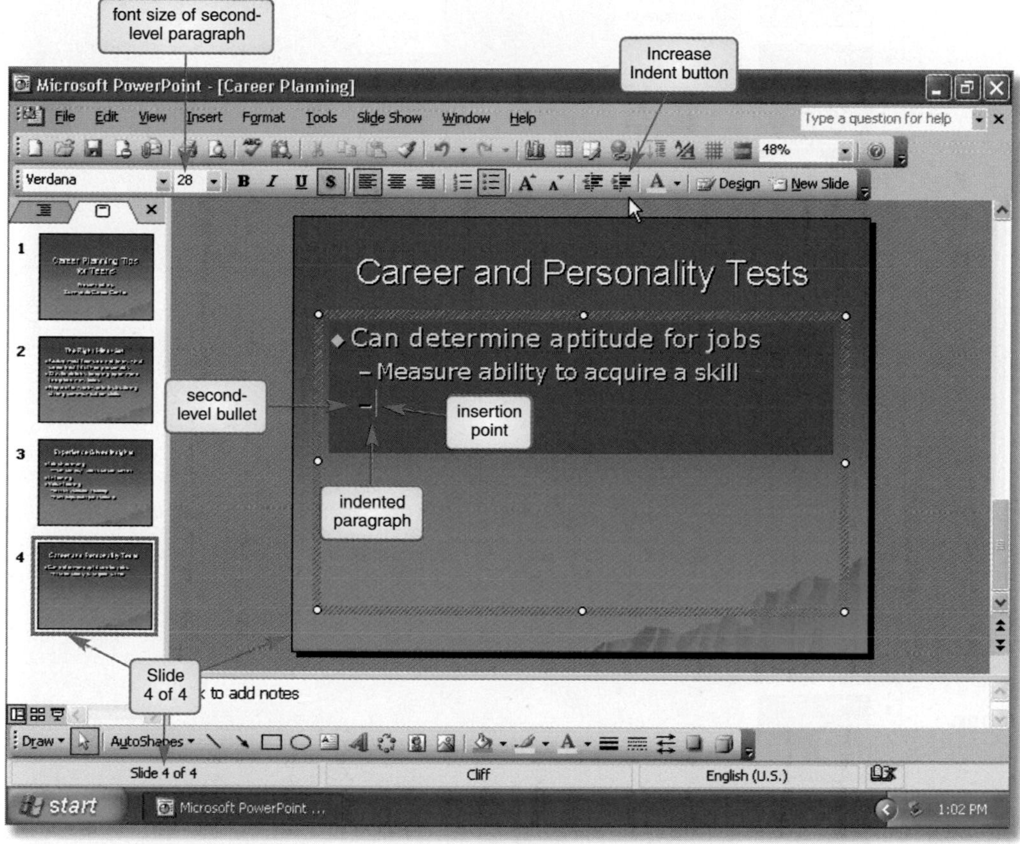

FIGURE 1-43

Creating a Third-Level Paragraph

The next line in Slide 4 is indented an additional level, to the third level. The steps on the next page create an additional level.

To Create a Third-Level Paragraph

1

• **Click the Increase Indent button on the Formatting toolbar.**

The second-level paragraph becomes a third-level paragraph (Figure 1-44). The bullet to the left of the new paragraph changes from a dash to a diamond, and the font size for the paragraph is 24. The insertion point appears after the third-level bullet.

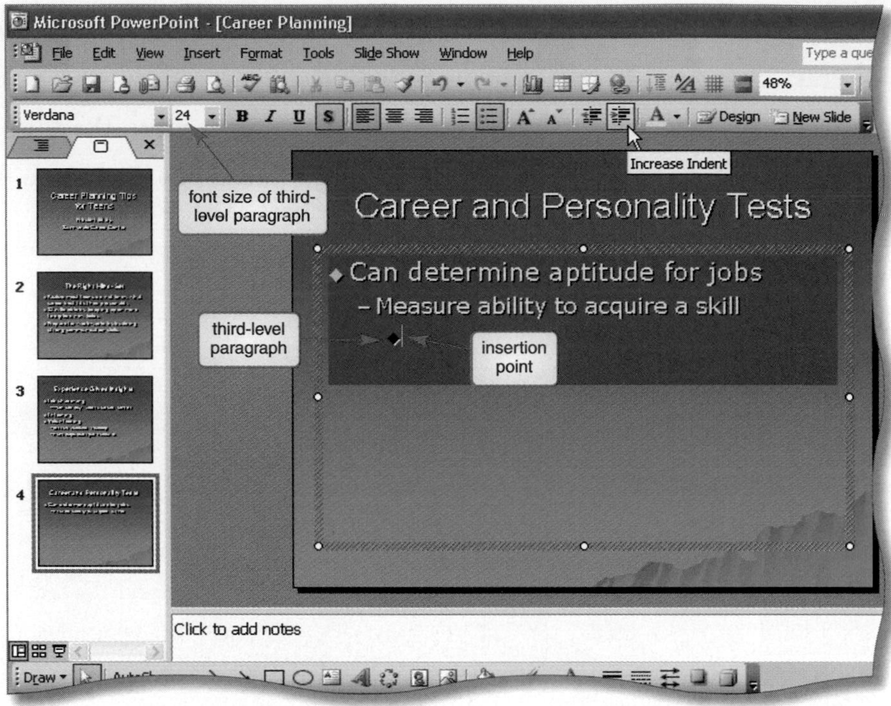

FIGURE 1-44

2

• **Type** `Employers use to screen job applicants` **and then press the ENTER key.**

• **Point to the Decrease Indent button on the Formatting toolbar.**

The first third-level paragraph, Employers use to screen job applicants, is displayed with the bullet for a second third-level paragraph (Figure 1-45).

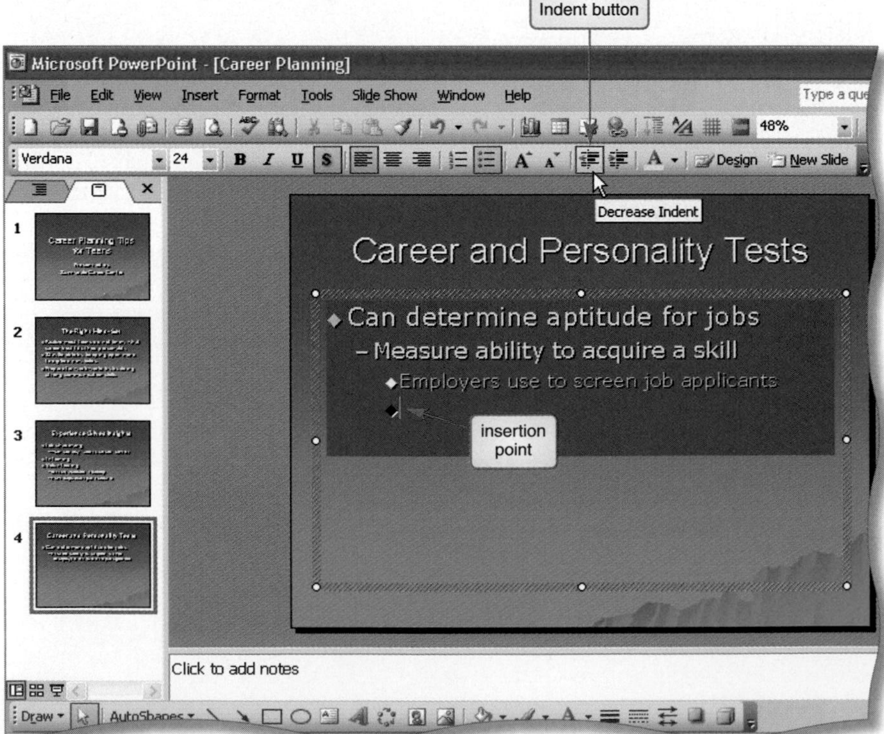

FIGURE 1-45

3

• **Click the Decrease Indent button two times.**

The insertion point appears at the first level (Figure 1-46).

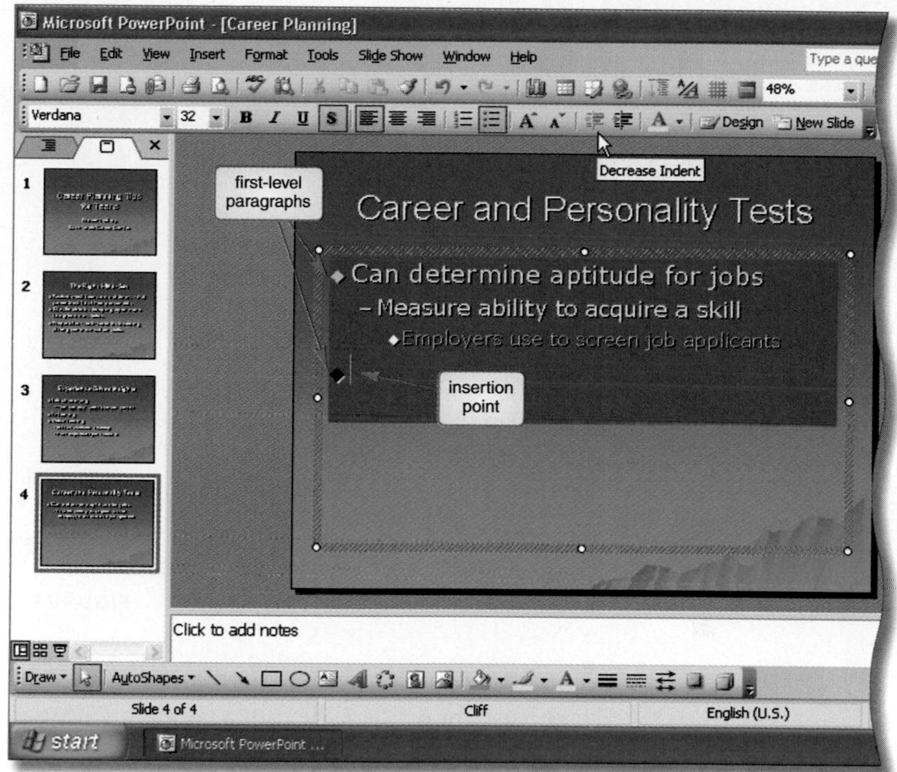

FIGURE 1-46

The title text and three levels of paragraphs discussing determining job aptitude are complete. The next three paragraphs concern planning tools. As an alternative to clicking the Increase Indent button, you can press the TAB key. Likewise, instead of clicking the Decrease Indent button, you can press the SHIFT+TAB keys. The following steps illustrate how to type the remaining text for Slide 4.

To Type the Remaining Text for Slide 4

1. **Type** `Use as tools for overall planning` **and then press the ENTER key.**
2. **Press the TAB key to increase the indent to the second level.**
3. **Type** `Results may vary greatly` **and then press the ENTER key.**
4. **Press the TAB key to increase the indent to the third level.**
5. **Type** `Many available online at no cost` **but do not press the ENTER key.**

The Slide 4 title text and body text are displayed in the slide pane and Slides tabs (Figure 1-47 on the next page). The insertion point appears after the t in cost.

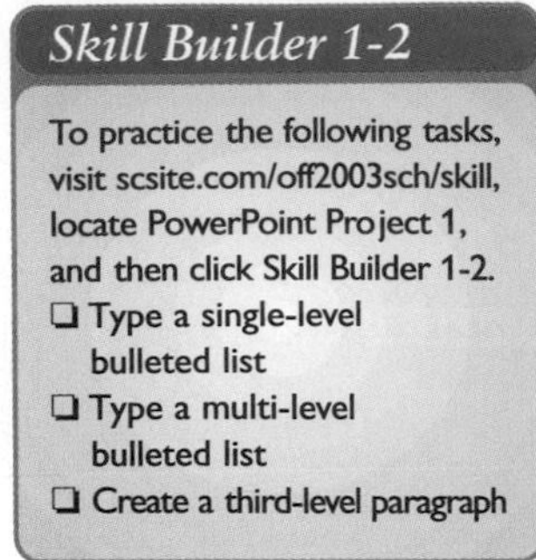

Skill Builder 1-2
To practice the following tasks, visit scsite.com/off2003sch/skill, locate PowerPoint Project 1, and then click Skill Builder 1-2.
❑ Type a single-level bulleted list
❑ Type a multi-level bulleted list
❑ Create a third-level paragraph

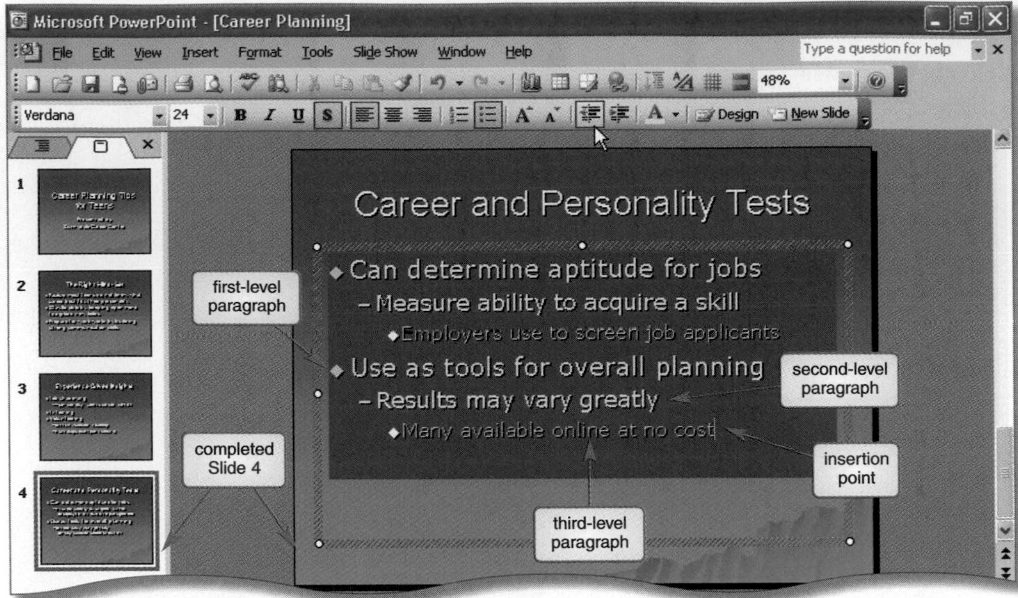

FIGURE 1-47

All the slides are created for the Career Planning slide show. This presentation consists of a title slide, one text slide with a single-level bulleted list, and two text slides with a multi-level bulleted list.

Ending a Slide Show with a Black Slide

After the last slide in the slide show appears, the default PowerPoint setting is to end the presentation with a black slide. This black slide appears only when the slide show is running and concludes the slide show gracefully so your audience never sees the PowerPoint window. A **black slide** ends all slide shows unless the option setting is deselected. The following steps verify that the End with black slide option is selected.

To End a Slide Show with a Black Slide

1

• **Click Tools on the menu bar and then point to Options (Figure 1-48).**

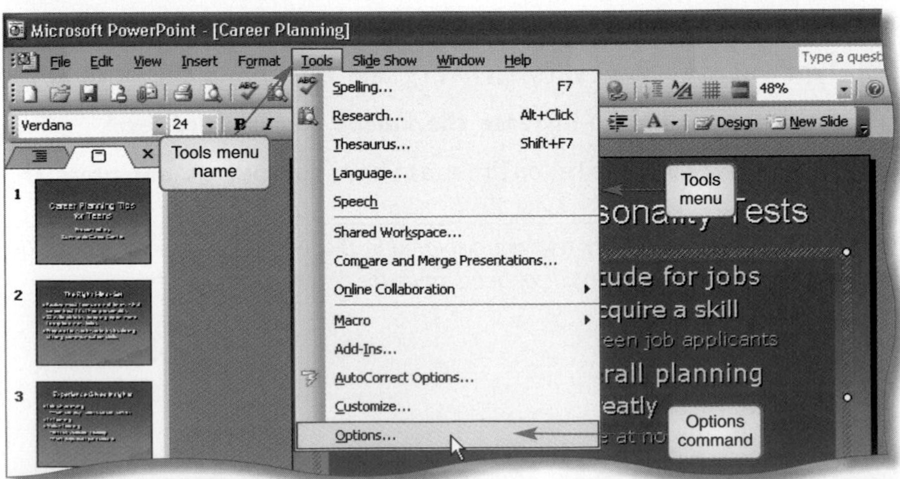

FIGURE 1-48

2

- **Click Options.**
- **If necessary, click the View tab when the Options dialog box appears.**
- **Verify that the End with black slide check box is selected.**
- **If a check mark does not show, click End with black slide.**
- **Point to the OK button.**

The Options dialog box appears (Figure 1-49). The View sheet contains settings for the overall PowerPoint display and for a particular slide show.

3

- **Click the OK button.**

The End with black slide option will cause the slide show to end with a black slide until it is deselected.

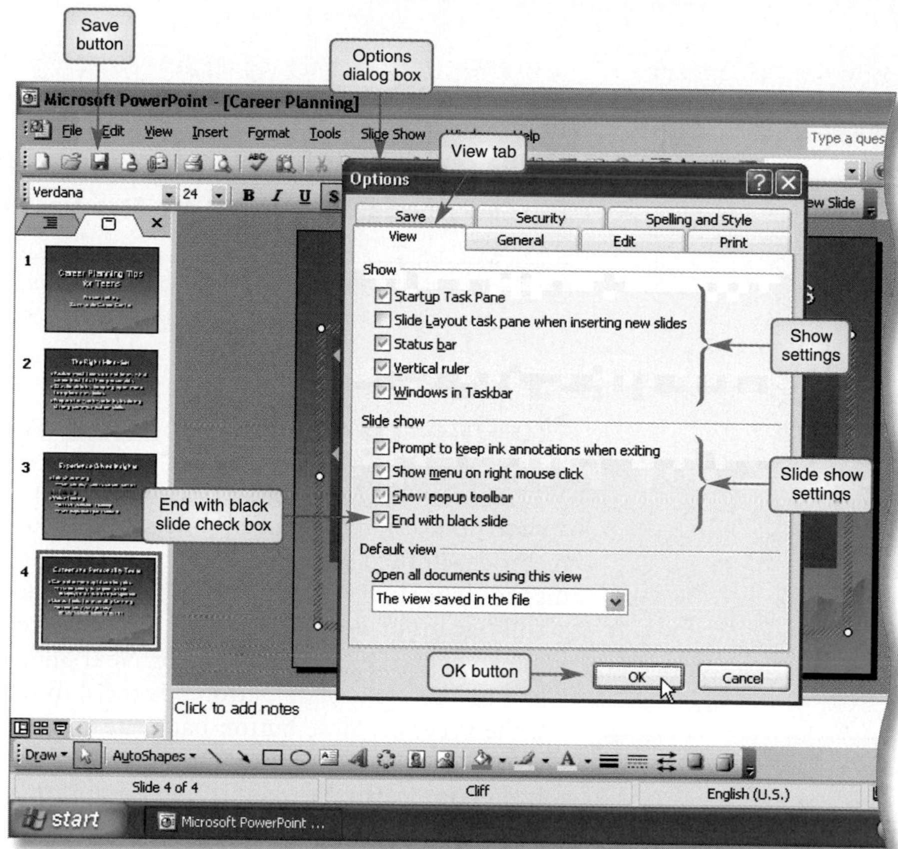

FIGURE 1-49

With all aspects of the presentation complete, it is important to save the additions and changes you have made to the Career Planning presentation.

Saving a Presentation with the Same File Name

Saving frequently cannot be overemphasized. When you first saved the presentation, you clicked the Save button on the Standard toolbar, and the Save dialog box appeared. When you want to save the changes made to the presentation after your last save, you again click the Save button. This time, however, the Save dialog box does not appear because PowerPoint updates the document called Career Planning.ppt on the USB flash drive. The steps on the next page illustrate how to save the presentation again.

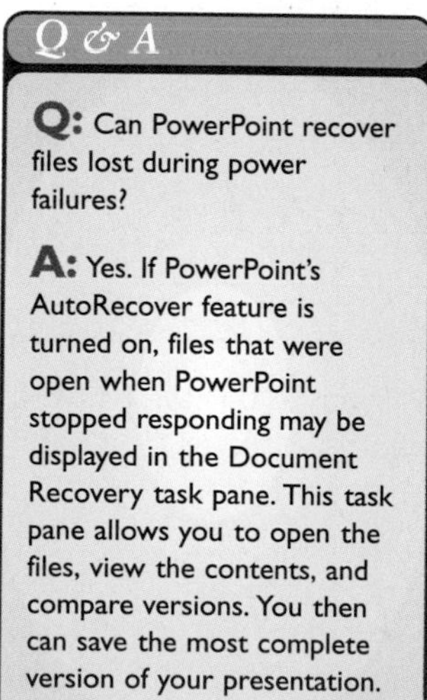

Q & A

Q: Can PowerPoint recover files lost during power failures?

A: Yes. If PowerPoint's AutoRecover feature is turned on, files that were open when PowerPoint stopped responding may be displayed in the Document Recovery task pane. This task pane allows you to open the files, view the contents, and compare versions. You then can save the most complete version of your presentation.

To Save a Presentation with the Same File Name

1. **Be certain your USB flash drive is connected to the computer's USB port.**
2. **Click the Save button on the Standard toolbar.**

PowerPoint overwrites the old Career Planning.ppt document on the USB flash drive with the revised presentation document. Slide 4 is displayed in the PowerPoint window.

Moving to Another Slide in Normal View

When creating or editing a presentation in normal view, you often want to display a slide other than the current one. You can move to another slide using several methods. In the Outline tab, you can point to any of the text in a particular slide to display that slide in the slide pane, or you can drag the scroll box on the vertical scroll bar up or down to move through the text in the presentation. In the slide pane, you can click the Previous Slide or Next Slide button on the vertical scroll bar. Clicking the Next Slide button advances to the next slide in the presentation. Clicking the Previous Slide button backs up to the slide preceding the current slide. You also can drag the scroll box on the vertical scroll bar. When you drag the scroll box, the **slide indicator** shows the number and title of the slide you are about to display. Releasing the mouse button shows the slide.

A slide's **Zoom setting** affects the portion of the slide displaying in the slide pane. PowerPoint defaults to a setting of approximately 50 percent so the entire slide is displayed. This percentage depends on the size and type of your monitor. If you want to display a small portion of the current slide, you would zoom in by clicking the **Zoom box arrow** and then clicking the desired magnification. You can display the entire slide in the slide pane by clicking **Fit** in the Zoom list. The Zoom setting affects the action of the vertical and horizontal scroll bars. If Zoom is set so the entire slide is not visible in the slide pane, clicking the up scroll arrow on the vertical scroll bar shows the next portion of the slide, not the previous slide.

Q & A

Q: Can I enlarge the slide size on my monitor?

A: Yes. You can increase your Zoom setting as large as 400% when you want to see details on small objects. Likewise, you can decrease your Zoom setting as small as 10%. When you want to redisplay the entire slide, click Fit in the Zoom list.

Using the Scroll Box on the Slide Pane to Move to Another Slide

Before continuing with Project 1, you want to display the title slide. The following steps show how to move from Slide 4 to Slide 1 using the scroll box on the slide pane vertical scroll bar.

To Use the Scroll Box on the Slide Pane to Move to Another Slide

1

- **Position the mouse pointer on the scroll box.**
- **Press and hold down the mouse button.**

Slide: 4 of 4 Career and Personality Tests appears in the slide indicator (Figure 1-50). When you click the scroll box, the Slide 4 thumbnail has no gray border in the Slides tab.

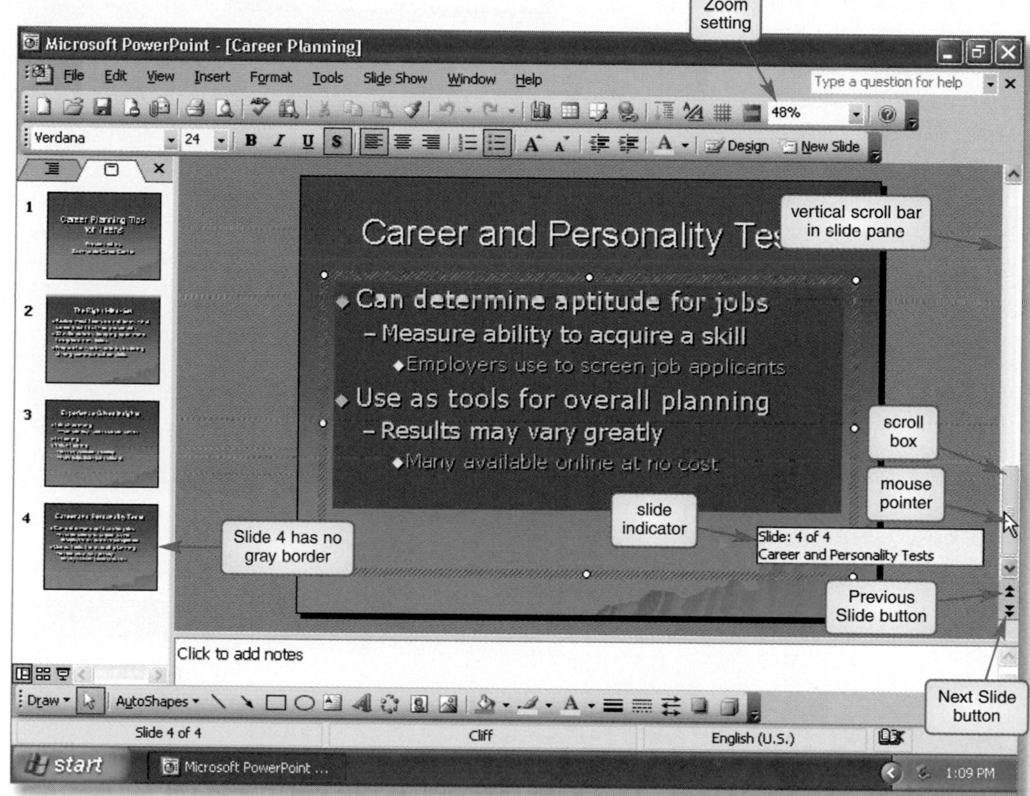

FIGURE 1-50

2

- **Drag the scroll box up the vertical scroll bar until Slide: 1 of 4 Career Planning Tips for Teens appears in the slide indicator.**

Slide: 1 of 4 Career Planning Tips for Teens appears in the slide indicator (Figure 1-51). Slide 4 still is displayed in the PowerPoint window.

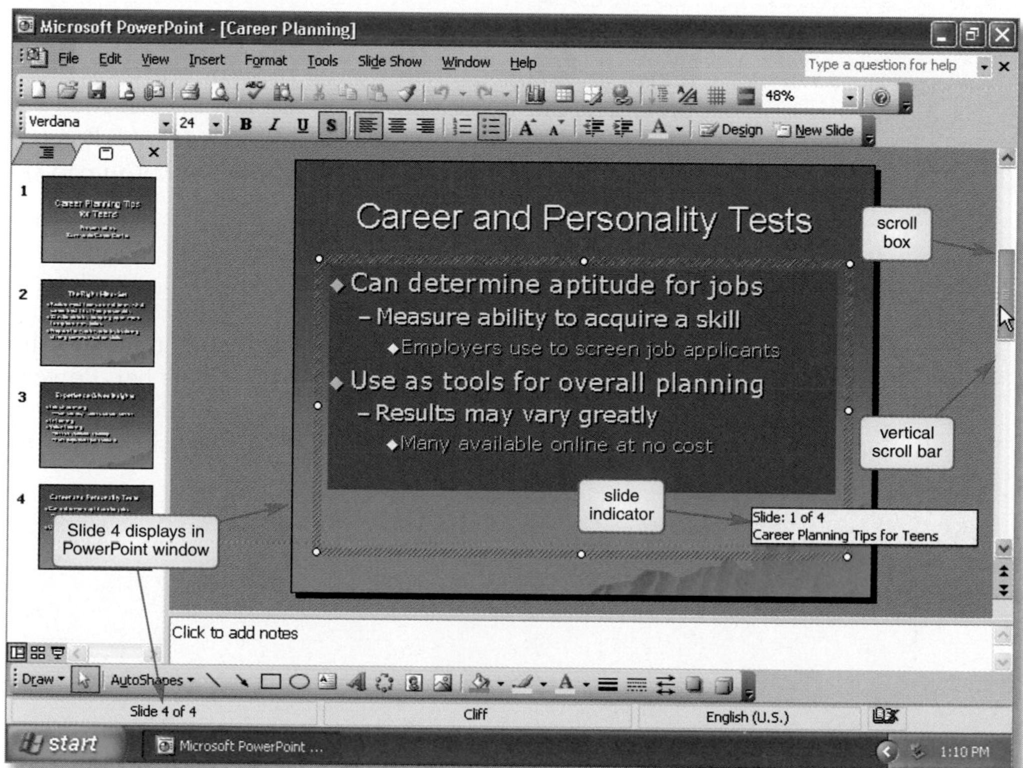

FIGURE 1-51

3

• **Release the mouse button.**

Slide 1, titled Career Planning Tips for Teens, appears in the PowerPoint window (Figure 1-52). The Slide 1 thumbnail has a gray border in the Slides tab, indicating it is selected.

FIGURE 1-52

Viewing the Presentation in Slide Show View

The Slide Show button, located in the lower-left corner of the PowerPoint window above the status bar, allows you to show a presentation using a computer. The computer acts like a slide projector, displaying each slide on a full screen. The full-screen slide hides the toolbars, menus, and other PowerPoint window elements. When making a presentation, you use **slide show view**. You can start slide show view from normal view or slide sorter view.

Starting Slide Show View

Slide show view begins when you click the Slide Show button in the lower-left of the PowerPoint window above the status bar. PowerPoint then shows the current slide on the full screen without any of the PowerPoint window objects, such as the menu bar or toolbars. The following steps show how to start slide show view.

To Start Slide Show View

1

- **Point to the Slide Show button in the lower-left corner of the PowerPoint window above the status bar (Figure 1-53).**

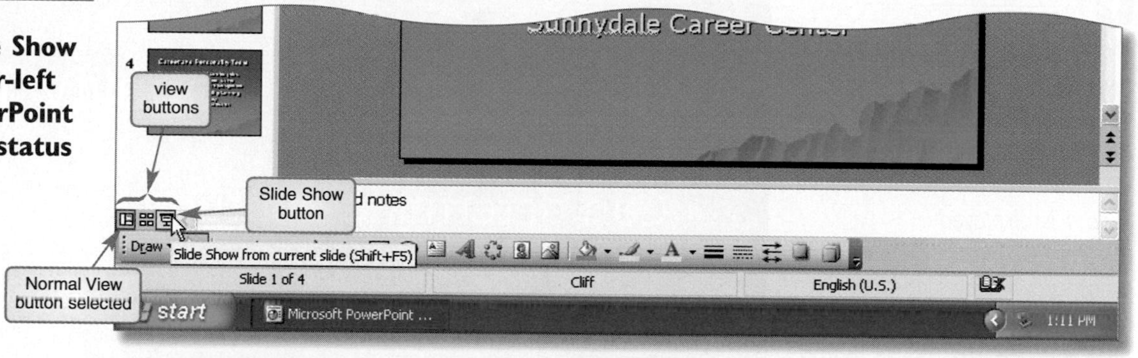

view buttons

Slide Show button

Normal View button selected

Slide Show from current slide (Shift+F5)

FIGURE 1-53

2

- **Click the Slide Show button.**

A starting slide show message may display momentarily, and then the title slide fills the screen (Figure 1-54). The PowerPoint window is hidden.

title slide in slide show view

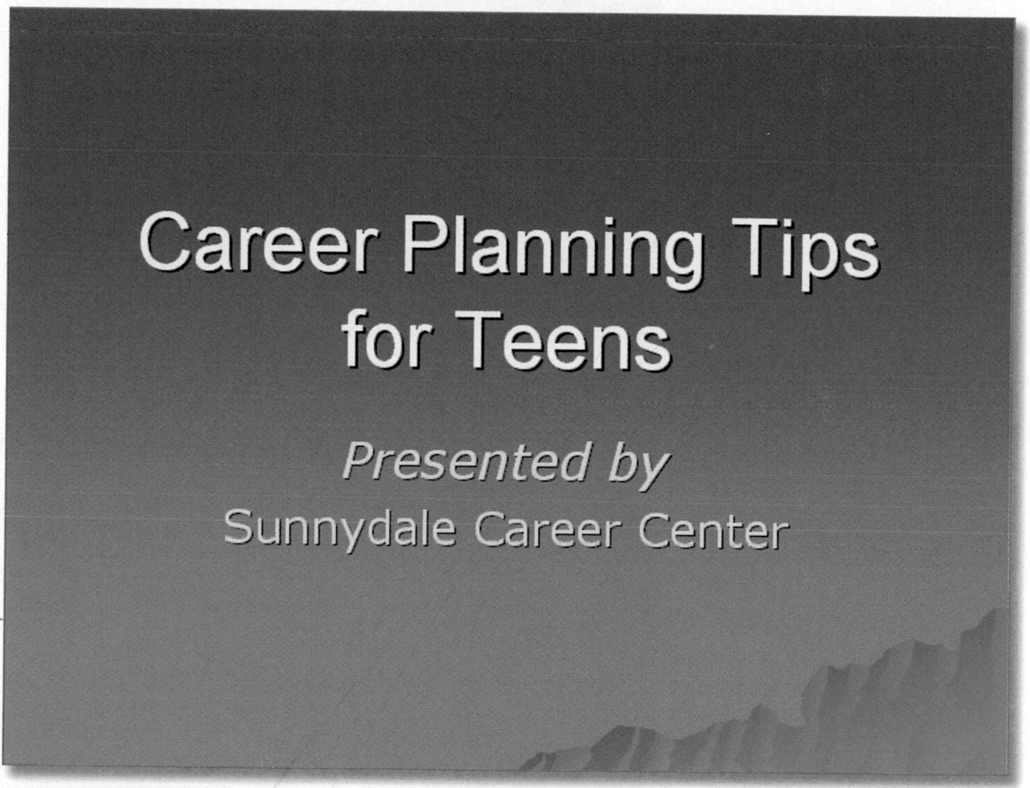

FIGURE 1-54

Advancing through a Slide Show Manually

After you begin slide show view, you can move forward or backward through the slides. PowerPoint allows you to advance through the slides manually or automatically. The steps on the next page illustrate how to move manually through the slides.

To Move Manually through Slides in a Slide Show

1

- **Click each slide until the Career and Personality Tests slide (Slide 4) is displayed.**

Slide 4 is displayed (Figure 1-55). Each slide in the presentation shows on the screen, one slide at a time. Each time you click the mouse button, the next slide appears.

Career and Personality Tests

- Can determine aptitude for jobs
  - Measure ability to acquire a skill
    - Employers use to screen job applicants
- Use as tools for overall planning
  - Results may vary greatly
    - Many available online at no cost

Slide 4 displays in slide show view

FIGURE 1-55

2

- **Click Slide 4.**

The black slide appears (Figure 1-56). The message at the top of the slide announces the end of the slide show. If you wanted to end the presentation at this point and return to normal view, you would click the black slide.

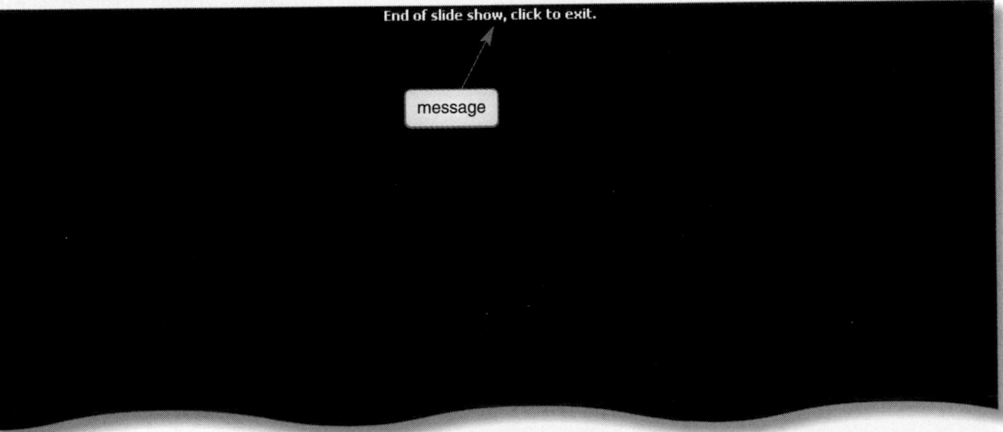
End of slide show, click to exit.
message

FIGURE 1-56

Using the Pop-Up Menu to Go to a Specific Slide

Slide show view has a shortcut menu, called a pop-up menu, that appears when you right-click a slide in slide show view. This menu contains commands to assist you during a slide show. For example, clicking the Next command moves to the next slide. Clicking the Previous command moves to the previous slide. Pointing to the Go to Slide command and then clicking the desired slide allows you to move to any slide in the presentation. The Go to Slide submenu contains a list of the slides in the presentation. You can go to the requested slide by clicking the name of that slide. The following steps illustrate how to go to the title slide (Slide 1) in the Career Planning presentation.

To Display the Pop-Up Menu and Go to a Specific Slide

1

- **With the black slide displaying in slide show view, right-click the slide.**
- **Point to Go to Slide on the pop-up menu, and then point to 1 Career Planning Tips for Teens in the Go to Slide submenu.**

The pop-up menu appears on the black slide, and the Go to Slide submenu shows a list of slides in the presentation (Figure 1-57). Your screen may look different because the pop-up menu appears near the location of the mouse pointer at the time you right-click.

2

- **Click 1 Career Planning Tips for Teens.**

The title slide, Career Planning Tips for Teens (shown in Figure 1-54 on page PPT 47), is displayed.

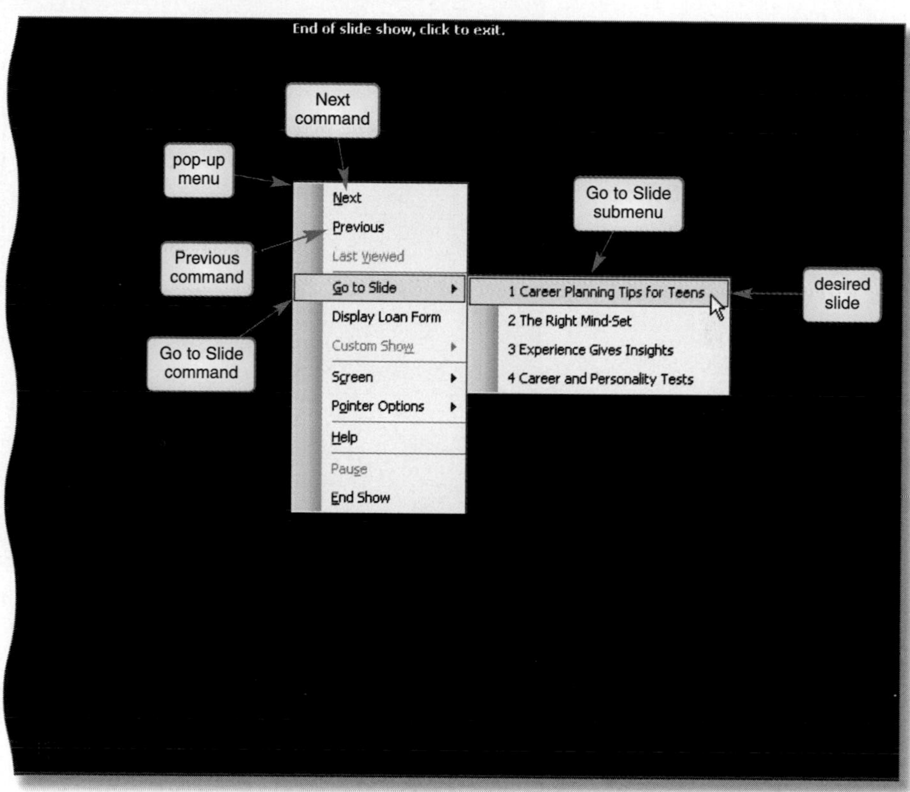

FIGURE 1-57

Additional pop-up menu commands allow you to change the mouse pointer to a ballpoint or felt tip pen or highlighter that draws in various colors, make the screen black or white, create speaker notes, and end the slide show. Pop-up menu commands are discussed as they are used.

Using the Pop-Up Menu to End a Slide Show

The End Show command on the pop-up menu ends slide show view and returns to the same view as when you clicked the Slide Show button. The steps on the next page show how to end slide show view and return to normal view.

To Use the Pop-Up Menu to End a Slide Show

1

• **Right-click the title slide and then point to End Show on the pop-up menu.**

The pop-up menu appears on Slide 1 (Figure 1-58).

2

• **Click End Show.**

• **If the Microsoft Office PowerPoint dialog box appears, click the Yes button.**

PowerPoint ends slide show view and returns to normal view (shown in Figure 1-59 below). Slide 1 is displayed because it is the last slide displayed in slide show view.

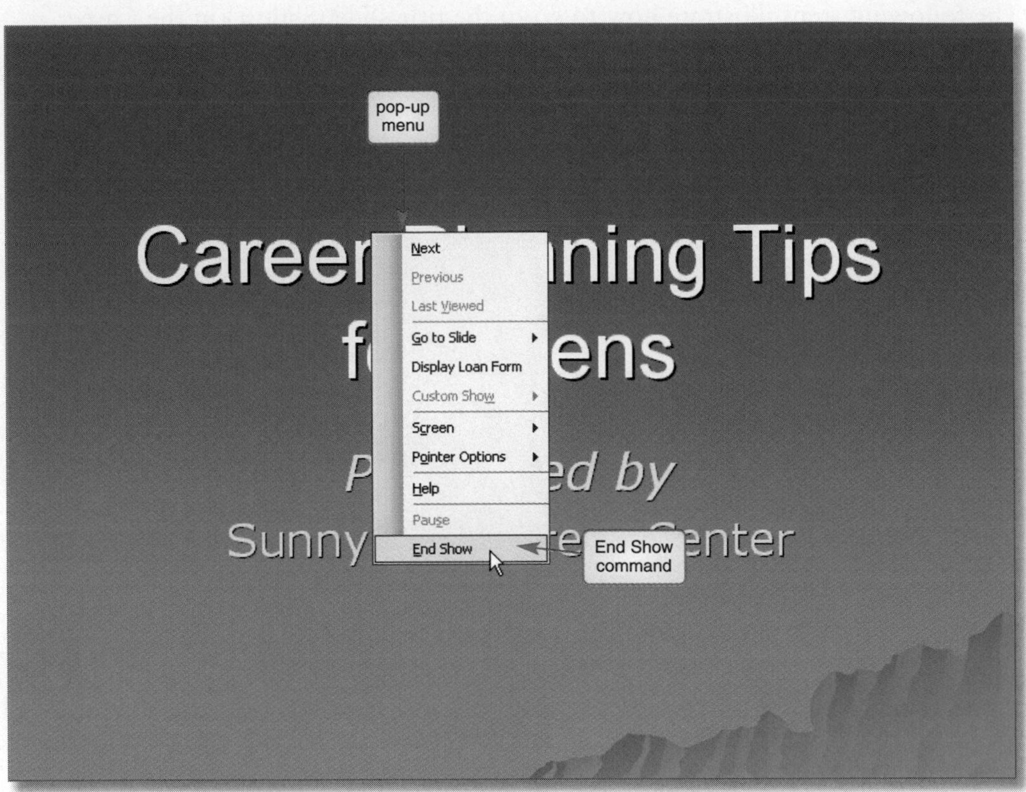

FIGURE 1-58

Quitting PowerPoint

The Career Planning presentation now is complete. When you quit PowerPoint, you are prompted to save any changes made to the presentation since the last save. The program then closes all PowerPoint windows, quits, and returns control to the desktop. The following steps quit PowerPoint.

To Quit PowerPoint

1

• **Point to the Close button on the PowerPoint title bar (Figure 1-59).**

FIGURE 1-59

2

- **Click the Close button.**

PowerPoint closes and the Windows desktop is displayed (Figure 1-60). If you made changes to the presentation since your last save, a Microsoft Office PowerPoint dialog box appears asking if you want to save changes. Clicking the Yes button saves the changes to the presentation before quitting PowerPoint. Clicking the No button quits PowerPoint without saving the changes. Clicking the Cancel button cancels the exit and returns control to the presentation.

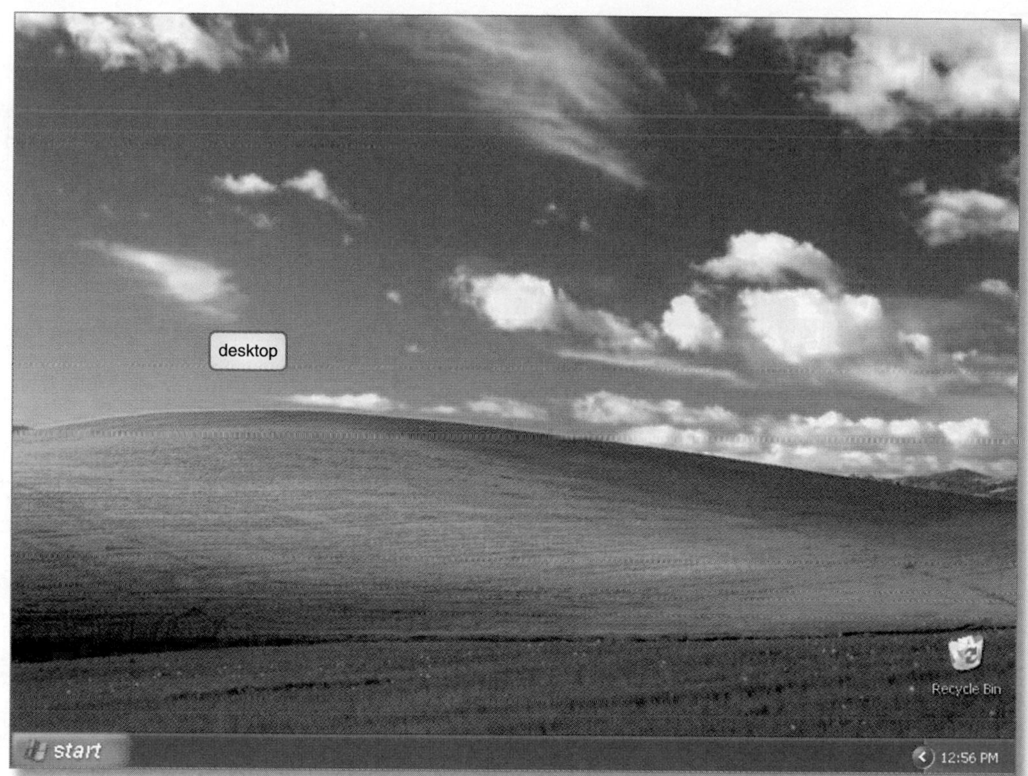

FIGURE 1-60

Starting PowerPoint and Opening a Presentation

Once you have created and saved a presentation, you may need to retrieve it from the USB flash drive to make changes. For example, you may want to replace the design template or modify some text. The steps on the next page assume PowerPoint is not running.

To Start PowerPoint and Open an Existing Presentation

1

- **With your USB flash drive connected to the computer's USB port, click the Start button on the taskbar, point to All Programs, point to Microsoft Office, and then click Microsoft Office PowerPoint 2003 on the Microsoft Office submenu.**
- **When the Getting Started task pane opens, point to the Open link in the Open area.**

PowerPoint starts. The Getting Started task pane opens (Figure 1-61).

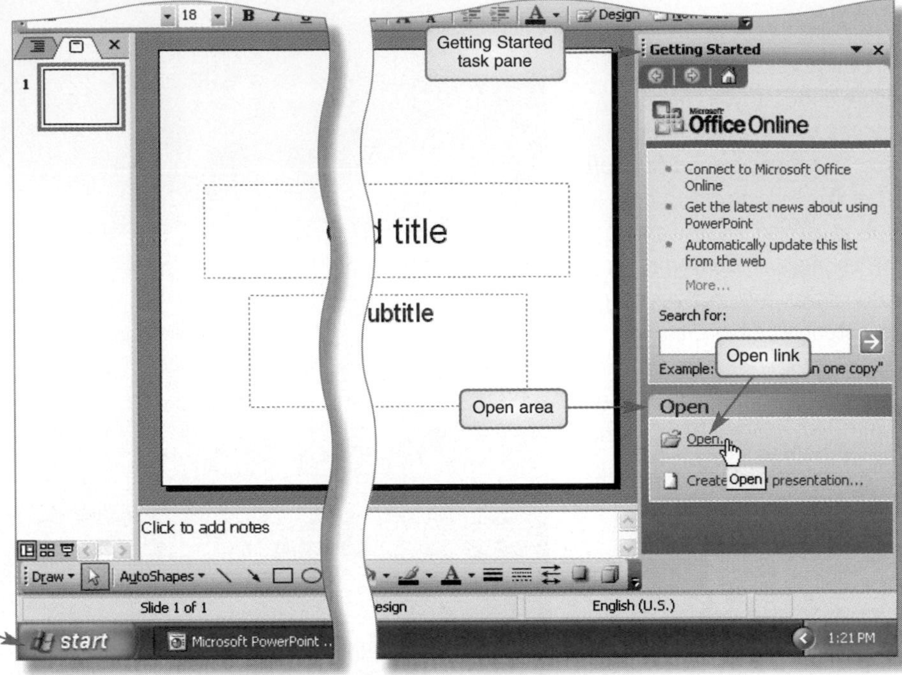

FIGURE 1-61

2

- **Click the Open link. Click the Look in box arrow, click UDISK (E:), and then double-click Career Planning.**

PowerPoint opens the presentation Career Planning and shows the first slide in the PowerPoint window (Figure 1-62). The presentation is displayed in normal view because PowerPoint opens a presentation in the same view in which it was saved. The Getting Started task pane disappears.

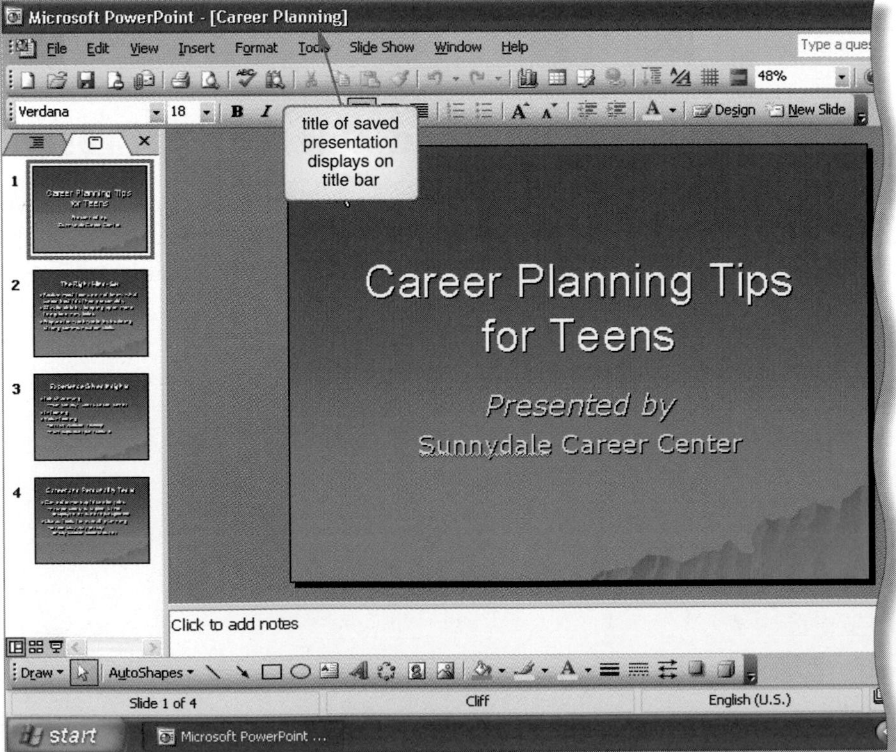

FIGURE 1-62

When you start PowerPoint and open the Career Planning file, the application name and file name are displayed on a recessed button on the Windows taskbar. When more than one application is open, you can switch between applications by clicking the appropriate application button. If you want to open a presentation other than a recent one, click the Open button on the Standard toolbar or in the Getting Started task pane. Either button lets you navigate to a slide show stored on a disk.

Checking a Presentation for Spelling and Consistency

After you create a presentation, you should check it visually for spelling errors and style consistency. In addition, you can use PowerPoint's Spelling and Style tools to identify possible misspellings and inconsistencies.

Checking a Presentation for Spelling Errors

PowerPoint checks the entire presentation for spelling mistakes using a standard dictionary contained in the Microsoft Office group. This dictionary is shared with the other Microsoft Office applications such as Word and Excel. A **custom dictionary** is available if you want to add special words such as proper names, cities, and acronyms. When checking a presentation for spelling errors, PowerPoint opens the standard dictionary and the custom dictionary file, if one exists. When a word appears in the Spelling dialog box, you perform one of the actions listed in Table 1-4.

Q & A

Q: Can I rely on the spelling checker?

A: While PowerPoint's spelling checker is a valuable tool, it is not infallible. You should proofread your presentation carefully by pointing to each word and saying it aloud as you point to it. Be mindful of commonly misused words such as its and it's, through and though, and to and too.

Table 1-4 Summary of Spelling Checker Actions

ACTION	DESCRIPTION
Ignore the word	Click the Ignore button when the word is spelled correctly but not found in the dictionaries. PowerPoint continues checking the rest of the presentation.
Ignore all occurrences of the word	Click the Ignore All button when the word is spelled correctly but not found in the dictionaries. PowerPoint ignores all occurrences of the word and continues checking the rest of the presentation.
Select a different spelling	Click the proper spelling of the word from the list in the Suggestions box. Click the Change button. PowerPoint corrects the word and continues checking the rest of the presentation.
Change all occurrences of the misspelling to a different spelling	Click the proper spelling of the word from the list in the Suggestions box. Click the Change All button. PowerPoint changes all occurrences of the misspelled word and continues checking the rest of the presentation.
Add a word to the custom dictionary	Click the Add button. PowerPoint opens the custom dictionary, adds the word, and continues checking the rest of the presentation.
View alternative spellings	Click the Suggest button. PowerPoint lists suggested spellings. Click the correct word from the Suggestions box or type the proper spelling. Then click the Change button. PowerPoint continues checking the rest of the presentation.
Add spelling error to AutoCorrect list	Click the AutoCorrect button. PowerPoint adds the spelling error and its correction to the AutoCorrect list. Any future misspelling of the word is corrected automatically as you type.
Close	Click the Close button to close the spelling checker and return to the PowerPoint window.

The standard dictionary contains commonly used English words. It does not, however, contain proper names, abbreviations, technical terms, poetic contractions, or antiquated terms. PowerPoint treats words not found in the dictionaries as misspellings.

Starting the Spelling Checker

The following steps illustrate how to start the spelling checker and check the entire presentation.

To Start the Spelling Checker

1

- **Point to the Spelling button on the Standard toolbar (Figure 1-63).**

FIGURE 1-63

2

- **Click the Spelling button.**
- **When the Spelling dialog box appears, point to the Ignore button.**

PowerPoint starts the spelling checker and displays the Spelling dialog box (Figure 1-64). The word, Sunnydale, appears in the Not in Dictionary box. Depending on the custom dictionary, Sunnydale may not be recognized as a misspelled word.

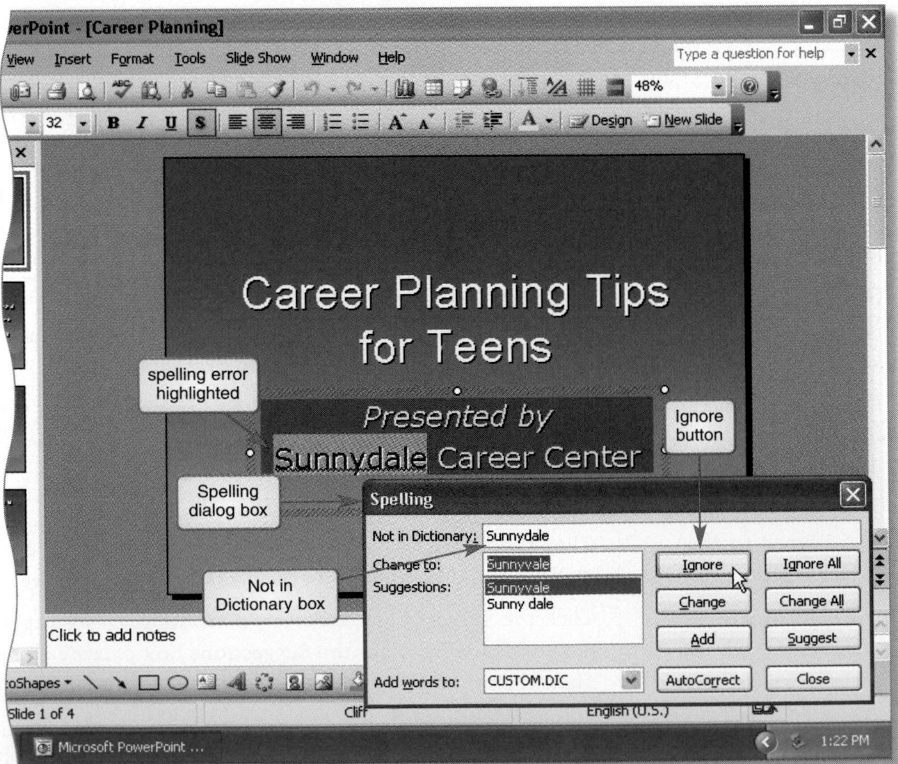

FIGURE 1-64

3

- **Click the Ignore button.**
- **When the Microsoft Office PowerPoint dialog box appears, point to the OK button.**

PowerPoint ignores the word, Sunnydale, and continues searching for additional misspelled words. PowerPoint may stop on additional words depending on your typing accuracy. When PowerPoint has checked all slides for misspellings, the Microsoft Office PowerPoint dialog box informs you that the spelling check is complete (Figure 1-65).

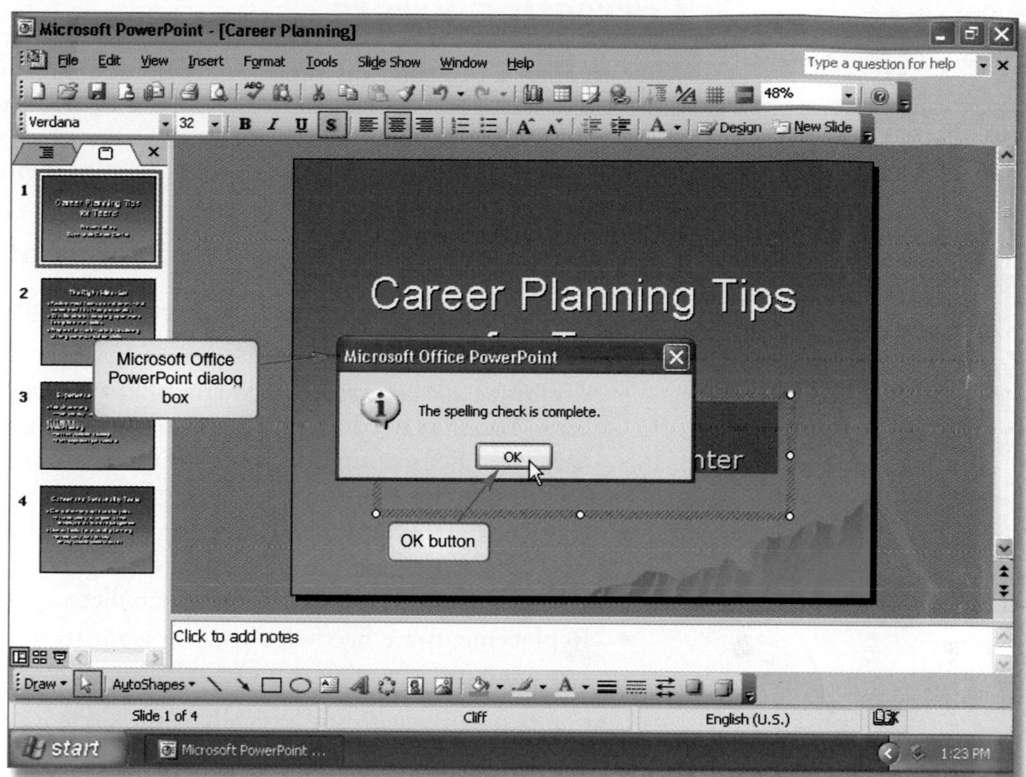

FIGURE 1-65

4

- **Click the OK button.**
- **Click the slide to remove the highlight from the word, Sunnydale.**

PowerPoint closes the spelling checker and returns to the current slide, Slide 1 (Figure 1-66), or to the slide where a possible misspelled word appeared.

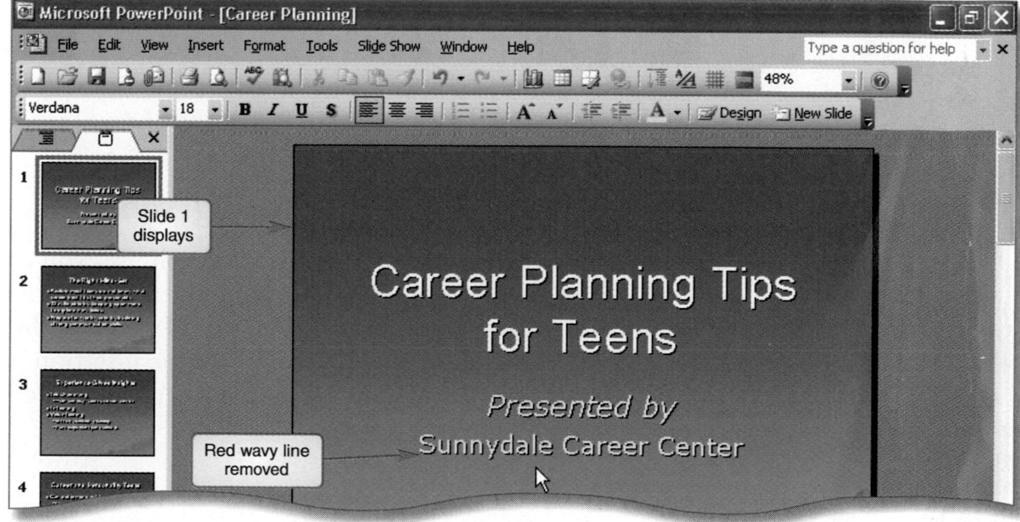

FIGURE 1-66

The red wavy line below the word, Sunnydale, is gone because you instructed PowerPoint to ignore that word, which does not appear in the standard dictionary. You also could have added that word to the dictionary so it would not be flagged as a possible misspelled word in subsequent presentations you create using that word.

Correcting Errors

After creating a presentation and running the spelling checker, you may find that you must make changes. Changes may be required because a slide contains an error, the scope of the presentation shifts, or the style is inconsistent. This section explains the types of errors that commonly occur when creating a presentation.

Types of Corrections Made to Presentations

Q & A

Q: Is there more than one way to invoke a command in PowerPoint?

A: Yes. For more information, see the Quick Reference Summary at the back of this book, or visit the Office 2003 Quick Reference Web page (scsite.com/off2003sch/qr).

You generally make three types of corrections to text in a presentation: additions, deletions, and replacements.

- Additions are necessary when you omit text from a slide and need to add it later. You may need to insert text in the form of a sentence, word, or single character. For example, you may want to add the presenter's middle name on the title slide.
- Deletions are required when text on a slide is incorrect or no longer is relevant to the presentation. For example, a slide may look cluttered. Therefore, you may want to remove one of the bulleted paragraphs to add more space.
- Replacements are needed when you want to revise the text in a presentation. For example, you may want to substitute the word, their, for the word, there.

Editing text in PowerPoint basically is the same as editing text in a word processing program. The following sections illustrate the most common changes made to text in a presentation.

Deleting Text

You can delete text using one of three methods. One is to use the BACKSPACE key to remove text just typed. The second is to position the insertion point to the left of the text you wish to delete and then press the DELETE key. The third method is to drag through the text you wish to delete and then press the DELETE key. (Use the third method when deleting large sections of text.)

Replacing Text in an Existing Slide

When you need to correct a word or phrase, you can replace the text by selecting the text to be replaced and then typing the new text. As soon as you press any key on the keyboard, the highlighted text is deleted and the new text is displayed.

PowerPoint inserts text to the left of the insertion point. The text to the right of the insertion point moves to the right (and shifts downward if necessary) to accommodate the added text.

Q & A

Q: What is the Microsoft Office Specialist Certification program?

A: The Microsoft Office Specialist Certification program provides an opportunity for you to obtain a valuable industry credential — proof that you have the PowerPoint skills required by employers. For more information, see Appendix E, or visit the Office 2003 Certification Web page (scsite.com/off2003sch/cert).

Displaying a Presentation in Black and White

Printing handouts of a presentation allows you to use them to make overhead transparencies. The Color/Grayscale button on the Standard toolbar shows the presentation in black and white before you print. Table 1-5 identifies how PowerPoint objects display in black and white.

Table 1-5 Appearance in Black and White View

OBJECT	APPEARANCE IN BLACK AND WHITE VIEW
Bitmaps	Grayscale
Embossing	Hidden
Fills	Grayscale
Frame	Black
Lines	Black
Object shadows	Grayscale
Pattern fills	Grayscale
Slide backgrounds	White
Text	Black
Text shadows	Hidden

The following steps show how to display the presentation in black and white.

To Display a Presentation in Black and White

1

• **Click the Color/Grayscale button on the Standard toolbar and then point to Pure Black and White in the list.**

The Color/Grayscale list is displayed (Figure 1-67). Pure Black and White alters the slides' appearance so that only black lines display on a white background. Grayscale shows varying degrees of gray.

FIGURE 1-67

2

• **Click Pure Black and White.**

Slide 1 is displayed in black and white in the slide pane (Figure 1-68). The four thumbnail slides are displayed in color in the Slides tab. The Grayscale View toolbar appears. The Color/Grayscale button on the Standard toolbar changes from color bars to black and white.

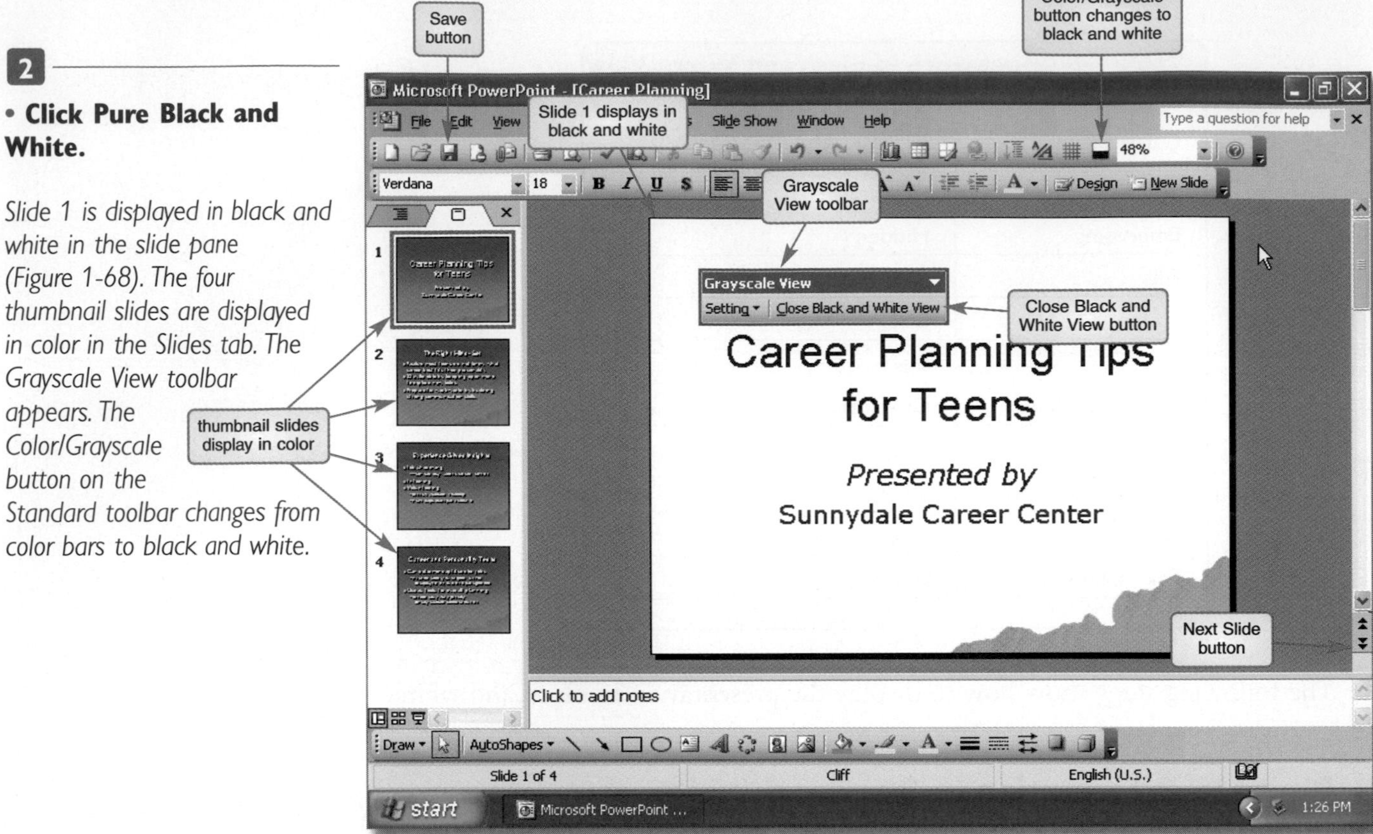

FIGURE 1-68

3

• **Click the Next Slide button three times to view all slides in the presentation in black and white.**

• **Point to the Close Black and White View button on the Grayscale View toolbar (Figure 1-69).**

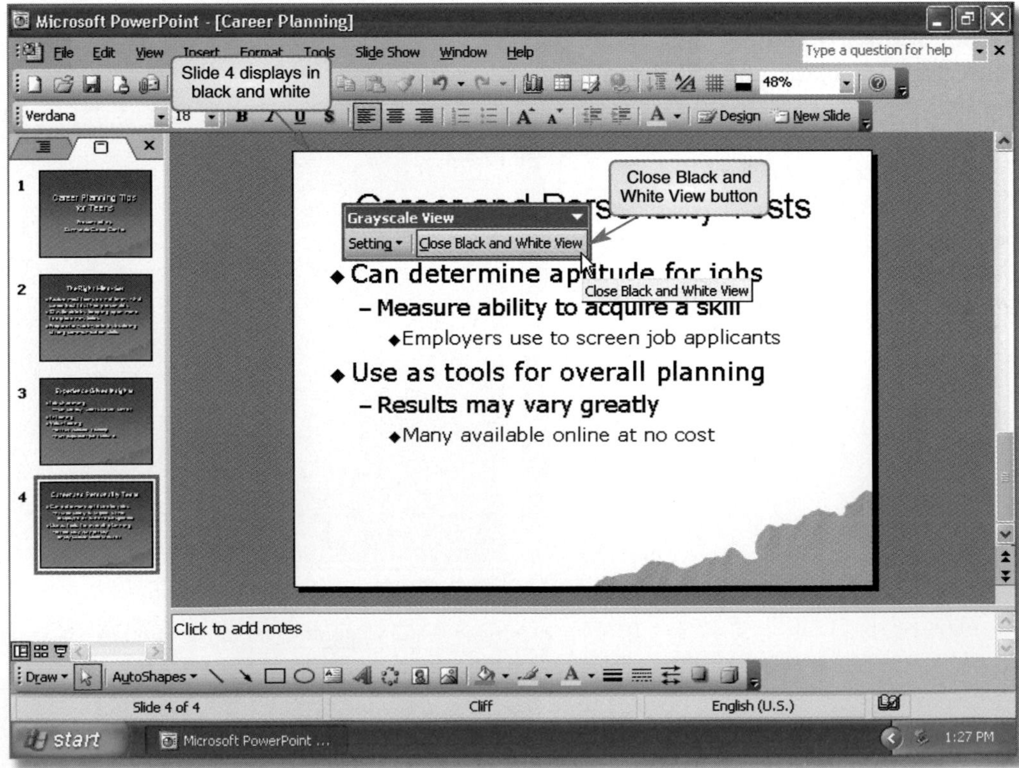

FIGURE 1-69

4

• **Click the Close Black and White View button.**

Slide 4 is displayed with the default Cliff color scheme (Figure 1-70).

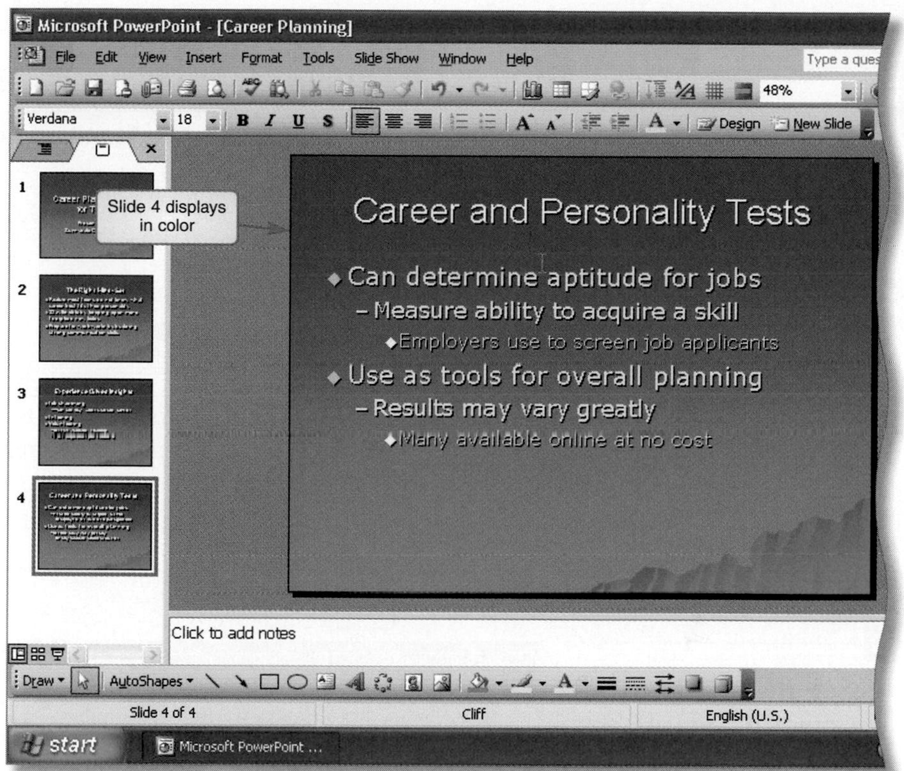

FIGURE 1-70

After you view the text objects in the presentation in black and white, you can make any changes that will enhance printouts produced from a black and white printer or photocopier.

Printing a Presentation

After you create a presentation, you often want to print it. A printed version of the presentation is called a **hard copy**, or **printout**. The first printing of the presentation is called a **rough draft**. The rough draft allows you to proofread the presentation to check for errors and readability. After correcting errors, you print the final copy of the presentation.

Saving Before Printing

Before printing a presentation, you should save your work in the event you experience difficulties with the printer. You occasionally may encounter system problems that can be resolved only by restarting the computer. In such an instance, you will need to reopen the presentation. As a precaution, always save the presentation before you print. The steps on the next page save the presentation before printing.

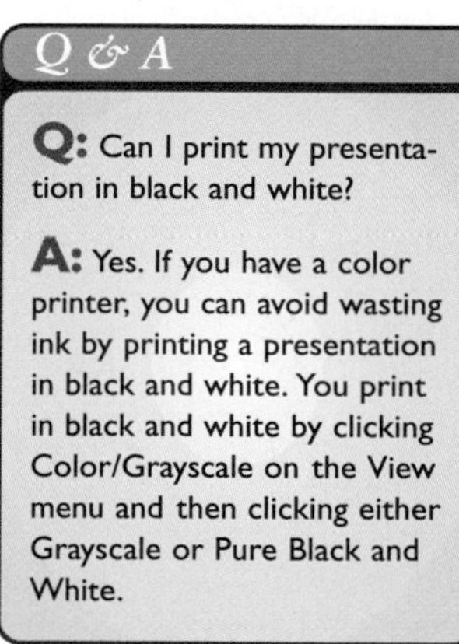

Q & A

Q: Can I print my presentation in black and white?

A: Yes. If you have a color printer, you can avoid wasting ink by printing a presentation in black and white. You print in black and white by clicking Color/Grayscale on the View menu and then clicking either Grayscale or Pure Black and White.

To Save a Presentation

1. **Verify that the USB flash drive is connected to the computer's USB port.**
2. **Click the Save button on the Standard toolbar.**

All changes made after your last save now are saved on the USB flash drive.

Printing the Presentation

After saving the presentation, you are ready to print. Clicking the Print button on the Standard toolbar causes PowerPoint to print all slides in the presentation. The following steps illustrate how to print the presentation slides.

To Print a Presentation

1.
- **Ready the printer according to the printer instructions.**
- **Click the Print button on the Standard toolbar.**

The printer icon in the tray status area on the Windows taskbar indicates a print job is processing (Figure 1-71). This icon may not be displayed on your system, or it may be displayed on your status bar. After several moments, the slide show begins printing on the printer. When the presentation is finished printing, the printer icon in the tray status area on the Windows taskbar no longer is displayed.

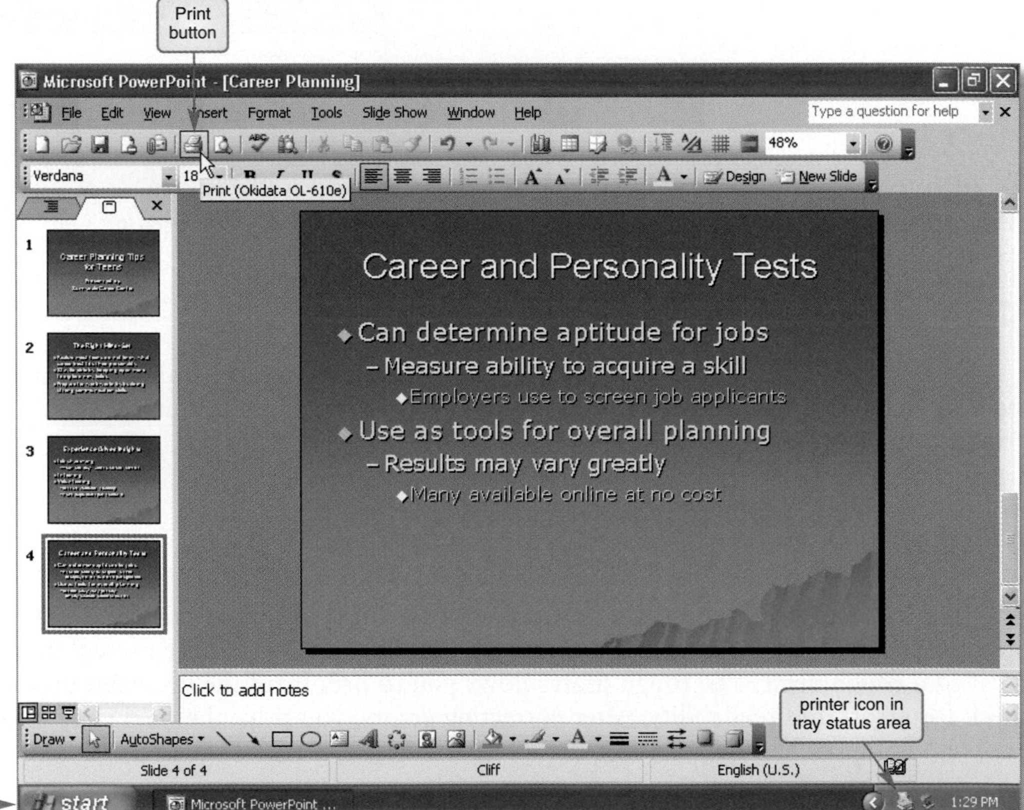

FIGURE 1-71

2

- **When the printer stops, retrieve the printouts of the slides.**

The presentation, Career Planning, prints on four pages (Figures 1-72a through 1-72d).

(a) Slide 1

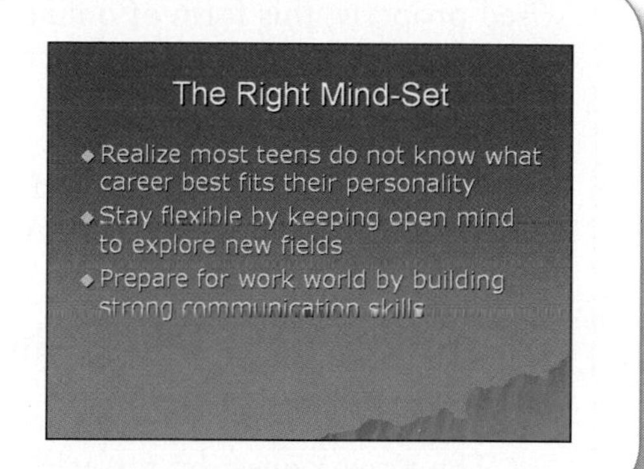

(b) Slide 2

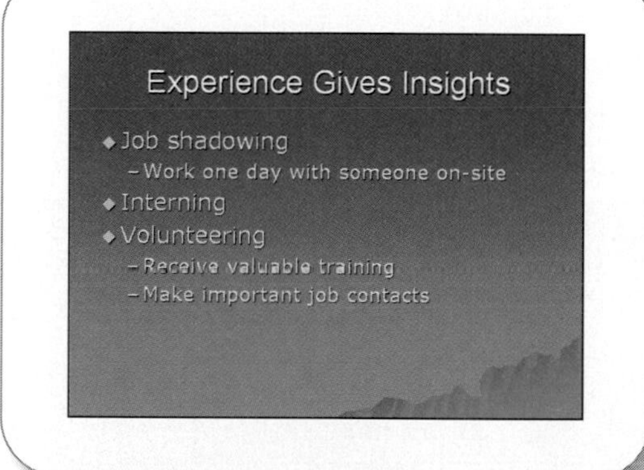

(c) Slide 3

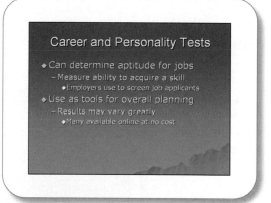

(d) Slide 4

FIGURE 1-72

You can click the printer icon next to the clock in the tray status area on the Windows taskbar to obtain information about the presentations printing on your printer and to delete files in the print queue that are waiting to be printed.

Making a Transparency

With the handouts printed, you now can make overhead transparencies using one of several devices. One device is a printer attached to your computer, such as an inkjet printer or a laser printer. Transparencies produced on a printer may be in black and white or color, depending on the printer. Another device is a photocopier. Because each of these devices requires a special transparency film, check the user's manual for the film requirement of your specific device, or ask your instructor.

> ***Skill Builder 1-3***
>
> To practice the following tasks, visit scsite.com/off2003sch/skill, locate PowerPoint Project 1, and then click Skill Builder 1-3.
> - ❑ Navigate through a slide show
> - ❑ Open an existing presentation
> - ❑ Check spelling
> - ❑ Correct errors
> - ❑ View a presentation in black and white
> - ❑ Print a presentation

> *Q & A*
>
> **Q:** Need help with PowerPoint?
>
> **A:** Help with PowerPoint is no further away than the Type a question for help box on the menu bar in the upper-right corner of the window. Click the box that contains the text, Type a question for help (Figure 1-73), type `help`, and then press the ENTER key. PowerPoint responds with a list of topics you can click to learn about obtaining help on any PowerPoint-related topic. To find out what is new in PowerPoint 2003, type `what is new in PowerPoint` in the Type a question for help box.

PowerPoint Help System

You can get answers to PowerPoint questions at any time by using the PowerPoint Help system. You can activate the PowerPoint Help system by using the Type a question for help box on the menu bar, by using the Microsoft PowerPoint Help button on the Standard toolbar, or by clicking Help on the menu bar (Figure 1-73). Used properly, this form of online assistance can increase your productivity and reduce your frustrations by minimizing the time you spend learning how to use PowerPoint.

The following section shows how to get answers to your questions using the Type a question for help box. Additional information on using the PowerPoint Help system is available in Appendix A and Table 1-6 on page PPT 65.

Obtaining Help Using the Type a Question for Help Box on the Menu Bar

The Type a question for help box on the right side of the menu bar lets you type free-form questions such as, *how do I save* or *how do I create a Web page*, or you can type terms such as, *copy*, *save*, or *format*. PowerPoint responds by displaying a list of topics related to what you typed. The following steps show how to use the Type a question for help box to obtain information on formatting bullets.

To Obtain Help Using the Type a Question for Help Box

1

- **Type** `bullet` **in the Type a question for help box on the right side of the menu bar (Figure 1-73).**

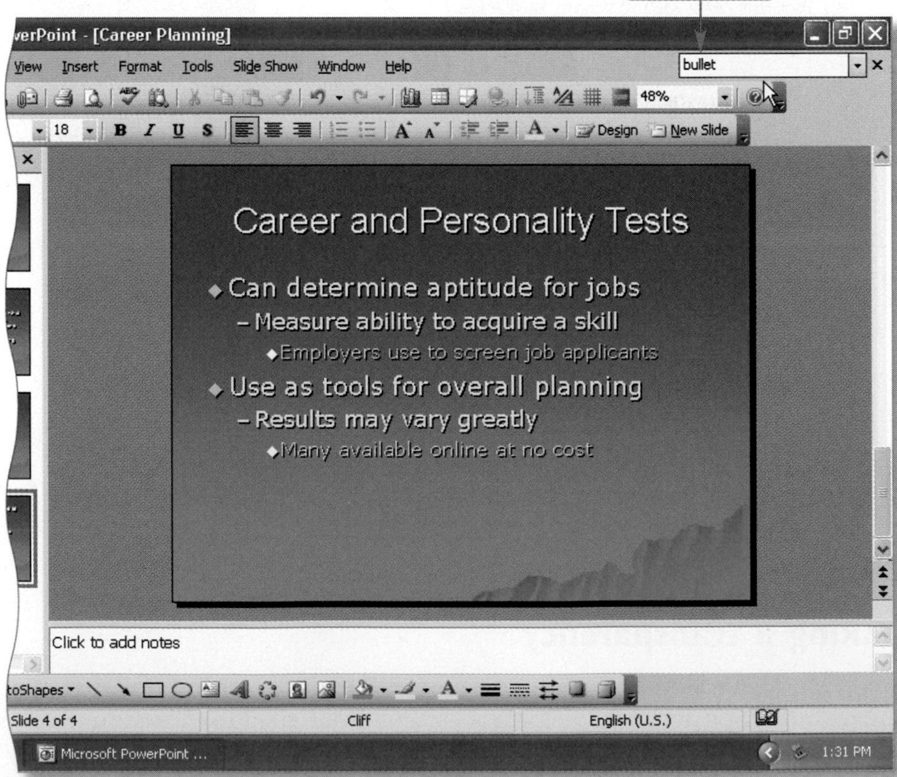

FIGURE 1-73

2

- **Press the ENTER key.**
- **When PowerPoint displays the Search Results task pane, scroll down and then point to the topic, Change the bullet style in a list.**

PowerPoint displays the Search Results task pane with a list of topics relating to the term, bullet. PowerPoint found 30 results from Microsoft Office Online. The mouse pointer changes to a hand, which indicates it is pointing to a link (Figure 1-74).

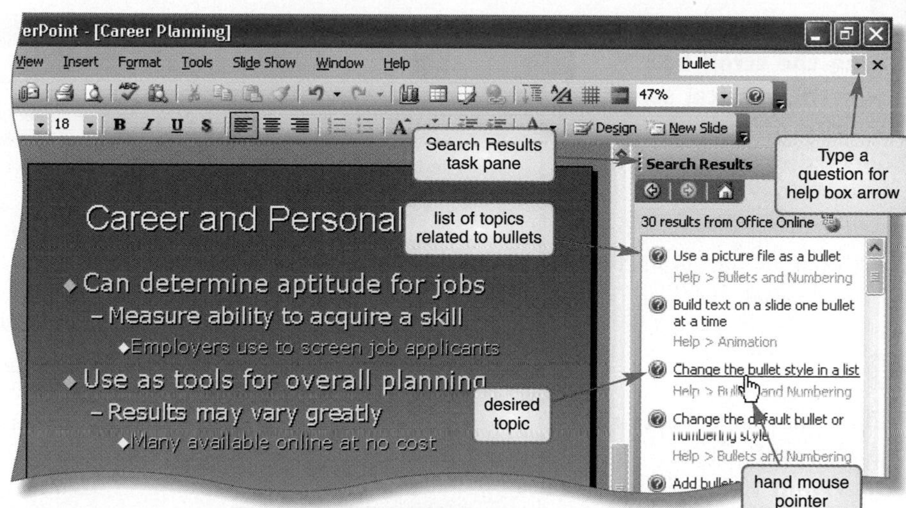

FIGURE 1-74

3

- **Click Change the bullet style in a list.**
- **When the Microsoft Office PowerPoint Help window is displayed, double-click its title bar to maximize it.**

A Microsoft Office PowerPoint Help window provides Help information about changing the bullet style in a list (Figure 1-75).

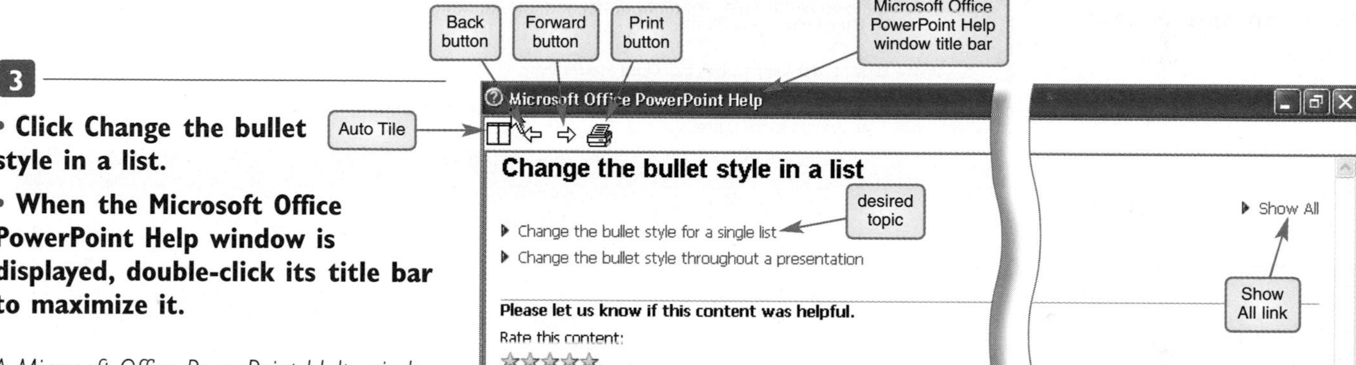

FIGURE 1-75

4

- **Click the Show All link.**

Directions for changing a bullet style for a single list are displayed. Options include change the bullet character, change the bullet size, and change the bullet color (Figure 1-76).

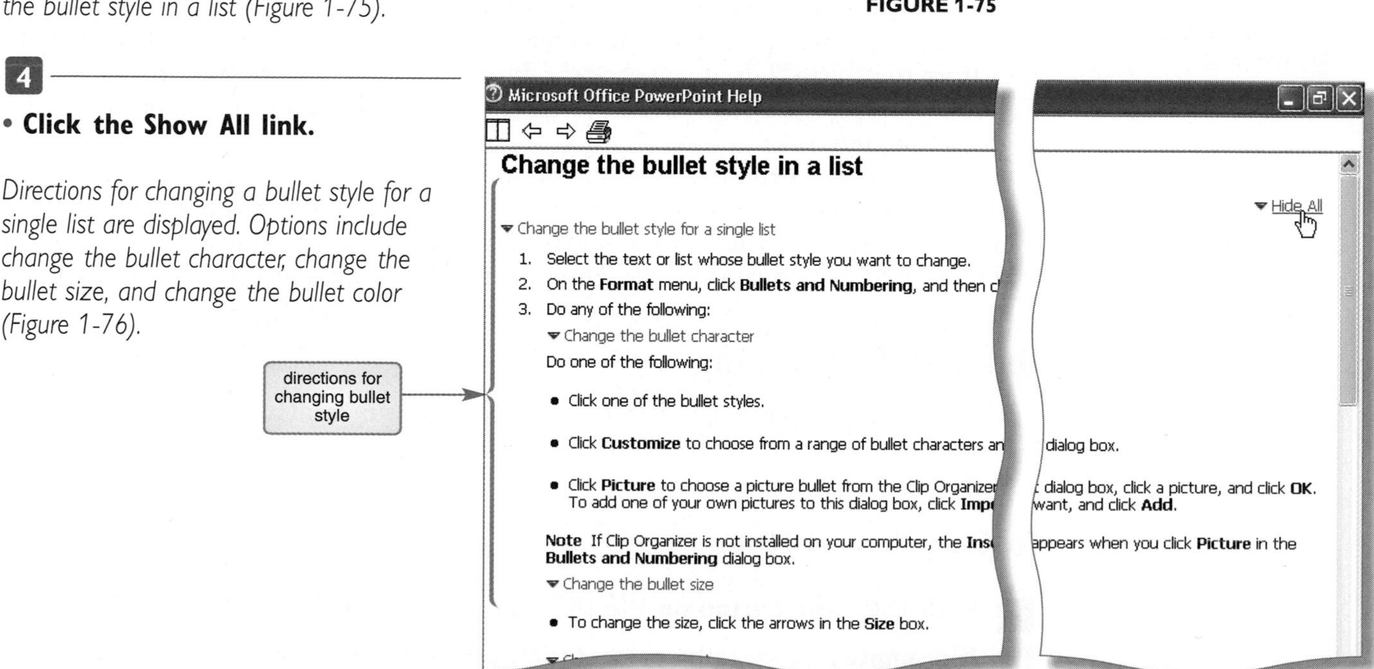

FIGURE 1-76

• Drag the scroll box down the vertical scroll bar until Change the bullet color is displayed.

PowerPoint displays specific details of changing the color of the bullets on a slide (Figure 1-77).

• Click the Close button on the Microsoft Office PowerPoint Help window title bar.

• Click the Close button on the Search Results task pane.

The PowerPoint Help window closes, and the PowerPoint presentation is displayed.

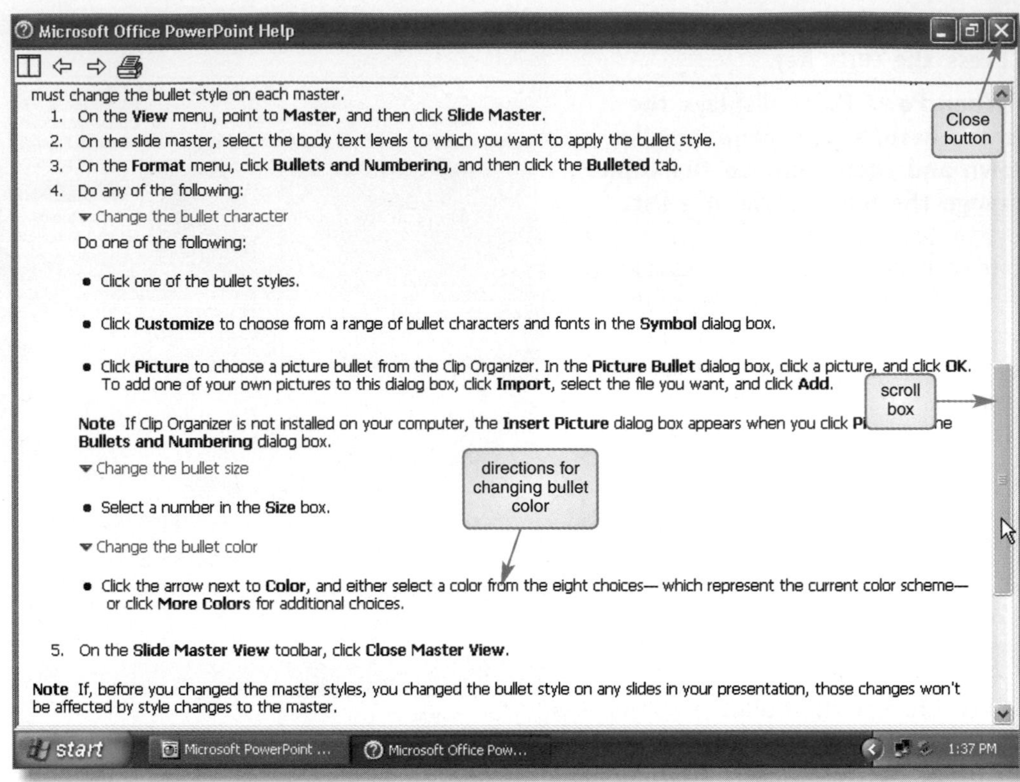

FIGURE 1-77

> ***Skill Builder 1-4***
>
> To practice the following tasks, visit scsite.com/off2003sch/skill, locate PowerPoint Project 1, and then click PowerPoint Skill Builder 1-4.
>
> ❑ Use the PowerPoint Help system

Use the buttons in the upper-left corner of the Microsoft Office PowerPoint Help window (Figure 1-75 on the previous page) to navigate through the Help system, change the display, and print the contents of the window.

As you enter questions and terms in the Type a question for help box, PowerPoint adds them to its list. Thus, if you click the Type a question for help box arrow (Figure 1-74 on the previous page), PowerPoint will display a list of previously asked questions and terms.

Table 1-6 summarizes the major categories of Help available to you. Because of the way the PowerPoint Help system works, be certain to review the rightmost column of Table 1-6 if you have difficulties activating the desired category of Help. Additional information on using the PowerPoint Help system is available in Appendix A.

Quitting PowerPoint

Project 1 is complete. The final task is to close the presentation and quit PowerPoint. The following steps quit PowerPoint.

To Quit PowerPoint

1. **Click the Close button on the title bar.**
2. **If prompted to save the presentation before quitting PowerPoint, click the Yes button in the Microsoft Office PowerPoint dialog box.**

Table 1-6 PowerPoint Help System

TYPE	DESCRIPTION	HOW TO ACTIVATE
Microsoft Office PowerPoint Help	Displays PowerPoint Help task pane. Answers questions or searches for terms that you type in your own words.	Click the Microsoft Office PowerPoint Help button on the Standard toolbar or click Microsoft Office PowerPoint Help on the Help menu.
Office Assistant	Similar to the Type a question for help box. The Office Assistant answers questions that you type in your own words, offers tips, and provides help for a variety of PowerPoint features.	Click the Office Assistant icon. If the Office Assistant does not appear, click Show the Office Assistant on the Help menu.
Type a question for help box	Answers questions or searches for terms that you type in your own words.	Type a question or term in the Type a question for help box on the menu bar and then press the ENTER key.
Table of Contents	Groups Help topics by general categories. Use when you know only the general category of the topic in question.	Click the Microsoft Office PowerPoint Help button on the Standard toolbar or click Microsoft Office PowerPoint Help on the Help menu, and then click the Table of Contents link on the PowerPoint Help task pane.
Microsoft Office Online	Used to access technical resources and download free product enhancements on the Web.	Click Microsoft Office Online on the Help menu.
Detect and Repair	Automatically finds and fixes errors in the application.	Click Detect and Repair on the Help menu.

Project Summary

In creating the Career Planning slide show in this project, you gained a broad knowledge of PowerPoint. First, you were introduced to starting PowerPoint and creating a presentation consisting of a title slide and single- and multi-level bulleted lists. You learned about PowerPoint design templates and text attributes.

This project illustrated how to create an interesting introduction to a presentation by changing the text font style to italic and increasing font size on the title slide. Completing these tasks, you saved the presentation. Then, you created three text slides with bulleted lists, two of which contained multi-level bullets. Next, you learned how to view the presentation in slide show view. Then, you learned how to quit PowerPoint and how to open an existing presentation. You used the spelling checker to search for spelling errors. You learned how to display the presentation in black and white. You also learned how to print hard copies of the slides in order to make handouts and overhead transparencies. Finally, you learned how to use the PowerPoint Help system to answer your questions.

If you have a SAM user profile, you may have access to hands-on instruction, practice, and assessment of the skills covered in this project. Log in to your SAM account and go to your assignments page to see what your instructor has assigned.

What You Should Know

Having completed this project, you should be able to perform the tasks below. The tasks are listed in the same order they were presented in this project. For a list of the buttons, menus, toolbars, and commands introduced in this project, see the Quick Reference Summary at the back of this book and refer to the Page Number column.

1. Start PowerPoint (PPT 7)
2. Customize the PowerPoint Window (PPT 9)
3. Choose a Design Template (PPT 18)
4. Enter the Presentation Title (PPT 21)
5. Enter the Presentation Subtitle (PPT 22)
6. Change the Text Font Style to Italic (PPT 24)
7. Increase Font Size (PPT 25)
8. Save a Presentation (PPT 27)
9. Add a New Text Slide with a Bulleted List (PPT 30)
10. Enter a Slide Title (PPT 32)
11. Select a Text Placeholder (PPT 32)
12. Type a Single-Level Bulleted List (PPT 33)
13. Add a New Slide and Enter a Slide Title (PPT 35)
14. Type a Multi-Level Bulleted List (PPT 36)
15. Type the Remaining Text for Slide 3 (PPT 38)
16. Create Slide 4 (PPT 39)
17. Create a Third-Level Paragraph (PPT 40)
18. Type the Remaining Text for Slide 4 (PPT 41)
19. End a Slide Show with a Black Slide (PPT 42)
20. Save a Presentation with the Same File Name (PPT 44)
21. Use the Scroll Box on the Slide Pane to Move to Another Slide (PPT 45)
22. Start Slide Show View (PPT 47)
23. Move Manually through Slides in a Slide Show (PPT 48)
24. Display the Pop-Up Menu and Go to a Specific Slide (PPT 49)
25. Use the Pop-Up Menu to End a Slide Show (PPT 50)
26. Quit PowerPoint (PPT 50)
27. Start PowerPoint and Open an Existing Presentation (PPT 52)
28. Start the Spelling Checker (PPT 54)
29. Display a Presentation in Black and White (PPT 57)
30. Save a Presentation (PPT 60)
31. Print a Presentation (PPT 60)
32. Obtain Help Using the Type a Question for Help Box (PPT 62)
33. Quit PowerPoint (PPT 64)

Career Corner

Graphic Designer/Illustrator

Graphic designers and *graphic illustrators* are artists, but many do not create original works. Instead, they portray visually the ideas of their clients. Illustrators create pictures for books and other publications and sometimes for commercial products, such as greeting cards. They work in fields such as fashion, technology, medicine, animation, or even cartoons. Illustrators often prepare their images on a computer. Designers combine practical skills with artistic talent to convert abstract concepts into designs for products and advertisements. Many use computer-aided design (CAD) tools to create, visualize, and modify designs. Designer careers usually are specialized in particular areas, such as:

- Graphic designers — book covers, stationery, and CD covers
- Commercial and industrial designers — products and equipment
- Costume and theater designers — costumes and settings for theater and television
- Interior designers — layout, decor, and furnishings of homes and buildings
- Merchandise displayers — commercial displays
- Fashion designers — clothing, shoes, and other fashion accessories

Certificate, two-year, four-year, and masters-level educational programs are available within design areas. About 30 percent of graphic illustrators/designers choose to freelance, while others work with advertising agencies, publishing companies, design studios, or specialized departments within large companies. Salaries range from $25,000 to $80,000-plus, based on experience and educational background. For more information, visit scsite.com/off2003sch/careers and then click Graphic Designer/Illustrator.

Learn It Online

Instructions: To complete the Learn It Online exercises, start your browser, click the Address bar, and then enter the Web address scsite.com/off2003sch/learn. When the Office 2003 Learn It Online page is displayed, follow the instructions in the exercises below. Each exercise has instructions for printing your results, either for your own records or for submission to your instructor.

1 Project Reinforcement TF, MC, and SA

Below PowerPoint Project 1, click the Project Reinforcement link. Print the quiz by clicking Print on the File menu for each page. Answer each question.

2 Flash Cards

Below PowerPoint Project 1, click the Flash Cards link and read the instructions. Type 20 (or a number specified by your instructor) in the Number of playing cards text box, type your name in the Enter your Name text box, and then click the Flip Card button. When the flash card is displayed, read the question and then click the ANSWER box arrow to select an answer. Flip through Flash Cards. If your score is 15 (75%) correct or greater, click Print on the File menu to print your results. If your score is less than 15 (75%) correct, then redo this exercise by clicking the Replay button.

3 Practice Test

Below PowerPoint Project 1, click the Practice Test link. Answer each question, enter your first and last name at the bottom of the page, and then click the Grade Test button. When the graded practice test is displayed on your screen, click Print on the File menu to print a hard copy. Continue to take practice tests until you score 80% or better.

4 Who Wants To Be a Computer Genius?

Below PowerPoint Project 1, click the Computer Genius link. Read the instructions, enter your first and last name at the bottom of the page, and then click the PLAY button. When your score is displayed, click the PRINT RESULTS link to print a hard copy.

5 Wheel of Terms

Below PowerPoint Project 1, click the Wheel of Terms link. Read the instructions, and then enter your first and last name and your school name. Click the PLAY button. When your score is displayed, right-click the score and then click Print on the shortcut menu to print a hard copy.

6 Crossword Puzzle Challenge

Below PowerPoint Project 1, click the Crossword Puzzle Challenge link. Read the instructions, and then enter your first and last name. Click the SUBMIT button. Work the crossword puzzle. When you are finished, click the Submit button. When the crossword puzzle is redisplayed, click the Print Puzzle button to print a hard copy.

7 Tips and Tricks

Below PowerPoint Project 1, click the Tips and Tricks link. Click a topic that pertains to Project 1. Right-click the information and then click Print on the shortcut menu. Construct a brief example of what the information relates to in PowerPoint to confirm you understand how to use the tip or trick.

8 Newsgroups

Below PowerPoint Project 1, click the Newsgroups link. Click a topic that pertains to Project 1. Print three comments.

9 Expanding Your Horizons

Below PowerPoint Project 1, click the Expanding Your Horizons link. Click a topic that pertains to Project 1. Print the information. Construct a brief example of what the information relates to in PowerPoint to confirm you understand the contents of the article.

10 Search Sleuth

Below PowerPoint Project 1, click the Search Sleuth link. To search for a term that pertains to this project, select a term below the Project 1 title and then use the Google search engine at google.com (or any major search engine) to display and print two Web pages that present information on the term.

11 PowerPoint Online Training

Below PowerPoint Project 1, click the PowerPoint Online Training link. When your browser displays the Microsoft Office Online Web page, click the PowerPoint link. Click one of the PowerPoint courses that covers one or more of the objectives listed at the beginning of the project on page PPT 4. Print the first page of the course before stepping through it.

12 Office Marketplace

Below PowerPoint Project 1, click the Office Marketplace link. When your browser displays the Microsoft Office Online Web page, click the Office Marketplace link. Click a topic that relates to PowerPoint. Print the first page.

13 You're Hired!

Below PowerPoint Project 1, click the You're Hired! link to embark on the path to a career in computers. Directions about how to play the game will be displayed. When you are ready to play, click the begin the game button. If required, submit your score to your instructor.

1 Searching on the World Wide Web

Instructions: Start PowerPoint. Open the presentation Apply 1-1 Wright Brothers. See page xxiv at the front of this book for instructions for downloading the Data Files for Students or see your instructor for information on accessing the files required for this book. The two slides in the presentation give information on Orville and Wilbur Wright and their experimental airplane. Make the following changes to the slides so they appear as shown in Figure 1-78.

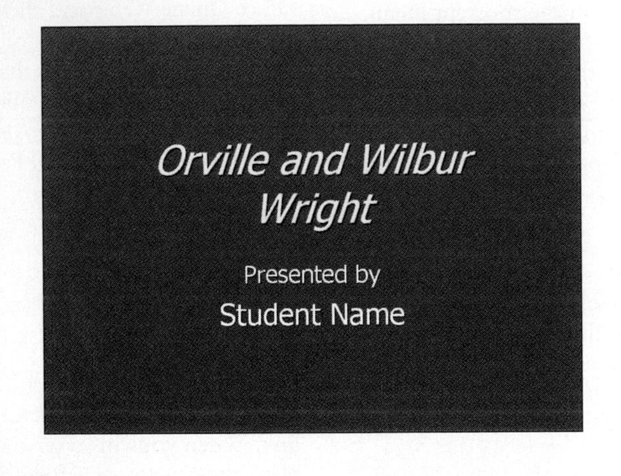

(a) Slide 1 (Title Slide)

(b) Slide 2 (Multi-Level Bulleted List)

FIGURE 1-78

Change the design template to Compass. On the title slide, use your name in place of Student Name and change the font size to 40. Italicize the title text.

On Slide 2, increase the indent of the second and fourth paragraphs, Experimented from 1899 – 1902, and Assembled in Kitty Hawk, North Carolina. Then change the last paragraph, Flew 12 seconds, 120 feet on Dec. 17, 1903, to a third-level paragraph.

Display the revised presentation in black and white, and then print the two slides.

Save the presentation using the file name, Apply 1-1 1903 Flyer. Hand in the hard copy to your instructor.

In the Lab

Note: These labs require you to create presentations based on notes. When you design these slide shows, use the 7 x 7 rule, which states that each line should have a maximum of seven words, and each slide should have a maximum of seven lines.

1 Road Testing Used Cars

Problem: Buying your first car is an exciting event. It makes good financial sense to buy a used car because a new car can lose at least 15 percent of its value the minute it is driven off the dealer's lot. Knowing how to road test a used car can save thousands of dollars and hours of aggravation. Mr. Rzepki is the auto mechanics teacher at your school. He has asked you to prepare a short PowerPoint presentation and handouts to educate students about how to test drive a used car. He hands you the outline shown in Figure 1-79 and asks you to create the presentation shown in Figures 1-80a through 1-80f.

I.) Buying a Used Car
Presented by
Joe Rzepki

II.) Used Cars Are Good Deals
- Save thousands of dollars in depreciation
- Low-mileage cars should last many years
- Services will provide vehicle history
- Dealers can give good warranties

III.) Inspect the Interior
- Driver's seat not torn, stained
- Driver's side door closes smoothly
- Rubber on pedals not worn

IV.) Start the Engine
- Should fire almost immediately
- Dashboard lights should go out soon
  - Oil pressure needle in middle or higher

V.) Listen for Clunking Sounds
- Automatic transmission
  - Shift from drive to reverse, park to reverse
- Drive shaft and axles
  - Accelerate and decelerate quickly

VI.) Inspect the Exterior
- Avoid worn tires
  - Rough edges suggest alignment problems
  - Insufficient tread increases stopping distance
- Press hard on trunk corners
  - As release pressure, car should rise smoothly
  - Shock absorbers, rear springs wear quickly

FIGURE 1-79

(continued)

In the Lab

Road Testing Used Cars *(continued)*

Buying a Used Car
Presented by
Mr. Rzepki

(a) Slide 1

Used Cars Are Good Deals

- Save thousands of dollars in depreciation
- Low-mileage cars should last many years
- Services will provide vehicle history
- Dealers can give good warranties

(b) Slide 2

Inspect the Interior

- Driver's seat not torn, stained
- Driver's side door closes smoothly
- Rubber on pedals not worn

(c) Slide 3

Start the Engine

- Should fire almost immediately
- Dashboard lights should turn off soon
  - Oil pressure needle in middle or higher

(d) Slide 4

FIGURE 1-80

In the Lab

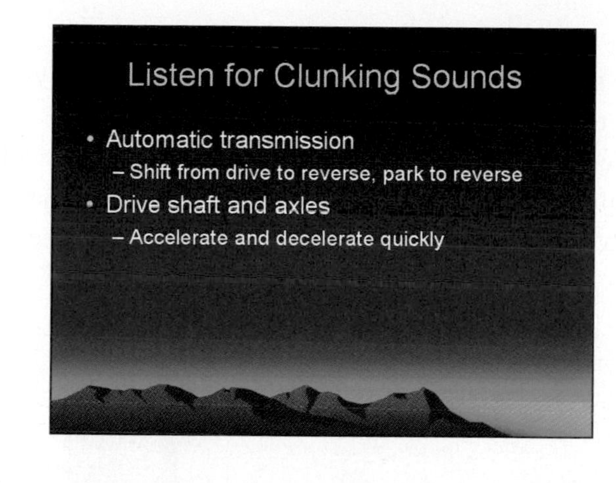

Listen for Clunking Sounds
• Automatic transmission
– Shift from drive to reverse, park to reverse
• Drive shaft and axles
– Accelerate and decelerate quickly

(e) Slide 5

Inspect the Exterior
• Avoid worn tires
– Rough edges suggest alignment problems
– Insufficient tread increases stopping distance
• Press hard on trunk corners
– As release pressure, car should rise smoothly
– Shock absorbers, rear springs wear quickly

(f) Slide 6

FIGURE 1-80 ***(continued)***

Instructions: Perform the following tasks.

1. Create a new presentation using the Mountain Top design template (row 7, column 1).
2. Using the typed notes illustrated in Figure 1-79, create the title slide shown in Figure 1-80a using your name in place of Mr. Rzepki. Italicize the title paragraph, Buying a Used Car, and increase the font size to 72. Increase the font size of the first paragraph of the subtitle text, Presented by, to 40. Italicize your name.
3. Using the typed notes in Figure 1-79, create the five text slides with bulleted lists shown in Figures 1-80b through 1-80f.
4. Click the Spelling button on the Standard toolbar. Correct any errors.
5. Drag the scroll box to display Slide 1. Click the Slide Show button to start slide show view. Then click to display each slide.
6. Save the presentation using the file name, Lab 1-1 Used Cars.
7. Display and print the presentation in black and white. Close the presentation. Hand in the hard copy to your instructor.

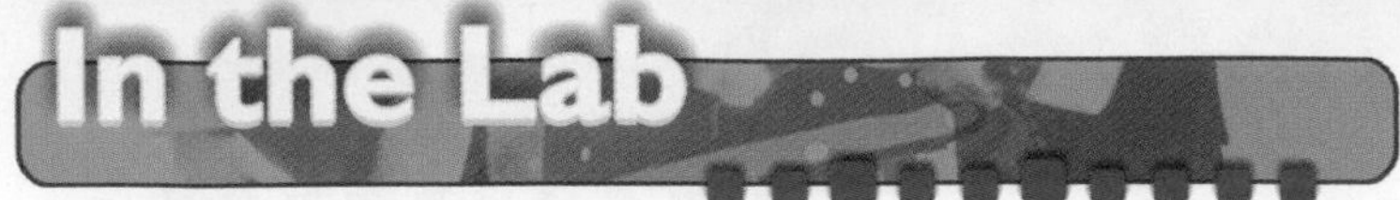

2 Natural Disasters Home Readiness

Problem: One of the units in your Earth Science class covers severe weather and natural disasters. You have been learning that families need to take personal responsibility to take action and reduce the effects of these weather emergencies. Your lab partner, Jason Black, and you decide to design a PowerPoint slide show that will help parents prepare their homes in advance of an emergency and plan to display it at the next Parent Teacher Association meeting. You type information with tips and supply suggestions (Figure 1-81) and then create the presentation shown in Figures 1-82a through 1-82d.

1) Preparing for Natural Disasters
A Guide for You and Your Family
Katie Anderson and Jason Black

2) Create Basic Supplies Kit
- Personal supplies
  - Batteries, first aid kit, work gloves
  - Trash bags, flashlights, utility knife
- Tools and recovery supplies
  - Generator, pliers, wrench
  - Cooler, rope, tarps, ladder

3) Develop Disaster Plan
- Identify two meeting locations
  - Outside the home
  - Outside the neighborhood
- Turn off water, gas, electricity
- Secure important papers in waterproof container and send copies to confidant

4) Gather in Safe Room
- Tornadoes
  - Interior room without windows on lowest floor
- Hurricanes
  - Room above ground without windows
- Earthquakes
  - Ground floor against inside wall

FIGURE 1-81

In the Lab

Preparing for
Natural Disasters
A Guide for You and Your Family
Katie Anderson and Jason Black

(a) Slide 1 (Title Slide)

Create Basic Supplies Kit
- Personal supplies
  - Batteries, first aid kit, work gloves
  - Trash bags, flashlights, utility knife
- Tools and recovery supplies
  - Generator, pliers, wrench
  - Cooler, rope, tarps, ladder

(b) Slide 2

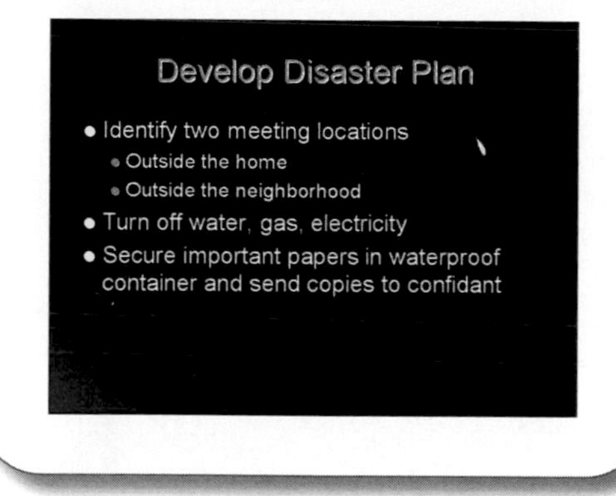
Develop Disaster Plan
Identify two meeting locations
Outside the home
Outside the neighborhood
Turn off water, gas, electricity
Secure important papers in waterproof container and send copies to confidant

(c) Slide 3

Gather in Safe Room
- Tornadoes
  - Interior room without windows on lowest floor
- Hurricanes
  - Room above ground without windows
- Earthquakes
  - Ground floor against inside wall

(d) Slide 4

FIGURE 1-82

Instructions: Perform the following tasks.

1. Create a new presentation using the Orbit design template (row 6, column 1).
2. Using the typed notes illustrated in Figure 1-81, create the title slide shown in Figure 1-82a using your name in place of Katie Anderson. Italicize both names. Increase the font size of the title paragraph, Preparing For Natural Disasters, to 72. Decrease the font size of the first paragraph of the subtitle text, A Guide for You and Your Family, to 28.
3. Using the typed notes in Figure 1-81, create the three text slides with bulleted lists shown in Figures 1-82b through 1-82d.
4. Click the Spelling button on the Standard toolbar. Correct any errors.
5. Save the presentation using the file name, Lab 1-2 Natural Disasters.
6. Display the presentation in black and white.
7. Print the black and white presentation. Close the presentation. Hand in the hard copy to your instructor.

3 New Courses Update

Problem: Every quarter the faculty and administrators at Thorn High School schedule new classes for returning students. For sophomores, the new classes are Introduction to Jazz, Meteorology, and Theater Appreciation. For juniors, the new offerings are Yoga and Introduction to African-American Music. Seniors can enroll in Introduction to Rock and Roll and Computer Animation.

Instructions Part 1: Using the outline in Figure 1-83, create the presentation shown in Figure 1-84a. Use the Slit design template. On the title slide, type your name in place of Mrs. Anderson, increase the font size of the title paragraph, Thorn High School, to 60 and change the text font style to italic. Increase the font size of the subtitle paragraph, New Fall Classes, to 40. Create the three text slides with multi-level bulleted lists shown in Figures 1-84b through 1-84d.

Correct any spelling mistakes, and then view the slide show. Save the presentation using the file name, Lab 1-3 Part One Fall Classes. Display and print the presentation in black and white.

1. Thorn High School
New Fall Classes
Mrs. Anderson, Principal

2. Sophomore Level
- Introduction to Jazz
    - o History and fundamental characteristics
- Meteorology
    - o Weather reports, maps, charts
- Theater Appreciation
    - o Stage elements, genres, history

3. Junior Level
- Introduction to Rock and Roll
    - o Trace pop music from early 1900s
    - o Sociological implications, messages conveyed
- Progressive Weight Training
    - o Improve muscle tone, range of motion
        - - Work on individual weaknesses, flexibility

4. Senior Level
- Introduction to African-American Music
    - o Style, performers, social influences
- Computer Animation
    - o Transfer art, design work into animation
        - - Add images, time sequencing, sound
    - o Use Macromedia Flash MX

FIGURE 1-83

In the Lab

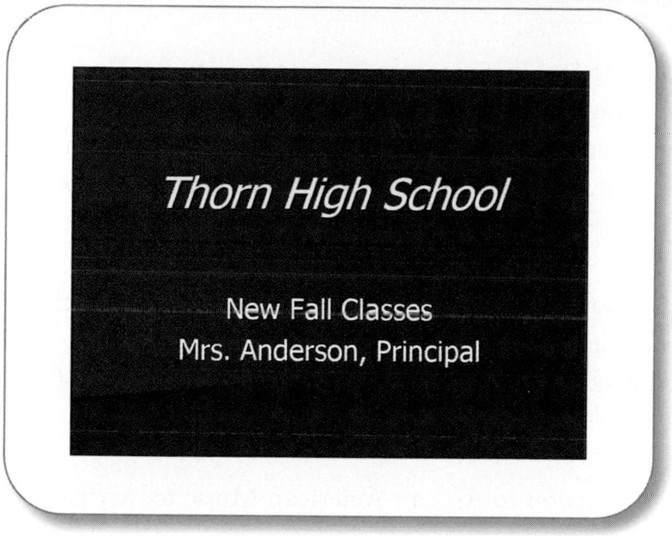

Thorn High School
New Fall Classes
Mrs. Anderson, Principal

(a) Slide 1 (Title Slide)

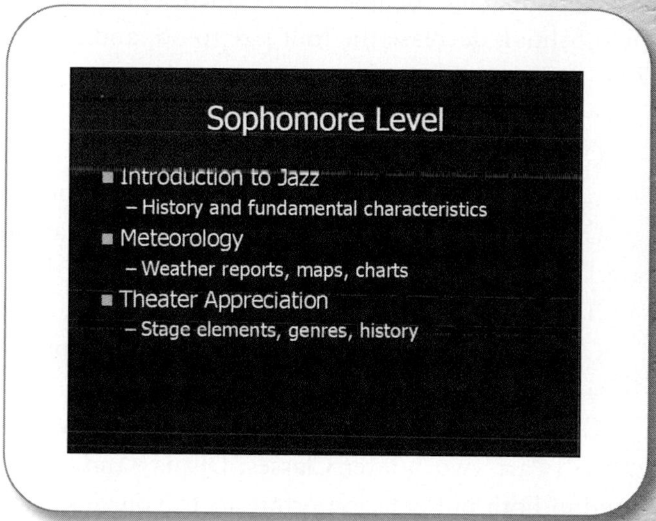

Sophomore Level
- Introduction to Jazz
  - History and fundamental characteristics
- Meteorology
  - Weather reports, maps, charts
- Theater Appreciation
  - Stage elements, genres, history

(b) Slide 2

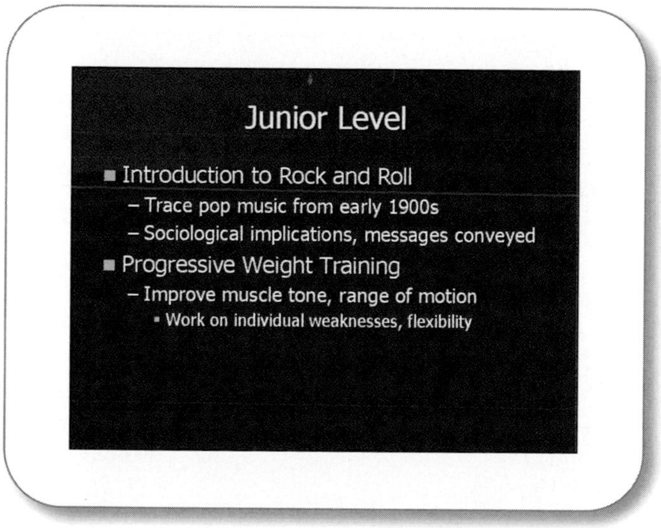

Junior Level
- Introduction to Rock and Roll
  - Trace pop music from early 1900s
  - Sociological implications, messages conveyed
- Progressive Weight Training
  - Improve muscle tone, range of motion
    - Work on individual weaknesses, flexibility

(c) Slide 3

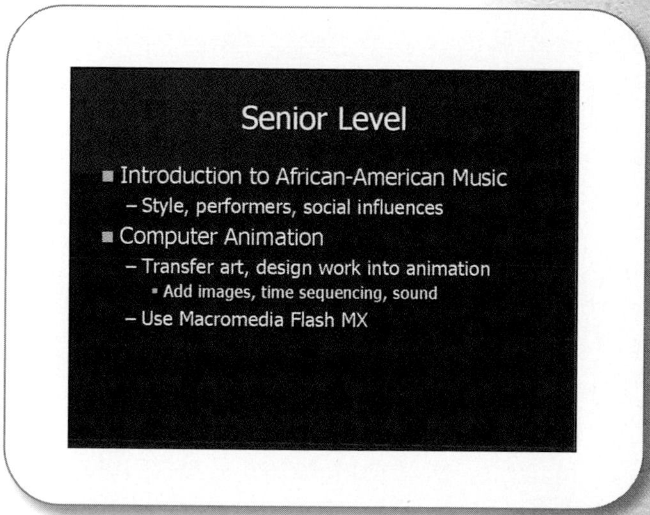

Senior Level
- Introduction to African-American Music
  - Style, performers, social influences
- Computer Animation
  - Transfer art, design work into animation
    - Add images, time sequencing, sound
  - Use Macromedia Flash MX

(d) Slide 4

FIGURE 1-84

(continued)

New Courses Update *(continued)*

Instructions Part 2: Thorn High School counselors want to update this presentation to promote the Winter class schedule. Modify the presentation created in Part 1 to create the presentation shown in Figure 1-85. Change the design template to Refined. On the title slide, remove the italics from the title paragraph, Thorn High School, decrease the font size to 60, and underline the text. Change the first subtitle paragraph to New Winter Classes. Then change your title in the second subtitle paragraph to Head Counselor and decrease the font size to 28.

On Slide 2, change the first first-level paragraph, Introduction to Jazz, to Advanced Jazz Music. Delete the last paragraph on the slide and replace it with the paragraph, Survey comedy, tragedy, farce, melodrama.

On Slide 3, change the first second-level paragraph under Introduction to Rock and Roll to, Influence of jazz, blues, rock on today's music. Then change the first second-level paragraph under Progressive Weight Training to, Part of overall, lifetime fitness plan.

On Slide 4, change the second-level paragraph under Introduction to African-American Music to, Stylistic characteristics of each time period.

Correct any spelling mistakes, and then view the slide show. Save the presentation using the file name, Lab 1-3 Part Two Winter Classes. Display and print the presentation in black and white. Close the presentation. Hand in both presentation printouts to your instructor.

In the Lab

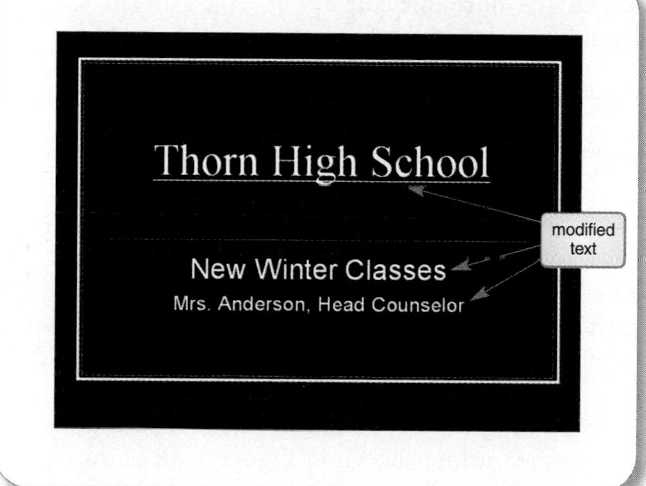

(a) Slide 1

Sophomore Level
- Advanced Jazz Music
  - History and fundamental characteristics
- Meteorology
  - Weather reports, maps, charts
- Theater Appreciation
  - Survey comedy, tragedy, farce, melodrama

modified text

(b) Slide 2

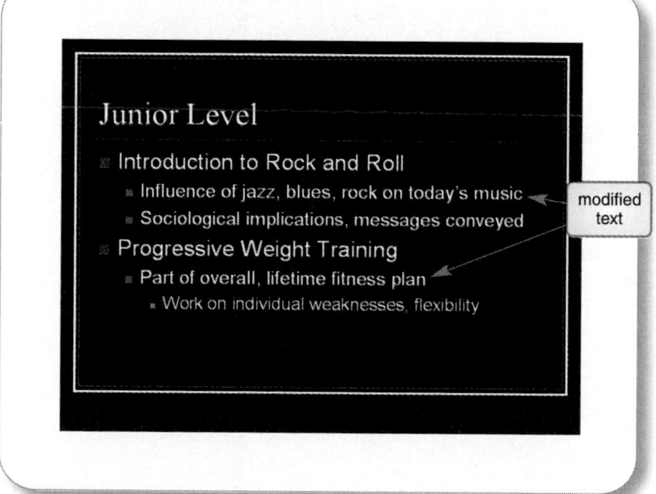

Junior Level
Introduction to Rock and Roll
Influence of jazz, blues, rock on today's music
Sociological implications, messages conveyed
Progressive Weight Training
Part of overall, lifetime fitness plan
Work on individual weaknesses, flexibility
modified text

(c) Slide 3

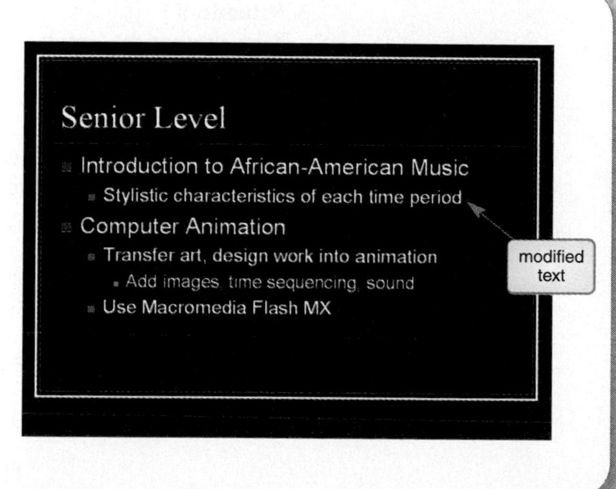

Senior Level
Introduction to African-American Music
Stylistic characteristics of each time period
Computer Animation
Transfer art, design work into animation
Add images, time sequencing, sound
Use Macromedia Flash MX
modified text

(d) Slide 4

FIGURE 1-85

Cases and Places

The difficulty of these case studies varies:
■ are the least difficult and ■■ are more difficult.
Each exercise has a cross-curricular designation.

Math Social Studies Science Language Arts Art/Music Business Health

Note: Remember to use the 7 x 7 rule as you design the presentations: a maximum of seven words on a line and a maximum of seven lines on one slide.

1 Eating junk foods seems a way of life for many active teens. Sometimes vending machine food is the only solution for curbing hunger pains. You are learning in health class that while fruit and vegetables are less costly than snack foods, many teens buy junk food rather than the vitamin-laden fruit and vegetable alternatives. Vitamins, particularly A, B, and C, are essential nutrients often missing in junk food. You decide to prepare a PowerPoint presentation explaining which foods contain these vitamins and how the body benefits from these nutrients. You create the outline shown in Figure 1-86 about vitamins A, B, and C. Using the concepts and techniques introduced in this project, use this outline to develop a slide show with a title slide and three text slides with bulleted lists. Print the slides so they can be distributed to your classmates.

1. A-B-C: Vitamins for Me
Presented by
Student Name
Health 1, Second Period

2. Vitamin A
Helps repair and grow skin tissues
Makes skin smooth and moist
Found in:
Oranges and dark green, leafy vegetables

3. Vitamin B
Helps prevent dry, cracking skin
Especially at the corners of the mouth
Especially necessary for active teens
Found in:
Bananas and sunflower seeds
Lentils and whole-grain cereals

4. Vitamin C
Helps body manufacture collagen
Protein that keeps skin firm
Found in:
Citrus juice and red peppers

FIGURE 1-86

Cases and Places

2 Samuel Langhorne Clemens, who is better known by his pen name Mark Twain, is one of America's most prominent writers. You are reading some of his works in your English II class, and you decide to prepare a PowerPoint presentation describing Twain's life and works for extra credit. You prepare the outline shown in Figure 1-87. Use this outline to design and create a presentation with a title slide and three text slides with bulleted lists.

1) Mark Twain: The Quintessential American Writer
- Presented by
- Student Name
- English II

2) Chronology
- Born November 30, 1835
- Worked as printer, riverboat pilot
- Traveled to Nevada, California, Hawaii
  - Had successful journalism career
    - Humorous works popular on lecture circuit
- Died April 21, 1910

3) Life Overview
- Fascinated with science
- Depressed in later life
  - Three children, wife died before him
  - Lost thousands of dollars
    - Typesetting machine never finished
    - Books were plagiarized

4) Noted Literary Works
- *The Celebrated Jumping Frog of Calaveras County*
- *The Adventures of Tom Sawyer*
- *The Prince and the Pauper*
- *Life on the Mississippi*
- *Adventures of Huckleberry Finn*

FIGURE 1-87

Cases and Places

3 Volcanoes are common occurrences throughout the Earth. As you are learning in Earth Science class, they take place when lava, or molten rocks, rises to the surface. It combines with gases that expand and fragment the lava into ash. Volcanoes can trigger tsunamis, earthquakes, mudslides, and flash floods. The three types of volcanoes are: active, which are erupting currently; dormant, which are not erupting at this time; and extinct, which cannot erupt. One of the largest eruptions occurred in 79 A.D. at Mount Vesuvius in Italy. Two cities were buried under 20 feet of ash. A second huge eruption occurred in 1883 at Krakatau in Indonesia. At that site, more than 163 villages were destroyed. You are writing a research paper on volcanoes for class, and you want to create a slide show on this topic to accompany an oral presentation that also is required. Prepare a short presentation to inform your classmates about volcanoes.

4 Throughout time, people have tried to determine the origins of the universe, why natural disasters occur, why people act in certain ways, and other difficult-to-answer questions. Myths involving gods and goddesses were developed as a means of explaining these topics. As part of your Ancient History class, you are studying myths, mythical places, and various gods and goddesses. You have been assigned an oral presentation on the topic, and you decide to focus on three gods and goddesses. Three Aztec gods are: Huitzilopochtli, god of the sun; Coatlicue, goddess of the earth; and Quetzalcoati, god of learning. Three Egyptian gods are: Ra-Atum, god of the sun; Nut, goddess of the sky; and Osiris, god of the underworld. The twelve Greek gods and goddesses are related and ruled the world from Mount Olympus in Greece. The most powerful is Zeus, and he is married to Hera. Aphrodite is the goddess of love and beauty. The Romans adopted and renamed the Olympian gods. Using the techniques introduced in the project, create a presentation to accompany your speech about gods and goddesses.

5 **Working Together** High school students can gain valuable experience and obtain insights about careers by volunteering in their communities. Many organizations and not-for-profit businesses frequently seek volunteers for various projects. Have each member of your team visit or telephone several local community groups to determine volunteer opportunities. Gather data about:

1. Duties and responsibilities
2. Required hours each week
3. Contact person
4. Telephone number
5. Address

After coordinating the data, create a presentation with at least one slide showcasing the charitable organization. As a group, critique each slide. Hand in a hard copy of the final presentation.

MICROSOFT OFFICE
PowerPoint 2003

Using the Outline Tab and Clip Art to Create a Slide Show

PROJECT 2

CASE PERSPECTIVE

Obtaining a driver's license is a goal for most high school students. Once they pass the test and receive their laminated card, they have the freedom to go wherever they want whenever time permits. With this license, however, come added risks and responsibilities. Mrs. Jessica Cantero, the coordinator of the drivers' education program at West Park High School, realizes that many new drivers neglect safe driving habits when they first get behind the wheel. While they have learned the skills needed to operate a car, they lack the firsthand experience needed for challenging situations. According to the National Center for Health Statistics, motor vehicle accidents are the leading cause of death for people from 15 to 20 years old.

Mrs. Cantero wants to develop a slide show to accompany her driving safety tips discussion during drivers' education class. She is hopeful her presentation will motivate new drivers to reflect upon their driving behavior and to establish good habits. It will include tips for driving to school, around town, and in inclement weather, along with other good guidelines to follow. She knows that PowerPoint slide shows enhance speakers' lectures, so she asks you to assist her in developing a presentation to accompany her talk. You mention to her that visuals, when used properly, can add interest and help reinforce the message. She would like you to add some relevant images to her slides.

As you read through this project, you will learn how to use PowerPoint to add clip art and animation to increase the presentation's visual interest. You also will e-mail the completed presentation to Mrs. Cantero.

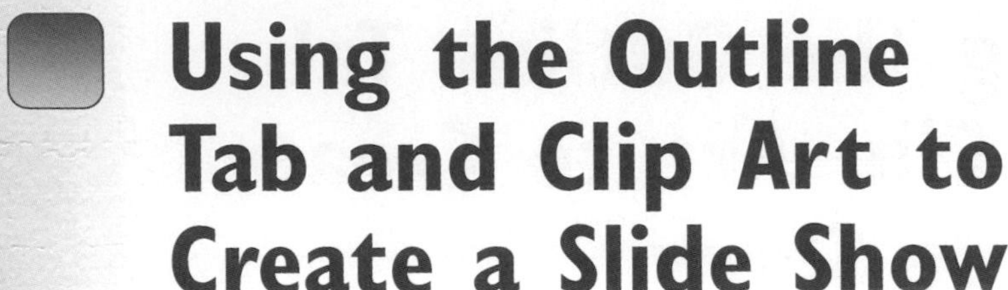

Using the Outline Tab and Clip Art to Create a Slide Show

PROJECT

Objectives

You will have mastered the material in this project when you can:

- Start and customize a new slide show from an outline
- Add a slide and create a closing slide on the Outline tab
- Create text slides with multi-level bulleted lists on the Outline tab
- Save and review a presentation
- Insert and move clip art and change its size
- Add a header and footer to outline pages
- Animate clip art
- Add an animation scheme and run an animated slide show
- Print a presentation outline
- E-mail a slide show from within PowerPoint

Introduction

At some time during either your academic or business life, you probably will make a presentation. The presentation may be informative by providing detailed information about a specific topic. Other presentations may be persuasive by selling a proposal or a product to a client, convincing management to approve a new project, or influencing the board of directors to accept the new fiscal budget. As an alternative to creating your presentation in the slide pane in normal view, as you did in Project 1, PowerPoint provides an outlining feature to help you organize your thoughts. When the outline is complete, it becomes the foundation for your presentation.

Project Two — New License, New Skills

Project 2 uses PowerPoint to create the five-slide New License, New Skills presentation shown in Figures 2-1a through 2-1e. You create the presentation from the outline shown in Figure 2-2 on page PPT 84.

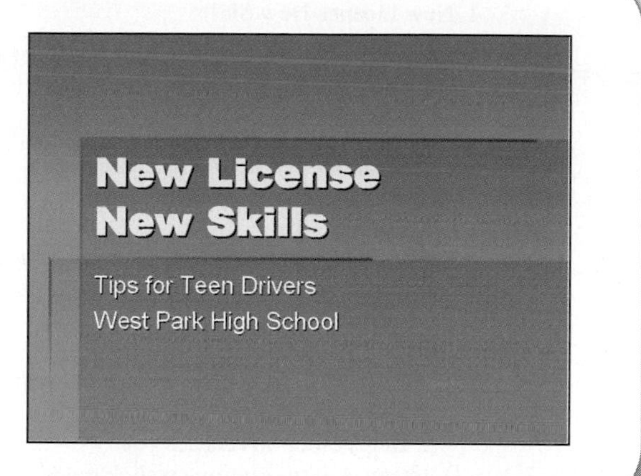

New License
New Skills
Tips for Teen Drivers
West Park High School

(a) Slide 1

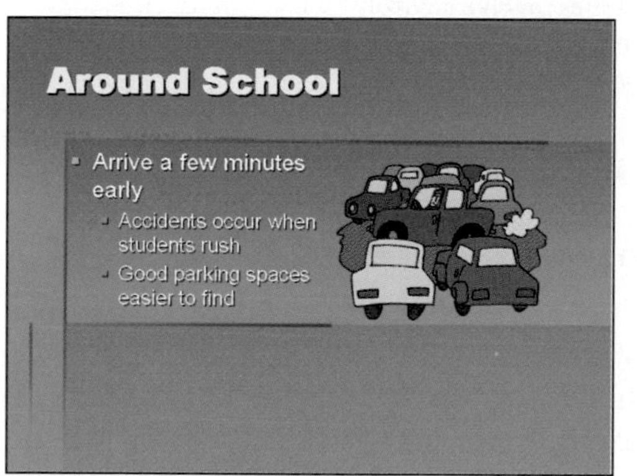

(b) Slide 2

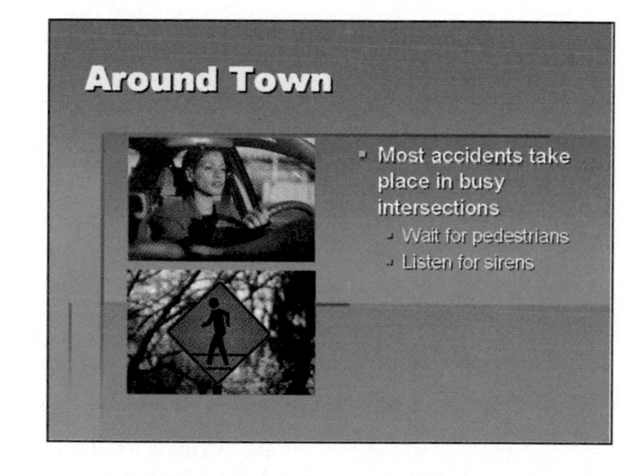

(c) Slide 3

Inclement Weather

- Turn on headlights and windshield wipers
  - Helps you see what is ahead
  - Helps other drivers see you
- Exercise extra caution on slick roads
  - Test brakes to determine stopping distance
  - Double space between car ahead of you

(d) Slide 4

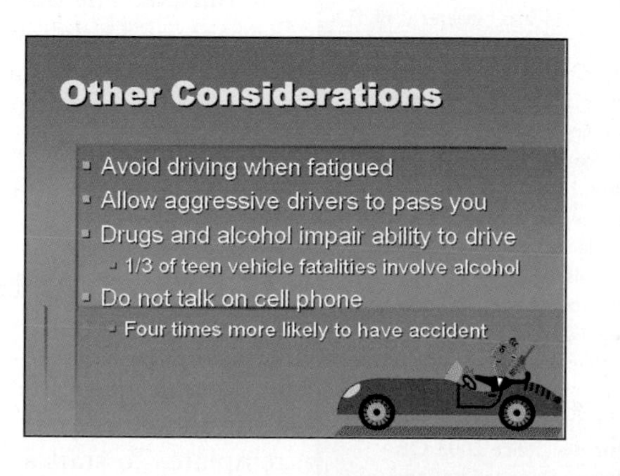

(e) Slide 5

FIGURE 2-1

I. New License New Skills
 A. Tips for Teen Drivers
 B. West Park High School
II. Around School
 A. Arrive a few minutes early
  1. Accidents occur when students rush
  2. Good parking spaces easier to find
III. Around Town
 A. Most accidents take place in busy intersections
  1. Wait for pedestrians
  2. Listen for sirens
IV. Inclement Weather
 A. Turn on headlights and windshield wipers
  1. Helps you see what is ahead
  2. Helps other drivers see you
 B. Exercise extra caution on slick roads
  1. Test brakes to determine stopping distance
  2. Double space between car ahead of you
V. Other Considerations
 A. Avoid driving when fatigued
 B. Allow aggressive drivers to pass you
 C. Drugs and alcohol impair ability to drive
  1. 1/3 of teen vehicle fatalities involve alcohol
 D. Do not talk on cell phone
  1. Four times more likely to have accident

FIGURE 2-2

You can create your presentation outline using the Outline tab. When you create an outline, you type all the text at one time, as if you were typing an outline on a sheet of paper. This technique differs from creating a presentation in the slide pane in normal view, where you type text as you create each individual slide and the text is displayed both in the slide pane and on the Outline tab. PowerPoint creates the presentation as you type the outline by evaluating the outline structure and displaying a miniature view of the slide. Regardless of how you build a presentation, PowerPoint automatically creates the three views discussed in Project 1: normal, slide sorter, and slide show.

The first step in creating a presentation on the Outline tab is to type a title for the outline. The **outline title** is the subject of the presentation and later becomes the presentation title text. Then, you type the remainder of the outline, indenting appropriately to establish a structure, or hierarchy. Once the outline is complete, you make your presentation more persuasive by adding **clips**, which are media files of art, animation, sound, and movies. This project uses outlining to create the presentation and clip art to support the text visually.

Q & A

Q: Why are outlines useful?

A: Outlining helps you plan, organize, and design your presentation. When you start to create an outline, you often begin to see new possibilities and find new ways to divide and group your ideas. You also find gaps where additional information is needed. A final glance at an outline can tell you if your plan is appropriate. For more information on outlining, visit the Office 2003 Q&A Web page (scsite.com/off2003sch/qa), locate PowerPoint Project 2, and click Outlining.

Starting and Customizing PowerPoint

Project 1 introduced you to starting a presentation document, choosing a layout, and applying a design template. The following steps summarize how to start a new presentation, customize the PowerPoint window, choose a layout, and apply a design template. To start and customize PowerPoint, Windows must be running. If you are stepping through this project on a computer and you want your screen to match the figures in this book, then you should change your computer's resolution to 800 × 600. For more information on how to change the resolution on your computer, see Appendix B.

To Start and Customize PowerPoint

1. **Click the Start button on the Windows taskbar, point to All Programs on the Start menu, point to Microsoft Office on the All Programs submenu, and then click Microsoft Office PowerPoint 2003 on the Microsoft Office submenu.**
2. **If the PowerPoint window is not maximized, double-click its title bar to maximize it.**
3. **If the Language bar appears, right-click it and then click Close the Language bar on the shortcut menu.**
4. **If the Getting Started task pane appears in the PowerPoint window, click its Close button in the upper-right corner.**
5. **If the Standard and Formatting toolbars are positioned on the same row, click the Toolbar Options button and then click Show Buttons on Two Rows.**
6. **Click the Slide Design button on the Formatting toolbar. When the Slide Design task pane is displayed, click the down scroll arrow in the Apply a design template list, and then click the Glass Layers template in the Available For Use area.**
7. **Click the Close button in the Slide Design task pane.**

If the Glass Layers template is not displayed in the Slide Design task pane, ask your instructor about installing additional templates. The PowerPoint window with the Standard and Formatting toolbars on two rows appears as shown in Figure 2-3. PowerPoint displays the Title Slide layout and the Glass Layers template on Slide 1 in normal view.

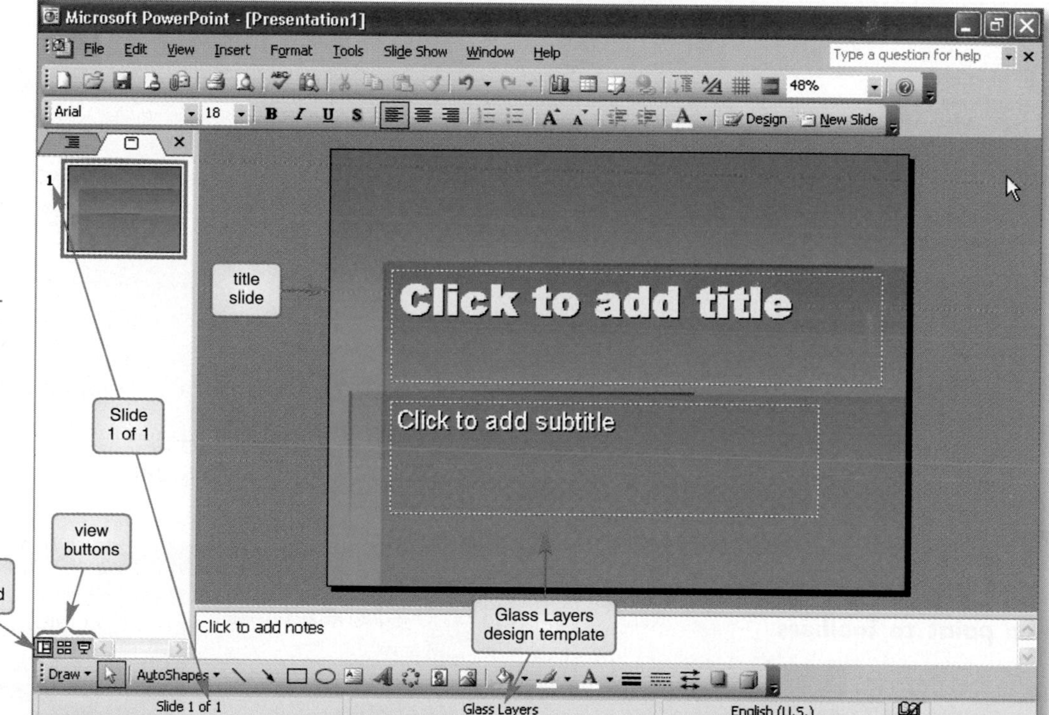

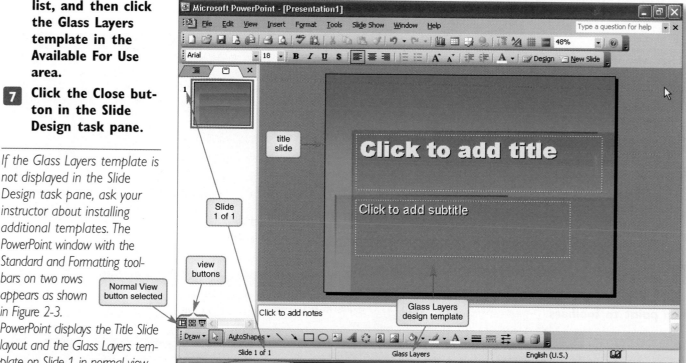

FIGURE 2-3

Using the Outline Tab

The **Outline tab** provides a quick, easy way to create a presentation. **Outlining** allows you to organize your thoughts in a structured format. An outline uses indentation to establish a **hierarchy**, which denotes levels of importance to the main topic. An outline is a summary of thoughts, presented as headings and subheadings, often used as a preliminary draft when you create a presentation.

The three panes — tabs, slide, and notes — shown in normal view also are displayed when you click the Outline tab. The notes pane is displayed below the slide pane. In the tabs pane, the slide text appears along with a slide number and a slide icon. Body text is indented below the title text. Objects, such as pictures, graphs, or tables, do not display. The slide icon is blank when a slide does not contain objects. The attributes for text on the Outline tab are the same as in normal view except for color and paragraph style.

PowerPoint formats a title style and five levels of body text in an outline. The outline begins with the slide title, which is not indented. The title is the main topic of the slide. Body text supporting the main topic begins on the first level and also is not indented. If desired, additional supporting text can be added on the second through fifth levels. Each level is indented. Levels four and five generally are used for very detailed scientific and engineering presentations. Business and sales presentations usually focus on summary information and use the first, second, and third levels.

PowerPoint initially displays in normal view when you start a new presentation. To type the outline, click the Outline tab in the tabs pane. The following steps show how to change to the Outline tab and display the Outlining toolbar.

To Change to the Outline Tab and Display the Outlining Toolbar

1

- **Click the Outline tab located in the tabs pane.**

The Outline tab is selected. The tabs pane increases and the slide pane decreases in size. The tabs pane consists of the Outline tab and the Slides tab (Figure 2-4).

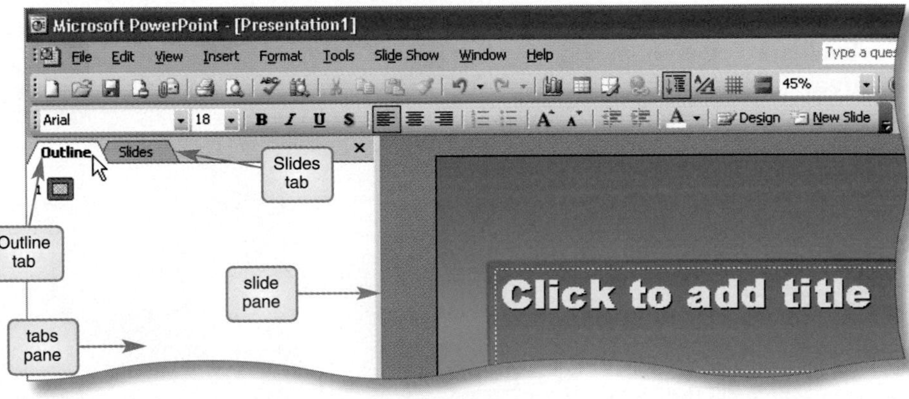

FIGURE 2-4

2

- **Click View on the menu bar and then point to Toolbars.**

The View menu and Toolbars submenu are displayed (Figure 2-5).

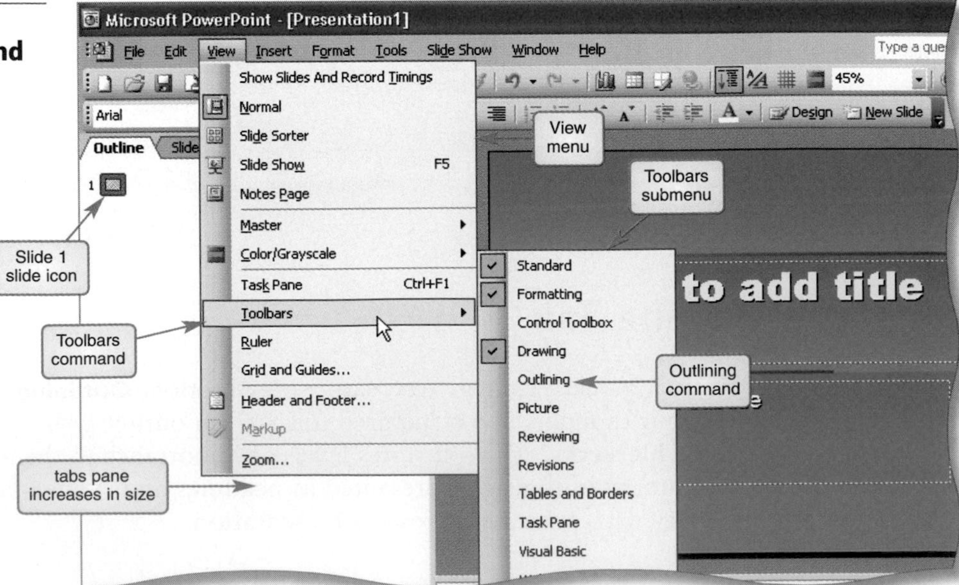

FIGURE 2-5

3

• **Click Outlining on the Toolbars submenu.**

The Outlining toolbar is displayed (Figure 2-6).

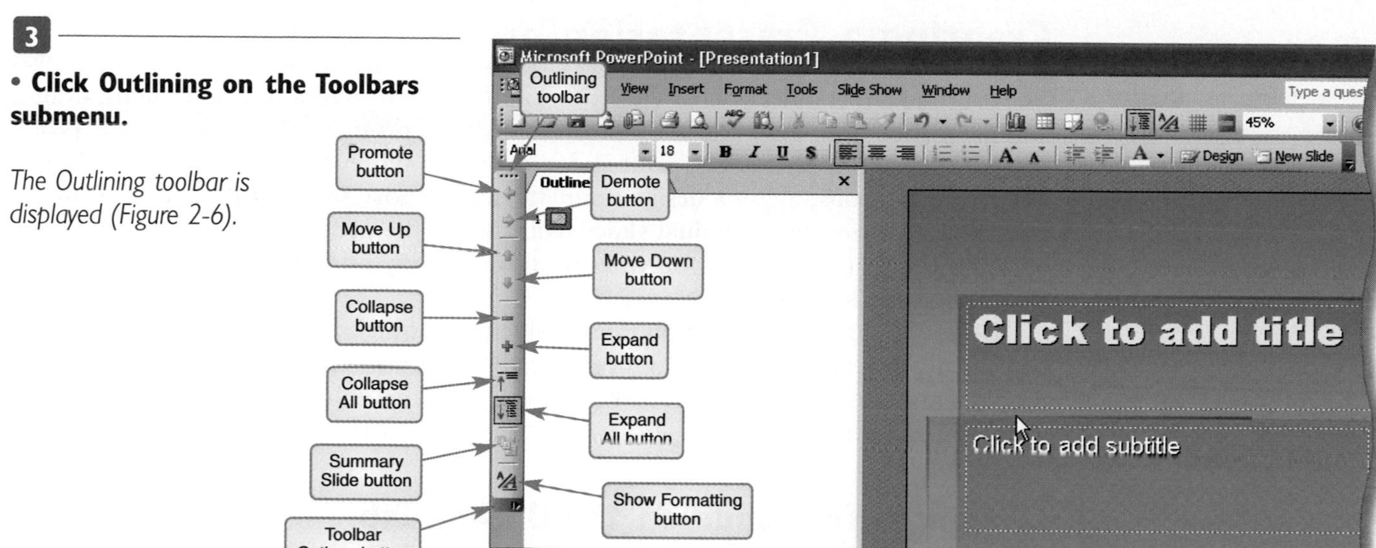

FIGURE 2-6

You can create and edit your presentation on the Outline tab. This tab also makes it easy to sequence slides and to relocate title text and body text from one slide to another. In addition to typing text to create a new presentation on the Outline tab, PowerPoint can produce slides from an outline created in Microsoft Word or another word processing application if you save the outline as an RTF file or as a plain text file. The file extension **RTF** stands for **R**ich **T**ext **F**ormat.

Table 2-1 describes the buttons on the Outlining toolbar.

Table 2-1 Buttons on the Outlining Toolbar

BUTTON	BUTTON NAME	DESCRIPTION
	Promote	Moves the selected paragraph to the next-higher level (up one level, to the left).
	Demote	Moves the selected paragraph to the next-lower level (down one level, to the right).
	Move Up	Moves a selected paragraph and its collapsed (temporarily hidden) subordinate text above the preceding displayed paragraph.
	Move Down	Moves a selected paragraph and its collapsed (temporarily hidden) subordinate text down, below the following displayed paragraph.
	Collapse	Hides all but the titles of selected slides. Collapsed text is represented by a gray line.
	Expand	Displays the titles and all collapsed text of selected slides.
	Collapse All	Displays only the title of each slide. Text other than the title is represented by a gray line below the title.
	Expand All	Displays the titles and all the body text for each slide.
	Summary Slide	Creates a new slide from the titles of the slides you select in slide sorter or normal view. The summary slide creates a bulleted list from the titles of the selected slides. PowerPoint inserts the summary slide in front of the first selected slide.
	Show Formatting	Shows or hides character formatting (such as bold and italic) in normal view. In slide sorter view, switches between showing all text and objects on each slide and displaying titles only.
	Toolbar Options	Allows you to select the particular buttons you want to display on the toolbar.

Creating a Presentation on the Outline Tab

The Outline tab enables you to view title and body text, add and delete slides, drag and drop slide text, drag and drop individual slides, promote and demote text, save a presentation, print an outline, print slides, copy and paste slides or text to and from other presentations, apply a design template, and import an outline. When you **drag and drop** slide text or individual slides, you change the order of the text or the slides by selecting the text or slide you want to move or copy and then dragging the text or slide to its new location.

Developing a presentation on the Outline tab is quick because you type the text for all slides on one screen. Once you type the outline, the presentation fundamentally is complete. If you choose, you then can enhance your presentation with objects in the slide pane.

> *Q & A*
>
> **Q:** What is drag-and-drop editing?
>
> **A:** PowerPoint's drag-and-drop editing setting helps you move text within a presentation, but it also can be used to move text from PowerPoint to another Microsoft Office program. To ensure the drag-and-drop editing setting is enabled, click Options on the Tools menu, click the Edit tab, and then click Drag-and-drop text editing if the check box is not checked.

Creating a Title Slide on the Outline Tab

Recall from Project 1 that the title slide introduces the presentation to the audience. In addition to introducing the presentation, Project 2 uses the title slide to capture the audience's attention by using a design template with an interesting title. The following steps show how to create a title slide on the Outline tab.

To Create a Title Slide on the Outline Tab

1

- **Click the Slide 1 slide icon on the Outline tab.**

The Slide 1 slide icon is selected. You also could click anywhere in the tabs pane to select the slide icon (Figure 2-7).

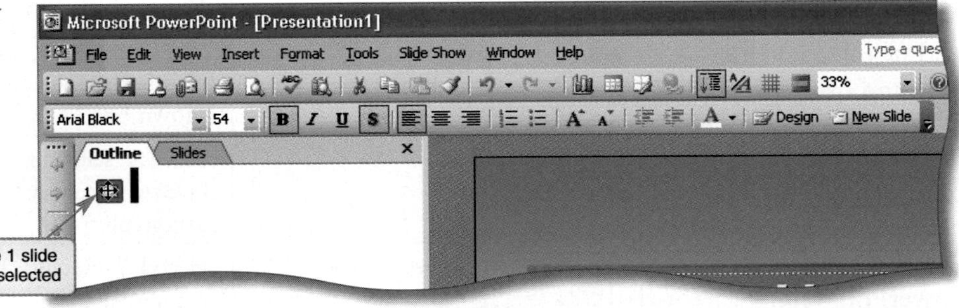

FIGURE 2-7

2

- **Type** `New License` **and then press the SHIFT+ENTER keys.**
- **Type** `New Skills` **and then press the ENTER key.**
- **Point to the Demote button on the Outlining toolbar.**

The Demote ScreenTip is displayed (Figure 2-8). Pressing the SHIFT+ENTER keys moves the insertion point to the next line and maintains the same first level. The insertion point is in position for typing the title for Slide 2. The first-level font is Arial Black and the font size for Slide 2 is 44 point.

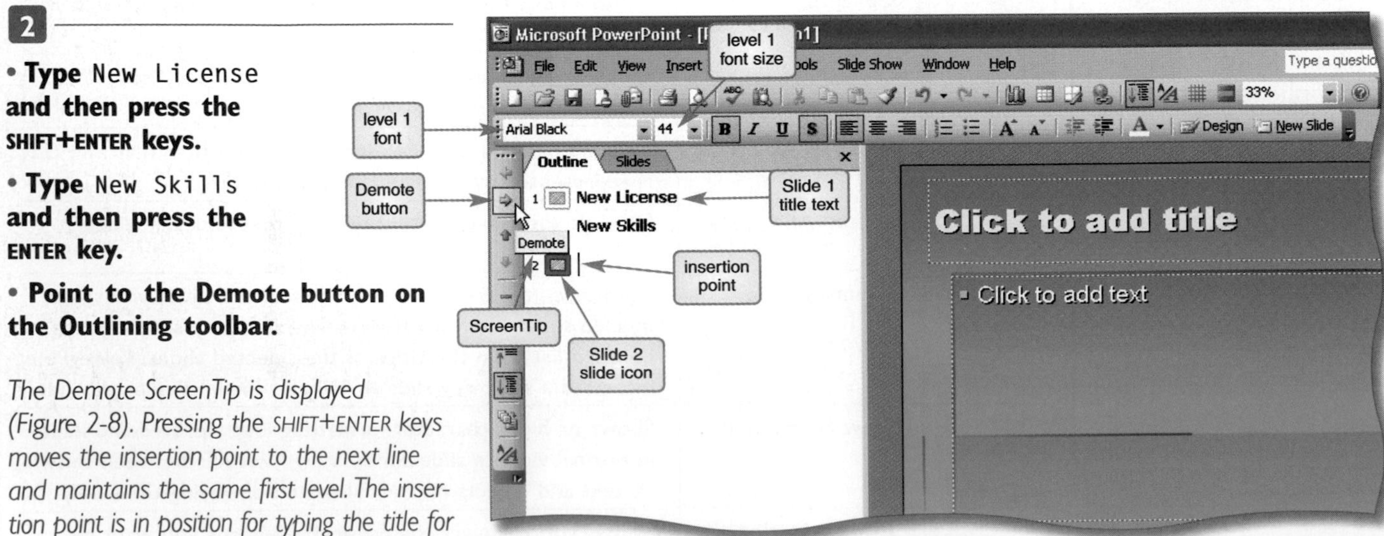

FIGURE 2-8

3

• **Click the Demote button on the Outlining toolbar.**

• **Type** `Tips for Teen Drivers` **and then press the ENTER key.**

• **Type** `West Park High School` **and then press the ENTER key.**

The paragraphs, Tips for Teen Drivers and West Park High School, are subtitles on the title slide (Slide 1) and demote to the second level (Figure 2-9). The second level is indented to the right below the first-level paragraph. The second-level font is Arial and the font size is 32 point.

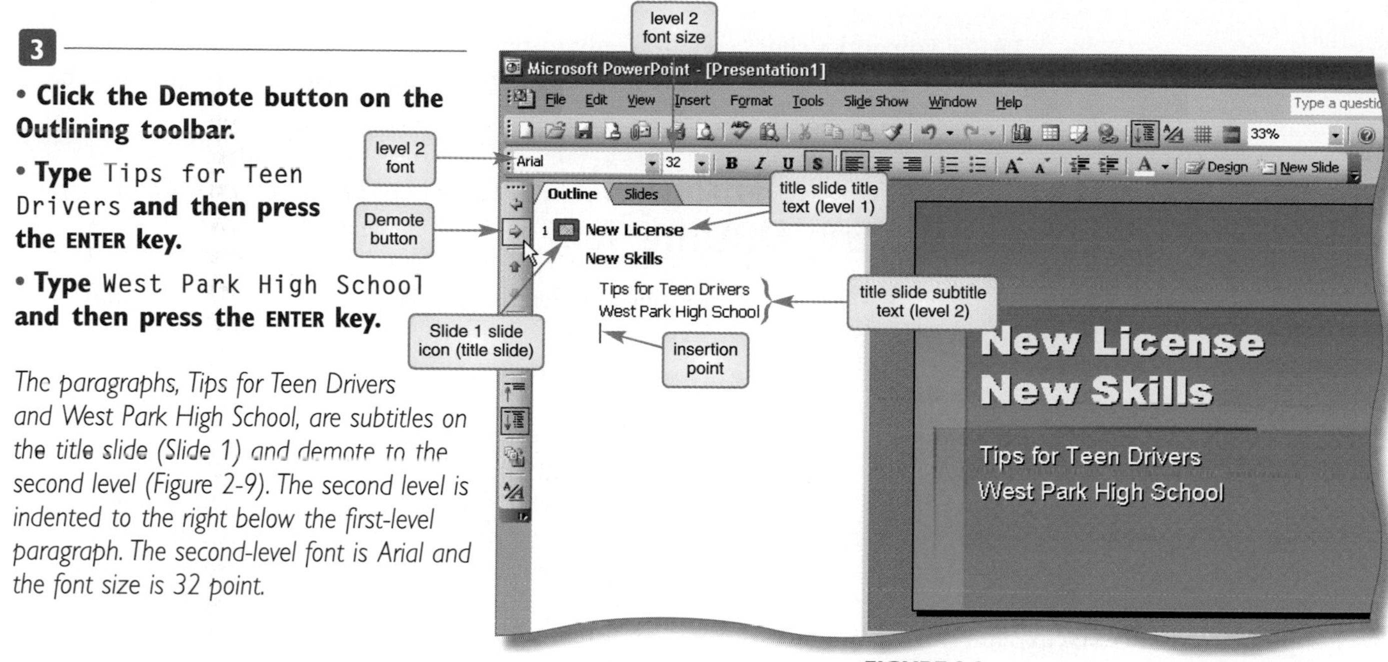

FIGURE 2-9

The title slide text for the New Licence, New Skills presentation is complete. The next section explains how to add a slide on the Outline tab.

Adding a Slide on the Outline Tab

Recall from Project 1 that when you add a new slide in normal view, PowerPoint defaults to a Text slide layout with a bulleted list. This action occurs on the Outline tab as well. One way to add a new slide on the Outline tab is to promote a paragraph to the first level by clicking the Promote button on the Outlining toolbar until the insertion point or the paragraph is displayed at the first level. A slide icon is displayed when the insertion point or paragraph reaches this level. The following step shows how to add a slide on the Outline tab.

To Add a Slide on the Outline Tab

1

• **Click the Promote button on the Outlining toolbar.**

The Slide 2 slide icon is displayed, indicating a new slide is added to the presentation (Figure 2-10). The insertion point is in position to type the title for Slide 2 at the first level.

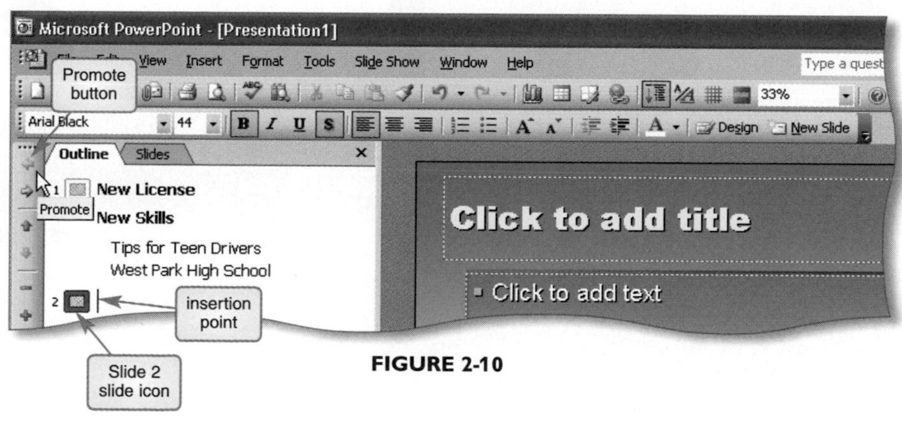

FIGURE 2-10

Skill Builder 2-1

To practice the following tasks, visit scsite.com/off2003sch/skill, locate PowerPoint Project 2, and then click Skill Builder 2-1.
- ❑ Start PowerPoint
- ❑ Apply a design template
- ❑ Create a title slide on the Outline tab

After you add a slide, you are ready to type the slide text. The next section explains how to create text slides with multi-level bulleted lists on the Outline tab.

Creating Text Slides with Multi-Level Bulleted Lists on the Outline Tab

To create a text slide with multi-level bulleted lists, you demote or promote the insertion point to the appropriate level and then type the paragraph text. Recall from Project 1 that when you demote a paragraph, PowerPoint adds a bullet to the left of each level. Depending on the design template, each level has a different bullet font. Also recall that the design template determines font attributes, including the bullet font.

The first text slide you create in Project 2 describes tips for driving around school. The slide title is displayed as a first-level paragraph on the Outline tab and in the slide pane, and the suggestion to arrive a few minutes early and reasons for this action are displayed as second- and third-level paragraphs. The following steps explain how to create a text slide with a multi-level bulleted list on the Outline tab.

To Create a Text Slide with a Multi-Level Bulleted List on the Outline Tab

1

- **Type** `Around School` **and then press the ENTER key.**
- **Click the Demote button on the Outlining toolbar to demote to the second level.**

The title for Slide 2, Around School, is displayed and the insertion point is in position to type the first bulleted paragraph (Figure 2-11). A bullet is displayed to the left of the insertion point.

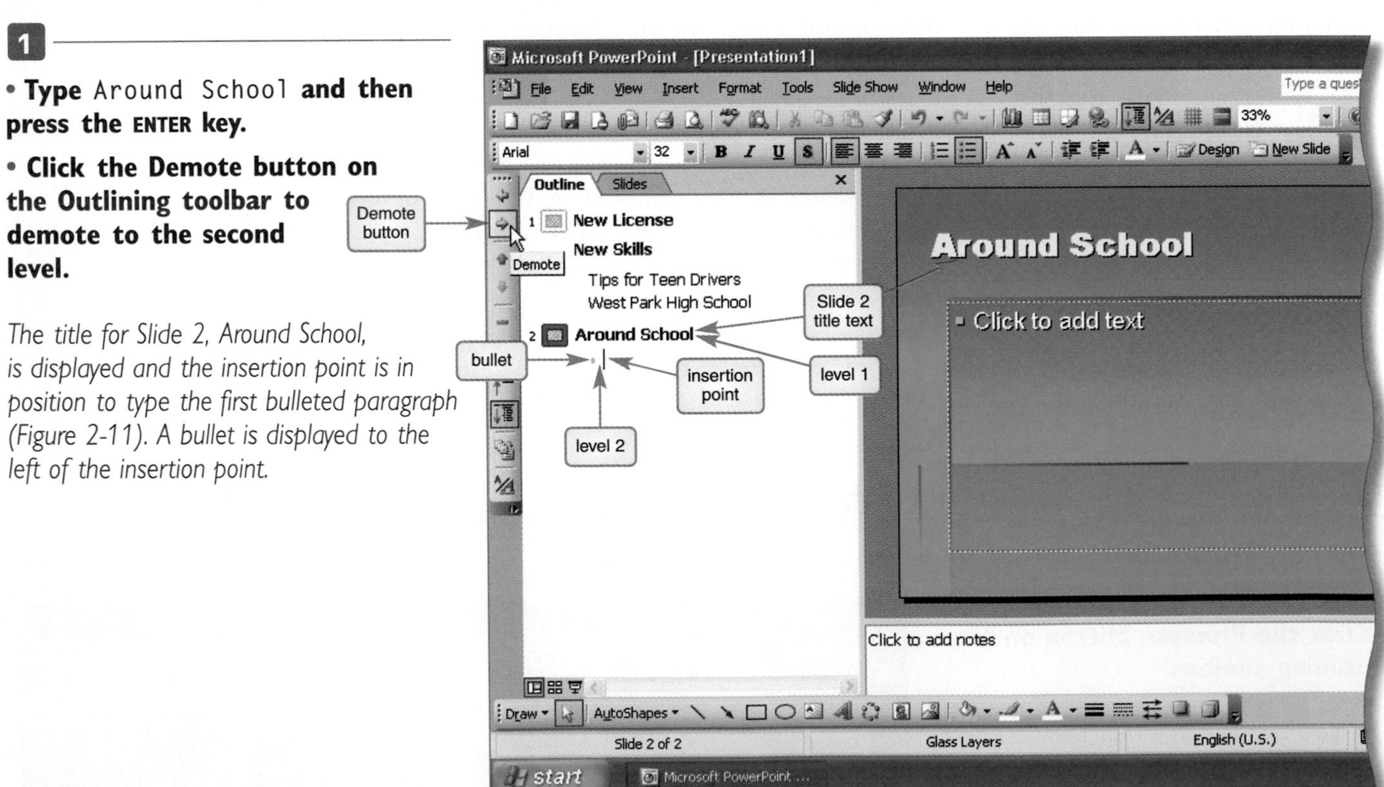

FIGURE 2-11

2

- **Type** `Arrive a few minutes early` **and then press the ENTER key.**
- **Click the Demote button on the Outlining toolbar to demote to the third level.**
- **Type** `Accidents occur when students rush` **and then press the ENTER key.**
- **Type** `Good parking spaces easier to find` **and then press the ENTER key.**

Slide 2 is displayed with three levels: the title, Around School, on the first level; the suggestion to arrive early on the second level; and two bulleted paragraphs and the insertion point on the third level (Figure 2-12).

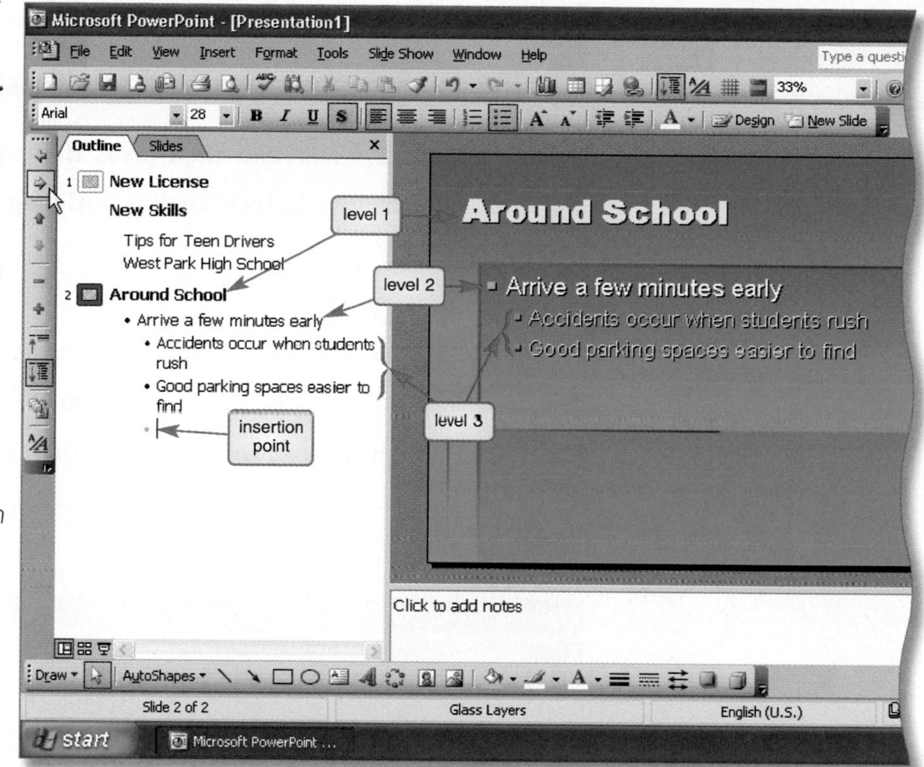
Microsoft PowerPoint - [Presentation1]
level 1
level 2
level 3
insertion point
New License
New Skills
Tips for Teen Drivers
West Park High School
Around School
Arrive a few minutes early
Accidents occur when students rush
Good parking spaces easier to find
Click to add notes
Slide 2 of 2
Glass Layers
English (U.S.)

FIGURE 2-12

Slide 2 is complete. The text on this slide abides by the 7 × 7 rule. As you learned in Project 1, this rule recommends that each line should have a maximum of seven words, and each slide should have a maximum of seven lines. All slides in this slide show use the 7 × 7 rule.

The remaining three slides in the presentation contain multi-level bulleted lists. Slide 3 provides information about driving around town, Slide 4 gives details about driving in bad weather, and Slide 5 lists other driving tips. It is easy and efficient to type the text for these slides on the Outline tab because you can view all the text you type in the outline in the tabs pane to check organization.

> *Q & A*
>
> **Q:** How many levels should a slide have?
>
> **A:** Three. Graphic designers recommend limiting the levels to three, although PowerPoint gives you five levels of body text to use on each slide. Details on all five levels may overwhelm audiences. If you find yourself needing more than three levels, consider combining content in one level or using two different slides.

Creating a Second Text Slide with a Multi-Level Bulleted List

The next slide, Slide 3, provides details about driving in the city. City driving requires a special set of skills, particularly when nearing intersections. The steps on the next page show how to create this slide.

To Create a Second Text Slide with a Multi-Level Bulleted List

1. **Click the Promote button on the Outlining toolbar two times so that Slide 3 is added after Slide 2.**
2. **Type** `Around Town` **and then press the ENTER key.**
3. **Click the Demote button on the Outlining toolbar to demote to the second level.**
4. **Type** `Most accidents take place in busy intersections` **and then press the ENTER key.**
5. **Click the Demote button to demote to the third level.**
6. **Type** `Wait for pedestrians` **and then press the ENTER key.**
7. **Type** `Listen for sirens` **and then press the ENTER key.**

The completed Slide 3 is displayed (Figure 2-13).

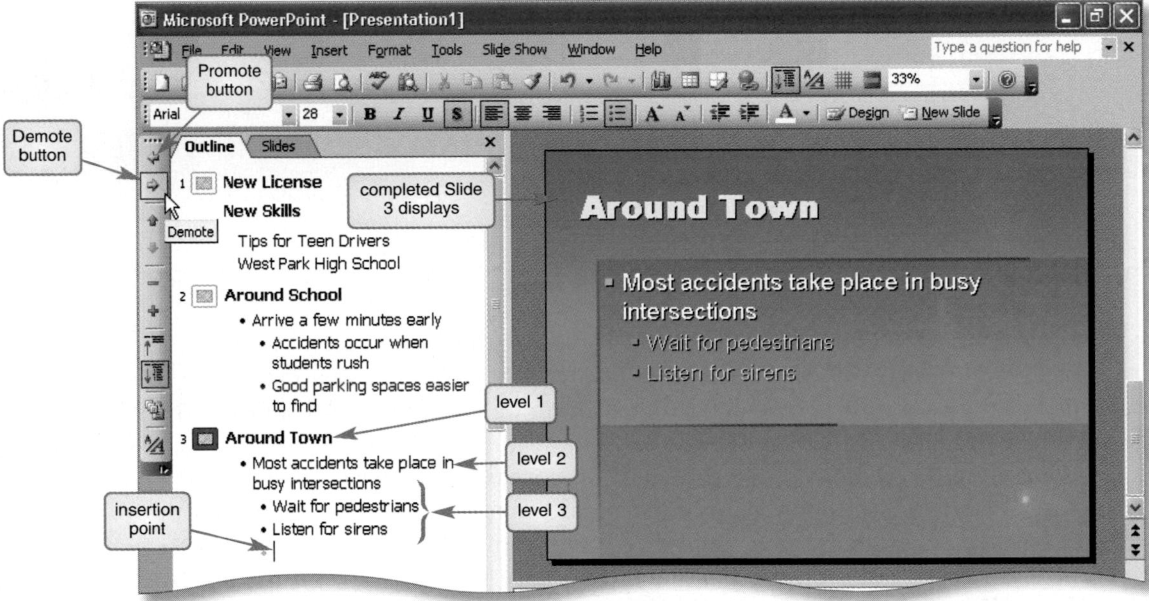
Microsoft PowerPoint - [Presentation1]
Promote button
Demote button
completed Slide 3 displays
New License
New Skills
Tips for Teen Drivers
West Park High School
Around School
Arrive a few minutes early
Accidents occur when students rush
Good parking spaces easier to find
Around Town
Most accidents take place in busy intersections
Wait for pedestrians
Listen for sirens
level 1
level 2
level 3
insertion point
Around Town
Most accidents take place in busy intersections
Wait for pedestrians
Listen for sirens

FIGURE 2-13

Creating a Third Text Slide with a Multi-Level Bulleted List

Slide 4 describes suggestions for driving in less-than-ideal conditions. The following steps show how to create this slide.

To Create a Third Text Slide with a Multi-Level Bulleted List

1. **Click the Promote button on the Outlining toolbar two times so that Slide 4 is added after Slide 3.**
2. **Type** `Inclement Weather` **and then press the ENTER key.**
3. **Click the Demote button on the Outlining toolbar to demote to the second level.**

4 **Type** `Turn on headlights and windshield wipers` **and then press the ENTER key.**

5 **Click the Demote button to demote to the third level.**

6 **Type** `Helps you see what is ahead` **and then press the ENTER key.**

7 **Type** `Helps other drivers see you` **and then press the ENTER key.**

8 **Click the Promote button to promote to the second level.**

9 **Type** `Exercise extra caution on slick roads` **and then press the ENTER key.**

10 **Click the Demote button to demote to the third level.**

11 **Type** `Test brakes to determine stopping distance` **and then press the ENTER key.**

12 **Type** `Double space between car ahead of you` **and then press the ENTER key.**

The completed Slide 4 is displayed (Figure 2-14).

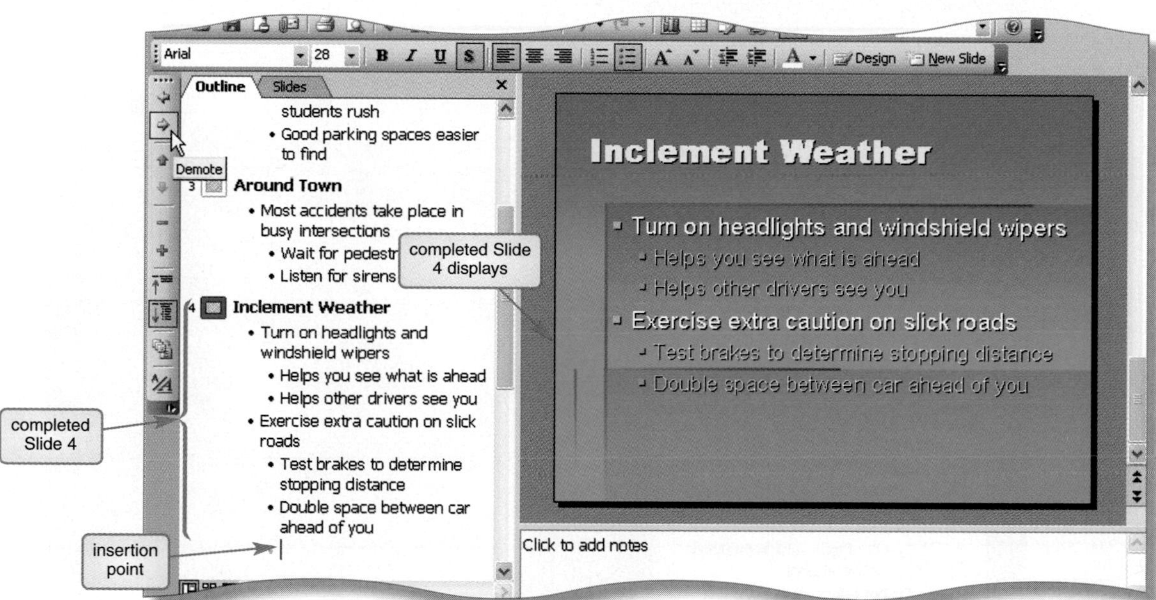

FIGURE 2-14

Creating a Closing Slide on the Outline Tab

The last slide in a presentation is the closing slide. A **closing slide** gracefully ends a presentation. Often used during a question and answer session, the closing slide usually remains on the screen to reinforce the message delivered during the presentation. Professional speakers design the closing slide with one or more of these methods:

1. List important information. Tell the audience what to do next.
2. Provide a memorable illustration or example to make a point.
3. Appeal to emotions. Remind the audience to take action or accept responsibility.
4. Summarize the main point of the presentation.
5. Cite a quotation that directly relates to the main point of the presentation. This technique is most effective if the presentation started with a quotation.

The last text slide you create in Project 2 provides additional suggestions for driving safely. The steps on the next page show how to create this closing slide.

Q & A

Q: What is a good starting point when developing a presentation?

A: Designing your conclusion is a good way to start creating a presentation. By developing the conclusion first, you focus on the objectives of the presentation and then design the rest of the slides to reach this ending.

To Create a Closing Slide on the Outline Tab

1. **Click the Promote button on the Outlining toolbar two times to add Slide 5 after Slide 4. Type** `Other Considerations` **and then press the ENTER key.**
2. **Click the Demote button on the Outlining toolbar to demote to the second level. Type** `Avoid driving when fatigued` **and then press the ENTER key.**
3. **Type** `Allow aggressive drivers to pass you` **and then press the ENTER key.**
4. **Type** `Drugs and alcohol impair ability to drive` **and then press the ENTER key.**
5. **Click the Demote button to demote to the third level. Type** `1/3 of teen vehicle fatalities involve alcohol` **and then press the ENTER key.**
6. **Click the Promote button to promote to the second level. Type** `Do not talk on cell phone` **and then press the ENTER key.**
7. **Click the Demote button. Type** `Four times more likely to have accident` **but do not press the ENTER key.**

The completed Slide 5 is displayed (Figure 2-15).

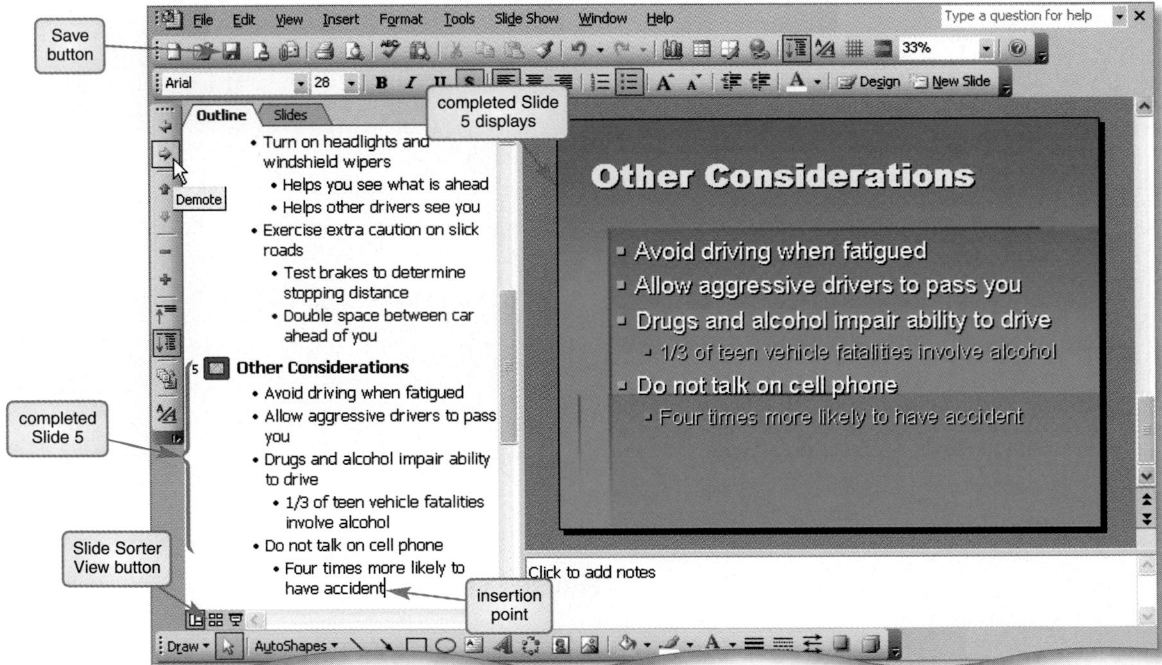

FIGURE 2-15

The outline now is complete, and you should save the presentation. The next section explains how to save the presentation.

Saving a Presentation

Recall from Project 1 that it is wise to save your presentation frequently. With all the text for your presentation created, save the presentation using the following steps.

To Save a Presentation

1 **Connect a USB flash drive to one of the computer's USB ports and then click the Save button on the Standard toolbar.**

2 **Type** `Driving Tips` **in the File name text box. Do not press the ENTER key after typing the file name. Click the Save in box arrow.**

3 **Click UDISK (E:) in the Save in list.**

4 **Click the Save button in the Save As dialog box.**

The presentation is saved with the file name, Driving Tips, on the USB flash drive connected to one of the computer's USB ports. PowerPoint uses the first text line in a presentation as the default file name. The file name is displayed on the title bar.

Reviewing a Presentation in Slide Sorter View

In Project 1, you displayed slides in slide show view to evaluate the presentation. Slide show view, however, restricts your evaluation to one slide at a time. The Outline tab is best for quickly reviewing all the text for a presentation. Recall from Project 1 that slide sorter view allows you to look at several slides at one time, which is why it is the best view to use to evaluate a presentation for content, organization, and overall appearance. The following step shows how to change from the Outline tab to slide sorter view.

To Change the View to Slide Sorter View

1

• **Click the Slide Sorter View button at the lower left of the PowerPoint window.**

PowerPoint displays the presentation in slide sorter view (Figure 2-16). Slide 5 is selected because it was the current slide on the Outline tab. The Slide Sorter View button is selected.

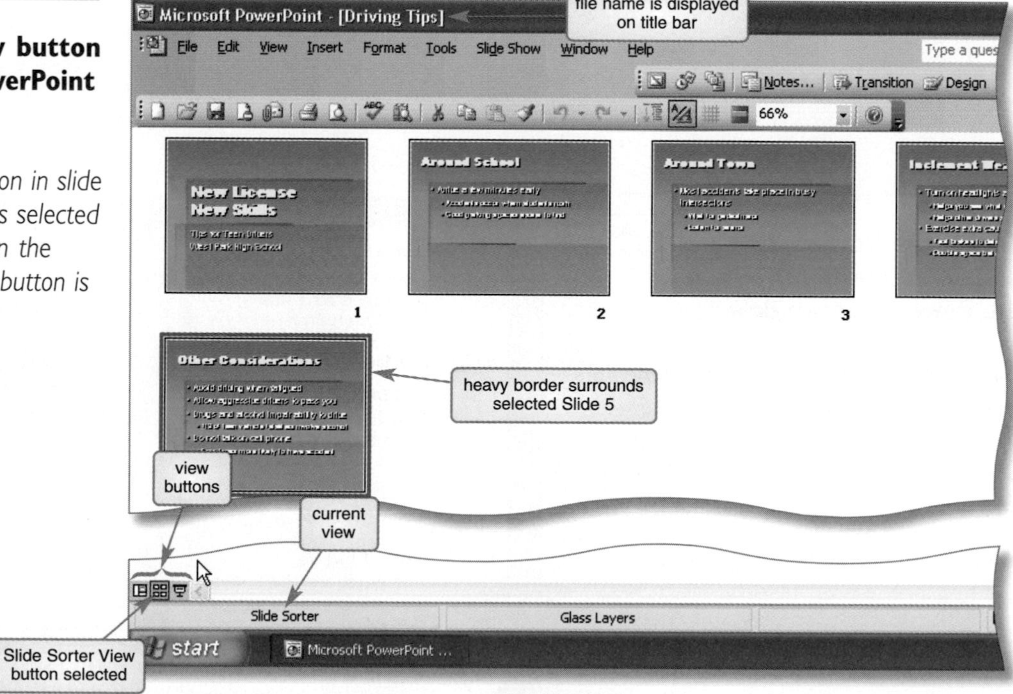

FIGURE 2-16

Skill Builder 2-2

To practice the following tasks, visit scsite.com/off2003sch/skill, locate PowerPoint Project 2, and then click Skill Builder 2-2.

❑ Add a slide on the Outline tab
❑ Create a closing slide
❑ Save a presentation

You can review the five slides in this presentation all in one window. Notice the slides have a significant amount of space and look plain. These observations indicate a need to add visual interest to the slides by using clips. The next several sections explain how to improve the presentation by changing slide layouts and adding clip art.

You can make changes to text in normal view and on the Outline tab. It is best, however, to change the view to normal view when altering the slide layouts so you can see the results of your changes. The following steps show how to change the view from slide sorter view to normal view.

To Change the View to Normal View

1

• **Click the Slide 2 slide thumbnail.**

Slide 2 is selected, as indicated by the thick blue border around that slide (Figure 2-17).

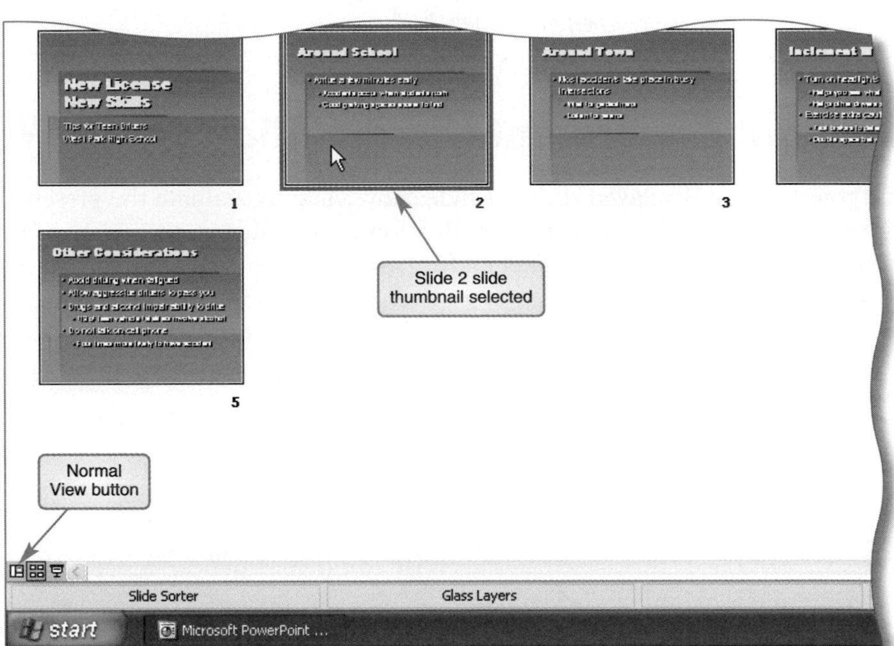

FIGURE 2-17

2

• **Click the Normal View button at the lower left of the PowerPoint window.**

The Normal View button is selected at the lower left of the PowerPoint window. The Slide 2 slide icon is selected in the tabs pane, and Slide 2 is displayed in the slide pane (Figure 2-18).

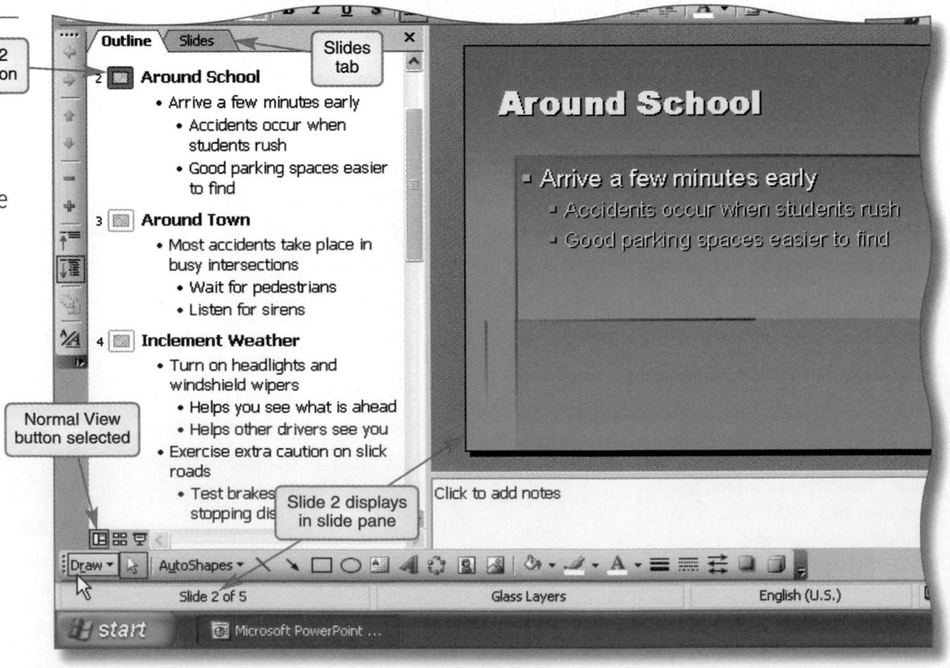

FIGURE 2-18

3

• **Click the Slides tab in the tabs pane.**

The tabs pane reduces in size. Slide thumbnails of the five slides are displayed (Figure 2-19).

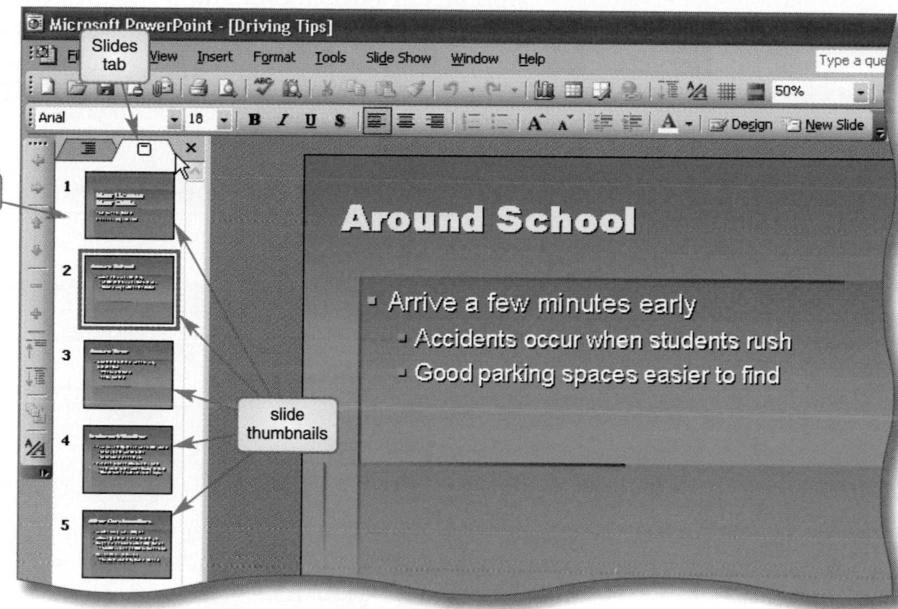
Microsoft PowerPoint - [Driving Tips]
Slides tab
tabs pane
Around School
Arrive a few minutes early
Accidents occur when students rush
Good parking spaces easier to find
slide thumbnails

FIGURE 2-19

Switching between slide sorter view and normal view helps you review your presentation and assess whether the slides have an attractive design and adequate content.

Changing Slide Layout

When you developed this presentation, PowerPoint applied the Title Slide layout for Slide 1 and the Title and Text layout for the other four slides in the presentation. These layouts are the default styles. A **layout** specifies the arrangement of placeholders on a slide. These placeholders are arranged in various configurations and can contain text, such as the slide title or a bulleted list, or they can contain content, such as clips, pictures, charts, tables, and shapes. The placement of the text, in relationship to content, depends on the slide layout. The content placeholders may be to the right or left of the text, above the text, or below the text. You can specify a particular slide layout when you add a new slide to a presentation or after you have created the slide.

Using the **Slide Layout task pane**, you can choose a slide layout. The layouts in this task pane are arranged in four areas: Text Layouts, Content Layouts, Text and Content Layouts, and Other Layouts. The two layouts you have used in this project — Title Slide and Title and Text — are included in the Text Layouts area, along with the Title Only and Title and 2-Column Text layouts. The Content Layouts area contains a blank slide and a variety of placeholder groupings for charts, tables, clip art, pictures, diagrams, and media clips. The Text and Content Layouts have placeholders for a title, a bulleted list, and content. The Other Layouts area has layouts with placeholders for a title and one object, such as clip art, charts, media clips, tables, organization charts, and charts.

When you change the layout of a slide, PowerPoint retains the text and objects and repositions them into the appropriate placeholders. Using slide layouts eliminates the need to resize objects and the font size because PowerPoint automatically sizes the objects and text to fit the placeholders. If the objects are in **landscape orientation**, meaning their width is greater than their height, PowerPoint sizes them to the width of the placeholders. If the objects are in **portrait orientation**, meaning their height is greater than their width, PowerPoint sizes them to the height of the placeholders.

Q & A

Q: Why is slide content indented?

A: Indentation identifies levels of importance. The more important the item, the closer it should be displayed to the left edge of the slide. Subordinate items must support the main topic under which they are placed. This means they must be less important in meaning while being related logically.

Adding clips to Slides 2 and 3 requires two steps. First, change the slide layout to Title, Text, and Content or to Title, 2 Content and Text. Then, insert clip art into the content placeholders. The following steps show how to change the slide layout on Slide 2 from Title and Text to Title, Text, and Content.

To Change the Slide Layout to Title, Text, and Content

1

- **Click Format on the menu bar (Figure 2-20).**

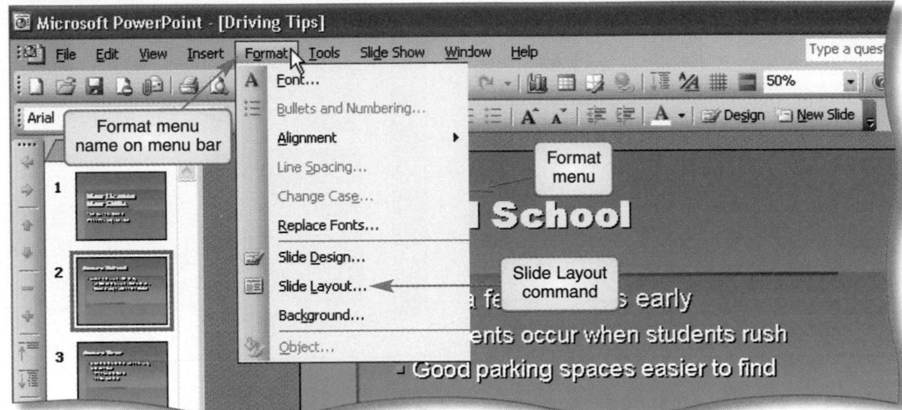

FIGURE 2-20

2

- **Click Slide Layout.**
- **Click the down scroll arrow in the Apply slide layout area and scroll down until the Text and Content Layouts area displays.**
- **Point to the Title, Text, and Content layout in the Text and Content Layouts area.**

The Slide Layout task pane is displayed (Figure 2-21). The Title, Text, and Content layout is selected, as indicated by the blue box around the template, the ScreenTip, and the arrow button on the right side.

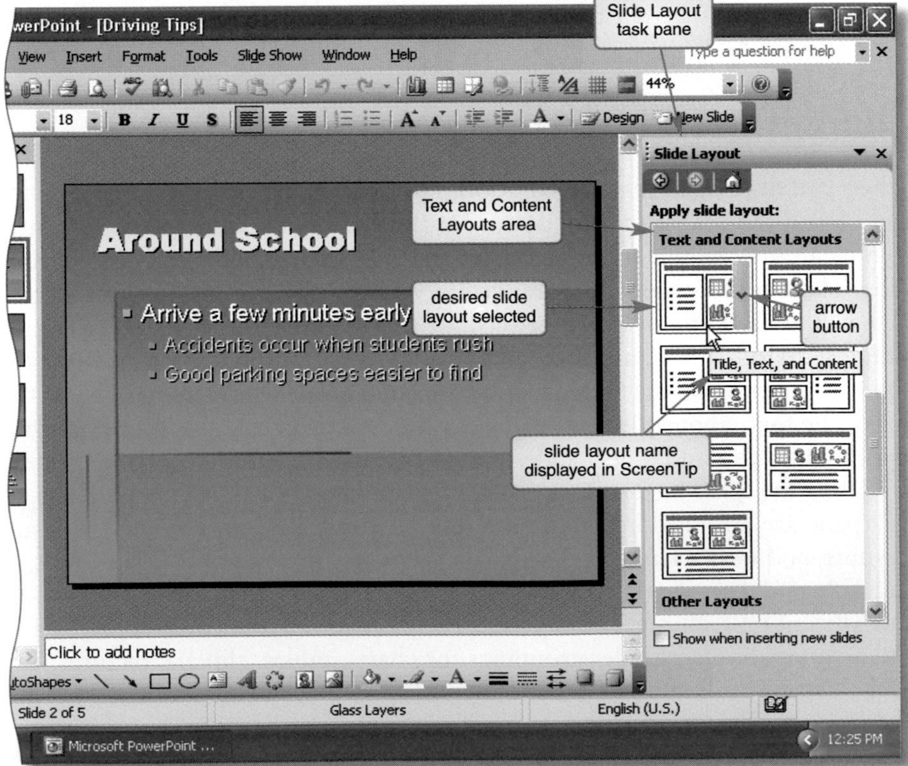

FIGURE 2-21

3

- **Click Title, Text, and Content.**

The layout is applied to Slide 2 (Figure 2-22). PowerPoint moves the text placeholder containing the bulleted list to the left side of the slide and automatically resizes the text. The content placeholder on the right side of the slide has the message, Click icon to add content.

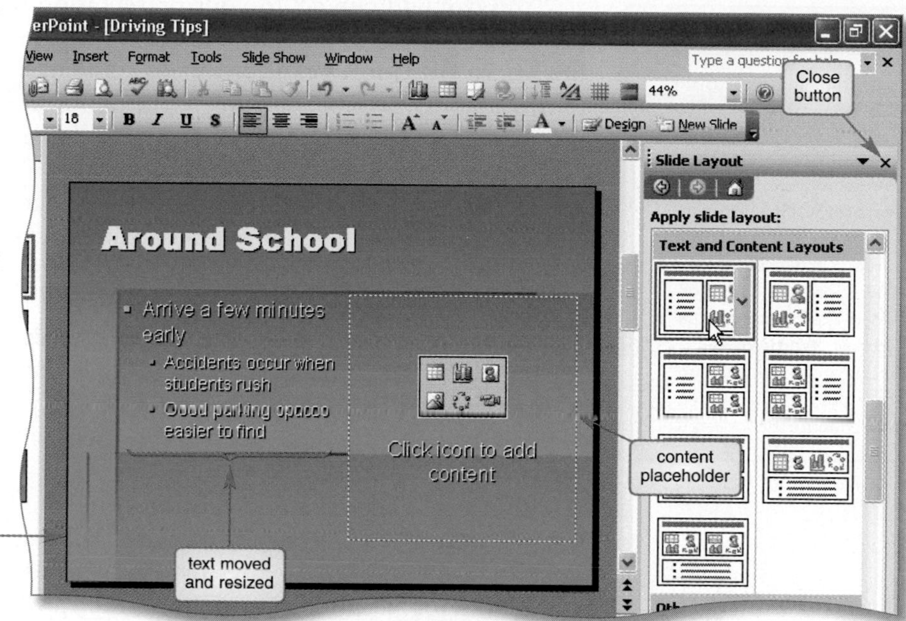

FIGURE 2-22

4

- **Click the Close button in the Slide Layout task pane.**

Slide 2 is displayed in normal view with the new slide layout applied (Figure 2-23).

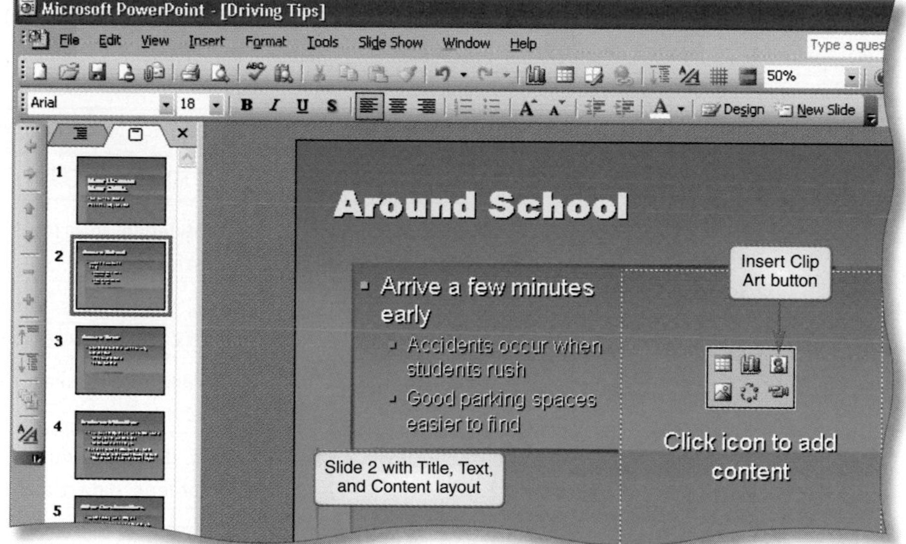

FIGURE 2-23

PowerPoint reduced the second-level text in the Slide 2 text placeholder from a font size of 28 point to 24 point so all the words fit into the placeholder.

Adding Clip Art to a Slide

Clip art helps the visual appeal of the Driving Tips slide show and offers a quick way to add professional-looking graphic images to a presentation without creating the images yourself. This art is contained in the **Microsoft Clip Organizer**, a collection of drawings, photographs, sounds, videos, and other media files shared with Microsoft Office applications.

Q & A

Q: Can I add clips to the Clip Organizer?

A: Yes. You can add media files and objects created in Microsoft Office programs. The media files are stored in a new subcollection in the My Collections clip collection folder. The objects can be pictures, WordArt, and AutoShapes, and you can store them in any desired collection folder.

You can add clip art to your presentation in two ways. One way is by selecting one of the slide layouts that includes a content placeholder with instructions to open the Microsoft Clip Organizer to add content. You will add art to Slides 2 and 3 in this manner. Double-clicking a button in the content placeholder activates the instructions to display the Select Picture dialog box, which allows you to enter keywords to search for clips.

The second method is by clicking the Insert Clip Art button on the Drawing toolbar to display the Clip Art task pane. The **Clip Art task pane** allows you to search for clips by using descriptive keywords, file names, media file formats, and clip collections. Specific file formats could be for clip art, photographs, movies, and sounds. Clips are organized in hierarchical **clip collections**, which combine topic-related clips into categories, such as Academic, Business, and Technology. You also can create your own collections for frequently used clips. You will insert clip art into Slides 4 and 5 using this process. You then will arrange the clips on the slides without using a placeholder for content.

Table 2-2 shows four categories from the Office Collections in the Microsoft Clip Organizer and keywords of various clip art files in those categories. Clip art images have one or more keywords associated with various entities, activities, labels, and emotions. In most instances, the keywords give the name of the clip and related categories. For example, an image of a cow in the Animals category has the keywords animals, cattle, cows, dairies, farms, and Holsteins. You can enter these keywords in the Search text box to find clips when you know one of the words associated with the image. Otherwise, you may find it necessary to scroll through several categories to find an appropriate clip.

Table 2-2 Microsoft Clip Organizer Category and Keyword Examples

CATEGORY	CLIP ART KEYWORDS
Academic	Books, knowledge, information, schools, school buses, apple for the teacher, professors
Business	Computers, inspirations, ideas, currencies, board meetings, conferences, teamwork, profits
Nature	Lakes, flowers, plants, seasons, wildlife, weather, trees, sunshine, rivers, leaves
Technology	Computers, diskettes, microchips, cellular telephones, e-commerce, office equipment, data exchanges

Depending on the installation of the Microsoft Clip Organizer on your computer, you may not have the clip art used in this project. Contact your instructor if you are missing clips used in the following steps. If you have an open connection to the Internet, clips from the Microsoft Web site will display automatically as the result of your search results.

Inserting Clip Art into a Content Placeholder

With the Title, Text, and Content layout applied to Slide 2, you insert clip art into the content placeholder. The following steps show how to insert clip art of a cornucopia into the content placeholder on Slide 2.

To Insert Clip Art into a Content Placeholder

1

- **Point to the Insert Clip Art button in the content placeholder.**

The Insert Clip Art button is selected (Figure 2-24). A ScreenTip describes its function.

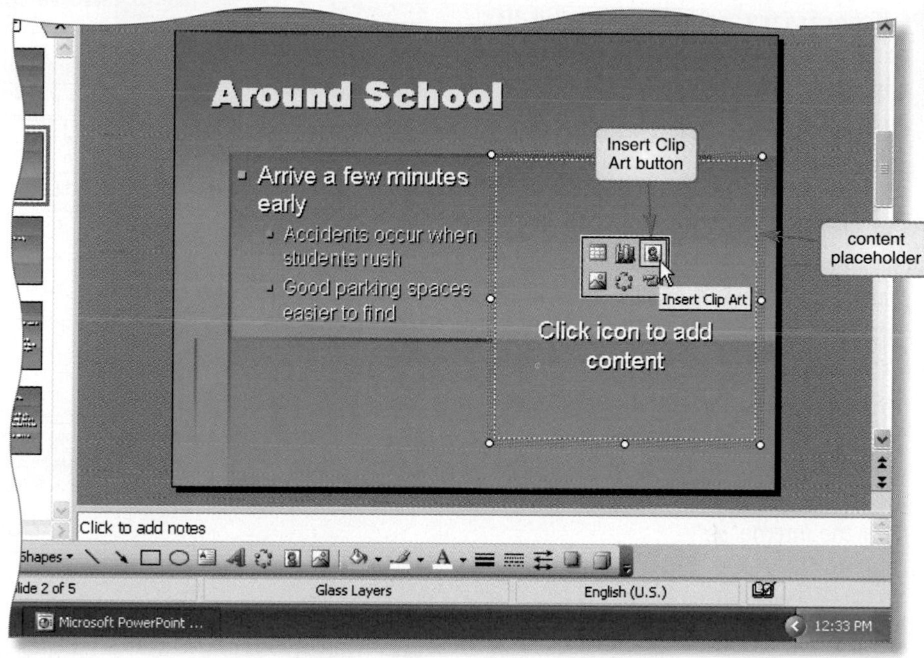

FIGURE 2-24

2

- **Click the Insert Clip Art button.**
- **Type** `parking lot` **in the Search text text box.**

The Select Picture dialog box is displayed (Figure 2-25). The clips displaying on your computer may vary.

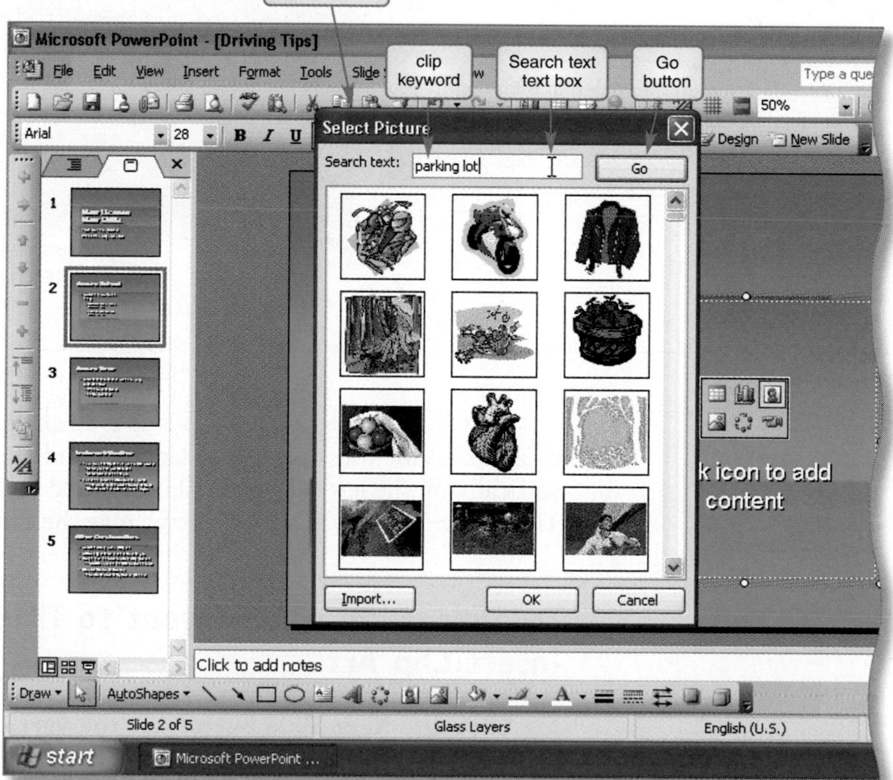

FIGURE 2-25

3

- **Click the Go button.**
- **If necessary, scroll down the list to display the cars in a parking lot clip shown in Figure 2-26.**
- **If necessary, click the clip to select it.**

The Microsoft Clip Organizer searches for and displays all pictures having the keyword, parking lot (Figure 2-26). The desired clip of cars in a parking lot is displayed with a blue box around it. Your clips may be different depending on the clips installed on your computer and if you have an open connection to the Internet, in which case you may need to obtain an appropriate clip from the Internet.

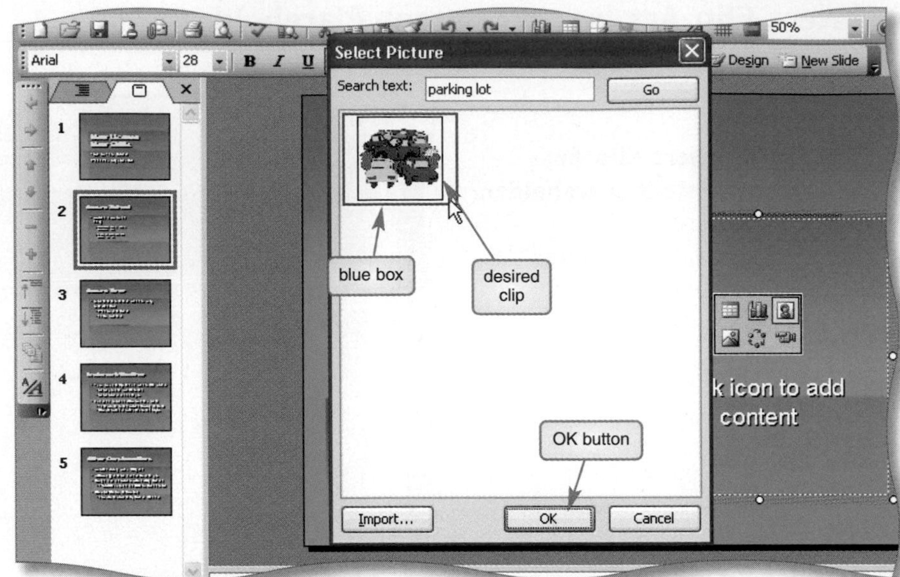

FIGURE 2-26

4

- **Click the OK button.**
- **If the Picture toolbar is displayed, click the Close button on the Picture toolbar.**

The selected clip is inserted into the top content placeholder on Slide 2 (Figure 2-27). PowerPoint sizes the clip automatically to fit the placeholder.

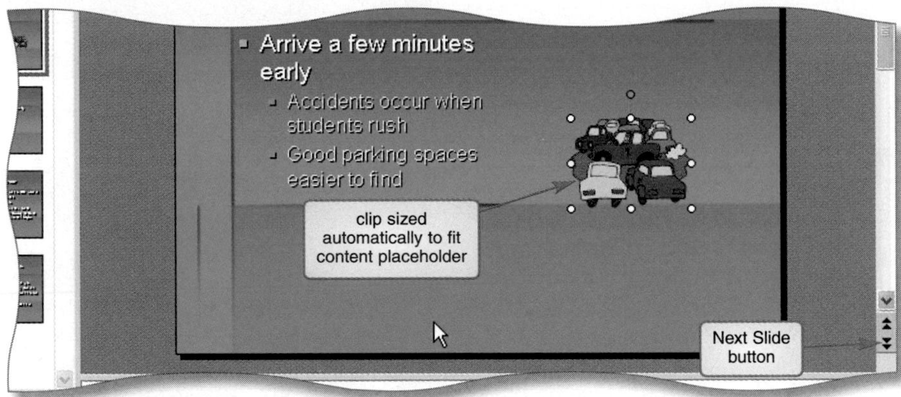

FIGURE 2-27

Slide 2 is complete. The next step is to change the Slide 3 layout and then add two clips. This slide uses the Title, 2 Content and Text slide layout so the two clips display vertically on the left side of the slide and the bulleted list is displayed on the right side. The following steps show how to change the slide layout and then add clip art to Slide 3.

To Change the Slide Layout to Title, 2 Content and Text and Insert Clip Art

1. **Click the Next Slide button on the vertical scroll bar to display Slide 3.**
2. **Click Format on the menu bar and then click Slide Layout.**
3. **Scroll to display the Title, 2 Content and Text slide layout located in the Text and Content Layouts area of the Slide Layout task pane.**
4. **Click the Title, 2 Content and Text slide layout and then click the Close button in the Slide Layout task pane.**

5 **Click the Insert Clip Art button in the top content placeholder. Type** `driving` **in the Search text text box and then click the Go button.**

6 **If necessary, scroll down the list to display the desired clip of a woman driving and then click the clip to select it. Click the OK button.**

The selected clip is inserted into the content placeholder on Slide 3 (Figure 2-28). The slide has the Title, 2 Content and Text slide layout. If the Picture toolbar is displayed, close it by clicking the Close button in the upper-right corner of the toolbar.

FIGURE 2-28

Inserting a Second Clip into a Slide

Another clip on Slide 3 is required to fill the bottom content placeholder. This clip should be the image of a pedestrian road sign. The following steps show how to insert the sign clip into the bottom placeholder on Slide 3.

To Insert a Second Clip into a Slide

1 **Click the Insert Clip Art button in the bottom content placeholder.**

2 **Type** `pedestrian` **in the Search text text box and then click the Go button.**

3 **If necessary, scroll down the list to display the desired clip of a yellow pedestrian road sign, click the clip to select it, and then click the OK button.**

The selected clip is inserted into the bottom content placeholder on Slide 3 (Figure 2-29). PowerPoint automatically sizes the clip to fit the placeholder.

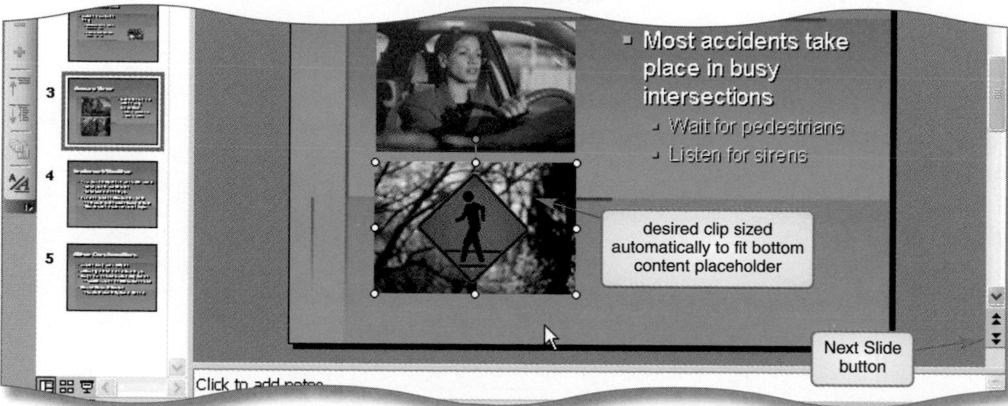

FIGURE 2-29

Skill Builder 2-3

To practice the following tasks, visit scsite.com/off2003sch/skill, locate PowerPoint Project 2, and then click Skill Builder 2-3.
- ❑ Review a presentation in slide sorter view
- ❑ Change the slide layout
- ❑ Insert clip art into a content placeholder

Slide 3 is complete. Your next step is to add a clip to Slide 4 without changing the slide layout.

Inserting Clip Art into a Slide without a Content Placeholder

PowerPoint does not require you to use a content placeholder to add clips to a slide. You can insert clips on any slide regardless of its slide layout. On Slides 2 and 3, you added clips that enhanced the message in the text. Recall that the slide layout on Slide 4 is Title and Text. Because this layout does not contain a content placeholder, you can use the Insert Clip Art button on the Drawing toolbar to start the Microsoft Clip Organizer. The clip for which you are searching has a blue storm cloud. A few of its keywords are clouds, rain clouds, raining, and rainy. The following steps show how to insert this clip into a slide that does not have a content placeholder.

To Insert Clip Art into a Slide without a Content Placeholder

1

- **Click the Next Slide button on the vertical scroll bar to display Slide 4.**
- **Click Tools on the menu bar and then click AutoCorrect Options.**
- **If necessary, when the AutoCorrect dialog box displays, click the AutoFormat As You Type tab.**
- **Click Automatic layout for inserted objects in the Apply as you work area if a check mark does not display.**
- **Click the OK button.**

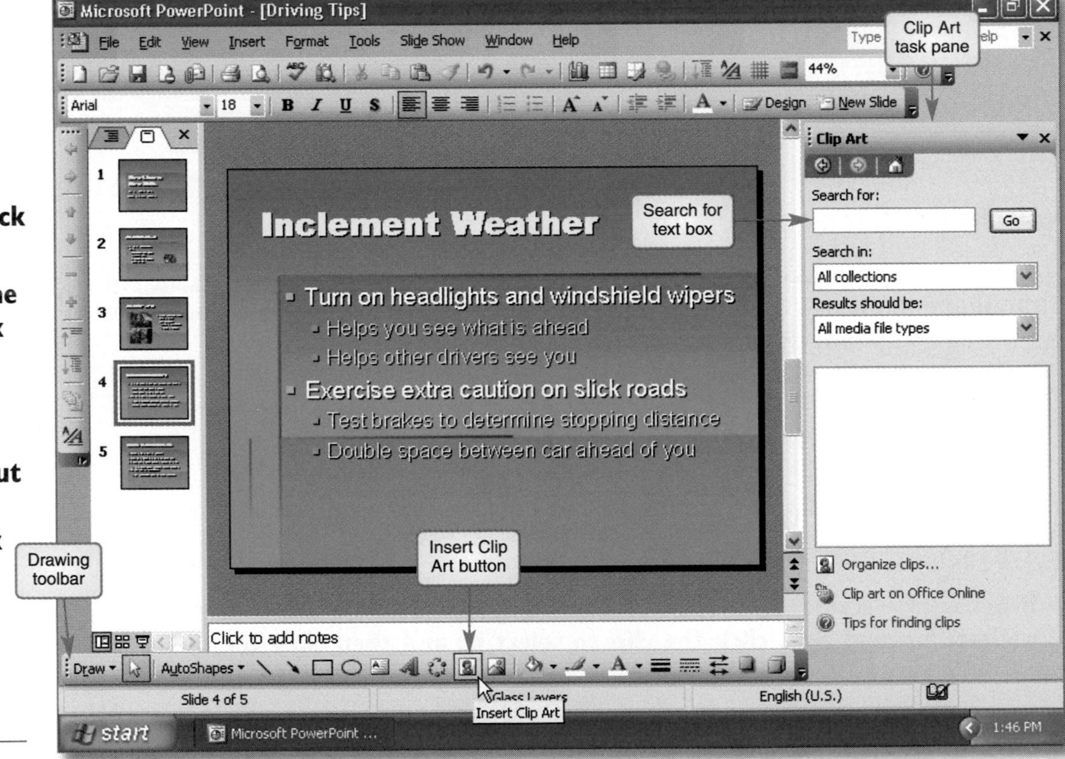

FIGURE 2-30

2

- **Click the Insert Clip Art button on the Drawing toolbar.**
- **If the Add Clips to Organizer dialog box displays asking if you want to catalog media files, click the Don't show this message again button, or, if you want to catalog later, click the Later button.**

The Clip Art task pane is displayed (Figure 2-30).

3

- **Click the Search for text box.**
- **If the Search for text box contains text, delete the letters.**
- **Type** `cloud` **and then press the ENTER key.**
- **If necessary, scroll to display the desired clip of a blue storm cloud.**
- **Point to this image.**

The clip of a blue storm cloud is displayed with any other clips sharing the keyword (Figure 2-31). Your clips may be different. The clip's keywords, size in pixels (245 x 258), file size (6 KB), and file type (WMF) are displayed.

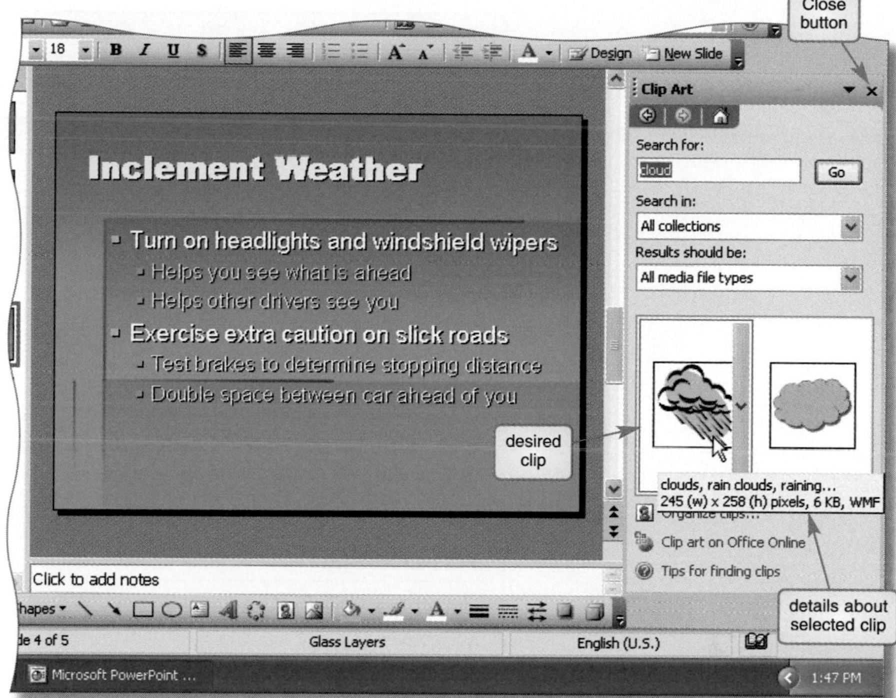

FIGURE 2-31

4

- **Click the desired clip.**
- **Click the Close button on the Clip Art task pane title bar.**

PowerPoint inserts the clip into Slide 4 (Figure 2-32). The slide layout changes automatically to Title, Text, and Content. The Automatic Layout Options button is displayed. If your slide layout does not change, then continue this project using the Moving Clip Art section on page PPT 108.

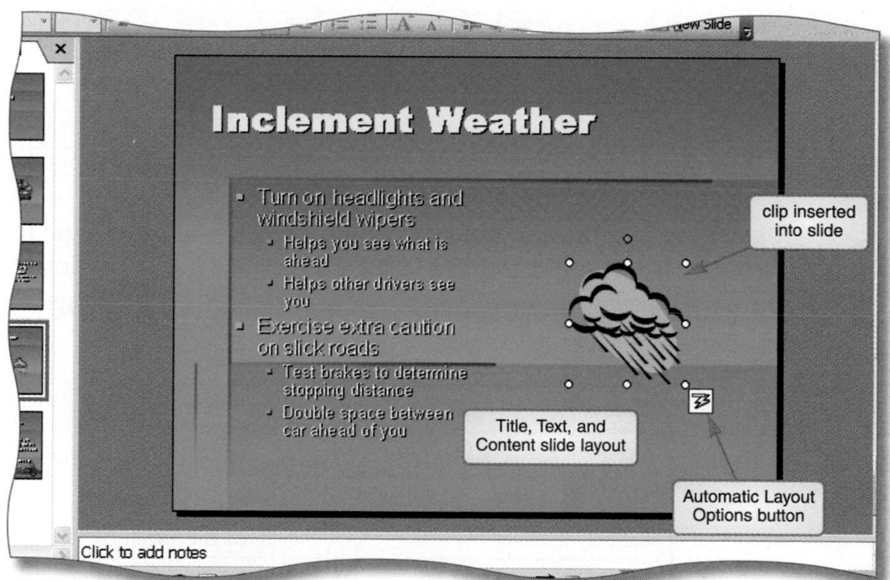

FIGURE 2-32

In addition to clip art, you can insert pictures into a presentation. These may include scanned photographs, line art, and artwork from compact discs. To insert a picture into a presentation, the picture must be saved in a format that PowerPoint can recognize. Table 2-3 (on the next page) identifies some of the formats PowerPoint recognizes.

You can import files saved with the .emf, .gif, .jpg, .png, .bmp, .rle, .dib, and .wmf formats directly into PowerPoint presentations. All other file formats require separate filters that are shipped with the PowerPoint installation software and must be installed. You can download additional filters from the Microsoft Office Online Web site.

Table 2-3 Primary File Formats PowerPoint Recognizes

FORMAT	FILE EXTENSION
Computer Graphics Metafile	.cgm
CorelDRAW	.cdr, .cdt, .cmx, and .pat
Encapsulated PostScript	.eps
Enhanced Metafile	.emf
FlashPix	.fpx
Graphics Interchange Format	.gif
Hanako	.jsh, .jah, and .jbh
Joint Photographic Experts Group (JPEG)	.jpg
Kodak PhotoCD	.pcd
Macintosh PICT	.pct
PC Paintbrush	.pcx
Portable Network Graphics	.png
Tagged Image File Format	.tif
Windows Bitmap	.bmp, .rle, .dib
Microsoft Windows Metafile	.wmf
WordPerfect Graphics	.wpg

Smart Tags

A **smart tag** is a button that PowerPoint automatically displays on the screen when performing a certain action. The Automatic Layout Options button in Figure 2-32 on the previous page is a smart tag. In addition to the Automatic Layout Options button, PowerPoint provides three other smart tags. Table 2-4 summarizes the smart tags available in PowerPoint.

Table 2-4 Smart Tags in PowerPoint

SMART TAG BUTTON	MENU FUNCTION
AutoCorrect Options	Undoes an automatic correction, stops future automatic corrections of this type, or displays the AutoCorrect Options dialog box.
Paste Options	Specifies how moved or pasted items should display (e.g., with original formatting, without formatting, or with different formatting.)
AutoFit Options	Undoes automatic text resizing to fit the current placeholder or changes single-column layouts to two-column layouts, inserts a new slide, or splits the text between two slides.
Automatic Layout Options	Adjusts the slide layout to accommodate an inserted object.

Clicking a smart tag button shows a menu that contains commands relative to the action performed at the location of the smart tag. For example, if you want PowerPoint to undo the layout change when you add a clip to a slide, click the Automatic Layout Options button to display the Smart Tag Actions menu, and then click Undo Automatic Layout on the Smart Tag Actions menu to display the initial layout.

Using the Automatic Layout Options Button to Undo a Layout Change

The Title and Text layout used in Slide 4 did not provide a content placeholder for the clip you inserted, so PowerPoint automatically changed the layout to Title, Text, and Content. If your slide layout did not change, then disregard this section and continue the project on the next page with the Moving Clip Art section. Because the text now violates the 7 × 7 rule with this layout and because you want to place the clip in a location other than the areas specified, you should change the layout to the Title and Text layout.

The Automatic Layout Options button is displayed because PowerPoint changed the layout automatically. If you move your mouse pointer near the changed object or text, the Automatic Layout Options button is displayed as an arrow, indicating that a list of options is available that allow you to undo the new layout, stop the automatic layout of inserted objects, or alter the AutoCorrect Options settings. The following steps show how to undo the layout change.

To Use the Automatic Layout Options Button to Undo a Layout Change

1

- **If your slide layout automatically changed to Title, Text, and Content, click the Automatic Layout Options button.**
- **Point to Undo Automatic Layout.**

The Automatic Layout Options list is displayed (Figure 2-33). Clicking Undo Automatic Layout will reverse the layout change.

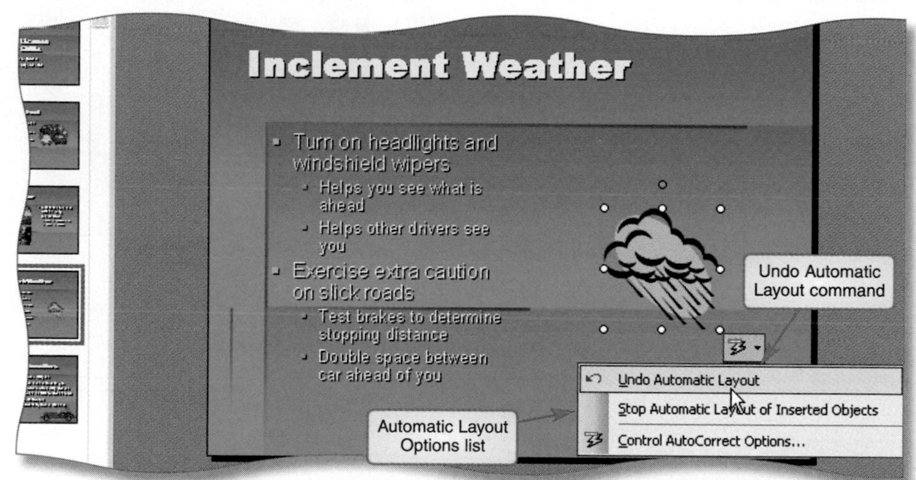

FIGURE 2-33

2

- **Click Undo Automatic Layout.**

The layout reverts to Title and Text (Figure 2-34).

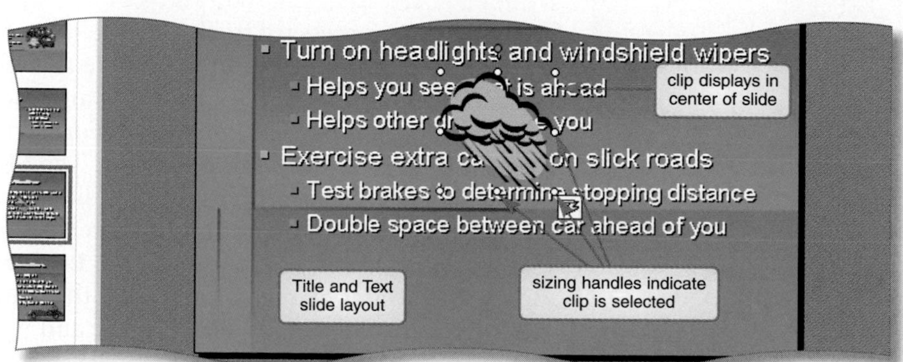

FIGURE 2-34

The desired clip is displayed in the center of Slide 4, which has the original Title and Text slide layout. The next step is to move the clip to the top-right corner of the slide.

Moving Clip Art

After you insert a clip into a slide, you may want to reposition it. The cloud clip on Slide 4 overlays the bulleted list. You want to move the clip away from the text to the upper-right corner of the slide. The following step shows how to move the clip to the upper-right corner of the slide.

To Move Clip Art

1

- **With the clip selected, point to the clip and then press and hold down the mouse button.**
- **Drag the clip to the upper-right corner of the slide.**
- **Release the mouse button.**

When you drag a clip, a dotted box is displayed. The dotted box indicates the clip's new position. When you release the left mouse button, the clip of the cloud is displayed in the new location and the dotted line disappears (Figure 2-35). Sizing handles display at the corners and along its edges.

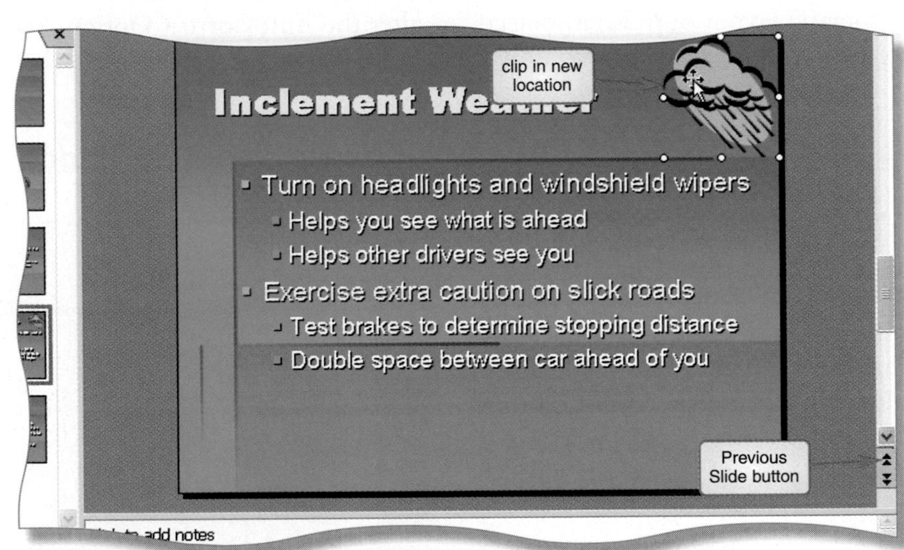

FIGURE 2-35

Q & A

Q: How can I use clips legally?

A: Be certain you have the legal right to use a desired clip in your presentation. Read the copyright notices that accompany the clip and are posted on the Web site. The owners of these images and files often ask you to give them credit for using their work, which may be satisfied by stating where you obtained the images. For more information on clip usage, visit the Office 2003 Q&A Web page (`scsite.com/off2003sch/qa`), locate PowerPoint Project 2, and click Legal.

Changing the Size of Clip Art

Sometimes it is necessary to change the size of clip art. For example, on Slide 2 much space appears around the clip. To make this object fit onto the slide, you increase its size. To change the size of a clip by an exact percentage, use the Format Picture command on the shortcut menu. The Format Picture dialog box contains six tabbed sheets with several formatting options. The **Size sheet** contains options for changing a clip's size. You either enter the exact height and width in the Size and rotate area, or enter the height and width as a percentage of the original clip in the Scale area. When a check mark is displayed in the **Lock aspect ratio check box**, the height and width settings change to maintain the original aspect ratio. **Aspect ratio** is the relationship between an object's height and width. For example, a 3-by-5-inch object scaled to 50 percent would become a 1½-by-2½-inch object. The following steps describe how to increase the size of the clip using the Format Picture dialog box.

To Change the Size of Clip Art

1

- **Click the Previous Slide button on the vertical scroll bar two times to display Slide 2.**
- **Right-click the clip.**

Sizing handles display at the clip's corners and along its edges (Figure 2-36).

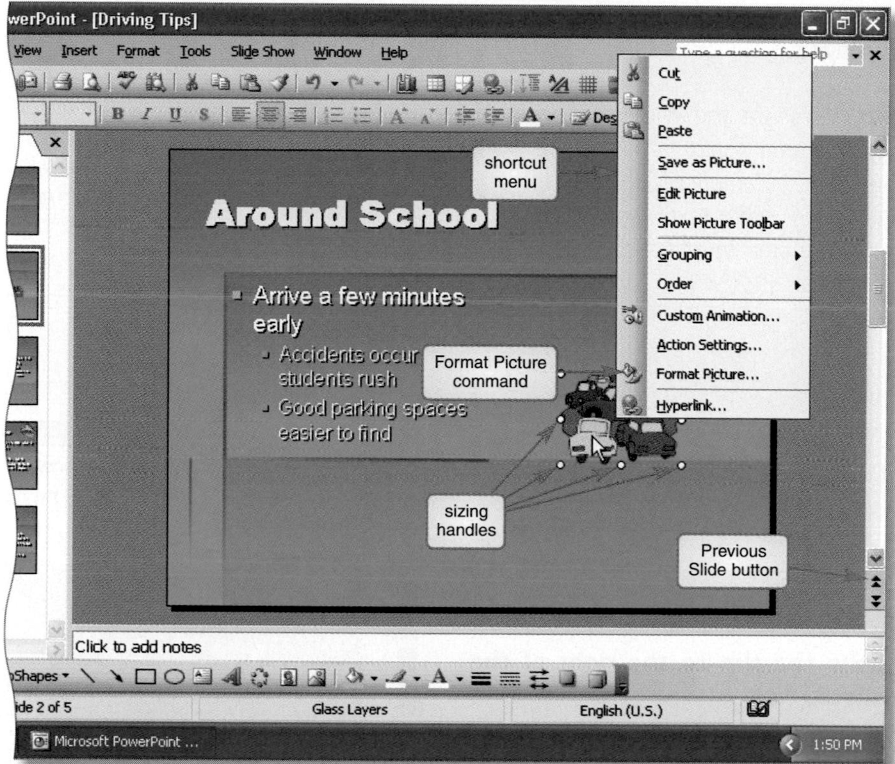

FIGURE 2-36

2

- **Click Format Picture on the shortcut menu.**
- **Click the Size tab when the Format Picture dialog box is displayed.**

The Size sheet in the Format Picture dialog box is displayed (Figure 2-37). The Height and Width text boxes in the Scale area display the current percentage of the clip, 100%. The Lock aspect ratio and Relative to original picture size check boxes are selected.

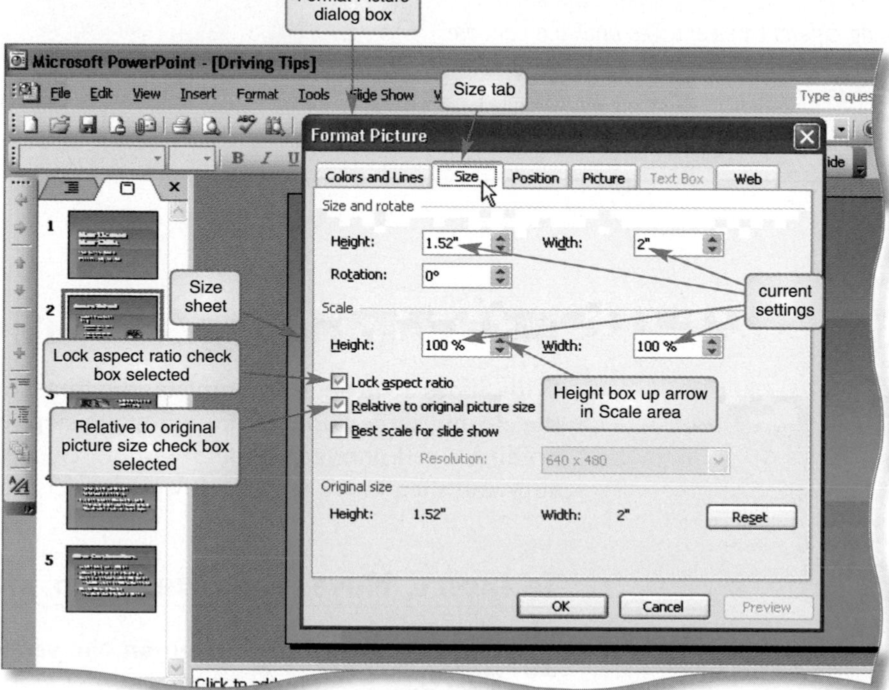

FIGURE 2-37

3

- **Click and hold down the mouse button on the Height box up arrow in the Scale area until 175% is displayed.**

Both the Height and Width text boxes in the Scale area display 175% (Figure 2-38). PowerPoint automatically changes the Height and Width text boxes in the Size and rotate area to reflect changes in the Scale area.

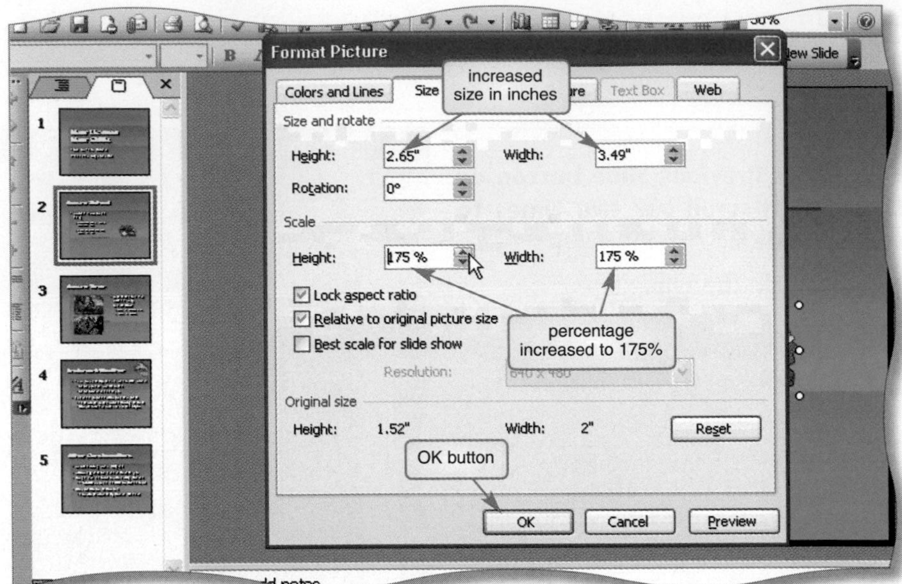

FIGURE 2-38

4

- **Click the OK button.**
- **Drag the clip to the right of the bulleted list.**

PowerPoint closes the Format Picture dialog box and displays the enlarged clip in the desired location (Figure 2-39). If your clip is too large or too small, repeat the steps using different percentages until the cars are the similar to those shown in Figure 2-39.

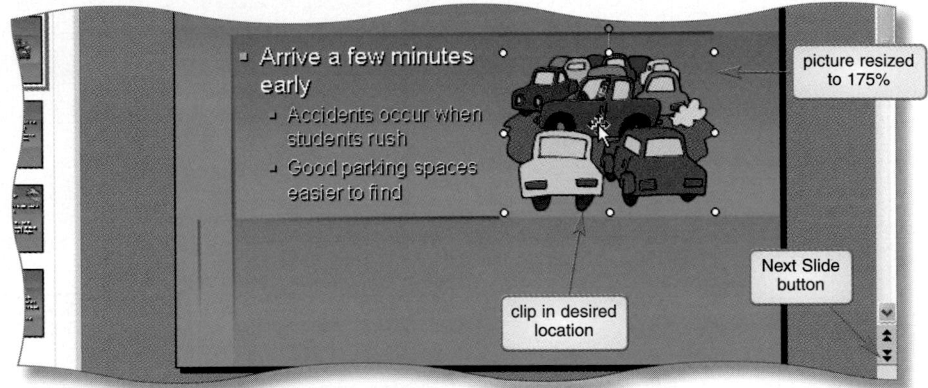

FIGURE 2-39

Inserting, Moving, and Sizing a Clip into a Slide

With Slides 1 through 4 complete, the final step is to add the cell phone user clip to the closing slide, Slide 5. The following steps show how to add a clip of a driver holding a cell phone to Slide 5 without changing the Title and Text layout, size the clip, and then move it to the lower-right corner of the slide.

To Insert, Move, and Size a Clip into a Slide

1. **Click the Next Slide button on the vertical scroll bar three times to display Slide 5.**
2. **Click the Insert Clip Art button on the Drawing toolbar. Delete the word, cloud, in the Search for text box, type** `cell phone`**, and then press the ENTER key. Click the cell phone user clip shown in Figure 2-40 or another appropriate clip. Click the Close button on the Clip Art task pane title bar.**

3 **If the layout changes, click the Automatic Layout Options button and then click Undo Automatic Layout.**

4 **Right-click the cell phone user clip and then click Format Picture on the shortcut menu. Click the Size tab in the Format Picture dialog box, click and hold down the mouse button on the Height box up arrow in the Scale area until 85% is displayed, and then click the OK button.**

5 **Drag the cell phone user clip to the lower-right corner of the slide.**

The cell phone user clip is inserted, moved, and sized into Slide 5 (Figure 2-40). If your clip is too large or too small, repeat the steps using different percentages until the cell phone user clip size is similar to the clip shown in Figure 2-40.

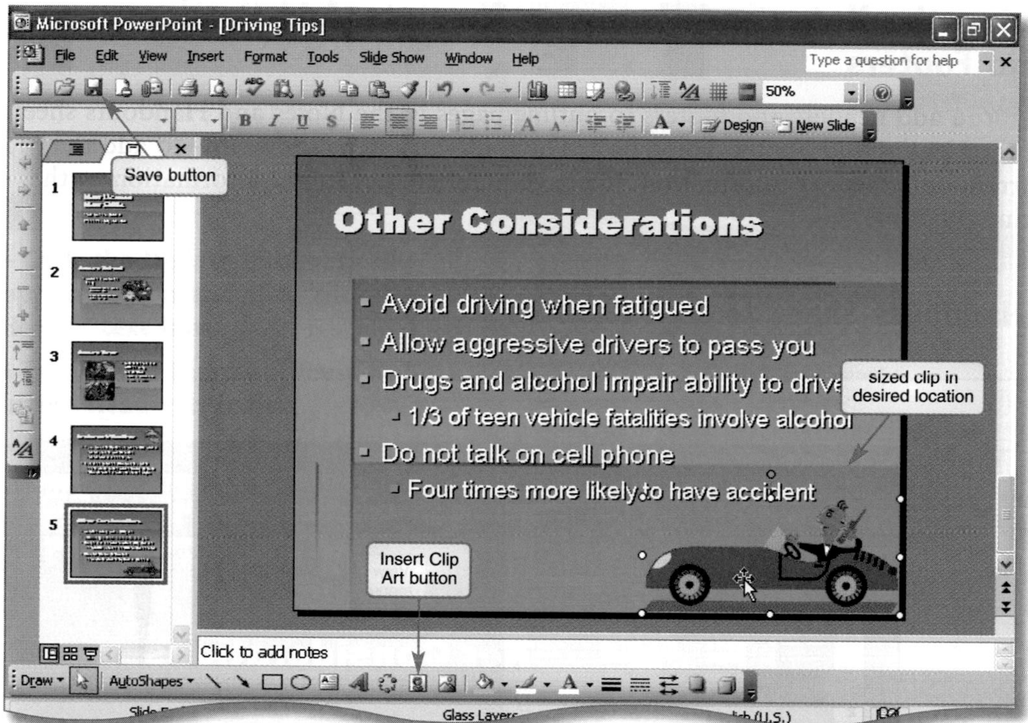
Microsoft PowerPoint - [Driving Tips]
File Edit View Insert Format Tools Slide Show Window Help
Type a question for help
50%
Design New Slide
Save button
Other Considerations
Avoid driving when fatigued
Allow aggressive drivers to pass you
Drugs and alcohol impair ability to drive
1/3 of teen vehicle fatalities involve alcohol
Do not talk on cell phone
Four times more likely to have accident
sized clip in desired location
Insert Clip Art button
Click to add notes
Draw AutoShapes

FIGURE 2-40

Saving the Presentation Again

To preserve the work completed, perform the following step to save the presentation again.

To Save a Presentation

1 **Click the Save button on the Standard toolbar.**

The changes made to the presentation after the previous save are saved on the USB flash drive.

A default setting in PowerPoint allows for **fast saves**, which saves only the changes made since the last time you saved. To save a full copy of the complete presentation, click Tools on the menu bar, click Options on the Tools menu, and then click the Save tab. Remove the check mark in the Allow fast saves check box by clicking the check box and then click the OK button.

4

• **Click the Apply to All Slides button.**

• **Click the Close button in the Slide Design task pane.**

The Float animation effect is applied to all slides in the presentation (Figure 2-48).

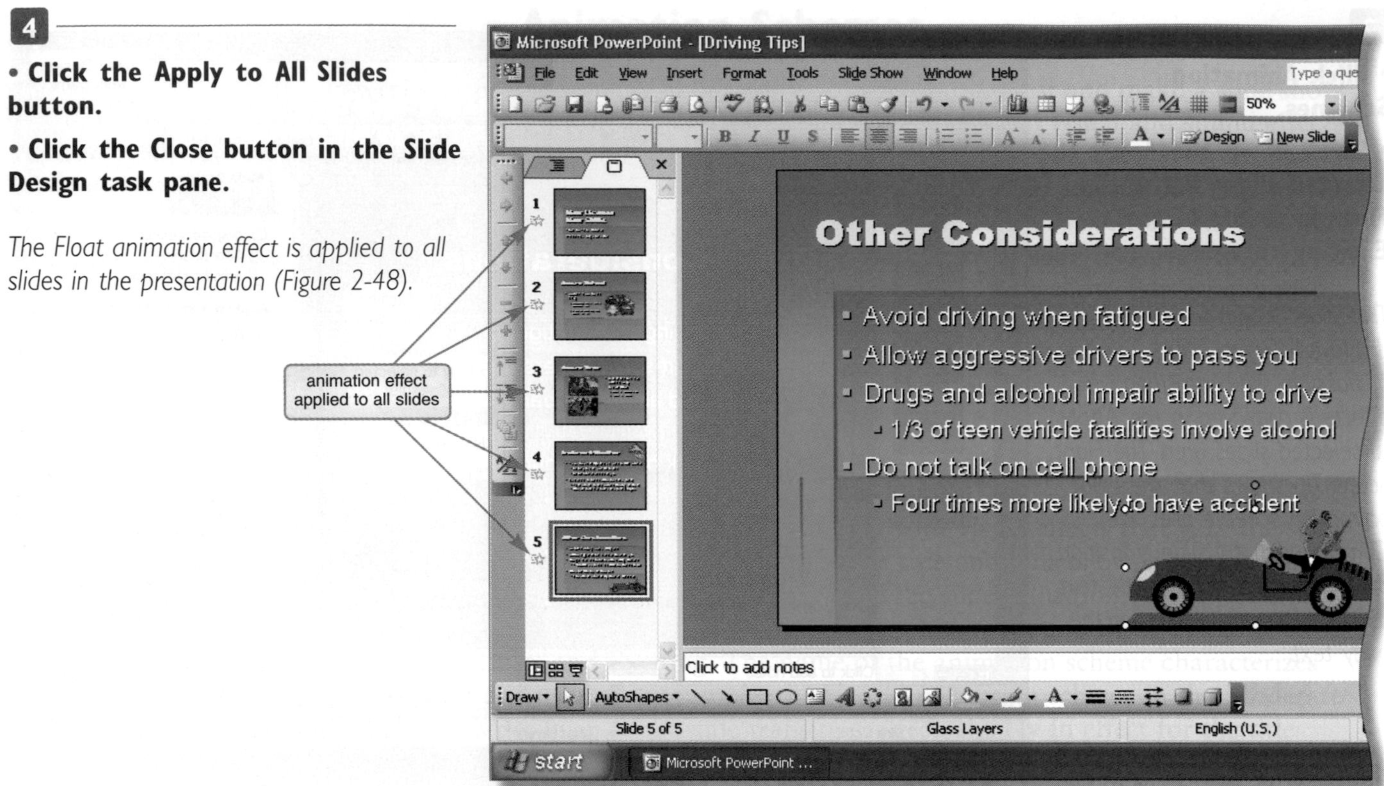
Microsoft PowerPoint - [Driving Tips]
animation effect applied to all slides
Other Considerations
Avoid driving when fatigued
Allow aggressive drivers to pass you
Drugs and alcohol impair ability to drive
1/3 of teen vehicle fatalities involve alcohol
Do not talk on cell phone
Four times more likely to have accident
Click to add notes
Slide 5 of 5
Glass Layers
English (U.S.)

FIGURE 2-48

Animating Clip Art

To add visual interest to a presentation, you can **animate** certain content. On Slide 5, for example, having the cell phone user appear in a diamond pattern on the screen will provide an interesting effect. Animating clip art takes several steps as described in the following sections.

Adding Animation Effects

PowerPoint allows you to animate clip art along with animating text. Because Slide 5 lists considerations every driver should follow, you want to emphasize these facts by having the clip appear on the screen in a diamond pattern. One way of animating clip art is to select options in the Custom Animation dialog box. The following steps show how to add the Diamond animation effect to the clip on Slide 5.

To Animate Clip Art

1

- **Right-click the clip.**

The shortcut menu is displayed (Figure 2-49). The clip is selected, as indicated by the sizing handles that display at the corners and along its edges.

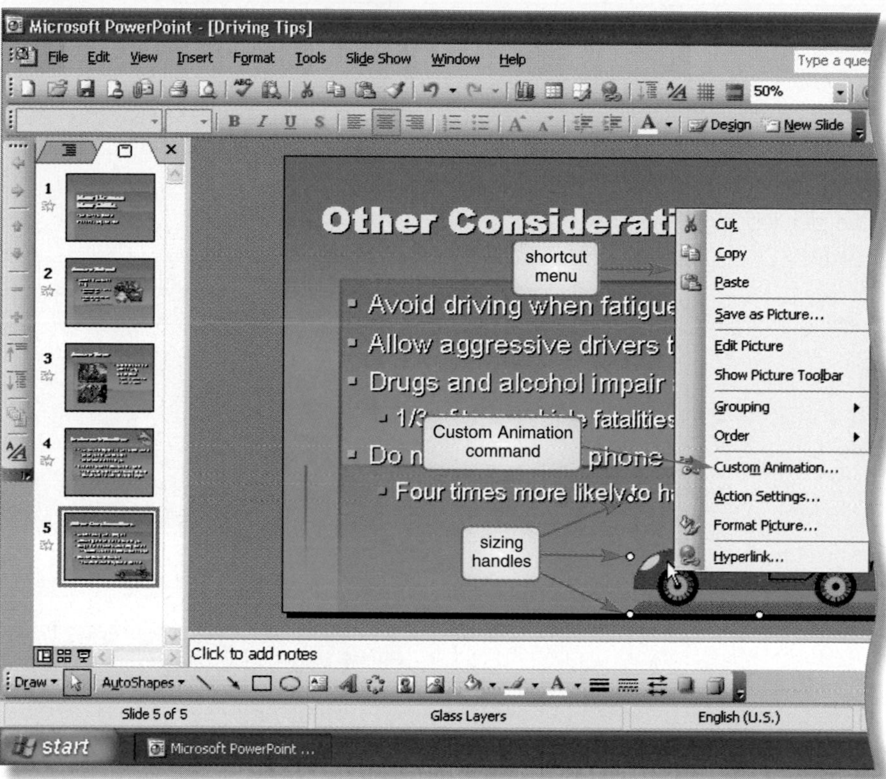

FIGURE 2-49

2

- **Click Custom Animation.**

The Custom Animation task pane is displayed (Figure 2-50). Two animation effects have been applied to the title and body of the slide previously.

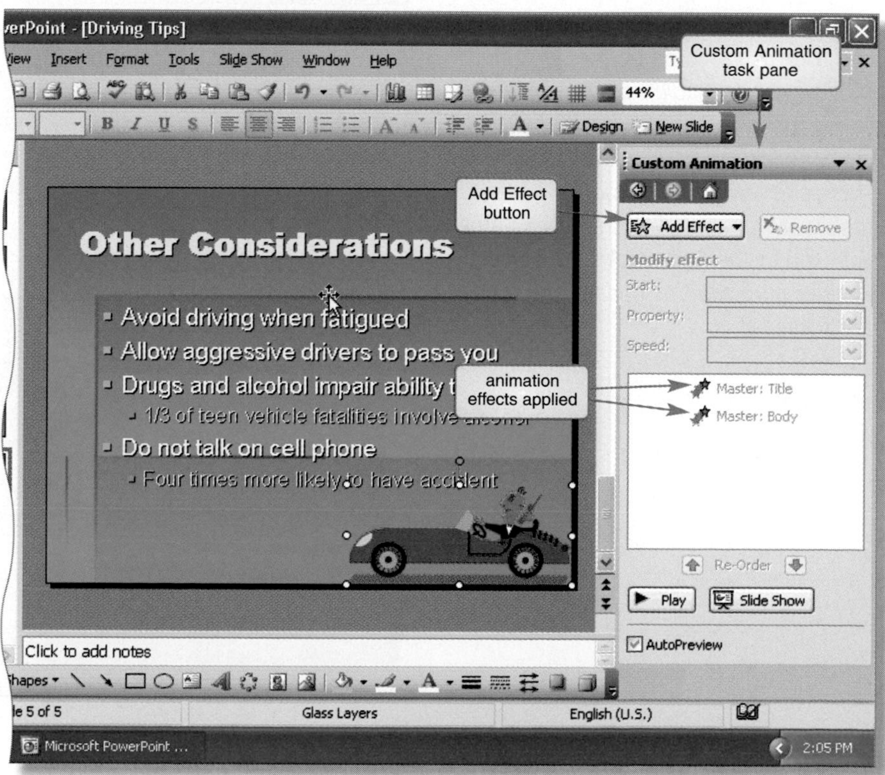

FIGURE 2-50

3

• **Click the Add Effect button, point to Entrance, and then point to Diamond in the Entrance effects list.**

A list of possible effects for the Entrance option is displayed (Figure 2-51). Your list may vary. You can apply a variety of effects to the clip, including how it enters and exits the slide.

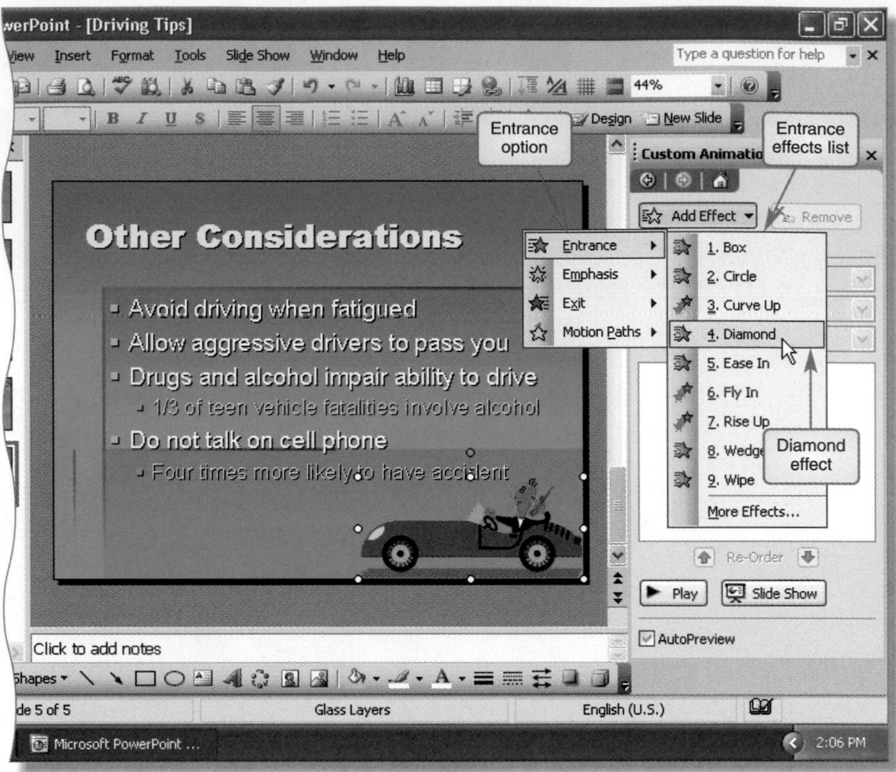

FIGURE 2-51

4

• **Click Diamond.**

The animation effect is applied to the cell phone user, as indicated by the number 1 icon displaying to the left of the clip and the corresponding 1 displaying in the Custom Animation list (Figure 2-52). You will see this effect when you click the mouse on that slide during your slide show. The name of your clip in the Custom Animation list may differ from the Cell phone name shown in the figure.

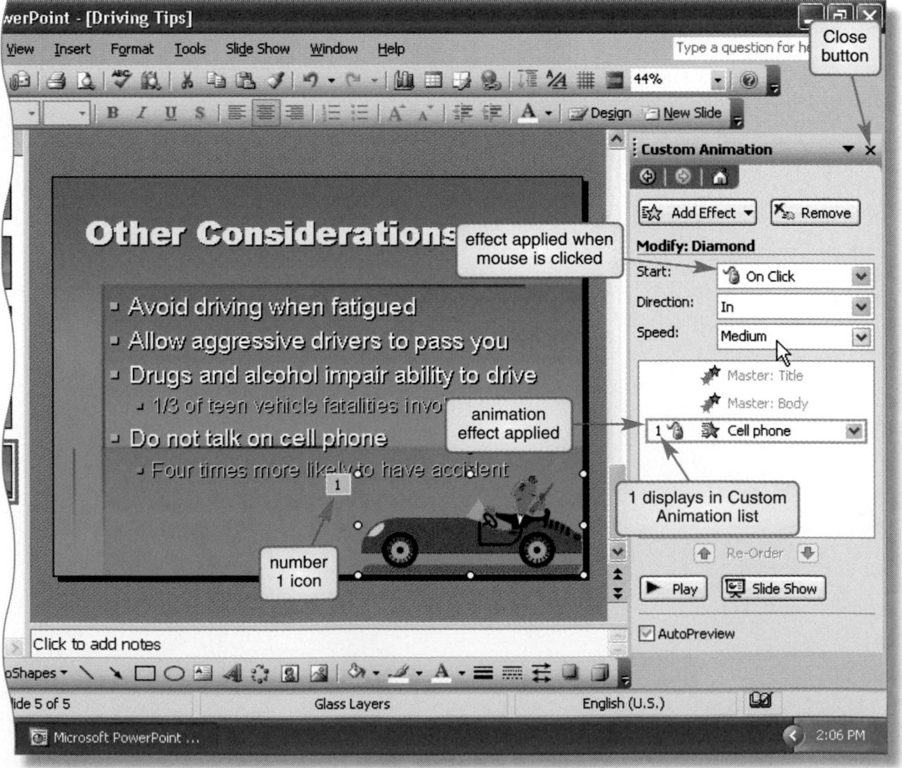

FIGURE 2-52

5

• **Click the Close button on the Custom Animation task pane title bar (Figure 2-53).**

The cell phone user clip will appear in the presentation using the Diamond animation effect during the slide show.

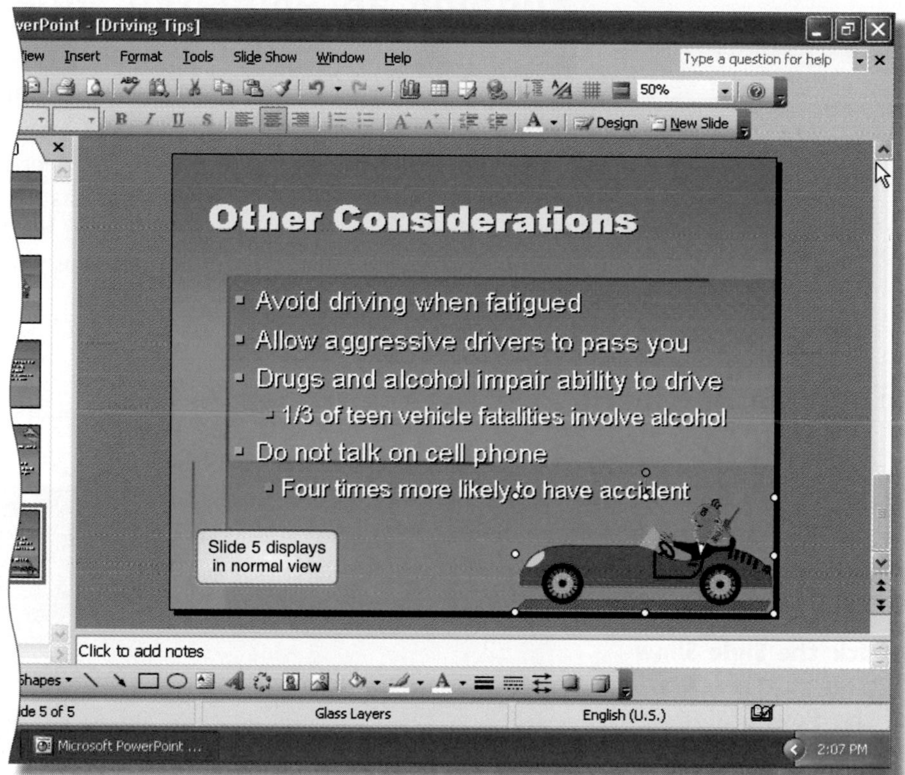

PowerPoint - [Driving Tips]
Other Considerations
Avoid driving when fatigued
Allow aggressive drivers to pass you
Drugs and alcohol impair ability to drive
1/3 of teen vehicle fatalities involve alcohol
Do not talk on cell phone
Four times more likely to have accident
Slide 5 displays in normal view
Click to add notes
Slide 5 of 5
Glass Layers
English (U.S.)

FIGURE 2-53

When you run the slide show, the bulleted-list paragraphs are displayed, and then the clip art will begin displaying on the slide in a diamond shape at the position where you inserted it into Slide 5.

Animation effects are complete for this presentation. You now can review the presentation in slide show view and correct any spelling errors.

Saving the Presentation Again

The presentation is complete. The following step shows how to save the finished presentation on a USB flash drive before running the slide show.

To Save a Presentation

1 **Click the Save button on the Standard toolbar.**

PowerPoint saves the presentation on your USB flash drive by saving the changes made to the presentation since the last save.

Running an Animated Slide Show

Project 1 introduced you to using slide show view to look at your presentation one slide at a time. This project introduces you to running a slide show with preset and custom animation effects. When you run a slide show with slide transition effects, PowerPoint displays the slide transition effect when you click the mouse button to advance to the next slide. When a slide has text animation effects, each paragraph level is displayed in the sequence specified by the animation settings in the Custom Animation dialog box. The following steps show how to run the animated Driving Tips presentation.

To Run an Animated Slide Show

1

- **Click the Slide 1 slide thumbnail on the Slides tab.**
- **Click the Slide Show button at the lower left of the PowerPoint window.**
- **When Slide 1 is displayed in slide show view, click the slide anywhere.**

PowerPoint applies the Comb Horizontal slide transition effect and shows the title slide title text, New License New Skills (Figure 2-54), using the Float animation effect. When you click the slide, the first paragraph in the subtitle text placeholder, Tips for Teen Drivers, is displayed using the Descend animation effect.

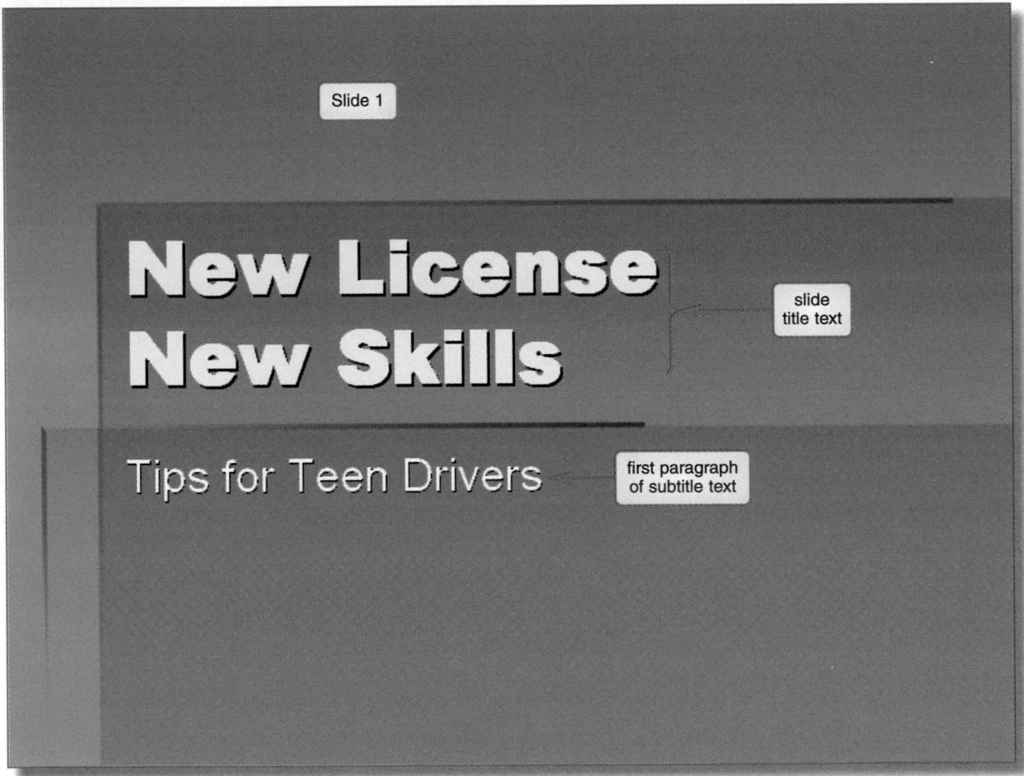

FIGURE 2-54

2

• **Click the slide again.**

PowerPoint displays the second paragraph in the subtitle text placeholder, West Park High School, using the Float animation effect (Figure 2-55).

If the pop-up menu buttons are displayed when you move the mouse pointer, do not click them.

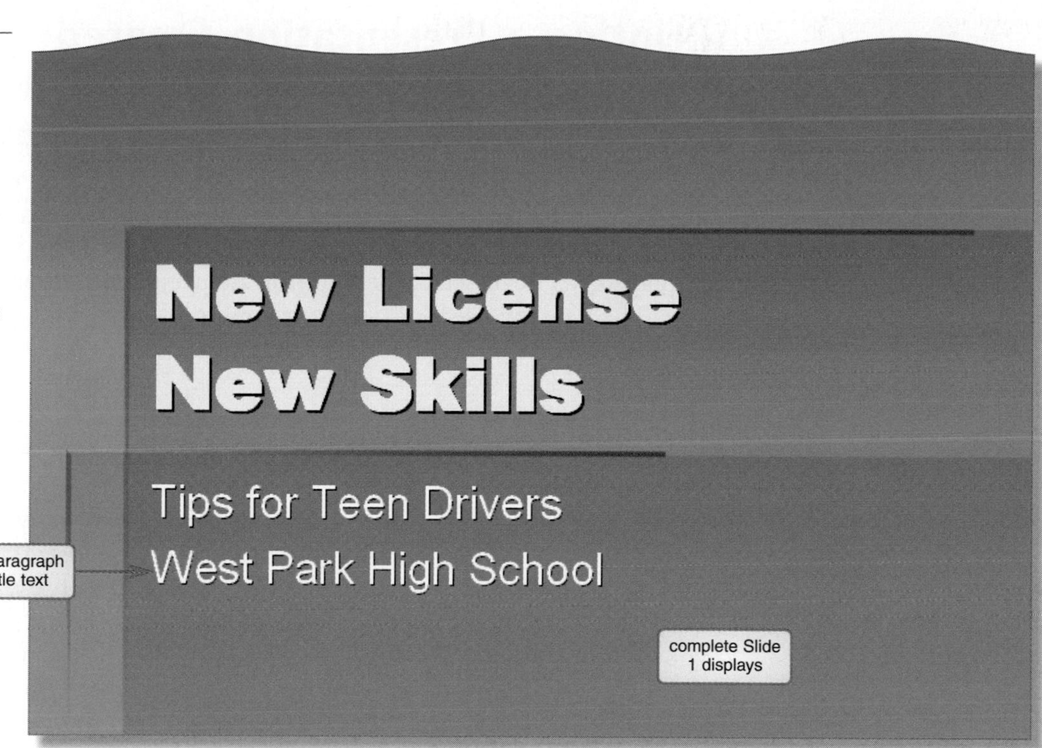

FIGURE 2-55

3

• **Continue clicking to finish running the slide show and return to normal view.**

Each time a new slide is displayed, PowerPoint first displays the Comb Horizontal slide transition effect and only the slide title using the Float effect. Then, PowerPoint builds each slide based on the animation settings. When you click the slide after the last paragraph is displayed on the last slide of the presentation, PowerPoint displays a blank slide. When you click again, PowerPoint exits slide show view and returns to normal view (Figure 2-56).

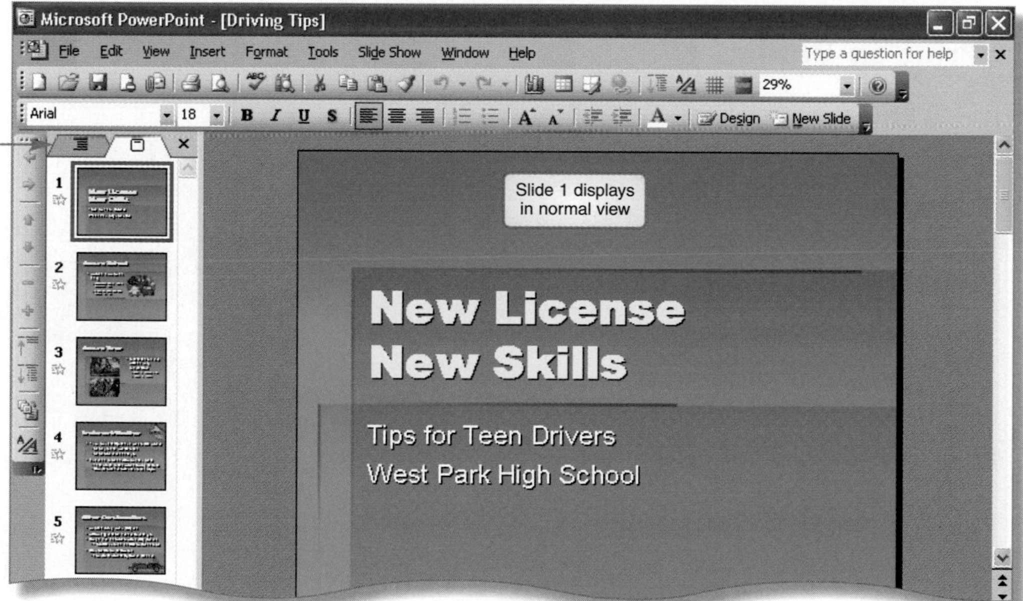

FIGURE 2-56

With the presentation complete and animation effects tested, the last step is to print the presentation outline and slides.

Printing a Presentation Created on the Outline Tab

When you click the Print button on the Standard toolbar, PowerPoint prints a hard copy of the presentation component last selected in the Print what box in the Print dialog box. To be certain to print the component you want, such as the presentation outline, use the Print command on the File menu. When the Print dialog box is displayed, you can select the appropriate presentation component in the Print what box. The next two sections explain how to use the Print command on the File menu to print the presentation outline and the presentation slides.

Q & A

Q: How much information does an audience member retain?

A: Handouts and slides help audience members remember what they hear. People remember 10 percent of what they read, 20 percent of what they hear, 30 percent of what they see, and 70 percent of what they see and hear.

Printing an Outline

During the development of a lengthy presentation, it often is easier to review your outline in print rather than on the screen. Printing your outline also is useful for audience handouts or when your supervisor or instructor wants to review your subject matter before you develop your presentation fully.

Recall that the Print dialog box shows print options. When you want to print your outline, select Outline View in the Print what list in the Print dialog box. The outline, however, prints as last viewed on the Outline tab. This means that you must select the Zoom setting to display the outline text as you want it to print. If you are uncertain of the Zoom setting, you should return to the Outline tab and review it before printing. The following steps show how to print an outline from normal view.

To Print an Outline

1

- **Click the Outline tab.**
- **Ready the printer according to the printer manufacturer's instructions.**
- **Click File on the menu bar.**

The File menu is displayed (Figure 2-57). The Expand All button on the Outlining toolbar is selected, so the entire outline will print. If you want to print only the slide titles, you would click the Collapse All button.

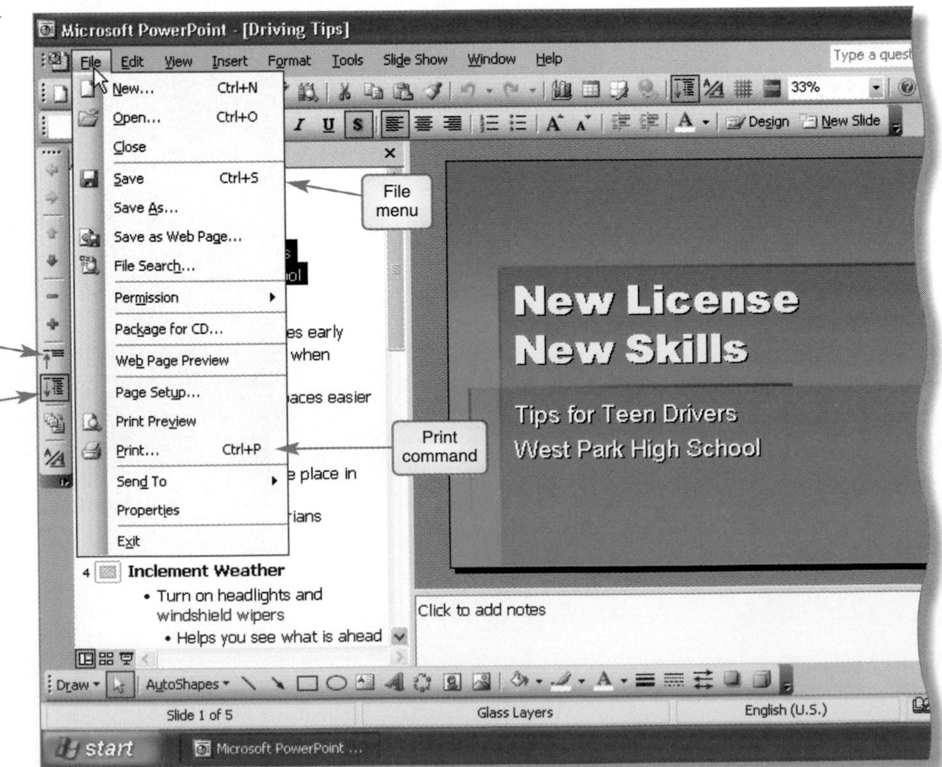

FIGURE 2-57

2

- **Click Print on the File menu.**
- **When the Print dialog box is displayed, click the Print what box arrow and then point to Outline View.**

The Print dialog box is displayed (Figure 2-58). Outline View is displayed highlighted in the Print what list.

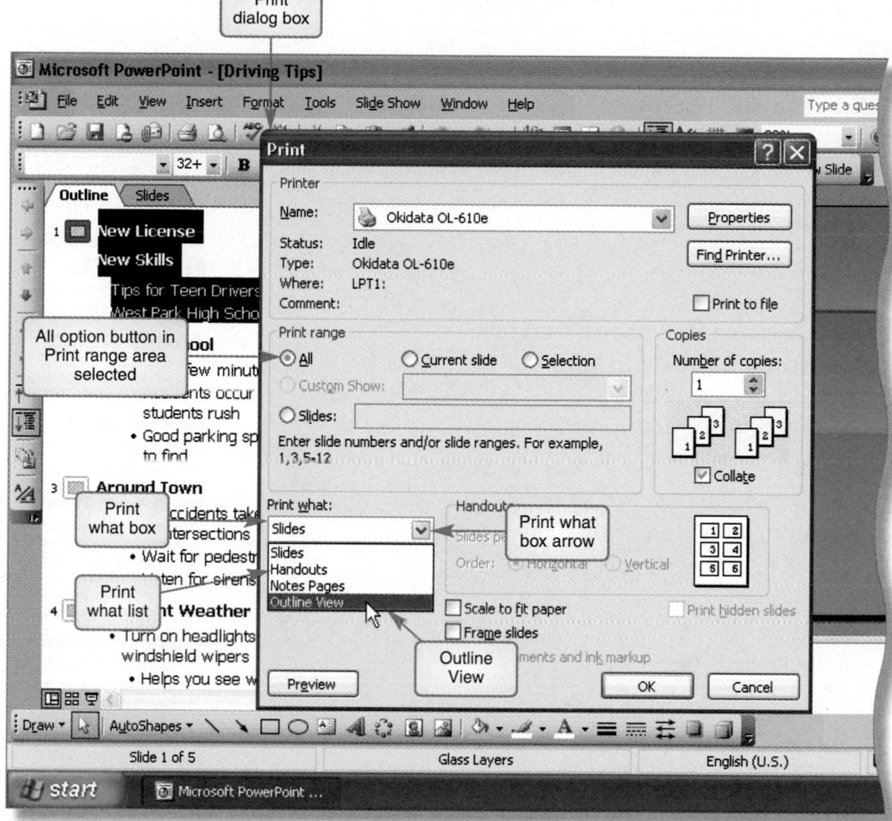

FIGURE 2-58

3

- **Click Outline View in the Print what list (Figure 2-59).**

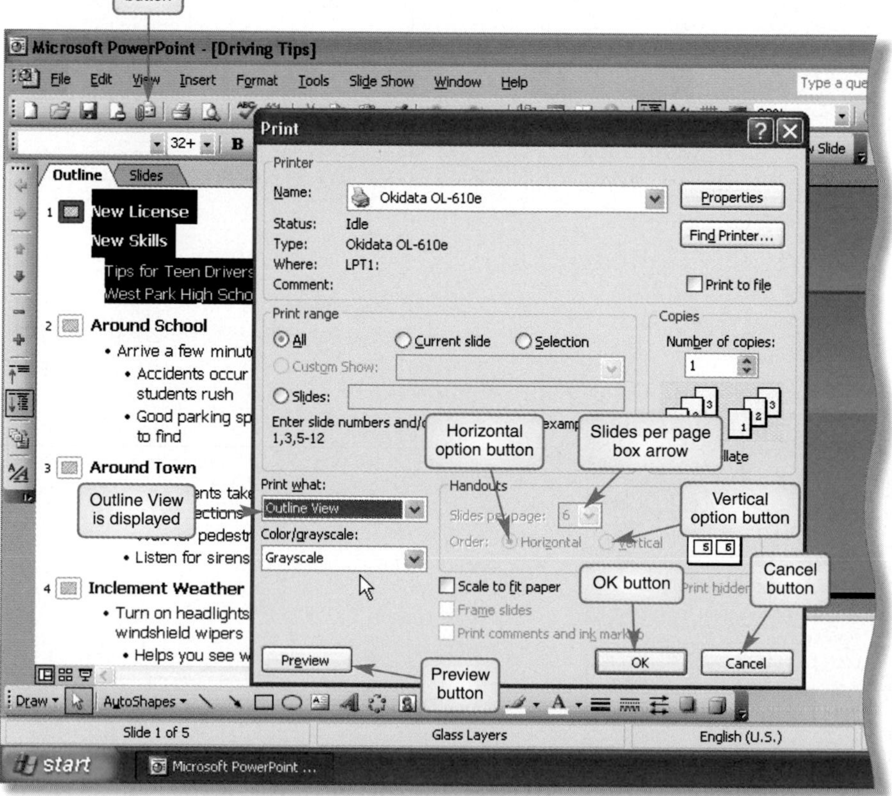

FIGURE 2-59

4

• **Click the OK button.**

To cancel the print request, click the Cancel button.

5

• **When the printer stops, retrieve the printout of the outline.**

PowerPoint displays the five slides in outline form (Figure 2-60). The words, New License New Skills, and the current date display in the header, and the words, West Park High School, and the page number display in the footer.

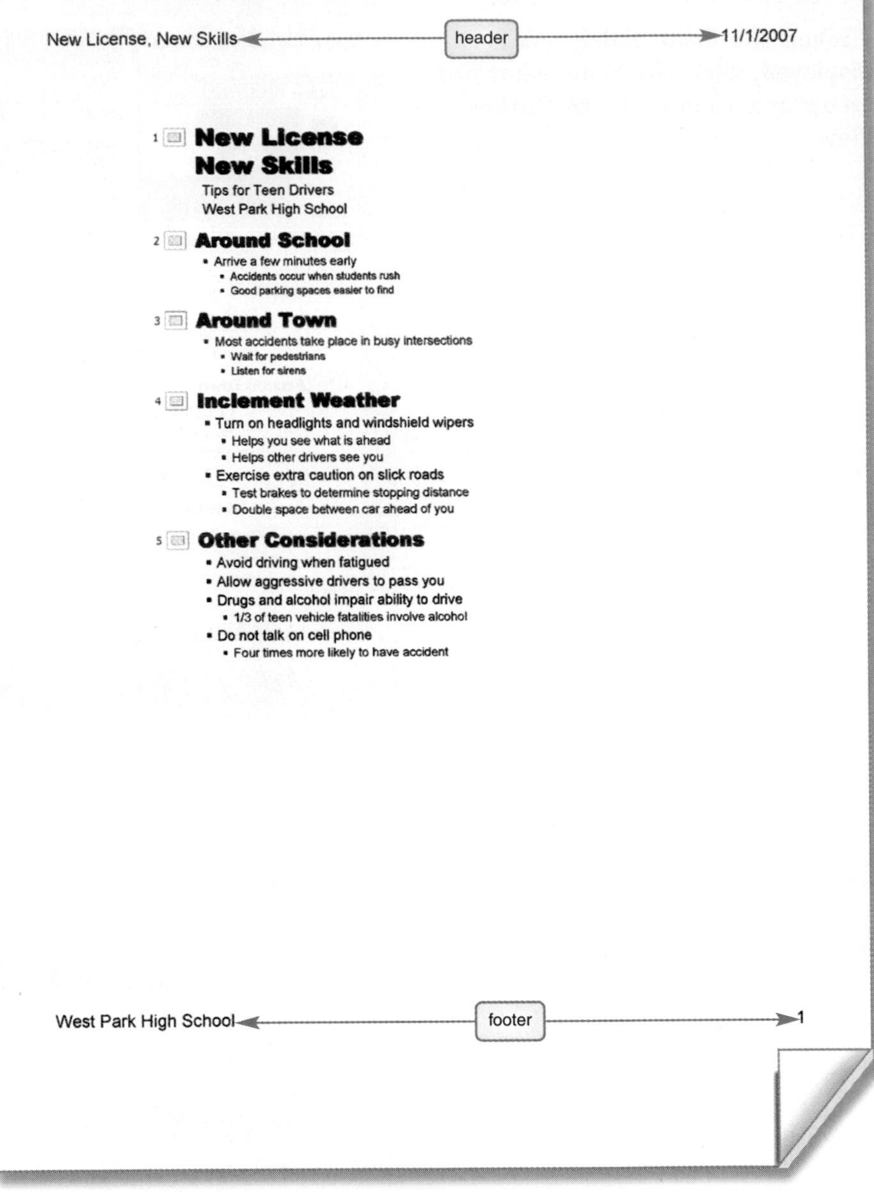
New License, New Skills
header
11/1/2007
1 New License
New Skills
Tips for Teen Drivers
West Park High School
2 Around School
• Arrive a few minutes early
• Accidents occur when students rush
• Good parking spaces easier to find
3 Around Town
• Most accidents take place in busy intersections
• Wait for pedestrians
• Listen for sirens
4 Inclement Weather
• Turn on headlights and windshield wipers
• Helps you see what is ahead
• Helps other drivers see you
• Exercise extra caution on slick roads
• Test brakes to determine stopping distance
• Double space between car ahead of you
5 Other Considerations
• Avoid driving when fatigued
• Allow aggressive drivers to pass you
• Drugs and alcohol impair ability to drive
• 1/3 of teen vehicle fatalities involve alcohol
• Do not talk on cell phone
• Four times more likely to have accident
West Park High School
footer
1

FIGURE 2-60

Skill Builder 2-4

To practice the following tasks, visit scsite.com/off2003sch/skill, locate PowerPoint Project 2, and then click Skill Builder 2-4.

❑ Change the size of clip art
❑ Add a header and footer to outline pages
❑ Add an animation scheme
❑ Animate clip art
❑ Print an outline

The **Print what list** in the Print dialog box contains options for printing slides, handouts, notes, and an outline. The Handouts area allows you to specify whether you want one, two, three, four, six, or nine slide images to display on each page. Printing handouts is useful for reviewing a presentation because you can analyze several slides displayed simultaneously on one page. Additionally, many businesses distribute handouts of the slide show before a presentation so the attendees can refer to a copy. To print handouts, click Handouts in the Print what box, click the Slides per page box arrow in the Handouts area, and then click 1, 2, 3, 4, 6, or 9. You can change the order in which the Driving Tips slides display on a page by clicking the Horizontal option button for Order in the Handouts area, which shows Slides 1 and 2, 3 and 4, and 5 and 6 adjacent to each other, or the Vertical option button for Order, which shows Slides 1 and 4, 2 and 5, and 3 and 6 adjacent to each other.

You also can click the Preview button if you want to see how your printout will look. After viewing the preview, click the Close button on the Preview window toolbar to return to normal view.

Q & A

Q: Can I change my handout's background?

A: Yes. First, display the Handout Master by pointing to Master on the View menu and then clicking Handout Master. Click the Handout Background command on the Format menu, and then change the Background fill. You can add a color, fill effect, or picture. To apply the background to the handout, click the Apply button.

Printing Presentation Slides

At this point, you may want to check the spelling in the entire presentation and instruct PowerPoint to ignore any words spelled correctly. After correcting errors, you will want to print a final copy of your presentation. If you made any changes to your presentation since your last save, be certain to save your presentation before you print.

The following steps show how to print the presentation.

To Print Presentation Slides

1. **Ready the printer according to the printer manufacturer's instructions.**
2. **Click File on the menu bar and then click Print.**
3. **When the Print dialog box is displayed, click the Print what box arrow.**
4. **Click Slides in the list.**
5. **Click the OK button. When the printer stops, retrieve the slide printouts.**

The printouts should resemble the slides in Figures 2-61a through 2-61e.

New License
New Skills
Tips for Teen Drivers
West Park High School

(a) Slide 1

Around School
Arrive a few minutes early

(b) Slide 2

FIGURE 2-61

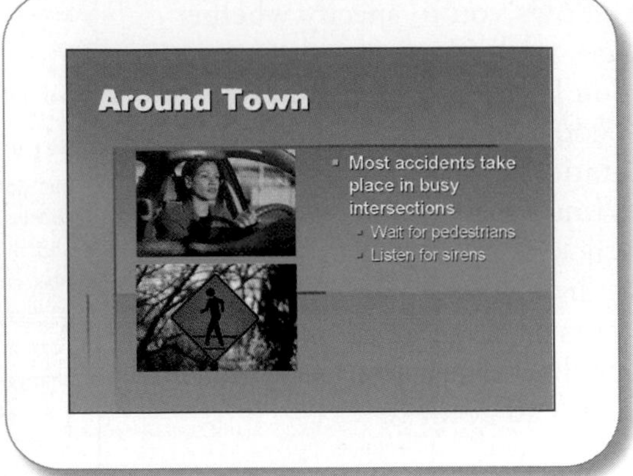
Around Town
Most accidents take place in busy intersections
Wait for pedestrians
Listen for sirens

(c) Slide 3

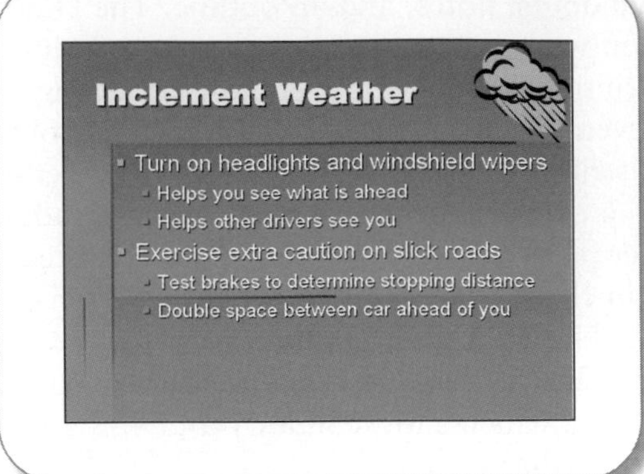
Inclement Weather
Turn on headlights and windshield wipers
Helps you see what is ahead
Helps other drivers see you
Exercise extra caution on slick roads
Test brakes to determine stopping distance
Double space between car ahead of you

(d) Slide 4

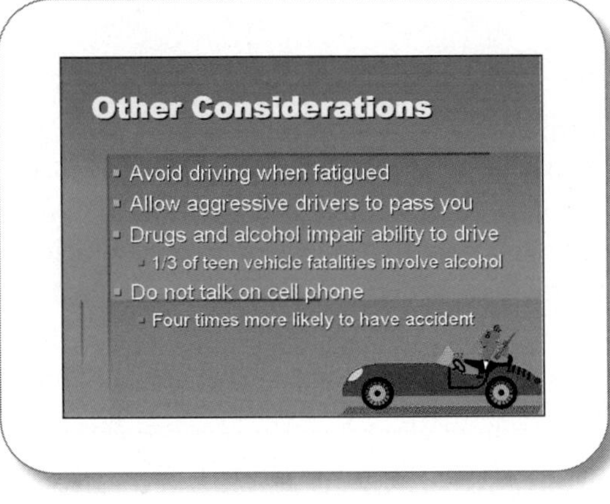
Other Considerations
Avoid driving when fatigued
Allow aggressive drivers to pass you
Drugs and alcohol impair ability to drive
1/3 of teen vehicle fatalities involve alcohol
Do not talk on cell phone
Four times more likely to have accident

(e) Slide 5

FIGURE 2-61 *(continued)*

E-Mailing a Slide Show from within PowerPoint

Billions of e-mail messages are sent throughout the world each day. Computer users use this popular service on the Internet to send and receive plain text e-mail or to send and receive e-mail content that includes objects, links to other Web pages, and file attachments. These attachments can include Office files, such as PowerPoint slide shows or Word documents. Using Microsoft Office, you can e-mail the presentation directly from within PowerPoint.

For these steps to work properly, users need an e-mail address and a 32-bit e-mail program compatible with a Messaging Application Programming Interface, such as Outlook, Outlook Express, or Microsoft Exchange Client. Free e-mail accounts are available at hotmail.com. The following steps show how to e-mail the slide show from within PowerPoint to Jessica Cantero. Assume her e-mail address is jessica_cantero@hotmail.com. Your screens may differ from those in this book depending upon your default e-mail program. If you do not have an E-mail button on the Standard toolbar, then this activity is not available to you.

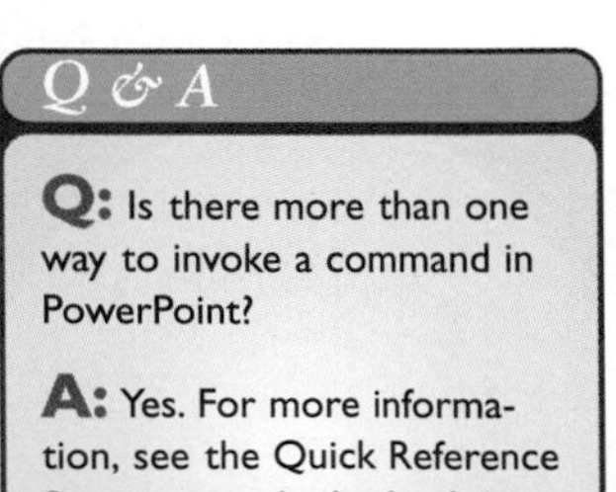
Q & A

Q: Is there more than one way to invoke a command in PowerPoint?

A: Yes. For more information, see the Quick Reference Summary at the back of this book, or visit the Office 2003 Quick Reference Web page (`scsite.com/off2003sch/qr`).

To E-Mail a Slide Show from within PowerPoint

1

- **Click the E-mail (as Attachment) button on the Standard toolbar. See your instructor if the Choose Profile dialog box displays.**
- **When the e-mail Message window is displayed, type** `jessica_cantero@hotmail.com` **in the To text box.**
- **Select the text in the Subject text box and then type** `Tips for Teen Drivers slide show` **in the Subject text box.**
- **Click the message body.**

PowerPoint displays the e-mail Message window (Figure 2-62). The insertion point is in the message body so you can type a message to Jessica Cantero.

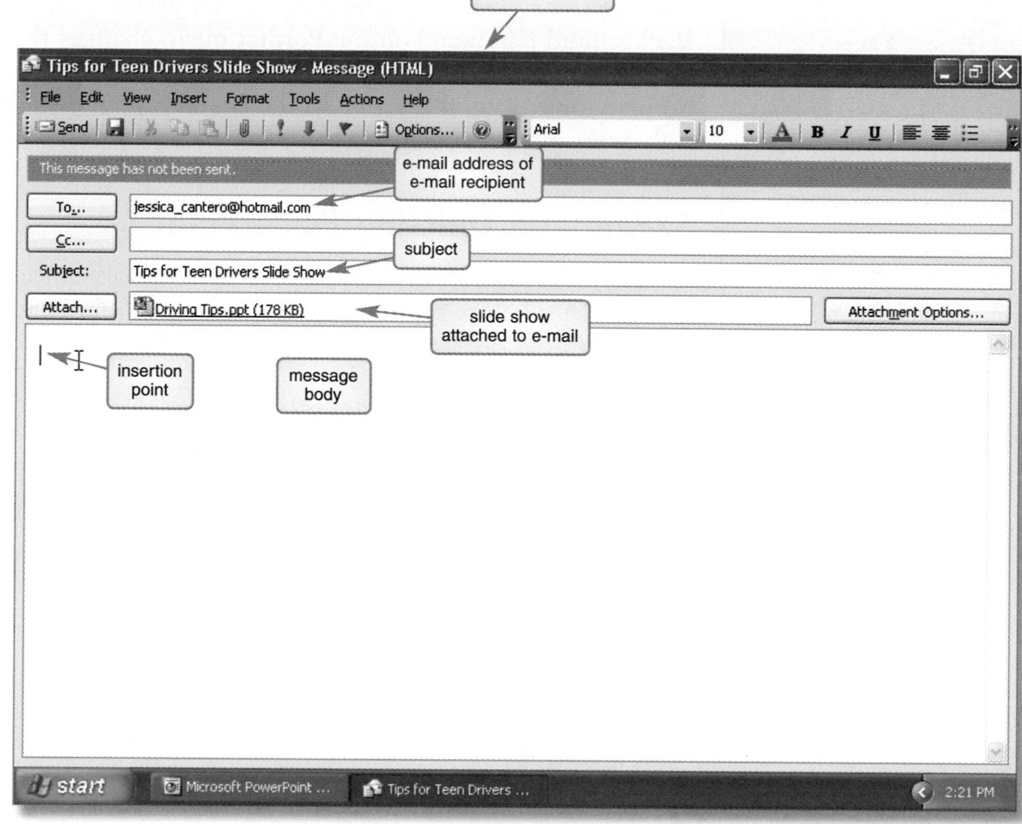

FIGURE 2-62

2

- **Type** `Attached is the PowerPoint presentation you can use during your class discussion.` **in the message body.**
- **Point to the Send button.**

The message is intended to help the recipient of the e-mail understand the purpose of your e-mail (Figure 2-63).

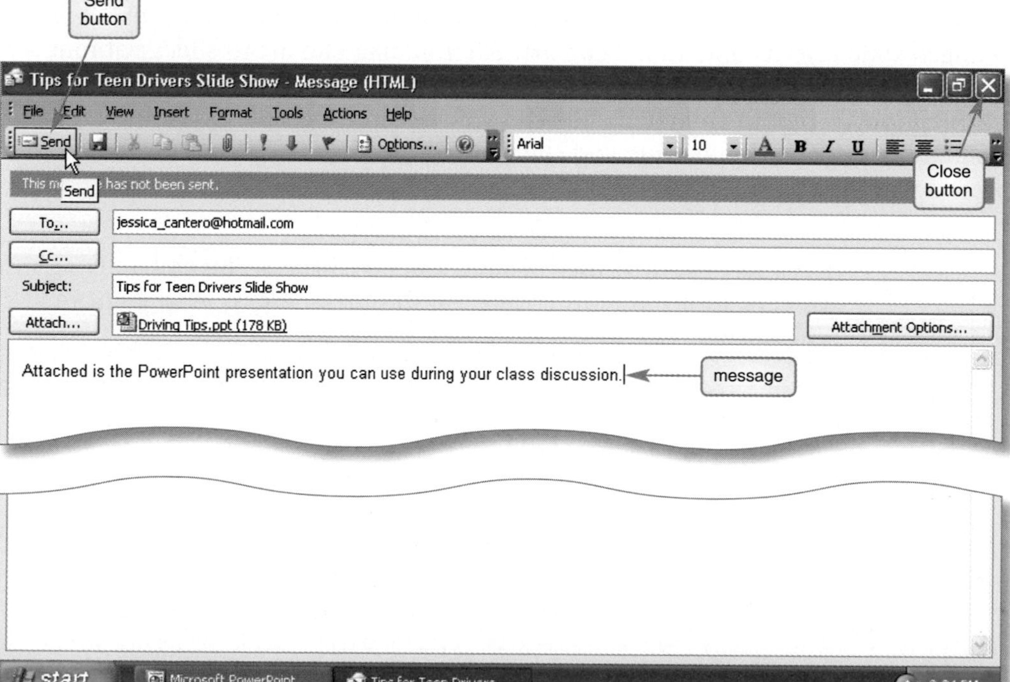

FIGURE 2-63

**3**

- **Click the Send button on the Standard toolbar.**

The e-mail with the attached presentation is sent to jessica_cantero@hotmail.com.

Q: When did people begin sending e-mail messages?

A: The first e-mail message was sent in 1969 from Professor Leonard Kleinrock to a colleague at Stanford University. Researchers estimate that the average computer user sends approximately 35 e-mail messages daily, seven with attachments. For more information on e-mail messages, visit the Office 2003 More About Web page (scsite.com/off2003sch/qa) and click E-Mail.

Because the slide show was sent as an attachment, Jessica Cantero can save the attachment and then open the presentation in PowerPoint. You can choose many more options when you send e-mail from within PowerPoint. For example, the Background command on the Format menu changes the colors of the message background and lets you add a picture to use as the background. In addition, the Security button on the Standard toolbar allows you to send secure messages that only your intended recipient can read.

Saving and Quitting PowerPoint

If you made any changes to your presentation since your last save, you should save it again before quitting PowerPoint. The following steps show how to save changes to the presentation and quit PowerPoint.

To Save Changes and Quit PowerPoint

1. **Click the Close button on the Microsoft PowerPoint window title bar.**
2. **If prompted, click the Yes button in the Microsoft PowerPoint dialog box.**

PowerPoint saves any changes made to the presentation since the last save and then quits PowerPoint.

Project Summary

In creating the New License, New Skills slide show in this project, you increased your knowledge of PowerPoint. You created a slide presentation on the Outline tab where you entered all the text in the form of an outline. You arranged the text using the Promote and Demote buttons. Once the outline was complete, you changed slide layouts and added clip art. After adding clip art to slides without using a content placeholder, you moved and sized the clips. You added preset animation effects and applied animation effects to a clip. You learned how to run an animated slide show demonstrating slide transition and animation effects. Finally, you printed the presentation outline and slides using the Print command on the File menu and e-mailed the presentation.

If you have a SAM user profile, you may have access to hands-on instruction, practice, and assessment of the skills covered in this project. Log in to your SAM account and go to your assignments page to see what your instructor has assigned.

What You Should Know

Having completed this project, you should be able to perform the tasks below. The tasks are listed in the same order they were presented in this project. For a list of the buttons, menus, toolbars, and commands introduced in this project, see the Quick Reference Summary at the back of this book and refer to the Page Number column.

1. Start and Customize PowerPoint (PPT 85)
2. Change to the Outline Tab and Display the Outlining Toolbar (PPT 86)
3. Create a Title Slide on the Outline Tab (PPT 88)
4. Add a Slide on the Outline Tab (PPT 89)
5. Create a Text Slide with a Multi-Level Bulleted List on the Outline Tab (PPT 90)
6. Create a Second Text Slide with a Multi-Level Bulleted List (PPT 92)
7. Create a Third Text Slide with a Multi-Level Bulleted List (PPT 92)
8. Create a Closing Slide on the Outline Tab (PPT 94)
9. Save a Presentation (PPT 95)
10. Change the View to Slide Sorter View (PPT 95)
11. Change the View to Normal View (PPT 96)
12. Change the Slide Layout to Title, Text, and Content (PPT 98)
13. Insert Clip Art into a Content Placeholder (PPT 101)
14. Change the Slide Layout to Title, 2 Content and Text and Insert Clip Art (PPT 102)
15. Insert a Second Clip into a Slide (PPT 103)
16. Insert Clip Art into a Slide without a Content Placeholder (PPT 104)
17. Use the Automatic Layout Options Button to Undo a Layout Change (PPT 107)
18. Move Clip Art (PPT 108)
19. Change the Size of Clip Art (PPT 109)
20. Insert, Move, and Size a Clip into a Slide (PPT 110)
21. Save a Presentation (PPT 111)
22. Use the Notes and Handouts Sheet to Add Headers and Footers (PPT 112)
23. Add an Animation Scheme to a Slide Show (PPT 114)
24. Animate Clip Art (PPT 117)
25. Save a Presentation (PPT 119)
26. Run an Animated Slide Show (PPT 120)
27. Print an Outline (PPT 122)
28. Print Presentation Slides (PPT 125)
29. E-Mail a Slide Show from within PowerPoint (PPT 127)
30. Save Changes and Quit PowerPoint (PPT 128)

Career Corner

Computer Science/IT Instructor

Computer science/IT instructors are in demand. In both the educational and business sectors, skilled teachers are reaping the many benefits and rewards of being in a highly sought after occupation.

Instructors in K-12 usually teach computer literacy or specific computer applications. Teaching in K-12 requires at least a bachelor's degree with some computer related courses. Instructors in higher education teach basic computer courses in addition to specialized classes such as computer engineering, Internet development, networking, programming, or systems analysis and design. Generally, these instructors have at least a master's degree with 18 graduate hours in the subject area. Teaching software and/or hardware design usually requires a master's degree and/or a Ph.D. in software engineering or electrical engineering.

Corporate trainers teach employees systems development, programming, and other computer-related skills. They also lead continuing education classes and introduce new software. Many companies have their own training departments. Qualifications for the corporate world are less stringent than those for educational institutions. Often, companies hire instructors with trainer certifications, such as the Microsoft Certified Trainer (MCT) and Cisco Certified Trainer.

Salaries range widely. In a traditional educational setting, salaries vary from about $40,000 to $75,000, depending on the area of expertise, years of experience, and location. In the corporate world, salaries are considerably higher, ranging up to $100,000 and beyond. For more information, visit scsite.com/off2003sch/careers and then click Computer Science/IT Instructor.

Learn It Online

Instructions: To complete the Learn It Online exercises, start your browser, click the Address bar, and then enter the Web address scsite.com/off2003sch/learn. When the Office 2003 Learn It Online page is displayed, follow the instructions in the exercises below. Each exercise has instructions for printing your results, either for your own records or for submission to your instructor.

1 Project Reinforcement TF, MC, and SA

Below PowerPoint Project 2, click the Project Reinforcement link. Print the quiz by clicking Print on the File menu for each page. Answer each question.

2 Flash Cards

Below PowerPoint Project 2, click the Flash Cards link and read the instructions. Type 20 (or a number specified by your instructor) in the Number of playing cards text box, type your name in the Enter your Name text box, and then click the Flip Card button. When the flash card is displayed, read the question and then click the ANSWER box arrow to select an answer. Flip through Flash Cards. If your score is 15 (75%) correct or greater, click Print on the File menu to print your results. If your score is less than 15 (75%) correct, then redo this exercise by clicking the Replay button.

3 Practice Test

Below PowerPoint Project 2, click the Practice Test link. Answer each question, enter your first and last name at the bottom of the page, and then click the Grade Test button. When the graded practice test is displayed on your screen, click Print on the File menu to print a hard copy. Continue to take practice tests until you score 80% or better.

4 Who Wants To Be a Computer Genius?

Below PowerPoint Project 2, click the Computer Genius link. Read the instructions, enter your first and last name at the bottom of the page, and then click the PLAY button. When your score is displayed, click the PRINT RESULTS link to print a hard copy.

5 Wheel of Terms

Below PowerPoint Project 2, click the Wheel of Terms link. Read the instructions, and then enter your first and last name and your school name. Click the PLAY button. When your score is displayed, right-click the score and then click Print on the shortcut menu to print a hard copy.

6 Crossword Puzzle Challenge

Below PowerPoint Project 2, click the Crossword Puzzle Challenge link. Read the instructions, and then enter your first and last name. Click the SUBMIT button. Work the crossword puzzle. When you are finished, click the Submit button. When the crossword puzzle is redisplayed, click the Print Puzzle button to print a hard copy.

7 Tips and Tricks

Below PowerPoint Project 2, click the Tips and Tricks link. Click a topic that pertains to Project 2. Right-click the information and then click Print on the shortcut menu. Construct a brief example of what the information relates to in PowerPoint to confirm you understand how to use the tip or trick.

8 Newsgroups

Below PowerPoint Project 2, click the Newsgroups link. Click a topic that pertains to Project 2. Print three comments.

9 Expanding Your Horizons

Below PowerPoint Project 2, click the Expanding Your Horizons link. Click a topic that pertains to Project 2. Print the information. Construct a brief example of what the information relates to in PowerPoint to confirm you understand the contents of the article.

10 Search Sleuth

Below PowerPoint Project 2, click the Search Sleuth link. To search for a term that pertains to this project, select a term below the Project 2 title and then use the Google search engine at google.com (or any major search engine) to display and print two Web pages that present information on the term.

11 PowerPoint Online Training

Below PowerPoint Project 2, click the PowerPoint Online Training link. When your browser displays the Microsoft Office Online Web page, click the PowerPoint link. Click one of the PowerPoint courses that covers one or more of the objectives listed at the beginning of the project on page PPT 82. Print the first page of the course before stepping through it.

12 Office Marketplace

Below PowerPoint Project 2, click the Office Marketplace link. When your browser displays the Microsoft Office Online Web page, click the Office Marketplace link. Click a topic that relates to PowerPoint. Print the first page.

13 You're Hired!

Below PowerPoint Project 2, click the You're Hired! link to embark on the path to a career in computers. Directions about how to play the game will be displayed. When you are ready to play, click the begin the game button. If required, submit your score to your instructor.

Apply Your Knowledge

1 Hemingway's Fascination with Bullfights

Instructions: Start PowerPoint. Open the presentation Apply 2-1 Bullfighting. See page xxiv at the front of this book for instructions for downloading the Data Files for Students or see your instructor for information on accessing the files required for this book. The four slides in the presentation give information on Earnest Hemingway's description of bullfighting in Pamplona, Spain, in his classic novel, *Death in the Afternoon*, and his description of the San Fermín Festival, which includes the running of the bulls, in *The Sun Also Rises*. Make the following changes to the slides so they appear as shown in Figures 2-64a through 2-64d. If you cannot locate the clips shown in the figures, see your instructor.

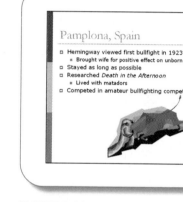

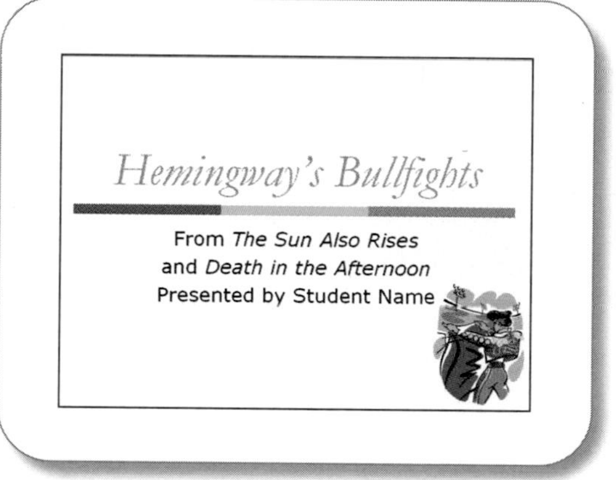

FIGURE 2-64a

Pamplona, Spain
- Hemingway viewed first bullfight in 1923
  - Brought wife for positive effect on unborn son
- Stayed as long as possible
- Researched *Death in the Afternoon*
  - Lived with matadors
- Competed in amateur bullfighting competitions

FIGURE 2-64b

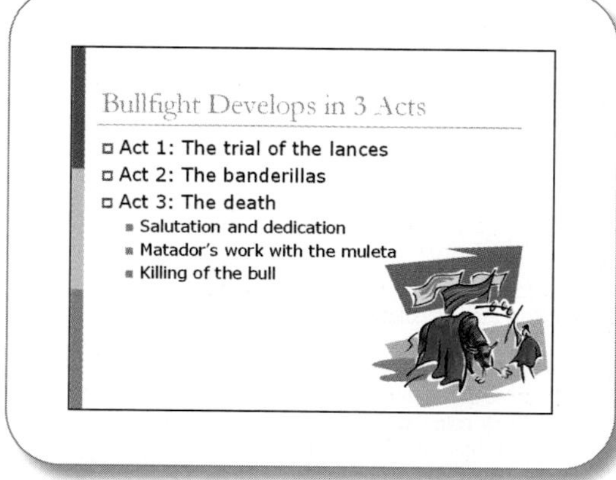

FIGURE 2-64c

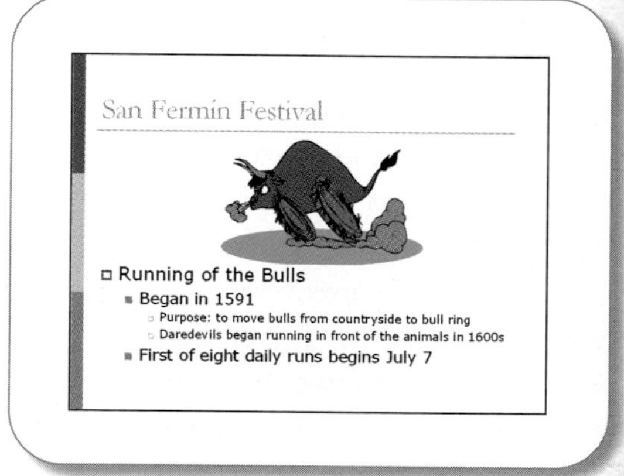

FIGURE 2-64d

FIGURE 2-64

Change the design template to Level. On the title slide, replace the words, Student Name, with your name. Then add the current date, page number, and your name to the notes and handouts footer.

On Slide 1, increase the font size of the Hemingway's Bullfights paragraph to 72 point and then italicize this text. Insert the bullfighting clip shown in Figure 2-64a. Scale the clip art to 90% and then drag the clip to the lower-right corner of the slide. Apply the Box Entrance custom animation effect to the clip.

(continued)

Apply Your Knowledge

Hemingway's Fascination with Bullfights *(continued)*

On Slide 2, change the slide layout to Title and Text over Content. Insert the bull clip shown in Figure 2-64b on the previous page. Change the size of the clip to 135% and then drag the clip to the bottom center of the slide.

On Slide 3, insert the matador clip shown in Figure 2-64c. Decrease the clip size to 90%, and then drag it to the lower-right corner of the slide. Apply the Blinds Entrance custom animation effect to the clip.

On Slide 4, change the slide layout to Title and Content over Text. Insert the running bull clip shown in Figure 2-64d and then change the size of the clip to 85%. Apply the Wheel custom animation effect to the clip. Increase the font size of the level 1 body text paragraph to 28 point and the level 2 body text paragraphs to 24 point.

Apply the Descend animation scheme in the Moderate category list to all slides.

Save the presentation using the file name, Apply 2-1 Hemingway. Print the presentation with all four slides on one page and the outline, and then hand in the hard copies to your instructor.

1 Home Schooling

Problem: Many parents believe their children can receive a better education at home than at school. During the past 25 years, home schooling has become a national trend. Your social studies teacher has assigned a research paper and a five-minute presentation on the topic of the perceived advantages of home schooling. You generate the outline shown in Figure 2-65 to prepare the presentation. You use the outline to create the presentation shown in Figures 2-66a through 2-66d. If you cannot locate the clips shown in the figures, see your instructor.

I. An Education at Home
- Support of Home Schooling
- Jason Harris

II. Well-Rounded Children
- A. Pursue interesting projects instead of sitting all day
- B. Participate in outside activities
  - 1. Music, science

III. Safe Environment
- A. No peer pressure
  - 1. Alcohol, drug use increasing among teens
- B. Protection against classroom violence

IV. Individual Attention
- A. Children learn at own pace
  - 1. Work one-on-one
  - 2. Flexible schedules, due dates

FIGURE 2-65

In the Lab

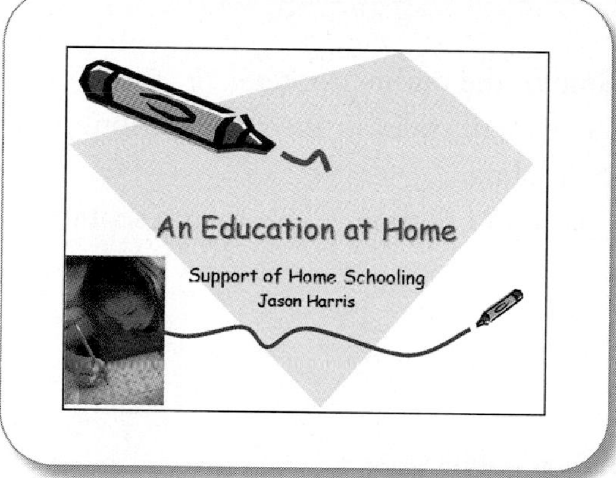

FIGURE 2-66a

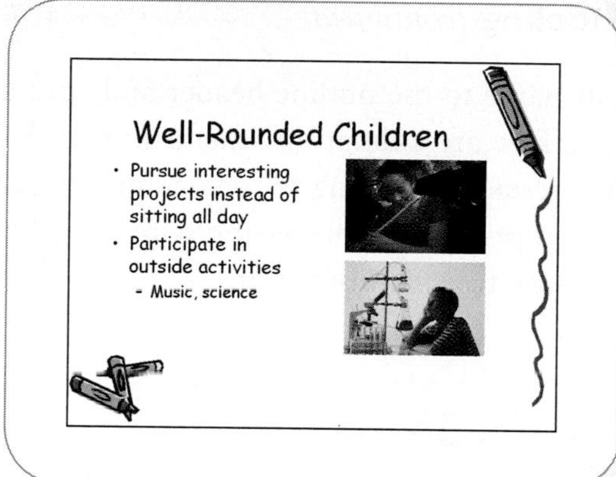

FIGURE 2-66b

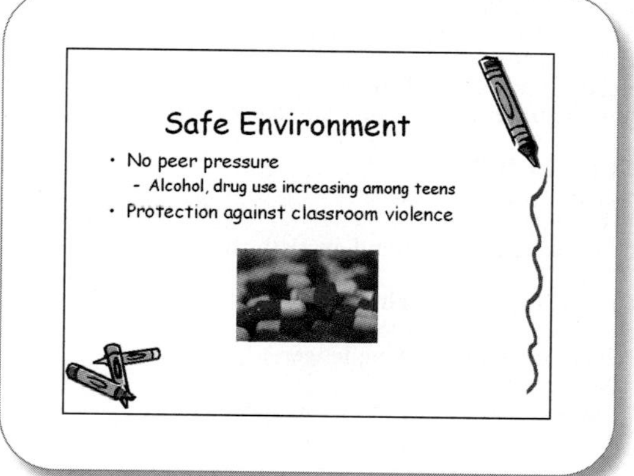

FIGURE 2-66c

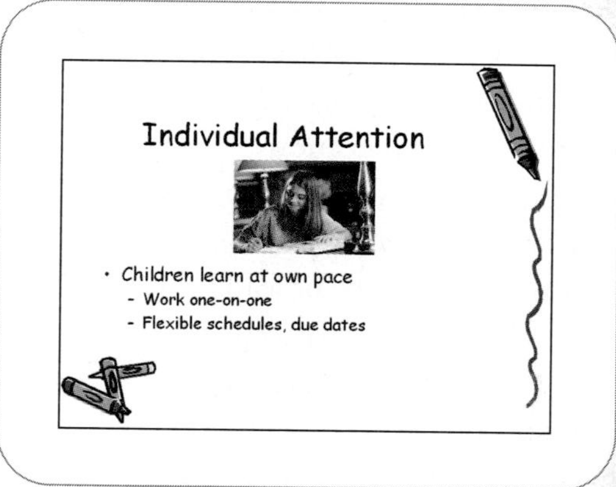

FIGURE 2-66d

FIGURE 2-66

Instructions: Perform the following tasks.

1. Use the Outline tab to create a new presentation. Apply the Crayons design template.
2. Using the outline shown in Figure 2-65, create the title slide shown in Figure 2-66a. Use your name instead of the text, Jason Harris. Decrease the font size of the your name to 24 point. Insert the homework clip art. Scale the clip to 90% and then drag the clip to the lower-left corner of the slide. Add the Blinds Entrance custom animation effect to the clip.
3. Insert a new slide. Change the slide layout on Slide 2 to Title, Text, and 2 Content. Using the outline in Figure 2-65, type the text for Slide 2. Insert the flute and science clip art shown in Figure 2-66b.
4. Using the outline shown in Figure 2-65, create the Slides 3 and 4 with the bulleted lists shown in Figures 2-66c and 2-66d.
5. Change the slide layout on Slide 3 to Title and Text over Content. Insert the drugs clip art shown in Figure 2-66c. Scale the clip art if necessary and then center it in the space under the text. Add the Diamond Entrance custom animation effect to the clip.
6. On Slide 4, change the slide layout to Title and Content over Text. Insert the clip art shown in Figure 2-66d, scale it if necessary, and then center it in the space above the text. Add the Box Entrance custom animation effect.

(continued)

Home Schooling *(continued)*

7. Add your name to the outline header and your school's name to the outline footer.
8. Apply the Title arc animation scheme in the Exciting category to all slides in the presentation.
9. Save the presentation using the file name, Lab 2-1 Home Schooling.
10. Display and print the presentation with two slides on one page and outline. Close the presentation. Hand in the hard copy to your instructor.

2 Getting in Shape

Problem: More than 15 percent of teenagers are overweight, and this number is increasing yearly. In addition, the growing incidence of teens' low levels of good cholesterol, high blood pressure, and elevated triglycerides is evidence of dangerous complications. You have been learning in health class that having a sensible diet and exercising regularly during your teen years are the best methods of leading a healthy adult life. You decide to design a PowerPoint slide show to accompany a required oral report on the best methods of getting in shape. You type information with sensible exercise suggestions (Figure 2-67) and then create the presentation shown in Figures 2-68a through 2-68d. If you cannot locate the clips shown in the figures, see your instructor.

1. **No Excuses - Get in Shape**
   Sensible Exercise Plan
   Presented by
   Jon Rowand

2. **But I Am Too Busy**
   You do not have time not to exercise
      20 minutes daily is sufficient
   Exercise gives increased energy
   Take stairs instead of elevator, talk on cell phone while walking at trac

3. **But Exercise Is Boring**
   Try sports-specific classes
      Running, golf
   Fusion classes calm the mind, work the body

4. **But I Am Not Overweight**
   Exercise helps prevent injuries
      Increases odds of living longer
      Reduces stress
      Boosts self-esteem

FIGURE 2-67

FIGURE 2-68a

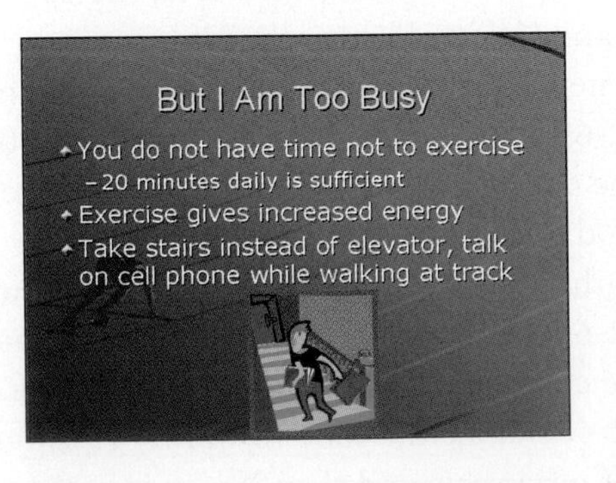

FIGURE 2-68b

FIGURE 2-68

In the Lab

FIGURE 2-68c

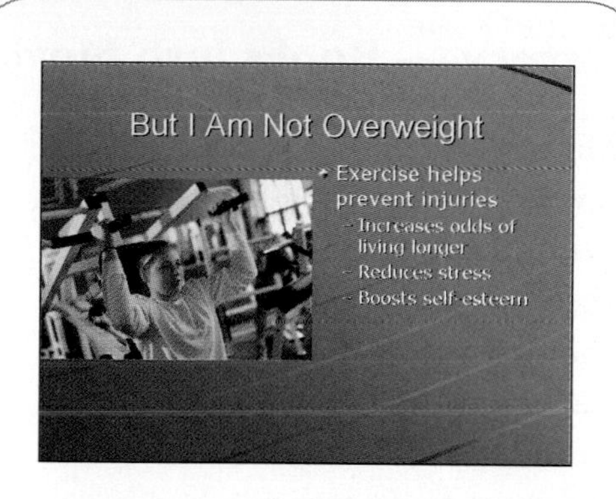

FIGURE 2-68d

FIGURE 2-68 *(continued)*

Instructions: Perform the following tasks.

1. Use the Outline tab to create a new presentation from the outline shown in Figure 2-67. Apply the Competition design template.
2. On the title slide, italicize the title text, No Excuses - Get in Shape and increase the font size to 48 point. Using Figure 2-68a as a reference, insert the jump rope clip art shown, scale it to 85%, and then drag it to the lower-right corner of the slide. Replace the name, Jon Rowand, with your name.
3. On Slide 2, insert the stairs clip art shown in Figure 2-68b. Scale the clip to 125% and then center it below the text.
4. On Slide 3, change the slide layout to Title, Content and Text. Insert the exercise clip art shown in Figure 2-68c. Scale the clip to 40% and then move it to the location shown in the figure.
5. On Slide 4, change the slide layout to Title, Content and Text. Insert the weight training clip art shown in Figure 2-68d, scale the clip to 120%, and then move it to the location shown in the figure.
6. Add the current date and your name to the outline header. Include No Excuses and the page number on the outline footer.
7. Apply the Compress animation scheme in the Moderate category to all slides.
8. Animate the clip on Slide 1 using the Spin Emphasis custom animation effect, the clip on Slide 2 using the Fly In Entrance effect, and the clip on Slide 3 using the Box Entrance effect. Do not animate the clip on Slide 4.
9. Save the presentation using the file name, Lab 2-2 Get In Shape.
10. Display and print the presentation with two slides on one page and the outline. Close the presentation. Hand in the hard copy to your instructor.

In the Lab

3 Reel History — Books into Movies

Problem: Many classic novels are based on historical events that occurred during the 1800s. In turn, Hollywood producers have turned these books into award-winning movies that have withstood the test of time. You have read many of these books in your American Literature class, and for extra credit you want to prepare a PowerPoint presentation showing the historical nature of the films and the novels. You discuss your project with your teacher, Miss Mary Halen, and develop the outline shown in Figure 2-69. You create the text for the presentation on the Outline tab and then search for appropriate clip art to add to the slides. If you cannot locate the clips shown in Figures 2-70a through 2-70d, see your instructor. You refine the presentation using an animation scheme and custom animation effects and then e-mail the presentation to Miss Halen.

Reel History
- Books into Movies
- Presented by
- Jennifer Askew

Moby Dick
- Based on novel by Herman Melville
- Captain Ahab obsessed with great white whale
  - Caused loss of leg

The Secret Garden
- Based on novel by Frances Hodgson Burnett
- Uncle's walled garden becomes secret world for three characters

Little Women
- Based on novel by Louisa May Alcott
- Sisters grow up under mother's guidance
- Theme: Quest for contentedness of family life

FIGURE 2-69

FIGURE 2-70a

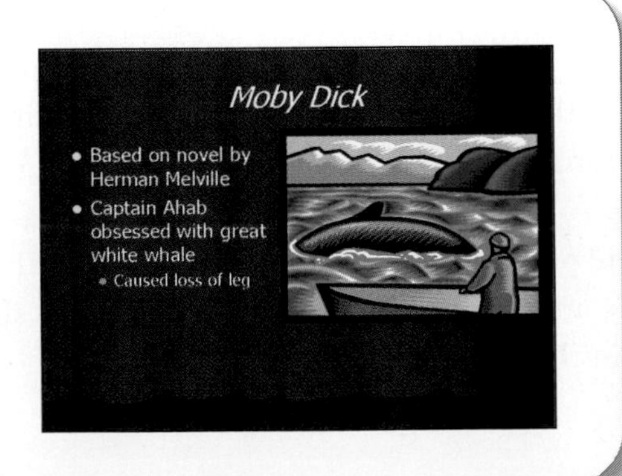

FIGURE 2-70b

FIGURE 2-70

In the Lab

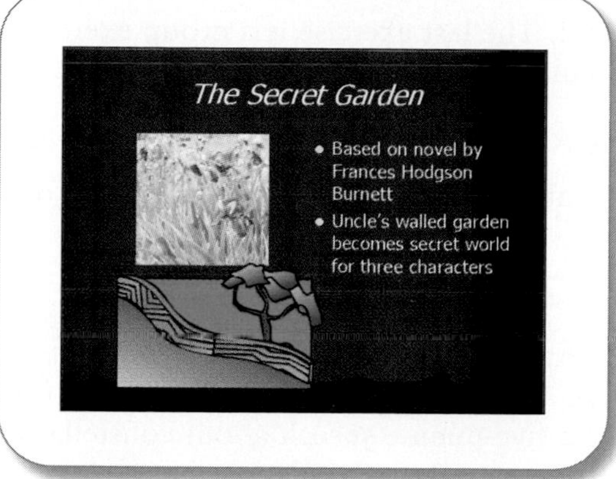

FIGURE 2-70c

FIGURE 2-70d

FIGURE 2-70 ***(continued)***

Instructions: Perform the following tasks.

1. Using the Outline tab, create a new presentation using the outline in Figure 2-69. Apply the Curtain Call design template.
2. On the title slide, insert and size the clip art image shown in Figure 2-70a. Add the Fly In Entrance custom animation effect and change the speed to Medium.
3. On Slide 2, change the slide layout to Title, Text, and Content. Insert the clip shown in Figure 2-70b. Add the Fly In Entrance custom animation effect and change the Direction to From Right. Size the clip if necessary. Italicize the slide title text, *Moby Dick*.
4. On Slide 3, change the slide layout to Title, 2 Content and Text. Insert the clips shown in Figure 2-70c. Add the Ease In Entrance custom animation effect for the top image and change the speed to Medium. Add the Curve Up Entrance custom animation effect for the bottom image and change the speed to Slow. Size the clips if necessary. Italicize the slide title text, *The Secret Garden*.
5. Change the slide layout on Slide 4 (Figure 2-70d) to Title and Content over Text. Insert the clip art image shown. Add the Transparency Emphasis custom animation effect using the default amount and duration settings. Size the clip if necessary. Italicize the slide title text, *Little Women*.
6. Display your name and the current date on the outline header, and display the page number and the name of your school on the outline footer.
7. Apply the Unfold animation scheme in the Moderate category to all slides.
8. Save the presentation using the file name, Lab 2-3 Reel History.
9. E-mail the presentation to Miss Halen using the address mary_halen@hotmail.com.
10. Display and print the presentation with all four slides on one page and the outline. Close the presentation. Hand in the hard copy to your instructor.

Cases and Places

The case studies are identified by discipline. The difficulty of these case studies varies: ▮ are the least difficult and ▮▮ are more difficult. The last exercise is a group exercise. Each exercise has a cross-curricular designation:

Math Social Studies Science Language Arts Art/Music Business Health

Note: Remember to use the 7 × 7 rule as you design the presentations: a maximum of seven words on a line and a maximum of seven lines on one slide.

1 Throughout the ages, people have stared at the nighttime sky and grouped the stars into meaningful figures. The stories associated the constellations are an integral part of mythology and folklore. One of your earth science class assignments is to prepare a five-minute speech about constellations. You develop the speech outline shown in Figure 2-71. Using the concepts and techniques introduced in this project, together with your outline, develop slides for a PowerPoint presentation to accompany your talk. Include clip art, animation effects, and an animation scheme. Print the outline and slides as handouts so they can be distributed to your teacher and classmates.

1. Constellation Revelations
- Presented by
- Student Name
- Earth Science 1

2. See the Stars
- 88 constellations recognized in past 5,000 years
- Asterisms are unofficial constellations
  - Part of official constellations
  - Easily identified stars
    - Big Dipper
    - Summer Triangle

3. Ursa Major and Minor
- Ursa Major
  - Large Bear
    - Includes the Big Dipper
- Ursa Minor
  - Small Bear
    - Includes the Little Dipper

4. Other Popular Constellations
- Andromeda (Princess of Ethiopia)
  - Impressive in winter sky
    - High overhead in November and December
- Orion (Great hunter)
  - Largest constellation
    - Companions are Gemini and Taurus

FIGURE 2-71

Cases and Places

2 All art forms are based on fundamental visual elements. You have been studying these concepts in your Art 1 class and decide to use them as the basis of an informative speech in your Speech 1 class. You develop the outline shown in Figure 2-72 and then develop a presentation that includes information about the color wheel, color principles, and art types. Using the concepts and techniques introduced in this project, together with the outline, develop slides for a presentation. Include clip art, animation effects, and an animation scheme. Display the presentation title in the outline header and your name in the outline footer. Print the outline and slides as handouts.

A. Art Fundamentals
- Visual Elements
- Student Name
- Art 1

B. Color Wheel
- Primary colors
  - Red, yellow, blue
- Secondary colors
  - Orange, green, violet
- Intermediate
  - Examples: red-orange, blue-violet

C. Color Principles
- Basic premise: color is light
- Black surface absorbs all light
  - Shading: Combining color with black
- White pigment absorbs no color rays
  - Tinting: Combining color with white

D. Art Types
- Always been part of life
  - Range from cave painting to graffiti
  - Include jewelry, baskets, masks
- New media
  - Video
  - Computer images

FIGURE 2-72

Cases and Places

3 Schizophrenia is a mental illness that usually develops in adolescence or early adulthood and affects teenagers especially hard. You have been studying this debilitating illness in your psychology class and decide to research the topic further for a required oral presentation in class. You learn that doctors have recognized the disease for many centuries, as early as the 1600s, and first named the illness in 1911. It affects both men and women and has many recognizable symptoms. People often have disconnected speech; when they change topics frequently during a conversation, they seem incoherent and incomprehensible. Their disturbed psychomotor behavior is characterized by very little movement, rigid posture, and frequent rocking and pacing. They have difficulty functioning in interpersonal situations and often seem self-centered and aloof. Their obsession with delusions, hallucinations, and illogical ideas results in detachment from friends and family. These behaviors often result in leaving school and jobs. Using this information, develop a slide show. Choose an appropriate design template and add clip art, animation effects, and an animation scheme. Print the presentation slides and outline to distribute as handouts for your classmates.

4 The United States Copyright Office has issued guidelines about reproducing, distributing, and performing intellectual works, including books, drama, music, and art. A copyright protects the work's creator from having others reproduce the work without permission. The laws vary depending upon whether the work was created before, on, or after January 1, 1978. Ask your school's librarian for a copy of the United States Copyright Office's rules, and then prepare a PowerPoint presentation explaining copyright registration, protections, and expiration. Include clip art, animation effects, and an animation scheme to add interest. Print the outline and slides as handouts so they can be posted at the library's photocopy machine.

5 **Working Together** An estimated 10 percent of high school girls suffer from the eating disorders anorexia nervosa and bulimia. High school boys also have this eating disorder, but in fewer numbers. Many high schools take an active role in counseling students to make healthy nutritional choices. Have each member of your team visit your guidance center and visit or telephone several local community agencies to gather information about nutritionists who provide nutrition counseling. Obtain data about:

1. Initial consultation
2. Follow-up sessions
3. Available services
4. Information provided

After coordinating the data, create a presentation with clip art, animation effects, and an animation scheme that describes the events that occur during counseling sessions. As a group, critique each slide. Hand in a hard copy of the final presentation.

MICROSOFT OFFICE
PowerPoint 2003

Creating a Presentation on the Web Using PowerPoint

CASE PERSPECTIVE

"A fool and his money are soon parted," according to British poet Thomas Tusser. Although he wrote this proverb in the mid-1500s, its message stressing the importance of knowing how to manage money is applicable today. The average high school graduate lacks basic skills in personal finance. Many students cannot balance a checkbook and are unaware of the fundamentals of balancing spending and saving, investing, and earning money.

Your Business 1 instructor, Miss Patty Schmitt, wants to teach her students the basics of personal finance. She is aware that one of the skills most critical for success is knowing how to manage money. Many teenagers fail early in their first credit experiences because they have poor financial management habits. Consequently, they are forced to correct these behaviors by trial and error or by asking their parents for assistance.

Miss Schmitt is developing a unit of her business class that will incorporate determining needs and wants, using credit cards, and budgeting. Her discussions will focus on the underlying principle that people should not spend money they do not have. By being aware of how much money is required for necessities and budgeting for those needs, students can learn to save prudently and spend carefully. If they use credit cards wisely and spend less than they earn, these habits will lay the foundation for a wealthy adult life. Miss Schmitt decides the most effective way to disseminate this information is to create a PowerPoint slide show (Figure 1) and then publish the presentation on the World Wide Web.

As you read through this Web feature, you will learn how to create and display a Web page from a PowerPoint presentation, edit the results using a browser, and then publish the presentation.

Objectives

You will have mastered the material in this project when you can:

- Preview and save a presentation as a Web page
- Create a new folder using file management tools
- View a Web page using a browser
- Edit the Web page content through a browser
- Publish a presentation as a Web page

Introduction

The graphic design power of PowerPoint allows you to create vibrant presentations that convey information in a clear, interesting manner. Some of these presentations are created for small, specific audiences, such as a subcommittee planning a department retreat. In this case, the presentation may be shown in an office conference room. Other presentations are designed for large, general audiences, such as workers at a corporation's various offices across the country learning about a new insurance benefits package. These employees can view the presentation on their company's **intranet**, which is an internal network that uses Internet technologies. On a grand scale, you can inform the entire world about the contents of your presentation by posting your slide show to the World Wide Web. To publish to the World Wide Web, you need a **File Transfer Protocol (FTP)** program to copy your presentation and related files to an **Internet service provider (ISP)** computer.

PowerPoint provides you with two ways to create a Web page. First, you can start a new presentation, as you did in Projects 1 and 2 when you produced the Career Planning and the Healthy Driving Tips presentations. PowerPoint provides a Web Presentation template in the **AutoContent Wizard** option when you start PowerPoint. The wizard provides design and content ideas to help you develop an effective slide show for an intranet or for the Internet by opening a sample presentation that you can alter by adding your own text and graphics.

Second, the Save as Web Page command on the File menu allows you to **publish** presentations, which is the process of making existing presentations available to others on the World Wide Web or on a company's intranet. If you have access to a Web server, you can publish Web pages by saving them to a Web folder or to an FTP location. To learn more about publishing Web pages to a Web folder or FTP location using Microsoft Office applications, refer to Appendix C.

The Publish command allows you to create a Web page from a single slide or from a multiple-slide presentation. This Web Feature illustrates opening the Dollars and Sense presentation on the Data Files for Students folder (Figure 1a) and then saving

FIGURE 1

the presentation as a Web page using the Save as Web Page command. You will save the Web pages and associated folders on a USB flash drive connected to one of the computer's USB ports rather than to a Web server. At times, this saving process may be slow and requires patience. See page xxiv at the front of this book for instructions for downloading the Data Files for Students or see your instructor for information on accessing the files required for this book.

Then, you will edit the presentation, save it again, and view it again in your default browser. Finally, you will publish your presentation, and PowerPoint will start your default browser and open your file so you can view the presentation (Figures 1b through 1e).

Q & A

Q: Why is it important to learn about personal finance now?

A: Learning money-smart skills is something you cannot delay until college. Nearly 80 percent of college students use a credit card and carry a balance of more than $3,200. In addition, more than 10 percent of these students have a balance of nearly $8,000. For more information on money management skills, visit the Office 2003 Q&A Web page (scsite.com/off2003sch/qa), locate PowerPoint Web Feature 1, and click Money.

Using Web Page Preview and Saving a PowerPoint Presentation as a Web Page

PowerPoint makes it easy to create a presentation and then preview how it will display on an intranet or on the World Wide Web. This action opens the presentation in your default Web browser without saving files. By previewing your slide show, you can decide which features look good and which need modification. The left side of the window includes the navigation frame, which is the outline of the presentation. The outline contains a table of contents consisting of each slide's title text. You can click the Expand/Collapse Outline button below the navigation frame to view the complete slide text. The right side of the window shows the complete slide in the slide frame. The speaker notes, if present, are displayed in the notes frame below the slide frame. Once the preview is acceptable, you then can save the presentation as a Web page.

Previewing the Presentation as a Web Page

Because you are converting the Dollars and Sense presentation on the USB flash drive to a Web page, the first step in this project is to open the Dollars and Sense file. At any time while developing a presentation, you can preview it as a Web page by using the Web Page Preview command on the File menu. When you use the Web Page Preview command, your browser starts and the presentation is displayed as a Web page. The steps on the next page show how to use the Web Page Preview command.

Q & A

Q: What are the advantages of saving a presentation as a Web page?

A: Saving the presentation in Web page format is an excellent vehicle for distributing in the slide show to many viewers. Another method of sharing your file is by broadcasting, which allows audience members to view the slide show in real time on their computers while you control precisely what they see. You also can record a broadcast so viewers can watch the presentation at their convenience.

To Preview the Presentation as a Web Page

1

- **Connect the USB flash drive to one of the computer's USB ports.**
- **Start PowerPoint and then open the presentation, Dollars and Sense, on the USB flash drive in drive E.**
- **Click File on the menu bar.**

PowerPoint starts and opens the slide show, Dollars and Sense, in normal view. The presentation is composed of four slides. PowerPoint displays the File menu (Figure 2).

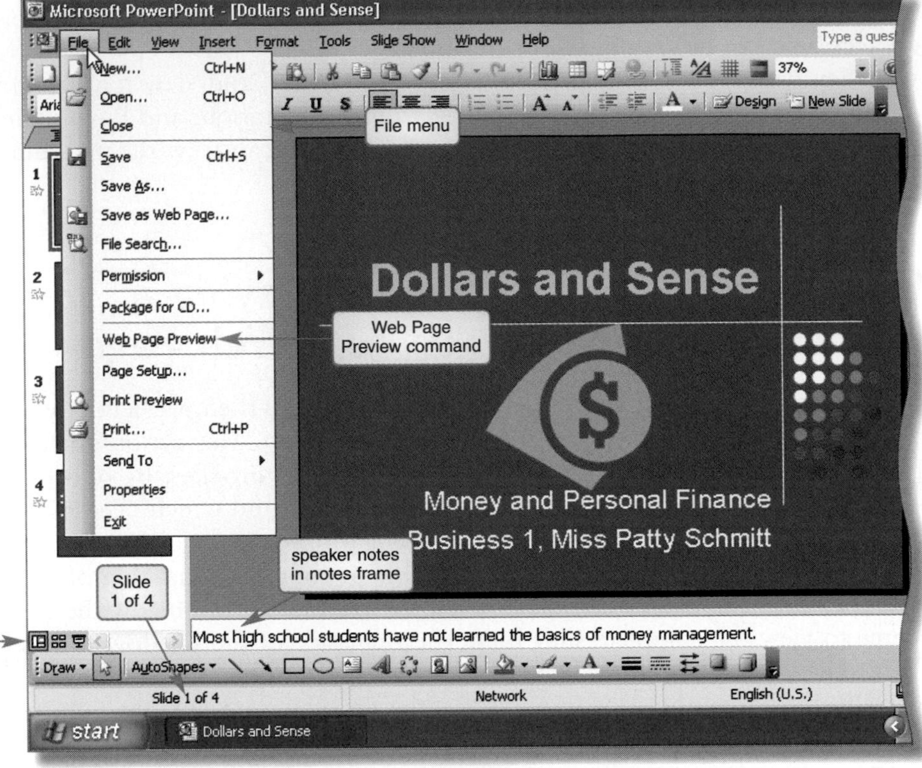

FIGURE 2

2

- **Click Web Page Preview.**

PowerPoint starts your browser. The browser displays a Web page preview of Slide 1 of the Dollars and Sense presentation in the slide frame in the browser window (Figure 3). The navigation frame contains the table of contents, which consists of the title text of each slide. The speaker notes are displayed in the notes frame. The Microsoft PowerPoint button on the taskbar no longer is selected. Windows displays a selected browser button on the taskbar, indicating it is active.

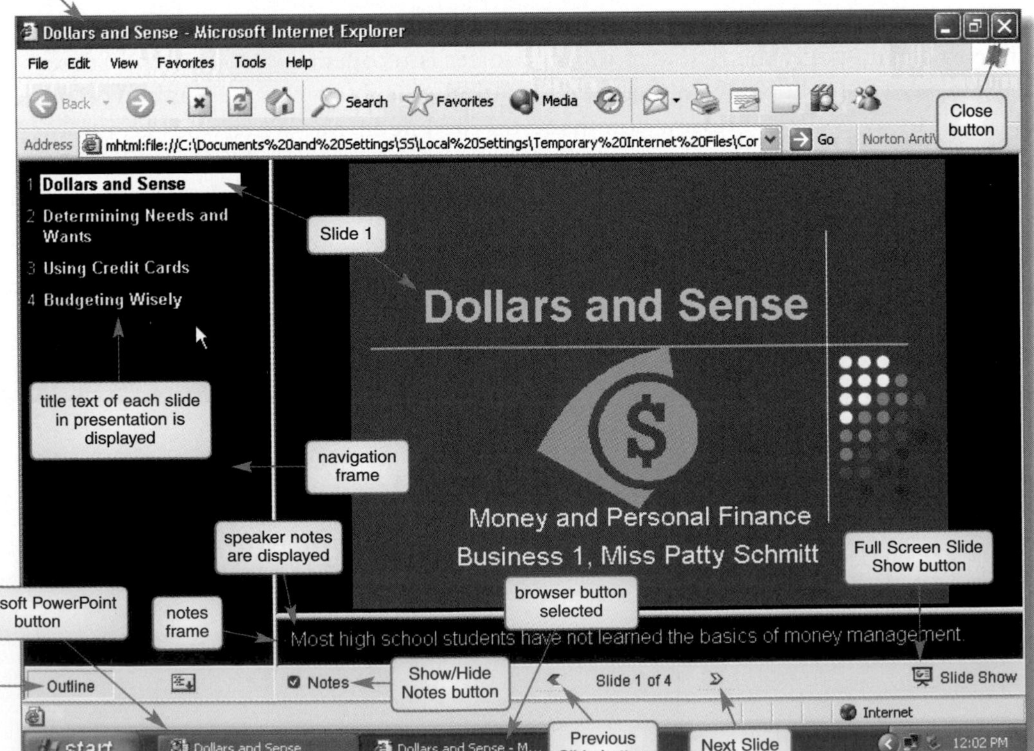

FIGURE 3

3

• Click the Full Screen Slide Show button.

Slide 1 fills the entire screen (Figure 4). The Slide 1 title text and clip art are displayed. The Web Page preview in the browser is nearly identical to the display of the presentation in PowerPoint.

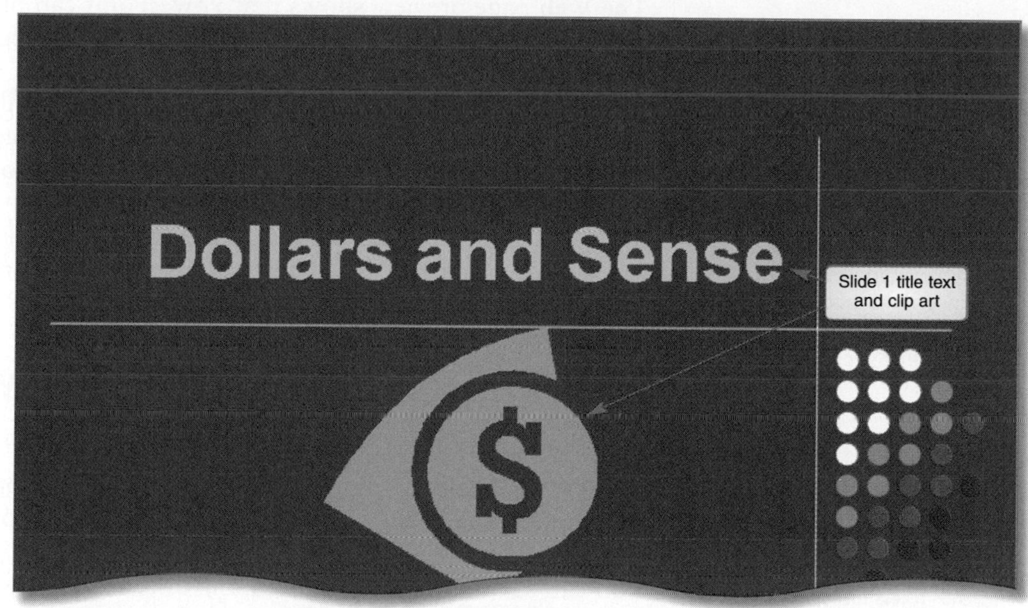

FIGURE 4

4

• Click to display the first line of the subtitle text.

The first line of the Slide 1 subtitle text is displayed.

5

• Continue clicking each slide in the presentation.

• When the black slide is displayed, click it.

Each of the four slides in the Dollars and Sense presentation is displayed. The message on the black slide, End of slide show, click to exit., indicates the conclusion of the slide show.

6

• Click the Close button on the right side of the browser title bar.

The browser closes, PowerPoint becomes active, and PowerPoint displays Slide 1 (Figure 5).

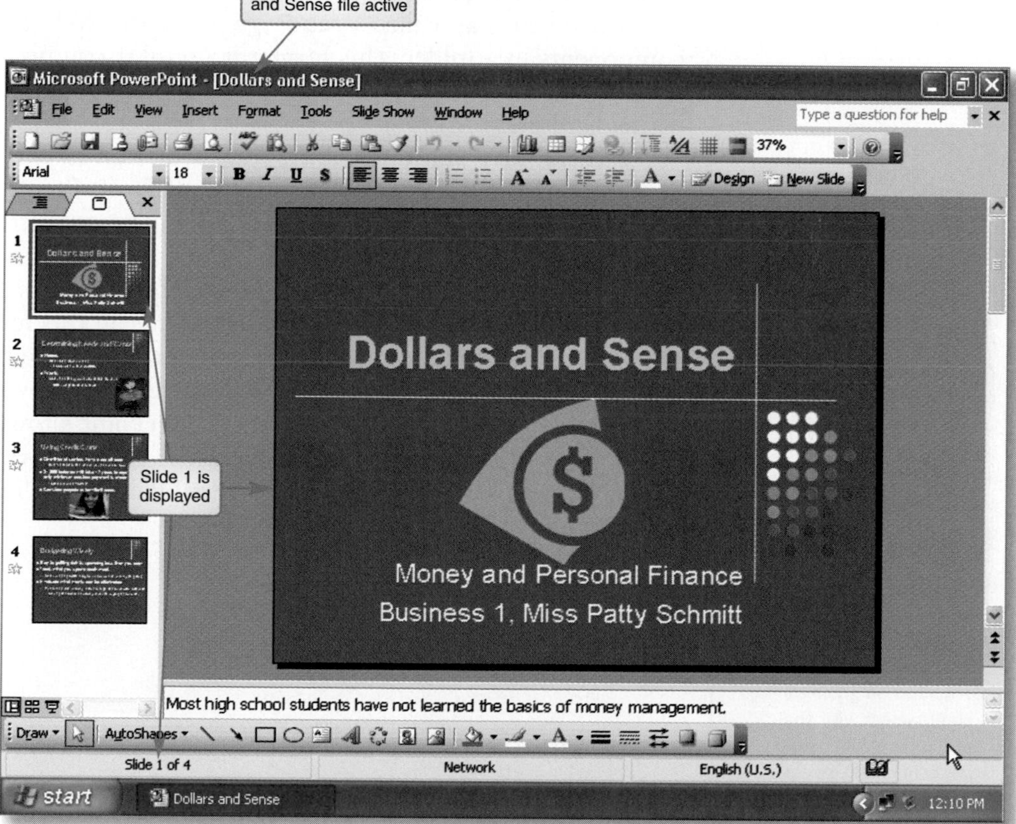

FIGURE 5

Q & A

Q: On what days are audience members most attentive?

A: Sundays, Mondays, and Tuesdays. Researchers believe these days are the best for delivering presentations because the viewers are more relaxed than at the middle and end of the week. As you choose to show or hide your outline and notes, consider your audience's attention span. You may need to provide more information via the outline and notes on the days when your audience is less focused.

The Web page preview shows that PowerPoint can produce professional-looking Web pages from presentations. You can alter the browser window by choosing to display or hide the navigation and notes frames. To hide the navigation frame, click the Show/Hide Outline button below the outline. Later, if you want to redisplay the navigation frame, click the Show/Hide Outline button again. Similarly, the Show/Hide Notes button below the slide frame allows you to display or conceal the speaker notes, if present, on a particular slide.

To advance through the Web page, you also can click the Next Slide button below the slide frame. Likewise, to display a slide appearing earlier in the slide show, click the Previous Slide button.

Saving a PowerPoint Presentation as a Web Page to a New Folder

Once the preview of a PowerPoint slide show is acceptable, you can save it as a Web page so you can view it in a Web browser. Microsoft Internet Explorer and Netscape Navigator are the two more common browsers installed on computers today.

You can save the presentation in one of two Web page formats. One format is called **Single File Web Page**, which saves all the Web page components in a single file with an .mht extension. This format is useful for e-mailing presentations in **hypertext markup language (HTML)**, which is a language browsers can interpret. The second format, called **Web Page**, saves the Web page in a file and some of its components in a folder. This format is useful if you need access to the components, such as clip art, that comprise the Web page. Both formats convert the slide show contents into HTML.

You can save and then view the presentation in two ways. First, you can save the entire presentation as a Web page, quit PowerPoint, open your browser, and open the Web page in your browser. Second, you can combine these steps by saving the presentation as a Web page, publishing the presentation, and then viewing the presentation as a Web page. In this case, PowerPoint will start the browser and display your presentation automatically. Later in this feature, the Publish button will be used to explain further how you can customize a Web page.

Experienced users organize their storage devices by creating folders and then save related files to a common folder. PowerPoint allows you to create folders in the Save As dialog box before saving a file. The following steps create a new folder on the USB flash drive and then save the Dollars and Sense presentation in the Web Page format to the new folder.

Q & A

Q: When was the first Web browser developed?

A: In 1993, computer science students at the University of Illinois developed Mosaic, one of the first graphical Web browsers. Marc Andreessen and a friend worked 18 hours a day for 6 weeks to develop this browser. This success led to the organization of the Netscape Communications Corporation. For more information on graphical Web browsers, visit the Office 2003 Q&A Web page (scsite.com/off2003sch/qa), locate PowerPoint Web Feature 1, and click Browsers.

To Save a Presentation in Web Page Format to a New Folder

1

- **With the Dollars and Sense presentation open, click the Next Slide button twice to view Slide 3.**
- **Click the notes pane and then type** `The proportion of bankruptcy filers under the age of 25 has risen from less than 1 percent in 1995 to more than 5 percent today.` **as the note.**
- **Click File on the menu bar.**

PowerPoint displays the File menu (Figure 6). The last two words of the speaker notes you typed appear in the notes pane.

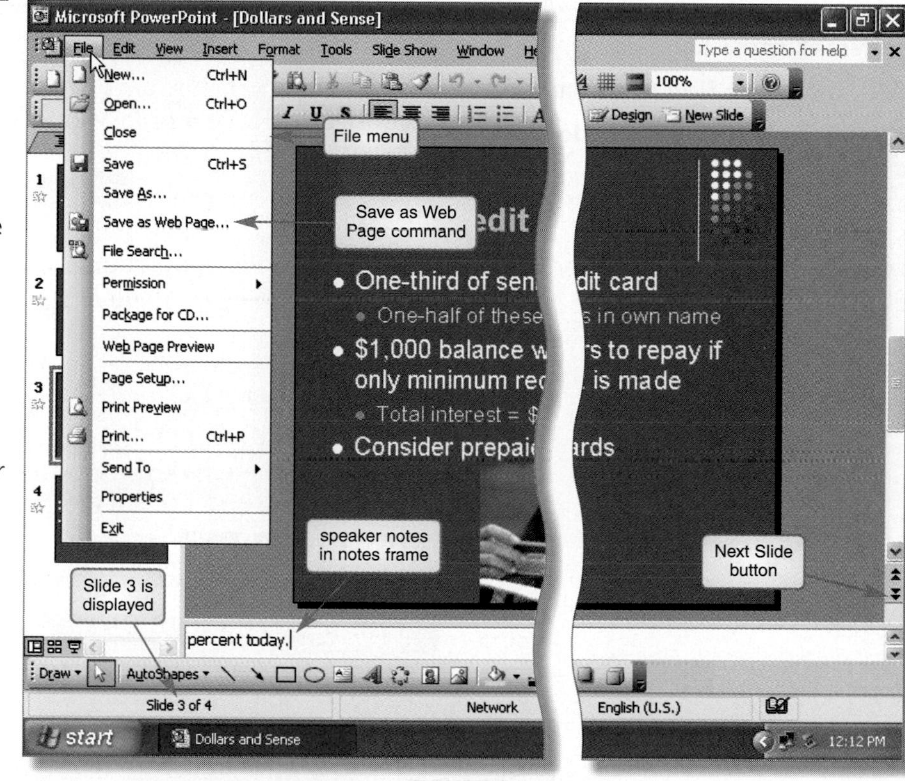

FIGURE 6

2

- **Click Save as Web Page.**
- **When the Save As dialog box is displayed, type** `Dollars and Sense Web Page` **in the File name text box so that the file name is Dollars and Sense Web Page.**
- **Click the Save as type box arrow and then click Web Page.**

PowerPoint displays the Save As dialog box (Figure 7). The default file format type is Single File Web Page.

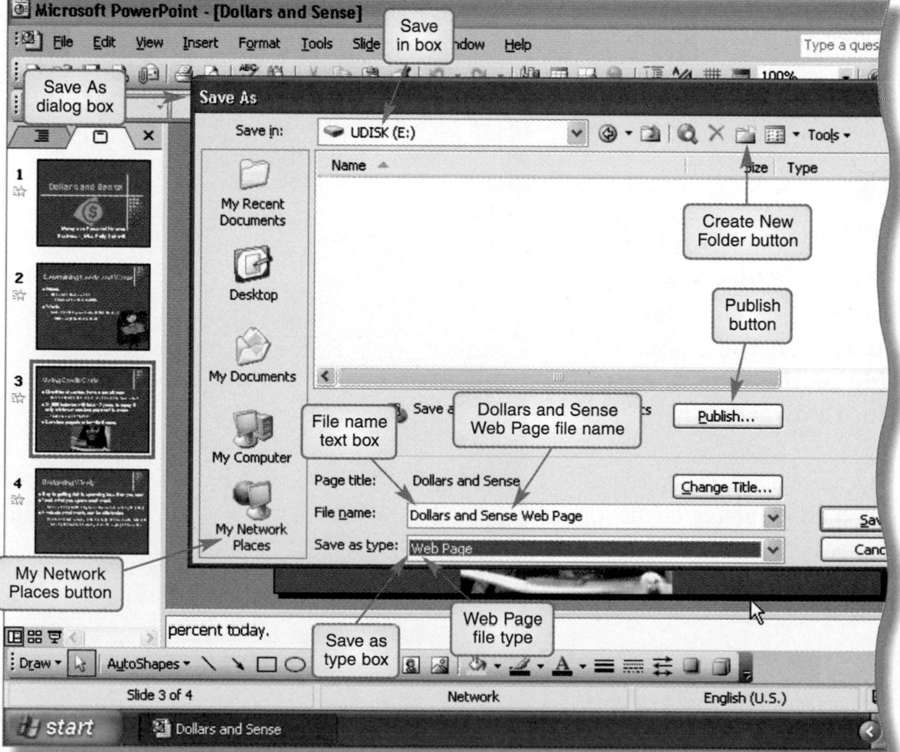

FIGURE 7

3

- **If necessary, click the Save in box arrow and select UDISK (E:). (Your USB flash drive may have a different name and letter.)**
- **Click the Create New Folder button.**
- **When the New Folder dialog box is displayed, type** `Web Feature` **in the Name text box.**

PowerPoint displays the New Folder dialog box (Figure 8).

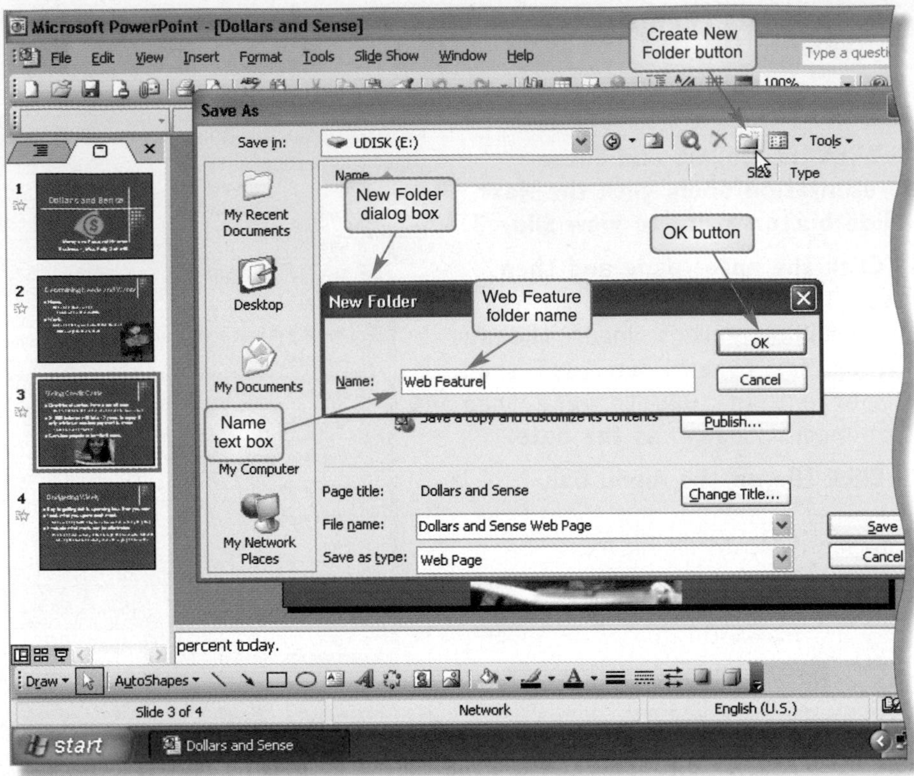

FIGURE 8

4

- **Click the OK button in the New Folder dialog box.**

PowerPoint automatically selects the new Web Feature folder in the Save in box.

5

- **Click the Save button.**
- **After all files are saved, click the Close button on the right side of the title bar to close PowerPoint.**

PowerPoint saves the presentation in HTML format on the USB flash drive in the Web Feature folder using the file name Dollars and Sense Web Page.htm. PowerPoint closes (Figure 9).

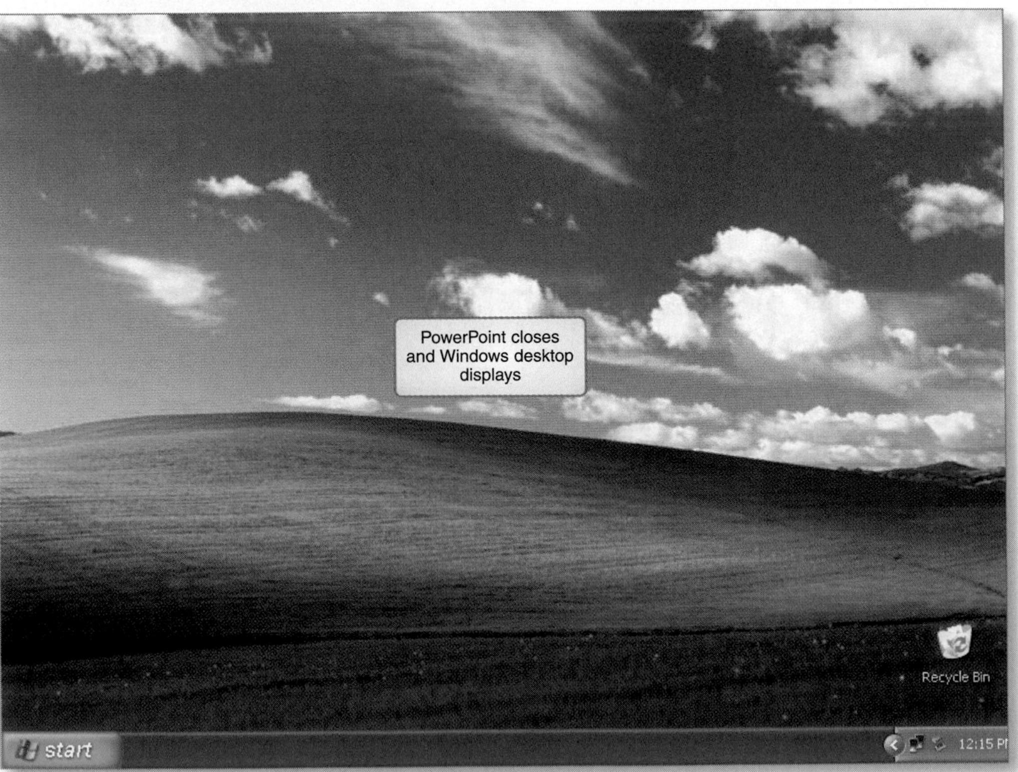

FIGURE 9

The Save As dialog box that displays when you use the Save as Web Page command is slightly different from the Save As dialog box that displays when you use the Save As command. The Publish button in the Save As dialog box in Figure 7 on page PPT 147 is an alternative to the Save button and allows you to customize the Web page further. In the previous set of steps, the Save button was used to complete the save. Later in this feature, the Publish button will be used to explain further how you can customize a Web page.

Q & A

Q: When is the PowerPoint Show format used for saving files?

A: PowerPoint provides many file formats for saving presentations. One useful format that allows viewers to see, but not alter, a presentation is the PowerPoint Show (.pps) format. A slide show saved as a PowerPoint Show always will open as a slide show presentation.

File Management Tools in PowerPoint

Creating a new folder allows you to organize your work. PowerPoint automatically inserts the new folder name in the Save in box when you click the OK button in the New Folder dialog box (Figure 8). Once you create a folder, you can right-click it while the Save As dialog box is active and perform many file management tasks directly in PowerPoint. For example, once the shortcut menu is displayed, you can rename the selected folder, delete it, copy it, display its properties, and perform other file management functions.

If you have access to a Web server that allows you to save files to a Web folder, then you can save the Web page directly to the Web server by clicking the My Network Places button in the lower-left corner of the Save As dialog box (Figure 7). If you have access to a Web server that allows you to save to an FTP site, then you can select the FTP site under FTP locations in the Save in box just as you select any folder in which to save a file. To save a presentation to a Web server, see Appendix C.

After PowerPoint saves the presentation in Step 5, it displays the HTML file — not the presentation — in the PowerPoint window. PowerPoint can continue to display the presentation in HTML format because within the HTML file that was created, PowerPoint also saved the formats to display the HTML file. This is referred to as **round tripping** the HTML file back to the application in which it was created.

Q & A

Q: What PowerPoint features will not work when a presentation is viewed as a Web page?

A: Several PowerPoint features do not work when a presentation is viewed as a Web page. These features include embossed and shadow effects for fonts, text that is animated by the letter or word rather than by the paragraph, and special effects on charts. In addition, music will not play throughout a Web presentation because moving to another slide stops the sound.

Viewing the Web Page Using Your Browser

With the Dollars and Sense Web page saved to the folder, Web Feature, on the USB flash drive, the next step is to view it using a browser, such as Microsoft Internet Explorer or Netscape, as shown in the steps on the next page.

Skill Builder WF-1

To practice the following tasks, visit scsite.com/off2003sch/skill, locate PowerPoint Web Feature, and then click Skill Builder WF-1.

- ❑ Preview a presentation as a Web page.
- ❑ Save presentation as a Web page to a new folder.
- ❑ View a Web page using a browser.

To View the Web Page Using Your Browser

1

- **If necessary, connect the USB flash drive to one of the computer's USB ports.**
- **Click the Start button on the taskbar, point to All Programs, and then click Internet Explorer.**
- **When the Internet Explorer window displays, type** `e:\web feature\dollars and sense web page.htm` **in the Address bar and then press the ENTER key. (Your USB flash drive may have a different name and letter.)**

The browser displays Slide 1 in the Web page, Dollars and Sense Web Page.htm (Figure 10).

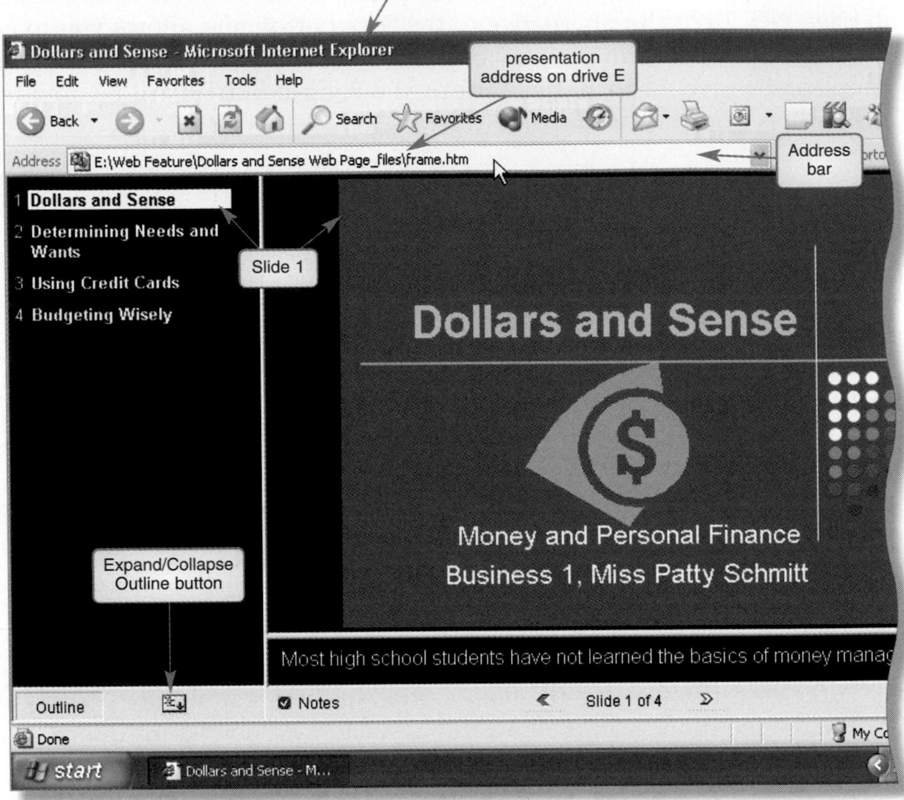

FIGURE 10

2

- **Click the Expand/Collapse Outline button at the bottom of the window.**

The text of each slide in an outline appears in the navigation frame (Figure 11). To display only the title of each slide, you would click the Expand/Collapse Outline button again.

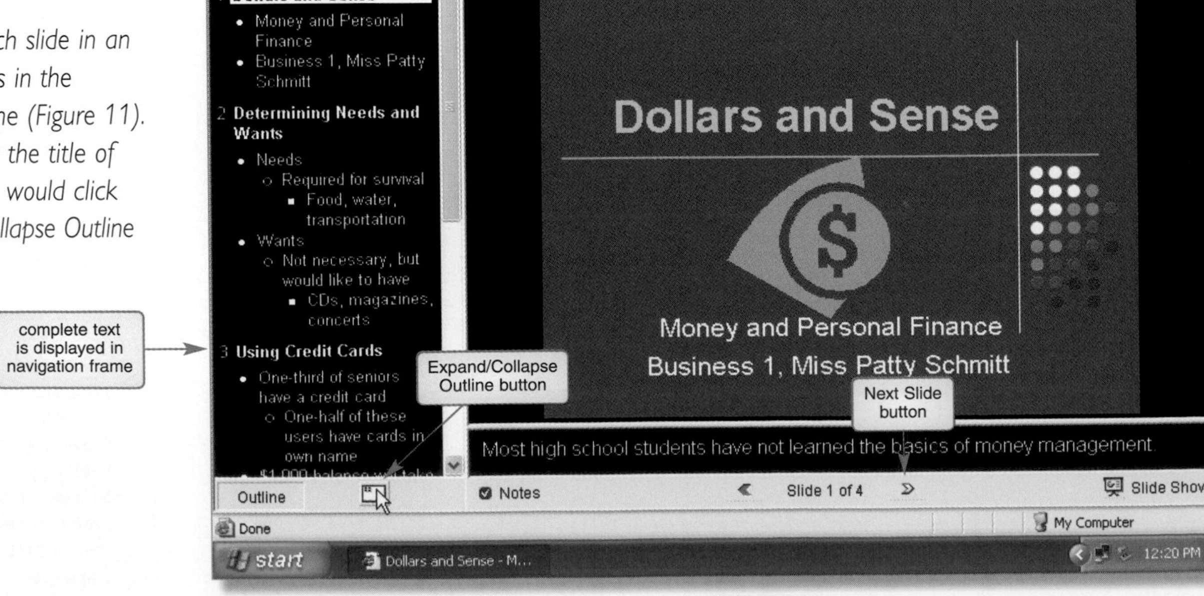

FIGURE 11

3

• **Click the Next Slide button three times to view all four slides.**

The browser displays each of the slides in the Dollars and Sense presentation. Slide 4 is displayed in the browser (Figure 12).

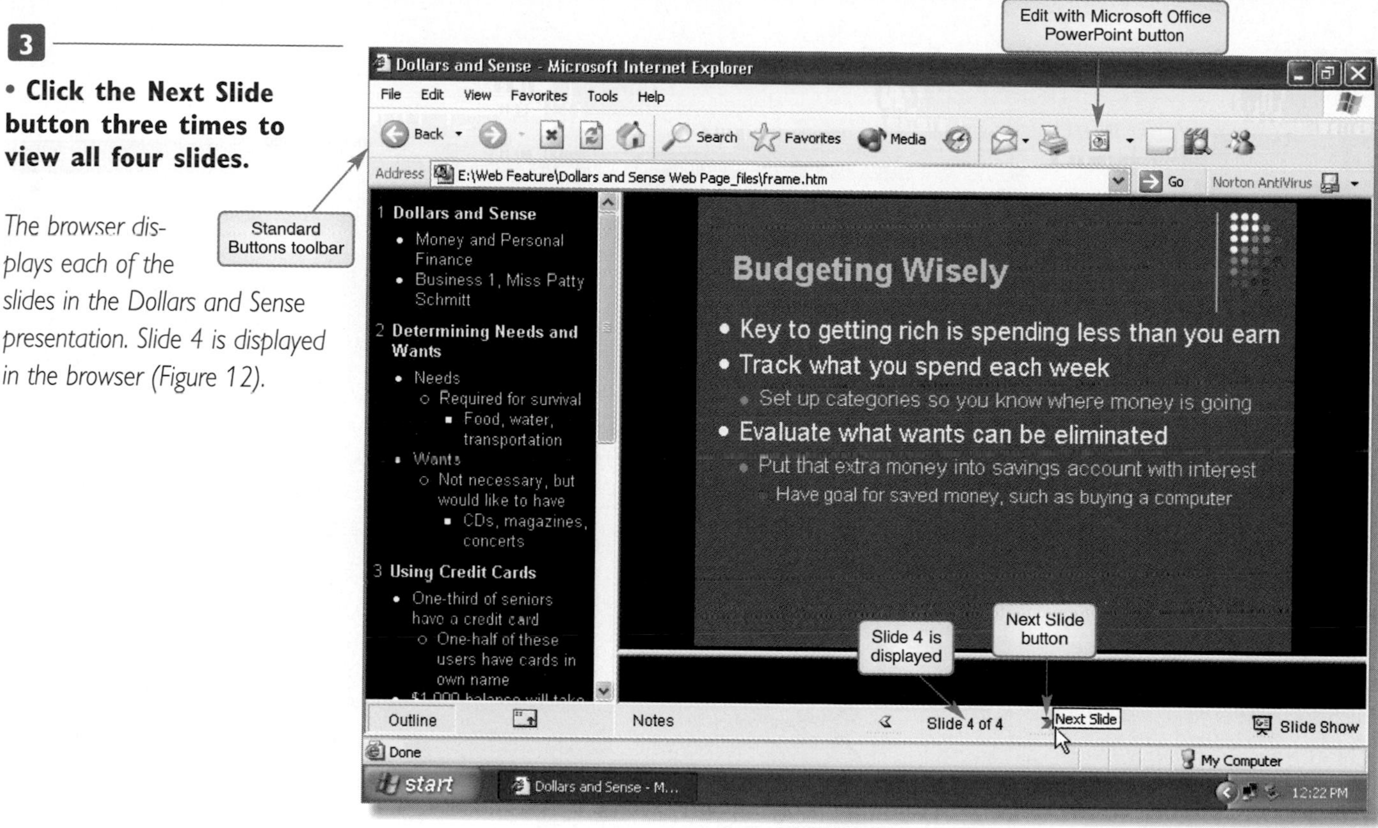

FIGURE 12

Figures 11 and 12 show that a Web page is an ideal medium for distributing information to a large group of people. The Web page can be made available to anyone with a computer, browser, and the address. The Web page also can be e-mailed easily because it resides in a single file, rather than in a file and folder.

If you want, you can use the Print command on the File menu in your browser to print the slides one at a time. You also can view the HTML source PowerPoint created by clicking Source on the View menu in Internet Explorer or Page Source on the View menu in Netscape.

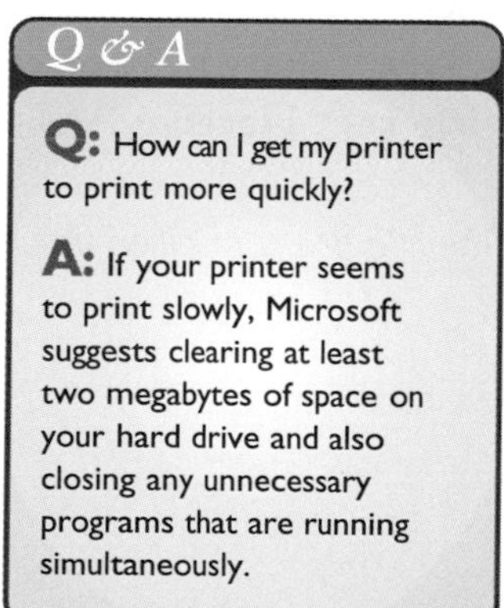

Q & A

Q: How can I get my printer to print more quickly?

A: If your printer seems to print slowly, Microsoft suggests clearing at least two megabytes of space on your hard drive and also closing any unnecessary programs that are running simultaneously.

Editing a Web Page through a Browser

You may want to modify your Web page by making small changes to the text or art on some slides. In this presentation, you want to change the title text in Slide 1 to reflect the fact that the teenage years are a good time to learn how to manage money responsibly. You can modify the presentation using PowerPoint directly in the browser window. Your computer may indicate other editing options, such as using Windows Notepad. The steps on the next page modify the Title Slide title text.

To Edit a Web Page through a Browser

1

- **Click the Edit with Microsoft Office PowerPoint button on the Standard Buttons toolbar.**
- **Select the words, Dollars and Sense, in the title text placeholder.**

When you click the Edit button, PowerPoint opens a new presentation with the same file name as the Web presentation file name, as indicated by the title bar and the selected Microsoft PowerPoint - [Dollars and Sense Web Page] button on the Windows taskbar (Figure 13). A selection rectangle appears around the title text placeholder. The three words are highlighted.

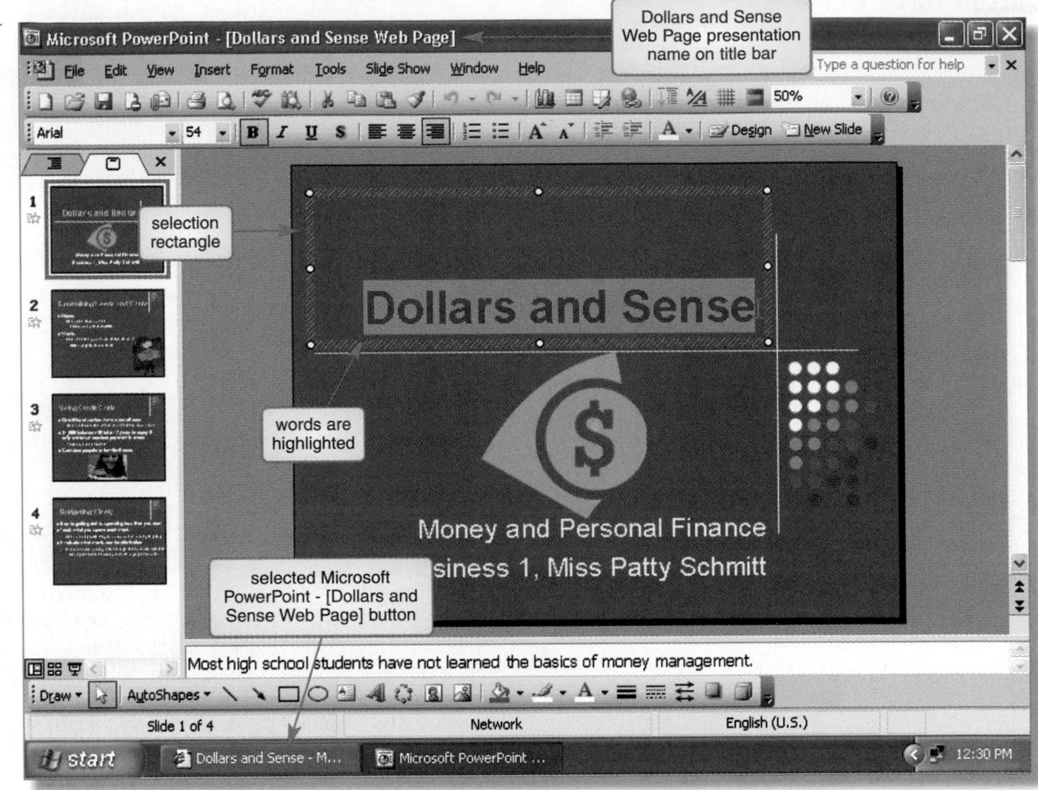

FIGURE 13

2

- **Type** `Sensible Spending` **in the title text placeholder.**

The title text is modified (Figure 14).

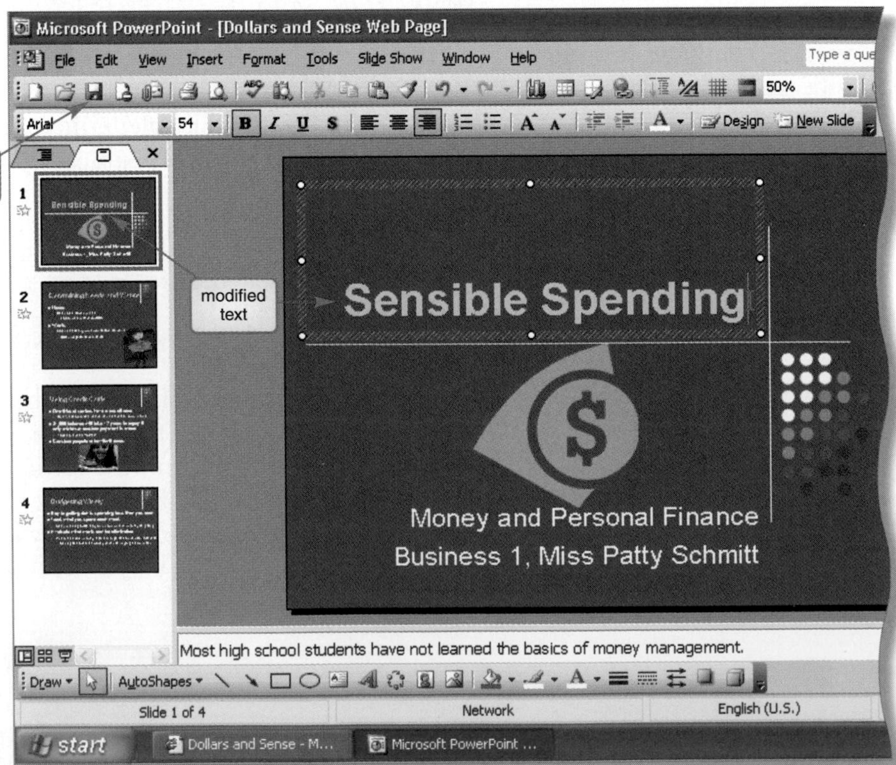

FIGURE 14

3

• **Click the Save button on the Standard toolbar.**

It takes several minutes for PowerPoint to save the changes to the Dollars and Sense Web Page.htm file on the USB flash drive. The buttons on the taskbar indicate that the PowerPoint presentation and the browser are open.

4

• **Click the Dollars and Sense - Microsoft Internet Explorer button on the taskbar.**

• **Click the Previous Slide button three times to display Slide 1.**

The browser displays the revised title text on Slide 1 (Figure 15). If the revised text does not display, click the Refresh button on the Standard Buttons toolbar.

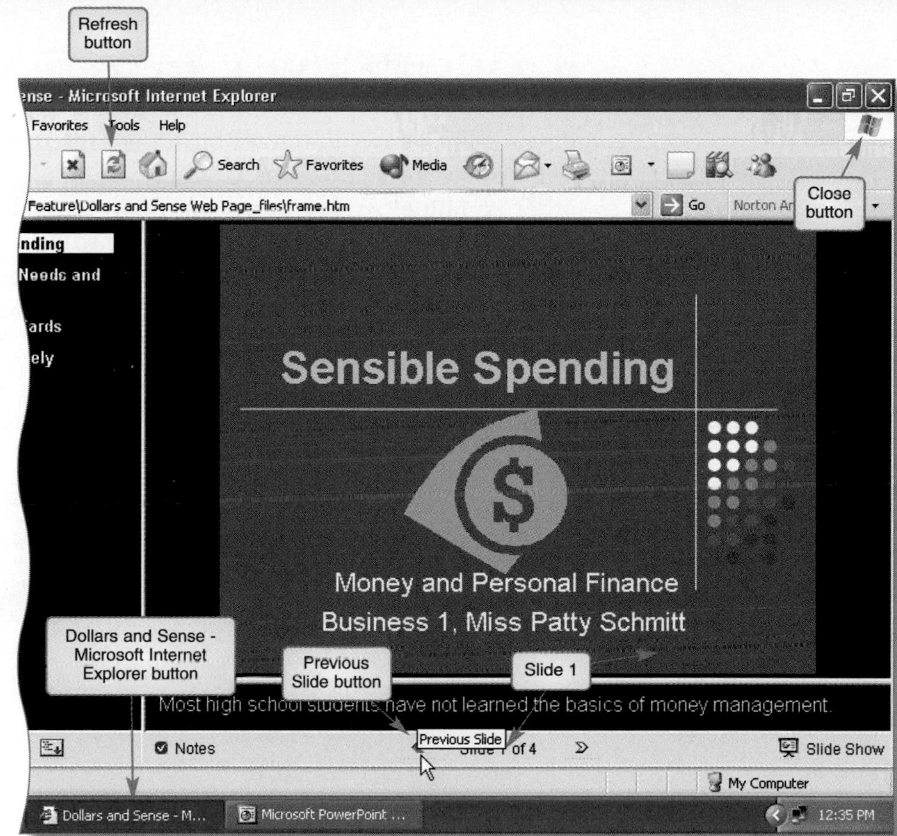

FIGURE 15

5

• **Click the Close button on the browser title bar.**

• **Click the Save button to save the revised PowerPoint Dollars and Sense Web Page.**

The browser closes, and the PowerPoint window displays in normal view with the modified Slide 1 of the Dollars and Sense Web Page presentation active (Figure 16).

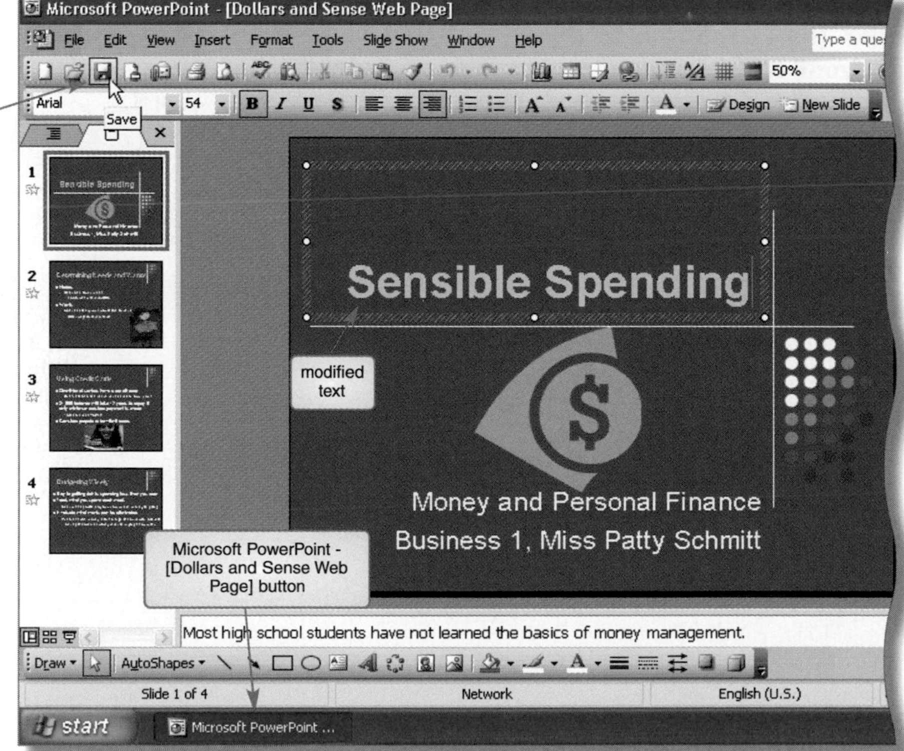

FIGURE 16

Publishing a Web Page

PowerPoint allows you to publish the presentation by saving the pages to a Web folder or to an FTP location. When you publish your presentation, it is available for other computer users to view on the Internet or by other means. Publishing a Web page of a presentation is an alternative to distributing printed copies of the slides. The following section uses the Publish button in the Save As dialog box, rather than the Save button, to illustrate PowerPoint's additional publishing capabilities.

To Publish a PowerPoint Presentation

1

- **Click File on the menu bar and then click Save as Web Page.**
- **Click the Save as type box arrow and then click Single File Web Page.**
- **Type** `Dollars and Sense Single File Web Page` **in the File name text box.**
- **If necessary, click the Save in box arrow, select UDISK (E:) in the Save in list (your USB flash drive may have a different name and letter), and then select the folder, Web Feature.**

The Save As dialog box is displayed (Figure 17). When you use the Publish button, PowerPoint will save the Web page in a single file.

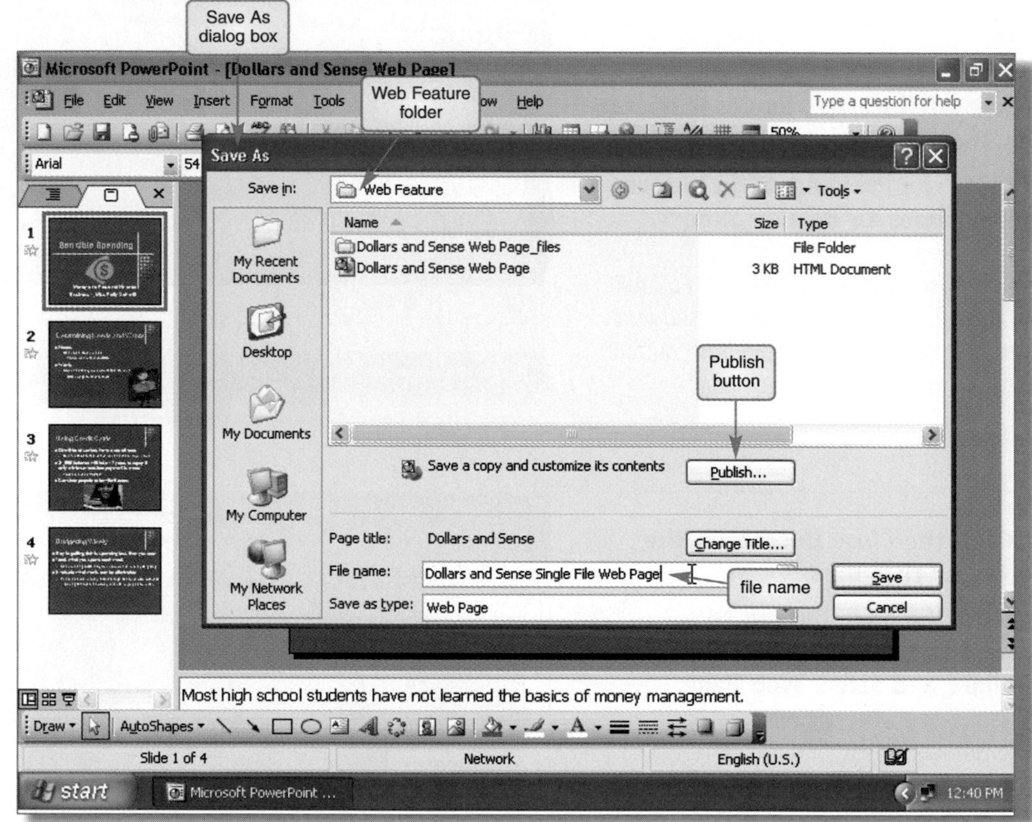

FIGURE 17

2

- **Click the Publish button.**
- **If the Office Assistant appears, click No, don't provide help now.**
- **If necessary, click Open published Web page in browser to select it.**

The Publish as Web Page dialog box is displayed (Figure 18). PowerPoint defaults to publishing the complete presentation, although you can choose to publish one or a range of slides. The Open published Web page in browser check box is selected, which means the Dollars and Sense Single File Web Page presentation will open in your default browser when you click the Publish button.

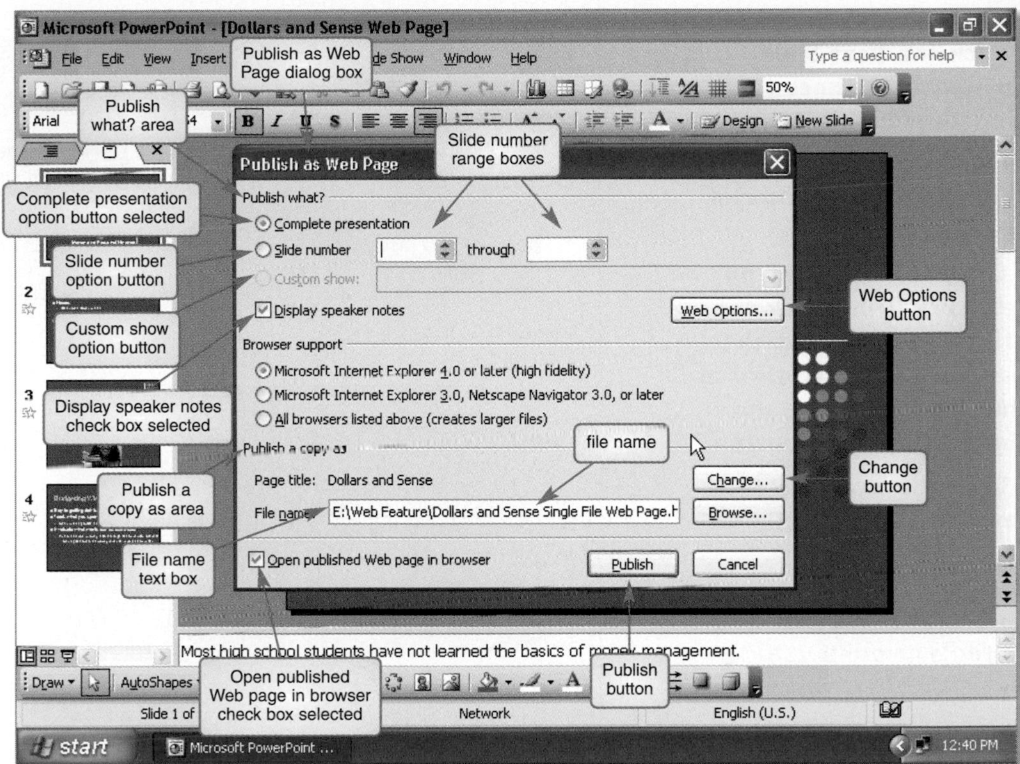

FIGURE 18

3

- **Click the Publish button.**

PowerPoint saves the presentation as a single file, Dollars and Sense Single File Web Page.mht, in the Web Feature folder on the USB flash drive. After a few minutes, PowerPoint opens your default Web browser in a separate window (Figure 19). If the browser does not open, click the Dollars and Sense - Microsoft Internet Explorer button on the Windows taskbar.

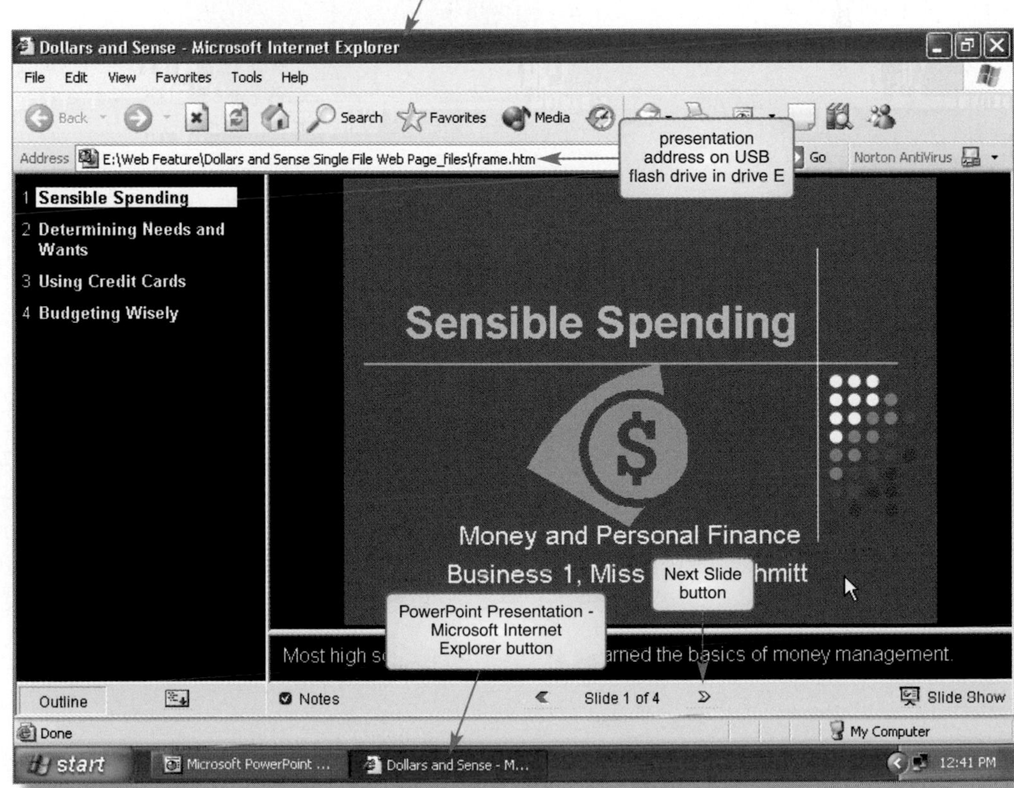

FIGURE 19

4

- **Click the Next Slide button three times to view the four slides.**
- **Click the Close button in the upper-right corner of the browser window.**
- **Click File on the menu bar, click Print, click the Print what arrow, click Handouts, click Vertical in the Handouts area, and then click the OK button.**
- **Click the Save button to save the revised Dollars and Sense Web Page.**

The browser closes, and PowerPoint prints the four slides as a handout (Figure 20). PowerPoint takes a few minutes to save the file to the USB flash drive.

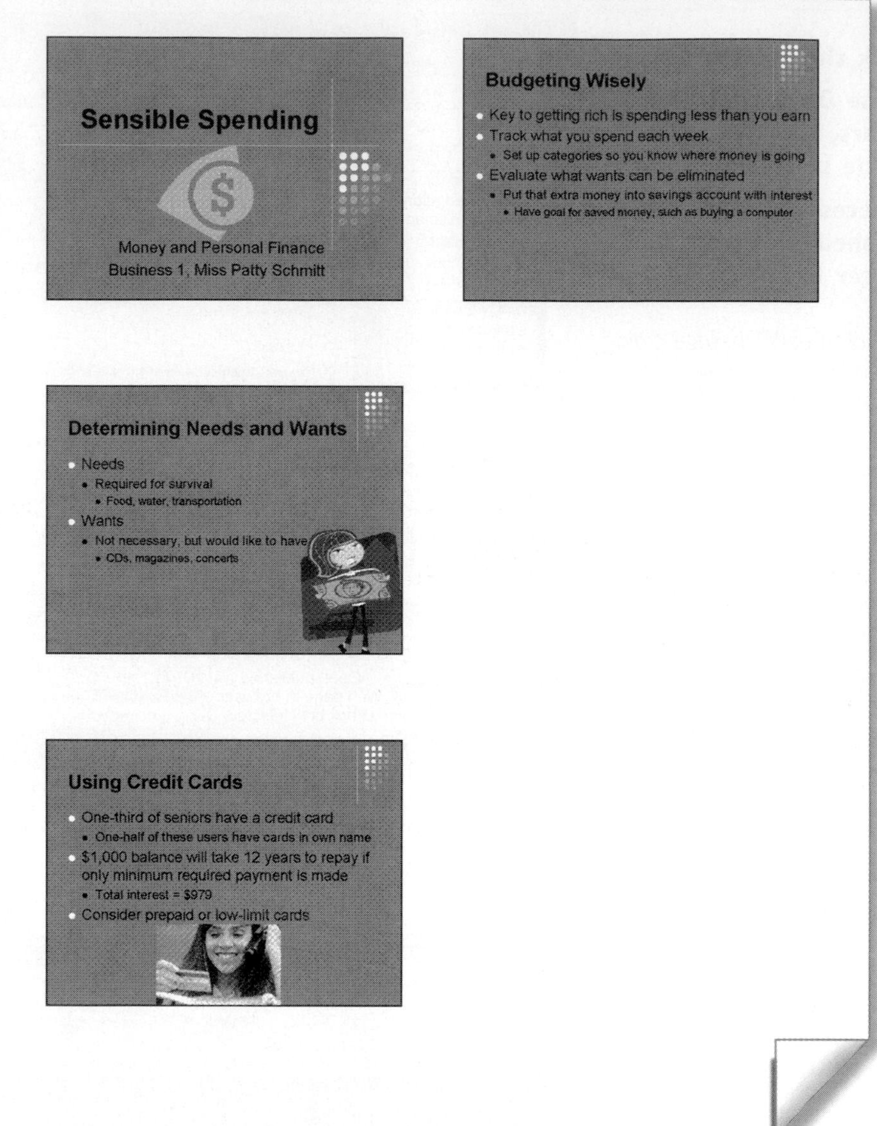

FIGURE 20

Skill Builder WF-2

To practice the following tasks, visit scsite.com/off2003sch/skill, locate PowerPoint Web Feature, and then click Skill Builder WF-2.

- ❑ Edit a Web page through a browser
- ❑ Publish a PowerPoint presentation

Publishing provides customizing options that are not available when you simply save the entire presentation and then start your browser. The Publish as Web Page dialog box provides several options to customize your Web page. For example, you can change the page title that displays on the browser's title bar and in the history list. People visiting your Web site can store a link to your Web page, which will display in their favorites list. To change the page title, you click the Change button in the Publish a copy as area (Figure 18 on the previous page) and then type a new title.

The Publish what? area of the Publish as Web Page dialog box allows you to publish parts of your presentation. PowerPoint defaults to publishing the complete presentation, but you can select specific slides by clicking the Slide number option button and then entering the range of desired slide numbers in the range boxes. In addition, you can publish a custom show you have created previously. A **custom show** is a subset of your presentation that contains slides tailored for a specific audience. For example, you may want to show Slides 1, 2, and 4 to one group and Slides 1, 3, and 4 to another group.

You can choose to publish only the publication slides and not the accompanying speaker notes. By default, the Display speaker notes check box is selected in the Publish what? area. You typed speaker notes for Slide 1 of this presentation, so the speaker notes will appear in the browser window. If you do not want to make your notes available to users, click the Display speaker notes check box to remove the check mark.

The Web Options button in the Publish what? area allows you to select options to determine how your presentation will look when viewed in a Web browser. You can choose options such as allowing slide animation to show, selecting the screen size, and having the notes and outline panes display when viewing the presentation in a Web browser.

The Web page now is complete. The next step is to make your Web presentation available to others on your network, an intranet, or the World Wide Web. Ask your instructor how you can post your presentation.

Q & A

Q: What is the purpose of a Web archive?

A: Once a presentation is published, viewers can view the slide show and then offer comments about the document. Saving the presentationas an .htm or .mht Web-based format provides the most flexibility for these reviewers. The mht format combines multiple pictures and slides into a single file called a Web archive. A Web archive works in the same manner as a Web page does in .htm format. For more information on publishing Web presentations, visit the Office 2003 Q&A Web page (scsite.com/off2003sch/qa), locate PowerPoint Web Feature 1, and click Publishing.

Web Feature Summary

This Web feature introduced you to creating a Web page by viewing an existing presentation as a Web page in your default browser. The presentation then was saved as an HTML file. Next, you modified Slide 1. You then reviewed the Slide 1 change using your default browser and then published the slide show. With the Dollars and Sense presentation converted to a Web page, you can post the file to an intranet or to the World Wide Web.

If you have a SAM user profile, you may have access to hands-on instruction, practice, and assessment of the skills covered in this project. Log in to your SAM account and go to your assignments page to see what your instructor has assigned.

What You Should Know

Having completed this project, you should be able to perform the tasks below. The tasks are listed in the same order they were presented in this project. For a list of the buttons, menus, toolbars, and commands introduced in this project, see the Quick Reference Summary at the back of this book and refer to the Page Number column.

1. Preview the Presentation as a Web Page (PPT 144)
2. Save a Presentation in Web Page Format to a New Folder (PPT 147)
3. View the Web Page Using Your Browser (PPT 150)
4. Edit a Web Page through a Browser (PPT 152)
5. Publish a PowerPoint Presentation (PPT 154)

1 Creating a Web Page from the Career Planning Presentation

Problem: Mr. John Wendt, the director of the Career Center at Sunnydale High School, wants to expand the visibility of the Career Planning presentation you created for the Career Center in Project 1. Mr. Wendt believes the World Wide Web would be an excellent vehicle to help students both at Sunnydale and at other high schools, and he has asked you to help transfer the presentation to the Internet.

Instructions: Start PowerPoint and then perform the following steps.

1. Open the Career Planning presentation shown in Figure 1-1 on page PP 5 that you created in Project 1. (If you did not complete Project 1, see your instructor for a copy of the presentation.)
2. Use the Save as Web Page command on the File menu to save the presentation in Web page format. Create a new folder called Career Planning Exercise and then save the Web page with the file name, Lab WF 1-1 Sunnydale.
3. View the presentation in a browser.
4. Edit the Web page by using the words, Choosing a Career, as the Slide 1 title text.
5. Change the last paragraph to read, Earn academic credit, on Slide 3.
6. View the modified Web page in a browser.
7. Print the modified presentation as a handout with the slides arranged horizontally.
8. Ask your instructor for instructions on how to post your Web page so others may have access to it.

2 Creating a Web Page from the Driving Tips Presentation

Problem: The Driving Tips presentation you developed in Project 2 for Mrs. Jessica Cantero, the drivers' education program coordinator at West Park High School, is generating much interest. Students are interested in the information discussed in class and are inquiring about additional lectures. Mrs. Cantero has asked you to post the presentation to the school's intranet.

Instructions: Start PowerPoint and then perform the following steps.

1. Open the Driving Tips presentation shown in Figures 2-1a through 2-1e on page PP 83 that you created in Project 2. (If you did not complete Project 2, see your instructor for a copy of the presentation.)
2. Use the Save as Web Page command on the File menu to save the presentation in Web Page format. Create a new folder called Driving Tips and then save the Web page using the file name, Lab WF 1-2 Driving.
3. View the presentation in a browser.
4. Modify Slide 1 by italicizing both subtitle lines.
5. On Slide 1, type `Drivers' education classes are scheduled on Mondays and Wednesdays during April and May.` as the note.

6. Modify Slide 3 by adding the words, `Look for motorcycles`, as the last third-level paragraph.
7. On Slide 4, type `A vehicle is visible for nearly four times the distance with its headlights turned on.` as the note.
8. Save the presentation, and then view the modified Web page in a browser.
9. Print the modified presentation as a handout with the slides arranged vertically.
10. Ask your instructor for instructions on how to post your Web page so others may have access to it.

3 Creating a Personal Presentation

Problem: Your local library is starting a tutoring program for elementary school students. The reference librarian is seeking qualified high school students to work as tutors in the subjects of mathematics, English, and reading. You have decided to apply for one of these positions and want to develop a unique way to publicize your academic skills and personality traits. You decide to create a personalized PowerPoint presentation emphasizing your scholarly achievements and your interpersonal communication skills. You refer to this presentation in your application and inform the reference librarian that she can view this presentation because you have saved the presentation as a Web page and posted the pages on your school's Web server.

Instructions: Start PowerPoint and then perform the following steps.

1. Prepare a presentation highlighting your scholarly skills and personality strengths. Create a title slide and at least three additional slides. Use appropriate clip art and an animation scheme. Save the presentation using the file name, Lab WF 1-3 Library.
2. Use the Save as Web Page command to convert and publish the presentation as a single file Web page. Save the Web page in a folder named Library Web Files using the file name, Lab WF 1-3 Library.
3. View the presentation in a browser.
4. Print the presentation as a handout.
5. Ask your instructor for instructions on how to post your Web page so others may have access to it.

MICROSOFT OFFICE

OUTLOOK

MICROSOFT OFFICE

Outlook 2003

MICROSOFT OFFICE
Outlook 2003

E-Mail and Contact Management with Outlook

PROJECT

1

CASE PERSPECTIVE

Rachel Watson is the captain of the Central City High School Huskies girls basketball team. You attend several classes with Rachel, and you always support her by attending the games. Rachel's responsibilities as captain of the team include scheduling team meetings, notifying team members of schedule changes, and reporting team concerns and/or problems to the coach. She also likes to keep track of team and personal statistics, scores, standings, and home court winning streaks.

You work as a teacher's aide at the Central City High School computer lab, which has given you the opportunity to work with Outlook and become familiar with its information management and communications features. Rachel has visited the computer lab and has watched you easily manage e-mail, contacts, and appointments. She knows that using Outlook could help her to communicate with her teammates and coach and to simplify team scheduling, but she needs some direction in getting started.

Rachel has asked you to help her in familiarizing herself with Outlook's e-mail and contact management capabilities. She feels that becoming proficient with Outlook will make it easier to keep her teammates informed of team meetings and schedule changes, as well as other information they may need with respect to games and activities. You agree to help her accomplish her goals.

As you read through this project, you will learn how to use Outlook to open, read, create, and send e-mail and to organize messages. You will learn how to attach a file to an e-mail message and create and attach an electronic signature. In addition, you will learn how to create, organize, and print a contact list. Finally, you will learn how to create a distribution list and track activities of a contact.

MICROSOFT OFFICE
Outlook 2003

E-Mail and Contact Management with Outlook

PROJECT

Objectives

You will have mastered the material in this project when you can:

- Start Outlook
- Open, read, print, reply to, and delete electronic mail messages
- View a file attachment
- Create and insert an e-mail signature
- Compose, format, and send electronic mail messages
- Insert a file attachment in an e-mail message
- Flag and sort e-mail messages
- Set e-mail importance, sensitivity, and delivery options
- Create a personal folder
- Create and print a contact list
- Use the Find a Contact feature
- Organize the contact list
- Track activities of a contact
- Quit Outlook

What Is Microsoft Office Outlook 2003?

Microsoft Office Outlook 2003 is a powerful communications and scheduling program that helps you communicate with others (Figures 1-1a through 1-1d), keep track of your contacts, and organize your busy schedule. Outlook allows you to send and receive electronic mail and permits you to engage in real-time messaging with family, friends, or coworkers using instant messaging. Outlook also provides you with the means to organize your contacts. Users easily can track e-mail messages, meetings, and notes with a particular contact. Outlook's Calendar, Contacts, Tasks, and Notes components aid in this organization. Contact information readily is available from the Outlook Calendar, Mail, Contacts, and Task components by accessing the Find a Contact feature. Personal information management (PIM) programs such as Outlook provide a way for individuals and workgroups to organize, find, view, and share information easily.

This latest version of Outlook has many new features, including a completely new look. The new Reading Pane takes the place of the Preview pane and allows for viewing twice as much information. A Junk E-mail filter has been added to help prevent unwanted messages. Quick flags make it easy to categorize and find your messages. Search Folders make it easy to find specific messages. Another new feature in Outlook allows you to have a unique signature for each e-mail account.

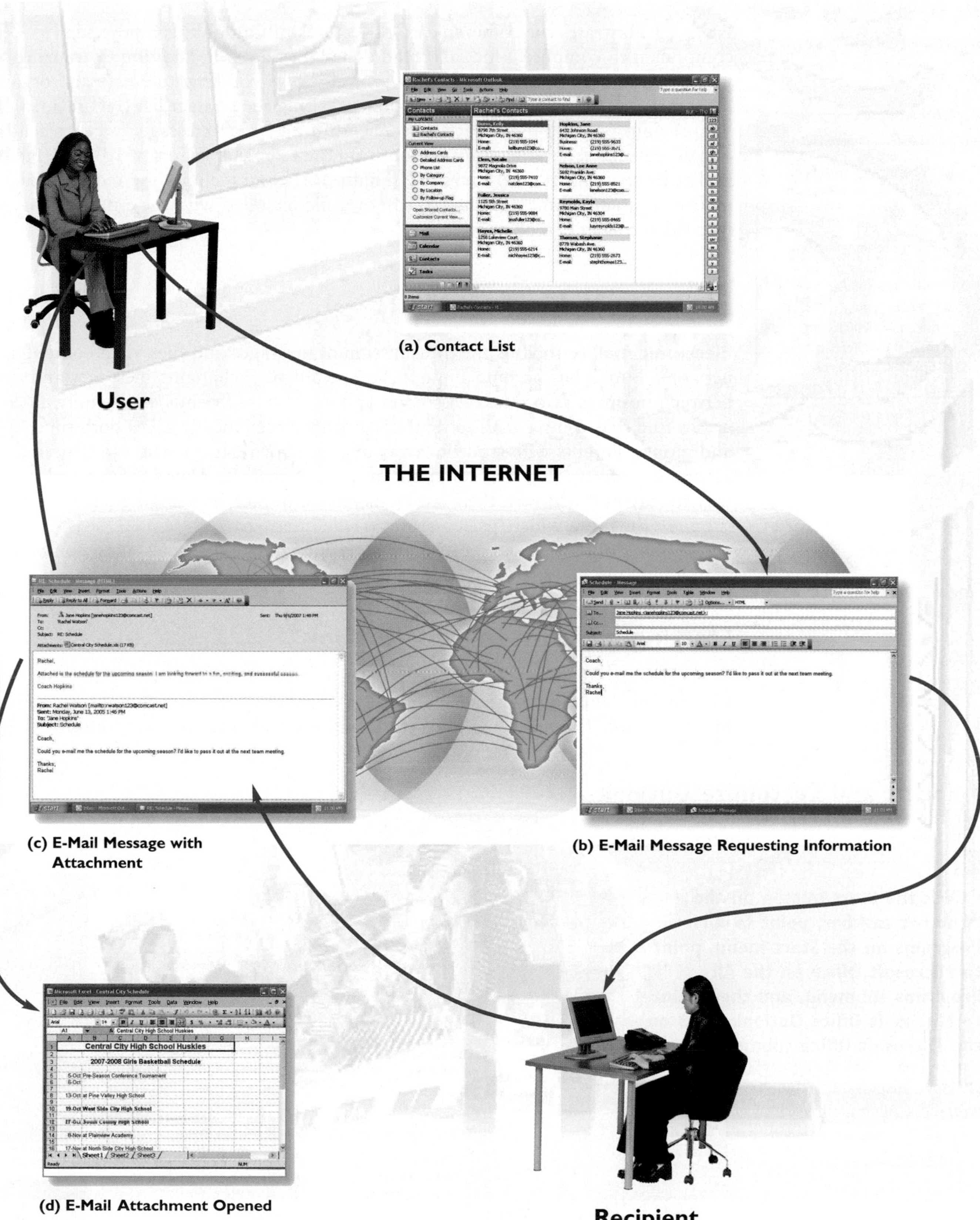
User
THE INTERNET
Recipient
(a) Contact List
(b) E-Mail Message Requesting Information
(c) E-Mail Message with Attachment
(d) E-Mail Attachment Opened

FIGURE 1-1

Project One — Communicating over the Internet

Project 1 illustrates the communications features of Outlook using the Mail component to compose, send, and read e-mail messages. In addition to utilizing Outlook's communications tools, this project shows you how to create and organize a contact list using the Contacts component. Using the contact list (Figure 1-1a on the previous page), a user selects a recipient for an e-mail message and then sends an e-mail message requesting information from the recipient (Figure 1-1b). The recipient replies by sending an e-mail message (Figure 1-1c) and includes the requested information as an attachment (Figure 1-1d), or a file included with the e-mail message, that the recipient can open.

Q & A

Q: Where can I find more information about Microsoft Outlook 2003?

A: For more information about the features of Outlook 2003, visit the Office 2003 Q&A Web page (scsite.com/ off2003sch/qa) and then click Microsoft Outlook 2003 Features.

Electronic Mail (E-Mail)

Electronic mail (**e-mail**) is the transmission of messages and files via a computer network. E-mail has become an important means of exchanging messages and files between business associates, classmates and instructors, friends, and family. Businesses find that using e-mail to send documents electronically saves both time and money. Parents with students away at college or relatives who are scattered across the country find that communicating via e-mail is an inexpensive and easy way to stay in touch with their family members. In fact, exchanging e-mail messages is one of the more widely used features of the Internet.

Outlook allows you to receive and store incoming e-mail messages, compose and send e-mail messages, and maintain a list of frequently used e-mail addresses.

Starting and Customizing Outlook

If you are stepping through this project on a computer and you want your screen to agree with the figures in this book, then you should set your computer's resolution to 800 × 600. The following steps start Outlook and customize its window.

To Start and Customize Outlook

1

- **Click the Start button on the Windows taskbar, point to All Programs on the Start menu, point to Microsoft Office on the All Programs submenu, and then point to Microsoft Office Outlook 2003 on the Microsoft Office submenu.**

Windows displays the Start menu, the All Programs submenu, and the Microsoft Office submenu (Figure 1-2).

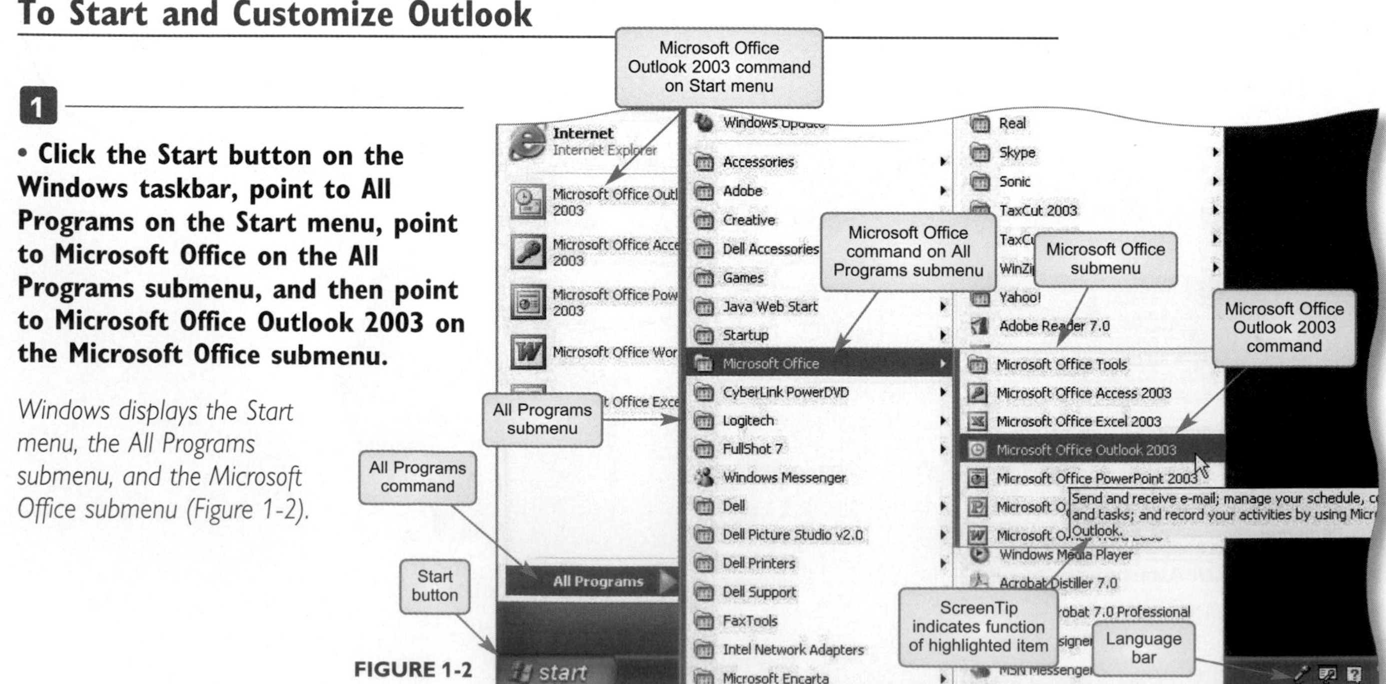

FIGURE 1-2

2

- **Click Microsoft Office Outlook 2003. If necessary, click the Mail button in the Navigation Pane and then click the Inbox folder in the All Mail Folders pane.**
- **If the Inbox - Microsoft Office Outlook window is not maximized, double-click its title bar to maximize it.**
- **Drag the right border of the Inbox message pane to the right so that the Inbox message pane and Reading Pane have the same width.**
- **If the Language bar shows, right-click it and then click Close the Language bar on the shortcut menu.**

Outlook starts and displays the Inbox - Microsoft Outlook window as shown in Figure 1-3.

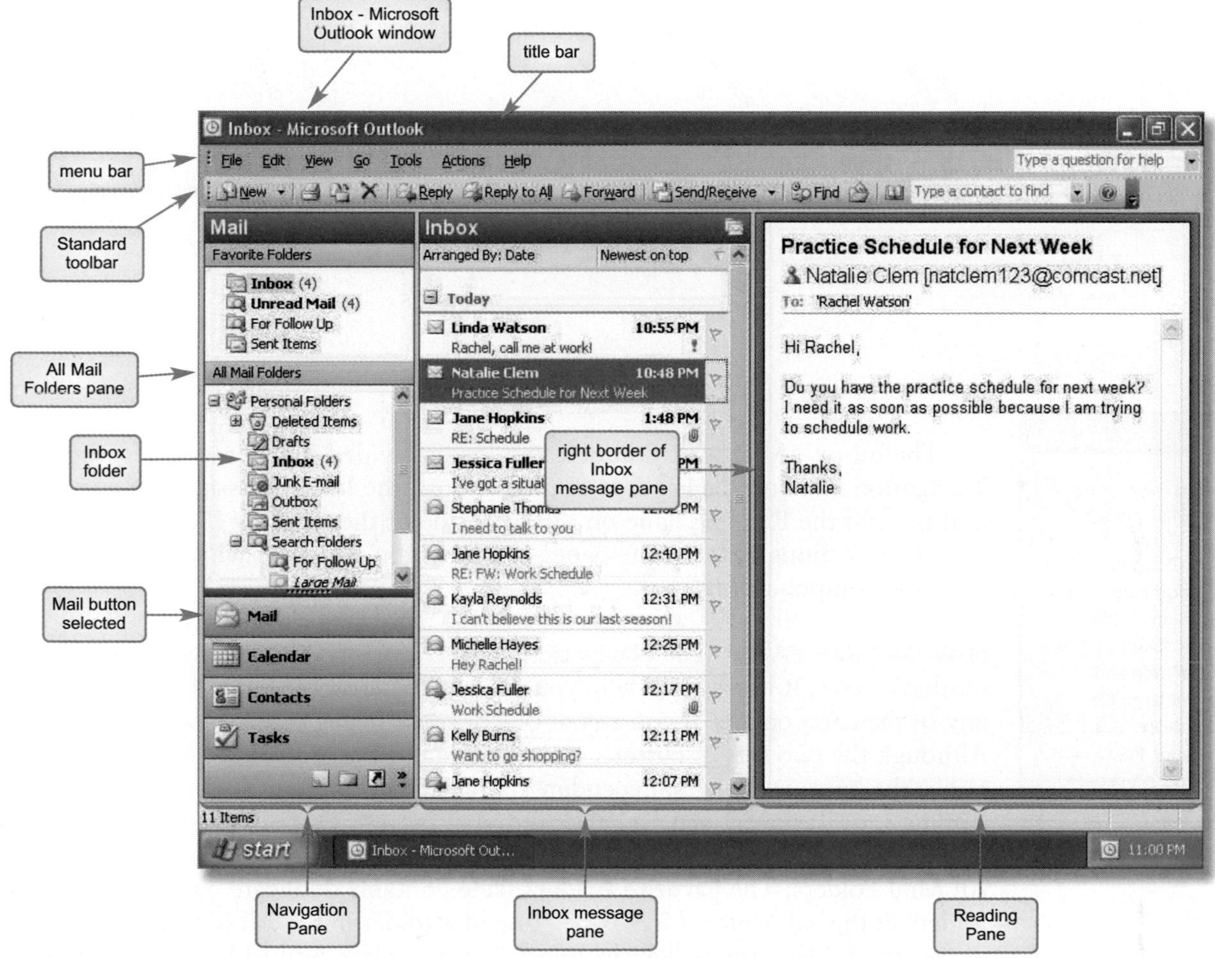

FIGURE 1-3

The screen shown in Figure 1-3 illustrates how the Outlook window looks the first time you start Outlook after setting up an e-mail account on most computers. If the Office Speech Recognition software is installed and active on your computer, then when you start Outlook, the Language bar may appear on the screen (Figure 1-2). The **Language bar** allows you to speak commands and dictate text. It usually is located on the right side of the Windows taskbar next to the notification area and changes to include the speech recognition functions available in Outlook. In this book, the Language bar is closed because it takes up computer resources and with the Language bar active, the microphone can be turned on accidentally, causing your computer to act in an unstable manner.

The Inbox - Microsoft Outlook Window

The Inbox - Microsoft Outlook window shown in Figure 1-3 on the previous page contains a number of elements that you will use consistently as you work in the Outlook environment. Figure 1-4 illustrates the Standard toolbar, located below the title bar and the menu bar. The Standard toolbar contains buttons specific to Outlook. The button names indicate their functions. Each button can be clicked to perform a frequently used task, such as creating a new mail message, printing, or sending and receiving mail.

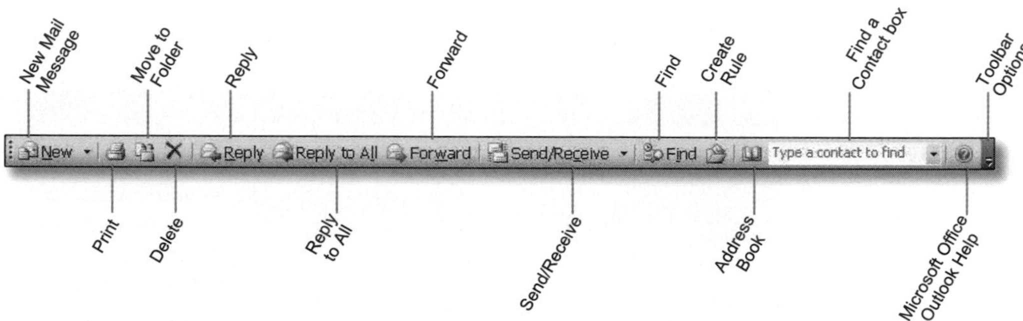

FIGURE 1-4

> **Q & A**
>
> **Q:** Can I find the Outlook folders on my hard disk?
>
> **A:** No. The Outlook folders in the Navigation Pane do not correspond to any folders on your hard disk. Outlook takes all your information and stores it in one large file based on the properties specified for your Personal Folders information service.

The Inbox - Microsoft Outlook window is divided into three panes: the Navigation Pane on the left side of the window, the Inbox message pane in the middle, and the Reading Pane on the right side of the window (Figure 1-5a). The following sections describe the panes and how you use them while working within the Mail component.

NAVIGATION PANE The **Navigation Pane** (Figure 1-5a) is a new feature in Outlook 2003. It is set up to help you navigate Microsoft Outlook while using any of the components. It consists of one or more panes and two sets of buttons. Although the two sets of buttons remain constant, the area of the Navigation Pane above the buttons changes, depending on the active component (Mail, Calendar, Contacts, or Tasks). When you click the Mail button, Outlook displays Mail in the title bar of the Navigation Pane. This pane includes two panes: Favorite Folders and All Mail Folders. The **Favorite Folders pane** contains duplicate names of your favorite folders in the All Mail Folders pane. To add a folder in the All Mail Folders to the list of favorite folders, right-click the folder and then click Add to Favorite Folders.

Below the Favorite Folders pane, the **All Mail Folders** pane contains a set of folders associated with the communications tools of Outlook Mail (Deleted Items, Drafts, Inbox, Junk E-mail, Outbox, Sent Items, and Search Folders).

The **Deleted Items folder** holds messages that you have deleted. As a safety precaution, you can retrieve deleted messages from the Deleted Items folder if you later decide to keep them. Deleting messages from the Deleted Items folder removes the messages permanently. The **Drafts folder** retains copies of messages that you are not yet ready to send. The **Inbox folder** is the destination for incoming mail. The **Junk E-mail folder** is the destination folder for unwanted messages or messages of an unknown origin. You can customize the settings in Outlook to direct only messages that meet certain criteria to the Inbox folder. Messages not meeting those criteria are sent to the Junk E-mail folder. The **Outbox folder** temporarily holds messages you

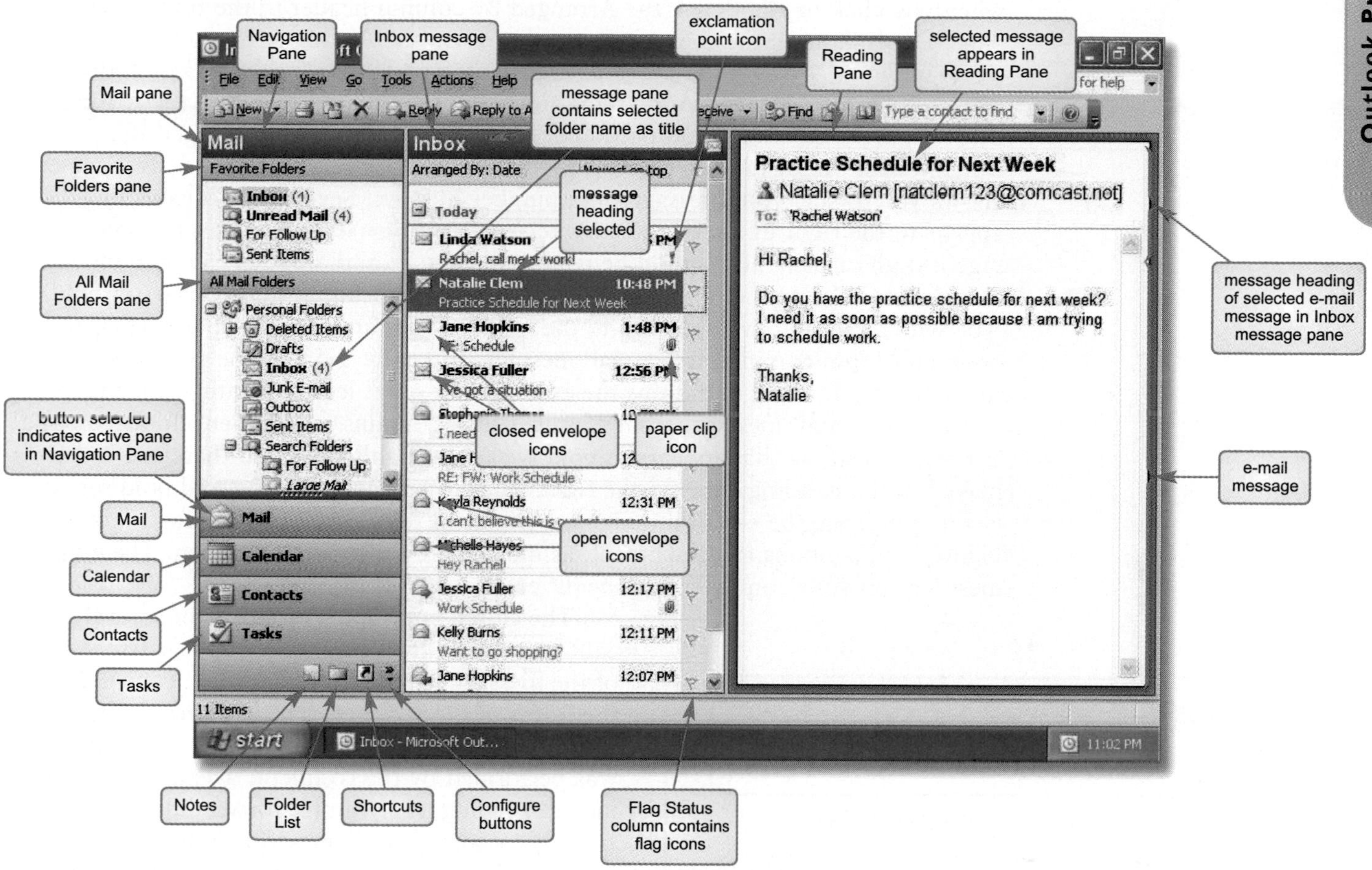

FIGURE 1-5a

send until Outlook delivers the messages. The **Sent Items folder** retains copies of messages that you have sent. The **Search Folders folder** actually is a group of folders that allows you to group your messages easily in one of three ways — messages for follow up, large messages, or unread messages.

Folders can contain e-mail messages, faxes, and files created in other Windows applications. Folders in bold type followed by a number in parentheses (**Inbox** (4)) indicate the number of messages in the folder that are unopened. Other folders may appear on your computer instead of or in addition to the folders shown in Figure 1-5a.

The two sets of buttons at the bottom of the Navigation Pane contain shortcuts to the major components of Outlook (Mail, Calendar, Contacts, Tasks, Notes, Folder List, Shortcuts, and Configure buttons).

MESSAGE PANE The Inbox **message pane** (shown in Figure 1-5a) lists the contents of the folder selected in the All Mail Folders pane. In Figure 1-5a, the Inbox folder is selected. Thus, the message pane lists the e-mails received. Figure 1-5b shows the Arranged By shortcut menu that appears

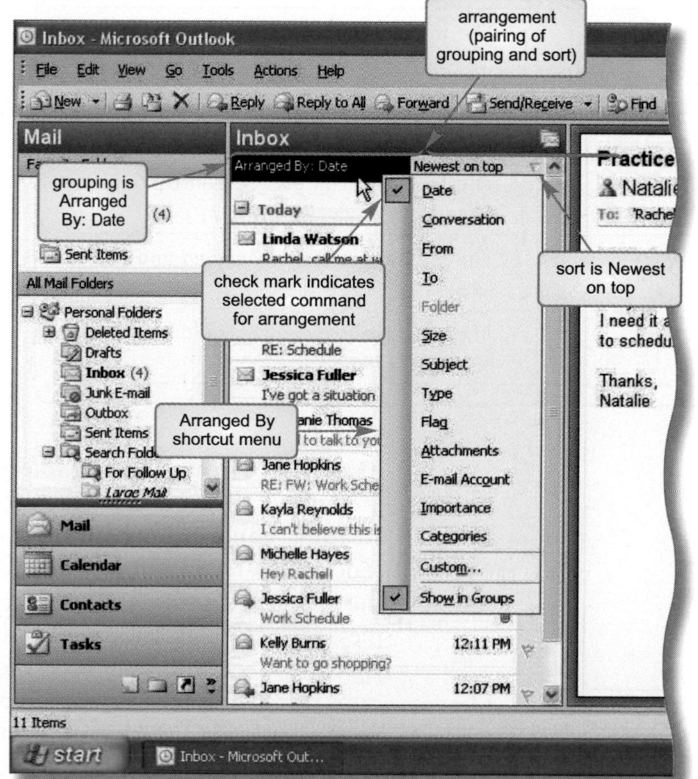

FIGURE 1-5b

when you click or right-click the Arranged By column header in the Inbox message pane. Depending on the command you choose on the Arranged By shortcut menu (Date in Figure 1-5b on the previous page indicated by the check mark), Outlook displays a column header to the right indicating the sort order within the Arranged By grouping. This predefined pairing of a grouping and a sort (Arranged By: Date/Newest on top) is called an **arrangement**. Using these predefined arrangements allows you to sort your messages in a number of ways. Several small icons may appear to the right of a message: an **exclamation point icon** indicates that the message is high priority and should be read immediately, and a **paper clip icon** indicates that the message contains an attachment. A message heading that appears in bold type with a **closed envelope icon** to the left identifies an unread e-mail message. An **open envelope icon** indicates a read message. In Figure 1-5a on the previous page, the first e-mail message contains the exclamation point icon indicating it is urgent. The second e-mail message, from Natalie Clem, contains a closed envelope icon and a message heading that appears in bold type. It is highlighted and therefore is displayed in the Reading Pane on the right. The closed envelope icon and bold message heading indicate the e-mail message has not been read. The third message shown in Figure 1-5a contains an attachment, as indicated by the paper clip icon. The e-mail messages on your computer may be different.

The closed envelope icon is one of several icons, called **message list icons**, which appear to the left of the message heading. Message list icons indicate the status of the message. The icon may indicate an action that was performed by the sender or one that was performed by the recipient. The actions may include reading, replying to, forwarding, digitally signing, or encrypting a message. Table 1-1 contains a partial list of message list icons and the action performed on the mail message.

Table 1-1 Message List Icons and Actions

MESSAGE LIST ICON	ACTION
	The message has been opened.
	The message has not been opened.
	The message has been replied to.
	The message has been forwarded.
	The message is in progress in the Drafts folder.
	The message is digitally signed and unopened.
	The message is digitally signed and has been opened.

Flag icons are displayed when the Flag Status column is visible (Figure 1-5a). To the right of the message header, a **flag icon** indicates the status of the message. Outlook allows you to prioritize messages in a manner you choose using message flags. To set priorities, you right-click a flag icon and then choose colors and notes on the shortcut menu. To view the information about the message flag, point to the flag in the message heading, and Outlook will display information about the message in a ScreenTip. Flagging and sorting e-mail messages using the Flag Status column are discussed later in this project.

READING PANE The **Reading Pane** (Figure 1-5a) contains the text of the selected e-mail message (Natalie Clem). The **message header** appears at the top of the Reading Pane and contains the e-mail subject (Practice Schedule for Next Week), the sender's name and/or e-mail address (Natalie Clem [natclem123@comcast.net]), and the recipient's name (Rachel Watson). Outlook displays the text of the highlighted e-mail message below the message header. The new Reading Pane is designed to provide almost twice as much information as the preview pane in previous versions of Outlook. In addition, using the View menu, you can display the Reading Pane to the right of the message pane (vertically), as shown in Figure 1-5a, or you can display it at the bottom of the message pane (horizontally), according to your personal preference.

Note: If you are stepping through this project on a computer and you want your screen to appear the same as the figures in the Mail Component section of this project, then you should ask your instructor to assist you (or see page OUT 61) to import Rachel's Inbox from the Data Files for Students. Once you have imported Rachel's Inbox, click the plus sign (+) next to the Inbox folder in the All Mail Folders list, and then select the Rachel's Inbox folder. See page xxiv at the front of this book for instructions for downloading the Data Files for Students or see you instructor for information about accessing files for this book.

Opening and Reading E-Mail Messages

In Figure 1-5a on page OUT 9, the message headings for each message appear in the message pane. Double-clicking the closed envelope icon in any heading opens the e-mail message and displays the text of the message in a separate window. The following step shows how to open the e-mail message from Natalie Clem.

To Open (Read) an E-Mail Message

1

- **Double-click the Natalie Clem message heading in the Inbox Message pane (Figure 1-5a) and then maximize the Practice Schedule for Next Week window.**

Outlook displays the maximized Message window (Figure 1-6). The Message window contains a menu bar, Standard toolbar, identifying information about the e-mail message, and message pane. The subject of the e-mail message (Practice Schedule for Next Week) becomes the window title.

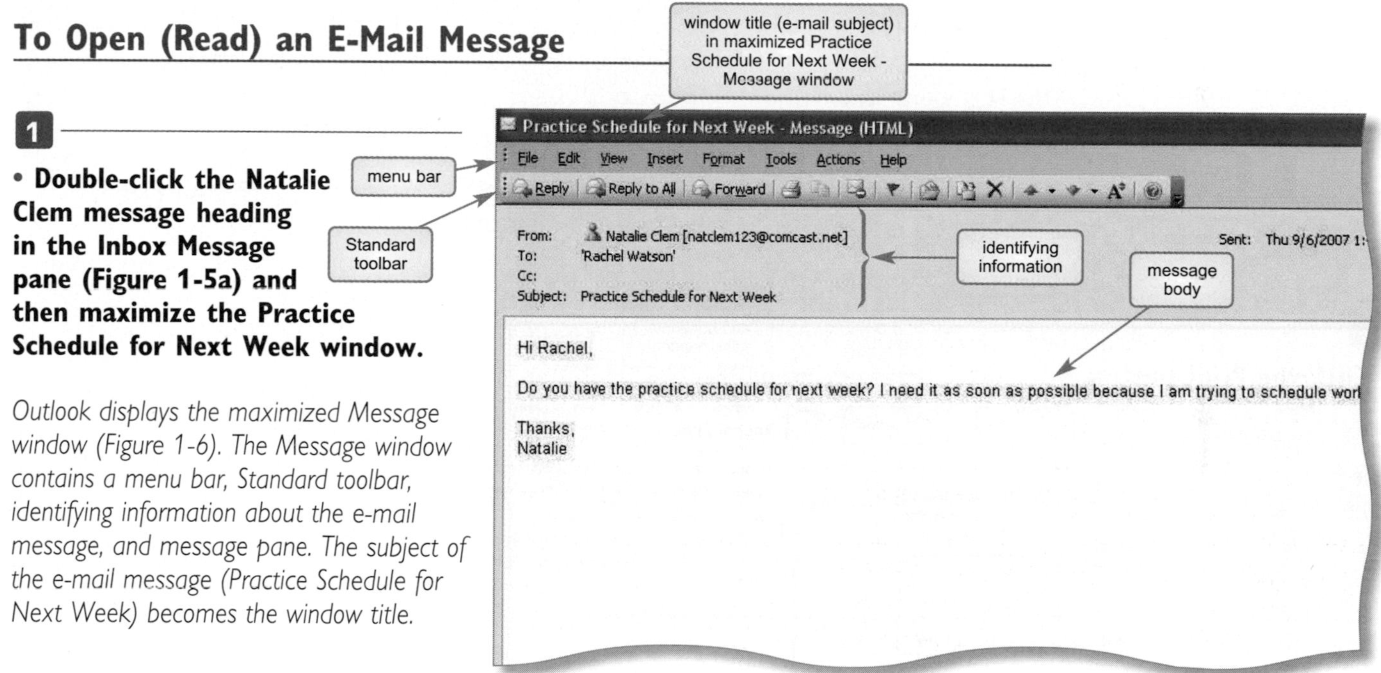

FIGURE 1-6

When you double-click a message heading in the message pane, Outlook displays the message in a separate window, changes the closed envelope icon to an opened envelope icon, and no longer displays the message heading in bold type.

Figure 1-7 illustrates the Standard toolbar in the Message window. The Standard toolbar is located below the title bar and menu bar. The buttons on the Standard toolbar allow you to select easily from a list of the most common responses to an e-mail.

Reply
Forward
Copy
Follow Up
Move to Folder
Previous Item
Font Size
Toolbar Options
Reply | Reply to All | Forward
Reply to All
Print
Permission
Create Rule
Delete
Next Item
Microsoft Office Outlook Help

FIGURE 1-7

Printing an E-Mail Message

You can print the contents of an e-mail message before or after opening the message. The following steps describe how to print an opened e-mail message.

To Print an Opened E-Mail Message

1

- **Point to the Print button on the Standard toolbar (Figure 1-8).**

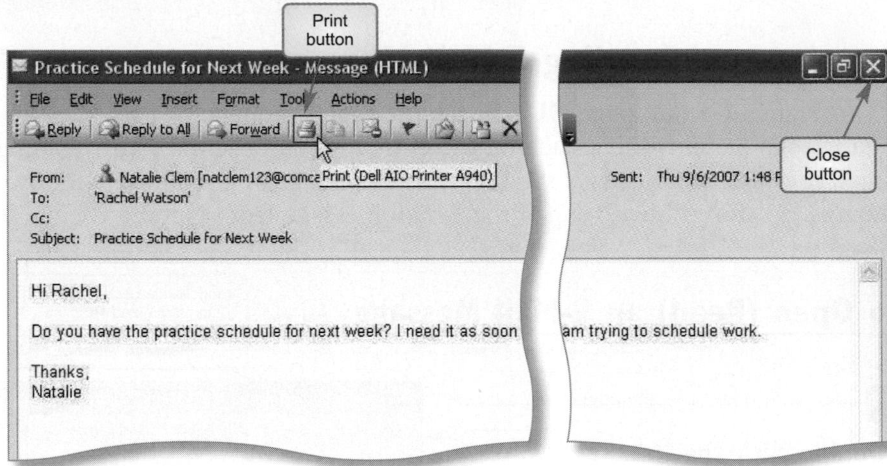

FIGURE 1-8

2

- **Click the Print button.**

Outlook prints the message (Figure 1-9). The printed message consists of a header at the top of the page, the recipient's name (Rachel Watson), and a horizontal line. Below the recipient's name are the From, Sent, To, and Subject entries, and the e-mail message. A footer at the bottom of the page contains the page number. The contents of the header and footer on your printout may be different.

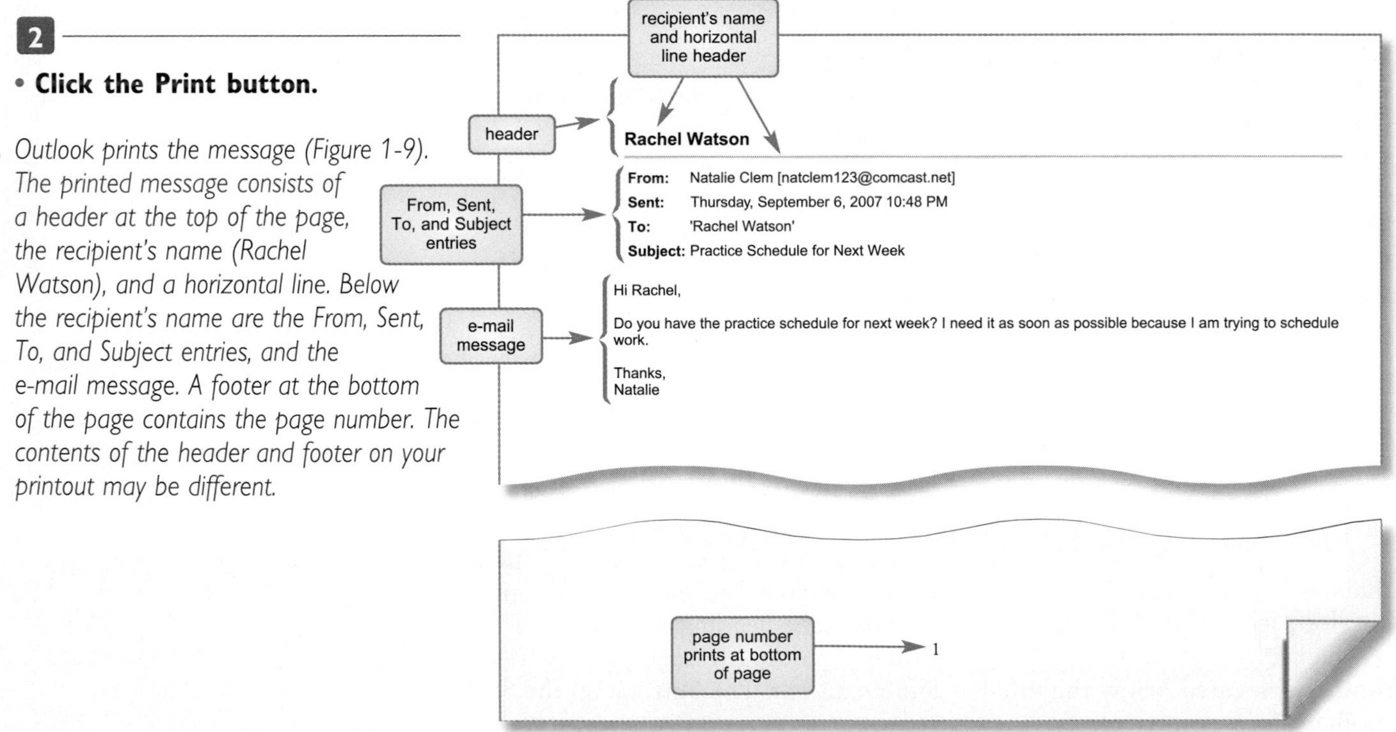

FIGURE 1-9

Closing an E-Mail Message

The following step shows how to close the Message window.

To Close an E-Mail Message

1

• **Click the Close button on the title bar (Figure 1-8).**

Outlook closes the Message window and displays the Inbox window (Figure 1-10).

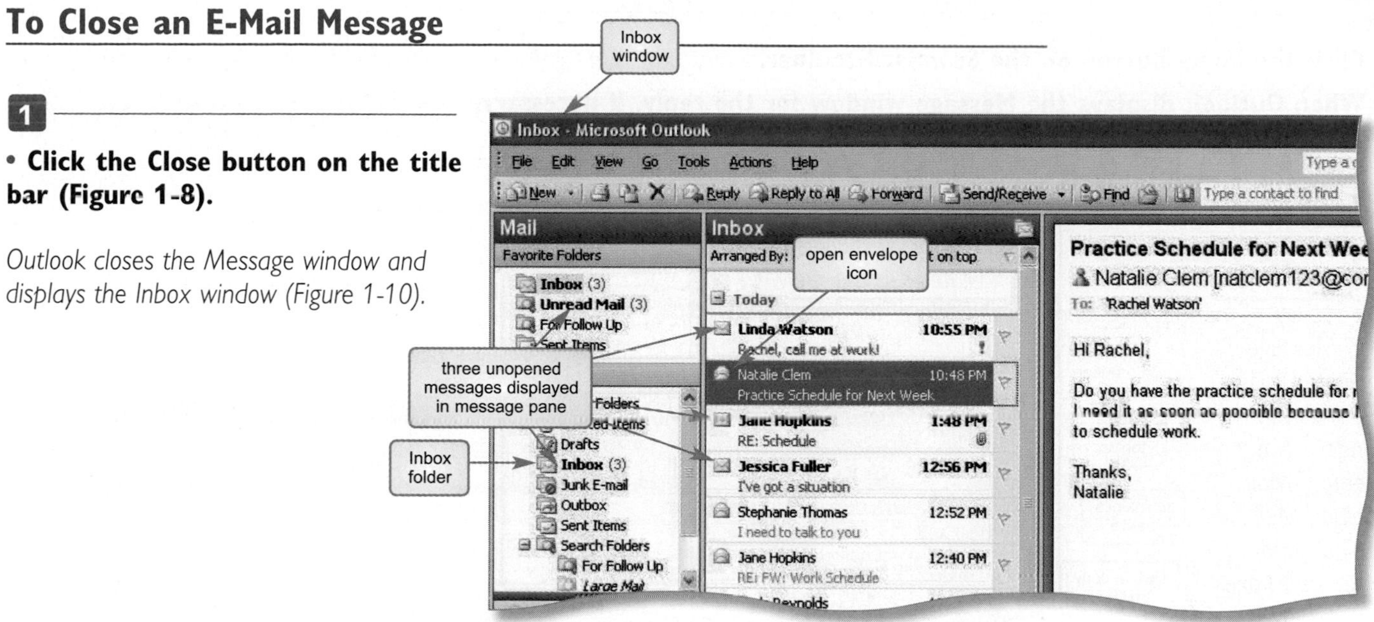

FIGURE 1-10

When you double-click a message heading with a closed envelope icon in the message pane, Outlook displays the corresponding message in the Message window. When you close the Message window, the Natalie Clem message heading in the message pane no longer appears in bold type, and the closed envelope icon changes to an open envelope icon to indicate the e-mail message has been opened. In addition, the Inbox folder in the All Mail Folders pane (Inbox (3)) indicates three e-mail messages remain unopened.

Replying to an E-Mail Message

The next step is to reply to the e-mail message from Natalie Clem. The Reply button on the Standard toolbar in the Inbox window allows you to reply quickly to an e-mail message using the sender's e-mail address, as shown in the following steps.

To Reply to an E-Mail Message

1

• **If necessary, click the Natalie Clem message heading in the message pane (Figure 1-11).**

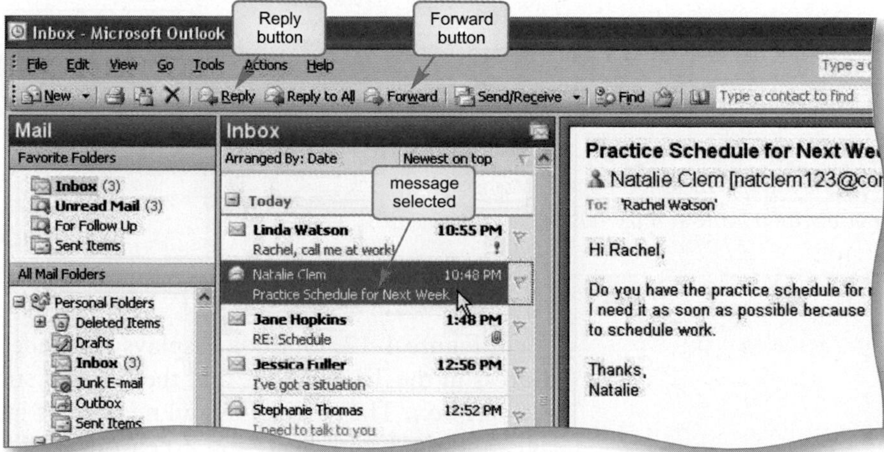

FIGURE 1-11

2

- **Click the Reply button on the Standard toolbar.**
- **When Outlook displays the Message window for the reply, if necessary, double-click the title bar to maximize the window.**
- **Type the e-mail reply as shown in Figure 1-12.**

Outlook displays the RE: Practice Schedule for Next Week - Message window (Figure 1-12). RE: indicates it is the reply, the subject of the message identifies the title of the window, and Message indicates it is the Message window. The menu, E-Mail toolbar, Mail toolbar, and three text boxes are displayed at the top of the window. The RE: entry and subject appear in the window title and Subject text box. The e-mail reply and original message appear in the message body.

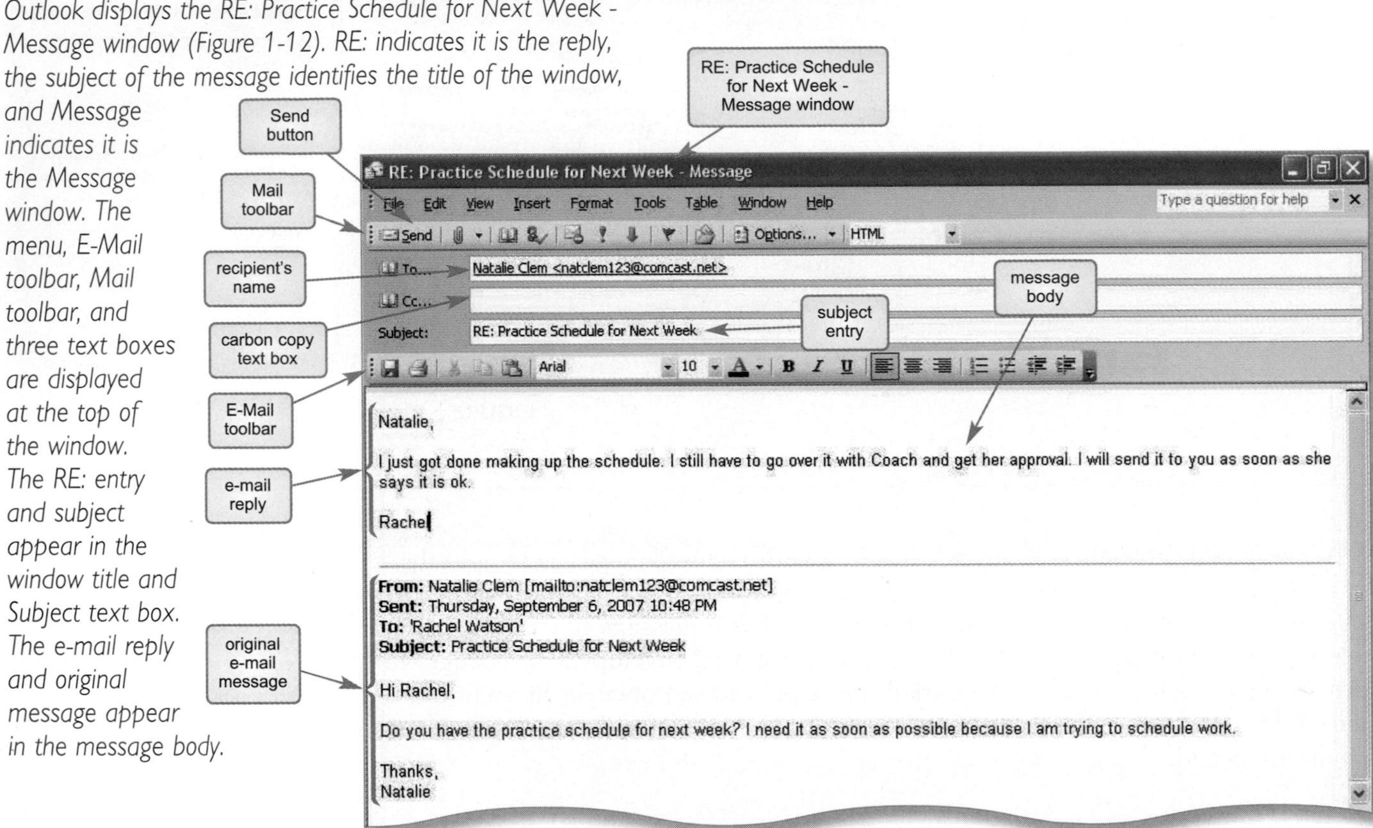

FIGURE 1-12

3

- **Click the Send button.**

Outlook closes the Message window, stores the reply e-mail in the Outbox folder while it sends the message, moves the message to the Sent Items folder, and displays the Inbox window (Figure 1-13). The opened envelope icon to the left of the Natalie Clem entry in the message pane contains an arrow to indicate a reply has been sent.

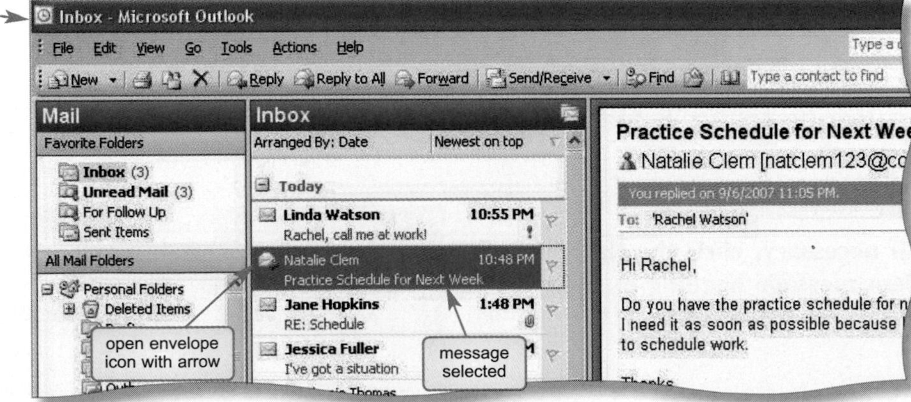

FIGURE 1-13

In Figure 1-12, Outlook displays the underlined Natalie Clem name and e-mail address in the To text box, and the original subject is added automatically to the Subject text box. The original e-mail message is identified by the words, Original Message, and the From, Sent, and To entries in the message body. In addition, the window contains two toolbars. The E-Mail toolbar and Mail toolbar appear below the menu bar. The **E-Mail toolbar**, shown in Figure 1-14a, allows you to change the appearance, size, and color of text; bold, italicize, or underline text; create a numbered or bulleted list; change paragraph indentation or align text; and create a link or insert a picture in an e-mail message. Figure 1-14b illustrates the **Mail toolbar**, which includes buttons that are useful when replying to a message.

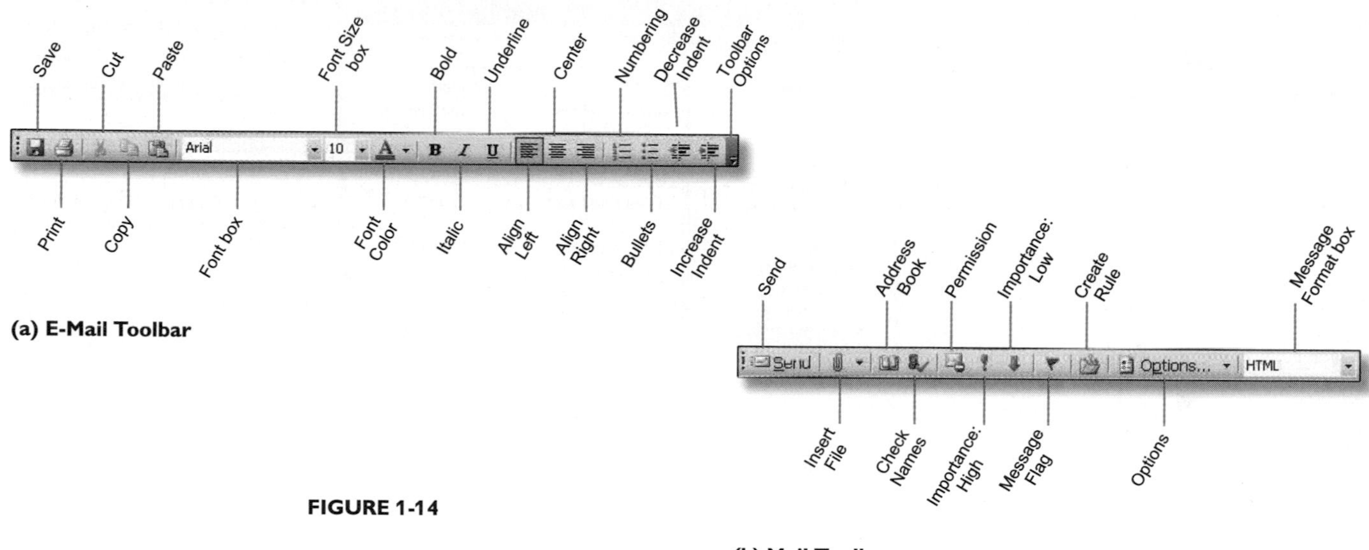

FIGURE 1-14

The Message Format box on the right side of the Mail toolbar is important because it allows you to change the format of the message. The options are HTML, Plain Text, and Rich Text and are summarized in Table 1-2. It is recommended that you use HTML format for your messages.

Table 1-2 Message Formats

MESSAGE FORMAT	DESCRIPTION
HTML	HTML format is the default format used when you create a message in Outlook. HTML supports the inclusion of pictures and basic formatting, such as text formatting, numbering, bullets, and alignment. HTML is the recommended format for Internet mail because the most popular e-mail programs use it.
Plain Text	Plain Text format is understood by all e-mail programs and is the most likely format to make it through a company's virus-filtering program. Plain text does not support basic formatting, such as bold, italic, colored fonts, or other text formatting. It also does not support pictures displayed directly in the message.
Rich Text	Rich Text Format (RTF) is a Microsoft format that only the latest versions of Microsoft Exchange Client and Outlook understand. RTF supports more formats than HTML or Plain Text, as well as linked objects and pictures.

Q & A

Q: How do I remove the original message when replying to an e-mail message?

A: To remove the original message from all e-mail replies, click Tools on the menu bar, click Options, and then click the E-mail Options button in the Preferences sheet in the Options dialog box. In the E-mail Options dialog box, select Do not include original message in the When replying to a message list.

Forwarding an E-Mail Message

In addition to replying to a message, you also can forward the message to additional recipients with or without adding additional comments, as shown in the steps on the next page.

To Forward an E-Mail Message

1

- **With the Inbox window active, click the Natalie Clem message header in the message pane.**
- **Click the Forward button on the Standard toolbar (Figure 1-15).**

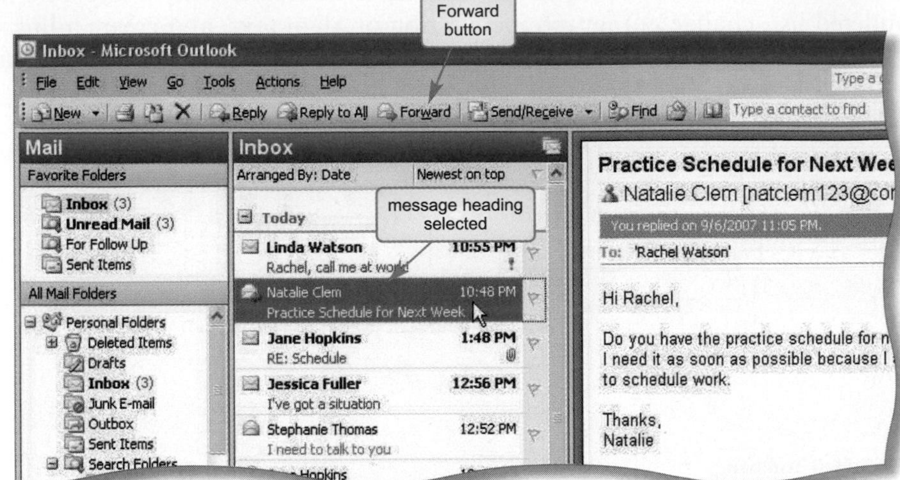

FIGURE 1-15

2

- **When Outlook displays the Message window for the forwarded message, type** `janehopkins123@comcast.net` **in the To text box as the recipient's e-mail address. (If you are stepping through this task, use an actual e-mail address in the To text box.)**
- **Enter the forwarding message in the message body as shown in Figure 1-16.**

Outlook displays the FW: Practice Schedule for Next Week - Message window as shown in Figure 1-16.

3

- **Click the Send button.**

Outlook closes the Message window, stores the reply e-mail in the Outbox folder while it sends the message, moves the message to the Sent Items folder, and displays the Inbox window.

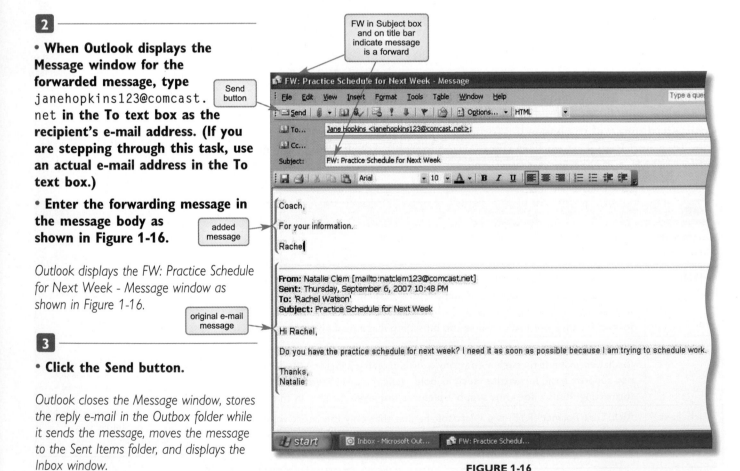

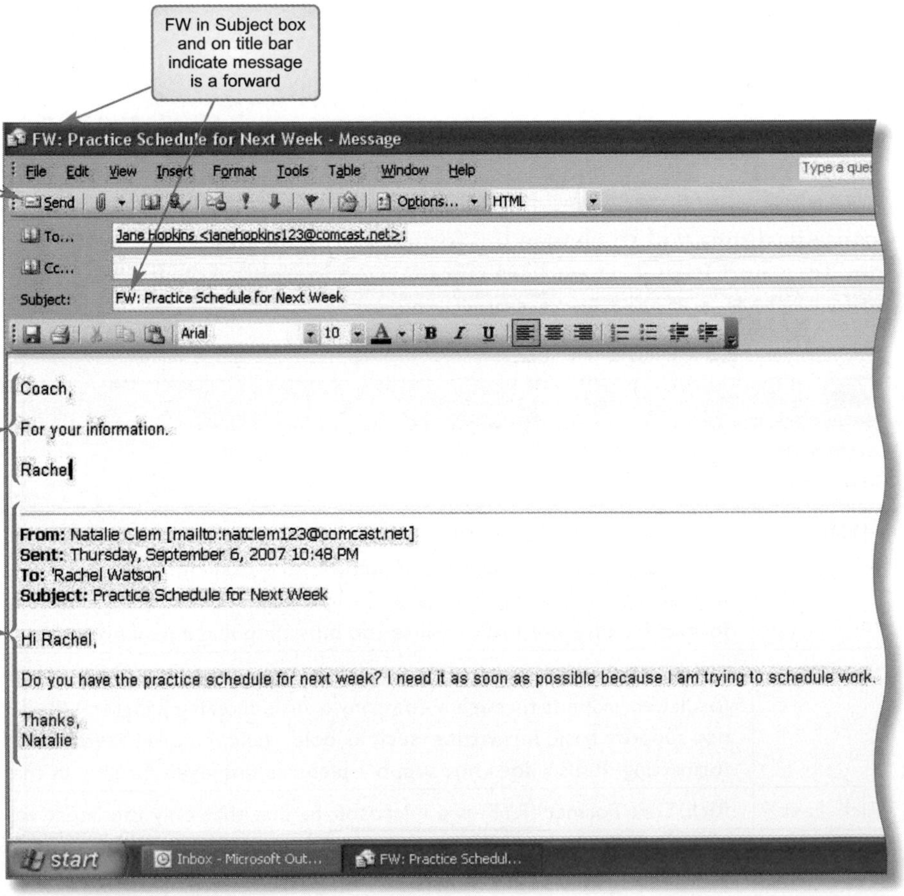

FIGURE 1-16

Deleting an E-Mail Message

After reading and replying to an e-mail message, you may want to delete the original e-mail message from the message list. Deleting a message removes the e-mail message from the Inbox folder. If you do not delete unwanted messages, large numbers of messages in the Inbox folder make it difficult to find and read new messages and wastes disk space. The following steps show how to delete the e-mail message from Natalie Clem.

To Delete an E-Mail Message

1

• With the Inbox window active, click the Natalie Clem message heading in the message pane.

The highlighted Natalie Clem message heading appears in the message pane, and the e-mail message appears in the Reading Pane (Figure 1-17). The open envelope icon contains an arrow to indicate you have forwarded the message.

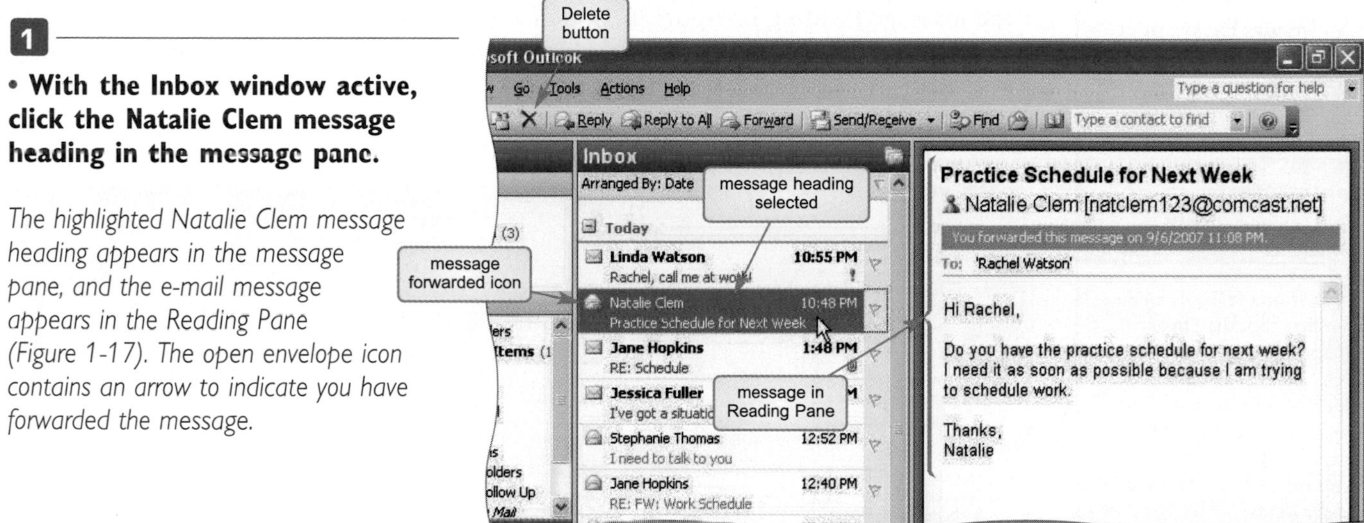

FIGURE 1-17

2

• Click the Delete button on the Standard toolbar.

Outlook moves the Natalie Clem e-mail message from the Inbox folder to the Deleted Items folder and removes the e-mail entry from the message pane (Figure 1-18).

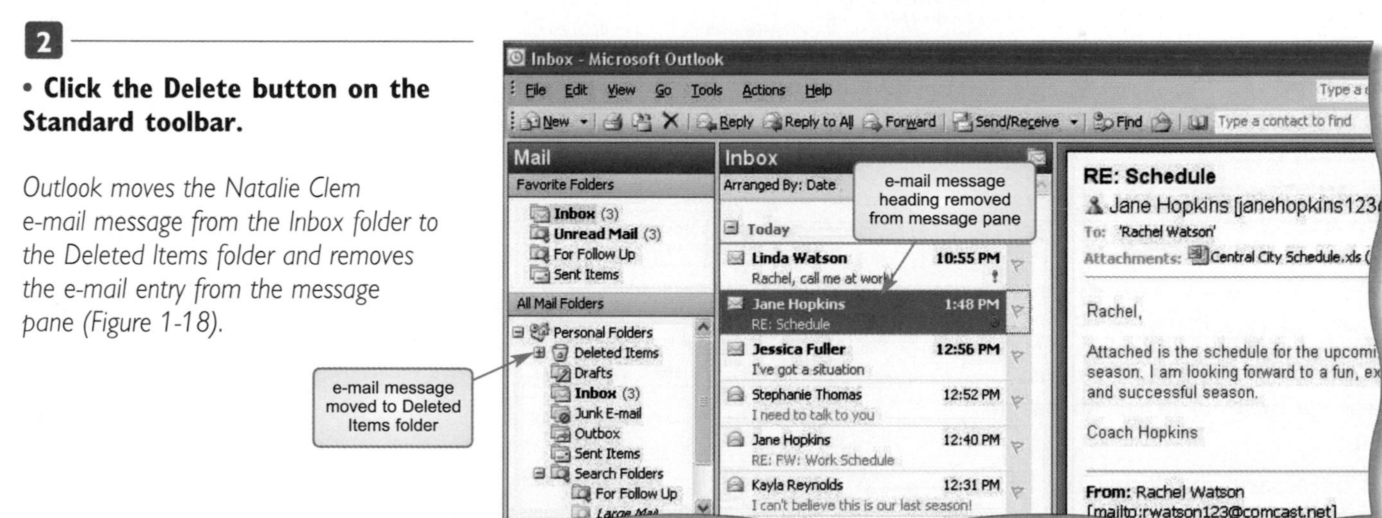

FIGURE 1-18

As you delete messages from the Inbox or Sent Items folders, the number of messages in the Deleted Items folder increases. To delete an e-mail message from the Deleted Items folder, click the Deleted Items folder icon in the All Mail Folders pane, highlight the message in the Deleted Items message pane, click the Delete button on the Standard toolbar, and then click the Yes button in the Microsoft Office Outlook dialog box. You also can delete multiple messages at one time by clicking the first message and then holding down the SHIFT key or CTRL key to click one or more messages. Use the SHIFT key to select a list of adjacent messages. Use the CTRL key to select nonadjacent messages. Once the messages are selected, click the Delete button on the Standard toolbar or press the DELETE key.

Q & A

Q: How can I use Outlook to protect against viruses?

A: Changing the format of an e-mail message can help prevent the possibility of virus infection. Many viruses are found in HTML-formatted messages. To help protect against viruses, you can configure Outlook to display opened messages automatically in plain text. Click Options on the Tools menu and then click the E-mail Options button in the Preferences sheet in the Options dialog box. In the E-mail Options dialog box, select Read all standard mail in plain text in the Message handling area.

Viewing a File Attachment

The message from Jane Hopkins contains a file attachment. The paper clip icon in the message heading in Figure 1-19 indicates the e-mail message contains a file attachment (file or object). The Attachments line in the Reading Pane indicates an attachment as well. The following steps show how to open the message and view the contents of the file attachment.

FIGURE 1-19

To View a File Attachment

1

- **With the Inbox window active, double-click the Jane Hopkins message heading in the message pane.**
- **If necessary, maximize the Re: Schedule - Message window.**

Outlook displays the Message window (Figure 1-20). The Attachments entry, containing an Excel icon, the file name (Central City Schedule.xls), and the file size (17 KB) appear above the message body on the Attachments line.

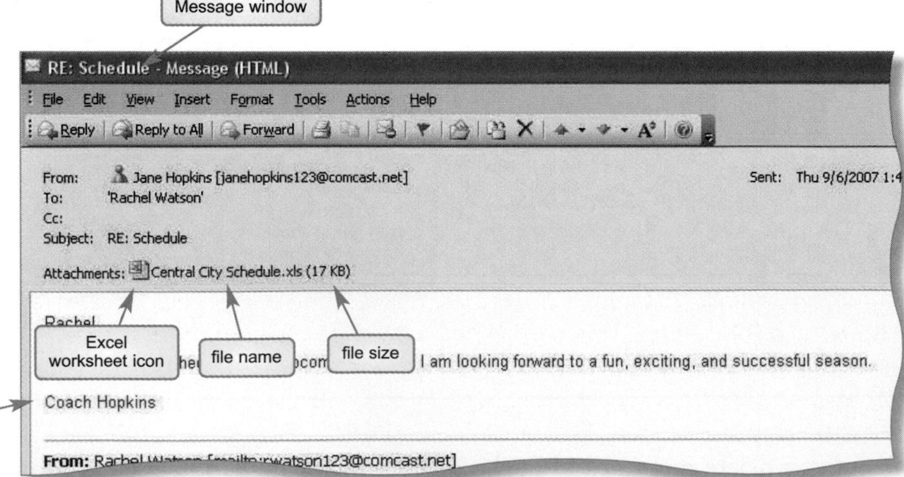

FIGURE 1-20

2

- **Double-click the Central City Schedule.xls icon on the Attachments line.**
- **If Outlook displays the Opening Mail Attachment dialog box, click the Open button.**

The Microsoft Excel - Central City Schedule window containing the schedule opens (Figure 1-21).

3

- **After viewing the worksheet, click the Close button on the right side of the title bar in the Excel window.**
- **Click the Close button in Message window.**

The Excel window and Message window close.

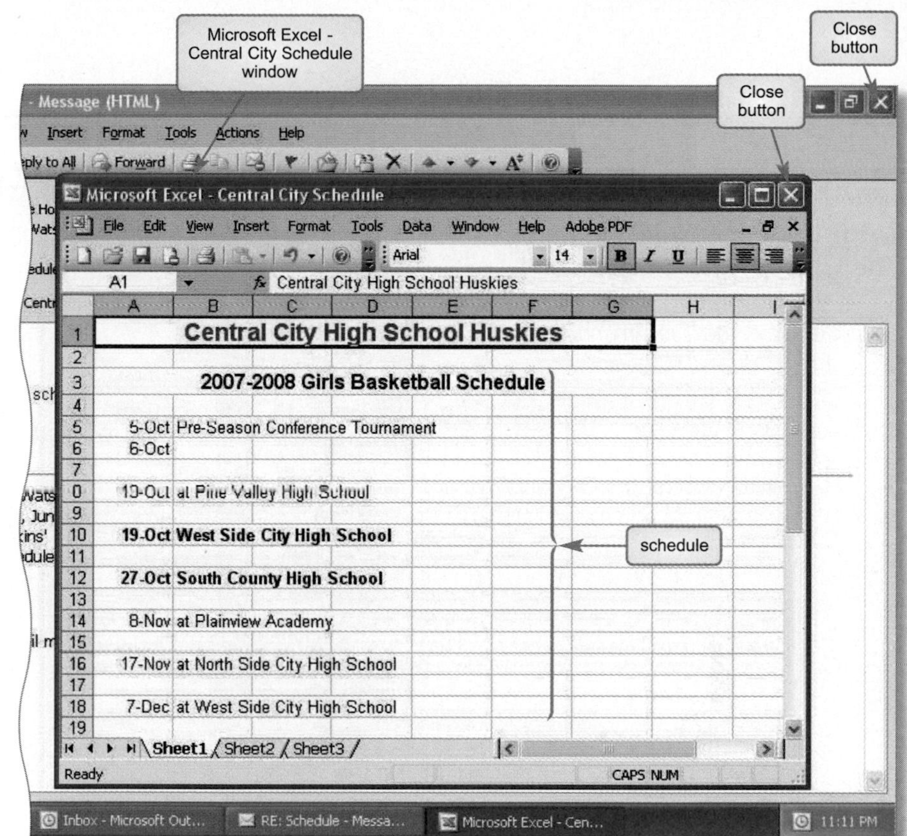

FIGURE 1-21

File attachments can be any type of file from worksheets to documents to presentations to pictures. Files can be viewed only if your computer has the appropriate software. For example, if your computer does not have Excel installed, then you cannot view an Excel file attachment. The Opening Mail Attachment dialog box in Step 2 gives you the option of viewing the attachment as you read the e-mail or saving it on disk to view at another time.

Creating an E-Mail Signature

An **e-mail signature** is a unique message automatically added to the end of an outgoing e-mail message. An e-mail signature can be much more than adding your name to the end of a message. It can consist of text and/or pictures. The type of signature you add may depend on the recipient of the message. For messages to family and friends, a first name may be sufficient, while messages to business contacts may include your full name, address, telephone number, and other business information. Outlook allows you to create a different signature for each e-mail account created in Outlook. The steps on the next page create and insert an e-mail signature in an e-mail message.

To Create and Insert an E-Mail Signature

1

- **With the Inbox window active, click Tools on the menu bar.**

Outlook displays the Tools menu (Figure 1-22).

FIGURE 1-22

2

- **Click Options on the Tools menu.**
- **When Outlook displays the Options dialog box, click the Mail Format tab.**

Outlook displays the Mail Format sheet in the Options dialog box (Figure 1-23).

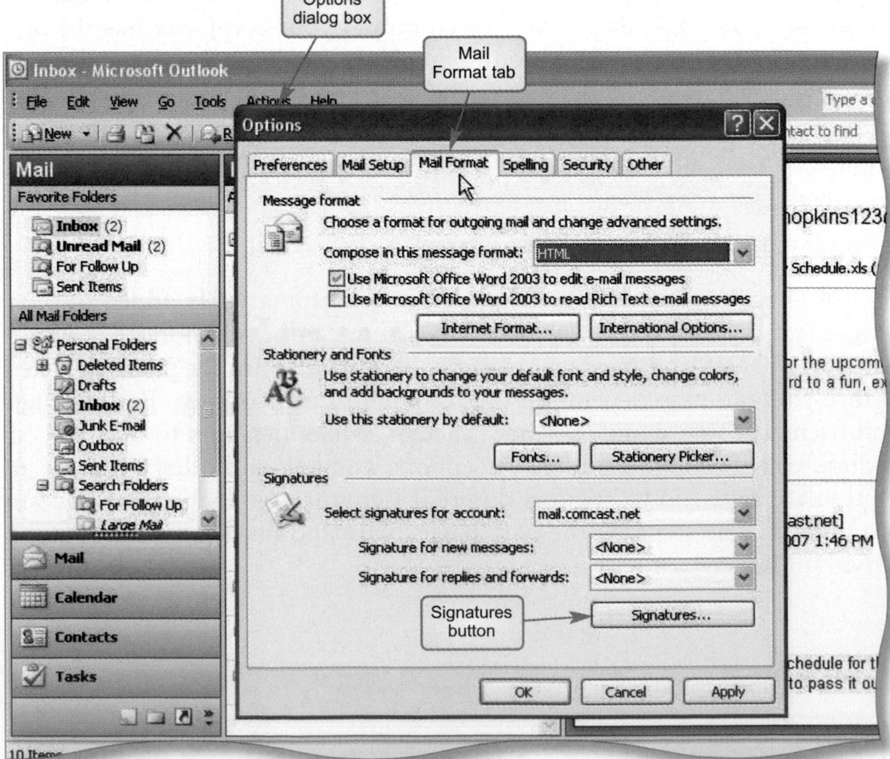

FIGURE 1-23

3

- **Click the Signatures button.**

Outlook displays the Create Signature dialog box (Figure 1-24).

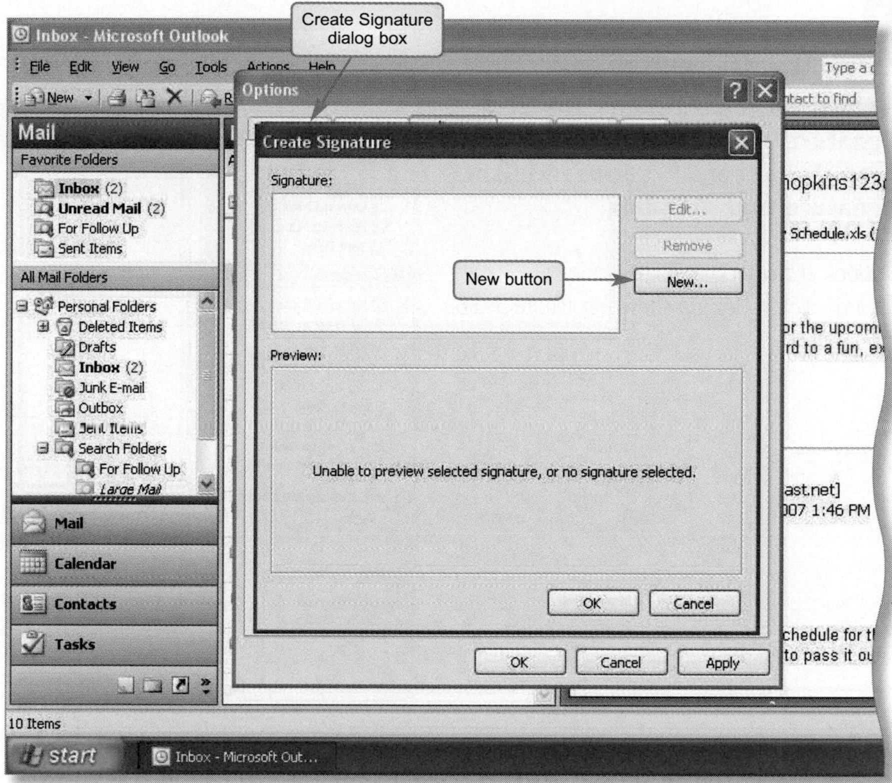

FIGURE 1-24

4

- **Click the New button.**
- **When Outlook displays the Create New Signature dialog box, type** `Team` **in the Enter a name for your new signature text box.**

Outlook displays the Create New Signature dialog box. Team is the name of the signature being created (Figure 1-25).

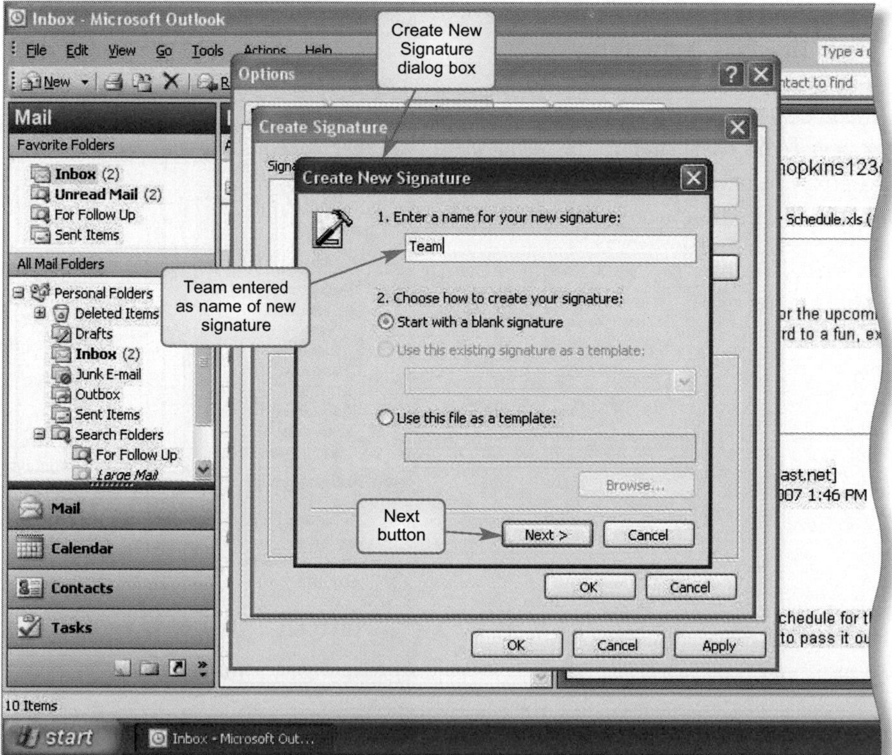

FIGURE 1-25

5

- **Click the Next button.**
- **When Outlook displays the Edit Signature - [Team] dialog box, type** `Rachel Watson - Captain` **in the Signature text text box.**

Outlook displays the Edit Signature - [Team] dialog box as shown in Figure 1-26.

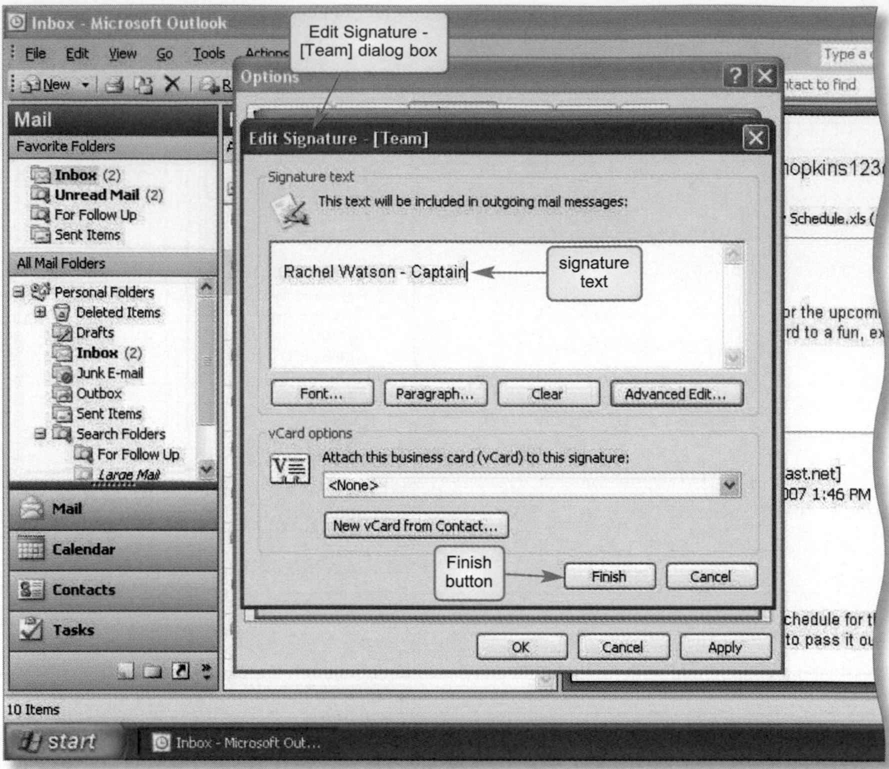

FIGURE 1-26

6

- **Click the Finish button.**

Outlook displays the Create Signature dialog box with Team highlighted in the Signature text box. The newly created signature appears in the Preview area (Figure 1-27).

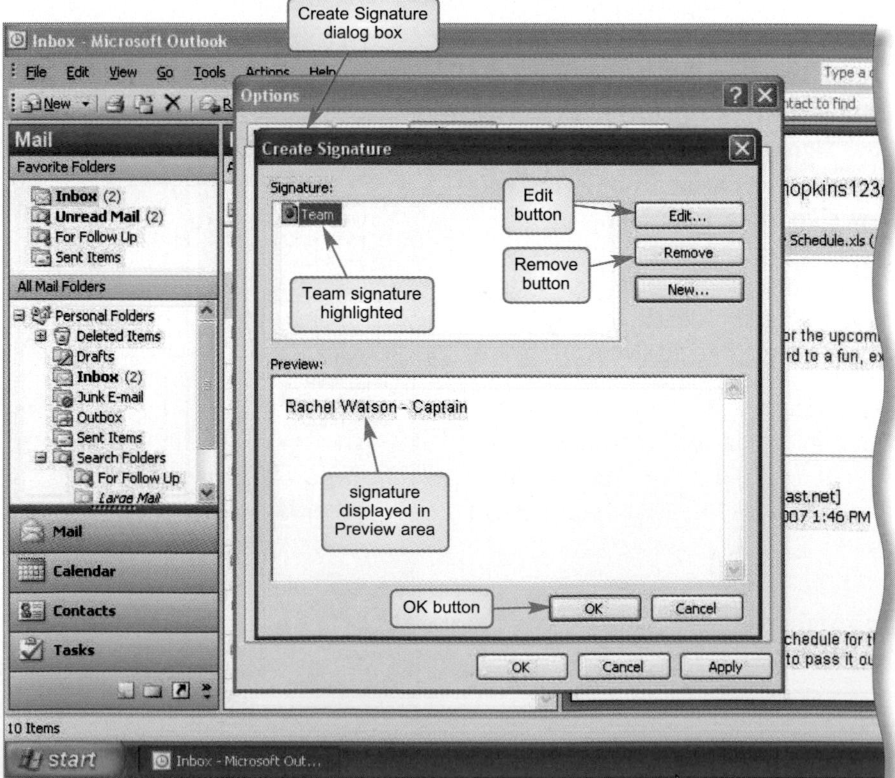

FIGURE 1-27

7

- **Click the OK button.**
- **In the Signatures area of the Options dialog box, select the appropriate e-mail account (if you are stepping through this project, ask your instructor for the appropriate e-mail account).**
- **If necessary, select Team in the Signature for new messages box and the Signature for replies and forwards box.**

Outlook displays the Options dialog box as shown in Figure 1-28. Team is selected as the signature for new messages and for replies and forwards.

8

- **Click the OK button.**

The signature settings are applied.

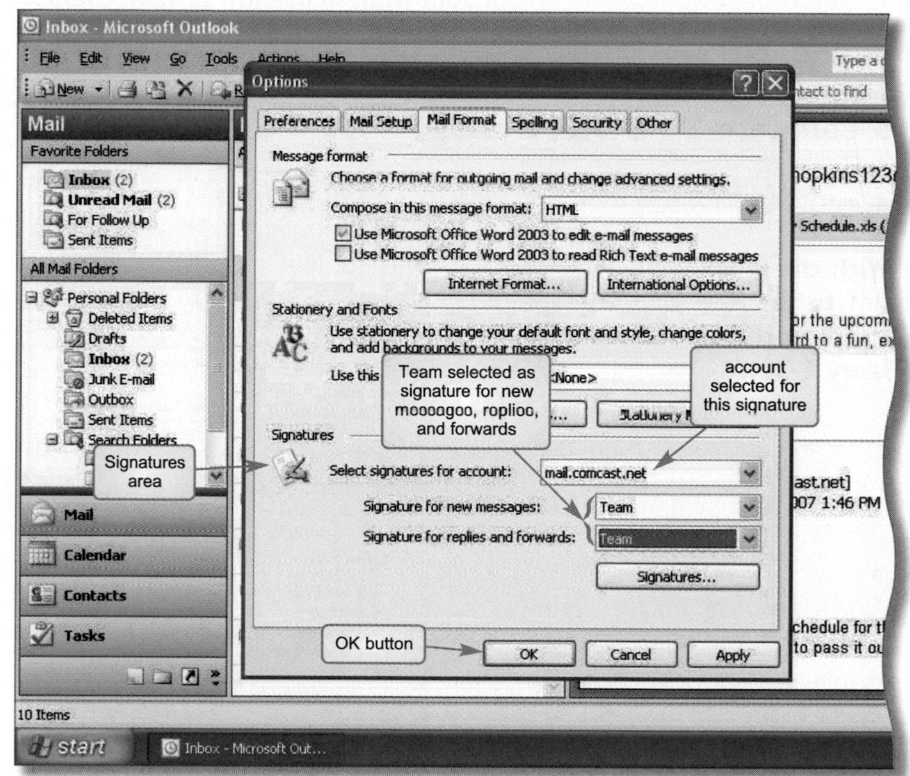

FIGURE 1-28

The signature Rachel Watson – Captain now will be inserted automatically in all new messages, as well as reply messages and forward messages. Signatures can be modified or removed at any time by clicking the Edit or Remove buttons in the Create Signature dialog box (Figure 1-27). You can add a variety of signatures to Outlook for different purposes that include any specific characteristics that you desire.

Creating Unique E-Mail Signatures for Multiple Accounts

You can create unique signatures for different accounts by adding new signatures and selecting a different account in the Signatures area in the Options dialog box (Figure 1-28). For one account, you may want to insert a personal signature. In another, you may want to include a business or professional signature with contact and other information.

Composing a New Mail Message

In addition to opening and reading, replying to, forwarding, and deleting e-mail messages, you will have many occasions to compose and send new e-mail messages. When you compose an e-mail message, you must know the e-mail address of the recipient of the message, enter a brief one-line subject that identifies the purpose or contents of the message, and then type the message in the message body.

You also can **format** an e-mail message to enhance the appearance of the message. Formatting attributes include changing the style, size, and color of the text in the document. As indicated earlier, Outlook allows you to choose from three formats: HTML, Plain Text, or Rich Text.

The following steps show how to compose a formatted e-mail message to Jane Hopkins with an attachment.

To Compose an E-Mail Message

1

• With the Inbox window active, point to the New Mail Message button on the Standard toolbar (Figure 1-29).

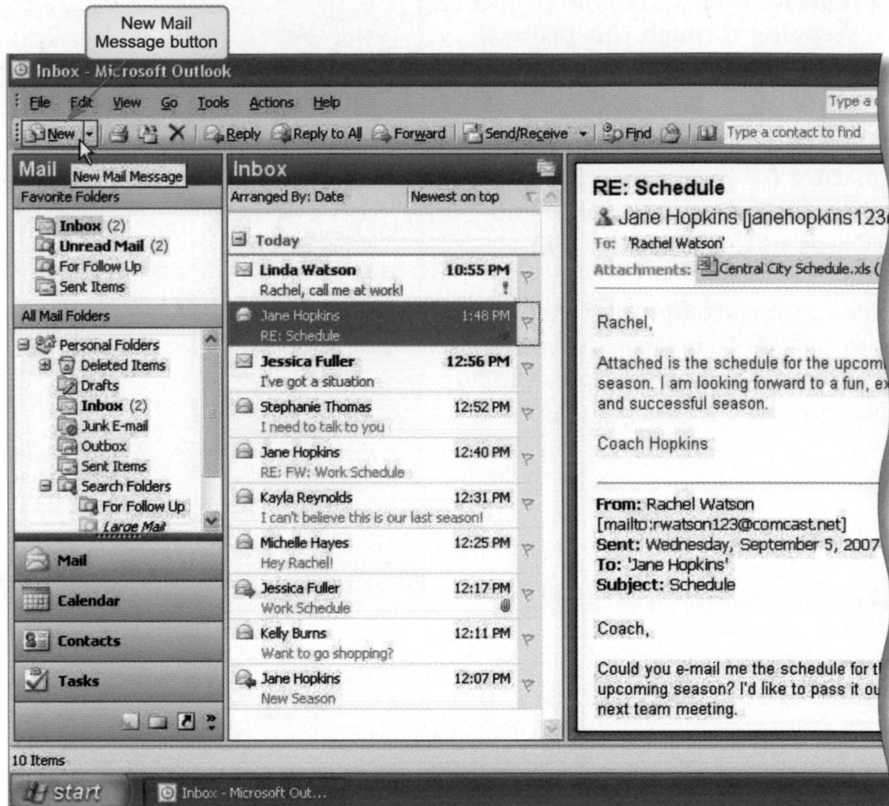

FIGURE 1-29

2

• Click the New Mail Message button.

Outlook displays the Untitled - Message window with the signature Rachel Watson - Captain (Figure 1-30). The Message window contains a menu bar, two toolbars, three text boxes, and the message body. Outlook positions the insertion point in the To text box.

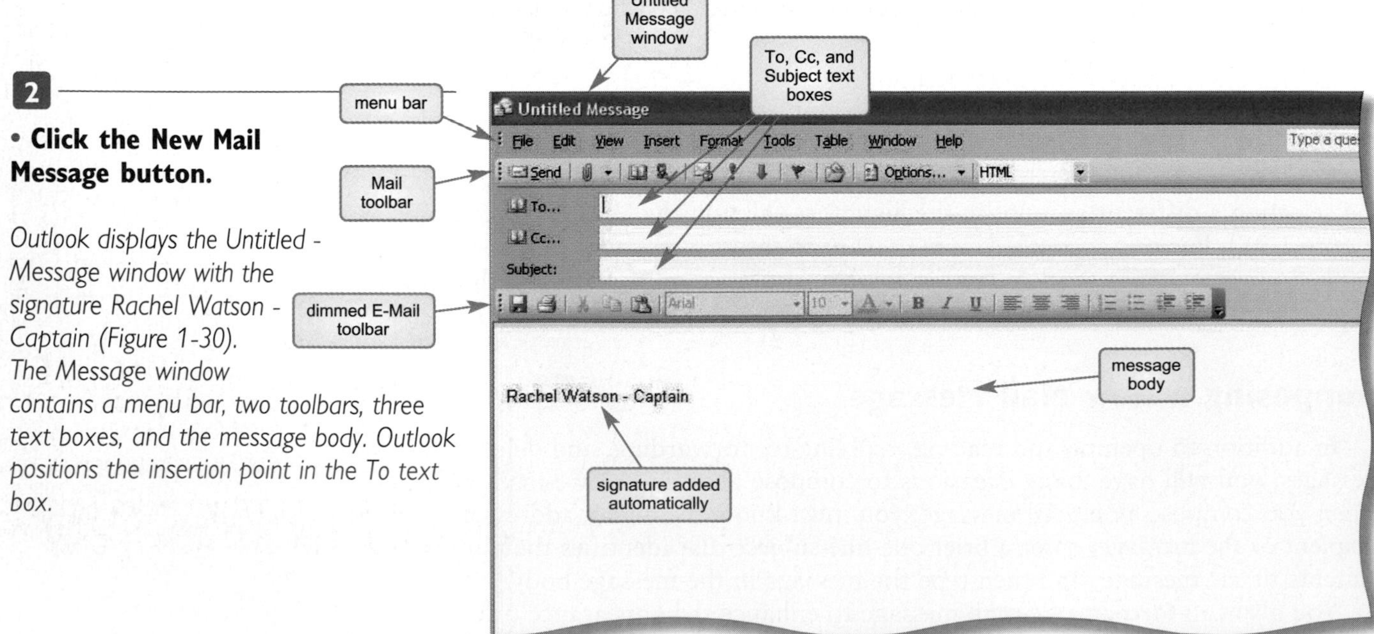

FIGURE 1-30

3

• **Type** janehopkins123@comcast.net **in the To text box, click the Subject text box, and then type** Updated Practice Schedule **in the Subject text box.**

• **Press the TAB key.**

The destination e-mail address appears in the To text box, and the subject of the message appears in the Subject text box (Figure 1-31). The title bar of the Untitled Message window now appears with the subject of the e-mail message (Updated Practice Schedule). The insertion point appears in the message body.

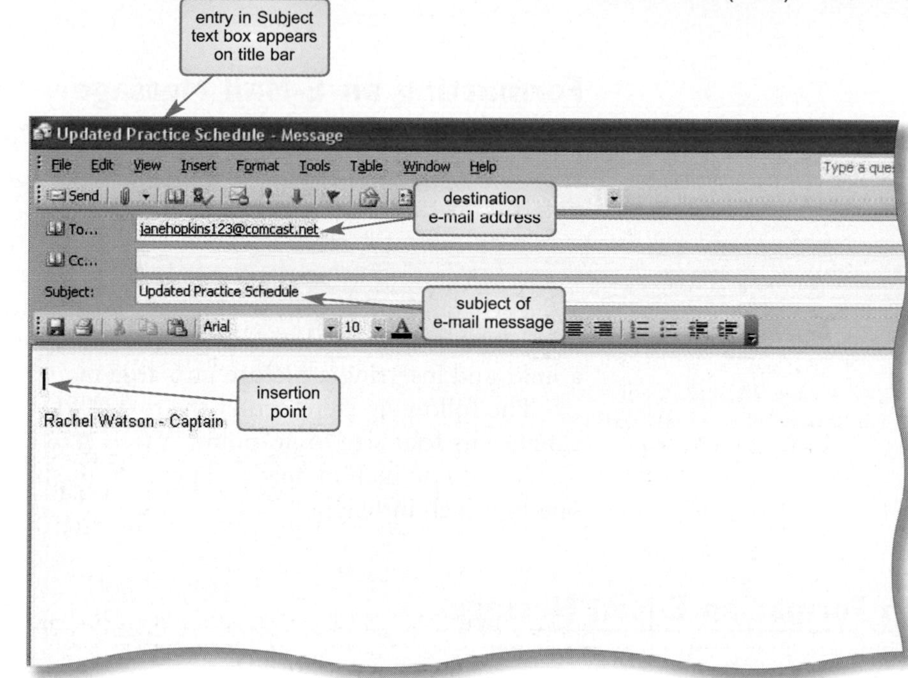

FIGURE 1-31

4

• **Type the e-mail message shown in Figure 1-32.**

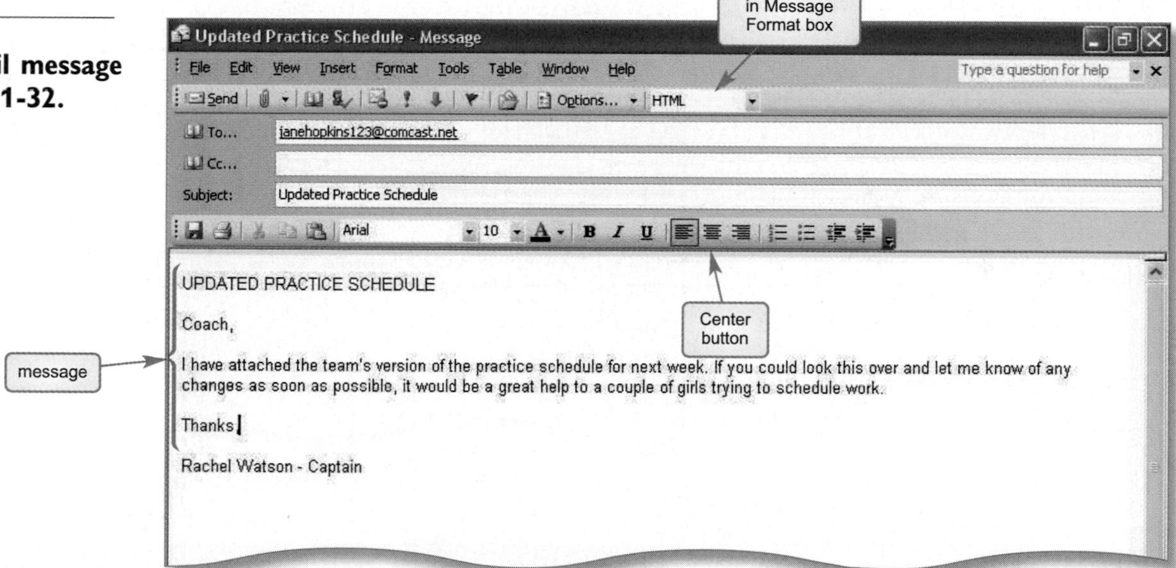

FIGURE 1-32

When you enter a message, you can use the DELETE key and BACKSPACE key to correct errors. Before pressing the DELETE key, select words, sentences, or paragraphs using the mouse. If you are using Microsoft Word as your e-mail editor and you have the appropriate Spelling options selected, then the spell checker will flag the misspelled words with a red wavy underline. Furthermore, the message will be spell checked before it is sent. To set the Spelling options, activate the Inbox window, click Tools on the menu bar, click Options on the Tools menu, and then click the Spelling tab in the Options dialog box.

Formatting an E-Mail Message

When you compose a message in Outlook, the default message format is **HTML** (**Hypertext Markup Language**). This format allows you to do text formatting, numbering, bullets, alignment, signatures, and linking to Web pages.

In addition to selecting the message format, Outlook allows you to apply additional formatting using the E-Mail toolbar. Formatting includes changing the appearance, size, and color of text; applying bold, italic, and underlines to text; creating a numbered or bulleted list; changing paragraph indentation or aligning text; creating a link; and inserting a picture into an e-mail message.

The following steps center the text, UPDATED PRACTICE SCHEDULE, and changes its font size to 36-point. A **font size** is measured in points. A **point** is equal to 1/72 of one inch in height. Thus, a font size of 36 points is approximately one-half inch in height.

To Format an E-Mail Message

1

- **Drag to select the text, UPDATED PRACTICE SCHEDULE, in the message body.**

The text, UPDATED PRACTICE SCHEDULE, is selected (Figure 1-33).

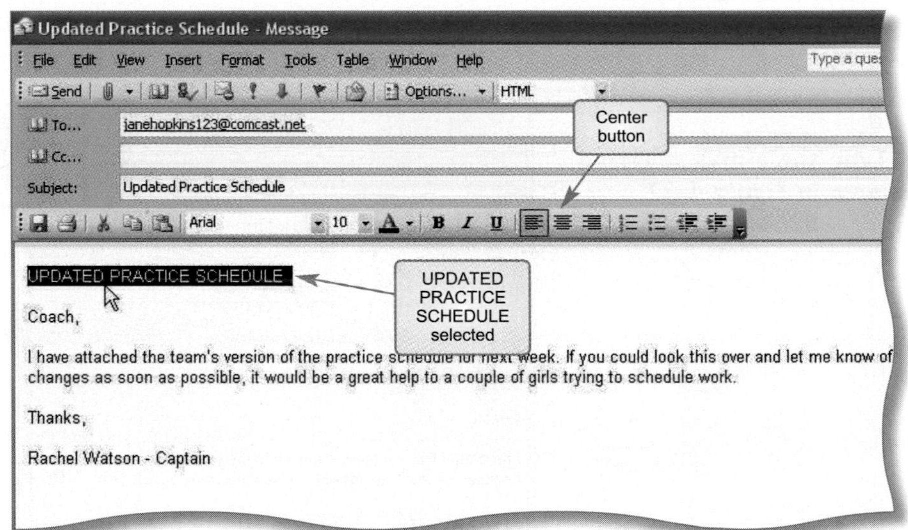

FIGURE 1-33

2

- **Click the Center button on the E-Mail toolbar.**

Outlook centers the text, UPDATED PRACTICE SCHEDULE, on the first line of the e-mail message (Figure 1-34). The current font size is the default 10 point.

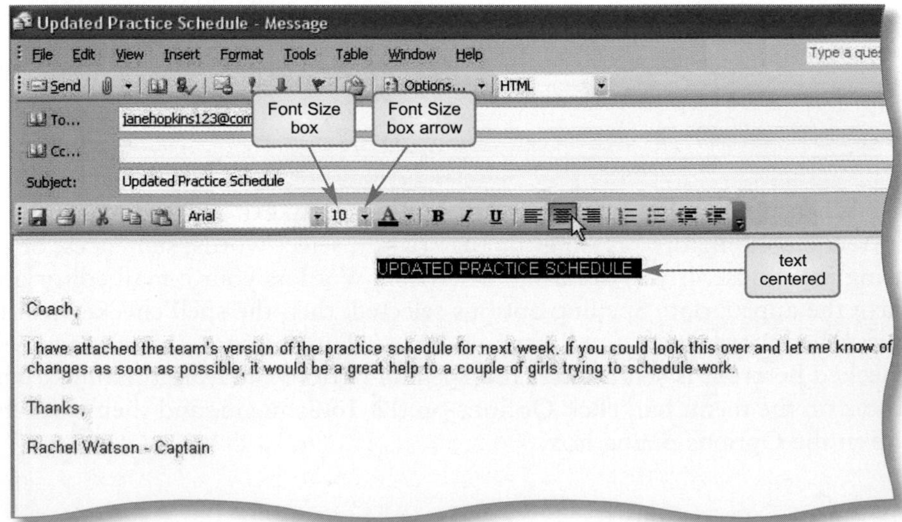

FIGURE 1-34

3

• Click the Font Size box arrow on the E-Mail toolbar.

Outlook displays the Font Size list (Figure 1-35).

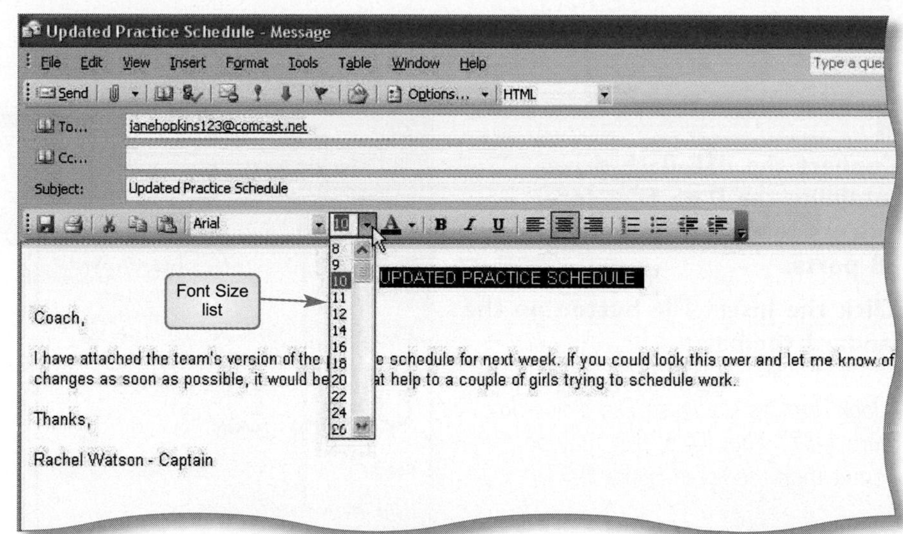

FIGURE 1-35

4

• Scroll down the Font Size list, click 36, and then click the selected text to remove the selection.

Outlook displays the text, UPDATED PRACTICE SCHEDULE, in 36-point font size (Figure 1-36).

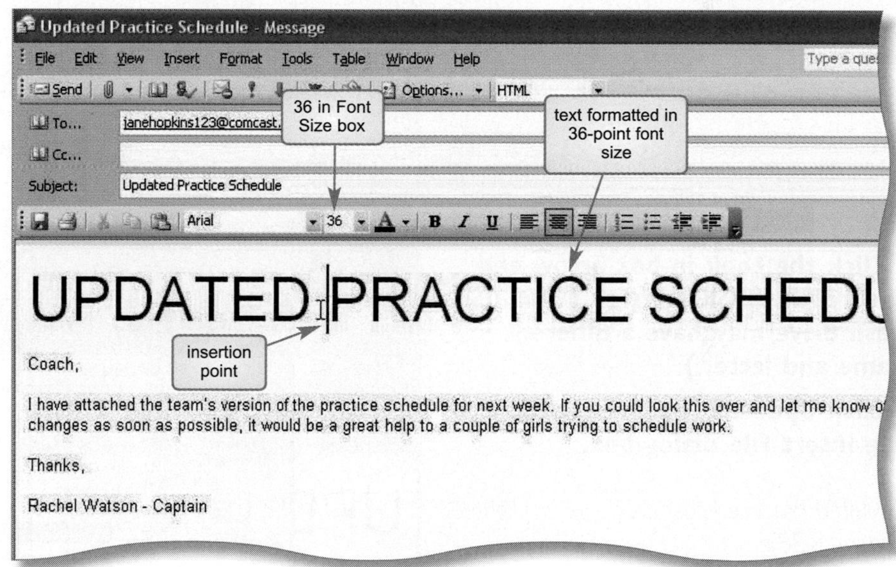

FIGURE 1-36

You do not have to select the text UPDATED PRACTICE SCHEDULE to center it on the line because centering is a paragraph format. All you have to do is click within the text, then click the Center button on the E-Mail toolbar. Font size, however, is a character format; therefore, you must select all the characters in the text before you select the new font size.

Attaching a File to an E-Mail Message

In some situations, a simple e-mail message is not sufficient to get the required information to the recipient. In these cases, you may want to attach a file to your e-mail message. Outlook allows you to attach almost any kind of file to your message. You may need to send a Word document, an Excel worksheet, a picture, or any number of file types. The steps on the next page show how to attach the Updated Practice Schedule.xls file to the e-mail message.

To Attach a File to an E-Mail Message

1

- **Connect the USB flash drive containing the Data Files for Students to one of the computer's USB ports.**
- **Click the Insert File button on the Standard toolbar.**

Outlook displays the Insert File dialog box (Figure 1-37). Your list of files may be different than the list in Figure 1-37.

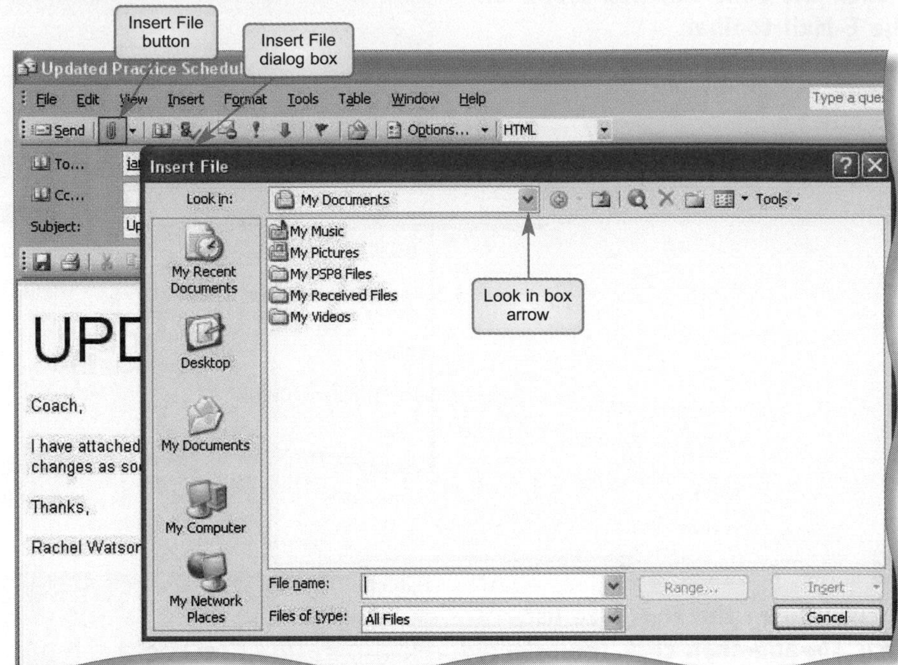

FIGURE 1-37

2

- **Click the Look in box arrow and then click UDISK 2.0 (F:). (Your USB flash drive may have a different name and letter.)**
- **Click Updated Practice Schedule in the Insert File dialog box.**

Updated Practice Schedule file is highlighted (Figure 1-38).

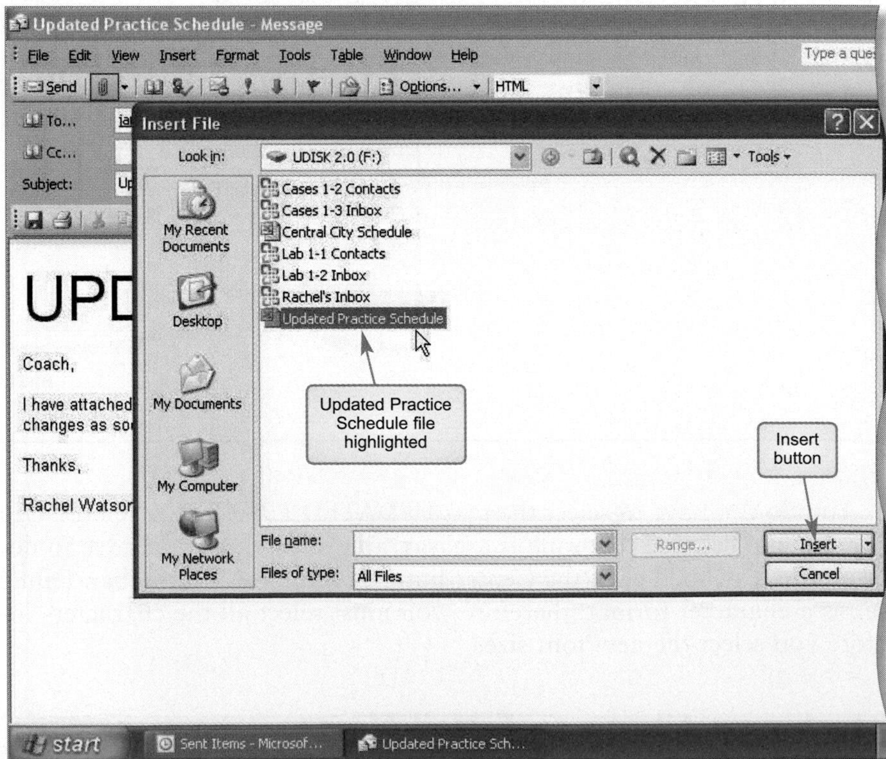

FIGURE 1-38

3

• **Click the Insert button in the Insert File dialog box.**

Outlook displays the name of the file, Updated Practice Schedule.xls, in the Attachment box, along with an Excel icon and the file size (Figure 1-39).

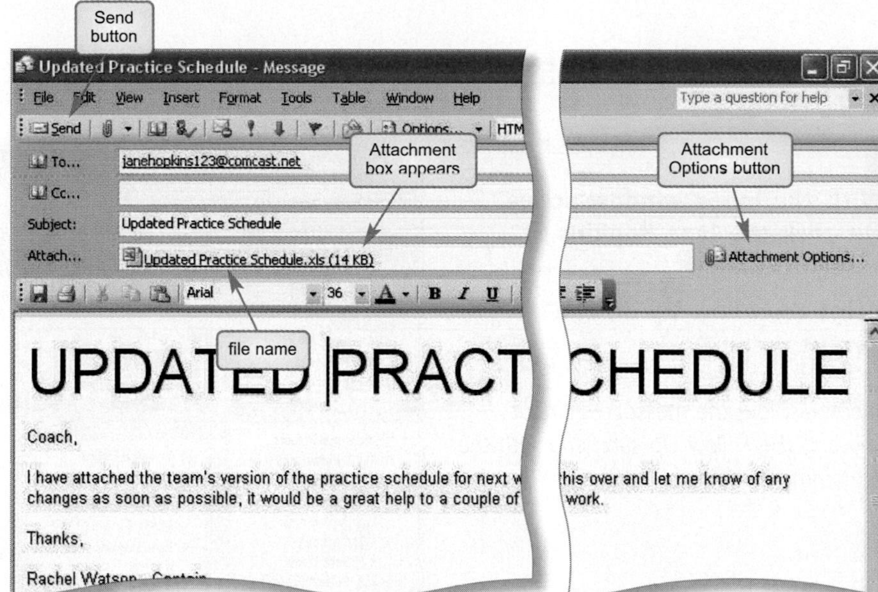

FIGURE 1-39

You can attach multiple documents to the same e-mail message. Simply perform the previous steps for each attachment. Keep in mind, however, that some Internet service providers have limits on the total size of e-mail messages they will accept. For example, if you attach pictures, which often are quite large, to an e-mail message, the recipient's service provider may not allow it to go through. In such cases, the sender is not informed that the e-mail message did not get through to the recipient. It is recommended that you keep the sum of the file sizes attached to an e-mail message less than 500 kilobytes.

Q & A

Q: How can I filter out unwanted e-mail messages?

A: A new feature in Outlook is the Junk E-mail Filter. The filter is on by default. It automatically evaluates whether an unread message should be sent to the Junk E-mail folder. You can configure the Junk E-mail Filter to your own personal settings. To change junk e-mail settings, click Options on the Tools menu, and then click the Junk E-mail button in the Preferences sheet in the Options dialog box. Make the preferred changes in the Junk E-mail Options dialog box.

Sending an E-Mail Message

After composing, formatting, and adding an attachment to an e-mail message, the next step is to send the message as illustrated in the following step.

To Send an E-Mail Message

1 **Click the Send button on the Standard toolbar.**

Outlook closes the Message window and temporarily stores the e-mail message in the Outbox folder while it sends the message, and then it moves the message to the Sent Items folder.

Flagging, Sorting, and Filtering E-Mail Messages

To the right of the message heading is the Flag Status column. The **Flag Status column** contains flags that can be assigned one of six different colors. One use for these flags could be to remind you to follow up on an issue. Color selection and the meaning of each color are entirely at the discretion of the user. For example, a red flag could mean the message needs immediate attention, a yellow flag may mean a response requires some information before you can reply, and a green flag simply may mean that the message requires a reply at your convenience (non-urgent). The steps on the next page show how to flag and sort e-mail messages.

Skill Builder 1-1

To practice the following tasks, visit scsite.com/off2003sch/skill, locate Outlook Project 1, and then click Skill Builder 1-1.

- ❑ Start Outlook
- ❑ Create an e-mail signature
- ❑ Compose a new e-mail message
- ❑ Format an e-mail message
- ❑ Attach a file to an e-mail message

To Flag E-Mail Messages

1

- **With the Inbox window active, right-click the Jane Hopkins message heading.**
- **Point to Follow Up on the shortcut menu.**

Outlook displays the message shortcut menu and the Follow Up submenu with the Flag commands (Figure 1-40).

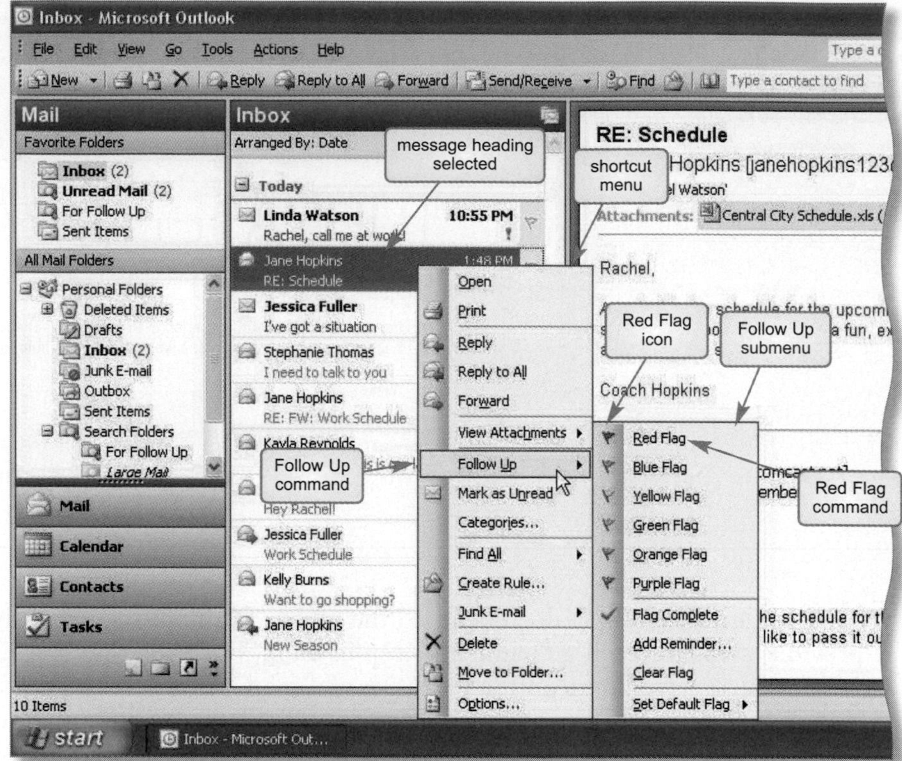

FIGURE 1-40

2

- **Click Red Flag on the Follow Up submenu.**
- **Repeat the Steps 1 and 2 to flag the remaining messages in the message pane.**
- **Select different colors as necessary.**

The Jane Hopkins message now displays a red flag icon in the Flag Status column (Figure 1-41). The remaining messages also display colored flag icons.

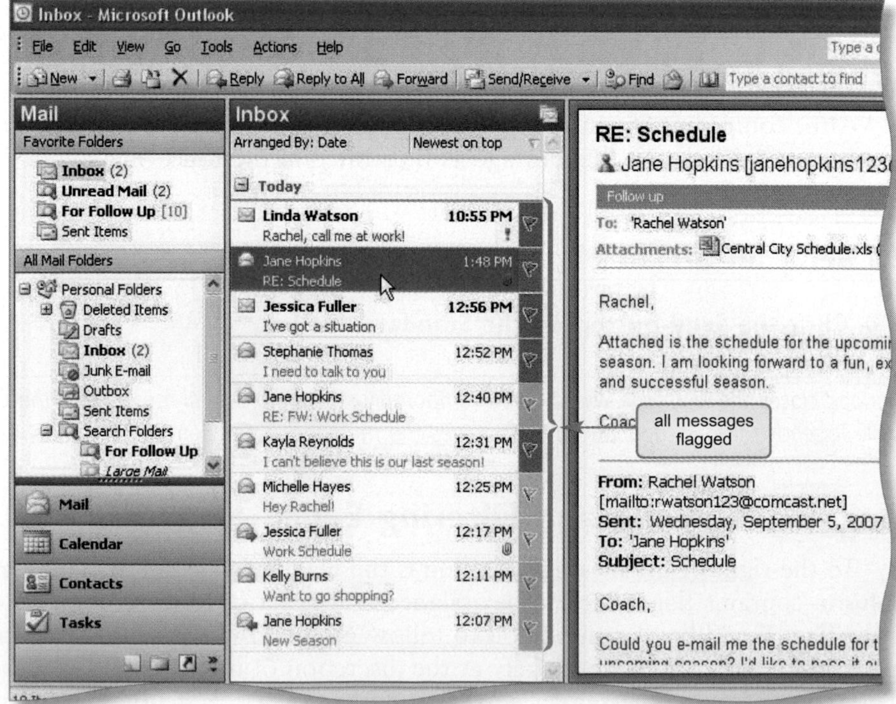

FIGURE 1-41

After flagging the appropriate messages, you can sort the messages by flag color. This is useful for grouping all the messages that require immediate attention as opposed to those messages that can be replied to at your convenience. The following steps show how to sort the messages by flag color.

To Sort E-Mail Messages by Flag Color

1

- **With the Inbox window active, click View on the menu bar and then point to Arrange By.**

Outlook displays the View menu and the Arrange By submenu (Figure 1-42).

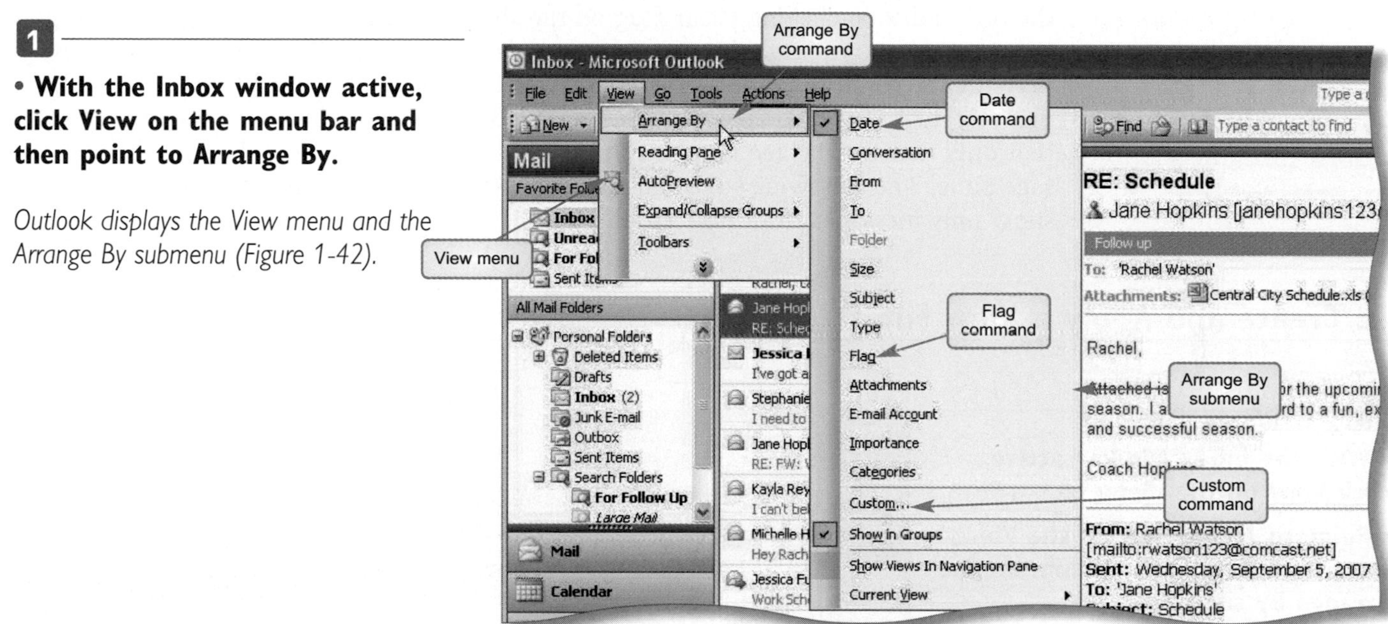

FIGURE 1-42

2

- **Click Flag on the Arrange By submenu.**

Outlook displays the Inbox window with messages arranged by flag and sorted by color (red on top) (Figure 1-43).

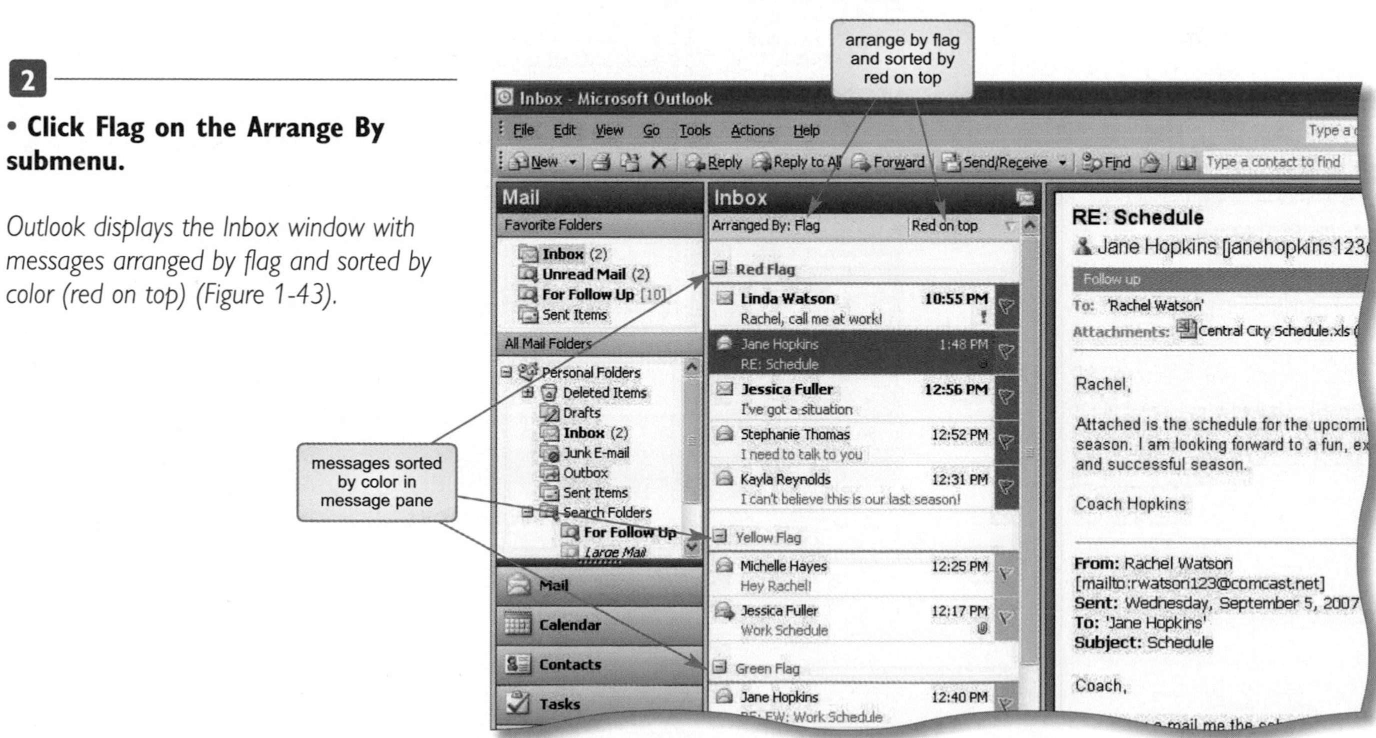

FIGURE 1-43

Outlook allows you to sort your messages several different ways using the Arrange By submenu (Figure 1-42 on the previous page). For example, you might want to see one particular person's messages. In this case, you would choose From on the Arrange By submenu. To return the messages to the default view, click Date on the Arrange By submenu.

After you have taken the appropriate action on a flagged message, you can indicate that no further action is required by changing the flag to a check mark simply by clicking the flag for that message. You also can remove the flag by right-clicking the flag and then clicking Clear Flag on the shortcut menu.

Another way to organize your messages is to use a view filter. A **view filter** displays items stored in Outlook folders that meet your specific conditions. For example, you might want to view only messages from Jane Hopkins. You would specify that only items with Jane Hopkins in the From text box should appear in the message pane. The following steps illustrate how to create and apply a view filter to show only messages from Jane Hopkins.

To Create and Apply a View Filter

1

- **With the Inbox window active, click View on the menu bar.**
- **Point to Arrange By on the View menu and then click Custom on the Arrange By submenu.**

Outlook displays the Customize View: Messages dialog box (Figure 1-44).

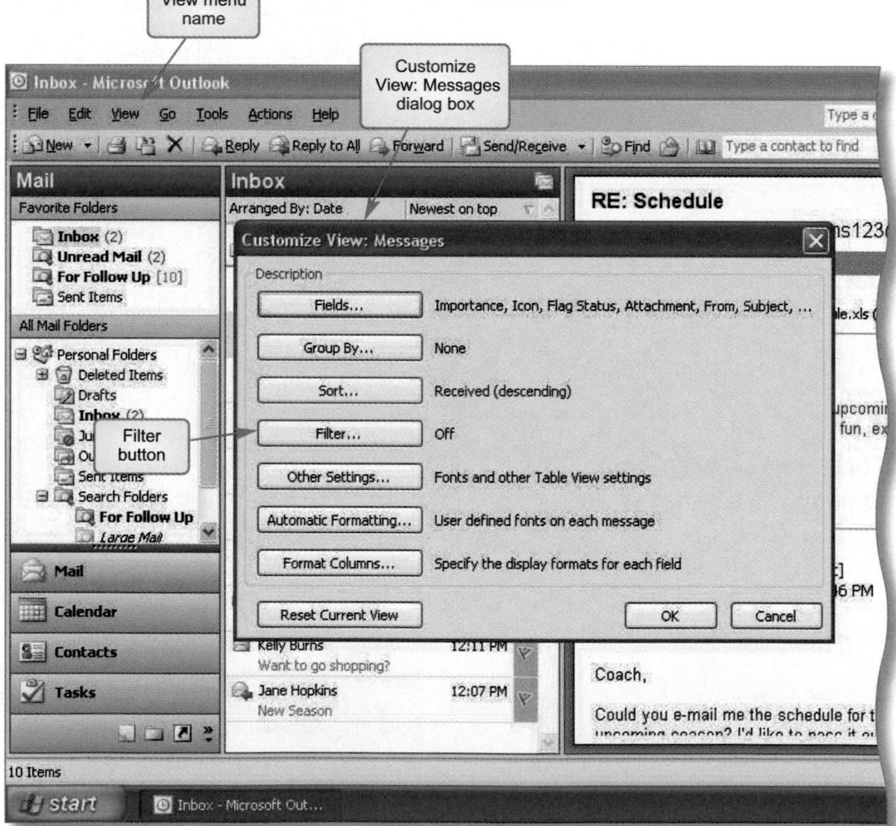

FIGURE 1-44

2

- **Click the Filter button.**
- **When Outlook displays the Filter dialog box, click the From text box.**
- **Type** `Jane Hopkins` **in the From text box.**

Outlook displays the Filter dialog box. The name, Jane Hopkins, appears in the From text box (Figure 1-45).

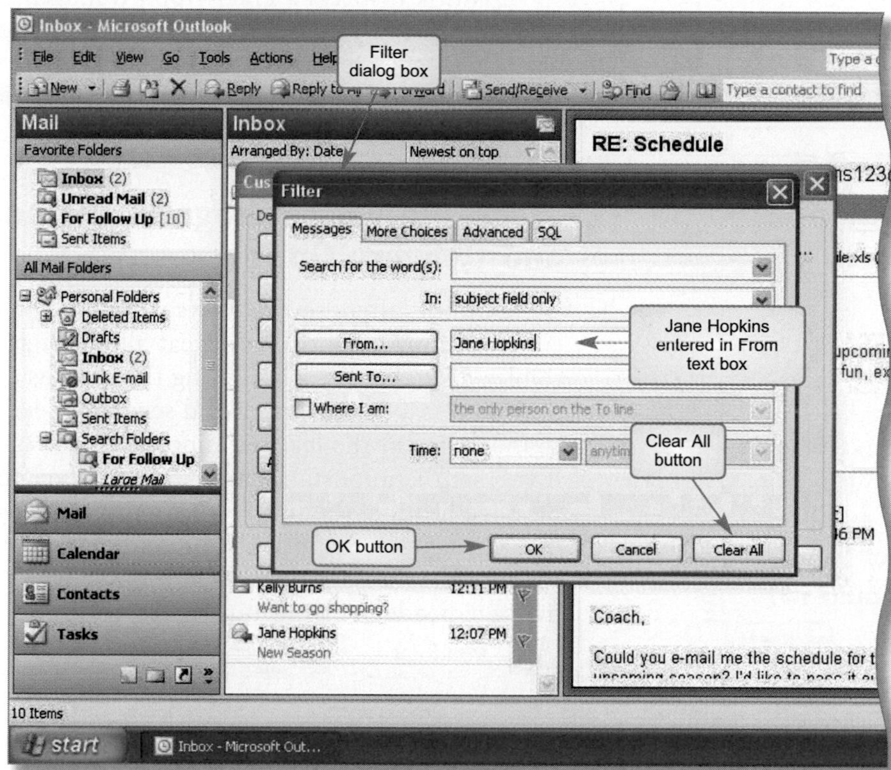

FIGURE 1-45

3

- **Click the OK button in the Filter dialog box and the Customize View: Messages dialog box.**

The Inbox window is redisplayed with only messages from Jane Hopkins showing in the message pane (Figure 1-46). The words, Filter Applied, appear on the status bar in the lower-left corner of the window.

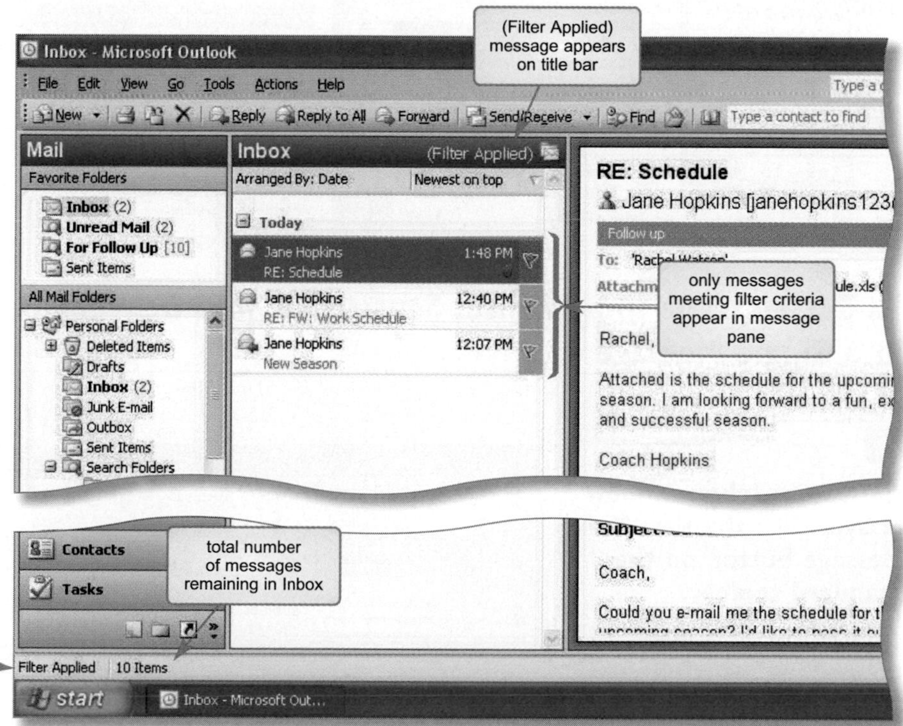

FIGURE 1-46

Outlook displays a Filter Applied message on the status bar and the Inbox pane title bar when a view filter is applied to a selected folder. It also shows the total number of messages remaining in the Inbox folder on the status bar. To remove a view filter, click the Clear All button in the Filter dialog box (Figure 1-45 on the previous page).

Setting E-Mail Message Importance, Sensitivity, and Delivery Options

Outlook offers several ways in which you can customize your e-mail. You can either customize Outlook to treat all messages in the same manner, or you can customize a single message. Among the options available through Outlook are setting e-mail message importance and sensitivity. Setting **message importance** will indicate to the recipient the level of importance you have given to the message. For example, if you set the importance at high, a red exclamation point icon will appear with the message heading (Figure 1-47). Setting **message sensitivity** indicates whether the message is personal, private, or confidential. A message banner indicating the sensitivity of the message appears in the Reading Pane below the sender's name in the message header as shown in Figure 1-47.

FIGURE 1-47

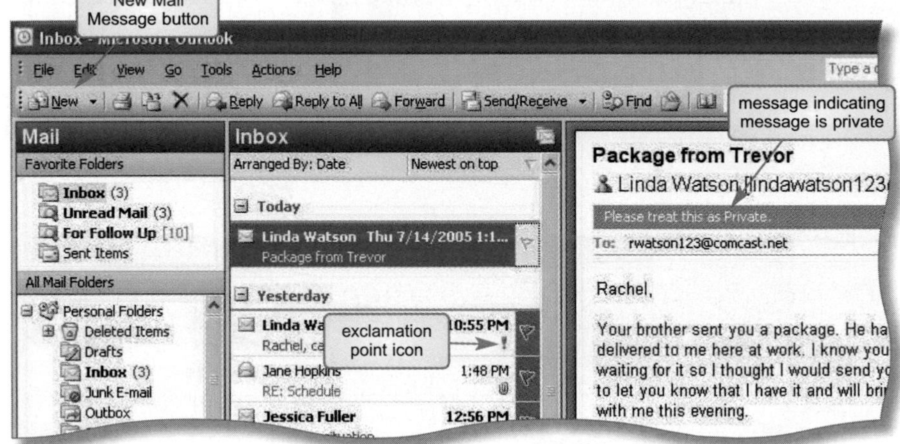

Along with setting importance and sensitivity, Outlook also offers several delivery options. You can have replies to your message automatically forwarded, save sent messages in a location of your choice (default is Sent Items folder), or delay delivering a message until a specified date and time.

The following steps illustrate how to set message importance, sensitivity, and delivery options in a single message.

To Set Message Importance, Sensitivity, and Delivery Options in a Single Message

1

- **With the Inbox window active, click the New Mail Message button on the Standard toolbar.**
- **Enter the appropriate message information as shown in Figure 1-48.**

Outlook displays the Jessica - Message window with the new message entered (Figure 1-48).

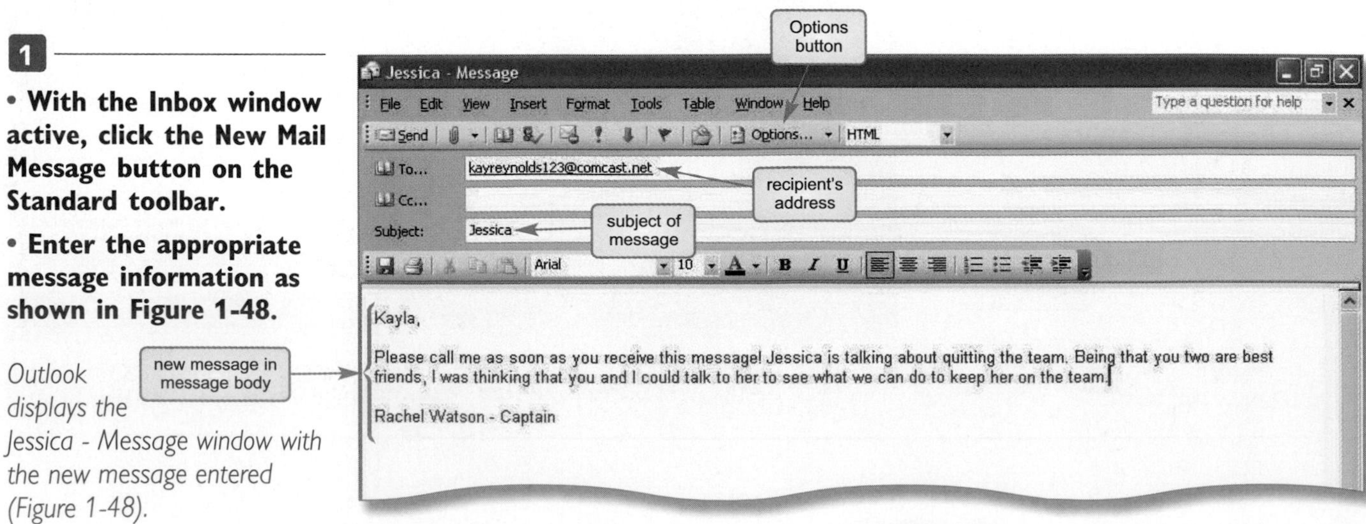

FIGURE 1-48

2

- **Click the Options button on the Mail toolbar (Figure 1-48).**

Outlook displays the Message Options dialog box (Figure 1-49).

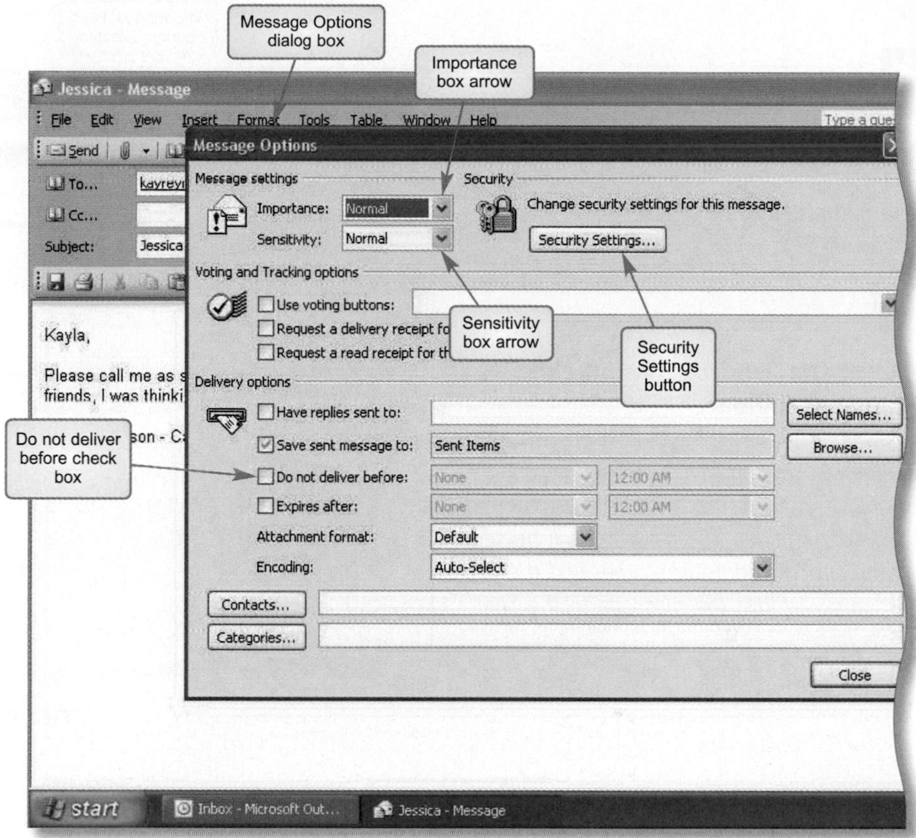

FIGURE 1-49

3

- **Click the Importance box arrow and then select High in the Importance list.**
- **Click the Sensitivity box arrow and then select Private in the Sensitivity list.**
- **Click Do not deliver before in the Delivery options area to select it.**
- **Select September 10, 2007 in the calendar and 12:00 PM as the time in the respective delivery boxes.**

Outlook displays the Message Options dialog box as shown in Figure 1-50. High is selected in the Importance box, Private is selected in the Sensitivity box, and the message delivery is set for 9/10/2007 at 12:00 PM in the date and time boxes.

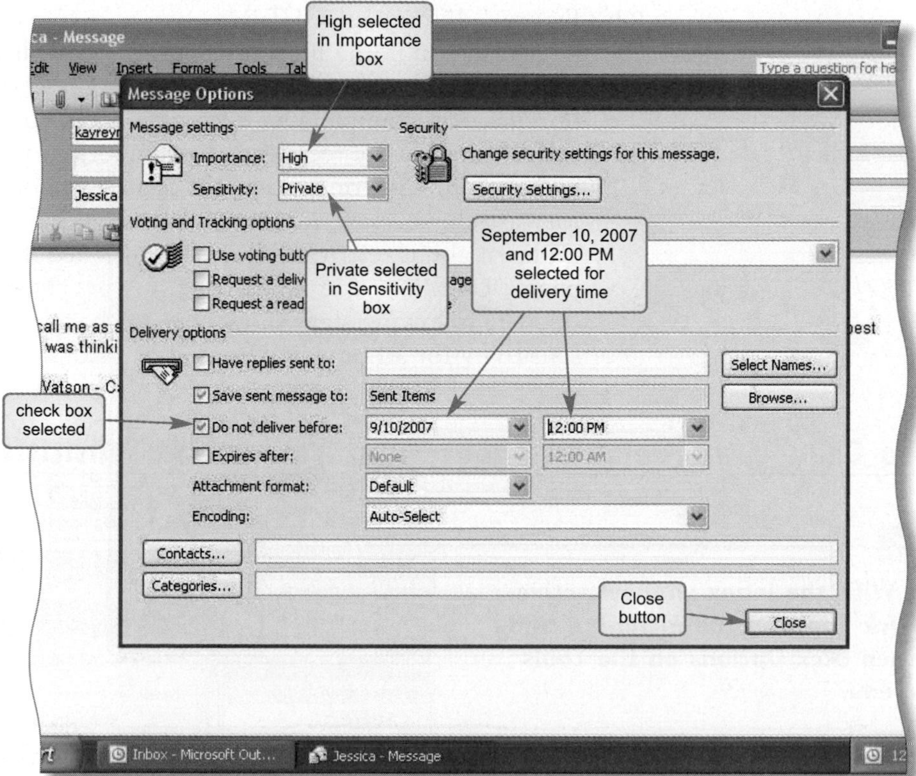

FIGURE 1-50

4

• **Click the Close button.**

Outlook closes the Message Options dialog box and displays the Message window (Figure 1-51).

5

• **Click the Send button on the Standard toolbar.**

Outlook closes the Message window and temporarily stores the e-mail message in the Outbox folder. The message will be sent on the specified date and time, and then Outlook will move the message to the Sent Items folder.

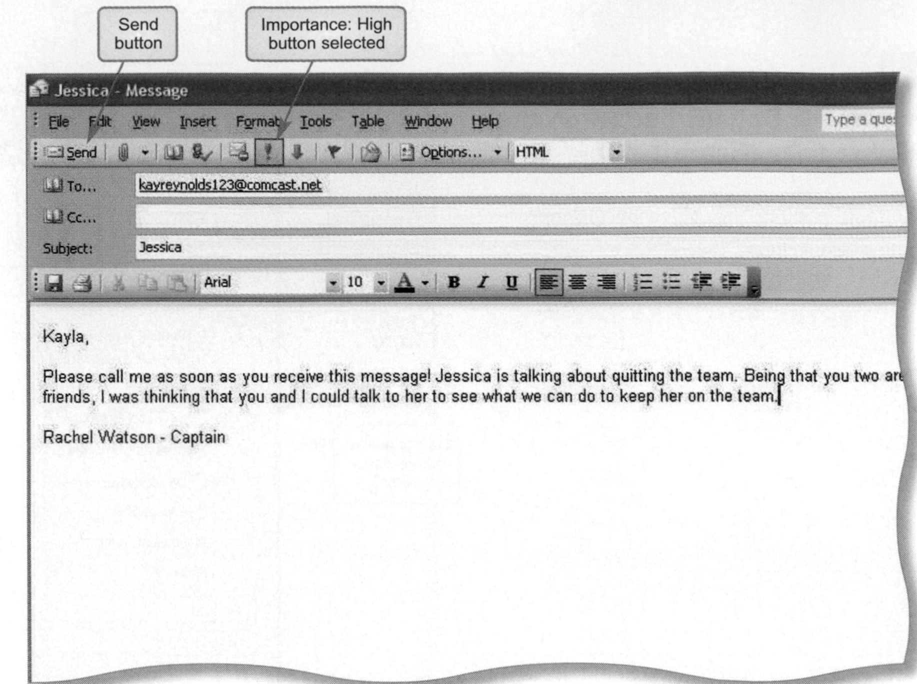

FIGURE 1-51

The recipient of the message will receive the message with the red exclamation point icon and the message indicating the e-mail is private like the one shown in Figure 1-47 on page OUT 34.

As shown in the previous steps, the default level of importance and sensitivity is Normal. Outlook allows you to change the default level for either or both of these options. For example, you may want all of your outgoing messages to be treated as confidential by the recipients. It is important to know that marking an e-mail as personal, private, or confidential is advisory only. The recipient still will be able to forward the message to another person or copy the message into another e-mail. To learn about restricting the recipient's actions on a message, see the Q&A on page OUT 38.

The following steps show how to change the default level of importance and sensitivity for all outgoing messages.

To Change the Default Level of Importance and Sensitivity

1

• **With the Inbox window active, click Tools on the menu bar and then click Options on the Tools menu.**

Outlook displays the Options dialog box (Figure 1-52).

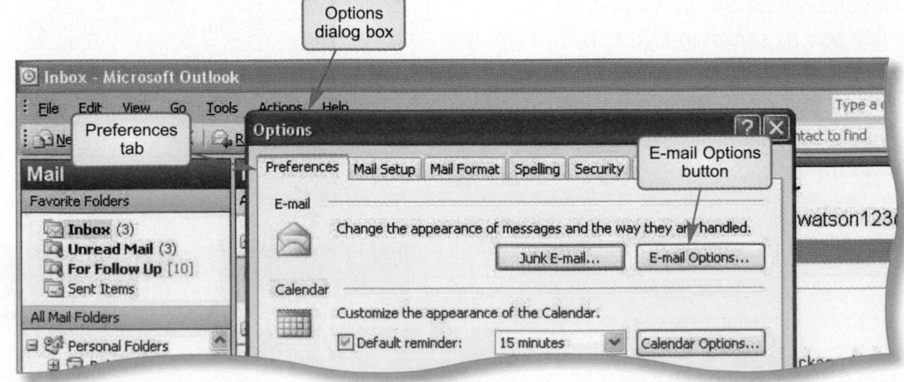

FIGURE 1-52

2

• **In the Preferences sheet, click the E-mail Options button.**

Outlook displays the E-mail Options dialog box (Figure 1-53).

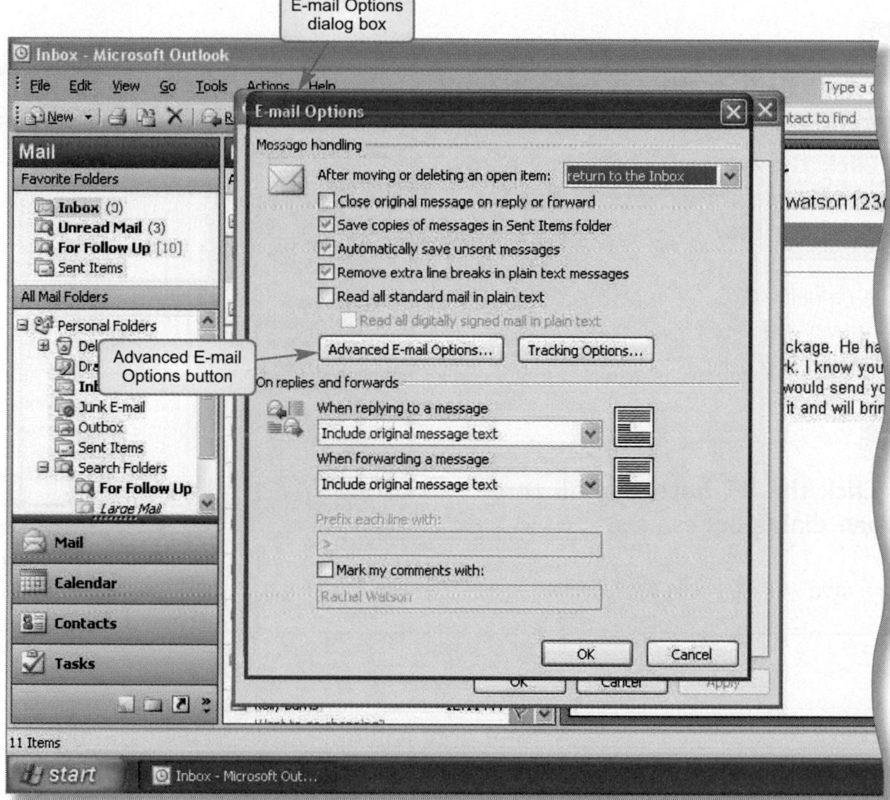

FIGURE 1-53

3

• **Click the Advanced E-mail Options button.**

• **When Outlook displays the Advanced E-mail Options dialog box, click the Set importance box arrow.**

Outlook displays the Advance E-mail Options dialog box with the Set importance list showing the available importance settings (Figure 1-54).

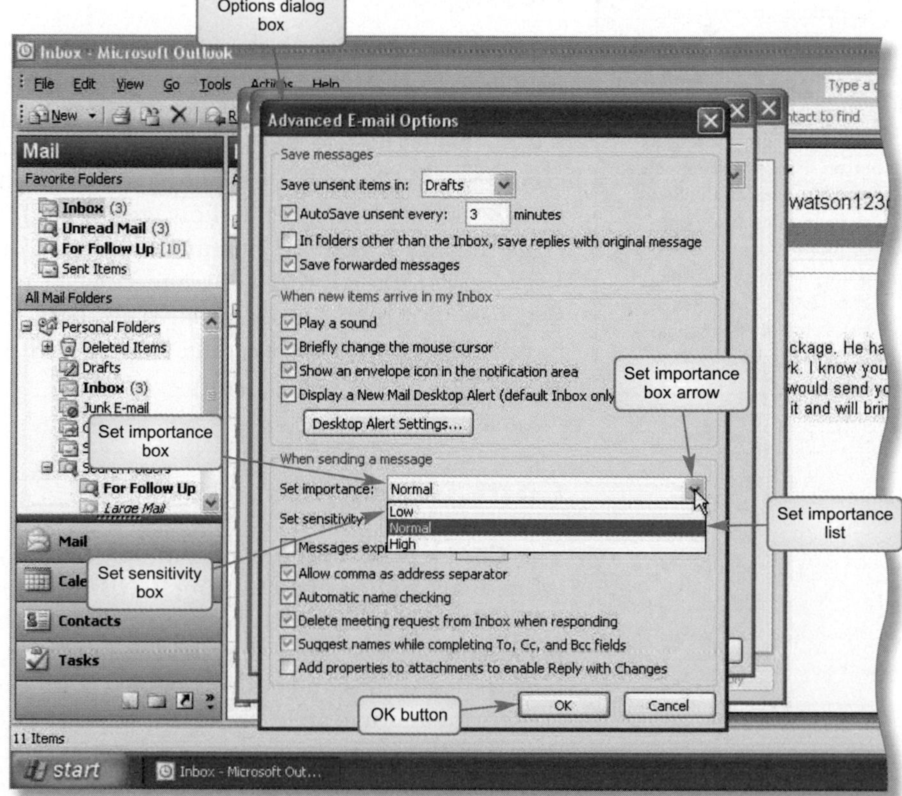

FIGURE 1-54

• **Select High in the Set importance list.**

• **Click the Set sensitivity box arrow and then select Private in the Set sensitivity list.**

The default values for importance and sensitivity are set at High and Private, respectively (Figure 1-55).

5

• **Click the OK button in all three open dialog boxes.**

The Inbox window is redisplayed.

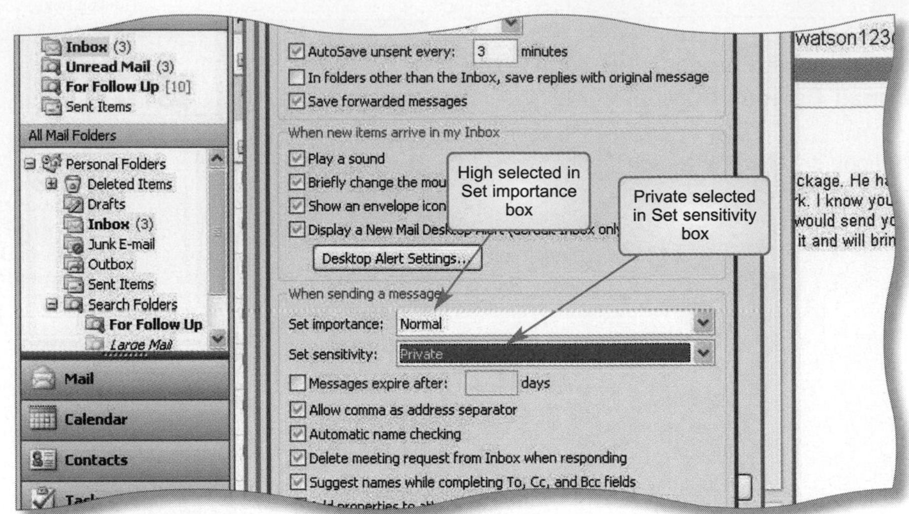

FIGURE 1-55

The default importance and sensitivity settings have been changed. Any outgoing e-mail now will appear with the high importance icon and the message indicating the message is private in the recipient's Inbox.

Q & A

Q: How can I set security restrictions on my e-mail messages?

A: To apply certain security restrictions on a message, click the Security Settings button (Figure 1-49 on page OUT 35) to open the Security Properties dialog box. For more information about security settings, visit the Office 2003 Q&A Web page (scsite.com/off2003sch/qa) and click Security Settings.

Using Search Folders to Display Categories of E-Mail Messages

A new feature in Outlook is the Search Folders folder in the All Mail Folders pane (Figure 1-56). The **Search Folders folder** includes a group of folders that allows you to group and view your messages quickly in one of three ways: (1) For Follow Up, (2) Large Mail, and (3) Unread Mail. **For Follow Up** messages are messages that you have flagged but have not taken action. These messages are sorted further by flag color (red, yellow, green, etc.). **Large Mail** contains messages with large file attachments. These messages are grouped by size: Large (100 to 500 KB), Very Large (500 KB to 1 MB), and Huge (1 to 5 MB). **Unread Mail** contains messages that have not been opened or have not been marked as read, even though you may have read them via the Reading Pane. Figure 1-56 shows messages in the For Follow Up folder.

Contacts

The **Contacts component** of Outlook allows you to store information about individuals and companies. People with whom you communicate for school, business, or personal reasons are your **contacts**. To help organize information about personal contacts, some people keep names, addresses, and telephone numbers in business-card files and address books. With the Outlook Contacts component, you can create and maintain important contact information in a **contact list**, which is stored in the Contacts folder. Your contact list is like an electronic address book that allows you to store names, addresses, e-mail addresses, and more. Once the information has been entered, your contact list can be retrieved, sorted, edited, organized, or printed. Outlook also includes a **Find option** that lets you search for a contact name in your address book while you are using the Calendar, Inbox, or other Outlook components.

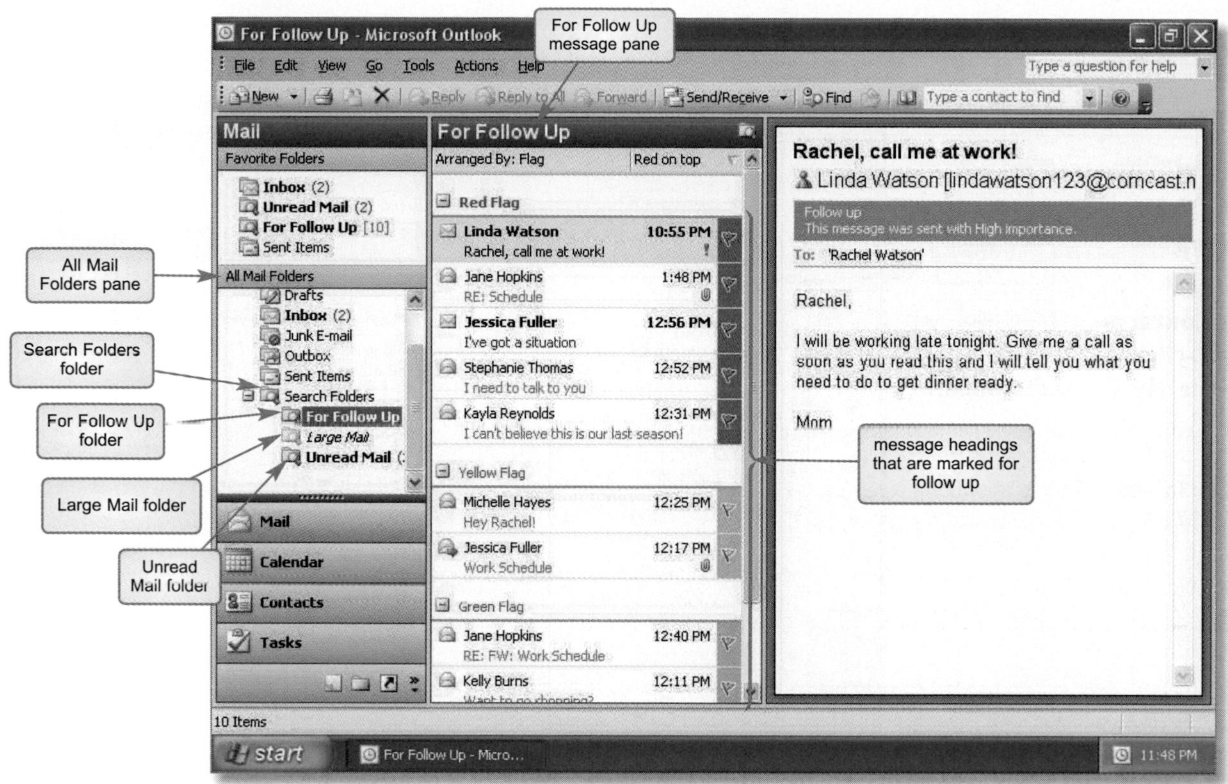

FIGURE 1-56

When the Contacts folder is open, information about each contact appears on an address card in the default **Address Cards view**. Each address card includes fields such as name, address, and various telephone numbers, as well as e-mail and Web page addresses. Choose which fields are displayed on the cards using the View menu.

Previously, an e-mail message was composed, signed, formatted, and sent to Jane Hopkins. Jane's e-mail address was typed into the To text box (see Figure 1-31 on page OUT 25). The following sections show how to: (1) create a personal folder, (2) create a contact list, (3) edit contact information, (4) print contact information, (5) send an e-mail to a contact, and (6) delete a contact.

Q & A

Q: Can I create my own Search Folders to meet my personal specifications?

A: Yes. Besides the three default Search Folders that Outlook provides, you also can create your own personal Search Folders using search criteria that you specify. To create a personal Search Folder, right-click Search Folders in the All Mail Folders pane, click New Search Folder on the shortcut menu, scroll down to the Custom category in the New Search Folder dialog box, and then select Create a custom Search Folder. Click the OK button. From this point on, you select criteria to meet your particular needs.

Creating a Personal Folder

The first step in creating the contact list is to create a personal folder in which the contact list will be stored. When only one person is working on a computer, a contact list can be stored in Outlook's Contacts folder. If you share your computer with a family member, lab partner, or coworker, you likely will want to store your contact list in a personal folder, which usually is added as a subfolder within the Contacts folder. The steps on the next page create a personal folder for Rachel Watson.

To Create a Personal Folder

1

- **Click the Contacts button in the Navigation Pane.**
- **When Outlook displays the Contacts window, right-click Contacts in the My Contacts pane.**

Outlook displays the Contacts - Microsoft Outlook window and the Contacts shortcut menu (Figure 1-57).

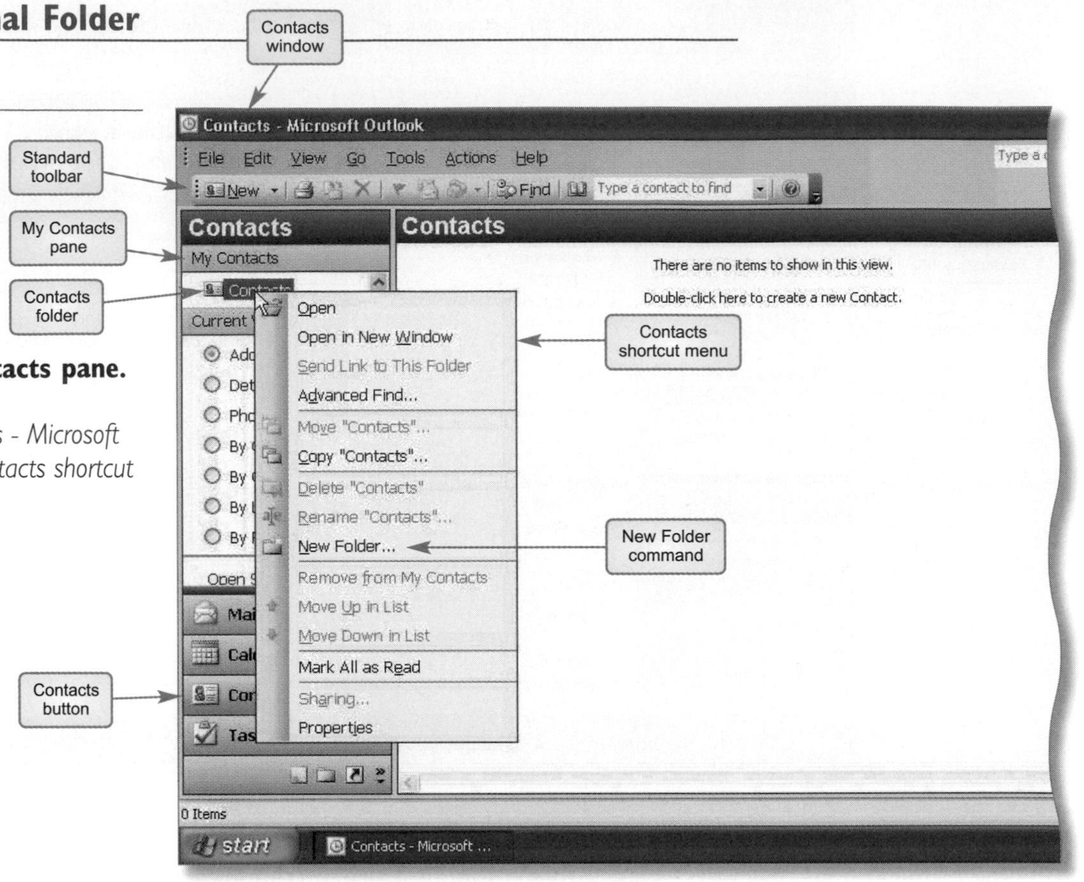

FIGURE 1-57

2

- **Click New Folder on the My Contacts shortcut menu.**
- **When Outlook displays the Create New Folder dialog box, type** `Rachel's Contacts` **in the Name text box.**
- **If necessary, select Contact Items in the Folder contains list.**
- **Click Contacts in the Select where to place the folder list.**

The new folder, Rachel's Contacts, becomes a subfolder of the Contacts folder (Figure 1-58). Rachel's Contacts appears in the Name text box.

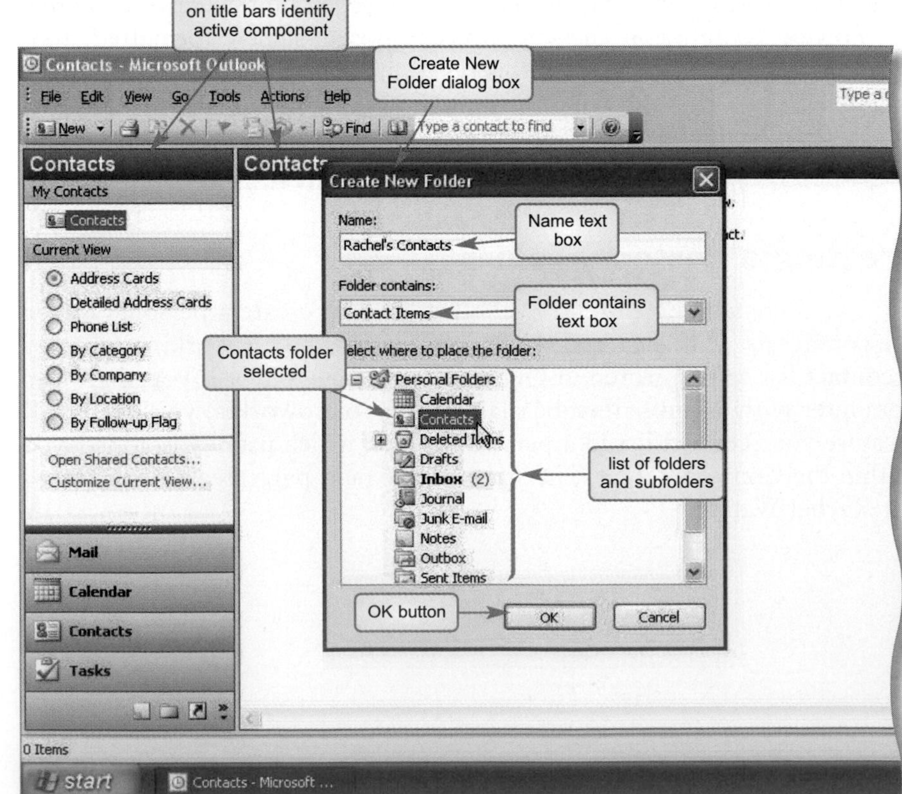

FIGURE 1-58

3

- **Click the OK button.**
- **Click Rachel's Contacts in the My Contacts list.**

Outlook displays a list of available folders in the My Contacts pane and displays an empty Contacts pane (Figure 1-59).

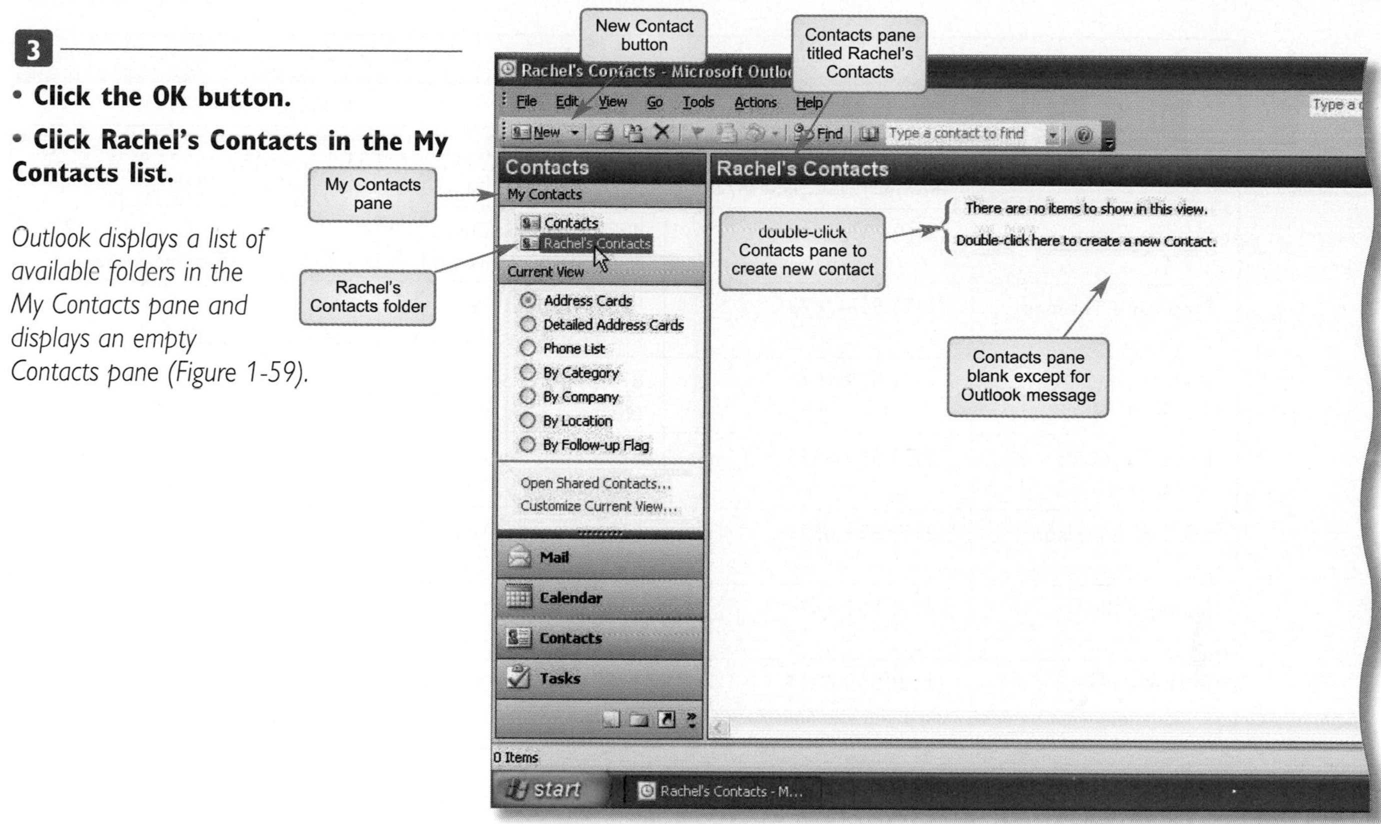

FIGURE 1-59

As indicated in the previous steps, it is relatively easy to create folders for your contacts. Most Outlook users have one folder for all their contacts. But you can create a folder for your family, another for friends, another for business associates, and so on. The number of folders you use for your contacts will depend on what works best for you.

Figure 1-60 illustrates the Standard toolbar located below the menu bar in the Contacts window.

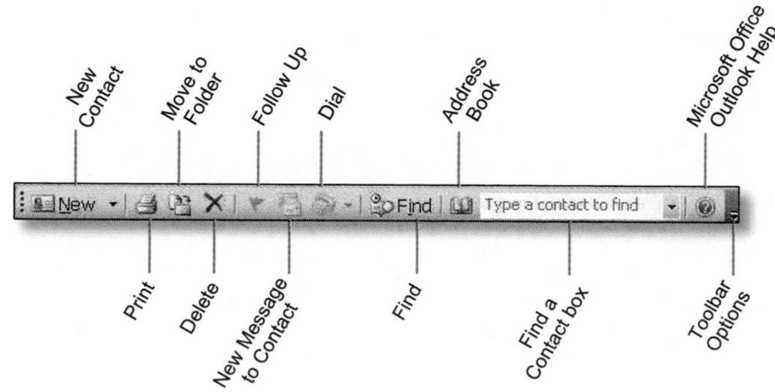

FIGURE 1-60

Creating a Contact List

The steps on the next page describe how to enter the contact information in Table 1-3 on the next page into the contact list.

Table 1-3 Contact Information

NAME	TELEPHONE	ADDRESS	E-MAIL ADDRESS
Jane Hopkins	Business: (219) 555-9633 Home: (219) 555-3571	6432 Johnson Road Michigan City, IN 46360	janehopkins123@comcast.net
Natalie Clem	(219) 555-7410	9872 Magnolia Drive Michigan City, IN 46360	natclem123@comcast.net
Stephanie Thomas	(219) 555-2673	8778 Wabash Ave. Michigan City, IN 46360	stephthomas123@comcast.net
Kelly Burns	(219) 555-1044	8798 7th Street Michigan City, IN 46360	kellburns123@comcast.net
Kayla Reynolds	(219) 555-8465	9780 Main Street Michigan City, IN 46360	kayreynolds123@comcast.net
Lee Anne Nelson	(219) 555-8521	5692 Franklin Ave. Michigan City, IN 46360	lanelson123@comcast.net
Jessica Fuller	(219) 555-9884	1125 5th Street Michigan City, IN 46360	jessfuller123@comcast.net
Michelle Hayes	(219) 555-6214	1258 Lakeview Court Michigan City, IN 46360	michhayes123@comcast.net

To Create a Contact List

1

- **With the Contacts window active and Rachel's Contacts folder selected, click the New button on the Standard toolbar (Figure 1-59 on the previous page).**
- **When Outlook displays the Untitled - Contact window, if necessary, maximize the window.**
- **Type** `Jane Hopkins` **in the Full Name text box.**
- **Click the Business text box in the Phone numbers area.**

Notice that Outlook automatically fills in the File as box, last name first (Figure 1-61). The name on the title bar of the Contact window changes to the Jane Hopkins - Contact window.

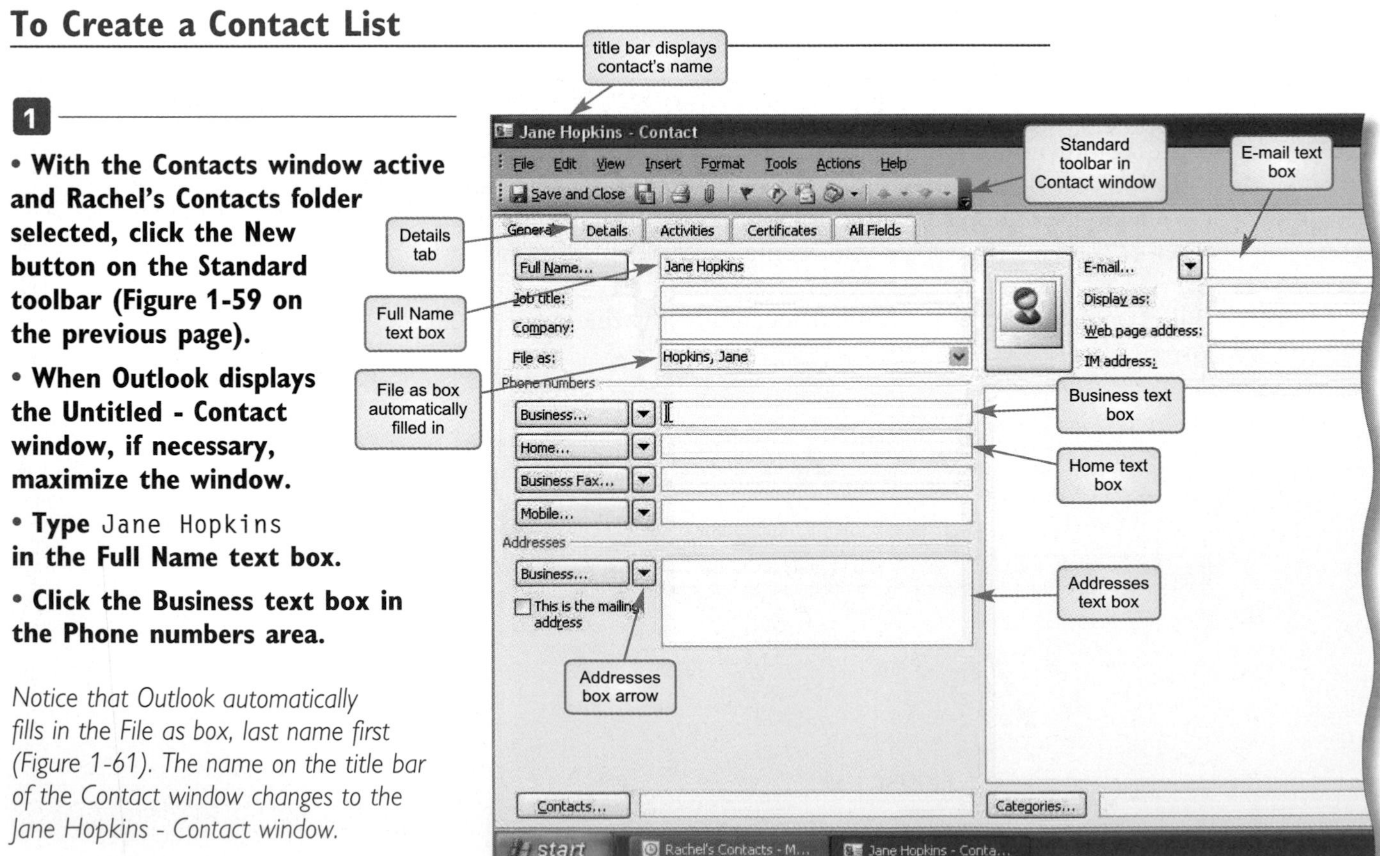

FIGURE 1-61

2

- **Type** 2195559633 **as the business telephone number and then click the Home text box.**
- **Type** 2195553571 **as the Home telephone number.**
- **Click the Addresses box arrow and select Home.**
- **Click the text box in the Addresses area, type** 6432 Johnson Road **and then press the ENTER key.**
- **Type** Michigan City, IN 46360 **to complete the address entry.**
- **Click the E-mail text box.**
- **Type** janehopkins123@comcast.net **as the e-mail address.**

Outlook displays the Jane Hopkins - Contact window as shown in Figure 1-62.

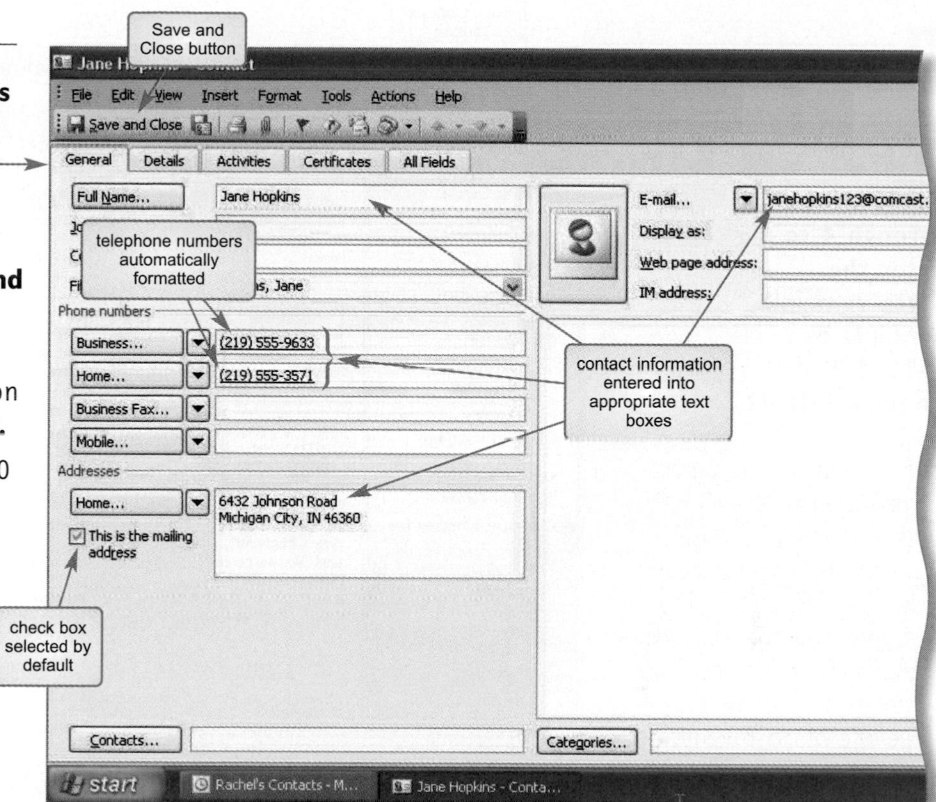

FIGURE 1-62

3

- **Click the Save and Close button on the Standard toolbar.**

Outlook displays the Jane Hopkins address card in Address Cards view in the Rachel's Contacts pane (Figure 1-63). Address Cards is the current view by default.

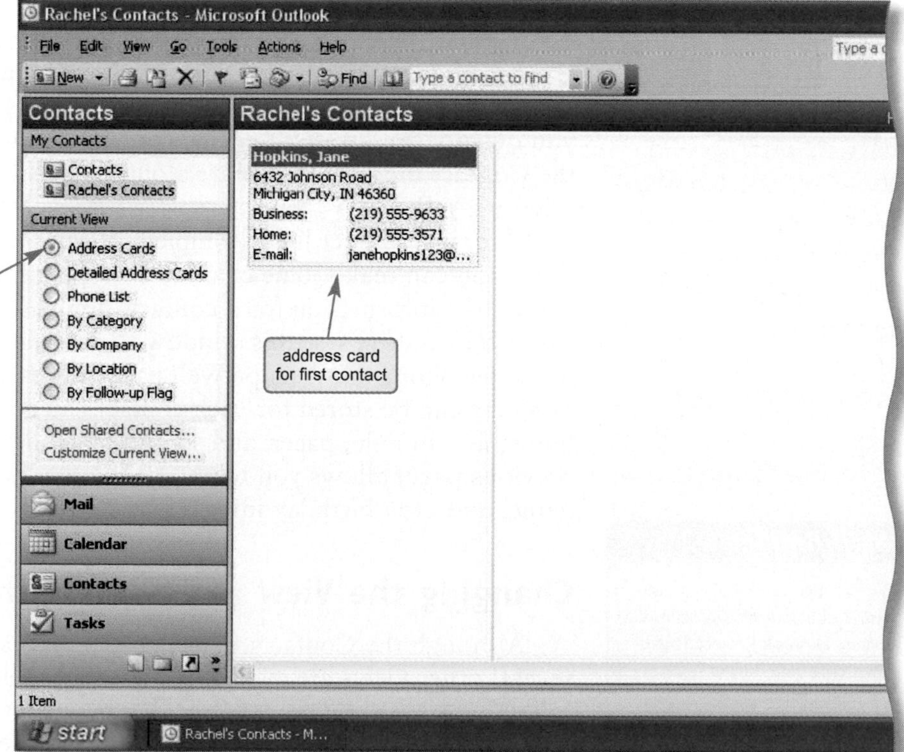

FIGURE 1-63

4

- **Click the New Contact button on the Standard toolbar.**
- **Repeat Steps 2 through 4 to enter the seven remaining contacts in Table 1-3 on page OUT 42.**

Outlook displays the contact list as shown in Figure 1-64. Outlook automatically lists the contacts in alphabetical order. The letters, Bur - Tho, that appear on the right side of the Rachel's Contacts pane title bar indicate the range of contacts currently displayed (Burns to Thomas).

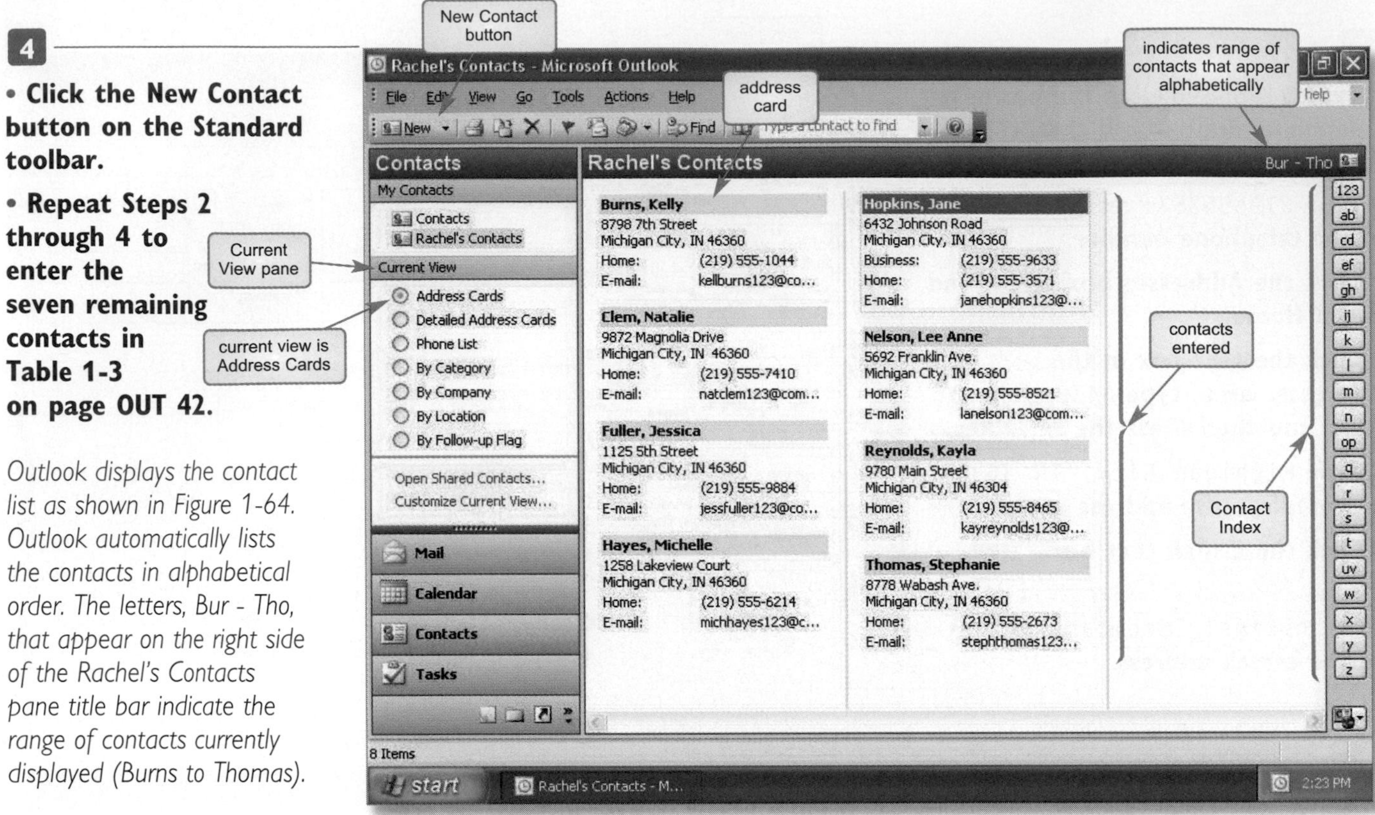

FIGURE 1-64

Because this contact list consists of only eight names, Outlook displays all of the contact names. The default view is Address Cards. With longer lists, however, you quickly can locate a specific contact by clicking a letters or numbers button on the **Contact Index** that appears along the right side of the Contacts window (Figure 1-64).

After the contact list is complete, it can be viewed, edited, or updated at any time. You can make some changes by typing inside the card itself. To display and edit all the information for a contact, double-click the address card to display the Contacts window. Use this window to enter information about a contact, such as home telephone numbers or Web page addresses. Up to 19 different telephone numbers can be stored for each contact categorized by location and type (business, home, fax, mobile, pager, and so on). Clicking the Details tab (Figure 1-62 on the previous page) allows you to enter a contact's department, manager's name, nickname, and even birthday information.

Skill Builder 1-2

To practice the following tasks, visit scsite.com/off2003sch/skill, locate Outlook Project 1, and then click Skill Builder 1-2.
- ❑ Start Outlook
- ❑ Create a personal folder
- ❑ Create a contact list

Changing the View and Sorting the Contacts List

Although the Contacts folder is displayed in Address Cards view by default, several other views are available and can be selected in the Navigation Pane. The following steps show how to change the view from Address Cards to Phone List, sort the contact list in descending sequence, and then change back to Address Cards view.

To Change the View and Sort the Contact List

1

- **With the Rachel's Contacts - Microsoft Outlook window active, click Phone List in the Current View pane of the Navigation Pane.**
- **With the Phone List in ascending sequence by the File As field, click the File As column heading in the Contacts pane.**

Outlook changes the contact list view from Address Cards to Phone List and displays the contact list in descending sequence by last name (Figure 1-65). Notice the direction of the small arrow in the File As column heading.

2

- **After reviewing the contact list in Phone List view, click Address Cards in the Current View pane in the Navigation Pane.**

Outlook displays the contact list in ascending sequence in Address Cards view (Figure 1-64).

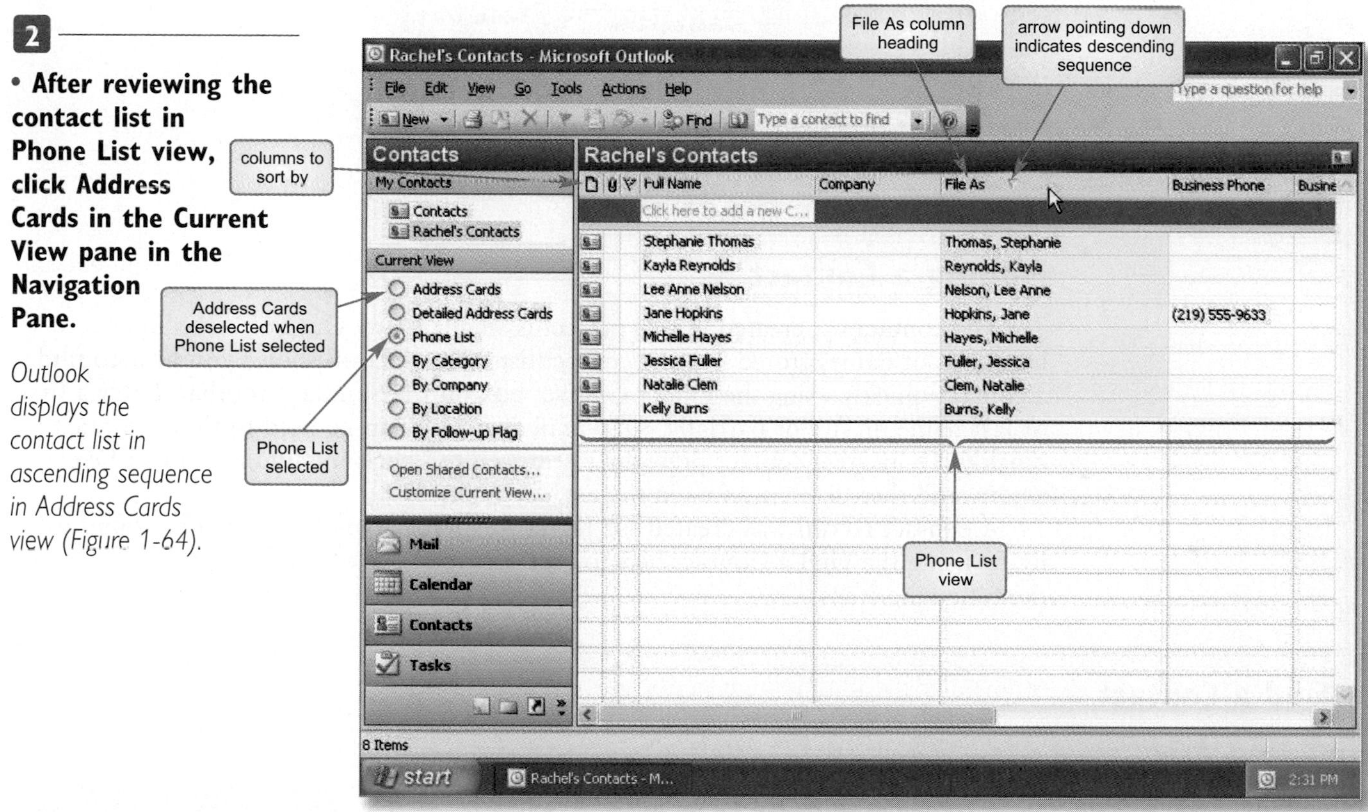

FIGURE 1-65

To see how easy it is to change views of the contact list, click one of the view options in the Current View pane in the Navigation Pane. You also can sort by any one of the column headings in the Contacts pane (Icon, Attachment, Flag Status, Full Name, Company, File As, Business Phone, etc.) just by clicking the column heading (see Figure 1-65). Click a column heading once and Outlook sorts the contacts list into descending sequence. Click the same column heading again and Outlook sorts the contact list into ascending sequence. The arrow in the middle of the column heading indicates whether the contact list is in ascending sequence or descending sequence. When you switch from one view to another, the sequence of the contact list reverts to what it was the last time the view was used.

You can sort the views of the contact list, e-mail messages, and other Outlook information in many different ways. If you right-click a column heading in any Outlook component and point to the Arrange By command on the shortcut menu (Figure 1-66 on the next page), you can see the Arrange By commands.

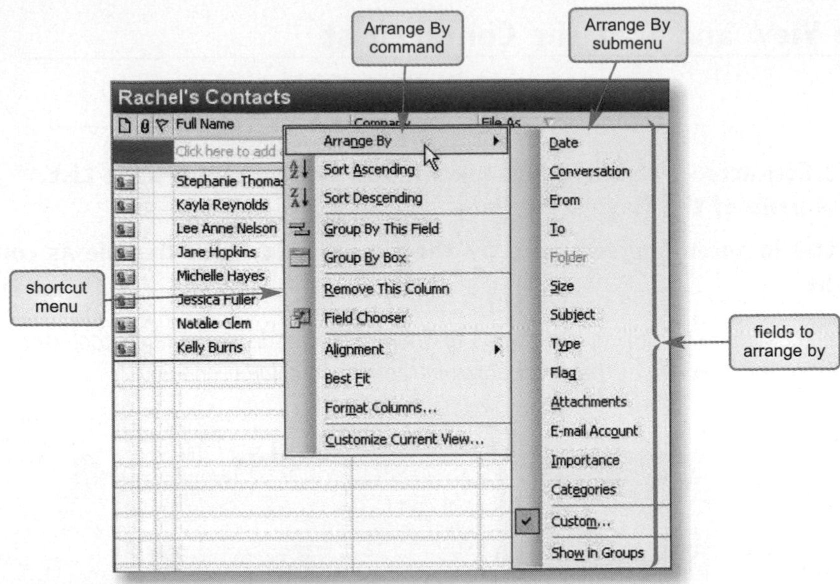

FIGURE 1-66

Finding a Contact

The contact list created in this project is small. Many Outlook users have hundreds of names stored in their contact lists. This section shows you how to find a contact quickly using the Find a Contact box on the Standard toolbar. Enter a first or last name, in full or partially. An e-mail alias also can be used to find a contact quickly. To locate a contact previously searched for, click the find a Contact box arrow, and then select a name in the list.

A contact record was created for Kayla Reynolds. This record can be found easily by using the Find a Contact box to type a part of the contact name, as shown in the following steps.

To Find a Contact

1

- **Click the Find a Contact box on the Standard toolbar.**
- **Type** `rey` **in the text box.**

The letters appear in the Find a Contact box (Figure 1-67). The letters, rey, are used to find the contact beginning with those letters.

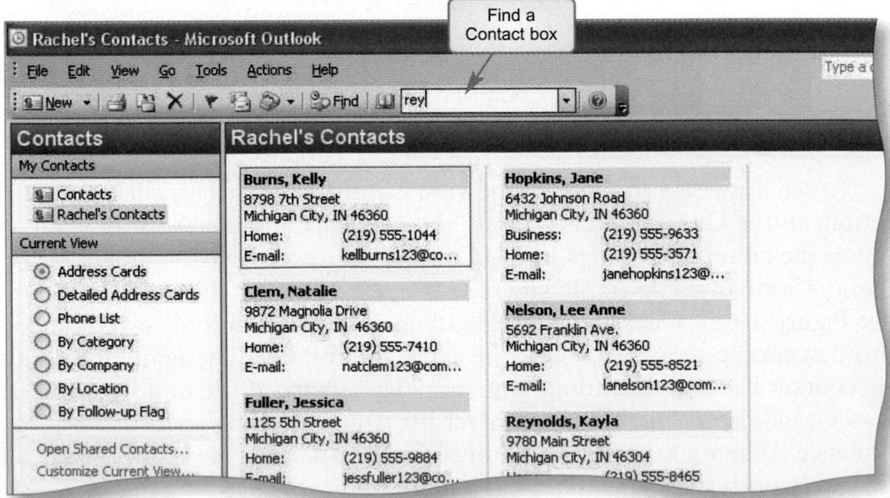

FIGURE 1-67

2

• **Press the ENTER key.**

Outlook opens the Contact window (Figure 1-68). Currently, only one contact exists with the letters rey in its name.

3

• **Click the Close button on the right side of the title bar in the Contact window.**

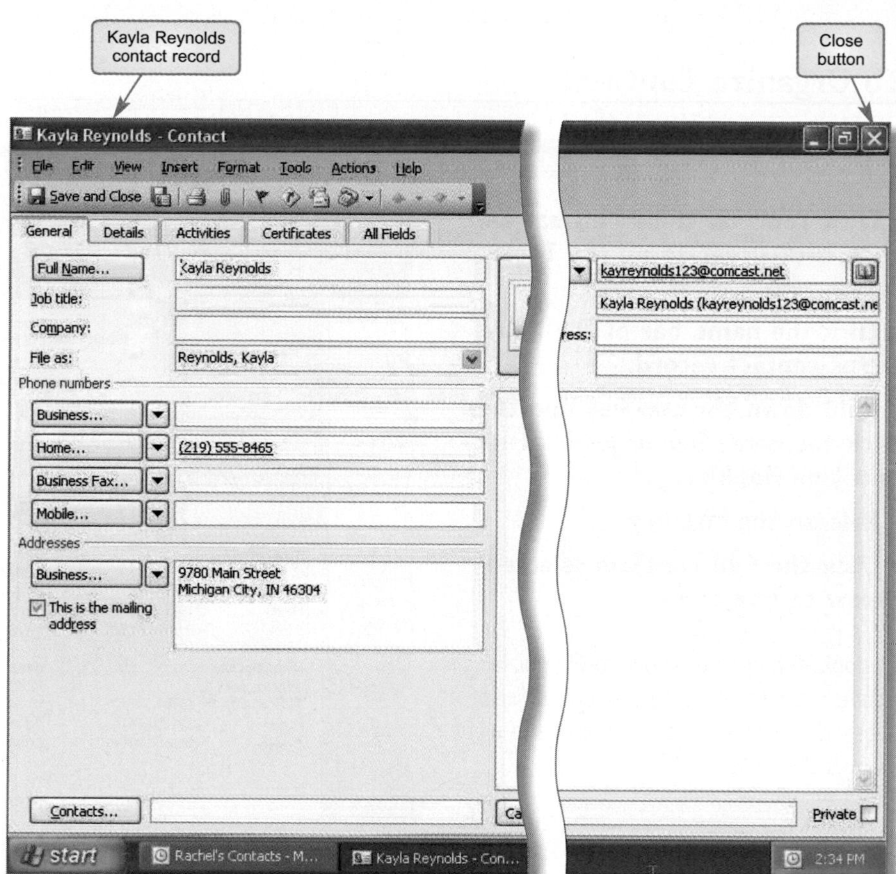

FIGURE 1-68

If more than one contact with the starting letters, rey, exists, Outlook displays a Choose Contact dialog box with the list of all contacts beginning with the string, rey. You then can select the appropriate contact from the Choose Contact dialog box.

Organizing Contacts

To help manage your contacts further, the contact list can be categorized and sorted in several ways. For example, you can group contacts into categories, such as Key Customer, Business, Hot Contact, or even Ideas, Competition, and Strategies. In addition, you may want to create your own categories to group contacts by company, department, a particular project, a specific class, and so on. You also can sort by any part of the address; for example, you can sort by postal code for bulk mailings.

For the contact list created in this project, it is appropriate to organize the contacts in a personal category. You can do this by selecting the contacts and then adding them to the personal category of the contact list. The steps on the next page illustrate this procedure.

To Organize Contacts

1

- **Click Tools on the menu bar and then click Organize on the Tools menu.**
- **Click the name bar of the Kelly Burns contact record.**
- **Hold down the CTRL key and then click the name bar of Jessica Fuller and Jane Hopkins.**
- **Release the CTRL key.**
- **Click the Add contacts selected below to box arrow.**

Outlook displays the Ways to Organize Rachel's Contacts dialog box and a list of categories (Figure 1-69). Three of the eight records are selected.

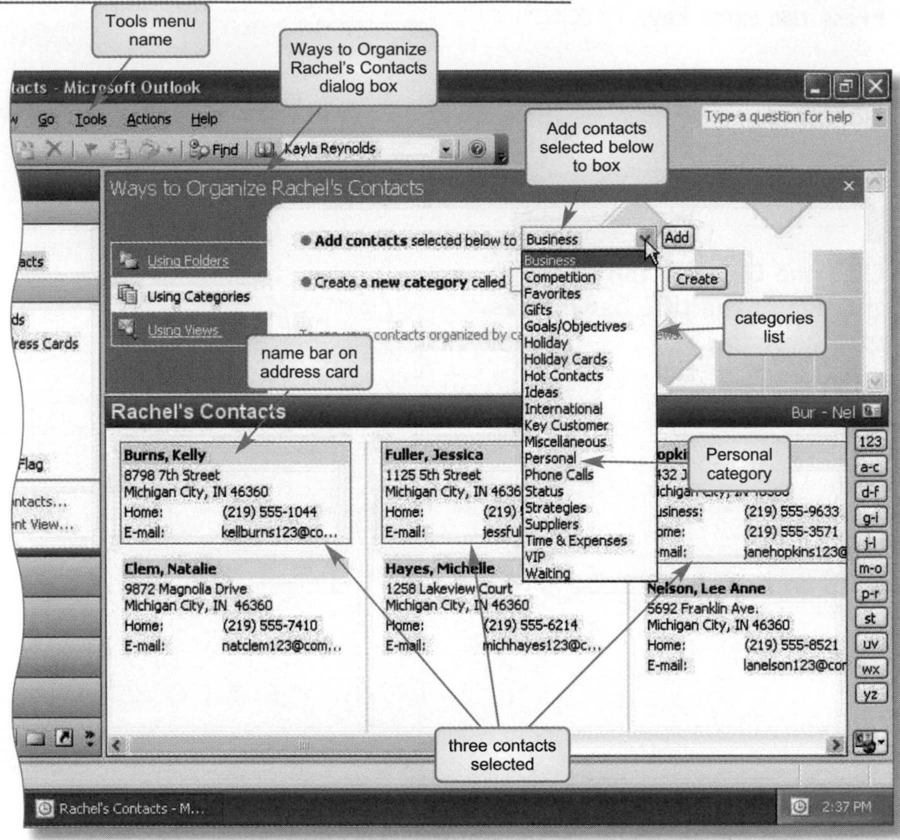

FIGURE 1-69

2

- **Click Personal in the list.**
- **Click the Add button.**

Outlook adds the selected records to the Personal category and the word Done! appears next to the Add button (Figure 1-70).

- **Click the Close button on the Ways to Organize Rachel's Contacts dialog box.**

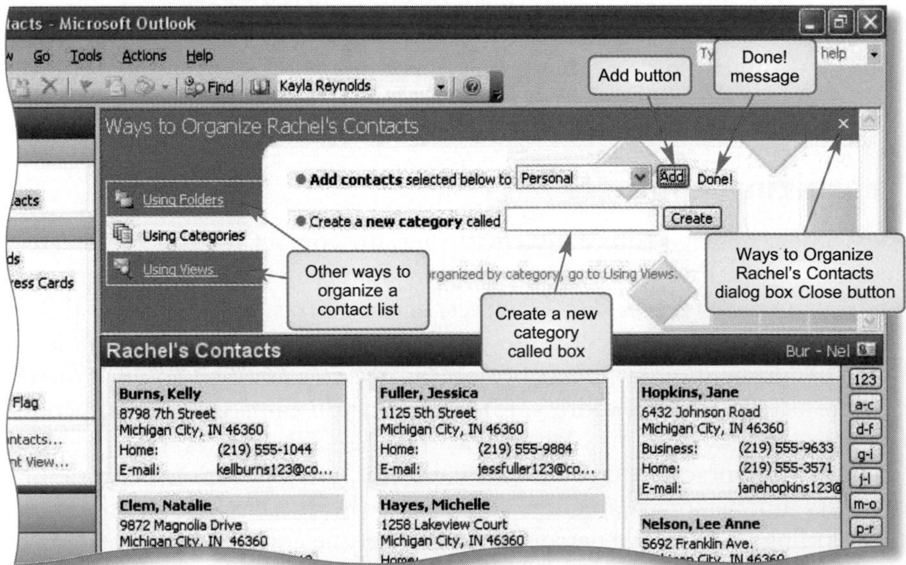

FIGURE 1-70

The three contacts are organized into a category called Personal. Organizing contacts in different categories helps make searching for groups of names easier.

Displaying the Contacts in a Category

By assigning the three contacts to a personal category, you can instruct Outlook to display only those contacts that belong to the category shown in the following steps.

To Display the Contacts in a Category

1

- **With the Contacts window active, click the Find button on the Standard toolbar.**
- **When Outlook displays the Find toolbar above the Contacts pane, type** `Personal` **in the Look for box.**
- **If necessary, click Rachel's Contacts in the My Contacts pane so it appears in the Search In box.**
- **Click the Find Now button on the Find toolbar.**

Outlook displays the three contacts that belong in the Personal category (Figure 1-71).

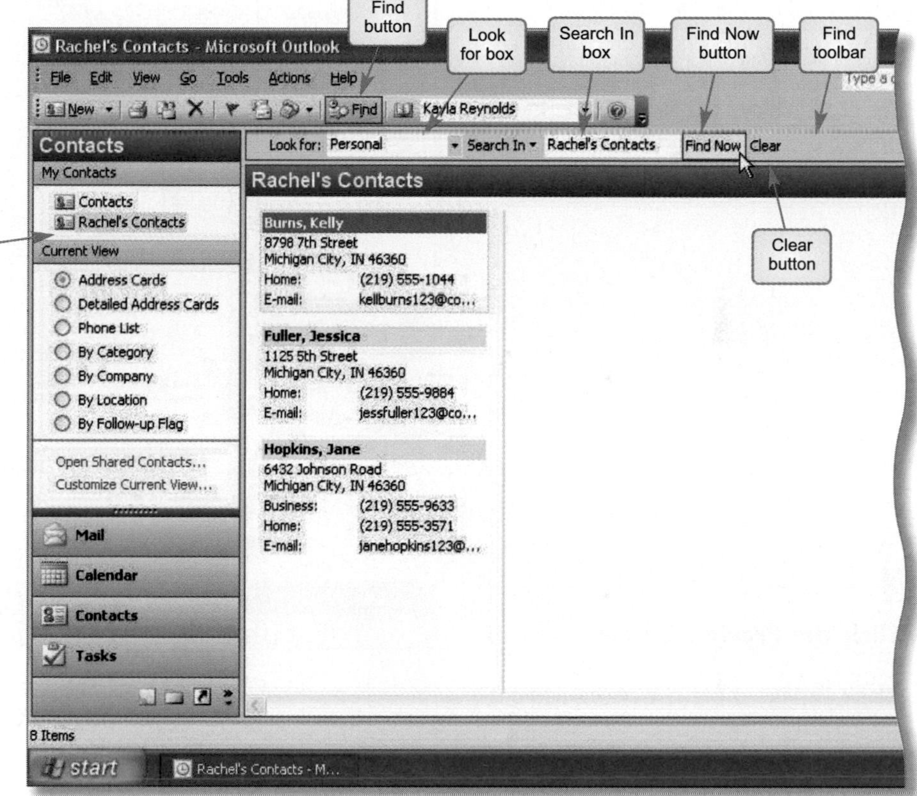

FIGURE 1-71

2

- **After viewing the contacts in the Personal category, click the Find button on the Standard toolbar.**

Outlook displays all the contacts in the Rachel's Contacts folder.

You can use the Find button on the Standard toolbar to find contacts when the Contacts component is active, messages when the Mail component is active, appointments when the Calendar component is active, and tasks when the Tasks component is active.

Previewing and Printing the Contact List

Printing the contact list is an easy way to obtain a listing of people you frequently contact. Previewing the contact list before you print it helps ensure the printed list can be used for business mailings, invitations to social gatherings, or even a telephone or Christmas card list. The steps on the next page describe how to preview and print the contact list.

Skill Builder 1-3

To practice the following tasks, visit scsite.com/off2003sch/skill, locate Outlook Project 1, and then click Skill Builder 1-3.

- ❑ Change the view of the contact list
- ❑ Sort the contact list
- ❑ Organize the contact list
- ❑ Display the contacts in a category

To Preview and Print the Contact List

1

- **With the Contacts window active, click the Print button on the Standard toolbar.**

Outlook displays the Print dialog box (Figure 1-72). In the Print dialog box you can select a format for the printout, print range, and number of copies. You also can change the orientation from portrait to landscape through the use of the Page Setup button.

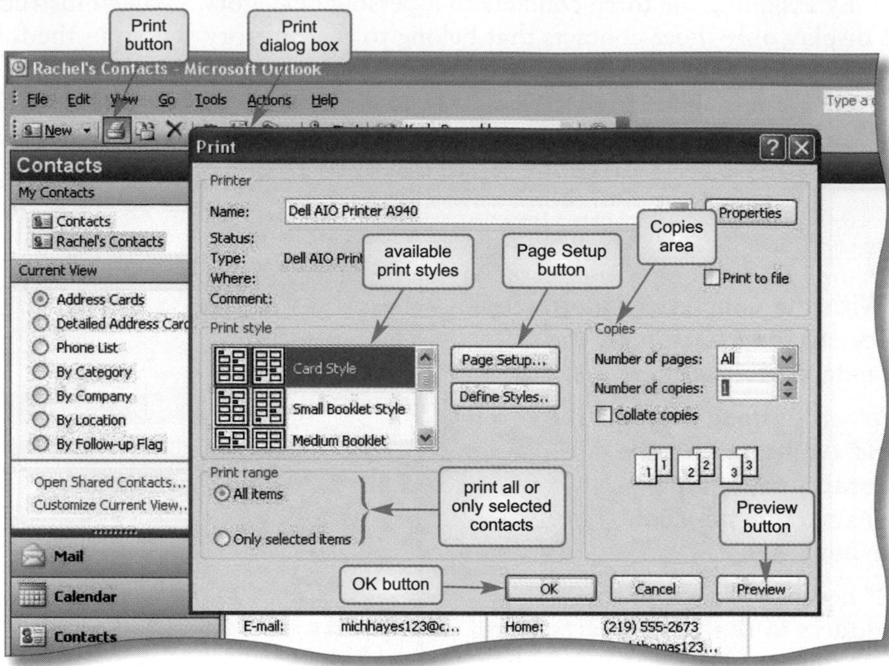

FIGURE 1-72

2

- **Click the Preview button.**

Outlook displays a preview of the printout (Figure 1-73).

3

- **After viewing the preview of the printed contacts list, click the Close button.**
- **If the preview is acceptable, ready the printer.**
- **Click the Print button on the Standard toolbar.**
- **When Outlook displays the Print dialog box, click the OK button.**

Outlook prints the contact list. The printout should resemble the preview in Figure 1-73.

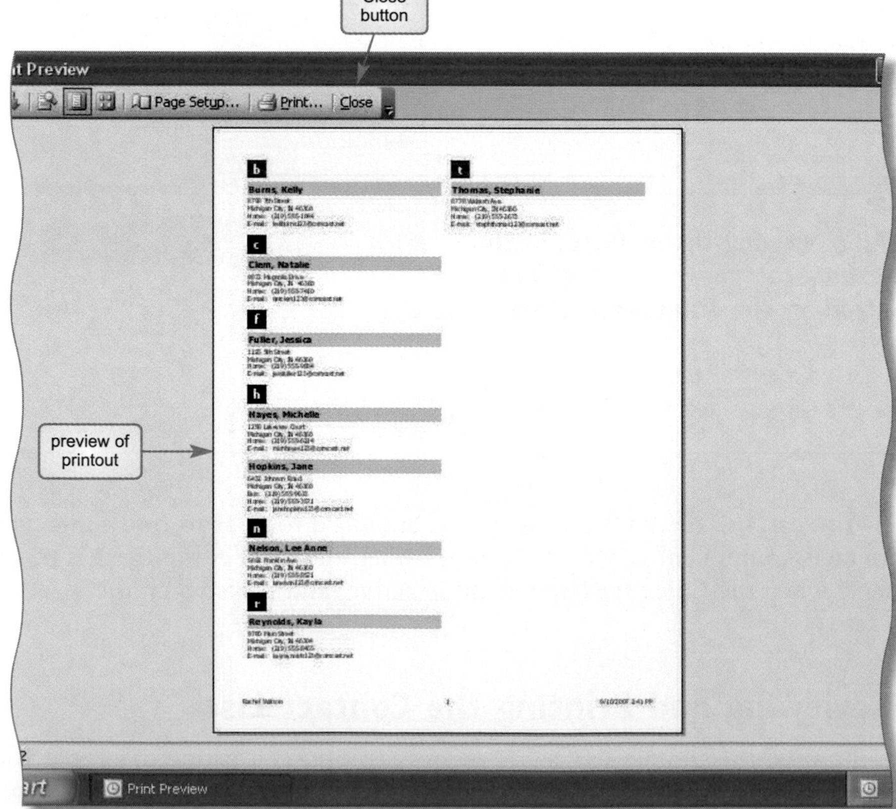

FIGURE 1-73

If you display a category of contacts and then click the Print button, Outlook will print only the contacts in that category. A printout can be customized by changing the Print style in the Print dialog box. These styles let you choose from a variety of formats along with choices for paper orientation and size.

Using the Contact List to Address an E-Mail Message

When you address an e-mail message, you must know the e-mail address of the recipient of the message. Previously, when an e-mail message was addressed, the e-mail address was typed in the To text box in the Message window (see Figure 1-31 on page OUT 25). In addition to entering the e-mail address by typing the e-mail address, an e-mail address can be entered using the contact list. The following steps show how to use the contact list to address an e-mail message to Kelly Burns.

To Use the Contact List to Address an E-Mail Message

1

- **Click the Mail button in the Navigation Pane to display the Inbox window.**
- **Click the New Mail Message button on the Standard toolbar.**
- **When Outlook displays the Untitled Message window, if necessary, double-click its title bar to maximize it.**

Outlook displays the Untitled Message window (Figure 1-74) with the insertion point in the To text box.

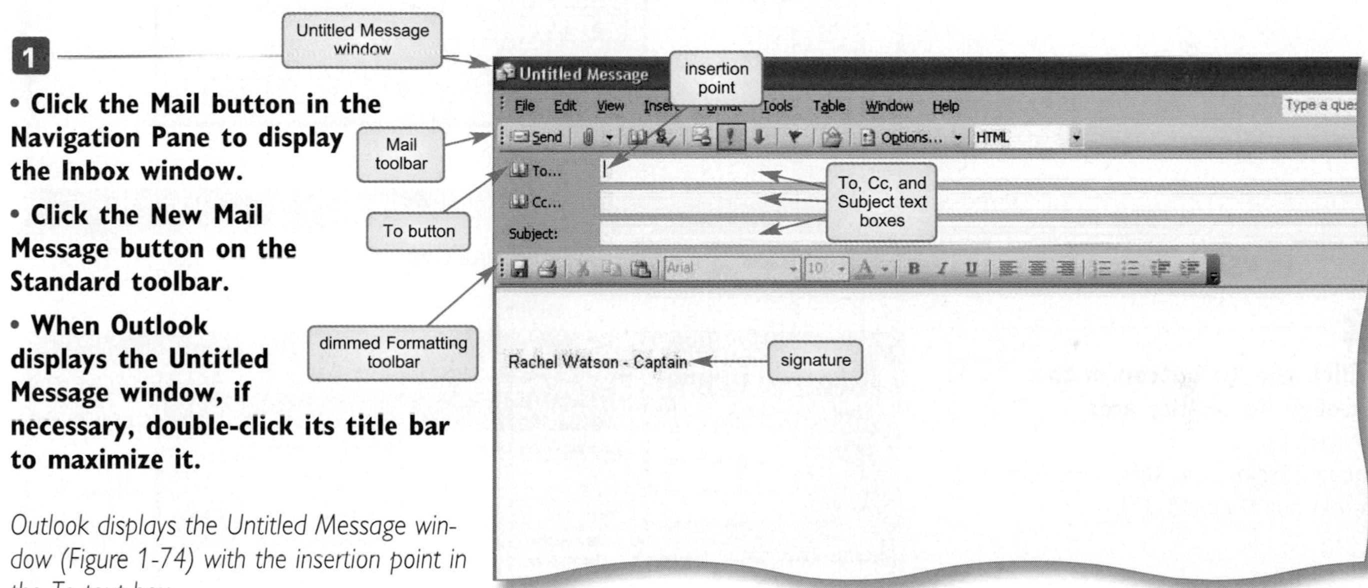

FIGURE 1-74

2

- **Click the To button on the left side of the Message window.**
- **When Outlook displays the Select Names dialog box, click the Show Names from the box arrow.**

Outlook displays the Select Names dialog box (Figure 1-75). The Show Names from the list displays the available contact lists from which to choose.

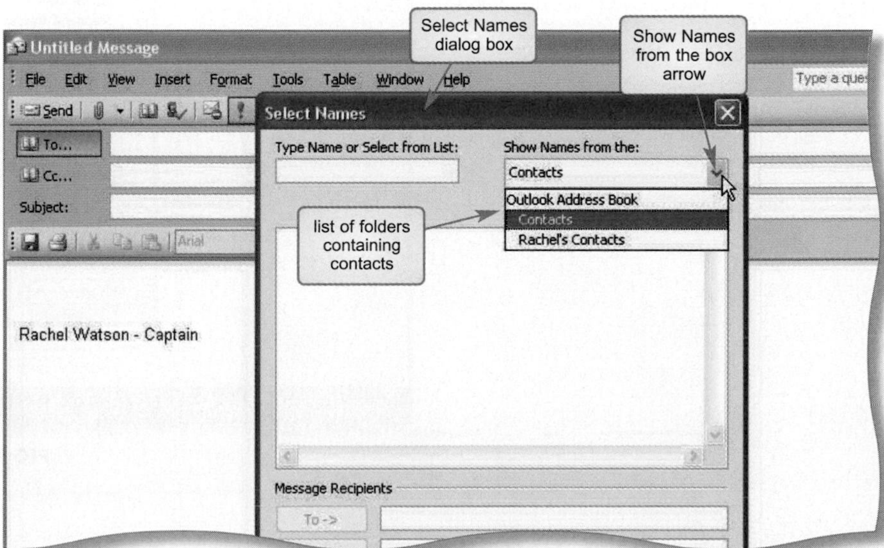

FIGURE 1-75

3

- **Click Rachel's Contacts in the list.**
- **Click the Kelly Burns entry in the list.**

The Kelly Burns entry in the E-mail Address list box is selected (Figure 1-76).

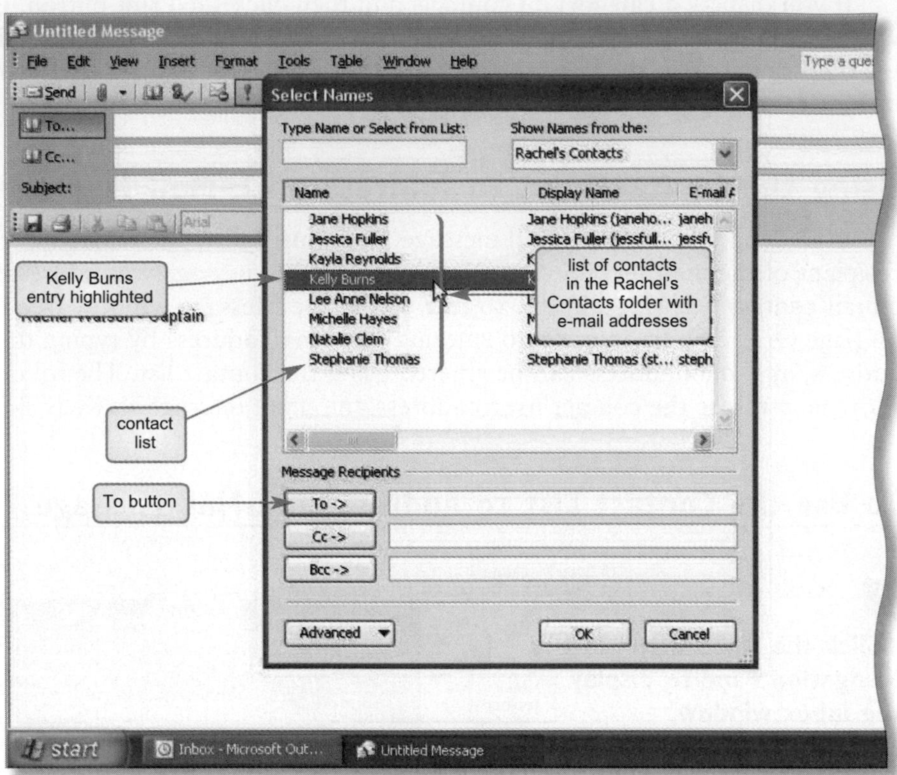

FIGURE 1-76

4

- **Click the To button in the Message Recipients area.**

Outlook displays the Kelly Burns entry in the To text box (Figure 1-77).

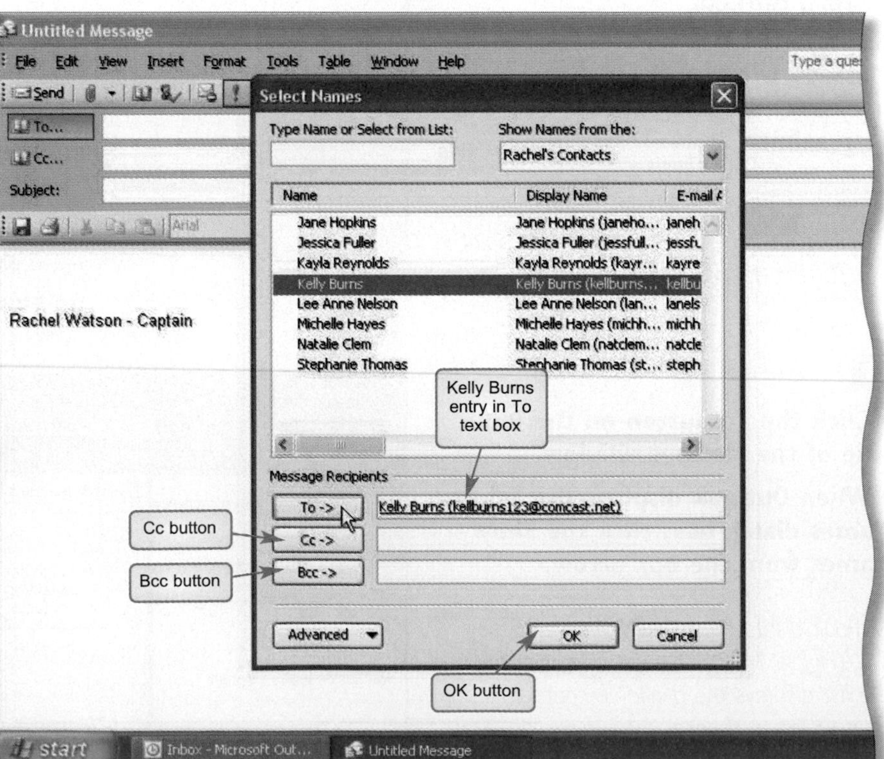

FIGURE 1-77

- **Click the OK button.**
- **Click the Subject text box and then type** `Fund-raiser T-Shirts` **as the entry.**
- **Press the TAB key.**

Outlook closes the Select Names dialog box and displays the Kelly Burns entry in the To text box in the Message window (Figure 1-78).

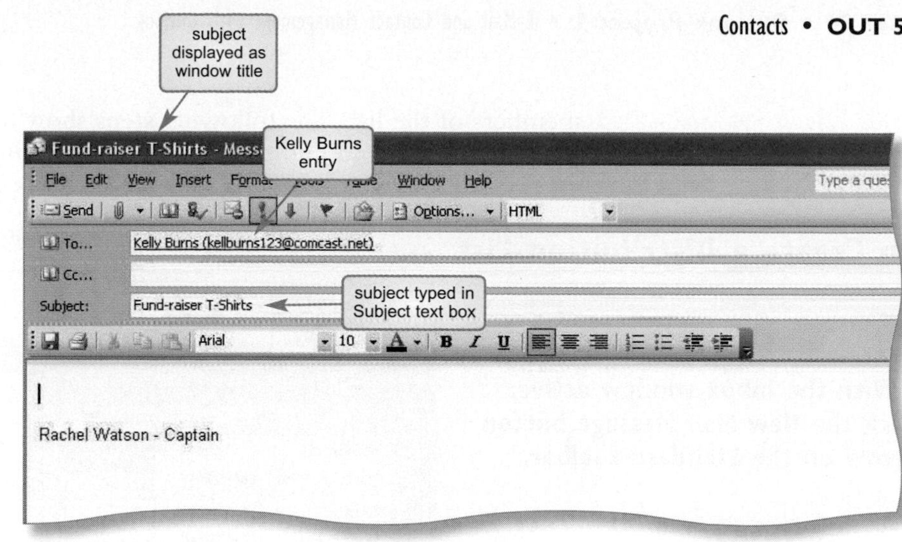

FIGURE 1-78

- **Type** `Kelly, I need help!` **and then press the ENTER key twice.**
- **Type** `The T-shirts for the team fund-raiser will be ready at 5:00 p.m. on Friday. I have a dentist appointment at that time, so I will need you to pick them up.`

Outlook displays the e-mail message in the message body (Figure 1-79).

7

- **Click the Send button.**

Outlook closes the Message window, displays the Inbox window, stores the e-mail message in the Outbox folder temporarily while it sends the message, and then moves the message to the Sent Items folder.

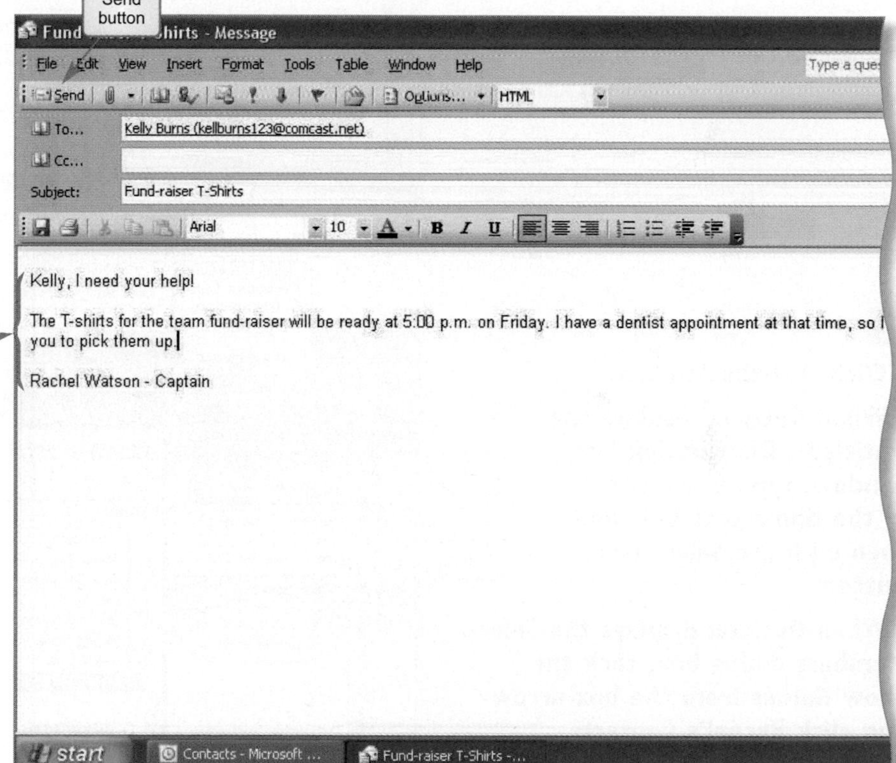

FIGURE 1-79

You can add as many names as you want to the To text box in Figure 1-77. You also can add names to the Cc text box. If you do not want those listed in the To text box or Cc text box to know you sent a copy to someone else, send a **blind copy** by adding the name to the Bcc text box.

Creating and Modifying a Distribution List

If you find yourself sending e-mail messages to the same group of people over and over, then you should consider creating a distribution list. A **distribution list** is similar to a category of contacts in that when you select the name of the distribution list as the recipient of an e-mail message, Outlook will send the message to all the members of the list. The following steps show how to create a distribution list titled Computer Club and add three members from the Rachel's Contacts list.

To Create a Distribution List

1

- **With the Inbox window active, click the New Mail Message button arrow on the Standard toolbar.**

Outlook displays the New Mail Message menu (Figure 1-80).

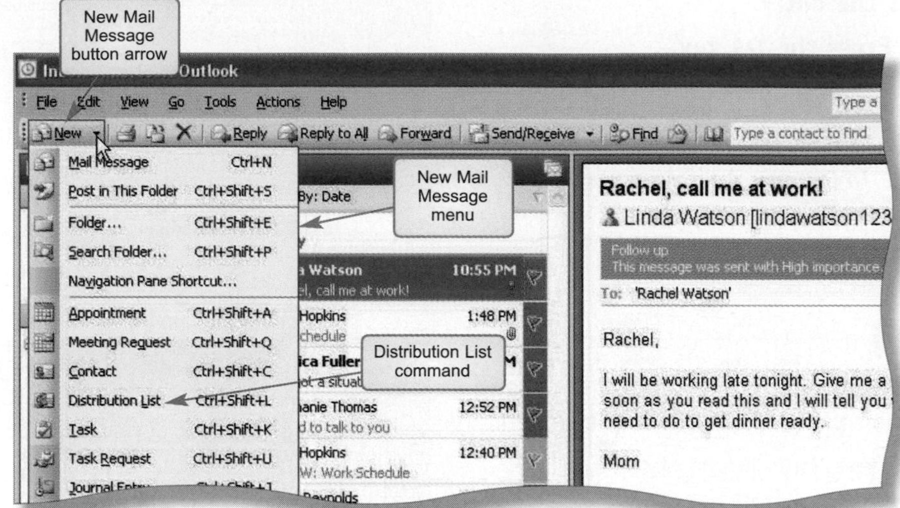

FIGURE 1-80

2

- **Click Distribution List.**
- **When Outlook displays the Untitled - Distribution List window, type** `Computer Club` **in the Name text box, and then click the Select Members button.**
- **When Outlook displays the Select Members dialog box, click the Show Names from the box arrow and click Rachel's Contacts.**
- **Select Michelle Hayes and then click the Members button.**
- **Add Jessica Fuller and Stephanie Thomas in the same manner to the Members list in the Add to distribution list area.**

Outlook displays the three members to add to the Computer Club Members list (Figure 1-81). The Members list is displayed in the Add to distribution list area at the bottom of the Select Members dialog box.

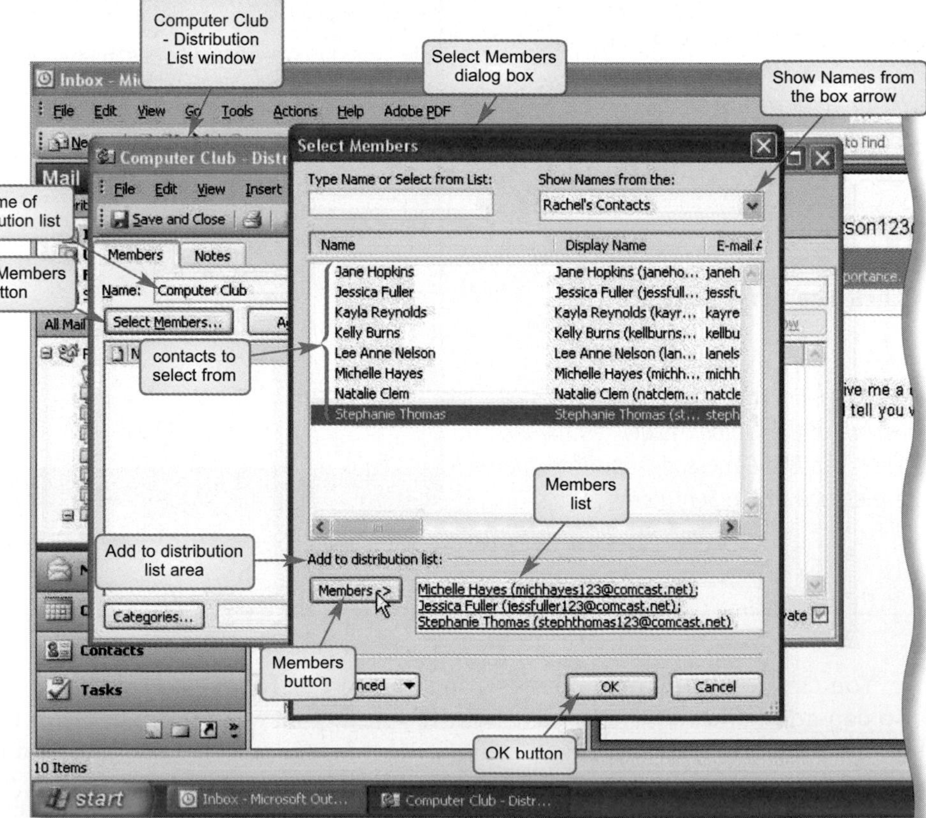

FIGURE 1-81

3

• **Click the OK button.**

Outlook displays the members of the Computer Club distribution list in the Untitled - Distribution List window (Figure 1-82).

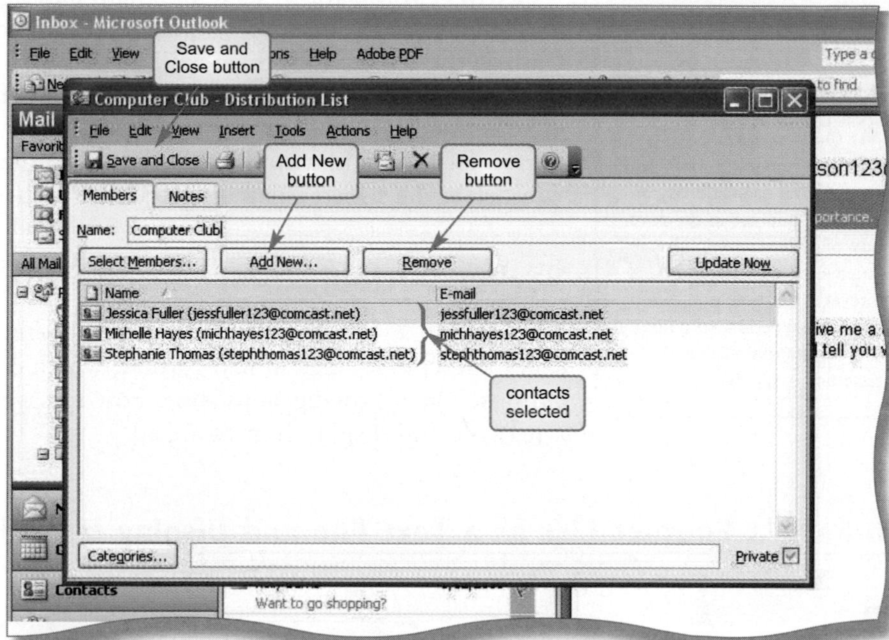

FIGURE 1-82

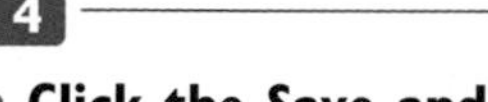

4

• **Click the Save and Close button on the Standard toolbar.**

Outlook closes the Untitled - Distribution List window, adds the new distribution list to the contact list, and activates the Inbox window.

5

• **Click the Address Book button on the Standard toolbar.**

Outlook displays the Address Book window, which includes the Computer Club distribution list (Figure 1-83).

6

• **Click the Close button on the right side of the title bar in the Address Book window.**

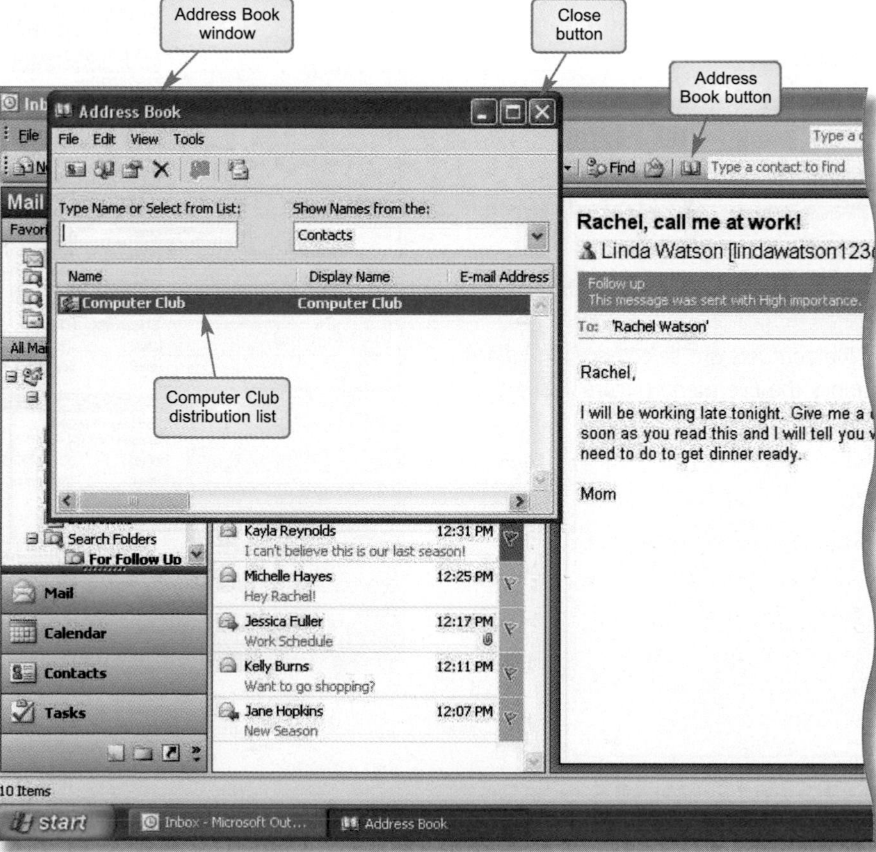

FIGURE 1-83

> **Q & A**
>
> **Q:** Can I create hyperlinks in a Contact window?
>
> **A:** Outlook automatically creates a hyperlink when you type a Web page address or an e-mail address in the text box of a Contact window. If you are connected to an Internet browser, you can click the hyperlink to go to the destination quickly or send an e-mail message.

Now if you want to send an e-mail message to Michelle Hayes, Jessica Fuller, and Stephanie Thomas, all you have to do is select the distribution list Computer Club as the recipient of the e-mail message.

The Untitled - Distribution List window in Figure 1-82 on the previous page includes two buttons that are useful for modifying a distribution list. The Add New button lets you add a contact that is not in the contact list. The Remove button lets you delete the selected names in the distribution list.

Saving Outlook Information in Different Formats

You can save Outlook files in several formats. For example, you can save messages and contact lists in text format, which can be read or copied into other applications. The following steps show how to save a contact list on a USB flash drive as a text file and display it in Notepad.

To Save a Contact List as a Text File and Display It in Notepad

1

- **Connect the USB flash drive containing the Data Files for Students to one of the computer's USB ports.**
- **With the Contacts window active, click the name bar of the first contact in the contact list.**
- **Press CTRL+A to select all the contacts.**
- **Click File on the menu bar.**

All the contacts are selected and Outlook displays the File menu (Figure 1-84).

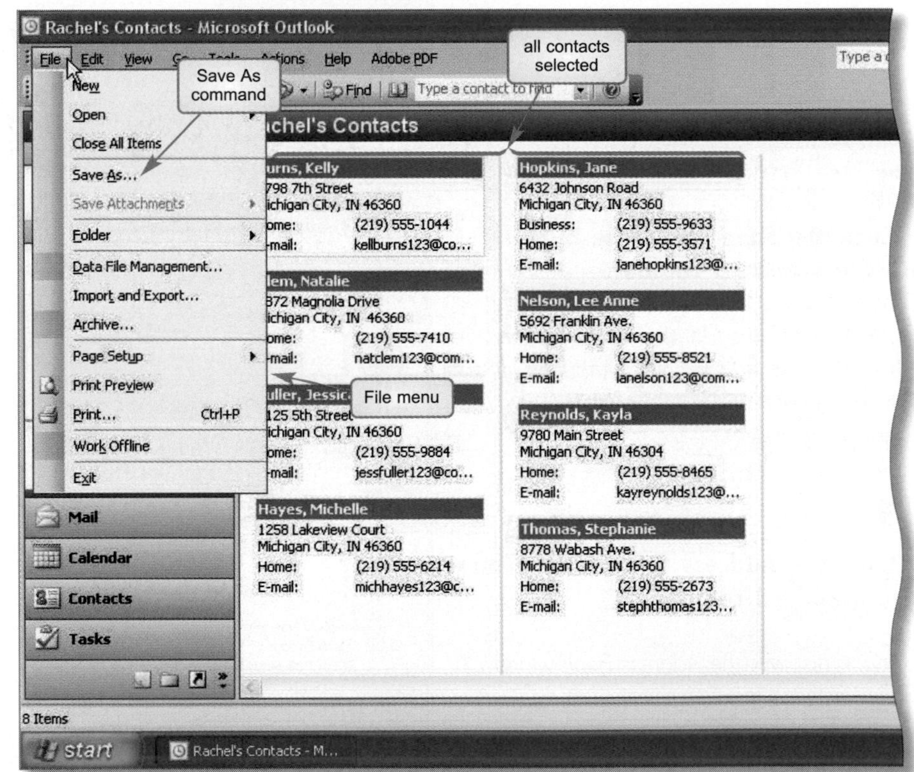

FIGURE 1-84

> **Skill Builder 1-4**
>
> To practice the following tasks, visit scsite.com/off2003sch/skill, locate Outlook Project 1, and then click Skill Builder 1-4.
>
> ❑ Create a distribution list
>
> ❑ Save and Print the content list as a text file

2

- **Click Save As on the File menu.**
- **When Outlook displays the Save As dialog box, type** `Rachel's Contacts` **in the File name text box.**
- **If necessary, select Text Only in the Save as type box.**
- **Click the Save in box arrow and then select UDISK 2.0 (F:). (Your USB flash drive may have a different name and letter.)**

Outlook displays the Save As dialog box as shown in Figure 1-85.

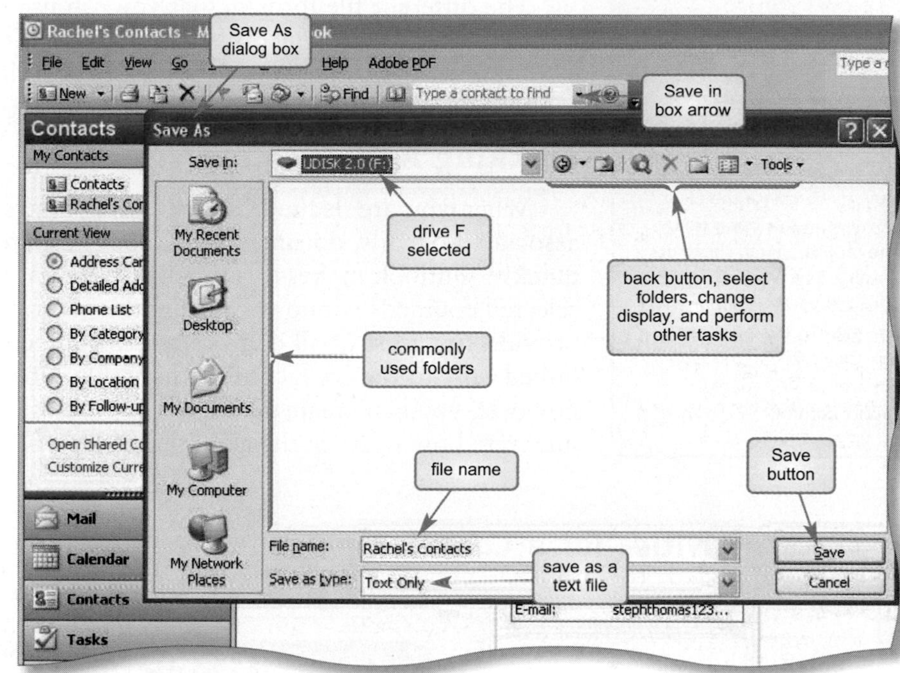

FIGURE 1-85

3

- **Click the Save button in the Save As dialog box.**
- **Click the Start button on the Windows taskbar, point to All Programs on the Start menu, point to Accessories on the All Programs submenu, and then click Notepad on the Accessories submenu.**
- **When Notepad starts, click the Maximize button on the title bar, click File on the menu bar, and then click Open.**
- **When Outlook displays the Open dialog box, click the Files of type box arrow, click All Files, click the Look in box arrow, and then click UDISK 2.0 (F:) (your USB flash drive may have a different name and letter) in the Look in list.**
- **Double-click Rachel's Contacts.**

Notepad displays Rachel's Contacts as a text file (Figure 1-86).

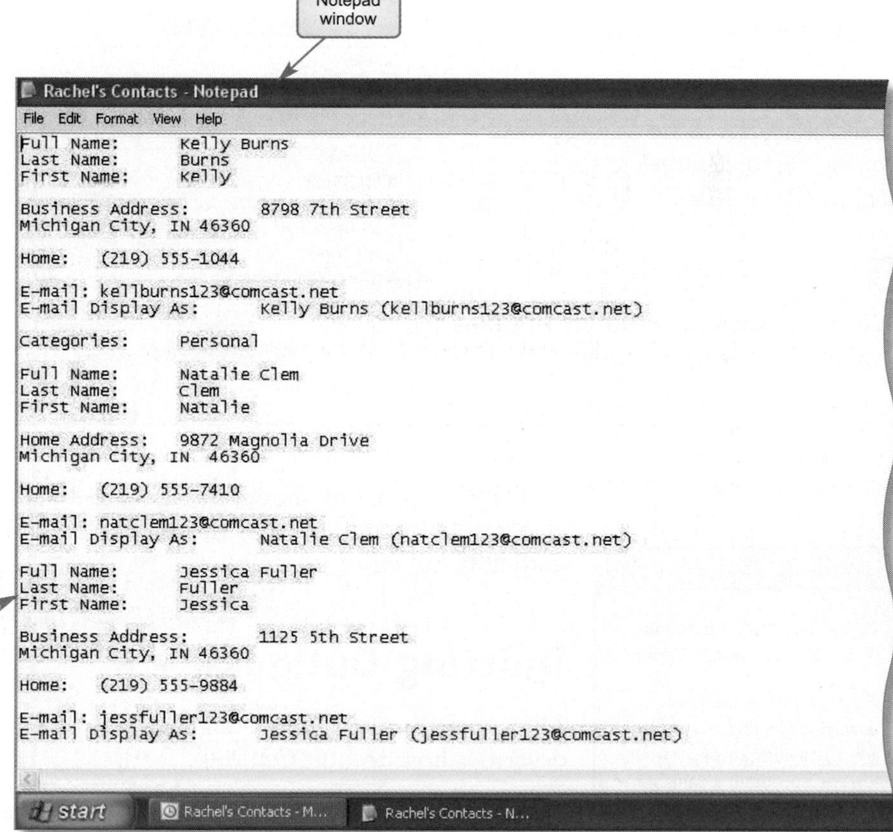

FIGURE 1-86

4

- **After viewing the text file, click the Close button on the right side of the Notepad title bar.**

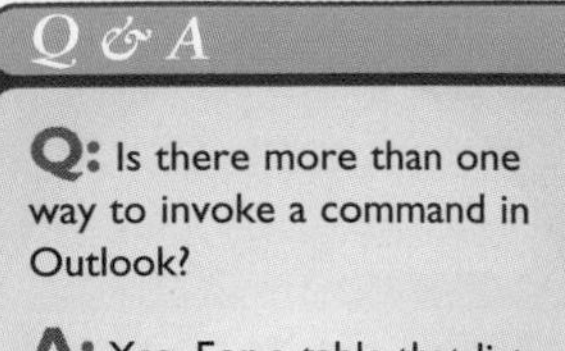

Q & A

Q: Is there more than one way to invoke a command in Outlook?

A: Yes. For a table that lists how to complete the tasks covered in this book using the mouse, menu, shortcut menu, and keyboard, see the Quick Reference Summary at the back of this book, or visit the Office 2003 Quick Reference Web page (scsite.com/off2003sch/qr).

The different file formats that you can use to save information is dependent on the component with which you are working. To view the different file formats for a component, click the Save as type arrow in the Save As dialog box.

Tracking Activities for Contacts

When you are dealing with several contacts, it can be useful to have all associated e-mails, documents, or other items related to the contact available quickly. Outlook makes this possible through the use of the Activities tab in the selected contact's window. Clicking this tab for any contact in your contact list will provide you a list of all items related to that contact. Outlook searches for items linked only to the contact in the main Outlook folders (Contacts, Calendar, etc.); however, you can create and add new folders to be searched. The following steps illustrate how to track the activities of Jane Hopkins.

To Track Activities for a Contact

1

- **With Contacts window active, double-click the Jane Hopkins contact heading.**
- **Click the Activities tab.**

Outlook displays the Jane Hopkins - Contact window with the Activities sheet showing a list of items related to Jane Hopkins (Figure 1-87).

2

- **Click the Close button on the Jane Hopkins - Contact window.**

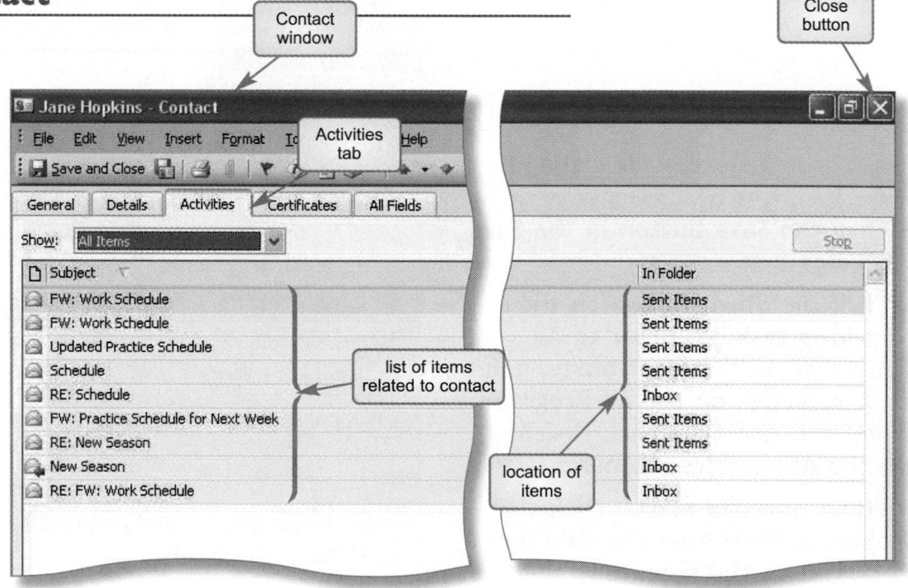

FIGURE 1-87

The list of items shown in Figure 1-87 consists entirely of e-mail messages. You also can link items, such as files, tasks, and appointments. E-mail messages are automatically linked to the contact.

Q & A

Q: What is the Microsoft Office Certification Program?

A: The Microsoft Office Specialist Certification program provides an opportunity for you to obtain a valuable industry credential — proof that you have the Outlook 2003 skills required by employers. For more information, see Appendix E or visit the Office 2003 Certification Web page (scsite.com/off2003sch/cert).

Quitting Outlook

The project now is complete and you are ready to quit Outlook. The following step describes how to quit Outlook.

To Quit Outlook

1 **Click the Close button on the Outlook title bar.**

Outlook is closed, and the Windows desktop appears.

Project Summary

In this project, you learned to use Outlook to open, read, print, reply to, forward, delete, sign, compose, format, and send e-mail messages. You opened and viewed file attachments as well as attached a file to an e-mail message. You learned how to flag, sort, and set importance and delivery options to e-mail messages. You added and deleted contacts to a contact list. Finally, you used the contact list to create a distribution list and track activities of a contact.

What You Should Know

Having completed this project, you should be able to perform the tasks below. The tasks are listed in the same order they were presented in this project. For a list of the buttons, menus, toolbars, and commands introduced in this project, see the Quick Reference Summary at the back of this book and refer to the Page Number column.

1. Start and Customize Outlook (OUT 6)
2. Open (Read) an E-Mail Message (OUT 11)
3. Print an Opened E-Mail Message (OUT 12)
4. Close an E-Mail Message (OUT 13)
5. Reply to an E-Mail Message (OUT 13)
6. Forward an E-Mail Message (OUT 16)
7. Delete an E-Mail Message (OUT 17)
8. View a File Attachment (OUT 18)
9. Create and Insert an E-Mail Signature (OUT 20)
10. Compose an E-Mail Message (OUT 24)
11. Format an E-Mail Message (OUT 26)
12. Attach a File to an E-Mail Message (OUT 28)
13. Send an E-Mail Message (OUT 29)
14. Flag E-Mail Messages (OUT 30)
15. Sort E-Mail Messages by Flag Color (OUT 31)
16. Create and Apply a View Filter (OUT 32)
17. Set Message Importance, Sensitivity, and Delivery Options in a Single Message (OUT 34)
18. Change the Default Level of Importance and Sensitivity (OUT 36)
19. Create a Personal Folder (OUT 40)
20. Create a Contact List (OUT 42)
21. Change the View and Sort the Contact List (OUT 45)
22. Find a Contact (OUT 46)
23. Organize Contacts (OUT 48)
24. Display the Contacts in a Category (OUT 49)
25. Preview and Print the Contact List (OUT 50)
26. Use the Contact List to Address an E-Mail Message (OUT 51)
27. Create a Distribution List (OUT 54)
28. Save a Contact List as a Text File and Display It in Notepad (OUT 56)
29. Track Activities for a Contact (OUT 58)
30. Quit Outlook (OUT 58)

Career Corner

CIO

CIO (chief information officer) is the highest-ranking position in an information technology (IT) department. The CIO manages all of a company's information systems and computer resources. In large organizations, the CIO typically is a vice president and reports directly to the organization's CEO.

Depending on the organization, a CIO can be called an MIS (management information systems) manager, an IS (information systems) manager, or an IT (information technology) manager. Regardless of the title, the CIO determines an organization's information needs and provides the systems to meet those needs. The CIO sets an IT department's goals, policies, and procedures. In addition, the CIO evaluates technology, hires and supervises staff, oversees the network, directs user services, develops backup and disaster recovery plans, and manages the department budget. Perhaps most important, the CIO provides leadership, creating a vision for an IT department and helping the department deliver that vision.

Some CIOs work as consultants, providing corporate IT departments with short-term or long-term guidance. Most CIOs rise through the department ranks of an organization's IT department. Generally, CIOs have a bachelor's degree or higher in computer science and at least ten years of experience in an IT department. Today, many CIOs also have an MBA. Pay reflects the importance of the CIO, with average salaries in excess of $180,000. For more information, visit scsite.com/off2003sch/careers and then click CIO.

Learn It Online

Instructions: To complete the Learn It Online exercises, start your browser, click the Address bar, and then enter the Web address scsite.com/off2003sch/learn. When the Office 2003 Learn It Online page is displayed, follow the instructions in the exercises below. Each exercise has instructions for printing your results, either for your own records or for submission to your instructor.

1 Project Reinforcement TF, MC, and SA

Below Outlook Project 1, click the Project Reinforcement link. Print the quiz by clicking Print on the File menu for each page. Answer each question.

2 Flash Cards

Below Outlook Project 1, click the Flash Cards link and read the instructions. Type 20 (or a number specified by your instructor) in the Number of playing cards text box, type your name in the Enter your Name text box, and then click the Flip Card button. When the flash card is displayed, read the question and then click the ANSWER box arrow to select an answer. Flip through Flash Cards. If your score is 15 (75%) correct or greater, click Print on the File menu to print your results. If your score is less than 15 (75%) correct, then redo this exercise by clicking the Replay button.

3 Practice Test

Below Outlook Project 1, click the Practice Test link. Answer each question, enter your first and last name at the bottom of the page, and then click the Grade Test button. When the graded practice test is displayed on your screen, click Print on the File menu to print a hard copy. Continue to take practice tests until you score 80% or better.

4 Who Wants To Be a Computer Genius?

Below Outlook Project 1, click the Computer Genius link. Read the instructions, enter your first and last name at the bottom of the page, and then click the PLAY button. When your score is displayed, click the PRINT RESULTS link to print a hard copy.

5 Wheel of Terms

Below Outlook Project 1, click the Wheel of Terms link. Read the instructions, and then enter your first and last name and your school name. Click the PLAY button. When your score is displayed, right-click the score and then click Print on the shortcut menu to print a hard copy.

6 Crossword Puzzle Challenge

Below Outlook Project 1, click the Crossword Puzzle Challenge link. Read the instructions, and then enter your first and last name. Click the SUBMIT button. Work the crossword puzzle. When you are finished, click the Submit button. When the crossword puzzle is redisplayed, click the Print Puzzle button to print a hard copy.

7 Tips and Tricks

Below Outlook Project 1, click the Tips and Tricks link. Click a topic that pertains to Project 1. Right-click the information and then click Print on the shortcut menu. Construct a brief example of what the information relates to in Outlook to confirm you understand how to use the tip or trick.

8 Newsgroups

Below Outlook Project 1, click the Newsgroups link. Click a topic that pertains to Project 1. Print three comments.

9 Expanding Your Horizons

Below Outlook Project 1, click the Expanding Your Horizons link. Click a topic that pertains to Project 1. Print the information. Construct a brief example of what the information relates to in Outlook to confirm you understand the contents of the article.

10 Search Sleuth

Below Outlook Project 1, click the Search Sleuth link. To search for a term that pertains to this project, select a term below the Project 1 title and then use the Google search engine at google.com (or any major search engine) to display and print two Web pages that present information on the term.

11 Outlook Online Training

Below Outlook Project 1, click the Outlook Online Training link. When your browser displays the Microsoft Office Online Web page, click the Outlook link. Click one of the Outlook courses that covers one or more of the objectives listed at the beginning of the project on page OUT 4. Print the first page of the course before stepping through it.

12 Office Marketplace

Below Outlook Project 1, click the Office Marketplace link. When your browser displays the Microsoft Office Online Web page, click the Office Marketplace link. Click a topic that relates to Outlook. Print the first page.

13 You're Hired!

Below Office Outlook Project 1, click the You're Hired! link to embark on the path to a career in computers. Directions about how to play the game will be displayed. When you are ready to play, click the begin the game button. If required, submit your score to your instructor.

Apply Your Knowledge

1 Creating a Contact List

Instructions: Start Outlook. Create a Contacts folder using your name as the name of the new folder. Create a contact list using the people listed in Table 1-4. Use the Department text box in the Details sheet to enter the student's grade level.

Create a distribution list consisting of freshmen and juniors. Sort the list by last name in descending sequence. When the list is complete, print the list in Card Style view and submit to your instructor.

Table 1-4 Contact Information

NAME	TELEPHONE	ADDRESS	E-MAIL ADDRESS	GRADE LEVEL
Shannon Olson	(219) 555-5246	6543 Ashford	solson@isp.com	Junior
Katie Young	(219) 555-6871	621 W. 13th	kyoung@isp.com	Freshman
Steve Woods	(219) 555-1582	872 Broadmore	swoods@isp.com	Freshman
Manuel Perez	(219) 555-3471	3489 Melody	mperez@isp.com	Senior
Lori Stone	(219) 555-9147	5474 Cherry	lstone@isp.com	Junior
Andrew Carter	(219) 555-8632	7850 E. 22nd	acarter@isp.com	Sophomore

Importing Subfolders for the In the Lab Exercises — Follow these steps to import subfolders for the following In the Lab Exercises:

1. Connect the USB flash drive containing the Data Files for Students to your computer.
2. Click File on the Outlook menu bar and then click Import and Export.
3. In the Import and Export Wizard dialog box, click Import from another program or file and then click the Next button.
4. In the Import a File dialog box, click Personal Folder File (.pst) and then click the Next button.
5. In the Import Personal Folders dialog box, click the Browse button to access drive F, select the appropriate subfolder, click Open, and then click the Next button.
6. In the Import Personal Folders dialog box, select the appropriate folder to import from and then click the Finish button.

1 Creating a Distribution List and Sending E-Mail

Problem: You are the chairperson for your class float for the upcoming Homecoming parade. Part of your responsibilities is to solicit and organize material donations for the float and food donations for the people that work on the float. To do so, you need to maintain and contact a list of past and potential donors.

Instructions Part 1: Import the Lab 1-1 Contacts folder (Figure 1-88 on the next page) into Outlook. Create two distribution lists, one consisting of past and potential material donors, and the other consisting of past and potential food donors. The donor type and status of each contact can be found in the Categories text box. Print each distribution list and submit to your instructor.

(continued)

Creating a Distribution List and Sending E-Mail *(continued)*

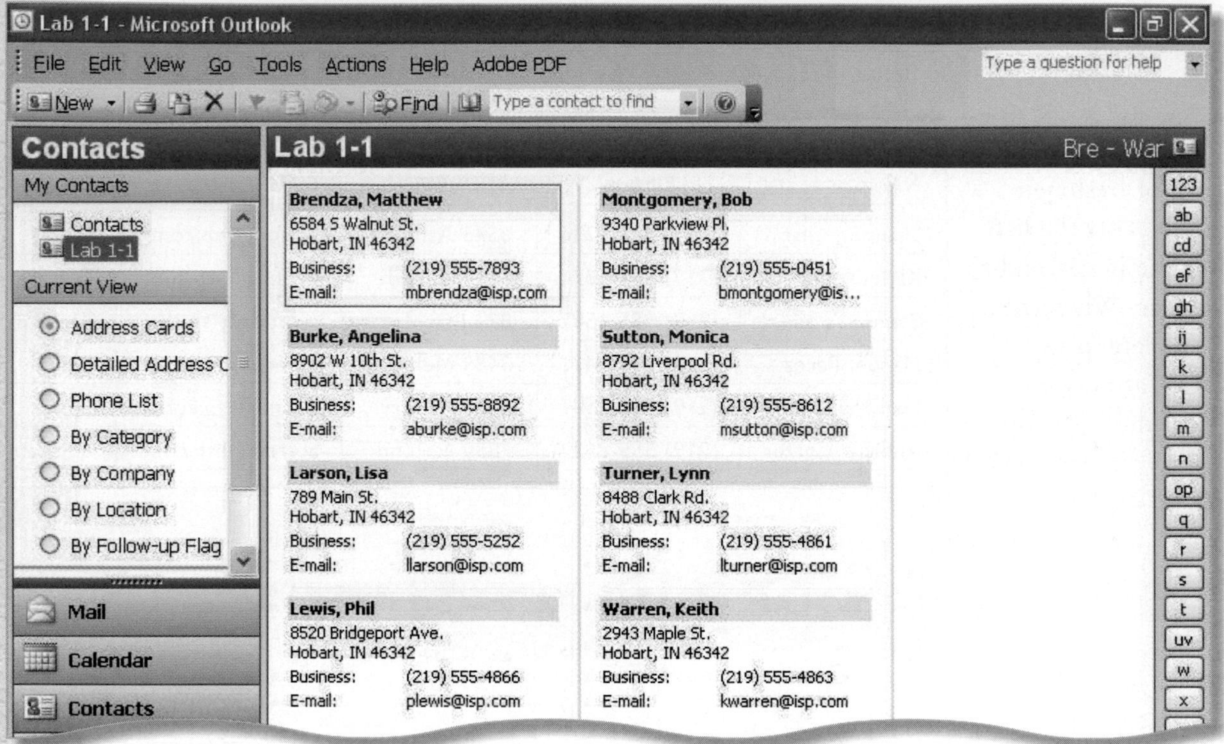

FIGURE 1-88

Instructions Part 2: Do the following:

1. Compose a message to each group created in Part 1. The message to past donors should thank them for their past support and request donations for this year's float. The message to potential donors should include a few examples of how their material or food donations help with float building.
2. Set the sensitivity for each message as confidential.
3. Using Microsoft Word, create a document called Homecoming Float Ideas, and include this file as an attachment with your e-mail messages.
4. Set the delivery for each message to November 1, 2007 at 9:00 a.m.
5. Format your messages to past donors as Plain Text and your messages to potential donors as HTML.
6. Print each e-mail message and hand them in to your instructor.

Instructions Part 3: Save the Lab 1-1 contact list as a text file. Open the file using Notepad. Print the contact list from Notepad and hand it in to your instructor.

2 Flagging and Sorting Messages

Problem: As president of the Computer Club, you are responsible for responding to questions about computer problems received via e-mail from your fellow students. Some questions require a more timely response than others do, so you need a way to sort the questions first by urgency and then by when they were received. At that point, you will be able to address the questions in an orderly manner.

Instructions: Import the Lab 1-2 Inbox folder (Figure 1-89) into Outlook. Read through each message and appropriately flag each one. Use a red flag for messages requiring immediate attention, yellow for messages requiring information before you can respond, and green for non-urgent, general questions. After you have flagged each message, sort the messages based on flag color.

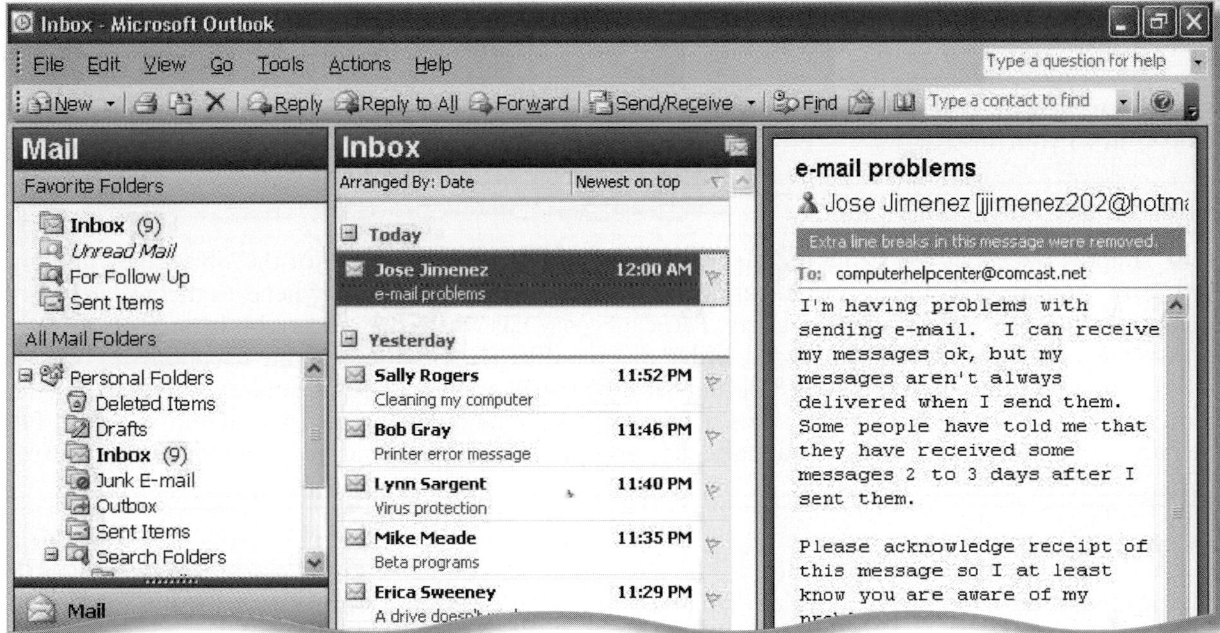

FIGURE 1-89

3 Creating an E-Mail Signature, Replying To, and Forwarding Messages

Problem: With all the messages sorted and flagged, you now have to respond to the messages. You need to perform this task in an efficient manner as it is the Computer Club's policy to respond to questions within 4 hours. It is also required that the name of the person responding, their telephone number, and the hours they can be reached appear on every reply.

Instructions Part 1: Create an e-mail signature consisting of your name, a telephone number (555-1234), and hours you can be reached (6:00 p.m. – 10:00 p.m., Mon – Thu). Click the New Message button on the Standard toolbar. Print the blank message containing the signature and hand it in to your instructor.

Instructions Part 2: Send a reply with the importance set at high to the messages flagged red. Forward the messages flagged yellow. You may use fictitious e-mail addresses for this exercise as the messages will not actually be sent. Hand in printouts of the replies and forwards to your instructor.

Instructions Part 3: Do the following:

1. Clear all the green flags from the non-urgent messages. Use Search Folders to display only the messages flagged for follow-up. Make a list of the sender's name, subject, and flag color and hand it in to your instructor.
2. Using information from Microsoft Outlook Help, create a unique signature for a separate e-mail account. See your instructor about setting up a separate e-mail account.
3. Print a blank message containing the signature and hand it in to your instructor.

Cases and Places

The difficulty of the case studies varies:
are the least difficult and are more difficult.
Each exercise has a cross-curricular designation:

Math Social Studies Science Language Arts Art/Music Business Health

1 Create a contact list of members of your math class. Include their names, addresses, telephone numbers, e-mail addresses (if any), and IM address (if any). Enter the employer for each one if appropriate. Use the Categories text box to list extracurricular activities (if any). Print the contact list and hand it in to your instructor.

2 Import the Cases 1-2 Contacts folder into Outlook. You are an intern for the Chicago Symphony Orchestra. Your responsibilities include updating the Symphony's contact list whenever there is a personnel change, someone receives a promotion, etc. Patricia Feeney has received a promotion from first chair violin to assistant conductor and was rewarded with a private office (Room 505), private telephone ((312) 555-6484) and fax number ((312) 555-6485), and her own e-mail address (pfeeney@chicagosymph.com). The information in her current record contains the general telephone number and the symphony's e-mail. Find the Patricia Feeney contact record and make the appropriate changes. Hand in a printout to your instructor.

3 Import the Cases 1-3 Inbox folder into Outlook. You work as an assistant to a medical consultant for a local newspaper. Every day you receive several e-mail messages about various health problems. One subscriber, Tom Black, has been sending several e-mail messages to your department complaining that his questions never get addressed. You are responsible for addressing his questions. Apply a filter to the Cases 1-3 Inbox folder to display only the messages from Tom Black. Respond to his latest e-mail message while sending a copy to the editor to show that you have answered Tom's questions. Hand in a printout of your reply to your instructor. Add Tom Black to your contact list. Track the activities for Tom Black. List the first five entries from the Activities list and hand it in to your instructor. After printing your reply message, delete all the messages from Tom Black and remove the filter.

4 You recently accepted a part-time summer position with an international law firm. Your first assignment is to make the main telephone and address file available to everyone in the firm. The file, which currently is maintained in a three-ring binder, contains names, addresses, telephone numbers, fax numbers, e-mail addresses, Web site addresses, and main language of your firm's clients. You decide to create a contact list using Outlook so everyone can access the same information and automatically dial and send e-mail and access Web sites. Create a contact list that includes at least the names, addresses, Web site URLs, and main language of seven corporations. Use fictitious company names and addresses or look up international companies on the Web using an Internet search engine. Create a Contacts subfolder in which to store the contact list. Categorize the contacts by language. Print the contact list and submit to your instructor.

5 **Working Together** Have each member of your team submit a design form for collecting contact information for employees of a new company you are starting. Have them base the form on the available fields in the General and Details sheets in the Contact window. Have the team select the best form design. After selecting a form, make copies for the entire class. Have your classmates fill out the form as employees. Collect the forms and create a contact list from the collected information. Hand in printouts of the final contact list.

MICROSOFT OFFICE 2003

Integration

MICROSOFT OFFICE 2003
INTEGRATION

MICROSOFT OFFICE 2003

Integration

Integrating Office 2003 Applications and the World Wide Web

PROJECT

1

CASE PERSPECTIVE

The Farley High School Travel Club organizes several trips each year for its student members. In addition to fund-raising activities, the club's leaders communicate with students and various destinations to provide fun and educational travel experiences. Kimberly Dewirt acts as the club's communication director and is responsible for raising the club's awareness within the school. Recently, the club's president assigned Kimberly the task of forming a new strategy to help inform students of the organization's structure and to promote the organization's mission.

Kimberly believes that interest in the club would increase if she sets out to provide more information about the club's members, finances, and goals. The travel club strives to provide unique education opportunities that students can highlight in their backgrounds when applying to colleges. In addition, the club's members have diverse backgrounds, including students from every grade level. Kimberly is investigating ways to publicize these benefits in an efficient and cost-effective way. She thinks that a Web site would be the answer, but she is inexperienced with Web site creation. Kimberly knows you have taken the school's Web design course and asks you to help her create a Web site that promotes the travel club.

Kimberly provides you with several files to get started, including the club's letterhead in a Word document, an Excel workbook that includes a chart, an Access database of the club's roster, and a PowerPoint presentation that provides an overview of the club's mission. Using the information provided in these files, you are confident that you can create a compelling Web site that highlights the club's strengths.

As you read through this project, you will learn how to use Office 2003 applications together to create a Web site.

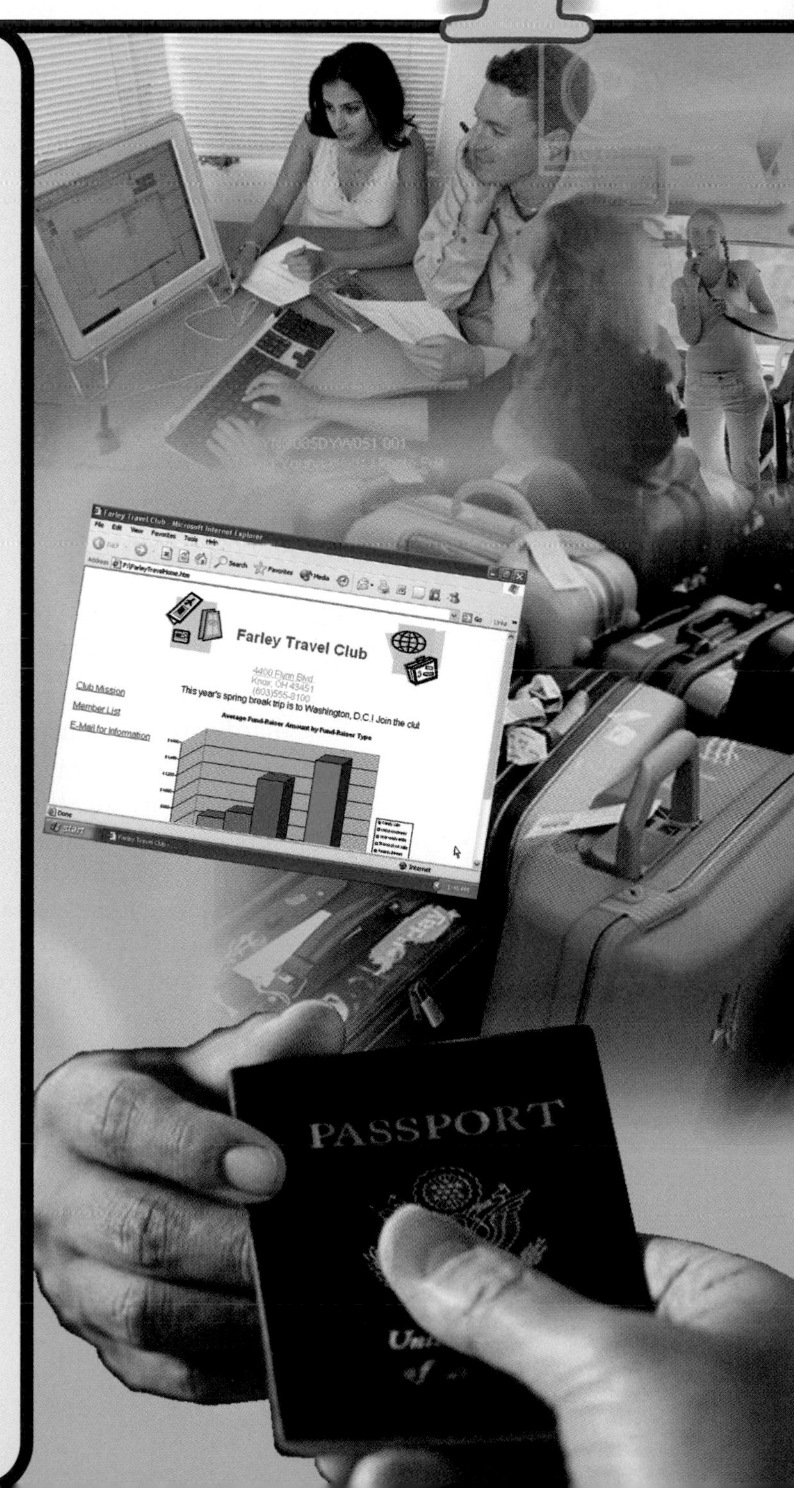

MICROSOFT OFFICE 2003

Integration

Integrating Office 2003 Applications and the World Wide Web

PROJECT

Objectives

You will have mastered the material in this project when you can:

- Integrate the Office 2003 applications to create a Web site
- Add hyperlinks to a Word document
- Embed an Excel chart into a Word document
- Add scrolling text to a Web page created in Word
- Add a hyperlink to a PowerPoint slide
- Create Web pages from a PowerPoint presentation
- Create a data access page from an Access database
- Test a Web site in a browser

Introduction

Integration means joining parts so they work together or form a whole. In information technology, common usages can include the following:

1. Integration during product development combines activities, programs, or hardware components into a functional unit.
2. Integration in companies can bring different manufacturers' products together into an efficiently working system.
3. Integration in marketing combines products or components to meet objectives, such as sharing a common purpose or creating demand. It includes such matters as consistent product pricing and packaging, advertising, and sales campaigns.
4. Integration in product design allows a unifying purpose and/or architecture, such as the Microsoft Office System. (The products also are sold individually, but they are designed with the same larger objectives and/or architecture.)

This Integration project will show you how you can use the functionality and productivity tools of the Microsoft Office System.

Integration Project — Farley High School Travel Club Web Site

Many businesses and organizations advertise their products and services on the Internet. Organizations find it easy to create Web pages using information already saved in word processing, spreadsheet, database, or presentation software formats. The Web page creation capabilities of Microsoft Office 2003 make it simple for you to create an entire Web site using the information available. Word allows you to create and save a document as a Web page. PowerPoint provides the same capability and adds a navigation structure for browsing. In addition, an Access wizard helps you create data access pages that enable the Web page visitor to navigate through the database.

This project supplies the following four files of information to help you get started:

1. A Word document that contains the club letterhead, including logo images, club name, and school address (Figure 1-1a on page INT 6).
2. An Excel workbook with a Bar chart graphically illustrating the club's breakdown of fund-raiser amount type by fund-raiser type (Figure 1-1b on page INT 6).
3. A PowerPoint slide show that contains general information about the club (Figure 1-1g on page INT 7).
4. An Access database that contains club member information (Figure 1-1c on page INT 6).

The Farley High School Travel Club Web site should include the following:

1. A home page with a Bar chart that contains the fund-raiser type by fund-raiser amount (Figure 1-1e on page INT 7). Three hypertext links also are included on the home page: Club Mission, Member List, and E-Mail for Information.
2. The Travel Club Members data access page (Figure 1-1d on page INT 6) is created from the Access file. Clicking the Member List link on the home page accesses this Web page. On this Web page, visitors can scroll through the club members, categorized by grade level.
3. The PowerPoint Web page (Figure 1-1g on page INT 7) displays information about the club's mission and information about how members can participate. Clicking the Club Mission link on the home page accesses this Web page.
4. Using the E-Mail for Information hyperlink, you can create an e-mail message (Figure 1-1f on page INT 7). E-mail is sent to the e-mail address travelclub@farleyhsus.edu.

The following pages contain a detailed explanation of these tasks.

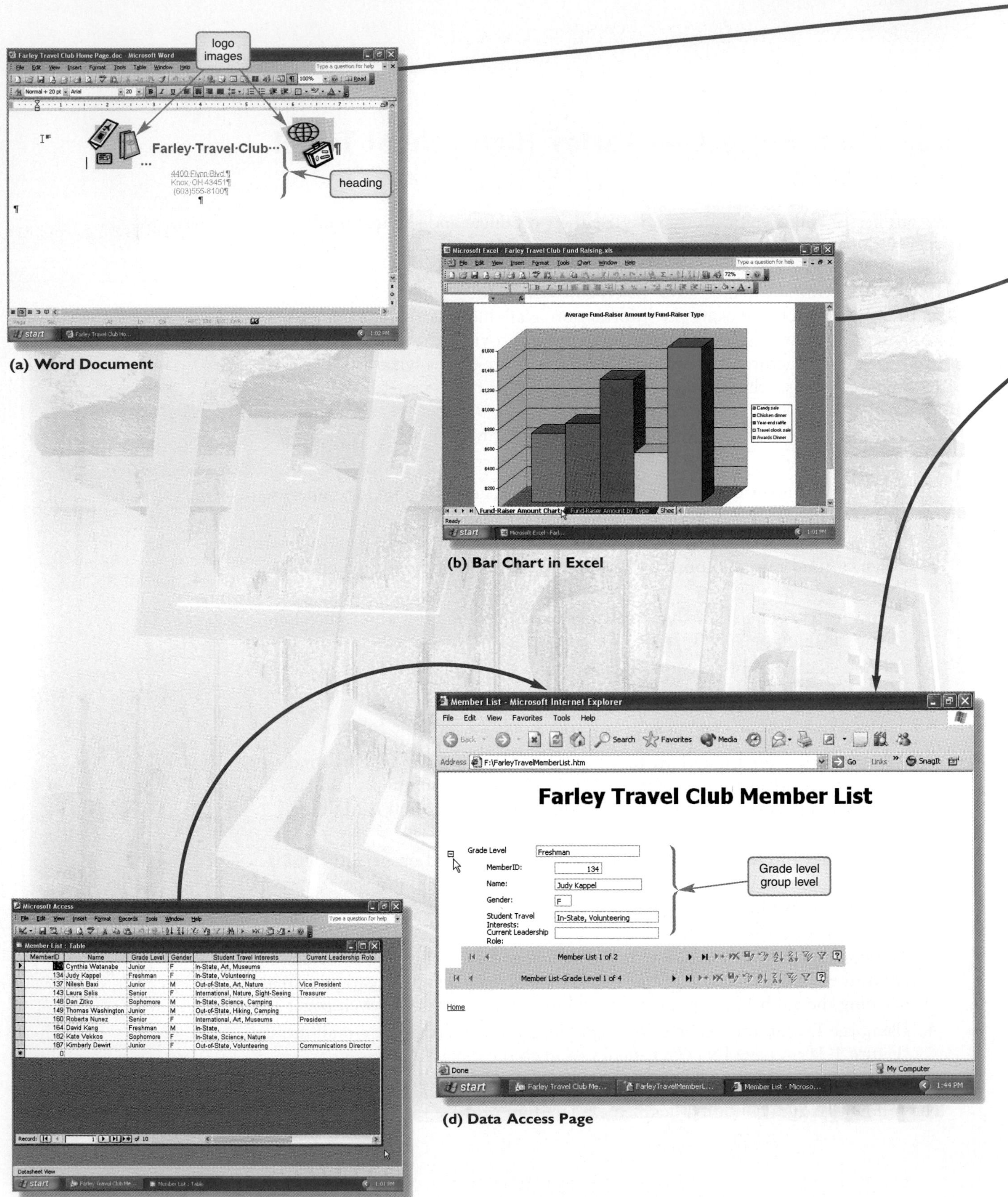

(a) Word Document

(b) Bar Chart in Excel

(c) Access Table

(d) Data Access Page

FIGURE 1-1

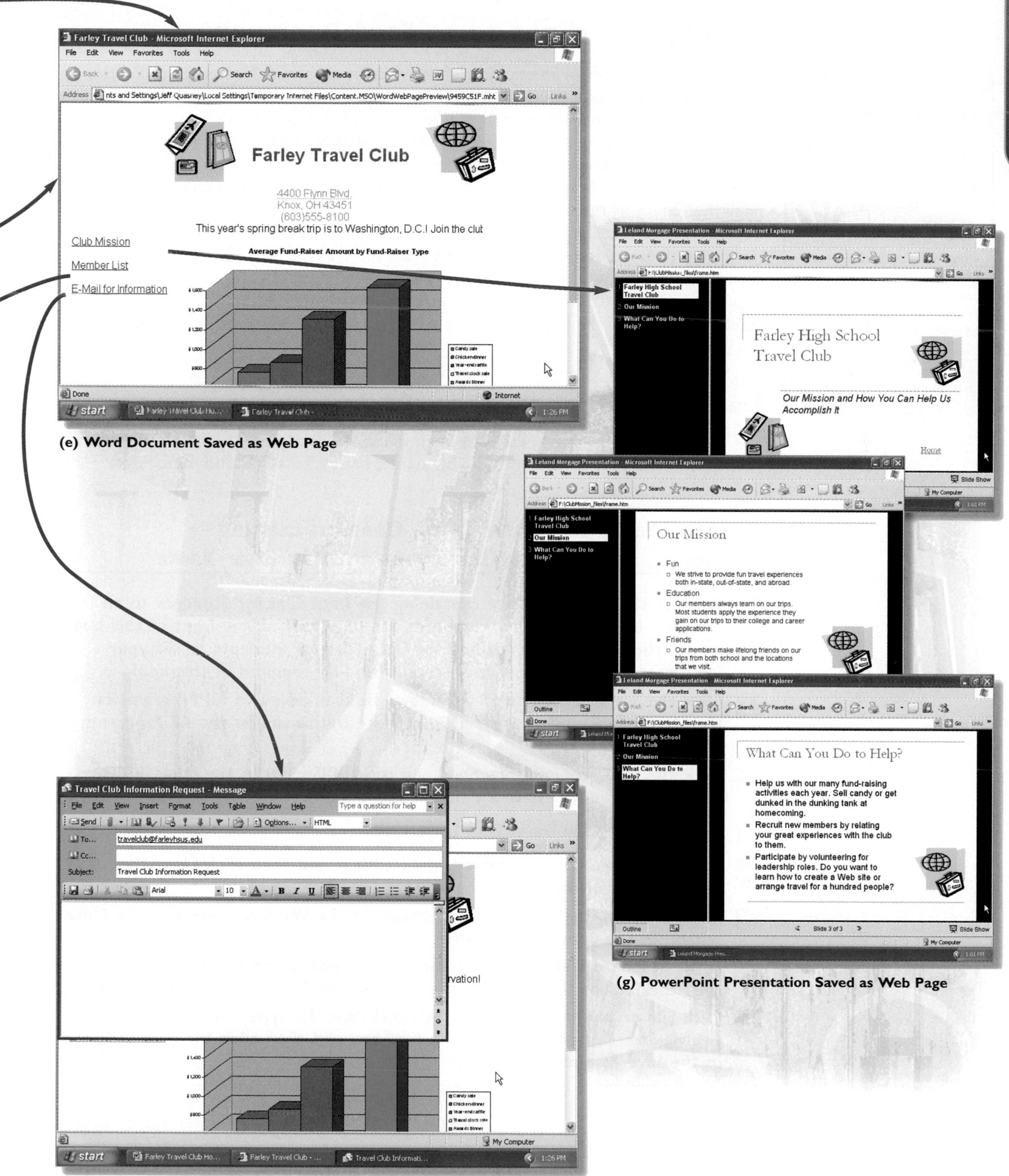

(e) **Word Document Saved as Web Page**

(g) **PowerPoint Presentation Saved as Web Page**

(f) **New E-Mail Message Created from Hyperlink**

Adding Hyperlinks to a Word Document

Q & A

Q: Can Office 2003 documents be converted to Web pages?

A: Yes. Making information available on the Internet is a key aspect of business today. To facilitate this trend, the Office 2003 applications easily allow you to generate Web pages from existing files. An entire Web site can be created with files from Word, Excel, PowerPoint, or Access, using the Save as Web Page command on the File menu.

The Web site created for the travel club consists of an initial Web page, called the **home page**, with two hyperlinks to other Web pages, an e-mail link, and a Bar chart. Clicking a **hyperlink**, which can be text or an image, allows you to jump to another location. Text is used (Club Mission, Member List, E-Mail for Information) for the three hyperlinks on the Farley Travel Club home page (Figure 1-1e on the previous page). The first hyperlink (Club Mission) jumps to a PowerPoint Web page that contains three Web pages that explain the travel club's mission. A second hyperlink (Member List) jumps to a data access page that provides inquiry capabilities for students to access the Farley High School Travel Club's member list database. This Web page allows inquiries only; updating the database is prohibited. The third hyperlink (E-Mail for Information) creates an e-mail message. In order to place the three hyperlinks to the left of the Bar chart, a table will be created in the Word document.

Starting Word and Opening a Document

The first step in this project is to open the Word document, Farley Travel Club Letterhead, and save it with the new file name, Farley Travel Club Home Page.

To Start Word, Customize Word, Open an Existing Document, and Save the Document with Another Name

1. **Connect the USB flash drive containing the Data Files for Students to an available USB port on your computer. See page xxiv at the front of this book for instructions for downloading the Data Files for Students or see your instructor for information on accessing the files required in this book.**
2. **Click the Start button on the Windows taskbar, point to All Programs on the Start menu, and then click Open Office Document on the All Programs submenu.**
3. **Click the Look in box arrow and then click UDISK (F:) in the Look in list. (Your USB drive may have a different name and letter.)**
4. **Double-click Farley Travel Club Letterhead.**
5. **If the Language bar is displayed, right-click it and then click Close the Language bar on the shortcut menu.**
6. **If the Getting Started task pane appears in the Word window, click its Close button in the upper-right corner.**
7. **If the Standard and Formatting toolbars are positioned on the same row, click the Toolbar Options button and then click Show Buttons on Two Rows.**
8. **Click File on the menu bar and then click Save As. Type** `Farley Travel Club Home Page` **in the File name text box and then click the Save button in the Save As dialog box.**

The document is saved as Farley Travel Club Home Page (Figure 1-2).

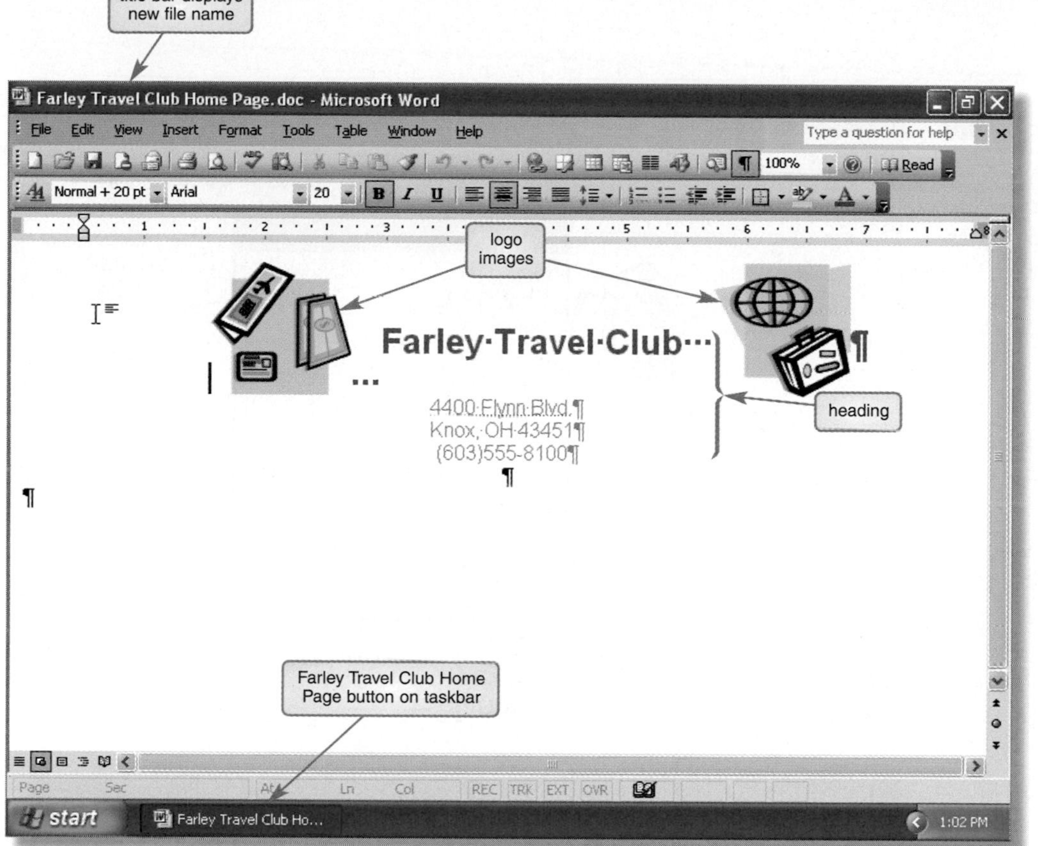

FIGURE 1-2

Inserting a Table into a Word Document

The next step is to insert a table with two columns and one row. The left column will contain three hyperlinks. The right column will contain the Bar chart.

The following steps add a table to the Farley Travel Club Home Page document.

To Insert a Table into a Word Document

1

- **Position the insertion point on the second paragraph mark below the club telephone number.**
- **Click Table on the menu bar, point to Insert, and then click Table.**

Word displays the Insert Table dialog box (Figure 1-3).

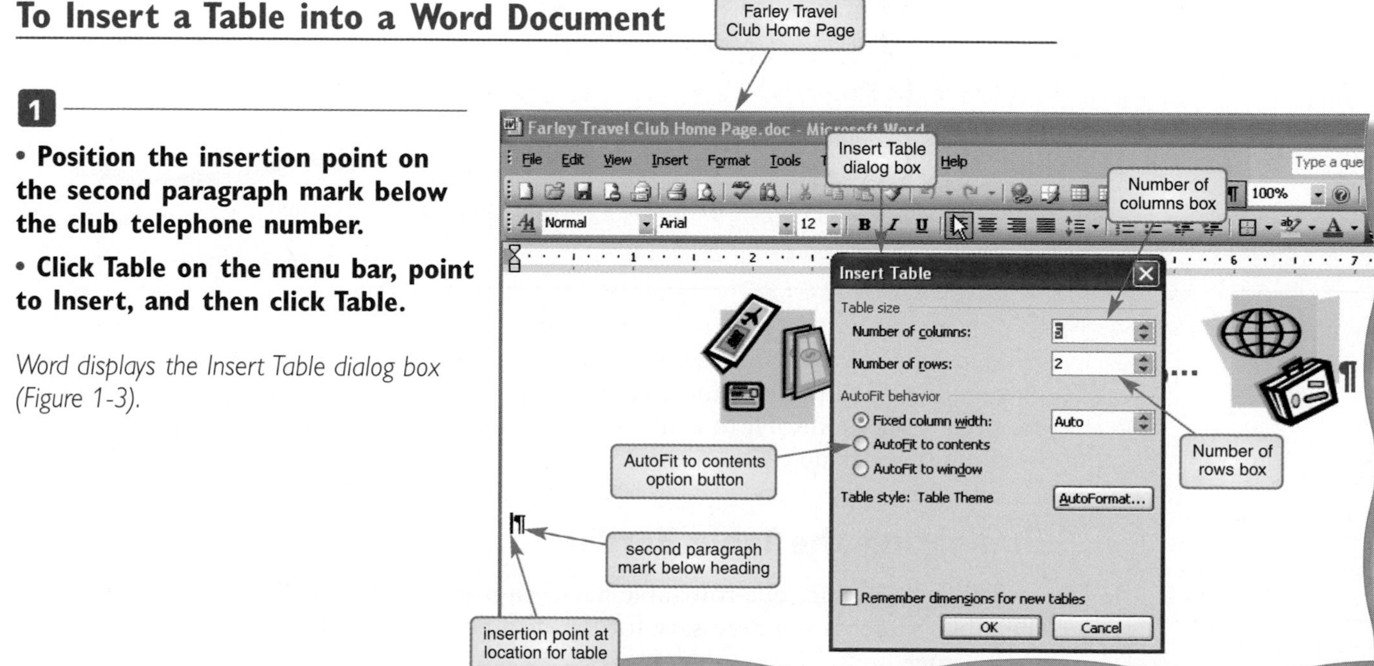

FIGURE 1-3

2

- **Type** 2 **in the Number of columns box and then press the TAB key.**
- **Type** 1 **in the Number of rows box and then click AutoFit to contents in the AutoFit behavior area.**

The new settings appear in the Insert Table dialog box (Figure 1-4).

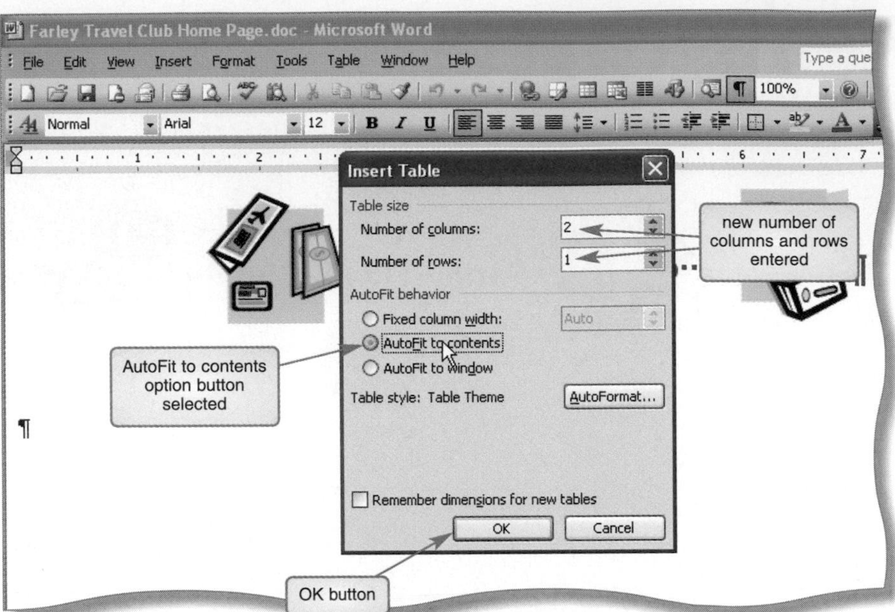

FIGURE 1-4

3

- **Click the OK button.**

Word displays the table in the document (Figure 1-5).

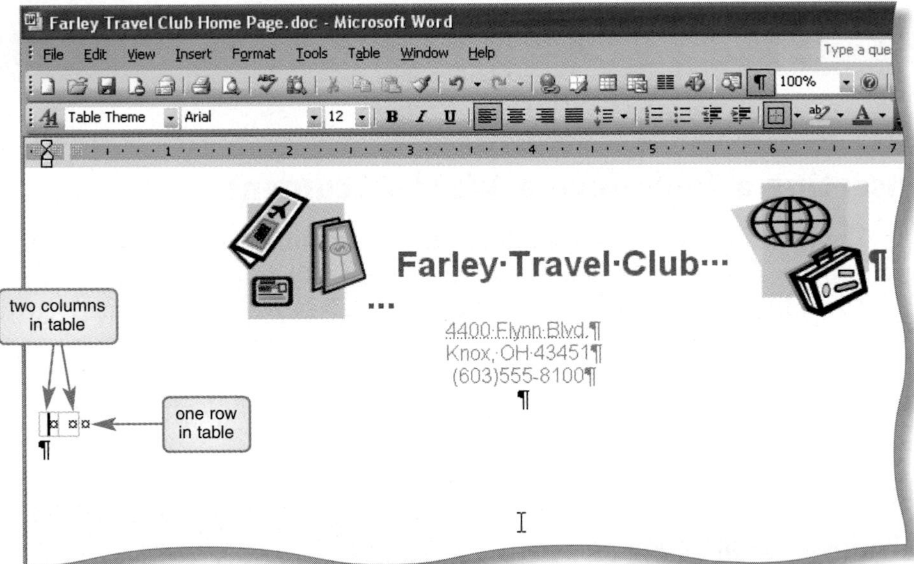

FIGURE 1-5

Step 2 instructed you to select AutoFit to contents. The **AutoFit to contents** option allows you to make the columns in a table fit the contents automatically. If you do not select AutoFit to contents, you can adjust the column widths manually using the sizing handles.

Eliminating the Table Border

The two-column, one-row table has been inserted into the Word document. The table border is not necessary for the Web page. The next steps remove the table border.

To Remove the Table Border

1

- **Click Table on the menu bar and then click Table Properties.**
- **Click the Borders and Shading button in the Table sheet.**
- **When the Borders and Shading dialog box displays, if necessary, click the Borders tab.**

Word displays the Borders and Shading dialog box (Figure 1-6).

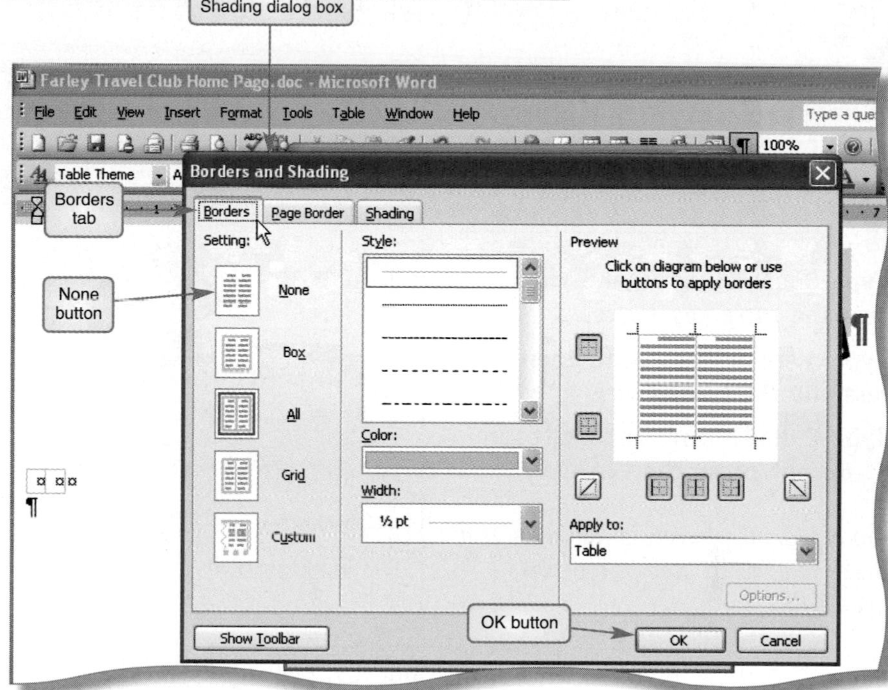

FIGURE 1-6

2

- **Click the None button in the Setting area and then click the OK button in the Borders and Shading dialog box.**
- **Click the OK button in the Table Properties dialog box.**

Word displays the borderless table (Figure 1-7).

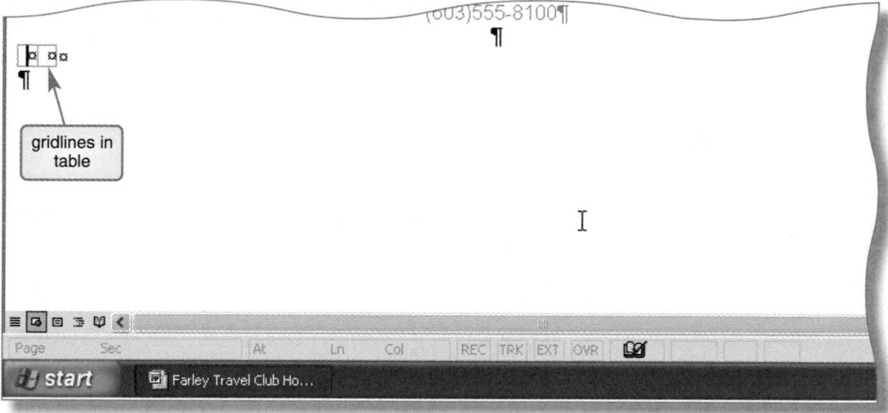

FIGURE 1-7

The border of the table displays with gridlines in the Word document. **Gridlines** can be used as a guide when entering text or images. When the document is viewed in your browser or printed, the gridlines do not display or print.

Inserting the Text for the Hyperlinks

After creating the borderless table, you must insert the three text phrases that will be used as hyperlinks on the home page. These phrases (Club Mission, Member List, and E-Mail for Information) allow the Web page visitor to jump to two other Web pages and create an e-mail message. The steps on the next page add the text phrases that are used as hyperlinks.

To Insert Text for Hyperlinks

1

- **If necessary, click the leftmost cell in the table.**

2

- **Type** `Club Mission` **and then press the ENTER key twice.**
- **Type** `Member List` **and then press the ENTER key twice.**
- **Type** `E-Mail for Information` **but do not press the ENTER key.**

Word displays the table with the three text phrases that will be used as hyperlinks (Figure 1-8).

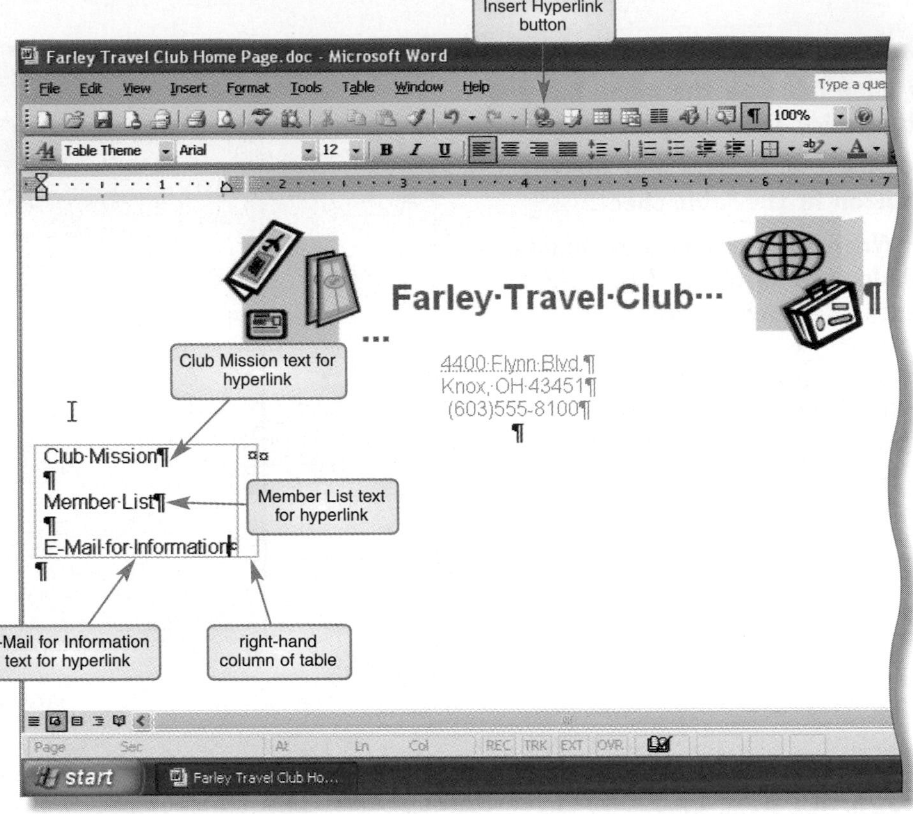

FIGURE 1-8

With the text phrases added, the next step is to select each text phrase and then insert the corresponding hyperlink.

> **Q & A**
>
> **Q:** Can hyperlinks link to both external and internal locations within the current document?
>
> **A:** Yes. To link to a location inside the current document, select the Place in This Document option in the Link to bar in the Insert Hyperlink dialog box. The Microsoft Office 2003 application then will provide a list of locations within the current document to which you can link.

Inserting a Hyperlink to PowerPoint Web Pages

The **Insert Hyperlink feature** provides the capability of linking to an existing file or Web page, to a place within the current document, to a newly created document, or to an e-mail address. In this project, two hyperlinks (Club Mission and Member List) will be created that link to Web pages. The Club Mission hyperlink will jump to a PowerPoint presentation that is saved as a Web page using the Web page name ClubMission.htm. The Member List hyperlink will jump to a data access page using the Web page name FarleyTravelMemberList.htm. You will create the data access page later from an existing Access database. The third text phrase (E-Mail for Information) links to an e-mail address, allowing the Web page visitor to send an e-mail message to the company's manager.

The following steps create a hyperlink for the first text phrase.

To Create a Hyperlink to PowerPoint Web Pages

1

- **Drag through the text, Club Mission, in the table.**
- **Click the Insert Hyperlink button on the Standard toolbar.**

2

- **If necessary, click the Existing File or Web Page button on the Link to bar.**
- **Type** `ClubMission.htm` **in the Address text box.**

The Insert Hyperlink dialog box is displayed with the name of the Web page in the Address text box (Figure 1-9).

3

- **Click the OK button.**

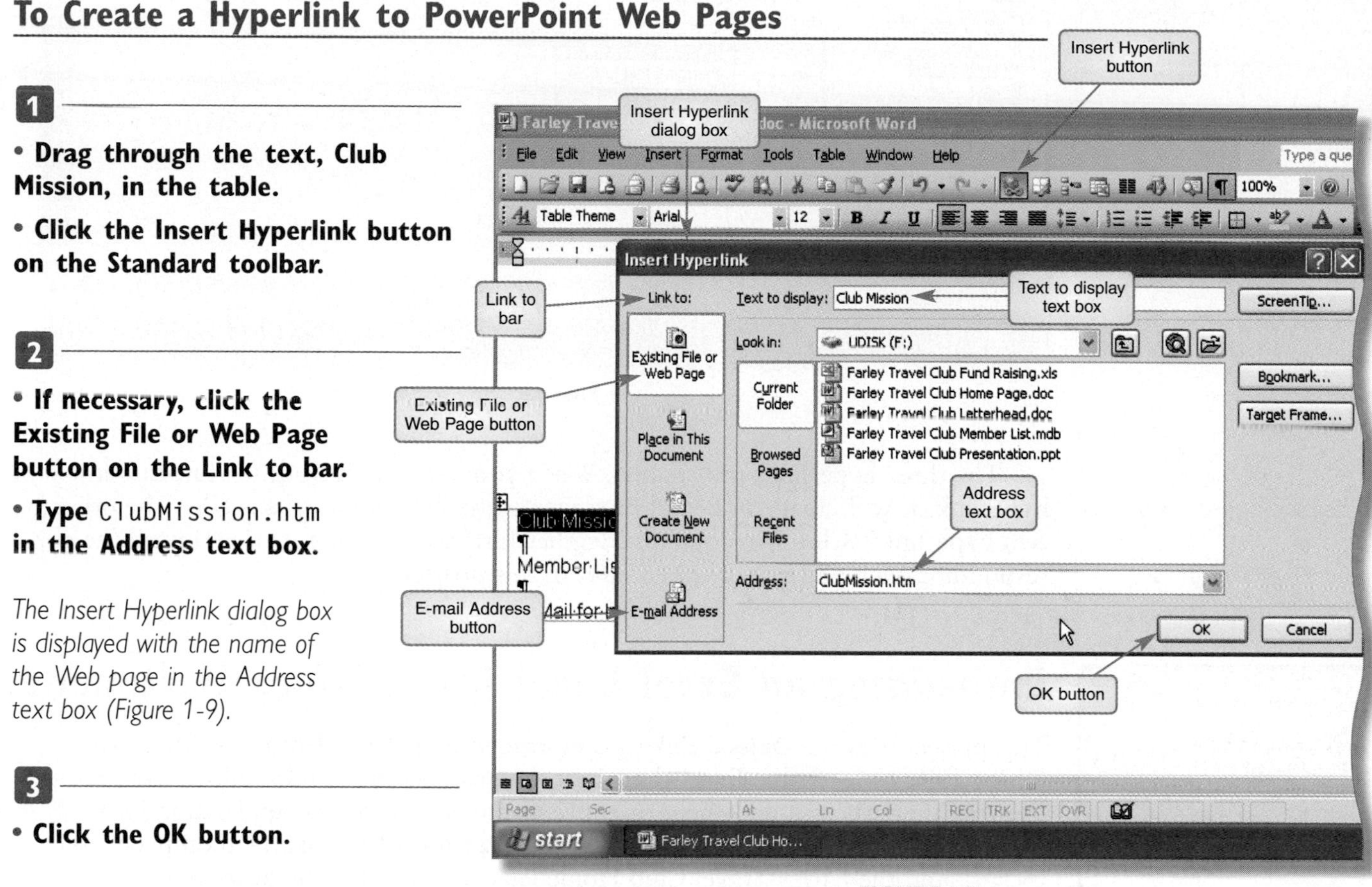

FIGURE 1-9

The hyperlink is assigned to the Club Mission text phrase. After the Word document is saved as a Web page and the visitor clicks the text, Club Mission, the ClubMission.htm file on the USB flash drive is displayed. The following steps add the other two hyperlinks.

To Insert the Remaining Hyperlinks

1. **Drag through the text, Member List, in the table. Click the Insert Hyperlink button on the Standard toolbar.**
2. **Type** `FarleyTravelMemberList.htm` **in the Address text box and then click the OK button.**
3. **Drag through the text, E-Mail for Information. Click the Insert Hyperlink button on the Standard toolbar and then click the E-mail Address button on the Link to bar.**
4. **Type** `travelclub@farleyhsus.edu` **in the E-mail address text box.**
5. **Type** `Travel Club Information Request` **in the Subject box and then click the OK button.**

Word displays the table as shown in Figure 1-10 on the next page.

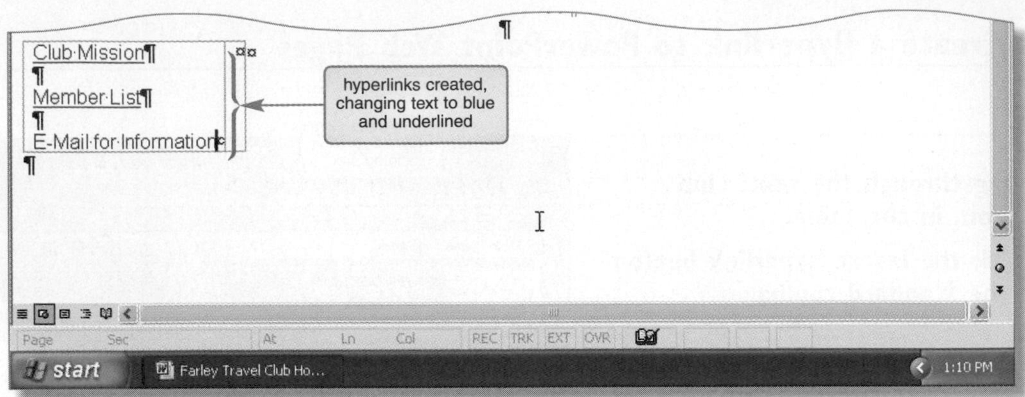

FIGURE 1-10

The three hyperlinks are created. When you click the E-Mail for Information hyperlink, it will create an e-mail message to travelclub@farleyhsus.edu. The other two hyperlinks (Club Mission and Member List) will not be functional until the corresponding Web pages are created later in this project.

Embedding an Excel Chart into a Word Document

This project uses the **Object Linking and Embedding** (**OLE**) feature of Microsoft Office 2003 to insert the Excel chart into a Word document. OLE allows you to incorporate parts of a document or entire documents from one application into another. The Bar chart in Excel is called a **source object** (Figure 1-1b on page INT 6), and the Farley Travel Club Home Page document is the **destination document**. After an object is embedded, it becomes part of the destination document. This project illustrates using the Paste Special command on the Edit menu to embed the Excel object. **Paste Special** inserts an object into Word, but still recognizes the **source program**, the program in which the object was created. When you double-click an embedded object, such as the Fund-Raiser Amount by Fund-Raiser Type worksheet, the source program starts and allows you to make changes. In this example, Excel is the source program. With the hyperlinks added to the Word document, the next step is to embed the Bar chart into the Word document. The following steps open the Excel workbook.

Q & A

Q: What are some advantages of OLE?

A: The advantage of using an integrated set of applications, such as Office 2003, is the capability of sharing information among applications. The Object Linking and Embedding (OLE) features of Office 2003 make the integration process more efficient. A chart created in Excel can be included in a Word document using OLE. To edit the embedded object, double-click it. The source program then starts and opens the source object for editing.

To Start Excel, Customize Excel, and Open an Existing Workbook

1. **Click the Start button on the Windows taskbar, point to All Programs on the Start menu, and then click Open Office Document on the All Programs submenu.**
2. **If necessary, click the Look in box arrow and then click UDISK (F:) in the Look in list. (Your USB flash drive may have a different name and letter.)**
3. **Double-click the Farley Travel Club Fund-Raising workbook.**
4. **If the Language bar is displayed, right-click it and then click Close the Language bar on the shortcut menu.**
5. **If the Getting Started task pane is displayed in the Excel window, click its Close button in the upper-right corner. If the Chart toolbar is displayed, click its Close button.**
6. **If the Standard and Formatting toolbars are positioned on the same row, click the Toolbar Options button and then click Show Buttons on Two Rows.**

The next two sections explain how to embed an Excel chart into a Word document and then resize it. The first section explains embedding a chart into a Word document. The following steps embed the Excel Bar chart into the Word document.

To Embed an Excel Chart into a Word Document

1

- **If necessary, click the Fund-Raiser Amount Chart tab.**

The Bar chart is active and is displayed (Figure 1-11).

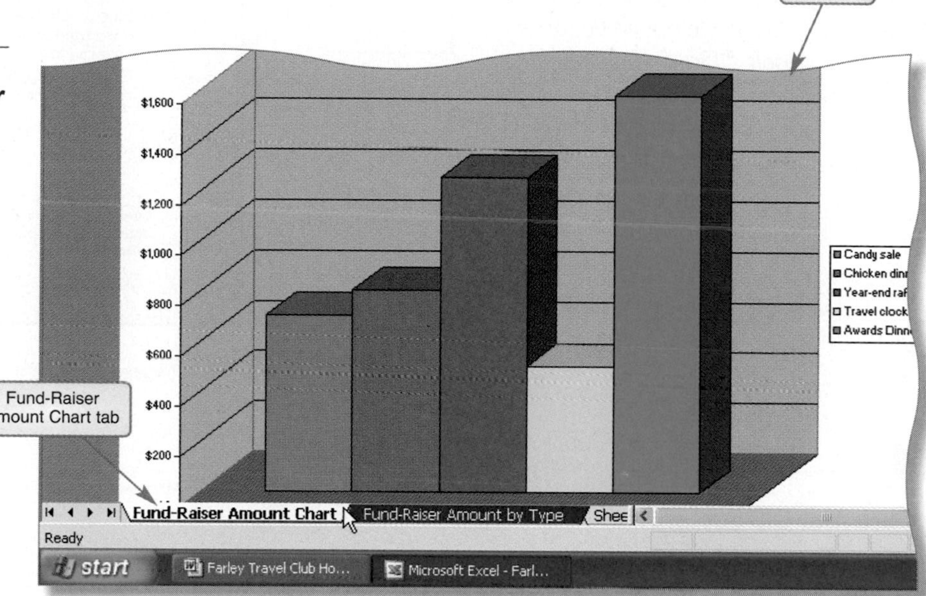

FIGURE 1-11

2

- **Click the white area around the chart area to select the chart and then click the Copy button on the Standard toolbar.**

Excel places a copy of the Bar chart on the Office Clipboard. A scrolling marquee is displayed around the chart area (Figure 1-12).

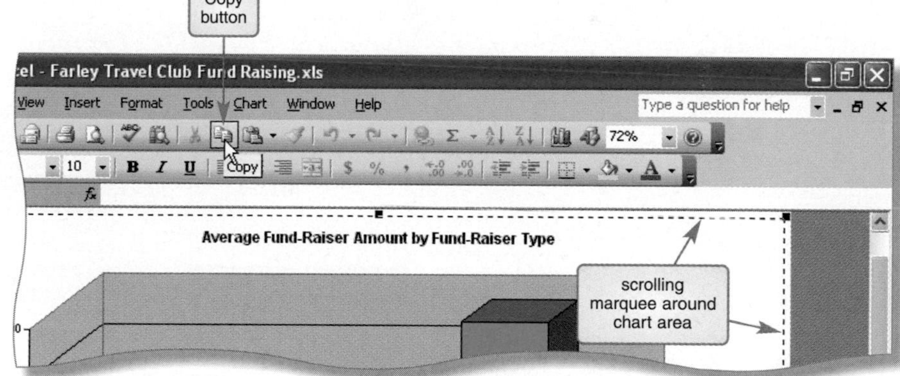

FIGURE 1-12

3

- **Click the Farley Travel Club Home Page button on the taskbar.**
- **If necessary, click the right column of the table.**

4

- **Click Edit on the menu bar.**

The Edit menu is displayed (Figure 1-13).

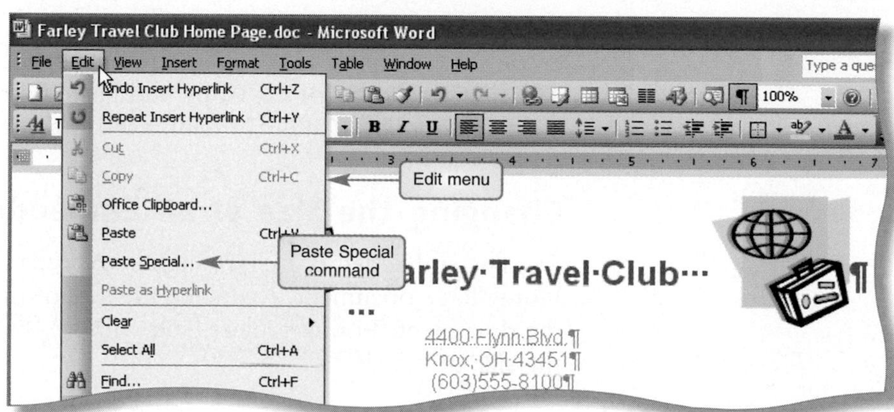

FIGURE 1-13

5

- **Click Paste Special.**
- **If necessary, click Microsoft Office Excel Chart Object in the As list.**

Word displays the Paste Special dialog box (Figure 1-14). The Paste option button is selected. Microsoft Office Excel Chart Object is selected in the As list.

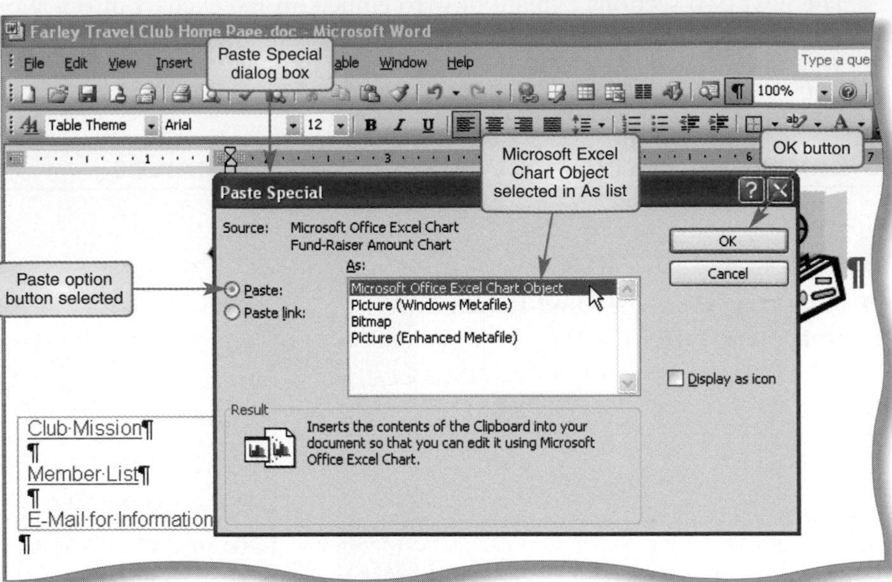

FIGURE 1-14

6

- **Click the OK button.**

Word embeds the Bar chart into the document (Figure 1-15).

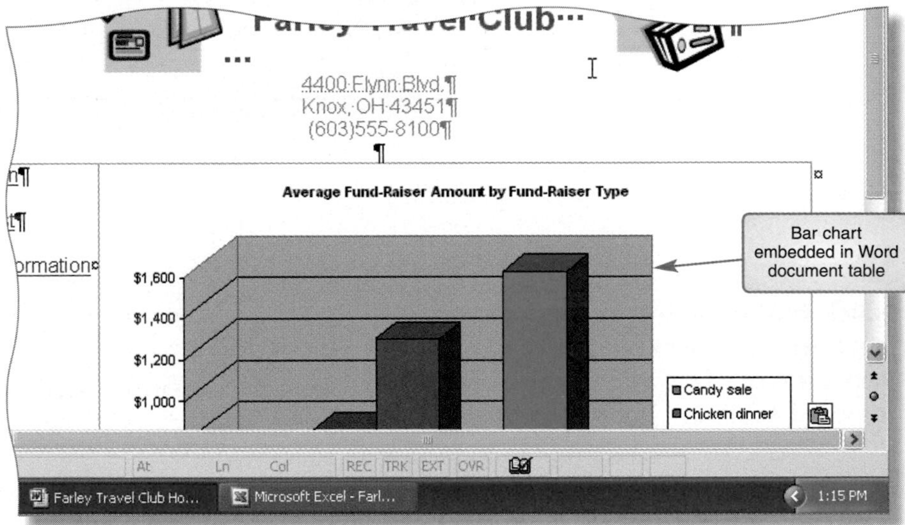

FIGURE 1-15

All Office 2003 applications allow you to use three methods to copy objects among applications: (1) copy and paste; (2) copy and embed; and (3) copy and link. The first method uses the Copy and Paste buttons. The latter two use the Paste Special command. Table 1-1 summarizes the differences among the three methods.

Changing the Size of an Embedded Object

The embedded Bar chart slightly exceeds the margins of the Farley Travel Club Home Page document. Reducing the size of the Bar chart will improve the layout of the document. In this project, you will use the Format Object dialog box to change the size of the chart.

Table 1-1 Copy Methods

METHOD	CHARACTERISTICS
Copy and paste	The source document becomes part of the destination document. An object may be edited, but the editing features are limited to those of the destination application. An Excel worksheet becomes a Word table. If changes are made to values in the Word table, any original Excel formulas are not recalculated.
Copy and embed	The source document becomes part of the destination document. An object may be edited in the destination document using source editing features. The Excel worksheet remains a worksheet in Word. If you make changes to values in the worksheet with Word active, Excel formulas will be recalculated. If you change the worksheet in Excel without the document open in Word, however, these changes will not be displayed in the Word document the next time you open it.
Copy and link	The source document does not become part of the destination document, even though it appears to be. Instead, a link is established between the two documents, so that when you open the Word document, the worksheet displays within the document, as though it were a part of it. When you attempt to edit a linked worksheet in Word, the system activates Excel. If you change the worksheet in Excel, the changes also will be displayed in the Word document the next time you open it.

Q & A

Q: What is an object in Office 2003?

A: Objects can be nearly any part of an Office 2003 application or other Windows application. Some examples are Excel worksheets, a paragraph in a Word document, and a slide in a PowerPoint presentation. As long as you use the Paste Special command to paste data in the Clipboard, you can keep data in its native format.

The following steps reduce the size of the chart using the Object command on the Format menu.

To Change the Size of an Embedded Object

1

- **If necessary, click the Bar chart to select it.**
- **Click Format on the menu bar.**

The Bar chart is selected as indicated by sizing handles on the selection rectangle. The Format menu is displayed (Figure 1-16).

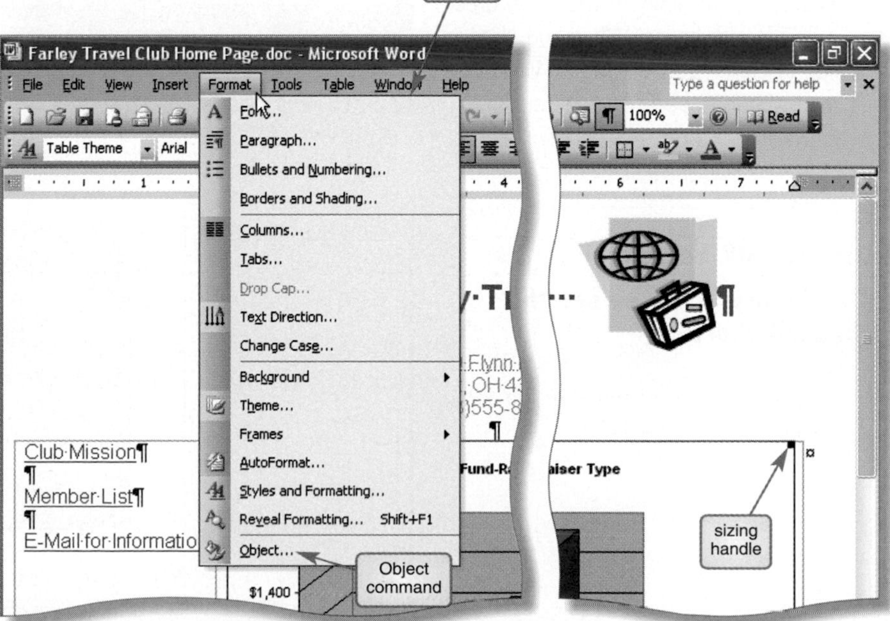

FIGURE 1-16

2

- **Click Object.**
- **If necessary, click the Size tab.**

The Format Object dialog box with the Size sheet selected is displayed (Figure 1-17).

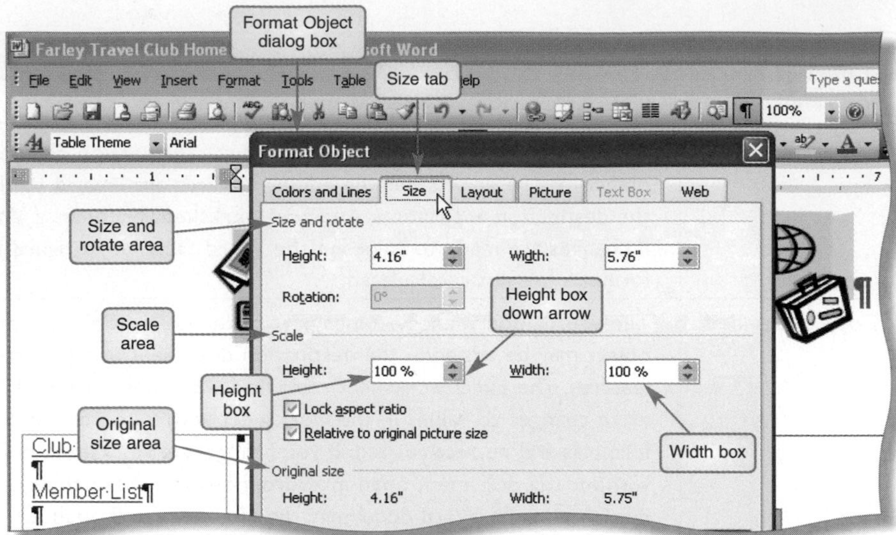

FIGURE 1-17

3

- **In the Scale area, if necessary, click the Height box up or down arrow or the Width box up or down arrow until 90 % appears in both the Height box and the Width box.**

The Height box and the Width box both display 90 % (Figure 1-18). Depending on the size of the object when it was pasted into the Word document, you either may need to scale up or down in the Scale area Height and Width boxes. When you change the value in either the Height or Width box, both values change because the Lock aspect ratio check box is selected.

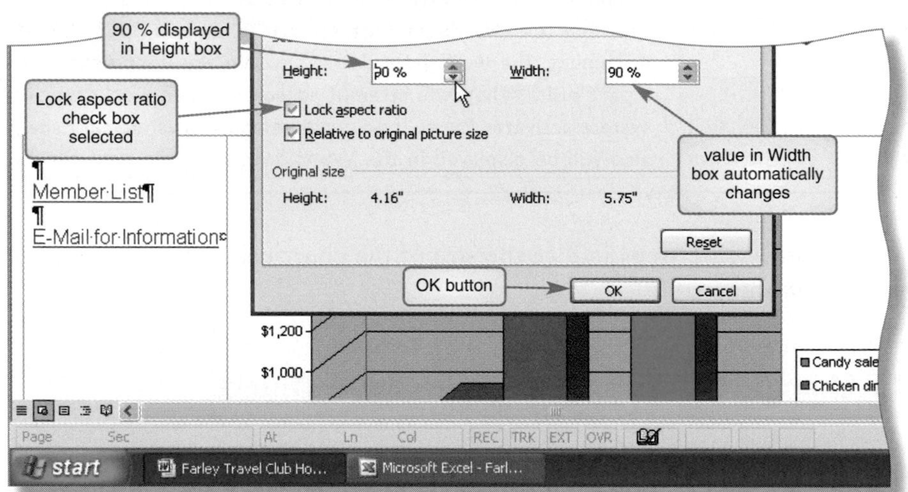

FIGURE 1-18

4

- **Click the OK button.**
- **If necessary, scroll to see the embedded chart.**

Word reduces the size of the chart to 90% of its original size (Figure 1-19).

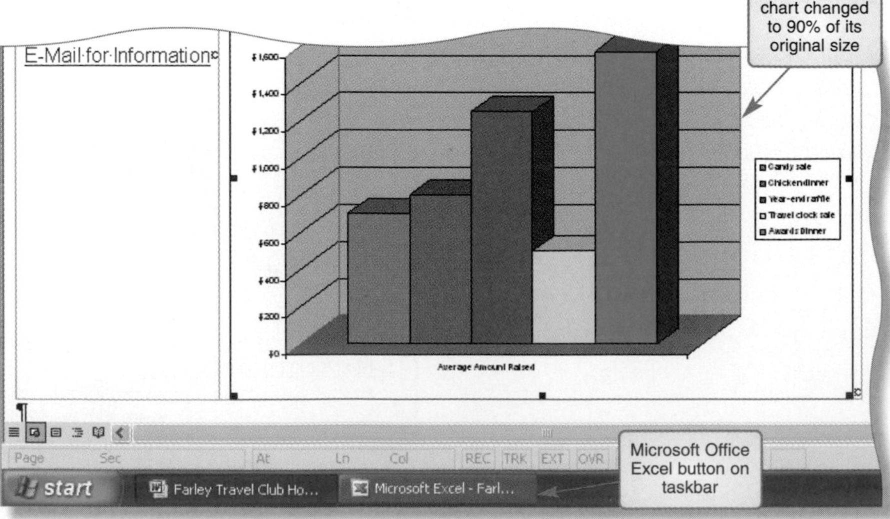

FIGURE 1-19

The Format Object dialog box (see Figure 1-17) contains two areas that can change the size of an object. The **Size and rotate area** allows you to increase or decrease the height or width of an object in inches. When available, it also allows you to rotate the object in degrees around an axis. The **Scale area** allows you to change the size of an object by a specific percentage while maintaining the height-to-width ratio. The height-to-width ratio is referred to as **aspect ratio.** You change the height and width independently by deselecting the Lock aspect ratio check box. The **Original size area** at the bottom of the Format Object dialog box displays the original height and width of the selected object.

Q & A

Q: What are some other methods to resize objects?

A: To resize an image proportionally from a corner, you can press and hold down the SHIFT key while dragging a corner sizing handle. To resize vertically, horizontally, or diagonally from the center outward, press and hold down the CTRL key while dragging a sizing handle. To resize proportionally from the center outward, press and hold down the CTRL+SHIFT keys and drag a corner sizing handle.

Quitting Excel

With the Bar chart embedded in the Word document, you no longer need the Farley Travel Club Fund-Raising workbook open. The following steps quit Excel.

To Quit Excel

1. **Right-click the Microsoft Office Excel - Farley Travel Club Fund-Raising button on the taskbar. Click Close on the shortcut menu. If prompted to save changes, click the No button.**
2. **If the Microsoft Excel dialog box appears regarding saving the large amount of information on the Clipboard, click the No button.**

Skill Builder 1-1

To practice the following tasks, visit scsite.com/off2003sch/skill, locate Integration Project 1, and then click Skill Builder 1-1.

- ❑ Embed an Excel chart into a Word document
- ❑ Change the size of an embedded object

Adding Scrolling Text to a Word Document

The Word document is almost ready to be saved as a Web page. The final item that needs to be added is an element that will capture the attention of your Web page visitors. One of the attention-grabbing techniques that Web developers use is scrolling text. **Scrolling text** is a line of text that moves across the Web page. Generally, scrolling text is used to highlight information about the Web site. With Word 2003, you can create scrolling text using the Scrolling Text button on the Web Tools toolbar. A scrolling marquee will be created just below the Farley Travel Club heading.

To create scrolling text, the Web Tools toolbar must display. The steps on the next page display the Web Tools toolbar.

Note: If you are stepping through this project on a computer and your computer has Service Pack 2 for Windows XP installed, then do not perform the steps on pages INT 20 through INT 23. Windows XP Service Pack 2 does not allow for the use of the Scrolling Text Web Tool.

To Display the Web Tools Toolbar

1

- **If necessary, scroll to see the top of the document.**
- **Click View on the menu bar, point to Toolbars, and then click Web Tools on the Toolbars submenu.**

2

- **If necessary, point to the Web Tools toolbar title bar and then drag the toolbar to the center, right side of the window.**

The Web Tools toolbar is displayed (Figure 1-20).

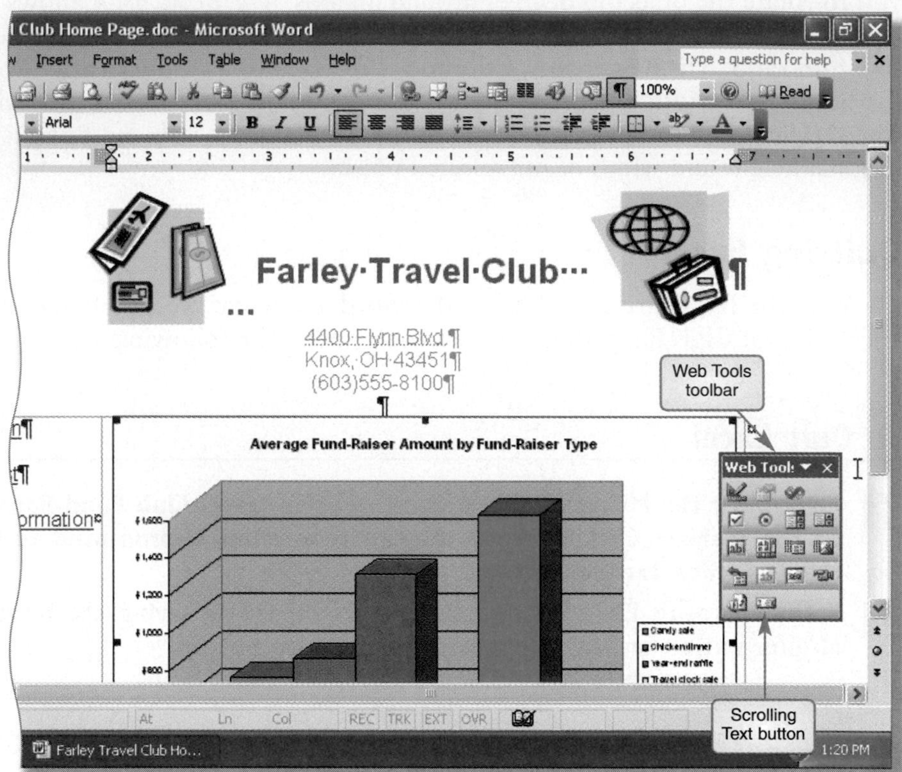

FIGURE 1-20

The Web Tools toolbar is used to create the scrolling text that moves below the Web page heading.

Inserting Scrolling Text

A number of options are available for scrolling text. The **behavior** of the text specifies the manner in which the text moves on the Web page. By default, the behavior of the line of text is to scroll. **Scrolling** moves the text in from one side and off the other side of the Web page. Another behavior option is to slide the text. Setting the behavior to **slide** moves the text in from one side of the Web page and stops as soon as the text touches the opposite side. The third option is to set text behavior to alternate. **Alternate** bounces the text back and forth in the margins of the marquee. The default behavior is scrolling text. In this project, the scrolling text behavior is changed to slide, as shown in the following steps.

Q & A

Q: Can I format scrolling text?

A: Yes. To format the text, use the Font command on the Format menu while you are in Design mode. You turn off Design mode to see the results. In browsers that do not support scrolling text, the text will display but it will not be scrolling.

To Insert Scrolling Text into a Word Document

1

- **Click the paragraph mark below the telephone number in the Farley Travel Club heading, and then click the Scrolling Text button on the Web Tools toolbar.**

Word displays the Scrolling Text dialog box (Figure 1-21).

2

- **Click the Behavior box arrow and then click Slide in the list.**

3

- **Drag through the text, Scrolling Text, in the Type the scrolling text here text box.**
- **Type** `This year's spring break trip is to Washington, D.C.! Join the club today and make your reservation!` **as the scrolling text.**

4

- **Drag the Speed slide one speed marker to the left, and then click the OK button.**

The scrolling text is displayed (Figure 1-22).

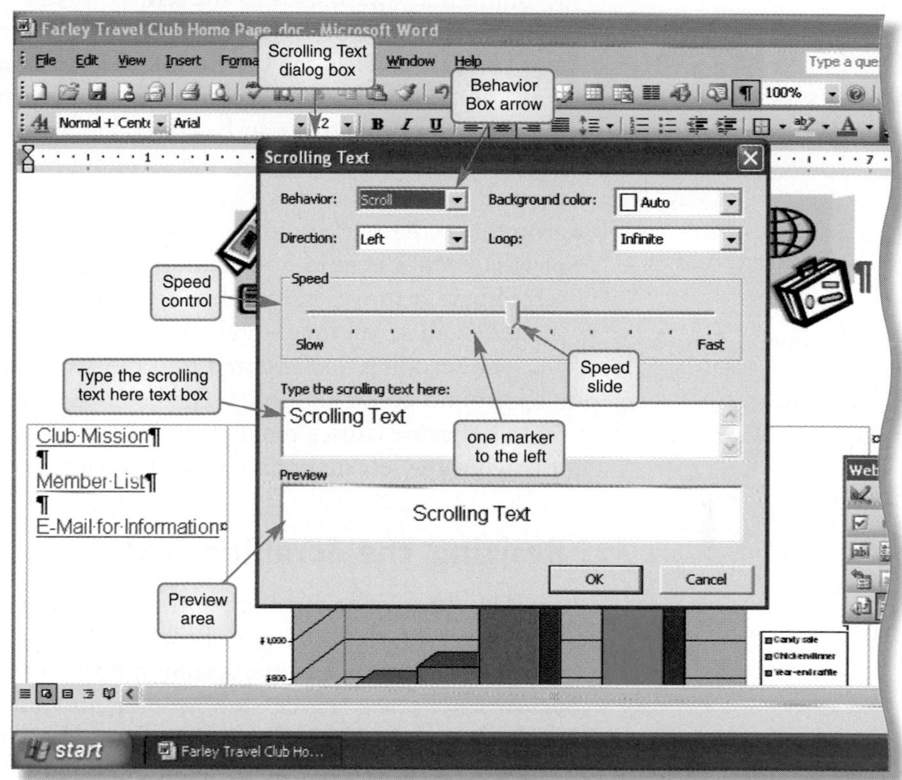

FIGURE 1-21

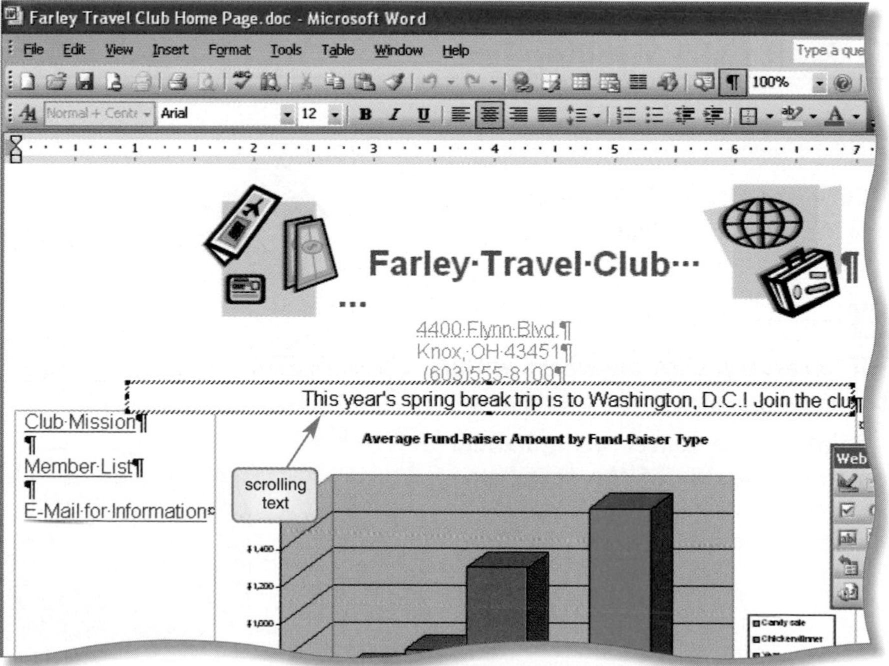

FIGURE 1-22

The **direction** of the text movement can be left to right or right to left. The direction attribute in the scrolling text options controls this movement. The default direction is to move right to left, so the text begins in the right margin of the line of scrolling text and moves to the left.

The **speed** of the scrolling text also can be varied from slow to fast. Scrolling the text too fast cancels the benefits of the scrolling text. If the Web page visitor cannot read the text because it scrolls too fast, the text serves no purpose.

Other options that can be controlled in scrolling text are background colors and the number of times to loop the scrolling text. The **background** attribute determines the color of the line of scrolling text. The background default is a transparent background, so the background of the line of scrolling text displays the background color of whatever is behind it. The **loop** attribute determines the number of times that the scrolling text moves across the Web page. The default is an **infinite loop**, which means the text will scroll indefinitely, but the loop can be set to a specific number of times.

The scrolling text inserted into the Word document uses the default direction, background color, and loop. The behavior selected for the scrolling text is Slide. The **Slide behavior** causes the text to scroll from the right margin and stop scrolling when it reaches the left margin. The next section explains how to resize the scrolling text.

Resizing the Scrolling Text

The default for scrolling text is to move the text all the way across the Web page from the right margin of the page to the left margin. Sometimes, it is better to shorten the distance of the scrolling text. In this project, the scrolling text is centered below the Farley Travel Club heading and address of the Word document. The Web page visitor sees the club name with address and telephone number information below it, followed by the scrolling message. This project uses the Design mode to change the size of the scrolling text. In general, **Design mode** allows you to rearrange and design the page in a user-friendly manner.

The following steps change the size of the scrolling text.

To Resize the Scrolling Text

1

- **Click the Design Mode button on the Web Tools toolbar.**

2

- **If necessary, click anywhere within the scrolling text box to select it.**
- **Point to the center sizing handle on the right side of the text box.**

The text box is displayed as shown in Figure 1-23.

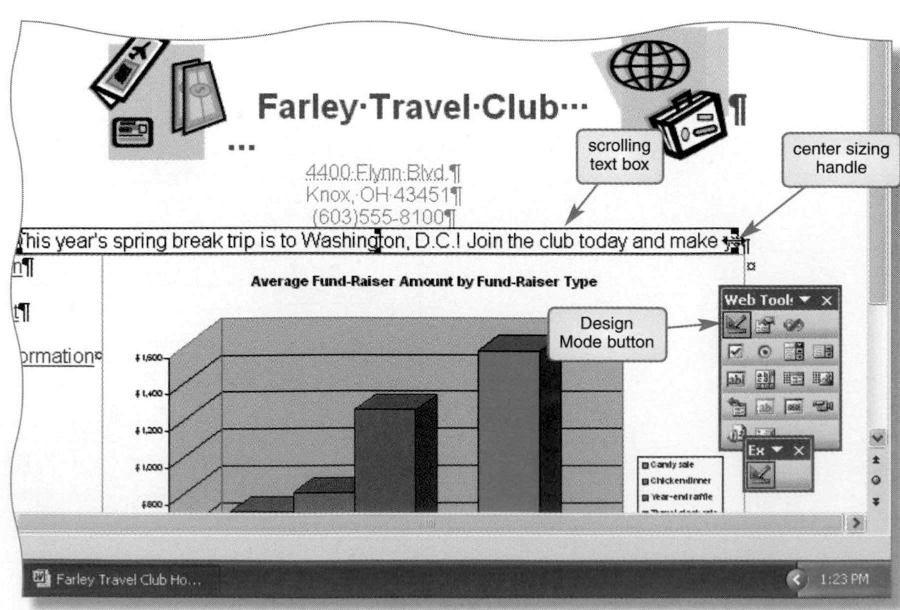

FIGURE 1-23

3

- **Drag the center sizing handle to the left, so that it is positioned approximately as shown in Figure 1-24, but do not release the mouse button.**

The dotted line shows the proposed size for the scrolling text.

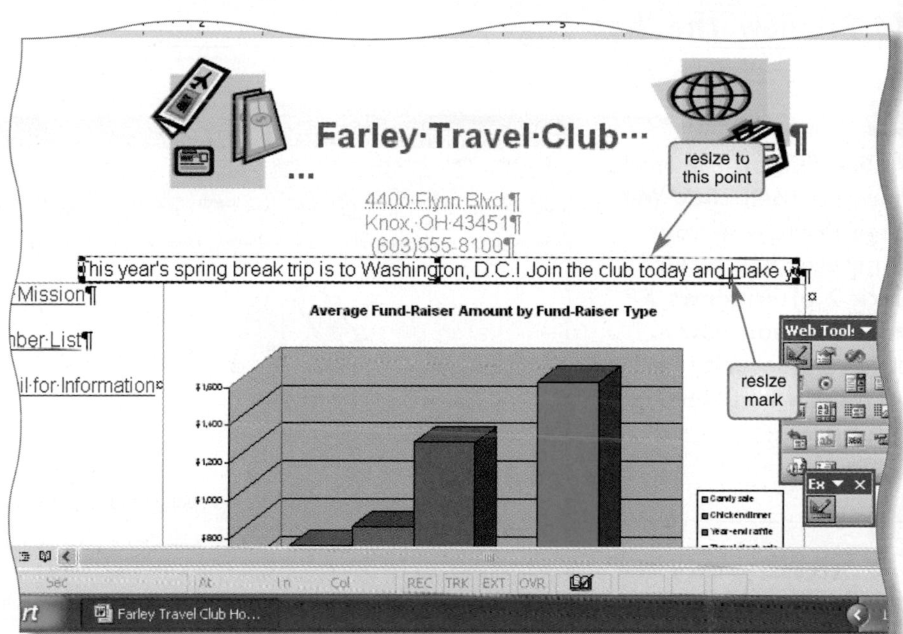

FIGURE 1-24

4

- **Release the mouse button.**

The scrolling text box is resized (Figure 1-25).

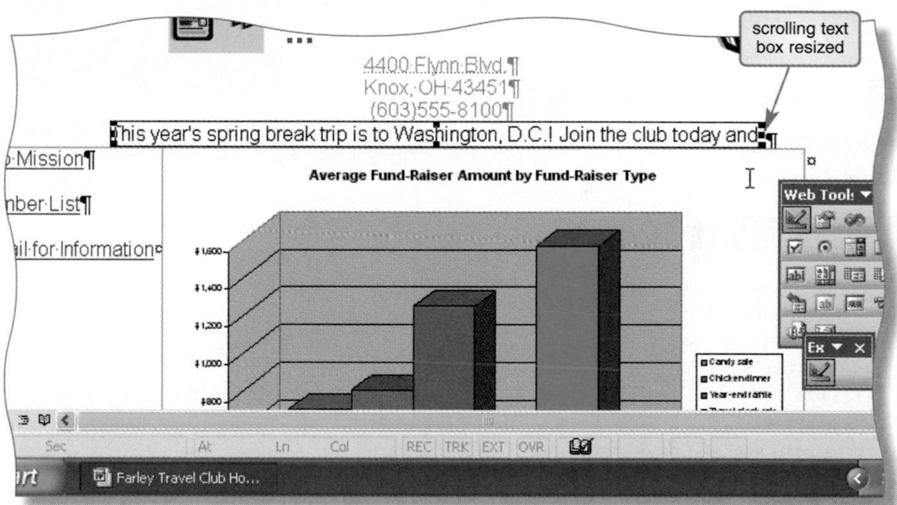

FIGURE 1-25

The home page for the Farley Travel Club Web site is complete.

Viewing the Word Document in Your Browser and Saving It as a Web Page

The next step is to view the Word document in your browser to verify that all information is accurate. After verifying its accuracy, you then can save the Word document as an HTML file. Saving the Word document as an HTML file makes it possible for it to be viewed using a browser, such as Internet Explorer.

The steps on the next page preview the document in the browser and then save the Word document as an HTML file.

Q & A

Q: Will my Web page look exactly like my Word document?

A: It depends. Because Word provides formatting options that most Web browsers do not support, some text and graphics may look different when you view them on a Web page. When creating documents for the Web, using Web layout view will ensure that your graphics look the way you want them to when they are viewed as Web pages in a Web browser.

To Preview the Web Page

1

• **Click File on the menu bar and then click Web Page Preview. If your computer has Service Pack 2 of Windows XP installed, you may receive a security warning when viewing the page.**

2

• **If necessary, click the Maximize button on your browser's title bar.**

The browser displays the Web page (Figure 1-26).

3

• **Click the browser's Close button.**

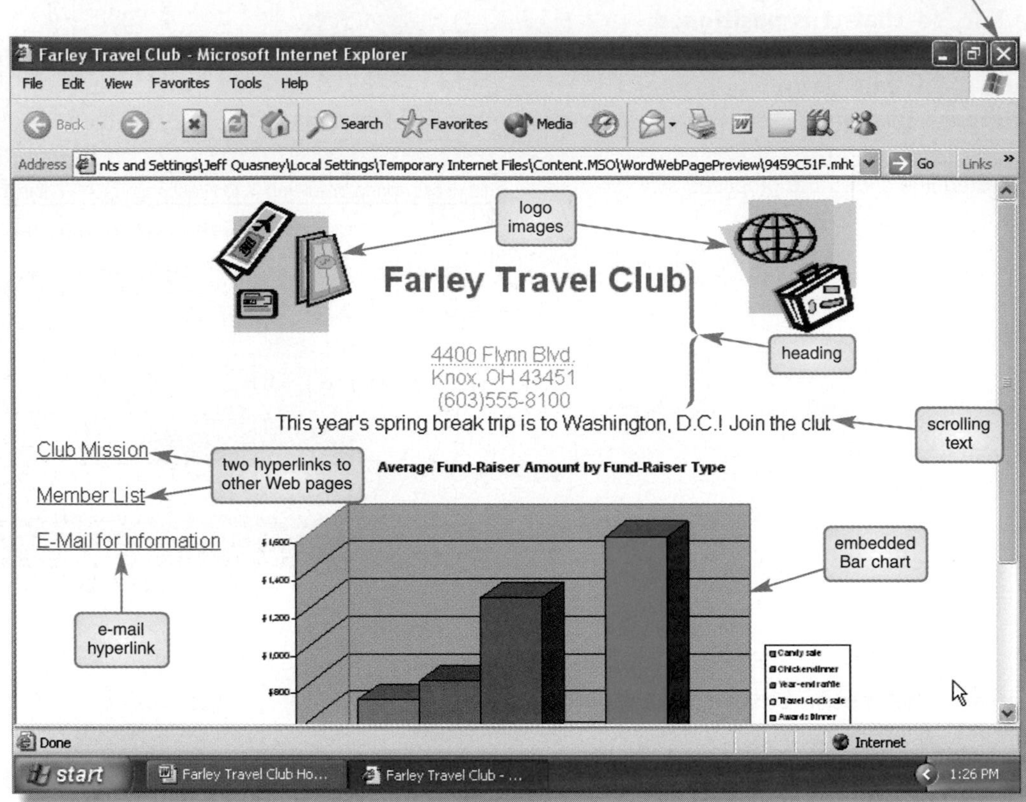

FIGURE 1-26

Skill Builder 1-2

To practice the following tasks, visit scsite.com/off2003sch/skill, locate Integration Project 1, and then click Skill Builder 1-2.

- ❑ Display the Web Tools toolbar
- ❑ Insert scrolling text into a Word document
- ❑ Resize scrolling text
- ❑ Preview a Web page in Word
- ❑ Save a Web page in Word

Verify that the Web page contains all information necessary and is displayed as shown in Figure 1-26. The Web page consists of a heading with images and the club name, address, and telephone number. Below that is a single line of scrolling text that scrolls in from the right margin and stops when it reaches the left margin. A borderless table displays three hyperlinks in the left column and a Bar chart in the right column. The E-Mail for Information hyperlink should work appropriately when you click it, displaying a new message. The other two links, Club Mission and Member List, do not work because the corresponding Web pages are not available until later in this project.

If the Web page is correct, save it on the USB flash drive as an HTML file. If changes need to be made to the Web page, return to the Word document and correct it. The following steps save the document as a Web page.

To Save a Document with a New File Name

1. **Click File on the menu bar and then click Save as Web Page. If the Microsoft Office Word dialog box displays, click the Continue button.**
2. **Type** `FarleyTravelHome` **in the File name text box.**
3. **Select Web Page in the Save as type box.**

4 **If necessary, click the Save in box arrow and then click UDISK (F:) in the Save in list. (Your USB flash drive may have a different name and letter.)**

5 **Click the Save button in the Save As dialog box. If the Microsoft Office Word dialog box displays, click the Continue button.**

Word displays the FarleyTravelHome Web page in the Word window (Figure 1-27).

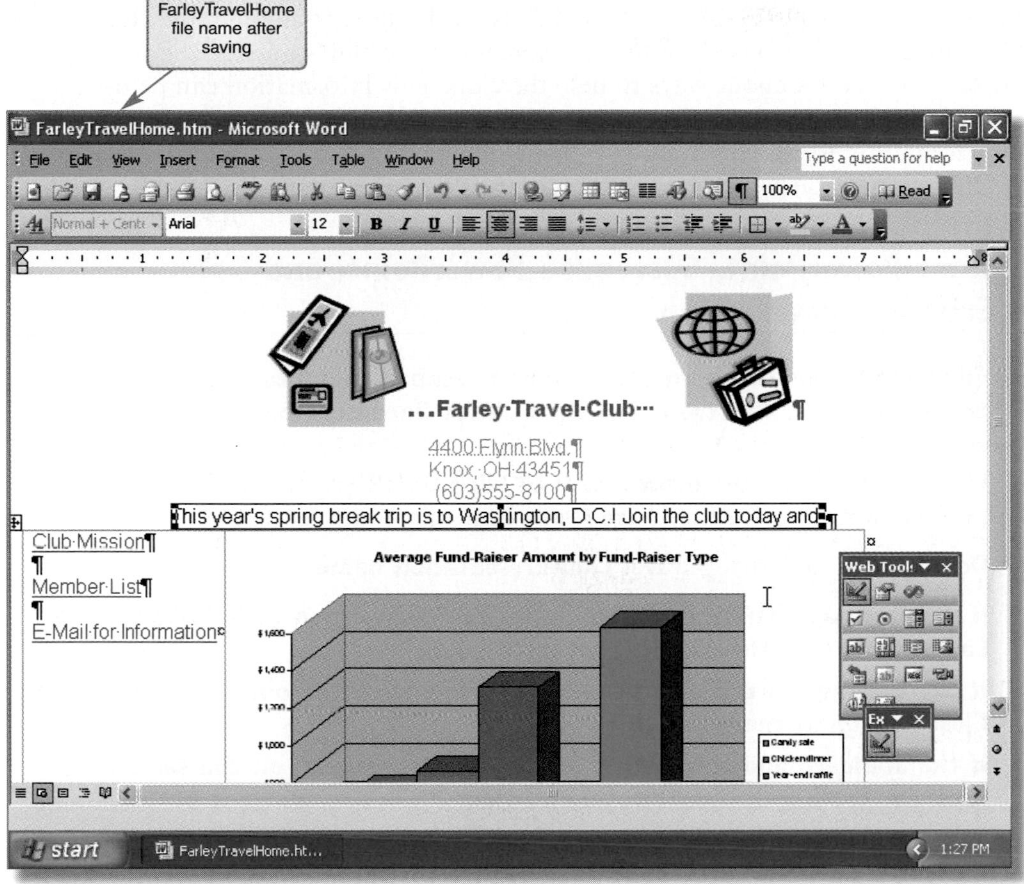

FIGURE 1-27

Saving an existing Word document as a Web page allows you quickly to get a Word document ready for copying to the Web or to an intranet. One alternative to this is to write the Hypertext Markup Language (HTML) to develop the Web pages. **HTML** is a programming language used for Web page creation. The home page created earlier in this project could be created by writing HTML tags (code). For documents that already are in Word format, the easier method is to use the Word Save as Web Page command. This essentially creates the HTML code for you and saves it in a file. The following step quits Word.

To Quit Word

1 **Click the Close button on the Microsoft Word title bar.**

The next step in creating the Web site for the Farley High School Travel Club is to save a PowerPoint presentation as an HTML file. The sections on the next pages describe how to open a PowerPoint presentation, add a hyperlink to the first page, and save the presentation as an HTML file.

Creating a PowerPoint Presentation Web Page

PowerPoint is a powerful software tool often used to assist in the presentation of information to groups of people. **PowerPoint 2003** allows you to create Web pages from an existing PowerPoint presentation, using the Save as Web Page command. The presentation then can be viewed using your browser.

The PowerPoint presentation used in this project consists of three slides (Figure 1-1g on page INT 7). The first slide is a title slide, containing the club's name and graphics. Slide 2 consists of information about the club's mission. Slide 3 includes information about ways to help the club. This information can be used in its present format to enhance a presentation about the club. As Web pages, you can use this presentation to address a much wider, global audience on the World Wide Web.

The following steps open an existing PowerPoint presentation.

To Start PowerPoint, Customize PowerPoint, and Open an Existing Presentation

1. **Click the Start button on the Windows taskbar, point to All Programs on the Start menu, and then click Open Office Document on the All Programs submenu.**
2. **Click the Look in box arrow and then click UDISK (F:) in the Look in list. (Your USB flash drive may have a different name and letter.)**
3. **Double-click the Farley Travel Club Presentation name.**
4. **If the Language bar is displayed, right-click it and then click Close the Language bar on the shortcut menu.**
5. **If the Getting Started task pane appears in the PowerPoint window, click its Close button in the upper-right corner.**
6. **If the Standard and Formatting toolbars are positioned on the same row, click the Toolbar Options button and then click Show Buttons on Two Rows.**

PowerPoint displays Slide 1 of the PowerPoint presentation (Figure 1-28).

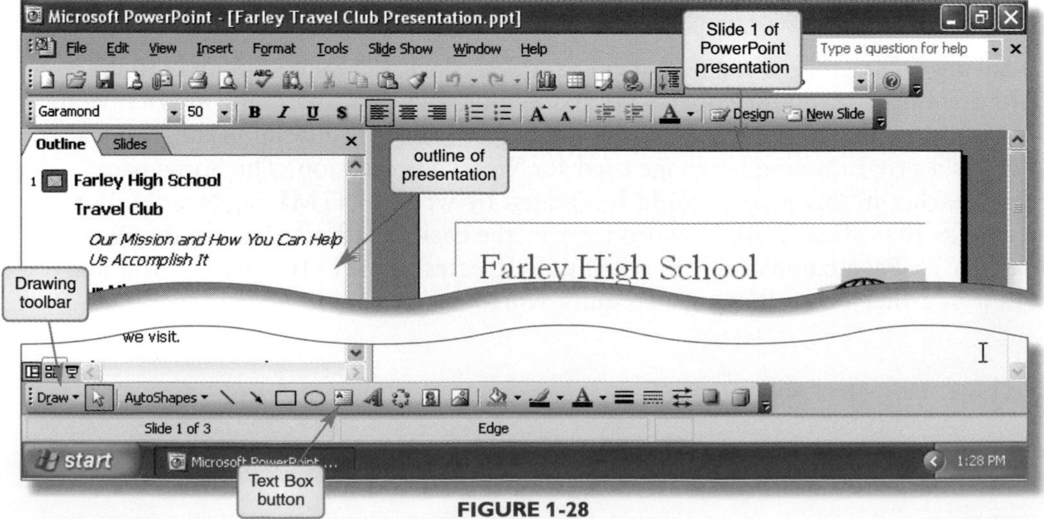

FIGURE 1-28

The PowerPoint presentation now is open. The next step is to add a hyperlink on Slide 1 that allows the Web page visitor to return to the Farley Travel Club home page.

Adding Text for a Hyperlink

One of the more important features of Web sites is their capability of linking from one Web page to another using hyperlinks. In earlier steps in this project, you added three hyperlinks to the Farley Travel Club home page. Once Web page visitors link to the PowerPoint Web pages, however, they cannot return to the home page without using the Back button on the browser's toolbar. This is not a convenient way for Web page visitors to navigate through the Web site. In this section, you will add a Home link to the first slide of the PowerPoint presentation (Figure 1-1g on page INT 7).

The following steps add the text that will be used as a hyperlink on the PowerPoint Web page.

Q & A

Q: What is a stale link?

A: When you create a Web page, it is important to make sure that all of your hyperlinks are functional as time goes on. Links to other pages can become stale, or nonfunctional, if another Web page creator or an external site takes a page offline. Automated tools can help you identify when pages to which you are hyperlinking no longer are available.

To Add Text for a Hyperlink into a PowerPoint Presentation

1. **Click the Text Box button on the Drawing toolbar.**
2. **Click in the lower-right corner of Slide 1.**
3. **Type** `Home` **as the hyperlink text.**

The text box is displayed with Home as the text for the hyperlink (Figure 1-29).

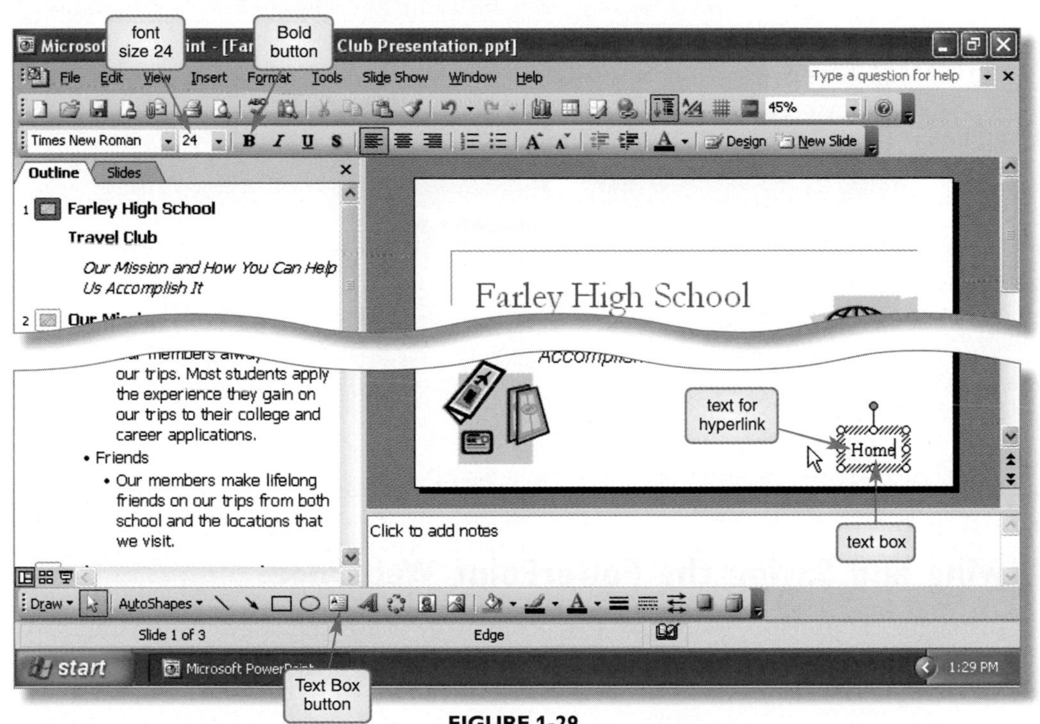

FIGURE 1-29

Creating a Hyperlink

After you enter the text for the hyperlink, you can create the hyperlink itself. When clicked, the hyperlink jumps to the Farley Travel Club home page created previously in this project and saved on the USB flash drive. To create the hyperlink, you will use the Insert Hyperlink button on the Standard toolbar.

The steps on the next page create the PowerPoint hyperlink.

To Insert a Hyperlink into a PowerPoint Presentation

1

- **Double-click the word, Home, inside the text box you just inserted.**

2

- **If necessary, click the Font Size box arrow on the Formatting toolbar and then click 24.**
- **Click the Bold button on the Formatting toolbar.**

3

- **Click the Insert Hyperlink button on the Standard toolbar.**

4

- **If necessary, click the Existing File or Web Page button on the Link to bar.**
- **Type** `f:\FarleyTravelHome.htm` **in the Address text box. Click the OK button.**

Slide 1 of the presentation is displayed as shown in Figure 1-30.

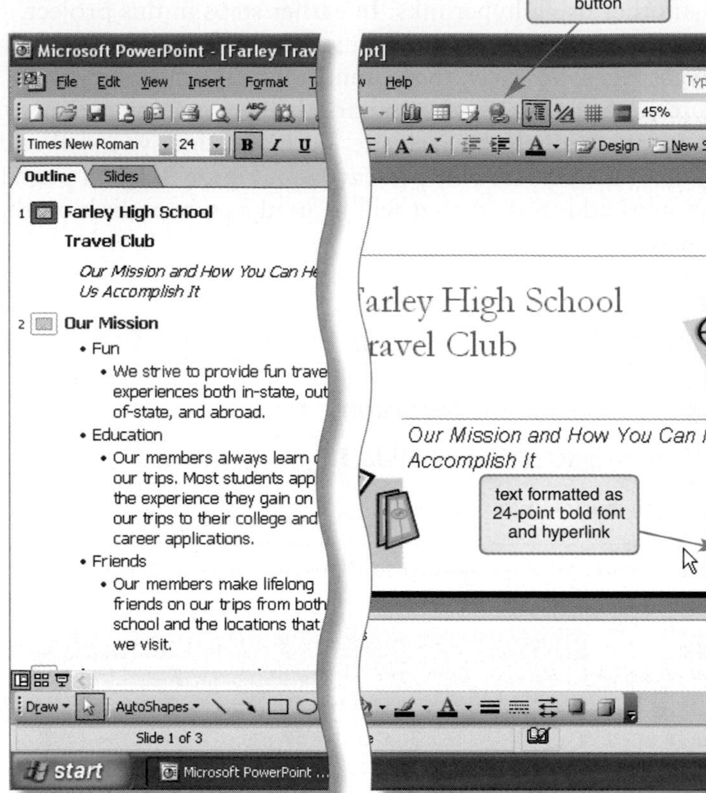

FIGURE 1-30

Viewing and Saving the PowerPoint Web Page

Just as in the previous section of this project, the following steps display the Web page before saving it. It is important to verify all of the Web page navigation features before saving the file.

To View the Web Page in Your Browser

1. **Click File on the menu bar.**
2. **Click Web Page Preview.**
3. **If necessary, click the Maximize button on your browser's title bar.**

The browser displays the PowerPoint Web page (Figure 1-31).

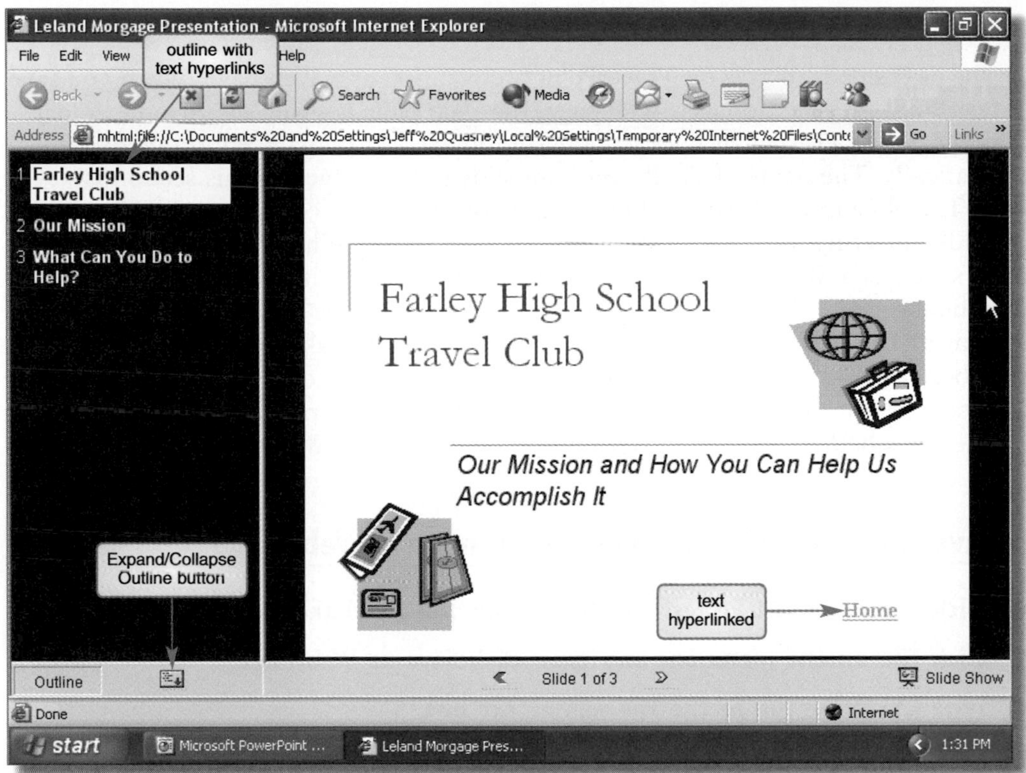

FIGURE 1-31

Slide 1 of the PowerPoint presentation Web page contains a hyperlink to the home page of the Farley Travel Club Web site. Although you created this hyperlink by adding a text box to the first slide, you also can create hyperlinks from existing text or images in a PowerPoint presentation. For example, one of the logo images on slide 1 could be used as a hyperlink to the home page of the Web site. Using one of those images, however, does not give the Web page visitor a clear idea of where the hyperlink will lead. It is more appropriate to create a hyperlink to the home page from text — for example, Home — that makes sense to the visitor.

In addition to any hyperlinks that are added to the presentation, PowerPoint automatically creates hyperlinks in the left column of the Web page, called the **outline**. Using the Expand/Collapse Outline button below the outline pane, you can expand or collapse the outline and navigate through the Web page presentation (Figure 1-31). The text in the heading of each slide is used as the phrases for these hyperlinks. When you click a link, you jump to that particular slide within the presentation. The ease of navigation within a PowerPoint Web page is valuable to the Web page visitor.

As well as being able to add your own hyperlink text, PowerPoint provides some ready-made action buttons that you can insert into your Web pages. **Action buttons** contain shapes, such as left and right arrows, that can be used to hyperlink to other Web pages within the presentation. You can insert symbols on the action buttons for going to the next (right arrow), previous (left arrow), first (beginning arrow), and last (end arrow) slides. PowerPoint also includes action buttons for playing movies or sounds. You insert these action buttons using the slide master feature of PowerPoint.

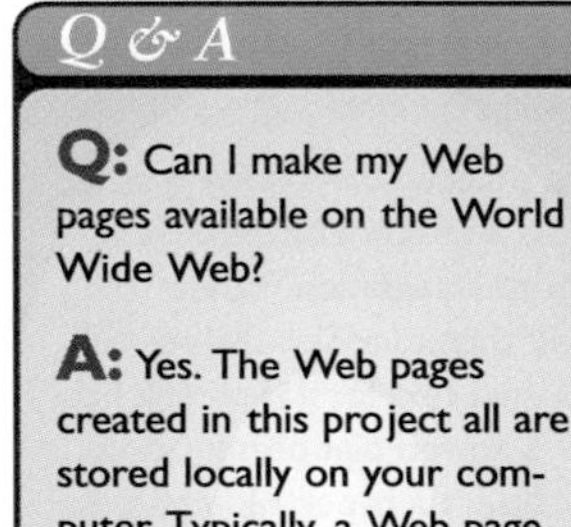

Q & A

Q: Can I make my Web pages available on the World Wide Web?

A: Yes. The Web pages created in this project all are stored locally on your computer. Typically, a Web page must be published to a server inside the organization or at your ISP. Microsoft offers a Web Page Publishing Wizard to assist in moving all of the related files and directories that comprise a Web site.

Saving the PowerPoint Presentation as a Web Page

The next step is to save the PowerPoint presentation as a Web page. When you save a PowerPoint presentation as a Web page, the Web page is saved in a default folder. All supporting files, such as backgrounds and images, are organized in this folder automatically. The name of the PowerPoint slide show opened in this section is Farley Travel Club Presentation. PowerPoint uses the name of the saved Web page and adds the string, files, for the name of the new folder. When the current presentation is saved as a Web page, the folder name that PowerPoint Web creates is ClubMission_files. The default name for the first slide in the presentation is frame.htm. The structure used in the folder organization makes Web page publishing easier because you can keep track of all of the files associated with the Web page. You also can edit the files manually, rather than using PowerPoint.

The steps below save the PowerPoint presentation as a Web page.

Q & A

Q: Can I hide the outline pane when viewing the presentation in a browser?

A: Yes. The outline pane is displayed by default when you view a presentation in a browser. To hide this pane, click the Outline button while in the browser. Click the Outline button again to redisplay the outline pane.

To Save the PowerPoint Presentation as a Web Page

1. **Click the Microsoft PowerPoint button on the taskbar.**
2. **Click File on the menu bar and then click Save as Web Page.**
3. **Type** `ClubMission` **in the File name text box.**
4. **Select Web Page in the Save as type box.**
5. **If necessary, click the Save in box arrow and then click UDISK (F:) in the Save in list. (Your USB flash drive may have a different name and letter.)**
6. **Click the Save button in the Save As dialog box.**

The PowerPoint presentation is saved as a Web page.

The task of saving the PowerPoint presentation as a Web page is complete. The hyperlink has been added to Slide 1 of the presentation that jumps to the Web site home page when clicked. Standard Web page navigation was added automatically to the presentation that allows the Web page visitor to jump to any slide in the Web page presentation. All of the files necessary for the Web page were saved in a folder named ClubMission_files.

After saving the PowerPoint presentation as a Web page, you can quit PowerPoint and close your browser, as shown in the following steps.

Skill Builder 1-3

To practice the following tasks, visit scsite.com/off2003sch/skill, locate Integration Project 1, and then click Skill Builder 1-3.

- ❑ Add text for a hyperlink into a PowerPoint presentation
- ❑ Insert a hyperlink into a PowerPoint presentation
- ❑ View a PowerPoint Web page in your browser
- ❑ Save a PowerPoint presentation as a Web page

To Quit PowerPoint and Close Your Browser

1. **Click the Close button on the PowerPoint title bar.**
2. **Click the Close button on the browser title bar.**

Creating a Data Access Page from an Access Database

The next step in the Farley High School Travel Club Web site creation is to use an Access database to create a data access page. A **data access page** is a special type of Web page that is designed for viewing and working with data. Similar to a form, a data access page is connected, or bound, directly to an Access database.

You can use data access pages to analyze data, enter and edit data, make projections, and review data. In addition, you can create a chart using the chart component to analyze trends, show patterns, and make comparisons on the data in the database. Then, you can add spreadsheet controls to allow the inclusion of formulas for calculations.

One of the more common purposes of data access pages is for viewing records in a database via a company's intranet or the World Wide Web. Data access pages provide a method to make inquiries of large amounts of data in a selective way. Groups of records can be expanded or collapsed so that Web page visitors can view the data they want to see.

The following steps open an Access database.

To Start Access and Open an Existing Database

1. **Click the Start button on the Windows taskbar, point to All Programs on the Start menu, and then click Open Office Document on the All Programs submenu.**
2. **If necessary, click the Look in box arrow and then click UDISK (F:) in the Look in list. (Your USB flash drive may have a different name and letter.)**
3. **Double-click the Farley Travel Club Member List database name. If the Microsoft Office Access dialog box appears, click the Yes button.**
4. **If the Language bar is displayed, right-click it and then click Close the Language bar on the shortcut menu.**
5. **If the Getting Started task pane appears in the Access window, click its Close button in the upper-right corner.**

Access starts and opens the Farley Travel Club Member List : Database window (Figure 1-32).

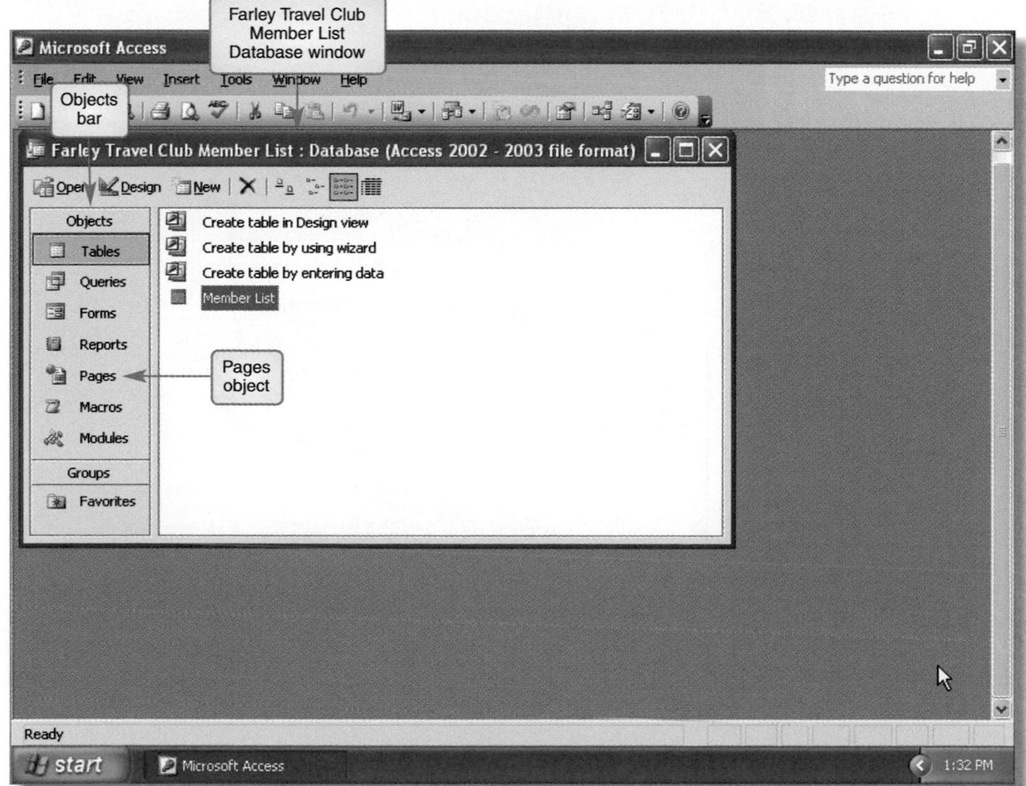

FIGURE 1-32

Creating a Data Access Page Using the Page Wizard

For the Farley High School Travel Club Web site, you do not want the database to be altered by the Web page visitor in any way. The visitors should be allowed to view only the data. Because of this, you must add a grouping level to the data access page. Adding **grouping levels** results in a read-only page. The Web page visitors can view all data and alter that view, but they cannot change the data itself.

The following steps use the Page Wizard to create a data access page.

To Create a Data Access Page Using the Page Wizard

1

• **Click the Pages object on the Objects bar.**

2

• **Double-click Create data access page by using wizard.**

Access displays the Page Wizard dialog box that includes options for setting up data access pages (Figure 1-33). The Member List table is selected automatically because it is the only table in the database. If more than one table exists, you would need to click the Tables object on the Objects bar and then select the appropriate table before clicking the Pages object in Step 1.

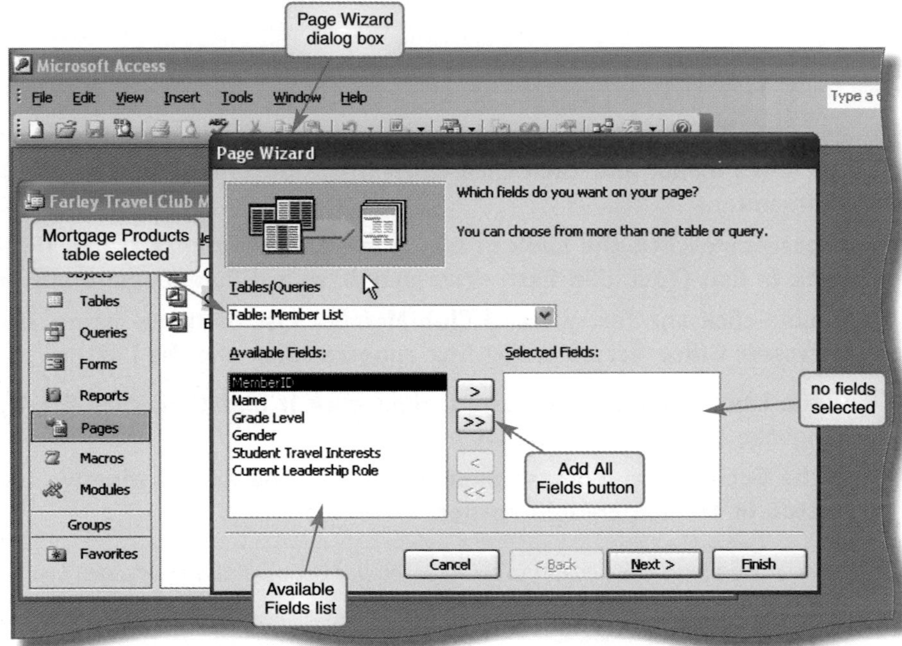

FIGURE 1-33

3

• **Click the Add All Fields button to add all the fields.**

The Selected Fields list displays all the fields in the table (Figure 1-34). This means you want to display all the fields on the data access page.

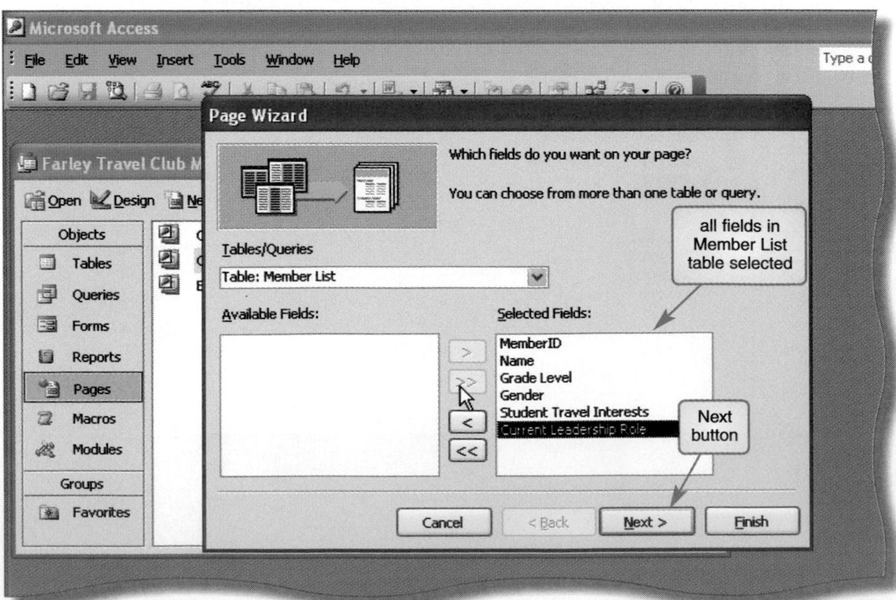

FIGURE 1-34

4

- **Click the Next button.**
- **Double-click Grade Level in the box on the left.**

Adding a grouping level, such as Grade Level, prohibits the data access page from being updated. Grade Level is displayed in the upper-right box, indicating it has been selected (Figure 1-35).

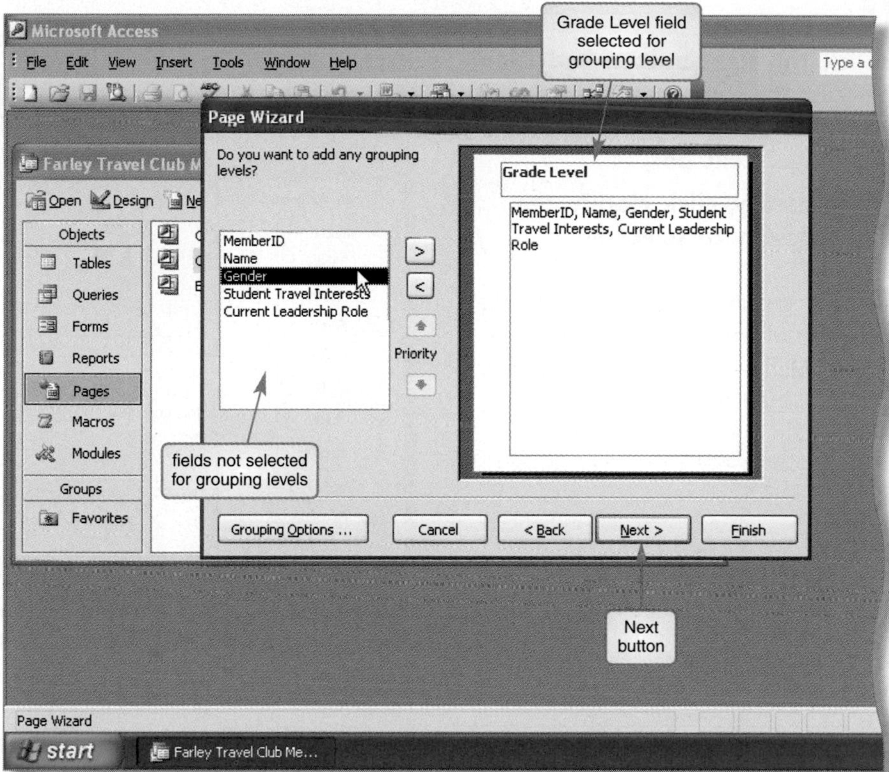

FIGURE 1-35

5

- **Click the Next button.**

The Page Wizard dialog box displays options for sorting records (Figure 1-36). No changes are required.

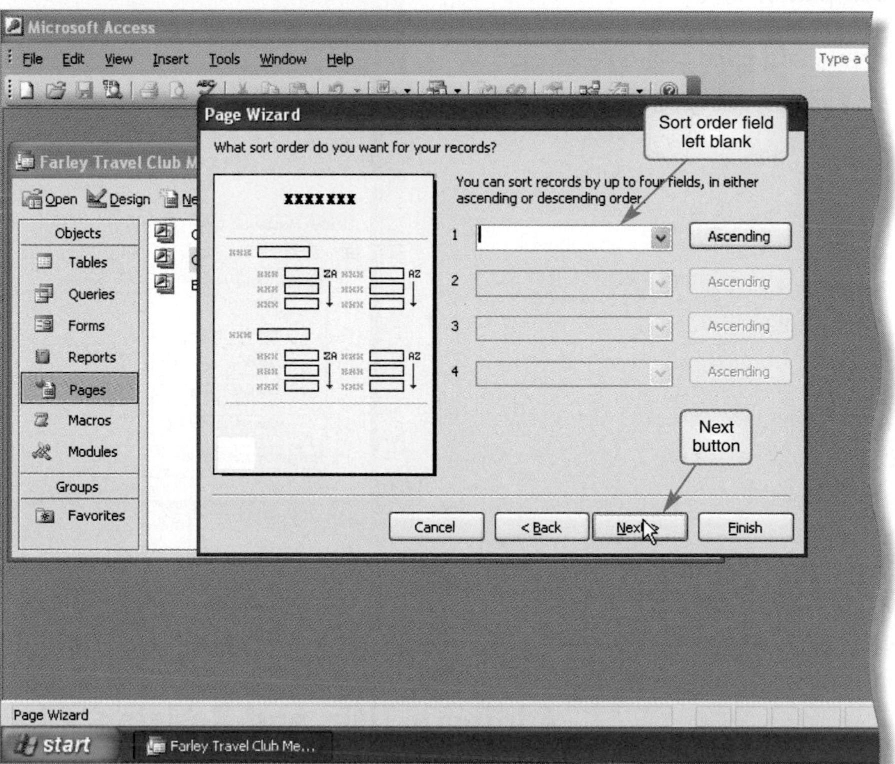

FIGURE 1-36

6

- **Click the Next button and then, if necessary, type** `Member List` **in the What title do you want for your page? text box.**
- **If necessary, click Modify the page's design to select it.**

The Page Wizard dialog box displays the page title, Member List, in the text box, and the Modify the page's design option button selected (Figure 1-37).

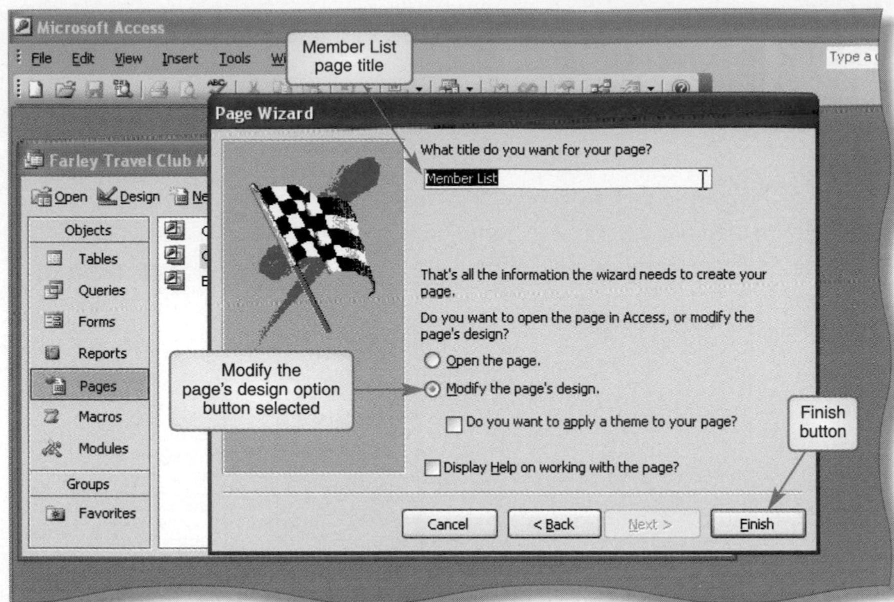

FIGURE 1-37

7

- **Click the Finish button.**
- **If necessary, close the Field List task pane.**

Access displays the data access page in Design view (Figure 1-38).

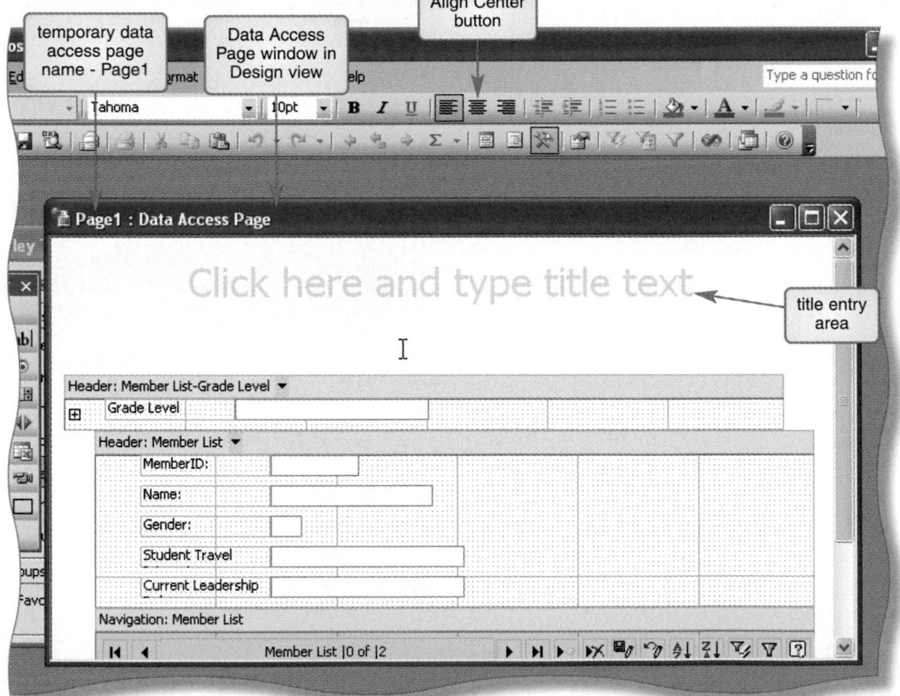

FIGURE 1-38

Adding a Title and Resizing a Label on a Data Access Page

The data access page is created, but additional information can be helpful for the Web page visitor. It is customary to insert a title at the top of the page that tells the visitor the purpose of the Web page. Resizing the Student Travel Interests label and the Current Leadership Role label is necessary because the entire text of these labels does not show after completing the Data Access Page Wizard. The following steps add a title and resize two labels.

To Add a Title and Resize Labels on a Data Access Page

1

- **If necessary, scroll to the top of the data access page.**
- **With the data access page in Design view, click anywhere in the Click here and type title text entry area.**
- **Type** `Farley Travel Club Member List` **as the title.**

Access displays the data access page as shown in Figure 1-39.

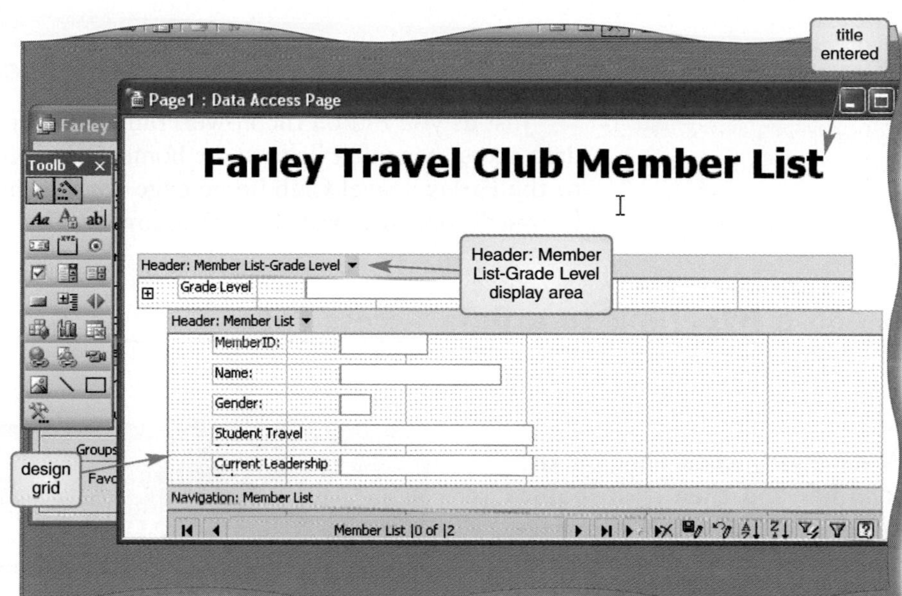

FIGURE 1-39

2

- **Click anywhere within the Student Travel Interests label in the Member List area of the data access page to select the label.**
- **Point to the lower-right sizing handle on the label.**

3

- **Drag the sizing handle straight down and to the left so that it doubles in height and the word Interests appears below the word Student.**

4

- **Click anywhere within the Current Leadership Role label in the Member List area of the data access page to select the label.**
- **Point to the lower-right sizing handle on the label.**

5

- **Drag the sizing handle straight down and to the left so that it doubles in height and the word Role appears below the word Current.**

The Student Travel Interests label and the Current Leadership Role label are resized, and Access displays the data access page as shown in Figure 1-40.

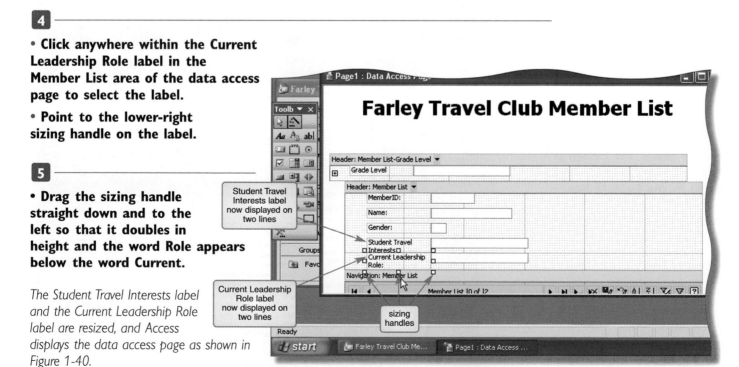

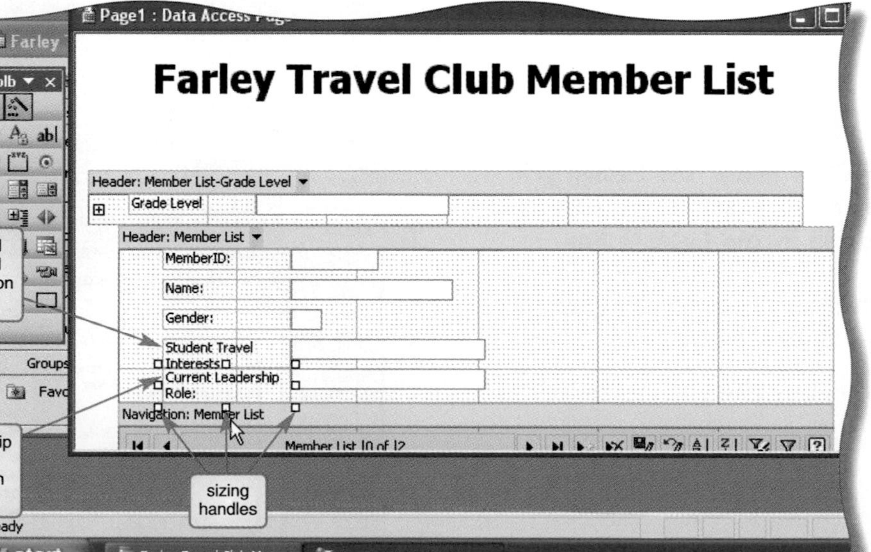

FIGURE 1-40

The data access page is created, a heading is positioned in the header, and the labels are resized as shown in Figure 1-1d on page INT 6. The next step is to add a hyperlink that returns the visitor to the Web site home page.

Adding a Hyperlink to a Data Access Page

Just as you did on the PowerPoint Web page, you should add a hyperlink on the data access page that links to the home page. This allows the Web page visitor to return to the Farley Travel Club home page without having to click the Back button on the browser's toolbar repeatedly. The following steps add a hyperlink to the data access page.

To Add a Hyperlink to a Data Access Page

1

- **If necessary, click View on the menu bar and then click Toolbox to display the Toolbox. If necessary, scroll down so the bottom of the data access page displays.**
- **Click the Hyperlink button on the Toolbox and then point below the design grid.**

The hyperlink mouse pointer is displayed as shown in Figure 1-41.

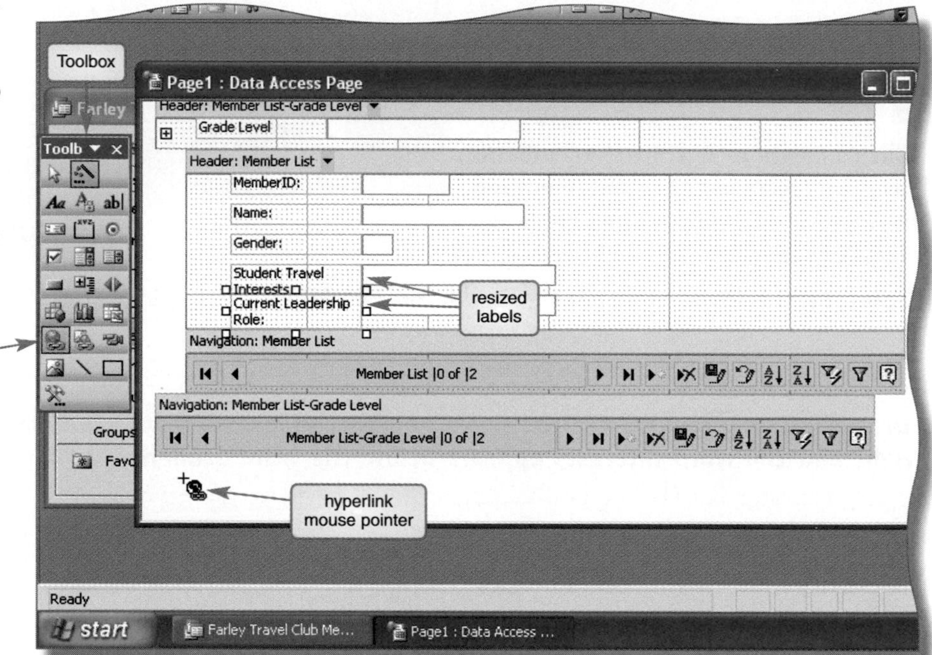

FIGURE 1-41

2

- **Click below the Design grid. If necessary, select the USB flash drive in the Look in box.**

The Insert Hyperlink dialog box is displayed (Figure 1-42).

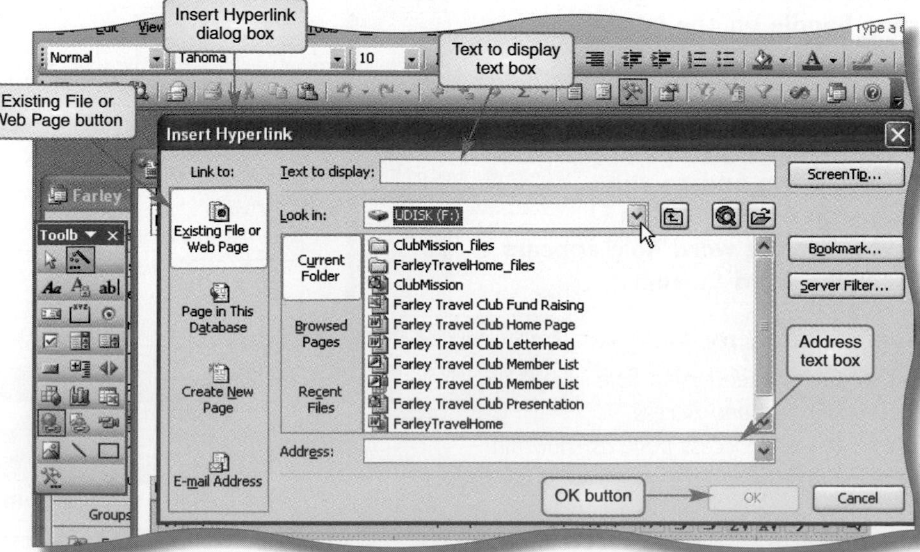

FIGURE 1-42

3

- **If necessary, click the Existing File or Web Page button on the Link to bar.**
- **Type** `Home` **in the Text to display text box.**
- **Type** `FarleyTravelHome.htm` **in the Address text box and then click the OK button.**
- **If the Microsoft Office Access dialog box appears, click the OK button.**

4

- **Click anywhere on the data access page to deselect the hyperlink box.**

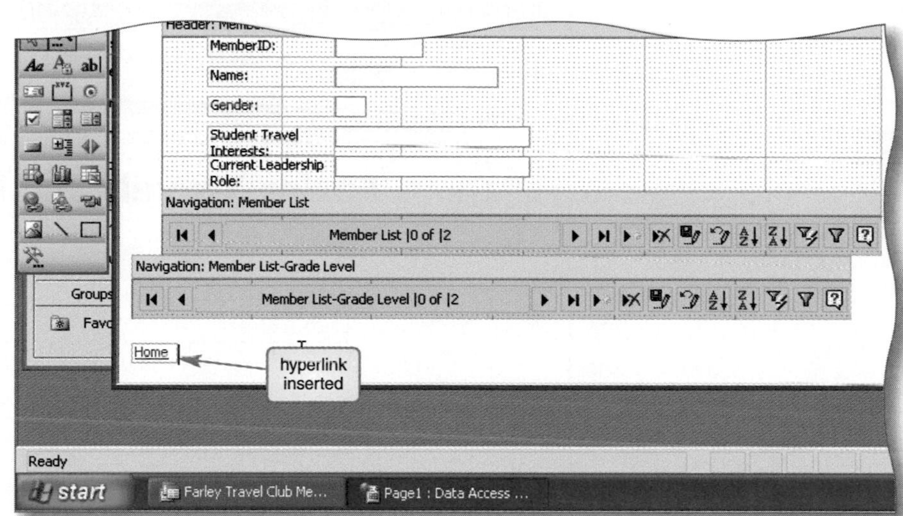

FIGURE 1-43

Access displays the data access page as shown in Figure 1-43.

The data access page is complete. In the next section, you will save the page to the USB flash drive and view it in the browser.

Saving the Data Access Page and Viewing It

In other sections of this project, you have viewed the Web page, verified that it is correct, and then saved it on a USB flash drive. Unlike Word and PowerPoint, you must save a data access page before you can preview it in your browser. As the Web page is being opened in your browser, Access displays a Databinding message on the status bar of your browser. This indicates that the data access page is connecting to the database that was open when the page was created (Farley Travel Club Member List).

The following steps save the file on the USB flash drive and then open it for viewing in the browser.

> ***Skill Builder 1-4***
>
> To practice the following tasks, visit scsite.com/off2003sch/skill, locate Integration Project 1, and then click Skill Builder 1-4.
> - ❑ Create a data access page using the Page Wizard
> - ❑ Add a title and resize labels on a data access page
> - ❑ Add a hyperlink to a data access page
> - ❑ Save a data access page and view it in your browser

To Save the Data Access Page and View It in Your Browser

1. **Click File on the menu bar and then click Web Page Preview. When the Microsoft Office Access dialog box displays, click the Yes button.**
2. **When the Save As Data Access Page dialog box displays, if necessary, type** `FarleyTravelMemberList` **in the File name text box. If necessary, click UDISK (F:) in the Save in list. (Your USB flash drive may have a different name and letter.)**
3. **Click the Save button in the Save As Data Access Page dialog box. If your computer has Service Pack 2 for Windows XP installed, you may receive a security warning when viewing the page. If the warning appears, click OK to close the dialog box.**
4. **Click the Expand indicator to the left of the Grade Level label to expand the display.**

The browser displays the expanded data access page (Figure 1-44 on the next page).

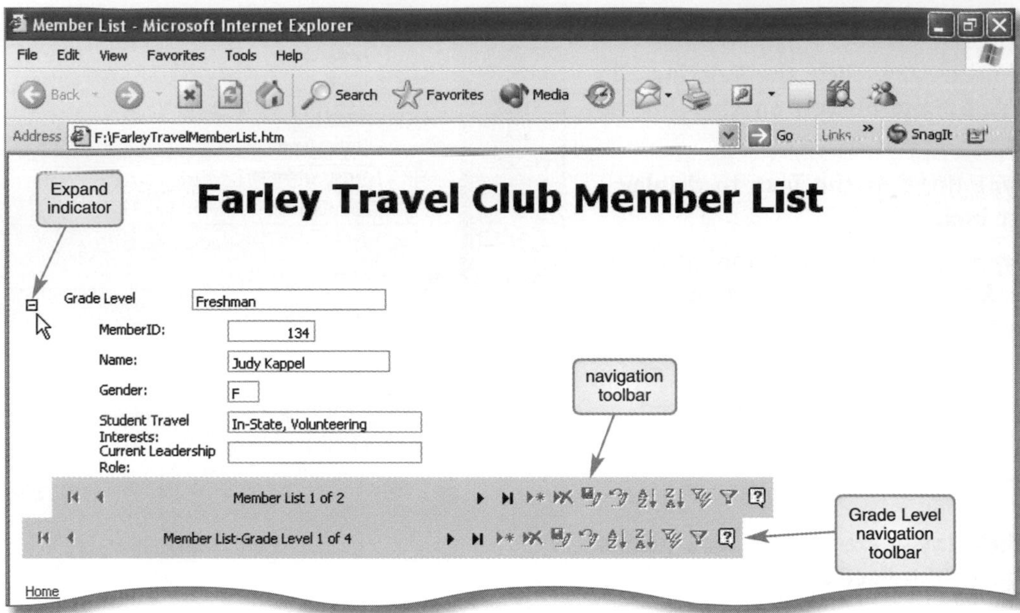

FIGURE 1-44

After you preview the data access page, you then quit Access and close your browser, as shown in the following steps.

To Close Your Browser and Quit Access

1 **Right-click the Member List - Microsoft Explorer button on the taskbar and then click Close on the shortcut menu.**

2 **Click the Close button on the Access title bar to quit Access.**

Q & A

Q: What is the Microsoft Office Specialist Certification program?

A: The Microsoft Office Specialist Certification program provides an opportunity for you to obtain a valuable industry credential — proof that you have the Office 2003 skills required by employers. For more information, see Appendix E, or visit the Office 2003 Certification Web page (scsite.com/off2003sch/cert).

Grouping records on a data access page is similar to grouping records on a report. You can group the data on this data access page in different ways, but the user cannot edit the data. The records in the data access page can be expanded or collapsed, using the **Expand and Collapse indicators**. This allows users to customize their view of the data and remove extra data from view that may not interest them. Using the **navigation toolbars** on the data access page, you can move, sort, and filter records and obtain Help.

Use the navigation toolbar to verify that the information in the database displays correctly. Click the link to the home page of the Web site to verify it.

Testing the Web Site

The Farley High School Travel Club site is complete. To ensure that all the links in the Web site are viable, the following steps open the home page and then thoroughly test the entire Web site.

To Test the Web Site

1 **Start your browser.**

2 **Click the Address bar of your browser.**

3 **Type** f:\FarleyTravelHome.htm **in the text box, and then press the ENTER key.**

The browser displays the home page of the Farley Travel Club Web site as shown in Figure 1-45.

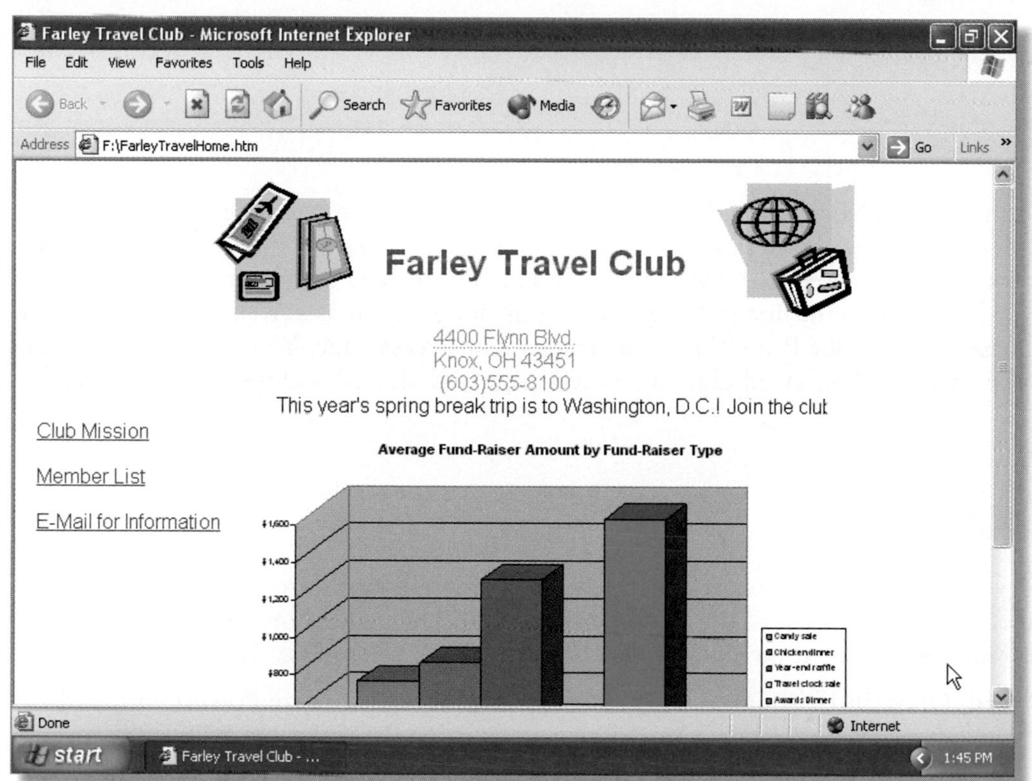

FIGURE 1-45

Verifying the Hyperlinks in Your Browser

All hyperlinks should be tested by clicking them and verifying that they jump to the correct Web page. Three hyperlinks are on the home page: Club Mission, Member List, and E-Mail for Information. The following steps test the links.

To Verify the Hyperlinks

1 **Click the Club Mission hyperlink.**

2 **Click the navigation buttons to view all slides on the Web page.**

3 **On the first slide on the PowerPoint Web page, click the Home hyperlink.**

4 **Click the Member List hyperlink. Click the Expand and Collapse indicators and then scroll through the database using the navigation toolbars.**

5 **On the data access page, click the Home hyperlink.**

6 **Click the E-Mail for Information hyperlink.**

A new e-mail message displays with travelclub@farleyhsus.edu in the To text box.

With the hyperlinks verified, the steps on the next page quit the e-mail program and the browser.

To Quit E-Mail and Close Your Browser

1. **Click the Close button on your e-mail program. Click No if asked to save changes.**
2. **Click the Close button on your browser's title bar.**

Project Summary

This project introduced you to integrating Microsoft Office 2003 applications. You opened an existing Word document and created a two-column, one-row, borderless table. You then inserted three hyperlinks, embedded a Bar chart from an existing Excel worksheet, and saved that document as an HTML file. You then opened an existing PowerPoint presentation, added a hyperlink to the first slide, and saved this presentation as a Web page. Finally, you opened an existing Access database and used the Page Wizard to create a data access page. You created a grouping level so the database could not be changed. You saved that data access page and viewed and tested all Web pages and hyperlinks.

What You Should Know

Having completed this project, you should be able to perform the tasks below. The tasks are listed in the same order they were presented in this project. For a list of the buttons, menus, toolbars, and commands introduced in this project, see the Quick Reference Summary at the back of this book and refer to the Page Number column.

1. Start Word, Customize Word, Open an Existing Document, and Save the Document with Another Name (INT 8)
2. Insert a Table into a Word Document (INT 9)
3. Remove the Table Border (INT 11)
4. Insert Text for Hyperlinks (INT 12)
5. Create a Hyperlink to PowerPoint Web Pages (INT 13)
6. Insert the Remaining Hyperlinks (INT 13)
7. Start Excel, Customize Excel, and Open an Existing Workbook (INT 14)
8. Embed an Excel Chart into a Word Document (INT 15)
9. Change the Size of an Embedded Object (INT 17)
10. Quit Excel (INT 19)
11. Display the Web Tools Toolbar (INT 20)
12. Insert Scrolling Text into a Word Document (INT 21)
13. Resize the Scrolling Text (INT 22)
14. Preview the Web Page (INT 24)
15. Save a Document with a New File Name (INT 24)
16. Quit Word (INT 25)
17. Start PowerPoint, Customize PowerPoint, and Open an Existing Presentation (INT 26)
18. Add Text for a Hyperlink into a PowerPoint Presentation (INT 27)
19. Insert a Hyperlink into a PowerPoint Presentation (INT 28)
20. View the Web Page in Your Browser (INT 28)
21. Save the PowerPoint Presentation as a Web Page (INT 30)
22. Quit PowerPoint and Close Your Browser (INT 30)
23. Start Access and Open an Existing Database (INT 31)
24. Create a Data Access Page Using the Page Wizard (INT 32)
25. Add a Title and Resize Labels on a Data Access Page (INT 35)
26. Add a Hyperlink to a Data Access Page (INT 36)
27. Save the Data Access Page and View It in Your Browser (INT 37)
28. Close Your Browser and Quit Access (INT 38)
29. Test the Web Site (INT 38)
30. Verify the Hyperlinks (INT 39)
31. Quit E-Mail and Close Your Browser (INT 40)

Learn It Online

Instructions: To complete the Learn It Online exercises, start your browser, click the Address bar, and then enter the Web address `scsite.com/off2003sch/learn`. When the Office 2003 Learn It Online page is displayed, follow the instructions in the exercises below. Each exercise has instructions for printing your results, either for your own records or for submission to your instructor.

1 Project Reinforcement TF, MC, and SA

Below Office Integration Project 1, click the Project Reinforcement link. Print the quiz by clicking Print on the File menu for each page. Answer each question.

2 Flash Cards

Below Office Integration Project 1, click the Flash Cards link and read the instructions. Type 20 (or a number specified by your instructor) in the Number of playing cards text box, type your name in the Enter your Name text box, and then click the Flip Card button. When the flash card is displayed, read the question and then click the ANSWER box arrow to select an answer. Flip through Flash Cards. If your score is 15 (75%) correct or greater, click Print on the File menu to print your results. If your score is less than 15 (75%) correct, then redo this exercise by clicking the Replay button.

3 Practice Test

Below Office Integration Project 1, click the Practice Test link. Answer each question, enter your first and last name at the bottom of the page, and then click the Grade Test button. When the graded practice test is displayed on your screen, click Print on the File menu to print a hard copy. Continue to take practice tests until you score 80% or better.

4 Who Wants To Be a Computer Genius?

Below Office Integration Project 1, click the Computer Genius link. Read the instructions, enter your first and last name at the bottom of the page, and then click the PLAY button. When your score is displayed, click the PRINT RESULTS link to print a hard copy.

5 Wheel of Terms

Below Office Integration Project 1, click the Wheel of Terms link. Read the instructions, and then enter your first and last name and your school name. Click the PLAY button. When your score is displayed, right-click the score and then click Print on the shortcut menu to print a hard copy.

6 Crossword Puzzle Challenge

Below Office Integration Project 1, click the Crossword Puzzle Challenge link. Read the instructions, and then enter your first and last name. Click the SUBMIT button. Work the crossword puzzle. When you are finished, click the Submit button. When the crossword puzzle is redisplayed, click the Print Puzzle button to print a hard copy.

7 Tips and Tricks

Below Office Integration Project 1, click the Tips and Tricks link. Click a topic that pertains to Project 1. Right-click the information and then click Print on the shortcut menu. Construct a brief example of what the information relates to in Office Integration to confirm you understand how to use the tip or trick.

8 Newsgroups

Below Office Integration Project 1, click the Newsgroups link. Click a topic that pertains to Project 1. Print three comments.

9 Expanding Your Horizons

Below Office Integration Project 1, click the Expanding Your Horizons link. Click a topic that pertains to Project 1. Print the information. Construct a brief example of what the information relates to in Office Integration to confirm you understand the contents of the article.

10 Search Sleuth

Below Office Integration Project 1, click the Search Sleuth link. To search for a term that pertains to this project, select a term below the Project 1 title and then use the Google search engine at google.com (or any major search engine) to display and print two Web pages that present information on the term.

11 Office Integration Online Training

Below Office Integration Project 1, click the Office Integration Online Training link. When your browser displays the Microsoft Office Online Web page, click the Office Integration link. Click one of the Office Integration courses that covers one or more of the objectives listed at the beginning of the project on page INT 4. Print the first page of the course before stepping through it.

12 Office Marketplace

Below Office Integration Project 1, click the Office Marketplace link. When your browser displays the Microsoft Office Online Web page, click the Office Marketplace link. Click a topic that relates to Office Integration. Print the first page.

13 You're Hired!

Below Office Integration Project 1, click the You're Hired! link to embark on the path to a career in computers. Directions about how to play the game will be displayed. When you are ready to play, click the begin the game button. If required, submit your score to your instructor.

1 Creating a Web Page in Word with an Embedded Excel Chart

Problem: As an employee of CreatiMusic, a local music publisher, you have created a worksheet and chart in Excel to analyze the sales for the past year. Create a Web page in Word and embed the chart from the CreatiMusic workbook on the home page. Add a link to a second Web page and an e-mail link to creatimusic@isp.com below the chart. Create a second Web page in Word by embedding the CreatiMusic worksheet.

Instructions: Perform the following tasks.

1. Start Excel by opening the Lab 1-1 CreatiMusic workbook.
2. Start Word and create a new Web page. Add a title as shown in Figure 1-46. Select the CreatiMusic chart in Excel, copy it, and use the Paste Special command in Word to embed the Excel Chart Object. Resize the chart to 84% of its original size. Center the chart on the Web page.

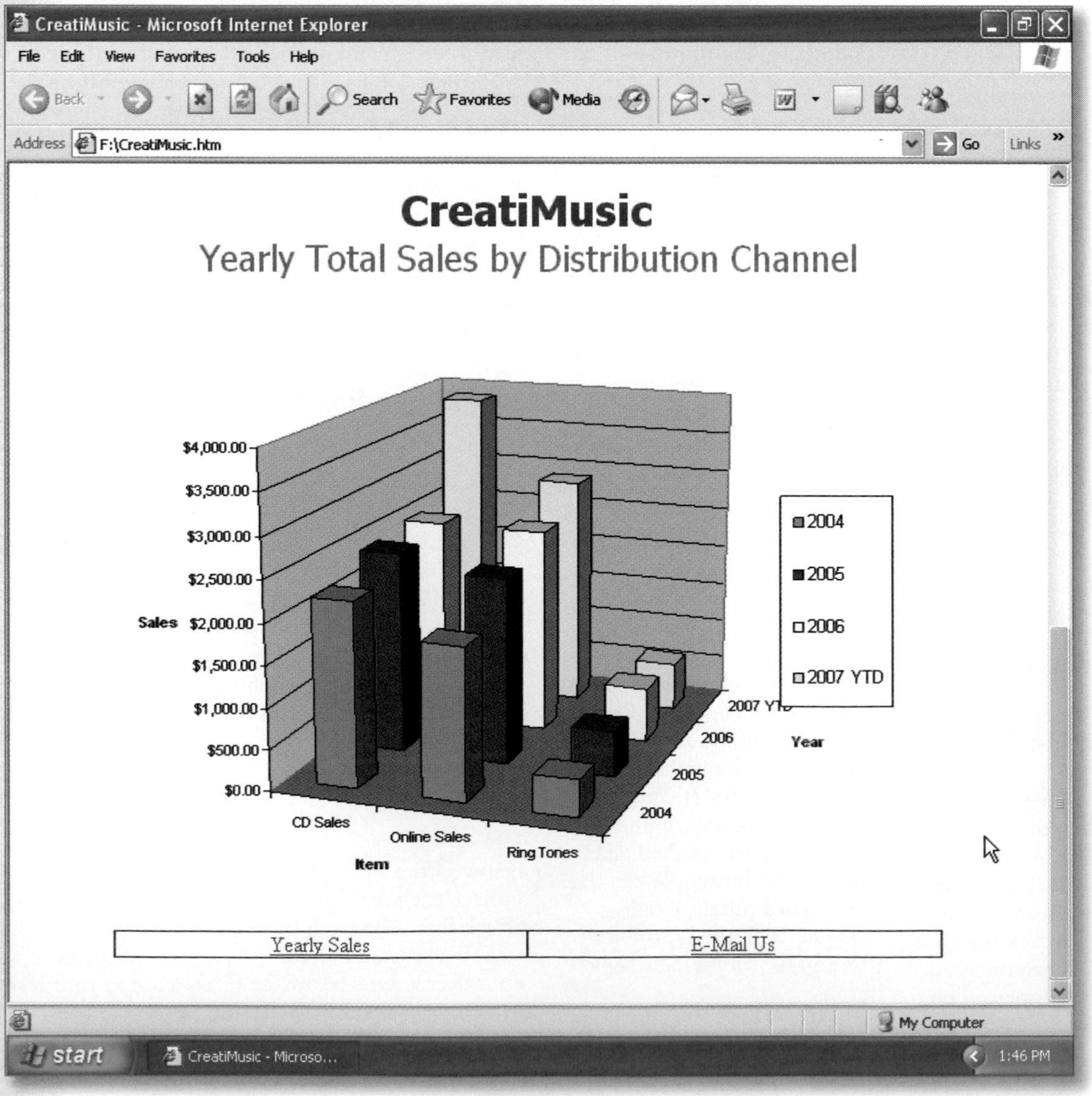

FIGURE 1-46

3. Add two hyperlinks to the bottom of the page in a centered table. The first hyperlink should jump to the Web page CreatiMusicSales.htm, which is created next. The second hyperlink creates an e-mail message to creatimusic@isp.com with the subject About Our Company.
4. Save this file as CreatiMusic.htm.
5. Create a new Web page in Word.
6. Embed the Excel worksheet into the Word page. That is, switch to Excel, select the CreatiMusic worksheet, copy the worksheet to the Clipboard, switch to Word, and use the Paste Special command on the Edit menu in Word to embed the Excel Worksheet Object.
7. Save this file as CreatiMusicSales.htm.
8. View the CreatiMusic.htm file in your browser (Figure 1-46). Print the Web page. Click the Yearly Sales link to navigate to the CreatiMusicSales.htm page (Figure 1-47) and print it.

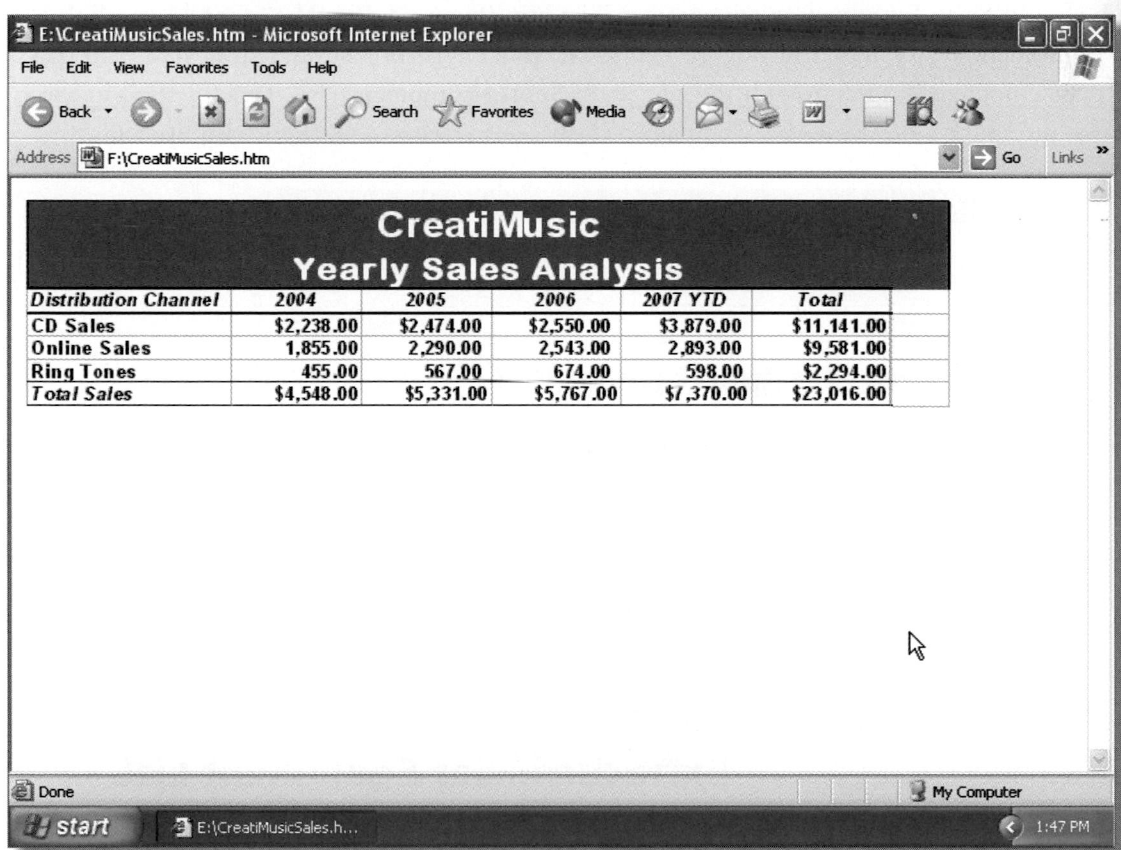

Distribution Channel	2004	2005	2006	2007 YTD	Total
CD Sales	$2,238.00	$2,474.00	$2,550.00	$3,879.00	$11,141.00
Online Sales	1,855.00	2,290.00	2,543.00	2,893.00	$9,581.00
Ring Tones	455.00	567.00	674.00	598.00	$2,294.00
Total Sales	$4,548.00	$5,331.00	$5,767.00	$7,370.00	$23,016.00

FIGURE 1-47

2 Extracurricular Sports Equipment Web Site with a Data Access Page and an Excel Worksheet

Problem: As the student manager of your school's extracurricular sports program, Allison Seidel is responsible for keeping track of sports equipment that is used by student groups on a per-day basis. She would like you to design a Web site that allows students to view the availability of equipment for use. She also wants an e-mail link for questions.

Instructions: Perform the following tasks.

1. Start Word. Create a home page for the Extracurricular Sports Equipment Web site (Figure 1-48). Add a title and a borderless, two-column table below the title. In the left column, insert three hyperlinks. The first hyperlink should go to ExtracurricularEquipmentList.htm (Figure 1-49). The second hyperlink should go to Lab 1-2 EquipmentAvailability.htm (Figure 1-50). The third hyperlink should start an e-mail message to extracurricularmanager@isp.com with the subject of Sports Equipment Use. Type the text in the right column shown in Figure 1-48. Save the Web page as Lab 1-2 ExtracurricularSportsEquipment.htm.

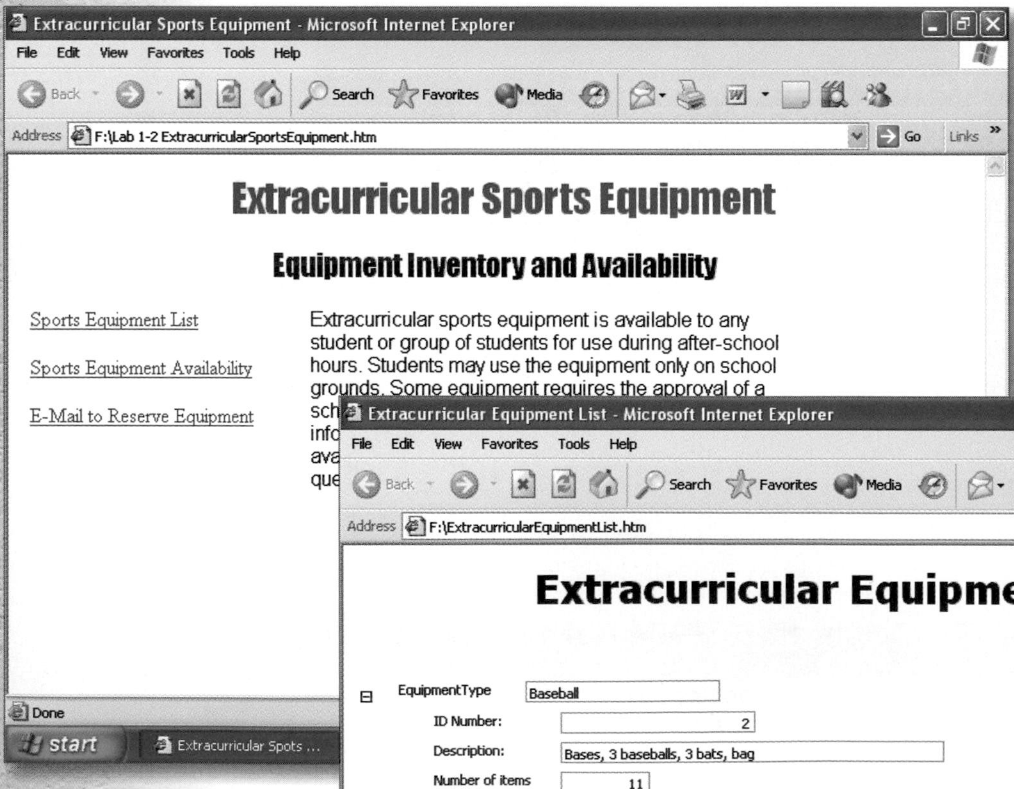

Extracurricular Sports Equipment - Microsoft Internet Explorer

Address F:\Lab 1-2 ExtracurricularSportsEquipment.htm

Extracurricular Sports Equipment

Equipment Inventory and Availability

Sports Equipment List

Sports Equipment Availability

E-Mail to Reserve Equipment

Extracurricular sports equipment is available to any student or group of students for use during after-school hours. Students may use the equipment only on school grounds. Some equipment requires the approval of a

FIGURE 1-48

Extracurricular Equipment List - Microsoft Internet Explorer

Address F:\ExtracurricularEquipmentList.htm

Extracurricular Equipment List

EquipmentType Baseball

ID Number: 2

Description: Bases, 3 baseballs, 3 bats, bag

Number of items included: 11

Number of days allowed: 1

Staff permission required

ExtracurricularEquipment 1 of 3

ExtracurricularEquipment-EquipmentType 1 of 5

Home

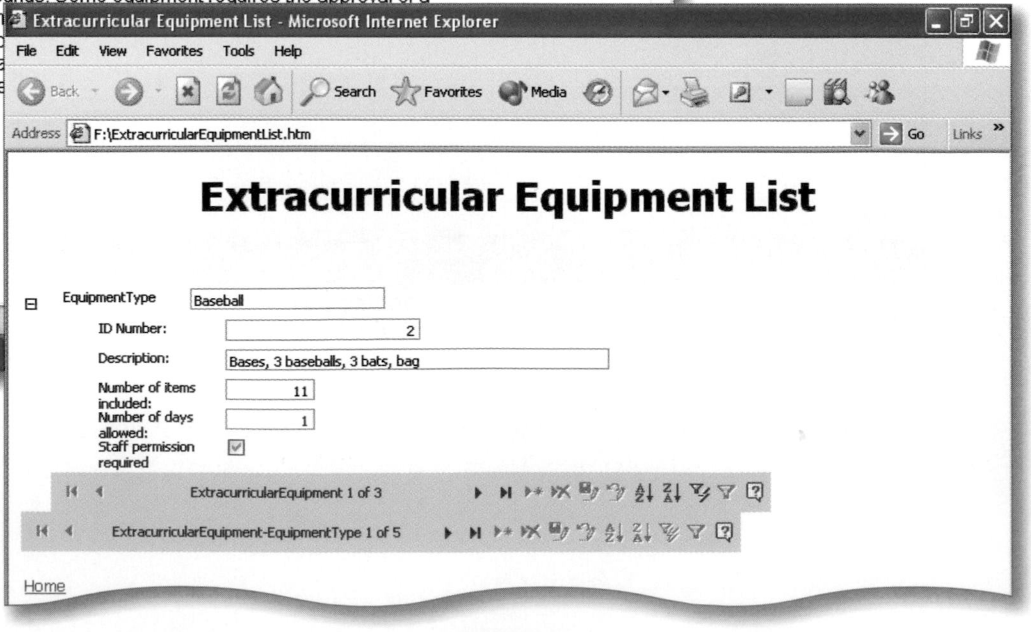

FIGURE 1-49

2. Start Access by opening the Lab 1-2 ExtracurricularEquipment.mdb database from the Student Data Files. Create a data access page from the ExtracurricularEquipment table. Create a grouping level using the EquipmentType field. Add a title as shown in Figure 1-49. Add a link named Home that links to the Lab 1-2 ExtracurricularSportsEquipment.htm home page at the bottom of the data access page. Save the data access page as ExtracurricularEquipmentList.htm.
3. Start Excel by opening the Lab 1-2 EquipmentAvailability.xls workbook from Data Files for Students. Create a Web page from the workbook by using the Save as a Web Page command on the File menu. Use the file name, Lab 1-2 EquipmentAvailability.htm.
4. View the Lab 1-2 ExtracurricularSportsEquipment.htm Web page in your browser. Verify that all links operate properly by clicking each one. Print all Web pages.

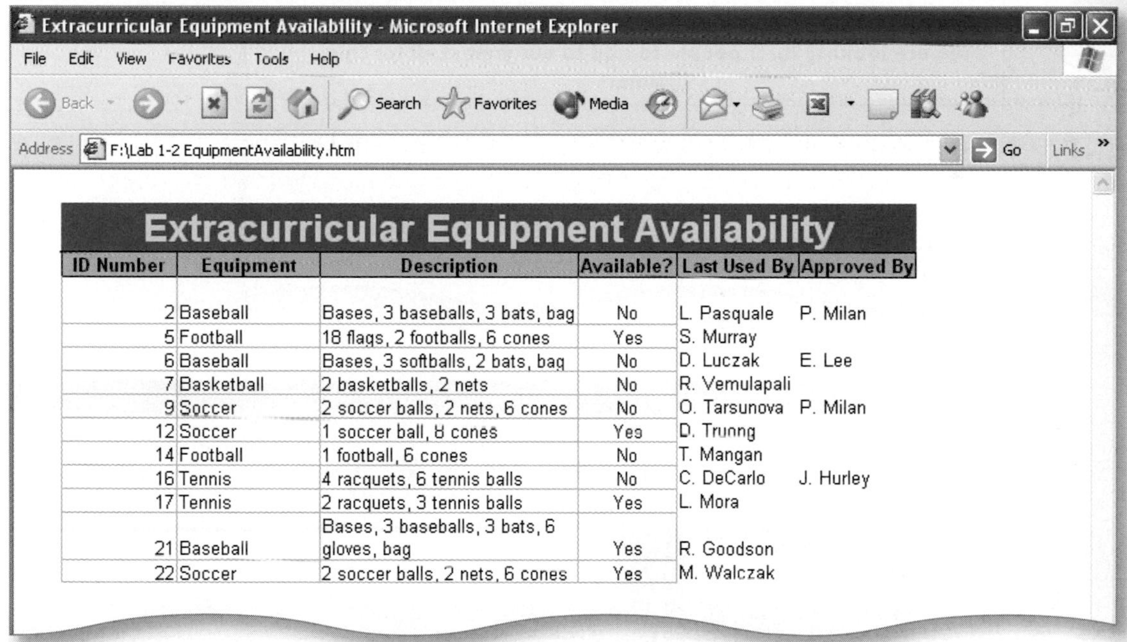

Extracurricular Equipment Availability

ID Number	Equipment	Description	Available?	Last Used By	Approved By
2	Baseball	Bases, 3 baseballs, 3 bats, bag	No	L. Pasquale	P. Milan
5	Football	18 flags, 2 footballs, 6 cones	Yes	S. Murray	
6	Baseball	Bases, 3 softballs, 2 bats, bag	No	D. Luczak	E. Lee
7	Basketball	2 basketballs, 2 nets	No	R. Vemulapali	
9	Soccer	2 soccer balls, 2 nets, 6 cones	No	O. Tarsunova	P. Milan
12	Soccer	1 soccer ball, 8 cones	Yes	D. Truong	
14	Football	1 football, 6 cones	No	T. Mangan	
16	Tennis	4 racquets, 6 tennis balls	No	C. DeCarlo	J. Hurley
17	Tennis	2 racquets, 3 tennis balls	Yes	L. Mora	
21	Baseball	Bases, 3 baseballs, 3 bats, 6 gloves, bag	Yes	R. Goodson	
22	Soccer	2 soccer balls, 2 nets, 6 cones	Yes	M. Walczak	

FIGURE 1-50

3 Cheryl's Place Job Openings Web Site Incorporating PowerPoint Web Pages

Problem: As an assistant manager at the Cheryl's Place restaurant, you have offered to create a Web page to recruit summer help for wait staff (Figures 1-51 and 1-52 on the next page). The specific information for the job openings is located in a PowerPoint presentation, which has four pages.

Instructions: Perform the following tasks.

1. Start Word. Create the Web page as shown in Figure 1-51. Include scrolling text or plain text below the Web page title. Insert two hyperlinks. The first hyperlink should link to Lab 1-3 CherylsPlace.htm, and the second should link to an e-mail address at cherylsplace@isp.com and create a new e-mail message with a subject of Job Information. Use clip art to insert the picture of a waitress or a similar graphic. Sav page as CherylsPlaceSummerHelp.htm.

(c

Cheryl's Place Job Openings Web Site Incorporating PowerPoint Web Pages *(continued)*

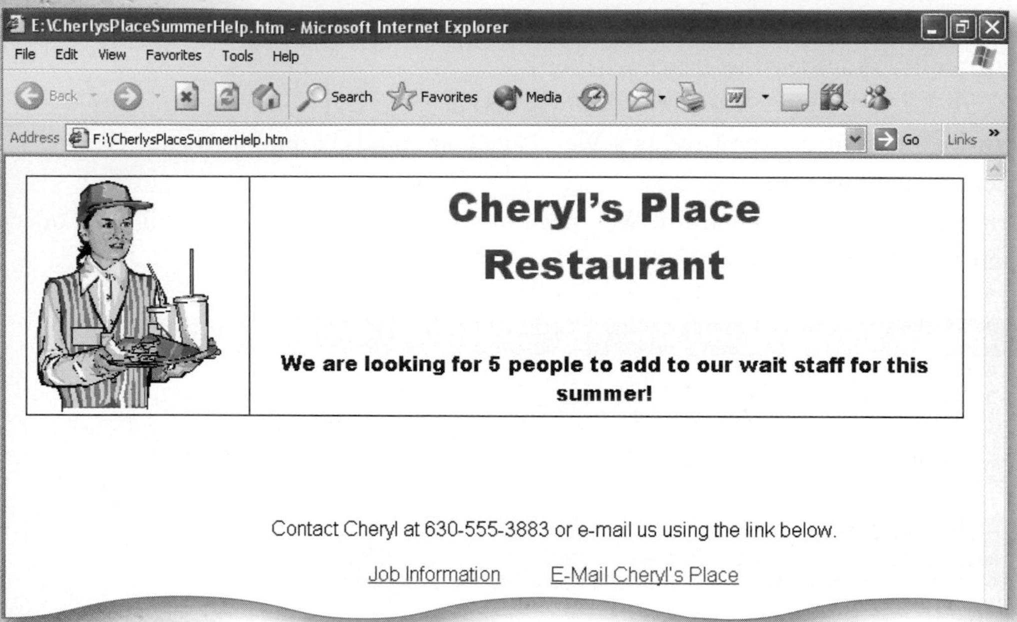

FIGURE 1-51

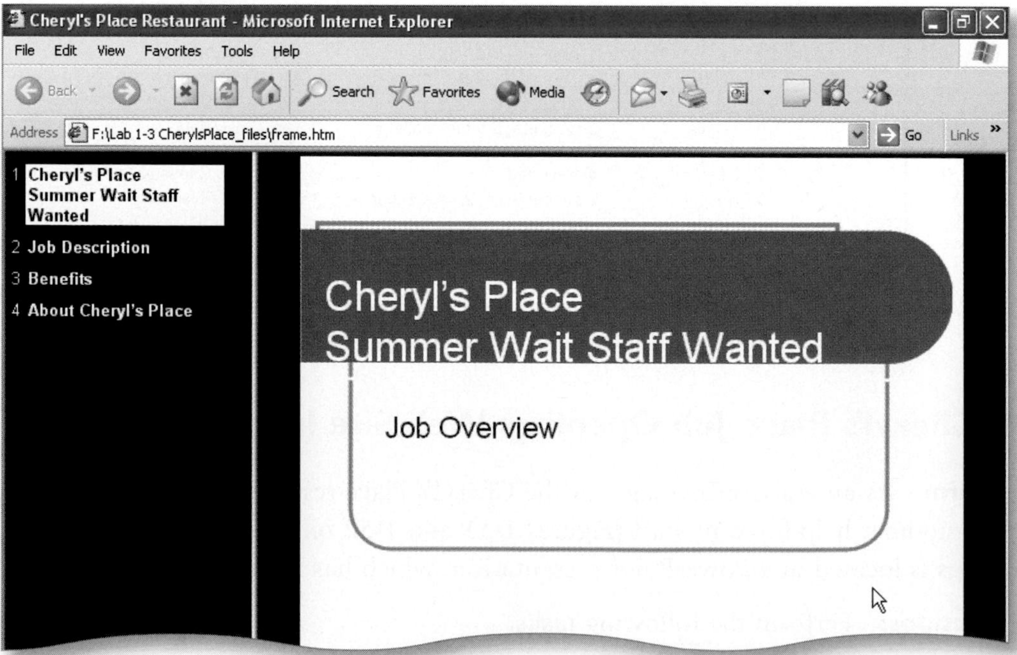

FIGURE 1-52

2. Open the Lab 1-3 PowerPoint presentation Lab 1-3 CherylsPlace.ppt. Add a link named Home at the bottom of the first page of the presentation that jumps to the CherylsPlaceSummerHelp.htm Web page. Save the PowerPoint presentation as Web pages on the USB flash drive. Name the Web pages Lab 1-3 CherylsPlace.htm.
3. View the Web pages in your browser. Print each page.

Cases and Places

The case studies are identified by discipline. The difficulty of these case studies varies:
are the least difficult and are more difficult. The last exercise is a group exercise.
Each exercise has a cross-curricular designation:

Math Social Studies Science Language Arts Art/Music Business Health

1 During your summer break, you and your friends decide to put your computer skills to work and start a video conversion business to help people convert their family videos to DVDs. You plan to offer four services, each at a different rate. To convert older VHS tapes to DVD, you will charge $20 for each hour of tape. To convert newer compact VHS-C tapes, you will charge $15 for each hour of tape. To convert digital video to DVD, you will charge $10 per hour of tape. Basic video editing services will cost $15 per hour of time that you spend editing the video. Create a worksheet in Excel that summarizes each service. Create a Web page using Word that embeds the Excel worksheet; the goal of the Web site is to inform new customers of your business and the services it provides. Make the Web site as informational as possible. Make sure to include an e-mail address on the Web page with a hyperlink that starts a new e-mail message.

2 A local merchant provides a yearly preventative health screening clinic for her customers. To advertise the service, she wants you to create a Web site that highlights the focus of the screening and historical information about past screenings. Using the data in Table 1-2, create an Excel worksheet and charts summarizing the data and graphing the number of people who participated each year and the number who were referred to a physician each year. Using Word, create a Web page and embed the worksheet on the home page of the Web site, and include information about the screening. Create another Web page, and embed the charts from Excel. Create a link to the Excel chart Web page and an e-mail link to your e-mail address.

Table 1-2 Preventative Health Screening History

YEAR	NUMBER OF SCREENINGS	REFERRALS TO PHYSICIAN
2002	53	4
2003	65	6
2004	81	8
2005	105	12
2006	131	15

Cases and Places

3 You are working on a science project with a group of classmates to study the effects of video game play on the body by taking measurements of heart rate, breathing rate, and blood sugar level. Because of the complexity of the experiment, you have decided to create a database for storing a list of issues, or problems, with the experiment. Create an Access database and add eight items to it with the following information for each issue with the experiment: issue number, type of issue, description, team member assigned to the issue, resolution date of the issue, and how the issue was resolved. From this table, create a data access page with inquiry capability only, using the issue type as the grouping level. Include issue number, description, team member assigned to the issue, resolution date of the issue, and how the issue was resolved in the data access page. Use a search engine to find at least four relevant links about topics relating to the science project, and create links to Web pages at the bottom of the data access page.

4 Your art instructor has assigned you the task of finding information on local artistic summer programs for high school students. Create an Access database and add information about local summer programs. Include the following fields: location, location type (such as local colleges, museums, art studios, libraries, and theatres), name of program, cost, experience required, and age range. From this table, create a data access page with inquiry capability only, using the location type as the grouping level. Create a Web page using Word that will act as the Web page for the program list, and create a link to the data access page. Be sure to include a link to your e-mail address on the Web page.

5 **Working Together** As a group, choose a book with which each team member is familiar. The purpose of this exercise is to create a book-review Web site of the book that you chose. Have one member of your team gather rating information from each team member, rating the following parameters on a scale from 1 to 10: plot, writing style, and how strongly you would rate this book to a friend. Create an Excel 3-D Bar chart to summarize the reviews by group member name. Have another member create a PowerPoint presentation that contains at least four pages of the group's main review of the book, including a plot summary, reviews, and the group's interpretation of the meaning of the book. A third member should create a data access Web page that includes information about the main characters in the book, including name, relevance, and a summary of the character's actions. Embed the Excel chart into one of the PowerPoint slides. Create a link from one of the PowerPoint pages to the data access Web page. Save the PowerPoint presentation as Web pages. Include relevant links to Web pages regarding the book and topics relevant to the book.

Appendix A

Microsoft Office Help System

Using the Microsoft Office Help System

This appendix shows you how to use the Microsoft Office Help system. At any time while you are using one of the Microsoft Office 2003 applications, you can interact with its Help system and display information on any topic associated with the application. To illustrate the use of the Office Help system, you will use the Microsoft Word application in this appendix. The Help systems in other Office applications respond in a similar fashion.

As shown in Figure A-1, five methods for accessing Word's Help system are available:

1. Microsoft Office Word Help button on the Standard toolbar
2. Microsoft Office Word Help command on the Help menu
3. Function key F1 on the keyboard
4. Type a question for help box on the menu bar
5. Office Assistant

1 MICROSOFT OFFICE WORD HELP BUTTON ON STANDARD TOOLBAR

2 MICROSOFT OFFICE WORD HELP COMMAND ON HELP MENU

3 FUNCTION KEY F1 ON KEYBOARD

4 TYPE A QUESTION FOR HELP BOX ON MENU BAR

5 OFFICE ASSISTANT

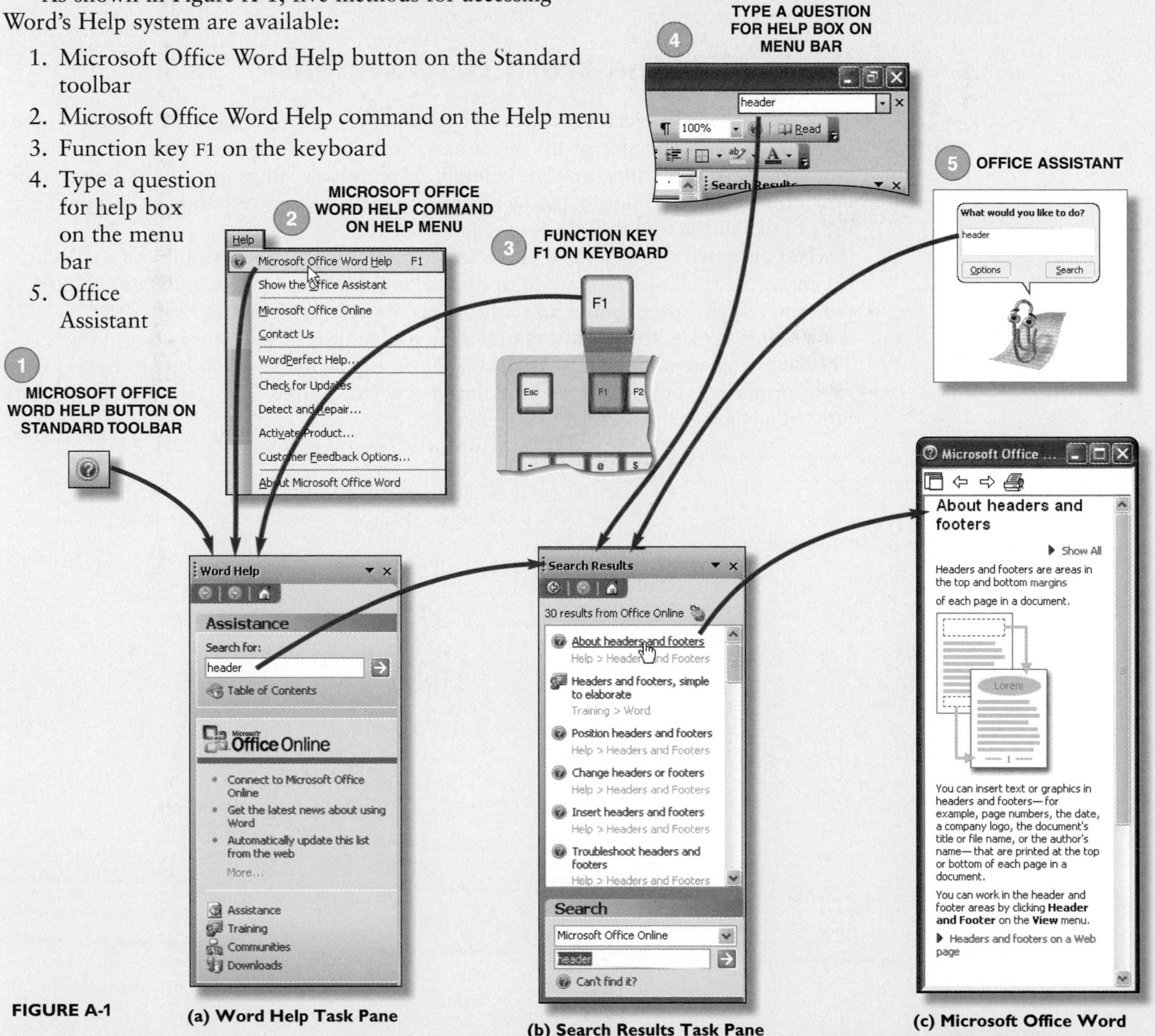

FIGURE A-1

(a) Word Help Task Pane

(b) Search Results Task Pane

(c) Microsoft Office Word Help Window

All five methods result in the Word Help system displaying a task pane on the right side of the Word window. The first three methods cause the **Word Help task pane** to display (Figure A-1a on the previous page). This task pane includes a Search text box in which you can enter a word or phrase on which you want help. Once you enter the word or phrase, the Word Help system displays the Search Results task pane (Figure A-1b on the previous page). With the Search Results task pane displayed, you can select specific Help topics.

As shown in Figure A-1, methods 4 and 5 bypass the Word Help task pane and display the **Search Results task pane** (Figure A-1b) with a list of links that pertain to the selected topic. Thus, any of the five methods for accessing the Word Help system results in displaying the Search Results task pane. Once the Word Help system displays this task pane, you can choose links that relate to the word or phrase on which you searched. In Figure A-1, for example, header was the searched topic (About headers and footers), which resulted in the Word Help system displaying the Microsoft Office Word Help window with information about headers and footers (Figure A-1c on the previous page).

Navigating the Word Help System

The quickest way to access the Word Help system is through the Type a question for help box on the right side of the menu bar at the top of the screen. Here you can type words, such as ruler, font, or column, or phrases, such as justify a paragraph, or how do I display formatting marks. The Word Help system responds by displaying a list of links in the Search Results task pane.

Here are two tips regarding the words or phrases you enter to initiate a search: (1) check the spelling of the word or phrase; and (2) keep your search very specific, with fewer than seven words, to return the most accurate results.

Assume for the following example that you want to know more about tables. The following steps show how to use the Type a question for help box to obtain useful information about tables by entering the keyword table. The steps also show you how to navigate the Word Help system.

To Obtain Help Using the Type a Question for Help Box

1

• **Click the Type a question for help box on the right side of the menu bar, type** `table`**, and then press the ENTER key (Figure A-2).**

The Word Help system displays the Search Results task pane on the right side of the window. The Search Results task pane contains a list of 30 links (Figure A-2). If you do not find what you are looking for, you can modify or refine the search in the Search area at the bottom of the task pane. The topics displayed in your Search Results task pane may be different.

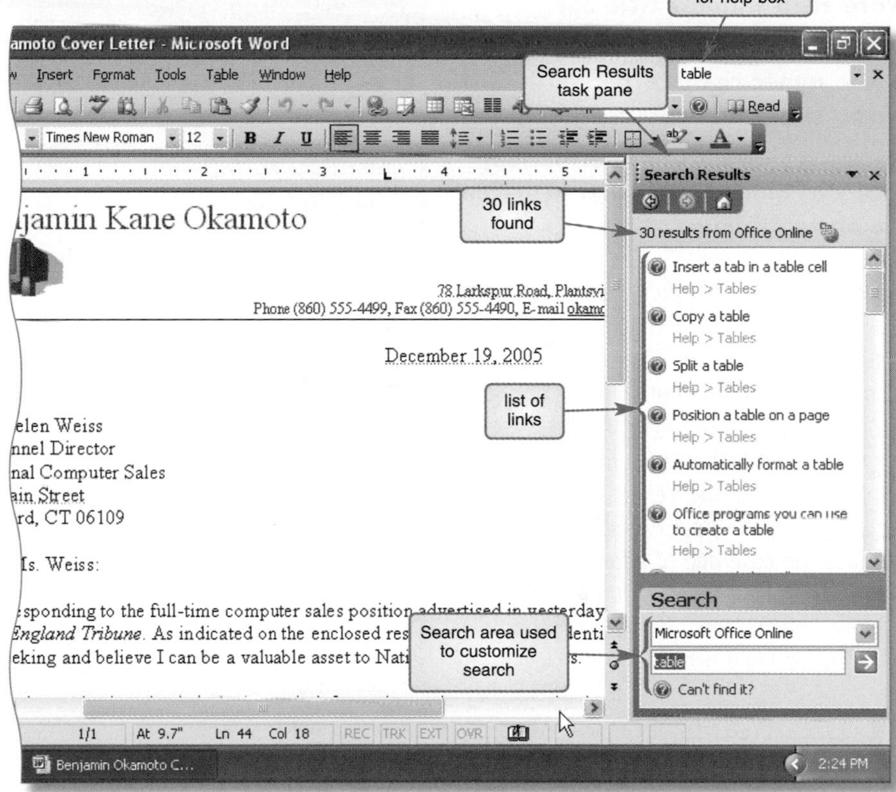

FIGURE A-2

2

Scroll down the list of links in the Search Results task pane, and then click the About tables link.

• **When Word displays the Microsoft Office Help Word window, click its Auto Tile button in the upper-left corner of the window (Figure A-4 on the next page), if necessary, to tile the windows.**

Word displays the Microsoft Office Word Help window with the desired information about tables (Figure A-3). With the Microsoft Office Word Help window and Microsoft Word window tiled, you can read the information in one window and complete the task in the other window.

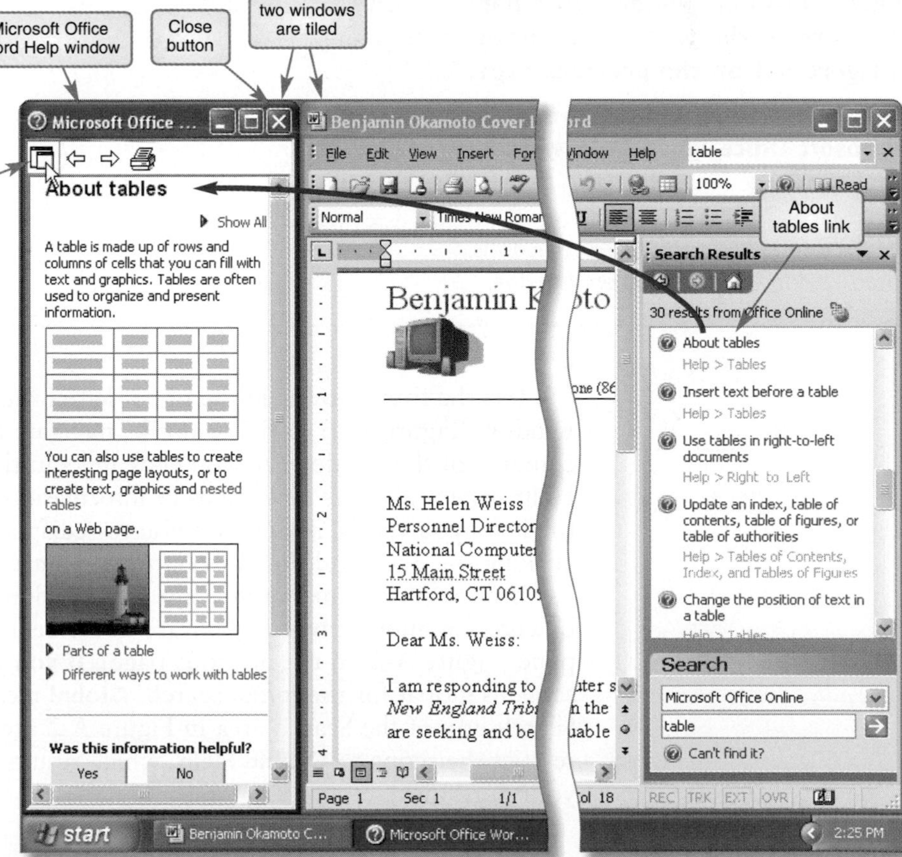

FIGURE A-3

3

- **Double-click the Microsoft Office Word Help window title bar.**
- **Click the Show All link in the upper-right corner of the window.**
- **After reviewing the information, click the Hide All link that replaced the Show All link.**

The Microsoft Office Word Help window is maximized so it fills the entire screen (Figure A-4). If you are connected to the Internet, you can give Microsoft your opinion as to whether the information was helpful by clicking the Yes or No button at the bottom of the page. The Show All link expands the coverage of information, and the Hide all link condenses the information displayed on the topic in the Microsoft Office Word Help window.

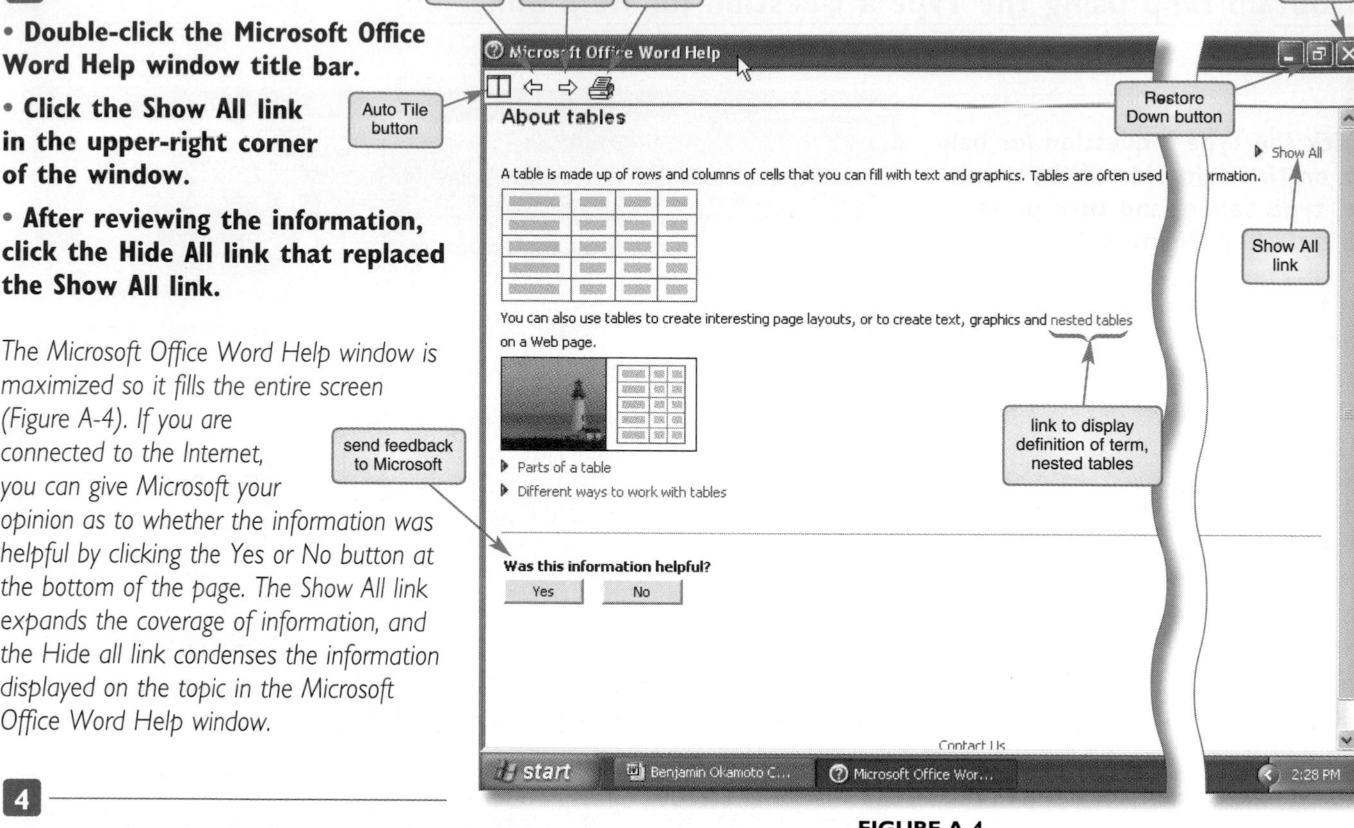

FIGURE A-4

4

- **Click the Restore Down button on the right side of the Microsoft Office Word Help window title bar to return to the tiled state shown in Figure A-3 on the previous page.**
- **Click the Close button on the Microsoft Office Word Help window title bar.**

The Microsoft Office Word Help window is closed, and the Word document is active.

Use the four buttons in the upper-left corner of the Microsoft Office Word Help window (Figure A-4) to tile or untile, navigate through the Help system, or print the contents of the window. As you click links in the Search Results task pane, the Word Help system displays new pages of information. The Word Help System remembers the links you visited and allows you to redisplay the pages visited during a session by clicking the Back and Forward buttons (Figure A-4).

If none of the links present the information you want, you can refine the search by entering another word or phrase in the Search text box in the Search Results task pane (Figure A-2 on the previous page). If you have access to the Web, then the scope is global for the initial search. **Global** means all of the categories listed in the Search box of the Search area in Figure A-2 are searched. For example, you can restrict the scope to **Offline Help**, which results in a search of related links only on your hard disk.

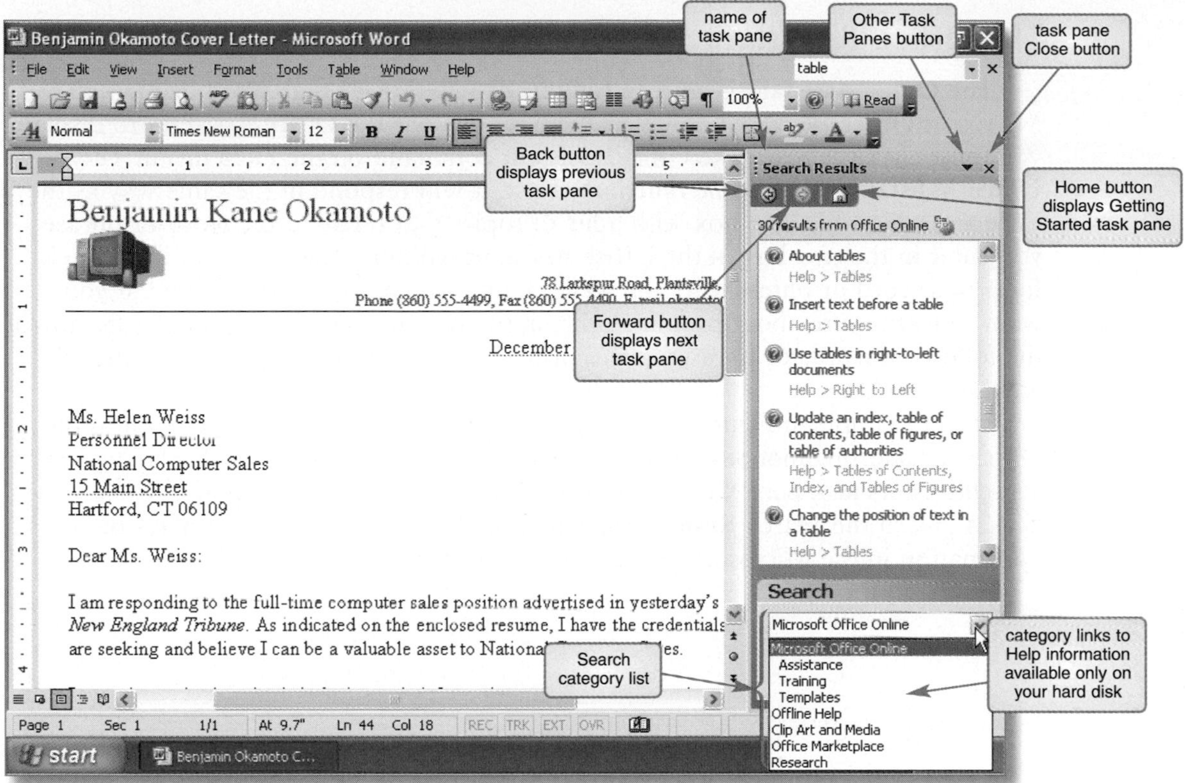

FIGURE A-5

Figure A-5 shows several additional features of the Search Results task pane. The Other Task Panes button and Close button on the Search Results task pane title bar allow you to display other task panes and close the Search Results task pane. The three buttons below the Search Results task pane title bar allow you to navigate between task panes (Back button and Forward button) and display the Getting Started task pane (Home button).

As you enter words and phrases in the Type a question for help box, the Word Help system adds them to the Type a question for help list. To display the list of previously typed words and phrases, click the Type a question for help box arrow (Figure A-6).

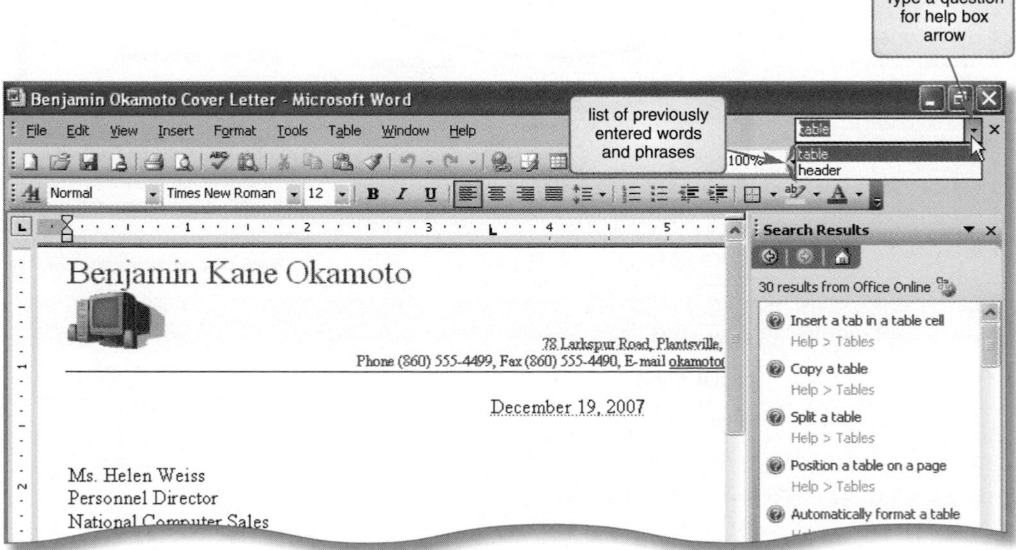

FIGURE A-6

The Office Assistant

The **Office Assistant** is an icon (middle of Figure A-7) that Word displays in the Microsoft Office Word window while you work. For the Office Assistant to display, you must click the Show the Office Assistant command on the Help menu. The Office Assistant has multiple functions. First, it will respond in the same way as the Type a question for help box with a list of topics that relate to the word or phrase you enter in the text box in the Office Assistant balloon. The entry can be in the form of a word or phrase as if you were talking to a person. For example, if you want to learn more about printing a file, in the balloon text box, you can type any of the following words or phrases: print, print a document, how do I print a file, or anything similar.

In the example in Figure A-7, the phrase, print a document, is entered into the Office Assistant balloon text box. The Office Assistant responds by displaying the Search Results task pane with a list of links from which you can choose. Once you click a link in the Search Results task pane, the Word Help system displays the information in the Microsoft Office Word Help window (Figure A-7).

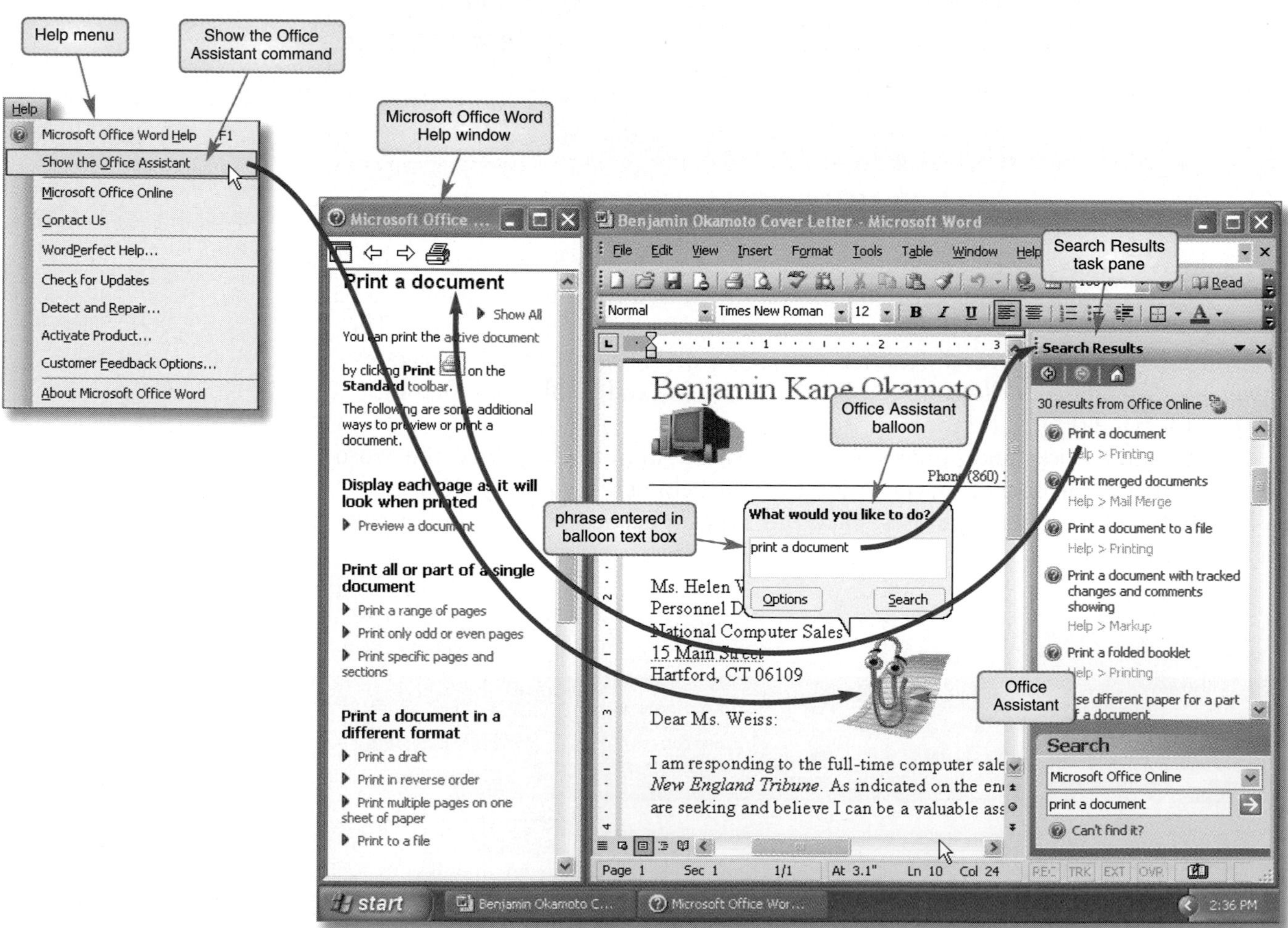

FIGURE A-7

In addition, the Office Assistant monitors your work and accumulates tips during a session on how you might increase your productivity and efficiency. The accumulation of tips must be enabled. You enable the accumulation of tips by right-clicking the Office Assistant, clicking Options on the shortcut menu, and then selecting the types of tips you want accumulated. You can view the tips at any time. The accumulated tips appear when you activate the Office Assistant balloon. Also, if at any time you see a light bulb above the Office Assistant, click it to display the most recent tip. If the Office Assistant is hidden, then the light bulb shows on the Microsoft Office Word Help button on the Standard toolbar.

You hide the Office Assistant by invoking the Hide the Office Assistant command on the Help menu or by right-clicking the Office Assistant and then clicking Hide on the shortcut menu. The Hide the Office Assistant command shows on the Help menu only when the Office Assistant is active in the Word window. If the Office Assistant begins showing up on your screen without you instructing it to show, then right-click the Office Assistant, click Options on the shortcut menu, click the Use the Office Assistant check box to remove the check mark, and then click the OK button.

If the Office Assistant is active in the Word window, then Word displays all program and system messages in the Office Assistant balloon.

You may or may not want the Office Assistant to display on the screen at all times. As indicated earlier, you can hide it and then show it later through the Help menu. For more information about the Office Assistant, type `office assistant` in the Type a question for help box and then click the links in the Search Results task pane.

Question Mark Button in Dialog Boxes and Help Icon in Task Panes

You use the Question Mark button with dialog boxes. It is located in the upper-right corner on the title bar of the dialog boxes, next to the Close button. For example, in Figure A-8 on the next page, the Print dialog box appears on the screen. If you click the Question Mark button in the upper-right corner of the dialog box, the Microsoft Office Word Help window is displayed and provides information about the options in the Print dialog box.

Some task panes include a Help icon. It can be located in various places within the task pane. For example, in the Clip Art task pane shown in Figure A-8, the Help icon appears at the bottom of the task pane and the Tips for finding clips link appears to the right of the Help icon. When you click the link, the Microsoft Office Word Help window is displayed and provides tips for finding clip art.

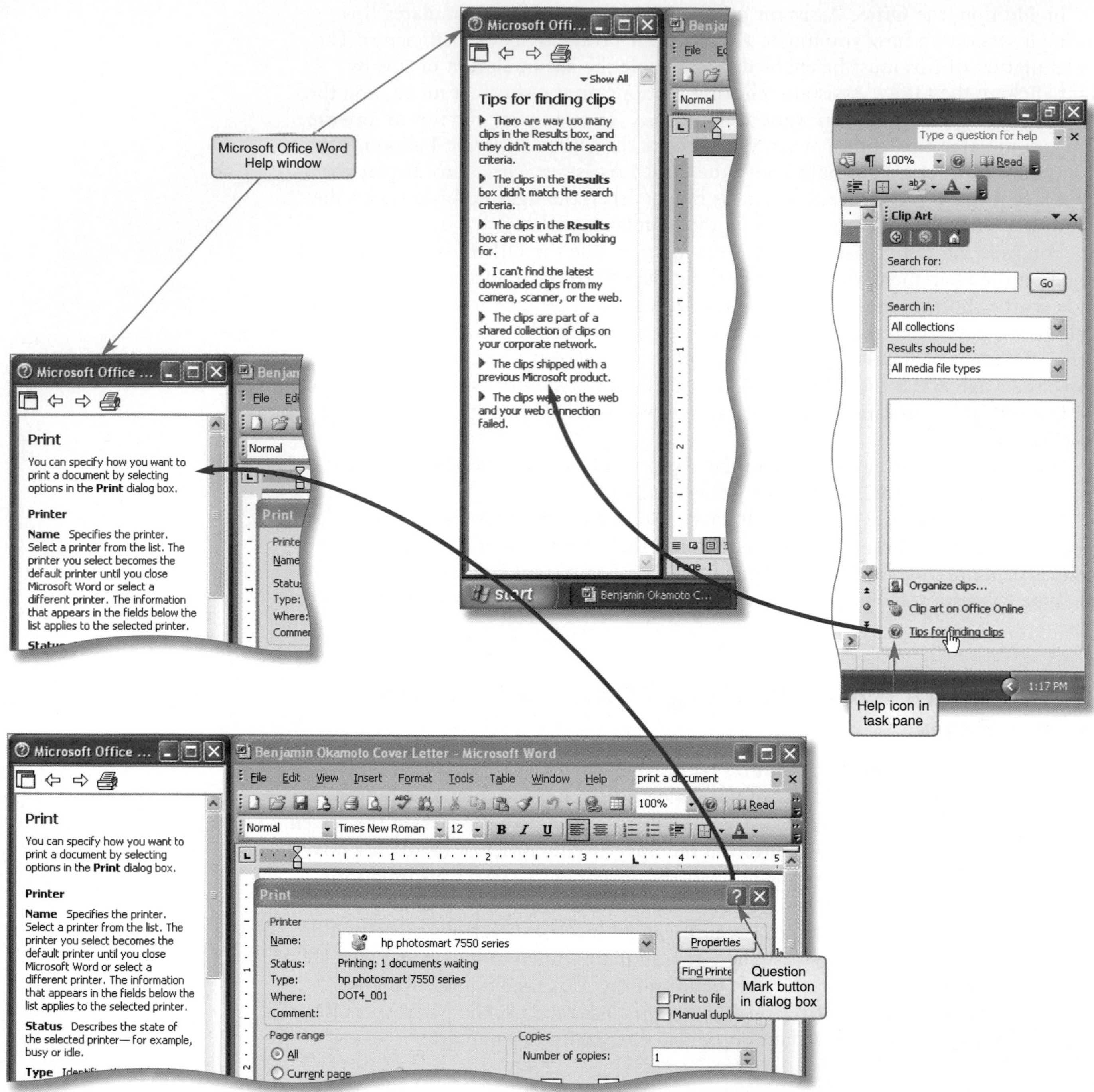

FIGURE A-8

Other Help Commands on the Help Menu

Thus far, this appendix has discussed the first two commands on the Help menu: (1) the Microsoft Office Word Help command (Figure A-1 on page APP 1) and (2) the Show the Office Assistant command (Figure A-7 on page APP 6). Several additional commands are available on the Help menu, as shown in Figure A-9. Table A-1 summarizes these commands.

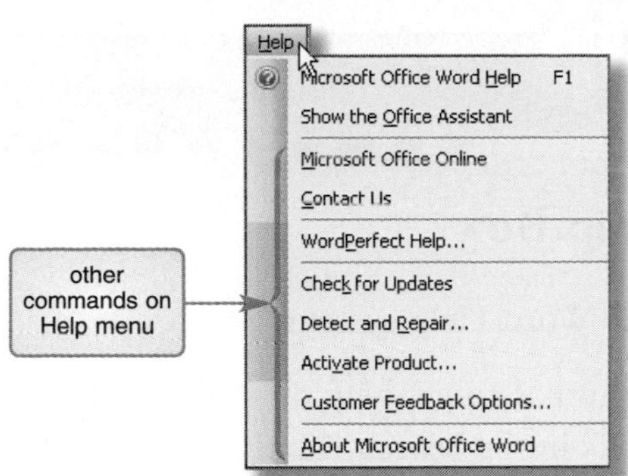

FIGURE A-9

Table A-1 Summary of Other Help Commands on the Help Menu

COMMAND ON HELP MENU	FUNCTION
Microsoft Office Online	Activates the browser, which displays the Microsoft Office Online Home page. The Microsoft Office Online Home page contains links that can improve Office productivity.
Contact Us	Activates the browser, which displays Microsoft contact information and a list of useful links.
WordPerfect Help	Displays the Help for WordPerfect Users dialog box, which includes information about carrying out commands in Word.
Check for Updates	Activates the browser, which displays a list of updates to Office 2003. These updates can be downloaded and installed to improve the efficiency of Office or to fix an error in one or more of the Office applications.
Detect and Repair	Detects and repairs errors in the Word program.
Activate Product	Activates Word if it has not already been activated.
Customer Feedback Options	Gives or denies Microsoft permission to collect anonymous information about the hardware.
About Microsoft Office Word	Displays the About Microsoft Word dialog box. The dialog box lists the owner of the software and the product identification. You need to know the product identification if you call Microsoft for assistance. The three buttons below the OK button are the System Info button, Tech Support button, and Disabled Items button. The System Info button displays system information, including hardware resources, components, software environment, and applications. The Tech Support button displays technical assistance information. The Disabled Items button displays a list of disabled items that prevents Word from functioning properly.

1 Using the Type a Question for Help Box

Instructions: Perform the following tasks using the Word Help system.

1. Use the Type a question for help box on the menu bar to get help on adding a bullet.
2. Click Add bullets or numbering in the list of links in the Search Results task pane. If necessary, tile the windows. Double-click the Microsoft Office Word Help window title bar to maximize it. Click the Show All link. Read and print the information. At the top of the printout, write down the number of links the Word Help system found.
3. Click the Restore Down button on the Microsoft Office Word Help title bar to restore the Microsoft Office Word Help window.
4. One at a time, click two additional links in the Search Results task pane and print the information. Hand in the printouts to your instructor. Use the Back and Forward buttons to return to the original page.
5. Use the Type a question for help box to search for information on adjusting line spacing. Click the Adjust line or paragraph spacing link in the Search Results task pane. Maximize the Microsoft Office Word Help window. Read and print the contents of the window. One at a time, click the links on the page and print the contents of the window. Close the Microsoft Office Word Help window.
6. For each of the following words and phrases, click one link in the Search Results task pane, click the Show All link, and then print the page: page zoom; date; print preview; office clipboard; word count; and themes.

2 Expanding on the Word Help System Basics

Instructions: Use the Word Help system to understand the topics better and answer the questions listed below. Answer the questions on your own paper, or hand in the printed Help information to your instructor.

1. Show the Office Assistant. Right-click the Office Assistant and then click Animate! on the shortcut menu. Repeat invoking the Animate! command to see various animations.
2. Right-click the Office Assistant, click Options on the shortcut menu, click the Reset my tips button, and then click the OK button. If necessary, repeatedly click the Office Assistant and then click off the Office Assistant until a light bulb appears above the Office Assistant. When you see the light bulb, it indicates that the Office Assistant has a tip to share with you.
3. Use the Office Assistant to find help on undoing. Click the Undo mistakes link and then print the contents of the Microsoft Office Word Help window. Close the window. Hand in the printouts to your instructor. Hide the Office Assistant.
4. Press the F1 key. Search for information on Help. Click the first two links in the Search Results task pane. Read and print the information for both links.
5. Display the Help menu. One at a time, click the Microsoft Office Online, Contact Us, and Check for Updates commands. Print the contents of each Internet Explorer window that displays and then close the window. Hand in the printouts to your instructor.
6. Click About Microsoft Office Word on the Help menu. Click the Tech Support button, print the contents of the Microsoft Office Word Help window, and then close the window. Click the System Info button. If necessary, click the plus sign to the left of Components in the System Summary list to display the Components category. Click CD-ROM and then print the information. Click Display and then print the information. Hand in the printouts to your instructor.

Appendix B

Speech and Handwriting Recognition and Speech Playback

Introduction

This appendix discusses the Office capability that allows users to create and modify worksheets using its alternative input technologies available through **text services**. Office provides a variety of text services, which enable you to speak commands and enter text in an application. The most common text service is the keyboard. Other text services include speech recognition and handwriting recognition.

The Language Bar

The **Language bar** allows you to use text services in the Office applications. You can utilize the Language bar in one of three states: (1) in a restored state as a floating toolbar in the Word window (Figure B-1a or Figure B-1b if Text Labels are enabled); (2) in a minimized state docked next to the notification area on the Windows taskbar (Figure B-1c); or (3) hidden (temporarily closed and out of the way). If the Language bar is hidden, you can activate it by right-clicking the Windows taskbar, pointing to Toolbars on the shortcut menu (Figure B-1d), and then clicking Language bar on the Toolbars submenu. If you want to close the Language bar, right-click the Language bar and then click Close the Language bar on the shortcut menu (Figure B-1e).

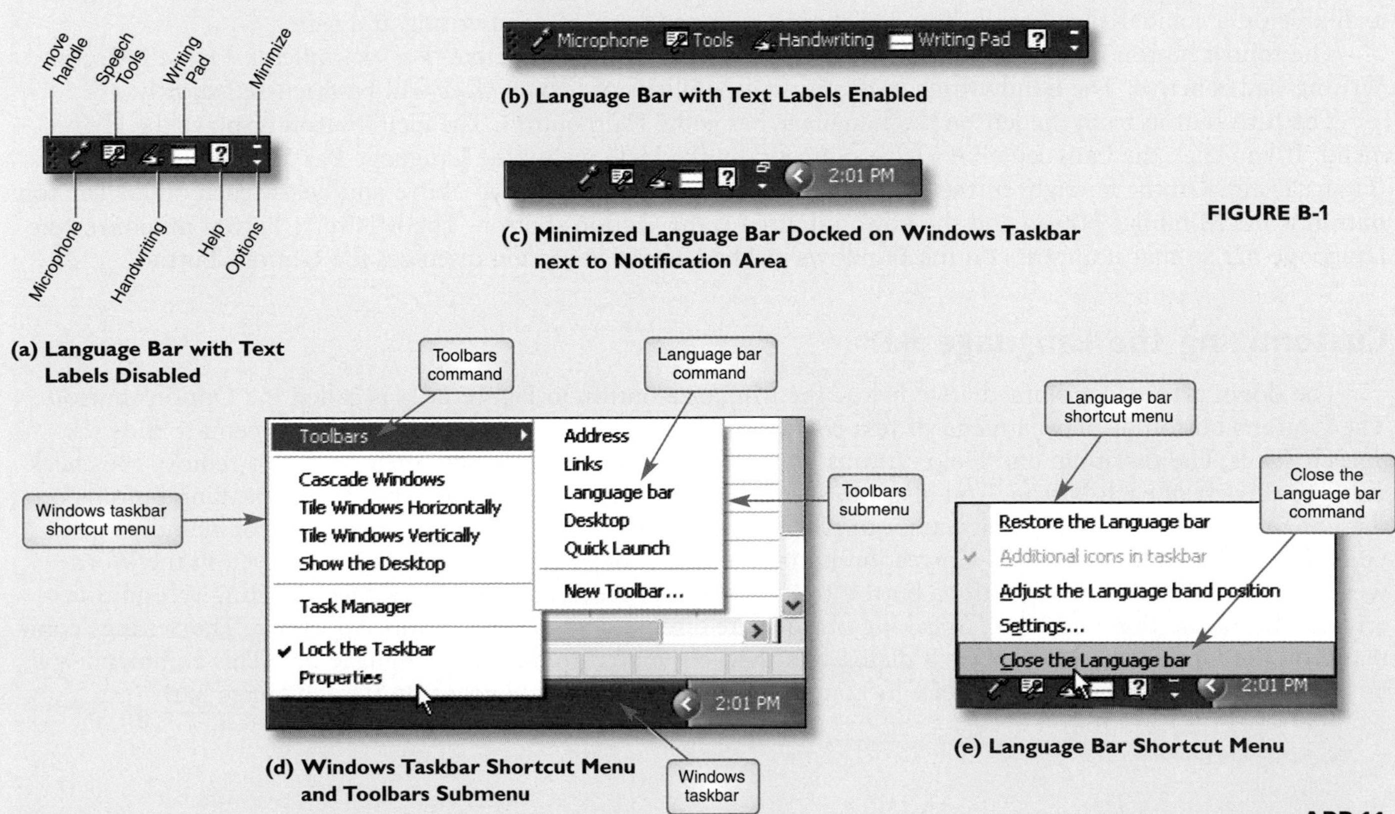

(a) Language Bar with Text Labels Disabled

(b) Language Bar with Text Labels Enabled

(c) Minimized Language Bar Docked on Windows Taskbar next to Notification Area

(d) Windows Taskbar Shortcut Menu and Toolbars Submenu

(e) Language Bar Shortcut Menu

FIGURE B-1

When Windows was installed on your computer, the installer specified a default language. For example, most users in the United States select English (United States) as the default language. You can add more than 90 additional languages and varying dialects, such as Basque, English (Zimbabwe), French (France), French (Canada), German (Germany), German (Austria), and Swahili. With multiple languages available, you can switch from one language to another while working in Word. If you change the language or dialect, then text services may change the functions of the keys on the keyboard, adjust speech recognition, and alter handwriting recognition. If a second language is activated, then a Language icon appears immediately to the right of the move handle on the Language bar and the language name is displayed on the Word status bar. This appendix assumes that English (United States) is the only language installed. Thus, the Language icon does not appear in the examples in Figure B-1 on the previous page.

Buttons on the Language Bar

The Language bar shown in Figure B-2a contains seven buttons. The number of buttons on your Language bar may be different. These buttons are used to select the language, customize the Language bar, control the microphone, control handwriting, and obtain help.

The first button on the left is the Microphone button, which enables and disables the microphone. When the microphone is enabled, text services adds two buttons and a balloon to the Language bar (Figure B-2b). These additional buttons and the balloon will be discussed shortly.

The second button from the left is the Speech Tools button. The Speech Tools button displays a menu of commands (Figure B-2c) that allow you to scan the current document looking for words to add to the speech recognition dictionary; hide or show the balloon on the Language bar; train the Speech Recognition service so that it can interpret your voice better; add and delete specific words to and from its dictionary, such as names and other words not understood easily; and change the user profile so more than one person can use the microphone on the same computer.

The third button from the left on the Language bar is the Handwriting button. The Handwriting button displays the Handwriting menu (Figure B-2d), which lets you choose the Writing Pad (Figure B-2e), Write Anywhere (Figure B-2f), or the on-screen keyboard (Figure B-2g). The On-Screen Symbol Keyboard command on the Handwriting menu displays an on-screen keyboard that allows you to enter special symbols that are not available on a standard keyboard. You can choose only one form of handwriting at a time.

The fourth button indicates which one of the handwriting forms is active. For example, in Figure B-2a, the Writing Pad is active. The handwriting recognition capabilities of text services will be discussed shortly.

The fifth button from the left on the Language bar is the Help button. The Help button displays the Help menu. If you click the Language Bar Help command on the Help menu, the Language Bar Help window appears (Figure B-2h). On the far right of the Language bar are two buttons stacked above and below each other. The top button is the Minimize button and the bottom button is the Options button. The Minimize button minimizes the Language bar so that it appears on the Windows taskbar. The next section discusses the Options button.

Customizing the Language Bar

The down arrow icon immediately below the Minimize button in Figure B-2a is called the Options button. The Options button displays a menu of text services options (Figure B-2i). You can use this menu to hide the Speech Tools, Handwriting, and Help buttons on the Language bar by clicking their names to remove the check mark to the left of each button. You also can show the Correction, Speak Text, and Pause Speaking buttons on the Language bar by clicking their names to place a check mark to the left of the respective command. When you select text and then click the Correction button, a list of correction alternatives is displayed in the Word window. You can use the Corrections button to correct both speech recognition and handwriting recognition errors. The Speak Text and Pause Speaking buttons are discussed at the end of this Appendix. The Settings command on the Options menu displays a dialog box that lets you customize the Language bar. This command will be discussed shortly. The Restore Defaults command redisplays hidden buttons on the Language bar.

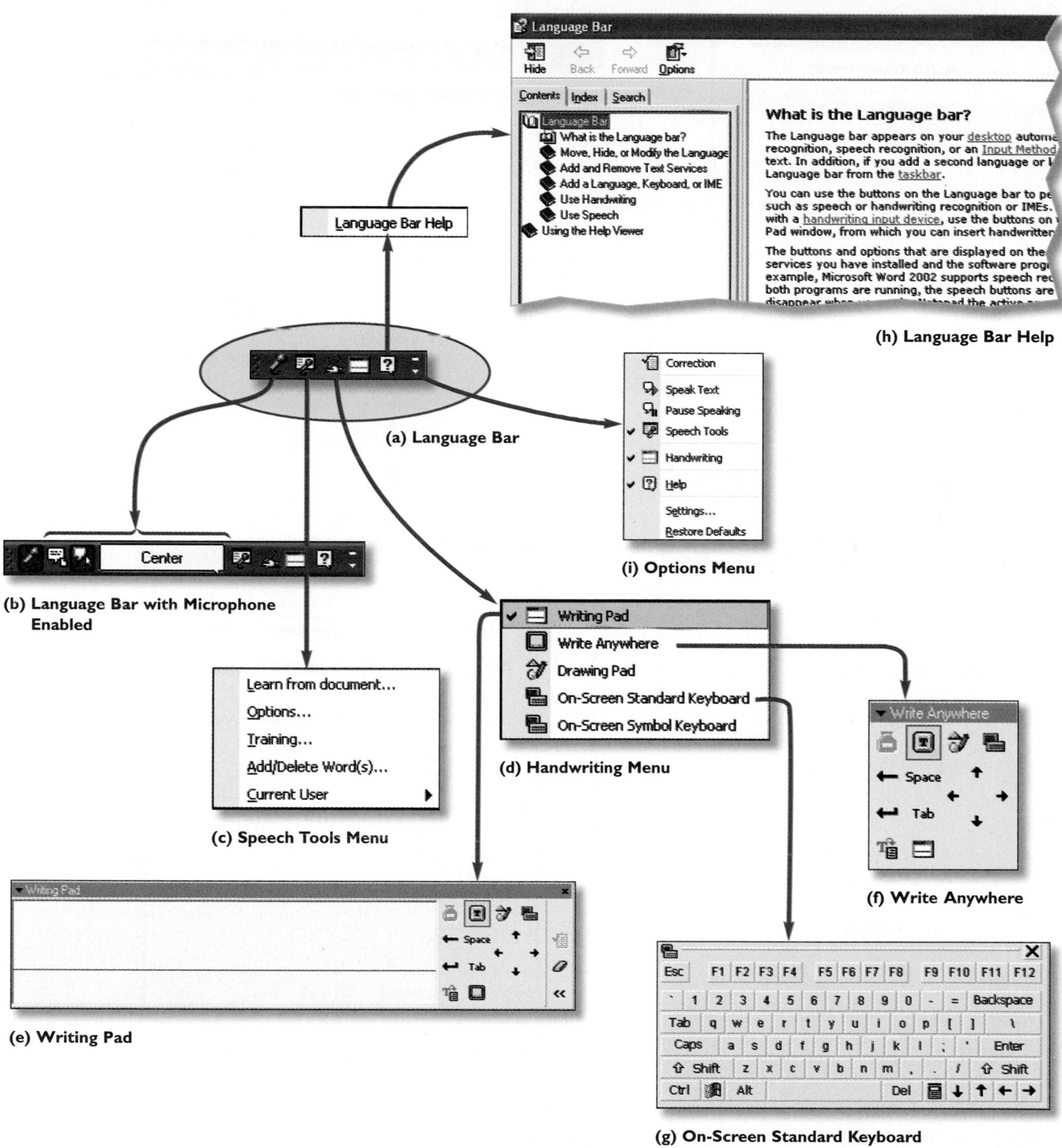

FIGURE B-2

If you right-click the Language bar, a shortcut menu appears (Figure B-3a on the next page). This shortcut menu lets you further customize the Language bar. The Minimize command on the shortcut menu docks the Language bar on the Windows taskbar. The Transparency command in Figure B-3a toggles the Language bar between being solid and transparent. You can see through a transparent Language bar (Figure B-3b). The Text Labels command toggles on text labels on the Language bar (Figure B-3c) and off (Figure B-3b). The Vertical command displays the Language bar vertically on the screen (Figure B-3d).

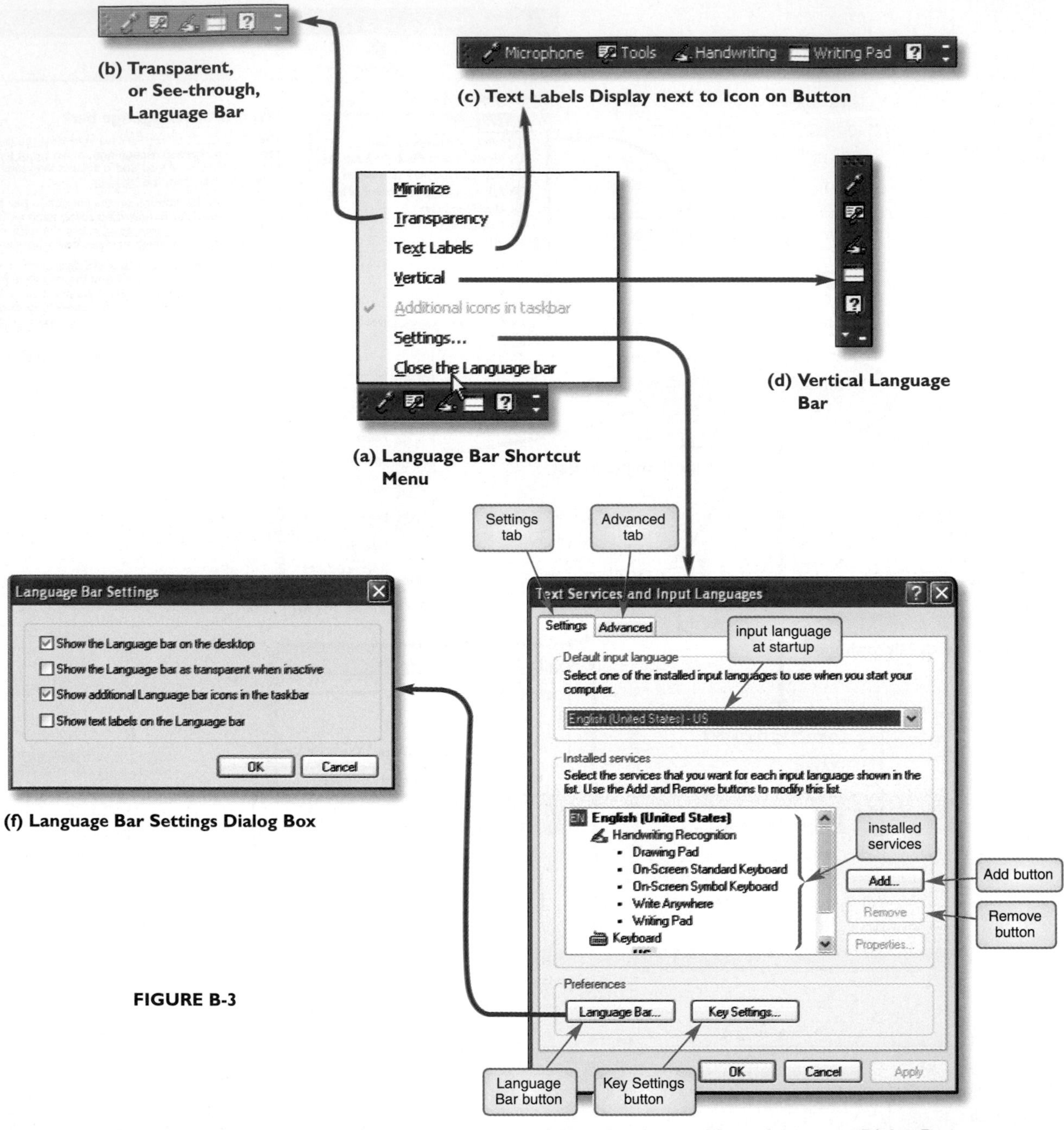

FIGURE B-3

The Settings command in Figure B-3a displays the Text Services and Input Languages dialog box (Figure B-3e). The Text Services and Input Languages dialog box allows you to add additonal languages, add and remove text services, modify keys on the keyboard, modify the Language bar, and extend support of advanced text services to all programs, including Notepad and other programs that normally do not support text services (through the Advanced tab). If you want to remove any one of the services in the Installed services list, select the service, and then click the Remove button. If you want to add a service, click the Add button. The Key Settings button allows you to modify the keyboard. If you click the Language Bar button in the Text Services and Input Languages dialog box, the Language Bar Settings dialog box appears (Figure B-3f). This dialog box contains Language bar options, some of which are the same as the commands on the Language bar shortcut menu shown in Figure B-3a.

The Close the Language bar command on the shortcut menu shown in Figure B-3a closes or hides the Language bar. If you close the Language bar and want to redisplay it, see Figure B-1d on page APP 11.

Speech Recognition

The **Speech Recognition service** available with Office enables your computer to recognize human speech through a microphone. The microphone has two modes: dictation and voice command (Figure B-4). You switch between the two modes by clicking the Dictation button and the Voice Command button on the Language bar. These buttons appear only when you turn on Speech Recognition by clicking the Microphone button on the Language bar (Figure B-5a on the next page). If you are using the Microphone button for the very first time in Word, it will require that you check your microphone settings and step through voice training before activating the Speech Recognition service.

The Dictation button places the microphone in Dictation mode. In **Dictation mode**, whatever you speak is entered as text at the location of the insertion point. The Voice Command button places the microphone in Voice Command mode. In **Voice Command mode**, whatever you speak is interpreted as a command. If you want to turn off the microphone, click the Microphone button on the Language bar or in Voice Command mode say, "Mic off" (pronounced mike off). It is important to remember that minimizing the Language bar does not turn off the microphone.

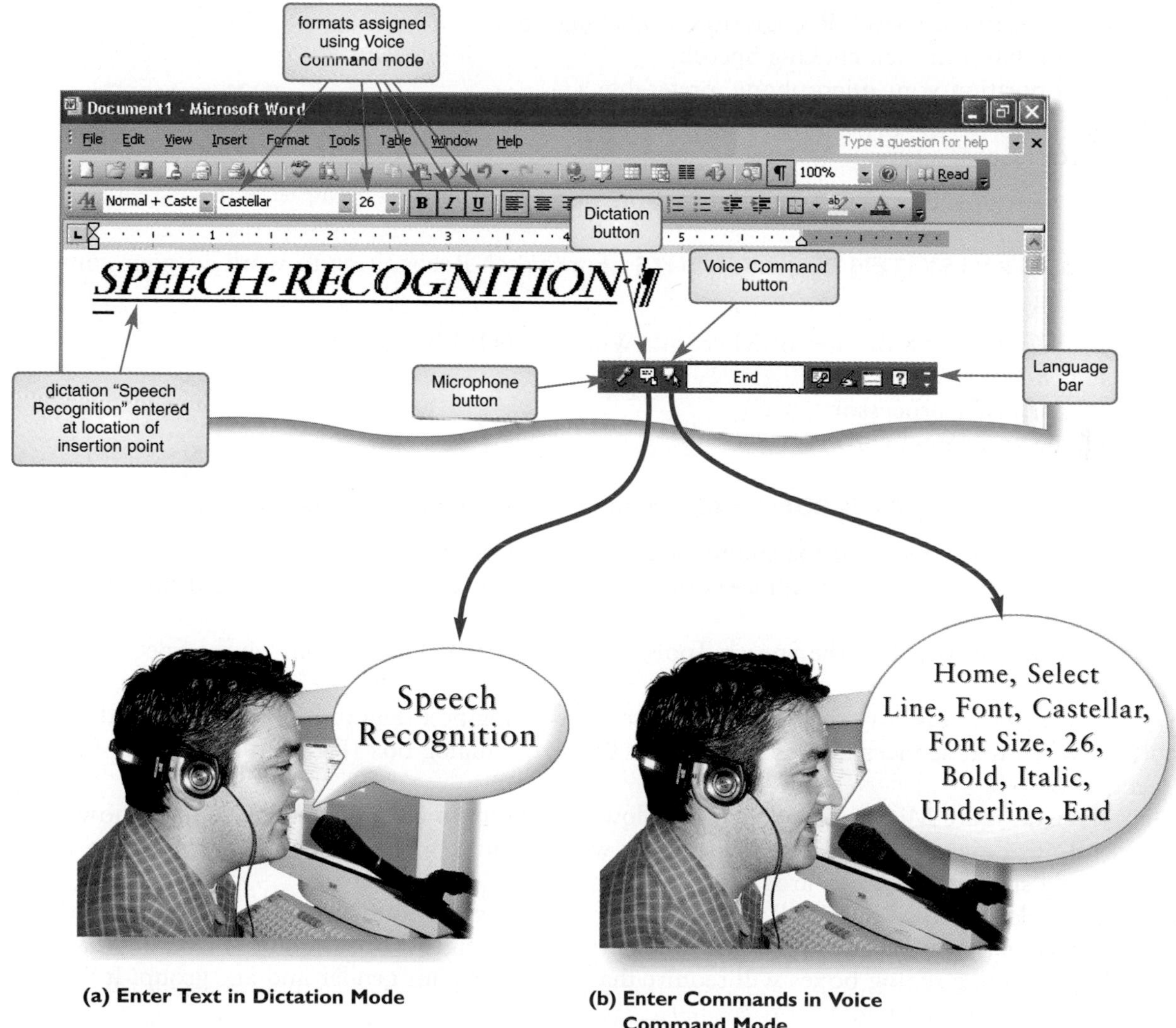

(a) Enter Text in Dictation Mode

(b) Enter Commands in Voice Command Mode

FIGURE B-4

The Language bar speech message balloon shown in Figure B-5b displays messages that may offer help or hints. In Voice Command mode, the name of the last recognized command you said appears. If you use the mouse or keyboard instead of the microphone, a message will appear in the Language bar speech message balloon indicating the word you could say. In Dictation mode, the message, Dictating, usually appears. The Speech Recognition service, however, will display messages to inform you that you are talking too soft, too loud, too fast, or to ask you to repeat what you said by displaying, What was that?

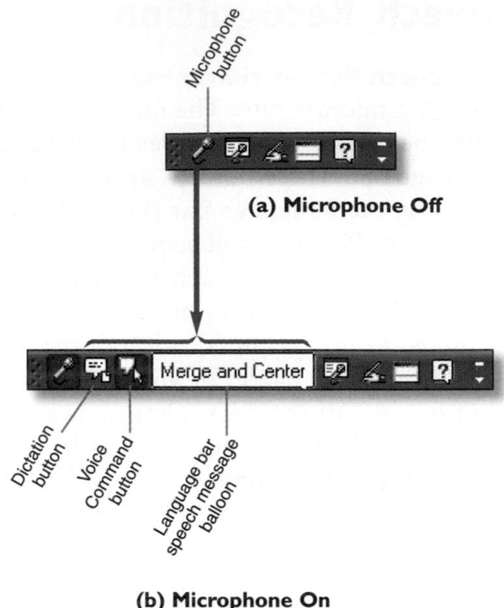

FIGURE B-5

Getting Started with Speech Recognition

For the microphone to function properly, you should follow these steps:

1. Make sure your computer meets the minimum requirements.
2. Start Word. Activate Speech Recognition by clicking Tools on the menu bar and then clicking Speech.
3. Set up and position your microphone, preferably a close-talk headset with gain adjustment support.
4. Train Speech Recognition.

The following sections describe these steps in more detail.

SPEECH RECOGNITION SYSTEM REQUIREMENTS For Speech Recognition to work on your computer, it needs the following:

1. Microsoft Windows 98 or later or Microsoft Windows NT 4.0 or later
2. At least 128 MB RAM
3. 400 MHz or faster processor
4. Microphone and sound card

SETUP AND POSITION YOUR MICROPHONE Set up your microphone as follows:

1. Connect your microphone to the sound card in the back of the computer.
2. Position the microphone approximately one inch out from, and to the side of, your mouth. Position it so you are not breathing into it.
3. On the Language bar, click the Speech Tools button and then click Options on the Speech Tools menu (Figure B-6a).
4. When text services displays the Speech input settings dialog box (Figure B-6b), click the Advanced Speech button. When text services displays the Speech Properties dialog box (Figure B-6c), click the Speech Recognition tab.
5. Click the Configure Microphone button. Follow the Microphone Wizard directions as shown in Figures B-6d, B-6e, and B-6f. The Next button will remain dimmed in Figure B-6e until the volume meter consistently stays in the green area.
6. If someone else installed Speech Recognition, click the New button in the Speech Properties dialog box and enter your name. Click the Train Profile button and step through the Voice Training dialog boxes. The Voice Training dialog boxes will require that you enter your gender and age group. It then will step you through voice training.

You can adjust the microphone further by clicking the Settings button in the Speech Properties dialog box (Figure B-6c). The Settings button displays the Recognition Profile Settings dialog box that allows you to adjust the pronunciation sensitivity and accuracy versus recognition response time.

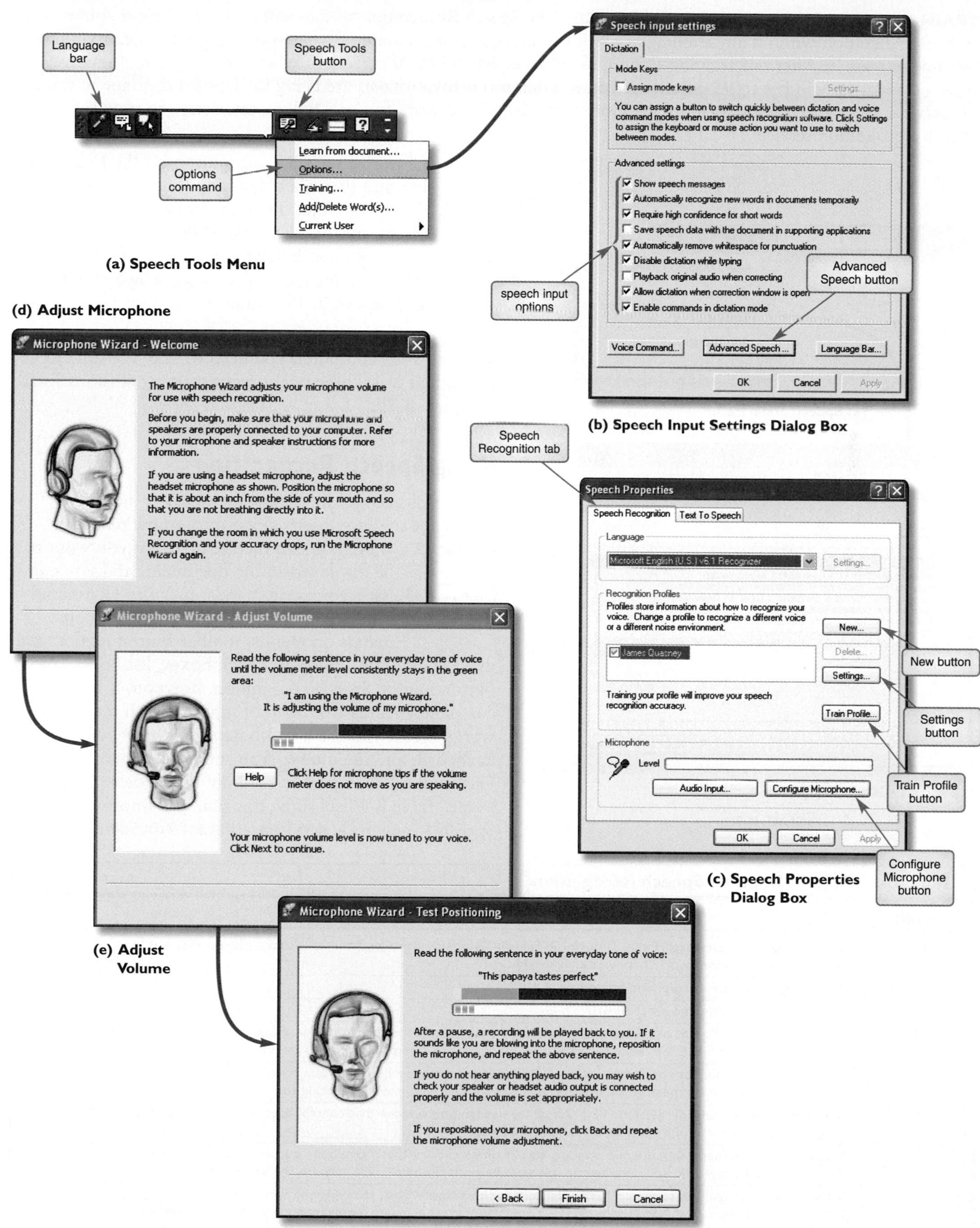

(a) Speech Tools Menu

(b) Speech Input Settings Dialog Box

(c) Speech Properties Dialog Box

(d) Adjust Microphone

(e) Adjust Volume

(f) Test Microphone

FIGURE B-6

TRAIN THE SPEECH RECOGNITION SERVICE The Speech Recognition service will understand most commands and some dictation without any training at all. It will recognize much more of what you speak, however, if you take the time to train it. After one training session, it will recognize 85 to 90 percent of your words. As you do more training, accuracy will rise to 95 percent. If you feel that too many mistakes are being made, then continue to train the service. The more training you do, the more accurately it will work for you. Follow these steps to train the Speech Recognition service:

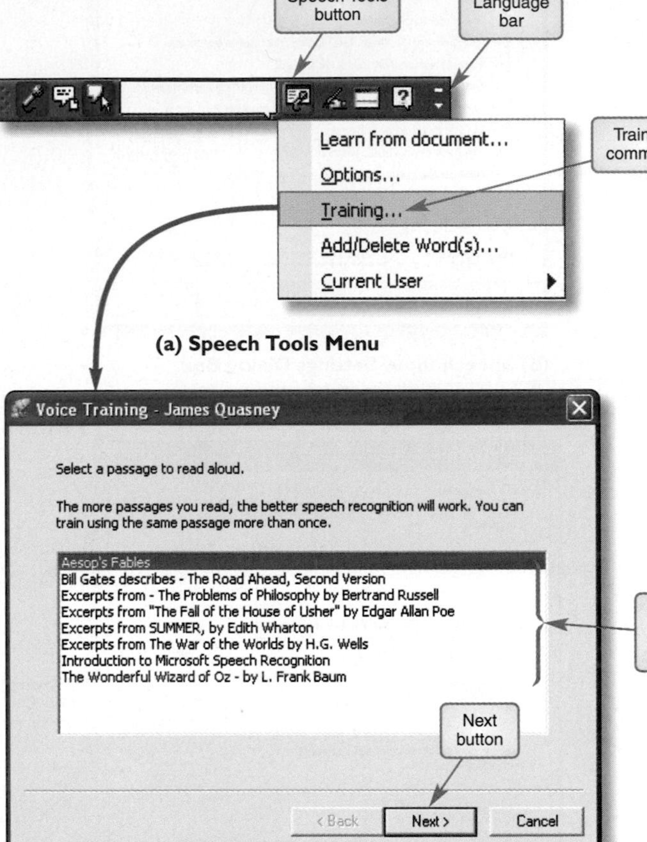

(a) Speech Tools Menu

(b) Voice Training Dialog Box

FIGURE B-7

1. Click the Speech Tools button on the Language bar and then click Training (Figure B-7a).
2. When the Voice Training dialog box appears (Figure B-7b), click one of the sessions and then click the Next button.
3. Complete the training session, which should take less than 15 minutes.

If you are serious about using a microphone to speak to your computer, you need to take the time to go through at least three of the eight training sessions listed in Figure B-7b.

Using Speech Recognition

Speech recognition lets you enter text into a document similarly to speaking into a tape recorder. Instead of typing, you can dictate text that you want to be displayed in the document, and you can issue voice commands. In Voice Command mode, you can speak menu names, commands on menus, toolbar button names, and dialog box option buttons, check boxes, list boxes, and button names. Speech recognition, however, is not a completely hands-free form of input. Speech recognition works best if you use a combination of your voice, the keyboard, and the mouse. You soon will discover that Dictation mode is far less accurate than Voice Command mode. Table B-1 lists some tips that will improve the Speech Recognition service's accuracy considerably.

Table B-1 Tips to Improve Speech Recognition

NUMBER	TIP
1	The microphone hears everything. Though the Speech Recognition service filters out background noise, it is recommended that you work in a quiet environment.
2	Try not to move the microphone around once it is adjusted.
3	Speak in a steady tone and speak clearly.
4	In Dictation mode, do not pause between words. A phrase is easier to interpret than a word. Sounding out syllables in a word will make it more difficult for the Speech Recognition service to interpret what you are saying.
5	If you speak too loudly or too softly, it makes it difficult for the Speech Recognition service to interpret what you said. Check the Language bar speech message balloon for an indication that you may be speaking too loudly or too softly.
6	If you experience problems after training, adjust the recognition options that control accuracy and rejection by clicking the Settings button shown in Figure B-6c on the previous page.
7	When you are finished using the microphone, turn it off by clicking the Microphone button on the Language bar or, in Voice Command mode, say "Mic off." Leaving the microphone on is the same as leaning on the keyboard.
8	If the Speech Recognition service is having difficulty with unusual words, then add the words to its dictionary by using the Learn from document and Add/Delete Word(s) commands on the Speech Tools menu (Figure B-8a). The last names of individuals and the names of companies are good examples of the types of words you should add to the dictionary.
9	Training will improve accuracy; practice will improve confidence.

The last command on the Speech Tools menu is the Current User command (Figure B-8a). The Current User command is useful for multiple users who share a computer. It allows them to configure their own individual profiles and then switch between users as they use the computer.

For additional information about the Speech Recognition service, enter `speech recognition` in the Type a question for help box on the menu bar.

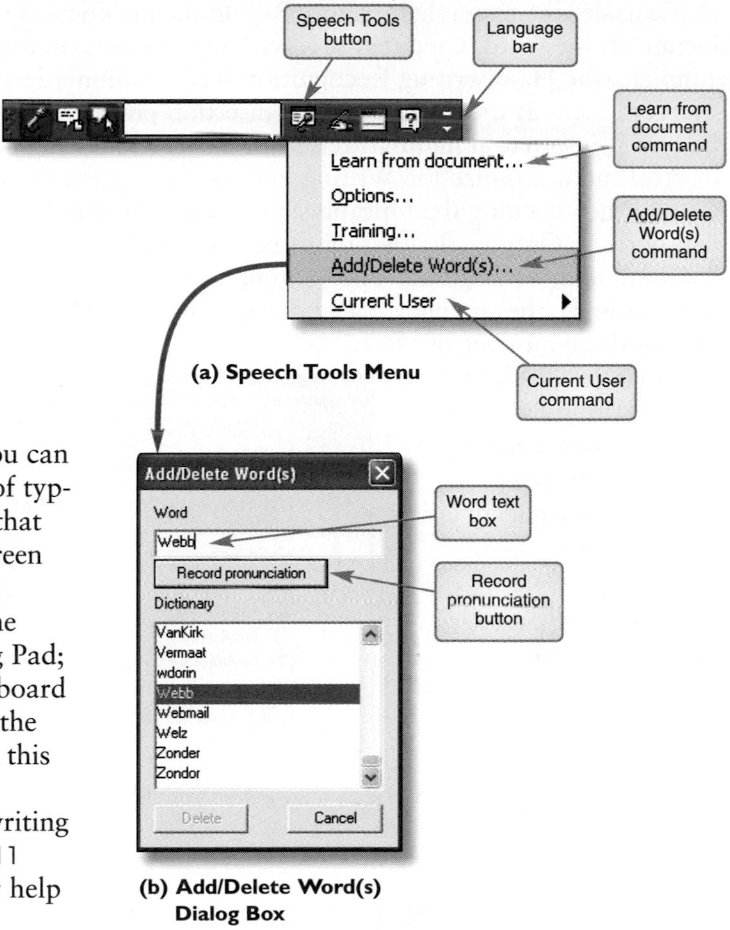

(a) Speech Tools Menu

(b) Add/Delete Word(s) Dialog Box

FIGURE B-8

Handwriting Recognition

Using the Office **Handwriting Recognition service**, you can enter text and numbers into Word by writing instead of typing. You can write using a special handwriting device that connects to your computer or you can write on the screen using your mouse. Four basic methods of handwriting are available by clicking the Handwriting button on the Language bar: Writing Pad; Write Anywhere; Drawing Pad; and On-Screen Keyboard. Although the on-screen keyboard does not involve handwriting recognition, it is part of the Handwriting menu and, therefore, will be discussed in this section.

If your Language bar does not include the Handwriting button, then for installation instructions, enter `install handwriting recognition` in the Type a question for help box on the menu bar.

Writing Pad

To display the Writing Pad, click the Handwriting button on the Language bar and then click Writing Pad (Figure B-9). The **Writing Pad** resembles a notepad with one or more lines on which you can use freehand to print or write in cursive. With the Text button enabled, you can form letters on the line by moving the mouse while holding down the mouse button. To the right of the notepad is a rectangular toolbar. Use the buttons on this toolbar to adjust the Writing Pad, select cells, and activate other handwriting applications.

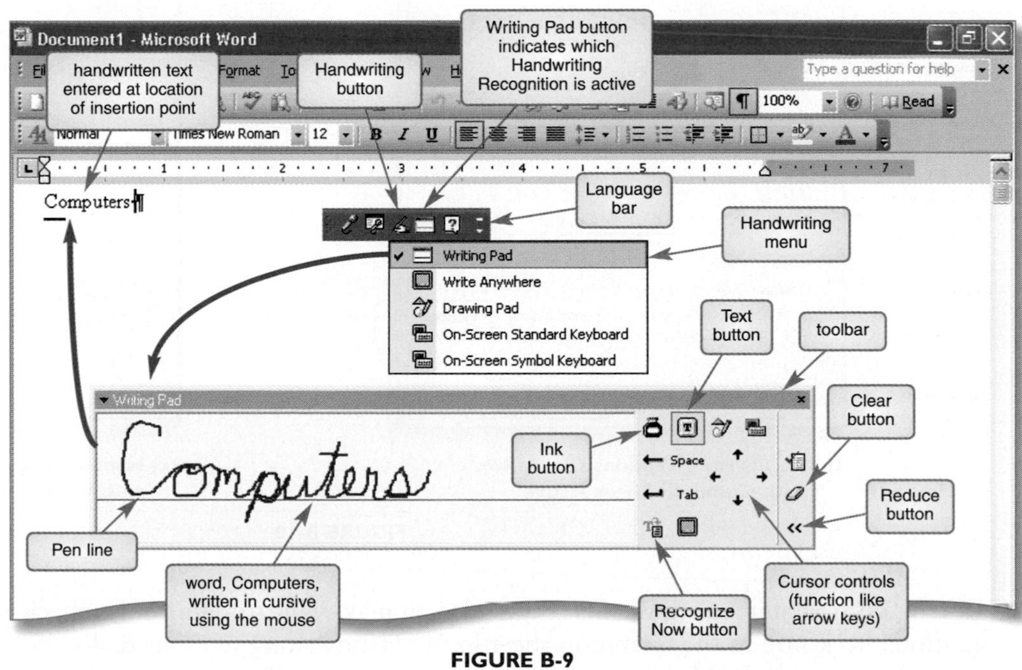

FIGURE B-9

Consider the example in Figure B-9 on the previous page. With the insertion point at the top of the document, the word, Computers, is written in cursive on the **Pen line** in the Writing Pad. As soon as the word is complete, the Handwriting Recognition service automatically converts the handwriting to typed characters and inserts the text at the location of the insertion point. With the Ink button enabled, instead of the Text button, the text is inserted in handwritten form in the document.

You can customize the Writing Pad by clicking the Options button on the left side of the Writing Pad title bar and then clicking the Options command (Figure B-10a). Invoking the Options command causes the Handwriting Options dialog box to be displayed. The Handwriting Options dialog box contains two sheets: Common and Writing Pad. The Common sheet lets you change the pen color and pen width, adjust recognition, and customize the toolbar area of the Writing Pad. The Writing Pad sheet allows you to change the background color and the number of lines that are displayed in the Writing Pad. Both sheets contain a Restore Default button to restore the settings to what they were when the software was installed initially.

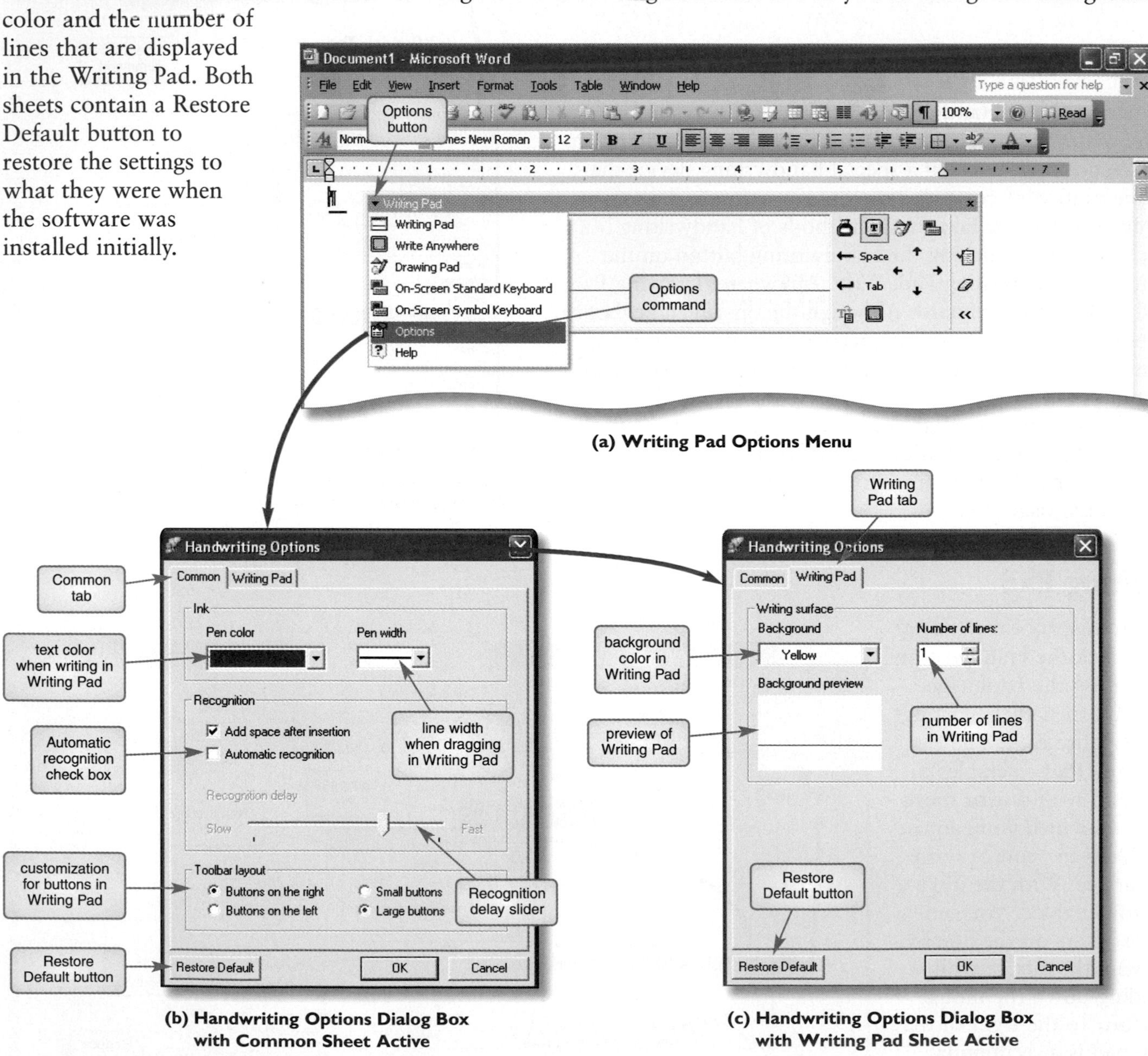

(a) Writing Pad Options Menu

(b) Handwriting Options Dialog Box with Common Sheet Active

(c) Handwriting Options Dialog Box with Writing Pad Sheet Active

FIGURE B-10

When you first start using the Writing Pad, you may want to remove the check mark from the Automatic recognition check box in the Common sheet in the Handwriting Options dialog box (Figure B-10b). With the check mark removed, the Handwriting Recognition service will not interpret what you write in the Writing Pad until you click the Recognize Now button on the toolbar (Figure B-9 on the previous page). This allows you to pause and adjust your writing.

The best way to learn how to use the Writing Pad is to practice with it. Also, for more information, enter `handwriting recognition` in the Type a question for help box on the menu bar.

Write Anywhere

Rather than use Writing Pad, you can write anywhere on the screen by invoking the Write Anywhere command on the Handwriting menu (Figure B-11) that appears when you click the Handwriting button on the Language bar. In this case, the entire window is your writing pad.

In Figure B-11, the word, `Report`, is written in cursive using the mouse button. Shortly after the word is written, the Handwriting Recognition service interprets it, assigns it to the location of the insertion point, and erases what was written.

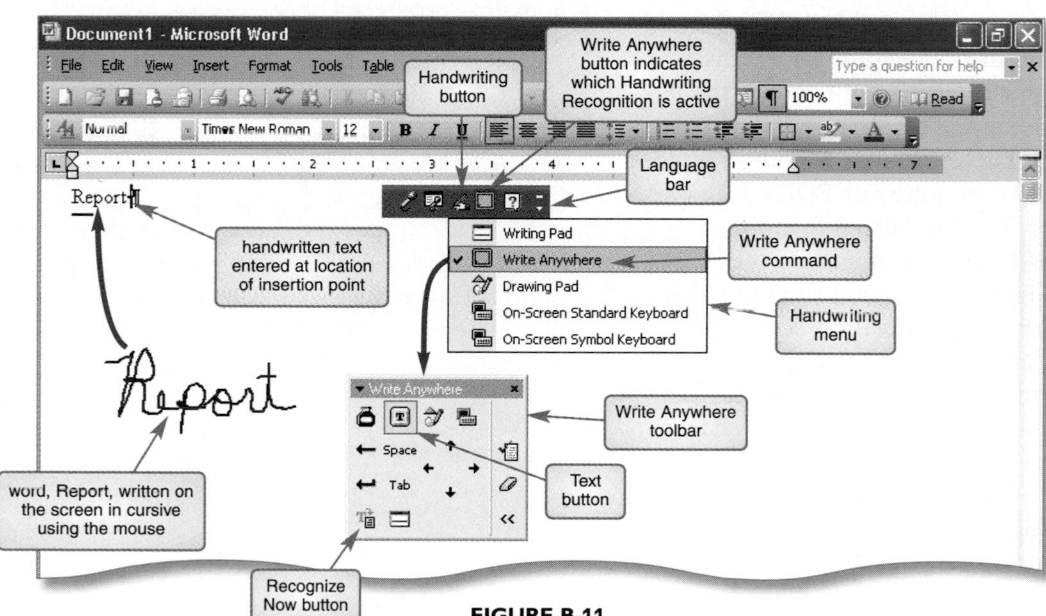

FIGURE B-11

It is recommended that when you first start using the Write Anywhere service that you remove the check mark from the Automatic recognition check box in the Common sheet in the Handwriting Options dialog box (Figure B-10b). With the check mark removed, the Handwriting Recognition service will not interpret what you write on the screen until you click the Recognize Now button on the toolbar (Figure B-11).

Write Anywhere is more difficult to use than the Writing Pad, because when you click the mouse button, Word may interpret the action as moving the insertion point rather than starting to write. For this reason, it is recommended that you use the Writing Pad.

Drawing Pad

With the Drawing Pad, you can insert a freehand drawing or sketch in a Word document. To display the Drawing Pad, click the Handwriting button on the Language bar and then click Drawing Pad (Figure B-12). Create a drawing by dragging the mouse in the Drawing Pad. In Figure B-12, the mouse was used to draw a tic-tac-toe game. When you click the Insert Drawing button on the Drawing Pad toolbar, Word inserts the drawing in the document at the location of the insertion point. Other buttons on the toolbar allow you to erase a drawing, erase your last drawing stroke, copy the drawing to the Office Clipboard, or activate the Writing Pad.

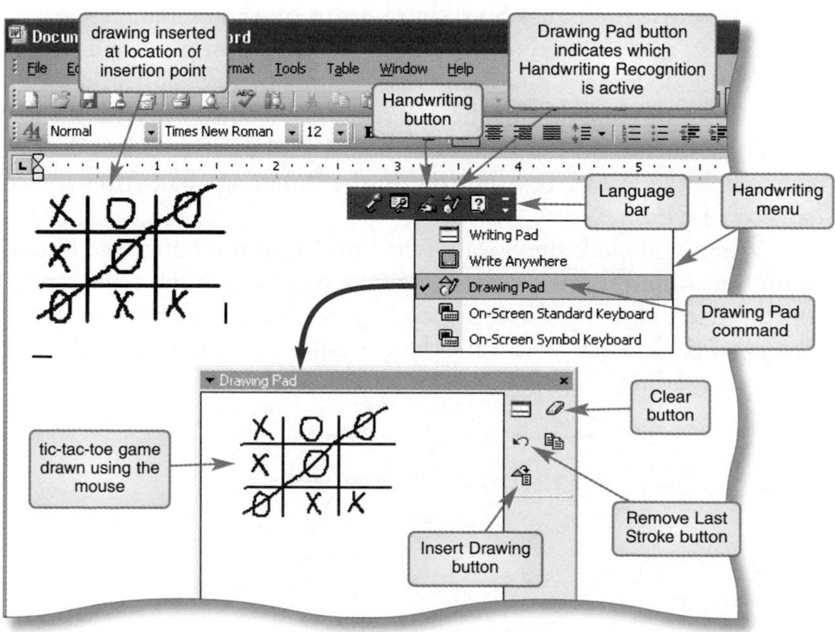

FIGURE B-12

The best way to learn how to use the Drawing Pad is to practice with it. Also, for more information, enter `drawing pad` in the Type a question for help box on the menu bar.

On-Screen Keyboard

The On-Screen Standard Keyboard command on the Handwriting menu (Figure B-13) displays an on-screen keyboard. The **on-screen keyboard** lets you enter data at the location of the insertion point by using your mouse to click the keys. The on-screen keyboard is similar to the type found on hand-held computers or PDAs.

The On-Screen Symbol Keyboard command on the Handwriting menu (Figure B-13) displays a special on-screen keyboard that allows you to enter symbols that are not on your keyboard, as well as Unicode characters. **Unicode characters** use a coding scheme capable of representing all the world's current languages.

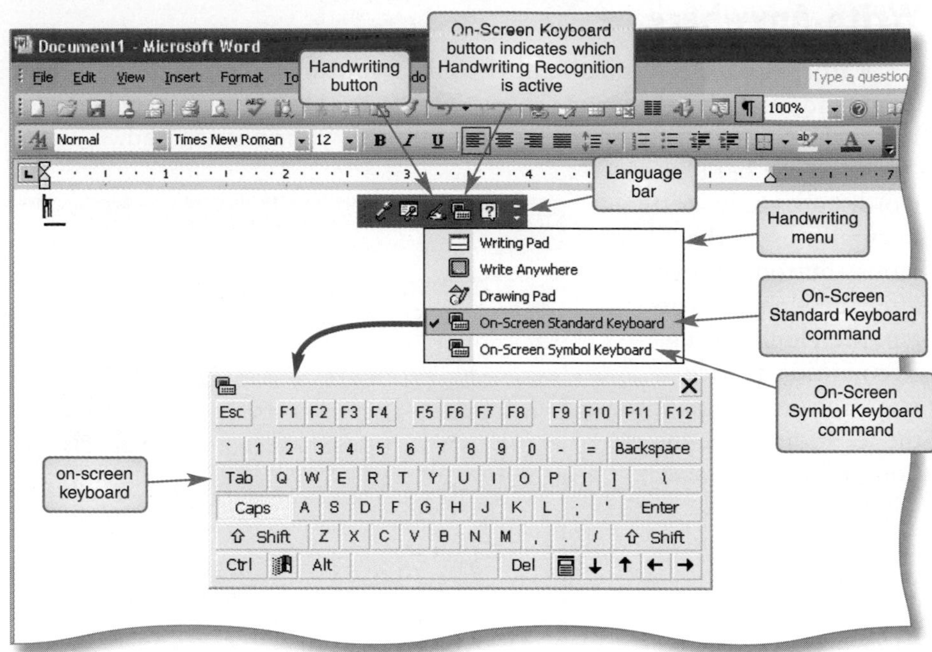

FIGURE B-13

Speech Playback

Using **speech playback**, you can have your computer read back the text in a document. Word provides two buttons for speech playback: Speak Text and Pause Speaking. To show the Speak Text button on the Language bar, click the Options button on the Language bar (Figure B-14) and then click Speak Text on the Options menu. Similarly, click the Options button on the Language bar and then click Pause Speaking on the Options menu to show the Pause Speaking button on the Language bar.

To use speech playback, position the insertion point where you want the computer to start reading back the text in the document and then click the Speak Text button on the Language bar (Figure B-14). The computer reads from the location of the insertion point until the end of the document or until you click the Pause Speaking button on the Language bar. An alternative is to select the text you want the computer to read and then click the Speak Text button on the Language bar. After the computer reads back the selected text, it stops speech playback.

When you click the Speak Text button on the Language bar, it changes to a Stop Speaking button. Click the Stop Speaking button on the Language bar to stop the speech playback. If you click the Pause Speaking button on the Language bar to stop speech playback, the Pause Speaking button changes to a Resume Speaking button that you click when you want the computer to continue reading the document from the location at which it stopped reading.

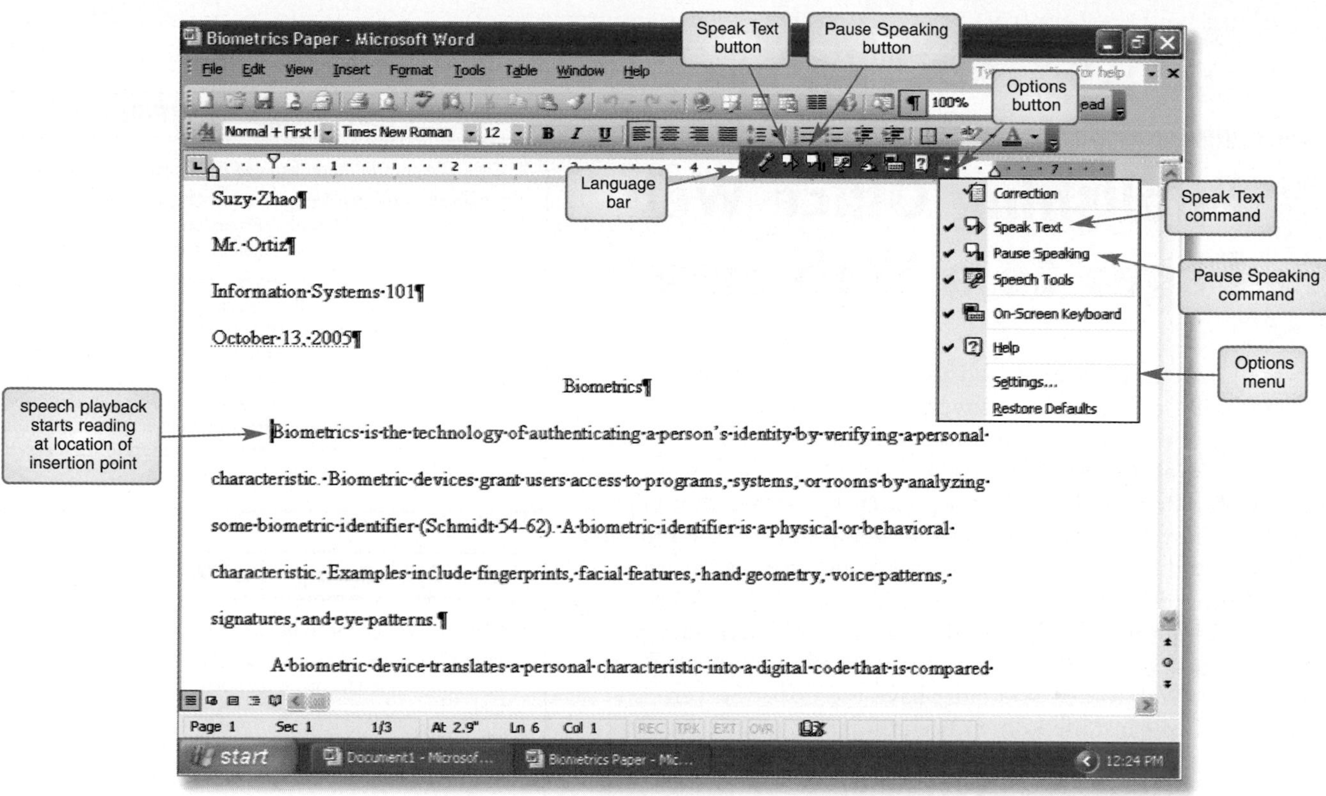

FIGURE B-14

Customizing Speech Playback

You can customize speech playback through the Speech Properties dialog box. Click the Speech Tools button on the Language bar and then click Options on the Speech Tools menu (Figure B-6a on page APP 17). When text services displays the Speech input settings dialog box (Figure B-6b), click the Advanced Speech button. When text services displays the Speech Properties dialog box, click the Text To Speech tab (Figure B-15). The Text To Speech sheet has two areas: Voice selection and Voice speed. The Voice selection area lets you choose between two male voices and one female voice. You can click the Preview Voice button to hear a sample of the voice. The Voice speed area contains a slider. Drag the slider to slow down or speed up the pace of the speaking voice.

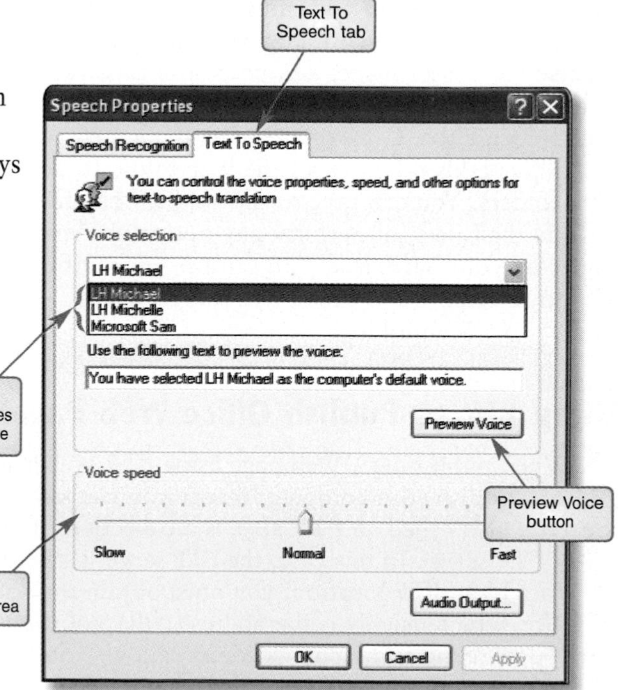

FIGURE B-15

Appendix C

Publishing Office Web Pages to a Web Server

With the Office applications, you use the Save as Web Page command on the File menu to save the Web page to a Web server using one of two techniques: Web folders or File Transfer Protocol. A **Web folder** is an Office shortcut to a Web server. **File Transfer Protocol** (**FTP**) is an Internet standard that allows computers to exchange files with other computers on the Internet.

You should contact your network system administrator or technical support staff at your ISP to determine if their Web server supports Web folders, FTP, or both and to obtain necessary permissions to access the Web server. If you decide to publish Web pages using a Web folder, you must have the Office Server Extensions (OSE) installed on your computer.

Using Web Folders to Publish Office Web Pages

When publishing to a Web folder, someone first must create the Web folder before you can save to it. If you are granted permission to create a Web folder, you must obtain the URL of the Web server, a user name, and possibly a password that allows you to access the Web server. You also must decide on a name for the Web folder. Table C-1 explains how to create a Web folder.

Office adds the name of the Web folder to the list of current Web folders. You can save to this folder, open files in the folder, rename the folder, or perform any operations you would to a folder on your hard disk. You can use your Office program or Windows Explorer to access this folder. Table C-2 explains how to save to a Web folder.

Using FTP to Publish Office Web Pages

When publishing a Web page using FTP, you first must add the FTP location to your computer before you can save to it. An FTP location, also called an **FTP site**, is a collection of files that reside on an FTP server. In this case, the FTP server is the Web server.

To add an FTP location, you must obtain the name of the FTP site, which usually is the address (URL) of the FTP server, and a user name and a password that allows you to access the FTP server. You save and open the Web pages on the FTP server using the name of the FTP site. Table C-3 explains how to add an FTP site.

Office adds the name of the FTP site to the FTP locations list in the Save As and Open dialog boxes. You can open and save files using this list. Table C-4 explains how to save to an FTP location.

Table C-1 Creating a Web Folder

1. Click File on the menu bar and then click Save As (or Open).
2. When the Save As dialog box (or Open dialog box) appears, click My Network Places on the My Places bar, and then click the Create New Folder button on the toolbar.
3. When the Add Network Place Wizard dialog box appears, click the Next button. If necessary, click Choose another network location. Click the Next button. Click the View some examples link, type the Internet or network address, and then click the Next button. Click Log on anonymously to deselect the check box, type your user name in the User name text box, and then click the Next button. Enter the name you want to call this network place and then click the Next button. Click the Finish button.

Table C-2 Saving to a Web Folder

1. Click File on the menu bar and then click Save As.
2. When the Save As dialog box appears, type the Web page file name in the File name text box. Do not press the ENTER key.
3. Click My Network Places on the My Places bar.
4. Double-click the Web folder name in the Save in list.
5. If the Enter Network Password dialog box appears, type the user name and password in the respective text boxes and then click the OK button.
6. Click the Save button in the Save As dialog box.

Table C-3 Adding an FTP Location

1. Click File on the menu bar and then click Save As (or Open).
2. In the Save As dialog box, click the Save in box arrow and then click Add/Modify FTP Locations in the Save in list; or in the Open dialog box, click the Look in box arrow and then click Add/Modify FTP Locations in the Look in list.
3. When the Add/Modify FTP Locations dialog box appears, type the name of the FTP site in the Name of FTP site text box. If the site allows anonymous logon, click Anonymous in the Log on as area; if you have a user name for the site, click User in the Log on as area and then enter the user name. Enter the password in the Password text box. Click the OK button.
4. Close the Save As or the Open dialog box.

Table C-4 Saving to an FTP Location

1. Click File on the menu bar and then click Save As.
2. When the Save As dialog box appears, type the Web page file name in the File name text box. Do not press the ENTER key.
3. Click the Save in box arrow and then click FTP Locations.
4. Double-click the name of the FTP site to which you wish to save.
5. When the FTP Log On dialog box appears, enter your user name and password and then click the OK button.
6. Click the Save button in the Save As dialog box.

Appendix D

Changing Screen Resolution and Resetting the Word Toolbars and Menus

This appendix explains how to change your screen resolution in Windows to the resolution used in this book. It also describes how to reset the Word toolbars and menus to their installation settings.

Changing Screen Resolution

The **screen resolution** indicates the number of pixels (dots) that your computer uses to display the letters, numbers, graphics, and background you see on your screen. The screen resolution usually is stated as the product of two numbers, such as 800 × 600 (pronounced 800 by 600). An 800 × 600 screen resolution results in a display of 800 distinct pixels on each of 600 lines, or about 480,000 pixels. The figures in this book were created using a screen resolution of 800 × 600.

The screen resolutions most commonly used today are 800 × 600 and 1024 × 768, although some Office specialists operate their computers at a much higher screen resolution, such as 2048 × 1536. The following steps show how to change the screen resolution from 1024 × 768 to 800 × 600.

To Change the Screen Resolution

1

- **If necessary, minimize all applications so that the Windows desktop appears.**
- **Right-click the Windows desktop.**

Windows displays the Windows desktop shortcut menu (Figure D-1).

Windows desktop shown at 1024 × 768 screen resolution

FIGURE D-1

2

• **Click Properties on the shortcut menu.**

• **When Windows displays the Display Properties dialog box, click the Settings tab.**

Windows displays the Settings sheet in the Display Properties dialog box (Figure D-2). The Settings sheet shows a preview of the Windows desktop using the current screen resolution (1024 x 768). The Settings sheet also shows the screen resolution and the color quality settings.

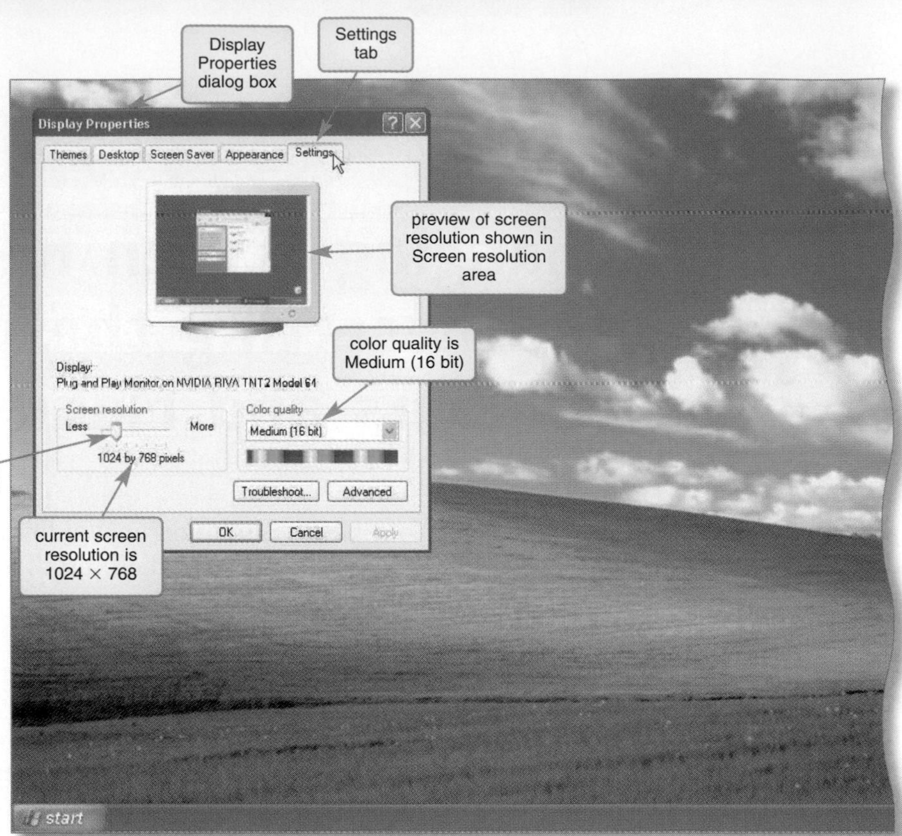

FIGURE D-2

3

• **Drag the slider in the Screen resolution area to the left so that the screen resolution changes to 800 x 600.**

The screen resolution in the Screen resolution area changes to 800 × 600 (Figure D-3). The Settings sheet shows a preview of the Windows desktop using the new screen resolution (800 × 600).

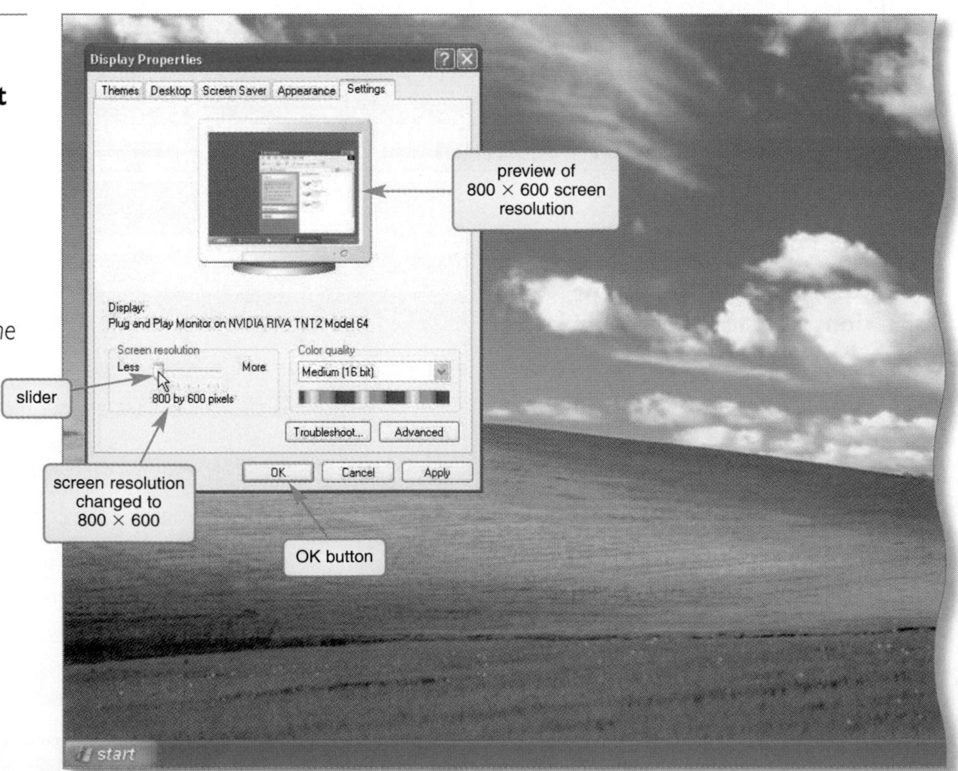

FIGURE D-3

4

- **Click the OK button.**
- **If Windows displays the Monitor Settings dialog box, click the Yes button.**

Windows changes the screen resolution from 1024 × 768 to 800 × 600 (Figure D-4).

FIGURE D-4

As shown in the previous steps, as you decrease the screen resolution, Windows displays less information on your screen, but the information increases in size. The reverse also is true: as you increase the screen resolution, Windows displays more information on your screen, but the information decreases in size.

Resetting the Word Toolbars and Menus

Word customization capabilities allow you to create custom toolbars by adding and deleting buttons and personalize menus based on their usage. Each time you start Word, the toolbars and menus are displayed using the same settings as the last time you used it. The figures in this book were created with the Word toolbars and menus set to the original, or installation, settings.

Resetting the Standard and Formatting Toolbars

The steps on the next page show how to reset the Standard and Formatting toolbars.

To Reset the Standard and Formatting Toolbars

1

- **Start Word.**
- **Click the Toolbar Options button on the Standard toolbar, and then point to Add or Remove Buttons on the Toolbar Options menu.**

Word displays the Toolbar Options menu and the Add or Remove Buttons submenu (Figure D-5).

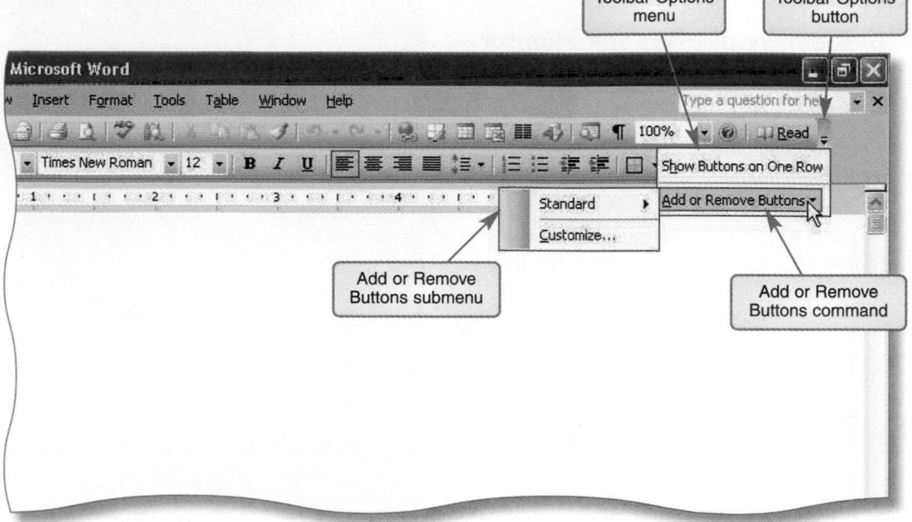

FIGURE D-5

2

- **Point to Standard on the Add or Remove Buttons submenu.**
- **When Word displays the Standard submenu, scroll down and then point to Reset Toolbar.**

The Standard submenu indicates the buttons and boxes that are displayed on the Standard toolbar (Figure D-6). To remove a button from the Standard toolbar, click a button name with a check mark to the left of the name to remove the check mark.

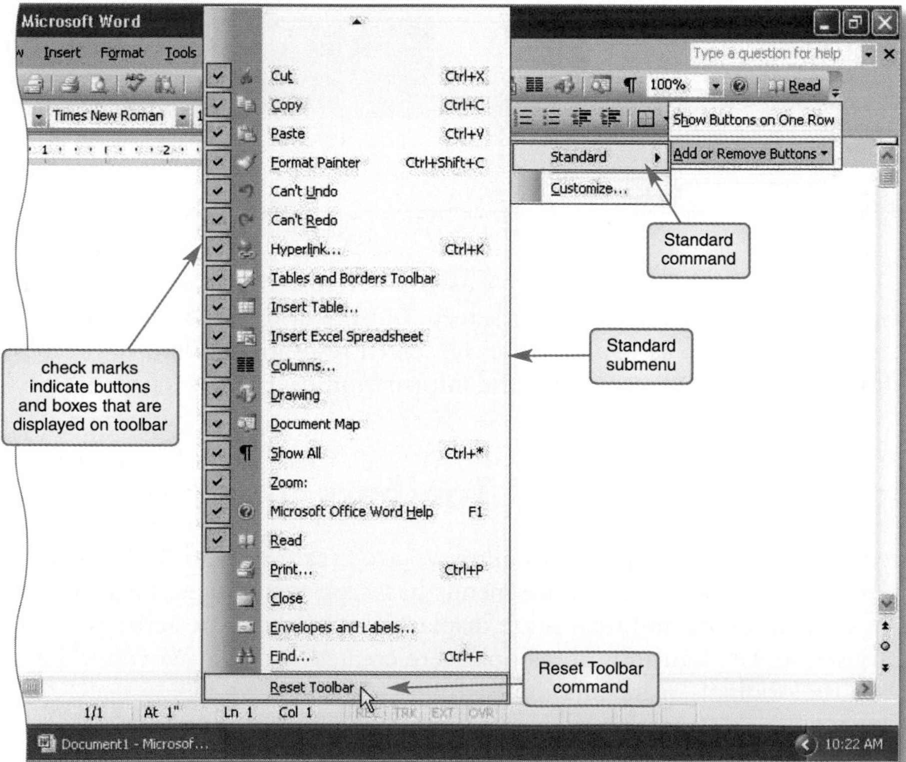

FIGURE D-6

3

- **Click Reset Toolbar.**
- **If a Microsoft Word dialog box is displayed, click the Yes button.**

Word resets the Standard toolbar to its original settings.

4

- **Reset the Formatting toolbar by following Steps 1 through 3 and replacing any reference to the Standard toolbar with the Formatting toolbar.**

Not only can you use the Standard submenu shown in Figure D-6 to reset the Standard toolbar to its original settings, but you also can use it to customize the Standard toolbar by adding and deleting buttons. To add or delete buttons, click the button name on the Standard submenu to add or remove the check mark. Buttons with a check mark to the left currently are displayed on the Standard toolbar; buttons without a check mark are not displayed on the Standard toolbar. You can complete the same tasks for the Formatting toolbar, using the Formatting submenu to add and delete buttons from the Formatting toolbar.

Resetting the Word Menus

The following steps show how to reset the Word menus to their original settings.

To Reset the Word Menus

1

- **Click the Toolbar Options button on the Standard toolbar, and then point to Add or Remove Buttons on the Toolbar Options menu.**

Word displays the Toolbar Options menu and the Add or Remove Buttons submenu (Figure D-7).

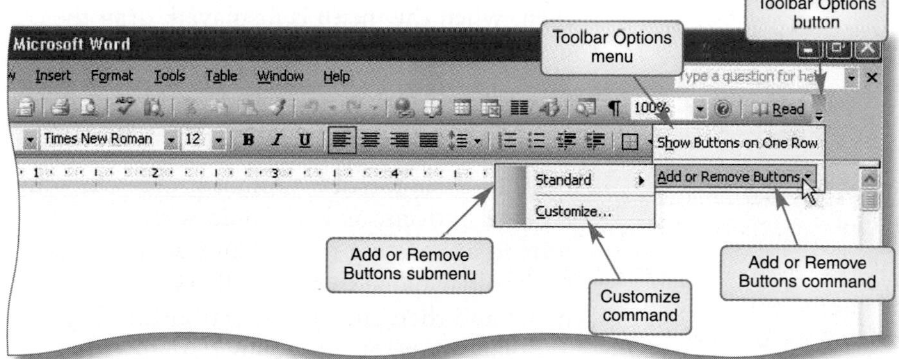

FIGURE D-7

2

- **Click Customize on the Add or Remove Buttons submenu.**
- **When Word displays the Customize dialog box, click the Options tab.**

The Customize dialog box contains three sheets used for customizing the Word toolbars and menus (Figure D-8).

3

- **Click the Reset menu and toolbar usage data button.**
- **When Word displays the Microsoft Word dialog box, click the Yes button.**
- **Click the Close button in the Customize dialog box.**

Word resets the menus to the original settings.

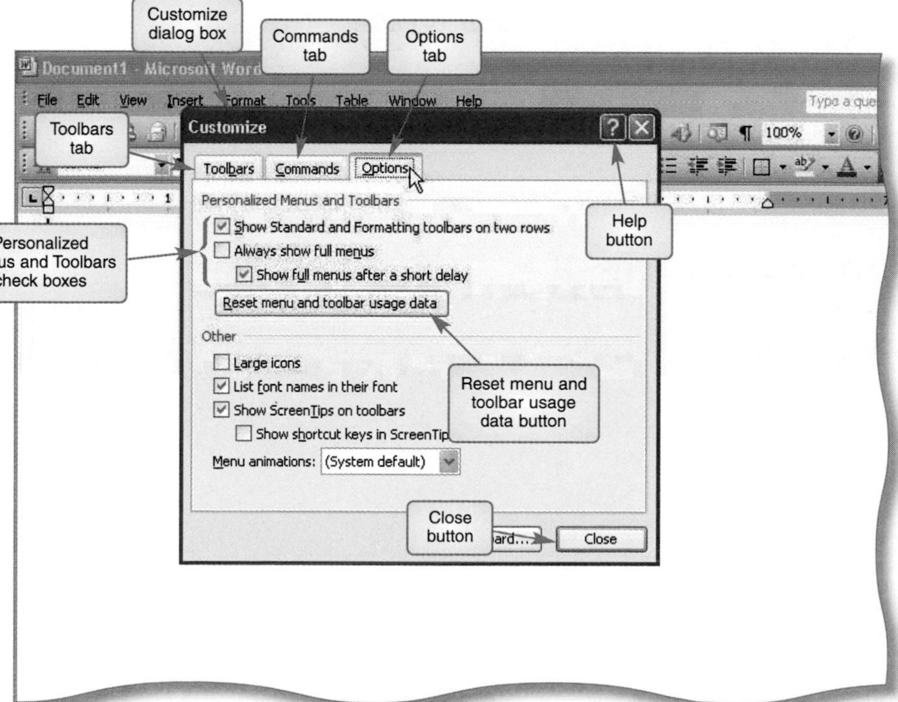

FIGURE D-8

Using the Options sheet in the Customize dialog box, as shown in Figure D-8 on the previous page, you can select options to personalize menus and toolbars. For example, you can select or deselect a check mark that instructs Word to display the Standard and Formatting toolbars on two rows. You also can select whether Word always displays full menus or displays short menus followed by full menus, after a short delay. Other options available on the Options sheet include settings to instruct Word to display toolbars with large icons; to use the appropriate font to display font names in the Font list; and to display a ScreenTip when a user points to a toolbar button. Clicking the Help button in the upper-right corner of the Customize dialog box displays Help topics that will assist you in customizing toolbars and menus.

Using the Commands sheet in the Customize dialog box, you can add buttons to toolbars and commands to menus. Recall that the menu bar at the top of the Word window is a special toolbar. To add buttons to a toolbar, click a category name in the Categories list and then drag the command name in the Commands list to a toolbar. To add commands to a menu, click a category name in the Categories list, drag the command name in the Commands list to a menu name on the menu bar, and then, when the menu is displayed, drag the command to the desired location in the list of menu commands.

Using the Toolbars sheet in the Customize dialog box, you can add new toolbars and reset existing toolbars and the menu. To add a new toolbar, click the New button, enter a toolbar name in the New Toolbar dialog box, and then click the OK button. Once the new toolbar is created, you can use the Commands sheet to add or remove buttons, as you would with any other toolbar. If you add one or more buttons to an existing toolbar and want to reset the toolbar to its original settings, click the toolbar name in the Toolbars list so a check mark is displayed to the left of the name and then click the Reset button. If you add commands to one or more menus and want to reset the menus to their default settings, click Menu Bar in the Toolbars list on the Toolbars sheet so a check mark is displayed to the left of the name and then click the Reset button. When you have finished, click the Close button to close the Customize dialog box.

Appendix E

Microsoft Office Specialist Certification

What Is Microsoft Office Specialist Certification?

Microsoft Office Specialist certification provides a framework for measuring your proficiency with the Microsoft Office 2003 applications, such as Microsoft Office Word 2003, Microsoft Office Excel 2003, Microsoft Office Access 2003, Microsoft Office PowerPoint 2003, and Microsoft Office Outlook 2003. The levels of certification are described in Table E-1.

Table E-1 Levels of Microsoft Office Specialist Certification

LEVEL	DESCRIPTION	REQUIREMENTS	CREDENTIAL AWARDED
Microsoft Office Specialist	Indicates that you have an understanding of the basic features in a specific Microsoft Office 2003 application	Pass any ONE of the following: Microsoft Office Word 2003 Microsoft Office Excel 2003 Microsoft Office Access 2003 Microsoft Office PowerPoint 2003 Microsoft Office Outlook 2003	Candidates will be awarded one certificate for each of the Specialist-level exams they have passed: Microsoft Office Word 2003 Microsoft Office Excel 2003 Microsoft Office Access 2003 Microsoft Office PowerPoint 2003 Microsoft Office Outlook 2003
Microsoft Office Expert	Indicates that you have an understanding of the advanced features in a specific Microsoft Office 2003 application	Pass any ONE of the following: Microsoft Office Word 2003 Expert Microsoft Office Excel 2003 Expert	Candidates will be awarded one certificate for each of the Expert-level exams they have passed: Microsoft Office Word 2003 Expert Microsoft Office Excel 2003 Expert
Microsoft Office Master	Indicates that you have a comprehensive understanding of the features of four of the five primary Microsoft Office 2003 applications	Pass the following: Microsoft Office Word 2003 Expert Microsoft Office Excel 2003 Expert Microsoft Office PowerPoint 2003 And pass ONE of the following: Microsoft Office Access 2003 or Microsoft Office Outlook 2003	Candidates will be awarded the Microsoft Office Master certificate for fulfilling the requirements.

Why Should You Be Certified?

Being Microsoft Office certified provides a valuable industry credential — proof that you have the Office 2003 applications skills required by employers. By passing one or more Microsoft Office Specialist certification exams, you demonstrate your proficiency in a given Office 2003 application to employers. With more than 400 million people in 175 nations and 70 languages using Office applications, Microsoft is targeting Office 2003 certification to a wide variety of companies. These companies include temporary employment agencies that want to prove the expertise of their workers, large corporations looking for a way to measure the skill set of employees, and training companies and educational institutions seeking Microsoft Office 2003 teachers with appropriate credentials.

The Microsoft Office Specialist Certification Exams

You pay $50 to $100 each time you take an exam, whether you pass or fail. The fee varies among testing centers. The **Microsoft Office Expert** exams, which you can take up to 60 minutes to complete, consist of between 40 and 60 tasks that you perform on a personal computer in a simulated environment. The tasks require you to use the application just as you would in doing your job. The **Microsoft Office Specialist** exams contain fewer tasks, and you will have slightly less time to complete them. The tasks you will perform differ on the two types of exams. After passing designated Expert and Specialist exams, candidates are awarded the **Microsoft Office Master** certificate (see the requirements in Table E-1 on the previous page).

How to Prepare for the Microsoft Office Specialist Certification Exams

The Shelly Cashman Series offers several Microsoft-approved textbooks that cover the required objectives of the Microsoft Office Specialist certification exams. For a listing of the textbooks, visit the Shelly Cashman Series Microsoft Office Specialist Center at scsite.com/off2003sch/cert. Click the link Shelly Cashman Series Microsoft Office 2003-Approved Microsoft Office Textbooks (Figure E-1). After using any of the books listed in an instructor-led course, you should be prepared to take the indicated Microsoft Office Specialist certification exam.

How to Find an Authorized Testing Center

To locate a testing center, call 1-800-933-4493 in North America, or visit the Shelly Cashman Series Microsoft Office Specialist Center at scsite.com/off2003sch/cert. Click the link Locate an Authorized Testing Center Near You (Figure E-1). At this Web site, you can look for testing centers around the world.

Shelly Cashman Series Microsoft Office Specialist Center

The Shelly Cashman Series Microsoft Office Specialist Center (Figure E-1) lists more than 15 Web sites you can visit to obtain additional information about certification. The Web page (scsite.com/off2003sch/cert) includes links to general information about certification, choosing an application for certification, preparing for the certification exam, and taking and passing the certification exam.

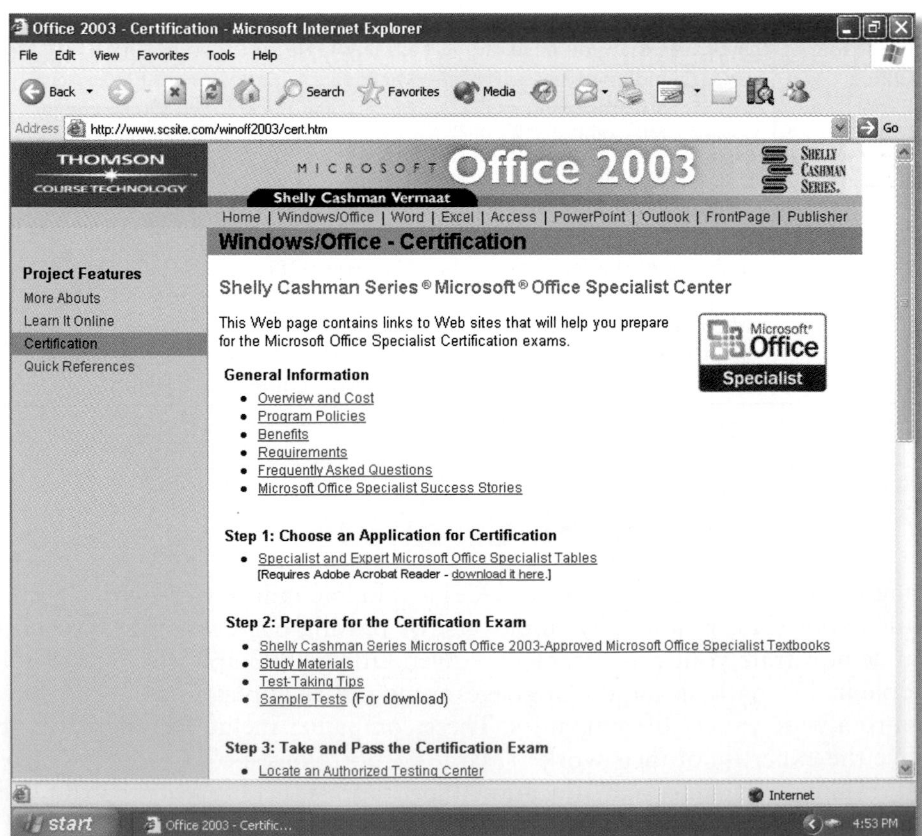

FIGURE E-1

Microsoft Office Specialist Certification Maps

The tables on the following pages list the skill sets and activities you should be familiar with if you plan to take one of the Microsoft Office Specialist certification examinations. Each activity is accompanied by page numbers on which the activity is illustrated and page numbers on which the activity is part of an exercise.

Microsoft Office Word 2003

Table E-2 lists the skill sets and activities you should be familiar with if you plan to take the Microsoft Office Specialist examination for Microsoft Office Word 2003. Table E-3 on the next page lists the skill sets and activities you should be familiar with if you plan to take the Microsoft Office Expert examination for Microsoft Office Word 2003. **ADV** means that the activity is demonstrated in the companion textbook, *Microsoft Office 2003: Advanced Concepts and Techniques* (ISBN 0-619-20025-1 or ISBN 0-619-20026-X). **POST-ADV** means that the activity is demonstrated in the companion textbook, *Microsoft Office 2003: Post-Advanced Concepts and Techniques* (ISBN 0-619-20027-8).

Table E-2 Microsoft Office Specialist Skill Sets, Activities, and Locations in Book for Microsoft Office Word 2003

SKILL SET	SKILL BEING MEASURED	SKILL DEMONSTRATED IN BOOK	SKILL EXERCISE IN BOOK
I. Creating Content	A. Insert and edit text, symbols and special characters	WD 18-20, WD 22-27, WD 57, WD 58-59, WD 83, WD 107, WD 112-114, WD 118-120, WD 125, WD 152, WD 156-157, WD 154-155, WD 166-172, WD 180, **ADV**	WD 65 (Apply Your Knowledge Steps 1-4), WD 67 (In the Lab 1 Step 3), WD 69 (In the Lab 2 Step 3), WD 70 (In the Lab 3 Step 1), WD 78 (Cases and Places 1-3, last sentence), WD 129 (Apply Your Knowledge Steps 1, 7-8, and 10 - 3rd sentence), WD 131 (In the Lab 1 Steps 8-9), WD 133 (In the Lab 2, Part 1 Steps 3b and 4, Part 2 Step 1), WD 134 (In the Lab 3 Steps 2-3), WD 136 (Cases and Places 5 - 4th sentence from end), WD 199 (In the Lab 1 Steps 1-2), WD 202 (Cases and Places 5 - 3rd sentence from end), **ADV**
	B. Insert frequently used and pre-defined text	WD 84 (2nd paragraph), WD 89-90, WD 91-93, WD 177-179, WD 181-182	WD 129 (Apply Your Knowledge Step 10 - 4th sentence), WD 134 (In the Lab 3 Step 1 - 4th sentence), WD 135 (Cases and Places 1 - 2nd to last sentence), WD 200 (In the Lab 2 Step 2 - 3rd and 4th sentences)
	C. Navigate to specific content	WD 110-112, WD 116-117, **ADV**	WD 129 (Apply Your Knowledge Step 6), WD 131 (In the Lab 1 Step 11), WD 133 (In the Lab 2 Part 2 Steps 2 and 4), **ADV**
	D. Insert, position and size graphics	WD 46-50, **ADV**	WD 65 (Apply Your Knowledge Step 15), WD 68 (In the Lab 1 Steps 13-14), WD 60 (In the Lab 2 Steps 12-13), WD 70 (In the Lab 3 Steps 6-7), **ADV**
	E. Create and modify diagrams and charts	**ADV**	**ADV**
	F. Locate, select and insert supporting information	WD 118, WD 124, WD 125	WD 129 (Apply Your Knowledge Step 13), WD 134 (In the Lab 3 Step 3), WD 135 (Cases and Places 2-4)
II. Organizing Content	A. Insert and modify tables	WD 150-151, WD 182-187, **ADV**	WD 198 (Apply Your Knowledge Steps 4-13), WD 200 (In the Lab 2 Step 2), WD 200 (In the Lab 3 Step 2), **ADV**
	B. Create bulleted lists, numbered lists and outlines	WD 153-154, WD 156, WD 187-189, **ADV**	WD 70 (In the Lab 1 Step 5), WD 72 (Cases and Places 4 - next to last sentence), WD 199 (In the Lab 1), WD 200 (In the Lab 2), WD 200 (In the Lab 3 Step 2), WD 202 (Cases and Places 5 - 4th sentence), **ADV**
	C. Insert and modify hyperlinks	WD 108, WD 122, WD 174, WD 207, WD 212-213	WD 131 (In the Lab 1 Step 8), WD 133 (In the Lab 2 Step 3b), WD 200 (In the Lab 2 Step 2 - 2nd to last sentence), WD 216 (In the Lab 2 Steps 2 and 4)

Table E-2 Microsoft Office Specialist Skill Sets, Activities, and Locations in Book for Microsoft Office Word 2003 *(continued)*

SKILL SET	SKILL BEING MEASURED	SKILL DEMONSTRATED IN BOOK	SKILL EXERCISE IN BOOK
III. Formatting Content	A. Format text	WD 17, WD 34-36, WD 40-42, WD 44, WD 87, WD 117, WD 161, WD 173, WD 213, **ADV**	WD 65 (Apply Your Knowledge Steps 5-6, and 8-13), WD 67-68 (In the Lab 1 Steps 1, 5, and 8-11), WD 68-69 (In the Lab 2 Steps 1, 5, and 8-10), WD 70 (In the Lab 3 Steps 1, 3-4), WD 71 (Cases and Places 3 - 3rd and 4th sentences from end), WD 72 (Cases and Places 4 - 4th and 5th sentences from end), WD 129 (Apply Your Knowledge Steps 2 and 9), WD 198 (Apply Your Knowledge Steps 3 and 9), WD 200 (In the Lab 2 Step 2), **ADV**
	B. Format paragraphs	WD 37-38, WD 79-80, WD 82-83, WD 86-89, WD 104-105, WD 163-165, WD 172-173, WD 176-177, **ADV**	WD 65 (Apply Your Knowledge Steps 7 and 14), WD 67 (In the Lab 1 Steps 6-7, 12), WD 69 (In the Lab 2 Steps 6-7, 11), WD 129 (Apply Your Knowledge Steps 3-4), WD 131 (In the Lab 1 Steps 3, 5-8), WD 133 (In the Lab 2 Part 1 Steps 1-3, Part 2 Step 2), WD 134 (In the Lab 3), WD 135-136 (Cases and Places 1-5), WD 198 (Apply Your Knowledge Steps 1-2), WD 199-200 (In the Lab 2 Step 2), **ADV**
	C. Apply and format columns	**ADV**	**ADV**
	D. Insert and modify content in headers and footers	WD 81-84, **ADV**	WD 129 (Apply Your Knowledge Step 10), WD 131 (In the Lab 1 Step 4), WD 133 (In the Lab 2 Part 1 Step 1 - Part 3 Step 2), WD 134 (In the Lab 3 Step 1), WD 135-136 (Cases and Places 1-5), **ADV**
	E. Modify document layout and page setup	WD 77-79, WD 103, **ADV**	WD 131 (In the Lab 1 Steps 2 and 7), WD 133 (In the Lab 2 Part 1 Steps 1 and 2, Part 3 Step 2), WD 134 (In the Lab 3), WD 135-136 (Cases and Places 1-5), **ADV**
IV. Collaborating	A. Circulate documents for review	WD 123, **ADV**	WD 134 (In the Lab 3 Step 5), **ADV**
	B. Compare and merge documents	**ADV**	**ADV**
	C. Insert, view and edit comments	**ADV**	**ADV**
	D. Track, accept and reject proposed changes	**ADV**	**ADV**
V. Formatting and Managing Documents	A. Create new documents using templates	WD 142-148, WD 175 (More About Saving), **ADV**	WD 199 (In the Lab 1 Steps 1 and 2), WD 201-202 (Cases and Places 1-5), **ADV**
	B. Review and modify document properties	WD 100-101, WD 102, WD 193-194	WD 131 (In the Lab 1 Step 12), WD 133 (In the Lab 2 Part 1 Step 7, Part 2 Step 6, Part 3 Step 5), WD 134 (In the Lab 3 Step 4), WD 200 (In the Lab 2 Steps 3 and 6)
	C. Organize documents using file folders	**ADV**	**ADV**
	D. Save documents in appropriate formats for different uses	WD 30, WD 205, WD 206, **ADV**	WD 216 (In the Lab 1 Steps 2, 5-6), WD 216 (In the Lab 2 Step 2)
	E. Print documents, envelopes and labels	WD 53, WD 190-191, **ADV**	WD 65 (Apply Your Knowledge Step 17), WD 68 (In the Lab 1 Step 16), WD 69 (In the Lab 2 Step 15), WD 70 (In the Lab 3 Step 9), WD 131 (In the Lab 1 Step 12), WD 200 (In the Lab 2 Step 7), WD 200 (In the Lab 3 Step 3), **ADV**
	F. Preview documents and Web pages	WD 52, WD 158-159, WD 208-209	WD 70 (In the Lab 3 Step 7), WD 199 (In the Lab 1 Step 5), WD 200 (In the Lab 2 Step 5), WD 216 (In the Lab 1 Step 3), WD 216 (In the Lab 2 Step 5), **ADV**
	G. Change and organize document views and windows	WD 9 Step 4, WD 20-21, WD 77, WD 148-149, WD 169-170, WD 172, **ADV**	WD 67 (In the Lab 1 Step 2), WD 68 (In the Lab 2 Step 2), WD 71-72 (Cases and Places 1-5), WD 133 (In the Lab 2 Part 3 Step 1), WD 135-136 (Cases and Places 1-5), WD 199 (In the Lab 1 Step 2), **ADV**

Table E-3 Microsoft Office Expert Skill Sets, Activities, and Locations in Book for Microsoft Office Word 2003

SKILL SET	SKILL BEING MEASURED	SKILL DEMONSTRATED IN BOOK	SKILL EXERCISE IN BOOK
I. Formatting Content	A. Create custom styles for text, tables and lists	WD 96-98, **ADV**, **POST-ADV**	WD 133 (In the Lab 2 Part 1 Step 2, Part 2 Step 2), WD 135-136 (Cases and Places 2-5), **ADV**, **POST-ADV**
	B. Control pagination	WD 103, WD 154-155, **ADV**, **POST-ADV**	WD 131 (In the Lab 1 Step 7), WD 133 (In the Lab 2 Part 1 Step 2, Part 3 Step 2), WD 134 (In the Lab 3 Step 1), WD 135-136 (Cases and Places 1-5), WD 199 (In the Lab 1 Step 2), **ADV**, **POST-ADV**
	C. Format, position and resize graphics using advanced layout features	WD 49-51, **ADV**, **POST-ADV**	WD 69 (In the Lab 2 Step 13), WD 70 (In the Lab 3 Step 7), WD 199-200 (In the Lab 2 Step 1), WD 201 (Cases and Places 1), **ADV**, **POST-ADV**
	D. Insert and modify objects	**ADV**, **POST-ADV**	**ADV**, **POST-ADV**
	E. Create and modify diagrams and charts using data from other sources	**POST-ADV**	**POST-ADV**
II. Organizing Content	A. Sort content in lists and tables	WD 109-110, **ADV**, **POST-ADV**	WD 133 (In the Lab 2 Part 1, Step 3), WD 134 (In the Lab 3 Step 1 last sentence), WD 135-136 (Cases and Places 1-5), **ADV**, **POST-ADV**
	B. Perform calculations in tables	**ADV**	WD 198 (Apply Your Knowledge Step 7), **ADV**
	C. Modify table formats	**ADV**, **POST-ADV**	**ADV**, **POST-ADV**
	D. Summarize document content using automated tools	**POST-ADV**	**POST-ADV**
	E. Use automated tools for document navigation	**POST-ADV**	**POST-ADV**
	F. Merge letters with other data sources	**ADV**	**ADV**
	G. Merge labels with other data sources	**ADV**	**ADV**
	H. Structure documents using XML	**POST-ADV**	**POST-ADV**
III. Formatting Documents	A. Create and modify forms	**POST-ADV**	**POST-ADV**
	B. Create and modify document background	WD 207-208, **ADV**, **POST-ADV**	WD 216 (In the Lab 2 Steps 2-3), **ADV**, **POST-ADV**
	C. Create and modify document indexes and tables	**POST-ADV**	**POST-ADV**
	D. Insert and modify endnotes, footnotes, captions, and cross-references	WD 93-99, **POST-ADV**	WD 131 (In the Lab 1 Step 7), WD 133 (In the Lab 2 Part 1 Step 2, Part 2 Steps 3 and 4, Part 3 Steps 1-3), WD 134 (In the Lab 3 Step 1), WD 135-136 (Cases and Places 1-5), **POST-ADV**
	E. Create and manage master documents and subdocuments	**POST-ADV**	**POST-ADV**
IV. Collaborating	A. Modify track changes options	**ADV**	**ADV**
	B. Publish and edit Web documents	WD 205-215, WD 209-212, Appendix C	WD 216 (In the Lab 1 Steps 2-5), WD 216 (In the Lab 2 Steps 2, 7)
	C. Manage document versions	**POST-ADV**	**POST-ADV**
	D. Protect and restrict forms and documents	**POST-ADV**	**POST-ADV**
	E. Attach digital signatures to documents	**POST-ADV**	**POST-ADV**
	F. Customize document properties	**POST-ADV**	**POST-ADV**
V. Customizing Word	A. Create, edit, and run macros	**POST-ADV**	**POST-ADV**
	B. Customize menus and toolbars	**POST-ADV**	**POST-ADV**
	C. Modify Word default settings	WD 121, **ADV**, **POST-ADV**	WD 136 (Cases and Places 5), **ADV**, **POST-ADV**

Microsoft Office Excel 2003

Table E-4 lists the skill sets and activities you should be familiar with if you plan to take the Microsoft Office Specialist examination for Microsoft Office Excel 2003. Table E-5 on the next page lists the skill sets and activities you should be familiar with if you plan to take the Microsoft Office Expert examination for Microsoft Office Excel 2003. **ADV** means that the activity is demonstrated in the companion textbook, *Microsoft Office 2003: Advanced Concepts and Techniques* (ISBN 0-619-20025-1 or ISBN 0-619-20026-X). **POST-ADV** means that the activity is demonstrated in the companion textbook, *Microsoft Office 2003: Post-Advanced Concepts and Techniques* (ISBN 0-619-20027-8).

Table E-4 Microsoft Office Specialist Skill Sets, Activities, and Locations in Book for Microsoft Office Excel 2003

SKILL SET	SKILL BEING MEASURED	SKILL DEMONSTRATED IN BOOK	SKILL EXERCISE IN BOOK
I. Creating Data and Content	A. Enter and edit cell content	EX 16-23, EX 50-53, EX 72-88, EX 151-154, **ADV**	EX 57 (Apply Your Knowledge 1), EX 58-64 (In the Labs 1-3 and Cases and Places 1-5), EX 212 (In the Lab 1 Step 2), **ADV**
	B. Navigate to specific cell content	EX 36-37, **ADV**	EX 57 (Apply Your Knowledge 1), EX 58-64 (In the Labs 1-3 and Cases and Places 1-5), **ADV**
	C. Locate, select and insert supporting information	**ADV**	**ADV**
	D. Insert, position, and size graphics	**ADV**	**ADV**
II. Analyzing Data	A. Filter lists using AutoFilter	**ADV**	**ADV**
	B. Sort lists	**ADV**	**ADV**
	C. Insert and modify formulas	EX 72-77, EX 79-80, EX 80-87, EX 168-172, EX 173, EX 174-175, **ADV**	EX 62 (In the Lab Part 3), EX 130 (In the Lab 1 Part 1), EX 130 (In the Lab 1 Part 1), EX 133 (In the Lab 1 Part 1 Steps 2 and 4), EX 135 (In the Lab 2 Part 1 Steps 3 and 5), EX 140-143 (Cases and Places 1-5), EX 211 (Apply Your Knowledge 1 Steps 5-8), EX 212 (In the Lab 1 Part 1), EX 217 (In the Lab 2 Part 1), EX 220 (In the Lab 3 Part 1 Step 11), **ADV**
	D. Use statistical, date and time, financial, and logical functions	EX 23-24, EX 26-27, EX 80-87, EX 165-167, EX 170-172, **ADV**	EX 59 (In the Lab 1 Step 2), EX 59 (In the Lab 2 Step 2), EX 130 (Apply Your Knowledge 1 Part 1), EX 133 (In the Lab 1 Part 1 Step 4), EX 135 (In the Lab 2 Part 1 Step 5), EX 212 (In the Lab 1 Part 1 Step 1), EX 216 (In the Lab 2 Part 1 Step 1), **ADV**
	E. Create, modify, and position diagrams and charts based on worksheet data	EX 38-41, EX 187-199, **ADV**	EX 59 (In the Lab 1 Step 6), EX 60 (In the Lab 2 Step 5), EX 62 (In the Lab 3 Part 2), EX 214 (In the Lab 1 Part 2), EX 217 (In the Lab 2 Part 2), **ADV**
III. Formatting Data and Content	A. Apply and modify cell formats	EX 28-36, EX 90-110, EX 177-186, **ADV**	EX 59 (In the Lab 1 Step 5), EX 60 (In the Lab 2 Step 5), EX 61 (In the Lab 3 Part 1), EX 63-64 (Cases and Places 1-5), EX 131 (Apply Your Knowledge 1), EX 133 (In the Lab 1 Steps 6-8), EX 135 (In the Lab 2 Part 1 Steps 6-9), EX 140-143 (Cases and Places 1-5), EX 214 (In the Lab 1 Step 8), EX 217 (In the Lab 2 Steps 8-10), **ADV**
	B. Apply and modify cell styles	**ADV**	**ADV**
	C. Modify row and column formats	EX 32-33, EX 91-94, EX 96-97, EX 107-111, EX 155-156, EX 159-162, **ADV**	EX 59 (In the Lab 1 Step 4), EX 60 (In the Lab 2 Step 3), EX 133 (In the Lab 1 Steps 6 and 7), EX 135 (In the Lab 3 Step 1), EX 135 (In the Lab 2 Step 6), EX 212 (In the Lab 1 Step 4), EX 216 (In the Lab 2 Steps 3 and 4), EX 219 (In the Lab 3 Steps 1-3), **ADV**
	D. Format worksheets	EX 124, EX 197-199, **ADV**	EX 135 (In the Lab 2 Step 10), EX 137-139 (In the Lab 3 Parts 1-4), EX 214 (In the Lab 1 Part 2), EX 217 (In the Lab 2 Step 11), **ADV**

Table E-4 Microsoft Office Specialist Skill Sets, Activities, and Locations in Book for Microsoft Office Excel 2003

SKILL SET	SKILL BEING MEASURED	SKILL DEMONSTRATED IN BOOK	SKILL EXERCISE IN BOOK
IV. Collaborating	A. Insert, view and edit comments	**ADV**	**ADV**
V. Managing Workbooks	A. Create new workbooks from templates	**ADV**	**ADV**
	B. Insert, delete and move cells	EX 24-27, EX 157-159, EX 161-162, EX 174-175, **ADV**	EX 62 (In the Lab 3 Part 3), EX 212 (In the Lab 1 Step 7), EX 216 (In the Lab 2 Step 6), EX 221 (In the Lab 3 Steps 1-3), **ADV**
	C. Create and modify hyperlinks	**ADV**	**ADV**
	D. Organize worksheets	EX 197-199, **ADV**	EX 214 (In the Lab 1 Part 2), EX 217 (In the Lab 2 Step 11), **ADV**
	E. Preview data in other views	EX 113-116, EX 228-230, **ADV**	EX 133 (In the Lab 1 Step 10), EX 137 (In the Lab 3 Part 2), EX 138 (In the Lab 2 Part 3), EX 239 (In the Lab 1 Part 1 Step 1), EX 240 (In the Lab 2 Part 1 Step 1), **ADV**
	F. Customize Window layout	EX 163-164, EX 175-176, EX 202-207, **ADV**	EX 215 (In the Lab 1 Part 3), EX 216-217 (In the Lab 2 Steps 2, 11, and 14), EX 219-220 (In the Lab 3 Steps 6 and 17), **ADV**
	G. Set up pages for printing	EX 113-116, **ADV**	EX 131 (Apply Your Knowledge 1), EX 133 (In the Lab 1 Step 11), EX 137 (In the Lab 3 Part 1), **ADV**
	H. Print data	EX 113-120, **ADV**	**ADV**
	I. Organize workbooks using file folders	EX 230-232	EX 240 (In the Lab 3)
	J. Save data in appropriate formats for different uses	EX 228-238, **ADV**	EX 239 (In the Lab 1 Parts 1 and 2), EX 240 (In the Lab 2 Parts 1 and 2), **ADV**

Table E-5 Microsoft Office Expert Skill Sets, Activities, and Locations in Book for Microsoft Office Excel 2003

SKILL SET	SKILL BEING MEASURED	SKILL DEMONSTRATED IN BOOK	SKILL EXERCISE IN BOOK
I. Organizing and Analyzing Data	A. Use subtotals	**ADV**	**ADV**
	B. Define and apply advanced filters	**ADV**	**ADV**
	C. Group and outline data	**ADV**	**ADV**
	D. Use data validation	**ADV, POST-ADV**	**ADV, POST-ADV**
	E. Create and modify list ranges	**ADV**	**ADV**
	F. Add, show, close, edit, merge and summarize scenarios	**POST-ADV**	**POST-ADV**
	G. Perform data analysis using automated tools	EX 204-208, **ADV, POST-ADV**	EX 215 (In the Lab 1 Part 3), EX 218 (In the Lab 2 Part 3), EX 221 (In the Lab 3 Part 2), EX 223-224 (Cases and Places 3-5), **ADV**, **POST-ADV**
	H. Create PivotTable and PivotChart reports	**POST-ADV**	**POST-ADV**
	I. Use Lookup and Reference functions	**ADV**	**ADV**
	J. Use Database functions	**ADV**	**ADV**
	K. Trace formula precedents, dependents and errors	**POST-ADV**	**POST-ADV**
	L. Locate invalid data and formulas	EX 89-90, EX 292-294, **POST-ADV**	EX 131 (Apply Your Knowledge 1 Part 1), **ADV, POST-ADV**

Table E-5 Microsoft Office Expert Skill Sets, Activities, and Locations in Book for Microsoft Office Excel 2003 *(continued)*

SKILL SET	SKILL BEING MEASURED	SKILL DEMONSTRATED IN BOOK	SKILL EXERCISE IN BOOK
	M. Watch and evaluate formulas	**POST-ADV**	**POST-ADV**
	N. Define, modify and use named ranges	**ADV**	**ADV**
	O. Structure workbooks using XML	**POST-ADV**	**POST-ADV**
II. Formatting Data and Content	A. Create and modify custom data formats	**ADV**	**ADV**
	B. Use conditional formatting	EX 103-106, **ADV**	EX 133 (In the Lab 1 Step 8), EX 135 (In the Lab 2 Step 8), **ADV**
	C. Format and resize graphics	**ADV**	ADV
	D. Format charts and diagrams	EX 192-198, **ADV**	EX 214 (In the Lab 1, Part 2), EX 217-218, (In the Lab 2 Part 2), **ADV**
III. Collaborating	A. Protect cells, worksheets, and workbooks	**ADV, POST-ADV**	**ADV, POST-ADV**
	B. Apply workbook security settings	**POST-ADV**	**POST-ADV**
	C. Share workbooks	**POST-ADV**	**POST-ADV**
	D. Merge workbooks	**POST-ADV**	**POST-ADV**
	E. Track, accept, and reject changes to workbooks	**POST-ADV**	**POST-ADV**
IV. Managing Data and Workbooks	A. Import data to Excel	EX 120-123, **POST-ADV**	EX 136-139 (In the Lab 3), EX 143 (Cases and Places 5), **ADV, POST-ADV**
	B. Export data from Excel	**POST-ADV**	**POST-ADV**
	C. Publish and edit Web worksheets and workbooks	EX 225-239, **POST-ADV**	EX 239 (In the Lab 1), EX 240 (In the Lab 2), **POST-ADV**
	D. Create and edit templates	**ADV**	**ADV**
	E. Consolidate data	**ADV**	**ADV**
	F. Define and modify workbook properties	**POST-ADV**	**POST-ADV**
V. Customizing Excel	A. Customize toolbars and menus	**POST-ADV**	**POST-ADV**
	B. Create, edit, and run macros	**POST-ADV**	**POST-ADV**
	C. Modify Excel default settings	**ADV**	**ADV**

Microsoft Office Access 2003

Table E-6 lists the skill sets and activities you should be familiar with if you plan to take the Microsoft Office Specialist examination for Microsoft Office Access 2003. **ADV** means that the activity is demonstrated in the companion textbook, *Microsoft Office 2003: Advanced Concepts and Techniques* (ISBN 0-619-20025-1 or ISBN 0-619-20026-X). Expert certification is not available for Microsoft Office Access 2003.

Table E-6 Microsoft Office Specialist Skill Sets, Activities, and Locations in Book for Microsoft Office Access 2003

SKILL SET	SKILL BEING MEASURED	SKILL DEMONSTRATED IN BOOK	SKILL EXERCISE IN BOOK
I. Structuring Databases	A. Create Access databases	AC 10	AC 56-64 (In The Labs 1, 2, 3; Cases and Places 1-5)
	B. Create and modify tables	AC 15, AC 159, AC 127-130	AC 63 (Cases and Places 3), AC 171 (Cases and Places 3), AC 167-172 (All Exercises)

Table E-6 Microsoft Office Specialist Skill Sets, Activities, and Locations in Book for Microsoft Office Access 2003

SKILL SET	SKILL BEING MEASURED	SKILL DEMONSTRATED IN BOOK	SKILL EXERCISE IN BOOK
	C. Define and modify field types	AC 130, AC 147	AC 169 (In The Lab 2 Step 5f, In The Lab 3 part 1), AC 172 (Cases and Places 5)
	D. Modify field properties	AC 127-128, AC 140, AC 141, AC 143, AC 142, AC 144, AC 160, **ADV**	AC 167-172 (All Exercises), **ADV**
	E. Create and modify one-to-many relationships	AC 151, AC 342	AC 171-172 (Cases and Places 1-4), **ADV**
	F. Enforce referential integrity	AC 152, **ADV**	AC 167 (Apply Your Knowledge Step 17), AC 169 (In The Lab 1 Step 13), AC 170 (In The Lab 2 Step 11), AC 170 (In The Lab 3 part 3), AC 171-172 (Cases and Places 1-4), **ADV**
	G. Create and modify queries	AC 34, AC 37, AC 104, AC 154,	AC 55 (Apply Your Knowledge Steps 3-6), AC 60 (In The Lab 2 Step 2), AC 62 (In The Lab Part 3), AC 63-64 (Cases and Places 3, 4), AC 109 (Apply Your Knowledge Step 8), AC 111 (In The Lab 2 Step 12), AC 112 (Cases and Places 5), AC 172 (Cases and Places 4), AC 171 (Cases and Places 3), AC 172 (Cases and Places 5), **ADV**
	H. Create forms	AC 38, **ADV**	AC 57 (In The Lab 1 Step 8), AC 61 (In the Lab 3 Part 1), AC 64 (Cases and Places 4), **ADV**
	I. Add and modify form controls and properties	**ADV**	**ADV**
	J. Create reports	AC 43, **ADV**	AC 55-64 (All Exercises), **ADV**
	K. Add and modify report control properties	**ADV**	**ADV**
	L. Create a data access page	**ADV**	**ADV**
II. Entering Data	A. Enter, edit and delete records	AC 23, AC 28, AC 116, AC 119, AC 125	AC 54-64 (All Exercises), AC 167-172 (All Exercises)
	B. Find and move among records	AC 77	AC 55 (Apply Your Knowledge Step 1), AC 57 (In The Lab 1 Step 9), AC 60 (In The Lab 2 Step 3), AC 62 (In The Lab 3 part 2)
	C. Import data to Access	AC 176-180	AC 191 (In The Lab 1)
III. Organizing Data	A. Create and modify calculated fields and aggregate functions	AC 96-97, AC 99-103	AC 110 (In The Lab 1 Step 11), AC 111 (In The Lab 3 part 3), AC 112 (Cases and Places 3), AC 110 (In The Lab 1 Steps 12 and 13), AC 111 (In The Lab 2 Step 11, In The Lab 3 part 3), AC 112 (Cases and Places 1-4)
	B. Modify form layout	**ADV**	**ADV**
	C. Modify report layout and page setup	AC 30-31, **ADV**	AC 170 (In The Lab 3 Parts 2-3), **ADV**
	D. Format datasheets	AC 131-135	AC 171 (Cases and Places 2)
	E. Sort records	AC 86-89, AC 155, **ADV**	AC 167 (Apply Your Knowledge Step 15), AC 171-172 (Cases and Places 2 and 4), **ADV**
	F. Filter records	AC 121, AC 123	AC 167 (Apply Your Knowledge Step 13), AC 169 (In The Lab 2 Step 9)
IV. Managing Databases	A. Identify object dependencies	**ADV**	**ADV**
	B. View objects and object data in other views	AC 23, AC 29-31, AC 42, **ADV**	AC 54-64 (All Exercises), AC 170 (In The Lab 3), **ADV**
	C. Print database objects and data	AC 29-31, AC 47, AC 72, **ADV**	AC 54-64 (All Exercises), AC 109-112 (All Exercises), **ADV**
	D. Export data from Access	AC 181, AC 183, AC 184, AC 185-187	AC 192 (In The Lab 2)
	E. Back up a database	AC 162-163	AC 167 (Apply Your Knowledge Step 18), AC 170 (In The Lab 2 Step 12), AC 171 (Cases and Places 1-2)
	F. Compact and repair databases	AC 163-164	AC 169 (In The Lab 1 Step 14), AC 170 (In The Lab 2 Step 12), AC 171 (Cases and Places 1-2)

Microsoft Office PowerPoint 2003

Table E-7 lists the skill sets and activities you should be familiar with if you plan to take the Microsoft Office Specialist examination for Microsoft Office PowerPoint 2003. **ADV** means that the activity is demonstrated in the companion textbook, *Microsoft Office 2003: Advanced Concepts and Techniques* (ISBN 0-619-20025-1 or ISBN 0-619-20026-X). Expert certification is not available for Microsoft Office PowerPoint 2003.

Table E-7 Microsoft Office Specialist Skill Sets, Activities, and Locations in Book for Microsoft Office PowerPoint 2003

SKILL SET	SKILL BEING MEASURED	SKILL DEMONSTRATED IN BOOK	SKILL EXERCISE IN BOOK
I. Creating Content	A. Create new presentations from templates	PPT 18-43, PPT 85-11, PPT 111, **ADV**	PPT 69-71 (In the Lab 1 Steps 1-3), PPT 132-133 (In the Lab 1 Steps 1-4), **ADV**
	B. Insert and edit text-based content	PPT 20-24, PPT 31-42, PPT 53-55, PPT 56, PPT 88-94, **ADV**	PPT 69-71 (In the Lab 1 Steps 2-4), PPT 72-73 (In the Lab 2 Step 4), PPT 74-77 (In the Lab 3 Parts 1 and 2), PPT 132-134 (In the Lab 1 Steps 2-4), **ADV**
	C. Insert tables, charts and diagrams	**ADV**	**ADV**
	D. Insert pictures, shapes and graphics	PPT 99-106, **ADV**	PPT 132-134 (In the Lab 1 Steps 2-3, 5-6), PPT 134-135 (In the Lab 2 Steps 2-5), **ADV**
	E. Insert objects	**ADV**	**ADV**
II. Formatting Content	A. Format text-based content	PPT 23-27, PPT 153-155, **ADV**	PPT 69-71 (In the Lab 1 Step 2), PPT 72-73 (In the Lab 2 Step 2), **ADV**
	B. Format pictures, shapes and graphics	PPT 108-111, PPT 116-119, **ADV**	PPT 132-134 (In the Lab 1 Steps 2-3, 5-6), PPT 134-135 (In the Lab 2 Steps 2-5, and 8), PPT 136-137 (In the Lab 3 Steps 2-5), **ADV**
	C. Format slides	PPT 17-20, PPT 85, PPT 97-99, PPT 144, **ADV**	PPT 69-71 (In the Lab 1 Step 1), PPT 131-132 (Apply Your Knowledge 1 Steps 3 and 5), PPT 132-134 (In the Lab 1 Steps 3, 5, 6), PPT 134-135 (In the Lab 2 Step 1), **ADV**
	D. Apply animation schemes	PPT 114-116, **ADV**	PPT 131-132 (Apply Your Knowledge 1 Step 6), PT 136-137 (In the Lab 3 Step 7), **ADV**
	E. Apply slide transitions	**ADV**	**ADV**
	F. Customize slide templates	**ADV**	**ADV**
	G. Work with masters	PPT 112-113, **ADV**	PPT 132-134 (In the Lab 1 Step 7), PPT 134-135 (In the Lab 2 Step 6), PPT 136-137 (In the Lab 3 Step 6), **ADV**
III. Collaborating	A. Track, accept and reject changes in a presentation	**ADV**	**ADV**
	B. Add, edit and delete comments in a presentation	**ADV**	**ADV**
	C. Compare and merge presentations	**ADV**	**ADV**
IV. Managing and Delivering Presentations	A. Organize a presentation	PPT 30-31, PPT 89-97, **ADV**	PPT 69-71 (In the Lab 1 Step 3), PPT 132-134 (In the Lab 1 Steps 3-4), **ADV**
	B. Set up slide shows for delivery	**ADV**	**ADV**
	C. Rehearse timing	**ADV**	**ADV**
	D. Deliver presentations	PPT 46-50, **ADV**	PPT 74-77 (In the Lab 3 Part 1 Step 2, Part 2 Step 6), **ADV**
	E. Prepare presentations for remote delivery	**ADV**	**ADV**

Table E-7 Microsoft Office Specialist Skill Sets, Activities, and Locations in Book for Microsoft Office PowerPoint 2003

SKILL SET	SKILL BEING MEASURED	SKILL DEMONSTRATED IN BOOK	SKILL EXERCISE IN BOOK
	F. Save and publish presentations	PPT 146-149, PPT 154-157, Appendix C, **ADV**	PPT 158 (In the Lab 1 Steps 2-3, and 6), PPT 158 (In the Lab 2 Steps 2-3, and 8), PPT 159 (In the Lab 3 Steps 2-3), **ADV**
	G. Print slides, outlines, handouts, and speaker notes	PPT 56-61, PPT 122-126, **ADV**	PPT 69-71 (In the Lab 1 Step 7), PPT 72-73 (In the Lab 2 Steps 6-8), PPT 158 (In the Lab 1 Step 7), **ADV**
	H. Export a presentation to another Microsoft Office program	**ADV**	**ADV**

Microsoft Office Outlook 2003

Table E-8 lists the skill sets and activities you should be familiar with if you plan to take the Microsoft Office Specialist examination for Microsoft Office Outlook 2003. **ADV** means that the activity is demonstrated in the companion textbook, *Microsoft Office 2003: Advanced Concepts and Techniques* (ISBN 0-619-20025-1 or ISBN 0-619-20026-X). Expert certification is not available for Microsoft Office Outlook 2003.

Table E-8 Microsoft Office Specialist Skill Sets, Activities, and Locations in Book for Microsoft Office Outlook 2003

SKILL SET	SKILL BEING MEASURED	SKILL DEMONSTRATED IN BOOK	SKILL EXERCISE IN BOOK
I. Messaging	A. Originate and respond to e-mail and instant messages	OUT 13-16, OUT 23-25, OUT 51-53, **ADV**	OUT 62 (In the Lab 1 Part 2 Step 1), OUT 63 (In the Lab 3 Part 2), OUT 64 (Cases and Places 3), **ADV**
	B. Attach files to items	OUT 27-29, **ADV**	OUT 62 (In the Lab 1 Part 2 Step 3), **ADV**
	C. Create and modify a personal signature for messages	OUT 19-23	OUT 63 (In the Lab 3 Part 1, Part 3 Step 4)
	D. Modify e-mail message settings and delivery options	OUT 15, OUT 29-31, OUT 34-38	OUT 62 (In the Lab 1 Part 2 Steps 2, 4-5), OUT 62 (In the Lab 2), OUT 63 (In the Lab 3 Part 2)
	E. Create and edit contacts	OUT 41-44, **ADV**	OUT 61 (Apply Your Knowledge 1), OUT 64 (Cases and Places 1-5), **ADV**
	F. Accept, decline, and delegate tasks	**ADV**	**ADV**
II. Scheduling	A. Create and modify appointments, meetings, and events	**ADV**	**ADV**
	B. Update, cancel, and respond to meeting requests	**ADV**	**ADV**
	C. Customize Calendar settings	**ADV**	**ADV**
	D. Create, modify, and assign tasks	**ADV**	**ADV**
III. Organizing	A. Create and modify distribution lists	OUT 53-56	OUT 61 (Apply Your Knowledge 1, In the Lab 1 Part 1)
	B. Link contacts to other items	OUT 58	OUT 64 (Cases and Places 3)
	C. Create and modify notes	**ADV**	**ADV**
	D. Organize items	OUT 31-34, OUT 44-48, **ADV**	OUT 61 (Apply Your Knowledge 1), OUT 62 (In the Lab 2), OUT 64 (Cases and Places 3 and 5), **ADV**
	E. Organize items using folders	OUT 39-41, **ADV**	OUT 61 (Apply Your Knowledge 1), OUT 64 (Cases and Places 4), **ADV**
	F. Search for items	OUT 38, OUT 46-47	OUT 63 (In the Lab 3 Part 3 Step 2), OUT 64 (Cases and Places 2)

Table E-8 Microsoft Office Specialist Skill Sets, Activities, and Locations in Book for Microsoft Office Outlook 2003 *(continued)*

SKILL SET	SKILL BEING MEASURED	SKILL DEMONSTRATED IN BOOK	SKILL EXERCISE IN BOOK
	G. Save items in different file formats	OUT 56-58	OUT 62 (In the Lab 1 Part 3)
	H. Assign items to categories	OUT 47-49	OUT 64 (Cases and Places 4)
	I. Preview and print items	OUT 12, OUT 49-50, **ADV**	OUT 61-62 (Apply Your Knowledge 1, In the Lab 1 Part 1, and Part 2 Step 6), OUT 63 (In the Lab 3 Part 1, Part 2, and Part 3 Step 5), OUT 64 (Cases and Places 1-5), **ADV**

Index

Quick Reference Summary

In the Microsoft Office 2003 applications, you can accomplish a task in a number of ways. The following five tables (one each for Microsoft Office Word 2003, Microsoft Office Excel 2003, Microsoft Office Access 2003, Microsoft Office PowerPoint 2003, and Microsoft Office Outlook 2003) provide a quick reference to each task presented in this textbook. The first column identifies the task. The second column indicates the page number on which the task is discussed in the book. The subsequent four columns list the different ways the task in column one can be carried out. You can invoke the commands listed in the MOUSE, MENU BAR, and SHORTCUT MENU columns using Voice commands.

Table 1 Microsoft Office Word 2003 Quick Reference Summary

TASK	PAGE NUMBER	MOUSE	MENU BAR	SHORTCUT MENU	KEYBOARD SHORTCUT
1.5 Line Spacing	WD 87	Line Spacing button arrow on Formatting toolbar	Format | Paragraph | Indents and Spacing tab	Paragraph | Indents and Spacing tab	CTRL+5
AutoCorrect Entry, Create	WD 91		Tools | AutoCorrect Options | AutoCorrect tab		
AutoCorrect Options	WD 90	AutoCorrect Options button			
AutoText Entry, Create	WD 179		Insert | AutoText | New		ALT+F3
AutoText Entry, Insert	WD 181		Insert | AutoText		Type entry, then F3
Blank Line Above Paragraph	WD 87		Format | Paragraph | Indents and Spacing tab	Paragraph | Indents and Spacing tab	CTRL+0 (zero)
Bold	WD 44	Bold button on Formatting toolbar	Format | Font | Font tab	Font | Font tab	CTRL+B
Border, Bottom	WD 172	Border button arrow on Formatting toolbar	Format | Borders and Shading | Borders tab		
Bulleted List	WD 187	Bullets button on Formatting toolbar	Format | Bullets and Numbering Bulleted tab	Bullets and Numbering | Bulleted tab	* and then space, type text, ENTER
Capitalize Letters	WD 87		Format | Font | Font tab	Font | Font tab	CTRL+SHIFT+A
Case of Letters	WD 87				SHIFT+F3
Center	WD 38	Center button on Formatting toolbar	Format | Paragraph | Indents and Spacing tab	Paragraph | Indents and Spacing tab	CTRL+E
Center Vertically	WD 38		File | Page Setup | Layout tab		
Clip Art, Insert	WD 46		Insert | Picture | Clip Art		
Clipboard Task Pane, Display	WD 169	Double-click Office Clipboard icon in tray	Edit | Office Clipboard		
Close Document	WD 59	Close button on menu bar	File | Close		CTRL+W
Color Characters	WD 161	Font Color button arrow on Formatting toolbar	Format | Font | Font tab	Font | Font tab	
Copy (Collect Items)	WD 166	Copy button on Standard toolbar	Edit | Copy	Copy	CTRL+C
Count Words	WD 100	Recount button on Word Count toolbar	Tools | Word Count		
Custom Dictionary	WD 121		Tools | Options | Spelling and Grammar tab		
Date, Insert	WD 177		Insert | Date and Time		
Delete (Cut) Text	WD 59	Cut button on Standard toolbar	Edit | Cut	Cut	CTRL+X or DELETE
Demote List Item	WD 189	Decrease Indent button on Formatting toolbar			
Document Summary, Modify	WD 193		File | Properties | Summary tab		
Document Window, Open New	WD 160	New Blank Document button on Standard toolbar		File | New | Blank document	CTRL+N

Table 1 Microsoft Office Word 2003 Quick Reference Summary *(continued)*

TASK	PAGE NUMBER	MOUSE	MENU BAR	SHORTCUT MENU	KEYBOARD SHORTCUT
Double-Space Text	WD 80	Line Spacing button on Formatting toolbar	Format | Paragraph | Indents and Spacing tab	Paragraph | Indents and Spacing tab	CTRL+2
Double-Underline	WD 87		Format | Font | Font tab	Font | Font tab	CTRL+SHIFT+D
E-Mail Document	WD 123	E-mail button on Standard toolbar	File | Send To | Mail Recipient		
Envelope, Address	WD 190		Tools | Letters and Mailings | Envelopes and Labels		
Find	WD 117	Select Browse Object button on vertical scroll bar	Edit | Find		CTRL+F
Find and Replace	WD 116	Double-click left side of status bar	Edit | Replace		CTRL+H
File Properties, Display	WD 194	Views button arrow in Open dialog box			
First-Line Indent	WD 88	Drag First Line Indent marker on ruler	Format | Paragraph | Indents and Spacing tab	Paragraph | Indents and Spacing tab	
Font	WD 36	Font box arrow on Formatting toolbar	Format | Font | Font tab	Font | Font tab	CTRL+SHIFT+F
Font Size	WD 17	Font Size box arrow on Formatting toolbar	Format | Font | Font tab	Font | Font tab	CTRL+SHIFT+P
Footnote, Create	WD 94		Insert | Reference | Footnote		
Footnote, Delete	WD 99	Delete note reference mark			
Footnote, Edit	WD 99	Double-click note reference mark	View | Footnotes		
Footnotes to Endnotes, Convert	WD 99		Insert | Reference | Footnote		
Formatting Marks	WD 21	Show/Hide ¶ button on Standard toolbar	Tools | Options | View tab		CTRL+SHIFT+*
Formatting, Clear	WD 173	Style box arrow on Formatting toolbar			CTRL+SPACEBAR; CTRL+Q
Frame, New	WD 210	Desired button on Frames toolbar			
Frames Page, Create	WD 210		Format | Frames | New Frames Page		
Frame Properties, Modify	WD 214	Frame Properties button on Frames toolbar	Format | Frames | Frame Properties	Frame Properties	
Full Menu	WD 13	Double-click menu name	Click menu name and wait		
Go To	WD 111	Select Browse Object button on vertical scroll bar	Edit | Go To		CTRL+G
Hanging Indent, Create	WD 105	Drag Hanging Indent marker on ruler	Format | Paragraph | Indents and Spacing tab	Paragraph | Indents and Spacing tab	CTRL+T
Hanging Indent, Remove	WD 87	Drag Hanging Indent marker on ruler	Format | Paragraph | Indents and Spacing tab	Paragraph | Indents and Spacing tab	CTRL+SHIFT+T
Header, Display	WD 81		View | Header and Footer		
Help	WD 60 and Appendix A	Microsoft Office Word Help button on Standard toolbar	Help | Microsoft Office Word Help		F1
Highlight Text	WD 213	Highlight button arrow on Formatting toolbar			
HTML Source	WD 206		View | HTML Source		
Hyperlink, Convert to Regular Text	WD 174	AutoCorrect Options button | Undo Hyperlink		Remove Hyperlink	CTRL+Z
Hyperlink, Create	WD 108 and WD 212	Insert Hyperlink button on Standard toolbar		Hyperlink	Web address then ENTER or SPACEBAR
Hyperlink, Edit	WD 207	Insert Hyperlink button on Standard toolbar		Hyperlink	CTRL+K
Indent, Decrease	WD 87	Decrease Indent button on Formatting toolbar	Format | Paragraph | Indents and Spacing tab	Paragraph | Indents and Spacing tab	CTRL+SHIFT+M
Indent, Increase	WD 87	Increase Indent button on Formatting toolbar	Format | Paragraph | Indents and Spacing tab	Paragraph | Indents and Spacing tab	CTRL+M
Italicize	WD 41	Italic button on Formatting toolbar	Format | Font | Font tab	Font | Font tab	CTRL+I
Justify Paragraph	WD 87	Justify button on Formatting toolbar	Format | Paragraph | Indents and Spacing tab	Paragraph | Indents and Spacing tab	CTRL+J

Table 1 Microsoft Office Word 2003 Quick Reference Summary

TASK	PAGE NUMBER	MOUSE	MENU BAR	SHORTCUT MENU	KEYBOARD SHORTCUT
Leader Characters	WD 164		Format | Tabs		
Left-Align	WD 86	Align Left button on Formatting toolbar	Format | Paragraph | Indents and Spacing tab	Paragraph | Indents and Spacing tab	CTRL+L
Line Break, Enter	WD 154				SHIFT+ENTER
Mailing Label, Address	WD 191		Tools | Letters and Mailings | Envelopes and Labels		
Margins	WD 78	In print layout view, drag margin boundary on ruler	File | Page Setup | Margins tab		
Move Selected Text	WD 113	Drag and drop	Edit | Cut; Edit | Paste	Cut; Paste	CTRL+X; CTRL+V
Nonbreaking Hyphen	WD 180		Insert | Symbol | Special Characters tab		CTRL+SHIFT+HYPHEN
Nonbreaking Space	WD 180		Insert | Symbol | Special Characters tab		CTRL+SHIFT+SPACEBAR
Numbered List	WD 189	Numbering button on Formatting toolbar	Format | Bullets and Numbering | Numbered tab	Bullets and Numbering | Numbered tab	1. and then space, type text, ENTER
Open Document	WD 55	Open button on Standard toolbar	File | Open		CTRL+O
Outline Numbered List	WD 189		Format | Bullets and Numbering | Outline Numbered tab		
Page Break	WD 103		Insert | Break		CTRL+ENTER
Page Numbers, Insert	WD 83	Insert Page Number button on Header and Footer toolbar	Insert | Page Numbers		
Paste	WD 170	Paste button on Standard toolbar	Edit | Paste	Paste	CTRL+V
Paste Options, Menu	WD 115	Paste Options button			
Print Document	WD 53	Print button on Standard toolbar	File | Print		CTRL+P
Print Preview	WD 158	Print Preview button on Standard toolbar	File | Print Preview		CTRL+F2
Promote List Item	WD 189	Increase Indent button on Formatting toolbar			
Quit Word	WD 54	Close button on title bar	File | Exit		ALT+F4
Redo Action	WD 39	Redo button on Standard toolbar	Edit | Redo		
Repeat Command	WD 39		Edit | Repeat		
Research Task Pane	WD 124	ALT+click word in document	Tools | Research		
Research Task Pane, Insert text from	WD 125			Right-click selected text in task pane, click Copy; right-click document, click Paste	Select text in task pane, CTRL+C; click document, CTRL+V
Resize Graphic	WD 50	Drag sizing handle	Format | Picture | Size tab	Format Picture | Size tab	
Restore Graphic	WD 51	Format Picture button on Picture toolbar	Format | Picture | Size tab	Format Picture | Size tab	
Resume Wizard	WD 142		File | New | On my computer | Other Documents tab		
Right-Align	WD 37	Align Right button on Formatting toolbar	Format | Paragraph | Indents and Spacing tab	Paragraph | Indents and Spacing tab	CTRL+R
Ruler, Show or Hide	WD 11		View | Ruler		
Save as Web Page	WD 205		File | Save as Web Page		
Save Document - New Name or Format	WD 52		File | Save As		F12
Save Document - Same Name	WD 52	Save button on Standard toolbar	File | Save		CTRL+S
Save New Document	WD 28	Save button on Standard toolbar	File | Save		CTRL+S
Select Document	WD 113	Point to left and triple-click	Edit | Select All		CTRL+A
Select Graphic	WD 49	Click graphic			
Select Group of Words	WD 43	Drag through words			CTRL+SHIFT+ARROW
Select Line	WD 40	Point to left of line and click			SHIFT+DOWN ARROW
Select Multiple Paragraphs	WD 33	Point to left of first paragraph and drag down			CTRL+SHIFT+DOWN ARROW

Table 1 Microsoft Office Word 2003 Quick Reference Summary *(continued)*

TASK	PAGE NUMBER	MOUSE	MENU BAR	SHORTCUT MENU	KEYBOARD SHORTCUT
Select Paragraph	WD 113	Triple-click paragraph			
Select Sentence	WD 112	CTRL+click sentence			CTRL+SHIFT+ARROW
Select Word	WD 58	Double-click word			CTRL+SHIFT+ARROW
Single-Space Text	WD 87	Line Spacing button arrow on Formatting toolbar	Format | Paragraph | Indents and Spacing tab	Paragraph | Indents and Spacing tab	CTRL+1
Small Uppercase Letters	WD 87		Format | Font | Font tab	Font | Font tab	CTRL+SHIFT+K
Smart Tag Actions, Display Menu	WD 192	Point to smart tag indicator, click Smart Tag Actions button			
Sort Paragraphs	WD 109		Table | Sort		
Spelling and Grammar Check At Once	WD 119	Spelling and Grammar button on Standard toolbar	Tools | Spelling and Grammar	Spelling	F7
Spelling Check as You Type	WD 26	Double-click Spelling and Grammar Status icon on status bar		Right-click flagged word, click word on shortcut menu	
Style, Modify	WD 96	Styles and Formatting button on Formatting toolbar	Format | Styles and Formatting		
Styles and Formatting Task Pane, Display	WD 152	Styles and Formatting button on Formatting toolbar	View | Task Pane		
Subscript	WD 87		Format | Font | Font tab	Font | Font tab	CTRL+=
Superscript	WD 87		Format | Font | Font tab	Font | Font tab	CTRL+SHIFT+PLUS SIGN
Switch to Open Document	WD 166	Program button on taskbar	Window | document name		ALT+TAB
Synonym	WD 118		Tools | Language | Thesaurus	Synonyms | desired word	SHIFT+F7
Tab Stops, Set	WD 164	Click location on ruler	Format | Tabs		
Table AutoFormat	WD 187	AutoFormat button on Tables and Borders toolbar	Table | Table AutoFormat		
Table, Fit Columns to Table Contents	WD 185	Double-click column boundary	Table | AutoFit | AutoFit to Contents	AutoFit | AutoFit to Contents	
Table, Insert Empty	WD 183	Insert Table button on Standard toolbar	Table | Insert | Table		
Table, Insert Row	WD 184		Table | Insert | Rows Above/Below	Right-click selected row; Insert Rows	TAB from lower-right cell
Table, Resize Column	WD 186	Drag column boundary	Table | Table Properties | Column tab	Table Properties | Column tab	
Table, Select	WD 186	Click table move handle	Table | Select | Table		ALT+5 (on keypad)
Table, Select Cell	WD 186	Click left edge of cell			TAB
Table, Select Column	WD 186	Click top border of column			
Table, Select Cells	WD 186	Drag through cells			
Table, Select Row	WD 186	Click to left of row			
Task Pane, Display Different	WD 10	Other Task Panes button on task pane			
Template, Open	WD 175		File | New | On my computer		
Theme, Apply	WD 208		Format | Theme		
Toolbar, Dock	WD 82	Double-click toolbar title bar			
Toolbar, Float	WD 82	Drag toolbar move handle			
Toolbar, Show Entire	WD 14	Double-click toolbar move handle	Tools | Customize | Options tab		
Underline	WD 42	Underline button on Formatting toolbar	Format | Font | Font tab	Font | Font tab	CTRL+U
Underline Words	WD 87		Format | Font | Font tab	Font | Font tab	CTRL+SHIFT+W
Undo	WD 39	Undo button on Standard toolbar	Edit | Undo		CTRL+Z
User Information, Change	WD 194		Tools | Options | User Information tab		
Web Page Frame, Resize	WD 211	Drag frame border	Format | Frames | Frame Properties | Frame tab		
Web Page, Preview	WD 209		File | Web Page Preview		
White Space	WD 149	Hide or Show White Space button	Tools | Options | View tab		
Zoom	WD 21 and WD 169	Zoom box arrow on Formatting toolbar	View | Zoom		

Table 2 Microsoft Excel 2003 Quick Reference Summary

TASK	PAGE NUMBER	MOUSE	MENU BAR	SHORTCUT MENU	KEYBOARD SHORTCUT
AutoFormat	EX 34		Format | AutoFormat		ALT+O | A
AutoSum	EX 23	AutoSum button on Standard toolbar	Insert | Function		ALT+=
Bold	EX 30	Bold button on Formatting toolbar	Format | Cells | Font tab	Format Cells | Font tab	CTRL+B
Borders	EX 96	Borders button on Formatting toolbar	Format | Cells | Border tab	Format Cells | Border tab	CTRL+1 | B
Center	EX 97	Center button on Formatting toolbar	Format | Cells | Alignment tab	Format Cells | Alignment tab	CTRL+1 | A
Center Across Columns	EX 33	Merge and Center button on Formatting toolbar	Format | Cells | Alignment tab	Format Cells | Alignment tab	CTRL+1 | A
Chart	EX 39	Chart Wizard button on Standard toolbar	Insert | Chart		F11
Clear Cell	EX 52	Drag fill handle back	Edit | Clear | All	Clear Contents	DELETE
Close Workbook	EX 46	Close button on menu bar or workbook Control-menu icon	File | Close		CTRL+W
Color Background	EX 94	Fill Color button on Formatting toolbar	Format | Cells | Patterns tab	Format Cells | Patterns tab	CTRL+1 | P
Color Tab	EX 198			Tab Color	
Column Width	EX 107	Drag column heading boundary	Format | Column | Width	Column Width	ALT+O | C | W
Comma Style Format	EX 108	Comma Style button on Formatting toolbar	Format | Cells | Number tab | Accounting	Format Cells | Number tab | Accounting	CTRL+1 | N
Conditional Formatting	EX 104		Format | Conditional Formatting		ALT+O | D
Copy and Paste	EX 157	Copy button and Paste button on Standard toolbar	Edit | Copy; Edit | Paste	Copy to copy; Paste to paste	CTRL+C; CTRL+V
Currency Style Format	EX 98	Currency Style button on Formatting toolbar	Format | Cells | Number | Currency	Format Cells | Number | Currency	CTRL+1 | N
Cut	EX 159	Cut button on Standard toolbar	Edit | Cut	Cut	CTRL+X
Date	EX 166	Insert Function box in formula bar	Insert | Function		CTRL+SEMICOLON
Decimal Place, Decrease	EX 100	Decrease Decimal button on Formatting toolbar	Format | Cells | Number tab | Currency	Format Cells | Number tab | Currency	CTRL+1 | N
Decimal Place, Increase	EX 99	Increase Decimal button on Formatting toolbar	Format | Cells | Number tab | Currency	Format Cells | Number tab | Currency	CTRL+1 | N
Delete Rows or Columns	EX 161		Edit | Delete	Delete	
Drop Shadow	EX 184	Shadow Style button on Drawing toolbar			
E-Mail from Excel	EX 125	E-mail button on Standard toolbar	File | Send To | Mail Recipient		ALT+F | D | A
File Management	EX 232		File | Save As, right-click file name		ALT+F | A, right-click file name
Fit to Print	EX 118		File | Page Setup | Page tab		ALT+F | U | P
Folder, New	EX 230		File | Save As		ALT+F | A
Font Color	EX 32	Font Color button on Formatting toolbar	Format | Cells | Font tab	Format Cells | Font tab	CTRL+1 | F
Font Size	EX 31	Font Size box arrow on Formatting toolbar	Format | Cells | Font tab	Format Cells | Font tab	CTRL+1 | F
Font Type	EX 29	Font box arrow on Formatting toolbar	Format | Cells | Font tab	Format Cells | Font tab	CTRL+1 | F
Formula Assistance	EX 83	Insert Function box in formula bar	Insert | Function		CTRL+A after you type function name

Table 2 Microsoft Excel 2003 Quick Reference Summary *(continued)*

TASK	PAGE NUMBER	MOUSE	MENU BAR	SHORTCUT MENU	KEYBOARD SHORTCUT
Formulas Version	EX 118		Tools | Options | View tab | Formulas		CTRL+ACCENT MARK
Freeze Worksheet Titles	EX 163		Window | Freeze Panes		ALT+W | F
Full Screen	EX 11		View | Full Screen		ALT+V | U
Function	EX 81	Insert Function box in formula bar	Insert | Function		SHIFT+F3
Go To	EX 37	Click cell	Edit | Go To		F5
Goal Seek	EX 206		Tools | Goal Seek		ALT+T | G
Help	EX 53 and Appendix A	Microsoft Excel Help button on Standard toolbar	Help | Microsoft Excel Help		F1
Hide Column	EX 109	Drag column heading boundary	Format | Column | Hide	Hide	CTRL+0 (zero) to hide CTRL+SHIFT+) to display
Hide Row	EX 111	Drag row heading boundary	Format | Row | Hide	Hide	CTRL+9 to hide CTRL+SHIFT+(to display
In-Cell Editing	EX 50	Double-click cell			F2
Insert Rows or Columns	EX 160		Insert | Rows or Insert | Columns	Insert	ALT+I | R or C
Italicize	EX 186	Italic button on Formatting toolbar	Format | Cells | Font tab	Format Cells | Font tab	CTRL+I
Language Bar	EX 15 and Appendix B		Tools | Speech | Speech Recognition	Toolbars | Language bar	ALT+T | H | H
Merge Cells	EX 33	Merge and Center button on Formatting toolbar	Format | Cells | Alignment tab	Format Cells | Font tab | Alignment tab	ALT+O | E | A
Move Cells	EX 159	Point to border and drag	Edit | Cut; Edit | Paste	Cut; Paste	CTRL+X; CTRL+V
Name Cells	EX 37	Click Name box in formula bar, type name	Insert | Name | Define		ALT+I | N | D
New Workbook	EX 53	New button on Standard toolbar	File | New		CTRL+N
Open Workbook	EX 47	Open button on Standard toolbar	File | Open		CTRL+O
Percent Style Format	EX 103	Percent Style button on Formatting toolbar	Format | Cells | Number tab | Percentage	Format Cells | Number tab | Percentage	CTRL+1 | N
Preview Worksheet	EX 114	Print Preview button on Standard toolbar	File | Print Preview		ALT+F | V
Print Worksheet	EX 113	Print button on Standard toolbar	File | Print		CTRL+P
Quit Excel	EX 46	Close button on title bar	File | Exit		ALT+F4
Range Finder	EX 89	Double-click cell			
Redo	EX 52	Redo button on Standard toolbar	Edit | Redo		ALT+E | R
Remove Splits	EX 204	Double-click split bar	Window | Split		ALT+W | S
Rename Sheet Tab	EX 198	Double-click sheet tab		Rename	
Rotate Text	EX 151		Format | Cells | Alignment tab	Format Cells | Alignment tab	ALT+O | E | A
Row Height	EX 110	Drag row heading boundary	Format | Row | Height	Row Height	ALT+O | R | E
Save as Web Page	EX 230		File | Save as Web Page		ALT+F | G
Save Workbook, New Name	EX 42		File | Save As		ALT+F | A
Save Workbook, Same Name	EX 89	Save button on Standard toolbar	File | Save		CTRL+S
Select All of Worksheet	EX 53	Select All button on worksheet			CTRL+A
Select Cell	EX 16	Click cell			Use arrow keys

Table 2 Microsoft Excel 2003 Quick Reference Summary

TASK	PAGE NUMBER	MOUSE	MENU BAR	SHORTCUT MENU	KEYBOARD SHORTCUT
Select Multiple Sheets	EX 200	CTRL+click tab or SHIFT+click tab		Select All Sheets	
Series	EX 151	Drag fill handle	Edit | Fill | Series		ALT+E | I | S
Shortcut Menu	EX 92	Right-click object			SHIFT+F10
Spell Check	EX 112	Spelling button on Standard toolbar	Tools | Spelling		F7
Split Cell	EX 33	Merge and Center button on Formatting toolbar	Format | Cells | Alignment tab	Format Cells | Alignment tab	ALT+O | E | A
Split Window into Panes	EX 203	Drag vertical or horizontal split box	Window | Split		ALT+W | S
Stock Quotes	EX 121		Data | Import External Data | Import Data		ALT+D | D | D
Task Pane	EX 8		View | Task Pane		ALT+V | K
Toolbar, Dock	EX 182	Drag toolbar to dock			
Toolbar, Reset	Appendix D	Toolbar Options button on toolbar, Add or Remove Buttons, Customize, Toolbars tab		Customize | Toolbars	ALT+V | T | C | B
Toolbar, Show Entire	EX 13	Double-click move handle			
Toolbar, Show or Hide	EX 182	Right-click toolbar, click toolbar name	View | Toolbars		ALT+V | T
Underline	EX 187	Underline button on Formatting toolbar	Format | Cells | Font tab	Format Cells | Font tab	CTRL+U
Undo	EX 51	Undo button on Standard toolbar	Edit | Undo		CTRL+Z
Unfreeze Worksheet Titles	EX 176		Windows | Unfreeze Panes		ALT+W | F
Unhide Column	EX 109	Drag hidden column heading boundary to right	Format | Column | Unhide	Unhide	ALT+O | C | U
Unhide Row	EX 111	Drag hidden row heading boundary down	Format | Row | Unhide	Unhide	ALT+O | R | U
Web Page Preview	EX 228		File | Web Page Preview		ALT+F | B
Zoom	EX 201	Zoom box on Standard toolbar	View | Zoom		ALT+V | Z

Table 3 Microsoft Office Access 2003 Quick Reference Summary

TASK	PAGE NUMBER	MOUSE	MENU BAR	SHORTCUT MENU	KEYBOARD SHORTCUT
Add Field	AC 129	Insert Rows button	Insert | Rows	Insert Rows	INSERT
Add Group of Records	AC 139	Query Type button arrow | Append Query	Query | Append Query	Query Type | Append Query	
Add Record	AC 23, AC 116	New Record button	Insert | New Record		
Add Table to Query	AC 92	Show Table button	Query | Show Table	Show Table	
Advanced Filter/Sort	AC 124		Records | Filter | Advanced Filter Sort		
Apply Filter	AC 121, AC 123	Filter By Selection or Filter By Form button	Records | Filter		
Calculate Statistics	AC 100	Totals button	View | Totals	Totals	
Change Group of Records	AC 136	Query Type button arrow | Update Query	Query | Update Query	Query Type | Update Query	

Table 3 Microsoft Office Access 2003 Quick Reference Summary *(continued)*

TASK	PAGE NUMBER	MOUSE	MENU BAR	SHORTCUT MENU	KEYBOARD SHORTCUT
Clear Query	AC 75		Edit | Clear Grid		
Close Database	AC 26	Close Window button	File | Close		
Close Form	AC 39	Close Window button	File | Close		
Close Query	AC 73	Close Window button	File | Close		
Close Table	AC 21	Close Window button	File | Close		
Collapse Subdatasheet	AC 153	Expand indicator (-)			
Create Calculated Field	AC 96			Zoom	SHIFT+F2
Create Database	AC 10	New button	File | New		CTRL+N
Create Form	AC 38	New Object button arrow | AutoForm	Insert | AutoForm		
Create Index	AC 161	Indexes button	View | Indexes		
Create Query	AC 68	New Object button arrow | Query	Insert | Query		
Create Report	AC 43	New Object button arrow | Report	Insert | Report		
Create Snapshot	AC 184		File | Export, select SNP as file type	Export, select SNP as file type	
Create Table	AC 17	Tables object | Create table in Design view or Create table by using wizard	Insert | Table		
Crosstab Query	AC 104	New Object button arrow | Query	Insert | Query		
Default Value	AC 142	Default Value property box			
Delete Field	AC 130	Delete Rows button	Edit | Delete	Delete Rows	DELETE
Delete Group of Records	AC 138	Query Type button arrow | Delete Query	Query | Delete Query	Query Type | Delete Query	
Delete Record	AC 125	Delete Record button	Edit | Delete Record	Delete Record	DELETE
Exclude Duplicates	AC 87	Properties button	View | Properties | Unique Values Only	Properties | Unique Values Only	
Exclude Field from Query Results	AC 78	Show check box			
Expand Subdatasheet	AC 153	Expand indicator (+)			
Export Using Drag-and-Drop	AC 182	Drag object, then drop			
Export Using Export Command	AC 183		File | Export	Export	
Field Size	AC 19, AC 127	Field Size property box			
Field Type	AC 20	Data Type box arrow | appropriate type			Appropriate letter
Filter Records	AC 121, AC 123	Filter By Selection or Filter By Form button	Records | Filter		
Font in Datasheet	AC 133		Format | Font	Font	
Format	AC 144	Format property box			
Format a Calculated Field	AC 98	Properties button	View | Properties	Properties	
Format Datasheet	AC 134		Format | Datasheet	Datasheet	
Group in Query	AC 103	Totals button	View | Totals		

Table 3 Microsoft Office Access 2003 Quick Reference Summary

TASK	PAGE NUMBER	MOUSE	MENU BAR	SHORTCUT MENU	KEYBOARD SHORTCUT
Import	AC 177		File | Get External Data | Import	Import	
Include All Fields in Query	AC 74	Double-click asterisk in field list			
Include Field in Query	AC 71	Double-click field in field list			
Join Properties	AC 94		View | Join Properties	Join Properties	
Key Field	AC 19	Primary Key button	Edit | Primary Key	Primary Key	
Link	AC 180		File | Get External Data | Link Table	Link Tables	
Lookup Field	AC 147	Text box arrow | Lookup Wizard			
Move to First Record	AC 27	First Record button			CTRL+UP ARROW
Move to Last Record	AC 27	Last Record button			CTRL+DOWN ARROW
Move to Next Record	AC 27	Next Record button			DOWN ARROW
Move to Previous Record	AC 27	Previous Record button			UP ARROW
Open Database	AC 26	Open button	File | Open		CTRL+O
Open Form	AC 116	Forms object | Open button		Open	Use ARROW keys to move highlight to name, then press ENTER key
Open Table	AC 26	Tables object | Open button		Open	Use ARROW keys to move highlight to name, then press ENTER key
Preview Table	AC 30	Print Preview button	File | Print Preview	Print Preview	
Print Relationships	AC 151		File | Print Relationships		
Print Report	AC 47	Print button	File | Print	Print	CTRL+P
Print Results of Query	AC 72	Print button	File | Print	Print	CTRL+P
Print Table	AC 30	Print button	File | Print	Print	CTRL+P
Quit Access	AC 50	Close button	File | Exit		ALT+F4
Relationships (Referential Integrity)	AC 150	Relationships button	Tools | Relationships		
Remove Filter	AC 122	Remove Filter button	Records | Remove Filter/Sort		
Resize Column	AC 131	Drag right boundary of field selector	Format | Column Width	Column Width	
Restructure Table	AC 126	Tables object | Design button		Design View	
Return to Select Query Window	AC 72	View button arrow	View | Design View		
Run Query	AC 71	Run button	Query | Run		
Save Form	AC 39	Save button	File | Save		CTRL+S
Save Query	AC 80	Save button	File | Save		CTRL+S
Save Table	AC 21	Save button	File | Save		CTRL+S
Search for Record	AC 117	Find button	Edit | Find		CTRL+F
Select Fields for Report	AC 44	Add Field button or Add All Fields button			
Simple Query Wizard	AC 34	New Object button arrow | Query	Insert | Query		
Sort Data in Query	AC 86	Sort row | Sort row arrow | type of sort			
Sort Records	AC 155	Sort Ascending or Sort Descending button	Records | Sort | Sort Ascending or Sort Descending	Sort Ascending or Sort Descending	

Table 3 Microsoft Office Access 2003 Quick Reference Summary *(continued)*

TASK	PAGE NUMBER	MOUSE	MENU BAR	SHORTCUT MENU	KEYBOARD SHORTCUT
Switch Between Form and Datasheet Views	AC 41, AC 120	View button arrow	View | Datasheet View		
Top-Values Query	AC 89	Top Values button	View | Properties	Properties	
Use AND Criterion	AC 84				Place criteria on same line
Use OR Criterion	AC 85				Place criteria on separate lines
Validation Rule	AC 141	Validation Rule property box			
Validation Text	AC 141	Validation Text property box			

Table 4 Microsoft Office PowerPoint 2003 Quick Reference Summary

TASK	PAGE NUMBER	MOUSE	MENU BAR	SHORTCUT MENU	KEYBOARD SHORTCUT
Animate Text	PPT 114		Slide Show | Custom Animation | Add Effect button		ALT+D | M
Black Slide, End Show	PPT 42		Tools | Options | End with black slide		ALT+T | O | E
Check Spelling	PPT 54	Spelling button on Standard toolbar	Tools | Spelling		F7
Clip Art, Add Animation Effects	PPT 117		Slide Show | Custom Animation		ALT+D | M
Clip Art, Change Size	PPT 109	Format Picture button on Picture toolbar | Size tab	Format | Picture | Size tab	Format Picture | Size tab	ALT+O | I | Size tab
Clip Art, Insert	PPT 101, PPT 104	Insert Clip Art button on Drawing toolbar	Insert | Picture | Clip Art		ALT+I | P | C
Clip Art, Move	PPT 108	Drag			
Delete Text	PPT 56	Cut button on Standard toolbar	Edit | Cut	Cut	CTRL+X or BACKSPACE or DELETE
Demote a Paragraph on Outline tab	PPT 90	Demote button on Outlining toolbar			TAB or ALT+SHIFT+RIGHT ARROW
Design Template	PPT 18	Slide Design button on Formatting toolbar	Format | Slide Design	Slide Design	ALT+O | D
Display a Presentation in Black and White	PPT 57	Color/Grayscale button on Standard toolbar	View | Color/Grayscale | Pure Black and White		ALT+V | C | U
Edit Web Page through Browser	PPT 152	Edit button on Internet Explorer Standard Buttons toolbar	File on browser menu bar | Edit with Microsoft PowerPoint in browser window		ALT+F | D in browser window
E-Mail from PowerPoint	PPT 127	E-mail button on Standard toolbar	File | Send To | Mail Recipient		ALT+F | D | A
End Slide Show	PPT 50			End Show	ESC
Font	PPT 24	Font box arrow on Formatting toolbar	Format | Font	Font	ALT+O | F
Font Color	PPT 24	Font Color button arrow on Formatting toolbar, desired color	Format | Font	Font | Color	ALT+O | F | ALT+C | DOWN ARROW

Table 4 Microsoft Office PowerPoint 2003 Quick Reference Summary

TASK	PAGE NUMBER	MOUSE	MENU BAR	SHORTCUT MENU	KEYBOARD SHORTCUT
Font Size, Decrease	PPT 27	Decrease Font Size button on Formatting toolbar	Format | Font	Font | Size	CTRL+SHIFT+LEFT CARET (<)
Font Size, Increase	PPT 25	Increase Font Size button on Formatting toolbar	Format | Font	Font | Size	CTRL+SHIFT+RIGHT CARET (>)
Header and Footer, Add to Outline Page	PPT 112		View | Header and Footer | Notes and Handouts tab		ALT+V | H | Notes and Handouts tab
Help	PPT 62 and Appendix A	Microsoft PowerPoint Help button on Standard toolbar	Help | Microsoft PowerPoint Help		F1
Italicize	PPT 24	Italic button on Formatting toolbar	Format | Font | Font style	Font | Font style	CTRL+I
Language Bar	PPT 16 and Appendix B	Language Indicator button in tray	Tools | Speech | Speech Recognition		ALT+T | H | H
Move a Paragraph Down	PPT 87	Move Down button on Outlining toolbar			ALT+SHIFT+DOWN ARROW
Move a Paragraph Up	PPT 87	Move Up button on Outlining toolbar			ALT+SHIFT+UP ARROW
New Slide	PPT 30	New Slide button on Formatting toolbar	Insert | New Slide		CTRL+M
Next Slide	PPT 45	Next Slide button on vertical scroll bar			PAGE DOWN
Normal View	PPT 96	Normal View button at lower-left PowerPoint window	View | Normal		ALT+V | N
Open Presentation	PPT 52	Open button on Standard toolbar	File | Open		CTRL+O
Paragraph Indent, Decrease	PPT 37	Decrease Indent button on Formatting toolbar			SHIFT+TAB or ALT+ SHIFT+LEFT ARROW
Paragraph Indent, Increase	PPT 36	Increase Indent button on Formatting toolbar			TAB or ALT+SHIFT+ RIGHT ARROW
Preview Presentation as Web Page	PPT 144		File | Web Page Preview		ALT+F | B
Previous Slide	PPT 45	Previous Slide button on vertical scroll bar			PAGE UP
Print a Presentation	PPT 60	Print button on Standard toolbar	File | Print		CTRL+P
Print an Outline	PPT 122		File | Print | Print what box arrow | Outline View		CTRL+P | TAB | TAB | DOWN ARROW | Outline View
Promote a Paragraph on Outline tab	PPT 89	Promote button on Outlining toolbar			SHIFT+TAB or ALT+ SHIFT+LEFT ARROW
Publish a Presentation	PPT 154		File | Save as Web Page | Publish | Publish		ALT+F | G | ALT+P | ALT+P
Quit PowerPoint	PPT 50	Close button on title bar or double-click control icon on title bar	File | Exit		ALT+F4 or CTRL+Q
Redo Action	PPT 22	Redo button on Standard toolbar	Edit | Redo		CTRL+Y or ALT+E | R
Save a Presentation	PPT 27	Save button on Standard toolbar	File | Save		CTRL+S
Save as Web Page	PPT 147		File | Save as Web Page		ALT+F | G
Slide Layout	PPT 98		Format | Slide Layout	Slide Layout	ALT+O | L
Slide Show View	PPT 47	Slide Show button at lower-left PowerPoint window	View | Slide Show		F5 or ALT+V | W

Table 4 Microsoft Office PowerPoint 2003 Quick Reference Summary *(continued)*

TASK	PAGE NUMBER	MOUSE	MENU BAR	SHORTCUT MENU	KEYBOARD SHORTCUT
Slide Sorter View	PPT 95	Slide Sorter View button at lower-left PowerPoint window	View | Slide Sorter		ALT+V | D
Spelling Check	PPT 54	Spelling button on Standard toolbar	Tools | Spelling	Spelling	F7
Task Pane	PPT 11		View | Task Pane		ALT+V | K
Toolbar, Reset	Appendix D	Toolbar Options button on toolbar, Add or Remove Buttons, Customize, Toolbars tab		Customize | Toolbars tab	ALT+V | T | C | B
Toolbar, Show Entire	PPT 9	Double-click move handle			
Undo Action	PPT 22	Undo button on Standard toolbar	Edit | Undo		CTRL+Z or ALT+E | U
Web Page, Preview	PPT 144		File | Web Page Preview		ALT+F | B
Zoom Percentage, Increase	PPT 44	Zoom Box arrow on Standard toolbar	View | Zoom		ALT+V | Z

Table 5 Microsoft Office Outlook 2003 Quick Reference Summary

TASK	PAGE NUMBER	MOUSE	MENU BAR	SHORTCUT MENU	KEYBOARD SHORTCUT
Address E-Mail Message	OUT 51	To button			CTRL+SHIFT+B
Attach File to E-Mail Message	OUT 28	Insert File button	Insert | File		ALT+I, L
Compose E-Mail Message	OUT 24	New button	File | New | Mail Message		CTRL+N
Create Contact List	OUT 42	New button	Actions | New Contact	New Contact	CTRL+N | ALT+A, N
Create Distribution List	OUT 54	New button	File | New | Distribution List		CTRL+SHIFT+L
Create E-Mail Signature	OUT 20		Tools | Options		ALT+T, O
Create Personal Folder	OUT 40		File | New | Folder	New Folder	CTRL+SHIFT+E
Create View Filter	OUT 32		View | Arrange By	Custom	ALT+V, A, M
Delete E-Mail Message	OUT 17	Delete button	Edit | Delete	Delete	CTRL+D
Display Contacts in a Category	OUT 49	Find button	Tools | Find		CTRL+E
Find a Contact	OUT 46	Find button	Tools | Find		CTRL+E
Flag E-Mail Messages	OUT 30		Actions | Follow Up	Follow Up	ALT+A, U
Forward E-Mail Message	OUT 16	Forward button	Actions | Forward	Forward	ALT+W
Open E-Mail Message	OUT 11		File | Open	Open	ALT+F, O
Organize Contacts	OUT 48	Organize button	Tools | Organize		ALT+T, Z
Print Contact List	OUT 50	Print button	File | Print		CTRL+P
Print E-Mail Message	OUT 12	Print button	File | Print		CTRL+P
Reply to E-Mail Message	OUT 13	Reply button	Actions | Reply	Reply	ALT+R
Save Contact List as Text File	OUT 56		File | Save As		ALT+F, A
Send E-Mail Message	OUT 29	Send button	File | Send To		ALT+S
Set Message Delivery Options	OUT 34	Options button			ALT+P
Set Message Importance and Sensitivity	OUT 34	Options button			ALT+P
Sort E-Mail Messages	OUT 31		View | Arrange By		ALT+V, A